Encyclopædia Britannica

Anonymous

Nabu Public Domain Reprints:

You are holding a reproduction of an original work published before 1923 that is in the public domain in the United States of America, and possibly other countries. You may freely copy and distribute this work as no entity (individual or corporate) has a copyright on the body of the work. This book may contain prior copyright references, and library stamps (as most of these works were scanned from library copies). These have been scanned and retained as part of the historical artifact.

This book may have occasional imperfections such as missing or blurred pages, poor pictures, errant marks, etc. that were either part of the original artifact, or were introduced by the scanning process. We believe this work is culturally important, and despite the imperfections, have elected to bring it back into print as part of our continuing commitment to the preservation of printed works worldwide. We appreciate your understanding of the imperfections in the preservation process, and hope you enjoy this valuable book.

SUPPLEMENT.

TO

ENCYCLOPÆDIA BRITANNICA.

(NINTH EDITION.)

A DICTIONARY

OF

ARTS, SCIENCES, AND GENERAL LITERATURE.

ILLUSTRATED.

VOLUME III.

THE HENRY G. ALLEN COMPANY,
NEW YORK.
1889.

Entered, according to Act of Congress, in the year 1889, by
HUBBARD BROTHERS,
In the Office of the Librarian of Congress, at Washington.

PREFATORY NOTE TO VOLUME III.

THE Third Volume of the American Supplement to the *Encyclopædia Britannica* has been prepared on the same general plan which had been laid down at the outset of the work. Both the previous volumes have been cordially received by an ever-widening circle of subscribers, who have frequently assured the Publishers of their gratification at the successful prosecution of this important undertaking. Critics of the highest rank in both hemispheres have passed encomiums on the former volumes. It has been the aim of the Publishers and Editors to continue to deserve these praises. For this purpose, not only have valued contributors to the former volumes been retained, but additions have been made to their number as the subjects to be treated appeared to demand. Attention is, therefore, called to the list of contributors to the present volume, as indicating at a glance the value of the present portion of a work, whose reputation has already been established on a firm basis.

As in the former volumes especial regard has been had to subjects relating to the United States, whether in biography, history, geography, science, politics, or religion. The development of the resources of our vast and rich inheritance has been treated in various articles with such fulness as the pressure of other important topics would allow. The social problems which have arisen from the rapid development of the country, and from the changes in transportation and industries, have been carefully attended to. In subjects even of a wider range care has been taken to discuss the questions on the lines most directly affecting American interests.

While in statements of fact and matters of general information in science and philosophy it has been the uniform rule of the Editors to avoid repetition of what is contained in the *Encyclopædia Britannica*, it has been felt that writers on certain topics in that valuable work had prepared articles which, however able, were so one-sided that fairness and justice demanded the presentation of the opposite views. This has been done, not only in case of certain subjects relating to the Bible, but in regard to Free Trade, Homœopathy, Freemasonry, and some topics of less prominence. In every such case the statements of this work should be compared with those ~nding title in *Encyclopædia Britannica*, before drawing conclusions.

Efforts have not been wanting to maintain the high standard of typographical and mechanical excellence which has hitherto characterized this work. Indeed, the Publishers have felt justified in going to greater expense in providing illustrations for the articles in this volume, hoping thereby not only to enrich the appearance of the volume, but to make still clearer the statements of the text.

With the hope of receiving renewed expressions of approval the present volume is respectfully submitted to the judgment of its final arbiter—an impartial public.

LIST OF CONTRIBUTORS TO THE SUPPLEMENT.
VOLUME III.

This list embraces the names of those contributors whose names are signed (by their initials) to articles in the present volume.

Where two or more contributors have the same initials, a distinction has been made in printing them, which will enable the reader to assign to each his own work.

The writers whose names are marked with an asterisk (*) have exercised more or less editorial supervision in their respective departments.

HOWARD CROSBY, D. D., LL. D., *Editor-in-Chief.*

Prof. JOHN P. LAMBERTON, A. M., *Associate Editor.*

HENRY E. ALVORD, Mountainville, New York.
   Ensilage.

Hon. RASMUS B. ANDERSON, U. S. Minister to Denmark.
   Drachmann, H. H. H.,
      and other articles connected with Scandinavian and Danish history and literature.

W. B. ATKINSON, M. D., Secretary American Medical Association, Philadelphia.
   Hospitals in the United States.

Capt. F. J. BABSON, Gloucester, Mass.
   Fisheries.

CHARLES BARNARD, *Century Magazine*, New York.
   Electrotyping,   Elevators.

Rev. WILLIS J. BEECHER, D. D., Auburn Theological Seminary, N. Y.
   Ecclesiastes.

JOHN S. BILLINGS, M. D., Washington, D. C.
   Dietetics,   Epidemics.
   Empiricism,

F. J. BIRD, Brooklyn, N. Y.
   Dyeing.

Rev. FREDERIC M. BIRD, South Bethlehem, Pa.
   Hymns.

JOHN BIRKINBINE, M. E., Philadelphia.
   Fuel.

WILFRID BLUNT, M. P., London.
   Egypt.

Prof. ALBERT S. BOLLES, Editor *Banker's Magazine*, New York.
   Debts, National,   Finance.

Justice JOSEPH P. BRADLEY, LL. D., U. S. Supreme Court, Washington, D. C.
   Government.

LINUS P. BROCKETT, M. D., Brooklyn, N. Y.
   Denmark,   Georgia.
   Florida,

ARNOLD BURGESS, Hillsdale, Michigan.
   Dog.

ADDISON B. BURK, *Public Ledger*, Philadelphia.
   Design, Schools of.

Rev. H. K. CARROLL, D. D., *The Independent*, New York.
   Dunkers.

*WILLIAM J. CLARK, JR., *Evening Telegraph*, Philadelphia.
   Doré, Paul Gustave,   Doyle, Richard,
      and other biographical sketches of distinguished artists.

Prof. PHILIP DE COMPIGNY, Paris.
   France.

ANTHONY COMSTOCK, Superintendent Society for Suppression of Vice, New York.
   Gambling.

THOMAS M. COOLEY, LL. D., formerly Chief-Justice Supreme Court of Michigan.
   Husband and Wife,   Impeachment.

*Prof. HENRY COPPÉE, LL. D., Lehigh University, Pa.
   Della Crusca,   Dettingen,
   Delphin Classics,   Fort Donelson,
      and other articles in American and European history and literature.

ELLIS COTTET, Philadelphia.
   Hotels,   Hypothecation.

*HOWARD CROSBY, D. D., LL. D., New York.
   Faith,   Hades,
   Faith-Cure,   High-Church,
   Future State,   Imputation,
   Grace,   Incarnation.

J. P. DAVENPORT, *New York Tribune*.
   Immigration.

A. M. DICKIE, M. D., Doylestown, Pa.
   Fowl.

EUGENE L. DIDIER, Baltimore.
   Dubois, John,   Early, Jubal A.,
   England, John,
      and other biographical articles.

GEORGE B. DIXWELL, Boston.
   Free Trade.

Prof. A. E. DOLBEAR, Tufts College, Mass.,
   Electricity.

Rev. LEWIS M. DORMAN, Brooklyn, N. Y.
   Deaconesses.

Prof. MORTON W. EASTON, University of Pennsylvania.
   Dialect.

LIST OF CONTRIBUTORS.

Rev. Benjamin Franklin, D. D., Shrewsbury, N. J.
Church.

Rev. George S. Fullerton, Ph. D., University of Pennsylvania.
Clairvoyance.

Major Asa Bird Gardner, U. S. A.
Cincinnati, Society of,   Courts-martial.

Prof. F. A. Genth, Ph. D., University of Pennsylvania.
Corundum.

E. L. Godkin, Editor *The Nation*, New York.
Civil Service Reform.

Harold Godwin, New York.
Bryant, William Cullen.

Plutarco Gonzalez, Matanzas, Cuba.
Cuba.

Prof. William Henry Goodyear, Metropolitan Museum of Art, New York.
Cypriote Art.

*Dr. Charles W. Greene, Merchantville, N. J.
Cherokees,   Corea,
Choctaws,   Cotton Culture in the U. S.,
Cliff-Dwellings,   Creek Indians,
Columbia, British,   Damian, Peter,
and other biographical and geographical articles.

Prof. Richard T. Greener, Howard University, Washington, D. C.
Cuffee, Paul.

George Butler Griffin, C. E., Los Angeles, California.
Colombia, United States of.

Col. Martin J. Griffin, Toronto, Canada.
Canada.

R. A. Guild, Brown University, Providence, R. I.
Brown University.

Henry Hall, *New York Tribune*, New York.
Clipper Ships.

William A. Harris, Editor *Carpet Trade Review*, New York.
Carpet Making in America.

Prof. Angelo Heilprin, Academy of Natural Sciences, Philadelphia.
Clam.

Edward Heintz, Philadelphia.
Confectionery.

Frank Henkels, Esq., Philadelphia.
Conspiracy,   Damages.
Criminal Law,

Albert F. Hill, *The Iron Age*, New York.
Cigar,   Cork,
Copper,   Crucibles,
and other articles on manufactures.

Rev. D. W. C. Huntingdon, D. D., Buffalo, N. Y.
Cartwright, Rev. Peter.

*Howard M. Jenkins, *The American*, Philadelphia.
Clayton, John M.,   Clayton-Bulwer Treaty.

*Prof. Alexander Johnston, author of *History of American Politics*, etc., Princeton, N. J.
Colonization Society, American,   Constitution of the U. S.,
Confederate States,   Davis, Jefferson.

Hon. John A. Kasson, Iowa.
Congress.

Rev. John S. Kedney, D. D., Faribault, Minn.
Conscience.

Dr. D. Otis Kellogg, Vineland, N. J.
Charity Organization.

Peter D. Keyser, M. D., Philadelphia.
Color-Blindness.

Philip C. Knapp, Jr., M. D., Boston.
Dante in America.

Dr. George A. Koenig, Professor of Geology, University of Pennsylvania.
Clay,
and other articles in geology and mineralogy.

*Prof. John P. Lamberton, Philadelphia.
Chancellorsville,   Crittenden Family,
Christian Commission,   Cushman, Charlotte S.,
Clay, Henry,   Cutler, Manasseh,
Clemens, Samuel L.,   Dallas, Alexander James,
Clinton, De Witt,   Dallas, George Mifflin,
Cooper, Peter,   Davis, Henry Winter,
and other articles in American and European biography.

George T. Lanigan, New York.
Circus,   Cremation.

Prof. Émile Laveleye, Liége.
Crisis, Commercial.

Alfred Lee, Jr., Esq., Philadelphia.
Courts of the United States,   Courts, State,
and other legal articles.

Lawrence Lewis, Jr., Esq., Philadelphia.
Civil Rights,   Comptroller,
Client,   Conveyancing,
Common Law,   Curtesy.
and numerous articles on legal subjects.

W. N. Lockington, Philadelphia.
Cochin China,   Congo Region.
Cod,

Rev. Albert G. McCoy, Ph. D., Monmouth, Ill.
Chicago.

Frederick G. Mather, Albany, N. Y.
Cavalry,   Cleveland, Ohio.
Champlain, Lake,

Brander Matthews, author of *French Dramatists of the Nineteenth Century*, New York.
Coquelin, Benoit C.,
and other articles in literary and dramatic biography.

*Thomas Meehan, Philadelphia, author of *Native Flowers and Ferns of the United States*.
Cherry,   Clematis,
Chestnut,   Currant,
Chicory,   Cypress,
Chrysanthemum,   Daisy,
and numerous articles in botany.

William M. Meigs, Esq., Philadelphia.
Clarendon, Constitutions of,   Confiscation,
Condonation,
and other legal articles.

N. C. Moak, Esq., Albany, N. Y.
Capital Punishment.

*Charles Morris, Academy of Natural Sciences, Philadelphia.
Climate,   Comanches,
Clouds,   Currents, Ocean,
Cheyennes,   Dakota Indians,
and numerous articles on American Indians and European biography.

Prof. George S. Morris, Johns Hopkins University, Baltimore.
Causation,   Consciousness,
Conception,
and other philosophical articles.

Rev. R. Heber Newton, D. D., New York.
Co-operation.

W. L. Nicholson, Washington, D. C.
Chesapeake Bay.

LIST OF CONTRIBUTORS.

Rev. JOSEPH V. O'CONNOR, D. D., Philadelphia.
Capuchins.

J. RODMAN PAUL, Esq., Philadelphia.
County.

*S. AUSTEN PEARCE, Mus. D., New York.
Catalani, Angelica,　　Costa, Sir Michael,
Chopin, François Frederic,　Curwen, John,
and other articles on music and musicians.

GEORGE PELLEW, Boston.
Browning, Robert.

THOMAS S. PERRY, Boston, author of *English Literature of the Eighteenth Century.*
"George Eliot."

EDWARD F. PUGH, Philadelphia.
Courts of Admiralty.

J. M. QUINN, Bismarck, Dakota.
Dakota.

C. V. RILEY, Ph. D., Entomologist U. S. Agricultural Department, Washington.
Codling Moth,　　Cotton Worm,
Colorado Potato Beetle,　Curculio, Plum.

ROBERT B. ROOSEVELT, New York.
Cookery, American.

Dr. J. T. ROTHROCK, Professor of Botany, University of Pennsylvania.
Cereals.

GEORGE W. RUSSELL, Philadelphia.
Clocks.

*S. P. SADTLER, Professor of Chemistry, University of Pennsylvania.
Chemical Analysis,
and articles on chemical subjects.

F. B. SANBORN, Concord, Mass., Secretary of the American Social Science Association.
Channing, William Ellery,　Concord, Mass,
Channing, William Henry,　Coroner.

EDWIN F. SCHIVELY, Esq., Philadelphia.
Charter,　　By-Laws,
Corporation (in Law),
and other legal articles.

Rev. J. B. SCOULLER, D. D., Newville, Pa.
Cuthbertson, John.

F. LAMSON SCRIBNER, University of Tennessee.
Cereals (under Agriculture).

MONSIGNOR ROBERT SETON, D. D., LL. D., Jersey City, N. J.
Charity, Sisters of, in the U. S.,　Encyclical,
Coadjutor,
and other ecclesiastical articles.

P. W. SHEAFER, C. E., Pottsville, Pa.
Coal.

ALFRED B. SHEPPARSON, New York.
Cotton Manufacture in the United States.

R. MEADE SMITH, M. D., Philadelphia.
Circulation.

*A. P. SPRAGUE, Esq., New York.
Code,　　Consuls,
Contraband of War,
and other articles on international law.

ADOLPH STRAUCH (since deceased), Cincinnati
Cemeteries.

Mrs. MARGARET F. SULLIVAN, Chicago.
Darwin, Charles Robert,
and other biographical articles.

*Prof. LEWIS SWIFT, Warner Observatory Rochester, N. Y.
Chronograph,　　Comet,
Clark, Alvan,
and other astronomical articles.

LINDSAY SWIFT, Boston.
Carlyle, Thomas.

CYRUS THOMAS, Washington, D. C.
Chinch Bug.

*Prof. ROBERT ELLIS THOMPSON, Ph. D., University of Pennsylvania.
China,　　Colwell, Stephen,
Circassia,　　Communism,
and other articles in biography, history, political economy, etc.

Rev. CHARLES F. THWING, Cambridge, Mass.
Colleges in America,　Common Schools.

Prof. ROBERT H. THURSTON, Stevens Institute, Hoboken, N. J.
Cotton Seed Products.

O. H. TITTMANN, Washington, D. C.
Coast and Geodetic Survey.

JAMES TYSON, M. D., University of Pennsylvania.
Cold.

*SAMUEL WAGNER, Esq., Philadelphia.
Check,　　Contract,
and other legal articles.

HENRY GALBRAITH WARD, Esq., New York.
Charter Party,　　Collision,
and other articles on maritime law.

WILLIAM B. WEEDEN, Providence, R. I., author of *The Social Law of Labor.*
Capital,　　Corporation.

J. WILLIAM WHITE, M. D., University of Pennsylvania.
Concussion.

XENOPHON A. WILLARD, Little Falls, N. Y.
Dairy Products.

F. HOWARD WILLIAMS, Philadelphia.
Clarke, John S.

Prof. ALEXANDER WINCHELL, University of Michigan.
Darwinism.

H. C. WOOD, M. D., University of Pennsylvania.
Cathartics,　　Cinchona.

Col. CARROLL D. WRIGHT, U. S. Commissioner of Labor.
Cotton Manufacture,　Factory.

SUPPLEMENT TO ENCYCLOPÆDIA BRITANNICA.

DEACONESSES.

DEACONESSES, an order of women in the early Church corresponding to that of deacons. (See vol. VII. p. 8 Am. ed. (p. 1 Edin. ed.).) In the West the office was shorn of its clerical character in the fifth century, but was continued in the Eastern Church down to the twelfth or thirteenth. During the Middle Ages the duties appertaining to the office, such as caring for the poor, nursing, teaching, etc., were performed by the nuns and Sisters of Charity. In the revival within the present century which we propose to consider in connection with the Lutheran Church, the Church of England, and the Episcopal Church in this country, the office is not strictly identical with that in the primitive Church. In the latter it was a regular standing office in every Christian congregation, but in modern times it has assumed the form of associations. In Germany and France these associations, as a rule, have borne the name of deaconesses, but in England and America that of sisterhoods. The two act in a like capacity as servants of the Church, but differ somewhat in point of organization, government, and discipline. Speaking in a general way, a band of deaconesses is more flexible and simple, and is directly responsible to the pastor or bishop. A sisterhood, on the other hand, is more highly organized and rather assumes the form of an autonomy.

A representative and by far the largest deaconess institution connected with the Lutheran Church is that at Kaiserswerth on the Rhine, founded by the Rev. Theodore Fliedner. After making himself familiar with religious and charitable institutions by travelling in England and Holland, he opened an asylum for discharged female prisoners in 1833. This was the beginning of a group of institutions which came to include a deaconess or mother-house, where the sisters live, a hospital, a deaconess school, to which girls who wish to become deaconesses are received after confirmation, an infant school, an orphan asylum for girls, an asylum for fallen women, a seminary for teachers, a house of rest for infirm and sick sisters, together with out-stations in all parts of the world.

In 1836 the deaconess house was opened without deaconesses, a single sister, however, offering herself the same year. Other aspirants to the office soon followed, and such were the additions that in 1867 some five hundred sisters belonged to the institution. Of these, over three hundred were deaconesses and the others probationers. Of the whole number, about ninety were employed as teaching sisters, and the rest as nursing sisters. As a rule, the seminary course of training for the teaching office in the infant school embraces one year; for the office of elementary teaching, two years; for that of teaching in the higher girls' school, three years. In thirty years over eleven hundred pupils had been instructed, and the demand was three times greater than the supply. The course of probation and instruction for the office of nursing sisters embraced from six to twelve months, and, if required, two or three years. For admission to the office of deaconess in either department certain conditions are required in the way of Christian character and experience, mental qualifications, bodily health, etc., together with such special gifts and dispositions as the office may require. Probationers who have proven acceptable must pledge themselves to continue in the office at least five years. They are also required to declare before admission that they intend to adopt the office for life. The consecration service, which was drawn up by Pastor Fliedner, consists of a short discourse on the history and duties of the office, a promise to faithfully fulfil its requirements, which is confirmed by giving the right hand, a form of benediction by the pastor, the candidates kneeling, a prayer in their behalf by the pastor and congregation, a short exhortation, concluding with the Lord's Supper, in which the newly-consecrated members partake. After the consecration they are required to sign the rule and give a pledge to keep it faithfully, to maintain a Christian and dignified demeanor, to avoid making or continuing any intimate acquaintance with men or contracting other earthly ties, not to indulge in unbecoming and even unnecessary correspondence, and to devote themselves with all their powers exclusively to their office.

The Rhenish Westphalian Society, so called, for the training and employment of evangelical deaconesses, was formally recognized, and the laws fixing its constitution approved, by the king of Prussia in 1846. It is governed by a council consisting of members of the Lutheran or Evangelical Church, the internal management of the institution, however, being in the hands of an inspector and superintendent or mother, as the latter is called. According to the report of the triennial conference held at Kaiserswerth in 1868, institutions, mostly in association with the mother-house, had been opened at Paris in 1841; at Strasburg and Echallens in French Switzerland in 1842; at Dresden and Utrecht in 1844; at Bethanie, in Berlin, in 1847; at Pittsburg, America, in 1849; at Bethanie in Breslau and Königsberg, in Prussia, in 1850; at Stettin, Ludwigslust, Stockholm, and Carlsruhe in 1851; at Riehen, near Basle, in 1852; at Neuendettelsau and Stuttgart in 1854; at Augsburg in 1856; at Halle in 1857; at Darmstadt and Zurich in 1858; at Hamburg, Berne, and Hanover in 1859; in London in 1861; and at Copenhagen and Dantzic in 1862. In addition to these and several others, four institutions have been opened in Asia, and one each in Jerusalem and Africa. The number of mother-houses in 1868 was 42, and the total number of deaconesses, 2106. Of these, more than a fourth part belonged to the institution at Kaiserswerth. The number of establishments of various kinds, including mother-houses, with which the deaconesses were connected, amounted to 566. The important institution at Neuendettelsau, Bavaria, founded by Father Löhe, includes two girls' reformatories, a Magdalen institution, a house for incurables, the largest asylum for idiots in Bavaria, and in the village a district hospital and mission-house. Self-abnegation is practised by the sisters as a rule of life.

In addition to thirty or forty sisterhoods connected with the Church of England, centres of Church deaconess work now exist at Maidstone, Chester, Bedford, Salisbury, Farnham, and Hackney. Representative of the work is the London Diocesan Deaconess Institution, opened in Burton Crescent in 1861, and removed twelve years later to Westbourne Park. The object of the institution, as stated in its last annual report, is to train educated women to serve as deaconesses, with commission from the bishop, in the Church of England. In the various departments of labor the deaconesses are assisted by churchwomen and communicants, who act as associates. As many of the deaconesses as can possibly be spared work with success and favor in seven or eight parishes, while other unattached members of the order, trained in the institution, are employed in five or six parishes elsewhere. The institution is under the immediate control of the bishop of London, and grants are made towards the support of deaconesses by the Bishop of London's Fund. The movement is warmly advocated by the archbishop of Canterbury and the bishops of London, Durham, Winchester, Salisbury, Peterborough, and Bedford. Some ten years since a conference of bishops was held in London, when general principles and proposed rules were set forth and concurred in by which the various deaconess institutions should be guided.

A much larger and very successful institution, but not so strictly under episcopal control, is the Deaconess Home at Mildmay Park, organized in 1860, and now under the management of Mrs. Pennefather. Connected with the institution is the deaconess house, six houses for probationers, a nursing home, cottage hospital, invalids' home, orphanage, invalids' kitchen, and various societies and missions. In 1873, from one hundred and fifty to two hundred women had been trained in the institution for various spheres of mission work in England, Scotland and Ireland, as also in India, China, and Japan. In 1880 the home had one hundred and fifty deaconesses and fifty nurses under training. In London the sisters do work among the most degraded classes in the way of house visitation, supplying dinners, nursing, teaching, etc. Bodily and spiritual wants are equally cared for. In its general spirit the Mildmay institution follows the system observed at Kaiserswerth, but admits of great freedom and simplicity. No vow is required but that of punctuality. The sum annually required to carry on the work is from $111,000 to $120,000, of which about $60,000 are received in voluntary gifts from the "Christian Church."

Of deaconess institutions connected with the Protestant Episcopal Church in the United States there are three, together with nine or ten sisterhoods. Of the former, by far the largest is the order of deaconesses for the diocese of Long Island, established in 1872. It now numbers seventeen deaconesses and one associate, all of whom are under the immediate direction of the bishop. The community has charge of the Church Charity Foundation in Brooklyn, an institution which includes a hospital, an orphanage, and a home for the aged. It also has charge of St. Catharine's Hall, a boarding and day school for girls, the Homœopathic Hospital, Brooklyn, while a number of sisters are "loaned" to carry on a home and orphanage in Buffalo, N. Y. Other sisters do work under the missionary committee of the diocese of Long Island, while others again do missionary work in several Brooklyn parishes under the direction of their rectors. At the end of a year probationers, if they so desire and are approved of, are received into full fellowship. While perpetual vows are not required, there is an understanding that the work is to be for life. The other institutions are the order of deaconesses for the diocese of Maryland, having its head-quarters at Baltimore, and a similar order in the diocese of Alabama, which was organized at Mobile in 1864. In all these institutions, as at Kaiserswerth and in connection with the English Church, probationers are consecrated to the office according to a prescribed form which answers as a kind of ordination. (L. M. D.)

DEADWOOD, the county-seat of Lawrence co., Dakota, is among the Black Hills, 250 miles S.W. of Bismarck, and 250 miles N.N.E. of Cheyenne, Wyoming. It has a fine court-house, 8 hotels, 2 national banks, 2 daily and 2 weekly newspapers, 4 churches, and 3 schools. Gold and silver were discovered in this vicinity in 1874, and soon large numbers of adventurers moved to Deadwood. It was settled in 1876, and incorporated in 1881. It has grown rapidly, and is the chief city of the Black Hills. Its property is valued at $1,200,000, and it is free of debt. It has water-works, but no manufactures of importance. Population, 3777.

DEAF-MUTES, EDUCATION OF. The first attempt, of which any record now appears, to teach the deaf in America, was made by Rev. John Stanford, about the year 1810. He was then acting as chaplain to the almshouse of the city of New York, and found in that establishment several deaf-mute children, whom he undertook to teach by causing them to write the names of familiar objects on slates. Finding the work of imparting a knowledge of language to the deaf and dumb more difficult than he had expected, demanding more time than he could afford, he was compelled to relinquish his undertaking. His interest, however, in the education of the deaf continued, and he was a few years later one of the founders of the New York Institution for the Instruction of the Deaf and Dumb.

See Vol. VII. p. 5 Am. ed. (p. 3 Edin. ed.).

The first effort to teach deaf-mutes in the United States in any systematic manner was made in Goochland co., Va., in 1812, in the family of Col. William Bolling, who had three deaf children, and whose brother and sister had been taught some years before in Edinburgh, in the school established by Thomas Braidwood, and carried on there by the Braidwood family. John Braidwood, a grandson of Thomas, came to

America in 1812, with the design of establishing an institution for the instruction of the deaf on a large scale. Col. Bolling invited young Braidwood to take charge of the training of his three children, and later advanced funds to aid in the organization of a permanent school in Baltimore. But Braidwood, though possessed of skill and ability as a teacher, squandered the funds intrusted to him in an irregular manner of life. He was twice assisted by Col. Bolling in efforts to set up a private school in Virginia; he made a feeble attempt at carrying on a school in New York city, and finally died a victim to intemperance.

The establishment of the first actual school for the deaf in America grew out of the interest manifested by the late Rev. Thomas H. Gallaudet, LL.D., of Hartford, Conn., in a deaf-mute daughter of Dr. Mason F. Cogswell, of that city, in 1814. Dr. Gallaudet had just graduated from the Andover Theological Seminary, and was expecting to enter the Congregational ministry. Having some months of leisure during the winter of 1814-15, he devoted considerable time to the instruction of the child, Alice Cogswell, and succeeded in imparting to her a knowledge of many simple words and sentences. This success led her father, Dr. M. F. Cogswell, to entertain the idea of the establishment of a school for the deaf in his own town, where his child, with others similarly afflicted, might be educated. A number of gentlemen met at Dr. Cogswell's house, March 13, 1815, to consider the suggestion, and these gentlemen appointed Dr. Cogswell and Mr. Ward Woodbridge a committee to raise funds to defray the expense of sending a suitable person to Europe for the purpose of acquiring the art of teaching deaf-mutes. Mr. Woodbridge, heading the list with a liberal subscription, secured the pledge of a sufficient sum in a single day. Dr. Gallaudet was urged to undertake the labor of establishing the proposed institution, and after some hesitation consented to do so. He sailed for Europe on the 25th of April, 1815, was unsuccessful in his efforts to obtain the necessary training in Great Britain, but was cordially received by the Abbé Sicard, the Director of the Institution for Deaf-mutes in Paris. After acquainting himself with the method pursued by that eminent teacher Dr. Gallaudet returned to Hartford in August, 1816.

He devoted his time during the following autumn and winter to the collection of funds for the new institution, and the school was opened April 15, 1817, in Hartford, with about twenty pupils. The first grant of public funds in behalf of the education of the deaf in this country was an appropriation made in October, 1816, by the legislature of Connecticut, of $5000 in aid of the new institution. During the winter of 1818-19 the Congress of the United States made a grant of a township of land (more than 23,000 acres) to the institution. This was sold to good advantage, yielding a fund of more than $300,000, the income from which has accrued to the benefit, mainly, of the New England States, by diminishing the *per capita* cost of educating the deaf of that section of the country. The institution thus established remained under the management of Dr. Gallaudet fourteen years. It has been sustained in a course of unbroken prosperity, and holds a place at the present time of highest rank among the local schools of the country. More than 2000 children have been educated to lives of usefulness within its walls, many of its teachers have been called upon to organize and take charge of schools in various parts of the country, many persons have come to it to fit themselves to become teachers of the deaf, and this now venerable institution is justly looked up to and honored as the *mother-school* of the fifty-five in which the education of the deaf is provided for in the United States at the present time.

The second school for the education of the deaf in America was opened in New York city, in May, 1818. The suggestion for its establishment came from the unsuccessful effort of John Braidwood, already referred to, in which the interest of Dr. Samuel Akerly was excited. With the co-operation of Dr. Samuel L. Mitchell, a society was organized with the distinguished De Witt Clinton at its head, which was incorporated by the legislature of New York, April 15, 1817, under the name of the New York Institution for the Instruction of the Deaf and Dumb.

The means for the support of the institution were, at first, subscriptions and donations, with payments from such parents of pupils as had means. The city of New York soon provided for ten day-scholars, and the legislature of the State promptly followed, first with donations of money, but soon (in 1821) with a permanent and specific provision for thirty-two State pupils. The liberality of the legislature has continued without interruption, increasing from year to year, and now embraces six institutions located within the limits of the State, in which more than 1200 children are receiving education.

The New York institution was for several years after its opening under the charge of Dr. Akerly. In 1821 Mr. Horace Loofborrow became the principal teacher and occupied that position for ten years.

The work of the institution had many difficulties and drawbacks, arising in part from the lack of well-qualified and competent teachers, and from the irregular attendance of pupils, a large proportion of whom were day-scholars. But in 1831 the institution made a new departure by securing the services of the late Harvey P. Peet, LL.D., as principal, in which office were united the duties previously delegated to the superintendent and the principal teacher.

Dr. Peet had been for seven years connected with the institution at Hartford, in the capacity of steward, and possessed qualifications, both natural and acquired, which well fitted him to assume the direction of such an establishment. As an assistant of Dr. Gallaudet, at Hartford, he had come to understand that the task of teaching the deaf demanded for its successful performance persons of exceptional ability and zeal. And the excellent results that followed his administration were owing in a large degree to his selection of his assistants. Among them were a number of young men of great talent, several of whom, after devoting years to teaching the deaf, left the profession to become distinguished in science, literature, and the work of general education.

The institution remained under the able and energetic control of Dr. Peet for nearly thirty-six years, and at the time of his resignation in 1867 the institution had educated nearly 2000 children. Under the management of Dr. Isaac Lewis Peet, who succeeded his father in the office of principal, the New York institution has held its place in public esteem, and for many years enjoyed the distinction of being the largest school for the deaf in the world. Within a short time, however, the numbers of the Illinois institution have exceeded those of the New York, the latter recording 481 as present in December, 1881, while the former reported 508.

Massachusetts was the next State to provide for the

education of the deaf at public expense; making an appropriation, in 1819, for the support of twenty beneficiaries in the school at Hartford. Pennsylvania followed the example of her eastern sisters in 1820. The Board of Directors of the Pennsylvania Institution for the Deaf and Dumb was organized April 20, 1820, under the presidency of the Right Rev. William White, D. D. Some months previously Mr. David G. Seixas had opened a private day-school for the deaf, in his own house in Philadelphia. Among his first pupils was John Carlin, who has attained distinction as an artist, and as the only congenital deaf-mute who has ever succeeded in composing poetry. This school was adopted by the organization just alluded to. Mr. Seixas was appointed principal; funds were freely advanced by benevolent persons in Philadelphia, and the infant institution well provided for during the summer, fall, and winter of 1820–21. In February, 1821, the legislature of Pennsylvania passed an act incorporating the institution, and authorized the education of fifty children at the expense of the State.

Mr. Seixas, after filling the office of principal for eighteen months, was succeeded temporarily by Mr. Laurent Clerc, the distinguished deaf-mute pupil of Sicard, who accompanied Dr. Gallaudet on his return from France, and rendered valuable services for many years as a teacher in the institution at Hartford. Mr. Clerc, after remaining seven months in Philadelphia, systematizing the work and methods of the school, returned to his labors at Hartford, and was succeeded by Mr. Lewis Weld, who had acquired the art of teaching the deaf as an assistant of Dr. Gallaudet at Hartford. Under the management of Mr. Weld, which continued until 1830, when he was called to succeed Dr. Gallaudet as principal of the Hartford school, the institution became well established. Its usefulness has increased during the years of its existence, and it now has accommodations for more than 300 pupils.

The State of New Hampshire made provision in 1821 for the education of ten deaf-mutes in the Hartford institution; and in the same year the legislature of New Jersey passed an act making an annual appropriation for the education of the deaf and dumb of the State "in some suitable and convenient institution." Under the provisions of this law the deaf of New Jersey have been educated at New York and Philadelphia up to the present time.

In Kentucky the fourth school was established in 1823. The legislature passed an act, Dec. 7, 1822, establishing a school for deaf-mutes, and providing for its support. The passage of this act was mainly due to the efforts of Gen. Elias Barbee. The school was opened for pupils at Danville, April 27, 1823, and placed in charge of Rev. John R. Kerr, a gentleman of good education, but without experience in teaching the deaf. Two deaf-mutes, young men, were successively employed as teachers, but were found to be incompetent. The board of directors, finding it impossible to secure the services of an experienced instructor of deaf-mutes, engaged John A. Jacobs, a young man of unusual ability, who was then pursuing his studies at Centre College, Danville, Ky. Mr. Jacobs went to Hartford to seek the aid of Dr. Gallaudet and his assistants, in acquiring the art of teaching the deaf. He remained an inmate of the Hartford institution for eighteen months, and then, before he had completed his twentieth year, returned to Kentucky to assume the direction of the school at Danville. He conducted the affairs of the Kentucky institution with marked ability and success for a period of forty-four years.

In this connection we take occasion to condemn the mistake of placing at the head of institutions for the deaf, men without previous knowledge of the art of teaching that class of persons. No censure can be too severe on such action, at once seriously injurious to the interests of pupils, and insulting to the body of teachers employed in the various institutions, among whom may be found men fitted by experience and natural ability to assume the direction of an institution. If, indeed, it prove a matter of difficulty to secure the services of such a man, then let the wise example of the directors of the Kentucky institution be followed, and the crime avoided of appointing, for political or personal considerations, inexperienced men to positions which can only be properly filled by specialists.

Maine and Vermont were the next States to provide for the education of the deaf, each making appropriations in 1825, to maintain beneficiaries at the Hartford institution. During the same year a school for the deaf was opened in Canajoharie, N. Y., the establishment of which was authorized by an act of the legislature, passed in 1822. Mr. Wm. Reid, a graduate of Union College, spent some time at the New York institution in 1825, preparing himself to be principal of this school, and assumed the direction of it at its opening. This institution was kept up until the year 1836, when it was discontinued and its pupils, together with Mr. Oran W. Morris, were transferred to the New York institution, Mr. Morris becoming an instructor therein. Mr. Levi S. Backus, one of the earliest pupils of the Hartford institution, was an instructor in this school, and, when it was closed, Mr. Backus became the editor of *The Radii*, a weekly newspaper published at Fort Plain, N. Y., and for many years was the only deaf-mute editor in the world.

In December, 1825, an act was passed by the legislature of New Jersey to "incorporate and endow the New Jersey Institution for the Deaf and Dumb," but the institution was never organized, the provision by the State, previously made for maintaining beneficiaries in the New York and Philadelphia schools, being deemed adequate to the wants of the deaf of New Jersey. In 1882, however, measures were inaugurated for the establishment of a school for the deaf in New Jersey, which will probably prove successful.

In May, 1827, a school for the deaf was opened at Tallmadge, Summit co., Ohio, where in the family of Mr. Justus Bradley were three deaf-mute girls. These with eight other deaf-mutes were placed under the instruction of Mr. C. Smith, a deaf-mute, who had been for six years a pupil in the Hartford institution. The school was sustained by private charity, with the exception of $100 granted by the legislature of Ohio in 1828. An unsuccessful effort had been made in Ohio to provide for the education of the deaf by citizens of Cincinnati in 1821, who went so far as to send the Rev. James Chute to Hartford to acquire the art of teaching from Dr. Gallaudet.

This enterprise was opposed in the legislature mainly on account of the proposed location of the school, which was not a central one. In January, 1827, the legislature of Ohio passed an act providing for the establishment of an institution for the deaf. The organization of the board of directors was effected in July following. ~~~~~~~~~~~ Hoge, D.D., as president. In Ma~~~~~~~~~ atio N. Hubbell, who had been ~~~~~~~~~~~ to

Hartford to secure a knowledge of the art of teaching the deaf, remaining there about a year and a half. In January, 1829, the legislature located the institution at Columbus, and it was opened for pupils in October of that year. This school has continued in successful operation, and now stands third in the country in point of numbers. Mr. Hubbell, the first principal, presided over the institution with honor and success for twenty-four years, when he voluntarily retired.

In 1835 the States of South Carolina and Georgia made provision for the maintenance of beneficiaries at the Hartford institution, continuing to send pupils thither until schools were organized within their own limits; the latter State establishing an institution in 1846, and the former in 1849.

In 1839 an institution for the education, under the same roof, of the two classes, the deaf and the blind, was opened at Staunton, Va., receiving the bounty of the State from the outset. The department for deaf-mutes was placed under the charge of Rev. Joseph D. Tyler, who had been for seven years an instructor in the Hartford institution. Mr. Tyler's able management, which continued until his death, in 1851, did much to settle the institution on firm foundations. During the civil war its operations were restricted by lack of funds, and by the diversion of its buildings to the uses of a military hospital.

In the year 1842 a deaf-mute young man, who had been a pupil in the school at New York, collected a half dozen deaf-mutes in Parke co., Indiana, and began teaching them. Not being well fitted for the work, his school was continued only a year. Attention was, however, directed by his undertaking to the importance of deaf-mute education in Indiana, and the legislature voted him $200 as a compensation for his services.

In 1843 a law was enacted with great unanimity, as a preliminary measure, by which a tax was levied of two mills on each $100, for the purpose of supporting an institution for the education of the deaf. In May of that year Mr. William Willard, a well-educated deaf-mute, who had been an instructor for twelve years in the school at Columbus, visited Indianapolis and interested himself in the organization of the new institution. With the indorsement of prominent citizens of the State Mr. Willard spent the summer in travelling over the State in search of pupils, and in October a school was opened under his direction with 16 pupils. An act incorporating the new institution was passed Jan. 15, 1844, and a board of directors was organized. Mr. Willard's school was adopted by the board, and he remained in charge a second year, when Mr. James S. Brown, who had been for four years an instructor in the Ohio institution, was placed at the head of the institution. Mr. Willard continued to teach for many years. Under Mr. Brown's management the institution enjoyed a healthy and rapid development. Liberal appropriations were judiciously expended under his direction, and by the end of 1851 commodious buildings, capable of accommodating 200 pupils, were completed.

In 1845 Rhode Island made provision for the education of her deaf-mutes in the Hartford institution.

The Tennessee school for the deaf and dumb was incorporated in the winter of 1843–4. Rev. R. B. McMullen was the first president of the board of trustees. The organization of the institution was due to the strong rivalry then existing between Middle and East Tennessee. A bill was proposed to the legislature by a member from Middle Tennessee for the establishment of an institution for the blind at Nashville, when Gen. Cocke, a prominent member from East Tennessee, immediately arose and proposed an amendment providing for a school for the deaf, to be located at Knoxville. Rev. Thomas MacIntire, Ph. D., for four years previously an instructor in the Ohio institution, was appointed principal, Jan. 1, 1845, and the school was opened at Knoxville April 14, but no pupil applied for admission. This was partly owing to the fact that payment for board and tuition was expected, but mainly to an indisposition on the part of parents to allow their deaf children to leave home. After waiting a month, without obtaining pupils, the board determined to issue new circulars offering free board and tuition to a limited number. This brought six pupils, whose instruction was commenced early in June. The number of pupils increased to ten, and the school was closed in February, 1846, for lack of funds. In the absence of funds from the State private benevolence was successfully appealed to, and during the summer of 1846 suitable grounds and buildings were secured, and the school was reopened with thirteen pupils. Circumstances led Dr. MacIntire, since become well known as the successful superintendent for many years of the Indiana institution, and later of the Michigan institution, to resign in August, 1850, after having done much to build up the school in Tennessee. This institution has passed through many vicissitudes, being suspended and much injured during the civil war; but it was reopened after the war, and has since received liberal aid from the State. It is now in a flourishing condition.

During the summer of 1843 Mr. William D. Cooke, then connected with the school at Staunton, Va., made a tour in North Carolina accompanied by a young deaf-mute, for the purpose of exciting an interest in the education of the deaf. He gave exhibitions of the manner of teaching, and urged in a number of public meetings the importance of providing for the instruction of the deaf. As a result of his efforts the legislature passed an act in January, 1845, establishing an institution and providing for its support. Mr. Cooke was appointed principal, and the school was opened May 1, 1845, with seven pupils, which number increased to seventeen before the close of the session. In April, 1848, the corner-stone of a permanent building was laid by the Masonic fraternity, and Dr. Peet, the principal of the New York institution, delivered an address. This institution was continued without interruption during the civil war, and is now in a flourishing condition.

The legislature of Illinois passed an act establishing an institution for the deaf Feb. 23, 1839, and appropriating one quarter per cent. of the interest upon the school, college, and seminary fund to the institution. The board of directors was organized under the presidency of Joseph Duncan, Esq., June 29, 1839, but owing to a variety of causes, especially the disturbance in the value of bank currency which was widespread at that period, the completion of the buildings of the institution was delayed until the autumn of 1845. The school was located at Jacksonville, and was opened for pupils Dec. 1, 1845. Mr. Thomas Officer, for five years previous an instructor in the Ohio institution, was appointed principal. In the first year the number of pupils was 9, and in the following year 14. Mr. Officer proved an eminently capable principal, and during the ten years he continued in charge of the institution its growth was rapid and healthy. At the time of his resignation in 1855 permanent buildings for the institution were completed, and the number of pupils had risen beyond 150. Philip G. Gillett, LL.D., was appointed principal of the institution in 1856, and is still in office. Dr. Gillett had been for four years an instructor in the Indiana institution. Under his very energetic and able management the Illinois institution has had a growth unparalleled in the history of schools for the deaf. Liberal appropriations from the State have provided for the improvement and enlargement of the buildings; the moneys granted have been so well expended that the school at Jacksonville is to-day probably superior in the convenience of its arrangements and appointments to any other establishment for the education of the deaf; and in the number of its pupils it leads the world, 508 being reported in December, 1881.

Of the institutions, the story of whose origin has now been briefly sketched, 10 are in full operation, and these 10 were established within 30 years from the time when Dr. Thomas H. Gallaudet began his pioneer work at Hartford.

During the 35 years which have followed the opening of the Illinois institution more than 50 schools for the deaf have been established in our country, and 45 of them are now in operation, as will appear from the tables.

Of these 50 schools 3 are deserving of particular notice for the reason that in connection with their development new and important features in deaf-mute education have been perfected.

In 1856 an adventurer from the city of New York brought with him to Washington, D. C., 5 little deaf-mute children whom he had gathered from the alms-houses and streets of the metropolis. With the aid of a number of benevolent citizens he succeeded in setting up a school and in collecting half a score of deaf and blind children belonging to the District of Columbia. Most prominent among the friends of the school was the Hon. Amos Kendall, who soon discovered that the would-be founder of the new institution was a man wholly unworthy of confidence. A little investigation showed that he had been maltreating the children under his care, and misusing the funds intrusted to his hands. Mr. Kendall preferred charges against him in the criminal court of the District, and was constituted by the court the legal guardian of the children brought from New York. The others having been removed from the school by their parents, Mr. Kendall took measures for the organization of an institution in due and proper form. An act of Congress was approved Feb. 16, 1857, incorporating the Columbia institution for the instruction of the deaf and dumb and the blind, naming a provisional board of directors, with Mr. Kendall as its president. In May of the same year the board appointed Edward M. Gallaudet and Mrs. Sophia Gallaudet, the youngest son and the widow of Dr. Gallaudet, of Hartford, as superintendent and matron of the new institution. Mr. Gallaudet had been for eighteen months an instructor in the Hartford school. On the 13th of June, in temporary buildings provided by the liberality of Mr. Kendall, the school was opened with five pupils. In the spring of 1859 Mr. Kendall added to his former benefactions by erecting a substantial brick structure, and deeding this, together with two acres of ground, to the institution. The total value of his gifts to the institution amounted to about $13,000. In 1862 Congress appropriated $9,000 for the enlargement of buildings, and by this act enabled the institution to provide fully for the education of the deaf and blind of the district.

In their report for 1862 the directors laid before Congress a proposal for the enlargement of the scope of the institution by the establishment of a collegiate department, which might afford the deaf of the country an opportunity to engage in the higher courses of study open to other youth in colleges. The desirableness of providing a college for the deaf had been urged for several years by prominent instructors, foremost among whom was the Rev. Wm. W. Turner, for many years an instructor in the Hartford institution, and for ten years its principal. Congress acted favorably on the suggestion of the directors of the Columbia institution, and in 1864 passed an act authorizing the board to confer collegiate degrees. An addition of $3100 was made to the annual grant of Congress for the support of the institution, and the sum of $26,000 was appropriated to enlarge the grounds and buildings.

The collegiate department, under the name of the *National Deaf-Mute College*, was publicly inaugurated June 28, 1864—the honorary degree of Master of Arts being conferred on John Carlin, to whom reference has been made. Mr. Carlin delivered an oration on this occasion, as did also the venerable and distinguished deaf-mute, Laurent Clerc, M. A., who had assisted the elder Dr. Gallaudet in organizing the Hartford school. At the same time Edward M. Gallaudet, who had filled the office of superintendent of the institution from its opening in 1857, was installed as president of the corporation and of the board of directors.

The development of the College for the Deaf, still the only one in the world, has been most gratifying. Opening with 7 students in September, 1864, it had during the year last reported 62, representing 26 States and the Federal district. More than 300 young men have availed themselves of its advantages, leaving its walls to enter upon lives of usefulness as teachers, editors, lawyers, farmers, business men, specialists in science, and officials in government departments. Private benevolence in the cities of Washington, Philadelphia, Boston, and Hartford, Conn., responded liberally to appeals in behalf of the college in its early days, upwards of $15,000 having been contributed in these cities by individuals. Congress has supplemented these private benefactions by liberal appropriations for buildings and grounds, besides granting an annual sum for the payment of the salaries of the professors and for the assistance of students unable to meet their own expenses. An able faculty of seven professors affords the students an opportunity of pursuing study in the several courses usually open in colleges. The primary department of the Columbia institution has flourished, although its numbers are naturally small.

The department for the blind, organized when the institution was opened in 1857, and never containing more than ten pupils, was discontinued in 1865, Congress making provision for the education of the blind of the District in the Maryland institution at Baltimore.

During the first half century of deaf-mute education the method pursued was, with very inconsiderable exceptions, that derived by the elder Dr. Gallaudet from the Abbé Sicard in Paris. This was the manual which is well described by Prof. E. A. Fay as "The course of instruction which employs the sign-language, the manual alphabet, and writing as the chief means in the education of the deaf, and has facility in the comprehension and use of written language as the principal object. The degree of relative importance given to these three means varies in different schools, but it is a difference only of degree, and the end aimed at is the same in all. If the pupils have some power of speech before coming to school, or if they possess a considerable degree of hearing, their teachers usually try to improve their utterance by practice; but no special teachers are employed for this purpose, and comparatively little attention is given to articulation."

Prior to the year 1867 the importance and feasibility of teaching deaf-mutes to speak orally had been urged by several American writers, notably by Horace Mann, who made a tour of Europe in 1843, when he visited some of the German schools for the deaf, in which articulation was the prominent feature. Mr. Mann urged the superiority of the German method over that pursued in America. His report excited so much interest that the Hartford and New York schools sent gentlemen abroad, who visited many schools where the oral method was practised. They reported that the manual method produced better results than the oral. Some little effort was, however, made to teach articulation to semi-mute and semi-deaf pupils; but this was not long continued. Although the suggestions of Horace Mann led to no immediate practical result, they were not forgotten. Dr. Samuel G. Howe, the distinguished teacher of the blind (still better known as the instructor of the blind deaf-mutes Laura Bridgman and Oliver Caswell), was Mann's travelling companion in Europe in 1843, and shared his views as to the importance of oral teaching for the deaf. In 1864, seconded by Mr. Gardiner Green Hubbard, of Cambridge, one of whose children was deaf, by Frank B. Sanborn and others, Dr. Howe made an effort to secure the incorporation of an oral school for the deaf in Massachusetts. This was successfully opposed by the friends of the Hartford school, in which the beneficiaries of Massachusetts were then educated, on the ground that for the mass of deaf-mutes, if one method were to be chosen to the exclusion of the other, which was what the oralists urged, the manual method would accomplish the most beneficial results. The controversy between these two parties was brought to an end, as many a similar struggle has been, by the discovery that each was demanding too much, and that a *juste milieu* of practicability could be found. In the autumn of 1864 Miss Harriet B. Rogers, a sister of the lady who, under Dr. Howe's direction, taught Laura Bridgman and Oliver Caswell, undertook to teach a deaf-mute child to speak. Meeting with encouraging success, she advertised in November, 1865, for other pupils, limiting the number to seven. In June, 1866, she opened her school at Chelmsford, Mass., with five scholars. In 1866 and 1867 the board of State charities, of which Dr. Howe was chairman, and F. B. Sanborn secretary, continued to press the importance of oral teaching for the deaf upon the attention of the legislature of Massachusetts. At this juncture John Clarke, Esq., of Northampton, Mass., proposed to contribute towards the endowment of a school for deaf-mutes in Massachusetts. His generous offer was communicated to the legislature by Gov. Bullock in January, 1867. In June following the Clarke Institution for the Instruction of Deaf-Mutes, at Northampton, was incorporated, and organized on the 15th of July with G. G. Hubbard as president. Miss Rogers, of Chelmsford, accepted an invitation to take charge of the new institution, and, having transferred her pupils to Northampton, the Clarke Institution was formally opened Oct. 1, and at the date of the first annual report—Jan. 21, 1868—had 20 pupils. The purpose, as to method and scope, as to the kind of pupils desired, of the institution, was made clear in the first report: "The Clarke Institution differs from all other American institutions [for the deaf] in this, that it receives pupils at as early an age as they are admitted in our common schools, and in teaching by articulation and lip-reading only." "This institution is especially adapted for the education of the semi-deaf and semi-mute pupils, but others may be admitted."

The success of the Clarke Institution has been marked in every particular. Never having claimed to be able to teach *all* deaf-mutes to speak and read from the lips, it has developed the speech of the semi-deaf and the semi-mute, besides imparting the power of speech to many congenital deaf-mutes in a very satisfactory manner. The endowment of the school by Mr. Clarke was munificent, and in 1877 the value of its real and personal estate was reported to be over $350,000. The number of its pupils in December, 1881, was 88.

In the city of New York during the year 1866 Mr. Bernhard Engelsmann, who had had several years' experience as an instructor in the Hebrew (oral) school for the deaf in Vienna, undertook to instruct a few deaf-mute children by the German or oral method. The parents of these children, together with a number of prominent Hebrew gentlemen of the city, met on Feb. 27, 1867, at the residence of Mr. Isaac Rosenfeld with the purpose of extending the advantages of Mr. Engelsmann's school to the children of parents who might be unable to pay the necessary expenses. So promptly were measures taken for the raising of funds that Mr. Engelsmann's school, under a formal organization, was opened with ten pupils on March 1, 1867, at No. 134 West Twenty-seventh street, antedating the opening of the Clarke institution by exactly seven months. The school, which was sustained wholly by private subscriptions and the payment of tuition by parents until 1870, was not incorporated, however, until Jan. 11, 1869. In 1870 the legislature of New York provided for the education of beneficiaries in the institution on the same terms and conditions as those prescribed for the old New York institution, making also a special appropriation to enable the institution to prepare for the reception of State and county pupils. In 1871 another special appropriation, this time of $25,000, was made by the legislature. Mr. Engelsmann was succeeded in 1869 by Mr. F. A. Rising, and he in 1873 by Mr. D. Greenberger, who, like Mr. Engelsmann, had been a teacher in the Hebrew School for the Deaf at Vienna.

The growth of the institution has been rapid and healthy. The number of pupils reported as present in December, 1881, was 137. The permanent buildings of the institution, erected at a cost of $134,904.53, on Lexington Avenue between Sixty-seventh and Sixty-eighth Streets, were formally dedicated Nov. 29, 1881.

Still a third event, which gave an added and most influential impetus to the movement in favor of oral teaching, occurred during the year 1867. The directors of the Columbia institution at Washington, having their attention called to the movements on foot in Massachusetts, in behalf of the oral method, and the persistent assertions there made that the oral method was to be preferred to the manual, which claims were stoutly disputed by the authorities of the Hartford institution, decided to send their president, Edward M. Gallaudet, LL. D., to Europe, for the purpose of making a thorough examination of all the methods pursued in that part of the world. President Gallaudet spent six months abroad and visited about forty institutions, including in his tour all the countries of Europe except Spain, Portugal, Greece, and Turkey.

In his report to the board of directors, Oct. 23, 1867, President Gallaudet took very different ground with reference to the oral method from that maintained by the gentlemen who had been sent out by the New York and Hartford schools some twenty years before. Giving the preference, as his father did, to the manual method, if the whole body of the deaf are to be restricted to one kind of instruction, he admitted the practicability of teaching a large proportion of the deaf and dumb to speak and to read from the lips, and advocated the introduction of articulation as a branch of instruction in all the schools of this country. Influenced by the recommendations of President Gallaudet, the directors of the Washington institution authorized the calling together of a conference of the principals of all the American schools for the deaf to be held at Washington in the spring of 1868. In response to this invitation the principals of fifteen institutions out of the twenty-five then existing in the country, together with one vice-principal and two ex-principals (Drs. Peet and Turner), met on May 12, 1868, and remained in session five days. Many subjects of interest and importance to the cause of deaf-mute education were considered by the conference, that of articulation occupying a prominent place. After full discussion the following was unanimously adopted:

"*Resolved*, That in the opinion of this conference it is the duty of all institutions for the education of the deaf and dumb to provide adequate means for imparting instruction in articulation and in lip-reading, to such of their pupils as may be able to engage with profit in exercises of this nature."

The action of this conference, taken in connection with the establishment at about the same time of the oral schools at Northampton and New York, gave a great impulse to the cause of the oral teaching of the deaf in America.

In nearly all the large schools, and in many of the smaller ones, classes in articulation were soon formed. So rapidly has this branch of instruction found favor in this country that to-day, among the fifty-five schools, only ten are to be found where speech is not taught. And these ten schools contain only 408 pupils out of the 7019 that were under instruction during the year 1881. The strictly oral schools are twelve in number and had in that year 527 pupils. It will be seen therefore that at the present time a majority of the schools in this country sustain the combined system, and that this latter class of schools includes more than six-sevenths of the whole number of pupils under instruction during 1881.

The distinctive features of the "manual method" have already been given. For a brief and clear explanation of the other two we quote again from Professor Fay in the *American Annals of the Deaf and Dumb* (January, 1882).

"By the *oral method* is meant that in which signs are used as little as possible; the manual alphabet is generally discarded altogether; and articulation and lip-reading, together with writing, are made the chief means as well as the end of instruction. Here too there is a difference in different schools in the extent to which the use of signs is allowed in the early part of the course; but it is a difference only of degree, and the end aimed at is the same in all.

"The *combined method* is not so easy to define, as the term is applied to several distinct methods, such as (1) the free use of both signs and articulation, with the same pupils and by the same teachers, throughout the course of instruction; (2) the general instruction of all the pupils by means of the manual method, with the special training of a part of them in articulation and lip-reading as an accomplishment; (3) the instruction of some pupils by the manual method and others by the oral method in the same institution; (4)—though this is rather a combined *system*—the employment of the manual method and the oral method in separate schools under the same general management, pupils being sent to one establishment or the other, as seems best with regard to each individual case."

The following tables will be found to include all the countries of the world where schools for the deaf are in existence. In preparing them, the figures of Professor Fay in the *Annals* (January, 1882) have been followed, with corrections and additions secured from various publications which have become available since January, 1882.

In conclusion it may be stated that in no country of the world is the education of the deaf so well provided for as in the United States, and in no country have public appropriations in aid of this object been as liberal as in our own.

STATISTICS OF THE INSTITUTIONS FOR THE EDUCATION OF THE DEAF.

Location.	Date of Establishment.	Principal.	No. of Pupils.
AUSTRALIA, 1879.			
Sidney, New South Wales	1860	Samuel Watson	53
Melbourne, Victoria	1860	Frederick J. Rose	99
Brighton, S. Australia	1874	Robert Hogg	14
Three schools in Australia.			167
AUSTRIA-HUNGARY, 1878.			
Vienna	1799	Alexander Venus	117
Waizen (Hungary)	1802	M. Fekete	
St. Pölten	1846	Johann Hollrigel	49
Linz	1813	Johann Brandstätter	50
Prague	1786	M. Hemet	135
Hall (Tyrol)	1830	I. Zampredi	26
Lemberg	1830	C. Pogonowsky	70
Gratz	1831	M. Fyringer	86
Görs	1840	M. Pauletic	99
Trent	1843	P. Don Amech	38
Vienna (Hebrew)	1844	J. Deutsch	107
Klagenfurt	1849	Ritt. V. Gallenstein	22
Brünn	1852	K. Partisch	123
Budweis	1859	M. Sedlak	64
Leitmeritz	1867	G. A. Demuth	30
Hürteldorf	1870	A. Lehfold	16
Buda Pest	1876	L. Grünberger	37
Seventeen schools in Austria-Hungary.			1129
BELGIUM, 1879.			
Ghent (Boys)	1822	Brothers of Charity	50
" (Girls)	1822	Sisters of Charity	64
Liége	1830	Lay Committee	243
Antwerp (Boys)	1835	Society of Family Fathers	44
Brussels (Boys)	1835	Brothers of Charity	99
" (Girls)	1835	Sisters of Charity	112
Bruges	1836		127
Namur	1840	{ Mme. V. Jourdin / Abbé E. Rieffel }	96
Masseyck (Girls)	1840	Sisters of Charity	14
" (Boys)	1844	Brothers of Pity	19
Ten schools in Belgium.			864
BRAZIL, 1879.			
Rio de Janeiro (Boys)	1857	T. R. Leite	32

DEAF-MUTES.

Location.	Date of Establishment.	Principal.	No. of Pupils.	Location.	Date of Establishment.	Principal.	No. of Pupils.
CANADA, 1881.				Paris	1875	M. Magnat	60
Montreal (Boys) (Roman Catholic)	1848	Rev. A Belanger	171	Villeneuve-lès-Avignon		Abbé Grimaud	25
Montreal (Girls) (Roman Catholic)	1851	Sister Philippe	215	St. Laurent-en-Royans		Sœurs Providence	70
Halifax, N. S.	1857	A. F. Woodbridge	76	Pupils in 7 common schools under the system of Dr. Blanchet	1849-55 In Paris		60
Belleville, Ont.	1870	R. Mathison	206				
Montreal, Mackay Inst. (Protestant)	1870	Thos. Widd	34	Pupils in 42 common schools under the system of M. Grosselin	1865-80 In Paris		88
Portland, N. B.	1873	A. H. Abell	18	Ditto	1865-80 In the Departments		70
Six schools in Canada.			810	Sixty-two schools in France.			3896
DENMARK, 1880.				**GERMANY, 1881.**			
Copenhagen (Royal Inst.)	1807	Rev. R. M. Hansen	142	*PRUSSIA.*			
" (School)	1850	J. Keller	144	*East Prussia.*			
" (School for children of the higher classes)	1871	J. Keller and Miss C. A. Mathison	6	Königsberg	1817	Gotsch	85
				Angerburg	1838	Stockman	128
				Braunsberg	1844	Helnick	77
Copenhagen (Home for adult girls)	1869		34	Königsberg	1873	Schön	108
				Tilsit	1881	Richter	18
Four schools in Denmark.			326	*West Prussia.*			
				Marienburg	1833	Hollenwager	117
FINLAND, 1882.				Elbing	1870	Wendt	34
Borga	1846	A. Sirén	30	Schlochat	1873	Eimert	72
Abo	1860	A. E. Nordman	66	Graudenz	1876	Radomski	53
Kuopio	1862	K. Killinen	19	Danzig	1881	Hahn	30
Bedesåre	1863	Anna Heikel	26	Oliva	1881	Spohn	27
Four schools in Finland.			141	*Brandenburg.*			
				Berlin	1788	Dr. Treibel	84
FRANCE, 1882.				Berlin	1875	Dr. Berndt	136
Paris (Boys)	1765	Dr. Peyron	270	Wriezen	1881	Walther	33
Angers	1777	Sœur Charnaci	50	*Pomerania.*			
Bordeaux (Girls)	1783	J. Huriot	200	Stralsund	1837	Junge	24
Nogent le Rotrou	1806	Abbé Perrebois	50	Stettin	1839	Erdmann	93
Auray	1812	Sœurs Sagesse	59	Cöslin	1861	Ottersdorf	59
Rhodes	1814	Abbé Roquette	43	Bütow	1865	Nüske	19
St. Etienne (Boys)	1815	Frère Virmire	80	Laurenburg	1867	Dehne	23
Caen	1817	Aug. Cavé	79	Demmin	1881	Genss	10
Arras	1817	M'lle Teissier	101	Berlinchen	1881	Marquardt	68
Le Puy	1818	Frère Marie-Pierre	81	*Posen.*			
Besançon (Girls)	1819	Sœurs Sagesse	70	Posen	1831	Matussewski	124
Marseilles	1819	Abbé Guerin	57	Schneidmühl	1872	Reimer	111
Lyons	1824	C. Forestier	90	Bromberg	1881	Lehmann	43
Besançon (Boys)	1824	Frère Romule	70	*Silesia.*			
Toulouse	1826	Abbé Duhagon	150	Breslau	1821	Bergmann	160
Clermont (Girls)	1827	Sœur Beatrix	22	Liegnitz	1831	Kratz	82
Nancy	1828	M. Pironx	115	Ratibor	1836	Schwarz	160
St. Etienne (Girls)	1828	Sœurs de Nevers	108	*Saxony.*			
Laval	1830	Sœur Augustine	71	Erfurt	1822	Rode	61
Albi	1832	Sœur Massol	59	Halerstadt	1828	Keil	56
Chaumont	1833	M. A. Hugonnet	27	Weissenfels	1829	Köbrick	48
Ronchin, Lille (Boys)	1834	M. Mesmin	95	Halle-on-the-Saal	1835	Klotz	56
Fives (Girls)	1835	Sœur Ste. Synclétique	40	Osterburg	1878	Kuhne	20
Orléans (Girls)	1836	Sœurs Sagesse	50	*Schleswig-Holstein.*			
Rouen	1835	M'lle Lefebvre	42	Schleswig	1787	Engelke	115
St. Brieux	1836	Abbé Bartho	90	"		Köhler	
Pont l'Abbé	1838	Abbé Ecroun	46	*Hanover.*			
Poitiers (Boys)	1838	Frère Médéric	94	Hildesheim	1829	Rössler	101
Orléans (Boys)	1839	Frère Joachim-Mie	52	Emden	1844	Frese	43
Paris	1840	M. Dubois	6	Stade	1857	Gude	89
Saint-Médard lès-Soissons	1840	Casmoine Bourse	178	Osnabrück	1857	Schroder	81
Grenoble (Boys)	1840	M. Rauh	12	*Hessen Nassau.*			
Chambéry	1840	Abbé Jouty	94	Camberg	1820	Wehrheim	84
Vanjours (Boys)	1843	M. Bidron	6	Frankfort-on-the-Main	1827	Vatter	25
Déols (Girls)	1846		8	Homberg	1837	Kessler	84
Aurillac	1846	M. Maitin	24	*Westphalia.*			
Fougères	1846	M. Brislère	49	Büren	1830	Dornseifer	39
Vieille (Girls)	1847	M'lle Lentilon	23	Soest	1831	Plöger	90
Bourg (Girls)	1847	Sœur Esperance	80	Petershagen	1839	Bökenkamp	66
Bron (Girls)	1847	Abbé Convert	40	Langenhorst	1841	Stahm	74
Larnay (Girls)	1847	Sœurs Sagesse	76	*Rhine Provinces.*			
Fontainebleau (Girls)	1848	M'lle Drouville	5	Cologne	1828	Weinsweiler	80
Montpellier	1850	Sœur Charite	70	Aachen	1838	Linnarts	73
Alençon	1852	Abbé Lebecq	49	Kempen	1841	Kirfel	57
Cahors (Girls)	1854	Sœur Marie-Bernard	15	Brühl	1864	Fleth	86
Paris	1854	Auguste Houdin	29	Neuwied	1854	Günther	89
Bourg (Boys)	1856	Abbé Goyotton	30	Trier	1881	Cüppers	75
St. Hippolyte du-Fort (Protestant)	1856	Rev. E. Bayroux	55	Elberfeld	1881	Hilger	36
				Essen	1881	Ochs	47
Nantes (Boys)	1856	Frère Louis	70	*BAVARIA.*			
Gap (Girls)	1856	Sœur Theodosie	10	Bayreuth	1823	Dr. Kranzold	18
Embrun	1856	M'lle Guien	8	Frankenthal	1825	Johann Reiss	38
Bourg-la-Reine	1861	Sœurs N. D. Calvaire	36	Munich	1828	Rev. Joseph Gunkel	74
Moingt (Girls)	1864	Abbé Dessaignes	25	Altdorf	1831	C. A. Zohn	9
Veyre-Monton (Girls)	1866	Sœurs St. Dominique	80	Nuremberg	1832	Pastor Michahelles	33
Saint Laurent-du-Pont (Boys)	1870	Frère Paul	40	Bamberg	1834	Rev. N. Eichhorn	20
Bordeaux (Boys)	1870	Abbé Gauressu	52	Straubling	1835	Ed. Mutzl	61
Algiers	1872	M. Chargebœuf	15	Würzburg	1835	Gregor Fischer	54
Lyons	1872	M. Hugentobler	19	Regensburg	1839	Johann Döring	30
Clermont-Ferrand (Boys)	1873	Frère Jacques	31	Dillingen (Girls)	1847	F. S. Wankmüller	52
				Augsburg (Boys)	1851	Sebastian Koch	60

Location.	Date of Establishment.	Principal.	No. of Pupils.	Location.	Date of Establishment.	Principal.	No. of Pupils.
Zell (Girls)	1872	Johann E Wagner	56	*With the two following Training Colleges for Teachers in London:*			
Fürth	1875	M. Hüchetetter	11	Fitzroy Square, W.	1871	Wm. Van Praagh	5
Hohenwart (Girls)	1877	Mrs. Schmalholz	55	Ealing, W.	1878	A. A. Kinsey	15
Saxony.							
Leipsic	1778	Dr. Eichler	128			ITALY.	
Dresden	1828	} Councillor Jenke	199	Genoa	1801	C. A. Boselli	86
Plauen	1872		37	Milan	1805	Sac. Cav. Kl. Ghislandi	88
Wurtemberg.				Modena (Girls)	1822	Sac. L. Giannasi	82
Gmünd	1817	} Wilhelm Hirzel	56	Siena	1828	Comm. T. Pendola	57
"	1869		40	Verona	1830	G. Mioritori	29
Winnenden	1824	M. Bellen	31	Palermo	1834	Sac. P. Conti	45
Esslingen	1825	M. Pfisterer	39	Turin	1835	Sac. L. Lazzeri	88
Wilhelmsdorf	1837	M. Ziegler	39	Brescia (Boys)	1836	Sac. Q. Metelli	24
Nürtingen	1846	Dr. Gunder	...	Cremia (Girls)	1840	Superiora Ferni	21
Heiligenbronn	1860	M. Fuchs	94	Vicenza (Girls)	1840	Ab. A. Demarchi	6
Baden.				Rome	1841	Sac. L. Bertaccini	81
Meersburg, formerly Pforzheim	} 1826	Jacob Stein	107	Bergamo	1844	Sac. G. Ghislandi	54
				Modena (Boys)	1846	Sac. G. Pollastri	22
Gerlachsheim	1874	M. Willareth	101	Cremona (Girls)	1847	Canon Ariel	29
Hesse.				Venice (Girls)	1849		29
Friedberg	1837	Ludwig Wodäge	68	Bologna	1850	Sacs. C. and G. Gualandi	103
Bendheim	1840	Jacob Buchinger	82	" (Girls)	1850	Sig. Anna Monti	26
Mecklenburg-Schwerin.				Como (Girls)	1852	Sac. S. Balestra	20
Ludwigslust	1840	M. Muslow	55	Oneglia (Boys)	1852	Sac. A. Capetta	29
Oldenburg.				Milan (Boys)	1853	Cav. Sac. G. Tarra	60
Wildeshausen	1820		46	" (Girls)	1853		53
Saxe-Weimar.				Mantua (Girls)	1853	Suor. A. T. Rota	10
Weimar	1820	Karl Okhlwein	30	Naples	1855	Sac. L. Apicella	83
Brunswick.				Pavia	1856	Sig. A. Beccalli	49
Brunswick	1823	Otto Danger	47	Brescia (Girls)	1856	Suora G. Fantasia	11
Hamburg	1827	J. H. Süder	63	Lodi	1856	Sac. G. Savare	74
Lübeck	1828	J. C. A. Bengoe	10	Catanzaro (Boys)	1859	A. L. Spadola	22
Bremen	1827		20	Casoria (Girls)	1860		29
Alsace-Lorraine.				Molfetta (Boys)	1863	Sac. L. Ajiello	29
Ruprechtsau (formerly Colmar)	} 1826	Ch. Jacoutot	92	" (Girls)	1863		18
				Genoa (Girls)	1866	Suoradi S. Vincenzo da Paola	44
Strasburg	1880	V. Paul	17	Cagliari	1869	A. V. Cane	
Metz	1875	M. Erbich	46	Venia (Boys)	1870	Sig. N. Crovato	30
Ninety schools in Germany.			5614	Assisi (Boys)	1872	Sig. D. di S. Francesco	10
				Chiavari (Boys)	1874	P. L. Revelli	11
GREAT BRITAIN AND IRELAND, 1882.				Naples (Boys)	1877		91
London (Old Kent Road S. E.)	} 1792	Richard Elliott, M. A.	70	Thirty-six schools in Italy.			1484
Edinburgh (Henderson Row)	1810	James Bryden	60			JAPAN, 1880.	
Birmingham (Edgbaston)	1812	Arthur Hopper, B. A.	106	Funa yamachi, Jokio Ku, Kioto	} 1878	Furukawa Toshiro	40
Dublin (Claremont)	1816	E. W. Chidley	43				
Glasgow	1819	John Thomson	140	Hoyensaka machi, Higashi Ku, Osaka	} 1879	Hiyanigi Seisaku	25
Manchester	1823	A. Patterson	160				
Liverpool	1825	James Gibbs	107	Two schools in Japan.			65
Exeter	1826	J. T. Hobbah	32				
Aberdeen	1826	Franklin Bill	18			MEXICO, 1882.	
Doncaster	1829	James Howard	152	Mexico	1873	C. R. I. Alcaraz	39
Belfast	1831	Rev. J. Kinghan	105	Zacatecas	1881		20
Newcastle-on-Tyne	1838	William Neill	95				
Brighton	1842	W. Sleight	85	Two schools in Mexico.			59
Bristol	1844	W. B. Smith	43				
Bath	1844	Miss Elwin (Hon. Sec.)	13			NEW ZEALAND, 1882.	
Dublin (R. C.) St. Joseph's (Boys)	} 1846	Rev. Bro. P. M. Wickham	190	Sumner (near Christ Church)	} 1879	G. Van Asch	22
Dublin (R. C.) St. Mary's (Girls)	} 1846	The Dominican Sisterhood	207			NETHERLANDS, 1880.	
Dundee	1846	James Barland	19	Groningen	1790	A. W. Alings, Ph. D.	202
Swansea	1847	B. H. Payne	40	St. Michiels-gestel	1840	C. J. A. Terwindt	145
Edinburgh (Donaldson's Hosp'l)	} endowed 1850	Alfred Large	118	Rotterdam	1853	D. Hirsch	118
London (Finsbury Park, N. Boys)	} 1856	Rev. W. Stainer	8	Three schools in the Netherlands.			365
London (Lower Clapton)	1861	D. Murray, B. A.	34			NORWAY, 1880.	
Northampton	1860	Rev. Thomas Arnold	9	Trondhjem	1824	H. Finch	80
Llandoff	1862	Alex. Melville	19	Christiania	1848	Fred G. Balchen	94
Margate	1862	Richard Elliott, M. A.	241	Christiansand	1850	E. H. Zeisler	70
London, Holland Road	1862	Miss S. E. Hull	12	Bergen	1850	N. C. Waagle	60
London (Inglefield)	1866	John Barber	12	Christiania	1881	Mrs. H. Rosing	40
Walmer Road, W.	1864	S. Schöntheil	25	Hamar	1882	E. H. Hofgaard	20
Hull	1869	Edward Bill	19	Trondhjem	1882	J. Lyng	15
Bristol	1869	Mrs. Thomas	7				
Boston Spa (Yorkshire)	1870	{Sisters of Charity of St. Vincent de Paul, under direction of Mgr. De Haerne}	97	Seven schools in Norway.			399
						PORTUGAL, 1861.	
Smyllum Orphanage Lanark (R. C.)	} 1871	Sister Teresa Farrell	27	Oporto	1870	R. de Aguillar	8
London, Fitzroy Square, W.	1871	Wm. Van Praagh	66			RUSSIA, 1882.	
London School Board	1874–9	Rev. William Stainer	183	St. Petersburg	1806	C. Sélesneff	200
" (Ealing)	1878	A. A. Kinsey	11	Warsaw	1817	J. Paplonski	105
Greenock	1878	S. Littlefield	4	Odessa	1843	Mrs. L. Mitrevitsh	26
London (Brixton)	1878	Miss Rhind	12	Moscow	1860	D. Organoff	134
Sheffield	1879	Geo. Stephenson	29				
Leeds	1881	Joseph Morton	20	Four schools in Russia.			465
Glasgow	1881	Miss Griffiths	9				
						SPAIN, 1881.	
Forty schools in Great Britain and Ireland.			2646	Madrid	1805	M. F. Villabrille	25

Location.	Date of Establishment.	Principal.	No. of Pupils.	Location.	Date of Establishment.	Principal.	No. of Pupils.
Barcelona	1416	F. Ronquillo	65	*Providence, R. I.	1877	J. W. Homer	29
Salamanca	1863	L. Rodrigues	11	*Baltimore, Md.	1877	F. Knapp	30
Santiago	1864	M. L. Navalon	13	*Milwaukee, Wis.	1878	A. Stettner	21
Burgos	1868	A. Sadam	27	†St. Louis, Mo. (Day School)	1878	D. A. Simpson, B. A.	44
Saragossa	1871	A. Trellam	8	*Marquette, Mich.	1879	Mrs. M. A. Kelsey	3
Seville (Boys)	1873	A. P. y Casado	22	Beverly, Mass.	1880	W. B. Swett	16
			——	†Scranton, Pa. (Day School)	1880	J. M. Koehler	13
Seven schools in Spain.			222	†Sioux Falls, D. T.	1880	James Simpson	19
	SWEDEN, 1881.			*Philadelphia, Pa.	1881	Miss E. Garrett	20
Stockholm	1812	O. Kyhlberg, Ph. D.	129				——
Karlskrona	1856	Sofia Ulfsparre	30	Fifty-five schools in the United States.			7055
Guttenburg	1850	S. Sjögren	34	National Deaf-Mute College, included in the Columbia Inst., D. C., Washington, D. C.	1864	E. M. Gallaudet, Ph. D., LL. D., Pres.	62
Hjorted	1858	J. A. Ortberg	31				
Stockholm	1860	Jeanette Berglind	17				
Gottenburg	1862	P. Brodahl	22				
Rephutt	1862	L. B. Faltenborg	30	Schools noted in Italics depend entirely on private support.
Hernösand	1867	S. Lagerström	33	* Exclusively oral schools.
Lund	1871	A. G. Flodin	60	† Schools in which the manual method is pursued.
Fulan	1873	A. A. Berg	20	All not specially marked follow the combined method.
Gumpetan	1874	T. Kaijser	35	
Hamre	1874	J. Prawitz	12	SUMMARY.
Orebro	1875	J. P. Blomkvist	26	
Wenersborg	1877	S. Kinman	23	

Country.	Number of Institutions.	Number of Pupils.
Australia	3	147
Austria-Hungary	17	1,129
Belgium	10	864
Brazil	1	33
Canada	6	610
Denmark	4	336
Finland	4	141
France	62	3,596
Germany	90	5,614
Great Britain and Ireland	40	2,649
Italy	36	1,430
Japan	2	65
Mexico	2	80
New Zealand	1	22
Netherlands	3	646
Norway	7	356
Portugal	1	8
Russia	4	400
Spain	7	222
Sweden	17	690
Switzerland	11	330
United States of America	55	7,056
Total	383	26,989

Great Britain has two training colleges for teachers. United States have one college for the higher education of deaf-mutes.

(E. M. G.)

DEAN, Amos, LL.D. (1803–1868), an American jurist, was born at Barnard, Vt., Jan. 16, 1803. He graduated at Union College, N. Y., in 1826, studied law, and became eminent in his profession. In 1838 he was made professor of medical jurisprudence in the Medical College at Albany, and in 1851 he joined in establishing the Albany Law School. In 1855 he was elected chancellor and professor of history in the University of Iowa, and spent three summers there in organizing the university. In 1859 he resigned his chair in the Medical College to devote himself more completely to his historical studies. He was of retired, studious disposition, and avoided public assemblies and duties. He died at Albany, Jan. 26, 1868. He published *Lectures on Political Economy* (1835), *Philosophy of Human Life* (1839), *Principles of Medical Jurisprudence* (1854). After his death his *History of Civilization* was published in seven octavo volumes. He had begun to labor on this in 1833, and after thirty years had completed it in 1863; he then spent three years in revising it, so that it was ready for the press, though he still delayed its publication.

DEANE, Silas (1737–1789), an American diplomatist, was born at Groton, Conn., Dec. 24, 1737. He graduated at Yale College in 1758, and became a merchant at Wethersfield, Conn. He was elected to the State legislature in 1768, and became a member of the first Continental Congress in 1774. He served on several important committees; purchased the first vessel for the American navy, and on account of his general ability was sent to France in 1776, ostensibly as a merchant, but really as a commercial and political agent. With the secret aid of the French Government large supplies of military stores were shipped to America. In Jan., 1777, when Franklin and Arthur Lee joined him as commissioners to ask for the recognition of American independence, the king ordered 2,000,000 livres to be paid them as token of his good-will. Deane had exceeded his instructions, and by liberal promises of high positions in the army had induced several officers in the French service to come to America, where their great expectations produced embarrassment to Congress and dissatisfaction in the army. Congress, having ordered his recall Nov. 21, 1777, afterwards added a request for information of the state of affairs in Europe, and directed him to return as soon as possible. He arrived July 10, 1778, and on the 13th reported to Congress, but six weeks passed before any notice was taken of him. In the mean time, Arthur Lee had accused him of extravagance and embezzlement of public funds, and Congress asked for a detailed statement of his financial transactions. This it was impossible for him to give without returning to France, but his honesty was vouched for by Franklin, and he was defended in this country by Robert Morris. In Aug., 1779, he was discharged from further attendance on Congress, and published a letter fiercely attacking his opponents, to which a reply was made by Lee on his return in 1780. Deane went to France, where a person had been appointed by Congress to audit and settle his accounts, but was subjected to many delays. Certain letters written by him to his brother and others, which charged the French court with intrigue and duplicity, were intercepted and published by Rivington, New York, 1781. Deane was in consequence obliged to retire to the Netherlands, where he lived in poverty. In 1784 he published at Hartford *An Address to the Free and Independent Citizens of the United States*; another edition, containing additional matter, was published in London in the same year. Finding his efforts to obtain a settlement of his accounts and payment of what he claimed to be due him entirely fruitless, he went to England, where he died in extreme poverty at Deal, Aug. 23, 1789. His official letters are published in Sparks's *Diplomatic Correspondence of the American Revolution*, vol. i., and Deane's *Narrative* was published in 1855. His heirs presented a memorial to Congress in 1835, and after a thorough investigation his long-disputed claims were adjusted in 1842, and a large sum ordered to be paid to the heirs.

DEARBORN, HENRY (1751-1829), an American general, was born at Hampton, N. H., March, 1751. He was a physician at Portsmouth when he heard of the battle of Lexington, and immediately marched with sixty volunteers, arriving at Cambridge, sixty-five miles off, early the next morning, April 24, 1775. He was a captain in Col. Stark's regiment, and took part in the battle of Bunker's Hill. He accompanied Arnold in his expedition through the woods of Maine to Quebec. He was captured in the attack on that city, Dec. 31, 1775, and after being closely confined was permitted to return on parole, May, 1776, and finally exchanged in March, 1777. He was a major in Gates's army at the capture of Burgoyne, and distinguished himself at the battle of Monmouth, June 28, 1778. He accompanied Sullivan in his expedition against the Indians in 1779, was with the army in New Jersey in 1780, and went with Washington to Yorktown in 1781. After the war he removed to Maine, and in 1789, Washington appointed him marshal of that district. He was elected member of Congress in 1793, and served two terms. In 1801, Jefferson appointed him Secretary of War, which position he retained till 1809, when he was made collector of the port of Boston. In 1812 he was commissioned as senior major-general in the United States army, and took command of the department of the North, intending to invade Canada. But as the militia refused to cross the border, and the administration seemed not urgent or earnest in prosecuting the war, Gen. Dearborn accepted, provisionally, the offer of an armistice made by the governor-general, Sir George Prevost, which was rejected by President Madison. In April, 1813, Gen. Dearborn's army was carried across Lake Ontario, and captured York (now Toronto), the capital of Upper Canada. Three days later the town was burned, and the army was transported to the mouth of the Niagara River, where Fort George was taken. In July, Gen. Dearborn was permitted by the Secretary of War to retire from Canada, and was placed in command of the military district of New York City. He resigned his commission in 1815. In 1822, President Monroe appointed him minister to Portugal, but two years later he was recalled at his own request. He died at Roxbury, Mass., June 6, 1829.

DEARBORN, HENRY ALEXANDER SCAMMELL (1783-1851), son of the preceding, was born at Exeter, N. H., March 3, 1783. He was educated partly at Williams College, and graduated at William and Mary College in 1803. Having studied law first in Washington, D. C., and afterwards with Judge Story at Salem, Mass., he commenced practice in Portland, Maine, but was soon after appointed to superintend the erection of forts in Portland harbor. He afterwards became an officer in the Boston custom-house, and in 1812 succeeded his father as collector of the port of Boston. He remained in that office till 1829, when he was elected to the Massachusetts legislature. The next year he became a State senator, and in 1831 was elected to Congress, where he served one term. In 1835 he was made adjutant-general of Massachusetts, and during Dorr's rebellion furnished arms to Rhode Island, for which act he was removed in 1843. He was mayor of Roxbury from 1847 till his death, July 29, 1851. The foundation and remarkable success of the Massachusetts Horticultural Society are due mainly to him. He was also active in establishing Mount Auburn and Forest Hill Cemeteries near Boston. He published a *Memoir on the Commerce and Navigation of the Black Sea*, 1819; *Internal Improvements and Commerce of the West*, 1809. He left a *Memoir of his Father*, a *Biography of Commodore Bainbridge*, and other works in manuscript amounting to forty-five volumes.

DEATH. This word has acquired a variety of meanings; it may signify (1) the time when an organized body loses its characteristic properties. In this sense of the word death implies the opposite of birth, or, more strictly, the time when the organism, as such, commences its existence. (2) The word death may refer to the transformed condition into which an organism passes when the processes which characterized its life have ceased. In this sense of the word death is the opposite of life. (3) It may mean the *act*, or transition stage, of passing from the condition of life to that of death; that is, the act of dying. (4) It may refer in man to the separation of the soul from the body.

In this article will be considered, *first*, the nature of death as a condition opposed to life; *second*, the cause and nature of the act of dying; *third*, the signs by which the near advent of death may be foretold; and *fourth*, the signs by which its actual occurrence may be recognized.

I. *The Nature of Death.*—Death, like life, is a condition which admits of no short definition. For the present we may say that death is the extinction in an organized body of its vital properties; consequently, in the most restricted sense of the word, death means the abolition of all those properties which distinguish animate from inanimate organized matter.

In lower forms of life, both animal and vegetable, the definition applies with considerable strictness. The properties of protoplasm, which we are accustomed to describe as vital properties, depend upon the integrity of the vehicle through which they are manifested; hence, in animals and plants which are composed of simple masses of undifferentiated protoplasm, we can conceive that as long as the elements carbon, hydrogen, oxygen, nitrogen, and sulphur are combined in certain definite proportions and molecular arrangements, the resulting compound possesses the vital properties. That is, it possesses the power of taking foreign material, suitable to its nutritive needs, into its interior, elaborating that matter into protoplasm, throwing out the waste, while the original matter composing the individual breaks up into simpler compounds which are cast off; it is also capable of carrying on the process of respiration, which is essentially a process of oxidation, while carbon dioxide is a constant result of this form of chemical change; it is also reproductive; that is, when the nutritive processes are in excess of activity over the processes of waste, it is capable by fission, or by some other simple process, of reproducing itself in a separate individual; it is finally contractile and capable of automatic movements.

Coincident with the disappearance of these vital properties of such an unit of protoplasm we find that the chemical elements of which it was composed tend to arrange themselves into simpler, more stable forms; but as to whether death—that is, the inability of carrying on these vital processes—depends upon the rearrangement of the molecules of the protoplasm, or whether the decomposition (in a chemical sense), and this is the older view, depends upon the death of the protoplasm, are points which have long been subjects of contention.

It had long been surmised that there existed some difference in the molecular constitution of living and dead protoplasm, but it is only recently that this difference has been demonstrated. It has been found that in living protoplasm the elements carbon, hydrogen, and oxygen are arranged in combination, analogous if not identical with the aldehyde group, and that on the death of the protoplasm this grouping is lost. As a consequence of the presence of this aldehyde group, living protoplasm possesses in the highest degree the property of reducing the noble metals out of alkaline solutions; but when the *life* of the protoplasm is destroyed, as by short exposure to a temperature of only 50° C. for some of the fresh water algæ, this property is lost; life therefore depends upon the presence of this aldehyde group, and its disappearance, as evidenced by the loss of reducing power, is the first sign of death.

We may then logically say that the so-called vital properties of protoplasm depend upon a certain definite arrangement of certain molecules, and that as long as these molecules are so arranged life is present. Under such circumstances protoplasm is a stable compound; for while, if we may admit the paradox, it is continually changing its constituents, replacing the old by new matter, its composition always remains the same, and it is only when no longer manifesting the characteristic properties that protoplasm is an unstable compound. Since, therefore, we never have a certain definite compound without attributing its properties to the elements composing it and to the mode of arrangement of its molecules, we must, to be consistent, attribute the vital properties of protoplasm to its chemical arrangement, plus, in all probability, a certain molecular movement or impact. Death therefore in such simple organism, as in the amœba, may be said to be simply the rearrangement of its molecules by which its components break up into simpler compounds. Death is therefore decomposition in the strict sense of the word.

Higher forms of animal and vegetable life may be regarded as merely associations of such simple masses of protoplasm, but so arranged that there is a division of labor; for while every individual cell possesses the vital properties inherent to protoplasm—that is, is capable of carrying on, in a certain sense, its own nutritive, respiratory, and reproductive processes—a number of cells are associated in the form of organs which are specialized to carry on certain functions. These specialized groups of protoplasmic cells receive the name of tissues; thus we have certain cells in which the reproductive functions are exalted, while they depend largely for nutritive material on other tissues whose main function is the elaboration of ingested food; then we have other tissues devoted to respiration; and others in which the contractile element predominates. So we may regard a complex animal as composed of tissues in each one of which one of the general properties of protoplasm has become specialized, the protoplasm in complex as in simple organism being equally the physical basis of life. It follows, therefore, that with this complex association of protoplasmic units, each fulfilling its own separate share of labor as a means of attaining a common end, the preservation of the individual and species, the phenomena of death, or loss of protoplasmic energy, must differ in accordance with the extent and functional importance of the part involved. We are compelled, therefore, to draw a distinction in the higher animals between *molecular death*, or the particular destruction of protoplasm, and *somatic death*, in which the vital properties are extinguished throughout the entire organism.

When an animal is said to be dead, when the last breath has been drawn and the last pulsation of the heart has taken place, even to a superficial observer it is evident that many of the phenomena which are associated with life may still be detected. Thus the muscular fibre, particularly the unstriped muscular fibre of the alimentary canal, may still manifest spontaneous contractions; the blood may continue to move in the blood-vessels; heat may still be produced, glands may secrete, and the nails and hair may be noticed to increase in length.

It is therefore evident that a distinction must be made between the popular and scientific use of the term death. General systemic or somatic death can never exist except as a result of general molecular death. Indeed, if we admit that life is simply a manifestation of the properties of protoplasm, we can conceive of no loss of function without the disorganization of the protoplasm with which that function is normally associated; hence we see that the old distinction between somatic and molecular death, in which the former referred to death occurring in one or more of the vital organs, is simply one of degree of functional importance of the disabled tissue, while general molecular death is the true scientific conception of death. In the representation we have given as to the formation of a complex animal out of a number of associated tissues, each carrying on a definite function, it is evident that the effect produced on the entire organism by the destruction of any tissue will depend upon the importance of the function possessed by that tissue and on the amount of tissue incapacitated. We know that oxidation is essential to the life of all forms of protoplasm; when, therefore, we find that the tissue whose function is to facilitate the supply of oxygen to all the tissues fails to act—in other words, when respiration by the lungs ceases—the other tissues must necessarily die. Or when the tissue, the blood, whose province is to bear this oxygen to the system at large and to carry away the products of waste, ceases to fulfil its office, death *in toto*, or true somatic death, as invariably results. And as the respiratory movements and the pulsation of the heart, the signs by which the functional activities of these two specialized tissues are manifested, are readily discernible; and as we know by experience that neither one nor the other can in the higher animals be arrested without ultimately causing the death of the organism, we have come to speak of these phenomena, the arrest of the heart or respiration, as systemic or somatic death, though we have already shown that many evidences of vitality may be manifested even after their arrest; cessation of respiration and circulation are, therefore, *per se* only instances of molecular death limited to special tissues.

But when, on the other hand, we have a loss of function in some less essential tissue, the occurrence of general death of the organism, or true somatic death, will depend upon the importance of the tissue and the extent involved. Thus caries of teeth or bone are examples of what is termed loss of molecular vitality; suppuration, as in the production of abscesses, or local gangrene and ulceration—all are instances of the loss of protoplasmic vitality; but the general life of the organism is evidently not threatened unless these changes are so extensive as to react on or implicate some vital organ.

II. *The causes and nature of the act of dying.*—The above considerations naturally lead to the examination of the means by which systemic or somatic death is produced, these terms being retained with the reminder that by somatic death we mean not the popular conception of death, but the entire extinction of vitality in the organism, brought about by the molecular death of those tissues whose functions are to maintain or to govern the functional activity of subordinate tissues. We consequently see that we must divide animal tissues into two classes: *first*, a class whose life depends upon that of the *second*, which, again, is one whose destruction necessitates the death of all other tissues, and whose death may be occasioned by death of the subordinate tissues.

We have therefore one or more governing tissues, upon whose death the death of all subordinate tissues necessarily ultimately follows; and subordinate tissues whose vitality is dependent upon the chief tissues and whose death does not necessarily imply death of that chief tissue. We have already given examples of death occurring in the subordinate tissues; we will now consider the latter more particularly.

According to older views, the maintenance of existence, in the higher forms of life, depended upon the integrity of three factors: the maintenance of the circulation; the functional activity of the respiratory centre; and the constant oxygenation of the hæmoglobin of the blood. Thus Bichat's tripod of life was the heart, the brain, and the lungs; the failure of any one overthrew the life of the organism. In reality, however, the invariable cause of somatic death on close analysis can be found in the stoppage of the heart and the consequent arrest of the circulation. We know that the functions of all tissues depend upon their steady supply with normal arterial blood; interference with that supply necessitates the death of those tissues. And while this result may apparently be directly due to interference with some other mechanism, the final result of that interference and the ultimate cause of death lies invariably in the loss of function of the central organ of the circulation. While, therefore, death invariably is due to the arrest of the circulation, that failure may be due to several causes, any one of which may thus indirectly be the cause of death. We will examine some of these in detail.

As the activities of the body are the result of oxidation processes, there may be three ways in which these processes are interfered with: (1) Deficiency of the material to be oxidized, or want of those organic and inorganic matters which are indispensable to nutrition; hence, *defective nutrition*. (2) Deficiency in supply of oxygenated blood. (3) Absence of the conditions necessary to oxidation. (Hermann.)

1. *Imperfect nutritive changes.*—In all periods of existence there is a constant molecular death and a constant interstitial repair by which the constancy of composition of the protoplasmic molecule is maintained, but it is inherent to the very nature of such action that it can be sustained throughout only a short space of time. In youth, the nutritive reparative processes are in excess of the waste; youth, therefore, is the season of growth and development. In maturity equilibrium is maintained by a balance between waste and repair; but when old age approaches there is a gradual falling off of reparative energy and a consequent decline in vigor. In maturity there occurs the greatest degree of actual waste because maturity is the time of greatest energy, and there can be no cell energy without cell death; but maturity is also the season of greatest actual nutritive activity, and a nutritive balance is maintained. In old age we have a gradually increasing relative excess of waste over repair; old age is therefore a gradually increasing disease—the disturbed balance between waste and repair, although the waste may be actually less than at any other period. Death from old age will thus fall into the class in which imperfect nutrition constitutes a remote cause of death, life being prolonged until the heart no longer has sufficient vigor to propel the blood into the arteries, and respiratory changes are too sluggish to permit the proper oxygenation of the blood and the removal of all the products of retrograde metamorphosis of the tissues. Death is then finally caused by the arrest of the heart after the functions of the organs of relation have been extinguished one by one.

In old age the organs all decline in functional activity until at last by imperceptible gradation they reach their lowest term. Drowsiness increases with the decline of the powers, life passes into sleep, sleep into death,—death from old age, or *natural death*. Generally the aged individual sinks gradually and silently into death, totally unconscious of all that surrounds him. At other times he may retain his sensorial faculties to the last, and even his locomotive powers, until owing, perhaps, to some oppression of one of the vital functions his sleep becomes the sleep of death. Bichat called attention to a most interesting characteristic of this kind of death, viz., that *animal life* terminates long before *organic life*. Death takes place in detail, the animal functions which connect the aged with the objects around them being destroyed long before those concerned in their nutrition. In other words, death in old age takes place from the circumference towards the centre; in *accidental* or *premature death*, from the centre towards the periphery.

Death from starvation will also fall into this class, in which the remote cause of death is imperfect nutritive supply, the ultimate cause being arrest of the circulation.

2. *Defective supply of arterial blood.*—Death may be caused by an insufficient supply, or entire absence of, oxygenated blood in the tissues. This condition may occur either as a consequence of hemorrhage, by which so much blood is lost that the remainder is insufficient to supply the needs of the organism, the motions of the heart are therefore arrested, and death results; or the circulation may itself be primarily arrested, either by direct arrest of the heart's action, or locally by closure of the arteries going to, or the veins coming from, a part, by ligature, rupture, embolism, or thrombosis, when local death may result; or when such accidents occur in vital organs, or in one of the large vascular trunks, they may react on the heart and so cause its stoppage and general death. Arrest of the heart may be directly due to injury, to defective nutrition of the heart's substance, to obstructed circulation in the coronary arteries, to some failure in function of its inherent or extrinsic nervous mechanism, or to defect in the valvular mechanism of the heart.

Defective supply of oxygenated blood may also result from all causes which hinder the free access and retention of oxygen in the blood. All forms of suffocation will fall into this category, either when there is an absence of oxygen in the inspired air, as when attempts at inspiration are made in a vacuum or under water; or when the proper oxidation of the hæmoglobin is interfered with by changes in the blood, such as are caused by the inhalation of carbon-monoxide, sulphuretted hydrogen, etc.; or the cutaneous or pulmonary respiration may be interrupted; the former by anything which interferes with the functions of the skin, as burns or scalds, or covering the skin with a layer of varnish, etc.; the latter by paralysis of the respiratory centre, as in apoplexy,—by insufficient or abnormal blood, or paralyzing poisons,—by interference with the functions of the respiratory nerves, as in section or compression of the phrenic nerve, or in curare poisoning,—or by paralysis or tetanus (as in strychnia poisoning) of the respiratory muscles; or, finally, by some mechanical obstruction to the expansion of the thorax.

3. *Absence of the conditions necessary to oxidation.*—As regards the production of death from disturbance of the conditions necessary to oxidation, very little can be said; about all that we know is that there are certain conditions essential to such processes. Modifications of these conditions may produce disease or modified vitality; their absence results in death. The most important of these conditions necessary to the proper oxidation of protoplasm is a certain degree of temperature, varying in the most marked degree for different members of the animal and vegetable kingdoms, but marked by strict limitations for each species, beyond which elevations or depressions of temperature must lead to depressed (as in hybernation) or suspended animation. A certain quantity of moisture appears to be also essential to the oxidation processes of protoplasm, a fact not strange to us when we recollect the composition of protoplasm itself, and demonstrated by the altered conditions of vitality which in the lower organisms follows the disturbance of the normal supply of water (latent vitality). Finally, the nutritive processes of oxidation which occur in protoplasm are, in the higher animals, directly under the control of the nervous system, and it is to disturbance of this controlling influence that the remarkable cases of suspended animation in man (trance, catalepsy) may be attributed.

III. *Signs of impending death.*—For some time before death the indications of the fatal event usually become more and more apparent; speech becomes thick and labored; the hands, if raised, fall inertly; the labored respiration causes insufficient oxygenation of the blood, and the distress excites an attempt at inspiration which debility renders nearly ineffectual; hence gasping, sighs, yawning. The heart loses its power to propel the blood into the extremities, they become cold, and a clammy moisture oozes through the skin. Irregular action of the heart and lungs takes place, until at last the contractility of the vital organs is entirely gone. Respiration ceases by a strong expulsion of air from the chest, and in the very act of expiring the person dies. While such is the ordinary sequence of events which precede the death of an individual, they must necessarily vary with the circumstances under which death occurs. Delirium, restlessness, and dementia often occur; or the dying man, as in apoplexy, old age, and many febrile diseases, may remain feelingless, motionless, mindless for many days before the cessation of the organic functions, or perfect consciousness may be possessed up to the last. The process of dying should not necessarily be considered one of physical distress and anguish; for no matter what may have been the previous torture, it must be all over when once those changes begin in which death consists; with the failure of the circulation the function of the brain declines. If the fatal process begins in the respiratory apparatus unconsciousness precedes the arrest of the circulation; and if in the brain, any injury sufficient to affect the lungs and heart fatally must destroy its own consciousness. Convulsion is not the sign of pain; it is an affection of the motific, not of the sensory, part of the nervous system, and is due, under such circumstances, to insufficient supply of oxygen to the medulla oblongata. Temporary faintings and asphyxia, and the convulsions of epilepsy, the nearest approach to actual death, have nothing formidable in sensation.

IV. *Signs of actual death.*—The recognition of the signs of death is important; in the first place, to enable the determination of the reality of death; and, in the second, on medico-legal grounds, to enable the formation of an opinion as to the length of time during which life has been extinct. We will examine in detail some of the various signs of death.

The *continuous and entire cessation of the circulation* is a positive sign of death: the difficulty, however, lies in obtaining such proof, since mere feeling of the pulse, or auscultation and palpation of the heart, may, from the weakness of pulsation, or some abnormality in situation or character, fail to reveal any action, and a temporary suspension of the heart's action has been known to occur without the production of death. Several accessory tests of the condition of the circulation have therefore been proposed. Thus, when a thread is tied tightly around the finger, if the person be living, the part beyond the ligature will become bluish-red in hue, while a narrow white ring will surround the finger where the ligature was applied: after the cessation of the circulation no such appearance will be found. Then if bright steel needles are thrust into the flesh during life they will become tarnished from oxidation: after death they will retain their brightness unchanged. If ammonia be injected under the skin during life it will cause a deep red congestion of the part: no such change occurs after death.

The *entire and continuous cessation of respiration* is also, when capable of demonstration, an incontestable sign of death, since, as a rule, life is destroyed by any cause which arrests respiration of atmospheric air for more than a few minutes. While auscultation will be generally relied upon for the determination of the existence or absence of respiratory movements, a number of accessory tests have been proposed. Thus, the popular test of holding a mirror before the mouth and nostrils, when the condensation of moisture on its surface is regarded as a sign of the presence of respiration; but this test, as well as the holding of feathers before the nose, or the standing of a glass of water on the chest, are more valuable as furnishing positive proof of life than the absence of the characteristic results is a sign of death, as they may all fail to show the presence of respiratory movements in hibernating animals.

There are certain other signs which may prove of confirmatory value as to the presence or absence of death. Thus, when heat is applied to the skin until a vesicle forms, if the contents of the vesicle contain albumen, and the cutis vera, after removal of the cuticle, appears red, and particularly if a red line forms after a short time around the blister, absolute evidence is furnished as to the life of the part, and hence strong presumptive evidence of the life of the individual. While if the vesicle so formed contains gas-bubbles, and only a little non-albuminous serum, and if the cutis vera appears dry and glazed, and no red line forms, the evidence is strong that the part is dead. So, also, caustic produces a reddish-brown eschar when applied to living skin, while the skin merely turns yellow or transparent without forming an eschar when the part is dead. Certain changes which occur in and about the eye may also be valuable confirmatory signs of death. Thus, at death, the pupil loses its mobility; the cornea loses its transparency, lustre, and sensibility; and the face assumes the well-known expression described as the *facies Hippocratica*.

After death the body is subject to a gradual and progressive loss of heat, until ultimately the body becomes of about the same temperature as the surrounding media, and as this loss of heat is progressive, it may serve as an indication of the time a body has been dead. Thus, under ordinary circumstances, a body becomes cold in from fifteen to twenty hours after death. In some cases, however, there may be a post-mortem elevation of temperature from chemical action, in which oxygen combines with the elements of the body with extraordinary energy.

Some of the most important signs of death are to be found in the condition of the muscular system. These conditions are marked by three stages: (1) When the muscles become flaccid, but still preserve their irritability. The duration of this stage, which sets in immediately after the arrest of the heart, or after death, in the popular conception of the word, may last for only a few minutes or for several hours, depending upon the cause of death. When contractility is present in *any* muscle, the person is either not dead or has recently died; when absent in *all* muscles, it may be stated positively that death has taken place. (2) *Rigor mortis*, or cadaveric rigidity, soon succeeds the first stage. In this condition the muscles become stiff and rigid, and the limbs retain the position they occupied at the time rigidity supervened. Rigor mortis is due to the coagulation of the myjosin of muscles, and is a process entirely analogous to the coagulation of the blood. On the occurrence of rigor mortis muscles lose their alkalinity and become acid: they also lose their elasticity and transparency. Rigor is also associated with the development of heat, partly due to the physical changes in density, and partly to the chemical changes.

Rigor mortis ordinarily commences about three or four hours after death, though the time of its occurrence will depend upon the mode of death. Thus, in cases of sudden death in robust muscular subjects, not having been exposed to fatigue, rigor may be delayed for twelve hours or more. On the other hand the first stage of muscular change may apparently be absent, and rigor occur almost immediately after death: such cases are seen in subjects which have been exposed to great fatigue before death, as in hunted animals, in strychnia poisoning, and in instant death at the close of the action on the battle-field. Rigor mortis passes from above downwards; it begins in the back of the neck and lower jaw, passes then to the facial muscles, the front of the neck, the chest and the upper extremities, and last of all to the lower extremities. Usually it passes off in the same order, and when once gone, whether from the natural progress of changes, or from forced movements, it never returns, and the body becomes as flexible as it formerly was. Rigor mortis usually lasts for twenty-four or thirty-six hours, though when death has been caused by long continued exhausting diseases it may not last longer than an hour or two, or it may be very much prolonged: as a rule the longer its advent is delayed, the greater its duration and intensity.

(3) After rigor mortis has disappeared the muscles again become flaccid and alkaline in reaction, and the third stage of change, that of *putrefaction*, sets in, unless prevented by rapid desiccation, or by the use of agents which prevent putrefaction. Putrefaction, which furnishes the sole absolute sign of death, consists in a slow oxidation of the organic constituents of the body, brought about by the action of the air under the influence of bacterial organisms. The marks of post-mortem lividity (*Suggilations, livores*), which are precursors of putrefaction, are caused by the diffusion of the blood coloring matter out of the corpuscles, first into the serum, and afterwards into the fluids of the different organs.

(R. M. S.)

DE BOW, JAMES DUNWOODY BROWNSON (1820–

1867), an eminent Southern editor and statistician, was born at Charleston, S. C., July 10, 1820. His father, Garret De Bow, a native of New Jersey, had settled in Charleston as a merchant, and was for a time successful, but afterwards sank into poverty. At an early age the son was employed in mercantile business, but as soon as he obtained the necessary means went to Cokesburg Institute, and thence to Charleston College, from which he graduated in 1843. Having studied law, he was admitted to the bar in 1844, but had already entered upon a literary career by contributing to the *Southern Quarterly Review*, then published at Charleston by D. K. Whitaker. De Bow soon became editor of the *Review*, and among his articles was one on *Oregon and the Oregon Question*, which attracted attention throughout the country, and was the occasion of a debate in the French Chamber of Deputies. In 1845 he was secretary of the convention held at Memphis, Tenn., to promote the interests of the South. John C. Calhoun presided over the convention, and De Bow prepared an elaborate report of its proceedings. He had also previously published some articles in the Charleston *Courier* advocating the holding of this convention, and while preparing them first felt the need in the Southern States of a monthly magazine, commercial rather than literary. For the purpose of establishing such a magazine he removed to New Orleans towards the close of 1845, and the first number of *De Bow's Commercial Review* was issued in the following January. For a time its existence was precarious, but eventually it became the leading periodical of the South-west. In 1848 he was appointed professor of political economy and commercial statistics in the University of Louisiana, and in the same year, when that State established a bureau of statistics, Mr. De Bow was placed in charge, and issued a valuable report in 1849. He assisted in founding the Louisiana Historical Society, and was a member of the New Orleans Academy of Sciences. He gathered material with a view of writing a history of Louisiana, but afterwards abandoned this intention, though he published a series of articles in his *Review* on "The Early Times of Louisiana." In 1853, Pres. Pierce appointed De Bow superintendent of the United States census, which position he held for two years, editing and completing the census report for 1850 in a superior manner, yet at reduced cost to the Government. In 1853 he issued *The Industrial Resources of the Southern and Western States*, in three volumes, compiled from his *Review*, and published an *Encyclopædia of the Trade and Commerce of the United States*. He was always an ardent advocate of Southern conventions, political, agricultural, mercantile, and educational. In most of those which were held he was a delegate, was several times secretary, and was president of the Knoxville convention of 1857. In these, as in the pages of his *Review*, he urged the perpetuation of slavery as it existed in the Southern States; and fiercely denounced all attempts at its abolition. Becoming more extreme in his views as time passed on, he even proposed the revival of the slave-trade. He was of course an advocate of the secession of the South, and in 1858, in an address before the alumni of Charleston College, he maintained that the only salvation of the interests of that section lay in an immediate dissolution of the Union. When secession was accomplished he held several important positions under the Confederacy, especially that of chief agent for the purchase and sale of cotton on behalf of the Government. His *Review* was suspended for two years, but he was still active with voice and pen in behalf of the Southern cause. After the close of the war he resumed the publication of his *Review* at Nashville, and, accepting the results of the conflict, urged the Southern States to encourage immigration from Europe, to make a fair trial of the system of free labor, and to introduce manufactures. He became president of the Tennessee and Pacific Railroad, and used every effort to advance this great undertaking. Learning that his younger brother was lying at the point of death in New Jersey, Mr. De Bow hastened from the South to be near him. On the journey he caught a severe cold that terminated in pleurisy, of which he died at Elizabeth, N. J., Feb. 27, 1867. His brother died a month later. The *Review* was continued by his heirs for two years after his death. Mr. De Bow's characteristics were self-reliance, diligence, application, integrity, and devotion to what he believed to be the true interests of his country.

DEBTS, NATIONAL. National debts of long duration were unknown among the nations of antiquity. They carried on wars either by preparing for them in times of peace, or by subsisting on the enemy.

See Vol. XVII. p. 249 Am. ed. (p. 243 Edin. ed.).

When Alexander overthrew Darius on the plains of Arbela an immense amount of treasure was taken. In most cases the nation which first declared war invaded the country attacked, where to a considerable degree its armies were supported. Napoleon adopted this policy, otherwise his military operations would not have been so favorably regarded by the French people. Debts were often contracted in anticipation of taxes; but the first permanent national debt is comparatively of modern date. The modern idea seems to be to incur the obligation requiring the expenditure, and raise the means to fulfil it afterward; the ancient idea was the reverse. It cannot be unhesitatingly asserted that the modern policy is the wisest. "Pay as you go" is one of the soundest rules that can be observed by nations as well as by individuals.

The first permanent national debt was created by the papal government. However loud were the complaints of extortion heard in Rome in the fifteenth century, the fact cannot be disputed that only a very small portion of the money raised for the pope was put into his treasury. All the nations of Europe were obedient to Pius II., yet he was so greatly in need of money that he could afford only one meal a day to himself and his dependents for a long time, and was obliged to borrow 200,000 ducats to prepare for the war with Turkey which he meditated. Whenever costly enterprises were undertaken the pope resorted to extraordinary expedients, and among these were jubilees and indulgences. Another mode of raising money was to create and sell offices. A certain sum was immediately paid for the office, and the official received at stated times thereafter a fixed sum or interest during his life. These arrangements were essentially annuities. The interest was raised by increasing the imposts of the church. There existed in the year 1471 nearly six hundred and fifty salable offices, the income from which amounted to 100,000 scudi. These were, says Ranke, chiefly held by procurators, registrars, abbreviators, correctors, notaries, clerks, even messengers and doorkeepers, whose increasing numbers continually raised the costs of a bull or a brief. This was, indeed, the very object of appointing them.

Sixtus IV., adopting the plan proposed by his prothonotary, Sinolfo, established whole colleges by a single act, the places in which were sold for 200 or 300 ducats each. These institutions bore singular titles; one of them was called the "college of a hundred janissaries." Sixtus IV. carried the system so far that he has been regarded its real author; but, as we have seen, it was invented long before his day. Under him, however, the system was worked to its utmost capacity. His successors did not hesitate to employ the system as occasion required. Innocent VIII. founded a new college of twenty-six secretaries for 60,000 scudi, with a complement of other officers. Alexander VI. appointed eighty writers of briefs, each writer paying 750 scudi for his appointment; and Julius II., on the same terms, added one hundred writers of archives. He also established a college consisting of a hundred and forty-one presidents of the annona, or bodies which received the different taxes, all of whom were paid by the state. His success in raising money was so great as to excite the admiration of other princes, whatever they might have thought of him as the religious head of the church. Leo X., who squandered the revenues of the church in a shameful manner, not content with selling the existing offices, raised a large sum by nominating additional cardinals. He created more than twelve hundred offices. Their sale yielded the sum of 900,000 scudi. The interest amounted to an eighth of the capital, and was raised by slightly increasing the church dues, but chiefly by contributions from the surplus of the municipal administrations paid into the coffers of the state from the produce of the alumworks, the sale of salt, and the *dogana*, or customs revenues of Rome.

"However censurable this prodigality," says Ranke, "Leo was doubtless encouraged in it by finding that it produced for the time advantageous rather than mischievous effects. It was partly owing to this system of finance that Rome, at the period in question, rose to such an unexampled height of prosperity, since there was no place in the world where capital could be invested to so much advantage. The multitude of new offices, the vacancies and consequent reappointments, kept up a continual stir in the curia and held out to all the prospect of easy advancement. Another consequence was that there was no necessity for burdening the public with new taxes; it is indisputable that the states of the church compared with other provinces, and Rome with other cities, in Italy, were charged with the smallest amount of taxation. The Romans had already been told that whilst other cities furnished to their princes heavy loans and vexatious taxes, their master, the pope, on the contrary, made his subjects very rich."

But this pleasant state of things could last no longer than while a surplus remained in the public treasury. Leo did not live to fund all his loans, and his successors were obliged to tax the people more heavily. In 1526 Clement VII. took up arms against Charles V. and new loans became necessary. Until this time the money paid to the state on the sale of an office was returned in the way of interest, but when the lender died the obligation of the state to pay ceased. Clement proposed to raise 200,000 scudi by paying ten per cent. to the lender during his lifetime and continuing the payment to his successors. This was the first national loan in the modern sense of the term. The interest was charged on the dogana or custom-house revenues, and the loan was made more secure by giving a share in the management of the institution to the creditors. The old form of borrowing, however, was not wholly abandoned, for the lenders constituted a college; a few undertakers of the loan paid the whole amount into the treasury, and then disposed of the shares among their own college-members. Thus the lenders became participants in the management of the government to a certain extent, and Ranke says that "no capitalist would lend his money without the form of such participation."

Although this mode of obtaining loans had been devised, the former one of getting them by the sale of offices was not abandoned. Subsequent popes resorted sometimes to one mode and sometimes to the other. When interest ceased on the death of the creditor, which was the case with the loans called *vacabili* and received for offices, the rate was higher than on those loans whose interest was perpetual. These loans were called the *non vacabili*. For a long period the popes exerted themselves to the utmost to raise money by these modes, chiefly to aid in prosecuting wars in which the states of the church were usually engaged in company with other nations. The Turks for centuries were a menace to Europe, and the pope was often zealous in raising men and money to beat back the dreaded Moslem. But after a time so many loans had been issued that the taxes grew very high and were among the most oppressive in Europe. Many of these had been assigned to the lenders to receive their advances, and they, of course, insisted on their collection, and were usually successful. By this method they made sure of getting their money: indeed, without having such power, probably no loans could have been negotiated in those days. The honesty and efficiency of the government were not so well established as to induce lenders to part with their money on the simple promise of the government that it should be repaid in regular annual payments. They insisted that certain revenues should be pledged to them, and, moreover, that the farmers of taxes should pay the portion thus assigned directly to the lenders without first putting it into the state treasury.

For centuries the people living under the most enlightened governments have had more faith in them and have trusted them to collect the revenues and pay their obligations. But one feature of this system has survived to our day—namely, the pledging of a certain revenue for the payment of a particular debt. That great financier, Pitt, strongly recommended Parliament to do this when authorizing some of the war loans during the war with Napoleon; and Alexander Hamilton, who had studied the British system of finance closely, recommended a similar policy for adoption by the American Congress. This was done in many instances. Pitt and Hamilton both believed that the possessors of money would lend more freely if the sources whence payments were to be made were described and specifically pledged for that purpose. But the custom of the lender to participate in the collection of the revenue, and to receive it directly from the tax-gatherer, has long since passed away, save in a few recent instances, as when Turkey and Egypt were compelled to allow some share of foreign interference in the administration of their finances.

The next states to imitate the pope in borrowing were Genoa and Venice. In both states taxes were assigned to the creditors, who participated largely in their collection. One revenue after another was thus assigned to them until only a very small sum flowed into the public treasury. The first mode of contracting a permanent national debt, therefore, was this: the state borrowed money, pledging certain revenues in payment which were collected by the creditors or largely through their instrumentality. A more minute account of the loans of Genoa and Venice will be found in the article on BANKING.

In Florence government loans were made during the first half of the thirteenth century. There were two modes of making them. By one mode the treasurers of the commune made an agreement with one or more great banking-houses, who, on receiving an assignment of the custom-duties, advanced the money and distributed the loan among their customers and friends. By the other mode the government itself announced the loan and allotted it to the citizens in proportion to their income, which was recorded on the *esturio* or assessment of real and personal property. The security given in this case also was the custom-duties for a fixed period.

Spain followed next. Then her Dutch child, Holland, followed her example. Her debt was contracted in the 16th and 17th centuries when contending so heroically against the might and tyranny of Spain, and also in consequence of the wars with Cromwell, Charles II., and Louis XIV. They attained their greatest height about the end of the 17th century, when the debt of England was beginning.

This was the time when the stadtholder of the Netherlands and his wife acceded to the throne of England. Many of the people were disaffected by the event, and William III. was obliged to guard his possession at no inconsiderable expense, and yet if possible to prevent his new subjects from feeling the cost. One of his first acts was to abolish the tax of hearth-money, thereby surrendering $1,200,000 per annum, although the national income was considerably below expenditures. Obliged to defend his kingdom within, and to enlist forces for war with France, and deeming it impolitic to impose new taxes, he could not do otherwise than to borrow. Other English monarchs had done the same thing before, but the credit of the state had never been pledged. The loans were personal, not national. In 1694, for the first time in English accounts, appears the item, "Interest and Management of the Public Debt."

The first funded debt was $6,000,000, borrowed from the Bank of England in 1694. At that time the word "fund" meant the special tax or fund which was set apart for meeting the charge on the money borrowed, whereas now the word has come to mean that money itself. After this followed the East India Company's loan of $10,000,000. Four years afterward the debt of Charles II. to the bankers and goldsmiths was compounded and added to the funded debt. This still forms a part of the national indebtedness. (For history of English debt see FINANCE, in ENCYCLOPÆDIA BRITANNICA.)

France created a debt in the reign of Charles V. in 1375, which was increased in ransoming Francis I. But when Sully became the chief minister of Henry IV. in 1597 he reformed the financial system, and during his administration paid the public debt, which amounted to 332,000,000 livres, besides remitting 20,000,000 of taxes in arrears and collecting a reserve of 17,000,000 livres, which were deposited in the Bastile. This reserve was squandered by Henry's successors, and the nation plunged deeply into debt during the reign of subsequent kings. At the death of Louis XIV. in September, 1715, the debt, says Cohen, amounted to $620,000,000; but another author more accurately states that "as to the amount and nature of the obligations which the state had incurred, the most vague notions prevailed; even among financiers. One author states that they were thought to exceed the intrinsic value of the whole country; the fact was that, except so far as the rents upon the Hôtel de Ville were concerned, there were no regular means of ascertaining what money had been borrowed by the state and from whom. The country was flooded with state bills of endless variety in point of amount, date, and security. Some were for millions of livres, others for tens, hundreds, thousands. The date of some was a century old, that of others did not extend beyond the existing year. Many were payable at the national treasury, not a few were drawn upon receivers-general; and the whole formed a mass of confusion, out of which it seemed impossible to evolve anything like order, in accordance with the principles of justice. The grossest frauds had been practised upon the state and its creditors; debts had been contracted, although no money had been received; those by whom money had been really advanced had been compelled to sell their securities at one-half or one-fourth of their nominal value." The only well-authenticated fact about the debt at this time is that the sum annually required to pay the interest exceeded 89,000,000 livres. A more particular description of the indebtedness of France at this date will be found in Murray's *French Finance and Financiers under Louis XV.*

France was not the only European state the amount of whose debt for a long period was involved in obscurity. The debts of Spain and Russia, until a recent period, have been an unfathomable mystery. Several reasons may be given for keeping them in this way. One is neglect and inefficiency on the part of officials. Another is that frauds could be more easily perpetrated and the treasury, with less difficulty, robbed. It has been considered a wise policy in some cases to keep the subject in darkness through fear that a full exhibit of the national indebtedness would impair public credit. So long as the real amount was unknown it was easier to make such representations concerning it as the public interests seemed to demand. Of course this could not be done if the record were accurately kept and published.

There are four ways of stating national debts. The most usual way is to state them by their nominal capital. Thus we say that the debt of the United States on Dec. 31, 1881, less the cash in the treasury, was $1,765,491,717. This way is inaccurate for comparing debts because the difference in interest is not considered, nor that of population or national wealth. But it is the easiest way, and conveys to the reader some idea of the subject. The second way, which is in general use on the continent of Europe, consists in stating debts by their annual rents or interest. This, it is said, measures more accurately the burden on a nation; though it does not when a portion of its debt consists of terminable annuities, which is the case with England. This way is not perfect, for it takes no account of population or wealth, and consequently of the pressure of taxation. The third way marks an advance by dividing the annual charge of the debt by the population, and the last way consists in ascertaining the proportion or percentage of the annual charge of the debt to the gross income of the population. But as Baxter, who has treated of this subject quite fully, says, "materials are seldom available for arriving at this comparison, and its general adoption must be left for an age of more complete statistical knowledge."

It is startling to think what a large proportion of national debts is contracted for war expenditure. The four debts incurred by the United States were for this purpose. The debt of Great Britain was similarly contracted. So was the larger part of the debt of France and the Netherlands, Russia, Austria-Hungary, and Italy. The debt of Germany represents a larger outlay for building railroads, and making other improvements, than the debt of any other European nation. A considerable sum has been expended by Italy and France for railroads and canals. A very large sum has been borrowed to meet annual deficits. This is true more particularly with respect to Austria-Hungary, Russia, Italy, and Spain.

The earliest account that can be given with any degree of accuracy of the debts of nations is for 1715. At that period the French debt was $700,000,000; the Netherlands owed $450,000,000; England, $180,000,000; and Spain, the Italian republics, and other states, about $250,000,000. The total national indebtedness of the world was therefore $1,500,000,000—being somewhat less than the debt of the United States.

The debt of France was so enormous, and a large portion was so well known to have been fraudulently contracted, that steps were immediately taken after the death of Louis XIV. to reduce the amount. The debt was of three kinds: state bills, the amount of which was estimated at 700,000,000 livres, another sum of 800,000,000 livres, which represented the purchase-money paid for judicial and other offices, and a third sum of 500,000,000 livres, which was properly the funded debt of the nation. This entire sum, as nearly as can be ascertained, was about $700,000,000. As the grossest frauds had been perpetrated in issuing the state bills payment of them was suspended until they could be examined and verified. The brothers Paris, who had acquired a great reputation for their financial skill, were appointed to perform this delicate task. The amount presented for examination was $210,000,000. It is not known on what principles the examiners proceeded in making their determination; but their result is known, for this portion of the public debt was reduced to $65,000,000. The proceedings appear to have been quite satisfactory, for when persons were asked to present complaints, if they had any, because of the decisions rendered, the total amount of the claims then presented was only 14,000,000 livres. Of this amount 8,000,000 livres were allowed. This was the beginning of national debt scaling—a process with which in these days we are painfully becoming too familiar.

The next step of the kind was taken by Spain. When Philip V. died in 1745 his debts amounted to $45,000,000. Ferdinand VI., who succeeded him, was frightened at the burdens. He assembled a junta composed of bishops, ministers, and lawyers, and asked them to declare whether a king was obliged to discharge the debts of his predecessor. The question was decided in the negative in accordance with the king's hope and expectation. His conscience was quieted and bankruptcy was declared. But he was no spendthrift; on the contrary was industrious in saving. All branches of the government became less effective in consequence of his parsimony. When Charles III. succeeded him he found nearly $35,000,000 in the treasury. He repaired the act of Ferdinand and in 1762 paid six per cent. on account of the debts of Philip V., and continued to do so for the next four years. In 1767 the loans bearing six per cent. interest were reduced to four per cent. loans. The year following 60,000,000 reals were divided among the creditors. In 1769 his situation obliged him to discontinue payments. The result was the complete destruction of the royal credit. In 1783 Charles tried to negotiate a loan of 180,000,000 reals, the creditors of Philip III. taking one-third at par. At the end of two years the experiment was given up, as hardly 12,000,000 had been taken.

Of all the countries in Europe carrying debts during the period under immediate review, the Low Countries were by far the most heavily burdened. But the people never for a moment thought of repudiating the debt. They struggled unflinchingly to pay it. So heavy was it that the price of bread in the towns was doubled, and it was a common saying at Amsterdam that every dish of fish brought to table was paid for once to the fisherman and six times to the state. For a short period her commerce, fisheries, and manufactures increased notwithstanding the burden. After 1672 the country began to decline, and its condition was very serious by 1715. "Wages," says McCulloch, "having been raised so as to enable the laborers to exist, the weight of taxation fell principally on the capitalist. Profits were in consequence reduced below their level in surrounding countries, and the United Provinces lost their ascendency; their fisheries and manufactures were undermined; and their capitalists chose in the end rather to transfer their stocks to the foreigner than to employ them at home."

During the next eighty years after 1715 the debt of England increased more than that of any other nation. One of the heavy items of indebtedness was the cost of attempting to subdue the American colonies. This period covered the long administration of Sir Robert Walpole, who established, with the concurrence of Parliament, a sinking fund, by the operation of which he was confident that within a reasonable period the national debt would be paid. It was composed of a few million pounds, which, by a wondrous manipulation not exactly understood by those less wise in finance than himself, would be sufficient in due time to pay a vastly larger amount of indebtedness. No wonder this brilliant discovery was hailed with delight, for the prospect of discharging a heavy debt by the payment of a small sum is, next to discharging such a debt by the payment of nothing, doubtless one of the most pleasing illusions in which the burdened debt-payer can indulge. For a considerable period Walpole's sinking-fund annually expanded. Within twenty years, however, from the date of its creation, the accumulated treasure was applied toward defraying the ordinary expenses of the government. Such was the fate of the first sinking-fund. Fifty years afterward Pitt established another, which was destined to play a more important part in the history of English finance, and excited many a grave discussion before the fatal error of the system was clearly seen.

In 1793 the following were the debts of the nations of the world:

Great Britain (with value of annuities)	$1,296,750,740
The Low Countries	500,000,000
Austria	175,000,000
France	160,000,000
Russia	85,000,000
Prussia and German States	50,000,000
Spain	40,000,000
Portugal	4,500,000
United States	80,352,634
British India	40,000,000

It will be seen, therefore, that since 1715 national indebtedness had increased more than $1,000,000,000. Borrowing had become more general. Yet the debt of Great Britain was more than half the entire amount. It had been augmented during the Wars of the Succession, and though a long and pacific administration followed that period, no sensible reduction of the amount was effected. Then came the checkered contest of 1739, and the more triumphant campaigns of the Seven Years' War, both of which added to the burden. But a far heavier weight was added by engaging in the contest with the United States. At its close in 1783 the national burdens were so greatly increased that both David Hume and Adam Smith believed that they would prove fatal to the nation. At that time the interest was no less than $47,258,860. The cost of the struggle with the United States was $487,997,480.

Pitt came into office in 1784. "The interest of the debt," says Alison, "absorbed now more than two-thirds of the public revenue. It was impossible to conceal that such a state of things was in the highest degree alarming, not only as affording no reasonable prospect that the existing engagements could ever be liquidated, but as threatening at no distant period to render it impossible for the nation to make those efforts which its honor or independence might require." The situation was deeply pondered by Mr. Pitt. Public attention had been directed by Dr. Price to the prodigious powers of the accumulation of money at compound interest, and he had demonstrated with mathematical certainty that any sum, however small, increasing in that way, would, in a given time, extinguish any debt. Pitt, accepting the views of Dr. Price, proposed to establish a plan for discharging the British debt. "All former sinking-funds had failed of producing great effects because they were directed to the annual discharge of a certain portion of debt, not the formation by compound interest of a fund destined to its future and progressive liquidation; they advanced, therefore, by addition, not multiplication, in an arithmetical, not a geometrical progression.... The wonderful powers of compound interest, the vast lever of geometrical progression, so long and sorely felt by debtors, were now to be applied to creditors."

Accordingly Pitt proposed that a million pounds should be vested in certain commissioners annually, which should be derived partly from savings effected in various branches of the service and partly from new taxes. The payments were to be made quarterly, and with the sums thus put into the hands of the commissioners they were to purchase stock, the dividends on which were to be invested in like manner. By thus setting apart a million pounds annually, and applying its interest to the purchase of stock, the success of the plan was regarded as a demonstrated certainty. The future accumulations would spring, not from any additional burdens imposed on the people, but from the dividends on the stock thus purchased. The powers of compound interest were thus to shift from the side of the creditor to that of the debtor, from the fundholders to the nation. The bill passed the house without a dissenting vote, and on the 26th of May, 1786, the king gave it the royal assent in person to mark his sense of the importance of the measure.

The fact that every dollar of debt discharged must come from the people in the way of taxation was a truth as obvious to Pitt as to Robert Hamilton, whose work on the National debt, first published in 1813, exploded the sinking-fund theory. Of course there was no magical power in the sinking-fund to draw money for paying the debt, but Pitt knew this as well as Hamilton. He knew that what came into the hands of the sinking-fund commissioners must be drawn from the tax-payer. But, as Alison truly says, "Pitt was perfectly aware of the natural impatience of taxation in general, and the especial desire always felt that, when the excitement of war ceased, its expenditure should draw to a termination. He foresaw, therefore, that it would be impossible to get the popular representatives at the conclusion of the war to lay on new taxes, and provide for a sinking-fund to pay off the debt which had been contracted during its continuance. The only way, therefore, to secure that inestimable object was to have the whole machinery constructed and in full activity during the war, so that it might be at once brought forward into full and efficient operation upon the conclusion of hostilities, without any legislative act or fresh imposition whatever." And although the true nature of the sinking-fund was after a time generally understood, yet through this machinery a large amount of indebtedness was discharged, far more probably than would have been if the people had clearly known how the reduction was effected. In other words this device blinded them; they did not know how much they were contributing toward paying the debt; if they had known, they would have set aside the plan at an earlier day.

It will be noticed in the foregoing table that old debts had increased in amount and new ones had been added. The debt of the United States had been created in contending against Great Britain. The debt of Russia consisted of notes issued by the Russian bank, which had been founded by the Empress Catherine in 1768. The finances of Prussia have been managed with great economy ever since the founding of the kingdom in 1700, and more than one king left a goodly treasure to his successor; but in the foregoing statement Prussia was a debtor to a small amount. The most noteworthy change beside the vast increase of the English debt was the diminution of the debt of France. That wonderful country, thrifty beyond comparison, has never done anything toward paying its debts, but on several occasions it has reduced them in a more speedy if less honorable manner. The first reduction while the Duke of Orleans was regent has been already described. It was frequently reduced and expanded during the reign of the two subsequent kings, and suffered a tremendous diminution amid the terrors of the Revolution of 1789. A vast amount of paper money was issued at that time. There were two kinds, the assignats and mandats. (See MONEY.) Of the former kind $6,125,000,000 were issued; of the mandats $480,000,000. The funded debt was also swelled to $480,000,000. This amount was afterward reduced two-thirds, and was consequently called the "Tiers Consolidés." A vast amount of paper money was issued in the time of John Law; for the history of his experiments see BANKING.

The next table of debts represents the indebtedness of the nations in 1820:

Great Britain...	$4,510,000,000	Russia............	$250,000,000
Low Countries.	720,000,000	Naples............	100,000,000
France	700,000,000	Portugal..........	40,000,000
Austria...........	493,500,000	Denmark........	21,500,000
Prussia and		United States...	91,015,566
German States	265,000,000	South America.	15,000,000
Spain	260,000,000	British India...	145,000,000

This period shows an enormous increase (above $5,000,000,000), more than two-thirds of which had been incurred by England. She now owed nearly three-fifths of the aggregate national debt of the world. This addition represented part of the expense to subdue Napoleon. The wars of that period mark a momentous epoch in English history. "Their effects and consequences," says Wilson, "are felt by us still, and, so far as one can see, will continue to be felt as long as England exists. Compared with what they cost us, all other outlays on our previous wars seem as nothing. Their charges led to the remodeling of our fiscal system, spurred the nation to great exertions, developed its trade, increased the poverty of its poor, and the wealth of its rich. We can form no intelligent conception of our financial position to-day, unless we can grasp some idea of what these wars meant and still mean for England."

Notwithstanding Pitt's greatness as a minister, he committed two errors from which his country has severely suffered. The first was in not waging the war against Napoleon with sufficient vigor during its early stages. Money and men enough were raised, but instead of sending the latter to the Continent to act in conjunction with the allies in putting down the common enemy, they were transported to India, where they performed a splendid service in winning an empire for the British crown; this, however, was a work which might have been postponed without much loss, while the delay to crush Napoleon in 1793, when it might have been done had Pitt employed all the resources at his command, entailed on his country a vastly greater burden which is destined to be felt by many succeeding generations.

The other mistake consisted in not borrowing more money at 5 instead of 3 per cent. interest. To clearly understand the serious consequences of this shortsighted policy it is only necessary to state that when loans were contracted bearing 3 per cent. interest the nation agreed to give 100 pounds for the 60 pounds which it received, whereas on the loans which bore 5 per cent. interest the nation received 100 pounds—the same sum which it agreed to pay. There was borrowed $3,000,000,000 of stock in the 3 per cents., and consequently the nation must pay $1,200,000,000 more than it ever received from the public creditors. Though the difference in the rate of interest was very considerable, yet on the return of peace the state acquired the power of lowering the rate of interest on its debts to the current rate by threatening to pay off the principal, an operation which was successfully performed by later administrations with the 4 and 5 per cents. By lowering the interest on the 5 per cents. in 1824 to 4, and in 1829 to 3½ per cent., no less than $12,000,000 annually was saved to the nation on that stock alone, though it amounted only to $785,000,000. Had the $1,800,000,000 which was actually paid by the public creditors for the $3,000,000,000 in the 3 per cents. been subjected to the same operation, the saving effected without doing injustice to any creditor would have been $27,500,000 a year. Besides, the 3 per cent. paid on the nominal amount of $3,000,000,000 received by the government was equivalent to 5 per cent. on the actual amount of $1,800,000,000. The national burden, therefore, was no lighter during the war by issuing 3 per cents. than it would have been had 5 per cents. been issued, and the greater burden afterward borne in consequence of adopting such a policy is very apparent.

It will be noticed that while France was the central figure in all the wars of this period her indebtedness did not increase with anything like the rapidity of that of England. It did not grow much beyond $500,000,000, although the empire was almost constantly engaged in war. Of this sum, too, $260,000,000 were levied for war contributions and the army of occupation after declaring peace. The reason for the small increase was that the French armies were fed, clothed, lodged, and paid very largely by foreign states. The revenues of France, as a good authority has stated, did not furnish more than half the total sum required to maintain the expensive and gigantic military establishment of the emperor, while its inhabitants received almost the whole benefit from its expenditure. This explains why he was constantly attempting to make fresh conquests and why the French people were so attached to his government. It also explains the internal prosperity of the country as well as the hatred with which France came to be regarded by foreign states.

Of all the nations of Europe which suffered by this system, Holland suffered most. Invaded and conquered by the French, she lost her commerce, her colonies, and her independence, and was obliged to pay war contributions to the French from 1794 to 1814, which amounted to nearly $500,000,000. Her funded debt also increased $220,000,000. Once a rich and brave people, they were enabled by borrowing to conquer their independence from Spain, to resist the encroachments of France, to carry on naval wars with England, and to rank as a first-rate power in Europe. But after 1715 her contest against the larger states was ended by exhaustion. She lost her commercial pre-eminence and resources through excessive taxation, and was weighed down by debt and competition with less burdened traders.

The increase of the debts of other European states during this period was caused mainly by the wars of Napoleon. The debt of the United States had been increased in consequence of engaging in a second war with Great Britain. After the amount of the Revolutionary debt was determined and funded, Congress devised a mode of reducing it; but, during the closing years of the 18th century, so many special and unexpected expenditures occurred that the amount remained about the same as it was when first funded. But in 1800 all untoward events within and without which had occasioned an increase of the army, the building of naval ships, and other preparations for threatened war passed away, and the debt-paying which then began continued without interruption until the opening of the second war with Great Britain. When this was ended in 1815 the debt had grown to $127,334,933; but the work of liquidation was again renewed, and by 1820 the national indebtedness had been reduced to the amount above mentioned.

The next table represents the national debts in 1848.

Great Britain	$4,019,145,810
France	910,000,000
Austria	625,000,000
Spain	565,000,000
Russia	500,000,000
The Netherlands	500,000,000
Prussia and German States	200,000,000
Italian States	150,000,000
Belgium	87,000,000
Portugal	85,000,000
Denmark	56,500,000
Greece	50,000,000
Sweden and Norway	3,000,000
United States	47,044,862
Mexico and South America	300,000,000
British Colonies	33,000,000
British India	250,000,000

For these thirty years the total indebtedness of nations was not very largely augmented, and only Sweden and Norway, Greece, and some British colonies were added to the roll of national debtors. The two most remarkable features in this statement are the reductions made in the English and Dutch debts. The principal reduction in the former was rapidly made after 1815. "If the sinking-fund had been let alone," said an able writer in 1832, "it would, since the year 1813, have paid off above £400,000,000; and even after deducting the immense loans of 1814 and 1815, the national debt would have been upwards of £300,000,000 less than it is now. In the year 1847, supposing no new debt contracted, it would have been entirely extinguished."

Turning now to the Netherlands, it may be remarked that when Napoleon took possession of the country he incorporated it with France, and reduced the debt to one-third of the former amount. Order was partly restored toward the end of 1813, after the arrival of the king, and on May 14, 1814, he presented to the States-General a new law for the regulation of the debt, by which the uniform rate of interest on all the stocks was fixed at 2½ per cent. Previously they had borne twelve different rates, varying from 1¼ to 7 per cent. Another provision of the law restored to the creditors the debt which Napoleon attempted to abolish. The nominal amount of the debt, therefore, was preserved, but the rate of interest was in the aggregate considerably reduced. Although new loans became necessary, yet by the operation of a sinking-fund, which was established at the time when the debt was restored and the rate of interest changed, and by the employment of surpluses in the same way, the debt was reduced at the beginning of 1851 to $512,300,000. The sum of $50,000,000 was transferred to Belgium after 1830, but a loan for as much more was negotiated to maintain the Belgian war.

In marked contrast with the action of the Dutch government in undoing the work of Napoleon and restoring the rights of its creditors was the action of the pope with respect to the creditors of the Roman state after the re-establishing of papal rule. When Napoleon invaded the latter state its debt amounted to $148,300,000. By a series of arbitrary orders it was declared to be extinguished. Napoleon realized that it was easier for him to impose new exactions if he could relieve those whom he conquered of their former burdens. When the pope regained power he did not recognize the existence of the old debt. It had become badly tangled, it is true, but the pope could have disentangled it if he had desired. He declared, however, that the debt had been extinguished by the action of the French emperor. Whatever regrets the pope may have had over other orders of Napoleon, there is no reason for believing that he was displeased with the great conqueror for his summary mode of relieving the Roman state of its obligations.

It will be noticed that France added $210,000,000 to her debt during the Orleans reign. Of this sum $150,000,000 were required to meet the deficits of the first four years after the Revolution. The addition to the Austrian debt was occasioned by annual deficits which have appeared without exception ever since 1789. With respect to Spain a commission was appointed in 1820 to examine into the public debt, and make recommendations concerning it. They reported the amount to be $700,000,000. This enormous increase since the time of Charles III. had come from the issue of bank and government notes. (See BANKING and MONEY.) Two years afterward the matter was reconsidered, and the amount was declared to be $260,000,000,—a wide departure from the former result. The doubling of the Russian debt was occasioned by war and by annual deficiencies. The increase consisted of paper money. The United States had paid off the debts of two wars, but had begun to accumulate debt in a time of profound peace, with no extraordinary expenditure, until 1846, when war broke out with Mexico, which gave rise to new loans for a considerable amount.

In 1870 we find the following figures of national indebtedness:

Great Britain	$3,989,718,300
France	2,277,522,000
Austria-Hungary	1,654,610,000
Russia	1,970,680,000
Italy	1,900,000,000
Spain	1,386,952,500
German Empire	720,242,000
Turkey	603,446,000
Netherlands	399,854,000
Portugal	294,990,000
Belgium	136,800,000
Smaller States	251,975,000
United States	2,480,672,427
British Colonies	101,600,000
Mexico and South America	1,060,000,000
British India	515,000,000
Japan, Ceylon, Hong-Kong	6,500,000
Australasia	178,720,000
Africa, Egypt, Morocco, etc.	198,275,000

What an enormous increase these figures show! And what a large number of states are now found in the company of debtors! Borrowing has become fashionable all over the world. At first confined to the older and richer countries, the fever has spread to the youngest and most impecunious. We hardly know which will surprise the reader most, the inclination of so many states to borrow, or the willingness of lenders to part with their money. The folly of much of this borrowing has long since been realized; but sweeping as national bankruptcy has been, it is feared that the list may be further enlarged.

Beginning with England, what do the figures show? A small decrease of $100,000,000,—a sum not so large as the United States, in several instances, has paid in a single year. England increased enormously during this period in wealth and population; but, instead of paying the national debt, the nation adopted the policy of remitting taxes and keeping up the interest account. It is true that an additional expense of $175,000,000 was incurred in 1855–56 for the Crimean war, and the expenditures were heavy for the Chinese and Abyssinian wars. Mr. Baxter has prepared the following table, which shows the total amount of capital paid off or expired from 1815 to 1870, not including the expense of the two wars just mentioned, which was paid out of the regular revenues:

1834, Negro Emancipation	$100,000,000
1846–47, Irish Famine	35,000,000
1855–56, Crimean War	175,000,000
1865, Fortifications	30,000,000
1869, Purchase of Telegraphs	35,000,000
Further balance paid off, being the difference between the total of $4,510,000,000 in 1815, and $4,000,000,000, in 1870	510,000,000
Total for the 55 years	$885,000,000
Being per year	$16,100,000

"But," says Baxter, "these figures take credit for $205,000,000, the value of the annuities existing before 1815, which were not created as a sinking fund; and they also take credit for the failure to meet the extraordinary emergencies during that period. The true reduction of the debt of 1815, by the efforts of the nation during the last fifty-five years, after providing for the expenditure of those years, is only

  Clear reduction $305,000,000
  Being per year 5,500,000

Such has been the progress of the English nation in the task of reducing the nominal capital of the national debt, a rate of progress that would require seven hundred more years to effect the final extinction of the debt existing in 1815."

While England reduced her debt somewhat during this period, the Netherlands did far more, comparatively, for she reduced hers $109,100,000. Thus in fifty-four years it has been diminished $320,000,000, a larger reduction than Great Britain effected during that time, although the latter country possessed tenfold more wealth and population.

But France added largely to her indebtedness. While the second republic lasted from March 1, 1848, to December 31, 1851, the deficit was $71,874,800, to cover which loans were necessary. The financial situation was not improved by establishing the second empire. The deficits continued. Extensive internal improvements were undertaken. Then there was a series of wars; the Crimean, Italian, Chinese, Anamite, and Mexican. These wars, beside other expenditures, occasioned deficits to the amount of $447,707,900. The total indebtedness of the nation, therefore, ran up to the very high figures above given previous to the outbreak of the Franco-German war.

Another marked change is noticeable in the Italian debt. Before annexation took place the debt of the kingdom of Sardinia in 1847 did not exceed $25,000,000. The difficulties of 1848 and the wars with Austria and Russia increased the debt within ten years to $200,000,000. When the kingdom of Italy was formed in 1861, the debt swelled to $420,000,000, including the Neapolitan debt of $125,000,000. But nine years afterwards the debt had reached the enormous sum of $1,857,300,000. Its increase had been more rapid than that of any other state. Every year after the formation of the Italian kingdom, March 17, 1861, ended with a deficiency until 1875. Perhaps no debt in Europe presses more severely on the people.

The United States now appears as the third on the list of borrowers, approaching very nearly to France. Great Britain, France, and the United States owed almost half the entire amount. The debt of the latter country was created with amazing rapidity; no nation ever spent so much for war purposes in so brief a period. This vast mass of indebtedness was accumulated in four years, for when the war broke out the national debt was only about $60,000,000. The money was borrowed at varying rates of interest from 5 to 7 7/10 per cent. A very large portion of the debt consisted of legal tender notes and other obligations bearing no interest.

On investigating the unexampled national borrowing which occurred in these twenty years, we find that the larger portion was spent to carry on wars and prepare for them; no inconsiderable sum was borrowed to pay constantly accruing deficiencies; a much smaller sum was expended for national improvements. A vast amount was spent in a most wasteful manner; and when the money was gone, more than one nation had but little to show for the expenditure. This was especially the case with Turkey, Egypt, Spain, Portugal, and the South American states. Borrowed money usually, as the world knows, is spent more recklessly than any other; this trite truth has been shockingly illustrated in the history of national spending.

We now come to the last date for tabulating the history of national borrowing, 1880. England no longer leads the nations; that unenviable distinction has passed to France.

France	$3,829,982,399
England	3,766,671,000
Russia	5,318,953,000
Spain	2,579,345,000
Italy	2,540,313,000
United States	2,120,415,370
Austria-Hungary	1,881,115,350
Turkey	1,376,486,500
Portugal	457,451,000
Netherlands	397,738,270
Belgium	508,269,490
German Empire	261,476,890
Roumania	118,742,600
Greece (1881)	71,540,155
Denmark	48,665,000
India	758,640,325
Australia	442,851,500
New Zealand	137,113,055
Japan	857,708,095
China	11,100,000
South America and Mexico	
Egypt	491,990,010

In this last decade the Franco-German and the Turkish wars have occurred, and a very short war between Germany and Austria, but no other costly operations of the kind have taken place in Europe, yet the growth of its national indebtedness has been truly fearful. Much of the money borrowed has been expended in building fortifications, ships, and in other warlike preparations. Something has been expended for internal improvements. Germany can give the most satisfactory account of her borrowings. It is said that her public property is quite sufficient to reimburse her debt. Her finances have been managed with great economy. Notwithstanding the heavy cost of the recent war to France she has been borrowing quite freely since to pay for building railroads and canals. Her budgets are made up in such a way that it is difficult to ascertain what are the yearly receipts and expenditures; what portion of the money borrowed has been spent in paying annual deficits is not publicly known. One thing is now certain: instead of having annual surpluses, as the finance ministers from time to time have announced, deficits have been constantly occurring, which were paid from loans contracted to pay for internal improvements. It may be added that the debts created in the Australian quarter of the world were for railroads, water-works, and other useful improvements, and the people living there have much to show for their expenditure. The debt of Japan was principally incurred in extinguishing the pensions which the nobles and priests drew from the government. Another portion was created to pay for building a railroad. The debt of China consists of two loans, one contracted in December, 1874, for $3,138,375, bearing eight per cent. interest; and the other in July, 1878, for $8,021,380 at the same rate.

Canada	286,112,295
Japan	249,108,517
South America (except as specified)	227,884,730
Mexico	203,244,300
Roumania	171,292,560
Sweden and Norway	104,008,358
Greece	91,618,340
Servia	62,550,000
Denmark	54,369,325
China	38,500,000
Switzerland	7,543,273

It will be seen from the above statement that the debt-making movement continues in many countries to advance, and that the total debt of the world has become terrible to contemplate, being in all over $35,000,000,000. These figures are, however, somewhat misleading, particularly in the case of the United States, whose net debt is greatly below that given, while much of the actual debt bears no interest. The gross debt is offset by large deposits of gold, silver, and notes in the treasury, the total net debt being $873,435,939, and the total interest-bearing debt, exclusive of bonds issued to Pacific railroads, $629,492,590. When it is remembered that on Aug. 1, 1865, the interest-bearing debt was $2,381,530,295, and that the rate of interest has been greatly decreased, it will be seen that the United States presents an instance of debt reduction unexampled in the history of the world. Only her rapid development of resources could have rendered such a result possible.

In contracting debts it is a very important question whether the money is advanced at home or comes from abroad. One reason why the English and French debts are cheerfully borne and the burden lightly felt is because almost the entire amount is held in the country which created the debt. In the United States a large portion of the debt was held abroad for several years, but the process of refunding it at lower rates of interest, and the movements of trade in favor of this country, have had the good effect of transferring nearly all the debt once held abroad to America. Less than $200,000,000 are owned probably by foreign creditors. The debt of Holland has also been owned at home. Indeed, in 1778, when the debt of that country was very large, the Dutch still owned more than $300,000,000 of the obligations of France and England.

But the case is very different with many nations. Nearly all the loans of Mexico and the South American states, those of Egypt, Turkey, Greece, Spain, and Portugal have been contracted with foreigners. Russia has contracted nineteen foreign loans since 1822, aggregating $734,900,000. It will be readily seen what a constant drain is going on in those countries to discharge the annual interest account. We might add, too, the British loans to India and to many English colonies. Of course the payment of so much interest abroad impoverishes a country. It can have no other effect. If there be a large trade-balance due to the interest-paying country, the effect of paying interest abroad may be counteracted; unhappily the nations which have borrowed the most freely from other countries have usually the smallest trade with them. So the account is kept perpetually on the wrong side for the debtor nations.

It is not singular, therefore, that such nations getting tired of paying, and knowing that the failure to pay will not cause loss at home, finally repudiate their obligations. France was perhaps the first nation to do this, but she has had many imitators in modern times. Over and over again Spain has compounded with her creditors. Greece has drawn a pretty wide line between her foreign and home creditors, paying the demands of the latter and ignoring those of the former. Many of the South American states long ago joined the ignoble but somewhat fashionable army of repudiators. Portugal belongs to the same category. Where a national debt is owned at home, a strong influence can be exerted to enforce its payment. Repudiation in that case at once creates a class of sufferers in the nation itself who, of course, will do their utmost to prevent it. But when the debt is held abroad too often all classes join in relieving themselves from the obligation of paying it.

One may ask how have so many nations been able to borrow so easily, especially after showing a disinclination to fulfil their obligations. This is one of the most curious chapters in the history of national borrowing. The brief answer is, many of these loans have been effected through the machinery which cunning bankers have devised. They have been offered large sums to negotiate loans, and the reward to be received in the event of success has been a sufficient stimulant to produce striking results. Hence bankers have almost always been found who were willing, nay, eager, to undertake these operations. A few years ago an investigation of this subject was made by a committee of the British Parliament and a flood of light was turned upon it.

In defence of the policy of paying a national debt slowly, it has been often urged with respect to Great Britain and some other nations that they were increasing in wealth and numbers, and consequently the burden grew lighter every year. Tables have been constructed from time to time showing the amount of debt, income, and population, and how the burden was diminishing. One of these, perhaps the most carefully calculated, may be found in that excellent work, Mulhall's *Progress of the World*.

But there is a great deal of delusion in these calculations. In the first place while it is perfectly clear that if the amount of debt is unchanged and the population increases, the average amount which one must pay is diminished, it does not follow that the amount is in any sense diminished for those who must pay. If the addition to the population be paupers or persons who are unable to pay, the burden of the others is not lightened. It remains the same. Now while the population in all countries is increasing, pauperism in some of them is increasing with frightful rapidity, so that an increase of their numbers does not diminish their burden of debt. This however is not true with respect to all nations, as a writer in a recent number of the *Contemporary Review* has shown.

Of course an increase of wealth diminishes the burden. This is true in one sense, though not in another. Two conditions must exist to make debt-paying possible: first, the means; secondly, the inclination. The truth is in countries where the theory of deferring the payment of their national debts is advocated that their citizens may increase in wealth and numbers, the way is solidly paved either for making their debts perpetual or for repudiating them. The desire to pay ceases. No country better illustrates this truth than Great Britain. While a certain class, and among them her ablest and best men, strongly favor a more rapid reduction of the debt, the idea is not popular. Mr. Gladstone has advocated a speedier reduction on many occasions. And, to effect this end, a kind of securities known as terminable annuities have been devised. These are formed by converting portions of debt into a security the annual payment on which is considerably higher than the rate of interest on the former security, but after a certain number of years the payment ceases and the debt itself is extinguished. As people are willing to discharge the interest on the debt, these conversions are made in order to blind the people into paying what they would not pay in the ordinary way by direct purchase.

While the policy of the English government in reducing taxes after the close of the Napoleonic wars was a wise one, yet not a few thoughtful persons have contended that the reductions were carried too far; that England ought to have proceeded more rapidly in cutting down her debt. Now the opposition to reducing the debt is so strong that it is very difficult to accomplish much. Nothing can be truer than that the best time to pay debts is when the people are in the mood for paying them. Possibly they might be richer at a future time, but if the inclination does not then exist, debt-paying is far more difficult. If any reduction were effected it would be an unwilling one, and would be regarded as a greater burden than the payment of the same or greater sum when the willingness to pay it prevailed.

Mr. Baxter in his work on *National Debts* reached sundry conclusions on this subject which are so valuable and weighty that we shall reproduce them. "A national debt is a mortgage of the future income and earnings of a nation, and shifts the burden from the borrowing generation to materially different property and earners. Hence it is only justifiable in case of great emergencies, with which the state is unable otherwise to cope; but it is then able to render great services to the nation. It generally leads to much greater and less economical expenditure, and is raised on onerous terms. It weakens a nation by withdrawing capital from productive employment and improvements, and also by necessitating additional and often injurious taxation. Its bad effect is modified by the growth of the nation, which gradually diminishes its pressure and burden. But great wars from time to time arise, requiring large increases of debt, so that national growth cannot be depended on to wipe out a national debt. In time of peace the industrial competition of nations gives a great advantage in the market of the world to the nation least weighted by debt. The removal of prejudicial taxation, so long as it exists, must be the principal object of exertion. But for war reasons, and also for peace reasons, it is always the true policy of a nation to keep steadily in view, and persevere in efforts for, the reduction of its national debt."

Having considered the national debts of the world, perhaps something ought to be added concerning the debts of the States composing the American Union. During the Revolutionary war they contracted debts to a considerable amount for war purposes. The contributions made by them were very unequal, but the Congress of the Confederation promised that justice should be rendered to all in the end. When the war was over, and the subject of funding the Revolutionary debt was discussed in Congress, there was a very strong opposition to assuming the debts of any States. Hamilton contended that when the debts were contracted the various States expected the Federal government to discharge them. There was another reason why the government should do it. Previous to entering into the permanent union the States on the seaboard collected taxes on imports, but this right was relinquished to the general government when the Constitution was adopted. Since they had parted with their richest sources of revenue the government was clearly bound to take the State burdens at that time existing. To take the taxes, or the right to receive them, and not pay the debts when due, was an unjustifiable proceeding. The motion to assume was carried by only two votes, and even this slim majority was obtained only by a consent on the part of Northern members to locate the capital on the banks of the Potomac. Besides, not the entire amount was assumed, but an arbitrary sum which was fixed at $21,500,000. A balance of about $4,000,000 was left which Congress would never consent should be paid by the government, although several efforts were made to secure the public assumption of the entire amount.

The balance that was not assumed was so small, however, that it formed no burden to the States, so that they really began under the present Constitution with no debts worth mentioning. For many years, too, they remained in that happy condition. Some of them assisted the Federal government in the way of loans during the war of 1812, but not until 1820, or more than 30 years after the adoption of the Constitution, did they incur much indebtedness. After that date they began to borrow, and during the next 20 years they piled up $200,000,000 of indebtedness. In this sum, however, is included $28,101,644.91 deposited with the States by the general government which had accrued as surplus revenue after discharging the national debt. Leaving out this advance to the States they had borrowed more than $170,000,000 in these 20 years. What did they do with the money? Mr. Flagg, once the comptroller of New York, declared it was spent essentially in the following manner: about 31 per cent., or $52,640,000, were expended in aiding State banks; $60,201,551 were expended for canals; nearly 25 per cent., or $42,871,084, were furnished to railroads, and $6,618,958 for turnpikes and macadamized roads, and the balance was expended for several objects. Over $100,000,000 therefore were spent for internal improvements.

These debts were chiefly due to British creditors. They were converted into stock, and held in shares, and passed through many hands, but after a short time some States became negligent about paying. The States finally turned toward the Federal government for relief. We have just remarked that the government deposited a large sum with the States in 1837, but this was not the entire amount of the surplus which Congress had ordered to be disposed of in this manner. It was three-quarters of it, but in consequence of the panic which swept over the country before the close of 1837, the government was not able to deposit the other quarter. Woodbury, the secretary of the treasury, recommended that Congress should ask the States to refund the money, inasmuch as the government was in sore need of it. But Congress had no thought of heeding his advice. On the other hand, it insisted at a little later period that the remaining quarter of the surplus should be deposited with them, but if the government complied it must borrow the money, for after 1837 for several years there was an annual deficit. Congress had temporarily stopped the payment of this quarter, and was angry with the president afterward because he would not consent to the legislation needed for paying this sum to the States. Failing to get that they sought to obtain the income from the sales of public lands. They were truly in great need of money, but the president was inflexible. Then William Cost Johnson, of Maryland, in 1842, introduced a new scheme which was nothing less than the assumption of the State debts by the government. This plan emanated from the other side of the Atlantic. Benton says that "these British capitalists, connected with capitalists in the United States, possessed a weight on this point which was felt in the halls of Congress. The disguised attempts at this assumption were in the various modes of conveying Federal money to the States in the shape of distributing surplus revenue, of dividing the public land money, and of bestowing money on the States under the fallacious title of a deposit. But a more direct provision in their behalf was wanted by these capitalists, and in the course of the year 1839 a movement to that effect was openly made through the columns of their regular organ, *The London Banker's Circular*, emanating from the most respectable and opulent house of the Messrs. Baring Brothers and Company."

A special committee was appointed to consider the matter, who reported in March, 1843. Johnson was chairman. Their appointment was based on numerous memorials for relief presented to the house desiring the issue of $200,000,000 of stock, which should be divided among all the States, Territories, and the District of Columbia. The memorialists desired also that the stock should be issued on the faith of the general government, and that the proceeds of the public lands should be specifically pledged for the payment of interest and principal. The industries of the country were then suffering an eclipse, and those who favored the assumption of the State debts believed 'that things would not improve until the States were relieved of their burdens. The committee also believed that the principal cause of the embarrassment then existing arose from the heavy State indebtedness. "At so late a period as 1830," the committee remarked, "very few of the States were indebted, and those few to a very moderate amount, whilst most of them had surplus revenues in their treasuries. Animated by a spirit of enterprise, in some cases perhaps imprudent, to develop their resurces, and encouraged for a time by the aid of the national treasury, some of the States embarked in systems of internal improvement too vast in design and too extensive for immediate accomplishment with their limited means, and, when suddenly all aid from the national treasury was withheld, had recourse to their own separate credit to effect what only the joint action of the States and the general government should perhaps have attempted, and which, by their united capacities alone, could have been successfully accomplished."

The interest on the State debts was payable abroad in specie or its equivalent. The States had no power to raise a revenue except by direct taxation. Some of them had already failed to comply with their engagements, because, as they declared, of their inability. The foreign holders were willing to reduce the rate of interest one-half if the government would assume the debts, and the saving thus effected, as the committee remarked, "set apart as a sinking-fund, at six per centum, would liquidate the principal of $200,000,000 in 18¾ years." The committee did not propose simply that the government should assume the obligations of the debtor States: the injustice of doing this was seen from the outset. What they did propose, therefore, was "to place all the States upon an equality in the benefit of the distribution of the stock, of the interest thereon as well as the principal."

The following table represents the State indebtedness on Sept. 2, 1842:

Maine	$1,734,861.47
Massachusetts	5,424,137.00
Pennsylvania	36,336,044.00
New York	21,797,267.91
Maryland	15,214,761.49
Virginia	6,994,307.54
South Carolina	5,691,234.41
Georgia	1,309,750.00
Alabama	15,400,000.00
Louisiana	23,985,000.00
Mississippi	7,000,000.00
Arkansas	2,676,000.00
Florida Territory	4,000,000.00
Tennessee	3,198,166.00
Kentucky	3,085,500.00
Michigan	5,611,000.00
Ohio	10,924,123.00
Indiana	12,751,000.00
Illinois	13,527,292.53
Missouri	842,261.00
District of Columbia	1,316,030.00
Total	$198,818,736.35

Although State indebtedness had spread over the country, very different views existed in the several sections about paying it. In the East, for example, no one thought of such a thing as not paying the obligations incurred. Massachusetts had created her debt chiefly in aiding a railroad enterprise; the investment was deemed wise, and no general regret was expressed because it had been made. A large portion of the indebtedness of New York had been incurred for building the Erie Canal. While, therefore, some States were very strenuous in having their burdens put on the shoulders of the general government, there was strong opposition to the measure, and it did not pass the house. A great deal was said during the debate about the assumption of the State debts in 1790, but the nature of these was entirely different. They had been created for the general good, and it was just that the government should assume them; but the debts since incurred were strictly of a local nature, and there was no reason why the government should be burdened with them. The amount, it will be noticed, was greater than that accruing from either war with Great Britain.

From that period until the outbreak of the war in 1861 the debts of the States did not increase much. Nothing more was heard about the federal assumption of them. Several of the States repudiated their debts, others reduced theirs, and in a few instances new debts were contracted. The following table gives a sectional view of State indebtedness from 1842 to 1860:

	1842.	1852.	1860.
New England States	$7,153,274	$6,862,265	$7,398,069
Middle States	73,348,072	79,510,726	86,416,045
Southern States	73,340,017	64,499,726	93,046,934
Western States	59,931,553	42,993,185	49,395,325
Pacific States		2,159,403	
Total	$213,777,916	$196,025,305	$236,256,364

During the war from 1861-65 the debts of the States were considerably increased by that event, but the indebtedness of the Southern section was swelled far more during a brief period afterward than were the debts of all the other sections by the war itself. Under the guise of internal improvements the debts of the Southern States after reconstruction had taken place increased at a rapid pace. Many of their bonds were negotiated under suspicious circumstances. In 1870 and in 1880 the debts of the States stood thus:

	1870.	1880.
New England States	$50,348,550	$49,969,514
Middle States	79,834,481	45,672,575
Southern States	174,486,452	113,967,243
Western States	44,018,911	36,565,360
Pacific States	4,178,504	4,547,389
Total	$352,866,898	$250,722,081

The reductions shown for 1880 were made by the Middle and Western States by actual payments, but this was not the case with the Southern States. Their sixty millions of reduction were effected by the much easier mode of repudiation. In nearly all of the States the policy of a gradual reduction has been established, the total bonded debt of 1890 being $194,954,207, a reduction since 1880 of over $55,000,000.

Authorities.—From Maurice Block's valuable *Statistique de la France* much may be gathered, not only concerning France, but other European countries. R. Dudley Baxter's *National Debts* (London, 1871) is also noteworthy. General papers on this subject have been read before the London Statistical Society, which are rich in facts and deductions. The first was read by Leone Levi in 1862 (vol. xxv., p. 313); the second by R. Dudley Baxter in 1874 (vol. xxxvii., p. 1); the third, and perhaps the ablest, by Hyde Clark in 1878 (vol. xli., p. 299). A very concise account of the national debts of Europe in 1840 may be found in *Hunt's Merchants' Magazine* (vol. viii., p. 397). The *Statesman's Year-Book* is a valuable repertory. Concerning the debt incurred by the Franco-German war of 1870-71, how the money was raised and paid, see Robert Giffen's excellent essay in his *Essays in Finance*; also another in *Blackwood's Magazine*, Feb., 1875, entitled "The Payment of the Five Milliards." Additional facts respecting the Italian debt are given by Leone Levi in a paper on "The Economic Progress of Italy during the last Twenty Years," which was read before the London Statistical Society in March, 1882. More complete information, however, is furnished by Mr. Herries in his report of 1876 as secretary of the English embassy and legation to Italy. A clear statement of the Japanese debt was made by Consul-General Van Buren in No. 15 of the *Reports from the Consuls of the U.S.*, Jan., 1882. For statistics of debt of the United States and the debts of the States see R. P. Porter's Special Report in the Census for 1880. Two papers on "Modern Public Debts and the Payment of Them," by Henry C. Adams, in the *International Review*, March and September, 1881, are worthy of mention in this connection.

(A. S. B.)

DE CANDOLLE, ALPHONSE LOUIS PIERRE PYRAMUS, a Swiss botanist, was born at Paris, Oct. 27, 1806. He is the son of the celebrated botanist, Augustin Pyramus de Candolle. He was educated at Geneva, to which city his father had returned in 1816. Having studied law he received the degree of doctor for his thesis on *The Law of Purdon*, which was published at Geneva in 1829. Yet he preferred to devote himself to the science in which his father had become famous, and in the study of which his father's instructions, library, and herbarium afforded him great advantages. One of his earliest publications was a *Monographe des Campanulées*, Paris, 1830. In the next year he was appointed professor of botany in the Academy of Geneva, and soon after prepared an elementary work, *Introduction à l'étude de la botanique*, 1835. He also assisted his father in the celebrated work, *Prodromus systematis naturalis regni vegetabilis*, and after his father's death in 1841 continued the work with the aid of botanists of various countries. Volumes vii. to xvii. contain many monographs of families prepared by him. After a time changes in the administration at Geneva obliged him to resign his position as professor and as director of the botanic garden. He then engaged chiefly in original research in his chosen field, and in 1835 published a valuable work entitled *Géographie botanique raisonnée*, which has procured for him a world-wide reputation. In 1866 he was elected president of the International Botanical Congress at London, and in the following year of a similar congress at Paris. In the latter a summary of laws on botanical nomenclature presented by him was adopted and has been published with notes in French, German, and English. Having already been a correspondent of the French Academy of Sciences, De Candolle was in 1874 chosen a foreign associate of that body, succeeding Prof. Agassiz. As the entire number of such associates is limited to eight, this position is one of the highest scientific honors of the present day. De Candolle has also been elected a member of the most eminent European scientific bodies as well as of the American Academy of Science. His labors in the cause of science have not prevented him from taking part in the public affairs of his city; he has several times been a member of its legislature and twice of its constituent assembly, acting with the liberal party. He is also president of the Geneva Society of Arts.

Besides a large number of memoirs and the works already mentioned he has published a *Histoire des Sciences et des Savants depuis deux siècles, suivie d'autres études sur des sujets scientifiques*, Geneva, 1873. This work has already become rare. A later practical work is his *Phytographie, ou l'art de décrire les végétaux considérés sous differents points de vue*, Paris, 1880. His latest work is *Origine des Plantes cultivées*, Paris, 1883.

DE CANDOLLE, ANNE CASIMIR PYRAMUS, a Swiss botanist, son of the preceding, was born at Geneva, Feb. 20, 1836. He completed his literary and classical studies at the University of Geneva, from which he received the degree of doctor of philosophy. He assisted his father in editing the *Prodromus*, as well as a continuation of that work in four volumes. These contain numerous monographs on families of plants written by him. He has given especial attention to the arrangement and formation of leaves; his most important treatise on this subject is *Considerations sur l'étude de la phyllotaxie* (1881).

DECATUR, a city of Illinois, county-seat of Macon co., is on Sangamon River, 39 miles E. of Springfield. It is on the main line of the Wabash, St. Louis, and Pacific Railroad, at the junction of the St. Louis, the Chicago, and the Champaign divisions; also on the Illinois Central, the Illinois Midland, the Peoria, Decatur, and Evansville, and a branch of the Indianapolis, Bloomington, and Western Railroad. Decatur has a national and 3 other banks, 4 weekly and 3 daily newspapers, 14 churches, 6 public-school buildings, also 2 large flour-mills, furniture-works, an iron-mill, and manufactories of farm implements and castings. It is thriving and pleasant, with gas- and water-works, and a park. The city debt is about $100,000, and the annual public expense about $60,000. Decatur was settled in 1820 and incorporated in 1829. Population, 16,481.

DECATUR, STEPHEN (1751-1808), an American naval officer, was born at Newport, R. I., in 1751. During the Revolutionary war he commanded several privateers and captured many English vessels. In 1798, when the navy was reorganized on account of trouble with France, he was appointed captain and placed in command of the Delaware, 20 guns, and cruised in the West Indies, where he captured some French privateers. He was afterwards placed in command of a squadron of thirteen sail on the Guadeloupe station. When the navy was reduced in 1801 he was discharged, and engaged in commerce in Philadelphia, where he died Nov. 14, 1808.

DECATUR, STEPHEN, JR. (1779-1820), son of the preceding, a distinguished American commodore, was born at Sinnepuxent, Md., Jan. 5, 1779. The family resided in Philadelphia, but his mother had taken refuge at this place when the British army occupied that city in 1777. After a brief experience in merchant vessels, Stephen entered the navy as a midshipman in 1798, and served in the West Indies under Com. John Barry. In the next year he was made a lieutenant, and in May, 1801, sailed in the Essex, under Capt. William Bainbridge, to Tripoli. Having been transferred to the frigate New York, Capt. James Barron, he acted as second in a duel at Malta in which an English officer was killed. When the governor of the island demanded the surrender of all concerned in the affair, Decatur was permitted to return to the United States. In November, 1803, he rejoined the fleet at Tripoli under Com. Preble, and was placed in command of the Enterprise. He soon formed a project of destroying the frigate Philadelphia, which had been captured by the Tripolitans, and was then lying in the harbor close by the castle and batteries. For this purpose he sailed into the harbor on the night of Feb. 15, 1804, with seventy men and thirteen officers in a small vessel that had been captured from the Tripolitans and named the Intrepid. When hailed and ordered to anchor, he directed his Maltese pilot to answer that he had lost his anchor. He was thus permitted to reach and board the frigate, when he quickly overpowered the Turkish crew, some of whom swam ashore, while at least twenty were slain. Spreading combustibles throughout the frigate, he set it on fire, and sailed back in the Intrepid without losing a man. For this exploit he was promoted to be captain. Congress presented to him a sword and voted two months' extra pay to all who had shared in the adventure. He continued to serve in the blockading fleet, and when Com. Preble bombarded the town and attacked the shore-batteries with his frigates, Aug. 3, 1804, Decatur led three gunboats in an engagement with a much larger number. With twenty-seven men he boarded a boat containing forty, and in ten minutes made it a prize. Meantime, his brother, Lieut. James Decatur, commanding another boat, was shot by a Turkish captain as he stepped on a vessel that had pretended to surrender. Stephen hastened in pursuit, boarded the vessel with eleven men, and after a desperate struggle killed the Turk. Of the eighty men in the two boats thus captured, fifty-two were killed or wounded, while the loss of the Americans was only fourteen. At the close of the war Decatur returned to America, and was employed in superintending the building of the gunboats ordered by Jefferson's administration until he superseded Com. Barron in command of the Chesapeake. In 1812 he was removed to the frigate United States, 44 guns, in which, on Oct. 25, he encountered the British frigate Macedonian, 49 guns, and captured her after a fight of an hour and a half, in which his loss was twelve and that of the enemy 104. Capt. Decatur, however, as an acknowledgment of the bravery of Capt. Carden of the Macedonian, refused to take his sword. His vessel was carried into New York, and Congress voted a gold medal to Decatur and a silver one to each officer under him. In 1813, the harbor of New York being closely blockaded, Decatur, attempting to pass to sea by Long Island Sound, was intercepted by the British fleet and driven into New London, where he remained over a year closely shut up in spite of his attempts to break the blockade. Decatur asserted that persons on shore gave warning to the ships outside of his movements by burning blue lights, and on account of this charge the political opponents of the war were henceforth called "Blue Lights." In the summer of 1814 he was transferred to the command of a squadron intended to sail from New York for a cruise in the East Indies, but here also was unable to leave the port until Jan. 15, 1815, when he sailed on a tempestuous night in the President, a 44-gun ship. Having grounded while crossing the bar, his vessel was injured, and when espied by the blockading squadron was chased for fifty miles. After a severe engagement with the Endymion, 40 guns, the President, being surrounded by three others, was obliged to surrender, and was carried into Bermuda. Decatur was paroled, and on his return to the United States was honorably acquitted by a court of inquiry for the loss of his ship. In May he was despatched with a squadron of nine vessels to the Mediterranean, and on June 17, off Cape de Gatte, fought and captured an Algerine frigate, 46 guns, the Algerine admiral, Rais Hammida, being killed in the action. Two days later Decatur captured another vessel of 22 guns, and on June 28 anchored with his whole squadron in the harbor of Algiers and demanded the immediate negotiation of a treaty. The dey, compelled to submit, surrendered all demands for tribute from the United States, restored all prisoners and property taken during the war, and received the vessels that had been captured a few days before. Decatur, then proceeding to Tunis and Tripoli, demanded and obtained satisfaction for past offences and the release of all American captives. He thus effectually showed the nations of Europe how to put an end to the piracy and insolence of the Barbary States, which had lasted for nearly three centuries. On his return to the United States he was appointed naval commissioner, residing in Washington. He was mortally wounded in a duel with Com. Barron, near Bladensburg, and died at Washington, D. C., March 22, 1820.

DECHAMPS, AUGUSTE ISIDORE VICTOR (1810-1882), a Belgian cardinal, born at Melle, East Flanders, Dec. 6, 1810, a brother of Adolphe Dechamps, a noted statesman, with whom he was educated at the Musée of Brussels. In youth he joined his brother in writing liberal articles for l'Emancipation and the Journal des Flandres. At that time he professed himself a disciple of Lamennais, a master whom he did not long follow. He studied divinity at the Tournay Seminary, at Mechlin, and the University of Louvain, and after joining the Redemptorists studied six years longer at Wittem, in the Netherlands. Thereafter he began a distinguished career as a pulpit orator, taking rank as a preacher with Dupanloup and Lacordaire. In 1865 he was consecrated bishop of Namur in 1867 he was translated to the archiepiscopal see of Mechlin (Malines), and in 1875 he was made a cardinal-priest. In the struggle of 1879 between the liberals of Belgium and the Ultramontanes regarding the secularizing of the public schools, Dechamps was the leader of the church party. Pope Leo XIII. addressed to Dechamps his celebrated letter of Dec. 20, 1880, on the Thomist philosophy. The cardinal was also a strenuous opponent of freemasonry. He died Sept. 29, 1883. Among his books are, *Le Christ et les antichrists* (1858); *La Question religieuse résolue par les faits* (1860); *Lettres théologiques* (1861); *Pie IX. et les erreurs contemporaines* (1865); *St. Vincent de Paul et les Misérables* (1865); *Appel et défi* (1865); *l' Infaillibilité et le concile général* (1869); and *La franc-maçonnerie* (1875).

The cardinal's elder brother, ADOLPHE DECHAMPS (1807-1875), was in early life a Liberal Catholic of republican proclivities, later a moderate liberal, and after 1851 a leader of the party of the episcopate He took a very important part in Belgian politics, in the cabinet and the legislative chambers, and as editor of the *Revue de Bruxelles* and the ultramontane *Revue Generale*. Among his writings are *Le second empire* (1859); *L'empire et l'Angleterre* (1860); *Jules César, l'empire jugé par l'empereur* (1865); *Les partis en Belgique* (1866).

DECORAH, the county-seat of Winneshiek co., Iowa, is on the Upper Iowa River, crossed here by two bridges, and on a branch of the Chicago, Milwaukee, and St. Paul Railroad, 30 miles W. of the Mississippi River, and 13 miles S. of the Minnesota line. It has 3 banks (1 national), 4 hotels, 7 churches, an academy and public schools, and is the seat of the Norwegian Luther College of the Northwest, a Lutheran institution with fine buildings, founded in 1861. Decorah has 5 weekly newspapers (1 Norwegian), and 3 literary and religious periodicals issued by the college. It has abundant water-power, which is used in a woollen-mill, agricultural implement factory, and flour-mills. It has also a scale-manufactory, 2 creameries, and other industries. It was settled in 1859, being named from Decorah, a Winnebago chief, and incorporated in 1867. Population, 3223.

DEDHAM, a town of Massachusetts, county-seat of Norfolk co., 10 miles S. W. of Boston, with which it is connected by two lines of the Boston and Providence Railroad, and by the New York and New England Railroad. It contains a granite court-house with a dome; a jail and house of correction, also of granite; a town-hall of stone (erected as a memorial of Dedham soldiers who fell in the war of 1861-65), a handsome stone railroad station, 10 churches (several of the number being fine structures), a national bank with a capital of $300,000, a savings bank (fund and surplus, $1,600,000), 2 fire insurance companies, a public library (8,000 volumes), a historical society, an asylum for its discharged female prisoners of the State, high and graded schools, a manufactory of woollens, with 3 large mills, various minor industrial establishments, gas- and water-works, and 2 weekly newspapers. "Mother Brook," a stream of water 3 miles long and partly artificial (made about the year 1639), diverts one-third of the water of Charles River and takes it to a branch of the Neponset, affording to Dedham and East Dedham very valuable water-power. Valuation in 1883, $4,966,250; yearly expenses, $78,000. There is no public debt. Dedham was settled in 1635 and was for a time called Contentment. Population of township 7119.

DE DONIS, THE STATUTE, more properly, the statute *De Donis conditionalibus*, being chapter i. of the Statute of Westminster the Second, passed in 13 Edw. I., A. D. 1285. The object of this statute was to prevent the alienation of landed property by those who held only limited estates therein, so as to defeat the estates of those who would otherwise take subsequently.

It was not uncommon during the general prevalence of the feudal system for a grant of land to be made in such form that upon the death of the original feoffee the same should descend only to the heirs of his body, and not to any of his collateral relatives. It is indeed supposed by many, and with much reason, that this was the universal form of the original feudal grants. An estate of this kind being, however, a restricted or limited feud, because it did not descend to all of the heirs, was called *feudum talliatum*, from *tailler*, to cut or mutilate, and in English a "fee-tail." Fee-tails existed among the Saxons in very early times, and were continued by the Normans after the Conquest. By a curious subtlety, however, they seem to have lost in England much of their distinguishing character. Where an estate was given in such a form, it was held to be in effect a conditional fee; *i. e.*, if the donee should not have heirs or issue according to the prescribed description, the land was held to revert to the donor: if, however, the condition of the grant was performed by the birth of such heirs presumptive or issue, then the donee was held to be immediately seised in fee simple, so that he might charge or alien the land as he could a fee-simple estate.

The barons of the realm, to whom this doctrine of conditional fees was peculiarly distasteful, appealed to King Edward I. for a restoration of the ancient strictness of the *feudum talliatum*. The result was the passage of the statute *De Donis*, the provisions of which substantially were, that in every case the will of the donor, according to the form in the deed of gift (*secundum formam in charta sui doni*), manifestly expressed, should be thenceforth observed, so that they to whom the land was given should have no power to alien the same, but that it should descend to their issue, or, in default of such issue, revert to the donor and his heirs.

The statute, being regarded as a remedial one by the courts, was liberally construed, and as a consequence a serious check was put to the alienation of lands throughout the realm. The obscure doctrine of collateral warranty afforded relief in some cases by authorizing alienation by a tenant in tail. No perfect system for evading the statute was, however, devised until near two hundred years afterwards. But at length, in 12 Edw. IV., A. D. 1472, the King's Bench in Taltarum's Case indicated that by the solemn farce of a common recovery a tenant in tail might alien his lands in fee, notwithstanding the provisions of the statute *De Donis*. Fines came a little later to be held capable of producing the same effect. Both these devices have now, however, been done away with by 3 & 4 Wm. IV. c. 104, and a tenant in tail is now enabled to alienate in fee by executing an ordinary deed reciting his intention to bar the entail and attended by certain simple formalities.

The statute *De Donis* is believed to have been originally in force in all the American colonies except South Carolina, fines and recoveries being commonly used to evade its provisions. In Virginia, so solicitous were the authorities to carry out its intent that fines and recoveries were expressly abolished by statute

In some of the United States statutes have been passed which virtually repeal the statute *De Donis*. This is the case in Alabama, California, Florida, Georgia, Indiana, Iowa, Kentucky, Maryland, Michigan, Minnesota, Mississippi, New York, North Carolina, South Carolina, Tennessee, Texas, Wisconsin, Virginia, West Virginia, and Dakota. In others the original tenant in tail is made tenant for life, with remainder to his heirs in fee. This is the law in Arkansas, Illinois, and Vermont. In all the rest of the States, where estates tail still exist, they may be barred at any time by deeds properly executed and enrolled.

(L. L., JR.)

DEED, in law, any contract or agreement in writing under seal. The term is usually applied to an instrument whereby lands, tenements, and hereditaments are conveyed from one person to another.

See Vol. VII. p. 22 Am. ed. (p. 23 Edin. ed.).

Deeds for the conveyance of real estate are either deeds poll or indentures. A deed poll is one executed by one person only, and is so called because it is polled or shaven quite even at the top. An indenture is a deed which is either actually or in contemplation of law made by and between two or more parties. It is so called because in early times two copies of the deed were usually written upon the same skin and subsequently cut apart in a sinuous or indented line, thus giving to each party a copy of the instrument.

The requisites of a good deed are said to be, (1) Competent parties and a sufficient thing or subject-matter. (2) Consideration, either good or valuable, though this in some of the common law conveyances seems not to be necessary. (3) The deed must be written or printed on parchment or paper. (4) It must contain sufficient and orderly parts. (5) It must be signed and sealed. (6) It must be delivered. (7) It ought properly to be executed in the presence of witnesses.

The regular and orderly parts of a deed are: (1) The premises, setting forth the number and names of the parties, together with such recitals as are essential or desirable to a complete understanding of the instrument. (2) The operative words of the deed, together with the *habendum* and *tenendum*, the former being intended to indicate what estate or interest is granted by the deed. (3) The description of the premises conveyed, which should be accurately set forth by metes and bounds. (4) The *reddendum* or statement of what reservation, of rent, etc., is created. (5) The conditions on which the grant is made, if any such there be. (6) The covenants entered into by the parties, *first*, those of the grantor; *second*, those of the grantee. (7) The conclusion, including the date of the execution of the instrument.

Deeds are divided into (1) those which derive their efficacy from the common law. These are deeds of feoffment, gift, grant, lease, exchange, partition, release, confirmation, surrender, assignment, and defeasance. (2) Those which derive their efficacy from the statute of uses. These are deeds covenanting to stand seised to uses, deeds of bargain and sale, deeds of lease and release, and deeds to lead, declare, or revoke uses.

In England, until recently, deeds of lease and release were most commonly used to transfer title to real estate, but by Stat. 8 & 9 Vict., c. 106, a deed of grant alone is made sufficient to convey all sorts of lands, tenements, and hereditaments, whether corporeal or incorporeal.

In many of the United States similar statutes have been passed, and where this is not the case deeds of bargain and sale are generally in use. (See BARGAIN AND SALE.)

In this country the universal adoption of the system of acknowledging and recording deeds has done away with many difficult legal questions formerly raised in this connection. (See ACKNOWLEDGMENT.) (L. L., JR.)

DEEMS, CHARLES FORCE, D. D., LL.D., was born in Baltimore, Md., Dec. 4, 1820. He graduated at Dickinson College in 1839, and in 1841 became the agent of the American Bible Society for North Carolina. In the same year he was elected to a professorship in the University of that State, and five years later was elected professor of natural science in Randolph-Macon College, Va. On his return to North Carolina he became president of Greensboro' Female College, and subsequently entered the pastorate. He had charge of churches in Newberne, Wilmington, and Goldsboro', and was repeatedly presiding elder of districts in North Carolina and delegate to the General Conference of the Methodist Episcopal Church, South. After the war he went to New York and established an independent church, called "The Church of the Strangers," which was organized in Jan., 1868, and of which he is still pastor. He has been much engaged in journalism, and is the founder of Leslie's *Sunday Magazine*. He is also the founder of the "American Institute of Christian Philosophy." Besides many sermons, addresses, and reviews, he is the author of *What Now?* (1869), *The Home Altar* (1867), and *Who was Jesus?* (1879), the last being an inquiry into the relation of Jesus to history.

DEERFIELD, a village of Franklin co., Mass., near the W. bank of the Connecticut River, 33 miles N. of Springfield. The Connecticut River Railroad and a branch of the New Haven and Hoosac Tunnel Railroad pass through the village. The Deerfield River flows through the town into the Connecticut River, making the Deerfield meadows noted for their tobacco. The town has several hotels, 6 churches, 2 high schools, an academy, and other schools. It was settled in 1670, and in 1704 was surprised and burnt by the French and Indians, who carried into captivity in Canada the family of Rev. John Williams, the pastor of the town. Population, 3543.

SOUTH DEERFIELD (a distinct village) is 5 miles S. of Deerfield village, and is on the Connecticut River Railroad, and on the Hoosac Tunnel extension of the New Haven and Northampton Railroad, at the junction of the branch to Turner's Falls. It has several churches, a pocket-book manufactory, and other factories. It is noted for the "Bloody Brook massacre" in 1675, when Capt. Lathrop and 76 men were killed by the Indians. A marble monument commemorates the fact. The scenery in the neighborhood is picturesque, and Deerfield Mount, 700 feet high, and the Sugar-Loaf, 500 feet high, afford fine views of the Connecticut Valley.

DEFIANCE, a city of Ohio, and county-seat of Defiance co., is on the right bank of the Maumee River, at the mouth of the Auglaize, 50 miles W S.W. of Toledo. It is on the Baltimore and Ohio Railroad, and on the St. Louis, Wabash, and Pacific Railroad. It is at the head of navigation on the Maumee River, which is here crossed by 7 bridges. It has a court-house, opera-house, 8 hotels, 3 banks (2 national), 3 weekly newspapers, 10 churches, and 6 schools. Its industrial works comprise a foundry, 2 flour-mills, woollen-mills, and manufactories of agricultural implements, furniture, doors, sash, etc. Here Gen. Anthony Wayne built Fort Defiance in 1794, and about 50 years later the settlement was made. The city was incorporated in 1882; its property is valued at $1,700,000; its public debt is $14,000; and its annual expenses about $30,000. The surrounding country is fertile, and is especially noted for its valuable ship-oak timber, which is sent from Defiance to Quebec by water. Population, 7386; chiefly of German origin.

DE FOREST, JOHN WILLIAM, an American novelist, was born in Seymour, Conn., March 31, 1826. At the age of twenty he travelled in Syria and the Levant for eighteen months, collecting material subsequently used in literature. On his return home he wrote and published the *History of the Indians of Connecticut*, intended as a trial work, his inclination being then towards history. He then resumed his travels, and remained for four years in Europe. Returning in 1856, he published two books of travel, *Oriental Acquaintance* and *European Acquaintance*, and two novels, *Witching Times* and *Seacliff*. On the breaking out of the Civil War he raised a company and entered the national service as a captain in the Twelfth regiment of Connecticut volunteers, serving for two years and a half in Louisiana and about six months in Virginia. He was engaged in forty-six days of fighting, and was once wounded. Late in the war he was transferred to the invalid corps, and after the war to the bureau of freedmen and refugees. He was at different times inspector-general of division, aide-de-camp on the staff of the Nineteenth corps, adjutant-general of the invalid corps, and chief of a district under the Freedmen's Bureau. Three years after the war he left the army and settled in New Haven, Conn., since which he has devoted himself to literature, producing, in addition to the works above mentioned, the novels of *Miss Ravenel, Overland, The Wetherell Affair, Kate Beaumont, Honest John Vane, Justine Vane, Irene the Missionary*, and *The Oddest of Courtships*, besides a large number of magazine stories, articles, reviews, and fugitive poems.

DE HAAS, MAURITZ FREDERIK HENDRIK, a Dutch-American artist, was born in Rotterdam, Holland, Dec. 12, 1832. He studied painting at the Academy of Fine Arts in that city, and for five years under Louis Meyer, the celebrated marine painter, at the Hague. He made several voyages in pilot-boats in the North Sea and English Channel, and also studied along the coasts of Holland, France, and England. In 1858 he was appointed artist in the Dutch navy, but resigned in the following year to come to America. Arriving at New York in October, 1859, he opened a studio and exhibited, for the first time, at the exhibition in the New York Academy of Design, in 1860. He was elected an associate of the academy in 1863, and an academician in 1867. His pictures are brilliant and vigorous in treatment, and show the sea under every aspect.

DE HAAS, WILHELM FREDERIK (1830-1880), a Dutch-American painter, elder brother of the preceding, was born at Rotterdam, Holland, in 1830. He studied at the Academy of Fine Arts, Rotterdam, and afterwards under Bosboom at the Hague. In 1854 he came to New York, and devoted himself to painting coast-scenery. Among his works are Scene on the Coast of Maine, Old Orchard Beach, Fishing-Boats off Mt. Desert, Boon Island, Midsummer Noon at Biddeford Beach, Evening at Halifax, and Narragansett Pier.

DE KALB, JOHN, BARON (1721-1780), general in the Revolutionary army, was born at Huttendorf in Bayreuth, Germany, June 29, 1721. He entered the French army in 1743, and rose by successive promotions to be brigadier-general, May, 1761. After the Seven Years' war the French minister, Choiseul, wishing to learn the resources of the colonies and their feeling towards Great Britain, sent De Kalb on a secret mission to America. He embarked in December, 1767, was shipwrecked near Staten Island, Jan. 28, 1768, and suffered great hardship. He executed his trust with ability, and, though arrested on one occasion, escaped detection. He returned to France at the close of 1768, and henceforth continued to feel great interest in American affairs. In 1776 he was engaged by Silas Deane to serve in the Revolutionary army, and in company with La Fayette arrived at Georgetown, S. C., early in April, 1777.

Having been appointed major-general by Congress, he took part in the battles of Brandywine and Germantown. After spending the winter at Valley Forge, he served in New Jersey and Maryland. In April, 1780, he was sent to the aid of Gen. Lincoln in South Carolina, but before he arrived the Southern army had surrendered at Charleston, and the further direction of affairs devolved upon De Kalb until the appointment of Gen. Gates in June. At the disastrous battle of Camden, De Kalb commanded the right wing, and with a Maryland regiment firmly held his ground against superior numbers until Lord Cornwallis, having defeated the militia, concentrated his forces against the Continental troops. De Kalb fought on foot, and fell pierced with eleven wounds. He died three days after the battle, Aug. 19, 1780. La Fayette, on his second visit to America in 1825, laid the corner-stone of a marble monument which Congress had ordered to be erected to his memory in Camden, S. C.

Friedrich Kapp, the latest biographer of De Kalb, was the first to bring to light the circumstances of his birth and early life. He shows that he belonged not to a noble but to a wealthy yeoman family. The prefix De and the rank of Baron seem to have been assumed to enable the wearer to obtain position in the French army, and the right to them passed unchallenged. See F. Kapp's *Life of Gen. John Kalb* (New York, 1884), which is enlarged from the German edition (Stuttgart, 1862).

DEKKER, EDWARD DOUWES, a Dutch author, was born at Amsterdam, March 2, 1820. He went to Java, in 1841, to take part in the administration of that county, becoming assistant resident of Lebak. But the reforms which he sought to introduce into the relations between the government and the natives were received with little favor, and he resigned his position. Then returning to Amsterdam, he denounced, in a series of articles which attracted much attention, the abuses which he had witnessed. He has published besides: *Max Havelaar of de Koffyveilingen* (Amsterdam, 1860); *Minnebrieven* (1861); *Ideën* (4 vols., 1862); two dramas—*De Bruid daarboven* (1864), and *De Vortenschool; Bloemlezing* (1865); *Nog eens* (1871); *Millionen studien* (1872), and several works on the Dutch Indies.

DE KOVEN, JAMES, D. D. (1831-1879), an American clergyman of the Protestant Episcopal church, was born at Middletown, Conn., Sept. 19, 1831. He graduated at Columbia College, New York, in 1851, and at the General Theological Seminary in 1854. He was admitted to deacon's orders in 1854, and was ordained priest in 1855. He had charge of a church in Delafield, Wis., and in 1859 was made warden of Racine College. He was earnest, eloquent, and uncompromising in his advocacy of High Church views. On account of his extreme position, though he was elected bishop of Illinois in 1875, the election was not confirmed by the house of bishops. He died suddenly at Racine, March 19, 1879. A volume of his *Sermons* was published in 1880.

DE LANCEY, WILLIAM HEATHCOTE, D. D., LL. D., D. C. L. (1797-1865), Protestant Episcopal bishop of Western New York, was born at Mamaroneck, Westchester co., N. Y., Oct. 8, 1797. He graduated at Yale College in 1817, studied theology under Bishop Hobart, and was ordained deacon in 1819. Being ordained to the priesthood in 1822, he became assistant of Bishop William White in Philadelphia. He was provost of the University of Pennsylvania from 1828 to 1833, when he became assistant minister of St. Peter's Church, Philadelphia, and after the death of Bishop White in 1835 he was made rector of that church. In 1838, when the diocese of Western New York was formed, he was chosen bishop and was consecrated May 9, 1839. He made his residence at Geneva, where Hobart College was founded and chiefly supported by his efforts. In 1852 he was commissioned by the American bishops as a delegate to England, and received the degree of D. C. L. from the University of Oxford. He died at Geneva, N. Y., April 5, 1865. His only publications were sermons and addresses.

DE LA RAMÉE, LOUISA, an English novelist, better known by her pseudonym "Ouida," was born at Bury St. Edmunds in 1840. She is of French descent, and at an early age removed to London, where she began to write for periodicals, under the name of "Ouida" (a child's mispronunciation of Louisa). Her first novel was published in *Colburn's Monthly* under the name *Granville de Vigne*, but when issued in book-form was called *Held in Bondage* (1863). This was followed by *Strathmore* (1865); *Chandos* (1866); *Tricotrin* (1868); *Under Two Flags* (1868); *Puck* (1869); *Folle Farine* (1871); *Pascarel* (1873); *Signa* (1875); *Ariadne* (1877); *Friendship* (1878); *Princess Napraxine* (1884). Her novels, full of exaggerations and improbable incidents, are written in a meretricious style, and are often objectionable in moral tone.

DELANO, COLUMBUS, an American statesman, was born in Shoreham, Vt., in 1809. He removed to Mount Vernon, Ohio, in 1817, studied law, and was admitted to the bar in 1831. He was eminently successful both as a criminal prosecutor and as an advocate. In 1844 he was elected to Congress as a Whig, and strongly opposed the war with Mexico. Having joined the Republican party, he was in 1860 a delegate to the Chicago convention, in which he advocated the nomination of Lincoln as President. In 1861 he was appointed commissary-general of Ohio, and discharged this duty until the national Government assumed the subsistence of all State troops. In 1863 he was a member of the Ohio legislature, and in 1864 was a delegate to the Republican national convention at Baltimore which nominated Pres. Lincoln for a second term. In the same year he was again elected to Congress, served as chairman of the committee on claims, and was re-elected in 1866. He was appointed by Pres. Grant in March, 1869, commissioner of internal revenue, and largely increased its receipts. In the following November, Pres. Grant made him Secretary of the Department of the Interior, which office he held till Oct. 19, 1875, the longest time this office has been held by one person. Mr. Delano has since been extensively engaged in agricultural pursuits and in banking. He has been an earnest advocate of liberal education, and has endowed a hall in Kenyon Grammar School at Gambier, Ohio. He has also been a prominent member of the Protestant Episcopal Church, representing the diocese of Ohio in all the recent triennial conventions of that Church. He resides at Lakeholm, near Mount Vernon, Ohio. His speeches never have been published in collected form.

DELAWARE, one of the States of the United States, contains 1960 square miles, being the smallest except Rhode Island. The surface is generally low and level, but the extreme northern portion, composing about one-fourteenth of the whole, is hilly, overlying azoic rocks, and resembling precisely the adjoining surface of Pennsylvania. Gneiss and felspar are found here, with limestone, serpentine, and granite in circumscribed localities. The limit of this rolling surface may be said to be the Christiana River. South of it the level lands are found, and these sink gradually until along the shores of Delaware Bay and in the southern part of the State there is much marsh- and swamp-land, requiring drainage before it can be used for agricultural purposes. A red-clay region lies next to the northern hills, and covers some ten or twelve miles. The southern border of this passes into the green-sand formation, usually a very productive soil. South of it is a tertiary formation, presenting an alternation of clay and sand, and abounding in organic remains, chiefly shells; while still farther south, and occupying about two-fifths of the State, is the light sandy country, which may be considered of recent formation. The northern hill country has a stony surface and deep-banked and quick-flowing streams; south of the Christiana the slopes are gentle, and the streams low-banked and slow. The drainage in the latter portion frequently requires artificial aid, and there are large "ponds" in the interior, and wide shallow lagoons near the bay and sea-shore, while on the southern border is the "cypress swamp," an extensive area below the drainage level. Taking for more particular description the central county, Kent, containing 682 square miles, a strip of 65,000 acres along the bay-shore contains what are called the salt marshes, subject to occasional overflow at high tide. Next inland is another and wider strip, covering about 180,000 acres, embracing rich alluvial lands in what are called the "necks"—*i. e.*, the spaces between the streams. Still farther inland, and extending along the Maryland line, is the third strip, usually called "the forest," and containing about 200,000 acres. This "forest" region lies along the whole western side of the State south of the Christiana River, and forms the water-shed of the peninsula. It is a wooded elevation, nowhere more than 100 feet above the sea, containing many springs and a number of marshes, from which issue streams that flow eastward to the Delaware and westward to the Chesapeake.

See Vol. VII. p. 39 Am. ed. (p. 44 Edin. ed.).

Influenced by the two great bays that almost surround it, the peninsula has a climate modified and moderated in an important degree; and this proves to be especially adapted, in combination with suitable soils, to the culture of fruits. In the southern half of Delaware nearly all the annual cultivated plants will perfect themselves, and in nearly the whole, except the northern hill section, the peach tree flourishes in a remarkable degree, giving the State a special reputation by its crops. For agricultural purposes much remains to be done by extensive works of systematic drainage in the central and lower parts of the State, and a public work of this kind, under general laws and directed by competent engineers, has been strongly urged by intelligent and scientific observers. Numerous local "ditch companies," to drain limited areas for local benefit, are in existence under the charter of the legislature.

There are no mineral deposits of importance, except iron ore and kaolin in the northern section, and some bog-iron ore in the southern. The two former are profitably worked. The chief interest of the people naturally is agriculture, developed largely within the last twenty years into fruit- and vegetable-growing. The climate is mild and the winters short; stock in the middle and southern sections requires little shelter. The streams are stocked with fish, and resorted to by wild fowl, while crabs, oysters, and other shell-fish abound in the waters of the southern part of the State.

By the census of 1890 Delaware had a population of 167,871, showing a gain of 14.5 per cent. since 1880. The distribution by counties in the latter year and 1870, was as follows:

	1880.	1870.	Increase.	Inc. per cent.
Kent	32,874	29,804	3,070	10.3+
New Castle	77,716	63,515	14,201	22.3+
Sussex	36,018	31,696	4,322	13.6+
Totals	146,608	125,015	21,593	17.2+

The comparison as to color and nativity with the census of 1870 is shown as follows:

	1880.	1870.	Increase.
White	120,160	102,221	17,967
Colored	26,448	22,794	3,626
Native	137,140	115,879	21,261
Foreign	9,468	9,136	332

Of the foreign-born 5791 were natives of Ireland, 1433 of England, 1179 of the German empire, 285 of Scotland, 208 of Canada, 138 of France, 71 of Sweden, 51 of Wales, 48 of Switzerland, 43 of Italy, and 221 of other countries. Of those born in the United States 26,497 were not natives of Delaware, 11,009 being from Pennsylvania, 9562 from Maryland, 2238 from New Jersey, 1321 from New York, and the remainder from other States of the Union.

There were in the State in 1880 38,298 males of twenty-one years old and upward, of whom 27,447 were native- and 4455 foreign-born whites, and 6396 were colored. There were 28,253 families, occupying 27,215 dwellings. The average number of dwellings to each square mile was 13.89, this density of population being exceeded in eight other States—Connecticut, Maryland, Massachusetts, New Jersey, New York, Ohio, Pennsylvania, and Rhode Island. The average number of acres of land to each family was 44.40. The whole number of farms was 8749 (as against 7615 in 1870, and 6658 in 1860). Of this number 5041 were worked by their owners, 511 were leased for a fixed money-rental, and 3197 were leased for shares of the produce. The crops of the State in 1880 were as follows:

Crops.	Acres planted.	Product.
Tobacco	4	1,278 pounds.
Barley	19	523 bushels.
Buckwheat	397	5,857 "
Indian corn	202,159	3,894,264 "
Oats	17,158	378,508 "
Rye	773	5,953 "
Wheat	87,539	1,175,272 "

Sorghum was also planted, yielding 25,136 gallons of molasses.

Strawberries, blackberries, raspberries, and whortleberries furnish, in most years, large crops, though the quantity varies with the season. The peach crop is still more irregular, being subject to injury by severe or unseasonable cold. It may be expected to fail entirely one year in five. The shipments of this fruit, however, as well as of the "small fruits," are large, and their consumption by canneries and drying-houses established within the State has greatly developed in the last few years. The routes of shipment for fruit are chiefly as follows: by rail northward to Philadelphia and New York, by water to Philadelphia and Baltimore, and by steamers running from Lewes to New York. Referring only to the first named route, there were sent out of the State over it in the five years 1879–83 inclusive, 8,228,495 "baskets" (about 5,000,000 bushels) of peaches. The total crop of that fruit in the State for 1879 was estimated at 4,000,000 baskets, and for 1883 at 3,500,000 baskets. Tomatoes are grown in large quantities, chiefly in Kent county, and numerous canneries operate on them during the crop season.

The live-stock of the State in 1880 was reported as follows: horses, 21,933; mules and asses, 3931; working oxen, 5818; milk-cows, 27,284; other cattle, 20,450; swine, 48,186. The wool-clip of 1880 was 97,946 pounds. The dairy products for 1879 were 1,132,434 gallons of milk, 1,876,275 pounds of butter, and 1712 pounds of cheese.

The State is divided into three counties, originally formed by William Penn: New Castle (north), Kent (central), and Sussex (south); and these are subdivided into "hundreds," corresponding substantially with the townships of other States. Hundreds are again divided for school purposes into school districts. The principal place in the State is Wilmington, whose population in 1860 was 21,258; in 1870, 30,841; and in 1880, 42,478 (to which may properly be added the closely connected suburbs of Browntown, Bancroft's Banks, Dupont's Banks, and Edgemoor, making an addition of 2640, and a total for the city of 45,118). From the earliest colonial times until 1881 New Castle had been the county-seat of New Castle county, but in pursuance of State and local legislation the court-house and offices of record are now at Wilmington. The towns in the State with a population over 500 are: New Castle 3700, Middletown 1280, Newark 1148, Delaware City 1085, Odessa 675, and Newport 535, in New Castle county; Dover (State capital and county-seat) 2811, Smyrna 2423, Milford 1240, Harrington 745, Camden 702, and Frederica 696, in Kent county; Seaford 1542, South Milford 1034, Milton 1026, Laurel 1022, and Georgetown (county-seat) 895, in Sussex county.

The governor is chosen for four years, and is not immediately eligible for re-election. He has no approval or veto in connection with laws passed by the legislature. He appoints the secretary of state (for a term

DELAWARE.

corresponding with his own), the chancellor and judges (for life or during good behavior), the attorney-general (for five years), the State superintendent of free schools, the county record officers, justices of the peace, notaries public, etc.; and he has power to remit fines and penalties and grant reprieves and pardons. The elections are held biennially, in the even-number years, on the Tuesday after the first Monday of November. The legislature sits biennially at Dover, beginning its sessions on the first Tuesday of January in the odd-numbered years. The senate has 9 members, 3 from each county, and the house of representatives 21 members, 7 from each county—there being no regard to population in the apportionment. Senators are chosen for four years (3 being elected in the year of the presidential election, and 6 the second year thereafter), and representatives for two years. The senate constitutes the court in the trial of impeachments, and two-thirds of the senators must concur in order to convict. The State treasurer and the auditor of State are elected by the legislature for terms of two years. The judiciary includes a chancellor and a chief-justice and 3 associate justices (one of these residing in each county), of the superior court, the courts of general sessions, and oyer and terminer. The chancellor, with the associate justice of the county, holds the orphans' court in each county. The chief-justice, with two associates, holds the superior court and court of general sessions in each county. The court of last resort, called the court of errors and appeals, is composed of the chancellor and the chief-justice and associate justices.

The debt of the State at Jan. 1, 1884, was stated as follows: 4-per cent. bonds, $625,000; school bonds, bearing 6 per cent. interest, due 1906, $156,750; Delaware College land-grant fund, bearing 6 per cent. interest, $83,000—total, $864,750. Against this gross amount assets of the State were credited as follows: mortgage on Junction and Breakwater Railroad, $400,000; mortgage on Breakwater and Frankford Railroad, $200,000; investments in bank-stock, $73,050—total, $673,050. The State also credits as assets the investments of the school fund, which, exclusive of a bond of the State itself for $156,750, amount to $338,999 in bank-stocks, etc. The revenue of the State for the year 1883, from taxes, interest, and dividends, and other sources not special in their character, amounted as follows: from licenses, $74,223.83; Philadelphia, Wilmington, and Baltimore Railroad taxation, $40,000; other railroads, $1,184.73; interest from Junction and Breakwater and Frankford and Breakwater Railroads, $24,000; the total, including sums from other sources, being $149,069.56. The disbursements for the year from the general fund were stated to be $138,183.11, the principal items being: executive, $2000; judiciary, $10,075; salaries of other State officers, $7787.50; Delaware State bonds and coupons, $24,250; interest on school-fund bonds, $9405; amount of appropriation for schools, $25,000; interest on debt to Delaware College, $2490; school-books, $2842.78; expenses of the general assembly, $46,701.56; appropriation to colored schools, $5000.

The annual valuation of Delaware in 1880 for tax purposes was as follows, according to the U. S. census: real property, $50,302,739, personal, $9,648,904—total, $59,951,643. There was no direct State tax on the people (the derivation of the revenue from special sources being mostly shown above); the county taxes amounting to $248,27⸺ wns, etc., to $223,574.

The public-school system, which up to 1875 had remained unchanged for many years, and was much neglected except in Wilmington and a few other localities, was in that year materially amended by act of the legislature, and is now in an improved condition. The schools are supported by local taxation, raised in each school district upon a vote of the people to that effect, and the distribution of the State fund. The State fund was begun in 1796 from the proceeds of marriage and tavern licenses. In 1829 it had accumulated to $158,160.15. In 1836 the State received its share of the surplus funds of the United States Treasury, amounting to $286,751.49, and this was added to the school fund, which in 1890 amounted to $495,749. The proceeds of the investment of this amount, with the revenue derived from certain licenses appropriated to school purposes, amounted in 1880 to a total revenue for distribution to the districts of $26,606.95. Besides this, the tax levied and collected locally in 1880 was $151,044.94, making a total expenditure for school purposes of $177,651.89. According to the report of the State superintendent, in 1880, there were in the State 512 schools, with 25,053 white children and 2216 colored children in attendance. The average number of months per year in which the schools were open was 7.53. There were 423 teachers employed (248 male, 175 female), with salaries amounting to $138,818.97, the average monthly salary of male teachers being $30.83, and of female $24.79. The total value of school property was $440,788, as follows: houses, $331,260; grounds, $75,669; furniture, $31,505. The education of colored children is not a part of the general system, and is not under the charge of the State superintendent. The school-taxes paid by persons of color are set apart for the education of colored children, and to these is added a specific annual sum (in 1884, $5000) appropriated by the legislature from moneys in the State treasury. This money is paid to the treasurer of the "Delaware Association for the Education of the Colored People," a voluntary organization formed soon after the war, and which established, in co-operation with the United States Freedmen's Bureau, a system of schools for colored children in this State. The taxes derived from colored people are also paid over by the several county treasurers to the treasurer of the Delaware Association, and from his hands they are distributed to the schools. It is required under the law that the taxes paid from each hundred shall be expended for schools therein, and that the sum annually appropriated from the State treasury shall be expended in equal shares in the three counties. During the school year 1883–84 there were in the State 65 schools open, under the supervision of the actuary of the Delaware Association above named, and 4 others, in Wilmington, in charge of the board of education of that city. The highest number of pupils enrolled in the 69 schools, in any month, was 3409. The total expenditure for the 67 schools of funds derived from taxes and from the State treasury was $8243.46. Delaware College, at Newark, an old institution, but reorganized upon its present basis in 1870, received from the State as an endowment the income of the proceeds ($83,000) of the sale of the State's share (90,000 acres) of the agricultural land-grant made by Congress under the act of 1862. This college receives students of both sexes. By the census of 1880 the population of the State, ten years old and upward, numbered 110,850 and of these 16,912 were returned as unable to read, and 19,414 as unable to write. Of the latter class, 6630 were native whites,

1716 foreign-born whites, and 11,068 native colored.

Delaware forms a diocese of the Protestant Episcopal Church, the bishop residing at Wilmington. It composes, with the remainder of the peninsula, the Roman Catholic diocese of Wilmington, whose bishop also resides in that city.

There is no penitentiary, and no asylum for the deaf and dumb, blind, or insane. Convicts are kept in the county jails, and the indigent afflicted classes in the county almshouses. Provision is made for the instruction of the blind, feeble-minded, and deaf-mute children in the training-schools of other States, usually of Pennsylvania. The pillory and whipping-post are maintained as part of the penal methods of the State, and are set up at each of the three county-seats convenient to the jail. The punishment, under the law, is chiefly imposed for larceny and other grades of theft, and is not administered to females.

The manufacturing interests of Delaware are proportionately large, and have increased rapidly since 1860. They are mostly located in the northern section of the State, at and near Wilmington. By the census of 1880 there were in the State 10,250 males, 16 years old or over; 1426 females, 15 years old or over; and 962 children, engaged in manufactures. There were 746 manufacturing establishments, with an invested capital of $15,655,822, and an annual product of $20,514,438. There were 8 establishments devoted specifically to the manufacture of cotton goods, having a capital of $874,570, running 46,188 spindles and 822 looms, and giving employment to 797 persons. There were 9 establishments engaged in the manufacture of iron, with a capital of $1,431,469 and employing 867 persons. There are at Wilmington two large "yards" for the building of iron ships, three car-shops, four rolling-mills, numerous carriage- and morocco-manufactories, and a variety of other establishments. At New Castle there are large iron-works, and also factories of textile goods. On the Brandywine, above Wilmington, are several cotton-manufactories and two paper-mills of large productive capacity, besides the very extensive gunpowder-manufactories of the Messrs. DuPont, the first of any note established in the United States. At Newark and Newport there are also paper-mills, textile factories, etc., while there are canneries of fruits, vegetables, game, etc., at many points in the State.

The railroads of the State are as follows: (1) The Philadelphia, Wilmington, and Baltimore, traversing the northern portion diagonally from Claymont, 23 miles south-westward, to the Maryland line; (2) the Delaware Railroad, from Wilmington south-eastward to New Castle, and thence traversing the central part of the State south to Delaware, on the Maryland line, in all about 97 miles; (3) branches of the Delaware Railroad, including on the west side the Dorchester and Delaware, the Delaware and Chesapeake, and the Townsend branches, and on the east side the Smyrna branch, the whole having 28¼ miles of road within the State; (4) the Junction and Breakwater and associated lines, connected with the Delaware Railroad at Harrington, and having an ocean and bay outlet—chiefly for New York trade—at Lewes (the Delaware Breakwater), the whole of this system having about 64½ miles within the State; (5) the Kent County and Smyrna and Delaware Bay Railroad, with 18 miles; (6) the Wilmington and Northern, with about 13 miles; (7) the Delaware Western, with about 17½ miles; and (8) the Pomeroy, Newark, and Delaware City line, with about 17½ miles within the State. These, with some later additions, made the total length of railroad in 1889 314.54 miles.

The Chesapeake and Delaware Canal, one of the oldest canals in the country, extends from Delaware Bay across the State, and thence into the "Eastern Shore" of Maryland to waters connected with Chesapeake Bay; its length is 13¼ miles. It was completed in 1829 at a cost of $2,250,000, partly by aid of the general government. In crossing the water-shed elevation it has a long summit level in a deep cut, the extreme depth of this being 90 feet. This canal is largely used by steamboats and sailing vessels engaged in the trade between Chesapeake and Delaware Bays. It is now proposed, however, to make a ship-canal, capable of accommodating the largest ocean-going vessels, across the peninsula, to connect the two bays, and numerous surveys have been made of routes crossing Delaware south of the present canal. Its construction has lately been declared to be assured at a near time. The State of Delaware constitutes one customs district under the United States laws, with a collector located at Wilmington and deputies at New Castle and Lewes. The commerce is not extensive; whatever foreign trade there is mainly enters and leaves the port of Wilmington. The coastwise trade is of more importance, and many cargoes of fruit, grain, timber, etc., go in small vessels out of the numerous navigable streams that flow into Delaware Bay.

The expedition of the Swedes which effected the first permanent settlement of Europeans within what is now the State of Delaware—and the first anywhere on the western banks of the Delaware River—was under command of Peter Minuit. (The several spellings of his name, Menewe, Minnewitz, etc., are due probably to the different ways of pronouncing it, but careful writers on Delaware history usually give it as above.) The expedition came over early in the year 1638, having left, probably, at the close of 1637. It arrived at Christina (now Wilmington), where the settlement was made, in the month of April. Previously, however—from 1631 to 1632—there had been a small settlement of Dutch, landed by David Petersen De Vries, at the Hoorn-kill, now Lewes, just within the entrance to Delaware Bay. The settlers were all killed by the Indians the next year after their arrival, and though De Vries revisited the place near the end of 1632 he made no attempt to resume the settlement.

The Indians who occupied lower Delaware were known later to the English as Nanticokes; toward the middle of the eighteenth century the survivors of them left Delaware in a body and went to the north branch of the Susquehanna River in Pennsylvania. Heckewelder, the Moravian missionary, relates that in his boyhood he had seen some of them pass through Bethlehem, carrying the bones of their principal chiefs, disinterred in lower Delaware, on their backs. This was about 1748, and these were probably the last Indians in the State. The tribes in the northern section were chiefly known as Minquas, and belonged to the family usually spoken of in Pennsylvania history as the Lenni Lenape. Their relations with the whites—Swedes, Dutch, and English successively—appear to have been uniformly friendly.

The period of Swedish control in Delaware extended from 1638 to 1655, when Gov. Stuyvesant, of Manhattan, with his expedition, celebrated in the humorous pages of Washington Irving's *Knickerbocker*, took

Fort Casimir, at New Castle, and Fort Christina (Wilmington), and brought the colony under Dutch rule. In 1664 it passed into control of the English under the Duke of York's general authority, and the government was administered by his governors and their deputies from New York until the arrival of William Penn in 1682. The "three counties on Delaware," then known as New Castle, St. Jones, and Whorekill (Hoorn-Kill), or New Deal, having passed by the Duke of York's deed to Penn into the proprietary control of the latter, they joined with the Pennsylvania counties in one legislative body, and so remained until 1703, when they set up their own assembly, which met at New Castle until about the time of the revolution, when the capital was fixed at Dover. Like Pennsylvania, they continued under the Penn proprietary and the English colonial system until the revolution. A new constitution was then framed (1776) and the old government set aside. In 1791 a new Constitution was adopted, and in 1831 this was revised, since which time until now (1883) there has been no change in the fundamental law, though in 1852–53 an earnest but abortive effort was made to secure its material amendment, a convention being held and a new constitution framed and submitted to the people; it was, however, not adopted by such a majority of votes as was required under the existing constitution, and so fell. Delaware was the first of the States (1787) that voted to adopt the federal constitution.

In the revolution Delaware bore a somewhat conspicuous part. At the adoption of the Declaration of Independence the majority in favor of the step substantially depended upon the decision of the Delaware delegates, who voted yea at a critical time. Besides the troops sent to the field at the beginning of the conflict, and which served temporarily, the State raised a regiment of the "Continental" establishment, which served with much credit throughout the war subsequent to the battle of Trenton, the remnant of it fighting almost to the end in the battles in the South. No engagement of note took place within the State, though Washington's army lay for a short time along Red Clay Creek, near Wilmington, facing the British under Gen. Howe, and a conflict there was avoided only by the flank march of the former into Pennsylvania just before the battle at Brandywine in September, 1777.

Until after the Revolution the population of Delaware was almost entirely of English descent, with the exception of the Swedish and Dutch infusion which had survived by descent from the original colonists. In the lower counties especially the purity of the English blood is still notable. After the troubles in San Domingo and the Revolution in France a number of French families of distinction settled in northern Delaware, and since the war of 1812 the inflow from other States, as well as the arrival of European immigrants, has much changed, as well as increased, the population of New Castle county.

At the outbreak of the rebellion, Delaware, though urged by commissioners from the seceding States to join in it, refused to do so and remained loyal to the Union. There were sent to the national army from the State, during the war, 10 regiments of infantry, 1 regiment of cavalry, 1 troop of cavalry ("emergency" service), 1 battery of heavy- and 1 battery of light-artillery.

For details, descriptive and historical, relating to Delaware, the following works are of importance: *A History of the Original Settlements on the Delaware*, by Benjamin Ferris (Wilmington, 1846); *A History of New Sweden*, by Israel Acrelius (Historical Society of Pennsylvania, 1874); *Annals of Pennsylvania [including the Delaware counties] from 1609 to 1682*, by Samuel Hazard (Philada., 1850); *Life and Correspondence of George Read*, by William Thompson Read (Philada., 1870); *A History of the State of Delaware*, by Francis Vincent (vol. I., Philada., 1870); *Reminiscences of Wilmington*, by Elizabeth Montgomery (2d ed., Wilmington, 1872); *Memoirs of John M. Clayton*, by Joseph P. Comegys (Historical Society of Delaware, 1882); Huffington's *Delaware Register* (Dover, 1838); *Annals of the Swedes*, by Jehu C. Clay (Philada., 1835).

In addition to these the collections of the Delaware Historical Society at Wilmington, and the Pennsylvania Historical Society at Philadelphia, contain a large amount of documentary and other information, and the New York volumes of Dutch records, translated by Brodhead and O'Callaghan, furnish abundant references to the Colonial period until the overthrow of the Dutch power at Manhattan. Among pamphlets of value upon special Delaware topics may be named Professor James C. Booth's report (1837–8) on the State's geology; a report by Dr. L. P. Bush (1872) on the climatology and diseases of Delaware; an address (1876) on *Delaware's Revolutionary Soldiers*, by W. G. Whiteley; *Lives of the Chancellors*, by Daniel M. Bates; *Report of the Proceedings in the Pea-Patch Case, before Hon. John Sergeant, arbitrator*; *Argument* (1874) *of the Delaware Commissioners in the Fishery Question* [with New Jersey]; Foote's *Historical Sketch of Drawyer's Presbyterian Church, Odessa, Del.* (1842).   (H. M. J.)

DELAWARE, a city of Ohio, county-seat of Delaware co., on the W. bank of Olentangy River, here crossed by 4 bridges, 20 miles N. of Columbus. It is on the Cleveland, Columbus, Cincinnati, and Indianapolis Railroad, at the junction of the Springfield branch; also on the Columbus, Hocking Valley, and Toledo Railroad. It is a handsome city, with fine county-buildings, an opera-house, 3 banks (2 national), 1 daily and 4 weekly newspapers, 13 churches, and 2 handsome public school-houses; also railway-shops and manufactories of woollens, flour, wagons, chairs, cigars, castings, etc. Delaware is the seat of the Ohio Wesleyan University, which is one of the leading schools of the Methodist denomination. There are theological, normal, and medical schools, and a female college connected with the university. Near the town is a State reform-school for girls. Within and near the city are several chalybeate springs, and there is a fine sulphur-spring, giving the town a reputation as a sanitary resort. Delaware is the birthplace of ex-President R. B. Hayes. It was founded in 1808; incorporated as a city in 1873; valuation, $3,500,000; public debt, $80,000; yearly expenses, $25,000. Population in 1880, 6894; in 1890, 8202.

DELAWARES. A tribe of American Indians who, on the settlement of Pennsylvania, were found established on the Delaware Bay and River, while closely affiliated tribes stretched from the Potomac on the south to and beyond the Hudson on the north. They were of Algonkin descent, and claimed to be the source of all the Algonkin tribes—a claim that was admitted by the other tribes in the title of "grandfathers" which they gave the Delawares. They were in many respects one of the most interesting of Indian tribes, both from their traditional history and the peculiar relations which they bore to the whites.

The Lenni Lenape, as the Delawares named themselves, had a tradition to the effect that, hundreds of years ago, they resided in a distant country on the west of the continent. Migrating eastward they found the country east of the Mississippi in possession of a powerful people called the Alligewi, who had many large towns. A great war ensued, the Alligewi were defeated and fled down the Mississippi, and the Lenni Lenape occupied their country in common with a tribe called the Mengwe or Minquas, who had followed them from the West. They finally became settled on the eastern coast, centring on the Delaware, while branching tribes stretched north and south, the Mohegans of the east being a direct outgrowth from the Delawares.

The tradition goes on to relate that wars broke out between them and the Mengwe, or Iroquois, as they were known to the English. In these wars the Iroquois confederacy was opposed by a yet stronger alliance between the Delawares and their related tribes. Finally the Iroquois, pressed by the French settlers in Canada on the one hand and the Delawares on the other, sought to relieve themselves of the enmity of the latter by inducing them to lay down their arms and assume the position of mediators between the warring tribes. The Delawares claim to have heard this scheme favorably, and to have consented to become "women," as all unwarlike tribes were scornfully denominated. This story is denied by the Iroquois, who claim to have conquered the Delawares in battle and forced them to become "women." The latter story is far more probable, as the former seems alien to the Indian character, while the Iroquois are known to have dominated the tribes throughout a wide territory. This position of the Delawares is an interesting anomaly in the history of Indian tribes.

It was with the Delawares that the European settlers of the Middle States first came into contact. The Dutch began to trade with them in 1616 on the Delaware. The Swedish settlers were well received, and made missionary efforts among the Indians, Luther's *Catechism* being translated into the Delaware language by Campanius. The Quaker settlers, under William Penn, by their fair and peaceful dealings, established still more friendly relations. The story of Penn's treaty—by which, it is said, he purchased his province from the Indians as the rightful owners—describes one of the most picturesque incidents in early American history. The relations between the Quakers and the Indians continued amicable. Penn's memory was long venerated by the tribes, and it is claimed that no Indian ever injured a Quaker within the limits of Pennsylvania. Another venerated character in the history of the Delawares is their great sachem, called Tamanend—Anglicised as Tammany. Little of his history is known, and he is perhaps wholly a traditional character; but the legendary memory of his wisdom and virtue is still warmly entertained. The name is still employed as a political designation.

In 1742 some trouble arose with the Delawares, who declared that they had been defrauded in a treaty called the "walking treaty." In settlement of this dispute an Iroquois chief was called in, who sharply rebuked the Delawares for presuming to treat for land. They were *women*, and had no claim to the land, which belonged to their masters. He ordered them to vacate the disputed territory and remove to Wyoming or Shamokin on the Susquehanna. His peremptory command was meekly obeyed. After this retreat the Delawares gave up their peaceful habits and became warlike and energetic. In 1755 many of them, irritated by outrages of the whites, joined the French in their war with the English, and took part in the battle of that year, known as Braddock's defeat. The enmity of the Pennsylvanians thus aroused finally resulted in an unprovoked massacre of the inhabitants of a small settlement known as the Conestoga Indians. Efforts were made to protect these inoffensive people, but the incensed borderers slaughtered them under the very eyes of the authorities. After this murderous outbreak the Delawares withdrew for safety into the wilds of the Susquehanna region.

Early efforts had been made to Christianize the Delawares, in which the Moravians were particularly successful. Settlements of Moravian converts were made in 1741 at Bethlehem and Nazareth. These Christian Indians always continued peaceful and friendly to the whites, although they were subjected to brutal outrages from lawless settlers during the exasperation of the French and Indian wars. The warlike Delawares took part in the celebrated "Pontiac conspiracy" of 1763, in which the lake tribes attacked Detroit, while the Delawares and some other tribes besieged Fort Pitt, the present Pittsburg. Their raids extended along the whole frontier, and great outrages were committed. Gen. Bouquet, marching to the relief of Fort Pitt, was ambushed by a party of Delawares at Bushy Run. A fierce fight ensued, which ended in a disastrous defeat of the Indians and the relief of the border. In 1774 an unprovoked invasion of the Indian country took place by a party of land-hunters, said by some to have been led by Col. Cresap. A Delaware chief, named Bald Eagle, was causelessly killed, scalped, and his body set adrift in his canoe. Terrible reprisals were made by the Delawares, Shawnees, and other tribes, led by a celebrated chief called Logan, whose family had been ruthlessly butchered. The war that ensued spread along the whole border, the settlements suffered severely, but the Indians were finally defeated and forced to peace.

The pressure on the Delawares had before this time caused a general migration westward. By 1768 they had all removed beyond the Alleghenies. The Moravian missionaries emigrated with their flock to Ohio, where the number of Christian Indians increased. During the revolutionary war a part of the Delawares joined the British, others remaining neutral. They all made peace after the fall of Fort Duquesne. A treaty between the Delawares and the government was signed in 1778, the first treaty ever made between the United States and an Indian tribe. The Christian Indians, who then had three towns on the Muskingum, the Delaware town being at Gnadenhütten, continued peaceful but friendly to the colonists during the Revolution. The hostile Indians, angry at the neutrality of the Christians, seized them and removed them to Sandusky, Ohio, in 1781. Thence, when they grew short of food, a party returned to save some of their crops. The neighboring settlers, hearing that Indians had appeared on the Muskingum, attacked them, and, though no resistance was made, ninety of them were brutally massacred. This unprovoked outrage threw the Christian Indians into despair. Most of them removed to Canada, where their descendants still remain.

The warlike Delawares, continuing hostile to the Americans, participated in all the Indian wars of the remainder of the century. Four hundred Delaware warriors took part in the disastrous defeat of the St. Clair expedition of 1791, which resulted in the loss of 894 whites. They were present also in the Indian defe— — —ayne in 1794, and were forced the su— —onclude peace. In the war with E— —Delawares remained faithful to the United States. In 1818 they ceded all their lands by treaty to the United States, and removed, with the exception of a small band, to a reservation on the White River, Missouri. By a further treaty, made in 1829, they agreed to move still farther west, and to accept a reservation in Kansas at the fork of the Kansas and Missouri Rivers. This was to be secured to them forever as a permanent home. Their reservation in Kansas consisted of 375,000 acres, which they employed in agriculture and stock-raising, and gained an excellent reputation. In 1853 they sold the United States all their lands except a limited reservation in Kansas, on which they gave up the most of their Indian habits, built themselves comfortable houses, and progressed in agriculture. Yet their experience in Kansas was like that of many other tribes. They suffered from incursions of the wild tribes and of lawless whites. A party of settlers entered their reservation, seized a piece of land on the Missouri, and laid out a town which they called the city of Leavenworth, without interference from the commander of the adjoining Fort Leavenworth. Other parties quickly followed, and were defended by the military in their aggressions. The Indians were personally maltreated, their property stolen, their timber destroyed, etc. Yet they quietly submitted, trusting to the government for redress, which failed to come. In 1860 and 1862 a treaty was made with them by which most of their lands were conveyed to the Leavenworth, Pawnee, and Western Railroad, they receiving payment in bonds of the company. In 1866 they finally sold the remainder of their reservation to the Missouri River Railroad, and in 1868 removed to the Indian Territory, where they settled on lands on the Verdigris and Caney, bought from the Cherokees. Here they were induced to give up their tribal organization, accept lands in severalty, and become citizens of the United States. This they did, receiving farms of 160 acres each. Thus the ancient tribe of the Delawares ceased to exist, though their old clan divisions of the Turkey, Turtle, and Wolf are still retained. When first known they numbered about 6000, but they are now reduced to about 1000. The Delaware language is one of the best known of the Algonkin dialects, its study having given rise to a number of works on the subject. The greater part of the Delawares at present are members of the Cherokee nationality, but some are settled with the Kiowas and Comanches. (C. M.)

DELBRÜCK, MARTIN FRIEDRICH RUDOLPH, a German statesman, was born at Berlin, April 16, 1817, and was the son of the preceptor of the two children of Frederick William III., who afterwards became Frederick William IV. and the Emperor William. He studied in the schools of Zeitz, Magdeburg, and Halle, in which latter city he commenced the study of law, which he completed at the Universities of Bonn, Göttingen, and Berlin. He practised at the bar of Halle during 1839 and 1840, after which he entered the civil service, becoming, after two years' provincial service, assistant in the ministry of finances, and then in that of commerce. He devoted himself specially to the study of economic questions, and became, in 1859, a director of the division of commerce and industry. To him principally are due the commercial separation of Prussia and Austria, and the commercial treaties of the smaller German states with Prussia, which put the latter at the head of a sort of customs confederation, very favorable to its political preponderance. In 1862 Bismarck, on being raised to the presidency of the ministry, declared himself in favor of Delbrück's ideas, and gave them a powerful support. The latter now extended his operations, obtained the assent of all the governments of the Zollverein to the commercial treaty already concluded, and made treaties of commerce with France, England, Belgium, and Italy. In acknowledgment of these and other services he was made president of the federal chancery, August, 1867. He employed the great influence given him by this position to aid the growth and transformation of the Prussian monarchy. During the events of 1870 he visited the various states of Northern Germany, and concluded with their rulers a new series of treaties, which completed the German unity, in advance of the proclamation of King William as Emperor of Germany. He prepared the constitution of the new empire, presented it to the parliament in the name of the Confederated States, and had it adopted without amendment, and almost without debate, in December, 1870. He continued, during the succeeding five years, president of the imperial chancery. His great reputation declined during this period. He was accused of a prodigal use of the French war contribution in unfortunate industrial enterprises, and his resignation in April, 1876, was attributed to these financial errors. During 1874 and 1875 he was a member of the Chamber of Deputies, but resigned his membership as incompatible with his other duties. Elected later to the Reichstag he there vigorously combated, in the question of the tariff, the change of opinion of Bismarck towards protectionist ideas (May, 1879), and also in 1880 vigorously opposed the Elbe navigation act, presented by Bismarck. In 1873 he received from the University of Leipsic the degree of LL. D.

DELEPIERRE, JOSEPH OCTAVE (1802–1879), a Belgian historian and antiquary, was born at Bruges, April 12, 1802. He studied law at the University of Ghent, practised as an advocate at Brussels, and entered the diplomatic service. In August, 1849, he received the appointment of Secretary of Legation and Consul-General for Belgium, at London. He died in London, August 17, 1879. Among his works are: *Histoire du Règne de Charles-le-Bon*, in collaboration with I. Perneel (Brussels, 1830); *Les Traditions et Légendes de Flandre* (Lille, 1834), translated into English by the author, as *Old Flanders* (London, 1845); *Précis des Annals de Bruges, depuis les temps les plus reculé, jusqu'au commencement du XVIIe siècle* (Bruges, 1835); *Le Roman de Renard*, from an ancient Flemish MS. (1838); *De l' Origine des Flamands*, with a sketch of Flemish literature; *La Belgique illustrée par les Sciences, les Arts, et les Lettres* (1840); *Galerie des Artistes Brugeois*, since Van Eyck (1840); *Marie de Bourgogne* (1841); *Examen de ce que renferme la Bibliotheque du Musée Britannique* (1846); *Histoire Littéraire des Fous* (1860); *Analyse des Travaux de la Société des Philobiblions de Londres* (1862); *Essai historique sur les Rébus* (1874); *Tableau de la Littérature du centon chez les Anciens et chez les Modernes* (1875, 2 vols.), etc. He has also published reprints of rare texts, and of macaronic pieces, such as: *Aventures de Tiel-Ulenspiegel* (1835); *Vision de Tyndalus*, a mystic narrative of the 13th century; *Macaroneana, ou Mélanges de littérature Macaronique des differents peuples de l' Europe* (Paris, 1852); *Nouveaux Mélanges de Littérature Macaronique* (London, 1862); with other works on like subjects.

DELITZSCH, FRANZ, a German exegete and Hebraist, was born of poor parents at Leipsic, Feb. 23,

1813. He studied divinity in the University of Leipsic; and took a professorship in theology at Rostock in 1846, at Erlangen in 1850, and at Leipsic in 1867. By persevering study he had become master of the great body of rabbinical and Jewish literature. Among his works are *Geschichte der Jüdischen Poesie* (1836); *Beiträge zur mittelalterlichen Scholastik unter juden und Moslemen* (1841); *Jesurum* (1838); and a large number of exegetical works, including commentaries on Habakkuk (1843); Canticles (1851); Genesis (1852; 4th vol., 1872); Hebrews (1857); Psalms (3 vols., 1859–74); Isaiah (3d ed., 1879); Job (2d ed., 1876); the Solomonic writings (1873, 1875); *Biblisch-theologischen und apologetisch-kritischen Studien* (with the aid of Caspari, 1845–48); *Biblischen Psychologie* (1855); *Neue Untersuchungen über Entstehen und Anlage der Kanonischen Evangelien* (1853); *System der christlichen Apologetik* (1869); *Handschriftliche Funde* (1861–62); *Sakrament des wahren Leibes und Blutes Jesu Christi* (1844; 6th ed. 1876); *Jesus und Hillel* (1867); *Jüdische Handwerkerleben zur Zeit Jesu* (1868); *Ein Tag in Kapernaum* (1871); and many other works. His Hebrew version of the New Testament is of vast importance, and has been adopted by the British and Foreign Bible Society. His son, JOHANNES DELITZSCH, born in 1846, died at Rapallo, Italy, Feb. 3, 1876. He was author of *Lehr-system der römischen Kirche* (1875). Another son, FRIEDRICH, born at Erlangen, Sept. 3, 1850, is author of *Assyrische Studien* (1874); *Assyrische Lesestücke* (1878); and *Wo lag das Paradies?* (1881); and is since 1877 professor of Assyriology in Leipsic.

DELIUS, NICOLAUS, a German author, especially noted as a critic of Shakespeare, was born at Bremen, Sept. 19, 1813. From the gymnasium of his native city he passed to the University of Bonn and afterwards to that of Berlin, where he devoted himself to linguistic studies. He also visited France and England before entering upon his professorial career. In 1841 he began to deliver lectures at Berlin, and after a year's experience as editor of a newspaper in Bremen settled in Bonn in 1846. Here he was made professor extraordinary in 1855; and ten years later became full professor. Delius lectured for some time on Sanscrit, but afterwards gave more attention to romance literature and especially to Shakespeare. His first publication was *Radices Pracriticæ* (Bonn, 1839), an appendix to a grammatical work by Lassen, but two years later appeared his first essay in the field in which he was to acquire renown. This was an edition of *Macbeth* (Bremen, 1841), and was followed by various works on Shakespeare's text, his critics, and the English stage in his time. His edition of Shakespeare's works (7 vols., 1854–61) has been enlarged and improved (1882). Besides his books on this subject Delius has been a frequent contributor to the periodical press, treating both of Shakespeare and of the early literature of France. He has published editions of Wace's Old French poem, *Saint Nicolas* (Bonn, 1850), and of *Provençalischen Liedern* (Bonn, 1853); and a treatise on the Sardinian dialect of the 13th century (Bonn, 1868).

DELLA CRUSCA, the name of an Italian academy of literature and philology, founded at Florence, Italy, in 1582. Such academies were numerous in that period, and this one seems to have been an outgrowth from the Florentine Academy, founded by Cosmo I., primarily for the study of the works of Plato. They bore curious names: two later ones were called *Dei Lyncei* ("of the Lynxes"), to indicate that they were sharp-eyed and unrelenting in their contest with falsehood and error; and *Del Cimento* ("of the Experiment"), because they used the Baconian method. Thus we have the *Academia della Crusca* ("of the Sieve"), indicating the purpose to sift the wheat from the chaff, especially with reference to the Italian language, which was being sadly corrupted. It had not a long life, but it has marked a period in Italian philology by its publication, in 1613, of the *Vocabolario della Crusca*. As might be expected, it gives undue importance to the Tuscan dialect, and it was severely criticised by Beni in his *Anti-Crusca*. It also published valuable editions of the ancient poets. It assailed the poet Tasso, but was so prejudiced and unjust that critics have sided with the poet in the controversy between them. The short life of the academy was a brilliant one; it eclipsed all other Italian associations of a similar kind.

The name *Della Crusca* was also adopted by an association of English poets under the patronage of Mrs. Piozzi (Thrale) during a residence at Florence in 1785–86. They printed, but did not publish, *The Florentine Miscellany*. Their high-flown and sentimental poetry awoke the anger of William Gifford, who ridiculed them in his satires, *The Baviad* and *The Mæviad*, particularly the former. (H. C.)

DEL MAR, ALEXANDER, an American mining engineer, statistician, and political economist, was born in New York, Aug. 9, 1836. His father, Jacques Del Mar, a Spanish mining engineer, had become a resident and citizen of the United States. Alexander, however, was educated in Spain, returning to the United States in 1849, and spending two years in mercantile business in New York. He then went back to Europe to complete his education. When he returned in 1854 he became connected with the New York press, writing chiefly on financial subjects. He edited for some time *Hunt's Merchants' Magazine*, the *New York Social Science Review*, and the *Commercial and Financial Chronicle*, which he originated, and contributed to *De Bow's Review* and other periodicals. In 1862 he published *Gold Money and Paper Money*; in 1865 *History and Principles of Taxation*; and in 1866 *Essays in Political Economy and Statistics of the World*. In the latter year Pres. Johnson appointed him director of the bureau of statistics, which position he held for four years, issuing meantime reports on American navigation interests and on the customs revenues. In 1872 he published a *History of the Rate of Interest*, and in the same year went to Russia as the American delegate to the Statistical Congress held in St. Petersburg. In 1875 he was one of the supervisors of the census of the city of New York. In 1876 he aroused an agitation against the demonetization of silver, which had been quietly effected in Congress. He was made a member of the silver commission, and helped to remonetize the silver dollar. His *Report on the Comstock Lode* (Washington. 1876), in which he predicted its speedy exhaustion, greatly enhanced his professional reputation. He has since resided in San Francisco, and has explored all the mining districts of the Pacific States. He has charge of various hydraulic mining-works in California and Brazil, but besides these professional duties spends much time in literary work on kindred subjects. His *History of the Precious Metals* (London, 1880) was begun in 1855, and embodies the researches of twenty-five years. His latest completed work is a *History of Gold-Mining in Brazil* (London, 1882).

DELPHI, a city of Indiana, county-seat of Carroll co., is on the left bank of the Wabash River, on the Wabash, St. Louis, and Pacific Railroad, and the Indianapolis, Delphi, and Chicago Air Line Railroad, 18 miles N.E. of Lafayette. It is also on the Wabash and Erie Canal. It has a court-house, jail, 2 opera-houses, odd fellows' hall, 3 hotels, 2 banks, 2 weekly newspapers, 6 churches, a graded school, and high-school. Its industries comprise factories making bent-wood furniture, staves, spokes and hubs, carriages, wagons, and portable-engines; 3 flour-mills, and 7 patent lime-kilns, which burn 1,500,000 bushels of lime annually. Delphi was settled in 1840, and incorporated in 1868. Its property is valued at $1,525,000, and its public debt is $45,000. Its inhabitants are almost entirely of American birth. The surrounding country furnishes excellent brick-clay and limestone, and the buildings of the city are chiefly of brick. Population, 2750.

DELPHIN CLASSICS, the name given to an edition of all the important writers of Greece and Rome, prepared for the use of the dauphin of France, the son of Louis XIV., whence the title reads *in usum serenissimi Delphini*. It was prepared under the direction of Bossuet and Huet, the tutor and sub-tutor of the prince, by thirty-nine of the best scholars of France. The series was re-edited in England in 141 volumes 8vo, between the years 1819 and 1830, by Abraham John Valpy, with the assistance of George Dyer, who prepared all the original matter except the preface. This reissue was criticised because, although good when published, the Delphin Classics had been already superseded and were of little value except as rare books. The Virgil and Horace, however, are exceptions, and have been used until almost the present time. (H. C.)

DEMOCRATIC-REPUBLICAN PARTY. The overthrow of the Anti-Federal party in 1788 left practically but one, the Federal party, in the country (see ANTI-FEDERAL, and FEDERAL). For the first three years after the inauguration of the new Government in 1789 all the public men of the country were nominally Federalists. In States like Massachusetts, where the Anti-Federalists had made their strongest opposition, they had announced at the end of the struggle their intention to support the Constitution before the people; that is, to become Federalists for the time. Jefferson, Madison, Edmund Randolph, Burr, all were nominally Federalists in 1790; indeed, the idea prevailed that there was thereafter to be but one party in the United States, and that the Government was to be administered without party contests.

Hamilton's project for the assumption of State debts by the Federal Government in 1790 brought out the first semblance of party opposition, which was fanned to a flame by his plan for the formation of a national bank in 1791. These, however, were but prominent instances of a general course of nationalizing policy, in which Jefferson could see only a design to finally subvert the State governments and establish a strong central government controlled by a single interest, that of commerce, and subjecting all other interests and the rights of individuals to that. It was for this reason that he and his party associates at once attacked the Hamilton party as monarchists: the king feared by them was not Washington, or Hamilton, or any other single man, but a clique of men united by a common interest. And it must be remembered that, at the worst, the idea of a king, perhaps disguised under another title, as in the case of the stadtholder of Holland, was by no means startling to the generation of 1783-93, and was very often suggested as a possible solution of the difficulties of the Confederation. It was formally broached to Washington by Jay in 1787, though only as a possible final resort. Steuben was sounded as to the willingness of Prince Henry of Prussia to become stadtholder of the United States. When the secret deliberations of the Convention of 1787 were ended, the impression was common that one of their recommendations would be the establishment of an English prince of the blood, the so-called bishop of Osnaburg, as "permanent President," or with some such title equivalent to that of king. The title of "king," in short, was so little hateful at the time that the appellation of "monarchist" was by no means startling. Hamilton, indeed, was no monarchist, though he had urged in the Convention the establishment of a President for life; it was patently absurd to attempt to establish any one but Washington as king, and impossible to induce him to accept such an office. Nevertheless, the assertion of monarchical designs against Hamilton and his supporters, the idea that they were monarchists in theory, and only waited for an opportunity to put their theory into practice, clung, and remained the principal party weapon for many years.

The opening scenes of the French Revolution, from which Jefferson had just returned, suggested a countername. If the opponents of monarchy in France were Republicans, the opponents of monarchy in the United States had a fair claim to the same name. So we find Jefferson, in his letter of May 13, 1792, to Washington, claiming the name of Republicans for his followers, "who wished to preserve the Government in its present form;" and for nearly twenty years the name of Republican was the only one acknowledged by the new party. In its first form (1792-93) the party was exceedingly small, without defined principles or limits, with but two or three leaders of national reputation—Jefferson, Madison, and Edmund Randolph—supported by a few Congressmen, Bland, Giles, and Page—and the whole drawn from Virginia. Indeed, the whole was at first a Virginia interest, and may be considered the Virginia type of Federalism, the Virginia method of supporting the Constitution.

The treaty of alliance between France and the United States, concluded in 1778, purported to be defensive only, but a provision in it for guaranteeing the French possessions in America, and the natural feeling of gratitude for French assistance in the Revolution, inclined many Americans to take part with France in the European wars which that republic declared in 1792-93, particularly against Great Britain. The policy of the Federal party was neutrality, since the ties of its controlling commercial interests were mainly with Great Britain; and the natural feeling of opposition, intensified in Jefferson's case by his theoretical sympathy with the French revolutionists, inclined the Republicans to favor France as far as that could be done without drifting into war. In April, 1793, the whole course of party conflict was mightily influenced by the arrival of Edmond Charles Genet, the envoy from the French Republic. The sending of such an envoy into a foreign country for the purpose of forming a French party, denouncing all opponents as enemies of the people, and finally either overturning the Government or compelling it to assist France, was the ordinary method of the French leaders at the time; and, though not directly successful in the United States, it had indirect effects beyond calculation. The first effect was the formation of "Democratic clubs" all over the country from Boston to Kentucky. They imitated all the follies of their Jacobin prototypes of France—cut their hair short, affected a new simplicity in dress and manners, changed the aristocratic title of "Mr." to the more modest name of "Citizen," and with all the zeal of new converts not only approved to the full all the doings of the French revolutionists, but made the most desperate efforts to discover tyrants in their own country in order to signalize their patriotism. It is hard to say which is the more amusing, the half-hearted Quixotism with which a Democrat of 1793–95 assimilated himself to Brutus by hinting a doubt of Washington's financial honesty, or the horror with which his Federalist neighbor regarded him as a Jacobin and revolutionist, with a list of suspects in his pocket and a guillotine in his back yard. But the real offence and the real work of the Democratic clubs lay in an entirely different direction. Heretofore, suffrage and political discussion were equally the province of the middle and upper classes, the former confined to freeholders, the latter to their abler representatives. When the right of suffrage was allowed to wealth without a freehold, it was allowed with a sort of protest; and the American feeling was thus spoken by Franklin in 1766: "Many who have no freeholds have nevertheless a vote; *which, indeed, I don't think was necessary to be allowed*" (italics as in original). With all their follies, the Democratic clubs introduced universal political discussion; and that, if unchecked, meant universal suffrage in the near future. Here lay the real point of contact and union between them and the Republicans, and the impassable barrier between them and the Federalists. The Democratic club was the New England caucus spreading into other States, and its deliberations were regarded by the Federalists very much as Hutchinson and Gage regarded those of the New England caucus—as an unwarranted intrusion into matters that did not concern it.

The coalescence of the Republicans and Democrats into a single national party was effected by the so-called "Whiskey Insurrection" in 1794 and the conclusion of Jay's treaty with Great Britain in 1795. If the Democrats did not favor the former, they at least did not severely condemn it, since one of their cardinal principles was that any general repugnance to a law argued the iniquity of the law. Washington's direct condemnation of the Democratic clubs as the instigators of the insurrection diminished the number of clubs without diminishing the number of Democrats; these were driven into tacit alliance with the Republicans. Jay's treaty, which secured a ten years' safety to American commerce, and with it to American neutrality, completed the union, and in effect formed the Democratic-Republican party. The name "Republican" still was used exclusively by its members, while the name "Democrat" was applied by its opponents as a term of contempt, equivalent to Jacobin or revolutionist; but the latter name was much more appropriate than the former, for the new party had no predilection for the idea of the United States as a unified republic, while its only logical growth was toward universal suffrage, an elective judiciary, exemption of the individual from governmental interference, the preference of the smaller and more democratic units of society to the larger and more republican, and all the methods by which weaker or individual interests are to be preserved against larger or combined interests. In this sense the names are now (1884) properly taken by the opposing Republican and Democratic parties, but the former follows Democratic methods, and the latter accepts Republican theory so far that it is often hard to find a line of division between them.

By the union of the two elements Jefferson was now the head of a national party, and no longer of a simple Virginia faction; and it speaks much for his political capacity that the reins never slipped from his fingers during the transformation. Indeed, his seat was firmer than before. His prominence in the outbreak of the French Revolution gave him a claim upon the allegiance of the Democratic leaders which Madison, his only rival in ability, could not dispute; and Monroe, his only possible competitor in this respect, was, like all the other Democratic leaders, a man of very inferior ability. Throughout the Union every man who felt the pressure of Church, State, or classes bearing heavily upon him looked to Jefferson in his hopes of relief. Electors until about 1824–28 were generally chosen by State legislatures, so that there is no record of the general popular vote at the Presidential elections of 1789 and the following thirty-five years. We can only know that when Washington refused to be a candidate for a third term Jefferson narrowly missed being his successor. Instead of the four votes of Kentucky, which had been given to him in 1792, he had now all the votes south of the Potomac and Ohio, except one from North Carolina and one from Virginia; and north of the Potomac he had fourteen of Pennsylvania's fifteen votes, and four of Maryland's seven votes. In the aggregate he received 68 votes to 71 for John Adams, and became Vice-President; nothing but the two straggling Southern votes prevented the positions of the two men from being reversed.

This defeat, so amazingly near to a victory, like the Republican party's defeat in 1856, gave Jefferson's party a standing which it had not before. It had been a matter of extreme difficulty for the nation to assert its existence even in foreign affairs by the adoption of the Constitution, and the country was not at all ready for even the indirect methods of asserting its existence in domestic affairs which made up Hamilton's Federalist policy. Without some such methods of conciliating State feeling as were afterwards followed by the Whig, and still more by the Republican, party, it should have been evident that every occasion of discussion would only increase Jefferson's strength toward the North, now that Washington, the Federalist pillar of support in the North, was out of politics. Unfortunately for the Federalists, the "X, Y, Z mission" to France (see FEDERAL PARTY) in 1797–98 roused an American storm of indignation against France, which comprehended the Democratic party also. In Congress their party force melted away. Some acted perforce with the Federalists; others found urgent business to attend to at home; only Gallatin showed a nerve and power in politics which, but for his foreign birth, would have made him a serious competitor to Jefferson for the party leadership. For a little space the Democratic party was out of the combat, and the triumphant Federalist majority pressed on to the organization of a standing army, the passage of the alien laws, and the passage of a sedition law. All these three steps were, in the view of the Democrats, directly levelled at them. The first they thought unwarranted by any danger of French invasion or of slave insurrection, and only designed to support the Government in arbitrary arrests of Democrats. The second, with their provisions for fourteen years' residence as an essential to citizenship, and for the arrest and transportation, at the President's order, of any alien whom he should consider dangerous, they looked upon as a direct attack upon a large mass of their own party. The third, which made it a crime to print or publish any "false, scandalous, or malicious" writings tending to defame the Government, President, or Congress, to bring them into contempt, or to excite the hatred of the good people of the United States against them, was certainly a direct attempt to stop party-newspaper criticism. And it was certain, while the machinery of Government was in Federalist hands, to be directed only against one party: Hamilton was to be at liberty to print the most contumelious personal attacks on the President himself, while "Judge" Peck was to be arrested for circulating a Democratic petition against the sedition law. But how were they to be resisted? In Congress alone? The whole series of laws was expressly modelled on the English precedent of 1791–93, and the arrest of members of the British Parliament for seditious language so late as 1882 may serve to show us why the Democrats of 1798 apprehended a possible wholesale arrest of Democratic members of Congress for the same offence, if such a step should prove necessary for perpetuating the Federalist hold on power. There was but one stronghold left—the State legislatures—from which to resist the supposed intentions of the Federalists, and but two of the State legislatures, those of Kentucky and Virginia—allied by blood, political sympathy, and former connection—were available at the moment. Two series of resolutions, the famous Virginia and Kentucky resolutions of 1798, were at once prepared, the former by Madison and the latter by Jefferson, and passed with little opposition, except in Virginia. They form the first declaration of principles of the new party. Both assert State sovereignty plainly; and, as State sovereignty is not only the putative but the real father of nullification and secession, a few words of explanation seem to be in place before analyzing the resolutions.

State sovereignty, the idea that the States had voluntarily formed the Union, and only voluntarily remained in it, was the formal belief of nearly all public men, and the hearty belief of many of them, until 1861. It was not until 1830, when a State's sovereign right to nullify national laws was first plainly asserted, that Jackson, Edward Livingston, and the other Democratic leaders modified the right of secession into a right of revolution under intolerable misgovernment, with a correlative right in the Federal Government to resist such a revolution. It was not until 1861, when the attempt to secede was openly made, that a hitherto unsuspected popular force compelled the national leaders to treat secession as rebellion. And yet neither Jefferson nor Madison, when they said State sovereignty, appear to have really meant State sovereignty to the full. The private correspondence of both, particularly of the former, shows that their governing desire was to have constitutional questions settled by a convention of the States. If a majority of the States pronounced against a State's claim that the Federal Government had transcended its powers, the State must yield and obey. But in that case what becomes of the State's "sovereignty"? Calhoun was more logical. When he said State sovereignty he meant it, and secession was a part of his possible train of action. Jefferson's "nullification" is to be effected by a convention of the States; Calhoun's, by the sovereign power of the State itself. To both secession seemed a possible calamity, but to Jefferson's thinking it was to be avoided by the maintenance of individual rights and the avoidance of class-government; while to Calhoun's it was to be avoided by an impossible yielding to the demands of a single section and of the interest of slavery which controlled it. The assertion of State sovereignty, then, in these resolutions is only the assertion of a particularist feeling, made in the only way in which such an assertion could be made at the time.

The Virginia resolutions were eight in number. They express the State's condemnation of the alien and sedition laws, its regret that the general phrases of the Constitution have been so perverted as to allow of their passage, and its desire that other States should concur with it in arresting the evil. The third resolution is the essential one. It is as follows: "That this assembly doth explicitly and peremptorily declare that it views the powers of the Federal Government as resulting from the compact to which the States are parties, as limited by the plain sense and intention of the instrument constituting that compact, as no further valid than they are authorized by the grants enumerated in that compact; and that in case of a deliberate, palpable, and dangerous exercise of other powers not granted by the said compact the States who are parties thereto have the right and are in duty bound to interpose for arresting the progress of the evil, and for maintaining within their respective limits the authorities, rights, and liberties appertaining to them." The word "interpose" has been most vigorously attacked by Von Holst as equivalent to Calhoun's idea of nullification. It is therefore fair to remind the reader of the different manner in which the two "interpositions" were to be effected, and to admit, on the other hand, that the word "respective" is at least a very awkward word for an apologist for the resolution.

The Kentucky resolutions were nine in number, the first being the essential one, as follows: "That the several States composing the United States of America are not united on the principle of unlimited submission to their general Government; but that by compact, under the style and title of a Constitution for the United States and of amendments thereto, they constituted a general Government for special purposes, and delegated to that Government certain definite powers, reserving, each State to itself, the residuary mass of right to their own self-government; and that, whensoever the general Government assumes undelegated powers its acts are unauthoritative, void, and of no force; that to this compact each State acceded as a State, and is an integral party; that this Government, created by this compact, was not made the exclusive or final judge of the extent of the powers delegated to itself, since that would have made its discretion, and not the Constitution, the measure of its powers; but that, as in all other cases of compact among parties having no common judge, each party has an equal right to judge for itself as well of infractions as of the mode and measure of redress." The fallacious idea here is in the word "compact:" the whole history of the country proves that the existence of the States is not due to their own power, but to the fixed preference of the whole country for the State form of local government, and that the whole country, by its own settled method of amending the Constitution, may at any time modify, diminish, or increase the powers of the States at its discretion. If the whole country chooses to give each State an opportunity of pronouncing on the change, that certainly does not make "each State an integral party," for we can hardly imagine a voluntary party to a "compact" who may be compelled to diminish his own powers. A line of citations from Jefferson's own correspondence is therefore given below to show that he himself was hampered by the indwelling consciousness of this fact; that a convention of the States was the real "party" which was to judge of infractions and the mode and measure of redress; and that his mythical State sovereignty was only particularism in a more ambitious dress than it has yet ventured to assume in other constitutional countries.

Both the Kentucky and the Virginia resolutions were sent to the other States, but received no support from them. In the following year Virginia reiterated her resolutions and followed them with a long commentary by a committee of which Madison was the chairman—the once celebrated "Report of 1800." It defends the resolutions as containing nothing dangerous or revolutionary, but quietly assumes the existence of a "compact" between the States. Jefferson made no defence of the Kentucky resolutions, which, indeed, were then passing under the name of George Nicholas of Kentucky, but in the following year (1799) procured the passage of a supplementary resolution containing this clause: "That the several States who formed that instrument [the Constitution], being sovereign and independent, have the unquestionable right to judge of the infraction, and that a nullification by those sovereignties of all unauthorized acts done under color of that instrument is the rightful remedy." The last paragraph, standing alone, can easily and naturally be referred to the idea of "nullification" by the convention of States, but the word "several" in the preceding paragraph is difficult to reconcile with this view. And the difficulty is increased by the paragraph which followed the word "remedy" in Jefferson's original draft: "That every State has a natural right, in cases not within the compact [*casus non foederis*], to nullify of their own authority all assumptions of power by others within their limits." It is not known whether Jefferson himself omitted this paragraph from the final draft, but the extracts from his correspondence below seem to show a flat opposition between this paragraph and his subsequent opinions. If the paragraph is admitted to be Jefferson's settled doctrine, he must be considered the father of nullification, even in the form given it by Calhoun.

In spite of the popular excitement over the hostilities with France, the last two years of Adams's administration show a steady increase of Democratic strength in the doubtful Middle States, Pennsylvania, New Jersey, and New York, owing to the unwise prosecutions in those States under the sedition law. The first test election came in New York in April, 1800, for the legislature which was to choose presidential electors. In that State, Aaron Burr had assumed control of the Democratic machine, and he managed it so well as to carry the State. In the presidential election Democratic electors were chosen by the whole South except Delaware, by Kentucky and New York, and eight of Pennsylvania's fifteen electors were Democrats. Jefferson and Burr received 73 electoral votes to 65 for their opponents, but the equality of their vote rendered a further contest in Congress necessary, in which Jefferson was finally chosen President (see FEDERAL PARTY). The Congress which met in 1801 was also Democratic in both branches, and before the end of Jefferson's first term the tide had set so strongly that the Federalists could depend on but three States—Massachusetts, Connecticut, and Delaware.

From the victory of 1800–01 the national history of the party becomes absorbed in the history of the country (see UNITED STATES), which it governed very steadily until 1840. Its policy was that for which the key-note was struck in Jefferson's first inaugural: "A wise and frugal Government, which shall restrain men from injuring one another, which shall leave them otherwise free to regulate their own pursuits of industry and improvement,—this is the sum of good government, and this is necessary to close the circle of our felicities." To this test every proposed measure was to be brought. There was to be no protection of any interest, no "paternal government;" and the less the Government did, the better it fulfilled its functions. The specifications of the general principle in the inaugural and elsewhere are as follows: universal suffrage, on the principle that "every man who pays or fights shall vote;" peace, commerce, and honest friendship with all nations, entangling alliances with none; the support of the State governments in domestic concerns, and of the general Government in foreign affairs; absolute acquiescence in the decisions of the majority; the supremacy of the civil over the military authority; economy in the public expenses; the payment of the public debt; direct taxes in preference to customs; and avoidance of standing armies and of navies. In carrying out this policy Jefferson and Madison (his Secretary of State) were assisted by a corps of new men, mostly brought into prominence by the elections of 1800–01. Prominent among them were Albert Gallatin of Pennsylvania, a naturalized Swiss, who remained Secretary of the Treasury until 1814, and then went into the diplomatic service; James Monroe of Virginia and Robert R. Livingston of New York, who together accomplished the cession of Louisiana in 1803; Aaron Burr, president of the Senate, soon to be driven from the party for suspected treachery in the election of 1800; George Clinton, governor of New York; his greater nephew, De Witt Clinton, the founder of the New York canal system; and Eldridge Gerry of Massachusetts, afterwards governor of his State and Vice-President. In Congress, for the next dozen years, the party was not ably represented. In 1803, John Quincy Adams, the son of the late President, left his former party and gave strength to his new party friends; Henry Clay was in the Senate for a time (1806–07), and in 1807, William H. Crawford of Georgia entered the Senate. Outside of these names the main party strength still came from Virginia. From this State came the eccentric John Randolph, for four years the party-leader in the House, and thereafter independent of, and often opposed to, the party; John W. Eppes and Thomas Mann Randolph, sons-in-law of the President; and William B. Giles, Wilson C. Nicholas, and John Taylor, his confidential friends. Joseph B. Varnum, a managing Massachusetts politician; Samuel Mitchill of New York, who mingled natural science with politics; Michael Leib, an ultra Pennsylvania Democrat; Nathaniel Macon, a rigidly and severely honest politician, who served as a Representative and Senator from North Carolina for thirty-seven years (1791–1828); and Stephen Roe Bradley of Vermont, make up the list of men who managed the party until 1811. In their management of it they found at once that their strict construction of the Constitution must be modified in practice. Their acquisition of Louisiana in 1803 and the embargo in 1807 had absolutely no constitutional warrant; both were evidently exercises of the sovereignty which the Democrats denied to the Federal Government in home affairs. But in their real party purpose, the extension of the right of suffrage, th   successful in all the States against   the Federalists.

State after State repealed its property or other qualifications, and, though the restrictions had never been severe, their repeal was sufficient to give quite a new character to politics and to bring in new men as leaders in the course of the next decade. In their purpose to reduce expenses and pay off the debt the party-leaders were successful in the most unstatesmanlike fashion. In Europe, Great Britain and Napoleon had become chronic antagonists, the former respecting no law on the ocean, and the latter respecting no law upon the land. All the world with the exception of the United States had been drawn into the whirlpool of their contests, and only a strong navy could gain from Great Britain any respect for the commerce of the United States. But the support of a navy would have checked the payment of the debt, and the party-managers took strong ground against a navy. Most of the vessels which the Federalists had built were broken up and sold; cheap and useless gunboats were substituted for them; and support of the "gunboat system" and opposition to a navy became the touchstone of Democracy until the Constitution's victory over the Guerriere in 1812. To take the place of a navy, the Democratic majority in 1807 enacted the Embargo Law, which prohibited commerce altogether. When this had aroused a dangerous discontent in New England, the commercial district of the country, the "Non-Intercourse Law" was substituted in 1809. It forbade commerce with Great Britain and France until one or both should withdraw their edicts against American commerce. In this way the party mismanaged foreign affairs until it was forced into war in 1812.

In 1809, Madison took Jefferson's place as President There had been much opposition to his nomination. Monroe estimated his claims to the Presidency as equal to Madison's, and George Clinton and his New York supporters felt that Virginia had no exclusive claim to the Presidency. Federalist opposition was so weak that Madison's nomination for the Presidency by the Congressional caucus was decisive. The same body gave Clinton the second place on the ticket. But in 1812, when Madison and Gerry were nominated by the caucus, discontent became revolt. De Witt Clinton had succeeded to his uncle's leadership in New York and to his uncle's aspirations. The Federalists adopted him as their candidate for the Presidency, and he thus obtained the votes of New England (except Vermont), New York, New Jersey, Delaware, and five of Maryland's eleven votes. Though he was defeated by 89 votes to 128 for Madison, yet the whole revolt had depended on Pennsylvania's twenty-five votes. The increase of Pennsylvania's western vote saved the whole vote of the State to Madison: had it gone to Clinton, it would have made him President by 114 votes to 103. A part of the bargain which had secured Madison's nomination by the caucus had been an agreement that he would abandon the peace policy and declare for war against Great Britain, for the system of no navy and restrictions on commerce had confessedly failed. New party-leaders had entered Congress with popular support behind them—William H. Crawford in the Senate, and Henry Clay of Kentucky, Felix Grundy of Tennessee, Langdon Cheves, William Lowndes, and John C. Calhoun of South Carolina, and Peter B. Porter of New York, in the House, being the leaders of the "War-hawks." These made their party a war party, and war was declared June 18, 1812 (see UNITED STATES).

The end of the war of 1812 left the country in severe straits. The long delay to prepare for war, the attempt to support it wholly by means of loans, and the pronounced hostility to the loans in New England, where alone they could be floated, had brought the national credit very low, and the first step of the dominant party was to charter a new national bank to take the place of Hamilton's, whose charter had been allowed to expire in 1811. This was not accomplished until April 10, 1816; the charter was to run twenty years; the capital was to be $35,000,000, one-fifth cash, four-fifths Government stocks; the Government was to have the appointment of five of the twenty-five directors; and the bank was to have the custody of the public funds, except in cases when the Secretary of the Treasury should decide to place them elsewhere, when he was to report his reasons at once to Congress. In the same year a slightly protective tariff on woollen and cotton goods became law. This was also a departure from Jeffersonian canons. But manufacturers were still a part of the Democratic party, and looked to it for protection. Jefferson himself, in his correspondence at this time, acknowledges a considerable change of feeling in regard to protection, and accepts its theory to a considerable extent as a preparation for possible war and the means of national independence. In 1819–20 a still more protective tariff passed the House, but failed in the Senate; and in 1824 and 1828 new tariffs were passed which raised the average duty to about 37 per cent. in the former year and nearly 50 in the latter. In a third respect the Jeffersonian theory was abandoned. About 1822 the policy of improving rivers and harbors and of building roads and canals at national expense was fairly begun, and during Adams's administration (1825–29) was carried out very thoroughly. The check which was given to the process in 1829 is curious and instructive.

The political history of New York, the largest State in the Union, with the greatest diversity of interests, is a good example of the development of Democracy While the suffrage was limited to freeholders political contest was limited to three great families, the Clintons, Livingstones, and Schuylers, and their adherents by blood or marriage. The influence of the last-named disappeared with Hamilton's death in 1804. The other two maintained for years after 1800 a war of varying successes, in which the State civil service was made open use of as a political weapon. De Witt Clinton usually maintained a superiority, but his self-confidence steadily drove from him his leading supporters, who gradually coalesced into the Bucktail or Tammany faction, and overthrew him. By this time the suffrage had been so far widened that no one man could manage a party in the State; and about 1821 the little knot of Bucktail leaders, soon to be known as the "Albany Regency," made its appearance. Their first principle was always to control the State by the political use of its civil service; and their second, to throw their leading men from time to time into the national service, there to maintain that theory of State rights which would leave the State of New York to manage its own concerns under the guidance of the Regency. Strict discipline, faithfulness to friends, unsparing punishment of desertion, made up the Regency's code of action. In 1825 the Regency was in favor of William H. Crawford for President as he had been the "regular candidate" of the Congressional caucus, the customary nominating body since 1797. But there were then other candidates, all nominally Democrats: Henry Clay, Speaker of the House, John Quincy Adams, Monroe's Secretary of State, and Andrew Jackson, a private citizen of Tennessee nom-

lasted by the legislature of his State. The friends of these candidates refused to take part in or be bound by the action of the caucus, and the electors made no choice, Jackson having 99 votes, Adams 84, Crawford 41, and Clay 37. In the following February the House of Representatives was to choose between the three highest on the list. Crawford was now so paralyzed as to be a hopeless candidate, and his vote in the House was but four States. The Clay vote went to Adams, and he was chosen by thirteen States to seven for Jackson. The fact that Jackson had had a plurality of both the popular and the electoral vote, and yet had failed of the election, woke to life the spirit of democracy, which had been accumulating under the gradual widening of the right of suffrage, and it soon became evident that Jackson was to be the "popular" candidate in 1828. Until this became evident the Regency trimmed between Adams and Jackson, with a strong inclination to the former; Sept. 26, 1827, Tammany Hall suddenly "pronounced" in favor of Jackson, and the whole Regency influence in the State went with it. Already the Regency had a member ready for national service. Martin Van Buren had in 1821 been elected to the United States Senate, and he conscientiously held all the "strict-construction" views of the Constitution which were so necessary for the continuance of the Regency's power. Van Buren's natural powers and the importance of New York's accession recommended him to the Jackson party and its head. In 1828, Jackson received a majority of the popular and electoral vote, and became President. Van Buren became his Secretary of State, and his appearance in the Cabinet marks the beginning of a development of Jackson's views in the direction of orthodox "strict construction." Before his election he had been no opponent of the Bank of the United States or of internal improvements or of a protective tariff, and had tried to induce Monroe to make the civil service non-partisan; after his election his whole drift is in the opposite direction. The conclusion seems inevitable that advancing democracy in New York had successfully secured, through one of its members, the lead of the national Democracy, and that it had thus reasserted the original Jeffersonian theory, together with that of rotation in office, which had hardly been more than a speculation with Jefferson.

For this period see, in general, Hildreth's *United States;* Schouler's *United States;* Tucker's *United States;* Hammond's *Political History of New York;* Statesman's *Manual;* 1–9 Benton's *Debates of Congress;* Ingersoll's *Second War with Great Britain;* Van Buren's *Political Parties in the United States;* Gillet's *Democracy in the United States;* Jefferson's *Works;* Madison's *Writings.* For biography see Randall's *Life of Jefferson;* Rives's *Life of Madison;* Parton's *Life of Burr* and *Life of Jefferson;* Adams's *Life of Gallatin;* Austin's *Life of Gerry;* Garland's *Life of Randolph;* Pinckney's *Life of Pinckney;* Dallas's *Writings of Dallas;* Adams's *Memoir of John Quincy Adams.* For authorities of an opposite cast see FEDERAL PARTY. The "Kentucky and Virginia resolutions" and Madison's "Report of 1800" are in 4 Elliot's *Debates,* 528–580. The authorized Democratic defence of them is in 1 Benton's *Thirty Years' View,* 347–360; the severest criticism of them in Von Holst's *United States,* 144–171. In connection with this latter, to show that Jefferson's thought was a "nullification" by national convention, and not, as Von Holst assumes, by a single State, the reader is referred to 3 Jefferson's *Works* (the edition of 1853, in four volumes), 429, 452, 453, 462, and 4: 103, 199, 221, 306, 374, 396. The last two citations are as follows: "But the chief-justice says, 'There must be an ultimate arbiter somewhere.' True, there must; but does that prove that it is either party [the Federal Government or a State]? The ultimate arbiter is the people of the Union, assembled by their deputies in convention at the call of Congress or of two-thirds of the States. Let them decide to which they mean to give an authority claimed by two of their organs." "If the two departments [Federal and State] should claim each the same subject of power, where is the common umpire to decide ultimately between them? In cases of little importance or urgency the prudence of both parties will keep them aloof from the questionable ground; but if it can neither be avoided nor compromised, a convention of the States must be called to ascribe the doubtful power to that department which they may think best." But see also the proposed protest of 1825 at page 415 of the same volume.

II. (1825–60). One of Jefferson's theories (which he had never thoroughly put into practice) was that an essential part of the republican system was a popular control of all officials through frequent elections. But the national civil service was different from that of a village or town: its officials were appointed, not elected. How were these to be reached? Evidently through removal by the President: when the people "desired a change" they could obtain it by changing the President, and could reach appointive officers through his power of removal. On this specious basis, this attempt to limit the administrative machinery of a great republic to the simple methods of a New England town, was built the Democratic theory of "rotation in office," slightly enforced by Jefferson, long familiar in New York and Pennsylvania, and finally enforced to the full by Jackson and Van Buren. Within the first year of the new Administration the removals of department officers, marshals, district attorneys, revenue officers, and land agents numbered 176, and of postmasters 491. Removals under former Administrations had been as follows: Washington (eight years), 9; John Adams (four years), 10; Jefferson (eight years), 39; Madison (eight years), 5; Monroe (eight years), 9; and John Q. Adams (four years), 2. Within three years the Administration had thoroughly "reformed" its civil service.

In the course of this process the Administration came into collision with the national bank, which refused, in June, 1829, to remove one of its subordinate officers for political reasons. Jackson was prepared by nature to see in any such institution one of "deadly hostility to republican institutions;" and this refusal of the bank to obey the will of the Democracy, as expressed in his election, only served to draw him to notice the bank as he had not noticed it before, and to bring out his natural opinion of its nature. His first annual message (in December, 1829) expressed doubts as to the constitutionality of the bank's charter, and the committees of both Houses reported that the charter was constitutional. The next year he renewed the suggestion more strongly, and no attention was paid to it. In 1831 he again renewed it, and this time brought conflict. His open opposition to the bank had prepared all the elements of the opposition (see WHIG PARTY) to support the bank. A presidential election was impending, and the opposition hoped that a conflict would alienate from him all his supporters who believed in the bank, and that this defection would defeat him. The bill to recharter the bank was at once prepared, ostentatiously introduced by an Administration Senator from Pennsylvania, passed the Senate June 11, 1832, and the House July 3, and was vetoed by the President July 10. The constitutional reason assigned was the want of power in Congress to charter any such institution, but a more popular and comprehensible reason was the one word "monopoly," which occurs sixteen times in the message, besides many other synonymous words, such as "exclusive privileges," "special favors," etc. A two-thirds majority could not be obtained to pass the bill over the veto, and the whole question was relegated to the presidential election in November. In this Jackson was re-elected, and this result he looked upon as a popular decision in his favor. He allowed the Congress then in existence to expire in March, 1833, and then proceeded to obtain by removal and appointment a Secretary of the Treasury who would do his will against the bank. The charter of 1816 directed the public funds to be deposited in the bank or its branches, "unless the Secretary of the Treasury shall at any time otherwise order and direct," in which case he was to give his reasons to Congress as soon as it should meet. Such cases had often arisen in Southern and Western towns where the bank had no branches: Jackson used it to attack the "mother bank." Oct. 1, 1833, the new Secretary of the Treasury, Taney, by direction of the President, suspended further deposits in the bank, and at the next session of Congress assigned as his main reason the suspected insolvency of the bank. However contrary to the spirit of the law, this "removal of the deposits" was certainly a political master-stroke. In the new Congress the House was in favor of the President, but the removal avoided all need of management or discussion to get a verdict in his favor. It presented the verdict signed and sealed, and threw upon the opposition the labor of reversing it. This was never done. Succeeding Congresses were Democratic, and refused to help the bank, and it secured a charter from Pennsylvania. The Senate of 1833-34 was anti-Jackson, and passed a vote of censure upon him, March 28, 1834; but this vote was expunged from the record Jan. 16, 1837, when the political majority had changed. During all this contest there were subsidiary events—investigations, charges and counter-charges of bribery and corruption, and commercial distress—but the only process here considered is that by which the President made his party an anti-bank party.

In other matters Jackson applied similar discipline to the party, but he possessed the Tudor characteristic of knowing when it was necessary to yield. His veto of the Maysville road bill, May 27, 1830, really ended the internal improvement system, and yet he was compelled several times afterward to yield and sign such bills. When they were passed within the last ten days of the session he disposed of them by a "pocket veto," retaining them without signing them; when a veto could win support he used the veto; but even when he yielded, his influence went against the system so strongly that under his successor, Van Buren, the tools held by the Government were finally sold off at auction. His policy was much the same in the matter of the tariff. He declared strongly against protection, but when the protective tariff of 1832 was passed by the assistance of Democratic votes, he signed it. When South Carolina undertook to nullify the law, he declared his intention to suppress by force any resistance to it, but at the same time the whole influence of the Administration in Congress was thrown in favor of the Verplanck bill, reducing duties to a revenue standard. In this manner the President managed his party, perpetually quarrelling with sections of it, never with the whole; always applying a steady pressure to influence its course, and yet always ready to yield for the moment; and as a result there was behind him at the close of his second term of office in 1837 a completely organized party, the Regency's conception enlarged into national proportions. New men had come in at or shortly before the political revolution of 1829, and in leadership the party was almost entirely new. Chief among the leaders were Van Buren, Jackson's Vice-President and destined successor: Hugh L. White, a Tennessee aspirant to the Presidency, whose disappointment at the President's antagonism to him was already driving him over to the opposition; and Thomas H. Benton, once a bitter Tennessee enemy of Jackson, now a Senator from Missouri and Jackson's trusted lieutenant, honest, verbose, and self-sufficient. Other leaders, prominent already or soon to be so, were John Holmes, an old leader in Maine; in New Hampshire, Levi Woodbury, Jackson's Secretary of the Navy and Treasury, Isaac Hill, an editor and the party manager of the State, Franklin Pierce, afterwards President, and Charles G. Atherton, whose name is connected mainly with the "gag resolutions" by which he endeavored to check slavery debate; in Connecticut, Isaac Toucey and John M. Niles; in New York, C. C. Cambreleng, the special advocate of free trade, and the leaders of the "Regency" (see BARNBURNERS); in New Jersey, Garret D. Wall and Peter D. Vroom; in Pennsylvania, James Buchanan, afterwards President, George M. Dallas, afterwards Vice-President, and Henry A. Muhlenberg, the most popular leader in his State; in Virginia, Philip P. Barbour and Andrew Stevenson, in Mississippi, Robert J. Walker, a Pennsylvanian by birth and education and the framer of the "revenue tariff" of 1846; in Tennessee, Felix Grundy, Cave Johnson, and James K. Polk; in Kentucky, Richard M. Johnson, the supposed slayer of Tecumseh and the avowed foe of imprisonment for debt; and in Ohio, William Allen, who disappeared from politics in 1849 until his election as governor of the State in 1874. This was the school of politicians which received the control of the party from Jackson, and kept it until slavery proved too strong for them. Their leading characteristic was caution: Van Buren's reported unwillingness to say positively whether the sun rose in the east or in the west, on the ground that east and west were "only relative terms," is not a violent exaggeration of his school's characteristic. On the surface all was a cautious watchfulness of and deference to the general sentiment of the party; under the surface was the vigorous direction of the expression of the sentiment which was to be obeyed. For this purpose the system of nominating conventions was carefully elaborated. This method of nomination occurs but a few times in our history before 1825, and these exceptional instances were the first blind gropings of the New York "Bucktails" towards the future development. When the Congressional caucus broke down in 1824 as a presidential nominating body, that function was appropriated for a few years by State legislatures. In 1831-32 the first national nominating conventions were held by the Anti-Masons and National Republicans, but nominations of a lower grade were still the result of mob caucuses. Before 1836 the Democratic party-leaders had fairly completed that national organization which succeeding parties have only copied, local conventions sending delegates to county, district, or State conventions, and district conventions being the unit of national conventions. In this way the party was so marshalled that in 1836 Van Buren was elected Jackson's successor over all the elements of the opposition (see WHIG PARTY).

In warring upon the bank Jackson's only alternative had been to make deposits in selected State banks, commonly known as "pet banks." This sudden influx of available wealth led all the banks to increase issues, and new banks, often without capital, imitated them.

All these notes were received for public lands until the "specie circular" of July 11, 1836, directing agents to receive only gold and silver for lands, sent the whole tide of paper-money back to the Eastern States for redemption. The result was the "panic of 1837." Throughout it Van Buren and the other leaders held the party to the *laissez faire* policy, refused to interfere with the business of the country, and bent all their energies to the passage of the "Independent Treasury" or "Sub-Treasury" Act. This made each official responsible, under bonds, for the safe-keeping and transfer of the public moneys which he should collect, and made the Government its own banker. On all points the party was now at one, and its national convention at Baltimore, May 5, 1840, for the first time formulated a platform. It defined the Federal Government as "one of limited powers, derived solely from the Constitution," and declared that "the grants of power shown therein ought to be strictly construed by all the departments and agents of the Government, and that it is inexpedient and dangerous to exercise doubtful constitutional powers." It opposed the expenditure of the national revenues for any system of public improvements, the charter of a United States bank, or the protection of manufacturers by the tariff, and favored a tariff for revenue only and an independent Treasury. The leading points of this platform were repeated by every succeeding convention until 1864, and form the only historical basis of the party. Of the other leading Jeffersonian ideas, universal suffrage was now accepted by all parties, and "rotation in office" has proved to be successful only in cheating the people and debauching the politicians.

Van Buren was nominated for the Presidency, but the Whigs succeeded in beating him and gaining control of the new House of Representatives. Nevertheless, the party's organization kept it well in hand throughout the trying term of John Tyler. It regained control of both Houses in 1842, and Tyler himself, like Calhoun and the other South Carolina and Virginia nullifiers of 1830-32, had drifted fairly back to the Democratic party. But this latter faction had none of the caution which marked the leaders of 1828-36. To the one the party was all, and slavery only an incident; to the other slavery was all, and the party only an incident. The new accession brought with it one controlling desire for the annexation of Texas. With this object Calhoun had entered the Cabinet, and this object he succeeded in accomplishing. Delegates from Southern States to the Democratic convention were pledged to annexation; and when Van Buren declined to support it he cut himself off from any chance to obtain the Democratic nomination, since a two-thirds majority was necessary for that purpose, according to the time-honored rule in Democratic conventions. Polk was nominated; the votes of New York and Michigan were given to him by the refusal of the abolitionists to vote for Clay; the vote of Pennsylvania was given to him through a letter from him to Kane of that State, in which he declared himself a free-trader with a leaning toward protection; the vote of Louisiana was given to him by unblushing frauds in Plaquemines parish; but only the vote of New York was a necessity, and he was elected.

Texas was annexed, and the war with Mexico followed. Texas was a slave State when annexed, but the other annexed territory, California, Utah (including Nevada), and New Mexico (including Arizona), brought with it the seeds of division and war. A large part of the Northern wing of the party approved the Wilmot proviso of 1846, excluding slavery from the new territory (see FREE-SOIL PARTY); but to the Northern leaders the party was still everything, and the Southern wing, which was necessary to the party, would not tolerate the proviso. The Wilmot-proviso men were "read out of the party," and the doctrine of "popular sovereignty," the natural, not constitutional, right of the people of a Territory to decide the status of slavery within their limits, made its appearance instead of the proviso. Of course it was only a device to throw the burden of decision off the Democratic party, but it was for the time a successful device. The Whig party split gradually into two parts: the Democratic party not only remained united, but gained continual accessions from Southern Whigs. A State schism in New York (see BARNBURNERS) defeated its nominees, Cass and Butler, in 1848; but in 1852 this schism had skinned over, the Whig party had gone to pieces, and the Democratic nominees, Pierce and King, received the electoral votes of all but four States, and were elected.

The position of the party at Pierce's inauguration was one of triumphant success and of imminent peril. It was the only national party, for the Southern Whigs had nearly all abandoned their former organization; but the unnatural growth of its Southern wing had thrown the party out of all natural proportion. To be sure, it had carried one more State in the North and West than in the South in 1852, but the majorities in the former sections were regularly small, and due mainly to the Free-Soil and Whig divisions, while in the latter they were heavy and reliable. This one circumstance was sufficient to give the South a new claim to the control of the party, and from this time until 1860 the proportion of Southern leaders in the party steadily increased. A large part of them were moderate men, but even the Whig accessions, such as A. H. Stephens and Robert Toombs of Georgia, and Clingman of North Carolina, had little of the old Democratic caution; while the new Southern element—JEFFERSON DAVIS of Mississippi (see his name) and Robert C. Breckinridge of Kentucky being the most conspicuous representatives—was distinctly aggressive and altogether wanting in caution. In the North and West there was nothing to balance these influences. There was now a heavy vote there, one great leader, Stephen A. Douglas of Illinois, and a number of second- and third-rate men: the old Northern leadership had disappeared. Douglas was the putative father of the doctrine of "popular sovereignty" which had saved his party from the fate of the Whigs, and he valued it far above its deserts. In the cases of Utah and New Mexico he had endeavored to apply it because the status of slavery in those sections had not been settled, and could not be settled without a sectional conflict. When the Territories of Kansas and Nebraska came to be organized in 1854, no such difficulty was in the way. Both lay north of latitude 36° 30′, and slavery had been forbidden in both by the Missouri compromise of 1820. But there was a difficulty in getting Southern votes to extinguish the Indian title in the new Territories; and, further, the desire to be consistent moved Douglas to apply his pet doctrine of popular sovereignty in this case also, the Missouri compromise and its positive prohibition of slavery to the contrary notwithstanding. Moved by both influences, he introduced in the Senate, in Jan., 1854, his "Kansas-Nebraska Bill," the most pregnant in consequences of all our national legislation. It organized the two Territories in the usual manner, but declared that the Constitution and laws of the United States were in force in them, except section 8 of the Missouri Compromise Act (the prohibition of slavery), "which, being inconsistent with the principle of non-intervention by Congress with slavery in the States and Territories, as recognized by the legislation of 1850, commonly called 'the compromise measures,' is hereby declared inoperative and void." It has been denied that this was a "repeal" of the Missouri compromise; but the voiding of the Missouri compromise, being based on subsequent legislation, and not on the antecedent Constitution, is evidently a repeal, and nothing else; and it cannot be held the repeal was in the legislation of 1850, for that had no assertedly exclusive constitutional ground, and was only a measure of expediency. From every point of view it flung again into the political arena a question once disposed of, and the final result was the disruption of the Democratic party, just as the Whig party had been disrupted over the status of slavery in the Mexican annexation.

The passage of the Kansas-Nebraska Bill in the Senate was not a difficult matter. Fifteen of the thirty-one States were slave States; their Senators were unanimous on any question relating to slavery; and but two Northern votes were necessary to give them a majority in any event. The House was a different field, and here the passage of the bill was not effected until May 22, 1854, by a vote of 113 to 100. In the affirmative were 44 Northern votes, all Democrats, and all the Southern votes but those of 9 border-State members; in the negative, 91 Northern votes, mainly Whigs. But the passage of the bill roused an excitement in the North greater and deeper than had before been known there. A section of the Northern Democratic party broke off from the organization; new and ambitious leaders came forward to head the revolt; the great body of Northern Whigs joined them; and the Republican party, with Whig principles and Democratic methods, was born (see REPUBLICAN PARTY). In the elections of 1854-55 Democratic candidates were defeated everywhere, and their leaders were dismayed to find that their opponents, "a mushroom and mongrel" organization, as yet hardly named, were strong enough to elect the Speaker of the House in 1855. From this time there was but one question: Would the whole body of Northern Whigs join the new party? If so, the Republicans would have a solid Northern vote, and could elect the President and control the House. If not, the Democrats could still hope for sufficient Northern strength to control the country. The latter event occurred. A respectable part of the Northern Whigs were conciliated by the nomination of Buchanan, a Pennsylvania man and very cautious in the expression of any views on protection; a still larger portion went into the "Know-Nothing" organization; and the electoral votes of Pennsylvania and Illinois made Buchanan President, though without a complete majority of the popular vote. The four years from 1852 to 1856 had certainly been no successful years for the party.

It is doubtful whether any party-leadership could have successfully directed the storm which the Kansas-Nebraska Bill had now evoked, but it must be confessed that the Democratic leaders did not deserve success by the courses they adopted. In Kansas, Missouri squatters had instantly gained control of the Territorial government. The Free-State settlers therefore organized a State government under the Topeka constitution in 1855, and in the following year the President dispersed it by armed force. Two years later the Free-State settlers gained control of the Territorial legislature, and proceeded in the formation of a State government to which no exception could be taken. But in the closing hours of the pro-slavery legislature a State government had been arranged under the Lecompton constitution, which was not to be submitted to popular vote excepting as to the single question, "With or without slavery?" Douglas and a part of the little remnant of Northern Democrats in Congress here halted, and would go no further; but the Congressional control of the party was now almost entirely Southern, and support of the Lecompton Bill became the test of party fealty. Few as were the leaders of the "anti-Lecompton" faction in Congress, the mass of the Northern Democratic vote was behind it. The furthest concession it could obtain was the submission of the Lecompton constitution to a new popular vote in Kansas, at which it was summarily rejected.

When the national convention met at Charleston, S. C., April 23, 1860, there was division from the start. The Northern delegates came prepared to declare that they had not changed their opinions as to "popular sovereignty" in the Territories, but that they would yield to and abide by the decisions of the Supreme Court [in the Dred Scott case] (see DRED SCOTT CASE). The Southern delegates came prepared to insist on the logical consequences of the Dred Scott decision: that slavery was legal in every Territory; that it could not be abolished or interfered with by Congress or by the Territorial legislature; and that popular control over it only began at the admission of the Territory as a State. Here the convention split. To have gone before the country on the Southern platform would have been political suicide for every Northern Democratic aspirant to State office or Congress; and the convention adopted the platform reported by the Douglas minority of the committee on resolutions. Thereupon the Southern delegations seceded from the convention, April 30 and May 1, and organized a convention of their own. The border-State delegations remained in the convention, and there took part in fifty-seven unavailing ballots for a candidate. Douglas had about 150 votes, and various border-State candidates about 100, but no candidate had a two-thirds majority of the original (303) votes of the convention. May 3 the convention adjourned to meet again at Baltimore, June 18. There the majority admitted several Douglas delegations to fill vacancies, and the border-State delegates withdrew and unanimously nominated John C. Breckinridge and Joseph Lane, June 28. Their nomination was ratified the next day by the original seceding convention, now in session at Richmond. In the mean time the residuum of the convention had held two ballots, the vote on the second (fifty-ninth) ballot standing 181½ for Douglas, 7½ for Breckinridge, and 5½ for Guthrie of Kentucky. It seems then to have occurred to its leaders that, as there were not 202 votes now in the convention, it would be difficult at least to give Douglas two-thirds of the original number of votes. It was therefore decided that Douglas was nominated, having two-thirds of the present number of votes. Benjamin Fitzpatrick of Alabama was nominated for the second place, but declined it, and Herschel V. Johnson of Georgia was substituted. The secession of the Southern delegations has been denounced as an intentional disruption of the Democratic party in order to secure Lincoln's election as a fair excuse for State secession. The political excuses for their action may be thus stated: Buchanan's experience in 1856 had shown that the party could no longer command a majority of the popular vote, and the chances were now worse for a majority of the electoral vote. Douglas could carry no Southern States, and Breckinridge no Northern States. Then let each poll his full strength in his own section, while the Bell and Everett ticket draws the old Whig strength away from the Republicans: there will be no choice of the electors, and in the House, voting by States, the South can force in Breckinridge in order to save the Union. Some such idea was in the heads of most of the Southern managers; and, though it failed and Lincoln was elected by 180 electoral votes out of 303, it is well to remember that if the "fusion ticket" of the combined opposition had carried New York with its thirty-five votes, or Pennsylvania and New Jersey with their thirty-one Republican votes, the plan would have been so far successful. Whether it would have been successfully carried out to the end may be doubted, but the running of fusion tickets in these three States shows how close had been the calculations of the managers.

See Von Holst's *United States*; Tucker's *United States* (to 1840); Benton's *Thirty Years' View* (to 1850) and *Debates of Congress* (to 1850); Woodbury's *Writings*; Niles's *Weekly Register*; *Democratic Review* (1838-59); 1 A. H. Stephens's *War between the States*; Chase's *Administration of Polk*; Buchanan's *Administration*; Cluskey's *Political Text-Book of 1860*; 1 Greeley's *American Conflict*; *Statesman's Manual* (for Presidents' messages to 1859); Fowler's *Sectional Controversy*. For authorities of an opposite cast see WHIG PARTY and REPUBLICAN PARTY. Electoral and popular votes are most conveniently collected in Spofford's *American Almanac* (1878), 119-169. In biography, see Parton's *Life of Jackson*, Sumner's *Life of Jackson*, Von Holst's *Life of Calhoun*, Hunt's *Life of Livingston*, Amos Kendall's *Autobiography*, J. A. Hamilton's *Reminiscences*, Holland's *Life of Van Buren*, Hammond's *Life of Silas Wright*, Scott's *Life of Hugh L. White*, Hamilton's *Memoir of Rantoul*, Dickinson's *Life of D. S. Dickinson*. Mackenzie's *Life and Times of Van Buren* and *Lives of Butler and Hoyt* are only useful for the confidential letters stolen and published by Mackenzie. The party platforms from 1840 until 1860 and the proceedings of the Charleston convention are in Greeley's *Political Text-Book of 1860*. See also authorities under BARNBURNERS; DAVIS, JEFFERSON.

III. (1860-82). Since 1860 the national history of the party has been one of opposition, and any sketch of it must be merely complementary to that of the dominant party (see REPUBLICAN PARTY). At the outbreak of the rebellion in 1861 its members and leaders were as eager for the suppression of the rebellion by arms as their opponents. Democrats like Douglas, John A. Dix of New York, Edwin M. Stanton, and Andrew Johnson at once took the name of "War Democrats," and were soon practically Republicans. As the war went on, as its expenses became greater, and as it began to strike at slavery (see ABOLITION), Democrats began to revert to the memories of the anti-slavery conflict and to detest an "anti-slavery war." Their first thought was the assembling of a Federal convention, like that which had formed the Constitution, in order to end the conflict; and this, though as evidently inopportune as an attempt to read the riot act to the contending armies at Gettysburg, became the desideratum of the great mass of the party throughout the war. It could not strike at slavery; it would not consent to the ultimatum of the South, independence; and thus, still striving to maintain its traditions, the party worked its way through the war until 1864, beaten in almost all State elections, and yet maintaining its proportion of the popular vote and of the lower House of Congress. But within the party there were two smaller elements—one which desired peace, even at the price of Southern independence, and another, mainly along the Ohio and Potomac rivers, which desired Southern independence itself as ardently as Southern leaders could have done. "Peace meetings" became the weapon of the one, and secret societies, such as the "Knights of the Golden Circle," were formed by the other. In order to suppress both of these "fires in the rear" the President suspended the privilege of the writ of *habeas-corpus*—at first, in April, 1861, as a local military measure, then generally, Sept. 24, 1862, as commander-in-chief, and finally, Sept. 15, 1863, by virtue of an act of Congress of March 3, 1863. The victims of "arbitrary arrest" under this suspension were regularly of the two classes above specified; but as these were all of one party, the conviction that the object of the *habeas corpus* suspension was entirely partisan spread, until the Democratic party was controlled by an active hatred of the "executive despotism" of Pres. Lincoln. When the national convention met at Chicago, Aug. 29, 1864, the platform for the first time dropped the resolutions of 1840, and was solely devoted to an attack on the management of the war. It "explicitly declared, as the sense of the American people, that, after four years of failure to restore the Union by the experiment of war," "justice, humanity, liberty, and the public welfare demand that immediate efforts be made for a cessation of hostilities, with a view to an ultimate convention of all the States or other peaceable means, to the end that at the earliest practicable moment peace may be restored on the basis of the federal union of the States." The phrase "convention of all the States," which sugar-coated the "failure of the war" to the convention itself, was not so successful to the country at large: the nominees, George B. McClellan of New Jersey and George H. Pendleton of Ohio, though they received 45 per cent. of the popular vote, carried but three States, New Jersey, Delaware, and Kentucky, with 21 of the 233 electoral votes, and were defeated. Such a defeat presaged greater evil for the future: that portion of the doubtful vote which loves to be upon the winning side at once concluded that the Democratic party was practically dead; its Congressional representation sank lower and lower; and the only policy of the party seemed to be a chronic readiness to oppose any measure introduced by a Republican. It was only able to enter a formal protest against the method adopted by the dominant party to reconstruct the lately rebellious States, and its passionate protest only served to make the terms of reconstruction more severe. It could only see that the war was over, that the Constitution's war powers had therefore ceased to apply, and that Congress had no constitutional power to interfere with the right of suffrage in a State. It could not be persuaded that war does not cease at the demand of the conquered or until the demands of the conquerors are satisfied; that some political penalty was to be paid for secession; and that the good offices of a mediator who demanded the entire remission of the penalty were hardly likely to be of much effect. During the period of reconstruction almost the only case in which the Democratic opposition achieved the result which it desired was the acquittal of Pres. Johnson on his impeachment trial by the united vote of the Democratic Senators, assisted by seven of their opponents.

Since 1850 the party had been constantly engaged in struggles with which its fundamental principles had no connection: universal suffrage, individual liberty, opposition to governmental protection in any form, and the preference of State to central government in fairly doubtful matters, had been dimmed in the eyes of Democrats themselves by the long contest against abolition, war, and reconstruction. When the national convention met at New York, July 4, 1868, it for the first time in the party's history pronounced against universal suffrage and "hard money." Compelled to choose between the admission of the enfranchised negroes to the right of suffrage and the jurisdiction of the States over that privilege, it chose the latter. Its leaders had opposed the issue of legal-tender paper money in 1862–63 as destructive to the interests of the mass of citizens. But the money had been issued; it had been used in the purchase of bonds; the "five-twenties" did not state on their face that the principal was to be paid in coin; and the convention proposed that they should be paid in "lawful money of the United States"—that is, in greenbacks. As both five-twenties and gold were then at a premium, the former of about 10 per cent. and the latter of about 38 per cent., and as they came to an equality in the course of the following year, it must be confessed that the party proposed to sell one of its fundamental principles, its denial of the "legality" of Government paper money, at a very low rate. Pendleton, Gen. Hancock, Thomas A. Hendricks of Indiana, and Andrew Johnson were the leading candidates before the convention, but no one seemed able to command the requisite vote. On the twenty-second ballot the Ohio delegation stampeded the convention into nominating its president, Gov. Horatio Seymour of New York, one of the most trusted party-leaders. His letter of acceptance was a temperate appeal to doubtful voters to elect a Democratic President as a counterpoise to the absolute power of the dominant party in Congress. But the nominee for Vice-President, Frank P. Blair of Missouri, had already publicly declared that a Democratic President must "trample into dust the usurpations of Congress known as the Reconstruction Acts," "compel the army to undo its usurpations at the South, and disperse the carpet-bag governments." No such programme was desired by the country, and the nominees were defeated, receiving 80 of the 294 electoral votes, but retaining their proportion of the popular vote.

This election ended the party's resistance to reconstruction, and the work was finished under its silent protest. But the thoroughness of the work had prepared the way for a reaction. The forcible means by which many of the reconstructed State governments had to be supported, the manner in which many of the reconstructed constitutions had disfranchised all persons prohibited from holding office by the fourteenth amendment—that is, most of the influential whites—and the consequent future difficulty of "supporting the pyramid for ever on its apex," had wearied and disgusted many of the Republicans. A successful movement was begun in Missouri in 1870 to obtain "universal amnesty and universal suffrage" by a union of Democrats and "Liberal" Republicans, and in the two following years it took larger proportions. A "Liberal Republican" convention was held in Cincinnati, May 1, 1872; but instead of nominating a leading candidate acceptable to all Democrats, it chose Horace Greeley of New York, a man of great ability, unselfishness, and honesty, but a veteran Whig and Republican editor, who had been the Black Douglas of every political battle against the Democrats since 1840.

Hard as the road was, the Democratic party was obliged to take it. It was easier to sign a platform offered from another convention, accepting the results of the war, than to offer it as an original contribution to American politics; and the convention at Baltimore, July 9, adopted the Cincinnati platform and ratified the Cincinnati nominations of Greeley and B. Gratz Brown of Missouri. As might have been expected, Democratic refusals to vote more than counterbalanced any Republican accessions, and the nominees received but 66 out of 352 electoral votes. About 30,000 "straight-out" Democrats abandoned the nominations altogether, voting for Charles O'Conor of New York and John Quincy Adams of Massachusetts. Some Democrats still take pride in declaring that they "took no part in the Greeley movement," thereby really meaning that they left all the inevitable humble pie to be eaten by their more unselfish party associates. Released from the incubus of unavailing opposition to accomplished facts, the party at once began to show signs of returning vitality. The State and Congressional elections of 1874–75, the "tidal wave," resulted in general Democratic success through the North, even Massachusetts electing a Democratic governor; and at the meeting of the Forty-fourth Congress, in Dec., 1875, the House of Representatives had a Democratic majority of over 60. In this House the party maintained a majority until 1881, and for the last two years of this period it controlled the Senate also; and yet it succeeded in making hardly any change in the general policy of the dominant party. Of course, one great reason for this was that it controlled but one House during most of the time, and a professed apologist might assert that the abuses which had grown up were too great for reformation except by an entire change in the control of the Government. But in either case the real reason would be untouched. In the Southern States the government had been transferred, by the reconstruction acts of March, 1867, to such persons as were not ineligible to office by the fourteenth amendment. Most of the States thus passed at once under control of negroes and of a few white Republicans, who were called by their opponents "scalawags" if of native birth, and "carpet-baggers" if immigrants from the North. By removal of disabilities, and the consequent increase of the white vote; by the entrance to politics of a new generation of whites free from disfranchisement; by the employment of every engine of interest, force, and even fraud,—the masterful white race had in 1875 regained its supremacy in every State but South Carolina, Florida, and Louisiana, and these three followed in 1877. But this supremacy was, in its way, as precarious as that of the antecedent negro governments: to maintain it the whole white vote had to remain united, and all whites, whatever their real opinions, whether they were old Whigs, Native Americans, Secessionists, Union men, Protectionists, or Greenbackers, had but one common name—Democrats. In the Forty-fourth Congress the Democrats would have had a majority in the House without the 58 Democratic votes from the lately rebellious States; but in subsequent Congresses the party majority depended altogether on its growing Southern representation. This was entirely Democratic in but one respect—its desire for State government. in any other respect there was always a fraction of the Southern vote which could not be depended on. Even in the two years (1879–81) in which both Houses were nominally Democratic no bill was framed to reduce the tariff, a measure to which the party was bound. This useless Southern majority has only brought the party into a condition of helpless dependence upon it.

In 1876, for the first time in half a generation, the convention at St. Louis, June 27, began to come back to its ancient moorings. Its platform denounced the tariff as "a masterpiece of injustice, inequality, and false pretence;" it demanded a tariff "only for revenue," preparation for resumption in 1879 by the accumulation of a sufficient reserve, the postponement of the date of resumption until such a reserve should be accumulated, and a general reduction of expenses. Gov. Samuel J. Tilden of New York was nominated for President, and Thomas A. Hendricks of Indiana for Vice-President. In the North the nominees carried Connecticut, New Jersey, New York, and Indiana; in the South all the States but South Carolina, Florida, and Louisiana. South Carolina was at first claimed for them, but the claim was soon abandoned. They thus had 184 electoral votes, 185 being necessary. In Florida and Louisiana the popular vote, as cast, showed a majority for the Tilden electors. Custom and the growth of Democracy have gradually made the popular vote decisive in the choice of electors; but the form of the Constitution orders electors to be chosen in such manner as the legislature of the State shall direct. In both the States named the legislatures had created bodies called "returning boards," and, by giving them absolute power to alter returns as they should consider just, had practically given them the power to choose all State officers as well as presidential electors. The power of the legislature to do so must be denied in the case of State officers, but admitted in the case of electors: in the latter case the legislature is omnipotent while it follows the forms of the Constitution. In Florida and in Louisiana the returning boards reversed the popular majority on the ground of force or fraud, and the Democratic nominees thus failed of an election. The anger of the party at this result, and its members' personal feeling that they had been defrauded, were very strong, and made the Congressional session of 1876–77 one of the most dangerous in our history. Congress had gradually assumed, since 1817, a power to decide especially on the validity of electoral votes; but Congress could do nothing now, for the House was Democratic and the Senate Republican. All that Congress could do was to create an extra-constitutional commission of five justices of the Supreme Court, five Senators, and five Representatives to report on disputed votes, their decision to be final unless reversed by both Houses. Seven of the electoral commission were Democrats and seven Republicans, and in every case of doubt the responsibility of decision was thrown upon the "odd man," Justice J. P. Bradley. In the cases of Florida and Louisiana the commission decided that the governors had correctly certified the action of the legislature's agent; in the case of a single disputed vote in Oregon it decided that the governor had not so certified. The Democratic candidates were thus finally defeated, to the intensified disgust and anger of the party. The "great fraud of 1876" engrossed all its thought, and would have been the means of Tilden's renomination in 1880 but for an accident. During the consequent investigations a mass of "cipher despatches" came to light, showing attempts to bribe the returning boards in the interest of Tilden, though, as he declared, without his knowledge. The discovery made Tilden assailable, and he was not renominated; but the party is indebted to him at least thus far, that his nomination in 1876 gave the party an economic policy for the first time since 1860.

In 1878 the Western and Southern members of the party yielded for the time to the "silver mania." They had felt in 1868 that the bondholders were making a hard bargain with the Government in insisting on payment in "coin" where coin was not specifically promised. When the relative value of the silver coin, as compared with gold, began to decrease, silver was "demonetized," or made no longer legal tender, in 1873. In 1878 the Bland bill, supported by all parties, but rather more generally and warmly by the Democrats, became a law over the President's veto: it remonetized the silver dollar and directed its coinage. In the following year the party at last united on a policy, though its dependence on its Southern vote evidently controlled its selection. In cities of over 20,000 inhabitants a Federal election law was in force authorizing the appointment of supervisors of Federal elections; and under this the supervisors claimed powers over any other elections occurring at the same time and place. Federal marshals and deputies exercised the power of arrest at the polls on an attempt to vote; and in New York City this feature of process was certainly made use of for party ends. The further Southern grievances were that Federal troops were alleged to have been used to overawe voters, and that the selections of Federal juries by court officers were partisan and unfair. In the winter of 1878–79 the Democratic House insisted on attaching repealers of these various points to the appropriation bills, knowing that after March 4 the new House and Senate would both be Democratic, and believing that the Republicans would not be willing to change a contest between the House and the President and Senate into a contest between Congress and the President. In March this Congress expired without passing the appropriation bills, and the President called an extra session of the new Congress. Instead of passing the repealers as distinct legislation, and appealing to the country on the vetoes, the majority persisted in adding the repealers as "riders" to the appropriation bills. These were vetoed; a two-thirds vote could not be obtained to override the veto; and if Congress should adjourn without passing the appropriation bills the President had the dangerous power to renew indefinitely his calls to extra sessions until a tractable majority should be found. In the event, the appropriation bills were passed without riders, excepting a fraction of one of them. But the good effects of even these poor attempts at party contest were seen in the platform adopted by the convention which met at Cincinnati, June 22, 1880. Its economic principles are thus stated: "No sumptuary laws; separation of Church and State, for the good of each; home rule [State government]; honest money, consisting of gold and silver and paper convertible into coin on demand; a tariff for revenue only; free ships [free trade in ships]; no discrimination in favor of transportation lines, corporations, or monopolies; and public land for actual settlers." On this platform Winfield S. Hancock of Pennsylvania and William H. English of Indiana were nominated. The popular vote was extremely close, the Democratic candidates falling about 7000 votes behind their opponents in a total vote of 9,000,000. In such a delicate balance party management told heavily, and the Democratic leaders succeeded in losing votes in two opposite directions on the tariff issue. The tariff statement in their platform cost them the votes of protectionists, and their weakness in even ing discussion of it when forced on them by their opponents cost them the votes of many of their own party, who naturally took evasion to be a confession of inability to defend successfully. Thus Hancock received but 155 of the 359 electoral votes, and was defeated.

The attitude of the mass of the party during the war may be found in S. S. Cox's *Eight Years in Congress*, from p. 303; W. H. Hurlburt's *McClellan and the Conduct of the War*; and 2 B. R. Curtis's *Works*, 306 ("Executive Power"). A much more extreme view, with an evident desire to be judicial, is in Harris's *Political Conflict in America* (down to August, 1868). The views of the extreme peace party will be found in the writings of H. C. Dean; Vallandigham's *Speeches*; Van Evrie's *Youth's History of the Civil War*; Bledsoe's *Is Davis a Traitor?* and "Centz's" *Davis and Lee* and *Republic of Republics*. See also Spencer's *Life of Bayard*; McPherson's *Political History of the Rebellion, History of the Reconstruction*, and *Political Manuals*; *Tribune Almanac*; Pike's *Prostrate State*; *The Nation* (1865-82).

(A. J.)

The general elections of 1882 showed great and sudden changes, justifying the common appellation, "a tidal wave." In Connecticut, New York, New Jersey, Pennsylvania, Nevada, Colorado, and California, the Democratic party elected the governors and made large gains in the legislatures. In New York their candidate, Grover Cleveland, obtained a majority of 193,825, the largest ever recorded in a State election, and was thus pointed out for the Presidential nomination in the convention of 1884. Hon. James G. Blaine was the Republican nominee. The ensuing national campaign was marked by disgraceful personalities, and the bitter contest was decided by a close vote in the city of New York, where Tammany Hall was disaffected towards Cleveland, while Independent Republicans, derisively styled Mugwumps, refused to support Mr. Blaine. The chapter of accidents finally gave Cleveland a plurality of 1047 votes in that city. His electoral vote, however, was 219 to Blaine's 182. Thus after twenty-four weary years of exile, the Democratic party again saw its candidate seated in the Presidential chair. In the Forty-ninth Congress the Democratic majority in the House was slightly reduced, there being 182 Democrats to 142 Republicans. The Senate in 1880 had a marked Democratic majority, but this was gradually lost, and now the Republicans had a decisive majority.

Pres. Cleveland displayed in his administration the fearless courage and self-reliance which had raised him in a few years from being mayor of Buffalo to the chief magistracy of the nation. For a time he did not manifest his position in regard to the important question of the tariff, and seemed disposed to conciliate that wing of his party, led by Hon. S. J. Randall, which still maintained the policy of incidental protection. A bill for the "horizontal" reduction of the tariff, introduced into the House by Col. William Morrison, of Illinois, had been defeated early in 1884. He introduced a similar bill in 1886, which shared the same fate. The aggressive tariff-reformers now claimed the president's aid in order that something might be accomplished in that direction. When the Fiftieth Congress assembled in December, 1887, the House consisted of 168 Democrats and 152 Republicans, while the Senate had 38 Republicans and 37 Democrats with one "Readjuster" from Virginia. To this Congress Pres. Cleveland addressed his first strongly outspoken utterance on the tariff problem. Arguing that a vast and dangerous surplus was accumulating in the National Treasury, he proposed that tariff rates on certain manufactured imports should be reduced and that various raw materials should be admitted duty free. Hon. Roger Q. Mills, of Texas, introduced a low tariff bill in strict accordance with the president's suggestions, and this was passed in the House. Mr. Randall's recalcitrant followers were threatened with non-recognition by their party, and were reduced to submission. The Senate, however, defeated the Mills bill and replaced it with a substitute, prepared by Mr. Aldrich, embodying protective principles, which the House declined to consider.

Tariff reform, as stated in the President's Message, and exemplified in the Mills' bill, became the vital issue in the next national campaign. On this platform Pres. Cleveland was unanimously renominated at the convention at St. Louis in 1888, and ex-Senator Allen G. Thurman, of Ohio, was made candidate for the vice-presidency. Benjamin Harrison, of Indiana, became the Republican candidate for the presidency, since Mr. Blaine firmly refused to allow his name to be used. In the ensuing contest the State of New York, to which Cleveland owed his election in 1884, gave a plurality of 13,002 in favor of Harrison, deciding the contest in his favor, though in the popular vote Cleveland had a plurality of over 95,000. For the first time for many years the Republicans secured also a majority of both Houses of Congress. The House had 161 Democrats to 169 Republicans, and the Senate had 37 Democrats and eventually 45 Republicans, two seats being vacant. Four new States admitted by this Congress had returned eight Republican Senators, and in its second session Idaho and Wyoming were also admitted, giving four more Senators to that side. The Republicans proceeded to frame a high tariff bill, which, after months of labor, was presented by Major William McKinley, of Ohio, and passed in 1890 at the close of a tedious session against the most strenuous opposition of the Democrats. Mr. Thomas B. Reed, of Maine, who had been chosen Speaker of the House, set himself to reverse its previous practice by new rules and new interpretations to overcome dilatory motions and filibustering. The most drastic of these was establishing a quorum by direct count of the members present instead of the number voting. The Lodge bill, which was intended to establish Federal supervision over national elections, met with such determined resistance from the Democrats, that it was first postponed to the second session and then finally laid aside by the Senate, the Republican vote being seriously divided.

The Congressional elections of November, 1890, were full of surprises to both parties. The people disappointed in the glittering hopes held out to them of prosperity as the effect of the tariff, and astonished to learn that the menacing surplus was already exhausted by appropriations, veered suddenly to the Democratic side. The Fifty-first Congress ended its existence with a Republican majority of 24 in the House. The roll of the Fifty-second Congress shows a Democratic majority of 149, while there are 8 representatives of the Farmers' Alliance who seem likely to act substantially with the Democrats. The Republicans will be as powerless here as the Democrats were in the reconstruction era. The Senate, however, will still remain under Republican control, though the Western Republican Senators have already shown signs of dissatisfaction with the financial policy which has heretofore prevailed. They advocate the free coinage of silver, which was strongly pressed by the

Farmers' Alliance, and approved by the masses of the Democratic party. Ex-President Cleveland, however, with his customary frankness, pronounced the experiment dangerous, and has thereby somewhat diminished his prospects of securing the presidential nomination in 1892. The Democratic party, under his leadership, has a revival of genuine enthusiasm; its danger lies in possible reckless action by its overwhelming majority in the House.

DEMOGEOT, JACQUES CLAUDE, a French author, was born in Paris, July 5, 1808. After teaching for two years in the seminary in which he had received his early education, he entered the University of Paris in 1828. He was afterwards professor in the colleges of Beauvais, Rennes, Bordeaux, and Lyons. In 1834 he became professor of rhetoric at the Lycée Saint-Louis in Paris, and still remains in this position, though he has also at times supplied the place of other professors. He has published an essay on *Ausonius*, a history of the College of Lyons, a French version of Shakespeare's *Romeo and Juliet*, and a poetical translation of Lucan's *Pharsalia*. His essay on *Les Lettres et l'Homme de Lettres au XIXe Siècle* (1856) was crowned by the Society of Authors. His *Histoire de la Littérature française* (1852) is a brilliant sketch of his countrymen's achievements in literature. It has reached its nineteenth edition, and has been translated into English by C. Bridge (1874). Demogeot has also prepared an *Histoire des Littératures étrangères* (1880), as well as good text-books on French literature. Selections from his numerous historical and literary contributions to the *Revue des Deux Mondes* and other periodicals have been published under the title *Notes sur diverses Questions de Metaphysique et de Littérature* (1877). Under the pseudonym of "Jacques" he has published some works.

DENISON, a city of Grayson co., Tex., 4 miles S. of the Red River and 9 miles N. of Sherman. It is a terminus of the Houston and Texas Central Railroad, and of 4 lines of the Missouri Pacific system. It has a handsome opera-house, 5 hotels, 2 daily and 3 weekly newspapers, and 9 churches; also flouring- and cotton-ginning-mills, manufactures of ice, of artificial stone, of carriages, brooms, etc. It is a fast-growing city, the centre of large railroad interests. Vast quantities of fruit are shipped northward from this point. The town has gas- and water-works. In 1883 the property valuation was $5,000,000, the public debt $52,000, and the annual expenses $18,000. Denison was founded in 1872, incorporated in 1873. In 1880 the population was 3975; in 1890, 10,959.

DENISON, GEORGE ANTHONY, an English clergyman, was born at Osington, Nottinghamshire, Dec. 11, 1805. He was educated at Eton and Christ Church College, Oxford, where he graduated, in 1826, with high classical honors. In 1828 he was elected a Fellow of Oriel College, Oxford, and also obtained the university prize for a Latin essay. In January, 1830, he became a tutor at Oriel, and in 1832 was ordained. He then held the curacy of Cuddesden, Oxfordshire, still retaining his tutorship for four years. In 1838 he became vicar of Broadwindsor, Dorset. In August, 1845, he was appointed vicar of East Brent, Somerset, and soon after examining chaplain to the Right Rev. Richard Bagot, bishop of Bath and Wells. About this time the modifications of the relation of the established church to the state, resulting from parliamentary reform, began to manifest themselves. One of the first questions which arose was that of national education. On this Mr. Denison took decided ground: believing that the education of the people belonged solely to the church, he opposed all schemes of government education. He strenuously resisted every attempt made to subordinate the church to the state, and even published objections to the presence of the bishops in the House of Lords, as tending to that result. In 1850 he joined in the protest of several high-church clergymen against the decision in the Gorham case. Two years later he was successful in procuring the revival of Convocation, after 135 years of abeyance, though its powers were now limited. In 1851 Bishop Bagot had appointed Mr. Denison archdeacon of Taunton, but in 1853, the latter being charged with unsoundness in doctrine with reference to the Eucharist, resigned his chaplaincy. To show his belief, he then preached and published three sermons on *The Real Presence*. In 1854 proceedings were commenced against him on account of these sermons, and two years later an ecclesiastical court convicted him and deprived him of all his church preferments. Appeal was taken to the Court of Arches and the judgment set aside on a point of law, and this decision was finally confirmed by the judicial committee of the Privy Council in February, 1858. The dean, who had always been affectionately regarded by his parishioners, was triumphantly welcomed by them on his return. In the previous autumn he had established among them the beautiful custom of Harvest Home, and for this, in 1868, he prepared a special service. Still continuing his protest against the tendency of the age to indifferentism and secularism he had, in 1855, withdrawn from the diocesan education board on account of its acceptance of compromises which he opposed. He returned occasionally, in later years, when there seemed some prospect of effectually resisting the government policy. On account of these questions he declared against Mr. Gladstone in 1853, and twelve years later was one of the most active in causing the University of Oxford to reject him as its representative. When ritualism began to appear in the Church of England, Dean Denison claimed for it a right to exist, though he adopted ritual only in part. After many years of active service in Convocation he finally withdrew from it in 1878, on account of its treatment of ritual and other important questions. In his autobiography, *Notes of My Life* (1878; 3d ed., 1882), he sets forth fully his position on the questions which have agitated the Church of England in his time, and candidly acknowledges that in most cases he has been the champion of a losing cause.

DENISON UNIVERSITY, at Granville, Licking co., Ohio, was established in 1831 by the Ohio Baptist Education Society. In its earlier years it was only a literary or higher academic school, with a theological department. For a considerable time it was conducted on the industrial plan, a large farm affording employment to those who were not skilled in any trade. Rev. John Pratt, a graduate of Brown University, first had charge of the institution, and remained in connection with it till 1859. In 1842 the scope of the school was enlarged, and a new charter obtained by which it became known as Granville College. Rev. Jonathan Going, D. D., was its first president. He was followed in 1846 by Rev. Silas Bailey, D. D., who in turn was succeeded in 1853 by Rev. Jeremiah Hall, D. D. Rev. Samson Talbot, D. D., was president from 1863 till his death in 1873. In 1875, Rev. E. Benjamin Andrews, D. D., became president, and was succeeded by Rev. Alfred Owen, D. D., in 1879.

The college for the first twenty-five years occupied

a farm 1½ miles west of Granville village. It was removed in 1856 to the hill overlooking the town, where it still remains. It has passed through many vicissitudes, and at times has seemed near extinction, but it has always rallied and become stronger than before. During the incumbency of Dr. Bailey the question of its removal to Lebanon was agitated, and the controversy that followed resulted in his resignation. For a part of one year the work of the college ceased entirely. During the incumbency of Dr. Hall considerable additions were made to its resources, and in consideration of a subscription of $10,000 by Hon. Wm. Denison of Adamsville, Ohio, the name was changed to Denison University.

The expenses, however, had so exceeded the endowment that in 1866, after thirty-five years of effort, the value of the property was estimated at only $40,000. At that time fresh exertions were made to put the university on a sound financial basis. During the next five years $175,000 were added to the endowment, and new buildings were erected, worth at least $35,000. In 1878, Mr. W. H. Doane erected a building for the use of the library at an expense of $12,000. In 1881, the fiftieth anniversary of the opening of the institution, another $100,000 was added to the endowment. The present value of the property, now wholly free from debt, is given in the last report of the treasurer as $400,691.29.

The college has ever maintained a high reputation for thoroughness and excellence of instruction, having numbered among its professors such men as John Stevens, Paschal Carter, W. H. Stevens, F. O. Marsh, and others who are affectionately remembered by hosts of former pupils. It has also maintained a high religious character, broad and catholic in spirit, but positive and earnest in its support of the tenets of revealed religion and of the Holy Scriptures as the authoritative revelation of God. It has passed through the period of its weakness and struggles, and has gained a foundation and character that make its future assured. (A. O.)

DENMARK. The transference of the Duchies of Sleavig and Holstein to Prussia has not marred the prosperity of the Danish Kingdom. The small sea-girt state, with apparently few natural elements of prosperity, maintains a position of greater independence, and perhaps greater influence, than other European states of much larger area and population. The alliances of its royal house with other reigning families of Europe have exceeded in extent and rank even the famous marriages of the Coburgs or the Hohenzollerns. Its present king, who came to the Danish throne in 1863, by appointment of the great powers of Europe, ratified by the Danish *Rigsdag*, or Legislature, has six children; the eldest, a son, is heir apparent, and has married the Princess Louisa, daughter of the late King of Sweden and Norway, and niece of the reigning king; the second, a daughter, Alexandra, is the wife of Albert Edward, Prince of Wales; the third, a son, is King of Greece, and his queen is the Grand Duchess Olga Constantinovna, a cousin of Alexander III., the reigning Czar of Russia; the fourth, a daughter, is married to Alexander III., Czar of Russia; the fifth, a daughter, the Princess Thyra, is married to Ernest August, Duke of Cumberland, a cousin of the Queen of England. Happily freed from the cares of a vast domain, ruling over an intelligent and loyal people, and not harassed by the anxieties and intrigues which are almost inevitable in larger states, and themselves generally not men of inordinate ambition, some of the kings of Denmark have found time to indulge in antiquarian and archæological pursuits, as well as in art studies. Their capital, Copenhagen, has more archæological collections of great value than any other city in Europe; and its art galleries have no superior, and but few equals on the continent. The government is a constitutional monarchy, in which the Rigsdag or Diet of two Houses—the Landsthing, or Senate, and the Folkething, or House of Representatives, make and amend the laws, and have a partial control over the action of the Sovereign and Council, in executing and enforcing them. The Council or Cabinet are, individually and collectively, responsible for their acts, and, if impeached and found guilty, cannot be pardoned, without the consent of the Folkething, or House of Representatives.

Rarely are there any items of historic interest in the political management of the country. The sessions of the Rigsdag are usually occupied with local affairs—the reduction of the national debt, the appropriations for military and naval purposes, the erection of fortifications, or the building of ships of war, appropriations for national museums or educational institutions, and for the personal expenditures of the royal family.

Yet, even here, great principles will sometimes agitate the people and the popular branch of the Rigsdag. The ministry were not in 1880-81 in sympathy with the Folkething, and the latter demanded, as the English House of Commons did long ago, that the Constitution should be interpreted as giving them the exclusive right to vote the budget, and that their votes on money bills should be simply registered in the Landsthing. This demand the ministry opposed strongly, and the king dissolved the Folkething; a new election showed a larger opposition; two more successive Folkethings were dissolved with no better result, and in 1883 the constitutional crisis came, the ministry resigned, and the Folkething gained its point.

The ports of Denmark are very well fortified, and the navy, though small, is efficient. The army, under the law of July, 1867, and the supplementary law of 1880, consists of all the able-bodied young men of the kingdom who have reached the age of twenty-two years; they are liable to service for eight years in the regular army, and for eight years subsequently in the army of reserve. While the law, if rigorously enforced, would cripple seriously the industrial ability of the kingdom, it is practically so managed as not to prove so heavy and crushing in its effect as the military laws of the German states. Every corps is required to drill each year, during from thirty to forty-five days; and during the eight years of service in the regular army there are two periods of drill; the first lasting six months for the infantry, five months for the field-artillery and engineers, nine months and two weeks for the cavalry, and four months for the siege artillery and technic corps. The second period of drill is only for a portion of the recruits of each branch of arms, especially those who have profited least by the first course. This lasts nine months for infantry, eleven months for the cavalry, and one year for the artillery and engineers. The army of reserve has only a brief annual drill.

The kingdom is divided into five territorial brigades, so distributed that the burden does not come more heavily upon one section of the population than upon another. The cavalry are distributed in the proportion of one regiment to each territorial brigade, and one-half of the artillery is furnished by the first two territorial brigades, and the other half by the other three. The total strength of the army was as follows in September, 1881;

	Regular Army.		Army of Reserve.	
	Officers.	Rank and File.	Officers.	Rank and File.
Infantry	774	26,992	245	10,925
Cavalry	128	2,180		
Artillery	145	4,755	41	2,068
Engineers	59	624		
Total	1,106	34,551	286	12,993

In 1889 the peace strength of the army was 16,318 men and 335 officers; the war strength about 60,000, with an extra reserve of 14,000.

The navy consisted, in December, 1889, of 32 steamers, of which 8 were armor-clad ships, and the rest unarmed vessels, mostly of small size. The 8 armor-clads had, respectively, the following thickness of armor—steel generally—at the water-line, 12 inches, 8 inches (two), 5 inches (two), 4½ inches (two), and 4 inches. There were in addition 3 protected cruisers, 1 armored torpedo ship, and a number of torpedo boats. The Danish navy is manned by 1025 men, and officered by 1 admiral, 16 commanders, 36 captains, and 181 lieutenants.

Churches and Education.—The established religion in Denmark is Lutheran, and more than 99 per cent. of the population are professedly adherents to it. There are seven bishops of the Lutheran Church, whose duties and privileges are generally similar to those of the bishops of the Church of England, except that they have no political character, and are not allowed to vote in the legislature. There is complete religious toleration for all religious denominations, except that they must not offend morality or public order. Only 17,670 persons were reported by the census of 1880 as dissenters from the Lutheran Church. Of these 3946 were Jews, 3000 Roman Catholics, 1363 Calvinists of the Reformed Church, 1722 Mormons, 3687 Baptists, 792 Irvingites, 1919 other sects, and 1241 without creed, or of unknown creed. The emigration of Mormons from Denmark to Utah has nearly ceased. Elementary education is widely diffused in Denmark, attendance at school from the age of seven to fourteen is compulsory, and is gratuitous in the public schools to children whose parents cannot afford to pay for their teaching. In higher education there is the great and liberally endowed University of Copenhagen, with its library of 250,000 volumes, its fifty or more professors, and more than a thousand students, and the Royal Library of over half a million volumes. There are 2940 parochial schools of excellent character, very many middle schools, fitting youth of the working classes for the gymnasia or colleges, and 13 public gymnasia, or collegiate schools of high order. About half of the students at the university are in the theological classes.

Area and Population.—The area of Denmark was diminished by the transfer of the Duchies of Slesvig, Holstein, and Lauenburg to Prussia, to the extent of 8524 square miles. The following table gives the present area as officially stated, the population in 1870, 1875, and 1880; and in the lower division, the area and population of the Danish colonies:

Divisions.	Area in square miles.	Population, 1870.	Population, 1875.	Population, 1880.
Copenhagen (Kjöbenhavn) and suburbs.	13	181,291		235,254
Islands in the Baltic	8,364	815,331	349,000	865,709
Peninsula of Jutland	13,290	788,119	836,100	862,492
Total	21,667	1,784,741	1,880,100	1,962,454

Colonies.	Area in square miles.	Population, 1870.	Population, 1880.
Færoe Islands (17 inhabited)	510	9,992	11,221
Iceland	39,756	69,763	72,000
Greenland	46,740	9,825	9,531
West Indies { Santa Cruz	74		
{ St. Thomas	23	} 37,821	37,609
{ St. John	21		
Total	87,124	127,401	130,362

Copenhagen (*Kjöbenhavn*, i.e., the Merchants' Haven) is the only large city in Denmark; its population in 1870 was 181,291; in 1880, 235,254; in 1887, 286,900. It has an admirable harbor, one of the finest in Europe, and is a city of great commercial activity. Its libraries, museums, and collections of art are very attractive. The other towns of note are Odense, which had a population in 1870 of 16,721, and nearly 20,000 in 1880; Aarhuus, 13,020 in 1870, and 16,000 in 1880; and Aalborg, 11,953 in 1870, and 14,300 in 1880. The land of Denmark is subdivided into great numbers of small estates, the law interdicting the union of small farms into a large landed property; 395 out of each 1000 of its inhabitants live exclusively by agriculture.

Emigration prevents any rapid increase of the population. The number of emigrants, chiefly to the United States, in the decade of 1871-1880 was 38,665; in 60 years ending Dec. 31, 1880, Danish emigration to the United States alone had been 58,606. This current of emigration has steadily increased. From 1881 to 1888 inclusive there were in all 63,482 emigrants to the United States, a larger number than the total of the previous sixty years.

Finances.—The estimated revenue of the Danish Kingdom, from all sources, for the year ending March 31, 1890, was 54,457,514 kroner (the krone or crown being of the value of 26.8 cents in our currency). The revenue consequently amounted to $14,194,613.75. The expenditure for the same year was 57,251,480 kroner = $15,343,396.64.

An important feature in the administration of the finances of the kingdom is the maintenance of a reserve fund of a comparatively large amount, the object being to provide means by which the government could, on sudden emergencies, command the necessary funds. In March, 1868, this reserve amounted to about $31,500,000, but it has been gradually reduced, mainly in paying off the national debt. The national debt of Denmark was incurred in part by large deficits in former years, before the establishment of parliamentary government; and, in part, by railway undertakings, and the construction of harbors, lighthouses, and other works of public importance. It has been gradually diminishing since 1866. In that year it amounted to 264,221,604 kroner = $70,811,390; in 1870 it was 234,740,700 kroner = $62,910,508; in 1875 it was 185,835,623 kroner = $49,803,947; in 1880 it was reduced to 173,326,628 kroner = $46,451,536. By the year 1890 it had somewhat increased, being about $57,870,000.

The largest sources of revenue are custom-house dues, excise on distilleries, and direct taxes; these constitute about five-eighths of the whole revenue; the remainder is made up of stamp duty and duty on inheritance the surplus on domains, posts, telegraphs, State railways, law-fees, interest and contribution from reserve fund. The revenue for 1881 showed a surplus of over $1,500,000.

Commerce, Trade, and Industry.—The commerce of Denmark and its West Indian colonies is carried on mostly with three countries, Germany, Great Britain, and the United States. In 1879 the total imports into Denmark from all quarters were 199,053,000 kroner = $53,346,204, of which $19,499,680 came from Germany; $13,106,665 from Great Britain, and $3,187,378 from the United States. The exports the same year were 158,063,000 kroner = $42,360,884, of which $15,007,500 were sent to Germany, $17,662,500 to Great Britain, and $464,265 to the United States. The remaining imports and exports came from and were sent to France, Belgium, Holland, Austria-Hungary, Sweden and Norway, and Russia. The aggregate of exports and imports, which was $95,707,088 in that year, was materially increased in 1880 and 1881, both years of very large crops of grain and very favorable to the production of live-stock. The imports from Great Britain in 1880 were about $9,500,000, and from the United States $4,160,308. The exports to Great Britain the same year were $26,428,835, and those to the United States only $641,796. In 1881 the imports from the United States were $7,126,249, and the exports $366,408. The exports of Denmark are of butter, grain and flour, live animals, and some manufactured goods. The imports are varied, consisting of cotton, woollen, and silk goods, coal, petroleum, iron, agricultural machinery, sewing-machines, etc. The agricultural crops of Denmark in 1880 were large, producing a calculated value of $91,388,000, consisting largely of barley, rye, oats, hay, wheat, potatoes, and seed. The harvest in 1881 was still larger, and was said to have been the largest gathered in Denmark for fifty years, and coming at a time when the crop of cereals in most of the countries of Europe was short, commanded high prices. The manufactures of Denmark and its West Indian colonies are of very considerable extent, comprising leather, woollen goods, train oil, refined (and in the colonies raw) sugar, molasses, and syrups, beer, ale, distilled liquors, etc. The Danes are a very industrious people, and the wealth of the kingdom *per capita* is large.

Railways, etc.—In January, 1883, there were 1915 miles of railway open for traffic, of which 810 miles belonged to the state. The length of telegraph lines at the same date was 2200 miles, and the length of wires 5840 miles. There were at the same date 354 telegraph offices, of which 160 belonged to the railway companies and 194 to the state.

On Jan. 1, 1880, the commercial fleet of Denmark consisted of 3271 vessels, of an aggregate burthen of 257,546 tons, an increase in 6 years of 401 vessels with 44,864 tons burthen. Of the whole number 193 were steamers of 48,826 tons. Only 135 of the 3271 vessels exceeded 300 tons burthen.

Money, Weights and Measures.—On Jan. 1, 1875, the decimal system of currency was introduced in Denmark, though with a different unit from that of other countries. The old unit was the *Rigsdaler* or Rix-dollar, whose value was 53.6 cents in our currency. It was divided into 96 shillings. This is now abolished and the new unit is the *Krone* (crown), which is just one-half the Rigsdaler and has a value of 26.8 cents in our currency. It is divided into 100 öre, the öre being worth about ¼ of a cent.

The other weights and measures are, the *pound*, which is divided into 100 koint, and is equal to 1.102 pounds avoirdupois; the ship-last = 2 tons; the tönde or barrel of grain and salt = 3.8 imperial bushels; the tönde of coal = 4.7 imperial bushels; the foot = 1.03 English foot; the viertel = 1.7 imperial gallon.

For further information in regard to Denmark see *Kongelig Dansk Hof og Statscalender* (Kjöbenhavn, 1882); *Résumé des principaux faits statistiques du Danemark* (Publié par le Bureau royal de Statistique, No. III., 8 Copenhague, 1881); *Trade of Denmark with the United Kingdom; Reports from the Consuls of the United States to the State Department* (1883 and 1884); Falbe-Hansen (V.) and Scharling (Wm.), *Danmark's Statistik*, 8, Kjöbenhavn, 1878–79; Frank Vincent, Jr., *Norsk, Lapp,* and *Finn*, 1881.

(L. P. B.)

DENNIE, JOSEPH (1768–1812), an American journalist, was born in Boston, Aug. 30, 1768. He graduated at Harvard College in 1790, studied law, and was admitted to the bar at Charlestown, N. H. He became a contributor to the newspapers, and in 1795 removed to Walpole, N. H., where he established the *Farmer's Weekly Museum*, in which he published a series of essays called "The Lay Preacher," which gave him a wide reputation as a graceful writer. In 1799 he was invited by Timothy Pickering, Secretary of State, to come to Philadelphia as his private secretary. This position he held a few months, then became editor of the *United States Gazette*, and finally established the *Port-Folio*, at first a weekly, afterwards a monthly magazine, to which many distinguished writers of the time contributed. Dennie's social qualities assisted in giving him a high reputation, and he was regarded in his time as the Addison of America. He died at Philadelphia, Jan. 7, 1812.

DENTISTRY. Among even the rudest and most barbarous of every age and nation the teeth, as organs of use and beauty, have claimed attention and been regarded of importance in giving expression and symmetry to the face, and in the preparation of food for the assimilative process.

See Vol. VII. p. 83 Am. ed. (p. 95 Edin. ed.).

Teeth.—Having their origin in the columnar epithelium, they are properly classed with the muco-dermal appendages, and when perfected may be defined as hard prominences projecting from the surface of the mucous membrane, located in the pre-assimilative portion of the alimentary canal. In the human family their most important function is to subserve nutrition by the mastication of food. Regarding them as tactile organs, and as organs of speech by aiding in the formation of articulate sounds, their impairment becomes still more serious, and their preservation, or replacement when lost, a matter of considerable moment.

Since the development of the teeth commences early in intra-uterine life, and continues through infancy and childhood, they may be subjected to certain imperfections in structure (vices of conformation) resulting from imperfect nutrition during this period. Subsequently, when erupted, they hold an important relation with the arterial and nervous system by means of the pulp within the tooth, the alveoli and the dental periosteum surrounding the root, which exposes them to abnormalities which in severity and persistence correspond with the morbid systemic conditions predominating at the time. In addition to this, they are continuously bathed in the oral secretions, which are liable to vitiation from constitutional disturbances as well as from the degeneration of particles of food remaining in the mouth. Add to these the serious and frequent abuse which the teeth receive both from improper use and want of use, and we have recognised some of the factors which contribute to their premature disease, disintegration, and loss, hence necessitating the practice of dentistry and the training of skilled dentists.

Practice of Dentistry.—That from a very remote period some attention was given to the treatment of diseases of the teeth by the Egyptians and Greeks is well attested by the writings of Herodotus, Hippocrates, Aristotle, Celsus, and others; but to the nineteenth century and to the United States of America has been reserved the honor of witnessing the present state of dental proficiency. This has been secured through the energy, industry, and genius of the native artisan, and for its maintenance it is essential that the future dental practitioner shall with unceasing effort pursue his anatomical, physiological, histological, and pathological studies. Familiarity with dental development and eruption, normal and abnormal, with the numerous and diversified anomalies to which the hard and soft tissues are liable, and the means essential for their protection and preservation, as well as of prosthetic dentistry, embracing the construction and adjustment of artificial substitutes where accident or disease has destroyed the natural organs, is of the utmost importance to those who would successfully practise dentistry.

The following statement embraces some of the more important points which require the attention of the dentist:

Abnormal conditions of the dental tissues :—Caries, necrosis, exostosis, abrasion.

Mechanical injuries of the hard tissues :—Fracture, dislocation, dilaceration.

Abnormal conditions of the dental pulp :—Irritation, inflammation, granulation or polypus, suppuration, death.

Abnormal conditions of the alveolo dental periosteum :—Irritation, inflammation, acute and chronic, hemorrhage, abscess.

Abnormal conditions of the aleveolar process :—Necrosis, exostosis, absorption.

Abnormal conditions of the gums, prior and subsequent to the eruption of the teeth :—Inflammation, ulceration, recedence, tumors.

Abnormal conditions of the antrum resulting from diseased teeth.

Tartar or salivary calculus :—Its origin, location, color, influence.

Extraction, replantation, and transplantation of teeth.

Construction of obturators and artificial palates.

Anæsthetics: their administration and influence.

Irregularity of the teeth: its cause and treatment.

Mechanical dentistry: manufacture of artificial teeth, taking impressions, base plates, attaching teeth to bases and securing the same in the mouth.

Dental anatomy.—Man, being both heterodont and diphyodont, has a deciduous and permanent set, which are dissimilar in their shape. The set belonging to childhood is twenty in number, equal in each jaw, and on each side of the median line, as follows: central incisors, 4; lateral incisors, 4; canines, 4; molars, 8—better written thus:

$$c.\ i.\ \frac{1-1}{1-1};\ l.\ i.\ \frac{1-1}{1-1};\ c.\ \frac{1-1}{1-1};\ m.\ \frac{2-2}{2-2}=\frac{10}{10}.$$

The central incisors, standing next to the median line of the mouth, are about one-third wider than the laterals, which are next in order; then the canines, followed by the molars.

The permanent set, or those of adult life, are thirty-two in number, as follows: central incisors, 4; lateral incisors, 4; canines, 4; bicuspids, or pre-molars, 4 first and 4 second, 8; and the true molars, 4 first, 4 second, 4 third, 12 in all—written thus:

$$c.\ i.\ \frac{1-1}{1-1};\ l.\ i.\ \frac{1-1}{1-1};\ c.\ \frac{1-1}{1-1};\ b.\ c.\ \frac{2-2}{2-2};\ m.\ \frac{3-3}{3-3}=\frac{16}{16}$$

Each tooth is so individualized by its peculiar morphology that one familiar with its shape can give its exact position in the mouth.

Hard tissues of teeth.—Enamel, dentine, and cement, the three hard tissues of which the tooth is composed, are widely different structures. The enamel, covering the exposed portion of the crown, is composed of dense hexagonal fibres compactly united and presenting on the surface a vitreous appearance. It is the most dense structure in the animal economy, consisting in the well-developed adult tooth of organic matter 3 per cent., of inorganic or earth salts 97 per cent. The dentine, of which the large body of the tooth is composed, is made up of tubular and intertubular tissue, much less dense than the enamel, containing 27 per cent. of organic matter and 73 per cent. of inorganic. The cement, covering the roots of the teeth from the neck where the enamel terminates to the apical end, is laminated and much like bone in structure, having within its tissue lacunæ and canaliculi. It is much less dense than either of the other tissues, consisting of 30 per cent. of organic matter and 70 per cent. of inorganic. The sensibility of these three tissues varies with their relative density and the amount of organic matter which they contain.

Tooth-pulp and nerve.—In the centre of the tooth, and having connection with each root, is a cavity known as the pulp-chamber; in this resides the pulp, a highly vascular tissue composed of nerves, blood-vessels, and the remains of the formative tissue; and to this the dentine is indebted for its connection with the nervous and arterial system.

Dental periosteum and alveolar process.—Covering the root, and lining the bony socket in which it is implanted, is the alveolo-dental periosteum, giving nourishment and sensibility to the cemental tissue, and to the alveolar process which forms the dental socket. This process, which surrounds the tooth as it comes into position, is the result of an exceedingly rapid development, and appears to be an outgrowth from the jawbone, stimulated into activity by the presence of the tooth, secondary entirely to it as it follows it into existence, and rapidly disappearing on its removal.

Arrangement and forms of the teeth.—The human teeth, when in normal position, are arranged around the margins of the jaws in two approximately parabolic curves, the superior being the larger of the two, and when closed and at rest it is external in its outer margin to the inferior teeth. The teeth stand side by side in close contact, without the diastemata or inter spaces which appear in most other animals; and no one tooth normally rises higher than its neighbor. As the teeth have a labio-lingual diameter which is slightly greater than their lateral, and stand in a curved line without interspaces, they must be wider in their labial or external than in their lingual or palatine aspect. By their peculiar shape, arrangement, and movement they are made most efficient in mastication, since no two teeth oppose each other only, but each tooth (as a rule) in closure of the jaws impinges upon two.

Incisors.—As has been stated, the incisors are four in each jaw. As seen from the front, the crowns are greater in their length than width, making them oblong in shape, with a slightly convex labial surface. Their labio-lingual diameter is greatest at the neck, from which it diminishes to the cutting edge, giving them a wedge or chisel shape, which facilitates the division of food. The crowns of the superior centrals are a third larger than the laterals, while the inferior centrals are a trifle smaller than the inferior laterals. The roots are single and tapering to the point or apical end, giving them a cone-shaped appearance. Of these teeth the superior centrals are the most cylindrical in their roots, all the others being flattened or compressed in their lateral diameter, as if making an abortive effort for a bifurcated fang. The teeth are wider at the cutting edge than at the neck, leaving a somewhat triangular space in that locality.

Canines.—The canines, four in number, are in every respect stronger and thicker teeth than the central incisors. The crown at the cutting edge terminates in a point or cusp, which is on a line with the axis of the root and a trifle nearer the median than the distal edge of the tooth. The labial surface is decidedly more convex than that of the incisors, and the lingual surface, instead of having the concave sweep of the incisors, is irregularly convex, with both diameters of the crown greatest a short distance from the neck. The root is longer and stronger than any other single root. The lower canines differ from the upper in the cusp being a little less pronounced and the root a trifle shorter.

Bicuspids.—The bicuspids are two on each side of the median line of both upper and lower jaws, making eight in all. They have upon their masticating surfaces, as their name would imply, two cusps, with a depression between them varying in depth, the outer or labial cusp of the superior teeth being the larger of the two. The shape of the crown is irregularly quadrilateral, with the lingual and labial surfaces decidedly convex, the latter slightly wider than the former. The root is usually single, though much compressed from side to side, and not infrequently is this depression sufficient to divide the pulp-chamber within the root; and in the first bicuspid a result in many instances is the bifurcation of one-third its length. The lower bicuspids differ in their cusps being less pronounced, the root less depressed from side to side, and without the tendency to division. It has much the appearance of a transitional tooth between the superior canine and first bicuspid.

Molars.—The first and second molars, superior and inferior, two on each side of the mouth, eight in all, are the most important in their triturating capacity. Each crown, approaching a square with rounded corners, offers five surfaces—masticating, buccal, lingual, mesial, and distal. The masticating surface is made up of cusps, ridges, and depressions, which aid the functions of the teeth and are utilized and modified by the upper and lower antagonizing each other. The buccal and lingual are slightly convex, with a depression on a line with the axes of the tooth, extending sometimes the whole length of the crown, and usually more marked on the buccal than lingual surface. The mesial and distal (sometimes termed approximating, because next to the adjoining teeth) are nearly flat, though somewhat modified in shape by the crowding of the teeth. The roots of the upper are three in number—two external or buccal, and one internal or palatal; those of the lower are two in number, an anterior and posterior, much flattened or compressed from front to back, showing a tendency to division. The roots of these teeth vary in their length, curvature, and divergence, and their peculiarities in these respects sometimes greatly complicate the operation of extraction.

The *third molars, dentes sapientiæ,* or wisdom teeth, are four in number, one on each side above and below. The crowns in general conformation are not unlike the first and second molars. They are usually smaller and extremely variable, both in form and position. The roots invariably converge, and not unfrequently form a confluent cone-shaped mass, with the apex curved abruptly backward.

Deciduous Teeth.—The deciduous or temporary set, 20 in number, are relatively smaller than their permanent successors, though resembling them in their general conformation. The deciduous molars, which precede the permanent bicuspids, have their roots diverging more abruptly and at a greater angle from the neck than do those of the permanent molars. This peculiarity gives room for the crypts, which contain their permanent successors, and lie directly beneath and contiguous to them. In all of the deciduous teeth the enamel terminates upon the neck with a thick edge, giving it a constricted appearance and constituting the most marked feature of dissimilarity between the deciduous and permanent teeth.

Dental development and eruption.—During the seventh week of intra-uterine existence there appear epithelial infoldings which are the enamel-germs for the twenty temporary teeth. During the ninth week, while the enamel-organs are progressing in their development, the germs for the future dentine make their appearance in close proximity with the former and almost simultaneously for all the temporary teeth. In the tenth week the walls of the follicle which enclose these germs become rapidly developed. During the fifteenth week the developing germs are progressing in their transformation into the future teeth, and the follicles enclosing them continue their growth. At this early period the enamel-germs for the four first permanent molars make their appearance. In the sixteenth week the follicles surrounding the germs of the temporary teeth are closed, the crypts encasing them lose their connection with the epithelial surface, and over each is a second inflection for the enamel-germs of their successors, which will constitute the ten anterior permanent teeth of each jaw—viz., four central incisors, four lateral incisors, four canines, four first bicuspids, and four second bicuspids. During the seventeenth and eighteenth weeks the enamel- and dentine-germs of the deciduous teeth commence the process of calcification. From the twentieth to the twenty-fifth week septa are formed between the deciduous teeth, connecting the external and internal plates of the alveolar process, and in them calcification begins. The enamel-organs for twenty-four permanent teeth which are in a progressive state of development, have established in close proximity to them the dentine-germs. From the twenty-eighth to the thirty-sixth week the crowns of the twenty deciduous teeth are rapidly calcifying, and the germs of the twenty-four permanent teeth, with their surrounding follicles, are progressing in development. At about the fortieth week, or at birth, the roots of the deciduous teeth are forming by the elongation and calcification of the dental pulp, and the follicles enclosing the germs of the permanent teeth have closed and are receding from their proximity to the mucous surface. Three months after birth the crowns of the deciduous teeth are advancing toward the mucous surface by the elongation and calcification of the dental pulp, and the adhesion to its surface of the dental sac, which had previously lined the follicle, forming the cemental matrix or germ. The enamel- and dentine-germs of the twenty-four permanent teeth are just beginning their calcification, and the epithelial inflections for the enamel-germs of the four second permanent molars are present. Seven to nine months after birth we have the eruption of the eight deciduous incisors, superior and inferior, the centrals preceding the laterals by about one month. At twelve to fourteen months the first four deciduous molars are erupted; at sixteen to eighteen months the eruption of the four deciduous canines takes place; at eighteen to twenty-four months of age the four second deciduous molars are erupted, and temporary dentition is complete. At three years of age the twenty-eight permanent teeth are within their bony crypts in various stages of progressive development, those for which provision was earliest made having their crowns well calcified, with the pulps elongating for the growth of the roots; posterior to these the epithelial inflections for the enamel-germ of the four third permanent molars, or wisdom-teeth, make their appearance.

At six years of age, and while the twenty deciduous teeth are still in position, the four first permanent molars are erupted, entirely posterior to them. From eight to ten years of age the eight deciduous incisors are removed by the absorption of their roots, and the permanent incisors gradually take their places. From ten to eleven years of age the eight permanent bicuspids take the place of the deciduous molars. From twelve to fourteen years of age the four permanent canines take the place of the deciduous ones, and the four second permanent molars are erupted. From eighteen to twenty-five years of age the four third molars, having passed through their various progressive stages of development, are erupted; and thus is completed permanent dentition.

The foregoing is the normal arrangement for the development of the teeth, but aberrations occur in the *time, order,* and *number* of teeth, sometimes giving rise to what is recognized as interrupted or pathological dentition.

Constitutional peculiarities.—In an effort to classify the peculiarities of tooth-forms and structures, in respect of shape, size, color, density, durability, sensibility, recuperative power, etc., we associate physical characteristics and idiosyncrasies with them; so that with careful study and observation of the one we must connect with it certain definite characteristics of the other. For instance: in one who is recognized as "lymphatic," with bulky organs—muscles and bones large, but possessing neither remarkable strength nor great density; actions slow, and recuperative power feeble—we shall find the teeth large in size, dull, opaque, and light in color, soft in structure, and loosely held in position by surrounding tissues, without a marked degree of beauty, strength, or recuperative power. Again, where the opposite physical characteristics exist—with structures dense, movements quick, nutrition and recuperation good, with bodily strength and great power of endurance—the teeth will be found to correspond by being firmly fixed in their sockets, dense in structure, well developed in shape and size, with yellowness of color and great strength.

Pathological dentition.—While dentition is unquestionably a physiological process, it is an undisputed fact that during this period occurs the largest number of deaths among children. Almost continuous irritation exists, and so often is the process subject to perversions that its effects often come within the domain of pathology. During the process of dentition there is an increased susceptibility to nervous, respiratory, and digestive troubles, demanding hygienic care, and not infrequently constitutional treatment, in the direction of sedatives and febrifuges. The general health, constitutional peculiarities, and predispositions, habitat, and surrounding conditions, all exert an influence which may aid in producing deviations from normality in dental evolution. The consideration, therefore, of pathological dentition must include disturbance of functional harmony in organs remote, as well as the expressions of abnormal conditions in the oral cavity; it must be credited with causing, modifying, or aggravating systemic disorders, as well as with being influenced by them. "Thus, while dentition is not to be held responsible for all the ills to which human infancy is heir, it is unsafe to ignore its possible pathological complications in any case."

Normal dentition depends upon an absolute correspondence between the elongation of the pulp and its calcification at the growing extremity of the tooth, and the absorption of the mucous membrane and subjacent tissue covering its crown. When the advance of the tooth is more rapid than the removal by absorption of the superimposed tissue, the latter acts as a mechanical obstacle, and the increased pressure may produce congestion, tumefaction, induration, and ulceration. But the direct pressure of the advancing tooth upon the overlying integuments is not the only nor the principal factor in the production of disturbance; the most serious complications result from the resisting gums inducing a backward pressure of the sharp edges of the calcifying tooth upon the nervous and vascular tissue, the uncalcified pulp giving rise to exquisite remitting pains, and a consequent irritability of the general system, which finds expression in sleeplessness, thirst, fever, nausea, diarrhœa, cutaneous eruptions, convulsions, paralysis, and other serious troubles. Under the above conditions it is rational, and in accord with analogy, to expect benefit, and often permanent relief, to follow the entire liberation of the advancing tooth by a thorough division of the resisting gum with the lancet. The manner in which this operation is performed has much to do with its success or failure. The object is not merely to induce a flow of blood, but rather to remove tension. The cuts should, therefore, be made with special reference to the form of the presenting tooth. The incisors and cuspids need only a division of the gum in the line of the arch; the molars require a crucial incision, thus, ×, the centre of the crown as near as possible indicating the point of intersection. The cuts should be sufficiently deep to each the advancing surface, extending fully up to or little beyond its boundaries, so as to insure the entire liberation of the organ. Usually there is but little inconvenience attending second dentition, yet occasionally considerable pain and swelling accompanies the eruption of the permanent molars; and especially is this true of the inferior third molars, or wisdom teeth, when they erupt close to, or become impacted in a horizontal position under, the coronoid process. In such cases the gums and adjacent soft tissues participate in the irritation, which extends into the fauces. Mastication becomes impossible, and deglutition difficult and painful; such lesions not unfrequently terminate in suppuration, and when accompanied by unfavorable idiosyncrasies or systemic conditions may cause necrosis, exostosis, ulceration, sloughing of the soft tissues, ankylosis of the jaw, facial paralysis, neuralgia, erysipelas, tetanus, and death. Until the third molars are all erupted it will be the part of wisdom to inspect the mouths of patients suffering from lesions not otherwise explainable in any locality to which filaments of the fifth pair of nerves are distributed, and in all such cases to count dentition as a possible factor. (See Dr. J. W. White's essay on *Pathological Dentition*.)

Dental caries.—Caries is molecular death and decomposition of the hard tissues of the teeth. The theories which have been advanced respecting its cause and progress have been numerous and diverse. At one time it was considered wholly due to chemical agents, acids especially, acting upon the salts of lime in the tooth; at another, an organic change, preceded by an exalted irritability, the result of systemic or local and external influences. Then came the chemicovital theory, vices of conformation from imperfect nutrition during the development of the tooth being considered a predisposing cause, while vitiated secretions, resulting from either systemic or local conditions, acted as an exciting cause. There has also been advanced a parasitic theory, as well as an electrical one. That the different tissues of the teeth were abnormally charged with negative and positive electricity, and hence were disintegrated by this antagonism, has found numerous advocates; and that some of the lower forms of life developed in the oral cavity were largely the cause of this retrograde metamorphosis, by their mycelium burrowing into the dental tissue, has been ably urged by many authors. No one theory has adequately explained these pathological phenomena; a better appreciation of the systemic and local conditions which contribute to this tooth-destruction might prove of value.

A study, carefully contrasting the teeth of those who live upon dry, solid food with those subsisting largely on fluids and semi-solids, would show a marked difference in favor of the former. The increasing predisposition to toothache and other dental annoyances, which many experience while laboring under mental or physical debility, or exhaustion; the exalted sensitiveness of the teeth during gestation and lactation; the almost uniform certainty of the loss of two or more teeth by the average mother for every child nursed; the greater predisposition of teeth to decay in youth over adult life; the uniformity with which the teeth of a child resemble in conformation and structure those of its ancestors; the certainty with which the influence of a specific taint transmitted from parent to progeny is shown upon the teeth; the recognized fact that dental caries always attacks the external surface of the tooth first, and in such localities as are difficult to keep clean, and from these points advances to the centre;—speak in unmistakable language of inefficiency of protective methods based entirely upon manipulative skill, and at the same time they point with unerring precision to the fact that there are certain physical, mental, moral, dietetic, hygienic, and hereditary causes which are contributing both directly and indirectly to the prevalence of dental caries.

Treatment of dental caries.—For convenience of description and treatment, dental caries has been divided into three stages, viz., superficial, or caries of enamel; middle, or caries of dentine; and deep-seated or penetrating, where the pulp is involved by exposure. The proficiency and dexterity with which this malady is treated to-day by excavating, shaping, and filling the cavity, is largely due to American genius as developed in the invention of mechanical devices, instruments, and appliances for keeping the operation dry and the cavity to be filled accessible; also for the preparation of the material with which the cavity is to be filled, and its insertion and condensation.

The successful treatment of teeth where the pulp is exposed, either by devitalization or by capping and preserving its vitality, and subsequently filling the crown-cavity, is largely due to American skill. In the former case an application of arsenious acid is made to the exposed organ, and subsequently the dead pulp is removed and the root filled; in the latter, a protective paste of oxide of zinc and creosote, or some other non-irritating substance, is placed over the exposed point, and upon this the permanent filling is condensed.

The varying density, sensibility, and recuperative power of the teeth of different individuals, and of the same individual at different periods of life, make the selection of a material for filling a matter of great importance. It is a well-recognized fact that teeth during the period of their lowest recuperative power and greatest metamorphic tendency will more readily tolerate and be best preserved by plastic fillings possessing a low conductive power and a maximum degree of adaptability.

Gold, tin, amalgams, gutta-percha, oxychloride-of-zinc cements, and phosphate-of-zinc cements constitute the materials now in use for filling; and while it cannot be claimed that any one of these is best fitted for the filling of all teeth, it is most evident that each has its use, and in many special cases some one is far preferable for accomplishing the desired result than either of the others.

A filling material must possess certain attributes, such as ease of introduction into the cavity; adaptability to the walls of the same; density, to withstand attrition in mastication; susceptibility of consolidation; resistance to chemical agents found in the mouth; non-susceptibility to thermal changes; harmony of color; and the absence of injurious influences, either local or constitutional.

In all filling operations the end to be obtained is the restoration of the conformation of the tooth and its functional qualities, the protection of the dentine from irritating and disintegrating agents, and the preservation of the organ for future use. These are secured by properly cleansing and shaping the cavity, careful and thorough insertion of the filling material, and an exact and artistic finish of the surface of the filling so as to be smooth and self-cleansing.

Dental necrosis.—Necrosis may be partial or complete. The dentine only may have lost its vitality by the death of the pulp, or the peri-dental membrane and cement may be involved and the whole vascular supply be cut off, resulting in complete necrosis. In either case the tooth loses its translucency, becomes dull and opaque in color, and may assume any shade from a blue to a dark reddish-brown, this varying with the density and structure of the tooth, age of patient, kind and quality of the dental operation.

This necrosed condition of the tooth may result from medicinal, local, or constitutional causes. When from the latter, with a chronic type of inflammation, treatment is rarely more than palliative, modifying the progress of the disease; in such cases, local applications of dilute sulphuric acid being often made to advantage.

Dental exostosis is a hyper-nutrition, an enlargement of the cement of the root of the tooth; in extent it may be circumscribed; in locality it may be confined to the apex of the root, to either side, or the whole root may be involved, depending in this somewhat upon the cause and its continuation. When confined to the end of the root, it frequently presents the appearance of a knob; if on one side only, the symmetry of the root is destroyed by the affected side being much thicker, or where the whole root is involved concentric layers are added to the normally developed root until the added cement completely invests it to the neck. Or if it be a multiple-rooted tooth, the two or three roots, as it may be, are united in an irregular cone-shaped mass. Its presence always implies previous irritation in the membrane covering the root, in which there is an abnormal quantity of blood, brought to the part by either local or constitutional conditions. Accumulations of foreign substances upon the necks of the teeth under the margin of the gums, cavities of decay in the same situation, biting off threads or other unnatural uses of the teeth, are all productive of hyper-nutrition. While this abnormal growth may, and often does, produce an uneasy sensation in the tooth and some soreness on pressure, the greater amount of discomfort is of a neuralgic nature, and frequently quite remote in its expression from the seat of the disease. This enlargement of the root, and the close adaptation to it of the walls of the alveolus, making in some instances almost a ball-and-socket joint, renders the removal of the affected teeth extremely difficult.

Abrasion of the teeth is a condition affecting only the cutting edges of the front teeth, usually the upper ones. It has never been satisfactorily explained. When fully developed, both the upper and lower are involved, and present the appearance of an elliptical span which somewhat corresponds with the boundary of the labial commissure when opened, as in the natural position of those who have the lips slightly unclosed. The cause of this abnormality has been attributed by the most careful authorities to an acidulated mucus from the glands of the tongue and the dental surface of the superior lips; the solvent in this case is supposed to be lactic and acetic acids, because both organic and inorganic substances are dissolved.

Mechanical injuries of the teeth, such as fracture, dislocation, and dilaceration, are the result usually of accidental injuries. A fracture of the tooth when the pulp-cavity is not involved, though unsightly and, if to any extent, impossible to remedy except by the substitution of a foreign substance for the lost tissue, does not in any appreciable degree necessitate the loss of the tooth or a diminution of its functions. All such teeth can sooner or later be filled with gold or some other material, to the complete restoration of its contour and functional use. Where the accident has fractured through the root, without displacement of the tooth, if the parts can be held perfectly quiet and in exact juxtaposition, a reunion is possible by the addition of cement, or if the tooth, without fracture, should be entirely dislodged, its replacement is practicable; and where conditions are favorable it becomes firm, with a re-establishment of its usefulness.

Dilaceration of the tooth consists in a forcible displacement of the cap of dentine and enamel of a partially developed tooth from the formative pulp; the development of the hard tissues, continuing in this abnormal position, presents, when completed, an appearance such as would be produced by twisting the coronal portion about its axis, until the corresponding surfaces of the crown and root do not lie in the same planes. A somewhat similar conformation may also be the result of deficiency of space in the alveolar arch at the time the tooth is developing. It is owing to this condition that the roots of the third molar or wisdom tooth are so frequently found presenting various positions divergent from a line with the axis of the tooth. Malformations and irregularities of structure are constantly found in both the root and crown of the tooth, and while not a few are the result of inherited tendencies, an interrupted nutritional process is probably responsible for the majority of such abnormal developments.

Abnormal conditions of the dental pulp.—The dental pulp occupies the cavity within the crown and the canal of the roots of each tooth; it is the germinal remains of the dentine and its organ of nourishment and sensation. In shape it corresponds with that of the tooth, dividing into as many radiating prolongations as there are roots to the tooth. It varies with age in its shape and anatomical character. It is richly supplied with nerves and blood-vessels, holding its connection with the nervous system through branches of the fifth pair (trifacial, trigeminus), and with the arterial system through the superior and inferior dental arteries—a branch of the internal maxillary. Small lateral processes (primitive dentinal fibrils) are supposed to form meshes and permeate the dentine; their presence there furnishes a rational, and probably a correct, explanation of the peculiar sensitiveness of that tissue.

The most conspicuous physiological change which the pulp undergoes in advancing age is its progressive calcification, which perceptibly diminishes its size and thickens the walls of the pulp-cavity. The pulp, like other vascular tissues, is subject to various lesions, nutritional and systemic as well as surgical and local. Surrounded as it is by an unyielding enclosure, which prohibits it from swelling, it becomes, when inflamed, the seat of severe pain, which may also find expression in parts quite remote. Its irritability may be caused by numerous local conditions, as also by slight or grave systemic disturbances. When in this morbid state the hard tissues surrounding it are exalted in their sensibility, and readily respond to thermal changes and the presence of certain articles of diet, which, were the pulp normal, would make no impression. This condition can usually be relieved by removing the cause and applying antiphlogistic treatment to the gum-tissue around the root of the tooth.

Inflammation of the pulp is attended by a throbbing, lancinating pain, which is usually increased by the patient's assuming a horizontal position. From this engorgement of the vessels the pulp-cavity becomes fused, and, if no relief is given by an artificial opening, degeneration and suppuration rapidly supervene.

Granulation, or polypus of the pulp, is a condition following long exposure by deep-seated caries and frequent wounding by contact with foreign substances; the appearance it presents is that of a vascular tumor filling up the cavity of decay, having its base at the opening into the pulp-cavity. Teeth so affected are susceptible of successful treatment.

Dental periosteum.—This lining and protective membrane occupies the space between the surface of the root and the inner walls of the alveolar socket, giving nourishment from its respective surfaces to each of those tissues. It is the germinal remains of the cement, and its organ of nourishment and sensation; when stimulated to a hyper-nutrition it causes a deposition of cement to the already completed root, this enlargement being recognized as dental exostosis. Like the dental pulp, it is confined between two unyielding surfaces, and when inflamed becomes the seat of severe pain. It holds its connection with the arterial and nervous system from the same source as does the pulp; its lateral processes permeate the cement and carry nourishment and sensation to the little lacunæ within the body of this tissue. The most frequent, unyielding, and persistent abnormal condition of this membrane is a chronic inflammation, which is accompanied by a thickened and vascular condition of the gums, a discharge of pus around the neck of the tooth, dissolution of the walls of the alveolus, a lengthening of the tooth, and finally its extrusion and loss. An acute and much more painful inflammatory condition is recognized as "alveolar abscess," an accumulation of pus around the end of the root, which, finding no means of exit either through the root-canal and pulp-cavity or along the surface of the root to the margin of the gum, is retained within the socket until its increasing quantity has by pressure upon the surrounding alveolar walls produced their dissolution so that the pus escapes either into the gum or maxillary sinus. If it takes the former course it rapidly burrows in the direction offering the least resistance, until it is discharged into the oral cavity or on to the external surface through a fistula established in the mucous membrane. During this pathological process, lasting thirty-six or forty-eight hours and sometimes longer, much redness, swelling, and pain is induced, which rapidly subside upon the liberation of the pus; the canal and fistula, having been secured by the previous inflammatory condition, remain as a means of exit for the continued accumulation. If this pus should be discharged into the antrum or maxillary sinus, its lining membrane becomes involved, and if neglected there is soon established a chronic case of diseased antrum with a purulent discharge into the nares and throat. A poultice should never be applied to the outside of the face during the progress of the abscess, as this has a tendency to induce the establishment of a fistula and the discharge of pus on the surface. The most frequent cause of this acute inflammatory condition of the peri-dental membrane is devitalization of the dental pulp.

Hæmorrhage from the alveolo-dental periosteum, whether subsequent to the extraction of a tooth, or a persistent oozing of blood from around the necks of the teeth *in situ*, never occurs in excess except there exists a hæmorrhagic diathesis or a temporary deficiency in tone of blood-vessels and quality of blood from constitutional disturbances. Where continuous bleeding follows the removal of a tooth, the only reliable remedy is a compress upon the lacerated membranes.

The alveolar process is a festooned ridge of spongy bone located upon the superior and inferior maxillæ, so as to form and maintain the elliptical figure characteristic of the human dental arch. It consists of two plates, an outer and an inner one, which are connected by numerous transverse septa, forming interspaces (sockets) in which are implanted the roots of the teeth. The mass of loose, spongy bone which makes up the alveolar socket is secondary to, and in its persistence dependent upon, the individual tooth which it surrounds. It is rapidly built up as the tooth is developed, and usually as promptly absorbed on the removal of the organ.

In a strumous diathesis necrosis of the process not infrequently follows the establishment of an acute alveolar abscess; and especially is this the case in children with diseased deciduous teeth. The process is also subject to a hyper-nutrition which may result in the filling up of the socket and extrusion of the tooth, or in thickening the external wall to the unsightly protrusion of the lips, without disturbance of the normality of the teeth. Its absorption or dissolution results from the extraction of the teeth, or, as previously stated, from chronic thickening and suppuration of the peri-dental membrane.

The gum, which is continuous with the mucous membrane of the inside of the lips, the floor of the mouth, and the palate, but differs from this principally in its greater density, is subject to lesions resulting wholly from the teeth, either in their evolution or abnormal conditions subsequent to eruption. The advancing tooth, whether it be of the deciduous or permanent set, may cause the inflammation and tumefaction of the superimposed tissue, with subsequent ulceration, or it may be white and indurated. With the progress of dental caries to the encroachment on the neck of the tooth, the sharp edges of the enamel may act as an irritant on the surrounding soft tissue; inflammation in the alveolo-dental periosteum would, from its continuity with the membrane covering the gums, induce an abnormal condition in the latter. Accumulations of foreign substance on the necks of the teeth, improper use of the brush, harsh and unsuitable dentifrices, as well as advancing years, all contribute to the recession of the gums from the necks of the teeth.

Tartar, or salivary calculus.—The teeth are constantly bathed in a fluid which is furnished by the salivary and mucous glands opening into the oral cavity. The character and quantity of this secretion are modified by systemic conditions and by articles of diet, but under all circumstances it is made up largely of water, holding in solution a small quantity of organic matter and a very variable amount of inorganic material, the latter being chiefly carbonate and phosphate of lime. The accumulation of solid matter found upon the necks of the teeth (varying in quantity, color, and density) is largely due to the constituents of the secretions in which they are constantly bathed, these being deposited upon those portions of the teeth where there is the least friction in mastication; hence tartar is found in the largest quantity on the lingual surface of the inferior incisors and external and buccal surfaces of the superior molars. The accumulation in these localities is also facilitated by the fact that the sublingual and submaxillary glands throw their secretions directly upon the former surface, and the parotid empties its supply upon the latter. The color of the tartar varies from a light cream to a dark brown or black; the density varies with the color, the lightest shades being the softest, and the hardness increasing as the color darkens. Its influence upon the hard tissues of the teeth is benign or protective, but when it has accumulated in large quantities and encroaches upon the surrounding soft tissues, or in smaller amounts under the margins of the gums, it causes inflammation of this tissue, and also of the alveolo-dental periosteum; both of these, together with the walls of the alveolar socket, are from the mechanical influence of the tartar finally absorbed and the tooth loosened and lost. Much of the discomfort resulting from this condition is of a neuralgic character, and frequently quite remote from the seat of the disease.

Extraction of teeth.—The removal of a tooth firmly implanted in its socket without the use of an anæsthetic is an operation attended with so much suffering that few submit to it except for the purpose of gaining relief from pain—present or prospective; but since the introduction of nitrous oxide gas, with its reputed comparative freedom from injurious influences, thousands of teeth are annually sacrificed which could with the aid of dental skill be made comfortable and serviceable for many years. To appreciate fully the extent of the injury done by this wanton sacrifice of human teeth would necessitate the collection and publishing of a complete record of the operations of those who perform only this one branch of dentistry. The flaming advertisements for the "painless extraction of teeth" are some of the most conspicuous relics of the charlatanism which has so successfully and unfortunately brought into disrepute the profession and retarded its advancement. When the extraction of a tooth is deemed advisable, three conditions are to be observed: first, the removal of the entire organ; second, to do this with as little injury as possible to the surrounding tissue; third, with no unnecessary pain to patient and without delay. To accomplish this, the operation should be divided into three stages: (1) properly and efficiently seizing the tooth: embraced in this must be the selection of the instrument; (2) the application of such force and in such direction as to break up the membranous connection the tooth holds with its socket; (3) the removal of the tooth from the mouth. To do these things effectually the operator must be familiar with the number and shape of the roots, the density of the surrounding alveolar tissue, and the condition of the alveolo-dental periosteum, the varying conditions of these structures adding much to the simplicity or complexity of the operation. The anterior single-rooted teeth, somewhat cylindrical and cone-shaped, admit of a rotary motion in breaking up their membranous connection, while the flattened or more compressed roots prohibit this, and must be loosened by an in-and-out motion or by elevating and depressing the hand. In the extraction of molars a recognition of the fact that the outer or external wall of the alveolus is less dense and less thick than the inner, and that these are multiple-rooted teeth, is all-important.

The necessity for tooth-extraction arises: (1) from a desire for relief from pain; (2) to anticipate or cure an external fistula; (3) to prepare the mouth for artificial substitutes; (4) to relieve and correct an overcrowded arch; (5) to remedy defects from malformed and misplaced supernumerary teeth; and (6) where the condition of the tooth, from disease or injury, precludes the possibility of reparation. The instruments in use are the key, the forceps, and the elevator. The use of the key is chiefly confined to the country physician, and, though usually effectual in its results, is poorly adapted to the purpose, because the force is applied at a right angle to the axis of the tooth; and where much resistance is offered considerable injury is done to the surrounding tissue. The forceps now in use are all constructed upon the principle of lengthening the crown of the tooth and applying the force on a line with its axis. The various shapes of the beaks correspond with the necks and bifurcations of the roots of the teeth; and when the application is made to the tooth or root to be removed, the pressure upon the tooth in closing the handles of the forceps is diffused over the greatest possible surface so as to avoid the danger of cutting or crushing it, or, in the effort of its removal, of its slipping off. In selecting forceps for a single-rooted tooth the edge of both beaks should be sharp so as to readily separate the gum from the neck of the tooth, and from the process also if necessary. They should be concave, with the external or labial beak slightly wider than the internal or lingual, to correspond with the shape of the tooth. For the upper molars, three-rooted teeth, the external beak should be wide, with a sharp point in the centre, and a concave sweep each side, so as to fit between and on the two buccal or outer roots, while the palatine beak should have a single concave sweep to fit the single palatine root. For the inferior molars, having an anterior and posterior root, both beaks are wide, with a sharp point in the centre, and concave each side. These teeth are frequently very difficult to extract, because of their bifurcation and the convergence of the end of the roots embracing within a strong section of alveolar process which must frequently be dislodged from its bed before the tooth can be removed. The undetermined shape of the roots of the third molar, with their abrupt curvature posteriorly and crowded condition between the second molar and base of the coronoid process below and tuberosity above, renders their extraction difficult. Especially is this so with the inferior molars when they become impacted. The forceps for these should have beaks of equal width, with concave sweep to fit the neck of the tooth. It is in the extraction of the inferior wisdom-tooth that Physic's forceps, used upon the principle of an elevator, often proves invaluable. Success in the extraction of either teeth or roots depends largely on forcing the instrument as near the apex of the root as possible; with this precaution less force is needed and much less liability of fracturing the root incurred. To secure this it often becomes necessary to pass the beak of the forceps up entirely outside of the alveolus, cutting the latter through and removing the loosened portions with the root. In selecting extracting instruments an efficient set for the removal of all roots and teeth could be comprised in twelve forceps and a heavy, lance-shaped elevator, those for the superior first and second molars being what are termed *right* and *left*.

The instruments most improved in every particular which can be procured for the extraction of teeth are the result of many modifications, with the view of an especial adaptation to each particular tooth with its complications. For the ease and success with which the dental surgeon performs his most difficult operations in the removal of teeth and roots he is indebted to the zeal and persistent efforts of the American dental instrument-maker and his desire to utilize the suggestions of the dental surgeon.

Replantation and transplantation of teeth.—Success or failure in this peculiar department of dentistry depends much upon the idiosyncrasies or peculiarities of constitution. With all favorable surroundings it is rarely possible to preserve the vitality of the pulp. The tooth having been dislodged, the vessels furnishing the vascular supply are necessarily broken, and a reunion of these can only take place under the most advantageous conditions. This being the case, it is preferable under all circumstances, where the dismemberment has been complete, before replacing the tooth in the socket to slightly enlarge the apical foramen and withdraw the entire pulp, and fill the cavity with a preparation of gutta-percha or some other indestructible material. This prevents the alveolar abscess which is almost sure to follow the disintegration of the devitalized pulp, and obviates the necessity of subsequently drilling into the tooth and filling the pulp-chamber from an external and artificial opening. In order to secure the inserted or replaced tooth firmly with the readjustment of the alveolus and gum, complete rest and freedom from motion must be obtained by the application of properly adjusted ligatures attached to the adjoining teeth. In the earlier days of American dentistry the transplantation of teeth was extensively practised, but the operation having proven so unsuccessful in the large majority of cases, it has grown into disuse, and now the effort is rarely made to place in an alveolar socket a tooth which had not previously grown there. In the replantation of teeth the result has been quite the reverse from that of the former operation, owing in a great measure to the necessity for exact adaptation of the tooth to the socket, and while transplantation has become almost obsolete, removal or dislodgement and replantation is yearly growing more in favor, many morbid conditions, as alveolar abscess, severe periodontitis, and exostosis, having all been successfully treated in this way.

Obturators and Artificial Palates.—The abnormal conditions which these mechanical appliances are intended to remedy are fissures of varying magnitude through the palate (cleft palate), arising from congenital or accidental causes, the former dating from birth, the latter the result of accident or disease. Where the deformity arises from an arrested development the fissure is always longitudinal and on the median line of the palate, while in those cases resulting from accident or disease the loss of tissue may be partial or entire, with scarcely a resemblance in any two cases. Nor does a congenital fissure necessarily bear any other resemblance to an acquired one than the fact that both represent loss of structure or a want of entirety in the palatine arch. When the defect is of such magnitude or the conditions are so unfavorable as to render surgical operations doubtful or impracticable, mechanism comes forward with properly adapted appliances and supplements the surgeon's skill. Obturators for the purpose of closing perforations of the palate are of an ancient date, and though crude and only partially effective, were valued. A piece of sponge, a cotton wad, or a thin piece of leather were all used as stoppings, serving a temporary purpose and being easily removed; but the impropriety of sustaining in position an obturator of any material by pressure upon the lateral walls of the opening will be readily recognized from the fact that absorption is thereby induced and the opening continuously enlarged, which necessitates repeated additions to the plug. Persistent and untiring effort on the part of a few who have pursued the subject in all its bearings has evolved a truer and more comprehensive appreciation of the functions to be restored and of the means adapted for that end; so that artistic and scientific skill has succeeded in the manufacture and adjustment of appliances which now so completely relieve the inconvenience of these lesions, whether congenital or acquired, that only critical inspection detects the imperfection.

Metallic plates, gold or silver, formerly constituted the material from which the majority of appliances used for closing lesions of the palate were made, and many ingenious pieces of mechanism were constructed for such purposes; but recently vulcanized rubber and celluloid have almost entirely superseded the use of metals. These substances being lighter and readily moulded into shape and adapted to openings and inequalities, much more artistic and efficient results can be obtained from their use. Dr. Kingsley, of New York, to whom the author is indebted for many suggestions on this subject, says: "It is of the greatest importance that all such instruments should be executed in the most perfect manner, and made to fit accurately all the parts with which they are to be in contact, so that they may not produce the slightest irritation or exert undue pressure upon any of the surrounding parts." Especially is this the case in acquired lesions, where the system is in a condition predisposed to inflammatory symptoms from slight irritations. In the construction of these appliances the methods are not unlike those used in the making of an artificial denture. An accurate impression of the parts, from which to secure a model of the opening and surrounding tissue, is the first and most essential step, and, in many cases, not the least difficult. Plaster of Paris being the only reliable substance with which to obtain an exact counterpart of the defect, much care is required in extemporizing an impression-cup of wax, block-tin, or sheet gutta-percha, in which the plaster in a plastic condition shall be gently pressed to the parts desired to be moulded. From the cast obtained from the impression a metal die can be secured; then upon this exact model the obturator must be constructed out of gutta-percha or celluloid. In many lesions, both acquired and congenital, the loss of tissue is confined to the posterior part of the soft palate; in such cases an unyielding appliance is not only undesirable, but inadmissible, where perfect articulation is to be attained. The constant vibration of these soft tissues would only tolerate with comfort a substitute possessing elasticity and flexibility; the elastic rubber is the material which is admirably adapted for this purpose.

The history of obturators for remedying defects in the hard palate dates back several hundred years, but that embracing the successful application of an artificial velum, which in a moderate degree fulfils the functions of the natural curtain of the palate, is a history of methods confined to the last forty years, developing the struggle of a few earnest men for an end which has only been attained by thought, ingenuity, and labor. A full recognition of the character, cause, and peculiarities of the lesion, as well as the function of the organ in health, was found to be an essential step towards success; a knowledge of the muscles to be propitiated and of the instruments they would tolerate was requisite to a successful artificial velum. "Muscular power cannot be given to a piece of mechanism, but the material of which it is made may be so soft, elastic, and flexible that it will yield to, and be under the control of, the muscles surrounding it, and thus measurably bestow upon it the function of the organ it represents."

Anæsthetics.—Anæsthesia, in the modern sense, was first induced at the suggestion of Dr. Horace Wells, a dentist of Hartford, Conn., who, on Sept. 11, 1844, inhaled nitrous oxide gas, and while under its influence submitted to the extraction of a tooth, the operation proving painless. In October, 1846, Dr. W. T. G. Morton, a practising dentist of Boston, Mass., first publicly demonstrated his discovery of the anæsthetic power of sulphuric ether upon a patient in the Massachusetts General Hospital. The use of ether and chloroform for many years entirely supplanted the anæsthetic originally employed, but during the past fifteen years the use of nitrous oxide gas has been revived, and it is now more generally used than any other anæsthetic agent in dental and other minor surgical operations. Its advantages are reputed safety, combined with great rapidity of action and the almost entire freedom from unpleasant sensations which it secures to the patient both during inhalation and subsequent to the operation. Headache, following the use of the gas, is, however, of frequent occurrence, and many cases are reported in which lifelong invalidism has been attributed to its influence. The impression produced upon the nervous system by anæsthetics is so profound that with susceptible constitutions unpleasant results will occasionally follow, whatever anæsthetic may be employed; and, as nitrous oxide gas is more frequently used than any other agent, the number of such cases may be absolutely greater, even while relatively less, than with ether or chloroform.

The fatality which has attended the administration of chloroform, owing to the heart-paralysis and brain-anæmia which it produces, has been so great—an aggregate of 500 deaths being now reported—that its use in general surgery, except in special cases, has by many been abandoned. In ordinary dental practice chloroform as an anæsthetic should be absolutely interdicted. In safety sulphuric ether compares favorably with nitrous oxide gas, very few fatal cases having resulted from its use, and it is claimed by many that when properly administered a fatal result is impossible.

The following rules should be observed in giving any anæsthetic: Loosen the clothing around the neck and chest, in order that respiration may be free. Be sure that the stomach contains neither solid nor liquid food; vomiting often occurs during the progress of anæsthesia, especially when ether is used, and food may, during this act, be drawn into the air-passages and death from suffocation ensue. With ether or chloroform the patient should be placed in a reclining or semi-reclining position, in order that the flow of blood to the brain may be favored by gravity, and the heart be thus relieved of a portion of its labor. Nitrous oxide gas weakens the force of the heart so little that with this agent this precaution is not necessary, and the upright position may be maintained throughout.

The first effect of all anæsthetic agents is decidedly exhilarating, all the forces being stimulated; this condition, however, is followed by a stage of depression more or less profound. Loss of consciousness, but not of sensation, comes very early in this stimulant stage, and then trifling surgical operations may often be performed without conscious suffering; but, except in the early part of that stage, it is unsafe to operate before anæsthesia is complete, otherwise the shock from the operation may, by reflex action, produce paralysis of the vital centres, weakened as they are by the narcotic effect of the anæsthetic employed. Neglect of this rule is chiefly responsible for the great mortality which has attended anæsthesia in dental operations.

Dr. W. F. Litch, of Philadelphia, to whom the author is indebted for valuable suggestions on this subject, says: "A good general test for complete anæsthesia is the entire muscular relaxation which usually attends total loss of sensibility; the arm of the patient when lifted drops heavily to the side. This test, however, does not apply to anæsthesia by nitrous oxide gas. Complete anæsthesia by that agent is attended by muscular rigidity and twitching, with more or less lividness of the face and lips. A critical test is to touch with the finger the edge of the eyelid; the conjunctiva covering the eye being very slow to lose sensation, absence of movement when the eyelid is thus touched is full evidence that the anæsthesia of the general system is very profound."

With ether, and especially with chloroform, a due proportion of air must be given with the vapor. Nitrous oxide gas must, on the contrary, be given as nearly as possible absolutely free from air. When dangerous symptoms arise, suspend the anæsthetic at once, place the head of the patient lower than the body, draw the tongue forward, dash cold water in the face, and, if necessary, resort to artificial respiration and the use of the electric battery.

Dental irregularities.—The deviations from the normal positions are, in the permanent set, of almost every conceivable variety, and when they occur are properly designated "dental irregularities." In the deciduous set, unless associated with some other deformity, abnormal arrangement of the teeth is very rare, seldom amounting to more than a slight malposition of one or two of the incisors, either of a congenital origin or resulting from the mischievous habit of thumb-sucking or the prolonged use of an artificial nipple; in neither case need they occasion any uneasiness regarding the position of their successors or be considered of sufficient importance to warrant an effort for their correction. Abnormal arrangement of the permanent teeth is of a much more serious character, and, whether involving one or two only or all of the anterior teeth, interferes more or less with their functions, both in regard to mastication and the formation of articulate sounds. It predisposes them to disease, endangers their durability, and may very seriously interfere with their beauty, and greatly impair and distort the expression of the countenance. The causes which contribute to the great variety of malpositions which they assume may be hereditary and congenital or from various mechanical influences, as follows: Prolonged retention or premature extraction of the deciduous teeth; accidental mechanical influences, such as disproportion of the size of the teeth and jaws, imperfect development of the maxillary bones, concomitant variations, thumb-sucking, tumors on the gums, injury to the jaw, persistent nursing in infancy from the one breast, cicatricial tissue from a burn or scald; abnormal development in one organ or locality, modifying the condition of structures subsequently perfected. This is verified in the fact that congenitally enlarged tonsils—which necessitate the continuous opening of the mouth for breathing—invariably induce a narrow and deep arch and protruding front teeth. The foregoing conditions, each of which may contribute to the malposition of one or more of the permanent teeth, can very properly be classified under two influences—developmental and accidental. The former operates prior to the eruption of the teeth, the latter subsequently and wholly through mechanical influences. Of developmental causes Dr. N. W. Kingsley says: "No one of extended observation will hesitate in believing that there is a faculty or power at work modifying materially the physique of the present generation, . . . and that it is in the accumulated, the intensified, effect produced by the law of inheritance that the most striking and destructive results are to be witnessed."

"The primary cause of any general disturbance in the development of the permanent teeth, showing itself particularly in their malposition, is directly traceable to a lesion of the trigeminal nerve; it is an interference, more or less prolonged, with one of the prominent functions of that nerve. The function of the trigeminus, whether stimulated or interrupted, is that which supports, regulates, and governs the nutrition of the tissues to which its terminal branches are distributed." Essential, therefore, to a perfect dental development is a well-balanced physical and nervous system without hereditary taint.

In the correction of irregularities in the position of the teeth appliances as varied in construction as are the malpositions may be used; but in all cases the first and most important object to be secured is a fixed point from which the force is to be exerted. This is to be obtained by plates of metal or hard rubber firmly attached to the teeth in position; with these a force either direct and positive or gradual and continuous is applied to the mal-placed teeth to pull or push them into the position they should occupy. In the application of force two systems are in vogue, which may be designated by the terms "positive" and "gradual." In the former a nut or screw is turned; the force is direct and complete for the time; the tooth is moved and held at rest for a period of twenty-four or forty-eight hours, when another turn of the nut brings the tooth nearer the desired position; and the process is thus continued until the tooth occupies its place in the arch. In the gradual system elastic ligatures and wires, in combination with springing- and section-plates, are used; the force is constant from the time of its application until the appliance is removed for renewal, and so, by lengthening or shortening the springs and ligatures as the tooth has been pulled or pushed, the force is renewed, and increased if desired, until the deformity is corrected. When this is effected by either method, if the natural occlusion of the opposing tooth does not maintain the correction, it must be held in position by a fixed plate or ligature until the alveolar process around the root of the tooth has become adapted to its new position.

Preliminary to the effort for correcting the malposition of teeth some important considerations are to be noted, which must be influential in deciding for or against the operation—namely, age, health, endurance, and desire of the patient; the probable durability of the teeth and extent of the deformity; the resistance offered by the density of surrounding structures, and the crowding of the adjoining and occlusion of the opposing teeth; the tendency to return to their original position, and the possibility of keeping them, when corrected, in their normal place in the arch.

In the extraction of the natural teeth for the purpose of procuring room for correcting an irregularity the tooth selected should invariably be one of the bicuspids. These teeth are less durable than either of the six anterior, and can be removed with little detriment to either speech or expression of countenance.

Mechanical dentistry.—The present application of this term includes the construction and adaptation of substitutes for the natural teeth, also the manufacture of appliances for the correction of every class of oral deformity, whether it be fissure in the hard and soft palate, malplaced teeth, or fracture requiring surgico-mechanical treatment. The mechanical dentist should be able to construct every mechanical appliance for the restoration of function or the concealment of deformities. The materials which have been used for the construction of dental substitutes within the present century are bone, ivory, the teeth of sheep, human teeth, and porcelain. These have been placed upon bases of ivory, the metals silver, gold and platinum, porcelain, hard rubber, and celluloid; and retained in the mouth by ligatures and clasps attached to natural teeth *in situ* or by adaptation to the gums and hard palate, with or without an air-chamber in the plate. When the latter is supplied, it is called a suction- or atmospheric-pressure-plate. If both an upper and lower denture were constructed, they were held in position by means of springs uniting them upon the principle of a hinge. Where practicable, a single tooth is still attached to a natural root by means of a wood or metal pivot; and this has for many centuries been the custom.

Modifications and improvements in materials and methods have simplified and made more successful many operations. The introduction of porcelain and gold crowns has made valuable many roots that were previously considered worthless, and has also increased the durability of the operation of pivoting more than twofold. Formerly, pivoting was confined to single roots, and the preparation of the root and the crown for its attachment was all done while the patient remained in the chair; now, after the root is prepared, an impression is taken of it and the adjoining teeth in calcined plaster; from this a cast is made which accurately represents the condition of the mouth. In the laboratory with this cast the tooth and pivot are put into complete readiness for insertion, which is usually done in a comparatively short time, and quite as successfully and readily upon multiple as single roots.

The work of dental prosthesis should begin immediately upon the loss of the teeth, and be continued to the full accomplishment of its purpose. It is not enough to make what is known as a "temporary set," and allow it to be worn as long as it can be endured, but to make a denture that shall fulfil every requirement in form, color, and expression, conserving to the best possible limit the functions of mastication and articulate speech. The bases of hard rubber and celluloid, with the addition of continuous gum-work, afford the opportunity and make this aim incumbent upon every worker in prosthetic dentistry.

A tendency to decomposition is a very serious objection to teeth and plates constructed of animal substances, but notwithstanding this the teeth of such materials were used long after the manufacture of those made from porcelain. In fact, human teeth are still largely used, because of the inability in many special cases to find mineral substitutes which present anything but a conspicuously artificial appearance. In the manufacture of artificial dentures, whether partial or complete, of porcelain teeth upon metal or other basis, from the primary through all the progressive steps to their completion, the utmost care is essential. The accurate impression is only to be had in plaster of Paris; the cast from this must be a fac-simile of the mouth; the die and counter-die must be accurate representatives of that; and every subsequent act must be with a skilled hand and an artistic eye if the result is to be more than an apology for a substitute for the natural organs. As the essential steps for the construction of an ordinary denture upon a metal base have been described in the ENCYCLOPÆDIA BRITANNICA under DENTISTRY its repetition is unnecessary here.

Continuous gum.—This term is used to designate the fastening of porcelain teeth to plates by means of a fusible compound applied on the base-plate and around the teeth, moulded and colored to represent the natural gum, and finally fused, thus making an almost homogeneous mass of the teeth, gums, and plate. Though not wholly of American origin, it has only in this country been brought to a degree of perfection that places it without a rival in all of the essential characteristics which inhere in a faultless denture. In its construction the preliminary steps, such as taking the impression, making the cast, die and counter-die, and swedging the plate, are the same as in any ordinary metal-base plate. The plate itself must be of platinum, the teeth moulded single and without gums, and of a peculiar shape and adaptation to the process. In their selection and arrangement upon the plate is offered an opportunity for a display of the utmost artistic skill, that their color, shape, and position shall all harmonize with the complexion, conformation, and expression of the countenance. The "body," composed of finely-pulverized feldspar, quartz, and kaolin colored to a proper tint with titanium, now in a plastic condition, is built upon the plate and around the teeth to a degree of fulness corresponding with the absorption of the alveoli and gums; upon this, after biscuiting, is placed the gum-enamel, made largely of pulverized feldspar colored with gold oxide. Again placed in the furnace, it is fused at a heat of about 280° Fahr. To complete the work, it is necessary that the case be subjected two or three times to the furnace-heat, with an addition each time of the gum-enamel to the surface; and when finished it represents in adaptation, durability, and beauty as complete a denture as it is possible to construct.

Vulcanite.—The announcement in 1851 of Nelson Goodyear's process for making the hard-rubber compound subsequently termed "vulcanite" turned the attention of those interested in the manufacture of various small articles for use and ornament to the adaptation of this material, which was announced to be a substitute for horn, bone, and ivory, susceptible of being colored, and possessing the plasticity of gutta-percha, while it was exempt from the action of heat, cold, and acids. In 1855 the first patent was obtained for making a dental plate in hard rubber, in which the teeth were secured before the compound was vulcanized. This was the first published suggestion of this use of the new material, which contained not only the adaptation of vulcanite, but also the use of the mould as now employed.

Vulcanite is used in dentistry for making base-plates for artificial dentures, obturators, and inter-dental splints. In making a piece of rubber-work for the purpose of supplying a denture or concealing a defect, the greatest possible care is necessary in order to procure an accurate impression of the parts upon which the appliance is to rest. For this purpose plaster-of-Paris is preferable wherever it can be used. The impression-mould obtained by it must be so prepared that the model made from it can be readily separated. The cast is now trimmed, and the points corresponding with the soft spots in the mouth slightly scraped. The trial-plate is next to be made of paraffine and wax. The articulation is taken as for metal-work, using the trial-plate as a metallic one. There are teeth especially designed for rubber-work, arranged in sectional blocks or single, with porcelain gums, the joints being at convenient places to give proper shape and contour to the denture. Plain teeth without gums can be used where they rest upon the natural gums, or where the latter are concealed by the lips. These are preferable to teeth with artificial gums, where they can be used, because they are susceptible of a more natural and artistic arrangement. The denture in this condition should be tried in the mouth to ascertain its correctness, and if not satisfactory, the necessary alterations should be made. The set is now placed on the plaster cast, and the whole imbedded with much skill and care in the flask. The trial-plate of wax and paraffine is then to be removed and the rubber substituted. The sections of the flask are now brought together and gradually though firmly closed under a moderate heat, so that the rubber may be forced into the inequalities of the cast and teeth, and made to assume a fac-simile of the counterpart of the mouth. A minute description of this accurate and painstaking labor would require more space than can be appropriated to it in this article, but every progressive step must be made with precision and care in order to secure success.

The flask is now placed in the vulcanizer, with water just sufficient to cover it. The top of the vulcanizer is tightly screwed on, and the temperature gradually raised during a space of not less than a half hour. When the vulcanizing point, 320° Fahr., is reached, the flame is lowered and the heat held uniform for an hour to an hour and a quarter, varying with the quantity and quality of the rubber.

The vulcanizing completed, the temperature is gradually lowered until the flask can be removed and the sections carefully separated; the denture is then subjected to the finishing process, which is done with files, chisels, scrapers, and sand-paper; the polishing being finally completed with a felt wheel upon a lathe with pulverized pumice, chalk, etc.

Celluloid.—Celluloid consists of white linen fibre reduced to a pulp by the action of nitric and sulphuric acids, with the addition of about 10 per cent. of camphor, and 3 per cent. of coloring matter, with which lead or zinc is added in quantity sufficient to tone it down and produce a pinkish color, well representing the gums and palate. The acids and volatile constituents are driven off, and the mass condensed into "blanks" by pressure in metal moulds, under a continuous heat of 180° Fahr. for some days.

In the construction of dentures from this material the utmost care must be observed in all preliminary work, so that from the impression of the mouth shall be made plaster casts and block-tin dies, representing accurately not only the alveolar ridge, but the surrounding depression, as well as of the rugæ covering the anterior part of the palate. Upon this metal cast is constructed a trial-plate of sheet-lead or paraffine and wax, and upon this the teeth, having been selected of the appropriate color, size, and form, are arranged, with paraffine and wax built around them, to represent the loss of alveoli and gum, and fulfil in every particular the prosthetic requirements of the case, the correctness of the model having been ascertained by its adjustment to the mouth. The proper investment of the cast, trial-plate, and teeth with plaster in a flask for the purpose, is a matter of great care, that the whole shall be maintained in the desired position without possible danger of disarrangement. The opening of the flask, the removal of the trial-plate from the matrix, the substitution of the celluloid, making suitable provision for the escape of the surplus material, the necessity of freedom from moisture and grease while in a plastic condition, and for a gradual, firm, and constant pressure while under a proper degree of heat in the furnace, are all matters to be observed and executed with the utmost care and accuracy. The success or failure of celluloid as a base for artificial teeth depends wholly upon its proper manipulation. It is a fibrous substance, and every effort should be made to keep its fibres closed, and sufficient heat used in altering its form by the moulding process to make it thoroughly plastic and remove all tendency to return to a previous shape or condition. As the cast or model is of tin, and the matrix lined with the same, it is not necessary to make the plaster investment absolutely dry, but all excess of water must be driven off; and this will have been accomplished when the steam ceases to rise through the "steam-escape" of the heater. If the heater compressing the celluloid be a closed one, a heat of 320° Fahr. may be attained, but to do this with safety and freedom from the danger of combustion all air or oxygen must be completely cut off from the celluloid. If the machine be not air-tight, 250° Fahr. is the limit to which the heat can with safety be raised; with this lower temperature the material cannot be rendered quite so plastic. Pressure must in all cases be gradual, constant, and even; and if the dryness be maintained the celluloid will be increased in density, toughness, and durability.

The advantages claimed for celluloid by those most familiar with its use and working are its unlimited artistic possibilities, resemblance in color to the natural tissues, ready toleration by the mucous membrane and soft tissues, elasticity under strain, adaptability for partial or complete dentures, and the readiness with which it can be applied to the correction or concealment of all oral deformities. For information on celluloid and its working, we are indebted to Dr. E. M. Flagg, of New York.

Attaching artificial teeth to bases.—The method first practised in securing teeth to the base was by rivets through the tooth. This was first applied to human, animal, and ivory teeth, but subsequently to those of porcelain, single and in sections or blocks. The imperfection of this method was soon shown by the loosening of the teeth from friction of the plate and rivet; to correct this fault many ingenious devices were attempted, each one approaching the end desired, until after repeated experiments the result was a complete revolution in tooth fabrication, and the present plan of fixing a platinum pin in the substance before baking was evolved. (This plan is wholly of American origin.) To these pins were soldered pieces of "backing" or plate, and this was again soldered to the base-plate if of metal; if vulcanite or celluloid, the pins were bent, split, or headed, and served directly for the attachment without further preparation.

Securing dentures in the mouth.—In securing artificial dentures in the mouth the methods of ligatures, clasps, pivots, and springs have already been mentioned. In 1835 Dr. C. A. Harris, of Baltimore, designed what he called an "air-chamber," being simply a depression in the surface of the plate projecting downward from the palatine arch. This has been subjected to many modifications, in position in the plate, shape, manner of construction, etc.; but the principle involved has remained the same. Its application and utility have been universally recognized, and it forms one of the greatest advances in prosthetic dentistry. Until quite recently it was thought useful only for dentures in the upper jaw, but now its adaptation to lower plates, in a modified form, is spoken of with much confidence.

The attachment of one or more teeth to the natural organs without clasp or plate is a modern device, and has been very successfully practised. It consists in the selection of plain plate-teeth, with color, shape, and size adapted to the locality; a backing fitted to the pins and soldered, with a wire attached thereto, and extending beyond the lateral sides; the free ends of this line are adjusted to holes drilled in the palatine or proximal surfaces of the adjoining teeth, and there secured by packing gold-foil or amalgam around the wire and thoroughly filling the holes made for its retention. The advantage of this, where it can be done without injury to the natural teeth, is freedom from plate or other annoyances in the mouth, and its firmness and durability.

The mechanical devices and various labor-saving appliances and materials of American origin which have contributed to the advancement of dentistry are numerous and important. For impressions there are preparations of wax, plaster, gutta-percha, and several compositions. For casts and dies are flasks, antagonizing casts, and articulators; also furnaces and muffles, vulcanizers, celluloid apparatus, lathes, grinding-wheels, scrapers, files, disks, and burr-wheels, as well as an almost endless variety of wheels, cones, cylinders, and disks of felt and other substances, for polishing and finishing cases of every variety of shape and material. For use in the office, and to aid in the operative department, for drying the mouth and cavities and protecting the operation from moisture, are napkins, paper, saliva-pumps and ejectors, duct-compressors, tongue-holders, air-syringes, rubber tubes, and Barnum's rubber-dam, the latter one of the most valuable inventions given to the profession. Cutting and drilling instruments, almost unlimited in shape and design, including corundum-wheels and disks of numberless sizes and various thickness, with Green's, Morrison's, Beer's, Bonwill's, Elliott's, and S. S. White's engine; also water and electrical motors; Foote's, Taylor's, Hodge's, Salmon's, Snow and Lewis', Baxter's, Banister's, Green's, Gaylord's, Buckingham's, and Pomroy's automatic mallets; Bonwill's electric mallet; hand-mallets of wood, rubber, steel, lead, and ivory; operating-chairs, possessing every conceivable movement, with the possibility of adaptation to patients of any size and in any position.

The operative and mechanical departments of dentistry, though still regarded by the majority of practitioners as industries not sufficiently dissimilar in their processes to prevent the pursuit of both by the same person, must, as competition necessitates and stimulates proficiency, gradually gravitate into the hands of artisans practising exclusively one or the other as a specialty. The laboratory-work essential to the construction of artificial dentures necessarily interferes with that delicacy of touch which is so indispensable to the skilful treatment of the natural teeth; and in like manner do the repeated and exacting demands of an operative practice intrude upon the work in the laboratory.

Porcelain teeth.—As an outgrowth from mechanical dentistry a new industry has arisen in the manufacture of porcelain teeth. These, in size, shape, and color, so nearly resemble the natural ones that when selected and arranged with artistic skill they are not easily detected. Though of French origin, their perfection is due entirely to the efforts of the American manufacturer. To Dr. A. A. Planton and Mr. Charles W. Peale, of Philadelphia, must be awarded the credit of manufacturing, in 1819 and 1820, the first porcelain teeth made in this country; but Samuel W. Stockton, of Philadelphia, and James Alcock, of New York, in 1835 began their production upon a more extended scale and for the purpose of supplying the profession at large, and thus initiated an industry which has attained remarkable proportions. The present degree of proficiency in moulding and enamelling the teeth was not attained until some years later, nor was the color so lifelike or the shades so varied. These improvements in the fabrication of porcelain teeth, which have so admirably displayed the possibilities of the manufacturer, in the transparency of the tooth, the granulated appearance and flesh-like tint of the gum, and the almost unlimited variety of shades, were due to the persistent and untiring efforts of Dr. Elias Wildman, of Philadelphia, who began his experiments in 1837. The employment of purple of Cassius, or oxide of gold, now exclusively used in the production of gum-color, was also attained wholly through his labors. In 1844 Samuel S. White, a nephew of Samuel W. Stockton, began the production of these teeth in Philadelphia; and this was the initiatory step in an enterprise which has since become the largest of its kind in the world. Numerous improvements are accredited to Mr. White, the most important of which are various modifications in the forms of the platinum pins and a studied effort to recognize and imitate the anatomical and physiological differences in natural teeth. An artificial tooth must possess certain characteristics respecting size, shape, and color; it must on its external surface resemble the external covering of the natural tooth; it must possess toughness, which permits the use of the hammer in riveting without fracture and the use of the blowpipe in soldering without liability to crack. If the tooth were a homogeneous mass, vitrification necessary to imitate the enamel surface would render it brittle. A nice adjustment of materials is necessary that beauty shall not be sacrificed to strength. The clear cutting edge of enamel projecting over the point, with the yellow or brown at the base, must be so nicely blended with the colors of the body of the tooth that the line of union cannot be determined. These and many other indispensable results have been secured by patient research, experiment, and artistic skill.

The principal materials entering into the composition of mineral teeth are feldspar, silex, kaolin, with various fluxes, characterized as glasses. The general tone or tint of these materials is white or light yellow, so that coloring forms an important adjunct in the process. The substances used are titanium for yellow, platinum sponge for gray, oxide of cobalt for bright blue, and gold oxide for red. These, with their varying combinations, are used to color the body, point, and surface enamels. There are over forty shades in the bodies used, and a greater number in the point and outside enamels. Starting with the lightest shade of body, known as "a," forty different grades may be produced by using a different point-enamel, and on each of these again a modified effect by the employment of surface enamels; so that with a single body of any given color may be produced 64,000 modifications; and as this is only one of the forty different bodies, a mathematical effort would determine the number of shades of which they are capable. For the production of these colors a muffle glowing with an incandescent heat is essential.

An establishment in Philadelphia produces over 400,000 teeth per month, or little less than 5,000,000 per year—about one-half of the whole number used in the world.

Origin of dentistry in the United States.—From the most reliable information attainable, we learn that Mr. John Woofendale, of England, was the first dentist in the United States. He practised in New York and Philadelphia from 1766 to 1768, at which time he returned to England. His successor was Mr. Joseph Le Maire, of France, who came with the French army during the period of the Revolutionary struggle; he was soon followed by one Whitelock in 1784. Mr. Isaac Greenwood was the first dentist established in Boston, and his son, John Greenwood, who was the first native American dentist, commenced practice in New York in 1788, and soon after constructed for Gen. Washington an entire denture, which for neatness of execution was said to have been unequalled. The teeth were carved from ivory, and secured in the mouth with spiral springs. From this time until 1820 accessions from Europe, and adoption of the profession by native Americans, increased the number of practitioners in the United States to more than 100. In the next decade they numbered 300, and in ten years more they exceeded 1200. The census of 1860 gave the United States 5000; in 1873 there were 10,000; and in 1882 not less than 15,000.

With this great increase in the number of practitioners the progress of dentistry as a science has been conspicuous. From comparatively elementary operations it has extended to a thorough and scientific treatment of the oral cavity. The desire on the part of the more liberally educated men in the profession that their specialty should attain and maintain a commanding position has created an interest in the education of students, and a corresponding desire for a more extended and liberal curriculum in the colleges. There are also those who believe that a thorough medical education, preparatory to studying the manipulative and artistic branch of dentistry, would make more efficient and useful practitioners, enabling the operator to treat an oral disease of any complexity without danger of meeting with disaster from the absence of surgical knowledge and skill; in fact, that dentistry should be practised as a specialty of medicine, the practitioner understanding and fully appreciating the influence morbific systemic conditions exert upon the teeth, and to what extent certain lesions of the mouth and teeth exalt or modify constitutional disturbances.

The progress so readily recognized has been stimulated not a little by the publication of journals, formetion of societies and associations, and the organization of colleges. Dental legislation, the establishment of State boards of examiners, and the organization of a national association of college faculties will also doubtless exert an influence in behalf of dental education.

Dental journals.—An important event in the history of dental surgery in the United States was the establishment of the *American Journal and Library of Dental Science* in Baltimore in 1839. Members of the profession widely separated, and almost wholly unknown to each other, found through this journal a medium of communication. Following its publication, and up to the present time, there have been about forty periodicals established ostensibly in the interests of dentistry. While many of these had an ephemeral existence, others have rendered a worthy service to the profession. Among the latter are the *Dental Cosmos*, the *Dental Register of the West*, *Missouri Dental Journal*, and others in New England and the South.

Dental societies.—Little more than forty years ago no organization of dentists had been effected; now every State has its State Dental Society and many minor organizations within its limits, while of national organizations there are three; the American Dental Association, being a delegated body, is the most important.

Dental colleges.—The origin of institutions for teaching dentistry was the result of the necessity for a radical change in the method of imparting instruction. The schools now granting dental degrees number twenty; the older and more important ones are the Baltimore College of Dental Surgery, chartered in 1839; the Ohio Dental College, chartered in 1845; the Philadelphia (afterwards the Pennsylvania) College of Dental Surgery, chartered in 1850; the Philadelphia Dental College in 1863; and the New York College of Dentistry in 1865. (C. N. P.)

DENVER, the capital of the State of Colorado and county-seat of Arapahoe co., is situated on the South Platte River, 15 miles E. of the foot of the Rocky Mountains, 39° 47′ N. lat. and 105° W. long. It is the metropolis of a very large region of country, made productive since 1860 by the discovery of precious metals and by the use of the prairie ranges for the herding of cattle. In 1858 a settlement called Aurania was made on the west side of Cherry Creek, Colorado being then a county of Kansas Territory. The following year Denver (named after Gen. James W. Denver, then governor of Kansas Territory) was laid out on the east side of the creek, and shortly after the two settlements were united. During the early years of Colorado Territory the seat of government was changed several times, but Denver was finally decided upon. In 1876, when the Territory was admitted into the Union, Denver was made the temporary capital; and in election of November, 1881, the city was chosen as the permanent seat of government. In the meantime Denver had shown unprecedented growth of population. In 1860 the region of which the city has become the trade centre was marked on the map as the Great American Desert, Denver being then but a frontier camp. In 1870 the population, by census, was 4800. During the decade from 1870 to 1880 the resources of the Territory developed rapidly, and a good agricultural product was added to the yield of mineral and live-stock. In 1877 the valuable deposits of mineral at Leadville were discovered, and Denver, as the commercial centre whence the mountain camps drew their supplies, grew from a frontier town into a city; so that,

in 1880, the census showed a population of 35,630. Estimating by the increased business, school population, and other elements, the population was placed in 1884 at 60,000. The growth of the city has been assisted by judicious exhibitions of the products of the State, the first of importance being at the World's Exposition at Paris in 1871. This was followed by a tasteful and attractive display at the Centennial Exhibition at Philadelphia in 1876. Finally a highly successful exhibition was held in Denver itself in 1882, which was attended by thousands of visitors from all parts of the United States, and even from foreign countries.

Denver to-day presents the appearance of a well-established, prosperous city. The site is nearly level, sloping slightly towards the Rocky Mountains, whose snow-clad peaks are in full view on the west. By means of irrigating ditches along the streets a fine growth of shade-trees has been secured, which, in summer, give the city a park-like appearance. The elevation of 5370 feet (over one mile above sea-level) makes the atmosphere rare, dry, and clear, there being on an average less than six days each year without sunshine. The large buildings of the city are of recent construction, the finest having been erected since 1880. The Tabor Grand Opera-House, one of the finest theatres in the United States, was built in 1881, by H. A. W. Tabor, who became a millionaire through successful mining. The Tabor Block was also built by him. Of the large hotels, the Windsor was constructed by the Denver Mansion company (limited), composed of English capitalists, who have invested very largely in land, buildings, and irrigating ditches. These buildings, and other large blocks, were erected during the two years from 1880 to 1882, and these years are notable in the city's history because of incessant building operations, winter as well as summer.

The public buildings of Denver were not begun until 1882. The court-house, built of Colorado stone, was completed in January, 1883. The city hall, also of Colorado stone, was completed the same year. A State capitol, on ground donated to the State, has been begun, as also the buildings of the National Government, for which Congress appropriated $300,000. A branch mint of the United States is located here, which in 1883 manufactured gold bars valued at $1,374,685.

Denver has a Chamber of Commerce, composed of merchants, manufacturers, mining-stock-brokers, and other business men. Its transactions for 1883 exceeded $31,000,000, showing an increase of $8,000,000 in two years. There are 6 national banks, and several private banks. The interests of the city have been mainly commercial, as this is the trading centre for the State and adjacent regions. In 1882 Denver was made by Congress a port of delivery for foreign goods, and already it has considerable direct importation. Manufactures have also been established, and in 1883 employed 5091 hands. The value of their products was $10,472,200, while the value of the plants was $4,502,600. There are two smelting-establishments, iron-works, agricultural-implement-factories, gunpowder-works, flour-mills, and breweries, while other works for the manufacture of cement, glass, chemicals—all depending on easily available resources—are being introduced. The city is the junction of a number of important systems of railway. Of these four go to the East—the Union Pacific, to Omaha; the Burlington and Missouri River, to Omaha and Chicago; the Kansas Pacific, to Kansas City; the Atchison, Topeka, and Santa Fé, via Pueblo, over the Denver and Rio Grande and the Denver and New Orleans to Kansas City. Other broad-gauge lines are the Denver Pacific and the Colorado Central to Cheyenne, and the Denver and Boulder Valley to Boulder. By way of Cheyenne Denver has lines of broad-gauge railways through the North-west. To the mountains there are three narrow-gauge roads—the Denver and Rio Grande, the South Park, and the narrow-gauge branch of the Colorado Central. Of the railways now in course of construction the most important is the Denver and New Orleans, which, already completed to Colorado Springs and Pueblo, is to run into New Mexico and Texas, where, on the Canadian river, it will join the Fort Worth and Denver City, thus becoming a through line to the cotton country and to the Gulf, giving Denver direct access to Southern products, and bringing the city a thousand miles nearer to tidewater. The Denver City Railway has 15 miles of track, 210 horses, and 38 cars in use now, and constantly increasing to meet the demand of travel.

The educational facilities of Denver are ample. There are 16 public schools, including a high-school. The value of public school property is $547,328, with a bonded indebtedness of $228,000. The seating capacity is 5607; enrolment of pupils, 6601; number of teachers, 110; average yearly cost of tuition, $2.09. The University of Denver, having a complete faculty and a medical department, is under Methodist auspices; Jarvis Hall and Wolfe Hall are Episcopal academies; Brinker Institute is an independent academy; and St. Mary's is Roman Catholic. Denver is the residence of three bishops, of the Roman Catholic, Protestant Episcopal, and Methodist Episcopal churches respectively. There are more than 30 churches, all the leading denominations being represented, and many of them having fine structures. There are 5 daily and 15 weekly newspapers.

Denver occupies a surface of about four miles square, and including its suburbs is six miles square. The area within corporate limits is 13½ square miles. The rapidity of its growth is shown by the following statement of the value of the public and private buildings erected each year since 1878:

Cost of buildings erected in	1879	. . . .	$2,068,894
"	"	1880	. . . .	3,917,362
"	"	1881	. . . .	4,739,000
"	"	1882	. . . .	4,039,554
"	"	1883	. . . .	2,257,695
Total cost of buildings		. . . .	$16,662,505

The assessed valuation of taxable property in 1883 was $30,597,855. The death-rate during 1883 was 17.98. This included consumptives who came in the last stages of that disease. Deducting these, the rate was 15.76. The sewers of Denver are constructed on the separate system, with glazed stoneware pipe, deep enough to drain cellars, carefully ventilated, and supplied with flushing apparatus. The city has gas and water-works. In 1883 pure water was obtained here from an artesian well, and there are now 65 such wells in various parts of the city, furnishing an abundant supply. The country near the city has been made very productive by a canal, constructed with English capital, extending a distance of over a hundred miles, and irrigating a vast tract of prairie adjacent to the city limits. The Denver City ditch is also an extensive irrigating canal, the water for these canals, as well as for the water-works supply, being drawn from the Platte river.

DE PEYSTER. Members of this family have been prominent in New York City since 1640. JOHANNES DE PEYSTER, the first of the name in America, was a member of a Huguenot family, and came from Holland to New Amsterdam about 1640. He held several city offices from 1655 to 1677 under both Dutch and English rule, and acquired great wealth. His eldest son, Abraham (1657–1728), was mayor of New York City and judge of the supreme court of the province. In 1700 he became president of the council and acting governor of the colony, and in 1706 treasurer of New York and New Jersey, which position he held till his death, in 1721. The eldest son, Abraham II., noted for his wealth, benevolence, and personal influence, succeeded him as treasurer, and retained the position till his death, in 1767. When the Revolutionary War broke out the family adhered to the king's cause, and three grandsons of Abraham II. became officers in the loyal or Tory regiments. Frederick, the youngest of these, was a captain at the age of eighteen, and was wounded in 1780 in the campaign in the Carolinas. His son, Frederick II. (1796–1882), graduated at Columbia College, studied law, and was for many years a master in chancery. He was also in early life active in connection with the State militia, and was an aide to Gov. De Witt Clinton. In later life he was a member and officer of many charitable, religious, and benevolent societies. For sixty years he was prominently connected with the New York Historical Society, and published several addresses on historical and antiquarian subjects. His son, JOHN WATTS DE PEYSTER, LL.D., was born at New York, March 9, 1821. In 1851 he visited Europe and investigated the military systems of the Continent. He embodied in several reports many valuable suggestions, which resulted in improvements of the militia system of the State of New York and in the establishment of the paid fire department of the city of New York. He has devoted much attention to the early history of the Dutch in America, and is one of the best military writers in this country. He published in 1855 a *Life of the Swedish Field-marshal Torstensen*, for which he received three medals from the king of Sweden. He has also published *The Dutch at the North Pole and the Dutch in Maine* (1857), *Early Settlement of Acadia by the Dutch* (1858), *The Dutch Battle of the Baltic* (1858), *History of Carausius* (1858), *Ancient, Mediæval, and Modern Netherlands* (1859), *Life of Lieutenant-General Menno, Baron Cohorn* (1860), *Winter Campaigns the Test of Generalship* (1862), *Practical Strategy* (1863), *Secession in Switzerland and the United States Compared* (1864), *Decisive Conflicts of the Late Civil War* (1868), *The History of the Third Corps, Army of the Potomac* (1868), *Local Memorials relating to the De Peyster and Watts Families* (1881), *Mary, Queen of Scots, a Study* (1882). Besides these separate publications, Gen. De Peyster has contributed frequently to military and other periodicals, and was editor of the *Ficlaireur* (1854–58). He is noted for his thoroughness of research in the subjects he has chosen, his sound judgment, and extensive knowledge of military affairs. His three sons—J. Watts, Jr., Frederic, Jr., and Johnston Livingston—were officers in the Union army during the Civil War, and the youngest, then a lieutenant on Gen. Weitzel's staff, received the brevet of lieutenant-colonel for hoisting the first United States flag over Richmond upon its evacuation by the Confederate troops, April 3, 1865.

DEPPING, GEORGES BERNARD (1784–1853), a French geographer and historian, was born at Münster, in Westphalia, May 11, 1784. In 1803 he removed to Paris, and was soon busily employed in teaching German and writing for the press. In 1827 he was naturalized as a French citizen. He died at Paris, Sept. 6, 1853. His earliest work of importance was *Histoire générale de l' Espagne* (2 vols., 1811). About the same time he made a collection of the best old Spanish romances. Afterwards he prepared some works for the young, designed to impart geographical knowledge in a pleasant guise. The success of these led to his preparing more ambitious descriptions of Switzerland, Greece, France, and England, which passed through several editions and were translated into other languages. Having formed acquaintance with Baggesen and Oehlenschläger, he began to study the history of the north of Europe, and some works which were the fruits of this study were crowned by the academy. His principal works are *Histoire des expéditions maritimes des Normands et 'eur établissement en France* (1826; 2d ed. 1844); *Histoire du commerce entre l' Europe et le Levant* (2 vols., 1830); *Les Juifs dans le moyen-âge* (1834); *Histoire de la Normandie* from 1066 to 1204 (2 vols., 1835). He also edited *Reglements sur les arts et métiers de Paris au treizième siècle* (1837), and *Correspondance administrative sous le règne de Louis XIV.* (4 vols., 1850–55). He published in German an autobiographic sketch under the title, *Erinnerungen aus dem Leben eines Deutschen in Paris* (Leipsic, 1832), and some minor historical works.

DERBY, EDWARD HENRY SMITH STANLEY, 15TH EARL OF, an English statesman, son of the 14th Earl of Derby, was born at Knowsley Park, in Lancashire, July 21, 1826. His mother was Emma Caroline, a daughter of Edward Bootle-Wilbraham, the first Lord Skelmersdale. He was educated at Rugby and graduated in 1848 from Trinity College, Cambridge, with high honors in classics. From his father, "the Rupert of debate" and the most finished parliamentary orator of his time, he inherited what may be called the profession of politics. In 1848 he failed of an election as representative for Lancashire; but during his absence (1848–50) on a tour in America he was returned to Parliament for Lynn-Regis, which borough he represented without a break for nineteen years, until in 1869 his father died, and the son (previously known as Lord Stanley) succeeded to the earldom. He at once took a marked position as one of the strongest men among the moderate conservatives of the House of Commons. While on a journey in India, in 1852, he was made under secretary of state for foreign affairs in his father's administration, and in 1853 brought forward a plan for reform in Indian affairs, substantially the same that was adopted in 1858. In 1855 he declined a cabinet office under Palmerston, but in 1858 entered his father's second administration as colonial secretary, and soon after was made president of the board of control and commissioner for India. He was secretary of state for India, 1858–59, and managed the transfer of British India from the East India Company's control to the crown officers. As secretary of state for foreign affairs (1866–68 and 1874–78) he won the reputation of a safe and industrious man, without any of his father's brilliancy and dash, but with admirable capacity for the details of that difficult position. Derby's mind is of the judicial quality, with no partisan bias, with no fire, with no faculty for constructive statesmanship. He is a pre-eminently plain and safe man, of phlegmatic and slow temperament, almost a non-combatant in Parliament—in short, the very reverse of what his brilliant father was. His retirement in 1878 from Beaconsfield's cabinet was caused by differences with his fellow-ministers regarding the occupation of Cyprus. In 1870 he married the Lady Mary, dowager-marchioness of Salisbury, and daughter of the fifth Earl De La Warr. While in the lower house he served on many important commissions. In 1874 he was chosen Lord-Rector of the Edinburgh University. In 1879 he announced the severance of his connection with the Conservative party. He afterwards became colonial secretary under Mr. Gladstone.

DERBY, a family prominent in the commercial affairs of Massachusetts for three generations.

DERBY, ELIAS HASKET, I. (1739–1799), a merchant of Salem, Mass., was born there Aug. 16, 1739. He was descended from Roger Derby (1643–1698), who was born at Topsham, England, and, being a Friend, emigrated to America to enjoy religious freedom. Capt. Richard (1712–1783), grandson of Roger, was a successful merchant, a member of the general court of Massachusetts and of the council from 1774 to 1777. Elias, the second son of Capt. Richard, in early life kept his father's accounts and conducted correspondence. At the commencement of the Revolution he had several vessels engaged in the West India trade. As the war destroyed American commerce, he united with his townsmen in fitting out privateers to prey upon British traders. No less than 158 were sent out, mounting more than 2000 cannon, and 445 vessels were captured from the enemy. The rate of insurance on English vessels rose to 23 per cent., and the British were compelled to employ their navy in convoying merchant-vessels. Perceiving the necessity of attaining the utmost speed, Mr. Derby studied naval architecture, and suggested many improvements in the models. His vessels were superior in size and speed to any previously launched in America. In 1775 his younger brother, John, by the swiftness of his ship carried to England the first news of the battle of Lexington, and at the close of the war brought home from France the first news of peace. Just after the battle of Lexington, and at other critical times in the Revolutionary War, Elias showed his patriotism by advancing to the Government large supplies. After the war, returning to peaceful pursuits, Elias showed spirit in opening up new channels for American commerce. In June, 1784, he despatched a vessel to St. Petersburg, and in November another to the Cape of Good Hope. Capt. Ingersoll, in command of the latter, refused to take a cargo of slaves from the Guinea coast, although the slave-trade was then allowed by law, but sailed in ballast to the West Indies. In Dec., 1785, Mr. Derby sent the first vessel from New England to India and China. In 1790, when his vessels brought 700,000 pounds of tea to America, just after a heavy duty had been imposed, he protested against being compelled to pay immediately, and was allowed time. In his correspondence with the Government he suggested the great importance of a system of drawbacks to a commercial people. The commerce of Salem, which had remained stationary from 1771 to 1791, greatly revived under the stimulus of the India trade, and in the last fourteen years of Mr. Derby's life his vessels numbered 37, making in that time 125 voyages, including 45 to the East Indies. Of these vessels but one was lost, and his good fortune may be partly attributed to his prudent order that none of his ships should come on the New England coast between November and March. In 1798 he liberally helped the Government in forming a navy. He died at Salem, Mass., Sept. 8, 1799.

DERBY, ELIAS HASKET, II. (1766–1826), son of the preceding, a merchant of Salem, Mass., was born there Jan. 10, 1766. At the close of the Revolutionary War he left college, visited England and France, and, learning something of the East India trade, induced his father to embark in it, and in 1785 went himself to the Isle of France, where he spent a year; then went to India, where he remained for three years. Returning in 1789, he brought the first cargo of Bombay cotton to America. He then devoted himself to commercial pursuits until the war of 1812, when he set up the first broadcloth loom in Massachusetts. In furtherance of the woollen manufacture he gathered a flock of 1100 merino sheep in Spain, and landed two-thirds of them in New York. A few merinos had been brought to the United States in 1802 by Gen. David Humphreys, American minister to Spain, but the practical introduction belongs to Mr. Derby. He was for several years a brigadier-general in the State militia, and was generally referred to by this title. He died at Londonderry, N. H., Sept. 16, 1826.

DERBY, ELIAS HASKET, III. (1803–1880), an American lawyer and author, was born at Salem, Mass., Sept. 24, 1803. He was a son of Gen. E. H. Derby, and graduated at Harvard College in 1824. Having studied law with Daniel Webster, he was admitted to the bar in 1827. He practised in Boston, and became eminent in his profession, especially in railroad cases. He was active in promoting the commercial interests of Boston, and was president of the Old Colony Railroad. During the Civil War he labored zealously to secure the construction of iron-clad vessels. He contributed frequently to the newspapers of Boston under the signature of "Massachusetts," treating of both national and local topics. He died at Boston, March 31, 1880. He published several articles in the *Atlantic Monthly*, *Edinburgh Review*, and other periodicals. He was also the author of *Two Months Abroad* (1844), *The Catholic*, *The Overland Route to the Pacific*, and many reports on *The Fisheries*, *The British Provinces*, and other subjects.

DERBY, GEORGE H. (1824–1861), an American soldier and humorist, was born in Norfolk co., Mass., in 1824. He was a descendant of Elias H. Derby, I., merchant of Salem. He graduated at West Point in 1846, and served in the Mexican War, being severely wounded at Cerro Gordo. He was afterwards employed in various surveys, explorations, and public works. While stationed in California he wrote a number of humorous sketches under the name of "John Phoenix," which obtained great popularity and led to many imitations. His sketches were collected and published in 1860 under the title *Phoenixiana*. In 1859, while employed by the Government in erecting lighthouses on the coast of Florida, he was sunstruck. A softening of the brain ensued, and he died insane at New York, May 15, 1861. After his death several of his sketches were published as *The Squibob Papers* (1861).

DESCANT, IN MUSIC. Descant was an early attempt to add to some existing melody a second part or subsidiary melody, to be sung simultaneously. The art of descant came into existence about the year 1095, or later, and gradually led to that of counterpoint in many parts, and in many forms. It is said that two musicians, amusing themselves by singing against one another, found that occasionally good effects resulted, and that on singing at the same time a slow church tune and a ribald song the contrasted motions and the various intervals gave a singular sort of pleasure alternating with displeasure, which was of course due to the incidental consonances and dissonances that resulted. They found at last certain tunes sung in certain ways united better than others and formed agreeable duets. One can understand that attempts would be made to reduce such combinations to writing, to form a basis for future experiments, or to preserve them for future use. But the difficulty of writing such singular combinations of melodies must have been exceedingly great, for the notation was not so perfect as it is now; the science of harmony had not progressed beyond the use of octaves, fifths, and fourths (the most perfect concords), and, as the tunes were often greatly dissimilar, it was necessary to make elaborate calculations respecting speed and rhythm, in order that the melodies might be made to move together as required. That such extremely difficult operations were attempted at this early period may be seen by consulting the complex diagram prepared by Thomas Morley in his *Plaine and Easie Introduction to Practical Musicke* (London, 1597). These combinations of rhythms were enormously difficult to express in writing, and are almost incapable of performance by executants of the present day.

The modern art of music appears as if born of two opposite principles. First, of harmony, which began with using the most perfect intervals, as regards consonance, and caused the added part to conform in its motions to the principal part (in a way similar to that adopted by certain singers now, who "make a second," by singing uniformly a third or a sixth below the principal tune). The early attempts of harmonists were variously called *diaphonia*, *cantilena*, or *organum*. The opposing principle was that of independent song, with its rhythm and series of sounds preserved intact, whatever were the motions of the associated melody. By degrees more dissonant intervals were introduced into harmony, and also contrary motion, which was no doubt due to the good effect noticeable in descants; and in descants the proportions of notes, as regards length, were simplified into halves, quarters, eighths, etc., in simple geometrical proportions, as they are at the present day. Although in modern music two or three rhythmic formations are simultaneously performed, these are so planned that the principal accents of each are synchronous. In the ball-room scene in Mozart's *Don Giovanni* one orchestra plays a Minuet in three-quarter time, a second plays a Gavotte in two-quarter time, and a third a Valse in three-eighth time, to provide music for the three sets of dancers; but the conductor has no difficulty in making the required beats with one baton, since the different speeds are regulated in such a way that the principal accents coalesce.

Descant was originally an extemporaneous performance, with or without words, which employed "divisions," like those found in Händel's choruses, where sixty or more notes are sung to one syllable. But, although for the most part descant was unwritten, many rules had to be obeyed. The principal melody of the music was originally sung by men in the church. Later, the "plain song" was given to the bass part, and was then called "ground." Favorite "grounds" were called after the writers' names, as "Purcell's Ground," "Farinelli's Ground," etc. When instruments were used, a second copy of the ground was given to a viol player, who, at each repetition of its few simple notes, made different extemporaneous variations upon it. Thus a certain "unity and variety" was secured for instrumental music. Certain passages from Shakespeare's plays, which refer to such operations, not only illustrate them, but also Shakespeare's meaning, singularly well:—

"Ah! what a world of *descant* makes my soul
Upon this voluntary *ground* of love."

"For *burden-wise*, I'll hum on Tarquin still,
While thou on Tereus *descantest* better still."

"And stand between two churchmen, good my lord;
For on that *ground* I'll make a holy *descant*."

(S. A. P.)

DESERTION. The act of abandoning, or forsaking, in a general sense. Legally, it is an offence consisting in the abandonment of the public service in the army or navy without permission; or, the act of a husband or wife in leaving his or her consort with the deliberate intention of causing a permanent separation, and without just cause.

1. *As a military or naval offence.*—By act of Congress, dated March 16, 1802, it is enacted that if any non-commissioned officer, musician, or private shall desert the service of the United States, he shall, in addition to the penalties prescribed in the articles of war, be liable to serve for such period as shall, with the time he may have served before his desertion, amount to the full term of his enlistment; and by the articles of war it is provided that desertion shall be punished at the discretion of a court-martial. The provision in the rules for government of the navy are substantially the same, and include those who solicit others to desert as well as actual deserters. The time after which absence becomes desertion is considered as being ten days, before the expiration of which the absentee is considered as a straggler and may return without penalty, unless wrongful intention be proved.

2. *As an offence against the marital relation*, desertion in most States constitutes a ground of divorce, though they all differ as to the period of time which must elapse before the action may be brought by the party deserted. For the varieties of State law on this subject, see DIVORCE.

A seaman who, after engaging for a voyage, deserts before its completion, is liable for damages, according to the nature of his shipping articles, and also forfeits his wages previously earned, unless he be able to prove cruel and inhuman treatment on the part of the captain. 2 Rob. Adm. R. 232.

DESIGN, SCHOOLS OF. The development of Schools of Design in England, which followed the International Exhibition of 1851, when English manufacturers first became convinced that in the arts of industrial design they had fallen behind their neighbors on the Continent, was not without its effect in the United States, in stimulating the study of drawing in its relation to industries. Prior to that time nearly all of the schools where drawing was taught gave attention chiefly to the Fine or pictorial arts; and in colleges, seminaries, and other private schools, drawing was at best an elective study, the art being treated as an accomplishment only, and one of little practical value. The few schools of design, proper, were small in size, and, being poorly supported, accomplished very little in the way of educating either industrial draughtsmen and designers or teachers of the art. In 1870 a movement was made in Massachusetts to have drawing taught in the public schools, not as an accomplishment, but with direct relation to its usefulness to workmen in various trades and professions. The fruits of that movement were just beginning to be made known when the Centennial Exhibition was opened at Philadelphia in 1876. Americans then had brought home to them the lesson learned by England in 1851, that a manufacturing nation, to keep its place in competition with others, or to advance in rank, must provide education in drawing for its workmen. There are two branches of the art of design—one dealing chiefly with form as limited by mechanical necessities and utility, the other chiefly with ornamentation and surface decoration. The one may be wholly or in greater part mechanical, the other is for the greater part a free-hand accomplishment. Although there were few industrial drawing-schools or schools of design in the United States prior to 1876, some instruction was afforded by various schools in the elements of these two branches of design. Thus, in mechanics' institutes, geometry and mechanical and architectural drawing were taught, generally to night classes, and very imperfectly; and in the academies of the fine arts in the larger cities opportunities were afforded the students for self-instruction in free-hand drawing, though not with the definite purpose of making them industrial draughtsmen. Design is so closely related to invention that it would scarcely have been possible for Americans to have won the distinction they have attained as inventors if they had not also acquired some skill as designers. The Centennial Exhibition showed that they had in fact developed a high degree of skill in mechanical drawing and in that branch of design which treats chiefly of form as related to the uses to which it is to be put. The necessities of the growing nation, sparsely settled over a broad expanse of territory, impelled the construction of tools combining lightness, strength, and adaptability, qualities of the highest value in industrial design. Thus, without any attempt being made by mechanics to give an art value as such to their productions, the makers of tools and machinery, by giving close attention to the mechanical requirements they had to meet, fulfilled a primary law of industrial design, and produced forms that compared favorably, from an art point of view, with similar productions from nations where academic art education had been much more highly developed than in the United States. But the moment one turned from exhibits of tools and machinery to exhibits where skill in free-hand design, color combination, and ornamentation is of more importance than accuracy in instrumental drawing, it was seen that the United States was far behind England and France and Germany, and indeed most of the smaller nations of Europe, in this branch of the art of design. In textile fabrics of all kinds, paper-hangings, oil-cloths, pottery, glass, and merely ornamental metal work, the American products were generally either mere imitations or very inferior attempts at original design. It was this discovery that greatly stimulated the organization of schools of design in manufacturing cities, and the enlargement and more liberal endowment of those already in existence, as well as the founding of museums of industrial art, where artisans might see the best results of human handicraft.

Although there is a broad line of distinction between pictorial art and industrial art, even where the former is used for surface ornamentation, it is not easy to separate the art-schools of the country into two classes, one training artists only, and the other artisans and designers. The training afforded by the higher art schools fits the pupils to become designers by a little special study, and the elementary training in all the schools is, or should be, the same. It is necessary, therefore, in describing the schools of design of the United States, to mention institutions which do not aim to produce industrial draughtsmen and designers, but have been established primarily for the education of artists. The earliest institutions of this kind in the country were the Pennsylvania Academy of the Fine Arts, Philadelphia (1806); the Public Library and Department of Fine Arts, Boston (1807); the New York Academy of Fine Arts (1808); and the National Academy of Design, New York (1820). These institutions were established with the sole purpose of educating public taste by art exhibitions, and to afford pupils opportunities to practise drawing from the cast and from life. Instruction, as carried on in modern art schools, was not attempted. In 1824 the Franklin Institute of Philadelphia was established. It was a mechanics' institute, and one of its purposes was the maintenance of schools for the education of young men in mechanical and architectural drawing. It was the earliest of a number of mechanics' institutes established in the larger cities with similar aims and having similar schools. The instruction was generally given to night classes, and was chiefly elementary. But schools of this kind represented for nearly fifty years almost the only means afforded in the United States for education in industrial drawing. The earliest institution established for the express purpose of teaching the arts of design was the Philadelphia School of Design for Women (1847). It was soon followed by the Schools of Art and Design of the Maryland Institute (1848). Their history apparently shows that the manufactures of the country were not at that time, nor for some years afterwards, far enough advanced to require such schools. They struggled along, accomplishing but little until recent years, when both schools were reorganized and shared with newer institutions the impulse given to industrial training by experiments in Massachusetts, and by the lessons of the Centennial Exhibition. It will be observed that up to this time Philadelphia had taken the lead in the three branches of art education—the fine arts, instrumental drawing, and designing. Within the last ten years Boston and Massachusetts have become more prominent in this respect, and also that the schools of Philadelphia have been improved and increased in number as a direct result of the Centennial Exhibition. Industrial education has probably at this day reached a higher development in Boston than in any other American city. In 1877 there were only eight institutions in the country professionally engaged in the work of art education, pictorial and industrial, the Boston Art Club (1855), and the Cooper Institute, New York (1857), being additional to the six first named. There were, however, in all the larger cities institutes and associations of mechanics where instrumental drawing was taught, Boston alone having four such organizations. But at that time the public school system itself was thoroughly developed, and many of the mechanics' institutes volunteered to teach reading, writing, and arithmetic in night classes to supplement the work of the public schools. When the want for such instruction was felt, it was supplied by public night-schools, opportunity was afforded to teach drawing at night in the rooms of these associations, the pupils having already acquired a common school education.

In 1861 the Massachusetts Institute of Technology was established. Its course of instruction adopted some years afterwards included a more thorough education in industrial art than had then been attempted in the United States, and was the starting-point of the newer class of schools of design. In 1870, in answer to petitions of manufacturers setting forth the disadvantages under which they had to compete with foreign manufacturers, for want of workmen skilled "in drawing and other arts of design," the legislature of Massachusetts passed an act providing that "any city or town may, and every city and town having more than 10,000 inhabitants shall, annually make provision for giving free instruction in industrial or mechanical drawing to persons over fifteen years of age." In 1874 twenty of the twenty-three cities and large towns of the State had complied with the law, in form at least, although there was a great want of qualified teachers of drawing—a fact which of itself most plainly shows that the art had been hitherto greatly neglected. Boston, which acted as the pioneer city in the introduction of the new public school study, engaged as director of art instruction Mr. Walter Smith, at that time head-master of the school of art in Leeds, England, who had (in his own language) "studied this matter for the last twenty-five years with the incentive of love and the opportunity given by having nothing else to do." In 1873 a State Normal Art School was established in Boston under Mr. Smith's direction, the purpose being to qualify the teachers in the public schools to act as instructors in elementary drawing; and it is largely through his exertions and skill as an instructor that the art education of the public schools of Massachusetts and of other States has been developed. New York followed the example of Massachusetts in 1875 by providing for instruction in drawing in the public schools. The foundation had thus been laid for a great development of schools of design and drawing when the Centennial Exhibition awakened widespread interest in the subject by exposing the need of such education. Among the direct results of that exhibition was the founding of the Pennsylvania Museum and School of Industrial Art, Philadelphia, which collected chiefly from the exhibits of foreign countries, one of the finest museums of industrial art works in the country, now displayed in Memorial Hall (the art gallery of the Exhibition), on the Centennial Exhibition grounds in Philadelphia. It has since established a school of industrial art, which, not having had permanent quarters, is as yet too small to make proper use of the rich museum with which it is endowed. A great impetus was also given by the exhibition to existing art-institutions in Philadelphia. The schools of the Academy of the Fine Arts were reorganized with instructors in all branches of art; the School of Design for Women removed to new and larger quarters, and was greatly improved; the Spring Garden Institute revived its old classes in mechanical drawing, opened a new school in free-hand-drawing and design for both day and night classes, and established mechanical hand work classes, where the principles of design were practically applied; the Franklin Institute enlarged its facilities for teaching drawing; and the West Philadelphia Institute re-established its drawing classes. In other cities similar activity was displayed. Boston, with its public school children trained in elementary drawing, had no difficulty in finding pupils for its art schools, and established new schools. Cincinnati organized important schools of decorative art which have rivalled those of Boston in providing teachers for other cities; Baltimore reorganized the schools of the Maryland Institute and put them in the front rank of schools of design; and New York established new schools connected with the Metropolitan Museum of Art, and also substituted instruction in drawing for instruction in other studies in some of its mechanics' institutes.

In 1857, as has been shown, there were only eight prominent art institutions in the country affording instruction which might be of benefit to designers and draughtsmen in industrial works. The report of the United States Bureau of Education for 1874 gives a list of twenty-six art-schools, ten being for the special education of artists and three others voluntary associations of artists for mutual practice and help. The report for 1880 gives a list of thirty-eight similar institutions, an increase of twelve. Eight of the new schools were established in the years 1876 and 1877, and of these the avowed purpose of six was to give instruction in design and industrial art. But this list is very imperfect. It is known that at this time (1884) there are in the United States at least eighty-three art schools, including seventeen universities with departments of the fine arts, where the study of drawing is a part of the regular course. There are twelve schools of pictorial art and fifty-four schools, nearly all of recent organization, established as industrial art-schools or schools of design. Mechanical drawing is also taught in many industrial schools as a basis for training in handiwork. They are in this respect schools of design, and should be classed as such, though their main purpose is mechanical training. Such institutions are the Institute of Technology, of Boston, Mass.; the Mechanics' School of the State College of Maine; the department of mechanic arts belonging to the Purdue University, Indiana; the Manual Training School of St. Louis, Mo.; and the mechanical handiwork school of the Spring Garden Institute, Philadelphia. There are also many colleges, seminaries, and universities where drawing from copies was formerly taught merely as an accomplishment, which have recently adopted the modern system and teach drawing with special reference to its educational influence upon eye and hand and memory. Drawing is also taught in the public schools of many cities; Philadelphia has adopted the Boston plan of training its teachers to teach elementary drawing to all the pupils, and thus to qualify them to enter the higher schools established by private bounty.

Information respecting the art-schools of the United States cannot well be tabulated so as to give a true conception of their history and present standing, because many of those which bear early dates of incorporation have only recently opened drawing-schools or have so changed their character as to make the date of their organization as applied to existing schools misleading. A brief account is here given of the facilities afforded for art instruction in the principal cities of the Union.

New York.—In New York instruction in pictorial art is given at the National Academy of Design and by the Art Students' League, the latter a new organization, founded in 1875 and incorporated in 1878, which has a large staff of teachers. Industrial drawing and the arts of design are taught at the Cooper Institute, which had over 2000 pupils in 1881-2; by the General Society of Mechanics and Tradesmen of the City of New York, 300 pupils; by the New York Turnverein, 750 pupils; and in the technical schools of the Metropolitan Museum of Art with about 300 pupils. In 1883 the last-named schools were reorganized with 100 pupils, but with ample accommodations for 1000. Drawing is also taught in the public schools of New York, and there are many societies of artists which maintain schools, as well as organizations, like the Society of Decorative Art established primarily for the sale of the works of members, but which give instruction to pupils in various branches of decorative art.

Philadelphia.—In Philadelphia instruction in the fine arts is provided at the Academy of the Fine Arts, which in recent years has occupied a new building and greatly enlarged its facilities for giving such instruction. The School of Design for Women, 293 pupils; the Spring Garden Institute, 653 pupils; the Franklin Institute, 200 pupils; and the Pennsylvania Museum and School of Industrial Art, 79 pupils, give instruction chiefly in industrial drawing; and all except the first have night-classes. The Pennsylvania Museum was founded in 1876 and has a valuable museum of objects of art. The other institutions are much older, but have been greatly improved and developed recently. There are also decorative art clubs and artists' associations similar to those of New York. Drawing is taught in the public schools. In Girard College and the House of Refuge mechanical handiwork schools have recently been organized, in which drawing is a primary study.

Brooklyn, N. Y.—The Brooklyn Art Association for a time maintained drawing-schools, but discontinued them in 1881. In 1883 it took charge of schools which had been established by the Art Guild in 1880. The Ladies' Art Association of New York maintains a Brooklyn branch which had 124 pupils in 1883. The Brooklyn Institute has an evening school with 50 pupils, and Packer Collegiate Institute has classes in drawing.

Chicago.—Chicago has an Academy of Design which still maintains classes in pictorial and industrial art, though its building was destroyed in the fire of 1870. The Art Institute, formerly the Academy of Fine Arts, organized in 1879, has a school of 300 pupils, including night-classes. The Chicago Society of Decorative Art, organized in 1877, gives instruction in industrial art, including embroidery and wood-carving, and there are two artists' associations with classes for self-help. A manual training-school where industrial drawing is taught was established in 1883.

Boston.—Boston has taken the lead among American cities in the development of industrial drawing. The Massachusetts Institute of Technology requires the pupils in all departments to learn mechanical and freehand drawing during the first year, and in most of the departments this study is carried through the whole of the four years' course. There are special classes in architectural drawing and the mechanic arts, and a free school in drawing and architecture, meeting at night, is supported by the institute. The State Normal Art School of Massachusetts is a training-school for teachers of industrial drawing, and was founded in 1870. In 1881 there were 222 pupils in the day-school and 72 in the night-classes. The latter have since been discontinued. The Museum of Fine Arts also maintains an art-school. The Young Men's Christian Association maintains night-classes in drawing, and the Boston School of Sculpture gives instruction in modelling to a few pupils. There are also many clubs and societies of artists for self-help, and a society of decorative art which maintains a school.

St. Louis.—The St. Louis School and Museum of the Fine Arts, forming the art department of Washington University, was organized in 1879, and in 1883 had about 300 pupils. Instruction in drawing is also given to pupils in other departments of the university. There are several artists' societies and sketch clubs.

Baltimore.—Baltimore has an old institute (the Maryland Institute), established for the promotion of mechanic arts, which was thoroughly reorganized in 1879, and now maintains both day and night-classes in drawing and painting, chiefly industrial. In 1883–84 there were 177 pupils in the day-classes and 497 in the night-classes. There is also a Decorative Art Society, for the sale of works of art, which maintains classes in drawing, design, and china-painting.

Cincinnati.—The Ohio Mechanics' Institute, established in 1856, maintains free schools, with 280 pupils, confining its instruction at present to drawing applied to the industrial arts, though the design is to supplement instruction in drawing with practical lessons in a school of technology. The University of Cincinnati had an art department with 411 pupils in 1883, but in January, 1884, it was transferred to the Cincinnati Art Museum Association, which is richly endowed.

San Francisco.—San Francisco has an art association, organized in 1871, which maintains classes in pictorial drawing, and also a Decorative Art Society, with 89 pupils.

New Orleans.—The Southern Art Union and Woman's Industrial Association of New Orleans, organized in 1880, is similar in organization and aims to the Decorative Art Societies in other cities, having a salesroom for the sale of works of art, but it also maintains day and evening classes in drawing and the decorative arts.

Cleveland, Ohio.—The Cleveland Academy of Art, organized in 1881, opened day and evening classes in 1883. The Western Reserve School of Design for Women, organized in 1882, had 60 pupils in 1884.

Pittsburg, Pa.—Pittsburg has had a School of Design for Women since 1865, which gives instruction to women and also to boys under the age of fifteen.

Buffalo, N. Y.—Buffalo has a Decorative Art Society, with schools for women and children.

Of the cities, having less than 150,000 inhabitants, the following are known to have schools of design and drawing: Charleston, S. C., the Carolina Art Association having organized a school in 1882; Columbia, Mo., where the Missouri University requires a study of art as a condition of graduation; Columbus, Ohio, an art-school founded in 1875, and having, in 1881–2, over 200 pupils; Denver, Col., a College of Fine Arts attached to the University of Denver, with 60 pupils; Elgin, Ill.; Fordham, N. Y.; Hartford, Conn., a School of Design, founded in 1872, which has loaned its casts, etc., to the Society of Decorative Art organized in 1877, which maintains classes in industrial art; Indianapolis, Ind.; Jacksonville, Ill.; Le Roy, N. Y., the Art College of Ingham University; Louisville, Ky., the Polytechnic Society, with art classes in drawing and painting; Manchester, N. H.; Meadville, Pa.; Milwaukee, Wis.; Newark, N. J., the Essex Art Association, which organized classes in 1884; Norwich, Conn., the art department of the Norwich Free Academy; Peoria, Ill., classes attached to the Ladies' Art Society; Portland, Me., the Portland Art League; Providence, R. I.; Richmond, Va.; Rochester, N. Y.; Springfield, Ill.; Springfield, Mass.; Syracuse, N. Y.; Urbana, Ill.; Washington, D. C.; Wellesley, Mass., the department of art attached to Wellesley College; and Worcester, Mass., the Worcester County Free Institute of Industrial Science, in the latter place, teaching drawing to the pupils in its technical schools.

Industrial drawing is also taught in the United States Military Academy, West Point, N. Y., in the United States Naval Academy, Annapolis, Md., and in the principal universities, colleges, and preparatory schools of the country, where it is no longer treated as a mere accomplishment but as a necessary part of general education. See *Reports of the Bureau of Education*, 1873–80; *Circulars of Information*, published by the Bureau; *The United States Art Directory and Year Book* (New York, 1882); *Modern Art Education* (Boston, 1875).

DES MOINES, the capital of Iowa, and county-seat of Polk co., is on the Des Moines River, 175 miles W. of Davenport, 138 miles E. of Omaha, and 357 miles W. of Chicago. It is also on the following railroads: the Chicago, Rock Island, and Pacific, the St. Louis, Keokuk, and North-west, the Des Moines and Fort Dodge, and branches of the Chicago, Burlington, and Quincy, and the Chicago and North-west. The entire city comprises an area of eight square miles, nearly equally divided by the Des Moines River, flowing from N. to S.; the "West Side" being again divided by the Raccoon River, which here joins the former. The sections of the city are united by six bridges. The northern section of the West Side is the main business part of the city, though there are many business houses also on the East Side, the ground in each section rising with easy slope from the river, the business portion being on an average 15 feet above the river. In the West Side are the county court-house, the principal hotels, railroad depots, and banks, as well as the post-office, a handsome marble structure, erected in 1870, which furnishes accommodations also for the United States courts and other offices of the Federal Government. Farther back from the river are many fine private residences, and in the extreme north-western part of the city is a park of 40 acres. There is also a large park on the Raccoon River, owned by a private association, in which agricultural fairs are held. On the East Side is the State Capitol, erected on an elevated site, and surrounded by a park of 10 acres. The State Arsenal is a large building, which contains equipments for the militia and many memorials of the civil war. The State library contains 30,000 volumes, and there is another public library with about 6000 volumes. In the West Side there are 5 public school-houses, 1 of which is a high-school, 2 are grammar-schools, and 2 are primary-schools. These furnish instruction to about 3000 pupils, and 600 more are taught in private schools. The University of Des Moines, a Baptist institution, chartered in 1865, has a commodious brick building, 80 by 250 feet, in a conspicuous position. Des Moines has 15 churches, belonging to the Methodist, Presbyterian, Congregational, Lutheran, Baptist, Christian, Roman Catholic, Episcopalian, and Universalist denominations. There are published here 2 daily, 10 weekly, and 3 monthly periodicals. There are 2 national banks and 4 other banks, a life-insurance and 2 fire-insurance companies. The industries of the city comprise iron-foundries, machine-shops, scale-works, agricultural-implement-works, woollen-mills, an oil-mill, and a paper-mill. For these industries the rivers furnish abundant water-power. The city is lighted with gas, and furnished with water by the Holly system from the Raccoon River. In the vicinity are found bituminous coal, potters' clay, fire-clay, lime, etc. The site was laid out in 1846, and a town was incorporated in 1851 under the name Fort Des Moines. In 1855 the State legislature resolved to remove the capital to this location, and in 1857 the transfer was effected and the city obtained a new charter under its present name. It has grown steadily in numbers and importance. Population in 1860, 3965; in 1870, 12,035; and in 1880, 22,048.

DETERMINISM, a word now generally used to designate that system of thinking which, upon whatever grounds, denies the freedom of the human will; maintaining, variously, that such apparent freedom is only concealed necessity. Any statement or defence of this scheme of opinion is, of course, in its last ground, philosophic, yet it will be conducive to clearness of view to distinguish, first, *Religious* determinism, depending on dogmatic grounds, and second, *Psychologic* determinism, in its various modes of statement. The first will occupy us but briefly, and then we will notice the chief variations of the other.

Religious determinism, first fully formulated by Augustine in opposition to the Pelagian heresy, reproduced in subsequent writers and intensified by writers of the older school of Calvinism, holds that in consequence of the fall of man, and the inherited sinful propensity arising therefrom, the human will has become enslaved; that man is in a condition utterly helpless, and can only be roused therefrom by an act of grace, which is of itself entirely deterministic, and entirely unconditioned by anything that, except by courtesy, could be called human freedom. This view is fortified by texts from the Christian Scriptures.

The dogmatic grounds for opposing it consist in the asseveration with equal earnestness that the Christian Church and the Christian Scriptures everywhere take for granted human responsibility and guilt, and offer the gospel of Christ to be freely accepted or rejected. Nay, it is asserted that the heathen, to whom the knowledge of the gospel offer has not come, are still responsible and will be judged by a law of their own.

Whenever this question is argued by religionists, except as a question of exegesis (into which we do not propose at all to enter), it is always and inevitably also argued as a question of psychology, and ultimately of philosophy. Indeed, the doctrine of *grace* is strictly philosophic, and consists in holding that the various influences brought to bear upon human nature that can be followed by the intellect (Providential), and the subtler influences working beneath consciousness (mystical) are ruled by the category of final cause, itself a part of a universal design in which the individual intelligence is a constituent element. The denial of grace resolves itself into pure indifferentism (one of the shallowest tentatives of human thinking), which will be noticed below. Such doctrine of grace may be made to consist either with the admission or denial of human freedom, though perhaps only in the former case does it deserve the name.

Let us then, as a question of psychology and philosophy, note the possible modes in which human freedom may be denied, and what are the positive schemes which make such a denial imperative. There are really only two such philosophies—(1) Materialistic and (2) Idealistic Necessitarianism.

Determinism everywhere opposes itself, and victoriously, to its favorite adversary, pure indifferentism. This latter scheme represents the human will as always *in æquilibrio*, that it looks at, sifts, and accepts or rejects all motives, is indifferent to them all, can at any time make a new beginning. Such seems to have been the thesis of Pelagius. Something like it seems to have been defended by Duns Scotus. It is defended by the Anglican Bishop King (*De origine Mali*), and expressions implying it are not infrequently to be found in writers of lesser note. According to the psychology implied in this scheme the human *will* seems to be thought as something apart from, superadded to, or enclosed within human *nature*, is regarded as an abstract entity, or as pure Ego; and therefore is indifferent, or may be indifferent, or at least was once indifferent. But determinists may and do always urge in opposition to this, that we know nothing of any such *will*, that we have no evidence of the existence of any such will, that we only know the Ego as concrete, and therefore as determined; that, indeed, the will is the nature itself, the entire nature, with all its past behind it, and becomes *will* when focussed, and *quoad* any possible activity (not denying, however, that as movement it is *prius*, and that pure activity is the first element of any concrete). It points, likewise, to the fact that we do not and cannot dissociate will from *character;* that there is no mere arbitrariness in human choices, that the "titillation of arbitrariness" is itself a motive for choice, that the motives or ends which the will constructs out of the material supplied by its environment, by the essential conditions of its existence, are always ruled by the prevailing traits of the character.

We may say here that the old attempt to represent the human will as an indifferent force-centre, in the concrete ruled inevitably by forces *ab extra* coming in the shape of motives—the stale maxim of which is, or was, that *the will is governed by the strongest motive*—seems to have been pretty much abandoned by able writers of late days in the interests of determinism; it being clearly seen at length, that motives are not *ab extra*, but creations of the will's own, that motives are only the self-mediation, and not the producing cause of free volition. Thus they have as a consequence of such abandonment found a deeper basis for their scheme.

The sort of determinism we have just above alluded to has been upheld by Buckle, J. S. Mill, by Schopenhauer, and other modern writers. It relies upon the testimony the experience of life furnishes as to the reliableness of human *character*, tells us that as a man is at bottom so will he act; that however artificial disguises may make him seem other than he is, the real self will be sure to break through on a sufficient emergency; and that this character is the creation of influences determining it *ab initio* and *ab extra*, that if there are innate determinations, and derived through the principle of heredity, they are still *ab extra*, and part of the dialectic movement of the universe, whether that be thought as materialistic or idealistic.

A critique of such determinism, while acknowledging that man does never act from a groundless freedom of choice, yet maintains that human volitions cannot be explained as the product of such forces *ab extra;* that beside the determinations derived from heredity or environment, whether belonging to the unconscious or the conscious processes, there are unsounded depths in human nature itself, modifying, and bringing forth new and unexpected results; that the human will, *i.e.*

human nature, is not measured by its conscious experience, that there is within it an incalculable possibility of self-movement, therefore that man is subtly related beyond all traceable relations, that his normal dimension is commensurate with the universe, that he reflects within himself the *whole* of it, and thus that he himself is a true universal, and so far an image of the first principle.

We have not the space here to adduce the facts resulting from an analysis of human experience, confirmatory of this view, and will content ourselves by merely stating an argument from analogy.

As science goes more and more to show the unity of the physical universe, and that every concrete thing is a system of relations, from which there is no evidence whatever that anything is excluded, so we may on grounds as valid infer, that man as an intelligent reflecting the laws of the universe, preadapted to them as they to him, must have the same universality, and that his ideal bound is the infinite.

Thus it comes to be held not only that human volitions require this universal ground for that basis, but that character itself is not only a *principle* of determinations of will, but also a *result* of determinations of will; that, in the words of Julius Müller, "its self-determinings condense themselves to determinations of self."

The question might now arise whether this view, which seems to steer between and along a depth profounder than the shallow currents of pure indifferentism, and superficial determinism, on either side, is not after all only a more recondite form of determinism still. Allowing that the highest possible idea of self-being is one in which there is a relation to the whole universe beside, that there is nothing indifferent to it, and which cannot amplify and enrich it—this same self may be thought as one determination of the universal; thus is in itself determinate essential being—essence—and its self-determination is just the necessary activity and consequence of this determined essence of being; that conscious self-determination, *i.e. will*, is not necessarily therefore *free*, and that self-consciousness may be only a link in the chain of necessity.

It is urged, in opposition to this, that it leaves unexplained indubitable facts of human nature which cannot possibly be brought under any category of necessity; *e. g.*, the sense of responsibility, the judgment and feeling of obligation, self-accusation, and guilt. And, while we cannot here enter into the argument, we may say that no plausible scheme of necessity, purporting or professing to explain these facts, has proved itself satisfying and compelled adherents. Mere mechanical (materialistic) determinism, for some time of late indulged in as a speculation, is giving way before the deeper study of the organism, and of the notion of development, for organism shows us the idea, the *scheme*, which the life-force is actualizing; and all development is synthetic, rather than analytic, making even more of itself by assimilating the food of the universe, yet preserving unimpaired its own unity.

Many writers—among whom may be named Kant, Schelling, Schopenhauer, and Julius Müller, while acknowledging that in the temporal sphere human actions and volitions are, on one side, ruled by the physical *nexus*, and therefore necessary, and on the other by the prevailing bent of the character (for which no origin in time can be posited), therefore also necessary—think to conserve the principle of freedom by speaking of it as a transcendent act. Schopenhauer teaches that by an act which lies before all time, and Julius Müller that by an extra-temporal act (*in forma æternitatis*) every individual has made himself once for all what he is, and that his life, in time, with the whole range of his proceedings, is merely the detailed performance of his pre-existent, or extra-existent, act. And thus we have a strict temporal determinism originating in an eternal act of freedom. Thus the consciousness of freedom is retained throughout the temporal experience; yet all volitions and actions are still thus and thereby inevitably determined. The sense of guilt is the haunting memory of that prior decision, and finds therein its only possible explanation.

The intellectual difficulties of this scheme are immense. It may be questioned, first, whether this so-called extra-temporal state can be concretely thought except as a pre-existent state, and whether we have got beyond the category of time. Be that as it may, we have thrown upon us the task of accounting for this transcendent act of freedom. It must either be thought after the manner of pure indifferentism; or else, this extra-temporal existence, if not absolutely barren, and a nothing in the semblance of something, must be thought as a state so rudimental that responsibility, and the tremendous consequences hanging upon choice, seem hardly to flow from so inadequate a source. As the choice, so far as is known, seems to have been in every case a wrong choice, this is only another form of presenting the question of the mystery of evil; of locating it for examination in a realm of shadows and unimaginable possibilities, instead of bringing it into the twilight of our actual knowledge. We note it, however, without discussion, as a phase of thought that has not yet vindicated for itself a philosophic basis. We may add, too, that possibly the sense of guilt is of *a posteriori* origin and entirely explicable within the temporal sphere.

There is a modification of determinism which, while denying freedom of choice, yet thinks it has found a way to admit essential liberty—teaching that essential free-will is fettered by the natural restrictions of the individual, yet is sometimes realized, or seemingly realized, and that by a higher or deeper natural process breaking out from the depths and changing the whole life. Thus, sudden conversions. But if this is a *natural* process it is no more, and the essential liberty must be still only a delusion. But, indeed, the facts to be explained do not wear the look of a natural process. They are, for our knowledge, moments in a process of ideal self-government. Such changes in the character, in our experience, come from the illumination of the moral or religious ideal, and the supply of some profounder and more powerful motive-spring. The consciousness that however conditions of nature or of grace may be thought necessary, this is still the soul's own act, is so profound and utter that no scientific or philosophic scheme can ever eradicate it or permanently disguise it. It will ever hold this to be a *prius*, if not a *primum*, of the whole process of thought, which anything else proves its own falsity or insufficiency by contradicting.

It is well known that some determinists, *e. g.*, Buckle, have endeavored to fortify their opinion by appealing to *statistics*, showing that in the aggregate human actions may be very well classified, and in the lump, therefore, predicted; that there will be in as so many murders, suicides, and even indifferent or trifling actions, annually, etc. But, in short, the fluctuations in such tables of statistics from movements originating in human free-will, by moral and religious activities, and not by hygienic or other physical ones merely, is enough to show the little worth of this appeal, and that it must not be taken for granted that these fluctuations can be explained from the physical *nexus*.

Again, determinism sometimes appeals to the confessions of certain criminals that they could not have done otherwise than as they did (which, if they are sane, nobody believes but hunters of paradoxes) and that if they had the opportunity they would do the same over again. To counterbalance the weight of such testimony may be set another kind of testimony—of those who have acknowledged their guilt and sought to make what reparation they could, even acknowledging the justness of the punishment they were receiving.

After all, this whole question of freedom and necessity will be decided in and for each intelligent mind by the system of philosophy adopted, according to whether the material or the mental is thought the *prius*, and if the mental, whether life is explained from the standpoint of the logical or the ethical. The position of the advocate of freedom is impregnable, and may be seen to be so. He may be willing to admit that freedom and necessity are but aspects of all concrete existence, and, therefore, in their deepest ground identical; but he is perfectly sure that the so-called necessity is a form of freedom, and not the reverse, and he sees no reason to lower his definition of freedom. There is nothing higher in our thought than the principle of self-determination. We feel that we ourselves are degraded in our own regard if we think of ourselves under any lower category. We feel that our conception of the First Principle is no longer the Highest, or any Absolute, if it is thought as anything other than freedom, pure self-determination. Determinism, as a mode of thinking and feeling, always shuts man in an intellectual dungeon, and inevitably leads to pessimistic views. Wronged human nature revolts and rises towards the optimistic sky only on the wings of freedom.

Yet the truth in determinism should by all means be conserved for the highest ethical interests; and what that is, as the result of the thinking of the present writer, he will state in some sentences as condensed as possible, thus.

1. Our whole essential being is derived, and therefore determined, for us. 2. Our environment, and therefore the whole range of possibilities which we can realize, the material which we may combine, constructing ends or motives, is determined for us. Therefore, 3, our idiosyncratic development, through heredity, education, and culture, is determined for us. 4. The matter or content of all our actions, when they pass out of the pure spiritual realm, is determined for us. It proceeds, according to the laws of the universe, not only outside our own bodies, but in our brains, nervous and muscular systems. Any physical liberty we have is only borrowed; may be lost utterly or granted in its fulness. Freedom, if it exist at all, must belong to the very centre of the spiritual soul. Even the ideal ends we can set ourselves, though innumerable, are not infinite, but limited in number, and therefore determined for us. They have not the exhaustlessness which belongs to absolute freedom; and the relative freedom, if we have it, is fettered by these bonds. What then is left for freedom if all this is abandoned to determinism? Nothing, but that the spiritual soul *can* either yield itself to the eternal, infinite, absolute ideal, however imperfectly or inadequately apprehended; or, abide in some one of the multitudinous lower ones which it can construct out of the material and within the range that is set it; that is, it is *morally* free. That to all appearance men do take one or the other of these alternatives is a proof *a posteriori* of their moral freedom. The last ground of this difference of choice is an insoluble mystery. It is no other than one of the forms of statement of the problem of *evil*. If the form of the universal, instead of the form of isolation, independency, is taken, then the spiritual soul is on the way to *real* freedom, to the removal of all physical limitations, to liberty, to the removal of all contradictions, when freedom is indistinguishable ethically from necessity, yet maintains itself in perennial consciousness as freedom. Here the ethical has merged into the æsthetical. Here beauty reigns. Here the soul can forever enrich itself, and find amplest activity in its expansion to fill the measure to which it can never become perfectly commensurate.   (J. S. K.)

DE TROBRIAND, PHILIP REGIS, a French author and officer in the American army, was born at Tours, France, June 4, 1816. He belongs to a noble French family, and is a baron by inheritance. He graduated at the University of Orleans and studied law. In 1841 he came to New York for the first time, and in 1849 published there the *Revue du Nouveau-monde*. In 1854 he became editor of the *Courier des Etats-Unis*, the leading journal in the French language in America. In July, 1861, he entered the Union army as colonel of the Fifty-fifth New York volunteers, and in 1862 commanded a brigade in the Third corps. He was promoted to be brigadier-general in Jan., 1864, and soon after was entrusted for a few months with the command of the defences of New York. At a later period of the war he was brevet major-general of volunteers, commanding a division, and after its close was appointed colonel and brevet brigadier-general in the regular army. He was afterwards engaged principally in frontier duty, and in Jan., 1870, organized the successful expedition which put an end to the depredations of the Piegans in Montana. After serving some time in Utah, he was ordered to Louisiana, in Oct., 1874, to command the United States troops concentrated in New Orleans in consequence of political disturbances which had culminated in the overthrow of the State government by an armed organization of citizens. When the next legislature met, in Jan., 1875, some seats were contested with such violence that the military was again appealed to, and Gen. de Trobriand expelled some of the contestants. He retired from active service in 1879. He published in Paris *Les Gentilshommes de l' Ouest* (1841) and *Quatre ans de Campagnes à l'Armée du Potomac* (1867).

DETROIT, the chief city of Michigan, is the county-seat of Wayne co., and, until 1847, was the capital of the State. It is situated in 42° 20′ N. lat., 82° 58′ W. long, on the North-west bank of the Strait (Fr. *Détroit*) or River, connecting Lake St. Clair 7 miles distant N. with Lake Erie 20 miles distant S. At this point the river has a width of ¾ mile, an average depth of 30 feet, and a current of 2¼ miles per hour. Nearly 40,000 vessels, with an aggregate tonnage of 19,000,000, pass here every year. Including the suburbs of Hamtramck and Spring Wells, from which the city is only municipally separated, Detroit stretches along the river for 6¼ miles, extending back 2¾ miles. Except for a gentle rise at the bank of the river the site is a level plain, broken on its extreme east and west limits by ravines and ancient water-courses, one of which, known as Bloody Run, was the scene of a massacre of British soldiers in an attack upon the famous Indian chieftain Pontiac, in 1763. Woodward Avenue, running northerly from the river, divides the city almost equally. For the most part the streets intersect each other at right angles, but from the Campus Martius—an open space of 3 acres, ⅛ mile from the river—and two quadrant parks, known as the Grand Circus ⅛ mile beyond, both of which are cut by Woodward Avenue, several diagonal avenues radiate—some of them to the city limits and beyond. These diagonal avenues, together with parallel circular streets conforming to the semi-circumference of the Grand Circus Park, create throughout the city at all intersections with the rectangular plan a somewhat perplexing intricacy of highways, many triangular parks, plots, and buildings. The principal avenues are from 100 to 200 feet wide, bordered by one and even two rows of elm or maple trees, and by broad plats of grass extending from the houses to the roadway. Nearly all of the residence streets are lined with trees, and in many quarters this natural beauty is enhanced by the absence of fences. The population of the city in 1880 was 116,342; including the manufacturing suburbs of Spring Wells and Hamtramck, 128,742, which in 1884 was estimated at 150,000. The population in 1810 was 770; in 1850, 21,019; 1860, 45,619; 1870, 79,599. In 1880 there were 17,292 of German birth, 10,754 Canadian, 6775 Irish. There were 20,493 dwellings, and 5.68 persons to a dwelling—the lowest number in any city of the United States having more than 100,000 inhabitants. The government of the city consists of a mayor elected every 2 years; a city council of 12 members, elected on a general ticket for terms of 4 years; and a common council of 26 members, 2 from each ward. Connected with the police department are 8 stations—the central situated in East Park—and 175 men. The annual expenses are $180,000. In the fire department there are 11 steam-fire engines, and 2 reserve, 3 chemical engines, 3 hook and ladder, 1 protection wagon, 1 fire escape, 129 alarm-boxes, 130 miles of wire, 893 street hydrants, 190 reservoirs, 65 horses, and 170 men. The annual expense is $142,538 (1884). Water is supplied to the city from Lake St. Clair by 3 pumping-engines and 242 miles of pipe, whose daily capacity is 72,000,000 gallons. In 1884 the daily consumption was 20,000,000 gallons, or 150 gallons to each inhabitant. The works are valued at $3,315,989. The schools have 12 grades with 14,385 sittings; a total enrollment of 300 teachers, and 18,971 pupils in attendance. The school census shows a population of 43,728 between the ages of five and twenty years. There is an average attendance of 400 at the night schools in winter; and connected with the department is a special school for vagrant, truant, and disorderly pupils. The annual expenditures (1884) are $256,013. The public library, consisting of 50,605 volumes, had, in 1884, an annual circulation of 102,610 volumes, and 31,428 volumes were consulted in the library building, erected for the purpose on the park bounded by Gratiot Avenue, Farmer and Farrar streets. The annual expenditures (1884) are $20,137, $6000 of which were derived from fines in the central station court. Between $15,000 and $20,000 are annually expended for the support of the poor. Belle Isle Park, an island of 650 acres and situated in the middle of the river 2 miles above the centre of the city, was bought in 1880 at a cost of $200,000 for purposes of a public park. It is more than a mile long and nearly half a mile wide, covered with a thick growth of native forest timber. Under the direction of Frederick Law Olmsted, architect of New York Central and Brooklyn Prospect parks, this has been transformed into a natural park, with water-ways for drainage and boating, and characterized by forest scenery, open parade-grounds, bathing facilities, drives, avenues, meadows, and woodland paths. The house of correction with 600 inmates—a few of them United States prisoners for life—is devoted, for the benefit of the city, to the manufacture of chairs. It has turned over to the city treasury as high as $50,000 annual profits. All these departments are governed by boards or commissions, whose members are, with two or three exceptions, appointed by the mayor and confirmed by the common council. The police commissioners are appointed by the governor of Michigan, the board of education is elected by the people on a general ticket, the commissioners of the public library are appointed by the board of education. In addition to the departments mentioned there is a board of public works, which, in 1884, had 100 miles of sewers and 97 miles of paved streets in charge, building inspectors, and a board of public health. The number of deaths in 1883 was 2884. The judiciary of the city consists of a police court, recorder's court, superior court, and circuit court of three judges. The United States District Court for the eastern district of Michigan is also held in Detroit.

The city is lighted by 20 electric lights and 3600 gas and naphtha lamps. In 1883, 7,046,192 letters, 1,142,408 drop letters, and 2,332,973 postal cards were delivered in the mails. There are 90 churches, 17 of which are Catholic, 2 Jewish, the rest Protestant. The Fort Street Presbyterian Church, the Central Methodist, and the Church of our Father (Universalist), both facing the Grand Circus Park, St. Joseph's (R. C.), on Orleans Street, St. Paul's (P. E.), on Congress Street, St. John's (P. E.), on Woodward Avenue, are distinguished for architectural attractions. The principal public building is the City Hall, on the west side of the Campus Martius. It is built of gray sandstone—three stories and a basement—in the Italian renaissance style with mansard roof surmounted by a cupola, the summit of which is 180 feet from the ground. It was finished in 1871 at a cost of $700,000. Four colossal statues of Cadillac, Lasalle, Hennepin, and Richard—the pioneers of the Lake region—adorn the roof. In front is a large grass-plat furnished with trees and fountains, and two British cannon captured in 1812 at the naval battle won by Commodore Perry on Lake Erie. On the east side of the Campus Martius is the market building, erected in 1881 at a cost of $75,000. The upper stories are occupied for city courts and offices. Between these two buildings is the soldiers' monument, designed and executed at Munich by Randolph Rogers, and erected at a cost of $70,000 by the people of Michigan to the memory of the soldiers who fell in the civil war of 1861-65. It consists of a granite base and shaft surmounted by a colossal female warrior in bronze with shield and sword, and surrounded by symbolical bronze human figures representing the navy and the cavalry, infantry, and artillery service. On the sides are medallions in relief of Grant, Sherman, Lincoln, and Farragut. The United States Government building on Griswold Street is (1884) in process of demolition preparatory to the erection of a new one. Another fine building is the station of the Michigan Central Railroad, on the corner of Jefferson Avenue and Third Street. It is 280 ft. long by 182 ft. wide; the front and side walls are low; the roof is broken into numerous gables, all subordinated to a tower at the corner 157 ft. high. It is built of pressed brick and terra-cotta, adorned with blue and red slate, and cost $175,000. Immediately south the freight building of this road extends along the river in for a quarter of a mile, the iron roof consisting of a single arch. Four grain-elevators along the river front have a united capacity of 2,375,000 bushels.

The principal benevolent institutions are the Detroit Industrial School, for the instruction of poor children; Harper Hospital (Prot.), with accommodation for 200 patients; Home of the Friendless (Prot.); House of Providence, Infant Asylum, and Lying-in Hospital (Cath.); Little Sisters of the Poor (Cath.); Retreat Insane Asylum (Cath.); Protestant Orphan Asylum; St. Vincent's (Cath.) Orphan Asylum; St. Luke's (Epis.) Hospital; St. Mary's (Cath.) Hospital, accommodating 150 patients; Thompson Home for Old Ladies (Prot.); United States Marine Hospital; Women's Hospital and Foundlings' Home (Prot.); House of the Good Shepherd (Cath.). The three principal cemeteries are Elmwood (Prot.) on Elmwood Avenue; Mt. Elliot (Cath.) just east of Elmwood; Woodmere (Prot.) 5 miles W. of the City Hall. There are also 1 Lutheran and 4 Jewish cemeteries. Detroit has 4 theatres and about 50 public halls; 26 miles of street railways, employing 300 men and 750 horses; 7 daily newspapers (2 German) and 40 other newspaper and other publications; 45 telephone stations with 1500 subscribers, connected with all the principal towns and cities within a radius of 100 miles. At Grosse Pointe on Lake St. Clair 8 miles N., and Grosse Isle 12 miles S. on the river, are many summer residences of the citizens. The river is the favorite resort during the hot months. Scores of steamboats ply to the towns on the Detroit and St. Clair rivers, at the mouth of which latter, and near the ship-canal of St. Clair Flats, are hotels, private houses, and fishing-club houses built over the water. Ferry-boats to Windsor, Ontario, opposite Detroit, and to Belle Isle Park, are during the hot months the daily resort of thousands, who, on payment of a few cents, may remain on the boats, without landing, all day and evening for the enjoyment of the cool breezes always to be found on the river. Detroit is connected with Chicago and Buffalo by the Michigan Central, the Wabash, the Grand Trunk, and the Lake Shore and Michigan Southern Railroads and their branches; with Mackinac by the Michigan Central Railroad; with the Grand Rapids and Indiana Railroad at Howard City by the Detroit, Lansing, and Northern; with St. Louis by the Wabash Railroad; with Toledo by the Michigan Central and the Lake Shore; with Bay City by a branch of the Michigan Central, and with Port Huron by the Grand Trunk; with Ludington on Lake Michigan by the Flint and Pere Marquette; with Grand Rapids by the Grand River Division of the Michigan Central; and with Grand Haven on Lake Michigan by the Detroit and Milwaukee Railroad.

The assessed valuation of the city was in 1883 $105,910,925, of which $78,982,170 was real estate and $26,928,755 personal property. There was a tax levy of 10.88 mills on the dollar, from which $1,113,222 were collected. The total receipts were $2,473,960; the expenditures $1,611,008. The total bonded debt, Jan. 1, 1884, was $1,056,500, for the redemption of which there were $941,322 in the sinking fund, leaving a net debt of only $115,178.

There are (1884) 5 national and 8 savings or other corporate banks, with an aggregate capital of $4,100,000; deposits, $21,745,000; loans and discounts, $18,113,000. The weekly clearing-house figures for 1883 range from $2,175,722 to $3,461,688.

The average annual entries and clearances at the custom-house are about 12,000 vessels and 2,000,000 tonnage. The value of imports in 1883 was $1,914,453; duties on imports and other receipts $21,917. The arrivals included 334,943 immigrants, and 176,308 animals for breeding. The total value of exports was $3,131,490.

The amount of capital invested in manufactures is $22,000,000; the annual value of the product, $50,000,000; wages paid, $10,000,000. Among the more important industries are boots and shoes, with $500,000 capital; cars, $500,000; clothing, $1,300,000; flour and feed, $550,000; hats and caps, $350,000; iron, steel, and castings, $1,800,000; leather, $750,000; machinery, $1,950,000; meat-packing, $1,650,000; safes, $300,000; stoves, $900,000; seeds, $762,000; tobacco and cigars, $1,500,000; malt liquors, $400,000. The amount of lumber manufactured was 125,000.000 feet. There are also large manufactories of iron, steel, copper, tobacco, stoves, cars, pins, etc., just outside of the city limits, owned and operated by Detroit citizens. Receipts of wheat have varied from 6,357,866 bu. in 1883 to 12,045,020 bu. in 1879; shipments from 6,260,480 bu. in 1883 to 10,964,183 in 1878. Receipts of corn have varied from 1,823,087 bu. in 1883 to 265,551 bu. in 1879; shipments from 1,572.627 bu. in 1883 to 60,629 bu. in 1879. Receipts of oats have ranged from 1,553,249 bu. in 1883 to 411,381 bu. in 1879; shipments from 670,882 bu. in 1883 to 62,891 bu. in 1880. Receipts of beans from 5,771,143 bu. in 1883 to 2,981,792 bu. in 1878; shipments from 5,255,291 bu. in 1883 to 978,952 in 1878. Receipts of barley, 765,531 bu. in 1883. The total capital invested in the wholesale business and manufacturing establishments of the city is $60,000,000; annual sales about $90,000,000. The retail and commission houses sell $40,000,000, making a total of $130,000,000.

The site of Detroit was first visited by civilised man in 1610, ten years before the landing of the Pilgrims at Plymouth. In 1705 there were 2000 souls in the Indian villages on its site. It was founded in 1701 by La Mothe Cadillac under the government of France; was transferred to England in 1763; was occupied by British troops during the revolutionary war; and was transferred to the United States by treaty in 1783, but not taken possession of until 1796. When the Territory of Michigan was organized in 1805, Detroit was made the seat of government. It was surrendered by Gen. Hull to the British in 1812, and retaken by the United States in 1813. It was twice besieged by Indians, eleven months by Pontiac in 1763, once captured in war, and once in 1805 burned to the ground. The present city was laid out in 1807; incorporated as a village in 1815, and as a city in 1824. When Michigan was admitted as a State in 1837, Detroit continued until 1847 to be the capital. It suffered from destructive fires in 1836, 1840, 1848, and 1849. (E. G. H.)

DETTINGEN, a village of Bavaria, in the circle of Lower Franconia, on the right bank of the river Mayn, the scene of a battle fought June 27, 1743, between the allied Austrians and English, commanded by George II., king of England and elector of Hanover, and the French forces under the marshal Duc de Noailles. The war is known as that of the Austrian Succession, incident to the death of Charles VI., the father of Maria Theresa. On the 20th of April, 1743, King George II. prorogued the British Parliament and went over to Hanover, taking with him his second son, the duke of Cumberland, and his secretary of state, Lord Carteret. In his youth the king had fought in person in the battle of Oudenarde, and had conceived a hearty and constant hatred to the French, which he was eager to gratify again in the field. In contrast to this activity, the young French king, Louis XV., was indolent and luxurious, taking little personal interest in the conduct of his armies, which supported the election of the elector of Bavaria to the imperial throne. The imperial forces had suffered greatly; they had ceased to threaten Hanover, and after marching to the relief of Prague had wintered in Northern Bavaria. To aid them a large French army now took the field, and all the troops were placed under the command of the marshal de Noailles. They marched full of hope and ardor, superior in numbers and equipment, to give the finishing-stroke to the allies and their cause. To meet them, the British forces proceeded early in February from Flanders into Germany, under the earl of Stair. They were joined by an Austrian force under D'Ahrenberg and 16,000 Hanoverian soldiers in the pay of the English government. The military conduct of Lord Stair, which has been lauded by the French, has been severely censured by English writers. His movements were very slow, and he did not cross the Rhine until the middle of May. At Hochst he awaited the arrival of another Hanoverian contingent, 6000 strong, who were paid by the electorate of Hanover. Thus the allied army, composed of English, Austrians, Hanoverians, Hessians, and a few troops from the Low Countries, numbered about 37,000. Lord Stair might have carried great prestige by capturing the emperor at Frankfort, whither he had fled, but Frankfort was a free city and its neutrality was respected. The peace was usual condition of affairs was curious. Although French and English armies were arrayed against each other in the field, the two countries still maintained the semblance of peace, the British ambassador was still in Paris and the French at the English court.

The army of De Noailles was 60,000 strong, [unreadable] were reinforcements expected. It crossed the Rhine and surrounded the Mayn by the southern bank, so as to watch the movements. Lord Stair, now of [unreadable] as he perceived that the army of [unreadable]

escape were blocked—above Aschaffenburg, below Dettingen, and along the banks of the river between the two. The most feasible plan was to break through the toils by countermarching down the stream in hope of reaching Hanau. This counsel was adopted, and the retreat from Aschaffenburg commenced. To meet and crush them, De Noailles, advancing his main body to Seligenstadt, threw two bridges over the river, and sent his nephew, Lieut.-Gen. the duc de Grammont, across with 23,000 men to secure the defile in front of Dettingen through which the allies must pass in carrying out their hazardous design. The village is divided by a small stream which empties into the Mayn and forms a ravine. Six French batteries were posted on the riverbank to play upon the flank and rear of the allies in passing through this ravine.

Before the dawn of the 27th of June the allied forces began their march, formed in two close columns. King George was at first with the rear column, which was considered the post of danger, as Aschaffenburg was, upon its evacuation, at once occupied by 12,000 French troops. But the troops of De Grammont were soon descried in front, and the king hurried thither to form the line of battle. Nothing could have saved the allies but the blunder of the French commander, who, impregnably posted in the village, had been ordered to wait and not attack the enemy until he should enter the ravine.

De Noailles having given these orders, and having everything arranged for the speedy destruction of the allies, left the front and recrossed the Mayn to hurry forward some tardy detachments. No sooner had he gone than De Grammont, with a rashness that was to prove fatal, crossed the ravine which protected his position and was designed to be the fatal trap for the allies, with considerable delay in getting his cavalry over, and gave battle to the enemy on equal terms. His whole command followed, and the encounter was waged with a rather more than even chance of success to the allies. King George was mounted upon a fiery horse, which ran away and carried him almost into the French lines. Fortunately stopped in this headlong career, the king put himself at the head of the advanced English regiment; he shouted, "Now, boys, for the honor of England, fire: behave well, and the French will soon run;" and after a volley led them to the charge. The repeated charges of the French cavalry could not break the English line: the French batteries along the bank were obliged to cease firing because their own troops were endangered. The Austrian troops under Neuperg having seconded the English, and when the astonished De Noailles returned he found his troops disheartened and disorganized and the allies on an irresistible advance. He could do nothing but order a retreat, which soon became a disastrous rout; the bridges were soon choked by the fugitives; many threw themselves into the river to escape by swimming; numbers fled to the mountains. The allied batteries played upon the flying masses. Victory had been snatched from the jaws of defeat. The fighting lasted until four o'clock; the king would not leave the field and did not leave it until ten. The allied army pursued its march unmolested to Hanau. The French losses amounted to about 6000, with an unusual proportion of officers, who had fallen in an attempt to stem the retreat. The loss of the allies was about [unreadable], and they left their wounded upon the field, [unreadable] to the French writers say "chivalrous [unreadable] a memory of the French [unreadable] notwithstanding the superior numbers of the French in the entire field, in the actual engagement on the restricted ground the allies were in somewhat greater force. Dettingen is notable as the last battle in which an English king has commanded in the field. (H. C.)

DEVASTAVIT, in law, a wasting or mismanagement of the estate and effects of a person deceased by the executor or administrator into whose hands the same have been committed. The term is also used to indicate an entry or suggestion of waste filed by a plaintiff in a suit against an executor or administrator.

Devastavits may arise in several ways: (1) By direct abuse, as where an executor or administrator sells, embezzles, or converts to his own use the goods entrusted to him; (2) by mal-administration, as where such a one pays a claim not actually due or does not distribute the assets in the order fixed by the law; (3) by neglect, as where he fails to sell goods at a proper time, or to collect a doubtful debt which by the exercise of due diligence might have been gotten in.

The law requires from an executor or administrator in the foregoing cases the exercise of honesty, care, and forethought; and if he be lacking in these respects he will be adjudged guilty of a *devastavit*. In such case said party will be held personally liable to make up the loss out of his own estate. (L. L., JR.)

DEVENS, CHARLES, an American general and jurist, was born at Charlestown, Mass., April 4, 1820. He graduated at Harvard College in 1838, and was admitted to the bar in 1841. He practised law in Franklin co., Mass., until 1849, and was a member of the State senate during the years 1848 and 1849. From 1849 to 1853 he held the office of United States Marshal for Massachusetts, after which he resumed the practice of law in Worcester. On the outbreak of the civil war he was commissioned as a major, but was soon made colonel of the Fifteenth regiment Massachusetts Infantry. In the unfortunate affair at Ball's Bluff this regiment won distinguished honor. Col. Devens was appointed a brigadier-general in April, 1862, and commanded a brigade during the Peninsular campaign. In 1863 he had command of the First division of the Eleventh corps, and in 1864 he commanded a division in the Eighteenth corps and afterwards a division in the Twenty-fourth army corps, which division was the first to enter Richmond when it was evacuated in April, 1865. Gen. Devens was three times wounded, slightly at Ball's Bluff, and severely at Fair Oaks and Chancellorsville. He participated in most of the battles of the Army of the Potomac, and at the request of Gen. Grant was breveted major-general for gallantry and meritorious conduct at the taking of Richmond. While at the front in 1862 he was nominated for governor of Massachusetts by what was termed the People's party, but was defeated by Gov. Andrew. After the surrender of Lee in 1865 Gen. Devens was ordered to a command in South Carolina, where he remained until 1866, when he was mustered out of service. Gen. Devens resumed the practice of law in Massachusetts, but in 1867 was appointed one of the justices of the Superior Court of that State, and in 1873 was made one of the justices of the Supreme Court of Massachusetts. In March, 1877, he was selected by President Hayes as attorney-general of the United States, and served as such until the close of that administration. In April, 1883, he was reappointed one of the justices of the Supreme Court of that State, which office he now holds. Except his judicial opinions and those given as attorney-general, his only publications have been occasional addresses, among which are an oration at Bunker Hill on the centennial anniversary of the battle, and one upon Gen. G. G. Meade, delivered before the Society of the Army of the Potomac.

DE VERE, SIR AUBREY (1788–1846), an Irish poet, was born at Curragh Chase, county Limerick, in 1788. The family was founded by Vere Hunt, an English soldier of noble descent, who went from Essex to Ireland in Cromwell's army, and afterwards settled there. A descendant, also named Vere Hunt, was made a baronet in 1784. His son, Aubrey, on succeeding to the title in 1818, dropped the name Hunt and assumed the name and arms of De Vere. At an early age he had married Mary Rice, sister of Lord Monteagle. He wrote little till he reached his thirtieth year, when he produced in succession two dramatic poems, *Julian, the Apostate*, and *The Duke of Mercia*. He was a friend and admirer of Wordsworth, and dedicated to him *A Song of Faith; Devout Exercises and Sonnets* (1842). This was followed by *The Waldenses* (1842), and *The Search After Proserpine* (1843). De Vere especially cultivated the sonnet, studying Petrarch and Filicaja. He was of a deeply religious nature and firmly attached to the Church of England, but favored the introduction of religious equality in Ireland. In the last year of his life he composed his longest dramatic poem, *Mary Tudor*, which was published after his death. He died in 1846.

DE VERE, AUBREY THOMAS, an Irish poet, third son of the preceding, was born at Curragh Chase, county Limerick, Jan. 10, 1814. He was educated at Trinity College, Dublin, but did not graduate. At an early age he wrote poetry which closely resembled his father's in thought and style. When famine fell on Ireland with all its horrors De Vere devoted himself to active charitable work, and his sad experience at that time led him to publish a pamphlet on *English Misrule and Irish Misdeeds* (1848). He was also led to engage in religious studies which resulted in his conversion to the Roman Catholic Church in 1851. He then began again to write poetry, partly to illustrate Irish history and partly to contribute to the aid of religion. In 1854 he was made honorary professor of political and social science in the Catholic University of Dublin. He afterwards took part in the agitation for the disestablishment of the Church of Ireland. Among his publications are *Picturesque Sketches of Greece and Turkey* (1850); *Poems, Miscellaneous and Sacred* (1856); *May Carols* (1857); *The Sisters, Innisfail, and Other Poems* (1861); *The Infant Bridal* (1864); *Irish Odes* (1869); *Legends of St. Patrick* (1872); *Alexander the Great* (1874); *St. Thomas of Canterbury* (1876); *Legends of the Saxon Saints* (1879); *The Foray of Queen Meave* (1882).

DE VERE, MAXIMILIAN SCHELE, LL.D., an American philologist, was born in Sweden, Nov. 1, 1820. His ancestors, the Barons von Schele, owned estates in Pomerania, and his father entered the Prussian military service and rose to high rank. The son was mainly educated in Germany, studied law at Berlin and Bonn, became referendarius in the Prussian department of justice, and entered the diplomatic service. He had also served the customary year in the army and was appointed lieutenant in the Landwehr. At the age of twenty-two he came to America and spent a year travelling through the United States, part of time in the far West. He was then invited to settle in Cambridge, Mass., and being generously assisted by

Longfellow and others, became a teacher of modern languages in Boston, but was soon called to a professorship in the University of Virginia, entering upon his duties there in November, 1844. He has since completely identified himself with his adopted country, and during the civil war remained in performance of his duties at the university. His literary career began with the publication of a work on Anglo-Saxon left in manuscript by President Jefferson, the founder of the university. Then follows his *Comparative Philology* (1865), *Studies in English* (1866), *Americanisms* (1871), and *Leaves from the Book of Nature* (1872), which has been republished in England with illustrations. His *Myths of the Rhine*, illustrated by Doré, appeared in 1874, as an *edition de luxe*. His minor works are the *Romance of American History* (1872), *Modern Magic* (1872), *Wonders of the Deep* (1869). In the *Great Empress* he sketches the life of Agrippina, the mother of Nero (1880). Besides contributing to leading magazines he translated several works, among which those of Spielhagen have been received with special favor. He has lectured before the Smithsonian Institution, the Peabody Institute, and other audiences. He has published school grammars of French and Spanish. He was one of the founders of the American Philological Association, and is a member of many learned societies at home and abroad.

DEWEES, WILLIAM POTTS (1768–1841), an American physician, was born at Pottsgrove, Pa., May 5, 1768. On his father's side he was of Swedish descent. He studied medicine with Dr. William Smith, and after attending lectures at the University of Pennsylvania, but without obtaining a degree, began to practise at Abington, Pa., in 1789. In December, 1793, he removed to Philadelphia, where, by his talent and diligence, he secured the favor of Dr. Rush. Dewees made obstetrics his specialty, and obtained extensive practice and high reputation. Feeling the necessity of having a degree in order to secure professional honors, he applied to the university and obtained it in 1806. In 1810 he was a prominent though unsuccessful competitor with T. C. James for the newly founded professorship of obstetrics in the University of Pennsylvania, the first of the kind in this country. In 1812, partly on account of ill health, he gave up his profession and devoted himself for five years to farming at Philipsburg. Having returned to Philadelphia in 1817, he became connected with the Medical Institute of Philadelphia, founded by Dr. Chapman. He was elected in 1825 adjunct professor, and in 1834 professor of obstetrics and of diseases of women and children in the University of Pennsylvania. A year later he was obliged to resign on account of ill health, and went to Cuba and thence to Mobile, where he resided for nearly two years, practising to some extent. Having returned to Philadelphia in 1841, he died there May 20, 1841. He published *Inaugural Essay on Means of Moderating Pains of Labor* (1806), *Treatise on Physical and Medical Treatment of Children* (1825), *System of Midwifery* (1825), *Diseases of Females* (1826). His several works have passed through several editions. His *System of Midwifery* was the first original American treatise on the subject, and it was pronounced equal to that of Baudelocque. It was not only a popular work. Dr. Dewees was a member of the American Philosophical Society and several many other learned and honorary institutions, at home and abroad.

DEWEY, CHESTER, D.D. (1784–1867), an American Congregationalist preacher and botanist, was born at Sheffield, Mass., Oct. 25, 1784. He graduated at Williams College in 1806, and in 1808 was licensed to preach, but soon after became a tutor in his *alma mater* and in 1810 was made professor of mathematics and natural philosophy in the same. In 1827 he took charge of an academy at Pittsfield, Mass., and was also professor of botany and chemistry in the medical college there. In 1836 he was made principal of the collegiate institute at Rochester, N. Y., and when the University of Rochester was erected, in 1850, he was made professor of chemistry and natural history. He retired from this position in 1860 and died at Rochester Dec. 15, 1867. He was especially eminent as a botanist, and his *History of the Herbaceous Plants of Massachusetts* was published by that State. He also contributed many articles to the *American Journal of Science and Arts*, and to the secular and religious papers.

DEWEY, ORVILLE, D. D., LL.D. (1794–1882), an American Unitarian minister, was born at Sheffield, Mass., March 28, 1794. He graduated at Williams College in 1814 at the head of his class, and became first a teacher, then a clerk, in New York. Afterwards he studied theology at Andover, finishing his course in 1819. He was for some months an agent of the American Education Society, and then took temporary charge of a congregation at Gloucester, Mass. In 1821 he became a Unitarian, and was appointed assistant to Dr. Channing in Boston. On Dec. 17, 1823, he was ordained pastor of a Unitarian church in New Bedford, Mass., and while there frequently contributed to the *Christian Examiner* and the *North American Review*. In 1833, on account of ill-health, he went to Europe, where he spent two years. When he returned he took charge of the Unitarian church of the Messiah in New York, which became large and prosperous under his ministry; but in 1842 he was obliged again to seek relief in travel. Two years later he resumed his charge, but resigned in 1848, and retired to a farm in Sheffield. He afterwards delivered in several places courses of lectures on *The Problem of Human Life and Destiny* and on *The Education of the Human Race*. He also took temporary charge of Unitarian churches in Albany and Washington, and from 1858 to 1862 was pastor of a church in Boston. He then retired to his native place, and, feeling that his work was accomplished, looked forth on the better world with kindly, unselfish interest. He died in the house in which he was born, in Sheffield, Mass., March 21, 1882.

Dr. Dewey was undoubtedly the greatest Unitarian preacher—equal to Dr. Channing in earnest and effective pulpit oratory, and superior to him in the grasp and profundity of his mental powers. He was unsurpassed in the attention he commanded, in the fervor and depth of the emotions he excited, in the power with which he brought home to the conscience the precepts of moral and religious truth. The uniform ability with which week after week he presented the momentous themes of the pulpit and showed the spiritual laws underlying and pervading human life was remarkable; but the long-continued intensity of the mind proved too much for the body, and obliged him frequently to suspend his labors and finally to retire from a devoted congregation. Although a firm believer in the Unitarian doctrines which he embraced early in his ministerial course, he never lost his sympathy with the great body of Christian believers. He was himself an embodiment of the noble character he loved to portray and impress upon his hearers.

His first book, *Letters on Revivals*, was published in 1830, and attracted attention. In 1835 he gathered into a volume *Discourses on Various Subjects*, and in 1836 he published the results of his travels in Europe in *The Old World and the New*. In later years his discourses were collected from time to time, and published in England as well as America, under the titles *Human Nature, Human Life, The Nature of Religion, Commerce and Business, The Unitarian Belief.*

DEXTER, HENRY MARTYN, an American Congregationalist minister, editor, and author, was born at Plympton, Mass., Aug. 13, 1821. He is on the father's side of the sixth generation from Thomas Dexter of Lynn, and on the mother's side of the seventh generation from George Morton of Plymouth, the presumed author of *Mourt's Relation*. His father, Rev. Elijah Dexter, prepared him for Brown University, which he entered in 1836, but two years later he removed to Yale College, where he graduated in 1840. After teaching for a year in Dorchester Academy, he studied theology, and graduated at Andover in 1844. He became the first pastor of the Franklin Street Congregational Church in Manchester, N. H., and in 1849 succeeded Rev. Austin Phelps, D. D., in charge of the Berkeley Street Church, Boston. After being for a year the weekly correspondent of the New York *Independent*, he became in 1851 an associate editor, and in 1856 the chief editor, of the *Congregationalist*. In 1866 his church had grown so large that he was compelled to resign his editorial position, but in the following May, when the Boston *Recorder* was merged in the *Congregationalist*, Dr. Dexter resigned his pastoral charge and returned to his editorial labors. He still holds this position, residing in New Bedford, but spending half of each week in Boston. Besides his journalistic work, Dr. Dexter was one of the founders of the *Congregational Quarterly*, and has largely contributed to its pages. He has also contributed to other reviews and magazines, and has published—*Street Thoughts* (1859), *Twelve Discourses* (1860), *Future Punishment* (1865), *Congregationalism* (1865; 5th ed., 1879), *New England Ecclesiastical Councils* (1867), *The Polity of the Pilgrims* (1870), *Pilgrim Memoranda* (1870), *As to Roger Williams and his Banishment from Massachusetts* (1876), *Congregationalism of the Last Two Hundred Years as Seen in its Literature*, with a copious bibliography (N. Y., 1880), *Hand-book of Congregationalism* (1880), *The True Story of John Smyth, the Se-Baptist*, with bibliography of the Baptist controversy (1881). He also edited in 1865 an exact reprint of *Mourt's Relation* and Capt. Benjamin Church's *Philip's War* and *Eastern Expeditions*. He has received the degree of D. D. from Iowa College and from Yale College. He has long been engaged upon a new history of the Plymouth colony of 1620, founded upon original researches.

DIALECT. In language there is a constant tendency to variation. This tendency manifests itself in very various ways—in the addition of new words and the loss of the old, in the change of form or of meaning of the same word, or in change of form combined with change of meaning. Nor do these processes, singly or in combination, affect always the whole of the word; on the contrary, a very important factor is the alteration of single syllables, especially final syllables and those by which the relations of inflection are denoted.

These tendencies are most clearly seen and best known in the comparison of documents produced at one period in the life of a people with those produced at a much later date, provided this people has not in the mean time changed its own speech for that of any other. Thus a comparison of the Latin with the Italian clearly shows how great the ultimate result of a long-continued succession of individual alterations may come to be, so that one tongue, through a large portion of its original area, has been altogether superseded by another that has grown out of it. Of certain precautions to be observed in making this comparison we shall speak farther on.

But these tendencies to change are never altogether the same over the whole district occupied by a language: they differ more or less widely in different sections, and thus tend not merely to change, but to differentiation. Where these differences affect any great number of words or forms, especially forms of inflection, the various contemporaneous local forms are called, with reference to each other, "dialects," the whole group of allied languages being termed a "family." Thus, the Latin split up into Italian, French, Spanish, Portuguese, and other less important forms of speech, collectively called the "Romance tongues," so that any one of these, as the Spanish, is properly described as "a dialect of the Romance family of languages."

This is the strictly scientific use of the term, and in this sense every tongue ever spoken, when considered in its relation to some kindred form of speech, may be described as a "dialect;" and, in consequence, the terms "language" and "dialect" are often quite synonymous terms, or at least seem to be such.

The term "dialect" is not, however, used to describe the special speech peculiarities of individuals, although the mutual relations between the forms peculiar to single persons are exactly the same as the mutual relations between those greater sums of difference to which the term is applied. Furthermore, when the region concerned is very limited, a single mountain-valley, for instance, although the term "dialect" is often used, it is more commonly displaced by the less familiar word "patois," which commonly implies that the variation is too unimportant, in some way, to receive special consideration. And yet in some of these cases the sum of differences between a "patois" and its allied forms of speech may be greater than those subsisting between two forms of speech classified as "languages."

These limitations, illogical as they are, bring us to the consideration of the less accurate use of the word "dialect"—a use that is very often found even in books of strict scientific content, and one that rests on a purely political or literary basis. Where a certain form of speech has, from the political circumstances of those that use it, or from its literary content, become a special subject of study, it is commonly spoken of as a "language," and related forms are generally described as its "dialects," unless some of these last have similar claims to special attention. Thus we speak of a "Spanish language," and describe certain provincial forms of speech as "dialects" of this. Yet the Portuguese, which closely resembles the Spanish, is termed a "language," and on very intelligible grounds.

The test of mutual intelligibility between two speakers has been sometimes proposed as a basis of exact definition, but it is valueless, as the degree of intelligibility often depends partly on the speakers and partly on the subject; and the proposed test altogether fails when confronted with the actual use of the word, for a party of three can get along fairly well although one may use the "Swedish language," another the "Danish language," and the third the Icelandic.

To describe, in all its phases, the continually fluctuating use of the two terms is impossible, and no definition will hold good if tested by all the quotable cases where they are found. The difficulty is one common to all cases of evolution; and it will be found that students of biological science, accustomed as they are to the parallel fluctuating use of the terms "family," "species," and "variety," often grasp the relation under discussion more readily than the average student of philosophy or even of philology.

The extent of the territorial range of a dialect depends upon political circumstances, but in primitive times the territory of each community, and in consequence of each dialect, was very limited. Thus, the Attic, the leading literary dialect of Greece, was originally the dialect of Attica alone, or probably of a very small portion of this small state. So also the classical Latin first appears at the city of Rome; and in the case of both languages it is not unlikely that the starting-point was the patois of a single village clustered on a single hilltop.

The vocabulary of such a community, however, by no means suffices for the needs of a great or a cultivated people. As it grows it makes new words; these new words alter the aspect of the sum of analogies, both for external phonetic form and internal content or signification, so that the mechanical deduction of a dialect from any form of speech standing even in the direct line of its ancestry is impossible. In addition to this, it is daily becoming more and more evident that dialects may be mixed, although this is by no means assented to by all good authorities, and the special investigations that may enable the philologist to speak of such mixtures with precision are as yet incomplete.

So, while the student must remember that every language is evolved from some dialect of limited area, he must beware of the conclusion that this evolution is one to be compared with the development of the oak from the seed; that is, one that is necessarily determined by the original content of the parent tongue. No such deduction by fixed processes is to be thought of in connection with languages.

In the case of the origin of most modern literary languages the districts concerned were somewhat more extensive than for the Greek and Latin. They arose at a time when the village community was superseded by a mere extensive social organization. They were still, however, "dialects," and nothing else, in the somewhat depreciatory sense of the term. Thus, in the history of the Germanic stock of speech in England there are found, at the outset, at least two important dialects occupying the soil—one the Anglian, in the north; the other the Saxon, in the south. The paucity of documents renders it impossible to decide upon the degree of uniformity with which these were spoken over their whole areas, nor indeed can a full account of the differences between them be given. There were, however, a number of dialects of each, and for a long time the written language in every part of England was, in each case, the more or less faithful phonetic rendering of the speech of the locality where the author lived. The Scottish, mediæval and modern, belongs to the Anglian. Between the two, in mid-England, lay the tract called Mercia. This, too, while it differed materially from the Anglian on the one side and still more from the Saxon on the other, presented a mass of dialects extending as far south as London. Out of the Mercian came the modern English, thus descending, at any rate, from but one of three local forms of speech. How much farther than this we can go, whether the literary English fairly represents only one patois of the Mercian or whether it is the result of the union of many distinct patois, cannot be certainly known. Of course no one needs to be reminded of the borrowed Norman element of the vocabulary. In passing, it may be noted that among the great number of dialects still existing in England the three great ancient divisions, North, Middle, and South, are still represented.

Finally, it should be noted that the limitation of the term "dialect" to *contemporaneous* forms of speech, however useful such restriction may be, may possibly mislead. From the point of view of the student of the dynamics of the growth of speech, the relation between the Sanskrit of the Vedas and the English of Tennyson is exactly the same, except in degree, as that subsisting between the language of Burns and that again of Tennyson.
(M. W. E.)

DIAZ, PORFIRIO, a Mexican general and statesman, of humble origin, first became noted during Maximilian's occupancy of Mexico in 1866. At the head of a republican army raised in the northern provinces, he laid siege to Pueblo, and after defeating the imperial Gen. Marquez, who was hastening to its relief, took the city by storm, April 5, 1867. He then proceeded to the capital, which made a stubborn resistance, but was obliged to capitulate, June 21, after Gen. Marquez had withdrawn. Having acquired a military reputation, Diaz aspired to the presidency in 1871 as a rival of Juarez. After the death of the latter in July, 1872, Diaz put himself at the head of a military insurrection, but was obliged to submit to Sebastian Lerdo, the chief-justice, who, according to the constitution, had succeeded to the office in the interim. Lerdo was afterwards elected president, Oct. 27, 1872; but before his term of four years expired Diaz was again in rebellion and seized the city of Matamoras. After a number of desperate adventures and hairbreadth escapes he succeeded in driving Lerdo from the country. On May 5, 1877, Diaz was proclaimed president by Congress till Nov. 30, 1880. During his presidency peace was maintained, the tariff revised, smuggling diminished, the finances improved, and several important lines of railway established. Much was done to invite the investment of foreign capital in mines and railroads. When Gen. Grant visited the country Pres. Diaz was assiduous in his attention to the distinguished chieftain. In 1880 an international exhibition was held in the city of Mexico, which gave abundant evidence of the resources and prosperity of the country. On the expiry of his term Diaz transferred his power to his friend, Gen. Manuel Gonzalez, inasmuch as the constitution forbids any person to hold the presidency for two successive terms. In order to carry on the system of internal improvements which he had inaugurated Diaz became the minister of public works, but resigned this position in June, 1881, and became governor of the province of Oaxaca. He has always been popular with the lower classes, and, after attaining the presidency, succeeded by his tact and good fortune in conciliating the aristocratic and conservative portion of the community.

DICEY, EDWARD, an English editor, was born in Leicestershire, May, 1832, and was educated at Trinity Hall, Cambridge, where he graduated B. A. in 1854. He has contributed largely to the *Fortnightly Review*, *St. Paul's*, *Macmillan's Magazine*, and other periodicals, and for several years wrote constantly for the *Daily Telegraph*, for which he has also acted as special correspondent. During his travels in the East he accepted the editorship of the *Daily News*, but after holding it three months resigned and in 1870 became editor of the *Observer*. His published works include *A Memoir of Cavour; Rome in 1860; The Schleswig-Holstein War* (1864); *Six Months in the Federal States* (1863); *The Battle-Fields of 1866* (1866); *A Month in Russia* (1867); *The Morning Land*, the story of a three months' tour in the East (1870); *England and Egypt* (London, 1881).

DICKINSON, JOHN, LL.D. (1732-1808), an American statesman well known as "The Pennsylvania Farmer," was born at Crosia, Talbot co., Md., Nov. 13, 1732. His father, Samuel Dickinson, had an estate in Kent co., Del., as well as that in Maryland, and was soon after appointed chief-justice of Delaware. He was a member of the Society of Friends. The son, having commenced the study of law at Philadelphia, went to London, where he completed his studies in the Temple. Returning to America after three years' absence he entered on the practice of his profession in Philadelphia, and in 1770 was married to Mary, daughter of Isaac Norris, usually called "the Speaker,"- as having held that position in the Pennsylvania Assembly for fifteen years. From his father-in-law Dickinson obtained Fair Hill, a handsome country residence on the northern border of Philadelphia. Here he lived in elegant style, refreshing his mind and cultivating his taste with one of the finest libraries in the colonies. In 1763 he was elected to the assembly, where he opposed the petition to Parliament asking that Pennsylvania be changed from a proprietary to a royal province, and demanded that some assurance should first be given that the change would be beneficial. Yet he did not hesitate to rebuke the selfishness of the proprietaries, who vetoed grants for the public service unless their estates should be exempted from taxes. When sent by the assembly as a delegate to the General Congress which met in New York in October, 1765, he found abundant opportunity for showing his love of constitutional liberty. Fluent in speech and ready in debate, his talents were acknowledged by his associates, and the resolutions adopted by the Congress were drafted by him. In plain yet dignified language they asserted that the American colonists had by their circumstances lost none of the rights and liberties of native-born Englishmen. But the protest was in vain. The British Parliament persisted in its determination to tax the colonies without their consent, and in 1768 he published his famous *Letters to the Inhabitants of the British Colonies, by a Pennsylvania Farmer*. The *Letters* clearly showed that while Parliament had power to regulate trade in the colonies, it had no right to impose duties on them for the purpose of raising a revenue, nor had such an attempt ever been made before. The "Farmer" called upon the people, therefore, to resist the "dangerous innovation" and "to exert themselves in the most firm but the most peaceable manner for obtaining relief." To him is due the famous phrase: "No taxation without representation." Franklin, then in London as the agent of Pennsylvania, published the *Letters* with a preface, as the best presentation of the case of the colonies. They were at a later date translated into French and published in Paris. Their arguments conciliated the wisest statesmen of Great Britain, while their tone and style were highly commended by Voltaire. The immediate effect of the *Letters* in America was to prepare the minds of the people for a firm maintenance of their rights and resistance to the encroachments of the British Parliament. In 1774, when the affairs of the colonies had reached a crisis in Boston, Dickinson endeavored to secure unity in action on the part of Pennsylvania, but, on account of the reluctance of the Quakers and of the friends of the proprietary, was obliged to act very cautiously. More eager patriots in the Philadelphia committee were vexed at the slow movements of the assembly, and wished a convention called to supersede it; while Dickinson's efforts were directed to getting Pennsylvania into line with Massachusetts without any overthrow of the existing government. This was felt to be difficult, and eventually proved impossible. When the assembly met in July, 1774, to elect delegates to the Continental Congress, first suggested by Virginia a year before, it passed over Dickinson and chose the ultra-royalist Galloway. But a few weeks after this first Continental Congress assembled in Carpenters' Hall, Philadelphia, Dickinson was substituted, and thenceforth his influence was seen and felt in all its actions and deliberations. As the drafts of various public documents previously proposed by committees had failed to express the judgment of the Congress, Dickinson was added to the committees and drew up the "Petition to the King," the "Declaration to the Armies," and the "Address to the States." These documents received the highest praise on both sides of the Atlantic. Their vigorous defence of the rights of America convinced all whose minds were open to reason. But the king and his ministers were obstinate, and when the second "petition," which Dickinson had drafted and insisted on sending, was presented by Richard Penn, it was rejected because it came from the Congress. Two days after the delivery of a copy of it to the ministry the king issued a proclamation declaring that open and avowed rebellion existed in the colonies, and calling on all his subjects to assist in bringing to condign punishment the authors of these traitorous designs. The proclamation arrived in Philadelphia, Nov. 1, 1775, and on the 4th the assembly chose nine delegates to Congress. Of these Dickinson, who had been elected almost unanimously to the assembly, was one, and Franklin another. Before the end of the month both were appointed members of a secret committee of correspondence with their friends abroad. Dickinson still continued to be a member of the Pennsylvania assembly, and, though the Quakers had there a majority, his cautious policy served so well that it was agreed to arm the people, for which purpose 5000 new muskets were ordered and bills of credit were issued amounting to £35,000. When the assembly of New Jersey proposed soon after to make a separate address to the king, Dickinson, as the chief advocate of united action, was sent to urge them to rest on the petition already sent in the name of united America. After the committee to draft the Declaration of Independence was appointed in June, 1776, Dickinson was made a member of the committees to arrange the form of confederation for the colonies and to prepare a plan of treaties with foreign powers. Meantime the proprietary government of Pennsylvania, which he had done so much to uphold, fell irretrievably, unable to endure the first shock of the conflict which had now begun. The plan of confederation proposed by Dickinson was not accepted. Firmly convinced by his knowledge of history that concentration of power was the cause of instability in previous republics, he was anxious to preserve the sovereignty of individual colonies. He allowed the general government no direct authority to raise a revenue, and in other ways restricted too much its necessary powers. Before the Declaration of Independence was formally signed, in August, he had ceased to be a member of Congress. Dickinson had opposed the declaration as being premature until the terms of confederation between the colonies were settled, unanimity assured, and the promise of foreign assistance obtained. But the temper of the American people had been roused beyond such cautious calculations. A few months later, when the seat of war was shifted from New England to the Middle States, he proved his unflinching devotion to his country by entering the army as a private, and, after serving for a time in New Jersey, was made a brigadier-general. His name and character were so well known to the British employed in subduing America that after the battle of Germantown—Oct. 4, 1777—his house was burned and his property laid waste. His family had retired to his paternal estate in Delaware, and his subsequent career shows that he was regarded as equally a citizen of either State. In April, 1779, he was unanimously elected to Congress from Delaware, and had further opportunity of displaying his ability in the field in which he had already achieved fame. He prepared, on behalf of the overburdened Congress, "An Address to the States," designed to rouse the people to renewed exertion at that time of despondency and peril. In 1780 he became a member of the assembly of Delaware, and was soon afterward chosen president of that State. In 1782 he was elected also president of the supreme executive council of Pennsylvania, being the candidate of the party which favored a revision of the State constitution to adapt it to the altered condition of affairs. During his administration he assisted liberally in establishing a college at Carlisle, and in gratitude for his services the institution received the name of Dickinson College. He was made president of the trustees, and continued in that position till his death. From 1785 he resided at Wilmington, Delaware, and in 1786 he was president of a convention of delegates from five States, which met at Annapolis to devise a uniform system of commercial relations between the States. In the next year he was a member of the convention which framed the Constitution of the United States. Representing a small State, yet having close connection with the great State of Pennsylvania, he was peculiarly fitted for adjusting the compromises necessary to secure harmony between the larger and the smaller States. He urged that considerable power should be left to each State, and that in one of the two branches of the national legislature the States should have equal votes without regard to their size or population. These provisions were incorporated, and Delaware was the first to ratify the constitution (Dec. 7, 1787), closely followed by Pennsylvania (Dec. 12). This result was largely due to the nine letters in which Dickinson, under the signature of "Fabius," set forth the features and advantages of the new bond of union. In 1792, at the convention to revise the constitution of Delaware, he was the most prominent and active member. In 1797, while serving as America was highly aroused against the French republic on account of its reported violation of the treaty of 1778. Resolved from his retirement by the general alarm at the prospect of another war, Dickinson published a second series of letters under the signature of "Fabius," commending to renewed trust our ancient ally and sympathizing greatly with her struggle for liberty. In 1801 he collected and published his various political writings. He died at Wilmington, Del., Feb. 14, 1808.

John Adams, when attending the first Continental Congress, visited Dickinson at his handsome residence, Fair Hill, and thus describes his personal appearance: "He is a shadow; tall, but slender as a reed; pale as ashes; one would think at first sight he could not live a month, yet upon a more attentive inspection, he looks as if the springs of life were strong enough to last many years." His character and abilities are readily seen in this sketch of his career. He was a man of thought and learning rather than of action; an able reasoner, an agreeable conversationalist, and a devout Christian. Wisely conservative, yet a friend of human rights, he had courage to set forth his views on all public questions that came before him, even at the expense of his own popularity. The American people still owe him a debt of gratitude, and the ideas which he proclaimed have long been imbedded in the national character.
J. F. L.

DICKINSON, JONATHAN (1688–1747), a Presbyterian minister of New Jersey, was born at Hatfield, Mass., April 22, 1688. He graduated at Yale College in 1706, studied theology, and was ordained pastor at Elizabethtown, N. J., Sept. 29, 1709. Here he labored for nearly forty years, taking part also in the various controversies which agitated the Presbyterian Church in that time, especially that concerning the revival under Whitefield. A pamphlet on this subject written by Dickinson, but at first published anonymously, was widely circulated, and commended by the most eminent Presbyterian divines. When the Presbyterian Church was divided in 1741 into the Synods of New York and Philadelphia, the former synod proposed to establish a college in New Jersey, and Mr. Dickinson, as an acknowledged leader in the denomination, was entrusted with the matter. A charter was procured in 1746 from John Hamilton, the acting governor of New Jersey, and the new institution went into operation at Elizabethtown under the name of Nassau Hall. Mr. Dickinson had long been engaged in the work of training young men for the ministry, and his new duties did not vary much from those in which he had been employed. He died of pleurisy at Elizabethtown, N. J., Oct. 7, 1747. He was an able defender of Calvinism, and his publications consisted entirely of sermons and pamphlets, many of them being controversial. A collection of his writings was published at Edinburgh in 1793.

DICKINSON COLLEGE, an institution of learning, at Carlisle, Pa., now under the patronage of the Methodist Episcopal Church, was chartered by the legislature of Pennsylvania, Sept. 8, 1783, and was named in honor of John Dickinson, who was then governor of the State. One week later Gov. Dickinson, who had taken great interest in the project, was elected president of the board of trustees. In order of time it was the second college in Pennsylvania and the eleventh in the United States. As communication between different sections of the country was then difficult, it was intended especially to afford the advantages of liberal education to the persons living west of the Susquehanna.

As was the case with all the early colleges, religious motives were prominent in leading to its organization, and although it was not limited by its charter to any denomination, the Presbyterians were for half a century most prominent in its management. The first president was Rev. Charles Nisbet, D. D., who was called from Montrose, Scotland, and was inaugurated

July 4, 1785. The other professors were Rev. Robert Davidson, D.D., pastor of the Presbyterian Church in Carlisle, and James Ross, whose *Latin Grammar* was a favorite text-book until the middle of this century. Mr. Ross had already begun a preparatory school in 1783, and on this foundation the college rested. Dr. Nisbet was indefatigable in his labors, but was not able to make the institution what he desired. It was crippled by want of means. The aid expected from the State was tardily given, and the chief dependence was on private contributions. Large donations of unimproved land were received, but as a purchaser could rarely be found these did little good. For nearly twenty years the exercises were conducted in a small two-story building with four rooms. The first commencement was held Sept. 27, 1787, when nine young men received "the first degree in arts." The students were first divided into three regular classes in 1796. In 1798 a lot of ground was purchased of the Penn family, and the erection of a new building commenced, but before it was completed it was destroyed by fire, Feb. 3, 1803. This misfortune enured to the benefit of the college, by enlisting the sympathies of prominent men and allaying the bitterness heretofore felt towards it on account of the strong sympathy its officers and students had shown for the Federalists. Pres. Nisbet died Jan. 18, 1804, aged 68. He was a man of great learning, lenient in discipline, but a master of sarcasm, which deterred those inclined to be disorderly. Dr. Robert Davidson, his colleague from the foundation, became acting president for five years, but in 1808 he resigned to devote himself wholly to the pastoral work. In June, 1809, Rev. Jeremiah Atwater, D.D., president of Middleburg College, Vt., was elected to the presidency of Dickinson. In 1811 the versatile and ingenious but eccentric Dr. Thomas Cooper was made professor of chemistry and mineralogy. In 1814 another year was added to the regular course, but on account of the war the senior class was called to the defence of Philadelphia, and the degrees were conferred *in absentia*. In June, 1815, in consequence of difficulties between the faculty and trustees in regard to discipline, President Atwater and some of his colleagues resigned, and soon after the operations of the college were suspended. In 1821 a new policy was inaugurated by the trustees; the land received from the State in 1786 was reconveyed to it for $6000, and this sum enabled them to pay off the debts, to repair the buildings, and complete West College. Rev. John M. Mason, D.D., was elected president, and with him an able faculty, consisting of Henry Vethake, Rev. Alexander McClelland, D.D., Rev. Joseph Spencer, Rev. Louis Mayer. The classes filled rapidly, but in 1824 Dr. Mason resigned on account of impaired health, and Rev. William Neill, D.D., succeeded him. Troubles again arose between the trustees and professors, and in 1829 the whole faculty resigned. A new faculty was organized in the following year, under the presidency of Rev. Samuel B. How, D.D. Though the institution was practically free of debt, the old trouble, arising from joint administration of discipline, soon again threatened its life.

The Baltimore Conference of the Methodist Episcopal Church was then considering the propriety of establishing a college within its bounds, and began to negotiate with the trustees of Dickinson College. The latter in April, 1833, agreed to transfer the institution to the Baltimore and Philadelphia Conferences, who obligated themselves to support it as a college. This was accomplished in June by the resignation of the majority of the trustees, the vacancies being filled by a committee of the conferences. The good effects of the change were speedily seen. Political and sectarian controversies which had vexed the former management were henceforth unknown.. The grounds were improved and beautified, and an endowment of about $40,000 was soon raised. Rev. John P. Durbin, D.D., editor of the *Christian Advocate*, and noted for his eloquence, was elected president, and Merritt Caldwell and Robery Emory were made professors. They did not enter on their duties here till September, 1834, by which time important changes in the charter had been obtained from the legislature, making the principal also president of the board of trustees, and giving the final decision in cases of discipline to the faculty, thus removing the stumbling-block which had so often caused trouble. Thus the college entered upon its second half century under new auspices, with new vigor, with an amended charter, and many external improvements.

Among the professors added about this time were William H. Allen, afterwards president of Girard College, and Rev. John McClintock, afterwards widely known as an author of excellent classical text-books, and joint editor of *McClintock and Strong's Religious Cyclopædia*. Dr. Durbin was a man of eminent prudence, tact, and wisdom, who treated the opinions of his associates with the utmost respect, while he impressed them with the excellence of his own plans. In 1845 he resigned and resumed the pastorate in Philadelphia; and his colleague, Rev. Robert Emory, an excellent disciplinarian, succeeded him. Mr. Spencer F. Baird, the eminent naturalist, who has since become secretary of the Smithsonian Institute at Washington, and Dr. George R. Crooks were now added to the faculty. In 1847 Pres. Emory and Prof. Caldwell died, and Professors McClintock and Crooks resigned. Rev. Dr. Jesse T. Peck was then elected president, and other changes were made in the faculty. Dr. Peck, though a dignified and amiable man, was not a college graduate, and did not find his new position congenial. After a trial of three years he resigned, and was succeeded by Rev. Charles Collins, D.D., in 1852. Under the latter the college, by the sale of scholarships at low rates, greatly increased the number of its students, while its reputation was fully maintained by the ability of the professors and their devotion to the interests of education. Dr. Collins, after a highly successful career, resigned in 1860, and removed to Tennessee. Prof. H. M. Johnson, who had first suggested the issue of scholarships, and who was noted as a stimulating teacher of philosophy and literature, now became president. The civil war, however, brought great discouragement by diminishing the number of students and the productiveness of investments in Western real estate. Yet the work was carried on, and every year a class was graduated. In 1863 the borough of Carlisle was occupied for a short time by the Confederate troops, who did no injury to the college then, though a few days later some shells were thrown in the grounds. At the close of the war the prospects of the college seemed to brighten, and in 1866, during the centennial of American Methodism, $100,000 were added to its endowment. An elective scientific course, including practical laboratory work, was introduced, and has proved highly successful. In April, 1868, Pres. Johnson died after a brief illness, and in September following, Rev. Robert L. Dashiell, D.D., an alumnus of the college, was elected president. After an administration of four years Dr. Dashiell was chosen missionary secretary by the General Conference; Rev. James A. McCauley, D.D., also an alumnus, was then elected president, and still retains the position. The preparatory school, which had been suspended in 1869, was revived in 1877, and is now in successful operation.

In connection with the college there have been two literary societies, the Belles Lettres Society, founded in 1786, and the Union Philosophical Society, founded in 1789. With varying fortunes they have continued to exert influence on the minds and habits of successive classes. They have gradually accumulated libraries, which now combined include 21,000 volumes, which are open twice a week to the members. The Scientific Society was formed in 1867, and is under the direction of the professor of chemistry. It affords an excellent means of training the members in power of scientific expression, as well as in advancing their knowledge.

In addition to the regular classical course, Dickinson College now furnishes a Biblical elective course for those preparing to enter the Christian ministry; two scientific courses, in one of which the study of Greek is entirely dispensed with, while in the other the full classical course is pursued to the end of the second year. Provision is also made for additional elective studies.

There is also in connection with the college a preparatory school, which has been in operation several years, and has proved an efficient aid to the main institution.

In 1883 the faculty consisted of seven professors, including the president, and there were 111 students in all the courses.

Among the more distinguished persons who have been professors in Dickinson College, but have not been mentioned in this sketch of its history, are Prof. C. D. Cleveland, the author of several *Compendiums of Literature*, John M. Keagy, Rev. Otis H. Tiffany, Alexander J. Schem, Charles F. Himes, Charles J. Little.

Among its distinguished graduates are President James Buchanan, Chief-Justice Roger B. Taney, several senators, judges, and many prominent clergymen.

DICKINSON, ANNA ELIZABETH, an American orator, was born in Philadelphia, Oct. 28, 1842. Her father died when she was only two years old, and the family was left to struggle with poverty. Anna was educated in the Friends' free schools, and showed great avidity for books. She readily accepted any means of making an honest living. In January, 1860, an address at a meeting of the Progressive Friends on "Woman's rights and wrongs" gave her a wide reputation. She was then a school-teacher, but a year later she obtained employment in the United States Mint in Philadelphia. From the outbreak of the Rebellion she frequently spoke on the questions of the day, and in December, 1861, she was dismissed from her position in the Mint for denouncing Gen. McClellan as a traitor. She then devoted herself entirely to political addresses, and rendered great service to the Republican party. She also visited the hospitals of the army and labored in behalf of the freedmen. After the war she continued her political addresses, discussing at first Southern reconstruction, but gradually turned her attention exclusively to woman's work and suffrage. In 1868, with the same object, she published a novel, *What Answer?* Afterwards, as the demand for lyceum oratory declined, she turned her thoughts to the stage, and in 1879 she appeared on the stage in several cities, but without marked success. Her attempt to render the character of Hamlet did not meet popular favor. She has since lived in retirement.

DICKSON, SAMUEL HENRY (1798–1872), an American physician, was born at Charleston, S. C., September, 1798. He graduated at Yale College in 1814, and studied medicine in Charleston and at the University of Pennsylvania. He assisted in establishing a medical college in Charleston in 1824, and became professor of the institutes and practice of medicine. In 1832 he retired, but when the college was reorganized in 1833 he was re-elected. In 1847 he became professor in the University of New York, but returned in 1850 to his professorship in South Carolina. In 1858 he was made professor of the practice of medicine in Jefferson Medical College, Philadelphia, which position he held till his death, March 31, 1872. His first work was *Dengue: its History, Pathology, and Treatment* (Philadelphia, 1826), and he subsequently published several articles on the same subject. Besides contributing to various medical journals, he published *Essays on Pathology and Therapeutics*, 1845; *Essays on Life, Sleep, Pain, etc.* 1852; *Elements of Medicine*, 1855. In his *Essays on Slavery* (1845) he maintained the essential inferiority of the negro race. He was not only a thorough scholar but one of the most graceful and elegant writers on medical subjects.

DICTIONARY. The recent additions to this important class of books are as follows:

See Vol. VII. p. 155 Am. ed. (p. 179 Edin. ed.).

EUROPE.

Ancient Greek.—Sophocles, Boston, 1870, 8vo; Rost, Braunschweig, 1871, 8vo; Buttmann, Andover, 1873, 8vo; Vanicek, Leipzig, 1877–79, 8vo, 2 vols.

Modern Greek.—Lass d'Agnen, Paris, 1874, 12mo; Contopoulos, London, 1880, 8vo, 2 vols.

Latin.—Forcellini, new ed., Prati, 1880–81, 4to, pts. 1–17; Georges, 7th ed., Leipzig, 1870–80, 8vo, 4 vols.; Lewis and Short, New York, 1879, 4to; Vanicek, Leipzig, 1877–79, 8vo, 2 vols.

Romance Languages.

Romance Languages generally.—Diez, 4th ed., Bonn, 1878, 8vo; Jarnik, Berlin, 1878, 8vo.

French.—Boissière, 3d ed., Paris, 1872, 8vo; Nugent, London, 1875, 24mo; Hamilton and Legros, Paris, 1876, 8vo, 2 vols.; Smith, Hamilton, and Legros, Paris, 1876, 8vo, 2 vols.; Brachet, Paris, 1878, 12mo; Fleming and Tibbins, Paris, 1878, 4to, 2 vols.; French Academy, 7th ed., Paris, 1878, 4to, 2 vols.; Bellows, 2d ed., London, 1880, 32mo; Sachs, 3d ed., Berlin, 1881, 8vo, 2 vols. *Slang:* Larchey, 8th ed., Paris, 1880, 8vo; Rigaud, Paris, 1881, 8vo. *Old French:* Bartsch, 4th ed., Leipzig, 1880, 8vo; Godefroy, Paris, 1880–81, 4to, pts. 1–9. *Dialects:* Metivier, London, 1870, 8vo; Meyer, Paris, 1871, 8vo; Boucoiran, Nîmes, 1875–77, 8vo, pts. 1–3; Andrews, Nice, 1877, 12mo.

Provençal.—Bartsch, 4th ed., Elberfeld, 1880, 8vo.

Spanish.—Gildo, 7th ed., Paris, 1870, 8vo, 2 vols.; Saura, Barcelona, 1870–78, 12mo, 2 vols.; Booch-Arkossy, Leipzig, 1874, 8vo, 2 vols.; Spanish Academy, Madrid, 1875, 4to; Salvá, redigé par Noriega, Paris, 1876, 8vo; abrégé, Paris, 1878, 18mo; Bustamente, Paris, 1878, 18mo, 2 vols.; Lopes and Bensley, Paris, 1878, 8vo; Velasquez, London, 1878, 8vo; 2 vols., London, 1880, 8vo; Franceson, Leipzig, 1879, 8vo, 2 vols.

Portuguese.—Constancio, 10th ed., Paris, 1873, 4to; Vieyra, Porto, 1873-75, 4to, 5 vols.: abridged, Paris, 1878, 12mo, 2 vols.; Fonseca, 3d ed., Leipzig, 1877, 12mo; Valdez, 2d ed., Rio de Janeiro, 1879, 12mo, 2 vols.

Italian.—Tommaséo, 6th ed., Milano, 1872, 8vo; Feller, Lipsia, 1873, 12mo; Valentini, Leipzig, 1873, 12mo, 2 vols.; Ferarari and Caccia, Paris, 1874, 8vo; Roberts, London, 1874, 8vo; Baretti, London, 1877, 8vo, 2 vols.; Millhouse, 4th ed., London, 1877, 8vo, 2 vols.; Scarabelli, Firenze, 1878, 4to, 8 vols.; Fanfani, Milano, 1879, 12mo; Michaelis, Leipzig, 1881, 8vo, 2 vols.; *Vocabulario degli Accademici della Crusca*, 5th ed., Firenze, 1881, fol., 12 vols.

Wallachian.—Laurianus and Massimu, Bucuresci, 1871-76, 4to, 7 pts.; Cihac, Francfort, 1879, 8vo.

Scandinavian.

Swedish.—*Ordbok öfver Svenska spraket*, Stockholm, 1870, 4to; Oman, Stockholm, 1872, 12mo; Lönnrot, Helsingfors, 1874-80, 8vo, 14 pts.; Berndtson, Stockholm, 1879, pt. 1; *Pocket Dictionary*, Leipzig, 1880, 16mo.

Danish and Norwegian.—Rosing, 5th ed., Copenhagen, 1874, 18mo; Helms, 3d ed., Leipzig, 1876; Kaper, 2d ed., Kopenhagen, 1880, 8vo; Larsen, Kopenhagen, 1880, 8vo.

Teutonic.

Anglo-Saxon.—Bosworth, London, 1881, 8vo.

English.—Jenkins, London, 1879, 64mo; Ogilvie, new ed., London, 1880-82, 8vo, vols. 1-3; Webster, new ed., Springfield, Mass., 1880, 4to; Worcester, new ed., Philadelphia, 1880, 4to; Walker, ed. by Sowerby, London, 1881, 8vo. *Americanisms:* Bartlett, 4th ed., Boston, 1877, 8vo; De Vere, new ed., New York, 1872, 8vo. *Synonymes:* Klöpper, Rostock, 1881, 8vo. *Etymology:* Wedgwood, 3d ed., London, 1878, 8vo; Müller, 2d ed., Cöthen, 1879, 8vo, 2 vols.; Skeat, London, 1882, 8vo. *Old English:* Stratmann, 3d ed., Crefeld, 1878, 4to. *German:* Mätzner, Berlin, 1872-76, 8vo, pts. 1-7. *Dialects: Glossary of North of England Words*, London, 1873; Ray (*Unusual*), ed. by Skeat, London, 1874; Elworthy (*West Somerset*), London, 1875; Halliwell (*Archaic and Provincial*), London, 1876; Bonaparte (*Southern and South-Western*), London, 1877; Ross, Stead, and Holderness (*Holderness*), London, 1877; Dickinson (*Cumberland*), London, 1878: supplement, 1879; Jackson (*Shropshire*), London, 1879, pt. 1; Skeat (*Five Glossaries*), London, 1879; Britten (*Old Country and Farming*), London, 1880; Charnock (*Essex*), London, 1880; Courtney and Couch (*Cornwall*), London, 1880; Patterson (*Antrim and Down*), London, 1880; Evans (*Leicestershire*), London, 1881.

Frisic.—Doornkaat Koolman, Norden, 1877-78, 8vo, pts. 1-6.

Dutch.—Oudemans, Arnheem, 1872-80, 8vo, pts. 1-7; Calisch, Tiel, 1875, 8vo, 2 vols.; Kramers, London, 1876, 12mo; *Pocket Dictionary*, Leipzig, 1878, 16mo.

German.—Weigand, 4th ed., Giessen, 1872-76, 8vo, 2 vols.; Sanders, 2d ed., Leipzig, 1876, 4to, 3 vols.; *Handwörterbuch*, 2d ed., ib., 1878, 8vo; *Ergänzungswörterbuch*, Stuttgart, 1879-80, 4to, pts. 1-4; *Wörterbuch der Hauptschwierigkeiten*, Berlin, 1881, 8vo; Duden, Leipzig, 1880, 8vo. *English:* Grieb, 8th ed., Stuttgart, 1881, 8vo, 2 vols. *Middle High German:* Martin, Berlin, 1878, 8vo; Lexer, 2d ed., Leipzig, 1881, 12mo. *Old High German:* Wackernagel, 5th ed., Basel, 1878, 8vo; Schade, 2d ed., Halle, 1873-80, 8vo, pts. 1-8. *Dialects: Wörterbuch der Mecklenburgisch-Vorpommerschen Mundart*, Leipzig, 1876, 8vo; Berghaus, Berlin, 1878-81, 8vo, pts. 1-6; Albrecht, Leipzig, 1881, 8vo; Staub and Tobler, Frauenfeld, 1881, 4to, pt. 1.

Celtic.

Celtic generally.—Obermüller, Berlin, 1867-72, 8vo, 2 vols.; Molloy, Eblanæ, 1878, 8vo; Zeuss, Lipsiæ, 1881, 8vo.

Irish.—Windisch, Leipzig, 1880, 8vo.

Welsh.—Spurrell, 3d ed., Caerfyrddin, 1872, 8vo.

Slavonic.

Russian.—*New Pocket Dictionary of English and Russian*, Leipzig, 1874, 12mo; Reiff, Karlsruhe, 1875-78, 8vo, 4 vols.; *Wörterbuch Deutsch-Russisches und Russisch-Deutsches*, St. Petersburg, 1878, 4to, pt. 1; Alexandrow, St. Petersburg, 1879, 8vo, 2 vols.; Pawlowsky, Riga, 1879, 8vo; Schmidt, 3d ed., Leipzig, 1880, 8vo; Booch, Frey, and Messer, 2d ed., Leipzig, 1881, 8vo; Potocki, 2d ed., Leipzig, 1881, 8vo.

Polish.—Lukasscwski and Mosbach, Berlin, 1881, 8vo.

Bohemian.—Faster, Prag, 1875, 16mo; Kott, Prague, 1878-80, 8vo, vols. 1-3; Mourek, Prague, 1879, 8vo, pt. 1; Spatny, Prag, 1879, 8vo; Konecny, Wien, 1882, 12mo, 2 vols.

Servian and Croatian.—Parcic, Zadru, 1874, 8vo; Filipovic, Agram, 1877, 12mo, 2 vols.; Karadschitsch, Wien, 1877, 8vo; Popovic, Pancova, 1879-81, 8vo, 2 vols.; Danicic, Zagreb, 1880, 8vo, vol. 1.

Slovene.—Sket, Klagenfurt, 1879, 8vo.

Ugrian.

Finnish.—Ahlman, Helsingfors, 1872, 8vo; Donner, Helsingfors, 1876, 8vo; Meurmann, Helsingfors, 1877, 8vo.

Hungarian.—Fongarasi, Budapest, 1870, 8vo, 2 vols.; Mártonffy, Budapest, 1879, 8vo, vol. 1.

Gipsy.—Leitner, Lahore, 1880, fol.; Leland, Palmer, and Tuckey. London. 1875. 8vo.

Albanian.—Rossi, Roma, 1875, 8vo; Dozon, Paris, 1878, 8vo.

Turkish.—Calligaris (*Polyglot*), Turin, 1870, 4to, 2 vols.; Bálint, Pesth, 1877, 8vo; Ruzicka-Ostoic, Wien, 1879, 8vo; *Dictionnaire Française-Turc-Italien-Arabe*, Jerusalem, 1880, 8vo; Redhouse, 2d ed., London, 1880, 8vo; Shaw, Calcutta, 1878-80, 8vo, 2 vols.; Barbier de Meynard, Paris, 1881, 8vo, pt. 1; Mallouf, 3d ed., Paris, 1881, 8vo.

ASIA.
Semitic.

Hebrew.—Gesenius, 21st ed., Boston, 1880, 8vo; Tedeschi, Padova, 1880, 8vo; Schulbaum, Lemberg, 1881, 8vo.

Chaldee.—Fürst, 3d ed., Lipsiæ, 1876, 8vo, 2 vols.; ib., trans. by Davidson, 4th ed., London, 1871, 8vo; *Aruch Completum*, Vienna, 1878-80, 4to, vols. 1-2.

Samaritan.—Petermann, Berolini, 1873, 12mo.

Assyrian and Accadian.—Talbot, London, 1868-69, 8vo, 2 vols.; Sayce, London, 1875, 4to.

Syriac.—*Thesaurus Syriacus*, Oxford, 1868-80, fol., pts. 1-5.

Arabic.—*Dizionario Italiano-Arabo*, Gerusalemme, 1878, 4to; Fleury (*French*), new ed., Beyrouth, 1878, 12mo; Dozy (*French*), Leyde, 1879-80, 4to, 8 pts.; Jamati (*French, Technical*), Le Caire, 1879, 8vo; Guaselin (*French*), Paris, 1880-81, 4to, pts. 1-9; Badger (*English*), London, 1881, 4to; Dieterici (*German*), Leipzig, 1881, 8vo.

Armenian.—Aucher, Paris, 1872, 8vo, 2 vols.; Nar Bey, 2d ed., Paris, 1872, 12mo; Petermann, new ed., Berolini, 1872, 12mo; Bedrossian, Venice, 1875-79, 8vo; Prispuchow, 2d ed., Petersburg, 1876, 8vo.
Kurd.—Jaba, St. Petersburg, 1879, 8vo.
Brahoe.—Bellew, London, 1874, 8vo.
Persian.—Farhang Djahangiri, Lucknow, 1876, 8vo, 2 vols.; Spiegel, 2d ed., Leipzig, 1881, 8vo.
Biluchi.—Gladstone, Lahore, 1874, fol.; Marston, Bombay, 1877, 8vo; Dames, Calcutta, 1881, 8vo.
Zend.—Geiger, Erlangen, 1879, 8vo; Harlez, Paris, 1882, 8vo.
Pahlavi.—Minocheherji, Bombay, 1877-79, 8vo, vols. 1-2; Harlez, Paris, 1880, 8vo.

Indian Languages.

Indian Languages generally.—Biddulph, Calcutta, 1880, 8vo.
Sanskrit.—Wilson, 3d ed., Calcutta, 1874, 4to; Amarakosha, ed. by Kielhorn, Bombay, 1877, 8vo; Borooah, Calcutta, 1877-81, 8vo, 3 vols.; Böhtlingk, St. Petersburg, 1879-81, 4to, 3 vols.
Bengali.—Mendies, abridg. of *Johnson's Dictionary*, 2d ed., Calcutta, 1872, 8vo.
Garo.—Keith, Julpigoree, 1873, 8vo.
Canarese.—*Polyglot Vocabulary*, Mangalore, 1880, 8vo.
Guzarati.—Minocheherji, Bombay, 1877-79, 8vo, vols. 1-2; Moos, 3d ed., Bombay, 1880, 8vo.
Hindi.—Thompson, 2d ed., Calcutta, 1870, 8vo; Bate, Benares, 1875, 8vo.
Hindustani.—*Vocabulary of Common Words*, etc., Roorke, 1871, 8vo; Forbes, London, 1876, 16mo; Blochmann, 8th ed., Calcutta, 1877, 12mo; Fallon, Benares, 1880-81, 8vo, pts. 1-4; Platts, London, 1881, 8vo, pt. 1; Small, London, 1882, 8vo.
Shan.—Cushing, Rangoon, 1881, 8vo.
Malayalim.—*School Dictionary*, Mangalore, 1870, 8vo.
Peguan.—Haswell, Rangoon, 1874, 8vo.
Marathi.—Godbole, Bombay, 1870, 16mo.
Multani.—Glossary, Lahore, 1881, 8vo.
Sindhi.—Shirt, Kurrachee, 1879, 4to.
Mikir.—Neighbor, Calcutta, 1878, 8vo.
Somali.—Hunter, Bombay, 1880, 16mo.
Indo-Chinese Languages.—*Annamese*: Taberd, Ninh Phu, 1877, 4to; *Dictionnaire Annamite-Français*, Tân-Dinh, 1879, 8vo; Ravier. Ninh Phu, 1880, 4to. *Cambodian*: Aymonier, Saigon, 1878, 4to; Moura, Paris, 1878, 8vo.
Malay.—Marsden, London, 1872, 4to, 2 vols.; Roorda van Eysinga, Leiden, 1875, 8vo; Clercq, Batavia, 1876, 4to; Badings, 3d ed., Schoonheim, 1879, 8vo; Morel, Haarlem, 1879, 8vo, 2 vols.; Kriens, 's Hage, 1880, 8vo.
Indian Archipelago.—*Javanese*: Janss, 3d ed., Samarang, 1877, 8vo. *Balinese*: Eck, Utrecht, 1876, 8vo. *Sunda*: Grashuis, 2d ed., Leiden, 1879, 8vo; Oosting, Batavia, 1879, 8vo, pts. 1-3. *Formosa*: Guérin, Paris, 1868, 8vo. *Nicobar and Andaman Isles*: Roepstorff, Fort Blair, 1874, fol.
Chinese.—Stent, Shanghai, 1874, 16mo; *Dictionarium Linguæ Sinico-Latinum*, Ho-kian-fou, 1877, 8vo; Eitel, Hong Kong, 1877-78, 8vo, pts. 1-2; Hamelin, Paris, 1877, 8vo; Gonçalves, new ed., Pe-t'ang, 1879, 8vo. *Pidgin-English*: Leland, London, 1876, 8vo.
Corean.—*Dictionnaire Corées-Français*, Yokohama, 1880, 4to.
Japanese.—*Lexicon Latino-Japonicum*, Roma, 1870, 4to; Hepburn, Shanghai, 1873, 4to; Hyan-go ri-ayo, Tokio, 1880, 8vo.
Aino.—Dobrotvorskij, Kasan, 1875, 8vo.
Northern and Central Asia.—*Ostiak*: Ahlqvist, Helsingfors, 1880, 8vo. *Tartar*: Vámbéry, Leipzig, 1878, 8vo.

AFRICA.

Egyptian.—Brugsch, Leipzig, 1880, 4to, vols. 5-6; Levi, Torino, 1880, 4to.
Nubian.—Reinisch, Wien, 1879, 8vo, 2 vols.; Lepsius, Berlin, 1880, 8vo.
Amharic.—D'Abbadie, Paris, 1881, 8vo.
Kiniassa.—Rebman, Basle, 1877, 8vo.
Galla.—Mayer, Basel, 1878, 8vo.
Malagasy.—Sewell, Antananarivo, 1875, 8vo; *Vocubulaire Français-Malgache*, Tananarive, 1880, 8vo.
Kalasha.—Leitner, Lahore, 1880, 8vo.
Zulu-Kaffre.—Davis, London, 1877, 8vo; Roberts, London, 1880, 8vo.
Chinyanja.—Riddel, Edinburgh, 1880, 16mo.
Mpongwe.—*Dictionnaire Français-Pongoué*, Paris, 1877, 12mo; *Dictionnaire Pongoué-Français*, Paris, 1881, 8vo.
Ashantee.—Christaller, Basel, 1881, 8vo.
Dinka.—Beltrame, Roma, 1881, 8vo.
Haussa.—Schön, London, 1876, 8vo.

AUSTRALIA AND POLYNESIA.

Australia.—Ridley, London, 1877, 4to; Smith, Adelaide, 1880, 8vo.
Samoan.—Pratt, 2d ed., London, 1878, 8vo; Violette, Paris, 1880, 8vo.
Papuan.—Hasselt, Utrecht, 1876, 8vo.
Maori.—Williams, London, 1872, 8vo.

AMERICA.

North America.—Platzmann, Leipzig, 1876, 8vo; Powell, 2d ed., Washington, 1881, 4to. *Hidatsa*: Matthews, Washington, 1877, 8vo. *Cree*: Lacombe, Montreal, 1874, 8vo. *Otchipwe*: Baraga, new ed., Montreal, 1879, 8vo.
Mexico and Central America.—*Mexican*: Molina, Leipzig, 1880, 4to. *Maya*: Perez, Merida de Yucatan, 1866-77, 4to.
South America.—*Guarani*: Montoya, Vienna, 1876-77, 4to, 2 vols. *Quichua*: Ellis, London, 1875, 8vo. *Aymara*: Bertonio, Leipzig, 1879, 8vo, 2 vols. *Paez*: *Vocabulario Paéz-Castellano*, Paris, 1877, 8vo. (I. E. J.

DIEFENBACH, LORENZ, a German philologist, was born at Ostheim, in Hesse, July 29, 1806. He was educated at Giessen, and studied theology and philosophy. In 1823 he removed to Frankfort-on-the-Main, where he studied modern languages and music. For some years he was pastor of a church and librarian at Solms-Laubach, and later lived in other parts of Germany. In 1845 he assisted in forming a German-Catholic congregation at Offenbach, and in 1848 was elected as delegate from that town to the Parliament at Frankfort. He was also made counsellor to Prince Leiningen, president of the imperial ministry. Having settled in Frankfort on account of his official duties, he lectured in the commercial academy, and displayed great literary activity, publishing several novels as well as scientific, literary, critical, and political articles and books. From 1865 to 1876 he was city librarian; he then removed to Darmstadt, and has since been engaged exclusively in literary work. Among his novels may be mentioned *Ein Pilger und seine Genossen* (1851), *Die Pfarrerskinder* (1867), *Arbeit macht Frei* (

His more important works have been on ethnographical and philological subjects, one of the earliest being *Ueber die Romanischen Schriftsprachen* (1837). This was followed by *Celtica* (3 vols., 1839–40), and several dictionaries, among which were supplements to the great work of Ducange on mediæval Latin, *Glossarium Latino-germanicum* (Frankfort, 1857), and *Novum glossarium* (Frankfort, 1867). Among his ethnographical works are *Origines Europææ* (1861), *Vorschule der Völkerkunde* (1864), and *Völkerkunde Osteuropas* (Darmstadt, 1878). Dr. Diefenbach is a member of the Berlin Academy and of several other literary societies.

DIES NON JURIDICUS, in law, a day upon which courts do not transact business and upon which no ordinary legal proceeding can be taken. Sunday is universally considered, both in England and in the United States, as *dies non juridicus*. Its observance as such is supposed to have been common to the Normans and Saxons, and will be found to be mentioned in the very earliest treatises on the common law. Hence the origin of the maxim, "Dies Dominicus non est juridicus." No judgment can therefore be entered in a cause on Sunday, nor can an award be made and published on that day. A return of process, a notice or demand, or levy of execution made on Sunday is void. Service of process in a civil case cannot be effected upon the defendant on Sunday, nor in general can any official charged with civil duties discharge them on that day.

The foundation of the maxim just referred to is based, however, solely upon the ground that it is improper to allow a violation of a period of time peculiarly set apart for repose and divine worship, when the same purpose can be as easily effected at another time. Hence, where there is any pressing necessity, or where the particular act in question tends to facilitate the transaction of business or to establish and maintain peace and order in the community, legal proceedings may be carried on upon Sunday. A verdict may therefore be rendered and received on Sunday, and so of an award where the deliberations of the arbitrators have extended continuously through the preceding night. Ministerial acts may also be lawfully executed on Sunday, for otherwise, peradventure, they can never be executed. An information may therefore be filed on that day or a recognizance taken. An injunction in a pressing case may be issued and served on Sunday. An arrest may also, without doubt, be effected in a criminal case on that day. In New Hampshire it is said that a writ may be issued on Sunday in a civil case, if not done "to the disturbance of others."

In addition to Sundays, the stat. 5 & 6 Edw. VI. § 3, prescribed a number of holidays, which had already prior to that time been observed, as *dies non*. These were the Feast of the Circumcision (Jan. 1), the Epiphany (Jan. 6), the Purification of the Virgin Mary (Feb. 2), the Feast of St. Matthias (Feb. 24), the Annunciation (March 25), the Feasts of St. Mark (April 25) and of St. Philip and St. James (May 1), of the Ascension, of the Nativity, of St. John the Baptist (June 24), of St. Peter (June 29), of St. James (July 25), of St. Bartholomew (Aug. 24), of St. Matthew (Sept. 21), of St. Michael (Sept. 28), of St. Luke (Oct. 18), of St. Simon and St. Jude (Oct. 28), of All Saints (Nov. 1), of St. Andrew (Nov. 30), of St. Thomas (Dec. 21), Christmas Day and the three following days, and Monday and Tuesday in Easter and Whitsun weeks. Good Friday was also generally observed, though not mentioned in the statute.

By stat. 3 & 4 Wm. IV. c. 42, § 43, the *dies non* in England are reduced to Sundays, Easter Monday and Tuesday, Christmas Day and the three following days, and so they stand at the present time. It should be observed that the English courts have always been extremely liberal in admitting the validity of all legal proceedings transacted on *dies non* other than Sunday.

In the United States the courts and court offices are generally closed on the following days besides Sundays: January 1st, or New-Year's Day; February 22d, or Washington's Birthday; May 30th, or Decoration Day; July 4th, or Independence Day; December 25th, or Christmas Day; and also on Good Friday and Thanksgiving Day, which latter usually falls on the last Thursday in November. In some of the States it is particularly provided by statute that those days shall be taken and considered as Sunday, in which case it is to be presumed that they are accounted *dies non* to all intents and purposes. In other States provision is only made that bills or notes maturing on those days shall be considered as due on the day preceding or following. Where this is the case it is presumed that they are not to be accounted as *dies non*, strictly speaking. (L. L., JR.)

DIETERICI, FRIEDRICH, a German Orientalist, was born at Berlin, July 6, 1821, and is the son of the noted statistician, K. F. W. Dieterici. He studied theology at Halle and Berlin, and then devoted himself to the study of Oriental languages under Rödiger and Fleischer. After obtaining, in 1846, permission to teach as professor, he went to London in 1847 and thence to the East, where he spent eighteen months in Cairo under the instruction of a learned sheik. He then visited Upper Egypt and Palestine and returned to Germany by way of Constantinople and Athens. In 1850 he was made professor extraordinary in the University of Berlin, and still holds this position. He published the text of *Alfiyyah*, an original Arabic Grammar, with the commentary of Ibn-Akil, and a translation of the same into German (Leipsic, 1852); a *Chrestomathie Ottomane* (Berlin, 1854), and an edition of the works of the poet Mutanabbi (Berlin, 1858–61). Turning his attention to the Arabic philosophy of the tenth century, he published *Die Propädeutik der Araber* (Berlin, 1865); *Logik und Psychologie* (Leipsic, 1868); *Naturanschauung und Naturphilosophie* (2d ed., Leipsic, 1878); *Der Streit Zwischen Mensch und Thier* (Berlin, 1858), Arabic edition, Leipsic, 1879); *Anthropologie* (Leipsic, 1871); *Die Lehre von der Weltseele* (Leipsic, 1873); *Die Philosophie der Araber* (Leipsic, 1876–79). He has also published an Arabic German dictionary (Leipsic, 1881), and the so-called *Theology of Aristotle* (1882), an Arabic version of a lost Greek work of special importance in the history of philosophy. Among his other works are volumes of travels and an essay on *Der Darwinismus im 10. und 19. Jahrhundert* (Leipsic, 1878).

DIETETICS. See Vol. VII. p. 174 Am. ed. (p. 203 Edin. ed.) No two nations use the same food or prepare it in the same way. In the United States the raw materials of food are abundant, and of great variety, but they are rarely turned to the best account, the waste is great, the cooking often bad, and the diet of a large part of the people is comparatively monotonous. Among farmers, the laboring classes, and those who do not keep servants—where the cooking is done by the wife and daughters of the householder—the faults of cooking are largely due to the desire to save labor. Dr. Derby's remarks on the food of Massachusetts laborers apply to a large part of the country. "Whatever can be made in one day and kept for use in several succeeding days is preferred. The quickest way to cook fresh meat is to put it in the frying-pan. The laborious kneading of fermented bread is dispensed with and its substitutes are prepared by the hasty stirring-in of chemical powders." Dr. Barnch in a paper on the cause of dyspepsia (or so-called liver complaint) among the rural and laboring population of South Carolina (*Second Report State Board of Health, S. C.*, Charleston, 1881, p. 273) comments on the excessive use of salted and smoked meats and the sameness of the "hog and hominy" diet of the average Southern laborer, and regards the general and almost constant use of fried meats as the cause of much of the sickness met with in rural districts. The supply of vegetables and fruits is more abundant and varied in the United States than it is in Europe, and the use of meat among the middle and lower classes is much more common here than it is abroad. Diseases due to insufficient food are rarely observed by dispensary and hospital physicians in this country.

The United States army ration is now composed as follows: 12 ounces of pork or bacon, or 20 ounces of fresh beef, or 22 ounces of salt beef; 18 ounces of soft bread on flour, or 16 ounces of hard bread, or 20 ounces of corn-meal. To every 100 rations, 15 pounds of beans or peas, or 10 pounds of rice or hominy; 10 pounds of green coffee, or 8 pounds of roasted (or roasted and ground) coffee, or 2 pounds of tea; 15 pounds of sugar, 4 quarts of vinegar, 24 ounces of adamantine or star candles, 4 pounds of soap, 4 pounds of salt, 4 ounces of pepper; and to troops in the field, when necessary, 4 pounds of yeast powder to the 100 rations of flour.

The component parts of the ration are subject to change at the discretion of the President of the United States. Fresh mutton may be issued in lieu of, and at the same rate as, fresh beef, when the cost of the former does not exceed that of the latter. 14 ounces of dried fish, or 18 ounces of pickled or fresh fish, may be issued in lieu of the meat components of a ration. Molasses or syrup may be issued in lieu of sugar, at the rate of 2 gallons for 15 pounds of sugar. When it is impracticable for troops in the field, or those travelling upon cars or transports, to draw or cook beans or rice, equivalents in money value of bread or meat may be issued.

The following issues may be made to troops per 100 rations: in lieu of the usual meat portion of the ration 75 pounds canned fresh beef, or 75 pounds canned corn-beef. In lieu of the dry vegetable portion of the ration 33 one-pound cans baked beans, or 25 pounds cheese.

The navy ration is as follows: 1 pound of salt pork, with ½ pint of beans or peas, or 1 pound of salt beef with ½ pound of flour, and 2 ounces of dried apples, or other dried fruit, or ¾ pound of preserved meat, with ½ pound of rice, 2 ounces of butter, and 1 ounce of desiccated "mixed vegetables," or ¾ pound of preserved meat, 2 ounces of butter, and 12 ounces of tomatoes, together with 14 ounces of biscuit, ¼ ounce of tea, or 1 ounce of coffee or cocoa, and 2 ounces of sugar, and a weekly allowance of ½ pound of pickles, ½ pint of molasses, and ½ pint of vinegar. Fresh or preserved meat may be substituted for salt beef or pork, and vegetables for the other articles usually issued with the salted meats, allowing 1¼ pounds of fresh or ¾ pound of preserved meat for 1 pound of salted beef or pork; and regulating the quantity of vegetables so as to equal the value of the articles for which they may be substituted.

Should it be necessary to vary the above-described daily allowance, it is lawful to substitute 1 pound of soft bread, or 1 pound of flour, or ½ pound of rice for 14 ounces of biscuit; ½ pound of rice for ½ pint of beans or peas; ½ pint of peas or beans for ½ pound of rice. The weekly quantity is valued at $2.10.

A valuable work on dietetics by Dr. C. A. Meinert, entitled *Armee- und Volks-ernährung* (2 vols., Berlin, 1880), contains a large and valuable collection of statistical information with regard to the food-supply of various countries, and should be consulted by those who wish to study the details.

DIETRICHSON, LORENTZ SEGELKE, a Norwegian poet and critic, was born Jan. 1, 1834, in Bergen. He was educated at Christiania, and in 1861 became an instructor in the University of Upsala. He has travelled extensively; in 1858 in Sweden; in 1860 in Germany; in 1861 in Finland; in 1862–65 in Germany and Italy; in 1867–68 in Denmark and France; in 1869–70 in Hungary, Turkey, Asia Minor, Greece, and Italy. In 1862 he married J. M. Bonnevie, a Norwegian painter, in Düsseldorf, who by accompanying him on his travels has found abundant opportunity to gather materials for her art, and she has also successfully illustrated some of her husband's books. In 1875 Dietrichson became professor of the history of fine arts in Christiania. His books are written partly in Norwegian, partly in Swedish. In 1862–63 he edited *Nordisk Tidskrift for Literatur og Kunst*, published in Copenhagen. In 1864 appeared his biography of the Finnish poet, Runeberg, which was followed by *Omrids af den norske Literaturs Historie* (2 vols., 1866–69). His chief work, written in Swedish, is *Det Skönas Werld* (2 vols., 1867–69). It is a comprehensive treatise on art and its history. His drama *Madonnabilden* was produced on the Stockholm stage in 1870 with great success. Sketches of his extensive travels are found in his *På Studieresor* (2 vols., 1875). Two other dramas from his pen are *En Arbetare* (1872), and *Karl Folkunge* (1874). His latest works are *Kivleslåtten* and *Den norske Træskjærerkunst*.

DIGBY, KENELM HENRY (1800–1880), an English author, was born in 1800, being the youngest son of Rev. William Digby, Dean of Clonfert, of the Established Church of Ireland. He was of the same family as Sir Kenelm Digby. He graduated at Trinity College, Cambridge, in 1823, but had already gained reputation by his *Broadstone of Honoure, or Rules for the Gentlemen of England* (1822). This work was not only an enthusiastic vindication of the principles and institutions of chivalry, but it showed a strong predilection for the teachings of the Roman Church, which he soon afterwards entered. He then rewrote his work, enlarging it to four volumes, each with a separate title (1828–29). He had closely studied the scholastic theology and the history of the middle ages, and embodied the fruit of his studies in his *Mores Catholici; or Ages of Faith* (1831–42), in which he depicted the victory of the church over the barbarians. After an interval of several years he published *Compitum; or the Meeting of Ways in the Catholic Church* (1848–54). These were his principal works, but in later years he issued *The Lover's Seat* (1856); *Children's Bower* (1858); *Evenings on the Thames* ([illegible]); *The Chapel of St. John* (1861), a memorial of his deceased wife; and *The Epilogue* (1876). He died

March 22, 1880. His first work was pronounced by Julius Hare, "That noble manual for gentlemen," but the author's conversion to the Catholic faith restricted his fame and influence. His style is diffuse, and his writings are pervaded with a pleasing melancholy and regard for the past.

DIGGER INDIANS, a name applied to the Pi-Utes, Goshutes, Washoes, Pah-Utes, and other minor tribes, of the Utah branch of the Shoshone family of American Indians. Its application is somewhat indefinite, however, and covers all those Indians of Nevada, Utah, and California, without respect to tribal designation, whose habits render the title of Root-Digger applicable. Many of the minor California tribes are genuine Diggers. They are among the lowest and most degraded of human beings, living in a comparatively mild climate, on nearly barren plains, where little food is to be obtained beyond the roots which they dig from the ground, and the berries, seeds, insects, fish, and small game, sparsely found in their territory. They are a cowardly, dull, poorly developed, half-starved phase of humanity, with filthy and beastly habits. The food is chiefly obtained by the women, the men being utterly indolent. Among their common articles of food are lizards, snakes, grasshoppers, and ants, which are thrown together into a dish of hot embers, and tossed about till roasted. Rats and rabbits are singed, and then cooked without removing the intestines. In the spring, when reduced to destitution by the winter lack of food, they will eat dead bodies, and even kill their children for food. Their only protection from wintry winds consists of circular heaps of brush, except that occasionally they dwell in caves or in fissures of the rocks, whence they crawl in the spring, often too weak to stand upright.

They know nothing of their past history, have no marriage ceremony, and no trace of religious observance, and are destitute of arts and weapons beyond the bow and arrow. Tattooing is commonly practised. The females wear their hair short, and the males quite long. They burn the bodies of their dead, with all the effects of the deceased, and indulge in wild mourning over the corpse. Their idea of their origin displays a peculiar evolutionary notion. The first Indians were coyotes. These first walked on all-fours, then gained human members, as one finger, toe, eye, ear, etc.; then two of these members; gained the habit of sitting, and so lost their tails; and finally became human beings. They regret the loss of the tail, which they consider an ornamental appendage.

The Diggers roam throughout Nevada, and into Oregon and California. Their degradation is largely a result of their destitution, since other members of the same tribes, who dwell in more fertile regions, are much less debased, and the Bannacks, who are closely related to them, are a proud, brave, and self-respecting tribe. The Pi-Utes, Winnemuccas, and Pah-Utes have made considerable progress of late.

DILKE, Sir Charles Wentworth, an English statesman and author, was born at Chelsea, Sept. 4, 1843. His grandfather, bearing the same name, was editor and proprietor of the *Athenæum*, and was distinguished as a critic. The grandson was educated at Trinity Hall, Cambridge, where he graduated as senior legalist in January, 1866. In the same year he was admitted to the bar in the Middle Temple, London, and set out on an extensive tour. After travelling alone for some months through Canada and the United States, he met Mr. W. Hepworth Dixon in St. Louis, and in his company crossed the Great Plains and the Rocky Mountains. Leaving Mr. Dixon at Salt Lake City, Mr. Dilke continued his journey to San Francisco. Thence he sailed to Panama, then to New Zealand, Tasmania, and Australia. He carefully examined these colonies both as to their present condition and future prospects, political and commercial. He then passed to Calcutta, visited Upper India, sailed down the Indus, and returned to England by way of Egypt. In 1868 he published the result of his observations in *Greater Britain: a Record of Travel in English-Speaking Countries during 1866–67*. This work attained a remarkable success, passing through four editions in one year in England and being republished by two firms in America, where it had a still larger number of editions. It was not merely a record of what he had seen, but also an attempt to show the effect of climatic conditions on the race and the influence of race upon government. Immediately after its publication the author was elected to Parliament from the new borough of Chelsea as a Radical, being the youngest man who ever represented a metropolitan constituency. He succeeded his father and grandfather in the proprietorship of the *Athenæum*, and is also proprietor of *Notes and Queries*, and principal proprietor of the *Gardener's Chronicle*. In 1871 he openly avowed his preference for a republican form of government over a constitutional monarchy, and in 1874 an effort was made to defeat his re-election at Chelsea on that ground, but he was returned at the head of the poll. In the same year he published anonymously a vigorous satire called *The Fall of Prince Florestan of Monaco*, which passed through several editions, and was translated into French. In 1875 he edited the writings of his grandfather, with a memoir, under the title *Papers of a Critic*. In the same year he made a second journey round the world, and published in the monthly magazines his observations in China and Japan. In his parliamentary career he has succeeded in introducing several reforms, among which are amendment to the education bill, by which the school-boards are directly elected by the rate-payers; conferring the municipal franchise on women; abolishing the barbarous penalty of drawing and quartering; the amendment of the registration law, and extension of the hours of polling at parliamentary elections in London. In April, 1880, he was again re-elected for Chelsea at the head of the poll, and on the formation of Mr. Gladstone's government was appointed under-secretary of state for foreign affairs.

DILLMANN, Christian Friedrich August, D. D., a German theologian, commentator, and Orientalist, was born at Illingen, in Würtemberg, April 25, 1823. After a preliminary education at Stuttgart and Schönthal, he studied philosophy and theology at Tübingen. In 1844, under the direction of Prof. Ewald, he devoted himself to Oriental languages, and in the next year, while pursuing his studies, had charge of a church at Tersheim. In 1846, having obtained the degrees of M. A. and of Ph. D. from the University of Tübingen, he went to France and England for the purpose of examining Æthiopic manuscripts in the public libraries. While in England he was invited by the authorities of the British Museum and of the Bodleian Library to prepare catalogues of such manuscripts in their possession. The offer was accepted, and the volumes containing the results of his labor appeared at London in 1847 and at Oxford in

1848. Returning to Tübingen, in the latter year, he became a theological repetent, and after the departure of Ewald performed the duties of professor of Old-Testament exegesis. In 1852 he became a privat docent, and the next year professor extraordinarius. In 1854, a similar position having been offered to him at Kiel in Holstein, he removed thither, and in 1859 was made professor of Oriental languages. In 1862 he received the degree of D. D. from the University of Leipsic. In 1864 he was called to Giessen in Hesse as professor of Old-Testament exegesis, and during his residence there was twice rector of the university. In 1869 he succeeded Hengstenberg as professor of Old-Testament exegesis in the University of Berlin. In March, 1877, he was elected a member of the Royal Academy of Science at Berlin. In September, 1881, he was president of the fifth international Orientalist congress, and as such published the proceedings of the congress in two volumes (1881–82). He is the highest authority in the department of Æthiopic (Geez) language and literature. His translation of the *Book of Jubilees, or the Little Genesis*, appeared in Ewald's *Jahrbücher der biblischen Wissenschaft* (1849–51), and his edition of the original Æthiopic text was published at Leipsic in 1859. He had already edited the famous *Book of Enoch* (Leipsic, 1851), and added a German commentary, with a translation, in 1853. In the latter year he published in Ewald's *Jahrbücher* a translation from the Æthiopic of the Christian *Book of Adam*. His greatest undertaking in this department is his edition of the entire Old Testament in Æthiopic, *Biblia Veteris Testamenti Æthiopica* (Leipsic, vol. i., 1853; vol. ii., 1861–72). To facilitate the studies of others he has prepared an Æthiopic grammar, *Grammatik der Æthiopischen Sprache* (1857); a lexicon, *Lexicon Linguæ Æthiopicæ cum indice Latino* (1865); and a chrestomathy, *Chrestomathia Æthiopica, edita et glossario explanata* (1866). His most recent publications in this department are the *Ascensio Isaiæ* in Æthiopic and Latin (Leipsic, 1877), and a catalogue of the Æthiopic manuscripts in the Royal Library at Berlin (1878). Of his theological works the most important are those on the *Origin of the Old-Testament Religion* (*Ueber den Ursprung der alttestamentlichen Religion* (Giessen, 1865) and *The Prophets of the Old Covenant in their Political Activity* (*Ueber die Propheten des Alten Bundes nach ihren politischen Wirksamkeit* (Giessen, 1868). He has also published several commentaries, the first being a new edition of Hirzel's *Commentary on Job* (1869), and the next a revision of Knobel's *Commentary on Genesis* (1875). His later exegetical works are original commentaries on *Exodus and Leviticus* (Leipsic, 1880) and on *Genesis* (1882). Valuable articles from his pen have appeared in the *Jahrbücher für deutsche Theologie*, in Herzog's *Real-Encyclopædie*, in Schenkel's *Bibel-lexikon*, and in the publications of the Royal Academy of Berlin. Prof. Dillmann is the most distinguished disciple of Prof. Ewald, and has followed his master in his treatment of the Old-Testament literature and history. While firmly maintaining that those ancient writings must be submitted to all the tests and requirements of modern criticism, he has strongly expressed his dissent from the results arrived at by Kuenen, Wellhausen, and Prof. W. Robertson Smith.

DILLON, JOHN, an Irish politician, is the son of John Blake Dillon, an Irish revolutionist of 1848, and was born in 1851. He was educated at the Catholic University, Dublin, studied medicine, and was licensed as a surgeon, but was prevented by ill health from practising his profession. In 1879 he accompanied Mr. Charles S. Parnell to the United States for the purpose of explaining the principles of the Land League and arousing sympathy for the Irish peasantry, who were suffering from famine. Elected member of parliament for Tipperary, in 1880, he won considerable distinction by his fearless defence of the claims of his country. He was then indicted with others for seditious conspiracy, but on the trial the jury disagreed. In 1881 he was arrested under the coercion act, placed in Kilmainham jail, denied bail or trial, and kept in durance until 1882, when he and others similarly imprisoned were unconditionally released. Mr. Gladstone paid a high tribute to Mr. Dillon's patriotism and purity of motive, but the latter indignantly spurned the eulogy, fearing that the real purpose of the premier was to asperse the motives of his colleagues. (M. F. S.)

DIMAN, JEREMIAH LEWIS, D. D. (1831–81), an American Congregationalist minister and educator, was born at Bristol, R. I., May 1, 1831. His father, Gov. Byron Diman, was well versed in history, and in early life the son showed similar tastes, contributing to the village journal articles on local history. He graduated at Brown University in 1851, and, after spending two years at Andover Theological Seminary, went to Germany, where he pursued various studies at Halle, Munich, Heidelberg, and Berlin. Returning, in the spring of 1856, he graduated at Andover, and in the autumn of that year was ordained pastor of the First Congregational Church at Fall River, Mass. In February, 1860, he removed to Brookline, Mass., and, after four years of pastoral labor there, was called to be professor of history and political economy in Brown University. In this department he was highly successful, being not only a careful investigator and an original thinker, but inspiring his pupils with his own enthusiasm. Having enjoyed while abroad familiar intercourse with Baron Bunsen, he fully accepted Bunsen's view, that "all history is instinct with a divine presence," and held that Jonathan Edwards, in his *History of Redemption*, had marked the true path of the deepest historical investigation. Besides his labors in Brown University he delivered several courses of lectures in other places, the chief of which were those on *The Thirty Years' War* before the Johns Hopkins University in 1879, and the Lowell lectures in the same year on *The Theistic Argument*. He died at Providence, R. I., Feb. 3, 1881. His work on *The Theistic Argument* is a valuable contribution to philosophy. A memorial-volume of Dr. Diman has also been published under the title *Orations and Essays, with selected Parish Sermons* (1882).

DINDORF, WILHELM (1802–1883), a German philologist, was born at Leipsic, Jan. 21, 1802. His father, Gottlieb Immanuel Dindorf (1755–1812), was a professor of Hebrew and Oriental languages. The son was educated at the University of Leipsic, and began his literary career in 1819 by assisting in an edition of Aristophanes. In 1828 he was made professor of literary history in his *alma mater*, but in 1833 he resigned and went to Paris, where he joined his younger brother Ludwig (born Jan. 3, 1805, died Sept. 6, 1871) and K. B. Hase (1780–1864) in preparing a new edition of Stephanus's great work, *Thesaurus Linguæ Græcæ* (1829–63). He also edited many Greek classics for Didot's *Bibliothèque*, and for the Oxford and Leipsic series. His principal works are *Demosthenes* (9 vols., Oxford, 1846-51); *Poetæ Scænici Græci* (1830; 5th ed., Leipsic, 1867); his Commentary on the Greek tragic poets and on Aristophanes (7 vols., Oxford, 1836-42). Unfortunate financial speculations in 1879 compelled him to sell his library and unfitted him for further work. He died at Leipsic, Aug. 7, 1883. His brother Ludwig, above mentioned, published editions of Xenophon, Diodorus Siculus, Polybius, Dion Cassius, and other historians.

DINGELSTEDT, FRANZ VON (1814-1881), a German poet and novelist, was born at Halsdorf in Hesse, June 30, 1814. He studied philology and theology in the University of Marburg, 1831-35, and became professor at Cassel in 1836. Here he gave offence by his liberal opinions. He published in 1841 a collection of poems entitled *Lieder eines Kosmopolitischen Nachtwächters*, which are remarkable for fine irony, poetical fancies, and exquisite humor. He became, in 1843, keeper of the royal library of Würtemburg at Stuttgart, and in 1850 intendant of the royal theatre at Munich. He was appointed director of the imperial opera-house in Vienna in 1867, and director of the great *Burgtheater* in Vienna in 1871. He received the title of baron from the emperor of Austria in 1876. He died at Vienna, May 15, 1881. Among his works are *Wanderbuch* (2 vols., 1839-43); a novel entitled *Unter der Erde* (1840); *Licht und Schatten in der Liebe* (1838); *Heptameron* (1841); *Gedichte* (1845); *Das Haus des Barneveldt*, a tragedy (1850); and *Nacht und Morgen* (1851). In 1840 he married Jenny Lutzer, a popular singer. He translated into German Shakespeare's *Tempest*, *As You Like It*, and *Twelfth Night*, and several historical plays.

DINWIDDIE, ROBERT (1690-1770), lieutenant-governor of Virginia, was born in Scotland in 1690. He became clerk to a collector of customs in the West Indies, and having exposed frauds committed by his employer, was rewarded by being appointed lieutenant-governor of Virginia in 1752. On assuming this position he divided the militia of the colony into four districts, assigning Major George Washington to the command of one of them. Having learned that the French were establishing military posts south of Lake Erie, he sent Major Washington to order their commandant to leave the British territory. The chief effect of this mission was to hasten the approaching conflict. Dinwiddie urged the assembly of Virginia to appropriate money for the public defence, and called upon the other governors to unite in efforts against the French encroachments. After much delay the Virginia Assembly voted £10,000 to be spent under the supervision of commissioners, and the other colonies did little or nothing. Dinwiddie increased the number of troops and promoted Washington to be lieutenant-colonel, nominally second, but really first, in command. The attempt to establish a fort on the Ohio River was unsuccessful, and Dinwiddie, having by urgent entreaties obtained more supplies, resolved to place the new forces under royal officers, allowing no native-born officer to take higher rank than captain. Washington forthwith resigned, but when Gen. Braddock arrived in 1754 consented to act as a volunteer aide-de-camp with his former rank. After Braddock's defeat the defence of the colony devolved upon Washington, who was frequently annoyed by Dinwiddie's ill-judged efforts at vigorous operations against the enemy. The governor also had frequent disputes with the Assembly, and was charged with avarice, embezzlement, and exaction of illegal fees. In 1758 he returned to England with great wealth. He died at Clifton, England, Aug. 7, 1770.

DIOCESE (διοίκησις), a term in general signifying administration, was applied, in the civil administration of the Roman empire, at first to a single province and later to an aggregation of provinces, and in the Catholic Church to the jurisdiction of a Bishop. In the reign of Constantine the empire was remodelled and divided into 117 provinces. For purposes of administration these provinces were grouped into 13 aggregates, to each of which the name diocese was applied. In the East lay the Oriental diocese (containing 15 provinces), Egypt (with 6), the Asiatic (with 10), the Pontic (with 11), and Thrace (with 6 provinces); these dioceses again being grouped under the control of the *Præfectus Prætorio Orientis*. To the westward, under the *Præfectus Prætorio* of Illyricum, were the diocese of Macedonia (containing 6 provinces), and the frontier diocese of Dacia (with 5). The three dioceses of Italy (with 17 provinces), Illyricum (with 6), and Africa (with 6), were under Præfectus-Prætorio of Italy. In the West, under the Præfectus-Prætorio Galliarum, were the 3 dioceses of Hispania (with 7 provinces), Gallia (with 17), and Britannia (with 5). In this way the 117 provinces of the Roman Empire were grouped into 13 dioceses, and these again placed under the jurisdiction of 4 *Præfecti-Prætorio*.

In accordance with the civil arrangement of the empire, the Christian Church perfected her organization. Every city where there was a civil magistracy seated became also the seat of a bishop; and as the metropolis of a province exercised jurisdiction over all its cities, so the bishop seated in the metropolis possessed a supervision over the bishop of the provincial cities and was thence designated as a metropolitan or archbishop.

The supervision of the bishop extended to the civil whole region lying round the city over which the magistracy exercised jurisdiction, called the προάστεια or παροικία, the Parish. The relation of this outlying region to the government of the city bishop varied in different parts of the empire. In the Oriental diocese, Syria and Asia Minor, in the country districts, especially in those localities where lay numerous villages, bishops were consecrated in subordination to the city bishop, and called χωρεπίσκοποι, country bishops. This system fell gradually into desuetude, and an attempt in the ninth century under the renewed empire of Charlemagne to establish it in the West was unsuccessful. Among the tribes of Arabia the bishop was itinerant, περιοδευτής, while in the neighborhood of the greater cities, as Alexandria, and always in the West, the administration was exercised directly by the city bishop through presbyters appointed for the purpose either permanently or for a time, and so called Cardinal, as at Rome.

In further conformity to the civil system, the different metropolitans of a civil diocese were grouped together under the care of an Exarch or Patriarch, πατριάρχης, an ecclesiastical Præfectus-Prætorio, who was usually the bishop of the civil capital of the diocese. But in this, as in some other respects, the conformity was not complete; Jerusalem being also erected into a patriarchate. So that the metropolitans of the Catholic Church within the empire were under the supervision of the five patriarchs (in the order of their precedence) of Rome, Constantinople, Alexandria, Antioch, and Jerusalem.

A few provinces were exempt from the authority of the patriarch, and to these the title autocephalous (αὐτοκέφαλοι) was applied. These included the Island of Cyprus and such Christian countries as Armenia not under the control of the empire. The same name was also given to the bishops of 41 cities in the empire exempted from the control of the metropolitans, and immediately under the authority of the patriarch, while in the civil diocese of Africa the primate or metropolitan of the provinces of Numidia and Mauritania was the bishop senior in consecration and not, according to the otherwise universal rule, the bishop of the metropolis of the province.

According to the canonical rule a diocese might have but one bishop and each bishop was limited to his own diocese. Occasionally an exception was made, as when a vacant diocese was committed to the care of a neighboring bishop or the metropolitan. The large profit accruing from this practice led to a flagrant abuse in the Middle Ages when the jurisdiction and revenues of two or more sees were accumulated upon one person with provision for life; a less objectionable practice existed in the "commendæ militares," when a portion of the revenues of the diocese was assigned to a great lay-noble in return for his protection. The canon law provided that in the diocese of another a bishop might perform the divine offices and use his episcopal habit, without leave, but exercise no jurisdiction; and should consent to exercise such jurisdiction be granted, yet it would be valid only with such as might willingly submit themselves to his authority.

It is to be observed that the view here presented of the organization of the church on the analogy of the empire is combated by a large school of Anglican writers, as Bishop Beveridge, and by the greater part of the Roman authorities, who carry back the metropolitans and patriarchs to apostolic authority, while others of that communion complete the analogy by placing one patriarch, as emperor, above the others, yet differ as to his apostolic or later foundation.

Bibliography.—W. Beveridge, D. D., *Synodicon, sive Pandecta Canonum*, etc. (Oxon., 1772); J. Bingham, *The Antiquities of the Christian Church*, book ix.; E. Brerewood, *Patriarchal Government of the Ancient Church* (London, 1687); Ayliffe, *Parergon Juris Canonici*; Barrow, *Treatise on the Pope's Supremacy*; W. Coxe, D.D., *A Dissertation Concerning the Government of the Ancient Church by Bishops, Metropolitans, and Patriarchs* (London, 1683); Du Pin, *De Antiqua Eccles. Disciplina, Dissert*; E. Hatch, *The Organization of the Early Christian Churches* (Oxford, 1881); J. Leunclavius, *Jus Græco-Romanum* (Frankfort, 1594); H. Maurice, D.D., *A Defence of Diocesan Episcopacy* (2d ed., London, 1700); Carolus a Sancto Paulo, *Geographia Sacra*, etc.; *cum notis et animadversionibus Lucae Holstenici* (Amstel., 1703); Suicer, *Thesaurus*; Thomassinus, *Vetus et Nova Ecclesia Disciplina*; Von Espen, *Jus Eccles. Universum*.
(P. H. H.)

DIPHTHERIA. Recent investigations cast light on the etiology or causation of the disease, and, as closely connected with this, the nature of the affection. The clinical facts which are well established, and which must here be considered, are as follows: First, in many cases the disease seems to originate entirely within the person of the patient, no exposure to contagion or epidemic influence being perceptible; second, in other cases the disease seems to be locally epidemic—for example, a single house will have an outbreak of diphtheria which may be of a very fatal nature and be confined absolutely to the one house; thirdly, the disease may occur as a widespread epidemic; and fourthly, diphtheria in some cases seems to be eminently contagious, and in other cases it fails to spread from person to person. There has long been, in the medical profession, a controversy concerning the relation of the two diseases known as pseudo-membranous croup and diphtheria, some physicians believing that the two affections are entirely distinct, and others that they are closely connected or even the same disease. It seems indisputable that a case may begin as one of croup or simple inflammation of the larynx and trachea, and gradually take on the features of diphtheria until it ends with all the well-known evidences of blood-poisoning; whilst in other instances the type of a simple inflammation is maintained throughout the attack, although a membrane is formed in the larynx or trachea which cannot be distinguished microscopically or in any other way from the membrane so prominent in cases of diphtheria, and death results.

Very abundantly, in the membrane of diphtheria, there is to be found a peculiar fungal organism known as the *micrococcus*. It occurs usually in irregular masses composed of innumerable exceedingly minute cells, but sometimes these cells are scattered, and sometimes they are collected into round balls, and in other cases they are in irregular masses known as *zooglœa*. The nature of these organisms and their relation to disease have been the subject of much controversy.

In an investigation lasting for some years made under the auspices of the National Board of Health, Drs. H. C. Wood and H. F. Formad have studied the subject very thoroughly, and have arrived at conclusions which seem positive. They find, in the first place, that the formation of the membrane in the throat, which has been supposed to be characteristic of diphtheria, is simply the result of a high degree of inflammation, and may be produced by the application of any caustic or irritant capable of producing inflammation of sufficient intensity. The membrane is not, therefore, peculiar to the disease, but may be formed in the throat of any individual who is suffering from a severe inflammation, the result of exposure to cold or other causes. They have also found that the micrococci or fungal organisms exist in the membrane which is produced by cold, although when this inflammatory membrane is first formed the organisms are very few in number, but later they become more abundant.

In regard to cases of diphtheria, they determined that the organisms are always abundant in the membranes about the throat, and that in malignant cases the same organisms are to be found in the blood and in the internal organs, especially in the spleen, the marrow of the bones, and the kidneys. In the kidneys they exist in such masses as to completely occlude some of the blood-vessels, and no doubt cause the peculiar inflammation of the organ so characteristic of the disorder. These organisms do not always exist in the blood of patients suffering from so-called diphtheria, but are always found in the throat; and the question naturally arises, Are they the cause of the disorder, or do they simply flourish in the throat because they find suitable nourishment and surrounding circumstances?

In order to determine this, experiments were made by inoculating the lower animals with the membrane taken from the throat of a diphtheritic patient, and it was found that when the case was malignant a disease was produced in the animals in all respects similar to human diphtheria. The disease was always primarily local. As an example, in the case of a pig which ate some the membrane death resulted from diphtheria of the stomach, the mucous membrane of the lower œsophagus and of the stomach being covered with a dense membrane full of micrococci. It was also found possible to pass the disease from animal to animal. Experiments were then undertaken by rubbing up the membrane with water and filtering out the solid particles, when it was found that the poison of the disease was the solid portion of the membrane, and was insoluble in water. It was also found that boiling the membrane for longer than fifteen minutes destroyed its noxious powers.

The micrococcus was then cultivated in various kinds of soups, entirely away from the animal body, according to the method of Sternberg, Koch, and others It was found that the cultivated micrococcus was not prone to develop the disease, but in a number of instances, by the third or fourth generation of the cultivated plant, diphtheria was produced in the lower animals. It was further discovered that when the micrococcus was taken from a case of malignant diphtheria its power of developing and growing was excessive, and was maintained for nine or ten generations, whereas when it was taken from a case of simple sore throat the power of growth was very slight; and finally, that the power of growth and development of the plant was always in direct proportion to the malignancy of the disorder.

It is evident that the micrococcus is either the immediate cause of the disorder, or else that it bears the same relation to the poison of diphtheria that the yeast-plant does to alcohol, producing the poison of diphtheria out of the fluids and tissues of the body at whose expense it grows. Under these circumstances a study of the life-history of the micrococcus becomes very important. It was cultivated in all kinds of liquids under very various circumstances, but our authors failed to develop from it any other form of plant, except that in certain cases of rats poisoned with the micrococcus, bacilli appeared in the blood, and it is possible, though scarcely probable, that the micrococcus altered its form. The mode of growth of the micrococcus inside of the body was distinctly made out. It usually first develops in the membrane, and forces its way into the submucous layer, and from thence into the blood; whether it ever primarily exists in the blood, so that the disease is constitutional before it is local, or not, is uncertain; but it is perfectly sure that in the great majority of cases the disease is primarily local.

In the blood, the micrococcus was found to especially attack the white blood-corpuscle. A few of the organisms would be noted inside of these corpuscles in a condition of vibratile movement. They would rapidly increase in number, and peculiar vacuoles would appear in the white blood-corpuscles. Whenever these vacuoles can be seen in the blood of a patient affected with this disease the prognosis is exceedingly grave, as in nearly every instance witnessed death followed. As the micrococcus multiplied in the blood-corpuscle, they finally filled it entirely, until at last the corpuscle or leucocyte is changed into a round ball composed simply of a mass of micrococci grouped together. It is in this way the micrococci balls are formed which have been so long known as existing in the throat. A little later the corpuscle bursts; the internal mass of micrococci escapes, leaving an outer thin membranous collapsed portion; the extruded mass continues to grow, and forms the irregular so-called zoogloea masses of micrococci. The micrococcus which has thus been studied does not differ in any appreciable way from the micrococcus which is found in the mouths of all healthy persons, except in its tendency to grow; and it will be remembered that an unbroken series in growth-power can be found between the micrococcus of the healthy mouth and the micrococcus of the most malignant diphtheria, the power of developing being always in direct proportion to the malignancy of the disease.

It has been shown by Pasteur, Koch, and other French and German investigators, in regard to certain other diseases, that fungal organisms which produce them are capable of passing into an inert condition, and in this inert state or condition they fail to develop in culture-fluids, and that the malignant power of the organism is always in direct proportion to its ability to grow in a culture-fluid where it gets little or no oxygen. It would seem, therefore, that the same fact is true of the organism that produces diphtheria. Its infective power is in direct proportion to its power of developing. These facts being established, the explanation of the clinical facts spoken of at the beginning of this article is very evident. A child gets a severe cold, and has as a consequence a catarrhal sore throat; the micrococci are present in this child's mouth in an inert condition, and by the abundance of food they find in the catarrhal exudation they are stimulated to growth: if, now, the vitality of the child be low, the conflict, which follows between the ever-increasing vitality of the micrococcus and that of the child, ends in the micrococcus getting a lodgment in the mucous membrane, and finally forcing its way into the blood; and that which was at first a simple case of sore throat or croup is converted into one of general blood-poisoning—i. e., diphtheria.

In the early stages of such a case, or when the micrococcus has not gained great vitality, the contagion is very feeble, but when the micrococcus has assumed its malignant powers, any of it, escaping with the breath from the mouth, coming in contact with the throat of another child or a wound in the finger of a doctor, finds lodgment, commences to grow, and gives origin to a new case of diphtheritic infection. It can be understood, therefore, why the contagiousness of diphtheria varies so infinitely. Again, a house will have some foul water-closet or similar local condition which favors the development of the micrococcus outside of the human body, and finally the whole air of that house becomes loaded with the poison, although the house is not able to infect the whole neighborhood. If, however, people pass from this house into other houses which contain suitable lodging-places for the plant, the epidemic may spread, and that which was purely a local may finally become a general epidemic. In the case of Luddington, in Michigan, the whole subsoil of the town was composed of rotting sawdust, and apparently the micrococcus found suitable conditions for its growth everywhere, so that a general epidemic was produced which attacked almost every child in the affected area. The micrococcus of diphtheria is not distinguishable from that which is found in various other diseases. The sore throat of advanced scarlet fever is exactly similar in its structural change, and in the organisms which it contains, with that of diphtheria, and it is not therefore surprising to find in malignant scarlet fever, after the lapse of some days, the blood presenting exactly the same lesions or changes that are found in the blood of diphtheria, and the kidneys and marrow of bones and other organs loaded with micrococci as in malignant diphtheria.

Drs. H. C. Wood and H. F. Formad have also found an abundance of micrococci present in the blood of women ——— ———eral infection, and in the blood of patients suffering from erysipelas, malignant measles, and in some cases of septic diseases. These micrococci are at present indistinguishable from those of diphtheria, which in turn are indistinguishable from the *Micrococcus septicus* of Koch, the plant which is supposed to be the poison of septicæmia. Whether future researches will show the micrococcus of diphtheria to be peculiar or not is of course uncertain, but at present it does not seem probable; and it must, therefore, be considered that the blood-changes which occur in diphtheria, and occur also in advanced scarlet fever, measles, erysipelas, etc., are simply the result of septicæmia, and that diphtheria is not in itself a specific disease, but that it is simply a sore throat plus septicæmia, it being understood that a sore throat may commence as a catarrh, or may be a septic sore throat from the beginning, the result of a poison coming from without the body.

The important practical deductions from these facts are: the great importance of attending to the simplest sore throat in children of low vitality; the importance of local treatment in cases of diphtheria for the purpose of checking inflammation, and also of killing organisms that develop in the throat; and finally, the maintenance of strict isolation in cases of diphtheria, and the prevention of the development of local foci of the disease in houses. (H. C. W., JR.)

DIRECTORY, a book containing an alphabetical list of the principal inhabitants of a city, town, State, etc., with their places of abode, business, etc. In all populous urban communities a directory has become an indispensable adjunct to business, an it is of necessity published yearly. Every city and town of any pretensions in the United States has its directory, but in a decreasing number of the smaller towns they are issued less often than once a year. Before published books came into use for this purpose other devices were used. Thus, in ancient Rome a class of nomenclators existed, whose business it was to know every citizen by sight, and the quarter of the city to which he belonged. We hear of these only with reference to their services in election times, when they accompanied the candidates through the streets, but there is a probability that knowledge so extensive, and acquired with so much difficulty by its possessors, was not allowed to remain useless in the intervals between elections.

Somewhat similar to these were the "caddies" of Edinburgh. They are described by Topham (1776) as "a society of men who constantly attended the Cross in High Street, and whose office it is to do anything that anybody can want, and discharge any kind of business. On this account it is necessary for them to make themselves acquainted with the residence and occupation of all the inhabitants; and they are of great utility, as without them it would be very difficult to find anybody, on account of the great height of the houses and the number of families in every building. The society is under particular regulations, and it requires some interest to become a member of it." Capt. Birt (1754) speaks of the "caddies" as "useful blackguards, who attend the coffee-houses and public places to go of errands. These boys know everybody we know who is of any note."

The necessity for such a class was probably greater in Edinburgh than in other cities. But everywhere the need for it must have been felt whenever a city outgrew the bounds of a large, mutually acquainted neighborhood. The next step was the establishment of intelligence-offices, at which written records were kept of the name and address of every citizen. It is from these offices that our modern directories originated. While a printed directory had been in use in London, England, in 1677, it was not until 1785 that a similar work made its appearance in America. In the latter year a directory was published in the city of Philadelphia—then the capital and chief city of the country—by Francis White, a broker and keeper of an intelligence-office. It made a volume of 83 pages, contained the names of about 3570 householders, and sold at half a dollar. It must have been remunerative, for a rival directory was published the same year by Capt. John Macpherson, who printed the occupation of his subscribers only, and specified the houses at which he was refused information. In these directories, as the houses were not numbered, residences are designated with reference to the nearest intersections of streets. But in 1790, Clement Biddle, while taking the census as U. S. marshal, procured the numbering of the houses, and also collected the names for a third directory, which he published in 1791. From this date a city directory has been published every year, with eight sporadic exceptions, and in eight years two were published. The directories of 1795 and 1801 have the names arranged, not alphabetically, but according to localities, with an alphabetical index at the end. Between 1823 and 1837 ten were published by R. Desilver. From 1837 till 1867, A. McElroy published every year except 1838. Since 1867, James Gopsill has been the publisher.

In 1786 a directory was published in New York by David Franks, a conveyancer and accountant, who had an office at No. 66 Broadway. In 1784 the want of such a guide was greatly felt, owing to the disarrangement of residences caused by the exodus of the "Loyalists" from the city and the return of many of the partisans of the British, to say nothing of the sudden development of New York. The first attempt at a directory was made by Cornelius Bradford, the keeper of the Merchants' Coffee-house, then the resort of the business community. On March 11 of that year he posted a notice in his coffee-house which read as follows: "For the accommodation of the public, to prevent the many disappointments that daily happen to returned citizens and others inquiring for their friends, connections, or those they may have business with, I have opened a book as a 'City Register,' alphabetically arranged, at the bar of the coffee-house, where any gentleman now resident in the city, either as a housekeeper or lodger, or those who may hereafter arrive, may insert their names and places of residence. The said register will always lay open at the bar of the coffee-house, by which means the disappointments so frequently happening to those who inquire or are inquired after will be prevented.—N. B. The constant opportunity the subscriber has of knowing how numerous these disappointments are has, for the convenience of the public, suggested to him the above-mentioned plan. CORNELIUS BRADFORD." It was the great success with which this plan of the keeper of the coffee-house met that induced Mr. Franks to undertake the publication of a printed directory. His book contained 821 names, and he boasted subsequently that the names of only four men of business had been omitted from its pages. He found a printer in Shepard Kollock, who had an office at Wall and Water Streets. In addition to the names of the inhabitants of New York, the book contained an almanac, tables of the different coins then in circulation in the United States, the names of the members of Congress, the departments of the United States for administering public accounts, the names of the members of the State senate and assembly, the names of the judges, aldermen, and other civil officers, the public State offices and by whom kept, counsellors-at-law, ministers of the gospel, physicians and surgeons, the president and directors of the Bank of New York (the only institution of the kind then in existence in the city), the names of the professors of Columbia College, the rates of postage, and the arrival and departure of the local mails. Mr. Franks reissued his directory the following year, but in 1788 New York was for the first and only time since then without a directory. Hodge, Allan, and Campbell were his successors, and they conducted the publication until 1792, when William Duncan undertook it. Four years later, David Longworth, the publisher of Washington Irving's works, assumed the responsibility, and the directory remained in his family until the death of his son Thomas in 1842. Then John Doggett, Jr., Thomas Longworth's legal representative, continued the publication until 1851, when, upon his death, H. Wilson and John F. Trow purchased the work and continued to issue it until The Trow City Directory Company was formed in 1871, by which corporation the book has since been published.

In 1804 the first directory of Boston was published in that city. In 1796 a directory of the city of Brooklyn, containing 126 names, was printed with the New York book. The residents were described as living "on the main road," "on the new ferry road," "at Sand's dock," and "near the Methodist church," Brooklyn in those days not having been laid out in streets.

The names in the early directories, while they were grouped alphabetically, were not so arranged in regard to each other. Before the publication of directories in the city of New York information concerning the residents was to be had principally from the tax-lists. As far back as 1697 there was a list of the members of the Dutch Reformed Church, originally made by Dominie Selyns, which included their residences. The census of New York, taken about 1710, gives the names arranged by wards.

The makers of directories have always experienced difficulty in obtaining the names of a certain class of people, who for one reason or another have objected to their names being included in the list of the residents of a city. In the beginning of the century one publisher wrote, "We would suppose that, each person being anxious to see his name in print, less trouble would be experienced in collecting them." The desire to appear in print is perhaps no inducement at the present day, while the wish to avoid jury duty and the payment of taxes, the jury- and the tax-lists being frequently augmented by the use of the directory, is to many persons a potent reason why their names should be withheld.

The canvassing for and the compiling and printing of a directory are most difficult and complicated undertakings. In New York City an office staff is always maintained by the publishers of the directory, and the work of preparing for the coming book is ever in progress. But the actual canvass for the names occupies only about six weeks' time. The book is published about June 25, and the canvassing begins on May 2, after the annual "moving day." About one hundred and thirty men are employed to make the canvass. Before it is begun the men receive a regular course of instruction in classes as to their duties, and when they are ready to go out upon the work they are given slips of paper about two inches wide and seven inches long on which to write the names. Only one name is written on each slip. The city is divided into not less than five hundred districts, and each canvasser has to cover about four districts. The men are in the first place sent to the outlying parts of the city, so that by the time the business centres are reached they have become thoroughly acquainted with their work, and are consequently not so liable to make errors. On an average each man turns in 160 names a day. Clerks in the office compare the names on the slips with the old directory, and where changes are found they are noted on the slip, and another canvasser is sent out to verify the work of the first one. A canvasser may return a slip like this: "Smith, John, painter, 2002 Forsyth st.," while last year's directory may show that James Smith, a paperhanger, lived at the address given. There is sufficient similarity here to suggest an error, and to avoid the blunder both names are written on a slip. The whole district having been examined in this way, the "discrepancy" slips are given to another canvasser to verify and correct. In this way comparatively few blunders escape detection. When the work of the canvassers is finished the slips which they have brought to the office are assorted alphabetically and pasted on long sheets of paper, which are sent to the printers. The proof-reading of the work is also done with much care. There are first proofs, revises, and re-revises. The printing of the edition then follows, and when the binder has done his work the volume, which this year (1882) numbers 1802 pages and contains 289,724 names, is distributed to subscribers. The same system, with variations of greater or less importance, is followed in all other cities, local considerations sometimes modifying the scheme. The preparation of the Chicago city directory occupies 120 canvassers three weeks. In St. Louis the work is in some respects simplified, in others rendered more difficult, by the fact that May 1 is not a general moving-day. Though it is sometimes alleged that the compilers of directories are apt to flatter local pride by the undue expansion of their lists, experience has shown that the directory canvass is more close and trustworthy than that made by the census agents of the municipal, State, or General Government, omissions or errors being instantly exposed under the operation of an interested and public check system; and the statistics of a city directory may be accepted in the great majority of cases as affording an accurate picture of its growth and condition. Thus, the figures of the Chicago directory for 1880, at first regarded as excessive, were proved even less than the actual population by the subsequent enumeration. The average ratio of population varies with the closeness of the enumeration, some directories excluding laborers and artisans in tenements and such classes, but it may be stated generally as ranging between three and a half to one, and four and a half to one.

Besides the ordinary local directories there are commercial directories of the Union or of a State; trade directories, including all the important dealers in a certain line of business, as druggists or dealers in hardware; élite directories, giving the names and residences of the well-to-do alone, and excluding merchants and business-men generally; and in fact all that array of books to be looked for in a highly-organized society of enterprising and labor-saving members. The utility of the modern directory can best be realized by reflecting upon the difficulty with which the functions of urban existence, the postal and telegraph system, the delivery of express parcels and baggage, would be carried on did none of these useful publications exist. A striking instance of the utility of such works even outside of their own direct sphere is afforded at the post-offices in the great cities, where files of directories are kept to be consulted in the case of letters imperfectly addressed or bearing the name of another place than that for which they were in reality intended, many thousands of letters thus reaching their destinations with but a trifling delay. (E. P. B.)

DISCIPLES OF CHRIST, popularly known as "Campbellites," or "Campbellite Baptists," though these designations are disowned by them; it being a religious principle with them to wear only such names as all Christians can wear, thus avoiding an obstacle to that union of Christians which they so earnestly advocate. They prefer to be known simply as "Christians," or "Disciples of Christ;" and in their church capacity—being congregational in government, and having no ecclesiastical organization other than that which belongs to each individual church—as "churches of Christ."

1. *History*.—As a distinct people, the Disciples came into public notice about 1830 under the leadership of Alexander Campbell; hence the popular name "Campbellites." But before that there had been out-croppings in Great Britain and Ireland, as well as in the United States, of the sentiments which finally found advocacy in the writings and addresses of Alexander Campbell and others associated with him. There is, indeed, not one feature of the doctrine or practice of the Disciples that was not taught in the writings of eminent men, and set forth in the orthodox symbols of former times. Their distinctive views, in fragmentary portions, had been advocated by many religious teachers. The first volume of Dr. R. Richardson's *Memoirs of A. Campbell* gives interesting sketches of various progressive movements, especially in Scotland, some of which had a marked influence in shaping the religious principles of Mr. Campbell. In the city of New York, as early as 1811, Mr. Henry Errett published a book entitled *The Constitution of the Apostolic Churches*, in which most of the principles now taught by the Disciples were clearly set forth. In 1818, as one of the bishops of a Church of Christ in New York city, Mr. Errett prepared a circular setting forth the faith and practice of that church, which was sent out with a request for answers from churches of similar faith and order. Answers came from eighteen churches in England, Ireland, and Scotland, three in the United States, and one in Upper Canada. These, together with the circular and an introduction and appendix from the pen of Henry Errett, were published in a small volume. Several letters came to hand after the volume was published; so that in all about thirty churches were known to have an existence at that time, mainly alike in doctrine and in order, though previously there had been no communication between any of them, nor were they under the guidance of any leading mind. These churches were essentially orthodox in faith. They had their rise in no dissent from the doctrine of the Trinity, or of the Atonement, but in their opposition to the assertion of human authority in matters of faith; to corruptions in ritual and government, which they regarded as the commandments and traditions of men; and to systems of speculative theology which, as they thought, had supplanted the simple gospel of the New Testament.

The reformatory movement of Thomas Campbell, Alexander Campbell, and others, sprang from no direct acquaintance or connection with these churches.

Some of the initial steps in the reformatory movement of the Campbells and their early associates are noticed in the article ALEXANDER CAMPBELL. Thomas Campbell, a native of Ireland, and a minister in that branch of the Seceders known as Anti-Burghers, came to the United States in 1807, and settled in Washington co., Pa. Deeply impressed with the mischiefs of sectarianism, he devoted himself to the task of recovering Christians out of sectarian strifes and uniting them in fellowship simply as Christians. This involved the abandonment of party names, human creeds, and ecclesiastical organizations; the acceptance of the Bible as an all-sufficient rule of faith and practice, and an agreement on the part of Christians to walk together in that on which they are agreed, and to bear with each other where they fail of agreement—studying the Holy Scriptures with a view to reach a final agreement in all that relates to faith or duty. In 1809 his son Alexander followed him to this country and joined him in this effort. They soon formed a Christian association, into which all were received who sympathized with its object, and began to leaven the public mind by tracts, lectures, sermons, etc., hoping to bring Christians of all denominations to see the evils of sectarianism.

But the free investigation led most of the members of this association to the conclusion that infant membership in the church, and sprinkling as baptism, were unauthorized by the word of God. This led to their separation from all pedobaptists by their adoption of immersion, as the only form of baptism, and the formation, in 1812, of a church of immersed believers. This church soon united with the Redstone Baptist Association, but with a written stipulation that "no standard of doctrine or bond of church union, other than the Holy Scriptures, should be required." The leading ministers in that Baptist association were Antinomians. Alexander Campbell was much their superior in scriptural knowledge, classical learning, and oratorical power. He took at once a leading position, and attracted general attention by the freshness and power of his sermons, which were sometimes startling in the boldness and novelty of their utterances, and always remarkable for their clearness of scripture exposition. While he was regarded with suspicion by many of the Baptist preachers, many others were brought into sympathy with his views, and Bible reading, investigation, and discussion became the order of the day. In 1823 Alexander Campbell began the publication of a monthly magazine, called *The Christian Baptist*, in which he and his co-workers set forth what they regarded as the true features of Primitive Christianity, in contrast with modern ecclesiasticism; and also what they held to be necessary to a restoration of the gospel and the Church of the New Testament. A widespread opposition being awakened among the Baptists—especially when, after 1827, Alexander Campbell and Walter Scott openly proclaimed the immersion of the penitent believer to be "for the remission of sins"—a separation gradually resulted, especially in Virginia and Kentucky, though many of the Baptists took their stand with the Reformers. Their numbers were largely increased in 1831 by a union with another body of immersed believers, known as "Christians," who, under the guidance of

Barton W. Stone and others, were pleading for the union of Christians on the Bible alone, and had become numerous in Kentucky and some other Western States. Friendly conferences between the leading men of both parties led to a common agreement to be silent on all questions of speculative theology, and to adhere closely to the language of the Bible on all controverted questions. From that time their progress has been rapid; their plea for Christian union brought in multitudes from the various Protestant denominations, and their plain and powerful preaching "turned many to righteousness."

II. Distinctive Teaching.—The Disciples hold that the Christian religion, as set forth in the New Testament, is the perfection of divine wisdom and philanthropy, to which, as announcing the conditions of salvation, and as instituting terms of Christian fellowship, nothing should be added, and from which nothing should be subtracted. This religion was gradually corrupted in a variety of ways—these corruptions culminating in a great apostasy from the simplicity, spirituality, unity, and true catholicity that marked the churches of the apostolic age. The attempts of Protestantism to recover the gospel and the church out of these corruptions have been but partially successful, resulting th far in numerous jarring sects. These sectarian divisions hinder the development of a pure Christianity. The Disciples now urge that loyalty to Jesus, the Christ, demands the abandonment of party names, party creeds, and party usages, and the restoration, in letter and in spirit, of the gospel and the church of the apostolic age. As a basis for such restoration, they submit the following to the consideration of Protestant Christendom:

1. The Old and New Testaments the only authoritative revelation of spiritual truth and source of Christian faith.

2. That the New Testament, as embodying what God has spoken by his Son, contains all that is binding on us as of divine authority; and, studied in the light of Old-Testament revelations, is a complete guide in all that pertains to salvation, duty, and destiny.

3. That the first complete proclamation of the gospel, and the planting of the first church of Christ, are recorded in Acts of the Apostles; so that from this, as a central point, we are to study the Old Testament as preparing the way for Christ; the four Gospels as furnishing a knowledge of Jesus and the means of faith in him as a divine Saviour; the Acts as showing how to preach Christ and how to obey the gospel—how sinners were turned to Christ, brought to rejoice in salvation and gathered into the church of Christ; the Epistles as teaching Christians and churches how to live; and the Apocalypse as unfolding the vicissitudes of the cause of Christ in this world, and to the eternal triumph of truth and righteousness.

4. That in the light of the Scriptures, thus studied, it is evident (1) that the faith of the heart in Jesus as the divine Lord and Saviour (accompanied, of course, with genuine repentance) is the sole condition of acceptance to baptism, and entrance, through baptism, into Christian fellowship; (2) that obedience to Christ in all things is the sole condition of continuance in that fellowship. In other words, faith in Christ and Christian character are the only conditions of fellowship.

5. As essential to the union of Christians, the Disciples insist on (1) the only book that all Christians agree in—the Bible. (2) The only leader and sovereign they all agree in, and whose name is the only name they will agree to wear—Christ Jesus. (3) The only faith they all regard as essential to salvation—faith in Jesus, the Christ, the Son of God. (4) The only baptism they all agree in—the immersion of the believer into the name of the Father, and of the Son, and of the 'y Spirit. (5) The only test of fellowship they all agree in—obedience to Christ. (6) The only church they all agree in—the church of God, built upon the foundation of apostles and prophets, Jesus Christ himself being the chief corner-stone.

The Disciples are essentially trinitarian in faith, but reject all creed formulations, and insist on a rigid adherence to the language of revelation concerning Father, Son, and Holy Spirit, repudiating all speculations on a subject of which we know only what is revealed. They rejoice in Christ crucified as a sin-offering, as the sinner's only hope; but they refuse to adopt any *theory* of the atonement. They regard the Holy Spirit as the revealer and demonstrator of spiritual truth, and as the divine guest of every purified heart; but the work of the Spirit must be tested by the word of God, and the facts of the Spirit's presence in the heart must be proved by the fruits of righteousness. To the believing penitent they regard baptism as conveying the divine assurance of the forgiveness of sins, and repentance, confession, and prayer as the conditions of pardon to the erring Christian.

In church government they are congregational. They have associations—district, State, and national—for missionary and other benevolent purposes; but these meddle not with questions of doctrine or of church government.

While they recognize all Christians as anointed priests of God, and make no distinction of clergy and laity, they appoint bishops to rule and teach, deacons to minister in financial affairs and works of mercy, and evangelists to go forth as missionaries to preach the gospel, plant churches and care for them.

III. Their Achievements and Present Condition.—A mere handful in 1830, the Disciples had according to the returns made in 1880—not in all cases accurate, but not far from the truth—a membership of 592,016, and their annual increase for several years past has been about 40,000. They have 5175 churches and 3787 ministers. They are enthusiastic in Sunday-school work, but it is not possible to give accurate Sunday-school statistics. In the British provinces they number about 5000; in Great Britain and Ireland about 4000; in Australia and New Zealand over 3000. They have 2 universities, 20 colleges, 8 collegiate institutes, 2 orphan schools. They publish in this country 12 weekly papers, 6 monthlies, 1 quarterly; also, 8 Sunday-school weeklies and 4 monthly Sunday-school magazines; also Lesson Leaves and Bible Lessons for Sunday-school teachers and pupils.

For missionary work, in addition to district and State organizations, they have: 1. The General Christian Missionary Convention, with headquarters at Cincinnati, O., which has in charge the destitute regions of our own country, which is now in the thirty-third year of its existence. 2. The Foreign Christian Missionary Society, with headquarters at Cincinnati, O., now in its seventh year. It has missions in England, France, Denmark, Norway, Turkey, 7 missionaries with their families being employed, who have established 8 churches, with 700 members, and about 800 scholars in Sunday-schools. In 1882 2 missionaries with their families were sent to Central India. 3. The Christian Woman's Board of Missions, with headquarters at Indianapolis, Ind., which employs several missionaries in Jamaica, W. I., and has planted several churches and schools in that island, with a church membership of 760. This board is now engaging in home work in the Western States and Territories. (See *Memoirs of Alexander Campbell, embracing a View of the Origin, Progress, and Principles of the Religious Reformation which he advocated*, by Robert Richardson. 2 vols., Philadelphia, 1868. (L. L.)

DISCLAIMER, in law, an act or declaration by which one denies, disavows, or renounces some claim, interest, or right which he has formerly alleged or which has been imputed or offered to him.

Where an estate is devised to a person or conveyed to him without his knowledge or consent, he is at liberty to *disclaim* all rights therein. Thus, a trustee of real property is said to *disclaim* when he declines to act as such. A tenant is also said to *disclaim* who denies the title of his landlord. The right of a patentee under sec. 4917 of the Revised Statutes of the United States to withdraw a part of his specification in the event of the same being too broad is termed the right of *disclaimer*. This right is allowed in order that patentees may be enabled to protect themselves against the defence being set up, in suits brought by them for infringement of their patents, that the specifications thereof are too broad.

In pleading, a *disclaimer* is a renunciation by the defendant of all right, title, or interest in the subject-matter of litigation. In law, *disclaimers* occur only in real actions, and practically amount to a confession of judgment. In equity, they claim that the defendant should be dismissed with costs because he has no interest or right in the subject. A *disclaimer* in equity must, in general, be accompanied by an answer. This is always the case where the defendant has so connected himself with the matter that justice cannot otherwise be done. (L. L., JR.)

DISCOVERY. (See ANNEXATION.)

DISFRANCHISEMENT, in law, the removal or expulsion of a member of a corporation, so as to deprive him of his corporate rights as such.

The right of disfranchisement vested in corporations is either expressed or implied. It is express when conferred in terms by the charter. In such case it may be exercised for whatever cause and in whatever manner the charter stipulates. The implied right of disfranchisement is that which is inferred from the simple fact of the corporate existence. There is no implied right of disfranchisement from moneyed corporations. The implied right of disfranchisement can only be exercised for certain specified causes. These are—1. Where a member has committed some crime so gross as to unfit him for the society of honest men, and has been duly convicted thereof by a jury. 2. Where a member has committed some act which is contrary to his duty as a corporator and manifestly prejudicial to the interests of the corporation. 3. Where a member has committed an offence of a mixed nature, both contrary to law and contrary to his duty as a corporator.

For any of the above causes a member may be disfranchised by vote of the corporation, but if the second cause be the one specified, only after the due observance of the following regulations: 1. The offender must be notified of the charges made against him, and must be summoned to appear on a particular day and at a particular place to answer them. 2. The place must be such as it is possible for the offender to attend, and the time must be at a sufficient distance from the notice to enable the offender to prepare his defence. 3. The offence must be proved by competent witnesses. 4. The defendant must be permitted a full and fair hearing. 5. He must be expelled either by a vote of the corporate body, or of such part of it as may be by the law of the corporation designated for that purpose. 6. The persons before whom the question is tried must not have any undue bias or prejudice against the defendant.

Where a member of a corporation has been unjustly disfranchised he may have resort to the courts. These will consider—1, whether there has been sufficient cause for disfranchisement; 2, whether the disfranchisement has been effected in a regular and orderly manner. If they are of opinion that there has not been sufficient cause or that the proceedings have been faulty, they will restore the person expelled by a mandamus. In the States of Maryland and Illinois such relief will not, however, it seems, be afforded in the case of incorporated beneficial societies and kindred bodies.

The aid of courts of equity is frequently invoked to assist disfranchised members of corporations, either by means of simple injunctions or through mandatory injunctions. It is the better opinion, however, that their jurisdiction does not extend to such cases.

(L. L. JR.)

DISINFECTANTS. There are certain principles which underlie the proper use of disinfectant substances which ought to be clearly understood by every person. There are very few, if any, poisons whose power is not destroyed by dilution, and in the great majority of cases dilution is nature's method of rendering innocuous disease-poisons. Thus in winter small-pox and other contagious diseases are more rife than in summer because during cold weather the poisons are concentrated in the air of enclosed rooms or houses and adhering to furniture, articles of dress, etc., are carried *en masse* from place to place; while in summer, through open doors and windows, the disease-germs are swept out and scattered so widely in the boundless atmospheric ocean as to be lost. Again, most of these disease-poisons are very lowly organized beings, with strong resistive powers. All powerful germ-killers are even more poisonous to man than to the germs, and consequently it is folly to attempt to disinfect any air in which a man is immersed. The man would be killed before the disease-germs would be seriously affected.

The only way of disinfecting the air of a sick-room is by quick *ventilation*, i. e., free dilution of the poison. Saucers of chlorinated lime and other disinfectants are an abomination in a sick-room, doing no good and hiding by their own stench the smell which is the natural warning of danger. They thus directly as well as indirectly produce a false sense of security. No folly can be more ridiculous than the attempt sometimes made in times of epidemic to disinfect the air of a city.

It is, however, possible to destroy germs held in suspension by liquids or adhering into solid masses. The excretions of a man suffering from contagious disease are loaded down with the germs, and therefore all the discharges in the sick-room should be received into vessels containing disinfecting solutions, so as to at once destroy the disease-germs before they stream out into the atmosphere. This precaution will not altogether avail, as many of the organisms are thrown out with the breath, and can only be combated by ventilation and the scrubber's brush. Hence all surfaces in the sick-room should be hard and of such character that they can be frequently washed with an abundance of weak disinfectant solutions, so as to overcome danger by the dilution and destruction of the adherent germs. Carpets, pictures, upholstered furniture, etc., should at once be removed when a contagious disease is to be received into a room.

When it comes to the selection of a disinfectant for practical purposes the object to be attained must always influence the choice. Thus for use about the mouth thymol is the best disinfectant on account of its pleasant taste and odor, but for the treatment of wounds it is unfit, partly on account of its great costliness and partly because it attracts innumerable flies. For ordinary purposes it is not the absolute disinfecting power of a substance which should direct selection, but it is the power compared with the cost. A second very important consideration is the poisonous properties of the agent as regards man.

Disinfectants are well divided into germicides or germ destroyers and chemical substances which simply oxidize and thereby remove the organic matter in which the germs develop. For purifying cesspools, sewage, and other large collections of organic material, agents of the latter class are chiefly used. The most important of these are lime, copperas, and chlorinated lime. Of these lime is the cheapest, and is very efficient when a slow action is alone necessary. In closed receptacles it has the great disadvantage of liberating organic alkaloids and ammoniacal compounds by the removal of their acids, and thereby at first increasing the emanations. In water-closets and similar situations copperas seems to be the most available of the class; it may be used in solution when an immediate action is required, or in coarse powder when a very persistent influence is to be exerted. Chlorinated lime is much used, and is undoubtedly efficient.

For disinfecting the discharges of a person sick with a contagious disease a germicide should always be selected. Carbolic acid and its congener, cresylic acid, are amongst the most important. Even superior to them is a solution of corrosive sublimate. It must be remembered that all of these substances are very deadly poisons, and if a malodorous principle be added to the mercurial solution as a means of warning, such solution would be as little liable to cause accidents as are the coal-tar acids. The sulphites are certainly efficient germicides, but are not ordinarily as available as those just previously mentioned.

For disinfecting wounds benzoic acid and its preparations, especially the old compound tincture of benzoin, borax, iodoform (when its odor is not objected to), and salicylic acid are among the best drugs. Alcohol in sufficient concentration is an excellent germicide, and hence wounds continually bathed in whiskey are very apt to do well. As a dressing for ordinary small cuts and abrasions the compound tincture of benzoin is superior; a piece of patent lint may be placed over the raw surface, saturated with the tincture, and appropriately secured. When textile fabrics, such as clothing, carpets, etc., are infected, as a means of purification heat affords almost the only security against evil. Recent experiments have shown that exposure even to extreme cold is of little service. *Prolonged*

boiling is efficient, although disease-germs will resist for some minutes a temperature of 212° Fahr. even when immersed in water. When dry heat is used the temperature of the air should be not less than 250° Fahr., and an exposure of several hours should be insisted on. (H. C. W.)

DISPENSARY. This word is used to denote an institution supported by private contributors (unless otherwise designated) to supply the poor, free of charge, with medical advice, usually with medicine, and sometimes even with food, the patient continuing to live at home and only coming to an office for advice, or being visited at his home by the physician if too ill to go to the dispensary office. It is used to include also the out-patient department of hospitals, but usually the hospitals have no physicians who visit patients in their homes. As a rule dispensary physicians serve without payment, or are paid an amount so small in proportion to the labor performed that all dispensary work may be said to be gratuitous so far as direct remuneration is concerned.

The first regular dispensary was founded in London in 1770, and called the "General Dispensary," though for more than a century poor persons had received medical treatment on what was practically the dispensary system, both from physicians and apothecaries. For centuries also the monks had distributed medicines as alms at the monasteries, and other benevolent persons had given out medicines to the poor, apparently thinking medical knowledge of less importance than the medicine itself. Before the year 1800 five dispensaries are known to have been opened in England and three in America.

In 1801 Dr. Lettson stated that 50,000 patients were relieved yearly in London; in 1850 almost 150,000 were relieved (in 35 dispensaries). Now the number is believed to have risen to 800,000, if not to 1,000,000, out of a population of about 4,000,000. A similar proportion of free patients to the population is observed in large cities in this country. In Philadelphia in 1877, according to Dr. C. E. Cadwallader, of a population of 817,446, there were 132,549 out-patients, or one in 6.16. In New York at the same time, according to Dr. W. Gill Wylie, of a population of about 1,000,000, there were 307,060 out-patients, or about one in three, besides over 20,000 persons treated in their homes by dispensary physicians. In Boston, out of a population of about 360,000, the number of dispensary patients exceeds probably 80,000.

Dispensaries appear, in fact, to create patients, and it is rare that the number of the latter does not increase year by year, unless some particular effort is made to counteract this tendency. From an address given in 1877, by Sampson Gamgee, Surgeon to the Queen's Hospital at Birmingham, it appears that the ratio of persons relieved by the local medical charities in that city has increased as follows:

Years.	Population.	Persons relieved.	Ratio to population.
1867	325,895	66,671	1 in 5
1876	371,839	104,648	1 in 3.5

If the number still increases in the same ratio, in 1886 the number of persons relieved in proportion to the population will be as 1 to 2.6.

Thus, dispensaries give medical charity not only to persons who receive charity of other kinds, but also to a large number of persons who supply themselves with all other necessaries of life, and who but for the existence of dispensaries would not be expected to ask for charity in any form. Meanwhile the dispensaries are generally overcrowded, and the physicians are often overloaded with work which cannot be thoroughly done. Even in dispensaries used for the purposes of medical education where patients not suitable for medical charity may be wanted for the illustration or study of diseases, the presence of a great mass of patients often makes it difficult to select those that are of value from those who are not. These facts are plain to any one who looks into the matter, and the recognition of them long ago led to the formation of Provident Dispensaries.

Provident Dispensaries.—The first definite proposal to alter the dispensary system appears to have been made by Mr. W. H. Smith, of Southam, Warwickshire, where, in 1823, the first dispensary on the basis of payment by the patient was established, and in the course of the next ten years 16 dispensaries on the same plan had been established. Mr. Smith called them Self-supporting, Charitable and Parochial Dispensaries, the name being intended to show the various sources of income, and though by its contradictory adjectives this name exposed the plan to criticism, yet the movement was an earnest attempt to remove generally recognized evils, and it is a matter of regret that its aims were not generally appreciated.

The Charity Organization Society of London, which was not formed till 1869, has generally received the credit of originating the movement in favor of provident dispensaries. In March, 1870, at a meeting presided over by the late Sir William Ferguson, at which 156 members of the medical profession were present, the following resolutions were passed:

"That this meeting is of opinion, that there exists a great and increasing abuse of out-door relief at the various hospitals and dispensaries of the metropolis, which urgently requires a remedy.

"That, in the opinion of the meeting, the evils inseparable from the system of gratuitous medical relief administered at the out-door department of hospitals, and in free dispensaries, can be in great measure met by the establishment, on a large scale, of Provident Dispensaries, not only in the metropolis, but throughout the kingdom, and by improved administration of poor-law medical relief."

The provident dispensary system, which in this way received its first prominent indorsement, has gradually developed, so that there are now a large number of provident dispensaries scattered throughout England. In London alone, where there is great difficulty in establishing them on account of the many free dispensaries and hospitals, yet about forty are now in existence.

In 1879 the "Metropolitan Provident Dispensary Association" was formed to enable persons of every class who are intermediate between those who can pay the ordinary professional fees, and the paupers, whose medical treatment is provided for under the Poor Law, to become members of local associations, whereby they can obtain advantages similar to those possessed by the rich. The Council of this Society is also the medium of communication with the Metropolitan Provident Dispensaries Joint Stock Company, the object of which is to provide suitable buildings where a self-supporting dispensary can be started, including payment of rent, and to suggest to them such rules for their government as the experience of other provident dispensaries had found to be most convenient.

Membership in provident dispensaries is obtained by paying a small sum, varying somewhat in each dispensary; single cards about 4d. per month (entrance fee about 1s.); family cards about 1s. (entrance fee about 1s. 6d.); persons under 16 can only ordinarily become members with their parents or guardians. Ordinary members are not treated until one month after admission. All payments are made in advance. There are fines for arrears; after three months' arrears a person ceases to be a member. Applicants actually ill are generally required to pay an entrance fee of about 5 shillings. Several physicians are chosen to compose the medical staff, and a member can select any one of them to attend him. Each physician receives a proportion of the fees, set aside for the medical officers, corresponding to the number of patients who have chosen him.

Any person or family is eligible for membership whose whole earnings do not amount to more than 35 or 40 shillings per week, it being supposed that under ordinary circumstances any one earning more than this amount can pay such fees as physicians usually demand of families in moderate circumstances. Originally, also, and still to a certain extent, honorary members have added to their funds without participating in the benefits of the dispensary.

There appears to be but one regularly organized provident dispensary in the United States, at Milwaukee, Wis., and this has not existed long enough to show whether it will be successful or not. The fees, paid weekly, are, for a woman, 5 cents; for a man, 10 cents; for man and wife, 12 cents; for each child 2 cents; for 4 or more children, 8 cents. It is open to any resident of Milwaukee, over fourteen years of age, whose total income does not exceed six hundred dollars a year. Payments cover all attendance and medicine during illness, except in case of childbirth, for which there is required an additional payment of five dollars for a physician, or two dollars for a midwife. Thirty per cent. of all dues received for the previous quarter are quarterly divided among all the physicians in proportion to the number of visits paid (except for surgery and midwifery cases), a house visit being counted as two office visits. Surgery and midwifery cases are paid for according to special agreement.

Provident Dispensary System not Self-Protective.—It is plain that the provident dispensary is not really placed on a purely business basis. If it were, no objection could be made to the admission of any one who was willing to subscribe, whether rich or poor.

A well-known English physician, always an able advocate of dispensary reform, writes, ". . . under the provident system, persons unfitted by social position will by virtue of the payment made claim that as a right to which they are certainly not entitled. . . . It is stated that more than one-third of the population of the town of Northampton were members of the provident dispensary, entitled to attendance. Now considering that these 17,849 persons only contributed £2218 for a year's attendance, and that their illness during this year required 50,769 separate visits either to or from the medical offices, giving an average of 10d. per visit, there must, even in this case, which is quoted as a highly successful illustration, be some ground for the objection I have raised against the indiscriminate application of the provident system." It becomes thus evident that the provident dispensary system is open to criticism similar to that brought against free dispensaries, viz., that they provide medical services for a less price than many of the recipients can afford to pay, and thus tend to pauperize them in the same proportion that they undersell to them. Another eminent surgeon has said: "The wages test is unsatisfactory, however, unless the nature of the case is taken into consideration; for it is obvious at once that a man earning forty shilling a week, but laboring under some very obstinate affection, or one requiring some special means of treatment, is a far more deserving and a far more eligible candidate for dispensary relief than one earning thirty shillings a week whose ailment is of a trivial nature."

In other ways also efforts have been made to limit the use of the free dispensary to the class for which it was intended. Originally contributors to dispensaries were allowed to recommend a certain number of patients, on the supposition that those who supported the institution must know what persons would be most benefited by it. But this privilege has been greatly abused, whether intentionally or through negligence, and the plan has been almost if not wholly given up in the United States and to a certain extent even in England, where it was once almost universal. The number of patients in some dispensaries has been cut down by charging a small fee for admission, or registration, or for medicine. But though this may reduce the number of patients temporarily it cannot bring about a lasting reform, for those who ought not to come to the dispensary think little of paying the shilling, and are not to be deterred by the rule; while to those that are proper applicants it is a great burden.

The simple exclusion of patients found by investigation to be able to pay ordinary medical fees is a first step toward the solution of the difficulty, but it does not affect that great class, by far the most important, so far as their own well-being is concerned, who ought not to accept medical charity, yet are not provident enough to save money to pay for medical treatment, so long as they know how easily it may be obtained gratis.

In this connection it should be kept in mind that as regards the amount of wages earned, provident dispensary patients differ very little from patients at free dispensaries. In 1873 Dr. Ford Anderson found the total wages of one hundred families in a provident dispensary to be £120 2s. 8d.; of one hundred families in a free dispensary £111 12s.

The Proper Function of the Dispensary.—In its early history the free dispensary was a place where the expensive product, medical treatment, was given to persons too poor to purchase it; it acquired a value of another kind, when it became also a place for giving clinical teaching in medicine. Both its charitable and its educational aspects should be considered in studying its effects on society. If the dispensary enables the rich to lighten the burdens of the poor and weak, and helps them to take better care of themselves in future, it is fulfilling its proper function; if, on the other hand, it saps the energies of that portion of the population who need to husband their energies to the utmost—if it constantly invites those people, who are just above depending on their richer neighbors, to become dependent on them; and having drawn in one set, immediately goes to work on the next above—then it is certainly a curse instead of a blessing. Were a number of grocers to send their goods to be distributed to people unable to supply themselves, no doubt the system would develop like the dispensary system. First would come those out of work for sickness or some other accidental cause, unwillingly at the outset, and only because their children were suffering, but with less hesitation later as they found themselves kindly treated. On going to work again they would still find it just as well to deal at the free grocery; and their neighbors too would soon see the advantage of getting their supplies in the same way. And so more and more people would cease to make provision for groceries; would arrange for other expenses; or on the other hand, finding it cost less to live, would underbid their neighbors for work, and be underbid in turn themselves. Groceries free to every comer would be regarded as an absurdity, yet free medicine is as far as the patient is concerned equally absurd.

In seeking for the best dispensary system, attention must be given (1) to the most efficient means of providing kindly and timely medical treatment for the poor, and (2) proper material for educational purposes.

Dispensary Reform.—Among applicants at dispensaries are found four general classes: (1) those that are suitable recipients of alms and therefore of medical charity; (2) those that can do something for themselves, but must still, to a certain extent, depend on charitable aid; (3) those that could in the long run provide their medical treatment, but have not learned to regard it as a need for which provision should be made; and (4) those that need no aid for ordinary medical expenses, though perhaps they are not able to meet the extraordinary expenses which must be incurred to obtain advice in consultations.

As schools of practical medicine dispensaries are valuable, partly because the diseases which are met with there are of a kind different from those that are usually found in hospitals, yet are quite as important for study, and partly because the number of patients is so large that the cases can be selected. For out-patient departments of hospitals and other dispensaries used for educational purposes applicants should be considered not only with regard to their circumstances, but also with regard to the diseases which they illustrate.

No method of reforming dispensaries which does not recognize this demand will enable them to fulfil their proper function. "At present it is too much the fashion for lay-governors to pass over all matters connected with medical tuition as being merely technical, or as being the business of the doctors, not of themselves. The truth is that the function of hospitals and dispensaries in teaching medicine is a matter of equal, if not greater, importance to the public than their function in relieving a certain proportion of the sick in the community."

By adopting the recommendation of an eminent English surgeon that the educational dispensaries and out-patient departments should only take the place of consulting physicians, these institutions would obtain the cases they most desire without the disadvantage of having to treat a great many patients that they do not want; on the other hand, since the physicians holding appointments in dispensaries of this kind would be eminent physicians and surgeons, and often specialists, poor persons, and persons who, though not poor, are yet not able to pay extraordinary fees, could obtain valuable consultations in obscure or complicated illness. It has been suggested in furtherance of this plan that the educational dispensaries should receive patients only for one visit, with, however, the proviso that any cases may, at the request of the attending physician or surgeon, be kept under treatment and observation.

Supposing, then, that such of the out-patient departments of hospitals and dispensaries as are connected with medical colleges supply all needful extraordinary medical treatment, how shall the patients be distributed for that kind of treatment which corresponds to ordinary medical practice? (1) Those who can pay such fees as physicians ordinarily demand of families in moderate circumstances need not be considered at all. (2) Those who could pay all their medical expenses, if allowed to do so, by paying a little at a time, could either join what might be called medical insurance clubs, or could separately agree with a physician to assume the care of the family by the year for a certain sum. These insurance clubs would be like the provident dispensaries in England, except that the fees would be much higher, so as really to remunerate the physicians and pay other expenses. Of course the fees must vary in different clubs according to the amount of remuneration which the experience and reputation of the physicians connected with it could command.

For the second class mentioned, who must at times receive aid from others, there would have to be dispensaries which would have to be charitable in fact, and should be so in name. The members would pay a fee which would either not pay the expenses or not pay the physicians, as is really the case in the English provident dispensaries. Such dispensaries might be managed in part by the members, but being charitable institutions the controlling power would have to be vested to a considerable extent in the physicians and contributors, who would then make arrangements to keep acquainted with the circumstances of the members, and discharge them from the dispensary, or persuade them to enter one of the self-supporting insurance clubs, if their circumstances became sufficiently improved. These dispensaries should be used for medical teaching, and would be of special service to medical students.

The proper patients for free dispensaries would be (1) those above mentioned who are acknowledged objects for charity of all kinds; (2) all persons applying in an emergency, who, though they ought to have provided for themselves, have neglected to do so. Such patients should be warned, however, that they would not be received again, and should be shown what steps to take to provide for future emergencies. All the patients above mentioned, including those who can pay ordinary fees but not consulting fees, could, as has been suggested already, be referred to the hospital out-patient department and educational dispensaries whenever, on account of the severity or obscurity of the case, it seemed desirable to do so.

To carry out the plan satisfactorily all the leading dispensaries would have to combine in order (1) to investigate all cases; (2) to decline all able to pay for the disease actually in hand, unless the case was one properly recommended as a case for instruction or consultation; (3) to inform all applicants what their proper course would be for securing good treatment.

The expenses of investigation would at first be considerable, but they would rapidly diminish if some simple system of registration were adopted among the dispensaries, (1) because the place of the individual applicants would become established, and (2) because people would learn from each other the advantages of the insurance arrangements and the difficulty of getting treatment free. (C. P. P.)

DISTRESS, in old English law, denotes a taking of the personal chattel of a wrong-doer into the possession of the party aggrieved as a pledge for the performance of a duty or the satisfaction of a wrong committed. In modern law distress is a summary method whereby a landlord may seize upon and sell the property of his tenant for rent in arrear. (See Vol. VII. p. 231 Am. ed. (p. 266 Edin. ed.).)

The right of distress was imported by the early settlers of the United States and is still generally recognized. In the New England States it has, however, been superseded by the law of attachment on mesne process. In New York the right of distress has been abolished by statute. In North Carolina the courts have declared it to be inconsistent with the spirit of the laws and have, therefore, denied it to be in force. To the same effect are the decisions of the courts of Missouri. In Alabama the right of distress is confined to the city of Mobile. In Mississippi and Wisconsin it has been abolished. In the remaining States it is believed to be still in force, though much modified by statutory provision.

In order to entitle a landlord to distrain for rent, there must be an actual letting and not merely an agreement to let, but the lease may be either by parol or in writing. A distress cannot rightfully be made until the day after that on which the rent falls due. It seems, however, that there is no necessity for making a demand for the rent in arrear prior to issuing the distress as in the case of a re-entry. As a rule all chattels which are on the demised premises at the time of the levy are liable to be distrained. There are certain sorts of chattels which are, however, exempt from distress. By stat. 2 William and Mary, chap. 5, it was provided that if five days should expire after levying the distress without payment of the rent in arrear or replevying of the goods, then the said goods should be properly appraised and sold after five days' notice, the proceeds to be applied towards payment of the rent in arrear. This statute is regarded as in force in most of the United States. In some, statutory provisions substantially similar have been passed by the legislature. Acts have also been generally passed whereby the landlord is enabled to distrain upon goods clandestinely or fraudulently removed by the tenant from the premises out of which the rent distrained for issues. In case of an illegal distress the proper remedy is an action of replevin. See REPLEVIN and AVOWRY.

DISTRICT ATTORNEY. A title usual throughout the United States, designating the law officer of either the State or the national Government within a particular district or county, as distinguished from the attorney-general, whose powers are commensurate with the entire domain.

By the provisions of the Revised Statutes of the United States a United States district attorney is appointed by the President for each of the numerous judicial districts (fifty-eight) into which the country is divided, and is commissioned for a term of four years. It is his duty to prosecute in his district all delinquents for crime and offences cognizable under the authority of the United States, and all civil actions in which the United States are concerned, and, unless otherwise instructed by the Secretary of the Treasury, to appear on behalf of the defendants in all suits or proceedings pending in his district against collectors or other officers of the revenue for any act done by them or for the recovery of any money exacted by or paid to such officers and by them paid into the Treasury. He is also to represent the United States in all prize causes wherein hey are concerned, and from time to time must make official reports of the manner in which he has discharged his duties.

He is not, however, regarded as having a general authority to commence suit in the name of the United States, except in extraordinary cases where the remedy or lien of the national Government may be lost by delay. In all other cases he awaits the direction of the President, some head of a department, or the solicitor of the Treasury. The United States courts in any district will only recognize the United States as a party plaintiff in the record to a suit when it appears that the action has been instituted by the district attorney.

In the various States the office of district attorney also exists, although the officer is not always so designated. In Arizona, California, Colorado, Dakota, Georgia, Iowa, Louisiana, Massachusetts, Mississippi, Montana, Nebraska, Nevada, New Mexico, New York, Oregon, Pennsylvania, Tennessee, and Wisconsin the term "district attorney" is employed. In Arkansas, Indiana, Michigan, Missouri, Ohio, Utah, Wyoming, and Washington Territories the term "prosecuting attorney" is employed. In Connecticut, Florida, Illinois, Kentucky, Indiana, Vermont, and Virginia these officers are termed "State's" or "commonwealth's attorneys." In Kansas, Maine, and Minnesota they are termed "county attorneys," and in New Hampshire and North Carolina "county solicitors." In Alabama and South Carolina they are known as "circuit solicitors," and in New Jersey as "prosecutors of the pleas." In Delaware and Rhode Island the functions of these officers are discharged by the attorney-general and his assistants. In almost all of the States the office of district attorney is an elective one. In New Jersey, however, he is appointed by the governor, and in New York by the judges of the county courts. In Connecticut the State's attorneys for the whole commonwealth are nominated by the judges of the superior court.

The duties of the district attorneys in the various States are wholly regulated by statute. It is their province to draw up indictments in all criminal cases, to present them to the grand jury, and on the trial to conduct the prosecution. (L. L., JR.)

DISTRICT OF COLUMBIA is the territory of the United States of America which contains the national capital or seat of the general government. The term is also the legal designation of the local government established by act of Congress, and now existing, for municipal purposes, over this territory. In the choice of the name the memory of the great discoverer, Christopher Columbus, was honored.

(See Vol. VII. p. 150 Am. ed. (p. 168 Edin. ed.).)

The District of Columbia is situated on the eastern or left bank of the Potomac River, at and around its junction with a small affluent from the N. E., called the Anacostia or Eastern Branch—about 100 miles, by the channel of the river, from the Chesapeake Bay, and about 200 miles, by the river and bay, from the Atlantic Ocean. It lies between the parallels of 38° 47' and 39° 00' N. lat., and between the meridians of 76° 54' and 77° 07' W. long. from Greenwich. The centre of the dome of the capitol is in 38° 53' 20" N. lat. and 77° 00' 29" W. long. (or, in time, 5h. 8m. 2s.) from Greenwich. The present area of the District is about 70 square miles, including the river and water-courses (the city of Washington occupying about 11½ square miles), bounded on the W. and S. W. by the Potomac River, and surrounded on all other sides by the State of Maryland. The original intention was that the District, or "Federal Territory," as it was for some time called, should include a square of 10 miles to the side (100 square miles), lying on both sides of the Potomac River, in which the future city would be near its centre; but this original project was afterwards somewhat modified.

During the Revolution, Congress had met at various places, as constrained by military exigencies. Soon after the close of the war (1782) rivalry between several of the States sprang up as to a permanent seat for the new government. Although the city of Philadelphia had chiefly enjoyed the temporary advantage of the more frequent presence of Congress, urgent pleas were advanced in favor of sites both farther north and south. During the existence of this sectional strife the Federal Constitution was adopted, which gave Congress the power "to exercise exclusive legislation in all cases whatsoever over such district" (not exceeding 10 miles square) "as might be accepted for the seat of the government." The Federal government under the Constitution was inaugurated at the session of Congress in New York, March 4, 1789.

Meanwhile, by an act of its general assembly, Dec. 23, 1788, the State of Maryland offered to cede to the general government "any district" in that State not exceeding ten miles square—to which offer was afterwards added a grant of $72,000; and, on Dec. 3, 1789, the general assembly of the commonwealth of Virginia offered a similar cession of "a tract of country," adding afterwards a grant of $120,000. These moneys were to aid in the purchase of land and in the erection of public buildings. These offers were accepted by Congress, and a final decision of the vexed question as to site was attained by the passage of the act of July 16, 1790, the first section of which declares "that a district or territory not exceeding 10 miles square, to be located as hereafter directed on the river Potomac, at some space between the mouths of the Eastern branch and Conogocheague, be, and the same is hereby, accepted for the permanent seat of the government of the United States." It was also at the same time enacted that the President of the United States be authorized to appoint three commissioners to survey and define "a district of territory" under the limitations mentioned, and that these commissioners should have power to purchase or accept such quantity of land on the eastern side of said river within the said district as the President should deem proper and according to such plans as he should approve, and that they should, prior to the first Monday of December, 1800, provide suitable buildings for the accommodation of Congress, and of the President, and for the public offices of the government. Also, that prior to the first Monday in December, 1790, all the governmental offices should be removed to the city of Philadelphia, and should remain there until the first Monday in December, 1800, on which day the seat of government of the United States should be transferred to the district and place aforesaid. This act was approved by the President, George Washington, who all along had taken an earnest interest in the subject, and thereafter gave his active personal attention to carrying into effect its minutest requirements.

By virtue of this act, President Washington, on Jan. 22, 1791, appointed Thomas Johnson and Daniel Carroll, of Maryland, and David Stuart, of Virginia, commissioners, and also issued a proclamation, dated Jan. 24, 1791, designating the experimental boundary lines of the district to be accepted, and directing the commissioners that, after they had run the lines, they should survey and define, by proper metes and bounds, the part within the same for immediate location and acceptance. It may be stated here that the Conogocheague, named in this memorable act, is a small creek entering the Potomac River at Williamsport, in Washington co., Md. The boundary lines run by the commissioners were, commencing at Jones' Point at the mouth of Hunting Creek on the Virginia shore south of the city of Alexandria, first in a N. W. direction for 10 miles, then N. E. for 10 miles, then S. E. for 10 miles, thence S. W. for 10 miles to the place of beginning. But, as the original act of July 16, 1790, required the location of the district to be *above* the mouth of the Eastern Branch, and the fourth of the above-named lines was found to run *below* or on the south side of said mouth, an act to amend was passed, March 3, 1791, so as to include part of the lands lying below, also naming the town of Alexandria as to be included, and with the further important proviso that "nothing herein contained shall authorize the erection of the public buildings otherwise than on the Maryland side of the river Potomac."

To give his personal supervision the President soon after this left Philadelphia, and on March 28, 1791, he arrived at Georgetown, and on the next day he rode over the new district in company with the commissioners and the two surveyors, Andrew Ellicott and Major Peter Charles L'Enfant. On the evening of that day (March 29) a meeting was held for the purpose of effecting a friendly understanding between the property-holders in the new district and the United States commissioners, which was perfected by a written agreement signed next day by nineteen of these property-holders, representing interests in Georgetown, and in hamlets called Hamburgh or Funkstown near the present Observatory, and Carrollsburg near the present arsenal at Greenleaf's Point. On March 30, 1791, while still at Georgetown, the President issued his proclamation declaring the location of the territory of 10 miles square, in conformity with the amendatory act of Congress of March 3, 1791, and directing the commissioners to have the lines run, defined, and limited, and to make their report thereon, and that this should be the whole territory accepted as the district for the permanent seat of the government—the place of beginning being, as before, at Jones' Point, one of the diagonals of the square being directed due north, and the other diagonal west-east. This is the figure of the present District, with the important exception that all the land on the right bank of the Potomac River, including the county and city of Alexandria, was retroceded to the State of Virginia by act of Congress, July 9, 1846.

On April 15, 1791, the initial or corner-stone of the lines of the Federal territory was planted at Jones's Point, in the presence of the commissioners and the surveyor, Ellicott, with Masonic solemnities. Negotiations with the local property-holders were continued, and on June 29, 1791, a final settlement with them was made, certain lots being reserved by them or exchanged for part of the new public domain, while others were sold at public auction to defray the costs of the new buildings and other public structures. The plan of the city was prepared, under the direction of the President, by Major L'Enfant, and was carried out by Mr. Andrew Ellicott, the other surveyor employed.

At first the future capital was alluded to as the "Federal City," and it is not until Sept. 9, 1791, that we find in a letter of the commissioners of that date that they "have agreed that the Federal District shall be called the 'Territory of Columbia,' and the Federal city the 'City of Washington.'"

During the year 1800 the public archives were removed from Philadelphia to the new seat of the government, where Congress soon after met (Nov. 21, 1800). On May 3, 1802, the city of Washington was incorporated. Its neighbor, Georgetown, had been an incorporated city from Dec. 25, 1789, having been first laid out for a town in 1751.

These, however, remained distinct corporations until both were abolished by act of Congress, Feb. 21, 1871, as well as the county of Washington, the name until then applied to all the part of the District outside the bounds of these two cities. In the new city, gradually, various buildings were erected for the governmental offices, and on Sept. 18, 1793, the foundation-stone of the north wing of the capitol was laid by George Washington. This was completed in 1800, and the remaining portions—the south wing and the central building—were finally completed in 1827. Part of this was burned (Aug. 24, 1814) by the British troops during the war with Great Britain (1812-1815). For an account of the public buildings, parks, avenues and streets, monuments, and other features of the city, we must refer to the article WASHINGTON (CITY OF), as well as for a detailed account of the governmental departments, schools, colleges, and other public institutions, etc.

In this place we shall only add that on April 16, 1862, slavery was abolished in the District; on Jan. 1, 1863, the Emancipation Proclamation of President Lincoln took effect; and on Jan. 8, 1867, colored men were admitted to vote in the District.

Population.—The following table shows the population of the District at each decennial census, exclusive of that portion of the ten miles square originally belonging to and retroceded to Virginia in 1846:

Census.	White.	Free Colored.	Slave.	Total Pop
1800	5,672	460	2,072	8,144
1810	10,345	1,572	3,554	15,471
1820	16,056	2,758	4,520	23,336
1830	21,152	4,604	4,505	30,261
1840	21,936	6,699	3,320	33,745
1850	37,941	10,059	3,687	51,687
1860	60,764	11,131	3,185	75,080
1870	88,296	43,404	......	131,700
1880	118,028	59,596	......	177,624

In this table, in the column "white," are included, for 1860, 1 Indian; for 1870, 3 Chinese and 15 Indians; and for 1880, 13 Chinese, 4 Japanese, and 5 Indians.

The increase from 1870 to 1880 was 34.8 per cent. Of the total population in 1880 there were 83,578 males, and 94,046 females; native, 160,502 (of these 80,702 born in the District); foreign-born, 17,122. The density of the population to the square mile was 2960.4. There were 34,896 families, averaging 5.1 persons, and 28,687 dwellings, averaging 6.2 persons to each. There were 164 blind, 169 deaf and mute, 860 insane, and 13 idiotic; 184 paupers were supported during the year, and 581 persons were convicted of crimes. There were 1464 persons engaged in agriculture; 15,337 in manufactures and mechanical industries; 39,975 in professional and personal services; and 9848 in trade and transportation. Of the total population, in 1880, there were credited to the city of Washington 147,293; to the city of Georgetown 12,578; and to the remainder of the District, including 4 villages, 17,753.

The number of farms within the District in 1880 was 435; the area of improved land was 12,632 acres; value of farms, including land, buildings, and fences, $3,632,403. Estimated value of farm products (for 1879), $514,441. Of these there were 29,750 bushels of Indian corn, from 1032 acres; 17,546 bushels of oats, rye, and wheat, from 852 acres; and 3759 tons of hay, from 2361 acres. The principal industry, however, of this class is now in market-gardening. The number of manufacturing establishments was 971; average number of hands employed, 7146; capital, $5,552,526; value of products, $11,882,316.

The surface of the land of the District is generally undulating, and but little elevated above sea-level. Within the city limits it varies from about 20 feet up to about 90 feet above sea-level; the plateau on the western edge of which the capitol stands being from 60 feet to 90 feet: round the city the ground rises in the directions N. E., N., and N. W., to elevations of about 120, 360, and 300 feet respectively, at the District lines. Along the southeastern line there is a ridge about 150 to 200 feet in height.

Within the District there are two considerable creeks flowing into the Potomac River—Rock Creek and the so-called Eastern Branch. The former, entirely unnavigable, pursues a sinuous course from north to south, through a picturesque, well-wooded valley; while the latter, flowing from the N. E., though in early times it was navigable as far as Bladensburg, about 6 miles, whence was shipped much tobacco, is now silted up and disused. Near its outlet, however, the water is deep enough to afford a channel to the United States Navy Yard there situated. Between these two there runs into the Potomac a smaller one, bearing originally the name of Goose Creek, but now that of Tiber: tradition connecting with it one of the early land-owners by name of Pope, who, from mere whim, or with prophetic prescience, was accustomed to speak of his tract as another Rome, its rivulet as the Tiber, and the adjacent height as the Capitoline Hill.

The soil of the District is a light sandy loam, moderately fertile, reposing upon rocks of the cretaceous system, the surface covered by drift, consisting generally of sandstone, limestone, boulders and pebbles of quartz, gravel, sand, clay, and loam, affording in places a good brick-clay. West of Rock Creek gneiss appears and is quarried for building purposes.

The area of the District was in parts, in early times, well wooded, but is now generally bare and impoverished.

The climate of the District is that of its latitude, elevation, and distance from the ocean—the summers very warm—the winters in general mild, though subject to exceptional severity of cold. The climatological features of Washington City may be thus summarized: mean temperature of spring 52°; summer 75°; autumn 57°; winter 34°; mean temperature of the whole year 54½°. For a series of 28 years the rainfall has been found to average for the whole year 37.6 inches; spring 9.9 ins.; summer 11.0 ins.; autumn 8.6 ins.; winter 8.1 ins. Thunder-storms are frequent in some seasons, but this vicinity seems to be exempt from the violent windstorms which pass over regions farther west.

The District is generally healthy, although in places near the water-courses bilious and intermittent fevers during summer and autumn are experienced to some extent. These may be in the future subdued, by the extension of the drainage and sewerage systems, and by the improvements in progress on the lines of the river's channel and shores.

The mortality statistics of the District compare favorably with those of other large cities. As exhibited in the report of Dr. Smith Townshend, health officer of the District, for the year 1880 the death-rate was—for whites 17.63 per 1000; for the colored population 35.71; average for all 23.68 per 1000. For the year ending June 30, 1883, in an estimated population of 191,980, the deaths were 4286, being at the rate of 17.98 for whites and 30.68 for colored; for all 22.33. The average death-rate of the whole population for 8 years ending in 1883 was 24.42 per 1000 per annum.

The commerce of the District, from Washington and its port of entry, Georgetown, is comparatively small—the brisk trade which the latter enjoyed in early times with Great Britain, the West India Islands, and coastwise having fallen off almost entirely. Lines of steamboats run now to Baltimore, Norfolk, and New York. The Chesapeake and Ohio Canal (built between 1828 and 1850) connects the coal-field at Cumberland, Md., with the head of tide-water at Georgetown, and is continued, under another company, to Alexandria, Va. It is 184½ miles in length.

Four lines of railroad traverse the District: the Baltimore and Ohio Railroad by its Washington and Metropolitan branches, and by a branch to Shepherd on the Potomac opposite Alexandria; and the Baltimore and Potomac Railroad, which has its southern terminus in Washington. With these the Virginia railway system is joined by a bridge over the Potomac.

The water-supply of the city of Washington is furnished from the Potomac River—taken off by a dam above the Great Falls, about 14 miles above the city, and thence led by a conduit and pipes to a receiving reservoir on the N. W. line of the District, thence to a distributing reservoir, and carried across Rock Creek by an arched bridge of 200 feet span formed by the great main pipes (see article BRIDGES, Vol. I., p. 634), and around the northern part of the city, where another distributing reservoir is being constructed. The daily supply per capita is now larger than for any other city in the world, the total supply being upwards of 24,300,000 gallons in June, 1883. With a proposed public park on the banks of Rock Creek is conjoined the project for another storage reservoir of large capacity.

Government of the District.—We have already given the history of the establishment of the governmental control over the District of Columbia up to 1800. On May 3, 1802, the city of Washington was incorporated under a mayor, board of aldermen, council, and the requisite officers for municipal management. Congress still, as empowered by the organic law, claimed the right of "exclusive jurisdiction," but the laws of the two States from which the federal district was formed remained in force in the respective parts taken from each. The people of the District had no delegate or representative in Congress, and no voice in the choosing of the presidential electors. The city of Georgetown had likewise its municipal officers, and the remaining portion of the District outside the limits of these two cities was known as the county of Washington, and matters relating to it were referred to a managing body known as the levy court. These incorporations, with amendments from time to time in their details, continued to exist for nearly three-quarters of a century, during which, though assisted occasionally by Congress, they contrived to create a considerable debt, until they were abolished by an act of Congress (Feb. 21, 1871).

By the same act of Congress a territorial form of government was substituted, under which the citizens were granted the right of electing a delegate to Congress with the same privileges as the delegates of other Territories. The charters of the cities of Washington and Georgetown were repealed from June 1, 1871, and the levy court of the county was abolished, but the act provided that the portions of the District included within the limits of the two cities should continue to be known as the cities of Washington and Georgetown respectively. This territorial government, under the name of District of Columbia, had a governor, nominated by the President of the United States and confirmed by the Senate; a legislative assembly, composed of a council of 11 members, nominated by the President and confirmed by the Senate, and a house of delegates of 22 members, elected by the people. The wants and claims of the citizens were represented in Congress by the delegate. There were a board of health and a board of public works. This latter board, of which the governor was *ex officio* president, was in reality the most influential under the new arrangement, and projected and carried into execution a vast scheme of improvements in and around the city of Washington, adding at the same time enormously to the debt and to the temporary embarrassment of the property-holders.

This increase of debt, together with other reasons, led to the sweeping away, in its turn, of the territorial form of government by the passage of an act of Congress, June 20, 1874, substituting what was termed a "provisional" government, which was finally superseded, in 1878, by the "permanent" government constituted by act of Congress approved June 11, 1878, which has continued to the present time (1884). Under this the local government is known as the "District of Columbia," a municipal corporation whose jurisdiction extends over what were the municipalities of the "city of Washington," the "city of Georgetown," and the levy court of the "county of Washington." It is administered by a board of three commissioners, two of whom are appointed from civil life by the President of the United States, by and with the advice and consent of the Senate. The other commissioner is an officer of the corps of engineers of the army, detailed by the President of the United States. There is no local legislative body. Congress, as required by the Constitution of the United States, exercises exclusive legislation.

The District has no code. The District judiciary (or Supreme Court of the District of Columbia) consists of a chief justice and five associate justices, with a district attorney, United States marshal, register of wills, and recorder of deeds. There is also a police court, with a judge. Under the control of the commissioners are the metropolitan police, the fire department, the health department, a collector of taxes, assessor, auditor and comptroller, coroner, surveyor, inspector of buildings, and the superintendent of the public schools. These schools, forty-five in number, are for whites and colored separately, and are in a high state of efficiency. They have XXX teachers, and a total enrolment of about XX,XXX scholars.

The revenues of the District are derived from two sources: first, from taxes levied on private property and privileges, and, second, from appropriations by Congress of an amount equal to the receipts from private sources. In 1882 the assessed value of real property used for agricultural purposes was $4,471,865 (rate of tax $1 per $100); other real property (exclusive of property of the United States), $85,836,630 (rate of tax $1.50 per $100); personal property, $9,666,272 (rate of tax $1.50 per $100); valuation of real property belonging to the United States (exclusive of the streets and avenues in the city of Washington, the fee-simple of which is in the United States), $83,416,117.

For the year ending June 30, 1883, the receipts of the District of Columbia were $4,184,376.23, and the expenditures $3,722,795.94. There is no floating debt. The indebtedness is funded as a sinking-fund, of which the treasurer of the United States is *ex officio* commissioner. The debt at June 1, 1882, was $21,888,790.18.

(W. L. N.)

DITTANY (Lat. *dictamnus*; Gr. δίκταμνος. Old writers derive the name from Mount Dicte in Crete.) A powerfully fragrant herb of the order *Rutaceæ*, and also called FRAXINELLA, which see. The dittany of ancient writers is thought to be *Origanum dictamnus*, a species of marjoram. To it they ascribed remarkable virtues. The *Cunila mariana* is sometimes called dittany in the United States. It is a pleasantly fragrant herb, somewhat used in domestic medicine, and having diaphoretic and carminative qualities.

DIVORCE, as it comes under the purview and operation of civil law, has relations to public virtue which depend upon acknowledged common principles of public opinion. The public opinion of America in relation to divorce had its germinal origin in New England. Indeed most of the seeds of civic public opinion, as well as their natural forces of evolution, have sprung from that soil.

See Vol. VII. p. 260 Am. ed. (p. 300 Edin. ed.).

The naturalistic opinion that marriage is a civil contract merely was wisdom in old pagan and philosophic Rome, and doubtless promoted that fundamental patriotism on which rested not only loyalty but the whole structure also of the state-religion. This was revived in the earliest form of Puritan law. Among the Puritans the belief that marriage was a divine institution was mingled with and affected by the conception that the state is a politico-religious commonwealth. The early New England idea of the state gave way before the pressure of immigration, but the widespread public opinion that marriage is "simply a civil contract," and that it only confers "purely a civil right," is an outgrowth of early New England teaching. Of course this principle did not do away, from the first, with all use of religious marriage ceremonies. The traditions were too strong in favor of solemn sanctions to the union; while a devout recognition of God's presence in every formal renewal of His own appointment of marriage, demanded, among religious people, that a religious ceremony should bless, and among cultivated people that it should grace, the occasion.

Still the leaves of the idea of "a merely civil contract" worked in the public mind. Hence at first legislatures were empowered to grant divorces. They who bound civil contracts could of course loose them. While legislatures kept this authority in their own hands divorces remained comparatively rare. But the acknowledged principle of the "civil contract," working naturally in the public mind, compelled legislatures to put marriage on the same ground with other civil contracts, and to allow or grant divorces.

While the theocratic opinions of the early Puritans prevailed, marriage was kept from degradation to the rank of a *secular* contract. The civil government itself was regarded by the Puritans as a divine institution: not formally indeed, but essentially. Hence the existing government was reverenced and obeyed as God's ministrant. While marriage, therefore, was counted a civil contract, it was not entirely shorn of religious obligation. This old view, however, has now very nearly died out, even in New England. The legislatures show very slight signs of consciously acting as under Divine authority. They have become so secularized that a civil contract is regarded by them as merely a secular contract. Even marriage itself has fallen into the latter category. As a secular contract, however, it still remains at the basis of social order and political stability. Hence it is a subject for statesmen to consider, and for governments to handle carefully; for the family, which marriage only forms, is the taproot of the tree of national existence; indeed the basis of all social order.

This important and serious connection between marriage and all good public order seems to have been strangely overlooked by our State legislatures. Instead of retaining divorce within their own jurisdiction, they have committed it to the courts. Even here action is not confined to the courts of higher jurisdiction where learning and wisdom are supposed to prevail, but divorces may be granted in some mere county courts. The grounds of divorce also are extended beyond causes that vitiate the marriage itself, and made to include even such trivial points as alleged incompatibility of temper, neglect, or even desertion—this latter in some cases for only one year.

It will be observed, in the Digest of Divorce Laws, which is appended to this article, that the largest liberty of divorce exists in Maine. There, in addition to all other causes, a divorce may be granted "when the judge deems it reasonable and proper, and consistent with peace and morality." Either party also may be a witness, and either may marry again.

In South Carolina, since 1878, no divorces have been legal. In New Mexico divorces to 1872 confirmed; none lawful since, except for adultery, inhuman treatment, or abandonment.

In Connecticut the divorce laws were extended in 1849, so as to include "general misconduct." A sudden increase of the number of divorces ensued; so that a popular pressure compelled the legislature, in 1878, to rescind this "omnibus clause." An equally sudden diminution in number of divorces followed.

It will be noticed that a great difference appears between the North and the South. In New England, and along the whole western course of northern migration, the State laws upon divorce are most lax. The extreme North-west responds to the extreme North-east, and Maine and Montana Territory lead the flank-wings of progress, in laxity of the marriage-bond. In the latter, divorce may be granted if the party "leaves the petitioner and the Territory without intention of returning." Utah perhaps contests the palm, in a clause granting divorce, "when it is proved that parties cannot live together amicably and separation is desired."

Every State has its own code and practice in divorce. Some confine jurisdiction to the Supreme Courts of State or county, some extend it to Common Pleas and Probate Courts. Some require assurance of due notice to the other party, and never "decree" a divorce by default; while others only require proof of diligence in sending copies of published notice to the last address of the absent party, and do grant divorces upon *ex parte* testimony. The legal causes of divorce begin at incest and adultery, and run down to impotency, force and fraud used in effecting marriage, crime against nature, gross neglect of marital duty, pregnancy by another at time of marriage, insupportable cruelty of either party, insanity or idiocy at marriage or in some cases after it, absence from seven years to one year, habitual drunkenness sometimes for only one year, habitual and wilful neglect, intolerable severity, neglect of husband for two years to support his wife unless great poverty is proved, refusal to provide wife with "necessaries of life," joining society adverse to marriage and refusing cohabitation, and finally, difference of color, including negroes, and in one case Chinese.

Divorces granted in one State do not legally extend to others. In Ohio, however, and probably in other States, a decree of divorce in another State is a valid plea for the same release to a petitioner bound by such decree. In Massachusetts an appeal lies in all cases to the governor in council.

The legislation which has resulted in the existing lax law of divorce has been partly a cause and partly an effect of laxity of public principles, both moral and political. Indeed the growth is remarkable of the idea that marriage is a simple bargain between man and woman; and that, like any other bargain, it may be closed or changed according to the wills, fancies, or even convenience of the parties. In fact, the relation of marriage to the permanent order of society is fast going out of popular knowledge; and the law-makers also are leaving it out of view. The popular mind is concentrating upon the individual instead of upon both the individual and the organisms of family, society, and state. It is, of course, difficult to keep these two correlative principles in view. It is easier for every person to think of what may benefit himself, or give him least annoyance, than of what may be necessary for the security, preservation, and good order of the body politic. Hence the drift of public opinion, and the consequent course of legal development, in codes and cases, is towards such enlargement of license in relation to marriage as may impose the least possible restraint upon individual choice and changes of feeling or fancy.

Philanthropists are combining, and through the press and otherwise are making earnest efforts to check, if possible, the growing moral laxity touching the relations of the sexes. They are pointing out upon philosophico-economical grounds the exceeding importance for the stability of society and for the preservation of culture with the amenities of life, of the stability, inviolability and permanence of marriage. Statesmen are siding with the philanthropists. Unfortunately, however, the politicians who make, and the judges who administer, our laws, are not always statesmen and not often philanthropists. The honorable members of the bar are generally on the side of the permanency of marriage; though it is true that some lawyers of talent and even of high moral and social reputation do not scruple to aid in procuring very unnecessary and, in some cases, quite scandalous divorces. The confusion arising from differences in the laws of marriage have led to important movements towards securing uniformity of code between the States.

In Dr. Woolsey's learned and valuable work upon *Divorce and Divorce Legislation*, some important tables are given. One shows the average of divorces to the whole number of marriages in the State of Ohio, from 1865 to 1874, to have been as 1 to 26.7. In the first year it was 1:26, and in the last 1:23. The year 1867 showed 1:30, and 1868, 1:33.2. The close of the war explains this. Dr. Woolsey adds, "I am informed that the ratio of divorces to marriages in the year from July 1, 1878, to July 1, 1879, is as 1 to 18, which would imply a considerable increase since 1874." In the 12 western counties of Ohio, settled by New Englanders, especially from Connecticut, the ratio of divorce to marriage is as 1 to 11; it is in Cuyahoga co., 1 to 9.9; in Ashtabula, 1 to 8.5; and in Lake co., 1 to 7. In Gallia co., where Welshmen and Southerners form the bulk of the population, the ratio is 1 to 50, and in Coshocton co., 1 to 47." Pages 243-4.

In a comparative table between marriages and divorces for 1878, in the States of Massachusetts, Connecticut, Vermont, and Rhode Island, Dr. Woolsey gives the whole ratio respectively at 1 to 21.4, 1 to 10.76, 1 to 14, 1 to 11.8. If, however, the marriages of Roman Catholics be deducted—they not being allowed divorce for any cause—the ratio would stand for Massachusetts, 1 to 14.86; for Connecticut, 1 to 8.22; for Vermont, 1 to 12.4; and for Rhode Island, 1 to 8.5. This he proceeds to show may not be quite fair, since some Romanists do get divorced, yet upon the whole it is not far wrong.

In the annual address of Bishop Williams to his diocese of Connecticut, June 14, 1881, occurs the following quotation:

"If we sum up for New England, there were in the year of grace 1878, in Maine, 478 divorces; in New Hampshire, 241; in Vermont, 197; in Massachusetts, 600; in Connecticut, 401; and in Rhode Island, 196; making a total of 2113, and a larger ratio in proportion to the population than in France in the days of the revolution, though far less than in the city of Paris. On the basis of population by the present census, there was 1 divorce to every 1357 inhabitants in Maine; 1 to every 1439 in New Hampshire; 1 to every 1687 in Vermont; 1 to every 2971 in Massachusetts; 1 to every 1553 in Connecticut; and 1 to every 1411 in Rhode Island."

The statistics of the whole country are not available. Enough has been given to show the direction of the current in law, public opinion, and the prevailing moral sentiments, both personal and social. It is evident that the fundamental principle or idea—in the minds of the law-makers and administrators, and in that of the multitude who are their electors—is, that all questions of public importance and general interest must be settled, not upon enlarged views of what may best conduce to the purity of society and the good of the whole, but upon the bearing of each case upon the comfort, convenience, feeling, or will of the parties directly interested. The result of this course is evidently not yet. The possibilities of license, which lie in the line of this downward progress, may soon become actual. Then, of course, our law-makers and administrators, with their constituents, will be brought face to face, not with a merely theoretic problem, but with a real mortal conflict, in which public good order will be at stake, family purity imperilled—perhaps its exclusive right invaded—political stability shaken, and our whole civilization tried as by fire. (B. F.)

II. DIVORCE LAWS IN THE UNITED STATES.—Divorce, under various conditions, is legal in every State and Territory of the Union, with the exception of South Carolina. In this State, by act of Dec. 20, 1878, all previous divorces were legalized, and none allowed after that date.

Divorce is of two kinds: the complete and total, called divorce *a vinculo matrimonii*, which usually restores both parties to their condition before marriage; and the partial, called divorce *a mensa et thoro*, which is simply legalized separation, and never involves any restoration of original condition, or dissolution of marital obligations as to support, etc. Of course, while the divorce *a mensa* can be granted alone, it is always included in our *a vinculo*. The differences of practice in the several States will be shown under the various headings which follow.

I. *Jurisdiction and kinds of divorce.*—Jurisdiction of divorce, until within recent years, lay with the legislatures of most of the States, but at the present time is not expressly conferred on them in any State, and is constitutionally prohibited in nearly all. The only legislatures which exercise jurisdiction in divorce at present are those of Delaware, Idaho, Washington Territory, and one or two others—in all these co-ordinately with the courts. It is conferred on any Court in Chancery in Alabama, Kentucky, Maryland, Mississippi, New Jersey, New York, Oregon, Tennessee, and Wyoming; on the Courts of Common Pleas in Indiana, Ohio, and Pennsylvania; on the District Courts in Arizona, Dakota, Idaho, Iowa, Kansas, Louisiana, Minnesota, Montana, Nebraska, New Mexico, Texas, and Washington Territory; on the Circuit Courts in Florida, Illinois, Indiana, Iowa, Michigan, and Missouri; on Circuit Court in Chancery in Arkansas, Tennessee, Virginia, West Virginia, and Wisconsin; on Probate Courts in Nevada and Utah; on Supreme Courts in the District of Columbia, Massachusetts, and Rhode Island; on the Superior Courts in California, Connecticut, Delaware, Georgia, Indiana, Maine, New Hampshire, North Carolina, and Vermont; and on the District Court in Chancery in Colorado.

Both kinds of divorce are legal in Alabama, Arizona, California, Dakota, District of Columbia, Georgia, Kentucky, Maine, Maryland, Michigan, Nebraska, New Jersey, New York, North Carolina, Pennsylvania, Rhode Island, Tennessee, Virginia, West Virginia, and Wisconsin. In Louisiana and Utah no total divorce is granted until preceded by separation *a mensa et thoro* for one year (except for an infamous crime or adultery), and in Minnesota, though both kinds are legal, the partial divorce is granted only on petition of wife. A declaration by the court that a marriage is null and void *ab initio* is legal in some States for causes which in others are grounds of divorce.

Only one kind of divorce—that *a vinculo*—is legal in Arkansas, Colorado, Connecticut, Florida, Idaho, Illinois, Indiana, Iowa, Kansas, Massachusetts, Mississippi, Montana, Nevada, New Hampshire, New Mexico, Vermont, and Washington Territory.

II. *Causes for which divorce may be granted.*—At the head of this list stands (1) *Adultery* and (2) *Natural impotency at marriage*, which are valid grounds in every State. (3) *Bigamy*, either wilful or ignorant, is ground for a decree of nullity in most States, but of divorce in Arkansas, Colorado, Florida, Kansas, Ohio, Pennsylvania, Tennessee, Montana, and New Jersey. (4) *Abandonment or desertion*. This must continue for one year in Arizona, Arkansas, California, Colorado, Dakota, Florida, Idaho, Kansas, Kentucky, Missouri, Montana, Nevada, Utah, Washington Territory, and Wisconsin; for two years in Alabama, Illinois, Indi ana, Iowa, Michigan, Mississippi, Nebraska, Pennsylvania, and Tennessee; for three years in Connecticut, Delaware, District of Columbia, Georgia, Maine, Maryland, Massachusetts, Minnesota, New Jersey, Ohio, Oregon, Texas, Vermont, and West Virginia; for five years in Rhode Island and Virginia, and without specification of time in Louisiana, North Carolina, and New Mexico. (5) *Simple unexplained absence* is a good ground in Connecticut and Vermont, after seven years' duration; after three years in New Hampshire, and in Montana for any length of time, if intention of desertion is proved; also simple separation after five years in Kentucky and Wisconsin. (6) *Inhuman treatment* of varying degrees of aggravation is a valid cause in every State for either total or partial divorce. Intimately connected with this is (7) an *attempt on the life* of one consort by the other, specified as a cause in Illinois, Louisiana, and Tennessee. (8) *Habitual drunkenness* is valid in very many States, mostly unrestricted in time, but specified as two years in Idaho, Illinois, and Oregon; one year in Arkansas, California, Colorado, Dakota, Florida, Kentucky, Minnesota, Missouri, Montana, and Wisconsin, and three years in New Hampshire and Ohio. (9) *Neglect to provide support* is a good cause, if prolonged for three years, in Delaware; for two years in Idaho, Indiana, and Kansas; for one year in California, Colorado, Dakota, and Nevada; and without restriction of time in Massachusetts, Michigan, Minnesota, Nebraska, Rhode Island, Utah, Vermont, Virginia, West Virginia, and Wisconsin. (10) *Imprisonment for crime* can divorce after five years in Massachusetts; three years in Michigan, Nebraska, Vermont, and Wisconsin; two years in Alabama, Georgia, and Idaho; more than two years in Pennsylvania; and without limitation in Minnesota, Mississippi, Ohio, Virginia, and Washington Territory. Very similar is (11) *Conviction of felony*, which is a cause in Arizona, Arkansas, California, Colorado, Connecticut, Dakota, Delaware, Illinois, Indiana, Iowa, Kansas, Kentucky, Louisiana, Missouri, Nevada, Oregon, Tennessee, Texas (twelve months afterward), Utah, Virginia, West Virginia, and Montana. In Rhode Island marriage is voidable on "civil death," *i.e.*, a conviction of arson or homicide. (12) *Pregnancy of wife at marriage without agency or consent of husband* is a valid ground in Alabama, Georgia, Kansas, Kentucky, Missouri, North Carolina, Tennessee, Virginia, and West Virginia; so also in Iowa, unless the wife can prove that an illegitimate child of husband was alive at their marriage. (13) *Marriage within the prohibited degrees* in many States is invalidated *ab initio* without special proceedings, but in Florida, Georgia, Mississippi, Pennsylvania, Virginia, and New Jersey, it is merely a ground of divorce; so if (14) *the female is under age* and marries without consent of parent or guardian, in Arizona, Delaware, and Idaho, an action of divorce will lie; in most other States the marriage is invalid *ab initio*, unless confirmed by subsequent cohabitation after age was attained. (15) *Force or fraud* in contracting the marriage justifies divorce in Arizona, Connecticut, Delaware, Georgia, Idaho, Kansas, Kentucky, Ohio, Pennsylvania, and Washington Territory; in most other States such marriage is void. A divorce for (16) *lunacy* or *idiocy* may be had in the District of Columbia, Georgia, Mississippi, Virginia, and Wisconsin. (17) *Vagrancy* is a ground in Missouri; "any cause rendering cohabitation impossible," in Washington Territory. (18) *Uniting with any society which discountenances the marriage relation* is a valid ground in Kentucky, Massachusetts, and New Hampshire; so is "gross misbehavior" in Rhode Island, and the contracting or concealing of any loathsome disease in Kentucky. Finally, *absolute discretion* as to the propriety of granting divorce in each individual case is conferred upon the court in Arizona and Maine.

III. *Conditions under which divorce will be refused.*—These are practically the same in all the States, though the local methods of interpretation vary slightly. 1. *Connivance.* If it be proved in any way that a conspiracy was entered into by the parties to obtain a divorce by collusion (see COLLUSION), such divorce will uniformly be refused. 2. *Condonation* bars divorce. This, in nearly every State, may be either (*a*) expressed, as by written or verbal contract in the presence of witnesses, or (*b*) implied, by such continued and voluntary cohabitation after the act complained of as will reasonably raise the presumption of forgiveness. 3. *Recrimination* will bar divorce. In most States this extends only to a recrimination of a similar offence—thus a counter charge of cruelty will not bar a divorce for adultery. This custom is not universal, however, and there is no definite statute on the subject.

Lastly, *lapse of time without entering suit* bars divorce. This is consonant with the doctrine of the statute of limitations. It is defined as one year in Oregon and Washington Territory; two years in California, Dakota, Idaho, Indiana, Nebraska, and New York, the application of the statute in the last four States being to divorce for impotency only; three years in Minnesota and Wisconsin, and five years in Arkansas, Michigan, New York, and Virginia. In Massachusetts it is defined as "unreasonable delay." In the other States, even where no statute exists on the subject, unreasonable delay will operate unfavorably against the plaintiff.

IV. *Residence of petitioner and notice to respondent.*—The majority of States favor a residence of one year before filing petition; such is the case in Alabama, Arkansas, Colorado, Illinois, Iowa, Kansas, Kentucky, Maine, Michigan, Minnesota, Mississippi, Missouri, Montana, New York, Ohio, Oregon, Pennsylvania, Utah, and Wisconsin, excepting in special cases. Two years is the limit in Florida, Maryland, Vermont, and Indiana (where six months in county is also required), three years in Connecticut, Massachusetts, and New Jersey (if for desertion), six months in Arizona, California, Idaho, Nebraska, and Wyoming; ninety days in Dakota; residence at time of cause in New Jersey; "*bona fide* residence" in New Hampshire and Texas; and no particular specification in the statutes of other States. Nearly all the above are with exceptions in particular cases, such as desertion, etc. In every State the notice of suit must be personal if possible, as in other civil cases, with time specified in the respective codes of civil procedure. This is particularly set forth as ten days in Indiana, twelve days in Vermont, fourteen days in Maine, thirty days in Nevada, and six weeks in Ohio. If personal service is impossible, on account of non-residence or uncertainty of defendant's whereabouts, publication in one or more county newspapers is generally had, the time for this being not stated in Alabama and California; specified as three months in Florida and Nevada; one month in Missouri; four weeks in Illinois, Iowa, and Pennsylvania; three weeks in Indiana and Vermont; six weeks in Rhode Island; six weeks and thirty days interval in Dakota, and at "discretion of court" in Connecticut, District of Columbia, Massachusetts, and New Hampshire. In other States local usages prevail.

V. *Legitimacy of issue.*—There is a continually increasing tendency throughout the United States toward refusing to allow divorce to bastardize previous issue. In many States divorce does not affect legitimacy in any case, and in nearly all in only one or two cases. These are as follows: in divorce for wilful bigamy in Colorado, Delaware, District of Columbia, Florida, Illinois, Indiana, Iowa, Maine, Massachusetts, Michigan, Mississippi, New Jersey, and Vermont; at discretion of court for adultery in California, Nebraska, Wyoming, District of Columbia, and New Hampshire; expressly for adultery of wife only in Alabama, Idaho, and Louisiana; for pregnancy of wife at marriage without consent of husband in Georgia, Kentucky, and Mississippi; for incest and impotency in Iowa, and for incest only in Kentucky, Louisiana, and Maine. In some of the other States, in the case of void marriage, issue is illegitimate, but the above comprise the only instances of bastardy as the result of divorce.

VI. *Alimony.*—The discretion as to the amount and character of the alimony granted lies with the court exercising jurisdiction in every State. Decrees of alimony may also be revised or otherwise altered at any time subsequent to the decree of divorce. As to the distribution of joint-property there is considerable diversity of statutes, with the general disposition to award in favor of the injured party. Special State practice on this point may be noted as follows: Arkansas statutes direct an equal division of joint property; so in California. Connecticut allows alimony not exceeding one-third of husband's estate; Florida prohibits alimony in suits for adultery of wife. A favorite rule seems to be to grant husband all of real estate of wife and so much of her personal estate as is not absolutely required for her support, if the fault is hers, but if his, then she is to have all her own property and part of his beside. This is the law in Delaware, Rhode Island, and Vermont; also in Ohio as to the latter clause. In Louisiana each take their original property and one-half of community. In Massachusetts real estate and part of personal goes to wife, except in case of her adultery; so in Minnesota and Nebraska. In North Carolina defendant loses all dower right estate by curtesy and estate of any kind derived from marriage, but in Texas "no person can be compelled to surrender title to real estate."

VII. *Other effects of divorce and miscellaneous points of practice.*—The general effect of absolute divorce in the various States may be said to be a restoration of both parties to their condition previous to marriage, and remarriage without restriction is usually allowed. Exceptions to this may be noted in Delaware, where defendant for adultery may not marry *particeps criminis*, and in Indiana, if divorce was decreed by default, defendant may not remarry at all for two years. In Georgia remarriage depends on discretion of court decreeing divorce, while in Virginia such discretion operates only against defendant. If divorce was through fault of wife, she may not remarry for ten months in Louisiana, while remarriage of the guilty party may be absolutely prohibited in Mississippi. In Massachusetts defendant may not remarry for two years; Vermont says three years, and Missouri five years, except by special permission of court. New York prohibits remarriage of defendant for five years, unless plaintiff has married again. Of course, in the event of the death of either of the parties subsequent to the divorce, any disability of the survivor as to remarriage is removed.

The various points of practice are as numerous as the States of the Union. Proceedings are usually the same as in other civil cases, following the formalities of a suit at equity if the statute indicates a court of equity as the proper tribunal; otherwise those characteristic of an ordinary suit at law. In Louisiana, except for adultery or crime, no absolute divorce is granted until one year from the entering of a decree of divorce *a mensa*, and every opportunity is thereby afforded for reconciliation in the intervening time. Similarly an absolute decree in Massachusetts is made *nisi*; *i. e.*, conditional, for six months after date, for the same purpose, and in Utah discretion is granted to the court to defer absolute decree for one year. In many States a divorced wife may resume her maiden name if petition to that effect be included in her pleading. In most of the populous States a decree of divorce may be entered on an *ex parte* hearing, without defendant's presence; but in most of the smaller ones such a course is prohibited. In New York a decree of *nullity of marriage* is made to serve many of the purposes of a decree of divorce in the other States, while in Oregon divorce proceedings are denominated a "suit for the dissolution of the marriage contract." A few States allow an appeal of either party to the Supreme Court of the State, and in almost every State, on proof of reconciliation and joint petition of both parties, a decree of divorce will be revoked by the courts. In most cases, also, an affidavit declaring that the cause is *bona fide*, and not the result of collusion, is required to make the petition valid. (R. F. S.)

DIX, DOROTHEA LYNDE, an American philanthropist, was born in Worcester, Mass. Her father was a physician, but died when she was quite young. She then went to Boston, where she established a select school for young ladies. Learning of the neglected condition of the inmates of the State prison at Charlestown, she devoted much time and attention to their instruction and moral welfare. About 1834 she inherited an estate which rendered her independent, and, as her health demanded rest, she gave up her school and went to Europe, where she remained till 1837. She then returned, and with the encouragement and assistance of Rev. Dr. Channing began an investigation of the condition of paupers, lunatics, and prisoners. In carrying out her plans she visited every State of the Union east of the Rocky Mountains, and sought to arouse the legislatures to their duty to the afflicted classes. Her exertions contributed to the founding of asylums for the insane in many States. She repeatedly asked from Congress grants of public lands in aid of the indigent insane, and a measure for this object was finally passed in 1854, but was vetoed by Pres. Pierce as unconstitutional. She continued her labors, however, with success among the States until the outbreak of the civil war. She then hastened to Washington, where she engaged at once in nursing wounded soldiers. Her administrative ability, as well as her philanthropic zeal, caused her to be appointed by Secretary Cameron as Superintendent of Female Nurses, July 10, 1861. She established excellent regulations, which were strictly carried out, but sometimes led to unpleasant controversies with others in authority. Miss Dix persevered to the end, carefully inspected the hospitals and the work of the nurses commissioned by her, and maintained a high standard of discipline among them. She served indefatigably and without salary, but made ample provision for the health of those laboring under her. When the war closed she resumed her efforts in behalf of the insane. She resides at Trenton, N. J., but for some years has been unable to continue her work with the same ardor as formerly. In early life she published *The Garland of Flora* (1829) and several books for children. In later years she wrote some tracts for prisoners and many memorials to legislatures on behalf of the insane.

DIX, JOHN ADAMS (1798-1879), an American statesman and soldier, was born at Boscawen, N. H., on July 24, 1798. At fourteen years of age, in consequence of the impending war, his father, Timothy Dix, then lieutenant-colonel in the United States army, removed him from the College of the Sulpicians in Montreal, and having procured him a cadetship with duties assigned at Baltimore, obtained his society and co-operation while engaged there on recruiting service. At St. Mary's College, in that city, the son continued his studies in Spanish, Greek, Latin, and mathematics. In March, 1813, he became ensign in the Fourteenth infantry, and was then the youngest officer in the United States army. But his position was far from enviable. There were reverses in the field, and there was also disease in the camp, to which his father fell a victim, leaving a widow and eight children and an estate that had long been neglected while he was serving his country in the field. In March, 1814, John A. Dix became third lieutenant in the Twenty-third infantry, and in June, 1814, was placed on the staff of artillery. Previous to the close of this war, while adjutant of an independent battalion of nine companies, he carried through an expedition on the St. Lawrence River that was attended throughout with difficulties, dangers, misfortunes, and privations. In 1816 he became first lieutenant, and in 1819 was aide-de-camp to Gen. Brown. In 1821 he was transferred to the First artillery, then to the Third artillery, and in 1825 became captain of this regiment. The following year, the war being ended, and the young soldier having seen fourteen years' continuous and active service, retired, married, studied law, and in 1828 was admitted to the bar.

In 1833 Capt. Dix became secretary of state for New York; in 1842 he was elected to State assembly; in 1845 he was made senator in Congress; in 1853 he was appointed assistant treasurer of the United States at New York; and in 1859 was made postmaster of New York. The following year, when the secession of the Southern States was impending, he became secretary of treasury in Buchanan's administration. Within one month after accepting this appointment he sent to the special treasury agent at New Orleans the celebrated telegraphic order, "If any one attempts to haul down the American flag, shoot him on the spot." In a time of indecision and consequent inaction, the bold, even fierce, determination and defiance of this soldier-like command would naturally embolden the weak and timid, and stimulate and inspire the strong. It seems natural also that such intrepidity should lead its possessor once more into the field. Therefore the time of thought being past and that of action having arrived, he re-entered the military service under President Lincoln.

In 1861 this gallant soldier was raised to the rank of brigadier-general and major-general of volunteers, and then of the regular army. After having charge of the department of Maryland, he was transferred to Fortress Monroe, with command of the Seventh army corps. In 1863 he was transferred to New York, where he was military commandant during the riots that ensued upon President Lincoln's order for the draft of men in 1864 and the following year. General Dix was appointed minister at Paris, September, 1866, and in 1872 was elected governor of the State of New York. Gen. Dix died in the city of New York, April 21, 1870.

Being born while Washington was living, he long connected the past with the present. Gen. Dix was active in politics, a strong abolitionist, and favored schemes of general education, free libraries, etc. He interested himself in commercial law, in the annexation of Texas, in the structure and preservation of canals, and specially in the exposure of city frauds. Ten millions of dollars that were missing when he was made governor had been stolen. He edited a literary journal, called the *Northern Light*, published various original works and translations, including one of the celebrated *Dies Iræ*, and gratified his artistic instincts by violin-playing. While aide-de-camp to Gen. Brown he was fond of playing duets with ex-President Jefferson. His religious character was firmly marked. He took conspicuous interest in the affairs of the Protestant Episcopal Church and of Trinity Church, of which he was a member and officer for many years. His *Speeches and Addresses* are published in two volumes. His *Winter in Madeira* and *A Summer in Spain and Florence* are among his best known writings. An excellent biography of him by his son, Rev. Morgan Dix, D.D., has been published (N. Y., 1883).

(S. A. P.)

DIX, MORGAN, S. T. D., an American theologian, son of Gen. John Adams Dix, was born Nov. 1, 1827, at Albany, N. Y. His education was conducted with great care in that city until 1842, when he matriculated at Columbia College, New York, graduating there A. B. in 1848 and A. M. in 1851. After a course of study in the General Theological Seminary he was made deacon, and the following year ordained priest by Bishop Alonzo Potter. Dr. Dix became assistant minister in Trinity parish, New York, in September, 1855, assistant rector in 1859, and was appointed rector Nov. 10, 1862. Dr. Dix is a trustee of Columbia College, member of the standing committee of the General Theological Seminary of the Protestant Episcopal Church of America, and has been intrusted with many other responsible duties in the church. In 1883 he was a prominent candidate for the office of assistant bishop of New York. His published works include *A Guide for Candidates for Adult Baptism; Lectures on the Pantheistic Idea of an Impersonal Substance Deity, as contrasted with the Christian Faith concerning God; Lecture on the Two Estates: of the Wedded in the Lord, and of the Single for the Kingdom of Heaven's Sake; Manual for the Young People of the Church, with Prayers and Hymns; Manual of Christian Life; The Christian Altar; Manual of Instruction for Confirmation Classes; Historical Recollections of St. Paul's Chapel, New York; Thoughts on the Lost Unity of the Christian World, and on the Steps Necessary to Secure its Recovery; Commentaries on St. Paul's Epistle to the Romans; Expositions of the Epistle to the Galatians and Colossians; Christian Women;* and many sermons, lectures, etc. The time and thoughts of the Rev. Dr. Dix are necessarily greatly occupied with the duties that devolve upon a priest, and in the harmonious adjustment and conduct of the many affairs of his very large, highly endowed, and influential parish. (S. A. P.)

DIXON, the county-seat of Lee co., Ill., is on both sides of Rock River, 89 miles W. of Chicago, on the Illinois Central Railroad and the Chicago and Northwestern Railroad. Wagon and railroad bridges cross the river. The city has 2 national banks, 6 hotels, 2 weekly newspapers, 6 churches, and 4 schools, and is the seat of Northern Illinois College. The river furnishes water-power for several industries, comprising 2 flour-mills, planing-mill, an agricultural-implement works, a foundry, manufactures of ploughs, doors, spring-beds, buttons. It has gas- and water-works, and a small park. Its property is valued at $3,000,000, and the debt is $84,000. It was settled in 1832. Population, 3658.

DIXON, JOSEPH (1799–1869), an American inventor, was born Jan. 19, 1799. He learned the trade of a shoemaker, but did not work at it. While yet a boy he constructed a machine for cutting files. He also learned the printer's trade, then lithography, and afterwards studied medicine. He invented friction-matches, originated the process for transferring on stone in 1841, and published his process for photo-lithography in 1854, several years before its value was understood. He originated the printing of colors on bank-notes to prevent counterfeiting, and originated the anti-friction metal known as "Babbitt metal," for which Babbitt obtained a patent. He was the first successful steel-melter in the United States, taught melters to use anthracite, and invented the present system of converting iron into steel in the crucible, thus avoiding the converting-furnace. He was an accomplished optician, and taught Prof. Morse the use of a reflector to prevent objects from being reversed; and was one of the first, if not the very first, to apply Daguerre's process to the taking of portraits. He perfected the preparation of collodion for photographers, and gave his process for public use. He was one of the most thorough chemists this country has produced. He originated the plumbago crucible as it is made in America. He built for his own amusement the largest orchestrion in the country, with cylinders ten feet in length. He died at Jersey City, N. J., June 14, 1869.

DIXON, WILLIAM HEPWORTH (1821–1879), an English author, was born in Yorkshire, June 30, 1821. Brought up in the country, he was early employed in business in Manchester, but soon displayed literary ability and became editor of a paper at Cheltenham. He went to London in 1846 and commenced the study of law, but still continued to write for the newspapers. Among his more important contributions was *London Prisons* (1850), originally published in the *Daily News*. He also prepared a very popular *Life of John Howard* (1849), and afterwards wrote the biographies of *William Penn* (1851), and *Admiral Blake* (1852). He was a commissioner at the World's Fair in London in 1851, and travelled through Europe in 1852. He was then made chief editor of the *Athenæum*, and while still holding this position he travelled in the East, in the United States, and in Russia. In all of these he made careful studies of various phases of society which had been neglected by other observers; and he afterwards published his views in brilliant narratives. In 1869 he resigned his editorial connection with the *Athenæum*. He afterwards held some official positions in the city of London. He died Dec. 27, 1879. Among his publications are *The Personal History of Lord Bacon* (1861); *The Holy Land* (1858); *New America* (1867), in which he gave prominence to the socialistic attempts in the United States; *Spiritual Wives* (1868), which treated of life among the Mormons and similar communities; *Free Russia* (1870); *Her Majesty's Tower* (4 vols., 1869–71); *The Switzers* (1872); *History of Two Queens, Catharine of Arragon and Anne Boleyn* (1873); *White Conquest* (1876), in which he depicted the struggle of the white, red, and black races in America. His works were popular and were translated into most of the European languages.

DOANE, GEORGE WASHINGTON, D.D. (1799–1859), an American bishop, was born at Trenton, N. J., May 27, 1799. He was educated in New York city, and afterwards at Geneva, N. Y., and graduated at Union College in 1818. He began the study of law, but soon turned to theology. He was ordained deacon by Bishop Hobart in 1821, and became assistant minister in Trinity Church, New York. When Washington (now Trinity) College was founded at Hartford in 1824 he was appointed professor of rhetoric and belles-lettres. In 1828 he went to Boston as assistant minister of Trinity Church, and in 1830 became its rector. He was consecrated bishop of New Jersey Oct. 31, 1832, and removing to Burlington, N. J., became rector of St. Mary's Church. He devoted himself especially to the cause of education, establishing in 1837, at Burlington, St. Mary's Hall, a school of high order for the education of young ladies, and in 1840 Burlington College. Under his influence the former of these institutions especially obtained a high reputation and extensive patronage. In 1841 Bishop Doane visited Europe and preached at the consecration of a church in Leeds, this being the first instance of an American bishop preaching in an English church. In the following year a volume of his sermons was published in London. In 1824 he published *Songs by the Way, chiefly Devotional, with Translations and Imitations*. He was frequently engaged in theological controversy, and was an earnest advocate of high-church views. His style was scholarly, elegant, and spirited. He died at Burlington, N. J., April 27, 1859. His *Life* has been written by his son, Rev. W. Croswell Doane, who has also edited his *Poetical Works, Sermons, and Miscellaneous Writings* (5 vols., 1860).

DOBSON, AUSTIN, an English poet and critic, was born at Plymouth, England, Jan. 18, 1840. He is of French extraction, and his father, M. Georges Clarisse Dobson, a French civil engineer, of an English family, did not come to England until late in life. Mr. Austin Dobson was destined for the profession of his father. He was educated at Beaumaris, at Coventry, and at Strasburg. On his return to England at the age of sixteen, he received an appointment at the Board of Trade, and there he has remained since Dec., 1856, rising steadily if slowly, until now he is at the head of an important bureau. His early ambition had been to be a painter; he designed on wood a little; but the training at the South Kensington schools of art did not in any way help the native faculty, if indeed it was not injurious. This early tendency has been of great service to the student of Hogarth and of Bewick. Mr. Dobson did not begin to write until he was twenty-four, and it was not until Mr. Anthony Trollope started *St. Paul's Magazine* that

Mr. Dobson wrote much. Mr. Trollope was an excellent though an exacting editor; he appreciated Mr. Dobson's abilities, and he stimulated him to do his best. At the very first Mr. Dobson struck the true note of his talents, yet after a little he went afield in the imitation of Rossetti. This vagary lasted for a brief period only, and the poet returned to his old love—the poetry of society, of human nature as it is seen in modern civilization. It was soon noted that Mr. Dobson had great natural abilities, and that he had very carefully cultivated them by the study of the long line of English poets who have written brightly and brilliantly of man as he moves among his mates—Suckling, and Pope, and Gay, and Prior, and Praed. Gay's serio-comic verse and Tennyson's "Will Waterproof" were seemingly models for the young poet. In 1873 he gathered his poems into his first book, *Vignettes in Rhyme*, which was instantly and widely successful. Steadily in search of new tools fit for his handling, Mr. Dobson attempted to acclimatize in English the old French metrical forms which M. de Banville had revived in France. His were the first really good *rondeaux, ballades*, and *triolets* in our language, and on the models set by him has been based nearly all subsequent work in these forms by English and American poets.

Mr. Dobson also wrote a set of airily graceful dialogues which gave the name to his second volume of verse, *Proverbs in Porcelain*, published in 1877. A selection from these two volumes, with the addition of certain later poems, was published in America in 1880 under the title of *Vignettes in Rhyme*, accompanied by an introductory essay by Mr. E. C. Stedman, in which the rare qualities of Mr. Dobson's genius were dwelt upon at length and with all the critic's wonted acuteness. Of late, Mr. Dobson has taken to the writing of fables, though without giving up the poems at once brilliant and tender by which he made his mark. His last work is as impeccable as Gautier's, but it has more heart and soul. There is the perfection of workmanship in the telling, and the story is always one worthy to be told. His style and taste are flawless, and behind his dexterity is a wit, a tenderness, a knowledge of humanity, very rarely found in conjunction. His satire is gentle, his humor is lambent, his pathos is never obtruded or unduly prolonged. His tone is the tone of Horace, of Thackeray, of Steele. He has ease and abundance and grace, and his verse never shows effort or reveals the labor spent to bring it to the utmost polish and point. It is with Praed that most critics have compared Mr. Dobson, but the comparison is plainly unfair to the later poet, who has at once a variety and a depth unknown to his predecessor. Mr. Stedman's criticism was juster when he said that "there is an English Horace in every generation, and Mr. Dobson is unquestionably the present holder of the title, if not of the Sabine farm." Where Mr. Dobson is unique—in the exact sense of that much-abused word—is in the extraordinary art with which he manages to fill a poem with the very color and time of the epoch when its story passes. His French poems are purely French. His eighteenth-century poems are such as Pope or Prior or Goldsmith might have signed with pleasure. His Elizabethan "Ballad of the Armada" contains no word not in use in the time, and this accuracy is not secured by a loss of spirit—far from it. There is life and fire in all his ballad-work. In short, Mr. Dobson, though he seeks not the uppermost heights of Parnassus, has pre-empted a very pretty section on the side of the twin peaks, and this delightful garden, carefully tended and watered, is all his own.

As a prose-writer Mr. Dobson has not published much. In 1879 he wrote a *Life of Hogarth* for the "Great Artists" series; in 1881 he wrote a chapter on "Illustrated Books" for his friend Mr. Andrew Lang's volume on *The Library* in the "Art-at-Home" series; in 1882 he prepared and prefaced a selection of *Eighteenth-Century Essays* for the "Parchment Library;" and he has since written the biography of Fielding for the "English-Men-of-Letters" series. A sketch of Bewick contributed to an American magazine in the fall of 1882 is likely to appear again somewhat enlarged as a book by itself. (J. B. M.)

DOCKET (apparently kindred in origin with the Germ. *docke*, a little bundle; Icel. *dockr*, a short tail, and derived from the verb *dock*, to cut off, abridge), in general, a brief or abstract in writing, usually of some larger document. In a legal sense the word has several modifications. In its most important meaning it denotes a formal record of judicial proceedings, giving the names of parties and their counsel, and a brief entry of every proceeding in the case. Such dockets are kept by the clerk or prothonotary of every court of record (though the presence of such a docket will not necessarily constitute a court of record), and are official evidence before the law. A list or calendar of causes ready for trial prepared for the use of courts and lawyers is also sometimes called a docket.

DODGE, MARY ABIGAIL, an American authoress, who writes under the name of Gail Hamilton, was born in Hamilton, Mass., about 1838. Her father was a farmer, and she was for some years an instructor in physical science in the high school at Hartford, Conn. Afterwards, while a governess in the family of Dr. Gamaliel Bailey, of Washington, D. C., she became a contributor to the *National Era*, a weekly anti-slavery paper, published by him. In 1862 she began to contribute to the *Atlantic Monthly*, and she has since written for *Harper's Bazar*, the *North American Review*, and other periodicals, treating of social, religious, and political subjects. Her style is vigorous and epigrammatic, and she delights in handling vexed questions. Her books have been chiefly collections of her magazine articles. The principal are *Country Living and Country Thinking* (1862); *Gala Days* (1863); *A New Atmosphere* (1864); *Stumbling-Blocks* (1865); *Summer Rest* (1866); *Wool-gathering* (1866), a sketch of a journey to Wisconsin and Minnesota; *Skirmishes and Sketches* (1867); *Woman's Wrongs, a Counter-Irritant* (1868), a reply to Rev. Dr. Bushnell's book on *Woman's Rights*; *Red-Letter Days* (1869); *Battle of the Books* (1870), which is a sketch of her quarrel with her former publishers; *Little Folk Life* (1871); *The Child World* (1872); *Twelve Miles from a Lemon* (1873); *Nursery Noonings* (1874); *First Love is Best* (1875); *Woman's Worth and Worthlessness* (1875); *What Think Ye of Christ?* (1876).

DOG. Upon the origin of the dog there has been great diversity of opinion, some writers declaring him a distinct species, and others simply a wolf, fox, or jackal, changed by domestication and subsequent breeding into his present form. Buffon claimed the shepherd dog as the parent of the race, while Pennant maintained it the result of crosses between the jackal and wolves or foxes. Bell, who wrote in 1837, thus upholds the wolf descent in his British Quadru-

See Vol. VII. P. 281 Am. ed. (p. 324 Edin. ed.).

peds: "In order to come to any rational conclusion on this head, it will be necessary to ascertain to what type the animal approaches most nearly, after having for many successive generations existed in a wild state, removed from the influence of domestication, and association with mankind. Now we find that there are several instances of the existence in dogs of such a state of wildness as to have lost even that common character of domestication, variety of color and marking. Of these two very remarkable ones are the dhole of India and the dingo of Australia. There is, besides, a half-reclaimed race amongst the Indians of North America, and another also partially tamed in South America, which deserve attention. And it is found that these races in different degrees, and in greater degree as they are more wild, exhibit the lank and gaunt form, the lengthened limbs, the long and slender muzzle, and the comparative strength which characterize the wolf; and the tail of the Australian dog, which may be considered as the most remote from a state of domestication, assumes the slightly bushy form of that animal.

"We have here a remarkable approximation to a well-known wild animal of the same genus, in races which, though doubtless descended from domesticated ancestors, have gradually assumed the wild condition; and it is worthy of special remark that the anatomy of the wolf, and its osteology in particular, does not differ from that of the dog in general, more than the different kinds of dogs do from each other. The cranium is absolutely similar, and so are all, or nearly all, the other essential parts; and to strengthen still further the probability of their identity, the dog and wolf will readily breed together, and their progeny is fertile. The obliquity of the position of the eyes in the wolf is one of the characters in which it differs from the dog; and although it is very desirable not to rest too much upon the effects of habit on structure, it is not perhaps straining the point to attribute the forward direction of the eyes in the dog to the constant habit, for many generations, of looking forward to his master, and obeying his voice." The fertility of the offspring of the dog and wolf herein claimed, though denied by many writers, has been amply proved by late investigation of the dogs belonging to Indians upon the Western frontier to which Bell alludes, it being now well established that these are the result of crosses between dogs, gray wolves, and coyotés, yet, though displaying a mixture of the forms and characteristics of their several ancestors, they breed freely together. As it is unquestionable that the offspring of dissimilar species are hybrids incapable of propagation *inter se*, this fertility must be accepted as settling the question of kinship between these races. The great variety in dogs, however, precludes the supposition that they are descended from any one ancestor, and scientific men now consequently hold, with scarcely any exception, that the race sprang from a combination of crosses between wolves, foxes, and jackals in different parts of the world; that the dog, in short, is neither a natural species nor yet a modified descendant of any one species which exists in nature, but a purely artificial product of domestication, the result of endless crossing and recrossing with various *Canidæ* of different parts of the world, and further modified to an extraordinary extent by systematic breeding and training, until the various breeds of dogs now known differ more from one another than most species, and even many genera of wild animals do. Were a naturalist supplied with a series of the skins and skulls of the animals exhibited at one of our large dog-shows, and desired to classify them as he would the same animals in a state of nature, he would divide them into some six or eight *genera* and fifteen or twenty *species*, as distinct from each other as recognised genera and species usually are in nature.

Upon the reversion to which Bell refers modern investigators have made many comments, regarding it as not only confirming present theories of origin, but also as showing the highly artificial state to which the race has been brought by breeding. This tendency is common to all domesticated animals, and under favorable circumstances is very rapid in action, a few generations being sufficient to produce an almost total loss of the characteristics acquired by domestication.

Association with man.—From the earliest times of which we have any record the dog has been associated with man in all the familiar relations of the present day. The Mosaic law refers to him, and writers both sacred and profane mention him, sometimes as a term of reproach and again as a synonym of faithfulness. The most ancient sculptures exhumed from buried cities represent him as an inmate of his master's house and his companion in the chase. With the primitive weapons used in war and the chase the pursuit of game would have proved an almost total failure but for the sagacity, speed, and courage of the dog, and as in the early ages of the world men were largely dependent upon hunting for their subsistence, the value of his services cannot be overestimated. When men came to dwell together one of the first forms of property was in their flocks, and as these were of necessity imperfectly protected, they were constantly exposed to attacks of the wild beasts of the field, who would have scattered and wholly destroyed them but for the watchfulness of their canine guards. Nor did the dog serve his master in these ways alone, for by the Greeks and Romans—as by the Chinese of modern times—his flesh was esteemed a delicacy, and was served up at their feasts. Hippocrates speaks of it with commendation, and other writers bear testimony to its quality, so that altogether it may be claimed with justice no other animal has been so closely associated with man, or has ministered in so many different ways to his wants.

Habitat and Physical Characteristics.—The dog is confined to no portion of the globe, but is thoroughly cosmopolitan, and finds a home in nearly every section inhabited by man. In the wild state he is found in packs like his ancestor the wolf, and like him lives upon the flesh of animals, which his powers of scent and speed enable him to run down, or his cunning to outwit. The dog is of course carnivorous, belonging to the order *Feræ*, and family *Canidæ*. Domestication, however, has so changed him that he will subsist upon the crumbs that fall from his master's table, and thrives better upon a mixed diet than upon meat alone. Dogs brought up upon the seacoast also become very fond of fish; and, in short, association with man has induced as great changes in the canine nature in this as in other respects.

The dog is known to naturalists as *Canis familiaris*. By the ancients he was classed according to his uses, as *pugnaces*, *sagaces*, and *celeres*,—a division, of course, not recognized in modern times.

Promiscuous breeding in early days resulted in the production of a great many varieties, which in time came to be regarded as distinct breeds, and gave rise to the necessity for classification. Cuvier divided them into three primary classes, distinguished by the shape of the skull, as follows:

"I. *Matins*, characterized by head more or less

elongated; parietal bones insensibly approaching each other; condyles of the lower jaw placed in a horizontal line with the upper molar teeth, exemplified by—Section 1. Half-reclaimed dogs, hunting in packs, such as the dingo, the dhole, the pariah, etc. Section 2. Domesticated dogs, hunting in packs or singly, but using the eye in preference to the nose, as for instance the Albanian dog, deerhound, etc. Section 3. Domesticated dogs, which hunt singly, and almost entirely by the eye. Example: the greyhound.

"II. *Spaniels.*—Characteristics—Head moderately elongated; parietal bones do not approach each other above the temples, but diverge and swell out, so as to enlarge the forehead and cavity of the brain. Section 4. Pastoral dogs, or such as are employed for domestic purposes. Example: Shepherd's dog. Section 5. Water-dogs, which delight in swimming. Examples: Newfoundland dog, water-spaniels, etc. Section 6. Fowlers, or such as have an inclination to chase or point birds by scenting only, and not killing. Examples: the setter, the pointer, the field-spaniel, etc. Section 7. Hounds, which hunt in packs by scent, and kill their game. Examples: the fox-hound, the harrier, etc. Section 8. Cross breeds for sporting purposes. Example: the retriever.

"III. *House Dogs.*—Characteristics—Muzzle more or less shortened; skull high; frontal sinuses considerable; condyle of the lower jaw extending above the line of the upper cheek teeth. Cranium smaller in this group than in the first or second, in consequence of its peculiar formation. Section 9. Watch-dogs, which have no propensity to hunt, but are employed solely in the defence of man or his property. Examples: the mastiff, the bull-dog, the pug-dog, etc.

Commenting upon this division, "Stonehenge," the great sporting authority, calls attention to some anomalies as follows: "For instance, the greyhound is quite as ready to hunt in packs as any other hound, and is only prevented from doing so by the hand of his master. The same restraint keeps him from using his nose, or he could soon be nearly as good with that organ as with the eye. So also Cuvier defines his sixth section as having an inclination to chase and point birds, whereas they have as great and often a greater desire for hares and rabbits." These exceptions Stonehenge makes in considering the dog in his sporting works, but otherwise follows Cuvier's classification.

The size of bone and consequent weight of frame should be proportional to the uses to which the dog is put. Those kept for fast and long continued work, involving a severe strain upon the physical system, should have sufficient bone to insure strength, but no more, as the extra weight serves only as a burden without any corresponding benefit. In the greyhound, where speed is of the first consideration, and whose endurance is very seldom severely tested, the frame may be proportionally lighter than in the setter, pointer, or hound. With these, bones of medium weight are very essential, as the heavier tend to slowness in action and brevity in endurance, while the lighter, though they permit of a flashy turn of speed, are very apt to give out in the joints or suffer injury from blows received in hunting. The extremes of physical formation are met with in dogs bred for great size, and in their opposites the toys, which should be as small as possible; the former requiring the most massive bones, and the latter the lightest and most delicate.

The dog has a chest-action directly opposite to that of man. That is, while the man's chest rises and falls, varying its measurements from front to rear, the dog's dilates and contracts laterally. The ribs enclosing the lungs are curved, which not only facilitates this action, but also by their shape makes the good or bad formation of the chest when regarded in its adaptation to speed and endurance, as well as grace in movement. The more easily the dog can breathe when undergoing severe exertion the less he will be distressed thereby. The chest and ribs should, therefore, be of a formation favorable to the most perfect dilation and contraction, and this is found to exist in a chest of moderate width with ribs proportionally sprung. With ribs excessively curved the expansion must necessarily be small, while with those that are too straight the contracting power will be limited. The medium chest on the contrary is capable of both dilation and contraction of the highest degree, which enables it to receive and utilize the largest volume of air, and proportionally to promote the comfort of the dog under the most trying circumstances. A wide chest also produces a rolling gait in the gallop, and this, though it may not affect the endurance, is certainly detrimental to speed and ungraceful in appearance.

The shoulder is fastened to the body by strong muscles attached to the top of the shoulder-blade and the lower ribs, the motion forwards and backwards being controlled by other muscles extending to the neck and the spine. This arrangement, with the absence of a collar-bone, allows of the greatest freedom of action, and is a safeguard against accidents which might occur to a rigidly fastened shoulder in an animal used as the dog is to travel at speed over every variety of surface.

The dog has forty-two teeth, viz.: six incisors in front, two canines or tusks and twelve molars in the upper jaw, with six incisors, two canines, and fourteen molars in the lower. Two of the teeth behind the canines are tubercular, and serve to distinguish the sub-family Canina from the rest of the family. There are two sets of teeth, the first or milk teeth lasting only till the dog is five or six months old, when the second set are developed.

The dog is also distinguished by having a round pupil in the eye, while the fox, which belongs to the same group, has a perpendicular slit in place of this.

The coat varies according to the breed. With some it is close and short, and with others long, accompanied by a fringe upon the backs of the legs and the lower edge of the tail, technically known as "feather." Some of the water-dogs are covered with close crisp curls, having an under-coat of thick short hair, admirably adapted for their protection when exposed to wet and cold. Modern breeding has also produced coats of opposite character in varieties of the same family, examples of this being found in the retrievers, the rough and smooth terriers, and the rough and smooth St. Bernards.

Though the dog does not arrive at full maturity till from eighteen to twenty-four months old, puberty is generally reached by the end of the first year, and the bitch comes in season at intervals of six months thereafter. In exceptional instances these intervals are shortened or lengthened according to the peculiarities of the individual. The season lasts about twenty-one days, the ѣ ng service after the first week, or as ng ceases, and carrying her whelp xty-three days.

The greater the development of the higher senses by breeding the more sensitive the nervous system becomes, and the more prone the dog is to diseases of a severe and dangerous character. The curs that run the streets uncared for escape most of the ills to which their aristocratic brothers are liable, and when attacked by disease it is generally of a comparatively mild character, from which the dog recovers unaided. In this the dog does not differ from other domesticated animals, the higher and more valuable classes having to pay the penalty of their refinement and the care with which they are treated by extra predisposition to disease and less power of resistance to it.

That new maladies occasionally appear is unquestionably true, but these are not so common as many persons suppose, the new names and apparent new phases being due to greater study of cases, and consequent better discrimination and classification according to symptoms, formerly overlooked or comprehended under a general name. The dog has many of the diseases from which human beings suffer, and should be treated in precisely the same way, only varying the remedies prescribed in quantity according to their peculiar action upon the canine system. Medical authorities declare that no specific for any disease has been discovered, and that each case must be treated according to its symptoms. This is a death-blow to the empirics who advertise their nostrums as unfailing cures or preventives, but the falsehood of whose pretensions is made apparent in canine distemper, which may attack the lungs, the bowels, or the brain, and evidently cannot be controlled in all these widely different types by any one remedy. It is only within a few years that canine diseases have been deemed worthy of the attention of the better class of practitioners. Before that they were given over to ignorant quacks of the lowest character, and to such may be traced most of the false theories and pretentious cure-alls which still retain a hold upon the confidence of inexperienced and credulous dog-owners. The important part now taken by dogs in the service or pleasures of their masters, with the increased value and attention to breeding resulting from this, has made them the subject of scientific study, and as a consequence past errors have been exposed, and a practice based upon scientific principles substituted in their stead.

Development.—The improvement of the dog upon his primary type, and the development of his character and instincts, have been accomplished in two ways; viz., first, by association with man, and second, by breeding for certain qualities. The association of a lower with a higher animal must of itself be beneficial to the inferior, and, when the superior is man, the acknowledged lord of creation, the influence exerted by him upon any of the lower orders from which he selects a companion must be in proportion to the natural comparative rank of the two races. Man has not simply accepted the dog as a hanger-on, but in return for food and shelter he demands service from him. To fit him for that service instruction has been needed, and this instruction, increased from generation to generation as the pupil has shown capacity to receive, and the advanced demands of the service have rendered greater knowledge necessary for the accomplishment of the desired ends, has resulted in making the dog an educated animal. The more intimate the association between man and dog, the greater has been the improvement of the latter, till educated instinct has raised its possessor almost to the altitude of a reasoning being. No animal displays so high a degree of intelligence as the colley, yet we have no reason to suppose him originally superior to other dogs, and we have only the alternative of crediting his present ability to his constant association, day and night, with his master, and the multitude and variety of the services demanded from him in herding the sheep intrusted to his care. The other classes of what may properly be called useful dogs are generally kept for some single and specific purpose; and, when the duties pertaining to it have been performed, they are released from attendance upon their masters and left to their own devices, the consequence of which is that, however highly accomplished in their particular line they may be, they are not so generally educated, or brought up to so high a standard in point of general intelligence and ability to perform any service occasion may make necessary, as the dogs which are seldom if ever out of their master's presence. Instances of rare intelligence and wonderful capacity for general service have been related of all classes of dogs, but, in such cases, the individual has almost invariably been the property of a man endowed with both a faculty for instruction and the inclination to make the dog his companion; so that the ability displayed by the latter has been the natural result of these combined influences. There is no reason why any other breed possessed of ordinary intelligence cannot be brought up to the colley standard by the same course of association and instruction to which he owes his goodness; but it is not to be expected that dogs which do not enjoy equal advantages will manifest equal powers. Though the characteristics displayed by the different varieties of dogs were doubtless originally due to accident or climatic influences, it is certain that when the value of these came to be recognized they were systematically bred for, and thus were developed far in excess of those possessed by dogs of earlier days. This improvement was not, however, effected in a short time, but was the work of many years, carried on through successive generations, since, in order to obtain the desired qualities in such degree that they could be relied on to reproduce themselves, it was not only necessary to intensify these, but also to breed out other qualities antagonistic to them. Great as was the change, there was still a too general ignorance of the laws of breeding, and too much carelessness or indifference in their application to the continued development of breeds, for the improvement to be more than comparative, and it has only been within the last quarter of a century that the dog has been brought up to his present perfection. During this time the demands of fashion, the institution of bench-shows, and the increase in field-sports, have given dogs of the highest quality a value never before known, and have stimulated breeders to study the laws governing reproduction, and to exercise such care in mating their breeding stock that the dogs of the present day have been made superior to those of any other time. For all this, it is not supposable that the possibilities of the race have yet been reached. Many imperfections exist in even the most highly developed breeds, and, as these are in the line where some of the greatest improvements have been wrought, it is only reasonable to expect that time and persistence in the methods already so successful will eventually produce a class of dogs proportionally better than those we have now.

Uses.—The uses to which the dog is put vary with circumstances, and are too numerous for specific mention. From the cold and barren regions of the North, where he draws his master's sledge, it is a long step to the boudoir of the fashionable lady, yet the dog, in appropriate form, is found there, the pet and plaything of his mistress. Whether watching the flocks upon a thousand hills; acting as a beast of burden to the poor; guarding the house; accompanying the sportsman in all his pursuits in field and forest; furnishing a study to the savant; an employment for the leisure hours of the fancier, or even, by the exhibition of his savage passions, ministering to the pleasures of men more brutal than himself, the dog is attached to every rank and station of human life in some useful or ornamental capacity.

Show Classification.—Apart from scientific divisions, custom has classed the dog according to his uses and the classification of bench-shows as sporting and non-sporting, each variety of the several groups having a certain recognized standard by which it is judged, and to as close approximation as possible with which it is bred. This standard is based upon what experience has demonstrated to be the best form, having due regard for the preservation of original types, so far as this is compatible with necessary improvements. The standard accepted in England and this country is that laid down by Stonehenge in his "Dogs of the British Isles." In the sporting class he places the "dogs used with the gun, and hounds and their allies." The first division comprises setters, pointers, spaniels, and retrievers. The setters are the English, the black-and-tan or Gordon, and the Irish. The pointer has but one variety, but is divided into classes according to weight. The spaniels are the modern field-spaniel, the modern cocker, the Sussex, the Clumber, and the Irish and English water-spaniels. The retrievers are the wavy- and curly-coated black retrievers; retrievers other than black, wild-fowl retrievers, and the deer-hound.

"Hounds and their allies" comprise the greyhound; "modern hounds hunting by nose," viz., the blood-hound, the fox-hound, the harrier, the beagle, and the otter-hound. The fox-terriers, both rough and smooth, and the dachshund, or German badger-dog, complete the class.

The non-sporting division comprises watch-dogs, sheep- and cattle-dogs, terriers—other than fox and toy—and the toy-dogs. The watch-dogs are the bull-dog, the mastiff, the Newfoundland, the Labrador, or lesser Newfoundland, the St. Bernards—both rough and smooth—and the Dalmation. The sheep- and cattle-dogs are the colley, the bob-tailed sheep-dog, and the Pomeranian or Spitz. The terriers are the nondescripts, the rough terriers, including the Skye—both drop- and prick-eared—the Dandie Dinmont, the Bedlington, the Yorkshire, and the Irish. The smooth terriers are the black-and-tan, or Manchester, the white English, and the bull-terrier. The toy-dogs are the rough-coated, including the King-Charles and Blenheim spaniels, the Maltese dog, and the rough toy-terrier. The smooth-coated include the pug, the Italian greyhound, and the smooth toy-terrier.

In an appendix Stonehenge also mentions the poodles, both French and Russian, the truffle dog, the Chinese crested dog, and the great Dane, these not being properly dogs of the country, though occasional specimens are met with.

The apparent inconsistency of classing the deer-hound with the retrievers is explained by the use to which this dog is put, viz., to pursue the deer after he is wounded, and, by bringing him to bay, secure his being retrieved. As his services are not required upon unwounded game, he cannot be properly associated with dogs used in the chase, as other hounds are used.

The greyhound is also excluded from the list of true hounds which hunt by nose, as he follows his quarry by sight. Stonehenge says: "From the latter half of the word greyhound and deerhound it might naturally be inferred that they should be considered hounds, but in sportsman's language they are not so, and if a man was heard to say that he saw a lot of hounds out on a certain farm, when it turned out that they were greyhounds he would at once be set down as ignorant of sport and its belongings. The term is therefore confined in the present day to the blood-hound, stag-hound, fox-hound, harrier, beagle, and otter-hound." The greyhound is so closely allied to the true hounds that he is classed with them. His manner of hunting is simply the result of education, but, as it has become habitual, it must be considered as constituting a distinction between himself and other dogs of his class.

The fox-terriers and the dachshund are also allied to the hounds, the former being used to balk the fox from his earth when driven into it by the hounds; and the latter, although he follows by scent, differs from the hounds in that he digs out his quarry when it takes to earth. He is also used for hunting the badger, which the true hound does not follow.

Dogs used in America.—Owing to the fact that sporting matters and canine-breeding are things of comparatively recent interest in this country, some of the dogs used in England are but little or not at all known here, and even these are kept for house or toy purposes rather than for their legitimate pursuits. We have no otter-hounds, stag-hounds, or harriers, and the fox-terrier, though coming into favor, is not used as a sporting-dog. The greyhound is found in limited numbers, and upon the plains and the Pacific coast is somewhat used for coursing. The bloodhound and dachshund are occasionally seen, and now and then a retriever, but none of these dogs can be said to be largely represented in this country, though they are recognized and have classes assigned to them at the principal shows. Sporting-dogs in America are confined to setters in their three varieties, viz., English, Irish, and Gordon; pointers; spaniels, chiefly the cocker; Irish water-spaniels, which are used for duck retrieving; fox-hounds, which are generally so mixed that the class may be said to embrace all varieties of large hounds, and which are also used for hunting the rabbit, as the small hare is called here, and a few beagles. The retriever is not popular in this country, despite the efforts of his admirers to make him so, owing to the breaking of setters and pointers to perform that as well as their peculiar duty, thus combining the qualities of two breeds in one and obviating the necessity for keeping a number of dogs, which would be very inconvenient to the great majority of sportsmen.

The non-sporting class embraces nearly all the varieties mentioned by Stonehenge. The colley is, however, the only recognized cattle-dog, as the bob-tailed sheep-dog is practically unknown, and the Spitz is kept only as a house-pet.

Breaking and Training.—These terms, often improperly used synonymously, have, in sporting parlance, very different significations, the former being restricted to mere education, and the latter to fitting the dog physically for his work. Setters, pointers, spaniels, and retrievers are broken; that is, taught to find game, point or flush it, and to retrieve from land and water, with such other matters as tend to the performance of these duties in the manner most promotive of sport. Hounds are broken to obey the horn and commands of the huntsman, and to follow the trail of the quarry. Sheep-dogs are broken to watch, collect, and drive the cattle or sheep intrusted to them. Trick-dogs are also broken in their own line. Greyhounds, with whom speed and wind are all-important, are prepared for their matches by a systematic course of exercise, medicine, and food, which is purely physical in its effects, and is known as training. Fighting dogs and ratters are trained before they are put into the pit, just as prize-fighters go into training to prepare themselves for the ring. Of course setters or pointers may at times get so out of condition that they are incapable of efficient work, but the course by which this is remedied certainly cannot with propriety be called breaking, and there is no more reason for the misapplication of one term than of the other.

Importations.—The narrow limits to which American sporting was restricted prior to the last few years naturally precluded proper attention to canine breeding and the preservation of pure strains. Anything that would work fairly well in the field was deemed good enough; and the indiscriminate mating of individuals solely on account of their field qualities, and without any consideration for their fitness for each other, resulted, as might be expected, in such mixture of blood that not only was there a great preponderance of dogs of inferior quality, but even the best became wholly unreliable as producers of progeny equal to themselves. The first effort of the pioneers in canine reformation was directed to obtaining blood which, from its purity, could be relied on to transmit the qualities of its possessors, and this led to importations from the most celebrated kennels in England, where the different strains had been kept pure, and their representatives brought up to the highest standard by intelligent breeding, designed to intensify desirable qualities and eradicate those which were undesirable. The superiority of the imported dogs was speedily recognized, and the interest awakened by them led to other importations and to the elevation of canine breeding to an equality with the breeding of fine horses and cattle, so that it was taken up by gentlemen of means, education, and position, and as a result we have now in the descendants of the various imported strains a class of dogs equal to those of any other country.

Bench-shows and Field-trials.—The benefits which English breeders had derived from shows and trials was too apparent to be overlooked by those interested in the improvement of American dogs, and about the time of the first importations of our present blood, these were instituted and have since become very popular. It is certainly not unjust to say that, prior to the institution of shows, comparatively very few men knew what constituted good form in any breed. The acceptance of a standard which was framed by the experience of the best recognized authorities, and the judging of dogs by it, very quickly exposed physical defects not hitherto suspected, and by educating breeders, led to the production of far superior dogs, so that at any prominent show of to-day one will scarcely find a single specimen as defective in form or lacking in quality as were the majority of the dogs exhibited a decade ago. Bench-shows are mere beauty exhibitions. They are intended solely to promote breeding for the best physical form, and have nothing to do with field-quality, so that an utterly worthless dog with correct form will beat a crack fielder that is not up to show standard. Field-trials on the other hand are intended to test the working abilities of the competitors, by running them on game and judging by a scale of merit and demerit, tending to show both the natural quality and breaking of each individual. With well-devised rules all qualities except endurance can be fairly tested, but this the brevity of time which can be given to the running forbids, thus leaving trials open to the objection that a dog may win at them, which would utterly fail if subjected to the test of severe field-work. This objection cannot be done away with, but with this field trials still afford a sufficiently reliable exhibition of quality to be of great value to breeders and sportsmen generally. There are now in this country, besides the National Kennel Club, associations in the East and South, which hold their trials annually upon quails, besides an association in California, which holds its trials upon the quails of that section. With some slight variations the rules of the National Club have been generally adopted by the Eastern and Southern associations, so that a dog can compete at any and all trials without having his chances for success imperilled by great diversity of the different scales by which he is judged.

While the importance of bench-shows must not be undervalued, the awards of trials naturally take a higher rank with those who look first of all to the working abilities of a dog; but over and above either is the combination of both show and field qualities in the same individual, and to this *summum bonum* the attention of the best breeders is directed. Winners of the double event have been produced, and the possibilities of the race will not be accomplished till dogs of this high character become proportionally common.

(A. B.)

DOGGETT, DAVID SETH, D.D. (1810–1880), one of the bishops of the Methodist Episcopal Church South, was born in Lancaster co., Va., Jan. 23, 1810, being the youngest child of John Doggett, a local preacher, who had been a Revolutionary soldier. The younger Doggett had few educational advantages, but of them he made the most. He united with the Methodist Church in his seventeenth year; when he was nineteen he became an itinerant preacher in the Virginia Conference. In 1839 he was chaplain to the University of Virginia; from 1840 to 1846 he was professor in Randolph-Macon College, Virginia. From 1850 to 1856 he was editor of the *Southern Methodist Quarterly Review*. In 1865 he founded, in connection with the Rev. John E. Edwards, D.D., the *Episcopal Methodist*, a weekly newspaper published in the interests of his church. During his itinerant ministry he served as pastor the most important churches in his conference, and had the reputation of being an eloquent and useful preacher. In 1866, at the session of the general conference that met in New Orleans, La., he was elected one of the bishops of the Methodist Episcopal Church South. He performed the duties of his office till his death in the city of Richmond, Va., Oct. 27, 1880. Bishop Doggett wrote much for the periodicals published by his church.

there is a posthumous volume of *Sermons* (Nashville, 1881).

DOGSBANE. Dogsbane is the familiar name given to the natural order *Apocynaceæ*, of which the genus *Apocynum* is the type. In many respects it is one of the most remarkable orders in the vegetable kingdom. The order is closely related to the gentians on the one hand, and has many characters in common with milkworts, or *Asclepiadaceæ*. The plants of the order are well marked by a peculiar pistil, which has the stigmas collected into a comparatively large head, expanded at the base in the form of a ring, and contracted in the middle, and the style usually tapering from the head of the stigmas to the base. The flowers are monopetalous, but more or less deeply five-lobed, the lobes twisted in the bud, the five stamens inserted on the corolla, the anthers adhering to the stigma, though the filaments are distinct; the two ovaries are also usually distinct, though the stigmas are united. The species in nearly the whole of the order have mostly opposite and entire leaves, without stipules, and with a milky, acrid juice, which occasionally furnishes some of the most active poisons known. The name *Apocynum* is an ancient one, and significant of the virulent character of the plant. It is employed by Pliny, who says, "*Canes et omnis quadrupedes necat in cibo datum*" ("Given in their food, it kills dogs and quadrupeds"). It seems to have been generally employed to destroy worthless dogs, as strychnine now often is; and in this way arose the familiar name of "dogsbane." The most celebrated plant of the order is the Tanghin bean of Madagascar, *Tanghinia venenifera*. The bean is no larger than an almond-kernel, but one is sufficient to destroy twenty men. It is said that the priests of Madagascar possessed a secret antidote, causing vomiting, by which the poison could be taken in safety, and that the poison was cunningly made a test of innocence and in this way obnoxious persons were murdered under the guise of a religious ceremony. Another virulent plant of the order is the *Nerium*, the common oleander of our gardens. It is evidently confounded by modern commentators with the *rhododendron* of ancient writers, and the poisonous character often attributed to the azalea and rhododendron was intended for the oleander. Rat-poison is still made of its powdered wood and bark, and it is on record that in 1809, when the French troops were lying before Madrid, a soldier used the wood for skewers in roasting meat, and of twelve who ate the meat all were taken ill, and eight died. The beauty of the flowers, however, renders the plant very popular in gardens, and it is extremely rare that any ill results of this culture are reported.

When the acridity is moderated the properties become nutritious. *Tabernæmontana utilis* in tropical America is a "cow tree," the sap being used as we use milk. Many species have delicate forms of caoutchouc prepared from the milk. Mr. Thistleton Dyer has recently stated that in Africa the natives smear the juices of a number of species of Apocynaceous plants over their arms and breasts, and in this way sheets of caoutchouc of much value are prepared.

The order is chiefly a tropical one. About nine genera and twenty species enter the United States, and of these two, *Apocynum androsæmifolium* and *A. cannabinum*, are found in the northern parts, and are the plants generally known as "dogsbane" in that region. Besides dogsbane, they are known as "Indian hemp," and in South Carolina they go by the name of "Amyer Marion's root," from having been a favorite medicinal plant with the famous Revolutionary general Marion of South Carolina. They are also known as "fly-catchers," in common with other species of the order. The flowers secrete a sweet liquid. The insect inserts its proboscis between the filaments; in withdrawing it, it is often caught between the anthers, which, as already noted, are united to the stigmas. Drawing the proboscis up into these narrowing spaces, of course the insect is held the tighter for its struggles. Though often referred to in modern times by fresh observers, the fly-catching ability was recorded by Erasmus Darwin, who in his notes to the *Botanic Garden* gives the observations of some of his correspondents made in 1788; and it is mentioned by Ray in his *Historia Plantarum*, which was issued in that year. Insects are believed by many to be specially designed for effecting the cross-fertilization of flowers, or rather flowers are believed to be specially adapted to the visits of insects in regard to cross-fertilization. In his works on cross-fertilization no reference is made to *Apocynaceæ* by Mr. C. Darwin, as this destruction of insect friends on their useful mission is necessarily an anomaly such as is often met with by those engaged in the endeavor to interpret the laws of Nature.

The name "Indian hemp" is derived from its use by the North American Indians. The bark-fibre is extremely fine and tough, and the natives used it for cordage, fishing-nets, baskets, coarse cloth, and indeed for almost all purposes that our hemp would be put to. It is much finer than hemp, whiter, and much more durable. It is remarkable that the moderns have not given this fibre more attention. Recently a German author has called attention to its value, enumerating it among other "new" substances, such as *Abutilon Avicennæ, Laportea pustulata*, and *Asclepias Cornuti* (see Fuehling's *Landw. Zeitung*, 1880). But similar observations were made by Gerard, who wrote in 1597. He says: "The cods of the greater upright broad-leaved American plant are stuffed full with a most pure silk of a shining white color; and every nerve or sinew, wherewith the nerves are ribbed, are likewise most pure silk; as also are the Peelings or Bark of the Stems or Branches, like as is the Peeling or Bark of Flax or Hemp Cordage for making Linnen. But the Indians have not the Understanding in them to make use of it so as to cover their Nakedness, notwithstanding the Earth is covered over with this Silk. This they daily tread under their Feet, which would be sufficient to Cloath many Kingdoms if it was carefully Cherished and Manured."

The two species are widely spread over the United States. *A. androsæmifolium* is found from Canada to Georgia, and across from New Mexico and California to British Columbia. *A. cannabinum* has smaller flowers than the other, and a rather more southern range. It has had a good chance to hold its own, as no animal is known to eat its leaves. Some authors and encyclopædias quote Kalm as saying that the plant is poisonous to some people and not to others, but Kalm refers to the *Rhus* or "poison-vine," and not to the dogsbane. *Apocynum* yields a peculiar principle known as *apocynin*. The juice of the plant has been used medicinally as an emeto-cathartic. It induces drowsiness. In doses of 15 to 20 grains it produces vomiting. When employed it is usually given in six-grain doses, but in modern times other drugs have almost superseded it.

A European species, *Apocynum venetum*, is believed to

have been the one referred to by the ancients. (T. M.)

DOGWOOD. This is the common name of the plants represented by the genus *Cornus*, which name is derived from the old English word *dagge*; that is to say, a dagger or skewer, the wood being from time immemorial used in connection with bows and arrows, javelins, lances, skewers, and wherever a strong, light wood was desirable. The European species, *Cornus mascula* and *Cornus sanguinea*, are still used when wood of such character is needed. The last-named species is still known among the English peasantry as "arrow-wood" and "skewer-wood." In Latin and Greek classics *Cornus mascula* is the species generally referred to, the name *Cornus* being supposed also to refer to the hard and horny character of the wood. The berries of this species were classed among the fruits, and are referred to as the cornelian cherry, or the cherry of the cornus or cornel tree. It grows to be a tree 20 feet high, and is wild in Asia Minor. It has oval red berries about the size of a cherry, and with a single stone inside. The Romans used the fruits in a fresh condition, as well as dried, and put them up in salt. They also fed them freely to their hogs. They have been freely used to the present time, but have had to give way to better things. The tree is, however, very ornamental, and will always be popular for its early flowers and handsome red berries. The berries of the *Cornus sanguinea*, female or English red dogwood, are often employed in adulterating buckthorn-berries.

In America by "dogwood" is generally understood *Cornus florida*, the flowering dogwood, so called from the series of white leaves or bracts which form an involucre under the real flowers. This peculiarity is shared by a species on the Pacific coast, *Cornus Nuttalli*, which was so named and figured by Audubon in his *Birds of America*, plate 467. This species has the bracts nearly six inches wide, or double the size of its Eastern relative. Besides these there are sixteen other species natives of North America—namely, *C. alternifolia*, which also makes a small tree, sometimes 20 feet high; *asperifolia*; *Californica*; *Canadensis*, an herbaceous species, which by its numerous red berries, often covering the ground in the greatest abundance, gives so much attraction to Northern forest scenery; *circinatum*; *Drummondii*; *glabra*; *paniculata*, interesting from its pure white berries; *pubescens*, also almost a tree, and the prevailing species of the mountains of Colorado and Utah, sometimes growing in dense masses and forming excellent covers for mountain-bears, which are fond of the berries; *sericea*, a species common along river-banks in the eastern parts of the United States: according to B. S. Barton, the Indians used its bark for flavoring tobacco, made baskets of the young twigs, and prepared a scarlet dye from the branches and the roots; *sessilis*; *stolonifera*, which is known in gardens as the white-berried dogwood, from its large white berries, though other species have smaller white berries, and which has had many other names, now given as synonyms; it is also called red dogwood, which name confuses it with *Cornus sanguinea* of Europe, the twigs being much more entitled to the name of red than the European; *striata*; *Suecica*; *Torreyi*; and *Unalaskensis*.

Though not a large tree, the common dogwood serves many useful purposes. The wood is very hard and light, and bends considerably before breaking. It is in common use for lumbermen's levers, for making cogs for mill-wheels, wedges, and the handles of many tools and implements. It splits easily, and thus makes excellent hoops for small kegs. The specific gravity of the wood, taking hickory at 1000, is 815, and it gives 765 pounds of charcoal to a cord of wood. It is in good demand for the finer kinds of gunpowder. The wood has been used for coarse engravings. The young branches are employed as a dentifrice. The bark has been extensively used in intermittent fevers. Nuttall says of *Cornus Nuttallii*, "An extract of the bark, boiled down to a solid consistence, contains in a very concentrated state the vegetable principle *cornine*, which we found of singular service in the settlement of Wahlamet, where in the autumn of 1835 the intermittent fever prevailed. In most cases pills of this extract, timely administered, gave perfect relief." Medical authorities regard 35 grains of the bark as equal to 30 grains of cinchona, but it is liable to produce pain in the bowels unless carefully administered. During the war of the rebellion in the United States the bark and berries were freely used in the South when quinine became scarce. The berries are sometimes steeped in brandy, and then give "dogwood bitters." Birds are very fond of the berries of all the species. Dr. Walker makes an excellent ink thus: Half an ounce of dogwood bark, 40 grains of sulphate of iron, 40 grains of gum-arabic, in 16 ounces of rain-water. It is said that an oil fit for table use or burning has been obtained from the American red-twigged dogwood, but it was more probably from the *Cornus sanguinea* of Europe. *Cornus florida* extends from Canada to Florida, and its analogue, *Cornus Nuttallii*, has about the same range of latitude on the Pacific coast.

DOGWOOD, Jamaica or West Indian. Unlike the common dogwood, this seems to have derived its name from real service to the canine race, being used in the West Indies to cure the mange in dogs. It is, botanically, *Piscidia Erythrina*, the generic name being from *piscis*, a fish, and the specific (once a generic name) from the Greek *erythros*, red. The powdered bark of the root when thrown into water makes it red, and according to Jacquin, who wrote a history of American plants in 1763, "the leaves and branches, when thrown into the water, intoxicate the fish, which then float on the surface of the water, and may be captured by hand. Many other American plants have this virtue." This early observation has been confirmed by modern authorities. While the larger fish are simply intoxicated, the smaller ones are killed. The narcotic property of the plant has been the theme of many able essays by medical men. Some assert that it is much safer than opium, leaving none of the unpleasant results of that drug. As with laudanum, when dipped in cotton and put into a hollow tooth it relieves the toothache. It grows in South Florida as well as in the West Indies, forming a straggling tree of about 20 feet in height; the flowers appear before the leaves, in April, and have much the appearance of the common locust-flowers, *Robinia pseud-acacia*. They are white, with a purplish tinge. The seed-pods are singular among the rest of the family, *Leguminosæ*, in having four strong wings along the entire length, giving them the appearance of being almost square. The pod is about two or three inches long, the lower portion being very slender, indeed thread-like, and about half an inch in length. (T. M.)

DOLLAR. See MONEY.

DÖLLINGER, JOHANN JOSEPH IGNAZ VON, a German theologian, leader of the "Old Catholic" movement, was born at Bamberg, Bavaria, Feb. 28, 1799.

being the son of the celebrated anatomist and physiologist, Ignaz Döllinger (1770-1841). He studied theology at Würzburg and Bamberg, and immediately after he received priestly orders; in 1822 he was made chaplain and in the next year became professor in the Lyceum at Aschaffenburg. His first theological work, *The Doctrine of the Eucharist in the First Three Centuries*, was published in 1826; and in the same year he was called to the University of Munich as professor of church history and canon law. His course of lectures was published in 1828 under the title of *Manual of the History of the Church*. This work was afterwards enlarged into a *Treatise on the History of the Church* (1836-38). In 1845, as the representative of the University of Munich, he entered the Bavarian Parliament, and in 1849, while a delegate to the Frankfort Diet, he voted for the entire separation of church and state. In 1861 he discussed the question of the temporal power of the pope in some writings which attracted much attention. In his work, *The Papacy and the State of the Church*, he counselled the abandonment of the temporal power, and thus gave occasion for a lively polemical discussion. His name became still more widely known by his opposition to the decrees of the Vatican Council of 1868-70, and particularly to the one relating to the infallibility of the pope. In a series of articles published in the *Augsburg Gazette* he demanded liberty of discussion in the Œcumenical Council, and argued that the new decisions, to have authority, should be adopted almost unanimously. Certain anonymous writings vigorously attacking the infallibility of the pope were attributed to him, and the *Roemische Briefe vom Council* brought against him an energetic attack. As he resolutely refused to submit to the decrees of the Vatican Council, he was, on April 17, 1871, formally excommunicated by the archbishop of Munich. By this, however, his popularity in Bavaria was increased. His resistance was sustained by the government, and he became the acknowledged leader of those who, holding the previous teachings of the church, have become disaffected toward the Holy See. The University of Oxford conferred on him the degree of D.C.L., Jan 6, 1871, and on July 29 he was elected rector of the University of Munich by a vote of fifty-four to six. He took a leading part in the "Old Catholic" congresses of Munich in 1871 and Cologne in 1872: but while firm on the question of doctrines he avoided any association in the political tendencies of the party. Since then he has presided, at Bonn, over several conferences of Old Catholics, with representatives of English, American, and oriental churches, with the purpose of effecting a unity of doctrine and to prepare for the fusion of all the Christian churches. In 1873 he was nominated, by King Louis of Bavaria, president of the Royal Academy of Sciences of Munich and conservator-general of the scientific collections of the kingdom.

In addition to the works named he has published: *Origins of Christianity* (1833-35); *The Religion of Mohammed* (1838); *The Reformation, its Interior Development and its Effects* (3 vols., 1846-8); *A Sketch of Luther* (1851); *Hippolytus and Callistus, or the Roman Church in the First Half of the Third Century* (1854); *Paganism and Judaism* (1857); *Christianity and the Church* (1860); *The Papacy and the Temporal Power* (1861); *Papacy Legends of the Middle Ages* (1863); and *History of the Religious Sects of the Middle Ages* (3 vols., 1870); *Lectures on the Reunion of the Churches* (1872); with numerous pamphlets and periodical articles, several of which have been collected under the title, *Essays on the Political, Ecclesiastical, and Social History of the last Six Centuries* (1862-82).

DOMINICAN REPUBLIC, or SAN DOMINGO (Spanish *Republica Dominicana*, or *Santo Domingo*), a republic of the West Indies, comprising the eastern two-thirds of the island of Hayti (Santo Domingo), of which the western one-third constitutes the republic of Hayti (Haiti). The Dominican Republic has an area stated at 20,597 square miles, while that of the Haytian Republic is but 9232 square miles. The Dominicans are a Spanish-speaking people of negro origin, with a large admixture of white and Indian blood; the Haytians speak a French *patois*, and are of more purely African stock. In the report of the United States commission of 1871 it is stated that in Santo Domingo there is a marked preponderance of white blood over the negro. Very few pure-blooded negroes are found; one-tenth of the people are of pure Spanish descent.

See Vol. XI. p. 485 Am. ed. (p. 543 Edin. ed.).

Mountains and Valleys.—The central range or backbone of the island (*Sierra del Cibao*) lies chiefly in Dominican territory, and has a general course from W. N. W. to E. S. E., and then turns to the E., extending to Cape Engaño, the E. point of the island. Northwardly this range is separated by the noble plain or valley of Cibao (called la Vega Real) from the northern coast-range (or Sierra de Monte Cristi). This plain is watered by the Gran Yaqui (the largest river of the island), flowing W. N. W., and by the Yuna, flowing E. S. E. The third or southernmost range lies mostly in the Haytian territory, but also occupies the S. W. parts of the Dominican republic. Between this and the central range is a valley broken by hill-ranges, and traversed by the head-streams of the Haytian river Artibonite, flowing generally westward, and by the Neyba, or Lesser Yaqui, flowing S. S. E. The central range is the highest, several of its peaks, according to some authorities, exceeding 9000 feet in height; but Mount Yaqui, the highest point, has been recently stated not to exceed 7560 feet. The southern range is not quite so high as the first; while the Sierra de Monte Cristi on the N. is believed to have no peak reaching 4000 feet. Yaqui, the highest mountain, is near the centre of the island.

Rivers.—The rivers comprise (1) the Artibonite (chiefly Haytian); (2) the Great Yaqui (called also Yacki, Yaque, Northern Yaqui, and Monte Cristi); it is the largest Dominican stream, yet has a shoal mouth, and is boatable rather than navigable; (3) the Yuna, flowing into the head of Samaná Bay; it has a sand-bar at the mouth, with only four feet of water, but boats can ascend it forty miles, nearly to the town of Cotuy; (4) the Neyba, Neyva, Neiva, or Lesser Yaqui, also called South Yacki; (5) the Nisao, a swift stream with a bad bar, scarcely passable for boats; (6) the Ozama, on the S. coast, and on which is the city of Santo Domingo; this stream at low tide can receive vessels of eleven to thirteen feet draught; inside the bar the water is twenty feet deep for some distance; (7) the four little rivers called Yeguada, Guanabo, Real, and Jayan; these all flow into the port of Jicaco, or English Port, eleven miles W. of Cape Rafael, as do also small streams called Capiton, Culebras, and Magüa; (8) the Higuey, or Yuma, whose mouth is near the S. E. point of the island; it has eight feet on the bar and twelve feet within; not far off are the Añamuya, Maymon, and Nisibon; (9) the Quiabon, with a bar often dry, and never more than three feet under water; (10) the Romana, a deep stream, whose mouth makes a good anchorage; ten feet may be carried for two miles up; (11) the Cumayaso, which may be entered by large ships; (12) the Soco, large but shallow, though passable for boats; (13) the Macroris, whose mouth forms the port of the same name; (14) the Jaina, which is not properly navigable, though mahogany is shipped from it; (15) the Nigua, Najallo, Nisao, Via, or Bya, Tabara, Nisaito, Agujero-Chico, Trou-Jacob, and Pedernales, all small streams of the south coast; (16) the small rivers of the north coast, the Estillero, Lateriana, Yasica, Bobo, San Marco, and Dajabon or Massacre River.

Boundaries, Coast-lines, Harbors.—The Dominican Republic is bounded W. by Hayti, the river Dajabon (Daxabon, or Massacre) marking the limit on the N. and the Pedernales that on the S. coast. Between the heads of these rivers the boundary line is not clearly established, though in part it follows the crest of a range called the Black Mountains. The only outlying islands worth naming are Saona, Catalina, and Beata, all to the S. The peninsula of Samana on the E. was an island in the colonial period. Cape Engaño, the E. point, is in lat. 18° 35' 51" N., lon. 68° 20' 40" W. The island of Beata, the southernmost point in the republic, is in 17° 36' 45" N., 71° 32' 54" W. The republic has few good harbors, but there are many tolerable anchorages and roadsteads.

Climate, Productions, etc.—The climate of course varies with altitude. The ports and low plains are hot and sickly, the yellow fever being endemic. The rainy season lasts from May till November, and is the worst time for strangers to visit the country. The dry season has strong N. E. and N. W. winds, while the violent winds of the rainy season are oftenest from the S.; most of the hurricanes pass N. of the island, but they are not very unfrequent between July 1 and the end of October. The mineral wealth is great; gold, silver, mercury, copper, platinum, iron, tin, sulphur, salt, antimony, and manganese are reported. Gold was formerly wrought on an important scale; it is now collected in a very small way. There are fisheries of some local importance. The forests yield oak, pine, mahogany of finest quality, lignum vitæ, satinwood, fustic, logwood, etc.; and nearly all tropical fruits can be grown in perfection. Charcoal and firewood are exported to some extent, but the principal exports are of hides, cattle, sugar, rum, tobacco, coffee, cacao, lignum vitæ, logwood extract, tortoise shell, honey, wax, mahogany, furniture-woods, and especially dyewoods. Santo Domingo, Puerto Plata, Samaná, Azua, and Monte Cristi are the chief ports for trade. The raising of cattle and of swine are leading industries. There is of late an active shipment of guano from the coast islets. Much of the soil is of unsurpassed fertility, but there are large barren tracts towards the west; while in the east agriculture is of the most slovenly description. There is little real industry, yet the people are in general happy and careless, and the criminal class is small.

Government, social life.—The government is republican in form, the president being chosen for six years. The republic is divided into five provinces and four maritime districts, each province or district having its governor. The provinces are Santo Domingo (with capital of the same name). Santiago (capital, Santiago de los Caballeros), La Vega (capital, Concepcion de la Vega), Azua de Compostela (capital, Azua), and El Seybo (capital, Santa Cruz del Seybo). The maritime districts are Puerto Plato, Monte Cristi, Samaná, and Barahona, each with a capital and seaport of the same name.

There is a national congress, in two houses, and each province has a legislature. There is a small standing army, rendered necessary by frequent Haytian trespasses on the west frontier. The general outlook for Santo Domingo is rather encouraging. The country is more quiet and prosperous than is Hayti, and the recent increase of sugar-production is in part a cause, in part an effect, of increased tranquillity.

The state religion is Roman Catholic. The capital city is an archiepiscopal see, now under the charge of a delegate apostolic. There is an institution called the University of Santo Domingo; but schools are not numerous or important, although there is a department of public instruction. There are few decent roads, and no railways except one in construction from Samaná to Santiago; another is to be made from Barahona to certain salt mines. Canoes carry freights on some of the rivers, but transportation is mostly by mules and pack-horses, which travel over mere bridle-paths in the forests and mountains. The only *towns* of importance are Santo Domingo (the capital-population 16,000), Santiago de los Caballeros, Concepcion de la Vega, Azua, Santa Cruz del Seybo, Puerto Plata, Monte Cristi, Samaná, and Barahona.

Finances.—The receipts for 1882 (chiefly from import duties) were about $1,500,000, the expenses somewhat less. A government debt of £757,000 was contracted in London in 1869, of which only a part is recognized by the Dominican government. There is also a home debt of $2,000,000, towards the extinction of which 15 *per centum* of the entry duties is applied. The population is variously estimated, but probably does not exceed 180,000. (C. W. G.)

DONALDSON, JAMES, LL.D., a Scotch classical scholar, was born at Aberdeen, April 26, 1831. He was educated in Marischal College, Aberdeen, New College, London, and the University of Berlin. He was appointed Greek tutor in Edinburgh University in 1852, rector of the High-school of Stirling in 1854, classical master in the High-school of Edinburgh in 1856, and rector of the latter school in 1866. In 1881 he was appointed professor of humanity in the University of Aberdeen. He has contributed to the ENCYCLOPÆDIA BRITANNICA, and to several periodicals. Among his works are a *Modern Greek Grammar for the use of Classical Students* (1853); *Lyra Græca: Specimens of the Greek Lyric Poets from Callinus to Soutsos, with Critical Notes* (1854); *Critical History of Christian Literature and Doctrine from the Death of the Apostles to the Nicene Council* (3 vols., 1864-66); *The Expiatory and Substitutionary Sacrifices of the Greeks* (1875); and *On the Position of Women in Greece.* In conjunction with the Rev. Alexander Roberts he edited *The Ante-Nicene Christian Library* (24 vols., 1867-72).

DONALDSON, JAMES LOWRY, an American general, was born in Baltimore, March 17, 1814. He graduated at West Point in 1836, then served in the Florida war and in removing the Cherokee Indians to the West. During the controversy about the boundary of Maine he served in that State, and in 1844 he was engaged in the survey of the line agreed upon, having previously furnished the maps upon which the treaty was principally drawn. He took part in the military occupation of Texas in 1846, and in the Mexican War.

He was engaged on duty as chief quartermaster of the department of New Mexico when the Civil War broke out. In 1862 he was ordered to Pittsburg, Pa., and became chief quartermaster of the Middle department. He established the great dépôt at Nashville, which furnished Gen. Sherman's supplies during the Atlanta campaign and the susequent "March to the Sea." Under the orders of Maj.-Gen. George H. Thomas, commanding the military division of the Tennessee, he established the system of national cemeteries, which was afterwards adopted by the quartermaster's department and approved by Congress. Gen. Donaldson became by successive promotions major-general of volunteers and brevet major-general in the regular army. He retired voluntarily from active service March 15, 1869, and from the army Jan. 1, 1874. He published in 1871 a tale of the Florida war called *Sergeant Atkins*.

DONALDSONVILLE, a town of Louisiana, the county-seat of Ascension co., is on the right bank of the Mississippi River at the head of Bayou Lafourche. It is 78 miles from New Orleans by river, and 65 by the Southern Pacific Railroad. It has a court-house, market-house, 4 hotels, 2 weekly newspapers, 5 churches, 2 public and 4 private schools. St. Vincent's Orphan Asylum occupies a fine building. Donaldsonville is the third oldest town in the State, and was incorporated in 1836. Its property is valued at $600,000. The population is 2600, about half of whom are colored. Bayou Lafourche flows from the Mississippi into Barataria Bay, an arm of the Gulf of Mexico. Population of Donaldsonville, 2600.

DONDERS, FRANTS CORNELIS, a Dutch physician, was born at Tilburg, in Northern Brabant, May 27, 1818. He was educated at the university and military medical school of Utrecht, and became physician at the hospital of Haag, and afterwards professor at the Utrecht school. In 1847 he was made professor in the University of Utrecht, where he taught physiology and histology, to which he added a course in ophthalmology, and a clinic on maladies of the eye. In 1863 he received the title of ordinary professor, and with the assistance of the government established a physiological laboratory, which was inaugurated in 1867. His works include: *Micro-chemical Researches upon the Animal Tissues* (1846); *Forms, Combinations, and Functions of the Primitive Tissue* (1849); and, in ophthalmic science, *Study of the Movements of the Eyes* (1847); *Astigmatism* (1862); *Anomalies of Accommodation and Refraction of the Eye, and their results* (1865); (an English translation of which was published by the New Sydenham Society). He has, besides, contributed numerous papers to medical journals, and has edited the *Researches made in the Laboratory of the University of Utrecht* (Utrecht, 1849-57; 2d series, 1867).

DONELSON, ANDREW JACKSON, LL. D. (1800-1871), an American diplomatist and politician, was born near Nashville, Tenn., Aug. 25, 1800. He graduated at West Point in 1820, and became aide-de-camp to his uncle, Gen. Andrew Jackson, then governor of Florida, which had recently been obtained from Spain. He resigned from the army in 1822, and studied law at Nashville. Gen. Jackson, on his accession to the presidency in 1829, appointed Donelson his private secretary, but the latter finally withdrew from Washington in consequence of the trouble caused by Pres. Jackson's insisting on the social recognition of Mrs. Eaton. In 1844 Donelson was sent by Pres. Tyler to Texas as chargé d'affaires, and negotiated its annexation to the United States. He was United States minister to Prussia in 1846. Returning to this country in 1849 he took an active part in the political discussions concerning slavery, and in 1851 became editor of the *Washington Union*. In 1856 he was nominated by the American party as their candidate for Vice-President, but was defeated. He then retired from public life, and lived as a planter in Mississippi. He died at Memphis, Tenn., June 26, 1871.

DONGAN, THOMAS (1634-1715), colonial governor of New York, and afterwards Earl of Limerick, was born in 1634, at Castletown, county Kildare, Ireland, being the second son of Sir John Dongan. Having adopted the military profession, he was, by the influence of his uncle Talbot, Earl of Tyrconnel, soon promoted to a colonelcy. He afterwards entered the service of France with the same rank, but in 1678, when Charles II. ordered all British subjects home, Dongan returned at considerable sacrifice. For this he was compensated by an English pension, and was appointed lieutenant-governor of Tangier. In 1682, when Sir Edmund Andros was recalled from the governorship of New York, Col. Dongan was appointed by the Duke of York to succeed him. He arrived Aug. 25, 1683, but was met with some distrust on account of his being a Roman Catholic. His firm and judicious policy as well as his pleasing address soon conciliated all classes. He had brought instructions under which the first general assembly of the colony was convened in New York city, Oct. 17, 1683. When the Duke of York became king, Dongan was continued in office, and April 27, 1686, he granted a charter to the city of New York, which has remained for two centuries the basis of its municipal rights. He also chartered the city of Albany, and endeavored to unite New Jersey and Connecticut with his own province. His policy with the Indians was to continue their instruction in Christianity which had been commenced by French missionaries, but to have the work carried on by English Catholic priests, so that French political influence might be restrained. But these views did not meet the king's approval, and in April, 1688, Dongan, resigning his office, retired to private life in New York and on Staten Island. In 1691 he returned to England, and in 1698 he succeeded to the title of Earl of Limerick by the death of his elder brother, but the estates had been forfeited by the adherence of the latter to James II. after the revolution of 1688. An act of parliament for his relief was passed May 25, 1702. He died in London, Dec. 14, 1715, without issue.

DONIPHAN, ALEXANDER WILLIAM, an American general, was born in Mason co., Ky., July 9, 1808, the youngest of ten children. When he was five years old, his father died. He was carefully trained and graduated from Augusta College at the age of eighteen. Having studied law, he was admitted to the bar in 1830 and removed to Lexington, Mo., where he began the practice of his profession. In 1833 he removed to Liberty, in Clay co., then on the verge of civilization. His eloquence and ability not only gave him prominence as a lawyer, but caused him to be elected to the Missouri legislature in 1836, in 1840, and again in 1854. When the State militia were called out in 1838 to enforce the law against the Mormons, Doniphan was in command of the First brigade and secured the surrender of their prophet, Joseph Smith; yet he was afterwards employed as the counsel of the prophet, who, however, escaped from jail and joined his people in Illinois. In 1846, at the outbreak of the Mexican war, a regiment of mounted volunteers from Missouri was organized June 18, with Doniphan as colonel. This regiment with some infantry, rangers, and artillery from Missouri, and six troops of United States dragoons, amounting in all to 1658 men, formed the Army of the West, under command of Col. S. W. Kearney, U. S. A. They marched 900 miles to Santa Fé, and took peaceable possession of New Mexico. On Sept. 25 Gen. Kearney set out for California, with his dragoons, and ordered Doniphan to march to Chihuahua to report to Gen. Wool, but afterwards directed him first to reduce the unruly Navajos to submission. In spite of the difficulties of a campaign late in the autumn, this was done. Then on Dec. 14 Doniphan set out from Valverde to seek Gen. Wool, far to the southward. His regiment had been reinforced and had two batteries. In bitterly cold weather they crossed a treeless desert of 90 miles, and on Christmas day the advance party of 500 encountered a Mexican army on the banks of the Bracito. The Missourians were summoned to surrender with a threat of "no quarter," but Doniphan refused. After a sharp contest of 30 minutes the Mexicans fled, leaving 63 dead and 150 wounded, while of the Missourians only 7 were wounded. On Dec. 27 Doniphan entered El Paso, but he still had 250 miles to march to Chihuahua; and in the meantime Gen. Wool had left that place to reinforce Gen. Taylor. On Feb. 8, 1847, Doniphan resumed his march with 954 men, pushed on through a sandy desert, and finally, on Feb. 28, encountered an army of 4000 men in front of Chihuahua. After three hours of hard fighting the Mexicans were routed, leaving 304 killed and nearly 500 wounded. The loss of the Missourians was 1 killed and 11 wounded. On March 1, 1847, Doniphan entered Chihuahua in triumph. He immediately despatched scouts in search of Gen. Wool, who was found on April 2, at Saltillo, 700 miles distant. Thither the Missourians were ordered to march, and on May 21 they joined Gen. Wool near Buena Vista. Their term of enlistment had now nearly expired, and it was decided by the commanding general that they should return home by way of New Orleans. At St. Louis they had a public reception, in which Col. T. H. Benton welcomed them back to their native State. This arduous and memorable march was the means of largely increasing the extent of the United States, being the ground of the annexation of New Mexico and other Territories, rich in the precious metals. Col. Doniphan returned to the practice of law in Liberty, but in 1854, during the troubles in Kansas, he was elected to the Missouri legislature, and in February, 1861, he was a commissioner from his State to the Peace Convention at Washington which vainly sought to avert civil war. He took no part in the dreadful strife that ensued, but awaited the result with deep anxiety. He still lives in Western Missouri, highly respected by the community.

DORAN, JOHN, PH. D. (1807-1878), an English miscellaneous author, was born in London, March 11, 1807. His family had long held an honorable position in Drogheda, Ireland, but his father, having taken part in the rebellion of 1798, removed to London after the failure of that attempt. Here, becoming a merchant, he made a contract to supply the Channel fleet with provisions during the war with Napoleon, and while so engaged was seized and carried to France. After a captivity of two years he was restored to his family. The son was well taught by his father and in a private school in London, and at an early age showed literary talent. His play of *The Wandering Jew* was performed at the Surrey Theatre when the author was only fifteen. On account of his proficiency in French, acquired from his father, he was selected while still quite young to take charge of the son of Lord Glenlyon (afterwards duke of Athole) during his residence in France. A series of letters from Paris, contributed by him at this time to the London *Literary Chronicle*, was reprinted in 1828 under the title *Sketches and Reminiscences*. For some years he was tutor in the family of Mr. Lascelles (afterwards earl of Harewood), and did much miscellaneous reading and writing. Part of this related to the *History and Antiquities of Reading in Berkshire*, which was published in 1835. He then spent two years on the Continent, during which he received on examination the degree of Ph. D. from the University of Marburg. Returning to England, he determined to devote himself to literature, and took up his residence in London. For eleven years he was connected with the *Church-and-State Gazette*, at first as literary editor, but afterwards doing all the work. Though the father had been a rebel, the son, who cherished his memory, was a Tory, full of hatred and scorn for political agitators, and also of tenderest regard for old laws and institutions. While editor of the *Gazette* he published *Filia Dolorosa, Memoirs of the Duchess of Angoulême* (1852), and wrote a *Life of Dr. Young* for a new edition of Young's *Poems* in 1854. He then began to write for *The Athenæum*, and was soon regularly employed on that journal. For fifteen years scarcely a number of it appeared without an important article from his pen, and at times he was the acting editor. During this period also he produced most of his books, whose titles show the wide range and curious character of their contents. They comprise—*Table Traits, and Something on Them* (1854), *Habits and Men* (1854), *Lives of the Queens of England of the House of Hanover* (1855), *Knights and their Days* (1856), *Monarchs Retired from Business* (1857), *History of Court Fools* (1858), *New Pictures and Old Panels* (1859), *Lives of the Princes of Wales* (1860), *Saints and Sinners* (1868). He also edited *The Last Journals of Horace Walpole* (1859) and *The Bentley Ballads, with original Poems by the Editor* (1861). His most important work was a history of the English stage, published under the title *Their Majesties' Servants* (1864). In the same year he was associated with Mr. W. Hepworth Dixon in editing *Court and Society*, which appeared, however, under the name of the Duke of Manchester, who had furnished the material for the volumes from the "Kimbolton Papers." In 1869 Dr. Doran became editor of *Notes and Queries*, a position for which he was eminently suited by taste and multifarious knowledge. He also contributed to the leading reviews and magazines of the times. In 1873 he published *A Lady of the Last Century—Mrs. Elizabeth Montague*, and in 1877 appeared his last work, *London in Jacobite Times*. He died in London, Jan. 25, 1878.

DORÉ, PAUL GUSTAVE (1832-1883), a French artist celebrated for his originality, his imaginative powers, his grotesque talent, and the enormous number of designs which he has made, was born at Strasburg, Jan. 6, 1832. It is said that before he was eight years of age he made satirical and other sketches which indicated great and original talent. He began his education at the College of Bourg, but in 1847 was taken to Paris

by his father and entered at the Lycée Charlemagne. While still at school he had a regular engagement as contributor to the *Journal pour Rire*, and by 1850, when he left the Lycée, he had produced many hundreds of drawings, and had established a reputation as an original and prolific designer of grotesque and satirical sketches. It was only four years after this that he published his first set of illustrations of the works of Rabelais. The grim and boisterous humor of the curé of Mendon was interpreted with so much sympathy and with such entire adequacy in this series of drawings that the peculiar genius of Doré obtained through them recognition of a portion of the public which had given but little consideration to his contributions to the *Journal pour Rire*. Doré, nearly twenty years later, returned to this subject, but the second set of Rabelaisian designs scarcely equalled the first in the peculiar qualities of excellence which had enabled the youth of twenty-two to win fame by a single stroke. It was evidently a labor of love for Doré to illustrate Rabelais, and it was equally so for him, two years later, to illustrate *Les Contes drôlatiques* of Balzac. The edition of this work containing Doré's designs has frequently been referred to as a remarkable instance of entire sympathy between author and artist. That there was abundant sympathy in certain respects is true enough, but Doré's genius is different in many essential particulars from Balzac's, and there is much in Doré's designs beyond what Balzac ever imagined. Balzac, in this work, attempted a deliberate imitation of Rabelais, but the designs of Doré have the true Rabelaisian flavor to a far greater extent than does Balzac's text. In truth, however, Doré was indebted to neither author for much more than hints and fillips to his fancy, and he gave to them quite as much as he received from them. To this period also belongs the singular series of drawings illustrative of the Wandering Jew legend, in which the pathetic and the grotesque are most audaciously combined. If we except certain of his landscapes and a comparatively small list of particularly powerful and original drawings that are scattered here and there through the immense number of books which he has illustrated, then these sets of designs may be regarded as the best expressions of the peculiar genius of Doré. He has never surpassed them, while he has many times fallen far below these special excellences, and that, too, in the treatment of themes which apparently should have stimulated him to put forth all his powers. From this time Doré was full of employment as a book-illustrator and contributor to the illustrated newspapers, and as a painter of pictures.

He first exhibited at the Salon in 1848; and thenceforth he nearly always contributed one or more works —often of huge dimensions—to the annual exhibition at Paris. His pictures represented Alpine and Spanish scenery, episodes of the *Divine Comedy*, scriptural incident, and what-not. Meanwhile he was busily engaged in illustrating books—now Perrault, now Montaigne, now Dante, now *Don Quixote*, now La Fontaine, until the promises of his publishers induced him to take up such uncongenial subjects as Tennyson's Arthurian poems, and the Scriptures and *Paradise Lost*. The illustrations of Perrault and La Fontaine are many of them admirable, while those to *Don Quixote*, although of uneven merit, frequently exhibit author and artist in entire accord. A few of the biblical designs are fine, but the series, as a whole, has a catchpenny appearance, and does the artist no particular credit. The Tennysonian illustrations are perfunctory, and of those made for the *Divine Comedy*, with few exceptions, the landscapes are the best. There is more of the real spirit of Dante in the two pictures painted by Ary Scheffer, and in the one great painting of a Dantean theme by Eugene Delacroix, than in all of the multitude of drawings made by Doré. Doré might possibly have received an inspiration from Coleridge's *Ancient Mariner*, had it been a French poem, but it is certain that the English work did not inspire him. With *Paradise Lost* he was equally unsuccessful: Milton was even further beyond his reach than Dante. The drawings made from Chateaubriand's *Atala* (published in 1863) are among the best by Doré that attempt to deal seriously with serious subjects. Many of the landscapes in this series are finely imaginative treatment of imposing subjects.

In addition to the works mentioned Doré made illustrations for the *Voyage aux Pyrénées* of M. Taine, *L'Espagne* of Baron Davillier, *Roland Furieux* and *London* by Louis Enault and Blanchard Jerrold. Insufficient as many of these drawings are, all of the series mentioned contain pieces that have extraordinary merit. In the *London*, for instance, are some effects which would not have done discredit to Rembrandt, and which could not have been produced except by an artist of real and very exceptional genius. The truth about Doré is that he permitted himself to be ruled too much by his publishers, and especially by his English publishers, and he not only undertook tasks for which he had no special qualifications, but he did more than it was possible for any man to do and at the same time maintain a high standard of excellence. The wonder with regard to him, considering his ceaseless activity and the enormous number of elaborate designs which he made, is not that he should have produced so much that is comparatively worthless as that he should have accomplished so much that is really excellent; for if all the manifestly inferior performances for which he is responsible were to be rejected, there would still remain many hundreds of designs marked by qualities which would stamp their author as one of the greatest artists of the age. In fact, the very multitude of this artist's designs, of one sort or another, has had the effect of preventing many persons of good artistic judgment from giving him the credit which is his due. Despite his manifold shortcomings, despite his lack of artistic conscience, and despite his fecundity, he is entitled to be regarded as a great artist, with exceptional and peculiar gifts, and with imaginative powers of all but the highest order.

Of the many huge canvases that Doré painted the most celebrated, if not the best, are his representation of a gambling-scene at Baden, his *Triumph of Christianity*, and his *Christ Leaving the Prætorium*. Doré's color is bad and his handling coarse, and although some of his paintings have impressive passages in them, they have added little or nothing to his real reputation. In the way of sculpture, also, he produced several pieces, among which may be mentioned the composition entitled *The Vine*—a huge flagon-shaped vase upon which a multitude of figures in violent action are modelled—which was shown at the Paris Exhibition of 1878, and a group entitled *Fate*. This last is a much more dignified and serious work than was to have been expected from the hand of the author. Fate is represented as a rather cadaverous woman, with a look of pitiless serenity on her countenance, who is about to snap the thread which an Eros with troubled countenance, who rests between her knees, holds in his hands. It is perhaps not a very great work, if we measure its worth by the standard of the greatest performances of the greatest sculptors. It is both in matter and manner far removed from the commonplace, however, and, whatever its strictly technical demerits may be, it has a real impressiveness such as belongs to very few contemporary sculptures.

Doré died suddenly in Paris, Jan. 22, 1883, having barely reached the age of fifty-one. (W. J. C., JR.)

DORN, JOHANN ALBRECHT BERNHARD (1805–1881), a German orientalist, was born May 11, 1805, at Schœnerfeld, Saxe-Coburg. He was educated in the Universities of Halle and Leipsic, and after his graduation in divinity travelled in France and England, becoming in 1829 ordinary professor of oriental languages at the Russian University of Charkow. Six years afterward he was called to St. Petersburg, where he became, first, professor of history and of Asiatic geography at the Oriental Institute, and in 1843 keeper of the Imperial Library and director of the Asiatic Museum. He was a member of the Imperial Academy of Sciences and of the French Academy of Inscriptions. His studies and works were principally devoted to the history and language of the Afghans (Pushtu), the history and geography of the Caucasus and of the regions bordering the Caspian Sea. He died at St. Petersburg, May 18, 1881. He published an English translation of Neamet-Ullah's *History of the Afghans* (London, 1829–36, 2 vols.); *Grammatical Observations upon the Language of the Afghans* (St. Petersburg, 1840); *Chrestomathy of the Pushtu or Afghan Language*, with glossary (1847); a German translation and the Persian text of Sehir-ed-din's *History of Tabaristan, of Rujan, and of Masenderan* (2 vols., 1850); of Chrondemir's *History of Tabaristan* (1850), and various other translations of oriental works on history and geography. In 1860–61 he made a scientific journey to the Caucasus, and obtained a rich collection of inscriptions of great importance in the history of the Caucasian dialects. He published the results in an important work entitled *Caspia, Invasion of the Ancient Russians in Tabaristan* (1875).

DORNER, ISAAC AUGUST (1809–1884), a German Lutheran theologian, was born June 20, 1809, at Neuhausen-ob-Eck, Würtemburg, where his father was pastor. He received his preliminary education at Maulbronn, and in 1827 entered the University of Tübingen, where he studied philosophy and theology. In 1832 he returned to Neuhausen to become vicar of his father's church. In 1834 he became a repetent at Tübingen, and in 1836 he received the degree of doctor. He then travelled through Holland and Great Britain to make a personal examination of the state of the Reformed churches. He was made extraordinary professor of theology at Tübingen in 1838, and ordinary professor at Kiel in 1839. In 1843 he took a similar position at Königsburg, and in 1847 at Bonn. From 1853 he taught in the University of Göttingen, and from 1861 in Berlin. In 1873 he visited the United States as a delegate to the meeting of the Evangelical Alliance in New York. He died at Wiesbaden, July 9, 1884. His principal work is *The History of the Development of the Doctrine of the Person of Christ*, which was originally published in the *Tübingen Zeitschrift für Theologie* in 1835, and was subsequently elaborated in four volumes (1845–56). An English translation appeared in 1859. The work is a model of historical learning and critical speculation, while it also bears witness to the firm faith of the writer. Among his other works are *Der Pietismus* (Hamburg, 1840); *Das Prinzip unserer Kirche* (Kiel, 1841); *De oratione Christi eschatologica*, Matt. xxiv. (Stuttgart, 1844); *Geschichte der Protestantischen Theologie* (2d ed., Munich, 1868); *Augustinus: Sein Theologisches System* (1873); *Christliche Glaubenslehre* (2 vols., Berlin, 1880–81); *Gesammelte Schriften aus dem Gebiet der systematischen Theologie, Exegese und Geschichte* (1883). Dr. Dorner died at Wiesbaden, July 8, 1884. By his teaching and writing he did much to turn the current of German thought from rationalism to belief in orthodox Christianity.

DORR, BENJAMIN, D.D. (1796–1869), an American Episcopalian clergyman and author, was born at Salisbury, Mass., March 22, 1796. He graduated at Dartmouth College in 1817, and commenced the study of law at Troy, N. Y., but in 1819 went to New York city, where he became one of the first class in the General Theological Seminary of the Protestant Episcopal Church. He was ordained by Bishop Hobart in 1820, and had charge of the churches of Lansingburg and Waterford, N. Y. In 1829 he became rector of Trinity Church, Utica, and in 1835 he was appointed general agent of the domestic committee of the board of missions. In discharge of his duties he visited most of the churches and missionary-stations in the United States, travelling 15,000 miles in eighteen months. In 1837 he was called to be rector of Christ Church, Philadelphia, succeeding the venerable Bishop White. In the next year the degree of D. D. was conferred on him by the University of Pennsylvania. In 1853 he made an extensive tour in Europe and the East, an account of which he published in 1856 under the title *Notes of Travel in Egypt, the Holy Land, Turkey, and Greece*. His other publications were— *The Churchman's Manual, an Exposition of the Doctrines, Ministry, and Worship of the Protestant Episcopal Church; The Recognition of Friends in Another World; Prophecies and Types relative to Christ; The History of a Pocket Prayer-Book, written by Itself; An Historical Account of Christ Church, Philadelphia, from its Foundation in 1695 to 1841*, and a *Memoir of John Fanning Watson, the Annalist of Philadelphia and New York* (1861). Dr. Dorr died at Germantown, Pa., Sept. 18, 1869.

DORR, THOMAS WILSON (1805–1854), a Rhode Island politician, was born at Providence, R. I., Nov. 5, 1805. His father, Sullivan Dorr, was a successful manufacturer. Thomas graduated at Harvard College in 1823, studied law with Chancellor James Kent, and was admitted to the bar in 1827. He was elected to the Rhode Island legislature in 1833, and soon began his efforts to obtain a new constitution for the State, instead of the colonial charter granted by Charles II. in 1663, which was still the fundamental law. Under it the right of suffrage was restricted to the holders of real estate valued at not less than $134 and to their eldest sons. The apportionment of representatives in the legislature had become very unequal. In 1834 a convention called by the legislature framed a constitution which was rejected by the legal voters. Another convention was called in 1834, but broke up without completing its task. In January, 1841, the legislature called a convention to meet in the following November, the delegates to be chosen by the legal voters. But the advocates of the extension of the right of suffrage, of whom Dorr was the most prominent, despaired of ever effecting a reform in the way proposed, and called upon the adult male population to elect delegates to a convention to be held at Providence in October. This was done, and a constitution was prepared and voted upon by the people, and declared to be accepted by a small majority. The other convention met at the appointed time, and in March, 1842, the constitution framed by them, which still somewhat restricted the elective franchise, was submitted to the people and rejected. In April the people, acting under the constitution informally constructed and ratified, elected Mr. Dorr governor of the State, and also elected senators and representatives to form a legislature. Appeal was made by both parties to the Federal Government for support, but President Tyler declared himself bound to respect the requisitions of the existing government. In May, Mr. Dorr and his government attempted to organize and get possession of the State arsenal and other property. The legal governor, Samuel W. King, successfully resisted the attempt and dispersed Dorr's legislature. Dorr himself escaped arrest, and on June 25 renewed his effort with 700 men, and intrenched himself at Chepachet. Gov. King now proclaimed martial law and called out 3000 militia, whereupon Dorr's partisans deserted their camp, and he fled to Connecticut, and afterwards to New Hampshire. A reward of $4000 having been offered for his apprehension, he returned, was arrested, tried, and convicted of high treason. He was sentenced to imprisonment for life, but three years later was released under a general amnesty. In 1851 the legislature restored him to full citizenship, and ordered the record of his sentence expunged. In June, 1842, the legislature called a convention to meet in September, and a new constitution was framed and ratified in November, and went into operation May, 1843. Mr. Dorr died at Providence, Dec. 27, 1854.

DOUGLASS, FREDERICK, the foremost representative of the colored race in the United States, was born in Tuckahoe, near Easton, Md., about 1817. His father was a white man and his mother was a negro slave, who, though a field-hand, had learned to read. Frederick was brought up on the plantation of Col. Edward Lloyd. When he was ten years old he was sent to Baltimore to be a servant in the house of Mrs. Sophia Auld, who taught him the alphabet, and he soon learned to read and write. He was said to be difficult to manage, and afterwards allowed to hire his own time and found employment as a caulker in a ship-yard. He had, however, determined to escape from slavery, and at last put his resolution in practice, fleeing from Baltimore Sept. 3, 1838. He found his way to New York, whence he soon removed to New Bedford, where he first assumed the name Douglass. He was steady and industrious, and, using every opportunity for intellectual advancement, became an exhorter in the colored Methodist church. He subscribed to William Lloyd Garrison's paper, *The Liberator*, and in 1841 he attended an anti-slavery meeting in Nantucket under direction of Mr. Garrison. Here Douglass was induced to make an address, which first revealed his gift of eloquence. He was engaged as an agent of the Anti-Slavery Society. At first he told simply his own experience, though concealing the place, but gradually his oratory took a wider range and he became a prophet of denunciation against the whole system of slavery. After having visited the greater part of New England he went to Europe in 1845, and spent nearly two years in Great Britain and Ireland. He then published his first book, *Life of an American Slave* (London, 1847). While he was abroad some of his friends purchased his freedom from his former owner. After his return to America he dissolved his connection with Mr. Garrison, and settled in Rochester, N. Y., where he began, with the assistance of Gerrit Smith, to publish a weekly paper called *The North Star*. After a time he became sole proprietor and changed its title to *Frederick Douglass's Paper*. He continued also his work as a lecturer and debater of public questions. He enlarged his autobiographical sketch into a volume called *My Bondage and Freedom* (1855). To escape annoyance on account of John Brown's raid on Harper's Ferry, he went again to England in 1860. During the civil war he strongly urged Pres. Lincoln to issue the proclamation of emancipation and to employ colored troops. As soon as this was done he sent his three sons into the service and took an active part in raising colored regiments. At the close of the war he moved to Washington and labored zealously in behalf of the freedmen. He was still frequently called upon to deliver lectures in various parts of the country. In September, 1870, he became editor of the *New National Era*, which he afterwards transferred to his sons. When Gen. Grant recommended the annexation of San Domingo, Douglass was appointed secretary of the commission to visit the island. He afterwards served as one of the territorial council of the District of Columbia. In 1872 he was elected presidential elector at large for the State of New York. He was a trustee of Howard University, and of the Freedmen's Savings Bank and Trust Company, being president of the latter at the time of its failure. In 1877 Pres. Hayes appointed Douglass United States marshal for the District of Columbia, and in 1881 Pres. Garfield appointed him recorder of deeds for the same district, which position he held till 1885. While he has done much to elevate the race to which he belongs his views have not always been favorably accepted by them. In 1879 he remonstrated against the "exodus" of the colored people from the South. In 1884 he was married to a white lady who had been a clerk in his office. Throughout his diversified career he has been honest, industrious, and honorable; his character is without a stain, and his success has won for him a memorable place in American history.

DOVÉ, HEINRICH WILHELM (1803–1879), a German physicist, was born at Liegnitz, in Silesia, Oct. 6, 1803. He was educated at Breslau and Berlin, where he studied the physical and mathematical sciences, and graduating as doctor in 1826, with a thesis, *De Barometricis mutationibus*. He became, in 1828, assistant professor of natural philosophy at Königsberg, and in 1829 at Berlin, where his works on meteorology brought him, in 1845, the title of full professor and a seat in the Royal Academy of Sciences. He investigated the movements of the winds, and sought to establish a theory of cyclones. Close attention was also given to the principles of electricity and the properties of polarized light. He became very popular from the interesting character of his lectures. He died in Berlin, April 4, 1879. His principal works are—*Ueber Mass und Messen* (2d ed., Berlin, 1835), which compares the different metric systems of civilized states; *Meteorologische Untersu-*

chungen (1837); *Ueber die nicht periodischen Aenderungen der Temperaturvertheilung* (6 vols., 1840–59); *Untersuchungen im Gebiete der Inductionselectricitnet* (1843); *Ueber den Zusammenhang der Waermeveraenderungen der Atmosphære mit der Entwickelung der Pflanzen* (1846). His work on *Heat Distribution* was published in English by the British Association in 1853. Among his optical discoveries, one of practical importance is the application of the stereoscope to the detection of forged bank-notes. As director of all the Prussian observatories, he published, annually, an account of their work.

DOVER, a town of Delaware, capital of the State, and county-seat of Kent co., is on Jones River, 4 miles W. of Delaware Bay, and 48 miles by rail S. of Wilmington. It is on the Delaware division of the Philadelphia, Wilmington, and Baltimore Railroad. It is neatly built, with wide and well-shaded streets, and is lighted with gas. It contains the state-house and other State and county buildings, has 2 banks (1 national), 2 weekly newspapers, 7 churches, 8 public and several private schools and an academy; railroad shops, flour-mills, fruit-drying and canning-works, and manufactories of fertilizers. Its property is valued at $1,600,000; its public debt is $25,000, and yearly expenses, $7000. It was settled in 1687 and incorporated about 1720. Population, 2811.

See Vol. VII. p. 330 Am. ed. (p. 381 Edin. ed.).

DOVER, a city of New Hampshire, county-seat of Strafford co., on both sides of the river Cocheco, up to this point a navigable tidal stream, being an affluent of the Piscataqua. It is 11 miles N. N. W. of Portsmouth by the Portsmouth and Dover Railroad, and is on the Boston and Maine Railroad, at the junction of the branch leading to Alton Bay on Lake Winnipisaukee. The site is somewhat uneven, but the city is laid out with considerable regularity. It has a fine city-hall, a court-house, a good high-school building, an academy, 12 churches, 3 national banks, 3 savings banks, 1 daily, 4 weekly, and 2 other newspapers, a subscription library with 6000 volumes, and abundant water-power furnished by the Cocheco and Black rivers. It has several large cotton-mills, print-works, and manufactures of woollens, shoes, leather, castings, and other goods. Settled in 1623, Dover is the oldest town in the State. It became a city in 1855. Population, 11,687.

See Vol. VII. p. 330 Am. ed. (p. 381 Edin. ed.)

DOWAGIAC, a city of Cass co., Mich., is on the Dowagiac River and on the Michigan Central Railroad, 178 miles W. of Detroit and 106 E. of Chicago. It has a national bank, 2 weekly newspapers, 3 hotels, 6 churches, good schools, and a public library. It was settled about the year 1840, was incorporated as a village in 1847, and received a city charter in 1877. It is chiefly supported by trade with the surrounding country, though since 1880 considerable interest has been taken in manufacturing, for which the Dowagiac River gives good water-power. It has 2 agricultural-works, stove-works, flour-mills, planing-mills, broom-factories, and saw-mills. Population, 2100.

DOWDEN, EDWARD, LL.D., an Irish poet and critic, was born at Cork, May 3, 1843. He is of English descent, and was educated at Trinity College, Dublin, in which also, in 1867, he was made professor of oratory and English literature. His work on *Shakespeare, his Mind and Art* (1872; 5th ed., 1880) is a valuable contribution to Shakespearian criticism. He also published a volume of *Poems* (1876); *Studies in Literature, 1789–1877* (1878); *Southey* (1879); *Goethe* (1880), and has edited *Shakespeare's Sonnets* (1881) and *The Correspondence of Southey and Caroline Bowles* (1881).

DOWER, the provision which the law makes for a widow out of the lands and tenements of her husband. The various writers on the subject of dower differ widely as to its origin. Mr. Cruise is of opinion that it was an ancient Teutonic custom in use among the Saxons, and thus transplanted into the common law. Blackstone holds, on the contrary, that it was first imported into England by the Danes. Sir Martin Wright finds no traces of its existence prior to the Conquest, and supposes it, therefore, to have been of Norman origin. Mr. Maine ascribes it to the influence of the Church. No thoroughly satisfactory account of its origin has as yet been given.

As early as the reign of Henry III. the right of dower was firmly settled in the English law, an express provision being inserted in the great charter obtained from that king to guard the widow's rights. The right of dower has been much affected in England by Stat. 3 & 4 Wm. IV. c. 105, known as the Dower Act, by which many of its peculiar features have been altered.

In the United States the right of dower still generally exists, though it has been modified from time to time by statute in the several States so as to suit the supposed wants and condition of their citizens. In Louisiana the right of dower has never existed. In Iowa, Kansas, Indiana, Nevada, and Dakota the right of dower is abolished.

Dower in the ancient English law was of five sorts: (1) Dower by the common law, by virtue of which the widow was entitled to a life estate in one-third of the lands, tenements, and hereditaments whereof her husband was seised in fee or in tail during the marriage. (2) Dower by particular custom, by virtue whereof the widow became entitled to either a greater or less interest in her husband's estate than was secured to her by the common law. (3) Dower *ad ostium ecclesiæ* (at the church-door), where a freeholder endowed his wife of certain lands immediately after the marriage. (4) Dower *ex assensu patris*, which was merely a species of dower *ad ostium ecclesiæ*, where, the husband's father being alive, the wife was endowed of specific lands whereof said husband was the heir, with his father's consent. (5) Dower *de la plus belle*, where a widow, on suing the guardian in chivalry for dower, was required by him to endow herself of the fairest portion of any lands she might hold as guardian in socage, and thus release from her dower all lands of her husband held in chivalry. The latter form of dower was abolished by 12 Chas. II. c. 24. All the remaining forms above mentioned, except dower at the common law and dower by special custom, are also abolished by Stat. 3 & 4 Wm. IV. c. 105, already referred to.

A widow was at common law dowable only of lands and tenements whereof her husband was seised in fee or in fee-tail during the marriage. She was therefore not entitled to dower in estates for years. This is still generally the law. In Missouri, however, a widow may claim dower in leasehold estates of twenty years or over. An estate in common is subject to dower, but not an estate in joint tenancy, strictly speaking, for the right of survivorship is superior to the right of dower. Where there is an exchange of lands, a widow may claim dower in either of the properties, but not in both. Actual seisin or possession of the land on the part of the husband is no longer very strictly required.

Constructive possession is enough, at least in the United States. Where the husband is seised of lands as a trustee merely, the widow has no right of dower therein. Formerly, this right did not attach where the husband was the *cestui que trust* of land, but this restriction is now generally abandoned. A widow is accordingly held dowable of an equity of redemption and of the interest of a vendee under articles of agreement. In some States a widow can only claim dower out of those lands whereof her husband died seised. Where there are no children the right of dower is very generally extended so as to embrace one-half of the husband's land.

The right to dower may be barred in several ways at common law. Alienage on the part of either husband or wife produced this effect, but by Stat. 7 & 8 Vict. c. 66 the disability of alienage has been almost entirely removed. Similar statutes are in force in all of the United States. At common law the widow of an attainted traitor could not claim dower of his lands. This principle has not, however, been imported into the United States. By the Stat. Westminster the Second, 13 Edw. I. c. 34, it was provided that the elopement and adultery of the wife should constitute a bar to her claim of dower. In some of the United States, as in Virginia, Missouri, and South Carolina, this statute has been re-enacted; in others it is considered as part of the common law. In Massachusetts, New York, Rhode Island, and Delaware, however, elopement and adultery unaccompanied by a divorce will not bar dower. A divorce *a vinculo matrimonii* bars dower, but not a divorce *a mensa et thoro* merely. Where a title paramount to that of the husband is set up, the right of dower will not of course attach; nor can it be claimed as against a vendee at a foreclosure sale upon a mortgage given by the husband before marriage. In almost all of the United States dower will not be divested by a judicial sale for the debts of the husband. In Pennsylvania, however, this result follows.

A married woman could anciently release her right of dower in land by suffering with her husband a fine or recovery. By the custom of London she might, however, effect the same result by simply joining her husband in the deed, to which a certificate of some magistrate was appended to the effect that the married woman had executed the deed of her own free will and consent. This custom was imported into the United States, and is still in general use. By 3 & 4 Wm. IV. c. 74 a similar system was introduced in England. The joinder of a married woman in a mortgage by her husband of his lands is generally essential to bar her dower. In Pennsylvania, however, this is not the case. The common method formerly employed to bar dower was a jointure. This consisted of a settlement of certain lands to the use of the wife from and after her husband's death for and during the term of her life. By Stat. 27 Hen. VIII. c. 10, known as the Statute of Uses, it was provided that where such a jointure was made before marriage the widow should have no right to claim dower. Where it was made after marriage it was provided that the widow might claim either the jointure or the dower, but not both. Jointures are occasionally, but not often, employed in the United States.

By the provisions of Stat. 3 & 4 Wm. IV. c. 105 a husband may now in England prevent his wife's right of dower from attaching to any of his land by inserting a clause to that effect in the deed or will by which he alienates the same. In the United States generally he has no such power. Where, however, there is a testamentary provision made for the wife, this will generally be presumed to be in lieu of dower, unless a contrary intention appear from the terms of the will; and in such case the widow is put to her election within a certain limited time whether she will accept the benefit under the will and forego her dower, or claim her dower and renounce her rights under the will.

The right of the widow to have her dower assigned to her accrues immediately upon the death of the husband. It was provided by Magna Charta that she should be allowed to remain in her husband's mansion for forty days after his death ("the widow's quarantine"), during which time it was the duty of the heir at law to apportion and set out to her her dower-land by metes and bounds. If he failed to do so, she had her action of *dower unde nihil habet*, or, in the event of the allotment being insufficient, an action of *dower*. The action of dower also lay against any alienee of the husband during coverture holding lands as to which the right of dower attached. In certain cases a bill in equity will also lie to set out dower-lands. Where an action of dower is brought against the heir, the rights of the plaintiff are ascertained by the value of the land in question at the time of the assignment. But where the action is against the husband's alienee, such rights are determined by the value of the property at the time of the alienation. In no case can the dowress avail herself of the enhanced value communicated to the land by the buildings and improvements erected thereon by the alienee. It seems, however, that she may avail herself of any enhancement of value caused by extraneous circumstances since the alienation—such, for example, as the general improvement of the neighborhood. Where the land has deteriorated in the hands of the alienee the widow has no remedy. In many of the States statutory provisions have been adopted whereby new remedies have been adopted in lieu of the action of dower. (L. L., JR.)

DOWNING, ANDREW JACKSON (1815–52), an American landscape-gardener and author, was born at Newburg, N. Y., Oct. 31, 1815. His father was a nurseryman, and from an early age the son showed strong inclination for the natural sciences. He was educated at an academy in Montgomery, N. Y., but left it at the age of sixteen to assist his brother in the management of the nursery. Having resolved to become a rural architect, he used every opportunity to improve his knowledge and his natural good taste. In 1838 he built an elegant mansion on his estate, in which he showed what he considered the true idea of an American country home. In 1841 he published a *Treatise on the Theory and Practice of Landscape-Gardening*, which at once attracted attention both in America and in England. In 1842 he published *Cottage Residences*, and was henceforth universally regarded as the highest American authority on the construction and embellishment of country residences. In 1845 he published his *Fruits and Fruit Trees of America*, and in the next year became the editor of the *Horticulturist*, a monthly magazine published at Albany. In 1850 he visited the chief country-seats in England, and wrote good descriptions of them. In 1851 he was appointed to lay out the public grounds of Washington, and was still engaged in this work when he sailed from Newburg on the steamer Henry Clay, July 28, 1852. The steamer took fire near Yonkers, and he was drowned in his efforts to save other passengers. Several of his contributions to the

Horticulturist were collected and published in 1854, under the title *Rural Essays*, together with a memoir by George W. Curtis. His works are still highly esteemed.

DOYLE, RICHARD (1826–1883), an English artist and book-illustrator, was born in London in 1826. His father, John Doyle, was of Irish descent, and had some celebrity in his day as the maker of certain political sketches signed "H. B." Doyle was one of the earliest artistic contributors to *Punch*, and began those humorous delineations of every-day English life which, more than any other feature, have given the publication celebrity, and which have been continued successfully by Leech, Keen, and Du Maurier. The well-known title-page of *Punch* is his design. In 1850, Doyle severed his connection with *Punch* on account of its anti-Catholic course, and especially on account of the unmerciful lampoons on Cardinal Wiseman which it published. Doyle's most important independent publications are *The Continental Tour of Messrs. Brown, Jones, and Robinson* (1854) and a Christmas book entitled *In Fairy-Land: Pictures of the Elf-World* (1869). He contributed illustrations to Leigh Hunt's *Jar of Honey*, Ruskin's *King of the Golden River*, Montalba's *Fairy-Tales of All Nations*, Thackeray's *Newcomes*, *Jack the Giant-Killer* and other fairy stories, and *The Cornhill Magazine*. Doyle's most pleasing designs have been made in illustration of grotesque and fanciful themes, such as the fairy-stories above mentioned. His illustrations to *The Newcomes*, although not without merit, are, most of them, too much in the nature of caricatures, and fail to do justice to the subject. The title-page of *Punch* is a favorable example of Doyle's manner. This composition and the *Newcomes* series very adequately represent his style and the range of his abilities. Personally he was a favorite in London society. He died Dec. 11, 1883.

DOYLESTOWN, a borough of Pennsylvania, the county-seat of Bucks co., is 25 miles N. of Philadelphia, and 10 miles W. of the Delaware River. It is the terminus of the Doylestown branch of the North Pennsylvania Railroad. It is on a high plateau, 600 feet above tide-water, and commanding a fine view of the surrounding country, which is highly cultivated.

Its streets are well shaded and the side-walks paved and curbed. It has gas- and water-works, a fine court-house, a jail, a hall and market-house, 2 banks, 7 weekly newspapers (3 German), a Masonic hall, 9 churches, an academy, graded public schools, and a Catholic parochial school. The industries are manufactories of agricultural machinery, sash and blinds, cheese-boxes, spokes and shirts, etc. Doylestown has the finest agricultural fair-grounds in the State, with suitable buildings. In the centre of the town there is a handsome monument erected to the memory of the officers and men of the 104th Pennsylvania Regiment, who fell in the war for the Union. Doylestown was settled by the Doyle family from the North of Ireland about 1730; in 1812 it became the county-seat; in 1833 it was made a borough. Population, 2070.

DOZY, REINHART (1820–1883), a Dutch orientalist and historian, was born at Leyden, Feb. 21, 1820, being descended from a Huguenot family, which had sought refuge in the Low Countries after the revocation of the Edict of Nantes. He studied history and philology in the University of Leyden, graduated as doctor in 1844, and became in 1850 extraordinary professor of history in the same university, attaining the full professorship in 1857. He died June 6, 1883. His works relate chiefly to the history, language, and literature of the Arabs in Spain and Africa. Among them are *Scriptorum Arabum loci de Abbaditis* (3 vols., 1846–63); *Recherches sur l'histoire et la littérature d'Espagne pendant le Moyen-âge* (1849; enlarged ed., 1881), a work which shed a flood of new light on its subject; *Al-Makkari, Analectes sur l'histoire et la littérature des Arabes d'Espagne* (2 vols., 1855–61), prepared in conjunction with Dugat, Krehl, and Wright; *Histoire des Musulmans d'Espagne jusqu'à la Conquête de l'Andalousie par les Almoravides* (4 vols., 1861; last ed., 1881); *Het Islamismus* (1863); *De Israeliten zu Mekka* (1864). He also edited several Arabic historical and geographical works. His excellent *Supplément aux dictionnaires Arabes* (2 vols., 1877–81) takes rank among the best works on Arabic lexicography.

DRACHMANN, HOLGER HENRIK HERHOLDT, a Danish poet and novelist, was born Oct. 9, 1846, in Copenhagen. He studied at the academy of fine arts, 1866–70, and his marine views became very celebrated. Since 1870 he has devoted himself chiefly to literature, though he still paints occasionally a landscape or marine view. As a poet and novelist he must be classed as a realist of the highest rank and is probably the most popular Danish writer now living. He began his literary career with a small volume, *Digte* (1872). In 1875 he published *Dæmpede Melodier*, illustrated by the author himself; *Ranker og Roser* (1879); *Ungdom i digt og Sang* (1879); *Princessen og det halve Kongerige* (1878), an epic poem, as is also *Østenfor Sol og vestenfor Maane* (1880). Drachmann has been particularly productive as a novelist. In rapid succession have appeared *En Overcomplet* (1876); *Tannhäuser* (1877); *Ungt Blod* (1877); *Paa Sømands Tro og Love* (1878); *Paul og Virgine* (1879); *Under nordlig Bredde* (1879); *Derovre fra Grænsen* (1871; 8th ed. 1882). His latest works are: *Peder Tordenskjold* (1881); a translation of Byron's *Don Juan* (1881–82); *Puppe og Sommerfugl* (1882); and *Reisebilleder* (1882). Since 1879 Drachmann has been honored with a literary pension from the Danish Parliament.

DRAKE, DANIEL (1785–1852), an American physician and author, was born at Plainfield, N. J., Oct. 20, 1785. His father, Isaac Drake, removed to Kentucky in 1788, where Daniel was brought up amid all the hardships to which settlers in the backwoods were then exposed. At the age of fifteen he went to Cincinnati, then a village of four hundred inhabitants, to study medicine under Dr. William Goforth. In 1805 he journeyed to Philadelphia to attend the lectures at the University of Pennsylvania, and on his return he practised for a year at Mayslick, Ky., his father's home, and then settled at Cincinnati. In 1810 Dr. Drake published *Notices Concerning Cincinnati*, and afterwards helped in movements from which in 1819 sprang the Cincinnati College. He also published a *Picture of Cincinnati and Miami County* (1815), which attracted attention to that region. In 1816 he obtained from the University of Pennsylvania the first diploma ever given to a resident of Cincinnati. In 1817 he was chosen professor of materia medica and medical botany in the Transylvania University, then newly established at Lexington, Ky. Resigning this position in 1818, he obtained a charter for the Medical College of Ohio, at Cincinnati, which went into operation in November, 1820, with twenty-four students, Dr. Drake being professor of the institutes and practice of medicine and obstetrics. But he soon resumed his professorship in Transylvania University, where he continued to lecture till April, 1827, though still residing in Cincinnati. He established there an eye-and-ear infirmary, and became editor of the *Western Medical and Physical Journal*, a monthly magazine whose name was afterwards changed to *The Western Journal of Medical and Physical Science*. In the winter of 1830–31 he lectured in Jefferson Medical College, Philadelphia, and in the following lectured on clinical medicine in the Medical College of Ohio. In June, 1835, he joined with others in forming a medical department in connection with Cincinnati College, which continued four years, and then accepted a professorship in the Louisville, Ky., Medical Institute, which he held for ten years till 1852, with the exception of the winter of 1849–50, when he lectured in the Medical College of Ohio. He died, after a brief illness, at Cincinnati, Nov. 5, 1852. His chief work was a *Treatise on the Principal Diseases of the Interior Valley of North America*, the first volume of which was published in 1850, after laborious researches extending over thirty years. After his death the second volume of this work was edited by Dr. S. Hanbury Smith, of Cincinnati, and Dr. F. Gurney Smith, of Philadelphia. His other publications were *Essays on Medical Education and the Medical Profession in the United States* (1832), and addresses before literary societies.

DRAKE, SAMUEL GARDNER (1798–1875), an American antiquary, was born at Pittsfield, N. H., Oct. 11, 1798. He received his education in a common schools and at the age of twenty became a teacher in them. In 1825 he removed to Boston and republished with notes Capt. Church's *Entertaining History of King Philip's War*. In 1828 he opened an antiquarian bookstore, the first of its kind in the United States. He was one of the founders of the New England Historical and Genealogical Society, and was its president in 1858. He then resided in London for two years. He died at Boston, June 14, 1875. His historical and antiquarian publications were numerous. Among them are *Indian Biography* (1832); *Book of the Indians* (1833), often republished; *Old Indian Chronicles* (1836); *Indian Captivities* (1839); *Drake Family* (1845); *History and Antiquities of Boston* (1856); *Researches among the British Archives* (1860); *Memoir of Sir Walter Raleigh* (1862); *Annals of Witchcraft in the United States* (1869); and *History of the Five Years' French and Indian War* (1870). He also edited with care some early New England works.

His son, FRANCIS SAMUEL, born at Northwood, N. H., Feb. 22, 1828, has published a very complete and accurate *Dictionary of American Biography* (1872).

DRAMA, AMERICAN. The beginnings of the drama in America are very obscure and almost impossible now to define with precision. Probably the first theatrical performances in the New World were given in those parts of America early colonized by the Spaniards. The Spanish stage was at the height of its glory at the very time when Spanish adventure was spreading itself abroad. There was no antagonism between church and stage in Spain; on the contrary there was almost an alliance. Lope de Vega was a priest and a familiar of the Inquisition, and Calderon's finest plays turn, as on a pivot, about the peculiar tenets of his creed. It is highly probable that at least some of the *Autos sacramentales*, or religious interludes, of Calderon or Lope de Vega were acted in Mexico, Cuba, Peru, or Florida. One

See Vol. VII. p. 338 Am. ed. (p. 39. Edin. ed.).

at least of the chief Spanish dramatists was born in Spanish America. This was Alarcon, born in Mexico, and best known to us as the author of the *Verdad Suspiciosa*, imitated by Corneille in his *Menteur*, which again was copied by Foote in his *Liar*. Such Spanish plays as may have been acted in America in the early days of colonization were no doubt performed by amateur actors, and the first theatrical performances in North America of which there seems to be any trustworthy record were also by amateur players; these were given at Quebec in 1694, when New France was under the government of Count Frontenac. In Mr. Parkman's history there is an account of the performance of Corneille's *Nicomède* and *Mithridate*, and of an attempt, or at least a threat, to act *Tartuffe* as an attack on the local Jesuits, with whom the governor had a deadly feud. It was a company of amateur actors, again, who gave the first performances in America in English; this was in 1745, in the island of Jamaica, and among them was Moody, who afterward became famous as an actor of Irish characters. Their success was so great (so John Bernard tells us in the posthumous papers on the *Early Days of the American Stage*, edited by his son, Bayle Bernard) that Moody went to England to bring out a regular company of actors, with whom he seems to have returned in 1746, and to have been very successful. It was a band of amateur actors, once more, who gave the first performance of an English play in English in what is now the United States. This was at the coffee-house in State Street in Boston, Mass., where Otway's *Orphan* was acted in 1749, some time before the first regular company of actors arrived on these shores. This attempt to introduce the drama into Puritan New England was received with deepest horror.

The next general court passed a strict law forbidding all theatrical performances, and fining the owner of any building used for such a purpose £20 "for each and every day or time," and fining the spectators and actors £5 apiece. This law prevented public acting for nearly fifty years, although private theatricals were not uncommon. In this same year (1749) a company of amateurs had also made an attempt to open a theatre in Philadelphia. William Dunlap, the author of an invaluable *History of the American Theatre*, refers humorously to this occurrence in these words: "As early as 1749 it is on record that the magistracy of the city [Philadelphia] had been disturbed by some idle young men perpetrating the murder of sundry plays in the skirts of the town, but the culprits had been arrested and bound over to their good behavior, after confessing their crime and promising to spare the poor poets for the future." According, however, to the highly probable surmise of Mr. Joseph N. Ireland, whose *Records of the New York Stage* is perhaps the most trustworthy and altogether admirable book of its kind ever written, it was this band of young Philadelphian amateurs who gave the first professional performances ever seen in New York. Judge Daly has discovered in *Bradford's Gazette* of October, 1733, an advertisement of a merchant who announces that his store is "next door to the Play-house," but his later and more minute researches led him to believe that this play-house of 1733 was used principally for puppet-shows and similar entertainments. But the performances given in 1750 by the Philadelphia company are beyond all doubt; and for the first time we are on the solid ground of assured fact. *The New York Gazette revived in the Weekly Post-Boy*, of Feb. 20,

1750, announced that "last week arrived here a company of comedians from Philadelphia, who we hear have taken a convenient room for their purpose in one of the buildings lately belonging to the Hon. Rip Van Dam, Esq., deceased, in Nassau Street, where they intend to perform as long as the season lasts, provided they meet with suitable encouragement." A later advertisement in the same paper declared that "By his Excellency's Permission, at the Theatre in Nassau Street, On Monday, the 5th day of March next (1750), Will be presented, the Historical Tragedy of King Richard 3d! Wrote originally by Shakspeare and altered by Colley Cibber, Esq. . . . To begin precisely at half an hour after 6 o'clock, and no person to be admitted behind the scenes." In the course of the season the company acted Otway's *Orphan*, the *Beaux' Stratagem*, *Love for Love*, Addison's *Cato*, the *Beggar's Opera*, the *Fair Penitent*, the *Busybody*, the *Distrest Mother*, *George Barnwell*, and the *Recruiting Officer*. The season lasted from March 5, 1750, to July 8, 1751, with the exception of six weeks in the summer of 1750. It speaks very highly for the character and ability of this company, whether they were originally amateurs from Philadelphia or not, that they were attractive enough to continue for so very long a season as this in a city which then had but ten thousand inhabitants. The managers of this company were named Murray and Kean, and they were also the chief actors. After this first long season the company seems to have disbanded, but the remains of it came together again under a Mr. Upton, and acted with but little fortune during the fall of 1751 and the winter of 1752, closing February 20.

Moody, about 1749, had returned to England for recruits, and was at once engaged by David Garrick for Drury Lane. But the rumor of his success had spread in London, and William Hallam, a brother of Admiral Hallam, and lately the manager of the Goodman Fields Theatre (at which Garrick had made his first great hit not long before, and in the management of which Hallam had failed), determined to send a company of London actors to America. He abandoned the West Indies to the company Moody had founded, and chose the more liberal Virginia as his objective point. The company sent there by William Hallam was ample and effective; it was headed by Mr. and Mrs. Lewis Hallam, and it had the advantage of the stock of scenery and costumes used at the Goodman Field's house. The company was what is known as a "commonwealth;" that is to say, the actors received no salaries, but divided the gross receipts among themselves, giving certain specified parts to the manager for the use of scenery, costumes, properties, etc., and for managerial expenses: this was the plan which obtained in England in Shakespeare's day, and in France in Molière's, and which now survives at the Théâtre Français in Paris. Hallam's company met in London, arranged a list of pieces, studied their parts, and, taking ship together, rehearsed on the way over, arriving at Yorktown, Va., late in June, 1752. Williamsburg was then the capital of Virginia, and here, by permission of Gov. Dinwiddie, Hallam altered an old storehouse into a theatre, and opened it, on Sept. 5, 1752, with the *Merchant of Venice* and Garrick's farce *Lethe*. There was also delivered a prologue composed at sea, probably by Mr. Singleton, who played *Gratiano*; it was spoken by Mr. Rigby, the actor of *Bassanio*. This prologue was a plea for the propriety of dramatic performances, and declared that the actors came

"to shew
Patterns of every virtue they should know,
Though gloomy minds through ignorance may rail,
Yet bold examples strike where languid precepts fail.
The world's a stage where mankind act their various parts,
The stage a world to show their various arts.

Yet, if the Muse, unfaithful to her trust,
Has sometimes strayed from what is pure and just,
Has she not oft, with awful, virtuous rage,
Struck home at vice and nobly trod the stage—
Made tyrants weep, the conscious murderer stand,
And drop the dagger from his trembling hand?
Then, as you treat a favorite fair's mistake,
Pray spare her foibles for her virtue's sake;
And while her chastest scenes are made appear
(For none but such will find admittance here),
The Muse's friends, we hope, will join our cause,
And crown our best endeavors with applause."

This prologue, written down by Dunlap from the lips of Lewis Hallam's son, a boy of ten or twelve years of age when it was delivered, shows that the actors feared to find in the New World that prejudice against the playhouse which exists in many respectable but dull communities to this day. In Virginia they met with no recorded opposition on moral grounds, and they took away with them when they left the colony a certificate from Gov. Dinwiddie, signed in council, recommending them as comedians, and testifying to the propriety of their behavior as men. From Virginia the actors went to Maryland, and at Annapolis acted in the first regular theatre erected in what is now the United States. In June, 1753, they went north to New York, and met with unexpected opposition. Lewis Hallam not only found that the Mr. Upton he had sent out to prepare a theatre had abused his trust, but that, partly perhaps on Upton's account, permission to perform was denied him. He plead his case before the public in the *New York Mercury* of July 2, 1753, and appealed to the authorities with Gov. Dinwiddie's certificate in his hand. At last he obtained the desired permission, and built a new theatre in Nassau Street, on the site of the old one. This was opened Sept. 17, 1753, with Steele's *Conscious Lovers*, a farce, a new occasional prologue spoken by Mr. Rigby, and an epilogue (addressed to the ladies), delivered by Mrs. Hallam. After a prosperous season of six months in New York the company went to Philadelphia, and here, too, they met with violent opposition. Petitions and counter-petitions were signed, and the city was rent in twain by the dispute. In the end the manager was favored by Gov. Hamilton, and permission was granted to perform twenty-four plays, with their attendant afterpieces, on condition that they "offered nothing indecent or immoral," and that the actors should give one night for the benefit of the poor of the city. "The storehouse of Mr. William Plumstead, at the corner of the first alley above Pine Street," so Dunlap tells us, was altered into a theatre, and there, in April, 1754, the company began to perform, appearing in Rowe's *Fair Penitent*. The season was very successful, and the governor added six nights to the original twenty-four. Acting three times a week, the company remained in Philadelphia until July. Then they went to the West Indies, where Lewis Hallam died, and his widow married a Mr. Douglass. In 1758 Mr. Douglass led the actors back to New York, and, after much opposition, built a new theatre on Cruger's wharf, the old one in Nassau Street having been turned into a church.

In the spring ensuing Douglass went to Philadelphia, where he had built a theatre on the corner of Vernon and South Streets, at a place called "Society Hill." This was the first regular theatre erected in Philadelphia; it was outside the precincts of the city authorities, but this did not prevent a renewal of the opposition of five years before. Shortly after a temporary theatre was built at Newport, R. I., and here, on Sept. 7, 1761, was acted *The Provoked Husband*. This was the first performance by professional actors in New England, and it is to be noted that it was given in spite of a formal vote at a town meeting. In 1762 the company visited Providence also. Thus was formed a theatrical circuit along which the comedians might find employment for the better part of the year. This circuit included Williamsburg, Annapolis, Philadelphia, New York, Newport, Providence, and a few smaller places where there was a court-house or other large building which might be made to serve as a temporary theatre; among these was Perth-Amboy. Along this American circuit, and with occasional visits to the West Indies, the company continued to play, headed now by the Lewis Hallam who had been but a boy when they first landed in this country. In New York a new theatre was built in Chapel Street, and during one of the disturbances caused by the Stamp Act (passed in March, 1765) this theatre was wrecked, but not totally destroyed. This seems to have been the first of the theatrical riots of which New York has had many. In 1767 a new and handsome theatre was built in John Street, New York. Albany was visited in July, 1769, the governor having authorized it "for one month only." The officers of a regiment quartered there had, in 1760, given private theatricals; to both amateurs and professionals was there much opposition. In September, 1773, a theatre was opened in Charleston, S. C., by invitation of the inhabitants and permission of the magistrates, and the season there lasted fifty-one performances, ending in June, 1774. Of course, in all these years changes had taken place in the company. Lewis Hallam's cousin Wignell arrived from England, and his future partner, Henry, had shown himself an admirable and versatile actor. The actors, assured of support in this country, called themselves "The American Company." It is highly probable that they were equal in histrionic ability to any company in England outside of the three London theatres.

But on Oct. 24, 1774, the Continental Congress, assembled in Philadelphia, recommended a suspension of all public amusements. The American Company was in New York, ready to begin the winter season. The resolution of Congress was conveyed to Douglass by the president, Peyton Randolph, and he was also notified by the New York committee. There was nothing left for the actors but to try their luck again in the loyal West Indies, where they were always welcome; and with their departure closes the record of professional performances in the colonies until after the declaration of peace had left them a free and prosperous people.

During the Revolutionary struggle the only theatrical performances were those given by the British officers. Burgoyne, who had written *The Maid of the Oaks* in 1775, was with the British troops in Boston, and there wrote his second play, seemingly of great contemporaneous human interest, as it was called *The Blockade of Boston*. While it was acting an alarm was given that the Americans had made an assault on the British works; and when a sergeant entered, saying, "The rebels have attacked the lines on the Neck," the audience applauded his spirited delivery, believing them to be part of the piece until the prompt cessation of the performance proved, as Dunlap neatly puts it, that the prompter was not behind the scenes, but behind the trenches. Driven from Boston, the British officers took possession of the John Street Theatre in New York, which they called the Theatre Royal, and in which they acted for the benefit of the military poor. Major André was among the chief actors. When the British army held Philadelphia also, the officers opened the Southwark Theatre, and here Major André was not only an actor, but the scene-painter as well. Certain of the scenes painted by him lasted for many years, and it is recorded that on July 4, 1807, a play on the capture of André (probably Dunlap's) was produced with the aid of scenery painted by the ill-fated spy himself, and signed with his name in bold black letters. Although we have here referred only to the private theatricals of the British in Boston, New York, and Philadelphia, it is probable that they gratified their histrionic tastes elsewhere also.

After the peace the players came back. Hallam came first to spy out the land, bringing but a weak detachment with him. He opened the Southwark Theatre in Philadelphia, March 11, 1785. He acted with profit, and then went to New York, where he announced a course of lectures, each followed by a farce, beginning Aug. 24, 1785. After he left Philadelphia the legislature of Pennsylvania discussed the prohibition of all plays, but the fatal clause was at last stricken out. In New York there was also some trouble with the city authorities. But Hallam, who had taken in Henry as a partner, felt encouraged, and, sending for the rest of the actors, he opened the John Street Theatre, Nov. 19, 1785, when *The Gamester* was performed by "the old American Company," for so it called itself on the bills. The legislature of New York was at this time petitioned to forbid the theatre, but counter-petitions in its favor prevailed. In 1786 a new theatre was built in Charleston, S. C.; and in August of that year the first playhouse was opened in Baltimore, then rapidly growing ahead of Annapolis. In October the company went to Richmond, Va., which in like manner was surpassing Williamsburg. The old American Company were alone in serving the circuit thus laid out for nearly forty years from the time of their first arrival in 1752. But in 1792 Wignell found that he could no longer agree amicably with Hallam and Henry, and he withdrew, taking with him two of the chief members of the company, Mr. and Mrs. Morris. He went to England for recruits, and organized a company superior to that he had deserted, although this was also strengthened, especially by the addition of Hodgkinson, the most versatile actor of his day, with the possible exception of Elliston in England. After much dispute and many delays Wignell opened the new theatre he had built for himself in Chestnut Street, Philadelphia, on Feb. 17, 1794. From this time forth the United States had two stock companies of very extraordinary merit, surpassed only by the companies at the three patent houses in London. In Wignell's company, for example, were Fennell, Harwood, Darley, and Mrs. Whitlock, the sister of John Kemble and Sarah Siddons.

After Wignell had laid hands on Philadelphia, Hallam and Henry turned their attention to Boston, where in 1792 a new exhibition room had been opened with a variety performance, rope-dancing, gymnastics, etc. A later playbill announced "A moral lecture in five parts, in which the dreadful effects of conspiracy will be exemplified." This was an underhand way of advertising Otway's *Venice Preserved*. *Hamlet* and *Romeo and Juliet* were also given as "moral lectures" or "moral dialogues." But this flagrant violation of the law was not long allowed, and in December, 1792, the exhibition room was closed. Hallam and Henry had in June, 1790, petitioned for a repeal of the prohibitory law of 1750, but in vain. In 1791 a petition was presented to the selectmen of Boston, who debated it, and instructed the representatives of Boston in the legislature to endeavor to effect a repeal of the law, at least as regards Boston. In January, 1792, the subject came before the house of representatives; a committee reported that a repeal was inexpedient; and this report was accepted, in spite of strenuous efforts. It was after this that the attempt to get around the law had been made at the exhibition room. In 1793, however, the legislature of Massachusetts repealed the law against the theatre, and on Feb. 4, 1794, the Federal Street Theatre was opened with a prologue by Robert Treat Paine, Jr.; and it remained open until July 4. In Hartford, Conn., a theatre was opened in August, 1795, by Hodgkinson and a part of the old American Company.

Thus far the attempt has here been made to show the difficulties under which the early actors labored, and to give the exact dates on which the first theatrical performances were given in each town. But with the beginning of this century the drama found itself firmly established, and spread itself with such rapidity as to make a minute chronicle of its growth too tedious to be inserted here. A few more dates of beginnings, and we leave the playhouses to consider the players and the playwrights. In New Orleans the first performances seem to have been given in 1791 in French by a company fleeing from the insurrection in St. Domingo. The first theatre seems to have been built about 1808. Dec. 24, 1817, was acted the first English play given by a regular company; and in 1822 James H. Caldwell, the manager of this company, began to build the first American theatre in New Orleans. In 1817 Caldwell had managed a theatre at Washington, D. C.; in 1818 he built a playhouse at Petersburg, Va.; in 1826 he opened theatres at Nashville, Tenn., and in Huntsville, Ala.; and in 1828 he built a brick theatre in Natchez, Miss. In 1819 N. M. Ludlow gave the first dramatic performance in St. Louis. The first performance in Cincinnati is said to have been given in October, 1801, but the first company of any consequence appeared there in 1815.

The first play on record written by an American is the *Prince of Parthia*, by Thomas Godfrey, of Philadelphia, the son of the inventor of the quadrant. This was published in 1765, but never acted. The first play written and acted in America seems to have been Burgoyne's *Blockade of Boston*, already referred to. Almost contemporaneous with this, however, was a polemic play called the *Americans Roused, or A Cure for the Spleen*, which was printed in New York by Rivington; it was a Tory pamphlet, and probably not intended to be acted. The first play written in America and by an American, and acted by a professional company, was the *Contrast* of Royal Tyler, some time chief-justice of Vermont; this play was performed at the John Street Theatre in New York by the old American Company, on April 16, 1786. It is a comedy in five acts, and it contains the first Yankee part ever seen on the stage. Its success led the author to write a farce called *May-day, or New York in an Uproar*. And it was the popularity of the *Contrast* which incited to playwriting the first professional dramatist of this country, William Dunlap. His first play, *The Modest Soldier; or Love in New York*, although accepted, was never acted. His second, *The Father of an Only Child*, was produced Sept. 7, 1789; and for years thereafter Dunlap was one of the most fertile of playmakers. William Dunlap had been born in Perth-Amboy in 1766; showing a taste for painting, he had been sent to England when seventeen to study under Benjamin West. He returned in 1787, having seen the best acting of London and with a strong liking for the stage. His *Father of an Only Child* so pleased Wigwell that he induced the author to write a farce for his benefit, a sequel to the *Poor Soldier*, called *Darby's Return*. In 1794 Dunlap's tragedy of *Leicester* was acted, and in 1795 a second tragedy, *Fountainville Abbey*. The next year he wrote a musical piece, called the *Archers*, and founded on the story of William Tell. By the persuasion of Hodgkinson he was induced to take an interest in the management of the theatre in 1796; two years later he became sole director. In 1805 he gave it up, having lost all he had, but in 1810 and 1811 he was again connected with the theatre. He was one of the founders of the National Academy of Design, and he wrote a *History of the Arts of Design in America*. His *History of the American Theatre* is an excellent book and an invaluable authority. A biography of George Frederick Cooke also attests his interest in the stage. He died in New York in 1839, at the age of seventy-three. He was the author, adaptor, or translator of fifty plays. One was *André*, afterwards revised as *The Glory of Columbia, her Yeomanry*. Many of Dunlap's pieces were versions of Kotzebue's plays, bearing the same titles as the English adaptations acted in London, and not seldom surpassing them in theatrical effect. Probably half of Dunlap's dramas were published by Longworth in the quaint little pamphlets familiar to all dramatic collectors.

Another dramatist whose plays may be found occasionally was John D. Burk, the historian of Virginia, who was killed in a duel in 1808. His *Bunker Hill; or the Death of General Warren*, was acted in both Boston and New York in 1797, and a *Joan of Arc* and half-a-dozen other pieces of varying merit were also tried by the light of the lamps. J. N. Barker wrote *Tears and Smiles*, a comedy, acted March 4, 1807, and, besides other plays, *The Indian Princess* (i. e., Pocahontas), acted April 6, 1808; his *Marmion*, a dramatization from Scott, was announced in 1812 as an English play—so strong was the belief that nothing good could come from an American dramatist. Richard Penn Smith wrote *William Penn*, acted in Philadelphia, and also made various adaptations from the German. The most prominent American dramatist after Dunlap was, however, John Howard Payne, the author of "Home, Sweet Home." Born in New York in 1792, he had gone on the stage at the age of seventeen, making almost as great a success as "Master Payne," as was made by his predecessor, "Master Betty," the English "Infant Roscius." He wrote some sixteen plays, mostly adaptations from the French.

Clari, a melodrama, is remembered now chiefly because it contains his famous song, for which Bishop adapted a Sicilian air. Payne's tragedy of *Brutus*, written originally for Kean, was often acted by Booth, and holds the stage to this day. Most of Payne's plays were originally produced in England, and even now the majority of Englishmen do not know that the author of "Home, Sweet Home" was an American. Appointed United States consul to Tunis in 1841, Payne died there in 1852. Another American songwriter, Samuel Woodworth, the author of "The Old Oaken Bucket," was also a writer of plays, among which the *Forest Rose*, acted in 1825, was the most successful. George P. Morris, the author of "Woodman, Spare that Tree!" also tried his hand at playmaking, and his *Briercliff*, produced in 1826, kept the stage for years. When to these plays we add *Metamora*, written by John A. Stone and acted in 1829 by Edwin Forrest, we have briefly passed in review the native drama as it had existed up to 1833, when Dunlap published his *History of the American Theatre*, to which he appended a list of the plays written by Americans. In this list he was able to set down the names of a hundred writers of plays and of nearly three hundred pieces. Yet we must not be led astray by his massing of figures. Even as late as 1833 the American dramatist was seen but seldom on the boards of an American theatre. The enormous majority of the plays acted in this country were imported from England. The latest London success was always soon reproduced in the chief theatres of the United States. In time the number of American dramatists increased, and it became no longer a disadvantage to a comedy that it had been written on this side of the Atlantic. But before considering the plays and playwrights of the past half century since Dunlap published his *History*, it may be well first to set forth the players who had come on the scene.

The Park Theatre of New York, built after the designs of Brunel, the engineer of the Thames tunnel, was opened in January, 1798, and for a quarter of a century it remained the foremost theatre of the United States, although there were years when the company at the Chestnut Street Theatre of Philadelphia excelled the company at the Park of New York. The Park Theatre Company included at one time or another, Hallam, Henry, Hodgkinson, Conway, and Cooper. The Chestnut had Wignell, W. B. Wood, Warren, and Jefferson (the father and grandfather of the William Warren and Joseph Jefferson, known to all play-goers of to-day). The Boston Theatre was headed by John Bernard. These were all remarkable actors. Perhaps the foremost was Thomas Abthorpe Cooper, born in England in 1776, brought up by Godwin, the author of *Caleb Williams*, and advised by Holcroft, the dramatist. He acted in Edinburgh first without success, but he studied and worked hard, and before he was nineteen he acted Hamlet and Macbeth in London with great applause. In 1796 he came to America, acting Macbeth, December 9, in Philadelphia. He first appeared in New York, Feb. 28, 1798, as Hamlet. For years he was the first actor of America; and when he went back to act for a season in England he was treated coldly as an American. He died in 1849, at the age of seventy-three. Cooper was the first actor in America to "star;" that is to say, he attached himself to no company, but went in turn to each of the chief cities, playing the chief parts in tragedy. In itself this early starring was not injurious.

The presence of Mr. Cooper strengthened the company, which, however, had to be strong enough to play the very same pieces without him, before and after Cooper's visit. Performances were given at first only three nights a week, and even after the theatre was opened every night but Sunday, the same play was rarely acted twice in succession; the star might appear in tragedy two or three times a week, and a comedy with a farce or two would fill the bill on the other nights. This is the system once universal, which still obtains at the Théâtre Français in Paris, where the most successful play is never acted oftener than three nights out of six. At the Park and the Chestnut, and the other theatres modelled on these, every actor was supposed to be perfect and ready in every part in his "line of business;" and the theatre had thus a repertory on which it could draw at will. As time passed on, the "star" became of more and more importance, and the company of less. Instead of going to see a good performance of a play by a competent company, with a very fine actor in the chief part, audiences were contented with the fine actor in a bad performance by a poor company.

But the evil effects of this starring system were not visible in Cooper's day. The first great actor to come to this country after Cooper was George Frederick Cooke, who acted Richard III. at the Park Theatre, Nov. 21, 1809, being then fifty-four years old, erratic, obstinate, fiery, and worn with drink. Yet he was a genius, and was welcomed as one. His brief but brilliant career in this country was ended by his death in New York, Sept. 26, 1812. Eleven years after Cooke came Edmund Kean, who also appeared as Richard III., Nov. 29, 1820, at the Anthony Street Theatre in New York, where the Park Theatre Company was acting, their own house being in ruins. In Boston, Kean refused to act one night because there was only a small audience. This was so much resented that Kean quit the country. He returned, and on Nov. 14, 1825, reappeared at the Park as Richard III., the recollection of his slight to a Boston audience causing one of the worst riots known to theatrical history. Kean apologized and filled his engagement in New York. But when he appeared in Boston, Dec. 21, a riot broke out there, and almost all the audience part of the theatre was destroyed. Kean made no further attempt to play in Boston, but he acted in the other cities without causing trouble. While in New York he put up a monument over Cooke's grave in St. Paul's church-yard. A year after Kean came his English rival, Junius Brutus Booth, and he also made his first appearance before an American audience as Richard III. in the theatre at Richmond, July 13, 1821. He appeared at the Park Theatre, New York, later in the season, and was at once acknowledged as a master.

He bought a farm in Maryland, and, although he returned to England for a brief visit, he was ever after an American, playing all over the country, even going to California in 1851. He died Nov. 23, 1852, on a steamboat bound for Cincinnati from New Orleans, where he had made his last appearance four days before. No actor ever exerted as much influence on acting in America as Junius Brutus Booth. Forgotten in England except as the actor whom Kean crushed, he was received here, coming after Kean, as Kean's equal. It is not a little curious to note how quickly the American public took to the lively style of Cooke, Kean, and Booth, who were all plainly of the same fiery school; yet Cooper was as plainly of the scholarly and more reflective school of John Philip Kemble. Certainly it was a great good-fortune for the young stage of the United States that tragic actors of the value of Cooper, Cooke, Kean, and Booth should be seen here to serve as models to the histrionic student. It was upon Cooper, apparently, that the first native actor who achieved eminence had modelled himself, yet it can hardly be doubted that Edwin Forrest was almost as much influenced by Kean, with whom he acted in Albany in 1825, and by Booth, whom he had many opportunities of observing.

Edwin Forrest was born in Philadelphia, March 9, 1806. He first appeared as Douglas when he was only fourteen. Two years later he played on a Southern and Western circuit, proving himself. In 1825 he was the leading actor of the Albany Theatre, playing Iago to Kean's Othello so well that Kean at a public dinner in Philadelphia took special occasion to praise him. It was as Othello that Forrest made his first appearance at the New York Park, June 23, 1826; he was chief actor at the Bowery and the Park for several years. Then he starred, playing Metamora in Stone's Indian drama and Spartacus in Dr. Bird's *Gladiator*, both parts having been written for him and exactly suiting his stalwart and massive style. In 1834, after a public dinner and the presentation of a gold medal, he went to Europe to travel, and in 1836 he acted Spartacus at Drury Lane Theatre, London. In England he was married. On his return he received another public dinner. In 1845 he again visited England, and then began his quarrel with Macready, whom he accused of having had him hissed, and whom he himself hissed openly. Forrest was a strong and headstrong man, and he brooked no opposition. The trouble with Macready ended in a riot in New York in 1849, by which many people lost their lives. Three years later came the discreditable divorce proceedings between Forrest and his wife. After these events the better class of people fell away from Forrest, and he resented the abandonment. As an actor and as a man he had been bold and forcible, but lacking wholly in refinement. After his scandals he became surly and almost morose. His acting, to say the least, was not improved by the change in his character, although by some law of compensation certain personifications, notably King Lear, became mellowed and more poetic. He died Dec. 12, 1872, leaving his fortune to found a home for the decayed members of his profession. The critical verdict that he was best in parts of physical rather than of mental display was not far out. Yet so shrewd and unprejudiced an observer as Mr. Ireland declares that portions of Forrest's Othello, Macbeth, and Lear thrilled to the very soul and made one stand aghast with horror. Beyond all peradventure, Forrest was a great actor, but he might have been much greater than he was.

Here, indeed, was the marked difference between Forrest and Macready, who was less gifted by nature and owed far more to art and to a dogged determination to conquer at any cost. William Charles Macready, born in 1793, and therefore thirteen years older than Forrest, first appeared in America as Virginius, Oct. 2, 1826, and was at once accepted as the best actor of the colder and more classical school seen in America since Cooper in his prime. In 1843 Macready came a second time to this country, and in 1848 he arrived here for the third time, and after his first engagement at the Astor Place Opera House he made a tour of the smaller cities, receiving a public dinner at New Orleans. In May, 1849, he was announced to play Macbeth in New York again; a riot ensued, excited by the fierce partisanship of Forrest's friends, who had taken his cause to heart. The militia fired on the mob and left twenty-two dead and thirty-six wounded on the pavement. Both actors were to blame in the unseemly quarrel which had this fatal end; but on Forrest lies the heavier burden, for he did nothing to check the violence of his riotous supporters.

Nor were the actresses seen on the earlier stage inferior to the actors. Mrs. Merry, especially, was the equal of any contemporary English actress except Mrs. Siddons, and possibly Miss O'Neil, in her best parts. Mrs. Duff, a sister of the wife of Thomas Moore, the poet, came after Mrs. Merry, and surpassed her in some parts. Her life has been told with loving care by Mr. J. N. Ireland, and we can no longer doubt that she was an actress of very remarkable powers, equalled rarely, and excelled only by Fanny Kemble at the best, and by Charlotte Cushman in the parts she had made her own. Mrs. Duff's first appearance in America was made in Boston, Dec. 31, 1810, when she acted Juliet for the first time. She afterward joined the Chestnut Street Theatre, and at intervals played in New York. While she was on the stage she was the foremost actress of America. She left the theatre in 1838, and lived until 1857 in an obscurity of her own seeking, for she had become deeply religious and felt no desire to recall the days of her histrionic triumphs.

A year before Mrs. Duff retired Charlotte Cushman was engaged in the stock company of the Park Theatre. Born in Boston, in 1815, of straight Puritan stock, she set out when only fifteen to help her family by her voice. When she was twenty she was prima donna at New Orleans, but unfortunately, as it seemed then, the change of climate and injudicious advice ruined her singing voice. Self-reliant, she appeared for a benefit as Lady Macbeth, and, having been well received, she determined to be an actress. After many rebuffs and trials she was engaged at the Park in 1837, and here in time she made her mark. Macready gave her good counsel, and after acting with him in 1844 she determined to play in London, which she did the next year, after many a hard struggle. But she made a brilliant success, and her engagement lasted eighty-four nights. In 1850 she played again throughout the United States, and for the next twenty-five years, during which she appeared at irregular intervals, she was acknowledged by all as the greatest actress of America. She died Feb. 18, 1876. Charlotte Cushman's first great hits were as Nancy in a version of *Oliver Twist*, and as Meg Merrilies in the melodrama of *Guy Mannering*. Later, Lady Macbeth, Queen Katherine, Emilia, and Bianca in *Fazio* were her most striking characters. Sturdy, strong, with a man's figure and a man's strength, she was fond of playing male parts: Wolsey was one; Cherubino was another; and the best of them was Romeo.

Between Mrs. Duff's earlier successes and Charlotte Cushman's came Fanny Kemble's. In September, 1832, Mr. Charles Kemble, the younger brother of John Kemble and Sarah Siddons, made his first appearance in America, accompanied by his daughter, Frances Anne Kemble. Charles Kemble was an actor of great skill, and in comedy he had no equal in his day. Miss Fanny Kemble, though almost a novice (she was only twenty years old when she appeared here), had the personal charm which made everything she did seem just the right thing to be done. She was hailed as a beauty and as a genius, and her sway there was none to dispute. She had the fire and impetuosity and fascination of a very clever young woman who builded better than she knew, and whose instinct was a true dramatic touchstone. In June, 1834, she left the stage and married Mr. Pierce Butler, of Philadelphia, in which city she has since resided more often than anywhere else. In time incompatibility of temper led to a divorce between her and her husband, and she resumed her father's name. Afterward Mrs. Kemble appeared a few times on the stage in England, but the personal exhibition of the theatre was always repulsive to her, and she gave up acting and confined herself to occasional courses of readings, generally from Shakespeare. One of these readings called forth one of Longfellow's best sonnets. Mrs. Kemble has written several plays, of which *Francis the First* is the best known. Most of her writing has been autobiographical. Her *Journal in America*, published just after her first visit, caused great and needless dissatisfaction, for the Americans were a very thin-skinned people in those days, and Miss Kemble was a lively young lady. Within the last few years she has published *Recollections of a Girlhood* and *Recollections of Later Years*, two as charming autobiographic books as it is possible to find in modern literature.

Before Charles Kemble had come Charles Mathews, whose eccentric comedy was as highly esteemed in England as Kemble's light comedy. Charles Mathews, born in 1776, first appeared in America in 1822. He acted Goldfinch in the *Road to Ruin*, Dr. Ollapod, and a variety of farces, and he gave his celebrated entertainment, "Mathews at Home." His trip here was profitable and pleasant, and on his return to England he utilized his experiences on this side of the water in a new entertainment, called "Mathews in America," some of the caricatures in which gave offence to a few highly sensitive Americans. Yet, when he returned in 1834 and produced his entertainment before the American people, no cause of complaint was found. His son, Charles James Mathews, the foremost light comedian of his day, first came to this country in 1838 in company with Madame Vestris, whom he had married just before his departure. Madame Vestris was over forty years of age when she appeared here, and this fact no doubt accounts for the general disappointment of play-goers, who had heard much of her great beauty. C. J. Mathews made more of a hit than his wife, and after her death he returned here in 1857 and married Mrs. A. H. Davenport, with whom he came here again in 1871. Charles Mathews "the younger," as he was generally called, was a comedian of extraordinary lightness and ease, and his influence on the younger generation of comedians survives to this day.

It must not be supposed, because mention is here made of the chief English comedians who crossed the Atlantic from time to time, that there were not American comedians of conspicuous merit. In the early days Hallam and Henry and Hodgkinson, especially the latter, were performers of great comic force. Then came Wignell, Prigmore, Bernard, Wood, Warren, Jefferson, Nelson, Barnes, and many more. Many of them were born in England, although they had settled here for life and considered themselves good Americans. In 1826 James H. Hackett, a merchant of New York who had married an actress, took to the stage himself, and became one of the foremost of American comedians. He was the first to make a specialty of Yankee parts, and although he repeatedly acted Richard III., Hamlet, and King Lear, it was as a comedian, and especially as an actor of dialect characters, that he was best received. He acted in England in 1827, and again in 1830, 1840, 1845, and 1851; and he was the first to introduce the stage Yankee to the English public. Hackett was probably the earliest performer of Rip Van Winkle, and in John K. Paulding's comedy, the *Lion of the West*, he appeared as Col. Nimrod Wildfire. It was possibly the success of a Yankee part in Woodworth's *Forest Rose* which turned Hackett's attention to the New England dialect; but this part was soon appropriated by an experienced comedian, George Handel Hill, who took advantage of Hackett's second trip to England to push himself forward as an actor of Yankee characters. Hill too went to England in 1836, personating the dramatic Down-Easter at Drury Lane and the Haymarket; he even acted twice in Paris, but the French did not understand the Solomon Swop of 1837 any better than they comprehended Asa Trenchard when Mr. John T. Raymond acted it there in 1867. After Hackett and Hill came Dan Marble, a coarser comedian, whose hit was made in *Sam Patch*; he acted also in *Yankee-Land* and the *Vermont Wool-dealer*, both written for him by Cornelius Logan, a brother of Senator Logan and the father of Eliza Logan. Ten years later (in 1848) Mr. F. S. Chanfrau set on the stage Mose, the New York fireman and the Bowery boy, and for ten years this type maintained its popularity and appeared in many pieces. Mr. Chanfrau achieved over a score of years later a second success in *Kit, the Arkansaw Traveller*, in which he has been acting now for the past twelve years or so: it is very rarely that an actor is ever able to make as decided a hit in a second part as broadly marked as the first. Other types of American character have been seen in the Salem Scudder and Asa Trenchard of Mr. Joseph Jefferson, in the Solon Shingle of Mr. John E. Owens, in the Colonel Sellers of Mr. John T. Raymond, the Judge Bardwell Slote of Mr. W. J. Florence, and the Davy Crockett of Mr. Frank Mayo. More famous than any of these is the Rip Van Winkle of Mr. Joseph Jefferson. After Hackett had acted in a dramatization of Irving's folk-tale many other actors attempted it, and among them were Mr. Chanfrau and Charles Burke, Mr. Jefferson's half-brother, who made a new version of the play. This version Mr. Jefferson acted many times, and it grew under his loving touch. In 1865, when he was about to act at the Adelphi Theatre, London, he got Mr. Dion Boucicault to put the play into shape, and in its new form Mr. Jefferson made one of the most remarkable successes ever known in the history of the stage.

During all these years, as these actors were coming forward in succession, there was a great growth in the number of theatres throughout the country. Nearly every town had its playhouse, called a theatre or an opera-house, or haply an academy of music. Theatres which had formed part of a circuit served by a company from a larger city came in time to have companies of their own. In the earlier days the manager depended on his own actors to attract audiences; in time he began to rely more and more on wandering stars. Cooper was the first of these; then came the great English actors Cooke and Kean and Booth, who could not well be expected to join a stock company. Following in Cooper's footsteps came Forrest and others now more or less forgotten. Mrs. Duff was starred now and again, and after her great hit Charlotte Cushman was a star only. So it was with others who had less right—Hackett, Hill, Marble. With the increase in the number of theatres it began to be difficult to get a good stock company together; and the difficulty was increased by the pecuniary temptation a profitable starring-trip offered to a favorite actor. At first stars only acted on special nights, the regular company appearing alone the other nights of the week. In the end, the star, for his own profit, was willing to act every night, and this made the regular company of less importance. Then the number of stars increased, so that instead of having half a dozen very eminent performers strengthening the company at intervals during the year, it became possible to engage a constant succession of stars following close on each other's heels. When this had come about the manager speedily discovered that it was the name of the star which attracted a large audience, and not the excellent performance of the whole company. Obviously it was possible to economize on the company, as a star supported as best he could be drew nearly as well as a star playing with a stock company. Then the star, seeing that the manager relied on him to get people into the house, demanded the lion's share of the profits; and the result of all this was that, except in four or five large cities, there were no stock companies able to give a creditable performance of any of the stock plays. The really capable and conscientious actors were forced either to star or to remain in the few surviving stock companies. Of course this process and this progression were slow in their action. Cooper did not begin to star until after 1800, and it was quite 1860 before things had come to the pass depicted above. And equally of course there were exceptions. In the large cities—in New York, Boston, Philadelphia, and later in New Orleans, Chicago, and San Francisco—the theatres kept fine companies, most of them admitting stars, but always with discretion and only at intervals, as when the system began. In Philadelphia the Chestnut Street Theatre held its own, and had for its chief rival the Walnut Street Theatre. In Boston the Boston Theatre and the Museum maintained a worthy rivalry; to this day the Boston Museum is one of the best-managed theatres in the country, and it has one of the most capable companies. In New York the first real rival of the Park Theatre was the Bowery, but it was not until James W. Wallack took in hand the National Theatre that the supremacy of the elder house was shaken. Wallack was a handsome, dashing actor, gentlemanly and popular in the best society, and fashion was ready to follow him; but the theatre was burnt in 1839. What Wallack had begun was finished by William E. Burton, perhaps the best actor of broad, low comedy parts yet seen here. In 1848 he opened as Burton's Theatre what had been the Palmer Opera House in Chamber street, and within a few months the Park Theatre was burnt down. Burton was a man of education, and for a while edited the Philadelphia *Gentleman's Magazine*. He continued to manage Burton's Theatre until 1856, when he moved uptown for two years. Then he left the field to Mr. Wallack, who had in 1852 taken Brougham's Lyceum and called it Wallack's Theatre. John Brougham was a genial and generous Irish-American actor and author, who had originally been part author of *London Assurance*, and who had written the version of *Dombey and Son* which had been the first great success at Burton's Theatre. He wrote many plays, all easy and amusing; among them the comedy of *Romance and Reality*, the burlesque of *Pocahontas*, and the adaptation of *The Duke's Motto*. He attempted management several times, but never with good fortune; he lacked the stern firmness of a business man. When Brougham failed Wallack took his theatre, and from that day to this there has been a Wallack's Theatre in New York. Ten years later a new house was built at the corner of Broadway and Thirteenth Street. In this Wallack never acted, but it was managed by his son, Mr. John Lester Wallack, a light comedian trained in the best school. In 1881 this house was found to be too far down town, and Wallack's Theatre was again moved up, this time to Broadway and Thirtieth Street. With the lapse of time, however, has come a distinct deterioration both in the company and in the class of plays presented, and Wallack's is no longer the first theatre in America.

Just as Wallack had taken Brougham's Lyceum in 1852 to rival Burton's Theatre and to seize the succession of the old Park Theatre, so in 1869 Mr. Augustin Daly took another house Brougham had opened in Twenty-fourth Street, and began at once a strong opposition to Wallack's. For eight years Mr. Daly engaged a very strong company; it is on record that he gave the *School for Scandal* at Newark and *London Assurance* at his own theatre on the same evening without enlarging his company; and he mounted his plays with lavish beauty. While Mr. Wallack, inheriting his traditions from his father, relied almost exclusively on the London stage for his plays, even if they were adaptations from the French, Mr. Daly imported his foreign dramas himself, and threw before the American public French and German comedy, drama, and farce in rapid succession. A dramatist himself of no little force and of great skill, Mr. Daly also brought forward other American authors—notably Mr. Bronson Howard, whose *Saratoga* proved a most amusing farce, equal in ingenuity to a Frenchman's work. It may be noted that this play was acted several hundred times in London, and was translated into German and played in Berlin. In 1870 was opened the Union Square Theatre, managed by Mr. A. M. Palmer, who followed Mr. Daly in relying on America and on France for his pieces, and not on England. Its most noted plays have been the *Two Orphans*, by MM. Dennery and Cormon, and Mr. Bronson Howard's *Banker's Daughter*, which, like his *Saratoga*, has been acted in London with popular approval equal to that bestowed on it here. For twelve years the Union Square Theatre has had a strong and varied company, most of the members of which were native Americans, and therefore capable of appreciating the American character and of giving full effect to American plays. About the same time that Mr. Daly opened the Fifth Avenue and Mr. Palmer the Union Square Mr. Edwin Booth opened the theatre he had erected for himself. Acting in 1864 in a fine revival of *Hamlet* at the Winter Garden Theatre, Mr. Edwin Booth, the son of Junius Brutus Booth, and an heir of much of his histrionic genius, was so acceptable to the public of New York that the tragedy was acted for one hundred consecutive nights, anticipating in a city of 600,000 inhabitants the later run of Mr. Henry Irving's Hamlet in London with 3,000,000 inhabitants. In 1866 Mr. Booth presented *Richelieu* with the same beauty of adornment, and in 1867 the *Merchant of Venice*, and then the theatre was burnt. It was on Feb. 3, 1869, that Mr. Booth opened Booth's Theatre, a playhouse magnificent in its proportions and noble in its structure. The first play was *Romeo and Juliet*, and the chief tragedies of Shakespeare followed. Mr. Edwin Adams and Mr. Lawrence Barrett were the chief actors who appeared with Mr. Booth, and as stars appeared Charlotte Cushman, Joseph Jefferson, W. J. Florence, J. S. Clarke, Adelaide Neilson, Miss "Lotta" Crabtree, and others of first-rate theatrical importance. But the house was very expensive, and Mr. Booth was not as good a manager as he was actor; and in time he found himself obliged to give the theatre up. It has since been leased by many managers, some of whom gave performances worthy of the house—notably a revival of *Julius Cæsar*—while others merely tried to make as much money as might be. Changing hands in this way from year to year, and not served by a permanent stock company, Booth's Theatre was finally torn down in 1884. The Madison Square Theatre is a small but perfectly built and beautifully decorated house, erected by Mr. J. Steele Mackaye, and opened by him in 1880 with his own drama, *Hazel Kirke*. Mr. Mackaye had been a pupil of Delsarte, and an actor and a teacher of acting, and he had written several plays, one of which, *Won at Last*, had had an honorable career. For the Madison Square Theatre he devised a mechanical novelty of much future value; this is a double stage. There are two stages, one over the other, like two shelves in a dumb-waiter, so hung on wire-ropes, and so carefully counterbalanced, that they may change places in a few seconds. The advantage of this is that while one act is being played on one stage the scenery for the next act can be made ready on the other stage, which is then either above or below; and thus no time is lost between the acts, and much more elaborate scenes are possible. It is probable also that in time the double stage may be utilised in furthering the action of the drama. Among the other theatres in New York, hitherto passed over, are to be mentioned Niblo's Garden, where a spectacular piece called the *Black Crook* was acted several hundred times in 1867 and since; and the Standard, where the English comic opera of *H. M. S. Pinafore* made its long stay in 1879. At a theatre called the Olympic, and now torn down, a comic actor of much humor, George L. Fox, appeared in 1867 as Bottom in *A Midsummer Night's Dream*, and as Humpty Dumpty the clown in a pantomime of the same name. This last was a delightful performance, free and unforced in its fun.

Space fails to mention in detail even the names of all the American actors who have appeared in the chief towns, or of the English artists who have crossed the ocean from time to time to try their fortunes here. Among the first Mr. John McCulloch must not be omitted, nor Mr. Lawrence Barrett, a tragic actor with a constant desire to enrich the stage with new plays, including *Pendragon* of Mr. Wm. Young and *Francesca da Rimini* of Mr. G. H. Boker. Among the latter may be noted Mr. and Mrs. Keeley, Mr. and Mrs. Charles Kean, Mr. Barry Sullivan, Mr. Buckstone, Mr. Charles Coghlan, and Mrs. John Wood, one of the few actresses with a sense of broad humor. Besides these English-speaking performers there have been here many French, Italian, and German histrionic artists of renown—Rachel, Ristori, Seebach, Salvini, Fechter, Sarah Bernhardt, Rossi, Janauschek, and others of minor importance. Most of these actors brought with them full foreign companies. Partly to these foreign companies, partly to the various operatic troupes—Italian, French, and English; partly to the desire of the manager of an attractive spectacle, play, or player to make himself all he could of the possible profit; partly to other minor circumstances, is due the rise of the "combination" system, which throughout the United States has now superseded the system of stock companies. In the earlier days of the American stage, as we have seen, there were no stars, and the local company was all-sufficient. In time stars began to revolve, and the stock company became of secondary importance; now, except in four New York theatres, one in Boston, and perhaps two or three elsewhere in the United States, there are no more stock companies. The star now travels from town to town, accompanied by his own company. The new play is now acted throughout the country by one or more "combinations" of actors chosen specially for the purpose and sent out from New York. The local manager is now merely the janitor of his own theatre, and has to attend only to the lighting, the ushers, and the advertising, the manager of the travelling combination furnishing the play, the players, and more often than not the scenery also. This change has come since 1876, and it is too early to see exactly what its effects will be on the drama. The better opinion is that it is an unmixed evil, and that there must in time be a reaction. It is to be noted, however, that a similar change has taken place in England and is taking place in France; as yet Germany is not affected, and in Italy something very like the combination system has always obtained. One result of the new state of affairs is that the country town and the metropolis are put on an equality, the country town seeing the most of the combinations which appear in the metropolis.

In the course of this sketch of the history of the stage in the United States, references have been made to many of the native dramatists who have from time to time revealed themselves. Other than incidentally it is impossible to treat American dramatic literature, because, although there have been many American plays, there is not, of a truth, any American dramatic literature to treat, as there is an English or a French dramatic literature. Until very recently the English dramatist alone supplied our stage; of late he has received some little aid from the Frenchman and the German. The appearance of the American dramatist even now is only sporadic. Thus, any account of the American drama cannot be the continuous story of a steady growth; it can only be a list of individual names.

In 1837 was acted *Bianca Visconti*, written by N. P. Willis, in his well-known style of verse. In 1845 was acted Mrs. Mowatt's *Fashion*, a lively enough comedy, but pretentious, although it is the best of its author's plays. John Brougham's plays have already been referred to. Mr. Dion Boucicault, with whom Brougham had been associated in the authorship of *London Assurance*, was an English dramatist of Irish birth, who became an American by adoption. The best of his plays are Irish in subject—*The Colleen Bawn*, *Arrah-na-Pogue*, and *The Shaughraun*, all of which were first acted in America. Another play of his, *The Octoroon*, made a very skilful use of the slavery question. Mr. Charles Gayler wrote *The Magic*

Marriage, a comedy of merit acted at Wallack's in 1861; and Mr. Lester Wallack himself has produced several plays, adapted from the French or dramatized from English novels; of these, the best is *Rosedale*. Mr. S. L. Clemens (Mark Twain) and Mr. Bret Harte have each written a play apiece, and another in collaboration.

Mr. Joaquin Miller is very widely known as the author of an effective melodrama of Western life and adventure called *The Danites*; and Mr. Bartley Campbell has written many plays, of which the best is also a drama of the West, called *My Partner*. *Conscience*, by Messrs. Julian Magnus and A. E. Lancaster; *The False Friend*, by Mr. Edgar Fawcett; *Clouds*, by Mr. Frederic Marsden; *The Rajah*, by Mr. William Young; *Two Nights in Rome*, by Mr. A. C. Gunter; *May Blossom*, by Mr. D. Belasco, are the most successful plays of writers from whom good work may fairly be expected in the future. The newer school of novelists have also turned their attention to the stage: Mrs. Burnett saw her *Lass o' Lowrie's* dramatized three or four times, and has herself produced a comedy called *Esmeralda*; and Mr. W. D. Howells has written two or three original comedies, besides making for Mr. Lawrence Barrett a very strong version of a Spanish play acted here as *Yorick's Love*. Mr. Augustin Daly and Mr. Bronson Howard have already been mentioned; Mr. Howard's *Young Mrs. Winthrop* is a fine and noble play. For the first time in the history of the American stage is there a band of young men desirous of writing for the theatre—clever, ardent, capable of taking pains, and willing to take pattern by the best models. It is surely justifiable to hope that in the next twenty years there may be as great an advance in the quality and quantity of our plays as there has been in the past twenty years in our novels. (B. M.)

DRAPER, HENRY (1837–1882), an American scientist, was born in Prince Edward co., Va., March 7, 1837. Two years later, his father, Prof. J. W. Draper, removed to New York, to become professor of chemistry in the University of New York. Henry graduated from the medical department of this university in 1858, taking for thesis the *functions* of the spleen, and illustrating it by microscopic photography. After a year's practice in connection with the Bellevue Hospital, he was made professor of physiology in the academic department of his *alma mater*, and in 1866 was advanced to the same department in the medical school. Resigning this position in 1873, he taught analytical chemistry in the academic department, and on the death of his father in January, 1882, was appointed his successor as professor of chemistry. At the close of the term he withdrew from the university, and in the summer he made an excursion to the Rocky Mountains. Here he contracted a severe cold, which on his return to New York resulted in pneumonia, from which he died Nov. 20, 1882. Prof. Draper had inherited his father's skill and enthusiasm in the cause of natural science, and in his brief career made several important discoveries. He devoted much attention to photographing the heavenly bodies and their spectra, in which he attained remarkable success. He published a *Text-book of Chemistry* (1864), and valuable papers in the scientific periodicals.

DRAPER, JOHN WILLIAM, M. D., LL. D. (1811–1882), was born May 5, 1811, at St. Helens, near Liverpool, and received his early education mostly from private tutors; he studied chemistry under Dr. Turner at the University of London. In 1833 he came to America, having relatives in Virginia, and in 1836 he graduated in medicine at the University of Pennsylvania with so much distinction that his inaugural thesis received the unusual compliment of being published by the faculty. Shortly afterward he was made professor of chemistry in Hampden-Sidney College, Virginia, and in 1839 received the appointment to the chair of chemistry in the University of New York. He was one of the founders of the medical department of the University of New York, and eventually became its president. At a later date he was made president also of the scientific department. He died Jan. 4, 1882.

Dr. Draper's earliest chemical publications were on the chemical action of light, and many of his subsequent memoirs were on radiant energy. Altogether, he published nearly forty of these memoirs in the *American Journal of Science and Arts*, the *Franklin Institute Journal*, the *American Journal of Medical Sciences*, and the *London, Edinburgh, and Dublin Philosophical Magazine*, and for them he received the Rumford medal of the American Academy of Science. Among the subjects treated of were an investigation of the temperature at which bodies become red hot, the nature of the light they emit at various degrees, the connection between their condition as to vibration and their heat. It was shown that incandescent solids yield a spectrum that is continuous, not interrupted. This has become one of the fundamental facts in astronomical spectroscopy. At this time (1847) no one in America had given attention to the spectroscope, and except Fraunhofer, few in Europe. Draper showed that the fixed lines might be photographed, doubled their number, and found new ones at both the violet and red ends of the spectrum. The facts thus discovered were applied to an investigation of the nature of flame and the condition of the sun's surface. He proved that under certain circumstances rays antagonize each other, and that the diffraction spectrum has great advantages over the prismatic, which is necessarily distorted. He attempted to ascertain the distribution of heat in the diffraction spectrum, and pointed out that advantages arise if wave-lengths are used in describing photographic phenomena, publishing steel engravings of the spectrum so arranged. He made investigations on phosphorescence, and obtained phosphorescent pictures of the moon. Up to 1840 it had been supposed that the great natural phenomena of the decomposition of carbonic acid by plants was accomplished by the violet rays, but by performing that decomposition in the spectrum itself, he showed that it is mainly effected by the yellow.

Dr. Draper was the first person who succeeded in taking portraits of the human face by photography. This was in 1839. He published a minute account of the process at a time when in Europe it was regarded as altogether impracticable. He was also the first to take photographs of the moon in 1840. When Daguerre's process was published he gave it critical examination, and described the analogies existing between the phenomena of chemical radiations and those of heat. For the purpose of obtaining more accurate results in these various inquiries, he invented the chlor-hydrogen photometer and examined the allotropic modifications that chlorine undergoes. Since in such researches most delicate thermometers are required, he investigated the electro-motive power of heat and described improvements in the thermopile. He discovered the true cause of the movement of camphor toward the light. In a physiological digression respecting interstitial movements he examined the passage of gases through thin films, such as soap-bubbles, and the force with which these movements are accomplished, applying the facts so gathered to an explanation of the circulation of the sap in plants and the blood in animals. Returning to an inquiry as to the distribution of heat and chemical force in the spectrum, he found, in opposition to the current opinion, that all the colored spaces are equally-warm and that chemical effects can be produced by every ray.

Though in his earlier years Draper was a skilful mathematical analyst, he published but few mathematical papers, the most important being an investigation of the electrical conducting-power of wires. This was undertaken at the request of Morse at the time he was inventing the electric telegraph.

The experimental investigations of Dr. Draper were collected together—once in 1844, in a volume *On the Forces that Produce the Organization of Plants*, and again in 1878, in a work entitled *Scientific Memoirs*. He also published an edition of Kane's *Chemistry*, a text-book on Chemistry, and a text-book on Natural Philosophy. In his work on *Physiology*, published in 1856, he showed the tone his mind had taken in regard to man in his social relations as under the dominion of law, and his subsequent works in this direction have given him worldwide celebrity. His *History of the Intellectual Development of Europe* was published in 1862. Few philosophical works have attained so quickly to fame. Many editions have been published in America and England, and it has been translated into almost every European language. The *Westminster Review* says: "It is one of the not least remarkable achievements in the progress of positive philosophy. A noble and even magnificent attempt to frame an induction from all the recorded phenomena of European, Asiatic, and North African history." This was followed by *Thoughts on the Civil Policy of America*, *A History of the American Civil War*, in 3 vols. 8vo, and a *History of the Conflict between Science and Religion*. This work has passed through many American and English editions, and has been translated into French, German, Spanish, Russian, Polish, Italian Servian, etc. (H. D.)

DRAPER, LYMAN C., LL. D., an American antiquary, was born in Evans, N. Y., Sept. 4, 1815 After receiving an academic education, he became editor of a paper at Pontotoc, Miss., but since 1834 he has largely devoted his time to gathering original materials for the biography and history of the Ohio and Mississippi valleys. From the recollections of pioneers, Indian fighters, and frontier leaders, he has gathered the largest and most complete collection of this kind ever made. In 1852 Mr. Draper settled in Madison, Wis., where, as secretary of the Wisconsin State Historical Society, he has collected a library of 100,000 volumes and pamphlets, and issued 9 volumes of collections. Besides editing these volumes, Mr. Draper was State superintendent of public instruction in 1858-59, and with the assistance of W. S. Croffut prepared in 1869 a work on farming and domestic economy. In 1881 he published *King's Mountain and Its Heroes*. He is now engaged on a life of Gen. George Rogers Clark, for which he has a rich collection of materials. In 1871 the University of Wisconsin conferred on Mr. Draper the degree of LL. D. He is a member of the principal historical and antiquarian societies of the country.

DRAYTON, WILLIAM HENRY (1742-1779), an American statesman, was born at Drayton Hall, on Ashley River, S. C., September, 1742. He went to England in 1753, and was educated at Westminster School and Balliol College, Oxford. He returned to Carolina in 1764, and was an active writer on political affairs, taking the side of the government. Having revisited England, he was in 1771 appointed privy councillor for the province of South Carolina. He afterwards espoused the popular cause, and protested against the proceedings of his colleagues. In 1774 he was appointed judge of the province, and under the name of "Freeman" wrote a pamphlet addressed to the first Continental Congress, then in session, setting forth the grievances of the colonies and proposing a bill of rights. The line of conduct thus marked was substantially followed by the Congress. Being suspended from his office under the Crown, he was made a member of the popular committee of safety, and advised the seizure of the provincial arsenals. In 1775 he was president of the provincial congress, and was reinstated in his office under the State Constitution. In 1776 he was made chief-justice of the State, and a charge which he delivered to the grand-jury in April on the subject of independence being published, had great influence throughout the country. He was president of South Carolina in 1777, and a member of the Continental Congress in 1778-79. He died at Philadelphia, Sept. 3, 1779. He left a manuscript history of the revolution to the end of the year 1778, which was published by his son, Gov. John Drayton, in 1821.

DRED SCOTT CASE, THE. This case, one of the most important in American history, was originally one of assault and battery. Dred Scott was the slave of Dr. Emerson, of the regular army, who in 1834 took him to Illinois, and thence in 1836 to Wisconsin. In 1838 the owner brought Dred back to Missouri. The line of Missouri decisions had held that such a transfer by the owner to free territory made the slave a free man, and that the conditions of servitude would not reattach on a return to slave soil. In 1848 Dred brought suit against his owner for assault and battery, and obtained a verdict in a State court. The case was appealed to the State Supreme Court, which in 1852 reversed the former line of decisions, and sent the case back to the lower court. Here it remained in abeyance, for the case had passed into the Federal Courts. Emerson had sold Dred and his family to John F. A. Sandford, of New York; and, as Dred and Sandford were "citizens of different States," Dred transferred the suit to the Federal Circuit Court for Missouri. Sandford pleaded to the jurisdiction of the court, asserting that Dred was not a citizen of Missouri, but "a negro of African descent; his ancestors were of pure African blood, and were brought into this country and sold as negro slaves." Dred answered this by a demurrer; that is, he claimed legal status as a citizen, even on defendant's own showing, and the demurrer was sustained. Sandford answered over, and pleaded in bar that Dred was his slave, and that he had only "gently laid hands" on him to restrain him, as he had a right to do. The court charged in Sandford's favor, and Dred carried the case, by exception, to the Supreme Court. (See Dred Scott *vs.* Emerson, 15 Missouri *Rep.*, 682, and authorities cited at the end of this article.)

By this time circumstances had made the case a pivot of national importance. When the United States acquired the vast territory of Louisiana in 1803, no steps were taken to prevent the custom of slavery from spreading through it. Louisiana was admitted in 1812 as a slave State, and when Missouri applied for admission it also came as a slave State. Here Congress attempted to retrace its steps, and a struggle was begun for the purpose of compelling Missouri to come in as a free State. For the first time a united North and a united South were opposed on a question of slavery; but the South had the nine points of possession in its favor, and Missouri entered as a slave State in 1820, on a compromise. Slavery was thereafter forever prohibited in the province of Louisiana, north of latitude 36° 30′, outside of Missouri. Now Fort Snelling, to which Dred had been taken by his owner in 1836, was in this part of Louisiana, in which Congress had prohibited slavery in 1820; and the Missouri Supreme Court had really only decided that Emerson had not intended to change his domicile, and that the local law of Missouri had reattached upon Dred when he returned to that State. This question of reattachment, then, would seem to have been the question before the United States Supreme Court, since the Federal Circuit Court was bound by the judiciary act of 1789 to follow State court constructions, when not in conflict with the Constitution. On this point the Supreme Court (Justices McLean and Curtis dissenting) sustained the State court, and directed the Federal Circuit Court to dismiss the case for want of jurisdiction.

Intervening events, however, had dove-tailed in so exactly with various features of the Dred Scott case that the individual justices were carried far beyond the main question in their opinions. During the years 1846–48 every attempt to vote money for the purchase of territory from Mexico had been met with the "Wilmot proviso," so called from David Wilmot, of Pennsylvania, who first introduced it, that slavery should be prohibited in any territory thus to be acquired. For two-and-a-half years after the acquisition of California and New Mexico in 1848, the organization of civil governments in those Territories had been prevented by a persistent attempt to add the Wilmot proviso. Finally, in 1850, this struggle ended in another compromise. California was admitted as a free State; Utah and New Mexico were organized as Territories without mention of slavery; the fugitive slave law was made far more stringent; and the sale of slaves in the District of Columbia was forbidden. The territorial feature of the compromise seems to have meant all things to all men; some alleged, some denied, that it meant to give the territorial legislature complete control of slavery. It seems to have given such control in fact, in this way: Territorial legislatures have the power of legislation within their spheres, unless vetoed by act of Congress; this compromise gave them an initiative power which it would be difficult to unite both houses in vetoing; and, as a result, both Utah and New Mexico allowed slavery before 1860, while the United States Senate balked every attempt to veto their action. In so far, the Wilmot proviso was a failure, except in California.

Until 1854 the power of Congress to forbid slavery in the Territories seems to have been quite generally admitted. There was no plain denial of the power of Congress to forbid slavery in the north-west territory in 1787, or in Louisiana, north of 36° 30′, in 1820. The special feeling of the South in 1850 seems to have been that the North had not favored the Mexican war, that the South had done most of the fighting to win the Mexican acquisitions, and that this was a special case in which positive prohibition of slavery would be unfair. The northern Democratic party, led by Cass and Douglas, sympathized with this feeling far enough to induce it simply to refrain from prohibiting slavery in Utah and New Mexico. It took but four years to carry this point of pure expediency up to a constitutional *obligation* to refrain from prohibiting slavery in any Territory whatever. And thus, when the Territories of Kansas and Nebraska came to be organized in 1854, although they lay within the limits where slavery had been prohibited in 1820, Douglas led his party in repudiating the compromise of 1820 as unconstitutional and void, and in formally handing over all powers of slavery legislation to the territorial legislature. The result was the inauguration of a desperate struggle, rising at times to a local civil war, between North and South, for the control of Kansas. (See KANSAS.)

Before the Kansas struggle had gone very far, it was apparent that the South was at a disadvantage so great as to be insuperable. Slavery could only obtain a secure foothold anywhere as a *custom*, fortifying itself slowly by the building up of vested interests until the mass became too great for interference. But the attempt to establish such a custom in Kansas was a hazarding of valuable property on the issue of a doubtful struggle. There were no border States between freedom and slavery in Kansas, and few slaves were sent there. As the result of the struggle became more evident, the influential Southerners drifted steadily to the ground which had been maintained by Calhoun from 1837 until his death, that slaves were property, that the Constitution was intended to protect property, and that Congress, the creature of the Constitution, was bound to protect the rights of property in the Territories. A negative refusal to suppress slavery in the Territories was no longer sufficient. Congress must actively protect slavery in the Territories.

On the main point, the denial of jurisdiction, the majority of the court was coherent. On the other points, dragged into the case by the peculiar state of political discussion, and by the wide sweep of the arguments on both sides, the majority was altogether incoherent, and it is not easy to say how far the various opinions have authority, and how far they are mere *obiter dicta*. The longest and most important opinion was that of Chief-Justice Taney. Its leading feature was its attempt to prove historically that, as negroes had not come to the United States voluntarily as persons, but involuntarily as merchandise and property, and as they had not been regarded as citizens when the Constitution was framed, they could never, even by emancipation, acquire the status of citizens. This point was so strongly made and supported that, after the ratification of the Thirteenth Amendment in 1865, it was felt to be necessary to ratify the Fourteenth Amendment, to establish the status of the freedmen as citizens. It was in this part of the opinion that the chief-justice used the phrase, so often misquoted, that, for more than a century before the Declaration of Independence, negroes had been regarded as beings of an order "so far inferior that they had no rights which the white man was bound to respect."

On the other point, not directly involved in the case, if the main point as to jurisdiction was correctly held, the chief-justice was equally emphatic. He held that "the only power conferred" on Congress in regard to slavery in the Territories was "the power, coupled with the duty, of guarding and protecting the owner in his rights." The Calhoun doctrine could have asked no more definite indorsement than this; and, as a consequence, the opinion of the court went on to declare that "the act of Congress [of 1820] which prohibited a citizen from holding and owning property of this kind in the territory of the United States north of the line therein mentioned [lat. 36° 30'] is not warranted by the Constitution, and is therefore void; and that neither Dred Scott himself, nor any of his family, were made free by being carried into this territory, even if they had been carried there by the owner with the intention of becoming a permanent resident." To appreciate fully the violence with which this point was dragged into the opinion, the reader must remember that the court had already decided that it had no jurisdiction of the case in any event, even if Dred Scott had been freed, which meant in effect that the Missouri compromise had nothing to do with the case.

The case was argued finally before the court at December term, 1856, but judgment was deferred until March 6, 1857. From that time the South felt that its position in regard to slavery in the Territories was supported by the highest judicial authority in the United States. One great reason for secession was the fear that a Republican president and Congress, by new appointments or by an increase in the number of justices, would change the majority of the Supreme Court and overturn the Dred Scott decision.

See Dred Scott vs. Sandford, 19 Howard's *Rep.*, 393; Tyler's *Life of R. B. Taney*, 373, 578; 2 B. R. Curtis's *Works*, 213; 9 Curtis's *Rep.*, 72; Benton's *Examination of the Dred Scott Decision*; Hurd's *Law of Freedom and Bondage*; 13 Benton's *Debates of Congress*, 577; 1 Draper's *Civil War*, 407; 2 A. H. Stephens's *War Between the States*, 260; Buchanan's *Administration*, 48; 2 Wilson's *Rise and Fall of the Slave Power*, 523.   (A. J.)

DRILL. This is a tool or instrument for making round holes in hard substances. A drill for metal consists of three parts, the shank, the body, and the cutting-edges. The *shank* is that portion which serves as a means of attachment to the spindle of the apparatus used for rotating the drill, and through which the motion and force are imparted. A common form of shank, for rough work, is of square section, each side being tapered towards the end at the rate of about one in twelve, thus being in the shape of a frustum of a square pyramid. It enters into a corresponding cavity or mortise in the end of the spindle or chuck, and makes a strong and efficient means of imparting the force of rotation to the drill. An advantage of this form of shank is, that it can be readily forged from a square bar of steel and fitted to the chuck. The objection to it is the difficulty of making the mortise in the chuck correctly, either as to the equality of its sides or the coincidence of its axis with the axis of rotation.

Another common form of shank is cylindrical. The tool is fitted to a cylindrical hole in the chuck, and held there by means of a set-screw bearing against a flat place on the side of the cylindrical shank. This form is the most easily made, whether in the rough or turned. The objection to it is, that the shank cannot be made to fit the hole exactly, and consequently, when the set-screw is tightened, the axis of the former will be forced away from that of the latter, and then, no matter how accurately the drill may have been made to have its cutting-edges of equal lengths and at equal angles with its axis, the latter cannot exactly correspond with the axis of rotation. Another objection is the continual bruising of the flat on the cylinder and the upsetting of the end of the set-screw. This form of shank is good if used in a clamping chuck, the jaws of which will always hold it concentrically with the spindle, but as such a chuck holds merely by friction, its use is confined to small drills.

An improvement on this form of shank was effected by tapering it, or making it the frustum of a cone instead of a cylinder, the flat on the side and the set-screw being the same as before. In this case the fit of the shank in the chuck can be made perfect, but, in tightening the set-screw, the shank is liable to be forced forward in the socket. The taper of this shank should be outside of the angle of friction, so that it will readily come out on releasing the set-screw.

Another form of shank, and the one most generally used with accurately made drills and for good work, is also in the form of a frustum of a cone, but with the sides more nearly parallel than in the preceding, the taper being such that the friction will hold it firmly in the chuck. From one-half to three-quarters of an inch taper to the foot is generally used. The small end of the shank is flattened on two opposite sides for a short distance, forming a tenon, which fits into a corresponding mortise in the bottom of the taper hole in the chuck. The force of rotation is imparted through this mortise and tenon. The mortise is extended entirely through the diameter of the chuck, and is made enough longer than the tenon to admit of a taper wedge being driven in behind the tenon in order to force the shank out of the hole whenever desired. An efficient system of shanks and chucks of this kind is very largely used for drills from one-quarter of an inch diameter up. A set of drills, say from one-quarter to two inches, are arranged in four divisions, all the drills of each division having one standard size of shank. If, now, the spindles of the drilling machines and lathes in an establishment have similar taper sockets, and the chucks for the drills have shanks to fit these spindles, an interchangeable system of great value is provided. Although this form of shank is good still it is open to the objection that the tenons frequently fail by being twisted off. To overcome this, one of the best engineering establishments omits the tenon, but cuts a key-seat the entire length of the taper shank, and inserts a corresponding key in the taper hole of the chuck. A mortise is cut through the chuck at the bottom of the hole as before, but only for the purpose of inserting a taper wedge to remove the drill.

Another excellent form of shank, particularly adapted to large drills and boring-bars, has a more obtuse taper with a short parallel screw-thread at one or the other end. The taper parts of shank and chuck are accurately fitted together to secure proper allignment, while the screw threads are loosely fitted, their functions being merely to draw the taper parts firmly together, and to receive the torsional strain.

The *body* of the *drill* is that portion between the shank and the cutting-edges. In *flat* drills or *fly* drills, which are forged to shape, the part next the shank is usually of the form of the original bar of steel for a short distance, then is gradually drawn down smaller than the size of the drill, and afterwards flattened and spread laterally until the size is slightly exceeded, the width of this flat being kept parallel for a short distance at the end of the drill, to prevent the size being diminished by the grinding away of the cutting-edges. The thickness of this flat at the point varies from one-fourth to one-eighth of its width, according to the size of the drill. The forging is not hardened, but is first centred at both ends. And the shank is turned and tenoned or key-seated to fit the chuck. The edges of the flat part are filed or ground to size, and the drill is then rotated with the chuck and straightened until the axes of the two coincide. It is then hardened and tempered to the right degree for a short distance at the point, and is complete except the cutting-edges. Many modifications of this style of body are in use, depending on the purposes intended and the tastes of the makers; but such frequent re-dressings are required to maintain the standard size that it probably costs more in the end than the more complete and finished forms to be described hereafter. Forged drills are sometimes made by drawing down the body to a flat somewhat narrower than the size of the drill, and extending from the shank to the point, and then twisting this flat into a spiral for its entire length.

The best modern drills are entirely machine-made, and possess many advantages, among which may be mentioned: 1st, the straightness of the body and the coincidence of its axis and point with the axis of rotation, so that, on inserting the shank into the chuck, the drill will be sure to revolve concentrically; 2d, their adaptation to a system of standard sizes; 3d, their ultimate cheapness, due to the smaller number required in proportion to the aggregate work performed, the greater care with which they are used, and the much less attention they demand to maintain them in good condition and of standard size.

Machine-made drills.—In the *Flat* or *Fly-Drill*, the body is turned, for its whole length, slightly above the required size. Flats are milled on two opposite sides, leaving the thickness tapering from the point nearly to the shank, in order to increase the strength. It is then hardened, straightened, and tempered, and the body is ground accurately to size in a lathe, or preferably in a machine which gives a very slight clearance to the edges of the body. With proper facilities for grinding the cutting-edges such a drill will last a long time, will always be straight and true, and in condition for accurate work, and will drill holes of an approximately uniform size until it is almost entirely used up by the grinding of the cutting edges.

The *Straight-fluted Drill* is one whose body is turned as before, but has two grooves instead of flats, milled on the opposite sides. These grooves are of such shape as to make each cutting-edge a straight line, while the other edge at the end of the groove is a curve. It is claimed that these drills are stronger than flat drills, that they preserve their sizes better, cut more rapidly, make straighter holes, and possess many advantages; but opinions differ as to these claims. Both kinds make good drills, particularly for use in a horizontal position.

The *Twist Drill* is very largely used on account of its being adapted for almost any requirement. In this drill the body is turned and is fluted with two *spiral grooves*, the pitch of the spiral depending on the diameter of the drill. These grooves are also of such shape as to make each cutting-edge a straight line. The portion of the cylindrical surface which is left between the grooves is rather less than the width of the groove, so that the width of each groove at the circumference is more than one-fourth of this circumference. The spiral of the grooves gives the cutting-edges a slight under-cut or lip, which is not found in either the straight-fluted or flat drills, and which in many kinds of work is advantageous. In some twist-drills the spiral has an increasing pitch, being less at the point and increasing towards the shank; but no good reason can be given for this, and experience has shown no advantage arising from it. The bodies of these drills have a slight clearance on the cylindrical surface between the grooves, which is usually filed in them before hardening but should be ground by a machine after hardening, in order to insure its being uniform.

The *Cannon Drill* is used for very long holes, particularly in wrought-iron or steel. In this drill the body is cylindrical for a distance of from three to six diameters from the point, and has but one groove and one cutting-edge. The groove has straight sides at an angle of from 90° to 120° with each other, and is made by first drilling a hole of small diameter, but of considerable length, along the axis of the cylinder, and milling the groove to this hole. The end of the cylinder is turned conical, with the included angle about 140°, and, after the groove is made, is ground or filed with a clearance from the cutting-edge in the form of a spiral of an angle of from 3° to 5°. In using this drill a hole of slight depth, but of the exact size and central with the axis of rotation, is first made, and, the drill being started in this hole, will follow a remarkably straight path, being guided entirely by the fit of its short cylindrical body. Beyond this part of the body, with its groove, the remainder is of smaller diameter, to make room for the chips or cuttings, and to permit the ready introduction of lubricants.

There are several other special forms of bodies of drills, the limited use of which renders it unnecessary to enumerate them.

The *Cutting-edges* are the most important part of all drills, and the most difficult to make in a correct and accurate manner. To understand their requirements and to comprehend the principles involved it is best to analyze the work they perform or the surfaces they produce. If we examine the bottom of a hole which has been drilled partially through a piece of metal, we shall find its surface to have the form of the frustum of a cone. If we turn a bar of steel to fit this hole (that is, with a conical end and flat circle at the point), and then mill off two opposite sides, leaving the thickness equal to the circle at the point, we shall have advanced in the direction of a correct drill. The body will be of the correct size, and the end edges, or what are eventually to be the cutting-edges, will be of equal lengths, and will make the same angle with the axis. On revolving this in the hole and forcing it down the end will not cut, but merely rub, as it conforms exactly to the shape of the bottom of the hole. To make it cut the edges must be given a proper clearance, precisely as in a turning-tool or planing-tool for cutting metal. In the latter we make the face form an angle of from 3° to 5° with the work, while the included angle of the two faces of the tool itself ranges from 45° to 90°, according to its purposes. In the present case the surface to be cut is that of a hollow cone. If we make the face of the cutter with a similar conical surface, but with clearance—that is to say, if a normal to the conical surface of the cutter makes an angle of about 5° with a normal to the conical surface of the work, the face of the cutter will be in the best possible shape for drilling iron or steel. For drilling brass a greater angle should be used. If now we give to each end-face of the drill this conical shape, with the same eccentricity, their surfaces will intersect, forming a wedge-shaped point or what is called a chisel-point, which is the best disposition that can be made of the thickness of the drill at the point. This chisel-point does not cut, but merely scrapes, and in large drills, which have considerable thickness, it consumes quite an amount of the force required to rotate and to feed the drill. The shape of the front face of the drill, the intersection of which with the conical face just considered forms the cutting-edge, depends on the shape of the body. In flat drills this face makes an angle of more than 90° with the surface being cut. This form is good for brass and steel, but for general purposes a less angle is desirable; and this is obtained in flat drills by forging them with a lip at each cutting-edge, while in twist-drills the spiral groove accomplishes the same result, with the advantage that successive grindings do not alter it, as the angle of the spiral continues for almost the entire length of the body of the drill.

The requirements of correct cutting-edges for drills are such as to make their production a difficult matter, particularly if ground by hand. Unless both cutting-edges are precisely the same, not only in length, but also in the angle made with the axis and in the kind and amount of clearance, the size and form of the hole drilled will not be reliable. The difficulty of correctly grinding twist-drills by hand is greater than that of flat drills, and this at one time threatened to be a serious obstacle to the general introduction of the former. The invention of drill-grinding machines has gradually and progressively overcome the difficulties of the case, until there is now a machine which will grind the cutting-edges of drills of any kind or size, within its capacity, in a theoretically perfect manner. In this machine the drill is held by the two opposite corners of the cutting-edges and by the centre at the end of the shank; so that, after grinding one edge, the drill can be turned over and the other edge ground of the same length, angle, and clearance, regardless of any crookedness or imperfection in the body. The mechanism which holds the drill is contained in a frame which can be partially rotated about an axis at an angle with the flat face of a grinding-wheel, so that the surface ground will be that of a cone about this axis. The axis of the drill does not coincide with this axis, but bears such a relationship to it that the conical surface has the proper eccentricity. The relationship between these two axes adjusts itself automatically to suit the diameter of the drill being ground. Drills ground on a machine of this kind can be depended on to make holes of uniform size with a minimum expenditure of power and waste of drill.

Drilling Machines, in which are used the drills already considered, are of various designs, the essential features being: a strong stiff spindle to hold the drill; a means of rotating this spindle at varying speeds to suit the different sizes of drills and with sufficient force to make the drill cut the metal; a means of traversing this spindle lengthwise, during the rotation, to maintain the proper amount of cut for each revolution; a means of varying this traverse or feed to suit the character of the material being drilled; and a means of firmly holding the work in the best manner to resist the thrust and the torsional strain of the cut, and to adjust it to the desired position. The various forms of drill used in boring stone are shown in the article COAL. (W. H. T.)

DROSERACEÆ. In this natural order of plants are found the remarkable "Venus's flytrap," *Dionœa muscipula*, and the no less curious and interesting genus *Drosera*, or the "sundew." The order has been a difficult one to understand in regard to its relation to other orders of plants. Dr. Lindley in his arrangement places it in his Berberidal alliance, and suggests a relationship with grapes and fumitories; Professor Asa Gray places it between violets and rock-roses on the one side and St. John's worts on the other. The order *Droseraceæ*, as defined by Prof. Gray, consists of bog-herbs, mostly glandular-haired, with regular hypogynous flowers, pentamerous and withering; persistent calyx, corolla, and stamens, the anthers fixed by their middle and turned outward; and a one-celled pod, with twice as many styles or stigmas as there are parietal placentæ. The leaves are circinate in the bud; that is, rolled up from the apex to the base, as in ferns. There are but seven genera in the order—*Drosera, Aldrovanda, Dionœa, Byblis, Drosophyllum, Roridula*, and *Sondera*—found by some representative in North and South America, Europe, Cape of Good Hope, Madagascar, New Holland, China, and the East Indies, generally in bogs and morasses or in moist, sandy places. Of these, only the three first named have found a place in popular literature, but the history of *Drosera*, and *Dionœa* particularly, has been one of great interest.

The *Dionœa*, or Venus's flytrap, is found only in North Carolina, in one comparatively limited area. It is an acaulescent plant, sending up a flower-stalk of from two to four inches high, and having comparatively small and by no means attractive white flowers. The leaves form a rosette around the base of the flower-stalks, and are about two inches long, formed of a narrow, flattened leaf-stalk, and with a broad, two-lobed lamina at the apex. This blade is somewhat thick and fleshy, and is furnished with long tapering ciliæ or teeth. When an insect or any substance falls on this fleshy face the lobes instantly close and capture whatever may have excited them. The name "flytrap" is derived from this behavior. It is singular that the history of the discovery of this remarkable plant should be unknown. Mr. William Canby, in an able paper contributed to the *Gardener's Monthly*, August, 1868, remarks: "It was discovered about one hundred years since, probably by John Bartram, as Ellis, the English naturalist, who first brought the plant into notice and gave it its botanical name, states in his letter to Linnæus that in 1765 his friend Peter Collinson had given him a dried specimen which he had received from Bartram." But Sir James Smith (*Selections of the Correspondence of Linnæus*, vols. i. and ii.) states that "the *Dionœa* was first brought to this country in the summer of 1768 by Mr. Young, gardener to the queen; and Mr. Ellis described it, and had a drawing and a plate engraved from a plant which flowered in his chambers the following August. It was from this plate and his characters of the plant that Linnæus's description was drawn up for his *Mantissa*." Little is known of Young's travels. From a note in *The American Handbook of Ornamental Trees*, p. 117, it appears he was known in America as the "king's botanist," that he was regarded as a sort of rival to John Bartram, and owned a place contiguous to Bartram's near Philadelphia, on which he planted a few trees, some of which survived to be referred to in the work cited. William Bartram, in his *Travels*, published in 1791, says, referring to *Dionœa:* "This wonderful plant seems to be distinguished in the creation by the Author of Nature with faculties eminently superior to every other vegetable production; specimens of it were first communicated to the curious of the Old World by John Bartram, the American botanist and traveller, who contributed as much if not more than any other man towards enriching the North American botanical nomenclature, as well as its natural history." It may be Bartram sent the dried, and Young carried the living, plants. It has been a question whether the plant derives any benefit from the insects caught. Kirby and Spence (*Introduction to Entomology* (1818), vol. i. p. 295) give the experiments of "a gardener, Mr. Knight," who put raw beef on the leaves, and the plant was more luxuriant than others not so treated. This Mr. Knight was afterwards the founder of the celebrated nurseries of Knight & Perry of Chelsea, often referred to in Mr. Loudon's works. The same experiment was tried by Mr. Wm. Canby in 1868, and reported in the magazine already cited, and with like results. Mr. Darwin (*Insectivorous Plants*, ch. xiii. p. 301, Am. ed.) tried a few experiments on *Dionæa*, which "were amply sufficient to prove that it [the leaf] digests." Mr. Peter Henderson, a well-known plant-grower of New York, published an account of some experiments differing from these conclusions, but the general belief is that the plant actually eats the insects it captures.

The sundews, species of *Drosera*, are also famous in connection with the history of insectivorous plants. They are small perennial plants, sometimes tufted, at other times branching, with the flowers ranged on one side of a short scape; and with the glands, which usually cover the whole plant, but especially the leaves, exuding drops of viscid liquid. It is from this fact that the name *Drosera* is derived, the Greek *droseros* signifying dewy. Unlike the other representative of the order *Dionæa*, which is limited to so small an area, droseras are found in most of the temperate regions of the earth, and some of the individual species are common alike to Europe and America. Over one hundred species have been described, but the genus is variable, and many species will probably be reduced to mere varieties. The species of the United States are *D. Anglica, D. brevifolia, D. capillaris, D. filiformis, D. rotundifolia, D. linearis,* and *D. intermedia*. Of these, *D. Anglica* and *D. rotundifolia* not only grow in the Atlantic United States, as well as in Europe, but are also found on the Pacific coast; *D. brevifolia* and *D. capillaris* are confined to the South and South-west; *D. linearis* and *D. intermedia* are Northern species; and the curious *D. filiformis* is found only along the sea-coast from Massachusetts to Florida.

The chief interest attaches to their insect-catching and insect-eating proclivities, which have been so clearly made manifest by Charles Darwin's famous work on *Insectivorous Plants*. That the viscid glands are means by which the plant captures insects and uses them for food was suspected before Charles Darwin undertook the proof of it. His grandfather, Erasmus Darwin, supposed these glands were for the purpose of preventing small insects from infesting the leaves, but he adds, "Mr. Wheatley, an eminent surgeon in Cateaton Street, London, observed these leaves to bend upward when an insect settled on them, like the leaves of the *Muscipula veneris* (Venus's flytrap), and pointing all their globules of mucus to the centre—that they completely entangled and destroyed it" (*Botanic Garden*, canto i., note to line 230). It is remarkable that, so far as it appears from Mr. Charles Darwin's elaborate work on the *Drosera*, he had wholly overlooked this observation of his grandfather made three-quarters of a century before, which his own experiment tended so remarkably to confirm. The great practical value of Mr. Darwin's researches in *Drosera* is that he shows that the viscid glands of plants have a use never before suspected—namely, that of absorbing for the use of the plant nitrogen from the atmosphere, instead of by the roots solely, as had been the belief hitherto. Darwin's observations have been confirmed by observers in America. Mrs. Mary Treat of Vineland, N. J., having shown that the long, slender-leaved species of that section coils back over an insect when caught till it looks like the uncoiled frond of a fern. Dr. Hooker has found in an Australian species an attempt to form an appendage as in *Dionæa*, from which it may be inferred that the latter is a develop ment from a Droseraceous parent. (T. M.)

DROYSEN, JOHANN GUSTAV (1808–1884), a German historian, was born at Treptow, July 6, 1808. He graduated at Berlin, and became in 1829 a teacher in a gymnasium, in 1833 a private lecturer, and in 1835 a professor extraordinarius. In 1840 he was appointed professor of history at Kiel, where he soon took an active part on the German side in the Schleswig-Holstein controversy. He assisted in composing the *Staats und Erbrecht des Herzogthums Schleswig* (Kiel, 1846), and the *Aktenmässige Geschichte der dänischen Politik* (Hamburg, 1850). He was a representative of the provisional government of the duchies in the German Diet at Frankfort, and was afterward elected to the National Assembly. In 1851 he accepted a call as professor in the University of Jena, and devoted himself to historical studies. In 1859 he became professor in the University of Berlin, where he remained till his death, June 19, 1884.

Droysen's literary career was remarkable for its variety and productiveness. His first work, a translation of Æschylus, was published in 1832, and reached its third edition in 1868, while his translation of Aristophanes, published in 1836, reached its second edition in 1871. They are the standard German translations of these authors. Continuing his labors in ancient literature, he prepared a *History of Alexander the Great* (1833), a *History of Hellenism* (1836–43), and several essays on Greek subjects. While at Kiel, besides some political works written in company with others, he published lectures on the *History of the War for Freedom* (1846). While at Jena he published an excellent *Life of Field-marshal York of Wartenburg* (Berlin, 1851; 8th ed., 1878), which obtained great popularity. He also published several historical investigations and essays. These were chiefly preliminary to his great work, *Geschichte der preussischen Politik* (5 vols., 1855–81). In these, from original sources previously unused, he sets forth fully the development of Prussia which has resulted in the formation of the present German Empire. Among his other writings are—*Das Testament des Grossen Kurfürsten* (Leipsic, 1866), *Grundriss der Historik* (1868; 3d ed., 1882), and *Gustav Adolf* (1870). Under his editorial care many documents relating to the history of Frederick the Great were published. In his later years he resumed his investigations of Greek history, and issued some valuable dissertations. Throughout his career he was noted for his elegant style in speaking and writing, and for his persuasive and enthusiastic eloquence.

DRUPACEÆ. This is a name suggested by De Candolle, and adopted by Lindley, for a distinct natural order of plants to include the almond, peach, cherry, and plum, as distinct from the order *Rosaceæ*, defined by other botanists. In like manner he adopts *Pomaceæ* to cover the apple, pear, quince, and a few allied genera, while for *Rosaceæ* proper he reserves such plants as the rose, blackberry, raspberry, strawberry, cinquefoil, spiræa, and similar plants. A drupe is a fruit with one or two stones with kernels, which fruit, when ripening, has the outer portion of the pericarp fleshy; and it may be readily seen how the order *Drupaceæ* suggested itself for the plants named. The peach, however, not unfrequently has flowers with four, or even five, carpels, which they often will perfect. This is seen very often in the case of the semi-double flowered varieties. Again, the almond has a comparatively dry fruit. Dr. Asa Gray does not regard the distinction as of more than sectional value. He places all these plants under one order, *Rosaceæ*, subdividing it into *Amygdalæ, Rosaceæ*, and *Pomaceæ*. *Drupaceæ* of some authors will therefore come under Dr. Gray's sub-order *Amygdalæ*.

It is worthy of note that while the order *Rosaceæ* in general is wholly free from noxious qualities, the Drupaceous section is in many respects poisonous. The leaves and kernels yield large quantities of hydrocyanic acid. In a case known to the writer peach-leaves were fed one evening to several rabbits, which were all found dead the next morning. Oil of bitter almonds is a deadly poison, and prussic acid is abundant in peach-kernels. It is remarkable therefore that the flesh around the stones is always very wholesome.

(T. M.)

DUALISM. Dualism may be viewed as either (1) an ontological principle, or (2) a psychological assumption, or (3) a moral theory in practical philosophy.

I. *Moral Dualism* is grounded in a metaphysical principle (unconsciously assumed,) but it is of so great antiquity, and through religious sects has exerted so marked an influence on the progress of thought, that it will be convenient to consider it in the first place.

Parseism is, perhaps, the most thorough practical dualism, of ethical and religious content, of which we have any record; through Gnosticism and Manicheism it may be traced into the Middle Ages (e. g., the Albigenses; see Mosheim, 10th and 11th Cent.), if it be not even recognizable in sects and opinions of our own day.

The earliest distinct form of it is found in the Avesta, ascribed to Zoroaster (6th Cent. B. C.). In the first "Fargard," Ahura-Mazda (Ormuzd) speaks to holy Zarathustra (Zoroaster), recounting his creations, and opposing them to the creations of Angro-Mainyus (Ahriman) which he made through the Devas. The first created fertile lands, useful animals, summer, fire, light, and all good things; the other made deserts and winter, cattle-destroying wasps, injurious insects and devouring beasts, evil thoughts, unbelief, sloth, poverty, worship of idols, uncleanness, murder, the burning of the dead, and burying of corpses, plagues, war, pillage, snow, and earthquakes.

Here is already intimated that there are two eternal sources of good and of evil. Ormuzd is (figuratively) pure infinite light, creator of all that is good. His symbol is fire, and fire-worship is the ritual way of approaching and adoring him. Ahriman is the opposite of all this—impure darkness, the source of all evil. The dualism, as we observe, extends through all moral and physical nature, the soul, and the universe. Souls are created by Ormuzd, but, in leaving heaven, their native place, and entering earthly bodies, the struggle with Ahriman begins. This dualism is a simple and natural explanation of the existing and perplexing antinomies of the world and of human life. (See J. S. Mill, *Essays on Religion*, I.) If a subtle metaphysics attempted to reduce this dualism to monism, by the emanation of both Ormuzd and Ahriman from an undefinable first principle, or, the decline of Ahriman from good, this must be regarded as later, and it was of no permanent influence or value.

Persian influence may be recognized in early Christian sects, and most notably among the Manichees. The Gnostics, at Alexandria, Antioch, etc., in the time of Hadrian and succeeding emperors, show the results of a crude syncretism of Greek Philosophy, Christianity, and Persian dualism. Saturninus, Basilides, Marcion, Valentinus, etc., through all their fantastic forms of "Gnosis," agree in their practical, ethical dualism of God and Matter. The first-begotten emanation from Deity had only the semblance of humanity, and could not really suffer death upon a cross. For the material world is evil, and nature itself is the evil principle standing over against spirit and what is good in complete opposition. It follows that the flesh of man is the home of this evil, and hence comes a perpetual struggle between the spirit of man which is an emanation from the realm of light, and its corrupted material tabernacle. Emancipation by death, or by a stern asceticism, alone releases the soul from its bondage. Marriage is Satan's work. Only the souls of men are immortal; the body perishes forever.

Manicheism was a more consistent dualism, linked more directly with that of Persia, and of wider and more permanent influence. We know it best through the eloquent St. Augustine, at first a disciple, and then an earnest opponent, but extracting freely from Manichean documents, most of which are otherwise not extant. See especially in his works the book of Faustus the Manichean, with his refutation of it (Op. tom. viii.), and the Epistola Fundamenti of Manes himself, also quoted by St. Augustine in his reply to it. Manes appears to have belonged to the race of the Magi, and to have been skilled in their learning. We find him at the court of Sapor, highly successful in making converts, until jealousy on the part of the Magi seems to have brought about his death (about 278 A. D.).

The Lord of Light (GOD) and the Lord of Darkness (Hyle) are both eternal, self-existent, unchangeable. But the worlds of light and darkness, it would seem, were co-eternal with these principles. (Eternal emanations? If so, the dualism extends throughout all existences, as in Parseism.) The Lord of Light is called GOD, but it is evident that to the Manichees He cannot be infinite, for, on one side at least, He is limited by evil, by darkness. In fact we find this inference to have been accepted by them.

From both principles proceed emanations; the children of light, dwelling happily in the world of light; the offspring of darkness (demons) in perpetual discord and war. On this earth, and in men, continually goes on the great struggle between light and darkness. For man has a soul, the life of his body, derived from the evil, and a soul of light, which is an emanation from the good.

Man, then, is composed of matter from the world of darkness, in which dwell two souls, one being this evil animal principle; the other rational, immortal. The first man was descended from the Prince of Darkness, who had captured a portion of the light, and marriage is his device for perpetuating his sway.

As the body, together with the irrational soul, is evil and the work of the spirit of darkness, it is plain that the law of a true life requires an extirpation of all appetites. Dropping the fantastic drapery which enwraps the oriental thought and language, as we have done, it is not difficult to recognize popular ideas of our own age. The "*signaculum oris*" requires an abstinence from flesh and wine, and from the blasphemy which asserts one first cause for all things, and that the animal body is created by God, and that the Son of God was actually incarnate and died. The "*signaculum manuum*" requires abstinence from killing anima'-, and from acts of natural affection, and from labor for wealth. Finally, the "*signaculum sinûs*" enjoins perfect celibacy. For whoever procreates a body produces a new prison for a soul of light.

All this, however, belongs to the "*elect*." Souls thus perfect will return at death to the kingdom of light but those not purified must pass into other bodies until they shall have expiated their guilt, and been thoroughly cleansed. As for the "*auditors*," they may hope in a future life to pass into the bodies of the elect, and reach perfect bliss the sooner. (See Mosheim, *Comment.*, cent. iii., §§ 39–56, who discusses at great length and with copious quotations the fantastic oriental fables through which Manes and his followers presented their ethical principle.)

From this dualism, whether metaphysical or moral, Christian philosophy escaped by the doctrine of creation, together with that of the essentially *negative* character of evil. The one, absolute, infinite, and eternal Being needed no pre-existent matter (against the Peripatetic dualism of form or intelligence, and matter), from which to produce the multiplicity of finite beings. Yet they are not emanations from Him, but products of His will, wisdom, and love; that is, of Himself, who is known to us as one under those different relations. An existing dualism, therefore, of the finite and the infinite is grounded on the absolute and eternal One. The finite and sensible finds its unity with the other in that it is made after the pattern of the eternal Logos, who is, in eternity, generated by the one eternal principle. (S. Aug., *Confess.*, b. xi.)

The dualism of practical philosophy, also, was denied. There is no evil substance, for God made all things by nature good. Moral evil is a voluntary deprivation of good on the part of a creature possessed of freedom of choice, as darkness is privation of light, cold of heat, blindness of the power of sight. (S. Aug., *Confess.*, b. vii.; *De Ordine*, i. 6, 7; ii. 4.) Consequently, there is no perfectly evil being. Such would be a mere negation of existence. How or why any creatures voluntarily deprived themselves of part of the good which they had by nature, reason cannot explain; but the result is a higher good for the universe considered as a whole.

Mediæval ethics, as a part of Christian philosophy, without extending these principles, reduced them to more systematic form; ethical dualism, in opposition to Manichean influences still prevalent, being avoided in the same manner.

Good and being are in essence one; the difference is relative to us, the good adding to the concept of being the attribute of desirableness (rationem appetibilis; Aquinas, *Sum. Theol.*, I., v. 1). Every entity, as entity, is good (3), and is called evil in being deprived of what it has by nature. A kingdom of darkness, ruled over by an absolutely evil being, is denied; for such would directly conflict with the principle of creation, and involve a concept contradictory to that of the Divine Infinity (I. 49, 3). There is no existing being evil by nature (I. 63, 4); and when Christian ethics speak of a devil, they simply indicate subordination among the ranks of corrupted (spiritual, intellectual) creatures called demons.

A metaphysical principle underlies these propositions (monism), but they are made a part of ethics.

In the moral sphere, indeed, is found an existing dualism; viz., in the voluntary exterior or interior acts of a rational creature. But these, if evil, are so through *deficiency*, (1) in being imperfect as actions (*Prim. Sec.*, xviii. 1); (2) in that the action itself (objectum) is not that which is due and proper (conveniens, not in itself, but) relatively to the agent; (3) in wanting due circumstances or accidents; (4) in being directed to an inferior good (relatively to the agent) in place of a higher.

Against Manichean dualism, also, the animal passions in themselves have no ethical character (xxiv. 1); and virtue is a habit (voluntary) directed to these as well as to the other parts of human nature (lv.). It follows that vice is contrary to nature (lxxi. 2).

Does moral evil, then, conflict with the unity of the first principle? Or do good and evil both proceed from God? Both are denied: the first, because evil is only deficiency; the second, because, although the act, as entity, is from God, the evil deficiency is not, but from the free choice of a rational creature. Further than this mediæval thought did not proceed. Neither can it be said that, following these lines, philosophy has since made any development. Our view of ethical dualism is, therefore, arrested at this point.

The problem still remains, viz., to bring the moral dualism of the empirical sphere into harmony with the fundamental monism founded on Being, one, infinite, perfect, absolute.

II. *Ontological Dualism.*—Metaphysical dualism rests upon the fundamental antithesis found in all thought, in all knowledge, etc., that if we know or think anything, in every judgment, even the most primary, the most elementary, there must be an object-thought or notion, which is distinguished, in the very act of thinking, from the subject thinker. Without this distinction of subject and object, of ego and non-ego, thought itself becomes impossible; for identification of the two, says the dualist, is the annihilation of all distinction, and in it, of knowledge and thought. Truth and falsehood are merged in the abyss of the indistinguishable and the unconscious. Even in denying this duality, we should still be asserting it; in trying to escape from it, shadowy though it be, like our own shadow it would still pursue us.

The final demand of reason, it may be admitted, is for unity. But dualism asserts that anything beyond its principles transcends our limited faculties, is simply unprovable assumption, difficult to be expressed, impossible to be defined. Proofs are out of the question, and the seeker after truth is offered only a collection of incoherent propositions, whose contradictories may often be predicated with equal probability, since there is no evidence of either, no logical sequence, and, sometimes, little, if any, clear sense.

Monism, however, replies that distinction belongs to the logical understanding with its discursive processes of thought; but only the higher intuitions of reason can satisfy the mind. It does not deny the practical distinctions of dualism, but seeks to explain their origin, rising on reason's wings into a higher sphere.

Taking up, then, the problem of knowledge by asking what we can know of permanent and substantial being, there seem to be three possible answers to the question:

(1) We can know nothing but appearances. If anything lie beyond them, it is also beyond all human power of knowledge. But a more critical investigation leads us to observe that appearances must be *appearances to some subject*, and, consequently, that our first statement must be modified thus: "All knowing and all that is known, all intelligence and all intelligible reality indifferently consist in a relation between subject and object" (Prof. Green, *Contemporary Review*, December, 1877). It is evident, then, that nothing but relativity can be known, and we are limited to this fundamental dualism of subject and object. Anything beyond it will be purely transcendent hypothesis, however necessary this hypothesis may be.

(2) At the opposite extreme of thought monism asserts that we may know the substantial unity of all that is. Beneath all appearances is found one permanent, changeless reality, their ground, their unity, the fixed and only true being which reveals itself in and through all change. This may be ego or matter, God or the universe, or simply an inconceivable x, of which we can predicate nothing but that it is, even if existence itself do not unduly determine it.

(3) We find what Sir William Hamilton (*Met. Lect.*, xvi.) calls "natural dualism," or "natural realism." This recognizes the duality of ego and non-ego as given directly in consciousness, "in equal counterpoise and independence."

Realists, if also dualists, assume, in opposition to pure idealism, that we know the existence of substantial beings of two wholly different natures, in and through their phenomenal appearances, viz., spirit and matter (*Reid's Inquiry*, etc. cii. § 7; Essay, ii., passim). But, as this theory will lead us to "psychological dualism," it may, for the present, be deferred.

But the realist may be a monist. (a) His only (formal) dualism may be that of Bishop Berkeley (*Princ. Hum. Knowledge*, §§ 1, 7), viz., of ideas and a sentient spirit, the only substance which can be known. This, consequently, is a pure monism, substance being one only. The dualism of subject and object may still seem to be preserved as the Ultima Thule of knowledge, but the former, as substantial being, comprehends the latter as a modification of it. If, as Berkeley maintained (avoiding Fichte's later egoistic monism), ideas have, necessarily, an objective source, since they are not the product of simple spontaneity of thought, we shall reach an existing dualism once more, viz., that of finite and infinite spirit, the latter a being who stands over against the subject, and is distinguished, at least negatively, from the conscious mind which knows these ideas. But, of course, this present dualism is grounded in the absolute eternal One.

(b) The monistic realist may be found at the opposite extreme which the good bishop so earnestly opposed. The one substance is matter; and spirit, so called, is but a name for an aggregate of certain phenomena of this one reality.

This materialism was a natural form of thought when the early Ionian thinker looked out upon the world, entirely ignoring himself who was contemplating it. His only inquiry, then, could be, What is the primitive form of matter which underlies all appearances? Is it water, air, fire, or many material elements with permanent distinctions for us, though essentially one? But this childish speculation must, sooner or later, yield to the deeper thought of Anaxagoras; and Nous (intelligence), as a co-existing, co-eternal principle, directing and arranging eternal matter, supplies the other element of an objective dualism which emerges from the Ionian (empirical) school. Monism must find a surer support in purely ontological speculation; and Parmenides by identifying all thought and all being paved the way for the widespread, influential, and permanent monism of the Neo-Platonic thinkers.

(c) But the concept of matter itself will need definition. Is it extended substance? Is it passive force, resistance? Is it both? Is it (local) centres of action and passive force? And the result of this criticism will be that the one substance will be called indifferently mind or matter, since its phenomena are two-sided; and when, by a sort of mental squinting, or, rather, in avoiding this, by a one-eyed view, we regard the subjective side of the phenomena, we shall speak of mind; and when we regard the objective side, we shall speak of matter (H. Spencer's *Psychology*, § 63).

Such, in various forms, are the ordinary realist dualisms and monisms of modern philosophy, until, at least, we reach those ontological speculations which endeavor to establish the fundamental unity of all being and all knowledge.

(a) The subject itself, the conscious ego, may be regarded as the only known substance, and the object as its product evolved from it. In which case an extreme idealism will end in egoistic monism (Fichte), the absolute antipodes of that theoretic materialism, now practically expelled from the most modern schools of thought, which regards mind as a function of extended substance.

(b) It is possible to maintain a direct intuition of the absolute as the unity of subject and object (*Philosophy of Identity*). These are only the differentiated revelations of the one only substance. Nature is the objective manifestation of God; thought in us the subjective manifestation (*Pantheistic Idealism*).

(c) Finally, we may try to avoid metaphysical dualism through the philosophy of the absolute (Hegel) in which thought = being; and the process and evolution of thought is the process and evolution of being. It is certainly possible to construct a highly logical and well-connected edifice of this ontological monism, for Hegel has done so, and it has proved wonderfully fertile in practical results. But if, unfortunately, it has been evolved out of a conscious mind, and, possessing logical truth, fails to establish itself by any other criterion of concrete reality—if, in Hegel's thought, as in all conscious acts of knowledge, the self and not-self are still mutually conditioning one another, even in his elaborate evolution of the all from the one, we shall not seem to have made much progress in actual knowledge, when we contemplate this ingenious edifice of dreamland. For we are still able to assume that the ego has built this logical edifice; or that this thought itself is but a manifestation of an absolute being, the only eternal reality, becoming conscious in man. However logically the parts of our scheme are dovetailed together, in transcending consciousness, we shall not only reach a sphere of contradictions between facts of experience and our ontology, but a sphere where fixed concepts and definitions have no place. Anything may be derived from anything, because we have no criterion of the certainty of our original assumption, or of the reality and validity of what we assume. Grant to Spinoza his primal notion of substance ("Id quod in se est, et per se concipitur; hoc est id cujus conceptus non indiget conceptu alterius rei a quo formari debeat." Ethica, I. Def. 3) as the only objective reality, and logic will carry him to the end. But one who wishes to know the truth will first compare the definition with his experience of an actual world, or else hold it as only a provisional hypothesis, whose results are to be tested and verified. So, also, if thought is being and being is thought, all thoughts may claim equal reality; and we may deny Hegel's assumptions with warrant equal to his.

III. *Psychological Dualism.*—It is possible to pursue a strictly psychological method in philosophy, endeavoring to examine with strict accuracy, and to analyze with impartial fidelity the facts given in consciousness, and on these as a basis to erect the final and harmonious structure of our knowledge. But empirical psychology, which we thus make our starting point in philosophy, like any other empirical science, will need its assumptions, not derived from the science itself, but assumed as the explanation of primary facts in the science. It may be maintained, indeed, that the object in every thought or feeling or act of will is only a modification of the subject itself which feels, thinks, or wills; and this idealism will thus be our primary assumption. Whether it will meet the demands of our science is another question. Or again we may assume that all these states or acts of the subject, viewed as it were objectively, are phenomena of brain; in which case our psychology will ignore the consciousness, which is the first warrant for the facts out of which we are trying to construct a science, or, finally, we may accept a dualism based on the facts, which will serve the purposes of our science, whatever may be its metaphysical warrant.

Thus considering the phenomena of consciousness, we shall see that no one can help distinguishing between those which he can attribute wholly to himself and those which he must ascribe to another source; *e. g.*, between the phenomena of anger in his conscious experience, and what he regards as signs of it in another. Paleness or redness, whatever may be its cause, he refers to another; pain, desire to injure, etc., to self. This is direct knowledge, if anything is. To distinguish these merely as "vivid" and "faint" feelings, as H. Spencer does (Princ. Psych.), is to nullify the primary interest of consciousness itself.

Psychology begins with this dualism in phenomena, proceeds from it to the dualism of ego and non-ego, by analogy infers other selfs; and so reaches a universal dualism of mind and matter, which will probably prove to be the "Natural Dualism" before mentioned (See Dr. Porter's *Human Intellect*, §§ 644, *et seq.*).

Modern psychological dualism may be said to date from Des Cartes. Defining substance as "that which so exists that it needs nothing else in order to its existence," he finds, by his "Method," two kinds of substances, mind and matter, to each of which pertains a class of things, the one intellectual, the other corporeal. Each of these is distinguished by a peculiar quality, the one by (active and spontaneous) thinking, the other by (passive and inert) extension. The relation between the two, and their mutual influence, with the problem how spirit can affect matter, as body, spirit, is left wholly unexplained. In order to serve the useful purpose of a "deus ex machina," the unscientific hypothesis of Divine assistance, like Leibnitz's "pre-established harmony" (concursus), is introduced.

If Kant declined, the hopeless task of presenting a pure metaphysic, ontological dualism or monism was, of course, out of the question. He starts, however, from a dualistic theory of knowledge, viz., ideal forms *à priori* furnished by the ego, and real phenomena, as materials of knowledge, *à posteriori*, which are of objective origin, indeed, while their source is unknown. And so, if we must rest contented within the limits of our faculties, as he defined them, the problem after the various monistic theories, egoistic, pantheistic, absolute, still remains unsolved: Is it possible for our knowledge to go beyond the natural dualism of consciousness? (J. J. E.)

DUANE, WILLIAM (1760–1835), an American politician and journalist, was born in 1760 near Lake Champlain, in New York. His father, a native of Ireland, had settled there a short time before, and died soon after. His mother removed to Philadelphia, and in 1771 returned to Ireland, where she gave William, her only son, a liberal education. At the age of nineteen he lost her favor by marrying a Presbyterian, as she was a Roman Catholic. Having learned the art of printing to support his family he went to London, and afterwards to Calcutta, where he established a newspaper called *The World*, but after a brief success offended the Government, was seized, and sent back to England, while his property was confiscated. His attempt to obtain redress from Parliament and the East India Company having failed, he became a parliamentary reporter and writer for the *General Advertiser*, a paper which has since attained celebrity as the *London Times*. In 1795 Duane returned to Philadelphia, and engaged in literary and journalistic work, editing for a time the *True American*. In 1798, on the death of Benjamin Franklin Bache, he became editor of the *Aurora*, and by his vigorous management made it the leading organ of the Republican party. His violent attacks on Pres. Adams's administration roused the resentment of the Federalists, and in 1799 he was tried with others for seditious riot. His offence consisted in posting on the walls of a Roman Catholic Church notices requesting the members of the congregation to meet in the churchyard and sign petitions against the alien law. These notices were removed, then replaced, and a slight disturbance followed. On his trial he was ably defended by A. J. Dallas, and acquitted. In 1800 he was charged by the United States Senate with defamatory publication, but avoided arrest by the sergeant-at-arms. To the vigor with which Duane conducted his paper Jefferson ascribed his own election to the Presidency. In 1805 Duane, with others, organised a society called the "Friends of the People," to bring about radical democratic changes in the constitution of Pennsylvania, but they were defeated by the constitutional Republicans; and from this time his paper, more abusive than ever, declined in influence. In 1811 even Jefferson, in his retirement still watchful of politics, found it necessary to rebuke Duane for his attacks on Madison's administration. In the war of 1812 Duane was made adjutant-general for the district of Pennsylvania. In 1822 he sold out his paper, and went to South America as the representative of the creditors of the new republics established there. Though he had received the thanks of the congress of Colombia for aid in their struggle for independence, he was unable to collect the debts. On his return he was appointed prothonotary of the supreme court of Pennsylvania, and retained this position till his death, which occurred at Philadelphia, Nov. 24, 1835. Besides his newspaper writings he published a *Military Dictionary* (1810), and *A Visit to Colombia in 1822–1823*.

DUANE, William John (1780–1865), an American lawyer, son of the preceding, was born at Clonmel, Ireland, May 9, 1780. When his father went to India the family returned from London, where they had been residing, to Clonmel, where the son was taught for fifteen months by the Rev. Dr. Carey. He accompanied his father to America in 1796, and assisted him as clerk. In 1805 he married Deborah Bache, a granddaughter of Benjamin Franklin, with whom he lived happily for fifty-seven years. In 1809 he became a member of the Pennsylvania legislature, and was re-elected in 1813. Having studied law with Judge Joseph Hopkinson, he was admitted to the bar in 1815, and obtained extensive practice. In 1819 he was again elected to the legislature, and was afterwards attorney of the mayor's court in Philadelphia for three years. He ardently supported Jackson for the Presidency, and in 1831 was nominated commissioner under the treaty with Denmark. In his second term Jackson appointed Duane Secretary of the Treasury, but when the latter refused to remove the government deposits from the United States Bank without authority from Congress, he dismissed him, Sept. 21, 1833. From this time Mr. Duane held no public position, but having been Stephen Girard's lawyer, and having drawn up his will, he was made one of the executors. The last time he left his house was in order to vote at the presidential election in 1864. He died at Philadelphia, Sept. 26, 1865. He published *The Law of Nations Investigated in a Popular Manner* (1809), and *Internal Improvements of the Commonwealth* (1811).

DU BOIS, a borough of Clearfield co., Pennsylvania, is 127 miles N.E. of Pittsburg, on the Alleghany Valley Railroad, and another railroad is in construction. It has 7 hotels, 1 bank, a weekly newspaper, 5 churches, and 9 schools. Its industrial works comprise large iron-works, box-factories, saw-mills, grist-mills, and coke-works. It was settled in 1873, when the Alleghany Valley Railroad was opened, and was incorporated in 1881. Population, 6137.

DUBOIS, John (1764–1842), the founder of Mt. St. Mary's College, Emmittsburg, Md., the first superior of the Sisters of Charity in the United States and second bishop of New York, was born in Paris, Aug. 24, 1764. His education was completed at the College of Louis le Grand, the Alma Mater of so many distinguished men of France. Among his teachers was the Abbé Delille, the poet, and among his fellow-students were Camille Desmoulins and Robespierre. Young Dubois was a diligent student, and passed through college with great distinction. His father had destined him for the army, but he at an early age showed a preference for the ecclesiastical state, and after completing his college course he entered the seminary of St. Magloire. So admirable were his theses, which he sustained at the Sorbonne, that while yet a student he received a benefice in the neighborhood of Paris. Ordained in 1787, his first position was that of assistant priest of St. Sulpice. When the French Revolution broke out he firmly refused to yield to its requirements, and was obliged to fly from France, which he did in the disguise of a layman. He sailed from Havre in the summer of 1791, and arrived at Norfolk, Va., in August of that year. He brought with him letters from La Fayette, and was cordially received by Bishop Carroll, who had recently been appointed the first American Catholic prelate, with his see at Baltimore. Mr. Dubois was first stationed at Norfolk, but was soon removed to Richmond. His letters were addressed to some of the leading men of Virginia, among others to James Monroe, Patrick Henry, and to the Randolphs, Lees, etc. He was received most cordially, and resided for a time in the family of Mr. Monroe, and was taught English by Patrick Henry. There being no Catholic church at that time in Richmond, he was invited to use the Capitol as his chapel. The most distinguised citizens bestowed marked attentions upon the exiled priest, who was so poor that he was obliged to teach French for a support.

At the end of a few months Bishop Carroll called him to Frederick, Md. His mission included Emmittsburg and Frederick in Maryland and Winchester and Martinsburg in Virginia, and he was for several years the only priest between Baltimore and St. Louis. He occupied a room in a house in Frederick as his chapel, and when the increase in his flock required the building of a church the people thought him mad; even Roger B. Taney, the most prominent of his congregation, thought it was a hopeless undertaking. But Mr. Dubois persevered; the church was built, paid for, and filled. He was an indefatigable worker, and having an iron constitution he often did the work of three men; he swam rivers, climbed mountains, and rode sometimes fifty miles on a sick call; cheerfully he endured the greatest hardships and inconveniences. Accustomed to the most polished and refined society, he met the rude and illiterate mountaineers on an even footing, and made them feel at home in his presence. A man of exalted dignity, he did not hesitate to share the roughest toils of his people, "following the ponderous wains over difficult and dangerous roads, cheering the woodman as his axe made the forest ring, plying the spade with hands more fit to wield the crosier, and presiding at a rural feast in honor of a successful raising of a log building with manners that would have graced the salons of his native city."

In the spring of 1806, Mr. Dubois, having selected a spot of great beauty in the midst of the wild mountain-forest, erected there the first brick church that was ever seen in that region. In 1809 he founded the secular and ecclesiastical seminary so long known as Mt. St. Mary's College—an institution that has sent forth in three quarters of a century one cardinal, four archbishops, twenty bishops, and more than two hundred priests and three thousand youths to occupy the various walks of life. Mr. Dubois was president of the college, pastor of the mountain congregation and the church at Emmittsburg, superior of St. Joseph's Academy, professor of Latin and French at the college, and occasionally of theology in the seminary, superintendent of the farm attached to the college, and general manager of the out-door business of the institution. He was also the chaplain and director of the Sisters of Charity, who were established at Emmittsburg under his auspices; he gave Mother Seton a home when she and her companions first arrived at the mountain, and furnished them with food when their necessities were so great that they were thinking of abandoning the foundation. It has been truly said that "the two institutions, the seminary and sisterhood, like brother and sister, have grown up together."

In 1826, Mr. Dubois was appointed bishop of New York. Although over sixty years old, he left his beloved mountain-home and repaired to the new field of labor. He was consecrated in the Baltimore cathedral on the 29th of October, 1826, the ceremony being performed by Archbishop Maréchal of Baltimore. The venerable Charles Carroll of Carrollton presented him with the episcopal ring and cross. On the 9th of November he was installed at St. Peter's cathedral, New York, in the presence of four thousand persons.

The diocese of New York at that time embraced the whole State of New York and a part of New Jersey, the entire Catholic population being one hundred and fifty thousand, with eight churches and eighteen priests. It was necessary for the bishop to perform not only the duties of the episcopal office, but also those of a missionary priest. Having made the visitation of his whole diocese, he discovered the need of more churches, educational establishments, and other institutions of learning and piety. Finding it impossible to raise the necessary funds in the United States, he went to Europe in quest of assistance, which he obtained, and returned to carry on the work of building up the Church in New York. In eight years eight churches were erected, and schools and colleges established and seminaries founded. In 1837, Bishop Dubois's health began to decline, and he asked for a coadjutor bishop, naming the Rev. John Hughes as his choice. Having consecrated Bishop Hughes in the New York cathedral, January 9, 1838, he was two weeks afterwards partially paralyzed, and was prevented from taking further part in the active government of his diocese. Bishop Dubois died Dec. 20, 1842. (E. L. D.)

DU BOIS-REYMOND, EMIL, a German physiologist, was born in Berlin, Nov. 7, 1818. His father, a native of Neufchâtel, Switzerland, was at that time in Government employ in Berlin, but afterwards returned to Neufchâtel, and Emil, who had attended the French college in his native city, was educated at the college of Neufchâtel. At the age of eighteen he went to the University of Berlin to study theology, but, attracted by the lectures of Mitscherlick on chemistry, he turned to the natural sciences and became a student of medicine. In 1841 his preceptor, Prof. John Müller, suggested to him the investigation of animal electricity, and he soon published a brief account of his experiments on frogs and electric fish, as well as a Latin essay on the references to such subjects in ancient authors. After seven years of patient labor he published his celebrated work, *Untersuchungen über thierische Elektricität* (Berlin, 1848–49). The apparatus employed in his experiments was for the most part invented by himself, and was remarkable for its delicacy. When the correctness of some of his statements was called in question by French scientists, he went to Paris in 1850 with his apparatus and proved them satisfactorily. He was then elected a member of the Royal Academy of Sciences of Berlin, and in 1867 became its secretary. Having established a high reputation as a lecturer, and being well acquainted with the English language, he was frequently invited to lecture at the London Royal Institution. In 1858 he succeeded Prof. Müller as professor of physiology in the University of Berlin, and under his superintendence one of the finest physiological laboratories in the world has since been erected in connection with the university. He has continued to labor in the field in which he early achieved success, and has published several memoirs, addresses, and larger works. They include *Ueber thierische Bewegung* (1851), *Gedächt-nisrede auf Johannes Müller* (1860), *De fibrae muscularis reactione ut chemicis visa est acida* (1859), *Ueber das Barrenturnen und über die rationelle Gymnastik* (1862), *Beschreibung einiger Vorrichtungen und Versuchweisen zu elektrophysiologischen Zweckes* (1863), *Voltaire in seiner Beziehung zur Naturwissenschaft* (1868), *Ueber Universitätseinrichtungen* (1869), *Ueber den deutschen Krieg* (1870), *Leibnizische Gedanken in der neuern Naturwissenschaft* (1870), *Ueber die Grenzen des Naturerkennens* (1872), *Ueber eine Akademie der deutschen Sprache* (1874). Other writings have been collected in two volumes under the title *Gesammelte Abhandlungen zur allgemeinen Muskel und Nervenphysik* (Leipsic, 1877). From 1859 to 1877 he was one of the editors of the Berlin *Archiv für Anatomie und Physiologie*, and since that time he has been sole editor of a similar periodical at Leipsic.

DUBUQUE, a city of Iowa, the county-seat of Dubuque co., and after Des Moines the largest city in that State by the census of 1880. It is situated on the W. bank of the Mississippi River, about midway between St. Paul, Minn., and St. Louis, Mo., and 200 miles W. of Chicago. Dubuque was the first place permanently occupied by white men in the State of Iowa. It derives its name from Julien Dubuque, who in 1778 obtained an Indian grant to mine for lead ore within an area now included inside the corporate limits of the city. The first permanent settlement of Dubuque dates from 1833, when about five hundred miners located at that place and commenced a search for lead ore which abounded in that portion of Iowa and has since been its chief product. It was incorporated as a town in 1837, and became a city in 1841. The original corporate limits of Dubuque included only a single square mile. The limits were extended in 1852 and again in 1854, and now include eleven square miles, being about four miles on the river front, and an average of nearly three miles wide, including much picturesque scenery, arising from the variety and combination of bluffs, ravines, level places, and beautiful groves. Many of the gardens rise in terraces to the tops of the bluffs, on the summits of which are built handsome houses. The bluffs at an average of half a mile from the main channel of the river are about 230 feet high, and are intersected by ravines, out of which pass the seven thoroughfares leading to the larger area of corporate space and to the country beyond. Dubuque is one of the most important commercial centres in the north-west, and abounds in wholesale houses, manufactories, and other business enterprises. Its lumber interests are extensive, the sales from this branch aggregating in 1883 upwards of $2,000,000. The river and railroad commerce of Dubuque exceeds that of any other city on the Mississippi between St. Louis and St. Paul, and is annually increasing. Dubuque has now 20 organized churches and several religious societies. There are 16 houses of public worship, many of them large, elegant, and commodious. The most costly is St. Mary's (Roman Catholic) Cathedral, which was completed in 1867. Dubuque has also a custom-house and post-office, built by the United States at a cost of $200,000, a fine three-story brick city-hall, 12 hotels, an opera-house, and several public halls, 7 large public-school buildings, the aggregate cost of which was $200,000; a theological seminary, commercial college, institute of science and arts, United States Marine Hospital, home for the friendless, orphan asylum, Catholic convent, and several other institutions of importance. It has 6 Masonic bodies, 4 of Odd-fellowship, and a number of other benevolent orders. Its railroads are the Illinois Central, which crosses the Mississippi at Dubuque on its own bridge; the Chicago, Milwaukee, and St. Paul, whose machine-shops are located in the city; and the Dubuque and North-western, now under construction. The population of Dubuque in 1880 was 22,254, of which 16,107 were native- and 6147 foreign-born. In 1890 the population was 30,147.

DU CHAILLU, PAUL BELLONI, a French traveller, naturalized as a citizen of the United States under the name of Chaylion, was born in Paris, July 31, 1835. He is the son of a French merchant of Equatorial Africa, trading near the mouth of the river Gaboon, where he was educated in a Jesuit mission. Having become familiar in his youth with the neighboring tribes, he undertook an exploring expedition in 1855 into the interior of the country. For four years he explored the equatorial region of the African continent, and discovered, in a thickly wooded region, a chain of high mountains extending east and west, with one peak 12,000 feet in height. He was one of the first travellers to describe the gorilla, of which he killed and brought back some specimens. He also collected many previously unknown birds. He has since then made long journeys of exploration in Sweden, Lapland, and Finland. He has published the following works: *Explorations and Adventures in Equatorial Africa* (1861), with a chart of the country explored; *A Journey to Ashango Land* (1867); *Stories of the Gorilla Country* (1868); *Wild Life under the Equator* (1869); *Lost in the Jungle* (1869); *My Apingi Kingdom* (1870); *The Country of the Dwarfs* (1871); and *Western Africa* (1874); and *The Land of the Midnight Sun* (1881), descriptive of his travels in the north of Europe.

DUCHE, JACOB, D. D. (1738–1798), an American Episcopalian clergyman, first chaplain of Congress, was born at Philadelphia, Jan. 31, 1738. His grandfather, Anthony Duché, was a French Huguenot refugee and one of the early settlers of Philadelphia. In 1757 Jacob was the first graduate of the College of Philadelphia, since known as the University of Pennsylvania. He went to England to study theology, and after spending some time at Clare Hall, Cambridge, was ordained in 1759 by the bishop of London and licensed as assistant minister of Christ Church, Philadelphia. He was also appointed professor of oratory in the College of Philadelphia, and in 1768 was made a trustee of the institution while still holding his professorship. He was an earnest preacher, good orator, and ready versifier, though somewhat mystical, being a follower of Jacob Boehmen and William Law. He contributed to a Philadelphia newspaper a series of letters, which he afterwards collected and published in 1771 under the title of *The Letters of Tamoc Caspipina*, this name being formed from the initials of his official designation as "the assistant minister of Christ Church and St. Peter's in Philadelphia in North America." These letters were reprinted in England in 1787, and also appeared in a German translation at Leipsic in 1778. During the political agitation which preceded the Revolution, Duché favored the cause of the colonists, and when, in 1774, the first continental congress met in Carpenter's Hall, Philadelphia, he was invited, on the motion of Samuel Adams, to open its session with prayer. For this purpose he came with his clerk Sept. 7, and, after reading several prayers and the thirty-fifth Psalm, prescribed for the day, he suddenly offered a fervent extempory prayer for America and the congress. The whole service made a profound impression, and the psalm was regarded as especially appropriate to the time. In the next year Duché, having succeeded Rev. Richard Peters as rector of Christ Church, opened the second Congress with prayer, and published a sermon preached before Congress on "The American Vine," the text being Psalm lxxx. 14. As soon as the Declaration of Independence was resolved upon the vestry of Christ Church agreed to omit the petition in the liturgy for the king of Great Britain, and on July 8, 1776, Duché was appointed chaplain of Congress. This position he resigned in October, and directed that the salary which had been offered to him should be given to the families of Pennsylvania officers who had fallen in battle. When the British army under Lord Howe occupied Philadelphia in 1777, Duché resolved to remain at his post in the city, and resumed the established form of worship, praying for the king. Naturally timid and oppressed with the gloomy aspect of American affairs, he wrote to Gen. Washington (Oct. 8, 1777) urging him to abandon the cause of independence as hopeless. The letter was immediately transmitted by Washington to Congress, and Francis Hopkinson, Duché's brother-in-law, replied to it with great spirit. In December Duché sailed to England, and when the British evacuated Philadelphia the next year his property was confiscated by the Pennsylvania assembly. In 1780 his wife joined him in England, where he had been well received, and was honored with the degree of D. D. He published two volumes of *Discourses on Various Subjects* (London, 1779), which were highly praised for their eloquent style. He served for a time as secretary and chaplain of a female orphan asylum in London, but on the conclusion of peace he desired to return to Philadelphia, where his father was still living. He wrote to Washington, disclaiming any intention of giving him pain in his unfortunate letter, and asking his influence with the authorities in Pennsylvania. Duché's friends, however, opposed his return, and he then sent for his aged father, who joined him and died in England. In 1787 Duché was present in Lambeth at the consecration of Bishop William White, who had succeeded him in his rectorate. As time passed on he became still more a mystic, and was deeply interested in the visions of Swedenborg. He relinquished all church preferment and would accept no pay for preaching. His wife and two daughters were devoted Christian women; his only son, Thomas Spence Duché, was a pupil of Benjamin West and painted the portraits of Bishops Seabury and Provoost. Thomas died in London, March 31, 1789, at the age of twenty-six. In May, 1792, Duché returned to Philadelphia and lived there in retirement until his death, Jan. 3, 1798.

DUCHOBORTZI ("Spirit-wrestlers"), a Russian mystical sect, which originated in the eighteenth century. Their doctrines are stated at some length by Krasinski. They say that in the Divine Trinity the Father is light, the Son is life, and the Holy Ghost is peace, and in the human soul, which is the image of God, there is a corresponding trinity of the memory, reason, and will. The human soul had existed and fallen before the creation of the visible world. It was then enclosed in the body, partly for punishment and partly that it might in this new state seek purification. Aid is given by the Spirit of God to those that strive for it, but there is no need to seek outer help. To this part of their belief the sect owes its name. They say that Christ, the Son of God, is in the Old Testament the Heavenly Wisdom, and in the New the incarnate Spirit. He descends into each believer, being spiritually received, and lives a spiritual life as in the Gospels a natural one. His miracles are again performed in the believer's spirit.

Ilarion Pobirochin is said to have led the sect to separate from the more numerous Malakans (milk-eaters), and, representing himself as a son of God, to have chosen twelve archangels to rule the society and twelve death-angels to dispose of backsliders. As the members of the sect refused to serve in the army they were much persecuted under Catharine II. Alexander I. granted them a settlement near the sea of Azof in the early part of this century, and here they were afterwards joined by Kapustin, a discharged military officer, who introduced many changes into their doctrines and practices. He claimed to be in a special sense the representative of Christ, or, indeed, Christ returned to earth. Under his rule they practised community of goods and had flourishing manufactures. In 1839 the government declared that a secret tribunal had been discovered among them, and ordered them to be transported beyond the Caucasus. About 2500 were allowed to remain, having conformed to the Greek Church. Those among the Caucasus are said to be decreasing in numbers.

DUCKWEED, usually *Lemna*, though, according to Dr. Peyre Porcher, *Podophyllum peltatum*, the May-apple of the northern portion of the United States, is sometimes called duckweed in the southern part of the country. In many respects the duckweeds are among the best known, as well as among the most interesting, of all plants. In still and somewhat stagnant waters they thickly cover the whole surface, giving the water a velvety-green appearance, which has often excited poetic admiration. When this green mass is examined it is found to be composed of very minute fronds little more than a line wide, from the under surface of which a single root, or in some species more than one root, will appear. Occasionally the little frond makes no root at all. The flowers are very minute and rarely seen. They are almost imbedded in the green surface of the frond, but under a microscope are seen to be composed of a small membranous spathe, as if they were small arum-flowers, only, instead of a spadix in each spathe, there are but two small flowers, one of which is male and the other female. The manner of growth and fructification of these minute plants has been the theme of many learned treatises; one of the latest and most clear is by Prof. Wm. Barbeck in the *Proceedings of the Academy of Natural Sciences of Philadelphia* for 1880. It is there stated that the plant does not flower until just before it finishes its season's work at the end of summer. When the seed matures it falls into the mud beneath. In April these seeds either absorb some heat, exude gelatine, or in some other way are enabled to float to the surface, where they germinate. After the first plant is formed it continues to make new ones in successive generations by a sort of bulblet which proceeds from a cleft in the parent frond. Prof. Asa Gray does not mention that the seed sinks in the autumn, but states that "the bulblets sink to the bottom of the water, but rise and vegetate in the spring." There are about a dozen species, some of which are found in almost all parts of the world. (T. M.)

DUDLEY, Benjamin Winslow, LL.D. (1785-1870), an American surgeon, was born in Spottsylvania co., Va., April 12, 1785. He was educated at Transylvania University, and received the degree of M.D. at the University of Pennsylvania in 1806. In 1810 he went to Europe, where he studied in London under Sir Astley Cooper and other eminent surgeons, and in Paris under Larrey, Dubois, and Boyer. In 1814 he returned to America with an established reputation. He settled at Lexington, Ky., and remained there, in active practice, till 1854, being regarded as the ablest surgeon west of the Alleghanies. He was the first professor of surgery in Transylvania University, was highly distinguished as an instructor, and published a number of medical essays. He died at Lexington, Ky., Jan. 20, 1870. He was especially eminent as a lithotomist.

DUER, John, LL.D. (1782-1858), an American jurist and author, was born at Albany, N. Y., Oct. 7, 1782. His father was Col. William Duer, of the American Revolutionary army, and his mother was a daughter of Gen. William Alexander, titular Lord Stirling. After two years' service in the army he studied law, and commenced practice at Goshen, N. Y. In 1820 he removed to New York, where he acquired high reputation and extensive practice. In 1821 he was a delegate to the State constitutional convention. In 1825 he was appointed one of the commissioners to revise the statute law of the State, but resigned before the work was completed. In 1849 he was elected an associate justice of the superior court of New York city, and in 1857 became the presiding justice. He died on Staten Island, Aug. 8, 1858. His principal works are—*The Law of Representations in Marine Insurance* (1845), *The Law and Practice of Marine Insurance* (1846), and *Duer's Reports of the Decisions of the Superior Court*, the sixth volume of which he left incomplete.

DUFF, Alexander, D.D. (1806-1878), an eminent Scotch Presbyterian missionary, was born at Moulin, Perthshire, April 25, 1806. He studied at the University of St. Andrew's, and, being licensed to preach in 1829, was appointed the first missionary of the Church of Scotland to India. He was shipwrecked on his voyage near the Cape of Good Hope, but persevered in his mission. As an essential part of his plan of operations he established a school of a high order in Calcutta, but encountered much opposition from the East India Company and its friends, who wished not to disturb the Hindoo traditions, while he required the Bible to be read in every class sufficiently advanced, and modern science to be taught in the English language. His school was very successful and popular with the natives, and a number of the scholars became Christians. In 1834 he was obliged to relinquish his work for a time, but, returning to Scotland, made a tour through the country, which greatly stimulated missionary efforts. He returned to his work, but when the Scotch Church was divided in 1843 he and his fellow-missionaries all went with the Free Church, though they thereby lost the use of the mission property, which legally belonged to the Established Church. Starting afresh they were enabled by the liberality of the church at home to found and equip new institutions equal to the old. Their labors were also remarkably successful in overthrowing Hindoo superstitions and producing conversions to Christianity. In 1850 he returned to Scotland to arouse the Free Church to yet greater efforts on behalf of the India mission, and in the general assembly of 1851 he was elected moderator. He was also induced to visit the United States and Canada, and by his quence and earnestness increased the missionary zeal of the Presbyterian churches. He again went to India and continued his labors with self-sacrificing zeal until 1864, when his failing health compelled him to return to Scotland. The chief direction of the foreign missions of the Free Church was then intrusted to him, and he showed deep interest in the work in South Africa. In 1867 he was made professor of evangelistic theology in the Free Church, the endowment of which chair had been raised by his personal efforts, and during his incumbency the proceeds were devoted to special missionary objects. In all his labors he displayed a truly catholic spirit, and in his later years especially aimed to secure a union of the various branches of the Presbyterian Church of Scotland. He died in Edinburgh, Feb. 12, 1878. Among his published works are *New Era for the English Language and Literature in India* (1837); *India and India Missions* (1839); *Missions the Chief End of the Christian Church* (1854); *The Qualifications, Duties, and Trials of an Indian Missionary* (1839); *Letters on the Indian Rebellion* (1858). He was for many years editor of the *Calcutta Review*, and wrote several pamphlets on miscellaneous subjects.

DUFFERIN, FREDERICK TEMPLE BLACKWOOD, EARL OF, an English statesman, diplomatist, and author, was born at Florence, Italy, June 21, 1826. He is the only son of Price, fourth baron Dufferin, and Helen Selina, grand-daughter of the famous wit, orator, and dramatist, Richard Brinsley Sheridan. His mother was noted for her beauty and accomplishments, though perhaps not so beautiful as her sister, the duchess of Somerset, nor so highly gifted intellectually as her other sister, the Hon. Mrs. Norton. She was the author of some favorite Irish songs. After twenty-one years of widowhood she became the countess of Gifford in 1862; she died in 1867. Lord Dufferin was educated at Eton and Christ Church, Oxford, but did not take a degree. On July 21, 1841, he had succeeded to his father's title, and in 1850 he was created peer of the united kingdom by the title of Lord Clandeboye. In 1846 he visited the south of Ireland, and on his return to England published his *Narrative of a Journey from Oxford to Skibbereen during the Year of the Irish Famine* (1847). Under Lord John Russell's administration in 1849 he was made one of the lords-in-waiting. His speeches and writings on the Irish question early attracted much attention. Among these writings was a valuable work entitled *Irish Emigration and the Tenure of Land in Ireland*. In 1855 he was appointed special *attaché* to the Vienna mission of Lord John Russell. In 1856 he visited Iceland and Jan Mayen in his yacht, and in 1860 published his well-known *Letters from High Latitudes*. In 1860 he was appointed British commissioner to inquire into the massacres (1858-60) of Christians in Syria, and succeeded in securing a great improvement in the government of Mount Lebanon. In 1862 he married the accomplished Harriet Georgina Hamilton, known as a writer of much humor and talent. In 1864 he became lord-lieutenant and *custos rotulorum* for the county Down; was under-secretary for India, 1864-66; under-secretary for war, 1866; was chancellor of the duchy of Lancaster, 1868-72, under Mr. Gladstone; was sworn of the privy council and made paymaster-general in 1868. He was raised to the earldom in 1871. From 1872 to 1878 Lord Dufferin held the important office of governor-general of the Dominion of Canada. In 1879 (though classed as a Liberal) he was sent by Beaconsfield as ambassador to St. Petersburg, and in 1881 he was transferred to Constantinople as ambassador extraordinary.

In each successive position his diplomatic ability became more conspicuous; the greater the difficulty of the situation the more his genius shone forth. In a troublous time he guarded skilfully the interests of Great Britain in the East, and when Egypt became the scene of an exciting and important struggle, Earl Dufferin was despatched as a special commissioner to Cairo. In a few months general tranquillity was restored, and administrative reform inaugurated. He resumed his place at Constantinople, and remained there till October, 1884, when he was appointed viceroy of India. Here his administration was equally successful, but he resigned in 1888 and returned to England. He was then raised to the rank of Marquis with the title Marquis of Dufferin and Ava.

DUFFIELD, GEORGE (1732-90), an American Presbyterian minister, was born in Lancaster co., Pa., Oct. 7, 1732. He graduated at Princeton College, and, after studying theology, became a tutor there for two years. In 1756 he was licensed to preach, and in 1761 he was settled as pastor of the congregations of Carlisle, Big Spring, and Monahan, Pa. He was a zealous promoter of revivals of religion, and went on missionary journeys through neglected districts. In 1770 he became pastor of the Second Presbyterian Church, Philadelphia, and he was afterwards for a short time chaplain of the Colonial Congress. He was noted for his devotion to the cause of American independence, and in 1777 he ministered to the soldiers of the Revolutionary army. He died at Philadelphia Feb. 2, 1790. His sons and grandsons have also held honorable positions as ministers of the same denomination.

DUFFY, SIR CHARLES GAVAN, an Irish journalist, lawyer, and statesman was born in Monaghan, in 1816. He is descended from an eminent native family, and is the son of a farmer. He entered the field of journalism at the age of eighteen, being first connected with a Dublin paper, and afterwards editor of the *Belfast Vindicator*, an ultra Roman Catholic paper. Returning to Dublin, he joined with Thomas Davis and John Dillon in establishing the *Nation*, the first number of which was issued Oct. 15, 1842. The Young Ireland party which it represented sprang from the movement which Daniel O'Connell had started, but aimed to secure in a different way the repeal of the union between England and Ireland. The new party, consisting of young men of ability and culture, urged a united action on the part of Protestants and Catholics, and in political matters ignored religious differences. From poetical contributions to the *Nation*, Duffy compiled the *Ballad Poetry of Ireland*, a volume which has had a remarkable success, having passed through nearly fifty editions. The powerful effect which the constant succession of able articles in the *Nation* had in encouraging and stimulating the people to resist the domination of the party in power led the Government to include its editors in the indictment for treason brought against O'Connell in 1844. They were tried, convicted, and sent to jail, but there were such serious faults in the indictment and in the method of trial that when appeal was taken to the House of Lords the judgment was reversed. Some time after the deliverance from jail thus brought about the more violent Catholics induced O'Connell to quarrel with the Young Ireland party, on the ground that they were seeking to subvert religion. The latter then reorganized under the name of the Irish Confederation, but soon divided into two factions, one under William Smith O'Brien, and the other under John Mitchel. The latter advocated insurrection as the only policy to secure redress of grievances, and the *United Irishman* was established to advocate that policy. The prevalence and temporary triumphs of the revolutionary spirit throughout Europe induced the Government to take prompt and stern measures to prevent any outbreak in Ireland. Within two months Mitchel was seized, tried, convicted, and transported. Then the Habeas Corpus Act was suspended, Duffy was arrested in Dublin, and the police broke into the office of the *Nation*. The chief leaders of the intended insurrection were either arrested and transported or went into voluntary exile. Duffy was tried thrice, but, being ably defended by Mr. Isaac Butt, it was found impossible to secure conviction. He then revived the *Nation* and advocated the movement for "tenant right." For this purpose the Irish Tenant League was formed, and when the Irish Liberal members of Parliament showed little inclination to favor the movement, others were elected in their place. Mr. Duffy thus became the member for New Ross in July, 1852, and with a few friends established the Independent Irish party in the House of Commons. On account, however, of dissensions caused by the ultra Catholics, Mr. Duffy resigned in 1856, and emigrated to Australia with the intention of practising law, as he had been admitted to the bar in 1846. In a short time he was drawn into a new political career and made minister of public works in the first administration under "responsible government" in Victoria. In the next year he became minister of lands. When a parliamentary commission was appointed on the subject of federation of the Australian colonies, Mr. Duffy was made chairman, and also served in the same capacity on the royal commission which followed. Both of these reported in favor of the federation of all the states of Australia and New Zealand, a project not yet accomplished. Mr. Duffy then spent two years in Europe, and on his return entered Parliament in Victoria. He became prime minister in 1871, and in the following year, being defeated on an important measure, wished to dissolve Parliament, but Viscount Canterbury, the royal governor, having refused to allow this, he resigned. Afterward, upon repeated request, he accepted the offer of knighthood, May 31, 1873. He then visited Europe, spending two years in travel. In 1876 he again became a member of the legislature of Victoria, and at the beginning of the next session he was unanimously elected Speaker of the legislative assembly. He has taken great interest in promoting art, literature, and industrial enterprises in Victoria. He has been twice married, and now resides in the south of France. He has published a volume containing the history of *Young Ireland* (1881).

DÜHRING, EUGEN KARL, a German philosopher and political economist, was born at Berlin, Jan. 12, 1833. He was educated in the gymnasium and university of that city, and studied jurisprudence from 1853 to 1856. He was then appointed referendary in the court of justice, but in consequence of a disease of the eyes, which eventually resulted in total blindness, he resigned this office and turned to the study of philosophy and national economy. In 1864 he became a privat docent in both branches in the Berlin University. After holding this position for some years, he engaged in a serious conflict with the university authorities, whom he accused of nepotism, and in 1877 withdrew from connection with that institution. He is the foremost German disciple of Henry C. Carey, and has endeavored to connect political economy with the exact sciences. In philosophy he inclines to materialism. His economical works include *Kapital und Arbeit* (1865); *Der Werth des Lebens* (1865; 3d ed., Leipsic, 1881); *Natürliche Dialektik* (1865); *Kritische Grundlegung der Volkswirthschaftslehre* (1866); *Die Verkleinerer Careys und die Krisis der Nationalökonomie* (1867). But the most important is *Kritische Geschichte der Nationalökonomie und des Sozialismus* (3d ed., 1879). He has also published *Kursus der National und Sozialökonomie* (2d ed., 1876). Among his works on philosophical and scientific subjects are *Kritische Geschichte der Philosophie* (1869; 3d ed., Leipsic, 1878); *Kritische Geschichte der Allgemeinen Prinzipien der Mechanik* (1872; 2d ed., Leipsic, 1877); *Kursus der Philosophie als streng wissenschaftlicher Weltanschauung* (Leipsic, 1874); *Neue Grundsätze zur rationellen Physik und Chemie* (1878); *Logik und Wissenschafts theorie* (1878). Prof. Dühring has taken an active part in discussing the social questions of the day, especially the higher education of women, and the Jewish question. On these he has published *Der Weg zur höhern Berufsbildung der Frauen und die Lehrweise der Universitäten* (1877); *Die Judenfrage als Racen Sitten und Culturfrage* (1881). Finally, as a key to all his other works, he has published an autobiography under the title *Sache, Leben und Feinde* (Karlsruhe, 1882).

DUKE CENTRE. A borough of McKean co., Penna., near the New York line, and 63 miles S.S.E. of Buffalo. It has a bank, a weekly newspaper, 4 churches, saw-mill, machine-shops, and other industries connected with the petroleum business. It was settled in 1868, and when petroleum was discovered in the neighborhood in 1877 it grew rapidly. In 1880 it was incorporated. Population, 2068.

DULSE, called also DILLISH by the Irish, is the dried frond or leaf of a seaweed known to botanists as *Rhodymenia palmata*, which is found on both sides of the Northern Atlantic ocean, and which extends on our coast as far south as Long Island Sound; though our market supply comes mostly from the British provinces. In appearance the fronds are "purplish-red, broadly wedge-shaped, six to twelve inches long and four to eight broad, irregularly cleft, palmate or dichotomous, sometimes repeatedly laciniate, the margin often winged with leaflets" (Farlow).

It grows on other seaweeds, extending from high water-mark out into deep water. Only the non-sexual fruit appears to be known. As a food dulse is eaten from choice mostly by the sailors and the Irish; though it is eaten thankfully enough by all in the marine districts where it is found, during times of scarcity. The flavor is decidedly of the sea; so much so as to make it unpleasant to the palate unaccustomed to its use; but for the Irish peasant it is the chief and often only relish to his potatoes. Ordinarily it is taken raw, sometimes fried, but it is said that even the genius of Soyer failed during famine years to render it popular in Ireland as a soup. The cooking probably rendered the unpleasant sea-taste more decided. The dulse most prized is that which grows among the mussels near low-water mark and hence is known as shell dillish.

Besides the above plant, *Iridœa edulis* is known as dulse in Scotland and is eaten raw there. It does not grow on our coast. Neither indeed does the so-called pepper dulse, which is the *Laurencia pinnatifida* of botanists.

(J. T. R.)

DULUTH, a city of Minnesota, county-seat of St. Louis co., situated near the W. end of Lake Superior, 156 miles N. N. E. of St. Paul, lat. 46° 48′ N., long. 92° 6′ W. It is one of the eastern termini of the Northern Pacific Railroad. It stands on a hill-side picturesquely overlooking Duluth Bay, a fine natural harbor, enclosed by Minnesota Point; and on the outside of this point is the outer harbor, protected by a breakwater. The access of vessels to the inner port has been rendered more feasible by costly improvements. The Northern Pacific and other railways have also terminal facilities at Superior, Wis., a town on the S. side of Superior Bay, an extension of Duluth Bay, seven miles S. E. of Duluth; and the St. Paul and Duluth Railway connects with the Northern Pacific at a point twenty-four miles W. of Duluth. The town is named for Jean du Luth, a French gentleman who in 1679 travelled in this region. In 1860 it was chosen as the lake terminus of the Northern Pacific Railroad, there being already a few inhabitants on and near its site. Several other railroads now extend branch lines to Duluth, and six lines of steamers connect it with other lake-ports. It is the outlet for a vast lumber and wheat region, and ships large quantities of iron and copper ore from the Lake Superior mines. It has a court-house, board of trade, produce exchange, 2 national and 6 other banks, 27 churches, a masonic temple, opera-house, water-works, gas and electric light, immense grain elevators, lumber-mills, stock-yards, and iron-works. Population, 32,725.

DUMAS, ALEXANDRE, *fils*, a French dramatist, was born in Paris, July 26, 1824. He was the illegitimate son of Alexandre Dumas, the novelist and dramatist, who died in 1870. In his boyhood the elder Dumas recognized his son and gave him the legal right to bear his father's name. The younger Dumas was brought up partly by his mother and partly at a school kept by Goubaux, one of the authors of *Thirty Years; or, A Gambler's Life*, and of other plays less known to the American public. When he left school he mingled at once in the very mixed society which surrounded his prodigal father. At seventeen he wrote a volume of poems published in 1847 as *Pechés de jeunesse*; they are of very slight importance. He went with his father to Spain and Africa, and on his return he began to write novels in imitation of his father's; they are of almost as little importance as the early poems. He soon saw that he had not the inexhaustible imagination which made his father's success possible, and he gave up fantasy for fact, and thereafter relied on his observation to furnish forth his fictions. He studied the questionable life around him, and in 1848 published a novel called the *Dame aux Camélias*, partly founded on personal experience. This story succeeded at once, and it was followed by others. The popularity of the *Dame aux Camélias* as a novel suggested its dramatization, and by a very few days of hard labor the author turned it into a play, only to find its performance forbidden by the censors. When the duke of Morny came into power under Napoleon III. in 1852, it was acted at the Vaudeville Theatre, and was instantly successful; after thirty years it still holds its popularity and is frequently seen on the French stage. It has been used as the basis of the libretto of Verdi's *Traviata*, and as a deodorized English adaptation was prepared by Miss Jean Davenport (afterwards the wife of Gen. Lander) under the name of *Camille*, and in a modification of this anodyned adaptation the late Matilda Heron made her first great hit; since which time the play has been a favorite with American actresses. The *Dame aux Camélias* is not a wholesome piece, and its artistic quality is not of the highest order, but it is vigorous and affecting. It was followed on the stage by another hasty dramatization of a novel, *Diane de Lys*, acted at the Gymnase Theatre in 1853. Like the earlier play, *Diane de Lys* was in part at least the result of a personal experience, fortunately not so fatal in life as that which befell the hero on the stage. It was not as strong a play as the *Dame aux Camélias*, and its attraction has not endured. Yet by these two plays M. Dumas had made money enough to pay off the debts he had contracted in the reckless life of his youth, and so was enabled to take time and pains with his third piece, the *Demi-Monde*, acted two years later, in 1855. This is a comedy of manners in five acts, and it is not only the best play of its author, but one of the best French comedies of this century. It depicted a stratum of society which M. Dumas was the first to discover. By the phrase *demi-monde* he meant not the class of courtesans (to whom it is now generally applied), but the class of exiles from society. The half-world he discovered is peopled not by those who have always been outcasts and sinners, but by those who have fallen from grace. It is for the most part an association of repudiated wives, who have admitted to fellowship a few brevet widows and wives by courtesy only. There is a distinct boundary-line between these women once in society, but now fallen from it while still keeping up a semblance of its usages,—there is a sharp line between these and the venal courtesans who now call themselves members of the *demi-monde*. The play in which these people were first set on the stage is not altogether pleasing, but it is powerful and brilliant beyond all question. It is now in the repertory of the Comédie Française. In 1857, M. Dumas brought out the *Question d'Argent*, in 1858 the *Fils Naturel*, and in 1859 the *Père Prodigue*, three serious comedies in which he studied social questions. There is no denying the distinct want of taste shown in his choice of such titles as the *Natural Son* and the *Prodigal Father*, but M. Dumas is not greatly gifted with good taste; and no further evidence of this deficiency may be asked than his next play, the *Ami des Femmes*, acted in 1864, the subject of which is singularly indelicate. In 1868 he brought out the *Idées de Madame Aubray*, an exceedingly clever plea for the rehabilitation of the woman who has fallen once and through ignorance. In 1871 he produced the *Visite de Noces*, a psychologic and physiologic study in one act—a repulsive play, and yet probably not untrue to nature. In the same year he put on the stage the *Princesse Georges*, a comedy-drama in three acts. In these later plays it could be seen that the dramatist was slowly yielding place to the theorist, and that the comedy was becoming a sermon. In the next play, the *Femme de Claude*, this tendency was even more marked, and though greatly talked about the drama failed to attract. In the same year, however, he brought out *Monsieur Alphonse*, one of his simplest and strongest plays, acted in America with much success. In 1878 his *Étrangère* was performed at the Théâtre Français for many nights, and in 1881 his *Princesse de Bagdad* was acted there for very few nights; neither play is on the line of progress. Besides these pieces signed with M. Dumas's name he has had a hand in the writing of half a dozen others. Among them were the *Supplice d'une Femme* (1865), with Émile de Girardin; *Héloise Paranquet* (1866), with M. Armand Durantin; and the *Danicheff* (1876), with M. Corvin. He has revised with success his father's *Jeunesse de*

Louis XIV. (1874), and without success his father's *Joseph Balsamo* (1878). He tried one play anonymously; this was the *Filleul de Pompignac.* He began to collect his plays into a *Théâtre Complet* in 1868, prefixing to each piece a preface in which he discussed either the drama itself or the theories it suggested: six volumes of this collected edition have now appeared. Having begun to write critically and didactically in these prefaces, M. Dumas developed a great fondness for preaching. In 1872 he published *L'Homme-Femme,* a discussion of the woman question (translated into English, with an introduction, by Mr. George Vandenhoff); in 1880 a plea for *Divorce;* in 1881 *Les Femmes qui tuent et les femmes qui votent,* another woman's rights argument; and in 1882 a letter to M. Naquet, in which he declared his hostility to the Republic. He has also written a number of prefaces and essays and letters of one kind or another, all of which he is gathering into volumes with the apt title of *Entr' Actes.* Three volumes of these have already appeared. Mention should also be made of *L'Affaire Clémenceau,* a novel, in part autobiographic, published in 1867; it is a study of modern Parisian life, or rather a dissection of a French career, identical in manner and method with his later plays. When the chair of M. Joseph Lebrun became vacant in the French Academy, M. Dumas presented himself, and was elected Jan. 30, 1874, by twenty-two votes against eleven, Victor Hugo being present for the first time in years to vote for the son of his old adversary. M. Dumas took his seat in February, 1875, and in his speech declared that he felt that the honor of an election among the Forty Immortals had been conferred on him only because his father was no longer alive to receive it. M. d'Haussonville in his reply courteously but keenly criticised the works and theories of M. Dumas.

And these works and theories are of a truth strange. M. Dumas is a bundle of contradictions. Brought up amid vice, he has discovered the value of virtue, and he proclaims it abroad from the housetop in the language he heard in his unregenerate days. Uneducated, he sees the future of science and fills his prefaces with a parade of scientific erudition. As a moralist he is queer, as a theorist he is cranky, and as a sociologist he is wholly untrustworthy and erratic. But as a dramatist, as a mere maker of plays, he is marvellous. His skill in handling a delicate question on the stage, his tact in anticipating the objections to an unpalatable solution of a dramatic difficulty, his faculty of developing a situation of tense emotion in the briefest dialogue and with the utmost effect, his gift of epigram, and his power of being even eloquent for a moment if need be,—in all these things he is incomparable, in all these he has no rival on the French stage. His influence on the drama of the day has been very marked. After the production of Hugo's *Hernani* in 1830 the Romantics had run riot on the French stage for five or ten years, until they began rapidly to go to seed. The production of the *Dame aux Camélias* in 1852 changed the whole front of the contemporary drama: it revealed to the many competent and clever dramatists of the day the possibilities of modern life, and it suggested the best method of treating the problems of modern life in the theatre. M. Emile Augier, for instance, was writing pretty and poetic plays before 1852, but it was after 1852 that he wrote the fine series of social satires, scorching and severe, which have made him the first dramatist of our day. And on others, on the late Théodore Barrière, on M. Victorien Sardou, on MM. Meilhac and Halévy, his influence has not been less marked. M. Dumas has been called immoral, but unjustly. To the innocent and ignorant his works are no doubt demoralizing. To the audience for which he writes, to Parisian playgoers, he appears as a stern moralist. He is sincere and earnest in his exhortations to quit evil and cleave to the good; and if his views as to evil and good in morals may at times seem confused to an English or American spectator, it must be remembered that M. Dumas is a recent convert to morality—that he only began to go to Sunday-school when he was thirty, and that some of his early and earthly notions cling to him still.

(B. M.)

DUMAS, JEAN BAPTISTE ANDRÉ (1800-1884), the most prominent French chemist during the last half century, was born at Alais in the department of the Gard, July 14, 1800. His father came of an ancient family, which at the revocation of the Edict of Nantes had separated into two branches, of which the Protestant branch emigrated, while the Catholic, to which his immediate ancestors belonged, remained in France. The father was clerk to the municipality of Alais. The son pursued the study of the classics as the foundation of his education, the numerous monuments of the Roman period in the vicinity of Alais contributing to the interest of such studies. At the same time the numerous industrial establishments in the neighborhood, such as glass-works, coal and antimony mines, tile- and earthenware-manufactories, became familiar to him in his early youth. He was preparing for an examination for entrance into the navy when the political events of 1814-15 obliged the family to select another career for him. He was therefore entered as an apprentice to an apothecary in Alais, but in 1816 left for Geneva, where he hoped for a wider field for his activities. He obtained the superintendency of a large laboratory belonging to the Le Royer pharmacy, and at the same time was enabled to hear lectures on botany by De Candolle, on physics by Pictèt, and on chemistry by Gaspard De la Rive. His attention was first turned to chemical study and research by the appearance of Biot's work on physics and the papers of Berzelius, Davy, Gay Lussac, and Thenard. His first individual research was upon the presence of water of crystallization in salts. When he showed his results to De la Rive he was told that Berzelius had anticipated him. He next worked out a method for determining experimentally the density of simple and compound bodies. De la Rive did not think much of it. Dumas said "the first time my experiments were good but they were not new; this time they are new but they do not appear to be good. I shall have to try again." Nevertheless, the method of vapor-density determination, whereby the varying weight of a constant volume of vapor is ascertained, still in current use under the name of Dumas' method, is practically the same with that originated by him at this early age. He next carried out several researches in physiological chemistry with Prevost, which were published and became widely known. An event which had a deciding influence upon his life was his meeting at this date with Alexander von Humboldt, the great naturalist and traveller. Humboldt's account of the scientific life in Paris and of the great advantages of constant intercourse and association with the leaders in chemical research led Dumas to give up his idea of settling in Geneva and brought him to Paris in 1821. Here he was kindly received by Thenard, Ampère, Gay Lussac, and others. His marriage in 1826 with the daughter of Alexander

Brogniart, the geologist, also aided in his advancement in scientific circles. Through the efforts of Ampère, the great physicist, he was appointed to two lectureships in succession, and soon became known as one of the most original and active workers in the domain of chemistry. His name will always be linked in the history of chemistry with what is known as the substitution theory, which he opposed to Berzelius' dualistic hypothesis. The views then accepted had been founded upon the relatively simple study of mineral compounds. All compounds were supposed to be formed of two proximate elements, which might be either simple bodies or combinations of a low order. The illustrious Swedish chemist, Berzelius, exercised at this time an uncontested authority, and to doubt his explanations of chemical phenomena implied great temerity. Nevertheless Dumas found that chlorine "possessed the singular power of combining with the hydrogen of organic bodies and at the same time of replacing it, atom for atom." This was the first announcement of a law, which is now proved by thousands of analogous facts, and which is the keystone of the theory of substitution. While Laurent and Gerhardt ably assisted in the elaboration of the new doctrine, Berzelius opposed it from the first with the weight of his ability and widespread influence. It may be of interest to note, on the authority of Prof. A. W. Hofmann, what a trival circumstance led Dumas into his study of these substitution phenomena. At a soiree of Charles X., the wax candles in burning not only gave a smoky flame but developed fumes of hydrochloric acid gas. Brogniart, as the director of the government porcelain manufactory at Sevres, was asked to investigate the matter and he intrusted it to his son-in-law, Dumas, who found that the wax of the candles had been bleached with chlorine, and that some of this element had combined chemically with the wax and was only liberated in the burning of the wax as hydrochloric acid. Dumas' interpretation of his results in the study of new organic compounds not only led him into antagonism with Berzelius, but also with Liebig, who occupied the foremost position in Germany as authority in the domain of organic chemistry. Liebig's theory of the part which compound radicals or groups of elements played in organic chemistry was only a modification of the dualistic theory of Berzelius, and could not be reconciled with Dumas' substitution results, so the two great leaders carried on for years a controversy, which was sharp, indeed almost acrimonious. Dumas gradually built up from his first views the great theory of chemical types or family groups as found among organic compounds. This theory, which allows of the widest substitution change and yet preserves a unity and class resemblance among the groups, somewhat modified in its modes of application, is still largely used in the classification of organic compounds. In the end Dumas may be said to have triumphed. Long after both Liebig and he had outlived the heat and ardor of their youthful contests, this was virtually acknowledged by Liebig, when at the Paris Exposition of 1867, at a dinner given by French chemists to their foreign brethren, he was asked by Dumas, who was presiding, why he had given so large a portion of his later years to agricultural chemistry instead of pure chemistry. Liebig replied that "since the theory of substitution was accepted, masters were no longer necessary, that workmen could build the edifice as well."

In later years Dumas withdrew from active research and teaching and occupied himself with his duties at the academy of sciences and in serving on numerous scientific commissions. In the early part of the past winter he went to Cannes in the south of France by the advice of his physician, and there he died on the 11th of April of this year. Dumas had received the highest scientific honors both of his own and of foreign countries. Entering the academy of sciences in his thirty-second year, on the death of Flourens, he was elected one of its permanent secretaries. On the decease of Guizot, he succeeded to his vacant chair at the Academie Française. He received from the Emperor Napoleon, in 1863, the grand cross of the Legion of Honor, and under the present republic became a life-senator. From England he received the Copley medal of the Royal Society in 1843, and the Faraday medal of the Chemical Society in 1869. (S. P. S.)

DÜMICHEN, JOHANNES, a German Egyptologist, was born Oct. 15, 1833, at Weissholz, near Grossglogau, Silesia, where his father was pastor of the church. He was educated at home, and afterwards in the gymnasium at Glogau. By his father's wish he studied theology and philology at the universities of Berlin and Breslau from 1852 to 1855, and then resolved to devote himself to the study of Egyptian antiquities. For this purpose he attended the University of Berlin from 1859 to 1862, where he enjoyed the instruction of Lepsius and Brugsch. Thus prepared for his lifework, he set out in Oct., 1862, on his first Egyptian journey, intending to spend six months in the examination of monuments in the valley of the Nile, but when in the country extended the time to three years, during which he visited not only Egypt proper and the adjoining desert, but also Lower and Upper Nubia, and even the plains of Soudan. The city El Efun in the province of Sennaar, on the banks of the Bahr-el-Azrak, beyond Soba, where are the ruins of the capital of the ancient Christian kingdom of Aloa, was the southern limit of his travels. Dümichen and his master, Lepsius, are the only Egyptologists of modern times who have travelled throughout the wide dominions of the ancient kingdom of Ethiopia. From this journey, Dümichen returned in the summer of 1865 with a valuable collection of hieroglyphic inscriptions, drawings of monuments, and notes. In 1868 the photographic corps of the Prussian expedition sent to Aden to observe the solar eclipse was ordered on its return in August to visit Egypt and take views of the temples and tombs, under the direction of Herr Dümichen. Although the work was thus performed in a season generally unfavorable in Egypt for such purposes, the results were of great value. In 1869, at the request of the khedive, Ismail Pacha, Dümichen attended the ceremonies at the opening of the Suez Canal, and sailed up the Nile as far as Nubia. On the re-establishment of the University of Strassburg in 1872, Dümichen was made professor extraordinarius of Egyptology, and in 1879 he became, by imperial order, a professor in the philosophical faculty of that university. In August, 1875, he made his fifth visit to Egypt, returning in the following April. Four months were spent in removing the rubbish in which the great temple of Dendera had been buried to the pediment, and thus a large number of inscriptions was uncovered; two months more were spent in work among the tombs at Thebes. Since that time Dümichen has remained in Germany, actively engaged in the duties of his professorship and in authorship. He has published the results of his investigations not only in the *Zeitschrift für Ægyptische Sprache* and other journals, but in a long series of valuable works. Among these are *Bauurkunde des Tempelanlagen von Dendera* (Leipsic, 1865); *Geographische Inschriften Altägypter Denkmäler* (2 vols. of plates, with another of explanation (Leipsic, 1865); *Altägypt. Kalenderinschr.* (Leipsic, 1866); *Historische Inschriften* (Leipsic, 1869); *Altägypt. Tempelinschr. Edfu und Dendera* (Leipsic, 2 vols., 1867); *Die Flotte einer Ægypt. Königin aus dem 17 Jahr. v. Ch.* (Leipsic, 1868); *Der Felsentempel von Abu-Simbel* (Berlin, 1869); *Resultate der archäolog-photographischen Expedition* (2 vols., Leipsic, 1870, and Berlin, 1871). The first volume of this work contains the hieroglyphic plates, with preface and explanation by the author, besides an essay on *The Ancient Egyptian Naval Affairs*, by Graser, and another on *The Pictures of Animals*, by R. Hartmann. The second volume contains 57 photographs with descriptions. Later works by Dümichen are, *Ueber der Tempel und Gräber im alten Ægypten* (Leipsic, 1872); *Ueber die Regierungszeit einer Ægypt. Königs* (Leipsic, 1874); *Baugeschichte der Denderatempels* (Strassburg, 1877); *Die Oasen der libyschen Wüste* (Strassburg, 1877); *Der grosse Thebanische Fest Kalender* (Leipsic, 1881); *Geschichte des alten Ægyptens* (Berlin, 1880).

DUMMER, JEREMIAH (1680–1739), an American scholar and author, was born at Boston in 1680. He graduated at Harvard College in 1699, studied theology, and began to preach, but was not popular. He spent some years at the University of Utrecht, and obtained there the doctor's degree. After his return to America he was sent to England as agent of the colony of Massachusetts, and remained there from 1710 to 1721. When the charters of the New England colonies were threatened in 1721 he wrote an eloquent defence of them, which was published in London (1728). He also published some Latin philosophical and theological treatises at Utrecht. He procured for the library of Yale College a donation of 800 volumes. He died at Plaiston, England, May 19, 1739.

DUNCAN, JOHN, LL. D. (1796–1870), a Scotch Presbyterian clergyman and Orientalist, was born at Gilcomston, near Aberdeen, in 1796. He graduated at the University of Aberdeen in 1814, and after studying theology at Edinburgh was licensed to preach in 1825. In the next year he came under the influence of Cæsar Malan, and afterwards, though subject to periods of depression and even skepticism, was truly pious. In 1831 he became pastor of a church in Glasgow, but in 1841 he went to Pesth, Hungary, as a missionary to the Jews. He returned to Scotland in 1843, and was made professor of Hebrew and Oriental languages in New College, Edinburgh, which position he held till his death, Feb. 26, 1870. He was not only an eminently learned man, but was a profound thinker on the most abstruse problems of philosophy and theology, yet was noted for his simple piety. Many of his sayings have been collected in W. Knight's *Colloquia Peripatetica by the late John Duncan* (Edin., 1870), in his *Life*, by David Brown (1872), in *Recollections of Dr. John Duncan*, by Rev. A. Moody Stuart, and in another volume, *John Duncan in the Pulpit and at the Communion Table* (Edin., 1874).

DUNCKER, MAXIMILIAN WOLFGANG THEODOR, a German historian, was born at Berlin, Oct. 15, 1811. He is a son of the celebrated book publisher, Karl Duncker, and studied at Bonn and Berlin from 1830 to 1834. By his essay on *Origines Germanica* (1840) he became a candidate for a professorship and in 1842 he was appointed to a position in the University at Halle. Here he engaged in literary work also, editing a journal and publishing an essay on *The Crisis of the Reformation* (1846). In 1848 he was elected a delegate to the National Parliament and acted with the party which favored the union of Germany under the leadership of Prussia. His pamphlet on the history of that parliament (1849) set forth the principles of his party; and these were further illustrated in his biographical sketch of Heinrich von Gagern (1850). He took part in the revision of the constitution of 1848, and in the German diet at Erfurt in 1850 acted with the national constitutional party. In a pamphlet called *Four Months of Foreign Politics* he criticised severely the policy of the Prussian minister Manteuffel, charging on him the loss of Olmütz. Withdrawing from state affairs he devoted himself to his great historical work, *Geschichte des Alterthums*, which appeared in four volumes from 1852 to 1857, and has in its fifth edition been enlarged to seven volumes. In 1857 he accepted a professorship in Tübingen University, but two years later was called to Berlin as a member of the council of Prince von Hohenzollern. In 1861 he was made a councillor of the Crown Prince, and from 1867 to 1874 had charge of the Prussian State-archives. In this position he labored diligently, establishing depositories for the archives in various cities and erecting new buildings for the purpose in Berlin, Düsseldorf, and Breslau. In 1874 he retired from office and he has since devoted himself to historical labors, the chief result of which is *Aus der Zeit Friedrichs II. und Friedrich Wilhelms III.*, though he has also treated of the times of Friedrich Wilhelm II., the ministry of Count Haugwitz and of Prince Hardenberg. As a member of the Berlin Academy since 1873 he has contributed to its proceedings several discussions of difficult questions in Greek history.

DUNGLISON, ROBLEY (1798–1869), an American physician and author, was born at Keswick, Cumberland, England, Jan. 4, 1798. His mother, a woman of remarkable intellectual power, bestowed unusual care on his education. At the age of seventeen he commenced the study of medicine, and afterwards pursued it in London, Edinburgh, and in Paris. He was admitted to practice by the Royal College of Surgeons in 1819, and established himself in London, at the same time lecturing on obstetrics and contributing to medical journals. He became editor of the *London Medical Repository* and the *Medical Intelligencer*. Having visited Germany to complete his medical education, he graduated at Erlangen in 1823. His reputation attracted the attention of F. W. Walker, who had been sent to England by ex-Pres. Jefferson to select professors for the newly founded University of Virginia. Dr. Dunglison accepted the professorship in that institution, and removed to Virginia in October of that year. During the nine years he spent there he delivered lectures on every branch of medical science and published a large number of treatises. He became the professional adviser of Jefferson and Madison, and his house at Charlottesville, Va., was the centre of a refined circle. In 1833 he accepted the professorship of therapeutics and materia medica in the University of Maryland, and removed to Baltimore. After spending three years there he removed to Philadelphia to become professor of the institutes of medicine in the Jefferson Medical College. Owing to his talents, reputation, and personal influence this college had an unprecedented career of success, his class in 1860 numbering 630 students. Dr. Dunglison remained in this position until June, 1868, when he resigned on account of ill-health. He died at

Philadelphia, April 1, 1869. He received in 1825, from Yale College, the honorary degree of M.D., and in 1852, from Jefferson College, that of LL.D. He was also the recipient of numerous testimonials and marks of respect from medical, scientific, and literary institutions in Europe and America. Dr. Dunglison was a member of many literary societies and vice-president of the American Philosophical Society. He was also vice-president of the Philadelphia Institution for the Blind, and besides devoting much time and attention to that class of unfortunates published a large dictionary specially prepared for their use. He was noted for his liberal spirit and freedom from prejudice. He was a frequent contributor to the leading medical, surgical, and scientific journals of the United States and Great Britain. His most important work is his *Dictionary of Medical Science and Literature*, which was first issued in 1833, and attained a success almost unparalleled in that department of literature. Among his other publications are: *Diseases of the Stomach and Bowels of Children* (London, 1824), *The Principles of Human Physiology* (1832), *General Therapeutics and Materia Medica* (1836), *The Medical Student* (1837), *New Remedies* (1839), *Human Health* (1844). He also edited new editions of *Magendie's Formulary*, *The Cyclopædia of Practical Medicine*, *Roget's Physiology*, *Traill's Medical Jurisprudence*, and other works. In 1870 his son, Dr. R. J. Dunglison, published a *Memoir of Dr. Robley Dunglison*, and in 1872 he edited the *History of Medicine*, left incomplete by his father.

DUNHAM, CARROLL (1828-1877), an American homœopathic physician, was born in New York city, Oct. 29, 1828. He graduated in 1847 at Columbia College, and received the degree of M.D. from the College of Physicians and Surgeons of New York in 1850. Having been cured of a dangerous illness by a homœopathic physician, he began to investigate the "new system." He next went abroad seeking instruction from the most eminent teachers in Dublin, Paris, Berlin, and Vienna. Under Bornninghausen at Münster he studied the "new method" of prescribing drugs. On his return to America in 1852 he began the practice of homœopathy in Brooklyn. In 1858 a severe attack of illness caused him to remove to Newburg, N. Y., where his patients followed him, and he was soon again professionally busy. In 1864 he removed to Irvington-on-the-Hudson, making his home there until his death. He was professor of materia medica in the New York Homœopathic Medical College for several years, and was dean of the faculty. During his last visit to Europe in 1874 he conceived the idea of a world's convention of homœopathy, and secured the co-operation of foreign physicians. In 1875 the American Institute of Homœopathy elected him to preside at this convention in Philadelphia in 1876. He also edited its *Transactions*, but overwork in behalf of the convention exhausted his strength. He died Feb. 18, 1877. Dr. Dunham contributed frequently to American and foreign journals, and since his death his lectures have been published under the titles *Lectures on Materia Medica* and *Homœopathy the Science of Therapeutics*.

DUNKERS. The rise of this denomination, which has been variously known as "Dunkards," "Dunkers," "Tunkers" (derived from the German *Tunken*, to dip), "Tumblers," "German Baptists," and "Brethren," was in Schwarzenau, on the Edder, in Witgenstein, Germany, in 1708, in a meeting of a number of Pietists to whom the teaching and practices of the Lutheran and Reformed Churches had become unsatisfactory. Seven of them met privately to read and study the Bible, and resolved to be guided by the light which they received from it. Believing that it taught baptism by immersion, government by the congregation, and separation from the world, they made these principles the basis of their system. Their minister, Alexander Mack, having first been baptized by a member of the company, immersed in turn the brethren and sisters in the Edder. This congregation increased and soon gave rise to others. Severe persecutions scattered the members widely, and in 1719 the original congregation, which had migrated to Friesland, sailed for America, whither the others came ten years later. Four years after the arrival of the first party at Germantown, Pa., the Brethren held their first love-feast. There had been differences among them which had prevented them from instituting a church with authority to administer the sacraments. These differences being settled, new converts were baptized and received into fellowship, and a love-feast was held. It is supposed that a church council, according to the usual course, was held the day before the love-feast; and that during the first thirty or forty years this plan was adhered to. In that period the congregations were all within the territory lying between the Delaware and the Schuylkill. Gradually this territory extended to the Susquehanna and beyond, and into New Jersey and Maryland. As the churches multiplied and became farther apart, it was found impracticable to have them all represented at every ordinary love-feast, so a "big meeting" or council was appointed to be held annually. The first of these councils was held between 1750 and 1760. The Annual Meeting, the most important of the gatherings of the Brethren, assembles on the anniversary of Pentecost. At first it was held alternately east and west of the Susquehanna; next the Allegheny mountains were regarded as the dividing line, and finally the Ohio River was chosen. One year the council meets somewhere east of the Ohio; the next year west of it. This indicates the westward march of the denomination.

They made no effort to number their churches or members until 1877, when a census was taken which showed that there were between 300 and 400 churches and about 60,000 members. Many of the churches are small, but each has two or more ministers, the average being about four, according to the statistics. A fourth or more of the total membership is in Pennsylvania. About 8000 are in Indiana, 6000 in Illinois, and upwards of 7000 in Virginia and West Virginia. The earlier converts were Germans, and all the congregations used the German language. Though that tongue is still extensively employed, the English congregations are multiplying. The list of over 1500 ministers is composed chiefly of names of German origin. It is said that some of the earlier immigrants among the Brethren were men of education; but the denomination has given little or no attention to the training of their children beyond the rudimentary branches. It is only within a few years that they have successfully established a high school. Thirty years ago the annual council in reply to the question whether Brethren might patronize high schools, advised them to be "very cautious and not mind high things, but condescend to men of low estate." They generally send their children to public schools, but do not think college life is wholesome for them. They have a normal school at Huntingdon, Pa., of some years' standing, in which the English branches and drawing and music are taught; also seminaries at Ashland, O., and Mount Morris, Ill.

The Brethren, like other denominations, have had several divisions. Before their first congregation had been in Pennsylvania a decade there was a schism in it, Conrad Peysel (or Beissel) and six other members withdrawing and forming the branch known as the Seventh Day German Baptists, a monastic institution at Ephrata being one of the features of the movement which is now nearly if not quite extinct. In 1790 occurred another secession, led by John Ham, who held Universalist ideas. This division, which was never very strong in members, has died out. The most important separation, amounting, indeed, almost to a disruption of the communion, took place a few years ago, the result being three distinct branches. The cause of this division, or divisions, was chiefly, if not wholly, differences concerning the treatment of disciplinary questions and the character of the decisions of the annual council. In order to understand these questions it will be necessary to state as briefly as possible some of the principles of the Brethren. They have held quite strictly until recent years to the principle of nonconformity to the world. Simplicity in dress has been so strenuously insisted on that a kind of uniform for men and women has always been distinctive of the denomination. Decisions have been promulgated by the council against various articles of apparel, against the shaving of the beard, the parting of the hair on one side, "fashionable hats" for the sisters, etc. Many a council has wrestled with the question whether the "old order" required a "standing" or a "rolling" collar to the coat, which as commonly worn by the Brethren was wont to be fastened with hooks and eyes, instead of buttons, whence they came to be nicknamed "Hookers." The principle of simplicity in dress was applied to other things, and new ideas and appliances, such as carpets, pianos, and costly articles in households, were discouraged, at least until they became common. Insurance, the taking of interest, serving on juries, voting or accepting public office, legal oaths, have all been prohibited to the Brethren. In recent years a more liberal feeling respecting these and kindred matters has obtained place in the denomination. Sunday-schools, high schools, missions, and other features not countenanced in former times have been introduced. These evidences of conformity to the spirit of the age alarmed the more conservative Brethren, and they demanded that those refusing to observe the "old order" strictly, not only in matters of conduct and dress but in questions of religious teaching and discipline, should be rigorously dealt with. On the one side there was the extreme conservative party, on the other the progressives, who while holding to the principle of plainness contended that a particular form need not be enjoined. Between these two parties was the great majority of the Brethren, who tried but unsuccessfully to bring the two wings together on the middle ground. The conservatives, as this middle party may be called, defend themselves against the attacks of the "old order" Brethren, first by charging that the latter are more rigorous in their requirements than were the fathers of the church, and secondly by contending that in the introduction of Sunday-schools they have only made a new application of the principle held by the fathers, namely, that the youth should be religiously educated, and assert that if the fathers were living now they would approve the educational enterprises which have grown out of the needs of the Brethren. They claim to have made progress with the age and rejoice in it as salutary, but they believe they are going as rapidly in this direction as the best interests of the church will permit. The progressives wished to get on faster, but they specially protested against the act of the annual council of 1882, by which the decisions of that body, which had always been regarded as simply advisory, were made mandatory.

The progressives hold no regular annual council, but they meet occasionally in convention. They are more strictly congregational than the other bodies. They believe in an educated ministry, and hold that ministers should be supported by the congregations. They have about seventy congregations and 5000 members. Their organ is the *Brethren's Evangelist*, of Ashland, Ohio.

The "old order" Brethren number, it is estimated, 3000 or 4000 members. They held their yearly meeting in 1884, in June, at Beaverdam, Md., where several deliverances, indicating their position on disputed questions, were adopted. These deliverances were against holding prayer-meetings except in cases of peril or persecution or famine; against revival meetings, bells in churches, school exhibitions, lyceums, against investing in government bonds, against lightning-rods.

The conservatives, or middle party, held their annual council in 1884 in Stillwater, near Dayton, O. Their chief organ is *The Gospel Messenger*, published at Mount Morris, Ill., and at Huntingdon, Pa.

The creed of the Brethren is in substance that held by all evangelical denominations. They have, however, peculiar usages. They baptize by trine immersion, and they observe the communion after the Lord's Supper, which is always held in the evening, and in connection with which the ordinance of feet-washing is celebrated and the holy kiss given. In discipline they use the "ban." In polity they are congregational. The churches are gathered into district meetings, which are represented in the annual meeting, or council.

Their ministers are selected by vote of the male and female members of churches, and are of three degrees, the third and highest being that of elder or bishop. Those of the first degree are on probation; those of the second have authority to hold meetings, administer baptism, and solemnize marriages. It is only those of the third degree who are ordained. They are the highest officers of the church, and are called overseers or householders. Women have equal rights with the men except in conducting church services. A ritual has in late years been observed in the administration of baptism. The order of worship resembles that of other non-ritualistic denominations. Singing, exhortation, and prayer, all brief, open the services, and after sermons from two or more preachers the meetings close with the same exercises, no benediction being given.

The Brethren have always been strong anti-slavery men and consistent teetotalers. (H. K. C.)

DUNKIRK, a city of New York, in Chautauqua co., is on Dunkirk harbor, Lake Erie. It is the western terminus of the main line of the New York, Lake Erie, and Western Railway, and the northern terminus of the Dunkirk, Allegheny Valley, and Pittsburg

(See Vol. VI. P. 469 Am. ed. (p. 544 Edin. ed.)

Railway. It is 40 miles from Buffalo and 130 from Cleveland. The New York, Chicago, and St. Louis, the Buffalo, New York, and Philadelphia (Pittsburg Division), and the Lake Shore Railways also pass through the city. The town was first settled in 1805, and was originally called Chadwick's Bay. It was first incorporated as a village in 1837, under its present name, and as a city in 1880. When the Erie Railway was first built much of the lake traffic for New York came by boat to Dunkirk, where freight was transferred to the cars. The Brooks Locomotive Works here have a capacity of 18 locomotives per month, and employ 1100 men. The other manufactures are machinery, boilers, knit-goods, flour, plaster, springs, cigars, beer-barrels, tanks, and agricultural implements. There are 10 churches in the city, 10 public schools and 2 church schools, a fire and a police department. There are 15 hotels, 2 national banks and 1 private, 1 daily newspaper and 4 weeklies. The city has gas-works, Holly water-works, two parks, a street-railway, and a good system of sewerage. The harbor is artificial, and is protected by a pier 1650 feet long. There are 2 light-houses and 4 docks. The total valuation of property is $1,609,470. The public debt is about $212,000. Population, 9402.

DUNMORE, a borough of Pennsylvania, in Lackawanna co., is on the Delaware, Lackawanna, and Western Railroad and the Pennsylvania Coal Company's Railroad, 1½ miles east of Scranton, the county-seat, with which it is connected by a horse-car railway. It has 5 churches, 8 schools, large machine-shops, and a good trade. It is mainly supported by the coal-mining of Lackawanna Valley. It was incorporated as a borough in 1851, and is free from debt. Its water supply is furnished by the Dunmore Gas and Water Company, which has a reservoir with a capacity of 1,000,000 gallons. Population, 8288.

DÜNTZER, JOHANN HEINRICH JOSEPH, a German philologist and literary historian, was born at Cologne, July 12, 1813. He studied in the gymnasium at Cologne and in the Universities of Bonn and Berlin, devoting himself in the latter to the study of Sanskrit. His first publication was *Die Lehre von der Lateinischen Wortbildung* (1836), but in the same year he issued the first of his critical essays, *Goethes Faust in seiner Einheit und Ganzheit*. He graduated as doctor of philosophy in 1836, and became a privat-docent in Bonn, but afterwards, disagreeing with the faculty there, he went to Cologne in 1846 to take charge of the library of the Catholic gymnasium. His philological works include *Homer und der epische Cyklus* (1839); *Kritik und Erklärung der Horazischen Gedichte* (5 vols., 1840-44); *Die Römische Satiriker* (1846); *Aristarch* (1862); *Homerische Abhandlungen* (1872); *Die Homerischen Fragen* (1874); with school-editions of Homer and Horace. Düntzer has also written a long series on works of Goethe, among which are *Goethe als Dramatiker* (1837); *Goethes Prometheus und Pandora* (1850); *Goethes Faust* (2 vols., 1850-51); *Frauenbilder aus Goethes Jugendzeit* (1852); *Freundesbilder aus Goethes Leben* (1853); *Schiller und Goethe* (1859); *Neue Goethe-Studien* (1861); *Aus Goethes Freundeskreise* (1868); *Zwei Bekerte, Zacharias Werner und Sophie von Schardt* (1873); *Charlotte von Stein* (1874). Düntzer has also published *Erläuterungen zu den deutschen Klassikern* (1855-82), and has assisted in a complete edition of Goethe's works. He has also edited collections of letters of Goethe, Schiller, Herder, and others eminent in literature.

DUPANLOUP, FÉLIX ANTOINE PHILIBERT (1802-1878), a French bishop, born at St. Félix, Savoy, Jan. 3, 1802. In early childhood he chose the clerical profession, and when seven years old was sent to Paris to be educated. He was ordained priest in 1825, and in 1827 became chaplain to the Count de Chambord, in 1828 a catechist of the Orleans princes, and afterwards was a chaplain and almoner in the dauphin's household. In 1837 he became vicar-general to the archbishop of Paris and head of the diocesan seminary. He was a superb pulpit orator, austere in private life, and towards the poor he was charitable to a fault. In 1838 he attended the death-bed of Talleyrand, who had entertained a warm affection for him and predicted his rise to eminence. In 1841 he took a theological professorship in the Sorbonne, but his lectures at the Sorbonne were unpopular in all parts of the Latin quarter, and he did not long retain that place. In 1849 the Abbé Dupanloup was consecrated bishop of Orléans. Here, as elsewhere throughout his life, he took an active part in the work of education, both opposing the government plan of sustaining schools not distinctly religious in their tone and at the same time combating those who, with the Abbé Gaume, wished to exclude from the schools the writings of pagan or non-Christian writers. In May, 1854, he was admitted to the French Academy and wielded considerable influence, but in 1871, when Littré, whose admission he had strongly opposed, at last gained an entrance, the bishop withdrew. In the National Assembly he was for years one of the most prominent and influential of the deputies, taking a chief part in all educational questions and acting as the leader of the clerical party. He was an active defender of the temporal power of the pope, but at the Vatican Council, as well as before it, he opposed the decree of papal infallibility, which, however, he at once accepted when it was officially proclaimed. During the German occupation of Orléans in 1870 he did much to soften the rigor of the invaders. At the same time he warmly welcomed the English ladies who came under the red cross flag to assist in caring for the wounded. He was a man of noble presence and generous nature. In politics he was regarded as a moderate legitimist. Under the third republic he was a member of the superior council of public instruction. He died at Laincey, Oct. 11, 1878. Among his works are an *Exposition of the Principal Truths of the Faith* (1832); *Elements of Sacred Rhetoric* (1841); a *Treatise on Education* (3 vols., 1855-57); and another *On the Higher Education*; ten volumes of pastoral, ecclesiastical, and oratorical studies; a treatise *On Pontifical Sovereignty*; *Souvenirs of Rome*; an Essay on *Popular Preaching*; a *Defence of the Liberty of the Church*; a pamphlet on Freemasonry; and many minor essays and papers. Sketches of his life have been published by Pelletier (1876), by Clerc, and by Hairdet (1878).

DUPONCEAU, PETER STEPHEN, LL.D. (1760-1844), an American jurist and philologist, was born June 3, 1760, on the Isle of Rhé, France, where his father held a military command. He studied at colleges St. Jean d'Angély and Bressuire, and after the death of his father went to Paris in December, 1775, where he was employed by Count de Gébelin in translating English and Italian books. In 1777 he came to the United States as private secretary to Baron Steuben, and on Feb. 18, 1778, was made captain by brevet in the Revolutionary army. His first military experience was at Valley Forge, where he assisted Steuben in preparing his system of army discipline. At the close of the campaign of 1779 a disease of the lungs obliged him to remain inactive for some months, but in 1780 he went with Steuben to the South. Returning to Philadelphia, he was employed by Robert R. Livingstone, Secretary of Foreign Affairs, from October, 1781, till June 4, 1783. Having become a citizen of Pennsylvania, he studied law, and was admitted to the Philadelphia bar in 1785. He soon rose to eminence in his profession, being especially skilful in questions of civil and foreign law, and was frequently employed in the Supreme Court of the United States. When the Federal Constitution was under discussion in Pennsylvania in 1788, he opposed it, but afterwards confessed that subsequent events had proved him wrong in this. When the United States acquired Louisiana in 1803, President Jefferson offered him the position of chief-justice of that Territory, but he declined it.

Duponceau was an ardent admirer of the political and social institutions of his adopted country, and delighted to show his reverence for William Penn. He established a society to commemorate Penn's landing, and wished that event to be celebrated annually. He was president of the American Philosophical Society, of the Athenæum, and of the Pennsylvania Historical Society, and was a member of many other literary and scientific societies. Besides general labors in connection with these, he especially devoted himself to philology. In 1819 he published an essay on the *Structure of the Indian Languages*, and in 1835 the French Institute awarded him the Volney prize for a *Memoir on the Indian Languages of North America*, and elected him a corresponding member of the Institute. In 1838 he published a *Dissertation on the Nature and Character of the Chinese System of Writing*, in which he maintained that the written characters represented sounds and not ideas. Believing that this country affords great facilities for the culture of the silkworm and of the mulberry tree, he induced M. d'Homergue of Nismes, France, to establish the manufacture of silk in Philadelphia, and spent much labor and money in the effort to make it successful. He died at Philadelphia, April 1, 1844.

Among his numerous publications are a translation of Bynkershoek's *Laws of War* (1810); a treatise on *The Nature and Extent of the Jurisdiction of the Courts of the United States* (1824); a *Brief View of the Constitution of the United States* (1834); and a translation of *A Description of New Sweden*, by Thomas Campanius Holm.

DUPONT, SAMUEL FRANCIS (1803–1865), an American naval officer, was born at Bergen Point, N. J., Sept. 27, 1803. His father, who was the son of the distinguished French publicist and statesman, Pierre Samuel DuPont de Nemours, had left France in 1799, and for a time resided in New Jersey, at Bergen Point—before undertaking in Delaware the establishment of the great gunpowder works with which various members of his family have since been connected. Samuel Francis was appointed a midshipman in the United States navy Dec. 19, 1815, and his service was continuous from that time until near the close of his life. In 1826 he reached the grade of lieutenant, and in 1842 that of commander. In 1845 he was sent to the Pacific in command of the frigate Congress, the flag-ship of Commodore Stockton's squadron, and he reached Monterey, in California, in 1846, just at the beginning of the war with Mexico. Placed in command of the sloop-of-war Cyane, he helped to clear the Gulf of California of Mexican armed vessels. In November, 1847, when Com. Shubrick took Mazatlan, DuPont headed the line of boats which made the attack, and in the following February he landed a force of sailors and marines and relieved Lieut. Heywood, who had been surrounded by a large number of Mexicans. DuPont reached the grade of captain in 1855, and in 1857 was sent on special duty to China in command of the steam-frigate Minnesota, returning two years later, after a cruise to Japan, India, and Arabia.

At the outbreak of the civil war in 1861 he was in command of the navy-yard at Philadelphia, and he rendered valuable service to the Government in the organization and equipment of its naval force. In September he was appointed flag-officer, and assigned to the command of the South Atlantic squadron. He proceeded at once to this important station, and on October 29 moved from Hampton Roads with a fleet of 75 vessels of all sorts, carrying a land-force of about 10,000 men, commanded by Gen. W. T. Sherman. The object of the expedition was the capture of Port Royal, S. C., and after encountering severe storms the force gathered off the harbor, November 4–6. On the 7th DuPont attacked the two defensive works—Fort Walker on Hilton Head and Fort Beauregard on the point opposite. Leading himself in the flag-ship Wabash, his ships passed three times around between the forts in an elliptic course, firing in turn as they passed; by keeping them thus in motion he avoided serious damage from the guns of the enemy. After a severe engagement, lasting over four hours, the forts were evacuated. This signal success at an important juncture served to maintain the courage of the national Government and of the friends of the Union, as well as to inspire confidence in the efficiency of the navy and the skill and courage of its officers. In February and March following, with his flag-ship and some other armed vessels, DuPont moved down the coast, taking Fort Clinch on Amelia Island and the town of Fernandina, St. Mary's, Brunswick, Darien, Jacksonville, and St. Augustine, thus regaining nearly the whole of this part of the coast. He was subsequently engaged in movements designed to effect the reduction of Charleston by moving through the waters in its rear, but there, though entirely successful so far as the naval part was concerned, he failed for want of effective co-operation by the land-force. In August, 1862, he was appointed a rear-admiral upon the creation of that rank by act of Congress. In March, 1863, his iron-clads made a demonstration upon Fort McAllister in the Ogeechee River, Ga., but were unable, on account of obstructions, to take a position from which they could effectually attack the work. Preparations were also made for a combined land and naval attack upon Charleston, and after an unseemly dispute over etiquette among the army officers concerned, the expedition under DuPont's command gathered in the mouth of the North Edisto River on April 3, and on the 5th proceeded to Charleston harbor with nine iron-clad vessels, besides five gunboats placed in reserve. On the 7th, shortly after noon, he advanced to the attack, the iron-clad Weehawken leading, and the other eight following in single file. At 4 o'clock the fire of the heavy barbette guns of Fort Sumter was encountered. The plan of DuPont had been to disregard the fire of the batteries, and to move into the harbor far enough to fire upon the left or north-west face of Sumter, that side being the weakest; but it was found impossible to get the desired position on account of torpedoes and obstructions, which detained the assailants and exposed them to the heaviest fire of the Confederates. The contest was thus altogether to the advantage of the latter, and at 5 o'clock Admiral DuPont signalled the withdrawal of his squadron, one of them, the Keokuk, being so disabled that she sank after leaving the scene of action. The failure of this brave endeavor convinced DuPont that any similar naval attempt would accomplish no better result, the enemy's works and obstructions being too strong to be overcome by such means. In July, 1863, he was relieved by Admiral Dahlgren, and returned to Wilmington, Del. He died while on a visit to Philadelphia, June 23, 1865, from disease incurred by his cruise in the East Indies seventeen years before. In the intervals of his service at sea he was engaged in various professional duties. In 1855 he was appointed a member of the naval retiring board. He was the author of a treatise on the use of floating batteries for coast defence, which has been republished with commendation in other countries. (H. M. J.)

DU QUOIN, a city of Perry co., Ill., is at the junction of the Illinois Central Railroad, Cairo Short Line Railroad, and Eldorado division of the Belleville and Southern Illinois Railroad, 71 miles S. E. of St. Louis, and 77 north of Cairo. It has a bank, a park, a public library, a weekly newspaper, 6 churches, a graded school. Its industries comprise 3 grist-mills, a foundry, and machine-shop. It is surrounded by rich fields of bituminous coal, and the salt-, coal-, and coke-works of St. Johns, a manufacturing suburb, contribute to its prosperity. Population, 4000.

DURBIN, JOHN PRICE, D.D. (1800-1876), an American Methodist preacher and author, was born in Bourbon co., Ky., in 1800. Trained by pious parents, he was converted at the age of eighteen and joined the Methodist Church. He was forthwith licensed to preach, but, being too vehement, his voice failed, and he was obliged to desist from public work. However, he still labored in private, and after six months again entered the pulpit, though he henceforth used a more conversational style. In 1820 he joined the Ohio conference and travelled on a circuit of 200 miles. While still preaching regularly he attended Miami University in 1822, and afterwards graduated at Cincinnati College. In 1826 he was made professor of languages in Augusta College, Ky., and was for a time employed as agent in securing funds for that institution. Becoming widely known for eloquence, he was chosen chaplain of the United States Senate in 1831, and on the centennial anniversary of the birthday of Washington preached a sermon which was regarded as a masterpiece. The next year he removed to New York to become editor of the *Christian Advocate*, the leading paper of his denomination. In 1834 the Philadelphia and Baltimore conferences of the Methodist Episcopal Church obtained control of Dickinson College at Carlisle, Pa., which, after an honorable career of fifty years, had fallen into difficulties. Mr. Durbin was elected president of the college, and for eleven years devoted himself zealously to the task of placing it on a firm basis, and by wise and prudent management succeeded in so doing. In 1842 he made an extensive tour abroad, the results of which were afterwards published under the title *Observations in Europe* and *Observations in the East*. In 1844 he was a member of the General Conference, and took part in the discussion of the slavery question then agitating the church. He was a member of six succeeding conferences, and was prominent in all matters pertaining to the welfare and prosperity of the church. In 1845 he resigned the presidency of Dickinson College and became pastor of a church in Philadelphia. He was afterwards, for one year, presiding elder in that city, and in 1850 he was appointed missionary secretary to fill a vacancy. The General Conference of 1852 elected him to that position, and he continued to hold it by successive elections till 1872, when he declined on account of his age. All the foreign missions of the church except those to Liberia and China grew up under his administration. By his executive ability, his rare tact, great popularity, and stirring eloquence he aroused the church to liberality and energy in the mission cause. The annual receipts rose from $100,000 to $700,000. After resigning his position he lived in retirement in Philadelphia, and died there Oct. 18, 1876. Besides his work for the cause of education and of missions in his own denomination, he raised Methodism to a higher place in general esteem among American people.

DURESS, in law, restraint or compulsion whereby a person is forced to commit some act or to omit the doing thereof contrary to his own wishes and free will in the premises.

Duress is either by imprisonment or *per minas*. Duress by imprisonment exists where a man has in any manner lost his personal liberty. A legal imprisonment for the purpose of obliging a party to sign a deed or enter into a contract will not, however, be considered as duress, unless, indeed, the legal proceedings be a mere pretext.

Duress *per minas* consists of any line of conduct calculated to put a person in reasonable fear of loss of life, limb, liberty, health, reputation, or property. It may be either by actions or by words. Such actions or words must, however, in order to constitute duress, be of such a character as are calculated to inspire with just fear a person of ordinary firmness. By the ancient law they were required to be of such a kind as might reasonably be expected thus to affect an average man, but the strictness of this rule is now somewhat laid aside. The age, sex, state of health, temper, and disposition of the party, together with other circumstances calculated to give greater or less effect to the violence or threats, are in every case taken into consideration.

By the common law, a deed or contract made under duress is not void, but voidable only. The person upon whom the duress has been practised may avail himself thereof as a defence, but the person who has employed the force or threats cannot set them up as a defence if the performance of the contract be insisted on by the other party.

Courts of equity are invariably peculiarly careful to guard the rights of persons who have acted, or who are supposed to have acted, under duress. If there be the slightest ground to suspect oppression or imposition in such cases, they will afford instant relief. Circumstances also of extreme necessity and distress of the party, although unaccompanied by any direct restraint or compulsion, will in some cases be held so entirely to have overcome a party's free agency as to justify the court in granting relief.

Duress *per minas* is also an excuse for the commission of some crimes. Where, for example, a man is violently assaulted, and has no way of escaping death save killing his adversary, he will be held justified in so doing. (L. L., JR.)

DURFEE, Job, LL.D. (1790–1847), an American jurist and philosopher, was born at Tiverton, R. I., Sept. 20, 1790. His father, Thomas Durfee (1759–1829), had gained some knowledge of law, and for the last nine years of his life was judge of Newport county. The son graduated at Brown University in 1813, and at his graduation delivered a poem on "The Powers of Fancy." He studied law, and was admitted to the bar in 1817. A year previous, however, he had been elected a member of the State assembly, in which he continued till he was elected in 1820, almost unanimously, to Congress, where he served two terms. While in the assembly he had succeeded in securing the abolition of the special privileges formerly allowed to banks as creditors. In Congress he delivered an able speech in 1822 against the new Apportionment Bill, which would have reduced his State to a single Representative. He was again a member of the State assembly from 1826 to 1829, and was Speaker of the House most of the time. He then declined a re-election, but in 1833 he was chosen a judge of the supreme court of the State, and in 1835 became chief-justice. While in the assembly he had favored the extension of the right of suffrage, which had been unduly restricted in Rhode Island by the colonial charter, but when, in 1840, an attempt was made, under the leadership of Thomas W. Dorr, to form a new constitution without regarding the requirements of the old law, he joined with his associates on the bench in declaring the "people's constitution" void, and warned all citizens against taking any part in the treasonable movement. In his charge to the grand-jury, and afterwards on the trial of Dorr for treason against the State, Chief-Justice Durfee laid down the principles which were on appeal sustained by the United States Supreme Court. In 1845 he received the degree of LL.D. from Brown University. He died at Quaket, R. I., July 26, 1847. He always took great interest in aboriginal and colonial history, and in 1832 published a poem, *What Cheer, or Roger Williams in Banishment*. Though not of lofty style, it was favorably received, and was republished in England. He also delivered some lectures on the history and beliefs of the Indians. His most remarkable publication was *The Panidea, or an Omnipresent Reason considered as the Creative and Sustaining Logos* (1846). He seems to have been indebted to Swedenborg for some of the ideas set forth in this treatise, and he acknowledged that a Swedenborgian saying, "The Divine fills all things without space," first started him on some of his subtlest speculations. He also studied Cousin and Coleridge, and was affected by the Transcendental movement in New England. His complete works, with a memoir by his son, were published at Providence, R. I., in 1849.

DURHAM, an incorporated town in Durham co., N. C., is 26 miles N. W. of Raleigh, on the North Carolina Railroad. It has a bank, a hotel, 3 weekly newspapers, 7 churches, 3 schools, and a Methodist female seminary. It has a machine-shop, planing-, saw-, and grist-mills, carriage-factories, cotton-gins, and especially large tobacco-works. At this place Gen. W. T. Sherman and Gen. J. E. Johnston made a treaty at the close of the civil war, but the terms were afterwards rejected by the President. In 1869 tobacco manufacture was commenced here on an extensive scale. The property of the town is valued at $1,600,000; its public debt is $1500. Population, 4231.

DURUY, Victor, a French historian and educator, was born at Paris, Sept. 11, 1811. He belonged to a family of artists employed at the Gobelins, and at first was intended to pursue the same career, but in 1823 he commenced a course of classical study at the college Sainte Barbe, and in 1830 passed to the normal school. Three years later he began his work as an instructor in history in the college Henri IV. at Paris, and assisted in preparing historical text-books. In 1853 he received the degree of doctor in letters, taking for his thesis "The State of the Roman World at the foundation of the Empire." In 1861 his work, hitherto confined to secondary instruction, was enlarged; he became, in turn, inspector of the academy of Paris, master of conferences at the normal school, inspector-general of secondary education, professor of history in the polytechnic school, and in June, 1863, was made minister of public instruction, which department was then separated from that of worship. He had already prepared some historical works, and brought to his new duties a rare professional competence. The measures instituted by him tended to improve the position of professors, to enlarge the scope of public instruction, and to extend to a greater number the advantages of education. In July, 1869, he was removed from his position as minister and was made a senator. He had been a member of the Legion of Honor since 1845, and by successive promotions had arisen to the rank of a grand officer in 1867. In 1873 he was chosen a member of the Academy of Inscriptions, and in 1879 a member of the Academy of Sciences, Moral and Political. His publications have been chiefly text-books on geography and history. Beginning with the geography of the Roman Empire (1839), he next treated that of the Middle Ages (1839), then France (1840), then published a universal historical atlas (1841). In history proper, his first work was an *Histoire des Romains* (2 vols., 1843–44), followed by an *Histoire de France* (1852), and an *Histoire de la Grèce Ancienne* (1862), which was crowned by the Academy. He has also written a popular history of France (1863), and an introduction to the history of France (1865). A new edition of his Roman history, in four volumes, has been issued (1870–79), and another handsomely illustrated edition appeared in 1882.

DUYCKINCK, Evert Augustus (1816–1878), an American author, was born in New York, Nov. 23, 1816. The family had resided in that city since the time of Dutch rule, and his father, Evert Duyckinck (1765–1833), had been a prominent book publisher for thirty years. His son graduated at Columbia College in 1835, studied law, and was admitted to the bar in 1837. He had already entered upon a literary career by contributing to the *New York Review*, and after spending a year in Europe joined with Cornelius Matthews in 1840 in editing a monthly magazine called *Arcturus, a Journal of Books and Opinions*, which closed in May, 1842. *The Literary World*, a weekly paper, was established by Mr. Duyckinck in 1847, but after the issue of a few numbers it was transferred to Charles F. Hoffman, who conducted it for eighteen months. Evert and his brother George then took charge of it until the close of 1853, when they were induced to undertake the preparation of the *Cyclopædia of American Literature*. This valuable work was first issued in 1856. The conscientious spirit and diligent labor manifested in its preparation were rewarded by the approval of the best critics as well as of the general public. In 1865 a *Supplement* was added by Evert A. Duyckinck, and in 1875 a new edition, by M Laird Simons, was published. Mr. Duyckinck also edited, in 1856, *The Wit and Wisdom of Rev. Sydney Smith*, with a memoir. During the progress of the Civil War he edited a *History of the War for the Union*, which was completed in three quarto volumes (1861-65). He was also engaged at the same time in the preparation of the *National Portrait Gallery of Eminent Americans* (1865). He edited, with a memoir and notes, *Poems Relating to the American Revolution, by Philip Freneau* (1865). He compiled a *History of the World* (1870), in four volumes. In 1874 he published two large volumes of biographical sketches of *Eminent Men and Women of Europe and America*. All of his writings are marked by careful statement of facts and a liberal spirit. He died at New York, Aug. 13, 1878.

DUYCKINCK, GEORGE LONG (1823-1863), an American author, brother of the preceding, was born in New York, Oct. 17, 1823. He was educated partly at Geneva College, New York, and graduated at the University of the City of New York in 1843. Like his brother, he studied law and was admitted to the bar, but his tastes and associations inclined him to a literary career. After an extended tour in Europe in 1847 and 1848 he joined with his brother Evert in editing the *Literary World*, and when it was discontinued in 1853 they united in preparing the *Cyclopædia of American Literature*. After its publication in 1856 he visited Europe, and upon his return became treasurer of the Church Book Society, in connection with which he prepared a series of biographies of worthies of the Church of England, including Bishop Ken, George Herbert, Jeremy Taylor, and Latimer. Though brief, these memoirs are characterized by good sense, piety, and careful statement of facts. He also contributed to various periodicals and had projected other biographies. He died at New York, March 30, 1863.

DWIGHT, HARRISON GRAY OTIS, D.D. (1803-1862), an American missionary and author, was born at Conway, Mass., Nov. 22, 1803. He graduated at Hamilton College, N. Y., in 1825, and studied theology at Andover, Mass. In 1830 he was sent by the American Board of Commissioners of Foreign Missions to labor among the Armenians, making Constantinople his headquarters. He was eminently successful in his work, not only preaching, but establishing schools and editing a religious paper. Besides books and tracts in oriental languages he published *Researches of Smith and Dwight in Armenia, Christianity Revived in the East, Memoir of Mrs. Elizabeth O. Dwight* (1840), *A Complete Catalogue of the Literature of Armenia, Christianity brought Home from the East*. Having returned to his native land for a brief visit, he was accidentally killed on the Northern Vermont Railroad Jan. 25, 1862.

DWIGHT, JOHN SULLIVAN, an American musical critic, was born at Boston, Mass., May 13, 1813. After graduating at Harvard College, he prepared himself for the ministry in the Cambridge Theological School. After six years' church work, however, he determined to make the study of literature and music his chief occupation for life. In 1842 he joined the "Brook Farm" community. In 1852 he established and edited the periodical called *Dwight's Journal of Music*, which during the twenty-nine years of its existence was uniformly respected in both Europe and America.

Mr. Dwight drew around him some of the most accomplished musicians of the country, and induced them to contribute papers on interesting subjects connected with their art in its varied phases; and exercised great discrimination in reprinting from time to time articles of value to students, and caused many of these in the German, French, and Italian languages to be translated for the benefit of English-speaking peoples. The general excellence of the *Journal* led musicians of the first rank in Europe to the belief and knowledge that America was ready to receive them and appreciate whatever they could accomplish. It may, therefore, be said that this periodical not only helped to form public opinion in the United States, and led persons to perceive the high artistic aims of the best musicians who came hither, but was to some extent the means of inducing the latter to come. With reference to compositions, it is noteworthy that the critic occupies a position similar to that of an orchestral conductor; he stands midway between the composer and the public, rendering equal service to both. In this respect Mr. Dwight accomplished much. He worked hard and unceasingly to gain for Beethoven, among the symphony writers, and Handel, among the oratorio composers, the respect due to their exalted genius.

As presiding officer of the Harvard Musical Association, he also exercised an influence over local musical affairs which was highly salutary. He had a noteworthy poetical talent. (S. A. P.)

DWIGHT, NATHANIEL (1770-1831), an American author, was born at Northampton, Mass., Jan. 31, 1770. He was a brother of Pres. Timothy Dwight, of Yale College. Nathaniel published the first school geography issued in America. It was in the form of question and answer, and was extensively used. He also published *The Great Question Answered* and a *Compendious History of the Signers of the Declaration of Independence*. He died at Oswego, N. Y., June 11, 1831.

DWIGHT, SERENO EDWARDS, D.D. (1786-1850), an American Congregationalist minister and author, was born at Greenfield Hill, Conn., May 18, 1786. He was a son of Pres. Timothy Dwight, of Yale College. He graduated at Yale in 1803, and was tutor there from 1806 to 1810. Having studied law, he was admitted to the bar in 1810 and practised for five years. He then studied theology, and, having been licensed as a preacher in October, 1816, was elected chaplain of the United States Senate. In September, 1817, he was ordained pastor of the Park Street Congregationalist Church, Boston, but was obliged to resign in 1826 on account of ill-health. He then took up his residence in New Haven, and in 1828 opened a school there on the plan of the German gymnasia. In 1833 he became president of Hamilton College, N. Y., but resigned in 1835. He resided for a time in New York, and died in Philadelphia, Nov. 13, 1850, having gone there for medical advice. He published *The Life of David Brainerd, Missionary to the Indians* (1822), a treatise on *The Atonement* (1826), *Life of Jonathan Edwards* (1830), and *The Hebrew Wife* (1836). He also edited *The Works of President Edwards*, in ten volumes (1829), and published several sermons. A volume of his *Select Discourses*, with a memoir by his brother, Rev. Dr. W. T. Dwight, was published in 1851.

DWIGHT, THEODORE, I (1764-1846), an American lawyer and journalist, was born at Northampton, Mass., Dec. 15, 1764. He was a brother of Pres. Timothy

Dwight, of Yale College, and studied law with his uncle, Judge Pierpont Edwards, at Hartford, Conn. He became eminent in his profession, and engaged in the political controversies of the time as a Federalist. He was for several years a State senator, and in 1806 was elected to Congress. During the war of 1812 he was editor of the *Hartford Mirror*, the leading organ of the Federal party, and was secretary of the famous but unfortunate Hartford Convention in 1814. In the next year he became editor of the *Albany Daily Advertiser*, and in 1817 removed to New York, where he founded the *New York Daily Advertiser*, of which he remained editor till 1836. He then retired to Hartford, but subsequently returned to New York, where he died July 12, 1846. He published a *History of the Hartford Convention* (1833), and the *Character of Thomas Jefferson as Exhibited in his Own Writings* (1839), both books being of a partisan political character.

DWIGHT, THEODORE, II. (1796–1866), an American author, son of the preceding, was born at Hartford, Conn., March 3, 1796. He graduated at Yale College in 1814, went to Europe, and spent some years in travel. After his return he published *A Tour in Italy* (1824). In 1833 he removed to Brooklyn, and assisted his father in editing the *New York Daily Advertiser*. He also published the *New York Presbyterian*, and prepared a large number of educational and popular books. He was a good linguist, and at the time of his death was preparing a series of educational works in Spanish to be used in Mexico and South America. He died at Brooklyn, N. Y., Oct. 16, 1866. His principal works were—*A Dictionary of Roots and Derivatives*, *History of Connecticut* (1841), *The Roman Republic of 1849*, *Life of Garibaldi* (1859), a *Tour of New England*, *The Kansas War*.

DYEING. Before the discovery of America the principal articles used in dyeing were indigo and kermes, and the colors produced were much less brilliant than those obtained to-day from aniline dyes. The New World furnished two important additions to the dyer's resources—cochineal and logwood—the latter of which continues indispensable in spite of the advance made through chemical research. During the eighteenth century chemical dyes were introduced, and in the present century they have reached great prominence, gradually supplanting indigo, madder, and other natural dye-stuffs.

See Vol. VII. p. 492 Am. ed. (p. 570 Edin. ed.).

The first important product within recent times was picric acid, then "Perkins' mauve," next magenta, otherwise called roseine and fuchsine, and then came violet and blue dyes, which eclipsed the brilliancy of all ancient art. Madder has been compelled to give way before alizarine, and cochineal before azo scarlet, articles dyed with the latter having the advantage that they will not oxidize when worn next the body.

We shall now consider some inventions of marked value for the various colors.

Blue.—*Nicholson's Blue* produces the purest colors imaginable, from the lightest azure to the darkest Guernsey blue. It requires to be worked in at least the same weight of alkali (soda or borax) as of color; with acid the surface only of the goods is dyed, the color not penetrating into the fibre. After being boiled for half an hour in the alkaline they should be washed in cold water, and are then of a pale-gray color. They are then placed in an acidulated bath, in which they are well opened, and the color is regulated by using from 4 to 6 B. Blue for light shades, and from 4 to 1 B. (Guernsey) for dark shades. The goods are then faster than others, yet they can be further improved by being washed, then passed through a soap-bath and again placed in the acid bath. This dye is used chiefly for silk and wool. If cotton is present it should be laid in a tannin-bath, then in muriate of tin, and then in cold blue.

Acid Blues are so called because they impart their color clearly and evenly upon silk or wool in an acid bath. The lighter shades are night, pure and soluble blue; the darker shades are distinguished as No. 2 of the same, and include also serge, navy, and several others.

Neutral Blues include methyl, methyline, and Victoria blue. They will fix upon silk and wool in hot water solutions. Glauber salts are sometimes used to make them even. Cotton can also be dyed with them, if prepared with tannin mordant.

Cotton Blues are specially adapted for cotton or mixed goods, producing in many cases as bright colors as in silk or wool, and requiring but little acid. Thus 4 pounds of alum, 8 pounds of glauber salts, and 1 pound of soda to 8 ounces of color will dye 100 pounds of carpet yarn. Tannin, acetate of tin, sugar of lead, and "red liquor" are sometimes used as mordants. They can be dyed at very moderate heat, or even boiled without injury, and require no washing from the dye.

Violet.—Methyl and Hoffman are both neutral, and will dye any material, either animal or vegetable; the latter, however, requiring a mordant, for which tannin, acetate of tin, red liquor, stannat soda, oil, starch, etc., are used. *Alkali Violet* is used in the same way as alkali blue, and can be used in conjunction with the deep shades of these blues to darken them. *Acid Violet* is worked on with sulphuric acid used with cardinals, garnets, etc., to darken and produce bluer shades. *Humboldt Violet* will also work on in the presence of sulphuric acid, and stand exposure better than any other. *Mauve* is a distinct shade from any of the violets, being only about one-half as dark, yet can be obtained from any of them, but in that case will not be really so fast as when *Perkins' Genuine Mauve* is used.

Green.—For this Iodine was formerly used, although its use was somewhat circumscribed from the cost of the color. Then followed *Methyl Green*, which was made from methyl violet. It was a good color and much cheaper than the former, but on the application of too much heat a reaction set in, changing it into the violet shade. Next in importance was *Malachite Green*, which is worked in the same way as methyl and produces nearly the same shade. It has this highly important characteristic: it stands boiling without change. Some grades of silk and wool will take up the color without any assistance, while borax is needed with others. Most other materials require a little assistance in the shape of a preparation, not only to enable it to take up a full color, but to permanently fix it. For this purpose tannin and sometimes an addition of muriate of tin is used, and after this a washing is required, since otherwise the color would not only precipitate in part, but the dyed work would in time turn dark by oxydation. This is true also in every case where tin salts are used on cotton goods, whatever the color may be. *Acid Green* dyes with sulphuric acid and with pure blue will form any shade of peacock

Alkali Green works like alkali blue, and with it will produce shades of peacock.

Pink and Rose Color were chiefly produced by the use of safflower. A carmine made from this and cochineal had largely the preference over all attempts to produce the same from Brazil wood, cudbear, archil, etc., as the shades were not only much brighter but faster. Considerable expense and time however was required for the preparation of them, so that the introduction of saffranine was hailed with considerable satisfaction, as it is both economical and gives good results. Eosine was also introduced about the same time, which gives a yellower tone than saffranine, so that in its fullest tone it produces a fine scarlet and in its lowest form flesh color. For delicacy of shade eosine has never been surpassed. From the first no difficulty was found in fixing the color on silk and wool, but it had three serious drawbacks—its expansiveness, its tendency to crock, and its inability to stand the light. In spite of these defects, however, considerable quantities are still used because of its beauty. Cotton has no affinity for it and difficulty was experienced in getting a proper mordant. Now good results are obtained by first giving the cotton a good bath of soap, drying it off, then running it through acetate of lead. Besides these we have erythrosin, a shade approaching eosine, and phloxine, a shade approaching to saffranine, and Bengalic pink, a shade bluer than saffranine, all very bright colors, capable of fixing on all materials of vegetable and animal fibres.

Cotton Scarlets have also been put upon the market. Those made from 5 parts saffranine, 3 parts crysodine, or 4 parts cotton orange are as bright and fast as any. The mordant is tannin and tin salts. Azo, or, as it is commonly called, "wool scarlet," can be successfully applied to cotton, by using first a good soap-bath and drying up, then passing it through red liquor, from which it is taken directly to a bath of color, at any temperature from 120° to 200° Fahr., in which 3 pounds of color are given at the start to 100 pounds goods; from this it is wrung and dried. By this process a very bright color is obtained that does not crock much, but which sheds if washed in soap. Several patents have been taken out in England, by Thomas Holiday, for the fixing of fast washable scarlets with the azo color, by the use of stannit of soda, an alkaline bath, etc., for which see *Chemical Review* (London, May and June, 1882). Fast Reds, Maroons, Clarets, etc., called acid colors, dye with sulphuric acid and glauber salts on silk and wool, and on cotton with the preparations as described for azo scarlet.

Yellows.—*Fast Yellow* or napthaline yellow is a bright canary color. It is worked with acid on silk and wool. It is liable, like picric acid, to stain other light goods it may come in pressure contact with. *Acid Yellow* is worked on in the same manner, but produces a shade more inclined to amber, and is used also to mix with acid green to produce apple green and with indigo to produce dark greens or bronze. *Acid Amber* is a full rich amber color worked the same as acid yellow. Chrysodine and tropæoline are other forms of yellow which have to a great extent displaced the previous ingredients used for producing these different shades.

Orange is a magnificent color, worked in the same manner as azo scarlet, and with archil and indigo for heavy shades of bronze and with indigotine, induline, or indigo for clarets and browns.

Brown.—Bismarck is a shade midway between orange and cinnamon brown. It will take on silk and wool in a neutral bath and on cotton after a tannin preparation. Acid or napthaline brown is a later invention, and is worked either in a neutral or acid bath. It has the decided advantages that it contains much less insoluble matter than Bismarck, and can be used to give tone to other acid colors, as with acid green and yellow to produce olive.

Seal is generally made with say 3 parts of induline, 1 part orange, and for redder shades inclining to garnet with 1 part fast red. It has been little used on account of its costliness, as it takes about 6 pounds of color for 100 pounds of wool to color seal-brown. F. J. Bird, of Brooklyn, has succeeded in manufacturing seal browns from aniline commercially practicable, as his acid color for wool will only take 2 pounds for a good shade and 3 pounds for a deep seal, and a cotton brown neutral that requires a tannin mordant only. One pound will dye 100 pounds twice as dark as Bismarck, 2 pounds a full shade, and 3 pounds a seal-brown. This neutral color will take on silk without a mordant and color it much quicker than any other means. It will also dye woollens or mixed goods full seal-brown, so as to bear soaping.

Black, as a direct color from aniline, has not been a commercial success, except in the printing of cotton goods.

An important fact in the tinctorial art is that all colors and shades are capable of being produced from red, blue, and yellow, yet the writer has met with but one dyer who knew enough of his art to keep but three colors in anilines, and from them produced everything required. Under ordinary circumstances it is at least convenient to be able to procure ready at hand just what is required, especially if it can always be accurately repeated at the same standard.

The direct colors obtained from aniline dyes are fairly understood, and the secondary colors are also moderately understood; as, for instance, that red and blue make purple, yellow and red orange, blue and yellow green; but they can go a step farther to-day and say, violet and green will make blue, brown and violet slate, magenta and violet claret, scarlet and acid magenta, cardinal red and acid magenta, and orange maroon induline and orange, brown orange and violet, claret, or garnet, etc. The only difficulties with these last are to be able to choose the colors that unite, and what proportions are relatively required for a given shade. A spirit-lamp with experiments would soon determine this, but for a guide the writer advises the order given above. It must be remembered, however, that more of one and less of the other anilines will change the balance of any shade.

Blue.—Take 2 parts of strongest malachite crystal green, and 1 part of 4 to 6 B. methyl violet, powder them well, and the mixture will dye a fine blue on silk or wool. Glauber salts may be used to even it; with a slight tannin mordant, cotton will take the color well. Methyl violet 3 parts, and Bismarck brown 1 part, will make slate, or reverse the order and you will get a shade redder, but much darker in brown than Bismarck.

Maroon.—4 parts magenta and 1 part 4 B. violet will make a good neutral claret, and it will take on cotton with tannin as in case of the blue. Acid cardinal, 4 parts 3 B. scarlet, and 1 part acid magenta will make the shade called fast red or B. cardinal; for blue shades reverse the order.

Acid Maroon.—Take equal parts of acid magenta and orange. *Acid Brown.*—Take equal parts of napthaline or acid brown and induline.

Acid Claret.—Equal parts of acid violet and orange, or for darker shades 1 part violet, 2 parts napthaline brown.

Acid Garnet.—3 parts violet, 1 part orange, or 1 part orange and 1 part violet if wanted fiery.

It will be seen by the above that acid colors should be taken to unite with other acid colors, and on the same principle neutral colors with neutral; there should be as few exceptions to this rule as possible. It is undesirable to attempt the use of alkali colors with either the acid or neutral colors, as the elements of adhesion and assimilation are wanting. The result is a precipitation of the colors, it may be to the bottom of the vessel, or if on to the surface of the goods, it is at best but a loose color.

Compound colors, properly speaking, are those which contain at least three kinds of colors, and these are necessarily more difficult to produce from aniline dyes, but, though difficult, it is not impossible except in the case of black, which has not yet been thus obtained. In 1879 considerable attention was drawn to this subject by the publication of patterns and articles upon dark colors and compound shades by F. J. Bird, of Brooklyn, who was the first to systematize this particular branch of aniline development, making it possible to compound the ordinary shades so as to produce very much deeper results than could otherwise be obtained except by the use of woods, roots, chemicals, etc., as in the old methods. It is not claimed that dyeing with anilines thus compounded is any cheaper than the old method, but that much time is saved. Two distinct classes of colors were thus made, the first called "acid colors," because they would take up the color and fix the same comparatively fast upon silk and wool, the others "neutral colors," because they will color wool, silk, or cotton in a bath in which the color was simply dissolved, in which glauber salts may be used to even it, the cotton requiring a slight mordant of tannin.

These discoveries awakened considerable solicitude amongst the various color-houses to be able to produce the like results, and in many cases they have succeeded. It also stimulated effort amongst dyers to learn how to mix their own colors, so that many to-day at the largest works do this, or else a color-mixer is employed.

Some illustrations will here be given, commencing with the acid colors. Bismarck had been the darkest aniline brown; much darker was now made with acid orange and induline, for redder shades adding dark acid claret, for darker shades on a flat hue some acid green, which gives darker shades than acid yellow, although this can be used. *Dark Green.*—Take, according to shade, acid green, and add to it acid yellow for light and fast yellow, for dark shades use serge blue to shade. *Bottle Green.*—2 parts acid green, 1 part fast yellow, 1 part acid brown and induline to shade. *Plum.*—2 parts acid violet, 1 part acid claret, 1 part acid brown. *Prune.*—2 parts acid violet, 1 part acid green, 1 part acid brown. *Claret.*—Fast red and violet to shade. *Bronze* and *Olive.*—Acid green, acid brown, and fast yellow. *Heavy Bronze.*—Acid orange, green, and 4 B. or serge blue. *Cardinal.*—All light shades with fast red and acid magenta. *Cardinal.*—All dark shades by adding acid claret or Bordeaux. *Navy Blue.*—3 parts induline, 1 part serge blue, etc.

Neutral Colors.—*Dark Brown.*—2 parts strongest crystal malachite green, 4 parts of 4 B. violet, 12 parts Bismarck. *Maroon.*—3 parts magenta, 1 part Bismarck. *Claret.*—3 parts magenta, 1 part violet. *Dark Bronze.*—Bismarck, violet, and green, in about the proportions of 2 parts brown, 2 parts green, 1 part violet. *Light Bronze.*—Equal parts Bismarck and green, or otherwise as to shade. *Drab.*—8 brown, 2 green, 1 violet, 1 cotton blue, to be worked with alum. *Plum.*—4 Bismarck, 2 violet, 1 green. *Prune.*—2 violet, 1 green, 1 Bismarck. *Cinnamon.*—4 Bismarck, 1 green. *Chestnut.*—10 parts Bismarck, 1 violet, 1 green, 1 magenta. *Slate.*—2 Bismarck, 2 violet, 1 green, 1 cotton blue, worked with alum. *Peacock.*—12 parts green, 1 part violet, or regulate to shade.

Alkaline Colors.—Of these there are only three. (1.) *Alkaline* or *Nicholson blues*, which are worked on silk or wool only, in an alkaline bath made so with soda or borax to 1 lb. of color, from 1 to 6 lbs., according to the hardness or softness of the water. (2.) *Alkaline Green.*—This can be worked in the same manner as alkali blue, and is intended for goods in wool or silk requiring to be washed. Peacocks of any shade are obtained by using parts of the alkali blue and green together, and are doubtless faster than any other peacock dyed with anilines. (3.) *Alkali Violet.*—This is worked in the same manner as alkali blue, and may be used on woollen goods that will require washing, or mixed with the deep shades of alkali blue to darken them, or with the blue and green to darken peacock colors. These three are called alkaline, not because they will bear washing in alkaline soap-baths, but because they are dyed in alkaline bath.

The improvements in machinery have nearly, if not quite, equalled the improvements in dyeing. If goods can be dyed faster they require to be finished faster to keep the manufacture running. It is a fact that improvements always pinch somewhere; in this case it has affected the finishing department, as old machinery has had to be turned out for new, which, though expensive, nevertheless pays, as it brings quicker returns and enables the manufacturer to place a much larger outcome upon the market and with increased profit to him, and at the same time a considerable advantage to the consumer.

Two questions arise: (1) Are the colors as fast, bright, and permanent, by these rapid methods as by the former ones, with woods, chemicals, etc.? It cannot be said that they are as fast, having reference to exposure (sunlight), but in the other sense with reference to smutting or crocking many of them are as fast. For examples, prussiate blue and aniline blues are equally fast.

Then, again, compared with violets dyed with tin and logwood, aniline violet is as fast and much brighter; and most others, if properly finished from the dye, should be equally good. If the color, even in neutral anilines, is allowed to boil for a few minutes, when the color is full enough it will be fixed very fairly. Many acid colors are absolutely fast, while "union" goods, that is, mixture of wool and cotton, should, after dyeing, be run through thin-boiled starch and finished from this, which will help to fix them. The starch, if not too thick, will not hurt any color.

(2) Are they as bright? In most cases they are brighter. Especially is this the case with "union" goods, in which the cotton will take at the same time as the wool, if mordanted first with tannin, and in especially bright colors, then put through a tin liquor, from which it is washed; and, in the case of dark colors, after a stronger tannin preparation then through nitrate of iron liquor, from which it is also well washed. It is by this time a dark drab, or slate, according to the amount of mordant received, which must be regulated by the depth of shade required. The cotton is somewhat darker than the wool, which is an advantage, inasmuch as the wool takes the color more freely.

All neutral anilines will follow this preparation, and, if proper attention is given to start at 150° Fahr., and gradually raise to boiling. the cotton and wool should be a more perfect match than most of the shots or union goods dyed in the old way, that required the wool to be colored first and the cotton after, thus often making the wool dull.

The question of "permanency" has been partly answered in what has been said on fastness, but it also follows that if the warp and weft are more uniformly dyed than was the case by the old process, that the cotton part at least will stand better, being more fully dyed, and, as a consequence, will not so soon present a shabby appearance, as when the color had left the cotton through being thinly dyed it soon presented an impoverished appearance. As the acid colors, or alkaline, can be used on all woollen goods, they ought to be fairly fast, and in the case of reds ought to be perfectly so. It must, however, be candidly admitted that the question of permanency does not count nearly so much as it ought, as the tropical heat of this country in the summer-time demands all the unfadable colors we have to be used; and to the honor of some firms be it said they say, "Give us the very best colors, even if they are dearer." But the most say, "Give us a bright color, that will take easily and not cost much."

This leads to so many blues being dyed with logwood in place of indigo, or its fast substitutes, as the former costs from two to three cents and the latter about forty cents per pound to color; the former looks quite as good, and is as fast, if not faster, as regards smutting, than the latter, but, as is well known, the indigo will last to its last thread, while logwood in one season will become half blue and half red, caused by the tin salts used in the mordant having acted upon the hematine (coloring-matter of the logwood), and, possessing more vitality, raised it from its assumed dark to its natural red shade. (F. J. B.)

DYER, THOMAS HENRY, an English historian, was born in London, May 4, 1804. He became a partner in an important commercial house in the West India trade. But the emancipation of the slaves so affected the business of the house that it was closed, and Mr. Dyer employed his leisure in a journey to Athens, Rome, and Pompeii, and in the study of the ancient topography of these cities. His publications consist of a *Life of Calvin* (1850); *History of Modern Europe* (5 vols. 1865–1877); *History of the City of Rome* (1867); *Pompeii* (1849); *Ancient Athens* (1873); *History of the Kings of Rome* (1868); *Roma Regalis* (1872); *A Plea for Livy* (1873); to which may be added articles in Smith's Dictionaries of Biography and Geography, and in other works.

DYNAMITE. See EXPLOSIVES.

E.

EADS, JAMES BUCHANAN, an American engineer, was born at Lawrenceburg, Ind., May 23, 1820. At the age of thirteen he went with his parents to St. Louis, where he has since resided. Leaving school at an early age, he was employed in a store and afterwards became a clerk on a Mississippi steamboat. Here he devoted his leisure to the study of engineering, and in 1842 he constructed a diving-bell boat for the recovery of cargoes of sunken steamers. He next designed other vessels with powerful machinery for removing sand from sunken boats and raising the entire hull and cargo. In 1845 he erected at St. Louis the first glass-works west of the Mississippi. He afterwards formed a plan for the improvement of navigation on western rivers, but failing to get the necessary support from the government it was not put in operation. In 1861, being consulted by Pres. Lincoln as to the best means for opening up the navigation of the Mississippi, he designed and completed for the government a squadron of eight light-draught iron-clad vessels for service on that river. These, the first iron-clads constructed by the United States, were completed and made ready for their guns within 100 days. They were first employed in the capture of Fort Henry, on the Tennessee River, Feb. 6, 1862. During that year and the next Capt. Eads designed and constructed six iron-clad vessels, heavily plated and having turrets worked by steam. This was the first application of steam to the manipulation of heavy guns. In 1867–74 Capt. Eads designed and constructed the famous steel bridge crossing the Mississippi at St. Louis. (See BRIDGES, vol. I., p. 726.) Many ingenious devices were invented and used in constructing the foundation for the piers and throughout the entire work. About this time the national government had begun to give special attention to the improvement of the channel of the Mississippi below New Orleans, which was seriously obstructed, especially by the bars at its mouth. A commission of army engineers had recommended that a canal be built from Fort St. Philip to Breton Bay, by which the bar would be avoided. Capt. Eads vigorously opposed this plan and undertook to increase the depth of the channel in the southwest pass (then only fourteen feet) to thirty feet, and thus to maintain an open mouth for the river. This he proposed to do by the jetty system, and he further engaged not to demand any pay for the services of himself and his associates until a stable depth of twenty feet should have been secured. By persistent effort he obtained a partial approval of his plans, first from a new commission of engineers and afterwards from Congress at different times. He was required by the bill which finally passed to apply his system to the South pass, which had two bars, one with a depth of eight feet, and the other of fourteen feet. In the course of five years he here secured to commerce a channel 200 feet wide and 26 feet deep, with a central depth of not less than 30 feet. This channel has since been maintained at a moderate expense in excellent condition, as testified by the government inspectors. Capt. Eads has also advocated the application of the jetty system to the improvement of the channel of the Mississippi as far north as St. Louis, believing that by making a uniformity of width a uniformity of depth could also be maintained. This plan has been approved by the Mississippi River Commission, composed of civil and military engineers appointed by the government, and work has been commenced in accordance with it. Another important project which has been urged by Capt. Eads is the construction of a ship-railway across the Isthmus of Tehuantepec. He argues that this will be cheaper in construction and maintenance and more convenient for commerce than the Panama canal. In 1884 Capt.

Eads turned his efforts chiefly to this project, but died at Nassau, March 8, 1887.

EAR. In this article we present only some considerations in regard to the relation of music to the ear in addition to, or in modification of, those given in the ENCYCLOPÆDIA BRITANNICA under EAR and ACOUSTICS. The powers of the human ear to discriminate between concord and discord, etc., are rarely properly estimated. The conclusions arrived at by Helmholtz and other great physicists, though apparently satisfactory, being borne out by experiment or mathematically demonstrated, are not really so, certain factors being left out of consideration. For this reason organ-builders and musical-instrument-makers generally find it next to impossible to follow the teachings of scientists; while practical musicians in their compositions and performances have learned by experience to recognize many modifying conditions that are unnoticed in books. The powers of the human ear are greater than usually believed, and may be increased by training to a degree scarcely credible or imaginable; yet at the same time the sense of hearing has limitations and also defects. It is the special province of the musician to decide how far he may hope to be appreciated in introducing complexities, and how far he may deceive the ear by causing it to accept, as consonant, intervals that are really dissonant.

Beat Theory.—The theory of beats, though satisfactory as far as it goes, does not (in deciding what the measurements of intervals should be to affect the ear as consonant) account for the whole musical world being content to employ "equal temperament," and listen complacently to the myriads of dissonances that thereby attend all performances. Physicists study one or two intervals at a time and decide on their characteristics, leaving for the most part unnoticed the combined effect of many such intervals (as in the massive chords of an organ, etc.), the quality of the tones, the temperament (causing conflicting overtones), the mental effect, the condition of the ear after listening for some minutes, etc.

Residual sensation.—One theory, for example, makes consonance and dissonance depend on pitch; whereas it is well known to organists that quality of tone is a factor that must not be disregarded. A chord of four notes playable with one hand will be accepted as completely satisfactory on a sweet-toned flute stop at a much higher pitch than it would on trumpet stops at the same altitude; and a similar chord which if played low in the bass will be too dull and muffled, to be accepted as harmony, will, on this flute stop, be perfectly satisfactory if played even in the lowest octave of the keyboard on a delicately voiced oboe.

Quality of tone.—The organ in the church of St. Leo in New York, which has remarkably good acoustic qualities, is made to speak on a very low pressure of wind (2¼ inches), and is "voiced" very smoothly and delicately, the resonance of the building adding additional power. The unpleasant effect of the beats, due to "equal temperament" in this instrument, is so slight as to be scarcely perceptible, or to resemble agreeable undulations or waves similar to those that are peculiar to the tones of instruments swung, as the bell harp, or those in which sympathetic vibrations are set up, as in the viola d'amore, or the undulations peculiar to the human voice, very slightly trembling with emotion; whereas an organ that from being placed in a church that is defective acoustically, or put away in a recess, or from whatever cause, must have the tone forced out of it by high wind-pressure, is distressingly unpleasant to tune or scrutinize as regards perfect consonance.

Beats due to overtones.—An organ has a number of compound stops that are intended to build up the typical or space-filling tone of the instrument. These are Nature's harmonies or overtones, reinforced by actual speaking-pipes, that are operated on the same clavier-key as the fundamental tone, and are tuned "in tune;" while the notes obtained by the different clavier-keys are all tuned "out of tune." Yet all this apparently horrible discord is accepted without protest by both musicians and audiences. These are some few instances in which the ear accepts as consonant, dissonant intervals, and consonant intervals, at extremely high and low pitches, both of which science teaches are not endurable.

Mental influence.—If this were a treatise on art it would be competent to show that the mental or psychologic effect of music renders the ear able to bear most distressing dissonances and enjoy them as much as consonances, certainly to take greater interest in them, for they are exciting rather than cloying and create expectation. It would also be in order to show that the musician, by cultivating a "polyphonic ear," is enabled to follow the many simultaneous streams of melody that are intertwined to form the plexus of a symphony for full orchestra, or other highly developed composition; to say nothing of his ability to detect the slightest errors in such a work proceeding at a high speed, whether of a technical and mechanical nature, or due to a want of sympathy in the performers with themselves, or the work or the conductor's direction of it, as shown by an indifferent quality of tone, proper adjustment of the relative degrees of power, etc. All such facts are astounding and defy explanation. They puzzle the psychologist when contending that the human mind really entertains but one thought at a time. Yet strange to say our modern music is rendered possible by a systematic deception of the ear. That the great physicist Helmholtz is himself deceived in this is known from the argument sustained in his elaborate work "*On the Sensations of Tone as a Physiological Basis for the Theory of Music,*" which has the following passage: "We often hear four musical amateurs, who have practised much together, singing quartets in perfectly just intonation." This error has led Ellis, Bosanquet, and others (who though professing to work scientifically allow their senses to mislead them) to try to construct instruments on "duodenal" and other systems, in the belief that our modern music may be rendered in tune. They are attempting the impossible. If musicians adopt an extremely complex system, based upon the laws of absolute truth, they must be content with very simple music. If they devise a very simple system they may produce most elaborate music. The great oriental nations of antiquity adopted the former, and all Christendom has accepted the latter alternative. Yet a composer's mind is not more biased or warped by his working habitually with a tempered intonation than our notions of a straight line are by living on a globe. If the Greek architects had not known the defects of the eye, and learned to deceive it, their works would not have been so entirely satisfactory. If modern musicians had not learned to deceive the ear, their marvellous productions would have been impossible. As in the Parthenon there are everywhere visible most subtle convex curves lying in vertical planes and no dead levels except in the subbasement which was unnoticed, so in modern music there is little slavish adherence to so-called truth except in the interval of the octave, which is so nearly like a unison as to be similarly unobserved. And even this is not always perfect; for tuners of piano-fortes make the octaves too large in the seven or eight highest notes when they extend to high C to enhance the brilliancy of the instrument and remove the insipidity of the tones at this pitch.

It was discovered in 1837 that not only were there certain irregularities and optical illusions in the greatest works of the greatest Greek architects, but that these were a source of expression as well as tending to correct the appearances of hollowness, chiaroscuro, etc. They knew well that a long horizontal line viewed from below would appear to be curved and many similar peculiarities. The fact of deviations, the determinations of their exact nature, the theories on which they were founded, and the consequent proofs of optical refinements of which the modern world had hitherto been in ignorance being set forth by Mr. Penrose, were published by the Society of Dilettanti, in London, in 1852. In the arts of Greece generally may be particularly noted limited aim and perfect achievement. In Christendom an ideal of impossible attainment is striven after in religion and morality, as in the imitation of the life of the Founder of Christianity, and also in the fine arts. Hence the apparent simplicity of Grecian as compared with Gothic architecture, of the Classic drama as compared with the Shakespearian, of the homophonic music of the Orient as compared with the polyphony of the West. The Greeks preferred delicacy of treatment to powerful effects and variety of range. Their music formed no exception. It was not limited in scope from want of invention but by design. The public singers did not force their voices to produce very loud or very high notes, to give the thrilling effects that opera-goers now applaud. All was artistically restrained. Vitruvius was taught by the Greek architects, but the modernizing spirit of Plutarch's time (one hundred years later) led to all such delicacy or subtlety of proportions being regarded as old-fashioned, pedantic, and even unintelligible. In the general decadence of all Greek art, loss of sensibility is similarly perceived. The indifference with which the imitations of Greek architecture in London, Paris, and Berlin were regarded was not simply because there were no sculptures or imitations of animal forms to impart life, but because all was stiff, cold, hard, and merely geometrically true.

Whereas the keen artistic perceptions, the fine sense of discrimination, of delicate variations of the best Greek architects, and the length of time during which they worked out their ideas, concentrating their highest intellects upon the various problems that arose and the appreciation of their labors by observers, led to results far different from our contract work. The being made conscious of this is an important event in the artistic experience of the modern world. It is now seen that in the Parthenon and Theseum, the absence of perfectly straight lines which do not return into themselves, lead to the sense of unity or completion as well as that of security or permanence.

It must be specially noted here that the works were to be contemplated as wholes and not studied by a relic or single column. For in this musicians find the chief point on which to base the analogy and show the impossibility of following the advice of Helmholtz. They are compelled to produce compositions as complete wholes, and not as a series of chords detached by silences.

The harmonies must move and form compact tonal structures. They must also be linked together. Were it not for this it would be easy to exhibit all chords with the most perfect proportions. By devices similar to those of the Greek architects, the musician hides every *apotome*, and with such success that even Helmholtz himself is deceived. His misconceptions are fully demonstrated in "Imperfections of Modern Harmony" in the *Popular Science Monthly*, vol. xvi., p. 510. They are referred to here, not to expatiate on the errors of learned men, but to prevent designers of musical instruments from wasting time and thought. Prof. Airy, in his celebrated work "*On Sound and Atmospheric Vibrations,*" quotes the music of "God Save the Queen" in numbers, but omits certain notes that seem to have puzzled him. If now these notes, with their numbers, are inserted, his dilemma will be seen, and a convenient illustration found in proof of the unsuspected or disbelieved fact that there are five fundamental ways of attempting to deceive the ear in the performance of this well-known and comparatively simple strain, but that its perfect intonation is impossible. 1st. The errors may be systematized, as by the adoption of any one or many forms of "temperament" (as on a piano-forte). 2d. The errors may be glossed over and atoned for by disarming the coldly critical faculty, by appeals to the feelings, and a general giving and taking, mutual compromises being made between the singers, etc.; in which case they will be undefined and unacknowledged; yet they must be variations of the following schemes. 3d. When the four melodies are correct, the chords are incorrect.

	God	Save	Our	Gra
Soprano or melody..	C 48	C 48	D 54	B 45
Contr'alto...........	G 36	A 40	A 40	G 36
Tenor...............	E 30	E 30	F 32	D 27
Bass................	C 24	A 20	D 27	G 18

At "our" the chord is out of tune for D:A (27:40) is not in the required ratio of 2 to 3. See "ACOUSTICS," sec. 45, in ENCYCLOPÆDIA BRITANNICA, p. 101, Am. Ed.

4th. If now the chords are in the required ratio the four melodies must be slightly tampered with. To avoid complication the keynote C will here be represented by 128.

C 128	C' 129¼	D 144	B 120	C 128
G 96	A' 108	A' 108	G 96	G 96
E 80	E' 81	F 86⅔	D 72	E 80
C 64	A' 54	D 72	G 48	C 64

The notes marked (') are altered from the proportions established for the diatonic scale, that the proportions of the combined notes in each column, that form chords, may be correct.

But this form of variation is hardly possible in actual performance, for the singers would sustain or repeat notes at the same pitch (being ignorant of the requirements of the harmony), unless they modified them as in the second case hypothecated above. Therefore the errors would not allow the singers to return to the pitch at which they started, if the chords were sung with perfect intonation. 5th. They would proceed in this manner:

C 129$\frac{3}{5}$	C 129$\frac{3}{5}$	D 144	B 120	C 128
G 97$\frac{1}{5}$	A 108	A 108	G 96	G 96
E 81	E 81	F 86$\frac{2}{5}$	D 72	E 80
C 64$\frac{4}{5}$	A 54	D 72	G 48	C 64

In an ordinary brick wall any one brick rests on one-half of two others. A similar "division of the difference" is noted in quartet music, by which unconnected or, more correctly speaking, distantly related harmonies are bound together. By the use of such "ligatures" the most novel and strange combinations of tones are literally welded together in elaborate music.

If the present harmony be only slightly enriched the divergencies must be more numerous, and partake also of the nature of those shown in 4; while as already stated in actual performance they would be rendered as in 1 or 2. Here is a simple illustration in C being represented by 336:

C 336	C 336	D 384	B 320	C 341$\frac{1}{3}$
G 252	F Sharp 240	F Sharp 240	G 256	G 256
E 210	E 216	C 168	D 192	E 213$\frac{1}{3}$
C 168	A 144	A Flat 134$\frac{2}{5}$	G 128	C 170$\frac{2}{3}$

The third C of the top line, the second G of the second line, the second E of the third line, and the second C of the fourth line are higher than the corresponding notes in the first column. The melodies are untrue. Although the second C of the top line is retained at the same pitch in the second column, it is necessary to change the altitude of the second E of the third line that this column or chord may be in the required ratio of 6 : 9 : 10 : 14.

These figures not only prove the variations, but give the exact measure of the variations. And these must occur whenever the harmonies pass the boundaries of the great triune system of triads, in any key. This consists of the chord of the tonic, with its dominant (found by multiplying the vibration numbers of the tonic triad by three and dividing by two), and its subdominant (found by dividing the same numbers by three and multiplying by two). The mere use of the relative minor chords of these major harmonies leads to the necessity of a compromise, as shown above.

It is, therefore, possible for some simple negro-melodies to be sung in tune in four-part harmony, but not music rising even to the very low level of an ordinary hymn. Helmholtz and Ellis, by their arguments, refer to music intended for the gratification of musically intelligent persons. It must here be noted that the greater the brilliancy and splendor of the harmony the greater latitude the ear allows the musician in his departures from strict mathematical proportion. This does not wholly account for the predominance of discords in modern music of the best kind. One must look deeper for the causes of artistic phases. Yet the knowledge of the fact has given a freedom to composers in projecting their mighty harmonies, representing the passionate strivings, aspirations, disappointments, etc., of noble souls (as in the truly heroic "Eroica" Symphony by Beethoven, or the psychologic studies of a Wagner or Liszt), and to gain a certain onward sweep or dynamic power in an elaborate movement. Dissonant compounds of tones demand "resolution," or progress. They indicate unrest, and hold us spellbound as they pass points of comparative rest. Hence it is incorrect to say that the proportions given in sections 45 and 46 in ACOUSTICS in ENCYCLOPÆDIA BRITANNICA can be preserved in ordinary quartet music. The best executants strive to hide such unavoidable discrepancies with subtile skill, and an art-concealing art worthy of the best Greek architects.

Yet the difficulties they have had to overcome must not be underestimated now that they are surmounted. Occasionally among amateurs they reappear and cause perplexity. For instance, the violin is tuned to the key of "D." If now a composition is to be played in some other key, the open strings of this instrument are avoided, not because they yield a different quality of tone from the notes made with the fingers, but because of their pitch being incorrect. The cello is tuned like the viola—to the key of "G," and hence corresponding peculiarities are noticed when this key is not used for them.

When tuning such instruments to the piano-forte, to perform piece in a key with two or three more sharps, it is important that the pitch of "A" be carefully adjusted, so that it may not be ever so small a degree above the corresponding note of the piano-forte. When preparing to play in a composition with several flats this "A" should be tuned a very little above the pitch of the piano-forte. In both cases the other strings are tuned, as usual, on the Pythagorean system. If these conditions are not observed the unsatisfactoriness of the accords will become unpleasant to the performers. To explain the reasons here would be to occupy space for a subject that falls under the head of "temperament." In the present article it is intended simply to point to the fact that the ear being deceivable, modern musicians have learned to deceive it, and put together the marvellously elaborate architectonic forms, or gossamer sound-fabrics, such as are found in the organ fugues of Bach or the orchestral scores of Wagner. To honor musicians let it be said that "they prefer creating an art with the imperfect proportions that are attainable, to indulging in useless sighs for perfect proportions that are unattainable."

Having seen that such art-works would be impossible without deviations from absolute truth, as regards the proportions of intervals, it is well to point out that some variations are made by musicians during performance that are not unavoidable, but voluntary, and simply to heighten the effect. Their aims in this respect are precisely analogous to those of the Greek architects. For, as obedience to mathematical truth for art-works of stone rendered them "hard and dry," in a particular sense, so, in tone-works, obedience to metronomic time-beats, and the observance of perfect proportions for intervals (in those cases where deviations are optional), lead to an inartistic, mechanical delivery that is immediately stigmatized. Hence the variations of *tempo* that a good conductor makes in a symphonic movement by Beethoven, with such gradations that they do not attract attention, or the *nuances* (*tempo rubato*, etc.) a good pianist makes in a nocturne by Chopin, or the gradual raising or depressing the pitch on a penultimate note as it gradually approaches the tonic, in accordance with the character of the emotion expressed.

Psychologic principles override mathematical principles in all such cases; and the sense of hearing is not offended, but excited, in the desired manner. The ear accepts as true that which is a true revelation of a soul-state, rather than mere symmetry of speeds of vibrations or recurring musical accents or phrases. These motions, to resemble emotions, must necessarily be subject to delicate and constant fluctuations.

The ability to remember the actual pitch of tones so well as to dispense with a tuning-fork distinguishes some musicians from early childhood. An extraordinary fastidiousness, as regards quality of tone (timbre), is common in China among the Musical Mandarins. Instruments of extremely soft and gentle tones—such as the neck flute—are highly prized in India. Some orientals employ musical intervals smaller than our semitone, and the Maories perceive most delicate variations of pitch.

To estimate rightly the powers of the human ear it is necessary to review the highly elaborated systems of music that were brought to perfection by ancient nations, and especially that of the Chinese. Their knowledge of acoustics and the particular effect of various modes of causing strings to vibrate was so marvellously great as to be out of all proportion to the art-works created to display such beautiful tones. Hence, their best music appeals more to the sensuous nature and understanding than the imagination and the emotions.

A few hours from birth, when the skin of the newly-born infant is not sensitive to the prick of a pin, and the eyes are unaffected by flashed lights, the ears are open to impressions. Through these gates the mental perceptions are first aroused. The sense of hearing is the first to awake and the last to sink to sleep. The cry of the young child, animal, or bird goes straight to the heart of the mother, and needs no theory to explain its meaning. It is most truly interpreted there. We recognize our friends by their voices, and learn their moods by the music of their speech, yet not by studying the overtones that cause the particular quality of their voices, or by consciously analyzing the variations of pitch in sentences, but, as it were, by instinct. Musical tones, as a means of expression, are similarly significant, and thus the art of music obtains its justification. (S. A. P.)

EARLY, JUBAL A., a lieutenant-general in the Confederate army, was born in Franklin co., Va., Nov. 3, 1816. He entered West Point in June, 1833; after graduating in 1837 was appointed second-lieutenant in the Third artillery, and served in the Seminole War in 1837–8. In July, 1838, he resigned his commission, studied law, and practised at the bar of his native county from the beginning of 1840. He was a member of the legislature of Virginia in 1841–2. When the Mexican War broke out, he was made major of the regiment of Virginia volunteers, and served with great gallantry in several important engagements.

He was a delegate to the convention of 1861, opposed and voted against the ordinance of secession; but, when it was adopted, he signed it, and entered the service of the Confederate States as colonel of the Twenty-fourth Virginia regiment. As colonel he commanded a brigade at the action of Blackburn's Ford on Bull Run, on the 18th of July, 1861, and at the battle of Manassas, on the 21st of July. For his gallantry on the latter occasion he was promoted to a brigadier-generalship, to rank from the day of battle. He was engaged in the battle of Williamsburg on the 5th of May, 1862, where he was severely wounded. After his return to duty during the seven days' battles around Richmond, in June and July, 1862, he was assigned to the command of a brigade in Ewell's division, Jackson's corps, and was engaged in the battle of Malvern Hill, on the 1st of July; also in the battle of Cedar Run or Slaughter's Mountain, on the 9th of August, 1862; and in the subsequent operations against Pope on the Rappahannock and around Manassas. At the battle of Sharpsburg, or Antietam, on the 17th of September, he succeeded to the command of the division by reason of the wounding of the division commanders (Ewell on the 28th of August, and Lawton in the battle), and he commanded the division at the battle of Fredericksburg, on the 13th of December, 1862. He was subsequently promoted to the rank of major-general, and assigned to the command of Ewell's division. During the battle of Chancellorsville, on the 1st of May, 1863, Gen. Early held the lines at Fredericksburg, and had several engagements with Sedgwick's corps. He led the attack which resulted in the capture of Winchester in June, 1863, and took an active and conspicuous part in the Pennsylvania campaign which immediately followed that event, leading the van of the Confederate army, which reached Chambersburg, Pa., June 16, and participating in the decisive battle of Gettysburg. He was engaged in all the subsequent operations of the army of Northern Virginia in the fall of 1863, and at Mine Run commanded Ewell's corps.

In the winter of 1863–4 Gen. Early was sent to the Valley of Virginia at the time of Averill's raid, and remained in command there until March, 1864, when he returned to his division, and was engaged in all the battles in the Wilderness, beginning on the 5th of May, 1864. On the 8th of May he was assigned to the command of A. P. Hill's corps, by reason of the sickness of that general, and remained in command until the 21st of May, which period embraced all the operations around Spotsylvania Court-house. Gen. Early was engaged in the operations about Hanover Junction, in command of his division, but at their close (May 26) he assumed command of Ewell's corps, that officer being unfit for duty on account of severe sickness.

On the 31st of May Early was made a lieutenant-general, and participated in the important operations about Cold Harbor, until the 12th of June, when he was detached and sent in pursuit of the Federal general Hunter, whom he intercepted at Lynchburg, when, after a slight engagement, the latter retreated precipitately, and was pursued into the mountains back of the town. Then, having been joined by Gen. Breckinridge's command, Early moved rapidly down the valley, crossed the Potomac into Maryland, defeated Gen. Lewis Wallace at Monocacy Junction July 9, and then threatened Washington on the 11th. After demonstrating in front of Washington until the night of July 12—during which time he arrived in sight of the dome of the capitol—when, finding the works had been heavily reinforced from Grant's army, and it was not practicable to make an attack with his small force of less than 8000 men, Early retired, and returned to the Valley of Virginia. Here, until late in the winter, he maintained a protracted and eventful campaign against Sheridan. Gen. Early displayed his usual pluck and dashing military skill, but the result of the long and active campaign was unfavorable to the Confederates. On the 30th of March, 1865, Gen. Early was relieved of his command. Upon this occasion Gen. Lee wrote him a letter, in which he expressed the fullest confidence in Gen. Early's "ability, zeal, and devotion to the cause," and thanked him for "the fidelity and energy" with which he had always supported Gen. Lee's efforts, and for "the courage and energy" which he had always manifested in the service of the South.

After the surrender of the Confederate armies Gen. Early succeeded in reaching Mexico, where he remained for several months; he then went to Cuba, and finally to Canada, and did not return to Virginia until the spring of 1869. In 1870 he resumed the practice of the law at Lynchburg. He has published a valuable historical work, *Memoirs of the Last Year of the War* (1867). (E. L. D.)

EARTH-ALMOND, CHUFA. This is one of the *Cyperaceæ*, or sedge-grasses, and stands almost alone among this numerous family in being of service to man. It is a native of the south of Europe, where it has long been known for its small tubers, which are produced in great abundance. From these a drink called *orchata de chufas* is made, which is very popular with the lower classes in Spain. To make the drink the tubers are beaten to a paste, mixed with a little sugar in water, and then strained, when it looks like milk. The tubers, however, according to Prof. Jackson of Boston, contain a peculiar form of sugar. On analysis he found in them—

Water	15·40
Fibrous matter	21·45
Starch	·27
A form of sugar	12·25
Wax	·50
Fat oil	16·65
Mucilage	6·65

Eaten raw, the tubers taste like chestnuts or cocoanuts. They were introduced to America in 1845 by the United States Patent Office, and, unlike many new introductions, achieved at once a popularity in the Southern States. The tubers are planted two feet apart each way, a number in a hill, and the produce of one bushel to the acre has been from 200 to 500 bushels. They are somewhat troublesome to harvest, and the most profitable way is to let swine gather the crop. A native species, *Cyperus Hydra*, also makes tubers, much smaller than those of the earth-almond, besides having numerous creeping roots, which make the species a terror to the Southern farmer. The earth-almond resembles the *Hydra*, or "nut-grass," in appearance, but is free from its vices. Repeated attempts have been made to introduce it in the place of coffee. John Ludwig Christ issued an octavo volume in 1801 at Frankfort-on-the-Main to show the immense amount of money which Germans might save by the universal use of this instead of coffee. Those who have experimented with it in America regard it as the best of the many substitutes suggested, but not likely ever to be as popular as the original. It seems to thrive well in many parts of the United States, even in Minnesota, but the best results have been obtained in rich and rather damp sandy soil in Alabama.

(T. M.)

EARTH-WORM (*Lumbricus*, L.), a genus of Annelid animals of the order *Oligochæta* and family *Lumbricina*. The body is cylindrical, attenuated at both extremities, and composed of a number of narrow rings or segments (in some cases upwards of 150), the most anterior of which shows on its ventral surface the oral aperture; there is no true differentiated head. A thickened, flesh-colored zone, formed by the union of 6–8 of the anterior segments, and designated the *cingulum* or *clitellum*, is present in the adult. The mouth is edentulous, and conducts into a muscular pharynx extending as far back as the seventh segment; upon this follows a narrow œsophagus, a crop or "proventriculus," and the muscular gizzard, succeeded at about the eighteenth segment by the straight sacculated intestine. The circulatory system consists of three principal longitudinal trunks (one dorsal, or *supra-intestinal*, one ventral, or *sub-intestinal*, and one situated underneath the nerve-cord, *sub-neural*) and their branches, which carry a deep-red, non-corpusculated blood-fluid. Five to eight pairs of so-called hearts, formed by the expansions of the commissural vessels, are situated in the anterior region. A colorless corpusculated fluid, answering to the blood of other invertebrate animals, occupies the body-cavity. The nervous system consists essentially of a pair of cephalic ganglia lodged over the pharynx in the third segment, and a ventral ganglionic chain and its branches. A pair of greatly convoluted tubes, known as the *segmental organs*, subserving either a respiratory or renal function, and opening internally into the perivisceral cavity by means of wide funnel-shaped apertures, and externally by superficial pores, is situated laterally in every segment except the first. The sexes are united in the same individual, but mutual fecundation takes place. The generative organs consist of two pairs of testes, opening on the ventral aspect of the fifteenth segment, one pair of minute ovaries, whose oviducts open on the fourteenth segment, and two pairs of spermathecæ, or seminal receptacles, situated in the tenth and eleventh segments. The eggs are deposited in chitinous capsules, from one to fifty or more in a capsule, and the young undergo no metamorphosis. Locomotion in the earth-worm is effected by eight rows of short bristles or setæ, four of which are developed not far from the median line of the ventral surface, and the other four laterally.

The various species of the genus *Lumbricus*, while they are to be met with over the greater portion of the earth's surface, are yet governed in their local distribution by certain particular conditions of the soil, which are not always readily apparent. Localities which retain for a considerable length of time the moisture of the earth, such as fields, meadows, and paved court-yards, are much more populously frequented than dry, sandy, or gravelly spots, where but a scanty vegetation is supported, and localities where the depth of soil does not afford sufficient protection from the cold of winter are usually deserted. Perrier found that exposure to the dry air of a room for only a single night was fatal to the animal, while, on the other hand, individuals retained their vitality after being completely submerged in water for a period of nearly four months. Earth-worms are nocturnal in their habits, and but rarely, except in the pairing season, expose their bodies during the daytime, lying usually concealed in their burrows at some distance from the surface; even during their nocturnal wanderings they but rarely emerge completely from their subterranean abodes; and indeed it has been asserted that in a perfectly healthy condition they never leave them. The senses are but feebly developed, that of hearing being completely absent. Darwin found that while these animals were entirely indifferent to the deepest and loudest tones emanating from the human voice, a bassoon, piano, or metallic whistle, and consequently to those undulations of the atmosphere which convey the impression of sound to the human ear, they were extremely sensitive to the vibrations transmitted through any solid body. Worms that under ordinary circumstances appeared indifferent to the sound of a piano retreated instantly into their burrows when the pots containing them were placed on the instrument and the note C on the bass clef or G above the line in the treble was struck. The visual organs are completely absent, yet the observations of both Hoffmeister and Darwin seem to prove that not only are these organisms cognizant of the difference between night and day, but that even minor changes of luminosity are keenly appreciated by them. The power of distinguishing between the various degrees of luminous intensities resides in the anterior portion of the body, or what corresponds to the head, and hence it is conjectured that for the exercise of this power the worm is dependent upon the rays of light passing through the skin and in some manner exciting the cerebral ganglia. The sense of smell is but imperfectly developed, and appears to be restricted to certain odors.

That the earth-worms possess a certain amount of intelligence appears to be almost indisputably proved by the manner in which they habitually plug up (probably for the purpose of protecting their bodies from the cold moisture of the adjacent earth) their burrows with leaves, their method of procedure, as observed by Darwin, being almost precisely that which would be employed by a man in plugging up a tube with similar objects. In a vast majority of cases it was found that the leaves were drawn in such a way as to encounter the least possible amount of resistance, those with broad bases being seized at the tips, and, *per contra*, those which separated (pines) or spread out towards their apices being seized at their basal ends.

One of the most interesting facts connected with the lives of these lowly organisms, and perhaps one of the most surprising in the entire range of physiographic science, is the important part played by them in the economy of the earth's history—namely, the formation of vegetable mould. From the observations of Mr. Darwin it would appear that the entire vegetable mould covering a country has been, and constantly is being, subjected to a species of animal digestion, it being at successive periods passed through the intestinal canals of worms. It has long been known that small objects scattered over the surface of a field or meadow disappear in course of time beneath a superficial layer of mould or turf, apparently undergoing a process of sinking, as induced by the force of gravity drawing toward the centre of the earth. And, similarly, fields that were at one time stony and considered unfit to be worked, have been found after a number of years to be covered with a comparatively deep deposit of soil, and in some cases to such an extent as to leave no superficial traces of the previously existing stones. In like manner, paved walks and the floors of ancient ruined buildings have, after a lapse of years, been buried beneath a greater or less depth of soil, and human relics and utensils that had doubtless been left exposed on the surface have been turned up by the ploughshare from varying depths of a first-sown field. This disappearance has been conclusively shown by Mr. Darwin to be due in great measure, if not almost exclusively, to the quantity of fresh earth that is constantly being brought to the surface in the form of "worm-castings"—i.e., the earth that is periodically being passed through and ejected from the intestinal canals of worms as a result of their burrowing operations. From data accumulated from various sources, and largely as the result of his own personal observations, Darwin estimates the quantity of worm-castings annually thrown up over each square acre of land to be equal in weight to no less than fifteen tons; and if this fifteen tons' weight of material were equally distributed over the surface of the acre, it would raise the general level by about fourteen-hundredths of an inch. In other words, about one inch of fresh soil would be deposited in the course of seven years. Assuming with Darwin that there are, on an average, 26,800 worms to each acre of land—which is about one-half the number claimed by Hensen for the most favored localities—then each single individual in the above period of seven years must have brought to the surface no less than one hundred and forty ounces of material! When it is borne in mind that worms live only in the top layer of the soil, and usually at depths from the surface of from four to twelve inches, and since they are constantly reburrowing and throwing up their castings, it is self-evident that in the course of every few years this top soil, or what constitutes the vegetable mould, must pass in rotation through the intestinal canals of these creatures. Through this process of intestinal rotation, it is contended, the ground is brought into a suitable condition for vegetable development. By the constant breaking up and loosening of the earthy material free access is given to the penetration of the air and the atmospheric waters, and the soil rendered fit for the retention of moisture and for the absorption by it of all soluble substances. The bones, shells, and other hard parts of animals, as well as the leaves, stems, and branches of plants, are rapidly buried beneath the surface, and are there, in a slowly decomposing condition, brought within the assimilating influence of the living roots.

The specific determination of the various forms of *Lumbricus* has not yet been satisfactorily accomplished, nor has it yet been absolutely determined to what extent the American forms are identical with those of the Eastern hemisphere. (A. H.)

EASTBURN, MANTON (1801-1872), an American bishop of the Protestant Episcopal Church, was born at Leeds, England, Feb. 9, 1801. He came to America while a child with his parents, and graduated at Columbia College, N. Y., in 1817. After studying theology at the Episcopal seminary in New York, he was ordained deacon in 1822, and made assistant minister of Christ Church, New York. In 1825 he was ordained priest, and became rector of the Church of the Ascension in 1827. He was consecrated assistant bishop of Massachusetts Dec. 29, 1842, and in the following February became bishop of that diocese. In his doctrinal views he was decidedly Low Church, and severely rebuked some mildly ritualistic practices introduced by Rev. Dr. Croswell in the Church of the Advent, Boston. He co-operated with other denominations in religious and benevolent work. He died at Boston, Sept. 12, 1872. Besides sermons and pastoral charges he published *Lectures on Hebrew, Latin, and English Poetry* (1825); *Essays in Biblical Literature* (1829); *Lectures on the Epistle to the Philippians* (1833); and edited with notes *Thornton's Family Prayers* (1836). His elder brother, JAMES WALLIS EASTBURN (1797-1819), was also a minister of the Episcopal Church, and was associated with Robert C. Sands in literary work, but died at an early age. His chief poem, *Yamoyden*, (1818), was founded on the story of the Indian King Philip.

EAST GREENWICH, the county-seat of Kent co., Rhode Island, is on the west shore of Narragansett Bay, and on the New York Providence, and Boston Railroad, 14 miles south It has a court-house, two banks a weekly newspaper, five churches, an academy, public schools, and a public library. It has two cotton-mills, a woollen-mill, print-works. It was incorporated Oct. 31, 1677. Population, 2887.

EASTHAMPTON, a town of Hampshire co., Mass., 5 miles S. of Northampton, and 16 miles N. of Springfield. It is on the New Haven and Northampton Railroad, and on the Mount Tom branch of the Connecticut River Railroad. It is a handsome village, picturesquely situated at the foot of Mount Tom, and the Mankan River affords water-power. Easthampton has a town hall, a good public library, the well-endowed Williston seminary for boys, a national bank, 4 churches, and a weekly newspaper. Among the industrial works (which are extensive) are manufactories of buttons, rubber goods, suspenders, steam-pumps, iron castings and cotton yarn. Valuation of the township, $2,340,500; annual public expenditure, $25,397. There is no town debt. Easthampton was settled about 1657, and was incorporated in 1785. Population of township, 4206.

EAST LIVERPOOL, a city of Columbiana co., Ohio, is on the Ohio River, 24 miles above Steubenville, and 44 miles W. N. W. of Pittsburg, on the Cleveland and Pittsburg Railroad. It has two national banks, 4 hotels, 3 weekly newspapers, 9 churches, and 5 schools. Its chief manufacture is pottery, for which there are about 30 works, besides brick-yards and a fire-brick-factory. The other industries are a foundry, glass-factory, two stave-mills, a flour-mill, and planing-mill. It has water-works and gas-works. It was settled in 1810 and incorporated in 1837. Its property is assessed at $1,750,000, its public debt is $30,000, and its yearly expenses $25,000. Population, 5568.

EASTMAN, SETH (1808–1875), an American army officer, was born at Brunswick, Me., Jan. 24, 1808. He graduated at West Point in 1829, and served in the infantry on the western frontier. In 1833 he became professor of drawing at West Point, and remained there seven years. He then served in the Florida War, and after spending some years in Minnesota and Texas, in 1850 went to Washington, and was employed for five years in the bureau of Indian affairs. He served in Utah in 1857–58, and after the outbreak of the civil war was employed as a mustering-officer at various points in the North. In 1863 he was retired from active service with the rank of lieutenant-colonel and brevet brigadier-general. He continued, however, to discharge such duty as was assigned to him till his death, at Washington, D. C., Aug. 31, 1875. He prepared a *Treatise on Topographical Drawing* (1857), but his most important publication was the illustrated work on the *History, Condition, and Future Prospects of the Indian Tribes in the United States*, which was published by order of Congress (Washington, 1850–57).

EASTMAN, MARY, an American novelist, wife of Col. Seth Eastman, was born at Warrenton, Va., in 1818. She was the daughter of Dr. Thomas Henderson, and was married in 1835. Having become familiar with Indian life through a residence of many years on the frontier, she published *Dacotah, or Life and Legends of the Sioux* (1849), *Romance of Indian Life* (1852), *Chicora* (1854). When Mrs. Stowe attacked American slavery in *Uncle Tom's Cabin*, Mrs. Eastman published *Aunt Phillis's Cabin* (1852), which was considered the most successful attempt at a reply. She also contributed many shorter tales and sketches to magazines, some of which were collected in book-form.

EASTON, the county-seat of Talbot co., Md., is on the head waters of Third Haven River, a navigable inlet of Chesapeake Bay, 50 miles south of Baltimore. It is on the Delaware and Chesapeake Railroad, 81 miles south of Wilmington. It was settled in 1737 and incorporated in 1787. In colonial times it was known as Talbot Court-house, and was the centre of social life of a large district. Evidences of its former importance are to be seen in the handsome suburban residences of the olden style. It is the seat of a Protestant Episcopal bishop. Besides the court-house, Easton has several fine buildings, among which are the music hall, Masonic and Odd-Fellows' halls. It has 3 hotels, a national bank, 3 weekly newspapers, 8 churches, 5 schools, an academy, a female seminary, and orphans' home. The industrial works are a paper-mill, 3 foundries, 2 flour-mills, 2 fertilizer-factories. Its property is valued at $1,200,000; its public debt is $5000, and its yearly expenses about $4800. It is the largest town on the eastern shore of Maryland. Population, 3005.

EASTON, a city of Pennsylvania, county-seat of Northampton co., at the confluence of the Lehigh River with the Delaware, 67 miles by rail N. of Philadelphia. Across the Delaware lies Phillipsburg, in New Jersey; and on the opposite side of the Lehigh is the borough of South Easton. The town is regularly laid out upon a site somewhat hilly. Situated in an iron-ore region, and near the best basins of Pennsylvania anthracite, Easton and its vicinity have many large and important iron-works. Business is facilitated by the Morris, the Lehigh Navigation, and the Delaware canals. The following railways either end here or pass through or very near the city: the Delaware, Lackawanna, and Western, the Lehigh Valley, the Central Railroad of New Jersey, the Delaware Belvidere, the Easton and Amboy, and the Lehigh and Susquehanna. Besides its iron-works, Easton has a large number of other manufactories, including tanneries, machine-shops, paint-works, and manufactures of cordage, pottery, furniture, etc. It is the seat of Lafayette College (Presbyterian), has an opera-house, a library association, 9 public-school buildings, newspapers, national banks, street railways, gas-works, and an abundant water-supply. The adjacent borough of South Easton has large railway shops, iron- and wire-works, a cotton-mill, and other industrial works. A chain bridge and other bridges connect it with Easton. Population of Easton, 11,924; of South Easton, 4534. This town was founded in 1728, and incorporated as a borough in 1789. In early times its site was known as the Forks of the Delaware.

(See Vol. VII. p. 533 Am. ed. (p. 616 Edin. ed.).)

EASTON, NICHOLAS (1593–1675), a colonial governor of Rhode Island, was born in England in 1593. He was by trade a tanner, and being a man of strong religious feeling, emigrated with his two sons, Peter and John, to the Puritan settlements in New England. Landing in May, 1634, he lived for a short time at Ipswich, Mass., but in the next spring commenced Agawam or Newbery. In 1638 he built the first house in Hampton, but in consequence of the Antinomian controversy withdrew to Pocasset, R. I. where he was admitted a citizen in August, 1638. In the following May he removed to Newport, where he built the first house, which however was burnt by the

Indians two years later. He had already been chosen a magistrate of the colony, and during the time of the English Commonwealth is said to have favored a republican form of government. In 1650 and again in 1654 he was chosen president of the council. In 1663 he erected the first wind-mill on the island. In 1665 he adopted the principles of the Society of Friends, but this did not prevent his being chosen deputy governor in the next year. This position he held for four years, and in 1672 he was made governor, and was re-elected in 1673. He died at Newport, R. I., Aug. 15, 1675.

His son, JOHN EASTON, was for many years attorney-general of Rhode Island and in 1674 was chosen deputy governor. In 1690 he was elected governor, and during the five years in which he held this office strenuously resisted the encroachments of Sir William Phipps, the royal governor of Massachusetts. He also wrote a *Narrative of the Causes which led to Philip's Indian War of* 1675, which was published at Albany in 1858.

EASTPORT, a town and island of Washington co., Me., is on Passamaquoddy Bay, and is the extreme eastern point of the United States. It is connected with the mainland at the north by a bridge, 1280 feet long. The island was formerly called Moose Island, and is separated from Lubec in Maine by Cobscook Bay, and from Campobello and other islands of the Province of New Brunswick by Passamaquoddy Bay. The spacious and well-protected harbor is never closed with ice, as the tide rises here 25 feet. Eastport has 2 banks (1 national), a custom-house, United States signal-station, a weekly newspaper, 8 churches, a public library, a high-school, and other schools. The inhabitants are largely employed in connection with the fisheries. Within a few years past much attention has been given to sardine canning, there being 13 factories in operation, which pack nearly 4,000,000 cans yearly. The other industries of the town comprise 2 saw-mills, with ship-yard and dry-docks, stove-factory, and other factories. Eastport has daily steam communication with Portland, Boston, St. Johns, N. B., and Calais, Me. In July, 1814, it was captured by a British fleet from Halifax, and remained in possession of the British for some months. Population, 4006.

EAST SAGINAW, a city and port of entry of Michigan, in Saginaw co., on the left bank of the navigable Saginaw River, nearly opposite Saginaw City, 15 miles from Saginaw Bay, and 90 miles N. N. W. of Detroit. It has a river-front of 4½ miles, and an area of 3905 acres. It is on 5 lines of railway—the Flint and Pere Marquette, the Saginaw, Huron, and Tuscola, the Port Huron and North-western, the Detroit and Bay City, and the Michigan Central—and it is the terminus of some lines of branch-railway, and has extensive commerce on the lakes. It has street-railways, well-paved streets, Holly water-works, gas and electric lights, and is one of the best-built cities in the State. It is the headquarters of vast lumbering interests, and has numerous manufacturing and industrial works connected with that trade. The city is well sewered. It has 11 public and several Catholic school-houses, a public library of 6000 volumes, well-endowed, a home for the friendless, an orphanage, a hospital, 14 churches, 6 banks (4 national), with $700,000 capital, and over $275,000 surplus. The manufactures include wooden-wares, axes, tools, saws,

See Vol. VII. p. 533 Am. ed. (p. 616 Edin. ed.).

files, boats and other vessels, oars, dairy salt (from wells), flour, belting, carriages, machinery, and a great variety of other goods. East Saginaw has also a large wholesale and distributing trade, and is a great shipping-point for farm-products and for horses. It has 5 daily and 3 weekly newspapers. The valuation is about $12,000,000, and the public debt is $600,000. East Saginaw was settled in 1836, and became a city in 1859. The population has increased from 3001 in 1860 to 19,016 in 1880.

EAST SAINT LOUIS, a town of Illinois, St. Clair co., is on the Mississippi, opposite the city of St. Louis, Mo. It is the converging point of a great number of railways, and is connected with St. Louis by a splendid bridge of steel. Adjoining East St. Louis are the great national stock-yards, one of the largest cattle-markets in the world, covering several hundred acres, and having a bank, an exchange building, and large hotel accommodations. The town has car-works, iron-works, 2 newspapers, several banks, a free public library and reading-room (5000 volumes), public and Catholic schools, the Howe Literary Institute (Baptist), and large grain-elevators. Communication is had with St. Louis by ferry and by tramway over the bridge. Population, 9185.

EATON, the county-seat of Preble co., Ohio, is on the Cincinnati and Chicago Air-line Railway, 53 miles N. of Cincinnati. It has 2 banks (1 national), a fine opera-house, 2 weekly newspapers, 8 churches, 2 good graded schools. It has an iron-foundry and machine-shop, 3 saw-mills, a grist-mill. It is 1200 feet above the sea-level and is geologically at the outcrop of the Niagara and Clinton formations, and is noted for its beauty and salubrity. On the west side of the village is St. Clair's (or Seven-mile) Creek, with two or three cascades, making a fall of 20 feet within 100 rods. A mile west is the site of Fort St. Clair, built by Gen. Arthur St. Clair, in his campaign against the North-western Indians in 1791, and afterwards maintained by Gen. Anthony Wayne till the treaty of Greenville in 1795. During this war a supply-train on its way to Gen. Wayne encamped here, and was furiously attacked by a force of Indians under Little Turtle, but the latter were driven off. The village of Eaton was laid out in 1806 by William Bruce, and, when Preble county was organized in 1808, was made the county-seat. In and around it are several chalybeate springs and flowing wells. Population, 2143.

EATON, DANIEL CADY, an American botanist, was born at Fort Gratiot, Mich., Sept. 12, 1834, son of Amos B. Eaton and grandson of Amos Eaton, also a botanist. He graduated at Yale College in 1857, and at Lawrence Scientific School of Harvard University in 1860. In 1864 he was made professor of botany in Yale College. Besides various scientific articles published in periodicals, he has contributed to Chapman's *Flora of the Southern States* (1860) and to Gray's *Manual* (8th ed., 1868), and has published an excellent work on *Ferns of North America* (1878–79). He is also a joint author of *Algae Americanae Boreales Exsiccatae* (1879).

EATON, WILLIAM (1764–1811), an American general and adventurer, was born at Woodstock, Conn., Feb. 23, 1764. When only sixteen years of age he enlisted in the Revolutionary army, and was discharged when peace was proclaimed. He afterwards obtained a liberal education, graduating at Dartmouth College in 1790. He was clerk of the Vermont house of delegates in 1791, but entered the army again in 1792 with the rank of captain, and served five years in the North-west. He was then appointed consul to Tunis, and arrived there in March, 1799. He was successful in procuring for American vessels immunity from depredations of Tunisian cruisers. Having returned to the United States in 1803, he was appointed navy-agent of the United States for the Barbary states. He again sailed with the American fleet to the Mediterranean in 1804. A romantic project was now formed. Eaton sought out Hamet Caramelli, who had been driven from the government of Tripoli, and with him gathered a motley band of troops amounting to 500 men. These he led across the desert 600 miles against Derne, capital of a province of Tripoli, and on April 27, 1805, with assistance of the American fleet, assaulted and captured the place. Eaton was wounded, but continued to hold the city in spite of fierce assaults by the reigning bey. In June the attacking party was completely defeated, and Eaton was preparing to march on Tripoli when he learned that the American consul-general at Algiers had concluded a peace, agreeing to pay a ransom for the Americans yet held in bondage. Eaton returned to the United States, and received many marks of popular favor, while the legislature of Massachusetts granted him 10,000 acres of land in Maine. He presented claims to the United States government for losses incurred in his expedition, but obtained no satisfaction until Aaron Burr, taking advantage of his discontent, tried to enlist him in his schemes. Pres. Jefferson then caused Eaton to be paid, and the latter testified against Burr on his trial at Richmond. Afterwards, failing to obtain such employment as his services and talents led him to expect from the Government, he retired to Brimfield, Mass., and was for a time a member of the State legislature, but became a victim of intemperance. He died at Brimfield, June 1, 1811.

EAU CLAIRE, the county-seat of Eau Claire co., Wis., is at the head of steamboat-navigation on the Chippewa River, at the mouth of the Eau Claire River, 75 miles by water from the Mississippi River and 89 miles E. of St. Paul, Minn. It is on the Chicago, St. Paul, and Minneapolis Railway, and is the terminus of the Wisconsin and Minnesota Railroad and of the Chippewa Valley and Superior Railroad. It is divided by its 2 rivers into 3 parts, which are connected by 3 bridges. It has a court-house, a city-hall, 3 banks (1 national), 12 hotels, 2 daily and 4 weekly newspapers, 12 churches, 6 public schools, a public library, gas-works, street-railway, and telephone-exchange. Its industries comprise 12 saw-mills, cutting annually 250,000,000 feet of lumber, 6 planing-mills, a paper-mill, 3 flour-mills, 2 foundries, 3 machine-shops, 5 grain-elevators. It was laid out in 1855, and incorporated in 1872. Population, 10,119.

EBEL, JOHANNES WILHELM (1784-1861), a German clergyman, was born March 4, 1784, at Passenheim, in East Prussia. He studied theology at Königsberg University and came under the influence of J. H. Schönherr, whose dualistic theosophy he embraced. After receiving his degree he taught in the gymnasium at Königsberg, and in 1807 became pastor at Hermsdorf. In 1810 he returned to Königsberg as preacher and religious teacher in Friedrich college, and in 1816 became preacher in the Old Town church there. The earnest and thoroughly evangelical tone of his preaching excited opposition among the rationalistic clergy. Ebel, by his personal piety and mystical views, had attracted a number of devoted followers, among whom were several ladies of noble families. A ministerial rescript issued in 1826, and warning congregations against mysticism and separatism, was made the basis of persecution against Ebel, who was charged with holding secret meetings and founding a sect of immoral tendency (the Königsberg *Mücker* or Pietists). The investigation was intrusted to his personal foes. Ebel having refused to submit to the trial as illegally conducted, was condemned and suspended from his office by the consistory in Oct., 1835, and his friend Diestel was similarly punished in December following. A criminal suit was then instituted against them which was conducted secretly, but after four years the accused were acquitted of all charges except founding a sect. For this Ebel was deposed and imprisoned; on appeal to a higher court he was in 1842 acquitted even of founding a sect, but was still deprived of his office. He then removed to Grunenfeld and in 1850 to Ludwigburg in Würtemburg, where he died Aug. 18, 1861. His character and life, which had long been the subject of gross misrepresentations, have been fully vindicated by Kanitz, *Aufklärung aus Aktenquellen über den 1835-42 zu Königsberg geführten Religionsprocess* (Basle, 1862). Ebel published several works, among which are *Die Weisheit von Oben* (1823; enlarged 1868). *Die Treue* (1835); *Gedeihliche Erziehung* (1825); *Die apostolische Predigt* (1835); *Verstand und Vernunft* (1837); *Grundzüge der Erkenntniss der Wahrheit* (1852); *Die Philosophie der heiligen Urkunde des Christenthums* (1854-56). Rev. J. I. Mombert has published a good biography of Ebel, with extracts from his works, under the title *Faith Victorious* (N. Y., 1882).

EBELING, CHRISTOPH DANIEL (1741-1817), a German geographer, was born near Hildesheim, Hanover, Nov. 20, 1741. He attended the University of Göttingen from 1763 to 1767, giving especial attention to the study of history and theology. A dulness of hearing which increased from year to year made him shrink from undertaking pastoral work, and in 1769 he became a teacher in a commercial school in Hamburg. He prepared some practical works for this institution, and soon obtained a wide reputation on account of his knowledge of ancient languages, the fine arts, and geography, especially of the New World. His reviews of musical works, published in the Hamburg journals, were highly esteemed. He contributed to the *Hanover Magazine* a brief history of the opera, and translated into German the first volume of Dr. Charles Burney's *Musical Tour*, treating of the state of music in France and Italy. This translation was published at Hamburg in 1772, but with the translation of the later volumes Ebeling had little to do. In 1784 he was appointed professor of Greek and history in the gymnasium at Hamburg, and afterwards was also superintendent of the city library. He published a large *Collection of Travels*, in ten volumes (Hamburg, 1780-'90). He contributed to Büsching's great work on geography, the volumes treating of the geography and history of America, and for this received the thanks of the United States Congress. In the last ten years of his life he became totally deaf and did little literary work. He died at Hamburg, June 30, 1817. His valuable collection of books and maps was purchased and presented to Harvard College in 1818.

EBERLE, JOHN (1787-1838), an American physician and author, was born at Hagerstown, Md., Dec. 10, 1787. He studied at Lancaster, Pa., and

Philadelphia, and graduated from the University of Pennsylvania in 1809. He first practised his profession at Manheim, Lancaster co., Pa., then at Lancaster. Removing to Philadelphia in 1815 he became editor of the Philadelphia *Medical Recorder*. He took an active part in founding Jefferson Medical College, and was appointed professor of the practice of physic in that institution in 1825, and in 1830 was transferred to the chair of materia medica. In 1831 he accepted the same position in the Ohio Medical College, and removed to Cincinnati. In 1837, becoming professor of the practice of medicine in Transylvania University, he changed his residence to Lexington, Ky., and died there Feb. 2, 1838. He published in 1823 the first edition of his work on *Therapeutics and Materia Medica*; in 1830 his *Practice of Physic*; in 1833 his *Treatise on Diseases of Children*. He was remarkably familiar with ancient medicine, and did much to diffuse sound medical knowledge in the West. His works passed through several editions and have been translated into German.

EBERS, GEORG MORITZ, a German Egyptologist and romance writer, was born in Berlin, March 1, 1837. He received his first instructions at Keilhau, Thuringia, then attended the gymnasium at Kottbus and Quedlinburg, and began the study of law at Göttingen in 1856. Two years later, having received an injury in his feet, he turned his attention to classical and oriental studies, and in 1859 removed to Berlin. When his health was fully restored he visited the principal museums in Europe and in 1865 obtained permission to teach in Jena. Here he was made professor extraordinary in 1868, and lectured on ancient Egyptian art, history, and language. In 1869 he started on an extensive tour, going to Egypt by way of Spain and Northern Africa, and also visiting Nubia and Petra. After an absence of fourteen months he returned to Germany and was made professor of Egyptian antiquity in the University of Leipsic. In the winter of 1872 he again visited Egypt, and in this journey discovered the Papyrus which bears his name. Besides a Latin thesis on the *Twenty-sixth Dynasty of the Egyptian Kings* (1865), he has published *Aegypten und die Bücher Moses* (Leipsic, 1868); *Durch Gosen zum Sinai* (1870; 2d ed., 1881); *Ueber das Altägyptische Schriftsystem* (2d ed., 1875). The *Papyros Ebers* (1874) is a hieratic treatise on the medical art. Prof. Ebers has also secured literary fame by his romances, the first of which, *Eine Aegyptische Königstochter* (Stuttgart, 1864), has passed through eleven editions in German and has been translated into the principal European languages. The story relates to the time of the conquest of Egypt by the Persians. His other romances relating to different periods of Egyptian history are *Uarda* (1877; 9th ed., 1881); *Homo sum* (1878); *Die Schwestern* (1880; 14th ed., 1883), and *Der Kaiser* (1881). He has also published two romances of modern life, *Die Frau Bürgemeisterin* (1882), and *Ein Wort* (1883); and an idyl, *Eine Frage* (1881). Ebers in his romances shows a wonderful power of setting forth the life of ancient times without burying the human interest under a mass of antiquarian details. Throughout his career he has contributed numerous papers on Egyptian and oriental subjects to various periodicals, to Bädeker's *Handbuch für Aegypten*, and to Riehm's *Biblische Realwörterbuch*, and has trained some scholars who are already doing good work in the same field. He has also furnished the text for finely illustrated works on Palestine and Egypt.

EBRARD, JOHANN HEINRICH AUGUST, a German theologian of the Reformed Church, was born at Erlangen, Bavaria, Jan. 18, 1818. He is descended from a noble Huguenot family, which left France at the revocation of the edict of Nantes. He was educated at the gymnasium of his native town, and, after studying theology at the university there and at Berlin, became an instructor in a French Reformed family at Friedrichsdorf, in Hesse-Homburg. In 1841 He obtained his degree of Ph.D. at Erlangen, and after lecturing privately for some time on theology he was in 1844 called to Zurich, Switzerland, as professor of theology. In 1847 he returned to Erlangen, where he was made professor of Reformed theology. In 1853 he became counsellor in the Royal Consistory of the Evangelical Church of the Palatinate at Spires. Here he came in conflict with a party which had adopted Lutheran views. The introduction of a revised hymn-book in 1860 especially excited great opposition, and in the following year he resigned his position because the government would not sustain the action of the consistory. Returning to Erlangen, he lectured on theology at the university, and was busily engaged in authorship. In 1875 he was elected pastor of the French colony at Erlangen, and since 1876 he has been president of the Reformed synod of Eastern Bavaria. As an author he has been remarkably prolific, producing works on all branches of theology—systematic, historical, exegetical, and practical—besides a large number of polemical pamphlets and sermons. His first work was *Scientific Criticism of the Gospel History* (1842; third ed., 1868), intended as a reply to Strauss. His other theological works are *The Doctrine of the Lord's Supper and its History* (1845); Continuation of Olshausen's *Commentaries; Christian Dogmatics* (1851; 2d ed., 1862); *Practical Theology* (1854); *History of the Christian Church and Doctrines* (4 vols., 1865–67); *The Irish-Scotch Mission Church from the Sixth to the Eighth Century* (1873); *Christian Apologetics* (2 vols., 1874; 2d ed., 1878); and *Bonifacius, the Destroyer of the Churches of Columbanus* (1882). Ebrard has also, generally under the assumed name of "Gottfried Flammberg," written several dramas: *Mornay-Duplessis* (1859); *Rudolph of the Palatinate* (1860); *Hermann* (1861); and *Stephen Klinger* (1872), the last appearing under the name of "Christian Deutsch." A number of short moral and religious stories have also appeared from his pen at intervals from 1860 to 1881. Among them are *The Rose of Urach; The File-cutter; The Golden Cup; The Bird-catcher of Eschlippthal*. His poems have been gathered in two volumes—*A Life in Songs* (1868), and *Ricordo, Impressions of a Journey in Italy*. Dr. Ebrard has given much attention to the Gaelic language, has translated Ossian's *Fingal* into German, adding an essay "On the Age and Genuineness of Ossian's Poems," and has prepared a *Grammar and Dictionary of the Mediæval Gaelic Language*.

ECCLESIASTES, BOOK OF. Dr. Ginsburg is bold enough to say: "On the Continent, where Biblical criticism has been cultivated to the highest degree, and where Old Testament exegesis has become an exact science, the attempt to prove that Solomon is not the author of Ecclesiastes would be viewed in the same light as adducing facts to demonstrate that the earth does not stand still. In England, however, some scholars of acknowledged repute still adhere to the Solomonic authorship." What is here stated of English scholars is also true of American scholars. The

See Vol. VII. p. 539 Am. ed. (p. 623 Edin. ed.)

slighting comparison made by Dr. Ginsburg justifies the retort that the more exact science is, if it be exact in opposition to the evidence, or without evidence, the more exactly wrong and silly it is. The assertion just cited as to the opinion concerning Ecclesiastes held by Continental scholars would be more exact if it were less sweeping. If the opinion that Ecclesiastes originated several centuries later than Solomon be correct, it is still a mistake to support it by mistaken arguments. And the proof of its correctness is not so overwhelming as to justify superciliousness toward those who hold a different opinion. Martin Luther wrote extensively on Ecclesiastes in German and Latin. He definitely held and taught that the Book of Ecclesiastes was composed of sayings publicly uttered by Solomon, but taken down and arranged by others. The scientific exactness which, in the face of this well-known fact, cites a careless and not very intelligible passage from Luther's *Table Talk*, apparently ascribing Ecclesiastes to Sirach and the times of Ptolemy Euergetes, as if this passage contained Luther's deliberate opinion on the subject, is not of a sort to which a large class of English and American scholars aspire.

Of the arguments commonly adduced to prove the late origin of this work the numerous Aramaic forms may be treated as a class by themselves. Aside from these, considerations like the following are mentioned: "The complaint about the multiplication of profane literature (chap. xii. 12) could only have been made at a time when the Jews became acquainted with the Greek writings and Alexandrian philosophy." This statement would have been more plausible several decades ago, when men disputed whether the hieroglyphs of Egypt and the cuneiform inscriptions of the Euphrates valley were really literary records, than it now is. Add what we now know of the literary activity in those countries previous to the time of Solomon to what the historical books of the Bible tell us of the numerous Israelitish sources whence they drew their material, and especially to what they tell us of Solomon's own achievements in the way of songs, proverbs, and studies in natural history, and we have abundant explanation of this passage without going to Alexandria for it.

Again, we are told that the "representation of Coheleth as indulging in sensual enjoyments and acquiring riches and fame, in order to ascertain what is good for the children of men (chap. ii. 3-9, iii. 12-22, etc.), making philosophical experiments to discover the *summum bonum*, is utterly at variance with the conduct of the historical Solomon, and is an idea of a much later period." But precisely the reverse will seem to most people to be the truth. With the modification that Coheleth is not represented as indulging in sensual pleasure and the like *merely* for the sake of philosophical experiment, the conduct here ascribed to him is decidedly such as we should expect in the historical Solomon. If Ecclesiastes be the production of a later age, its author has admirably mastered the literature of the Solomonic period and placed his Coheleth in the midst of the scenes of that period. As to the assertion that the idea of a philosophical search for the highest good belongs only to a later age, when did men ever begin to write their thoughts without beginning to philosophize concerning the highest good?

Apart from the Aramaisms, the supposed foreign terms in the book rather favor the idea of its Solomonic origin than otherwise. At what other period was Israel in Palestine ever brought into so direct and wide contact with the other populations of the earth? Considerations like these sufficiently represent this branch of the argument. On the whole, it certainly confirms the testimony of tradition to the effect that the book is from Solomon. Even one who holds to its later origin must see that its teachings belong to the period when Solomon reigned.

The argument from the Aramaisms of Ecclesiastes needs to be treated with more caution. On the philological theories now commonly held, these peculiarities have weight to prove that this book, in its present form, belongs with Ezra, Nehemiah, and Chronicles to the latest group of Old Testament writings. It is conceivable, and, indeed, not on the face of it improbable, that one who holds to the Solomonic authorship of Ecclesiastes might construct, upon that basis, a theory of the Aramaisms in Hebrew literature, and might vindicate its right to supersede those now current; but until this is done, the existence of an element of uncertainty as to the Solomonic authorship of Ecclesiastes must be admitted.

The argument from the Aramaisms, however, has no weight to prove that the book is much younger than those of Ezra, Nehemiah, and Chronicles, and none, therefore, to prove its date to be later than that fixed by the testimony in the case for the close of the canon. The early controversies as to its canonical authority do not show that it was of recent origin, or that it was only at a late date admitted into the canon, but merely that it was less familiarly known than the other *hokmah* books of the Old Testament, so that some investigation concerning it became necessary. (See BIBLE.) The result of these investigations by the Jewish scribes of the first Christian century was to convince them that Solomon wrote Ecclesiastes, and that it had ever since been a part of the Scriptures.

Literature.—Schaff's edition of Lange includes both a translation of Zöckler's commentary, by William Wells, and a metrical version, with notes, by Dr. Tayler Lewis. The introductory discussions are quite full and valuable. Renan's *L'Ecclésiaste* (1882) presents the most extreme view of the recent destructive criticisms. (W. J. B.)

ECCLESTON, SAMUEL (1801-1851), an American archbishop of the Roman Catholic Church, was born in Kent co., Md., June 27, 1801. He was the grandson of Sir John Eccleston, an English gentleman who settled in Maryland shortly before the American Revolution. His parents were Episcopalians, but, after the early death of his father, his mother married a Catholic, and young Eccleston was sent to St. Mary's College, Baltimore, where he became a Catholic, and was regarded as a shining light. At the age of eighteen he determined to study for the priesthood, and entered the seminary attached to the college, May 23, 1819. He was ordained April 24, 1825, by Archbishop Maréchal, and shortly afterwards went to France to continue his studies at the Sulpician Seminary at Issy, near Paris. He returned to the United States in July, 1827, and was appointed vice-president of St. Mary's College, and in 1829 president of the same institution. Under his wise and admirable administration St. Mary's prospered. In 1834 the health of the venerable Dr. Whitfield, the fourth archbishop of Baltimore, became so infirm that he consulted with his suffragan bishops as to the appointment of another and more vigorous ecclesiastic to assist him in his arduous labors, and to succeed him in the episcopal office. All concurred in recommending the president of St. Mary's College for this high dignity, although he was only thirty-three years old. In the summer of 1834 the papal brief was received appointing Dr. Eccleston coadjutor of Baltimore with the right of succession, and he was consecrated September 14 of the same year by Archbishop Whitfield. In a few months Archbishop Eccleston received the pallium from Rome, conferring upon him all the powers and honors of the metropolitan see of Baltimore.

Upon assuming the position of primate of the Catholic Church in the United States, Archbishop Eccleston made an exact examination of the affairs of his archdiocese. He had the satisfaction of finding a zealous and well-equipped body of clergy, and many religious institutions; but the Catholic population had so greatly increased that there was still much work for him to do. Under his wise and liberal administration the number of churches, schools, and religious orders was greatly multiplied. He introduced the Christian Brothers in the United States. The first school under these zealous teachers was opened at Baltimore in 1846. To meet the large increase of the German Catholic element Archbishop Eccleston brought into his diocese the priests of the Holy Redeemer in 1841. Their novitiate was first established at Annapolis, Md., in an old mansion which was once the residence of Charles Carroll of Carrollton, and which was presented to the order by his granddaughters. During the eighteen years that he presided over the archdiocese of Baltimore six large churches were built in Baltimore, and new churches in various parts of Maryland. One of the most important events of his administration was the establishment of St. Charles's Ecclesiastical Seminary, the original donation for which was from Charles Carroll.

Archbishop Eccleston presided over five provincial councils of Baltimore. The archbishop was deeply interested in the Baltimore Cathedral, to which he contributed liberally from his private means, and he had the satisfaction of seeing the edifice far advanced, and the improvement of the interior commenced. In the midst of his usefulness he was struck down by a mortal illness, while visiting Georgetown, D. C., in April, 1851, and expired on the 21st of the same month. (E. L. S.)

ECHIUM. The blue-weed, blue-thistle, blue devil, of North Carolina, Virginia, and Maryland is *Echium vulgare* of Europe, there commonly known as "viper's bugloss," "viper grass," and "snake-flower." We have here an illustration of the value of common names in helping to solve other than philological questions. The plant has been considered a native of England, but its common name, bugloss (Latin, *buglossa*), is evidently a Greek word signifying "ox-tongue." The plant is certainly a native of the islands in the Grecian Archipelago, and we may believe, from the evolution of its English name, that it travelled from Greece to Rome, and thence perhaps with the Romans to Britain, and, as we know, from the north of Europe to the United States. The original bugloss may have been the garden-plant borage, the rough, ox-tongue-like leaves suggesting the name. The botanical name, *Echium*, is from the Greek *echis*, "viper," and so also "viper's bugloss" is a common name for this plant. It was long in high estimation as a cure for snake-bites in Europe, and is believed to be the "alcibiadion" of some ancient Greek writers, so named from a certain Alcibiades, who, when bitten by a viper, chewed the leaves, swallowed the juice, rubbed the plant over the bitten place, and was saved. Down to comparatively modern times it was used in such cases, six spoonfuls of the juice being given in wine; but it is now believed, as in the case of many similar remedies, that the spirits in which the remedies were generally administered were more potent than the infusions they contained. Hence we find the explanation in most modern botanical works that "*Echium* is from *echis*, a viper, because the seed resembles the head of a viper," and not, as Sir William Hooker gives it, "because this or some allied plant was believed to cure a viper's bite."

It belongs to the natural order *Boraginaceæ*, an order well distinguished by the ovary being usually four-lobed and with the pistil rising in the centre from the base of these lobes. It has almost always rough leaves, and the flower-stalk uncoils after the manner in which the fronds of many ferns do. *Echium* has a tubular, bell-shaped corolla, with the limb almost two-lipped, and not regularly divided, as in the forget-me-not and other well-known plants of the same natural order. The flowers have a reddish tint when they first open, but afterwards change to a purplish blue. Sometimes they retain the red tint to the last. In the parts of the United States already noted they afford a pleasing variety to the eye of the traveller, who frequently passes acres of them, covering the whole surface with a sheet of reddish-blue. But they increase to this great extent only on comparatively neglected farms, and cannot be considered a troublesome weed in American agriculture.

Beyond its beauty it renders little service to man. So far as the honey is concerned, it is an excellent bee-plant, but complaints have been made that the rough hair with which the plant abounds tears the wings of the bees, which thus are prevented from reaching their hives. Rafinesque observes that a fine charcoal is made from the stems which is "useful to painters, as it does not soil paper." (T. M.)

ECKARDT, JULIUS, a German writer, was born in Wolmar, Livonia, Aug. 1, 1836. He was educated at St. Petersburg, Dorpat, and Berlin, studying chiefly law and history. He established himself at Riga, in 1860, as a consulting advocate, and afterwards became secretary of the Provincial Consistory of Livonia, and at the same time became one of the editors of the *Rigasche Zeitung*, the organ of the German party in the Baltic provinces. In 1867 he went to Germany, where he edited several journals—the *Grenzboten* (1867–70), the *Hamburgische Correspondent* (1870–74), the *Hamburgische Boersenhalle*, etc. He was secretary of the senate of Hamburg, 1870–82, and has since been in the Prussian state-service. His works treat principally of the Baltic provinces. Among them are—*The Baltic Provinces of Russia* (1869); *The Condition of Rural Russia since the Abolition of Serfdom* (1870); *Young Russians and Old Livonians* (1871); *The Society of St. Petersburg*, anonymous (1875); *Livonia in the Eighteenth Century* (1876); *Russia Before and After the War* (1879); *Berlin and St. Petersburg* (1880); *From Nicholas to Alexander III.* (1881); *Russian Transformations* (1882), and *The Prospects of German Parliamentary Government* (1882).

ECKERT, THOMAS THOMPSON, an American telegraphist, was born at St. Clairsville, O., April 23, 1824. In 1849 he was appointed postmaster at Wooster, O., and had charge of the telegraph-office there.

In 1852 he became a telegraph-superintendent. In 1859 he engaged in gold-mining in North Carolina, but, on account of the outbreak of the Rebellion, was obliged to abandon his property and remove to the North. He was then invited to Washington, where he gave considerable information in regard to Southern affairs. He was placed in charge of the military telegraph connected with the Army of the Potomac. So useful was this system found that it was afterwards extended to the whole country. Mr. Eckert's services in this connection were of the utmost value to his country. In 1864 he was made assistant-secretary of war, and remained in that position till August, 1866. He was then made general superintendent of the Western Union Telegraph, and he has since continued to direct the operations of this company.

ECLIPTIC, the great circle of the heavens which the sun apparently, but the earth really, describes in the course of a year—so called because eclipses only happen when the moon, in her monthly journey round the earth, is at or very near this circle. The centres of both the earth and sun are always in the plane of the ecliptic, but the moon's orbit, being inclined to it at an angle of about 5° 8', is in that plane only when in the act of crossing, which she does twice at each revolution around the earth.

See Vol. II. p. 674 Am. ed. (p. 771 Edin. ed.).

The plane on which the earth daily rotates (plane of the equator) is inclined to that on which it yearly revolves (plane of the ecliptic) at an angle of about 23° 27' 17", technically called the obliquity of the ecliptic. This angle in our age is decreasing at the very slow rate of a little less than 50" in one hundred years. At a very remote time in the future this decrease will cease, and be changed to an increase, to continue for ages, and then again to a decrease, and thus oscillating through a small arc of perhaps 1½°, will mark the flow of millenniums rather than of years or centuries.

That this angle is steadily decreasing the following facts will conclusively show. About 230 B. C. this angle, according to Eratosthenes, amounted to 23° 51' 20".

Ptolemy, 370 years later, found it 23° 35' 00".

In A. D. 1600, according to Flamsteed, it was 23° 29' 00".

At the beginning of the year 1882 it was about 23° 27' 17".

The refinements of astronomical calculations, to give which would be to exceed the scope and design of this article, have proved that these fluctuations are altogether too small to produce any perceptible variation in the normal changes of our seasons, and that with the hypothetical ice-age they could have had nothing to do.

The disturbing and ever-varying influences of the planets and satellites upon each other are very numerous and complicated, and to completely eliminate from the whole the effect which each exerts upon the others is beyond the reach of man's highest intellectual achievement.

When the sun and all the planets and satellites shall have been accurately weighed, their distances from each other measured, and their periods of revolution ascertained, it will be possible by mathematical analysis to compute the length of time required for a single oscillation of this plane and the extent of its vibratory arc.

One effect of the variation of the ecliptic's obliquity is to increase the latitude of all the stars in certain localities, and to lessen it in regions opposite. Another important effect of this change is, that the sun in one age does not, at the summer solstice, ascend as far north nor descend at the winter solstice as far south as in another, thus producing, as before stated, a very slight change in the seasons.

The ecliptic passes through the centre of the zodiac, a belt about 16° in breadth in which all the major planets and their satellites perform their journeys round the sun. Many of the asteroids, owing to their great inclinations, extend beyond the limits of the zodiac, and hence are called ultra-zodiacal planets.

The north pole of the ecliptic is situated in the constellation Draco, though somewhat remote from any conspicuous star, and is 66° 32' 43" north of the equator, or 23° 27' 17" south of its pole. The north pole of the equator is in the constellation Ursa Minor, distant at the present time about 1¼° from Alpha (called also Polaris) of that constellation. The south pole of the ecliptic is situated near Epsilon Doradus, a fifth-magnitude star, and is of course the same distance south of the equator that its north pole is north of it, they being exactly a semi-circumference, or 180°, apart. No star brighter than the sixth magnitude is within 6° of the south pole of the equator, and hence there is now no pole-star for the southern hemisphere.

The two points of intersection of the planes of the ecliptic and equator are called the equinoxes, or equinoctial points, and they also are 180° apart. The one crossed by the sun's centre in his annual journey from south to north is called the vernal, and that from north to south the autumnal, equinox. It is from the vernal —situated at the first point of the sign (not constellation) Aries—that right ascension on the equator and longitude on the ecliptic are reckoned (always eastward), from 0° to 360° on the ecliptic, and from 0ʰ to 24ʰ on the equator. Some astronomers, however, reckon by degrees instead of hours on the equator. (L. S.)

ECUADOR, a centralized republic of South America, has in undisputed possession a territory estimated at 180,000 square miles. The Galápagos Islands, lying on the equator at a distance of 600 miles from the mainland, belong to Ecuador; their area is 2950 square miles, and since 1832 some of them have been occupied by a penal colony, which furnishes supplies to whalers touching there.

See Vol. VII. p. 558 Am. ed. (p. 644 Edin. ed.).

Produce and industries.—The chief article of export is the *cacao* bean, of which chocolate is made. Of this there are two varieties, one of which has always been considered among the best in the market. Ever since the Spanish conquest great quantities have been sent to Spain, a great deal goes to Peru and Chili, while of the remainder England and Germany are the principal consumers. In 1880 nearly 15,000 tons, valued at $3,500,000, were exported; in 1882 the export was valued at $3,867,900. The introduction of aniline dyes destroyed the nascent industry of indigo-producing. The collection of india-rubber is becoming important, though in European markets, and those of the United States, the rubber is considered inferior to that of any other country whence it is brought. In 1880 nearly 4000 cwt. found its way across the isthmus of Panamá, chiefly to New York. The total export in 1882 was valued at $1,045,700. The exportation of cotton, which in 1874 was nearly half a million of quintals, has dwindled to almost nothing. In 1882 the other more important exports were cinchona bark to the value of $319,950; ivory-nuts, valued at $418,600; Panama hats, leather, and skins, and coffee. In addition, tobacco, rice, sarsaparilla, bamboos, mats, and a few other articles, in comparatively insignificant quantities, are exported, to the neighboring countries chiefly. The total exports in 1882 were valued at $5,469,790.

Constitution, government, etc.—The constitution of 1830 was supplemented by that of 1843, but this has been greatly modified—notably in 1861. According to this constitution the executive power is lodged in a president and vice-president, elected by a majority of 900 electors voted for by a majority of citizens, who must be Roman Catholics and able to read and write. The presidential term is six years, and the president cannot be re-elected; he has a veto, but cannot act officially at a greater distance from Quito than eight leagues. There are several other things he cannot do, but the man who gets into power is usually a dictator, who violates the constitution at his will. The cabinet consists of a home secretary, a minister of finance, and one of war and marine. There is also a council which passes upon certain executive acts; this consists of the vice-president, the cabinet, the president of the supreme court, a representative of the church, and one of the landed interest. The legislative power is vested in a congress of 16 senators and a lower house of 30 members, elected biennially by the people. Congress elects the supreme court, which is in permanent session at Quito. There is a lower court in each province; the alcaldes preside over municipal tribunals, and there are also parochial courts. Trial by jury obtains in criminal cases, but does not work very well. Slavery was abolished in 1854. The army in time of peace consists of 1500 men, and there is no navy other than two or three revenue vessels.

Gen. Ignacio de Veintemilla, who, in 1876, while holding command of Guayaquil, had caused himself to be proclaimed president, was declared dictator for an unlimited period by a convention, July 10, 1878. Again in 1882, when his term was properly drawing to a close, he incited a sham revolution, and then issued a pronunciamento (April 2), in which he styled himself "supreme chief by the will of the people." A real revolution ensued, and soon Veintemilla's power was restricted to Guayaquil and Esmeraldas. In January, 1883, the dictator's troops were driven from the latter town, but escaped by steamer to Guayaquil. The insurgents had formed a provisional government at Quito, and their cause found a steady increase of favor throughout the country. In May their several armies moved from different directions on Guayaquil, and Veintemilla, after having seized the deposits in the bank of Ecuador, was so convinced of the desperate state of his affairs that he offered to abdicate his dictatorship in favor of Señor Antonio Flores, son of the first President of Ecuador, but the latter declined. After a siege of two months, Gen. Rinaldo Flores on the morning of July 9 took Guayaquil by storm, and Veintemilla fled to Peru. Local governments were organized in several places, and a national convention was called for October 9. In this convention Señor José M. Caamaño, of Guayaquil, was elected provisional president of the republic.

Finances.—The finances of Ecuador are in a very rotten condition. In 1881 the public revenue was about £700,000; the expenditures £720,000. The national debt, home and foreign, is £3,800,000.

EDDY, THOMAS M., D. D. (1823–1874), an American minister of the Methodist Episcopal Church, was born Sept. 7, 1823, near Cincinnati, Ohio. He was educated at a classical academy at Greensboro', Ind., and in 1842 became an itinerant preacher in the Indiana Conference. He was a frequent contributor to the press, and in 1856 was appointed editor of the *North-western Christian Advocate*, which position he held for twelve years, during which time the circulation of that paper increased from 14,000 to 30,000. Besides his labors as editor he was still frequently called upon to preach on important occasions.

In 1868 he became pastor of a church in Baltimore, and after serving three years was appointed pastor of the Metropolitan Church in Washington, D. C. In 1872 he was a delegate to the General Conference, and was elected by that body a missionary secretary. In this capacity he labored assiduously till his death, which took place at New York, Oct. 7, 1874. He published a *History of Illinois During the Civil War*.

EDISON, THOMAS ALVA, an American inventor, was born at Milan, O., Feb. 11, 1847. The family soon afterwards removed to Port Huron, Mich., and Thomas, who had received all his education from his mother, was, at the age of twelve, a train-boy on a railroad. He learned something of printing, and started a newspaper in a baggage-car. A stationmaster, whose child he had rescued from death on the railroad track, in gratitude taught him the art of telegraphy. Edison then practised the art in many places in the United States and Canada, becoming noted for his skill and rapidity in transmission of messages. He also studied the principles of the science, and made various inventions of practical importance. He failed, however, in his attempts at duplex telegraphy. In 1868 he happened to be in New York when the indicator of the gold and stock company broke down, and, in the absence of a competent employé, volunteered his services, which were not only successful in adjusting the instruments, but suggested to his inventive mind a new device—the printing telegraph. The success and immediate usefulness of the new contrivance induced prominent telegraph companies to employ him in researches aiming at further inventions. He also established in Newark, N. J., the manufacture of printing telegraphs. This, however, he sold in 1876, and removed to Menlo Park, N. J., where he erected large workshops for the purpose of making experiments in the application of electricity to the wants of every-day life.

Altogether Mr. Edison has taken out nearly 400 patents, 29 of these having been issued in a single week in January, 1882. His most valuable inventions have been patented in other countries as well as in the United States. The American patents may be classified as follows: 35 relate to automatic and chemical telegraphs, 8 to duplex and quadruplex telegraphy, 38 to printing telegraph instruments, 14 to improvements in the Morse telegraph apparatus, while the others relate to electric signals, the electric light, district telegraphs, fire-alarms, etc. The electric pen is one of the most curious of his minor inventions in this department, while his electric railway at Menlo Park, three miles in length, opens a prospect of a change of incalculable proportions in the movements of modern civilization. On this railway a well-loaded train can be carried at the rate of 42 miles an hour on level ground. The locomotive is controlled by an ingenious electric brake, or by a reversal of the current. In a wider application of this invention stations along the line would contain the necessary engines, dynamos, etc., while the current would pass through the rails and the wheels of the locomotive to the motor inside Mr. Edison has also contrived electro-motors for running sewing machines and various domestic purposes.

Among his remarkable inventions relating to sound are the microphone, for the detection of faint sounds; the megaphone, by which ordinary sounds can be heard at a great distance; the phonograph, a marvellous instrument, by which the sounds of the voice can be registered and preserved; the carbon telephone, and the phonomotor. He also invented the microtasimeter, by which very minute variations of temperature can be measured; for instance, the heat of the corona of the sun and of the star Arcturus was thus measured in 1878.

The difficulties of duplex telegraphy—that is, transmitting messages in opposite directions on the same wire at the same time—were at last overcome by his untiring energy and inventive skill, and soon he was able to obtain quadruplex and sextuplex transmission of messages. This system has been acknowledged by the most prominent telegraph companies to have been the means of immense saving in the construction of their lines.

The pecuniary profits arising from his numerous patents have been largely expended in prosecuting further experiments with the aid of able assistants.

Mr. Edison's name has been most prominently connected with experiments in electric lighting. At first he used platinum for burners, but carefully sought for a better, more accessible, and less expensive material. After a protracted series of experiments among metals and minerals, carbon was found to have the greatest resisting power to the electric current. For the purpose of preventing its combustion by the access of oxygen from the air, it had to be placed in a vacuum as nearly perfect as could be made. But a further investigation was necessary to determine from what material the carbon should be obtained. Charcoal and other ordinary forms of carbon could not be used on account of their porosity. Vegetable fibres, silk, cotton, flax and others were carbonized and tried with various results, but none were satisfactory, chiefly on account of their looseness of structure and the want of tenacity in the carbonized fibre. For a time specially prepared cardboard seemed the most available substance. Finally, however, Mr. Edison pronounced carbonized bamboo to have all the requisite properties, so that now in each household lamp a small strip of bamboo will furnish light for at least 600 hours.

The search among the various metals and minerals and the attempts to lessen the expense of procuring platinum had incidentally led Mr. Edison to some extremely lucrative inventions, which, however, he readily abandoned to others in order to pursue diligently the main object of his investigation.

In all the exhibitions which have been made of various methods of applying the electric light to domestic uses Mr. Edison's displays have been noted for their brilliancy and utility. The great difficulty formerly experienced in the use of the electricity for such purposes was that, when the light was subdivided, the extinction of one light affected all the others. But Mr. Edison's invention has enabled one light to be raised, lowered, or extinguished without disturbing the others, and without producing waste heat elsewhere. His incandescent lamp may be said to combine economy, purity, steadiness, safety from fire, and simplicity in manipulation. It does not taint the atmosphere and gives out only a slight heat.

Mr. Edison still continues to prosecute his search for improvements in the various inventions he has sent forth for the benefit of the world. Though he has chiefly devoted his attention to electricity and its applications, his success has been as marked in other fields. He is very systematic in his habits, keeping a daily record of his experiments. He is modest and retiring, and his mode of life is very simple. In every respect he is an admirable representative of American mechanical genius and perseverance.

EDMONDS, John Worth (1799–1874), a New York jurist and spiritualist, was born at Hudson, N. Y., March 13, 1799. He graduated at Union College, Schenectady, N. Y., in 1826, studied law, and was admitted to the bar in 1819. After practising for some years with success in Hudson, he was elected to the State legislature in 1831, and in the next year to the State senate. In 1836 he was appointed by the United States government an Indian agent, and held the position for two years. In 1841 he removed to New York city, where he practised his profession with great success. In 1843 he was one of the inspectors of the State prisons, and introduced various reforms in the treatment of criminals. In 1845 he was appointed a circuit judge. In 1847 he became judge of the supreme court, and in 1852 a member of the court of appeals. In 1851 he had commenced an investigation of the phenomena of Spiritualism, and in 1853 openly avowed his faith in that system. In consequence of the popular prejudice against this belief, he retired from the bench and devoted himself to private practice. He continued firm in his adherence to the views he had professed in his work on *Spiritualism* (1853; 2d ed., 1865) and defended them in other publications. His moral character was above reproach, and his reputation as an able and learned lawyer remained unimpaired to the last. He died at New York, April 5, 1874.

EDMUNDS, Francis W. (1806–1863), an American painter, was born at Hudson, N. Y., Nov. 22, 1806. Though evincing a strong liking for art in his youth, he became a clerk in a bank, and after rising to the position of cashier removed to New York city, where he held a similar position in several banks until 1855. He joined with others in forming the Bank-Note Engraving Company of New York, and several country scenes painted by him were engraved on notes prepared by that establishment. Throughout his business career Edmunds practised painting diligently in his leisure hours, but had no regular art-training. In 1836 he exhibited a painting, Sammy the Tailor; in 1838 he was elected an associate of the national academy and afterwards an academician. He profited much in his knowledge of art by a visit to Italy in 1840. Among his pictures are Dominie Sampson (1837); City and Country Beaux (1840); Stealing Milk (1843); Vesuvius (1844); Florence (1844); Trial of Patience (1848); Taking the Census (1854); Thirsty Drover (1856); The New Bonnet (1859); Gil Blas and the Archbishop. He died at New York in 1863.

EDMUNDS, George Franklin, an American lawyer and senator, was born at Richmond, Vt., Feb. 1, 1828. The son of a farmer, he was educated in the village school and by a private tutor. Having studied law, he was admitted to the bar in 1849, and two years later removed to Burlington, the chief city of the State, where he practised his profession with diligence and success. Taking part in the movement which eventually led to the formation of the Republican party, he was elected to the State legislature in 1854, and, continuing there, was chosen speaker in 1857. From the lower house he passed in 1860 to the State senate, where he served two terms. After the outbreak of the rebellion a State convention was held in Burlington for the purpose of uniting members of all parties in support of the national government. The resolutions for this purpose were drawn up and presented by Mr. Edmunds and were unanimously adopted. On the death of United States Senator Foot in the spring of 1866 Mr. Edmunds was appointed by the governor to fill the vacancy, and his first speech was a eulogy of his predecessor. Though he thus entered the Senate without the usual previous experience in the House of Representatives, he soon showed himself admirably qualified for his position. From the start he has been remarkable for his devotion to public duty, studying carefully every measure brought before the Senate and endeavoring if possible to remedy its defects. When Pres. Johnson attempted to enforce a Southern reconstruction policy at variance with that intended by Congress, Senator Edmunds reported from the judiciary committee the Tenure of Office act, which effectually restrained the president's power. Though not approving all the measures of Pres. Grant's administration, he remained throughout on friendly terms with the president, while Sumner and others of his associates passed over to the opposition. He has always been devoted to the interests of the Republican party, but has refused to secure a temporary advantage at the sacrifice of any principles. In this way he opposed the admission of Colorado as a State under a constitution which confined the franchise to white men. During the trouble arising from the presidential election of 1876, Mr. Edmunds was prominent in devising and securing the reference of the disputed questions to the electoral commission, and afterwards served as a member of that commission. His fidelity in discharge of his duty has been honored by three elections to the Senate, in which he has served on the most important committees, and in March, 1883, he was elected president of that body. Tall and slender, bald with full gray beard, he looks older than he really is. In speaking he is deliberate and undemonstrative; his style is simple and weighty; he is especially noted for dry humor and sarcasm, and is strong in debate. His literary attainments are extensive, and in knowledge of civil and parliamentary law he is without a rival in the Senate. He has been prominently mentioned in national conventions of the Republican party as a candidate for the presidency, but has uniformly discountenanced such action.

EDUCATION, SECONDARY, or that which is intermediate between the elementary and the collegiate, is, in America, chiefly conducted by means of academies and high schools. These institutions belong to that grade often known in Europe as middle schools. They correspond to the "great public schools" of England, as Harrow, Eton, Westminster, and Rugby, to the grammar or high schools of Scotland, and to the gymnasia or "classical drill schools" of the continent.

The first institutions of secondary instruction founded in America were modelled on the "public or foundation schools of England." In Boston, Cambridge, Dorchester, Salem, Ipswich, and Hadley, of Massachusetts, and Hartford and New Haven, were these so-called grammar schools established in the seventeenth century. Their primary design was to fit students for college. They were supported both from the public fund and from endowments, as well as from small tuition fees. The town of New Haven paid its master, Ezekiel Cheever, the most distinguished teacher of early New England, at first £20 a year for his services, a sum that in 1644 was increased to £30. But the first endowments (of a large amount) coming from individuals were received from the estate of Edward Hopkins, who died in London in 1657. He had been governor of Connecticut seven times between 1640 and 1654; and bequeathed certain sums "to give encouragement," as expressed in his will, "in those foreign plantations for the breeding up of hopeful youths, both at the grammar school and college, for the public service of the country in future times." New Haven, Hartford, Cambridge, and Hadley received the larger portions of these bequests. Although the donations of Governor Hopkins were, particularly in Hartford and Hadley, used to maintain a common English school, yet in New Haven the support that was thus furnished to the pursuit of classical studies was great, so great that one in thirty of all the graduates of Harvard College prior to 1700 came from that town, although it at no time of this period had more than five hundred inhabitants. The schools so endowed do not seem to have been designed for the exclusive use of the towns in which they were situated. This doubtless was their primary purpose; but as Judge Shaw, of Massachusetts, decided in 1833 in reference to a contest which arose between the town of Hadley and the academy which succeeded the grammar school, that the Hadley school was founded for the benefit of "all the persons in that (then) newly-settled part of the country who desired to avail themselves of a grammar school adapted to instruct and qualify pupils for the university." This was doubtless true of all schools endowed by Hopkins.

Prior to the Revolution it would appear that the secondary schools were few, and that the support accorded them was slight and desultory. Many graduates of Harvard and Yale who desired to become teachers found little demand for their services. They were, therefore, compelled to enter the ministry. But while pursuing this vocation they were able to teach the classics, and they fitted a large number of students for college. In the middle of the eighteenth century, however, appeared a revival of interest in the intermediate school. In 1746 Samuel Moody graduated at Harvard College, and at once began his distinguished career as a teacher in the York Grammar School of Maine. Since the death of Ezekiel Cheever, in 1708, no teacher of equal celebrity with Master Moody had arisen. His school at York, though the only public school in town, became the resort of scholars. In 1763 was founded the Dummer School at Byfield, Mass., the first of the New England academies, and to it Master Moody was transferred. Under his administration there is reason to believe that it was the best school of its type in America, and that it had hardly been surpassed by the Boston Latin School, under the charge of Master Cheever. The success of the school at Byfield was doubtless of influence in the foundation of academies at Andover and at Exeter, N. H. Phillips' Academy at Andover and Phillips' Exeter Academy were founded by members of the family whose name they bear in 1778 and 1782; and they have for a century been regarded as the best schools in America preparatory for college. They have, to a degree, served as a model for other schools of secondary instruction, as the Williston Seminary of Easthampton, Mass., founded by Samuel Williston in 1841, and academies in Maine, Vermont, and a few other States. The establishment of other academies at once followed the foundations of Phillips': fifteen were incorporated in Massachusetts before 1797. Their relation to the public-school system, on their application for aid from the State, became a subject of debate, and it was affirmed that they "were to be regarded as, in many respects and to a considerable extent, public schools; as a part of an organized system of public and universal education." But, though the academy spread through New England, and obtained a footing in New York, and has in later years been represented in a few institutions of the West, it has remained pre-eminently a New England institution.

But by the side of the academy has arisen since 1840 in New England a public school, like the early grammar school, designed to prepare students for college. It is now almost universally known as the high school. Between 1830 and 1850 the interest in public schools greatly revived. (See COMMON SCHOOLS.) At the same time the small endowments of academies, and other reasons of a financial character, contributed to their decline, and although the stronger institutions flourished, the weaker either surrendered their charter or became incorporated into public schools. At the present time, therefore, in even New England the high school, as the instrument of secondary instruction, is relatively far more important than a generation since. Its usefulness differs greatly in different States and towns. The high schools of Massachusetts are of as good a grade as any, and a few of them are excellent fitting-schools.

Throughout the West, at the time of its settlement, the high school became the chief institution of intermediate instruction. The number of schools of this grade changes from year to year, and also with important changes in the school laws, but nearly all towns of Western States of 15,000 or more inhabitants have schools in which the classical studies, and the mathematics necessary for admission to college, can be pursued. It is not to be questioned that the general influence of these schools upon the higher education has not been favorable. They have not afforded opportunities for a thorough preparation for college. Many of the colleges, therefore, have been obliged to establish preparatory departments. But frequently these departments, since they naturally failed to receive the principal attention of officers, have languished. It is the common desire of a well-equipped college to be freed from the encumbrance of a fitting-school. In the lack of opportunities for secondary instruction is found one reason of the inefficiency of many colleges. Compelled to receive students, if they were to receive any, not qualified to enter upon collegiate studies, they have been obliged to spend a quarter or even a half of the course in completing the work that should have been finished in the preparatory school. This fact renders many colleges of the West and South institutions as much for secondary as for superior instruction.

In addition to high schools and academies there are in all parts of the United States various private institutions that afford secondary instruction. They are open both to day-scholars and boarders, and are especially designed for young women. They usually, though not always, bear the name of "seminary." For support they depend on both tuition-fees and endowments. (See COLLEGES IN AMERICA.) (C. F. T.)

EDWARDS, AMELIA BLANDFORD, an English author, was born in 1831. She was the daughter of an army officer, and while very young began her literary career. Among her works are short histories of France (1858) and of England (1856); numerous novels, *My Brother's Wife* (1855); *The Ladder of Life* (1857); *The Little Marquis* (1857); *Hand and Glove* (1859); *Barbara's History* (1864); *Miss Carew* (1865); *Half a Million of Money* (1865); *Debenham's Vow* (1870); *In the Days of my Youth* (1873); *Monsieur Maurice* (1873); *Lord Brackenbury* (1880); also a volume of *Ballads* (1865); and *Untrodden Peaks and Unfrequented Valleys* (1873). Her book entitled *A Thousand Miles up the Nile* (1877) is a production of high value, having copious illustrations drawn on the spot by the author. Other works of hers are *The Story of Cervantes* (1862); a *Poetry-book of the Elder Poets* (1879). She has given much attention to the study of Egyptian antiquities.

EDWARDS, BELA BATES, D.D. (1802-1852), an American Congregationalist theologian and author, was born at Southampton, Mass., July 4, 1802. He graduated at Amherst College in 1824, and after studying theology at Andover for a year became tutor in Amherst College. In 1828 he was made assistant secretary of the American Education Society, and in 1836 became professor of Hebrew in the Andover Theological Seminary. In 1848 he was transferred to the chair of biblical literature, which he held till his death. Besides the duties of the positions named, he was editor of the *American Quarterly Register* from 1828 to 1842, and of the *American Quarterly Observer*, which he founded in 1833. When this was united with the *Biblical Repository*, founded by Prof. Edward Robinson, Dr. Edwards remained as editor until 1838. He was also editor-in-chief of the *Bibliotheca Sacra* from 1844 till his death, which took place in Georgia, April 20, 1852. His most important work is to be found in the periodicals which he edited. Among his earlier publications were, *Biography of Self-taught Men*, *Missionary Gazetteer* (1832); *Memoirs of Elias Cornelius*, and a volume on *The Epistle to the Galatians*. After his death several of his sermons and addresses, with a memoir by Prof. E. A. Park, were published in 1853.

EDWARDS, JONATHAN, D.D. (1745-1801), an American Congregationalist divine, frequently called the "younger Edwards," as being a son of the more distinguished theologian of the same name, was born at Northampton, Mass., May 26, 1745. At an early age he had much intercourse with the Indians, and his father wished him to become a missionary to them. He lived for a time among the Six Nations, but before the outbreak of the French and Indian war returned home. He graduated at Princeton in 1765, and, having studied theology with Rev. Dr. Bellamy, was licensed to preach the next year. He was for a time a tutor in Princeton, and in 1769 was ordained pastor of the church at White Haven, near New Haven, Conn. After a pastorate of twenty-six years he resigned on account of difference in doctrinal views with his congregation. He was soon settled in Colebrook, but in May, 1799, was elected president of Union College, Schenectady, N. Y. After a brief service in this position he died at Schenectady, Aug. 1, 1801. He was a man of great learning, and carried on an extensive correspondence with learned men of Europe and America. His complete works, with a memoir by his grandson, Rev. Tryon Edwards, D.D., were published at Andover in 1842.

EDWARDS, MATILDA BARBARA BETHAM, an English novelist, a cousin of Miss Amelia B. Edwards and a niece of Sir W. Betham, was born at Westerfield, Suffolk, in 1836. When nineteen years old she published *The White House, by the Sea,* a very popular tale. Other works of hers are *Doctor Jacob; Kitty; A Winter with the Swallows in Algeria; A Year in Western France,* and *Mrs. Punch's Letters.* She wrote also a great number of papers on social and literary subjects, and contributed largely to *Punch* and the leading periodicals.

EDWARDSVILLE, the county-seat of Madison co., Ill., is on Cahokia Creek, 18 miles N. E. of St. Louis, on the Wabash, St. Louis, and Pacific Railway, the Toledo, Cincinnati, and St. Louis Railroad, and the Wabash Branch Railroad connecting with the Chicago, Alton, and St. Louis Railroad and the Indianapolis and St. Louis Railroad. It has a court-house, 2 banks, 5 hotels, 3 weekly newspapers, 10 churches, a high school and other good schools. It has 3 flour-mills, 3 carriage-factories, 2 saw-mills, 3 machine-shops, and within the city limits four shafts are sunk to a bed of bituminous coal 6 feet thick which underlies the country at a depth of from 80 to 200 feet. The surrounding country is fertile, producing fruit and sugar-cane as well as grain. It was first settled in 1805 by Thomas Kirkpatrick, and a mill and block-house served as nucleus for the town, which he laid out in 1816. It was named from Ninian Edwards, governor of Illinois Territory and also first governor of the State, who was a resident of the town. Population, 2887.

EFFINGHAM, the county-seat of Effingham co., Ill., is on a prairie east of Little Wabash River, 100 miles east of St. Louis, and 200 miles south of Chicago. It is on the Illinois Central Railroad, the St. Louis, Vandalia, and Terre Haute Railroad, the Wabash, St. Louis, and Pacific Railroad, the Springfield, Effingham, and South-eastern Railroad. It has a park, a fine court-house, 2 banks, 4 weekly newspapers, 6 churches, and 2 graded schools. It has machine-shops of the St. Louis, Vandalia, and Terre Haute Railroad, a foundry, 2 flour-mills, and other industries. It was settled in 1857, and incorporated as a city in 1869. Population, 3069.

EGGLESTON, EDWARD, an American author, was born at Vevay, Ind., Dec. 10, 1837. Owing to ill-health his education was irregular, but he entered the Methodist ministry when only nineteen years of age. Soon after he removed to Minnesota, where he spent some years in pastoral work, though his health repeatedly broke down. In 1866 he removed to Evanston, Ill., where he was chiefly engaged in work connected with Sunday-schools, editing *The Sunday-School Teacher* and contributing to other papers, especially stories for children. In May, 1870, he became literary editor of the *Independent* in New York, and in July, 1871, the editor of *Hearth and Home,* but resigned this position in October, 1872. He afterwards had charge of a Congregationalist church in Brooklyn, though chiefly engaged in literary labor, and since 1879 he has devoted himself entirely to the latter. His principal publications are *The Hoosier Schoolmaster* (1871); *The End of the World* (1872); *The Mystery of Metropolisville* (1873); *The Circuit Rider* (1875); *Roxy* (1878); *The Hoosier Schoolboy* (1883). These novels are vivid pictures of the frontier life amid which his boyhood was passed. Since 1880 he has been engaged in writing *A History of Life in the United States,* portions of which have appeared in serial form in *Harper's Magazine.*

EGG-PLANT, a well-known vegetable, *Solanum melongena* of botany, *melongena* being altered from the Arabic word *bydengan.* It is supposed to be a native of Arabia or of warmer parts of the East Indies, though not now known to be indigenous anywhere; but it has long been under culture, and certainly from the earliest Roman times. It is not distantly related to the mandragora, a noted narcotic, and hence received the name of mad-apple. By the Spaniards it is called belangela, by the Italians malanzana, and by the Germans tollapfel, —all suggesting the idea of insanity in connection with the fruit. There is one form, *Solanum ovigera* of some authors, which has a fruit about the size and color of a hen's egg, commonly grown for ornament in British gardens, and hence the American "egg-plant." In France it is known as *aubergine* as well as *melongene.*

The egg-plant requires a great deal of heat to bring it to perfection; hence it is almost unknown as a vegetable in England and the northern countries of Europe. Though in use in the warmer parts of the world, its culture reaches its greatest perfection in the United States. It is not unusual to see fruits measuring three feet in circumference, and sometimes six of these will be borne by a single plant. In the hot sandy soils of New Jersey, wherever it is possible to obtain quantities of rich fertilizing material, the raising of egg-plants is a profitable branch of market-gardening. It requires a great deal of heat and attention to raise the young plants, and care to preserve them in the earlier stages from the beetle *Doryphora decem-lineata;* but these difficulties make the growth more profitable to those who discover how to overcome them. In cooking the plant is sometimes stewed, but generally is cut in thin slices, soaked for a while in water with a little salt, and then fried, sometimes being first dipped in crumb-batter. The vegetable does not seem as popular in Europe, even when it grows well, as here. A leading French authority describes the variety popular in France as having "un fruit long et gros comme un concombre, dont l'écorce est purpurine et unie," and that it is "agréable quand il est apprêté avec du sel, du poivre, du vinaigre, et-cet.; mais en général il est venteux, malaisé à digérer." But this long kind, eaten like cucumbers and quite as indigestible according to this author, gives place in America to the large round variety, which is regarded as one of the most wholesome of American vegetables. (T. M.)

EGILSSON, SVEINBJÖRN (1791–1852), an Icelandic antiquary and lexicographer, was born March 12, 1791, at Innri-Njardvik, in the south-west of Iceland. He was the son of a peasant, but was brought up in the house of Magnus Stephensén and instructed by Arni Helgason, afterwards titular bishop. In 1814 Egilsson went to the University at Copenhagen, and in 1819 he was made assistant in the Latin school at Bessastadir. In 1846 he was called to the rectorate at Reikjavik, having already received the degree of Doctor of Theology from the University of Breslau. He resigned his post in 1851 and died Aug. 17, 1852. He was one of the founders of the Royal Society of Northern Antiquities in 1825, and until his death a member of its committee on old manuscripts. In 1816 he was one of the founders of the Icelandic Literary Society. His reputation is based on his scholarly dictionary of the words used in the poetry of the Old

Norse literature: *Lexicon poeticum antiquæ linguæ septentrionalis* (Copenhagen, 1860); on his Latin translations of the sagas of the Norse kings: *Scripta historica Islandorum*, and on his Icelandic translation of Homer. (R. B. A.)

EGYPT. In 1879 the English and French governments, anticipating bankruptcy at Cairo, urged on the Porte the necessity of appointing a new viceroy in Egypt, with the result that Ismail Pasha was deposed by an Imperial Hatte, and his son Mohammed Tewfik nominated khedive in his place. Sir Rivers Wilson then returned to Egypt to negotiate terms of liquidation with the state creditors, and in the following year a new law of liquidation was issued at Cairo, by which interest on all the state debts was reduced to an average of 4¼ per cent., the great powers of Europe signifying their assent to the arrangement, while England and France undertook a special joint control over the finances of the country. This law of liquidation formed the basis of English intervention two years later. Order in Egypt was first disturbed Feb. 1, 1881, by a military demonstration, headed by the colonels of the three regiments of guards at Cairo, Ali Fehmy, Abd el Aal, and Arabi, who, having some days previously signed a petition to the chief minister, Riaz Pasha, representing the grievances of the army, had been arrested at his instance, and had been forcibly released a few hours later by their men. The three regiments on that day marched to the Aledin Palace, and petitioned the khedive to appoint a new minister, and to reform certain abuses chiefly connected with the army administration, but including also matters of political interest. This bold action gave their leaders a prominent position with the public, and their names grew rapidly popular. Arabi especially, by his superior education and his gift of eloquence, attracted general attention, and he became the daily recipient of addresses and petitions from every part of Egypt, as well as the recognized spokesman of the party of constitutional reform, which now began to call itself the "National Party." A desire of reform in the direction of popular institutions had long existed among the better educated class in Egypt, and at his accession Tewfik Pasha had issued a decree promising the convocation of a chamber of notables, and other liberties essential to modern progress, which had, however, remained a dead letter. But now the popular desire was renewed, and in the summer of the same year Arabi was intrusted by the leaders of the party with the task of enforcing the fulfilment of his promise on the khedive.

A second military demonstration was accordingly made, Sept. 9, 1881, which may be distinguished from the first by the fact of its having been distinctly political. In it Arabi, for the first time, in the name of the Egyptian people, formulated their demands for a chamber of deputies, as well as for the dismissal of Riaz, and an increase of the national army to the full number allowed by law, 18,000 men. On this occasion the khedive being prepared for the demonstration and supported by the English consul and the English controller, made some attempt at evading the popular demands, but in the end yielded. Riaz was dismissed, a new promise was given of summoning a chamber, and the army also was to be increased. At the suggestion of the national leaders, Sherif Pasha, known as the author of a draft constitution, and believed, though a Turk by birth, to be a staunch reformer, was then named first minister, and Mahmud Sami (afterwards head of the nationalist cabinet), minister of war. A chamber of notables was also summoned, and met at Cairo, before the close of the year, while about the same time Arabi issued a manifesto, in which he stated the objects of the movement he had supported, and the position in it of the army as guardian of the popular rights. This was published in the London *Times*, Jan. 14, 1882, and attracted so much attention that it was thought advisable by the English and French governments to suggest his being included as under-secretary of war in the new-formed cabinet.

Up to this moment the national movement had been directed solely against the Circassian oligarchy, which had so long misruled the country. It looked to Europe, and especially to England, for support; and the English and the French governments had each by turns shown it some encouragement. But on the 8th of January Lord Granville and M. Gambetta, for reasons which have not yet transpired, delivered, through their agents at Cairo, a joint note to the Egyptian government, in which, assuming a tone of menace to the popular party, they recorded their guarantee of personal protection to the khedive against all danger which should menace him from without or from within Egypt. This turned the storm of popular indignation against themselves, and against Sherif Pasha, who supported them, and the excitement was considerably increased by the receipt of letters from the sultan's private secretary, in which Abdul Hamid, as caliph, called upon Arabi to defend the interests of the Mohammedan nation in Egypt, and alluded to the recent invasion of Tunis by the French as an episode about to be repeated on the Nile.

These letters arrived at a critical moment, when the newly assembled deputies were debating the terms of the constitution promised them, and it encouraged them to claim the control of that part of the budget not affecting the debt, as part of their prerogative. The claim was strongly resisted by the French and English controllers, and by Sherif Pasha, whom the latter had gained to their interests. Popular pressure, however, proved too powerful for them, and, on Feb. 2, Sherif Pasha resigned his office, and a new ministry was appointed, having Mahmud Sami and Arabi Pasha at its head, and giving the Nationalists, for the first time, full power in the government. The decree authorizing a constitution of the most advanced type was signed by the khedive Feb. 6, and from that date till the middle of May Egypt was governed according to the usage of constitutional government. Then, however, a quarrel broke out between the khedive and his ministers, on the subject of a sentence passed on certain Circassians who had been convicted of plotting the death of the ministers; and the incident was made use of by the controllers for an attempt to bring about a counter-revolution. On May 17 the English and French fleets were ordered to Alexandria to support the authority of the khedive, and simultaneously with its arrival Sir Edward Mallet and M. de Sinkiewitz, the English and French ministers, delivered an ultimatum to the Nationalist ministry, calling on them to resign their offices and demanding the exile of Arabi. This led to an open rupture. The ministers resigned, indeed, their offices, but a popular demonstration forced the khedive immediately to reinstate Arabi as minister of war and practical dictator of the country. The two powers, France and England, now appealed to the Porte. A conference was assembled at Constantinople, and the sultan despatched Dervish Pasha as his special commissioner to restore tranquillity to Egypt and reestablish his authority. The Nationalists, nevertheless, refused either to allow Arabi to leave Egypt or Turkish troops to land on Egyptian soil; and, though Dervish was received with great show of loyalty at Cairo, he was unable to effect the purpose of the powers.

Matters stood thus till June 11, when a serious riot occurred at Alexandria, in which 50 Europeans lost their lives, and over 400 natives of the town. Its origin has been variously stated as traceable to Arabi Pasha, to Dervish Pasha, and to the khedive himself, but the official account now accepted in England describes it as an accident caused by the violence of popular feeling, augmented by the presence of the fleet and connived in by the police. At the time, however, it was attributed by the English government to the secret action by the Nationalist leaders, and public indignation was violently inflamed against them by articles which appeared in the *Times* and other organs of London opinion. The European colony began to leave Egypt. Mercantile enterprise was checked, and the price of Egyptian bonds fell to 52. It is probably owing to financial pressure that armed European intervention was then decided on by Mr. Gladstone.

On July 11 a pretext was found for hostilities in the arming of certain forts in the Alexandrian harbor, which the English admiral, Sir Beauchamp Seymour, regarded as a menace to his position, and, after sending in his ultimatum, the town was bombarded, with the result that on the second day it was evacuated by the Egyptian troops, who set fire to the town as they retreated, thus burning down the European quarter of Alexandria, with a loss to property estimated at £4,000,000. The khedive now, although he had ordered the defence of Alexandria, went over to the English, taking refuge on board the admiral's flagship, while Arabi, with the army and a vast number of fugitives, entrenched himself at Kafr Dowar, some twelve miles off, in which position he repelled all attempts made to dislodge him.

Six weeks then elapsed, which were made use of by the Nationalists to organize a provisional government at Cairo. The Khedive Tewfik was deposed by a decree of the religious Sheykhs of the Azhar University, as a traitor to his country and his religion, and the executive government was intrusted to a council called the Mejtiss el Orfi, which maintained order, levied taxes, and raised recruits for the army. The task of national defence was intrusted to Arabi.

By the middle of August the attack on Kafr Dowar was abandoned, and an Anglo-Indian army, about 38,000 strong, was landed at Ismailia, on the Suez canal, which Arabi, confiding in M. de Lesseps' assurance that its neutrality would be maintained, had left unguarded. Sir Garnet Wolseley commanded the expedition, and advanced slowly along the line of the sweet water canal towards Tel el Kebir, where Mahmud Fehmy Pasha, the chief of Arabi's staff, had traced another line of entrenchments. Battles were fought at Shaluf, Nefish, Mahsameh, and Kassouin. At Mahsameh, Mahmud Fehmy was made prisoner, having advanced too far on a reconnoitring expedition, and at Kassouin the life-guards decided the day by a charge, the first that they had made since Waterloo. On Sept. 9 the Egyptians advanced in attack, and shelled the British camp, but the movement failed, their commander, Ali Fehmy Pasha, being wounded. Finally, on the 13th, Sir Garnet Wolseley moved forward his whole forces, and by a rapid night-march stormed the lines of Tel el Kebir. The Egyptians were surprised at daybreak and utterly routed, Arabi saving himself with difficulty by flight.

The battle was followed up by a brilliant forced march on Cairo; and at nightfall Gen. Drury Lowe reached the city gates, while the national council was still deliberating what course to pursue. The suddenness of his arrival disconcerted the leaders, and Arabi Pasha surrendered himself as prisoner of war to the English. Sir Garnet Wolseley, with the bulk of his forces, entered Cairo on the following morning, and a few days later the khedive was brought back to the city and reinstated in his office. The national army was disbanded, and Arabi's life was only spared by a sudden revulsion of public feeling in England, which insisted that the sentence of death intended for him should be commuted into one of perpetual exile. He and five of his companions left Egypt Jan. 4, 1883, for Ceylon. (W. B.)

Earl Dufferin, who had come from Constantinople as a special commissioner to Egypt, was the agent in effecting this change in policy. He found abundant room for his diplomatic skill in attempting to settle the complicated affairs of that ill-fated country. The dual control ceased in January, 1883, though France protested against the action of England. In February Sir Auckland Colvin was made financial counsellor to the khedive. Various political trials and executions took place in the former part of the year, but in October the khedive granted a general amnesty, and set free those imprisoned for participation in the outbreak. The restoration of tranquillity was in a measure due to the hopes inspired by the presence of Earl Dufferin. Yet the necessary expenses of the reforms in administration which he proposed actually increased the burdens of the people, who were already groaning under taxation, and Egypt was required to support in part the British army of occupation. The numbers of the latter, however, were steadily diminished, in accordance with Mr. Gladstone's promise of an early withdrawal, until the Soudan war, which he had tried to keep out of the problem, compelled him to reverse his policy. The Egyptian army had been reorganized under the English Gen. Wood, but the number of British officers was limited to 25, and one-half of the regiments were to be commanded by Egyptians. A separate constabulary force was organized under Baker Pasha for the preservation of domestic order. This was really a military force, and when Hicks Pasha's army of the Soudan was annihilated by El-Mahdi, November 3, it was despatched to the relief of the towns and garrisons in Soudan. England was now compelled to take an active part in this war, for events of which see SOUDAN.

II. RECENT ARCHÆOLOGICAL DISCOVERIES.

WITHIN a few years past there have been archæological discoveries of unusual importance. A remarkable causeway, presumably dating from the time of Khafra (Greek, Chephren), has been laid bare at Gheezeh; a large number of pyramids of different epochs have been opened at various points of the great pyramid-field, which extends from Memphis to the Fayoom; and the family vault of the priest-kings near Dayr-el-Baharee, Thebes, has yielded the most extraordinary treasure of mummies, papyri, and sepulchral objects of all kinds ever found in a single hiding-place. These discoveries, together with others of less magnitude, range over a period which may be roughly estimated at 3000 years.

The causeway of Khafra.—This causeway was discovered by Herr Emil Brugsch, assistant conservator of the Boolak Museum, in January, 1881. It connects the pyramid of Khafra (generally known as the

Second Pyramid) with the singular subterraneous structure commonly, but erroneously, called the "Temple of the Sphinx." This latter monument, discovered by the late Mariette-Pasha, in 1858, is situate about 250 feet to the S. E. of the Great Sphinx. In plan and general arrangement it resembles the *Mastabas*, or tomb-chapels, of the Ancient Empire, to which period it undoubtedly belongs. From these it is, however, distinguished by the splendor of its materials; namely, red granite and alabaster. The structure is rectangular and oblong, consisting of one long hall, two transverse halls, some side-chambers, and corridors. One of these chambers, built entirely of large blocks of alabaster, contains six horizontal niches, or *loculi*, evidently designed for the reception of mummies. At the bottom of a deep well, at the east end of the building, were found nine portrait-statues of Khafra, third Pharaoh of the IVth Dynasty, and builder of the second pyramid of Gheezeh. Eight of these statues were shattered. The ninth, magnificently sculptured in green diorite, and almost perfect, now occupies the place of honor in the museum at Boolak. Each statue was engraved with the cartouche of Khafra; but the building is wholly devoid of inscriptions. The discovery of a road of communication between this monument and the second pyramid shows, however, that the former was a dependency of the latter, and enables us to assign it with comparative certainty to the reign of Khafra. This road is paved, like the transport causeways of the first and third pyramids. It starts from the ruins of the funerary chapel attached to the east side of the second pyramid, and thence leads direct to the granite mausoleum; not descending to the actual level of that monument, but conducting apparently to an entrance in some superstructure now destroyed. At the upper end of this road, where it adjoins the chapel of the pyramid, the remains of a granite doorway have been found, and some fragments of a diorite statue of Khafra, similar to the statues previously discovered in the well of the mausoleum. The paved roadway is almost perfect, and does not seem to have been at any time enclosed between walls.

This remarkable discovery justifies archæologists in henceforth rejecting the name assigned by Mariette to the "Temple of the Sphinx." The granite and alabaster monument was evidently not a temple, and it had no connection with the sphinx. Its connection was with the funerary chapel and pyramid of Khafra, some 1500 feet away to the N. W.; and the *loculi* in its mortuary chamber distinctly point to the fact that it was a tomb. Seeing that it was at this period customary for the king's family to be buried around, or near, his pyramid, it seems reasonable to conclude that this mausoleum was designed for the family of Khafra.

Recently explored pyramids.—No less than fourteen pyramids have been explored since 1879. Of these, three were excavated in 1880 by order of the late Mariette-Pasha, and the remaining eleven in 1881 and 1882, under the direction of Professor Maspero, who, on the death of Mariette, in January, 1881, succeeded to the post of director-general of the museums of Egypt. We proceed to treat of these pyramids, not in order of discovery, but in chronological succession; beginning with the remarkable structure known as the pyramid of Meydoom.

The pyramid of Meydoom, situate about a mile and a half to the N. W. of the village of Meydoom, stands in the midst of a very ancient necropolis containing numerous tombs of the family and court functionaries of Seneferoo, last king of the IIId Dynasty. Here, Egyptologists have concurred in believing this magnificent monument to be the sepulchre of that Pharaoh. Built in stages, or tiers, like enormous steps, it towers more than 240 feet above the level of the desert. The débris of the upper stages, which must have been very lofty, forms an immense mound, like a natural hill, rising to a height of 120 feet around the base of the structure. This mound has now been cut through, and cleared down to the base of the pyramid, thus revealing the lower tiers, the masonry of which looks perfectly new, as if but just built. The whole revêtement of this pyramid consists of polished blocks of fine Mokattam limestone, so admirably fitted that the joints are scarcely traceable. Each tier, or stage, is inclined at an angle of 74° 10′. The three top tiers (which alone were visible before the late excavations) measure 69 feet, 20½ feet, and 32 feet. This pyramid is unlike every other in Egypt, and excels all in the excellence of its masonry. Prof. Maspero began his operations in November, 1881, by opening a vertical trench down the north face of the mound. On Dec. 13, precisely in the centre of the first stage, 20 metres above the level of the plain, the workmen uncovered a square aperture from which the facing-block had been extracted. The entrance—open, but choked with rubbish—was now disclosed to view. Up to this moment it had been believed that the pyramid was inviolate. The entrance passage, which measures 1.30 metre square, descends at a steep incline, strikes the living rock at a depth of 10 metres, and thence becomes an excavated shaft carried down at the same incline, and of the same dimensions, as before. The pyramid is, in fact, formed upon a core of rock, around which the stages are built. A "stopper" stone originally blocked the passage, 5 metres from the entrance; and that the pyramid must have been open at least 3000 years ago is proved by the discovery of three hieratic inscriptions of the XXth Dynasty, scribbled by Egyptian tourists on the ceiling of the passage at the precise spot once occupied by the "stopper." These *graffiti* merely record the visit of two scribes named Sokari and Amenmes. The passage, after descending for more than 40 metres, led to a central chamber which contained only some pieces of highly desiccated timber. Whether the passage took an upward incline before reaching this chamber has not been stated. It is possible that the true sepulchral chamber has not yet been found. The village of Meydoom (which stands high upon an ancient mound) perpetuates to this day the name of "*Metun*," which appears in a list of towns belonging to Prince Nefermat, a son, or, at all events, a near relative, of Seneferoo. In this inscription, which occurs in Nefermat's tomb, a little distance north of the pyramid, Metun is styled "Metun of the cattle."

It is not possible to assign a positive date to the pyramid of Meydoom, or to the king who is supposed to have built it. Mariette, following Manetho, places the beginning of the IIId Dynasty at B. C. 4449, and the beginning of the IVth at B. C. 4235. Brugsch gives B. C. 3966 and B. C. 3733. The death of Seneferoo, as last Pharaoh of the IIId Dynasty, would, in either case, synchronize with the commencement of the IVth line.

The Pyramid of Unas.—The huge, flat-topped structure called the *Mastabal el Faraoun*, in the necropolis of Sakkarah, was supposed by Mariette to be the tomb of Unas, ninth and last Pharaoh of the Vth Dynasty. The explorations of Prof. Maspero prove, however, that Unas was buried in the pyramid numbered XXXV. by Lepsius, and entered on Perring's plan as No. IV. It is situate a little to the S. W. of the famous step-pyramid of Sakkarah; is much ruined; has been stripped of its casing-stones, and is encumbered by mounds of débris, which prevent exact measurements being taken of its base. The length of each side is, however, approximately estimated at 220 feet, and it is supposed to have been 62 feet in height. Prof. Maspero commenced excavations on the north side of this pyramid about Feb. 10, 1881, and his workmen reached the sepulchral chamber on the 28th. Like the pyramid of Meydoom, it proved to have been violated long before; and an Arabic inscription on the ceiling of the entrance passage leads Prof. Maspero to believe that it was broken into about A. D. 820, at the time when the Great Pyramid of Gheezeh was rifled, and probably by the same band of marauders. The structure is built around and upon a core of limestone rock, through which a descending passage, more than 30 feet in length, running due south, leads to a first hall, the walls of which are bare. Then follows a level passage about 45 feet long, blocked at three points by three enormous portcullis stones of granite, still *in situ*. A similar portcullis-stone, also *in situ*, blocks the outer entrance. The ancient tomb-breakers, unable to remove or destroy these obstacles, had excavated a passage round the first, and made their way over the three last. It was in their footsteps that Prof. Maspero and his workmen followed, when the entrance was found. Beyond the last portcullis, the passage (here lined with hieroglyphic inscriptions) leads into the actual tomb, which consists of a central hall, a sepulchral chamber, and a chamber (*serdab*) with recesses for funeral statues. The two former are built with pointed roofs. The entire wall-space of the central hall, part of three sides of the sepulchral chamber, and the walls of the short corridors between the several chambers, are covered with hieroglyphed inscriptions in vertical columns, consisting of prayers, magical formulas, and ritualistic texts. These last contain a complete ceremonial of the last services for the dead at the period of the Vth Dynasty; and as an interesting evidence of the unbroken unity of tradition in matters of religion, it is to be noted that many of these texts occur, with but slight variation, in monuments of the XIIIth, XVIIIth, and XIXth Dynasties. Some of the magical formulas of the pyramid of Unas are actually identical not merely in substance, but in phrase and orthography, with texts of the XXVIth Dynasty; so proving that at this early period, instead of being still in course of formation, the language and religion had already passed into the crystalline stage. The upper end of the sepulchral chamber in this pyramid is lined with alabaster, and decorated with engraved ornamentation, filled in with green and black paint. The sarcophagus, which is of black basalt, remains *in situ*; its cover flung near the doorway. The shattered mummy and torn bandages of Unas strewed the floor. Some fragments of the skull, a tibia bone, some rib bones, and one perfect arm, being the only recognizable remains of this ancient Pharaoh, were removed to the museum at Boolak. A pot of black paint, a workman's plumb-line, and some bones of the sacrificial ox slain during the funeral service, were also found. If the tomb ever contained any objects of value, they were stolen by the early tomb-breakers, who likewise tore up part of the pavement of the sepulchral chamber, in search of treasure. The ancient name of the pyramid of Unas was "*Neferasu*," *i. e.*, "The most Beautiful of Places."

The hieroglyphic texts from this pyramid, with translations by Prof. Maspero, have been published. (See *Recueil des Travaux*, Vol. III., 1882.)

The Pyramid of Teta.—This pyramid, as it appears on Prof. Maspero's plan (see *Recueil des Travaux* as above), is considerably larger than the pyramid of Unas. It is situate to the N.E. of the Stepped Pyramid of Sakkarah, three other ruined pyramids intervening; and it stands nearest but one to the edge of the desert, near the Cat-mummy pits. This pyramid was opened by Prof. Maspero May 29, 1881. The early tomb-breakers had, as usual, been beforehand with the modern explorers, and in this instance had boldly attacked the massive portcullis stones which blocked the entrance-passage. Teta, first Pharaoh of the VIth Dynasty, was also the first Egyptian king who assumed the title of *Se Ra*, "Son of the Sun." His pyramid bore the name of *Tut-Asu*, "The most Stable of Places."

The Pyramid of Rameri Pepi I. is situate considerably to the S.S.E. of the Stepped Pyramid, and is numbered XXXVI. by Lepsius and 5 by Vyse. This pyramid was opened by direction of Mariette-Pasha in June, 1880. This pyramid is described as entirely destroyed in the upper part, and containing two chambers, one of which has been broken into through the roof. Both are built of fine Mokattam limestone, with pointed roofs. The entrance passage, as usual, is on the north side. The sepulchral chamber measures 25 feet 8 inches by 10 feet 3 inches. The walls were originally covered with inscriptions; those on the long side walls have, however, been destroyed at some remote period, and only those on the end walls remain. The hieroglyphs are finely cut, and colored a brilliant green; the roof, where perfect, is decorated with incised stars, white on a black ground. The basalt sarcophagus, though much damaged, is yet *in situ*. It bears the official cartouche of the king, "Ra-Meri," and is nearly 12 feet in length, the sides being more than 12 inches in thickness, and the bottom 20 inches. Some portions of the wooden mummy-case were found; also a quantity of brown and yellow bandages, and a well-embalmed hand, supposed to be the hand of the Pharaoh. The inscriptions are very archaic, and, although not historically important, are of great value in regard to the light which they throw upon the mythological development of the Egyptian religion at this remote period. The king is repeatedly said to be not dead, but living; fed with the viands of the gods; identified with Horus; dwelling among spirits; and one with Osiris. All the principal deities of the Egyptian Pantheon are mentioned. The antagonism of Horus and Set is distinctly alluded to; the name of Amen is found, which is remarkable at this early date; and a reference to Sothis points to a possible chronological date. The funeral inscription of Pepi-na, a priest of the pyramid of Pepi, informs us that the name of this structure was *Men-Nefer*, *i.e.*, "The Good Station," which was also the name of Memphis. In the famous inscription of Una, a functionary who flourished under the three first Pharaohs of the VIth Dynasty, it is stated that king Pepi sent him to a locality named Ruau, to fetch "a white stone sarcophagus," which command he duly executed, bringing the sarcophagus "with its cover" by water from Ruau to Memphis. The sarcophagus discovered in the pyramid of Pepi is evidently not the same, being of basalt; but the "white stone" sarcophagus fetched by Una may have been intended for some member of the royal family.

The Pyramid of Mer-en-Ra, elder son and successor of Rameri Pepi, lies to the S.W. of the pyramid of Pepi, in a direct line with the pyramid of Unas and the Matabat el Faraoun. It was opened by order of Mariette-Pasha in December, 1880. This pyramid has been not only broken into and plundered in ancient times, but has been despoiled of nearly half its masonry. The modern explorers entered it by way of a forced passage bored by the early tomb-breakers. This forced passage opened into the true entrance passage, which is very low, and covered with hieroglyphic texts in vertical and horizontal lines wherein occur the two cartouches of the king. A first chamber, built of fine white limestone, with a pointed roof, opens from the passage and leads into a second and larger chamber containing two rectangular sarcophagi of red granite. The walls of both chambers contain hieroglyphed texts very archaic in style, and of a mythological and ritualistic character, treating chiefly of the labors to be performed by the deceased in the fields of Aahlu (Elysium), and of his passage through the various gates of the lower world. The myths of Osiris, Ra, and Set are alluded to; and the gods are said to have been born of Nut, with crowns on their heads and collars of leaves upon their necks. Horus is spoken of as "the avenger of his father;" and the king is described as the twin-brother of Orion, rising with him in the east, and setting with him in the west of the heavens. The mummy of Mer-en-Ra had been dragged out of the sarcophagus and stripped of its bandages, which, however, were distinctly impressed upon the surface of the skin. The body (now removed to Boolak) is remarkably well preserved, only a portion of the lower jaw being gone. The features are almost perfect, the eyes are closed, the nose has fallen in. The discovery of this extremely ancient mummy (from 5000 to 5500 years old, according to the chronologies of Brugsch and Mariette) proves that the processes of embalmment during the VIth Dynasty were substantially identical with those employed in later times. In life Mer-en-Ra was a small man of the type of the modern fellah. That he was thin is shown by the tightness of the skin. He was between 30 and 40 years of age. His sarcophagus, which measures 6 feet 10 inches long and 4 feet 4 inches high, is engraved with the royal titles, i.e., "The living Horus, lord of diadems, king of Upper and Lower Egypt; Mer-en-Ra, the twofold Golden Hawk; Mer-en-Ra, heir of Khab; Mer-en-Ra, the Great God; Lord of the Horizon; Mer-en-Ra, Living like the Sun." From the inscription of Una, who received from Mer-en-Ra a commission such as he had previously executed for the king's father, we learn the name of this pyramid. "His majesty," says Una, "despatched me to Abha to bring for the Living Lord the sarcophagus of the living (Lord) with its cover and pyramidion, and a statue, for the pyramid *Kha-nefer* (i.e., 'The Beautiful Rising') of Mer-en-Ra, the Divine Ruler." The statue and pyramidion are gone, but the sarcophagus is most probably the one discovered in situ in 1880. The smaller sarcophagus was uninscribed.

The Pyramid of Nefer-ka-Ra Pepi II., younger brother and successor of Mer-en-Ra, was opened under the direction of Prof. Maspero, April 18, 1881. The ancient name of this pyramid was *Men-Ankh*, i.e., "The Permanent Life."

Six other pyramids, including a large one formerly opened and reclosed by Perring, have been excavated since 1880 in the Necropolis of Sakkarah. One of these (opened in December, 1880) proved completely blank. Also, at a point about 10 miles south of Esneh, in Upper Egypt, the ruined pyramid called by the Arabs *El-kodla* was attacked during the spring of 1882 but without success. Though levelled almost to the ground, this little pyramid, the base of which is only 60 feet square, kept its secret to the last. No entrance was found, and Prof. Maspero inclines to believe that none has ever existed. In such case the structure would probably have been only monumental, and a subterraneous vault may lie far below excavated in the rock. One of the two ruined pyramids of Lisht, near Kafr-el-Ayát, about 7 miles north of Meydoom, was taken in hand at about the same time. After seven months' labor the entrance was found, and the descending passage cleared for a distance of 50 feet. Just at this juncture, when another week or ten days would have crowned the work with success, the serious aspect assumed by the military rebellion in Egypt caused the excavations to be suspended. The pyramid had been violated in ancient times, and ruthlessly mutilated. The wall-surfaces of the passage had evidently been covered with inscriptions; but the inscriptions had been chipped off by the early treasure-seekers, and the sand which choked the passage was full of illegible fragments. From the appearance of these fragments and other indications Prof. Maspero pronounces the Lisht pyramid to belong to the XIIth Dynasty.

It must not be supposed that these pyramid explorations are made without a definite and important object. They are, on the contrary, the most important excavations which have, perhaps, ever yet been undertaken in Egypt; and they have for their object the restoration of the history of the early dynasties. In this history there occur two strange and ominous chasms, the earliest of which is not illustrated by a single monument. This chasm falls between the VIth and XIth Dynasties; the VIIth, VIIIth, IXth, and Xth Dynasties being an absolute blank. Historians have vainly sought to bridge this void by means of conjectures more or less ingenious, but Prof. Maspero differs from them all in believing that no such void exists. The great pyramid-field, he argues, reaches from Aboo-Roash, a little below Gheezeh, to the Fayoom; and the pyramids, which range in an irregular line from north to south, are, he maintains, chronologically classified in that order. The pyramids of Aboo-Roash, which are the most northerly, are also the most dilapidated, and look as if they might be the most ancient. There is nothing to show to what king or period they belonged. Next come the pyramids of Gheezeh, which date from the IVth Dynasty; next follow the pyramids of Abooseer (Vth Dynasty); next, those of Sakkarah, which, as these latest explorations show, belong to the VIth Dynasty. Between Sakkarah and the Fayoom lie many more, few of which have been explored, though all probably have been violated by ancient plunderers. These, according to Prof. Maspero's theory, should belong to the Pharaohs of that lost period, which comprises the VIIth, VIIIth, IXth, and Xth Dynasties. The Fayoom, with its pyramids, brings us to the XIIth Dynasty: the XIth being the dynasty of the Mentuhoteps and Entefs, who had their res-dence and tombs at Thebes. For many years Prof. Maspero has held by his opinion, and stood alone in so holding by it. As successor to the late Mariette-Pâsha he is now in a position to test the accuracy of his judgment, and it is his announced intention to open every pyramid from Sakkarah to the Fayoom. Whether his theory be proved or disproved, science cannot fail to benefit by his researches.

The Discovery of Royal Mummies at Dayr-el-Baharee, Thebes.—On July 2, 1881, the most extraordinary archæological treasure ever discovered in a single hiding-place was betrayed into the hands of the Egyptian government by a native fellah named Mohammed Abd-er-Rasoul. The existence of a sepulchral treasure of unusual value had long been suspected by the authorities. Objects of great historical and archæological interest, appertaining for the most part to the XXIst Dynasty, were annually brought to Europe by travellers who proved not only to have purchased them at the same place (Luxor), but also from the same persons. Among these objects were libation-vases, canopic jars, Osirian statuettes, or *Shabti*, and several superb papyri written for royal personages of the family of Her-Hor, first Pontiff-King of the Sacerdotal line. On succeeding to the post of director-general of the museum of Egypt, Prof. Maspero at once proceeded to investigate into the sources of this illicit traffic, which was found to be in the hands of four Arab brethren, one of whom—apparently the principal offender—was forthwith arrested, interrogated, and imprisoned. His dogged fortitude was, however, shaken by neither bribes, punishments, nor threats; and the secret would not even then have transpired but for Mohammed, eldest of the four, who turned "king's evidence," and claimed the £500 reward offered by the Egyptian government. Upon the information thus given two officers of the Boolak Museum were at once despatched in a Khedival steamer. These officers—Herr Emil Brugsch, assistant conservator of the museum, and Ahmed Effendi Kemal, secretary and interpreter to the same—were met a little above Luxor by the said Mohammed, and by him conducted to a lonely spot in that embayed recess in the great limestone range on the western bank of the Nile, which is commonly called after the ruins of the Christian convent of Dayr-el-Baharee. Here, at a short distance to the S. W. of the great temple of Hatasu (so admirably concealed that, according to Prof. Maspero's report, the keenest observer might have passed it twenty times without noticing it), they were shown the mouth of a small pit, and told that here was the place of the treasure. Being lowered into this pit, down a vertical shaft measuring 2 metres square by 11½ metres in depth, they found themselves landed in a subterranean passage along which they had to crawl upon their hands and knees. At the end of a distance of 7 metres this passage turned abruptly northward—that is to say, at right angles to its first direction—and after proceeding for a distance of 23 metres was interrupted by a flight of roughly hewn steps. At the foot of these steps the passage (still trending due north) was continued some 40 metres farther, and ended in a large sepulchral chamber measuring 7 metres in length by 4 metres in breadth. The entire length of the excavation, taken in a straight line from S. to N. and including the sepulchral chamber, is 74 metres; or, including also the first short passage from E. to W.; 81 metres. The height of the short passage was only 1.10 metre; the height of the long passage varied from 1.40 metre to 5 metres. This last was found strewn with fragments of mummy-cases and linen wrappings. Funereal vases, boxes, rush-woven baskets, etc., were piled against the walls. In one corner, rotting in a crumpled heap, lay the famous leather canopy of Queen Isi-em-kheb. Farther on, almost blocking the passage, were several enormous sarcophagi elaborately painted, and surmounted by recumbent effigies; while yet farther on there appeared a crowd of mummy-cases, mostly stacked upright, leaning against each other, and looking strangely human, with carved and painted masks, and hands piously crossed, as if in prayer. Upon each of these were painted bands of hieroglyphs, in which, accompanied by certain customary religious formulas, were stated the titles and names of the deceased. The amazement of Herr Brugsch and his companion may be conceived when, instead of a few petty princes of the sacerdotal line, such as they had expected to find, they read the names of nearly all the most famous sovereigns of the XVIIIth and XIXth Dynasties: Ahmes I., the patriot king who expelled the Hyksbos from Lower Egypt after a dominion of 500 years; Queen Ahmes-Nofretari, his wife; Amenhotep I., their son and successor; Thothmes II.; Thothmes III., perhaps the greatest of all the Pharaohs; Seti I., a mighty warrior; and Rameses II., the Sesostris of the Greek historians, commonly called "the Great." A still earlier hero, Sekenen-Ra Taaken, prince of Thebes, of the XVIIth Dynasty, one of the leaders of the great war of national independence, was also found in this passage; and Queen Hathor Hont-taui, wife of Pinotem I. of the XXIst Dynasty. Entering the mortuary chamber at the end, an extraordinary sight met their eyes. They beheld a vault stored from floor to roof with enormous sarcophagi, packed one upon another, gorgeous with color and glittering with varnish. These proved to be the coffins of the family of Her-Hor Se-Amen, who was High Priest of Amen at Thebes under the last Ramesside Pharaoh, and who (according to inscriptions found in the Temple of Khons at Karnak) finally assumed the style and title of royalty, and became the founder of the XXIst Dynasty. The mummy of this first priest-king was not found. He may possibly have been buried at Tanis, where monuments of his line and time have been discovered; or his remains and relics may have been dispersed by the Arabs. Here, however, was found the body of his mother Queen Notem-Maut, his grandson Pinotem I., his great-grandson Pinotem II., Queen Makara, Queen Isi-em-kheb, Prince-Pontiff Masahirti, Princess Nasi-Khonsu, and several other personages apparently of royal and priestly descent belonging to this dynasty. The members of the Her-Hor family were for the most part enclosed in two coffins; some in three. Those of the XVIIIth and XIXth Dynasties were, with but one exception, enclosed in a single mummy-case; that exception being Queen Ahmes-Nofretari, whose mummy in its crimson-painted inner coffin of "cartonnage" was again enclosed in a gigantic outer shell of the same material 7.17 metres high, fashioned in the form of an Osirian statue. This huge effigy represents the mummied queen, and the face bears every appearance of being a portrait. The arms are crossed, each hand grasping the *Ankh* ($\female$), symbolical of eternal life. The head is surmounted by the plumed headdress peculiar to the God Amen; and the plumes, which are of painted wood, measure 1.50 metre in height. The total height from the ground to the top of the plumes is therefore 8.67 metres. This cartonnage (made of many layers of linen saturated in some kind of resin, and coated with stucco) is stamped in part with a reticulated hexagonal pattern, resembling a section of honeycomb; the hollows being painted blue, and the rest of the surface yellow. A similar outer case of the same size and pattern, inscribed with the name of "The Royal Wife and Royal Mother, Aah-hotep," was also found here. It is to be remembered in connection with this circumstance that in 1859, at but a short distance from the mouth of the lately discovered vault, there was found, under some 12 or 15 feet of sand, the superb mummy-case, jewels, and mummy of a queen of this name. Among the jewels were a poniard and a pectoral ornament inscribed with the names of Ahmes Ranebpehti, first Pharaoh of the XVIIIth Dynasty, and a flabellum, or feather fan, bearing the name of Kames, a Theban prince of the XVIIth Dynasty, who is supposed to have been the husband of Queen Aah-hotep, and the father of Aahmes. The carelessness of the burial and the miscellaneous nature of the treasure found with the mummy have given rise to much learned speculation. The discovery of the queen's outer sarcophagus in the Her-Hor vault suggests, however, a simple explanation of the mystery. The jewels were doubtless the spoils of several royal mummies, secreted *en masse* in the inner coffin of Aah-hotep, and so removed from the vault; the whole being in all likelihood temporarily hidden in the sand, pending a safe opportunity for transporting the booty to Luxor. It seems impossible to doubt that the mummy of Ahmes (which is among those recovered) was originally arrayed with the poniard and pectoral ornament which bear his name; and the flabellum of Kames points to the probability that this prince's mummy has been destroyed or sold

Among other relics of personages, whose mummies may originally have been laid in the vault, must be noted the empty coffins of Thothmes I. and Rameses I.; while of the famous Queen-Pharaoh, Hatasu, daughter of Thothmes I., was discovered an extraordinary *memento* in the shape of a small cabinet containing a dried human liver, which we are fain to suppose is that of the great queen herself. The cabinet is made of wood and ivory, and is sculptured with both cartouches of Hatasu. A tiny model mummy-case, 10 inches in length, adorned with the royal fringe of asps, disks, and "tats," inscribed for a priest named Soutimes, contained a similar liver.

The following list, tabulated according to the chronology of Mariette (which is based on that of Manetho), gives the various mummies, empty coffins, and royal relics in their historical order. The exact succession of some numbers of the Her-Hor line is not, however, as yet finally determined.

XVIIth Dynasty.—(*Circa* B. C. 1750 to B. C. 1703.)
1. Sekenen-Ra Taaken (prince of Thebes) .... Mummy; mummy-case.
2. Queen Ansera (probably his wife) .... Mummy.
3. Queen Aah-hotep .... Outer sarcophagus.

XVIIIth Dynasty.—(*Circa* B. C. 1703 to B. C. 1462.)
4. King Ahmes-Ranrebpehti .... Mummy; mummy-case.
5. Queen Ahmes-Nofretari (his wife) .... Mummy; mummy-case; outer sarcophagus.
6. Queen Merit-Amen .... Mummy.
7. King Amenhotep I. .... Mummy; mummy-case.
8. Queen Hontimoohoo .... Mummy; mummy-case.
9. King Thothmes I. (son of Amenhotep I.) .... Mummy-case.
10. Queen Hatasu (daughter of Thothmes I.) .... { Small cabinet, containing a desiccated human liver.
11. King Thothmes II. (brother and husband of Hatasu) .... Mummy; mummy-case.
12. King Thothmes III. (second brother of Hatasu) .... Mummy; mummy-case.
13. Queen Sitka (?) .... Mummy.

XIXth Dynasty.—(*Circa* B. C. 1462 to B. C. 1288.)
14. King Rameses I. .... Mummy-case.
15. King Seti I. .... Mummy; mummy-case.
16. King Rameses II. .... Mummy; mummy-case.

XXth Dynasty.—(*Circa* B. C. 1288 to B. C. 1110.)
No mummies of this dynasty were found, unless the mummy of a prince named Tat-f Pthah-au-f-Ankh, styled "Royal son of Rameses," be of that period. He was possibly a son of one of the last *rois fainéants* of this line. Of Rameses IX. there was found some indication in the shape of various fragments of a chair, or stool, made of wood, bronze, and ivory.

XXIst Dynasty.—(*Circa* B. C. 1110 to B. C. (?).)
17. Queen Notem-Maut (mother or possibly wife of Her-Hor). .... Mummy; two mummy-cases.
18. Pinotem I. (Pontiff; apparently not styled king). .... Mummy; mummy-case.
19. Queen Hathor Hont-taui (wife of Pinotem I.) .... Mummy; two mummy-cases.
20. King Pinotem II. .... Mummy; mummy-case.
21. Queen Makara .... Mummy; two mummy-cases.
22. Prince-Pontiff Masahirti .... Mummy; three mummy-cases.
23. Princess Nasi-Khonsu .... Mummy; two mummy-cases.
24. Queen Isi-em-kheb .... Mummy; three mummy-cases.

Besides the foregoing there were found several mummies of royal children, including a young son of King Ahmes I.; also the mummy and mummy-case of one Nebsooni, a priest, grandfather of Queen Hont-taui and husband of a certain Queen Tentamen, of the XXIst Dynasty; the mummies of various royal ladies, also of this dynasty, who were priestesses of Amen; several mummy-cases of servants of the royal household, some mummy-cases without inscriptions, some mummies without mummy-cases, and some imitation mummies, consisting of pieces of wood bandaged to represent human forms, and enclosed in cases from which the original occupants had been abstracted. Of other sepulchral treasures there was found a vast store of funereal statuettes (*shabti*), bronze libation-jars, "canopic" vases for containing the viscera of the mummied dead, small vases, bottles and vessels in various materials, amulets, four papyri, etc., etc., numbering in all some 6000 objects.

The above list is separable into two parts or groups: the first group containing mummies and relics of the XVIIth, XVIIIth, XIXth, and XXth Dynasties; the second group consisting of mummies and relics of members of the family of Her-Hor. Had no names been painted on the coffins of these royal personages, Egyptologists could have classified them dynastically from the distinctive styles of their workmanship. Most of the earlier ones are white or yellow and decorated with simple bands of hieroglyphs; those of the XXIst Dynasty are covered with mythological designs, both inside and out, elaborately painted and gilded and highly varnished. As we have already remarked, none of the earlier mummies have more than one coffin; whereas, with but two exceptions, all the members of the Amenide group are enclosed in two coffins, and, in some instances, in three. Also, the greater part of the miscellaneous funereal objects and all the papyri belonged to the Amenides, the sepulchral furniture of the royalties of the earlier group being limited to some porcelain *shabti* found with Thothmes III., the alabaster canopic vases of Queen Ahmes-Nofretari, some *shabti* of Queen Hatasu, etc., etc.

That so many royal mummies of various epochs should be found in a single vault, and that the funereal equipments of some should be costly and numerous, while others were either quite destitute of such objects or but scantily supplied, was at first sight inexplicable. The most probable solution of the mystery seemed to be that a foreign invasion had taken place, and that all these royal dead had been hastily hidden in the best concealed "pit" that could be found for that purpose. The subsequent researches of Prof. Maspero have, however, brought to light three Mēratic inscriptions upon the jambs of the doorway of this vault, recording the dates of the interments of Pinotem II. and Princess Nasikhonsu, thus showing that the excavation was continuously in use, and that it was the family sepulchre of the priest-kings. It is also quite certain that the last interred was Queen Isi-em-kheb, daughter of Masahirti and Nasi-Khonsu, and wife of Menkheperra II. This king's broken seal, impressed on clay, was found upon the shattered floor of the mortuary chamber, where it had been placed by his own hand when the vault was closed at the burial of his queen. It was also found unbroken upon the lid of a very curious rush-hamper containing her funereal feast. This hamper contained gazelle-haunches, calves' heads, trussed geese, all mummified and bandaged, as well as a dessert of nuts, raisins, and dates. Four alabaster canopic vases, a set of libation vases, a complete toilet service of ointment bottles and goblets in variegated glass (probably of Phœnician make), and a curious collection of full-dress wigs highly curled and frizzed, each in a separate little hamper sealed with the seal of Menkheperra, were also found with this queen. To her likewise belonged the great funereal canopy in cut leather embroidery which has since been fully described and figured by Mr. J. Villiers Stuart. (See his work, *The Funeral Tent of an Egyptian Queen*, 1882.) This superb specimen of ancient needlework consists of a centre-piece of bluish gray leather ornamented with rosettes and emblematic vultures in appliqué work of colored leather, bordered with a frieze of hieroglyphed legends, royal cartouches, lotus bouquets, grotesque figures of birds and beasts, etc. From this centre-piece depend four flaps of a chess-board pattern, the whole being designed as a canopy for the double purpose of covering the bier during the procession by land and the cabin of the funereal galley by which the mummy was conveyed across the Nile. The centre-piece measures 2½ metres long and the four flaps 2¼ square metres each. The hieroglyphed frieze is of great historical importance, as showing that Menkheperra and Masahirti were sons of Pinotem II., and that Isi-em-Kheb, being wife to the one and daughter to the other, was in fact married to her uncle. These and other genealogical details, derived from inscriptions on objects found in the vault, have enabled Prof. Maspero to draw up the following provisional scheme of the succession of the family of Her-Hor:

1. Her-Hor .... { High Priest of Amen; afterwards King.
2. Piankhi .... High Priest of Amen.
3. Pinotem I .... High Priest of Amen.
4. Pinotem II .... King.
5. Masahirti .... High Priest of Amen.
6. Menkheperra II .... King.
7. Pinotem III .... High Priest.

All these, though some did not assume the title and cartouches of royalty, were sovereign rulers at Thebes, and probably also at Tanis. Those who took the kingly title are believed to be the sons of princesses of the old Ramesside line, styled Queens, who married Amenide rulers, and so (according to Egyptian law) transmitted royal rights to their male offspring. Queen Notem-maut, who was undoubtedly royal in her own right, enclosed her name in a regal cartouche. From her, Her-Hor, who was more probably her son than her husband, derived his right to the kingly title. The wife of Pinotem I. was Queen Hont-taui, whose son, Pinotem II., was therefore king. This second Pinotem married two wives, the Lady Nasitanebasneroo, mother of High Priest Masahirti, and Queen Makara, mother of King Menkheperra; the one son being priestly and the other royal. The mummies of both wives were found in this vault, the mummy of a little newly-born infant being enclosed in the coffin of Makara, who died, apparently, in childbed. A significant illustration of the maternal transmission of royalty is afforded by the fact that this infant is styled by all her mother's titles, including that of "principal Royal Wife," so showing that descendants of the old royal stock inherited from birth all the dignities which would be theirs on arriving at years of maturity. Seeing that this vault was no mere temporary hiding-place, but the family sepulchre of the Amenide dynasty, it may be concluded that the whole royal and sacerdotal family was originally interred here. There are, however, important gaps in the succession of the mummies actually discovered. Her-Hor, Piankhi, and the wife of Piankhi are missing. So, also, is the mummy of a certain Queen Tent-Amen, mother of Queen Hont-taui, of whose former presence in the vault we have distinct evidence in the shape of her funereal papyrus, which (evidently stolen from hence) was bought at Thebes in 1874 and resold to the Louvre. It may be assumed that all the mummies of the Her-Hor line were buried with papyri, vases, foo

ings and every due honor, and that these treasures have been on sale at least since 1859 (when the mummy and jewels of Aah-hotep were found in the sand), if not still earlier. It is indeed impossible to conjecture how many links in the history of the XVIIth, XVIIIth, XIXth and XXth Dynasties have been irretrievably lost during this time. Many objects undoubtedly abstracted from the vault of the priest-kings have, however, been traced of late to various public and private collections, among which are especially to be noted the funereal papyri of Queen Notem-Maut, Queen Tent-Amen, King Pinotem II., Queen Hont-taui and Prince Tat-f Pthah-au-f-Ankh, and the canopic vases of Pinotem I. and Nasi-Khonsu. Many more such objects must have found their way to America and to the Continent of Europe; and their possessors could render no greater service to science than by making known the nature of their purchases and publishing accurate copies of inscriptions, cartouches, and the like.

Something remains to be said in respect to the mummies of the earlier dynasties, and of their presence in the vault of the priest-kings. Seeing that the condition of Egypt during the reigns of Her Hor and his descendants would appear to have been one of profound peace, there exists no ground for supposing that these august mummies were removed hither from their own sepulchres in the Valley of the Tombs of the Kings, and elsewhere, in order to safeguard them against the sacrilegious hand of a foreign invader. A much more simple and satisfactory explanation is to be found in the social condition of Thebes itself, and the inefficiency of the Theban police, at this period. Not the foreign foe, but the native tomb-breaker, was the real source of danger to the dead. Then, and long before then, at least as early as the reign of Rameses IX., there existed bands of desperadoes who lived by plundering the city of tombs upon the western bank, and who respected a mummied Pharaoh no more than a mummied ibis. There are yet extant two papyri— the "Abbott papyrus" and the "Amherst papyrus" —both original documents of the time of Rameses IX. (XXth Dynasty), and both relating to these tomb-robberies. The "Abbott papyrus" is the actual draft of a report penned by the scribe of the commandant of police at Thebes, and it gives a circumstantial account of an official tour of inspection made through various parts of the Necropolis (chiefly among the royal tombs) from the 18th to the 21st day of the month Athyr, in the tenth year of Rameses IX. A list is given of the tombs found intact; of those unsuccessfully attempted and showing marks of violence; of others violated and sacked, where "the thieves had torn their occupants from the coffins and mummy-cases, and had cast them in the dust, and had stolen their funerary furniture, and also the gold and silver and the ornaments that were with them." The "Amherst papyrus" contains the confession of one of the robbers, as taken down by a scribe in attendance on the Governor of Thebes. The culprit admits having broken into the sepulchre of King Sevek-eon-saf and Queen Nubkhas his wife (XIIth Dynasty), and relates how he and his companions despoiled these royal mummies of their valuables, and then set fire to their mummy-cases. Other papyri of an earlier date, written in the reign of Rameses III., reveal a generally demoralized condition of society under the XXth dynasty, and show that not only did anarchy reign in the provinces, but that disaffection and conspiracy were rife among the priestly and military castes in Thebes itself. If such was the state of the capital under a powerful Pharaoh like Rameses III. there can be no doubt that the mischief must have largely increased under his feeble successors, in which case tomb-breaking would have flourished almost unchecked during the reigns of those later Ramessides who preceded the dynasty of the priest-kings. The marvel is indeed, not that so many Pharaohs of the earlier dynasties should have been removed from their sepulchres and reinterred in the tomb of the Her-Hor family, but that any royal mummies of those periods should have survived the century and more of warfare which had been waged against the dead. For there can be no question that it was for protection against theft and sacrilege that the remains of their illustrious predecessors had been gathered by their priest-kings into the shelter of their own sepulchre. The fact is indirectly proved by a number of inscriptions written in the hieratic script upon the mummy-cases and bandages of several of the Pharaohs of the XVIIIth and XIXth Dynasties. These inscriptions, though dated some in the reign of Her-Hor, some in the reign of Pinotem II., and some in the reign of Masahirti, are almost identical as to substance. Each purports to be the record of an official visit of inspection to a royal tomb; each is dated, and signed by numerous witnesses. These inspectors of tombs were careful to state how they "renewed the funerary appointments" of the royal dead; that is to say, how they swathed them in fresh outer bandages, garlanded their mummied forms with flowers, and repaired, or renewed, their coffins. They were also empowered to remove these ancestral Pharaohs from place to place, if necessary; and it is clear that this could only have been done with the object of baffling the tomb-breakers. Also, it is impossible that their coffins can have needed repair or renewal, unless wilfully injured. Mummy-cases of a much more ancient date than any found at Dayr-el-Baharee have come down to the present day, perfect even to the gilding and coloring of their surfaces. The dryness of the Egyptian climate, and the safety from insect ravages which was insured by the places and conditions of burial, render anything like natural decay wholly impossible. The rough treatment to which many of the Dayr-el-Baharee coffins had evidently been subjected at the period of these inspections can have arisen from no other cause than sacrilegious violence. Of the original coffins of Amenhotep I. and Thothmes II., only the lids remain; the lower part of both being of rougher and later work. From the mummy-case of Thothmes III. the gilding is scraped off, and the whole much battered and disfigured. The coffin of Rameses I. is a wreck, all but the lid, and was found empty. A very finely-bandaged mummy lying near by is supposed, however, to be the mummy of the founder of the XIXth Dynasty. The original mummy-case of Rameses the Great must have been either destroyed or injured beyond repair, as his mummy reposes in an entirely new and very handsome coffin of carved sycamore wood, of XXIst Dynasty workmanship. The hieratic inscriptions traced on the coffin and on the bandages of the mummy show that this famous Pharaoh was first visited by the inspectors when yet in his own sepulchre in the Valley of the Tombs of the Kings; and that after this inspection his mummy was at least four times shifted from tomb to tomb (i. e., to the tomb of Seti I., to the tomb of Queen Ansera, to the tomb of one of the Amenhoteps, and back to the tomb of Seti I.) before being finally deposited in the sepulchre of the priest-kings. Seti himself was twice shifted, and Rameses I. three times. All these facts are shown by the inspectors' entries. It seems singular that the only mummies which bear these entries are those of Amenhotep I., Thothmes II., Rameses I., Seti I., and Rameses II. The great Ahmes, who founded the XVIIIth Dynasty, his famous queen, Thothmes III., and the rest, though carefully rescued and sheltered, were either not periodically visited, or were left uninscribed. These examinations, as far as we have record of them, begin with the sixth year of Her-Hor, reappear under Pinotem II., and end with the sixteenth year of the pontificate of Masahirti. It must evidently have been at some date subsequent to that last entry, and before the interment of Queen Isi-em-kheb, that these defunct guests were received *en masse* into the family vault of the priest-kings. Prof. Maspero conjectures that this admission was the act of King Menkheperra II., and that the vault and passages became therefore so crowded that he sealed the sepulchre forever, and was, with his descendants, buried elsewhere. Prof. Maspero's exhaustive report (*La Trouvaille de Deir-el-Bahari*, Cairo, 1881) contains many more details of this discovery than we have space to quote; but the following measurements of the mummies of some of the most celebrated Pharaohs are too curious to be omitted:

	Metre.
Ahmes Ranebpehti (founder of the XVIIIth Dynasty)	1.67.
Queen Ahmes Nofretari (his wife)	1.68.
Amenhotep I.	1.65.
Thothmes III	1.60.
Seti I	1.75.
Rameses II	1.80.

From these measurements we learn that Queen Ahmes Nofretari was one inch and three-eighths taller than her husband; and that Thothmes III. and Rameses II., the two most famous Pharaohs of Egyptian history, were respectively the shortest and the tallest of all this illustrious company.

Having escaped depredators, ancient and modern, these royal mummies, and the treasure found with them, are now safely lodged in the Museum of Egyptian Antiquities at Boolak, near Cairo, where several additional rooms have been built for their reception. A new catalogue of the collection, including these acquisitions, has been published. (A. B. E.)

EHNINGER, JOHN WHETTON, an American artist, was born in New York, July 22, 1827. He was educated at Columbia College, and after graduating in 1847 he went to Paris, when he entered the atelier of Couture. He studied for several years in Paris and other European cities, and executed a number of pictures which were greatly admired when they were exhibited in the United States, several of them being selected by the Art Union as subjects for engravings to be issued to its subscribers. Ehninger has attempted many themes from the highest, such as Christ Healing the Sick, to the most familiar. His most popular as well as his best performances are representations of American country-life, such as A New England Farm-Yard, Love me, Love my Horse, and Yankee Peddler. He has been a frequent contributor to both the English and American illustrated papers, and has made etchings for Hood's "Bridge of Sighs," Washington Irving's "Dolph Heyliger," Longfellow's "Miles Standish," and other stories and poems.
(W. J. C., JR.)

EISENLOHR, AUGUST, a German Egyptologist, was born at Mannheim, Oct. 6, 1832. He studied theology at Heidelberg and Göttingen, but on account of a nervous disease was obliged to discontinue his studies in 1853. On his recovery in 1858 he devoted himself to agriculture, and afterwards to natural science, especially chemistry. From 1862 to 1865 he had a manufactory of aniline colors. In the latter year he was accidentally drawn to the study of Chinese, and then to Egyptian hieroglyphics, in the interpretation of which he followed Chabas and afterwards Brugsch. In 1869, having presented an analytical explanation of the Demotic part of the Rosetta Stone, he was admitted as an instructor in Egyptology in the University of Heidelberg. Having been sent by the Grand Duke of Baden to Egypt he ascended the Nile to the second cataract, and examined in Alexandria the great Harris papyrus, a document of Rameses II., 1320 B. C. He returned through Palestine, Syria, and Asia Minor. In 1872, having purchased from its owner, Miss Harris, for the British Museum, the papyrus, whose value he had ascertained, he published an essay on it (Leipsic, 1872), and a translation of it in the *Aegyptischen Zeitschrift*. In the same year he was made professor extraordinarius in the University of Heidelberg. He published in 1875 an explanation of the ancient Egyptian measures from a papyrus in the British Museum. He has also translated and explained another papyrus of the museum under the title, *Ein Mathematisches Handbuch des alten Aegypter*, Leipsic, 1877. The papyrus Rhind from which this is taken was probably written in the time of the Hykshos, 1700 B. C., and contains a summary of the mathematical knowledge and operations of that age.

EJECTMENT. The action of ejectment is still in use in some of the United States, stripped however almost entirely of the fictions and forms by which it was attended at the common law. In those States where it is still retained it is the sole method of settling the titles to land. The claimant issues a writ directed to the tenant actually in possession. All persons claiming a title adverse to the plaintiff are then permitted on application to come in and defend. On the trial it is incumbent on the plaintiff to prove (1) possession on the part of the defendant, and (2) his own superior title. It is believed to be a universal rule that the plaintiff must recover on the strength of his own title and not on the weakness of his adversary's. The judgment in ejectment is by statute generally made conclusive as to the title so far as the parties to the action are concerned, and all persons claiming from, through, or under them. In some States, however, it is made conclusive as to the right of possession only, and in Pennsylvania it has not even that effect, the judgment being only deemed conclusive as to such right when it has been preceded by another similar judgment between the same parties. In a few States the common law rule is retained, and any number of actions of ejectment may be brought for the same premises between the same parties until a court of equity intervenes to prevent vexations and repeated litigation. In those States where separate forms of action are abolished and a code is in force, ejectment as a distinctive action has of course disappeared. The

See Vol. VII. p. 687 Am. ed. (p. 792 Edin. ed.).

form of action, however, prescribed for the recovery of the possession of real estate is necessarily very similar to the action of ejectment, and is governed by much the same rules. Substantially the same evidence is required and the judgment is usually made conclusive with respect to the title involved. (L. L., JR.)

ELECTION LAWS, AMERICAN, prescribe and regulate the exercise by citizens of their rights of suffrage; they direct the manner and times of holding elections and declare who shall be entitled to vote at such elections.

See Vol. VIII. p. 4 Am. ed. (p. 2 Ed. ed.).

The jurisdiction of the election laws of the United States extend only to such officers of the Federal Government as are elective, viz.: the President, the Vice-President, and members of the House of Representatives; and have no application to the election of the officers of the several State governments, which are regulated by their own particular codes. They prescribe that the President and Vice-President shall be elected by a college of electors, which college shall be composed of as many electors as there shall be Senators and Representatives in Congress according to the appointment thereof at the time of the appointment of such electors. That the people shall vote directly for the electors, who in turn shall meet in college on the first Wednesday in December, in the year in which they are appointed, and at such place in each State as the legislature thereof shall direct, and after making a list of the names of the persons voted for by the electors for the offices of President and Vice-President, with the number of votes each received, make three certified copies of the same: one shall be delivered to the Vice-President at the seat of government, or, in case of his absence, to the Secretary of State, before the first Wednesday in January next ensuing; one shall be sent by the post-office to the President of the Senate at the seat of government, and the third one shall be delivered to the Judge of the District in which the electors shall assemble. That Congress shall be in session on the second Wednesday of February succeeding every meeting of the electors, and the certificates from them shall then be opened, the votes counted and the persons to fill the offices of President and Vice-President ascertained and declared agreeably to the Constitution. It provides also that no one shall be eligible to these offices unless he be 35 years old and be born in the United States. Members of the Congress are by the laws elected in the following manner: each State shall be entitled to two Senators in Congress, who shall be elected by the Senate and House of Representatives of the several States, on joint ballot; and that no person shall be eligible for the office of Senator unless he be 30 years of age and be 9 years a citizen of the United States, and be an inhabitant of the State for which he shall be elected. The members of the House of Representatives shall be elected directly by the people, and that there shall be one representative for every 30,000 inhabitants. That no person shall be eligible to this office unless he be 25 years of age and been a citizen of the United State 7 years, and a citizen of the State from which he shall be chosen. Under these laws all citizens of the United States are entitled to vote except citizens of the District of Columbia, who because of the District being the capital seat of the Federal Government are given no part in the elections. All the officers of its government are appointed by the President, and the United States courts exercise exclusive jurisdiction over the District. (See DISTRICT OF COLUMBIA.) The Enforcement Act of May 31, 1870, which was founded upon the Emancipation Proclamation, makes it indictable and punishable for any one to prevent persons of African descent from voting, or for refusing to register such votes.

The various States of the country have from time to time enacted laws for the regulation and management of their own local elections, embracing the public choice of the officers of the State, city, and county, and prescribing the punishment to be inflicted upon any one who violates them, and according a proper remedy for any one who may, by fraud in the election, be hindered from the occupancy of an office to which he was elected. This consists in a contest with the person claiming to hold the same, wherein he must show that the incumbent's tenure is a fraudulent one. The right of suffrage is the highest branch of the liberty of the American citizen—a right inherent with his birth, is the free exercise of which he elevates his fellow to power, or transfers that power to another, and becomes a most effectual check upon the improper exercise of power by those in authority. It is that sovereignty, so essential to the free institution of the government, whose fundamental principle is that all men are born free and equal. The constitutions of the States secure to the citizen this right, prescribe and declare the number and nature of the offices, whose incumbents shall preside over the State and municipal affairs, the manner and form in which they shall be chosen, but leave to the qualified citizen the exercise of that right of choice. The laws of each State, as enacted by the legislature, enlarge and provide the means of effecting the ends of the constitution, and forbid the doing of those things by the citizen which would be a violation of them: as, voting twice at any one election, bribing others to vote or not to vote, personating voters, defacing or destroying the ballots, false representations as to qualification to vote, or making false returns of the elections; and punish such offenders with fine, imprisonment, and the deprivation of the rights of citizenship for such period as the court may direct.

(F. H.)

State Qualifications of Electors.—In all the States the following qualifications may be properly classed as universal, viz., that the elector be a male, over twenty-one years of age, neither a lunatic nor a pauper, and prepared to take, if necessary, an oath of allegiance to the Federal Government. The only one of these conditions not absolutely universal is the first, to which there are a few exceptions in certain States for particular elections. For several years after the late civil war, a few of the States disfranchised those who had taken arms against the United States, but these disqualifications no longer exist.

As to *residence in the State* previous to an election, 2 years are required by Kentucky and Rhode Island; 1 year by Alabama, Delaware, Florida, Illinois, Louisiana, Maryland, Massachusetts, Missouri, New Jersey, New York, North Carolina, Ohio, Pennsylvania, South Carolina, Texas, Vermont, Virginia, West Virginia, and Wisconsin; 6 months by Arkansas, California, Georgia, Indiana, Iowa, Mississippi, Nebraska, Nevada, and Oregon; 4 months by Minnesota, and 3 months by Maine and Michigan. Oregon further requires United States citizenship for 1 year, Pennsylvania for 1 month, Massachusetts 2 years, and New York 10 days.

Previous residence in *county* is required for 1 year by Kentucky; 6 months by Connecticut, Florida, Maryland, Massachusetts, Rhode Island, Texas, Tennessee and Louisiana; 5 months by New Jersey; 4 by New York; 3 by Alabama, North Carolina, and Virginia; 2 by Iowa, Missouri, and South Carolina; 40 days by Nebraska; 30 days by California, Delaware, Georgia, Illinois, Mississippi, Nevada, Ohio, and West Virginia; and 10 days by Michigan and Minnesota. Besides these, a residence of 30 days in the district is required in New York, and 60 days in Pennsylvania; Kentucky requires 60 days' residence in the precinct, Louisiana 30, and Nebraska 10; Ohio requires 20 days in the township or village, while residence at time of election only is required by Arkansas and New Hampshire.

Disqualifications exist in the several States as follows: Conviction for treason, embezzlement of public funds, malfeasance, bribery, or fraud, in Alabama, Arkansas, Kansas, Virginia, West Virginia, and Wisconsin. Michigan, Georgia, Kansas, and Virginia also include duelling, or challenging to a duel. Conviction of any infamous crime disqualifies in California, Delaware, Florida, Georgia, Iowa, Maryland, Minnesota, Nevada, New Jersey, New York, North Carolina, Rhode Island, Tennessee, and Texas; also of bribery or election fraud in Pennsylvania for 4 years, and in New York for betting on an election. No person under guardianship can vote in Florida, Kansas, Maine, Maryland, Massachusetts, Minnesota, or Wisconsin, and to deny the existence of Almighty God disqualifies in North Carolina.

Foreigners not citizens can vote on declaring their intention of becoming such in Arkansas, Florida, Georgia, Indiana, Kansas, Minnesota, Missouri (where declaration is required at least 1 year previously), Oregon, Texas, and Wisconsin. A former citizen of Mexico prior to 1848, now a United States citizen, can vote in California. *Property* qualification is required only in Rhode Island, where at least $134 of real estate must be owned by each elector. Connecticut requires a good character and an ability to read any part of the constitution or State laws; Massachusetts does the same, and adds an ability to write name. Missouri requires all voters new after 1876 to be able to read and write. Two years' residence after naturalization is required in Massachusetts.

Tax is required from all over 22; to be paid not more than 2 years or less than 6 months before election, by Delaware; Massachusetts requires within 2 years, Rhode Island within 1 year, and Pennsylvania not less than 30 days. Georgia requires all taxes payable within the year. Persons excused from taxation are disfranchised in New Hampshire, and all electors must "certify to good behavior" in Vermont. The legislature is empowered to pass acts of disfranchisement for various crimes in Illinois, Indiana, North Carolina, and Oregon.

Primary Elections in Pennsylvania are regulated by two separate acts. The first, approved June 8, 1881, provides as follows: 1. That any candidate giving or offering, directly or indirectly, any gift or bribe of any nature to an elector at a primary or delegate election for the purpose of inducing him to cast his vote or use his influence for or against any particular candidate, shall be guilty of a misdemeanor, punishable by fine of not more than $300 and imprisonment for not longer than 3 months. 2. That any elector accepting such bribe or (3) offering to sell his vote or influence at such election or convention shall also be guilty as above and subject to same punishment. 4. That any disqualified person voting at such election, or person procuring such disqualified vote, or person voting twice on the same day for the same candidate, or procuring another to do so, shall be guilty as above. Penalty $200 and 3 months. 5. That any delegate to such election receiving or asking for any recompense to vote or abstain from voting for any person as candidate for office, shall be guilty as above. Penalty $100 and 3 months. 6. That any person having to do with the conducting of such election or convention who shall receive or solicit any bribe in connection therewith shall be guilty as above. Penalty, $100 and 3 months. 7. That any person offering to bribe or influence any officer of such election shall be guilty as above. Penalty, $200 and 6 months.

The second act, approved June 29, 1881, provides as follows: 1. That every officer of any primary election in Pennsylvania shall be sworn before entering on his duties by one of the inspectors, and may swear any elector offering to vote at such election. 2. That any officer presuming to act in an official capacity without being so sworn shall be liable to fine of $200; same penalty for his knowingly refusing any qualified vote or accepting any unqualified one, and for his wilful disregard of any party rule at such election; or if such officer be guilty of any wilful fraud in his duties, he shall be liable to fine of $500 or 1 years' imprisonment, or both or either at discretion of court. (E. F. S.)

ELECTRICITY.

See Vol. VIII. p. 4 Am. ed. (p. 3 Edin. ed.).

WITHIN the past forty years the great generalization known as the Conservation of Energy has been made, and the forms in which energy exhibits itself have been investigated with great diligence and success, with the result of making much more definite than was formerly possible the conceptions of what is really taking place in matter when it is exhibiting various phenomena, such as heat, light, electricity, and magnetism. All the old theories concerning each of these have been discarded, and as no one now thinks of speaking of caloric when referring to thermal phenomena, so no one speaks of the electric fluid when electrical phenomena are involved. Those who have investigated the subject have satisfied themselves that whatever may be the form of electrical energy it cannot be a fluid.

Before one can form a judgment as to the probability of any theory of the nature of electricity being true or an approximation to the truth, one must have some kind of a mechanical idea of the physical conditions known to be present when electrical phenomena present themselves, and then see how far additional assumptions are necessary. To this end it must be borne in mind that all electrical phenomena, so far as we *directly* can observe them, are phenomena of common matter, and it is from the behavior of common matter that all inferences are drawn as to there being something else in some way involved. By "matter" is here meant just what is meant by that word in the law of universal gravitation: "Every particle of matter in the universe attracts every other particle of matter." If there be any kind of matter in the universe that is not subject to the law of gravitation, then that law is not universal, and it should read, "Some particles of matter," etc. Such terms as "electric matter" and "magnetic matter," when used to designate a kind of matter not subject to gravitation, are inappropriate, and not in accordance with scientific terminology, as their use makes indefinite what otherwise would be definite and accurate.

The phenomena of heat and of light furnish abundant evidence of the existence of some medium that is not matter, but which fills space and apparently is continuous, and not atomic or molecular in its structure. This medium is so related to matter that the vibrations of atoms and molecules generate waves in it which travel outward in straight lines from the vibrating body with the velocity of 186,000 miles per second. The accompanying diagram will aid to a conception of the

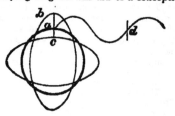

FIG. 1.

mechanical relations involved. Let the heavy-lined circle represent an atom of matter, and it is to be supposed to be surrounded by the continuous medium which is called "the luminiferous ether." If we adopt for the time the vortex-ring theory of matter—seeing that it has a stronger probability in its favor than any other that has yet been thought of—and we consider what happens when such an atom vibrates, that it must appreciably change its form, elongating into ellipses, the major axes of which are at right angles to each other as drawn, the point a of the atom vibrating between the limits b and c. The disturbance in the ether as a moves toward c incites a movement that will at once begin to be conducted outward, and if some direction, $a\ d$, be chosen, the complete vibration $a\ c\ b\ a$ will result in the undulation $a\ d$, and continuous vibration in a continuous line of undulations, called a ray, and wave-length $a\ d$, must obviously depend upon the rate at which such a disturbance is propagated in the medium, as well as upon the time of vibration of the atom. Such a line of undulations is called a "ray of light" when it happens to be of such a wave-length as is capable of affecting the eye and producing vision, and a "heat-ray" when of some other wave-length. It is also to be understood that when such undulations in the ether fall upon other atoms and molecules of matter, they are competent to set them vibrating in a way similar to the first or originating atom. This vibratory motion of the atom by which its form is changed constitutes the motion we call "heat," and is to be clearly distinguished from a change of position in space of the atom, the latter being called "free path motion," and is generally the effect of heat. Thus, a form of energy in matter is changed into a form of energy in the ether, and this latter may be again transformed into the original form in matter. We may speak of the vibrating atom as a source of energy, and the space about it which is affected by that energy as the field of force of the atom; and as these rays move in straight lines it is evident that such field is as extensive as is the universe. These facts from the phenomena of heat are chiefly of importance here in helping one to conceive such mechanical relations between atoms and the ether as are known to exist, that we may the better be able to conceive how other motions of atoms may affect the ether in a different way, and so develop still different phenomena.

Now, electrical phenomena are always developed whenever two different substances are brought into contact, or when two different substances in contact are heated, whether by friction or by the application of some source of heat. It is not essential that the two substances should be different kinds of substances; it is only necessary that the two should in some way be physically different. Thus, if a homogeneously constituted piece of wire, forming part of a circuit, be twisted at some point, its physical condition at that point will be different enough from the untwisted part to give rise to an electric current if the wire be heated adjacent to the twist. As we know the nature of the heat-motion, it is plain that two adjacent atoms or molecules, one of which is under constraint or differs from the other in mass or in complexity, cannot both vibrate at the same rate, the motions of each will be interfered with, and some differential motion must result, tending to force each molecule into some new position or to assume some other form of motion, as rotatory or other, which may react upon the ether.

The phenomena of induction and of attraction exhibited by electrified bodies, both of which are manifested in and through the most perfect vacuum that we can produce, and which also take place through bodies that are the most perfect non-conductors, such as glass and mica, prove incontestably that the electrified body does in some way affect some medium that surrounds it. The velocity of this movement in this medium has been measured in various ways, and has been found to be approximately the same as the velocity of light; and this leads one almost irresistibly to the conclusion that the medium must be the same in both cases, and that the velocity of propagation depends solely upon the properties of the medium itself. Suppose two bodies, A and B, be 186,000 miles apart; then, if A be suddenly electrified, the effect upon the ether will travel outward towards B and reach it in just one second. If A was made luminous at the same instant that it was electrified, the light-ray and the inductive ray would reach B at the same instant; the light-ray would make B vibrate, and the inductive ray would electrify it and make it tend to move towards A; it would be attracted. Suppose that B be in contact with A, then would there be no appreciable time between the electrification of A and the effect upon B. If B be separated by a short distance from A, nothing could be put between them that would prevent the inductive effect; and in this particular the electrical effect upon the ether is singularly unlike the heat-effect upon it, for if B should be shielded by interposing any substance between it and A, more or less of the light would fail to reach it; and if an opaque substance were placed between, no such rays could reach it at all; they would all be either absorbed or reflected.

The space about an electrified body within which inductive effects may be observed is called the "electric field," and the effect upon a body in that field is called the "inductive effect," or simply "induction;" and it is to be noted that no specific name has been given to the effect upon the ether or the condition into which it is thrown by an electrified mass of matter. The corresponding effect of a heated mass is known as "radiant energy." It is to be apprehended that for the lack of such distinctive name, and of the importance of having some mechanical conception of the nature of it, the notion has grown up that electricity is ether or something that is not matter. On the one hand, attention has been occupied with what happens in matter, and, on the other hand, with what happens in the ether; and hence confusion, and the failure to agree as to the nature of electricity. The ether never exhibits any electrical phenomena except when it is affected by matter subject to certain physical conditions. If we call the physical condition of matter "electricity," then we have no name for its effects upon the ether. If we call the physical condition induced in the ether "electricity," then we have no distinctive name for the matter exhibiting such properties.

Some of the ablest living physicists hold the opinion that "potential energy, like kinetic energy, depends .... upon motion" (see art. "Mechanics," § 297, vol. xv. ENC. BRIT.). Although in many cases of kinetic energy the form of the motion has not been clearly made out, yet it will add to clearness of conception if one will think out the various possible motions which a given body may have. Obviously a body may move in a straight or curved line or what is called its free path. It may vibrate with or without changing its form, or rotate on any axis, both of these without changing its position in space, and there may be various combinations of these motions, each involving energy, and, among atoms, each having its characteristic reaction upon the ether. The vibratory character of heat-energy has been clearly made out, and there is much reason for thinking that in like manner the characteristic of electrical energy is atomic or molecular rotation. If a current of electricity be passed through a long wire having one end free to move, the free end will be twisted, the torsion being right-handed or left-handed as the current goes this way or that. Imagine a rope-ring to be grasped by the hand anywhere and given a torsional strain. The rope will be twisted tighter on one side and untwisted to the same degree upon the other, and these two conditions will be conducted outwards through the ring, and one witnessing the advancing torsional movement might speak of it as a current if he chose, and, considering the whole ring of rope, the character of the motion would be what is called vortical. The above is a good mechanical analogy of what takes place in an electric circuit.

It is most in accordance with usage to speak of a battery as a generator of electricity, and the molecular physical disturbance that travels upon a conducting-wire as a current of electricity, implying in both cases that electricity is as much a property of the matter exhibiting such phenomena as is heat when it appears, and thus electricity may be defined as a physical condition of ordinary matter that manifests itself in two ways: 1st, by inducing in the adjacent ether a particular condition of the nature of a stress; and, 2d, by being propagated with great velocity in some kinds of matter which are hence called conductors. All the other observed effects are secondary; for instance, attraction is due to the reaction of the electrically-stressed ether upon the attracted body, and heat to the direct conversion of the electric motion into vibratory atomic motion.

Electrical conductability is that property of matter by which it assumes the electrical condition by contact and without transmutation. It is the essential condition for maintaining an electric current. A break in the continuity of a conductor absolutely stops the current. The ether is an absolute non-conductor. The so-called electric arc is maintained by the gaseous materials of the air, the volatilised carbon, or other material of the terminals. An electric spark that will jump two feet in the air will not jump a quarter of an inch in the best vacuum we can make, and that is nowhere near a perfect vacuum. Electrical induction, on the other hand, is always the result of transmutation. If a body be electrified by induction, the electrification is the result of the reaction of the electrically-stressed ether upon it, which in turn derived its stress from some electrified mass of matter. Radiant energy is transformed heat, and if a body be heated by radiant energy two transformations have taken place; the cases are analogous.

RESISTANCE is that property of a conductor which determines the amount of electricity that can traverse it in a given interval of time from a definite source of electricity. Resistance varies—
(a) with the quality of the conductor;
(b) with its physical condition;
(c) with its form.

By "quality" is meant the distinctions that are made between matter of different kinds—such, for example, as copper, platinum, and zinc. Each of these elements possesses the property of responding to electrical excitation with a certain velocity, each different from the others. Suppose a wire of each of these substances to be a mile long and one-tenth of an inch in diameter. If a battery should be attached to the copper wire so as to complete a circuit, and a measure made of the amount of electricity that passed through that circuit in, say, one minute; then if the platinum wire should be substituted for the copper, and a similar measurement made of the amount of electricity traversing the circuit in the same interval, a much less quantity would be found to have passed. If the amount traversing the copper wire be represented by 100, then that traversing the platinum wire would be represented by 16, and a similar experiment with the zinc would give about 30. What is true for these specific cases is true for all substances that will conduct.

By "physical condition" is meant the state of the body as to its density or compactness of molecules, and also their motions. The denser a given conductor is, the better will it conduct—that is, the less is its resistance. Also, the colder a body is, the less is its resistance; the resistance depends upon its temperature. In all probability this is due to the expansion, which is the result of heat, as expansion lessens the density of a substance, and so will increase resistance.

By "form" is meant the relative dimensions of a substance. The resistance of a conductor like a wire varies as its length. By doubling or trebling the length of a conductor the resistance is doubled or trebled. If the resistance of a mile of copper wire be 5 units, then the resistance of two miles of it will be 10, and three miles 15; and this is true for all materials and all conditions of it. Resistance also varies inversely as the cross-section of the conductors. If a copper wire a mile long and one-tenth of an inch in diameter has a resistance of 5 units, then if the wire be drawn to the twentieth of an inch in diameter the resistance of a mile of it will be 20 units, for the cross-section is but one-fourth that at first. It will take four such wires to be equal in cross-section to the one-tenth of an inch in diameter. To vary the diameter of a conductor of a given length is to vary its weight; and hence the greater the weight the less will be the resistance of it. This, too, is applicable to solid and liquid conductors.

Inasmuch as all kinds of matter have some resistance, it follows that in every electric circuit there must be some resistance in every part of it, the amount depending upon the quality of the material, the size of it, and its temperature.

As an example of the foregoing principles, suppose

that in the figure is represented an electric circuit consisting of a galvanic battery with two plates, one of copper, C, and the other of zinc, Z, with a connecting wire, &c. A current of electricity will traverse the circuit in the direction indicated by the arrow. Now, the circuit is made up of the several parts—copper plate, conducting wire, zinc plate, and the liquid between the plates. Each of these has its own resistance, depending upon quality, length, cross-section, and temperature. Suppose that the resistance in the connecting-wire be ignored, and the attention be directed to that in the battery alone. The resistance of every kind of a liquid is very many times greater than that of most metals—that is, when measured in equal lengths and cross-sections—and just as the resistance of a large wire is less than that of a small one of the same quality of matter, so will the resistance of a given length of liquid vary inversely as its cross-section. Let Z be moved towards C, and the liquid section will be shortened, and consequently the resistance in the cell will be lessened. This is one way of varying the resistance of a cell, or, as it is more generally called, the internal resistance of a battery. Again, suppose plate C to be made smaller and smaller, or, what will amount to the same thing, let it be slowly drawn out from the liquid; the cross-section of the liquid will be made smaller and smaller, and hence the resistance of the cell will be correspondingly increased. Thus, the internal resistance of a battery-cell may be varied in two ways.

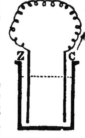

Fig. 2.

POTENTIAL AND ELECTRO-MOTIVE FORCE.—If a platinum wire P N have a few coils made in it by wrapping it about a lead pencil or otherwise, and then it be heated at some point A adjacent to the coil, the

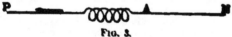

Fig. 3.

wire will become electrified in such a way that if it was suspended by its middle point, so as to swing freely, and an excited glass rod be brought near to it, the end P would be repelled and the end N would be attracted by the rod. If P and N should be bent round so as to be near each other, they will attract each other, while if the ends quite touch together a current of electricity will traverse the whole wire in the direction indicated by the arrow. The electrical condition of either end is called its potential, and the difference in potential between the ends is called the electro-motive force between them. The end P is said to have a higher potential than the end N, and electricity always flows from a point of higher to a point of lower potential. In a battery the two plates, being differently acted upon by the liquid, have a difference of potential between them which is called the electro-motive force of the cell. When copper or platinum are employed with zinc to form a battery, the zinc has the lower potential, and as a consequence the current in the conductor connecting them outside the cell flows towards the zinc. If magnesium or sodium took the place of the copper or the platinum, then the zinc would have the higher potential, and the current would flow from the zinc towards the other element. Whether

a substance is positively or negatively electrified depends upon what substance is employed with it. In the wire (fig. 3) the electro-motive force is maintained by the expenditure of the heat-energy. In the battery it is maintained through the solution of the surface molecules of one of the elements, in consonance with the general statement that electricity is developed upon contact of dissimilar substances. The surface molecules of the zinc that have acted are removed by the solvent action of the liquid, thus presenting a fresh surface of molecules.

CURRENT.—By "current" is meant the moving electricity in a conductor or a series of conductors—generally, that in a closed circuit. By "strength of current" is meant the amount of electricity that passes any point in a conductor in a given interval of time, generally one second. With any given source of electricity the current-strength will vary inversely as the resistance in the whole circuit. The greater the resistance the less will be the amount of electricity that can get through the circuit. Let B represent a battery-cell, Z the zinc, C the copper elements, and S a switch that may be swung about so as to touch either a or b, and let r be a coil of wire connecting a and b. When switch S is in the position shown there can be no current whatever, but the terminals, having a difference of potential, will attract each other. If S be made to touch upon a, then will the electric circuit be complete, and the current will flow in the direction indicated by the arrow. The strength of this current will depend upon the amount of resistance in the circuit, including the liquid in the battery and the wires. Let S be swung round so as to touch b, and the circuit will again be complete, and the current will flow as before, but the strength of the current will be greater, for there is less resistance in the circuit by the amount in r taken out.

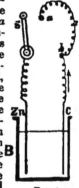

Fig. 4.

OHM'S LAW.—All of these conditions are expressed in a simple equation which is known as Ohm's Law. Let E be electro-motive force, R resistance, and C current; then

$$C = \frac{E}{R}$$

Now, electro-motive force is measured in volts, resistance in ohms, and current-strength in amperes. The electro-motive force of an ordinary copper-zinc cell, or Daniel cell, is very nearly one volt. Suppose such a cell to have an internal resistance of one ohm, and that a wire so large and short that its resistance need not be considered, because it is so small, then the strength of that current will be, as

$$\frac{\text{E in volts}}{\text{R in ohms}} = C \text{ in amperes}, \quad \frac{1 \text{ volt}}{1 \text{ ohm}} = 1 \text{ ampere}.$$

If, however, the connecting wire has a resistance of one ohm, the current strength will then be

$$\frac{1}{1+1} = .5 \text{ ampere}.$$

If the wire has nine ohms, then

$$\frac{1}{1+9} = .1 \text{ ampere},$$

for in every case R must express the whole of the resistance in the circuit.

INTERNAL RESISTANCE.—To illustrate the application of Ohm's law to the internal resistance of a battery:

I. Suppose the plates Z and C (fig. 2) be very large, but that they dip slightly into the liquid. Suppose the internal resistance be one ohm and the current strength one ampere; now dip the plates so as to immerse twice the surface; the resistance will be reduced one-half and the current-strength will be doubled, for

$$\frac{1}{.5} = 2 \text{ amperes.}$$

If the surface be increased by dipping to ten times the original surface or cross-section, then the current will be

$$\frac{1}{.1} = 10 \text{ amperes,}$$

and so on. If the plates could be made infinitely large the current could be infinitely great.

II. Let the plates be as shown, and one inch apart, the resistance of the cell one ohm. As resistance varies directly as the length of a conductor, if the plates are brought within half an inch of each other, the resistance will be reduced one-half, and the current will be doubled. If they are brought so near as the one-tenth of an inch, the current will be increased ten times; but there is a practical limit to this approach of plates in a battery, because for the proper action of the cell it is essential that the liquid shall have free access to the plates. If the plates are too near each other, the liquid between the plates cannot be renewed when exhausted, and the cell is brought to a stand-still.

ON EXTERNAL RESISTANCE IN RELATION TO SIZE OF CELL.—Let the internal resistance of the cell be again one ohm, and the external resistance of wires and other connections be 100 ohms; then the current-strength will be

$$\frac{1}{1+100} = \frac{1}{101} \text{ ampere.}$$

Suppose the plates now to be made so large that their resistance is nothing, the current would then be

$$\frac{1}{100} \text{ ampere,}$$

a quantity differing from the former quantity by less than 1 per cent. The only way the current-strength in such a circuit can be increased is to increase the electro-motive force, and so affect the numerator of the fraction. This may be done by increasing the number of cells, each one of which will have its own electro-motive force and resistance. Let there then be ten such cells as the first, the current-strength will be

$$\frac{10}{10+100} = \frac{1}{11} \text{ ampere.}$$

Thus, current strength may be increased in this way or in that, according as the resistance in the external circuit is large or small.

Whenever the earth is made part of an electric circuit by burying the metallic terminals in it, as is customary in telegraph-work, the resistance of these "grounds," as they are technically called, has to be considered, as one can seldom be made to be less than fifty ohms and often they are several hundred.

If a certain telegraph sounder requires a current of one-tenth of an ampere to work it promptly, then a single cell cannot be made to work it if part of the circuit be made in the earth, for if the electro-motive force of the cell be one volt, its internal resistance five ohms, that of the line and grounds be one hundred and that of the sounder itself be five ohms, then the current will be

$$\frac{1}{5+100+5} = .018 \text{ amperes,}$$

though without the line and grounds the current would be

$$\frac{1}{5+5} = .1 \text{ ampere.}$$

GENERATORS OF ELECTRICITY.—Electricity may be generated by direct and by indirect action. By direct action is meant that the energy spent in producing it is immediately transformed into electricity as in a battery or thermopile; and by indirect action when a second transformation of the energy is involved as in all cases of induction. Electricity is generated—

I. Whenever two dissimilar substances are brought into contact. The phenomenon appears to be simply one of surface action. It is true for solids and for liquids. Thus, if a piece of copper and a piece of zinc be touched together, one becomes positively, the other negatively, electrified. The source of the electrification is in the different rates of atomic motion of the two substances. They have different atomic weights, and for a given temperature their rates of vibration must be different, and when such surfaces are placed in contact there must be a rearrangement of the interfering molecules, which results in what we call electrification. The effect is transient unless a fresh surface or a supply of energy to maintain the condition be provided. The first may be effected

a. By friction, in which fresh surfaces are brought into contact by rotation or otherwise, and

b. By solution, as in common galvanic batteries when the surfaces are renewed by the dissolution of the surfaces that have acted.

Whether a given body will be positively or negatively electrified by contact or friction will depend upon what substance it is in contact with. If glass be rubbed with flannel the glass becomes positive, if flannel be rubbed on hard rubber the flannel becomes positive, and if hard rubber be rubbed on silver the hard rubber becomes positive. The electricity produced in this way is generally of very high electro-motive force, 50,000 volts being not uncommon. In the galvanic battery the electrification of the plates is maintained by the chemical action of some liquid that acts upon one of them, generally the zinc. The dissolution of the zinc stops when the circuit is broken, but there is still electrification, and the wire terminals attract each other.

II. Electricity is generated by heating the junction of dissimilar metals, as in the familiar thermopiles, the heat applied being transformed into electricity.

III. Electricity is generated by the proper motion of either part of a magneto-electric system. Such a system consists of a magnet, a wire helix, and an armature.

When the pole of a magnet is thrust into or drawn out from a helix the two ends of the helix assume different potentials, or an electro-motive force is induced between the ends. If the two ends are connected outside by a conductor, the electro-motive force induced will discharge itself as a current through such conductor. If the terminals of the helix do not touch, they will be electrified and will attract each other. The phenomenon is a transient one, lasting no longer than the motion of the magnet lasts. If the magnet be stationary and the coil be moved over it, the same result in the helix will follow as before; and if the helix be already about the pole of the magnet, and a piece of iron be brought near to the pole, a similar electric condition will be induced.

For example, let N S represent a magnet, H a helix of wire surrounding the pole, t the terminals of the

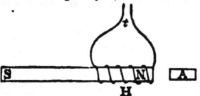

FIG. 5.

wire of the helix, and A a piece of iron. Now, if the magnet has its relative position to the coil changed, either by its own motions or the motion of the coil, or if with both magnet and coil stationary, and the attracted piece of iron, A, be moved either towards or away from the pole, an electrical disturbance in the coil will result, and the terminals t will attract each other; or, if they already touch each other, a current of electricity will pass through it. The field or space within which such effects will be produced is called the "magnetic field." It is the space occupied by the so-called lines of force of the magnet, such as may be traced by the lines assumed by iron filings when they are permitted to arrange themselves about a magnet. When any conductor of electricity is moved in this field in such a way as to cross these lines at right angles to them, the conductor is always electrified, its two ends having different potentials. The nearer it is to the poles of the magnet the greater will be the number of these lines which a given motion will cross and the greater will be the electro-motive force between the terminals, and the stronger will be the current, provided there is a completed circuit. When an armature of iron is used instead of moving magnet or coil, the strength of the magnet is varied, the magnetic strength being greatest when there is an open field and nothing to attract, and weakest when the armature is touching it and is large enough to engross all the lines of force; for the presence of the armature to a magnet rearranges and apparently absorbs these lines of force, enfeebling the magnet. The varying of the strength of the magnet has the same effect upon the encircling coil as the movement of the magnet within it.

When all of these parts are quiescent there is no electrical disturbance whatever. It is only while some mechanical energy is spent in moving some of them in this magnetic field that electricity appears; and all of the various forms of magneto-electric generators are but modifications of these essential conditions. When permanent magnets are employed, the machine is called a "magneto-electric machine." When an electro-magnet is substituted for the permanent magnet, it is called a "dynamo-electric machine." The current of electricity to maintain the strength of the electro-magnet and create a magnetic field is sometimes supplied by a separate machine, sometimes by making a part of the same machine furnish the needed current, and sometimes by making a part or the whole of the current from the machine go through its own coils. The magnets of any machine that maintain the magnetic field are called the "field magnets," whether these are permanent or electro.

THE MAGNETIC FIELD.—The lines of force, as traced by iron filings sprinkled about a straight bar-magnet, are seen to be curved, running from one pole to the other; and as these lines of force apparently repel each other, the shape of the field of such a magnet is oval. If the magnet is bent, so that its poles face each other, the lines of force are nearly straight lines between the poles, and the field is very dense; hence nearly all the forms of magneto and dynamo machines have their field-magnets made with their poles facing each other.

ARMATURES.—The piece of iron called a keeper that is furnished with a commercial permanent magnet is also called its armature. As this is inductively made a strong magnet when in the neighborhood of the poles, and as it is small compared with the magnet itself, it is found to be better to give to it the necessary motion rather than the larger mass. There are three specific methods of thus utilizing the magnetic field.

FIG. 6.

I. By making the armature in ordinary magnet form, surrounding it with a proper coil, and mounting it so that it may be rotated in front of the poles of the field-magnet. The common electro-magnetic engine of Page is a type of this method (fig. 6). If it be placed in circuit with a common galvanometer, and then it be rotated by friction of the hand upon the spindle, the generated electricity will manifest itself by the movements of the galvanometer needle. The common medical magneto machine, rotated with a crank by hand, is a familiar form of such machine. Some have been made very large, requiring an engine of several horse-power to run them, but they are now mostly superseded by the others.

II. The Siemens armature, in which the coil is wound longitudinally in deep grooves cut into the opposite sides of a spindle of iron.

III. The ring armature, in which a solid iron ring an inch or more in thickness, three or four or more inches broad, and the whole five or six inches or more in diameter, has its coil wound longitudinally in and out, completely covering the ring from sight. This is called the "gramme ring."

The distinctions between these three forms of armatures may be more easily perceived by comparing the accompanying diagrams, in which only the essential conditions are drawn.

In Fig. 7 N and S represent the poles of the field-

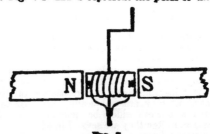

FIG. 7.

magnet, n and s the soft-iron bar armature with its coil, and an axis for rotation, indicated by the crank

The polarity of this armature will depend upon the pole of the adjacent field-magnet, and will always be the opposite of that. When one-quarter of an entire revolution has been made, the ends of the armature will be at right angles to the poles of the field-magnet, and, being equally solicited by each pole, will have no polarity. When half a revolution has been made, the end that is now marked *s* will have been brought to face S, and it will therefore be of *n* in polarity; the magnetism will be completely reversed, and on account of this change of magnetism in the bar an electro-motive force will be generated in the surrounding coil. The terminals of the coil are soldered to a commutator upon the axis of revolution, and a system of conductors beyond provides a way for a current of electricity to where it is wanted.

The Siemens armature is represented in Fig. 8,

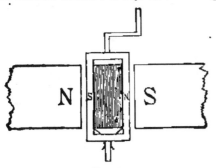

FIG. 8.

where N and S are the poles of the field-magnets, *n* and *s* the armature, with its coil *within it*, and mounted so as to rotate on a longitudinal axis. Polarity will be given to this by induction, as shown; and as this is rotated the sides will alternately be brought to face each pole of the field-magnet, and thus completely reverse the polarity of the armature. This will set up to-and-fro currents in the coil, the ends of which are connected to a proper commutator, as in the first case.

The third form, or the gramme ring, is shown in Fig. 9. The ring is so mounted as to be rotated be-

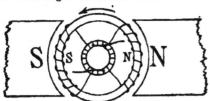

FIG. 9.

tween the poles of a powerful field-magnet S and N. These give inductive polarity to the parts of the ring adjacent to each pole, so that the outer part of the ring facing the pole N will have *s* polarity, while the inner part of the ring at the same place will have *n* polarity. This condition must evidently be reversed when the ring has made half a revolution, and hence there will be an electrical reaction within the coils while the motion goes on. In practice, several separate coils are fixed in each ring (sometimes thirty or forty), such an arrangement being highly advantageous. This third form of armature is the peculiarity of what is known as the Gramme machine. Each of these methods is capable of being varied in several ways. They also may be combined, these changes and combinations being the bases of numerous patents.

In every case where electricity is obtained by means of motion in a magnetic field, the electricity represents the mechanical energy expended, and is maintained at the expense of such energy. Suppose a large dynamo machine to have its external electric circuit open. The armature may be turned by the hands at considerable speed, but if, while it is still moving, the circuit be closed, it will at once come nearly to rest, as if a strong break had been applied, so that only a very small machine can be turned by hand. It requires a steam-engine or some other source of mechanical energy to maintain the proper speed; but the dynamo is such a perfect machine for the transformation of the energy that as much as 90, and even 95, per cent. of the expended energy appears as electricity. The amount that a given machine will produce depends upon its size, the strength of the field-magnets, the velocity of rotation, and the resistance.

MECHANICAL EQUIVALENT OF ELECTRICITY.—Inasmuch as electricity never appears save when energy in some other of its forms has been expended to produce it, it follows that there is a quantitative as well as a genetic relation between the energy expended and the electrical energy developed. The knowledge of this equivalent is important to those having a commercial interest in the transformation, and also to that class, still much too large, who appear to expect that a given amount of electricity is capable of doing almost any amount of work, that more can be got out of a machine than is put into it, provided only that what comes out be electricity. Energy is measured by the weight it can raise a given distance, which is expressed in foot-pounds or kilogrammetres. It is found experimentally that the heat energy required to heat a pound of water one centigrade degree will raise 1390 pounds one foot high if applied to that purpose in a suitable engine; 1390 foot-pounds is consequently the mechanical equivalent of heat. But electricity is most readily converted into heat, and again it is experimentally found that a unit current of electricity in a conductor of unit resistance will raise the temperature of a pound of water .000525° centigrade. As the mechanical equivalent of one degree is 1390 foot-pounds, the equivalent of the above fraction is $1390 \times .000525 = .733$, that is to say the energy of a unit current of electricity in a resistance of one ohm is capable of raising .733 of a pound one foot high in one second. In one minute it is obvious that it could do 60 times as much work, or 44 pounds one foot high. Now a horse-power can raise 33,000 pounds one foot in a minute and

$$\frac{44}{33000} = \frac{1}{746},$$

a fraction that represents the relation of electrical energy to horse-power. As a rule, the horse-power of a given current may be found by multiplying the current strength C in amperes, by the difference in potentials E in volts and dividing the product by 746.

$$\frac{E\,C}{746} = \text{Horse-power.}$$

The product E C is technically known as so many *watts.* An example will serve to show the application. What is the horse-power of an electric circuit of 48 bichromate cells, each having an electro-motive force of 2 volts, and an internal resistance of .25 ohms with ten ohms in external circuit? Suppose the cells to be arranged tandem, then $E = 48 \times 2 = 96$. $R = 48 \times .25 = 12$ ohms internal resistance and

$$\frac{96}{12+10} = 4.36 \text{ amperes} = C.$$

$$\frac{EC}{746} = \frac{96 \times 4.36}{746} = .56 \text{ horse-power.}$$

If arranged for maximum current with 16 sets of 3 cells then $E = 16 \times 2 = 32$.

$$R = \frac{.25}{3} \times 16 = 1.3 + 1 \text{ ohm.}$$

$$\frac{32}{2.3} = 13.8 \text{ amperes} = C.$$

$$\frac{32 \times 13.8}{746} = .59 \text{ horse-power.}$$

This does not represent the available energy, but the total in the circuit; more than half of it being expended in the battery itself, heating it, only .25 horse-power being available. These figures show how impracticable it is to get any considerable amount of work out of a battery. It also shows that current strength is not the measure of the ability of electricity to do work.

COST OF BATTERY.—The cost of electricity, when generated by a battery, is very great, when compared with its cost when generated in a dynamo-electric machine, run by steam- or water-power. A pound of zinc at five cents costs twenty times as much as a pound of coal. A pound of coal yields about 8000 heat-units when burnt, while a pound of zinc will yield but about 1300 such units—only one-sixth that of coal—which makes zinc to be 120 times more costly for mechanical work than coal. In the best steam-engines only about 25 per cent. of the energy of the fuel is made available for work; and although an engine may transform 90 per cent. of its energy into work, yet for an equal amount of work the battery costs nearly 25 times as much as the engine. Add to this the cost of other chemicals, such as sulphuric acid and bichromate of potash, with the labor of replacing them as they are used up, and the rapid consumption of the zinc itself requiring frequent renewal, and the battery becomes not only costly but very troublesome.

It is a curious circumstance that electrical phenomena are nearly all reversible with the physical conditions that produce electricity. That is to say, as electricity may be produced by heat, as in the thermopile, so may electricity produce heat by transformation. As electricity may be produced by chemical action, as with a battery, by magnetism, and by the motions of matter, as in dynamo machines and friction, so may electricity be spent in doing chemical work in making a magnet, or doing mechanical work. The chief commercial uses to which electricity is applied at present are:

1. Electric lighting.
2. Electro-plating and electrotyping.
3. Telegraph and telephone.
4. Heating.
5. Mechanical work.

1. ELECTRIC LIGHTING.—The passage of a current of electricity through any conductor always results in heating that conductor, and the heat developed in any part of a circuit will depend upon the resistance of that part; the greater the resistance the higher will be the temperature with a current of given strength. The best conductors, such as copper and silver, may be fused and converted into vapor by a strong current, while in the heat in the so-called electric arc all substances, even the most refractory, are speedily vaporized.

Carbon is an element having a greater variety and range of properties than any other known substance. Its electrical resistance may vary from a fraction of a ohm in such sticks as are used for electric arc-lights to infinity as in the diamond, which is an excellent electric, friction developing upon it strong electrical excitation and the consequent attractive property. On account of the extremely high temperature needed to volatilize it—that its resistance decreases within limits as its temperature rises, and also that at about 300° C. its radiations are of all wave-lengths, and gives the sensation of white light to the eyes—it is the substance chiefly employed in electric lighting.

It was about the year 1809 that Sir Humphrey Davy discovered that an electric current might be maintained between two sticks of carbon when they were separated by a short space. The carbons were placed horizontally in his experiment, and so high an electro-motive force had his battery that he was able to separate the points four inches. The luminous band between the points consists of incandescent particles passing from one electrode to the other, and the band itself is flexible and easily deflected. On account of the great heat, there is a rising current of air past it, which gives the band an upward curve or arc form, and on that account it was called the electric arc. When the carbons are arranged one above the other, as is common now, there is nothing of the sort to be seen; there is no proper arc, though the name is still retained. The resistance of the arc is generally no more than four or five ohms, but the high temperature developed shows a great expenditure of energy.

With the best machines now made it requires nearly a horse-power to maintain a single arc light. Now, it happens that the positive carbon is always heated to a higher temperature than the negative one; and, as has already been explained, whenever there is a physical difference between adjacent parts of an electric circuit there is an electro-motive force set up, so in this case there is an electro-motive force developed at the carbon points, tending to oppose that in the rest of the circuit, and it amounts to something like thirty volts for a strong light. In order, then, to maintain the arc, it is necessary to overcome this developed electro-motive force by a still greater difference of potential, so that in practice an electro-motive force of about fifty volts is employed for each light. When a series of arc lights is maintained in one circuit, the electro-motive force must be proportional to the number of lights. Thus, a Brush machine maintaining forty lights in one circuit must have an electro-motive force of $50 \times 40 = 2000$ volts, and generally is somewhat in excess of that. In an arc lamp where there is a difference of potential of 50 volts between the carbons, and a horse-power is expended in maintaining the light, the current strength will be found by applying formula,

$$\frac{EC}{746} = \text{horse-power (see p. 276).}$$

$$\left(\frac{50 \; C}{746} = 1\right) = 14.9 \text{ amperes.}$$

THE INCANDESCENT ELECTRIC LIGHT.—When the carbon rods giving an arc light are brought together, the resistance to the current is reduced so much at that place that the points of the rods lose their brightness, and unless the current is an exceedingly strong one they will cease to be luminous. If now the rods be supposed to be reduced in thickness while the current passes, they would again begin to glow as the resistance became greater on account of the lessened diameter, and when it became of the thickness of a thread it would give out a light equal to a bright gas-jet. But red-hot carbon burns up in the air, being converted into carbonic acid gas, and is dissipated. If such a light from a thread of carbon is to be maintained, it must be protected from the air, which may be done by enclosing it in a glass receiver that has had the air removed from it. Incandescent electric lamps have been known and employed for demonstrative purposes in schools for many years, but all such were not adapted for house illumination, because they were costly, cumbersome, and without any durability.

The great advance in this kind of electric lighting that has taken place within a few years has not been due to any new electrical or optical discovery whatever, but to the reduction of the aforementioned principles to a more economical basis—

1st. By the improved dynamo-electric machines, giving a stronger, steadier current, and at a cheaper rate;

2d. By making the lamp itself smaller and the vacuum more perfect;

3d. By the production of a better quality of carbon, securing toughness, elasticity, and involatility; and

4th. By making them with much higher resistance than was formerly attempted.

Instead of charcoal, coke, or gas-retort carbon, it has been found that some specially prepared for the purpose is superior. For this purpose Edison used a fine quality of bamboo. A filament of this but little larger than a horse-hair is cut of proper length, placed in a mould, and then raised to a very high temperature in a furnace. The filament comes out properly shaped and carbonized, possessing also remarkable density, tenacity, and elasticity. It is then by special method made fast at its two ends to the copper terminals, and hermetically fastened into a small globular or pear-shaped glass receiver, which is hermetically sealed after the air has been as completely removed as is practicable. A standard lamp of this pattern has a filament six inches long bent into the form of a horseshoe. It may have a resistance of upwards of two hundred ohms when it is cold, and not more than half that when very hot. A current of one ampere or less may give a light equal to sixteen candles.

Other inventors use different materials for the filament. Thus Maxim carbonizes a strip of paper card-board; Swan, a cotton thread that has been subjected to a chemical treatment that makes it of the texture of parchment. As has before been stated, the resistance of carbon when in this form decreases when it is heated up to a certain limit, which is near to its point of vaporisation, and hence all incandescent lamps have less resistance when lighted than when cold. About ten such lamps of sixteen-candle power may be obtained from one horse-power, in which case the electro-motive force, which would be measured by finding the difference of potentials at the two terminals of the lamp when lighted, may be no more than one hundred volts, and need be no more with a large number of lamps than with one; for, unlike the arc system described, the current is not sent through the whole of the lamps seriatim, but the lamps are fixed in cross circuits somewhat like the steps upon a ladder.

That the limit of efficiency in electric lamps has not been reached by either the incandescent or the arc systems the following considerations will show:

When any substance like iron or carbon is heated it will begin to be visible as a luminous body when its temperature rises to 977° Fahr., as was shown by Dr. John W. Draper in 1847. The rays that are emitted at that temperature are of such a wave-length as to give the sensation of redness to the eye, and they take their place at one extreme of the visible spectrum. As the temperature is made to rise, shorter and shorter waves are emitted *in addition to those already* given out, until not only all of the rays constituting the visible spectrum, but also a great quantity beyond the other extremity of the visible spectrum, when the body is said to emit white light. In other words, a body that is white hot is giving off rays of all wave-lengths, while the eye is capable of being affected by only a small fraction of them, and the greatest amount of energy is spent in producing rays that have no luminous property whatever, and so far are wasted. If it were true that such radiations as are competent to produce the sensation of light could be produced only by such superheating of a substance, than there would be no remedy; but it is not true that heating is an essential condition for luminosity. The phenomena of phosphorescence and fluorescence, such as are exhibited by some worms and insects, by Bailman's luminous paint, decaying wood, by the residual gases in Gusèler tubes, and in the aurora, all prove that high temperature is not an essential for the production of light, and there is great room for invention and the cheapening of light-producers by working from this so-called chemical end of the spectrum rather than from the heat end.

HEATING.—The heat that may be developed in an electric arc is so great that the most refractory substances may be either fused or volatilized. It is the highest temperature that can be produced artificially. It has therefore been thought that electricity might in some way be used as a source of heat. As a competitor with other sources it is evidently a matter of either convenience or economy. For common purposes only economy need be considered. If a steam-engine is to furnish the electricity, the energy must be transformed several times, the series being heat, mechanical motion, electricity, heat; in each stage there is inevitably some loss and it is apparent that it will be more economical to use the fuel at once as a source of heat rather than after the energy has been lessened by a series of changes. This relative cost must remain to the disadvantage of electricity until some cheaper method of developing it can be found than by turning a wheel, which is not probable. It is not to be expected that electrical energy can be much cheapened from its present figures, for with such dynamos as we now have as much as 90 per cent. of the expended mechanical energy appears as electrical energy, a degree of efficiency that surpasses most other kinds of transformations. Even the turbine waterwheel does not exceed it. The monopoly of a good waterfall will always keep the cost of the supplied energy very near what it would be if supplied by a steam-engine. If one imagines that some one may discover some cheaper method of producing electricity than we at present possess he should remember that it would be a competitor with coal, and the price of the latter would fall. Available energy can nowhere be had for nothing.

ELECTRICAL STORAGE OF ENERGY.—Where an ordinary battery cell is furnishing a current of electricity the zinc is dissolved in the liquid, which is generally sulphuric acid forming sulphate of zinc. If, after that has taken place for a time, a current of electricity having a higher electro-motive force than the cell could give was sent through the cell in a direction opposed to that the cell would give, the sulphate of zinc would be decomposed and the zinc would be deposited upon the surface from which it was removed, when the cell would be again ready to furnish a current as at first. If instead of the ordinary cell two strips of sheet-lead be taken and rolled together, having a strip of coarse cloth between them to keep them from metallic contact, and these placed in a vessel containing dilute sulphuric acid, and a current of electricity passed between them as in the first case, hydrogen will be set free on one strip and oxygen on the other. The free oxygen at once combines with the lead of the strip, forming what is called lead peroxide, and this over the whole surface of the strip, which becomes physically unlike the other strip, a condition already explained as being essential for the development of electricity. When this coating has formed, if the cell be disconnected from the source of the current of electricity that has done the chemical work in it, and the two strips be connected by a wire—a strong current of electricity will be maintained until the original condition of the strips is attained. It should be noted that it is not the electricity that has been stored in the cell that is yielding the current, but it is the chemical energy of the cell that yields it, the chemical energy being the result of the original current. It is therefore not correct to speak of such a source of electricity as stored electricity. It is no more so than is an ordinary battery cell. It is more appropriate to speak of it as a *secondary cell*. Secondary cells are now generally made by filling the space between two plates of lead with the red lead of commerce, or by perforating the plates with holes and filling them with the same materials. The charging current deposits lead on one plate and peroxidizes the other. Such a cell has, when properly charged, an electro-motive force of about 2.25 volts, and as the plates are large—eight or ten inches square—and are so close together that the internal resistance is very small, less than the thousandth of an ohm, and is quite ignored in most computations. Such secondary cells are large and heavy when compared with ordinary battery cells. The industrial type weighs as much as fifty pounds, and frequently two or three times that amount. Their capacity is reckoned by the amount of electricity required to charge them to saturation. Now the quantity of electricity in a circuit is measured in amperes per second, and the unit is called a *coulomb*. A cell may require 500,000 coulombs or more to properly charge it. A dynamo that would give a current of twenty-five amperes would charge it in

$$\frac{500,000}{25} \text{ seconds} = 20,000 = 5\tfrac{1}{2} \text{ hours.}$$

The time of the discharge depends upon the resistance of the circuit provided. If it was allowed to discharge through a short, thick wire with such resistance as to admit a current of 25 amperes, it would obviously maintain that current for the same time that was required for charging it if there was no waste, but practically there is a rather large margin of waste, which, however, depends in a measure upon the external circuit provided for it. It could maintain a current of 10 amperes for about 14 hours under similar conditions:

$$\frac{500,000}{10} = 50,000 \text{ seconds} = 14 \text{ hours,}$$

but a cell charged with 500,000 coulombs will not give back but about 80 per cent. of its quantity, and hence would yield at that rate of 10 amperes for between 11 and 12 hours. As for the energy of the current, it must be remembered that it is measured by the product of the electro-motive force into the current strength, and hence the yield of such a cell will be at the rate of

$$\frac{2.25 \times 10}{746} = .03 \text{ of a horse-power.}$$

In other words, it would be able to do about 650,000 foot-pounds of work. One horse-power will in 11 hours do $33,000 \times 60 \times 11 = 21,780,000$ foot-pounds of work, and .03 of this is 653,400. Of course, such secondary cells may be coupled in series with the same advantages as the common battery cells, and thus the electro-motive force adjusted to any requirement. It is customary to indicate the requirements of an incandescent electric lamp by specifying the number of volts necessary to make it yield the stated candle-power. Thus a sixteen-candle-power lamp might require 100 volts to make it yield that amount of light. If its resistance was 100 ohms it would have a current strength of one ampere when lighted. Such a lamp would require not less than 45 secondary cells to make to give its sixteen-candle light. At the same time, however, the same number of cells could keep an indefinite number of such lamps lighted. Suppose there were an hundred, then each would be provided with the same electro-motive force, and the battery would be providing a current of 100 amperes per second, and would be exhausting at that rate. Hitherto secondary cells have not been durable. When they are perfected in that particular they will be most valuable adjuncts to many electrical enterprises.

ELECTRICAL TRANSMISSION OF ENERGY.—In an ordinary electrical circuit the energy is uniformly distributed in it, and one may utilize it at any point of the circuit, whether it be only a few feet or a hundred miles or more away. The common Morse telegraph is one device for the transmission of energy, for the latter is employed to move an armature to produce concerted signals. The same current might be employed to turn a wheel or produce any other kind of mechanical motion. Such a device as is illustrated in Fig. 5, was invented nearly fifty years ago by Dr. C. G. Page, and contains in principle the electric motors of to-day. Soon after the invention of the Grove battery attempts were made to propel boats and cars by electricity. Page in 1850 made an electric locomotive which with its battery weighed 10½ tons, and run it on a railroad in the neighborhood of Washington city at the rate of 19 miles per hour. He estimated the horse-power of his engine to be about 12, but we now know it was greatly overestimated. The writer tried in 1855 to make one magneto-electric machine furnish current to drive another one, but did not succeed. With some of the modern dynamos driven by steam- or water-power it is possible to drive another similar machine and get a yield in work of about 40 per cent. of the original expenditure. With such motors cars have been run, fields have been ploughed, and various other kinds of mechanical work performed. The distance to which it is possible to transmit energy in this way economically is not very great. A dynamo using sixteen horse-power has driven an electro-motor yielding six horse-power at a distance of 30 miles with an ordinary telegraph wire as a conductor. This is a recovery of 37.5 per cent. of the expended energy. In places where energy of water-power may be cheaply had, but where it is inconvenient to utilize it, it is possible to place a dynamo and lead a wire to the electro-motor in the convenient place. In this way it has been proposed to utilize the Falls of Niagara, where something like 9,000,000 horse-power is wasted; the conducting wires stretching out to various cities and towns where it is to be used.

Telpherage is the name given by the inventor, Prof. Fleming Jenkin, of Edwinboro, Scotland, to a new method for employing electrical energy for transportation. The scheme consists in utilizing a series of small motors to run upon an elevated conductor, each motor capable of doing from one to two horse-power, and dragging a series of vehicles loaded with two or three hundred pounds. A variety of ways for doing this have been invented. One of them is to provide two parallel conductors of stout enough wire to sustain the weight of the loading. These are to be strung upon the ends of a cross-arm fixed upon the top of a post like two telegraph-wires, but without the ordinary fixtures for insulation, as they would interfere with and prevent the rolling of a grooved wheel upon it, which is one of the conditions of telpherage. One of these wires is for the outgoing and the other for the returning telphers. The electricity for the circuit is provided at one end of the line by a suitable dynamo driven by steam- or water-power. The inventor describes a train as being 120 feet long and consisting of seven buckets and a locomotive motor, each of these when loaded weighing about 300 pounds. The buckets, or skips, as they are now called, hang belong the line on two V-shaped wheels, supported by arms that project out sideways so as to clear the supports at the posts. The locomotive motor also hangs below the line, and is driven by two specially-made grip-wheels. The advantages of such a system are said to be that within its limits of working it is independent of grade, for lines can be carried over hills and across rivers; that it can go round sharp curves, and the road will not be subject to deterioration and right of way will be the same as for telegraph wires. The capacity of such a road, reckoned at 15 hundredweight for each alternate section of 120 feet, is 16¼ tons per mile, which may be run at the rate of 5 miles per hour. This would deliver goods at the rate of 925 tons in ten hours.

OTHER ELECTRICAL PHENOMENA.—In pursuing his investigations in radiometry, Crookes observed that as the vacuum became more and more perfect the stratifications in an ordinary Geissler tube became fewer in number, being separated from each other by longer and still longer spaces, until none were apparent. When one of the terminals of a tube was made into a disk, or concave surface, the effect of the excitation of it was to impel the residual-gas molecules from it with greater energy than they possessed before; that is to say, its velocity in its free path was greater after impact with such electrified surface; and if its free path is long, compared with what it is in air at ordinary pressure, the energy of its movements, instead of being distributed as pressure, manifests itself in other ways, such as making a light paddle-wheel to revolve, or making a disk of platinum red hot, or developing fluorescent phenomena by impact upon the sulphide of calcium or aluminum. Such phenomena show that the molecules of the electrified surface are intensely agitated, as they would be if they were heated in any way; and the same reactions may be produced by heating the terminals in the tube in any way. In an ordinary radiometer the heated vanes beat off the molecules with greater energy than they were struck, and the reaction makes the vanes to revolve. If the free path in a tube is very long, and only one terminal be attached to the electrifying source, which is generally an induction coil, the result is that the gaseous molecules, impelled from the excited surface to a considerable distance, may be seen to return towards the same terminal. If both terminals are attached, the different potentials induce motions of the matter between them, but not in such a sense as to make a straight-moving molecule to go in a curved line.

The first law of motion holds good for a molecule as well as for a body of visible magnitude, and tubes are constructed to show that such molecular movements cannot be made to go round a corner. The fluorescent phenomena are such as appear when the same substances are subjected to radiant energy, especially such as has the wave-lengths of the blue end of the spectrum. Such an effect might be expected when it is known that the violence of the gaseous impacts is great enough to produce luminousness of the molecules themselves, which must set up corresponding undulations in the ether adjacent to each one, and all in proximity to substances so constituted as to absorb and transform them into longer-period waves. The phenomenon, then, is due, not to a peculiar electrical action, but to the heat-vibrations set up, as has been explained.

It has been stated that electricity is developed upon the simple contact of dissimilar substances. The ordinary apparatus for proving it is costly, and requires considerable skill to successfully use it. It may easily be done by connecting the terminals of a telephone to two different kinds of metals and connecting them by touching while the telephone is held to the ear, or, better still, if one of the metals be a tuning-fork, which, while it vibrates, is permitted to gently touch a piece of zinc or copper. The series of pulses will give a distinct sound. The changes in strength of an electric field may also be easily perceived by employing a telephone with a single wire, three or four feet long, attached to one terminal, and one end hanging in free air; any change in the electric field may be heard, especially if the changes recur with frequency enough to give a continuous sensation. By insulating the wire the end may be moved about as an explorer and thus the shape of the field determined. Prof. Trowbridge, of Harvard College, has been able to detect differences in potential in the ground produced by the buried terminals of a battery when the circuit was completed and broken by the pendulum of a seconds clock. The beats of the clock could be detected a mile away from the buried terminals by simply sticking the two terminals of a magneto-telephone into the ground at a distance of fifty feet apart. He suggests the possibility of thus telegraphing across a river by providing a battery-circuit on one side, with terminals a mile or two apart, and a short parallel telephonic-circuit upon the other side. Morse signals sent on the battery-circuit would be heard in the other circuit. Some years ago Edison discovered that friction between surfaces where one was an electrolitic substance was considerably lessened when an electric current was passing between them, and he has developed this into a new telegraphic method and a new telephonic method.

Mr. E. H. Hall has discovered that when a magnet is presented to a thin strip of metal, through which a current of electricity is passing, that the current is deflected. He has also discovered that the direction of the deflected current is different for different metals. Thus iron, cobalt, and zinc have the reaction in the same direction as the conductor itself would move if free to do so, while silver, copper, and some others deflect the current in the opposite direction. Sir William Thomson has declared this to be comparable with the greatest discoveries made by Faraday.

We are now familiar with a great variety of effects which electricity can produce in solids, liquids, gases, and even in vacuous space, and it is highly probable that other effects will be discovered, for no one thinks that the possibilities of electrical phenomena have been exhausted. But all should know that there are two kinds of possibilities—*qualitative* and *quantitative*. It is hazardous for any one to deny qualitative possibilities prior to experiment; neither so-called common sense nor mathematics have determining weight in the untested field. If they had been heeded in the past, some of the most important scientific and commercial interests would have had no beginning. On the other hand there is no better established fact in the whole range of science than what is known as the *conservation of energy*. That no collocation of matter can create it or annihilate it, and that it never appears in any form except an equal amount in some other form has been spent to produce it. A definite amount of electrical energy will do no more work than the same amount of heat energy or mechanical energy, yet there are some who expect a duty from some electrical device quite beyond that of the energy that is furnished to it. It follows that the possibilities of any electrical apparatus are quantitatively fixed by the supply of energy in any form that may be provided, and hence one may always know the maximum work possible. In all commercial enterprises it is energy that is paid for, and it is best that the sanguine investor should bear in mind that no more can be got out of an electrical machine than is put into it.

(A. E. D.)

ELECTROTYPING, the art of making copies in metal from types, stereotypes, or engravings, and making them ready for use in printing on paper or woven fabrics. While the art of making electrotypes appears to have been invented at almost the same time in London, St. Petersburg, and the United States, it was here that it was first brought to a commercial success. Joseph A. Adams of New York made and used an electrotype of an engraving in 1841. Daniel Davis of Boston first made and used electrotype plates in printing a book, and Mr. Wilcox of New York started the business of making electrotypes, or "electros," as they are commonly called. Mr. Wilcox and others made many improvements in the processes, and the art now ranks next to the art of printing.

The assembling of the types, leads, rules, engraved blocks, etc., or the composition of the form, is an art quite distinct from electrotyping. The composed matter, properly corrected, justified, and locked in the chase, comes to the electrotype-foundry in the same condition as if prepared for the printing-press, except that special pains must be taken to secure great evenness in the face or surface of the types and firmness and rigidity in the chase. On receiving the forms at the foundry they are washed in water if new and not much stained, and in naphtha or benzene if soiled with ink, and carefully planed to bring the face of the type to an even and uniform surface. After being dried, the forms are carefully coated with a thin film of black lead, laid on by means a soft brush. Meanwhile, pure yellow beeswax is melted and poured into a shallow pan having a raised edge and made of brass. This is the moulding-pan, and holds the sheet of wax in which an impression is to be taken from the form containing the types or blocks to be copied. In pouring the hot wax into the pan care is taken to have the pan level and to prevent the formation of cracks and bubbles in the wax. Should any appear, they are touched with a hot iron and melted down smooth. When in cooling the hot wax reaches just the required consistency, it is brushed over with black lead and placed with the type-form in a powerful press. Pressure is applied to force the type into the wax till an impression is obtained, the amount of pressure varying with the character of the work. There appears to be no exact limit of pressure, experience alone deciding what it shall be in each case. After the impression has been obtained the moulding-pan is removed from the press, and if, on examination, the impression appears to be perfect, the sheet of wax is cut from the pan and made ready for the electro-plating bath.

In the United States both hand and power tools are used in this part of the work. The first are—the steam-jacketed melting-kettle, a shallow brass pan called the moulding-case, and a steam-heated table on which the metallic plates on which the moulds are formed may be heated. The presses in which the impressions of the form are taken in the wax are of two kinds. Toggle-joint presses moved by screws controlled by hand-wheels are used for low powers, and hydraulic presses where more pressure is needed for deeper impressions. In all the presses the lift is upward, one style of press having a movable head for convenience in getting the work in place. Shelves or supporting rails are also provided at the side on which the forms or moulds may be placed. The toggle presses give a pressure of about 10 tons; the hydraulic presses will give as high as 80 tons.

Before the impressed mould can be placed in the electro-plating bath it must be "built up." By means of a hot iron tool called a "building-iron" and strips of wax the blank spaces in the mould between the pages or paragraphs are built up or raised in relief by flowing wax, precisely as in soldering soft metals, over the blank spaces.

On removing the form and mould from the press they are carefully separated, and the mould, now deeply impressed with the type and engravings, is made ready for the plating bath. By means of a hot iron, called the "building-iron," and strips of wax the blank parts of the mould are "built up" or raised by spreading the soft wax over the blanks. The mould is then thoroughly coated with a finer quality of black lead to give it a metallic surface, on which the current of electricity is conducted to start the deposit of copper which forms in the bath. Two processes are employed, the wet and the dry. In the dry way the moulds are placed in a machine having an iron grid that travels backward and forward on top of the machine. Above this is a brush fixed to a vibrating arm. An apron is arranged below to catch the waste lead, and a hood is placed over th tain the dust. In this machine the mould, well covered with lead, travels under the vibrating brush till it is covered with a thin and uniform film. After being coated with the dry powder the mould is removed from the machine and the superfluous dust is brushed off by hand. The next step is to clean out the fine dust lodged in the minute bowls or depressions of the letters, and the mould is submitted to a powerful blast of air, which effectually removes all the loose particles of black lead, leaving only a thin firm film on the mould.

By the wet process, which was invented by Silas P. Knight of New York, the moulds are placed on shelves in a chest and washed with a mixture of black lead and water delivered by a fine rose-nozzle.

The next step by the dry process is to "stop out" those parts of the mould that need not be copied in the electrotype. This is readily performed by painting over the blank portions with hot wax. The black lead is thus covered again with wax upon which the copper refuses to lodge. The face of the mould is then dusted over with fine powdered iron filings. Sulphate of copper is poured over the powder. The reaction that follows leaves a thin film of copper on the mould that serves to save time in the bath and forms a basis or starting-point on which the plating may begin. This operation may be repeated a number of times if a thicker film is required.

The electro deposition of the copper on the mould then follows. Batteries have been used until within the last few years, when the dynamo machines were introduced, and these machines are now being used in all electro-plating works. (See ELECTRICITY.) The copper film deposited in the bath is usually sufficiently thick for ordinary printing in from three to seven hours. For fine book and illustrated work longer time is given and a thicker film is obtained. The film is then taken from the bath and laid on an inclined board while hot water is poured over the back of the copper mould. This causes the wax to melt and frees the copper shell. The shell is then placed on an iron grid, and boiling potash is poured over it to remove all traces of the wax. It is then rinsed in clean water and brushed over with a solution of sal-ammoniac and chloride of zinc, and the face of the shell is brushed with a fine quality of French lac varnish.

The shell is then placed face downward in the backing-pan or metal dish in which it is to receive the metal backing. More of the solution of chloride of zinc is brushed over the back, and sheets of tin-foil are spread over the entire back, the tin serving as a solder to unite the copper with the type-metal. A pot of molten backing-metal (type-metal) has been in the mean while prepared, and the backing-pan containing the shell is then placed in the melting-pot and allowed to float on the hot metal till the tin-foil begins to melt, when it is removed and placed on a level table. The molten metal from the pot is then poured over the back of the shell till it is filled and brought up to the required thickness. When the metal sets the shell may be taken up. It is now an electrotype—a sheet of type-metal having a copper face bearing an exact copy of the types or blocks in the original form.

The electro is then washed and scoured, and taken to a circular saw and trimmed into shape to fit it for the printing-press. It is then rough finished by hand or brought into shape for the first cutting. It is then re-examined by the finisher, and sent to the planer for the final finishing work, sawing straight, bevelling the edges, and routing.

Wooden blocks are then fastened with screws to the back of the electro to make the work "type-high," or as high as ordinary type in a form. In this final work shaving, sawing, and planing machines, both hand and power, are used. In 1878, Michael Crane of New York received a patent for casting curved electrotypes, or copper shells designed to fit the cylinder of a rotary press. Curved forms, or "turtle-backs," used in newspaper presses, are now copied by electro-plating, and within a short time the forms used in printing curtains and on fabrics have been successfully reproduced in electrotypes. The work and tools here described are the same as may be found in any first-class electro-plating plant in the United States. (C. B.)

ELEVATOR, OR LIFT. An apparatus for hoisting or elevating goods or passengers from one level to another. In the United States the word elevator has come to mean all kinds of lifts and hoists, either movable or stationary, excepting those machines that come under the general names of *cranes*, *derricks*, *sheers*, and *winches*. It also includes structures for handling and storing grain and other loose material in bulk. An elevator may be a simple dumb-waiter moved by hand, or a vast structure hundreds of feet long, and holding many thousand bushels of grain. The high cost of labor and the value of land in cities has led to the invention of a great number of appliances to be used in lifting men and materials from one level to another. Some of these inventions are of considerable scientific interest, and have become of the greatest value in business and trade. (See EVANS, OLIVER.)

See Vol. XIV. p. 577 Am. ed. (p. 573 Edin. ed.).

Elevators may be broadly divided into two classes—those for handling and storing materials, as a grain elevator, and those used for simply lifting, as a hotel or warehouse elevator, car elevator, ice elevator, hod elevator, canal elevator, etc. The hoisting elevators are divided into classes according to the power employed, as steam elevators, pneumatic elevators, and hydraulic elevators.

Grain elevators.—While a grain elevator now means a structure for storing grain, the original meaning of the word was an apparatus for lifting grain, oats, flour, corn, meal, etc., from one part of a mill to another. This apparatus consisted essentially of an endless belt or band provided with caps or buckets fastened to one side. The band was carried over two wheels, pulleys or drums, one above and the other below, and when at work it continually travelled in one direction over the drums. Loose wheat, corn, or other grain placed over the lower drum was lifted by the cups or buckets. As each bucket moved upward it scooped up and raised a small quantity of the grain. On reaching the upper drum, the buckets passed over the drum and throwing out the loads into a bin prepared to receive it, passed down empty on the other side. This simple piece of mechanism makes the principal feature of a grain elevator, and gives its name to quite another thing. Grain elevators are built of wood, some having outside walls of brick as a protection against the weather and fire. Where brick walls are used, the main wooden structure within is practically a separate building. This is made necessary by the shrinkage of the wood-work, that in the mass amounts to several inches, and which would tend to crush the brick walls, if connected directly with them. When brick is not used the outer surface of the wood-work is usually covered with slates. As an elevator is essentially a place of storage it is constructed upon a somewhat peculiar system. The first or lower story is formed of massive timbers set up on end and designed to form columns for supporting the bins above. Aisles are arranged between these columns for railroad tracks for the cars that enter the building, and for the conveyers used to move the grain horizontally from one part of the building to another. Upon these columns are laid planks, one over the other, and crossing each other at right angles. Planks are laid one over the other in this way till the intended height is reached. The structure thus becomes a honey-combed mass, with solid wooden walls crossing at right angles, and leaving square or oblong spaces between the walls. These spaces or wells extend from the top to the bottom of the mass and form the bins. The bins are usually from ten to twenty feet square, or ten by twenty feet, and sixty feet deep. The lower end of each is provided with a hopper and gate for taking the contents out from below whenever desired. At the top all the bins are open, the roof of the building forming a hood over them all. At different points in the structure are placed the elevators proper, or, as they are sometimes called, the "lofters." These are endless belts studded with buckets, and they are usually of great size and strength. The material of the belt is india-rubber reinforced by heavy canvas. In an elevator at Milwaukee, 280 feet long and 80 feet wide, with a storage capacity of 1,500,000 bushels, the elevator belt is 280 feet long and 36 inches wide. The drums over which the belt turns are 140 feet apart, and the belt lifts, when all the buckets are full, 25 bushels at once. The elevator discharges the grain in a continuous stream into a weighing bin at the top-story of the building. After weighing in large lots, the grain is diverted by means of movable spouts into a bin ready to receive it. The grain falls by its own weight into the bottom of the bin, from which it may be drawn for delivery to car or boat.

In connection with the elevation of the grain, there is also in all elevators cleaning machinery. This is of two kinds—sieves or riddles, over which the grain flows in a stream, while the sieves are violently shaken from side to side, and blowers. The heavier refuse, sand, straw, etc., is extracted by the sieves, and the lighter dust is blown out by allowing the grain to fall in a thin film past the inlet of a powerful exhaust. The waste, after passing through the fan, is thrown out through pipes in the lower part of the building.

Elevators are placed beside railroads for storing grain for local consumption, or beside docks for unloading cars, storage and reloading into canal-boats or vessels, or from vessels into cars. In unloading grain from cars, the grain is shoveled out of the car into pits beside the track and in which the lower drum of the belt is placed. This unloading is usually done from the tracks under the building. Where elevators are placed on docks and the grain is raised from the holds of canal-boats or vessels, a movable apparatus, called an elevator leg, must be used. The belt and its drums are placed within a wooden frame-work, pivoted at the top and supported by ropes, and by this means the belt is swung outside of the building and lowered into the hold of the canal-boat. When the work is finished the elevator leg is drawn back into the building and protected by a long narrow door that covers the slot in the wall through which it moves.

In transferring grain from one bin to another a number of appliances are used. If the elevator is a small one, the grain is simply led by means of spouts from the bottom of the bin to the foot of the lofter. It is then raised to the top of the building and diverted by means of the spouts into another bin. Grains are mixed in the same way by allowing the contents of two bins to run into the elevator, and then raising the mixture and placing it in another bin. In small elevators the grain for delivery is drawn from the bins and placed in bags. To convey these bags to the door, a belt conveyer is sometimes used. This is an endless belt stretched over drums and laid down flat and near the floor. At intervals are rollers for supporting the belt as it moves. The loaded bags of grain are thrown upon this belt while it is moving rapidly, and are moved or conveyed to the door. As the belt passes over the last drum, the bags are shot off by the momentum into a spout that leads to the wagon in the street below. This same system of horizontal belts or conveyers is also used to move grain in bulk from one part of an elevator to another. The belts are of great strength and are often many hundreds of feet long, and move with great rapidity. The grain falling on a belt from the spout of a bin, or from an elevator, is carried along in a solid stream till the point of discharge is reached. As the belt turns over the last drum, the grain shoots ahead into a spout prepared to receive it. By breaking the belt at different points (by having a series of short belts in line) the grain can be taken off at a number of different points. Another form of conveyer consists of a round pipe of wood or metal, in which turns a long screw. The turning of the screw forces the grain along the pipe, and to draw it off, openings, closed by valves, are placed at intervals along the pipe. Belt conveyers are placed at the bottom of stationary elevators under the bins. Screw conveyers are sometimes placed in the upper story to move grain from the lofter to the distant bins. They are also used in the holds of floating elevators.

The largest grain elevator in the world is said to be at Brooklyn, N. Y. It is known as Dow's, and forms a conspicuous landmark in the southern part of the city. This elevator consists of nine lofty brick stores, each containing a large number of bins, and a long wooden structure extending to the end of the dock below the stores. Above the stores are three wooden towers, each containing an elevator. On the dock is another tower with two elevator legs, and in the second story of the long building are four lines of belt conveyers. The grain is lifted from the canal-boats at the dock, weighed, screened, blown, and delivered upon the conveyers. It moves on these up the dock and under the main stores to one of the three lofters. It is then raised to the top of one of the towers and distributed by means of long pipes, run on the outside of the towers, to the bins. This elevator, when fully employed, can receive, store, and deliver 60,000 bushels of grain in 60 minutes.

The delivery of grain in bulk from elevators into cars or vessels is through hinged pipes leading from the bottom of the bins through the walls into the holds of the vessels that lay longside.

Floating elevators are wooden towers built in the hull of the vessel, containing one or more elevator legs. The object is not so much to store grain as to transfer it. They are usually placed between a ship to be loaded with grain and a canal-boat. The elevator leg is placed in the hold of the canal-boat and the pipe is lowered into the hold of the ship and the grain is elevated, passed through the screens and blowers, elevated again, and poured into the ship's hold. In some floating elevators two legs are used, one being much longer than the other, and intended to reach over one canal-boat to another outside. Grain is also stored in the hold of the elevator, and screw conveyers are used to move the grain from one part of the hold to another. The floating elevators are usually provided with a marine engine and propeller for moving them from place to place. They are all self-contained, carrying their motive power for the machinery on the deck in the rear of the tower. Floating elevators are largely used in New York harbor, where they form a singular feature of the scene along the docks.

Coal elevators.—Next in point of size and capacity, in dealing with large quantities of loose material, are the coal elevators. While they are called "coal dumps" they are strictly elevators, because the coal is elevated and delivered through pipes, and because they are practically large hoisting-machines. Examples may be seen at Bergen Point, Jersey City, and Hoboken, near New York. The cars loaded with coal arrive at tidewater only a few feet above high tide, and to unload the coal into vessels without handling, the cars must be raised above the vessel's decks. To accomplish this, elevated structures are built upon the docks and connected with the railroad by means of inclined planes. Tracks are laid up the plane and on top of the elevator, and the cars are drawn up the incline by means of wire ropes. Pipes or chutes are provided for directing the coal into the holds of the vessels in the docks below. The cars are brought over the upper ends of these chutes and the loads are shot out into the vessels. The empty cars return by gravity down the incline. Where coal is to be taken from vessels and transferred to cars, as in many New England ports, coal elevators are used to both elevate and store the coal. The coal is hoisted by buckets to the top of the elevators and stored in bins or "pockets" (hence the word "coal-pocket"), or shot through pipes into cars under the elevators.

Ice elevators.—Between the grain elevator and the simple hoisting-machine or lift is a class of machines allied to both. In these, of which the ice elevator is an example, a chain, belt, or strap, of metal or fabric, is carried over two drums, and armed with spikes, claws, or boards. In the ice elevator the lower drum is placed under water and the upper drum at the top of the ice-house. The drums are turned by steam-power, and the chain, armed with spikes arranged in pairs, traverses up one side and down the other between an inclined railway. The cakes of ice are floated over the lower drum and are caught in the chain and dragged up the incline on the rails. Arriving at the top, the cakes slide off and run down inclined ways or tracks to the bottom of the ice-house. Similar apparatus are used to raise loose cotton in cotton-mills, and clay, drugs, and other loose materials, in mills and other works.

Car elevators.—Inclined planes or railways, where the cars are hoisted and lowered over the plane by means of ropes, are not strictly elevators. A car elevator is a hoisting-machine for lifting the car bodily upon a platform. An example can be seen at Hoboken, New Jersey. At this place there is a rocky bluff between the streets, built on the low land near tidewater and the streets on the hill. To connect the horse railroad systems of the two parts of the city an elevator is used to raise the cars and horses. An inclined railroad 430 feet long, with two tracks, is built upon the hillside. The incline has a rise of $104\frac{1}{2}$ feet, and is closely connected with the tracks above and below. At the lower end the two tracks of the incline run into a deep pit in the ground. At the upper end they enter the upper part of a building containing the engines, hoisting apparatus, etc. On each track is a large car having six wheels, one side of the car being higher than the other, so as to make the top level. Three steel ropes are attached to each car. Two enter the building and pass round the drum of a winding engine. The third rope passes over two large wheels at the top of the incline, and is connected with the other car. By this arrangement one car balances the other, one moving up while the other moves down. Tracks are laid on top of each platform. On arriving at the elevator the horse-car is driven upon the platform and locked upon the tracks, and the gates are closed. At a signal from the attendant the engine is started, and the car, horses, and passengers are raised or lowered to the other level, where the horse-car is driven off and goes on its way.

Passenger and freight elevators, called in England "lifts," are very largely used in the United States. They include everything in the way of a hoisting apparatus that has a platform or car moved up and down in a well or hoistway. The well is also sometimes called the elevator shaft or hatchway. Elevator shaft appears to be the most common name. If the car or cage is an open platform, and used only for freight, it is called the platform. When used for passengers, it is called the car, or sometimes the elevator.

The most simple form of freight elevator is the dumb-waiter, used in dwellings and apartment-houses. It consists of an enclosed shaft, in which is suspended by a rope some simple box or cage, with sometimes a shelf hinged at the back. The rope passes over a pulley at the top of the shaft, and carries a counterweight, moving in an enclosed shaft, at the other end. The cage or elevator is drawn up or down by means of rope. In apartment-houses signal bells are provided for calling attention to the elevator from the street floor.

Hod elevators, or builders' elevators, are open platforms suspended by a rope, and designed to run in guides placed in the open stairways of new buildings. Steam-power is often used to raise the platform. Another form of builders' elevator consists of an endless chain carried over a pulley, supported by wooden horses placed on the upper floor of a building in process of erection. The lower end of the chain passes over a pulley in the cellar or hangs loosely. The hods, filled with brick or mortar, are hooked on to the chain, and are thus carried up or down. These hod elevators are usually operated by hand-power, two men turning a crank at the top. As the floors are raised the chain is lengthened, and the upper pulley is raised to the next floor.

The simplest form of freight elevator (beyond a rope-tackle and fall) is an open platform suspended between guides in an open shaft or hatchway. The wire rope used to lift the platform is wound round a drum connected by gearing with pulleys, over which belts are taken from the source of power in the building. A hand-rope suspended in the shaft and passing through the platform is used to control a belt-shifting apparatus. On pulling the rope from the car the belts are changed, and the power is applied to the winding-drum. Another movement of the rope shifts the belts to cause the platform to move the other way. A second rope or hand-chain is provided for stopping the car.

The drum-gearing and belt-shifting device may be placed on any story of the building, and is usually suspended from the ceiling, so as to be out of the way. In one form of this apparatus the winding-drum is connected with the shaft bearing the pulleys by means of a worm-gear. This gear, instead of being cylindrical and straight, is curved, to fit the surface of the circular gear. By this arrangement a firmer hold is secured, as more teeth are brought into play at once, and giving opportunity for greater speed and a more rapid motion.

When steam-power is used exclusively for hoisting, as in warehouses and retail stores, the power is applied directly to the elevator. For this purpose a variety of hoisting-engines are used. Some of them are simply double or single horizontal engines connected directly with a winding-drum. The power is only used to lift the load, descending loads being brought down by their weight; held in check by a brake or by the engine. In some instances, however, the engine is reversed by an ordinary link-motion, and the power is used both ways.

One of the best forms of engines for hoisting heavy freight is the double upright engine connected by a belt with the winding-drum. The platform is raised or lowered by means of a hand-rope. This is connected with a lever that controls a three-way valve admitting steam to both cylinders. The movement of the valve starts the engine in one direction, another movement stops it, and a third reverses the engine and starts it in the new direction. These engines all have brakes and safety appliances.

Hydraulic elevators.—The general use of water under pressure in cities, and the introduction of simple forms of steam-pumps, has led to the employment of water-power in elevators. These are called hydraulic elevators. They may be divided into three classes, according to the way in which the power is applied. The first of these are simple hydraulic lifts, in which the car or platform is placed over the hydraulic cylinder, and resting directly on the piston-rod. In the second class the car is supported by a rope, the rope being connected by means of a pulley-block with the piston-rod. In the third class a series of pulleys are employed, so that a slow movement of the piston-rod may be converted into a rapid movement in the car.

Hydraulic lifting elevators.—These elevators are hydrostatic presses. An upright cylinder is set up in the lower part of the building under the elevator shaft. The piston-rod passes through the upper cylinder head and supports the car. Water under pressure is admitted below the piston, and its upward movement raises the car. For lofty buildings the cylinder is made telescopic, expanding as it is filled with water, and thus lifting the load to a greater height. The objections to this kind of hydraulic elevator are its tendency to leak at the telescopic joints, and the deep excavation that must be made under the building to hold the cylinder. For short lifts, say of twenty feet or less, and where power is of more value than speed, this class of elevator is very useful. It is often used in docks and in iron and steel furnaces, and in warehouses to raise goods from the basement to the street. They are then called sidewalk elevators. Where the hydrostatic press is used to lift a tank containing water, in which a boat may float, it is called a canal elevator. An example can be seen at Anderton, England.

Hydraulic hoisting elevators.—In this class the car is supported by a wire rope that is connected with a simple form of hydraulic engine. Two methods are used in connecting the rope with the source of power. In one it is direct, in the other sheaves pulleys are employed. In the first plan the cylinder is placed upright, and stands in a well or shaft adjoining the elevator. The rope is fastened to the top of the car, and is carried upward to a pulley at the top of the shaft. It then passes downward to a pulley at the upper end of the piston-rod of the hydraulic cylinder, and through this upward to the top of the building, where it is securely fastened. The cylinder is of comparatively small diameter, and is as long as one-half the whole height of the lift. If the pressure of the street mains is sufficient, the water may be used directly in the cylinder. If the pressure is low, two tanks must be provided, one at the top of the building and one in the cellar. A steam-pump must also be provided to lift the water from the lower to the upper tank. If the tanks are used, a pipe is laid from the upper tank to a three-way valve near the bottom of the cylinder. From this valve pipes extend to the top of the cylinder and from the top of the cylinder to the bottom, and also from the bottom to the lower tank. Supposing the car to be at the bottom of the shaft the piston will be at the top of the cylinder, resting on a column of water that fills the entire cylinder below it. On pulling the rope the exhaust-pipe at the lower end of the cylinder is opened, and the water is permitted to escape into the lower tank (or the drain, if the street mains are used direct). At the same time the water from the upper tank is admitted to the cylinder at the top, above the piston, and by its pressure forcing it downward, and thus raising the car. When the car is at the top the piston has sunk to the bottom of the cylinder, which is now filled with water. A pull on the hand-rope changes the valves, closing the exhaust, shutting off the supply from the upper tank and opening the connection between the upper and lower ends of the cylinder. The weight of the load now tends to lift the piston, and under this influence the water moves through the pipe from the upper to the lower end of the cylinder. As this pipe is small, the water cannot be transferred from above to below the piston very rapidly, and this tends to retard the too rapid descent of the elevator. The apparatus is now in the same position as before, one complete movement of the elevator consuming only enough water to fill the cylinder once. To counterbalance the weight of the car, weights are placed in the cylinder above the piston. Automatic devices are provided for stopping the car at top and bottom of the shaft. The column of water at all times, above or below the piston, also acts as a safety-brake to prevent the car from falling when stopped at the top, or at any floor.

By an improvement recently applied to this class of elevators, they can be operated without the aid of an attendant. Electrical connections are made with the interior of the car and with the door on each floor with the valve of the cylinder. A small hydraulic motor, controlled by an electro-magnet, is used to give sufficient power to move the valve. On pressing a button in the car the motor is started and the valves set to lift the car. On pressing a second button it is stopped, while pressure on a third reverses the motion. Automatic lock... applied to all the doors of the well ...nnot be opened from the outside till the car arrives opposite the door, nor can the car be moved till after the door has been closed again.

In the other plan of connecting the car with the hydraulic engine the cylinder is short, and to obtain speed and a larger movement of the car, multiplying sheaves are employed. In one form of elevator the cylinder is upright, and a cross-head or massive bar is placed at the end of the piston-rod, and from each end of this is hung a series of sheaves. Below, on each side of the cylinder, is second pair of sheaves, and the lifting ropes are taken through these. By this arrangement a movement of the piston of one foot causes the car to travel five, ten, or more feet, according to the ratio between the multiplying sheaves.

In another arrangement of this system the cylinder is horizontal, and the cross-head carrying the sheaves travels back and forth upon ways or guides.

Hydro-pneumatic system.—In this system the lifting apparatus is the same as in hydraulic elevators just described, the difference being in the employment of compressed air in connection with the hydraulic cylinder. Two tanks are prepared, either in one construction divided by a diaphragm, or placed close together, and, in addition to the hydraulic pump, an air-compressor is provided, the compressor being directly connected with the same motor that operates the pump. The design is to compress air in a tank to a considerable pressure, and to employ this pressure to move the motor. When it is desired to lift the elevator the rope is pulled by the attendant, and a valve is opened that admits the compressed air from the tank in which it is stored into the tank containing the water. Immediately after the valve is opened admitting the water into the hydraulic cylinder. The pressure of the air upon the surface of the water in the tank drives it into the cylinder, and thus the air-pressure is the indirect motive power. When the load is lifted the rope is pulled, and the air-valve and the water-valve are closed, and the piston stands still, the water in the cylinder acting as a firm support for the elevator. To lower the car the rope is pulled again, when valves are opened, allowing the compressed air over the water in the tank to pass into the cylinder above the piston. The hydraulic valve is, at the same time, opened to permit the water in the cylinder to return to the tank. It will be seen that the pressure is thus balanced on each side of the cylinder, the pressure of the air being equal to that of the water, the weight of the car serving to destroy this balance in part, and to move the piston till all the water is driven back to the tank, and the mechanism is restored to its original position. The air above the piston may be then exhausted into the atmosphere, or into the air compressor. As it has considerable pressure it reduces the power needed to work the compressor, and it is returned to its storage tank in an economical manner. By this arrangement the air is used over again continuously, and free air is required only to compensate for waste. By an ingenious arrangement of the valves the pressure of the air controls the steam compressor. The compressor starts automatically whenever the pressure in the tank is reduced, and continues to work till the maximum pressure is reached, when it stops automatically. By this arrangement the amount of the load controls the consumption of water used and power required. A light load only demands a light pressure on the water, and when enough pressure is obtained the elevator starts, and no more power is consumed. This form of elevator is reported to be very rapid in its movement.

Automatic elevator.—In a new form of elevator intended only for light freight, the hand-rope is replaced by a fixed rod. This rod can be moved up or down to start or stop the car by means of hand-levers placed at every floor. The load is put on the car and the lever is moved, when the car travels up or down alone to its destination. At each floor clogs or stops are placed in the rod, and by rotating the rod one of these stops may be brought into a position to meet the car. A lever is provided on each floor for rotating the rods and also an indicator for showing which stop is brought into action. The moving car meets the stop and lifts the rod, thus bringing itself to a stop. An alarm is also sounded to announce its arrival.

Safety appliances.—The universal use of elevators in the United States has brought out a great number of appliances for preventing the fall of the elevator in case the rope breaks, to prevent overwinding and to close the hatchways (to prevent the spread of fire and accidents) when the elevator is not in use. To prevent overwinding a stop is placed on the hand-rope, and the car in rising meets this and pulls on the rope, and thus stopping the engine or shutting off the water. Brakes are employed in all steam-engines to hold the car in one position, and in hydraulic elevators the column of water in the cylinder forms a secure support for the car. For checking the fall of the car, in case the rope breaks, a variety of clutches and stop-motions are employed. Some of these are controlled by springs that, as soon as the strain on the rope is slackened, cause bolts to fly out and engage in teeth placed on the guide-posts of the elevator shaft. Brakes are also brought into play by governors. A too rapid descent of the car throws out the arms of the governor and this puts on the brake. Cams, eccentrics, and wedges, designed to bite or clasp the guides, are also used. Automatic devices for opening and closing the hatchway covers are also largely used. (C. B.)

ELGIN, a city of Kane county, Illinois, is on Fox River, 36 miles W. of Chicago, on the Chicago and North-western Railroad, the Chicago, Milwaukee, and St. Paul Railroad, and the Fox River Branch of the former. It has 6 hotels, 3 banks (2 national), 3 weekly and 3 daily newspapers, 12 churches, 9 schools, and an academy. There is also a hospital for the insane, with fine building and grounds. The most important industry is the manufacture of watches, which is conducted on a very extensive scale by the National Watch Company. There are also 2 foundries, a large book-publishing-house, canning-works, flour-mills, lathe-manufactory, agricultural-implement-manufactory, etc. Fox River is here crossed by 2 bridges, and furnishes abundant water-power for the industries of the place. Besides being an important manufacturing city, it is the centre of the dairy interests of Illinois. Elgin was settled in 1835 and incorporated in 1855. Population, 17,429.

ELIOT, CHARLES WILLIAM, an American educator, was born in Boston, Mass., March 20, 1834. He was educated at the Boston Latin School and Harvard College, graduating in 1853. In the next year he was tutor in mathematics, and in 1858 he was made assistant professor of mathematics and chemistry and held this position till 1863. He was professor of analytical chemistry in the Massachusetts Institute of Technology from 1865 to 1869, and in the latter year was elected president of Harvard University. In this position his career has been distinguished by administrative ability, zeal in the cause of higher education, and an earnest effort to make the college curriculum perfectly fitted to prepare the students for the highest demands of American life and citizenship. His influence has reached far beyond the bounds of Harvard, and has stimulated into new vigor every institution for higher education in the United States. His annual reports as president have been eagerly sought and read by all friends of college education, and, though their suggestions have been criticised by the more conservative, their ability has been unquestioned. Besides these, reports and some essays on educational topics and two manuals of chemistry.

"ELIOT, GEORGE." See CROSS, MARY ANN.

ELIOT, JOHN, D.D. (1754-1813), an American Congregationalist minister and antiquarian, was born in Boston, May 31, 1754. He graduated at Harvard in 1772, studied theology, and was ordained pastor of the New North Church, Boston, as successor to his father, Nov. 3, 1779. He remained in this charge till his death. With his friend, Rev. Dr. Jeremy Belknap, he founded the Massachusetts Historical Society and contributed liberally to its collections and library. He was also a member of the American Academy of Arts and Sciences. His publications are chiefly the result of original research in New England history and biography; among them are an *Ecclesiastical History of Massachusetts and Plymouth*, and an *Account of John Eliot*. He also published a *New England Biographical Dictionary* (1809). He died at Boston, Feb. 14, 1813.

ELIOT, SAMUEL, LL.D., an American teacher and historian, was born in Boston, Dec. 22, 1821. He graduated at Harvard College in 1839 with the highest honors, spent two years in a counting room, and then went to Europe. While in Rome in 1843 he formed a plan of writing a history of liberty, and after his return published in Boston in 1847 a portion of his projected work, in which he treated of early European liberal movements. In 1849 he issued two volumes on *The Liberty of Rome*, which appeared again in revised form in 1853 under the title *The History of Liberty, Part I: The Ancient Romans*. Two volumes on *The Early Christians* were added in the same year.

part of the city, and Elizabethport, which lies on the bay and sound. The city is handsomely laid out, with broad, regular, and well-shaded streets. It is at the junction of several branch railways with the main line of the Pennsylvania Railroad (United Railroads of New Jersey) and of the Central Railroad of New Jersey. Elizabeth is noted for its schools and the wealth and refinement of its society. Elizabethport is an important point for the shipment of coal, and is the site of large manufactories, including potteries, foundries, extensive sewing-machine-works, etc. Street-railways connect the city with Newark. Elizabeth has county and city buildings, an orphan asylum, an old ladies' home, a high school, an academy, 2 young ladies' boarding-schools, besides 2 Catholic academies, 4 parish schools, and 3 convents. There are 6 public-school buildings. The banks are 5 in number (3 national), and 3 daily and weekly newspapers. The city was chartered in 1865. Population in 1870, 20,832; in 1880, 28,229; and in 1890, 37,670.

ELIZABETH CITY, a port of entry and the county-seat of Pasquotank co., N. C., is on Pasquotank River, 44 miles S. of Norfolk, Va., with which it is connected by the Elizabeth City and Norfolk Railroad. It has 3 hotels, 2 banks, 1 daily and 3 weekly newspapers, 5 churches, and 3 schools. It has 3 grist-mills, 4 saw-mills, a planing-mill, a cotton-factory, a sash- and door-factory, a carriage-factory, and 2 ship-yards. It was settled in 1800, and incorporated in 1850. Its property is valued at $1,500,000, and it is free of debt. Population, 4150.

ELIZABETHTOWN, the county-seat of Hardin co., Ky., is on the Louisville, Nashville, and Great Southern Railroad, 42 miles S. of Louisville, and is the eastern terminus of the Elizabethtown and Paducah Railroad. It has a fine court-house, a bank, 2 hotels, 8 churches, a weekly newspaper, a saw-mill, and flour-mill. It is one of the oldest towns in the State. Population, 2250.

ELKHART, a city of Elkhart co., Ind., is at the confluence of the St. Joseph and Elkhart Rivers, 101 miles E. of Chicago. It is on the Lake Shore and Michigan Southern Railroad, at the junction of the Air-Line Division with the main road, and on the Cincinnati, Wabash, and Michigan Railroad. There are 5 iron bridges over the adjoining streams. Elkhart has a fine city-hall, 4 hotels, 2 national banks and 1 other bank, 2 daily and 3 weekly newspapers, 12 churches, and 6 fine school-houses. The industrial works comprise a musical-instrument-factory, grist-mills and planing-mills, 4 paper-mills, 2 board-mills, 2 carriage-factories, a harrow-factory, 2 starch-mills, a foundry, and the car and locomotive-shops of the Lake Shore Railroad. The city was settled in 1832 and incorporated as a city in 1875. It is well laid out and presents a handsome appearance. It is lighted with gas and has a park. The property is valued at $3,000,000; its public debt is only $5000. Population.

and minor industries. It was incorporated in 1858. Population, 3450.

ELLERY, WILLIAM (1727-1820), an American statesman, was born at Newport, R. I., Dec. 22, 1727. He was the son of Lieut. Gov. Ellery, and graduated at Harvard College in 1747. He was at first a merchant, but in 1768 was made clerk of a court, and in 1770 began to practise law. In 1776 he was chosen a delegate from Rhode Island to the Continental Congress, and signed the Declaration of Independence and the Articles of Confederation. He continued to be a member of Congress till 1785, except in the years 1780 and 1782, and served on the marine and other important committees. He suffered great loss of property while the British occupied Newport in 1777. In 1786 he was chosen by Congress commissioner of the Continental loan-office for Rhode Island, and was afterwards chief-justice of the supreme court of that State. He exerted himself to procure the abolition of slavery throughout the United States. In 1790 he was appointed by Pres. Washington collector of Newport, which position he held till his death, Feb. 15, 1820.

ELLET, CHARLES, JR. (1810-1862), an American engineer, was born at Penn's Manor, Bucks co., Pa., Jan. 1, 1810. He was brought up on a farm, but, obtaining employment in the construction of the Chesapeake and Ohio Canal, at first as a rodman, he turned his attention to mathematics and engineering. He went to Europe, and studied at Paris privately, following the course of the Ecole Polytechnique. Returning to America, he was employed on the Utica and Schenectady Railroad, then on the Erie, and afterwards was chief-engineer of the James River and Kanawha Canal. In 1842 he planned and built the wire suspension-bridge across the Schuylkill River at Fairmount, Philadelphia, the first structure of its kind in this country, and considered at the time a triumph of engineering skill. In 1845 he announced that a railroad suspension-bridge could be built across the Niagara River below the Falls, and two years later planned and constructed the preliminary bridge of 759 feet span, the wire cables of which were afterwards used in the bridge built there in 1855 by John A. Roebling. In 1846 Mr. Ellet became president of the Schuylkill Navigation Company, and was afterwards engaged in important engineering works. In 1848 he built a suspension-bridge of 1010 feet span over the Ohio at Wheeling, which was blown down in 1854. (See article BRIDGES, Vol. I., pp. 701-41.) After improving the navigation of the Kanawha River Mr. Ellet carefully examined the channels of the Ohio and Mississippi Rivers, and prepared an elaborate work on the navigation of those rivers. He was one of the first to advocate the use of steam-rams, proposing to the Russian government in 1854 thus to destroy the fleet attacking Sebastopol. At the commencement of the Civil War in 1861 he presented his plans to the United States government, but received no encouragement from the Navy Department. He submitted to Gen. McClellan a plan for the capture of the Confederate army, and when it was rejected wrote two pamphlets in which he severely criticised that general's conduct of the war. After the famous conflict of the Monitor and the Merrimac in March, 1862, he was commissioned by the War Department as colonel of engineers, and sent to protect the Mississippi gunboats against the Confederate rams. In a short time he turned nine powerful light-draught steamboats into rams, which were placed under his command. With four of these he joined the fleet under Commodore Davis, and on June 6, 1862, when they approached Memphis, eight Confederate gunboats and rams came out to meet them, while thousands of spectators gathered on the shore to watch "the battle of the rams." In the end seven Confederate vessels were destroyed or disabled, and only one escaped. The next day the city of Memphis was surrendered by the civil authorities During the battle Col. Ellet was shot in the knee by a musket-ball, and, being already in feeble health, died from the effects of the wound, at Cairo, Ill., June 21, 1862. His publications were—*An Essay on the Laws of Trade* (1839); a paper on the *Physical Geography of the Mississippi Valley, with Suggestions as to the Improvement of the Navigation of the Ohio and other Rivers*, published by the Smithsonian Institute (1851); *The Mississippi and Ohio Rivers, with Plans for the Protection of the Delta from Inundation* (1853); a pamphlet on *Coast and Harbor Defences, or the Substitution of Steam Battering-Rams for Ships of War* (1855). He also published many scientific papers.

ELLICOTT, CHARLES JOHN, D.D., an English bishop, was born at Whitwell, near Stamford, April 25, 1819. He was educated at Oakham and Stamford Schools, and at St. John's College, Cambridge, where he graduated with honors in 1841, and became Fellow of his college. He obtained the first member's prize in 1842, and the Hulsean prize in 1843. In 1848 he was appointed to the small living of Pilton, in Rutlandshire, which he held until 1858, when he was appointed professor of divinity in King's College, London. In 1859 he became Hulsean lecturer, and in 1860 Hulsean professor of divinity at Cambridge; in 1861 was made dean of Exeter, and in 1863 bishop of Gloucester and Bristol. His *Critical and Grammatical Commentaries* upon the Epistles of St. Paul, which began to appear in 1854, and his *New-Testament Commentary* (1877), have put him into the front rank of biblical scholars. He is also the author of *Historical Lectures on the Life of our Lord Jesus Christ* (1860), which formed the Hulsean lectures for 1859. He was one of the company of revisers of the English New Testament.

ELLIOTT, ROBERT WOODWARD BARNWELL, D. D., an American bishop, was born at Beaufort, S. C., Aug. 16, 1840. He graduated in 1861 at South Carolina College, and was an officer in the Southern army throughout the civil war. He served (1861-62) on the staff of Gen. Lawton, as an aide-de-camp; was wounded in the second battle of Bull Run; and was adjutant-general to Gen. McLaws, 1864-65. He took deacon's orders in the Episcopal Church in 1868; became a presbyter in 1871, and in 1874 was consecrated bishop of Western Texas, having his cathedral church at San Antonio.

ELLIOTT, STEPHEN, LL. D. (1771-1830), an American botanist, was born at Beaufort, S. C., Nov. 11, 1771. He graduated at Yale College in 1791, and devoted himself to literature, natural science, and the cultivation of his estate. In 1796 he was elected to the legislature, and continued to be a member till 1812 when he became president of the State bank. In 1813 he founded the Literary and Philosophical Society, and in 1814 delivered the first annual address before it. In furtherance of its object he delivered a gratuitous course of lectures on botany. In 1819 he received the degree of LL. D. from Yale College, and in 1820 was elected president of South Carolina College, but declined the position. His most elaborate work was *The Botany of South Carolina and Georgia* (2 vols., 1821–24), in preparing which he was greatly assisted by James McBride, M. D. (1784–1817), of Pineville, S. C. Dr. Elliott aided in establishing the medical college of South Carolina at Charleston in 1825, and was appointed professor of natural history and botany. In 1827, in conjunction with Hugh S. Legaré, he established the *Southern Review*, for which he wrote in all thirteen articles. He died suddenly at Charleston, March 28, 1830. He left a number of works in manuscript, and his collection of objects in natural history was one of the most extensive of his time.

ELLIOTT, STEPHEN, D. D. (1806–1866), an American bishop, son of the preceding, was born at Beaufort, S. C., Aug. 31, 1806. His father having removed to Charleston in 1812, he was taught there by Mr. Hurlburt, and entered Harvard College in 1822, where he remained only a year. He graduated at South Carolina College in 1825, studied law, and began practice in Charleston. He also contributed to the *Southern Quarterly Review*, which his father had founded, and advocated the political doctrines of State sovereignty, to which he adhered throughout life. He afterwards removed to Beaufort, and in 1833 turned his attention to theology and was ordained deacon in 1835. He had scarcely entered on the charge of the parish of Wilton, S. C., when he was elected professor of evidences of Christianity and sacred literature, and also chaplain, in South Carolina College. He was tall and dignified in appearance, graceful in his manners, and earnestly devoted to the work of education. He was ordained priest June 22, 1838. In 1840, when the diocese of Georgia was formed, he was chosen bishop, and was consecrated at Savannah, Feb. 28, 1841. He devoted himself to the arduous duties of his position, carefully avoiding extremes in doctrine and worship. He gave earnest attention to the religious needs of the colored population, establishing missions and sending missionaries among them as far as possible. In the earlier part of his administration he sacrificed his private fortune in his efforts to establish a female high school at Montpelier, Ga., and he afterwards united with Bishops Otey and Polk in an attempt to establish a great Southern university, but this project was frustrated by the outbreak of the Civil War. During the war he gave cordial support to the struggle in which his State had engaged, and sent his sons to fight in the Confederate armies. He prepared the pastoral letter issued by the council of the bishops of the Protestant Episcopal Church in the seceded States, held at Augusta, Ga., in Nov., 1862. When the war was ended he devoted himself with renewed energy and faith to his labors for the church. He died suddenly at Savannah, Ga., Dec. 21, 1866. During his life some of his sermons had been published separately, and in 1867 fifty were selected and published in New York under the editorial care of Rev. J. H. Hopkins, Jr., with a memoir by T. M. Hanckel.

ELLIS, ALEXANDER JOHN, F. R. S., an English philologist and orthoepist, was born at Hoxton near London, June 14, 1814. In 1825 his name was changed by royal license from Sharpe to Ellis. He studied at Shrewsbury and Eton, graduated with high classical and mathematical honors at Trinity College, Cambridge, in 1837. He also studied law in the Middle Temple. In 1864 he was chosen a F. R. S., and he has at various times held offices of honor in the learned societies of England. Among his numerous works are *The Alphabet of Nature* (1845); *Essentials of Phonetics* (1848); *A Plea for Phonetic Spelling* (2d ed., 1848); *Early English Pronunciation* (in parts, 1869, sqq.); Treatises on Greek and Latin pronunciation; *Speech in Song* (1878), *Basis of Music*, *History of Musical Pitch*, besides many tracts and other writings on phonology, mathematics, and music. He has also owned, edited, and published the *Phonetic News*, a journal devoted to improved methods in spelling. His masterly translations of Ohm's *Spirit of Mathematical Analysis*, and of Helmholtz's *Sensations of Tone as a Physiological Basis for the Theory of Music* (with valuable notes by the translator) are of very high importance. Mr. Ellis is a man of multifarious learning and remarkable powers of analytic thought. His belief that modern music may be rendered in tune has led him to take infinite pains to devise arrangements by which instruments with keyboards may be made to produce perfect accords. In this he is incorrect (see article EAR), yet his labors are entitled to high consideration.

ELLIS, GEORGE EDWARD, D.D., an American Unitarian minister, was born in Boston, Aug. 8, 1814. He graduated at Harvard College in 1833; studied at the Cambridge divinity school, and in 1840 was ordained pastor of a church in Charlestown, Mass. He held this charge till 1869, and was also professor of doctrinal theology in the divinity school at Cambridge, 1857–64. He was for some years editor of the *Christian Register* and also one of the editors of the *Christian Examiner*. His writings include biographies of Ann Hutchinson, William Penn, and John Mason in "Sparks's American Biography;" *The Half-century of the Unitarian Controversy* (1857); *The Aims and Purposes of the Founders of Massachusetts* (1869); *A Memoir of Jared Sparks* (1869); *A Life of Count Rumford* (1871); *History of the Battle of Bunker's Hill* (1875); and *The Red Man and the White* (1883).

ELLIS, ROBINSON, an English classical scholar, was born at Barming, Kent, Sept. 5, 1834. He was educated at Walthamstow, at Elizabeth College, Guernsey, and at Rugby, and was elected to a scholarship at Balliol College, Oxford, in 1852. After graduating he was elected a fellow of Trinity College, Oxford, and continued there till 1870, when he was appointed professor of Latin in University College, London. In 1876 he returned to Oxford. He has published a critical edition of the text of Catullus (1867, 3d ed., 1878), a commentary on the same (1876); and a translation into the metres of the original (1877); a critical edition, with commentary, of the *Ibis* of Ovid (1881); and various philological articles in English, German, and American periodicals.

ELLSWORTH, the county-seat of Hancock co., Me., is on Union River, a few miles from the ocean, and 26 miles S. E. of Bangor. It has 4 hotels, 2 banks, a weekly newspaper, 5 churches, and several schools. It has a foundry, a woollen-mill, lumber- and grist-mills, and a machine-shop. It is lighted with gas. Its property is valued at $1,535,000; its public debt is $68,000. It was settled in 1763, incorporated in 1800 as a town, and in 1869 as a city. Population, 4785.

ELLSWORTH, OLIVER (1745–1807), an American statesman and jurist, was born at Windsor, Conn., April 29, 1745. He was educated by Rev. Dr. Bellamy, and after spending two years at Yale College went to the college of New Jersey at Princeton, where he graduated in 1766. Although he had been educated with a view of entering the ministry, he left theology after a year's study for the law. In the latter he was trained by Gov. Griswold and Judge Root He was admitted to the bar at Windsor in 1771, and a few years later removed to Hartford. Here he enjoyed a lucrative practice, and as an advocate stood at the head of the Connecticut bar. In 1775 he was elected to the General Assembly, and in October, 1777, was chosen by this body a delegate to the Continental Congress, but did not take his seat till a year later. He served on the committees on marine and on appeals. He was also a member of the Governor's council, holding by yearly election from 1780 to 1784, and in the latter year he was appointed a judge of the superior court. In 1787 he was a member of the convention which framed the Constitution of the United States, and was reckoned among the ablest advocates of States' rights in that body. He was afterwards a member of the State convention of Connecticut which ratified the Federal Constitution. He became a determined Federalist. In the first congress under the new Constitution, Ellsworth was one of the senators from Connecticut, and was appointed chairman of the committee to organize the judiciary of the United States. He was watchful over public expenditures, and was pronounced by John Adams the firmest pillar of Washington's administration in the Senate. The mission of John Jay to England was due to his suggestion, and when the treaty then negotiated met with serious opposition in this country Ellsworth was one of its foremost defenders. Pres. Washington appointed him chief-justice of the supreme court in 1796. By his dignity, impartiality, and firmness, as well as his ability and learning, he proved himself worthy of the high position. His opinions were concise and perspicuous, and were noted for their cogency of reasoning. In February, 1799, on account of the complications caused by various acts of the French government, Pres. Adams appointed Chief-Justice Ellsworth, with W. R. Davie and W. V. Murray, envoys extraordinary to France. Although he had not been hopeful of the results, he succeeded in negotiating a treaty with Napoleon, who was then first consul. This treaty had secured indemnity for French depredations on American commerce, but the article relating to this subject was expunged in the Senate. Ellsworth was already suffering from severe disease, and he visited Bath, England, but without receiving much benefit from its mineral waters. When he returned to America in 1800 he resigned his office of chief-justice. He was, however, elected again a member of the Governor's council, which acted as a supreme court of errors in Connecticut. In May, 1807, when the judiciary of the State was reorganized, he was appointed chief-justice of the State, but declined the position on account of failing health. He died at Windsor, Nov. 26, 1807. Throughout his career he was noted for his high moral and religious character, as well as his intellectual force and wisdom in the conduct of affairs.

ELM. If the English name "elm" be derived from the Latin *ulmus*, the ancient Plinian name, this would indicate that it is not aboriginal in England. But philologists are of opinion that the name is common originally to Latin and the Teutonic languages, and not derived from either into the other. The elm is now one of the commonest and most useful timber trees in Great Britain. Botanically, America seems to be the home of the elm, some half dozen good species having been identified in the district bordering or east of the Mississippi River. No species has been found on the Pacific coast. The most northern species is the *Ulmus Americana*, or white elm, and is the species most generally referred to in our literature as the elm. It is exclusively used for ornamental purposes, especially in New England, for a shade tree, and is often called "the New Haven elm." It often reaches a height of 100 feet, with a circumference of 12 feet, and is a tree of striking beauty, chiefly on account of its slender sub-pendulous branches, which are widely extended. Of late years its beauty has been marred by the rapid increase of a small European beetle, *Galeruca calmariensis*, which was first reported in America in 1837. The beetle deposits its eggs on the leaves in May, which hatch in a few days, and the larvæ eat out the whole of the cellular matter of the leaves, leaving little more than the principal nerves and midrib. As soon as full grown they descend to the ground by the trunk of the tree, at the base of which they enter the pupa state, and a few days after form a new generation of beetles. In this stage of their existence they may be so easily destroyed that the insect will not be a serious enemy wherever earnest efforts are made to protect the trees from it. Another serious insect enemy to the tree is the elm-borer, *Saperda tridentata*, which often destroys great numbers of trees. Another European enemy is the twig-borer, *Scolytus destructor*, but it does not as yet seem to have appeared in America, though very destructive in Europe. The elm is never found in forests, but usually in bottom-lands along streams or in the good soil collected in ravines. The timber is used in wagon-work and in shipbuilding, but not to a very great extent, as its place, as compared with the elm in the Old World, is taken by other trees of more value. Still, large quantities are exported from Canada, the value being estimated at from a quarter to half a million of dollars annually, and in commercial importance elm ranks second only to oak among the Canadian hard woods. The variety known as the rock elm is the most highly appreciated. When thoroughly dry it gives 666 feet to the ton of 2000 lbs., as against basswood 1000 and beech 571. The next best known species of America is the red or slippery elm, *Ulmus fulva*, or *Ulmus rubra* of Michaux. The name "slippery elm" is derived from the mucilaginous character of the inner bark, which is one of the most popular emollients for poultices. The Indians used a drachm of the bark to every pound of bear's fat, heating them a few moments together, and then straining the fat, which was thus permanently preserved from rancidity. Another interesting species is the wahoo, *Ulmus alata*, whose common name probably indicates some use in Indian economy now unknown. The bark is, however, hemp-like and tough, and an excellent rope for bagging cotton is made from it. It makes but a small tree, usually about 30 feet high and 3 or 4 feet in circumference, while the red or slippery elm reaches 50 or 60 feet by 4 or 5. The bark is covered with corky, wing-like excrescences, much as in the sweet gum, and hence the name *alata*—winged. The Thomas elm, *Ulmus racemosa*, has somewhat racemose flowers, and was discovered in the early part of the present century by David Thomas of New York. The branches have also somewhat the corky character of the wahoo. *Ulmus opaca*, with small thick leaves, was discovered in 1818 by Nuttall on the Red River. All of these have nearly the same character as regards their several uses. (T. M.)

ELMENDORF, John Jay, born in 1827, is descended from one of the old Dutch families which settled on the banks of the Hudson River. He received his degree of bachelor in arts from Columbia College, N. Y., in 1846. While pursuing scientific studies at the College of Physicians and Surgeons in his native city, and a theological course at the General Theological Seminary, N. Y., he was also tutor in mathematics, in the absence of the professor of that department, at Columbia College. In 1853 he established a free church in what was then a suburb of New York, and continued rector of the same until he was called to the professorship which he now (1882) holds. During this period he received his degree of S.T.D. from his own college. He published his monograph on Sir T. More (cited in App. to Ueberweg, *Hist. Phil.*, vol. ii. p. 518), and, besides various occasional tracts, his *Rites and Ritual*, an outline of the principles of ceremonial as applied to the sacrament of the altar by the Church of which he is a priest.

In 1869 he was called to be professor of mental philosophy and English literature at Racine College, Wis., which chair he has ever since occupied. Besides various essays on philosophical subjects in general, applying the principles of Kant to special questions (*e. g.*, "Nature and Freedom," in the *Transactions* of the Wisconsin Academy of Science and Arts; "Miracles" and "Prayer," in the same publication and in the *Church Eclectic*, Feb. and March, 1880, June, 1881; "Hallucinations, Delusions, etc.," in the *American Church Quarterly*, July, 1882), he published, in 1876, his *Manual of the History of Philosophy*, an outline of principles and references intended to accompany lectures upon the same subject.

ELSTER, Kristian (1841-1881), a Norwegian novelist, was born March 4, 1841. His first work, *Tora Trondal*, is full of issues that have never before been essayed in Norwegian elegant literature. His next work, *Farlige Folk* (1881), was a complete revelation of the author's great and rare genius. In the form of a fascinating story it deals tenderly but earnestly with the most vital religious, political, and social questions of the day. Before this work appeared in print the author died, April 11, 1881. After his death some short stories which he left in manuscript were published by Alexander Kjilland in a volume entitled *Solskyer* (1882). Mr. Kjilland has prepared the volume with a biographical sketch of Elster.

ELYRIA, the county-seat of Lorain co., O., is at the junction of the Northern and Southern divisions of the Lake Shore and Michigan Southern Railroad, and at the crossing of the Cleveland, Tuscarawas Valley, and Wheeling Railroad, 25 miles W. from Cleveland, and 7 miles S. of Lake Erie. It is between the two branches of the Black River, which, each falling over a perpendicular ledge 44 feet high, unite half a mile below the town. It has a fine court-house, 2 banks (1 national), 3 hotels, 2 weekly newspapers, 8 churches, good public schools, and a public library. It is lighted with gas and has good water-works. The chief industries are the manufacture of cheese, grindstones, screws, and tobacco. It was first settled in 1817. Population, 5500.

ELZE, Friedrich Karl, a German literary critic and historian, was born at Dessau, May 22, 1821. After preliminary training in the gymnasium of that place, he pursued classic studies in the Universities of Leipsic and Berlin. In 1843 he turned rather to the study of modern languages, especially English, and afterwards made several journeys to London and Edinburgh. For many years he was a professor in the gymnasium at Dessau, but in 1875 he was called to the newly founded chair of English philology in the University of Halle. He has done much to extend among his countrymen a knowledge of English literature, and especially of Shakespeare, Scott, and Byron. His first publication was *Englischer Liederschatz* (5th ed., 1869); in 1857 he issued a critical edition of *Hamlet*, which has since been superseded by his edition of 1882 (Halle and London), in which he has retained the old spelling. In 1853 he established a journal called *Atlantis*, to promote acquaintance with English and American life and literature, but this was suspended at the end of its second year. He has published critical editions of some other early English dramas and biographies of Sir Walter Scott (1864), Byron (1870), and Shakespeare (1876), the last being especially well done. For twelve years he was editor of the *Shakespeare-Jahrbuch*, and a selection of his contributions to this publication appeared under the title *Essays on Shakespeare* (London, 1874). Among his other publications are *Die englische Sprache und Literatur in Deutschland* (1864); *Eine Frühlingsfahrt nach Edinburgh* (1860); *Nach Westen* (1860), which contains translations of English and American poems; *Der englische Hexameter* (1867); *Vermischte Blätter* (1875), a selection of his literary essays; *Notes on Elizabethan Dramatists* (1880), and a volume of poems (1881).

EMANCIPATION is the act by which a person who was once in the power of another is rendered free. A minor who is permitted by his parents to govern and control his own actions is said in law to be emancipated. His earnings thereafter in such case belong to him and not to his parents. The term is, however, usually employed to indicate the act of giving freedom to a slave. Emancipation was in the Roman law accomplished by manumission.

In the territory now occupied by the United States slavery existed from the earliest colonial times. In the year 1620 a Dutch trader landed at Jamestown in Virginia a cargo of twenty negroes, who were sold to the planters and are supposed to have been the first slaves introduced into the colonies. The number, however, rapidly multiplied, and at the period of the Revolution there was not a colony from New Hampshire to Georgia which did not number negro slaves among its population. Several attempts were made in early colonial times to abolish slaveholding in the colonies. The assembly of Pennsylvania passed an act to this effect in 1712, which was, however, abrogated by the king in council. Other similar efforts were from time to time made, but with a like result. In 1776 the continental congress resolved that "no slaves be imported into any of the thirteen united colonies." The convention summoned in 1789 to frame the constitution of the United States was of the same opinion. It resolved unanimously that the clause be inserted in the constitution prohibiting the importation of slaves into this country after the year 1808.

The State of Pennsylvania was the first to take definite action for the abolition of negro slavery. On March 1, 1780, her assembly passed an act entitled "an act for the gradual abolition of slavery," by the terms of which it was in substance provided that the master of every slave in the commonwealth should, within a time certain, register the name, age, and description of all his slaves; otherwise they were to be deemed free; and, further, that no children of any slaves thereafter born in the commonwealth should be considered as in a state of servitude, but that on the contrary they should be considered free.

Massachusetts was but one day later. On March 2, 1780, the constitution of that State was adopted embodying the following clause: "All men are born free and equal, and have certain natural, essential, and unalienable rights, among which may be reckoned the right of enjoying and defending their lives and liberties; that of acquiring, possessing, and protecting property; in fine, that of seeking and obtaining their safety and happiness." This declaration was afterwards pronounced to have abolished slavery in Massachusetts forever. The example of Massachusetts in wholly emancipating its slave population was followed in 1792 by New Hampshire and in 1793 by Vermont. The remaining Northern States followed the example of Pennsylvania by passing laws for the gradual abolition of slavery much after the same fashion. This was accomplished in Connecticut in 1784, in Rhode Island in the same year, in New York in 1799, and in New Jersey 1804. Maine, in 1819, embodied in her constitution principles inconsistent with the existence of slavery. Ohio, Indiana, Illinois, Michigan, Wisconsin, and Iowa contained no slaves by virtue of the provisions of the act of Congress of July 13, 1787, known as the Ordinance for the Government of the North-western Territory. (See CUTLER, MANASSEH.)

In the Southern States, prior to the War of the Rebellion, slavery continued as a domestic institution, and emancipation could only be effected by the voluntary act of the master. The policy of those States led to many restraints upon such emancipation, which have now happily passed into matters rather of curiosity than of practical importance. Slaves being considered as property, no emancipation could be effected by the master, either by deed or will, as against his creditors, if, at the time of the emancipation, the person making it had not sufficient money to pay his debts. Where emancipation was in such cases effected the creditor of the emancipator might, notwithstanding, levy upon the slave and sell him anew into bondage. Where a testator emancipated his slaves by will, his widow was, nevertheless, entitled to her thirds of his personal estate therein, provided he did not leave other sufficient property to satisfy her claim. In South Carolina, Alabama, Mississippi, and Georgia no slave could be emancipated without the consent of the legislature, and in Georgia any master endeavoring to emancipate his slave without such consent was subjected to a penalty of five hundred dollars. In North Carolina a slave could, in early times, be emancipated only for meritorious services, to be admitted and allowed by the county court. By later laws, however, the master was authorized in any case to present a petition to the county court asking leave to emancipate his slave. The petition being allowed by the court, the master was then enabled, upon entering bond with surety for the slave's good behavior, to emancipate him. The freedman was, however, bound immediately after to leave the State and never to return thither. In Tennessee the law was substantially to the same effect, a discretion being, however, vested in the courts as to whether the emancipation was consistent with the interest and policy of the State. In Mississippi every emancipation had to be effected by an instrument under seal, attested by two witnesses and acknowledged in open court. In addition, satisfactory evidence had to be adduced to the general assembly that the slave had done some meritorious act for the benefit of his master, or rendered some distinguished services to the State. A special act of assembly had then to be procured sanctioning the proposed emancipation, otherwise the prior proceedings were inoperative. In Kentucky, Missouri, Virginia, Maryland, and Arkansas greater facility was afforded for emancipation. It was in those States provided that slaves might be emancipated either by deed or will, provided they were not infirm or diseased so as to be unable to provide for themselves. In Virginia an emancipated slave remaining in the State twelve months after he became actually free forfeited his freedom. In Louisiana slaves might be manumitted either by deed or will, but in no case could this be done where the slave in question was less than thirty years old, unless he had saved the life of his master, his master's wife, or one of his children.

Wherever statutory provisions existed in reference to the emancipation of slaves, it was necessary to comply strictly with such provisions. Such compliance was a condition precedent to a slave's freedom. Where emancipation by deed or will was lawful it was need that the intention to free the slave, in order to be operative, must be expressed in direct and unequivocal terms. Hence a mere permit to a slave "to go about his lawful business" was not held to amount to an emancipation. In some few cases it was held that the bringing of an action by the master against the slave, or the devise of property, real or personal, to the slave by the master, implied manumission. This was not, however, the law in Louisiana.

Upon the breaking out of the War of the Rebellion an agitation at once arose in the Northern States looking to the emancipation of the slaves in the southern part of the country. This was deemed by many a proper war measure admirably calculated to crush the rebellion and to restore peace to the nation. Pres. Lincoln, however, anxious if possible to bring about a reconciliation, and fully aware of the importance of the step which he was pressed to take, hesitated for a long time. At length, on Sept. 22, 1862, he issued a proclamation setting forth that he proposed on the first day of January of the ensuing year to declare all persons held as slaves within any State or designated part of a State, the people whereof should then be in rebellion against the United States, free thenceforward and forever. Accordingly, on Jan. 1, 1863, the rebellion still continuing, the president issued a further proclamation, reciting that above set forth, and declaring that by virtue of the power in him vested as commander-in-chief of the army and navy of the United States in time of actual armed rebellion against the authority and government of the United State, and as a fit and necessary war-measure for suppressing said rebellion, he did thereby order and declare that all slaves in the States of Arkansas, Texas, Louisiana (with the exception of certain parishes), Mississippi, Alabama, Florida, Georgia, South Carolina, North Carolina, and Virginia (the forty-eight counties designated as West Virginia and some others only excepted) were and henceforward should be free. The forces of the United States, both by land and by sea, were instructed to recognize and maintain the freedom of said persons. "And upon this act, sincerely believed to be an act of justice, warranted by the Constitution upon military necessity, I invoke (said the President) the considerate judgment of mankind and the gracious favor of Almighty God."

It was not, however, until somewhat later that the emancipation of all the slaves in the country was finally effected. On Feb. 1, 1865, Congress passed a resolution that a thirteenth amendment to the Constitution be proposed to the legislatures of the various States in the terms following:

SECTION 1. Neither slavery nor involuntary servitude, except as a punishment for crime, whereof the party shall have been duly convicted, shall exist within the United States or any place subject to their jurisdiction.

SECTION 2. Congress shall have power to enforce this article by appropriate legislation.

The proposed amendment was accordingly submitted to the various legislatures, and was duly ratified in Illinois, Rhode Island, Michigan, Maryland, New York, West Virginia, Maine, Kansas, Massachusetts, Pennsylvania, Virginia, Ohio, Missouri, Nevada, Indiana, Louisiana, Minnesota, Wisconsin, Vermont, Tennessee, Arkansas, Connecticut, New Hampshire, South Carolina, Alabama, North Carolina, and Georgia, in all twenty-seven States, or three-fourths of those constituting the Union. On Dec. 18, 1865, a proclamation was issued certifying that the consent of the requisite number of States had been obtained, and the amendment was accordingly declared part of the Constitution of the United States. (L. L., JR.)

EMBURY, PHILIP (1729–1775), the pioneer of Methodism in America, was born at Ballygaran, Limerick, Ireland, Sept. 21, 1729. His parents were natives of Germany, and he became a carpenter. Having been converted in 1752, he joined Wesley's society, and was made a local preacher in 1758. He emigrated to New York in 1760, and pursued his trade there. At the instance of Barbara Heck he began preaching there in 1766. On account of the strict laws against nonconformity the meetings were held at first in his own house, but afterwards in a rigging-loft in William street, which has since been known as the birthplace of American Methodism. In 1768 the first Methodist church was erected in John street. He worked on the building as a carpenter, and made the pulpit with his own hands. He preached the first sermon in it Oct. 30, 1768, and continued preaching without salary until the arrival of ministers sent by Wesley. He then removed to Camden, Washington co., N. Y., where he worked during the week as a carpenter and preached on Sundays. He organized a Methodist society at Ashgrove, near Camden, which was the first in the bounds of the Troy conference. He died, from an accident while mowing, at Camden, N. Y., August, 1775. He was buried in the neighborhood, but in 1832 his remains were moved to Ashgrove churchyard, and in 1866 to Cambridge, N. Y., where a monument, erected by Troy conference, commemorates his services.

EMERSON, RALPH WALDO (1803–1882), an American poet and philosopher, was born in Boston, May 25, 1803. He was a descendant of the founder of the Christian Church in Concord, Rev. Peter Bulkeley, who came to New England from the little parish of Odell, or Woodhill, in Bedfordshire, England, where the first clerical ancestor of Mr. Emerson, so far as we know, Rev. Edward Bulkeley, D. D., was rector from about 1580 to 1620. Rev. Peter Bulkeley was Dr. Bulkeley's son, born at Odell, Jan. 31, 1583; succeeded his father as rector in 1620; was driven away by Archbishop Laud about 1633; came to Cambridge, Mass., in 1634; settled in Concord in 1635, and died there March 5, 1659. Rev. William Emerson, of Concord (born May 21, 1743, died Oct. 20, 1776), was the grandfather of R. W. Emerson, and the first occupant of the famous "Old Manse," in Concord, where Emerson wrote *Nature* and Hawthorne his *Mosses*. Through this grandfather, who left an only son, Rev. William Emerson, of Harvard and Boston (born May 6, 1769, died May 12, 1811), R. W. Emerson traced his descent from Rev. Joseph Emerson, of Mendon, who married, in 1665, at Concord, Elizabeth, the daughter of Rev. Edward Bulkeley, and granddaughter of Rev. Peter Bulkeley, above mentioned. These three Bulkeleys, ancestors of R. W. Emerson, were clergymen at Odell and Concord, in lineal succession, from 1580 to 1696, when Rev. Edward Bulkeley died, his Emerson ancestors were ministers in Malden, Concord, and Boston for nearly one hundred years, terminating at his father's death in 1811; through a female ancestor he descended from Rev. Samuel Moody, of York, Me., who preached from 1698 to 1747, and through another ancestor, Rebecca Waldo, he descended from Peter Waldo, one of the early Reformed Christians known as Waldenses. His ancestors in all directions, therefore, were clerical persons for more than two centuries before his birth. His first ancestor of the name in New England, Thomas Emerson, of Ipswich, Mass., was a baker and farmer there as early as 1638; but two of Thomas Emerson's sons were ministers, and Thomas seems to have belonged to a younger branch of the family of Ralph Emerson, of Durham, who, in 1535, was ennobled by Henry VIII., and received by grant the heraldic arms which have been used since 1640 by the descendants of Thomas Emerson in America. The Bulkeleys were a family still more ancient in England, claiming descent from one Robert Bulkeley, who, in the reign of King John, was lord of the manor of Bulkeley, in the county palatine of Chester. The Rev. Peter Bulkeley had for his second wife Grace, daughter of Sir Richard Chetwode, of Odell, and was related to Oliver St. John, Cromwell's solicitor-general, whom Bulkeley called his "nephew." These genealogies are mentioned to show that the ancestors of the poet Emerson were technically "gentlemen" for many generations, and specially scholars and clergymen in those generations that dwelt in New England.

R. W. Emerson's father, Rev. William Emerson, of Boston, was born at Concord, in the "Old Manse," and his mother (the grandmother of R. W. Emerson) was Phebe Bliss, daughter of Rev. Daniel Bliss, minister of Concord from 1739 to 1765. This lady, after her first husband's death in 1776, married his successor, Rev. Ezra Ripley, minister of Concord from 1778 to 1841, and it was at Dr. Ripley's house that Rev. William Emerson, of Boston, spent his youth. He married Ruth Haskins, of Boston, a little before 1800, and had eight children, six of whom, five sons and a daughter (who died early), survived their father's death in 1811. R. W. Emerson was the second in age of these sons. At the death of their father he was minister of the First Church in Boston, a highly honorable position among the clergy of Massachusetts, to which he was called from the little town of Harvard in 1799. Ten years before that date Rev. William Emerson had taught the grammar school in Roxbury, where Rev. Charles Lowell, father of the poet Lowell, was one of his pupils. Dr. Lowell describes the father of R. W. Emerson as a "handsome man, rather tall, with a fair complexion, his cheeks slightly tinted, his motions easy, graceful, and gentleman-like, his manners bland and pleasant; he was an acceptable preacher; his delivery was distinct and correct, and was evidently the result of much care and discipline." His son in 1849 wrote of him: "He inclined obviously to what is ethical and universal in Christianity, very little to the personal and historical. I think I observe in his writings, as in the writings of Unitarians down to a recent date, a studied reserve on the nature and offices of Jesus. They had not made up their own minds on it. It was a mystery to them, and they let it remain so." This describes well the state of mind in which Rev. William Emerson's two eldest sons, William and Waldo, came to their theological studies about 1823. William, the elder, went abroad to study in Germany, and there, finding himself involved in doubts and perplexities, he visited Goethe at Weimar, and laid his difficulties before the old poet, who advised him to quiet his conscience, go home, and preach, whatever his doubts might be, and not frustrate the hopes of his family. William Emerson returned to America, but not to preach; he laid the case before his brother Waldo, who said afterward, "I was very sad to hear it, for I knew how much it would grieve my mother;" but he could not advise his brother to go into a pulpit, and William became a lawyer instead.

Although the death of his father had left Waldo Emerson poor, he had friends who provided for his education, and he was carefully instructed in the Boston Latin School and at home, where an aunt, Miss Mary Emerson, undertook to train his mind and direct the course of his studies, which she was well fitted to do by the acuteness and vigor of her own mind. A friend, Miss Sarah Bradford, afterwards Mrs. Ripley, set young Emerson, at the age of eleven, the task of finishing a translation of the fifth Eclogue of Virgil, which is the earliest known verse composed by the future poet. Miss Bradford wrote him (May, 1814): "You love to trifle in rhyme a little now and then; why will you not continue this versification of the fifth Bucolic? you will kill two birds with one stone: improve in your Latin as well as indulge a taste for poetry." The boy undertook the task, and produced some creditable lines. His aunt, when he grew older and had read something of Plato, caused him to write her a letter as if to Plato, which she answered in the name of that philosopher; and she also introduced him to the *Pensées* of Pascal and other books which boys of his age seldom read. He entered Harvard College in 1817, at the age of fourteen, and there came under the instruction of Caleb Cushing in mathematics, of Edward Everett in Greek, and of George Ticknor in belles-lettres. His rhetorical professor was Edward Channing. He was devoted to eloquence in public speakers and heard all the Boston preachers and orators he could—Dr. Channing, Harrison Gray Otis, John Quincy Adams, and especially Daniel Webster. In 1835, writing to his friend Carlyle in London about Webster, Emerson spoke of him as 'that great forehead which I followed about all my young days, from court-house to senate chamber, from caucus to street. I owe to him a hundred fine hours and two or three moments of eloquence." In his old age Emerson once said: "I have heard three Americans who spoke better than any of their contemporaries—Dr. Channing, Webster, and Wendell Phillips. I could never find in the hymns what I heard Dr. Channing read from them. Webster was never a heavy or a dull speaker—when he was sober." In 1834 he supported Webster as against Gen. Jackson, whom Emerson styled "a most unfit person in the presidency, doing the worst things; the worse he grew, the more popular." Leaving college in 1821, Emerson at first joined his brother William in a school for girls in Boston. He continued in this occupation for several years, but in the meantime, in 1823, began to study theology with a view to following his father's profession and that of his ancestors. He had not distinguished himself for scholarship in college, but he was a serious student, and had a gift of eloquence which soon made itself manifest. His father's church had been in Chauncy Place, not far from Dr. Channing's, and the doctor's house was near where Mrs. Emerson and her children lived in Boston.

Young Emerson then began to study divinity (nominally with Dr. Channing, whose sermons he had long heard, and who "possessed the mysterious endowment of natural eloquence," as Emerson once said). His chief instructor in divinity was at Cambridge, however—Andrews Norton, then a professor in the Unitarian theological school, whom Emerson described in 1835 as "one of our best heads, once a theological professor and a destroying critic, who lives upon a rich estate at Cambridge, and frigidly excludes Carlyle's 'Diderot' from his *select journal*, calling it 'another paper of the Teufelsdröckh school.'" This critic was an exact scholar, who could teach the young men much that they wished to know; and Emerson said in after years that he profited more by Norton in theology than by any other professor. His studies were interrupted by ill-health and by the necessity of teaching for his own support, and he was excused from very rigid examination on the books he read and the lectures he heard. "If the professors at Cambridge had examined me then," he used to say, "perhaps they would not have let me preach at all." He was "approbated" as a preacher by the Middlesex County Association of Congregational ministers in 1826, and in 1827 began to preach steadily as a candidate in various pulpits. In 1828 he took the place of his grandfather, old Dr. Ripley, in the parish church at Concord for a few weeks, and early in 1829 he was invited to settle in the Second Church of Boston, where Rev. Henry Ware, Jr., was the pastor. Mr. Emerson became his colleague, and soon found himself in fact the pastor of the church, Mr. Ware having duties as a professor at Cambridge after 1830. He held this position from March 11, 1829, to Dec. 22, 1832.

In September, 1829, he married Miss Ellen Tucker, of Boston, who soon became an invalid, and died in February, 1832. A year after his marriage he became sole pastor, and then in a letter to a kinsman he made this remark: "I stand alone, but there is, of course, no real change in my relations. The work was great enough before, and it is not more now." He had devoted himself with much zeal to sermon-writing, and in July, 1829, had written to his aunt Mary in excuse for the brevity of his letter: "I am striving hard to-day to establish the sovereignty and self-existent excellence of the moral law in popular argument, and *slay the Utility swine;* and so must run." It was apparently this sermon which Mr. Alcott heard him preach in Dr. Channing's church in the autumn of 1829—the first time his friend had listened to him. The subject was "The Universality of the Moral Sentiment," and Mr. Alcott was struck, as he has since said, "with the youth of the preacher, the beauty of his elocution, and the direct and sincere manner in which he addressed his hearers." He was much admired in the pulpit, but not by all who heard him, the wife of his friend, George Ripley, thus describing him on one occasion: "Waldo Emerson came last Sunday and preached a sermon for George, with his chin in the air, in scorn of the whole human race." His Boston ministry was passed chiefly in a house in Chardon Street, near Bowdoin Square, where the young minister and his delicate wife set up housekeeping in October, 1830, and where his mother and his brothers, one or more of them, generally lived with them. His brother Edward, who graduated at Cambridge in 1824, had studied law in Boston with Daniel Webster, and was tutor in 1827-28 to his son, Fletcher Webster. His youngest brother, Charles, who graduated in 1828, also taught school for a while, and then studied law; but both these brilliant young men died early—Edward in 1834, and Charles in 1836. Emerson admired his brothers greatly, mourned for them profoundly, and has borne witness to their character and talents in verse and prose. To Carlyle he wrote of his brother Charles's death in words which may in some respects be applied to himself: "Your last letter (in April, 1836) found me a mourner, as did your first. I have lost out of this world my brother Charles, the friend and companion of many years, the inmate of my house, a man of beautiful genius, born to speak well, whose conversation for these last years has treated every grave question of humanity and has been my daily bread. He built his foundation so large that it needed the full age of man to make evident the plan and proportion of his character. He postponed always a particular to a final and absolute success, so that his life was a silent appeal to the great and generous." The death of his wife, in 1832, had been a severe blow to Waldo Emerson, and after giving up his Boston parish he resolved to leave America for a time.

On this first voyage to Europe he sailed up the Mediterranean before visiting England, and spent the spring months of 1833 in Italy and France, going as far east as Malta, and passing some time in Sicily. Early in May, 1833, he was in Florence, where he met Horatio Greenough, the sculptor, and dined with Landor, then "living in a cloud of pictures at his Villa Gherardesca." The favorable impression then made upon him by Landor was never effaced, though Carlyle, and Landor himself, did what they could to change his mind. When Carlyle wrote to him in 1840, "Of Landor I have not got much benefit," Emerson replied, "I suspect you of very short and dashing reading in his books," but added, "His speech, I remember, was below his writing." An English friend in Italy had given Emerson a letter to Carlyle, then living in his wife's house in Scotland; and so, in July, 1833, after some weeks in Paris, he went to London, and towards the end of the summer visited Carlyle at Craigenputtock, sixteen miles from Dumfries, where, in a sort of exile, "amid desolate heathery hills, the lonely scholar nourished his mighty heart."

In sight of Wordsworth's country in August, 1833, Carlyle and Emerson "sat down and talked of the immortality of the soul." Had Goethe been living, Emerson "might have wandered into Germany also." He visited Coleridge and Wordsworth, and saw Wellington at the funeral of Wilberforce. Returning to New England, he resumed his scholastic life, and soon took up his residence in Concord, where his kindred were living.

In October, 1834, he went with his mother to live at the "Old Manse" with his grandfather, Dr. Ripley, which continued to be his home for a year or more, and until after his marriage to Miss Lilian Jackson, of Plymouth, in 1835. Then he bought and fitted up a house which had been built by a Boston merchant, on the Lexington road in Concord, and went there to live in October, 1835. It is on the eastern side of the village, and not far from where Alcott and Hawthorne afterwards dwelt side by side. There, with the exception of two visits to Europe—in 1847 and 1873—Emerson always afterwards lived, and there he died, April 27, 1882. All his four children were born there—his eldest son, Waldo, in October, 1836—and all his books were written there, except the first one, *Nature*, which was composed in the "Old Manse." His first born son died in this house in 1842, and, in the pathetic poem which he wrote soon after, Emerson described with a few touches the locality in which his home stands:

"His daily haunts I well discern—
The poultry-yard, the shed, the barn—
And every inch of garden ground
Paced by the blessed feet around;
From the road-side to the brook,
Whereunto he loved to look;
Step the meek birds where erst they ranged,
The wintry garden lies unchanged;
The brook into the stream runs on;
But the deep-eyed boy is gone."

Three other children of Emerson survive him—Ellen, Edith (Mrs. W. H. Forbes), and Edward the latter a physician in Concord and the heir to his father's manuscripts and books. There are also ten grandchildren living, most of whom bear the name of Forbes. All his children were of the second marriage.

The volume lately published by Prof. Norton containing the correspondence between Emerson and Carlyle, from 1834 to 1880 (Boston, 1883), is the fullest revelation yet made of the friendship between these men, and of the affectionate side of Emerson's life; of which, also, the letters give many indispensable particulars. Of the visit made by Emerson to Carlyle at Craigenpultock in 1833, which has been so often described, Mrs. Carlyle herself wrote to Emerson five years later·

"If there were nothing else to remember you by, I should never forget the visitor who years ago, in the Desert, descended on us, out of the clouds as it were, and made our day there look like enchantment for us, and left me weeping that it was only *one* day. When I think of America, as is of you; neither Harriet Martineau nor any one else succeeds in giving me a more extended idea of it."

The early letters throw light on the infancy of "Transcendentalism" in New England, and reveal the fact that Emerson and Dr. Hedge invited Carlyle in April, 1835, to come to Boston and edit there a proposed review, *The Transcendentalist or Spiritual Inquirer*, which never came to anything, but of which *The Dial*, in 1840, was the first visible manifestation. Dr. Channing told Miss Peabody, in March, 1835, "that he lay awake all night because he had learned in the evening that some young men proposed to issue a journal, to be called *The Transcendentalist*, as the organ of a spiritual philosophy;" and Dr. F———

ingham, whom Emerson describes as "a worthy, accomplished man, more like Erasmus than Luther," said to Emerson, "You cannot express in terms too extravagant my desire that your friend Carlyle should come to Boston." After such a glow of anticipation in 1835, it is painful to read what Emerson wrote to Carlyle in 1842, after *The Dial* had existed for two years: "I submitted to what seemed a necessity of petty literary patriotism, and took charge of the thankless little *Dial*, without subscribers enough to pay even a publisher, much less any laborer. It has no penny for editor or contributor—nothing but abuse in the newspapers, or at best silence; but it serves as a sort of portfolio to carry about a few poems or sentences which would otherwise be transcribed and circulated." In reply to an invitation from Emerson to write for the *Dial*, Carlyle, in August, 1842, rather ungraciously said: "I love your *Dial*, yet it is with a kind of shudder. You seem to me in danger of dividing yourself from the fact of this present universe—in which alone, ugly as it is, can I find any anchorage—and soaring away after ideas, beliefs, revelations, and such like, into perilous altitudes, as I think. Alas! it is so easy to screw one's self up into high and ever higher altitudes of transcendentalism; easy for you, for me, but whither does it lead?" To which Emerson generously replied: "For the *Dial* and its sins I have no defence to set up; we write as we can, and we know very little about it."

When the *Dial* had just begun (July, 1840), we find that in his diary for August 2 John Quincy Adams (for whom Emerson had cast his first presidential ballot, and whose eloquence he greatly admired) wrote thus: "After failing in the every-day vocations of Unitarian preacher and schoolmaster, Emerson starts a new doctrine of Transcendentalism, declares all the old revelations superannuated and worn out, and announces the approach of new revelations." Emerson's "failure," such as it was, in the two vocations named by Adams had taken place from seven to fifteen years earlier; for he never taught school after he began to preach, and he voluntarily withdrew from a pulpit where he was desired, in 1832, and never returned to preaching as a profession. In 1834, after his return from Europe, he began to create for himself and others the new profession of lecturing, which gave him an independent pulpit of his own. Despondent Carlyle, writing to him from Chelsea (Aug. 12, 1834), had said: "At last we have lived to see all manner of Poetics and Rhetorics and Sermonics—one may say, generally, all manner of *Pulpits* for addressing mankind from—as good as broken and abolished." But Emerson went on lecturing in Boston from 1835, while he was yet living a widower in the "Old Manse" at Concord, till a year or two before his death; and in April, 1836, he wrote to Carlyle: "The pulpit in our age certainly gives forth an obstructed and uncertain sound, and the faith of those in it, if men of genius, may differ so much from that of those under it as to embarrass the conscience of the speaker, because so much is attributed to him from the fact of standing here. In the Lyceum nothing is presupposed. The orator is only responsible for what his lips articulate. Then what scope it allows! I cannot remember that here are any other mouth-pieces that are specially vital at this time, except Criticism and Parliamentary Debate. I think this of ours would possess, in the hands of a great genius, great advantages over both." By 1837 he had persuaded Carlyle to attempt lecturing in London, and almost induced him to come to New England and give courses of lectures, as he was himself doing every winter. Emerson had thus made a profession for himself—not always agreeable, either, for in October, 1835, he spoke of "public lecturing" to Carlyle as something "I could recommend for medicine to any gentleman who finds the love of life too strong in him." But, whether pleasant or odious, he felt bound to continue it, writing to Carlyle in 1837:

"There are in this country so few scholars that the services of each studious person are needed to do what he can for the circulation of thought, to the end of making some counterweight to the money force and to give such food as he may to the nigh starving youth. So I religiously read lectures every winter, and at other times whenever summoned—last year 'The Philosophy of History,' twelve lectures; and now I meditate a course on what I call 'Ethics.'"

In June, 1835, Carlyle had so far been converted by Emerson as to say:

"It does seem next to certain to me that I could preach a very considerable quantity of things from that Boston Pulpit, such as it is" (the lecture platform), "were I once fairly started. If so, what an unspeakable relief were it, too!"

Failing to bring his friend bodily to Boston and Concord, Emerson then undertook to get Carlyle a hearing in America through his books. In the spring of 1836, before printing his own first volume (*Nature*), he had helped forward an American edition of *Sartor Resartus*, of which 500 copies were printed in Boston. The book went to a second edition soon after *Nature* was published (in September, 1836), and a year later 1200 copies of *Sartor* had been sold in America, while *Nature* was ten years in selling 500 copies. The *French Revolution* and Carlyle's *Miscellanies* were brought out in Boston editions by Emerson in 1838, and before the summer of 1839, in money and American printed volumes, Carlyle had received from Emerson for this American reprinting £250. In acknowledging the receipt of this sum, Carlyle said:

"Thanks to you and the books, and to Heaven over all, I am for the present no longer poor, but have a reasonable prospect of existing. Not for these twelve years—never since I have had a house to maintain with money—have I had as much money in my possession as even now."

While Carlyle was struggling with poverty from 1820 to 1840, Emerson, after the years of his boyhood and youth, found himself with a modest competence which he inherited, and could increase his income up to the limit of his wants by the exercise of his profession as lecturer. His books for many years were as unsuccessful as those of Carlyle; nor had he until past middle-life Carlyle's faculty of writing for the magazines. His first printed pamphlet was an address at the two hundredth anniversary of the founding of Concord (by his ancestor, Rev. Peter Bulkeley, in 1635). This was printed at Concord, and is now very rare. The first edition of *Nature*, printed by James Munroe (Carlyle's Boston publisher) in September, 1836, is also long out of print. He then published nothing but pamphlets until February, 1841, when the first series of *Essays* appeared in Boston, and was soon after republished in London with a commendatory preface by Carlyle. Privately, Carlyle wrote most warmly about this volume:

"Ah me! I feel as if in the wide world there were still

but this one voice that responded intelligently to my own; as if all the rest were hearsays, melodious or unmelodious echoes; as if this alone were true and alive. These voices of yours, which I censure sometimes for having no body, how can they have a body? They are light rays darting upward, in the east; they will yet make much and much to have a body."

Four or five years earlier, before he had read anything of Emerson's except his letters, so friendly and wise, Carlyle had written, in answer to an invitation from Emerson to visit him:

"Truly, Concord, which I have sought out on the map, seems worthy of its name; no dissonance comes to me from that side, but grief itself has acquired a harmony; in joy or grief a voice says to me, Behold there is one that loves thee; in thy loneliness, in thy darkness, see how a hospitable candle shines from far over seas, how a friendly heart watches! It is very good and precious for me. How gladly would I run to Concord. It is far within the verge of probabilities that I shall see Mrs. Emerson's face and eat of her bread, one day."

This expectation vanished after a few years, and all the hospitality of Emerson could not draw Carlyle away from London. The latter was alternately urging his American correspondent, now to be quiet, not to publish too fast, and again to produce some work of history or biography which would faithfully represent his genius. Thus, in 1839, Carlyle wrote:

"I long to see some concrete Thing, some Event, Man's Life, American Forest, or piece of Creation, which this Emerson loves and wonders at, well *Emersonized*—depictured by Emerson, filled with the life of Emerson, and cast forth from him then to live by itself."

To such exhortation Emerson replied, in 1840:

"Almost all my life has been passed alone. Within three or four years I have been drawing nearer to a few men and women whose love gives me in these days more happiness than I can write of. . . . I incline to write philosophy, poetry, possibility—anything but history. I dot evermore in my endless Journal a line on every knowable in nature; but the arrangement loiters long, and I get a brick-kiln instead of a house. My Journals are full of disjointed, dreamy audacities, unsystematic, irresponsible lampoons of systems, and all manner of rambling reveries."

In an earlier letter he had said—and this remained true of him through life—

"I think I shall never be killed by my ambition. I behold my failures and shortcomings with an equanimity which my worst enemy might be glad to see. My whole philosophy, which is very real, teaches acquiescence and optimism. Only when I see how much work is to be done, what room for a poet—for any spiritualist—in this great, intelligent, sensual, and avaricious America, I lament my fumbling fingers and stammering tongue."

Again he wrote: "I do not belong to the poets, but only to a low department of literature, the reporters—suburban men."

This was by no means the estimation in which the few readers and the many hearers of Emerson held him in 1840. He did not make himself known as a poet until some years later, when his verses, published in the *Dial*, had attracted the notice, not only of newspaper wits and critical reviewers, but of admirers and imitators; but he had become widely celebrated as an orator and radical thinker. With his native generosity he brought out the poems of his fantastic friend Jones Very in 1839, before he attempted to collect his own; and he encouraged his younger friend, Thoreau, in 1838-39 to write verses, some of which Emerson published in the *Dial*. But the Boston lectures of 1835-37, and the publication of *Nature*, had drawn attention to Emerson's philosophic position, for which, however, few cared in those days. His Phi Beta oration of 1837 had given high hopes of his eloquence and critical powers; but the Divinity School address, in the summer of 1838, was the first of his writings which made him generally known. Its occasion was very simple, and no great expectation or excitement seems to have attended its delivery. The Divinity College which had invited him to address its alumni was a small school of theology maintained by the Unitarians of Massachusetts, which had been founded less than twenty years before, and in which Andrews Norton had been a distinguished professor, as Moses Stuart still was in the opposing school of theology at Andover. Prof. Norton had retired from his chair soon after 1830, but was living near by Divinity Hall and still exercised a friendly oversight of the school at Cambridge. The delivery of the address was followed by a great stir in the Unitarian body in and around Boston, Mr. Norton being the most agitated by its heresies. Theodore Parker, then preaching in a suburb of Boston, a few miles from Cambridge, heard Emerson on that occasion, and soon wrote to his classmate Ellis, then in Europe:

"You know Emerson was to preach the sermon before the class. I heard it. It was the noblest of all his performances; a little exaggerated, with some philosophical untruth, it seems to me; but the noblest, the most inspiring strain I ever listened to. It is printed (Aug. 7, 1838), but not published. 'I took six,' as Major Crockett said of the ice-creams at the President's table, and I send you one. It caused a great outcry—one shouting 'The Philistines be upon us!' another, 'We be all dead men!' while the majority called out 'Atheism!'"

Parker again wrote to Ellis (Oct. 15, 1838): "Emerson's address has made a great noise. Mr. Norton opened the cannonade with a broadside aimed at Emerson, Cousin, Carlyle, Schleiermacher, Shelley, and 'a paper called the *Western Messenger*.' This provoked several replies—one of singular beauty from Theophilus Parsons, one from the iron pen of Brownson, in the *Post*, and one from J. F. Clarke in defence of the article in the *Messenger*. . . . Ministers preached on Emerson's sermon. Henry Ware delivered a sermon on the 'Personality of God,' which, it is said, Emerson denies; and the students of the Divinity School come out, cap in hand, and say, *Peccavimus omnes*, and the last class in particular, and request Henry Ware to publish his sermon. Chandler Robbins speaks mildly, as his manner is, and calls the common rant of denouncing Emerson 'a vulgar clamor,' and 'the popular roar.' All this makes a world of talk. For my own part, I see that the sun still shines, the rain rains, and the dogs bark; and I have serious doubts whether Emerson will overturn Christianity this time. The charm of all is that Abner Kneeland (your old friend) got Emerson's address, and read it to his followers one Sunday, as better infidelity than he could write himself." (Kneeland was a free-thinker, lately sentenced to jail for blasphemy, and for whose pardon Dr. Channing and Theodore Parker had petitioned.)

A few months later Parker reports to Ellis a scene in the Boston Association of Unitarian Ministers, where the question was debated whether Emerson was a Christian:

"Dr. Greenwood, of King's Chapel, said he was not, but defended his position rather poorly. John Pierpont maintained he was an atheist, a downright atheist. But nobody doubted he was a virtuous and most devout man

—one who would enter heaven when they were shut out. Of course they were in a queer predicament. Either they must acknowledge a man may be virtuous and yet no Christian (which most of them thought it a great heresy to suppose), and religious, yet an atheist—which is a contradiction—or else affirm that Emerson was neither virtuous nor religious, which they could not prove. Dr. Walker and Dr. Frothingham thought he should be called a Christian if he desired the name. Dr. (Francis) Parkman is one of the most charitable of men; he loves all men—even Bancroft (the historian) and Brownson—but he hates all their new notions. It is quite evident there are now two parties among the Unitarians: one is for progress, the other says 'our strength is to sit still.' Dr. Channing is the real head of the first party; the other has no head. The oyster, which never moves, has none and needs none."

These citations show how deeply the word of Emerson had stirred the waters. The controversy went on, and while Emerson declined to take part in it, by a manly letter to Henry Ware, his friends stood forward in his behalf. George Ripley undertook to answer Prof. Norton's *Latest Form of Infidelity*, and did so in a pamphlet which Parker, in September, 1839, pronounced "strong, clear, and very good," adding: "He will not say all that I wish might be said; but after we have seen that, I will handle certain other points not approached by Ripley." This Parker did under the name of "Levi Blodgett," and there were more replies and rejoinders; to all which Emerson answered nothing. But he was disturbed by the clamor, and wrote to Carlyle in 1838, a little regretting that he had asked his Scotch friend to join his fortunes with an American so unpopular as he then found himself. Carlyle replied with equal generosity, and said, among other things:

"I am older in years than you, but in humor I am older by centuries. What a hope is in that ever young heart, cheerful, healthful as the morning!"

But meantime Emerson was going on to make himself still more unpopular by connecting himself with the Abolitionists, who were greatly hated, and with the social reformers like Bronson Alcott, who favored a vegetable diet, life in communities, and withdrawal from the yoke of civil government. In the spring of 1840 Mr. Alcott, having failed with his Boston school in spite of the warm defence which Emerson had made for him, removed to Concord and took to labor in field and garden for his support. In October, 1840, Emerson wrote to Carlyle:

"We are all a little wild with numberless projects of social reform; not a reading man but has a draft of a new community in his waistcoat pocket. I am gently mad myself."

And in May, 1841, he again wrote:

"One reader and friend of yours dwells now in my house, Henry Thoreau, a poet whom you may one day be proud of—a noble, manly youth, full of melodies and inventions. We work together day by day in my garden, and I grow well and strong."

The same year the Brook Farm Community began its career, with George Ripley at its head and Hawthorne for one of its laborious members. Indeed, while Emerson and Thoreau were hoeing in the garden at Concord and Alcott was a wood-cutter near by, Hawthorne was milking cows and planting corn at Brook Farm. The next year he also went to live in Concord, whither Ellery Channing and Margaret Fuller had gone before him, and the Transcendental brotherhood was established in Emerson's neighborhood. They met frequently at his house and held their conversations by his fireside. "The house," wrote Emerson to Carlyle, "is not large, but convenient and very elastic. The more hearts, and especially great hearts, it holds, the better it looks and feels." Here the hunted slave and the unpopular reformer found shelter, and here the friendly guest had his time to himself—a privilege which Emerson exacted on his own behalf. When he invited Alcott, and, still earlier, Carlyle, to come and live with him, he wrote thus:

"If you will come here like a noble brother, you shall have your solid day undisturbed, except at the hours of eating and walking; and as I will abstain from you myself, so I will defend you from others."

Thoreau lived with him upon these terms, and it was from Emerson's house that he went forth in 1845 to build his hut beside Walden Pond in the midst of his friend's pine wood. It was Emerson's dream to build a lodge of his own on the opposite shore of the pond, with an outlook towards the New Hampshire mountains, and there to study and meditate in the midst of nature.

He had been pursuing his studies in many directions since leaving the pulpit, and, among other things, had conquered the German language. He wrote to Carlyle before 1840: "I have contrived to read almost every volume of Goethe—and I have fifty-five—but I have read nothing else in German." He had always cultivated biography, and in the spring of 1835 said: "I found much indulgence last winter in reading some biographical lectures which were meant for theories or portraits of Luther, Michael Angelo, Milton, George Fox, Burke, etc." To these he afterwards added those lectures on Plato, Swedenborg, Shakespeare, etc. which he included in courses read at Concord and Boston before 1847, and in that year and the next delivered before audiences in England and Scotland. They were published in 1850 under the title of *Representative Men*, but the lectures of 1835 were never published as a whole. It was his custom always to read as lectures what he afterwards printed as essays, but he by no means printed all his lectures, of which, between 1830 and 1880, he gave a hundred in his own town of Concord. In all he must have written two hundred lectures at least. Quite early in his career as lecturer (1836) he writes:

"I have written this year ten lectures; I had written as many last year, and for reading both these and those at places whither I was invited, I have received this last winter about $350. Had I, in lieu of receiving a lecturer-fee, myself advertised that I would deliver these in certain places, these receipts would have been greatly increased."

Afterwards he adopted this method in part, and for some years his chief income was derived from lecturing. In one of his earlier letters to Carlyle (May, 1838) Emerson describes frankly his way of life, including his income and domestic surroundings, of which he gives this picture:

"I occupy, or *improve*, as we Yankees say, two acres only of God's earth, on which is my house, my kitchen-garden, my orchard of thirty young trees, my empty barn. Besides my house, I have, I believe, $22,000, whose income in ordinary years is 6 per cent. I have no other tithe or glebe except the income of my winter lectures, which was last winter $800. Well, with this incor[...] home, I am a rich man. I stay at home and go abroad at my own expense. I have food, warmth, leisure, books, friends. Away from home, I am rich no longer. I never have a dollar to spend on a fancy. As no wise man, I suppose, ever was rich in the sense of freedom to spend, because of the inundation of claims, so neither am I, who am not wise. But at home I am rich—rich enough for ten brothers. My wife Lilian is an incarnation of Christianity, and keeps my philosophy from Antinomianism; my mother, whitest, mildest, most conservative of ladies, whose only exception to her universal preference for old things is her son; my boy, a piece of love and sunshine, well worth my watching from morning to night; these and three domestic women, who cook and sew and run for us, make all my household. Here I sit and read and write with very little system, and, as far as regards composition, with the most fragmentary result; paragraphs incomprehensible, each sentence an infinitely repellent particle. In summer, with the aid of a neighbor, I manage my garden; and a week ago I set out on the west side of my house forty young pine trees to protect me or my son from the wind of January. The ornament of the place is the occasional presence of some ten or twelve persons, good and wise, who visit us in the course of the year."

With the changes that time brought this picture would serve for the next forty years; but after 1878 he gave up lecturing abroad, though not the hospitality of his house.

As a citizen, the Concord philosopher was exemplary at all periods of his life. He served on the school-board of Boston in 1831, and for many years afterwards held the same office in Concord. He could sympathize with his socialist or separatist friends in their denunciation of society, and sometimes say, as he did:

"Even here it behooves every man to quit his dependency on society as much as he can, as he would learn to go without crutches that will soon be plucked away from him."

But he never detached himself from those mutual good offices of town and neighborhood which make up the social life of New England, seldom failed to vote in town-meeting, and scrupulously took part in many public assemblies, where he neither spoke nor listened to much profit. He allowed himself to be mobbed now and then at anti-slavery meetings, though nothing could be more annoying to him than public controversy. When Harriet Martineau in 1837 brought him forward in her book on America as a champion of free thought he wrote to Carlyle:

"Meaning to do me a signal kindness (and a kindness quite out of all measure of justice), she does me a great annoyance—to take away from me my privacy and thrust me before my time (if ever there be a time) into the arena of the gladiators to be stared at. I was ashamed to read, and am ashamed to remember."

Yet he never avoided the disagreeable duties of publicity if the cause of a friend or of the poor and persecuted was in question. As he said of one of his neighbors, so Emerson "returned from courts or congresses, to sit down with unaltered humility, in the church or in the town-house, on the plain wooden bench where honor came and sat down beside him."

The literary and philosophical work of Emerson was chiefly done between 1836, when he published *Nature*, and 1870, when he delivered at Harvard University his course of lectures on the "Natural History of the Intellect." Before 1836 he wrote little which has been published, and after 1872 he wrote scarcely anything, though he printed several books. He spoke of his first book, *Nature*, at the time, "as an entering-wedge for something more worthy and significant, only a naming of topics on which I would gladly speak and gladlier hear." He continued to speak on these topics all his life, having become, as he said of a friend, "that good despot which the virtuous orator is." Until his visit to England in 1847-48, he was much inclined to mysticism in that extreme or pure form which is seen in *Nature*. Thus he wrote in 1836:

"In God we meet, therein we are, thence we descend upon Time, and these infinitesimal facts of Christendom and trade and England, Old and New. Make the soul now drunk with a sleep, and we overleap, at a bound, the obstructions, the griefs, the mistakes of years, and the air we breathe is so vital that the Past serves to contribute nothing to the result."

It was such sentences as these which Carlyle told him in 1840 were "an utterance of what is purest, youngest in your land, pure, ethereal as the voices of the morning." To the same effect the old poet Rogers said when he first read one of Emerson's Cambridge orations: "It is German poetry given out in American prose."

The English visit changed perceptibly his point of view, rather than his manner of seeing and saying. He recognized now that there was a worldly or practical side which he had only seen by glimpses before, though he had from infancy a keen eye for whatever came under his notice. When he seated himself in Concord in 1835, he became a farmer in a small way, and gradually increased his acres, by the purchase of woodland chiefly. As a farmer he was watchful and sensible, even as he was in pruning his sentences and bettering his style. To a friend who had ditched his land and grafted his orchard he wrote:

"Our clover grew well on your patch between the dikes, and Reuben Brown adjudged that Cyrus Warren should pay $14 this year for my grass. Last year he paid $30. All your grafts of this year (1843) have lived and done well. The apple trees and plums speak of you in every wind. This sun without showers will perchance spoil our potatoes."

In all things he was a close observer, and when in Liverpool, Dec. 1, 1847, the day fixed for reducing all the varying clocks of England to Greenwich time for the railroads, he noted the fact, and that the Liverpool clocks were put forward just twelve minutes. In Manchester, two months later, he heard Cobden speak at a great Free Trade meeting, followed by "old Peyronet Thompson, the father of Free Trade, who spoke in a very vigorous rasp-like tone;" while George Thompson, who "brought up the rear," was "merely a piece of rhetoric, and not a man of facts and figures and English solidity like the rest." "I admire the English," he adds, "and I think never more than when I meet Americans; as, for example, at Mr. Bancroft's American soirée, which he holds every Sunday night. Great is the self-respect of Mr. Bull; he is very short-sighted, and without his eyeglass cannot see as far as your eyes to know how you like him so that he quite neglects that point. The Americans see very well—too well." He noted in England "the vulgar hatred and fear of France and the jealousy of America that pervade the newspapers;" but he did not the less reprove the odious faults of his own country; particularly its oppression of the negro in slavery, and the cowardly submission to public opinion which kept Americans otherwise virtuous from denouncing this sin. In addresses on emancipation given at Consord in 1844 and at Waltham in 1845, Emerson attacked slavery with no feeble weapon:

"It is certain that, if it should come to question, all just men, all intelligent agents, must take the part of the black against the white man. Then, I say, 'Never is the planter safe; his house is a den; a just man cannot go there except to tell him so.' Nature fights on the other side; and as power is always stealing from the idle to the busy hand, it seems inevitable that a revolution is preparing, at no distant day, to set these disjointed matters right."

In less than sixteen years after these words were uttered the predicted revolution came, and at the end of twenty years every slave in America was free.

In 1844 he had touched upon another crying evil, the seizure of colored sailors of Massachusetts when they went into the ports of Carolina:

"Gentlemen, I thought the deck of a Massachusetts ship was as much the territory of Massachusetts as the floor on which we stand. It should be as sacred as the temple of God. If such a damnable outrage can be committed on the person of a citizen with impunity, let the Governor break the broad seal of the State; he bears the sword in vain. The great-hearted Puritans have left no posterity. The rich men may walk in State street, but they walk without honor; and the farmers may brag their democracy in the country, but they are disgraced men."

From 1844 till the close of the civil war Emerson took an active part in the anti-slavery agitation, holding an opinion the exact opposite of Carlyle's on the enslavement of the blacks. This difference, though publicly manifested only after 1844, had existed much earlier; for in 1835 Emerson had shown his sympathy with the Abolitionists in Boston at the time they were mobbed and an attempt was made on Garrison's life; while Carlyle in 1837 had written to Emerson in the same scoffing tone about "Mungo the stupid slave" that he afterwards took in the *Latter-Day Pamphlets*. He even declared to Theodore Parker in 1843 that Emerson held the negro in the same estimate as himself; which Parker disputed, and afterwards sent Carlyle the emancipation address of 1844 to disprove. In 1850-52, after Daniel Webster had declared against the Abolitionists, Emerson, who had greatly admired him, denounced Webster as false to his country and to justice in a speech which he made at Cambridge. The college students went down to hear Emerson, and hissed him—the first time, perhaps, he had ever been received with hisses, though by no means the last time, for in the Boston anti-slavery convention of January, 1861, where Emerson spoke, there was a mob, and it was with difficulty he could make himself heard. When the civil war began a few months later, he took sides warmly with the North, and favored emancipation as a war measure. When Pres. Lincoln issued his first emancipation proclamation, in September, 1862, Emerson heartily supported it; indeed, he had addressed Lincoln, Seward, Stanton, and a great audience of public men at Washington six months before, pointing out to them that emancipation was the demand of civilization.

"That is a principle; everything else is an intrigue. Thus, while slavery makes and keeps disunion, emancipation removes the whole objection to Union. And this action, which costs so little, rids the world at one stroke of this degrading nuisance, the cause of war and ruin to nations."

No doubt this address aided Lincoln in reaching his slow conclusion that slavery must be abolished under the war power of the Constitution; and when he had issued the decree, none praised him more heartily for it than Emerson. In a funeral eulogy of Lincoln, in April, 1865, Emerson called him "a heroic figure in the centre of a heroic epoch," and said of his eloquence:

"His brief speech at Gettysburg will not easily be surpassed by words on any recorded occasion. This and one other American speech—that of John Brown to the court that tried him—and a part of Kossuth's speech at Birmingham, can only be compared with each other, and with no fourth."

This habit of Emerson, to stand forth and give public expression to the opinion of himself and others upon great national questions, began as early as 1838, when he addressed a letter to Pres. Van Buren protesting against the wrongs then endured by the Cherokee Indians at the hands of the Government. His anti-slavery speeches; his remarks on the attack made upon Charles Sumner in 1856; his speech in behalf of the Kansas farmers in the same year; his eulogies of John Brown in 1859; his speech of welcome to Kossuth at Concord Bridge in 1852; his speech at the centennial celebration of Concord Fight in 1875, and many other such brief addresses, are examples of this habit. These addresses were not collected until the year 1883, when most of them appeared among Emerson's collected works. Other occasional addresses, such as that on Burns, on Scott, on Carlyle, etc., belong properly among his literary papers; but his distinct political writing was considerable, and may be said to have begun with his first published work, the historical address in 1835 at the two-hundredth anniversary of the planting of Concord. He was an active citizen also in practical ways, and was punctual in his attendance at the town-meetings, where he often took part in debates. He liked to carry his English visitors to the Concord town-house and show them the village assembly in session on election-day. Yet he had sympathized to some extent in the no-government theories of his friends Alcott and Thoreau; and when they were taken to jail in 1842 for refusing to pay taxes to a government that sustained slavery, Emerson visited them, and perhaps paid the tax of Mr. Alcott, though this is said to have been done by Samuel Hoar.

The career of Emerson as an author may be said to have fairly begun in 1840 with the publication of the *Dial* and the preparation of his first book of essays for the press. His *Nature*, and the two or three orations previously printed, had been but occasional utterances, attracting notice, if at all, from the opinions they set forth and the circumstances of their publication. But his contributions to the *Dial* were distinctly literary in their character, and the *Essays* made a book which commanded attention in other countries than his own. It was published in March 1841, having been long in preparation; was reprinted in England, with a preface by Carlyle, in the summer of 1841, and was much read there; to some extent also in France and Germany. In 1844 he published a second volume of *Essays*, which was at once reprinted in England, where, in the meantime, the *Dial*, which came to an end in 1844, had found a few readers. When he visited England, three years afterward, he wrote home to Thoreau, who had been one of his most active contributors:

"The *Dial* is absurdly well known here. We at home, I think, are always a little ashamed of it. I am; and yet here it is spoken of with the utmost gravity, and I do not laugh."

He continued to publish his friends' books more rapidly than his own—Carlyle's *Chartism* in 1842, his *Past and Present* in 1843, and in the same year a volume of poems by Ellery Channing, which he not only aided in publishing, but reviewed in the *Democratic Review* of New York, to which magazine Hawthorne and Whittier were then contributing frequently. He caused John Sterling's poems to be reprinted in America, and finally, in 1847, published the first volume of his own *Poems*, many of which had already appeared in the *Dial*. In 1849 his *Nature* was reprinted in a volume with *Addresses and Lectures* from "The American Scholar" of 1837 (the first Phi Beta oration) to "The Young American" of 1844. In 1850 appeared *Representative Men;* in 1852 his *Memoirs of Margaret Fuller;* and in 1856 *English Traits*. In November, 1857, the *Atlantic Monthly* began, and for some years Emerson contributed often to its pages, as he had infrequently to the *Massachusetts Quarterly Review* from 1847 to 1850. In 1860 he published *The Conduct of Life;* in 1864 *Society and Solitude;* in 1867 a second volume of poems, entitled *May-Day;* in 1874 a collection of poetry by other authors, called *Parnassus;* and in 1876 a new selection of his own *Poems* and a collection of essays, called *Letters and Social Aims*. This was the last book which he printed, though he continued to furnish essays for the magazines until 1881, which have, since his death, appeared in one of the volumes of the new edition. His projected philosophical work, *The Natural History of the Intellect*—which he had been preparing for thirty or forty years, and which he partly threw into chapters for a course of university lectures at Cambridge in 1870—was never brought by him to a form suitable for publication, and must remain a fragment, if it is ever printed by his literary executors. They have published a new edition of his verses, with additional poems and fragments of poems which he left in manuscript. Among these unpublished verses is a college poem which he prepared for a Phi Beta anniversary at Cambridge nearly fifty years ago, and portions of a long work, which he called *The Discontented Poet, a Masque*, but from which he afterwards detached passages and printed them separately. Since his death his correspondence with Thomas Carlyle has been published (not quite complete) (Boston, 1883), edited by Prof. Norton, of Cambridge. His literary executor, J. Elliott Cabot, is writing a biography which will include passages from his diary and letters, and may be published in 1885. Other writings of his will be published hereafter, the amount of manuscript left by him being nearly as great as all that he published in volumes during his lifetime. He wrote little or nothing during the last ten years of his life, but devoted much time to revising and editing what he had written, and his biographer had been chosen, and some part of his life written, before his death in 1882. A memoir by Dr. O. W. Holmes, containing some of his letters, appeared in 1884.

Emerson may be considered in several aspects, for he was a man of varied and, in some degree, contradictory powers. He was a poet, a philosopher, an orator, a critic, and the head, if not the founder, of a school of thought and action, with disciples in both hemispheres. In this power of influencing the thought of others he resembled Goethe, to whom also he bore other resemblances, though widely differing from him in some of the most fundamental points of character and genius. Like Goethe he was a man of positive genius, which displayed itself in verse and prose, but most of all in the masculine power of fertilizing other minds by its influence—exerted not directly through elaborate works, but by a subtle and pervasive spirit analogous to what Matthew Arnold terms the *Zeitgeist*, but often in direct opposition to the apparent spirit of the times. Like Goethe he lived to old age, saw his country and the world pass through a great political revolution, and could look back over a broad field of literary and philosophic activity; and, like Goethe, he was originally and chiefly a poet—that is an idealist seeking naturally the image of beauty, and expressing himself easily in metrical form; though he lacked the constructive and artistic spirit so characteristic of the great German poet. On the other hand he wrote prose better than Goethe, though less copiously and systematically; and he possessed, too, the critical faculties of insight and discrimination in a remarkable degree. He lacked in some measure Goethe's broad wisdom and talent, by which he appeared as a perfect man of the world while holding the highest literary rank in Europe; but, as a compensation for this, Emerson was more perfectly related to the family and to the State as a citizen and an observer of all the social laws that guard domestic life. In this respect he resembled the other great European poet of that age, Wordsworth, who, standing apart from Goethe on the moral and religious side, yet influenced literature almost as forcibly, at least among those who speak the English tongue. Emerson may be said to stand, as a poet and as a man, between Wordsworth and Goethe—exhibiting likewise a distinct American quality in his genius, which before his time no literary man had shown.

It has not been customary to speak of Emerson as a poet, but rather as a philosopher or literary man in general, passing lightly over his poems as something odd and peculiar that must be tolerated but need not be understood nor generally read. Even Carlyle, when they first appeared, was compelled to apologise for them, promising to make them nearly all intelligible, if his friends would let him read them aloud and explain them. Yet it is certain that Emerson, whose judgment of men was so discriminating as to be called "fatal," regarded himself a poet, and he once said "I am not a great poet, but whatever there is of me at all is poet." He was well aware, however, of his want of facility in metrical expression, and that his poetic faculty was seldom under the control of his will; so that he wrote verse fitfully and at long intervals—beginning, as we have seen, at the age of 11—then from 21 to 30 writing but little which he thought worth preserving—but from 35 to 50 writing verse frequently and with delight; after which he wrote little poetry, but among the later pieces were some of his best. As now published by his executors, a single volume of some 300 pages contains his poetical work, but several of the poems he printed in his first collection (of 1847) are here omitted, and there remain in manuscript many verses which may yet be deemed worthy of publication, though he did not so regard them. Although Matthew Arnold in a recent essay on Emerson speaks slightingly of his poems, there is increasing testimony to their high value, not only as expressions of his philosophy, but as genuine poetic utterances—often oracular and dithyrambic, but belonging to that class of poems which is never forgotten though it may never become popular. There is much variety in his poems, notwithstanding the mystic and enigmatical character which many of them have; and passages of pure and charming description, of delicate satire, of lyric melody, and of plain sententious force are frequently found. No modern poet, and few of former times, have written so nobly of love as Emerson, who, like the Persian poets, elevates the human passion into a divine sentiment and even a mystery of religion. Thus he says in the fragments printed since his death:

"I saw the hid beginnings
  When Chaos and Order strove,
And I can date the morning prime
  And purple flame of Love.
When the purple flame shoots up,
  And Love ascends his throne,
I cannot hear your songs, O birds,
  For the witchery of my own."

He returns again and again to this theme, devoting one of his longest poems to the three aspects of love which he calls the "Initial, Dæmonic, and Celestial," and again summing up the whole matter in that epigram on "Eros" which first appeared in the *Dial*:

"The sense of the world is short,
  Long and various the report—
    To love and be beloved;
Men and gods have not outlearned it,
And, how oft soe'er they've turned it,
  'Tis not to be improved."

In epigram Emerson is the most successful of recent poets, and he often uses this form; indeed many of his poems are but a succession of epigrams, with here and there a wild melodious verse thrown in. It would not be easy to condense into a quatrain more meaning and persuasion than lurk in these four lines which he calls "Sacrifice:"

"Though love repine and reason chafe,
  There came a voice without reply—
'Tis man's perdition to be safe,
  When for the truth he ought to die."

Many of Emerson's lines are on the way to become proverbial, if not already so, like that one from "The Problem:"

"He builded better than he knew,"

and the close of "The Rhodora:"

"Beauty is its own excuse for being."

On the whole we must say that he is a high and rare poet, perhaps to be recognized hereafter as a great one. As a critic of other men's poetry he is among the best, and his collection or common-place book, called *Parnassus*, is more interesting than any other of its kind.

Emerson's immediate success and his first impression upon the world was as a prose-writer. Yet in prose as in verse this was produced by the instantaneous combination of force and beauty, thought and grace of diction, in what he wrote. Hence his style is inextricably blended with his philosophy like light and heat and chemical action in the rays of the sun; and as it is hard to define his philosophy in set terms, so is it to describe the excellence and the defects of his prose. When to this undefinable quality of his writing were added the graces of his oratory, a high and charming effect was the result. James Russell Lowell, who as a youth listened to some of his first lectures in Boston, has quoted as applicable to the young orator the praise of Sir Philip Sidney by Matthew Roydon:

"Was ever eye did see that face,
  Was ever ear did hear that tongue,
Was ever mind did mind his grace,
  That ever thought the travel long?
But eyes and ears and every thought
Were with his sweet perfections caught."

The fitness of this quotation was at once seen by those who had heard Emerson at his best; and yet he had not the manifest arts nor the ordinary eloquence of an orator. His gestures were not always graceful, nor his elocution regular; but the expression of his face, of his whole bearing, and the searching, thrilling tones of his manly voice, won from the hearer at once that prize of oratory, the whole soul of his audience, so that they followed him where he chose to lead them. They might not understand his meaning, but they were charmed and captivated by his periods, and the deep meaning which he evidently found in them. He took pleasure also wherein he gave pleasure, and very early in his correspondence with Carlyle he said: "I have a certain delight in speaking to a multitude," nor did he ever quite lose the delight even in his years of age and forgetfulness. It was as the vehicle of his thought, however, that he valued eloquence, and he sought no profit from his hearers that he did not return to them fourfold. In his writing he favored short and simple sentences; avoiding the cumbrous periods that were in vogue before his time, and following the example of Channing in breaking up the long sentence into several briefer ones. He wrote readily, yet revised and rewrote with infinite pains before he published anything—often keeping an essay in hand ten or twenty years before printing it, or allowing it to be verbally reported. His sermons, all written before 1835, were pillaged to enrich his lectures and essays.

The earliest expression of Emerson's philosophic insight—for it is hardly just to speak of his philosophic system—is his first little book, *Nature;* and from this delicate and world-embracing idealism he never departed, though he reinforced its poetic beauty with much plain ethical wisdom in later years. It had something in common, both on its metaphysical and its ethical side, with the transcendentalism of Kant; but nothing could be farther from the method of Emerson than the dry critical analysis of Kant. To suggest spiritual truth in images of beauty, and with love as its inspiration, was Emerson's ideal of a philosopher, and hence his admiration for Plato. Yet the Puritan was strong in him also; and he insisted, as rigidly as Milton or Calvin, on moral excellence and the deeds as well as the dreams of virtue. Nor did he fail to adorn, by his own noble and amiable life, the philosophic profession; and all men, whether they accepted his teachings or not, were struck with the beauty of his conduct in every emergency and towards every condition of men. He had the knightly and the saintly virtues, along with the poetic genius and the scholastic habit. In every relation of love and friendship, in all the duties of the family, the community, and the individual, he was so nearly faultless that the voice of those who knew is one unbroken chorus of praise. His writings are sometimes taxed with a coldness and distance towards the ordinary affairs of men and women which never appeared in his daily practice. A loving son, a devoted husband, a kind and wise father, a faithful friend, a good neighbor, an active and useful citizen—he passed through life solitary in his thought, but social and beneficent in all his affections. It is too early to assign his rank among philosophers and men of letters, as some have endeavored; but the deep impression which he made upon his age bespeaks for him an enduring fame among those who have enriched literature and made life better worth living. He died after a short illness, but a long period of decaying memory and advancing age —all which he endured sweetly, firmly, and in the confident hope of personal immortality. He is buried on a hill-top in Concord, amid oaks and pine trees, and near the graves of Thoreau and Hawthorne. (F. B. S.)

EMERY is an impure variety of corundum, mixed chiefly with magnetic oxyd of iron. On account of its extreme hardness, it has been long used in the arts for grinding and polishing hard stones, metals, and glass, but its mineralogical character was not determined until 1846, when Dr. J. Lawrence Smith, of the United States, then in the service of the Turkish government, investigated its occurrence and the various geological and mineralogical facts connected with it. At that time it was obtained only from the Island of Naxos, and the Greek government had granted a monopoly of it to an English merchant. Dr. Smith found it in six other localities in Asia Minor and the Greek archipelago, thus breaking up the monopoly and reducing the price from $140 to $50 a ton. His exact statement of its geology and of its associate minerals, made first to the French Academy of Sciences in 1850, eventually led to the discovery by Prof. C. T. Jackson of a vein of emery at Chester, Mass., in 1863, and afterwards to discoveries in other parts of the United States. Dr. Smith gives (*American Journal of Science*, Vol. xcii, p. 89) the following analyses of emery taken from different localities:

See Vol. VIII. p. 157 Am. ed. (p. 171 Edin. ed.)

Locality.	Alumina.	Oxyd of iron.	Lime.	Silica.	Water.	Specific gravity.
Kulah	63.50	32.25	0.92	1.61	1.90	4.28
Samos	70.10	23.21	0.62	4.00	2.10	3.98
Naxos	58.53	24.10	0.86	3.10	4.73	3.75
Ephesus	60.10	33.20	0.48	1.80	5.62	4.31
Chester 1	44.01	50.21		3.13		
" 2	74.22	19.31		5.48		

Taking the effective hardness of the sapphire of India as 100 he assigns the following degrees of hardness to the different varieties of emery analyzed above: Kulah, 57; Samos, 56; Naxos, 46; Ephesus, 42; Chester 1, 33; Chester 2, 45. The minerals always associated with emery are diaspore, emerylite, chlorite, and magnetic and titaniferous iron.

EMIGRATION. (See IMMIGRATION.)

EMMONS, NATHANAEL, D. D. (1745–1840), an eminent American theologian, was born at East Haddam, Conn., April 20, 1745. He graduated at Yale College in 1767, and was ordained pastor of the Congregational church at Franklin, Mass., in 1773. He remained pastor of this congregation till his death, though after 1827 he was assisted by others. Besides his pastoral labors he trained for the ministry eighty-seven students, and was one of the founders of the Massachusetts Missionary Society. He was also editor of a missionary magazine, and labored actively for the cause of foreign missions. He published many works in his lifetime, and after his death they were collected and edited, with a memoir, by Rev. Jacob Ide, D. D. (7 vols., Boston, 1842), and again by Prof. E. A. Park (6 vols., Boston, 1861). Dr. Emmons died in Franklin, Mass. Sept. 23, 1840. His system of theology was a modified Calvinism. In opposition to the doctrine of original sin, which had prevailed among the so-called orthodox divines, he maintained that the exercise of the will is necessary to either sin or holiness. He also maintained that God is the efficient cause of every act and thought of man, while yet man is in every moral act perfectly free. His sermons were noted for their dignity of style and power of thought, and in them, as well as in his theological treatises, he discussed the profound problems of "fate, free-will, foreknowledge absolute." He was one of the framers of the creed required to be subscribed by every professor in the Andover Theological Seminary.

EMORY, JOHN, D. D. (1789–1835), an American bishop of the Methodist Episcopal Church, was born at Spaniard's Neck, Queen Anne co., Md., April 11, 1789. He was educated at a classical school in that neighborhood, then at Lancaster, Pa., and finally graduated at Washington College, Chestertown, Md. His parents were members of the Methodist Church, and he had received religious training, but in 1806 he experienced what he considered a spiritual renovation. By his father's desire he had studied law, and was admitted to the bar when only nineteen years of age. His sense of duty soon led him to enter the ministry, and in 1810 he joined the Philadelphia Methodist conference. He served in Wilmington, Del., Washington, Philadelphia, and other places. In 1816 he was chosen delegate to the General Conference, and, except in 1824, was a member of every subsequent conference till his death. In 1820 he was sent as a delegate of the American Church to the British Wesleyan Conference. In 1824 he was appointed book-agent and editor in New York, and succeeded in freeing the Methodist Book Concern from the difficulties with which it was surrounded. He established a publication fund, and founded the *Methodist Quarterly Review*, in which for some time he was the principal writer. In 1832 he was chosen bishop, and, besides his other duties, labored especially to promote the educational interests of the church. He was influential in bringing Dickinson College, at Carlisle, Pa., under Methodist control, and in establishing the Wesleyan University at Middletown, Conn. Besides his articles in the *Methodist Review*, he had, in 1817, a pamphlet controversy with Bishop William White, of Pennsylvania, on *The Personal Assurance of the Holy Spirit*, and in 1830 he published a *Defence of the Original Organization of the Methodist Episcopal Church*. His writings were collected and published, together with a biography, by his son, Rev. Robert Emory, at New York (1841).

EMORY COLLEGE, located in the town of Oxford, Newton co., Ga., 40 miles east of Atlanta, was incorporated by an act of the general assembly of the State Dec. 10, 1836, during the administration of William Schley, governor. The charter-members of the board of trustees were all Methodists, nine of them being itinerant preachers. The act of incorporation was liberal, giving all the authority needful for founding and conducting a college of high grade. The trustees met and organized Feb. 6, 1837. They purchased a large tract of land near Covington, Ga., the county-town, and procured a charter for Oxford, the village that subsequently grew around the college. By special act of the State legislature "all drinking- and gaming-places" are excluded from the village, and have been from the beginning. Every deed to property in it came originally to private holders through the trustees, and has a "for feiture clause" in it setting forth that "the selling or permitting to be sold on said premises of intoxicating liquors" shall forfeit the title. There has never been a liquor- or gambling-saloon in the village.

The first faculty was elected at a meeting of the trustees held Dec. 8, 1837, and was composed as follows: Ignatius A. Few, president; Archelaus H. Mitchell, professor of moral and mental philosophy and belles-lettres; Alexander Means, professor of natural sciences; George W. Lane, professor of ancient languages; Harry B. Lane, professor of mathematics and civil engineering. These men began with much zeal, great faith, and little money. Unpretentious and inadequate buildings were erected; there was hardly a thought of endowment; they depended for the most part on patronage; and for forty-four years the college had a hard struggle, meantime doing good and honest work. The list of beneficiaries has always been large, averaging one-fourth of the whole number, and often one-third. Methodist itinerant preachers were the real fathers and founders of the college, and from the beginning their sons have been, by college law, entitled to free tuition. In this way hundreds of the pastors have been able to give their sons a liberal education. In the course of years the principle was extended to other denominations, and for a long time preceding 1882 the sons of all "pastors" have received tuition free of cost. Soon after the Civil War, to meet the wants of the impoverished people, several free scholarships were given for the benefit of laymen. By 1860 a considerable endowment had been collected; during the war a large amount of "Confederate money" was given to the college agents for endowment purposes. At the close of hostilities the endowment was so impaired by the destruction of property and by bankruptcies incident to the collapse of the Southern Confederacy that the total productive endowment barely reached $20,000. Some years prior to 1860 large and commodious buildings were erected; but about 1870 it became necessary, on account of the faulty construction of the main building, to take it down and build others. This was done, after great exertion, during the panic of 1873. Bishop George F. Pierce was the chief agent in raising the necessary funds for all these buildings.

During all these vicissitudes, as the records and the alumni show, a good standard of scholarship was maintained. About the year 1881, Mr. George I. Seney, president of the Metropolitan Bank, New York, became interested in the "cause of education in the South," and of his own motion gave to Emory College $75,000 to increase its endowment, $5000 to help pay a debt, and the cost of "Seney Hall," a large and elegant building finished during the summer of 1882, the whole amount being $125,000. (During the same period he gave $125,000 to Wesleyan Female College, Macon, Ga., and $10,000 to Lucy Cobb Female College, Athens, Ga.—his generous gifts awakening the gratitude of the whole South.) At the beginning of 1882 the productive endowment of Emory College amounted to $100,000. The annual catalogue for this year showed the names of 241 students, a faculty of 12, and an alumni list of 690. The students came from ten States, one Territory, and two foreign countries. In addition to the course of study common to colleges of high grade, Emory College has introduced vocal music and book-keeping. In the beginning of 1882, through a system of boarding-houses peculiar to the institution, nearly one hundred young men were maintaining themselves at a cost of $8 per month, many of them making enough money during the vacation, embracing the months of July, August, and September, to meet their expenses the ensuing year.

The following have been presidents of the college: Rev. Ignatius A. Few, D. D., LL.D.; Rev. A. B. Longstreet, D. D.; Rev. Bishop George F. Pierce, D. D., LL.D.; Rev. Alexander Means, D. D., LL.D.; Rev. J. R. Thomas, D. D., LL.D.; Rev. L. M. Smith, D. D.; Rev. O. L. Smith, D. D.; Rev. Atticus G. Haygood, D. D. (in office 1882).

The graduates of the college are found in all the Southern States. The majority of the graduates in professional pursuits are teachers; lawyers, preachers, physicians coming next in the order named. The college has furnished two U. S. Senators—Hon. Thomas M. Norwood of Georgia, from the class of 1850; Hon. L. Q. C. Lamar of Mississippi, from the class of 1845. A number have been members of the House of Representatives. Many of its alumni were among the officers in the Confederate army, and many died in its service. Among the most distinguished of the alumni is Rev. Young J. Allen, D. D., LL.D., of the class of 1858, a leading missionary in China, who began in December, 1881, a system of high schools in Shanghai, preliminary to the establishment of a thoroughly equipped Christian college under the care of the Methodist Episcopal Church, South. The college has always been characterized by a profound religious spirit singularly free from sectarianism. Its sessions have been continuous since its foundation except during 1863, 1864, and 1865, when the exercises were broken up by the war between the States. Few colleges in the Southern States have so promising a future. The spirit of its management and of its students is progressive and national. (A. G. H.)

EMPIRICISM. This word, derived from the Greek ἐμπειρία, "experience," is used in three senses. In the first it relates to the sect or school of medicine founded at Alexandria at the beginning of the third century B. C., by Philinus of Cos, and developed by Serapion. This school professed to reject all reasoning, and to make medicine consist only in the results of experience. It flourished for a very brief period, and had little or no influence,—its teachings being substantially a series of minute and subtle reasonings to prove the vanity of reasoning. In the second sense it is applied not only to medicine considered as an art, but to other things, to indicate that what is done is not the result of scientific deduction or reasoning, but is simply a following out what has been done before. A popular and expressive phrase for this is "to work by rule of thumb." In the third and most usual sense empiricism is used as equivalent to charlatanry or quackery, implying a mixture of ignorance and knavery in various proportions.

This vulgar empiricism is common to all times and all countries, for it is an attempt to satisfy a desire which is so universal that it has been claimed to be instinctive. This is the desire for a specific remedy, in case of pain or disease, based on the idea that diseases are specific entities, and is expressed in the phrase that "every disease must have its remedy."

Skilled physicians have ceased to seek for such specifics since the discoveries of modern physiology and pathology have shown the impossibility of success. Every case of disease is a problem by itself, yet the desire and the attempt to satisfy it remains, and a practice founded on it is alike agreeable to the patient and the practitioner. "To the one, if there be faith in the specific remedy or method, it administers a most cheering and effectual remedy; to the other it saves the trouble of thought; hence we may readily understand how many may enthusiastically receive and practise a system of empiricism independently of all sordid motives, and if the perceptive faculties predominate over the reason however wisely educated, that often talented persons may be carried away by a false system."

Some empiricists have but one specific, as hydropathists; others have, or attempt to find, a different specific for each disease, as was the case with the empirical school of Alexandria, and is the case with homœopathists. All empirics constantly appeal to *experience* in proof of their doctrines. An especial characteristic of empirics of all grades is the animosity displayed by them in their writings towards regular medicine. "It is also a general characteristic of empiricism that it appeals from the judgment of the educated profession to that of the uneducated public. This is in fact an essential element of the pure quackeries, being indispensable to their success. Attempts made from time to time to put quackery away by vilification or direct persecution have probably done more to encourage and promote it than anything else. The slightest persecution can be skillfully transmuted into a crown of martyrdom, and they assume the attitude before the public of being champions of truth and of political freedom, and the victims of professional dislike excited solely by pecuniary interest. Every man duly authorized has the undoubted moral right to practise his art to the best of his judgment. He should, however, be no party to the public expression of vaunts and assumption of superiority to any sect. Let him believe and practise as he thinks right, and publish the results, not as a sectarian but as a catholic member of the universal school of scientific investigation." A form of empiricism which especially flourishes in the United States is that which accepts each man's opinion of the nature of his disease and provides a remedy according to the name he gives it. This includes the so-called "patent medicines," of which, however, very few are really patented, since to do this it is necessary to reveal their composition. They come under the general definition of "nostrums," *i. e.*, "medicines the ingredients of which are kept secret for the purpose of restricting the profits of sale to the inventor or proprietor." Many of these nostrums are composed of inert and harmless ingredients, and the purchasers are simply cheated. Some of them, however, are dangerous poisons—such, for instance, as those advertised and sold for the purpose of procuring abortion. Advertisements of these are not uncommon, religious and family journals being a favorite medium, and their uses are generally well understood. The liquid forms usually contain oils of savine, tansy, or rue, and the chief ingredients of the potions which are sold for this purpose are solid extracts of the same substances together with ergot and aloes.

Some empirics pride themselves on their want of education, as, for instance, the so-called Indian doctors, Chinese doctors, etc., who boast that their remedies are eminently free from all speculation and hypothesis. Closely allied to these are the root doctors, herb doctors, etc. There is an absurd idea among the people that vegetable medicines are safer than those derived from the mineral kingdom, and there was at one time a law in the State of New York prohibiting all persons not regularly licensed to practise medicine from giving any medicines except those of a vegetable origin, which were the products of our own soil. This forbade a person from giving a dose of salts or of magnesia, but authorized him to administer the deadly stramonium, hemlock, etc. The widest and most lucrative field of quackery is that of patent medicines, which are sold in immense quantities. The favorite theory with the advertisers of these remedies is that all diseases are the result of impurity of the blood, and this impurity of the blood may be removed by one remedy which is the great panacea. It is a significant fact that in some instances the powers of secret medicines have been so highly esteemed that large sums of money have been given for a revelation of their composition, but as soon as the mystery disappears the charm disappears also and the remedy before regarded as so important is promptly consigned to oblivion.

One reason for the temporary success of the charlatan is that he takes care to hold out a prospect of cure without interfering with the pleasures and appetites of his patient. A skilled physician tells a person affected with a chronic disease that to recover his health he must practise self-denial, must be temperate and abstemious, keep regular hours, give up the use of tobacco, devote fewer hours to his business, etc. In such a case the patient is often inclined to regard the remedy as worse than the disease. If, then, he finds his symptoms described in the advertisement of an electrical or of a shampooing doctor, or of certain pills or bitters, promising speedy cure without change of diet or habits, he is very apt to try it.

The popular ignorance which promotes quackery is not so much the ignorance of what is known in medicine as of what is not known, of the fact that there is much that is beyond the reach of our present means of investigation, much that is doubtful and uncertain, and that a skilled physician who is honest must in many cases acknowledge his ignorance. (J. S. B.)

EMPORIA, the county-seat of Lyon co., Kan., is on the south bank of the Neosho River, and at the intersection of the Atchison, Topeka, and Santa Fé Railroad with the Missouri, Kansas, and Texas Railroad, 61 miles S. W. of Topeka. It has a fine courthouse, 2 opera-houses and public halls, 2 national banks, 1 daily and 3 weekly newspapers, 10 churches, a Franciscan convent, the State Normal School, with fine building, built in 1880, a high school, 4 graded schools, gas-works, and Holly system of water-works. Its manufactures comprise flour, furniture, carriages, soap, and woollen goods. It is surrounded by a good agricultural and stock-raising district. Population, 7500.

ENCYCLICAL. An ecclesiastical term, derived from the Greek, and meaning literally "in a circle." It is used of a letter sent to many persons or to a whole order of men. The first example, in church history, of an encyclical or circular letter, is found in the Acts of the Apostles, ch. xv., where the apostles assembled at Jerusalem instructed the converts from heathenism that they were not bound by the law of Moses. The use of encyclicals has been for many ages confined, in the Roman Catholic Church, to the sovereign pontiff. There is a slight distinction between an encyclical letter and apostolic letters, although they are sometimes used in the same sense. Both sorts of communications are restricted to the pope, but the former, which is always in the singular number (*Epistola Encyclica*), is addressed exclusively to the governing body in the church, or the hierarchy; whereas the latter, which are always used in the plural number (*Litteræ Apostolicæ*), are addressed as well to the inferior orders of the clergy and to the laity. They are always in Latin, and sealed with the Fisherman's Ring. (R. S.)

ENDICOTT, JOHN (1588-1665), a Puritan colonial governor of Massachusetts, was born in Dorchester, England, in 1588. When a number of English gentlemen in 1628 purchased from the Plymouth Company a tract of land near the Merrimack River, Endicott was chosen to lead a band of settlers there. He arrived at Naumkeag, or Salem, on Sept. 6, 1628, and in the next year, when a royal charter was obtained, was appointed by the Massachusetts Bay Company governor of their colony. This colony was composed of Puritans who claimed to belong to the Church of England, and were not separatists like the Pilgrims of Plymouth. Still they did not use the Book of Common Prayer, and when a few insisted upon it Endicott sent them back to England and secured quiet. He also cut down the May-pole that had been erected at Mount Wollaston, or Merry Mount, and administered a sharp rebuke to Thomas Morton, a roystering fellow, who had settled there and sold ammunition and strong drink to the Indians. In 1629 the government of the colony was entirely transferred to New England, and John Winthrop, "the Father of Boston," became governor in 1630. Trouble with the Indians having arisen, Endicott was sent with 90 men to attack the Pequots, and this expedition led to a war in which that tribe was exterminated. Endicott objected to the cross in the English flag as savoring of popery, and had it removed. He was made deputy-governor in 1641, and governor in 1644, when he removed from Salem to Boston. In 1645 he was made major-general of the troops of the colony. From 1649 till his death he was governor, except for two years in which he was deputy-governor. In 1652 he established a mint, which continued to coin money till the charter of the colony was abrogated in 1685. He was a stern Puritan, resolute to maintain with the sword what he believed to be the cause of God and truth. He persecuted the Quakers, and in a formal proclamation denounced the practice of wearing long hair. He was well educated, talented, keen in discernment and prompt in action, and under him the colony prospered. He died at Boston, March 15, 1665.

ENGELMANN, GEORGE (1809-1884), an American physician and botanist, was born at Frankfort-on-the-Main, Germany, Feb. 2, 1809. He was educated in his native city, then studied medicine and natural science in the universities of Berlin and Heidelberg, and emigrated to the United States in 1832. He settled first at Belleville, Ill., but in 1835 removed to St. Louis, where he practised his profession. He also founded *Das Westland*, a German periodical, which treated, in an interesting manner, American life and institutions. Amid the duties of his profession he gave much attention to botany, and published many monographs on the plants of North America. There are few descriptive works on that subject in which the authors do not acknowledge their indebtedness to Dr. Engelmann. He died at St. Louis, Feb. 13, 1884. His principal publications were "North American Cuscutineae," in *Silliman's Journal* (1842); "Cactaceae of the United States," in the *Proceedings of the American Academy of Arts and Sciences* (1852); "Supplement to Dr. Gray's Plants of the Rocky Mountains," in *Silliman's Journal*, vols. 33, 34; "Cactaceae," in Emory's *Mexican Boundary Survey* (1859); "Cactaceae," in Whipple's *Survey* (1856). In conjunction with Dr. Gray he published "Plantae Lindheimerianae," in the *Boston Journal of Natural History*, vol. v. Among his monographs were *The Genus Cuscuta* (1867); *The Cactus Flora of the Rocky Mountains* (1868); *North American Species of Juncus* (1868); *Notes on the Genus Yucca* (1873); *Notes on the Agave* (1875); *Oaks of the United States* (1876); *Revision of the Genus Pinus* (1880); *The Genus Isoëtes in North America* (1882).

ENGLAND. The lull in political affairs which followed the overthrow of Mr. Gladstone's reforming ministry in 1874, and the accession of the Conservatives to power, was of brief duration. From the torpor and indifference which succeeded an epoch of rapid change, the nation was roused, by events that took place in the distant East, to a degree of passion and excitement unknown in English political life since the repeal of the Corn Laws. In 1875 Bosnia and Herzegovina rose in rebellion against the Turk. In the following summer a report reached England that in putting down the beginnings of a similar rising in Bulgaria the Turks had been guilty of the most shocking cruelty. This report was treated in Parliament by Mr. Disraeli, the Prime Minister, with ill-judged levity, and characterized by him as coffee-house gossip. But others were not so easily satisfied. The representatives of the press made their way to Batak, and found among the miserable survivors and in the charred ruins of this and other villages the most heart-rending evidence of the storm of savage fury that had passed over the ill-fated district. The publication of details, verified by eye-witnesses, produced the deepest impression in England. Meetings held in every important town gave voice to the general sentiment of horror at these barbarities, and of sympathy with their victims. It was indeed subsequently alleged that the outburst of pity and indignation which, in the autumn of 1876, threw every daily care and interest of the English people into the background, was the result of a fictitious agitation set on foot by politicians out of office with the view of making capital for their party. This shallow and credulous representation is on a level with the old Continental theory that the vehemence of the English people against the slave-trade, in 1814, was an elaborate piece of commercial hypocrisy. Those who were in England in 1876, and who had the opportunity of moving among people of all grades of life, know how spontaneous, how widespread, and how passionate was the cry of indignation against the Turk, and how ardent the desire to employ the influence of England in rendering such outrages impossible in the future. The fault of the English at the present day is certainly not a deficiency of feeling when the sense of wrong is touched, but rather an over-excitability which is apt to spend itself before sufficient knowledge has been gained to result in useful action. In the case, however, of Turkey, the experience of 1876 did once and for all make an end of the illusions which had existed in England, since the Crimean War, as to the virtues of the Turk, and brought home to the nation, for the first time, the fact that five-sixths of the inhabitants of the so-called Turkey-in-Europe were not Turks at all, but Christians, and that the liberation of these races from Turkish misrule constituted the real Eastern question. Though the government of Lord Beaconsfield (Disraeli), following the same policy which had made Castlereagh the foe of Greek independence in 1821, and shutting its eyes and its heart to everything except the supposed danger to British interests in the extension of Russian power, declined to enter into any effective concert for the protection of the Christian subjects of the Sultan, there was now too strong a feeling in the country in favor of these Slavonic people and against their Turkish oppressors for the government to promise its assistance to the Porte in the event of war with Russia, though Lord Beaconsfield, according to his own statement, would have taken this course if public opinion had not prevented him. A conference was held in Constantinople in December, 1876, and attended by Lord Salisbury on behalf of Great Britain. Here all the proposals for reform made by the Great Powers were rejected by the Sultan. Lord Salisbury returned to England; Ignatieff, the Russian plenipotentiary, shortly followed him, and a protocol was signed at London on March 31, 1877, in which the Powers declared that in case of the failure of the Porte to improve the condition of its Christian subjects, they reserved to themselves the choice of means best fitted to secure that end. To this declaration the Porte replied by a protest. On the 26th of April Russia declared war, alleging as its grounds the failure of the conference and the rejection of the protocol. Lord Derby, the Foreign Secretary, replying in the name of his government to the statement of Russia, expressed disapproval of the war, and declared that the action of the Czar would "neither alleviate the difficulty of reform nor improve the condition of the Christian population throughout the Sultan's dominions." Resolutions brought forward by Mr. Gladstone, in the House of Commons, asserting that England had just cause of dissatisfaction and complaint in the conduct of the Ottoman Porte were rejected by a large majority. The government informed Russia that it would consider British interests threatened if any interference should take place with the Suez Canal, if Egypt should be made the scene of hostilities, or if Constantinople should be occupied for any considerable time: if its interests were not so menaced it would remain neutral. The Russian ambassador gave satisfactory assurances on these points, and shortly afterwards made Lord Derby acquainted with the terms of peace which Russia proposed to insist upon at the end of the war. No exception seems to have been taken to the terms by the cabinet. The Queen's speech at the prorogation of Parliament, on August 15, acknowledged the friendly disposition shown by the Czar's government, and expressed a desire to aid in the restoration of peace, if suitable opportunity should occur, on terms compatible with the honor of the belligerents. It was not until the autumn of 1877, when the obstinate defence of the Turks at Plevna, and the repeated victories won by them over blundering Russian generals, had excited some surprise and admiration, that a war-party sprang up in Great Britain, and that its leaders called for an alliance with the Turks. The fall of Plevna, on December 10, and the rapid advance of the Russians that followed it, caused a change in the tone of the English government. Parliament was summoned in January — a month before the usual time — and the Queen's speech, after announcing that communications had been made to the Czar in favor of peace, and that the conditions of British neutrality had not yet been infringed, continued in the following ominous words: "I cannot conceal from myself that should hostilities unfortunately be prolonged, some unexpected occurrence may render it incumbent upon me to adopt measures of precaution. I trust to the liberality of Parliament to supply the means that may be required for that purpose."

On the 20th of January the Russians occupied Adrianople; on the 23d orders were sent from London to Admiral Hornby to sail at once for the Dardanelles; on the 24th the government gave notice that they would ask for a vote of £6,000,000 for naval and military purposes. It was now known that there were dissensions in the cabinet; that Lord Carnarvon had resigned, and that Lord Derby, who, after the Premier, was the most important member of the ministry, had tendered, but afterwards withdrawn, his resignation. The vote of £6,000,000, as a direct menace of war, was opposed in the Commons by the leaders of the Liberal party; but, while the debate was proceeding, telegrams arrived from Mr. Layard, ambassador at Constantinople, which gave the impression that, in spite of an armistice, the Russian forces were on the point of entering the capital. A panic followed; the opposition to the proposals of the government collapsed, and the money was granted. It subsequently turned out that the movements of Russian troops, which had given rise to the ambassador's alarming reports, were in accordance with the stipulations of the armistice, which were not themselves unusual or unreasonable ones. The British fleet was now ordered to Constantinople, but, on its being stated by Prince Gortschakoff that if this step was taken the Russian army would enter the city, the fleet was directed to anchor about thirty miles off; and it was subsequently agreed that if the Russians refrained from occupying Gallipoli no British troops should be disembarked on either side of the Dardanelles. Nevertheless, it was felt at this time that the two countries were within a hairbreadth of war, and that the merest accident might result in hostilities. The danger from the close approach of the rival forces happily passed over; but danger enough remained in store from the growth and violence of the war-party in England, and from the difficulty of accommodating the Russian terms of peace with the claims which England justly enough put forward to a share in the settlement of the Eastern question. The treaty of San Stefano was signed by Russia and Turkey on March 3. It was agreed by the Czar's government that a congress of all the powers should be held at Berlin to take this treaty into consideration; but while Great Britain demanded that each and every article of the treaty should be submitted to the congress, Russia declared that it could only accept discussion on those portions of the treaty which affected general European interests. It would have been vain for England to attend a congress on these terms. The prospects of a peaceable settlement seemed faint, and the ministry, under the powers granted by an act for dealing with "occasions of great emergency," called out the reserve forces. Lord Derby now resigned office. His chief stated that the reason for this resignation was a difference of opinion as to calling out the reserves. Lord Derby declared that this was neither his sole nor his principal reason, adding that he could not divulge the other reasons until the propositions of the government relating to them were made known. It subsequently appeared that the proposition had been made in the cabinet to send a secret expedition from India to seize upon Cyprus and some harbor in Syria, with or without the Sultan's permission, as a basis for operations in the event of war against Russia, and that this proposed invasion and seizure of the territory of a friendly state had caused Lord Derby's resignation. He was succeeded in his duties by Lord Salisbury. A vigorous declaration against the treaty of San Stefano was published from the foreign office, and a contingent of native troops was ordered from India to Malta (April 17). Count Schouvaloff, ambassador at London, now went off to St. Petersburg to lay his views and those of the British government before the Czar. He returned on the 20th of May, and a few days later it was announced that the prospects of the meeting of a congress had materially improved. Early in June it was known that Russia had accepted the principle of a discussion of the entire treaty of San Stefano. The British ministry had triumphed; and in the midst of universal congratulations Lord Beaconsfield and his foreign secretary set out to represent Great Britain at the congress. Scarcely had they reached Berlin when, through the mischievousness of a copying-clerk, a secret agreement, signed by Lord Salisbury and Count Schouvaloff, was made public, which covered almost all the points nominally reserved for the consideration of all the great powers. There was, in reality, nothing objectionable in the making of such an agreement; on the contrary, it showed better statesmanship than the menace and bluster with which the government had hitherto proceeded. But, gaining publicity at the very climax of Lord Beaconsfield's performance as champion of the treaty-rights of Europe, and conceding, in the cession of Bessarabia and Batoum, the very points on which the war-party in England had raised the loudest outcry, it excited a fatal sense of the comic, while the equivocations made in Parliament as to its genuineness damaged the moral prestige of the government. The congress of Berlin, anticipated to a great extent by negotiation between the two rival powers, had for its principal task the settlement of the limits of Bulgaria. In the curtailment of the exaggerated area, given to this country by the treaty of San Stefano, England and Austria possibly achieved a useful result. The division of Bulgaria into two principalities was a measure of doubtful wisdom; and the stipulation insisted upon and carried by Lord Beaconsfield that the Sultan should have the right of maintaining garrisons in the Balkans was matter of ridicule to every one who considered it seriously, for the appearance of Turkish troops in any part of Bulgaria would certainly have opened up the whole Eastern question anew. One more surprise awaited the English public. The nation suddenly learned that by a secret convention the Sultan had ceded Cyprus to Great Britain, which in return had undertaken to defend his whole Asiatic territory against all future attack. The Sultan also promised in the same agreement to carry out a system of reform throughout his Asiatic dominions. When the congress was over Lord Beaconsfield and his colleague returned to England, and received an ovation in London, bringing back, as they said, "peace with honor." But the more the work of the ministry was examined the less it appeared to be in consonance with the instincts of the English people in favor of straightforward action and of the rights of nations. Greece, when on the point of entering into the Russo-Turkish war, had been held back by an assurance from England that its interests should not thereby suffer; and, when it was a question of curtailing Bulgaria, Lord Salisbury had made effective use of the claims of the Greek race in Macedonia. But no sooner had the Sultan agreed to cede Cyprus to England than the ministry practically abandoned the cause of Greece; and the congress of Berlin contented itself with recommending the Porte to accept a new frontier-line in Thessaly and Epirus, declining to provide means for enforcing its recommendation. This question, therefore, remained open, and a probable source of war in the East. What was done was perhaps worse than what was left undone. The acquisition of Cyprus was from the first viewed with suspicion in England. The guarantee given to the Sultan for the defence of his Asiatic dominions was regarded as either illusory or the acceptance of an enormous and intolerable responsibility; while the promise of reform, which alone could justify England's protection, had been too often made by the Porte to gain the slightest degree of confidence. In spite of the extraordinary fascination which at this time Lord Beaconsfield exercised over his sovereign, over the higher classes of England, the public service, the clergy, and the men of finance, as well as over the metropolitan press, there seems to be good reason to believe that the great mass of popular opinion was steadily, from first to last, against the government from the time when it allowed it to be seen that its sympathies were with the Turk, and not with the subject European races. The expressions of this deep-rooted conviction were no doubt overpowered for a while by the noise and vehemence of the so-called "Jingo" party, and in the metropolis itself physical force was sometimes called into play to suppress the free utterance of opinion. But in the provinces the voice of protest was never silent. It is, indeed, one of the most singular features of this agitated time that the supposed leaders of public opinion in the metropolitan press were utterly ignorant of what was passing in the country at large. Down to the day when the general election of 1880 swept Lord Beaconsfield's government from power they knew no more of the real current of English feeling than if they had been living at Constantinople. Public opinion has since begun to appreciate these organs at their true value. It is now understood that outside London, where political organization is less advanced than in the other large towns, they reflect nothing and influence nobody.

Towards the end of the year 1878 the Eastern Question passed into the background, to the intense relief of those who feared that England might be plunged into war, with Turkey for an ally. Troubles of a minor character, however, soon arose. The Zulu king, Cetewayo, had organised an army, which caused great alarm to the neighboring colonists, and especially to Sir Bartle Frere, the Queen's High Commissioner in South Africa. No evidence has ever been produced that Cetewayo actually intended to invade Natal. Sir Bartle Frere, however, declaring that attack could only be averted by taking up the offensive, ordered British troops to invade the Zulu territory. Lord Chelmsford was the commander, and through the incapacity of this general, or his subordinates, a body of about a thousand British soldiers was annihilated by the warriors of Cetewayo at Isandlana, on January 22, 1879. Severe fighting followed during the spring and summer. In this campaign the young Louis Napoleon, son of the Emperor Napoleon III., lost his life. It was found necessary to send out large reinforcements to overcome the resistance of the brave and energetic Zulus. Cetewayo was ultimately defeated at Ulundi, and, after being hunted down, was taken as a prisoner to Cape Town. The sympathy of the English, however, is easily won by a gallant enemy. Cetewayo excited much interest in his captivity; there were many who pleaded his cause in England, and maintained that the war had been unnecessarily begun; even the government had at first dissented from the policy of Sir Bartle Frere, and urged him to confine his action to measures of defence. Though Cetewayo remained a prisoner until the downfall of Lord Beaconsfield's administration, he was subsequently brought as a guest to England, received with kindness by the Queen, and restored to sovereignty over a part of his dominions. His return, and the division of Zululand into several petty states, were not followed by the advantages expected. His prestige was lost and he perished ignobly. It is doubtful whether, by the disintegration of that country, which Cetewayo seems to have governed before the war with more than the average ability of a savage chieftain, the welfare of the inhabitants has not been greatly injured. To England itself the affairs of South Africa are the source of nothing but anxiety and annoyance.

The inquiet spirit which animated Lord Beaconsfield's system of imperialism made itself felt in almost every quarter of the globe. Early in his ministry he conferred upon the Queen the title of Empress of India, and this appeal to the oriental imagination formed the prelude to a series of measures intended to advance English influence in the countries that lie between Hindostan and the Turkoman provinces, that had recently been conquered by Russia. The violation by Russia of an agreement that Afghanistan should remain outside the range of its diplomatic relations gave Lord Beaconsfield the occasion for carrying into execution plans that had already been discussed in the cabinet and communicated to Lord Lytton, the Viceroy of India. As Shere Ali, Ameer of Afghanistan, had allowed himself to be withdrawn from the isolation in which he ought to have remained, and had admitted a Russian legation to Cabul, England had the technical right to demand that a British legation should also be admitted to the capital. But before this demand was made the town of Quettah, beyond the frontier of British India, was occupied by the Queen's troops. The seizure of this post excited a strong protest on the part of Lord Lawrence, formerly Governor-General of India, and probably the highest authority of the time on Indian affairs. It seems also to have had an unfavorable effect on Shere Ali; and when Sir N. Chamberlain, accompanied by an escort of a thousand armed men, appeared on the road to Cabul, and demanded, through his subordinate, Cavagnari, to be admitted as the Queen's representative, he was informed that the Ameer declined to receive an embassy. It was telegraphed to England that Cavagnari had been threatened and insulted—a disgraceful fabrication, intended to justify, in the eyes of the English people, an immediate declaration of war. The zeal of Lord Lytton, however, outran that of the government, and he was compelled to wait until an ultimatum had been tendered to Shere Ali. In the meantime troops were massed upon the frontier; and again Lord Lawrence raised his warning voice, declaring that, in forcing a mission upon Afghanistan, the British government were playing Russia's game, and courting, in place of their rivals, the hostility of a savage people which resented all foreign intervention alike. No attention was paid by the ministry to this advice; and when Shere Ali, in vain reliance upon Russian support, had allowed the time for an answer to the ultimatum to expire, war was declared, and British troops marched upon Cabul (Nov. 20, 1878). No effective resistance was made by the Afghan forces. General Roberts gained a victory at the Peiwar Crest; Stewart occupied Candahar; and Shere Ali fled from his capital, leaving his son, Yakub Khan, in possession of the government. Yakub entered into negotiations with the English commanders, and finally signed a treaty at Gandamak, placing his foreign relations under British control, admitting an English resident to Cabul, and ceding a strip of territory on his eastern frontier (May 26, 1879). The object of the war seemed to have been attained by England. Cavagnari was received at the capital as British resident, and the process of evacuating the country was begun.

Suddenly there came an event which, in a striking and tragical manner, verified the prediction that had been made by Lord Lawrence. On the 23d of September Cavagnari was attacked and murdered with all his suite. The outbreak appears to have originated in a military tumult; it is doubtful whether Yakub Khan was in any way implicated in it, and the story that it was the result of a Russian intrigue was a mere invention of anti-Russian newspapers. There was, however, an end of the illusion that Afghanistan was pacified and won. General Stewart, who had just evacuated Candahar, reoccupied that city. Roberts marched upon Cabul, defeated the enemy, and entered the capital, where there was complete anarchy. Yakub, declaring that the murder of Cavagnari was the work of rebels, abdicated, and was sent as a prisoner into India. The murderers of Cavagnari were brought to justice; and in an order, which was severely criticised in England, General Roberts announced that he would execute, as rebels against Yakub, all persons taken in arms. A chief-priest and a great number of Afghan soldiers so taken were put to death. But whether in consequence of the severity or in spite of it, Roberts found that the whole country was now rising against him. His positions outside of Cabul were attacked, and a series of encounters took place, in one of which the British troops were so severely handled that Roberts found it necessary to evacuate the capital and await reinforcements. The houses of the adherents of the British were now destroyed by the National party. Reinforcements, however, soon arrived, and Roberts again occupied Cabul. Afghanistan, however, was not really conquered, nor could the English find any native chieftain to whom, in pursuance of the boasted intention of making a "strong, united, and friendly Afghanistan," they could with safety commit the government of the country. It was accordingly determined to divide Yakub's dominions into several provinces, and to incorporate Candahar with the system of Indian protected states.

Things were in this unsettled condition when events took place in England which gave an entirely different complexion to the affairs of the East. Lord Beaconsfield dissolved Parliament in the spring of 1880, and a general election immediately followed. The contest was fought with extraordinary passion and energy, and, turning almost wholly on the foreign policy of the government, it gave occasion for the clearest possible expression of the judgment of the nation upon that policy. On the one hand, it was said that Lord Beaconsfield had kept the Czar's armies out of Constantinople, and had forced Russia to modify the treaty of San Stefano without involving England in war; that something of the Ottoman Empire had been saved out of the general wreck; that the Zulu war had been unavoidably begun and successfully ended; and that the invasion of Afghanistan was no more than a measure of self-defence, forced upon Great Britain by the advances and the intrigues of Russia in the East. On the other hand it was charged upon the government that they had deliberately sided with the Turk, and opposed the liberation of the Christian races; that when there was not the least danger of Russia appropriating Constantinople, and when it was perfectly certain that Austria and Prussia would have prevented the execution of any such design, had it existed, Lord Beaconsfield's menaces and armaments had brought this country within an ace of war with Russia; that the claim, to have wrested back by diplomacy some of the fruits of Russia's victories, was mere bluster, for, by the secret agreement with Lord Salisbury, Russia had gained everything that it wanted; that Cyprus had been dishonorably acquired; that the invasion of Zululand was an act of unnecessary and wanton aggression; that the attack upon Afghanistan was a crime and a blunder, committed in spite of the most authoritative warning, and accompanied with every circumstance of harshness and injustice; and, finally, that throughout his administration Lord Beaconsfield had systematically kept Parliament and the nation in the dark, or misrepresented his intentions until they were carried into effect and it was too late to attempt to undo them. Such was the indictment—the gravest made against any English government since the Napoleonic wars—which in every quarter of Great Britain was raised against Lord Beaconsfield's ministry in the spring of 1880. It found its most eloquent and impressive enunciation in the speeches made by Mr. Gladstone during his candidature in Midlothian; but everywhere the drift of argument was the same; and never were political questions more thoroughly thrashed out, or the points at issue more completely understood by those who were about to vote upon them. The answer made by the nation to Lord Beaconsfield's appeal was summary and overwhelming. His followers were utterly routed, and his rival was called to power by one of the greatest majorities that has displaced or set up a government in recent times. Lord Beaconsfield, in conversation with a friend of the writer, who was then staying under the same roof with him, attributed the decisive character of his defeat to three causes: First, to the accidental winning of so many seats by the Liberals on the first day of the election, that their opponents became demoralized; secondly, to the irresistible energy and eloquence of his rival; and, thirdly, to the commercial and agricultural depression which had prevailed during the four preceding years. The first of these reasons only illustrates Lord Beaconsfield's own habit of making the most of the accidental; the second is assuredly no undeserved tribute to a statesman whom Lord Beaconsfield, in the intoxication of success, described in very different language; the third seems to be in great part disproved by the fact that the agricultural counties of Wales, where the government sustained its most crushing and most unexpected defeats, were precisely those where, in all Great Britain, the "bad times" had been the least felt. The plain reason for the overthrow of Lord Beaconsfield's government was that, from the moment when it began to have a distinct policy of its own, the mass of the nation disagreed with it.

The first task of the new ministry was to decide what they should do in Afghanistan. They had, while in opposition, condemned the principle of intervention in the affairs of that country; and, consistently with their earlier language, they now determined to withdraw from it as soon as the actual condition of affairs permitted them to do so. Lord Lytton resigned the vice-royalty as soon as he heard of the result of the elections, and was succeeded by Lord Ripon. From among the rival claimants to the Afghan throne Abdurrahman was recognized as Ameer, and preparations were made for quitting Cabul. But it is easier to begin an unjust enterprise than to relinquish it. A son of Shere Ali, Ayub Khan, had gathered an army round him at Herat, and now moved against Candahar. General Burrows, who set out with about 2500 men to oppose him, was totally defeated at Maiwand, June, 1880, and Candahar, with its British garrison, was besieged by Ayub's forces. Roberts was ordered to march from Cabul to its relief. This march of 318 miles, through a wild country and under an Indian sun, was executed with admirable energy and skill by the general and his troops within twenty-three days. The troops had to carry their supplies with them, for all communication with Cabul was abandoned, and the army struck into the mountains trusting to itself alone. Roberts reached Candahar on the 31st of August, combined his operations with those of the garrison, and, by one vigorous blow, dispersed the besieging army. This ended the Afghan war. In pursuance of the fixed policy of the government Cabul had already been evacuated, and Candahar was not long held. The victory over Ayub made the conqueror's withdrawal possible, and in the spring of 1881 the last British troops quitted Afghanistan. It was, of course, represented by Lord Beaconsfield's followers that this withdrawal from the country was an act of cowardice as well as an abandonment of the interests and of the allies of Great Britain, But the nation had formed its judgment upon the policy of the late minister, and the attempt to draw a "scientific frontier" for the Indian empire in the hornet's nest of Afghanistan is not likely to be soon repeated.

It would have been well for the credit of England if the new government had as frankly broken loose from the policy of their predecessors in Africa as they did in Asia. In the year 1877 the Transvaal republic, inhabited by Dutch Boers and by natives, had been annexed to the British empire by the colonial executive, in consequence of the supposed inability of the Boers to defend themselves against the warlike Zulus, and of acts of oppression alleged to have been practised by the Boers upon the natives. Very little attention was paid in England at the time to this annexation, and, although the Boers protested against it and declared that they would maintain their independence, they remained quiet during the Zulu war or even assisted England, not desiring a native alliance against a European power. But when the Zulu war was over they renewed their protests, and held a great meeting at Wonderfontein in December, 1879, at which they fixed upon the maximum of concession which they would make to England. In the meantime public opinion in Great Britain was becoming more busy with the Transvaal question. It was discussed in Parliament, and the annexation was generally condemned by the liberal party. After the overthrow of Lord Beaconsfield in the elections of 1880 it was anticipated by many in England and by the Boers themselves that the annexation would be peaceably undone by Mr. Gladstone's ministry. This hope, however, was disappointed. In the Queen's speech at the opening of the new Parliament the Transvaal question was thus handled: "In maintaining my supremacy over the Transvaal, with its diversified population, I desire both to make provision for the security of the indigenous races and to extend to the European settlers institutions based on large and liberal principles of self-government." The Boers sent a telegram to England as soon as the declaration of the ministry became known, expressing their dissatisfaction, and forcible resistance was now offered to the collection of taxes. On Dec. 16, 1880, the flag of independence was hoisted. A triumvirate was appointed to carry on the government of the republic provisionally, and hostilities with the British troops in the Transvaal began. A body of the Ninety-fourth regiment was attacked and suffered severely from the accurate firing of the Boers. Sir Owen Lanyon, the governor, was blockaded in Pretoria, and other garrisons were besieged. Gen. Colley, governor of Natal, made preparations for the relief of his countrymen. Though he had but 1500 men he took up the offensive, crossed the river Ingogo, and moved against the Boers, who were stationed at Laings Nek. Here on Jan. 28, 1881, he was repulsed with loss. His communications were threatened, and he fell back to protect them. In the meantime negotiations were being conducted with the English government through Mr. Brand, president of the Orange Free State. The ministry, who were anxious not to come to extremities with the Boers, telegraphed that if opposition ceased forthwith they believed an accommodation would be possible. Gen. Colley, however, who had received reinforcements, attacked the Boers at Majuba Hill without waiting for further negotiations. He was defeated and killed. An armistice followed, during which Sir Evelyn Wood conducted negotiations with the Boer leaders, which ended successfully. The suzerainty of the Queen was acknowledged; complete self-government was given to the Boers, the control of their foreign relations being reserved. It was agreed that a British resident should be placed at their capital, and that a royal commission should consider the provisions necessary to be made for the protection of native interests, and decide whether any portion of territory eastward should be severed from the Transvaal with the view of preventing disputes between the Boers and their neighbors. The commission sat from June 14 to August 3, when a convention was signed. This was ratified by the Volksraad of the Boers on Oct. 25. A certain number of disputed questions, however, still remained open, and the last difficulties between England and the Transvaal are yet scarcely settled.

While embroiled with Zulus, Afghans, Egyptians, and Boers, Great Britain has had to face a yet more painful and difficult problem in its dealings with Ireland. The discontent of a conquered nation, whose soil is owned by a handful of landlords, alien in religion and race, is not to be appeased by a generation, nor by a century, of palliative measures. The disestablishment of the Protestant Church in Ireland and the land act of 1870 failed to make many friends for England. The tenant was still in the power of his landlord, who could raise his rent and evict him when he declined to pay the increase. It needed only the failure of the harvest in 1879 to throw the whole country into the hands of agitators. The Land League, since become famous all over the world, was established in the autumn of that year; and, in order that nothing might be wanting to popular exasperation, the landlords continued to evict their tenants throughout the winter, when famine had actually begun. The coercion act, which expired in June, 1880, was, however, not renewed by Mr. Gladstone's ministry, which showed its good-will to the Irish peasantry by bringing in a measure temporarily preventing evictions. This bill, after passing the Commons, was thrown out by the Lords. Affairs now became much more serious. Agrarian outrages increased, and the payment of rent was very generally refused. The Land League became the dominant authority in Ireland, and the operation of boycotting, named after its first victim, the land-agent Boycott, proved itself wonderfully effective. More murderous crimes, however, which at a later period covered the managers of the Land League with infamy, were as yet rare. It was still hoped in England that a moderate tightening of the reins, combined with a liberal reform of the land laws, might restore order. In the spring of 1881 Mr. Gladstone submitted a coercion bill to Parliament, intending to follow it immediately with a land bill. The progress of the coercion bill brought to a climax that system of obstruction with which the Irish members had for some time past been endeavoring to extort home rule from England by rendering all legislation in the imperial Parliament impossible. After a series of sittings, extended over whole nights and days together, twenty-eight Irish members, brawling and vociferating, were thrust out of the house by main force. The coercion bill, empowering the executive to imprison without trial, was carried, and the way made clear for the introduction of the land act. This measure, which passed both Commons and Lords in the summer of 1881, was one of those few in modern English history in which Parliament, rising above the principle of *Laissez Faire* and the maxims of current political economy, has boldly faced a great social problem, and endeavored by resolute legislation to recast the social order of a people. The so-called freedom of contract, under which it was possible for the Irish landlord to extort whatever he pleased from his tenant, under the threat of expelling him from his home, was ruthlessly swept away. Law courts were established for the purpose of settling, on the tenant's appeal, what rent was a fair one for him to pay. The rent so named by the court was fixed for fifteen years, and at the end of that time the landlord could only raise it if the court should decide that agencies other than the tenant's own industry had added to the value of the land. The Government was empowered to advance three-fourths of the purchase-money to tenants who should arrange, under certain conditions, to purchase the land outright from their landlords and become peasant proprietors. These were the two leading provisions of the act, and although the second has as yet failed in its operation, the first has within two or three years reduced the rents paid by tenants by something representing a capital sum of over £5,000,000, and has made hundreds of thousands of families, who were hitherto at the mercy of their landlords, secure in the possession of their farms. Fair rents, free sale, fixity of tenure—the so-called three F's, long demanded as the minimum of reform by the more practical leaders of the Irish people—were virtually conceded in the land act of 1881, to the deep satisfaction of that numerous and increasing class in England which desire to see the Irish people secure, prosperous, and happy in their homes. If the Irish parliamentary leaders had been less inclined to methods of violence, or the mass of the people had understood how great a victory had been gained by their friends in England over the lately dominant class, they would probably have settled down under the new act and have trusted to time and conciliation for the winning of further concessions. This, however, was unfortunately not the case. Mr. C. S. Parnell and his colleagues set themselves against pacification. Ancient hatreds were rekindled, the peasantry were taught to distrust the land act, and, instead of the expected harvest of quiet, storms of agitation swept over the country. The British ministry now lost patience, and, under the powers given them by the new coercion act, arrested Mr. Parnell, with his colleagues Dillon and O'Kelly. They were confined in Kilmainham Gaol, and so unsparingly were the provisions of the coercion act put in force that during the winter of 1881-82 above 700 persons were imprisoned without trial. The Land League now published a manifesto calling upon the Irish farmers to pay no rent at all until their leaders were released. This was followed by a proclamation of the English government declaring the Land League an illicit society, and making membership in it a punishable offence. The meetings of the League were suppressed, and its organization appeared to dissolve under the armed hand of authority. But worse growths came in its place. Secret conspiracy was substituted for open combination, and homicide became the agency of those who, whether in hiding or from beyond the seas, kept up the agrarian conflict with the landlord and the political conflict with England. (C. A. F.)

The subsequent history of England has been very largely occupied with Irish affairs, the difficulty in settling which has caused several notable changes in the ministry, and given rise to a long series of dramatic events. The first of these followed the release of Mr. Parnell and his colleagues from Kilmainham Gaol and their return to Parliament, on the understanding that their influence would be exerted in favor of pacific measures. This action caused the viceroy and the chief-secretary of Ireland to resign, the the vacancy in the secretaryship thus caused being filled by Lord Frederick Cavendish, a son of the Duke of Devonshire, and brother of the Marquis of Hartington. This nobleman landed in Ireland on May 6, 1882, and on the evening of that day, he and the under-secretary, Mr. Burke, were attacked and murdered in front of the viceroy's lodge at Dublin. This foul assassination put an end to all immediate hopes of conciliation. Ireland was covered with police and troops, and the murderers sought with the most earnest vigilance. They were finally discovered through one of the gang turning state's-evidence, the actual assassins were executed, and their accomplices less stringently punished. Cary, the informer, while escaping the vengeance of the law, was killed at Cape Town by one O'Donnell, who in his turn paid the penalty of death.

The violence of the Irish party continued unabated. Dynamite was brought in as an aid to their views of justice to Ireland, and in 1884 several bold and partly successful endeavors were made to carry the war into the camp of the enemy by creating a feeling of terror in London. Attempts were made to blow up Victoria Station, Scotland Yard, London Bridge, the Nelson Monument, and even the Houses of Parliament and the Tower of London, with dynamite. Fortunately in no case did these nefarious attempts accomplish the injury that their projectors had intended. The explosions in the Houses of Parliament and the Tower took place Jan. 21, 1885. Twenty persons were hurt, and some degree of damage done.

The Home Rule element grew steadily larger in Parliament, and in 1885 showed its strength and determination by a sudden combination with the Conservatives, which defeated the Government. In consequence the Gladstone ministry resigned, and were succeeded on June 23 by a Conservative ministry, with Lord Salisbury as premier. Such a coalition, however, could not last. In the next session of Parliament the Conservative party was defeated, on a bill for the government of Ireland, and a new Gladstone ministry came into existence on Feb. 3, 1886. This, however, had even a shorter lease of life than its predecessor. The burning question of Irish Home Rule again came prominently forward, with Gladstone now as one of its warmest advocates. His former policy of mingled concession and repression was laid aside, and he strongly maintained that the demand of the Irish people to manage their own affairs was just and should be granted. His scheme for the autonomy of Ireland in its home affairs was unfolded in a vigorous speech on April 8, 1886. But it soon appeared that Parliament was not prepared to go the length which the ministry desired. A vote was taken on June 8 on the Home Rule question, and the ministry defeated. Lord Salisbury was again called to the head of affairs, and on July 21 a new Conservative ministry was formed, which, with some changes in its personnel, still holds the reins of government.

The next event of striking interest in the drama of Irish Home Rule was the charge made by the London *Times* against Parnell of criminal participation in the murder of Lord Cavendish. The *Times* intimated that it had evidence sufficient to prove that the assassination had been devised by him, and that the murderers were under his pay. This charge Parnell boldly and indignantly denied, and demanded a legal investigation, bringing counter-charge of libel against the *Times*. Before arrangements for a trial could be made, however, Parliament took the question in hand, and appointed a committee of investigation, whose sessions began in September, 1887, and continued till Nov. 22, 1889, the time of actual session being 129 days. Very many witnesses were examined, the investigation being widened from the original charge to take in the whole question of Irish crime and misdemeanor. Politically the court was hostile to Parnell, but his side of the case was conducted with the greatest adroitness and ability, and in the end it was conclusively proved that the letters on which the *Times* had depended in making its charges were forgeries, and that the great London journal had permitted itself to fall almost blindly into a trap, being rendered unduly credulous by its hatred to and desire to injure the Irish cause. Parnell was triumphantly acquitted, and Pigott, the forger, who had fled to Spain, soon after committed suicide.

The subsequent career of Parnell has been of the same dramatic character, though disgrace has replaced his former triumph, and his influence with the Irish people has greatly declined. In 1890 a Captain O'Shea brought a suit against his wife of adultery with Parnell, who virtually admitted the charge by declining to come forward to combat it. That he was guilty was so evident that he was strongly called upon to give up his leadership of the Irish Parliamentary party. This he persistently declined to do, and has since fought the host of enemies which his crime called up with a vigor, skill, and audacity which have enabled him as yet to withstand all their endeavors to oust him. Gladstone, who had sacrificed much in becoming his earnest co-laborer, has broken all connection with him. Ireland is divided into Parnellite and Anti-Parnellite parties. The Irish members of Parliament are similarly divided, Justin McCarthy heading a strong opposition section. But for the energy and determination of Parnell he would have ere this been dead politically, but he continues to fight his foes with a skill and persistence worthy of a better cause. Meanwhile the question of Irish reform stands still, quite lost sight of in this factional fight between Parnell and the host of foes whom his guilty relations with Mrs. O'Shea have raised against him.

Of the home events in England, the most important is the passage, in 1884, of the new Franchise Bill. This bill extends the borough franchise to the counties. Under it every citizen of England of full age who has occupied a house for a year, or can be classed as a lodger, including those who occupy dwellings for offices, employment, or service, can claim registry as a voter. Under its provisions there are added over 1,300,000 to the voting lists in England and Wales, 200,000 in Scotland, and over 400,000 in Ireland, thus constituting one of the most notable measures of reform passed for years in the British Parliament. In 1889 an important measure was brought before Parliament in consequence of the refusal of the tenant farmers in Wales to pay tithes to the clergy of the Established Church. A bill to coerce them into payment was brought in, but failed to pass. It was succeeded by a resolution in favor of disestablishment in Wales, which likewise failed. The question still remains unsettled.

In the same year broke out one of the greatest labor disturbances of recent years in England, the strike of the London dock laborers. Over 150,000 men, led by John Burns, took part in this strike, which enlisted the sympathies of the public, the justice of the demand of the laborers being evident, and their moderation of conduct commendable. Cardinal Manning gave effective support to the movement. It ended after about a month in the employers giving way and conceding the full demands of the laborers. The final result of the movement has been an extension of the principle of trade-unionism to a much lower range of employments than formerly took part in it. In 1888 Parliament passed a local government act of great importance, its effect being an entire transformation in the county governments of England and Wales. Most of the power formerly held by justices of the peace has been transferred to a council elected by freeholders, local government thus falling definitely into the hands of the people. A similar bill for Scotland was passed in 1889.

Imperial Federation has recently been earnestly advocated by a party of some strength. Its purpose is to combine England and her colonies in a federal union, with home rule in each member of the federation, and an imperial parliament to govern all general affairs. This scheme, however, is not favorably received in the colonies, who fear the preponderating influence of England in the parliament, and a loss of in some measure of the liberties they now enjoy. Meanwhile the Colonies of Australia are taking decided steps to form a federation of their own, a congress of delegates from the various colonies having formed a scheme of federal union, to be called the Commonwealth of Australia. The government devised will closely resemble that of the United States, the main difference being that England will have the appointment of a Governor-general for the Commonwealth.

During the period here considered the foreign relations of England have been of interest and importance. For English operations in Egypt, see EGYPT.

In November, 1885, a war with Burmah broke out which quickly ended in the defeat of the Burmese and the surrender of King Thebaw. On Jan. 1, 1886 Burmah was annexed to the British Empire. On May 1, 1887, Cyprus was ceded to Great Britain by Turkey. On May 12 Zululand was annexed. The process of annexation in Africa has since gone steadily on, a very large section of this Continent being now English territory. In 1890 a dispute as to colonial borders and navigation rights broke out with Portugal, which was settled with a strong hand by England, the smaller state being forced to withdraw its pretensions. The difficulty in the same year in regard to Samoa was settled by a tri-partite treaty of control by England, Germany, and the United States.

ENGLAND, JOHN, an American Bishop of the Roman Catholic Church, was born in the city of Cork, Ireland, Sept. 23, 1786. Until his fifteenth year he went to the best schools in his native city, and made considerable progress in his studies. He then studied at home for two years, and having determined to embrace the ecclesiastical state he was sent to the College of Carlow, where he remained five years, devoting himself to the study of the higher philosophy and moral and dogmatic theology. His shining virtues and brilliant talents won the admiration of both professors and students. While still a seminarian he gave instructions on the catechism to the children of the town, but so interesting were his discourses that they were attended by persons of all ages. He was instrumental in procuring the establishment at Carlow of a female prison, an asylum for unprotected females, and poor schools for both sexes. In 1808 he returned to Cork for ordination, a special dispensation having been obtained from Rome for that purpose, as he was only twenty-two years old. Soon after his ordination he was appointed to lecture on the Old and New Testament at the Cork Cathedral. His eloquent discourses attracted crowds of people of all religions. He established a Magdalen asylum, and gave his services as chaplain gratuitously to the city jail. In 1812 he was appointed president of the Theological Seminary of St. Mary's. His matchless eloquence, powerful pen, and patriotic devotion to Ireland caused his name to be mentioned as a fit candidate for a mitre. He did not shrink from the duties and responsibilities of the position, but declared he would never wear a mitre in any country subject to the British Government. The United States had already become a great and powerful republic, and as the Catholic Church grew with the growth of the country, new Sees were rapidly created. In 1820 Dr. England was appointed the first Bishop of Charleston, S. C. He was consecrated at Cork, Sept. 21, 1820, and, shortly afterwards sailing for America, arrived at Charleston, Dec. 31.

The new diocese of Charleston embraced Georgia, North and South Carolina, but had only two priests and two churches. The Catholic population was very limited in number, and consisted chiefly of poor Irish emigrants, ruined refugees from San Domingo, and their slaves. All the wealth, influence, culture, and respectability belonged to the Protestants. Bishop England devoted himself first to his own flock, which had been long neglected, and was scattered over a large extent of country. He succeeded in infusing into them some of his own zeal and enthusiasm. Churches were built, and the number of priests soon increased. The people of Charleston discovered that Bishop England possessed intellectual gifts worthy of their highest admiration. His learning and eloquence drew around his pulpit some of the most distinguished people of the South, who were delighted by his oratory, if they were not convinced by his logic. Bishop England opened a classical school at Charleston, which was attended by the sons of the first gentlemen of the city, and by this means a sufficient income was raised to support the theological students, and thus gradually able and zealous clergymen were secured for the diocese of Charleston. The scarcity of priests rendered the labors of the Bishop very arduous. Sometimes he went one hundred miles to administer the sacraments to a single individual. Bishop England identified himself with every good and useful movement of the community in which he lived. An elegant scholar, he revived a love of classical literature in South Carolina. He was an active member of the Philosophical and Literary Association of Charleston, and infused a new vigor into it by his eloquent addresses and scientific investigations. In order to check the barbarous practice of duelling, he formed, in conjunction with several influential gentlemen, an Anti-duelling Association, of which Gen. Thomas Pinckney, of Revolutionary fame, was president. Before this Society the Bishop delivered one of the most powerful and irresistible arguments against duelling ever written on that subject. He was also instrumental in preventing hostile meetings in a number of conspicuous instances. So great was his fame as an orator that, for the first time in the history of our country, a Catholic bishop was invited to preach in the House of Representatives at Washington, and he delivered a brilliant and forcible address, which a committee of the members, in a flattering letter, requested permission to print. Before the Washington Light Artillery of Charleston he delivered an oration, which was one of the noblest tributes to the character of Washington.

Bishop England was thoroughly imbued with the spirit of American institutions, and all his public addresses breathed the most exalted patriotism. Through his influence the provincial councils, composed of the American Catholic bishops, assembled at stated periods, for the promotion of friendly intercourse, for counsel, and for the transaction of important eclesiastical business. His learning, tact, and energy were of great service upon these occasions, and were so generally recognized that he was called the "Father of the Provincial Councils." Bishop England visited Europe three times during his episcopacy, and secured great assistance in priests, money, and female religious. So highly was he appreciated in Ireland that he was offered the bishopric of Ossory in that country, but he declined that high ecclesiastical dignity, which would have secured for him ease and luxury in his native country, saying he preferred to remain with the beloved church in America,—that he had become an American citizen and an American prelate, and intended to be both as long as he lived. When in Rome he was consulted on the ecclesiastical affairs of this country by the pope and cardinals, who were astonished at the great labors and extensive travels of the Bishop of Charleston. From the chambers of the Propaganda he would announce the very day he intended to administer confirmation in the interior of South Carolina, and the cardinals, impressed by the rapidity of his movements, called him "*il Vescovo a vapore*," or the "Steam Bishop."

In the diocese of Charleston he increased the number of churches from two to sixteen, organized a well-appointed and zealous clergy, and established many ecclesiastical, religious, and charitable institutions. He introduced the Ursuline Sisters into his diocese, where their school acquired a high reputation, and also the Sisters of Mercy to take charge of orphan children, visit the prisons, and nurse the sick.

On Bishop England's return, from his last visit to Europe in 1841, the voyage was long and stormy. With health broken down, he had to act as the physician and nurse of many persons who were really less ill than himself. Malignant dysentery broke out among the steerage passengers, and he attended them day and night, until he was taken down with the disease himself. When he landed at Philadelphia, instead of retiring to a sick-bed, he delivered a course of lectures, speaking for seventeen nights in succession; assisted at consecrations, and was kept busy sending to Charleston the numerous co-laborers whom he brought from Europe for the various institutions of his diocese. In failing health he went to Baltimore, where, although he remained only four days, he preached five times, and never in his palmiest days did he display more power, eloquence, and brilliancy. At length he arrived in Charleston, exhausted from travelling and constant work. His physicians pronounced his case hopeless, and, with calmness and resignation, he prepared for his death, which took place on April 11, 1842. As an evidence of the respect felt for the illustrious deceased, the bells of the Protestant churches tolled, the flags on the shipping were lowered, and persons of every denomination, class, and condition united in paying every mark of respect and affection to his memory. (E. L. D.)

ENGLEWOOD, a village of Cook co., Illinois, is a suburb of Chicago, from which it is distant 7 miles, on the Chicago, Rock Island, and Pacific Railroad; the Lake Shore and Michigan Southern Railroad; the Pittsburg, Fort Wayne, and Chicago; the Wabash, St. Louis, and Pacific Railroad; the Chicago and Eastern Illinois Railroad, and the Louisville, New Albany, and Chicago Railroad. Here many business men of Chicago reside, and there are more than forty trains each way daily. It has 9 churches, the Cook County Normal School, a high-school, and 3 other public schools. Population, 15,000.

ENGLISH, THOMAS DUNN, an American poet and journalist, was born in Philadelphia, June 29, 1819. He studied medicine at the University of Pennsylvania, receiving the degree of M. D. in 1839, but afterwards turned his attention to law, and was admitted to the bar in 1842. In that year he published in a New York paper a song called "Ben Bolt," which became widely popular. He has since published several novels, only three of which he has acknowledged. He has also composed several dramas, of which *The Mormons* has been printed. He has contributed numerous poems and prose sketches to journals and magazines in New York and elsewhere. He lived for some time in Virginia, but since 1856 has resided in New Jersey, near New York city, practising as a physician, and giving his leisure to writing for the magazines. He

ENGLISH LITERATURE. The death of Sir Walter Scott, in 1832, marks the close of an interesting era, for with him expired what we may call the original romantic movement in English literature. At its beginning, romanticism was the literary expression of a widespread reaction against the classicism which accompanied and followed the renaissance. The long-continued imitation of the ancient, and especially of the Roman, writers, had combined with the strong tendency of society to seek polish, and was at length outgrown after much of literature had become scarcely more than a sort of scholastic exercise. Early in the eighteenth century English and French writers had discovered how great a part of human nature was left without representation in the exact but arid methods of writing then current; yet it was not till shortly before the French Revolution that we see unmistakable signs of the existence of new models and wider interests.

See Vol. VIII. p. 360 Am. ed. (p. 403 Edin. ed.).

The Romanticists, of whom Scott is one of the most famous English representatives, gave the world brilliant pictures of the past as well as of the remote regions which had been somewhat contemptuously overlooked by those writers who cared most for polish. Yet, while Scott's influence long survived upon the Continent, in England he left no important successor, and almost the sole survivor of the army of knights and warriors who crowded his pages was G. P. R. James's long since forgotten "solitary horseman." The picturesqueness of romanticism was but one side of the movement. Already, before Scott's death, some of his contemporaries had indicated the lines on which his successors were about to do their work. He had shown the splendor of the past; other writers began to see that it was not necessary to go back four or five hundred years, or even fifty, to find impressive subjects. Miss Edgeworth's stories—and, for that matter, such of the Waverly novels as dealt with contemporary life in Scotland—showed that there was an abundance of material near home capable of interesting treatment. Moreover, there was a strong impulse toward utilitarianism, which was directly opposed to one side of romanticism, although later, as we shall see, the two influences amalgamated.

The Reform Bill of 1832 was an important step in the advance of England towards popular government, and the victory of the Liberals placed political power in the hands of a large number of inexperienced men. The successful reformers immediately interested themselves in popular instruction, and simultaneously a number of writers began to publish manuals full of lucid information on almost every conceivable subject. These manuals were what may be called secular tracts: they undertook to impart knowledge instead of religion. As early as 1825 Archibald Constable had led the way with his *Miscellany*; in the same year Lord Brougham wrote his *Education of the People*, and in 1826 the same indefatigable writer began to organize the Society for the Diffusion of Useful Knowledge. Charles Knight was appointed to superintend the publications of this society, and shortly after he started his own, *Library of Entertaining Knowledge*. Charles Knight continued this useful task by establishing the *Penny Magazine* in 1832, the year in which William and Robert Chambers began to publish *Chambers' Edinburgh Journal*. Charles Knight in 1838 brought out his *Pictorial History of England*, and in 1844-45 Prof. Craik's *Sketches of Literature and Learning in England*. Meanwhile *Chambers' Information for the People* began to appear in 1833, and was followed by various other works of a similar aim. This list, which might easily be made longer, will show how widespread was the general movement in the direction of popular instruction. In the previous century literature had been undeniably didactic. Phillip's *Cyder* and Dyer's *Fleece*, for example, had in their way echoed the *Georgics*, and the never-ending instruction in morality had done much toward civilizing a rude society. Now an effort was made to simplify for the populace the great discoveries in modern sciences. The effort extended into what we may call pure literature, traces of practical instruction indeed are to be found in Richardson, and it held a prominent place in Rousseau's novels. Miss Edgeworth, too, had followed Day's *Sandford and Merton* with *Frank*, the hero of which was dosed with early instruction. These books, however, were but the blind gropings of beginners. Miss Martineau, in her tales illustrative of political economy, developed the method which Miss Edgeworth had adopted in her *Evenings at Home* and her *Moral Tales*.

This outbreak of utilitarianism in literature seems very remote from the spirit of romanticism, which atoned for the long reign of good sense by concerning itself mainly with the picturesqueness of things. Indeed, in France, where all thought is carried to its logical extreme, Théophile Gautier had said with a youthful exaggeration, which, however, well expressed one of the animating principles of romanticism, that everything that was useful was hateful. "I had rather forswear potatoes than roses," he said; "and I do not think there is more than one utilitarian in the world capable of uprooting a bed of tulips in order to plant cabbages there." It is at first somewhat puzzling to find the landscape gardeners engaged in setting out cabbages picturesquely. Yet that is what happened, and we may understand it when we recall the double origin of romanticism in a feeling of the picturesqueness of man as well as of nature. That men were brothers was part of the new creed, and it at once became necessary to know what was to be done with these newly-discovered relatives. Sheer picturesqueness could scarcely ameliorate the pangs of suffering humanity; these appealed with a new zeal to writers, who at once set about rectifying what was wrong. Thus, in France, George Sand made use of romantic methods to do away with what she thought abuses. In the same way in England, the real home of compromise, we find Dickens beginning, in 1838, the war against social wrong with his *Oliver Twist*. William Henry Ainsworth was meanwhile busying himself with the already obsolescent historical novel, and Bulwer was busy with the romantic exposition of the moral superiority of criminals. Home-born evil-doers took the place which in Scott's time had been occupied by the heroes of the past; the crusaders gave way to more informal murderers. The study of lofty heroes was carried on, as we shall see, by philosophers and historians, while fiction, which for nearly a century and a half has been the most sensitive means of expressing the prevailing thought of the time in all its fluctuations, led the way in the more careful study of the populace. Here, however, it was the most striking and picturesque objects that were first studied. Dickens desired to bring out what he called "the romantic aspect of familiar things," and he began with the study of vicious poverty. Bulwer had tried to show how excellent were highwaymen like Paul Clifford and murderers like Eugene Aram. Dickens was dissatisfied with these novels, and he undertook to show how pardonable was law-breaking in the condition of society at that time. Before *Oliver Twist* (1837) appeared the *Posthumous Papers of the Pickwick Club* (1836), and the *Sketches by Boz*, in the same year. *Nicholas Nickleby* was begun in 1838 and finished in the next year. In this, as is well known, he turned his attention to the long infamous barbarities of Yorkshire schools. Most of Dickens' subsequent novels were inspired by a firm purpose to accomplish some reform. The intention of a novel, however, is something very different from the execution; and in Dickens we find his desire to represent "the romantic side of familiar things," leading him to exaggerate, to be sure with delightful humor, one side of almost all the many characters which he introduces into his novels. It would be quite possible that each thing uttered by his characters might really have been said, but a marked exaggeration of the salient points of the people he writes about is what most frequently strikes his readers. We notice this in *Our Mutual Friend* quite as much as in his earliest work. If his writing seems to a later generation to smack of excess, it is because other writers have shown that equal vividness may be attained by greater economy. The change of taste was obvious in Dickens' lifetime. We have seen how Dickens answered Bulwer's early work, and in Thackeray's *Catherine*, which is reprinted in a less violent form than that in which it was first published in *Fraser's Magazine*, we notice how the melo-dramatic tone of *Oliver Twist* struck him. In Thackeray's longer novels, too, we find him continually holding his hand, and taking just those pains to be deliberate and exact which Dickens was forever neglecting. The contrast between the two writers was not merely a personal one between two rival claimants for the popular favor; it was one between the fashion of the time and the fashion that was to succeed it—between romanticism and the realism that naturally and necessarily followed it. Just as, doubtless, Fielding was induced by Richardson's delicacy to add to the roystering tone of his own novels, so we may presume did Dickens' exaggeration tend to make Thackeray's work more polished. Already in *Bleak House* we see Dickens abandoning the study of a single hero and taking up the study of a careful plot. This was a change that the age was making. We see it in Thackeray, whose early picturesque sketches were followed by descriptions of masses of society, and in other writers.

Carlyle was the mouth-piece of the strongly-felt need of individual heroism, such as, with some modifications, had inspired this early literature. Kingsley in his first stories gave it full expression, but, after the revolutions of 1848, heroes, so to speak, went out and society came in. We see the change in Germany, perhaps, even more clearly than in England. Kingsley's fervid rhetoric has now a remote sound, and in the work of succeeding novelists we find less stress laid on the hero and more on the manifold influences and complications of society. In Trollope's novels we have the conventional, in George Eliot's the philosophical exposition, of modern life. What recent novelists have shown is the interdependence of human beings, the relation that every man bears to his surroundings. Fiction has thus kept in close connection with society, reflecting not only its mood, but also its important changes, showing thereby that it has real life and does not exist as a mere literary form at the present time, like the modern drama or a great deal of modern English poetry. Even such novels as Mr. William Black's—which are certainly not the best, clear as they are—have much more genuineness in their composition than many of the more famous verses of his contemporaries. In the novels, too, we see the steady inclination of modern literature towards realism.

The novels of Charlotte Brontë, published between 1847 and 1853, opened fresh stores of delight to the reader. The books are full of romantic interest, which is only intensified by its realistic setting, and few writers have shown such power of delineating passion. Mrs. Gaskell's novels lack that fierce intensity, but they are admirable books, and full of humor as well as pathos. Mrs. Oliphant, a most industrious writer, carries on the same tradition. Her excellent stories have left romanticism far behind them, and they show no trace of the struggle with social wrongs which inspired Mrs. Gaskell, as well as the other writers of her time; but the three writers are alike in the precision with which they represent the life of women. There is a touch of artificial grandeur about Charlotte Brontë's men, but the other two novelists draw admirably the domestic lives of their heroes.

The English poetry of the last fifty years has received much admiration. That is something, however, that has never been lacking, even in times of extreme poetical drought. Young readers are always ready to praise those of their contemporaries who repeat to them their own sensations in a novel form. Whether the fame of the poetry of this period will last is a question that time will answer, but it may be fair to doubt the importance of much modern verse. That a great deal of pains has been expended on expression cannot be denied, but whether the poetry that has been most admired has been burdened with an important message is still an open question. Tennyson began to write under the influence of Keats, and he gave the world a number of short pieces in which precision of phrase, careful workmanship, and some of the more immediately striking qualities of artistic taste are plainly visible. His method in these minor pieces shows the same traits of artificial grace and modern sentimental pathos that we see in the pictures of the once-famous pre-Raphaelite school of a few years ago. His *Maud* is an attempt to put into verse the tragedy of modern life, but it is scarcely a success. The *Enoch Arden* and the few short idylls of contemporary life in England abound with a cold, ornate simplicity which stands in the same relation to the work of the great poets of the latter half of the century that the poetry of the later followers of Pope does to that of their great master.

The remoteness of modern poetry from contemporary life is shown by nothing more vividly than by its artificial prolongation of romanticism, which was at one period a healthy, natural impulse, but is now a mere temporary diversion, like a back-eddy that one sees near the bank of a swift stream. The whole movement of the Neo-romantic school in England is a frank confession of inability to deal with modern life, an undisguised effort to imitate, as if through thin tracing-paper, once successful work. The tone of the age is towards critical examination of the legends of the past and precision in the treatment of antiquity; yet one of the leading poets of the day invokes the shadowy King Arthur and endows him with modern feelings. William Morris, again, with false modesty, considering his numerous volumes, calls himself "an idle singer," and denounces the present time as "an empty day," but the emptiness is not in the day. He chooses the most simple, unconscious poet that has ever sung in English verse for his model, and gives us deliberate studies in wilful simplicity. Rossetti, on the other hand, selected the masters of literary artificiality for imitation, and outdid them in decorative work. Painting in England, we may remark, has followed a similar direction.

Fortunately, however, the present time has produced some writers who have dared to be themselves instead of throwing all their energy into being some one else. Browning, for instance, has never followed the tempting path into which many of his contemporaries strayed. He has suffered somewhat from the fact that he possesses a rare dramatic imagination in a period when the drama is dead and buried. Then, too, in a natural reaction from the current alliterations and the euphuistic abuse of adjectives, he has kept much of his verse needlessly rugged, for excess in one direction always does additional harm by inspiring excess in the other. He has, nevertheless, not wanted admirers, and, indeed, he has within a few years, had an opportunity to enjoy honors which are generally delayed until after a great man is dead, and he has been able to see, doubtless to his surprise, how many interpretations pious disciples have been able to put on his writings.

Where Browning shows his modern spirit, his content with the air of his own time, is, of course, in his way of handling his subjects. For many of the things he writes about he is indebted to the romantic revival which unlocked vast amounts of unknown treasures, enriching literature in a way that it is hard for us to appreciate. Yet Browning is not a romanticist of the early kind, who were forever in peril of becoming melodramatic, nor yet one of the new kind, whose verses seem but one form of household decoration; but rather a poet of to-day, with the endless curiosity, combined with wide sympathy, such as are distinct traits of modern men. He neither tries to show that the most vicious person is thereby the most virtuous, nor does he shut himself up in a room with a dado to sing about pallid, wan-faced nymphs. Far from it: Browning writes about living people of flesh and blood, and he describes them with a realism which is far removed from mere petty precision of detail.

Clough's fame is not widespread in these days when much stress is laid on mechanical execution, yet there are few of his contemporaries whose verse so exactly expresses the thought that animated the controversies of his time. He and his friend, Mr. Matthew Arnold, will never be popular poets, but they will always have the admiration, and, what is better, the affection, of a certain number of readers who perceive the pathos of life. Much less known will always remain Ebenezer Jones, whose stammering measures gave but awkward expression to the utterances of an intense imagination. James Thomson, too, who died in 1882, had just published two volumes of verse which gave clear proof of the possession of technical skill and true feeling. It is to be hoped, and indeed expected, that in the future this sincerity of feeling will be more respected than it is when the public taste is temporarily perverted by undue praise of exaggerated but picturesque emotions.

It may not be unfair to say that Swinburne has done as much as any one to make these cloying measures fashionable. He possesses magnificent lyrical gifts which cannot fail to do good to the mechanical part of poetry, and, now that he has abandoned the lush wantonness of much of his earlier verse, he shows great power in interpreting some of the elemental feelings that animate the social system of the day. This is but a cool manner of describing Swinburne's passionate, dithyrambic verse, which is full of comprehension of the past and hope for the future. Yet the future which he sings is a very misty future, and very indistinct is the liberty which he chants so melodiously.

Chronologically, Landor of course belongs before Swinburne, but his absolute lack of connection with any time nearer than the Hellenic civilization permits mention of him here. He was truly a survival of ancient Greece, resembling one of those statues that are exhumed at times from beneath a street which has been a public way for centuries, and has lost all memory of the past amid the sordid needs of the present. His appearance in the full glory of the early romantic period was no stranger than it would have been in the time of the French classicism of a century earlier, for a Greek revival accompanied the birth of romanticism. He would always have been alone. His audience is small, but for those who admire the artful simplicity of his well-molded phrase, of his clear-cut epigrams, he is, and will always remain, a consummate master. His work is sculpture in verse, and his sonorous prose is an unattainable model. He seems to have been born to show an age of materialism what are purity of style and grandeur of phrase. He has had no equal followers, and it may be many centuries yet before another poet appears to show us in our own tongue what it was that people mean when they express admiration of the best work of the Greek classic writers, on which education has been based for four hundred years, with Landor for the only pupil who has learned his lesson.

In this brief sketch it has been necessary to overlook many things; such as, for instance, the transitory notoriety of the "spasmodic school," which barely lived long enough to receive the name that is now its epitaph. Alexander Smith wrote some pretty lines, but he had no significance as a poet, and P. J. Bailey, the author of *Festus*, suffers from the resemblance of the title of that poem to *Faust*. It might be interesting to examine with some clearness the vagaries of Arthur O'Shaughnessy, Mr. J. Payn, and Mr. Marzials, all of whom are very modern poets; and more serious attention is demanded by Mrs. Browning and Miss Rossetti. Mrs. Browning had considerable poetical feeling and an abundant vein of sentiment which was always ready to grow into sentimentality; her facility of expression too frequently became profusion. Yet she well repays study as one of the more important of the women who within a century have taken up literature. In the interchange of thought which makes up literature it is interesting to observe the direct influence of the women who write; and what we notice in her and in her more illustrious contemporaries, George Eliot and George Sand, is a swift application of the current thought to the practical questions of daily life. Abstract questions interest them mainly as possible solutions of the problems of, one might say, daily life. Thus, in the Italian war of independence, Mrs. Browning sees not the exultant joy in the market-place for a nation victorious over a detested enemy, but the mother who mourns her slain sons, and is yet proud of her sacrifice. George Sand, while busy with the discussion of the complete upheaval of society, applies every theory to some concrete instance of more or less domestic life. In George Eliot, too, we see morality taken out of the seclusion of books on ethics and put to the test of daily wear and tear. As the number of women who write increases, we shall doubtless see the growth of this tendency. Miss Rossetti has written some charming verses that are marked by much feeling, especially of a religious sort, and great technical skill. Certainly, English poetry with this abundant and, in many respects, rich showing is justified in not turning to the colder paths of criticism, as it has been recommended to do.

There is seldom a lack of critics and teachers in the world, and certainly if the present generation goes astray it will not be for want of advice. The man who has had the most influence on his contemporaries during the last forty years is probably Carlyle. His importance lies in this that he was by far the greatest of the Englishmen of his time who taught the value of sincerity, who inculcated admiration for heroic endeavor as distinguished from the barren emotion of the poets on the apathy of common life. His fervor, his eloquence, are familiar to us all, and after the reign of reason in the eighteenth century, and the vast tempestuous whirl of Byronism, Carlyle's stern voice crying out the command to be one's self, to do one's duty, was a new sound. Yet just where one's duty lay was not perfectly clear. To do right is excellent but sometimes vague advice, and Carlyle seldom defined his meaning. To all the fervor of the romanticists in teaching the importance of the individual as something in itself grand and admirable he added the romantic detestation of utility. He shared the abhorrence which the whole school felt for practical instruction, for science, for positive tangible improvement. Yet his eloquence fertilized and prepared the ground for the seed that was to fall on it. He refused to say that the seed was good, but he was forever fitting the soil for its reception. He aroused the love of duty, and there he stopped ; it was left to others to point out what the duty was. He reminded the world of the need to admire heroism ; and the value of a man who fills his generation with ardent enthusiasm for duty and warm love of greatness cannot be easily estimated. Yet the thrilling response to the prophet's eloquence is a transitory emotion, and the moment one begins to analyze or explain one's admiration half of their fervor is lost. We see in Carlyle's own fate the insufficiency of his way of looking at things. He finally became so enthusiastic for force that the quality itself, without regard to its object, seemed holy in his eyes. In his admiration of individual force, which, it will not be forgotten, was contemporaneous with Balzac's study of *l'homme fort*, he overlooked the way in which national forces work together for some great end, and also how even wider forces work together on all civilized men for the accomplishment of progress. We shall see later how the recognition of these facts affected modern thought.

Before we come to that, however, it will be necessary for us to consider another writer who has had an enormous influence on some of his contemporaries, and an influence that shares many of the peculiarities which we notice in that of Carlyle. This writer is John Ruskin, and the remoteness from the English people of any wise comprehension of art sufficiently explains the apparent anachronism of his appearance at this late day. For in Ruskin we find romanticism applied to the fine arts. We have seen it in poetry and in fiction ; Carlyle illustrates it applied to ethical thought ; it affected every interest, for is not imperialism in politics one of its manifestations ? However this may be, as it appears in Ruskin's writing it is as a vigorous denunciation of the pseudo-classical painters, extreme condemnation of the modern French school, and most enthusiastic praise of the glowing splendor of Turner. Ruskin's advocacy of Turner's work has been unwearied. His unrivalled eloquence has been directed to proving him the greatest of modern painters. This is very natural, for if Ruskin represents romanticism in critical writing about art, Turner represents in painting the melodramatic spirit which is so abundant in romantic literature. Ruskin takes Turner's work to pieces, and shows that this bit is true and that the other is also true, just as literary critics have shown that this and that sentence in Victor Hugo or Dickens might be uttered in certain circumstances ; but after all is done the impression still remains on the student of Turner that the whole sum of his work represents something beyond Nature—that he is a melodramatic painter.

Another instance of Ruskin's romanticism is his ardent admiration for the wilful attempts of the pre-Raphaelites to be mediæval, a movement which exactly corresponds with some of the forms of romanticism in literature. That past was discovered anew, and it seemed the most valuable model ; and in Ruskin's praise of the great Italian artists, Michael Angelo and Raphael, as well as the Venetian school, we see the equivalent of the renewed interest in Shakespeare and the whole Elizabethan drama. For this service romanticism deserves and receives all praise, but when we find it turning its back on the present in order to be a bad copy of the past, we see that it has outlived its best work. The most intelligent eclecticism, if not sterile, produces hybrids. The followers of Ruskin, who do not distinguish the wheat from the chaff in the copious writings of their master, look with considerable scorn on the sole natural, as distinguished from literary, art of the present day—that, for instance, of J. F. Millet—with very much the same impatience that a thorough-going romantic writer must feel when he tries to read the work of a realist—as if, in a word, the glory of life were wholly overlooked.

Yet the very grotesqueness of the romantic exaggerations is but proof of the original fervor. When we read Ruskin's curious medley of talk about pictures, political economy, the beauty of mountains, and of sincerity, one is impressed with the feeling that there are some things which the warmest *a-priori* inspiration cannot accomplish—that enthusiasm has its place, but that it is not omnipotent. It has done its work, and even if it has tried to do a great deal more, it should not be judged too harshly. When Mr. Ruskin denounces railroads and factories and science, he is talking pure romanticism, such as inspired Théophile Gautier when he wrote his preface to *Mademoiselle de*

Maupin—such as in later years inspired Carlyle; it was, in one way perhaps, intolerance of practical detail. Romanticism, we must not forget, stands wholly outside of the idea of growth. This is not a peculiarity of romanticism alone, but a distinguishing trait of all periods of great emotional excitement. The renaissance at first inspired pure intellectual ardor; then, when its first fury was extinct, it became a cold-blooded imitation of classicism as interpreted by pedants. It is not in periods of great religious fervor that one finds the narrow bonds and details of sects insisted on; they become prominent later, when faith is cool and trifles take the place of principles. In just the same manner the romantic writers swept away the rigid routine of the past and brought all manner of forgotten truths before the world, dissolving arid superstitions; it is only later, when questions begin to be asked, when the original impulse is growing cool, that we find the law applied to the new material. We now-a-days are but pruning, revising, correcting our predecessors, and we are but once more bringing into notice the law of growth which was stated by Herder a century ago, and overlooked everywhere, except in Germany, as a bit of cold and profitless eighteenth-century reasoning. The true romanticist would have nothing to do with it; he would wear no fetters, and consequently he has become a mere declaimer to deaf ears, who is left behind by men who acknowledge that romanticism must have a sequel.

This is all in accordance with the German proverb, that it is carefully provided that trees shall not grow into the sky. Each generation has its own message to deliver, and the fervor which enables it to struggle on against prejudice, opposition, and that deadliest foe to progress, indifference, hardens it against those who bring forward some modification or novel application of their own principles. They can answer all the arguments of the past, but they cannot cast their minds into the future; just as social reformers wish every one above them to be overthrown, and desire their own condition to be the norm, so do they believe that beyond them truth may not go.

We may see an illustration of this in the way the romantic leaders regarded John Stuart Mill, who represented the reaction against the emotional enthusiasm by which they were inspired. He had the same object in view as they had—namely, the amelioration of the race—but his method of attaining it was entirely different. He applied his reason to the discussion of similar problems. In the eighteenth century the object of interest had been a philosophical, abstract man; romanticism created the notion of what we take to be the real man, with failings as well as with aspirations. Carlyle appealed to the aspirations, Mill argued with the prejudices and convictions of a later generation; his influence was, and still is, very great.

Yet while in Mill we see beneath a cool exterior a warm nature that was not wholly suppressed by education and training, Macaulay represents in all its mechanical neatness the practical spirit and complacent content which Carlyle was forever denouncing in vain. Macaulay drew his vivid pictures in plain black and white, with no more consciousness of the mystery of things, of the baffling questions that gather about the study of life, whether in the present or the past, than have the color-blind of the majesty of sunset or the varying tints of the landscape. He treated bygone days with the easy assurance that a prophet displays when in full flood of eloquence about the future. He was proof against contradiction and argument. Yet his lucid style and his masterly arrangement of abundant facts must have fostered a love of reading among multitudes who, but for him, would never have approached the higher walks of literature. This is something for which Macaulay deserves respect; he carried out the principles that were warmly supported by poets like Wordsworth and Southey, and by what in distinction are called practical men, in doing his part in the education of the people.

In the hands of later writers literary criticism has become much more complex. Macaulay's dogmatism has been succeeded by the perception of the half-tints and shades that make the final appreciation of works of art a delicate and difficult matter. No English writer has more earnestly insisted on the need of carefully weighing all the various qualities that go to form a piece of literary work than has Mr. Matthew Arnold. This writer is not only a philosopher—not, to be sure, of the schools—but one who in his books on theology has examined the most serious problems of human life, and a poet who has remained firm in his allegiance to the higher subjects of poetry in a time when dexterity of execution has seemed the most important thing. He has brought to the discussion of literary matters the wide cultivation of a delicate taste. No one has done more than he, it may be safe to say, to open the ears of Englishmen to what is uttered in foreign lands. He has brought to his fellow-countrymen the results of the best French thought of modern times, and at times he has acted as an interpreter between Germany and England. In doing this service he has met with some opposition: a certain provincialism has inspired the objection that this course renders a man unfit to judge of what is done at home—that this enlargement of his vision cannot fail to obscure his mind. Mr. Arnold's essays are a sufficient answer to such statements, which might possibly have some weight in the unsupposable case that thought observed geographical limits, and never strayed from one country to another. It is sufficiently obvious to any one who has studied literature even superficially that such is very far from being the case. For a single instance, take the influence of the French Revolution on English literature in the first quarter of this century, and it at once becomes clear that the student is aided rather than confused by investigating what was done across the Channel. Moreover, even if this were not true, the study of the vicissitudes of any remote literature would be profitable, just as the study of any history is full of lessons to the thoughtful reader.

Possibly Mr. Arnold's ardor led him to more enthusiastic admiration of certain French methods than can command universal assent. There seems a lack of historical tact in commending the French Academy, as he has done, to English-speaking people, with their history behind them; but enthusiasm is a pardonable error in a reformer. It certainly has not led him to disloyalty to the magnificent abundance of English literature, or to raise up an altar to foreign provincialism in the place of that which is native to the soil. He is simply one of the leaders of thought who anticipate the practical men of the future in seeing that civilization is a unit, and not an accumulation of diverse and separate institutions.

The late Mr. Walter Bagehot was a valuable critic of moderate scope. Mr. Swinburne has given the world some prose essays which are interesting and often valuable, although at times marred by extravagance. His most important work has been the praise of English poets, of the past as well as of the present. For one thing, he is singularly and admirably free from petty jealousies. Mr. Leslie Stephen has written, and, fortunately, continues to write, papers of literary criticism which are always full of meaning, although at times they are marred by a note of crude, boyish indifference to delicate distinctions. Of course the boundary-line between delicacy and effeminacy is one not easily drawn, but in his reaction against the affectations of the lily-lovers, Mr. Stephen in his essays sometimes betrays what may be called an eighteenth-century violence. In his most important book, however, he is free from this fault. His *History of English Thought in the Eighteenth Century* is one of the more important works of recent date. It is a model of what is still rare in English literature of historical criticism which is not the expression of likes and dislikes or the defence of the decisions of taste, but the interpretation of the matter under discussion by the investigation of the causes and attendant phenomena. This method, which has long been familiar to Germany, is the result of the welding of science and literature, which is one of the more interesting modifications of modern thought.

Mr. John Morley's writings do an important service in widening the literary horizon of England. His lives of Voltaire, Rousseau, and Diderot are most valuable contributions to modern history, and have been of especial merit in correcting the narrowness with which the English were disposed to judge these three remarkable men, against whom there had existed a bitter prejudice, handed down from what we may call the stalwart conservatives of the last century. Mr. Morley's *Essays* are full of interest, not merely from the intelligent literary criticism which they contain, but also because the writer has a wide comprehension of the fact that literature is not merely an art by itself, but rather the vehicle in which are expressed the hopes, interests, and aspirations of the time. It is the perception of this connection between literature and humanity which makes Mr. Morley one of the most prominent writers of the present day. It is curious to notice, however, that he has not inspired most of the contributors to the "English Men-of-Letters Series," which he edits, with his own comprehension of the dependence of different authors on one another and on their own and earlier time. In most of the volumes we find the writer under discussion treated as if he were an absolutely singular phenomenon, unrelated to anything in the universe. Mr. Morley's volumes on Burke and Cobden abound with political wisdom, and it is one of the most marked traits of this author that his great intelligence and wide and careful training are mainly devoted to furthering the good of mankind. Many writers treat literature as if it were a remote thing, like painting on china; with him it is a means of civilization.

Mr. J. A. Symonds has discussed many chapters of literary history, and his *History of the Renaissance in Italy* carries him into deep waters. His discussion of this important period is marked by most intelligent sympathy and discreet criticism, and is an admirable proof of the wideness of the interests of the present day. The book is a masterpiece.

The consideration of the minor writers of promise would carry us too far. It is interesting to see in literature the widening of interest among the cultivated classes, and the way in which the modern spirit is gradually making its way into England. Much yet remains before its work is done with anything like thoroughness. There is now a wide chasm between the leaders and the huge untrained band of ordinary writers. England, the country that has made the most important contributions that the present century has seen to the arrangement of the accumulated knowledge of ages in Darwin's theory of evolution, has, though with some exceptions, remained singularly indifferent to the importance of this great step, which is meanwhile inspiring good work in Germany, where for a century the historical method had been followed in almost every department of work, and in France, where it is now taken up by the younger men.

Darwin's theory, which has made over again the classification of knowledge, need not be described here. It is curious to observe that the need of some systematic arrangement was felt by other investigators. Not only did Mr. Wallace contemporaneously light on one part of the truth, and Mr. Spencer advance towards it from another direction, but there had been other men shooting at the same mark. Comte's classification of human knowledge was an empirical attempt to accomplish the same end, but in its singular incoherence it bears the mark of being an ingenious guess rather than the result of generally convincing arguments. Buckle a few years later made another attempt, in which we see the confusion wrought by an exaggerated notion of the power of the metaphysical conception of law.

That literature has been influenced by the new vigor given to science is sufficiently clear to every one who has observed its course of late years. Every department of intellectual work has responded to the impulse which Darwin's theory gave to the thinking world. History has been made over, one may fairly say; criticism, which, rightly understood, is a subdivision of history, at last rests on a firm foundation, instead of being the expression of casual likes and dislikes; and men of science, like Huxley, Tyndall, and the late Professor Clifford, have all enriched literature by the application of scientific methods to topics of general interest. This, however, is but the smallest part of what the renewed interest in science is accomplishing. Its indirect influence on literature cannot fail to be productive of great results, for the men who are taught to regard Nature and humanity in a new way cannot fail to express their feelings in new forms, or at least in important modifications of the old forms. Every great change in human thought is an inspiration to literature, because literature is nothing more or less than one form of expression of the thoughts of a time. (T. S. P.)

ENSILAGE. This word, together with the term *silo*, has been adopted from the French, in connection with a system of providing cattle with green forage throughout the year. The word *silo* denotes the pit, *ensilo* the process of pitting, and *ensilage* the product, or pitted material. As different plants are preserved by this method, the single word ensilage is incomplete, and "ensilage of corn," "ensilage of clover," or the like, is necessary to a clear understanding of the article referred to; yet usage already makes "ensilage" alone mean pitted corn-plants. Prof. McBryde quotes passages from the writings of Cato, Varro, Columella, and Pliny, showing that the word *sirus* denoted an underground pit used for the storage of grain and green crops, at a very early period, by the people of Cappadocia, Thrace, Spain, different parts of Africa, and the East. The requirements for the ancient *sirus* were the same as those deemed essential for the modern *silo*, protection of the contents from contact with sides of pit, if of earth, by a straw lining, dryness, and perfect exclusion of the air.

It is not easy to trace this method of preserving green forage down to the present time. It is known to have been in practice in Hungary at the opening of the nineteenth century, and in Germany not many years later. The process in East Prussia was well described by Grieswald in 1842, and similar accounts exist of its application in Spain, France, and Mexico, to the preservation of different vegetable products, including the leaves of trees and vines. In Germany it was especially useful in keeping beet leaves and beet pulp in connection with the sugar industry. The French adopted it from the Germans and used it in the same way until a beet-sugar manufacturer, Adolph Reihlen, near Stuttgart, accidentally applied it to maize about the year 1855. Auguste Goffart began a series of experiments with the ensilage of maize, at his farm near Burtin, Loir-et-Cher, France, about the same time. These two, with their countrymen Crevat, Piret, Grandeau, and Leconteaux, have the credit of bringing the system, after years of trial, to a state of greater perfection and economy than exists elsewhere in Europe. It was mainly through the efforts of M. Goffart and the attention his work attracted, that the silo was introduced into the United States.

In the year 1873, and again in August, 1874, a description of the Hungarian method of making "sour fodder" in the crude trench form, appeared in *The American Agriculturist*. The same journal published in June, 1875, an illustrated account of the European experiments with ensilage, based upon reports in the *Journal d'Agriculture Practique* of Paris. The report of the United States Department of Agriculture for 1875 contained (pp. 397–408) a full description of "The French Mode of Curing Forage," its origin, the silos, the usual methods of cultivating crops for and making the ensilage, effects of fermentation in the silo, and value of the ensilage in stock-feeding. The general principles of ensilage were applied to the preservation of different products in numerous places in America, between 1870 and 1880. Prof. Manly Miles, at the Illinois Industrial University, kept broom-corn seed and the green corn plant, whole, in this way for months. In dairying districts brewers' grains were similarly preserved in pits. In September, 1877, *The American Agriculturist*, under the title "An American Silo," described and illustrated a dairy barn in Westchester co., N. Y., which contained a cellar or pit, especially constructed for storing brewers' grains and preventing their fermentation and decay by pressure and the exclusion of air. M. Goffart's book on *The Ensilage of Maize* (1877) was noticed in a paper read by ex-Gov. R. M. Price, of New Jersey, Dec. 6, 1878, at the International Dairy Fair, New York city, and subsequently printed in its *Proceedings*; the subject attracted much attention and was discussed by the farmers and dairymen present. This was undoubtedly the first presentation of ensilage in a public meeting in America. In 1879 a translation of Goffart's book was published in New York by J. B. Brown. Other American publications are: *The Book of Ensilage*, by Dr. John M. Bailey (Boston, 1880); *Ensilage of Green Forage Crops in Silos*, by H. R. Stevens (Boston, 1881); *Silos and Ensilage*, by Dr. Geo. Thurber (New York, 1881); and *Soiling, Summer and Winter*, by F. S. Peer (Rochester, 1882). Since 1880 the agricultural press of America has maintained an active discussion of the merits of ensilage, with many statements of practical trials. At least nine-tenths of all persons who have practised the system for a year or two give unqualified testimony in its favor, as being economical and advantageous.

The first person who built silos and made ensilage of corn in quantity for cattle food, in the United States, was Francis Morris, of Oakland Manor, Howard co., Md. Having read an account of the process in a French newspaper, early in 1876, he opened a correspondence with M. Goffart, and in the same year he raised five acres of corn in drills and preserved it in silos, repeating the trial the following year. It was his experience that was given at the Dairy Fair, as already noted. From this beginning, the system has rapidly spread in America; and in 1882 there were hundreds of silos, of varied forms and sizes, in use in different parts of the country. They are chiefly in the Eastern and Middle States, but also as far south as Georgia and as far west as Nebraska.

Silos may be built wholly above the surface of the ground, partly excavated, or entirely underground, and may be made of stone, brick, concrete, wood, or earth. The location, form, and material for any silo should be largely governed by the surrounding circumstances. Therefore only general directions can be given. The requirements in building a good ice-house apply well to a silo. It must be strong enough to hold its solid contents at 50 pounds per cubic foot and the weight or pressure placed upon the upper surface. It should be air-tight and water-tight. Whether it must be so placed as to protect the contents from the action of frost is still an open question, but ensilage is probably not liable to injury by freezing, while under pressure. When equally convenient, it is desirable to place a silo so as to maintain an even temperature of its contents at all seasons. The location should be such as to facilitate filling and also removing the ensilage. It is well to have the bottom on a level with, or not much below, the feeding floor, with a door into the silo from this floor, through which the ensilage is taken out. The opening must be made air-tight. The inner walls of the silo must be vertical and their surface smooth, to permit the ensilage to settle evenly in the pit and for the cover to follow. To avoid angles, silos have been built in Europe, and a few in America, of oval form, horizontally, but the usual form is rectangular. A large upper surface is not desirable, and the depth should be as much as either length or width, preferably more. Several small silos, independent or connecting, are better than one large one. A good size is that which, with accompanying facilities, enables the filling, covering, and weighting of a compartment to be done in one day, or in two days at the most. Yet such rapid work is not essential, and it will answer if, from the commencement of the filling, at least two feet in depth of ensilage over the whole surface can be put in daily until the work is done. In calculating the size for a silo, a rule approximately accurate is to allow one and one-half cubic feet of space, in the portion to be filled by the ensilage after its compression, for every day that it is desired to feed the material, as the only coarse fodder, to 1000 pounds live weight. Thus, a silo 12 feet long, 10 feet wide, and 16 feet deep, contents to be compressed to about 12 feet depth, will contain from 30 to 35 tons, or enough, allowing for waste, to feed three cows for a year. Forty-five cubic feet will generally hold a ton, and this is a maximum allowance for an animal for one month. A substantial masonry silo, by greater durability and better action, will generally be found true economy, yet cheaper structures, with walls of wood or earth, do very well. Silos are in use, and satisfactory, built wholly above ground, the walls of two thicknesses of inch boards, with and without tarred paper between. Under-ground silos, if not cement-lined, must have thorough drainage. Successful silos have been made by excavations in a heavy clay soil and in the side of a compact, well-drained gravel bank; in these cases the walls are coated with cement mortar, like a cistern, or the earth-walls left bare and simply a layer of straw, as a lining, placed between the earth and the ensilage. The crude form of the silo still in use, in parts of Europe, is a long, narrow trench, with sloping sides; this is filled with fodder, cut or uncut, and as much more piled above; the whole is then banked up and covered closely with earth, which serves both for pressure and sealing. This is, substantially, the kind of silo used by Mr. Morris, of Maryland.

Indian corn, rye, oats, the different millets and clovers, vetches, the cow-pea, beet tops and various grasses, can be successfully preserved green, as ensilage. But corn is so easily grown and is so much more productive on a given area than all other plants yet tried, that it is the ensilage crop *par excellence* in America. The large varieties with luxuriant foliage, regardless of grain, are those best adapted to the purpose. The corn is best grown in drills, three or four feet apart, on highly manured land, and thoroughly cultivated during growth. Crops of 20 to 30 tons of green fodder are commonly obtained; much larger crops have been claimed, but the average is rather below 20 tons than above it. The best time for cutting is when the plant is approaching maturity, after the ears have formed but before any part begins to dry.

In filling the silo, the fodder, whatever it be, should be cut and taken from the field without delay, to a chaffing machine placed near the silo, and then quickly cut into lengths of not less than ⅓ inch nor more than one inch. Experienced persons differ in judgment as to the length of cut; the greater number prefer to make it nearly one inch, if not quite. The chopped fodder should pass at once to the silo; carriers attached to the cutters are economical. In the silo the material must be spread of even thickness and moderately tramped down, as the filling proceeds; these are points of importance and require careful attention. The fresher the fodder when it goes into the silo and the sooner the compartment is filled, the better. No harm results from the material being quite wet with dew or rain at the time of pitting. In order to have the silo full, after settling, there should be an upward extension of the walls, one-fourth to one-third the depth of the silo, and the filling should be to the top of it. This curb or apron may be a temporary arrangement of boards, to be removed after the ensilage has fully settled. Immediately after the silo has been filled, a cover of stiff planks should be put on, closely fitting, yet just loose enough to prevent catching on the side walls during the settling. A second course of planks placed so as to cover the joints of the first is desirable. Upon the cover apply pressure in any convenient but effective form. The simplest method is by weights, using 150 to 250 pounds to the square foot of surface; these limits are safe without regard to the depth of the silo. The object is to force out air and prevent fermentation, and the weight is only needed for the uppermost six feet of ensilage, all below that depth being sufficiently compressed by the weight of the mass above. There are several devices in use for applying the pressure by screws and levers. A continuous following pressure is the best; the details are immaterial. When the cover rests directly upon the ensilage, it is usually found upon opening that two or three inches in depth has moulded and become unfit for food; this can be avoided by putting a layer of two inches thickness of cut straw upon the ensilage before covering the pit.

Harvesting the crop and filling the silo are the main items of labor in connection with ensilage, and it is in this work that the greatest opportunity occurs for system and economy. The location of the growing crop, with reference to the silo, and the arrangement for hauling, cutting, storing, and pressing, require good judgment. Ensilage in the silo costs from one to four dollars a ton, according to management; this includes seed, manure, use of land, and all labor. The average cost in the United States, during the season of 1884, was about $2.25 per ton. Ensilage being four-fifths water, the solid substance costs just about the same as its equivalent in dried fodder at usual market rates.

The silo should remain undisturbed long enough for the fermentation to reach its maximum, and the whole mass then to become cooled. In several practical tests the greatest heat has been found between the fourth and eighth days after closing the pit, and it has required several weeks to thoroughly cool. It is usually from ten to twelve weeks before the ensilage is in good condition for keeping and feeding, and it may be left as many months without injury. Upon opening a small part of the cover should be removed at a time, and the section thus exposed cut down from top to bottom like hay in a mow. If by cutting the exposed surface is changed daily in warm weather, and twice a week when cold, no decay occurs on the cut face of the ensilage. Corn ensilage comes from the silo in a moist condition, of a dark greenish-brown color, and with a pungent odor and more or less acid taste. The extent of the fermentation in the silo and the degree of acidity developed are very variable; these are important points not yet under control, and not likely to be until careful investigations throw more light upon the chemical processes of the silo.

As a rule, all horses, mules, cattle, sheep, swine, and poultry are fond of ensilage. Occasionally an animal will be found to refuse it when first offered, but these soon learn to like it and, with the rest, eat it with avidity. Most farm animals prefer ensilage to the best of dry forage, and many will eat it rather than good roots when both are placed before them. The acidity seems unobjectionable when the ensilage is fed fresh from the silo; but if kept loosened up for half a day or a day the material becomes less acid, its greenish hue brightens, and it is then eaten with more relish. That it is very palatable is shown by cattle eating a much greater weight of ensilage per day than the same animals do habitually of green grass or growing corn fodder. A cow or steer of 1000 pounds weight will often eat 120 pounds and sometimes 140 pounds ensilage in a day. From the many practical results on record it is plain that corn ensilage cannot be fed alone with profit, unless it be merely as a maintenance ration, and for a limited time. Store-hogs have been wintered upon ensilage alone without loss, but the corn plant is an incomplete food, both in its growing state and as ensilage. The best results have been those where ensilage has been fed in limited quantities, 40, 50, and not exceeding 60 pounds per day to 1000 pounds live weight, and in connection with liberal grain feeding to secure the proper nutritive ratio. Many careful feeders prefer that the ensilage should not constitute the only coarse forage, and so use only 40 or 30 pounds with 5 to 10 pounds of hay added, besides grain. Some well-conducted trials show most satisfactory results from using ensilage mainly as a condiment or addition to the usual dry winter diet and as a substitute for roots. In nearly all cases where ensilage is used as a considerable portion of the daily ration for horses and cattle, but not exclusively, its excellent hygienic effect is apparent in the thrifty appearance and action of the animals, their smooth coats, and the healthy condition of the bowels. Ensilage tends to maintain the flow of animals in milk, like any other succulent food. In the case of breeding ewes it has been substituted for turnips with satisfactory results, and their lambs have learned to eat it sooner than any other food. Milch cows on an ordinary winter diet show a marked gain in quantity of milk and some in quality, if a portion of ensilage be added to their daily ration. No such gains result from entirely substituting ensilage for other coarse fodder. Errors have arisen from comparing corn ensilage with hay, straw, and other kinds of food. No such comparison can be justly made until ensilage as a food has a more even quality, so that a standard may be fixed. The primary question is as to the effect of this process of preserving any forage plant. What is the feeding value of clover or rye as ensilage compared with the same plant in its growing state, or preserved by drying? Likewise corn ensilage must be compared with the green maize, cured corn fodder, or stover and grain. Chemical and practical comparisons made on this basis show that the nutritive value, digestibility, waste in feeding and result at the pail, are substantially alike in equal quantities of corn, whether cured as fodder or ensiloed. When such results are verified the whole problem is reduced to one of convenience and economy in the method of curing, storing, and feeding out the forage crops. With the exception of feeding, the advantages are on the side of ensilage when managed under the most favorable conditions. With well-cured corn-stalks 1¼ tons must be handled to give animals a ton of solid food; with ensilage of corn fully five tons are needed to make one of solid food. The large proportion of water in ensilage is not a direct loss, however, for animals fed largely upon it drink very little, and the effect is better when the water is thus combined with the food than when taken separately.

The chemistry of the silo is much in the dark. It is not known why ensilage from different silos varies so much, nor just what the course of chemical change is which occurs in the process, nor the effects upon the food value of the material. Opinions among good authorities range from the claim that the ensilage of any given plant is a better food than the same dried, or even in the growing state, because of greater digestibility, to the assertion of considerable losses in nutritive value by the destruction of carb-hydrates through fermentation. There is need of further investigation, carefully conducted, although the heat generated, and the smells, now of alcohol and now of vinegar, are sufficient evidence of the loss of sugar in the process. The degree and nature of the acidity developed is a matter of interest and importance. That free acid exists in ensilage, usually in considerable quantity, is agreed. But is it acetic acid or lactic? It makes a vast difference whether a milk-producing animal is fed saurkraut or pickles. The closest determination recorded gives an average of 3.69 per cent. of free acid in samples of corn ensilage analyzed, and classes it as acetic. If this be true, an animal eating 110 pounds of such ensilage a day consumes 3 quarts of strong vinegar, and a milch cow fed 50 or 60 pounds is given 3 pints of vinegar. This is hardly a proper diet to make "food for babes."

With such knowledge of the subject as is available up to present time, the conclusions in America are these: 1. That one or more silos, well built, and not too large, may be relied upon as convenient and economical on most farms, to preserve green any forage crop which circumstances prevent curing, or crops specially grown to supply succulent food for the winter season. 2. That this system of storing forage may be pursued almost regardless of the weather, and timed so that the labor will come at a season when other farm-work is not pressing. 3. That with due care the process of ensiloing will preserve green forage in an edible condition, but subject to an uncertain loss in its nutritive value. 4. That as cattle food it forms a good and cheap substitute for roots, but the crops generally thus used fail to fill the place of the root in a judicious farm rotation. 5. That in feeding ensilage to farm animals the best results follow a moderate ration, rather than its entire substitution for dry coarse fodder. 6. That the extensive use of ensilage upon any farm is mainly a question of convenience and economy to be decided by the local conditions. (H. E. A.)

ENTRY is, in law, the act of entering upon real estate in order to take possession thereof. It was at the common law an indispensable prerequisite to complete ownership. An heir could not have the absolute ownership of real estate until he had made an entry thereon; and, in case of his death before entering, the estate did not descend to his heirs, but to the heirs of the prior possessor. This doctrine was an outgrowth of the feudal system and its policy; in the earliest days, upon the conveyance of land, the parties always went upon the land together, and livery of seisin was given by the grantor to the grantee, whereby a clod of earth or a twig was handed by the former to the latter as a symbol of the delivery of the ownership of the whole tract of land, in the presence of witnesses of the neighborhood. This ceremony was formerly requisite to a conveyance, and, after deeds came into use, still continued to be a part of the formality attending such a conveyance. Its object was to give notoriety, so that those interested might know to whom lands belonged, and so that the owner might be able to prove his ownership. The necessity of an entry applied in England to the case of leases as well as to conveyances of the freehold. In America this doctrine has not been generally received very favorably. It was in early days recognized, and was the law of many or probably all of the States, but has been generally altered by statute; and it is now generally the law in this country that any interest of any kind to which an ancestor was entitled shall descend upon the heir; therefore, if an ancestor die without having the actual seisin of land, but having a claim thereto, the heir has the same claim the ancestor had, and can, in a proper case, gain complete possession by his own entry. An entry by a party turned out of possession was also a remedy for many cases where a person had a claim to real estate. The ancient law was very technical upon this subject, and drew many fine distinctions between actual possession, the apparent and actual right of possession, and the right of property. An entry by the party himself who had been turned out was generally a proper means of regaining possession for one who had the apparent right of possession, but not in any of the other cases; it was, in other words, generally a remedy against a mere wrong-doer; but, if the wrong-doer had died, the estate then, by virtue of his having had the seisin, descended upon his heir, and the heir thus gained an apparent right of possession, and could not be turned out merely by the act of the party who had been turned out by the ancestor of the heir. A *writ of entry* was one of the means to obtain possession in such a case as this, and was a regular suit, the object of which was to prove the plaintiff's right and how the defendant wrongfully obtained the possession. Moreover, when an entry was a remedy, it had to be pursued quietly and in a peaceable manner: the party could not go on the land and by force turn out the possessor, for he would thereby render himself liable both to a civil and a criminal action (forcible entry and detainer), but he could go upon the land quietly and break open an outer door of the house if necessary. These elaborate distinctions are for the most part done away with in this country, and now in England, and the actual possession and the right of property alone recognized; the right of property includes the ancient right of possession and right of property. The result of legislation, both in England and in this country, has been to extend the remedy by mere entry of the party dispossessed; thus in England a statute of Henry VIII. enacted that unless the ancestor had held the estate for five years its descent on the heir should not deprive the owner of his right to enter; and it is generally the law of this country that such a descent does not in any case bar the entry of the real owner, but in Pennsylvania the law is as established by the statute of Henry VIII. This old doctrine is known to lawyers as the tolling of an entry by a descent cast. For the meaning of entry in criminal law see article BURGLARY, vol. I., p. 678. For a stranger to enter upon lands is generally a trespass for which he will be liable to suit. But it is sometimes the case that a party has the right to enter upon lands for certain purposes, even when they are rightfully in the possession of another. Thus, a landlord may enter upon lands leased by him, in order to levy a distress, to see whether waste has been committed, etc.; one may enter upon land to pick up his goods which have gotten there without his default; every one has a right to enter a public inn; and every one may enter upon another's land in order to abate a public nuisance maintained thereon. So, too, the law often gives a right of entry for the purpose of protecting the community from crime or of bringing criminals to trial, as, *e. g.*, in cases of arrest.

The word *entry* is also frequently used in common language and in law proceedings to indicate the writing down by a merchant or person transacting any business of the details of his business, as of goods delivered, etc., etc. If there be original entries made at the time the business was transacted, they form competent evidence to establish the claim; they must, however, have been actually made at or about the time, and not be mere charges transferred from one book to another, as, *e. g.*, the ledger.

Another use of the word entry is to express the entering of goods imported at a custom-house, when they, together with the invoice and a statement, are submitted to the proper officer to estimate the amount of duties to be paid on them. (W. M. M.)

EPHOD, a Hebrew term denoting a sacred vestment originally worn only by the high-priest, but afterwards by other priests, and deemed characteristic of the office. It is fully described in Exodus, chapters xxviii. and xxxix. It was made of thin plates of gold, with blue, purple, scarlet, and fine linen. Its two parts—one covering the back, the other the breast—were clasped together on the shoulders by two large onyx-stones, each having engraved on it the names of six of the tribes of Israel. The parts were also fastened at the waist by a "curious girdle" of the same materials as the ephod. The wearer was said to be "girded with a linen ephod." Attached to the ephod of the high-priest was the breast-plate of judgment, with the Urim and Thummim, and to this the term sometimes specially refers. The nature of this part of the ephod, and the manner of its use, have never been satisfactorily explained. By means of the Urim and Thummim divine direction was sought, but how it was given we are not informed. The words themselves, it is generally agreed, mean "light and perfection," but beyond this commentators confess their ignorance or deal in conjectures. The breast-plate contained twelve precious stones, arranged in four rows, set in gold, and having the names of the children of Israel engraved upon them. Many have identified these with the Urim and Thummim, but the statements of Scripture rather make a distinction between them. The breast-plate was fastened at the top by rings and chains of gold to the onyx-stones on the shoulders, and below with rings and blue lace to corresponding rings in the ephod, so as to keep it above the curious girdle. The robe of the ephod was a longer blue garment, on which the ephod rested; it was without sleeves, but had slits for the arms and an opening for the head to pass through. Its skirt was trimmed with pomegranates in blue, purple, and scarlet, alternating with bells of gold. In a few instances the ephod is mentioned as worn by others than priests, but it was then of coarse linen. It is also sometimes mentioned as used in idolatrous worship.

EPIDEMICS (Gr. ἐπί, "upon," and δῆμος, "the people"). An epidemic, in the popular sense, is something which is general, prevalent, affecting many people at the same time. It is commonly applied only to disease, but is also used metaphorically, as an epidemic of speculation, etc. The term may be applied to any disease, since it denotes not a cause, but a result—it states not an essential characteristic of a disease, but one which may be either present or absent. An epidemic disease may or may not be endemic or specific. The older medical writers use the word in a narrower sense, which is perpetuated in the definition given by Dunglison, "A disease which attacks at the same time a number of individuals, and which is referred to some particular *constitutio aëris*, or epidemic constitution." In this sense an epidemic disease is one that is exceptional as well as widely diffused. The most extensively prevalent disease in the United States, and the one which has caused the greatest mortality, is consumption, yet it is not considered as an epidemic. Some French writers would limit the name "epidemic" to those diseases which never appear in isolated or sporadic cases in Europe unless imported—that is, to cholera, plague, and yellow fever. Others, as Monneret, characterize these as the "great epidemics." It is, however, impossible to maintain any essential distinction of this kind. A better classification is that of Leon Colin, who divides them into pestilential, endemic, and ordinary, corresponding very nearly with Dr. Guy's divisions of exotic, indigenous, and naturalized. The endemic diseases of Colin include only those which are confined to a limited locality beyond which they never extend.

In this article we shall consider only those forms of epidemic disease which are now generally supposed to be due to specific causes, and which are classed by modern German writers as the infective (not infectious) diseases. These have a special interest, not only because of their frequency and destructive effects, but because the belief is steadily gaining ground that they are all more or less preventable, and because such prevention requires something more than individual action. Few educated men now consider an epidemic as a manifestation of the anger of an offended Deity, which it is not only useless but impious to attempt to check, although there are still many who believe in the necessity of some mysterious entity called the epidemic constitution, or pandemic influence, to explain the course of extensive epidemics.

Epidemics have prevailed from the earliest times among all nations of which we have historic records. The Old Testament contains references to ten plagues, and the history of Rome before the Christian era includes thirty-two plagues. The first epidemic of which we have any definite account was the plague of Athens, 430–425 B. C., described by Thucydides, who ascribes its origin to Egypt. It is impossible to say positively what was the nature of this pestilence, but the probabilities are that it was a form of typhus. The first clear notice of the Oriental, or bubonic, plague is given by Rufus of Ephesus in the first century of our era. He refers to its existence in Libya, Syria, and Egypt. The Antoninian pest, 165–168 A. D., is described by Galen: it appears to have been a malignant form of small-pox by which, Ammianus Marcellinus says, the whole country, from Persia to the Rhine and Gaul, was filled with contagion and death. The next great epidemic recorded is the pest of 251–266 A. D., described by Cyprian. This appears to have been the Oriental plague, coming from Ethiopia and raging especially in Egypt. The sixth century after Christ was one of epidemics, including the great outbreak of the Justinian pest, which started from Egypt about 542 A. D., reached Italy in the following year, and spread through France and Germany in 545–546, recurring in 566.

Throughout the ninth, tenth, and eleventh centuries occurred a series of epidemics of a disease characterized by gangrene of the feet and hands. This affection, known to ancient writers as *Ignis sacer*, *Arsnea*, *Mal des Ardens*, and, after the twelfth century, as Saint Anthony's fire, is now known to have been, for the most part at least, what is now called ergotism, due to the use of bread made from rye affected with ergot, a peculiar fungoid parasitic growth. The suffering and mortality from some of these epidemics were frightful, especially in France. Passing over numerous outbreaks of small-pox, typhus, and plague occurring between the seventh and thirteenth centuries, we come to the most destructive epidemic of which there is any extended record. This is the great outbreak of the Oriental plague in the fourteenth century which desolated Europe, Asia, and Africa, and which is known as the *Black Death*, or *the great mortality*. The very extensive literature relating to this outbreak has been carefully summed up by Hecker, whose work on the *Epidemics of the Middle Ages* is the great storehouse of information on this subject.

He traces the origin of this epidemic to China, where it was preceded by violent earthquakes and inundations, and by repeated famines. The disease appeared in 1347 in Constantinople, Cyprus, Sicily, and Marseilles, and in January, 1348, it reached Avignon and other cities in Southern France and Northern Italy. It reached England in August; Poland and Sweden in 1349, and Russia in 1351. The mortality was enormous; for instance, Florence lost 60,000, Venice 100,000, Paris 50,000, London 100,000. In many places in France not more than two out of twenty of the inhabitants were left alive. In Avignon the pope found it necessary to consecrate the Rhone, that bodies might be thrown into the river without delay, as the church-yards would no longer hold them. Italy lost half of its inhabitants. Hecker's estimate is that about one-fourth of all the inhabitants of Europe were carried off, amounting to not less than 25,000,000 persons.

The moral, social, and political effects of this epidemic were great and far-reaching. One of the most curious was the epidemic of convulsions which closely followed it, and which was called the dance of St. John or of St. Vitus, and is now generally known as the dancing mania. This was not really a new disease, since similar small localized outbreaks had been known and recorded in the previous century, and the phenomena have been observed in our own time, as in the "jerks," in Kentucky religious revivals about 1840. The dancing mania prevailed in the Netherlands and in Germany in 1374, and the following years. About the same time a very similar epidemic occurred in Italy. This was known as tarantism, being supposed to be due to the bite of a species of spider—the tarantula.

Throughout the end of the fourteenth and fifteenth centuries a series of epidemics, of plague, typhus, etc., occurred in Europe. The most remarkable of these was what is known as the sweating sickness, a disease which broke out in England in August, 1485, becoming conspicuous just after the battle of Bosworth. It rapidly spread throughout England and Wales, and produced great mortality, but it did not extend to Scotland or cross the Channel. A second outbreak occurred in 1506, also confined to England, as was a third in 1517. But in 1528 it again appeared in a very intense form, so that "between health and death there lay but a brief term of five or six hours," and in the following year it broke out at Hamburg, and thence traversed Germany, the Netherlands, and Scandinavia, causing many deaths and a terror entirely disproportionate to its effects.

The first epidemic of diphtheria of which we have any definite record is that which occurred in Spain, 1583–1618, where it was known under the name of *garrotillo*. It had been described, however, as early as the second century after Christ by Aretæus, under the name of *malum Egyptiacum*. In 1701 the disease appeared in the Levant, and in 1735 it broke out in New England. In 1739 it was generally prevalent in Europe, and since that date has rarely or never been wholly absent from all parts of the country. Between 1845 and 1856 it appeared over the larger part of Europe and North America, and between 1856 and 1865 it assumed the proportions of an epidemic. Recently it has prevailed in epidemic form in Poland and Southern Russia, and also in various towns in the northern and western portions of the United States.

The epidemics of the nineteenth century, which are the most noteworthy, are those due to cholera, cerebro-spinal meningitis, relapsing fever, and yellow fever. While cholera had been known for a long time, it attracted little or no attention as a specific pestilential disease until the outbreak in Bengal in 1817. This spread over a large part of Asia during the next six years, and then subsided. In 1826 and 1827 it reappeared in epidemic form in India, from which it spread gradually, reaching Russia in 1829, Western Europe in 1831, and North America in 1832, where it raged as an epidemic during that and the following year.

The second great pandemic of cholera occurred in 1847-48, and reached New York in December, 1848. It lingered in the United States until 1850. The third outbreak commenced in 1852, reaching North America in 1854, and the fourth occupied the period from 1863 to 1873, reaching North America in 1865. The fifth and last cholera period extends from 1873 to the present time. Its last prevalence in the United States was in 1873. (See CHOLERA IN AMERICA.)

The history of epidemic cerebro-spinal meningitis begins with its appearance in France in 1805, prior to which time it had attracted no special attention. In 1806 it appeared at Medfield, Mass., and from that date until 1816 it extended throughout the United States and into Canada. The second outbreak of this disease began in France in 1837, and for two years was limited to that country. It then spread until 1850, appearing in the United States in 1842, and again in 1848-49. The third outbreak began in 1854 in Sweden, which had not before suffered from this disease. From 1860 to 1864 it appeared in epidemic forms in the United States, and since that time has never been entirely absent from the country. The peculiarity of this disease, which it shares with influenza, is that it is a true pandemic, not propagated by contagion. The first epidemic of influenza, definitely recorded, occurred in Europe, in 1602, since which time it has repeatedly spread over a large part of the earth.

The epidemic of 1757-58 and 1772 commenced in North America. That of 1781-82 spread over all Asia and Europe, and that of 1890-91 affected Europe and the United States, adding greatly to the death rate.

Yellow fever, which, with cholera and plague, completes the trio of pestilential epidemic diseases, has been known for over two hundred years; but the first clear and definite accounts of it are connected with the great epidemic which prevailed in New York, Philadelphia, and other cities on the Atlantic coast of the United States at the end of the last and beginning of the present century. The first recorded epidemic in New Orleans occurred in 1796, and since that time it has frequently appeared. The last extensive epidemic of this disease in the United States occurred in 1878, when it spread from New Orleans through the Mississippi Valley. According to the report of the board of experts, appointed to investigate this epidemic, yellow fever has invaded the present territorial limits of the United States in eighty-eight different years, commencing in 1693.

Relapsing fever, also called "famine fever," has only been distinctly recognized within the last forty years, attention having been called to it by the English, Scotch, and Irish epidemics which began in 1842. It had, however, been endemic in Ireland for more than a century before this. In 1847 it was brought to New York. Since 1863 it has prevailed in Russia, and several epidemics have occurred in Germany. It has also spread to India. In 1870 it was epidemic in New York and some other American cities, having been imported by foreign immigrants.

Each of the above-mentioned principal forms of epidemic disease, with the exception of influenza and cerebro-spinal meningitis, the peculiarities of which have already been referred to, has a certain limited local habitat where it is endemic. For the plague, this is the valley of the Nile; for cholera, the valley of the Ganges; for yellow fever, the West Indies; for relapsing fever, Ireland. From these points they occasionally spread far and wide, but do not become endemic elsewhere, and decline as rapidly as they spread. England is the country of scarlatina, France of typhoid fever, Russia of diphtheria and typhus. To explain these peculiarities some writers think that it is necessary to suppose the existence of what they call the epidemic constitution, a sort of cosmical influence, the nature and laws of which are unknown, but are supposed to depend upon changes in the earth. One of the most recent theories of this kind is that of Dr. Robert Lawson, who supposes that there is some influence connected with variations in terrestrial magnetism, forming what he calls pandemic waves, which gradually spread from south to north, and in the course of from three to five years pass from the latitude of the Cape of Good Hope to that of Ireland, giving rise to epidemics of yellow fever in the Gulf of Mexico and in Spain, pernicious malarial fevers in the southern part of the United States and in India, the plague in Asia, typhoid fever in the temperate zone, and typhus and relapsing fevers in the north.

The same theory in another form is advanced by Mr. Cushing in a paper entitled "Sun Spots, Cycles, and Epidemics," published in the *International Review*, April, 1880. The periodical variations of the so-called sun-spots have been shown to have a cycle of a little over eleven years, and to be connected with periodical variations in terrestrial magnetism and rainfall, the latter being connected with famines in India during the present century, such famines following after a drought occurring at the minimum of sun-spots. To put it in his own words: "Terrestrial epidemics depend largely on the disturbance in the economy of nature caused by the cyclical variation in the solar energy which coincides with the vast disturbances in the sun, appearing to us as spots on its disc." The last sun-spot minimum occurred in 1878, the maximum in 1881-2.

The great objection to these theories is that they do not take into account the influence of certain causes which are well known, and which certainly act in some, if not all epidemics. As a rule those who advance them practically overlook or deny the influence of contagion and infection, of insufficient and improper food, and of meteorological influences. The increase of susceptible, or, as they are sometimes termed, "epinosic" persons, in a locality, in the intervals of epidemics, explains, to some extent, the periodicity of those diseases which, as a rule, attack a person but once in his life, such as measles, small-pox, and yellow fever. A good illustration of this is found in the history of epidemics of small-pox in the last century. They came round in a given locality about once in five years—

when enough unprotected children had accumulated to furnish material. The disease occurred chiefly in children under five years of age, because the older children and adults were the survivors of a previous attack. The history of epidemics is closely connected with that of famines, and the fact that mortality varies with the price of wheat is well known to statisticians. Relapsing fever is so emphatically the famine fever that it is known by that name. Typhus is so invariably associated with poverty, over-crowding, insufficient food, and over-work, that it seems as if the combination of these causes were sufficient to produce it. It is a disease of armies, and especially of unsuccessful armies, of sieges, of prisons, and attacks especially those weakened by scurvy, malaria, etc. The supposed dependence of typhus upon climate, and its increase in cold weather, is probably due simply to the over-crowding caused by the efforts of the poor to obtain shelter. In short, the more each particular epidemic is studied, and the more complete the records with regard to it, the more we can see how its progress is influenced by well-known, every-day causes, and the less necessity appears for attributing it to a wholly mysterious thing like the epidemic constitution. One of the most interesting practical questions with regard to the larger number of those diseases liable to become epidemic, viz., the acute specific diseases which are capable of reproducing their own kind, being either contagious or infectious, or both, is whether they ever at the present time originate spontaneously, *i. e.*, independent of an antecedent case. The arguments on either side have been very well summed up by Dr. Thorne, who states them substantially as follows:

Those who think that such spontaneous origin cannot occur may be called the "contagionists." Their belief is grounded on the fact that such diseases do largely spread by mediate communication with other cases of the same disease. As this is the usual mode of spread, we are justified in assuming that often no direct proof as to the transmission of the specific poison, can be given. It must have passed in some undetected way. The opposite belief arises from negative evidence only. We are every day discovering new means by which the poisons of these specific diseases are either preserved through long periods of time, or conveyed from one person to another. It is now well known that typhoid fever and scarlet fever may be spread through the agency of milk. Numerous local epidemics of these diseases can now be explained in this manner. The same is true with regard to the spread of typhoid fever through an intermittent water surface leading to the specific poison being drawn into the mains during periods of intermission. In many cases where at first it might be supposed that the evidence was strong in favor of spontaneous origin, careful and skilled investigation has shown that it is due to infection from some prior case. The period of incubation, as it is called, for each specific disease is known to vary to a certain extent; but it seems likely that in exceptional cases this variation may be very great, and therefore form a series of errors in investigating the cause of a given outbreak. It may also be the case that the outbreak of an acute specific disease, apparently of spontaneous origin, may be really the result of infection from a case of the same disease which had occurred long previous. Some organisms do retain their vitality for long periods, and the organism in one of the acute specific diseases, viz., splenic fever, or malignant pustule, is found to exist in two states, in one of which it has great prevalence, and resists all ordinary influences of destruction. They can be reduced to dust, wetted and dried rapidly, and kept in liquids for weeks, and yet at the end of four years will still display an undiminished potency. There are many well-known instances where the poison of scarlet fever has remained dormant for a number of years and then acted with unabated virulence. Similar evidence is furnished with regard to typhoid fever. The long-continued and complete immunity from this specific disease which certain isolated countries have enjoyed, and the virulence which such diseases have exhibited when once introduced within them, is also an argument in the same direction. The freedom of the New World from small-pox prior to its discovery by Columbus, and the immunity of the Faroe Islands from measles for many years, with the disastrous results in each when these diseases were introduced, illustrate this fact. On the other hand there are many who, admitting that these diseases are self-propagating, assert that some of them are of spontaneous origin, and urge in proof of this view the outbreaks of typhus in ill-fed and over-crowded collections of men, especially in armies. The main argument, however, is that these specific diseases must at some time or other have had first cases, and that unless we are prepared to accept the view that the several contagia are the result of a definite act of creation, we must assume that they did arise independently of antecedent cases.

Dr. Thorne states, as the result of his experience in investigations into the origin of outbreaks of diphtheria, that he has been specially struck with the fact "that in isolated districts, and in houses situated at times miles away from other habitations, in some instances in lonely spots among mountain ranges, where a visit to or from the nearest town or village would be a circumstance too important to be forgotten, I have met with instances of what appeared to me to be nothing more than a simple inflammation of the throat, at times so trivial that it is passed almost unnoticed, and yet it has led by transmission through other persons to cases of very marked and severe diphtheria; and I have hardly been able to refrain from drawing the conclusion that conditions very similar to those under which genuine diphtheria was epidemic in a limited degree existed, and that these conditions, leading to a somewhat general predisposition to simple and apparently known infectious inflammatory sore-throat, had tended to produce an infection capable of taking on the property of infectiousness. The possible explanation of this is that minute organisms, capable of producing a minor and uncommunicable disease in particular stages of their growth may at other stages, or by subsequent development, become capable of producing a specific disease communicable from person to person—that is, the production by means of evolution of special properties in an already existing organism."

This idea of the gradual development of specific infectious properties in minute organisms is one of special importance at the present time. The question is stated by Dr. Airy as follows: "If we suppose a community exposed in an equal degree to a number of diseases of equal fatality; any one of these diseases, which has in any appreciable degree the property of infectiousness, will attack more persons than a non-infectious disease, and those who contract the disease in the more infectious form will be more likely to transmit it to others. In short, the more infectious the disease becomes the more numerous will be the persons attacked by it, and the greater, *ceteris paribus*, will be its chance of revival by continued reproduction. The conditions are practically the same as those of fever variation in animal and vegetable life, enabling its possessors to leave more offspring after their own likeness than other less favored forms."

This tendency is, however, self-limited, owing to the fact that in most of the specific diseases an individual ordinarily suffers but one attack, and, in case of survival, is protected against future attacks. Whether we assume that infectious diseases arise from the reception into the body of specific living organisms, the so-called "germ theory," or from the reception or formation in the body of a certain virus or poison, the so-called "glandular secretion theory" of Dr. Richardson, the influences of natural selection in the matter must be very great. Dr. Richardson's theory is that when the poison of a specific disease, as, for instance, small-pox, has entered the system, it does not propagate absolutely in the system, but that setting up a new series of chemical results the blood is so modified that, brought to the excretal surface, the normal secretion is simply prevented, and the new special albuminous excrete is the result; that the process of development of these poisons, whether occurring in the body or out of it, though manifest always by the agency of organic matter, is essentially a chemical process, and when this occurs in the body the new chemical products are the causes of the symptoms as well as the pathology of the disease excited; that the virus of this disease is purely incidental to a modified chemistry in the organism, being as necessarily an excrete under the modified conditions as urea is necessarily an excrete in perfect health. In other words, he considers this disease as due to zymosis in which the external conditions and the supply of matter susceptible of zymotic change being supplied, the quantity of ferment added as a starting-point is a matter of comparatively small importance.

The opinion at present prevailing among physicians and scientific men is that the peculiar phenomena of epidemics of cholera, plague, yellow fever, typhus, typhoid and relapsing fevers, diphtheria, measles, small-pox, scarlet fever, and whooping-cough are best explained on the hypothesis that they are caused by minute living organisms. As regards typhus, typhoid and relapsing fevers, and diphtheria, the organisms which produce them, and by means of which they are propagated, may be produced from certain very common and harmless organisms, which are found everywhere, by a process of development in which variations in the human body due to malnutrition play an important part. Such production is, however, rare, and as a rule a case of either of these diseases is due, directly or indirectly, to a preceding case of the same disease. As regards the other diseases mentioned above, there is no evidence of their spontaneous development in recent times. The influence of foul air and impure water upon their spread is very great, and their malignancy and contagiousness may be greatly increased by unsanitary surroundings—apparently upon somewhat the same principle as the increase in virulence which may be given by successive cultures to a given microzyme. The reverse of this is also true, and upon this fact depends the great interest which attaches to the recent investigations of Pasteur and Koch. For some of the contagious diseases it would seem that the contagion is subject to the laws of gravitation, and this is confirmed by the results of an investigation made by Dr. Power as to the effects of a small-pox hospital in spreading the disease in the vicinity. Dr. Buchanan has pointed out that the distribution of infection from a central point, if effected into space of three dimensions, will differ from that effected along a single plane. In the first case the relative force or probability of infection at a place will be inversely as the square of its distance from the centre; in the last case it will be inversely as the distance itself. When, however, we consider the frequency with which the contagia must be passing into the atmosphere at many different points in any large city—their small specific gravity, and the ease with which they may be carried by currents of air; and, on the other hand, the rarity of the diseases caused by them, and the fact that in most cases we can trace the causation of such diseases to comparatively close association with persons affected with them—it is evident that the virulent properties of the immense majority of such contagia must be speedily destroyed by exposure to air and light.

With regard to the origin and progress of epidemics, each disease has its own laws. The brief historical sketch given above shows the truth of the remark of Littré, that new diseases are developed, and that there is not only a geography, but a chronology, of disease. The ancient belief was that all great epidemics came from the east and travelled to the west, and this was borne out by the history of the plague, of small-pox, and of measles. When we remember, however, that all the civilized nations in whom there were persons competent to observe and record such events were denizens of Europe, and especially of Western Europe, so that they could only be invaded from the east, this is not strange, and it becomes still less remarkable when the character and habits of Asiatic nations are considered. The sweating sickness arose in England and travelled east and south. Yellow fever is a disease of the Western Hemisphere, and cholera has spread to the east as well as to the west. An epidemic of contagious and infectious diseases usually follows a tolerably uniform course of development in any given locality, so much so indeed that it has been made the subject of mathematical analysis. The following is the mode of calculation employed by Dr. Farr in estimating the probable course of an epidemic which is increasing with the gradually decreasing ratio of increase.

"Take nine weeks of the early course of the epidemic, in three groups of three weeks each; find the average deaths per week in each group; find the number by which you must multiply the first average to obtain the second, and the numbers by which you must multiply the second average to obtain the third; or, as simpler process, take the difference between the logarithms of the first and second, and between the logarithms of the second and third. The first of these differences may be called X, and the difference between these two differences, which should, to bear out this theory, be a negative quantity, may be called Z. We have now the data for constructing the series. The average of the first three weeks is the starting-point, and represents the centre week of those three. The next number in the series is obtained by adding to the logarithm of our first number a number composed of $\frac{X}{3} + \frac{Z}{9}$, remembering that Z is a negative quantity. We continue to add to the logarithm for each place in the series a number gradually diminished by the addition in each place of $\frac{Z}{9}$; after a time the number to be added becomes negative, and the series gradually diminishes."

The measures to be taken by a community to prevent the spread of epidemics may be divided into two classes. The first are those designed to prevent the appearance of the first cases. The second those intended to limit its spread and, to use a popular phrase, "to stamp it out." The preventives of the first class are cleanliness, quarantine, and, as regards small-pox, vaccination. Those of the second class are isolation and disinfection, with vaccination for small-pox. The form of cleanliness which is efficacious is that which prevents accumulations of decaying organic matter, of excreta in vaults and cesspools, of garbage in cellars and alleys, and which prevents the poilution of the water supply. It is especially useful against cholera, typhoid fever, and diarrhœal affections of all kinds, and also against diphtheria, typhus, erysipelas, and certain forms of inflammation of the lungs. Quarantine is of the greatest importance against yellow fever because that disease is terminated by frost, and every day's delay in its appearance is a decided gain, even if it passes the barrier at last. This is not the case with those diseases whose spread is not limited by temperature.

For preventing the spread of a contagious disease it is of the greatest importance that the first cases be promptly and effectually dealt with so as to prevent the spread of the virus. This implies early notification of the existence of such cases. The methods of treating the cases so as to protect the community vary with the different diseases. In cholera, for example, the poison is conveyed in the intestinal discharges; and hence attention is to be mainly directed to securing prompt and thorough disinfection of these and of whatever clothing, etc., has been soiled by them. In scarlet fever the poison is conveyed from the skin, throat, and perhaps also the excreta, especially the urine. In such a case the first object is to have the patient placed in a room by himself and to have in it no carpet, curtains, upholstered furniture, or anything which is not necessary. No one should enter this room but the nurse and the physician, and they should take special precautions. The patient should be kept thoroughly anointed from head to foot with some oily or fatty material, such as vaseline. The great object is to prevent the occurrence of dust in the room. All clothing, bed-linen, etc., should be placed in a disinfectant solution as soon as they are no longer needed. They should never be removed from the room while dry, and should not be shaken or disturbed more than is necessary before they are moistened. A good disinfectant solution for this purpose is composed of four ounces of sulphate of zinc and two ounces of common salt to the gallon of water. If this is not at hand place the articles at once in scalding water. All dust and dirt about the room should be removed by damp cloths, which are to be treated like the clothing. No sweeping or dusting in the ordinary way should be permitted. The excreta should be received in vessels containing a solution of sulphate of iron, $1\frac{1}{2}$ pounds to the gallon. Many other details might be given, but the above are probably sufficient to illustrate the principles involved, which apply also to diphtheria, measles, and smallpox. When the separate room and the constant intelligent care cannot be had, the best thing to be done is to remove the sick person to a hospital. This presupposes that proper hospitals for the reception of such cases have been provided, and without such hospitals a community is comparatively helpless.

The spread of scarlet fever and diphtheria is largely effected through schools, and it is sometimes thought necessary to close the schools in epidemics of these diseases. Such action, however, should be very rarely required. So long ago as 1793 Dr. Withering, speaking of scarlet fever, said: "For several years past I have never thought it necessary either to break up a school or to disperse a family. The allotting apartments or separate floors to the sick and the healthy, and prohibiting any communication between the sick and their attendants and the healthy, with positive orders to plunge into cold water all the linen, etc., used in the sick-chambers, has very universally been found to check the further progress of the infection.' The great difficulties are to secure effective isolation. Nothing but great care and tact is sufficient for this purpose. The majority of people are too apt to rely mainly upon the action of gaseous disinfectants, such as chlorine or burning sulphur, in place of minute and constant cleanliness in the sanitary sense.

As regards individual prophylaxis in the presence of contagious diseases, when these are epidemic, little is known. It has been recommended to make use of the sulphites with the idea of making the blood of such a character that the supposed germs will not develop in it. The use of chlorate of potash and local applications to the throat of solutions of the salts of iron have been recommended as a preventative of diphtheria. As yet, however, there is no satisfactory evidence of the utility of these measures. In case of the pestilential diseases, where the locality becomes infected, the most certain means of putting a stop to their ravages is to abandon the place temporarily and place the inhabitants in camps. It is not necessary to remove any great distance to secure the desired results. The experience of the camps near Memphis in 1879 was very satisfactory, and the same has always been the case when a post has been abandoned by troops on account of yellow fever. This evacuation of an infected locality for a time until the virus can be destroyed gives excellent results in plague, yellow fever, and typhus. It does not work so well in cholera; in fact, as Colin remarks, it may aggravate it in case of a mixed population. With troops, however, where discipline can be enforced, it gives good results even in cholera, but it cannot be relied on alone. To put an end to a typhus epidemic the great remedy is fresh air and plenty of it, and the only way to obtain this in most cases is to evacuate the infected premises. The time to prepare for an epidemic is when no epidemic is threatening, when there is no panic or confusion. Unfortunately the great mass of people and of municipal administrators are unwilling to take any precautions in this direction, such as the providing hospitals for infectious diseases, proper sewerage and other means of securing cleanliness, and a system of notification of infectious disease, until the epidemic is at their doors, when it is usually too late. (J. S. B.)

EPILEPSY. There are three distinct affections to which the name of epilepsy is commonly applied. The first of these is the so-called *idiopathic* or *essential* epilepsy. This ordinary or true epilepsy is treated with sufficient fulness in the ENCYCLOPÆDIA BRITANNICA. (See Vol. VIII. p. 425 Am. ed. (p. 479 Edin. ed.))

The second, called *reflex* or *eccentric* epilepsy, is related to the essential epilepsy in that it is capable of being converted into it, or, to speak more accurately, giving origin to it. In reflex epilepsy there is always a peripheral point of irritation in which lies the starting point of the convulsive paroxysm. This point is of various nature: thus it may be a scar, a tumor, an improperly developed genital organ, a parasitic intestinal affection, a developing tooth, etc. In such a case, so long as no secondary changes have been wrought in the nerve centres, the removal of the irritation puts an end to the series of convulsions.

The human nervous system has, however, a very strong tendency to be affected by habitual action: thus, if for a sufficient length of time the nerve centres have, under the influence of a peripheral irritation, developed frequent convulsive discharges of nerve force, a condition of the centres themselves is induced by virtue of which the discharges recur, although the original point of irritation is removed. Under such circumstances the reflex epilepsy has been converted into an essential epilepsy. The important practical deduction is that in reflex epilepsies the peripheral irritation should be removed immediately, even, if needs be, at much hazard.

The discoveries of Dr. Brown-Sequard have thrown much light upon these reflex epilepsies. He found that Guinea-pigs, after recovering from certain injuries to their nerves, were epileptic. In a particular region of the face the character of the hairs was at this time distinctly abnormal, and at any moment titillation of this portion of the skin produced violent epileptic convulsions. If the altered skin were cut out the epilepsy was cured. It appears, therefore, that section of a sciatic nerve will cause in the Guinea-pig such alteration in the nutrition of a distant part of the skin that stimulation of its peripheral nerve-endings provokes a general convulsion. The fact that, before removal of the diseased skin, the Guinea-pig may beget epileptic offspring, shows a relation between this reflex and essential epilepsy.

In some cases of reflex human epilepsy handling of the scar, or other point of irritation, will cause a paroxysm, but epilepsy has been cured by removal of a scar which was apparently entirely inert.

An epilepsy which is not reflex, and first develops after the age of thirty, is in the great majority of cases either *toxic* or *organic*.

In toxic epilepsies the convulsions are caused by the presence, in the blood, of a poison, which may have either been generated in the body or received from without. The autochthonic poisons are, with rare exceptions, due to disease of the kidneys. Epileptic form convulsions are not merely a symptom of chronic alcoholism, but lead and other poisons may cause such attacks.

Organic epilepsies are those which result from gross lesions of the brain, such as tumors, syphilitic disease, etc. They are frequently to be distinguished by being localized; thus only one-half of the body, or even one limb, may be convulsed. The cases are, however, exceptional in which the movements are thus restricted during the whole convulsion, as they usually rapidly spread so as to involve the whole person. When the epileptic attack has first appeared, years after the completion of puberty, and the paroxysms persistently begin in one extremity, the patient is almost invariably suffering from organic brain disease, and close scrutiny should be made so as to discover other symptoms, and to decide the nature of the lesion. (H. C. W.)

EPISCOPAL CHURCH, PROTESTANT. This is the legal title of that branch of the Catholic Church which had its origin from the Church of England, and which claims jurisdiction in the United States. The name "Protestant Episcopal" came into use popularly at first as a matter of convenience, and was afterwards acquiesced in, rather than adopted, as the legal and corporate title of this church. As the claims of the church came to be better understood by her own members, it was seen that this title does not adequately indicate those essential and permanent characteristics which are expressed in the creeds and other formularies. Of late years an agitation has sprung up to bring about a change of name. This was made a definite issue in the General Convention of 1877 and 1883, but failed to obtain a majority. It is no new thing for a particular branch of the church to assume a special designation. Thus, the Holy Eastern Church is commonly known as the "Orthodox Church," in distinction from the numerous heretical sects of the East. The titles, "Church of England" and "Church of Ireland," had their origin in the connection of church and state. It may be said also that the present title of the church in America expresses, in a measure, the peculiar mission which the state of religion here has imposed upon her.

The Protestant Episcopal Church is in entire accord with the Church of England in doctrine, accepting the same creeds and articles; in worship using services which are substantially identical, and in the essential principles of church government by bishops, priests, and deacons; but she is entirely independent of the state, and, as regards the law of the land, rests upon the same ground with other religious bodies. There are besides certain peculiarities in her constitution, which still further distinguish her from the mother church.

The history of this church exhibits, in a striking manner, "the vital energy of the episcopal system," and the tenacity of catholic principles under the most unfavorable circumstances. During the first 150 years, neglected by the authorities of the mother-country, her constitution left incomplete in the most essential particulars, her extension and welfare left almost entirely to individual and voluntary effort, the church nevertheless lived and grew. The adverse influences of the Revolution did not destroy her, and upon completing her organization with bishops of her own she soon entered upon a new period of rapid extension and vigorous life.

THE COLONIAL PERIOD (1607-1776).

The earliest expeditions fitted out in England, with the object of forming settlements in America, had in view the extension of the church as well as material interests. For example, in the expedition of Sir Humphrey Gilbert (1585) the religious objects proposed were, "compassion of poore infidels captived by the devil," and the establishment of a system of government "not against the true Christian faith professed in the Church of England." The letters patent granted to Sir Walter Raleigh contained similar provisions for the establishment of the "true Christian faith now professed in the Church of England." It was during the temporary occupation of the coast of North Carolina by one of Raleigh's expeditions that the first baptism of a native Indian took place, also the first recorded baptism of a white child.

Virginia.—The first permanent settlement was effected under a charter of 1606 at Jamestown, in Virginia. A decided religious feeling actuated its founders, and found expression in the letters-patent. The Rev. Robert Hunt accompanied the expedition, and did much to keep the spirit of true religion among the contentious and struggling colonists. The holy communion was celebrated by him for the first time in May or June, 1606. The services of the church were first held under an awning hung between the trees. "This," says the famous Capt. John Smith, "was our church till wee built a homely thing like a barne, set upon cratchets, covered with rafts, sedge, and earth." "Wee had daily common prayer, morning and evening, every Sunday two sermons, and every three moneths the holy communion, till our minister died. But our prayers daily, with an homily on Sundaies, wee continued two or three years after, till more preachers came." A new charter was granted in 1609 to a company which included a number of bishops, and counted among its names Sir Edwin Sandys and Nicholas Ferrar, the friend of George Herbert. Under the influence of such men the religious interests of the colony were sure to be provided for. The arrival of a new governor at a critical juncture, known as "the starving-time," was celebrated by a service in the church, "which was neatly trimmed with the wild flowers of the country." In 1619 the first legislature of Virginia set apart for each parish a glebe of 100 acres, and fixed a yearly stipend for the payment of the clergy. The bishop of London was applied to for a body of "pious, learned, and painful ministers," and was about this time appointed a member of the king's council for Virginia. Thus began the relation by which the bishop of London became, in a manner, the diocesan of the infant church in America. The charter of 1609 was annulled in 1625, and the company in which Sandys and Ferrar had been leading spirits was broken up. The whole property and government of the colony were assumed by the Crown. But the religious character originally impressed upon it was maintained until the period of the great Rebellion. Virginia had declared for the king, and during the troublous times which ensued became a place of refuge for the Cavaliers, many of whom were men of broken fortunes and reckless lives. During the Protectorate the church in Virginia became greatly demoralized. At the Restoration most of the parishes were without incumbents. Applications were now made to the mother-country "for help to preserve the Christian religion by supplying them with ministers." A new class of men made their appearance in answer to these petitions, "such as wore black coats and could babble in a pulpit, roare in a tavern, exact from their parishioners, and rather by their dissoluteness destroy than feed their flocks." Great scandals arose, and the urgent necessity for the presence of a bishop in America was clearly seen. A bishop was actually nominated, when the fall of Lord Clarendon put an end to the project. The bishop of London had been invested with formal jurisdiction over English congregations abroad since 1634. But this authority had, up to this time, never been effectively exercised in the American colonies. After the failure of the scheme for sending out a bishop, the bishop of London, as a partial substitute, in 1689 appointed the Rev. James Blair his commissary. This officer had power to hold visitations, to deliver charges, and, to a certain extent, enforce discipline, but he could not confirm, ordain, or consecrate, nor could he depose a priest from his office. Nevertheless, during the fifty-three years in which Blair held this position, he did much to remedy the prevailing laxity, and to improve the state of the church.

Early in the 18th century the external equipment of the church in Virginia seemed all that could be desired. There were fifty-four parishes, with about seventy places of worship. The supply of clergy was nearly sufficient, there were glebes and parsonages, and all wore a prosperous look. But, in reality, the state of affairs was far from satisfactory. The system, as an establishment, was very defective, and through certain evasions of the order provided by law the worst features of the voluntary system were introduced. By the act of 1642 a clergyman was to be inducted into his parish by the governor, and henceforth held a freehold in his living, and consequently could not be removed except after a fair trial upon charges regularly preferred. But the presentation was in the hands of the parish, and might be withheld indefinitely; this became the general practice, so that the majority of the clergy were hired from year to year. This, taken with the indifferent quality of many of those who came out from England after failure to obtain a living at home, and the fatal defect in organization by which it was rendered impossible to remedy existing evils, fully explains the low tone of the church in Virginia. The disuse of induction was in many cases accompanied by the withholding of the glebe by the vestry. This led to a legal contest, which was decided in favor of the clergy, and reaffirmed by an act of assembly in 1748. Another contest sprang up between the clergy and the provincial assembly in consequence of an attack made by the latter in 1757 upon the salaries of the former. An act was passed which compelled the clergy to accept a money-payment at a low valuation in lieu of the tobacco hitherto paid. This act was annulled by the king's council, and the clergy instituted suits for the recovery of the full amount of their stipends. One of these was brought to trial as a test case, and by the exertions of the celebrated Patrick Henry was decided against the church (1763). The relation of the vestries to the clergy in the first place, and these contests in which, first, the clergy and the parish authorities were arrayed against each other, and afterwards the clergy and the legislature, brought the laity into a position of influence in the management of ecclesiastical affairs which, taken with a similar state of things in Maryland, had an important part in the formation of the constitution of the American church of a later period.

A second project for the establishment of bishops in North America had received the sanction of Queen Anne, but was defeated by her death. Petitions for this purpose sent in by the churchmen of the colonies were of no effect. A last attempt of this kind was made a short time before the Revolution. At the solicitation of the clergy of the Northern and Middle colonies a meeting of the Virginia clergy was held in June, 1771, which decided against the design, and the chief opponents received a vote of thanks from the legislature.

Maryland.—The first settlers of Maryland in 1634 were Roman Catholics. Freedom of religion was, however, granted to all comers. This was secured, in the first place, by the oath of office. The colony soon had a very mixed population as regards religion, and in 1646 an act of toleration was passed by the assembly. Under the Protectorate, upon the submission of the colony after a struggle, a law was passed tolerating all forms of Christianity except "popery, prelacy, and quakerism." The earliest trace of the Church of England is in 1676, when it appears that there were four clergymen in the province supported by private means. From 1688 to 1692 occurred the "Protestant Revolution," which ended in the establishment of the Church of England by act of assembly in 1692. The territory of the colony was divided into parishes, and a tax payable in tobacco laid upon the people for the support of the church. Sir Francis Nicholson, appointed governor in 1694, exerted himself in behalf of the church and brought the new act into operation. The number of clergy rapidly increased. Following the same course as in Virginia, the bishop of London in 1696 appointed

Dr. Bray his commissary for Maryland. This officer arrived in 1700, and at a visitation held at Annapolis made a determined and partly successful effort to enforce discipline in the case of profligate clergy. At this meeting also arrangements were made to support a missionary among the Quakers of Pennsylvania. Dr. Bray was compelled in a short time to return to England in order to counteract attempts made to overthrow the Maryland establishment. In this he was at length successful. Although he never returned to America he did not relax his efforts in behalf of the church. One good work of his was the provision of numerous parish libraries for the colony, but by far the most important result of his labors was the foundation of the "Society for the Propagation of the Gospel," which is directly traceable to his influence. No new commissary was sent to Maryland until 1716, when two were appointed—Mr. Wilkinson for the Eastern Shore, and Mr. Henderson for the Western. The latter was a man of remarkable energy, but he was not able to contend successfully against the extraordinary difficulties in which he found himself involved, resulting from laxity of discipline within and hostile attacks from the civil power without. The contest in Maryland had two phases. The absence of any ecclesiastical authority empowered to enforce discipline induced the governor and assembly at different times to assert an undue control of the affairs of the church. This was carried so far as to resist all attempts to remedy existing evils through ecclesiastical channels; thus, in 1718, the assembly refused to recognize by a formal act the jurisdiction of the bishop of London, and in 1727, when the Rev. Mr. Colebatch was invited to come to England to receive consecration for the episcopal office, he was prevented by a writ of *ne exeat* from leaving the colony. On the other hand, here, as in Virginia, attacks were made upon church property and the support of the clergy. Henderson at last, worn out by the conflict, ceased to exercise his office as commissary, and matters were henceforth allowed to drift. The church in Maryland, during the whole period of its existence before the Revolution, was under the same disadvantage as to discipline with that of Virginia, although there were periods when, by the energy and faithfulness of such men as Bray and Henderson in their office as commissaries, the tone of clerical character was high. On the other hand, the church in Virginia was, perhaps, never subjected to such extreme claims on the part of the civil power as that asserted by the governor and assembly of Maryland on some occasions.

The Carolinas and Georgia.—The early history of the church in the Carolinas unfolds the same tale of mismanagement in its relation to the civil government. Much the same arrangement also existed as regards the incumbent and his parish which was so fraught with evil in Virginia. As early as 1704 an act of assembly constituted a lay commission for the trial of causes ecclesiastical. This law was afterwards annulled on appeal to the home government, chiefly through the exertions of the Society for the Propagation of the Gospel. In 1707 Gideon Johnstone was appointed commissary of the bishop of London in this region, succeeded soon afterwards by Alexander Gordon. The administration of Gordon was judicious and faithful, but was chiefly remarkable for his collision with Whitefield. This famous teacher was producing great confusion in the infant church, but upon admonition he defied the authority of the commissary and treated with contempt the proceedings of the ecclesiastical court which convened at Charleston for his trial in 1740.

The Colony of Georgia was established through the benevolence of Oglethorpe in 1732. The early history of religion in this region was marked by the labors of the Wesleys, who had been recommended to Gov. Oglethorpe as fit persons to aid in carrying out his plans. Charles was engaged as the governor's secretary, while John became the first missionary at Savannah. Charles was soon so involved in disputes with the governor that he felt that his usefulness was at an end, and left the colony four months after his arrival. John Wesley endeavored to introduce, above and beyond the requirements of the church, a system of rigid asceticism for which the society about him was utterly unprepared. After a career marked by intense ardor and devotion he became involved in an unfortunate lawsuit turning upon an injudicious attempt to administer discipline, and without waiting for its final settlement shook off the dust of his feet against the colony and departed, after a ministry of 21 months. It is interesting to remember that at this time the brothers appeared as very high churchmen, contending for an exact literalness in carrying out the law of the church which was unknown at that day.

The Middle Colonies.—In New Jersey, Delaware, Pennsylvania, and New York the church was never established. That was precluded by the character of the first settlements. The Swedes and Dutch, who colonized these regions from 1608, brought with them the religious rites and usages of the Swedish Lutheran and Dutch Presbyterian worship. The English element in New Jersey and Pennsylvania came in with the Quakers, who founded Burlington in 1677, and Philadelphia under William Penn in 1681. Large bodies of Scotch Covenanters also emigrated to East Jersey in consequence of the severities inflicted upon them at this period in their native country. This whole region, therefore, was settled under influences adverse to the Church of England. But while this was true, it does not appear that opposition to the church ever assumed an organized form or that laws were made of an intolerant character. In the charter of Penn it was expressly stipulated that whenever twenty inhabitants requested a Church of England minister, he should be allowed to dwell among them without molestation. In pursuance of this arrangement we find the first place of worship belonging to the Church of England erected in Philadelphia in 1695, and the Rev. Mr. Clayton appointed its first minister. But the growth of the church in these colonies, as in those of New England, was chiefly owing to the zeal of new converts to her fold and to the fostering care of the Society for the Propagation of the Gospel, founded in 1701. George Keith, a convert from the Quakers and the earliest missionary of the society, by his incessant activity in preaching, disputing, and the publication of tracts, spread the principles of the church and laid the foundation of many parishes in Pennsylvania and New Jersey. With him was associated John Talbot, who became rector of the church in Burlington, N. J., in 1704, and who remained a faithful and successful missionary of the society until 1725. The crying need of episcopal supervision, disregarded through so many years by the church at home, induced Mr. Talbot on a visit to England in 1624 to receive episcopal orders at the hands of the non-juring bishops. Dr. Welton, also consecrated by the non-jurors, came to America at the same time, and was made rector of Christ's Church, Philadelphia. This attempt to introduce episcopacy necessarily miscarried. The association of the non-jurors with the Jacobite party brought all connected with them under suspicion of disloyalty to the established government. The two bishops were compelled to keep their true position a secret, and it is not certain that they ever performed any episcopal acts, though there are traditions to that effect. When the facts became known, Welton was required to leave the colony and Talbot was discharged from the society and inhibited by the bishop of London. The latter, in obedience to the orders laid upon him, abstained from officiating in the public services of the church, and notwithstanding the unanimous petitions of the vestry of Christ Church, Philadelphia, and of his old congregation at Burlington, lived in retirement until his death two years later.

The province of New York was surrendered to the English by the Dutch authorities in 1664, but it was not until 1693 that any move was made in favor of the Church of England. An act was passed at that time for the maintenance of the clergy. In 1696 Trinity Church, then said to be "the finest church in North America," was built. The first rector was Mr. Vesey, previously a layman, but chosen by the governor and vestry and commended to the bishop of London for ordination, with the approval of all ranks of people. Vesey was rector from 1697 to 1756, and about 1713 was appointed commissary of the bishop of London. The parish was endowed soon after its foundation with the freehold of a neighboring property known as the "King's Farm." Vesey's assistant and successor, Barclay, opened St. George's as a chapel of ease, aided in the establishment of King's College, and designed St. Paul's, which was completed by his successor, Auchmuty. Under these rectors the church did effective work among the Indian tribes and the negroes. An earnest promoter of missionary work among the New York Indians was the celebrated Sir William Johnson, who was a faithful member of the church and conveyed to the Society for the Propagation of the Gospel shortly before his death 20,000 acres of land as a basis for the future endowment of the episcopate. Under the methods pursued in these Middle colonies —and the same is true of New England—the congregations were represented by vestries, who did not, however, in all cases, exercise the appointing power, but generally accepted the appointments of the bishop of London and the Society for the Propagation of the Gospel. In the case of Christ Church, Philadelphia, we meet with an exception to this in the election of Dr. Welton in 1624 without waiting for authority from England. In the case of Trinity, New York, the power of the vestry to elect its own rector was conceded from the first. The support of the ministry depended chiefly upon the society, eked out by such contributions as the people were able to afford. In the absence of any establishment the contests, which were so disastrous to the spirit of true religion to the southward, could not arise. Nor was there here any such laxity of discipline as in Maryland and elsewhere drew the civil authorities into attempts to regulate the conduct of the clergy. The bishop of London, with the aid of the Society for the Propagation of the Gospel, was able to exert a direct and wholesome authority by withdrawing the stipends and cancelling the appointment of any of the clergy who failed to fulfil the requirements of their position.

New England.—The Puritans of New England were the most violently opposed to the church of all the American colonists. Puritanism in that region was a theocracy in which church and state were identical. Penal laws were brought to bear upon dissenters, under which fines, imprisonment, and banishment were the principal penalties. Two brothers among the original settlers at Salem, Mass., ventured to "uphold" in their own house, "for such as would resort unto them, the common prayer worship," and were ignominiously expelled from the colony. There were attempts on the part of royal governors, under the favor of Charles II., to introduce the church service, but so little pains was taken to conciliate the prejudices of the people that they were rather the more exasperated against the whole system. This was especially the case under Gov. Andros in 1686, who took forcible possession of the Old South meeting-house. King's Chapel was built in 1689, and received many gifts from the king and queen, with a valuable library from the bishop of London. This church afterwards fell into the hands of the Unitarians, who have held possession ever since. For a long time the church remained to the people of the Eastern colonies an alien institution. But at length a spontaneous development, springing up in the heart of New England itself, changed the aspect of affairs and produced results of permanent importance. After the establishment of the Society for the Propagation of the Gospel Keith and Talbot had visited Connecticut, and in 1707 the parish at Stratford was organized by the Rev. Geo. Muirson, a missionary of the society. But the movement referred to sprang up within the precincts of Yale College, in 1722. Seven gentlemen connected with the college, including Timothy Cutler, the first president, and Samuel Johnson, the first president of King's College, N. Y. (now Columbia), were led by the perusal of certain theological works sent out from England for the college library to declare for the Church of England. They were all ordained pastors among the Independents, and were men of mark in the colony. Four of these men subsequently went to England for holy orders, and, one having died, three returned to exercise a strong and active influence in the formation of the church in New England. Cutler became rector of Trinity Church, Boston, while Johnson continued many years at Stratford. This movement spread rapidly, and, being grounded in the study of first principles and conducted in the face of violent opposition from the authorities of both church and state, it assumed a character of strength and vigor which made an indelible impression upon the State of Connecticut, and affected all New England.

Education in the Colonial Period.—The most important educational foundations to which church influences gave rise during this period were William and Mary College, Va., founded by Dr. Blair in 1693, and King's College, N. Y., established in 1754. King's College received as an endowment a portion of the "King's Farm" from Trinity Church, on condition that the "president forever, for the time being, should be in communion with the Church of England," and that the church service should be used in the college chapel. Churchmen were also largely concerned in the establishment of the University of Pennsylvania (1749), eighteen out of twenty-four members of the first board of trustees being attached to the church, while a large part of the funds was collected in England by the endeavors of Dr. William Smith, the first provost of the college. Dean (afterwards Bishop) Berkeley came out to America in 1728 in order to establish a college in the Bermuda Islands for training American missionaries, but, owing to the failure of the government grant, which had been promised, was unable to carry out his project. His residence of some years in Rhode Island was not without benefit to the cause of education, which he promoted by liberal donations of books and other property to Yale College, and subsequently by similar gifts to Harvard. He also gave valuable assistance in the establishment of King's College, N. Y. The Society for the Propagation of the Gospel from its foundation adopted education as a proper branch of its work, and sent out schoolmasters as well as missionaries. A considerable number of parochial schools were sustained from a very early date in Philadelphia and other places of Eastern Pennsylvania. In New York city, Trinity School, which still flourishes, was established by the aid of the society in 1709.

Summary.—Under the widely different conditions which existed in the Southern, Middle, and Eastern colonies respectively, the tone and character of the church were so far affected that three distinct phases are readily discerned. In the South the church was organized in feeble imitation of the church at home. The system had more than the faults and none of the merits of the English establishment. In the intermediate region the rise of the church proceeded from missionary effort, and as it met no determined hostility anywhere, it grew quietly and healthfully, but attention was rarely directed to first principles. In the Eastern colonies the real foundation of the church is due to the movement at Yale College. It proceeded from deep and candid study, and made its way in the face of a hostile religious establishment and amid the strongest popular prejudice. The result was a thorough knowledge of church principles and firm conviction of their truth.

THE ORGANIZATION OF THE PROTESTANT EPISCOPAL CHURCH.

The entire dependence of the American Church upon the mother country which her peculiar position entailed upon her prevented the growth of sentiments in accord with the principles of the Revolution. In the great national movement the clergy generally found themselves out of sympathy with their countrymen. The majority of the Northern clergy, as missionaries of the Society for the Propagation of the Gospel, were in constant communication with their superiors in England. Moreover, the theological principles accepted in the North, especially in New England, were of a High Church tendency, carrying with them at that period the strongest convictions of the duty of loyalty to legitimate authority. Especially they felt themselves hampered by their oath of allegiance taken at the time of ordination. The result was, that the majority of the clergy throughout the North were found on the loyal side. Many voluntarily resigned their cures, while others continued their ministrations until they were silenced by force. In the Middle region some influential churchmen, of whom Dr. William White was a representative, favored the cause of the Revolution. In the South the clergy did not, on the whole, maintain the same attitude as in the North. In fact, one-third of those in Virginia and Maryland advocated the Revolution. It was generally felt, however, that the tone and temper of the church was opposed to extreme measures, and though Virginia and Maryland might present exceptions to this, the church establishments which existed in those provinces were peculiarly odious to a majority of the people, both for their inefficiency and because they represented English ideas. In Virginia acts were soon passed repealing all former laws in favor of the church. Only the glebes and church edifices were preserved. The incomes of the clergy were summarily stopped at a time when it was impossible to make new provision. They were driven from the country unless they espoused the popular cause without reserve. Churches were everywhere abandoned, flocks broken up, and the sacraments continued to be administered only from time to time by a few zealous men who travelled through the country for the purpose. In Maryland the Declaration of Rights in 1776 secured to the church her property, but during the war a measure was proposed which threatened the very existence of the church as an episcopal body. This was the attempt on the part of the legislature, in 1782, to reorganize the church, and in particular to appoint ordainers to the ministry. This movement was defeated by the energy and earnestness of one man, the Rev. Samuel Keene, who obtained a hearing before the legislature and defended the cause of the church. The close of the war found the church utterly prostrate. In the North and East the work could only be resumed upon an entirely new basis, since the aid of the Society for the Propagation of the Gospel could no longer be obtained. In New York Trinity Church had been burned. A few scattered parishes remained in Pennsylvania and New Jersey. Virginia, from 164 churches and chapels, with 91 clergy, was reduced to 38 in actual operation, with only 28 clergymen. In Maryland the clergy had fallen from 44 to 20. Thus at the declaration of peace, in 1783, the church was disabled and utterly disorganized. The relation which had existed with the bishop of London was dissolved, and the bond of union with each other and with the mother church which the society had fostered among the clergy was now destroyed, so that nothing was left to constitute, or even symbolize, ecclesiastical unity. Without bishop or even provisional headship, without diocesan constitutions, every parish autocephalous, a slight impulse might have sent the congregations of some regions into the arms of the most congenial sect or might have led to the adoption of such a system as would have changed the character of the church in essential particulars. We have seen measures of this kind attempted in Maryland. About the same time, White, despairing of better things, proposed a scheme of organization without the episcopacy, committing to elective officers the powers of discipline and ordination.

But, depressed as the church was, her traditions were still strong enough to preserve her from destruction or perversion. The civil division of State lines and the fellow-feeling between the clergy of the same locality led to the first movement in the direction of harmonious organization. The earliest formal meeting of the clergy was in Connecticut, in March, 1783, which led to the selection of Seabury as bishop, and his departure for England to obtain episcopal ordination. The policy pursued here was to complete the organization by obtaining a bishop before any measures were taken for settling the constitution of the church. Seabury, unable to obtain his purpose in England without undue delay, was finally consecrated in Scotland by

Bishops Kilgour, Petrie, and Skinner, on Nov. 14, 1784. At meetings held in Maryland, in 1783-84, no steps were taken to obtain the episcopacy, but declarations were agreed to defining the inherent power of bishops and the rights of the clergy in a Low-Church direction; giving the appointment to a particular cure into the hands of the congregation; asserting the right of the laity to representation in ecclesiastical synods; and proposing that judicial and disciplinary powers be exercised only by such a body of clergy and laity. A meeting in Philadelphia, in 1784, took substantially the same ground, and issued a call for a general convention. The first convention of a general character assembled accordingly in Philadelphia in 1785. It represented seven States. Against the wish of Connecticut and Seabury, it was decided to proceed at once to the adoption of a permanent constitution and the revision of the Prayer Book. The constitution thus framed, in addition to the rights conferred upon the laity of sitting in council, made bishops amenable to their diocesan conventions. The Prayer Book was radically changed, and even its orthodoxy was brought into question. These measures delayed instead of hastening the desired union and the acquisition of bishops from England. Seabury and the church to the eastward declined to submit to this organization, and the English bishops refused to consecrate for America while fundamental principles were left in doubt. These difficulties being subsequently removed, Provoost of New York and White of Pennsylvania were finally consecrated in the chapel at Lambeth, Feb. 4, 1787. Connecticut was satisfied by the removal of the objectionable features from the constitution, and, at the convention of 1789, Bishop Seabury was present. At this time the Proposed Book was set aside, but two principles still contended—the one on the side of tradition and continuity, the other disregarding precedent and insisting upon proceeding *de novo* in the settlement of the Liturgy. The influence of the bishops turned the scale, and the more catholic position was maintained, as set forth in the Preface of the revised Book: "This Church is far from intending to depart from the Church of England in any essential point of doctrine, discipline, or worship; or further than local circumstances require." Two influences are traceable in this revision in the daily offices and litany, that of the Proposed Book, or rather of the remote attempt of the latitudinarian commission of 1689; in the Communion office the influence of Seabury prevailed, and the Scotch office was adopted, of even higher liturgical and doctrinal value than that of the Church of England. In 1792 the convention assembled in New York with three bishops of the English line—Provoost, White, and Madison—besides Seabury of the Scotch succession. The bishops now felt themselves authorized, consistently with engagements entered into with the English prelates, to perform consecrations. The first consecration to the episcopate, therefore, performed on these shores, took place at this convention, the candidate being the Rev. Thomas James Claggett of Maryland, and all four of the bishops present uniting in the act.

The organization of the Episcopal Church was completed in accordance with sound principles in all essential particulars. The peculiarities of this organization, while they have been defended on general principles, are easily seen to be based not upon theoretical schemes, but to be a natural development from causes previously existing. The constitution thus embraces ideas derived from the experience of the church in Virginia and Maryland and the South generally, modified by the church principles of the Northern clergy. The most radical innovation was the part assigned to the laity in the government of the church. It will readily be seen how naturally this grew out of the previously existing state of things. The subsequent history of the church seems to justify the experiment, and the laity have often been found to be more conservative than the clergy. The limits of lay-power in legislation and government have, however, been left to adjust themselves in accordance with general principles as they may be instinctively perceived. Such limits have never been expressly defined by legislation.

PERIOD SINCE THE REVOLUTION (1783-1882).

Growth of the Church.—The growth of the church after the organization was at last completed was for a long time exceedingly slow. The reputation which she had acquired during the Revolution, of sympathy with the mother-country, her necessary connection with the Church of England, the rigidity of her working system, and its lack of special adaptation to the conditions about her—all combined with the general prejudice against episcopacy to obstruct her influence and impede her growth. Many faithful churchmen almost despaired of the future. But, though progress was slow, it soon became apparent that the church was by no means dead. In New England there was always life and activity. Pennsylvania had the advantage of Bishop White's fatherly guidance for fifty years; he died in 1836. The episcopate of Bishop Moore (1814-41) did much to build up again the broken foundations of the church in Virginia. But the chief impulse to church life and growth was given by the influence of John Henry Hobart, D. D., bishop of New York (1811-30). His firm grasp of the distinctive principles of the church, and his ability in maintaining them, his activity and the vigor of his administration, produced permanent effects of the highest value to the whole church. The consecration of Bishop Philander Chase in 1819 marked the first great step in the advance of the church westward. He afterwards (1835) became first bishop of Illinois. An important step in the same direction was the consecration of Jackson Kemper in 1835 to be missionary bishop of the North-west. A voluntary movement of great interest and importance was the formation of the "Associate Mission" at Nashotah, Wis., under the leadership of James Lloyd Breck (1842). This association of young priests, fresh from the seminary, living in common, and devoting themselves to missionary work, evangelized Wisconsin and founded the famous theological school at Nashotah. Out of the same movement sprang subsequently the theological school at Faribault and the foundation of missions among the Indians of the North-west. Other bishops appointed over missionary jurisdictions were Kip (California, 1853) and Scott (Oregon and Washington Territory, 1854). But it was only from 1865 that the principle has been definitely acted upon that the bishop ought rather to lead than follow missionary enterprise, and the number of missionary jurisdictions has been increased as fast as circumstances seemed to warrant. The first domestic and foreign missionary society of the Protestant Episcopal Church was organized under the authority of the General Convention in 1822. It was reorganized in 1835, and became the "Board of Missions of the Protestant Episcopal Church," comprehending "all persons who are in baptism members of this church." Through this board the missionary bishops and their clergy are for the most part maintained. The earliest bishops consecrated for foreign work were Boone for China and Southgate for Constantinople (both in 1844). The board was reorganized in 1877, and a reconciliation effected with the American Church Missionary Society, a voluntary organisation founded under Low-Church auspices by those who disapproved of the general board. The most successful missionary work among the Indians has been carried on in the North-west. Such missions were commenced in Minnesota by Breck, and afterwards renewed and fostered with great zeal by the Rt. Rev. H. B. Whipple, of that diocese. From these efforts have sprung also a number of flourishing missions along the Missouri River in Nebraska and Dakota Territory, which now constitute the missionary jurisdiction of Southern Dakota. The numerical increase of the membership of the church has been constant, and often rapid. Meanwhile, there has been a constant struggle, as her mission has opened before her, to adapt her system to the needs of all sorts and conditions of men, and to escape whatever trammels obstruct her growth and extension. This is seen in the increasing number of free churches; in attempts to make the public services attractive; in the formation of various parochial agencies for effective work among all classes of society; in the establishment of guilds and societies for special ends, as, for instance, the promotion of temperance; in the rise of sisterhoods consecrated to a life of charity and devotion. The conservative spirit proper to a branch of the catholic church prevents sudden and radical changes, and secures thorough discussion of all questions which arise, but does not in the end defeat the great objects to be attained. During the trying period of the great Civil War the Episcopal Church was enabled to maintain an attitude of dignity, a general freedom from the bitterness of party spirit, which made her walls a refuge for many who were wearied and disheartened at the strife and confusion of the times. The church in the South, anticipating the success of the Southern arms, in pursuance of the principles asserted after the achievement of American independence, organized as a separate national body. But at the close of the war this arrangement was immediately dissolved, and at the convention of October, 1865, the reunion of the church was effected without difficulty. In 1873 occurred the defection of Dr. Cummins, assistant bishop of Kentucky, who withdrew from the church soon after a meeting of the "Evangelical Alliance," in New York city, in which he had taken part, and had united in a Presbyterian communion service, for which he was severely criticised. The reasons assigned in a published letter for his withdrawal from the Episcopal Church were the growth of "Ritualism" and the "Romanizing tendencies" which he discerned in the Prayer-Book and the life of the church. He was formally deposed by the presiding bishop, Dr. B. B. Smith, but shortly afterwards he instituted a new denomination called the "Reformed Episcopal Church," in which he continued to exercise the episcopal office by ordaining ministers and consecrating bishops. His most prominent associate was Dr. C. E. Cheney, of Chicago, who had been deposed in 1871 for contumacy after refusal to submit to the sentence of the ecclesiastical court of the diocese, which had tried him for mutilating the service for baptism by omitting the words "regenerate" and "regeneration" whenever they occur. It was supposed that they would be joined by a considerable number of influential members of the Low-Church party. But many leaders of that party promptly repudiated the movement, and it has had little perceptible effect upon the Episcopal Church.

Interesting and important circumstances in the later history of the church were the first "Pan-Anglican" conference at Lambeth in 1867, at which a majority of the bishops of the Anglican communion assembled for "fraternal council and spiritual communion;" also, the sympathy officially expressed by resolution of the House of Bishops with the Old-Catholic movement of Germany in 1871, and further exhibited in the presence of prominent bishops of the American church at the meetings of the Old-Catholic congress. The consecration of James Theodore Holly for Haiti in 1874, and of Henry Chauncey Riley for Mexico in 1879, were also events of considerable significance. Bishop Riley's subsequent course was not marked with that prudence which was necessary in his peculiar circumstances, and in 1884 he resigned his office and withdrew from further effort to establish the church in Mexico.

Ecclesiastical polity.—The ecclesiastical polity with which the church emerged from the conflicts and confusion of the Revolutionary period is as follows: The union of the whole church was maintained by a "General Convention," to meet every three years, consisting of two houses—that of the bishops and that of clerical and lay deputies elected from each diocese. This body has the power to pass general canons and under certain restrictions to make alterations in the liturgy and fundamental law. The senior bishop in order of consecration is called "the presiding bishop." He is president of the House of Bishops, and is "the presiding bishop for all other purposes contained in the canons." This rule, however, was not formally adopted until 1832. The organisation, therefore, represents, according to early precedents, a single province with its metropolitan and provincial council. With the spread of the church over the continent this arrangement has become inadequate. The General Convention has become too unwieldy to fulfil its proper functions satisfactorily. Questions of great importance are postponed from year to year. It is impossible that such a body should be able to hear appeals, while, on the other hand, it is an abnormal state of things that no appeal should be open from the decisions of diocesan courts. One result of this is a growing tendency to result to the civil courts whenever the case can be brought under their jurisdiction. Both legislative and judicial functions, therefore, are hampered and obstructed by the present constitution. These evils have led to the agitation of the "provincial system," which was first discussed in the convention of 1850, but without result. Two methods of provincial organization have been proposed—one looking to an association of the dioceses of several States; the other to the union under one system of the dioceses within a single State. The progress of the church within the several States meanwhile has been so great that the assignment of a single bishop to each State was soon found to be inadequate. The plan of appointing assistant bishops in such cases was tried and still meets with favor in some quarters, but a different expedient has met with much more general approval. This is the division of dioceses. The first instance of this kind was the formation of the diocese of Western New York in 1838. The division of the diocese of Pennsylvania followed after a long interval with the erection of the diocese of Pittsburg in 1865. Since that date the process of subdivision has gone on with rapidity. There are now (1884) in New York five dioceses, in Pennsylvania three, New Jersey two, Maryland two, Ohio two, Illinois three, Wisconsin two, California two, Texas three. This process has brought the second plan of provincial organization into prominence. It is natural that dioceses which have formed part of one whole should desire to remain in some sort united. Moreover, by this means the undue multiplication of organizations for special purposes may be avoided. This plan has also the advantage of bringing the associated dioceses under the laws of a single State. With this view a scheme for a "federal council" of the dioceses within a State was authorized by the General Convention of 1868, but was never brought into operation. The dioceses within the State of Illinois have now entered into a provincial arrangement which gives some promise of success. It includes provision for a court of appeals.

Doctrine and ceremonial.—The doctrines of the Protestant Episcopal Church are contained in the creeds and in the acts of the undisputed general councils. She has received them as expressed in the formularies of the mother-church of England. It is, nevertheless, true that the long period of imperfect or perverted organization, and the deep depression which she had experienced, had left her hardly conscious of her true character and claims. But the keynote had been struck with a firm hand by Seabury. Hobart revived and strengthened the spirit of the church. Long before the *Oxford Tracts* appeared he had defended the order of the church as apostolic, and upheld the doctrine of the sacraments. The Oxford movement in England (1833) met with a quick response in this country. The church was soon stirred to its foundations by the controversies to which it gave rise. The strife culminated in connection with the ordination of Arthur Carey in 1843 by Bishop B. T. Onderdonk, of New York, against the protest of two priests, who accused Carey of Romanizing tendencies. Bishop Onderdonk was brought to trial in 1844, and was suspended from his sacred office. The charges were directed against his moral character, but the case was inextricably connected with the party strife of the times. His own diocese petitioned, in 1850, for a remission of the sentence of suspension, but the effort was unsuccessful, and a provisional bishop was appointed in 1852. Bishop Onderdonk lived in retirement a blameless life, and died in 1861 protesting his innocence. Upon the defection of Newman, in 1845, some of his followers in this country, as in England, left the ministry of the church, but the whole number amounted only to about thirty in ten years, including Bishop Ives, of North Carolina. The effect of the movement, on the whole, was to spread the knowledge of church principles and to strengthen the conviction of their truth in the minds of churchmen themselves. The catholic character of the church and her mission in the world came to be apprehended with a thoroughness unknown before, and a new enthusiasm was aroused.

Closely connected with this great doctrinal revival came the so-called "Ritualistic movement." In the colonial days the architecture of the churches, the arrangement of the interior, and the mode of conducting the services, had naturally taken form from the contemporaneous fashions of the mother-church, chiefly in the period following the accession of William and Mary. This, as is well known, was a period of extraordinary coldness in the Church of England. Church architecture was ill-suited to its purpose. The arrangement within was rather with a view to private comfort than the common worship of God. The services were cold and perfunctory. The American church at the beginning of this century had inherited this state of things. Externally, the church edifice was hardly to be distinguished from the meeting-house; internally, the advantage was on the side of the latter. The pulpit, commonly what is known as the "three-decker" arrangement, completely overshadowed chancel and altar. The high, square pews were arranged primarily for the comfort of the worshipper and the exclusion of the stranger. Chanting was unknown; hymnology remained uncultivated. Gradual improvements were made as new life made its influence felt, but it was not until the great doctrinal movement of 1833 had made considerable progress that there was any marked change. A wise writer of the Church of England, many years before, had said: "Just and adequate views of the sacraments, the church, and the Scriptures must precede all subordinate auxiliaries; the latter must be regulated by the former. Labor to make religion impressive will be much worse than doing nothing until it be clearly ascertained what religion is." (*Alex. Knox*, 1820.)

The development of ceremonial followed naturally the revival of doctrine. There was an immediate improvement in church architecture. The internal arrangements began to exhibit more clearly the proper relations to each other of the different elements of divine service. Chanting and choral services, rendered by surpliced choirs, were introduced. Still later, as the study of patristic theology and the ancient liturgies brought the conviction that the Holy Eucharist was the central and all-important act of worship, great attention began to be paid to the ceremonial adjuncts of that office in particular. In England the movement took the "Ornaments' Rubric" as its authority. Six usages especially were insisted upon: "the eastward position," "vestments," "lights," "the mixed chalice," "unleavened bread," "incense." The legal position of the so-called "Ritualist" in the American church depends either upon the principle that English canon law must prevail here, except in so far as it is expressly repealed or modified, or, according to others, in the absence of explicit regulations regarding the ceremonial of divine worship, the church is thrown back upon the customs and usages of the Catholic Church in general. In 1865 appeared a tract, entitled *The Law of Ritualism*, by the venerable presiding bishop, Dr. Hopkins, of Vermont. In this little treatise, written in answer to the request of a number of eminent churchmen, lay and clerical, the author calmly considers and defends most of the usages above mentioned.

The advance of the ritualistic movement from this time was so rapid in all parts of the country that it soon aroused great opposition. In 1868 the subject was brought forward in general convention and referred to a committee of bishops to report to the next succeeding convention. At this time (1871) a repressive "canon of ritual" was proposed, but, after prolonged discussion, the convention contented itself with the passage of two resolutions of a general character. In 1874 the attempts at legislation culminated in a canon forbidding certain devotional acts which were considered as symbolizing "erroneous or doubtful doctrines." This canon has, however, remained inoperative, and is considered by many to be unconstitutional, since it contains directions for the proper mode of conducting the services of the church in addition to those contained in the Prayer-Book. The testimonials of the Rev. Dr. G. F. Seymour, bishop-elect of Illinois, came before this same convention. A determined attack was made upon him as a partisan of ritualism, and the convention, by a close vote, refused to accept the testimonials. In 1875 Dr. DeKoven was elected to the same episcopate, and in his case also the canonical testimonials were rejected, this time by the standing committees of a majority of the dioceses, to whom the testimonials of a newly-elected bishop are submitted when the general convention is not in session. This action called general attention to these officers, and a searching discussion took place as to their true position and the proper limits of their powers.

With regard to the ritualistic movement in general, it is now for the most part conceded that great good has resulted from it, whatever may have been the extravagances or the errors of individuals. It has in particular led to the movement for the enrichment of the Prayer-Book, in which all parties happily united in the General Convention of 1883.

Education.—The Episcopal Church has always been distinguished by the high importance assigned to education within her fold. Her share in the foundation of some of the most important institutions of learning in the early colonial days has already been referred to. The necessity of special efforts for the advancement of theological learning was strongly felt after the Revolutionary War, and in 1817 the organization of a general theological seminary was resolved upon. It was finally established in the city of New York in 1821. Other theological schools of importance are—that at Alexandria, Va., famous for the large number of missionaries among its graduates; the Berkeley Divinity School, Middletown, Conn.; the school in Kenyon College, at Gambier, O., founded by Bishop Chase; that at Nashotah, the result of the labors of Breck and his companions; and schools founded more recently at Philadelphia, Faribault, Minn., Cambridge, Mass., and the theological department of the University of the South. A great impulse was given to the cause of education in church schools by the zeal of Bishop Doane, of New Jersey (1832-59), who founded St. Mary's School for girls, and Burlington College for boys, both at Burlington, N. J.; and within thirty years schools of this character have multiplied rapidly in every part of the Union, many under diocesan authority, besides a great number under private management.

Educational statistics.—Theological seminaries and schools, 16; church colleges, 17; academic institutions, 99; other educational institutions, 56.

General statistics in 1883.—Dioceses, 48; missionary jurisdictions, 15; bishops, 68; priests and deacons, 3559; parishes, about 3000; ordinations of deacons, 146; priests, 132; total, 278; confirmations, 26,133; baptisms, 16,945; contributions, $8,319,191.39.

Books relating to the History of the Protestant Episcopal Church.—Anderson's *History of the Colonial Church;* Wilberforce's *History of the American Church;* Rev. Dr. Hawks's *Contributions to the Ecclesiastical History of the United States;* Fac-Similes *of Church Documents* (Historical Club); Bishop White's *Memoirs of the Protestant Episcopal Church;* Beardsley's *History of the Church in Connecticut;* Bishop Perry's *Handbook of the General Convention,* 1785-1877; Caswall's *America and the American Church;* Dr. Hills's *History of the Church in Burlington, N. J.;* G. G. Perry's *History of the Church of England* (Am. ed., with continuation by Dr. Spencer); Denison's *History of the Foreign Missionary Work of the Protestant Episcopal Church.* (W. J. G.)

ERCKMANN-CHATRIAN. Under this name two French writers—EMILE ERCKMANN and ALEXANDRE CHATRIAN—have published a long series of novels, sketches, and plays. Emile Erckmann was born May 20, 1822, at Phalsbourg (now Pfalzburg) in Lorraine. He was the son of a bookseller, and, after some study in the college of his native town, went to Paris in 1842. Although his intention had been to study law, he was drawn aside to literature. In 1847 he became acquainted with Chatrian, who was born at the hamlet of Soldatenthal, near Phalsbourg, Dec. 18, 1826, and was then an instructor in the college of that town. The two became fast friends, and soon formed a literary partnership. Their earliest efforts, published in local journals, met with little encouragement, and Erckmann, returning to the law, passed the examination in 1858, while Chatrian entered the employ of the Eastern Railway Company. In 1859 they achieved their first success by the publication of *L'Illustre Docteur Mathéus,* which gave some popularity to their combined name. Their reputation, however, rests on a series of simple stories describing faithfully and minutely the common life of their native province. With this was deftly interwoven the peasants' view of the military glory and subsequent reverses of the French Revolution and the First Empire. Among these works the chief were— *Madame Thérèse, ou les Volontaires de '92* (1863); *L'Ami Fritz* (1864); *Histoire d'un Conscrit de 1813* (1864); *L'Invasion, Waterloo* (1865); *Histoire d'un Homme du Peuple* (1865); *La Maison Forestière* (1866); *La Guerre* (1866); *Le Blocus de Phalsbourg* (1867); *Histoire d'un Paysan* (1868). These apparently simple sketches of peasants' lives and thoughts were really admirable artistic exposures of the hollowness and sham of imperial government, and contributed indirectly to the enlightenment of the French people in regard to the tendency of the Napoleonic system. After the downfall of the empire the authors were able to speak more freely of the system under which the French people had been crushed for years. Their *Histoire du Plébiscite racontée par un des 7,500,000 oui* (1872) was a graphic exposure of the devices by which the empire had been supported, and made a great sensation. Their later works comprise— *Le Brigadier Frederic* (1874); *Une Campagne en Algérie* (1874); *Maitre Gaspard Fix* (1876); *Souvenirs d'un chef de Chantier à l'Isthme de Suez* (1876); *Contes Vosgiens* (1877); *Le Grandpère Lebigre* (1879). Their play, *Le Juif Polonais,* founded on one of their stories, was highly successful in 1869, and *L'Ami Fritz,* in spite of newspaper denunciation, was well received in 1876. Later their literary partnership was broken, and unfriendly relations arose, owing to Chatrian's aberration of mind. He died Sept. 4, 1890. Their works have always been remarkably pure in moral tone, and free from sensationalism. They have been translated into several foreign languages.

ERDMAN, AXEL JOACHIM, Swedish geologist, born Aug. 12, 1814; died Dec. 1, 1869. In addition to numerous articles in scientific publications, he published as separate works: *Lärebok, Mineralogien* (1853; 2d ed., 1860); *Vägledning till bergarternos Kännedom* (1855); and *Bidrag till Kännedom om Sveriges quartära bildningar* (1868).

ERDMANN, JOHANN EDWARD, a German philosopher, was born at Molmar, in Livonia, June 13, 1805. He studied theology at the University of Dorpat from 1823 to 1826, and afterwards at Berlin, under Schleiermacher and Hegel. He returned in 1828 to his native town, where, the following year, he was appointed deacon, and, in 1831, pastor to the church. In 1832 he returned to Berlin, graduated in 1834, and being already favorably known by his writings, was appointed, in 1836, extraordinary professor of philosophy in the University of Halle, and in 1839 became professor. Erdmann's principal work is his very valuable *Versuch einer wissenschaftlichen Darstellung der Geschichte der neueren Philosophie* (3 vols., 1834–53). He has also written *Ueber Glauben und Wissen* (1837); *Natur oder Schöpfung* (1840); *Leib und Seele* (1837; 2d ed., 1848); *Grundriss der Psychologie* (1840; 4th ed., 1873); *Grundriss der Logik und Metaphysik* (1841; 4th ed., 1864); *Vermischte Aufsätze* (1847); *Vorlesungen über den Staat* (1851); *Psychologische Briefen* (1851; 6th ed., 1882); *Grundriss der Geschichte der Philosophie* (1866). He has also published a large number of sermons and addresses.

ERICSSON, JOHN, LL.D., an American engineer and inventor, was born in Wermeland, a province of Sweden, July 31, 1803. At a very early age he showed decided mechanical ability, and in 1814, having been appointed a cadet in the engineer corps by the favor of Count Platen, he was employed as a leveller in constructing the grand canal between the Baltic Sea and the German Ocean. In 1820 he entered the Swedish army as an ensign, and was employed in the northern part of Sweden. After rising to the rank of captain he resigned in 1826, and went to England to introduce his flame-engine, but though it had succeeded with a wood-fire it failed with coal. He now devoted himself entirely to mechanical pursuits, and did much to improve the steam-boiler. He introduced artificial draft, and though his original method was afterwards superseded the principle is still used. In 1829, when the directors of the Liverpool and Manchester railway offered a prize for the best locomotive-engine, the "Novelty," which Ericsson built and guided, was successful in the competition. It ran fifty miles an hour, and was the lightest engine exhibited. Applying the same principles, he next constructed a steam-fire-engine, which was highly successful. His caloric or hot-air engine, exhibited in London in 1833, attracted much attention among scientific men as well as the general public. In 1836 he first applied the screw to the propulsion of steam-vessels, but not receiving sufficient encouragement from the British admiralty he came to New York in 1839. Under his direction the United States steamer Princeton was built in 1841, and in it he displayed a wonderful fertility of invention. The propelling machinery was placed under the water-line, the steam-engine, though powerful, was simple and compact, the chimney could be raised or lowered at pleasure, and the recoil of the guns was counteracted by mechanical devices. He continued to produce inventions, some of the most practical kind, while others were for theoretical science. In 1852 he applied his caloric engine in a new form to the propulsion of vessels. The Ericsson, a ship of 2000 tons, sailed on a trial-trip from New York in February, 1853, and attained a moderate speed with a very small consumption of fuel. The caloric engine has been found better adapted to light work than steam, and Mr. Ericsson has spent years in making improvements in it to fit it for the work required. Soon after the outbreak of the civil war he was employed by the United States government to construct iron vessels with revolving turrets for guns. The first one, the famous Monitor, built in 100 days, reached Hampton Roads, in the Chesapeake Bay, March 8, 1862, just in time to save the United States fleet there from complete destruction by the Confederate iron-clad Virginia, which had been constructed out of the United States ship Merrimac. On the next morning the famous conflict took place, the Confederate vessel was defeated and driven into Norfolk harbor. Mr. Ericsson constructed several monitors, and has, since the war, been engaged in the construction and improvement of his numerous inventions. Among these are a pyrometer, an alarm barometer, a sea-lead, and a hydrostatic gauge. In recent years he has devoted much time to constructing a solar engine, whose motive power is to be concentrated solar heat.

ERICSSON, NILS (1802–1870), Swedish engineer, brother of the preceding, was born Jan. 31, 1802. He became a sub-lieutenant in the engineer corps of the Swedish army, and rose to the rank of major in 1832. He was afterwards transferred to the navy and was made head of the mechanical corps. From 1855 to 1863 he was chief of the Swedish railroads, in which time the most of the railroads in Sweden were built. The canal-locks at Trollhättan, the locks near Stockholm, and the Saima Canal in Finland were engineered by him. He was also in part the projector of the Dalsland Canal. For his eminent services he was knighted in 1854 and made a baron in 1860. He died at Stockholm Sept. 8, 1870.

ERIE, a city of Pennsylvania, county-seat of Erie co., is on Lake Erie, 117 miles N. of Pittsburg. It is on the following railroads—the Lake Shore and Michigan Southern, the Philadelphia and Erie, and the Erie and Pittsburg. A large and handsome Union dépôt, built of brick in the Romanesque style, affords facilities for the passengers and traffic of these roads. The New York, Chicago, and St. Louis Railroad also passes through Erie, and has a separate dépôt. The city is finely situated on a bluff, commanding an extensive view of the lake, and is regularly laid out with wide streets. The harbor, formed from a natural bay, which has been greatly improved, is protected by a breakwater and by Presque Isle, originally a peninsula, lying in front of the city. Two light-houses guard the entrance to the harbor, which is 3¼ miles long, more than a mile wide, and from 10 to 25 ft. deep. There are extensive docks, some of which have railroad-tracks for the direct transfer of freight between the cars and the vessels. The principal shipments are of coal, iron-ore, petroleum, and lumber. The total value of the exports from Erie for the year 1883 was $1885, and of the imports was $896. Of the vessels entering the port 8 were American, with a tonnage of 590, and 13

See Vol. VIII. p. 462 Am. ed. (p. 522 Edin. ed.).

were foreign, with a tonnage of 841. Of the vessels cleared for foreign trade 8 were American, with a tonnage of 581, and 12 were foreign, with a tonnage of 866.

Erie has 4 national banks, with an aggregate capital of $850,000, 3 savings banks, 4 insurance companies, and a safe deposit and trust company. There are 3 daily and 9 weekly newspapers, two of which are German. The leading industry is the manufacture of iron, including steam-engines, car-wheels, stoves, and machinery of various descriptions. There are several large rolling-mills, and also petroleum refineries, manufactories of leather, pumps, bricks, and several beer- and ale-breweries. Among the public buildings are the court-house, the custom-house, and post-office; there are also an opera-house, academy of music, marine hospital, and city hospital. There are 35 churches of various denominations, 57 schools, including a high school and 18 grammar schools, besides parochial schools and a female academy.

For municipal purposes the city is divided into 6 wards, each of which elects 2 members to the select council and 3 to the common council.

The city is lighted with gas, and has an excellent supply of water, pumped from the lake to the top of a tower 200 ft. high and thence distributed through the mains. There are several parks or squares, and near the city limits is the Erie cemetery, comprising 75 acres, laid out with good taste and carefully kept.

On the site of the present city of Erie the French built a fort about 1746, called Fort de la Presqu' isle, but the town was not laid out till 1795. In 1805 it was incorporated as a borough, and in 1851 as a city. At this place Com. O. H. Perry, in the summer of 1813, equipped a fleet of 9 vessels, which, on September 10, defeated the British squadron and established American supremacy on the lakes.

ERIE, LAKE, the most southern of the Great Lakes, on the boundary between the United States and the Dominion of Canada, is the last but one in the series. It receives at its upper end, through the Detroit River, the accumulated waters of the three upper lakes, and discharges them, through the Niagara River, into Lake Ontario, whence they are carried by the river St. Lawrence to the Atlantic Ocean. The axes of these two lower lakes are both nearly in the straight line of a prolongation of the St. Lawrence, in a general direction S.W. to N.E. Lake Erie is contained between the parallels of 41° 24' and 42° 54' N. lat., and between the meridians of 78° 55' and 83° 30' W. long. It is bounded on the N. by the Province of Ontario, on the S.E. and S. by the States of New York, Pennsylvania, and Ohio, and on the W. by the State of Michigan. It is nearly elliptical in form—the length about 250 miles; the mean width $38\frac{1}{2}$ miles; circumference about 650 miles; area about 9600 square miles.

It is the shallowest of the Great Lakes, its greatest depth being 204 ft., near its eastern end. Its bottom area may be regarded as consisting of three portions. The western, from a line between Detroit and Toledo to the line of the southward prolongation of Pointe Pelée—32 miles in length—has a mean width of 27 miles, and an average depth of 30 ft.; this is the only part of the lake containing islands (if we except that formed recently by the cut-off of Long Point). The five principal are Pointe Pelée, Kelley's, Put-in Bay, Middle Bass, and Isle St. George. Some of these are under good cultivation, have a fertile soil,

and are well wooded. The middle and larger portion of the lake, from Pointe Pelée to a line crossing the lake S. of Long Point—135 miles in length—has a mean width of 43 miles (maximum, 57 miles), and a depth from 60 to 80 ft. The eastern portion, ending at the outlet of the Niagara River, near the city of Buffalo, is 81 miles in length, has a mean width of $25\frac{1}{4}$ miles, and an average depth of 100 ft.

The ordinary elevation of the surface of the lake above mean sea-level has been determined to be 573 ft. Its level has been found to be variable—it has both an annual fluctuation and a general one extending over a series of years, known as the secular fluctuation. According to the observations and compilations of Col. Charles Whittlesey, the lowest known level was in February, 1819—after which time it rose more or less each year until June, 1838—in the extreme to 6 ft. 8 in.; the difference between 1819 and 1838 was 5 ft. 2 in. The average annual rise and fall (mean of 12 years) is 1 ft. $1\frac{1}{2}$ in. The surface is also acted upon by the winds, tending to drive the water from one end of the lake and to heap it up at the other.

The lake is surrounded by a surface formation of drift-clay and gravel—the deposits of the great glacial action from the north—covering the upper Silurian formation and strata of the Devonian system which appear—the former at the extremities; the latter around the greater part of the lake. The coast is generally low—rarely cliffs or bluffs are found. On the southern shore an elevated plateau surrounds the lake, at no great distance, the general dip of the strata and surface being to the southward. Through this plateau the rivers have cut deep channels, and the water-courses and the waves of the lake undermine it and keep up an incessant degradation, tending to fill up and shallow the basin.

The principal rivers and creeks, naming them from E. to W., are the Cattaraugus, Conneaut, Ashtabula, Grand, Chagrin, Cuyahoga, Rocky, Black, Vermilion, Huron, Sandusky, Portage, and Maumee. The coast is but little indented by bays, and there are but few harbors, natural or improved. The principal of these on the S. shore (from E. to W.) are those of Buffalo, Dunkirk, Erie, Ashtabula, Fairport, Cleveland, Sandusky, Port Clinton, and Toledo. Some of the foregoing have been greatly improved by the United States Government. On the north (or Canadian) shore the harbors are Ports Colborne, Maitland (at the mouth of Grand River, the only considerable stream on the Canadian side), Dover, Barwell, Stanley, and Talbot.

The meteorological elements affecting the climate of the shores of Lake Erie may be thus summarized: mean temperature of the year at the S.W. end of the lake, $48\frac{1}{2}°$; at the N.E. end, $46\frac{1}{2}°$; mean temperature of the three summer months, 70° and 68°, and of the three winter months, 28° and 27°, at these ends respectively. The mean annual rain-fall around the shores of the lake is about 34 in. The lake is usually closed by ice in the early part of December, and continues more or less frozen over until March or April.

During the season of navigation an enormous amount of transportation is carried through Lake Erie from the upper lakes, the outlets eastward and to the ocean being—at Buffalo, the Erie Canal, 352 miles long, to Albany, N. Y.; and at Port Colborne, in Canada, the Welland Canal, 27 miles long, which connects with Lake Ontario, avoiding the falls of Niagara. There are two other great canal systems on the southern shore of Lake Erie, crossing the State of Ohio—the Ohio and Erie Canal, from Cleveland to Portsmouth, and the Miami and Erie Canal, from Toledo to Cincinnati.

The larger cities on the southern shore are Buffalo, N. Y., and Cleveland and Toledo, O. Five lines of steamers connect these and other ports. There are no large cities on the Canadian shore. Great railway systems are run close to and parallel with both shores.

The fisheries of Lake Erie are very extensive, the catch exceeding that in any of the other lakes, that of Lake Michigan being next in amount. The census of 1880 gives for Lake Erie: number of fishermen, 1470; value of apparatus, etc., $503,500; number of steam-tugs, other vessels, and boats, 538; total catch in lbs., 26,607,300; value, $412,880—consisting principally of herring, white-fish, sturgeon, trout, pike, bass, muskalonge, catfish, and lake-shad.

It was in the western part of Lake Erie, near Put-in Bay, that on Sept. 10, 1813, the American commodore, O. H. Perry, with 9 vessels, carrying 54 guns and 490 men, gained a decisive victory over the British captain, Barclay, with 6 vessels, carrying 63 guns and 502 men. (W. L. N.)

ERIES, a tribe of American Indians, who formerly occupied the shores and islands of Lake Erie, but have entirely disappeared. Their history is of interest. They adjoined, and perhaps formed, the principal tribe in a confederacy known as the Neutral Nation, who were prominent in the region of Western New York at the date of the first French settlements in Canada. They occupied a position of neutrality between the Wyandottes or Hurons, the allies of the French, and the Iroquois, the allies of the English, and suffered the usual fate of neutrals. Great obscurity surrounds their history. The power to kindle the council-fire of peace, which they maintained, is said to have been held by female hands before its final extinction. The Eries, or Cats, as the French called them, were a powerful tribe, numbering about 12,000. They were attacked by the Iroquois about 1650, and a long and bloody war ended in their destruction or expulsion in 1655. In this war all the neutral tribes seem to have been involved, and the whole Neutral Nation disappeared. There are traditions of the Catawbas of South Carolina which render it possible that they were descendants of some of these tribes. West of the Neutral Nation was a cognate tribe, the Andastes, or Kahquas, who were next attacked by the Iroquois, and vanquished in 1672, after a well-sustained war, which lasted sixteen years. These powerful tribes, who stood first in the way of the vigorous and aggressive Iroquois confederacy, were utterly swept away, so that no positive trace of them now exists upon the earth.

ERRETT, ISAAC, A. M., an American theologian and author, was born in New York city, Jan. 2, 1820. When he was five years old, his father, Henry Errett, died, leaving a widow with seven children. His mother was married again in 1829 to Robert Sutor, and moved to New Jersey, where two or three years were spent on a farm. Then they removed to Pittsburg, Pa., where the rest of Isaac's boyhood was spent in hard work in grist- and saw-mill, farming, bookstore, printing-office, and school-teaching. His leisure hours were spent in study, and his winters in attendance at school. During five years in a printing-office his nights were given to reading and writing for the papers. His education was therefore largely self-conducted. In his thirteenth year he became a member of the Church of the Disciples, in which he had been reared, and in 1840 he was set apart to the Christian ministry. He spent three years in pulpit service in Pittsburg, Pa., five years at New Lisbon, O., two years at North Bloomfield, O., five years at Warren, O., ten years in Michigan—two at Detroit, and eight in Ionia county. Since 1866 he has had no regular charge, being engaged mainly in editing, in preaching on special occasions, or holding protracted meetings. He was one of the founders of the school at Hiram, O., which has grown into Hiram College. Three years were spent in the service of the Ohio Christian Missionary Society as corresponding secretary, and three years in the service of the National Christian Missionary Society in the same capacity. During these last three years, in addition to a large evangelizing work, and the care of a farm, he travelled about 10,000 miles a year in the service of the missionary society, lifting it out of its financial straits and starting it on a career of prosperity. He was also at this time a co-editor of Alexander Campbell's monthly, the *Millennial Harbinger*, and wrote for it regularly. Bethany College bestowed on him the honorary degree of A. M.

In 1866 he started a religious weekly in Cleveland, O., *The Christian Standard*, of which he still continues editor-in-chief. It has grown to be the largest, most widely circulated, and most influential of the journals published by the Disciples. In 1868 he was elected to the presidency of Alliance College, Ohio; but as the interests of his paper required its removal to Cincinnati, in 1869 he resigned this position, and has since declined similar offers. He was president of the Ohio Christian Missionary Society for six years, of the General Christian Missionary Society for three years, and since 1875 has been the president of the Foreign Christian Missionary Society. He has been largely engaged in all the general enterprises of the Disciples. He has published several volumes: a *Debate on Spiritualism* with Joel Tiffany; *Walks about Jerusalem*; *Talks to Bereans*; *Letters to a Young Christian*; *Letters to an Inquirer*, besides numerous pamphlets. He now lives in Cincinnati, O., still editing the *Christian Standard*, along with other religious periodicals.

ESCANABA, the county-seat of Delta co., Mich., is on the west shore of Little Bay de Noquette, a part of Lake Michigan, near the mouth of Escanaba River, and is on the Chicago and North-western Railroad, 325 miles north of Chicago. It has a fine harbor, with two iron docks, costing $400,000, and is the principal outlet for the iron ore mined in adjoining regions, as well as trade in lumber and fish. It has a foundry, furnace, and machine-shops, saw-mills, a weekly newspaper, a bank, 5 churches, and a graded school. It was laid out in 1863. Population, 7677.

ESCAPE is (1) the going away by one lawfully in custody from the place where he is confined, and (2) the allowing voluntarily or negligently of such prisoner to leave his confinement. It is the duty of every man to submit himself to the inquiry and judgment of the law, and therefore one who removes himself from its custody, though without the exertion of any force or breaking, is guilty of a misdemeanor; nor is it material whether or not he is guilty of the crime with which he is charged; it is sufficient that he is lawfully in custody to answer a charge. Where force is exerted in any way to effect the escape, the offence falls under the head of prison-breach or rescue. As said above, the name escape is also applied to the act of any one who voluntarily or negligently allows a prisoner in his custody to go at large; and the escape is complete when the prisoner is allowed to go beyond the limits of the place where he should be confined, nor is it remedied by a retaking of the prisoner. This offence may be committed by any one—even a private citizen—who has a prisoner lawfully in custody. If the party voluntarily allows his prisoner to escape, he makes himself an accessory after the fact in felonies; is guilty of treason, if the prisoner's crime was treason; and of a misdemeanor, if the prisoner's offence falls in that grade. The *negligent* allowing of an escape is a misdemeanor; and, so far is it considered the duty of the officer to retain the prisoner in custody (*salva et arcta custodia*) that it is not necessary on the trial of one for allowing an escape to prove negligence on his part, but it will be presumed from the mere fact of escape; and he cannot avoid the presumption of such negligence except by affirmatively proving that he had exerted all due diligence to prevent escape. Besides this criminal liability for an escape, the sheriff and jailer or bailiff, when a prisoner in custody in a civil case regained his freedom, were liable to a civil action by the plaintiff at whose suit the prisoner had been arrested. If the prisoner was in custody on mesne process, the plaintiff could recover in an action on the case against the sheriff or the under officer such damages as he could have recovered against the original defendant; but, if the officer could rearrest the prisoner, he escaped this liability. But in an escape from imprisonment on final process, the officer became liable in an action of debt for the full amount of the judgment which had been recovered against the defendant; and this, too, irrespective of the question of the solvency of the original defendant, and whether or not he was rearrested. This branch of the subject has, of course, been materially altered by the general abolition of imprisonment for debt. The law on the subject of escape is to-day in its general principles as above described, though its details have been more or less altered by statute in the different American States. (W. M. M.)

ESMARCH, JOHANNES FRIEDRICH AUGUST, the most eminent German surgeon of the present day, was born Jan. 9, 1823, at Tönning in Schleswig-Holstein. His father was a physician of considerable repute, and was also a local magistrate. The son, after passing through the usual course in the gymnasia at Rendsburg and Flensburg, studied medicine at Kiel and Göttingen. In 1846 he became Dr. Langenbeck's assistant in the surgical hospital at Kiel, and in the Danish war of 1848 he served first as a lieutenant and afterwards as assistant surgeon. Being then made chief physician of the citizens' hospital at Flensburg, he had abundant opportunity of acquiring proficiency in military surgery. During the armistice Dr. Esmarch returned to Kiel, but when hostilities were resumed he served in the two following campaigns as adjutant of Stromeyer, to whom he is greatly indebted for his success in his profession. He was promoted to be chief surgeon Aug. 8, 1850, and having meantime received from the state license to teach, he delivered lectures at Kiel on gun-shot wounds. The year 1851 he spent in visiting the medical institutions of the principal cities of Europe and attending the lectures of the great masters of surgery, but after his return the Danish government revoked his license. In February, 1854, he married the daughter of his preceptor, Stromeyer, and when his father-in-law a month later was called to Hanover as general staff surgeon of the army of that kingdom, Esmarch succeeded him in the surgical clinic. In October, 1857, the government was compelled to acknowledge his abilities, and he was appointed professor and director of the hospital at Kiel. His vacations were spent in various journeys to increase his knowledge of his art, and especially the management of hospitals. During the Schleswig-Holstein war of 1864 he held high official positions, serving in the hospitals at Flensburg, Sundewitt, and Kiel. In July, 1866, he was summoned to Berlin to become a member of the hospital commission, and, though he was not immediately successful in securing the adoption of many improvements suggested by the experience of the civil war in America, such as barrack-hospitals, sanitary trains, etc., yet his labors were not in vain. At the outbreak of the Franco-German war of 1870 Dr. Esmarch was just recovering from a serious and tedious illness, and therefore did not enter the campaign. In July, however, he was appointed surgeon-general and consulting surgeon of the army. He had already organized at Kiel a volunteer aid commission in behalf of the Schleswig-Holstein troops and assisted in a similar movement at Hamburg. He was again summoned to Berlin Aug. 3, 1870, to direct the construction of large hospital barracks in accordance with his former suggestions. Here he was unremittingly employed as consulting surgeon till the close of the war. In April, 1871, he resigned his position in order to enjoy a much-needed rest. Since his return to Kiel he has been constantly engaged in his work as professor and surgeon. At the surgical congress in the year 1873 he explained the great invention in surgery by which he is now known to the medical profession throughout the world, the bloodless method of operating on the extremities. By passing around the limb to be operated upon tight rubber bands gradually from the extremity to a point above the place of operation the amount of blood in the limb can be so much reduced that the formerly great risk of excessive bleeding is removed. In 1874 Dr. Esmarch visited Great Britain and was received with special honor by the surgeons of the country. In the hospitals he was more than once called to illustrate the method which already bore his name. He has in turn acknowledged the merit of the antiseptic method of Lister and has combined it with his own. His wide experience, his keen insight and his valuable inventions cause his suggestions in all matters pertaining to surgery, and especially on gun-shot wounds, to be received with great deference. Hence, too, his censure of the treatment of President Garfield after his assassination excited unusual interest in the surgical profession of both Europe and America. In February, 1872, some years after the death of his first wife, Dr. Esmarch married the Princess Henriette of Schleswig-Holstein.

Dr. Esmarch has published many professional works, among which are *Ueber Resektionen nach Schusswunden* (Kiel, 1851); *Beiträge zur praktischen Chirurgie* (Kiel, 1853–60); *Verbandplatz und Feldlazarett* (Berlin, 2d ed., 1871); *Der erste Verband auf dem Schlachtfelde* (Kiel, 1869); *Ueber künstliche Blutleere bei Operationen* (Leipsic, 1873); *Die erste Hilfe bei Verletzungen* (Hanover, 1875); *Die erste Hilfe bei plötzlichen Unglücksfällen* (Leipsic, 1882).

ESPARTERO, DON JOAQUIN BALDOMERO, duke of Vitoria, prince of Vergara (1792–1879), a Spanish general and statesman, was born at Granatula, in La Mancha, Feb. 27, 1792. Being the youngest of nine children of a wheelwright, he was on account of his weak constitution intended for the church, but during the French invasion of 1808 he enlisted as a volunteer in a battalion composed of students. In 1811 he was appointed a sub-lieutenant of engineers at Cadiz, but afterwards, not being able to pass the examination in that service, was transferred to the infantry. In January, 1815, he accompanied the expedition to South America under Gen. Morillo, and became his chief of staff. He fought in Venezuela and Peru, and was for some months a prisoner. During the ten years of his sojourn in America by successive promotions he rose to the rank of colonel, and also acquired considerable wealth. In 1824, after the capitulation of Ayacucho, by which Spain abandoned her possessions in South America, Espartero returned to his native land. Being stationed at Logroño, with the rank of brigadier-general, he married a daughter of a wealthy resident of that place. In 1832 Ferdinand VII. attempted to abolish the application of the Salic law to Spain, and Espartero declared in favor of the succession of the princess Isabella to the throne. On the death of the king (Sept. 29, 1833) the general offered to march against the northern provinces, which had risen in favor of Don Carlos, who claimed the throne under the former law. Espartero was made commander of Biscay and afterwards field-marshal and lieutenant-general. He displayed considerable ability, and in 1837 saved Madrid from capture by a raid of the Carlists. As a reward he was appointed general-in-chief of the Army of the North, viceroy of Navarre, and captain-general of the Basque provinces. Being chosen a member of the Cortes, he gave his approval to the new constitution of 1837, and was henceforth an advocate and supporter of constitutional liberty. In September, 1837, he saved Madrid from capture by Don Carlos himself, drove him across the Ebro, captured Lucana, and raised the siege of Bilbao. For these exploits he was made duke of Lucana, but his victorious career was embarrassed by quarrels with the ministry. He then undertook the difficult task of restoring discipline in the army and establishing order in the conquered provinces, which was effected only after severe executions at Pampeluna and elsewhere. He defeated the Carlist Generals Negri and Guergué, and in 1839, taking advantage of dissensions in that party, concluded with Gen. Maroto the famous convention of Vergara, in consequence of which Don Carlos retired to France, though Gen. Cabrera maintained his cause a few months longer. As a reward for his services Espartero was made a grandee of the first class and duke of Vitoria. His success led him to demand also rewards for his favorite aide-de-camp, Linage, which Narvaez, the minister of war, attempted to resist. The latter was compelled to resign, and the rest of the Cabinet in their blind rage aimed a blow at the liberties of the municipalities, which Espartero was known to favor. An insurrection ensued at Madrid, and the victorious general was called to be the head of a new ministry. In October, 1840, Queen Christina, who had still resisted all liberal movements, was compelled to abdicate the regency and retire to Paris. Espartero was elected to that position May 8, 1841, and displayed his accustomed energy in suppressing the republican movement in Valencia, crushing the insurrection of O'Donnel at Pampeluna in favor of Christina, as well as defeating the plots of Generals Concha and Diego-Leon, the latter of whom he caused to be shot. By severe measures he again restored order in the Basque provinces and made himself for a time master of the situation. He resisted the extreme demands of the Church party and prevented the abduction of the young queen. At the end of 1842 a new insurrection at Barcelona was excited by the partisans of Christina, and Espartero bombarded the city. In 1843 the progressive party, of which he had been the leader, united with the moderates, and his refusal to dismiss his secretary Linage and generals who had taken part in the conquest of Barcelona, brought on a crisis. His treaty of commerce with England was denounced as disadvantageous to Spain, and several of the provinces rose in revolt. A revolutionary junta at Barcelona, June 13, 1843, proclaimed that Isabella II., though only twelve years of age, had attained her majority, and a provisional government composed of Lopes, Caballero, and Serrano declared Espartero a traitor to his country and deprived him of all his dignities. Narvaez at the head of the insurgents marched on Madrid, and entered without resistance, July 22, 1843. Abandoned by his troops, Espartero embarked at Cadiz July 30, and sought refuge in England, where he was received with all the honor due to his former rank. In 1848, the queen having annulled the decree which had deprived him of his rank, he returned to Spain and resumed his place in the senate, but soon retired to his estate at Logroño. In July, 1854, when Christina was compelled to leave Spain, Queen Isabella sought to save her throne by calling the veteran statesman to be head of her ministry at the very time when the revolutionary junta at Saragossa had chosen him commander-in-chief of the national forces. He formed a new cabinet, in which, as the only means of saving the nation from bloodshed, O'Donnel, the leader of the partisans of Christina, was made minister of war and the queen was banished. But between these two leaders, the progressive and the reactionary, there could be no harmony. A financial crisis added to the difficulties of the situation, and the Cortes which met in November spent its time in discussing the constitutional limits of monarchy, even questioning its right to exist. Finally, after a struggle of two years, the whole ministry resigned, and O'Donnel, whom the queen favored, was requested to form a new cabinet. Fresh insurrections followed at Madrid, Barcelona, and Saragossa, but Espartero refused to engage in these contests made in his name. Resigning his dignity as senator, he again retired to Logroño. After the revolution of October, 1868, and the expulsion of Queen Isabella, he gave his adhesion to the provisional government under Marshal Serrano, but took no active part in affairs. While the question of the form of government to be adopted was still under discussion a deputy proposed to the Cortes in May, 1869, to restore the monarchy and place Espartero on the throne. Though the proposal met with little favor, it was renewed with no better success a year later. After a long period of suspense, Amadeus, Duke of Aosta, son of Victor Emmanuel, was elected king in the autumn of 1870. After his arrival in Spain the new king bestowed many marks of favor on Espartero, conferring on him the order of the Annunciation and visiting him at Logroño, Sept. 30, 1871. Espartero, on his part, declared his adherence to the new dynasty, yet he gave no assistance in the troubles with which the young king was surrounded, and was with difficulty induced to accept the title of prince of Vergara, January, 1872. After the abdication of Amadeus, when Castelar was at the height of his power in the short-lived republic, Espartero thanked that statesman for referring to him as "the veteran of liberty." Two years later the republic had passed away, and Espartero gave his approval of the accession of Alfonso XII. He took no further part in public affairs, and died at Logroño, Jan. 9, 1879.

ESPARTO. This material, well known in connection with paper-making, is derived from two different grasses—*Lygeum Spartum* and *Macrochloa tenacissima*. It was well known to the ancients in connection with cordage, basket-making, and other work. Pliny devotes considerable space to "Spartum" in his 19th book, and says that it was known long before his time. It seems, however, not to have been much noticed in modern times till the advent of the American war for the Union, when the scarcity of cotton from the Southern United States made an unusual demand for paper-making material. England uses over thirteen pounds of paper per head of her whole population, and esparto came in well to supply part of the deficiency of cotton. The demand once opened, increased to such an extent that by 1868 England was importing nearly 98,000 tons, 93,000 of which came from Spain. In 1870 England received 100,000 tons, and in 1871 150,000, notwithstanding the enormous increase in price. England paid for the little it bought the year before the American war about $20 per ton in American money; in 1870 it cost $50, and was still regarded as profitable. For a considerable time after the war above referred to, very large quantities were imported directly from Spain to the United States, but now the importation has measurably fallen off through the discovery of cheaper material in that country. Some paper-makers in Philadelphia who used it extensively at one time have wholly abandoned its use.

In the old world attention seems to be growing towards it, and countries which seemed able to do without it are gradually coming to regard it with favor. A large company was formed in Germany during 1881 for paper-making from esparto grass, the first in the empire. Esparto is Spanish for sedge. Sedge, as we now understand it, is confined to *Carex* or *Cyperus*, but the esparto plants are true grasses. The Spanish people seem to retain the name "Esparto" for the material, the two grasses being distinguished, the *Sygeum* as *alfa*, and the *Macrochloa* as *atocha*. The former is chiefly from strong clayey land in Spain; the latter grows farther west in dry sandy land, even extending to the Desert of Sahara. A most remarkable fact in its history is that it takes ten or fifteen years from seed before it is strong enough to pay for cutting, but after it has once come into use it will allow of an annual cropping for forty or fifty years without showing signs of depreciation. In consequence of the long time it takes to produce a paying crop, the French are looking to legislation to prevent the destruction of the esparto grounds in Algiers as they look for similar legislation in forestry elsewhere. Much is destroyed by wanton fires, and stealing from the esparto public grounds is also a matter for Algerine legislation. For the increase of young esparto plantations fire is used, as the seeds seem to vegetate and the young plants to come sooner into profit from burned land than from elsewhere. The gathering of the grass commences at once after the wheat harvest. At that time the leaves and stalks part readily from the rhizomes, which remain in the ground for future crops. The stalks are from six to ten feet high, and are gathered in large handfuls, the gatherer wearing leather gloves to protect the hand. Sometimes a short stick is used, the gatherer dexterously twisting the tops around the stick, when a slight pull upwards and sideways draws the stalks out without any damage to the roots. The material is tied in small bundles by a piece of the grass, dried a little, and then in burdens of about two hundred weight carried across the deserts on the backs of asses to the commercial dépôts. In Spain the town of Crevilente is the headquarters for the esparto trade, though much business with it is done in Madrid.

The manufacture of paper from esparto requires some peculiar management. The grass is laid on tables and weeds and foreign material sorted out, the refuse usually amounting to about four per cent. of the original weight. The cleaned grass is then boiled by steam, ten pounds of caustic soda being used with every one hundred pounds of grass. After being boiled and stirred for six hours the water is drawn off. It is then boiled again in fresh water for an hour. It then receives two washings with cold water. Two and a half hundred weight of bleaching powder to the ton is added, and the mass revolved through bleaching tubs till white. It is again washed to free it from all traces of the bleaching powder, pressed to clear out the liquor, when it is ready for use. The pulp yielded is about one-half the original weight of the grass. Large amounts of esparto are exported from Tripoli and Tunis.

Attempts have been made by the United States Department of Agriculture to introduce the plant into the United States, but its slow growth will always be against its value. In New Mexico are some native species, *Stipa Spartea* especially, closely allied to the European and African forms. In recent industrial literature there is some confusion made between esparto and the fibre of *Spartium junceum* or Spanish broom, a totally distinct plant. (T. M.)

ESPY, JAMES POLLARD (1785–1860), an American meteorologist, was born in Westmoreland co., Pa., May 9, 1785. Ten years later his father died and the family removed to Ohio, where young Espy worked on a farm, but did not learn to read till he was 17 years old. From that time he was eager in pursuit of knowledge, and before reaching manhood he was a school-teacher. He removed to Philadelphia, where he became professor of mathematics in the Franklin Institute. His scientific researches led him to investigate the origin of storms, and after a time he formed a theory on the subject and asserted the possibility of producing rain by artificial means. He had meantime sought aid from the national government to prosecute his experiments, but he was disappointed and his suggestions ridiculed. He then began to lecture in the principal cities and thus obtained the friends and the means necessary. In 1839 he went to England and was able to show sufficient confirmation of his theory to attract the notice of the British Association. In Paris, too, Prof. Arago made an extended report on it to the French Academy of Sciences. Encouraged by this aid he published his work, *The Philosophy of Storms* (1841), and at last in 1843 the United States government appointed him to a position in the Washington observatory that he might conduct meteorological researches, being   observers in various parts of the country. The results were published by the War Department in several volumes. Prof. Espy died at Cincinnati while on a visit, Jan. 24, 1860. Though his theory is discarded, some parts of it still hold an important place in meteorology, but by the aid of the telegraph and further investigation the science has been extended far in advance of what was thought possible in his time.

ESTRAY. In law, cattle found straying about from point to point, the owner of which is unknown. At common law all estrays belonged to the crown, unless there had been a special royal grant to the lord in whose manor the same were found of all estrays therein. In order to vest an absolute property in the king or his grantees it was necessary that the estrays should be proclaimed in the church and two market towns next adjoining to the place where they were found. If no man claimed them they became the property of the crown after the lapse of a year and a day. At any time before the expiration of that period they might be claimed by the owner, upon his paying the reasonable charges of finding, keeping, and proclaiming them. In the United States the right of the finder of an estray to detain it until his reasonable charges are paid by the owner is generally secured by statute. Provision is also made for the sale of all unclaimed estrays by the officers of the township in which they have been found, after due proclamation and advertisement. The proceeds are usually applied either for the support of the poor or some other public purpose. (L. L., JR.)

ETEX, ANTOINE, a French artist, was born at Paris, March 20, 1808. He is descended from a family of artists, and at an early age devoted himself to such pursuits. He frequented the studios of Dupaty and Pradier, and received instruction from Ingres and Duban. In 1828 he obtained the second *prix de Rome* by his Hyacinthus slain by Apollo. After spending two years in Italy he visited Algeria, Germany, and England. At the salon of 1833 he exhibited a colossal statue of Cain, the originality and boldness of which so impressed M. Thiers, then minister of public works, that he gave Etex a commission for two of the groups for the Arc de l'Etoile. Yet many of his works were rejected at the salons, and for a time he refused to compete. In 1841, however, his Tomb of Géricault obtained for him the decoration of the Legion of Honor. In the revolution of 1830 he fought, and in 1848 he presented himself as a Republican candidate for the Assembly, but without success. He has not confined himself to sculpture, but has also been a painter, engraver, and architect. Among his statues are—Hero and Leander, at the museum of Caen; Blanche of Castile, at Versailles; Charlemagne, at the Luxembourg; St. Augustine, at the Madeleine; St. Benedict (1865); the Genius of the 14th Century; the Shipwrecked, which was exhibited at the exposition of 1867; Sleeping Child; Susanna surprised at the Bath (1875). He has executed also a large number of bas-reliefs and busts of the principal men of France, both in marble and bronze. Among his paintings are—Joseph Relating his Dreams; Christ Preaching; Eurydice; Sappho; Romeo and Juliet; Dante and Beatrice; The Great Men of the United States (now in City Hall, New York); Jacob Going Down to Egypt; Jacob Blessing the Sons of Joseph; The Flight to Egypt; The Ancient Slave; The Modern Slave. He has also made many water-colors and pastels. As an architect he has executed designs for monuments and public works. Among these is the monument of Francis I. at Cognac. The principal of his engravings are comprised in *La Grèce tragique*, a series of designs from the Greek tragic poets. As an author he has contributed to various journals political and critical articles, and published *Essai sur le beau* (1851); *Cours élémentaire de dessin* (1859), and an autobiography, under the title *Les Souvenirs d'un Artiste*.

EUGENIE, empress of France and wife of Napoleon III., was born in Granada, Spain, May 5, 1826. Before marriage she was known as Eugenia Maria Guzman de Montijo, Countess of Teba, being the daughter of Count Montijo, a grandee of illustrious descent. Her mother was Doña Maria Manuela Kirkpatrick Closeburn, a lady sprung of an old Scottish family, expatriated at the fall of the Stuarts; her father was at one time British consul at Malaga. In 1851 Eugénie lived with her mother at Paris. Here her beauty and mental accomplishments, no less than the dignity and refinement of her manners, attracted much attention. The future emperor had known her during his residence in England, and was believed to be one of her admirers. After the failure of the project for a marriage with a Swedish princess, the emperor, on Jan. 2, 1853, apprised his ministers of his intended marriage to the Countess Montijo. The wedding was celebrated Jan. 29, 1853, at the church of Notre Dame. The imperial court owed much of its brilliancy to Eugénie's tastes; and she gave largely to charitable and pious enterprises. To the ultramontanes her support was unfailing, and her influence unquestionably affected the imperial policy at many important junctures. The affairs of Italy and of Rome (1859-65), and, later, the Mexican question and the disputes which ended in the Franco-German war of 1870-71, are believed to have been greatly complicated by her prejudices. But, though her political sagacity was often at fault, her high personal and moral qualities were never open to question. On the fall of the second empire (Sept. 3, 1870) she left Paris for England, where she was joined by the prince imperial (1856-79), her only child, and, in the following March, by her husband. The ex-emperor died Jan. 9, 1873, and her son was killed in the Zulu war, June 1, 1879. This event was a terrible blow to Eugénie and to the imperialist cause. Her residence in exile is at Chiselhurst, Kent.

EUPHORBIA. A well-known genus of plants, the type of the natural order *Euphorbiaceæ*, which probably embraces 3000 species, of which Boissier, in 1862, enumerated 720 species in *euphorbia* alone. The flowers are of separate sexes on the same peduncle. The female flower consists of little more than a three-lobed pistil, terminating a three-celled ovary elevated on a short pedicle, around which are several monostaminate male flowers; and beneath this an involucre often highly colored. Besides this, the plants abound with a milky, highly-acrid juice. There are some exceptions to these general characteristics; yet euphorbiaceous plants are readily recognized by them.

These plants abound in the warmer parts of America. Indeed, about one-fourth of all the species known are found on the American continent. Of the genus *euphorbia* there are 27 species found in the United States east of the Mississippi, and 19 recorded in the botany of California. Some of these are, however, common to both continents.

Plants of this genus have had a medical reputation from the earliest times on account of their great aperient powers. They have the common name of spurges, and the whole order is called spurgewort in Europe. These properties are said to have been discovered by Euphorbus, a physician to King Juba, of Mauritania; but, as the Greek *euphorbus* signifies well-fed, the name may have been derived from the fact that the African plants had thick, succulent stems, like our cactus, and were filled with milky juice. The juice of these euphorbias is extremely acrid, and its medical application is scarcely ever quite safe. Since the discovery of castor-oil, obtained from *Ricinus communis*, also a euphorbiaceous plant, the juice of the *euphorbia* has fallen into disrepute. At one time it was considered so important that a supply of euphorbia should be always on hand, that Charlemagne ordered *Euphorbia Lathyris* to be planted in all the monastic gardens of his empire. Perhaps among the most famous in its time has been the "cypress spurge," *Euphorbia cyparissia*, which, near two hundred years ago, was the basis of a popular medicine, known as Rulander's extract, which was to cure scurvy, dropsy, jaundice, gout, rheumatism, and other disorders. The belief in the medicinal value of this plant must have been very strong, for the early German settlers of Pennsylvania brought it with them from their fatherland, and we find it still in most of the farm gardens in the older portions of the Atlantic United States. Yet no one now regards the plant as good for anything but to destroy warts. Of American species *Euphorbia corollata* was in use by the Indians as an emetic. They called it "pehac," and it is yet known as "wild ipecac." The root of another species, *Euphorbia ipecacuanha*, has been used as ipecacuanha, but is not equal to it in medicinal properties. Some of the South American Indians use the juice of a species of that region to poison their arrows, and *Euphorbia maculata* of the United States has been charged with making the mouths of horses sore and inducing what is known as "slobbers." But heat seems to drive out the acrid properties, and from some of the more fleshy rooted kinds farinaceous food is prepared. One species—*Euphorbia edulis*—is boiled as greens in China. The albumen in the seeds is nutritious. The agriculturants of America make good use of them. In Colorado stores of *Euphorbia maculata* seeds have been found in the ant-nests, and in Texas the ant-granaries are largely supplied with croton seeds—croton being a very large genus of euphorbiaceous plants. Some of the tropical euphorbias are cultivated as greenhouse plants. Among the more interesting species are the tree-euphorbias, which abound in certain parts of Africa.

EUREKA, the county-seat of Eureka co., Nevada, is 90 miles south of the Central Pacific Railroad, with which it is connected by the Eureka and Palisade Railroad. It contains a court-house, costing $60,000, 2 banks, 2 daily papers, 3 churches, a good school. It was founded in 1871. The rich mines of silver in this vicinity have yielded altogether $60,000,000. Population, 4207 in 1880, but 3000 in 1890.

EUREKA SPRINGS, a city of Carroll co., Ark., is at the headwaters of a branch of White River, 8 miles south of the Missouri boundary and 250 miles S. W. of St. Louis. A branch railroad is now in construction from Seligman, 18 miles N. W. on the Arkansas division of the St. Louis and San Francisco Railroad. It was settled July 4, 1879, and has already become noted as a health-resort on account of its medicinal springs. Situated on the sides of the White River Mountains, in the midst of a wilderness, it is resorted to by thousands of invalids, for whose accommodation there are numerous hotels and boarding-houses. The city was organized in 1880 and has a bank, 2 daily and 3 weekly newspapers, 7 churches, and 5 schools. The following analysis of water from one of the medicinal springs was made by Potter and Riggs, of Washington University, St. Louis: chloride of sodium, .19; sulphate of soda, .09; bi-carbonate of soda, .15; sulphate of potash, .13; bi-carbonate of lime, .47; bi-carbonate of magnesia, 4.43; iron and alumina, .08; silica, .31; total solids, 5.85 grains. It contains also free and albuminoid ammonia; the gaseous contents are estimated at 28.52 cubic inches in each gallon of water. Resident population, 5000.

EVANS, FREDERICK WILLIAM, presiding elder of the community of Shakers at New Lebanon, Columbia co., N. Y., is the foremost representative of that religious body in America. He was born at Bromyard, Herfordshire, England, June 9, 1808. His mother having died when he was four years old, he lived for some years on his uncle's farm, and in 1820 his father brought him to America. After settling at Binghamton, N. Y., Frederick, who had formerly been considered stupid, showed eagerness for knowledge and became a materialist and an extreme Democrat. In 1829, accepting the socialistic theories then in vogue, he travelled on foot to Ohio to join a "community," which however disbanded two months after his arrival. He then paid a visit to his relatives in England, and returning to New York in Jan., 1830, went to New Lebanon, N. Y., where he joined the Shaker order. He then commenced a new study of the Bible, and has since claimed to find in it confirmation of his present belief. In 1838 he was appointed assistant elder in the young believer's order, and in 1855 he became first elder. The statements of doctrine put forth by him in numerous lectures and publications vary considerably from those made by the earlier Shakers. All however agree in maintaining the duality of God, represented as fatherhood and motherhood, the former manifested on earth in Jesus and the latter in Ann Lee, the founder of Shakerism. Celibacy is required of all members, and none are admitted to the community under twelve years of age except when parents join with their children. Evans has had great influence upon the internal management as well as the external relations of the society. In 1871 he went on a special mission to England, lecturing and publishing some books. He has been joint editor of the *Shaker and Shakeress*, a monthly journal, and has also published an *Autobiography* (1869), a *Life of Ann Lee* (1871), *Shaker Communism* (1871), and other works, in which he displays considerable literary power.

EVANS, OLIVER (1755-1819), American mechanician, especially remarkable for his improvements in flour-mills and for his introduction of the high-pressure steam-engine. He was born near Newport, Del., in 1755, and was a descendant of the Rev. Evan Evans. He served an apprenticeship to a wheelwright, and afterwards removed to Queen Anne county, Md., and there opened a store. He early developed a pronounced mechanical turn of mind, and possessed great ingenuity and fertility of resource. At the age of

See Vol. VIII. p. 637 Am. ed. (p. 726 Edin. ed.).

twenty-two he invented and perfected machines for making the teeth of wool-cards and for perforating the leather for their insertion, operations until that time (1777) performed exclusively by hand. In 1782 he contracted with two of his brothers who were practical millers to put up a merchant flour-mill in New Castle co., Del. The mill was completed and began to manufacture Sept. 5, 1785, but during its erection Evans became extremely dissatisfied with the cumbersome and laborious methods and machinery then in use, and devised many labor-saving contrivances which, after sturdy opposition from millers and mill-owners, were finally adopted almost universally, and have remained, with few essential changes, in use ever since. His chief aim was to reduce the manual labor required to transport the grain and flour from one place to another during the various operations to which they were subjected. Among those which he considered the most important of his inventions were the elevator, the conveyor, the hopper-boy, the drill, the descender, and the crane-spout. The elevator, which had its prototype in the "Persian wheel" of the Nile, and later in the chain-pump, was simply a series of buckets attached to an endless band passing over pulleys, so arranged that the buckets filled as they passed under the lower pulley and emptied as they went over the upper one; and was employed not only for the elevation of grain or meal from one story of the mill to another, but also for the removal of grain from the holds of vessels moored beside the mill. The hopper-boy spread the meal to cool it before bolting; while the drill, the descender, and the conveyor (which, Evans says, was suggested by the Archimedes screw) were devices for moving the meal or grain from one machine or one place to another. The crane-spout was pivoted so as to deflect the descending grain into any one of several receptacles into which it might be desired to send it. Together, they performed, in the inventor's words, "every necessary movement of the grain or meal through all the various operations from the time the grain is emptied from the wagoner's bag or from the measure on board the ship until it is manufactured into flour and separated ready for packing into barrels."

Although Evans's mill-machinery probably constituted the most valuable of his inventions, he is perhaps more widely known from his invention of a high-pressure steam-engine and his persistent efforts to secure its introduction. As early as 1772, when he was but seventeen years old, and still apprenticed to the wheelwright, he turned his attention to the discovery of "some means of propelling land-carriages without animal power." His attention being accidentally directed to the expansive force of steam, he fancied that he had discovered an original source of power, which, however, he saw at first no means of utilizing. About this time he met with a description of the atmospheric steam-engine, and was surprised to find that steam was only used to produce a vacuum, while the piston was moved by atmospheric pressure. This he believed to be an erroneous application of the force of steam, and he conceived the idea of a high-pressure steam-engine, using steam at perhaps 120 pounds pressure per square inch. The cylinder and piston did not at first satisfy him, as it did not immediately produce circular motion, and he invented and described four forms of rotary engines, the chief of which he called his "circular steam-engine No. 2." Having satisfied himself by much study and some experiments that he could make steam-wagons, and also steamboats driven by paddle-wheels, and having perfected his improvements in flour-mills, in 1786 he petitioned the legislature of Pennsylvania for the exclusive right to use his improvements in flour-mills and also "of propelling land-carriages by steam in that State for twenty-one years." In March, 1787, an act was passed granting the flour-mill patent, but ignoring the remainder of the petition. Delaware granted the same year like privileges, but the legislature of Maryland, May 21, 1787, granted both patents for a term of fourteen years, and New Hampshire granted them for seven years. The Maryland patent also gave him the exclusive right to use steamboats on the waters of that State. Evans then endeavored, unsuccessfully, to interest some capitalist in his invention, and up to 1801 had done little towards the perfection of his engine except to try a few experiments on a small scale. In 1791 he surrendered his State patents and took out United States patents, and in 1792 he filed drawings and specifications in the U. S. Patent Office. In 1794-95 he sent drawings and descriptions of his steam-engine to certain English engineers. In 1801 he began, unaided, the construction of his "steam-wagon," actuated, he affirmed, by the feeling that he owed it to the State of Maryland to accomplish, if possible, the undertaking for which he had been granted a patent. He had made some progress when it occurred to him that, as his engine differed from any then in use, he might obtain a patent for it as applied to driving mills of various sorts; he therefore changed his plans somewhat, and began the construction of a small high-pressure steam-engine of 6-inch cylinder, 18-inch stroke, and in the winter of 1802 he had his engine at work on Market Street, Philadelphia, sawing stone with a gang of twelve saws. In 1804 he constructed for the Board of Health of Philadelphia a steam-dredge which he called the "Orukter Amphibolos;" it consisted of a scow 30 feet long by 12 feet wide, carrying an endless chain of buckets to bring up the mud, and hooks to clear away stones, sticks, etc. This apparatus was actuated by a small vertical steam-engine of 5-inch cylinder and 9-inch stroke. Boat and machinery, together weighing about 43,000 pounds, were roughly mounted on wheels, to which the engine was connected by belts, and this unwieldy vehicle propelled itself to the Schuylkill River, a distance of one mile and a half. When launched, a simple paddle-wheel was rigged up at the stern, and the scow steamed down the river to its junction with the Delaware, and thence against a head wind back to Philadelphia. It is asserted that the drawings which Evans sent to England fell into the hands of Andrew Vivian, a mechanical engineer, and were incorporated in the high-pressure engine and locomotive of Trevithick & Vivian, which undoubtedly had many features in common with the Evans engine, notably the use of the exhaust steam to heat the feed-water. Their patent is dated 1802, and their locomotive was tried in 1804. Evans's mill-machinery was widely and successfully introduced during his lifetime, and many of his steam-engines were built for manufacturing and steamboat purposes; but the great goal of his ambition he never reached—that is, the construction of a locomotive to run on ordinary turnpike roads. He made a model engine somewhere about 1817 which would run perhaps 200 or 300 yards, but his most persistent efforts and convincing arguments never elicited the necessary means for the accomplishment of this scheme. He put himself on record, however, as a very early, if not the very earliest, projector of steam-locomotion, and demonstrated its feasibility as clearly as anything short of actual accomplishment could do. He even made offers to a turnpike company to accept its order for an engine, with the proviso that it should cost them nothing if it did not perform what was promised for it. Great success attended the introduction of his stationary and steamboat engines, and in 1816 he claimed between 50 and 100 engines in use. In 1817 one of his engines, 24″ × 48″, was employed in the Philadelphia Waterworks at Fairmount, and at an earlier date one was used successfully at the Centre Square Waterworks in the same city. The advantages which may be claimed for Evans's engine over the low-pressure condensing engine then in use consist chiefly in greater simplicity, diminution of weight, and consequent ease of construction and reduction of first cost—qualities which made it peculiarly adapted to the requirements of a sparsely-settled country, and especially to the needs of river-navigation. Evans's improvements consisted principally of the use of high-pressure steam; the use of the exhaust blast; the use of the exhaust to heat the feed-water; and the use of an excellent form of boiler, generally of cylindrical shape, with large internal flue containing the fire, return flues on the sides, and re-return flue underneath. He also applied the exhaust steam to the warming of apartments, and suggested the use of steam-power for the propulsion of fire-engines. The success attending the use of his engines, and his earnest advocacy in various publications of the use of high-pressure steam, dispelled in America at least the distrust with which it had since the time of Watt been regarded, and the high-pressure, high-speed, non-condensing engine of small cylinder and long stroke remained for many years the distinctively American engine.

Evans's first and most important work was *The Young Millwright's and Miller's Guide*, which first appeared in 1795, and has since been repeatedly republished. the fourteenth edition having been issued in 1853, while a French translation was issued in Paris in 1830. This work seems to have absorbed the author's whole attention for three years, to the neglect of his business and his family; so that, as he himself recorded, his faithful wife sold tow cloth of her own making to buy food for her children. The book was published by subscription at $2 a copy, assisted by a loan of $1000, and the first edition was of 2000 copies. The book contained, along with some questionable theories, a great deal of valuable practical information, and remained for many years the best authority on the design and erection of flour- and saw-mills, the construction of gearing and waterwheels, etc.

In 1804, Evans petitioned Congress for an extension of his patents on flour-mill improvements, claiming that a continuation of his fees and royalties would enable him to prosecute certain useful discoveries and inventions which he was about consummating; and during the favorable consideration of his bill he issued proposals for a new work to be entitled the *Young Steam Engineer's Guide*. The petition was, however, defeated on its third reading, and Evans, in the consequent period of despondency, declaring his hopes blasted and his new schemes abortive, called his family together and solemnly renouncing all further efforts for the benefit of a thankless generation, committed to the flames the drawings and specifications of eighty new inventions.

In 1805 he published his contemplated book in an abridged form, and called it *The Abortion of the Young Steam Engineer's Guide*. He therein explained the operation of the steam-engine as then understood, gave rules for the proportions of the various parts, and determined the proper point of cut-off, which he placed at from ⅛ to ¼ of the stroke, according to the steam-pressure and the work to be done. He also set forth at length the peculiar merits of his own form of steam-engine, and described various others of his useful inventions, including an ice-machine to work by mechanical evaporation and recondensation of ether; and finally forswore all further investigations for the benefit of an inappreciative public. In 1805 he had a somewhat bitter discussion, through the columns of the *Medical Repository*, with Col. John Stevens of Hoboken, N. J., wherein each writer claimed priority and pre-eminent importance for his own improvements in the steam-engine and in steam-navigation. The publication of the *Engineer's Guide* left Evans at fifty years of age again impoverished and with a large family to support. He applied himself strictly to business, and in three or four years claimed to have made himself "independent and saved $20,000." In the summer of 1807 he commenced as an iron-founder and steam-engineer, and opened the "Mars Works" in Philadelphia at the corner of Vine Street and the Ridge Road. The following year he advertised that he had "the necessary apparatus and machinery for an iron-foundry, a pattern-shop, a blacksmith-shop, a steam-mill for turning and boring heavy iron and grinding plaster, a steam-engineer's shop, a burr-millstone factory, a furnace, foundry, and shop for manufacturing iron castings, wrought-iron work, and machinery for flax, cotton, and wool spinning, for the construction of sugar-mills, patent steam-engines, etc." As early as 1800 Evans had a mill at No. 275 Market Street, and appeared also as a "manufacturer of burr-millstones and seller of bolting-cloths." He had a high reputation as a millwright, and seems to have done a good business in mill-machinery and supplies. Having been non-suited in a suit against some infringers on his mill-machinery patents, he again applied to Congress for relief, and after a hard struggle on both sides he got a bill, January 22, 1808, granting a reissue of his patents for a term of fourteen years.

During the proceedings Evans published a pamphlet entitled *Oliver Evans to his Counsel who are engaged in the Defence of his Patent Rights for the Improvements he has invented, containing a Short Account of Two out of Eighty of his Inventions, their Use and Progress in despite of all Opposition and Difficulty, and Two of his Patents, with Explanations* After the successful termination of his appeal to Congress he appears to have increased the price of his license, which, he argued, had been far too cheap, and then had cause to complain of the great difficulty he experienced in collecting from the mill-owners. The law appears to have been retrospective in its action, and the courts sustained him when he endeavored to collect royalties from those millers who had put in his improvements after the expiration of his original patents before their reissue. April 15, 1811, Evans obtained a patent for a saw-mill, and the following year he gave notice that he claimed a patent for a "cylinder or globular boiler," and warned infringers to desist.

Evans died of apoplexy in New York, Thursday, April 15, 1819, soon after he had heard of the complete destruction of the Mars Works by an incendiary fire four days previously. (C. S., JR.)

EVANSTON, a village of Cook co., Ill., is on Lake Michigan, 11 miles north of Chicago, on the Milwaukee division of the Chicago and North-western Railroad. It was commenced as an educational town in 1854 by some prominent Methodists, and is the seat of the Garrett Biblical Institute and the North-western University. The village has gas, good supply of lake water, good sewer system, and is a favorite place of residence for the business men of Chicago. It has a weekly and a bi-weekly newspaper. 2 banks, 7 churches, a high school and private schools. Population, 13,000.

EVARTS, JEREMIAH (1781–1831), an American editor and advocate of foreign missions, was born in Sunderland, Vt., Feb. 3, 1781. He graduated at Yale College in 1802, studied law, and was admitted to the bar in New Haven in 1806. He afterwards became editor of the *Panoplist*, a religious monthly magazine published in Boston. In 1812 he was chosen treasurer of the American Board of Commissioners for foreign missions, and still edited the *Panoplist* and its successor, the *Missionary Herald*. In 1821 he was appointed corresponding secretary of the board, and remained in that position till his death. He died at Charleston, S. C., May 10, 1831.

EVARTS, WILLIAM MAXWELL, LL. D., an eminent American lawyer and statesman, son of the preceding, was born in Boston, Feb. 6, 1818. He graduated at Yale College in 1837, studied at the Harvard Law School, and was admitted to the bar in New York in 1841. He soon became eminent in his profession, and is regarded as one of the most eloquent advocates in the United States. He has been a Republican in politics since the organization of that party. When Pres. Andrew Johnson was impeached before the Senate in the spring of 1868, Mr. Evarts was the leading counsel for the defence, and made a masterly argument in behalf of the President. On July 15, 1868, he was appointed attorney-general, and he held this seat in the cabinet till the end of Pres. Johnson's administration in March, 1869. Pres. Grant appointed him one of the counsel for the United States before the tribunal of arbitration on the Alabama claims at Geneva in 1872. In 1876, as an orator of the highest national reputation, he was appropriately selected to deliver the oration at the centennial celebration in Philadelphia. On the accession of Mr. Hayes to the Presidency in 1877, Mr. Evarts, who had made a strong argument in defence of the validity of his election before the electoral commission, was made Secretary of State. He remained in that position till 1881, discharging its duties with faithfulness and efficiency. In 1885 he was elected to the U. S. Senate, but in 1891, he was defeated for re-election by Governor D. B. Hill.

EVE, PAUL FITZSIMMONS (1806–1878), an American surgeon, was born near Augusta, Ga., June 27, 1806. He graduated at Franklin College, Athens, Ga., in 1826, and received the degree of M. D. from the University of Pennsylvania in 1828. After practising for a year in Georgia he went to Europe, where he studied in London and Paris. He was present and assisted professionally in the French Revolution of July, 1830, and he took part in the Polish Revolution of 1831. After the fall of Warsaw, Sept. 8, 1831, he was for a short time prisoner. Returning to America he was elected professor of surgery in the Medical College of Georgia in June, 1832. In 1850 he was called to the chair of surgery in the University of Louisville, and in the following year to a similar position in the University of Nashville, then being organized. In 1857 he was elected president of the American Medical Association. In 1859 he went to Europe, and, having visited the seat of war in Northern Italy, published the results of his observations in the *Nashville Medical and Surgical Journal*. After the outbreak of the American Civil War he was made surgeon-general of Tennessee, and held other positions in the Confederate service till the end of the war. In 1868 he was elected professor of surgery in the Missouri Medical College, but resigned a year later and returned to Nashville, where he resumed his professorship in the university. In 1877 he became a professor in the newly-established Nashville Medical College, and remained in connection with this institution till his death. He died at Nashville, Jan. 10, 1878. He was the foremost surgeon of the South-west, and at the international medical Congress in Philadelphia in 1876 was the most distinguished representative of his department. His publications comprise 600 articles. His most important works are—*Remarkable Cases in Surgery* (1857); *One Hundred Cases of Lithotomy* (1870); *What the South and West have done for American Surgery.*

EVERGREENS. In America "Evergreens" usually represent simply coniferous trees; when other evergreens are referred to, they are distinguished as "Broad-leaved Evergreens." Evergreens are so named because the trees always have leaves on them, though the leaves themselves mostly die annually. In the case of deciduous trees the leaves are developed in spring, and die when the autumn or winter approaches. But the leaves of the broad-leaved Evergreens have the power of resisting frost or drying winds, and retain some vital power till the new growth starts in the following year, when they gradually fall. In other words the fall of the leaf in deciduous trees is in the autumn, but in broad-leaved evergreens the fall of the leaf is not till the following spring. A large number of plants which are evergreens when protected by snow, or the shelter of woods, are deciduous when in exposed places. Some of the honeysuckles, oleasters and burning-bushes are illustrations of this class, hence we find the greater number of broad-leaved evergreens in those climates where but little frost prevails. Some trees have the leaves with the power of cohering with the bark. Many *Coniferæ*, such as arbor vitæ, cedars, juniper, some pines, and spruces, are illustrations. The leaves in all these are wholly or in part adnate with the stem. This gives them a greater power over the usual leaf-destroying elements, and they continue longer than one year. They in fact become a part of the bark, and partake of the comparative longevity common to the cortical system. Even with this advantage the cohering leaves do not often continue more than two years, as may be seen by examining the branches of arbor vitæ and some pines, where they may be found, at the end of that period, peeling off in the form of lanceolate and membraneous scales. The leaves of some spruces and firs, as we may suppose from analogy with pines, partly united with the stems, often last several years, as do the secondary leaves or bundles of needles of true pines. A large number of herbaceous plants preserve their leaves from one spring to another, the vicinity of the earth and proximity to the roots—the sources of food—aiding their vital power; and they are evergreens in the same sense as many trees and shrubs are; but the term is generally confined to plants of a ligneous character, and to the two classes described.

In America the greater number of broad-leaved evergreens are found in the beautiful natural order *Ericaceæ*. Some of the huckleberries and bilberries (*Gaylussacia* and *Vaccinium*) are evergreens. *Arbutus* and *Arctostaphylos* are also evergreens. *Epigæa*, the trailing arbutus, the *Ganetheria* or tea-berry, some andromedas—the old genus *Andromeda* being now divided into several others—are also evergreens. Then there is the beautiful section *Rhododendreæ*, in which, besides the well-known laurels *Rhododendron* and *Kalmia*, are *Ledum, Leiophyllum*, and other genera. Most of these are appreciated for the great beauty of the flowers as well as for their evergreen character. Some are found high up in the Arctic regions, and they extend thence down to the tropical regions. There are some evergreens among the berberries and hollies, and others scattered through other genera. (T. M.)

EVICTION. The original meaning of this word in Anglo-Saxon law was an expulsion of one holding real estate from such estate by legal process consequent upon the assertion of a paramount title. The word did not cover the case of one who was turned out by other means than legal process; such case would have fallen under ouster. But the word is undoubtedly not confined at present to so narrow a meaning, but covers the case of any expulsion from possession by a paramount title, whether by the aid of legal process or not. Total eviction occurs where one is wholly deprived of his right to the premises, partial where he is deprived of the possession of some part. There may be an eviction in cases where the purchaser or lessee has not made any actual entry into the lands, but found them in the actual and lawful possession of another when he went to them for the purpose of entering; it is, of course, necessary, in this case to show that the party in possession actually had a good title, paramount to that of the purchaser or lessee. An actual physical dispossession is not always necessary to an eviction; for, if a landlord erect a nuisance near the demised premises or in any way materially interfere with the tenant's rights under his lease, this also will constitute an eviction. The remedy for eviction in the case of a lessee is ordinarily simple, as the contract of lease falls at once, and he need pay no more rent. In the case of a purchaser, the remedy depends largely upon the covenants contained in the deed of purchase. Formerly the party had only a writ of *warrantia charta* upon his warranty, by which he could recover a recompense in lands of equal value with the freehold of which he had been deprived; now, this remedy is entirely replaced by a personal action in some one of the covenants which it is almost universally the custom to insert in deeds. This matter depends largely upon the covenants which exist in the special case, under the language of the deed, and under the statutory provisions which frequently exist, to define what shall be the exact effect of certain words commonly used in deeds, and it is impossible to go into it closely here. Some of these covenants are said to run with the land, *i. e.*, they enure to the benefit of purchasers from the first purchaser as well as to the benefit of that person himself; they may therefore be asserted by such second purchasers in case they are evicted. Other usual covenants do not run with the land but enure only to the benefit of the first purchaser. The measure of damages for a purchaser who has been evicted is ordinarily the price he paid for the land with interest. If the land has increased in value since his purchase, the increase does not belong to him but to the grantor; and this is the case even where the rise in value is due in whole or in part to improvements erected by the grantee—or the lessee, in a case between landlord and tenant—such improvements belong to the grantor or lessor, for he should not be burdened with the cost of may be expensive buildings which he would not himself have erected. (W. M. M.)

EWBANK, THOMAS (1792–1870), an American writer on mechanics, was born at Barnard Castle, Durham, England, March 11, 1792. When thirteen years of age he was apprenticed to a tin- and copper-smith, and worked for some years in London. He emigrated to New York about 1819, and in the next year began to manufacture metallic tubing, but in 1836 retired from business to devote himself to literature and science. In 1842 he published a *Descriptive and Historical Account of Hydraulic and other Machines* (last ed. 1872). In 1845 he went to Brazil, and afterwards published *Life in Brazil*, 1856. Pres. Taylor in 1849 appointed him commissioner of patents, and he held that office till 1852. He afterwards published *Reminiscences of the Patent Office* (1859), and other works. One of his discoveries was a method of increasing the resisting power of building-stones. He died at New York, Sept. 16, 1870.

EWELL, RICHARD STODDARD (1816–1872), an American Confederate general, was born in the District of Columbia in October, 1816. He graduated at West Point in 1840, and served on the Western frontier till 1846, when he was engaged for a time in the coast survey. During the war with Mexico he was brevetted captain for gallantry at Contreras and Churubusco, Aug. 20, 1847. Afterwards he served in New Mexico on expeditions against the Apaches. When the State of Virginia seceded he resigned, May 7, 1861, and entered the Confederate army as brigadier-general. He served in the Manassas campaign in 1861, and at the first battle of Bull Run his troops were twice repulsed. Yet he did not lose the esteem of his superiors, and was soon promoted to be major-general. He was at the battles of Union Church, White Oak Swamp, and Cedar Mountain, and was defeated at Kettle Run. He was engaged in the second battle of Bull Run, and was wounded in the Maryland campaign in 1862. He became lieutenant-general May 20, 1863, and, when Stonewall Jackson died, was, at his request, appointed to succeed him in command of the Second corps. He fought at Winchester, Gettysburg, and in the Wilderness, May, 1864. He was finally captured by Gen. Sheridan, April 6, 1865, at Sailor's Creek, near Appomattox River. When the war closed he accepted the result in good faith and lived a retired life. He died at Spring Hill, Tenn., Jan. 25, 1872. He was one of the ablest and bravest Confederate generals, yet expressed his desire that nothing might be placed on his tombstone reflecting upon the Government of the United States.

EWER, FERDINAND CARTWRIGHT, D.D. (1826–1883), an American Episcopalian divine, was born at Nantucket, Mass., May 22, 1826. He graduated at Harvard College in 1848. By birth a Unitarian, he became, before entering college, an enthusiastic Episcopalian of the Pusey, Keble, and Newman school, and intended entering the priesthood, but the onset of painful doubts regarding the truth of Christianity led him to adopt another profession. He studied civil-engineering, but went to California in 1849, and became a successful journalist. In 1857 the difficulties which had beset his faith were overcome, and he was ordained a deacon, and in 1858 a priest. In 1860 he removed to New York, where he was (1860–62) assistant-rector of St. Ann's Church. In 1864 he became rector of Christ Church, but resigned in 1871, on account of differences with some members of his vestry regarding ritualistic practices. In 1871 he took charge of the new parish of St. Ignatius, of which he remained rector till his death, which occurred at Montreal, Oct. 10, 1883. His published writings include—*The Failure of Protestantism* (1875); *Catholicity, Protestantism, and Romanism* (1878); *The Operation of the Holy Ghost* (1879); *The Grammar of Theology* (1880).

EWING, THOMAS, LL.D. (1789–1871), an American statesman, was born near West Liberty, Ohio co., Va., Dec. 28, 1789. His father had been an officer in the Revolution, and in 1792 removed to Ohio, where he was one of the settlers of Amestown. Thomas was taught at first by an elder sister, and, while employed in the Kanawha salt-works, prepared himself for college by study at night. In 1815 he graduated in the Ohio University at Athens, receiving the first degree of A.B. conferred by that institution. He studied law, was admitted to the bar in 1816, and practised with success in Ohio and before the Supreme Court of the United States. He was elected to the United States Senate in 1831, and acted with the Whig party. In March, 1841, he was appointed by Pres. Harrison Secretary of the Treasury, but in September, when Pres. Tyler vetoed the bill for a national bank, he resigned, with other members of the cabinet. He was Secretary of the Interior, under Pres. Taylor, from March, 1849, to July, 1850. In the latter part of that year he was appointed to the seat in the United States Senate left vacant by the appointment of Thomas Corwin to a position in the cabinet. He opposed the Clay compromise bill and the fugitive-slave law. Returning to private life in 1851, he resumed the practice of law at Lancaster, O. In February, 1861, he was a member of the peace convention at Washington. He died at Lancaster, O., Oct. 26, 1871.

EXPLOSIVES. An explosion is simply a chemical reaction between molecules, by which a volume of heated gas much larger than that of the original explosive substance is formed suddenly. Upon the degree of suddenness depends the possible intensity of the action. In *mechanical* mixtures, as gunpowder, these reactions can occur only after the lapse of sensible though very short intervals of time (0.01 seconds). With *chemical* compounds, like nitroglycerine, the atoms are already in position and the reaction may be said to take place instantaneously, producing a *detonation*. The relative values of all explosives, whether mechanical or chemical, depend largely upon the circumstances under which the explosion is produced, such as the nature of the resistance to be overcome, the condition of the explosive, the rapidity with which it is fired, etc.

See Vol. VIII. p. 705 Am. ed. (p. 806 Edin. ed.).

Gunpowder.—The Chinese are said to have possessed a knowledge of gunpowder prior to A.D. 80, but it is believed to have been invented in Europe in 1320 by Berthold Schwarz. In 1397 powder mines were used at the siege of Merat, but it was not until 1613 that Martin Weigel, mine superintendent of Freiberg, first proposed its use for ordinary mining operations.

In 100 parts of gunpowder there are from 80 to 60 parts of saltpetre, from 21 to 12 of charcoal, and from 19 to 8 of sulphur. The grains must be firm, hard, angular, free from dust, of uniform color, and should not readily absorb moisture. The explosive force of good blasting powder is about 64,500 pounds per square inch or 303,786 foot-pounds. Its specific gravity is about the same as water, hence 1 lb. = 28 cubic inches. The weight of powder required to fill one foot of hole of various diameters is given in the following table:

Weight of Powder in one foot Depth of Hole.

Diameter. Inches.	Weight. Avoirdupois.		Diameter. Inches.	Weight. Avoirdupois.	
	lbs.	oz.		lbs.	oz.
1	0	5.03	3½	3	12.6
1¼	0	7.86	4	5	0.4
1½	0	11.30	4½	6	5.3
2	1	4.11	5	7	12.7
2½	1	15.42	5½	9	8.1
3	2	13.24	6	11	5.0

Powder may be ignited by impact, but only with great difficulty and uncertainty. In such cases it is most readily fired by a blow from iron upon iron, and least readily from copper upon copper; hence the use of copper priming wires, etc.; but it is best ignited by rapid heating to a temperature of 578° to 608° F., by introducing a red-hot substance, as iron, tinder, a burning brand, wire, or by a fulminate surrounded by some sensitive powder in a cap. The gases evolved by combustion are carbonic acid, nitrogen, and carbonic oxide, which are so deleterious as to cause delays in mining until the air can be removed, or sufficiently diluted with fresh air, so as to be inhaled without discomfort or danger.

Powder is usually packed in 25 lb. kegs. Amongst the various grades of powder may be mentioned *mortar, musket, cannon, mammoth, orange, lightning,* and *Oliver*. The safety compound of the Oriental Powder Company, which consists of an intimate mixture of potassium-chlorate, and crude gamboge, is very sensitive to friction and is justly regarded as dangerous. It has been driven from the market by nitro-glycerine, which is both stronger and safer to handle.

Other Explosives.—A safer and stronger explosive than powder, known as *haloxyline*, is composed of charcoal, saltpetre, ferrocyanide of potassium, and some cyanide of potassium. It is granular, burns slowly in open air with a violet flame without exploding, is not ignited by pressure or impact even of powerful blows of iron on iron. Ignition is only effected by a spark or flame; no smoke results from combustion, and the gaseous products are neither unpleasant nor injurious. When rammed firmly into the bore hole its effect is said to be twice that of an equal weight of powder, although acting more slowly, so that the rock is not scattered but lifted and rent—that is, the cones of rupture and of projection are more nearly coincident.

A modification of haloxyline known as *Horsley's Powder* consists of chlorate of potassa mixed with resin or with powdered nut-galls, and, later, with 5 per cent. of nitro-glycerine.

Gun-cotton, discovered by Schönbein in 1846, is prepared by exposing dry cotton to a mixture of nitric and sulphuric acid, and then thoroughly washing the cotton to remove excess of acid. When kept wet and compressed it is one of the safest of explosives. It can be fired in this state by a primer made of a cake of the dry gun-cotton with a fulminating fuse attached. In soft rock it exerts twice, in hard rock five to six times, the energy of gunpowder. It is unaffected by moisture or cold and leaves no deleterious gases when completely exploded. *Glyxoline* is a preparation of gun-cotton pulp and saltpetre saturated with nitro-glycerine.

Nitro-Glycerine, or *Glonoine*, is the most important of all modern explosives. It was discovered in 1847 by Sobrero, but it was not until 1863 that Alfred Nobel brought it into general use as a blasting agent. Its use in the United States was greatly stimulated by its successful introduction at the Hoosac tunnel in Massachusetts in 1866. Three varieties are manufactured, known as mono-, di-, and tri-nitro-glycerine, between which there appears to be no difference in the intensity of the action, but for safety of storage and handling the tri-nitro-glycerine, as manufactured by Prof. George W. Mowbray, of Massachusetts, appears to be unrivalled. "It is a light yellow, clear, oily liquid, odorless, has a pleasant, sweet taste, is poisonous when inhaled, swallowed or introduced into the system through the pores, producing headache and sickness. It has a specific gravity of 1.6 and freezes at about 46° F." When pure it is said not to explode by friction or percussion, but when partially decomposed it is readily fired by a blow, and in such condition should never be stored nor transported in tin canisters, but in open frangible vessels covered with water.

The phenomena of explosion, according to Charles L. Kalmbach, who has had a long and intimate experience with it, can only be effected by any cause producing a temperature of 360° F. Percussive compression, as that produced by a blow from a hammer or pick, or by a bullet or rock fired into or dropped upon it, will invariably produce an explosion accompanied by enormous heat and the liberation of about 12,000 times its volume of gas.

The destruction of the Mosel at Bremerhaven, Jan. 8, 1876, was supposed to have been due to the small chest of nitro-glycerine, which had *congealed*, having been carelessly dropped on the pavement; hence it was inferred that in a frozen state it was exceedingly dangerous. This was only disproven by an effort to carry some fluid cartridges over the Hoosac Mountain in winter, when the sleigh was upset and the contents frozen. The journey was completed in great trepidation when it was discovered that in that condition a primer would not explode them until thawed out. The only absolutely safe rule appears to be "to pack it in non-metallic or frangible vessels, closed if need be, but holding, with the nitro-glycerine, at least an equal bulk of atmospheric air; and to store it when not in transit in perpendicular or flaring-sided open vessels of similar nature covered only by a film of water." Attention to these rules would doubtless have prevented the serious explosion at West Berkely, San Francisco Harbor, on Sunday, Jan. 21, 1883, by which 23 men were killed. The works were in full operation when at 4 P. M. an explosion took place in the packing house, followed a few minutes later by one in the mixing house, whereby eight tons of giant powder were destroyed. A magazine containing 200 tons of powder was fortunately saved, or the wreck of the works would have been complete.

Dynamite.—Numerous compounds of nitro-glycerine exist known under the generic term of *Dynamite* or *Giant Powder*, in which some absorbing material is mixed with the explosive to prevent leakage. For this purpose, silicious marl, tripoli, rotten stone, sawdust, corn-meal, sponge plaster, and "keiselguhr" (an infusorial earth) have been used with various success. Two grades of dynamite are manufactured, designated as No. 1 and No. 2, the first containing 75 per cent. by weight of nitro-glycerine with infusorial earth, and the second 40 per cent. of nitro-glycerine with other substances.

Fulgurite.—A mixture of four parts of corn-meal to six of nitro-glycerine is said to be stronger and more compact than dynamite or dualin. It makes a dough which can be inserted in holes inclined upward, without a cartridge. Being nearly pure starch it yields a large volume of gas; it is very porous and elastic, and consequently safer than pure nitro-glycerine; it freezes at 45° F., when it is practically inexplosive.

Dualin consists of nitro-glycerine, mixed with cellulose, nitro-cellulose, nitro-starch, or nitro-mannite, in various proportions, according to the strength required. Its best form is that containing nitro-cellulose (Schultze's powder) obtained by subjecting woody fibre to the joint action of nitro-sulphuric acid. It is generally prepared from sawdust, is sensitive to heat, cold, and friction, and can readily be exploded when frozen.

Lithofracteur, or *rendrock* (1866), contains nitro-glycerine, 52 per cent.; infusorial silica and sand, 30; carbon, 12; nitrate of soda, 4; and sulphur, 2. It is more sensitive to temperature than dynamite, exploding at 248° F., while that of dynamite is 356, while it is said to be inferior in power (*Trauzl*).

Vulcan powder is a mixture of from 16 to 33 per cent. of nitro-glycerine with mealed gunpowder, and is merely a modification of the general mixtures classed as dynamite No. 2.

Hercules powder consists of a mixture of 77 parts of nitro-glycerine; 20 of magnesium carbonate; 2 of wood pulp, and 1 of sodium nitrate. Numerous other mixtures exist, known as *Neptune*, *Thunderbolt*, *Vigorite*, *Potentia*, *Titan*, *Electric*, etc.

Mica powder is a No. 1 dynamite, in which the "keiselguhr" or sawdust is replaced by finely divided mica scales, which act as a carrier rather than as an absorbent. In this capacity it is found to contain only 52 per cent. of nitro-glycerine, while the keiselguhr will contain 75 per cent.

Of the *picrates*, the potassium and ammonium salts are the only ones that have been much used in explosive preparations; thus *Designolles*' blasting powder is a mixture of potassium nitrate (saltpetre) and potassium picrate, discovered in 1788. It decrepitates with violence when heated to 600°, is very sensitive to friction, and dangerous. Its chief use is as a fulminate rather than an explosive agent.

Brugere powder is a picric compound, in which ammonium picrate is substituted for the potassium salt. It is not liable to accidental explosion from rough handling, but when fired is much more violent than gunpowder.

Explosive gelatine is the latest invention in explosive agents. It is a peculiar kind of gun-cotton, entirely soluble in nitro-glycerine, and forming with it a gummy substance more powerful than nitro-glycerine. The proportions are 93 parts of nitro-glycerine and 7 of soluble gun-cotton. It is insensible to water, and the addition of a small percentage of camphor renders it proof against heavy blows or shocks. It requires a peculiarly powerful primer to insure its explosion. Other compounds may be derived from it. The difficulty of exploding and its great power render it peculiarly valuable as a blasting agent. It is exploded when in a soft state by a service fuse charged with 24 grains of fulminating mercury contained in a copper cap. The results of experiments to determine its strength, made by Gen. H. L. Abbot, U. S. Engineers, show it to be 1.17 stronger than dynamite in a horizontal plane; 1.13 stronger vertically over the charge, and 1.25 stronger under the charge, from which he concludes that for use in subaqueous explosions it is the strongest agent known to modern science. His experiments also disproved the assertion that an increased effect could be obtained by a mixture of several explosives over that produced by an equal weight of the several ingredients taken separately.

Fulminates are salts of fulminic acid. The mercury salt is the only one of practical value. They are easily exploded, and some are exceedingly sensitive. Fulminating mercury explodes violently when forcibly struck, when heated to 367° F., when touched with strong sulphuric or nitric acid, and by sparks from flint, steel, or electricity. When wet it is inexplosive. Its chief use is as a detonating powder in primers, where it is of great value in developing the full effect of high explosives.

The relative strength of explosives may practically be taken as follows: For gunpowder, 1; gun-cotton, from 4 to 6; dynamite, 6; and nitro-glycerine, 8. The distinction should also be made in practice between the slow-burning (explosive) agents used for rending, and the quick or detonating agents used for shattering rock, and their resisting effects. Thus it will always be found that around the crater or base of the *cone of projection* there is a mass which has been more or less disturbed and broken, but not ejected: this is known as the *cone of fracture*. The relation between these cones is a function of the material operated upon, the position and strength of the charge and other minor quantities. As the very high explosives throw more and loosen less than those of less intensity, these cones will be more nearly coincident in the first case than in the second. The general polar equations for the radii of the corresponding spheres of projection and rupture may be represented by $R = R_m \sqrt{\sin a}$ and $\rho = \rho_m \sqrt{\sin \beta}$ in which R and $\rho =$ the slant-heights of the cones or radii of the spheres; R_m and ρ_m the radii of the spheres of projection and rupture for a given medium and charge just sufficient to reach the surface, or to disturb a single central element, and a and β are the angles between the elements of the cones and their bases. The cone of fracture attains its *greatest volume* when $\beta = 48° 11' 23''$, but the crater, or base, will be the largest when $\beta = 35° 15' 30''$. To determine the charge for a cone of fracture for a given explosive and medium, we have only to determine experimentally the radius of the cone of rupture (r) produced by a given charge C, and substitute these values in the formula $C' = \dfrac{C}{r^3} r'^3$ in which C' is the desired charge, and r and r' the radii of the corresponding cones of rupture. The quantity $\dfrac{C}{r^3}$ is called the charge co-efficient and may be represented by K. If we represent that of any other explosive by K' and call W and W' the corresponding fracture values, and P and P' the market prices per unit of weight, then $\dfrac{K}{K'} = \dfrac{W}{W'}$ and if $\dfrac{W'}{W}$ is greater than $\dfrac{P'}{P}$ then the explosive whose price is P' should be selected in preference to that whose price is P. (*Höffer on Theory of Blasting*.) (L. M. H.)

EX POST FACTO LAW. A law whereby an act is declared a crime and made punishable as such, though it was not a crime when done; or whereby the act, if a crime, is aggravated in enormity or punishment; or whereby different or less evidence is required to convict the offender than was required when the act was committed.

By the Constitution of the United States (Art. I, sect. 9, ¿ 3) Congress is forbidden to pass any *ex post facto law*, and a like prohibition is imposed upon the legislatures of the various States (Art. I., sect. 10, ¿ 1). Like clauses occur in many of the State constitutions.

The phrase "*ex post facto law*" was in common use among lawyers and legislators long prior to the American Revolution. Hence it had acquired a distinct technical meaning quite separate and apart from that which it apparently possessed. It was very early decided that the intention of the framers of the Constitution was to apply the phrase to acts of a criminal nature merely, and such has been the construction since uniformly put upon it.

It must be carefully observed, however, that it is not essential in order to render a law invalid as *ex post facto* that it should expressly assume the action to which it relates to be criminal or provide for its punishment on that ground. Any law which subjects an individual to a pecuniary penalty for an act done which, when done, involved no such responsibility, or any law which deprives any party of any valuable right for acts which were innocent, or at least not punishable when the offence was committed, is *ex post facto* in the constitutional sense, notwithstanding it does not in terms declare the acts to which the penalty is attached criminal. A law is not *ex post facto* which merely alters the method of procedure with relation to crimes which have already taken place. The legislature may, therefore, wholly alter the constitution of a court before which a criminal is to be tried subsequent to the commission of the offence. It may also authorize amendments of indictments to a greater extent than before, and preclude the defendant from taking advantage of immaterial variances on the trial. It may authorize a change of venue, confer upon the government additional challenges, diminish the number of the prisoner's peremptory challenges, and modify, simplify, or reduce the essential parts of the indictment, provided the offence remain distinctly the same.

By far the most difficult question connected with this subject is, What is such an increase in the punishment for a past offence as to render the law enacting such increase void as an *ex post facto* law? No definite rule can be laid down which will apply in all cases, the matter depending to a great degree upon the sound discretion of the court. In Illinois the substitution of imprisonment in the penitentiary for a term not exceeding seven years, in place of a whipping not exceeding one hundred stripes, has been held not to be an increase of the punishment; and a law making such alteration was accordingly held applicable to an offence consummated prior to its passage. In Texas it has been held that the substitution of stripes for the death penalty was an increase in the punishment, while in South Carolina a directly contrary conclusion has been reached. In New York a law prefixing a year of hard labor in the State penitentiary to every sentence of capital punishment has been held an increase in the punishment, and therefore as applied to offences prior to its passage *ex post facto*, and this though the act was evidently designed for the benefit of parties convicted, and, among other things, to enable advantage to be taken for their benefit of any circumstances coming to light which might show the injustice of the judgment, or throw any more favorable light on the action of the accused. This decision has been several times since followed in New York, and it may now be regarded as the settled law of that State that any law changing the punishment for offences committed before its passage is *ex post facto* and void, unless the change consists in the remission of some separable part of the punishment before prescribed, or is referable to prison discipline or penal administration as its primary object. Laws providing for heavier penalties for a second or any subsequent offence than for the first have not been deemed objectionable, on the ground that they authorize a conviction to be taken into account in fixing the penalty which may have taken place before the law was passed. In such case it is the second or subsequent offence that is punished, not the first.

Extradition treaties providing for the surrender of persons charged with offences previously committed are not open to objection as *ex post facto* laws.

(L. L., JR.)

EXPRESS. The express business in America had its origin in the custom among the people of intrusting packages for delivery to travellers, stage-drivers, clerks of vessels, and conductors of trains, and giving them orders to execute. The absence of any systematized method of conducting business of this kind suggested to William F. Harnden, a railway employé in Boston, of talent and energy, the idea of arranging for the carriage of packages by special messenger between the great centres of industry and travel. Being encouraged by others, he contracted in 1838 with the Boston and Worcester Railroad for the carriage of packages over its line. Harnden at this time lived at Boston, and recorded himself as an "express package carrier." In 1839 he arranged with the Providence Road and the New York Steamboat Company to operate over their lines between New York and Boston four times a week. Harnden himself was the messenger, and carried his packages at first in a small hand-bag, afterwards in a stout trunk.

In 1840 Harnden extended his business to Philadelphia; he also established agencies in the great centres of Europe for the carriage of transatlantic packages, the soliciting of emigrants, and the purchase and sale of foreign exchange. In 1841 he extended his business to Albany, and contemplated its introduction throughout the West, but he devoted the greater part of his time and energies to his European enterprises. He seems not fully to have anticipated the possibilities of the inter-state business. He died Jan. 14, 1845.

Harnden's success and enterprise served to incite others to enter the business. Accordingly, Alvin Adams (the originator of the Adams Express Company) in 1841 commenced to operate an express line between New York and Boston. His business was for several years limited to New York, New London, Norwich, Worcester, and Boston. The Adams line slowly extended its business, and in 1861 occupied, through extension and by means of consolidation with local companies, the Southern States, a portion of New England, and the border country between the Northern and Southern States.

The American Express Company originated in Henry Wells, an employé of Harnden, who established a weekly line between Albany and Buffalo in 1841. In 1843 trips were made daily, and a line was opened on the Hudson River. About this time the express business was extended to Cincinnati, St. Louis, Chicago, and Detroit, and intermediate points, to the great convenience and profit of the public. The express carriers were greatly strengthened in their early efforts by the carriage of letters, the excessive rates charged by the government at that time enabling the express lines to do the business at about one-fourth government price with great profit to themselves. The American Express Company established a transatlantic line, with agencies in London and Paris, in 1846. Its lines extend throughout New England and the Northern and Western States and Territories, and included lines in Canada. The United States Express was originated in 1854 for the purpose of doing business over the New York and Erie Railway. It operates in the Middle, Northern, and Western States. The National, operating in Northern New York and Canada, was originated by one of the early operatives of the express business. Thompson & Co. operate the line between Boston, Springfield, and Albany, started in 1841 by Harnden. Wells, Fargo & Co. established in 1852 a line from New York to San Francisco by water, and about this period an overland express from the Missouri River to California. Subsequently, by purchase and extension, they monopolized practically the business of California and the Western Territories. The Southern Express Company was organized at the breaking out of the civil war in 1861 for the purpose of taking charge of the Adams Express business in the South. It has greatly extended and enlarged its business, and occupies the Southern and South-western States. The express business in Canada is largely performed by the Canadian Express Company.

The foregoing is a brief history of the origin and progress of our express system, which has suggested the parcel traffic in Europe. The general management of the express companies is intrusted to a president and a board of directors, under whom the business is directed by division superintendents and other officers, much as the local affairs of railroad companies are conducted. These officers have immediate charge of the servants of the company, regulate their salaries, adjust claims, fix the tariff rates, and perform other important functions. The property of the companies, including the valuables intrusted to them, is under the immediate care of the agents at the various stations, and they are responsible to the companies for its safe custody. The companies employ experts called route agents, whose duty it is to examine the affairs of the agencies and see that their accounts are kept in accordance with the prescribed form, and that they duly account for all moneys coming into their possession. The messenger has immediate charge of the property intrusted to it while it is being transported from the point of shipment to the place of destination. He receipts to the agents for the property they deliver to him at the various stations and exacts a similar receipt for the property turned over to them by him. The expedition with which the business is conducted renders it impossible at the time to methodically compare the articles with the receipts which pass between the different officials of the company. Hence the element of good faith between subordinates assumes an importance that cannot perhaps be found in any other business of equal magnitude. It thus becomes necessary that the greatest care should be exercised in introducing new men into the service. The various blanks employed by the express companies in connection with their business conform generally to those used in connection with the goods traffic of railroads, but with some necessary changes and modifications.

The methods of accounting pursued by express companies differ more or less in form, but the principles observed are the same with all companies.

The express business is the least bulky and relatively the most profitable that is handled by common carriers. It is made up of innumerable items that, while singly of little importance, are yet in the aggregate of great value and of a character that can pay a better price than ordinary freight. The business embraces the carriage and insurance of property and valuables (save baggage for which no special charge is made by the carrier) transported on passenger trains. It also embraces the collection of accounts and the execution of papers, and the carriage of valuable documents and letters. While the express business is still relatively very profitable, it is not now as productive as it was at one time. The introduction of the money-order department in connection with the postal service, whereby the people are able to remit small amounts of money through the mails for a merely nominal fee, with other concessions made by the government, has greatly reduced the demand upon the companies for services of this kind, and necessitated also an immediate and marked reduction in the rates asked for doing such business. The express business has also been greatly undermined by the use of refrigerator cars and the introduction of fast freight trains and other improvements and appliances in the freight department of railroads. The parcels that make up the traffic of our express companies embrace the articles requiring transportation that are too valuable to be intrusted to the comparatively rude appliances of the goods department of carriers. It includes a class of property that requires the constant guardianship of a trustworthy messenger. Much of the business that is done by this department of the service requires quickness of delivery. Especially is this the case with such articles as vegetables and fish and game. The most profitable branch of the express business is comprised in the collection of notes, drafts, and accounts; in the attention given to the execution of deeds, conveyances, and contracts; in the transportation of gold and silver coin, bank-notes, currency, deeds, contracts, bullion, precious stones, jewelry, watches, clocks, gold and silver ware, plated articles, costly pictures, statuary, and other articles of *virtu*; also musical instruments, laces, furs, silks, china, stained glass, birds, valuable animals, delicate fruits, fresh vegetables, and fish. The distribution of newspapers, magazines, and books is conducted largely through the medium of the express business, and yields a handsome income. All the great dailies and many of the weekly papers find their way to interior cities, towns, villages, and hamlets in this way. Promptness is here, also, one of the chief requirements of the service. The conduct of the business, therefore, requires watchfulness upon the part of the carrier, and it involves precision, harmonious action, and efficient service. All these are happily combined in the conduct of the service upon our different lines. In the large cities the carrier provides the facilities, including men and teams, required to traverse the streets from door to door for the purpose of collecting and delivering the goods consigned to his care. Convenient offices that are accessible to the business community are also needed in handling the traffic, and capacious and costly vaults must be at hand in which to store the more valuable articles. Agents, accountants, and laborers, of capacity and tried experience, are also required to transact its business and protect its dépôts, and finally the property while in transit must be accompanied by skilful and trustworthy messengers. The responsibilities attending the handling of the express business are so peculiar and so exceptionally great that there cannot be any wide division of the labor attending its operation. The traffic must in the main be regulated and carried on entirely by officials intrusted with its particular care, and those connected with the transportation service not immediately identified with the express business must be prohibited from attempting to discharge any of its functions or duties, more particularly those embraced in the carriage of valuable packages and the making of collections. The conduct of the express business by companies organized for the purpose is a tacit acknowledgment on the part of other carriers that the former are able to do the business with exceptional economy and efficiency. The measure of success that characterizes the conduct of the express business by separate organizations is, however, directly dependent upon the good-will and co-operation of the companies owning the lines over which they operate; and while the latter cannot perhaps exclude the express lines, still there is nothing that can prevent them from carrying on the business independently if they see fit; and the fact that this is so places the express companies at their mercy. The basis upon which the express companies do business with the railroad companies varies upon different roads according to the extent and character of the business done. Upon the bulk of our roads there is a minimum rate per diem for a stipulated amount of traffic, and when the amount of business it provides for is exceeded, an additional charge is made by the railroad companies. Of the measure of security that the express companies afford the public for the property intrusted to them there can be no question. They not only carry the valuables of the community, including the government, but in many instances those of the owners of the lines over which they operate as well. The principal express companies in the United States touch at all the great commercial centres, and are thus able individually to do most of the business that is offered them without the intervention or co-operation of other organizations. This fact adds greatly to the security and convenience they offer the public, as in the event of loss or damage settlements can be made without reference to other companies.

The basis for the rates charged for handling express matter are speed, distance, quantity, value and character of goods, the space occupied, the nature of the services rendered, and insurance. In determining the rate the value of the property and the speed with which it is transported are more important than any other two factors. The element of speed may be said to be the occasion of the most important differences in rates as between goods carried by passenger trains and those carried by freight trains. In the former case it may be said to operate uniformly upon all classes of goods. In the latter, however, the rate of speed varies according to the urgency or nature of the business, this variation in every case having its influence upon the rate charged by the carrier. In examining the published tariffs of the express companies we find that the rate charged for packages transported a thousand miles is about 25 per cent. less relatively than on packages transported half that distance. Where the goods are exceptionally bulky, or especially liable to damage, or require special attention in transit, a proportionate addition is made to the regular rates. Small packages and isolated shipments are charged greater rates relatively than large packages and regular shipments. The rate for transporting 100 pounds a given distance is usually made the unit, packages weighing more being charged on this basis, while on those weighing less the rates are relatively much higher. No package is taken any distance for less than a minimum sum—usually 25 cents. Having established a grade based on weight for the transportation of merchandise parcels of an average character (which rate may be said to be twice the ordinary rate for goods carried by freight trains), a certain additional charge (serving as insurance) is made on the basis of values when said values exceed a certain amount, say $50. On such articles as looking-glasses, pictures in frames, statuary, plate-glass, show-cases, poultry in coops, and live-stock, exceptionally high rates are charged. In making rates on money and valuable papers the charge is based primarily on the declared value of the same. Distance is also considered, but not to the same extent as in making rates on ordinary parcels. In practice the rate for transporting $1000 in currency is made the unit, sums over this amount being charged on this basis; on smaller sums an arbitrary rate is made which is proportionately higher, but is modified to meet somewhat the very low rates made by the government on postal money-orders and registered letters. The transportation of gold and silver brings a material element of weight into the problem. An additional rate per thousand dollars or fraction thereof as compared with currency is therefore made. The addition for gold is about 25 per cent., and for silver 50 per cent. Papers, the value of which is only nominal, or which can be replaced in case of loss, are usually charged only a fraction of the rate for currency and papers having intrinsic value. When papers are received for collection a fraction of the currency rate is charged for carrying the papers and making the collection, and full currency rates for returning the money. When, however, the papers taken for collection have a specific value, for which the carrier would be liable in case of loss, such as bonds and coupons, full currency rates are charged both ways. Where goods are sent to be collected for on delivery, the regular rates are usually charged for the transportation of the property and for the return of the money.

(M. M. K.)

EXTRADITION of criminals is now generally conceded to be dependent almost exclusively upon treaty regulations. Treaties on the subject exist between the United States and many other nations, including the following: Great Britain, Austria, France, Sweden and Norway, Germany, Italy, Switzerland, Mexico, Venezuela, and Belgium. The crimes for which extradition is usually granted are: Forgery, burglary, bigamy, embezzlement, counterfeiting, grand larceny, manslaughter and murder, perjury, rape, and other offences amounting to a felony. But different treaties specify different offences, and there is no uniform law of extradition applicable to all nations. Political offences are excluded from the category of extraditable offences, except in rare instances and under special conventions, and the exception occurs only when the offence partakes largely of the purely criminal character. Much discussion has arisen in recent times in regard to the *status* of the accused after answering the charge in the country to which he has been extradited. There is great diversity of opinion and practice as to whether the accused can be tried for any offence except that specified in the demand for extradition. The principle which is gradually becoming established is that the person surrendered cannot be prosecuted or punished for any offence not mentioned in the demand. Treaties between France and several other countries expressly affirm the doctrine that the person extradited can in no case be prosecuted for a political offence. The treaty between the United States and Italy recognizes the principle that the prosecution should be limited to the offences comprised in the demand.

See Vol. VIII. p. 711 Am. ed. (p. 813 Edin. ed.).

(A. P. S.)

EXTRA-TERRITORIALITY. See TERRITORY.

EYE, JOHANN LUDOLF AUGUST VON, a German art historian, was born at Fürstenau, in Hanover, May 24, 1825. He was educated at the gymnasium in Osnaburg and at the University of Göttingen, where he studied jurisprudence, philosophy, and history. He was a tutor in various parts of Germany, and in 1853 he was appointed director of the collection of art and antiquities in the newly-founded German museum at Nuremberg. Here, in company with J. Falke, he published the illustrated works, *Kunst und Leben der Vorzeit* (3 vols., 1854; 3d ed., 1868); *Galerie der Meisterwerke alt-deutscher Holzschneidekunst* (1857). He also published *Deutschland vor drei hundert Jahren in Leben und Kunst* (1857); *Leben und Wirken Albrecht Dürers* (1860); *Eine Menschenseele, Spiegelbild aus dem 18 Jahrhundert* (1863); *Wesen und Werth des Daseins* (1870). In 1874 he accepted a professorship in Rio Janeiro, but in the following year he was summoned by the Saxon government to take charge of the museum of the newly-founded art school in Dresden. While holding this position he published his long-meditated work, *Das Reich des Schönen* (Berlin, 1878), in which the whole system of æsthetics is treated in the inductive method. In 1881 Prof. von Eye returned to Brazil.

EYRE, EDWARD JOHN, an English colonial governor, was born in August, 1815. His father, Rev. Anthony William Eyre, was vicar of Hornsey, in Yorkshire; and the son, at the age of 17, went to Australia as a settler. Arriving at Sydney in 1833 he engaged in sheep-farming and the transportation of cattle. After some preliminary journeys, he undertook to explore the barren south coast of Australia from 134° to 118° E. long. On June 20, 1840, he started on an expedition to explore the region north of Lake Torrens. After suffering dreadful hardships, and having been given up as lost, his party reached Albany, in West Australia, July 7, 1841. A large lake which he discovered, but supposed to be part of Lake Torrens, has since been named Lake Eyre. He was, in 1841, made a resident magistrate, with special power to protect the aborigines. In 1845 he returned to England, and published his *Discoveries in Central Australia*, in which he calls special attention to the condition and needs of the natives. For these discoveries the gold medal of the Royal Geographical Society was awarded to him. In 1846 he was appointed by Earl Grey lieutenant-governor of New Zealand, with special charge of the administration of the Middle Island. In April, 1853, he returned to England, and in 1854 he was appointed lieutenant-governor of the island of St. Vincent, West Indies, and in 1859 was transferred to administer the government of Antigua and the Leeward Islands, but in 1860 he returned to England to recruit. In the spring of 1862 the duke of Newcastle commissioned him to administer the government of Jamaica; and July 15, 1864, he was appointed captain-general and governor-in-chief of that island. Its affairs had been in bad condition for many years, and were growing worse; and in October, 1865, a serious rebellion broke out at Morant's Bay, in which many Europeans were massacred. It spread rapidly over a large tract of country, and Gov. Eyre promptly proclaimed martial law. In addition to other severe measures of repression, George William Gordon, a mulatto of considerable wealth and influence, was tried by court-martial, condemned, and executed. While Gov. Eyre had succeeded in crushing the rebellion, the report of his arbitrary acts excited a fierce agitation in England. The government sent a commission of inquiry to Jamaica, which in June, 1866, exonerated him from the charges, and declared that the rebellion was put down by his "skill, promptitude, and vigor." He was, however, recalled from his post, and his opponents determined to prosecute him and some of his subordinates. Large sums were raised for the purpose, while his friends rallied to his defence. In the public discussion of the case, Carlyle was conspicuous for his support of Eyre and his denunciation of the negro and his friends. The local magistrates refused to commit Mr. Eyre on a charge of murder, and other proceedings which were instituted against him failed. He is now living at Steeple Aston, Oxfordshire, in receipt of a pension.

F.

FACTORY. The factory system of manufacture means the production of goods from the raw material by consecutive processes carried on as a harmonious whole, and necessitates the congregation of labor in large works in order to secure the combined operation of many orders of workpeople in tending a series of productive machines impelled by a central power. According to Dr. Ure (*Philosophy of Manufactures*, p. 13) the factory involves in its strictest sense the idea of a vast automaton, composed of various mechanical and intellectual organs, acting in an uninterrupted concert for the production of a common object, all of them being subordinated to a self-regulated moving force.

At the close of the American Revolution the domestic system of manufactures prevailed in this country. The results of the great inventions which had revolutionized labor in England had not reached across the Atlantic; in fact the legislation of England forbade the exportation of either machinery, models, or plans of machinery. These inventions, which related to spinning yarn, had been made by Hargreaves and Arkwright in 1767-9, and marked the inauguration of the regime of machinery and of the factory system of labor. The inventions of the spinning-frame, the spinning-jenny, and subsequently of the mule-spinning machine, could not of themselves have created a sudden and radical change in the existing system of labor; but the extension of the canal system of transportation, the improvements in the steam-engine, the release of capital caused by the suppression of the slave-trade, and the opening of the war with the colonies, the influence of Adam Smith's works on political economy—all these mechanical, political, and moral forces combined, made possible the rapid change in England from the domestic to the factory system of labor.

At the close of the war the States of the Union found themselves in want of fabrics, and the British manufacturers readily and rapidly supplied this market as soon as the American ports were opened. The power-loom, invented in England soon after, brought the completion of a series of inventions, which, for positive influence upon the politics and civilization of the world, must stand beside that of printing with movable types. When the people of the States saw that the treaty of Paris had not brought industrial independence to the United States their patriotism took a new form, and associations were formed, the members of which pledged themselves to use and to wear only domestic productions, and the State legislatures were besought to protect home manufactures. The Constitution of the United States, adopted in 1789, gave Congress the power to legislate on commercial affairs. This Constitution was really the outcome of the industrial necessities of the people, because it was on account of the difficulties and irritations growing out of the various commercial regulations of the several States that a convention of commissioners from five States was held at Annapolis in September, 1786, which convention recommended in turn the one that framed the present Constitution.

The non-importation resolves of the Continental Congress and the war itself had thrown the colonists upon their own resources, and had really laid the foundation of American manufactures. During the war some industries had failed, owing to the scarcity and high price of labor, while those whose products were called for by the necessities of the war were greatly stimulated; household industries became profitable, and were greatly extended. With peace came a reaction, and the temporary success engendered by the war gave place to a general depression, which was aggravated by the flooding of our markets with immense importations of the products of British workshops. This condition of affairs, the desire of the people to become independent of the mother country industrially as well as politically, and the appeals from the merchants and manufacturers for commercial restrictions upon imports, caused the first Congress which assembled under the new Constitution to turn its attention to the protection of manufactures, and its second act (passed July 4, 1789) was "for laying a duty on goods, wares, and merchandise imported into the United States." Patriotism and statute law thus paved the way for the importation of the factory system of labor; its institution here, as well as in England, was the result of both moral and economical influences.

The honor of the introduction of power-spinning machines in this country, and of their early use here, is shared by the States of Massachusetts and Rhode Island; for while the first-named State claims the first experiments in embodying the principles of Arkwright's inventions and the first cotton factory in America, Rhode Island claims the first factory in which perfected machinery, after the English models, was practically employed. This was the factory built by Samuel Slater in 1790. From that date progress in the establishment of the factory system of manufactures in America was uninterrupted, save by temporary causes. The invention of the power-loom, however, really gave the completing characteristic to the factory system. Francis Lowell, at Waltham, Mass., was the first man in the world, so far as record shows, to carry the raw material through all the manipulations and processes necessary to produce finished goods in one factory, and by one complete series of processes. (See Article COTTON, Chapter IV.)

The inauguration of the factory system in the United States was some fifteen years later than its birth in England; but the extension of the system here has been far more rapid, and its application has embraced many more industries than in the mother country. For many years the system embraced only textile manufactures, but as parties engaged in other branches saw the wonderful results of systematic labor by its division, they gradually adopted the factory system, until now, of nearly 3,000,000 people employed in the mechanical industries of the United States, at least four-fifths are working under the factory system; indeed, the statistics of the industries of the country are the statistics of that system. It is quite impossible to estimate accurately the number of persons the old individual system would require to produce the goods made by the present factory workers, but careful computations in some branches of work indicate that each factory employé in 1884 represents at least 100 workmen under the former system. Hence it would require 300,000,000 working under the old domestic system to produce the goods made by the 3,000,000 factory-workers of the United States.

The last quarter of a century has witnessed wonderful instances of the adoption of the factory system. The little shoe-shop has disappeared, and the shoe-factory has taken its place. The expensive hand-made watches, which only the few could buy, have been replaced by the better article, the product of the factory, which the many can afford. Pianos, house-organs, tapestry-carpets, in fact nearly all the articles which the rich only could enjoy, are now enjoyed by the masses, because they are produced under the factory system. Even the slaughtering of hogs is now accomplished under the system of consecutive processes, and dairy products now issue from the factory.

The rapid extension of the factory system, absorbing as it does small enterprises, and crushing out the ideal domestic system of labor, has not been accomplished without great social changes affecting the morals as well as the politics and the legislation of the countries in which it has been established. No one disputes the economic advantages of the modern system; few admit that it is a moral force in the actual progress of civilization, yet the system is and has been an active element in the upbuilding of the character of the people involved in the changes inaugurated by it.

A superficial study of the system usually reveals what appear to be great evils, and the result is an indictment of the system under various counts, among which will be found the following: (1) that the factory system necessitates the employment of women and children to an injurious extent; (2) that consequently its tendency is to destroy family ties and domestic habits, and ultimately the home; (3) that it is promotive of intemperance, unthrift, and poverty; (4) that it feeds prostitution and swells the criminal lists; (5) that it tends to intellectual degeneracy; (6) that factory employments are injurious to health. These are the leading disadvantages which many honestly believe to belong naturally to and to be inseparable from the system. The rise of a factory village is therefore contemplated with the same feelings that would follow the breaking out of a plague-spot.

While many disadvantages appear to attend the system, a careful study shows that they do not necessarily belong to it; that so-called factory evils cannot be attributed to the factory, but that existing evils may be congregated or brought to light by it. Whether the system inaugurates evils, or brings them out in the processes of the development of society, can be best understood by judging of the system in comparison with the separate or individual system which preceded it. To this end we will examine the separate items of alleged disadvantages already enumerated.

As to the assumption that the factory tends to destroy domestic ties and habits, it may be said that this charge against the factory grows out of another assumption: that the cottage of the domestic worker was the ideal home. It is poetry which calls such home a cottage; history rather calls it a hut. The home of the worker of old was the workshop also, and the wheels or looms disputed with the inmates for the room. Small, close, crowded, with bad air and bad surroundings, the hut was occupied day and night by a class which cannot find its kin under the factory system, for the operative of to-day, as a rule, occupies a home, even in the factory tenement or boarding-house, superior in every sense to the home of the domestic worker. The morals in all respects under the individual system were greatly below those of the factory operatives of to-day. The evils which became apparent during the early days of the factory system were simply the results of bringing together the labor which had become pauperized under the domestic system and in agricultural districts. The employment of children which so excited the philanthropists sixty years ago, while bad enough in itself, and while attended with many features which brought merited condemnation, really placed the children employed in a much better position than they occupied before, because it made them self-supporting. The congregation of bad elements under the new system enabled humane men to insist upon legislation which should correct evils.

The wrongs which accompanied the inauguration of the system never existed to such extent in this country as they did in England. But the home in the United States suffered more from the system than it did in England, for the reason that the factory there found a population ready to become factory workers, while here it was necessary to provide for a new population, and this gave rise to the tenement house and the factory boarding-house, two features of factory life quite unknown in England. Yet here the individual home is increasing in its influence in factory centres, for it is gradually taking the place of the tenement and boarding-house. With this growth there is a gradual decrease in the employment of married women in factories. In Massachusetts—a factory State—the married women employed in cotton-factories constitute but about 8 per cent. of the whole number of women so employed. The statistics in this direction are not available for other sections of the country. The employment of young children is now forbidden by law wherever the factory has gained a strong foothold. The factory has not so much destroyed the home as it has enabled members of broken families to earn a livelihood. If it has at times taken the mother from the care of her young children—the worst feature of the employment of married women—it has enabled more who had no home to become self-supporting.

Theft of material, drunkenness, laziness, and a state of morals now largely outgrown even by the lowest were accompaniments of the "ideal system" of labor. The worst factory was light and airy compared with the hand-weavers' huts. And yet the transition from the old to the new system brought the same untold misery which every step in the progress of society brings, even when slaves are made freemen. The employment of women and children, except married women during and after pregnancy, is no longer an evil, thanks to machinery and wise legislation, and so the better home is more generally coming to have a higher influence. More than has been might still be done in this direction, but it is satisfactory to know that manufacturers are more keenly alive at the present time than ever before to the absolute benefits, both moral and economical, which accrue from happy conditions. Admitting all possible domestic evils which accompany low social conditions—the neglect of young children, and consequent high rates of infant mortality, the physical degeneracy which follows mechanical employments when engaged in by married women—and yet none of these can be attributed to the factory system as the creator of such evils. They belong to the ignorance of the substratum of society which the factory system is constantly lifting to another and a higher plane, and thereby lessening instead of increasing the misery of the world. We are deceived because the factory, by and through the perfection of machinery and the development of the division of labor, is constantly employing a less and less cultivated class of operatives. We remember the farmers' daughters of a generation ago as constituting the factory population of Lowell and other towns, and contrast them with the present operatives, and are too apt to conclude that the factory degrades, when the fact is it has enabled the lower order to step up in the scale of employment, in living, and consequently in civilization. This process is constantly narrowing the limits of the class which occupies the lowest step in the progress of society. This mission alone stamps the factory system as an active element in the moral elevation of the race. Of course we speak of the factory under men who realize that they have some responsibility beyond declaring dividends. A narrow-minded, close-fisted employer, who regards his people as his machines, taking no pains relative to their moral well-being, never recognizing that by congregating labor for his own profit he owes it something besides wages, such an employer will have a factory which will convince any community that it is not an element in civilization. The man should be condemned, not the system.

If it could be shown that the factory leads to intemperate habits, it would follow conclusively that it is productive of unthrift and poverty—the sure conditions resulting from intemperance. It is true that a great deal of drunkenness exists in factory towns and among factory operatives; it is not true that the factory is the creator of this. On the other hand, the investigations of Louis Reybaud, a member of the institute of France, prove conclusively that the factory operatives are far more temperate than those engaged under the domestic system. The industries of France afford the very best opportunities for comparative study in this respect. In the United States drunkenness has never been much of an obstacle in the way of the success of the factory. Factory towns support a large number of common laborers, and the intemperance of this class is usually attributed to the factory. It must be frankly and freely admitted that whatever of unthrift there may be among factory operatives is to a very large degree due to the habit of beer-drinking; but employers, overseers, and even the operatives themselves, are creating a sentiment which does not allow a habitual drunkard to remain in a factory. This sentiment is on the increase, and, as soon as proprietors will shut their doors to all drunkards, the factory will become a most powerful agent for the prevention of intemperance. Its power in this direction is now far greater than is generally known.

The charge that the factory feeds prostitution and swells the criminal lists is absolutely unfounded. This impression first grew from the condition of Manchester, England, where a large cellarage population, which has entirely disappeared, was attributed to the factory. It has been shown by the returns from the penitentiary of Manchester that the ranks of prostitution were not fed from the factory, 8 only out of 50 coming from the factory, and 29 out of 50 from domestic service. An extensive examination of the criminal records of a large number of British factory towns discloses the fact that neither the ranks of prostitution nor the criminal lists are increased to such extent from a factory population of these towns as from other classes. This is equally true in this country. It should be borne in mind that regular employment is conducive to regular living, and that regular employment does not harmonize with a life of prostitution, intemperance, and crime. The virtue of the factory women of this country and of Europe will compare favorably with that of any other class, and much better than with many departments of social life. Certainly there is nothing in factory employment conducive to vicious lives.

The impression that the factory tends to intellectual degeneracy is a greater fallacy than the preceding. Through the simplification of mechanical process ignorant labor is congregated in factory centres, but as we have said, it is not created nor induced by the factory. The fact that ignorant masses are enabled by the factory to engage in what it once had skilled labor to perform has given the widespread impression that the factory has degraded the skill, when the truth is, it has lifted the unskilled; and this is the inevitable result of the factory everywhere. It is a curious fact that after the factory system was inaugurated in England, and the poor, degraded and excessively ignorant pauper labor of the southern agricultural districts were lifted up to respectable and self-supporting employment, and to comparative self-respect, the factory was held to be responsible for the ignorance which it found; and so the laws of England and America have insisted upon the education of children as a prerequisite to factory employment. This may explain the superior intelligence of the children of factory towns in England as compared with those of agricultural localities. The half-times of England and the factory children of America are laying a foundation, if proprietors will only recognize the power of moral forces in the conduct of individual enterprises, which will, in another quarter of a century, change the social complexion of our factory towns. If the advantages afforded in factory towns will stimulate rural districts to emulate the work of providing for the proper amusement and instruction of their children and young people, perhaps the constant depletion of such places may be checked and the inhabitants of crowded towns attracted to the soil. The mental friction of the factory is not without its healthful influences. Certainly it is better for the persons engaged than the filthy little shop, occupied by a few foul-talking people, which characterized the

14 weeks during the year preceding; the employer to a certificate of such school attendance. Eight hours titute a legal day's work, except for farm and domestic t, but overwork for extra compensation is permitted.

Jersey.—No child under 10 years of age shall be tted to work in any factory, and no minor shall be n or required to work more than ten hours on any day, xty hours in any week. The penalty for violation of latter provision is $50. Ten hours per day constitute al day's work in all cotton, woollen, silk, paper, glass, flax factories, and in manufactories of iron and brass.

nsylvania.—Eight hours constitute a legal day's work bsence of special contract, except for farm labor and r by the year, month, or week. Ten hours constitute al day's work in cotton, woollen, silk, paper, bagging, flax factories. No minor under 13 shall be employed ny such factory, under penalty of $50. No child be- n 13 and 16 years of age shall be employed more than months in any one year, who shall not have attended ol at least three consecutive months in the same year. ainor shall by any contract be employed in any of said ries for more than sixty hours per week or an average a hours per day; penalty for violation of this provision o exceed $50.

ctories in which employés are at work in the third or er stories must have permanent external fire-escapes, factory to the fire commissioners and fire marshal of listrict.

aryland.—The law prohibits the employment of chil- under 16 years of age in factories for more than ten s per day, under penalty not exceeding $50. .

ho.—No child under 14 shall be employed in mills or s during school-hours, unless he has received at least ve weeks' schooling during the year preceding, and loyers must have a certificate to that effect. Two weeks dance at a half-time or night-school is to be considered valent to one week at a day-school.

hoever compels a woman or a child under 18, or permits ild under 14, to labor in a mechanical or manufacturing ess more than ten hours per day, may be fined from $50.

(C. D. W.)

AED, JOHN, a Scotch painter, was born at Burlay l, in the stewartry of Kirkcudbright, in 1820. He the son of a millwright and in early boyhood ved a decided taste for art. In 1841 he removed Edinburgh, where his talent was soon recognised he was chosen an associate of the Royal Scottish demy. Among his early pictures are The Cotter's urday Night (1851), The Household Gods in Dan- (1856), The Scottish Justiciary (1857). He began hibit at the Royal Academy, London, in 1861, ling in that year Queen Margaret Refusing to De- the Keys. In 1862 he removed to London, where as since resided, though he exhibits also in Edin- h. His later pictures include The Gamekeeper's ghter (1871), The Hiring Fair (1871), The Morn- before Flodden (1874), Blenheim (1875), Gold- h in his Study (1877), The Old Basket-Maker 8). He is most successful in domestic and rural es of a cheerful character. His popularity has increased by the excellent engraving of some of paintings by his brother James.

AED, THOMAS, a Scotch painter, brother of the eding, was born at Burlay Mill, in 1826. He was wise early drawn to art and in 1843 was invited to burgh by his brother John, who was then rising notice. In 1849 Thomas exhibited his well-known ting of Sir Walter Scott and his Friends at Abbotts- which secured his admission as an associate of he Royal Academy, London, and in the next year oved to that city. Among his paintings executed at this time are Burns and Highland Mary (1852), The Patron's Visit to the School (1852), Morning— Reapers Going out (1854), and above all The Mither- less Bairn (1855), which still continues the unsur- passed type of his best works, though he has added a long series of pathetic pictures of Scotch domestic life and has occasionally ventured into other fields. It has been truly said that Thomas Faed has done for Scottish art what Burns did for Scottish song; he has made it attract universal interest and command universal respect. His pictures are generally elabor- ate in detail and full of sentiment which can be appre- ciated by all classes. They may sometimes be criticised as aiming at too much, as intended to tell a story rather than allowed to depend for their success on the strictly limited resources of the painter's art. Within his own field, the vivid delineation of Scotch humble life, Faed is unsurpassed.

FAIDHERBE, LOUIS LÉON CÉSAR, a French general, statesman, and archæologist, was born at Lille, June 3, 1818. He studied at the Ecole poly- technique in 1838, passing to Metz in 1840, and served as a military engineer in Algeria and the West Indies. In 1852 he went to Senegal, of which he was made governor in 1854. In 1863 he was promoted to be general of brigade, and in 1865 he was recalled to France at his own request. From 1867 to 1870 he had command of Bona in Algeria. When M. Gambetta was reorganizing the armies, Gen. Faidherbe offered his services, and in November, 1870, was appointed general of division and commander-in-chief of the Army of the North. A month later he fought the battle of Pont-Noyelles, and thus relieved Havre from siege. After movements in various directions he was compelled to retire towards Cambrai, where he re- mained with his army till after the signing of the armistice. He was elected to the national assembly in February, 1871, and again in July as a Republican, but soon resigned. He was afterwards sent on a scientific expedition to Upper Egypt, where he studied the Libyan monuments and inscriptions, which form the subject of some of his publications. For several years he was counsellor-general of the North for the canton of Lille, and in January, 1879, he was elected to the senate, though, on account of his infirm health, he was carried there in a reclining chair. He is grand- chancellor of the Legion of Honor. Gen. Faidherbe has published several works, some relating to his mili- tary career and the countries he has governed, and others on linguistic and archæological topics.

FAIR. See INDUSTRIAL EXHIBITIONS.

FAIRBAIRN, PATRICK (1805–1874), a Scotch divine, was born at Greenlaw, Berwickshire, Jan. 10, 1805. He graduated at the University of Edin- burgh, held several pastoral charges, and was made professor at Aberdeen University. In 1856 he was called to be principal of the Free Church Theological College at Glasgow, with the professorship of sys- tematic theology and New Testament exegesis. He died at Glasgow Aug. 6, 1874. His works are valu- able contributions to theological literature. They comprise *Typology of Scripture* (1847; 6th ed. 1880); *Ezekiel* (1851; 4th ed. 1876); *Prophecy* (1856; 2d ed. 1866); *Hermeneutical Manual* (1858); *Pastoral Epis- tles* (1874); *Pastoral Theology* (1875). He also edited *The Imperial Bible Dictionary* (1867).

FAIRBANKS, ERASTUS (1792–1864), an Ameri- can governor, was born at Brimfield, Mass., Oct. 28, 1792. He had a common school education and at the age of twenty settled in St. Johnsbury, Vt. In 1825 he formed a partnership with his brother Thaddeus, who in 1830 invented an improved scale for weighing heavy bodies. This platform scale, patented in 1831 and intended chiefly as a hay scale, was gradually improved, and its sale spread so widely that the whole town of St. Johnsbury shared in the resulting prosperity of its manufacturers. In 1836 Erastus was elected to the legislature, and in 1852 and 1860 he was chosen governor of Vermont, but served without salary. He showed great energy in raising troops for the Union army. He was remarkable for his piety and culture as well as for his diligence and business success. He died at St. Johnsbury, Vt., Nov. 20, 1864.

FAIRCHILD, LUCIUS, an American general, was born at Franklin Mills, Ohio, Dec. 27, 1831. He settled in Iowa and in June, 1861, became lieutenant-colonel of the Second Iowa infantry. In August he was made brigadier-general of volunteers. He served in Virginia under McClellan and Pope. On leaving the army he settled in Wisconsin, where he was elected secretary of state in 1864. He was governor of Wisconsin 1866–70, and was afterwards consul at Liverpool.

FAIRFAX FAMILY. Henry Fairfax of Tolston, the ancestor of the American Fairfaxes, was the second son of Henry, fourth Lord Fairfax. William Fairfax, the second son of Henry of Tolston, was the first of the family that came to America, where he arrived in 1717. He was collector of the customs at Salem, Mass., in 1725. In 1734 he removed to Virginia as agent of his cousin Thomas, the sixth Lord Fairfax, and built Belvoir on the Potomac, about two miles from Mt. Vernon, on the opposite side of the river. He was lord-lieutenant of Fairfax county, collector of South Potomac, and president of the council of Virginia. His eldest son, George William Fairfax of Belvoir in Virginia and Tolston in Yorkshire, was born in the Bahamas in 1724, and married in 1748 Sarah, daughter of Col. Wilson Cary of Ceeleys, near Hampton, Va. George William was the companion of Washington on his first surveying-tour, employed by Lord Fairfax of Greenway Court. He inherited Tolston from his uncle Henry, and went to England in 1773, passing in the Thames, on its way to America, the tea which caused the Revolution. When the American war broke out he received no more remittances, and was obliged to sell Tolston. He died at Bath, April 3, 1787, leaving his estates to his nephew, Ferdinando.

Thomas, the sixth Lord Fairfax, was born in 1690. Educated at Oxford, he possessed a cultivated literary taste, contributed to the *Spectator*, and was a man of wit and fashion; his bow was the most elegant at the court of Queen Anne, and he was one of the brightest ornaments of the famous Kit-Kat Club. He inherited from his mother, who was the daughter of Lord Culpeper, governor of Virginia between 1680–83, immense estates in that province, amounting in all to about 6,000,000 acres of land. A cruel disappointment in love drove him from the brilliant scenes where he had shone so long, and he sought in the wilds of Virginia a refuge for his wounded heart. He established himself at Greenway Court, near where Winchester now stands, and passed the last thirty-five years of his life in hunting, fishing, and out-door amusements.

Brian Fairfax, of Mt. Eagle in Virginia, the eldest son of William of Belvoir by his second wife, Deborah Clarke, was born in 1737. In 1759 he married Elizabeth, daughter of Col. Wilson Cary. His wife died in 1788, and he then entered holy orders. He was the rector of Christ Church in Alexandria, where Washington had a pew, and at the funeral of the latter he was the chief mourner. After the death of Lord Fairfax of Greenway Court and his brother Robert, the seventh Lord Fairfax, Rev. Brian Fairfax went to England and was recognized in May, 1800, by the House of Lords as the eighth Lord Fairfax, but he never assumed the title. He returned to America and died at Mt. Eagle in August, 1802. He was succeeded by his eldest son, Thomas Fairfax of Vaudus, a beautiful seat about three miles from Alexandria. It was situated in the midst of a park of grand old oaks, all of which were destroyed during the Civil War. Thomas Fairfax was born in 1762, and spent his life in superintending his paternal estates on the Potomac, and in exercising a genuine old Virginia hospitality. The family title is still vested in the American Fairfaxes, the tenth Baron Fairfax being John Contee Fairfax of Northampton, Prince George co., Md.

FAIR OAKS, a place in Henrico co., Va., seven miles E. of Richmond, having a station on the Richmond and York River Railroad. Here a battle was fought, May 31 and June 1, 1862, between Gen. G. B. McClellan's army, which had advanced from Yorktown, and a Confederate force under Gen. J. E. Johnston. The left wing of the former, comprising the corps under Gens. E. D. Keyes and S. Heintzelman, had crossed the Chickahominy about a week earlier. The creek here flowed through a heavily timbered swamp, which was a serious obstruction to the passage of artillery. Bottom's Bridge was the only practical means of communication between the right wing, which stretched for twenty miles on the east bank. Johnston on May 30 ordered an attack to be made the next day at dawn on Keyes' corps, which was six miles from the bridge. But a heavy rain prevented this plan from being executed. After 1 P. M. Gen. D. H. Hill came upon some troops of the other Union corps and compelled them to retire within their intrenchments. The firing attracted McClellan's attention, and he ordered Gen. Sumner to cross to Heintzelman's relief. Meantime the Union Gen. Couch had joined in the fight, and though separated from the main part of his own division determined to hold his position near Fair Oaks. At 4 P. M. Sumner came to his relief and endeavored to open up communication with Heintzelman. The Confederate charges were repulsed, and late in the day Gen. Johnston being wounded his command devolved on Gen. G. W. Smith. The Union troops under Hooker and some batteries of Sedgwick's division came up, but the divisions of Franklin and Porter 35,000 men in all, were allowed to remain on the east side throughout the next day. With dawn on June 1, the Confederates renewed the attack, chiefly on Richardson's division, but after an hour's fighting fell back. Meantime Hooker and Sickles had come into position to assist Richardson, who then charged with the bayonet. The Confederates retreated in confusion to Richmond, and the Union troops regained all they had lost on May 30. Their advanced pickets were within five miles of Richmond, and had Gen. McClellan ordered up his troops, which had not yet been engaged, he might readily have entered that city. This alone was wanting to render the victory complete, but the opportunity passed and never returned. The Union loss is officially stated at 890 killed, 3627 wounded, 1222 missing. The Confederate loss is estimated at 6500.

FAITH. This word is used theologically for the form of belief in God and divine things which a man may hold. It is often confined to the philosophical scheme of religion to which he gives an intellectual assent. In this way we speak of the Mohammedan, Buddhist, or Christian faith. It is also used in a more spiritual way for a heart-embrace of God himself, according to the individual conception of God.

In the Christian Scriptures faith is an adherence of the soul to the Lord Jesus Christ, from which union spring all Christian graces. Yet even in the Scriptures the word is used in a more general sense as indicating a firm reliance on God.

The *Rule of Faith* is a phrase expressive of the authoritative guide to the soul in the matter of faith. With some Christians it is the Church, with others the Bible, with others again the Church and Bible united. With Mohammedans it is the Koran. With many it is a priesthood. With many others it is the "inward light" of the conscience.

In the New Testament faith is united to hope and love as forming a trio of graces which abide forever. (1 Cor. xiii. 13.)

Saving Faith is that kind and degree of faith which is necessary to the soul's salvation from sin and eternal death. It is opposed to both an intellectual faith ("the devils believe and tremble," James ii. 19) and a speculative faith.

A *matter of faith* is sometimes contrasted with a matter of practice.

Degrees of faith have regard to the intensity of conviction and corresponding life.

FAITH-CURE is the name given to the doctrine founded on James v. 14, 15, that any one who is diseased may be cured by using the method prescribed in that passage. The holders of the doctrine declare that the passage is not to be confined to the apostolic age, or to the so-called "age of miracles," but is a promise for all time. In practice, however, they do not adhere to all the requirements of the passage. They do not "call for the elders of the church," but go to a *single* elder. Many faith-cure stations have been established in America, and multitudes flock to them, but without such results as have been convincing to the public mind. The believers in the system use prayer and oil-anointing, and forbid any use of medical means.

The objections to the doctrine are (1) that no clear evidence of a cure by this method has been furnished; (2) that it puts aside the use of means approved by God-given reason; and (3) that it asserts the continuance of miraculous power in the church, against which is all the evidence.

A fourth objection might be added, that it makes the matter of the body too prominent above the condition and needs of the soul.

FAITHFULL, EMILY, an English philanthropist, was born at Headley, in Surrey, 1835—the daughter of a clergyman. In early life she left the dissipations of the fashionable world of London, and devoted herself to the task of improving the condition of working-women. She began her labors as a member of the Social Science Association, learned the art of typesetting, and in 1860 established the Victoria Press, a printing-office where women were the only compositors. The publication of a handsome book, called *Victoria Regia*, led to Miss Faithfull's appointment, in 1862, as printer and publisher to the queen. She gave great attention to sanitary questions, and won a high reputation as a lecturer in England, and also in the United States, which she visited in 1872-73, and again in 1883-84. Among her writings are many tracts and pamphlets; *A Reed Shaken with the Wind*, a novel of social life (1873); *Change upon Change* (1868), and other works.

FALCON, a genus of the family *Falconidæ*, or diurnal birds of prey. All the members of the group *Falconinæ*, comprising several genera, are often called falcons, but the true falcons are restricted to the genus Falco. (See Vol. IX. p. 3 Am. ed. (p. 1 Edin. ed.).) Of these there are more than 50 species, whose distinguishing feature is a strong, projecting tooth, behind a notch in the edge of the upper mandible. They are birds of medium or small size, one being no larger than some sparrows, yet in build they are compact and powerful, and are bolder in proportion to their size than any other birds of prey. The wings are strong, long, and pointed, the power of flight great, and the prey taken by sudden and fierce assault. It is their habit to fly at lofty altitudes, and descend vertically on their prey, which consists of smaller birds, and of small land animals.

FIG. 1.—Duck Hawk (*Falco anatum*).

There are several North American species, of which the jerfalcon or gyrfalcon (*Falco gyrfalco*) is an arctic species, which descends to the United States in winter. It is of white color with dark markings, or ash colored with lighter bars, more than 2 feet long, and with wings 16 inches long. *F. candicans* is a pure white variety. There are several American varieties of the species, of which *F. labradorus* is marked by dark plumage. The duck hawk, or great-footed hawk (*F. anatum*), probably identical with the European *F. peregrinus* or *communis*, the bird used in falconry, is from 18 to 20 inches long, and a very powerful, courageous, and destructive bird. It builds its nest on inaccessible cliffs, and preys on the smaller ducks and other water birds, pigeons and other land birds, and small animals. It is generally distributed in the United States, but not abundant. The pigeon falcon or hawk (*F. columbarius*) is a common and generally distributed North American bird, about 13 inches long, of an ashy blue color above, and a pale fulvous shade below, with large, oblong dark spots. It is very destructive to the smaller birds. Richardson's falcon (*F. richardsonii*) is closely related to the last, though lighter colored. It is found from the Mississippi to the Rocky Mountains. The Lanier falcon (*F. mexicanus*) has its range in the Western United States, and southward. It is 18 inches long, of a plain brown hue above and white below, with brown patches and streaks. The sparrow hawk (*F. sparverius*) is an elegant little bird, very abundant throughout North America. It is about 11 inches long, of a cinnamon brown hue above, and whitish below, its plumage greatly varying in hue, and being peculiarly spotted and striped. It preys on mice and

FIG. 2.—Goshawk (*Falco palumbarius*).

young birds. *F. femoralis* is a widely distributed Central and South American species, and reaches just north of the Mexican border. It is 15 inches long, of an ashy brown or pale slate color, according to age, the wings and tail with numerous white bars, the throat and breast white or tawny, with a broad black zone below.
(C. M.)

FALK, PAUL LUDWIG ADALBERT, a German jurist and statesman, was born Aug. 10, 1827, at Metschkau in Silesia. He was educated at the Gymnasium and University of Breslau, and in 1847 he began his legal career in the state service. In 1862 he was made counsellor of the court of appeals at Glogau, where he also labored on the *Ergänzungen und Erläuterungen der preussischen Rechtsbücher*, popularly known as the "Fünfmännerbuch." On the formation of the North German Confederation in 1867, he was elected as representative of Glogau in the constituent assembly, in which he acted at first with the "Old Liberal" party, but finally with the National Liberals. In 1868 he was assigned as privy counsellor to the ministry of justice, and was employed in the codification of the laws of the German empire. In February, 1871, he was made a representative of Prussia in the imperial council. When Prince Bismarck had resolved to make an aggressive movement on the privileges of the Roman Catholic Church, Dr. Falk was made minister of public worship and instruction, Jan. 22, 1872, and brought forward, in the Prussian parliament, a series of repressive laws, intended to give the government control of ecclesiastical affairs. After an exciting struggle these laws were passed by both houses and promulgated in May, 1873, but the attempt to enforce them was stoutly resisted by the Catholic clergy. The widespread agitation, or *Kultur-Kampf*, which ensued, made Dr. Falk's name familiar throughout Christendom. The resistance of the clerical party led to still severer laws. Several bishops were arrested and imprisoned, Archbishop Ledochowski was removed from his office, and hundreds of parishes were deprived of priestly ministration. In January, 1875, a law passed making civil marriage obligatory, and also providing that Roman Catholic clergy and members of religious orders might contract legal marriage. The pope, Feb. 5, 1875, issued an encyclical declaring the May laws invalid, and forbidding the faithful to observe them. The Prussian government retorted by withdrawing from the refractory clergy all state endowments and support. Dr. Falk's activity was by no means confined to attacks on the legal position of the Catholic Church. He effected a considerable increase of schools, raised the salaries of teachers, and improved the methods of instruction. When Leo XIII. succeeded to the papal throne, and entered into negotiations with Prince Bismarck for a restoration of harmony between church and state, Dr. Falk found his position untenable. In June, 1879, he asked permission to retire from office, and this was granted July 14. A peerage was offered to him, and he accepted it for his son, then an army officer. His public activity was now limited to the Reichstag. In 1882 he was appointed to the presidency of the court at Hamm.

FALLOUX, ALFRED PIERRE, COMTE DE, a French statesman, was born at Angers, May 7, 1811. He first became known by his lives of Louis XVI. (1840) and of Pope Pius V. (1844). As a legitimist he was elected to the chamber of deputies in 1846, but when the republic was declared in February, 1848, he recognized its authority. He was a member of the Constituent Assembly, and took an active part in its discussions. When Louis Napoleon was elected president, Comte de Falloux was made minister of public instruction, but being censured by the legislative assembly for arbitrary measures he resigned. He was afterwards elected to the Assembly, but he did not long support the policy of Napoleon. After the *coup d'état* of December, 1851, Falloux withdrew from Paris unmolested, and devoted himself to agriculture. In 1855 he became assistant editor of the *Correspondant*, the leading Catholic review. In 1856 he was admitted to the French Academy. In 1867 he took part in the Catholic Congress at Mechlin, and supported the declarations of the *Syllabus*. He was twice an unsuccessful legislative candidate of the clerical opposition, and in 1871 he declined a nomination on account of his health. In 1872 he took part in the abortive attempt to get the Comte de Chambord to recognize the tricolor as the national flag. Among his later works are *Madame Swetchine, sa vie et ses œuvres* (1859); *Dix ans d'agriculture* (1863); and *Questions monarchiques* (1873). He has also edited a collection of the letters of Madame Swetchine (1866).

FALLOWS, SAMUEL, an American bishop, was born at Pendleton, near Manchester, England, Dec.

3, 1835. He removed to Wisconsin in 1845, and graduated at the University of Wisconsin in 1859. Entering the ministry of the Methodist Episcopal Church, he became a chaplain in the army, but afterwards was made colonel and brevet brigadier-general. He became State superintendent of public instruction in Wisconsin in 1870, and president of Illinois Wesleyan University, at Bloomington, in 1874. In 1875 he entered the Reformed Episcopal Church, became rector of St. Paul's Church, Chicago, and edited *The Appeal*. In July, 1876, at the general council held at Ottawa, Canada, he was chosen a bishop, and has continued since to hold also his rectorship.

FALL RIVER, a city and port of entry of Massachusetts, in Bristol co., is on the eastern shore of Mount Hope Bay, an arm of Narragansett Bay. It is the fifth in population among the cities of Massachusetts; it is compactly built, lying on a succession of granite ridges that skirt the bay, and on both sides of the Quequechan River, that flows from Watupha Pond, a lake lying nearly 3 miles E. of the bay. The city's area is 27¼ square miles, and, with its ponds, contains a little over 17,000 acres. The Watupha, though very short, formerly furnished a vast amount of water-power. It falls about 128 feet in the course of its last half mile, and as early as 1689 Captain Benjamin Church utilized the water-power by erecting a mill on the stream. In the early years of the 19th century iron-works were started for making nails and several grades of iron, and this enterprise was followed, in 1813, by the establishment of a small cotton-factory, which proved so successful that the city has pursued the development of that industry till now the corporations number 39, with 53 mills, including one woollen manufactory and the American Calico-printing Company. This last enterprise has struggled on through many reverses—having once been burned at the loss of $2,000,000—till now it ranks fifth in number of calico-printing machines among similar enterprises in the country, and second in capacity for producing calico fabrics. It runs 20 machines, and can turn out an aggregate of 75,000,000 yards per annum, and employs 000 persons in the various grades of work. The iron-works run 105 nail-machines and several sets of rollers or other manufactures. The machines turn out 20,000 kegs of nails annually.

The chief product of the mills has been print-cloth or calico, though now a more varied assortment of goods is turned out, mainly wide goods, fancy dress-goods, sheetings, silesias, yarns, merino underwear, lawns, towellings, ginghams, drills, Jersey coatings, and chambrays. The number of mills is 53; capital, $17,538,000, really worth $35,000,000; spindles in use, ,678,016; looms, 39,818; persons employed, 18,135; weekly pay-roll, $113,000; yards of cloth manufactured annually, 467,250,000; bales of cotton used, 194,650; capacity of power, 28,120 horse-power; coal used, 99,100 tons. Some of the mills, as well as other buildings in the city, are handsome structures of granite.

The harbor of Fall River, formed by a widening of the mouth of the Taunton River, is spacious, covering seven square miles of water, is easy of access and sufficiently deep for the largest vessels. A large coastwise trade is carried on in coal, lumber, and cotton centres here, and the Taunton River, which flows into the bay, has been deepened for some 14 miles, vessels of 1000 tons burthen easily ascend it to Somerset, Dighton, and Taunton. The coal traffic has grown to be a leading item of business here, about 500,000 tons being brought to the port annually. Lumber, grain, iron, and cotton form the chief articles of domestic commerce, and but little foreign trade is carried on from this port. In 1883 Fall River had 121 vessels enrolled and licensed, whose tonnage amounted to 44,817 tons; of these 22 were steamers, with a tonnage of 22,287 tons. The main line of the Old Colony and Newport Railroad passes through the city from Boston to Newport, R. I., and has its terminus here for steamers to New York. It is a very popular route between Boston and New York, especially for tourists during the summer season. There are railway connections also with Providence and New Bedford.

Fall River abounds in minor mechanical industries connected with her manufacturing enterprises. The local traffic is not extensive, and the rural districts are lacking in natural fertility, as granitic boulders cover most of the land. The chief feature of its surroundings is four beautiful ponds that lie within or near to the city. The largest—Watupha—covers 3500 acres, receives the water from two other ponds, and supplies the water for manufactories (all mainly driven by steam-power), and also for the use of the people. The mills are located close to the water-supply, are mostly built of granite, though some are of brick. These mills constitute a prominent feature of the view of the city from the bay in summer, which is seldom surpassed for beauty.

Fall River has about 52,000 inhabitants, having doubled since 1870, and increased eight-fold since 1840. Of these only one-third are of native origin. The Irish lead in numbers of the foreign-born, being 15,000; the Canadian French come next, 12,000; and the English and Scotch are numerous also.

Fall River has 27 churches, some of them very handsome structures. Of these 8 are Roman Catholic, 6 Methodist Episcopal, 3 Baptist, 3 Congregational, 2 Episcopalian, and the Christians, Unitarians, Friends, Presbyterians, and Primitive Methodists have one each.

The city is well provided with all the various grades of schools, in which 183 teachers are employed. A splendid high-school edifice, for classical, literary, and technical instruction, has been erected, the gift of Mrs. Mary B. Young. The city has also several beautiful cemeteries, a noble city hall, and other public edifices, a public farm of 110 acres for the poor, an orphan asylum, and many private edifices and blocks for business of great excellence. The most prominent public building is the United States custom-house and post-office. There are 2 daily and 4 weekly newspapers.

Fall River is part of an ancient purchase from the Indians in 1659, and down to 1803 was included in Freetown. The place was conspicuous in the war with the Indian King Philip in 1675-6. In 1803 it was set off as a separate town called Fall River. Its territory was enlarged in 1858, by having a strip of land set off from Rhode Island, when this part of the boundary line of that State and Massachusetts was finally settled. In 1804 its name was changed to Troy, and in 1834 it was changed back to Fall River. The Indian name of the place is said to have been Quequeteant, meaning "the place of quick-running water." (W. R.)

FANEUIL, PETER (1700–1743), an American merchant, was born at New Rochelle, N. Y., in 1700, of a Huguenot family. He settled at Boston, and was highly successful in his enterprises. The market at Boston was held in the open street until at a town-meeting, in 1740, Faneuil offered to erect at his own expense a suitable building, the second story to be used as a town-hall. The offer was accepted; the building was commenced in September, 1740, and completed in 1742. Faneuil died March 3, 1743. The original building being burned in 1761, it was rebuilt in 1763 at public expense. This second building, being much used by the patriots at the outbreak of the Revolution, obtained the name "The cradle of American liberty." While the British held Boston, in 1775, Faneuil Hall was used as a theatre. In 1805 the hall was much altered and enlarged.

"The Cradle of American Liberty"—1770.

FARIBAULT, the county-seat of Rice co., Minn., is on the Cannon River, at the mouth of the Straight River, and on the Chicago, Milwaukee, and St. Paul Railroad, 53 miles S. of St. Paul. It contains the State school for the deaf and dumb, the blind, and the school for the feeble-minded, Seabury Divinity School (Protestant Episcopal), Shattuck School for boys, and St. Mary's Hall for girls. It has also a Roman Catholic school for girls, a parochial school, a graded public school. It has fine public buildings, 2 parks, a public library, 2 weekly newspapers and 3 monthly publications, an opera-house, 11 churches. It has a fire department, is lighted with gas, and has no public debt. In 1855 it was an Indian trading-post, and in 1872 was incorporated as a city. Population, 5415.

FARM. The word "Farm" as used in America is thus defined in the United States Census Report: "A farm is what is owned or leased by one man and cultivated under his care. A distant wood-lot or sheep-pasture is treated as a part of the farm; but whenever there is a resident overseer or manager, there a farm is reported. Farms include all considerable nurseries, orchards, and market gardens, which are owned by separate parties, which are cultivated for pecuniary profit, and employ as much as the labor of one able-bodied man during the year." According to that report as shown in the table (p. 319), only about one-seventh of the land-surface of the United States was improved, and this amount was divided into 4,008,907 farms, thus giving each an average of 71 acres. There were 4352 farms with less than 3 acres; 134,889 with from 3 to 10 acres; 254,749 with from 10 to 20 acres; 781,474 with from 20 to 50 acres; 1,032,910 with from 50 to 100 acres; 1,695,983 with from 100 to 500 acres; 75,972 with from 500 to 1000 acres; 28,578 with more than 1000 acres. The farms contained besides the improved lands 251,310,773 acres of unimproved land, thus making the entire farming area 536,081,835 acres.

In 1870 there were 188,921,099 acres of improved land, valued at $7,410,243,089; the table shows an increase of 52 per cent. in area, and of 30.7 per cent. in value. Every State showed an increase, though in Virginia the percentage was only 0.42, and in Vermont 0.69, while Kansas showed an increase of 444 per cent, and Nebraska of 750 per cent. Even this percentage is exceeded by Wyoming Territory, which gives an increase of 24,492 per cent. The value of farming implements and machinery in 1870 was reported as $289,502,743, and in 1880 at $406,520,055, showing an increase of 52 per cent., being just the same ratio as that of the increase in area of improved land, but considerably greater than that of the increase in its value. This shows that the tendency is to use the improved implements of recent invention both on old and new farms.

The census of 1880 also gives the number of farmers, including stock-raisers, gardeners, etc., as 4,346,515, being 25 per cent. of the whole number of persons engaged in regular occupations. But if to the number of farmers we add 3,323,876 agricultural laborers, we shall find 44 per cent. of all having regular occupations to be engaged in tilling the soil. Indeed we may safely give a higher estimate, for it is noted that some agricultural districts "agricultural laborers" are reported simply as "laborers," and hence were not included in the above calculation. As regards the wealth of the farming class, the census report shows that while the assessed value of all the real estate in the country was $13,036,766,925, that of farms was $10,197,096,776, being 77 per cent. of the whole. The total personal property was assessed at $3,866,226,618; that of farmers, including live-stock, was $1,906,984,655, being 49.3 per cent. of the whole. Combining real and personal property, we find that out of a total assessed value of $16,902,993,543, farmers held $12,104,081,431, or 71 per cent., though they form only 25 per cent. of the population engaged in gainful occupations. It may be that their wealth, being in a more palpable form than some other kinds, is more fully assessed, yet it is not probable that the actual value varies very much from this estimate. It may safely be stated at two-thirds. Farming is proved then to be not only a necessary and honorable occupation, but lucrative, as compared with other occupations. It has been favored by legislation in the various States, especially by the homestead exemption laws. These laws give stability to the population, and encourage the farmer in his efforts to improve his land.

The average size of farms in the United States is 71 acres, and except in some of the Territories, where fertile unimproved land is still abundant, the tendency is to even smaller farms, from 40 to 50 acres. The quarter-section (160 acres) of land which is allowed by law to the actual settler is found to be more than one man can properly attend to, and it is readily divided

OLD STYLE SOWING.—"BONANZA" FARM STYLE OF PLOWING AND SOWING.

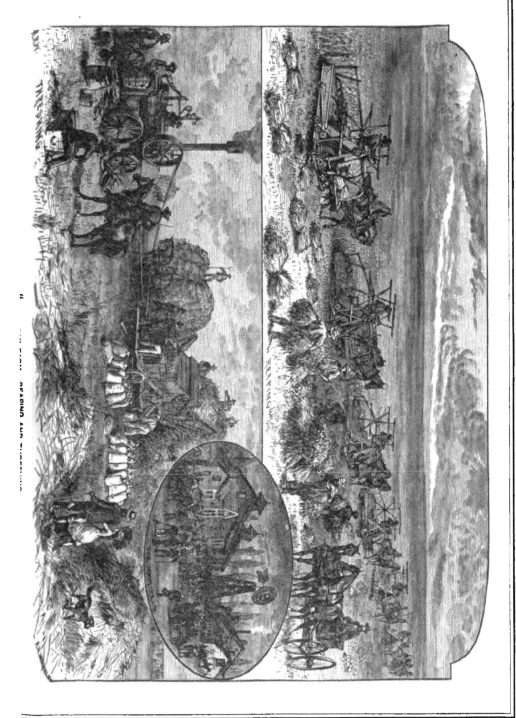

FARM. PLATE XX.

STATES.	Land Surface of the United States.	Number of Farms.	Improved Land.	Average Imp. Land in Farms.	Value of Farms.	Value of Implements.	Value of Products, 1879.
	Acres.		Acres.	Acres.	Dollars.	Dollars.	Dollars.
Alabama	32,985,600	135,864	6,375,706	47	78,954,648	3,788,978	56,872,994
Arkansas	33,948,800	94,433	3,595,603	38	74,249,655	4,637,497	43,796,261
California	99,827,200	35,934	10,669,698	296	262,051,282	8,447,744	59,721,425
Colorado	66,268,800	4,506	616,169	137	25,109,223	910,085	5,035,228
Connecticut	3,100,800	30,598	1,642,188	53	121,063,910	3,162,628	18,010,075
Delaware	1,254,400	8,794	746,958	85	36,789,672	1,504,576	6,320,345
District of Columbia	38,400	435	12,632	29	3,632,403	36,798	514,441
Florida	34,713,600	23,483	947,640	40	20,291,835	689,666	7,439,392
Georgia	37,747,200	138,626	8,204,720	59	111,910,540	5,317,416	67,028,929
Illinois	35,840,000	255,741	26,115,154	102	1,009,594,580	33,739,591	203,980,137
Indiana	22,982,400	194,013	13,933,738	72	635,236,111	20,476,988	114,707,082
Iowa	35,504,000	185,351	19,866,541	107	567,430,227	29,371,884	136,103,473
Kansas	52,288,000	138,561	10,739,566	77	235,178,936	15,652,848	52,240,301
Kentucky	25,600,000	166,453	10,731,683	65	299,298,631	9,734,634	63,850,155
Louisiana	29,068,800	48,292	2,739,972	57	58,989,117	5,435,525	42,883,522
Maine	19,132,800	64,309	3,484,908	54	102,357,615	4,948,048	21,945,489
Maryland	6,310,400	40,517	3,342,700	82	165,503,341	5,788,197	28,839,281
Massachusetts	5,145,800	38,406	2,128,311	55	146,197,415	5,134,537	24,160,881
Michigan	36,755,200	154,008	8,296,862	54	499,103,181	19,419,360	91,159,858
Minnesota	50,681,200	92,386	7,246,693	78	193,724,260	13,089,783	49,468,951
Mississippi	29,657,600	101,772	5,216,937	51	92,844,915	4,885,636	63,701,844
Missouri	43,990,400	215,575	16,745,031	78	375,633,307	18,103,074	95,912,660
Nebraska	46,758,400	63,387	5,504,702	87	105,932,541	7,820,917	31,708,914
Nevada	70,233,600	1,404	344,423	246	5,408,325	378,788	2,855,449
New Hampshire	5,763,200	32,181	2,308,112	72	75,834,389	3,069,240	13,474,330
New Jersey	4,771,200	34,307	2,096,297	61	190,895,833	6,921,085	29,650,756
New York	30,476,800	241,058	17,717,862	73	1,056,176,741	42,592,741	178,025,695
North Carolina	30,991,200	157,609	6,481,191	41	135,793,602	6,078,476	51,729,611
Ohio	26,086,400	247,189	18,081,091	73	1,127,497,353	30,521,180	156,777,152
Oregon	60,518,400	16,217	2,198,645	136	56,908,575	2,956,173	13,234,548
Pennsylvania	28,780,400	213,542	13,423,007	63	975,689,410	35,473,037	129,760,476
Rhode Island	694,400	6,216	298,486	48	25,882,079	902,825	3,670,135
South Carolina	19,308,800	93,864	4,132,050	44	68,677,482	3,202,710	41,969,749
Tennessee	26,720,000	165,650	8,496,556	51	206,749,837	9,054,863	62,076,311
Texas	166,865,600	174,184	12,650,314	72	170,468,886	9,051,491	65,204,329
Vermont	5,846,400	35,522	3,286,461	93	109,346,010	4,879,285	22,082,656
Virginia	25,681,000	118,517	8,510,113	72	216,028,107	5,495,114	45,726,221
West Virginia	15,772,800	62,674	3,792,327	60	133,147,175	2,669,163	19,360,049
Wisconsin	34,848,000	134,322	9,162,528	68	357,709,507	15,647,196	72,779,496
Arizona	7,226,800	767	56,071	73	1,127,946	88,811	614,327
Dakota	93,528,000	17,435	1,150,413	66	22,401,084	2,390,091	5,648,814
Idaho	53,945,600	1,885	197,407	106	2,832,890	363,390	1,515,314
Montana	92,978,400	1,519	262,611	175	3,234,504	401,185	2,024,923
New Mexico	78,374,000	5,053	237,392	47	5,514,399	255,162	1,897,974
Utah	52,601,600	9,452	416,105	44	14,015,178	946,753	3,337,410
Washington Territ'y	42,803,200	6,529	484,346	74	13,844,224	958,513	4,212,750
Wyoming Territory	62,448,000	457	83,122	184	835,895	95,482	372,391
Totals	1,900,800,000	4,008,907	284,771,042		10,197,096,776	406,520,055	2,213,402,564

into two or more farms, as the settler's sons grow up. The skilful management of moderate sized farms is found to bring better and quicker returns than the enlarging of their area, which was once the criterion of a successful farmer. Now the desire of the intelligent farmer is not so much to get more acres as to get more from each acre. (See AGRICULTURE, Vol. I.)

The famous exception to this rule is found in the prairies of the west and north-west, which are rapidly coming under cultivation. In Kansas, Nebraska, Minnesota, and more recently Dakota, the capitalist, availing himself of the latest inventions of American ingenuity in farming implements, draws from the apparently unlimited fertility of the virgin soil abundant harvests of wheat and maize, with which the transcontinental railway systems enable him to supply the markets of the world. The immense scale on which agricultural operations are there conducted is strikingly shown in the illustrations (Plates XIX. and XX.) taken from Dr. L. P. Brockett's work, *Our Western Empire* (Phila., 1881). Yet even in that region of "bonanza farms" the immigrant of small means finds room and opportunity to better his condition by diligence and thoughtful attention to the requirements of the soil in order to produce a satisfactory return of his outlay.

FARNHAM, ELIZA WOODSON (1815-1864), an American author and philanthropist, was born at Rensselaerville, N. Y., 1815, her maiden name being Burhaus. In 1835 she removed to Illinois, where she married Thomas Jefferson Farnham. In 1841 she returned to New York and devoted herself to philanthropic labors. From 1844 to 1848 she was matron in the State Prison at Sing Sing, and meantime published *Life in Prairie Land*. She spent some years in California, and organized a society to assist women in emigrating to the West. She published *California Indoors and Out* (1856), *My Early Days* (1859), and *Woman and her Era* (2 vols., 1864). She died at New York, Dec. 15, 1864. A posthumous work, *The Ideal Attained*, appeared in 1865.

Her husband, THOMAS JEFFERSON FARNHAM (1804-1848), was born in Vermont, studied law, and in 1839 organized an expedition across the continent to Oregon. He also visited California, and procured from the Mexican Government the release of several American and English prisoners. He published *Travels in Oregon Territory* (1842), *Travels in California and Scenes on the Pacific* (1845), *Mexico: Its Geography, People, and Institutions* (1846). He died in California, in September, 1848.

FARR, WILLIAM (1807-1883), an English medical statistician, was born at Kenley, Shropshire, Nov. 30, 1807. He studied medicine at the Universities of Paris and London, and graduated from University College in 1833. While practising in London he began to lecture on public health, and contributed frequently to the *British Annals of Medicine*. To McCulloch's *Statistical Account of the British Empire* (1837), he contributed a noted chapter on "Vital Statistics," which led to immense improvement in the collection of data for that department. The registration of all the deaths in England and their causes was then commenced, and Dr. Farr was appointed to a position in the Register's office. He continued to devote himself to the study of statistics, of epidemics, and of the duration of human life, and has written many official reports on these subjects. He was assistant commissioner in taking the censuses of Great Britain from 1851 to 1881. His researches have given greater precision to the science and practice of life insurance. His paper "On the Construction of Life Tables" (1859), his introduction to the *English Life Tables* (1864), and his *Statistical Nosology*, are of great value. In 1855 he was elected Fellow of the Royal Society, and in 1859 he received from the University of Oxford the degree of D.C.L. He died April 14, 1883.

FARRAR, FREDERIC WILLIAM, an English clergyman, was born at Bombay, India, Aug. 7, 1831. He was educated at King William's College, near Castletown, Isle of Man, and at King's College, London, where he first came under the influence of Prof. Frederic D. Maurice. He entered Trinity College, Cambridge, and graduated in 1854 with high honors. In 1856 he was made a fellow of Trinity College; in 1857 he received the degree of M. A., and was ordained priest. He had already entered on the educational work to which he devoted more than twenty years of his life. After a few months service as assistant master in Marlborough College, he spent fifteen years (1855-71) in the Harrow School, and then was recalled to be head master of the former. As a teacher, he not only had remarkable power of inciting intellectual exertion and of inculcating correct literary taste, but by both example and precept he trained his pupils to a high sense of duty. His sermons delivered in the school chapel are models for such purpose. His merits as a preacher were recognized in his appointment as a chaplain to the queen in 1873. He has also repeatedly been one of the University preachers, both at Cambridge and at Oxford. In 1874 he received the degree of D. D. from Cambridge University. In 1876 he was appointed canon of Westminster and rector of St. Margaret's Church. In 1883 he was made archdeacon of Westminster. He has taken an active part in various movements for the improvement of the lower classes, and has especially been an advocate of the total prohibition of the liquor traffic.

Archdeacon Farrar has been prominent in several departments of literary activity. He began with some works of fiction in which he depicted in vivid colors school and college life from his own experience. The first of these was *Eric, or Little by Little* (1858); then came *Julian Home: a Tale of College Life* (1859); and *St. Winifred's, or the World of School* (1863), the last being issued anonymously. These all have retained their popularity with the class for whom they were intended.

While actively engaged in school work, Mr. Farrar prepared some text-books in Greek grammar and some philological treatises, displaying learning and thought. The first of these was on *The Origin of Language* (1860), in which he maintained with considerable force of argument the interjectional theory. It was followed by *Chapters on Language* (1864), and afterwards by a treatise on *Families of Speech* (1870), which had already been delivered as lectures before the Royal Institution. He also contributed to the general discussion of the subject of education and especially of the proper place of the classics in modern liberal training.

The greater number of Archdeacon Farrar's works, however, have been produced in the line of his activity as a Christian preacher and theologian. At first simply collections of sermons, they have in later years become transcripts of his studies in the historical development of Christianity. His first volume of sermons appeared in 1865; in 1870 came his Hulsean lectures, *The Witness of History to Christ*; in 1873 *The Silence and the Voices of God*; in 1878 *Eternal Hope*. This last work, which set forth in part his view of the teachings of Scripture in regard to the future state, provoked an animated discussion. His works of a historical and biographical character include *Seekers after God* (1869); *The Life of Christ* (1874); *The Life and Work of St. Paul* (1879); *Saintly Workers* (1876); *The Early Days of Christianity* (1881).

Farrar's learning is ample; his thoughts are clear and well arranged; his style is brilliant and rhetorical. In theology he belongs to the Broad Church School. He shows thorough appreciation of the difficulties which the religion of Christ encounters from the materialistic philosophy, scientific dogmatism, and unsparing criticism of the present day, but equally plain are his unwavering faith in its ultimate triumph and his constant endeavor to remove the accretions and obstacles which impede its progress. In the history of the world he sees continual manifestation of the grace of God, and he tries to awaken others to the same view, the same hope, and the same earnestness in Christian work.

FARRER, HENRY, an American artist, was born in London, England, March 23, 1843. His parents removed to New York during his youth. He has given much attention to etching and water colors. In 1879 he was made secretary of the American Water Color Society, and in 1881 president of the New York Etching Club. Among his works may be mentioned A Calm Afternoon; The Silent Tongue (1872), which is a study of a deserted ferry wharf; The Old Homestead at Twilight (1875); A Windy Day (1876), exhibited at the Centennial Exhibition, Philadelphia; A Quiet Pool (1878), exhibited at the Paris Exposition of that year; Autumn (1883), exhibited in London. His pictures are careful, quiet studies of scenes which win regard the more closely they are examined.

FATALISM is a theory which affirms that all things are subject to an inflexible necessity lying outside of the human will. There is a popular form of fatalism existing as a fruit of ignorance and superstition by which determining phases of human life are ascribed to luck or chance. This irregular and irresponsible development of thought is hardly susceptible of further definition or classification. Fatalism ascribes the origin of its necessity to the will of a free deity, or to nature. In the latter case, that namely of circumstantial fatalism, the controlling necessity may be regarded as involving Deity itself in its compulsions. Fatalism originates sometimes as a religious dogma and as an actual or supposed part of a Divine revelation: this is termed religious fatalism. In the other case it arises as a product of certain phases of metaphysical inquiry, and is termed speculative or philosophical fatalism.

The Fates or Parcæ of the Greeks who, according to the prevailing mythology, supervised the affairs of the earth and punished its malefactors, bear only a remote and indefinite relation to the general doctrines of fatalism. Their work was a surprise and their purpose was generally effective: they thwarted human design and interfered with the sequence of cause and effect, and yet their operations were regarded rather as interferences than as laws. They effected an intrusion upon the ordinary and even course of nature, rather than an expression of a universal control. Many of the early Greek writers were evidently fatalists. Sophocles devotes one of his plays largely to the exposition of this conception of life. Even Plutarch in his *Morals* suffers his philosophy to be so largely influenced by his mythology, that Fate and Providence and Free Will become inextricably tangled. Among the Stoics, also, there existed a school whose followers regarded man as the creature of an absolute fate. By some careless writers fatalism is regarded as a prevalent doctrine among the Stoics. It is evident, however, from a careful reading of Epictetus, that this was far from being a universal doctrine among them, this writer going to the extent of affirming that even Jupiter himself cannot compel a man to act contrary to his personal choice.

The most prominent and unequivocal avowal of fatalism in religion is found in connection with Mohammedanism. According to the conception of this religion, every man's life is in all its details predetermined. His entire experience is a "destiny" which he works out in a way that is more or less mechanical. God or Allah is an absolute despot. He is limited by no necessities of his own nature. Whatever he does is right. He may give one law to the Moslem and another to the Christian. He even varies and changes his laws for the same people, and he fixes, arbitrarily, for every man, the course and the end of his life. Singularly enough, this fatalistic idea of Divine government is not regarded as impairing personal responsibility. The sovereignty of Allah is absolute and unlimited. He marks the manner and measure of life: in reference to thought and motive and every detail of its environment it is fixed and unalterable. To the inspiration of this conception of destiny is largely due the fanatical and matchless fearlessness of the Moslem soldiers. No terrors were too great for men who could not escape destiny, who would be wise only in fulfilling it, and who were fighting for Him that controlled fate itself. Sometimes, on the other hand, this same fatalism has paralyzed effort when men, anticipating doom, have refused to move hand or foot to avert or mitigate its power. The peril of calamity was apt to be regarded as its prophecy, and a doom which was simply threatened was regarded as an indication that it was fixed. "It is Allah," was an expression that usually indicated the end of effort and of hope. It is interesting to observe that among the early phases of sectarianism among the Moslems was the growth of a school which emphasized the apparent contradictions of the Koran in its teaching of absolute predestination on the one hand, and of free will on the other, the result of which has been the growth of a large body of believers who, placing the emphasis of their faith on the latter element of the creed, reject the grosser forms of fatalism (see MOHAMMEDANISM in the ENCYCLOPÆDIA BRITANNICA).

Fatalism is often charged upon certain phases of Christianity. John Calvin formulated a system of doctrine which lays prominent stress upon the ideas of the divine foreknowledge and foreordination. Starting with the idea of an absolute purpose on the part of God, all things are regarded as being involved in its conclusions, and even the minute events of personal life are by it fixed and determined. This form of statement is regarded as involving the same idea of a predominant necessity as the avowed fatalism of the East, differing prominently however in the substitution of a personal God for an impersonal and undefined destiny. We are not concerned in this article with anything more, however, than with the classification of these different schools of religious and scientific thought, which in scientific rather than popular phraseology are assigned to limits now under discussion. Jonathan Edwards is the foremost writer among all who have attempted to follow Calvin's position to legitimate metaphysical conclusions. He denied the freedom of the will and wrote an elaborate treatise in defence of his attitude. All spiritual advance on the part of man was made contingent upon an extraneous influence, which is imposed according to an eternally foreordained plan on the part of God. These facts were not regarded by him as impairing personal responsibility. So far as this is affirmed by those who follow him it is regarded as a perversion rather than a fair result of his theology. In certain parts of the United States and also in England there has arisen a class of religionists who are charged with pushing to undue limits the leading tenets of the Calvinistic theology, while they have utterly excluded everything that tends to modify their rigor. They are known as Antinomians. They affiliate in other dogmas with various sects. Such of them as associate with the Baptists are denominated "Old School," or in derision "Hardshell" Baptists. Consistently with their theories of the absoluteness and rigor of the sovereignty of God they refuse to acknowledge the need of intermediate agencies for influencing human will. This is directly moved and controlled by Divine power alone. Missionary societies and Sunday-schools, no less than direct appeals to men intended to secure their conversion, are regarded as useless attempts to invade a divine prerogative. In this entire realm man is regarded as being utterly helpless and simply at the disposal of a Sovereign and Divine power, which arbitrarily fixes the destiny of man apart altogether from any determining processes of his own will.

Necessitarianism or philosophical fatalism is found to be a logical result of two contrasted phases of metaphysical inquiry. Under certain modified forms it has been held and defended by foremost writers of their several schools in Europe and America. The term fatalism as applied to philosophy has reference rather to the predominating influence by which human action is decided than to the manner in which that decision may be pronounced. Outside of man's self we may conceive of two great powers as having either of them independent existence. They are God and nature. If self is entirely controlled and neutralized by deity, the result is religious fatalism. If on the other hand nature is the controlling power, the result is circumstantial fatalism. The philosopher does not necessarily exclude a personal deity from this latter view, but regards the whole realm of being as involved in the control of a fixed necessity. The existence of this necessity is affirmed by its relation to the human will. Fatalism, therefore, whether considered in its use with reference to philosophy or theology in this article, is not regarded as implying a personal power on the one hand or a blind chance or destiny on the other, but is the simple affirmation of a supposed law of sequences in which personal decision is overruled by a power lying outside of the province of the human will.

The sensational philosophy on the one hand when pushed to extreme logical conclusions seems to involve fatalism as a necessary consequence. Hobbes was one of the first English philosophers to accept this result. Following the method of induction which Bacon had introduced, he carried the theories of his master into metaphysical realms. He began by making sensation the real origin and medium of all ideas and consequently of all knowledge. Since sensation can come only by that which was material, nothing but what was material had real existence. Every thought even is the product of single or remembered sensations. Consequently good and evil are only words expressing the fact that sensations are agreeable or otherwise, and since our sensations are contingent upon our environments, and since their effects as to agreeableness or disagreeableness is not the result of our volition, and as this is itself perpetually determined from without, it follows that man is perpetually the helpless creature of something which the philosopher calls necessity. It is difficult to see where even a shadow of personal responsibility remains under such a theory. David Hartley, another prominent English philosopher, proclaimed with yet greater emphasis the same idea. As all our thoughts are the fruit of sensations, and excited directly by these or aroused indirectly by the laws of association of ideas, it follows that the power of the will is a nonentity, that man has no control over his own mind, and is the creature of an irresistible power outside himself. Hartley was a man of devout spirit and of a deeply religious life, and resisted strenuously the practical inferences which others derived from the logic of his philosophy. The sensational philosophy holds in short that desire and will are synonymous, that these are excited by sensation which are determined in their effects by our education, which in turn is the inevitable result of our experience. Since our will is thus mechanically excited, it is impossible that any man should act otherwise than he does under any given circumstances. It tends to establish along a line of natural law a theory of circumstantial fatalism.

Robert Owen, of Wales, who wrote a socialistic treatise entitled the *New Moral World* (1812), gave open expression to his belief in the ultimate conclusions of sensationalism as involving inevitable necessity. He regards man as a compound being whose character is formed "of his constitution or organization at birth and of the effects of external circumstances upon him from birth to death, such original organization and external influences continually acting and reacting each upon the other." He receives his feelings and convictions without the exercise of volition: indeed these feelings and convictions are regarded as creating the motive to action which Owen denominates the will. In short, the character of man is made for him and not by him. The first effect of Owen's necessitarian doctrine has been regarded to be subversive of morals and religion.

The ideal philosophy on the other hand pursues an opposite direction an investigation into the cause and nature of things which sometimes involves a similar result. Baruch Spinoza, of Holland, is the author of a system of objective idealism. His teaching began with an identification of the idea of substance with God. God is the free cause (*causa libera*) and the only thing that is free. He is also the immanent cause of all things. He does not stand apart from the universe and create. He simply is, and all things that are are simply the unfolding of himself. Man seems to be free only in a certain limited sense, and is involved in the absolute determinations which include the universe and the very nature and essence of the Deity itself. All individual beings, whether nations or men, are changing forms of substance, parts of God, as the wave is a part of the sea and the idea of the mind. The individual is absorbed in an infinite substance whose evolutions are determined and inevitable.

Among subjective ideal philosophers it would naturally be difficult to find any who avow a necessitarian or fatalistic theory—the tendency of this line of thought being naturally to exalt the liberty of the individual will. Hegel has been charged with necessitating by his absolute idealism a conclusion of fatalism, but this has arisen from his near approach to Spinoza in some of his conclusions, and the impression has arisen from a failure to observe the accurate line of demarcation between the two philosophies.

J. Stuart Mill has been classed among necessitarian writers, but he himself denies the term while seeming to avow the theory which is usually described by that use. In his *Examination of Sir William Hamilton's Philosophy*, while contending against the doctrine of free will and declaring that a volition follows as inexbly from corresponding moral causes as a physical ault from a physical cause, he avows this as a conclusion resulting from experience. He refuses to commit himself to the declaration that the nature of things demands such a sequence. He does not know, he says, that it *must* thus result. He seems to desire himself to be regarded as an agnostic with reference to the idea of necessity. His distinctions are subtle and many unsatisfactory. He declares that real fatalism of two kinds: "Pure or Asiatic fatalism—the fatalism of the Œdipus—holds that our actions do not depend upon our desires. Whatever our wishes may be, a superior power or an abstract destiny will override them and compel us to act not as we desire but in the manner predestined." "Modified fatalism holds that our actions are determined by our will, our will by our desires—these by the joint influence of the motives presented to us and of our individual character." He adds in substance, that we are not responsible for our actions or our character and should in vain attempt to alter either or both. Mill departs from this theory afterward so far as to attempt to establish responsibility while affirming that the motives which influence the will are necessarily determining and inevitable in their result.

The literature of this subject is very extensive, and embraces not only a wide range of Asiatic writings but almost all the recent works on philosophic subjects published in England and America. The following are among the most important: Caussin de Perceval, *Essai sur l'histoire des Arabes avant l'Islamisme pendant l'epoque de Mahomet, et usqu' à la reduction de toutes les tribus sous la loi musulmane* (Paris, 1848); J. J. Döllinger, *Muhammed's Religion nach ihrer innern Entwickelung und ihrem Einflusse auf das Leben der Völker* (Ratisbon, 1838); *Islam, its History, Character, and Relation to Christianity* (Boston, 1874); *Plutarch's Morals* (vol. v., pp. 293–308); Ralph Waldo Emerson, *Conduct of Life*, pp. 1–43 (Boston, 1860); A. Bain, *Mental and Moral Science*, pp. 369–428 (1868); C. Bray, *Philosophy of Necessity* (1841), a work of considerable interest; Jonathan Edwards, *A Careful and Strict Inquiry into the Prevailing Notions of the Freedom of Will*, in *Works*, pp. 3–93 (London, 1840); "Causality, Liberty, and Necessity," in the *Lectures of Sir Wm. Hamilton* (Vol. 2, p. 39–41); R. G. Hazard, *Freedom of Mind in Willing*; Thomas Hobbes, *Tripos Point of Liberty, Necessity, and Chance*, in *Works* (Eng., 1840), vols. 4 and 5; J. Stuart Mill, *Examination of Sir Wm. Hamilton's Philosophy*, vol. 2, pp. 275–304 (1865); J. Priestley, *Letters on Necessity*, in *Works*, vol. 4; Emanuel Kant, *Critique of Pure Reason*; Aristotle, *Nt. Ausc.*, II., ix. 1.; Robert Owen, *Book of the New Moral World* (1812).   (T. A. K. G.)

FAUGÉRE, ARMAND PROSPER, a French literary historian, was born at Bergerac, Dordogne, Feb. 10, 1810. In 1836 he founded the *Moniteur religieux*. In researches for his *Eloge de Blaise Pascal* (1842) he discovered several important documents, from which he was able to restore in their original form the *Pensées, Fragments et Lettres de Blaise Pascal* (1844). He also edited memoirs of Pascal's relatives, and in 1868 defended him against the attacks of M. Chasles. He was employed in the department of public instruction, and afterwards became director of the archives in the bureau of foreign affairs. Besides his works relating to Pascal he published *Mémoires de Madame Roland* (1864), *Fragments de littérature morale et politique* (1865), and some pamphlets on national economy.

FAUNA. The word "fauna" is now very generally used to express the entire assemblage of animals that inhabit any given locality. Thus we can speak of the fauna of Pennsylvania, of the United States, of North America, or of the Western Hemisphere. Every group of animals has its centre or head-quarters, where the species belonging to it are more abundant than they are elsewhere. In the same manner every species has its centre of distribution, and becomes less common as we recede from that centre. Thus every large tract of land bounded by mountain or oceanic barriers has some orders, families, or genera of animals peculiar to itself; and smaller areas, defined by less impassable barriers, such as rivers, deserts, or narrow seas, yet usually have their peculiar species, and are often the home of larger groups which do not occur elsewhere. These peculiar species, genera, or larger groups mark the distinctness of the fauna of any region. If political boundaries approximately followed natural ones, each country would have its peculiar fauna, but as the lines man has traced upon the globe are in great part artificial, a fauna which has distinctive characters may be divided up between several countries; while another country may include within its boundaries several more or less distinctive assemblages of animals. Thus, though we may speak of the fauna of Pennsylvania or of New York, the difference between these assemblages of animals is very small, and the same would be found to be the case with Nevada and Utah. The most distinct fauna of the United States is that of the Pacific coast; separated from the rest of the country by the Sierra Nevada and Rocky Mountains. The great basin and great plains have also their peculiar forms; the Gulf States, especially Florida, savor of the tropics; and the Mississippi basin has numerous fishes and shellfish which are either peculiar to it or have their centre of distribution there. The most peculiar fauna to be found upon the earth's surface is that of Australia, characterized by the egg-laying quadrupeds, the echidna and the ornithorhynchus; by an assemblage of pouched mammals or marsupials; by an abundance of pigeons and parrots; by the megapodes or mound-building birds and the bower birds; by strange forms of reptiles; and by the curious fish ceratodus. The next most peculiar fauna is that of South America, the land of armadillos, sloths, anteaters, and varied forms of gnawing mammals, and rich in birds, reptiles, fish, and insects not to be found elsewhere. The third in the list of peculiar faunas is that of South Africa and Madagascar. Here dwell the aardvark and the scaly anteaters, some singular carnivora, and the greater part of the monkey-like lemurs. Madagascar is the head-quarters of the lemurs, and the few forms not found there or in the adjacent continent are to be met with in the East Indian islands, which partake also of the peculiar creatures of Australia. It is an interesting fact that these three most peculiar faunas of the globe are all centred in the southern land masses. It is not unlikely that they are the remnants of the fauna of an antarctic continent which is now for the most part submerged. The animals of the rest of the world show fewer peculiarities. The great mammals of India and Central Africa, the elephant, the rhinoceros, the hippopotamus, the lion, etc., were in ages geologically not remote represented by kindred forms in the north temperate zone. They seem to be principally the descendants of a homogeneous fauna which once spread to the polar regions, and not improbably had its starting point there in an age when a more uniform climate prevailed. Subsequent evolution upon separated continents, coupled with climatic and other changes, have caused great variations; some southern forms, as the opossums, have spread northwards; and in North America most of the great ruminants perished before the present age set in, leaving their bones alone to tell of their existence; yet there is still sufficient resemblance to point to a common origin. The ocean has also its faunal regions, but differently distributed from those of the land. There are in the ocean three principal faunas: (1) that of the coast and shallow seas, (2) that of the ocean surface, (3) that of the deep seas. The first, or littoral fauna, may be divided into several sub-faunas, and to some extent reflects the conditions to be found on land; the second, or pelagic fauna, is richest within the tropics, but its forms are often widely spread; while the third, or abyssal fauna, is nearly cosmopolitan, as the conditions of existence at great depths do not differ greatly the world over.

(W. N. L.)

FAVRE, JULES CLAUDE GABRIEL (1809–1880), a French statesman, born in Lyons, March 21, 1809. He studied law in Paris, and took part in the revolution of 1830; became an advocate in Lyons, and both there, in 1834, and at Paris, in 1835, won fame for his successful defence of certain revolutionists and socialists. In 1836 he removed to Paris. He was for a time secretary-general of the interior in the republican ministry of 1848, and took an active part in the constituent assembly. Under the second empire he was a bold and outspoken opponent of the imperial policy on most of the great questions of the time, and in the *corps législatif* he was regarded as the chief of the democratic opposition. With Thiers, in 1870, he opposed the hostile preparations directed against Prussia; but when once the war was begun, he cordially supported the cause of the nation. After Sedan he became vice-president and minister of foreign affairs in the new republic. In the negotiations which preceded the definitive treaty of peace with Germany Favre did his best to prevent the cession of Alsace-Lorraine. Though personally the friend of Thiers, he left the ministry in July, 1871. In 1876 he was returned as senator for the department of Rhône. He died at Versailles, Jan. 20, 1880. Favre's reputation as a brilliant and finished orator was deservedly high, and the literary excellences of his style won him a place in the Academy in 1867. Many of his speeches and political writings have been printed in book-form.

FAWCETT, HENRY (1833–1884), an English publicist and statesman, was born at Salisbury in 1833; graduated at Trinity Hall, Cambridge, in 1856, with high mathematical honors, and in that year became a fellow of his hall. In 1858 an accident, which occurred while he was shooting, deprived him of sight. Yet with rare courage he persevered in the plan of life which he had already marked out for himself. In 1863 he was chosen professor of political economy in the University of Cambridge. After three defeats for parliament, he was returned, in 1865, as member for Brighton, which borough he represented till 1874, when he was elected for Hackney. In 1880 he was made postmaster-general, and greatly improved the postal service. In Parliament he was a frequent speaker, particularly on Indian finances; in politics he was an advanced liberal, favoring election by ballot and woman suffrage. Among his works are *A Manual of Political Economy* (1863; revised and enlarged ed., 1867); *The Economic Position of the British Laborer* (1865); *Pauperism* (1871); a volume of *Speeches* (1873); *Free Trade and Protection* (1878), and many magazine articles. He died Nov. 5, 1884. His wife (born in 1847) was his efficient helper in his remarkable career. She is author of *Political Economy for Beginners* (1870) and *Tales in Political Economy* (1874). See Leslie Stephen's *Life of Henry Fawcett* (1885).

FAY, THEODORE SEDGWICK, an American author, was born in New York city, Feb. 10, 1807. He was admitted to the bar in 1828, but devoted himself to literature. His contributions to the *New York Mirror*, of which he was for a time editor, were collected under the title *Dreams and Reveries of a Quiet Man.* In 1833 he went to Europe, and in 1837 he became secretary to the American Legation at Berlin. In 1853 he was appointed minister resident at Berne, Switzerland, which position he held till 1861. He published *The Minute Book* (1834), a journal of his travels; several romances, including *Norman Leslie* (1835; new ed. 1869); a long poem called *Ulric, or The Voices* (1851); and a *History of Switzerland* (1860). He also published a series of papers on Shakespeare.

FAYE, HERVÉ AUGUSTE ETIENNE ALBANS, a French astronomer, was born at Saint Benoît du Sault, Indre, Oct. 5, 1814. He studied mathematics at the École Polytechnique and in 1834 went to Holland, but afterwards returned to France, when Arago recommended him to the observatory. On Nov. 22, 1843, he discovered the comet which bears his name, and for this discovery obtained the Lalande prize. He was elected a member of the Academy of Sciences in 1847. In 1848 he was made professor of geodesy at the École Polytechnique, and in 1854 became rector of the Academy at Nancy. In 1873 he was made inspector general of scientific instruction in the department of secondary education. In 1877 he was elected to the chamber of deputies, and for a few weeks he was minister of public instruction. He has since been inspector general of higher instruction. He assisted in translating Humboldt's *Cosmos* into French (1846–1859), and published *Leçons de Cosmographie* (1864).

FAYRER, SIR JOSEPH, an English physician, was born at Plymouth, Dec. 6, 1824. He was educated at King's College, London, and the University of Edinburgh, and received the degree of M. D. both at Edinburgh and at the University of Rome, 1849. In 1847 he became assistant surgeon in the navy, in 1849 was transferred to the army, and in 1850 to the East India Company's service. In 1853 he was appointed civil surgeon at Rangoon, and in the same year was sent to Lucknow as residency surgeon. He served with great distinction during the great siege of Lucknow in 1857, and at the relief of Cawnpore. In 1859 he was appointed professor in the Calcutta Medical College, and afterwards held other distinguished positions. In 1872 he became president of the Indian Medical Board and surgeon-general. Among his writings are *Poisonous Snakes of India* (1872); *Tropical Diseases* (1881); *The Tiger; Journal with the Prince*, and various professional works, relating chiefly to questions of climate, to snake-bites, etc.

FAZY, JEAN JAMES (1794–1878), a Swiss statesman, was born at Geneva, May 17, 1794. He was of Huguenot descent and was educated at a Moravian school at Neuwied. He went to Paris to study jurisprudence and became a journalist, but in 1833 returned to Geneva, where he was head of the radical republican party. His efforts resulted in the adoption of a liberal constitution in June, 1842. In the struggle between the Protestant and Catholic cantons in 1846, under the influence of Fazy Geneva joined the former, and thus overcame the Sonderbund. Since Calvin's time no man has had so great power in Geneva as Fazy, yet as in Calvin's case there were ebbs and flows of his influence. Fazy's political career, while in some respects beneficial to the city, was marred by his selfishness and lust of power. From 1855 resistance to his rule increased, and in 1869 he retired from public life. He died at Geneva, Nov. 6, 1878. For many years he was professor of constitutional law in the University of Geneva. His principal publication is *De l' intelligence collective de sociétés* (Basle, 1874).

FECHNER, GUSTAV THEODOR, a German physicist, was born at Gross-Sährchen, in Lower Lusatia, April 19, 1801. He was educated at Soran and Dresden, and studied medicine at Leipsic, but soon devoted himself to the natural sciences. Some of his earliest writings treated scientific problems in a humorous way, and these were afterwards collected under the title *Kleine Schriften von Dr. Mises* (1875). His serious works related to galvanism and chemistry, and in 1834 he was made professor of physics in the University of Leipsic, but he was obliged to resign his chair in 1839, by a disease of the eyes. He then turned his attention to æsthetics and anthropology, and published some volumes of poems of considerable merit. His philosophical writings include *Ueber das höchste Gut* (1842); *Ueber die Seelenfrage* (1861); and *Vorschüle der Æsthetik* (1876). His principal work is *Elemente der Psychophysik* (1860), a scientific presentation of mental phenomena. He died at Leipsic, Nov. 18, 1887.

FECHTER, CHARLES ALBERT (1824–1879), a French actor, was born in London, Oct. 23, 1824. His father was a German, and his mother was French. He was educated chiefly in France, and became a sculptor. While thus employed, he appeared on the stage, and the drama soon became his chief occupation. He joined a company which made a tour in Italy, and in 1846 appeared at Berlin. From 1847 he was connected with various theatres in Paris. Among his noted characters was Duval in Dumas's *Dame aux Camélias*. In 1860 Fechter went to England, and gave striking representations of Hamlet, Othello, and other Shakespearian characters. In 1863 he leased the Lyceum theatre at London, but his career as manager involved him in debt. In 1870 he came to the United States, and appeared both in French and English plays. Though highly commended by Dickens and other English critics, he was received with only moderate favor by the American public. In 1872 he opened a theatre in New York for the production of French plays, but soon gave it up. He retired to a farm at Quakertown, Pa., where he died Aug. 5, 1879.

FEDERAL PARTY. The name assumed by that portion of the people of the United States who favored the adoption of the Federal Constitution, and after its ratification in 1789 organized the government and administered it for twelve years. It is difficult for us who are accustomed to view the Constitution as a production of extraordinary political wisdom, and its popular acceptance as an equally marvellous example of intelligent patriotism, to conceive of the difficulty with which it was formed, and the opposition it encountered. Its merits were reasoned before the people with great power in the essays by Hamilton, Madison, and Jay, published in the newspapers, and collected in *The Federalist*, a volume that will never lose its value while the Constitution it defended exists. But there is reason to believe that at the outset a majority of the people were either opposed or indifferent to it. In Pennsylvania, out of an estimated voting population of 70,000, not more than 13,000 votes were cast in the election of the convention which ratified it. The election in Virginia was closely contested. When the conventions met to act on the ratification, that of New York had only nineteen members favorable to the Constitution, to forty-six opposed. The Massachusetts convention, on assembling, had a majority in opposition. That it was finally ratified was due to the able reasoning and masterly tactics of the leading Federalists. If Mr. Jefferson, whose adverse opinion is on record, had been at home, it is doubtful if Virginia could have been carried in its favor; but he was absent as our envoy to France. In the New York convention, the task of turning a small minority into a small but sufficient majority was performed by Alexander Hamilton almost single-handed, and was one of the most memorable achievements even of his commanding genius. In the Massachusetts convention, a proposition for conditional ratification was dexterously modified into an unconditional ratification, with an appended resolution recommending additional articles, ten of which were afterwards adopted, and form the first ten of the existing "Articles of Amendment."

The first party division was thus into "Federalists" and "Anti-Federalists." The Federalists advocated a government having attributes of sovereignty, operating upon the people directly, and having all the powers necessary to its own effective action; the Anti-Federalists favored rather a union of sovereign States in a simple compact of confederation, acting by mutual agreement, not by law operating *proprio vigore*. When the Constitution was ratified further opposition ceased, and the adoption of the first ten amendments removed one of the chief objections that had been urged against it—the want of a bill of rights. The Anti-Federalists then assumed the title of "Republicans," intending, probably, to imply that the Federalists were anti-republican. They regarded it as their mission to defend the reserved rights of the States, by insisting on a very strict construction of all grants of power to the Federal government. The Federalists maintained that their policy asserted no more than the constitutional powers of the United States, and equally stood for the rights of the States. It is certain that the Tenth Article of Amendment— "The powers not delegated to the United States by the Constitution, nor prohibited to the States, are reserved to the States respectively or to the people"— which is the special charter of State rights, was drafted by that distinguished Federalist, Theophilus Parsons, of Massachusetts. In his first administration Washington had both parties represented in his cabinet. But since he adopted habitually the advice of Hamilton, Jefferson retired, and was soon after followed by Randolph, so that the administration became avowedly Federalist. The decorous distinction between the President's supposed impartiality and the party leanings of the cabinet was at length disregarded, and Washington was recognized as a party leader, exposed to the censure and disparagement of the opposition.

The first questions upon which the parties divided were financial: the funding of the national debt; the assumption of the State debts incurred in the struggle for independence; the imposition of taxes to pay the interest of the debt, and to carry on the government; and the establishment of a national bank. These measures were open to exceptions, which the Republicans did not fail to urge; but they prevailed, and received Washington's approval. This system of financial policy, it should be noted, received a double ratification, for the Republicans, when in power, after some tentative deviations, followed in the main these precedents of their former adversaries. Questions of foreign policy supervened, and for a considerable period divided the country, almost to the exclusion of domestic issues. Both parties sympathized with the opening acts of the French revolution, but the Federalists withdrew their sympathy when they proved to be the prelude of a European war, and the President's proclamation of neutrality expressed the determination to keep the United States out of the contest. The Republicans insisted that we were bound by ties of gratitude to France for aid extended in the Revolution, and France claimed that the United States were under treaty obligations to be her ally. It must be confessed that the French had some grounds for this claim, but it was plain that the nation could not, in the weakness of its infancy, cast itself into such a gigantic struggle, but must at any cost keep out of it. A few years later the obligation was acknowledged and the default atoned for. The negotiation of Jay's treaty with England, which secured some part of our just demands, leaving others unsatisfied, aggravated the discontent of the opposition, and an attempt of the House of Representatives to interfere with the constitutional prerogatives of the President and Senate, which the President firmly resisted, cost Washington a loss of popularity which he keenly felt.

John Adams succeeded to the Presidency by a majority of barely three electoral votes. The difficulties with France reached an acute stage under his administration. The French government, by a series of hostile decrees, plundered our commerce, and, when envoys were commissioned to demand satisfaction, refused to treat with them, except on terms too humiliating to be tolerated by national self-respect. The envoys returned, and reported that they had been required to purchase audience with money. The effect was to rouse almost the whole people to the support of the administration. Measures were taken to build a navy. A provisional army was set on foot, Washington was appointed to the chief command, and the enthusiasm of the people rose to a high pitch. At this time the Federal party was at the height of its power. Its downfall was, however, near, and was rapid. The passage of the Alien Act, by which the President was authorized to expel from the country any alien who was deemed dangerous to our peace, and of the Sedition Act, providing special penalties for libelling the President or the government, created wide-spread popular dissatisfaction, and led to the passage of the famous Virginia and Kentucky resolutions of 1798 (of which Mr. Jefferson was the then unknown author), in which the doctrines of nullification and of secession ever afterwards found their justification, until the twin heresies were subdued, at immense cost, in our civil war. These discontents would not, perhaps, have caused the political revolution that followed, had the Federalists continued to be a united party. But Mr Adams became convinced that Gen. Hamilton and the Federal leaders sympathizing with him desired war. Projects were ascribed to Hamilton for an alliance with Great Britain against France, and for hostile measures against Spain, looking to the seizure of the Floridas, Louisiana, and Mexico.

The President had made the announcement that no minister would be sent to France without an assurance that he would be received in a manner suited to the dignity of the United States. Such an assurance, in the very words of the President, was informally and circuitously given by Talleyrand, upon which Mr Adams nominated a minister; and, objection being made to him, named three commissioners to reopen negotiations with France. Peace was thus preserved, but, as Hamilton and his friends insisted, at the sacrifice of honor. For this they resolved to defeat the re-election of Mr. Adams. It was not difficult to do this, but it was at the price of the defeat of the Federal party—a fall from which it never rose. Mr. Jefferson's first administration was so tranquil, and the country so prosperous, that he was re-elected with very little opposition, Massachusetts giving him her vote. Then came the war upon our commerce, waged by England and France. In their life-and-death struggle with each other they disregarded the rights of neutral powers, of the United States especially. England added the grievance of kidnapping American seamen to man her navy, under pretence of reclaiming British subjects. We had no navy; the beginning of one in Mr. Adams' administration had been arrested by Mr. Jefferson, and we were in no condition to appeal to arms. Resort was had to an embargo; as its opponents expressed it, our enemies crippled our commerce, and our government killed it. Against this policy the Federal party rallied with much resolution and little strength of numbers. Its chief strength was in New England. When war with England was declared, in 1812, it was against the earnest resistance of Federalists, who found much also to complain of in the policy by which it was directed. Declared mainly on account of injuries to our commerce, in opposition to the commercial States, the defence of these States was neglected, their industries were paralysed, and they were compelled to bear the heaviest burdens of the contest. It is not to be wondered at as the years wearily passed over them, a passionate sense of wrong led to a doubt of the value of the Union. When a convention of delegates, commissioned by the legislatures of Massachusetts, Connecticut, and Rhode Island, and, with some local representatives from New Hampshire and Vermont, met at Hartford, in 1814, it was strongly suspected that a plot against the Union was hatching. But the delegates were commissioned to consider and declare their grievances, and to propose measures for redress "not repugnant to their obligations as members of the Union." The assertion that they had treasonable designs concealed under these professions was vehemently urged, and for a long time believed, but it rested on no evidence, and is not now credited. The grievances they alleged were the power over the State militia claimed by the Federal government; the raising of troops by conscription, and the enlistment of minors without the consent of parents. Amendments to the Constitution were proposed: to base representation on free population; to declare the President ineligible for a second term; disqualifying persons of foreign birth from holding office; limiting embargoes, in every case, to 30 days; requiring a two-thirds vote of both Houses of Congress to admit new States, to declare war, or to interdict commercial intercourse. Such were the sole devices of the famed Hartford Convention. Its members were among the most honored citizens of their respective States, but they became the objects of popular suspicion, and were ostracised from all other

tive offices. One or two of them sat in the Senate, or occupied honorable positions on the judicial bench, but many years elapsed before men's minds were calm enough to weigh their merits with candor. As for any political effect from their deliberations, their meeting was too late. They fulfilled the prediction of Josiah Quincy, that "the outcome of the convention would be—a great pamphlet." Their messenger, on his way to Washington with their memorials, was met with the tidings of peace with Great Britain. With this announcement the issues of war and embargo disappeared from our politics, to be speedily followed by the disappearance of party divisions in "the era of good feeling," which followed the election of Pres. Monroe.

The Federal party, as a party of administration, ended with the accession of Pres. Jefferson, in 1801. Its record up to that point, with the exception of the Alien and Sedition laws, was highly honorable. The party embraced a very large proportion of the constructive ability required for the formation, establishment, and practical operation of our constitutional system, and continued in power for a sufficient time to get the machine running smoothly. One of the last acts of Mr. Adams was to appoint John Marshall Chief-Justice of the Supreme Court, which, under the lead of his clear and massive intellect and eminent judicial faculty, became the defence of the Constitution and held the balance firmly between the powers granted to the nation and the powers reserved to the States. This administrative history is the brighter page in the record of the party. It is marred by some narrowness of judgment and some weaknesses of feeling. Abhorrence of demagogism led them into the opposite extreme of something like contempt or distrust of popular opinion. Some of them had an almost hysterical fear and dislike of the French. They so far identified Mr. Jefferson with the Jacobins of the French revolution as to predict, and, we may not doubt, in sad sincerity, that his election would be followed by a reign of terror and a war upon Christianity. The very excess of these alarmist outcries, when contrasted with the actual results of the change of administration, contributed to the reaction that followed. As a party of opposition, the Federalists were less wise and less fortunate. Their opposition was so indiscriminate as to be factious. Above all, when we were at war with England, a war that put in peril our very existence as a nation, opposition seemed unpatriotic. For twenty-five years after the peace, in the feeling of a large portion of the people, the name of Federalist was as odious as that of Tory had been in the Revolutionary war, and long afterward. Now that our great civil war has made obsolete all political issues of the preceding period, and it is possible to review our earlier party history with calmness and impartiality, the Federal party, as above all others, the framers of our national government, and of an administrative system which became traditional and survives essentially to this day, receives the honor that is due to so transcendent a public service.

For the adoption of the Constitution the chief authority is George Bancroft's *History of the Formation of the Constitution* (2 vols.). See also J. B. McMaster's *History of the People of the United States*, and *Life of Alexander Hamilton*, by J. T. Morse, Jr. Some interesting incidents of the Massachusetts Convention are given in the *Memoir of Chief-Justice Parsons*, by his son. For the administrations of Washington and Adams, see McMaster and Morse as above, *The Life of John Adams* (Vol. I. of his *Life and Works*), and Gibbs' *History of the Federal Administrations*. The Federal view of the embargo and the war of 1812, including the Hartford Convention, may be seen presented in an interesting way in the *Life of Josiah Quincy*, by Edmund Quincy, and more fully in the *History of the Hartford Convention*, by Theodore Dwight, and the *History of New England Federalism*, by Henry Adams.   (L. E. S.)

FENCES, LAW OF. Stone walls, hedges, and fences of board, pickets, rails, or wire fastened to posts driven into the ground, are corporeal hereditaments belonging to the land to which they are attached. When standing on division lines separating adjacent lands they are the joint property of adjoining land-owners, who are charged with the duty of keeping such partition fences in good repair; but portable fences of any kind are personal property the title to which does not pass with the land on which they rest.

In New York and other Eastern States land protected by a substantial fence and occupied by a claimant without title to the land is deemed in adverse possession, and a conveyance of such land by the owner thereof is void.

In most of the Western States a conveyance of land in adverse possession is not void, but no writ of ejectment will issue against the occupying claimant until his fences and other improvements have been appraised and paid for.

Wherever the common law has not been modified by statutory enactments or municipal ordinances permitting cattle to run at large, the owner of land is not bound to fence it against trespassing animals, and may distrain such animals, or recover damages from their owner; but against cattle lawfully grazing on common land and permitted to roam at large the land-owner must protect his crops by sufficient fences, and cannot recover for injuries done by cattle breaking into his close unless protected by a fence of the character described by statute, or one of equal capacity to turn cattle.

Statutory provisions regulating fences differ according to the character of the localities for which they are made; and the question of sufficiency, as well as all controversies about rights in fences and duties in relation to their erection, maintenance, and removal, are usually referred to fence-viewers, who are the trustees or selectmen of the townships for which they have been elected.

In Illinois justices of the peace have jurisdiction over fences and in all controversies between adjoining land-owners on this subject.

In Iowa a fence made of three rails of good substantial material, or three boards not less than 6 inches wide and ¾ inch thick, or of three barbed wires with not less than 36 iron barbs of 2 points each to the rod, or 26 iron barbs of 4 points each to the rod, or of four wires two of which are so barbed, the top wire, board, or rail not more than 54 inches and not less than 48 inches, and the bottom wire, board, or rail not more than 20 inches and not less than 16 inches from the ground, fastened to good substantial posts not more than 10 feet apart where rails are used, not more than 8 feet apart where boards are used, and not more than 2 rods apart with two stays between, or 1 rod apart with one stay between where wire is used, or any other kind of fence, which in the opinion of the fence-viewers is equivalent thereto, is deemed a lawful fence.

By act of Congress fences around the premises of distilleries must not exceed a height of 5 feet, and by act of the Iowa legislature barbed wire fences are forbidden on the grounds of public schools, and on private land within 10 feet of the boundaries of school-house lots since Sept. 1, 1884.

But dumb beasts following their natural instinct may still be lacerated and killed by such barbarous fences with impunity, and the annual loss, especially of horses, caused thereby is very considerable in the aggregate without redress to their owners.

In the absence of any special agreement between adjoining land-owners about their partition fences it is the duty of each, so long as he improves his land, to keep up and maintain such fences in equal shares; and in case of any one neglecting to do so the aggrieved party may make all necessary repairs and recover therefor from the delinquent party; but neglect cannot be imputed until after an assignment of shares and notice to repair by the fence-viewers, and an action of trespass cannot be maintained for injuries suffered from a neglect to repair fences.

In North Carolina and other Southern States all persons, not only planters, are subject to indictment for not keeping their fences in good repair as required by statute.

In Iowa and other Western States, when a controversy arises between the respective owners about the obligation to erect or maintain partition fences, either party may apply to the fence-viewers, who after due notice to each party may assign to each his share thereof, and designate the time within which each shall erect or repair his share in the manner designated by the fence-viewers, and for any neglect thereafter the aggrieved party may recover double costs of the repairs made by him for the other.

A land-owner not occupying his land, nor using it otherwise than in common is not obliged to contribute toward the erection or maintenance of fences between him and adjacent owners; but when he encloses his land for private use, and joins his fence to partition fences previously erected by adjacent owners, he becomes liable for one-half the value of such partition fences and for the future maintenance of his share thereof.

A person desiring to enclose his land independent of adjoining owners may do so by leaving a strip of not less than 20 feet wide all along his boundaries open for common use by the public; but before he can move his part of a partition fence for such purpose he must give the adjoining owner six months' notice of his intention to do so.

In some States only three months' notice is required in such case, and the removal of a division fence without such notice entitles the injured party not only to actual damages sustained in consequence of such removal, but empowers him also to restore the fence at the expense of the offending party.

When lands owned in severalty have been enclosed in common without a partition fence, and one of the owners desires to occupy his in severalty, and the other refuses or neglects to divide the line where the fence should be built, or build a sufficient fence on his part of the line when divided, the party desiring it may have the same divided and assigned by the fence-viewers, who may designate in writing the manner and time in which such fence shall be built; and either party neglecting to comply with the decisions of the viewers, the other party after making his own part of the fence may make the other part also at the expense of the delinquent party; but disputes about the true location of a boundary line cannot thus be settled by fence-viewers.

When a division of fences between adjoining owners has been made, either by fence-viewers or by agreement in writing recorded in the township where their lands are situated, the owners, their heirs and assigns are bound thereby and must support the fences accordingly; but if any one desires to lay his lands in common and not improve them along the fence so divided, he may give the required notice and then proceed as in the case where lands owned in severalty have been enclosed in common, and such proceedings remit the parties thereto to their common law rights.

In such cases the term "owner" applies to the occupant or tenant when the owner does not reside in the county, and such proceedings will not bind non-resident owners unless notified; and when the partition fence is on a township line, and the parties in controversy reside in different townships, one fence-viewer at least must be taken from that of the party complained against.

Fences may be placed so as to stand partly on one side and partly on the other side of a division line, and the owner of the fence may remove the same as if it was wholly upon his own land; and where a fence has by mistake been placed wholly upon the land of an adjoining owner, such fence may be removed by its owner after the true boundary line has been established and payment of any damages to the soil caused thereby, or a tender thereof, has been made; and, where parties cannot agree as to amount of such damages, the same may be determined by the fence-viewers; but such fences made of material taken from the land on which they stand must not be removed until such material also has been paid for, nor at a time when their removal would expose the crops of an adjoining land-owner.

For work done and material furnished for fences or other improvements and not paid for when due, a lien may be obtained on such improvements and on the land owned or occupied by the party for whom the improvements were made, which liens take precedence over prior incumbrances of the land.

Fences in public highways obstructing travel are deemed public nuisances, and may be abated as such, and parties maintaining them are subject to indictment; but, for the purpose of protecting growing hedges on abutting lands, fences may be set out into the highways 5 feet on each side, 6 months prior to planting such hedges, and may be maintained there for 10 years afterwards, before they become nuisances.

Travellers on a highway out of repair and fenced on both sides may open the fence on either side and go through an adjoining close around an impassable obstruction in the highway without being liable for trespass.

In controversies about the original location of lost corners and boundary lines, fences, hedges, and rows of trees set out when the original corners were still in existence are taken as *prima facie* evidence that they were set out by such corners on the true boundary line, and control the courses and distances of field-notes of surveys and descriptions in conveyances, but do not absolutely establish such boundaries except by prescription, and ordinarily only shift the burden of proof on the contesting party.

In California 16 years of acquiescence in a fence originally built as a division fence estops all parties from controverting the correctness of its location. In most other States the period is 20 years.

Railroad companies as a general rule are not bound to fence their tracks of way, but they are liable for injuries to   by their trains, which are sometimes wrecked, thereby causing more serious injuries to life and property, for which they are also liable; and, as a matter of self-protection and economy, railroad companies generally erect fences and provide crossings with cattle-guards as soon as practicable, whether obliged to by law or not. Provisions in their charters requiring fences are for the benefit of adjoining land-owners only, and merely place the corporation in the position of a proprietor who is bound by contract or prescription to build the fence between himself and adjoining owners.

The grantor of a right of way through his land to a railroad company is not bound to fence it, nor is the company under any legal obligation to do so, and neglect in this respect renders the company liable for injuries only arising solely from that cause.

Care and diligence required of railway companies in constructing fences and cattle-guards depend upon the locality of the road, and negligence for not fencing cannot be imputed where a road runs over common, vacant, or unenclosed lands, but where required to fence by municipal regulations and failing to do so, they are liable for injuries without contributory negligence.

Fences built by mistake or design upon government land are the property of the government, and pass to a subsequent patentee with the land on which they stand, and a removal of such fences by the party erecting them or any other unauthorized person is trespass.

Since 1875 immense tracts of public lands have been unlawfully enclosed in western States and Territories by a new species of nobility—cattle-barons and their cowboys—organized into powerful syndicates for the patriotic purpose of supplying the poor people of England and America with cheap beef, and appropriating the public lands of this country to their own exclusive uses as pastures for their large herds of cattle.

Upon the principle that the end justifies the means, leases were obtained by them from Indians; here and there isolated entries were made by roaming cowboys under the homestead, timber-culture, and desert-land acts, or with spurious land-scrip; now and then a Mexican land-grant of uncertain dimensions and a township or two of railroad land were added, and then the whole area, comprising entire counties and in some instances populous towns, was enclosed by substantial fences, barring highways, streams, lakes, and mountain passes and stopping free intercourse, until at last Pres. Cleveland issued a proclamation against their unlawful proceedings and ordered the army to remove from the public domain all trespassing herds of cattle and cowboys, and all fences which had become public nuisances. But the end of this struggle has not yet been reached. Similar encroachments upon the public lands of the ancient Roman republic by the patricians led to the enactment of agrarian laws designed to limit the individual right of pasturage upon public lands and of acquiring title thereto, and to arrest the absorption of small freeholds by large corporate estates.

The law of fences, growing ever more complicated with the progress of civilization, is with us to-day one of the many other causes which are gradually and silently undermining the existing small freeholds of the common people in this country, and rendering future acquisitions of such by people of small means ever more difficult. And with the loss of a people's hold upon the soil, their independence invariably disappears.

Under the Mosaic law every forfeited freehold was restored free and clear of all incumbrances to the original owner or his heirs in each year of jubilee, and a revival of some such custom seems necessary for a preservation of the free institutions of our republic.

References to Court Decisions on Fences. Alabama Reports.—8, 492; 24, 310; 28, 385.
Connecticut Reports.—14, 292; 16, 200; 24, 271; 28, 600; 28, 193; 29, 421; 32, 108; 15, 133.
Illinois Reports.—2, 178, 215; 10, 130; 15, 341; 20, 334; 39, 186; 45, 76.
Indiana Reports.—9, 290; 14, 371.
Iowa Reports.—3, 396; 9, 283; 20, 378; 22, 568, 572.
Kentucky Reports.—3 Dana, 154; C. Dana, 290; 3 Bush., 547.
Maine Reports.—2, 72; 5, 357; 13, 371, 428; 22, 541; 29, 282, 336; 34, 332; 39, 526; 50, 86.
Massachusetts Reports.—4, 471; 6, 90; 11, 294; 16, 36; 15 Pick., 123; 14 Pick., 276; 2 Metc., 180; 4 Metc., 589; 11 Metc., 496; 1 Cush., 11; 2 Cush., 536; 6 Cush., 396; 1 Allen, 450; 6 Allen, 437.
Michigan Reports.—2, 259; 3, 163; 17, 417.
Missouri Reports.—16, 154; 24, 199; 28, 558.
New Hampshire Reports.—7, 436, 518; 8, 378; 11, 421; 13, 399; 24, 204; 26, 132; 29, 280; 31, 147; 37, 331; 43, 260; 44, 458; 38, 160.
New Jersey Reports.—1 Law, 53; 3, 662; 5, 547; 9, 384; 13, 229; 18, 368; 18 Eq., 54.
New York Reports.—4 Johns., 414; 9, 136; 19, 385; 3 Wend., 142; 11, 46; 17, 320; 18, 213; 19, 102; 22, 132; 24, 188; 2 Hill, 472; 3, 38; 11 Barb., 409; 18, 397; 25, 19; 41, 150; 44, 134; 21 N. Y., 275.
North Carolina Reports.—2 Murp., 298; 3 Jones, L., 375; 7, 555; 8, 397; 3 Ired., L., 506; 6, 352; 8, 229; 13, 36; Busb., 197.
Ohio Reports.—3 O. St., 172.
Pennsylvania Reports.—2 Miles, 247; 2 Pa. St., 126, 488; 18, 367; 20, 138; 23, 316; 25, 187; 27, 95; 32, 55.
Rhode Island Reports.—6, 422.
South Carolina Reports.—2 Brev., 67.
Tennessee Reports.—1 Head, 156; 3 Coldw., 406.
Vermont Reports.—18, 425; 22, 480, 565; 25, 116; 31, 450; 34, 336; 38, 678.
Virginia Reports.—2 Rob., 657.
Wisconsin Reports.—1, 127; 2, 10; 14, 432; 15, 598; 19, 49.
Miscellaneous Reports.—6 Peters, 498; 6 Wheat., 580; 111 U. S., 228; 18 Cal., 351; 33 Cal., 351; 70 Maine, 305; 56 Iowa, 237; Am. Dec., 5, 586; 20, 678; 34, 50; 36, 556; 42, 648; 49, 268–272.
Code of Iowa and Session Laws.—1880–1884, Tit. XI, Chap. 4.

(F. H.)

FENTON, REUBEN E. (1819–1885), an American Senator, was born at Carroll, Chautauqua co., N. Y., July 1, 1819. He studied law, but early engaged in business. In 1853 he was elected to Congress as a Democrat, but he joined the Republican party on its formation in 1856. In Congress he took high rank, being chairman of the committee on ways and means. In 1863 he was elected governor of New York, and held this office till 1868, when he was chosen United States Senator. Through dissensions in his party he lost, in 1872, the political power he had held for many years. He was a member of the international monetary conference in 1878. He died Aug. 25, 1885.

FERGUSON, SIR SAMUEL, an Irish poet and story-writer, was born at Belfast in 1810. He was educated at Trinity College, Dublin, and became a lawyer. He attracted attention in 1832, by his poem, "The Forging of the Anchor." To *Blackwood's Magazine*, in which this appeared, he also contributed an amusing dialogue, called "Father Tom and the Pope," and to the *Dublin University Magazine* a series of stories, called *Hibernian Nights' Entertainment*. In 1859 he was made Queen's Counsel, and in 1865 received the degree of LL. D. from the University of Dublin. In that year he published *Lays of the Western Gael*, and in 1872 *Congal*, an epic poem. In 1878 he received the honor of knighthood.

FERGUSSON, JAMES, a Scotch writer on architecture, was born at Ayr, in 1808, and was educated at the High School of Edinburgh. Entering into commercial pursuits, he went to India, where he devoted much time to the rock-cut temples. In 1845 he published an illustrated work on this subject, and afterwards other works, whose chief features were finally embodied in his *Cave Temples of India* (1880). Besides his works on the architecture of India he published *Palaces of Nineveh and Persepolis Restored* (1851), and an *Essay on the Ancient Topography of Jerusalem*. His *Hand-book of Architecture* (1855) was afterwards enlarged into *A History of Ancient and Modern Architecture* (3 vols. 1865). His work on *Tree and Serpent Worship* (1866), magnificently illustrated, was published at the expense of the Indian Government. He advocated the substitution of earthworks for masonry in fortifications, and served on the commission on defences of Great Britain in 1859. He died Jan. 9, 1886.

FERLAND, JEAN BAPTIST ANTOINE (1805–1864), a Canadian historian, was born at Montreal, Dec. 25, 1805. He was educated at Kingston and the College of Nicollet and admitted to holy orders in 1823. After serving as secretary to Bishop Plessis and as professor in the College of Nicollet he was ordained priest in 1828. He held several charges until 1848, when he was called to the archbishop's palace at Quebec. In 1855 he was made professor of history in Laval University, and he was afterwards dean of the faculty. He published several works on the history of Canada, *A Voyage to Labrador*, *A Voyage to the Coast of Gaspé*, and a *Life of Bishop Plessis* (1863). He died at Quebec, Jan. 8, 1864.

FERNS. A large group of acrogenous plants, constituting the order *Filices* of De Jussieu. They are partly tree-like, with leaves or fronds rising from the apex; and partly herbs, with fronds rising from a rhizome or underground stem. The fruit consists of cases containing *spores*, most usually seated on the under surface or at the margin of the fronds. The spores differ radically from seeds, and develop, on reaching the ground, into a secondary organism, the *prothallium*, upon which the sexual organs arise. To these, by a subsequent act of fertilization, the fern plant is due. About 2500 species of ferns have been described, though probably many more exist. They are widely spread, ranging from the tropics to near the frigid limit of vegetable life, and to a height of 15,000 feet in the tropics. Most of them may be classed as herbaceous perennials, with seasons of growth and rest in accordance with the nature of their climate. They vary considerably in size, many being as small and as delicate in texture as mosses, some few of shrub-like aspect, while about 150 species resemble trees, some of them growing to a height of more than 50 feet. Ferns have few economical properties, either as food, as medicine, or in the arts. The pith of *Alsophila excelsa*, a large tree-fern, is greedily eaten by hogs, and the wood used for building, it being hard, fireproof, and exceedingly durable. The Maidenhair fern is said to derive its name from a syrup made from it called *Capillaire*, and used for hair-dressing; or perhaps from the slenderness and delicacy of its stems. The common *brake* is used as a food in some countries. There is a superstitious idea that the burning of it will bring down rain. Few ferns grow in dry or flat countries. They need moisture for abundant growth. Of North American ferns 70 species were named by Nuttall in 1820. Since then the number has been more than doubled. In 1879 the species known north of the Mexican boundary numbered 143. The peculiar climbing fern of the Eastern States is the only species of this genus found in the United States. About sixteen other species of this genus are known, mostly tropical, and none reaching so high a latitude as the one above named.

(C. M.)

FERRY. A passage across a river or stream, which, in the absence of a bridge, is traversed on a ferry-boat. The boats range all the way from the flat-bottomed scow, propelled by a pole, to the large and expensive steam ferry-boats seen on the New York ferries.

A *flying bridge* is a ferry where the boat is held by a rope fastened up stream, which, under the action of the current, is made to cross a river in the arc of a circle, the rope being made fast at the centre of the circle. Sometimes a wire rope is stretched across the stream, high enough to be out of the way of floating objects when the stream is swollen. On this cable runs a small trolley from which lead two ropes to the ends of the boat. By hauling in one rope till it is shorter than the other, the boat is placed at an angle with the direction of the current, so that there is a resultant force due to the action of the current, which propels the boat across the river toward the side of the shorter rope or upstream end of the boat. A bridge of pontoons or boats is also called a flying bridge, and is often quickly improvised in time of war for the passage of troops across streams that are not fordable.

Much of the same nature as the two first mentioned examples of flying bridges is what is termed the *floating bridge*. A good example of this type of bridge is to be seen at Portsmouth, England, where a large flat boat is drawn across the ferry to Gosport by means of a chain lying on the bottom of the river. This chain passes in at one end of the boat, thence around a sprocket wheel turned by steam, and out at the other end. By turning the wheel in the proper direction the boat is drawn across to the required side. Such a bridge does not, of course, depend on the action of the current, while the chain is out of the way of passing vessels.

FERRY, JULES FRANÇOIS CAMILLE, a French statesman, was born at Saint Dié, Vosges, April 5, 1832. He studied law at Paris and was admitted to the bar in 1854. He soon joined with other young lawyers in harassing the imperial government. After contributing for some time to the *Gazette des Tribunaux* he became, in 1865, one of the editors of the *Temps*, in which he exposed the extravagance of Baron Haussmann in the rebuilding of Paris. In 1869 Ferry was elected to the *Corps législatif* as a radical democrat. On the downfall of the empire in September, 1870, a government of national defence was formed, of which Ferry was made secretary. There were internal as well as external foes, and on Oct. 31 he displayed great energy in putting down the communist insurrection at the Hotel de Ville. After the capitulation of Paris he retired from the government, but was elected to the national assembly from the Vosges, and in May, 1872, he was sent as minister to Greece. Ferry returned to the national assembly in 1876, and he was more than once vice-president of that body. He was the leader of the Republican left and in numerous speeches insisted on radical changes in public education, elections, and municipal administrations. Cautiously but steadily the Republican party moved forward from one victory to another, until in January, 1879, they had a majority in both chambers and were able to compel the retirement of Marshal MacMahon. On Feb. 5, 1879, M. Grévy, the new president, called Ferry to his cabinet as minister of public instruction and of the fine arts. His new law for higher education, proposed in March, 1879, required the complete exclusion of the unrecognized religious orders from the work of education. Article 7 was especially aimed at the Jesuits, who then had 27 colleges in France with 848 teachers, though there were also other communities affected having a still larger teaching force. Article 7 was struck out in the Senate, and thus modified the bill became a law. However, M. de Freycinet, then prime minister, declared the purpose of the government to enforce the old laws against the Jesuits. Such difficulties were experienced that a ministerial crisis ensued, and in September, 1880, M. Ferry was made president of the council. In the beginning of 1881 the French government sent an expedition to Tunis. Though this movement brought Tunis completely under French control, the costly and corrupt management of army affairs produced a revulsion of popular feeling. M. Ferry was compelled to resign Nov. 10, 1881, and Gambetta was called to assume the responsibilities of prime minister, but before three months had elapsed he also retired. M. de Freycinet then formed a cabinet with M. Ferry as minister of public instruction and worship, but this ministry also resigned in July, 1882. M. Ferry, however, in Feb. 1883, was again made prime minister, and held this place more than two years, when the Radicals again drove him from power.

FERTILIZERS. Substances which, when applied to the soil of any locality, supply it with the elements in which it is deficient, are called fertilizers. Such substances may be of organic or of inorganic origin, and the applicability of any particular fertilizer depends chiefly upon the nature of the soil to which it is applied, but to some extent upon that of the crop which it is intended to raise.

Plant Food and its Sources.—All organic life, whether plant or animal, primarily depends upon the four elements, oxygen, hydrogen, carbon, and nitrogen. But in the solid tissues of both plants and animals other materials are required, and plants use variable quantities of potash, phosphorus, silicon, iron, calcium, magnesium, chlorine, and sodium. All these substances are procured either from the air or from the soil. The air is an inexhaustible source of oxygen; carbon is taken up by the leaves from the carbonic acid which is always present in the atmosphere; hydrogen is absorbed in the form of water, chiefly by the roots, but to a certain extent by the stems and leaves; and nitrogen is to a great extent derived from the compounds of nitrogen produced in comparatively small quantities in certain electrical conditions of the air. Although nitrogen forms the greater portion of the air, it seems that plants are quite unable to use it in its pure or uncompounded state, but are dependent for their supply entirely upon nitric acid, ammonia, and the nitrates—substances which are as a rule rare both in air and soil. The first essential of a soil, from an agricultural point of view, is, therefore, that it contain nitrogen; but certain soils may be poor in other necessary elements or compounds, and may therefore need a different treatment. As has been shown, the four elements which are present in all living tissue are derivable either directly or indirectly from the air, which supplies the rainfall, and is the source of the rare nitrogen compounds. But no plant can be brought to perfection unless nearly all of the elements before mentioned are present. Phosphorus is one of the most important of these; sulphur is, as well as nitrogen, an essential constituent of all the albuminoid bodies to be found in every growing plant-cell, and the compounds of the four metals, potassium, calcium, magnesium, and iron, are universally present in the ashes of plants, and no plant can be brought to maturity when any of them is absent, yet but little is known concerning their action. Potash is always present along with starch, cellulose, and other carbo-hydrates, and is most abundant where those compounds are in greatest proportion, but the real connection between the two is at present unknown. Iron seems to be essential to the proper development of the chlorophyll grains of the leaves.

Many plants contain other elements, which may, in some cases, serve useful purposes, but do not seem to be essential to the vital processes. Thus silicon is often deposited in the cells of certain plants, especially cereals, giving rigidity to their stems; chlorine seems to be of advantage to many plants by favoring the translocation of starch granules, yet is injurious in excess; and sodium, though present in the ashes of many plants, does not seem essential to the growth of any.

The Origin of Soils.—To understand why fertilizers are needed, it is necessary to know something of the origin and nature of soils. All exposed surfaces of the earth's crust, however hard, however tenacious, or however soft, are perpetually subjected to influences which decompose them or wear them away. Water and air, aided by carbonic acid, and by other substances present in them, perform the work of disintegration, and thus, if every particle stayed near the spot from which it came, the entire land surface would be covered by a layer of loosely compacted material or soil, which would be fitted or unfitted to support plant life, according to the substances which the local rocks might afford. But the action of gravity, of running waters, and to a smaller extent of winds, does not permit the disintegrated particles to remain where they were formed. Gradually they are washed or blown downwards into the hollows between the rocks or into the valleys, leaving the higher rocks bare and still exposed to the decomposing influences of the air and moisture. The mingled materials borne into the valleys are usually rich in plant food, and were the home of generation after generation of plants before man appeared upon the scene to claim the soil for the culture of plants specially suited to his wants. Uplands—that is to say the gentle slopes of rolling land, terraces, and the foothills of mountain ranges—have a thinner soil, yet are often covered in a state of nature with thick forest or luxuriant herbage. Many broad plains, though covered with disintegrated material, are barren, either from lack of water, or from the absence of some necessary constituent of the soil. The materials which are most common and most universal in most soils are silica or flint, alumina or clay, oxide of iron, and lime; for these are the most abundant materials in the rocks of which the earth's crust is composed. Soils which contain these materials very often have also an ample supply of magnesia, potash, and soda, for these also enter into the substance of all the older rocks of the globe. But over large areas of the land surface the surface rock may be composed chiefly of one mineral, which has during geological ages been separated from the others. Sandstones may cover one extensive tract, limestones another, while a third may be clay. Evidently a soil formed in a limestone area is likely to be rich in lime and carbonic acid, the materials of limestone, but poor in other necessary substances; while a soil derived from sandstone will be mainly powdered silica or sand—and so on. But in a large proportion of the soil-covered areas a sufficiency of the necessary elements to support plant life exists, and the growth and death of many generations of plants has added to the original soil a store of materials best fitted to supply other generations of plants. Animals, ever present where there are plants, upon which they mainly depend for sustenance, add, both during life and after death, their materials to the soil. By the action of life the rare nitrates are stored up in the surface soils ready for plant use. (See AGRICULTURAL GEOLOGY, Vol. I., p.)

The Needs of Soils.—Man, having become predominant upon the globe, needs an annual growth of certain plants to supply him with food, and also wishes to cultivate plants which yield fibres, timber, etc. Of many of these needs he has found a plenteous store provided, and has used it wastefully, so that he is now beginning to see the need of economy, and to study the laws of plant growth.

The fruits, vegetables, and cereals which are fitted to his use, man has long grown upon soils which at first possessed a sufficiency of the necessary elements. But as he each year took away from the soil, by harvesting his crops, a much larger portion of nitrogenous and other matter than was returned to it by plant decay, he long ago learned the need of applying some fertilizer which should prevent the soil from becoming utterly barren. The first fertilizer thought of, the only one which is of universal application, and the only one in universal use, was MANURE. (See Vol. I., p.) Under this term may be included every form of decomposing animal or vegetable matter, brought to such a condition that it is susceptible of ready mixture with the soil. As knowledge of the nature of soils progressed, it was found that other things than the presence of sufficient organic matter were needed to make a good soil, and gradually there grew up a demand for fertilizers which should supply to the soil the exact element it lacked. Moreover, as population increased, the need for additional food production prompted the effort to bring under cultivation lands which seemed barren. It was found that many such soils needed only water, hence IRRIGATION (q. v.) has been practised from very early ages. Other soils, however, needed phosphorus, others lime, while almost all soils could be stimulated to increased production by the application of nitrates.

From what has been said it is evident that there may be sandstone soils lying upon sandstone, sandy soils which no longer rest on the parent rock; clay soils from clay slate, shales, etc., either in situ or transported to a distance; limestone soils derived from the decomposition of limestone or dolomite; pebbly or gravelly soils from fragments of any kind of rock; loamy soils, containing mixtures of sand and clay; marly soils, mixtures of lime and clay; or admixtures of these in any proportion.

From this complexity in the nature of soils, coupled with the fact that different crops assimilate different proportions of the various constituents, it follows that it is no easy matter, in many cases, to properly regulate the use of fertilizers. A knowledge of chemical facts is far from universally diffused, while the practical application of those facts is known to comparatively few. Thus fertilizers are often misapplied. An excess of nitrogenous or phosphatic matter may be present in the soil, and the crops may be starved through the lack of one of the elements which they require in smaller quantity. Thus such fertilizers as guano and bone-dust do not supply a sufficiency of potash to the soil. So long as soil is dressed only with ordinary farmyard manure, there may be a deficiency in total quantity, but the relative quantity of each fertilizing element is that required by plants. When, therefore, guano or bone-dust is used for several years on soils containing their normal amount of potash, such soils necessarily in a few years become so poor in potash that they no longer yield a good crop. The addition of potash to such a soil, rich in nitrogen and phosphorus, will cause it to produce much larger crops than can be obtained by the use of any other fertilizer. Potash usually acts favorably upon a sandy soil, or on one which is non-absorbent, and has little effect on heavier soils which are likely to be rich in potash. Potash manures are usually employed mixed with lime or gypsum. These latter materials, as well as most marls, do not, like nitrogenous and phosphatic fertilizers, act directly as nutriment, but stimulate growth by their indirect action upon the soil. They benefit a crop by dissolving, setting free, or replacing substances that were before in a condition unavailable for use. Thus carbonic acid has a solvent effect on silicates and nitrates; and when a soil contains potash in an absorbed or insoluble state, a solution of lime will release a part of the potash, the lime being retained in its stead. The addition of the soluble salts of lime to the surface will set free other salts contained there, and these freed salts will then sink deeper, and be brought within reach of plants having deeply penetrating roots.

Quicklime, carbonate of lime, and marls also promote the decay of vegetable matter, and cause the production of humus with its peculiar acids. *Humus*, or vegetable matter in the soil, in process of decomposition, is not so directly a source of plant nutriment as was once thought, but acts *physically* by rendering the soil more porous, and a better absorber of heat and moisture; and *chemically* by introducing a ceaseless chemical activity by which those constituents of the soil which are capable of further change are decomposed, and the actual plant food (potash, phosphoric acid, etc.) they contain is set free and rendered available, and by which ultimately some at least of the nitrogen of the humus itself is converted into ammonia or nitric acid.

Natural Fertilizers. Guano.—On many islands and coasts comparatively unvisited by man sea-birds have lived in countless numbers for long ages, and their excrements, mingled with the remains of their bodies and of their food, form extensive accumulations. In similar situations seals and sea-lions have their breeding places, and their excretions and remains occasionally form appreciable beds. These beds of organic matter are exported under the name of guano. From its origin guano is rather a manure than a fertilizer, and it contains phosphorus and lime as well as nitrogen and some potash. The proportion of phosphates and nitrates contained in commercial guano depends chiefly upon the rainfall of the region in which it has accumulated. A group of small islands known as the Chinchas, situated in a rainless region off the coast of Peru, for ———— furnished nearly all the commercial guano. When the deposits found on these islands were practically exhausted, the Macabi and Huanape islands, and Ballestas group, etc., were worked, but these for the most part yielded a product inferior in nitrogen to Chincha guano. Nevertheless Peruvian guano is still acknowledged to be the most excellent of fertilizers, since it contains from 25 to 30 per cent. of ammonia and phosphoric acid.

Guano or "Huano" was used long ago by the Indians of Peru, but was not introduced into Europe until Liebig's writings had drawn attention to the importance of fertilizers. The regular trade commenced in 1842, and in 1862 there were 435,000 tons exported. England and France are the greatest consumers of Peruvian guano, but it is used to some extent in every quarter of the world. The best qualities of Peruvian guano are of a light yellow or coffee brown, do not weigh more than 60 lbs. per bushel, and consist of a fine grained powder containing small lumps. The softer lumps contain ammoniacal salts, while of the harder ones some are highly phosphatic and others highly siliceous. Analyses show considerable variation, but the presence of any considerable excess of moisture proves damage either by rain or by sea-water on the voyage, and is accompanied by a loss of ammonia.

From the coast of Bolivia a guano is exported which is rich in phosphates but comparatively poor in nitrogen, and other guanos of a similar nature are procured from the West Indian Islands, under the names of the Curacoa, the Sombrero, and the Navassa, and from Ichaboe and other islands on the west coast of Africa, as well as from the Pacific Islands. These guanos are to a large extent lime phosphate. The animal remains are exposed to rains, which wash out the ammonia and the phosphates, but when the deposit lies upon limestone phosphate of lime is formed below and is the chief ingredient in the exported material. Bat guano is often found in caverns, but does not exist in sufficient quantities to be of commercial importance.

The following will give an idea of the constituents of various Peruvian guanos, as compared with Bolivian phosphatic guano:

	Anguros	Chincha	Pabellon de Pica	Punta de Lobos	Bolivia
Moisture	11	16	17	16	13
Organic matter combined with water	53	52	45	34	23
Whereof is nitrogen equal to ammonia	17.5	17	12	7.5	4
Tricalcic phosphate	19	22	19	29	42
Phosphorous pentoxide in alkaline salts	1	3	4	3	3
Alkalies, etc., by difference	9	6	12	12	12

Bolivian guano is put up for the trade under five different brands, the best warranted to contain an average of 10 per cent. of ammonia, while the second is guaranteed to average 6 per cent. The lumps contained in guano must be crushed before using, and treatment with sulphuric acid is not only necessary with the more phosphatic varieties in order to convert the phosphate into superphosphate, but is also useful to render the ammonia non-volatile.

Guano may be applied broadcast, but a time should be chosen which will be followed by rain, and it should always be mixed with from two to four times its bulk of sifted earth, mould, plaster, etc., before use. This mixture renders certain its more equal distribution, and prevents it from being blown away by the wind. It should never be mixed with ashes or lime, with bone-dust, or with superphosphates, but may advantageously be combined with stable manure.

Nitrates.—Nitrate of soda exists native as part of an earth called *caliche* or *terra salitrosa*, which abounds in the district of Atacama and the formerly Peruvian but now Chilian province of Tarapaca. The caliche forms a layer from ten inches to five feet thick, stretching over a length of forty leagues, and is covered by "lostra," a hard conglomerate from half a metre to two metres in thickness. It contains from 48 to 75 per cent. of nitrate of soda, and from 20 to 40 of common salt, associated with small proportions of iodate of soda, organic matter, etc., suggesting the idea that the bed was formed from excrementitious animal matter, probably from the guano deposits which covered the shore of a great soda lake. The caliche is worked on the spot for crude nitrate of soda, which is exported under the name of "Chili saltpetre." Nitrate of soda occurs also in comparatively small quantity in Humboldt co., Nevada, and some other spots in the great basin, as well as near Chihuahua, in New Mexico and Mexico.

Nitrate of potash (saltpetre) occurs native in India and other parts of the world, including many of the western and south-western States, and the western Territories. It is in use as a fertilizer, but is more expensive than the sodium nitrate, from which the greater part of that used in this country is manufactured. The sodium nitrate is treated with German potassium chloride, and the two by interchange form saltpetre.

Phosphates.—*Apatite*, a phosphate of lime, occurs in many of the older crystalline rocks, but the great beds of phosphorites, as the "Phosphorites de Quercy" of France, and the phosphatic rocks of South Carolina and Florida, belong to a later age. Apatite is found in small quantities in many parts of the United States, and was formerly mined for agricultural purposes in Essex co., N. Y., and in Sussex co., N. Y. Extensive deposits exist in Ontario and Quebec, and in 1882 17,000 tons were shipped to Europe and 5000 to the United States for fertilizing purposes. (See APATITE, Vol. I., p. 292.) The supply of phosphates for this country now comes from an area on the coast of South Carolina, 70 miles long and 30 in greatest width. The most accessible deposits are situated at a radius of about eight miles from Charleston. The formation is of the upper eocene age, like that of the marls which lie below it. It is an ocean ooze which was raised above the surface, and in pliocene and post-pliocene ages formed the surface of the country. Thus the bones of various land animals became mingled with the casts of shells which are its proper fossils. It is believed by some that the bed owes its origin to the action of the fecal matters of extinct land quadrupeds upon the calcareous marl which lies below. The layer most used for fertilizers is one containing hard nodules of lime phosphate, the softer phosphate in which they occur being ignored. The composition is as follows:

	Per cent
Phosphoric acid	20–30
Carbonic acid	2–10
Lime	30–45

Magnesia	1— 2
Silica and sand	2—25
Organic matter	1— 7
Moisture and water of composition	1— 3

Together with small quantities of sulphuric and fluoric acids, sesquioxide of iron, and ammonia. Alumina may be present sometimes to 3 per cent. The phosphate of lime is in tribasic form and the average rock shipped contains 53 to 60 per cent. There have been recently discovered in Florida extensive beds of phosphatic deposits, as yet not largely developed, yet promising to become of high importance in the future. They extend through many counties of the State.

Phosphatic deposits have also been found in Alabama, both in the cretaceous strata and in two horizons of the tertiary, viz., the lower portion of the oligocene and the centre of the lignite eocene beds. The cretaceous phosphate beds extend into Mississippi.

Coprolites.—Coprolites are lumps of phosphate of lime which are really the fossilized excrements of extinct animals. They are found in considerable quantities in Bohemia, France, England, etc. They vary greatly in composition and usually contain much alumina and iron oxide. They are not used directly as phosphatic fertilizers, but are employed in the manufacture of low grade superphosphates.

Gypsum.—Sulphate of lime or gypsum, the material from which plaster of Paris is made, is tolerably abundant in most parts of the world, including the United States. Its use is chiefly in the arts, but it is also often employed as a fertilizer. Gypsum furnishes plants with two substances, lime and sulphuric acid, of which they need a small quantity, but as it is beneficial in soils which have an abundance of these substances, it must have some other action, either fixing the volatile salts of ammonia or replacing and setting free other bases as previously described.

Salt has in some cases been found valuable as a stimulant.

Marls are strictly calcareous clays, but the term has also been applied to the greensand or glauconitic beds which occur near the seacoast of the United States at various points from New Jersey through Delaware, Virginia, North and South Carolina to Alabama, Mississippi, and Louisiana. Along nearly all the Atlantic seaboard and Gulf States marine calcareous marls are also found, also in Arkansas and Texas. Greensand occurs also in Tennessee. These beds belong to the cretaceous and eocene formations, but small beds of marls of recent age are found in many of the Eastern States. Analyses of New Jersey marls gave the following result:

	Per cent.
Phosphoric acid	1.02— 3.87
Sulphuric acid	0— 1.89
Silicic acid and sand	37.70—59.80
Carbonic acid	0— 6.13
Potash	3.53— 6.32
Lime	1.26— 9.07
Magnesia	1.50— 3.95
Alumina	6.00—10.20
Oxides of iron	11.98—25.23
Water	6.85—10.00

From the presence of phosphoric acid and potash in notable proportions, it is evident that greensand marl is not merely a stimulant but an actual fertilizer.

The calcareous marine marls of South Carolina do not average above a third of one per cent. of phosphoric acid, and about one per cent. of potash. Their value is, therefore, chiefly due to the lime and carbonic acid which form more than 90 per cent. of their bulk, except where there is an admixture of silica. Apart from purely chemical properties, the application of marl may cause a desirable physical change in the soil, as when a clay marl is spread upon a sandy soil, or a sandy marl upon a heavy clay soil.

Kainite, etc.—Since 1858 large quantities of salts of potash have been exported from the salt mines at Stassfurth, Germany. The principal of these is a double sulphate of potash and magnesia known as *kainite*, and containing from 15 to 18 per cent. of potash. In its natural state it contains much chlorine, which is by treatment with alcohol separated as chloride of magnesium. This and other potash salts form the upper covering of the rock salt deposit at Stassfurth. Many preparations containing a higher percentage of potash are made by concentrating the crude salts.

Artificial Fertilizers.—Besides these natural fertilizers large quantities of artificial ones are now made from various kinds of organic waste, and also from the natural fertilizers. Among those valuable chiefly for the nitrogen they contain is "*fish guano*," consisting of the refuse of fish, crabs, and other marine animals. As a fertilizer this can be made to have a value little inferior to that of Peruvian guano. Unfortunately it is not made solely from waste materials, but from the product of a fishery which consumes a large quantity of edible fishes or of fishes which form the food of edible fishes. Other nitrogenous fertilizers are hides, hair, the flesh of animals, blood, hoofs, wool, and feathers. In some parts of South America, where animals are slaughtered for their hides alone, or for meat extract, the greater part of their bodies is worked up into a preparation which is called guano, and contains about 7 per cent. of nitrogen and 13 or more of phosphoric acid. Skin, horns, hair, hoofs, and similar substances, on account of the slowness with which they decompose, are before application subjected to the action of superheated steam, after which they are easily reduced to powder. Still another commercial fertilizer is "*poudrette*" or dried human excrements. This is largely used in France, and in smaller quantities in other countries. In amount of nitrogen it is far superior to farm-yard manure, and the comparatively small use made of a substance the disposal of which in every other way is dangerous to health, can only be attributed to lack of civilization. Manufactories of poudrette are supposed to be a nuisance, and it is certain they could not be tolerated near to a city, but a civilised society would utilize, either in a liquid or a solid form, the whole of the sewage which we in our proud barbarism pour into our drinking waters. In this respect we are far behind the Chinese and Japanese, who return all such material to the soil, and thus succeed in cultivating land for many centuries without impoverishing it as much as, for instance, the lands of California were impoverished by twenty years of constant cropping without fertilization.

Phosphatic blood guano is made by combining with dry powdered blood which yields 16 per cent. of ammonia, a quantity of bones dissolved in acid and ground with the addition of potash and soda. Vegetable refuse, such as cotton seed, oil-cake, the waste from breweries, starch-manufactories, sugar-works, etc., are also used as fertilizers. The oil-cake contains 3 to 4 per cent. of nitrogen, 3 to 4 of phosphoric acid, and 1 to 2 of the alkalies.

One of the chief phosphatic fertilizers is formed

from the bones of animals, which contain, when dry, about 60 per cent. of lime phosphate. These are used simply as bone-dust, or, by treatment with sulphuric or hydrochloric acids, have their bone phosphate converted into superphosphate, with the production of chloride or sulphate of calcium, according to the acid used. As the sulphate of calcium (gypsum) is more beneficial to the soil than the chloride, sulphuric acid is generally used.

The action of the superphosphates upon land is not simply nutritious, but stimulating, on account of the contained gypsum. It will, therefore, tend to exhaust a soil unless ammoniacal salts, greensand, potash salts, or other nitrogenous or alkaline materials are added, as is done in some commercial artificial fertilizers, the analysis of one of which (bone-dust phosphate) is appended:

			Per cent.
Soluble phosphoric acid			5.64
Insoluble	"	"	3.76
Reverted	"	"	6.47
Alkali			4.77
Ammonia			3.41

The advantage of the superphosphate is, that it is soluble in water, while bone phosphate is not. It is thus readily dissolved by the rains and evenly disseminated through the soil. Though it is speedily carried back again into the insoluble form by contact with the constituents of a normal soil, it is presented to the plant in a far more available state than can be attained by the finest state of mechanical division. What is known as reduced or reverted phosphoric acid is in combination with iron, alumina or lime, and though no longer soluble in water, is quite soluble in dilute acids. This reverted acid is considered by chemists nearly as valuable as the soluble portion.

Precipitated phosphate of lime is a by-product in the manufacture of glue, and like bone-dust is basic or bone phosphate. In some manufactures a more soluble neutral phosphate, with 35 to 42 per cent. of phosphoric acid, is produced.

The phosphates are very beneficial to pastures, and to crops which are cultivated for their roots or tubers.

Ashes.—Wood-ashes contain about 5 per cent. of potash; indeed, it is claimed that unleached wood-ashes from timber grown on strong land contain 7 per cent. Such ashes are also rich in lime, phosphoric acid, silica, magnesia, and iron. Ashes of turf or peat have but 3 per cent. of potash. Leached ashes are without potash, yet are still useful from the phosphoric acid they contain.

The production of artificial fertilizers in this country during 1880 amounted to 727,453 tons, with a value of $19,921,400. (W. N. L.)

FESSENDEN, WILLIAM PITT (1806–1869), an American statesman, was born at Boscawen, N. H., Oct. 16, 1806, being a son of Gen. Samuel Fessenden. He graduated at Bowdoin College in 1823, and was admitted to the bar in 1827. He began practice at Bridgeton, Me., but in 1829 removed to Portland, where he became noted in his profession. He was elected to the legislature in 1832 as a Whig, but afterwards declined political position until 1840, when he returned to the legislature. In the next year he was elected to Congress, and in 1843 was the Whig candidate for U. S. Senator, but was defeated. He served again in the State legislature in 1845, 1846, and in 1853. In 1854, during the movement to exclude slavery from the territories, the Free-Soil Democrats united with the Whigs in electing Fessenden to the U. S. Senate. In this body he achieved a prominent position as a speaker and a debater, and when the Republican party was organized he was one of its leaders. In February, 1861, he was a member of the Peace Congress at Washington which tried in vain to avert the war. He was then chairman of the finance committee of the Senate, and he succeeded S. P. Chase as secretary of the treasury in 1864. On account of impaired health he relinquished this position a year later and resumed his place in the Senate. He was still prominent in the councils of the Republican party until 1867, when, during the impeachment of Pres. Johnson, he was one of the seven Republicans that voted for his acquittal. He died at Portland, Me., Sept. 8, 1869.

FESSLER, JOSEPH (1813–1872), an Austrian prelate, was born at Lochau, Tyrol, Dec. 2, 1813. He studied theology at Brixen and was ordained priest in 1837. In 1841 he became professor of church history and canon law in the seminary at Brixen, in 1852 professor of church history in the University of Vienna, and in 1856 professor of the decretals. In 1861 he went to Rome to assist in conducting the affairs of the oriental churches. On April 7, 1862, he was nominated by the pope bishop of Nyssa *in partibus*. He was made bishop of St. Pölten March 27, 1865. He was general secretary of the Vatican Council in 1869, and afterwards published a defence of its action, *Die wahre und die falsche Unfehlbarkeit der Päpste* (Vienna, 1871). His principal work is *Institutiones patrologicæ* (2 vols., 1850–52). He also published *Sammlung vermischter Schriften* (Freiburg, 1869). He died April 25, 1872.

FEUILLET, OCTAVE, a French novelist and dramatist, was born at Saint Lô, department of Manche, Aug. 11, 1812. His father was secretary-general of the prefecture and sent his son to Paris, where he was educated at the College of Louis le Grand. In 1845 he was called to assist Bocage and Aubert in preparing *Le grand Vieillard*. Having once begun to write he poured forth a stream of novels, romances, vaudevilles, and comedies which were long received with favor. His most noted novel was *Le Roman d'un jeune homme pauvre* (1858), which by the excellence of its description of French provincial life and by the purity of its moral tone gained great popularity throughout Europe. *Histoire de Sibylle* (1862) was almost equally successful, and called forth from George Sand a reply. His later works, *Monsieur de Camors* (1867), *Julia de Trécoeur* (1872), *Un Mariage dans le Monde* (1875), were written in the realistic style which had come into vogue under the Empire. They attracted attention, but did not increase his reputation. He died Dec. 29, 1890.

FEVERS.—A. This name denotes disorders characterized by elevated temperature and hurried pulse. Those which belong particularly to warm climates are separately classified, and treated in this article. SMALL-POX and MEASLES, with the closely related Chicken-pox and Roseola, will be treated in separate articles. Fevers are all regarded as contagious, the contagium being enormously multiplied in the human body, to which it gains access mostly by the air-passages in breathing, but in some cases by the alimentary canal in food or drinks. The nature and mode of action of fever-poisons are not definitely settled. They are generally regarded as living entities, the favorite theory being that they are microscopic fungi, collectively known as bacteria, and classed according to form as micrococci, spirilla, and bacilli.

See Vol. IX. p. 109 Am. ed. (p. 125 Edin. ed.).

Each malady has regular periods of incubation, invasion, progress, and decline, but the later stages are more variable in symptoms and duration than the earlier. The most characteristic are the eruptive fevers, in which varied inflammatory conditions of skin and mucous surface are attributable to local action of specific poisons in escape from the superficial capillaries.

1. *Scarlet Fever* (*Scarlatina*).—Until about 200 years ago this eruptive fever was not distinguished from measles. It is less contagious than small-pox and measles, but the contagium is singularly persistent when undisturbed in fomites. Young children are more susceptible than adults, but the latter suffer more seriously. The period of incubation is short, but by no means uniform.

Like other eruptive diseases, it commonly begins with a chill, headache, and vomiting. Sore throat is a prominent symptom. In young and delicate children convulsions sometimes occur. The temperature is high and pulse very rapid. On the second day a scarlet rash appears on the chest and rapidly extends over the body, but the skin remains smooth. From the fourth to the sixth day the fever usually declines, the rash begins to fade, and on its disappearance desquamation takes place during a period varying from a few days to six weeks.

Three different types of scarlatina are recognized: 1. *S. simplex*, very mild, in which the rash is the prominent symptom, though there are cases in which it is scarcely noticeable; 2. *S. anginosa*, in which the throat is highly inflamed and sometimes ulcerated, the nasal-passages being also involved; 3. *S. maligna*, falling with greatest severity on the nervous centres, with delirium, stupor, or convulsions, and early dissolution.

The sequelæ of scarlatina are especially numerous and grave: such as ulcerations of the throat, extension of inflammation from throat to middle ear, resulting in chronic obstruction of the Eustachian tube, caries of bony structure, and permanent deafness; chronic nasal catarrh; chronic ophthalmia; rheumatism, affecting various joints and sometimes the valves of the heart; inflammation of the tubular structure of the kidneys, resulting in albuminuria, uræmic poisoning, and dropsy.

Mild cases do well without medication; severe ones require treatment adapted to special symptoms. Strict confinement in-doors during the period of desquamation should be enforced for the safety of the patient, and for preventing the infection of others. Oily applications to the skin prevent itching and irritation and the scattering of the infectious scales.

2. *Diphtheria* (*Membranous Croup?*).—There is presumptive evidence of the ancient prevalence of diphtheria, in the writings of many authors from the time of Aretæus (about A. D. 100); but the first clear description was made by Bretonneau of Tours in 1821, since which time its literature has grown voluminous. It is an open question whether diphtheria and membranous croup are varying forms of the same disorder, or two distinct maladies. The common symptoms are fever and a fibrinous exudation of a grayish-white color upon mucous surfaces. In croup the exudation is limited to the larynx and trachea. In diphtheria it commences in the fauces and may be confined to that tract, but often extends into the nares and trachea and appears sometimes on remote mucous surfaces, or even the abraded skin. Invasion of the larynx is known by huskiness of voice, advancing to total extinction, and a hoarse, ringing cough, with expulsion of moulded casts of false membrane.

In all cases the onset is insidious, and the first recognized appearance of illness may be invasion of the larynx, almost certainly resulting in suffocation. Under best opportunities for observation, it is found that the period of incubation is quite indefinite, and the course of the disease widely variable. That diphtheria is not merely a local disease is proved by early appearance of albuminuria in a majority of cases, and by frequent occurrence of local paralysis after subsidence of the acute symptoms. The disease is always attended with great prostration and convalescence is slow. The contagiousness of diphtheria is universally admitted, while those who hold membranous croup a distinct disease are not agreed upon its communicability. Young children are much more susceptible to both than adults, but one attack confers no immunity.

The most important measures of treatment consist in supporting the strength by appropriate food, tonics, and stimulants, and in dissolving the fibrinous membrane by a warm spray of lime-water or diluted lactic acid. The utility of tracheotomy for relief of impending suffocation is questionable. It does not arrest the malady, and consent to the operation is rarely obtained in season to do any good.

3. *Typhus Fever* (*Ship, Jail, Hospital*, or *Camp Fever. Spotted Fever*).—The conditions under which typhus arises and becomes epidemic are the crowding of people into badly ventilated quarters and the presence of animal filth. Undoubtedly infectious, it is communicable only for a short distance, through the breath of the sick and not their excretions; but the virus may be long preserved and carried far in fomites excluded from the air. Typhus is far less prevalent now than formerly, owing to better hygienic conditions, and has scarcely appeared in the United States for more than 20 years.

Persons are susceptible at all ages, but it is most common between 15 and 25 years. Immunity is almost certainly conferred by one attack. The latent period is commonly 5 to 12 days, but is not restricted to either limit.

The attack commences with chilliness, followed by fever seldom above 105° Fahr. From the fourth to the seventh day an eruption resembling that of measles appears on the chest and abdomen, and gradually extends over the whole surface. It begins to fade in 3 or 4 days and disappears about the end of the second week. The bowels remain rather constipated, the tongue becomes dry, sordes collect on the teeth, the intellect is dulled, and the patient often passes into a state of coma-vigil, unconscious, but with open eyes. During the third week, unless convalescence occurs earlier, the pulse becomes extremely feeble and quite rapid, the muscles tremulous, the prostration excessive, and control is lost over the evacuations. In rare instances the case terminates fatally within a week, with active delirium or profound stupor. Death may take place from exhaustion, or a refreshing sleep may supervene, followed by gradual recovery. Under the age of 30 years the mortality is usually only 5 or 6 per cent, while between 50 and 60 years it is nearly 50 per cent, and in old age much more.

Post-mortem examination shows the quality of the blood much impaired, but discloses no organic lesions. As the nature of the disease clearly indicates, the most important measures of treatment consist in the best practicable ventilation and the support of the vital powers by liquid nourishment, of which alcoholic drinks form a most important adjuvant. Removal of filth personal cleanliness, and free ventilation are effectual preventives.

The foregoing maladies are more prevalent and severe in cool climates than in warm, in the cold months than in the hot. The explanation is that under a high temperature free ventilation produces attenuation of contagia. The importance of thorough disinfection of apartments by sulphur fumigation, after termination of sickness, cannot be overestimated. All articles of bedding and clothing used about the sick must be included. Such as can be wet may be placed in a solution containing 4 oz. sulphate of zinc and 2 oz. common salt to a gallon of water and boiled. All discharges from the sick, particularly from the throat, should be disinfected with a stronger solution, or one of corrosive sublimate, 1 part to 500 of water. These precautions apply particularly to small-pox, scarlatina, diphtheria, and typhus fever.

4. *Enteric Fever (Typhoid Fever).*—The distinction between typhoid and typus fevers was made about 1830, by the discovery of an inflammatory affection of Peyer's glands in the small intestine as an essential lesion of enteric fever. In fatal cases these glands are found ulcerated, and in some instances the whole thickness of the intestinal walls is perforated. No period of life is exempt, but about four-fifths of the cases occur in persons under 25 years of age. The poison is undoubtedly reproduced in the bodies of the sick, and is communicated only by the alvine discharges. The usual mode of infection is through drinking water obtained from wells, springs, or small streams, which have been contaminated by the dejections of the sick.

The onset is marked by a few days of malaise. In the early stage there are irregular chills, alternating with flushes of heat, lassitude, and pains in the limbs and back, thirst and want of appetite, headache, with sometimes drowsiness by day and wakefulness at night, occasionally vomiting and diarrhœa. During the second week the fever becomes continued, the abdomen is tympanitic, with gurgling or pressure in the right iliac region, and at this time usually a few rose-colored spots, about the size of a pin's head, appear upon the abdominal surface, soon fading and succeeded by others. Throughout the course of the disease the alvine discharges are loose and have the appearance of pea-soup. The temperature varies from 102° to 106°. There is a daily remission from 12 P. M., succeeded by a corresponding elevation after 12 M. In severe and prolonged cases profound nervous disturbances ensue: delirium, tremors, picking at imaginary objects, deep stupor. Emaciation and prostration become extreme. Death results from gradual exhaustion, or from the rapid inflammation following intestinal perforation and escape of contents into the abdominal cavity; or the fever may abate any time from the 21st to the 60th day, and the patient slowly recover.

During adolescence light cases sometimes occur, terminating in 10 or 12 days, and these are often mistaken for febricula or remittent fever; while in young children it is probable that mild enteric often passes under such names as "worm fever," "gastric fever," "bilious fever," etc.

No specific treatment is appropriate. It is of vital importance to husband and sustain the vital powers. Milk and alcohol are invaluable resources. Medication must be adapted to each case as symptoms arise, not with a view of arresting the disease, but of conducting it to a safe termination. Thorough disinfection of the alvine discharges is an indispensable preventive measure.

5. *Relapsing Fever (Famine Fever).*—Until within the last half century typhus, typhoid, and relapsing fever were all included in the common term *continued fever*. Relapsing fever, like typhus, is epidemic in character, and associated with overcrowding, filth, and insufficient food. It is likewise highly contagious, through the breath of the sick, and transportable in fomites. Unlike typhus, it has no eruption, it is attended with enlargement of liver and spleen, and one attack does not confer immunity. It has prevailed in various parts of Europe and Africa and in India, and once in the United States during the winter of 1869–70.

After a latent period, varying from 2 to 16 days, the subject is seized with a chill, accompanied by severe pains in the head, trunk, and limbs. A fever follows, ranging from 104° to 108°, which declines in 3 to 6 days. In about a week subsequently another attack of fever similar to the first generally occurs, and sometimes a third after another interval. The average mortality is less than 5 per cent. Convalescence is protracted, but generally without sequelæ.

6. *Influenza (Epidemic Catarrh).*—This disorder prevails during the colder months, and few escape an attack as often as it appears, for immunity is never acquired. After a short but indefinite latent period, a moderate fever sets in, accompanied by severe nasal catarrh, gradually extending down the bronchial passages, with suffusion of eyes, headache, and cough. The attack usually lasts from 4 to 12 days, leaving protracted debility. It is never fatal, save as a complication or with feeble subjects.

7. *Hooping Cough (Pertussis).*—The respiratory organs are chiefly affected, but an essentially nervous character is indicated by the spasmodic cough. Few children escape it, but adults are susceptible, and in rare instances have it a second time. After an uncertain period of incubation, there is a slight febrile action, with an ordinary catarrh and cough. In about two weeks the cough becomes paroxysmal and spasmodic, recurring from 2 to 50 or 60 times in 24 hours, which seems to be provoked by the presence of tenacious mucus in the trachea. The cough consists of expiratory efforts to detach this mucus, so rapid as to nearly exhaust the lungs of air, followed by a long inspiratory act, with the peculiar sound which gives it name. In the warm season the cough runs its course in 4 to 6 weeks, but in winter it lasts until settled warm weather. The spells of coughing frequently end with vomiting, which seriously interferes with nutrition. On account of severe and repeated shocks to the chest and abdomen, from violence of cough, it becomes a grave complication of any intercurrent malady. Among direct effects of the cough are pulmonary congestion, running into lobular pneumonia, collapse of vesicular tracts, producing solidification, and rupture of air-cells, resulting in emphysema. Much of this mischief may be obviated by appropriate remedies and careful protection from the cold air.

8. *Mumps (Parotitis).*—This is also a disorder incident to children, on account of its great contagiousness, but all ages are susceptible. The period of incubation is believed to be about 14 days. The essential feature is inflammation of the parotid salivary glands, one only being occasionally affected. This gives rise to moderate fever, drowsiness, headache, swelling of neck and throat, with great difficulty of motion and pain in swallowing. The inflammation often extends to the submaxillary glands, tonsils, and fauces; rarely to the

testicles or mammary glands. The complaint runs its course in 1 to 2 weeks. As there is no danger of suppuration of the inflamed glands, warm fomentations or poultices are appropriate and alleviating to the pain.

B. FEVERS OF WARM CLIMATES.—These fevers belong especially to those regions where a warm temperature prevails throughout the entire year, and those portions of the temperate zones where a high temperature lasts during a great part of the year. Prolonged freezing weather surely arrests them, and where this prevails most of the year they are unknown.

1. *Malarial Fever.*—The term is derived from *malaria* (bad air), which has long been used to express the cause of the malady. *Paludal* and *miasmatic* have also been used as distinguishing terms, but with less propriety, inasmuch as the fever prevails in many localities far distant from marshes, and the word miasm includes all air-borne poisons. The distinguishing feature of the disease is periodicity, or recurrence in separate paroxysms. While the tendency of most disorders due to specific causes is to a single attack, terminating either in death or permanent and complete recovery, and in many instances pursuing a definite course regardless of remedial agents, this malady, if not positively interrupted, has an indefinite duration, with progressively aggravated symptoms.

The terms intermittent and remittent are applied to two types of the fever, which differ in severity and distinctness of paroxysmal character. The former, being less serious, is marked by total disappearance and reappearance of symptoms in regular order. The onset is sometimes abrupt, but generally preceded for several days by pains in the head, back, and muscles, constipation, and loss of appetite. The paroxysm is often ushered in with a short period of yawning and stretching, followed by a chill, which may last from a few minutes to several hours, and of every grade of severity from the faintest chilly sensation to the most violent rigor, icy coldness of surface, and total insensibility, sometimes running into coma and death without reaction. During this stage the superficial blood-vessels are contracted, and a corresponding accumulation of blood occurs in the interior organs, particularly the spleen and liver. The blood-vessels of the kidneys, lungs, brain, mesentery, and stomach are also liable to engorgement, resulting in albuminuria or hæmaturia, pulmonary congestion, sometimes developing into pneumonia, delirium or coma, dysentery or bloody vomiting, according to the organ congested. Repeated congestion in the spleen frequently results in such an enlargement of that organ as to have given rise to the term "ague-cake," and sometimes in the liver abscess of that organ occurs.

The fever which follows ague is a reactionary struggle to restore the circulation to its equilibrium, in which there is a determination of blood to the surface. This leads to excessive secretion of the sweat-glands, constituting the sweating stage, during which the temperature of the body declines and the paroxysm ends. The interval between the disappearance of fever and the next paroxysm is called the period of apyrexia, which varies according to duration of paroxysm. The period between the beginning of one paroxysm and the beginning of the next is called the interval. When this is 24 hours the intermittent is styled quotidian, when 48 hours, tertian, and when 72 hours, quartan. Irregular types occasionally occur, such as the double quotidian, with two paroxysms in 24 hours; the double tertian, with daily paroxysms, beginning at different hours, or, rarely, with two on one day and none on the next, etc. The relative frequency of the regular types of intermittent may be approximately stated as 52 per cent. of quotidian, 47 per cent. of tertian, and 1 per cent. of quartan; but this varies at different times and localities and in different persons. In intermittents not checked by suitable treatment, the interval of the paroxysm frequently becomes shorter, while retardation, or lengthening of the interval, is likely to follow insufficient doses of antiperiodics. Vomiting is quite frequent in the early stage, becoming bilious when often repeated. Great drowsiness ensues in the second stage. The chill generally takes place between sunrise and mid-day; rarely during the night.

The congestive or pernicious form of malarial fever, which may be either intermittent or remittent, is characterized by excessive determination of blood to such vital organs as the nervous centres, resulting in coma or convulsions sometimes suddenly fatal, or the kidneys, resulting in suppression or bloody urine. The term *dumb ague* is applied to those cases of intermittent in which the cold stage is imperceptible. Oft-repeated paroxysms of malarial fever are exceedingly destructive to the red blood-globules, attended with ashy pallor, great prostration, and frequently jaundice and dropsical swelling of the extremities.

The remittent form of malarial fever, often called bilious, or bilious remittent fever, generally begins with a cold stage, which is less violent and prolonged than in the intermittent. As in the other form, the body-temperature varies from 101° Fahr. to 108°, and this only partially declines before another access occurs. The duration of the paroxysm may vary from 12 to 72 hours, and the next one, if not modified by treatment, is likely to be more severe and prolonged. With suitable and timely management a remittent is speedily suppressed or moderated into an intermittent and then arrested, while a neglected remittent will run into a continued form, with only a slight decline in the early morning hours, lasting several weeks and rebellious to any medication. Bilious vomiting, headache, and delirium are more marked than in the intermittent form; anæmia, jaundice, and dropsical effusions are more pronounced; a chronic cachexia often ensues, and convalescence is liable to be slow.

Malarial complications occur with a great variety of other diseases in regions where this fever prevails. These are characterized by periodic access of fever or periodic aggravation of some symptoms belonging to the main ailment. Complication with typhoid fever produces the so-called "typho-malarial" fever, which was so common among the troops during the American civil war as to be regarded by some observers as a new and distinct disease. A periodic form of neuralgia, occasionally becoming continued, is a well-recognised result of malarial poisoning, often easily but sometimes with difficulty amenable to medication.

Malarial fever and malarial complications of other diseases are most prevalent in the later summer and autumn months, and in most parts of the temperate zones disappear or greatly decline during the winter season. In the low regions of the tropics, especially near sea-marshes, the shores of lakes, and sluggish streams, malaria is ever active. Strangers from high grounds and cooler climates are more susceptible to the malarial poison than those who have always breathed it, but it is doubtful if mankind ever becomes fully acclimatized to this miasm. Nothing is certain than the destructive effects of malaria upon the health and energies of those permanently subjected to it. This is proved by a high rate of mortality and general cachectic appearance of the inhabitants of malarious regions.

The settlement and cultivation of new grounds in most parts of the world have been effected with enormous cost of human health and life. Disturbance of the soil during the hot months is found far more detrimental to health than in the cold season, and in some localities this is regulated by law. The presence of primeval forests and of a luxuriant vegetation counteracts this miasm. Resinous trees are believed to afford great protection by the generation of ozone, and the planting of the *Eucalyptus globulus* especially has been found an important prophylactic in climates warm enough to favor its growth. But the thorough and prolonged cultivation of the soil, with drainage of the subsoil, has been found to bring about the gradual disappearance of malaria. On the other hand, the cultivation of lowland rice, which requires the flooding of grounds for a portion of the season, followed by their drying, has made regions malarious to a serious degree, which were before far less so, or were entirely exempt. A remarkable reappearance of malaria in the valley of the Connecticut River, after disappearance for several generations, is a recent fact which has not been satisfactorily accounted for.

Experience shows that the malarious influence may be carried by winds to the distance of several miles, and it has been found that the first hills some distance from rivers and lakes are more malarious than the grounds closely bordering. Malaria is far more active at night than by day. Crews of vessels land with impunity by day on the fever-stricken coast of Africa, but are ordered aboard before sunset some miles off shore. The citizens of Charleston, S. C., visit the country by day with confidence, but dare not pass the night out of town. A belt of forest, or an intervening expanse of water, will often give protection from the miasm. In malarious localities considerable immunity may be gained by avoidance of the outer air at night and by sleeping in upper rooms.

There seems to be a definite relation between the complexion of races of mankind and their susceptibility to malaria. The fair races of the North are most susceptible, and the African race least so. Negroes of pure blood are less liable than mulattoes, but the negroes of the United States have partially lost the immunity enjoyed by their ancestors in Africa.

The nature of malaria, save in relation to its effects, was a complete mystery until about the middle of the present century. The three conditions of heat, moisture, and vegetable decomposition have been commonly assigned as the efficient and indispensable causes. A temperature above 60° Fahr. is certainly necessary to render a region malarious, but fevers may occur after the temperature has fallen considerably lower. Malarial fevers have developed on arid grounds, though probably underlaid by abundant moisture, which indicates that vegetable decomposition is not an essential condition. The thorough desiccation of malarious grounds and their prolonged submergence have been found to eradicate malaria. The theory that gaseous emanations of any kind are the true essence of malaria is simply speculative. The same sulphuretted and carburetted gases which are accused, when inhaled in non-malarious localities produce no paroxysmal symptoms.

Prof. John K. Mitchell, M. D., of Philadelphia, has the credit of originating the theory of the cryptogamic origin of malarial fever, which he published in 1849. Prof. J. H. Salisbury, M. D., of Cleveland, Ohio, in 1866 published his researches on this subject, and announced the discovery of a palmella, which he cultivated and experimented with. Having taken some boxes of earth, in which he had planted this vegetation, to the sleeping-room of some young men in a healthy locality, they were soon affected with intermittent fever. It is proper to say that subsequent researches by other medical men in the same line of study have given negative results, until the remarkable announcement, in 1879, of the discov——— ——— malariæ in the neighborhood of Rom——— ———masi Crudeli. This bacillus is a microscopic fungus, found in the lower strata of atmosphere and soil of malarious localities, and has been cultivated in other soils. Inoculations of these bacilli under the skin of dogs are said to have been followed by the usual symptoms of intermittent fever, including enlargement of the spleen, and the bacilli have been found in that organ. They are also found in the blood of persons during the invasion of fever, but at the acme the spores only appear. Though this theory has not been fully confirmed by other investigators, it is quite in line with the accepted doctrine of the material cause of the specific contagious diseases. It is also in harmony with the recognized properties of the most efficient remedial agents for the cure of malarial disorders—the cinchona alkaloids and arsenic, which are destructive to low vegetal forms.

In the present state of our knowledge, the mode of action of these supposed bacilli must be conjectural. Inasmuch as malaria is found to be highly destructive to the red blood-globules, it may be supposed that the bacilli or their spores, having gained access to the body through the lungs or the alimentary canal, easily reach the capillaries, where they attach themselves to the blood-globules as a favorable soil for their growth. Their enormous multiplication and increase of bulk in a short time would obstruct the capillaries and cause the blood to accumulate in the larger vessels, producing the habitual congestion of certain organs; while the speedy decay of the bacilli, after their consumption of the blood-globules, would allow the circulation to return to the capillaries and the surface of the body. In the later stage spores only are found in the blood, which may soon germinate and produce a new crop of bacilli, followed by another paroxysm of fever, going through the several stages as before. It is possible that a period of about twenty-four hours suffices for the growth and maturity of a crop of the bacilli, coincident with the quotidian paroxysm, while two generations may be necessary in other cases, thus constituting the tertian type, and so on. In the remittent form we may suppose that the bacilli are in various stages of growth at the same time with some fluctuations, while in the continued form all regularity of growth and decay has disappeared, and all stages are in operation at the same time. During the cold stage, refrigeration of the body is confined to the surface, where the volume of blood is diminished. Elevation of temperature is partially explained by rapid oxydation or consumption of the bacilli, while they disappear from the blood in the intermittent form; whereas this process is constantly going on in the remittent and continued forms. This hypothesis accords with the known diminution of the red blood-globules, with the depletion of the capillaries and repletion of the large vessels, followed by reaction, and with the general laws which govern organized matter.

Other points relative to malarial fever must be barely alluded to. The cinchona alkaloids and arsenic are the most valuable curative and prophylactic remedies, while the former, together with strychnia as a general tonic, and preparations of iron as blood-restoratives, are important to establish convalescence. In many cases, however, no positive and permanent recovery can be gained without removal from the miasmatic clime.

2. *Yellow Fever.*—There is no evidence that this disease was known by Europeans prior to the discovery of America by Columbus. Historical indications exist of its presence in San Domingo in 1493, in Porto Rico in 1508, on the Isthmus of Panama in 1514, in Guadaloupe in 1635, at Havana in 1648 and 1655. It has been conjectured that this disease was brought to the West Indies in slave-ships from Africa, but it prevailed on several of the islands before slaves were brought from Africa, and hence it would appear to have pursued the opposite course. Yellow fever was first recognized as a distinct disease in the greater Antilles at or near the time they were first visited by white men, and from this region it has radiated ever since in the lines of commercial intercourse. In this way it has extended (at one time or another) along the

eastern coast of the mainland from Montevideo to Halifax and up the St. Lawrence to Quebec. It has repeatedly scourged Spain, extending far into the interior, has visited Marseilles, and reached as far eastward as Leghorn. England and France on the Atlantic have been touched by the disorder, but it has never gained a firm foothold in either country. All the West Indies have been more or less ravaged in earlier times. On the Pacific coast of America this fever has extended beyond the isthmus, only since the first third of the present century, to Callao on the south and Guaymas on the north.

In the United States yellow fever has visited New York 63 times, from 1668 to 1873, and has been six times epidemic; it has appeared 10 times at Boston, 1691-1858, and was epidemic in 1798; at Philadelphia 34 times, 1695-1870, and epidemic 9 times; at Charleston 52 times, 1699-1871, and epidemic 17 times; at Norfolk 18 times, 1747-1855, and epidemic twice; at Savannah 9 times, 1807-58, and epidemic in 1858; at Pensacola 23 times, 1764-1882; at Mobile 26 times, 1705-1878. There is some evidence that yellow fever appeared at New Orleans in 1769 and again in 1791, but it was first epidemic in 1796. Since the last date there have been few years without cases, but many in which the number has been very small, all traceable to direct importation. Since 1858 general epidemics have occurred in 1867 and 1878. In the United States its ravages have been mostly confined to seaports and towns in the interior accessible by steamboat navigation. In 1878 only it extended along railway lines in many directions through Mississippi, Tennessee, Kentucky, and Alabama.

In the United States yellow fever has never prevailed at a higher altitude than 500 feet above the sea. It has never occurred at Jalapa, Mexico, 4330 feet above sea-level, nor at Maroontown, Jamaica, at an elevation of 2000 feet; but has raged with great severity on the plateau of Caracas, 3000 feet above the sea, and at Cuzco, at an elevation of 11,000 feet.

The African race is far less susceptible to yellow fever than any other, and the fair nations of the white race most so. The aboriginal race of America and Mongolians are susceptible in rather less degree than the white race.

It has long been believed by residents of towns where yellow fever habitually prevails that natives of those places enjoy immunity from the disease. This notion was generally entertained by the creoles of New Orleans, and was termed creole immunity. Even Prof. S. H. Dickson, writing in 1855, expresses the same belief in regard to the natives of Charleston, S. C. As the fever has become less and less prevalent in these and other American cities, the idea has been gradually abandoned. In the most recent epidemics, which occurred after intervals of almost total absence of the disease for years, it has been found that young native children die in large numbers with the symptoms shown by others born at a distance. The explanation is, that children have the fever in infancy, where it prevails annually, and it is well known that nursing infants have great advantage over older subjects. This is attributable to the perfect quietude of their early existence.

A very prevalent and persistent belief, entertained in those cities most often afflicted with yellow fever, is that of its endemicity. There are physicians in New Orleans who still adhere to it, though all recent and undisputed appearances of the disease are unmistakably traceable to importation from its permanent seats. Yet there have been repeated instances of reappearance the following season after a general epidemic without fresh importation, of which the year 1879 afforded notable examples at Memphis and New Orleans. La Roche, writing in 1855, with special reference to Philadelphia, is unequivocal in denying the portability and communicability of yellow fever, and in insisting upon its originating in local causes, such as bad sanitary conditions connected with defects of drainage and accumulation of filth, together with some ill-defined and mysterious conditions of atmospheric humidity, electricity, and ozone. But it has not been explained in what respect these conditions have changed at Philadelphia and New Orleans, as to occasion total absence at the former place, and its appearance at the latter, only when imported from abroad. Neither has it been explained what local conditions obtain around the shores of the Gulf of Mexico different from those existing upon the shores of the Indian Ocean, which can account for the continual presence of yellow fever on the one, and its total absence on the other.

One meteorological condition is universally acknowledged to govern the existence of the fever, and this is the only one supported by evidence of any value. A continued temperature of not less than 80° Fahr. must have been maintained for a considerable time, to give the disease activity enough to spread. It is invariably checked by frost, and repeated frosts put a stop to the malady. But in every inhabited place where the temperature never falls below 20°, there are sheltered spots in which water does not freeze, and here the *materies morbi* may survive the winter.

There have been able advocates of the theory that yellow fever is of the same nature as malarial fever, differing only in degree or virulence. This opinion is based solely upon similarity of symptoms, without regard to the following discrepancies: yellow fever prevails especially in towns, malarial fever in the country; the one is abruptly checked by frost, the other is not; the one spreads from a focus of infection and becomes epidemic, while the other is endemic; a single attack confers immunity with the one, and predisposes to repeated attacks with the other; the one is a fever of a single paroxysm and rather definite duration, while the other has a tendency to repeated paroxysms and indefinite duration; quinine has no control over yellow fever and almost absolute control over malarial fever.

Since 1820 the extent of country ravaged by this disease has much diminished. In 1822 strict quarantine regulations were instituted in Spain and at the ports of New York, Philadelphia, and Baltimore, and from that time it has ceased to be epidemic in Europe and ports of the Union north of Norfolk. In 1761 it became domiciled at Havana, persisting continually to the present time, and most of the towns on the island of Cuba are permanently infected. Since 1849 it has constantly occupied Rio de Janeiro and frequently occurred at the other cities on the Brazilian coast. For many years it has not been absent from Vera Cruz, though clean bills of health are generally granted there in the winter season. Since 1865 it has been permanently fixed on the isthmus both at Panama and Colon. These important seaports are visited by strangers at all seasons, and they always afford the three indispensable conditions for the existence of yellow fever—a high temperature, the active cause of the disease, and susceptible people to take it. At all the important ports of the eastern coast of the United States quarantine regulations are in force, of such efficiency as to give protection under ordinary circumstances. The epidemic of 1878 at New Orleans, which spread more extensively over the great valley than any previous visitation, has been followed by measures of exclusion more rigorously enforced than any previously adopted, and these have been so thoroughly seconded by local sanitation on the appearance of the disease that no spread has followed the landing of single cases, which have several times occurred on vessels after leaving the quarantine station.

While the preponderance of evidence indicates that yellow fever is a specific disease, due to a peculiar poison; that this poison is transportable in porous articles; that it spreads from foci in all directions upon land, without regard to air-currents, but is arrested by high and unbroken walls; that the poison is indefinitely multiplied in a temperature from 100° down to 60°, when once fairly grounded; yet, unlike most spreading diseases, its contagium seems to propagate itself rather outside the human body than in the persons of the sick.

Experience shows that ships and their cargoes, and the personal effects of crews and passengers, coming from infected ports, are more dangerous than sick persons landed without other effects than the clothing on their bodies.

The period of incubation is rather indefinite, varying from one to five days, though a longer limit is allowed by some. The attack is abrupt, and oftener at night than by day. It is ushered in with violent pain in the forehead and back, generally with a moderate chill, followed by a high fever, flushed face, and injected eyes. Nausea and vomiting frequently appear early and become persistent. Restlessness and insomnia are marked features. The gums are red, tumid, and bleed on pressure. The eyes, at first glistening and fiery red, afterward become jaundiced. In ordinary cases the fever rapidly declines at the end of the third day (sometimes earlier), when the pain and restlessness also disappear. The patient passes into a stage of calm, with great muscular prostration; but, with good management, makes a rapid and complete recovery, often being able to rise from bed in a week. In other cases more profound symptoms then set in. The temperature rapidly rises higher than before; the previously moist skin becomes dry and pungent; the urine is albuminous, scanty, and often completely suppressed; the stomach will retain nothing; the respiration is sighing; eructations of gas are frequent, followed by mucus, soon colored with small dark specks, which afterward give place to copious vomiting without effort of a fluid loaded with a black deposit like coffee-grounds ("black-vomit"), which is blood, colored by the acids of the stomach. The pulse, full and soft from the beginning, now becomes gaseous and flickering, the intellect is rather dulled than distorted, the flush of the face deepens, and gives way to a lemon hue, and death takes place by exhaustion, usually on the fifth day. If recovery takes place after these severer symptoms, convalescence is tardy and apt to be complicated with abscesses.

Yellow fever is a specific and self-limited disease, and it is worse than useless to attempt to interrupt or control its natural course by drugs, as is done in many other disorders. Heavy prescribers generally lose most patients. At the onset it is important to evacuate the bowels, and also the stomach, if it contains undigested food. Drinks should be given frequently, but in moderation. The body should be sufficiently covered to produce steady perspiration; and when this is interrupted, warm foot-baths should be given to the patient in bed, from which he should not be allowed to rise from the horizontal posture for at least five days. During the three days of fever, it is important to allow no food—certainly no solid food. For several days afterward nourishment of the lightest character, and entirely fluid, should be given in small quantities, and at short intervals. During this period, the judicious use of alcoholic drinks, in some acceptable form, is of the highest advantage.

Ordinary cases actually require no medication after the purgative dose—the emetic being used only when the stomach contains undigested food. A faithful, attentive, and skilled nurse is of the highest importance. The more severe symptoms require treatment adapted to each individual case, according to discretion, which can be acquired best by personal experience.

The mortality is largest with those lately arrived in the stricken locality; with the intemperate, particularly if seized during a spell of indulgence; with those who fear the disease; with those who continue to go about while sick (walking cases all die); with the headstrong, who will not submit to restraint, nor follow directions; with those who are disturbed through rashness or officiousness of those around them; with those who are unstintingly physicked and injudiciously fed. On the other hand patients have been starved to death through excess of caution.

The mortality in yellow fever varies from 5 to 80 per cent., being highest in sporadic and early cases, since success in treatment demands early recognition and appropriate management from the start. At New Orleans, the mortality in the epidemic of 1867 was about 8 per cent. of all cases; in that of 1878, nearly 20 per cent.

Various prophylactic remedies have been recommended and used, among which quinine was the most prominent in 1878, but no one proved trustworthy. The recent claims of Freire and Carmona, in the subcutaneous injection of the attenuated virus of yellow fever, by which they profess to produce a mitigated type of the disease, which confers subsequent immunity, lack confirmation. Analogy favors the hypothesis that this virus is a special microbe, but most searchers acknowledge their failure to differentiate from the variety found in the blood and excreta a species constant and peculiar to yellow fever.

3. *Dengue.*—This disease, also known as "dandy fever," "breakbone fever," "scarlatina rheumatica," and "eruptive rheumatic fever," is said by Pozzio to have been brought to Spain from Africa in 1764. A disorder resembling it, in respect of general prevalence with uniform recovery, is recorded to have occurred on the Coromandel coast of India in 1780. The first authentic accounts of dengue are dated 1824, when it appeared at Rangoon, Mecca, and the island of St. Thomas. This visitation was traced from India to Aden, and thence to Zanzibar. The disease probably originated in Africa. Dengue reached Charleston, Savannah, and other Southern cities in 1828, and again appeared in 1848. Since the latter date it has been a frequent visitant of the Southern States of the Union.

Though it is generally agreed that dengue is both specific and infectious, its course and symptoms are more variable than those of other diseases of this class. It is essentially epidemic in character, resembling influenza in the very large numbers attacked, in rareness of fatality, in liability to secondary attacks, and in its catarrhal symptoms. The onset is usually abrupt, but sometimes preceded by a few days of malaise. A brief chill is followed by a fever, sometimes rising to 105° of body-temperature. The most characteristic symptom is the severe and general pain, which is often so intolerable as to demand free use of opiates. In the febrile movement, injection of eyes, flush of face, restlessness, pain in head and back, and moderate hemorrhagic tendency of the nose, stomach, and uterus, there is strong resemblance to yellow fever; but an attack of neither one affords protection against the other, while yellow fever has never appeared in Asia or Eastern Africa. In most cases, but not uniformly, an eruption resembling that of scarlatina, sometimes that of measles or nettle-rash, appears in the early stage. The fever is subject to remissions, and during its course the eruption disappears, and may reappear in the same or a different form. After complete subsidence of the fever, at the end of five or six days it often reappears, but runs a shorter course. The whole duration of the febrile and eruptive stages varies from three to eight days, leaving the subject greatly prostrated. Convalescence is peculiarly slow, and the rheumatic symptoms are often prolonged.

Most cases demand relief to the pain and restlessness, for which opiates, the bromides, and chloral hydrate generally suffice. Abortive and depletive measures during the acute stage are worse than useless. Want of autopsies in this remarkable malady has prevented accurate knowledge of its lesions, and the bacteriologists have not assigned its peculiar microbe.
(S. S. H.)

FEVER-BUSH is a common name of *Lindera Benzoin*, also called spice-bush and American Benjamin tree. It is of the natural order *Lauraceæ*, and was described under the name of *Benzoin odoriferum* by Nees. The flowers are bi-sexual and the four-parted calyx has permanent segments. The true Benzoin is a species of styrax, and the present species derives its name apparently from a mistake of Banister, who sent it from Virginia to Compton, Bishop of London, as a citron- or lemon-scented species of Benzoin. It has no relation to *Styracaceæ*, and is not even a gum-producing plant. John Clayton, the Virginian botanist, who furnished to Gronovius material for the *Flora Virginica* (1739), says, "It is a Virginian shrub, with the leaves of a persimmon, and berries redolent of benzoin. It is our wild allspice and wild pimento, famous for easing the soreness from colic pains." Rafinesque extends its beneficial uses to dysentery. As a febrifuge it has, however, derived its common name, yet it does not appear to have any more value than most aromatic herbs would have. Dr. Wm. Darlington, an eminent physician as well as botanist, makes no mention at all of it in connection with human diseases, but simply says that it is "a strongly aromatic shrub, of the twigs of which a decoction was formerly in great vogue as a medicinal drink for horned cattle in the spring of the year." The name Benzoin or Benjamin is of Malayan origin. The Cistercian monks dedicated the benzoin to St. Benjamin, a Persian martyr who died in 424, and whose festival is kept on March 31. This is about the flowering time of the American plant in the centre of its geographical area, which is in the low grounds of the Atlantic slope of the United States. The flowers are associated by the poet ornithologist Wilson with the arrival of the blue bird. The small, green flowers, on the bush of 10–12 feet, are succeeded in autumn by brilliant scarlet berries, and the bush itself is in some request as an ornamental plant for gardens. In this connection its only common name is spice-bush. (T. M.)

FIBRE. The main substances used as textile fibres, as is well known, are the wool of the sheep and the silk of the silk worm, of animal origin; and cotton, flax, and hemp, of vegetable origin. The hairs of some varieties of the goat, of the camel, and of some other animals, are also used in a lesser degree, while many plants yield fibres which are or may hereafter become important. Of these fibre-yielding plants about a dozen varieties which may yet be utilized are indigenous to North America. Of these the most important are *Abutilon* (Indian mallow or American jute), *Althea hibicus* (marsh mallow), *Yucca* (bear or dagger grass), and *Asclepia* (wild cotton, so called). To these may be added the introduced *Ramie* (China grass). In addition to flax, hemp, and cotton, these are our most important fibre plants. *Abutilon avicenna* is an annoying weed, which is frequently seen in corn and potato fields. It averages six feet in height, its fibre running the whole length of the bark, and being far superior to Indian jute in strength and dyeing qualities. It may be useful for fine cordage, carpet filling, matting, etc. *Althea hibiscus* is a similar, marsh-growing plant, of five feet in height, and yielding an excellent fibre. It is really a cotton plant without fruit, while the cotton plant itself possesses a good fibre in its bark, which has never been utilized. Steps towards its utilization are now being taken. *Yucca* belongs to the semi-tropical agave tribe, yet it resists Northern winters, and is grown from Pennsylvania to Florida. It has a large percentage of fibre, which resembles Manilla in strength

See Vol. IX. p. 115 Am. ed. (p. 131 Edin. ed.).

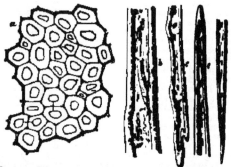

FIG. 1.—Fibres of Yucca (*Agave Americana*) magnified 37 times.
a. Sections of the fibre. *b.* Longitudinal views. *c.* End.

and quality, but not in length, and is suitable for cordage. *Asclepia* yields a pod whose seeds are furnished with a silky cotton-like hair over 1½ inches long, while the bark has a soft white fibre, of some value. The silky hairs are coated with so much silica that they could not be used without some silica-dissolving treat-

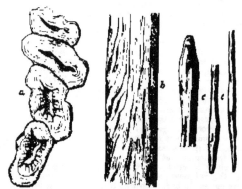

FIG. 2.—Fibres of Ramie (*Bœhmeria Nivea*) magnified 73 times.

ment. *Ramie* is of growing value as a fibre plant. It is well suited to our climate from New Jersey to the South, and is the most prolific of textile plants. Rooted in fair sandy soil its shoots increase at the rate of 100 annually for each one planted. The stalks measure 4 to 5 feet in length, and yield a fibre with the fineness, gloss, and almost the tensility of silk. It has been used in the East since before the Christian era. Its preparation is very difficult, needing a combination of chemistry and machinery, yet the American method of treating it is complete and radical, and its use is extending in this country. The ordinary textile plants, hemp, flax, and cotton, have been treated under their respective titles, yet the experiments made by Professor J. M. Ordway on cotton fibre, in connection with the 1880 census, call for some attention. The hair of the cotton seed is, when young, a cylinder filled with liquid. In ripening this disappears, and the cylinder contracts into a flat band, with thickened edges, and more or less of a spiral twist. To this peculiarity much of the value of cotton fibre is due, since it permits it to be easily spun even when very short. Its value in this respect depends upon the extent of the twist, the width, and the form of the edges.

FIG. 3.—Fibres of Cotton (*Gossypium*) magnified 275 times.

Cotton varies considerably in length, ranging ordinarily, according to Professor Ordway's measurements, from ⅞ to 1¼ inch, while the Sea Island staple ranges from 1¾ to 2 inches. The width averages about .001 inch. The breaking weight of the fibre varies from 61 grains for sandy upland growth to 214½ grains for the product of creek bottoms. The percentage of list on the seeds varies from 31.67 to 43.79. *Short staple* cotton signifies that which is under .98 inch in length; *medium*, from .98 to 1.17; *long*, from 1.18 to 1.57; and *extra*, 1.58 and over. The long and extra staples appear to come from what Todaro describes as *Gossypium maratimum* (Sea Island cotton). The short and medium correspond to *G. hirsutum* and *G. herbaceum*. Of the cotton-raising States Florida makes the best show as to quality, Sea Island cotton being predominantly grown. The fibre product of the United States in 1880, per the census reports, was: flax, 1,565,546 lbs.; cotton, 5,755,359 bales; and hemp, 5,025 tons. (C. M.)

FICHTE, IMMANUEL HERMANN (1797–1879), a German philosopher, son of the famous J. G. Fichte, was born at Jena, July 18, 1797. He studied philology at the University of Berlin, and early devoted himself to philosophy. In 1822 he began to teach at Saarbrücken, and he was afterwards director of the gymnasium at Düsseldorf. In 1836 he was called to the University of Bonn as professor extraordinary, and in 1840 was made ordinary professor. From 1842 to 1867 he held a similar position at Tübingen. He died at Stuttgart, Aug. 8, 1879. His first publication was *Sätze der Vorschule zur Theologie* (1826), and his first important work *Beiträge zur Characteristik der neuern Philosophie* (1829). He then published his father's *Life and Literary Letters* (Sulzbach, 1831), and at a later date edited his father's *Complete Works* (8 vols., Berlin, 1845–46). He also established at Tübingen, in 1837, the *Zeitschrift für Philosophie und Speculative Theologie*, which he edited until 1848. In 1852 it was revived by Fichte, Ulrici, and Wirth. His other publications comprise *Ueber Gegensatz, Wendepunkt und Ziel heutiger Philosophie* (3 vols., Heidelberg, 1832–36); *Speculative Theologie* (Heidelberg, 1847); *System der Ethik* (1850–53), which is his most important work; *Anthropologie* (2d ed., 1860); *Psychologie* (1864); *Philosophie, Theologie, und Ethik* (2 vols., 1869); *Die theistische Weltanschauung und ihre Berechtigung* (1873). His system was a continuation of his father's in the direction of Christian theism, of which he was for a time the most prominent champion.

FIELD. The name of an American family, noted in mercantile, professional, and public life.

I. FIELD, DAVID DUDLEY (1781–1867), an American clergyman, was born at East Guilford, Conn., May 20, 1781. He graduated at Yale College in 1802, studied theology under Rev. Dr. Backus, and was installed pastor at East Haddam in 1804. Here he remained until 1818, and in 1819 he accepted a call to Stockbridge, Mass., but in 1837 he returned to Haddam. In 1848 he travelled in Europe, and in 1851 he resigned his charge. He spent the remainder of his life at Stockbridge, where he died April 15, 1867. He published some works of local history and occasional sermons.

II. FIELD, DAVID DUDLEY, an American jurist, eldest son of the preceding, was born at Haddam, Conn., Feb. 13, 1805. He graduated at Williams College in 1825, studied law, and was admitted to the bar in 1828. He settled in New York city, and became one of the leaders of the bar. In 1839 he began his advocacy of reform in the modes of legal procedure, and as a result of his efforts the revised State constitution of 1846 provided for the codification of the laws. In 1847 he was appointed by the legislature a member of the commission to carry out this provision. For the reforms effected by this commission see CODE, Vol. II., p.

In 1857 Mr. Field was called by the legislature to continue and supplement his former work by preparing other codes, civil, penal, and political. These were completed in 1865 and 1866, and the penal code was finally enacted in 1882. In 1866 he induced the British Association for the Advancement of Science, at its meeting in Manchester, to appoint a committee of eminent jurists to revise and codify international law. In this case even more than in the former the chief labor fell upon himself. By 1873 he had prepared a large volume, called *Outlines of an International Code*. It was approved by a meeting of the most eminent European jurists held at Brussels in that year, and an association was there formed to advocate the decision of international disputes by arbitration, and to promote in each country the codification of the laws. Mr. Field has taken an active part in the discussion of the questions of the day, and has published several political pamphlets.

III. FIELD, CYRUS WEST, an American merchant, son of Rev. D. D. Field, D.D., was born at Stockbridge, Mass., Nov. 30, 1819. At the age of fifteen he went to New York, where he entered upon a mercantile career. In 1853 he spent six months in travelling in South America. On his return he was asked to assist in establishing a telegraph across Newfoundland. Being convinced that it would be practicable to lay a line across the ocean, he obtained from the legislature of Newfoundland the exclusive right for fifty years to connect that island by telegraph both with Europe and the continent of America. He then organized the New York, Newfoundland, and London Telegraph Company to carry out this plan. Two years were spent in building the necessary land lines, and the submarine cable was laid across the Gulf of St. Lawrence in 1856. Mr. Field then went to London, when he organized the Atlantic Telegraph Company to lay the cable across the ocean. Two attempts to lay the cable proved unsuccessful, and in August, 1858, when communication was at last established, the cable worked only a few days. Most of those who had been interested in the work became disheartened, but Mr. Field preserved his faith and made fresh efforts. The breaking out of war in America prevented anything from being done until 1865. In the meantime the art of telegraphy and all its appliances had been improved. The Great Eastern was employed to carry the cable across, and though unsuccessful in its first voyage in 1865, it accomplished the work in the next year, and even recovered the cable which had been lost the year before. A double line was thus obtained, and since that time communication has never been interrupted. Mr. Field was now the recipient of many marks of honor; Congress voted to him a gold medal with the thanks of the nation; the Paris Exposition of 1867 bestowed on him its highest prize, and the British Government testified its appreciation of his skill, courage, and perseverance. Mr. Field continued to devote attention to the improvement of the practical working of the ocean telegraph, and afterwards he used his time and wealth in the establishment of elevated railroads and other devices for the benefit of New York city.

IV. FIELD, STEPHEN JOHNSON, an American jurist, was born at Haddam, Conn., Nov. 4, 1816. He was the son of Rev. D. D. Field, D.D., and when only thirteen years old went to Smyrna and Athens, where he spent three years. He graduated at Williams College in 1837, studied law with his brother Dudley in New York, and became his partner. In 1848 he went to Europe and in the next year to California, where he settled at Marysville, and was elected alcalde, an office which then involved much care and responsibility. In 1851 he was a member of the first State legislature, and successfully exerted himself to establish satisfactory laws in regard to miners' claims and customs. In 1857 he was elected a judge of the Supreme Court of California, and in September, 1859, he became the chief justice of the State. His success in adjusting conflicting claims under Spanish and English laws was so great that, when these troublesome questions were brought by appeal before the Supreme Court of the United States, Pres. Lincoln in March, 1863, appointed Judge Field, though a Democrat, an associate justice of that court. He delivered dissenting opinions in several important cases relating to the powers of the national government.

V. FIELD, HENRY MARTYN, an American clergyman, son of Rev. D. D. Field, D.D., was born at Stockbridge, Mass., April 3, 1822. He graduated at Williams College in 1838, studied theology at East Windsor, Conn., and New Haven, and was pastor of a Presbyterian church in St. Louis from 1842 to 1847. He then spent a year in travelling through Europe, which furnished him material for a history of the Italian revolutions and other publications. In January, 1851, he was installed pastor at Springfield, Mass., but in 1854 he removed to New York to become editor of the *New York Evangelist*, of which he afterwards became proprietor. He has since spent much time in foreign travel, and in 1875–76 made a journey around the world. Among his publications are *Irish Confederates* and *The Rebellion of 1798* (1851); *History of the Atlantic Telegraph* (1866). His books of travel include *From the Lake of Killarney to the Golden Horn* (1877); *From Egypt to Japan* (1879); *On the Desert* (1882); *Among the Holy Hills* (1883); and *Turkey and the Greek Isles* (1885).

FIELD, KATE, an American journalist, was born at St. Louis. After receiving a careful education in Massachusetts and Europe she became foreign correspondent of leading American papers. She also contributed to the *Atlantic Monthly* and other periodicals. In 1874 she appeared on the stage in New York, but she has had more success as a lecturer. In 1883 she undertook the management of a Co-operative Dress Association in New York, but it failed within a year. She is a brilliant writer and an able dramatic critic.

FIELD MOUSE, the common name given to many species of small rodents of the family *Muridæ*, but more properly restricted to the members of the genus *Arvicola*. This genus includes about 50 species, of which 27 are North American. The field mice or voles probably far exceed in number of individuals any other mammal, and sometimes appear in such vast hosts as to be terribly destructive. In a single province in Germany 1,500,000 of them were captured in 14 days, in 1822. They frequent fields and woods, and have often destroyed extensive young plantations by gnawing the bark from trees, while their ravages on grain fields are often very severe. It is their habit to lay up a winter stock of food in their underground runs, and

Field Mice and Nest.

a vast quantity of nuts, grain seeds, and roots is sometimes thus accumulated. The field mice are spread all over the northern portion of the north temperate zone, where they seem to prefer the colder regions, while the true mice prefer the warmer. The most common of the United States species are the generally distributed red-backed mouse, the meadow mouse of the Northern and Middle States, and the gray and upland mice of the Eastern States. The meadow mouse (*A. xanthognatha*) is about 5 inches long, with fawn-colored back and ashy gray beneath. Another species, perhaps a variety of the above, the Pennsylvania meadow mouse (*A. Pennsylvanica*), is 4 inches long, tail 1 inch, of brownish fawn color above and grayish white below. It has very small eyes and short ears. It feeds on bulbous roots, and often injures river plantations by making holes in the banks. The genus *Arvicola* includes our common water rats, and several other excavating ratlike species. There are many species of other genera with habits similar to the field mice, the smallest being the harvest mouse (*Reithrodon humilis*), which is but 2¼ inches long, and closely resembles a small house mouse.

FIELDS, JAMES THOMAS (1817–1881), an American publisher and author, was born at Portsmouth, N. H., Dec. 31, 1817. At the age of 14 he found employment in a bookstore in Boston; and from 1837 to 1870 he was a member of a publishing firm. Thenceforth he devoted his time to lecturing and authorship. While a publisher, Mr. Fields had edited several valuable works, and he was editor of the *Atlantic Monthly* from 1861 to 1871. Volumes of his poems appeared in 1849, in 1854, and in 1858. He also wrote *Yesterdays with Authors* (1871); *Underbrush* (1877). He died in Boston, April 24, 1881.

FIGUIER, GUILLAUME LOUIS, a French scientific writer, was born at Montpellier, Feb. 15, 1819. Having studied chemistry in that city, he received, in 1841, the degree of M. D. In 1846 he was made professor of pharmacy at Montpellier, and he was afterwards connected with the school of pharmacy at Paris. He contributed a vast number of scientific articles to various periodicals. Among his more important works are *Exposition et histoire des principales découvertes scientifiques modernes* (1851); *L'Alchimie et les alchimistes* (1854); *Histoire du merveilleux dans les temps modernes* (1859–60). He has also published popular presentations of science and natural history which have been translated into English. Among these are *The Vegetable World; The Ocean World; The Insect World; The Wonders of Science; The Wonders of Industry*. In 1856 he founded *L'Annee scientifique et industrielle*, which he has since continued to edit with success.

FINANCE, AMERICAN.—Finance relates to the modes of raising and expending public revenue. It is true that bankers are not infrequently called financiers, but such a use of the term is an abuse of language. A banker is a dealer in money; a financier is an administrator of the public revenue, and this distinction should always be regarded. As the ENCYCLOPÆDIA BRITANNICA under this head treats the history of British finance, we shall here describe the modes of raising and expending the public revenue in the United States.

I. The subject may be conveniently divided into five periods; the first is the *Colonial*. Beginning with the oldest colony, Virginia, four sources of revenue may be mentioned. First, were the quit-rents, which were paid to the king; second, an export duty on tobacco and port duties on vessels arriving; third, a duty on tobacco exported to other colonies, which was paid to William and Mary College; and last, the money-tax raised by the assembly. There were also three levies: the parish levy which was assessed by the vestries; the county levies which the justices of the peace assessed; and the levy assessed by the assembly. All three were paid in tobacco, which formed the money of the colony, and were collected by the sheriff. They were assessed on the whole number of persons in the parish, county, or colony, and divided by the number of taxable persons. The governors of the colony often quarrelled with the assembly about the taxes, but the latter easily had their way unless the royal government interfered. As the expenditures, except in time of war, were small, the taxes were light and easily borne. No army or navy existed. The governor received a salary which was a charge on the export duties, and another sum was distributed among the councillors. The expenses for clerks, courts, etc., were light, and so were all salaries.

As Maryland was a proprietary government, the proprietary held the title to the land, and controlled all the patronage, both lay and clerical. To him belonged the quit-rents, the tobacco and tonnage duties, and the legal fines and forfeitures. The legislative body consisted of the council and the burgesses; the former were appointed by the governor, who represented the proprietary, while the latter were elected by the people. Before the Revolution the burgesses had succeeded in wringing from the proprietary the entire law-making power, and limited the exercise of his patronage by regulating the fees. The government was inexpensive, and consequently taxation was light. Quit-rents and church-dues were the only matters of complaint. The original charter contained exemptions from taxation, but in 1661 a revenue was raised for the crown by customs duties.

In North Carolina revenue was raised for the crown from "quit-rents, tonnage duties, and duties on rum and wine; while the expenses of the province were met by simple and direct taxation of tolls, tithables, free negroes and their intermarriage, and by an excise on spirits. There were, as in Virginia, public, county, and parish levies, collected by the sheriffs. Taxation was light; but it was sedulously avoided by the people, who were clearly of opinion that all taxes were an evil, and was only enforced with the greatest difficulty; so much so that the government found it necessary to get a portion of its revenue by compelling the inhabitants to work on the roads and keep the streets of the towns clean." In South Carolina revenue was raised chiefly from general duties on all things except British manufactures, and on deer-skins when exported. A direct real and personal tax was laid. The quit-rents, when collected, were paid to the crown, and so were the duties on negroes and liquors imported. The salaries and ordinary expenses of government were light, and taxation was not a burden. The assembly of that colony, like most of the others, held the purse-strings and possessed the patronage of the financial offices. In Georgia, also, taxation was light; the quit-rents were paid to the crown, and the revenues needed to pay the few and small salaries and other expenditures were raised on rum, negroes, and West India produce, supplemented by a small direct tax on lands, houses, and slaves.

The colonies of Pennsylvania and Delaware will be described together, as a single executive administered the affairs of both. With the exception of Maryland, they were the only proprietary governments among the thirteen. "The descendants of William Penn stood in a relation of quasi sovereignty, and drew a large revenue from the great colony which bore their name." The income to the proprietary came from the quit-rents reserved in all deeds, and which could be collected by distress, and from manor-lands. The taxation of these caused much contention. Other revenue was raised by direct taxes, excise, light customs, and tonnage duties. The latter were spent for the erection and maintenance of light-houses. No navy existed, and the small militia was organized and maintained without expense to the public. As the salaries were neither numerous nor heavy, it was not necessary to go far into the pockets of the people to maintain the government. Across the Delaware was New Jersey, whose government was so frugal that only a small revenue was needed, which was raised chiefly by taxing the land. When we reach the colony of New York the story is changed. The government was often ill-managed and expensive and sometimes corrupt; beside, the frontiers were greatly exposed to Indian attacks, and constant expenditures were needful to maintain a successful defence. Consequently, taxes were much higher than in the other colonies and were raised by duties on negroes and other importations, and by direct levies on real and personal estate. The method of levying them was unjust and oppressive, and caused no little irritation.

Although the forms of government in the New England colonies differed somewhat from each other, their points of resemblance were more numerous, and also their methods of administration. "The theory of taxation," says Lodge, "was simple and democratic—to levy on all property without distinction; and although a system suited to the condition of a colony has long been outgrown, it still prevails not only in New England, but in many parts of the United States, a monument of Puritan policy and of conservatism of thought and habit." Of course, in the long colonial period of more than 150 years, many changes occurred in the financial systems of the colonies which have not been mentioned. Only a few of the more general and permanent features have been sketched. The historian of New England, Dr. J. G. Palfrey, thus describes the revenue system of the Massachusetts colony after it had existed forty years. "The public charges continued to be met by a revenue chiefly derived from direct taxes upon property. Real estate and stock in trade were assessed according to an estimate of the value made by town magistrates. Cattle, sheep, goats, and swine were taxed according to a permanent legal valuation of each description of such property. Artisans and mechanics contributed to the public expenses in proportion to the estimated gains of their business. There was a capitation tax of 1s. 8d. for each male person 'from sixteen years old and upwards.' Assessments were made in the autumn of each year, but selectmen might in any month collect taxes from transient merchant strangers on property brought by them into the country. Ministers of religion were freed from all rates for the country, county, and church, so far as concerned such estate as was their own proper estate, and under their own custody and improvement. 'Taverners paid a duty for the wine which they sold, at the rate of 50s. by the butt or pipe, and proportionally for all other vessels;' and for the retail of 'strong waters,' at the rate of '2d. upon every quart.' Imported goods of all descriptions, 'excepting fish, sheep's wool, cotton wool, salt,' and a few others, had to pay an *ad valorem* duty of 5 per cent. on a valuation determined by adding 5 per cent. to the cost of the article at the place of exportation." In the Plymouth colony a premium was exacted for the privilege of taking bass and herrings with nets on the coast of Cape Cod, while the other colonies introduced some changes into the system above described, required by their different situation. With respect to their expenditures these were quite similar to the expenditures of the colonies outside New England. Those for the ordinary administration of the governments were light, and hence the amount of revenue required was small.

In all the colonies, however, additional expenditures were necessary for extraordinary purposes, such as resisting Indian aggressions, and especially for the French war. The outfit of the Massachusetts troops for the Port Royal expedition had been accomplished by borrowing money with the expectation of getting enough from the enemy to repay the lenders. When the expedition returned without achieving success, the government knew not what to do. The colonial treasurer had no money, the soldiers needed their pay and were near the edge of mutiny. A heavy tax was laid, but funds were necessary at once. The General Court, in 1690, "desirous to prove themselves just and honest," so they said, considering the "scarcity of money and the want of an adequate measure of commerce," authorized a committee to issue forthwith in the name of the colony £7000 in bills of credit, from 2s. to £5 each. They were essentially the same as the treasury notes issued at a later day, and were payable by a tax and also receivable for public dues. They fell in value as soon as issued, so that the soldiers who received them were losers. When the outcry was loudest the governor did something to lessen it by exchanging a considerable amount of specie for the notes. Two years afterwards their value was enhanced by the issuing of an order which declared that they should pass current within the colony in all payments at their face value, and in all public payments at 5 per cent. advance. The object of this action was to prevent their depreciation, and for 20 years it was effectual. When taxes became due they were worth more than specie because the 5 per cent. bonus was attached to them. When £40,000 had been emitted an order was passed limiting the amount to those figures, but the cry of the "scarcity of money" was constantly heard, and within 12 years, including re-emissions, £110,000 were issued. This increase, however, finally affected the prosperity of the colony. "During the first half of the eighteenth century," says Palfrey, "the prosperity of Massachusetts was kept down by her use of a vicious substitute for money. The paper-money drove almost all the coin abroad, leaving commerce without a sound currency whereon to base its transactions." The success of the colonies in dealing with so hazardous a thing greatly varied. Connecticut, after the disastrous attempt on Canada in 1709, issued paper-money to the amount of £8000. Four years afterward the issue of £20,000 more was ordered, but only a part of the amount was annually put in circulation, and the provisions for redeeming it were so judicious and well enforced that for many years no depreciation occurred. Indeed, it never became large. South Carolina, perhaps, carried the paper-money experiment further than any other colony. After the unsuccessful expedition against St. Augustine in 1703, "following the example of many great and rich countries, who have helped themselves in their exigencies with funds of credit, which have fully answered the ends of money," £6000 were issued bearing 12 per cent. interest. They were a legal tender, and if the creditor refused to receive them he lost his debt. "But such refusal never occurred, for the paper was hoarded for the sake of the interest." Afterward another issue was made which did not bear interest, and was exchangeable for the "old currency." A twofold object existed for this issue: to increase the volume of circulation, and to diminish the interest burden. "Notwithstanding this change, the bills remained at par until the subsequent issue of very large amounts caused their depreciation." In 1712 the colony established a public bank, which issued £48,000, called bank-bills, which were lent on landed or personal security for a year. By this mode the people were furnished with a circulation, and the government profited by the interest received. Pennsylvania adopted a similar mode of issuing paper-money, and continued it with marked success for a long period. The act first, authorizing the modest sum of £15,000, was passed in 1723. The bills were to be lent on land security or plate of treble value, deposited with the government at 5 per cent. interest. They were declared to be a legal tender in payment of all debts, and if the creditor refused them the obligation to pay ceased. The lenders were to pay annually one-eighth of the sum borrowed and the interest. A loan office was created at which the business was conducted by 4 trustees. In December, 1723, the issue of £30,000 more was authorized, and 3 years afterward an additional sum of £10,000 to replace the bills which had become torn or defaced. The most serious evil which attended their circulation was the counterfeiting of them. Notwithstanding the severe laws against the practice, large quantities of fraudulent bills were put into circulation. They were made chiefly in Ireland, and brought into the colony. The colony having thus amply provided for their redemption, the notes circulated freely at their face value and superseded the bills of other colonies, which, until that time, had formed the chief part of the circulating medium. The only trouble which arose from this paper-currency was due to the action of the proprietaries, who demanded and received in payment of their quit-rents the difference of exchange on England, and an annuity of £130 annually so long as the notes circulated. For 40 years the system worked well; so well, indeed, that Gov. Pownall declared "that there never was a wiser nor better measure, never one better calculated to serve the interests of our increasing country." But in 1756, in consequence of the immediate need of a large supply of public funds, £60,000 were voted for the king's use, which was to be redeemed by taxation. Subsequently, other issues were put into circulation redeemable in the same manner.

Three modes, therefore, were practised by the colonies in issuing paper-money: 1. The issuing of bills which were redeemed by receiving them in payment of taxes; 2. The issue of bills in the way of loans to individuals who paid interest thereon, and which were cancelled when the lenders returned the same; and 3. The issuing of bills which bore interest. The mode first mentioned was the most extensively practised; New Jersey adopted it at the outset, and afterward adopted the second. All the colonies issued paper-money, but not many before 1700. In truth, Massachusetts was the pioneer. During the Revolution they issued large quantities, and it depreciated enormously, causing untold distress. In this connection mention must be made of the colonial coinage. The Massachusetts "mint-house" was established in Boston in 1651. The mint-master, John Hull, coined by contract, charging 5 per cent. The coins thus struck did not go beyond the New England colonies. The institution was declared to be illegal, yet it continued in operation for more than 30 years. To conceal its business all the coins were dated 1652. The other mint was established in Maryland, in 1660, and silver-money was struck 9 pence to the shilling. In 1662 "the people were ordered to buy 10 shillings per poll of this sophisticated coin, and pay for it in good casked tobacco at 2s. per pound." This arbitrary measure was repealed in 1676.

II. *The Revolutionary Period.*—After the colonies declared themselves independent, the most serious difficulty they encountered was to provide the funds needful to equip and sustain an army. Men were forthcoming, but where could the means be obtained to pay them? The colonies themselves were poor, for they had just emerged from an exhaustive war on the northern frontier. As we have seen they had relied largely on paper-money, but the credit of every colony had been stretched to the utmost, and in most of the colonies their bills were depreciated. The Continental Congress had no credit, for it possessed no well-defined powers. The delegates had been sent by the respective colonies clothed with certain powers which were defined in their letters of appointment. They were, therefore, in every sense the representatives of the colonies, and were obliged to look to the appointing and not to a central power for authority. What could such a body do in the way of raising money? Who would trust the Continental Congress? Suppose the contest should prove unsuccessful, who would pay the indebtedness incurred? Lenders have never been swift to part with their money under such circumstances. Moreover, the people were not a unit in opposing Great Britain. Many tories flourished who were as active as they dared be in aiding the enemy. To raise the money required was therefore a most difficult task, and, considering the nature of it, one cannot help wondering that the Continental Congress should have dared raise the flag of rebellion. The truth was repeated, alike in the lives of nations and individuals, no one measured the full cost of the undertaking. Had those delegates been able to see all the hardships that were to be endured, probably they would have shrunk from trying the great experiment.

The first resource was the issue of paper-money. But Congress dared not lay a tax to provide for its payment. That body had no power to do such a thing. At a subsequent period the States were recommended to lay taxes for raising money to support the general government, and apportionments were made among them, but this was the furthest limit in the way of exercising general authority. Whether, therefore, the issue of paper-money was expedient to adopt, let it be remembered that it was the only resource in the beginning. Congress could get some means in this manner; moreover, the expedient was popular. Taxation, however, would not have been endured in the beginning, nor, indeed, at any time. Said one of the delegates during a debate on this subject: "Do you think, gentlemen, that I will consent to load my constituents with taxes when we can send to our printer and get a wagon-load of money, one quire of which will pay for the whole?" Nor was this view shared by him alone.

All the members knew that the colonies had issued paper-money in many cases without causing a depreciation in value, and why could not Congress do the same thing? This was the way the members reasoned. The first issue was for $2,000,000, and the second issue, which was authorized soon afterward, was for $1,000,000. The third issue for $3,000,000 soon appeared. Had no more been issued its value could have been easily sustained. But this was only a small portion of the revenue required. Within a year the bills began to depreciate. As soon as this was perceived some members who had favored the issue of paper-money urged Congress to try the experiment of borrowing. But there was no time to wait, and the printing-press was set agoing. Although independence had now been declared, Congress had no authority to tax, and therefore could raise no money by direct authority from the States. Congress did call on the States repeatedly to contribute, and apportionments were made on the basis of population. Of course this was a very weak way to get money, but what more could Congress do? Neither the amount of wealth nor the number of population was known. Congress, however, could guess more exactly concerning the latter than the former. From time to time addresses were issued to the States, urging them by the strongest arguments possible to contribute. If wrongs were done, they would be corrected in the end. New Hampshire made a census of her population, and, finding the number to be far below the estimate made by Congress, desired a reduction of the apportionment. The thoughtful reply was made that perhaps if the other States made an enumeration of their population it would appear that the estimates for them were equally high. So Congress refused to correct it. The States did contribute to some extent, but very fitfully and unequally. Congress continued to push out the paper-money into the fearfully swollen stream, and to sustain its sinking value by arguments addressed to the people showing its worth. On such matters the people of every country have always done their own thinking. The most remarkable of these addresses was issued in 1779. The amount issued had been enormous, and Congress proposed to stop when $200,000,000 had been put in circulation. Congress sought to show how small the debt would be, "perhaps not ten dollars" apiece; besides, as the debt would not be payable immediately, but probably twenty years allotted for it, the number of inhabitants by that time in America would be far more than double their present amount. Congress also added: "Let it be remembered that paper-money is the only kind of money which cannot make unto itself wings and fly away. It remains with us; it will not forsake us; it is always ready and at hand for the purpose of commerce or taxes, and every industrious man can find it." Many expedients were attempted to prevent it from sinking in value. One of these was the making of it a legal-tender so as to circulate as widely as possible. Another method was the fixing of the prices of the commodities usually bought and sold by law. This was the favorite remedy. The idea was not altogether new, for the colonies had established many regulations of that nature. The right to thus restrict the operations of trade seems not to have been questioned. When, therefore, prices had risen to a considerable height, representatives of the New England States assembled at Providence and formed a tariff, which was adopted by all the States represented in the convention. The plan was eagerly seized by Congress and recommended to other States for imitation, in order "to prevent the present fluctuating and exorbitant prices." A week before this action of Congress John Adams wrote to his wife that "the attempt of New England to regulate prices is extremely popular in Congress," but, "for my own part," he continues, "I expect only a partial and temporary relief from it, and I fear that after a time the evils will break out with greater violence. The matter will flow with greater rapidity for having been dammed up for a time," the truth of which opinion was soon seen. The rapid increase of prices was generally condemned as immoral and unpatriotic and deserving severe punishment. A French writer, who doubtless expressed the truth, wrote, "The country people are so exasperated at the high price everything bears that unless some change soon takes place they threaten not only to withhold provisions from the town, but to come down in a body and punish the leaders."

The depreciation was quickened by State issues of paper-money. As a considerable part of the cost of the war was maintained by the States they were obliged to raise funds. Of course they had the power to levy and collect taxes, but were slow in exercising this power. They preferred to rely on the paper-mill. These issues were in conflict with those issued by the Continental Congress and helped on the depreciation. Another cause which operated powerfully in the same manner was counterfeiting. The severest laws were enacted against counterfeiters, but without lessening the evil. The enemy engaged in the business. A ship laden with counterfeit money was lost during the voyage to our shore. These causes, and others which we have not space to mention, seriously affected the value of these issues and led many to fear that repudiation would be the end of the experiment. Congress, though, repelled this suspicion with lofty indignation, declaring that it was with great regret and reluctance they could prevail on themselves to take the least notice of a question which involved in it a doubt so injurious to the honor and dignity of America. "We should pay an ill compliment," they continued, "to the understanding and honor of every true American were we to adduce any arguments to show the baseness or bad policy of violating our national faith, or omitting to pursue the measures necessary to preserve it. A bankrupt, faithless republic would be a novelty in the political world, and appear among respectable nations like a common prostitute among chaste and respectable matrons." Yet this very thing did happen not long afterward. These issues continued to sink in value, and Congress finally acknowledged the depreciation. A scale of depreciation was established, but they continued to fall more and more in value until they disappeared from circulation. When this event happened, the government was better off than ever. The British government had applied the base arts of forgery to the utmost extent, confidently believing that if the paper-money fountain could be dried up, the rebellion would come to an end. Vain hope: having cast off this incubus, the government was in a better condition than before to continue the struggle. The truth is, the people had been paying for the money all through its course of depreciation. The tax was an enormous one, and occasioned much hardship and inequality. The debts of that period were paid in the depreciated paper-money, and many a pitiful story might be told of the losses to wards, schools, and the like through the operation of paper-money. The newspapers of that day contained letters written by the persons who had thus suffered through their guardians and trustees. Yet the end of the paper-money experiment was not quite come. Congress essayed another. It was for the States to make new bills which were to be countersigned by the general government. These were called bills of the new emission. Not many were issued, for the people had had enough of paper-money.

Besides paper-money Congress did borrow some money to carry on the war. Loan-offices were established in all the States, and the people were invited to lend. It was hoped that they would subscribe liberally enough to put an end to further issues of paper-money, and thus prevent its value from depreciating. The loan-office certificates issued were of two kinds. One kind bore interest payable in specie, and the other in paper-money. The former kind was the more popular. When the American commissioners in Europe gave assurance of their ability to borrow enough specie to pay interest on all sums which the government could probably borrow at home, and sustained their word by promptly paying all bills of exchange drawn on them for the discharge of such interest, the more patriotic citizens purchased a considerable quantity of certificates. In numerous instances property was sold and the sum received was invested in this manner.

When Congress authorized the certificates it was supposed they would be hoarded for the sake of the interest just as the interest-bearing bills of exchange had been. Unhappily they were not; their circulation became general, and they had essentially the same effect as the issue of an equal quantity of paper-money. Moreover, the very fact that they did bear interest led persons to take them in preference to continental paper-money, thus depreciating the value of the latter. Such an effect was not foreseen at the time their issue was authorized.

Beside a home loan of this nature money was borrowed from abroad. France disliked England and longed to witness her defeat and humiliation. The first money loaned to Congress was in secret, nor was this known for a long time. In 1778, after the surrender of Burgoyne, an alliance was formed with France and a loan was granted. It was from this source that a supply of specie was obtained for paying the interest on the specie-bearing loan-certificates. France continued to supply funds to some extent during the war, and became responsible for a loan contracted by John Adams with bankers in Holland. Toward the close of the war the Bank of North America was established, which also made loans to the government, while Robert Morris also used his own extensive personal credit in the same manner.

The machinery for administering the finances was crude in the extreme. A Board of Treasury was established in 1776, consisting of ten members of Congress, who employed such assistance as was needful for transacting the public business. As the members also had legislative duties it will be at once seen how inefficient their administration must have been. The mode of conducting the business was improved from time to time, but at best great dilatoriness was shown. Letters remained unanswered, and matters of pressing moment often received no attention. As the paper-money depreciated, and the unpaid requisitions increased, the affairs of the office became more disordered until Robert Morris was elected superintendent of finance, when the board was abolished. Morris insisted on having large powers, particularly with respect to the removal and appointment of men in his office. Several of the members of Congress objected to granting him such large powers, but he was inexorable. He knew that the inefficiency of the Treasury Board was due largely to divided responsibility. There was no head. There were two reasons why this state of things so long existed: the first was because Congress was afraid to bestow much authority on any one; they were afraid of power, and could not immediately forget how they had suffered from the exercise of it. The people had suffered too much from the exactions of the members of the British cabinet to put much authority in individuals, even if they were of their own number. The other reason was because no one had shown a marked aptitude for administering the finances. Morris had indeed displayed much patriotism, he had contributed generously to the needs of the government, and his influence had been potent in persuading others to do likewise. He was a man of large wealth, a successful merchant, and commanded the confidence of all. The time at length came in 1781 when Congress was willing to put the finances of the country in his hands. Morris was no believer in paper-money, nor in slipshod methods. He sought to reduce the public indebtedness to order, to find out the nature and amount of the unpaid requisitions, and to stop the practice which had been in operation for some time of making seizures of provisions and other things needed for the army and giving certificates therefor. He succeeded in doing this, in getting the supplies in regular ways, and in paying the obligations of the government far more promptly than before. Yet his sources of supply were limited—foreign loans to some extent; some aid from the Bank of North America, which he established; the use of his own means and credit, and the fitful and meagre supplies furnished by the States. Morris retired in 1784, and then the Board of Treasury was re-established, as there was no other person to whom Congress was willing to intrust so much power. The attention of the board was largely bestowed on the adjustment of the debt that had been incurred, but peace having been declared, no one was longer willing to do much; claims of all kinds remained unpaid; no authority indeed existed for anything, for the Confederation had no vitality, and thus the country drifted on in a miserable way, neglecting all its financial obligations, until the adoption of the Constitution in 1789.

III. *The Peace Period from* 1789 *to* 1861.—When the Constitution was adopted the experiment of maintaining a republican form of government for the first time was seriously begun. The Continental Congress was not a government—that body acted through sufferance and because the members were careful not to go beyond the limit of the popular will. The Articles of Confederation were without vitality. No government existed that could lay a tax for a dollar, and as the people would not give voluntarily to support the government, nor the States, nothing but disorder could exist. Out of this disorder and weakness arose the existing government. Sheer necessity forced people to unite. Their miseries were so great from self-destroying and also from outward forces that a plan of union was finally formed which has grown stronger with advancing years.

The first question that confronted Congress after assembling under the new Constitution was the funding and payment of the revolutionary debt. The greatness of the question was realized by some, who felt that the existence of the government was bound up with the settlement of it. Hamilton, the secretary of the treasury, was directed by Congress to consider the subject, and make a report thereon at the next session. During the Revolution he had furnished evidence of his financial genius by preparing a plan of a national bank which was submitted to Morris. When Washington was one day conversing with Morris about the finances of the country, he asked, "What are we going to do with this heavy debt?" to which Morris replied, "There is but one man in the United States who can tell you—that is Alexander Hamilton." Having been appointed secretary of the treasury, he now had the opportunity of telling Congress how to reduce the financial chaos then existing to order.

The debt was of two kinds, foreign and domestic. The foreign part was due to three nations, France, Holland, and a very small sum to Spain. The amount was known, and no one thought of doing other than faithfully fulfilling the contracts by which it had been obtained. The domestic debt was far more difficult to manage. It was composed of three branches. One branch covered the expenditures by the Continental Congress or general government. The evidences of this portion consisted of certificates of various kinds that were in the possession of creditors. In many cases, however, they had been transferred, and for varying sums, often far less than their face value. Two questions were raised concerning them: ought the government to pay more than the present holders paid for them? and, again, if the government ought to pay more, should not the additional sum be paid to the original holders? Hamilton contended that the government ought to pay the full value promised in the certificates and to their present holders. Jefferson and Madison differed from him, but his view was adopted. The second branch of expenditures pertained to the expenditures incurred by the States for maintaining the war. Congress repeatedly promised while the war was going on to equalise the burdens of the States and thus to do justice to them, and when they adopted the Constitution and relinquished the right to collect taxes on imports, they did so expecting that the government would relieve them of their war burdens. They maintained that it would be a gross injustice to deprive them of their most fruitful source of taxation, and do nothing in the way of relieving them of their war burden. The contest over the question was prolonged and bitter, and the final action of Congress was regarded with doubt and alarm. The amount of the State debt was supposed to be about $25,000,000. Congress finally agreed to assume $21,500,000, and apportion this sum among the States. The members from the Northern States, which were the heaviest creditors, were in favor of assumption, while those from the Southern States were opposed. Hamilton's recommendation in favor of assumption was finally carried by getting enough votes to favor the measure on condition that enough members from the North would vote in favor of locating the capital on the Potomac to carry that measure. Thus the national honor was saved by bargaining away the location of the capital. The third branch of the domestic debt consisted of money advanced to the States by the Continental Congress and to that body by the States. No one knew what these amounts were, and Congress appointed commissioners to determine what was due "according to the principles of general equity."

Congress determined to pay these three branches in the following manner: interest at the rate of 6 per cent. was to be paid on two-thirds of the principal of the first branch, or debt contracted directly by Congress, after 1790, and on the balance after 1800, and 3 per cent. interest was to be paid on the interest which had accumulated on this portion of the debt. The government could redeem 2 per cent. annually of the portion bearing 6 per cent. interest and the portion bearing 3 per cent. whenever it desired. The second branch, consisting of the State debts, were funded in the following manner: four-ninths of the amount bore 6 per cent. interest after the end of 1791, three-ninths 3 per cent., beginning at the same time, and the remainder, two-ninths, 6 per cent. interest after 1800. The third branch of the domestic debt, consisting of loans by the Continental Congress to the States, and by them to the Congress, was adjusted by the commissioners. As whatever the States owed was due to the other States, of course the two sides of the account balanced. It stood thus:

Creditor States.		Debtor States.	
New Hampshire..	$75,055	New York..........	$2,074,846
Massachusetts.....	1,248,881	Pennsylvania......	76,009
Rhode Island......	299,611	Delaware............	612,428
Connecticut........	619,121	Maryland............	151,640
New Jersey.........	49,630	Virginia............	100,879
South Carolina...	1,205,978	North Carolina...	501,082
Georgia.............	19,988		
Total...........	$3,517,584	Total............	$3,517,584

The balances due to the creditor States were funded in the same manner as the second branch of the domestic debt. But the debtor States never paid their indebtedness. Thus this great question was finally settled. It should be added, however, that the plan of funding adopted by Congress was more intricate in several respects than Hamilton's plan. It bears the marks all over of compromise. It was the outcome of contending interests and sections. The opposition among the people to funding was strong in many quarters. Having in mind the history of the British debt, they believed that funding meant the perpetuation of the burden. They vented their opinions through the newspapers and pamphlets. The most able critic of the plan was Albert Gallatin.

Having funded the debt the next thing was to provide a plan for extinguishing the principal and raising the means to do this. Prior to 1800 the means for effecting this end were cumbrous. Hamilton, who displayed a bold genius in extricating the government from financial chaos, was under the spell of Walpole's sinking-fund theory, and reported an elaborate scheme for paying the debt by the operation of the sinking-fund machinery. Robert Hamilton had not yet exposed the utter fallacy of extinguishing debts in that manner. Commissioners were appointed for receiving that portion of the public income obtained from taxes and loans, which were applicable for discharging the interest and principal of the public debt. But no annual reduction of the public debt had been fixed, nor had any taxation adequate enough to effect a reduction gone into operation. It may be added, though, that all the debt purchased and redeemed was regarded as drawing interest as though unpaid, and the amount was paid to the commissioners as a debt-redemption fund. This feature of debt-paying is still maintained by several of the States and cities of the Union, and is embedded in the national sinking-fund law. When Gallatin became secretary of the treasury in 1801, another law was passed providing that $7,300,000 should be set aside annually for reducing the debt. This sum was fixed not arbitrarily, but because it was needed for paying the interest and principal, which could be discharged during the next two years. When, in 1803, Louisiana was purchased, $700,000 were added to the annual sinking fund.

For the first ten years of our history the public debt was not diminished, because the ordinary and extraordinary expenditures were so heavy that no surplus was left for such application. There was a war with the Indians on the frontier, a whiskey insurrection in Pennsylvania, a difficulty with the Barbary powers, while the conduct of both England and France rendered some war preparations necessary. Besides, the revenues from internal sources were not faithfully collected; evasions were great, and at that early day the government could not enforce its collections with rigor. Everything was new, much jealousy toward the government existed, and it could not be expected that the financial or any other machinery so soon would work perfectly. When, however, the war-clouds rolled away, and the Indian aggressions were quelled, the expenditures were reduced and debt-paying began. As it was not necessary to continue to collect internal revenue in order to get the needful supply of funds, these taxes were abolished in 1801. In order to put the debt more perfectly under the control of the government, Gallatin recommended that, with the consent of the creditors, a portion of the debt on which annuities had been paid should be changed into paid-up stock for the balance, payable at a fixed time. Congress authorized the change, and many creditors availed themselves of the privilege. In eleven years $46,022,810 were paid, leaving $45,154,189 unpaid. Had the second war with Great Britain not occurred this sum would probably have been paid in about the same time.

With respect to taxes, these were levied on imports and also collected for the first ten years from internal sources. The second act passed by Congress provided for taxing imports. The law was crude, and could not be otherwise in the beginning. It was revised from time to time, but during the first twenty years of our government, taxation of this nature was not heavy. Internal taxation was less popular. Nevertheless, a large and intelligent class strongly favored the levying of such a tax for this reason, among others, that the people, feeling it more keenly than a tax levied on foreign goods, would be more watchful of the public expenditures. This certainly was a plausible supposition, but how completely negatived has it been by our experience in State and municipal taxation! One of the things that Jefferson promised to do if elected President was to repeal the internal taxes, and accordingly this was done, though contrary to the advice of his secretary. The revenues from imports, however, increased enough to cover the expenditures and reduce the debt, so no ill results followed their repeal.

In 1812 another war was on hand. The government long tried to escape, and various expedients were practised to maintain the national dignity, but they availed nothing. Gallatin was yet at the head of the treasury department, and the financial leader of his party, as much so as Hamilton had been of the other. His plan of finance for the emergency was very simple. He proposed that sufficient taxes should be laid to defray the ordinary expenses of the government, the interest on the old debt and the new one that might be created, while the war expenditures should be raised from loans. Six of these were made during the war, aggregating $80,952,800. They bore 6 per cent. interest. Gallatin thought that as our commerce would be idle, banks and individuals would readily lend their money to the government; and so they did, in those sections where the war was popular, which were the Southern and Middle States. After a short time, though, the credit of the government declined and lending was more difficult. The reason for this decline is easily explained: Congress would not adopt an adequate system of taxation. The members were willing for the secretary to borrow money to carry on the war, but unwilling to tax the people to pay the loan. The consequences of such a policy have always been the same at every age of the world: lenders are never willing to part with their money if it is to be lost; they are not more benevolent than other persons. They could not help seeing that the policy of Congress was utterly subversive of the national credit. The duties on imports were doubled; but as importations had greatly fallen away, not much revenue could be expected from this source. Gallatin strongly recommended the adoption of an internal revenue system, but his party, which had a majority in both Houses, were not prepared for the measure. They had always been opposed to such a system, and should they falsify their record? Nevertheless, they were obliged to do so. Every criticism they launched on the policy of the Federal party, when that was in power, could be repeated of the Republicans during the first sixteen years of their ascendency. They were obliged to increase the import duties, to restore the internal revenue system, and, finally, to charter another national bank. It should not be omitted that one reason why they so strongly opposed Gallatin's recommendations was, because they wished to destroy his influence and drive him from the treasury department. A strong cabal of his own party had been formed, which was under the leadership of Senator Smith, of Maryland, whose enmity sprung from Gallatin's condemnation of the wrong practices of his brother in the navy department. Gallatin was both honest and competent, and had his party adopted his recommendations, and laid adequate taxes at the outbreak of the war, and not frittered away the revenues of the government as they did for several years before this event, and contrary to his advice, and rechartered the United States Bank as he strongly desired, the credit of the government would have been maintained, and we should have been spared from chronicling the disgraceful fact that, in consequence of the wantonly wrong action of Congress, the $80,000,000 borrowed to carry on the war, after deducting discounts and depreciation, yielded only $34,000,000. Another expedient to raise money was to issue treasury notes; they bore 5$\frac{2}{5}$ per cent. interest, ran for a year, and were receivable by the government for all dues to it. They were not a legal-tender, and their circulation therefore was at the will of the receivers; they were issued really in anticipation of taxes, and the amount increased until the close of the war. The last quantity, authorized in 1815, differed from prior issues in this, that notes for less than $20 were payable to bearer and did not draw interest. They were convertible into stock bearing 7 per cent. interest, and it was soon found that, though well adapted to serve as a circulating medium, they were converted into such stock almost as soon as issued. This led to a restricting of their issue to occasions of peculiar urgency, like paying the army, and also dividends on the public debt when local currency could not be procured.

When Gallatin's influence had become much impaired he was sent abroad in company with two other commissioners to negotiate a treaty of peace. He did not resign his secretaryship, for even then the President was unwilling to part with him. Gallatin had desired to retire long before, but the President insisted on his remaining. Notwithstanding the opposition to him in his own party, he was so skilled in finance, and could be so fully trusted, that Madison clung to him as his sheet-anchor. When the President found that the secretary's endeavor to stem the tide was hopeless, he unwillingly let Gallatin go abroad. As he had not resigned, Mr. Jones, the secretary of the navy, was made acting secretary of the treasury. He knew nothing about finance, and soon showed his inefficiency for the place. That was a time when the strongest man truly was needed; the very opposite idea had prevailed in making the selection. Finally, Gallatin sent his resignation, and the President then selected George W. Campbell, a senator from Tennessee, who had been chairman of the committee of ways and means, for the office. He desired another, Alexander J. Dallas, of Philadelphia, but as the Pennsylvania senators were opposed to him, the President turned aside in deference to their wishes. Campbell was not the man for so trying an occasion. Besides, he was in ill-health, and on the chief clerk devolved much of the work and responsibility of the office. After a short trial Campbell resigned. When this event happened, "tell Dr. Madison," said Senator Lacock, of Pennsylvania, to the President's private secretary, "that we are now willing to submit to his Philadelphia lawyer for head of the treasury. The public patient is so very sick that we must swallow anything the doctor prescribes, however nauseous the bolus." "His intrepidity and firmness," says Ingersoll, "gave fresh impulse to the war for the few months that it lasted after his coming, . . . and rescued the treasury from the disgraceful inanition it had fallen to during the prior twenty-eight months of hostilities. Arms, revenues, national power and resource were just elevated to the proper war-standard, when it ended—never till then." Dallas was favored by the situation. Congress had come to see that strong measures were necessary to save the country from destruction. The currency was fearfully depreciated at this time because a numerous brood of State banks had grown up after Congress refused to recharter the first United States Bank. To restore the circulation to a sound condition Dallas recommended the establishing of another bank, which was done, and which, moreover, speedily accomplished that result. (See article BANKING, Vol. I.)

The war having ended debt-paying was resumed. The annual sinking fund was increased to $10,000,000, but the revenues were not always large enough to furnish a surplus to this extent. Portions of the debt when maturing were extended, but in 1834 the last was extinguished. The taxation of imports was largely reduced in 1816, but in 1824 they were raised, and four years afterward yet higher. But the internal revenue system was repealed in 1817, nor was it revived until 1861. After the discharge of the public debt the revenues accumulated in the treasury from taxation and the sale of public land, and Congress finally voted to distribute all the surplus except $5,000,000 among the States in proportion to their population. This was in 1837. The amount to be distributed was $37,468,819.97. It was to be deposited with the States and subject to recall by the government. One-quarter was to be paid at the end of the third month until the completion of the distribution. After paying three-fourths of the amount a financial cyclone swept over the land, prostrating all business and bringing the government to the edge of bankruptcy. The revenues of the government were in the keeping of the State banks, where they had been put after their withdrawal from the United States Bank by R. B. Taney, the secretary of the treasury. As they were all swept away by the storm, they could not respond to the demand of the treasury department, and the government which a few months before had presented the unexampled spectacle among nations of such a plethoric treasury that an enormous sum had been really given away in order to get it out of the treasury, was now unable to pay its ordinary bills! This was an extraordinary state of things surely, but if American finance has many a splendid episode, many a stroke of rare financial genius, darker and unpleasant features also appear intermingled. Van Buren was now President, having succeeded Pres. Jackson, in March, 1837; and he convened Congress in extra session and rehearsed the dismal story. Once more treasury notes were authorized to pay the public expenditures, and these were put out, with some intermissions, until the close of the Mexican war. New loans were also contracted for the expenditure thus incurred, payable at fixed periods. After the war closed payment began, but in consequence of the long time the bonds could run, the secretary was obliged to pay a high premium to get hold of them for redemption.

With a few exceptions the revenues were ample to pay the public expenditures during the long period from the close of the second war with Great Britain to the opening of the civil war in 1861. W. H. Crawford, of Georgia, was at the head of the treasury department during the eight years of Monroe's administration. The revenues during the earlier part of this period were rather light, owing to the falling off in the imports and the hard times which prevailed throughout the country. Before the close of Monroe's first term, however, the country had recovered, and during Pres. J. Q. Adams' administration, when Richard Rush was secretary of the treasury, business prospered, general contentment prevailed, and no difficult questions troubled the treasury department. The eight years of Jackson's administration were not so serene. His first secretary of the treasury was S. D. Ingham, of Pennsylvania, who resigned for social reasons, which need not here be rehearsed. Louis McLane, of Delaware, was a worthy successor. The President was now engaged in the controversy with the United States Bank concerning the removal of deposits, and insisted that Mr. McLane should do this. He refused.* Because he persisted in his refusal he was obliged to retire. He was succeeded by William J. Duane, of Pennsylvania, who was told by the President that if he would accept office he would not be asked to remove the deposits, and on this specific understanding accepted the office. No sooner had he been fairly installed in the treasury than the President asked him if he would not remove the deposits. When Duane reminded the President of his promise, the latter said he simply made the request; it was not compulsory, and hoped he would do as the President desired. It appears that the President thought that Mr. Duane was a flexible kind of man and would readily yield to his wishes. But Duane would not yield, nor would he resign his secretaryship. So the President removed him and transferred Mr. Taney, the attorney-general at that time, to the treasury department, where he was willing to do the President's bidding. The President afterward richly rewarded him by appointing him successor of the illustrious Marshall, chief-justice of the Supreme Court of the United States, over which he presided for thirty years, when he was succeeded by another secretary of the treasury, Salmon P. Chase. To fill the vacancy caused by Mr. Taney's retirement Senator Woodbury, of New Hampshire, was appointed, who served through the remainder of Pres. Jackson's second term and also during that of Mr. Van Buren. When Gen. Harrison became President he appointed Thomas Ewing, of Ohio, but the President's early death wrought serious changes in the cabinet. Ewing soon resigned after Mr. Tyler became President, and Walter Forward, who had been appointed first comptroller by Pres. Harrison, became secretary of the treasury. He remained in office long enough to make two annual reports and then the third appointment was made, John C. Spencer, of New York. The President sent in the name of Caleb Cushing, but the Senate refused to confirm him. Mr. Spencer remained in office a few months, and George M. Bibb, of Kentucky, served during the remainder of Pres. Tyler's troubled term. During the four years of Pres. Polk's administration Robert J. Walker, of Mississippi, was at the head of the treasury department. By many he is regarded as one of the ablest men who ever filled that office. He was succeeded by William M. Meredith at the opening of Pres. Taylor's administration, and on the death of the latter Mr. Fillmore appointed Thomas Corwin, of Ohio, secretary. James Guthrie, of Kentucky, served under Pres. Pierce, and Howell Cobb under Pres. Buchanan. In 1857 the tariff was reduced; soon afterward, however, a panic desolated the country, the revenues fell off, and were not sufficient to pay the ordinary expenditures. Several movements were made to increase the revenues, but all proved unavailing, and at the expiration of Mr. Buchanan's administration the government had increased its debt to $60,000,000.

IV. *The Civil War Period.*—We have thus traced the outline of our history to the civil war in 1861. Salmon P. Chase, of Ohio, was secretary of the treasury. He declined the appointment when it was first tendered to him, but finally accepted through the earnest solicitation of Horace Greeley and other friends. He was a lawyer by profession, had had no financial experience, and realized his unfitness for the place. Nevertheless, he accepted and entered on the duty at a most inauspicious time. Howell Cobb, above mentioned, had done his utmost to ruin the credit of the government, and though Gen. J. A. Dix served during the expiring months of Mr. Buchanan's administration, after Mr. Cobb's retirement, the time was too short to effect much of an improvement. He borrowed a small amount of money, paying 12 per cent. interest. To such a condition was the public credit reduced at the opening of the conflict. Congress, near the close of the session of 1860-61, had enacted a new tariff law increasing duties, and had also authorized the secretary to borrow more money. The uncertainties of the future led to great prudence among business men, and trade and business of every kind fell away. No one could foretell what was coming, and for a year after the war began business was timid, though the enormous operations of the government absorbed capital and every form of activity, and therefore the stagnation of trade was not so marked to the people. The imports revealed the story, for these fell off and the supply of revenue from that source was disappointing. Mr. Chase negotiated loans for a small amount under the authority already existing, and on the 4th day of July, 1861, Congress convened to enact further measures for suppressing the war. A loan of $250,000,000 was authorized, the duties were increased, an internal revenue system was adopted, and a direct tax of $20,000,000 was laid. The States were offered 15 per cent. reduction if they paid the tax, and this course was taken by all the States except those in rebellion, Delaware, and two of the Territories. Tax commissioners were appointed to enforce the law in the insurrectionary States, and they made levies and sold land, and after a long effort collected a portion of the tax assessed on them. As soon as the session closed Mr. Chase went to New York and negotiated a loan of $150,000,000 with the New York banks and those of Boston and Philadelphia. Never had such a large loan been contracted before in this country, but the banks were patriotic, the war fever was high, and though the figures were nearly as great as their associated capital they made the loan. The banks proposed that they should pay their respective portions over to one or two banks, and that the secretary should draw it out by issuing checks like an ordinary borrower. In that event they would pass through the clearing-house and be easily paid; indeed, would add only a million or so to the $20,000,000 that were daily passing through that institution for settlement. Congress had passed a law in the summer session of 1861 authorizing the secretary of the treasury to suspend the operation of the sub-treasury law, as it was called, which was passed in 1846, and prohibited the officers of the government from receiving anything beside specie from debtors. The banks were very desirous that the secretary of the treasury should exercise this authority, assuring him that if he did so they could easily make their payments, and that the loan, large as it was, would not disturb the money market. To their surprise he refused, and insisted that the banks should pay in gold. They undertook to do so, but sought a promise from him that the treasury notes, which he had been authorized to issue at the July session to the extent of $50,000,000, should not be issued. Though not making any formal promise he assured the banks that their wishes should be regarded. Very soon, however, the notes began to appear in circulation. The effect of this step was soon apparent. The banks could provide for the redemption of their own circulation, but as the government had only so much gold as the banks could furnish, which of course was soon paid out at the sub-treasuries for army and navy and other supplies, either the banks must provide for the redemption of the government notes, or they must circulate without any foundation to sustain them. Naturally the banks were afraid of them, and they caused trouble. They appeared in small quantities at first, and so long as this was the case the gold paid out by the banks to the government quickly came back again in the way of ordinary deposits, and all went well. But as soon as the quantity of the treasury issues became considerable the gold did not return to the banks as before, and seeing that it was rapidly disappearing the banks, on the 28th of December, 1861, concluded to suspend specie payments on the Monday following (30th). Of course, the government was obliged to do the same thing, and thus the secretary, by ignoring the advice of the banks and refusing to suspend the sub-treasury law, was quickly brought to the end of the road. It is the opinion of many that had Mr. Chase followed the advice of men not less patriotic than himself and comprehending far more perfectly the nature of the situation that the suspension of specie payments might have been averted, or deferred until near the end, in which event the evil consequences would have been fewer and less momentous than they were from the suspension so early in the struggle. The banks completed their engagement by paying in treasury notes, and after a considerable delay sold their bonds, and on some of them realized a considerable profit. But for a considerable period after getting them, contrary to their expectation, there was no market, and they were obliged to keep them or sell them at a sacrifice.

What was to be done now? Congress was in session, but knew not how to act. The business of the government could no longer be maintained on a specie basis, that was certain. Nor could the notes of suspended banks used for a circulating medium be used without danger. For, all responsibility for their redemption having ceased after suspension had been declared, what prevented them from issuing all they could get out? In some States there were severe laws against the issuing of notes by suspended banks, especially in New York, which was the leading banking State in the country. It was shown that the banks might continue to issue their notes in safety by the imposition of a heavy tax on all issues exceeding a safe amount. Public sentiment, however, rapidly centred on the plan of issuing more treasury notes, but possessing a legal-tender quality. A bill was introduced into the House for the issue of $50,000,000 of such notes. It was considered in committee, the amount was increased to $100,000,000, and reported favorably by one majority, and the vote of this member was thus cast in order that the bill might be reported, and not as an expression of his real opinion. A long debate ensued, relating chiefly to the constitutionality of the bill. The Constitution provides that Congress shall have power "to coin money, regulate the value thereof," and "no State shall . . . make anything but gold and silver coin a tender in payment of debts;" and it was strenuously maintained that such an act was a direct violation of it, yet the bill passed the House authorizing the issue of $150,000,000, and subsequently it passed the Senate, and was signed by the President. The House bill was amended in the Senate, one of the principal changes consisting in making customs dues an exception, and requiring importers to pay in gold as they had always done. This amendment, after a strong contention between the two Houses, prevailed. The amount issued was speedily absorbed, and a second bill was introduced for the issue of a similar amount. When the first bill was before the House, Mr. Hooper, of Massachusetts, one of the most intelligent members of that body, remarked: "It is said that when a government once assumes the power to issue a currency, the temptation to continue issuing it rather than resort to the more unpopular method of taxation is so great that it will not cease to issue it until it finds itself in a state of utter bankruptcy. The answer to this objection is, that the power of the government is limited by the law in this respect to $150,000,000, and consequently the government cannot, if it would, yield to any such temptation."

Yet how soon was this remark falsified! Many who voted for the first bill strongly opposed the second; but it passed through and became a law, and this amount, too, was soon issued, thus enormously swelling the volume of circulation. The banks, though prudently confining their issues for a time after suspending specie payments, turned a fresh issue into the swollen stream. As soon as the legal-tender notes appeared, the banks could legally use these for redeeming their own issues, and thus the way had been made easy for an enormous inflation. Some of the banks did, in truth, collect the legal-tender notes and substitute their own to a much larger amount. This was one of the causes of enmity on the part of Congress against the banks, and helped onward the creation of a rival system, and the imposition of the tax of 10 per cent. on the State bank issues, which finally drove them out of existence.

The same law which authorized the first issue of legal-tender notes also authorized the issue of $500,000,000 of bonds bearing 6 per cent. interest and payable after five and within twenty years. The interest was payable in gold collected from import duties, and at this early date Congress also provided that 1 per cent. of the public debt should be discharged annually. At first the bonds sold very slowly, but in the meantime the government procured considerable funds by two kinds of temporary loans. The first consisted of certificates of indebtedness, which were nothing more than certificates given to such creditors of the government as would take them, payable in a year, or sooner if it desired, and bearing 6 per cent. interest. The other kind of temporary loan consisted at first of $25,000,000, and finally increased to $100,000,000, of deposits of treasury notes by the banks to the government, which bore not exceeding 5 per cent. interest, and which they could demand after thirty days' notice. To some members of Congress this operation of the treasury seemed to be wholly for the benefit of banks, as the government could make no use of money which it was liable to pay at such a short notice. In truth, however, the government did use all of the money thus loaned, so that it was a highly favorable operation of the government. To provide more adequately for the payment of these deposits, if they should be demanded when the government was not able to respond, the secretary of the treasury was authorized to issue $50,000,000 of legal-tender notes, in the event that they should be wanted for that purpose.

When the country became deluged with paper-money and many had rapidly acquired wealth for investment, and the government bonds were considered as good as any other, their purchase began. Arrangements were made with a banking-house, Jay Cooke & Co., for the sale of them, and they, through commendable energy, succeeded in selling large quantities. They became very popular, and the secretary having now found a way for replenishing the treasury, ought to have continued so long as people were willing to buy and money was wanted. Instead of doing this, he discontinued their sale, and ordered the sale of another kind of bond bearing only 5 per cent. interest. He was besought not to try so hazardous an experiment, but he could not be dissuaded. The 5 per cent. bonds were put on the market, but fell flat. No one wanted them; it was an unusual rate of interest. The public indebtedness rapidly increased. Mr. Chase was besought to return to the 6 per cent. issues. But he was inflexible, and he would not acknowledge his mistake. The soldiers wanted their pay, and there was no money to pay them. In this dilemma, resort was once more had to the paper-mill. Another $100,000,000 of legal-tender notes were authorized beside the $50,000,000 above mentioned. Pres. Lincoln signed the bill with great reluctance, and said he would not have done so had the occasion been less urgent. It is unquestionably true that the country would have been spared this third issue had Mr. Chase continued to offer 6 per cent. bonds, instead of withdrawing them and offering 5 per cent. This experiment was the most costly to our government of any that has ever been tried.

At the end of the fiscal year 1864, Mr. Chase resigned and Senator Fessenden, of Maine, who had previously served as chairman of the finance committee of the Senate, was appointed. Confidence revived under his management, and bonds began to sell. Beside bonds another kind of loan had been tried, namely, treasury notes running for 1, 2, and 3 years, and bearing 6 per cent. interest in coin. The amount became so large, considering the other coin obligations, that the plan was adopted of issuing them bearing $7_{\frac{3}{10}}$ currency interest. Secretary Fessenden served only to the 4th of March, 1865, when he was succeeded by Hugh McCulloch, who paid the greater portion of the remainder of the war obligations in treasury notes of this nature. The principal acts authorizing loans beside the legal-tender notes were passed Feb. 25, 1862, which authorized $500,000,000 of bonds; the $900,000,000 loan act of March 3, 1863; the $200,000,000 loan act of March 3, 1864; the $400,000,000 act of June 30, 1864, and the $600,000,000 act of March 3, 1865. There were other acts, but these five contained the authority for making the great loans of the war.

Let us now briefly consider the war-taxation. Secretary Chase recommended, in his annual report at the close of 1862, the raising of $50,000,000 from internal sources. Congress more perfectly gauged public sentiment and the needs of the situation, and voted to raise from all sources $150,000,000. The committee of ways and means, through an able sub-committee, proceeded to prepare a bill. This work ought to have been done by the treasury department before the convening of Congress, and if it had been, several months of valuable time would have been saved and a revenue collected more quickly, and when the effect would have been most beneficial in sustaining the public credit. The bill was prepared as quickly as possible, but the discussion of it was elaborate, and not until July 1, 1862, did it become a law. It provided for the taxation of spirits and liquors of all kinds, of manufactures, for issuing licenses for conducting many kinds of business, for the taxation of incomes; in short, it swept over a wide field. Perhaps the most serious defect was that it did not provide for the immediate taxation of distilled spirits. The postponing of its operation in regard to them led to a series of gigantic speculations. The higher the tax, the more could be made by its imposition; and it is one of the singular facts of our war-history that, instead of looking with disfavor on it, many interests, perceiving how they would be benefited by increasing taxation, were eager for an advance. Just as the war closed the system became efficient, and for the fiscal year 1866 it yielded $310,906,984. With every increase in internal taxation the tax on imports was increased in order to prevent the manufacturer from suffering by the advance. Imports, nevertheless, were enormous, for money was abundant, every one was employed, wages and salaries were high, and consequently the demand for all kinds of commodities was great. All classes were flourishing, but there were persons who saw clearly that this period would come to an end, and wise were they who put their houses in order in season. The war closed in April, 1865; the debts paid during the next five months were enormous, and on the 1st of September of that year the debt reached its greatest height. Deducting the cash in the treasury, the amount was $2,756,431,571. The cost of the war, deducting for the expenditures that would probably have been incurred had the nation remained at peace, was, according to the best calculation, $6,189,929,908. Let us hope that this huge war-bill is the last.

V. *From the Close of the War to* 1891.—When Congress discussed the legal-tender bill, one of the leading objections to it was its unconstitutionality, G. H. Pendleton, of Ohio, making perhaps the strongest speech on that side. The State courts decided in favor of the law, with the single exception of the Supreme Court of Pennsylvania. The Court of Appeals of New York at an early day declared the law to be constitutional. But all felt that the question would not be settled until it reached the United States Supreme Court. When it finally came before that tribunal, in 1867, Mr. Chase was the chief-justice. He and three of his colleagues decided against the constitutionality of the law, the other three dissenting. At the time of rendering this decision two vacancies existed, which were soon after filled. The attorney-general, E. R. Hoar, then applied for a reargument of the question in another case. He claimed that the former decision had been made when the bench was not full, and that a question of such transcendent importance ought not to be declared as definitely settled until all the members had expressed an opinion. The judges who concurred in the opinion given were opposed to opening the question; but those who dissented uniting with the two new appointees, constituted a majority and decided in favor of another argument. The decision in the second case sustained the law. At a later period another question was raised, namely, that admitting it was constitutional to issue such notes in time of war, could this be legally done in a time of peace? The court in the second case maintained that if the issuing of such notes was necessary to supply the absolute necessities of the treasury, that if nothing else would have enabled the government to maintain its armies and navy, nothing else would have saved the government and the Constitution from destruction while the legal-tender acts would, could any one be so bold as to assert that Congress had transgressed its powers? Whether they were needful, the court declared, was a question for Congress to decide. If it was a question for Congress in the second case it was equally so in the last case, so the court decided, and thus the law stands. This case was decided in March, 1883. It was supposed by many that specie payments would be resumed soon after the war closed, and had this event happened the Supreme Court would not have been confronted with these questions. A long time was to pass, however, before they could be resumed. Mr. McCulloch favored their speedy return, and in his first report made some strong recommendations on the subject. Congress, after a long debate, authorized the secretary to retire $4,000,000 of treasury notes a month; but after he had executed this policy for a period of 22 months, Congress rescinded the law, and though the subject was constantly discussed in and out of Congress, not until 1875 was a law enacted for resuming specie payments, and even that put the time off until Jan. 1, 1879. The main features were the withdrawal of $80 of the legal-tender notes for each issue of $100 of national bank notes, until the aggregate amount should be reduced to $300,000,000 and the accumulation of coin from customs duties and the sale of bonds. One of the grave objections to the law was, could the treasury notes thus withdrawn be reissued? It was seen that if they could be the intent of the law could be defeated. It was a defective, double-faced law, but it was the best that could be enacted. Opposition in Congress to any kind of a resumption measure was strong. Happily, Senator Sherman, who framed the law, became secretary of the treasury in March, 1877, and through his wise efforts a sufficient quantity of coin was accumulated, and the long-delayed event came around without the disturbance of any interest. The premium on gold ran down, the foreign exchanges were in our favor, gold flowed here in large quantity to pay for exports, the banks cordially co-operated with the secretary, and when the day for resuming arrived no demand for coin occurred, nor has the treasury at any time suffered from the presentation of the treasury notes for payment.

Next to the resuming of specie payments the payment of the public debt has engaged the attention of Congress and the people. If the debt was heaped up with extraordinary rapidity its reduction has astounded the great nations of the old world. The first considerable portion of the debt to mature were the two and three-year treasury notes, amounting to $830,000,000. Before their maturity had arrived a portion had been paid and another portion had been converted into bonds running for a longer date. In 1870 a funding law was enacted whereby the treasury department was able to refund the obligations of the government into others bearing a lower rate of interest. The new bonds were sold by various arrangements with bankers, and, as the credit of the government improved, the secretary was able to sell them on better terms. Of these, $250,000,000 were sold at 4 per cent. interest; afterward Mr. Sherman sold $737,691,550 at 4 per cent.; finally a portion was continued, though at a lower rate of interest, 3½ per cent., and, lastly, a large quantity at 3 per cent. Payment has gone on with few interruptions since 1865. After 1873 there was a short period when debt reduction was slow, and now and then a monthly debt statement has shown an increase. The people very generally have favored this policy of debt-paying, and have rejoiced over the statements showing large reductions.

To reduce the debt so rapidly, however, heavy taxes have been necessary. The import duties were not much changed until 1883, though large reductions were made in internal taxation. When the war ceased, the demand for things speedily fell away. War is an exceedingly wasteful business. The various interests then felt the pressure of taxation and loudly clamored for relief. Of course, a system devised so hastily, and extending so widely, was very imperfect, and Congress would have acted more wisely if while throwing off taxes it had also in many instances readjusted them. This easy method of Congress, though affording relief, did not always remove inequalities. The following table shows the reduction in internal revenue taxation:

July	13, 1866	$65,000,000
March	2, 1867	40,000,000
Feb.	3, 1868	23,000,000
March 31, 1868, and		
July	20, 1868	$45,000,000
July	14, 1870	55,000,000
June	6, 1872	20,651,000
March	1, 1879	13,273,148
March	3, 1883	31,955,332

The revenues were so large that, notwithstanding the reduction of the debt, a large amount was left for expenditure in other ways. The ordinary expenditures had swelled from the expansion of the government; but, beside these, enormous sums were appropriated for pensions, river and harbor improvements, public buildings in many of the cities of the Union, and other purposes. Under the Pension Bill of 1879 enormous sums have been paid to the defenders of the Union. Still more extravagant Pension bills have since been passed to testify the exceptional gratitude of the American Republic to those who fought and suffered in its defence.

After the suspension of specie payments in 1861, Congress was not much troubled with coinage questions for many years. The size and composition of the cents were reduced during the war, and in 1870 the laws regulating coinage were revised. This work was first done, at the request of the secretary of the treasury, by Mr. Knox, the comptroller of the currency. Among other alterations which he reported as desirable was the discontinuing of the coinage of silver dollars. None had been coined since 1809, and none circulated; for this reason, among others, they were worth more than gold ones. The report was carefully considered by both Houses, far more so than reports usually of that nature. But slight opposition appeared to the recommendation in either House. Four years afterward, when the statutes of the United States were revised, the legal-tender quality was taken from the silver dollars in all payments exceeding $5. Hardly had this law gone into operation, when silver, as compared with gold, began to fall rapidly in price. Then a movement was started to restore the coinage and legal-tender power of silver. A monetary commission was appointed to examine the subject, which made one of the most elaborate investigations of the kind in our history. In 1876 a bill was introduced into the House providing for the free coinage of silver. The bill was amended, the amount was limited to $4,000,000 a month, and passed. In 1890 a bill for the free coinage of silver was actively pressed, but was defeated.

With respect to those who administered the finances of the government, it may be stated that Hugh McCulloch served during Pres. Johnson's administration, and George S. Boutwell during Pres. Grant's first term (1869-73). On being elected to the Senate from Massachusetts he resigned, and W. A. Richardson became secretary. After fifteen months' service he retired, and Benjamin H. Bristow filled the office for two years (1874-76), and was succeeded by Senator Lot M. Morrill, who served during the remainder of Pres. Grant's second term. During the next four years John Sherman was secretary of the treasury. Pres. Garfield appointed Senator Windom, of Minnesota, but when Mr. Arthur became President, Judge Folger, of New York, was made secretary of the treasury. After his death in September, 1884, W. Q. Gresham and Hugh McCulloch successively held this important office. Under Pres. Cleveland, Daniel Manning was secretary from 1885 to 1887, and Charles S. Fairchild to 1889, in which year Mr. Windom again became secretary, under Pres. Harrison. After the sudden death of Mr. Windom, in Jan. 1891, Charles Foster, of Ohio, was called to the office. (A. S. B.)

FINCH, the common name given to a very large family of birds, the *Fringillidæ*, which comprise one-eighth of North American birds, and include the several tribes of sparrow, linnet, bunting, crossbill, greenfinch, goldfinch, etc. As a rule they are plainly clad, though some are brightly colored. Their most common feature is their short, thick, cone-shaped bill, which is well adapted to crush seeds, their chief food, though they eat insects and worms to some extent. The true finches form a group, *Fringillinæ*, of which the typical genus is *Fringilla*. The members of this genus have long and pointed wings, and a slightly forked tail. They include the chaffinch, siskin, goldfinch, linnet, snow bird, yellow bird, etc. These birds are very widely distributed, and live in flocks, though they are not truly gregarious, feeding on seeds in winter, and on larvæ, grain, etc., in summer. The genus includes more than 80 species, according to Gray, some of which are very sweet singers. The Bramble finch or Brambling (*F. montifringilla*) is

See Vol. IX.
p. 167 Am.
ed. (p. 191
Edin. ed.).

The Bramble Finch (*Fringilla montifringilla*).

the type. Of the American species, the pine finch (*F. pinus*) is common in the pine forests throughout the United States. It is of a yellowish gray above, and whitish below, the wings and tail being dusky with white edges. Length 4¾ inches. The yellow bird, or American goldfinch (*F. Chrysomitris tristis*), is a beautiful species, closely resembling the European goldfinch, but with more yellow in its plumage. Among American finches of related genera may be named the grass finch, the sea-side finch, and Lincoln's finch, a bird with a sweet and loud song, that is found from Labrador to Guatemala. Of introduced species of finches, the best known are the canary, and the English sparrow, which is increasing so rapidly as to drive off many of the native species. The finches, as a rule, do not migrate, being hardy enough to bear the winter weather. Some, as the snow birds, are found in very cold climates.

VOL. III.—23

FINLAND. In recent years Finland has made steady if not rapid progress. The population, which at the end of 1875 was 1,912,647, was on Jan. 1, 1881, 2,081,612, showing an average increase of 33,793. There were at that date 43,238 more women than men. This is accounted for partly by emigration, partly by the effects of drink, but principally by accidents. Finland having an extensive sea-coast and great lakes, a large portion of her male population are engaged in hazardous marine enterprises, and about 550 men are drowned every year. In the above statistics the Russian soldiers temporarily stationed in Finland are not included. Neither are the Jews, as they are not considered to be citizens. The population of the four principal cities of Finland was, Oct. 1, 1880: Helsingfors, 43,142; Abo, 22,967; Wiborg, 14,668; Tammerfors, 13,750.

See Vol. IX.
p. 188 Am.
ed. (p. 216
Edin. ed.).

Religion.—Of the population of 2,081,612 the large proportion of 2,060,535 are Lutherans; 38,757 belong to the Orthodox or Russo-Greek Church, and 2,320 are Roman Catholics. These last two denominations are found almost exclusively in Helsingfors and Wiborg. The Lutheran clergy are a body of intelligent, faithful, and hard-working men. There are 900 of them, with two bishops and one archbishop. The Finns, both men and women, are a church-going people.

Commerce.—The exports, which in 1876 were of the value of about $19,200,000, had risen in 1882 to 19,873,130 marks, or $23,135,514. The imports in the same time had risen from about $27,000,000 to 167,054,387 marks, or $34,041,497. The commerce with Russia is of the greatest magnitude, and embraces nearly one-half of the whole, both of exports and imports. Next in importance comes the commerce with Germany, and then with Great Britain. The imports from the United States reach the value of 2,200,000 marks, or $424,600 per annum, and consist principally of cotton and petroleum.

The principal exports of Finland are wood in its various forms, such as fire-wood, boards, plank, lath, etc., etc.; butter, rye, and oats. The supply of wood is inexhaustible unless destroyed by fire, and this the government has taken efficient means to prevent; for the forestry laws of Finland are excellent, and are strictly enforced. A proprietor's woodland is divided by government officers into thirty sections. He may cut one of these sections each year, but no more. The butter is excellent, and is made in large quantities, being exported to Russia and to England. The pasturage is good, and, when that fails, the cows find nutritious food in browsing. The rye is probably the best in the market, and is largely exported to Sweden. The oats are shipped to Great Britain.

Debt.—The public debt, Jan. 1, 1883, was 70,085,739 marks, or $13,526,548. The finances are in excellent condition, the receipts being equal to the expenses. The currency is gold, silver, and paper, the paper being at par with gold, and consequently preferred. The unit of value is the mark, which is the equivalent of the franc, or $0.193, or about 19¼ cents. The penni is the $\frac{1}{100}$ part of the mark, and answers to the centime.

Language and Literature.—The official language is now Finnish. Until a very recent date it was Swedish. This is still the language of the better classes and of the higher orders of literature. The famous Finnish poet, Runeberg (died May 10, 1877), wrote in Swedish. His poems are remarkable for their imagery, for their beautiful descriptions of nature, and for the smoothness of the versification. Many of them have been translated into German, and some of them into English. Runeberg may be justly said to rank with Tennyson, and with other of the most eminent poets of modern times.

FINLEY, JAMES BRADLEY (1781–1856), an American clergyman, was born in North Carolina, July 1, 1781, being the son of Rev. R. W. Finley, a Presbyterian minister. In 1801 he removed to Ohio, and in 1809 he joined the Western Conference of the Methodist Episcopal Church. He itinerated for six years, and became presiding elder. He was a missionary among the Wyandot Indians on the Upper Sandusky, 1821–29, then preacher or presiding elder in Southern Ohio, 1829–45, and afterwards was chaplain of the Ohio penitentiary until 1849. He died Sept. 6, 1856. His works include *Wyandot Mission* (1840); *Life among the Indians* (1857); *Sketches of Western Methodism* (1857); *Prison Life* (1860); and an *Autobiography* (1854).

FINLEY, SAMUEL (1715–1766), an American Presbyterian minister and educator, was born in Armagh, Ireland, in 1715. He removed to Philadelphia in 1734, studied theology, and after ordination in October, 1742, was chiefly engaged as an itinerant in the "Great Revival." In 1744 he settled at Nottingham, Md., where he remained as pastor seventeen years, conducting also an academy of high reputation. On the death of President Davies of the College of New Jersey, Mr. Finley was chosen to succeed him, and removed to Princeton in 1761. He edited the sermons of President Davies, and published some of his own. His grandson, W. P. Finley, LL. D., was president of Charleston College, S. C., for some years.

FINNEY, CHARLES GRANDISON (1792–1875), an American preacher, was born at Warren, Litchfield co., Conn., Aug. 29, 1792. He reached manhood on his father's farm, then went to Jefferson co., N. Y., where he studied law, but in 1822 was ordained a minister. He labored with great fervency and success as a revival preacher and in 1835 accepted a professorship in Oberlin College, Ohio, then recently founded. In 1837 he became also pastor of the First Congregational Church in Oberlin. He spent three years (1849–51) in England and by his fervid eloquence exerted a powerful influence in the non-conformist churches. From 1852 to 1866 he was president of Oberlin College. He died at Oberlin, Aug. 16, 1875. Besides his prominence as a revivalist he was noted for his opposition to secret societies. His publications include *Sermons on Important Subjects* (1836); *Lectures on Revivals* (1835); *Lectures to Professing Christians* (1836); *On Sanctification* (1840); *Systematic Theology* (1847); *Guide to the Saviour*; all of which had a wide circulation. His theological system was largely based upon man's free will, and was severely criticized by Rev. Dr. Charles Hodge. See *Memoirs of Charles G. Finney, with an Autobiography* (1876).

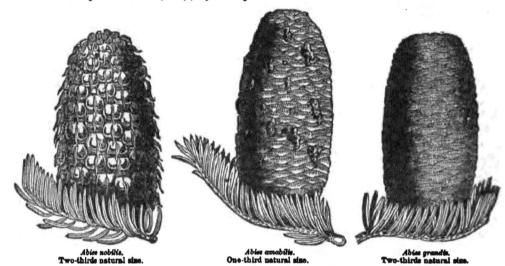

Abies nobilis. Two-thirds natural size.   *Abies amabilis.* One-third natural size.   *Abies grandis.* Two-thirds natural size.

Cones and Leaves of American Firs.

FIR, the common name given to many species of coniferous trees, often extended to include the genus *Pinus*, but more usually restricted to the genus *Abies*. The species of this genus are known somewhat indifferently by the common names of fir, spruce, and hemlock, but we restrict ourselves to those that are particularly known as firs. This genus bears its fertile flowers in catkins, consisting of open imbricated carpels in the form of scales subtended by a bract. The fruit forms a *strobile* or cone, whose scales are thin and flat, not thickened at the apex, nor with a prickly point. The seeds have a persistent wing. The leaves are not clustered like those of the pines and larches, but are scattered upon the shoots, needle-like in shape, and frequently two-ranked or doubled. The trees are usually of an attractive pyramidal shape, sending out annually a whorl of branches from the foot of the leading shoot. They are much used as ornamental shade trees. Those known specially as firs bear erect, lateral cones. Of these our most important Eastern species is the balsam or balm of Gilead fir (*A. balsamea*), the source of the well-known Canada balsam. It is a handsome, quick-growing, short-lived tree, from 40 to 60 feet high, with a slender trunk, and of little value as timber. The cones are cylindrical and large. The

(See Vol. IX. p. 193 Am. ed. (p. 222 Edin. ed.).)

bark is smooth, but covered with small sacs or blisters, filled with a transparent liquid resin, of honey-like consistency, which exudes on puncturing, and is caught in suitable vessels. It is used in making delicate varnishes, and is of great value as an agent in the mounting of microscopic objects. The tree grows in cold damp woods and swamps from New England to Wisconsin and northward. A. *Fraseri*, the small-fruited or double-balsam fir, is a tree which somewhat resembles the above, but has much smaller cones. It also yields the Canada balsam. It occurs on the mountains of Western New England and of Pennsylvania, and is common southward on the highest Alleghenies. The Western coast region of North America is remarkably rich in firs, often of immense size. Of these the most common is *Pseudotsuga (Abies) Douglasii*, the Douglas or red fir, which forms seven-eighths of all the forest growth in Oregon and Washington Territory, and extends from British Columbia to California, and along the mountain ranges into Mexico. It is a very large tree, growing from 200 to nearly 300 feet high, and 8 to 10 feet diameter, and is the most valuable timber tree of the Pacific region. It often forms extensive forests, almost to the exclusion of other species. The wood is hard, strong, and durable, in color from light red to yellow, and is largely manufactured into lumber, used for all kinds of general construction. The bark is found valuable in tanning leather. *A. concolor*, the white or balsam fir, is a tree of 100 feet in height, found on the moist slopes of the mountains from Oregon to Arizona, and to the Pike's Peak region of Colorado. It is greatly developed in the California sierras. The wood is light and soft, and of little value. *A. bracteata*, of the Santa Lucia Mountains of California, reaches a height of nearly 200 feet, and forms a heavy, compact though not hard wood. It will probably prove one of the most valuable of the North American Abies. *A. amabilis*, the lovely silver fir, is found from British Columbia to Oregon, and reaches a great development in the Cascade Mountains. It is from 100 to 200 feet high, its wood a light brown hue, hard, but not strong. *A. nobilis*, the noble silver fir, is a tree from 200 to 300 feet high, found in the mountains of Oregon. It forms, with *A. amabilis*, extensive forests along the slopes of the Cascade range. The wood is light, hard and strong, of a light brown color with red streaks. *A. magnifica*, the red fir, occurs on Mount Shasta, California, and along the west slope of the Sierra Nevada. It is a large tree, of over 200 feet high and 7 to 9 in diameter. The wood is light, soft, not strong, rather close grained, of a satiny, light red color. It is largely used for fuel, but is of little value for other purposes. *A. grandis*, the white fir, occurs from Vancouver's Island to California, reaching its greatest development in the moist bottom lands of West Washington and Oregon. It grows from 200 to 300 feet high and 5 feet diameter. The wood is light and soft, and is manufactured into lumber, and used for some building purposes. *A. subalpina* occurs from Alaska to North Oregon. It is a scattered tree, 100 feet high, and of little importance. These trees are remarkable for their perfect conical forms. Yet though perfect in outline they are less graceful than the spruces. Their timber, in most cases, is of little economical importance. (C. M.)

FIRE DEPARTMENTS. The fire departments of America are of two general classes: (1) the departments of large cities, composed of officers and men who devote their whole time to the calling, and are paid for their services;

See Vol. IX. p. 202 Am. ed. (p. 233 Edin. ed.).

and (2) those of smaller cities and villages, composed wholly or chiefly of volunteers, who pursue their own avocations but respond to calls for duty, and are not paid, but generally enjoy exemption from jury and militia duty during their service as firemen, and after discharge therefrom, and are also sometimes allowed a slight reduction in taxation. The first of these classes is commonly known as *paid*, and the second as *volunteer department*. In some of the minor cities there are also departments made up partly of full-paid firemen and partly of volunteers, or call-men, who are subject to duty during the day on call only, and to full duty at night, for which they receive suitable compensation. Such departments, unless the paid element preponderates over the volunteers in numbers, are considered as belonging to the second class.

The best organized fire departments of the United States provide not only for the extinguishing of fires but also for their prevention, by regulating the storage, sale, and transportation of combustibles and explosives, ascertaining the causes and origin of fires, and the detection of incendiaries.

In New York and Detroit the supervision of the construction of buildings and of their alteration and repair is also imposed upon the fire department. In the first-named city this important branch of the municipal service has been more economically administered (notwithstanding an enormous increase in its business), and is far more efficient, than it was as a separate and independent department of the city government. This result was foreseen and is not unnatural, for no other department or branch of the municipal service can have so great an interest in improving the stability and general security of structures as the fire department, the members of which are so often compelled to risk their lives in burning buildings in efforts to save the lives and property of others. Such adjuncts to the fire-extinguishing corps are valuable as preventives of fire, and necessary in all well-organized fire departments.

In the organization, equipment, and government of fire-extinguishing corps the climate, the topography of the city to be protected, the character of its industries, its water supply, the size, height, and general construction of its buildings, the proportion of buildings used wholly or partly for dwelling purposes to those used exclusively for business purposes, and the character of its inhabitants, are conditions to be considered. A striking example of the extreme dissimilarity of large American cities with respect to these conditions is afforded by the cities of New York and Brooklyn, which, though separated only by the East River, have nevertheless but one of these conditions, that of climate, in common.

The fire-extinguishing corps of the United States are superior in point of power, *i. e.*, size, number, and capacity of engines, to those of other countries. This is necessitated mainly by the fact that the laws and regulations relative to prevention of fires are less stringent than, for instance, in England, France, and

Germany; and, in a lesser degree, by the more rapid growth of American cities, naturally engendering a general spirit of carelessness. There can be no doubt that a very large proportion of the loss by fire in the United States would be prevented by the enactment and enforcement of laws compelling better construction of buildings; imposing proper restrictions upon the manufacture, storage, and transportation of combustible and explosive materials and compounds; requiring searching investigations into the causes and origin of fires, with suitable punishment of persons found guilty of carelessness resulting in fires as well as of incendiaries; and, lastly, by instituting very necessary reforms in fire-underwriting. Neglect of these fundamental principles necessitates the maintenance of large and expensive fire-extinguishing corps, causes great fire-losses, and thus entails a waste of the people's substance. All of these shortcomings may be immediately remedied by legislation except the proper construction of buildings; for the harm already inflicted by faulty construction, permitted or induced by inadequate or improper laws or negligent supervision, is unfortunately of a more permanent nature, and can only be gradually righted. While it is conceded that the vast majority of the large fires and disastrous conflagrations are due to this cause, the lesson taught by this experience and paid for with millions of treasure seems nevertheless to go unheeded. In the absence of these safeguards the efficiency of American fire-extinguishing corps becomes of paramount importance, and that depends upon the character of its personnel, its equipment, and management.

The paid fire-extinguishing corps of the United States are generally organized into companies of from 6 to 12 officers and men each, equipped either with a steam fire-engine and hose-tender or a chemical fire-engine (which are called engine companies); or with a hose-carriage only (called a hose company); or with a hook-and-ladder truck (called a hook-and-ladder company); each apparatus being drawn by horses. Some engine companies are also equipped with a hook-and-ladder truck and additional officers and men, and a water-tower is also sometimes added to either an engine or hook-and-ladder company, with additional men. Most cities are divided into company districts, in which the commander of each fire-company exercises a general control over the fire department material located in it, the fire-alarm boxes, fire-hydrants, etc., and by frequent inspections keeps himself informed as to the enforcement of all laws with the execution of which the department may be charged, and the plan and construction of the buildings. In some of the larger cities the companies are organized into battalions commanded by a chief of battalion, the whole being under the command of the highest officer, who is variously designated as "chief of department," "chief-engineer," or "fire-marshal." In a few of the larger cities the regular firemen, from the highest officer down to the humblest private, are appointed for life or during good behavior, being removable for misconduct only, and are therefore free from the baneful effects of local political changes. In others a "clean sweep," of the higher officers at least, is looked for as a matter of course after each revolution in local politics, and in some places is remorselessly ordered with but little regard to the efficiency of the service. It is needless to say that a high state of discipline and effectiveness cannot be attained in an organization the members of which feel dependent upon the political faction in power for the time, and that the effect of each political change is under such circumstances necessarily demoralizing and destructive of every condition of success.

Permanency in position, dependent only upon good conduct, was first assured to the members of its fire-extinguishing corps by the New York Fire Commissioners in 1867, and simultaneously the system of promotion after qualification before an examining board was inaugurated. So evident was the good effect of these provisions that the principle of a life-tenure was recognized by law in 1873, while the civil service reform legislation has, within the past few years, provided for examination and qualification before appointment or promotion. Physical qualifications had, however, also been required of candidates for appointment in that department since 1867; and in 1883 another important stride in advance was made by the fire commissioners, in requiring that every candidate for appointment or promotion must successfully pass through a course of practical instruction and drill in the use of scaling-ladders, life-lines, and other appliances, recently introduced for life-saving purposes. This is the crucial test, and it may be safely asserted that the candidate who successfully passes this examination possesses, so far as it can possibly be ascertained prior to actual service, all the requisites of courage, nerve, strength, and agility necessary to make a first-class fireman.

The best fire-extinguishing corps are unquestionably those in which these principles underlie the organization, and in which the arduous, wearing, and often very dangerous nature of the fireman's service is acknowledged in the form of liberal pay and provision for retirement upon becoming disabled for active service. Under such conditions the very best service can and should be exacted from the members. In both these conditions the New York department leads. The salaries paid are liberal compared with other cities, though the cost of living is higher and the service is considered to be more arduous. By a legislative enactment in 1871 a relief fund was created, from which pensions are paid to officers and men upon their retirement, or when partially disabled and relieved only from active service at fires but still held for lighter duties. For disability (whether total or partial) incurred in the line of duty, or after 10 years' continuous service, the law allows half pay; if not incurred in the line of duty, and before 10 years' continuous service, one-third pay. To those advantages are added rewards of merit (consisting of endowed medals) for courageous rescues at fires and other acts of heroism, and for general good deportment. The additional requirement might with great benefit be everywhere made, that officers and men should have their homes in the immediate vicinity of their respective company houses, and that transfers interfering with this condition, should not be made. Finally, strict discipline is essential to the effectiveness of a fire-extinguishing corps.

Apparatus.—The steam-fire-engine is the most important apparatus, except in the rare instances where the water pressure is effective for fire-extinguishing purposes without their use. These engines are generally classified according to the construction of the pumps, which are either piston or rotary, and may be either single or double; and as to the construction of the boilers, which are either flue, tubular, or coil, as shown by the accompanying illustrations. The tubular boiler is now made of two patterns, the drop-tube and the nest-tube, the latter being the latest form. Naturally the aim of all manufacturers is to produce engines of the greatest power and least weight compatible with necessary strength and durability. They are made of various sizes, but, as each manufacturer has adopted a classification independent of the others, there is no general fixed standard of size. About the heaviest engines now in use weigh, fully equipped, with water in boiler and men riding upon them, somewhat over 5 tons, while the lightest made to be drawn by horses, under the same conditions, weigh about 2¼ tons

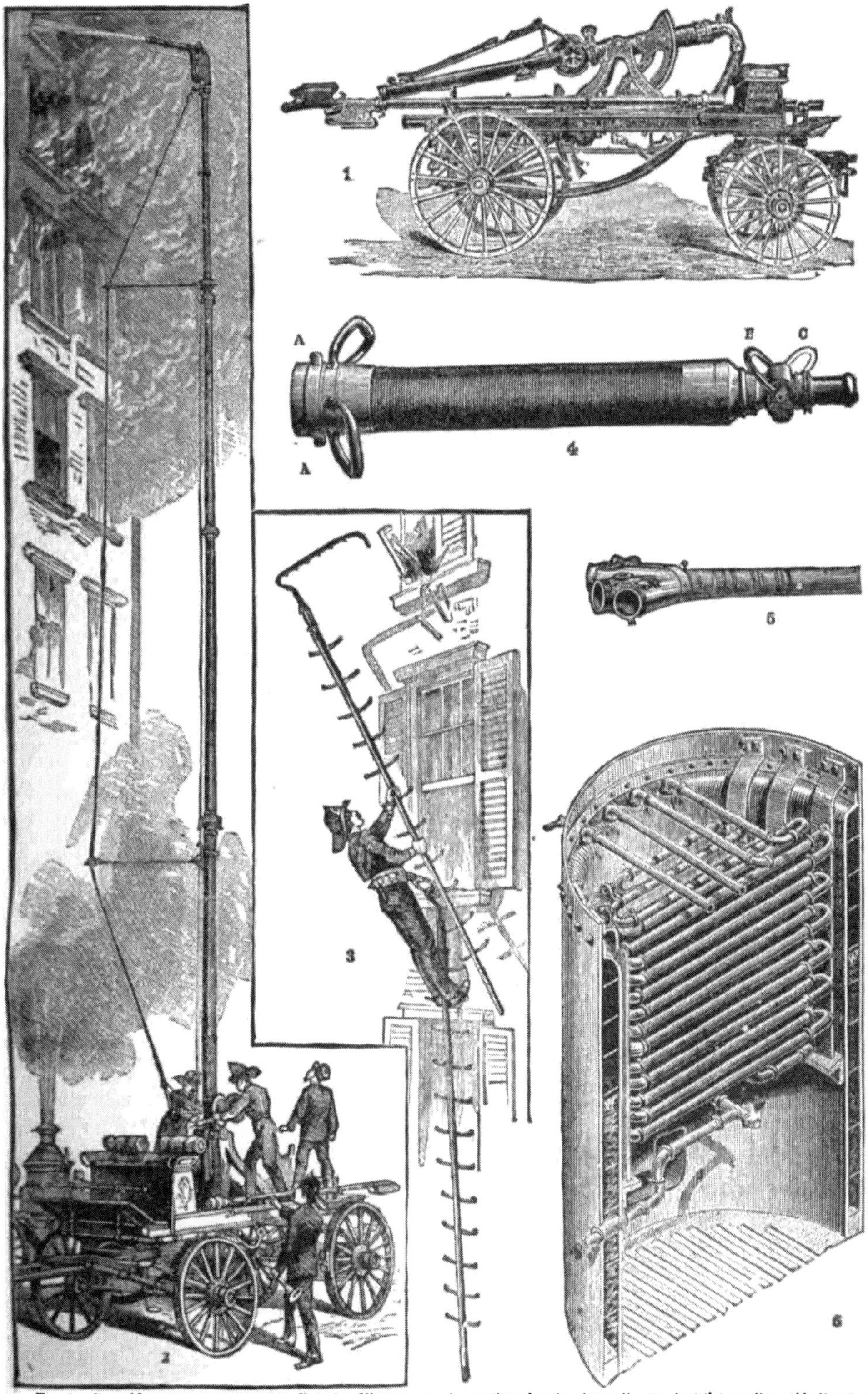

FIRE. PLATE XXI.

Fig. 1. Portable water-tower at rest. Fig. 2. Water-tower in service, showing brace-line against the recoil; guide-line for directing stream, etc. Fig. 3. Using the scaling-ladder. Fig. 4. Pipe and cut-off nozzle. (*A*, Grip-handles; *B*, Cut-off open; *C*, Cut-off closed.) Fig. 5. Siamese connection (4-way, with automatic valves). Fig. 6. Internal construction of coil fire-engine boiler.

Preference is now generally given to a light engine of about 3 tons weight, the heavier ones being used as reserve engines and during fires of long duration. In nearly all of the more important departments the water in the boilers is maintained at or somewhat above the steaming point while standing in quarters, to insure a working pressure on arrival, in case of fire in the immediate vicinity. This is effected by an attachment known as the heater, ordinarily placed in the basement or cellar of the engine-house, consisting of a stove with a coil of pipe through which water circulates and is converted into steam, passing thence through pipes into the boiler of the engine, to which it is connected in such a manner as to permit of instantaneous disconnection upon the sounding of an alarm.

The maximum capacity of the most powerful steam-fire-engines is about 900 gallons per minute; that of the smallest about 300 gallons. A most important improvement in the pumps of fire-engines was the invention of the automatic relief-valve, which enabled the pipe-man to shut off the flow of water at the point of discharge without communicating with the engineer running the engine. By means of this device the pipeman has complete control of the flow of water. The damage to property from the unnecessary use of water, formerly caused by the delays in stopping the engine, is thus entirely obviated.

The means of obtaining water for fire-extinguishing purposes consists principally of hydrants connected with the water-mains in streets, though all engines are also constructed to draw water from streams and other bodies of water, as well as from cisterns, etc., by means of flexible suction-pipes with which they are provided. Fire-hydrants are now placed much nearer together than formerly, especially in important sections of large cities, thereby obviating the necessity of long lines of hose, the consequent loss by friction, and wear and tear of both hose and engines. Fire-hydrants are of two distinctive kinds: the post hydrant, projecting above the sidewalk level, and the flush hydrant, which does not project above the sidewalk or street level, the opening to it being covered by an iron plate appropriately marked. The first named is most used and is of various patterns, while the use of the second is restricted to a few cities only.

The hose-cart or hose-tender is ordinarily built to carry from 750 to 1000 feet of hose upon a large coil, and with seats for 6 of the men. Most of these tenders are two-wheeled and drawn by one horse, but in the larger cities the four-wheeled tender drawn by two horses is now preferred, by reason of its greater carrying capacity and because the two-wheeled tender is too heavy for one horse. All tenders are fitted to carry wrenches and other necessary tools, and in New York some of the four-wheeled tenders also carry short scaling-ladders, for use if required before the arrival of a hook-and-ladder company.

The hose, and in fact nearly every apparatus, implement, and tool designed for fire-extinguishing purposes, should be as light in weight as is compatible with necessary strength and durability. But it is a question whether the quality of durability should be very strongly insisted upon, for if the article has the required strength, and is light and portable at the expense only of great durability, it would be true economy to replace it frequently. The pressure upon hose at fires rarely exceeds 250 pounds to the square inch, and any that will resist a pressure test of 300 pounds applied to a single length, selected at random from a lot, is deemed safe and reliable. It should, however, possess two other indispensable qualities, to wit: that it neither shortens in length nor twists under the test pressure. The hose now almost universally used in large cities is of two general kinds—the rubber or combination, made principally of rubber upon a body of cotton fabric, being both covered and lined with rubber; and the cotton, rubber lined, which is principally of cotton woven cylindrically and rubber lined. The various brands of the rubber or combination hose do not differ in construction as widely as the cotton fabric, which is of two distinct kinds—the ordinary single fabric, and the double or jacket pattern, which may be best described as consisting of a light cylindrically woven cotton hose, rubber lined, with another similar cotton hose without lining drawn over it. The ordinary fire-hose is 2½ inches in internal diameter, but for special apparatus, such as fire-boats, or water towers, and for "Siamesing" or combining two or more streams into one, 3, 3¼, 3½, and even 4-inch hose is made use of. The ordinary 2½-inch hose weighs about 65 pounds per length of fifty feet, inclusive of couplings; the rubber or combination of this weight being 3-ply, by which is meant the number of thicknesses of canvas between the outer coating and the interior lining of rubber; while the thickness and number of strands composing the cotton fabric hose are greater or less, according to weight.

The simplest coupling, the screw, is considered the best, as being the most reliable under all circumstances, though much ingenuity has been shown in devising couplings to lock quicker than it is possible to screw those of the kind first referred to together. As none of these improvements have so far been found to be without objections, rendering them not as positively reliable as the screw coupling, it has been deemed best to adhere to that pattern, at the expense of a little more time at the outset in making connection, but with the absolute certainty that, once properly made, it holds together. It has been the aim for many years past to have a standard coupling throughout the United States, so that, in the event of a conflagration, neighboring fire-extinguishing corps can readily render aid. So far as the larger cities are concerned this has been accomplished, mainly through the efforts of the chief officers of the country assembled in annual convention.

For cities having many high business structures the "water tower" has become an indispensable apparatus. It is in reality a portable stand-pipe, run upon wheels and drawn by horses; the pipe itself is easily and quickly put together in lengths varying in the aggregate from 33 to 51 feet, and is then as easily and quickly elevated to a perpendicular position. The hose supplying the water is attached to the bottom of the pipe or tube, which is made to revolve by a simple gearing, the end or top section having a flexible discharge-pipe with nozzle, which can be pointed at any required angle by means of a wire cord attached to it; and the whole apparatus, when in operation, is under the control of one man standing upon the truck, from which point he is enabled to give the stream any direction. The great advantage of having a powerful and steady stream of water delivered horizontally, or nearly so, and at short range, into the upper stories of a burning building, is manifest. It should be mentioned that the pipe, in whatever direction the water may be delivered, is always braced against the recoil. The accompanying illustrations show the apparatus.

A number of the large cities also have floating engines or fire-boats, fitted with more or less powerful fire-pumps. The latest addition to this branch of fire-extinguishing equipment is the one built for the city of Brooklyn, which is said to be an improvement on its predecessors in other cities. It is undoubtedly so in furnishing more steam-power, greater speed and facility in turning (having twin screws), more powerful pumps, and greater deck-room. These improvements are made possible mainly by dispensing with the quarters for the crew, usually built upon the deck, which, wherever it is practicable to provide them on shore in the vicinity of the boat's berth, are not necessary. A fire-boat should be built solely with a view to fighting fire most effectually under all possible circumstances. It is therefore requisite not only that it is powerful, swift, and easily handled, but also that it is as nearly fire-proof above the water-line as it can be made, the part of the hull below the water-line being constructed only with a view to securing the necessary strength and the maximum of buoyancy. The majority of fire-boats are built entirely of wood; a few have iron hulls, but all have upper works of wood, and, as a consequence, instead of being able to run close into a fire and deliver their streams at the shortest and most effective range, they are often obliged, if the fire be hot, either to keep away from it and do comparatively ineffectual work, or to devote a considerable part of their effort to protect themselves from burning.

The chemical fire-engine is by reason of its lightness much used in villages and smaller cities, and to some extent in larger cities, in the latter, however, principally in the suburban districts. The best form is the double tank, which enables the recharging of the tank first exhausted while the second is discharging, in that manner securing a continuous flow. These tanks are each from 60 to 100 gallons capacity, and contain a chemical mixture with water producing carbonic acid gas, which generates the pressure (about 125 lbs. at the maximum) necessary to force the mixture through hose about an inch in diameter, and throw it, through a $\frac{1}{4}$ to $\frac{3}{8}$ inch nozzle, a maximum distance of about 150 feet. Another pattern of this apparatus discharges hydrochloric acid and ammoniacal gases upon the fire by air pressure. These gases are effectual fire extinguishers, but there is much more claimed for their efficacy when employed in this manner than experience proves them to be entitled to, as but a fractional part of the gas generated is carried with the stream and reaches the fire. As the former apparatus furnishes its own discharging force, and the engine possesses the important requisite of lightness and consequent rapidity of movement, and is always ready for instant service (the mixture being also non-freezing at zero), it is for many localities a valuable apparatus.

The portable fire-extinguisher, a cylindrical vessel of about 7 gallons capacity, made to be carried upon the back of a man, is in principle of construction and operation like the chemical fire-engine, and uses the same mixture. It throws a stream of about $\frac{1}{4}$ of an inch diameter about 30 feet, for about 8 minutes. In the hands of a cool person it is capable of effective work, though necessarily its field of usefulness is circumscribed. But its importance and effectiveness in the hands of the inexperienced have been much exaggerated. A bucket of water is generally quite as good for extinguishing a small or incipient fire. It often happens, too, that from want of care and disuse the extinguisher is out of order and useless when needed. Firemen employ it to good advantage, after the large streams have done their work, in extinguishing the remnants of fire.

The hook-and-ladder truck, as now built and equipped, is made to carry ladders of various lengths, ranging from the shortest of 10 feet to the longest single ladder of 45 feet, and an extension ladder, which, when fully extended, is about 83 feet in length. Hooks, at the end of stout poles, of various lengths, 6 to 20 feet, axes, pick-axes, forks, shovels, a battering-ram, tools for prying open heavy doors and the like, scaling-ladders, life-lines and belts, fire-extinguishers, are also carried upon this apparatus. In the manufacture of the best fire-ladders great care is exercised in the selection of the timber, second-growth spruce or Oregon pine, entirely free from knots and other defects, which has been weather-seasoned (not kiln-dried), being the preferred material. A fully equipped large hook-and-ladder truck weighs about 8000 pounds, and is drawn by two horses. Its great length of 51 feet necessitates the tiller, attached to and situated over the hind axle, which turns the rear of the truck in either direction, in going around street corners, etc. The apparatus is about 8 feet high, and great care and experience is required on the part both of the driver and tillerman to prevent collisions and other accidents. Most of the long ladders each rest upon rollers in the frame of the truck, and are so placed that either can be taken out without unloading those placed above it.

Though they may not be charged by law with saving human life at fires, it is a duty voluntarily assumed by fire-extinguishing corps in the United States, and many of the appliances carried upon the improved hook-and-ladder trucks and elsewhere are mainly useful for that purpose. First among them is the scaling-ladder, of which illustrations are herein given. There is no limit to the height at which a scaling-ladder can be used, provided there are windows or other openings into which its hook can be inserted. Its great importance will be readily understood when it is stated that 14 per cent. of the buildings in New York city, at the close of 1885, were of such a height that the windows of the top floors could not be reached with the longest extension ladders in use. In the hands of active, courageous, and well-trained men the scaling-ladder is a most valuable appliance for life-saving as well as for ordinary work at fires. In New York city over one-half of all the officers and men of the fire-extinguishing corps have received thorough training in this important branch of the service; and though the large majority of them may never be called upon to apply the training thus acquired in rescuing human beings at fires, it has made them better firemen for the ordinary work they are called upon to do. To St. Louis belongs the credit of being the first American city to adopt these methods, and a few others besides New York have since followed the example.

The "jumping-sheet," designed to catch persons falling or jumping from a height at fires, which is employed as a last resort in life-saving, is ordinarily made of canvas with rope handles along the edges for holding it stretched out. A circular rope-net about 15 feet in diameter is the pattern now carried upon the tenders and hook-and-ladder trucks of New York.

To hoist lines of hose upon high buildings is a very laborious process by the primitive method now all but universally in vogue, which is to pull it up with a roof rope by main strength. An officer of the New York Fire Department has recently made a "hose-hoister," which has proved a success. It consists of a frame with two rollers, upon which the rope runs, and is so shaped that it readily adjusts itself to a projecting cornice or the plain coping of a wall. It effects a saving of time, labor, and wear and tear, and has also been utilized in hoisting ladders to roofs.

Apparatus Houses.—In the modern apparatus house of a large fire department everything is made subservient to the requirements of the service. The ground floor is occupied mainly by the apparatus and horses; the former stand with tongue or shafts, as the case may be, towards the street doors and with the harness suspended over them; the latter also face towards the street and stand in stalls along the side walls, opposite the wheels of the apparatus. The telegraph machinery is located at the side and near the street entrance. The basement or cellar is devoted to the storage of fuel, and in engine-houses the heater for maintaining steam-pressure in the boiler of the engine is there located as previously explained. The second floor is occupied as officers' quarters and dormitory, bath, etc. Upon the third floor is the sitting-room for the members (if the size of the house does not admit of its location on the first or second floor), and this floor is also used for men's clothing lockers, the storage of horse-feed, etc. In engine-houses, in lieu of the hose tower built upon the roof over the hose shaft, which is ordinarily located at either side of the building and near its front, a fourth story is now added to the front of the building, extending back from 20 to 25 feet. The hose shaft is for the purpose of hanging the hose not in use at full length, and serves the double purpose of thoroughly drying it and straightening it out after use. One or more poles connect the several stories with each other through openings in the floors, which are used for sliding down on when alarms are received.

In some cities two companies, an engine and a hook-and-ladder company, are located together. This is not desirable, for the reason that two companies located apart cover more territory in the same space of time. If time was not so important a factor in fire-extinguishing in American cities, a concentration of apparatus at a central point, as is the case in some European cities, would not be so objectionable. Apparatus houses are also located where possible in the centre of the most dangerous districts.

In choosing a site for a company, due regard is also had to the height of the location, so that in responding to alarms from any direction the ascent of hills may be avoided. Locations in hollows, or at the base of steep acclivities, are therefore not chosen.

Uniforms.—The uniform of the firemen should be neat, and, above all, serviceable and convenient. The dark blue in use by most paid departments is perhaps the best as to color, and the white metal button, for all below the grade of officers at least, seems most appropriate. The cut of the usual standard fireman's uniform is also proper, with the exception of the overcoat, the long skirts of which certainly interfere with and impede the free motion of the firemen. They are of course, rarely purposely but often perforce, worn at fires, and should be cut with short skirts or sack pattern to secure the utmost freedom of motion. Rubber coats, leggings, and boots are clearly a necessity, as well as the fire-cap of leather with its ribbed conical top and peculiar brim to protect the head. For the latter a helmet has been suggested as a substitute, but while perhaps more pleasing in appearance it affords hardly as much protection.

Horses.—A good fire-horse possesses many qualities of excellence, such as strength, speed, intelligence, and alertness. In size and weight they average 16 hands and 1300 pounds. The ordinary heavy draught or truck horse usually lacks some of the other requisites and is not suitable for fire purposes. In the New York Fire Department horses are taken on trial at the risk of the dealer, and are first sent to a training stable where they are accustomed to the sound of the telegraph alarm gong, the hitching with the various kinds of harness in use, and are driven before an apparatus. They are next sent for trial in active service to a company, and if the reports of both tests concur in showing them to be in every respect suitable for the service, they are purchased and receive a registered number, which is stamped upon a seal of lead, fastened to a round leather strap worn around the horse's neck. This serves to identify the horses, though a descriptive record of each horse is also kept. Some horses can be trained to stand unfastened in their stalls, but the majority are fastened with a halter strap by means of a bolt in the side of the stall which passes through a ring in the end of the strap. The first stroke of the gong withdraws the bolt and the horse is released. Horses, like men, though rigidly examined at the time of entering the service, frequently develop disease of the heart as a consequence of the exciting duty they are called upon to perform, and sudden deaths from that cause often occur. The average length of service of horses in the New York Fire Department is 6 years, and the age at which they are purchased varies from 4½ to 6 years. As a matter of course, a horse, though becoming unfitted for active fire-service, may still be useful for other purposes, and the policy therefore is to sell them as soon as it becomes apparent that their usefulness for the former is waning.

The harness for teams is, with the exception of the head-stall (which is worn by the horses continuously), suspended from the ceiling over the tongue of the apparatus, with the traces attached to the whiffletrees, so that, when the horses run under it, it is only necessary to snap the hinged collar together around the neck, to snap the pole chain and two reins, in all four snaps for each horse, while a simple jerk upon the reins from the driver's seat detaches the entire harness from the rig by which it is suspended. For one-horse apparatus the harness is arranged over the shafts, the ends of which are elevated so as to allow the horse to run under them, and the attaching of the two rein snaps, with the collar and the belly-band snaps, completes the hitching process. This is not merely a time-saving process, but a saving in horse-flesh and harness, compared to former methods.

Fire-alarm Telegraph.—The telegraph is in American cities an indispensable branch of the fire-service. Without the means of promptly furnishing information of the locality of fires which it affords, other more expensive and yet less effective methods would have to be employed, involving a considerable increase of the fire-extinguishing force, men and apparatus. The ordinary system consists in a central office, generally located at the head-quarters of the department, with metallic circuits radiating thence in all directions, and street boxes connected therewith, located at from two to six blocks or squares apart. Where practicable the circuits are so run that contiguous boxes are connected with different circuits, so that if one circuit is at any time out of order the nearest box will not be affected.

The majority of the boxes are of the locked door pattern, keys to open them being placed in prominent buildings in the immediate vicinity, and are also carried by firemen and policemen. In New York any reputable citizen can also have a key to be carried on the person, and a considerable number of them have been issued with very good results. All keys are registered by number and series. The locked door is, however, in New York, Chicago, Boston, and St. Louis, rapidly being replaced by the keyless door, which is opened by simply turning a handle. In this door, which is made double, is placed a loud gong with a striking mechanism, wound up by turning the handle in opening the door, thus sounding a local alarm and attracting the attention of persons in the vicinity. The gong continues to sound for about 5 seconds after the door is opened, and is intended to prevent interference with the boxes. In New York, where, before the introduction of the keyless door, much trouble had been experienced by interference with the locked-door boxes, the former has proven in every way satisfactory. It is manifest that an open box, accessible to all, from which an alarm can be sent without a key, the search for which necessarily sometimes results in delay, is a most valuable improvement. The street fire-alarm telegraph boxes principally in use do not differ materially in interior construction and mechanism. The one most used has an interior locked door upon which the hook or slide, by means of which the alarm is sent, is placed, so that, in the case of a box having either the locked or keyless door, it is necessary, after opening the outer door, to pull down the hook or slide upon the inner door to send the alarm. The inner door is opened by means of a key usually intrusted only to officers of the fire-extinguishing corps and telegraph employés, and inside of it is a Morse-key for use in sending second and third alarms and special calls. This inner-door key is also used in New York for releasing the key used in opening the outer door in locked boxes, the locks in which are so constructed as to prevent the withdrawal of the key after it has been turned in it, without the use of the inner-door key.

In addition to the box-circuits there are other circuits devoted exclusively to the transmission of alarms and other signals from the central office to the company houses, etc., in which they are sounded upon large gongs, and there are also so-called talking circuits (now telephonic in most cities), over which all except the first rounds of an alarm received at the central office are, by means of a lever switch, sent to the various apparatus houses, in advance of the regular gong circuit, signal and sound upon a small gong. This is popularly known as the combination, and is relied upon to such an extent as to almost entirely supersede the large gong circuit, when both are in working order.

New York has connected with its street fire-alarm telegraph system what is known as the special building system, under which any building can be connected directly with the central office for fire-alarm purposes, by means of a metallic wire loop running from a box circuit to the building and connected with an alarm-box therein. The expense of this is borne by the owners. All of the theatres and the public schools are thus connected, the latter having facilities for sending for the police and ambulances additionally. There is also in that city a private corporation which furnishes an automatic system of communicating alarms for fire by means of thermostats connected by wire and set to send an alarm when the temperature surrounding it attains a certain fixed degree. The alarms received by this company are also received and responded to by the fire department; and though the proportion of unnecessary alarms received by this method is very large, and there have been some instances of its entire failure, it has in a number of cases proved of great benefit in giving early notice of fires.

Service at Fires.—The usual system of assignments of companies to duty at fire-alarm stations is in the order of the proximity of their quarters to them. This, in case of large fires requiring the service of many companies, results in leaving large sections unprotected to such an extent that in case of another fire occurring therein it would be necessary to summon companies from a considerable distance, thus incurring the proverbial dangers of delay. Attempts have been made to remedy this in two ways: the first, by calling distant companies, one by one, to temporarily locate in and protect the denuded districts; the other expedient is the "double company," which is equipped with a duplicate set of apparatus, horses and hose, and has its force of officers and men increased 50 per cent. The double company is divided into two sections for fire-duty; the first being held in instant readiness for service, and is replaced by the second when it responds to an alarm, which in turn then responds to any subsequent call for the company. It has been suggested that a modification of the system of assignments would overcome the difficulty without additional expenditure. This in brief is, that where now, for instance, engine-companies Nos. 1, 2, and 3 are assigned to a certain station on first alarm, Nos. 4, 5, 6, and 7 on second alarm, and Nos. 8, 9, 10, and 11 on third alarm (all being placed in the order of their proximity to the station), the last one assigned on each alarm is taken out and held in reserve, the others being moved forward to take the vacant places; thus, first alarm, 1, 2, and 4 (3 in reserve); second alarm, 5, 6, 8, and 9 (7 in reserve); and third alarm, 10, 12, 13, and 14 (11 in reserve). The same principle, though necessarily limited in scope, is applicable to hook-and-ladder companies.

Upon the sounding of an alarm signal the entire company, men and horses, are instantly roused into activity, though at the time the house watchman may be alone on the apparatus floor. The horses rush to their places, the men slide quickly down the poles from the upper floors, and before the gong has ceased striking the first round (unless it be a very short signal), the horses are hitched, the doors opened, the men mounted upon the apparatus, and the company is ready to start, as soon as it is known by the completion of the signal whether it is to proceed to the station indicated or not. If it is, the company is off for the scene of the fire by the shortest or most practicable route. The operation, up to the crossing of the curb in front of quarters, consumes about 15 seconds of time from the first stroke of the gong, and, if it be an engine, the torch has already been applied to the carefully prepared fuel in the furnace, and when the apparatus has travelled a few blocks the steam-gauge indicates a working pressure.

No time is lost upon arrival at the fire; the engine is directed to the nearest hydrant, and attaches to it; the tender connects its hose to the engine, and reels off a sufficient quantity in the direction of the fire; the company commander who arrives first assumes command of the whole force until relieved by a chief officer; ladders are raised if required, doors are battered in, iron shutters opened, and lines of hose are carried into the burning building, up ladders or stairways, or down into basements and sub-cellars, in search of the seat of the fire. Smoke is generally first encountered, through which the firemen fight their way, blinding and stifling though it be, in their efforts to reach the point from which they can do effective work and reach the body of the fire with streams of water. The respirators and other contrivances to relieve the firemen from the effects of smoke have proved of little use. The hardest work is generally done out of sight of all except the officers, who are at the front aiding and guarding the safety of their men; and it is not easy for those who have not had the experience to fully appreciate the exhaustive nature of this service. Many a fire is stubbornly fought for hours in dense and suffocating smoke and heat, while hardly a tongue of flame is visible to the spectator. The approved modern method of fighting fire is always, where practicable, to attack it inside the burning structure and at the shortest possible range. In the vast majority of cases these tactics are successful; but it sometimes occurs that the firemen are driven from their first position to another, and, in rare cases, at once, or step by step, to the street. Though accustomed to face danger in many forms firemen are naturally not exempt from becoming panic-stricken, though seldom without justifiable cause. They are even then, however, readily controlled, and under competent and courageous leadership often quickly recover the lost position, and finally conquer the fire. There are also instances where the fire has already attained such headway when the fire-extinguishing corps arrives that the experienced officer sees at a glance that the burning structure is doomed to destruction, and determines that all the energy of the corps must be exerted to prevent the extension of the fire to the adjoining or neighboring property.

For the efficient carrying on of the work of the fire department in large cities, a classification of the structures in each district is essential. In New York three general classes are recognized: (1) The so-called fire-proof buildings; (2) Buildings principally of non-inflammable materials, but with wooden beams, floors, etc.; (3) Buildings chiefly of wood. They are further classed according to use, whether for residence or for business, or partly for each purpose, etc.   (C. J.)

FIRE-WEED. The *Erechtites hieracifolia*, a coarse American herbaceous plant of the order Compositæ, is called fire-weed from its vigorous growth on ground which has been burned over. When it has to struggle with other species of vegetation it is often not more than a few inches high, though it perfects seeds and perpetuates its race unnoticed; but after a fire it grows with very remarkable luxuriance. Hence rustic observers often believe it is wholly created by the fire. It usually reaches three and sometimes five feet high under these conditions. Its decoction has been found serviceable in dysentery. In the time of Linnæus it was classed with the groundsels, well-known composite plants of the genus *Senecio*, and was called *Senecio hieracifolius* by that eminent botanist. Its general appearance is more like a sow-thistle—*Sonchus*, though its botanical characters are much like *Senecio*. Rafinesque, in the *Flora Ludoviciana*, first separated it under the name of *Erechtites*. The flowers are all tubular (in *Senecio* generally radiate); those of the margin pistillate, of the disk perfect, involucre cylindrical, simple, slightly calyculate; receptacle naked; pappus of numerous, fine, capillary bristles. The involucre is comparatively large and turned at the base. Fire-weed in the north is very often *Epilobium angustifolium*, which, like the *Erechtites*, springs up in immense quantities, clothing the whole surface very soon after a fire, and giving even by its bright rosy flowers an igneous character to the scenery. (T. M.)

FIRKOWITSCH, ABRAHAM (1786–1874), a Jewish archæologist, was born at Lutzk, in the Crimea, Sept. 27, 1786. He belonged to the Karaites, and became a rabbi. After his sect established a printing press at Eupatoria in 1825 for the reproduction of manuscripts and works in support of Karaite teaching Firkowitsch became the leader in gathering documents for this purpose. He gave some account of his labors in *Massa u-Meriba* (1838) and in *Abne-Likkaron* (1872). After he had gathered more than 15,000 Hebrew manuscripts, Biblical, Talmudical, and other, he took them to St. Petersburg, where they were purchased for the imperial library. He also published several remarkable inscriptions which he professed to have discovered in the cemeteries of his sect. These and others of his publications tended to carry its antiquity back several centuries. At last the orthodox Jews were roused to investigate his claims, and soon succeeded in proving that many of his documents were untrustworthy and that some were absolute forgeries. Before this was established, however, Firkowitsch died at Tshufut-Kale, in the Crimea, June 7, 1874.

FISCHER, ERNST KUNO BERTHOLD, a German philosopher, was born at Sandewalde, Silesia, July 23, 1824. He was educated at Posen and Leipsic, and finally graduated at Halle in 1847. His lectures on philosophy at the University of Heidelberg began in 1850, but in July, 1853, his license to teach was revoked by the government of Baden. He remained, however, at Heidelberg until 1855, when he removed to Berlin. In September, 1856, the King of Prussia, on the request of the faculty of the Berlin University, granted him permission to lecture, but he went to Jena as professor of philosophy in December. His lectures were attended by a larger concourse of students than had ever been known since the time of Schiller and Fichte. In 1862 the Grand Duke of Weimar gave him the rank of privy councillor. In 1872 Fischer accepted a call to Heidelberg, where he has lectured with the same success as at Jena.

As a philosopher, he belongs to the school of Hegel, but he has been especially noted for his brilliant expositions of the schools and leaders of modern thought. His first work, *Diotima, Die Idee des Schönen* (1849), was a development of the principles of æsthetics, according to the Hegelian school. More important was his *Logik und Metaphysik, oder Wissenschaftslehre* (1852), which was a further exposition of the doctrines of the same school. His chief work is his *Geschichte der neuern Philosophie*, which began to appear in 1852, and after various revisions was completed in 1882. It includes a series of monographs on Descartes, Spinoza, Leibnitz, Kant, Fichte, and Schelling. He has also published *Francis Bacon und seine Nachfolger* (1856), and works on Schiller and Lessing, on Goethe's *Faust* and Shakespeare's *Richard III*. J. P. Mahaffy has translated and edited his *Commentary on Kant's Critick of the Pure Reason* (1866).

FISH. The general subject of Fish is fully presented under ICHTHYOLOGY in the ENCYCLOPÆDIA BRITANNICA, but Food-Fishes, being worthy of separate discussion, are here treated. By far the greater part, if not all, the backboned, cold-blooded inhabitants of the rivers and seas are fit for human food, yet for various reasons only a limited number are taken for that purpose in sufficient quantity to merit the title of food-fishes. Very small fishes, such as sticklebacks, are not usually fished for, and there are many fishes which, although they attain a larger size, seem to be almost entirely head, skin, fins, spines, and scales. There is a popular prejudice against many fishes, some of which are reputed poisonous, while others are loathed because of their hideous aspect or power to inflict wounds. A further large deduction must be made for the species which are too rare, or at least too seldom met with, to furnish material for a fishery.

There seems to be no doubt that persons have occasionally been poisoned by eating fish, and certain kinds seem to have a bad pre-eminence in this direction, yet it may fairly be doubted whether the flesh of any fresh and healthy fish is ever poisonous. Certain subtle chemical poisons, called "ptomaines," develop in the flesh of animals that have been killed, and fish are often kept too long. It must also be remembered that we know nothing of the diseases of fish. The flesh of diseased cattle is usually not eaten, but the flesh of fishes is partaken of indiscriminately. Thus there is, on the whole, more risk in a diet of fish than in one of flesh.

The tribes which furnish the chief food-fishes are the Salmonidæ, or salmon, trout, and whitefish family; the Gadidæ, or cod, pollock, and whiting family; the Clupeidæ, or herring and shad family; the Pleuronectidæ, or turbot, sole, and flounder family; the Scombridæ, or mackerel; and the Cyprinidæ, or carp and roach family. Less important, yet still supplying many food-fishes, are the Siluridæ, or cat-fish tribe; the Anguillidæ, or eel tribe; the Mugilidæ, or mullets; the Percidæ and Serranidæ, perch and sea-perch; the Sparidæ, snappers, porgies; the Sciænidæ, drumfish, sea-bass; the Labridæ, Scorpænidæ, etc. Sharks and skates are also eaten, especially by the poorer classes, while the oil, skin, or shagreen, and fins of some of them are articles of commerce: Sturgeons are eaten in all countries, but the repute in which they are held varies greatly.

The food-fishes of the world are beyond treatment here, but the principal species caught in the rivers and on the coasts of the United States are as follows.

Lampreys, often called lamprey eels or even eels, are sometimes eaten. They may be easily known by their round, sucking mouth and by the seven small gill-openings on each side of the body behind the head. Like salmon, they ascend the rivers (usually in spring) to deposit their spawn.

Among the rays those most often used for food belong to the genus *Raia*. All rays have huge pectoral fins, extending along each side of the body, which forms with it a flat disk, from which the hinder part of the body projects as a comparatively thin tail. In *Raia* the pectoral fins are not continued around the snout, as they are in some other rays, and the tail has two dorsal fins.

The dog-fish, or picked dog-fish (*Squalus acanthias*), is a small shark with a strong spine in front of each of its dorsal fins. Dog-fish oil is obtained from its liver, as it is also from those of *Galeorhinus galeus*, the oil-shark of the Pacific coast.

The sturgeons and their relatives are large fishes with a partly cartilaginous skeleton, a shark-like or heterocercal tail, and the mouth placed, as in sharks, upon the under side of the head. Most of them have no teeth, and the skin is either smooth, as in the paddle-fish, or beset with spinous bony plates. The paddle-fish (*Polyodon*) of the Mississippi Valley and rivers of the Southern States attains a length of five or six feet, and has its snout lengthened into a thin flat blade. Its mouth is set with fine teeth, and it has no barbels and no tongue. The true sturgeons (*Acipenser*) have a much less produced snout, five rows of bony bucklers on the body. each bearing a spine, no teeth, and a small mouth with thick lips, preceded by a row of four barbels on the under side of the snout. The two best known American species are *Acipenser sturio*, the common sturgeon of both shores of the Atlantic Ocean, and *A. transmontanus* of the Pacific coast. The latter species attains a length of nine or ten feet and a weight of 600 pounds. It ascends the Sacramento, Columbia, and Fraser Rivers in large numbers in spring. Its flesh is used both under its own name and as "sea-bass" and "tenderloin of sole" and its eggs are made into caviare. A somewhat smaller sturgeon of the Pacific coast is the green sturgeon, which, perhaps from the tint of its flesh, is reputed poisonous and is not eaten.

The Mississippi and its affluents, the great lakes and other fresh waters, are frequented by the black or lake sturgeon (*A. rubicundus*), which weighs from 50 to 100 pounds, and seldom descends to the sea. The shovel-nose sturgeon has a broad, shovel-like snout, and the tail is entirely mailed. It is common in the Mississippi Valley and in the rivers of the Southern States.

Very strange fishes are the gar pikes of the lakes and large rivers of the United States, with their bodies covered with hard, enamelled, diamond-shaped scales, running in rows obliquely backward across the body, and their long jaws set with many teeth. The long-nosed gar reaches a length of 5 feet, while the great alligator gar, which ranges from the Southern States to Cuba and Central America, attains 8 to 10 feet.

About 30 species of cat-fishes inhabit the waters of the United States, and of these two only are marine. Among those most used for food are the mud cat or yellow cat of the Mississippi Valley and Southern States, a fish which reaches a weight of from 50 to 75 pounds; *Amiurus catus*, the bull-head, horned pout, or cat-fish of the Schuylkill and most rivers and ponds of the Eastern States; the darker *Amiurus melas*, and two species of *Ictalurus* or channel cats. The Schuylkill cat-fish has been introduced into California, where it has rapidly multiplied, and also into some European countries. The great fork-tailed or Florida cat-fish (*Ictalurus lacustris*) reaches 100 pounds, and is abundant in all large bodies of water from British America to Florida and Texas, while the still larger *I. ponderosus*, or great cat-fish of the Mississippi, reaches 150 pounds. The channel cat-fish (*Ictalurus punctatus*) reaches a length of 2 or 3 feet and a weight of 15 to 20 pounds, but individuals exceeding 5 pounds are rare in the markets. The skin is thinner than in the common cat-fishes (*Amiurus*), and as the head is small and the body slender, there is less waste, while the flesh, when fresh, is very superior, being inferior only to the white-fish and trout and salmonoids generally.

The channel cat abounds in all flowing streams from western New York to Montana and southward to Florida and Texas. It seems, unlike others of its tribe, to prefer running waters. It is less tenacious of life than the *Amiuri*.

The cat-fishes and their numerous relatives, which swarm in South America and Africa, principally in fresh water, form the first order of a sub-class of bony fishes which have the air-bladder (if present) opening into the gullet, the ventral fins placed far back (on the abdomen), and the scales (as a rule) smooth-edged or cycloid. The next order consists of fishes which have no teeth in the mouth, but are furnished with comb-like teeth on the pharyngeal bones. The principal families are the fresh-water Cyprinidæ and Catostomidæ, containing many species that are used for food and a few that are highly prized. Nearly 60 species of the latter family inhabit the waters of North America. The mouth is directed downwards and usually has fleshy lips. The species are known as fresh-water suckers, and are not very highly valued as food. Those known as buffalo-fishes are natives of the Mississippi Valley. One species reaches a weight of 30 pounds. Five or 6 kinds of suckers (*Catostomus*) occur in California; Utah Lake has 2, and Arizona has 2 or 3 others. The genus *Chasmistes* has 2 species in the Klamath River and 1 in Utah Lake. The greater part of our fresh-water fishes belong to the Cyprinidæ. About 260 species of this tribe are given in Jordan and Gilbert's *Synopsis*, and others have since been described. The great development of the river and lake systems of North America has given opportunity to these fishes to develop into many more or less distinct forms, many of them restricted to limited areas. The smaller species are known as minnows, red-fins, and shiners; the larger as dace, chub, roach, bream, carp, etc. The fish known by these names are not specifically identical with those which bear these titles in Europe, except in the case of the carp, which are the European species introduced.

The largest of our native Cyprinidæ are Californian, and on account of the form of the head are commonly known as "pike." *Ptychochilus oregonensis* reaches a length of from 3 to 5 feet, while *Mylopharodon robustus* attains 18 inches. The species of Cyprinidæ which occur upon the Pacific coast are comparatively few (about 30) in number, but most of them are sufficiently large to be available as food-fishes. A large number of species inhabit the Gila and Colorado rivers, and the small lakes of the Great Basin are well provided with forms peculiar to them. The most important Cyprinidæ as food-fishes are, however, the two kinds of introduced carp, *Carassius auratus*, the

Crucian carp, and *Cyprinus carpio*, the true carp, especially the latter. (See FISH-CULTURE.) The carp has been an object of culture for many generations, and in its domesticated state is generally acknowledged to be a fine fish for the table. The most highly prized varieties are the scaleless or "leather" carp and the "mirror" carp, which is only partly covered with scales.

It is uncertain whether the original home of the carp is the Caspian or whether it originally belonged to the Danube, Rhine, and Main, but it was known to the Greeks and Romans, and has spread throughout Europe. England received it in 1521, Prussia in 1769, Denmark in 1560. Since 1877 a number, especially leather and mirror carp, have been sent to America by the German fishery association. In 1881 they were introduced into Canada, in 1882 into Brazil, Columbia, and Ecuador. Carp seem to increase faster in America than in Germany, growing 3 to 4 pounds in weight every year.

Nearly allied to the herrings or Clupeidæ are the lady-fish (*Albula conorhynchus*), a native of all warm seas and sparingly met with in California; the moon-eyes or fresh-water herring (*Hyodon*), of the fresh waters of the Eastern and Central States; and the Elopidæ or big-eyed herrings. *Elops saurus* is a handsome fish some 2 feet long, not rare on the Atlantic coast, while its near relative, *Megalops thrissoides*, attains dimensions exceeding those of a large salmon. This fish, usually called the Tarpum, and by the French the Grande Ecaille, ascends rivers, is common on the southern coasts of the Atlantic, and is remarkable for the great size of its scales. It is also famous for its propensity to spring from the water when attacked, a habit which renders its capture with hook and line a difficult feat. About eight species of the herrings occur on our coasts, viz.: the common herring (*Clupea harengus*) of both shores of the Atlantic, the young of which is known as whitebait; the California herring (*Clupea mirabilis*); the California sardine (*C. sagax*); the Ohio shad or skipjack (*C. chrysochloris*); the hickory shad (*C. mediocris*); the alewife (*C. vernalis*); the glut herring or blue-back (*C. æstivalis*); and the highly valued shad (*C. sapidissima*). The skipjack and alewife, as well as the shad, enter fresh waters. The menhaden or mossbunker (*Brevoortia tyrannus*) ranges the ocean from New England to Brazil, and is largely used in the manufacture of fish-guano and oil. The young are canned as sardines. All the true herrings have the belly sharp-edged and protected by a series of large bony scales. The anchovies (*Engraulidæ*) are near the herrings, from which they may be known by their relatively large mouth overhung by a bony snout. Three species occur on the Pacific coast and 3 on the Atlantic coast. The anchovy is made in Europe into a sauce for flavoring other fishes, but the American species are neglected. *Synodus fœtens*, the lizard fish, is occasionally found in the markets of San Francisco.

The salmon family contains the most important of food-fishes, except, perhaps, the Gadidæ or cod tribe. Out of about 125 species some 40 are North American. From the herrings all may be known not only by the rounded section of the belly, but by the presence on the back, behind the true dorsal fin, of a small fat-fin without fin-rays. The greater number of Salmonidæ are either natives of fresh water, or are anadromous, coming up from the sea to spawn in the river of their birth. The capelin (*Mallotus*) is a boreal marine species, occurring in New England and Alaska, as well as at intermediate points. The eulachon or candle-fish, of the coast of Oregon and Alaska, is so oily that when dried it will burn like a candle. It ascends the rivers in enormous numbers, and is highly prized as a pan-fish. The smelts (*Osmerus*) are represented by a common species on each of our ocean coasts; for though some still more common fishes of another family have in California usurped the name of smelt, a true smelt is found from San Francisco northward. The surf-smelts (*Hypomesus*) are excellent little firm-fleshed species of the Pacific coast. The genus *Coregonus* furnishes us with eleven kinds of white-fish, all of them confined to fresh waters. The eggs are smaller than those of salmon and trout, and the flesh is usually pale. One species is peculiar to the Rocky Mountain and Pacific region, while most of the others are found in the Great Lakes, three or four of them extending north-westward to Alaska. The black-fin (*C. nigripinnis*), one of the largest species, is confined to the deep waters of Lake Michigan. The grayling (*Thymallus signifer*) occurs on the northern borders of the United States, and thence to the Arctic Ocean.

The salmon of the Pacific coast belong to a genus (*Oncorhynchus*) distinguished from the true salmon by the greater length of the anal fin, and by the long and hooked jaws acquired by the adult males. Although all the five species are used as food, the salmon *par excellence* of the Pacific coast is the one which was becoming familiarly known as the *quinnat*, but has, by a too methodical ichthyologist, had its more ancient name of *chouicha* or *tshawytscha* restored to it. This is the species so extensively canned on the Columbia (see FISHERIES), where it usually reaches a weight of 22 lbs. Individuals of 70 to 100 lbs. have been taken. It is abundant in all the large rivers of the North Pacific from Ventura River, Cal., to Alaska and Northern China. The day salmon (*O. keta*) does not exceed 12 lbs., and spawns much nearer to the sea than the *quinnat*. The blue back (*O. nerka*) weighs 4 to 8 lbs., and in the fall is often found in mountain lakes, where it is known as the red-fish.

The most important well-marked forms of true salmon and trout are the rainbow trout or California brook trout (*Salmo irideus*), now introduced into Europe; the steel-head or salmon trout (*S. gairdneri*), probably identical with the Rocky Mountain trout (*S. purpuratus*), a variety of which is found in Lake Tahoe, Cal.; the mackinaw or great lake trout (*S. namaycush*), a lake species; the Dolly Varden trout of California and Alaska, red-spotted (*S. malma*); and the eastern brook trout (*S. fontinalis*). Besides these there is the well-known and highly valued true salmon (*S. salar*) of both coasts of the North Atlantic, with its lake-dwelling variety (*S. sebago*), the land-locked or Schoodic salmon. The pikes (*Esocidæ*) are a small family of voracious fresh-water fishes. One, the true pike (*Esox lucius*), is common to the northern parts of both the old world and the new, and reaches a length of from two to four feet. The still larger muskallunge (*E. nobilior*) lives in the great lake region and northward, and grows from four to eight feet in length. The three other species are known as pickerel.

The muræna and eel families are not represented by many species in North America, but the abundance of the common eel (*Anguilla rostrata*) of the Atlantic coast in all the streams from Maine to Mexico, and also in the Mississippi Valley, atones for this. The Conger eel (*Conger niger*) is common to both coasts of the Atlantic, while the Conger eel of the Pacific coast is a muræna (*M. mordax*). It reaches a length of five feet, has very large teeth, and is noted for its ferocity.

Until very recently it was believed that the common eel was hermaphrodite, but it is now known that the male eels are smaller than the female, and have the head somewhat differently formed. Microscopical examination of certain organs in these smaller adult eels leaves no doubt that they are truly the male generative glands.

We now arrive at the large sub-class *Physoclisti*, in which the air-bladder, if present, is entirely closed, while the ventral fins are usually placed close to, or even in front of, the pectorals, and the dorsal and anal fins consist to a greater or less extent of spines.

The gar-fish family (*Scomberesocidæ*) includes also the flying fishes (*Exocetus*). Some of the species of gar-fish reach lengths of three or four feet, and are marketable fishes.

Three species of mullet (*Mugil*) occur on our coasts. One of these (*M. brasiliensis*) is found in both oceans. The most important as a food-fish is *M. albula*, the striped mullet, which is very abundant southward on the Atlantic coasts. To the *Atherinidæ* or silversides belong the California smelts, two species of which attain respectable dimensions, and are excessively abundant on the Pacific coast.

The barracudas (*Sphyrænidæ*) furnish four food-fishes, the chief of which are *S. argentea* of the Pacific coast, and *S. picuda* of Florida and the West Indies. These are almost cylindrical, voracious, swift-moving, pike-like fishes, from three to three and a half feet long.

The great sword-fishes (*Xiphiidæ*) are the objects of a regular fishery. The common sword-fish of the Atlantic and Pacific has no ventral fins, nor any teeth, its long sword serving as its weapon of offence and defence. The spear-fish (*Tetrapterus*) and the sail-fish (*Histiophorus*) have ventral fins and small teeth, and the latter has a very high dorsal fin. The mackerel tribe is allied to the sword-fishes, and contains a considerable number of oceanic fishes, the most important of which is the common mackerel (*Scomber scombrus*). This beautiful fish is abundant on both coasts of the North Atlantic, and occasionally strays into the Pacific. Even more valued are the species of *Cybium* or *Scomberomorus*, commonly known as Spanish mackerel. One of these (*S. maculatus*) is found on the North American coasts of both oceans, though it does not appear to occur north of Lower California in the Pacific, while another, *S. concolor*, is a rare and valued fish of California. The Sierra (*S. caballa*) is found in the warm parts of the Atlantic, and occasionally on our coasts. It reaches a weight of 100 lbs. The Spanish mackerel are almost scaleless. A species of bonito (*Sarda*) occurs in the Atlantic and Mediterranean, another on both coasts of the Pacific. The albicore (*Orcynus alalonga*) is abundant in all warm seas, and though rare on the Atlantic coast, is frequently found around the Santa Barbara Islands (Cal.), and the tunny (*Orcynus thynnus*) or horse-mackerel visits our Atlantic coast. The tunny is larger even than the sword-fishes, reaching a length of ten feet and a weight of half a ton.

The true *Scombridæ* are rather elongated fishes and usually have a series of small finlets above and below the tail. The *Carangidæ* are an allied family, characterized by a more compressed, often very high and thin body, usually without finlets, and often covered with a row of plates. The most important North American food-fishes of this family are the horse-mackerel (*Trachurus saurus*), the various species of *Caranx*, better known as crevallés, the pompanos (*Trachynotus*), and the amber fishes (*Seriola*). *Caranx pisquetus* is the most abundant crevallé of the northern parts of the Atlantic. The common pompano (*T. carolinus*) is the most valued food-fish of the Gulf and Southern States. It ranges north to Cape Cod. The yellow-tail (*Seriola lalandi*) occurs on both coasts, and the rudder-fish (*S. zonata*) ranges from Cape Cod to Florida. In other small groups which are nearly allied to the mackerel come the well-known blue-fish or skipjack (*Pomatomis saltator*), the voracious and active destroyer of smaller food-fishes; and the harvest-fishes, one of which (*Stromateus triacanthus*) is very abundant from Maine to Cape Hatteras, while *S. simillimus* is not uncommon in summer on the Pacific coast, where it is known as pompano. Species of dolphin (*Coryphæna*) are occasional on the Southern Atlantic coasts. After the assemblage of mackerel-like fishes come the perch-like fishes, also divided into several sub-families. One of these (*Centrarchidæ*) consists exclusively of fresh-water fishes, and includes the crappie (*Pomoxys annularis*), calico bass (*P. sparoides*), Sacramento perch (*Archeoplites*), rock bass (*Ambloplites*), the various little fishes known as sun-fishes (*Lepomis*, etc.), and the black bass (*Micropterus*). The two species of *Pomoxys* are valued as food, and abound in the lakes and streams of the Mississippi Valley, etc., and the Sacramento perch is the only perch-like fish as yet discovered in the streams of California. There are two kinds of black bass, the large-mouthed (*M. salmoides*) and the small-mouthed (*M. dolomieu*). The first is usually rather the larger, but the latter is generally more valued as a game-fish. The true *Percidæ* are for the most part too small to be of much use as food, but the American or yellow perch (*Perca americana*), scarcely distinct from the European perch, and the pike-perch (*Stizostedium*) are exceptions. The common pike-perch of the Great Lakes, Upper Mississippi, and some Atlantic streams (*S. vitreum*) grows to a length of three feet, and is a highly valued food-fish of the inland regions. It has many names, as wall-eyed pike, dory, glass-eye, yellow pike, blue pike, and jack salmon. The lawyer, sand-pike, gray pike, or horn-fish (*S. canadense*) is a smaller fish of the same region.

Most of the *Serranidæ*, or sea-perch, are valued food-fishes of the warmer seas. Among them are the robalo (*Centropomus undecimalis*), found in the Gulf, and also in the coast of Lower California; the striped bass or rock-fish (*Roccus lineatus*), three other species of *Roccus* known as white bass, yellow bass, and white perch; the great Jew-fish, or black sea-bass of the Californian coast, five feet long, and 300 to 400 pounds in weight, and several species of *Serranus*. The black-fish, or black sea-bass (*S. atrarius*), is abundant from Cape Cod to Florida; the serrano or squirrel-fish (*S. fascicularis*) comes north to South Carolina; and three other species occur on the southern part of the Californian coast. The groupers (a corruption of the Portuguese name *garrupa*) are valued food-fishes of Florida and the Gulf. They belong to the genera *Trisotropis* and *Epinephalus*. The guasa (*Promicrops*) reaches a weight of 400 or 500 pounds, and ranges from the West Indies to Florida. The Sparidæ are well distinguished from the Serranidæ by the manner in which the lower jaw is received into a sheath when the mouth is closed, and by the larger and less comb-edged scales. The snappers (*Lutjanus*) are valued food-fishes of Florida, especially the red snapper (*L. campechianum*). The hog-fish (*Pomadasys fulvomaculatus*) occurs from New York southward, and is a food-fish of some importance. Two species of *Pomadasys* occur in California. The grunts (*Haemulon*) are another group of sparoid fishes which, like *Pomadasys*, are short and ovate in form. The genera *Sparus*, *Calamus*, and *Diplodus* have two or three series of large round-topped molar teeth in the jaws. The species are commonly known as porgies. Five species of *Calamus* occur in Florida, one of them the pez de pluma of the Spanish fishermen. The scup, scuppaug, or porgy (*Diplodus argyrops*), ranges from Cape Cod to Florida; and the sheepshead from Cape Cod to Texas. Both are among the most valued of our food-fishes. Other species of *Diplodus* are known as pin-fish and bream. The blue-fish of California (*Girella nigricans*), and *Pimelepterus bosci*, differ from the preceding Sparidæ in their herbivorous habits. The red surmullet (*Mullus barbatus*) and the bearded goat-fishes (*Upeneus*) are Floridian food-fishes. The Sciænidæ or croakers differ from the percoid and sparoid families in the absence of teeth on other bones of the mouth save the jaws, and in their generally less spinous aspect. Many are large, and nearly all are valued food-fishes. The drum, sheepshead, white perch or croaker of the great lakes, etc., the sea-drum (*Pogonias chromis*), the silver perch (*Sciæna punctata*), and channel-bass (*S. ocellata*) of the Atlantic coast; two species of Sciæna found in California, and known as Roncador; the spot or old wife (*Liostomus xanthurus*); the little roncador (*Genyonemus*) of California; the "whitings" of the Atlantic coast (three species of *Menticirrus*); the bagara of Southern California (*M. undulatus*); the large and highly valued white sea-bass of the Californian coast (*Atractoscion*); the weak-fish (*Cynoscion regale*) of the Atlantic coast; the corvina (*C. parvipinne*) of California; the spotted sea-trout (*C. maculatum*) of the Atlantic; and the king-fish or queen-fish (*Seriphus politus*) of California, belong to this family.

A very peculiar tribe of Pacific coast fishes is that known as Embiotocidæ. These are all viviparous, bearing a comparatively small number of young, which are at birth not unlike the parent: one kind lives in fresh waters. There are about 18 species, most of them sufficiently large and abundant to be used for food in considerable quantities, but none of them valued highly. In their cycloid or smooth-edged scales, well-developed lips, etc., these fishes resemble those of the larger family Labridæ, which yields the Cunner (*Ctenolabrus*), the tautog or black-fish (*Tautoga*), the hog-fish (*Lachnolaemus*), and the doncellas (*Platyglossus*) of the Atlantic coast; and the red-fish or flat-head of Southern California. *Ephippus faber*, the angel-fish or porgy, is a good food-fish of the warmer seas of both coasts. The blanquillo (*Caulolatilus chryops*) of the Southern Atlantic States, and the white-fish (*C. princeps*) of Southern California, are good food-fishes. A large tribe of fishes, now considered as forming several families, is distinguished by having a bony stay across the cheeks from the eye. One of the subordinate groups (*Chiridæ*) contains about 15 species, all found in the North Pacific, and almost all valued for food. Two species of *Hexagrammus* are common in California, and are known as rock-trout or sea-trout. Three others are more common in Alaska. The common green cod or blue cod of the Pacific coast (*Ophiodon elongatus*) is no cod at all, but is none the less a large and very valuable food-fish, reaching a weight of 30 to 40 pounds. Another valuable fish of this family, the coal-fish or black cod (*Anoplopoma fimbria*), is, like the rock-cod, and some other fishes called cod on the Pacific coast, no cod at all, but appears to be an excellent food-fish, whether broiled or roasted like planked shad. In deep water it attains a length of 40 inches, and a weight of 15 pounds. The Haidah Indians are successful fishers for this fish, and use lines made of the grout kelp (*Nereocystis*), and hooks made of splints of the knots of hemlock steamed and bent into shape. The rock-cod of the Pacific coast are the mailed-cheeked and spiny-headed Scorpænidæ. Twenty-seven species of the genus *Sebastodes* are distinguished by Jordan, all of them caught for food. They are exceedingly abundant along rocky coasts. The young are born alive in great numbers, but much less developed than the young of the Embiotocidæ. The rose-fish, red-fish, or snapper (*Sebastes marinus*), is an Atlantic species, and (*Scorpæna guttata*) is abundant in Southern California. The sculpin or bull-head family (*Cottidæ*) comprises both marine and fresh-water species, but few are of any value as food. *Scorpænichthys marmoratus*, a very common fish from Puget Sound to San Diego, and reaching a weight of 10 pounds, is an exception. The elongated blennies, which have no ventral fins, or but small ones, and a long dorsal and anal, furnish the San Francisco market with the kelp-fish (*Heterostichus rostratus*), and with what, in the lack of true eels, are sworn to as eels, viz., the green *Apodichthys flavidus*, and the olive *Cebedechthys*. The wolf-fish (*Anarrhichas*) of the Atlantic, and the exceedingly elongated wolf-eel (*Anarrhichthys ocellatus*) of the Pacific, are also blennies. The last-named species is from 4 to 8 feet long, and has a heavy head furnished with large seizing and grinding teeth. It feeds largely on sea-urchins. By far the greater part of the about 90 species of *Gadidæ* are valued highly as food. (See COD, Vol. II.) The burbot (*Lota*) is a native of the fresh waters of the northern parts of both hemispheres, while two genera are blind and inhabit the cave streams of Cuba. The other species are marine.

The flat fishes are peculiar in having the body flattened sideways, and both eyes upon the same side of the head. They swim with the eyed side uppermost. In very young individuals the head is symmetrical. Nearly 50 species occur on the coast of the United States. The genus *Citharichthys* includes five American species, mostly small, but *C. sordidus* of the Pacific coast is a food-fish. The halibut (*Hippoglossus*) is the largest of the flat fishes, sometimes reaching a weight of 400 lbs. The single species occurs in the northern seas of both hemispheres, ranging south to Cape Cod and San Francisco, and in Europe to France. Another very large species is known as the Greenland halibut. The Monterey halibut or bastard halibut (*Paralichthys californicus*) is an important food-fish, reaching a weight of 60 pounds. The common flounder of New England, ranging to Texas and the West Indies, is another species of *Paralichthys*, and five other species occur on the Atlantic coast, as well as *P. liolepis* on that of Southern California. The rough dab of the Atlantic coast, and four Pacific species, belong to the genus *Hippoglossoides*. Two species, *H. jordani* and *H. melanostictus*, are important food-fishes of the San

Francisco markets, and are commonly called "sole." To the genus *Pleuronichthys* belong three California species, which, together with *Hypsopsetta guttulata*, a spotted species, pass for "turbot." The plaices (*Parophrys*) furnish 12 American species, 8 of them peculiar to the Pacific coast. The most important is *P. stellatus*, a large species with black-banded fins, common from San Luis Obispo to Kamschatka, and known as "flounder." Next in importance is *P. bilineatus*. Several other species are eaten, and some of those of the Pacific coast are of exceedingly delicate flavor; but, though a small species of sole (*Achirus*) occurs in the Gulf of Mexico, the fishes known as sole and turbot in Europe, and famed for their delicacy, are absent from the markets of the United States.

(W. N. L.)

FISH COMMISSION. The United States Fish Commission was established for the double purpose of fostering the fishing industries of the country by the propagation and distribution of food-fishes, and of investigation into the habits, habitat, food, etc., of food-fishes. Both these ends have been fully kept in view with such success as to demonstrate that pisciculture can only be carried on effectively by operations conducted upon a large scale. For the fish-cultural operations of the Commission see FISH-CULTURE.

The total amount appropriated by Congress for the purposes of the Fish Commission since its inception in 1871-72 has been $1,679,415, besides $20,000 for the International Fishery Exhibition at Berlin in 1879-80, and $50,000 for that of London in 1883-84. Of the total amount $978,124 was expended upon the general work of propagation; $411,209 upon steam-vessels for the prosecution of research; $154,201 upon hatcheries, ponds, and distribution; and $54,500 upon the food-fishes inquiry. The remainder was divided among buildings at the station at Wood's Holl, railroad cars, illustrations, and rent.

The steamer recently built for the Fish Commission, the Albatross, 1300 tons, is a model of what a vessel should be for purposes of scientific research, while the Fish Hawk, 850 tons, is not good for heavy seas, but is well fitted for fish propagation.

There are now in operation, under the auspices of the Fish Commission, 17 hatching stations, of which the principal is at Wood's Holl, Mass. Here there are laboratories for research, hatching ponds for 2,000,000 young cod, etc.

Spencer F. Baird was the president of the Commission until his death in 1887. The present commissioner is Marshall McDonald.

State fish commissions are now established throughout the country, and aid greatly in the work of fish-culture and fish protection. Besides investigations in the rivers, lakes, and coasts, the fish commission has pushed inquiry into the deep seas. The exploration of the Gulf Stream region off the outer banks of the southern coast of New England has been carried on most thoroughly by the Albatross. Successful dredgings have been made at various depths from 40 to 2600 fathoms. The bottom of the ocean in this region consists in some parts of a more or less impure globigerina ooze, but between 500 and 1200 fathoms it was in many cases found to be a tough compact clay, with a consistency like hard Castile soap. The ooze, when present, is always mixed with some sand and clay-mud. In other localities, from 1000 to 1600 fathoms, the bottom is covered with hard crust-like concretions of clay and iron oxide with more or less manganese oxide in the crevices. The masses brought up varied in size from a few ounces to 20 lbs. or more. Rounded boulders and pebbles of granite, gneiss, and other crystalline rocks were found in some places. Between 2000 and 3000 fathoms the bottom met with was globigerina ooze. The "red clay" which at similar depths was found during the cruise of the Challenger was not observed.

The zoölogical results of these explorations have been most important. Of mollusca alone 336 species were added between 1880 and 1885. Forty-nine of these were dredged at depths exceeding 2000 fathoms, and 170 between 1000 and 2000 fathoms.

Huge spiny spider crabs over 3 feet across were taken; another very large crab (*Geryon*) occurred in abundance between 500 and 1000 fathoms, and a *Munidopsis* was taken in 2574 fathoms.

Two large sea-cucumbers or holothurians were obtained in abundance at great depths—one (*Benthodytes gigantea*) from 904 to 2033 fathoms; the other (*Euphronides cornuta*) from 861 to 1735 fathoms.

Sea-urchins of the curious genus *Phormosoma*, with flexible shells, were found up to 1230 fathoms. The irregular sea-urchin *Pourtalesia jeffreysii* was taken from 1253 to 1555 fathoms, and *Aerope rostrata* in 1608 fathoms. Two species of the beautiful star-fish *Brisinga*, both of them new to science, were obtained, and one of these ranged from 906 to 2021 fathoms. Three other star-fishes were found in more than 2000 fathoms, and two serpent-stars reached 2574 fathoms. Many before unknown fishes have also been taken— among them the fine food-fish known as the tile-fish (*Lopholatilus*), large numbers of which were for three summers found abundantly inside the Gulf Stream near 40° N. lat., and 70°-71° 20' E. long. In 1882 dead tile-fish were observed in large quantities floating upon the surface, and investigation seemed to show that the destruction was due to a sudden change of temperature.

(W. N. L.)

FISH-CULTURE, or PISCICULTURE, is an attempt upon the part of man to counteract the destructive effects of fisheries. Animal life is a constant struggle for existence, a warfare between reproduction and destruction. Even on the land a large portion of the forms of life live by preying upon other kinds, and in the sea this is still more the case, for there the vegetable world plays a less conspicuous part. The greater part of the fishes are carnivorous; and the safeguard of the weaker kinds consists chiefly in their greater powers of reproduction. Nearly all fishes are oviparous, laying an immense number of ova, yet, except under favorable circumstances, and within limited areas, the finny inhabitants of the seas do not increase in numbers. No sooner are the ova of even the most powerful fishes deposited than they are subject to the attacks of countless enemies. Not only do fishes, large and small, feed upon the eggs and just hatched young, but the invertebrate dwellers in the ocean do the same. The only advantage enjoyed by the most powerful predatory fish is that it has a chance of distancing its enemies by growth, and this chance is usually balanced by the fact that the ova of large fishes are more readily observed and attract a larger number of devourers.

See Vol. XIX. p. 135 Am. ed. (p. 126 Edin. ed.).

In any river, lake, or sea, a sort of balance between the forces of distribution and repair is observed until man interferes with his nets and lines, and causes the former to preponderate. It is comparatively difficult to exterminate a species, but persistent injudicious fishing has often destroyed the fishery. If the species, for the sake of which the fishery is carried on is confined to a limited area, it may even be thoroughly exterminated, or at least brought down to numbers so small that it stands no chance of recovery. This result has occurred with several species of the large marine mammals which are hunted for their oil or other products; while fishes have been locally exterminated by contrivances which, instead of securing only well-grown examples of the kinds eaten by man, have destroyed wholesale the young of the food-fish, and the adults and young of the fishes upon which they live.

In the open seas fisheries do not often lead to the destruction of a fishery, for the reason that the species consumed by man are many, and he destroys the destroyer as well as the destroyed. Every ray or skate that is taken gives the flat fishes a better chance to live, while the catch of the dog-fish, bonito, blue-fish, etc., is a distinct gain to the herring and other small fishes.

The destruction of fish in rivers and lakes may be effected without fishing. Though the larger fishes live to a great extent upon the smaller, and the smaller feed partly upon the ova of the larger, living beings of lower grade and smaller size than fishes form the food of the smaller species, and thus the existence of food-fishes depends upon that of the minute animals which form their food.

Life, whether vegetable or animal, can be preserved only in water that is comparatively pure. The death of both plants and animals tends to render the water impure, but the process of oxidation, constantly going on, will under normal conditions keep the waters fitted to supply the needs of fishes. But stagnant waters, and those into which a larger amount of decaying matter is poured than can be quickly oxidized, become incapable of supporting a supply of fish (1) on account of the death of the small organisms which form the basis of the food supply, and (2) by poisoning the fish themselves.

Harbors, estuaries, and more or less enclosed bays and gulfs, are to some extent under conditions similar to those of rivers. Although some of the great fisheries, such as those of the cod and mackerel, are carried on in open waters, a large part of the marine fishes taken for food consists of species which habitually live near shore. The effect of wasteful or immoderate fishing upon a shore-living species is to rapidly diminish its numbers, and, since it cannot at once be recruited by individuals from without, and has not the advantages afforded by migration, further fishing for it becomes unprofitable.

Fish-culture, therefore, in its broadest sense does not consist only of the art of fish-breeding, but includes (1) the preservation of rivers, lakes, harbors, estuaries, and shore waters in a normally pure condition; (2) the prohibition of methods and seasons of fishing which have been proved too destructive, or clearly would prove to be so; and (3) the destruction of such creatures as prey upon food-fishes, and the encouragement and growth of plants and animals which serve them for food.

The first of these aids to fish-culture has as yet scarcely been attempted. Every town befouls the neighboring streams with sewage and with the refuse products of manufactories, and the foreshore of every port and seaside resort is the cesspool of the inhabitants. The deposition of cinders from steamers has also an injurious effect in confined waters.

Various laws have, both in this country and in others, been enacted for the preservation of food-fishes during the spawning season, for the prevention of over-fishing, and for the prohibition of too effective engines of destruction. Such laws are, however, systematically evaded, and, as most fisheries can be carried on at spots remote from supervision, regulations of the most judicious kind fail to produce the effect expected from them. Thus the tendency, especially in this country, is to place most reliance upon actual fish-breeding, and upon the culture of the young fry in normally pure waters. In the case of many ocean fishes, and of all those which ascend rivers to spawn, the spawning season is the only one in which they can be caught.

The productiveness of any confined piece of water is limited by the amount of fish-food contained within it. In order to successfully rear a larger number of young fishes than could be under normal conditions supported by a pond or tank, artificial feeding has sometimes been resorted to, especially in Germany, with successful results. Small crustacea, as water-fleas (*Daphnia*) and *Cyclops*, are very acceptable food for young fish, and so also are the larvæ of small insects, such as gnats and mosquitoes, for which man can thus find a use. A supply of these animals can readily be obtained by placing decaying vegetable matter in a tub of water. Growing carp will thrive on cooked cereals and vegetables, kitchen scraps, etc.

Another method to promote the growth of fish is to encourage that of such water-plants as furnish shelter to protozoans, crustacea, etc. It has been found that the azolla, a cryptogam which covers the water with a variegated carpet formed by its imbricated leaves, and the water-chestnut (*Trapa natans*), a flowering plant with extensive fibrous roots, are excellent plants for carp-ponds on account of the harbor they afford to animalcules. The water-purslane (*Ludwigia palustris*), yellow and white water-lilies, Tuscarora rice (*Zizania*), and American lotus (*Nelumbium luteum*) are good plants for carp-ponds, as are most water-plants except pond weed and the water-shield (*Brasena*), which take possession of too large a part of the pond.

The enemies of food-fishes are by no means confined to creatures of their own class. In lakes and rivers large numbers of the young are destroyed by water-beetles, by the predaceous larvæ of dragon-flies, by frogs, which seem to have great fondness for small carp, and by turtles and snakes. Muskrats must be reckoned among their enemies; and even plant-life, which in most cases furnishes food and shelter to fishes, takes its turn at fish-destruction. It has been proved that the *Utricularia* or bladder wort, a common water-plant with finely divided leaves and conspicuous yellow flowers, has the power to seize and hold within its bladders the tiny fry, and to absorb the products of their decomposition. In the ocean there are numerous invertebrates sufficiently powerful to destroy small fishes, and some which devour large ones. Polyps of various kinds, free-swimming and fixed, furnished as they are with deadly lasso-cells, readily kill small fishes; the crustacea are active enemies; and squid, large and small, are voracious devourers of all that they can master. It has been proved that squid destroy large numbers of mackerel. To these enemies must be added the large carnivorous mammals of the sea, the sea-lions, seals, dolphins, and whales. A sea-lion in captivity will devour forty pounds of fish per diem, yet for many years the colony near the entrance of San Francisco harbor was protected by law. Evidently the fishes used for food can be rendered more abundant by the systematic destruction of their enemies. In small rivers and lakes, where the habits of the denizens are tolerably well known, and the area not too large to be controlled, something may be done in this direction; and even in harbors and bays it is manifestly in the power of mankind to keep down the numbers of seals; while the establishment of a shark-fishery, whether for flesh or oil, must relieve the food-fish of some of their most active foes.

Among methods of fish-culture, in the sense of preservation, one of the most important is that of fish-ways, *i. e.*, contrivances placed within the river-bed to enable migratory fishes to surmount a cascade or dam which otherwise would bar their passage. A large number of contrivances have been invented for this purpose, and many that have been erected at considerable expense have proved inadequate. One of the best known fish-ways used in this country is known as the McDonald.

The methods of fish-breeding now practised are comparatively new. The Chinese cultivate the eggs and fry, but do not seem to be acquainted with artificial fertilization—with the mode of stripping the ova from the female fish, and mingling them with the milt taken from the male—which has recently led to such important results, and has been extended even to oysters.

The art of artificial fertilization was discovered by Stephen Ludwig Jacobi, of Westphalia, in 1748, and was carried on by Shaw in England and Remy in France for several years before the now historic station of Huningue, in Alsace, was established. As knowledge of the sexes and habits of various food-fishes progressed, the practice of the art was extended, and the large numbers of ova and young fry rendered available by this means have been distributed far and wide, so that many food-fishes have not only been introduced to distant waters in their native country, but into far distant countries.

The United States.—Although this country was not the first to practise pisciculture, in no other country at the present time is the art carried on so successfully or so extensively. The fishes which have been most extensively hatched and introduced into new waters in this and other countries are the California salmon (*Oncorhynchus chouicha*), known also as the quinnat; the true salmon (*Salmo salar*), as well as its variety, the land-locked salmon (*S. sebago*); the eastern brook trout (*S. fontinalis*); the California brook trout (*S. irideus*); the white-fish (*Coregonus albus*); the cat-fish (*Amiurus albus* and *nebulosus*); the shad (*Clupea sapidissima*), and the carp (*Cyprinus carpio*). An establishment for the propagation of striped bass (*Roccus lineatus*) is in operation at Weldon, S. C.

No food-fish has received more attention than the shad. Some idea of the extent of the work done with this fish may be obtained from the fact that during the three years 1883-85 the number of shad eggs hatched at Central Station, Washington, was 53,089,000. Twenty-six millions of shad eggs have been planted in North Carolina since 1877. The plant of shad made in Georgia in 1880 and 1881 (2,800,000 shad fry) has been successful. The Chattahoochee, Ocmulgee, and Etowah Rivers have thus been stocked, and shad were taken out abundantly in 1884. The fish is rapidly becoming common in California since its introduction, but here it has preferred to frequent sheltered bays, such as that of Monterey, rather than to ascend the Sacramento, though it was first introduced in that river.

The great success which attends artificial propagation may be judged from the results of the shad-hatching operations at Battery Station, Md., from April 16 to June 11, 1885. During this period 3512 shad were taken, the total number of eggs from all sources was 13,357,000, and 10,725,000 of these were hatched. In the year 1886 there were distributed 92,679,000 shad fry, of which 21,618,000 were planted in Delaware River, and 52,835,000 in the tributaries of the Chesapeake. From Jan. 1, 1886, to June 3, 1887, 210,628,413 eggs and fry were taken, including 110,470,000 shad and 94,670,000 white-fish. The results have been evident. Not only has the decrease which was the result of persistent and skilful fishing been arrested, but a tangible increase has taken place.

Another fish to which great attention has been paid is the German carp (*Cyprinus*), which was first imported by Mr. Poppe, of Sonoma, Cal., in 1872. In 1882 those bred at Washington were distributed in lots of twenty to 10,000 applicants in different parts of the country. The fish has now been placed in 30,000 separate waters.

Attempts to introduce the California salmon on the Atlantic coast proved a failure, but not so the restocking of depleted California waters. The McCloud fish-hatching station, near Mt. Shasta, Cal., was established in 1872. In 1873 2,000,000 of eggs were taken by using seines, but in 1874 6,000,000 were obtained by putting a fence across the river to stop the upward course of the fish. To accommodate the eggs within a moderate area, several layers were stacked over each other in trays laid in troughs through which water had to force its way. In 1878 14,000,000 of salmon eggs were successfully taken, two car-loads of which were shipped to the Atlantic coast and several millions to foreign countries. In 1880 a trout-breeding station was established, and 338,000 trout eggs were taken. The floods of 1881 swept away the station, which was at once rebuilt, and 7,500,000 eggs taken and mostly hatched for the Sacramento River. In 1882 and 1883 the catch was small, and in 1884 the station was closed. The effect of the introduction of the artificially reared salmon into the Sacramento has been so great that, whereas in 1872 the canneries were closed, twelve years after there were 15 canneries running.

Very much has yet to be learned respecting fish-culture. It is practically a science of the past sixteen years. At most a few hundred people are interested in it, while every fisherman and the community generally are practically hostile to it. Comparatively little is yet known with reference to the embryonic life of fishes, suitable temperatures of water, the proper kind and necessary amount of food, and many other things. For these reasons it cannot be claimed that every introduction made has been a success. The conditions of life were not always favorable to the strangers, who either met with too many enemies, failed to find food, or were in some other way prevented from prospering.

Appliances for hatching fish-ova have gradually been perfected, and very few are now lost. To prevent destruction by fungus, constant movement is necessary. To effect this McDonald's fish-hatching jar, by which a current is sent among the eggs so as to impart to them a regular, rolling, boiling motion, and provided with an exit tube by which dead eggs can be removed at pleasure, has proved a great success. One of the greatest causes of the death of young fish is the appearance of fungus. This is always attendant when there is not sufficient change of water, and is also pretty certain to grow upon wounds.

The cost of production of shad at Central Station, Washington, has been at the rate of $330 for each million of shad fry furnished for distribution; or more than 30 for one cent.

Great Britain.—Although considerable interest has for many years been taken in fish-culture, very little has yet been done compared with the progress made in this country. The British fisherman still takes all that comes to his net, and, though the ocean fisheries still seem to keep up their average, many rivers and inland waters have been depleted. Salmon especially, once the most common of fish in Scotland, have become rare, the Scotch rivers not yielding half the quantity they once afforded. Yet no Scotch river, save the Tay, on which the establishment of Stormontville is situated, has been stocked with fry.

One of the most successful private fish-cultural establishments in Great Britain is that of Howietown, owned by Sir J. Gibson Maitland, of Stirling, Scotland. Upwards of 10,000,000 trout ova are annually incubated here. In 1884 90,000 yearling trout were delivered to various parts of Great Britain and Ireland, and two consignments of trout ova and one of salmon ova were successfully forwarded to New Zealand. Yearling trout are strong enough to find their own food, stand a journey well, and accommodate themselves readily to new water. A twenty hours' journey in ice water does not hurt them, but they must be introduced into water of the same temperature or the gills become inflamed. Eleven private fish-hatcheries are now in operation in Scotland, but the government does nothing.

Eggs of several American fishes have been sent to England. The brook trout does not seem to have become acclimatized, spite of several attempts. Considerable opposition is manifested to the introduction of the cat-fish, which is not acceptable to the large British angling fraternity.

Sir Lyon Playfair has put on record his belief that much of the lack of progress in fish-culture in England is to be attributed to the fact that commission after commission has examined fishermen and obtained from them a vast body of contradictory evidence, while the American commissioners, instead of seeking information from men who, though they gain their living by taking fish, know less about fishes than the community, have investigated nature directly and worked in a scientific manner.

Canada.—In 1883 Canada had eleven government hatcheries in operation, eight of which were occupied exclusively with salmon eggs. There are also two private fisheries engaged in salmon-hatching. The oldest of these hatcheries had then been in operation fifteen years, the latest two years. The entire cost to date was $259,400. Two hatcheries are employed in hatching salmon, white-fish, and trout, and one hatches pike, perch, and white-fish. The entire number of fish bred and distributed up to 1883 was about 105,000,000, of which about 20,500,000 were salmon and 60,500,000 white-fish.

Europe.—Preservative laws have in France proved inoperative, for when the "prohibited" nets are unproductive, lime and *Cocculus indicus* are used to poison the fish, or dynamite is employed. Nothing is really done, and both sedentary and migratory species are passing away from the rivers. On the other hand our eastern brook trout and the California salmon are in process of acclimatisation in France, and are increasing in many water-courses.

Intelligent interest in fish-culture is taken in the Netherlands, Switzerland, and Norway. In 1884 considerable numbers of various species of fishes, including American salmon, were placed in Lake Zurich by the fish-cultural establishment of the canton.

Among European countries Germany appears to take the lead in fish-culture. Carp have been extensively reared for centuries, and reports from various rivers show that success has attended the culture of salmon, sea trout, brook trout, lake trout, char, grayling, white-fish, carp, and eels. An attempt has been made to introduce the eel into the Danube, where it is not native. The eastern brook trout is already acclimatized in Germany, so much so that impregnated eggs have been sent from Pomerania and Mecklenburg to other parts. It flourishes also in Upper Hungary and in Bavaria. The California trout is doing well, and the same is true of the land-locked salmon and white-fish. Several other American species have been introduced into Germany and other European countries, but the success of the attempt is not assured.

Australia.—Salmonoids were not originally found in Australia. In 1852 an attempt was made to introduce salmon and salmon trout, but failed. The same result attended efforts made in 1860 and 1862, but in 1864 these fishes were successfully introduced. Other importations were made, and at the present time the salmon trout is well acclimated in the rivers of New Zealand, Tasmania, and Victoria. Both salmon and salmon trout are frequently taken, the first up to twenty-eight pounds. Several varieties of carp, perch, and other fresh-water fish have also been introduced, and the common tench (*Tinca vulgaris*) and perch (*Perca fluviatilis*) have greatly increased. The California salmon has also been introduced.

China.—Pisciculture in China is of early date. A treatise on rearing fish is ascribed to Fanli, who lived in Che-kiang in the fifth century B. C. A quotation from it, in a work written long before the commencement of our era, shows that fabulous ideas of the rate of increase were entertained. Carp and many other Cyprinidæ, bream, tench, gold-fish, etc., are cultivated. It is stated that ova hung up to dry near a chimney will hatch if cast into a pond in the spring, and this even after three years. Che-kiang is the original home of the golden carp, all the varieties of which come from a black species. Much of the art of changing their color consists in affording due amounts of shade and sunshine. The Chinese entrap male fish with imprisoned males, and in a similar way decoy the females. They do not in all cases cultivate the ova, but take very small fishes, and seem to impartially include all kinds. In other cases they catch the spawn in closely woven bags with wide mouths, the insides coated with paste of white of eggs and flour, to which the spawn adheres. In Southern China the fish-ponds are located on tidal rivers, streams, and creeks, and the fish are fed with human excrement, washed twice to extract the liquid fertilizers, and then mixed with finely cut young grass and fed to the fish. For this reason foreigners seldom have fresh-water fish on their tables.   (W. N. L.)

FISH, HAMILTON, an American statesman, was born in New York city, Aug. 3, 1808, being the son of Col. Nicholas Fish. He graduated at Columbia College in 1827, and was admitted to the bar in 1830. He was frequently a candidate of the Whig party, and in 1837 was elected to the State Assembly. He served one term in Congress 1843–45, and in 1847 he was elected lieutenant-governor of the State. He was next elected governor, serving from 1849 to 1851, when he was chosen United States senator. At the close of his term he went to Europe, where he resided until 1860. During the civil war he gave liberally of his means and influence in aid of the government. In 1862, by appointment of Secretary Seward, he took part in negotiations with the Confederate government, which led to the subsequent rules for exchange of prisoners. Gen. U. S. Grant, on becoming president in 1869, called Mr. Fish to be Secretary of State. The duties of this office he discharged with vigor and ability, until the close of President Grant's second term. The most memorable events of his administration were the negotiation of the Treaty of Washington, signed May 8, 1871, and the settlement of the Alabama claims by the Geneva tribunal of arbitration, Sept. 14, 1872.

FISH, NICHOLAS (1758-1833), an American military officer, was born in New York city, Aug. 28, 1758. He entered Princeton College, but soon left to study law under J. Morin Scott. His preceptor was made a general when the revolutionary war commenced, and Fish became his aide-de-camp. He was in both battles of Saratoga, commanded a corps of light infantry at Monmouth, served in Gen. Sullivan's expedition against the Indians in 1779, and in the operations at Yorktown in 1781, being then a lieutenant-colonel. In 1786 he was appointed adjutant-general of the State of New York, and held that office several years. In 1794 President Washington appointed him supervisor of the revenue, and in 1797 he became president of the New York Society of the Cincinnati. He died at New York, June 20, 1833.

FISHER, GEORGE JACKSON, an American physician, was born in Westchester co., N. Y., Nov. 27, 1825. He graduated from the medical department of New York University, March 1, 1849. He was physician of New York State prison at Sing Sing in 1853-54, president of the Westchester County Medical Society 1857-58, and president of the New York State Medical Society in 1874. He has published *Biographical Sketches of Physicians of Westchester County* (1861); *Animal Substances employed as medicines by the Ancients* (1862); *Diploteratology* (1865), and other professional works.

FISHER, GEORGE PARK, an American clergyman, was born at Wrentham, Mass., Aug. 10, 1827. He graduated at Brown University in 1847, studied theology at New Haven and at Andover. After further study in Germany, he was made professor of divinity in Yale College in 1854, and in 1861 became professor of ecclesiastical history. He has been a frequent contributor to the leading literary and theological reviews, and since 1866 one of the editors of the *New Englander*. He has published *Essays on the Supernatural Origin of Christianity* (1865); *Life of Benjamin Silliman* (1866); *History of the Reformation* (1873); *Beginnings of Christianity* (1877); *Discussions in History and Theology* (1880), relating chiefly to the Roman Catholic Church and to New England theology; *Grounds of Theistic and Christian Belief* (1883). Prof. Fisher combines in admirable proportion the best qualities of the historical essayist and the Christian philosopher.

FISHERIES. The systematic quest and capture of any animal which resides in water is popularly known as a fishery, the word being a survival of the old idea that all aquatic animals are fishes. Certain of the most important marine and fresh-water animals are made special objects of search; ships, boats, nets, and engines of destruction being manufactured specially for their capture. Thus there is a whale-fishery, a seal-fishery, a cod-fishery, a herring-fishery, a salmon-fishery. The majority of aquatic animals are not of sufficient importance to be thus made sole objects of search, but form part of the miscellaneous fishery carried on in a locality.

This article will be confined to the fisheries of the United States and British America, yet some idea of the great importance of the total harvest of the sea, a harvest gathered in wasteful fashion, from a crop that is neither sown nor tended, may be derived from statistics which show that nearly 150,000 vessels are engaged in fishing in Europe and America, and that between 600,000 and 700,000 men are employed. The total animal product is said to be not far short of 1,500,000 tons.

North Atlantic Fisheries.—Of these the cod-fishery in its generic sense is the most important. Though it has already been treated under COD, in Vol. II., the following statements give additional information about its methods as practised by American fishermen.

The banks most used by fishermen are Iceland Banks, Greenland Banks, Grand and Western Banks, Flemish Cap, Banquereau, La Have, Brown's Bank, St. George's Bank, and numerous smaller banks, all of which are outside of all national jurisdiction. On these banks are found the finest specimen of the cod, varying in size and quality. The St. George's Banks, lying 125 miles south-east from Cape Ann, affords the finest fish. The bank-fishery is pursued in vessels from 50 to 200 tons burthen, and the manner of taking the fish is principally the French trawl system, viz.: by the use of a long line extended along the bottom of the ocean, secured at either end by small anchors, which are buoyed to the surface by means of buoy-lines to which are attached empty wooden kegs with a short staff with a flag attached to mark the location. Hooks baited with short gangings are attached five feet apart on the main line of the trawl. These trawls are from 500 to 1500 feet in length. They are set and remain from 12 to 24 hours, when they are underrun, the fish taken from the hooks, a new bait put on the hooks, and the trawl left as before. In this way 300 hooks are used on one trawl. This kind of fishing is done in dories, small boats which are carried on the vessel, and are each manned by two men. This business is peculiarly hazardous, as the dories go quite a distance from the vessel and often go astray in the fog which prevails or are overloaded with fish and in case of sudden winds are swamped. The loss of life is very great.

On George's and other banks from Gloucester alone 419 vessels and 2249 men have been lost from 1830 to 1881. The old hand-line system and fishing direct from the vessel is almost entirely superseded by the trawl system.

The inshore cod-fishery is largely pursued in small boats that go out and return daily. Most of the British North American cod-fisheries are of this character. The fish taken are smaller than the bank fish and are well adapted to the West Indies market. During the existence of the Washington treaty the Dominion of Canada and Newfoundland have largely increased their bank fleet of vessels. The American fishermen take no fish except mackerel in so-called British waters. The entire bank fisheries are outside of all national jurisdiction.

Another method of taking cod lately come into use is the gill-net, with meshes large enough to take the larger fish but allowing the small fish to pass through. In the winter and early spring months the fish are readily taken by this method, but later they shun contact with the net, and the fishermen explain this by claiming that the sight of the fish is impaired at this time. It is a theory which seems to be sustained by observation that fish at the time of spawning are more reckless and less careful than at other times, and the fishermen hold that fish imbed themselves in the mud, and when they come out to frequent the banks or shores where they spawn a film has grown over the eye to protect it from contact with the mud, and it renders them partially blind for a short season, and, therefore, they do not avoid the net. These nets are set in the same manner as herring gill-nets and hang perpendicularly, being sustained by glass balls at the top with the lower line of the net resting on the bottom. This manner of setting is necessary, as the cod-fish swim near the bottom and their food, consisting of cockles, shell-fish, and shrimps, is found there. This method of sinking gill-nets to the bottom has proved very successful in other fisheries, and finer and better qualities of fish are taken by this process. The old method was to sustain the net at the surface with cork buoys and let it hang from them downward. This is well in shoal water, but in deep-water fishing the new method is far superior.

The other varieties of the fisheries, consisting of the halibut, haddock, pollock, hake, or ling, are taken similar to the cod-fish, although the halibut, which once was so plenty on all the banks and also frequenting the shore, is now becoming very scarce, and is mostly found in the deepest water where there is a divergence of the banks in the intervals between them. One hundred and fifty fathoms is the depth at which most of them are now taken. Pollock and hake are found mostly within a few miles of the shore and are taken at certain seasons of the year; but the cod-fish is perennial and is the grand basis of the fishing business, being available at all seasons.

The history of the treaties relating to the North Atlantic fisheries and their effect upon this industry will be given later in this article.

The great migrations of mackerel, herring, and menhaden, or porgies, represent a large interest in the prosecution of the Atlantic fisheries. The mackerel make their appearance near Cape Hatteras as early as the month of April, and pursue their way northward, and are found off the New England coast from June until November. It is a question as yet undecided whether the migration of mackerel is entirely from this direction, or whether they come in toward the shore from the borders of the Gulf Stream simultaneously north and south. It is claimed that an early school of mackerel make their appearance in the Gulf of St. Lawrence on Banks Bradelle and Orphan in the month of May, and it would appear that the Gulf of St. Lawrence was the northern limit of their migration, although at times mackerel of large size and coarse texture have been taken at Newfoundland. The mackerel-fishery as such did not assume any great distinction as a peculiar fishery by Americans until 1820, and the methods of taking have changed from the drailing process—that is, extending poles from the sides of the vessel with lines attached while the vessel under sail run through the schools—to the hand-line system and the distribution of bait ground fine to attract the fish to the surface. It was under this process that the mackerel-fisheries of the Gulf of St. Lawrence were so largely developed, and an Amer-

FIG. 1.—Cod Trawl-fishing.

ican fleet of 600 vessels usually resorted to the Gulf of St. Lawrence to take mackerel. Immense quantities of menhaden were used for bait in this fishery, each vessel taking, on an average, 50 barrels of slivers (which are the flesh of the menhaden cut from the vertebræ and salted in barrels for this purpose). This was ground fine by hand-mills and scattered on the surface to attract the fish. This immense feeding process with this peculiar oily bait was very attractive to the mackerel, kept them together in a great body, prevented their scattering for food, and thus made them available to the small boats as well as to the vessels, as the bait thrown kept the mackerel near the shore. The introduction of the purse seine and its universal adoption by the vessels changed the entire character of this fishery. The operation of these seines requires great depth of water in open sea, and, if used in cessant pursuit of the mackerel disturbs their migratory course and is gradually driving them farther from the shores, and the fishery is becoming more and more an ocean fishery. In addition to the seine methods for the capture of mackerel the shore weirs are being largely used, and when the mackerel are pursued by their natural enemies, the blue-fish, bonitos, or sharks, etc., they frequently endeavor to escape by swimming close to the shore. The weirs, constructed in shoal water of stakes and bushes and in deep water of walls of netting, intercept them by what is called a leader, which is an extension of the weir by a single wall of net reaching out 500 feet or more from the body of the weir. The fish meet this wall of netting, and instead of turning back they follow along the side, and are thus led into the weir, which is so constructed that the way to go out is never apparent to the fish. Many of these

FIG. 2.—Cod Gill-net fishing.

shoal water, requires a clean, sandy bottom, as rocks destroy the seine and the fish escape. The mackerel that heretofore were coaxed and enticed by bait to become victims were now ruthlessly assailed at the entrance of their migration north, enclosed before they were aware in the immense wall of net, the lower part of these walls being drawn together under them, forming a complete net purse of gigantic size. In this manner a thousand barrels are secured at one haul. The vessel is then brought alongside of the seine, and the fish bailed out and dressed at the convenience of the fishermen. This warfare, commencing off Cape Hatteras in March, is kept up unceasingly throughout the season, not only in the daytime but in the night. A fisherman at the masthead is able in the darkness to trace the movement of the fish in the water by the agitation of the phosphorescent particles in the water, and directs the operations of the boats and setting of the seine. Many fish are thus taken in the night that would be shy of the surface in the daytime. This inweirs are models of ingenuity and are patented. It has been questioned whether this wholesale destruction of mackerel would not in time be total destruction of the fishery, but scientific observation and statistics show that while locations may be temporarily affected, yet the impression made upon the great life of the ocean is not apparent. The shore-fisheries for mackerel on the American coast and in the Gulf of St. Lawrence have sensibly diminished under the operation of the seine and weir fisheries, and the fish are exhibiting a shyness which did not exist under the hook-and-line system.

The menhaden- or porgy-fishery is fast becoming a lost art in northern waters. The first use made of this fish was for bait for cod-fish, and during the summer months these fish were so abundant in the creeks, harbors, and rivers of New England, that they were used as a fertilizer by the farmers. After the mackerel-fishery became a staple business they were used for bait, and when ground fine the oily nature of the bait would float it near the surface and attract the mackerel so they could be taken with hook and line. The menhaden never went north farther than the shores of Maine and were not available to the provincial fishermen. They usually made their appearance at or near the mouth of the Chesapeake Bay and came north about the same time as the mackerel. They courted the shore in their migratory progress, and were very numerous in their season in Long Island Sound, along the New England coast, and especially in the waters of Maine. In their early advent they are poor in quality, like the mackerel, but if unmolested and allowed to come into the northern waters they become very fat and yield great quantities of oil. As the fishery is now conducted by means of seines and weirs, they are almost annihilated except in Long Island Sound, and a school of them is rarely seen north of Cape Cod in the harbors and creeks as formerly. But few are used for bait, none being necessary in the mackerel vessel fishery as all use seines, and the system of weirs furnishing small fish and herring which with the yield of clam-bait equips the cod-fishermen. The menhaden-fishery is now almost exclusively confined to the oil-producing factories, which use steamers and seines largely in their capture. The increase of this branch of the fishing business has been sudden and immense, and it bids fair to decrease from the extinction of the fish in the localities that abounded with them. In 1878 the menhaden oil and guano industry employed capital to the amount of $2,350,000, 3337 men, 64 steamers, 279 sailing vessels, and consumed 777,000,000 fish. There were 56 factories, which produced 1,392,644 gallons of oil, valued at $450,000, and 55,154 tons of crude guano, valued at $600,000: this was a poor year. In 1874 the number of gallons produced was 3,373,000; in 1875, 2,681,000; in 1876, 2,992,000; in 1877, 2,427,000. In 1874 the manufactured products were $1,809,000; in 1875, $1,582,000; in 1876, $1,671,000; in 1877, $1,608,000; in 1878, $1,050,000; in 1880 there were employed in this industry 3635 persons; capital invested $2,362,841; the value of products, $2,116,787; the fishermen numbered 2543; the factory hands, 1092; vessels employed, 456, of 12,905.71 tons; vessels' value, $1,009,650; value of outfits, exclusive of nets and boats, $143,819; number of boats, 648; value, $65,435; number of purse seines, 366; value, $138,400; value of factories with fixtures, $1,009,537; pounds of menhaden taken, 570,424,377; gallons of oil made, 2,066,396; value of oil, $733,424; tons of guano, 68,904; value of guano, $1,301,217; value of menhaden compost, $61,699.

The Atlantic herring-fishery is a shore-fishery. The only general use made of vessels is as a means of transportation. The herring strike in upon the coast of Massachusetts and Maine in the late fall and early winter to spawn; they are taken in gill-nets and weirs, and are salted, pickled, or sold fresh for food or bait to the cod-fishermen. Later in the season they are usually very abundant on the coast of New Brunswick, Grand Menan Island, Bay of Fundy, and in January in the bays and coves of Newfoundland. The usual process of taking by gill-nets has the effect to strangle the fish, causing a redness of the eyes which is detrimental to their appearance when fresh or frozen; and since the introduction of seines and traps or weirs, they are frozen or preserved in better condition after being taken from the seines. From 50 to 100 vessels pursue this business for about three months in the year. The fish are all taken by the local fishermen and sold to the vessels, which receive them fresh, and by means of freezing before being loaded in the vessel they are kept fresh and sweet for a number of weeks. In this condition they are brought to the United States and sold for food or bait for the fishermen's use. As this business is a mercantile transaction on the part of the Americans, the entire benefit of the production goes to the local British fishermen. This fishery occurring in the winter on these coasts where the only resource is in taking fish, affords a remuneration to the coast-fishermen which saves them from the extreme poverty and distress which characterizes the life of many of the fishermen on these coasts and the coasts of Ireland. Previous to this trade the government of the Provinces was often obliged to afford aid and sustenance to the poor fishermen of these localities, but, under the system of trade initiated by the Americans paying cash for bait-fish and herring, the people enjoy a prosperity unknown to them before. Under the Washington treaty the Americans had an undoubted right to use their own seines and nets in these waters. On Jan. 6, 1878, the Americans attempted to exercise this right at Fortune Bay, Newfoundland, but were resisted by the local fishermen, their seines destroyed, and the voyages broken up. Great Britain afterwards paid $75,000 as indemnity. The poor fishermen of the coast have nothing but these fisheries to sustain themselves and families, and no treaty will be acknowledged by them that takes these fisheries from them.

The preparation of small herring as sardines is an industry that has grown into large proportions. Experiments were made in this business as early as 1866, but its existence as a business dates from 1875. In 1880 it furnished employment to over 1500 fishermen and factory-hands, in addition to 376 fishermen belonging to New Brunswick; the whole capital employed is $560,000, and the value of the products, $825,000. The entire herring- and sardine-fisheries of the United States show a valuation of $1,130,000.

In the preparation of fish for market, great changes have taken place in mode and methods. Ice, formerly unknown to the operative fisherman as a preservative, now constitutes one of the greatest factors in his business. The canning process utilizes the small fish, and the entire absorption for fertilizers of every portion that constituted the waste shows a steady progress in the scientific development of this hitherto neglected industry. The researches and results of scientific investigation aided by the government and sustained by the indefatigable exertions of the Smithsonian corps of scientists, will in time develop not only new fisheries and locations, but establish reliable systems by which the fisherman may guide his business according to recognized authority rather than by luck. In no business are such high qualities of risk and daring displayed, and the sad record of continual loss of life and property shows the power of the element with which they contend. In this business, pre-eminently, labor and capital share mutual profit and loss, both are banded together for success, and need neither strike nor arbitration to adjust their relations.   (F. J. B).

The Southern Fisheries.—Pensacola and Key West are two important fishing-points in the Southern States, and the character of the fisheries there will give a good idea of the Southern fisheries in general. Besides the distinct fishery for the red snapper, a large amount of shore-fishing is done. the principal fishes being blue-fish, pompano, and Spanish mackerel. In 1885 the catch of Spanish mackerel at this point in the month of April was 121,931 pounds.

The history of almost all the Gulf fisheries shows that where pursuit has in any locality been vigorous the supply has rapidly diminished. This is true only of the bottom fishes, as sheepshead, channel bass, mullet, snappers, etc., and does not refer to migratory fishes, such as the pompanos and mackerel.

The mullet-fisheries carried on at Cedar Keys, Charlotte Harbor, and other points on the Florida coast are of considerable importance. At Cedar Keys the season begins about the end of November and continues until the first ten days of February, December and January being the best months. The fish weigh two or three pounds. They are taken in gill-nets, seines, and cast-nets. Eight men with a seine consider 10,000 a good day's take. Fresh fish find a ready market, and are shipped to Georgia and South Carolina in ice. Many are salted, and the roes cured. On the spot the fish are worth 2½ cents; roes 1 cent.

One of the most common fishes of the Gulf of Mexico is the red snapper (*Lutjanus campechianus*). It is gorgeously colored, averages 7 pounds weight, and lives in the strictly salt waters of the Gulf at depths of from 60 to 240 feet. Where there is a rock, coral, or gravel bottom this fish is sure to occur. The flesh is firm and sweet, and is good boiled, baked, broiled, or fried. It is caught with hook and line. Vessels carrying six to eight men go to sea with all appliances for both capture and preservation, and generally secure a load in about a week. The abiding places of the fish are found by sounding lines with baited hooks attached. The vessels are anchored over the spot or are allowed to drift across it, while the fishermen, each with a single line bearing two large hooks and loaded with several pounds of lead, work as rapidly as possible, for when the fish are hungry they bite as fast as the lines are lowered to them and even rise to the surface in their eagerness, biting at bare hooks or anything that is offered. This has given them the name of snappers. Yet at other times they take no notice of any bait or snare. The vessels go as far as 250 miles from home and 50 from shore. As the chief fishing-grounds of the Gulf are between Mobile Bay and Cedar Key, Pensacola is the most convenient shipping-point.

All the market fishing at Key West is done with hook and line. The great supply comes from bottom fishing, but some kinds are in the winter taken in large numbers by trolling. Among these are the king-fish (*Scomberomorus cavalla*), the dolphin (*Coryphæna hippurus*), the barracuda (*Sphyræna picuda*), the amber jack (*Seriola lalandi*), the albicore (*Seriola dumerili*), the jack (*Caranx*) and the bonito, as well as the sword-fish or spike-fish (*Histiophorus*) and the wahoo (*Acanthocybium*). The king-fish, one of the mackerel tribe, is in season from the first of December to April.

The most abundant of the bottom fishes, in quantity exceeding all others, is the common grunt or ronco grande (*Hæmulon plumieri*.) Next to this comes the red grouper (*Epinephelus morio*), and then the different snappers (*Lutjanus*), groupers (*Epinephelus*), porgies (*Calamus*), and grunts (*Hæmulon*), each of which groups contain several species. The gray snapper, the yellow-tail, the lane snapper, the mutton fish, the schoolmaster, and the dog snapper are common species of *Lutjanus*; the common groupers are the red, the Nassau, the gag, the black, the scamp, the rockhind, and the coney; the common porgies, the jolt-head, the saucer-eye, the littlemouth, and the shad or grass porgy; and the common grunts, the sailor's choice, the yellow grunt or ronco amarillo, the tom-tate, and the French grunt, besides the more common ronco grande. Other food-fishes are the hog-fish (*Lachnolæmus*), the pork-fish (*Pomadasys*), the turbot (*Balistes caroliniensis*), and the jack, horse-eye jack, and runner (species of *Caranx*). Less abundant, yet frequently seen in the markets, are the blue-fish, the goat-fishes (*Upeneus*), the breams (*Diplodus*), the pompanos (*Trachynotus*), 3 species, the pudding-wife (*Platyglossus*), the Spanish hog-fish (*Harpe rufa*), the moon-fish (*Selene*), the Spanish mackerel (*Scomberomorus*), with several others. The "Whiting" of Key West is no relative of the cod, but is *Pomadasys chrysopterus*.

These fishes are all brought to the market alive, in the wells of the smacks, and killed by a blow on the head when sold.

In deeper water, another fish called the red grouper is the leading fish, and next comes the red snapper (*Lutjanus campechianus*), with several species of *Epinephalus*, including the gigantic Jew-fish or guasa.

Not a seine is owned on the island, but during the run of the mullets (*Mugil*), several species of that fish are taken in cast-nets, together with some other fishes.

The names given to fishes at Key West are still used for the same species in the Bahamas, whence they were brought, and also at the Bermudas. They were in use more than 150 years ago, at the time of the visit of Mark Catesby, and each name usually applies to but one species.

British America. East Coast.—The chief fishery of Newfoundland is that of the cod. (See COD, Vol. II.) The total exports of fishery products from Newfoundland to all countries in the year ending Dec. 31, 1883, was $6,498,727, of which $4,725,960 was for dry cod-fish, and $364,157 for cod-fish oil. About $1,000,000 for seal-skins, oil, etc., are included in this amount. Out of 1,163,934 quintals of cod-fish, Spain and Portugal received 573,181, Russia 295,094, and the West Indies 98,913. The value of the product of the Newfoundland fisheries imported by the United States in the same year was $393,114. There are along the coast of Labrador, between Manicouangan and Blanc Sablon (500 miles), several large fishing-establishments, whose yearly catch of cod amounts to over 1000 quintals, or hundred weights. In 1878 this coast furnished 160,500 quintals, but about 104,000 of these were taken by vessels from the United States, Newfoundland, etc.

The salmon-fishery is, in Labrador, next in importance to that of the cod. The fish are caught in gill-nets, with a regulation mesh of 6 inches. The season is from about July 25 to August 25. Fish are plentiful in all the rivers: there is seldom one without several fisheries upon it. The catch is prepared for market by cleaning, skinning, soaking in fresh water, and afterwards in brine, and packing in barrels. Twenty-three fishes usually fill a barrel, which is worth $12 cash, first cost. Drying, smoking, and canning are also practised. The rod and line can be used with good results. It is on record that one man caught, in this manner, 3861 pounds of salmon in 18 days.

In trout-fishing long and narrow nets are used, with meshes 3½ to 4 inches wide, so as to allow the young to escape. The fish taken average 12 to 18 inches long, and 3½ to 4 pounds weight. The net is set across the mouth or along the shore of some small bay into which a stream runs. Trout are taken at all seasons, but are always most abundant just before high tide.

Two or three species of herring appear in the Labrador waters late in April, or early in May. They are fished for with nets and seines till some time in June, when, having deposited their spawn, the fish return to deep water. These "spring herring" are poor and thin, and are largely fed to the dogs. The "fall herring" appear on the coast about the middle of August, and stay about six weeks. They are equal to the best Scotch herring. Sometimes the fish remain till October, and these later fish are generally fine. What is known as "weir-fishing" consists in making, at ebb tide, a barrier of young fir-trees driven into the mud. When full tide comes the fish are caught in the interlacing branches, and are left stranded by the retreating tide. The total value of the north shore or Labrador fisheries for 1880 was $1,401,289, of which the codfishery amounted to $1,200,000. In 1881 the catch of cod was nearly double that of 1880.

Besides the salmon-fishery of Labrador, salmon are extensively taken at Restigouche, and in the Bay of Chaleur, on the southern shore of the Gulf of St. Lawrence.

The total catch of salmon in Canada was given by the census returns at 4,754,800 pounds in 1881, and of white-fish, 7,848,200 pounds. The exportation of salmon to the United States in 1890 was 853,963 pounds, and of all other fish 40,372,180 pounds.

Mackerel abound in the Gulf of St. Lawrence, but are rare in Labrador. They are taken from early in July to late in September.

Pacific Coast Fisheries.—The fisheries of the Pacific coast are at the present time of great importance, and only lack a wider market to become more so. In the extreme north, on the coast of Alaska and British Columbia, some of the leading fishes are identical with those of the Atlantic. Thus the cod and halibut are objects of special fishery. The streams and coasts of Alaska and British Columbia swarm with fish, and the Indians of the region are expert fishers.

The fisheries of British Columbia employed in 1884 10 steamers, 21 schooners, etc., and 1141 boats and canoes, giving occupation to 85 sailors, 1881 fishermen, and 1315 shore men. The total value of the yield was $1,358,267. The principal item was 541,242 cases (4 dozen pound cans) of canned salmon, but the list includes 367,000 pounds of smoked and 5636 barrels of salted salmon; 173,056 fresh salmon; sturgeon, 352,000 pounds; haddock, etc., 240,000 pounds, and 150,000 pounds of halibut.

The most important fishing industry of the Pacific coast is that of salmon-canning, carried on principally upon the Columbia, but to a considerable extent upon the Sacramento and other rivers. The first salmon-canning establishment was started on the Sacramento in 1864; and in 1865 the Columbia River salmon-fishery was commenced. The quality of the goods, and the convenient method of preservation adopted, in a few years enabled Pacific coast canned-salmon to make its way in all the markets of the world.

The salmon fleet of the Columbia now numbers about 1500 boats, with two men to each boat. The best material for a salmon net is Barbour's twine, made at Paterson, N. J. A single thread of this twine will bear a strain of 160 pounds. The season begins in April, and ends in August. The work of canning is principally performed by Chinamen, sometimes under the direction of an American superintendent. The salmon is placed in the cans raw, with some salt. The cans are covered, soldered, then boiled by steam-heat for an hour, and lastly, in order to cook the bones, placed for another hour in cylindrical iron retorts at a temperature of 133°. In 1884 the various establishments on the Columbia put up 620,000 cases of salmon, each containing 48 cans. The total number of cases shipped from Portland to San Francisco in the season of 1884–85 was 82,984, while there were exported to England between Aug. 25, 1883, and Sept. 7, 1884, 409,727 cases, valued at $2,023,830.

The next important fishing-point on the Pacific coast is San Francisco. Here extensive fisheries are carried on in the bay and also in the Pacific. The fisheries of the bay have been greatly injured by over-fishing, by the use of small-meshed nets, which are still employed by the Chinese fishermen, and by the depredations of the flourishing colony of sea-lions which has for ages been established on a rock just outside of the bay, and was for several years protected by law.

The most abundant fishes of San Francisco Bay are one or two species of rock-fish or rock-cod (*Sebastodes*); the large sculpin, *Scorpaenichthys marmoratus*; two species of *Hexagrammus*, sometimes called sea-trout; the California smelts or silversides, some embiotocidæ, and the great sturgeon. Large quantities of salmon are canned on the Sacramento, the yield having been restored by the operations of the United States salmon-hatchery on the McCloud River. In the ocean are taken the various species of rock-cod, *Hexagrammus*, green-cod (*Ophiodon*), viviparous perch or embiotocidæ, sea-bass (*Atractoscion nobile*), and other sciænoids, together with herring, sardines, and several species of flat-fish, which are sold as sole, turbot, flounder, etc., though in no case specifically identical with the fishes of the North Atlantic rightfully so called. The fishes of the Central Californian coast are, as a whole, distinct from those of the northern region and also from those of Lower California. In Monterey Bay the two faunas meet, and that point has thus the most abundant fish-fauna to be found on the Pacific coast of North America, and is also the seat of an active fishery. Farther south, at Santa Barbara, Wilmington, and San Diego, the character of the food-fishes becomes somewhat like that to be met with in the Gulf of Mexico, Serranidæ, Sparidæ, Sciænidæ, and Labridæ being prominent. (See FISH.)

The fresh-water fishes of the Pacific rivers belong chiefly to the Salmonidæ, Catostomidæ, and Cyprinidæ. Only one species of perch-like fishes exists. Most of the Cyprinidæ are large, are extensively eaten at Sacramento and other points in the interior, and are occasionally brought to San Francisco. Lake Tahoe yields a good supply of a large spotted trout, a variety of the widely distributed *Salmo purpuratus* or mountain trout, with which the "salmon-trout" of the Pacific coast is now believed to be identical. Sea-run specimens are more silvery, with finer spots and less red; they also grow larger. The species may always be known when fresh by a deep scarlet or crimson blotch on the membranes of the lower side of the lower jaw.

The exportation of fishery products (excluding whales, but including seals) from San Francisco in 1883 was not less than $4,000,000, or about 9 per cent. of the total exports of the city. Of this value $2,320,624 was for canned and $76,431 for pickled salmon. All other fish exports amounted to only about $140,000, the large remainder representing sealskins, shrimps, abalones, etc.

The shad, carp, and Schuylkill cat-fish have been successfully introduced into the waters of California.

Other Fisheries.—The most important food-fish of the large rivers of the Eastern United States is the shad (*Clupea sapidissima*), a large and savory member of the herring family. This fish is systematically taken upon the Delaware, Hudson, Potomac, etc. In 1883 the Potomac fisheries alone yielded 379,816 shad and 8,989,261 fresh-water herring. Other fishes of which large quantities are taken are blue-fish, mackerel, mullets, rock-fish, spot, white, and yellow perch, pike, cat-fish, and trout.

Considerable indignation has recently been exhibited by the fishermen of the Middle States at the operations of the makers of fish-guano, who, it is alleged, have destroyed the fisheries of some localities, both by taking food-fish and by consuming in immense quantities fishes which are the food of better food-fishes. Some idea of the extent to which the business alluded to is carried on may be obtained from the fact that during the quarter ending Sept. 30, 1884, the number of menhaden taken to factories and rendered into oil and guano was 117,000,000, besides 5,000,000 used for manure. From these 585,000 tons of oil were manufactured, as well as 81,000 tons of soap. Of edible fish 230 tons were marketed. Two hundred and one sailing vessels and 29 steamers are employed.

The great interior system of rivers formed by the Mississippi and its tributaries, as well as the Great Lakes, are abundantly furnished with fishes which are the object of local fisheries. Among the most valued are the trout, bass, white-fish, and wall-eyed pike or perch (*Stizostedion*). The crowd of Cyprinidæ and Catostomidæ or suckers are less valued. On the Great Lakes the fish supply has been much diminished by incessant fishing. The black bass is scarce, and those taken to market often weigh only from half to two and a half pounds. The wall-eyed pike, which twenty-five years ago was common and large, reaching 15 lbs., is now said to be brought to market at 1½ to 2 pounds.

(W. N. L.)

Statistics.—The great extent of the fishing and marine industries of the United States may be seen from a mere enumeration of the classes into which they are divided by government officials. They are as follows:

A. *Ocean fisheries* (fishermen living on the vessels and making long voyages when necessary).—1, whale; 2, Antarctic seal and sea-elephant; 3, Grand Bank cod; 4, George's Bank cod; 5, Alaskan cod; 6, winter haddock; 7, fresh halibut; 8, salt halibut; 9, mackerel; 10, sword-fish; 11, hake and cusk; 12, red snapper and grouper; 13, menhaden; 14, herring and sardine industry.

B. *Coast fisheries* (chiefly from small boats).—15, New England shore cod; 16, mullet; 17, eel; 18, New England pound and trap; 19, lobster; 20, crab; 21, prawn and shrimp; 22, oyster; 23, scallop; 24, sponge; 25, sea-otter; 26, New England shore fishery; 27, Middle States shore fishery; 28, South Atlantic shore fishery; 29, Gulf shore fishery; 30, California shore fishery.

C. *River and lake fisheries.*—31, shad and alewife; 32, western salmon; 33, eastern salmon; 34, great lake white-fish; 35, smelt; 36, river sturgeon; 37, lake sturgeon; 38, great lake general fishery; 39, inland lake and creek fishery.

D. *Strand fisheries and shore industries.*—40, Alaska seal; 41, turtle and terrapin; 42, clam; 43, quahog; 44, abalone; 45, Irish moss industry; 46, marine salt industry; 47, seaweed industry.

The accompanying table, taken from the Census Report of 1880, was prepared under the direction of Prof. G. Brown Goode, of the United States Fish Commission, and is a faithful presentation of the work, value, and results of American fisheries of all kinds, so far as these admit of enumeration.

The nationality of the American fishermen, excluding 5000 Negroes and 8000 Indians and Esquimaux, and including all naturalized citizens engaged in the business, is 88 per cent. American, and, taking into account the various industries directly affected by the fisheries, it can be said that directly and indirectly this industry gives employment to and sustains not less than 1,000,000 persons in the United States. The vessels are models of marine architecture, combining great speed with admirable strength and sea-going qualities, and the men who man them are by habit and training, endurance and exposure, the hardiest and finest seamen on the ocean.

Treaties.—The importance, both national and international, of the various treaties relating to the North American fisheries requires that they should be considered at some length. They date back to the Treaty of Versailles, in 1763, when France yielded to Great Britain all of her possessions in North America, and afterwards at the Treaty of Paris, 1783, obtained the cession of the islands St. Pierre and Miquelon as fishing-stations. This treaty, by which the independence of the United States was recognized by Great Britain, was also definitive as to the rights of American fishermen, both on the ocean, over which Great Britain had no dominion whatever, and also in the waters adjacent to the shores, where her jurisdiction was unquestioned. It was a full acknowledgment, freely given, and was as much a warranted deed as the transfer of the territory of the United States. The article is as follows:

"It is agreed that the people of the United States shall continue to enjoy, unmolested, the right to take fish of every kind on the Grand Bank and on all other banks of Newfoundland; also in the Gulf of St. Lawrence, and at all other places in the sea where the inhabitants of both countries used at any time heretofore to fish; and also that inhabitants of the United States shall have liberty to take fish of every kind on such parts of the coasts of Newfoundland as British fishermen shall use, but not to dry or cure the same on that island; and also on the coasts, bays, and creeks of all His Britannic Majesty's dominions in America; and that the American fishermen shall have liberty to dry and cure fish in any of the unsettled bays, harbors, and creeks of Nova Scotia, Magdalen Islands, and Labrador as long as the same shall remain unsettled. But as soon as the same, or either of them, shall be settled it shall not be lawful for said fishermen to dry or cure fish at such settlement without a previous agreement for that purpose with the inhabitants, proprietors, or possessors of the ground."

The war of 1812, which was terminated by the Treaty of Ghent, Dec. 24, 1814, was claimed by Great Britain as a termination of the provisions of the Treaty of 1783, admitting Americans to the inshore fisheries, and, as the commissioners were unable to agree, no settlement relative to these fisheries was made. Following this England assumed jurisdiction of the entire British North American shore fisheries, including all bays, claiming authority over all waters three miles outside of a line drawn from headland to headland. American vessels were captured and driven out from this assumed line until, in 1818, Richard Rush, Minister to England, and Albert Gallatin, Minister to France, were empowered by the President to treat with Great Britain on the subject of the fisheries

FISHERIES.

and other matters. The result of the conference was the Treaty of Oct. 20, 1818, Art. 1 defining the fisheries:

"Whereas differences have arisen respecting the liberty claimed by the United States for the inhabitants thereof to take, dry, and cure fish on certain coasts, bays, harbors, and creeks of His Britannic Majesty's dominions in America, it is agreed between the high contracting parties that the inhabitants of the said United States shall have forever, in common with the subjects of His Britannic Majesty, the liberty to take fish of any kind on that part of the southern coast of Newfoundland which extends from Cape Ray to the Ramean Islands, on the western and northern coasts of Newfoundland, from the said Cape Ray to the Quirpon Islands, on the shores of the Magdalen Islands, and also on the coasts, bays, harbors, and creeks from Mount Joly, on the southern coast of Labrador, to and through the straits of Belle Isle, and thence northwardly indefinitely along

FISHERIES OF THE UNITED STATES, 1880.

States	Persons Employed — Fishermen (No.)	Persons Employed — Shoresmen (No.)	Persons Employed — Total (No.)	Vessels — Number	Vessels — Tonnage	Vessels — Value (Dollars)	Boats — Number	Boats — Value (Dollars)	Value of outfits (Dollars)	All other capital (Dollars)	Total capital (Dollars)	General fisheries (Dollars)	Menhaden fishery (Dollars)	Total value of products (Dollars)
New England	29,838	7,205	37,043	2,066	113,602.59	4,562,131	14,787	739,970	5,038,171	9,597,335	19,937,607	10,014,645	539,722	14,370,393
Middle States	12,564	2,397	14,961	1,210	22,565.93	1,382,000	8,293	546,647	674,961	1,822,480	4,425,078	2,882,294	1,261,385	8,676,579
S. Atlantic States (exc. Great Lakes)	38,774	13,044	52,418	3,014	60,886.15	2,375,450	13,331	640,508	1,145,878	4,789,886	8,961,722	2,217,797	315,680	9,002,737
Gulf States	4,382	749	5,131	197	3,009.86	306,061	1,252	50,173	52,823	134,537	545,584	713,594	......	1,227,544
Pacific coast	11,613	6,190	16,803	64	5,463.42	546,450	5,547	404,696	467,238	1,330,000	2,748,383	4,792,538	......	7,484,750
Great Lakes	4,493	557	5,050	63	1,768.87	183,200	1,594	83,400	766,200	313,175	1,345,975	1,784,050	......	1,784,050
Alabama	545	90	635	24	317.20	14,685	119	10,216	7,000	6,400	38,200	74,325	......	119,275
Alaska	6,000	130	6,130	49	......	......	3,000	60,000	7,000	380,000	447,000	564,640	......	2,661,640
California	2,089	1,005	3,094	291	5,246.80	535,350	853	91,485	205,840	307,000	1,139,675	1,341,314	......	1,860,714
Connecticut	2,685	446	3,131	122	9,216.95	514,000	1,173	73,585	375,535	467,850	1,421,020	353,887	256,206	1,456,866
Delaware	1,662	317	1,979	69	1,226.00	51,000	889	33,227	70,324	113,060	268,231	309,029	941	907,845
Florida	2,294	196	2,490	124	2,152.97	272,646	1,066	28,508	89,927	65,087	406,117	426,527	......	643,227
Georgia	809	90	899	1	12.00	450	358	15,425	18,445	44,450	78,770	94,993	......	119,963
Illinois	295	35	330	3	209.73	8,500	101	2,000	11,900	61,000	83,400	60,100	......	60,100
Indiana	45	7	52	1	21.90	2,500	15	1,650	20,210	5,000	29,360	32,740	......	32,740
Louisiana	1,300	297	1,597	49	539.69	20,821	165	4,900	18,000	50,000	93,621	192,610	......	392,610
Maine	8,110	2,961	11,071	906	17,632.65	683,542	5,990	245,624	234,593	1,562,235	3,375,994	3,576,678	......	3,614,178
Maryland	15,873	10,135	26,008	1,450	43,500.00	1,760,000	2,825	186,448	297,145	4,108,850	6,342,443	479,388	11,851	5,221,716
Massachusetts	17,165	2,952	20,117	1,054	63,232.17	3,171,189	6,749	351,736	3,528,925	7,282,800	14,334,450	5,581,204	61,769	8,141,750
Michigan	1,000	181	1,181	98	914.42	98,500	454	10,345	272,920	60,900	442,665	716,170	......	716,170
Minnesota	30	5	35	1	33.59	5,000	10	900	3,760	500	10,160	5,200	......	5,200
Mississippi	110	76	186	23	1,019.06	61,500	58	4,600	1,600	2,600	8,800	12,640	......	22,540
New Hampshire	376	38	414	560	10,445.90	545,900	211	7,780	60,385	89,850	209,465	170,634	146,286	176,684
New Jersey	5,659	561	6,220	641	11,682.61	777,500	4,065	225,983	232,389	490,000	1,492,202	948,678	......	3,176,589
New York	5,650	1,616	7,266	95	1,457.90	39,000	3,441	289,885	390,000	1,171,900	2,829,685	1,689,357	1,114,158	4,380,565
North Carolina	4,729	545	5,274	9	359.51	38,400	2,714	123,175	225,436	118,950	506,561	785,287	......	845,995
Ohio	925	121	1,046	......	......	......	487	29,830	253,795	151,775	473,800	518,420	......	518,420
Oregon	2,795	4,040	6,835	11	321.99	10,500	1,386	246,500	245,750	639,000	1,131,350	2,776,724	......	2,781,024
Pennsylvania	511	41	552	92	2,502.77	191,850	156	13,272	40,638	55,500	119,810	132,550	......	320,050
Rhode Island	1,602	708	2,310	22	337.33	15,000	734	61,245	133,733	204,850	595,675	302,243	221,746	880,916
South Carolina	964	41	1,005	......	......	......	501	9,790	25,985	15,500	66,275	192,463	......	212,463
Texas	491	110	601	......	......	......	167	15,000	4,400	23,000	42,400	81,000	......	123,300
Virginia	16,051	2,813	18,864	1,446	15,578.93	671,000	6,618	292,720	560,763	489,636	1,914,119	602,259	503,329	3,124,444
Washington	729	15	744	7	216.62	11,100	334	6,510	8,648	4,000	30,358	109,960	......	181,373
Wisconsin	730	70	800	11	380.25	26,700	319	24,975	145,165	26,000	222,840	253,100	......	253,100
Total	101,664	29,742	131,426	6,605	206,297.83	9,357,282	44,804	2,465,333	8,145,361	17,987,413	37,965,849	22,405,018	2,116,787	43,044,053

the coast; and that the American fishermen shall also have the liberty forever to dry and cure fish in any of the unsettled bays, harbors, and creeks of the southern part of the coast of Newfoundland, hereinbefore described, and of the coast of Labrador. But as soon as the same, or any portion thereof, shall be settled it shall not be lawful for said fishermen to dry or cure fish at such portion so settled without previous agreement for such purpose with the inhabitants, proprietors, or possessors of the ground. And the United States hereby renounce forever any liberty heretofore enjoyed or claimed by the inhabitants thereof to take, dry, or cure fish on or within three marine miles of any of the coasts, bays, creeks, or harbors of His Britannic Majesty's dominions in America not included within the above-mentioned limits: Provided, however, that the American fishermen shall be admitted to enter such bays or harbors for the purpose of shelter, or repairing damages therein, of purchasing wood, and of obtaining water, and for no other purpose whatever; but they shall be under such restrictions as shall be necessary to prevent their taking, drying, or curing fish therein, or in any other manner whatever abusing the privileges hereby secured to them."

The surrender made by the American commissioners fully justified the action of Great Britain, and the peculiar provision limiting American fishermen to shelter, the repairing of damages, purchasing wood, obtaining water, and for no other purpose whatever, put the power into the hands of the local authorities to deny them all commercial privileges, and it is upon this unwritten but implied definition that much of the existing troubles depend. Under the provisions of the Treaty of 1818 American vessels were subjected to constant annoyance, until it culminated in the seizure of the schooner Washington in the Bay of Fundy for fishing within said bay ten miles from the shore. This seizure was the subject of a special message from President Tyler to Congress in 1845, and after a long correspondence between Mr. Everett, the American Minister, and Lord Aberdeen the matter was referred to Joshua Bates, of London, who decided against Great Britain. This decision did not affect the headland theory, as the mouth of the Bay of Fundy is contiguous to American territory; but, without relaxing anything of her original claim, Great Britain modified her instructions to her officials, making three miles from the shore line the boundary of jurisdiction. The negotiation of the reciprocity treaty between Lord Elgin and Mr. Marcy followed shortly after, and the Treaty of 1854 admitted British fish free to the American market, and the freedom of the British waters was allowed to American fishing vessels.

This treaty was terminated in 1866 by the act of the United States and Canada instituting a license system by which she received—

In 1866, from 454 vessels at 50 cts. per ton, $13,928
In 1867, " 295 " " $1.00 " " 15,714.92½
In 1868, " 61 " " 2.00 " " 5,824.75
In 1869, " 31 " " 2.00 " " 2,617.85½

While the license fee was 50 cents per ton, it was paid to be relieved from annoyance, and even $1 was paid, but when it was increased to $2 per ton it was more than the commercial privileges and the right to fish inshore was worth and the vessels could not afford to pay it. These were the seasons when mackerel were taken with the hook and line, before seines were generally used. After the repeal of the license act the provisions of the Treaty of 1818 were enforced to the letter, and in many cases beyond it, as it was publicly announced in the speeches in the Canadian parliament that the treaty was to be made aggressive until reciprocity was attained. This policy brought a strong message from President Grant, and nothing but the early arrangement of the Washington Treaty prevented retaliatory measures on the part of the United States. The Treaty of Washington, negotiated in 1871, and fully ratified in 1873, gave to American fishermen the right to fish inside of the three-mile limit without any enlargement of their commercial privileges; but it made provision for the Halifax Commission, which assembled at Halifax June 15, 1877. The object of this commission was to decide the relative value of the mutual concessions made by either government and name the amount to be paid in excess. The commission consisted of Sir Alexander T. Galt, on the part of Canada; Hon. Ensign H. Kelloge, on the part of the United States, and Maurice Delfosse, of Belgium, umpire. The British claim was for $14,880,000 for the privilege of fishing within three miles of the coast of the Dominion and Newfoundland. The claim of the United States was that the remission of duties on Canadian fish and oil with the privilege of free markets and free fishing on their coasts was more than an offset. It was apparent from the first that the British claim had a close relationship to the Geneva award of $15,000,000, allowed the United States for the depredations of the Alabama, and the award of $5,500,000 made by the commission in the light of subsequent history justifies the assertion. For the twelve years of the Washington Treaty 94,930 barrels of mackerel were taken within the three-mile limit, which sold in the United States for $778,582. This price includes the entire cost of production, salt, packing, barrels, inspection, and transportation. This is the entire benefit conferred by the treaty. The United States fishermen have paid the local British fishermen for herring bait-fish and ice over $2,000,000. The government of the United States has remitted to Canadian fishermen over $7,000,000 in duties, besides paying the $5,500,000 in gold as the award of the Halifax Commission.

The arbitrary and aggressive enforcement of the clause of the Treaty of 1818, by which American fishing vessels were not allowed to enter Canadian waters for any other purposes than to repair damages, gain shelter, or purchase wood and procure water, has been the cause of all the trouble in the vexed fishery question. Canadian vessels had the right to buy and sell without restriction in American ports, and American vessels claimed the same privilege in Canadian ports. On the expiration of the fishery provisions of the Treaty of Washington, July 1, 1885, a commission was appointed to consider the whole subject, and a new treaty prepared, its purpose being to fix the limit within which Americans could not fish in Canadian waters, and regulate the terms under which American vessels should be allowed within this limit, to refit, handle or sell fish in case of casualties, etc. This treaty, offered to the Senate in 1888, was rejected, there remaining only the power of the President to retaliate in case Canada should adopt new restrictive regulations.

A new aspect has been given to the fishery question by the Bering Sea fur-seal complication, fishing vessels from Canada having invaded the neighboring waters and killed seals without regard to American rights. Revenue vessels were stationed in those waters to prevent such invasion, and several of the Canadian craft taken. But new vessels were fitted out, which attacked the seals on their way to their rookeries. The fur-seals were fast disappearing under this indiscriminate onslaught, and an international question of great difficulty arose between the United States and Great Britain, in which Secretary Blaine and Lord Salisbury alike maintained their positions with great firmness. The main purpose of the United States is to save a valuable animal from extinction, and Great Britain has an industrial interest in its preservation.

The national necessity of maintaining the fisheries as a school and nursery for seamen is too apparent to be neglected. The foreign commerce of the country has largely passed from the hands of the American people, and the domestic coasting trade and the fisheries are the only marine resources on which to rely for a national marine militia, and it would now be suicidal to abandon national interest in the fisheries. The fisheries can furnish 60,000 men, the finest seamen in the world, for naval service. (F. J. B.)

FISH HAWK (*Pandion haliaëtus*), a species of the Falcon family widely spread in North America, and identical with the European osprey. It is distinguished from other birds of the family by the lack of aftershafts in its plumage, the peculiar conformation of its feet, the oiliness of its plumage, and its narrow, elongated form, all being adaptations to its habit of preying upon fish. The feet are large and strong, with naked tarsi, and very large claws. The wings are broad and powerful, and sharp-pointed at their extremities. In color, the under surface, with head and neck, is generally white, the upper surface a dark brown. The body is about 2 feet long, the wings more than 5 feet from tip to tip. The favorite haunt of the fish hawk is on the borders of the sea or of lakes, where it builds its huge nest of sticks and dried plants at the top of a dead or dying tree, the same nest being used year after year. When in search

Osprey or Fish Hawk.

of prey the bird soars in broad easy curves above the surface of the water. On seeing a fish the wings are closed, and it darts downwards, as if by its weight only. Sinking for an instant below the surface it quickly reappears, grasping its slippery prey in its strong talons with such firmness, that cases are known where fish hawks have been drowned by seizing too heavy a fish, from which they could not extricate their claws. Shaking the water from its plumage, the hawk soars aloft, often to be robbed of its prey by the bald eagle. This pirate dashes at the overladen bird, and forces it to drop its prey, which the eagle darts after and seizes ere it reaches the surface of the water. The hawks, however, do not always submit quietly to this robbery, but wage war on the eagle, and often drive him from their haunts by force of numbers and perseverance. The fish hawk is migratory on the Atlantic coast, reaching the Northern States about the end of March, and leaving for the South in late September.

FISK, WILBUR (1792-1839), an American educator, was born at Brattleboro', Vt., Aug. 31, 1792, being the son of Judge James Fisk (1762-1844). He graduated at Brown University in 1815. After some study of law, he entered the ministry of the Methodist Episcopal Church in 1818. He became presiding elder of the Vermont district in 1823, and delegate to the General Conference in 1824. Though eminent as a pulpit orator, he exerted himself especially in the cause of higher education. When the Wesleyan University was founded at Middletown, Conn., in 1830, Dr. Fisk was chosen its president. He declined the office of bishop in 1836. For the sake of his health he went to Italy in 1835, and to England in 1836. He died at Middletown, Conn., Feb. 22, 1839. He published *Notes of Travel in Europe* (1838); *The Calvinistic Controversy* (1837), and other controversial treatises.

FISKE, JOHN, an American author, was born at Hartford, Conn., March 30, 1842. He graduated from Harvard University in 1863, and studied law, but gave his chief attention to literature and philosophy. He lectured at Harvard University on philosophy 1869-71, and was afterwards assistant librarian until 1879. He has since been one of the overseers of the university, and has lectured in many places on history and philosophy. His publications include *Tobacco and Alcohol* (1868); *Myths and Mythmakers* (1872); *Outlines of Cosmic Philosophy* (1874); *The Unseen World* (1876); *Darwinism and other Essays* (1879); *Excursions of an Evolutionist* (1883); *The Destiny of Man* (1884); *The Idea of God* (1884); *American Political Ideas* (1885). Mr. Fiske is a profound thinker and a clear and brilliant writer. While a positivist in philosophy, he defends theism with marked ability. His discussions of American history are valuable contributions to the philosophy of history.

FITCH, ASA (1809-1879), an American entomologist, was born at Fitch's Point, Washington co., N. Y., Feb. 24, 1809. He was educated at Rensselaer Polytechnic Institute and afterwards studied medicine in New York and Albany. He was assistant professor of natural history in an expedition to Lake Erie in 1830. In 1831 he began the practice of medicine at Fort Miller, N. Y., removed to Stillwater in 1832, and returned to his native place in 1838. He then engaged in agriculture, and devoted much time to entomology, especially in its economic aspects. He contributed to Dr. Emmons' *American Quarterly Journal of Agriculture and Science* papers on the wheat midge, Hessian fly, etc. In 1854 he was made State entomologist, and his annual reports printed in the *Transactions of the State Agricultural Society* from 1854 to 1870 are his most valuable contributions to science. He died April 18, 1879.

FITCHBURG, a city of Massachusetts, half-shire of Worcester county, is 50 miles W. of Boston. The north branch of the Nashua River runs through the city, and there are 10 bridges in the vicinity, three railroads—Fitchburg, Cheshire, and Old Colony—centre in the town. The principal buildings are the courthouse, Wallace Library, and art building. There are 6 hotels, 4 national banks, 3 other banks, 1 daily and 2 weekly newspapers, 11 churches, a high school, and 18 other schools. The industrial works comprise iron- and brass-foundries, paper-, woollen-, and cotton-mills, manufactories of shoes, saws, rock-drills, etc. The city is lighted with gas and has water-works. Its property is valued at $11,000,000, and there is a net debt of $640,000. The town was settled in 1730, and incorporated in 1764, when it was set off from Lunenburg. Rollstone Hill, 300 feet high, with several granite quarries, is in the most thickly settled part of the city. On top of the hill is a large boulder weighing 100 tons, and of different formation from any rock within 30 miles. Besides the city proper, Fitchburg includes 5 villages. Its population in 1870 was 11,260; in 1880, 12,429; and in 1890, 22,007.

FIVE FORKS, a place in Dinwiddie co., Va., noted for a battle fought April 1, 1865, between the Union army under Gen. P. H. Sheridan, and part of Gen. Lee's army. Here three roads met, the White Oak, Ford's, and the Dinwiddie C. H. road. As the Southside Railroad could be reached by Ford's Road, Gen. Lee was anxious in prospect of leaving Richmond to retain this point, though it was nearly five miles from his main line. Gen. Sheridan had first attempted to take it on March 30, but had been driven back. Early on April 1 he renewed the attempt with about 13,000 men, first driving the Confederates into their works, then making a strong feint on his right, while the main attack by the Fifth corps under Gen. G. K. Warren was to be made on the left. The plan was carried out with great precision, but Gen. Sheridan, thinking that Warren had not been sufficiently prompt in his movements, removed him from command on the next day. The pursuit had been continued till dark, and 5000 prisoners were taken. The most important result of the battle was the evacuation of Petersburg April 2, followed closely by that of Richmond. The removal of Gen. Warren was afterwards the subject of a court of inquiry, and Gen. Sheridan's action was sustained as within his discretion. But many military critics exonerate Gen. Warren from any blame.

FLAG, the name given to several distinct endogenous plants, native to wet or marshy situations. It is mainly applied to members of the iris family, of which *Iris versicolor*, the large blue flag, is a plant with a stout stem, sword-shaped leaves, and large, showy flowers, of blue color, variegated with green, yellow, and white at base, and veined with purple. It is common in wet places, flowering in May and June. *I. Virginica*, the slender blue flag, has a slender stem with narrow leaves, and flowers much smaller than the preceding. It occurs in marshes from Maine to Virginia and southward, flowering in June. *I. cuprea* is a reddish-brown species, resembling *I. versicolor*, found in Illinois and southward. There are three species which grow only about six inches high, and bear blue flowers: *I. verna* and *I. cristata* in Virginia and southward, and *I. lacustris* on the great lakes. The violet-scented orris root of the shops is the dried rhizome of several European species. The sweet flag (*Acorus calamus*) is a plant of a different family, common to the United States, Europe, and Asia. It is the only native aromatic plant of northern climates, its creeping stem or rhizome having a warmly pungent taste. It is found on the borders of rivers and swamps, its stem from two to three feet high, the flowers densely crowded on a spadix, enclosed in a long, leaf-like spathe. The rhizome is used in the arts by perfumers and tanners, and is sometimes employed in medicine as a mild tonic and aromatic stimulant. The name flag is also given to certain flexible algæ, from their flag-like motion when stirred by the water.

FLAG, THE AMERICAN. The flags used by the American colonies prior to their separation from the mother country would naturally be those of England, though such does not appear to have been invariably the case. The red cross of St. George was without doubt hoisted over the Mayflower in 1620. Belonging to South Britain she may have displayed the king's colors from her main top, and a St. George's cross at the fore, as required by King James' proclamation of 1606. In November, 1634, we learn from the records of Massachusetts, complaint was entered "that the ensign at Salem had been defaced by cutting out one part of the red cross." When it was shown that "the mutilation complained of was done, not from disloyalty to the flag, but from an entire conscientious conviction that it was idolatrous to allow it to remain," the opinion of the ministers was asked, but they could not agree. The whole case was referred to the next general court, and the commissioners for military affairs in the meantime ordered that all ensigns should be laid aside. In the interim a flag having for an emblem the red and white roses was proposed, but in December, 1635, the commissioners appointed colors for every company, leaving out the cross, and appointing that the king's arms should be put into them. In 1643 the colonies of Plymouth, Massachusetts, and Connecticut were united in a league called "The United Colonies of New England." This union, the first on this continent, was declared to be perpetual, but no common flag was adopted until 1686, when Governor Andros received one from the king. This flag, as appears by a drawing of it in the British State-paper office, was the cross of St. George, borne on a white field occupying the whole flag, the centre of the cross emblazoned with a gilt crown over the cypher of the sovereign, James I. It was soon seen that a special flag to designate the merchant ships of the American colonies to distinguish them from the king's ships was desirable. An order was issued from the admiralty office, July 29, 1701, that merchant ships "wear no other Jack than that hereafter mentioned, viz., that worn by his majesty's ships, with the distinction of a white escutcheon in the middle thereof, and that said mark of distinction may extend itself to one-half the depth of the Jack, and on third part of the fly thereof according to the sample (drawing) hereunto annexed." The flag must have been worn by the American colonial vessels for many years, though we have no more than the official mention of it, and it is never depicted in the engravings of the time. A crimson

Colonial Flag.
Ordered for Merchant Service (1701).

flag, the Jack of which was a red St. George's cross on a white field, with sometimes a tree, at other times a globe, in the upper corner of the canton next the staff, was the ensign most generally in use in New England; occasionally the field or fly of the flag was blue. In a little book entitled *The Present State of the Universe* (London, 1704) there is a picture of a New England ensign with a tree in the canton. In a *Treatise on the Dominion and Laws of the Sea*, by Alex. Justice (London, 1705), there is a folding plate of national flags—one of which is a New England flag. It is difficult to say whether the device in the canton is a globe or a tree. Another work, 1701, has a representation of this New England ensign, and in still another there is a dark blue New England ensign with a white canton and red cross, having a globe in the upper corner of the latter. A French work on flags (La Haye, 1737) depicts and describes a *Pavillon de Nouvelle Angleterre en Amerique* "as *azure* on a canton *argent* quartered with the red cross of St. George, having a globe in the first quarter," in allusion to America, commonly called the New World. The departure from the authorised English flag and assuming standards of their own evinces a feeling of independence among the colonies. The absence of a desire for separation is evident in the allegiance implied by representing on them the colors of England, or, when from tenderness of conscience they were left out, the substitution of the arms of the king. In the newspapers for ten years preceding the commencement of our revolutionary struggle, liberty poles and trees, and Liberty and Union flags of various devices are frequently mentioned. These flags were party banners rather than colonial ensigns. On most of them the word "*Liberty*" was conspicuous. In the earliest days of the revolution each State seems to have set up its own banner. A green pine-tree was the favorite emblem of Massachusetts.

There were probably no colors worn by the handful of Americans hastily called together at the battle of Lexington, or on the night march to Bunker Hill and into the battle the next morning, though tradition seems to assert the contrary. Trumbull in his celebrated picture of that battle, now in the Capitol at Washington, has represented a red flag having a white canton and red cross, and a green pine-tree. On July 18, a month after the battle, Putnam assembled his division on Prospect Hill and unfurled the scarlet standard of the Third Connecticut regiment just received, bearing on one side the Connecticut motto, "*Qui transtulit sustinet*," and on the other the Massachusetts motto, "*An appeal to Heaven.*" The armed ships of New York had a black beaver on a white field for their flag. Those of Massachusetts and Pennsylvania carried a white flag on which was painted a pine-tree and the motto, "*An appeal to Heaven.*" In January, 1776, the American vessel Franklin, Capt. Samuel Tucker, wore the pine-tree flag. The first American flag displayed in the South was hoisted by Col. Moultrie on Fort Sullivan, afterwards named Moultrie for its gallant defender. It was a large blue flag with a white or silver crescent in the dexter corner, and the word *Liberty* blazoned across it. John Jay in a letter dated July, 1776, expressly states Congress had made no order at that date "concerning Continental colors, and that captains of armed vessels had followed their own fancies."

Bunker Hill Flag.
In Trumbull's picture.

The first legislation of Congress on the subject of a federal navy was October, 1775. Notwithstanding the equipment of this fleet the necessity of a common national flag seems not to have been thought of until Dr. Franklin, Mr. Lynch, and Mr. Harrison were appointed to consider the subject and assembled at Cambridge. The result of their conference was the retention of the Union Jack, representing the yet recognized sovereignty of England, but coupled to 13 stripes alternate red and white, emblematic of the Union of the 13 colonies against its tyranny and oppression, in place of the loyal red ensign. This new striped flag was first hoisted Jan. 2, 1776, over the camp at Cambridge and was saluted with 13 guns and 13 cheers. The only contemporary drawing of this flag is in a picture of the schooner Royal Savage, of Arnold's Lake Champlain fleet, found among the papers of Gen. Schuyler. The Massachusetts council passed a resolution that the State colors should be "a white flag with a green pine-tree and the inscription '*An appeal to Heaven.*'" A portrait of "Commodore Hopkins, commander-in-chief of the American fleet, published Aug. 22, 1776, by Thomas Hart, London," has represented on the ships in the background, on one side a white flag with green tree and over it "Liberty tree," underneath the motto "*An appeal to God;*" at his other

New England Flag (1737).

Flag of Massachusetts State Cruisers.

Pine-Tree Flag.
From a map published in Paris, 1776.

FLAG.

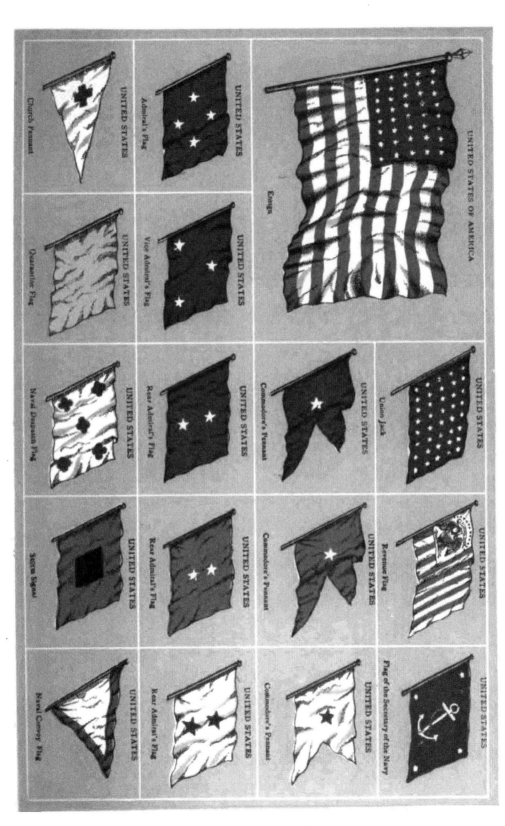

FLAG. PLATE XXII.

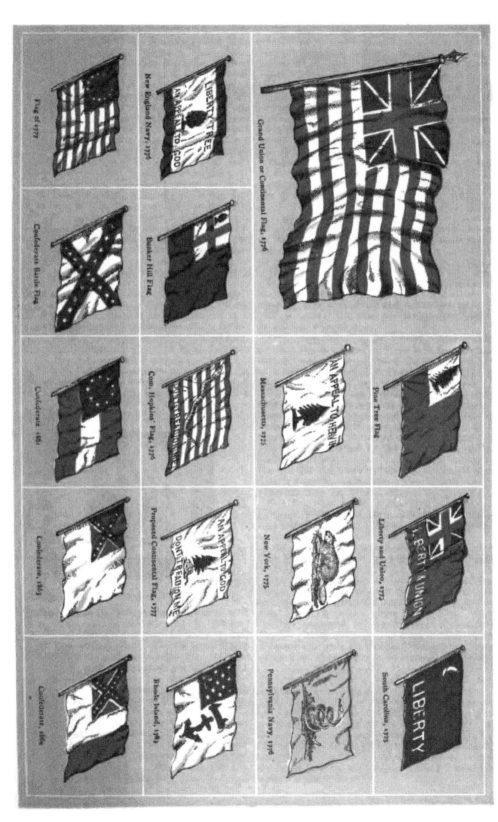

nor does it say whether the stripes are to be vertical or horizontal, though from the beginning they have invariably been horizontally placed. Paul Jones hoisted on the Serapis and Landais on the Alliance at the Texel in 1779, ensigns in which the stars had *eight* points, and the stripes of the flag of the Serapis were blue, red, and white, as appears from the official description preserved in the records of that place. As the arms of Washington are blazoned with stars and stripes it has been suggested that the design of our flag may have originated in a compliment to him, but Washington has not in his correspondence or writings mentioned any connection of his arms with our flag, as he would have been likely to do had there been any. The descendants of Mrs. Elizabeth, widow of John Ross, of Philadelphia, claim that she made the first pattern flag, and point to the house, still standing, No. 239 Arch street, as the place where it was made, and there is reasonable ground for the statement. Mrs. Ross was a flag-maker in Philadelphia, probably the only one; and, as appears by a bill in the *Pennsylvania Archives*, dated May 29, 1777, received 14*l*. 12*s*. 2*d*. for making ship's colors for the State navy of Pennsylvania.

The famous Paul Jones, commanding the Ranger, wrote to the naval committee of Congress, on Feb. 22, 1778: "I am happy to have it in my power to congratulate you on having seen the American flag, for the first time, recognized in the fullest and completest manner by the flag of France. The wind being contrary and blowing hard it was after sunset (on Feb. 13) before the Ranger was near enough to salute the La Motte Piquet with *thirteen* guns, which he returned with *nine*. However, to put the matter beyond a

Philadelphia City Troop—First stripes.

doubt I did not suffer the Independence to salute until the next morning, when I sent word to the admiral that I would sail through his fleet in the brig, and would salute him in open day. He was exceedingly pleasant, and returned the compliment also with nine guns." Jones had at first demanded gun for gun, but afterwards waived this point, when assured that the Admiral of Holland, then a republic, was saluted with nine guns, and the senior officer of the American republic was thus treated with the same respect.

Jones also reported in his letter to the commissioners that in the action between the Ranger and Drake fought on April 24, 1778, when the latter hoisted English colors "the *American stars* were displayed on board the Ranger." This is the first recorded naval action under the new flag.

The first military incident connected with the stars and stripes belongs to Fort Stanwix, afterwards known as Fort Schuyler, and now the site of the town of Rome, N. Y., Aug. 3, 1778. When the enemy appeared before it the garrison was without a flag, but their patriotism and ingenuity soon supplied one. Sheets were cut up to form the white stripes, bits of scarlet cloth were joined for the red, and the blue ground for the stars was composed of a camlet cloak furnished by Capt. Abraham Swartwout. Before sunset this curious mosaic standard was floating over one of the bastions.

Beyond a doubt the stars and stripes were unfurled at the battle of Brandywine, Sept. 11, 1777, and at Germantown the 4th of Oct., and witnessed the surrender of Burgoyne at Saratoga, Oct. 17, 1777, and the sight of the new constellation helped to cheer the patriots of the army amid their suffering around the camp-fires at Valley Forge. They waved triumphant at Yorktown, Sept. 19, 1781, looked down upon the evacuation of New York, Nov. 25, 1783, and shared in all the glories of the latter days of the revolution.

On Jan. 28, 1778, they waved for the first time over a foreign fortress, when Capt. John Rathburne, of the sloop-of-war Providence, landed at night 25 men on the island of New Providence and took possession of Fort Nassau, hoisted the stars and stripes over it, and held possession of it two days.

The independence of the United States of America having been recognized by Great Britain, the stars and stripes became henceforward the recognized symbol of a new nation, and their history is an exhibit of its military, naval, civil, and commercial progress.

The honor of having been first to hoist the stars and stripes in a British port has been claimed for several vessels, but must be assigned to the ship Bedford of Nantucket, which arrived at the Downs, Feb. 3, 1783, passed Gravesend the same day, and reported at the London custom house on the 6th. The honor of displaying our flag first in England must be awarded to Copley, the American painter, who, after listening to King's speech, recognizing the United States of America, Dec. 5, 1782, returned to his studio, and added to a ship in the background of a portrait of Elkanah Watson the stars and stripes. The ship Empress of China, of 360 tons, was the first vessel to carry the flag into the Chinese Sea. The ship Franklin, of Salem, Mass., was the first to carry it to Japan, 1798-99. The first to carry it around the world was the ship Columbia, Capt. Gray, 1789-90.

In 1794, in consequence of the admission of the new States, Vermont (1791) and Kentucky (1792), an act was passed increasing the stars and stripes on our flag from 13 to 15, to take effect May 1, 1795. This was the flag presented to the National Convention of France. It was worn by our ships in 1798-99 during the quasi war with France, and throughout the war of 1812-14, in all our battles, whether by land or sea, and was hoisted by Commodore Porter over Nookahiva or Madison Island, in the South Pacific, when he took possession of that island, Nov. 19, 1813.

The revenue flag of the United States was created by an act of Congress, March 2, 1799, which directed the president to prescribe an ensign and pennant for the revenue cutters and boats. Accordingly on Aug. 1 it was ordered that the ensign should consist of *sixteen* perpendicular stripes, alternate red and white, and the union bear the arms of the United States in dark blue on a white field.

The stripes represent the number of States in the Union, when this flag was prescribed, and the ensign has undergone no change since. In 1871 thirteen blue stars, in a white field, were substituted for the eagle in the union of the revenue pennant. Whenever revenue vessels are employed beyond our coast, or in conjunction with the navy, they are allowed to wear the national ensign.

On April 27, 1805, Lieut. O. Bannon of the marines hoisted over the Tripolitan fortress of Derne the first American flag planted upon a fortress of the Old World.

The flag of Fort McHenry, whose "broad stripes and bright stars" inspired Francis Scott Key to write our national song, "The Star-Spangled Banner," still exists in a tolerable state of preservation, and is in the possession of Mr. Eben Appleton, of Yonkers, N. Y., a grandson of Colonel Armstead, the gallant defender of Fort McHenry. It is a flag of 15 stars and 15 stripes, the broad stripes being each 2 feet wide, and its bright stars 2 feet from point to point. The flag is 30 feet wide, and was originally beyond doubt 40 feet long, but in its present curtailed dimensions is only 32 feet long. The admission of the new States of Tennessee, Ohio, Louisiana, and Indiana made a change in the flag desirable. Accordingly, on the admission of Indiana in 1816, it was resolved "that a committee be appointed to inquire into the expediency of altering the flag of the United States." While this committee had the matter under consideration, Capt. S. C. Reid, famous for his defence of the privateer General Armstrong in Fayal Roads, was requested to make a design for our flag, which would represent the increase of States without destroying its distinctive character. Capt. Reid at once recommended that the stripes be reduced to the original *thirteen*, and that the stars should be increased to the number of States, and formed into one great star, whose brilliancy should represent their Union; also that a star should be added to this constellation for every new State admitted. Accordingly, after considerable debate, it was enacted by Congress

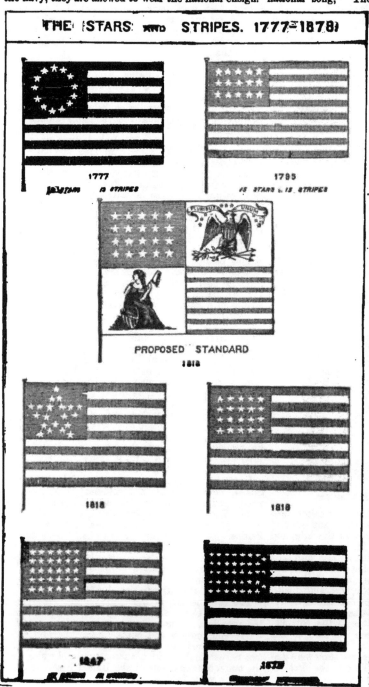

"That from and after the fourth day of July next the flag of the United States be thirteen *horizontal stripes*, alternate red and white; that the union have twenty stars, white, in a blue field."

And "That on the admission of every new State to the Union one star be added to the union of the flag, and that such addition shall take effect on the fourth of July next succeeding such admission."

This act was approved April 4, 1818. It prescribes, for the first time, that the stripes shall be horizontal, but does not designate the number of points the stars shall have, or how they must be placed in the union. Custom, however, has settled upon the stars being five-pointed, but the placing of the stars, whether in the irregular form of a constellation—as seems to have been the intent of the resolution of 1777, establishing the flag —or in a circle significant of an endless Union, or formed into one bright star, or arranged in parallel lines, or in any fanciful shape is still left a matter of choice and taste. The first flag flung to the breeze, under the new law, was made by Mrs. Reid, the wife of its gallant designer, and had the stars arranged as one great star. It was hoisted over the United States House of Representatives, April 14, 1818, though the law was not to go into effect until the 4th of July. The flags of the military department of our government have mostly had the stars similarly arranged. By direction of the President, orders were issued, May 18, 1818, and reiterated in September that the stars in "the flag to be worn by the vessels of the United States, and at our naval stations," should be arranged in parallel lines, and that order has never been rescinded. The new flag was first hoisted and saluted at our naval stations on the 18th of September, 1818.

The first State to add a star to the constellation of the new flag was Illinois, admitted Dec. 3, 1818. The original constellation has increased from 13 to 44; should this increase of States continue, as is inevitable, some new symbol will have to be adopted, as the stars of the union have already dropped from those of the first magnitude, and become indistinct and confusing.

The Flag of Fort McHenry.

WORKS ON THE FLAG.—*The History of the National Flag of the United States*. By Schuyler Hamilton, U. S. A. (Phila., 1853. Pp. 115.)
The History of Our Flag. By Ferdinand L. Sarmiento. (Phila., 1864. Pp. 96.)
Our Flag—Origin and Progress of the Flag of the United States. With an introductory account of the flags of ancient and modern nations. By George Henry Preble, U. S. N. (Albany, 1872. Pp. 535.)
Our National Flag—Its History in a Century. By General Schuyler Hamilton. (In the American Magazine of History, July, 1877.)
The History of the First United States Flag and the Patriotism of Betsey Ross. By Colonel J. Franklin Reigart. (Harrisburg, 1878. Pp. 25.) A worthless book.
History of the Flag of the United States of America and of the Naval and Yacht Club Signals, Seals, Arms, and Principal National Songs of the United States. By George Henry Preble, Rear Admiral U. S. N. Revised edition. (Boston, 1880. Pp. 814.) Third revised edition of the same illustrated with plates, engravings, maps, and autographs. (Boston, 1882.)

(G. H. P.)

FLAGET, BENEDICT JOSEPH (1763–1850), an American prelate, was born at Contournat, France, Nov. 7, 1763. He was educated at the College of Billon and the University of Clermont, and spent three years in theological study at Issy. After being ordained priest in 1789, he was made professor of dogmatic in the seminary at Nantes. On the outbreak of the French Revolution he emigrated to America, arriving at Baltimore in March, 1792. Bishop Carroll assigned him to the mission at Vincennes, Ind., which he reached on Christmas day. After more than two years of arduous labor he was recalled to become professor in Georgetown College. He was afterwards transferred to St. Mary's College, Baltimore. On Nov. 4, 1810, he was consecrated bishop of Bardstown, Ky., and arrived at that place June 9, 1811, making his first abode in a log-cabin. There being only seven priests in the vast diocese, Bishop Flaget had to make long journeys to supply the wants of his people. In 1819 the increase of the Roman Catholic population had made a coadjutor necessary, and Father David was appointed. In 1822 the diocese of Cincinnati was formed, Right Rev. E. D. Fenwick being its first bishop. In September, 1828, Bishop Flaget attended the first provincial council at Baltimore. In 1834 the diocese of Vincennes was formed, Dr. G. Bruté being the first bishop. Within twenty-five years Bishop Flaget established four colleges, three religious sisterhoods, a brotherhood, two religious orders, an orphan asylum, an infirmary, and eleven academies. Going to Europe in 1835, he spent four years chiefly in France. In 1841 his episcopal see was changed to Louisville, and after the death of his first coadjutor he was able, in September, 1848, to consecrate as second Right Rev. M. J. Spalding, this being the last official act of his career. However, he witnessed the laying of the corner-stone of the Louisville Cathedral, Aug. 19, 1849. He died Feb. 11, 1850.

FLAGG, GEORGE WHITING, an American artist, was born at New Haven, Conn., June 26, 1816. He spent his boyhood in Charleston and early evinced a love of art. He studied under the care of his uncle, Washington Allston, in Boston, and afterwards spent three years in further study in Europe. He resided in London for six years, devoting himself chiefly to portrait painting. After his return to New Haven he painted some historical scenes, among which are Landing of the Pilgrims, Landing of the Atlantic

Cable, Washington Receiving his Mother's Blessing, Columbus and the Egg.

FLAGG, JARED BRADLEY, an American artist and clergyman, was born at New Haven, Conn., June 16, 1820. He is a brother of G. W. Flagg, with whom he studied. In 1836 he exhibited at the National Academy a portrait of his father. He settled at Hartford, where he painted portraits, but in 1849 removed to New York. He afterwards studied theology, and in 1854 was ordained in the Episcopal Church. He has had charge of several churches, but has still given time to art. His portrait of Commodore Vanderbilt was at the Centennial Exhibition in Philadelphia.

FLAGG, WILSON (1805-1884), an American naturalist, was born at Beverly, Mass., Nov. 5, 1805. He was educated at Phillips Academy, Andover, and Harvard College, but did not graduate. He contributed to the *Atlantic Monthly* and other periodicals. His publications include *Studies in the Field and Forest* (1856); *Woods and Byways of New England* (1872); *Birds and Seasons of New England* (1874). In 1881 the latter two were enlarged and republished under the titles *Halcyon Days*, *A Year with the Birds*, and *A Year with the Trees*. Mr. Flagg was an ardent lover of nature, a careful observer, and enthusiastic writer. He died at North Cambridge, Mass., May 6, 1884.

FLAGSTONE, thin layers of stone, cut or split, much used in American cities for sidewalks. A stone is usually employed for this purpose that splits naturally into layers of 2 to 4 inches thickness and smooth enough to need little surface-dressing. They are used in sizes of from 10 to 100 or more square feet of area. Laminated sandstones are ordinarily chosen, but mica slate, hornblende slate, or granite are frequently employed. Limestone sometimes splits well, but becomes slippery by wear. The harder veins of slate quarries are also used, but are not very durable. The fine-grained sandstone used in New York, known as *bluestone*, is one of the best of flagstones. Recently an artificial stone, made of asphalt and other materials, has come into common use and bids fair to supplant the employment of the natural stone for this purpose.

FLAMINGO, the common name of a remarkable genus of birds (*Phœnicopterus*), comprising about seven tropical species, of which four are American. The Red flamingo (*P. ruber*) is the only one that visits the United States, it being found in Florida and on the borders of the Gulf States. These birds are remarkable not only for their brilliant scarlet color, but for their extreme length of neck and legs, and the peculiar form of the bill, which is used with the upper mandible turned downwards in feeding. They present external features of both the wading and the swimming birds, and have been placed in both groups, but their organization most nearly approaches that of the duck tribe. The Red flamingo stands nearly 5 feet high, the length of the body being about 4 feet, and spread of wings 5 feet. It weighs from 6 to 8 pounds. It seeks its food in the mud of river borders, where the birds stand in long lines, with posted sentinels, who give warning of danger by a trumpet-like note. The nest is made in irregular heaps of mud, 2 or 3 feet high, scratched up in the salt ponds, and entirely surrounded by water. Two eggs are usually laid, and the young, whose color is nearly white, are said to take to the water as soon as they are hatched. The hen's strange habit of standing while hatching her eggs is shown in the accompanying cut.

See Vol. IX.
p. 249 Am.
ed. (p. 286
Edin. ed.).

Flamingoes on their nests.

FLAMMARION, CAMILLE, a French astronomer, was born at Montigny-le-Roi, Feb. 25, 1842. After entering on a course of theological study he turned his attention to astronomy, and became an assistant in the Observatory at Paris. Retiring in 1865, he devoted himself to the popularization of science in newspapers and books. A mystical vein in some of his writings has helped their popularity. Among the principal publications are: *La Pluralité des mondes habités* (1862); *Les mondes imaginaires et les mondes réels* (1864); *Les Merveilles célestes* (1865); *Histoire du ciel* (1867); *L'Atmosphere* (1871). He made many balloon ascensions for the study of aerial phenomena, as described in his *Voyages aériens* (1868).

FLANDERS, HENRY, an American lawyer and author, was born at Plainfield, N. H. He is a prominent lawyer of Philadelphia. He has published treatises on *Maritime Law* (1852), *Law of Shipping* (1853), *Principles of Insurance* (1871), and other legal topics. He is also the author of the *Lives and Times of the Chief Justices of the United States* (2 vols., 1855-58), a standard work; and of *Memoirs of Cumberland* (1856).

FLATHEAD INDIANS, a popular name for the Selish, or Hopilpo, a tribe of North American Indians inhabiting the middle valley of the Columbia, and at present occupying mainly a reservation on the Jocko River, and on the Northern Pacific Railroad, in the north-west part of Montana. A considerable number of Flatheads have refused to go upon this reservation, but remain in their old home in Bitter Root Valley, surrounded by whites. The Selish proper are all Catholics, and are among the best and most intelligent of the native North American peoples. They do not flatten the heads of their children, and appear never to have done so; the name Flathead being at first applied to them by mistake. They are the representative tribe of the great Selish family of the Columbia Valley. On the Flathead reserve are found many Kootenai Indians and the Pend d' Oreilles (Kalispel or Kalispelm Indians), both speaking Selish dialects. Other tribes of the Selish stock are the Kwantlum and Haitlin, of British Columbia; the Shushwaps, Okanagans, Spokanes, the numerous small Nesqually tribes of Puget Sound, and the Chehalis of the Pacific coast. Father G. Mengarini's *Selish Grammar* (1861), his MS. dictionary, and the Jesuit fathers' *Kalispel Dictionary* (1879), are the best sources of information regarding the very difficult languages of this group of tribes. See also George Gibbs' vocabularies of the Lummi and Clallam languages, which are regarded as of the Selish stock, though another so-called Clallam language is assigned to the Haidah group.

The practice of flattening the heads of infants was once widely prevalent among American Indians. The ancient Mexicans and Peruvians, the Caribs, the Natches, the Chickasaws, Choctaws, and other tribes formerly compressed the heads of children either sidewise or on the forehead. Latterly the custom has prevailed among the Klicketals (Sahaptin or Nez Percé stock), and several of the Chinook or fish-eating tribes of the Lower Columbia Valley. The infant's head was compressed either by tying a flat piece of wood or a bunch of grass across the forehead. The Choctaws used a sand-bag for the same purpose. The practice is said not to have interfered with the health or intelligence of children upon whom it was practised; and the resulting deformity diminished to a greater or less degree, as adult life was approached.

FLAX, the name given to both the plant and the fibre of *Linum usitatissimum*, the basis of the linen manufacture, and of the flax-seed and the linseed-oil industries. The plant grows from two to over three feet in height, and bears small lanceolate leaves and bright blue flowers, which yield seed vessels containing each ten seeds. It has been very long cultivated for industrial purposes, and is now widely grown in Europe, Asia, and America, being congenial to a considerable diversity of soil and climate. For profitable cultivation it needs a good, deep soil, well drained and fertilized,

See Vol. IX. p. 256 Am. ed. (p. 262 Edin. ed.).

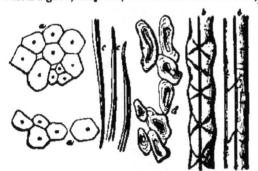

a Sections of the fibres. *b* Fibres seen longitudinally. *c* Ends of fibres. *d* Sections of fibres nearer butt of the plant.
Fibres of Flax (*Linum Usitatissimum*).
Magnified 275 times.

though too much manure gives coarseness to the fibre. The seeds are sown broadcast during April or May, and much more thickly for a fibre than for a seed crop. The after culture is chiefly confined to weeding. If grown for fibre the plant is pulled

the seeds begin to ripen; if for seed, when the stem is growing yellow and the leaves begin to fall. The after preparation consists in a process of *rippling*, with a sort of iron comb, to secure the seed; *rething*, or steeping in water, to produce fermentation and separate the fibre; breaking and *scutching*, to remove all woody particles; and *heckling*, by which the fibre is combed out, straightened, and the longer threads or *line* separated from the woolly mass of *tow*.

The use of flax fibre in linen-weaving is but one of the important results of flax cultivation. The seed is highly nutritive, and is beneficial to every species of animal. Given to calves in the form of a jelly, mixed with other substances, it is an excellent substitute for milk. It also yields about 22 per cent. of the highly valuable linseed oil, while the residue of the pressed seed is a valuable food for cattle, used alone or mixed with fodder. It is known as linseed meal or oil-cake. There is an enormous demand for both the fibre and the oil, yet of late years flax-culture has been neglected in America. In the early years of this country flax was a standard American farm-product, and continued so till the cotton-culture rose into importance. The fibre was prepared on the farm, and spun into cloth by the women of the family. But flax-culture was attended with much unpleasant labor, while its profits were small, and less attention has been paid to it since cotton goods have come largely into use. Recently, however, this labor has been much reduced. The old method was to pull the plants by hand. Now, reapers, or flax-pulling machines, have come into use. At present, however, flax is mainly grown in this country for seed, and its cultivation for fibre has greatly decreased. In 1870 the product of fibre amounted to 27,133,034 lbs., of which nearly 18,000,000 lbs. were produced in Ohio; and of seed 1,730,444 bushels, more than one-third of which came from Ohio. In 1880 a marked change is observable, the seed product being 7,170,951 bushels, and the fibre being reduced to 1,565,546 lbs. The centres of cultivation have also changed, the most important seed-raising States in 1880 being Illinois, Iowa, and Indiana, while New York is credited with more than one-half of the total product of fibre.

FLEA, a genus of wingless insects now ordinarily classed in the family *Diptera*, though it has been difficult to fix their true relations. They live by sucking the blood of various animals, on which they are, to a certain extent, parasitic. Several of our domestic animals are infested by species peculiar to themselves, those of the cat and dog, for instance, being, fortunately, very little disposed to attack man. All the species are very similar to the common *Pulex irritans*, which is found in all parts of the world, and is in some of the warmer countries an intolerable nuisance. Several of the European countries, such as Turkey and Italy, are the homes of countless myriads of fleas, as travellers find to their cost. The northern parts of the United States are not seriously affected by them in any place where reasonable cleanliness prevails. During the Centennial Exhibition, for instance, part of the Italian

See Vol. IX. p. 262 Am. ed. (p. 300 Edin. ed.).

1. Natural Size. 2. Magnified.
The Common Flea.

exhibit was a plentiful importation of fleas, which spread over Philadelphia, and proved a serious annoyance for a year or two. Yet they quickly vanished before careful housekeeping. Fleas have long been noted for their remarkable muscular powers, being able to leap to an astonishing distance, and to thirty-six times their own height. Their strength has been taken advantage of in exhibitions of so-called educated fleas, in which the only education is in the effort of the animal to escape from its tormentors. The most annoying of American species is the tropical *Pulex penetrans*, called by the natives chigoe, jigger, bicho, chique, or pique. The female of this species penetrates the feet, particularly beside the nails, where it becomes distended with eggs to the size of a pea, causing distressing and often dangerous sores.

FLEABANE, the common name given to various herbs belonging to the order *Compositæ*, and especially to the genus *Erigeron*, from their supposed power to drive away fleas. Several American species bear this common name, as *E. Philadelphicum*, *E. heterophyllum*, *E. annum*, and *E. strigosum*, the latter two species being known as the daisy fleabane. In England two allied genera, *Pulicaria* and *Conyza*, are known as fleabanes. The above-named species of *Erigeron* are all worthless weeds, found in pastures and waste places throughout the United States. They are perennial herbs, with alternate leaves, stems from two to four feet high, the flower with yellow disk, and white or purplish rays, narrow and numerous. The *Compositæ* most deadly to insects are certain species of *Pyrethrum*, of Asia and Europe. The leaves of these are used in the Persian insect powder.

FLETCHER, JOHN (JOHN WILLIAM DE LA FLECHERE) (1729-1785), a clergyman of the Church of England and prominent coadjutor of the Wesleys, was born in Nyon, Switzerland, Sept. 12, 1729. He was educated at the University of Geneva, and, contrary to the wishes of his parents, chose for himself the military profession. At the age of twenty he went to Lisbon and accepted a captain's commission in the army of Portugal, he and his company being assigned to a man-of-war then about to sail for Brazil. But an accident prevented his sailing, and when he procured a commission in the army of Holland his plans for a military career were again thwarted. At the age of twenty-three he went to London for the purpose of perfecting his knowledge of the English language. While there he engaged as tutor in the family of Thomas Hill, a member of Parliament from Shropshire. From Mrs. Hill he first heard of the Methodists, and seeking them out he joined the society. In 1757 he was ordained in the English church at Whitehall, and in 1760 settled at Madeley. Here he applied himself to the work of his ministry with self-consuming zeal, preaching in different parts of the parish, and employing many hours of the night in study and prayer. Failing in health, in 1769 he visited France, Switzerland, and Italy. On his returning to England he was chosen to take the direction of a school established by the countess of Huntingdon at Trevecca in Wales "for the education of pious young men" who desired to enter the Christian ministry. He accepted this position, however, with the understanding that he should be allowed still to serve his parish at Madeley. In 1771 Lady Huntingdon was induced to order that whoever did not fully disavow Wesley's views must quit the college. After some deliberation Mr. Fletcher resigned his office, and published his well-known *Checks to Antinomianism*. In 1778 he again visited Switzerland in pursuit of health, and remained there for nearly three years. On his return he applied himself to the work of his calling with unabated ardor until his death, Aug. 14, 1785.

Fletcher's life was one of uncommon purity and spiritual elevation, though at times bordering on asceticism. He lived in the most simple manner, and gave away all he could spare for the relief of the poor. As a preacher he was the Chrysostom of Methodism. He wrote in an easy, flowing style, though with great clearness and logical acuteness. For vigor of thought, force of argument, and the entire absence of bitterness his controversial writings have been pronounced one of the best models to be found in the literature of polemical theology. Fletcher's *Works* are published in this country in 4 vols. 8vo. His treatise upon human depravity, entitled *An Appeal to Matter-of-Fact and Common Sense*, and also his *Pastoral and Familiar Letters*, are published in separate volumes. (D. W. C. H.)

FLEURY, EMILE FÉLIX (1815-1884), a French general, was born in Paris, Dec. 23, 1815. He was educated at the Collège Rollin, and in 1837, after losing his fortune, joined the corps of Spahis, then just formed. He served in eleven campaigns in Algeria, and by his gallantry obtained rapid promotion. He returned to France in 1848 and ardently served the Bonapartist cause. In the *coup d'état* of Dec. 2, 1851, he was wounded in the head. He was made brigadier-general March, 1856, and general of division August, 1863. In 1866 he was sent on a diplomatic mission to Italy, and in September, 1869, was appointed minister to Russia. On the downfall of Napoleon III. in September, 1870, he retired to Switzerland, but still retained his rank in the French army. In October, 1879, he was placed on the retired list. He died Dec. 12, 1884.

FLINT, a city of Michigan, county-seat of Genesee co., is on the Flint River and at the intersection of the Flint and Pere Marquette Railroad with the Chicago and Grand Trunk Railroad, 64 miles N. W. of Detroit. It has a court-house, city-hall, 2 national banks, 2 daily and 6 weekly newspapers, 13 churches, a high school with fine building, 10 graded schools, and 2 public libraries. Its business was formerly altogether in lumber, but it has now a large woollen-mill, cotton-mill, paper-mill, wagon-factory, flour-mills, and grain-elevators, and other industries. It is lighted with electricity and gas, and has water-works. Its streets are well shaded with trees, and it has a park. Its property is assessed at $7,830,720. A trading-post was established here in 1819; the city was incorporated in 1885. Population in 1880, 8409; in 1890, 9845.

FLINT, AUSTIN, Sr., an American physician, was born at Petersham, Mass., Oct. 20, 1812. Both his grandfather and father were prominent physicians in that State. Austin was educated at Amherst and at Harvard College, and graduated from the medical department of the latter in 1833. After some practice in Massachusetts he settled at Buffalo in 1836, where he became eminent in his profession. In 1847 he assisted in founding the Buffalo Medical College, in which he was professor of the principles and practice of medicine. He had previously held a professorship in Chicago for a year, and in 1852 he accepted a position in the University of Louisville, but in 1856 returned to the college in Buffalo as professor of pathology and clinical medicine. From 1858 to 1860 he spent the winters in New Orleans as professor of clinical medicine in the medical school, and having also established practice in New York city, he was in 1861 appointed a physician of Bellevue hospital and professor in its college. In 1872 he was elected president of the New York Academy of Medicine. He was editor of the *Buffalo Medical Journal* (1846–56), and published *Physical Exploration of the Chest and Diagnosis of Diseases affecting the Respiratory Organs; Pathology, Diagnosis, and Treatment of Diseases of the Heart; Principles and Practice of Medicine* (1866; 3d ed., 1873); *Causation and Prevention of Disease* (1867); *Essays on Conservative Medicine* (1874); *Phthisis* (1875); *Manual of Percussion and Auscultation* (1876). He died March 15, 1886.

FLINT, AUSTIN, JR., an American physiologist, son of the preceding, was born at Northampton, Mass., March 28, 1836. He spent a year in Harvard College, then began the study of civil engineering, but in 1854 devoted himself to medicine, studying at Buffalo, Louisville, and Philadelphia, and graduating from the Jefferson Medical College in 1857. He then succeeded his father as editor of the *Buffalo Medical Journal*, and in 1858 was made professor of physiology in Buffalo Medical College. In 1859 he took a similar professorship in New York, and again in 1860 one in the New Orleans School of Medicine, but in the outbreak of the civil war resigned and went to Europe. With Charles Robin and Claude Bernard he studied physiology and then returned to assist in organizing the Bellevue Hospital Medical College, New York, in which he has since been professor of physiology. He was surgeon-general of the State of New York (1875–79). His whole career has been marked by original researches of great importance in physiology. In 1863 he published observations on the excretory function of the liver, which received from the French Academy of Sciences a prize of 1500 francs. He showed that one of the functions of the liver is to remove the waste nervous tissue (cholesterine). He has also published *Physiological Effects of Severe and Protracted Muscular Exercise* (1871), founded on observation of Weston the pedestrian; *Manual of Chemical Examination of the Urine* (1872); *Physiology of Man* (5 vols., 1866–72); and a *Text Book of Human Physiology* (1875).

FLORA. The term flora is used to designate the assemblage of plants found in any given region or country, and is the exact parallel of "fauna," which applies to animals. As is the case with animals, assemblages which present notable peculiarities have their limits determined by natural barriers, not by the artificial lines which separate countries, so that, though the plants of any district form its flora, distinctive floras have boundaries of their own. Plants, like animals, have their centres of distribution; while families are peculiar to certain regions, and are most abundant in a still narrower region. To a certain extent the distribution of plants parallels that of animals, yet there are great differences. Climate is a much more effectual barrier to plant life than it is to animals, many of which can bear considerable change of temperature provided they find food. Thus the plants of any region are a better index of its climate than its animals can be. The existence of a sub-tropical flora in British America and in Greenland, during the cretaceous and much of the tertiary ages, proves that a milder climate once reigned in those regions.

In the United States and British America two tolerably distinct floras exist: that of the Atlantic coast, with a preponderance of broad-leaved deciduous trees, and that of the Pacific coast, with a preponderance of cone-bearing trees. In both regions coniferæ form a larger proportion of the flora in the north than in the south, but the species of the two coasts are usually different. A small strip of country around the point of Florida has a tropical flora akin to that of the Antilles.

The most peculiar flora is the companion of the most peculiar fauna, and has its home in Australia. Eucalypti, casuarinas, banksias, and many other strange forms have their home here, but there is a lack of that rich variety which can be found in America, especially in the region of the Amazons, and also in India.

The flora of the ocean is unvaried, and is limited to depths to which light can penetrate. Its forms are algæ, commonly called seaweeds. (W. N. L.)

FLORICULTURE. In the United States floriculture has developed to a business of great commercial importance, while those who follow it as a labor of love have to pursue it by different methods from those adopted in most parts of the old world. (See Vol. XII. p. 215 Am. ed. (p. 247 Edin. ed.).)
In Europe a large capital is invested in the growth of pot-plants for the adornment of rooms, yards, and small conservatories, and the flower-markets of Paris and other cities of the continent are famous for the interest derived from these products of the florist's art. In America the heat of the summer's sun necessitates the darkening of rooms, while the dry and otherwise close atmosphere from the artificial heat required during long winters is much more unfavorable to the growth of plants in dwellings than on the other side of the Atlantic. The trade in pot-plants is, therefore, comparatively light and is mostly confined to small growers who can invest a few hundred dollars in a greenhouse in most of the larger cities and towns. There is, however, a widespread love for decorating home grounds, parks, and public gardens with flowers that will prove ornamental during the summer season, and an enormous capital is devoted to growing plants for these purposes. The taste for cut flowers is also universal, and the trade in these is now extremely large; and there are few of the larger towns in the United States that have not extensive cut-flower establishments. This has been fostered, in a great degree, by the introduction of steam-heating apparatus, instead of heating by hot water as still common in Europe. Very large areas of glass can thus be rapidly and easily warmed, and the chief expense in maintaining the establishment be reduced to a minimum. Each house is devoted to a single kind of flower, and frequently not more than a dozen kinds of plants are grown in the whole establishment. The skill to manage these few items is thus soon mastered, and the simplest form of labor under one intelligent head is all that is needed for success. Roses, carnations, bouvardias, lilies, heliotrope, richardia or calla lilies, pansies, violets, myrsiphyllum asparagoides, popularly known as smilax, and rare orchidæ are the leading staples in this trade. These are mostly grown in shallow benches of wood or slate, elevated so that the plants are brought as near to the glass as possible. Carnations, bouvardias, and similar plants are renewed every year. Raised from cuttings in spring, they are planted in the open ground during summer, and transferred to the benches before winter sets in. Roses are also grown largely in benches, but these remain two or three years before renewal. The houses for this class of

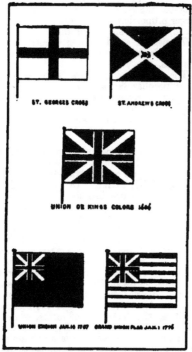

Formation of the Grand Union Flag of 1776.

Flag of the Royal Savage, 1776.

hand is a flag of 13 alternate red and white horizontal stripes with a rattlesnake undulating diagonally across them, and underneath the motto, "*Don't tread on me.*" This flag, as engraved, has no union, and it seems doubtful whether the first naval ensigns had one. Capt. Paul Jones, writing to Baron Vander Capellan, says: "I had the honor to hoist with my own hands the flag of freedom the first time it was displayed on the Delaware; and I have attended it with veneration ever since on the ocean."

Jones' commission is dated Dec. 7, 1775, but as the flag is said to have been first hoisted when Esek Hopkins, the commander-in-chief, embarked on the ship Alfred, and his commission was not issued until the 22d, it is probable that Christmas or New Year's day was selected for its display. The latter date would bring it to the same time as the raising of the striped union flag at Cambridge. A gentleman, however, writing to the Earl of Dartsmouth from Maryland, Dec. 20, 1775, says: "An admiral is appointed, and on the 3d inst. the Continental flag was hoisted on board the Black Prince (the Alfred) opposite Philadelphia." Commodore Joshua Barney claimed to have been the first to hoist the new American flag in Maryland. The brig Lexington, Capt. John Barry, was credited with having first borne it on the ocean, but on examination Capt. Barry's papers show that he was detained in the Delaware, and that Hopkins' squadron, which left Philadelphia, January, 1776, and got frozen up in the Delaware at Reedy Island, was the first to wear it on the ocean, Feb. 17, 1776. The first achievement of the squadron under the Continental flag was the capture of New Providence, with 100 cannon and other stores. Hoisting over it the striped flag, they held it a few days, and on leaving, March 17, brought away the governor and one or two men of note. The Reprisal, a brig of 16 guns, was the first to show the flag in European seas. The first vessel to obtain a salute for this flag was the brig Andrea Doria on her arrival at St. Eustatia, Nov. 16, 1776. She saluted the Dutch flag, and her salute was returned by the governor, who was subsequently removed for his indiscretion. In August, 1777, the General Mifflin, wearing the *Continental* colors, was saluted at Brest to the indignation of the British ambassador. This is the second salute to the striped flag of which we have any account.

We have now arrived at the period when the striped Union flag of continental colonies received added beauty and new significance by the erasure of the blended crosses of St. George and St. Andrew, displaying in their place a canopy of stars and a blue field representing a new constellation.

The earliest suggestion of stars as a device is found in the song written for the anniversary of the Boston massacre, and printed in the *Massachusetts Spy*, March 10, 1774:

"The American ensign now sparkles a star,
Which shall shortly flame wide through the skies."

It was probably a poetic flight and not designed by the writer to be prophetic. The earliest instance of the thirteen stripes being used upon an American banner is as a standard presented to the Philadelphia Troop of Light Horse in 1775, which is still preserved in the armory of that troop.

On June 14, 1777, nearly a year after the declaration of independence, the American Congress "*Resolved*, that the flag of the thirteen United States be thirteen stripes alternate red and white; that the union be thirteen stars white on a blue field, representing a new constellation." Thus without debate or previous legislation our flag was born and flung as a new constellation among the nations. A careful examination of the Rough and Smooth Journals of Congress and the files of the original drafts of nations shows this to have been the first, as it is the only record of the establishment of a national flag for the United States of America. This resolve was printed in the newspapers in August, but was not officially promulgated in Philadelphia until Sept. 3, and at other places still later. It will be observed the resolve does not prescribe how the stars are to be placed, or whether they shall have five, six, eight, or any other number of points, nor has the number of points been settled by any legislative enactment up to this time, though custom has established a star of five points.

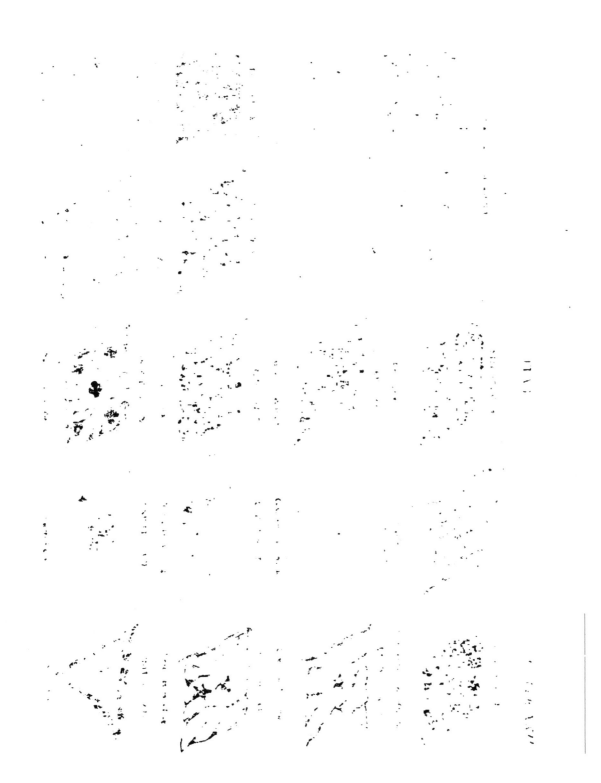

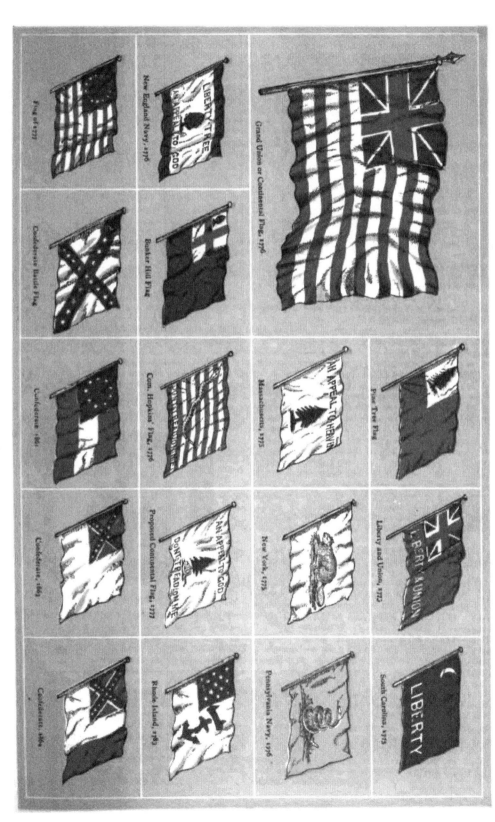

FLAG.

PLATE XXIII.

FLORIDA.

Florida is very level. It has no mountains, and in the north-west, where there are some hills, there is no elevation much exceeding 200 feet above the sea. In the peninsula, below the mouth of the Suwannee and St. Augustine on the east, the coast survey has been able to find but one elevation attaining to the height of 60 feet. Lake Okeechobee is from 16 to 22 feet above the sea, while most of the four southern counties range from nothing to 12 feet above the sea.

State Seal of Florida.

The Everglades form the expanded outlet of Lake Okeechobee, and in the rainy season are submerged, except the numerous islets with which they are studded. Florida has a coast-line of about 1200 miles, with numerous fine bays, harbors, and estuaries. The harbors on the Atlantic coast are Fernandina, St. Augustine, Daytona, and Port Orange, and Jacksonville on the St. John's River; on the S. Key West; and on the Gulf coast, Oyster Bay, Punta Rassa, Caloosahatchie River, Charlotte Bay, Tampa Bay, Cedar Keys, Deadman's Bay, St. Marks, Appalachee Bay, Appalachicola, Pensacola, Escambia, Perdido, etc. The principal rivers are, on the Atlantic side, the St. Mary's and the St. John's, with its large tributary the Ocklawaha, and the Kissimmee, which flows into Lake Okeechobee; on the Gulf side the Perdido, Escambia, Appalachicola, St. Mark's, Suwannee, Withlacoochee, Peace Creek, and Caloosahatchie, with their affluents. The so-called Indian River is not a river, but a long narrow sound with several inlets extending along the Atlantic coast for almost 100 miles, and separated from the ocean by sand-bars. Of the rivers, the St. John's is navigable to Sanford, and for large steamers to Palatka. The St. Mary's, the Appalachicola, Perdido, Escambia, Suwannee, Ocklawaha, Kissimmee, Caloosahatchie, and several other streams are navigable, the first six for large steamers.

Lakes are found everywhere. Lake Okeechobee, the largest, has an area of 650 square miles, and in a rainy season seems to extend over the entire Everglades, an area of 6400 square miles more. The other large lakes are Ahapopka, Istokpoga, Orange, Kissimmee, Cypress, Lake George, Lamona, Washington, Tohopokaliga, Alligator, Dunn's, Harris, Trati-apopka, Griffin, Jessup, Monroe, Santa Fe, Maitland, etc.

The islands are literally innumerable. The Everglades contain thousands; south of the peninsula, but belonging to it, and included in Monroe county, are the Florida Keys or *Cayes*, coral islands and islets, of which the group known as the Dry Tortugas (Turtle Islands) form the western termination. They extend 220 miles; many of the thousand or more are not inhabited, but some of them are of considerable size. Key Largo is the longest, and Key West contains an important city and naval station. On the south-west is a group called the Thousand Islands, and all along the Gulf coast, as well as the Atlantic coast of the peninsula, are numberless keys, coral islands, and sand banks, many of them inhabited by fishermen and others.

Geology.—The geology of Florida has until within a few years past been very generally misunderstood. The explorations of the United States Coast Survey since 1879 have thrown much light upon it. It is now conceded that the whole peninsula has for its base coral-reefs sufficiently close together to form a good and sufficient foundation, and that these extended, in the remote æons, to what was then the shore-line of the mainland, now the line of the Gulf coast of North-west and North Florida. By depressions and subsequent upheavals, what are now the Central Counties of the State received a deposit of greater or less thickness of the Vicksburg limestone of the Upper Eocene period. The peninsula was at this age more than twice its present breadth, but not much more than half its present length, from north to south; this increase of breadth being on the west or Gulf side. The lower part of the peninsula was still submerged, the coral reefs not having yet reached the surface. The broad plain of Central Florida was further elevated during the Miocene and Pliocene periods, and was subjected in common with the northern and north-western portions of the State, of which it then formed a part, to sub-aerial erosion, some of the rivers of North-western Florida probably making their way through the uplifted plains to a more southern outlet. The distribution of high and coast or gulf hammocks on the western half of the peninsula was probably caused by this erosion. During the period of the deposit of the beds of the Champlain strata (stratified drift or orange sand) there was another submergence, in which Central and Northern Florida, as well as the southern portions of what are now Alabama and Georgia, received deposits of pebbles, sand, and clay, varying in thickness from a few feet to two hundred feet. These beds were sediments from rapidly flowing, ever varying currents. In the northern and north-western parts of the State beds of red and yellow loam unstratified and without fossils are deposited directly upon this stratified drift. The axis of elevation was from north-east to south-west, coinciding probably very nearly with a line drawn from the mouth of the St. John's River to Bayport on the Gulf coast. During all this long Tertiary period Southern Florida had no existence above the waters. But in the Quaternary period there was again a partial elevation which brought the peninsula to nearly its present form. The southern portion of the peninsula and the keys and reefs which surround it now reached the surface and received a coating of the peculiar white sand which still characterizes them, probably from the waters of the Gulf, which still often washed over them, and from the floods and slow-moving streams, and the decaying vegetation, some acquired a deposit of loam and humus, which made them fertile. The streams of Central and Northern Florida began to flow in better defined channels, and some of them had sufficient descent in their course to furnish a moderate water-power. It will be seen from this brief history that Florida has no geological strata of earlier date than the Vicksburg limestone (Upper Eocene) of the Tertiary period. Aside from this limestone, of which there are seven varieties, there are no other Tertiary rocks except a Miocene limestone, not fossiliferous, on the eastern slope of the peninsula. The deposits of the Champlain era were, as has already been stated, stratified drift and a non-stratified loam. All the other deposits are of a later date and belong to the Quaternary or recent period. The Vicksburg limestone is cavernous, and where the cavernous strata are thin they frequently break through, forming those sinks which are common to this State and Alabama. The waters gathered in these caverns may pass by underground channels to the larger streams or to the sea; sometimes they reappear at the surface, after a subterraneous course of considerable length, as "boiling" or "blue springs," and flow thence by a short open run to the nearest large water-course to the sea.

In a State so recent geologically there are no minerals of importance. There is a bed of lignite or brown coal of the Tertiary period on the Suwannee River, but it is of poor quality, and though worked for a short time it is now abandoned. There are beds of marl at the head of Tampa Bay, and near the mouth of Manatee River, and phosphate rock, though of uncertain extent and commercial value, has been discovered in Clay, Alachua, Wakulla, Duval, and Gadsden counties, and a species of limestone called coquina stone, and much used for building in St. Augustine. The Vicksburg limestone, which is not so good for building, occurs in ten or twelve counties.

Most of the springs which abound in the State owe whatever medicinal value they have to the purity and sparkling character of their waters. A few, however, like the Newport Springs in Wakulla county, the Hampton Springs in Taylor, the White Sulphur Springs in Hamilton, the Suwannee Springs in Suwannee, the Green Cove Springs in Clay, and the Tarpon Springs in Hillsborough county, contain more or less sulphur, iron, and other substances.

Soil.—Florida has a great variety of soils, adapted to different classes of products. The best general classification is, perhaps, that of (1) the oak, hickory, and pine uplands; (2) that of the long-leaf pine lands; and (3) that of the pitch-pine, treeless, and alluvial lands; but each of these has many sub-divisions. I. The oak, hickory, and pine uplands have three distinct subdivisions: the red-loam lands, which are found only in Jackson county, with an area of 150 square miles; the brown-loam uplands, with oak, hickory, and short-leaf pine, occupying 1190 square miles; and the long-leaf pine ridge-lands, occupying 960 square miles. These are all in North-western Florida, on both sides of the Appalachicola River. The soil is fairly good; the forest trees which grow upon it are strong and vigorous, and the land where cultivated bears moderate, though very seldom large, crops of Indian corn, and in some places the small grains; vegetable and root crops yield moderately. In most of this region the orange grows well, but is liable to be injured by frosts. The pine, both the long and the short leaf, attain large proportions here, and so do most of the hard woods. Most of the subsoils are clay, though sand increases in the subsoils as we go southward.

II. Of the long-leaf pine lands proper there are three distinct varieties: the rolling lands, the flat pine lands, and the hammock lands. The rolling pine lands have generally sufficient elevation to secure good drainage, usually from fifty to sixty feet above the sea. They are the best orange lands in the State, but in general are not well adapted to the culture of grain or root crops. The soil is often a dark-colored, sandy loam, usually underlaid with a stiff, clayey loam; but at many points, with the same forest growths, the surface soil is a white, brilliant sand which, though it appears to be utterly destitute of humus, yet sustains heavy growths of long-leaf pine, Spanish and red oaks and hickory, and proves well adapted to orange-culture, though soon needing a large addition of wood-ashes and other fertilizers. These rolling pine lands are found in 24 counties, mostly of Northern and Central Florida, though of different degrees of fertility. They have an area of about 15,120 square miles. The flat pine lands form the margin of the rolling lands as the Atlantic and Gulf coasts are approached. They are badly drained, from their flatness, and become water-soaked and marshy in wet weather, and numerous lakes are found on them at all times. The soil is sandy, and is usually underlaid by a solid, clayey subsoil or one of densely-packed sand, either of which holds water, and prevents drainage, and swamps result. These lands cannot be profitably cultivated. Their principal forest growths are long-leaf pine, blackjack oak, saw-palmetto, and gallberry. They are found in 22 counties of Central and North-western Florida and have an area of about 11,250 square miles. There are also similar tracts of flat, marshy lands, but of higher elevation, in the seven North-eastern counties of the State, where they comprise an area of about 2230 square miles.

Hammock lands are either high hammocks, low hammocks, or Gulf hammocks.[1] Some of the high hammocks are very fertile, and have large forest-trees growing upon them; others, less productive, contain more sand, but are still fertilized by the crumbling limestone beneath. The Gulf hammocks are of greater size, and though apparently composed of a white or grayish-white sand, derive a certain fertility from the underlying limestone. They are adapted to orange-culture, but after a little time require additional fertilization. The hammocks are usually partially or entirely surrounded by water or marshes. The high hammocks support a vigorous growth of live-oaks and other oaks, hickory, magnolia, bay-laurel, sweet bay, long-leaf pine, cabbage-palmetto, cedar, elm, and red linden. The color of the soil varies from brownish-red to nearly black; it is always more or less sandy, and is from 8 to 12 inches thick. The subsoil is usually a marl or limestone, and the disintegrated Vicksburg limestone invariably underlies it. The low hammocks are found on the margins of many of the lakes and streams of Central Florida, and in some of the low, swampy areas, not connected with any lake or running water. The finest trees are usually those characteristic of a swampy region, the cypress and palmettoes predominating. The soil is white or grayish, but with a subsoil largely impregnated with lime from the underlying limestone. The low hammocks are good orange-lands, though less fertile than the high hammocks, but are not adapted to the culture of cereals, vegetables or root crops. Along the Gulf coast from Wakulla county to Hillsborough there are extensive patches of hammock land, known as Gulf hammocks, in which the white or very light-gray surface soil predominates, and the underlying limestone imparts fertility to it.

III. The pitch-pine, treeless, and alluvial lands of Florida include flat woods (pitch-pine), swamps, prairies, and savannas, everglades and marshes. The pitch-pine (a valuable timber) grows all along the Gulf coast. The coast marshes and swamps are not confined to the southern portion of the peninsula; the treeless portions are practically mere modifications of these marshes, brought about by varying degrees of moisture, and changes from salt to fresh water. This division of soils and vegetation embraces an area of about 23,290 square miles, of which 4850 square miles are swamp-lands; 5840 square miles, coast marshes and flat lands, timbered with pitch-pine; and 12,600

---

[1] The term "hammock," sometimes though improperly written "hummock," is peculiar to Florida, or at least to the Southern Gulf States. It signifies, there, an elevation of the surface, usually of no great extent, somewhat analogous to the "knoll" of the Northern States, but which is composed of humus, sand, and disintegrated limestone (the Vicksburg limestone).

square miles, prairies, savannas, and everglades. The area of the Everglades is estimated to be 6400 square miles. The pitch-pine not only replaces the long-leaf pine on the entire Gulf coast, and is equally frequent with it on the Atlantic coast, but below the latitude of 27° is the only species of pine throughout the peninsula. The prairies and savannas alternate with the flat woods in Manatee and Brevard counties, while the Everglades, which occupy most of Monroe and Dade counties, extend into Manatee also. Very little of this region is adapted to agriculture, but is used almost exclusively for grazing. To sum up then as to soils, the swamp-lands of Southern Florida are the most productive, and the most durable in their fertility, but are best adapted to tropical crops—sugar-cane, coffee, rice, anona or custard apple, pine-apples, guavas, bananas, and liquorice. The swamp-lands, farther north, are wet and not easily drained. The low hammocks and Gulf hammocks come next, and the high hammocks third. After these come the pine, oak, and hickory lands, and the pine barrens last. Muck, marl, humus, and phosphatic rock are accessible in many sections, and with the aid of these even the poorest lands may be made to produce good crops of the sorts which are adapted to culture in their several localities.

Vegetation.—Florida has a large proportion of forest. There are, at the present time, probably 25,000,000 acres of land, more or less densely covered with timber, and in this the yellow or pitch-pine largely predominates, occupying from three-fifths to three-fourths of the whole. The long-leaf pine comes next, though very much less in quantity. In the lower lands near rivers, lakes, and swamps, the live-oak and other species of oak, hickory, ash, beech, cedar, magnolia, bay-laurel, sweet-bay, gum, cypress, and, in Southern Florida, the saw-palmetto, cabbage-palm, date-palm, royal palm, mahogany, lignum-vitæ, green ebony, mangrove, the cork-tree, poplar, palm-tree, olive, cotton-tree, juniper, and red cedar; and many rare shrubs which do not thrive in a more northern climate. There are said to be nearly 200 species of arborescent plants in Florida, about one-half of all in the United States. In Northern and North-western Florida the sylvan growth is substantially that of the Middle States and the Mississippi Valley, the black-walnut, bass-wood, beech, birch, sugar-maple, cotton-wood, sycamore, elm, ash, and red maple predominating. Of cultivated fruit-trees, those belonging to the genus *Citrus* largely outnumber all others, the species *Citrus aurantium* (orange) having at least twenty subspecies or distinct varieties, while the shaddock of six varieties, bitter orange, lemon, lime, citron, and pomegranate are also found in the wild state.

The culture of the orange is one of the largest industries in the State; the crop was reported as being 140,000,000 oranges in 1883, 166,000,000 in 1884, and over 200,000,000 in 1885, while every year many thousands of new trees come into bearing, and those already in bearing yield larger crops. The Florida oranges have a higher reputation for excellence than any other oranges in the market, but there is great difference in these—a difference depending upon soil, temperature, and methods of cultivation. Figs, olives, English walnuts, Italian chestnuts, and, among the shrubs, the pine-apple, anona or custard apple, banana, and guava are cultivated in the central and southern counties. In the northern and north-western counties the apple, quince, and pear are favorite fruits, and the early summer and autumn varieties are much liked; the peach is cultivated for exportation, but is not of prime quality.

Animals.—The black or brown bear of the Southern States (and possibly the Mexican bear) are somewhat numerous; wolves are more rare, but the gray and possibly the black wolf exists there. There are red and gray foxes, cougars or panthers, and 2 or 3 of the smaller felines, opossums, raccoons, ground-hogs, the fisher or land otter, several species of rats, mice, and bats. Of game animals there is the white or cottontail deer, and probably the Virginia deer also, and rabbits, squirrels, etc., in great numbers. Among reptiles the alligator has been more numerous in Florida than anywhere else in the United States, frequenting the St. John's, Suwannee, Apalachicola, Caloosahatchie, and other rivers, and the larger lakes; but the persistent hunting of them, both for sport and for their hides, which have now a high commercial value, have greatly diminished their numbers. There is a true crocodile in South Florida, and the manatee or sea-cow is still found in the sounds and bays. The food-fishes of Florida have attracted great attention of late years. There had been for many years a considerable demand for fresh and salted mullet from Cuba, and even while Florida was a Spanish colony there were several mullet-fisheries on the west coast of Florida for the Cuban trade. This has greatly increased of late years, and there are fishing-stations on both the Atlantic and Gulf coasts, and about 5,000,000 pounds of mullet alone are exported, valued at $125,000; but the mullet-fishery is now only an item of the Florida fish production; the grouper, a favorite fish in the West Indies, abounds on the Gulf coast, and is taken with hook and line. The value of the export in some years has reached $141,000. The sea-trout, the Spanish mackerel, tarpum, and blue-fish, which are caught on both shores in large numbers, are in good demand at the North, and their capture employs many hands; but the finest food-fishes of the Florida coast are the pompano or pumpkin-fish, and the red snapper. The last named is now one of the most popular fish in the New York market. The export from West Florida in 1884 was over 3,500,000 pounds, and is constantly increasing. The beauty of the fish and its fine quality as a food-fish will give it a permanent place in the Northern markets. The pompano is not so well known, and does not bear transportation quite so well, but its consumption is increasing. Shad are exported early in the season, being found plentifully in all the larger rivers. The numerous keys and coral islets are the home of the sea-turtles, and the green turtle, so highly prized by epicures, is largely exported from Key West. The shark, the octopus, and other large species of cuttle-fish are common on the South Florida coasts.

There is a greater variety of birds in Florida than in any other State in the Union. Of the birds of prey, the king vulture, next in size to the condor, has been found only here and in Mexico, on the North American continent. There are many lesser vultures, and eagles, hawks, kites, and owls. Among the waders the scarlet ibis and the flamingo are the most noticeable, though there are herons, cranes, and other waders, and many species of ducks, teal, brant, etc., among the swimmers; the wild-turkey is the finest of game-birds, but there are also grouse, snipe, woodcock, rail, reed-birds, etc., in great numbers. The smaller birds are remarkable for the beauty of their plumage, and some of them, like the mocking-bird, for the melody and variety of their song. The insect pests, sand-flies, mosquitoes, black-flies, and chigoes, are plentiful enough, at certain seasons, in the swampy and marshy regions, but elsewhere in the State they are not abundant, and in some districts are unknown.

The domestic animals in the State in January, 1884, were, according to the report of the Agricultural Bureau, 27,202 horses and 11,221 mules, valued at $3,515,052; milch cows, 46,054, valued at $658,572; oxen and other cattle, 560,000, valued at $5,140,800; sheep, 98,940, valued at $173,145; swine, 313,600, valued at $671,104. In 1889 the numbers were: horses and mules, 41,113; cattle, 505,636; sheep and goats, 114,393; hogs, 201,812. The cattle are of small size and low value, but recently increasing attention has been paid to breeding from the best stocks, with very hopeful results. The sheep and swine have not been of particularly good breeds, and hence have not done the State much credit.

Agricultural Products.—In 1884 Florida produced 3,837,000 bushels of corn, valued at $3,069,600; no wheat was reported, either in 1883 or 1884, and none is believed to have been produced; 494,000 bushels of oats were reported, valued at $296,400; potatoes, about 160,000 bushels, of which more than five-sixths were sweet potatoes. This does not, however, represent fairly the sweet potato crop, which in 1880 was 1,687,613 bushels. They were valued at $150,000. The rice crop averages about 1,200,000 pounds, sugar not far from 1500 hogsheads, and molasses over a million gallons. The hay crop was insignificant; of cotton, the crop was estimated at 60,000 bales, but a considerable portion of this was Sea-island, and its estimated value exceeded $3,000,000. The orange crop is steadily on the increase, and is becoming one of the most valuable industries of the State. Attention is also being paid to other semi-tropical fruits—lemons, limes, shaddocks, anonas, bananas, guavas, pine-apples, and cocoanuts, as also to pears, grapes, etc., but these have not as yet been brought into the market in sufficient quantities to give them any great importance. From the north-eastern counties large quantities of market-garden vegetables, tomatoes, sweet potatoes, small fruits, etc., are sent to Northern markets, and this business is of growing importance. Among the industries of the State is a large business in the production of pine and other lumber, and of live-oak for ship-building. A recent industry is the development of the phosphate deposits.

Climate.—The range of temperature and the amount of rainfall in a year are important factors in their relation to the desirableness of a climate, yet there are others quite as important in deciding its healthfulness and adaptation to settlement. So far as temperature is concerned the range of the year throughout the State is not excessive. In Northern Florida the usual range is from 90° or 93° to 26°, or about 67°; in Central Florida, from 95° to 43°, or 52° (rarely there is a single day or night of frost); in Southern Florida there is seldom an approach to frost, and the annual range is from 96° to 46°, or 48°, or 48° to 50°. The annual mean temperature of the State is about 70°.05; for stations north of lat. 28° it is 69°.82, and, more in detail, for spring, 70°.66; for summer, 80°.10; for autumn, 70°.23; and for winter, 58°.29. For stations south of lat. 28° the annual mean is 74°.87; for spring, 74°.94; for summer, 81°.93; for autumn, 76°.27; for winter, 63°.69. Yet in this southern half there is a material difference; the western or Gulf coast maintaining a higher mean temperature than Key West; thus Punta Rassa, lat. 27°, has five or in most years six months from May to October, inclusive, in which the mean temperature ranges from 80°.10 to 83°.10, and the maximum temperature of nearly every day of those months is 90° or more; while at Key West, lat. 24° 36', but nearly 60 miles from the mainland, the mean temperature in the same months ranges from 78°.11 to 83°, and the maximum temperature of the same months does not average more than 85°. The continuous high heat of Southern or South-western Florida during six months of the year is an objectionable feature. The rainfall exhibits greater variations, though everywhere it is amply sufficient. On the Atlantic coasts it ranges from 47.86 inches at St. Augustine to 53.95 inches at Jacksonville; at Key West it varies from 42 to 50 inches; at Punta Rassa from 32 to 40 inches; at St. Marks, on Appalachee Bay, North-west Florida, from 73 to 77 inches.

As a winter resort for invalids, who require a mild and uniform climate during the cold months, especially to persons suffering from pulmonary diseases, almost all sections of Florida offer remarkably strong attractions; for rheumatic, bilious, and febrile affections it is not so well adapted, and for kidney diseases it is especially undesirable.

From the first of April to the middle of October all of Florida south of 28° 30', and we might, perhaps, safely say south of 29°, is objectionable, as a permanent residence, to persons from the North who have any tendencies to malarial or typhoid fevers. This might be expected from its geological structure, since its soil is alluvial, with a large admixture of decayed vegetation, and swamps and marshes abound at all points. The refreshing and health-giving breezes, which sweep across the peninsula, modify this condition somewhat, but it exists nevertheless, and is more strongly marked as the season progresses, and on the marshy savannas of South Florida it is perilous to Northern constitutions. North of 29° these diseases are less prevalent, but they exist to some extent even in North-western Florida. Those who are thoroughly acclimated may withstand these diseases even in South Florida, but careful and extended observation indicates that the period of acclimation is a very long one.

Aside from agriculture and the cultivation of the orange, lemon, and other semi-tropical fruits, and the market-garden products of Northern Florida, the industries of the State, though now increasing, have not attained very great magnitude. There is a rapidly growing demand for the yellow pitch-pine, known to the market as Georgia pine, which abounds in Florida; and Western and North-western Florida have many large saw-mills for the production of this valuable lumber and timber. Live-oak is prepared for the ship-builders in North-eastern as well as in South Florida, and the other oaks and hard woods are in demand for the railroad construction in progress there. The demand for houses and other buildings also causes considerable activity in lumber manufacture. The production of naval stores, turpentine, tar, rosin, and pitch, and the distilling of the turpentine, employ many hands; the manufacture of orange boxes has risen to be an important industry; the production of Havana cigars, now extensively conducted at Key West, and to some extent at other points in Florida, the evaporation of sea-salt, and cotton-seed-oil production, are the other principal manufactures. The *fisheries* are of growing importance. The capture of green and other turtles for the supply of Northern and foreign markets, the sponge- and coral-fisheries, and the rapidly growing trade in food-fishes, the mullet, grouper, sea-trout, blue-fish, Spanish mackerel, pompano, and red snapper, will soon give Florida the pre-eminence over the other Southern States in her fisheries. In 1880 the statistics of these industries, including the fisheries, was 426 establishments, $3,210,680 capital invested, 7984 persons employed, $5,546,448 annual value of products. It has doubled since then.

Railways.—In no Southern State has there been so proportionally rapid a development of railways as in Florida since 1880. At that time there were 554 miles operated. Since that date the extension of railroads throughout the State has been actively continued, various localities formerly almost inaccessible having by this means been opened to commercial traffic. At the end of 1889 the railroad mileage of the State was 2377.55, a growth of 1800 miles since 1880. In 1882 a consolidation of the roads of the Yulee system with several other roads formed the Florida Railway and Navigation, controlling more than 700 miles of railway, which extended to Pensacola on the west and to Plant City on the south. In 1888 this system, with other lines, was reorganized under the name of the Florida Central and Peninsular. Other important roads, which reach the leading points in the southern section of the State, are the Jacksonville, Tampa, and Key West, which, with its branches, has a length of 203 miles; and the Florida Southern Railroad, which has in all a length of 307.54 miles. To these may be added the Savannah, Florida, and Western, entering the State from Southern Georgia; the Orange Belt Railroad, 151.10 miles long; the Pensacola and Atlantic, 160.28 miles, and connecting at Pensacola with the extensive Louisville and Nashville system of roads; and a number of smaller roads. To these means of communication must be added an important system of inland navigation, traversing the St. John's and other navigable rivers of the State. Many fertile sections of Florida, previously neglected, have by these means been made desirable, and impetus has been given to settlement.

Canals.—A ship-canal across the peninsula, though long agitated and repeatedly chartered, has not yet been commenced. Another, known as the Barge Line, crossing through the St. Mary's River, Okeefinokee Swamp, and the Suwannee River, and by inland waterways to New Orleans, has also been projected but not built. There are several other canals along the Atlantic coast, and connecting with the slack-water and lake navigation in Southern Florida, which have an aggregate length of about 170 miles.

Four steamship lines leaving New York and having Havana and New Orleans as their ultimate destination stop at Fernandina both in going and returning; these are the Mallery, the Morgan, the Alexandre, and the Ward lines. Others running to Savannah as their port of destination connect with Florida by the railway lines noticed.

Land Companies.—No State in the Union has so large a portion of its area held by land companies as Florida; yet its prosperity within the past five years has been largely due to this very fact. In January, 1881, and for several years previous, from the lands owned by the State, patented to it by the National Government as swamp and overflowed lands, school and university lands, etc., etc., amounting originally to 14,442,464 acres, 1,684,725 acres had been sold, leaving unsold 12,757,739 acres. But under an act of the Florida Legislature, passed in 1855, the trustees of the Internal Improvement Fund were authorized to indorse the bonds of certain railroads to the extent in all of $20,000 per mile, these bonds being a first mortgage or lien to the State on the entire roads, and in case of the failure of the roads to pay the interest on the bonds, the State could sell the roads, but must pay the interest, unless their sale brought a sufficient sum to pay both principal and interest on the bonds. Under this act of Jan. 1, 1881, there had accumulated against this internal improvement fund, which held the public lands as security, arrearages of interest amounting to about $600,000, and with other indebtedness of the State to very nearly $1,000,000. This indebtedness was, by legal proceedings, in what was known as the Vose judgment, declared a first lien on all these State lands, and hence the State's finances were crippled and no aid could be extended to the new railroads and other measures of internal improvement needed for the development of the State. With a fine climate, and most of the elements needed for a rapid growth, the State seemed to be struck with paralysis. On June 1, 1881, relief came in the purchase by Hamilton Disston, of Philadelphia, and his associates, of 4,000,000 acres of these lands, to be selected by the purchasers from the more than 12,000,000 acres which the State possessed, for the sum of $1,000,000 in cash. The State, during the next year, sold also 296,574 acres to actual settlers or to companies in comparatively small holdings. With the money derived from these sales the State was able to liquidate its indebtedness, and has sold and granted about a million acres a year of its lands since 1882.

The first of these great land companies then was the *Florida Land and Improvement Company*, organized by Hamilton Disston and his associates for the disposal of the 4,000,000 acres which they had purchased. Very soon after the consummation of this purchase the Florida Land and Improvement Company sold 2,000,000 acres, or one-half of the whole, to Sir Edward Reed and his associates, English and Scotch capitalists, who organized under the name of the *Florida Land and Mortgage Company, Limited.* This company subsequently purchased other lands in various sections of the State to the extent of over 300,000 acres; their corporate name and directorship has been changed two or three times, and it is not now certain how much land they hold in the State. But Mr. Disston and his associates were disposed to invest still further in Florida lands, and they did so in a new way. They proposed to the trustees of the internal improvement fund of the State to undertake the draining of a portion of the Everglades, the lowering of Lakes Okeechobee, Kissimmee, and other smaller lakes of that region by means of navigable canals and ditches, at their own expense, on condition that one-half (the odd-numbered sections) of the lands so reclaimed should be patented to them. The trustees agreed to the proposition in the autumn of 1881, and active operations were begun at once. The new company was called The Atlantic and Gulf Coast Canal and Okeechobee Land Company. The undertaking was encompassed with many difficulties. Lake Okeechobee was in its best condition only 22 feet above the ocean, and it must be lowered permanently at least 6 or 8 feet before any considerable amount of land could be reclaimed. In October, 1884, the company claimed to have drained permanently about 2,500,000 acres and were to receive patents of 1,250,000 acres. The land is very rich and will yield fine crops of tropical products if it can be permanently freed from overflow; but whether this can be done cannot yet be definitely decided. The Disston companies have also acquired large landed interests on the Gulf coast of the State, some of which they have sold again to other companies, six or seven of which hold from 10,000 to 200,000 acres each in Southern and Central Florida. Recently they have also taken an interest in another great enterprise, which must depend largely for its success on the sale of these reclaimed lands—*The International Railroad and Steamship Company.*

Other land companies are the *Florida Railway and Navigation Company*, which holds at present and in prospect nearly 2,000,000 acres; the *Plant Investment Company*, which holds for itself and the South Florida and Florida Southern Railways, at present and in prospect, almost 3,000,000 acres, a part of its lands being in Southern Florida; the Sumter Land Company, an English company, holding about 50,000 acres, mostly in Sumter county. There are also several smaller holdings of an independent character in Marion, Volusia, and Orange counties; of these the most noted and popular are the De Land purchases in and around De Land, Volusia county, on which a young city has been built up, the Silver Springs Lake Company, at Silver Springs, in Marion county, the Lake Weir Settlement in the same county, and the Orlando Land Company in Orange county.

Education.—The public-school system of the State is increasing in efficiency. The school fund had, in 1888, a capital of about $500,000, yielding an income of nearly $40,000, to which must be added the product of the one mill annual school tax, and the sum required to be raised by the several counties for school purposes. In 1882 the total expenditure for public schools was $117,532; in 1888 it had increased to $484,110. The number of children enrolled for the public schools was, by the enumeration of 1888, 50,699 white and 33,572 colored. In 1880 there were 1135 schools, 1151 teachers, and 31,477 pupils. In 1888 there were 2249 schools with 2413 teachers, and 53,130 pupils. Of the schools about one-third were for colored children, and of the teachers 1793 were white and 620 colored. There is a State University at Tallahassee, organized in 1884, with good prospects of success; two collegiate schools, the East and West Florida Seminaries at Tallahassee and Gainesville, the latter with a normal department; an excellent classical academy at De Land, and a State Agricultural College at Lake City. There are also two institutes for the education of colored teachers and preachers—the Florida Institute at Live Oak, and the Cookman Institute at Jacksonville.

Religion.—There are in the State at least 55,000 members of the different Protestant denominations, implying at least 262,500 of adherent population, and adding the Catholic population there are 273,500 of the population belonging to some religious organization. Of these denominations the Baptists are in the lead, having, in 1883, 398 churches, 221 ordained preachers, 28,731 members. The different branches of the Methodist Church, of which four are represented in the State, had, in 1883–4, a membership, including probationers, of about 19,000. The Protestant Episcopal Church had 27 parishes, 27 clergymen, 1989 communicants. The Presbyterian Church South had 31 ministers, 36 churches, and about 1800 communicants. There are about 20 churches of other Protestant denominations, with a membership of about 3000. The Catholic population is estimated at 11,000.

Population.—The population of Florida in 1870 was 187,748, an increase of 33.7 per cent. from 1860; in 1880 it was 269,493, an increase of 43.6 per cent. from 1870; in 1890 it was 390,435, an increase during the decade 1880–90 of 44.9 per cent. The predominance of the native over the foreign population was about 25 to 1. The voting population in 1880 was 1 in a little over 4 of the inhabitants. After 1880, owing to the efforts of the land companies to advertise their lands, the conviction of the desirableness of the State as a winter resort, the multiplication of railway and steamship lines, and the great increase of the orange-culture, the population rapidly increased, and its growth still continues at a highly encouraging ratio. The State is divided into 39 counties. In 1884 the total assessed valuation of its property was $55,249,311, which had increased in 1888 to $87,552,447. The number of acres of land assessed in the latter year was 22,840,320, of which 652,353 were under cultivation. The total value of the land (except town lots) was $19,389,816. The bonded State debt was $1,032,500, while the yearly receipts and expenditures were each about $580,000.

Principal Towns.—Jacksonville is now the largest city in the State, its population in 1890 being 17,160. Key West, the most southern city, which is largely engaged in commerce, manufacture, and the fisheries, has a population of 16,058. Pensacola, a U. S. naval station, and a large lumber shipping port, has a population of 11,751. Tallahassee, the capital, has 2933; St. Augustine, the oldest town in the United States, 4612; and Tampa, about 6000. Other important towns are Cedar Keys, De Land, Lake City, Ocala, Fernandina, Palatka, Orlando, etc.

The history of Florida since 1879 has been one of rapid growth and development in all directions, but not of stirring incident in either its political or civil affairs. At that time George F. Drew was its governor, and the State was hampered with a debt, partly a heritage from former administrations, which seriously crippled this small State and prevented its growth. Its railroads were incomplete, and some of them bankrupt, its lands were locked up under the Vose judgment, and its taxes were insufficient to meet its current expenses and interest. The inauguration of Gov. William D. Bloxham in January, 1881, proved the epoch of a new and improved condition. The finances of the State were placed on a better basis by the sale of a portion of its lands to Hamilton Disston and his associates, and the subsequent sales to other parties; the railroads were reorganized, and, being enabled to obtain a portion of their land grants, pushed forward their lines to all parts of the State; new towns and cities were built almost by magic to accommodate the winter visitors. Orange-culture began to assume large proportions, capital flowed in rapidly, the fisheries of both the Gulf and the Atlantic coasts were rapidly developed and found new markets in Northern cities; education, which had hitherto been neglected, became an object of great interest. The State University, which had hitherto existed only on paper, was organized and equipped; academies and seminaries were established, and the public schools became objects of solicitude to the citizens. This advance all along the line was coincident with Governor Bloxham's administration, though not, probably, wholly the result of it. He was succeeded in 1885 by Governor E. A. Perry, and in 1889 by Frank P. Fleming. (L. P. B.)

FLOTOW, Friedrich von, Baron (1812-1883), a German composer, was born at Teutendorf, in Mecklenburg-Schwerin, April 26, 1812. His parents intended him for a diplomatic career, but at the age of sixteen he went to Paris to devote himself to music. Having studied under Reicha he composed some pieces for private presentation, and in 1839 published the opera *Le Naufrage de la Méduse*, in which he had the co-operation of Pilati. A series of operas quickly followed, among which *Stradella* (1844) and *Martha* (1847) obtained the greatest favor. These are the most characteristic of his works, being marked by fresh and pleasing melodies and brilliant instrumentation. Among his later works were *Die Grossfürstin, Rübezahl, Indra,* and *Albin.* In 1855 Flotow was made director of the theatre at Schwerin, but resigned the post in 1863. In 1864 he was made a corresponding member of the French Institute. He died at Darmstadt, Jan. 24, 1883.

FLOUR, Manufacture of. This article is entirely devoted to the recent improvements and inventions in flour-milling. As practised in the best American mills, the manufacture of flour consists in a gradual reduction of the wheat as here fully shown.

See Vol. IX. p. 306 Am. ed. (p. 343 Edin. ed.).

The Separator.—Thorough cleaning of the wheat is now universally recognized as the first great step in modern milling processes. By proper use of the fanning-mill the farmer may send his wheat to market in a reasonably clean condition, but farmers are not all careful in this matter; hence the inspection rules of all grain markets provide for whatever degree of dockage for dirt the inspector may determine as proper, after getting fair samples of the grain. The Separator here presented is a standard type of the efficient modern machine.

This is termed a Wheat Separator and Oat and Weed Extractor, and consists of a series of rotating sieves, or screens, mounted in a suitable frame, with a fan attachment, as shown in engraving (Fig. 1). Wheat is fed into the machine from bins, cars, or the farmer's wagon at a point above the upper sieve, being subjected at the same time to a strong air-current, which draws out dust, chaff, light oats, and other foreign matter of a lighter character than the wheat. The latter passes through the first sieve, the perforations of which permit this, while the foreign material tails over this sieve and is carried away. The operations of a second and third sieve are similar to the first. At the bottom of the machine is a fourth sieve, but with perforations so small that the wheat is carried over it, while small seeds and bits of clay, etc., which may have passed the other sieves, fall through it. At this stage the wheat is subjected to another air-draft, for the purpose of drawing out any light impurities that may have escaped the first air separation.

The Cockle Separator.—This machine occupies a place higher even than the separator in the estimation of millers. There are many varieties of cockle, but the one most troublesome to millers is that known as *Lychnis Githago.* It is a very hardy and prolific plant, and when the seeds are ground in with flour the latter has the effect of cantharides, a deadly poison, upon the human system; hence it is imperative that the cockle-seed be taken out of the wheat. The success of American inventive genius in this direction is matter for just pride and satisfaction. In Europe, of which cockle is a native, several methods of separating it were tried, but none proved so effective as the work of the American machine, the invention of Kurth, a German.

The machine which is here illustrated separates it almost entirely from the wheat and is simply indispensable in modern mills. The engraving shows the interior of the machine, which is enclosed when in operation, the cylinder being cut open and the entire internal economy of the machine being shown as in operation (Fig. 2).

There are no holes in the indented cylinder. The grain first falls on sieve A, the larger berries passing over the tail into division B, thence along spout B, and discharging into hopper C. The smaller grain and the cockle fall through sieve A, pass through division E, entering the indented cylinder F at the rear end, the cockle fitting into the indentations, and thus, by the revolving of the cylinder, being carried up past the catch-board, fall on the same and roll into the spout, being, by the shaking motion of the

Fig. 1.

same, discharged, as the cut shows. Only the ends of the kernels of wheat can stick into the indentations, thus: they consequently fall out before reaching the catch-board, slide back to the bottom, and at the same time are impelled by the motion and inclined position of the cylinder towards the hopper C, where they mix with the large wheat from the tail of sieve A, or can be kept separate, if desirable, thus making two grades of wheat.

The Scourer and Smutter.—After the wheat has been cleaned of what may be called field impurities, including cockle, it passes to graders, which separate the small, shrunken, or imperfect kernels from the plump and sound ones; thus enabling the miller to keep up his higher grades of flour by using only sound wheat, while the inferior quality may be kept separate and reduced to lower grade flour. This grading is, perhaps, more generally practised in mills using soft wheat exclusively than in those which use mainly hard wheat, with only a sufficient mixture of soft to expedite its reduction. Graders are of too common a type to require illustration or extended description.

The next operation is a radical one, consisting of the passing of the wheat through a machine known as the scourer and smutter, a large variety of these necessary adjuncts to milling having been invented. Crease dirt, while hardly perceptible to the casual observer, is peculiarly abhorrent to the good miller, and must be taken out before pure white flour can be made. The machine illustrated is the invention of Morgan, now a resident of Wisconsin. This scourer, one of his many valuable inventions, was first exhibited at the Wisconsin State Fair in 1845, where it was awarded first premium, though then regarded more as a curiosity than a practicable machine. It has since come into very general use, although there are many competitors, some of which are regarded as superior to it, in that the same work is done by gentler means. A sectional view of this scourer is here given. (Fig. 3).

Fig. 2.

The Scourer consists of a number of beaters, mounted on a vertical shaft, surrounded by a case of perforated metal with oval indentations on the inner side, presenting an uneven surface to the scouring case. The perforated metal case is surrounded by a tight wooden case, shaped as in the engraving, and at the top of this is a suction fan for the removal of the impurities taken off in the cleaning operation, which may be thus described: The grain being fed in at the top of the machine, passes through an air-current which draws out any light material or dust that may remain in the wheat, which then falls upon a disc that throws it to the scouring case, where it is caught by the beaters and carried around the machine at a high speed. Coming in contact with the uneven surface of the scouring case, the wheat is subjected to a severe rubbing, which removes the fuzz from the end of the berry, together with any dust or impurities that may adhere to the berry. In passing out of the machine the wheat is again subjected to a strong current of air, which separates light wheat and other light substances from the clean grain by specific gravity. The grain, while being subjected to the scouring process, is acted upon by a current of air coming into the machine in the centre at the bottom, passing through the grain and out through the perforated case, up and between it and the outer wooden case to the fan on top of the machine, taking with it all impurities detached from the wheat.

Another valuable machine has come into general use during the wheat-cleaning process as the direct result of the employment in the harvest-field of self-binding machines which use wire as a binder. It is inevitable that bits of wire should get into the wheat while going through the thresher, and before wire binders were used, nails, screws, and bits of iron often found their way into the grain. It will be readily seen that such things are a source of annoyance and loss of time and money to the miller. A simple machine known as the magnetic separator, built on several patterns, serves the purpose admirably. In them the wheat is passed over a series of strong magnets and all metallic substances are removed, the machine being so constructed as to allow of easy and frequent cleaning of the magnets.

The Roller Mill.—The necessity for this machine arose from the desire to produce the greatest possible amount of middlings in the breaking of wheat, and the smallest amount of flour, without rubbing the impurities into the material or comminuting the bran. It is superior to the millstone for this purpose, as being more gentle in action, more easily regulated to the demands of various products, and more susceptible of close and accurate adjustment. While attempts at using rollers for milling were made both in Europe and

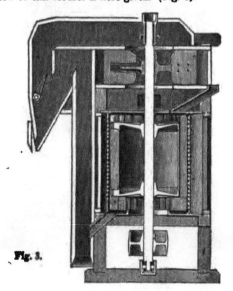

Fig. 3.

America prior to the invention of the middlings purifier, their success was extremely limited. Its real development was consequent upon the wide possibilities of gradual reduction as demonstrated by the purifier, and its spread proportionate to the comprehension and use of that machine.

Collier of Paris, Bollinger of Vienna, and Helfenberger of Switzerland, began experimenting with the roller mill about 1820. The Helfenberger mill had two grooved rolls, arranged side by side, with a board of hard wood fixed beneath and in close contact with them. Bollinger Bros. of Vienna made a mill with three hardened iron rolls, two side by side and having grooves winding in opposite directions, while a third roll was located beneath and parallel to the others. These rollers had differential speed, revolved in different directions, and were the most perfect of any made up to that time. Collier's rolls were conical, with axes parallel and the greater diameter of one roll adjacent to the smaller diameter of the other. A. Von Mueller, councillor of Warsaw, also invented a roller mill superior in some respects to Helfenberger's.

About 1830, Sulzberger, a Swiss milling engineer, succeeded in building a mill better than any which preceded it. This machine had three pairs of grooved rolls 6 inches in diameter, arranged one over the other. The grain was broken on the first, the middlings and finer material detached by the second, and reduced to flour by the third pair. Their speed was differential, the slow roll making 216 and the fast one 229 revolutions per minute. A company was formed by Sulzberger for introducing the mills, and establishments were built in Milan, Venice, Munich, Mayence, Stettin, Leipsic, Pesth, and other places, on his plan. It was, however, found difficult to procure intelligent workmen to operate the mills, and equally hard to accustom the public to the dry, roller-milled flour, and teach them how to use it. For this reason all the altered mills save one or two, notably the one at Pesth, returned wholly or partly to the use of stones. The Pesth mill was a success, and continued to use the same roller system for many years. The process was kept secret to a great degree, though it was known that the rollers frequently broke, necessitating many repairs.

Naeff of Pesth invented a roller mill which came prominently into use after that of Sulzberger, and was manufactured about 1864 by Escher, Wyss & Co., of Leesdorf, near Vienna. This machine had four rollers, placed one above the other. The use of these and the earlier rollers was, however, not at all general for some years. They were employed in a few large establishments for breaks, while the ending and flouring were done on stones. The reconstructed Pesth cylinder mill, in 1867, seems to have been the first successful exclusive roller establishment. There were in this mill 210 pairs of rolls, arranged in 5 sections, 2 of which were for making middlings, and the remaining 3 for their reduction into flour. Two or three other mills at various points adopted the same system on a smaller scale, but without as great success.

A difficulty in dealing with roller mills, which had been all along the greatest of any, was the impossibility of procuring any material for them which would prove alike durable and cheap. But about this date the manufacture of iron and steel was being fast developed, and erel ong the chilling or hardening process, applied to iron rolls, resulted in a surface comparatively durable and satisfactory, though at first far from cheap.

While the use of the improved iron roll was spreading very slowly, Franz Wegmann of Naples exhibited his porcelain roll at the World's Exposition in Vienna in 1873. Wegmann's roll, made of porcelain or biscuit china, had a fine, smooth, yet granular appearance. So great were its apparent virtues that it was adopted by various stone mills of Pesth, where it was originally used for sizing middlings, rather than for reducing them to flour. Wegmann also made rollers for Ganz & Co., of Budapest, but in chilled iron of which they were manufacturers, instead of porcelain. In 1875 the use of the rolls, of one sort or the other, spread rapidly in Germany, and at exhibitions at Vienna in 1875 and Nuremberg in 1876 many different makes were shown. It was at this time that the roller flour of Pesth began to obtain the wide reputation in Europe which it so fully achieved later on.

Of the two porcelain roller mills first brought to America by Oscar Oexle, a milling engineer, in 1873, E. T. Archibald, of Dundas, Minn., secured one, and, it is supposed, Hecker & Co., of New York city, the other.

As the fitting complement of the purifier, put in use in America but a few years before, the roller was favorably received and was disseminated with little delay. The experimental mill of 100 barrels' capacity, built in one end of the Washburn C mill, at Minneapolis, in the winter of 1878-79, was the first attempt at genuine roller milling made in America. This mill contained sharp corrugated iron, smooth iron, and porcelain rolls. It proved such a success as to give a powerful impetus to the general introduction of roller milling.

It should be said, in considering the employment of rollers in America, that they were used experimentally in some mills at a date nearly as early as that of their invention in Europe. A patent is recorded, issued before 1840, the claim of which embodies the use of rolls for reducing grain. Such rolls, first employed in crushing wheat, were clumsy affairs, many of them 30 to 40 inches long and 18 in diameter. Ordinary cast-iron, and, earlier, granite, stone, and marble were the materials employed. Afterwards chilled iron rolls were produced and used for making a germ separation, and, later on, for wheat reduction. Their construction was clumsy and faulty in all respects, their means of adjustment with regard to distance being so poor as to result in flattening instead of granulating the stock. With the importation of the first corrugated iron rolls for reducing wheat, a great change took place. The imported rolls being of very superior construction, our mill-builders quickly perceived their valuable points and set about to furnish better machines. So great was their success, that it may with perfect truth be said that American roller mills now surpass all others for convenience and ingenuity. From rolls of 30 and 36 inches in length and 10 and 12 in diameter, they were altered, after the change in grinding methods, to 18 inches in length and 9 in diameter. At present machines much smaller are made by way of supplying the requirements of small mills. Yet, though both longer and smaller rolls are made and much used, 9 by 18 may be considered the standard size. Among the foreign innovations was the belt drive, which was well received as being lighter-running and much less noisy.

According to early practice a single pair of rolls was customary in a frame, but the common and nearly universal practice of late years is the use of two pairs, as being more economical and convenient, as well as more perfect mechanically. Mills having four pairs of rolls are built, but their use is somewhat exceptional. An arrangement of three rolls placed one above the other, and designed to save space and power by doing the work of two pairs, originally invented by Daverio of Switzerland, after Wegmann's porcelain rolls, is also made in America and is finding many advocates.

The rollers, as employed in general practice, are grooved for reducing wheat to middlings and also for cleaning bran. The corrugations are of many angles and degrees of sharpness, each maker having patented a theory of his own on the subject. Ordinarily they have a slight spiral twist from end to end to prevent interference in differential driving. The fineness of corrugation depends on the material to be treated,

Figs. 4 and 5 show a roller mill with two pairs of rolls. The inside ones have stationary bearings; the outside ones movable bearings. D is a nut and hand-wheel which engages screw F, passing through a chamber in the frame and a coil-spring and attached to the bar B. By tightening the nut D the spring is compressed in the chamber and acts on the roll bearing through the fulcrum C, pressing the movable roll against the stationary roll. The hand-wheel G also engages a screw passing through a hole at H in the roller frame and connects the movable bearing A; by tightening the screw the rolls are held apart, the object being to prevent the rolls from coming together in case the feed accidentally runs out. K is a tightener pulley held in place by the movable plate M, moving in a chamber O; M and N, a screw and hand-wheel for adjusting the pulley just mentioned. Each roll has a driving pulley, the differential motion being arranged by the use of pulleys differing in

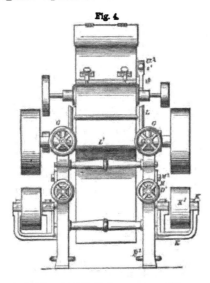

Fig. 4.

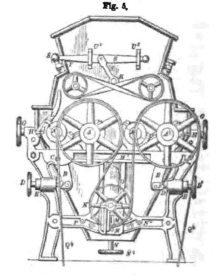

Fig. 5.

those on the first breaks being coarse, with a gradual change as the material is more and more reduced. The smooth rolls are employed mainly in the reduction of the purified middlings to flour, and are set closer and closer as the particles of stock grow finer, the same being true of corrugated rolls on breaks.

The object of the breaks of wheat in roller milling is to crush the grain so gradually and gently as to liberate the impurities and detach the bran from the granular fragments of the grain, making at the same time as little flour as possible. The object of the reduction of middlings is to so flatten the germ that it can be easily separated, and to powder the detached and purified particles by gentle and cool pressure, so that the flour resulting will be granular and strong, as well as white.

There are eighteen or twenty firms in the United States at present engaged in making roller mills. Of these some manufacture all styles and sizes, and others but one or two. The essential principles involved are the same in all, the difference on which the various patents rest being details of construction, drive, or adjustment. The engraving here given represents end and side sectional views of a modern type of roller mills, if a machine so recently come into general use can be styled modern.

diameter. R, a shaft running through the hopper of the machine and connecting with bars $S S S$, is a device for shutting off the feed.

After the wheat has been cleaned upon the usual separators, smutters, and brush machines (and cockle separators where necessary), it is spouted to the first pair of rolls, which sometimes have four to eight corrugations per inch of circumference, as shown in the accompanying engraving: (Fig. 6).

Fig. 6.

This is intended to split the wheat berry through the crease, for the purpose of liberating the germ and the impurities contained within the crease which are beyond the reach of the wheat-cleaners. This split wheat is then sent to a wire-covered scalping reel, to sift out all germ, crease impurities, and a very insignificant amount of middlings and flour; in good milling the proportion being 90 to 100 pounds for each hundred barrels of flour, so that it is after this break that the actual manufacture of flour commences. The second break is on the wheat which tails over the end of the reel above mentioned, and through spouts to the second pair of rolls, which have finer corrugations and are set closer together than the first set. This crushes the broken wheat slightly, resulting in a yield of middlings and a little break flour. This chop is then sent to the scalping reel, where the flour and middlings sift through, and the remainder passes over the tail of the reel to the third break. The break stock from the tail of the second scalping reel then passes to the next pair of break rolls, having still finer corrugations and set still closer together, and then to the third scalping reel, when the middlings and flour are separated from the chop as in the second break. The break stock from the tail of the third scalping reel then passes to the fourth pair of rolls, where it is still further reduced by finer corrugations and closer setting. From these two breaks is obtained the greatest quantity of middlings. The break stock from the tail of the fourth scalping reel, now nearly reduced to bran, is sent to the fifth break rolls, and thence to the fifth break scalping reel, where separations are made similar to those above outlined. The sixth break is the last step in the reduction of the wheat berry, and with it ends the use of the corrugated rolls, the process being the same as those preceding it, except that the bran passing over the tail of the sixth scalping reel may be sent to the bran duster, the middlings which have been made and separated on the six breaks outlined going through purifiers before again passing to rolls, and being then reduced on smooth instead of corrugated rolls. On some kinds of wheat, seven and eight breaks are deemed desirable, but commonly six is the highest number used. In small mills, to save expense in machinery, it is customary to reduce the wheat in four or five breaks only; but while even this is a long step in advance of the old style stone milling, it results in an increased percentage of flour from the breaks, and a decreased percentage of middlings, thus defeating, in a measure, the chief aim of gradual reduction milling.

In bolting, the flour and germ sifting through the first break and scalping reel are sometimes sent to the offal or feed bin, but in many cases are rebolted for a low grade of flour. The flour and middlings sifted through the bolting cloths of the second, third, fourth, fifth, and sixth break scalping reels are collected and sent to the proper reels for the purpose of separating the flour from the middlings. The resultant flour is then sent to other reels, properly clothed, and is redressed, the product being what is known as bakers' or the third highest grade of flour. The middlings, after being properly dusted and purified, are then gradually reduced to flour by a series of processes similar to the breaks of the wheat. That is, the coarser middlings are crushed on smooth rolls to finer middlings, and the flour being bolted out after each crushing until, in all roller mills, nothing remains but the feed. The germy middlings, the light fluffy materials, and other offal containing some traces of flour, which are taken out during the various stages of this gradual reduction of middlings, are further reduced to the lowest grades of flour and to offal.

There is yet considerable diversity of opinion among advanced millers as to the proper method of reducing a certain grade of fine middlings, when a point is reached where the smooth rolls flatten most of the stock and make a little poor flour, but the weight of opinion and usage is in favor of handling this stock on the millstones for which greater capacity is claimed as well as the obtaining of a granular flour of better color and strength and with less manipulation than by the reduction to the end on rolls. Most millers who use and advocate this use of the millstones say that if compelled to throw out the stones they would employ porcelain rolls to finish the fine middlings, but as to this there is much diversity of opinion, even among the most successful millers.

Flour and Middlings Graders.—The middlings and flour resulting from the first six breaks of the wheat are referred to as going to scalping reels, etc. These consist of a series of centrifugal or other reels, bolting chests or machines, of various patterns and covered with different numbers of wire cloth and silk gauze, the numbers representing the various degrees of fineness of mesh. These machines are of a common type, or so much so as not to require illustration or description, that given of the centrifugal reel being sufficient to indicate the office and style of construction of these machines, although some of them resemble the illustration of the centrifugal but slightly.

The Middlings Purifier.—The province of the purifier is to remove the impurities and fine material, and notably the bran particles, from granular product resulting from the gradual reduction of the wheat berry. Working by specific gravity and adjustable to middlings and impurities of varying degrees of fineness, it entirely eliminates the greater part of those foreign or discoloring substances for which there was no adequate remedy prior to its invention. Originally its use was peculiarly applicable to the reduction of very hard wheat, in which the middlings were the glutenous portion next the hull. These had invariably adhering particles of bran, which there was no rational way of removing. Yet in case they were ground together the resulting product was but little better than cattle-feed. The desire to improve this product suggested the invention of the middlings purifier. High grinding increased the quantity of middlings and made the need of such a machine more evident. Its invention and adoption marked an entire revolution in the art of milling, the roller mill being but its sequence, developed by high milling, which is simply the production of the least amount of flour and the large quantity of middlings in the preliminary breaking of wheat.

It may be said that the term middlings is now applied indiscriminately to the granular products resulting from the gradual reduction of wheat. The application of the machine in practice has thus become extremely broad, it being considered as much a necessity in winter wheat milling as among the hard wheat mills where it originated.

Ignaz Parr, or Paur, known as the father of high milling, and born at Tattendorf, Lower Austria, 1778, invented about 1810 the first purifier of which there is record. The machine was the result of an effort to facilitate the work of cleaning middlings, in order that more of the product known as "extract flour" might be made. The demand for this flour, which Paur produced by regrinding the purified middlings, was greater than he could supply with the use of hand sieves only in purifying. He therefore experimented, and finally, with the aid of Winter, a cabinet-maker, made machine, Fig. 7.

From this beginning the use and improvement of the purifier in Europe seems to have spread to some extent, and there is every reason to presume that it was considerably employed in the best Austrian, German, and French mills perhaps thirty years before any knowledge of it found its way across the Atlantic. G.

H. Christian, of the Washburn mill, Minneapolis, visiting France about 1870 in search of information with regard to purifying, saw the Cabanas purifier, invented in 1855, at work there, and brought home a machine of this patent which was used in the Washburn mill up to the time of the great explosion in 1878. This purifier had a sieve suspended, with both horizontal and vertical reciprocating movements, and enclosed in a box. It had a pendant cloth attached to its interior border in such a manner as to confine the air between the lower surface of the silk and the bottom of the box. The current of air produced passed from below upward through the silk, thus lifting the lighter particles and effecting a separation.

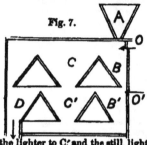

Fig. 7.

A is the hopper from which the broken grains fall into the purifier. O is an opening through which a current of air is drawn in upon the falling middlings. The heaviest fall through the division B, the next heavier fall at C. What falls through B encounters a current of air from O', which carries the lighter to C', and the still lighter is carried over to D. Thus the currents separate the middlings into three grades.

Until 1866 the only middlings purifying attempted in America was by means of sieves, or, as practised by Oliver Evans in 1836, on the ordinary bolting reel. This was done to clear the product so far as possible from bran and impurities, when, being reground, it occupied a place intermediate between flour and feed. But the production of middlings was carefully avoided by Evans and all other American millers, for, though they were known to contain rich and nutritious elements, there was an entire lack of means and knowledge to utilize them. As they formed comparatively a small proportion of the whole product prior to the practice of high milling, no strenuous efforts to turn them to account more satisfactorily were made in this country for many years.

In 1866 Jesse Ames & Sons, of Northfield, Minn., having accidentally discovered the virtues of high grinding, experimented with various devices to purify the large quantity of middlings resultant upon that mode of reduction. One method was in blowing a blast of air through a falling stream of middlings, but as they were not of the same size this did not work well. They were then run into an eight-sided reel into which a blast of air was blown, a plan proving the most successful of any tried. In 1868 Nicholas and E. N. LaCroix were experimenting with and operating in Faribault, Minn., a machine described as a box with a sieve on top of it and an air-blast under the sieve. This is the earliest account given of the use in this country of sieve and air-blast in middlings purification. Their machine was an imitation of the patent of one Perigault, which LaCroix had seen working in France. In February, 1870, La Croix built for George H. Christian, then manager of the Washburn mill at Minneapolis, an imitation of this Perigault purifier, and the machine was run several weeks in the Washburn mill, where it proved the value of the principles involved, but was not successful enough for practical use.

These experiments were carried on with the utmost secrecy, but E. T. Archibald, of Dundas, Minn., who had lately built a new mill, induced LaCroix to make another purifier for him, which, completed late in the year, he placed in his mill-attic and began also to experiment secretly. Having by hard and slow work accumulated 100 barrels of middlings, he had them ground on a stone. The flour resulting was shipped to New York and Boston, and was the first flour made by the middlings purifying process to be marketed in America. So great was its excellence that its price rose several dollars above that of what had previously been considered the best flour.

After LaCroix's purifier went out of use in the Washburn mill, because of its defects, George T. Smith, then head miller, began to experiment with it. He saw that the great need was a brush to keep the meshes of the cloth free, and this he successfully supplied. Profiting by his own study of the principles involved, he developed one improvement after another and embodied them in a purifier which was constructed under his personal supervision in that mill.

This machine contained the following new elements: An upward air-current through the covering of a reciprocating sieve, clothed with silk of progressively coarser mesh from head to tail; an enclosed air-space above the sieve, divided by transverse partitions into separate compartments, having practically no communication with each other, and each opening into the chamber of an exhaust fan through an adjustable valve so placed as to permit the regulation of the strength of the air-current through each compartment separately; a series of dust-settling chambers or testing drawers corresponding in number to the compartments above mentioned, and a brushing device automatically operated, and working against the under side of the sieve clothing. The principles of purification which this organization was adapted to carry out, and the general plan of construction followed by Mr. Smith in building his first purifier, have since been steadily preserved in the manufacture of this machine. The accompanying Fig. 8 gives a longitudinal vertical section.

A is the frame-work. H the hopper into which the middlings to be purified are spouted. K a feed roll for delivering them to the sieve M. Y is the brush carried by endless chains, and arranged to sweep the under side of the sieve cloth from head to tail. G, G, G, the compartments above the sieve. F, F, F, the dust-collecting chambers or drawers. E, E, E, the adjustable valves, opening into the air-chamber D; and B the exhaust fan. Motion imparted to the driving pulley R puts all parts of the machine into operation as follows: the sieve is rapidly reciprocated horizontally, and from the manner in which it is suspended has also a very slight rising and falling movement, which causes material delivered to it to flow from head to tail. The middlings are fed on to the sieve in a broad, thin stream by the feed roll K, at its head, where the silk covering is finest, and a very slight air-current, regulated by the valve E, is drawn upwards through the first compartment G, barely sufficient to float the lighter impurities, and not sufficient to prevent the small, fine middlings from passing through the silk, thus avoiding the loss which would follow an ungraded air-current, strong enough to remove the heavy impurities through such a current, carrying the small middlings with the impurities to the fan. As the middlings flow along the sieve, and pass from fine to coarser silk, the strength of the air-current through each succeeding compartment is increased as may be required to suit the stock being purified, the character of which constantly changes as the smaller middlings pass through the progressively coarser sections of silk. The continuous air-currents upwards through the sieve cause fine particles of dust and flour to adhere to the under side of the silk, and granules of middlings too large to pass through become wedged into its meshes on the upper side. These are removed by the brush Y, which is arranged to sweep the entire under surface of the sieve covering at intervals of a few minutes. The air-currents drawn up through the sieve carry a large quantity of dust and other impurities, and are made to pass across the open tops of the dust-settling chambers, or drawers, F, on their way to the fan, thus producing an eddy, which causes the heaviest and best portions of the material carried by the air to be deposited in these drawers. Access to them is conveniently had, and an examination of their contents will at once inform the operator whether any good material is being taken out by the fan, and if so, from which section of the sieve it comes, so that he may know where to reduce the current by means of valves E.

plicated and costly, but he expects to offset this drawback by the greatly improved value of the product.

The Jonathan Mills Flour Dresser.—In this machine, which is enclosed like all bolters and very similar in external appearance to the centrifugal, is a round reel, covered with suitable numbers of silk and supported on several flat, tempered, steel hoops running around the reel. The heads are cast solid and are fitted with V-shaped troughs in their circumferences. Into these and inside the silk are fitted 24 staves, so joined together that the cylinder is solid, but with a zigzag surface of V-shaped grooves throughout

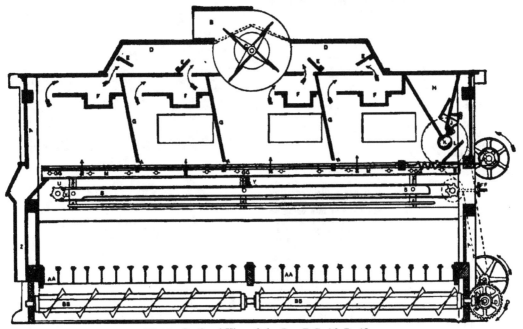

Fig. 8.—Sectional View of the Geo. T. Smith Purifier.

All of Smith's inventions were patented by him, and although some of his devices were claimed by Lacroix, Christian, Barter, and others, giving rise to much controversy and costly litigation, Smith was finally awarded priority over all contestants. Amongst the first to adopt Smith's purifier and system were C. A. Pillsbury, of Minneapolis, and E. T. Archibald, of Dundas, Minn. As is the usual experience of inventors, there were several imitations of Smith's machine, and efforts were made to break down his patents; but he was able not only to successfully defend himself against both classes of attacks but to organise and build up a great company on the basis of his patents, which under his management has grown into one of the largest manufactories of any kind in the United States, and the largest of its class in the world.

Flour Purifying.—The latest development of modern milling contemplates the application of the principle of purification by specific gravity to flour as well as to middlings. This process, which is as yet in an experimental state, aims at the production of a very large proportion of white flour. Its inventor assumes that when all possible impurities are eliminated from middlings, there still remain many which inevitably enter the flour, and he claims that it is practicable to take such worthless material out and thus lessen the proportion of low grade and increase the quantity and value of higher qualities. He admits that, by the use of this process, the already complicated and costly machinery of milling will be rendered still more com-

its length. Six or seven inches back from the reel head, at each end, every other stave is cut out, leaving apertures through which the stock is fed on the silk. Being fed in at the head by screw conveyer, it falls through the openings on the cloth and rapidly makes its way to the tail of the reel, where it drops through the slats and is carried away by conveyer. For keeping the cloth clear there is an arrangement of bristle brushes, so suspended over the top of the reel as to rest on the cloth.

The Jonathan Mills Disk Machine.—This reducer works on a principle combining the action of stones and rollers. Its grinding surface is furnished by two horizontally placed chilled iron disks, of which the lower is the runner and the upper is stationary. These disks have a depressed face to within a few inches of the periphery, leaving just space enough for the wheat to pass flat. The skirt of the disks is corrugated, and there are also several leading grooves, or corrugations, in the depressed face. The speed of the machine being high, the product works along the leading grooves by centrifugal force and passes on the corrugation of the skirt, where it is crushed, different adjustments and corrugations being made for varying degrees of fineness.

Other disk machines, either horizontal or vertical, and employing knives, rings, pegs, or other comminuting devices on their working surfaces, are also in use, though their employment is not extensive, comparatively.

The Morse Elevator Bolt.—As its name indicates, this apparatus consists of an elevator system in combination with a bolting sieve. The sieve is inclined at a slight angle and the stock is fed on it by a system of rows of buckets mounted on an endless belt running around the drums

The stock is fed into the buckets by a suitable device, elevated over the upper drum and delivered on a cantboard, whence it falls on the inclined screen, sliding down its whole length. Appropriate mechanism returns what remains upon the screen to the buckets, so that the operation may be repeated to any desirable extent. Stock of varying fineness or character may be fed into the different rows of buckets, the screen being, in such case, clothed to suit the material.

The Centrifugal Reel.—This reel, introduced into America by a Swiss inventor in 1880, differs from the ordinary bolter in employing various devices of beaters or wings on an axle in the centre of the cylinder, the design of which is to secure a tangential or throwing movement of the stock, instead of the sliding movement of the ordinary reel. As the beater action makes the bolting more intense, the centrifugal may be, and is, considerably smaller than the old bolt. Its length differs with different makers from 6½ to 11 or 12 feet over all; width of frame from 3 to 4 feet; height of frame from 4½ to 5½ feet. The beaters, of various shapes, length, and sizes, are arranged spirally about the central axle, and by their action in motion create a vacuum which prevents the stock from dropping to the bottom of the reel. The frame on which the cloth is stretched is in some cases six- or eight-sided, and in others circular. The ribs bracing the cloth are of various designs, some having in view supplementary effect in keeping the stock going from silk to beaters. Devices are now in use involving the use of shovels or scoops so fastened on the frame of the reel as to swing with its motion, and thus, after collecting the flour, throw it, as the reel passes around, again on the beaters. The centrifugal has been found especially applicable to stock of a flat, soft, or somewhat lifeless character, on which its rapid and vigorous action has a disintegrating effect. It is not regarded as likely to supersede the ordinary reels, though a few mills have been built of late using no other style of bolting. By millers in general it is considered a valuable supplement to the old reel, and a relief to the work of the purifiers. It is manufactured by several American mill-builders, the patents not referring to the principle, as in the case of those on roller mills, but to the details of construction. Much diversity exists in this way as to shape, size, and length of beaters, form of ribs, manner of clothing the cylinder, etc. The illustration shows the machine with a portion of the outer case, as well as of the cloth on the cylinder, removed to show the inner workings, while another reel in the background is reversed to show its drive-gearing. (Fig. 9).

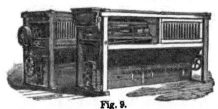

Fig. 9.

The Dust Collector.—Flour-dust, which is the inevitable attendant of the rudest milling, was vastly increased in quantity by the complicated reducing and sifting processes of gradual reduction. The use of the purifying and aspirating machinery, distinguished by the employment of air in rapid motion, kept vast quantities of fine dust constantly in suspension in the air of mills employing such devices. Although an effort was made to remove this substance by blowing it into rooms designed for the purpose, the process was more or less ineffectual, much dust escaping removal or finding its way back into the mill. When, after a time, a series of disastrous explosions occurred in great mills employing improved methods, it was discovered that the fine flour-dust was the cause of this lamentable destruction of life and property. Suspended in large amounts in the dry air of the mills and dust-rooms, it was shown to possess the explosive qualities of gunpowder. Efforts were at once made to replace the ineffectual dust-rooms by some better device, these efforts resulting in the machine known as the dust-collector.

It consists of an enclosed cylinder with inner and outer ribs, around which flannel is wound from one piece, so that when complete there is an air-space the width of each rib between two flannel surfaces. The dust and air are drawn into the machine by suction, and forced through the flannel into and through the spaces between the inner flannel surfaces and on to the centre of the machine or cylinder, whence the air passes out of either end, both being open. The cylinder is revolved slowly, rib by rib, by a ratchet, and as each rib reaches a point directly over the centre of the bottom of the collector, it is tapped lightly by a knocker, which causes the dust, arrested by the flannel, to drop into a conveyer which carries it away from the machine. By a peculiar construction of the machine a reverse current of air is drawn from the outside through the flannel in such a way as to facilitate the thorough cleaning of the cloth.

In addition to the merits of the dust collector as a preventive of explosions, it is effectual in saving the good material blown from the purifiers, as in the old dust-rooms a very large portion of this was blown out and wasted. The dust collector has also much shorter spouts for connection with the purifiers, if it is not, as in most cases, placed directly upon them. Thus the long spouts necessitated by the dust-room, which occupied much space, and acted as the most destructive of conductors in case of fire, have been to a great extent displaced by the device in question. The illustration shows the machine in perspective, with the doors removed, showing the "balloon," or cylinder, and the end section of the latter, clothed with flannel; the arrows indicating the course of the air-currents. (Figs. 10, 11).

Fig. 10.

Fig. 11.

The Bran Duster.—This is a machine which was long desired, but is of very recent invention and construction on correct principles, and has become another of the appliances indispensable in successful milling. A fair type of the several varieties in use is a machine with an upright cylinder, covered with a fine wire cloth, the cylinder having adjustable brushes on the inside, secured to the central arm in such a way as to very nearly touch the cloth. This cylinder revolves rapidly, usually about 300 revolutions per minute, and the bran, being fed into it from the top, must pass between the brushes and the sides of the cylinder. In getting through it is so thoroughly swept by the brushes as to remove from it all adhering particles of flour, which is forced through the wire cloth, while the cleaned bran falls down and is carried away to the feed-bins. An automatic knocker prevents the cylinder from becoming clogged, while the wooden case confines the material to the machine. Herewith is an illustration of the bran duster. (Fig. 12).

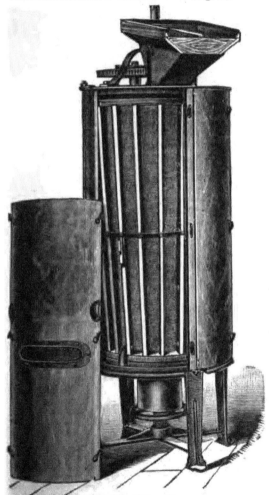

Fig. 12.—A Bran Duster.

When the flour of the various grades has been separated and carried to the bins provided for each, it is packed in barrels or sacks, as is desired. In all well-regulated flour-mills, the packing device is attached to the hopper of the bin, and when set in motion does its work rapidly and well, with little dust or waste. The packer is a simple yet ingenious device. It connects directly with the bin and has removable tubes, the lower ends of which are adaptable to sacks and barrels of various sizes. The general style of packers is the same, and it is equally well adapted to filling the 2 lb. sack, the half-barrel, or the 280 lb. export sack, the largest package used. Flour which goes abroad is put into jute sacks, mainly of 140 lbs. weight, but often in cental and in 280 lb. sacks. For domestic trade, paper and cotton sacks and oak or elm barrels are used exclusively, although of late attempts have been made to introduce a paper barrel. The handling of packed flour has been reduced to great precision in late years, the results being a marked reduction in the cost of operating mills.

Statistics.—In 1880 there were in the United States 24,338 flouring-mills, employing $177,361,878 capital and 58,407 operatives. The aggregate wages paid yearly was $17,422,316, making 99¼ cts. per day to each operative, estimating the working year at 300 days. Operating 59,612 runs of stone, these mills had, at that time, capacity to grind 4,730,106 bushels daily. The total value of all grain ground in 1880 was placed at $441,545,225, with resulting products worth $505,185,712. Partial statistics of the ten leading States at that time are shown in the following table:

	Mills.	Capital.	Wheat. (Bushels.)	Other grain.	Value of products.
New York	1,768	$19,545,994	19,904,896	34,814,643	$49,321,984
Illinois	1,024	13,579,680	34,287,427	15,721,729	47,471,558
Pennsylvania	2,873	20,238,601	19,081,580	25,860,258	41,522,662
Minnesota	436	10,510,362	35,264,005	2,040,064	41,519,004
Ohio	1,380	12,328,847	26,091,762	11,409,117	38,950,264
Missouri	872	7,853,675	24,402,229	9,471,767	32,438,851
Indiana	996	9,484,023	21,682,123	2,906,588	29,591,397
Wisconsin	705	9,199,735	19,616,905	9,698,086	27,609,430
Michigan	706	7,704,464	15,442,842	8,985,989	23,546,875
Iowa	713	7,890,859	14,604,382	11,509,181	19,089,401

The total export for 1890 from all American ports was, in wheat, 54,387,767 bushels; in flour, 12,231,711 barrels; of these the value was as follows: wheat, $45,275,906; flour, $57,036,168. Exports of wheat and flour estimated as wheat from all American ports for 1884 and three years preceding were, by months and years, as below in bushels, allowing four and a half bushels to a barrel of flour.

	1884.	1883.	1882.	1881.
January	8,864,386	11,214,983	8,915,157	11,592,874
February	6,808,511	9,727,883	7,687,428	10,145,202
March	7,242,876	9,805,474	8,534,585	14,680,652
April	9,392,155	7,110,523	6,971,948	13,580,167
May	7,745,191	5,696,784	7,217,656	12,904,013
June	7,146,871	6,254,120	6,421,221	12,763,667
July	9,194,892	6,425,799	12,570,229	11,618,246
August	15,609,225	12,690,128	23,863,614	17,072,696
September	12,932,343	11,305,765	20,853,888	13,122,662
October	11,046,067	10,058,515	12,808,304	8,850,438
November	10,857,808	10,902,528	11,708,584	11,884,887
December	12,862,001	9,268,889	12,861,854	10,208,957
Total	119,702,326	110,401,391	140,414,468	148,424,461

Of the flouring mills in operation at present, probably from one-third to one-half work on the new process or gradual reduction system, or some more or less complete attempt at its methods. While the whole number of mills has undoubtedly much increased, especially in the hard wheat section of the middle and extreme north-west, the increase in flour production is proportionately much greater. This is owing to the fact that in altering from the old process to the new, machinery sufficient for a greater output has usually been added, and also because a very large proportion of the new mills have been those of the merchant class. A careful compilation of returns from 430 principal merchant mills in seventeen chief milling States and Territories, with perhaps a few in other States, gives an aggregate daily capacity in 1885 of 146,031 barrels, with a flour product for the crop year of 24,563,364 barrels.

Experience has shown that in Minneapolis, the world's milling centre, the average consumption of flour *per capita* yearly is 1¼ barrels. It is probable that the average of the United States as a whole is from ¾ to 1 barrel.

Roller mills produce from four to ten grades of food materials, according to the machinery employed and the trade supplied. These may, however, be condensed as below, to illustrate conveniently the percentage of the various grades resulting from a certain amount of wheat:

Patent flour	18.125	per cent.
Clear flour	47.125	"
Low grade flour	7.250	"
Feed	24.6	"
Invisible loss	2.9	"

The amount of wheat used in making a barrel of flour varies from 4½ to 5¼ bushels, the former quantity being generally regarded as an ideal in good milling.

FLOWER, WILLIAM HENRY, an English zoölogist, was born at Stratford-on-Avon, Nov. 30, 1831. He was educated at University College, London, and at the Middlesex Hospital, graduating at London University in 1851. In 1854 he was admitted to the Royal College of Surgeons, and served with distinction in the Crimean war. In 1857 he became a fellow of the Royal College of Surgeons, and lecturer on comparative anatomy in the Middlesex Hospital. In 1858 he married a sister of Prof. Piazzi Smyth; in 1861 he was made curator of the Hunterian Museum. He also took Mr. Huxley's Hunterian professorship in 1869, and in 1879 he became president of the Zoölogical Society. He is the author of a very great number of scientific papers and of several volumes, chiefly on mammals.

FLOYD, JOHN BUCHANAN (1805–1863), an American statesman, was born in Montgomery co., Va., in 1805, being the son of Gov. John Floyd. He graduated at South Carolina College in 1826, and was admitted to the bar in 1828. He practised law at Helena, Ark., from 1836 to 1839, then returned to Virginia, and was member of the State legislature in 1847 and 1849. He was governor of Virginia from 1850 to 1853. He was secretary of war during President Buchanan's administration, and when the secession of the Southern States was imminent, he took advantage of his position to scatter the small national army, and to transfer arms and munitions in large quantities to the Southern arsenals. In December, 1860, he was indicted by the grand-jury of the District of Columbia as being privy to the abstraction of a large amount of Indian bonds from the Department of the Interior, but he left Washington without being brought to trial. On the secession of Virginia he was made a brigadier-general in the Confederate army, and commanded in West Virginia. He was defeated by Gen. J. D. Cox and driven out by Gen. W. S. Rosecrans in the fall of 1861, and afterwards was transferred to Kentucky. He commanded Fort Donelson during its siege, but on Feb. 16, 1862, he abdicated the command and with Gen. Pillow and 3000 men of the garrison escaped to Tennessee. For his abandonment of the fort he was censured by the Confederate Government, and afterwards held only nominal commands. He died at Abingdon, Va., Aug. 26, 1863.

FLUSHING, an incorporated village of Queens co., New York, is on Flushing Bay, on the north side of Long Island, 8 miles E. of New York, on the North Shore division of the Long Island Railroad. It has a town-hall, 2 banks, 2 hotels, 2 daily and 2 weekly newspapers, 8 churches, a high school and other schools and academies. It has also an iron-foundry, planing-mills, dye-factory, tool-works. It is a handsome town, rising gently from the bay, has well paved, flagged and macadamized streets, a park, gas, and water-works. Its property is valued at $3,500,000, and the public debt is $237,000. It was settled in 1643 by English Quakers, but these were soon joined by Dutch and French immigrants. The name is derived from Flushing (Vlissingen) in Holland. Long noted for its nurseries and gardens as well as its educational advantages, it is a favorite residence of New York merchants. Population 6683.

FOND DU LAC, a city of Wisconsin, county-seat of the county of the same name, is 60 miles N. by W. of Milwaukee, at the S. end of Winnebago Lake, at the entrance of Fox River. It is on the Chicago and Northwestern, the Chicago, Milwaukee, and St. Paul, and four other railroads. It has communication also by steamboat with towns on the Fox, Wolf, and Wisconsin Rivers. Among its principal buildings are a fine court-house, opera-house, and high school. It has 6 hotels, 4 banks (one national), 2 daily and 5 weekly newspapers, 12 churches, 13 schools, 2 convents, and a monastery. Its manufactures comprise threshing-machines, farm implements, wagons, furniture, shoes, doors, sashes, etc. It is lighted with gas and electricity and has water-works and many astesian wells. Its property is valued at $4,000,000 and the public debt is $130,000. It was settled in 1836 and incorporated in 1851. Its population in 1880 was 13,094, one-half being of American birth.

FOOTE, ANDREW HULL (1806–1863), an American admiral, was born at New Haven, Conn., Sept. 12, 1806. He was the son of Gov. Samuel A. Foote (1780–1846), and entered the navy as midshipman Dec. 4, 1822. He became lieutenant in May, 1830, and in 1833 was flag lieutenant of the Mediterranean squadron. In 1838, in the sloop-of-war John Adams, he circumnavigated the globe, and took part in an attack on the pirates of Sumatra. As superintendent of the naval asylum, 1841–43, and in the cruise of the Cumberland, 1843–45, he enforced total abstinence from intoxicating liquors. He also gave religious instruction and preached extemporaneously. From 1849 to 1852, in command of the brig Perry, he was engaged on the coast of Africa in suppressing the slave-trade. In 1856 while in command of the sloop Portsmouth he arrived at Canton just before the outbreak of hostilities between the English and the Chinese, and exerted himself to protect American property. While thus engaged he was fired upon by Chinese forts, and when an apology for this action was refused he attacked and captured the four forts, built of granite, and garrisoned with 5000 men. Out of his own force of 280 men he lost 40, while the garrison had 400 killed and wounded. At the outbreak of the civil war he was executive officer of the Brooklyn navy-yard. In July he was made captain, and in September was appointed flag officer of the flotilla intended to open the navigation of the Mississippi and its tributaries. With seven gunboats which had been built under his direction he sailed from Cairo, Ill., on Feb. 4, 1862. He first attacked Fort Henry on the Tennessee River on the 6th, and compelled it to surrender. On the 14th he attacked Fort Donelson on the Cumberland River, but after an action of an hour and a half was obliged to withdraw, two of his gunboats having become unmanageable. He himself was severely wounded in the ankle, but without waiting for proper treatment of the injury he sailed down the Mississippi, where he besieged and captured Island No. 10, which had been strongly fortified by the Confederates. He was then compelled to ask for leave of absence, and from the condition of his wound nearly lost his life. On June 16, 1862, he was promoted to be rear-admiral, and soon after was made chief of the bureau of equipment and recruiting. On June 4, 1863, he was ordered to take command of the South Atlantic squadron, but on his way was taken ill at New York, and died there June 26, 1863. He published *Africa and the American Flag* (1854), and *Letters from Japan.* See *Life of Admiral A. H. Foote* by J. M. Hoppin (1874).

FOOTE, HENRY STUART (1800-1880), an American statesman, was born in Fauquier co., Va., Sept. 20, 1800. He graduated at Washington College, Lexington, Va., in 1819, studied law, and was admitted to the bar in 1822. He soon after removed to Tuscumbia, Ala., where he edited a Democratic paper, and in 1826 he settled at Jackson, Miss. He took an active part in politics, and in 1847 he was elected to the United States Senate, where he was made chairman of the committee on foreign relations. He was a firm supporter of Clay's compromise, and in 1851 he was elected governor of Mississippi over Jefferson Davis, who had announced and advocated the policy of secession on account of the admission of California as a free State. In 1854 Foote removed to California, but he returned to Mississippi in 1858. He was still an adherent of the Union cause, and in the Southern Convention at Knoxville, Tenn., in 1859, spoke warmly in opposition to the policy of the Southern leaders. During the civil war he was a member of the Confederate Congress from Tennessee, and was noted for his hostility to Jefferson Davis' administration. He was engaged in several duels, in two of which he was slightly wounded. He died May 19, 1880. He published *Texas and the Texans* (1841); *The War of the Rebellion* (1866); *Bench and Bar of the South and South-west* (1876).

FOOTE, WILLIAM HENRY (1794-1869), an American clergyman, was born at Colchester, Conn., Dec. 20, 1794. He graduated at Yale College in 1816, and taught at Winchester, Va. After studying theology at Princeton, he was licensed to preach by the Presbytery of Winchester, and he became agent of the Central Board of Missions. Afterwards he was agent for Hampden-Sidney College, and during the civil war he was chaplain in the Confederate army. He died at Romney, Va., Nov. 28, 1869. His *Sketches of the Presbyterian Church in North Carolina* (1846), and in *Virginia* (two vols., 1850-55), are valuable contributions to the history of those States. After his death his work on *The Huguenots* appeared.

FOOT-WASHING, an ecclesiastical ceremony, founded on the act of our Saviour, described in John xiii. 4-14. It does not seem that our Lord's injunction in ver. 14, "Ye ought to wash one another's feet," contains any warrant for an ecclesiastical ceremony, but is an oriental method of enjoining humble helpfulness among believers. However, in Augustine's day (A. D. 400), the custom appears in the church, and through the ages since both popes and monarchs have used the Thursday of holy week (Maundy-Thursday: Maundy=*Mandatum*, John xiii. 34) for the washing of the feet of twelve poor persons. The custom is found not only in the Roman Church but among the Moravians and Dunkers. By all these the reciprocal character of our Lord's injunction is overlooked.

FORAGE CROPS. The grains or cereal grasses have been treated under CEREALS, Vol. II., and more fully in the article AGRICULTURE, Vol. I. There is another class of grasses less directly useful, but still no less important to man, for by their herbage they supply the food and nourishment of those animals that supply him with meat and raiment. These may be termed *agricultural grasses*, to distinguish them from the cereals and other groups of economic importance. They may be briefly characterized as comprising those kinds which furnish the food of the grass-eating animals of the farm, or those which may be cultivated for this purpose. As thus defined this group includes a large number of species which may be separated into (1) meadow or mowing grasses and (2) pasture grasses. The first division includes those cultivated for hay; the second, the kinds best adapted for pasturage or grazing:

The pasture grasses of this country, with a few exceptions in the older-settled portions, are wild or native species, that grow spontaneously without care or culture. Upon the vast grazing lands of the region beyond the Mississippi these wild species alone support 30,000,000 head of horned cattle and sheep. The so-called "artificial grasses," embracing the different kinds of clovers, etc., form a very considerable portion of the hay crop of the country, and are generally associated by the farmer with the true grasses. They belong to a very different class of plants, however, and will be treated separately.

Mention has been made of the fact that the cereals are frequently cultivated for winter pasturage, or are grown for hay. The first is a common practice in the South, while their use for hay is chiefly confined to California.

There are but few kinds of grasses which are actually cultivated for hay; and of those species which supply the great grazing interests of the country the average farmer knows little or nothing. The importance of an acquaintance with these may be inferred from the fact that in point of value they exceed many times that of the hay crop, which is estimated to be above $400,000,000. The number of kinds growing in the meadows and pastures of an ordinary farm is much larger than is generally supposed. To be able to distinguish these various kinds requires no great amount of study. It is an easy matter to learn the terms applied to the different parts of a grass sufficient to enable the farmer to distinguish those that are likely to come within the range of his observation, and, possessing this knowledge, he will soon discover the relative merits of each.

According to their habit of growth grasses may be classified as—1. *Bunch grasses*, or such as grow in bunches and do not form a sward. The "bunch grass" of the Rocky Mountain region and the common hair or hassock grass of the Eastern States are examples of this class. 2. *Gregarious grasses*, or such as grow crowded together, forming a compact turf or sward. This is the usual habit of the grasses of the temperate regions.

A further classification based upon the *place of growth* may be made, and we have, *a. Aquatic grasses*, those growing in the water, *e. g.*, wild rice (*Zizania aquatica*) ; *b. Salt grasses*, those growing only in alkaline soil or on salt marshes near the coast, *e. g.*, rush salt grass (*Spartina juncea*) ; *c. Meadow and pasture grasses*, embracing the greater number of the valuable species of the meadow and pastures ; *d. Agrarian grasses*, or those possessing the character of weeds.

Useful as the grasses are in general, there are a few species among them which can only be looked upon as weeds—not in the sense merely of "plants out of place," but weeds wherever and under whatever conditions they may be found. Hedgehog or burgrass (*Cenchrus tribuloides*) is a species of this character. In the same category belong chess (*Bromus secalinus*), and bearded darnel (*Lolium temulentum*), both frequent grasses in grain-fields. The seeds of the last named are believed to be poisonous, a character almost exceptional in the grass family. Bearded darnel is supposed to be the "tares" of the New Testament.

There are other grasses which are weeds only when "out of place," or when occupying land designed for the use of other plants. Couch grass at the North and Bermuda grass in the South are species which become weeds of the very worst character when growing among cultivated crops. Barn-yard grass (*Panicum crus-galli*) and crab grass (*Panicum sanguinale*) are considered worthless weeds at the North, while at the South they are prized both for hay and pasturage. There are other kinds that make excellent forage while young, but as they mature they become weeds of a dangerous nature by the development of sharp-pointed awns, which may seriously injure horses or other animals feeding upon them. Wild oat grass (*Avena fatua*) and porcupine grass (*Stipa spartea*) are species of this character.

In a territory so large as that embraced within the limits of the United States, covering 25 degrees of latitude and 60 of longitude, with a climate that is subarctic at one extreme and nearly tropical at the other, with a surface diversified by the greatest lakes and longest rivers in the world, by endless plains, numerous and lofty mountain ranges, and great deserts, the vegetation must needs be of a most varied character. This variety maintains in the grasses, 800 species and varieties being known to grow within our limits.

In considering the *agricultural grasses* which abound throughout this vast area, they may be arranged into four groups : first, those belonging to the Northern and Middle States east of the Mississippi ; second, those of the Southern States, ranging westward to Texas ; third, those of the great plains and Rocky Mountain region ; and, fourth, those of California. A list of the more common species, or those having recognized or probable value for forage, that grow in each of these districts, will be given. It will be observed that many of the species named are common to the whole region. Some of these are natives ; but the larger part are introduced species, or those which have been brought from foreign countries, either intentionally or by accident. Certain species seem to follow in the footsteps of civilized man, and wherever he makes his abode there they may be found.

NORTHERN AND MIDDLE STATES EAST OF THE MISSISSIPPI.—The country embraced in this district seems to be especially fitted for the growth of the grasses. The summers never have that protracted season of excessive heat and drought that is so fatal to the growth of the more valued kinds at the South, but the moderate temperature and usually abundant moisture keep the grasses fresh and green throughout the season. This region has long been the home of timothy and herds-grass, Kentucky blue-grass and orchard grass—varieties most highly prized for hay and pasturage. The number of native species is large, and in time some of these will doubtless dispute the claims of the now more favored European grasses.

The order in which the species are taken up is that of their botanical classification :

Paspalum.—Two species may be mentioned, smooth paspalum (*P. lœve*), frequent in moist meadows from New England southward, and setaceous paspalum (*P. setaceum*), having nearly the same range but found chiefly on sandy soil. They have not been sufficiently recognised to receive popular names, but their high nutritive value, that of the first named being equal to orchard grass, together with their general prevalence, entitle them to notice.

Panicum.—The genus *Panicum* is the largest among the genera of grasses. The species are chiefly tropical or subtropical. A number of kinds extend within the limits of this list and are included under the general name of panic grass. They possess little agricultural value. Barnyard grass (*Panicum crus-galli*) and old witch grass (*P. capillare*) are common everywhere in cultivated grounds and waste places, and are classed with the weeds.

Bristly Foxtail Grass (*Setaria*).—There are four or five species of Setaria, all introduced grasses and all weeds, excepting Setaria Italica, which, with its varieties, includes the Italian, German, and American millets. The true millet is a species of *Panicum*.

Fresh-water Cord Grass (*Spartina cynosuroides*).—Near the sea-shore and along the margins of lakes and rivers the fresh-water cord grass is quite common. It is not deemed of any agricultural value, but is mentioned here on account of its having been used with success in the manufacture of paper. Another species of *Spartina*, called salt reed grass, has a more robust habit than the last and is confined in its growth to salt or brackish marshes within tide-water. Rush salt grass (*Spartina juncea*) is common on salt marshes, forming a considerable bulk of the salt meadow hay of the coast. Salt marsh grass (*Spartina stricta*) is a very common species along the sea-coast. Cattle are very fond of it. It has a strong, rancid odor which is communicated to the milk, and even to the flesh of the animals that feed upon it. Salt marsh grass makes an excellent material for thatching, more durable than wheat straw. On account of this use of the grass it is sometimes called " thatch."

Indian Rice, Water Oats (*Zizania aquatica*).—This is a very tall reed-like grass, common in muddy or swampy borders of streams and rivers, growing frequently in shallow water. Extensive areas bordering the shores of the Delaware, below Philadelphia, are covered with this grass. (See CEREALS.)

Rice Cut Grass, Rice's Cousin (*Leersia oryzoides*).—This and white grass (*L. virginica*) are common in very wet meadows and along streams. They are late bloomers and may have some value for late summer feed in localities where they abound.

Meadow Foxtail (*Alopecurus pratensis*).—This is an introduced species of much agricultural value. The floating foxtail (*A. geniculatus*) is an allied native species, frequent in wet meadows. Although prized both for hay and pasturage in England, they are not so much esteemed in this country. The meadow foxtail has a striking resemblance to timothy (*Phleum pratense*), but is distinguished by certain botanical characters as well as by its preference to wet meadows and earlier blooming. It is an excellent grass for permanent pastures and is valuable as a mixture in lawns.

Reed Canary Grass (*Phalaris arundinacea*).—This is a widely distributed native species, growing on alluvial soils by the sides of rivers, lakes, etc. It yields a large bulk of scarce hay, little liked by cattle or other stock. Canary grass (*Phalaris canariensis*) is an introduced species, rather frequent in waste grounds, and is sometimes cultivated for the seed, which is the favorite food of canary birds.

Sweet Vernal Grass (*Anthoxanthum odoratum*).—A native of Europe, but naturalized here in meadows, pastures, etc. It is of no value for hay, but it is hardy and its early growth renders it desirable as a lawn or pasture grass when mixed with other varieties.

Wild or Native Millet (*Milium effusum*).—A perennial, rather slender grass, common to the northern portions of Europe and America. It grows naturally in cold, damp woods and on mountain meadows, but thrives well when transplanted to open and exposed situations. It yields largely and multiplies both by seed and by the roots, sending out horizontal shoots of considerable length, which root at the joints as they grow.

Drop-seed Grass (*Muhlenbergia*).—Seven species of *Muhlenbergia* are found within the limits embraced in this list. They all come into foliage and bloom in the latter part of summer, and are, perhaps, of some value in supplying forage in pastures and woods at a season when the herbage of more valuable grasses is withered or dead. In the western districts they occur in greater abundance than at the east, and not unfrequently form a considerable bulk of what is called wild or prairie hay.

Timothy (*Phleum pratense*).—Introduced from Europe and cultivated throughout the region as the most valuable of all grasses for hay. In New England it is very generally known as herds-grass, but this name had best be restricted to a species of *Agrostis* mentioned below.

Sporobolus is a genus including a number of species, more or less common, but none of sufficient recognized importance to have received familiar names. *Sporobolus heterolepis*, a valued grass on the western prairies, is found as far east as New York.

Herds-Grass (*Agrostis alba*). [See Plate XXV.]—This is a variable grass and has received a number of common names. In the Middle States it is called herds-grass, while in New England it is named "red top." *Agrostis vulgaris* is not regarded as a distinct species, it being united with *Agrostis alba*. This grass is a native of Europe and was probably introduced into cultivation from that country. It appears, however, to be a native along our northern borders. It is a valuable grass for moist meadows and pastures, and is very generally cultivated. There are several native species of this genus, one of which, hair grass (*Agrostis scabra*), often becomes a troublesome weed in cultivated fields.

Wood Reed Grass (genus *Cinna*).—A frequent grass in swamps and along the borders of moist thickets, where it affords some forage.

Blue Joint Grass (*Deyeuxia canadensis*). [See Plate XXIV., where it bears the name *Calamagrostis canadensis*.]—This is a common species in wet meadows, especially northward. It is one of the most highly valued of the native grasses. It yields a large amount of forage, and cattle are fond of it both in its green state and when made into hay. There are several other species of *Deyeuxia* found in this district, but none to compare with blue joint in point of value. The name "blue joint" is popularly applied to several other grasses.

Sea Sand Reed (*Ammophila arundinacea*).—Common on the sandy shores of the Atlantic coast and borders of the great lakes. It has no strictly agricultural value, but it serves an important purpose in protecting sandy beaches from the encroachments of the sea by binding together the loose sands with its strong, perennial roots, which often extend to the distance of twenty feet or more.

Common Hair Grass (*Deschampsia flexuosa*).—A common grass in dry, sandy soil and on rocky hill-sides. It has no value for hay, but sheep are very fond of feeding upon the short, radical tuft of leaves. It deserves notice as a pasture grass where the soil is light and sandy.

Velvet Grass (*Holcus lanatus*).—A native of Europe, naturalized here in moist meadows. Although easy of cultivation and quite productive, it is of little value either for hay or pasture. It has some claims as an ornamental grass, its attractive appearance having brought it into notice wherever it abounds. It has received many common names besides the one given above. In New England it is known as "Salem grass" and "white timothy;" in the South, "velvet lawn grass" and "velvet mesquit grass;" in England, "woolly soft grass" and "Yorkshire white." Meadow soft grass is another familiar name applied to it.

Wild Oat Grass (*Danthonia spicata*), also called "white-top" and "old fog."—This is a native and is common in dry fields and open pastures. Its presence in meadow lands is a sure indication of an impoverished soil. It makes a light yield, and its only recommendation is in the fact that it will grow on hard clay soils where little else will.

Mesquite Grass (*Bouteloua oligostachya*). [See Plate XXIV.]—This and two other species (*Bouteloua hirsuta* and *Bouteloua racemosa*) are found within the district covered by this list, but with the exception of *Bouteloua racemosa* are confined to the western borders. They are native grasses growing in dry, sandy soil.

Dog's-tail, or Wire Grass (*Eleusine indica*).—This is an introduced grass, common in the Middle States, growing in paths and in moist cultivated grounds about dwellings. It comes into full vigor late in the season, and is one of the latest flowering species, continuing to bloom until killed by the frosts.

Common Reed (*Phragmites communis*).—This grass is common to both the old and the new world. It is one of the largest of the grasses native to the United States, often growing to the height of twelve feet or more. It is only found in swamps or along the marshy borders of streams and lakes, and can scarcely be said to have any agricultural value although cattle will feed upon it while the plants are young and tender. In Great Britain it is used for thatch, and it may be utilized for the same purpose in this country.

Spike Grass, Salt Grass (*Distichlis maritima*), is common in the salt marshes along the coast, and in the alkaline districts of the Far West. It enters largely into the composition of marsh hay, but is deemed of little value.

Orchard Grass (*Dactylis glomerata*).—This is one of the very best grasses grown either for grazing or hay. It easily adapts itself to a variety of soils and climates, and in consequence has become widely distributed. It grows well in moderate shade, as in orchards, and its name (orchard grass) is probably due to this fact. Although a native of Europe, its first cultivation was in this country about the middle of the last century. Unless sown thickly or with a good mixture of other grasses, orchard grass will grow in clumps or tussocks, which is its natural habit and only objectionable character. [See Plate XXV.]

Kentucky Blue-grass (*Poa pratensis*). [See Plate XXV.]—The best known, and, at present, the most valued of the *Poas* is the Kentucky blue-grass, a native species, growing in meadows and along streams and rivers from Maine to Oregon and northward to Alaska. It is highly valued for hay, but it excels chiefly as a pasture grass. In the rich calcareous soils of Kentucky this grass appears to have attained to its greatest perfection: for this reason, probably, it has become generally known as Kentucky blue-grass. "June grass" and "green-grass" are names also applied to this species.

Rough Meadow Grass (*Poa trivialis*).—This is an introduced species of *Poa*, but has become very common in moist meadows. For such localities it is a valuable addition to the pasture grasses.

Wire Grass (*Poa compressa*).—A common grass in Europe, and probably introduced from that country along with the more valuable cultivated varieties. It is believed to be indigenous northward. The stems are flattened, and, unlike those of most grasses, are solid, and consequently it makes a hay very heavy in proportion to its bulk. It affects dry, sterile soils, and is regarded as a valuable pasture grass, since most grazing animals, especially sheep, are very fond of it. In color it has a decidedly bluish cast, and the name "blue-grass" is far more applicable to this species than to *Poa pratensis*.

Fowl Meadow Grass, False Red-top (*Poa serotina*). [See Plate XXIV.]—Common to Europe and America, growing naturally in moist meadows and along the low borders of streams. It is especially suited to the cool climate of New

England and northern portion of New York, and its cultivation is chiefly confined to that region. As long ago as 1749 Jared Elliott published an account of this grass, claiming that it was much superior to timothy (*Phleum*), making a more soft and more pliable hay, and, in consequence, better suited for pressing and shipping. It thrives best when mixed with other grasses, and deserves a place in all mixtures for rich, moist pastures. The name "fowl meadow" is also applied to *Glyceria nervata*, a grass very similar to the above.

The genus *Poa* is represented in all parts of the world by many species, growing in woodland, pasture, or meadow, and, almost without exception, they make valuable forage plants wherever they abound. There are thirteen species found in the district embraced by this list: the most common is the little annual *Poa*, or low "spear grass," found in cultivated and waste grounds everywhere.

Manna Grass (*Glyceria*).—Ten species are natives of this district, and all are aquatic or semi-aquatic in their habits. The native hay from moist meadows is often largely composed of one or more of these grasses. One species, *Glyceria distans*, popularly known as sea or marsh spear grass, is one of the most valuable kinds of the salt marshes along the coast. *Glyceria canadensis* has received the common name of rattlesnake grass, probably from the resemblance of the rather large spikelets to that snake's rattle. It is rather an ornamental grass, and is sought for winter bouquets. *G. fluitans*, Floating glyceria, or true "manna grass," is common in very wet, low grounds, usually growing in the water. The seeds have a sweetish taste, and are used by the poorer peasantry of some European countries for food. Reed meadow grass is a robust-growing species and yields a large bulk of hay. Nerved manna grass, *G. nervata*, sometimes called fowl meadow grass, is the most common species, and is, perhaps, the most valuable of all from an agricultural point of view.

Fescue Grass (*Festuca*).—Four native and two introduced species, the most valuable of which is the taller, or meadow fescue (*Festuca elatior*). [See Plate XXIII.] Common in rich pasture lands, meadows, and by the waysides. In Virginia it is called Randall grass. It is a hardy, perennial species, thriving equally well in dry and moist grounds. It deserves more attention than has been given it, especially as a permanent pasture grass. Sheep's fescue (*F. ovina*) is a low, densely tufted variety, and is valued in sheep pastures.

Brome Grass (*Bromus*).—Within the present district there are two native and six introduced species having little or no agricultural value; some of them are even troublesome weeds, as chess or cheat (*Bromus secalinus*) and upright chess or smooth brome grass (*Bromus racemosus*), both common in grain-fields.

Ray or Rye Grass (*Lolium perenne*). [See Plate XXV.]— This is a common grass in fields and by the wayside. It is sometimes cultivated here with other grasses, but it has received more attention and is more highly esteemed in Europe, from whence it was introduced, than it has in this country. Ray grass has a historical interest from the fact that it is the grass first mentioned as having been cultivated for agricultural purposes. As early as 1677 it was sown for the purpose of improving "cold, sour, clayey, weeping ground, unfit for saint-foin."

Couch Grass (*Agropyrum repens*).—This has been referred to under agrarian grasses. Although valued by some for hay its place in permanent meadows had better be occupied by species of really more worth, and its introduction among hoed crops is greatly to be dreaded, as it soon becomes a great pest exceedingly difficult to eradicate.

Wild Barley Grass (*Hordeum*).—There are two native species—one, wild field barley (*Hordeum pratense*), common on the prairies from Ohio westward, and the other abundant on the salt meadows along the coast and borders of the great lakes. The last is called squirrel-tail grass (*H. jubatum*). It is an ornamental species, and its seeds are sold by the florists.

Wild Rye, Lyme Grass (*Elymus*).—There are five native species found within the limits of this list, the most valuable of which is probably the Canadian wild rye (*E. canadensis*). It grows in rich alluvial soil along river banks, and yields a large bulk of hay. *E. virginicus* and *E. striatus* are smaller species, growing in similar situations.

GRASSES OF THE SOUTH.—In the Southern States there is a more marked diversity in the soils and climate than appears in the New England and Middle States, and consequently there is a more decided difference in the character of the plants which the various sections afford. In the upper districts and in the mountains of Georgia and the Carolinas many of the grasses of the higher latitudes abound, and some of the long-established cultivated varieties of Europe and the Northern States are successfully cultivated; but the sub-tropical character of the climate of the lowlands near the seaboard and along the Gulf coast is incompatible with their growth. To meet the demands of this portion of the country selections must be made from the more promising species native to the soil, or the cultivator must look to the introduction of valuable varieties from regions farther south. Johnson grass (*Sorghum halepense*) and Bermuda grass (*Cynodon dactylon*) [see both on Plate XXV.], two of the most highly valued grasses at the South, either for hay or pasturage, are examples of such introduced species. Cattle may be left to graze throughout the mild winter season, so that there is less demand for meadow grasses than in more northern latitudes. Permanent pasture grasses are the species most desired—such as will withstand the excessive heat and drought of summer. As has been stated, the cereals, especially barley, are largely grown for winter pasturage. Tall oat grass (*Arrhenatherum*) [see Plate XXV.] is highly prized and cultivated in some sections for winter forage, and standing next in value to this is orchard grass. Where timothy and herds-grass can be grown they are cultivated for hay.

Florida abounds in native grasses, some of which have the appearance of possessing much agricultural merit, and would probably prove valuable in that State if cultivated.

The grass flora of Texas is wonderfully rich in its variety and extent—well shown by the fact that 12,000,000 head of cattle (including horses and sheep) feed upon the native grasses alone. Among these Texan grasses the agriculturists at the South can hardly fail to find valuable species that will be to them all that could be desired.

There are about 250 species of this family found growing spontaneously in the Southern and Gulf States, of which about 125 extend beyond their limits northward. Those which have been more or less recognized in agriculture are named below:

Paspalum.—Nearly twenty varieties or species of *Paspalum* are found in the South. With one or two exceptions they are all perennials, and, where abundant, are valued both for permanent pasture and for hay. Some of the species yield a large amount of tender and nutritious herbage, which is relished by all kinds of stock. *Paspalum dilatatum* is found in Texas, growing on dry lands, and is there commended in the highest terms, as furnishing excellent green feed for stock at all seasons. *Paspalum distichum*, a low-growing species, with something of the habit of Bermuda grass, though usually growing where the soil is more moist, makes excellent forage, of which cattle are very fond. It is known in some localities as "joint grass."

Panicum.—The Panic grasses are very abundant in the Southern States, and represent a large number of species, of great diversity of habit, growing in every variety of soil. Crab grass (*Panicum sanguinale*) and Barnyard grass (*Panicum crus-galli*), both introduced species, are the two most widely known, and by some, the most highly valued. The first is abundant in all cultivated lands, and is regarded as one of the best grasses at the South for hay; the second, frequenting damp, rich soils, is of a much larger and coarser growth, but is very highly esteemed for pasturage during the latter part of summer. *Panicum virgatum* is a

GRASSES.

PLATE XXIV.

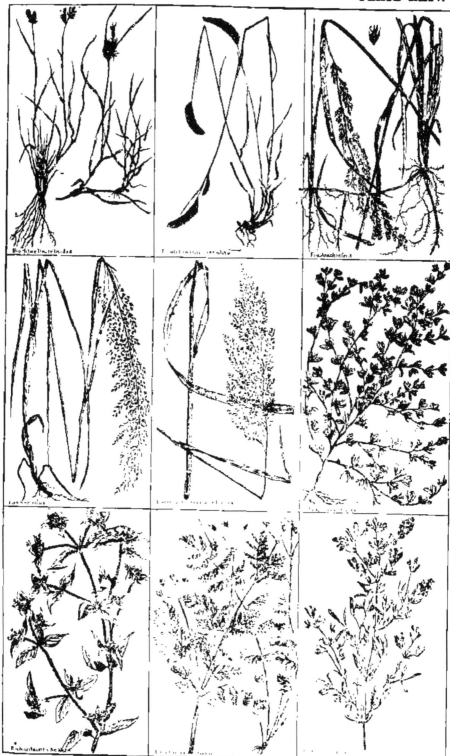

GRASSES. PLATE XXV.

tall-growing species, common on sandy soil, where there is moisture, and yields a large amount of nutritious forage if cut while young. Texan millet (*Panicum texanum*) is a tender and nutritious grass, of luxuriant and rapid growth, producing an abundant yield of hay or forage. It has been introduced into cultivation.

Guinea Grass (*Panicum maximum*) is an introduced grass from the tropics, but thrives well along the Gulf coast, especially near the sea-shore and on sandy lands, where other good grasses do not succeed. It is a coarse grass, but sweet and nutritious, and all kinds of cattle eat it with avidity. A gentleman who has cultivated "Guinea grass" in Florida states, that "with this grass I believe Florida, with its mild and pleasant climate, might be made one of the finest grazing States in the Union." In Jamaica, large districts that were barren and regarded as utterly worthless previous to the introduction of this grass, have become the most profitable parts of the island, supporting vast herds of cattle. It is a perennial, and is best propagated by root cuttings.

Fox-tail Grass (*Setaria glauca*) is common in cultivated grounds, and is regarded of some value. At the North this is classed with the weeds.

Spartina.—There are four native species, which grow either in sandy, saline swamps, or salt marshes along the coast. They yield an abundant supply of green pasturage in spring and summer.

Hard Grass (*Stenotaphrum*) is an evergreen grass of low habit, confined to the damp, sandy soils of the coast, from South Carolina southward, and supplies excellent winter-pasturage.

Gama Grass (*Tripsacum*) grows in rich, damp, clayey soil, frequent in some portions of the South, and formerly cultivated as a forage or soiling plant. It is very tall and rank in habit, and may be cut five or six times a year, under favorable circumstances. All kinds of stock are fond of it, both as green or dry fodder.

Teosinte, or Guatemala Grass (*Euchlæna luxurians*), is a tropical grass related to maize or Indian corn, that has been introduced into this country within the past few years, and promises to be the most valuable of all grasses in the South for soiling or ensilage. It "tillers" out largely, and a single seed sends up many leafy stalks to the height of twelve or fifteen feet. "Undoubtedly there is not a more prolific forage-plant known. Cattle delight in it in a fresh state; also when dry." It is estimated that a hundred tons might be produced from a single acre upon land that is best adapted to it.

Wild Rice (*Zizania aquatica*) is common in marshes and along the margins of ponds and rivers, in shallow water, from Florida northward. It is a tall, coarse grass, often growing to the height of ten feet, and has elongated, rice-like seeds, which were the "*folle avoine*" of the early French settlers of the Mississippi Valley. There is another species (*Z. miliacea*), of similar range and habits. Both may be, and are, utilized for hay in especially dry seasons. "An acre of wild rice is about equal in nutriment to an acre of wheat."

Rice Cut-Grass (*Leersia oryzoides*), also called "false rice," "rice's cousin," and "white grass," has already been mentioned.

Broom Sedge (*Andropogon*).—There are a number of species of Andropogon found at the South, including *A. furcatus*, *A. scoparius*, etc., but all are here regarded as worthless.

Indian Grass (*Chrysopogon nutans*) is common in dry, sandy fields, but has little value.

Johnson Grass (*Sorghum halepense*) [see plate], also known as "Means' grass," "Cuba grass," "Egyptian grass," "green valley grass," and "Guinea grass," is an introduced species, largely cultivated, and valued most highly, both for forage and hay. It is a perennial, of rapid and luxuriant growth, and is less affected by summer drought than other species. The name "Guinea grass," sometimes applied to this plant, belongs to a species of Panicum (*P. maximum*, Jacq., which is the same as *P. jumentorum*, Pers.)

Reed Canary Grass (*Phalaris arundinacea*) is frequent in marshy lands and along the borders of lakes and streams.

American Canary Grass (*Phalaris intermedia*) is a more strictly Southern species, although extending westward to the Pacific coast. Where it abounds, it is much esteemed for winter and spring grazing and for hay. A variety of this, of larger growth and closely resembling timothy in appearance, is still more highly valued by those who have experimented with it.

Sweet Vernal Grass (*Anthoxanthum odoratum*) is widely introduced, and similarly regarded as at the North.

Muhlenbergia.—There are a number of species of *Muhlenbergia* natives of the Southern States, but none of them have received any special attention. *M. diffusa*, called "wire grass" and "nimble Will," is perhaps the most valuable.

Timothy (*Phleum pratense*) grows spontaneously in some sections, and is cultivated for hay, as at the North.

Smut Grass (*Sporobolus indicus*).—This is the only one, among the several species of this genus which occur, that has attracted particular notice as a forage grass. It grows chiefly in waste grounds, and about dwellings where the soil is rich and undisturbed. If allowed to mature, it becomes tough and wiry, but if kept grazed down, it makes excellent forage throughout the summer season. *Sporobolus vaginæflorus* grows on sandy, barren soil, and is valuable as affording food for cattle where little else will grow.

Herds-Grass and White-top are varieties not now regarded botanically distinct, being both referred to *Agrostis alba*. They grow spontaneously in many parts of the country where the soil is sufficiently moist, and are esteemed for hay and pasturage. Southern bent grass (*Agrostis elata*) is taller and in every way more robust than herds-grass, growing abundantly in sandy swamps.

Velvet Grass (*Holcus lanatus*) is found in low ground as far south as North Carolina.

Tall Meadow Oat Grass (*Arrhenatherum avenaceum*) has been introduced naturally, and by cultivation, into several of the Southern States. It thrives well in a great variety of soils. Where it has been cultivated in the upper districts, it takes precedence over all other grasses for winter pasturage. It also makes a large yield of excellent hay.

Bermuda Grass (*Cynodon dactylon*).—This grass grows in all warm and temperate regions of the world, and has become thoroughly naturalized throughout the Southern States; probably introduced there from Bermuda, as the name suggests. It is one of the most valued grasses for permanent pastures, especially in the sandy regions along the borders of the Gulf coast, and it is one of the most troublesome of weeds when established upon lands designed for other crops.

Wire Grass, Yard Grass, or Dutch Grass (*Eleusine indica*).—This grass, supposed to have been introduced from India, is very common about gardens, and in rich soil near dwellings. It is nutritious, and by some is considered excellent for soiling, grazing, or for hay. Crowfoot Grass (*Eleusine ægyptiaca*) is a species allied to the last, growing in similar situations. By many it has been more highly esteemed for hay, for which purpose it has occasionally been cultivated.

Common Reed (*Phragmites communis*) is found in deep river marshes near the coast, from Florida northward.

Broad-Leaved Spike Grass (*Uniola latifolia*).—There are four native species of *Uniola*, but only the one here mentioned is considered of any agricultural merit. It grows in large tufts along the borders of streams as far north as Pennsylvania. Sea Oats (*Uniola paniculata*), growing in drifting sands along the coast, is ornamental, and is gathered for winter bouquets.

Perennial Rye Grass (*Lolium perenne*).—This and Italian rye grass, both valuable for pasturage or hay, are cultivated to some extent in the upper districts.

Wild Rye Grass (*Elymus*).—The species of *Elymus* are evergreen at the South, and are valued for winter grazing.

Cane (*Arundinaria*).—The large cane, which abounds in deep river swamps, forms a remarkable feature in the vegetation of the Southern States. Wide areas covered with this grass occur on the rich alluvial soil of the Santee swamp, forming thickets so dense as to be impenetrable by man or beast, and growing to the height of 20 to 30 feet, the stalks having a diameter of 2 inches or more at the base. A small variety of the above grows in swamps and low grounds. Both are evergreen, and grazing animals feed greedily upon the leaves in winter, and find protection from the driving rains and piercing winds under the dense roof of the canebrake or thicket.

Orchard Grass (*Dactylis*).—An introduced species already referred to.

Kentucky Blue-Grass (*Poa Pratensis*) is frequent in cultivated grounds. It is grown as a pasture grass, and is valued as a winter and spring grass at the South.

Manna Grass (*Glyceria*).—Several species that are common at the North come within the limits of this list. They have no recognised importance.

Fescue Grass (*Festuca*).—There are several species: Meadow (*Festuca elatior*) is cultivated as far south as the Carolinas. In Virginia it is locally called "Randall grass." It remains green throughout the winter months, and supplies excellent grazing throughout that season. Hard Fescue (*F. duriuscula*, L.), a variety of sheep's fescue, occurs as far south as Florida.

Brome Grass (*Bromus*) has one native and several introduced species. *Bromus unioloides*, called "rescue grass," has been cultivated in some sections, and grows spontaneously in the far South. It is a rapid grower, very tender and sweet, and is greedily eaten by cattle.

III. GRASSES OF THE GREAT PLAINS.—That vast area forming the eastern slope of the Rocky Mountains, embracing the States and Territories of Nebraska, Colorado, Kansas, Wyoming, Montana, the Indian Territory, and Eastern New Mexico, is the great grazing region of the country. Here abound in great variety the most nutritious native grasses, which yield ample forage to more than 20,000,000 head of cattle (including horses and sheep), besides supporting innumerable herds of buffalo and other wild grass-eating animals. The grazing resources of these "boundless, endless, gateless" pasture-lands are apparently unlimited. No labor is spent in the cultivation of these grasses, excepting that an occasional stream may be diverted from its course for the purpose of irrigation. During the rainy season, in May and June, vegetation grows luxuriantly; but when the rains cease, the grasses gradually dry on the ground, and before the winter season arrives they have become perfectly cured, uncut hay, as nutritious as the best of meadow hay. The principal varieties composing the herbage of these plains are "bunch grass" (including several species of *Poa, Festuca, Oryzopsis*, etc.), buffalo grass (*Buchloë*), grama grass, broom-sedge or prairie-grass, and mesquite. In some of the valleys blue-joint grass (*Calamagrostis*), native red-top, and wild-rye grass abound.

In the Rocky Mountain region, about the head waters of the Missouri, the most valuable grasses on the river bottoms and lower bench lands are *Poa tenuifolia, Kœleria cristata, Agropyrum glaucum, Bouteloua oligostachya*, and *Oryzopsis cuspidata*; on the upper benches and lower foothills these grasses gradually give way to *Agropyrum divergens* and the varieties of *Festuca ovina*; above these the "great bunch grass" of the Rocky Mountains (*Festuca scabrella*) becomes the prevailing and most important species.

The list given below includes the more important grasses found upon the plains. Mr. E. Hall, in the report of the U. S. Department of Agriculture for 1870, gives a more extended list, embracing 57 genera and 143 species, of which he states that 91 extend across the Missouri River, leaving 52 species belonging to the plains and mountain region proper. The relative value of the twelve most important species representing the great forage resources of the country is exhibited in the following table of percentum estimates, 100 representing the aggregate value of the twelve:

Name.	Missouri River Region.	Rocky Mountain Region.
Andropogon furcatus.....Broom sedge.........	40	16
Andropogon scoparius... " "	20	10
Chrysopogon nutans......Indian grass.......	20	12
Sporobolus heterolepis...................	12	1
Buchloë dactyloides......Buffalo grass.......	5	5
Bouteloua oligostachya..Grama grass........	0	10
Spartina cynosuroides...Fresh-water cord grass......	2	2
Festuca ovina..............Sheep's fescue......	0	20
Festuca microstachya	0	5
Bromus kalmii.............................	0	8
Poa serotina...............................	0	8
Stipa viridula.............................	0	5

Barn-yard Grass (*Panicum crus-galli*) occurs in rich soils about settlements. Crab grass (*Panicum sanguinale*) is found in similar situations.

Beckmannia erucæformis is frequent on the borders of mountain ponds, etc. It is a valuable forage grass in such localities.

Fresh-water Cord Grass (*Spartina cynosuroides*) is common in wet lands, but is a very poor substitute for hay, for which it is sometimes cut. Another species (*Spartina gracilis*) is not uncommon in alkaline soils.

Wild Rice (*Zizania aquatica*) grows near lakes and muddy river bottoms, and is especially common in the Northwest.

Broom Sedge (*Andropogon furcatus*).—This, with an allied species, *Andropogon scoparius*, grows in great abundance in the eastern portions of the district, and with Indian grass (*Chrysopogon nutans*) constitutes three-fourths of the grazing resources of that portion of the country. The first named is one of the principal hay grasses of the country, and is largely cut and cured for winter use. All three, however, enter into the composition of prairie hay, which is considered best when cut just before killing frosts, in early autumn.

Feather Grass (*Stipa*).—Several species occur, but only one (*S. viridula*) that has any value. In favorable localities this grows to the height of from four to six feet, and it furnishes a considerable amount of valuable grazing in the mountain districts.

Reed Canary Grass (*Phalaris arundinacea*) is common in wet situations.

Oryzopsis cuspidata is a handsome grass, growing in bunches on the sandy plains. It is one of the several kinds called "bunch grass," and is highly valued for grazing.

Muhlenbergia.—Five species are common on the plains or along mountain streams. *Muhlenbergia pungens* is perhaps the most valuable as a forage plant. In Arizona, where it is abundant, it is known as black grama, or grama China. *Muhlenbergia gracilis* is also an important species in grazing districts.

Sporobolus airoides is frequent in mountain valleys, growing chiefly in alkaline soils. When green it is readily eaten by stock.

Sporobolus heterolepis flourishes chiefly in the moister portions of the plains, and many local areas are almost exclusively occupied by it. It is especially liked by cattle, and in Kansas, where it abounds, it affords a rich winter-pasturage. It is sometimes cut for hay in the absence of more productive species, and makes an article of first quality. (Hall.)

False Red-top (*Agrostis exarata*).—A good pasture grass, frequent along mountain streams, etc.

Blue Joint Grass (*Deyeuxia canadensis*) is common in moist prairie land. It makes a very large yield in rich soil, and great quantities are cut for hay. *Deyeuxia stricta* and *sylvatica* are two other species of smaller habit, that supply more or less forage on the mountains.

Bouteloua oligostachya. [See Plate XXIV.]—A perennial grass, very common on the mountains and adjacent plains. Although too low in habit and too much scattered in its growth to be cut for hay, it is one of the most valuable species for grazing purposes, and much of the beef of the South-west is the product of this grass. It is commonly known as "grama grass," a name, however, that is applied, not only to other species of *Bouteloua*, but to grasses of other genera. In some places this grass is called meskit, or mesquite, which is another name that has been applied to several different species of grass, and, again, it is called buffalo grass.

Bouteloua hirsuta, a species closely resembling *B. oligostachya*, is valued for forage on the plains, where it is common, preferring sterile or sandy soil. *B. racemosa*, frequent in many localities on the plains and mountains, is a handsome and well-marked species, but of less value than the others for forage.

Buffalo Grass (*Buchloë dactyloides*). [See Plate XXIV.] —This is abundant on the central plains from Texas to the British possessions. This is a grass of low growth, rarely more than four or five inches in height, but it extends rapidly by means of its creeping stolons, and covers with a dense turf large areas, and affords rich and nutritious forage throughout the year, its stolons remaining green during the months of winter. In Texas it is called "mesquite."

Common Reed (*Phragmites communis*) occurs on the borders of lakes, etc.

Kœleria cristata is a perennial grass, very common on dry hills or sandy prairies, and forms a valuable addition to the forage of the drier regions, where it most abounds. In some localities this is called June grass.

Salt Grass (*Distichlis maritima*).—This is abundant on the alkaline meadows. It is but slightly nutritious, and when encrusted, as it often is, with the surrounding alkaline matter, it is positively injurious. Its stout creeping roots form a most compact sod, which is very difficult to break up with the plow.

Poa tenuifolia is one of the so-called "bunch grasses," and furnishes abundant and valuable forage in the mountain districts. It is usually associated with *Kœleria cristata*. *Poa nemoralis* is common on the higher as well as on the low mountain ranges. This, with *Poa pratensis*, which is indigenous to the mountain districts, affords valuable food for all kinds of stock. Several other species of *Poa* occur, but these here mentioned are the most important.

Nerved Manna Grass (*Glyceria nervata*) in swamps and wet lands, and *Glyceria pauciflora* by high mountain springs and brooks, make excellent forage where they abound, and are eaten by cattle with avidity.

Festuca scabrella is one of the largest and most valuable of the "bunch grasses" of the Rocky Mountains, cattle being very fond of it, especially in winter.

Sheep's fescue, in several varieties, is plentiful in the mountain regions and adjacent plains. It is a nutritious grass and contributes largely to the general forage crop of the country.

Festuca microstachya is a valuable annual species abundant in dry soil on the mountains and higher plains on the southern portion of the district. This is one of the so-called "grama grasses."

Bromus kalmii is confined chiefly to the mountain region. Although the species of this genus (*Bromus*) are usually regarded as worthless, Mr. Hall states that, where plentiful, *Bromus kalmii* affords excellent pasturage.

Couch Grass (*Agropyrum repens*) is truly indigenous in the Rocky Mountain region, presenting many forms. It is valued for forage, and is known to the herdsmen as bluejoint, bunch grass, and lagoon grass. One of the varieties is especially valued for hay in Montana.

Hordeum jubatum and *nodosum* are both common on the plains in moist land, and when young make tender and nutritious forage; but when allowed to mature they become a great nuisance, for when associated with other grasses the value of these for hay is entirely destroyed. The long and sharp-pointed beards stick fast in the nose or mouth of horses feeding upon them, often penetrating the flesh, sometimes causing death.

Wild Rye (*Elymus canadensis*) is a valuable grass frequent on the plains and mountains in moist localities; and *Elymus condensatus*, the more common species, makes valuable winter grazing for cattle.

THE GRASSES OF CALIFORNIA.—California, with an agricultural area exceeding that of Great Britain and Ireland, has done very little in the way of cultivating the agricultural grasses; in fact, the climate of that State is such as to preclude any system of grass-culture for meadows and pastures where artificial or natural irrigation cannot be maintained throughout the season. From about the 1st of May until the 1st of November no rains fall, and none of the grasses cultivated in the Eastern States can withstand so protracted a season of drought.

Almost the only grasses employed for hay are the cereals. These are cut before the grain has ripened, and the "wheat hay" and "barley hay," with oats similarly cured, constitute the mass of the hay crop. Where permanent pasturage is wanted, and where it is possible to secure and maintain this by irrigation, alfalfa (*Medicago sativa*), an "artificial grass," is employed almost exclusively. Kentucky blue-grass is used for lawns, but its verdure is only maintained at great labor and cost. In Oregon this grass, so highly prized in the East, is regarded as one of the most troublesome weeds in cultivated fields, its rapid propagation by means of root-stocks and stolons making it very difficult to eradicate.

Rye Grass (*Lolium*) is sufficiently abundant in some localities to be cut for "volunteer hay." This grass remains green all summer, without irrigation, in the bay climate, and at some points it is regularly cultivated as a meadow grass. In the higher valleys, that can be irrigated from mountain springs, there is an occasional field of timothy. Orchard grass has been introduced, and this, with soft meadow grass (*Holcus lanatus*), is found in the tule lands and in other naturally or artificially watered regions, and has come into some use for pasture as well as hay. Several species of sorghum and other large grasses have been introduced, and their culture is increasing. Especially is this true of Pearl millet (*Penicillaria spicata*). In winter and early spring the hills and plains are green with species of crane's bill (*Erodium cicutarium* [see Plate XXIV.] and *E. moschatum*). The first named is esteemed as one of the most important natural pasture plants, being about the only green thing available to stock throughout the dry season, and it is eagerly cropped by animals at all times. It is called by the Spanish "Alfilerilla." "Bur-clover" (*Medicago denticulata*) is another "artificial grass," which flourishes under difficulties that would discourage most other plants from attempting a growth, and forms a valuable ingredient of the dry pastures.

Wild Oat (*Avena fatua*) was formerly very abundant in the hills and valleys throughout the State, but it has been much reduced in extent by the depredations of sheep. In early times it was most highly prized for hay, and it is still employed for this purpose.

Herds-Grass, or Red Top (*Agrostis alba*), has been introduced in most of the cultivated portions of the State.

Sweet Vernal Grass is another introduced species; and so is the Tall Meadow Oat Grass, which has become naturalized as a weed.

Bermuda Grass (*Cynodon*) is found native in the southern part of the State.

The natural grasses of the State contribute but an insignificant portion towards the maintenance of the flocks and herds. On the open "ranges" cattle scour large areas, browsing upon every green thing which is not too repellant. To the eye of the herdsman from the East these grazing grounds appear to be little more than barren wastes, where cattle could only be left to starve: but they supply food and that sufficiently nourishing to bring the stock into fine condition. Between the wet and the dry season there is no gradual transition; but the change is sudden, and the grass and other herbage is cured *in situ* into a most nutritious hay.

The native grasses of California having more or less agricultural value are enumerated below:

Beckmannia erucaeformis forms the greater part of the herbage of the wet meadows in the northern part of the State.

Salt Marsh Grass (*Spartina stricta*) is common on the salt marshes along the coast.

Feather Grass (*Stipa setigera*) is a tufted grass, common on the dry hills and plains throughout the State. It is tender and nutritious in April and May. Another species (*Stipa speciosa*) grows in scattered bunches over the Mojave desert, and, with other species, furnishes an "occasional bite, palatable though tough to chew, to antelopes and to strolling cattle and sheep." It is a handsome grass, and would make a valuable addition to the ornamental species.

Hilaria rigida is a "striking species on account of its rigid, woody stems, in habit resembling some of the dwarf bamboos." It grows in the dry, sandy districts in the southern part of the State. Although it is tough and hard, mules eat it with avidity.

Reed Canary Grass (*Phalaris arundinacea*).—This and the more common *Phalaris intermedia* occur in wet grounds and along river banks. They are of little agricultural value. The first named is a very common plant in similar situations in the Eastern States. *Phalaris amethystina* is another Californian species, less common than the two above named, but is tenderer and more palatable than either of them.

Hierochloa macrophylloa is found in damp woods, and yields a small amount of tender herbage.

Silky "Bunch Grass" (*Oryzopsis cuspidata*) is a handsome grass, growing in tufts or bunches with *Stipa speciosa*, on the Mojave desert, and extending eastward from the Sierras.

Sporobolus airoides is scattered over the Mojave desert with *Stipa speciosa*, and, like that grass, yields a bite here and there to roving animals.

Blue-joint Grass (*Deyeuxia canadensis*) is common, especially in the Sierra Nevada Mountains, growing in moist places and producing a large amount of nutritious forage.

Deyeuxia aequivalvis is a tender and sweet grass, growing on the verge of mountain brooks.

Deyeuxia Aleutica is a coarse grass, growing in dense tufts. When sufficiently abundant it makes a valuable pasture grass, animals eating it with avidity. There are two other species of *Deyeuxia* that may be mentioned—*D. Bolanderi*, scattered through damp forests along with *Hierochloa macrophylla* and *Deyeuxia rubescens*, a "hard grass growing in thin, rare tufts, on pine-barren plains, where there is nothing else for deer to feed upon."

Deschampsia calycina is often so abundant in moist meadows as to constitute a large proportion of the herbage. It is a tender grass, and is eaten with avidity by animals. *Deschampsia holciformis* is a more robust species, growing in similar situations.

Mesquite, or Gramma Grass (*Bouteloua oligostachya*), referred to under GRASSES OF THE PLAINS, is rare in California.

Common Reed (*Phragmites communis*) grows in wet places along the margins of rivers, etc.

Golden Lamarkia (*Lamarkia aurea*) is a very pretty ornamental grass, found in the Colorado Desert.

Melica imperfecta is frequent on the hill-sides and in meadows. It makes tender and valuable forage in April and May.

Pleuropogon californica grows in valleys and moist meadows. Animals are very fond of it; and, according to Mr. Bolander, it is almost the only certainly indigenous grass deserving the attention of the agriculturist.

Poa tenuifolia is one of the most valuable of the "bunch grasses," and is frequent throughout the State.

Couch Grass (*Agropyrum repens*) is found in various parts of the State, and is valued for forage.

Squirrel Tail Grass (*Hordeum jubatum*), one of the earliest grasses, is common along roadsides and in waste grounds. While young it is much relished by cattle, but later, by the development of its barbed or awned flowers, it becomes a serious nuisance.

Elymus condensatus grows in small scattered patches or in clumps; and its leaves, though tough and hard, are stripped off by hungry cattle. Wild Rye Grass (*E. canadensis*), a more widely known and more valuable species, is found in moist low lands and along river borders.

"Throughout the mountains, where cattle cannot be herded so successfully, sheep are everywhere led by their herders, swarming like vermin and creeping up to the very pinnacles of rock to the snow-line, nibbling or trampling in the dust all vegetation. No grass, at ever so great an altitude, but must contribute its mite towards the sustenance of these flocks. Thus *Stipa stricta, Sporobolus depauperatus* and *gracillimus, Agrostis varians, Trisetum canescens, Melica stricta, Poa tenuifolia,* and *P. Pringlii* on bare mountain tops, or around mountain springs and rills, must all yield a dainty mouthful to the miserable, dust-begrimed sheep, compelled, in their ascent, to live on the foliage of shrubs and brittle herbs." (Pringle.)

ARIZONA AND SOUTHERN CALIFORNIA.—The soil and climate of Western New Mexico, Arizona, and Southern California are in many points unlike those of any other portion of the United States, and the peculiarities of the grass-flora are remarkable. The following sketch of the grasses of this region is from the pen of Mr. C. G. Pringle, a well-known botanist and collector, who has traversed this section of our country several times and carefully studied its vegetable productions.

In going into the South-west from New England, where all deforested areas are closely sodded with perennial grasses, one is struck with the insignificance of the permanent grasses there and the almost entire absence of sod.

In the bottom of the valleys and along the line of the water-courses (although water may not flow above the surface, except during the period of summer or winter rains), and in soil more or less impregnated with alkali, the traveller occasionally meets with natural meadows, chiefly formed by *Distichlis maritima*, its creeping roots forming a close net-work in the soil, and *Sporobolus wrightii*, growing in great clumps. The former has a wiry stem and its foliage is tough; but animals accustomed to subduing spiny opuntias and thorny shrubs thrive on it. The latter is rigid, coarse grass, its culms often four or five feet high and as thick as a goose-quill; when its stems are young animals browse away their upper portions, and cull out—from amongst the bristling stumps of the stems of former years, that remain standing dense and stiff and some two feet in height—the long radical leaves of the plant. To arrive after nightfall and a long forced drive to reach grass and water upon such a meadow, and be compelled to picket one's horses on its pastures, which have been closely grazed by the herds of ranches far and near, seems hard, but from May to August the valleys and plains furnish nothing better.

Sporobolus cryptandrus, var. *stricta,* scattered along the margins of streams, possesses much the habit of *S. wrightii* and is of equal economic value. *Sporobolus asperifolius* with a finer herbage than the last, occupies patches of wet soil, and its abundant and leafy sterile culms yield forage more easily appropriated by animals.

Panicum obtusum, growing in low lands, particularly in the partial shade of shrubs, contributes a trifle of forage, by its long, creeping, wiry, but leafy stems.

In low lands, scattered trifles of *Andropogon saccharoides* and *Trichloris fasciculata* contribute a little food to animals, as acceptable probably as any afforded by the perennial grasses. *Panicum leucophæum* and *Andropogon contortus*, growing in thin scattered tufts on the mesas and foot-hills, are of similar value. *Hilaria rigida* on sandy plains has hard stems and tough leaves, but animals are forced to consume it. *Panicum fuscum, verrucosum, capillare* var., and *colonum* are rather weeds of tilled fields, and as forage plants probably equal *Panicum crus-galli, P. sanguinale, Setaria viridis*, and *Setaria glauca*. With these may be classed *Helopus punctatus, Eragrostis purshii*, var. *diffusa, Chloris alba, Leptochloua mucronata*, grasses of tenderer substance that are eaten with avidity.

Agrostis verticillata, growing on the margins of watercourses, is a tender and nutritious morsel; so also are *Eatonia obtusata*, which, however, is less abundant in Arizona, *Agrostis exarata*, growing by brooks, and *Phalaris intermedia*, a species more widely scattered along streams and in wet cultivated soil.

To cattle straying over miles of arid wastes, nibbling at the leaves of thorny trees and shrubs, or pulling here and there a bitter weed, such grasses as *Setaria caudata, Tricuspis pulchella* and *mutica, Muhlenbergia debilis*, and even *Aristida americana*, and *A. humboldtiana, Bouteloua gracilis*, and other species, all scattered in thin tufts over hill and mesas, furnish dainty bits that are seized upon with avidity.

When the summer rains fall abundantly, these species renew their growth, or spring up from the seed, and grow so rapidly as to cover the soil with a pretty close growth of herbage, which furnishes abundant pasturage to fatten herds during the autumn months. Only a small part of this is consumed while green, but drying up in the droughts of October and November, and being little weather-beaten in that dry climate, it serves to sustain the herds through the winter and early spring months. The more densely covered areas are sometimes mown for hay.

Cottea makes its growth entirely during the summer rains. This and the two species of *Pappophorum* may be classed, in point of economic value, with the species of *Aristida* and *Bouteloua*, though apparently far less common than these.

Hilaria cenchroides, not rare on the hills, is a perennial, grows feebly, and fruits during the dry months from April to July, and contributes a little to save stock from starvation; so likewise does *Muhlenbergia pungens*. Both are wiry, but nutritious grasses. Under the summer rains they grow more luxuriantly, and the latter growing in bushy clumps, retains in its wiry stems much nutriment, so that it supplies the more common sort of hay in the towns and in the stop-stations, being pulled by the Mexicans or Indians, and brought in on the backs of donkeys or on carts, even as late as May, when it is gray with age hence "grama grass."

Poa annua, var. *stricta*, and *Festuca microstachya* furnish a few tender bits of food to cattle following up the mountain streams in the spring.

Beside streams of mountain cañons a species of *Imperata* furnishes tall leafy clumps that are eaten eagerly by animals at all seasons of the year.

On the higher slopes of the mountains, particularly on those turned away from the direct rays of the sun, and under the partial shade of pines and rocks, are found in May, *Atropis californica* and *Muhlenbergia virescens* growing in clumps, and standing so close together as to remind one of the northern meadows. The first named furnishes the tenderest and sweetest of pasturage; the last is a soft and leafy grass. These two species largely compose the "deer parks" of those mountains, but unfortunately their growth begins at such an altitude, some 6000 feet, that horses can seldom get the benefit of them.

In Arizona the coarse grass of the valleys is called "sacatone," a name applied to *Sporobolus wrightii* and similar species. There is another name in use among the Mexicans to distinguish the shorter, softer grasses of the mesas.

Works of Reference: Chapman, Dr. A. W.—*Flora of the Southern United States;* Flint, Chas. L.—*Grasses and Forage Plants;* Gould, John Stanton—*Grasses and their Culture* (1869); Gray, Dr. Asa—*Manual of Botany of the Northern United States;* Howard, C. W.—*Manual of the Cultivation of the Grasses and Forage Plants at the South;* Mohr, Dr. Chas.—*Grasses and Forage Plants of Alabama;* Phares, Dr. D. L.—*Farmer's Book of Grasses and other Forage Plants for the Southern United States* (1881); Scribner, F. Lamson—*Agricultural Grasses of Central Montana;* Thurber, Dr. Geo.—*S. Watson's Botany of California;* Vasey, Dr. Geo.—*Agricultural Grasses of the United States* (1884). (F. L. S.)

CLOVER, though not botanically classified among the grasses, is an important forage plant. It is represented chiefly by the genus *Trifolium*, though some species of allied genera, having similar leaves, get the popular name of clover applied to them. Thus the "bur clover" of California is *Medicago maculata*, and *M. lupulina* is "wolf clover." "Chili clover," also known as "alfalfa," is *Medicago sativa*. "Japan clover" is *Lespedeza striata*, and "Mexican clover" *Richardsonia scabra*. These are all shown on Plate XXIV. "Bokhara clover" is *Melilotus leucantha;* "Hart's clover," *M. officinalis*, which is also called "sweet clover;" and "prairie clover" is represented by various species of *Petalostemon*. The *Richardsonia*, however, has not leaves like the "trefoils," as the *Trifolium* family is commonly called. It is a plant of the Rubiaceous family, a native of Mexico, which has become naturalized near Mobile and other points in the Southern United States, and is found to do very well and to be acceptable to stock in places where genuine clover does not do well. The alfalfa is a famous plant for dry regions; even in places like those west of the Rocky Mountains and Utah it will afford two or three cuttings a year. The Bokhara clover is a famous bee-plant, as are indeed most of the trefoils; the white clover, *Trifolium repens*, and the Alsike clover, *Trifolium hybridum*, ranking also among the best for this purpose.

Of true trefoils, which comprise the genus *Trifolium*, there are about 200 species known, inhabiting the temperate regions of both the northern and southern hemispheres, some of them reaching to almost alpine heights. In the eastern parts of the United States there are only three truly indigenous species—*Trifolium carolinianum, T. stoloniferum*, and the "Buffalo clover," *T. reflexum*. The last named is strong enough in growth to make a field-crop; it does not seem to have been tested for agricultural purposes. West of the Mississippi the number of species increases, some forty having been described as indigenous between the Rocky Mountains and the Pacific coast. The European species are abundantly naturalized, the "red clover," *Trifolium pratense*, white or "Dutch" clover, *T. repens*, "hare's-foot" trefoil, *T. arvense*, and the "hop clover," *Trifolium procumbens*, being particularly abundant. In agriculture the red clover is the most popular, as yielding the heaviest amount of hay or forage; the white clover for permanent pastures, and the Alsike clover, *Trifolium hybridum*, where the ground may be either mown or pastured, and especially for cool climates. These are all perennials. In grassy places in Colorado, New Mexico, and Arizona an annual species, *Trifolium involucratum*, enters largely into the herbage. The Alsike clover is so named from the Swedish district where it was first found, and where, from the characters being intermediate between the red and white clovers, it was believed to be a hybrid. From this belief Linnæus gave it the name of *Trifolium hybridum*. Botanists, however, do not regard it as a real hybrid, chiefly perhaps from a prevalent belief that hybrids are sterile, which, however, is by no means always the case. Its exact native place is, however, not known. The seeds are much smaller than those of red clover, and are of a dark green tinged with yellow when ripe. In Sweden, where the seed is grown largely for exportation, the yield is about 135 pounds to the acre. Red clover is grown largely for the seed in the United States. The first crop rarely produces seed to any great extent. It was once thought that this was on account of the absence of humble-bees to fertilize the flowers, but it is now known that the bees visit the first crop of flowers as freely as the last, and that they have little part in the fertilization, as they bore into the corolla from the outside when gathering honey, and thus avoid the stamens. The pollen-gathering insects may aid fertilization. The second crop has lost some of its vegetative power, and this always assists reproduction. The seed is threshed by machines especially constructed for the work; about 1,500,000 bushels is the annual product of the United States. Western New York is a famous clover-seed district, some seasons producing as much as 30,000 bushels. The usual yield is from three to seven bushels per acre; one case is on record of a lot of 48 acres in Western New York yielding 315 bushels, which were sold for $2200. In France and England, where sheep-husbandry prevails, the scarlet or French clover, *Trifolium incarnatum*, is often grown, because it makes, with turnips, a very early herbage for sheep to feed on, but it is grown only for ornament in the United States. Red clover is often used where manure is scarce, to be ploughed down as a fertilizer. When a crop of about two tons to the acre is so used, it is believed to be equal to five cords of stable-manure. The Japan clover is believed to have been in some unknown way introduced from Japan about the middle of the present century. Its growth is small, but its advantages are that it will thrive on the poorest ground where other clovers will not, and cattle thrive very well on it. The bur clover, *Medicago maculata*, has become naturalized, and thrives wonderfully well in California and contiguous States. Cattle are very fond of it, but the seed-vessels are bur-like, and give the wool-raisers great annoyance. It seems to have spread in California from early times. The Indians are very fond of the seed. They also use the plant, which is gathered and placed between hot stones, first moistened, and sometimes a small quantity of a kind of onion is added. The Apaches used the plant boiled as greens.

Many other forage plants allied to the clovers might be enumerated. The White Lupine is of extreme value both as fodder and as a plant to be ploughed under in the green state for its fertilizing effects. Its culture is chiefly confined to the south of Europe. Vetches and Tares are highly prized in Europe for pasture plants. They are of the genera *Vicia* and *Orobus*. They have by no means received in the United States the attention they deserve. The Vetchlings are of the genus *Lathyrus*, and in some European places are highly valued. The same is true of the "Bird's-foot trefoils," small Old-World herbs, very nearly allied to the true clovers. They are of the genus *Lotus*. The Sainfoin (*Onobrychis sativa*), though adapted only to a very small range of soils, proves of high value in dry, chalky places in the south of England. (T. M.)

FORBES, ARCHIBALD, a British journalist, was born in Morayshire, Scotland, in 1838, being the son of a clergyman. After studying at the University of Aberdeen he enlisted in the Royal Dragoons, and served for some years. Then becoming connected with the London press, he was sent in 1870 to France as correspondent of the *Daily News*. In the same capacity he has visited India, Turkey, Cyprus, South Africa, and America. His practical knowledge of military affairs and his indomitable courage and perseverance have made him one of the ablest war-correspondents. Among his publications in book form are *Drawn from Life*, a novel; *My Experiences of the War between France and Germany; Soldiering and Scribbling;* and *Life of Chinese Gordon*.

FORBES, JOHN MURRAY (1807–1885), an American Episcopal clergyman, was born in New York, May 5, 1807. He graduated at Columbia College in 1827, and at the General Theological Seminary of the P. E. Church in 1830. In 1834 he became rector of St. Luke's Church, New York, and was also for a time professor of pastoral theology in the General Theological Seminary. In 1849, influenced by the tractarian movement, he entered the Roman Catholic Church, and was soon after made pastor of St. Ann's R. C. Church, New York city. In 1852 he attended the plenary council of the Roman Catholic Church at Baltimore, as the theologian of Bishop Reynolds, of Charleston. In 1854 he was theologian to Bishop J. B. Fitzpatrick, of Boston, in the provincial council held at New York. In 1859 he withdrew from the Roman Catholic Church, and in 1862 he was restored to the exercise of his ministry in the Protestant Episcopal Church. From 1869 to 1872 he was dean of the General Theological Seminary. He died at New York, 1885.

FORCE, PETER (1790–1868), an American antiquarian, was born at Passaic Falls, N. J., Nov. 26, 1790. His father was a revolutionary soldier, and in 1793 removed to New York city, where Peter became a printer. In 1815 he removed to Washington, and there published the *National Calendar*, an annual volume of statistics (1820–36). He also (from 1823 to 1830) published the *National Journal*, which supported the cause of John Quincy Adams, and during his presidency was the official journal of the administration. Having already devoted much time to the collection of documents illustrating American history, Force undertook by government authority the preparation of a documentary history of the American colonies. To this work he devoted thirty years, during which he published nine folio volumes called *American Archives*. A tenth volume was prepared, but remains unpublished. Force also gathered an immense and valuable collection of books, pamphlets, manuscripts, and maps relating to American history. From these he published four volumes of historical tracts. The entire collection was purchased by Congress in 1867 for $100,000. Mr. Force had also taken an active part in the affairs of the city of Washington, and from 1836 to 1840 was mayor of that city. He died at Washington, Jan. 23, 1868. Besides his historical works he published *Grinnell Land* (1852) and *Auroral Phenomena* (1856).

FORESTRY. The art of protecting, producing, and utilizing forest growth, though as a science almost unknown in America, has had for centuries a recognized place in Europe. It rose there to its present dignified position simply because it was found to be an essential element of national prosperity; and the time appears to be at hand when it will here be recognized as of great importance.

(See Vol. IX. p. 349 Am. ed. (p. 397 Edin. ed.))

More than 600 years ago Philip III. of France laid down a crude code of laws for the protection of the forests in his domain; and Louis XIV. in 1669 reduced the management of his forests to a system more perfect than had hitherto been attained. France in July, 1827, modernized her forest system, adapting it to the needs of the time. The Saxon King Ini, about the end of the seventh century, was rigid, but just as the age allowed, in enforcing forest regulations among his subjects in England, carrying his supervision down to a forest which comprised but a few acres. William the Conqueror, however, was oppressive, cruel, and in the last degree regardless of private rights in government of the forests of England. It is to be observed that under this monarch the forests were chiefly valued as accessories of royal luxury and because they held and hid the king's game. It has been truly said that the unauthorized killing of a hare then was a more serious offence than the killing of a man. It was only when war turned the attention of princes from hunting to ship-building that the timber came to be valued for itself. It is interesting also to observe how the forests, which originally were no man's land, became, first, after law asserted itself, the king's, for the king's sport; second, the king's, for the use of the realm when that was apt to mean the king's ambition; and, third, the realm's, for the highest good of the people. These may be regarded as marking distinct steps in the history of England.

Sweden demands that for each tree cut down two shall be planted, and in 1878 the forests returned to the public treasury, over and above cost of care, $450,000. Even Finland has her School of Forestry, and, unexpected as it may be, Spain has produced 1126 books and pamphlets on the subject. In Germany forest schools are as much fostered by the government as the most renowned university of the empire. An eminent legal writer in France broadly and exactly states the problem of the relations of the government and the individual to the wooded portion of the domain. "The preservation of forests is one of the first interests of society, and consequently one of the first duties of government." "The forests are actually more requisite to the state than to the individual. As to woods and forests the public interests demand that individuals shall not be free to clear them from the soil whenever they please." England, though among the first to enact forest laws, has as yet no school of forestry. The result is that her most inspiring young estate managers go to France or Germany to seek the higher special culture they desire.

For our purposes we may divide the science into the following heads:

I. The Original Timber.
II. Present Condition of our Forests.
III. Destruction of Timber, and need of Legislation.
IV. Proper Native and Introduced Forest Trees for Planting.
V. Effect of Forests on Rainfall and in Protecting the Surface of the Earth.
VI. Forests as Affording Protection against Extremes of Temperature.

I. THE ORIGINAL TIMBER.—Taken as a whole, North America can hardly be regarded as densely wooded. The fact that the eastern coast from Maine to the Gulf was covered with timber, good in quality and abundant in quantity, and that this condition extended west beyond the Alleghenies and in some instances even beyond the Mississippi River, has been misleading; for in the State of Texas alone there are areas larger than Pennsylvania without trees, and one may cross from the Pacific to the Gulf encountering no forests large enough to be represented on the map. Major J. W. Powell, in his report upon the "Arid Region," thus states the relations between timber and those regions: "The Arid Region of the United States is more than four-tenths of the entire country, excluding Alaska" (p. 23). "The timber regions constitute from 20 to 25 per cent. of the Arid Region" (*l. c.*) In other words, to start with, in four-tenths of the United States we have what corresponds, nearly, to one-tenth of one entire area in timber. Of the remaining six-tenths it is safe to say, in the absence of exact statistics, that not more than three-tenths are covered with original timber. This with the one-tenth above given would make, as an approximate estimate, four-tenths of the United States in timber; but out of this area so much of the original, the best, timber has been culled that we should be safe in saying this is equivalent to the removal of another tenth, thus leaving three-tenths of the entire area in available first-class timber.

Before the first crops could be planted, it was requisite to remove and destroy the timber. This has induced almost a tree-destroying tendency among Americans.

It is also surprising how small a portion of North America produces good, strong, durable timber in considerable quantity, even in the timber regions. The best oaks, all the hickories, most of the maples, the locust-trees of sufficient size to be valuable as timber, as well as the large wild cherry-trees, the beeches and the large birches, along with the elms, stop before they reach the Rocky Mountains, and but few of them reappear on the Pacific slope. The one oak of the Rocky Mountains is a mere bush which attains no commercial size, and though California, Oregon, and Arizona have several species, they are of less value than those of the Atlantic side. But rich as the East is in cone-bearing trees, it is far behind the West in the size of its species. The gigantic representatives of the order are the chief glory of the Rocky Mountain and the Pacific regions. When the central parts of the continent are reached timber ceases to be found on the lower levels. Vast areas there are absolutely devoid of tree growth until an altitude of 4000, 5000, or even 8000 feet above the sea is reached. Then forests largely of coniferous growth continue until, on the parallel of 40° N. lat., an average altitude of 11,500 feet is reached where trees disappear, and all above is a naked alpine region where cold excludes all vegetation save the hardy herbs, or still hardier lichens or mosses. Following Drs. Gray and Hooker in their paper on the vegetation of the Rocky Mountain region, we may say of the oak family in the United States that it comprises "21 oaks, 2 chestnuts, and a beech, in the Atlantic flora; 9 oaks and a Castanopsis in the Pacific flora; and 2 or 3 others [oaks] between the Rocky Mountains and Mexico." The following quotation from the same authors fully expresses the relations of the Coniferæ or Cone-bearing trees:

"*Taxineæ* are absent from the Rocky Mountain flora. The Atlantic flora has the depressed *Taxus Canadensis* at the north, and an upright arborescent and perhaps peculiar species in the northern part of Florida. There is a similar one in the woods of the Pacific side of the continent. The Atlantic flora possesses the original *Torreya*; California another; the two remaining species are of North-eastern Asia.

"*Cupressineæ.*—The amphigæan *Juniperus communis* traverses the continent at the north; and a prostrate form of *J. Sabina* probably does the same; also *J. Virginiana*, the eastern red cedar. But on a southern range the latter species hardly passes out of the Atlantic region. *J. occidentalis* and *J. Californica* are the characteristic species of the mountains bordering and traversing the southern part of the Great Basin and of California. *Cupressus* is wanting to the Atlantic and to the Rocky Mountain floras, but there are three species in the Pacific flora. *Chamæcyparis* is of one species in the Atlantic flora, two in the Pacific, the remainder in Japan. *Thuja* is of two species, one of the Atlantic flora, the other of the Pacific and of Japan. *Libocedrus* is represented by a peculiar species only in the Pacific flora.

"*Taxodineæ.*—Of *Taxodium distichum*, in the Atlantic flora; *Sequoia gigantea* and *S. sempervirens*, the Big Trees and Redwoods, in California.

"*Abietineæ* are more numerous in North America than elsewhere. Like the preceding, they prefer the sides to the centre of the continent, yet are not wanting to the mountains of the latter. *Pinus* is represented in the Atlantic flora by twelve species; in the Rocky Mountains and those of the Great Basin by six different species, not counting those of Arizona; in the Pacific flora by eleven species, four of which are in the preceding flora. *Larix* has a single Atlantic and two Pacific species, one or both of which occur in the Northern Rocky Mountains. *Picea*, the spruces, two in the Atlantic, two others in the Rocky Mountain, and two in the Pacific flora, one of the latter a Rocky Mountain species. *Tsuga*, one (hemlock spruce) in the Atlantic, and one almost the same in the Pacific flora, which has also the peculiar *T. Pattoniana* or *Williamsonii*. *Pseudotsuga Douglasii*, of the Pacific and Rocky Mountain flora, most abundant in Oregon. *Abies*, the firs or balsam firs, two in the Atlantic, two in the Rocky Mountain, and four or five in the Pacific flora, one of them common."

Or expressing the same thing with special reference to our subject, we may say there are on the Atlantic side 4 or 5 species of pine of greater or less commercial importance, 1 hemlock spruce, 1 larch or hackmatack, which does not extend South, an arborvitæ or Thuya likewise largest and commonest toward the North, a white cedar (*Cupressus*) which abounds in swamps from Massachusetts to Wisconsin, and along the coast to Florida, furnishing a light wood of great durability, and a bald cypress (*Taxodium*) commonest toward the South, where it becomes a large tree, and furnishes a lumber which year by year is becoming more popular in house-finishing.

The valuable trees of the Rocky Mountains are 1 or 2 pines; 1 fir (*Abies*); a hemlock (*Tsuga*); the so-called Oregon pine (*Pseudotsuga Douglasii*), which is of wide range and extreme importance to the wants of the West; and 1 or at most 2 cedars.

The trees of value to the Pacific region are, 1 yew; 2, or possibly 3, junipers; the so-called white cedar (*Libocedrus*), the 2 redwoods (*Sequoia*) or big trees, of which 1 is the largest, though not the tallest, known species of tree; 2 or 3 firs (*Abies*) belonging to a group of 7 species, of which 3 are 200 feet or more high; the *Pseudotsuga Douglasii*, which is the same as the "Oregon Pine" of the Rocky Mountain region; 2 hemlock spruces (*Tsuga*), which are both large trees; 1 genuine spruce (*Picea*) which reaches nearly 200 feet high, 3 or 4 (out of 8) pines of real importance to civilization; besides which there are 4 species of pine whose large edible nuts were of extreme value to the aborigines; and a Thuya or arbor-vitæ which grows 150 feet high, and ranges from Northern California to Sitka.

Then the East has a dozen or more species of oak which, in size, strength, and durability, meet the conditions of a vast range of utility, but the West has perhaps nothing equal among oaks to either the white or live-oak of the East. Maples give in the East 3 species, and in the West 1 species of value. Hickories belong exclusively to the East, and the locust also so far as size requisite for utility is concerned.

Value depends somewhat upon surroundings. Thus the cottonwoods (*Populus*), though of very little or no value in our well-timbered East, are of value in the desert areas of the West, where it is almost the only indigenous group of trees which fringes the banks of the streams in an otherwise treeless waste. To these the future population, scant though it may be, must look for its home supply of wood.

The object in enumerating so much in detail the locations and species of native trees is to furnish a sure foundation for any conclusion as to what the forestry of the future must rely upon. It will be seen that the range of choice is large enough to meet any future wants if the task of restoration be early and wisely undertaken.

The great danger lies in the fact (granting unusual rapidity of growth here) that men forget that from 30 years to a century is the time requisite for production of a tree crop, for as a crop requiring care trees must sooner or later be regarded.

II. PRESENT CONDITION OF OUR FORESTS.—The statements given above apply to areas and not to the quantity of timber on each surface. It is evident, however, that a division is possible here, into lands which are as yet practically in their original condition, and lands from which the original growth of most or at least the *best* of the timber has been taken. We might, so far as the Atlantic States are concerned, say that there has been, as we go from Maine to the Gulf, a constantly decreasing ratio of destruction in the timber. In some of the States a very large proportion of the best has already been taken, in others it is hardly sensibly diminished. Thus while along the shores of the Delaware and Chesapeake Bays the white oak has been very largely taken, in the mountains of Virginia and North Carolina, as well as in similar parts of adjacent States, it is still abundant, and of very superior quality. It should be added that the term quality is a variable one. Thus we may have timber actually of the very first class for one kind of work, and almost useless for another. To illustrate, it has been found by certain railroads that for ties whilst white oak from Ohio was good that from Pennsylvania was better, but that from Virginia was best of all, so far as durability was concerned. Timber taken from the island of the Grand Menan, in the Bay of Fundy, has for ship-building purposes about one-third more durability than that from the main land, but 10 miles to the west; and it is alleged that the best Susquehanna white-oak will rot vastly sooner than the same kind of wood from the Chesapeake shores of Maryland and Virginia. There is a rule which may be applied to discrimination between good and bad timber ordinarily. Thus, as between two specimens of the *same kind* of wood, that which has its medullary rays or silver grain the closer and which has the larger year's growth will be the stronger.

The following statistics have been collected under the direction of Prof. Sargent for the Census Office, and may be regarded as being the most reliable that can be obtained. The column headed "Standing Timber" means that which was standing in the respective States up to May 31, 1880, and the next column, headed "Cut Timber," shows what was ent during the year ending May 31, 1880. The fourth column gives the number of years it would require to exterminate the given species in each State at the rate of destruction indicated in the third column. The measure represents *board feet*.

State.	Kind of timber.	Standing timber.	Cut timber.	Duration.
Pennsylvania	White pine (*Pinus Strobus*).	1,800,000,000	380,000,000	4.7
"	Hemlock (*Tsuga Canadensis*).	4,500,000,000	300,000,000	15
Michigan, Lower penins.	White pine.	29,000,000,000	4,068,773,000	7.1
Upper penins.	"	6,000,000,000	328,438,000	18.2
Minnesota	"	6,100,000,000	540,997,000	11.2
Wisconsin	"	41,000,000,000	2,097,299,000	19.5
North Carolina	Long-leaved pine (*Pinus Australis*).	5,229,000,000	108,411,000	48.2
South Carolina	"	5,316,000,000	124,402,000	42.7
Florida	"	6,515,000,000	205,054,000	31.7
Georgia	"	16,778,000,000	272,743,000	61.5
"	Short-leaved pine (*Pinus mitis*).	....	23,335,000	
Mississippi	Long-leaved pine.	17,200,000,000	108,000,000	159.1
"	Short-leaved pine.	6,775,000,000	7,778,000	871.3
Louisiana	Long-leaved pine.	26,588,000,000	61,882,000	429.6
"	Short-leaved pine.	21,625,000,000	22,709,000	952.2
Texas	Long-leaved pine.	20,508,000,000	66,450,000	308.7
"	Short-leaved pine.	26,093,200,000	146,420,000	178.2
"	Loblolly pine (*Pinus taeda*).	20,907,100,000	61,570,000	339.5
Alabama	Long-leaved pine.	18,885,000,000	245,396,000	76.9
"	Short-leaved pine.	2,307,000,000		
Arkansas	Short-leaved pine.	41,315,000,000	129,781,000	318.2
California	Redwood (*Sequoia sempervirens*).	25,825,000,000	186,685,000	138.3

Michigan has also very large bodies of hemlock, white cedar, yellow cedar, and tamarack.

Minnesota has, beside white, red, and burr oaks, sugar maple, poplar, tamarack, cedar (*Thuya*), paper birch, and scrub pine (*Pinus Banksiana*).

Wisconsin has, beside considerable quantity of oak, tamarack, cedar (*Thuya*), fir spruces.

In North Carolina over large areas turpentine manufacture has caused a loss of 10 to 20 per cent. of the timber. The State has also considerable loblolly pine (*Pinus taeda*).

California has besides much valuable sugar pine and several inferior species of oaks.

The list of States is, as will be observed, by no means complete so far as such reliable data as the above go. Those given indicate that at present rates of decrease the average duration of these species for the whole area represented by those States mentioned would be 185.5 years.

III. DESTRUCTION OF TIMBER AND NEED OF LEGISLATION.—From the foregoing statistics it is evident that for the more Northern States the timbers which are most prized are in some States already nearly exhausted, and that in others they will be gone before a crop can be grown to take their place. But the Southern and South-western States appear as yet to have centuries ahead of them before this condition of affairs is reached. This, however, is only an apparent abundance, as will be clear when one remembers that, first, in addition to what we have hitherto removed from them the absolute coming dearth at the North must now be supplemented from the South; second, that building of new railways in the South will make new and heavy inroads upon the forests for ties, for building, and in coalless regions to a certain extent for fuel also; whilst at the same time it will afford new facilities for the removal of timber; third, that instead of the rate indicated marking the rapidity of timber disappearance, it will be a vastly greater and constantly increasing ratio to meet the wants of an increasing population. And further, that in opening new farms and settlements much of the timber, as hitherto, will be burned down to get rid of it instead of being made to serve some useful purpose. Hence with all these new factors we must conclude that the superabundance in the South indicates simply that with increasing dearth elsewhere and increasing facilities for reaching that section, all the tree-destroying agencies of the land will speedily be concentrated there and hasten, beyond what we can now think possible, the destruction of the forests. The above estimates give no clue to the disappearance in smaller ways of other valuable timber, for example the rock elm (*Ulmus racemosa*). The forests of Puget Sound are matchless in both the size and abundance of the timber they furnish, but the completion of one railroad after another will hasten their removal. Second natural growth will of course to a certain extent take the place of the timber removed, but thus far it has been precarious, or at least uncertain.

These facts and considerations prove that legislative action is needed, if not for the preservation of our forests, then at least for some protection against their reckless destruction. It is probably out of the question to prevent the individual owner doing as he will with what he has fully acquired by purchase; but it is evidently within the power of government to retain absolutely what forests it still holds, or to impose such conditions as may be deemed wisest when they are sold. Major Powell (*l. c.* p. 27) writes: "The timber lands cannot be acquired by any of the methods provided in the pre-emption, homestead, timber-culture, and desert land laws, from the fact that they are not agricultural lands. Climatic conditions make these methods inoperative. Under these laws 'dummy entries' are sometimes made. A man wishing to obtain the timber from a tract of land will make homestead or pre-emption entries by himself or through his employés without intending to complete the titles, being able thus to hold these lands for a time sufficient to strip them of their timber. The government still owns about 85,000,000 acres of forest land."

Among the most serious injuries to a country is the removal of timber recklessly in advance of the wants of a permanent settlement, because after the first rush of adventurers, who have come and gone, the final settler finds himself restricted at all points for want of that great requisite of civilization—lumber. Fires have become one of the most serious foes to our forests. The injury inflicted thus upon old and the number of young trees killed outright in some regions is simply incalculable. No penalty can be too severe for those who designedly start a fire through a wooded tract, and though legislation has already been had the penalty is entirely too light for the injury done. Prof. Sargent has estimated that in 1880 the country suffered a loss of $25,462,252 from forest fires.

Many States now place a reward upon trees planted. Especially in the Western States—Kansas, Nebraska, Iowa—is this done. It is fairly a question as to whether protection of trees already standing, whether of artificial or natural growth, is not entitled to more consideration than it has received. A thriving young tree saved from being cut down simply " to make a clearing" is as much a source of future good to the State as one planted. "If the individual is laboring to benefit the commonwealth by planting trees along the roadside and receives the State bonus in the form of lighter taxation, why should he not receive the same consideration when he allows his acres to go untilled in the interest of the State?" In other words why should forest land be taxed so long as it is unproductive to the individual but productive to the State? The legal bearings of this relation are worthy of consideration. A well-known U. S. Senator publicly stated that owing to the taxes on his white pine lands he was obliged to remove the timber. This means that such taxation is a premium placed upon the premature removal of one of the most important sources of future prosperity. Before leaving this part of the subject it may be allowable to anticipate and to say that inasmuch as trees act beneficially to the State by their mere presence and growth, it is not enough to meet the question of timber destruction by answering that with increasing facilities for transportation what lumber is required in the arts can be brought from where it abounds. This leaves a most important factor in the problem absolutely untouched. No area capable of producing trees should be without them in due proportion.

IV. PROPER NATIVE AND INTRODUCED FOREST TREES FOR PLANTING.—Large as our list of available native trees is, it by no means follows that we might not with advantage introduce others from other countries. Southern Europe furnishes now a notable illustration of the value introduced trees may be to a land. Thus our common locust, introduced there about the year 1600, is now a large, widely diffused, and most useful tree. In some of the arts it has won a special place, being for example largely used in manufacture of spokes for wheels, and for other purposes where strength and elasticity are required. Any wood is better than no wood, hence the Ailanthus, box elder (*Negundo*), and Catalpa, which in the East are regarded as of so little value, become on the western plains of prime importance, as they are, along with the cottonwoods, if not the only trees which will flourish there, at least those which do best there. (The western form of Catalpa, as we shall see, has new and important uses assigned it.) In California, though the native tree flora is large, the Australian Eucalyptus or blue gum appears to have a most important future. Its growth is rapid, its timber strong and durable, and considered as a crop the thinnings will, after the first five years, pay the cost of cultivation, and at the end of twenty years pay for the capital invested besides a liberal interest. Mr. Elwood Cooper says it will give larger returns than the cereals. Over how large a portion or in what parts of our South-west the blue gum will flourish must be decided upon trial.

The white poplar or abele, which has been introduced here from Europe and which multiplies so rapidly by *suckers* as to prove a nuisance, has a really good wood for many purposes, and like others above named especially commends itself to the western plains.

The rule to observe for each densely settled district is to see that enough young trees of the most desirable species in the native sylva are planted to keep at least one acre out of four or five in timber, unless it shall be proven that introduced trees are more desirable than the native. Another important rule is, keep the ridges and the mountains when unavailable for agriculture in forest growth.

We can specify but few out of the most important trees, though for the Middle Atlantic States we may safely name the following: white pine is rapidly disappearing; it will always have a value; it will grow on most diverse soils; it will grow (if properly cared for during the first ten years) to a marketable size inside of forty years (though of course a century would be better); it will pay for itself year by year, after the first five years, by the thinnings from the plantation.

The western Catalpa (*Catalpa speciosa*, Warder) is of rapid growth, attains a fair size, has wood of great durability, and is strong enough for such important purposes as railroad ties; besides it will grow over a large range of country, and in the most diverse soils.

The common locust (*Robinia Pseud-acacia*), which is a native of our rough mountain sides, will thrive as well in the rich soil of a "river bottom," and has all the merits of the Catalpa, besides being better known and more thoroughly tested. Beyond doubt the cultivation of this tree would pay large returns on the capital invested. Of late years it has become infested by a borer.

The same may be said of the chestnut, save that it is somewhat less durable and strong; it has however a large range of usefulness.

Black walnut (*Juglans nigra*) is now undergoing trial on a large scale by competent business men in West Virginia, and so far as information goes with satisfactory results.

For mature timber one must wait longer than the above species require if he would undertake growth of oak. Of these species the most desirable is beyond doubt the white oak (*Quercus alba*), to mature which at least a century would be requisite. That the time is coming in which a growing oak-grove will have a cash value long before it is ready for the axe hardly admits of a doubt. It may, it is true, be a "legacy for the grandchildren," but it will be one which can be converted into ready money.

One essential question is: Will forest-culture ever pay in the United States? Probably in another half century it will be as generally recognized over the whole country as it now is in Germany or in France. Already it has thoroughly commended itself to the citizens of Nebraska and Kansas, where it has reduced the price of wood for fuel from $8 to $4 a cord. In Nebraska one practical tree-grower asserts that as a business raising trees there ranks next to raising stock. In such otherwise waste grounds as certain parts of Cape Cod there can be no doubt as to the importance of immediate forest production. What is now true of such regions will speedily become true of much wider areas in our country.

The above may be regarded as the personal proprietary aspects of forestry. What follows is more nearly connected with State forestry, in which the general good rather than individual advantage is to be consulted.

V. EFFECTS OF FORESTS ON RAINFALL AND IN PROTECTING THE SURFACE OF THE EARTH.—The belief that forests actually increase the rainfall is widespread and general. However, no satisfactory evidence has been forthcoming. To form a correct conclusion required an examination of most carefully kept tables which embraced a long range of years. This has been done by Sir Gustav Wex, imperial and royal ministerial councillor and chief engineer of the improvement of the Danube at Vienna. He undertook a critical examination of the tables, in which were noted the height of the water five times a year for many years, and reached the following results:

The Rhine at Emmerich had from 1770 to 1802 a mean height of 10 feet 6.74 inches; but from 1803 to 1835 the mean was 9 feet 1.26 inches. At Cologne between 1782 and 1808 the same river had a mean of 9 feet 7.01 inches; but from 1809 to 1835 the mean was 9 feet 2.89 inches.

The Elbe at Magdeburg from 1728 to 1777 showed a mean of 8 feet 10 inches; but the mean from 1778 to 1827 was 7 feet 4.33 inches, and from 1828 to 1869 the mean was 6 feet 1.96 inches.

The Oder at Kustrin from 1778 to 1806 gave as a mean 4 feet 9.12 inches; from 1807 to 1835 the mean was 3 feet 10.69 inches.

The Vistula at Kursebrack gave from 1809 to 1840 a mean of 6 feet 10.64 inches; from 1841 to 1871 a mean of 5 feet 5.39 inches.

The Danube at Vienna gave from 1826 to 1848 a mean of 1 foot 7.97 inches; from 1849 to 1871 a mean of only 10.89 inches.

Here, then, we have five rivers whose flow has been most carefully considered and all leading to the same conclusion that there is a decrease in the water carried during the last period for which the observations were made. In order, however, to put a check upon any observations taken upon mean height alone, another set of observations was made with the result of showing that from 1840 to 1853 (13 years) the Rhine discharged at Germersheim an annual mean of 53,154,869,396 cubic yards of water, but during the ensuing 13 years (from 1854 to 1867) the mean annual discharge was only 44,061,059,828, thus showing a decrease in the second period of 9,093,809,568 cubic yards.

The important point now was to trace this decrease in the water carried to the destruction of the forests. Gathering his data from observations made and opinions formed by the most distinguished and capable observers over the globe, the author makes it almost impossible to doubt that the alleged connection is true. Becquerel, Boussingault, Herschel, Arago, Känits, Lecoq, Tchihateff, and the English Commission appointed in England in 1851 to investigate this subject, Blanqui, Marchaud, Meldrum at Mauritius Island, Dr. Graham at the Madeira Islands, Mathieu in a French imperial school of forestry, Dove, and Gräger, all bear direct testimony in favor of this connection.

In our own country it is well known that since Utah has been settled and tree-planting actively prosecuted by the Mormon population there has been a marked increase in the precipitation. It has become the custom to explain this by the statement, undoubtedly true, that Utah had for an unknown period been undergoing a period of increasing desiccation, but that a change had taken place, that the time for the periodic increase had come, and that to this cosmic relation and not to the tree-planting the increased precipitation is due. In the first place, granting such periods of greater or less rainfall, the application of the law in this case is absolutely gratuitous, and in the second place large portions of Arizona and New Mexico appear to have undergone a like desiccation, but no corresponding increase in precipitation has been noted, and we may just as rationally infer that this is because there has been little or no increase in the tree-producing areas. Still it must be said that there is yet no positive evidence that forests increase the rainfall of a region. Recent statistics from the Adirondack Mountains make it more doubtful than ever.

There is one more aspect from which this relation of rainfall to forests may be considered. Even if we did not regard as proven the greater rainfall in earlier years in the regions of Europe which we have considered, there can be no doubt but that the forests do in the most marked manner aid in utilizing what does fall. A comparison of a treeless with a well-timbered region will show that in the former the number of destructive freshets is greater even with the same precipitation than in the latter. There being no leaves, roots, and undergrowth to retard the flow of the water, it hurries along the lines of descent from stream to stream, hastening out of the country and producing extensive washes and inundations along its course. Besides this which is directly carried off as surface water much less finds its way along the roots into depths where it would be secure against speedy evaporation, and hence go to feed the perpetual springs and through them the smaller water-courses, and finally ensure a more even average depth of water in the navigable rivers above tide-water. This is a factor which evidently involves the most vital interests of the state, *i. e.*, destructive freshets on the one hand and excessive drought on the other. It may be added there is nothing hypothetical or doubtful in this latter aspect of the problem.

The well-known effects of forests and vegetation in general in fixing sandy soils against high winds, or in holding soil against the washing of swift currents, need but bare mention.

The history of the redemption of the Landes in France by planting the maritime pine is still so fresh that it affords the most available illustration of important public interests subserved by scientific forestry. In our own country, to show how efficient even low shrubby vegetation may be in retaining earth, we may well mention the dunes formed at Provincetown on the extremity of Cape Cod.

VI. FORESTS AS AFFORDING PROTECTION AGAINST EXTREMES OF TEMPERATURE.—This may be considered from the standpoint of the mere obstruction offered to driving storms, where a few lines of close evergreen growth will suffice for considerable areas. Nurserymen are thus in the habit of protecting more tender plants by hedges of hardier ones; and so well is the efficiency of this protection known and recognized that in Iowa and other North-western States the people have more than once appealed to their legislatures to have trees planted along the roadsides as a protection to human life against the sudden and terrible winter-storms to which the region is subject.

During summer, at least, forests may be regarded as tending to produce a mean rather than an extreme climate. The reasons appear to be obvious. Thus in summer the shade protects the ground from becoming so excessively heated, and both evaporation and atmospheric circulation are less rapid. This, with the moisture which the leaves draw up through the roots from great depths and which is constantly given off by the leaves, prevents a rapid radiation by night of what heat the earth received during the day. Contrast this with the climate of open desert areas where the earth becomes intensely heated by the sun's rays, but where absence of aqueous vapor in the atmosphere allows so free radiation of the heat by night that before morning ice may form in midsummer.

The popular idea that forests are warmer in winter than the open ground is, if recent experiments be reliable, not true. From time immemorial savage nations have sought shelter for themselves and their domestic animals in forests against inclemencies of weather. Nor can there be any doubt but that protection has been rendered. This, however, is to be explained otherwise than by a supposition that the temperature was higher among the trees, for thermometric observations prove that it is during winter often lower there than in the fields. The protection comes partly from the velocity of the wind being less than in the open ground, and hence the animal heat is less rapidly carried away. Just as burial in a snow-bank would afford protection in the same way for a time at least.

The literature of forestry in this country is meagre in the extreme. G. B. Emerson published in 1846 an important pioneer work, *Trees and Shrubs of Massachusetts*, which has recently been enlarged. Under the auspices of the general government Dr. Franklin B. Hough published two important *Reports upon Forestry* (1877 and 1878-9). These volumes as compilations of all the available literature and as giving the results of extended observation are marvels of well-executed labor, and are monuments to the industry of the author. The same writer has published a *Manual of Forestry* (1883). Prof. Sargent, director of the Arnold Arboretum, has for years been making our forest trees a subject of special study. His connection with the Census Office of the general government has resulted in the production of a work which in the completeness and exactness of its details is a credit to the nation as well as to the author and his associates. As a justification for this science, which is old in the old world and new in the new, one may well quote the words of the Hon. Mark Dunnell, of Minnesota: "In recent journals we see accounts of gigantic monopolies springing up for 'cornering' the great supplies of timber still in the hands of the government on the Pacific coast. Should we not 'corner' these monopolies in the interest of the government before we get 'cornered' by them?" We may also ask, of what special value would these timber lands be to shrewd private speculators if a scarcity of timber were not impending? William Penn was wise enough to anticipate a time when timber might become scarce even in his then densely wooded domain, and to stipulate that one acre in six should remain uncleared; especially that oak- and mulberry-trees should be spared in the interests of silk and shipping. The last ten years have witnessed an increasing interest in the protection of our forests. A national forestry congress has done much to call attention to the importance of the subject. Besides this there are now many State forestry associations. (J. T. R.)

FOREY, ÉLIE FRÉDÉRIC (1804-1872), a French marshal, was born at Paris, Jan. 10, 1804. Graduating at the military school of St. Cyr in 1822, he made campaigns in Algeria in 1830, in 1835, and again in 1840. Returning to France in 1844 with the rank of colonel, he became general in 1848. For his energetic support of the *coup d'état*, he was in 1852 made general of a division. For a short time in 1854 he had command of the French before Sebastopol. Invading Italy in 1859 he defeated the Austrians at the bloody battle of Montebello, May 20, and received many marks of honor from Napoleon III. In July, 1862, Forey was sent with reinforcements to the French army in Mexico, with full civil and military powers. He arrived at Vera Cruz Sept. 27, and soon suspended the government of Almonte. After some reverses Forey captured the city of Puebla, May 17, 1863, and entered the city of Mexico June 10. For these successes he was made a marshal of France, July 2. His confiscation of the property of all Mexicans who opposed the invasion and his arbitrary conduct necessitated his recall. Transferring his military authority to Marshal Bazaine he returned to France, where he had command of an army corps and of the camp at Chalons. He died at Paris June 20, 1872.

FORMES, KARL JOHANN, a German basso singer, was born at Mühlheim, on the Rhine, Aug. 7, 1818. He had already entered the priesthood, when the remarkable qualities of his voice induced him to prepare for the stage. He first appeared in January, 1842, at Cologne as Sarastro in Mozart's *Magic Flute*. His enthusiastic success procured an immediate engagement for three years. In 1845 he was called to the Imperial Theatre at Vienna as primo basso, but being implicated in the revolutionary movements there in 1848, he was obliged to retire to Hamburg, and afterwards went to England. He also visited Russia and Spain, and from 1852 to 1857 he appeared in the Italian opera at Covent Garden, London. In 1857 he came to the United States and appeared at the New York Academy of Music in December. His triumph here was as marked as in the European capitals, and he expressed his intention of making America his home. However, he again visited Europe, and in 1874 appeared on the stage at Berlin. But his voice had then lost its flexibility and power, and even his undoubted dramatic ability seemed to have declined. In the height of his career he was equally successful in comic and in tragic rôles, and he added to his reputation by singing in oratorio. His chief parts were Figaro, Bertram, and Plunkett. He died at San Francisco, Dec. 15, 1889.

His son, Ernst, born at Mühlheim, Jan. 30, 1841, has been highly successful as a comic actor, appearing at Berlin, Dresden, Hamburg, and other German cities.

FORNEY, JOHN WEISS (1817-1881), an American journalist, was born at Lancaster, Pa., Sept. 30, 1817. After learning the printer's trade he became editor of a paper when only twenty years of age. In 1845 he was made deputy-surveyor of the port of Philadelphia, and removing thither became editor of the *Pennsylvanian*. In 1851 he was chosen clerk of the United States House of Representatives, and was also editor of the *Union*, a Washington Democratic paper, till 1856. In that year he exerted himself for the nomination and election of James Buchanan to the Presidency. A year later, Forney, disappointed in his expectation of being elected United States senator from Pennsylvania, started in Philadelphia the *Press* as an independent Democratic paper. Before long he was an earnest opponent of Buchanan's policy in reference to slavery, and the *Press* became a leading organ of the new Republican party. In 1859 Forney was again clerk of the House, and in 1861 was chosen secretary of the Senate. Besides the *Press* he now conducted the Washington *Chronicle*, and throughout the civil war these papers were prominent and able representatives of northern public opinion. In 1868 Forney retired from his secretaryship, and in 1871 he was appointed collector of customs at Philadelphia. He then relinquished the *Chronicle*, and in 1877 the *Press*. He afterwards established *Progress*, a weekly paper, which he edited till his death, Dec. 9, 1881. He had published in book form *Letters from Europe* (1867), *Anecdotes of Public Men* (1873), and a novel.

FORREST, Edwin (1806–1872), an American tragedian, was born at Philadelphia, March 9, 1806. He early displayed dramatic talent, making his first appearance as Douglas at the Walnut Street Theatre, Philadelphia, Nov. 27, 1820. He then went on a professional tour through the West, and on his return was engaged at Albany and Philadelphia. His delineation of Shakespeare's characters gave him fame, and in 1826 he appeared at the Park Theatre, New York, as Othello. His splendid figure, hard study, and thorough determination to succeed gave him the foremost place on the New York stage. Plays were specially written to enable him to display his matchless powers. Among these were John H. Stone's *Metamora*, in which Forrest took the title role, Dr. R. M. Bird's *Gladiator*, in which he enacted Spartacus, and later R. T. Conrad's *Aylmere*, in which was his famous part Jack Cade. On visiting England in 1835, Forrest was warmly received by both actors and critics. On his second visit in 1837 he married Catharine Norton Sinclair, daughter of a ballad singer. His third visit in 1845 was marred by a violent quarrel with Macready, who had formerly befriended him. When Macready came to New York in 1849, Forrest's partisans banded against him, and a bloody riot ensued at the Astor Place Theatre. In the same year began the scandalous suits for divorce between him and wife. A divorce was granted to Mrs. Forrest in 1852, and the professional skill of her lawyer, Charles O'Conor, secured for her all her legal rights and $3000 a year as alimony. Forrest's conduct throughout the trial alienated the regard of society, though his dramatic ability drew large audiences whenever he appeared. After securing an ample fortune he purchased in 1850 an estate on the Hudson, where he built a stone mansion called Fonthill. This was afterwards sold for a convent, and Forrest removed to Philadelphia. In 1865 he purchased a handsome country-seat at Springbrook in that vicinity. Although he had retired from the stage in 1858, he was induced to reappear in 1863, and again in 1867. Among his later impersonations that of King Lear was the most noted. From his last engagement in 1871 illness compelled him to retire, yet in the autumn of 1872 he gave Shakespearian readings. He died of apoplexy at Philadelphia, Dec. 12, 1872. By his will the greater part of his fortune was left to establish a home for aged and destitute actors at his country-seat. His magnificent library, especially rich in Shakespearian literature, was almost entirely destroyed by fire in his house at Philadelphia, Jan. 15, 1873. Forrest was not only a great tragic actor, but an excellent critic, and possessed refined literary taste. His impetuous temper brought him into troubles which embittered his life, yet he was in general of a frank and social disposition. His *Life* has been written by James Rees and W. R. Alger.

FORREST, Nathan Bedford (1821–1877), an American general, was born in Bedford co., Tenn., July 13, 1821. He removed to Mississippi in 1834, and after managing a farm entered into business at Hernando, Miss. In 1842 he removed to Memphis, Tenn., where he dealt in slaves and land. In 1859 he became a cotton planter in Coahoma co., Miss. Soon after the outbreak of the civil war he raised a cavalry regiment, and being made lieutenant-colonel in October, 1861, led his men to Fort Donelson. He escaped from the fort before its surrender and reached Nashville, Feb. 18, 1862. He was afterwards engaged in the battle of Shiloh. In June he held command of the cavalry at Chattanooga, and in July was made brigadier-general. He fought at Chickamauga, Sept. 19–20, 1863. While commanding in Northern Mississippi he was appointed major-general, and in April, 1864, captured Fort Pillow, where the negro soldiers were inhumanly butchered. He was promoted to be lieutenant-general in February, 1865, and surrendered at Gainesville, May 9, 1865. He engaged in business after the war and became president of the Selma and Memphis Railroad, but resigned in 1874. He died Oct. 29, 1877.

FÖRSTER, Ernst Joachim (1800–1885), a German art-writer, was born at Münchengossenstädt, Bavaria, April 8, 1800. He studied theology and philosophy at Jena and Berlin, but in 1822 abandoned these for painting. He was instructed by Cornelius at Munich, and soon was employed in painting frescoes in the Aula at Bonn and in the Arcades at Munich. In 1826 he visited Italy and began the researches in art-history which he afterwards prosecuted in Germany, France, Belgium, and England. The results of his journeys and studies are given in a long series of publications, the first of which was *Beiträgen zur neuern Kunstgeschichte* (1835), and the most important *Geschichte der deutschen Kunst* (5 vols., 1851–62); *Denkmale der deutschen Baukunst, Bildernei und Malerei* (12 vols., 1855–69). After the completion of these works on German art he undertook a similar service for Italian art, and published *Geschichte der italienischen kunst* (5 vols., 1869–78), and *Denkmale italienischer Malerei* (4 vols., 1869–82). In his researches in Italy he made important discoveries and restorations, bringing to light works of Raphael and David. Förster assisted in editing the *Kunstblatt*, continued the translation of Vasari's *Lives of the Painters*, commenced by Schorn, and wrote the biographies of J. G. Müller, Raphael, and Peter Cornelius. Having married a daughter of Jean Paul Friedrich Richter, he published several books relating to his father-in-law, and edited his letters and remains. He died May 10, 1885.

FÖRSTER, Heinrich (1800–1881), a German prelate, was born at Grossglogau, Silesia, Nov. 24, 1800. He was the son of a painter and was educated at the University of Breslau. Having been ordained priest April 17, 1825, he was chaplain at Liegnitz and afterwards pastor at Landshut. For the excellence of his pulpit oratory he was in 1837 attached to the cathedral at Breslau and became inspector of the theological seminary there. In 1844 the movement of Ronge and others for a German Catholic Church, and again the revolutionary movements of 1848, called forth his powers as a preserver of ecclesiastical discipline. On the death of Diepenbrock, Prince-bishop of Breslau, Förster was chosen his successor, May 19, 1853. His biography of his predecessor was widely read. Bishop Förster had several controversies, especially with Baltzer, the founder of a free religious community at Nordhausen, and with the theological faculty at Breslau. Though he had declared his opposition to the doctrine of papal infallibility before the Vatican Council, yet he submitted on its promulgation and instituted severe measures against those who rejected it. During the *Kulturkampf* the efforts of the Prussian government to control ecclesiastical affairs were baffled by his obstructions. For such acts he was repeatedly fined and at last was suspended from his office, Oct. 6, 1875. He had, however, already removed his residence to Johannisberg, in the Austrian part of his diocese. He died there Oct. 20, 1881. Among his published works are: *Homilien auf die Sonntage des*

Katholischen Kirchenjahres (1851); *Der Ruf der Kirche in die Gegenwart* (1852); *Die Christliche Familie* (1854); *Kanzelvorträge* (1854).

FÖRSTER, WILHELM, a German astronomer, was born at Grünberg, in Silesia, Dec. 16, 1832. He studied mathematics and natural science at Berlin, and astronomy at Bonn, graduating in 1854. In October, 1855, he was made second assistant at the Berlin Observatory, in 1860 he became first assistant, and in 1863 professor extraordinary of astronomy in the University. In 1865 he succeeded Encke as director and has since been editor of the *Astronomisches Jahrbuch* and contributor to the *Europaisches Gradmessung*. At the end of 1868 he was appointed a director of the commission for the introduction of the metric system of weights and measures into Germany. Besides his scientific papers contributed to various journals he has published popular sketches of the history of astronomy and the lives of distinguished astronomers.

FORSTER, WILLIAM (1784–1854), an English philanthropist, was born at Tottenham, near London, March 23, 1784. He was of Quaker descent, and after becoming a minister of the Society in 1805, he spent much time in religious journeys to various parts of England. In 1816 he married Anna, a sister of Thomas Fowell Buxton, and settled at Bradpole. In 1820 he visited the Friends' meetings in the United States, travelling as far west as Indiana, and as far south as Georgia. In 1843 he went on a missionary tour in France, and in September, 1845, he was sent to the United States to endeavor to heal the division among the Friends in Indiana, due to the agitation of the slavery question. He afterwards travelled through Scotland and the north of England, and in 1846 he made a memorable visit to Ireland during the famine. In 1849 he was commissioned by the Yearly Meeting of London to present to the rulers of Christian countries an address on slavery and the slave-trade. With this object he visited most of the countries on the continent of Europe, being everywhere treated with great respect. Coming again to the United States in 1853, he had interviews with the President and with the governors of several of the Southern States. Before his mission was completed he died at Holston, Tenn., Jan. 27, 1854.

FORSTER, WILLIAM EDWARD, an English statesman, only son of the preceding, was born at Bradpole, Dorsetshire, July 11, 1818. He was educated at the Friends' School, Tottenham, and engaged in worsted manufacture at Bradford. In 1850 he married the eldest daughter of Dr. Thomas Arnold, of Rugby. He entered Parliament in 1861, being chosen from Bradford as a liberal. From November, 1865, to July, 1866, he was under-secretary of state for the colonies, and from 1868 to 1874 he was vice-president of the committee of council on education. Under his auspices the Education Bill of 1870 was passed, which greatly improved and extended public instruction in England. Mr. Forster was also a prominent advocate of suffrage by ballot, and assisted in passing the Ballot Bill of 1871. In 1874, after the Conservatives had regained power, Mr. Forster made a visit to the United States, where he was cordially welcomed. In 1878 he was chosen Lord Rector of Aberdeen University. In 1880, when Mr. Gladstone became prime minister again, Mr. Forster entered the cabinet as chief-secretary for Ireland. The difficulties of this position were greatly increased by the sufferings of the Irish people from bad harvests and the agitation of the Land League. With the utmost desire to relieve the distress of the people, by changes of the land laws, Mr. Forster felt it necessary first to pass the Coercion Bill, granting to the Lord Lieutenant of Ireland extraordinary powers for the suppression of disturbances. In 1881 he retired from the Cabinet, on account of the English interference in Egyptian affairs. He died April 5, 1886.

FORSYTH, JOHN (1780–1841), an American statesman, was born at Fredericksburg, Va., Oct. 22, 1780. He graduated at Princeton College in 1799, studied law, and began practice at Augusta, Ga., where his father had settled. He became attorney-general of Georgia in 1808, and was elected to Congress in 1813, and after serving three terms was elected United States senator in 1818. President Monroe sent him as Minister to Spain in 1819, and on his return in 1823 he was elected to Congress, and served two terms. He was governor of Georgia from 1827 to 1829, and then was again elected to the United States Senate. Before the expiration of his term he was appointed by President Jackson as secretary of state, and he held this position throughout Van Buren's administration. He died at Washington, D. C., Oct. 21, 1841.

His son, JOHN FORSYTH, was born at Augusta, Ga., Oct. 30, 1812. He graduated at Princeton College in 1822, removed to Mobile, Ala., where he became editor of the *Register*. He served as an officer in the Mexican war, and was United States Minister to Mexico from 1856 to 1858. After the formation of the Southern Confederacy, he was one of the commissioners appointed to treat with President Lincoln in March, 1861. He served on the staff of Gen. Bragg during the civil war, and afterwards resumed the publication of the *Register*. He died May 2, 1877.

FORSYTH, WILLIAM, an English lawyer and author, was born in 1812. He was educated at Trinity College, Cambridge, graduating in 1834. He was called to the bar in 1839, and became Queen's Counsel in 1857, and bencher of the Inner Temple in 1859. He was elected to Parliament from Cambridge in 1856, but was unseated on the ground that as standing counsel to the secretary of state for India he was holding an office of profit under the crown, and was thereby disqualified. He was however elected to Parliament from Marylebone in 1874. He has been a frequent contributor to the *Quarterly Review* and other periodicals, and is well known by his works on legal and historical subjects. In the former class are *The Law of Composition with Creditors* (1841); *Hortensius, or The Duty and Office of an Advocate* (1849); *The Custody of Infants* (1850); *The History of Trial by Jury* (1852). In the latter class we have *Napoleon at St. Helena* (1853); *Life of Cicero* (1864); *The Novels and Novelists of the Eighteenth Century* (1871).

FORT DONELSON was a large earthwork on the left bank of the Cumberland River, one mile below the town of Dover, Stewart co., Tenn. It was erected by the Confederates in 1861, and captured by the Union forces under Gen. U. S. Grant Feb. 16, 1862. The object of the United States military authorities at that time was to advance into Tennessee through Kentucky, principally by using the Tennessee and Cumberland Rivers. A large Federal force was collected in Paducah at the mouth of the former, and a fleet of gunboats at Cairo, the mouth of the Ohio. To circumvent the Federal plans, the Confederates had erected Fort Henry on the right bank of the Tennessee, very near the Kentucky border, and Fort Donelson on the left bank of the Cumberland about 12 miles to the S. E. Pursuant to orders from Gen. Halleck, Gen. Grant on Feb. 1 steamed up the Tennessee with 17,000 men on transports, convoyed by Flag-Officer Foote of the navy, with 7 gun-boats, 4 of which were iron-clad. Fort Henry was garrisoned with 2000 men under Gen. Lloyd Tilghman. The work had 5 bastions, with 12 guns on the river front, and 5-trained inward. Although it commanded a long stretch of the river, it was on low, marshy ground, and was dominated by higher points within cannon range; but Gen. Grant, after making a reconnoissance in a gun-boat, brought his whole force up to Bailey's Ferry, within 3 miles of Fort Henry, where all had debarked by nightfall of Feb. 5. McClernand was directed to move upon the communications leading to Fort Donelson and Dover. The gun-boats steamed up and opened fire. Tilghman soon saw that the place was untenable, and, therefore, ordering his infantry force to fall back, before they were cut off, he remained in the work with but 60 gunners to return the concentrated fire of the gun-boats. Com. Foote began the attack before noon, Feb. 6, and Tilghman responded with great vigor; but after making a gallant resistance he surrendered at 2 P. M. The work was given up to the navy; Gen. Grant's troops not arriving until after the flag was lowered. They were at once ordered to advance upon Fort Donelson. The cavalry pursued the escaping garrison, but only 38 prisoners and 2 guns were taken.

Fort Donelson was erected between the mouths of Indian and Hickman Creeks, which both fall into the Cumberland River, and form a strong natural enclosure. It was an earthwork of numerous bastions and crenates, forming an irregular oblong. It stood upon an elevation of 100 feet, above the ordinary water line, and enclosed in its *enceinte* 100 acres. A bend in the river gave its heavy guns a clean sweep of the channel beyond cannon range. Lower down, on the slope towards the river, were two water-batteries, 30 feet above the water level and with the same sweep: they were formed by a trench 20 feet wide, the earth from which was thrown up in front, and with sand-bag additions made a parapet with embrasures 12 feet wide. In the lower battery were 10 heavy guns, and in the upper 3; besides numerous field-batteries there were 8 heavy guns mounted in the fort. The position was indeed a strong one; it was protected by the river on the east; on the north by the batteries and by Hickman Creek, the back water of which was impassable except by boats or bridges; while all the way round, following the ridges, in an irregular convex, and encompassing the town of Dover, as well as the fort, was an outer line of works, intrenched batteries, and rifle-pits, lying from 1¼ to 2½ miles from the fort. All along in front of this line were rude *abatis* or tree-slashings. The Confederate garrison had originally been of 6000 men under Gen. Bushrod R. Johnson, but on Feb. 9 Gen. Gideon J. Pillow arrived with 2000 men to take command. Gen. Clarke's contingent of 2000 came immediately afterwards, and then on the 12th Gens. Floyd and Buckner arrived with 8000. Gen. Polk also sent 1860 men from Columbus, and thus the total of troops—a competent garrison—was about 20,000. Gen. Floyd assumed command as ranking officer. To attack this large garrison, fortified and intrenched, the Union army under Grant numbered only 15,000, and should have been met in the field with superior numbers. The heavy rains had produced such an overflow that Grant was obliged to leave his wagons behind, and all his stores, that he might double-team his artillery for the heavy roads. For two miles out from Fort Henry the country was under water. Leaving Gen. Lewis Wallace with 2500 men temporarily at Fort Henry, Gen. Grant moved the remainder of his force by the two roads running to Fort Donelson and Dover. The First division under Gen. McClernand was in three brigades, commanded respectively by Gen. Oglesby, Gen. W. H. L. Wallace, and Col. Morrison. This division comprised altogether 11 Illinois regiments of infantry, with a regiment and 4 companies of cavalry, and 2 batteries. The Second division, under Gen. Charles F. Smith, consisted of four brigades, commanded respectively by Gen. McArthur, Gen. Lewis Wallace, Gen. J. Cook, and Col. Lanman. Gen. Wallace's brigade had been left at Fort Henry. Besides it, this division comprised 5 regiments of Illinois troops, 3 from Indiana, 4 from Iowa. With these also was a battalion of Missouri artillery, and there were 8 light batteries. In the march to Fort Donelson McClernand was in advance. Smith's division was posted on the Federal left, his left resting on Hickman Creek. McClernand was instructed to push forward to the extreme left of the enemy's position, to the river bank if possible, in order to cut the communication south of Dover. This was the condition of affairs on Thursday morning, Feb. 13. Grant was anxiously awaiting the co-operation of the fleet, and the arrival of reinforcements. He had sent 6 regiments back from Fort Henry by the Tennessee to Paducah to stop the sending of troops up that river, but to have them sent up the Cumberland. These had not yet appeared. In order to prevent further reinforcement of the enemy from Columbus, he despatched a small body of men to destroy the railroad bridge across the Tennessee above Fort Henry. This done, he ordered Lewis Wallace to join him with his 2500 men. There was considerable desultory fighting while these dispositions were being made, and much suffering among the troops from the severity of the weather, the thermometer during the night sinking to 10°. By noon of the 14th Gen. Lewis Wallace had arrived from Fort Henry, and the troops which had come from Paducah under convoy of the fleet were all debarked, bringing the total of Grant's force to 27,000 men. A third division was formed and given to Gen. Wallace, consisting of 3 brigades. It included 2 regiments of Kentucky volunteers, 2 from Indiana, 3 from Ohio, 3 from Illinois, and 1 from Nebraska. This division was posted in the centre, between Smith and McClernand, completing the investment of the fort. It should be observed that the only professional officers with this command were Gens. Grant and Smith and Lieut.-Col. McPherson, who had been temporarily detached from Gen. Halleck's staff to accompany this expedition. By 3 P. M., Feb. 14, Flag-Officer Foote had brought up his gun-boats to the attack. The fleet consisted of 4 iron-clads, each of 13 guns, and 2 wooden gun-boats. After the iron-clad Carondelet had drawn the fire of the water-batteries, the rest steamed up in the form of a crescent, opening fire at the distance of 1½ miles, and halting when within 400 yards. They could only use their bow guns, and after a severe conflict of an hour and a quarter they were obliged to haul off, with material damage, and 54 killed and wounded, among the latter being Com. Foote.

The reinforcements which had come with the fleet were landed from the transports, and McArthur's brigade of Smith's division was ordered round to the Union right to act as a support to Oglesby's advance. The night of the 14th, like the preceding, was intensely cold, and the men were without food and fire. Gen. Floyd having called a council of war, consisting of Gens. Pillow and Buckner, and Col. Gilmer, engineer, the following plan was agreed upon: a sortie should be made the next morning to open a way by which the command could retreat across the Wynn's Ferry road. To effect this Pillow was to attack the right of McClernand with cavalry, Buckner was then to strike his centre, and roll his division back on Lewis Wallace. A clear space being thus made, the whole command, after destroying the stores and munitions, should leave the place, leaving bare earth walls to the besiegers. This plan almost succeeded. Before dawn of the 15th Pillow began the movement. Oglesby and McArthur were obliged to fall back. McClernand sent to Lewis Wallace for aid, which, at first, in the absence of Gen. Grant, he declined to render. But at last he sent Cruft's brigade. At this period of the battle there was dire confusion, in which the details are lost. Federal regiments fired into each other by mistake. Cruft, after a manful resistance, was obliged to retire. It was then that Pillow ordered Buckner to attack with his whole force: he advanced with three regiments. The brigade of W. H. L. Wallace, of McClernand's division, fell back, and the division retreated for half a mile. A mounted officer rode rapidly up, shouting, "We are cut to pieces." Lewis Wallace then ordered Thayer with the third brigade to the rescue; it received and broke a new advance of the enemy, and the sortie had expended its force. The open space, however, had been cleared, and the Confederate troops might have marched out, but Pillow, most unaccountably, ordered Buckner back into his lines, and the movement was abandoned. When the fleet hauled off, Com. Foote wrote a note begging Gen. Grant to visit him on board his ship, as he was disabled. The general started before day of the 15th, and was ignorant of what was passing on his right. On his return he stopped at C. F. Smith's position, and on receiving the reports, determined, with great judgment, to attack at once. Directing Smith to be ready to move at a moment's notice, he rode round to his right, and, undismayed by the disaster, ordered them to rectify their alignments so as to resume the offensive. "Whichever party," he said, "first attacks now will whip, and the rebels will have to be very quick if they beat me." Smith's assault was a model of coolness and dashing valor. He formed his command, Lanman in front, in column of battalions, five companies in each, with sharp-shooters in advance on the flanks, and supported by the fire of Major Cavender's batteries. The regiments rushed forward without firing, crushing down or surmounting the *abatis*, up to the outer works, over and in. Buckner hurried Hanson's regiment forward to repel them, but it was too late. The attacking column was at nightfall in a commanding position, and had two Parrott guns posted to enfilade and take in reverse the inner works of the enemy. Smith lost in his charge 61 killed and 321 wounded. Sixty years old, he spent the night on the ridge without shelter or fire. While this success was being achieved on the Union left, Grant was ordering the troops of Wallace forward, and witnessing the retirement of the Confederates after severe fighting.

On the night of the 15th Floyd called a second council of war at Pillow's head-quarters. There were criminations and recriminations, but it was finally decided to evacuate the place at once, marching out through the space which had been opened. An order was issued to the chief quartermaster to burn and destroy all stores: scouts were sent to see that the way was open. To the consternation of all they returned to report that the ground was almost entirely re-occupied. Pillow then proposed that they should cut their way out. Buckner declared that to be impossible; there was nothing left, he said, but surrender. Floyd and Pillow said they would not be taken. Forrest asked leave to cut his way out with the cavalry, which was granted. Floyd then transferred the command to Pillow, who passed it to Buckner, and these two generals, abandoning their troops to capture, escaped under cover of the night. Buckner, having assumed the command, countermanded the order to destroy the stores, and sent at once for a bugler and a white flag. On Sunday morning, Feb. 16, 1862, the men of Lanman's command heard a solitary bugle, and saw an officer approaching with a flag of truce. His message was from Gen. Buckner to Gen. Grant, proposing an armistice until noon and the appointment of commissioners to arrange for a capitulation. Grant's answer was: "No terms except unconditional and immediate surrender can be accepted; I propose to move immediately on your works." Although Buckner characterized these terms as ungenerous and unchivalrous, he immediately surrendered everything, including 65 guns and from 12,000 to 15,000 prisoners. Forrest had succeeded in getting his command out; it consisted almost entirely of cavalry. The landing place at Dover was thronged with men seeking to escape; the steamers had gone up the river; when they returned at daybreak, Floyd got his Virginia regiments on board, and made off so rapidly that he left his aide behind. "The men," says Badeau, "crowded to the shore, ... filling the steamers to their utmost capacity, those who remained cursing and hissing the officers who were leaving them to their fate." The number that escaped was between 2000 and 3000.

The total of Confederate losses was about 2000. The Union army lost 3329 in all. The results of the capture of Fort Donelson were great and far-reaching: the defensive line from Columbus to Bowling Green was broken, and both these places were soon after abandoned. As a consequence, also, Nashville was evacuated, and the war was carried into the heart of the Confederacy. There was great surprise and excitement in both sections of the country. When the news reached Washington Grant was at once promoted to be a major-general, dating from the day of the surrender; in March the same rank was conferred upon C. F. Smith, McClernand, and Lewis Wallace. (H. C.)

FORT FISHER was an earthwork erected by the Confederates on a low sandy peninsula between Cape Fear River and the Atlantic Ocean, and was intended to protect the entrance to Wilmington, N. C., one of the favorite resorts of blockade-runners. It had a sea-front of 1300 yards, and an arm at right angles to this, 480 yards long. Towards the close of the siege of Richmond, Wilmington was the only remaining source of supplies for that capital, and, therefore, in December, 1864, an expedition was sent against the fort from Hampton Roads. Gen. B. F. Butler, who commanded the expedition, had ordered a vessel to be filled with over 200 tons of powder, and taken as near the fort as possible. This was done early on the morning of Dec. 24, but when the vessel was exploded at the dis tance of 1000 yards no appreciable effect was produced on the fort. Later in the day the fleet opened fire on the fort, and this was continued next day. Troops were then landed, but the assault being considered impracticable, they were withdrawn and taken back to the James River. A week later another expedition was sent under Gen. A. H. Terry, which landed on the peninsula on Jan. 13, 1865, and protected itself with intrenchments from an attack in the rear. The fleet, which had still remained off the coast, kept up a heavy fire for two nights and throughout the morning of the 15th. The assault was made in the afternoon by the land forces at one end of the shorter side, and by a force of sailors and marines at the other. The latter were driven back by the heavy fire, but the former effected a lodgment, and steadily drove the enemy out of their defences in spite of their stubborn resistance. After six hours' hard fighting the whole of the works were in possession of the Union forces. Gen. Whiting, the Confederate commander, was captured, with 2083 men, 160 pieces of heavy artillery, and many small arms. The Union loss in the assault was 110 killed, 536 wounded, but on the next day by the explosion of the magazine 200 more lost their lives. The other defences of the Cape Fear River were speedily abandoned by the Confederates, though they held Wilmington until Feb. 21.

FORT SUMTER, a noted defensive work of the harbor of Charleston, S. C., occupies a shoal, artificially enlarged, on the south side of the entrance to the inner harbor, 1 mile south-west of Fort Moultrie, ⅜ mile north of the northern end of Morris Island, and 3½ miles from the city. It was constructed by the United States government according to plans made in 1827-8. It was built of brick on a rip-rap foundation, and was in form pentagonal with truncated salients. The exterior wall was 38 feet high, and 7½ feet thick. The full armament was to be 146 guns, two tiers being in casemates, and one in barbette. When South Carolina passed its ordinance of secession in December, 1860, the embrasures of the second tier were still unfinished, but the fort had 62 guns mounted, the largest being six 24-pounders, and three 10-inch columbiads. On Dec. 26, Major Robert Anderson (q. v.), who had command of the United States troops in Charleston harbor, prudently transferred his little garrison of about 80 men from the defenceless Fort Moultrie to the stronger Fort Sumter. South Carolina troops then occupied all the surrounding points, erected batteries, obstructed the harbor, and extinguished all the coast lights. Meantime the openings which had been left in the walls of the fort were closed, but the attempts of the United States government to introduce reinforcements or supplies failed. After two days' bombardment, which marked the commencement of the civil war, Major Anderson surrendered the fort, April 14, 1861. During its subsequent occupancy by the Confederates its strength was increased; many of the casemates were filled with sand; and its armament was raised to 72 guns and 4 mortars. No direct attempt was made to retake it until April 7, 1863, when Rear-Admiral S. F. Dupont, commanding the South Atlantic blockading squadron, attacked the fort with an iron-clad fleet, consisting of the frigate New Ironsides and eight monitors. After firing 139 shots from 23 guns in 2¼ hours, he withdrew the fleet. One of his vessels was sunk the next day, and others had been seriously injured, while the fort sustained but trifling damage. Seeing the necessity of using the heaviest siege-guns, Gen. Quincy A. Gillmore, on July 10, seized the southern end of Morris Island, and erected batteries, from which, on Aug. 17, he opened a terrific fire on the fort. The distance was about 4000 yards, but the Parrott rifled cannon proved effective, and at the end of a week much of the fort was demolished. The batteries had thrown 5009 projectiles, weighing from 100 to 300 pounds. The fort was silenced, but the Confederates still maintained possession, and were able to repulse a naval attack by boats on the night of Sept. 8. A second bombardment, begun on Oct. 26, from the northern end of Morris Island, was continued for 40 days, but though further damage was done, and many lives lost, the reduction of the fort was not effected. Again, on July 7, 1864, a heavy bombardment commenced, which lasted about two months. The commander of the fort was killed, and the number of guns mounted was reduced to 9. Yet not till after the city of Charleston was evacuated by the Confederates, Feb. 18, 1865, in consequence of Gen. Sherman's march through South Carolina, was the United States flag again raised over the ruins of the fort. By order of President Lincoln this was formally done on April 14, 1865, the fourth anniversary of the evacuation. The same flag which had been lowered was then raised again by Gen. Robert Anderson and saluted by the guns of the fort and of all the batteries which had taken part in the bombardment of 1861. In accordance with a plan approved by the United States government in 1870, there has been a partial restoration of the fort, fitting it for an armament of 35 cannon, besides 4 Gatling guns.

FORTUNE, ROBERT (1812-1880), a Scotch botanist and traveller, was born in Berwickshire, Sept. 16, 1812. Taught only at a village school he became a gardener. After being employed for some years in the botanical gardens at Edinburgh and at Chiswick, he was sent by the Horticultural Society of London in 1842 to collect plants in Northern China. In this work he was very successful, and after his return he published *Three Years' Wanderings in China* (1847), which gave a new insight into the condition of that country. He was now commissioned by the East India Company to make thorough investigation of the tea-plant, and returned to spend three years more in China. The result is recorded in his *Two Visits to the Tea Countries of China* (1852). After its publication he made a third visit from 1853 to 1856, which is described in his *Residence among the Chinese Islands, on the Coasts, and at Sea* (1857). When an effort was made to introduce the cultivation of tea in the United States in 1857, Fortune was employed by the United States Patent Office to collect the seeds of the tea shrub and other plants, and was thus engaged until 1863. He spent the latter years of his life on a small estate in Scotland. He died April 13, 1880.

FORTUNY, MARIANO (1838-1874), the greatest Spanish painter of the nineteenth century, was born at Reus, near Barcelona, June 11, 1838. He studied art at the Academy of Barcelona, then under the direction of Claudio Lorenzales, a pupil of Overbeck. But Fortuny soon swerved from the beaten track. By the excellence of some early designs he won a prize which enabled him to go to Rome in 1858. There he not only sketched from the old masters, but devoted much time to modern life as seen in the streets of Rome. In 1859 he accompanied Gen. Prim in his expedition to Morocco and filled his portfolio with sketches of its barbaric splendor and brilliant skies. He returned to Barcelona to put on canvas the essence of the materials he had gathered, but soon repaired to Rome. Henceforth his works showed him to be the legitimate successor of Velasquez and Goya. Renouncing entirely the classical traditions, he depicted with the utmost care but with startling vigor and matchless color what he had seen in Spain and Africa. Around him gathered a group of young and enthusiastic artists devoted to splendid realism. In 1866, his rank and fame being already established, Fortuny went to Paris, where he came into close relations with Meissonier, and, though their methods were widely distinct, the influence of the great French artist can be seen in the Spaniard's later works. Fortuny's paintings were now eagerly sought for, and American merchants vied with European nobles in purchasing them. Mr. A. T. Stewart, of New York, became the fortunate owner of some of the best, among which were The Serpent Charmer and A Fantasy of Morocco. In 1868 Fortuny went to Madrid, and while there married a daughter of Madrazo, the director of the royal museum, several of whose family had won distinction as artists. He was fortunate in his wife, and his marriage suggested to him one of his most famous paintings, The Spanish Marriage, in which appear the portraits of his wife and of his friend, the artist Regnault. In 1870 Fortuny took up his residence in Granada, where he devoted himself with fresh enthusiasm to painting, to sketching for new works and perfecting his former pieces. He also visited Morocco to revive and deepen his recollections of its life and scenery. To this visit are due The Fencing Lesson and The Tribunal of a Cadi. In 1872 Fortuny returned to Rome, where he lived in princely style, courted by travellers and surrounded by artists. At times he withdrew to other Italian cities to get the relief needed for the prosecution of his work. His health failed in 1873, but he seemed afterwards to have recovered entirely. By imprudently working in the open air in autumn he brought on a fever, of which he died at Rome, Nov. 21, 1874. Besides his oil-painting he gave attention to etching and to water-colors, manifesting in all the same originality and genius. These productions were eagerly sought for and commanded high prices, and engravings of all his famous pictures have been widely circulated.

FORT WAYNE, a city of Indiana, county-seat of Allen co., is at the head of the Maumee River, formed by the junction of the St. Mary's and St. Joseph's Rivers, 148 miles S. E. of Chicago. It is an important railroad centre, being on the Pittsburgh, Fort Wayne, and Chicago Railroad and on the Toledo, Wabash, and Western, with railroads also to Richmond, Grand Rapids, Muncie, Saginaw, and St. Louis. There are seven bridges in the vicinity. Being situated on an elevated plain, Fort Wayne is known as the "Summit City." Its principal buildings are the United States Government house, masonic temple, two hospitals, Catholic cathedral, and some fine churches. There are altogether 25 churches, 10 hotels, 3 national banks, 5 daily and 7 weekly newspapers, a high school, normal school, and 15 other schools. There are also two colleges, a Methodist and a Lutheran. Large railroad-works, machine-shops, and foundries give employment to thousands. There are also large establishments, manufacturing wagons, wheels, furniture, organs, etc. There are 6 flouring-mills, 6 saw-mills, and 15 factories. The city is lighted with gas and electric light; it has water-works and a park. Its property is valued at $16,000,000. The site was early occupied by a French trading-post, and in 1794 Gen. Anthony Wayne established there a fort, around which a town grew. It was laid out in 1825, and in 1839 was incorporated as a city. The completion of the Wabash and Erie Canal in 1842 increased its trade. In 1854 the railroad to Pittsburg was opened, and since that time the city has become a great railroad centre. Its population in 1840 was only 2080, in 1860 it had increased to 10,388; in 1880 to 26,880; and in 1890 to 36,600.

FORT WORTH, a city of Texas, county-seat of Tarrant co., is on the Trinity River, at the junction of the Clear and West Rivers, 200 miles N. of Austin. Here the Texas Pacific and Transcontinental Railways unite and form one line to El Paso. The Missouri, Kansas, and Texas Railroad from St. Louis, and the Gulf, Colorado, and Santa Fé also pass through the city. It has daily trains to New Orleans, Galveston, St. Louis, and to El Paso. A railroad intended to reach Denver has been built for 150 miles. There are 3 iron bridges within the city limits. Besides the court-house and other county buildings there are 6 hotels, 5 national banks, 4 weekly and 2 daily newspapers, 10 churches, 9 public schools, 5 private schools, and a college. The industrial works comprise a foundry, a cotton-compress, cottonseed-oil-mill, and flour-mills. The city is well laid out, is lighted with gas, and supplied with water-works. Its property is valued at $7,000,000, and its debt is $320,000. Settled in 1848, it was made the county-seat in 1857, and obtained a city charter in 1873. Yet its real development began only when the Texas Pacific Railway reached it in 1876. In 1880 its population was 6663, and in 1890 had increased to 20,719.

FORWARD, WALTER (1786-1852), an American statesman, was born in Connecticut in 1786. Removing to Pittsburg in 1803 he studied law and was admitted to the bar in 1806. He was elected to Congress in 1822, and in the presidential elections of 1824 and 1828 he was the supporter of John Quincy Adams. He was a member of the Pennsylvania Constitutional Convention of 1837. In March, 1841, he was appointed first comptroller of the U. S. Treasury, and in September following President Tyler appointed him secretary of the treasury. Forward resigned in March, 1843, and remained in private life until President Taylor appointed him *chargé d'affaires* to Denmark. He returned to America in 1852 and became presiding judge of the District Court of Allegheny co., Pa. He died at Pittsburg, Pa., Nov. 24, 1852.

FOSS, CYRUS DAVID, an American bishop, was born at Kingston, N. Y., Jan. 17, 1834. He graduated at Wesleyan University, Middletown, Conn., in 1854, and taught in Amenia Seminary, 1856-57. He then entered the New York Conference and was pastor of prominent churches until 1875, when he was made president of Wesleyan University. In 1878 he was the delegate from his denomination to the General Conference of the M. E. Church South. He was chosen bishop in 1880, and has since been active in discharge of the duties of that office.

FOSTER, BIRKET, an English artist, was born at North Shields, Feb. 4, 1825. He was of Quaker descent, and was apprenticed to a wood-engraver. Being confined to bed for seven months he spent the time in close study of engravings. His first work to attract attention was the illustration of Longfellow's *Evangeline* (1850). He afterwards illustrated most of the standard English poets. In 1859 he exhibited at the Royal Academy a water-color, The Mill at Arundel. He afterwards devoted himself to depicting child-life and rural scenes.

FOSTER, JOHN GRAY (1823-1874), an American general and engineer, was born at Whitefield, Coos co., N. H., May 27, 1823. He graduated at West Point in 1846, and entering the engineer corps served with Gen. Scott in Mexico. He was severely wounded at Molino del Rey. After the war he was engaged in the coast survey and at West Point. He was chief-engineer at Charleston Harbor when Fort Sumter was attacked in April, 1861. In October he was appointed brigadier-general of volunteers, and went with Gen. Burnside to North Carolina in February, 1862. In July following he was promoted major-general with command of the department of North Carolina. In December he defended New Berne against Gen. D. H. Hill. This department was afterwards enlarged, the head-quarters being removed to Fortress Monroe. In December, 1863, he was transferred to the department of the Ohio, but soon retired on account of wounds. From May, 1864, to February, 1865, he had command of the department of the South, and afterwards that of Florida, where he remained till September, 1866. He was then placed in charge of works at the harbors of Boston and Portsmouth, N. H. In the regular army he reached the grade of lieutenant-colonel of engineers, with the brevet of major-general. He died at Nashua, N. H., Sept. 2, 1874.

FOSTER, JOHN WELLS (1815-1873), an American geologist, was born at Brimfield, Mass., in 1815. He graduated at Wesleyan University, Middletown, Conn., in 1835, and soon after removed to Zanesville, Ohio, where he became a lawyer. He assisted in the geological survey of Ohio in 1837, making a report on the central district, which included the coal-fields. In 1845 he went to the copper region of Lake Superior, and in 1847 became associated with Prof. J. D. Whitney in the government survey of that district. Their Report was published in 1850-51. Mr. Foster afterwards resided in Massachusetts, but in 1858 he removed to Chicago. In connection with his geological researches he had gathered much valuable information in other departments, which he embodied in his works, *The Mississippi Valley* (1869) and *The Prehistoric Races of the United States* (1873). He also published several monographs on American ethnology and contributed to various scientific periodicals. He was for some time land commissioner for the Illinois Central Railroad, and was president of the American Association for the Advancement of Science. He died at Chicago, June 27, 1873.

FOSTER, RANDOLPH S., an American bishop, was born at Williamsburg, Ohio, Feb. 22, 1820. He was educated at Augusta College, Ky., and in 1837 became an itinerant in the Ohio Methodist Conference. He had charge of several churches in Ohio until 1850, and afterwards in New York city and Brooklyn. In 1857 he was made president of the North-western University at Evanston, Ill. In 1860 he returned to pastoral work in New York. In 1868 he was a delegate to the British Wesleyan Conference, and in the same year was made professor of systematic theology in Drew Theological Seminary, Madison, N. J. In 1872 he was elected bishop, and soon afterward went to visit the Methodist churches and missions in Europe and South America. He has published *Objections to Calvinism* (1849); *Christian Purity* (1851; new ed., 1869); *Ministry for the Times* (1855); *Theism* (1872).

FOUQUIERA, OCOTILLO, or JACOB'S WAND. One of the most remarkable shrubs or rather small trees of Western Texas and the great Colorado desert, attracting the attention of all travellers by the singularity of its growth, and the remarkable beauty of its flowers, is *Fouquiera splendens*, so named by Engelmann in the botany of Gregg's expedition, on which it was found by Dr. Wislizenus, the naturalist of the party. The genus was founded by Humboldt on two species discovered in Mexico, and dedicated to Dr. Peter Edward Fouquiere, a physician of Paris. These three are all yet known. It belongs to the natural order *Tamariscineæ*. The flower has five free sepals, petals united into a tube, the spreading lobes of the limb imbricated. The stamens are ten to fifteen, hypogynous, and exserted; filaments thickened at the base, ovary imperfectly three-celled; placentæ about six, ovuled; styles three, long, and somewhat united; seeds three to six, oblong, flattened, surrounded by a fringe of long white hairs or by a membranous ring.

F. splendens has a main trunk of only a foot and a half high and a foot in diameter, from which arises sometimes a single stem, but frequently ten or twelve erect wand-like branches, with a fan-like spread, generally from 10 to 15, but often 20 or 30 feet high. These branches, or branchless secondary stems, are clothed with gray recurved thorns about an inch long, apparently the bases of undeveloped leaves, and clusters of small secondary leaves appear in the axils. The flowers are scarlet, tubular, nearly an inch long, and terminate the stems in panicles 6 to 10 inches in length. It grows in the most sterile and stony places, and where the hot, dry atmosphere is almost stifling. It furnishes the "ocotillo" poles of the Mexicans. Out of these with strips of rawhide they make admirable fences; and for hedges they cut the pieces of stems into lengths and plant them, when they readily grow. The wood is extremely hard and durable. They are often planted so as to grow up into tall and impregnable barriers around yards and farm-buildings. The stems, according to Dr. Harvard, are impregnated with a resinous substance which makes them excellent fuel—the small scales or chips, which can readily be pulled off from the base of the stems, are invaluable for starting camp-fires. The leaves chewed are pleasantly acidulous. Its common name with American travellers is Jacob's wand and Jacob's staff. (T. M.)

FOWL. The original ancestry of the domestic fowl is involved in uncertainty. The traditions of the earliest peoples carry back a knowledge of poultry-keeping and cock-fighting to the remotest antiquity. Some naturalists have attributed to the *Gallus Bankiva*, a wild jungle-fowl of India, the origin of all our domestic breeds. On the other hand, naturalists of equal ability and acuteness refer it to the *Gallus giganteus*, another jungle-fowl. It is conceded that some species of the wild jungle-fowls were domesticated. But more knowledge of facts is necessary before the question of origin can be definitely settled. Whatever may have been the original, it was a very different bird from the one we know at present.

See Vol. IX. p. 433 Am. ed. (p. 491 Edin. ed.).

There are several races of fowls, the best known of which are the game-fowl, of Indo-European origin, noted for its beauty and courage; the Asiatic race, of Chinese origin, large in size, docile, abundantly covered with loose, fluffy plumage, and feathered on feet and legs; the East India fowls, close-feathered, clean-shanked, and mostly fierce and cruel in disposition; the European race, of rather spare and upright build, some crested with feathers, others with large combs, compact plumage, smooth shanks and feet, and all good layers.

The show standards for poultry recognize the following classes: 1, the American; 2, the Asiatic; 3, the Game; 4, the Spanish; 5, the French; 6, the Polish; 7, the English; 8, the turkey; 9, the duck; 10, the goose; 11, the miscellaneous or unclassified. Each of these so-called classes contains several sub-varieties or breeds, more or less modified in color, crests, combs, etc. The American standard of excellence recognizes about sixty varieties, to which new ones are added from time to time. But this multiplication is a work of fancy rather than of value. For instance, most of the Asiatics are merely variations of what were known forty years ago as the Shanghais. The endless varieties in the Game class are also much alike except in size and color. There are five varieties of Hamburgs, the same of Polish, Leghorns, Dorkings, Cochins, etc., each having the general characteristics of its class, but differing in some minor point of coloring, combs, claws, or in other trivial variations, which can be perpetuated only by the skilled art of the fancier. Some of the most valuable breeds of chickens are such as have been cross-bred from varieties possessing well-established characteristics; thus the Houdan combines some of the characteristics of the English Dorking, the Pomeranian Polish, and the native French stock. So, too, the American Plymouth Rock, a valuable fowl, has been recently produced by a cross of the native Dominique fowl with Asiatic hens.

Jungle Fowl.

The first Europeans who came to America brought fowls with them, but not much attention was paid to poultry-raising here until within the memory of men now living. There were always a few fanciers and poulterers in and near the seaboard cities, but not until 1850 was any special attention given to the subject, except in the case of a few of the old well-known breeds, as Games, white-faced Spanish, Hamburgs, and the native Dominique fowl and its crosses with the above, which were bred in a small way in the immediate neighborhood of the large cities. The year 1846 marked an epoch in the raising of poultry in the United States. In that year the first Asiatic fowls were introduced, and created an immediate sensation. By 1850 the "poultry craze" had fairly set in. The new breed was sent to England. An enterprising Yankee presented Her Majesty Queen Victoria with some of the famous birds, and an uncommon interest in poultry was soon manifested. Poultry clubs and societies were organized. The first poultry-show in America was held at Boston in 1857, but the first home of the Asiatic fowl on the Western continent was Philadelphia, whence it was soon distributed to New England, and thence to Western Europe. The interest in poultry being thus awakened, seafaring men brought fowls from different parts of the world, and several new foreign breeds were introduced. Among the most noted of these were the Leghorns from Italy, between 1855 and 1865. In 1867 the French breeds were introduced. The Dorking was brought from England, the Silkies from Japan, and many varieties from the Indian Archipelago and elsewhere, most of which, however, were more novel than useful. Thus, from 1855 to 1875 the world was searched and varieties more or less valuable were contributed to the general poultry-stock.

The really useful breeds are embraced in a short catalogue. They are the Asiatics, Brahmas and Cochins; the English, Dorkings and Hamburgs; the French, Houdans and Crevècœurs; the Spanish, including the Leghorns; the Dutch Hamburgs and crested Polish; and the old-fashioned native Dominique. In addition to these, Games and Bantams are an important ornamental class. With these as a basis the fowl-stock of the country has been made up, and since 1870 the interest in poultry has spread from the Atlantic to the Pacific.

The turkey is certainly a great acquisition to our poultry-stock. Its large size and great hardiness, after its early life of chickhood is passed, make it a desirable bird to raise. The turkey-hen lays 18 to 24 eggs. The first-laid ones are usually placed under ordinary hens for incubation; the remainder are hatched by the turkey-hen, and all the young are allowed to run and forage together when they are large enough to go abroad. The delicacy of the young poults is doubtless due to a want of fresh blood in the long domesticated strains. In the breeding of turkeys, as of fowls, new blood may easily be procured. Breeders have recently crossed their strains with the wild birds, and have greatly increased the size and vigor of the turkey. The best known of these recent crosses is the bronze turkey, a very fine, large bird, the heaviest of the hens weighing at maturity 25 pounds, and cocks as high as 40 pounds each. The best breeding-stock is two- and three-year-old hens and a full-sized cockbird not less than two years old. If the cock is very large and heavy, he should be penned up and fed sparingly to reduce his weight previous to the mating-season. With proper management, there is little if any more difficulty in rearing turkeys than chickens. The turkey-hen and her brood are kept in a large coop slatted in front and placed on a dry, sheltered grass-run facing the sun. The feeding and management are much the same as for other young broods. They must be kept dry and clean, fed often, and supplied with fresh water or milk two or three times a day. Well-drained curds, mixed with finely-chopped onion- or garlic-tops and dandelion-leaves, are excellent food for young turkeys, and the green food must not be omitted from the time the chicks are a few days old. The food must of course be out of reach of the mother-hen; and as young turkeys are sometimes very stupid about learning to eat, a newly-hatched chicken or two cooped with the turkey-chicks will soon teach them. When the broods are three or four weeks old the mother-hen may be let out on fair days, after the grass is dry, to go abroad with the brood, but all must be brought back to the coop before night or on the approach of rain. As soon as the young can go up to roost, they should be furnished with a proper perch in the turkey-house, and encouraged to use it. Turkeys dislike to roost with other fowls, and should have a house or high open shed of their own, with lofty perches. The American standard recognizes six varieties of turkeys—viz., the bronze, Narragansett, black, white, buff, and slate; mongrels are not recognized or classified. The turkey attains its full size in its third year, but all except breeding-stock are fattened and slaughtered under one year old at an average weight of 13 pounds for hens and 19 pounds for cocks. In many parts of the country, particularly east of the Susquehanna Valley, the turkey-crop is valuable and considered profitable, and in all except densely-populated districts it should be more largely cultivated. The turkey is an excellent forager, consuming innumerable insect pests, and, although disliked in the fields by those who are not well acquainted with it, does very little damage to growing crops.

The duck occupies a less prominent place in American poultry-yards than in those of England and France. There are several breeds of domestic ducks, all originating from the wild mallard. The larger and most useful breeds for domestic purposes are the Aylesbury, Rouen, Pekin, Cayuga, and Musk or Muscovy. The Aylesbury duck takes its name from the county-town of Buckinghamshire, England, where it has been bred from time immemorial. It is a beautiful pure white bird in both sexes, with orange-colored feet and legs, and in its native place a flesh-colored bill; in America the bill cannot be retained of this color, but becomes yellow. Except the Pekin duck, introduced from China in 1872, the Aylesbury is the best layer of all the ducks, and has been known to produce 120 eggs in a year. The young of all the ducks are mostly hatched under common hens. Two, and sometimes three, broods are given in charge of one hen, and are reared much as other young poultry. They need no water except for drink during the first month, after which they should have a shallow vessel of water to play in; but they may be allowed a running stream or pond after they are two months old, though they are often successfully reared with only a large trough or tub of water in their runs. The next best-known duck is the Rouen, supposed to have originated at the city of that name in France. This is also an excellent duck, and more nearly resembles the wild mallard in plumage than any other of the domestic breeds, the green head and the white band which nearly surrounds the neck of the drake being the same as those of the wild ancestor, and the general plumage in both the male and the female resembling that of the wild bird in many respects. The drake and the duck in this breed are quite unlike in color, and in this respect they differ from the other pure breeds of ducks in domestication. The feet and legs of the Rouen are of a bright orange, while the bill is dusky yellow tinged with green. The Rouen is heavier at maturity than the Aylesbury by a pound or more. The strong points of the latter are its early maturity and its early readiness for market. It is ready to kill at eight to ten weeks old, and with proper feeding weighs 5 to 6 pounds the pair at that age. The best food for ducks reared for early marketing is ground oats, corn, barley, and buckwheat made into gruel, and chandlers' greaves. The Pekin duck is pure white, somewhat tinged with a creamy yellow, with orange-colored legs, feet, and bill. It is a good duck, and valuable as a cross on either Aylesbury or Rouen breeds. The Cayuga duck is jet black, the male having a greenish metallic iridescence of plumage which is striking and beautiful. It is a good duck, but smaller than the preceding. The Musk or Muscovy duck comes from South America. It is particolored, of larger size than any other domestic duck, but inferior as a farm-bird. Ducks are all proverbially hardy, are easily reared, and should be more popular with American poultry-keepers.

The goose is a domestic bird of ancient lineage, but its ancestry is easily traced to the wild goose. The two chief domestic varieties are the Embden and the Toulouse. It is difficult to say which of these stands first in point of merit. The Embden goose takes its name from the city of Embden in Westphalia, where it originated. The bird is of spotless white plumage in both sexes, with dark flesh-colored bill and deep orange legs and feet, the eyes being bright blue. The Toulouse geese take their name from the city of Toulouse in France, where they are largely reared. They are gray in color in both sexes, darkest on the neck, shading off gradually to lighter gray on the breast and body, running to white on the belly and hinder parts. The bill is about the color of sun-tanned flesh, and the legs and feet are of a deep reddish orange. These two varieties are the best and most profitable. They are nearly equal in size and weight; the Embden is taller, and the Toulouse a better layer; both are easy to rear, and attain heavy weights by early winter. The goose never lays until she is a year old, and sometimes not until two years old. The eggs are very large and may be hatched under common hens, but the young should be cared for by the geese. They are easy to rear on the same food as other young poultry. They need green food when quite young, and when fledged will thrive on grass alone until fall, when they need some grain to fatten them. A large expanse or stream of water is not necessary for geese, but it is desirable. On every farm where there is a water-course, if it be but a rivulet or brook, a goose-paddock will be profitable, under fair management, both for the feathers and the flesh. The rearing of ducks and geese in this country has been retarded by the abundance of wild waterfowl. But these are rapidly diminishing, and soon the domestic ones will receive more attention. In Western Europe ducks and geese fill an important place in the poultry-market; $100,000 are annually returned to the town of Aylesbury and its vicinity for ducks, to say nothing of other points largely engaged in producing geese and ducks in Great Britain and on the Continent.

The Guinea-fowl comes from Northern Africa, and is well worth raising for its eggs and flesh; the latter is of superior quality. The Guinea-fowl fraternizes with common fowls in the poultry-yard; is somewhat domineering, and rather shy; conceals her nest in the grass; and lays 100 to 120 eggs in a year. The young are at first very tender and difficult to rear. They need careful attention and frequent feeding while very young, but when once started are hardy, healthy, alert, and watchful, and somewhat noisy. They are adapted only to farms or large poultry-yards. The eggs are small, brownish in color, and very rich and good. They are hatched under common hens.

Pigeons may also be considered domestic fowls, and may be kept profitably if systematically managed, but not otherwise. The popularity of pigeons on the farm is owing mainly to juvenile inclinations, and in cities to the fancy which finds amusement and profit in breeding them for show purposes and for racing. The Antwerp or homing pigeon, which is the one used for this sport, sometimes changes hands at high prices. But this kind of pigeon-culture is very different from that of breeding the birds for food.

Management of Poultry.—Except with fanciers and breeders who have given poultry special attention, methods of management are crude, and even primitive. Few practical poultry-keepers have commodious and proper quarters for their stock. Poultry should be furnished with houses devoted to them exclusively, well lighted and ventilated, and kept clean. To every poultry-house, however small, there should be an open-shed attachment for the use of the birds. The house proper need be only large enough to furnish comfortable roosting and laying room, but the shed should be as large and airy as possible, facing to the sun, with a hard, smooth, perfectly dry floor. This floor should be covered to a depth of three or four inches with clean sand, sifted coal-ashes, road-dust, or sifted garden-soil. The surface must be raked over occasionally, and the whole removed and renewed two or three times a year. The droppings from under the perches should be mixed with this dry absorbent, and the whole kept under cover until needed for fertilizing purposes, when it will be found to be very valuable. In the open shed are placed the feeding and watering vessels. The size of the quarters must be proportioned to the number of fowls accommodated. A poultry-house 4 feet by 6 feet, and a shed 6 feet by 10 feet, will be large enough for six hens and a cock, and with an adjoining open run it will accommodate ten hens and a cock. If chickens are to be reared, the laying- and hatching-places must be separated. This will save trouble and some loss, as sitting hens should never be disturbed by other hens. The real wants of poultry are few and simple, but it is essential that they be provided for. They need protection against the weather and vermin, and a sufficient amount and variety of food.

In the selection and mating of breeding fowls care and judgment are to be exercised, as it is unprofitable to breed inferior stock of any kind. Fowls should be mated early in the season, and in breeding pure stock cocks of other breeds must not be allowed to associate with the breeding hens at any time. Early hatching is desirable, as in the end it is always the most profitable. There is a good market for pure-bred fowls of all the useful sorts for stock purposes, and there will always be a fair margin of profit for the competent breeder. In every case in-and-in breeding must be avoided, for it soon deteriorates the vigor and usefulness of the strains.

The successful rearing of poultry involves much routine and attention to small details. The hen and her brood must be placed in a coop and properly looked after. The coop should be in a sheltered place, and near a grass-run when possible. The dam is confined to the coop, and the chickens are allowed to go out and in at will. The best food for the chicks for the first few days is hard-boiled eggs grated fine, mixed with bread-crumb, and moistened with sweet milk. This is gradually changed to more common food, and at the end of a week cracked corn, whole wheat, barley, or buckwheat may be gradually allowed, and after the tenth day may be substituted as the food, in connection with a little sweet milk. The young birds need frequent feeding. Wet, sloppy, or pasty food should not be given to young chickens. As they grow older—say at the age of three weeks—the hen may be allowed to go abroad with her brood. Good feeding is always advisable for growing chickens, and they must not be draggled in wet grass nor be out in rains.

Diseases of Poultry.—The most serious hindrance to rearing young poultry is the "gapes." It is caused by entozoic worms in the windpipe of the chicken, which obstruct respiration and cause the bird to gasp or gape for breath; whence the name of the disease. On infested grounds the disease is very troublesome and destructive. Every henwife has a theory for the cause of the gapes, but the real origin of the gape-worm is unknown. The way to avoid the difficulty is either to hatch the broods in winter, or to establish a sufficiently spacious *chicken-nursery* in which to rear the broods until they are weaned, after which there is less danger from the parasite. There must be plenty of dry open shedding in the nursery, some of it preferably covered with glass. All other fowls except the dams are to be rigidly excluded from the nursery, and the chicks must be confined within it. The coops and all utensils must be kept scrupulously clean. The general enclosure should be large enough to furnish some cultivated crops for green food for the young things confined to the nursery, where they should remain until they are six weeks or two months old, when they may be removed and colonized in suitable quarters. Every dam and her brood must be thoroughly cleared of vermin before being placed in the nursery. This is most easily done by carefully anointing them with a preparation made of an ounce of crystallized carbolic acid mixed with a pound of melted lard. A free use of carbolic acid or carbolate of lime about the coops, and an occasional dusting of the broods with Egyptian powder or pulverized pyrethrum ("Persian insect-powder"), will keep the young poultry clear of vermin of every kind. Such management, with proper feeding and protection against en-

FOWL PLATE XXVI

Dark Brahma. Light Brahma. Duck-Wing Game. Dorking. Japanese Bantam. Dominique.

FOWL. PLATE XXVII.

Light Bronze Turkeys.

Dark Bronze Turkeys.

Cayuga Black Duck.

Rouen Ducks.

Hong Kong Goose.

White China Goose.

mies like rats, cats, crows, hawks, etc., very much reduces the difficulty of rearing young poultry.

Other diseases attacking both young and adult poultry are roup and cholera. The first is an old disease, and has always been known to poultry-keepers. It is caused mainly by undue exposure to damp, cold weather. Pathologically, roup is a malignant catarrhal disease affecting the mucous membrane of the air-passages and the eyes. It is caused at first by the fowls taking cold, and progresses to the malignant stage, when it destroys the fowl. Stock weakened by vicious in-and-in breeding, or having weakened constitutions from any cause, are most likely to be attacked by roup. Careful breeding, the introduction every second year of fresh healthy blood, comfortable housing, cleanliness, the destruction of vermin, and proper feeding, will avoid trouble from roup.

Poultry cholera is a comparatively new disease; it was unknown in this country until 1867. It baffled and frightened both fanciers and ordinary poultry-keepers for some time, but is now well understood. Dr. A. M. Dickie, of Doylestown, Pa., made a careful study of the epidemic in 1873–74. He diagnosed the disease as zymotic in character, and as being caused by an organic germ introduced into the circulation through the food, drink, and respiratory act, but did not detect the germ. Pasteur, of Paris, in 1880 discovered, figured, and described the bacterium that causes the blood-poisoning, thus substantially confirming the results of Dickie's labors. Though still formidable and destructive in some sections, poultry cholera is much less so than when it first appeared. Upon the discovery of the very first symptoms of the malady prompt action must be taken, and the whole flock treated as if they had the cholera. Affected birds are to be isolated at once, and treated with a preparation of dissolved sulphate of iron, to which has been added a slight excess of sulphuric acid. This is to be administered in soft food, and if the fowl refuses to eat, it is to be put into the mouth and pushed into the crop with the finger, a few drops of the solution being poured down the throat at the same time. The poultry quarters and runs are to be copiously sprinkled with water acidulated with sulphuric acid, and the droppings of the birds drenched with the same. The whole premises may afterwards be sprayed with water slightly impregnated with carbolic acid, thus destroying the germs that cause the disease, which is preferable to Pasteur's method of vaccination in unskilled hands.

Poultry-Keeping as a Business.—Poultry-keeping, after a fashion, is common throughout the country, but the majority of successful poultry-keepers are villagers, persons occupying small holdings, and laborers. On their small places by far the greater number of eggs are produced, and even most of the market poultry, exclusive of turkeys and geese. In small establishments it is more profitable to produce eggs than flesh, and fowls are often kept only for the sake of the eggs. There is a difference in the laying qualities of breeds. The spare-built, close-feathered ones are the best layers, while the bulky Dorkings, Asiatics, and their crosses are the best to rear for their flesh. The recognized laying breeds are the Hamburg, Leghorns, Polish, and French. These all lay pure white eggs of good size and quality, the Hamburg eggs being the smallest, and the white-faced Spanish and Houdan the largest. The eggs of the so-called small breeds average as large as those of the Asiatics. These last and their crosses all lay brownish-colored eggs, which popular opinion has erroneously rated as of a better quality than the white eggs. There is no difference in the quality of eggs produced by different breeds with the same food and treatment; but the size, number, and quality of the eggs of any breed will vary with the food and care the fowls get. The laying breeds produce each an average of 150 eggs per annum, whereas the large or meaty breeds yield about 100 each. The smaller breeds are therefore to be selected where eggs are mainly wanted, the large breeds where flesh is required, and a medium-sized fowl, a cross between the large and the small, where both are desirable. It is usually preferable to keep pure breeds, but from the practical standpoint judicious crosses are always advantageous. In ordinary cases one cock is enough for twenty-five or thirty hens, but it is different where eggs are wanted for hatching. Then one cock should not have more than five to eight hens, unless on an unlimited run; and even then there should not be more than ten or twelve hens in one harem. If the breeding-stock is properly selected and given sufficient room and care, the eggs will all be fertile and the chicks strong and healthy. Disappointment is often experienced with eggs laid by hens closely confined and insufficiently supplied with green food.

Laying hens must be properly fed. Though a simple problem, this is by no means an easy one. Corn is the staple food of all poultry in this country, and, while it is the best for some purposes, it is not a good staple food for laying hens, being too heating and fattening. Good oats, barley, buckwheat, and wheat, all of which are richer in albuminoids, are better food for laying hens than corn. When practicable, the smaller grains should be alternated with corn and with one another. The early morning meal must be soft food, cooked or scalded. It may consist of any of the above grains, ground and mixed, half and half, with good sound wheat-bran, fed moderately warm, and in sufficient quantity to satisfy the fowls, but to that extent only. Fresh, clean water must be supplied at feeding-time, and calcareous matter, that the hens may get lime for the wants of the organism and to form the shells of the eggs. This lime-supply is important, and may be found cheaply in crushed oyster-shells. The birds may have a light feed of whole small grain at noon, and a more liberal one at evening. In winter the latter food may be whole corn. Green food and animal food in some form are necessary; the former may be supplied in the form of grass, cabbage, lettuce, cooked vegetables, etc.; the latter in sour milk when it can be had, offal meat from the butcher, and greaves from the tallow-chandler. All scraps and odds and ends from the table and kitchen should go to the fowls. Laying hens in confinement must be furnished with employment to divert them, or they will contract bad habits, as feather-plucking, egg-eating, and other mischief. They may be employed in searching for a part of their food, which has been hidden in a rubbish-pile or in the straw and litter of their quarters. Whole or broken grain, broken oyster-shells, small table-scraps, and the like may be thus secreted. A fresh sod or turf thrown into their quarters daily affords the hens much profitable amusement.

The cost of keeping a hen from the time she is hatched until she should be killed and eaten is about $2, if all her food is bought and fed to her in a confined run. The profit on this expenditure will depend upon the time at which the hen is hatched. If hatched in March or early April, she will begin to lay at about six months of age; if in June or July, she will not, under ordinary circumstances, lay until nine months old. From the economic standpoint, the hen should be hatched at least as early as April 1st, and be killed at sixteen or seventeen months old, when she is ready to moult. She is then to be disposed of, and her place filled with a six-months' old pullet ready to begin laying; thus no food and care are wasted. Most of the unsatisfactory results in poultry-keeping are traceable to a lack of knowledge in feeding, and to keeping birds that make no return for the care and food given.

As a source of food-supply eggs and poultry fill an important place. Statistics are difficult to get at, but from such as are available some idea of the poultry-products of the nation may be gained. The egg-trade of New York City, as shown by the reports of the Produce Exchange, amounts to between $8,000,000 and $9,000,000 a year. In Boston the trade is a little more than one-third as much, and in Philadelphia it is a little above two-thirds as much. The total for the egg-trade of the three cities is, in round numbers, $16,000,000 per annum. The trade in poultry is equal in value to that in eggs. Allowing the trade in these three cities to represent one-fourth of the total aggregate trade of the country at large, there is at least the enormous total of $130,000,000 worth of food-products derived from the poultry-yards of the nation. The industry is largely on the increase; new and systematic methods are being introduced and adopted. Improvements in artificial hatching and rearing are opening the door for an almost unlimited extension in the production of poultry. The canning industry, too, opens a vista of magnificent possibilities, and assures a poultry dinner anywhere on land or sea at any time of year. The cold-storage methods also open a new door for the poultry-keeper. When poultry and poultry-products are promoted to a place in the census reports the public will have a better chance to understand and appreciate the business.

Poultry-keeping will soon be attempted here, as it has been abroad, on a large scale (poultry-farming), and, let us hope, with success. The outlook for such an enterprise in competent hands is favorable. But as regards the increase of poultry-production, taken as a whole, in this country, less is to be expected from poultry-farming, pure and simple, than from the gradual growth of interest in the business on the part of ordinary farmers and poultry-keepers; and it will not be long until the Americans will equal the French as a nation of poultry-producers, consumers, and exporters.

Poultry-culture is largely assisted and stimulated by the literature pertaining to the subject. The first poultry periodical published in the world was issued in New York in 1869, under the title of *The Poultry, Pigeon, and Pet-Stock Bulletin*. This pioneer effort has been followed by the publication of a number of similar journals in America, Canada, and England. Most of these periodicals are fairly well conducted and supported. Besides these, every leading newspaper, religious, secular, and agricultural, gives some attention to poultry topics. The most comprehensive and excellent work on the subject is *The Book of Poultry*, edited by L. Wright (London, 1875). This exhaustive work is illustrated with fifty colored plates and numerous wood-engravings. There are books on poultry published in America, but none of them equal in value and authority to the one just named. (A. M. D.)

FOWLER, CHARLES HENRY, an American bishop, was born in Upper Canada in 1837, but his parents removed to the United States in 1840. He graduated at Genesee College in 1859, and studied theology at Evanston, Ill. He entered the itinerant ministry in 1872, serving churches in Chicago until 1872, when he was made president of the North-western University at Evanston. In 1876 he was appointed editor of the New York *Christian Advocate*, and in 1880 general missionary secretary of the M. E. Church. In 1884 he was chosen bishop, his residence being fixed at Atlanta. He has been highly esteemed as a pulpit orator.

FOWLER, ORSON SQUIRE, an American phrenologist and lecturer, was born at Cohocton, Steuben co., N. Y., Oct. 11, 1809. He graduated at Amherst College in 1834, and with his brother, Lorenzo Niles (born June 23, 1811), began the advocacy of phrenology and various projects for the promotion of education, health, and social reform. They wrote and published many books on these subjects. In 1863 they retired from publishing, Orson going to Boston and Lorenzo to England, but both continued to write and lecture on their favorite subjects. Orson died Aug. 18, 1887.

FOX. The dog family (*Canidæ*) may be divided into two series, one containing the dog-like, the other the fox-like forms. Certain cranial peculiarities characterize the foxes. The frontal bones are without the hollow or sinus found in the true dogs, and the cerebral hemispheres, instead of widening out abruptly a little behind their junction with the olfactory lobes, are narrow in front, being shaped like a pear with the narrow end forwards. The fennec of Africa is ranged with the foxes, which, besides the structural peculiarities noted, are distinguished by their bushy tail, elongated muzzle and pupils, and erect ears.

See Vol. IX. p. 435 Am. ed. (p. 493 Edin. ed.)

Besides the common red fox (*Vulpes fulvus*), which is very near to the European fox, and branches into several varieties, there are several other more or less distinct species of fox in North America. One of these is the gray fox (*V. cinereo-argentatus*) which is distributed throughout the United States. The hair of this species is stiff, coarse, and long, of a mixed silver-gray tint, or hoary and black, not unlike that of the badger, but darker. Black predominates on the upper surfaces of body and tail, while the underparts of the body are pale cinnamon, and the underside of the tail chestnut. The gray fox has a power of climbing trees not possessed by the red species, and is thus better adapted for a wooded region. The felling of the forests, combined with its lower brain-power as compared with the red fox, seems to cause it to give way to the latter in the more settled and cultivated districts. The bones of this fox have been exhumed from the caves of Pennsylvania, and thus it seems to be the aboriginal species.

Allied to the gray fox, and very possibly but a geographical variety of it, is the coast fox (*V. littoralis*) of the islands off the Pacific coast of North America from California to Costa Rica. This form is scarcely more than half the size of the gray fox, and has short, weak, slender legs, causing it to be a poor runner. The tail is about one-third the length of the body, and has a black stripe above. Black predominates also on the chin, sides of the muzzle, and back. Both these forms have small teeth and weak jaws, and are among the lowest of the foxes.

The silver fox or black fox, in which the fur is black, with the hairs of much of the back ringed with gray; the cross fox, which has a dark band between the shoulders, crossed by another passing over the shoulders, and the long-tailed fox (*V. macrurus*) of Utah, are all varieties of the common red fox.

Among the characters which distinguish this fox from the common fox of Europe (*V. vulgaris*) are a greater fineness of fur, a brighter color, and a narrower and more delicate head. The red fox will eat crabs or fish when near the seashore, and feed on crickets or carrion when hard pressed for food.

In Central North America, from the Cascade Mountains of Oregon to the timbered lands of the Lower Missouri, the kit fox, swift fox, or burrowing fox (*V. velox*), a small species about twenty inches in length without the tail, is common. In the basin of the Upper Columbia it seems to be the prevailing species, but is not on record north of the Saskatchewan. The face is broader and the nose shorter than that of the red fox. In color it is brownish gray, becoming reddish orange on the breast and flanks and fading to white below. The soles of the feet are covered with long woolly hair, hiding the callosities. In winter the fur is pale grayish-brown. It lives in holes in the ground, and is a dexterous burrower.

The well-known and beautiful little Arctic fox is another North American species. Among foreign species, besides the notorious European fox, may be mentioned the caama or asse (*V. caama*) of South Africa, which feeds largely upon the eggs of such birds as lay on the ground; the kokree or Bengal dog (*V. bengalensis*), the corsac or adive (*V. corsac*) of Tartary, Siberia, and other parts of Central Asia; the sobona or tahaleb (*V. niloticus*) of North Africa and Egypt; the canduc (*V. adusta*) of Caffraria and other parts of South Africa; the Cape jackal or tenlie, which ranges from Abyssinia to the Cape; the Persian fox (*V. flavescens*), found also in India; the hill fox of Nepal and Thibet (*V. montana*), *V. japonica* from Japan, and *V. cana* from Beluchistan.

The corsac was in the reign of Charles IX. kept as a pet by the fashionable Parisian ladies. Col. Prejevalsky states that it is abundant in Thibet, and is called karsa by the Mongols. It makes its own burrows, and in the breeding season is noted for its hideous cry, like the hooting of an owl.

Another and a rather exceptional species is the fennec (*V. zerda*), a pretty little pale fawn-colored animal, sometimes almost creamy white, and barely a foot in length without its tail, which has a black tip. The eyes are blue, the whiskers long and thick, the ears large and pointed, and the form slender. It lives by day in burrows scooped in the light sandy soil of the deserts of Northern Africa. It makes an admirable pet. The fennec is said to be able to climb the date palm for dates, of which it is very fond.

(W. N. L.)

FOX INDIANS. This tribe belongs to the Algonkin family, and was divided into two branches, the Outagamies, or Foxes proper, and the Musquakink. They were first found by the whites in Canada, near Lake St. John, but were gradually driven westward, and settled on Fox River, Wisconsin, about 1660. Their number was estimated by the Jesuit missionary in 1667 to be 500 warriors. They were excellent hunters, and brave in war, and cultivated Indian corn. At times they were friendly to the French, and again they joined combinations against them. In 1712 they attacked Detroit, but were afterwards severely punished by its commander. As they occupied part of the usual route of the French from Canada to Louisiana, and at times completely obstructed the passage, expeditions were sent against them. In the final struggle between the English and the French for Canada in 1763 the Foxes aided the latter. They resided at Prairie du Chien during the Revolutionary war, and so far as they took part in it they assisted the English. Their kindred the Sacs were involved in the Miami war, 1790-94, but the Foxes remained quiet. In 1804 both these tribes having crossed the Mississippi, ceded their lands to the United States. Some of them afterwards went to Canada and joined the British during the war of 1812, but they made peace in 1815, and gave up their prisoners. Treaties were again made with them in 1824 and 1830, but in 1831 a dispute about Rock Island led to the Black Hawk war. At the close of this war further cessions of land were made by them and they retired to Des Moines, Iowa. Here they gave constant trouble to their Indian neighbors, and in 1842 the United States government removed them to the Osage River. Later the Sacs and Foxes were in Kansas, but in 1859 they ceded their lands and were placed on a reservation between forks of the Canadian and Arkansas Rivers. It covers 483,800 acres, and is partly cultivated. A smaller band occupy a reservation on the boundary between Kansas and Nebraska. Both these branches receive annuities from the United States. Still another band of about 300 settled down in Iowa without aid from the government, and have made progress in agriculture.

FOX, GUSTAVUS VASA (1821–1883), an American naval officer, was born at Saugus, Mass., June 13, 1821. He entered the navy as midshipman in 1838, and served in the coast survey and in the Mexican war. He resigned in 1856, and became agent of a cotton-factory at Lawrence, Mass. Early in 1861 he was engaged in attempts to take supplies and reinforcements from New York to Fort Sumter, but through various delays was prevented from entering Charleston Harbor until after Major Anderson's surrender, when his vessel was used to take the garrison to New York. Fox immediately fitted out a steamer and sailed to the Chesapeake, where he assisted in restoring communication between Washington and the North. He was soon after made assistant secretary of the navy, and his prudence, good sense, and administrative ability were shown in the efficiency and success of that department throughout the war. In April, 1866, being about to resign his office, he was sent on a special mission to St. Petersburg to present to the Emperor Alexander II. congratulations on his escape from assassination. On his return to the United States in September he took charge of large woollen factories at Lowell, Mass. Afterwards he was engaged in business at Boston, where he died, 1883.

FRANCE. The Republic in France is the condition of all progress, yet its establishment is a work far greater and more difficult than was anticipated by its ardent friends. The old Europe of feudalism cannot at once disappear, the new Europe of the people cannot begin till the Republic is founded. Republicanism means the definite extinction of hereditary claims of every kind, the final admission of capacity and merit to every function in the state. This is the great political problem of modern Europe.

See Vol. IX. p. 445 Am. ed. (p. 505 Edin. ed.).

Early in 1879 the republican majority in the French assembly was once more face to face with a reactionary administration. Control of the army was an important subject in the dispute with Marshal MacMahon. It ought not to be of any consequence what are the politics of the commanders of the grand divisions of the French army, nor should it be a point of great moment what party the minister of war sympathizes with. But this point was forced upon the attention of republicans by the marshal's tactics when Gen. Borel was made minister of war. He was formerly chief of staff to Marshal MacMahon. No man of great talent was ever endured in that position. Borel owed his distinction to his readiness to lend himself in every way to any administration of his department that might give effect to his chief's ill will towards the Republic and the republicans. Moved by the facts of such an administration of the army the republicans made some demands. They asked for the removal of certain Bonapartist generals. But the very denial of their demand and the persistence in this denial assured them that the facts in the army to which they objected were not accidental, and the policy against which they had to strive was the same in nature as that of the De Broglie ministry; it was an attempt to govern without the majority. On Jan. 30, 1879, MacMahon being defeated in this attempt found himself at last compelled to resign. M. Jules Grévy was then elected president of the French Republic and Gambetta became president of the French assembly.

Gambetta had he chosen might have secured the presidency as the marshal's successor. But with that keen and wise foresight for which he was remarkable he saw that the time was not yet ripe. It is useless, perhaps, to ask where and when Léon Gambetta learned the arts of government and war. The fact remains that in the terrible crisis of 1870 an unknown, penniless lawyer of thirty-two became at once the absolute dictator of France, roused her from her slumber, upheld her banner against hopeless odds; he himself organized the army of the Loire, the only army which won a victory in that gloomy period of war with Prussia; he made the French people feel again they were a people and impressed on their hearts the image of Republic instead of the Empire. He alone gathered the discordant factions of the republican party into a compact and harmonious body. He restrained or let loose the ardor of his followers at will, each at the moment when the restraint or when the display would be most effective for the end in view. The Republic, as it is to-day, owes its very existence to Gambetta; to his audacity in 1868; to his resolution in 1870; to his sagacity in 1877. His mysterious death on Dec. 31, 1882, was to France what the death of Cavour was for Italy; what the death of Bismarck will be to Germany.

The death of the Prince Louis Napoleon, son of Napoleon III., on June 1, 1879, showed once more that the Bonapartists had no influence on the popular mind, and in spite of their combined attack with the non-compromising Left Centre and the Orleanists the ministry had no difficulty in pursuing its policy of non-intervention.

Meanwhile a sensation was created by Jules Ferry, the head of the ministry, in September, 1880. He put into vigorous operation the dormant law for the expulsion of the Jesuits from France. At the time the chambers adjourned for the Easter holidays it was announced that the contemplated decrees in reference to "unauthorized congregations" would appear in the official journal at once; but this publication was deferred after Easter, in order that a holy season, recognized by the whole Christian world, might not be disturbed by what is very apt to be called an assault upon religion. In discrediting the republican theory and in fighting the Republic in every way the Jesuits have distinguished themselves. Their open battle with the Republic on article 7 made a dangerous exhibition of their power. They were therefore expelled, and M. A. Ferry received credit for his tact and patience in that hazardous undertaking, in which he gave no chance to the enemies of the French Republic to raise the cry of persecution.

Despite many disappointing circumstances the French colonies have gained much by the substitution of a Republic for monarchy, and in regard to the new policy a few details are necessary. At the commencement of April, 1881, the expedition sent to explore the Sahara was entirely annihilated by a tribe called Kroumir, who crossed the Tunisian frontier and went back to their wilderness. M. Roustan, then French consul at Tunis, acted with uncommon vigor, and demanded redress of this hostile conduct. When no satisfaction was received from the bey, the General Forgemol at the head of 30,000 men invaded the Tunisian country and soon completed its conquest.

In addition to the advantages of general topography Tunis possesses an important condition of natural wealth, in having the finest position of North Africa and the control of the Mediterranean. Hence arise its attractions for the powers which strive for its possession or for its neutralization. It has an area of 60,000 square miles and a coast line of 550 miles. Its closeness to the interior of Africa made it once the most important market and commercial country of the African continent, and under favorable circumstances it might again become distinguished for its commerce. Such are the privileges which, with its admirable maritime position, necessarily predestined Tunis for long and glorious annals. The French Republic organized a regency in Tunis, March 30, 1882, which has since conducted the government of the province without serious difficulty.

The French and Tonquin war was occasioned by the alleged encroachments of the so-called "Black Flags" upon the foreigner and specially the Christians. A French fleet went up the Min River. A temporary panic in Southern China ensued and a popular uprising was felt, but this alarm soon passed away. The fleet under Rear Admiral Courbet subdued the Black Flags, and his triumph was peculiar and almost unexpected. A treaty was made with China giving to France the protectorate of that province, which is now under the control of M. Paul Bert as governor.

The French have also been active in Madagascar, where for the last 200 years they have had considerable influence. Here trouble broke out with the Hovas, the most intelligent and energetic of its numerous tribes, and troops were sent to protect the foreigners. Although Madagascar is known to be the third largest island in the world its actual condition is not very generally understood. Its importance may be fairly estimated by its size, it being nearly 1000 miles long by about 250 in average breadth, and reaching to 350 miles at its widest part. A barrier reef of coral extends from 200 to 300 miles along the south-east coast. There is a vast extent of country on the coast plains where the soil is most fertile, but which is only thinly peopled. At the present time this vast island is of peculiar interest to the world by a series of political changes. The Hovas have gradually obtained the supremacy over all the other tribes. The central province of Imerina occupied by them, and especially its capital city of Antananarivo, has been for several years past a centre of intelligence, civilization, and

Christianity. During the recent war the foreigners suffered no serious disturbance, and the treaty of Dec. 17, 1885, restored to France her former influence in that country.

The several changes of the ministry have not disturbed the harmony and permanency of the actual government. It has carried on a judicious policy of colonization and has conducted successful though expensive campaigns in Tunis, Tonquin, and Madagascar. M. Grévy, the model chief of the Republic, was strongly entrenched in the favor of the French people. When his first term of seven years was drawing to a close he was, in December, 1885, elected for a second term. In M. de Freycinet's ministry in 1886 Gen. Boulanger, the Radical minister of war, attained a prominence out of all proportion to his merits. He struck off the army roll all Bonaparte and Bourbon princes, and aroused a popular clamor for a war against Germany. When his measures were overruled he showed such insubordination that he was placed on the retired list, but he continued his political activity. In the midst of his intrigues, an inquiry in the autumn of 1887 revealed the shameful fact that Pres. Grévy's son-in-law, M. Wilson, had been trafficking in appointments to office. The venerable President was therefore compelled to resign Dec. 2, 1887, and the Republican, M. Sadi Carnot, was elected his successor. Gen. Boulanger redoubled his efforts to embarrass the Government, and as candidate for the chamber of Deputies, called for a revision of the Constitution. The monarchists who hoped for the overthrow of the Republic gave him substantial aid, and he was elected in several districts. Finally in Jan., 1889, the Government instituted a prosecution, and he fled from France. Gradually the agitation was quieted. In May, 1889, Pres. Carnot opened the Paris Exposition, which commemorated the hundredth anniversary of the French Revolution, and though the sovereigns of Europe withheld their countenance, the exhibition proved to be the greatest ever held in that city. The Republic, having successfully passed a dangerous crisis, has an assured vitality.

Statistics.—By the census taken Dec. 18, 1881, the population of France was 37,672,048, and its area 204,177 square miles, giving the ratio 184 inhabitants to a square mile, but in the department of the Seine (Paris) it is 14,670, and in the Basses-Alpes 49. The population present numbered 37,405,290, of whom 18,656,518 were males and 18,748,772 females, the excess of the latter being less than in any other state of Western Europe. The number of families was 10,399,885, and there were 7,609,464 dwelling-houses, containing 10,720,826 apartments. France is divided into 87 departments, which are subdivided into 362 arrondissements, 2865 cantons, and (in 1883) 36,097 communes. The stationary character of the French people is shown by the fact that of the total population 22,702,356 were born within their communes. There were 1,001,900 foreigners residing in the country, and 77,046 naturalized. The total emigration (exclusive of Algeria) was 4456. According to occupation the population was divided as follows:

Agriculture	18,249,209	Public forces	552,851
Trades and manufacture	9,324,107	Living on income	2,121,173
		Without occupation	737,088
Commerce	3,843,447		
Professions	1,585,358	Occupation unknown	191,316
Transportation	800,741		

The agricultural population was classed as follows: farming proprietors, 2,425,500; farmers, 1,010,999; small proprietors working for others, 772,339; foresters, 112,200; employés and domestics, 3,535,040; families of preceding, 10,393,131. The following 10 cities had each over 100,000 inhabitants:

Paris	2,239,928	Toulouse	140,289
Lyons	376,613	Nantes	124,319
Bordeaux	360,099	St. Etienne	123,813
Marseilles	221,305	Rouen	105,906
Lille	178,144	Havre	105,867

On May 30, 1886, the population was 38,218,903, averaging 187 to the square mile. That of Paris, in 1887, was 2,344,550. In the chamber of deputies there are 557 members; in the senate 300, of whom 75 originally held their seats for life, but in 1884 it was enacted that vacancies in the life-senatorships should be filled by election for the usual term of 9 years.

The financial statement for 1890 was as follows: Estimated revenue, $648,335,000; expenditure the same, with an additional expense budget for 1890-91 of $144,696,060. The debt had reached the enormous total of $6,427,500,000, on which the annual interest and sinking fund charge amounted to $258,458,895. The great debt left by the Franco-Prussian war has been materially enlarged, and now considerably surpasses that of any other nation. The total value of the imports of France for the fiscal year 1889 was $835,000,000; of the exports, $721,716,400.

FRANCHISE, a special privilege conferred by the government of a country upon an individual or body of individuals, which does not belong to the citizens of the country generally of common right. In England franchises were anciently granted by the crown and in modern times by authority of Parliament. In the United States franchises can only be granted by the legislature or by some other branch of the government by virtue of legislative authority.

Franchises are generally granted for a public or at least quasi-public use. The various rights conferred upon different classes of corporations are franchises. The right to erect and maintain a ferry, a bridge, or a turnpike road is in like manner a franchise. According to the ancient rule of the common law the obligation existing between the government and the person holding a franchise was mutual. It was the duty of the latter to furnish to the public all the facilities which the nature of the franchise granted to him called for. The owner of a ferry was, therefore, bound to continue to run his boats and the owner of a toll bridge to keep the same open and in repair. The penalty for failing to do this was forfeiture of the franchise. This is still the law.

On the other hand the government was anciently held bound not to grant to other parties franchises in conflict with those previously granted. In the United States this doctrine has not been distinctly repudiated, but the principle has been laid down that the grant of a franchise will always be construed strictly against the grantee. Hence the exclusive nature of a franchise will not be inferred unless expressed in terms.

The grant of franchises by the government when accepted and acted on by the party are within the purview of the constitutional prohibition of the impairment of contracts. The grant by the government on the one hand and its acceptance on the other are deemed to constitute a binding contract which the legislature cannot subsequently repudiate by withdrawing the franchise conferred. Where the charter conferring the franchise, however, contains a clause reserving to the legislature the right to annul or vary the franchise granted, or where the charter is granted subject to a constitutional provision or general act reserving to the legislature such a power, it may constitutionally be exercised.

Franchises are not alienable by the owner or owners thereof without express legislative authority. They cannot, therefore, be conveyed or mortgaged of common right. They cannot be taken in execution and sold so as to convey any title to the purchaser.

Elective Franchise.—In the United States the term "franchise" is commonly used as synonymous with "elective franchise." It indicates the right to vote at elections on matters ordinarily submitted to the people. All persons who are citizens are not necessarily invested with the franchise. It is a special privilege conferred upon certain individuals among the citizens of the country.

The Constitution of the United States as originally adopted does not contain any provisions as to who shall have the privilege of the franchise, but leaves the matter entirely to be determined by the laws of the several States. The fourteenth amendment to the Constitution provides that whenever by the law of any State the right of voting is denied to any male inhabitant over twenty-one years of age except for participation in rebellion or other crime, the basis of representation in the House of Representatives shall be reduced proportionally. The fifteenth amendment to the Constitution provides that the right of citizens of the United States to vote shall not be denied or abridged by the United States or by any State on account of race, color, or previous condition of servitude. This amendment does not take away from the various States the right of determining the qualifications of electors. It merely prohibits them from discriminating against parties for any of the causes specified.

The provision of the fourteenth amendment to the Constitution prohibiting the States from making laws abridging the privileges or immunities of citizens of the United States has been construed not to confer the privilege of the franchise upon any one. The right of citizenship and the right to vote are separate and distinct. The guarantee of one right does not in any way refer to the other.

In the early colonial days of the United States the right to exercise the franchise was very limited. There were numerous religious and property qualifications which it was requisite that a voter should possess.

At the time of the adoption of the Constitution the laws of almost every State conferred the right of exercising the elective franchise to citizens who were the owners of a certain amount of property. Such were the express provisions of the laws in Massachusetts, Connecticut, New York, New Jersey, Delaware, Maryland, Virginia, North Carolina, South Carolina, and Georgia. In New Hampshire each male inhabitant who was of age and possessed of town privileges, excepting paupers and persons excused from paying taxes at their own request, was entitled to vote. In Rhode Island "such as were admitted free of the company and society" of the colony. In Pennsylvania all freemen who had lived for two years in the State, and who had paid a State or county tax assessed six months before the election in question.

Since the adoption of the Constitution the laws have been so altered in the various States as to admit to the privilege of the elective franchise all male citizens of the United States who have attained lawful age. In the State of Wyoming women are permitted to exercise the elective franchise.

Residence within the State and election district for a certain specified time before the election, and the payment of a State or county tax within another certain specified time, are by law generally made prerequisites to the right to vote. In some States disability to vote for a limited period is an additional penalty imposed by law upon conviction of certain classes of crime. (See ELECTION LAWS.) (L. L., JR.)

FRANCIS, JOHN WAKEFIELD (1789–1861), an American physician, was born in New York city, Nov. 17, 1789. In early youth he learned printing, but afterwards entered Columbia College. Graduating in 1809, he studied medicine at the College of Physicians and Surgeons, and in 1811 received his medical degree, being the first conferred by that college. He became partner with his preceptor, Dr. Hosack. In 1813 he was made professor of materia medica in Columbia College, and in 1816 went to Europe, where he studied under Dr. Abernethy. After his return he held the chairs of the institutes of medicine, medical jurisprudence (1817), and obstetrics (1819) until 1826, when he withdrew with others of the faculty to form the Rutgers Medical School, in which he was professor of obstetrics and forensic medicine until the college was closed in 1830. Dr. Francis then devoted himself to professional, literary, and reformatory work. He published many professional, scientific, and biographical sketches. His latest work was *Old New York, or Reminiscences of the Past Sixty Years* (1857; new ed., 1865). He died Feb. 8, 1861.

FRANCIS JOSEPH, Emperor of Austria and King of Hungary, was born Aug. 18, 1830, being the son of Archduke Francis Charles (1802–1878) and of the Princess Sophia (1805–1872). He ascended the throne Dec. 2, 1849, on the abdication of his uncle Ferdinand. The war in Hungary had shaken the foundations of the empire. Although at the outset he promised a constitutional government, he soon found himself compelled to assume absolute power to prevent the dissolution of the empire. In Hungary, by the intervention of Russia, the republic established by Kossuth was overthrown. In Italy the military skill of Radetsky restored the Austrian supremacy. When order was thus established in his dominions, Francis promulgated the edict of Schönbrunn, Sept. 26, 1851, declaring the government responsible only to the emperor. A policy of centralization was enforced, while much attention was given to financial matters and to commercial reforms. During the Crimean war Austria remained neutral, and, though this policy was dictated by good reasons, she thereby incurred the displeasure of France. Napoleon III. at the earliest possible moment took his revenge by carrying the war into Italy. Lombardy was wrested from Austria, but the peace of Villafranca, July 8, 1859, stopped the advance of the French army, and left Venetia still under Austrian control. By the march of events and the force of public opinion the emperor was obliged to recede from his autocratic pretensions. First he enlarged the Reichsrath, and in 1862 he admitted the principle of the responsibility of the ministry. In 1864 Austria joined with Prussia in enforcing against Denmark the German claim to Schleswig-Holstein. But though these powers were thus banded together for a time, their divergent interests soon forced them apart. Napoleon III. fomented their jealousies, hoping to profit by their quarrel. On the other hand Francis Joseph had been able to conciliate to a remarkable extent the people of Hungary, and when war came in 1866 that kingdom proved the most loyal of his dominions. Although the best generals and troops of Austria had been marshalled on its northern borders in readiness for war, the skill and strategy of Von Moltke overthrew them in a few weeks. On the bloody field of Sadowa the superiority of the needle-gun was demonstrated for the first time. Count Beust, who had been prime minister of Saxony, now held that place in Francis Joseph's councils, and by his advice peace was promptly made. In recognition of the loyalty of Hungary in this time of trial, the emperor proceeded to Pesth and was formally crowned King of Hungary June 8, 1867. In a few years Count Bismarck found means to attract Francis Joseph, and in 1871 there was a friendly meeting of the two emperors, Francis Joseph and Wilhelm, at Gastein. In the next year the Czar of Russia met with the other two, and since that time there have been other interviews of the three emperors. These meetings seem to have had the effect of restraining the propensity to war on the part of their nations, though the condition of Turkey has been a constant incentive in that direction. The Congress of Berlin in 1880 revised the terms of the treaty of San Stefano and gave Austria a proper share in the territory taken from Turkey.

The Emperor Francis Joseph is tall and handsome. He is well educated, and in the Italian war was conspicuous by his bravery. He married, April 24, 1854, Elizabeth Amelia Eugenia, daughter of Duke Maximilian Joseph of Bavaria. They have one son, Archduke Rudolph (born Aug. 21, 1858), and three daughters.

FRANKFORT, a city, the capital of Kentucky and of Franklin county, is on both banks of the navigable Kentucky River, here crossed by a railroad and a highway bridge, 65 miles E. of Louisville. It is on the Louisville, Cincinnati, and Lexington Railroad. It is regularly laid out on a plain surrounded by hills, has public gas and water supply. The principal public buildings are the State capitol, the United States customhouse, State prison, and the other city, county, and State buildings. Among its institutions is the State school for feeble-minded children. Frankfort has 3 banks, 8 churches, and several schools, public, private, and parochial. It has manufactures of flour, hemp, spirits, machinery, and lumber; hard-wood timber being a leading article in the local trade. Tax valuation, $2,271,011; public debt, $146,076. Frankfort was settled in 1786, and became the State capital in 1792. Population in 1850, 3308; in 1860, 3702; in 1870, 5396; in 1890, 8500.

FRANKING PRIVILEGE. When the importance and independence of the British Parliament increased during the seventeenth century, its members obtained by favor of the crown the privilege of sending and receiving mail-matter free of charge. The abuses which grew around this practice, while the rates of postage were high, led to its formal recognition and regulation by act of Parliament in 1764. In America, after the declaration of independence, the Continental Congress conferred on its members while in actual attendance the same privilege for communications on public service. Certain civil and military officers also had this privilege, and army officers in actual service were allowed to send and receive single letters free of charge.

When the United States Post-Office was fully organized in 1792, the franking privilege was granted to the president, vice-president, the secretaries of state, treasury, and war, and certain of their assistants, the postmaster-general and his assistants, and the commissioners for settling the accounts of the individual States. The privilege was also granted to all members of Congress, to the secretary of the Senate, and the clerk of the House, during actual attendance in any session of Congress and for twenty days after. No person was allowed to frank or enclose any letter or packet not his own. Any enclosure to such a one for other persons was to be delivered to the post-office that postage might be charged. Under regulations of the postmaster-general newspaper publishers were allowed to send single copies of their papers to any other publisher free of charge. The franking privilege was afterwards extended to delegates to Congress from the Territories, to the cabinet officers, subsequently created, to ex-presidents and to their widows during life. In 1810 the list of franking officers was revised, and postmasters were allowed to send and receive without charge letters not exceeding ½ oz. in weight. All persons having franking power were allowed to receive newspapers free of postage. Members of Congress were allowed to transmit the president's message and its accompanying documents within the year of their issue. Afterwards all executive documents were allowed to be so sent without limit of time. In 1825, when the post-office laws were revised and re-enacted, the time of franking for members of Congress was extended to 60 days before and after any session of that body, but the weight of letters and packets was limited to 2 oz., and provision was made for payment of postage on the excess.

In the revision of the post-office laws by the act of March 3, 1845, the franking privilege was restricted to senators, members of Congress, delegates, secretary of the Senate, and clerk of the House, during each session of Congress and for 30 days before and after. On the excess in weight above 2 oz. of any package postage was to be charged and paid for out of the contingent fund of the Senate or House. Yet members were allowed to frank their own letters throughout the year. Offices of the government who formerly had the franking privilege were to be paid quarterly all postage on official letters and packages received by mail, but the president, ex-presidents, and widows of former presidents were still allowed to have the franking privilege. By the act of March 3, 1847, an annual appropriation of $200,000 was made for the transportation of mail matter of Congress and the departments of the government. In 1851 this appropriation was increased to $500,000, but probably did not cover the actual expense of transportation of the matter franked. Public documents, printed in excess of any possible demand, burdened the mails from Washington. The franking privilege was granted in 1854 to the superintendent of the coast survey, and in 1855 for life to any person who had held the office of vice-president. Publications required by law to be deposited in the library of Congress were allowed to be sent free of postage. By the act of March 3, 1863, the list of those having the franking privilege was again revised. It was limited to the chief officers of the government, but heads of bureaus, chief clerks of the executive departments, and postmasters could use it for official communications, which were to be placed in envelopes marked "Official" with the signature of the officer thereon. Fraudulent use of such envelopes involved a penalty of $300. The franking privilege was limited to packages not exceeding 4 oz. in weight, except petitions to Congress, and congressional and executive documents. The franking privilege of members of Congress was to begin with the term for which they were elected and continue till the December after its close. They were authorized to frank seeds, roots, etc., subject to regulations of the postmaster-general. In course of time it became common for persons having the franking privilege to use stamps with fac-similes of their signatures, but in 1869 this practice was prohibited. In 1873, in accordance with the repeated recommendations of successive postmaster-generals, the privilege was entirely abolished, the act for this purpose taking effect July 1, 1873. It was provided, however, that official stamps and stamped envelopes should be issued to the several executive departments, being sold at the same prices as stamps of the same value were sold at the post-office. This provision was abolished July 5, 1884, up to which time official stamps representing $8,049,609 had been used. In 1885 millions of such stamps were destroyed by burning in order to close the accounts of the government officers in relation thereto. Instead of these stamps, envelopes with a notice of the penalty incurred by using them except for official purposes, had already been authorized. These are now exclusively used by the various departments of the government. Newspapers are allowed to be carried free of postage in the county in which they are published.

In early times the abuse of the franking privilege was chiefly in the direction of its being used directly or indirectly by persons not authorized to enjoy it. In later times the chief abuse was the overweighting of the mails by the immense amount of printed matter and other articles sent by those who had the privilege and felt no restraint in using it. By them the government mail facilities were often used to do the work properly belonging to express companies. The reduction of the rate of postage and the wide extension of postal service have done away with all excuse for the existence of the privilege. Knowledge of the abuses with which it has always been accompanied will undoubtedly prevent any attempt at its restoration. (J. P. L.)

FRANKL, LUDWIG AUGUST, BARON, a German poet, was born Feb. 3, 1810, at Chrast, in Bohemia, of Jewish family. He was educated at Prague and Leitomischl, and in 1828 went to Vienna to study medicine. His first collection of historical ballads, *Habsburglied*, appeared in 1832, and was soon followed by *Epische und lyrische Dichtunge* (1833); *Sagen aus dem Morgenlande* (1834); and translations from Moore and Byron. His epics, *Cristoforo Colombo* (1836) and *Don Juan d' Austria* (1846), increased his reputation. He also published translations from the Servian, under the title *Gusle* (1852), and a history of the Jews in Vienna. He was an active journalist. His satirical poem *Der Universität* (1848) had great vogue. Another poem, published anonymously, *Ein Magyaren König* (1850), pleaded the cause of Hungary, and was for a time suppressed by the Austrian government. In 1851 Frankl was made professor of æsthetics in the Vienna Conservatory of Music. In 1856 he went to Jerusalem to found a school, and afterwards gave an account of his journey in *Nach Jerusalem* (1858) and *Aus Ægypten* (1860). In his *Helden und Liederbuch* (1861) many of his minor poems were gathered, while *Der Primator* (1862) was an important addition to his larger poems. The 500th anniversary of the University of Vienna in 1865 gave him another opportunity for satire. His *Gesammelte poetische Werke* were published in 1880, but he has since added a volume or two. In addition to his literary labors, Frankl has had charge of an institute for blind children, and in 1873 called at Vienna a congress of instructors of the blind, over which he presided. In February, 1877, the Emperor of Austria conferred on him the title of Baron of Hochwart.

FRANKLAND, EDWARD, an English chemist, was born Jan. 18, 1825, at Churchtown, Lancashire. He was educated at Lancaster, London, Marbury, and Giessen, and was a pupil of Bunsen and Liebig. In 1851 he was appointed professor of chemistry in Owens College, Manchester, and in 1857 took the chemical professorship in St. Bartholomew's Hospital, London. In the same year he received the Royal Society's gold medal for his brilliant discoveries relating to metallo-organic compounds. In 1863 he was made professor of chemistry in the Royal Institution, and afterwards in the Royal College of Chemistry. In 1871 he became president of the Chemical Society; in 1877 of the Institute of Chemistry. He is the author of important papers on chemical notation, on drainage, on rivers pollution, and a great variety of practical and theoretical questions connected with his specialty. Among his works are *Notes for Chemical Students* (2 vols., 1876); *How to Teach Chemistry*; *Experimental Researches* 1878); and a *Handbook of Water Analysis* (1880).

FRANKLIN, a city of Pennsylvania, county-seat of Venango county, is on Venango River, near its junction with the Allegheny River, 65 miles (123 by rail) north of Pittsburg. It is on a branch of the New York, Pittsburg, and Ohio Railroad, and on a branch of the Lake Shore Railway. It is also on the main line of the Allegheny Valley Railway. At proper stages of water small steamboats can reach the place. Franklin has a court-house, jail, and city-hall, 1 national and 4 other banks, a daily and 3 weekly newspapers, 12 churches, a flouring-mill, a brush-factory, a foundry, 3 machine-shops, and several oil-refineries, 2 of them of great extent. It is a well-built town, with streets well flagged. It has gas, water-works, and a fine park. It was settled in 1795, and was incorporated as a borough in 1827, and as a city in 1868. Population in 1880, 5010; and in 1890, 6000.

FRANKLIN, the county-seat of Williamson co., Tenn., is on Harpeth River, 18 miles south of Nashville. It has a national bank, some manufactories, and a weekly newspaper, and is the seat of Tennessee Female College. During the civil war Gen. Granger, while holding the town with Union troops, defeated Gen. Van Dorn, April 10, 1863. A still more important battle was fought here Nov. 30, 1864, in Gen. J. B. Hood's march on Nashville. Gen. J. M. Schofield, with the Twenty-third corps and other troops amounting to 17,000 men, had been sent back from Atlanta by Gen. W. T. Sherman to reinforce Gen. G. H. Thomas at Nashville. Hood overtook Schofield's corps before his wagon trains had crossed the Harpeth River, which surrounds the town on two sides. Schofield stationed his cavalry on the north bank, to guard the fords above and below the town. His infantry on the south side stretched from river to river, and was protected by breastworks and artillery. Hood attacked the advance guard about 4 P. M., and drove it back in such confusion that the centre of the main line was broken. Entering the gap, the Confederates captured some guns, but by the gallantry of Col. Opdyke were driven back, losing the guns again. The Confederates renewed the assault, but were repulsed with great loss. During the night Schofield crossed the river and reached Nashville. The total Union loss was 2300; that of the Confederates over 5000.

FRANKLIN, WILLIAM BUEL, an American general, was born at York, Pa., Feb. 27, 1823. He graduated at West Point in 1843, standing first in his class, and was engaged in the survey of the Northern lakes. In 1845 he accompanied Gen. Kearny's expedition to the South Pass of the Rocky Mountains. He served on Gen. Taylor's staff at the battle of Buena Vista, and obtained the brevet of first lieutenant. From June, 1848, to February, 1852, he was professor of natural philosophy at West Point, and for a few months held a similar position in the New York City Free Academy. Afterwards he was consulting engineer and inspector of various public works, including the capitol and other government buildings at Washington. In May, 1861, he was made colonel of the Twelfth United States Infantry, and soon after assigned to command of a brigade in Heintzelman's division. At the battle of Bull Run he was in the hottest of the fight. His commission as brigadier-general of volunteers, received in August, was to date from May 17, 1861. When the Army of the Potomac was reorganized in September, he received a division. Having transported his troops to West Point, on York River, he repulsed Gens. Whiting and G. W. Smith, who attempted to prevent his landing, May 8, 1862. He was now appointed to the command of the Sixth army corps, and took part in the operations before Richmond, fighting from June 27 to 30, and covering the retreat to the James River. He was made major-general of volunteers July 4. At the battle of South Mountain, Sept. 14, he stormed Crampton's Gap, and he fought in the battle of Antietam, Sept. 17. In November he was placed in command of the left grand division, and commanded it in the battle of Fredericksburg, Dec. 13. In July, 1863, he was transferred to the department of the Gulf, and he commanded the expedition to Sabine Pass, Texas, in September. In Gen. Banks' Red River expedition Gen. Franklin was second in command, and was wounded at Sabine Cross-roads, April 8, 1864. He was made brevet major-general in the United States army, March 13, 1865, and resigned March 15, 1866. He had become vice-president and consulting engineer of Colt's fire-arm manufacturing company at Hartford, Conn., in November, 1865.

FRANKLINIA, or FRANKLIN TREE, excites considerable interest among botanists. It belongs to the genus *Gordonia*, of the natural order *Ternstroemiaceæ*, to which the camellia and the tea-plant of China also belong. The allied genus *Stuartia* and *Gordonia* are the only representatives of the order on the American continent. One species, *Gordonia lasianthus*, was discovered in the early part of the last century, and named by Ellis and described by Linnæus in 1767 under this name in honor of James Gordon, a nurseryman near London, who corresponded with John Bartram, and planted many of the seeds Bartram sent to Peter Collinson. In 1760 John Bartram discovered this second species, and William Bartram, in the catalogue of the Botanic Gardens, called it *Franklinia*. It was not however till 1785 that the description necessary to secure priority to the name was given by Humphrey Marshall in his *Arbustum Americanum*. He names it there *Franklinia alatamaha*, and says: "It was first observed by John Bartram when on botanical researches on the Alatamaha River in Georgia in 1760, but was not brought into Pennsylvania till fifteen years after, when his son William, employed in like pursuits, revisited the place where it had been observed, and had the pleasing prospect of beholding it in its native soil, possessed with all its floral charms, and bearing ripe seeds at the same time, some of which he collected and brought home and raised several seeds therefrom. It seems nearly allied to *Gordonia*, to which it has in some late catalogues been joined; but William Bartram, who first introduced it, believing it to be a new genus, has chosen to honor it with the name of that great and distinguished character, Dr. Benjamin Franklin." It proved finally not distinct from *Gordonia*. It is the *Gordonia pubescens* of L'Heritier, a French author; but it has retained the name *Franklinia* as its common appellation. The most remarkable circumstance connected with its history is, that since William Bartram found it, over a hundred years ago, it has been seen in a wild condition by no one; and the general impression is that it no longer exists in a state of nature. It is generally conceded now that species are continually disappearing and others coming into existence to supply the vacant places. Whether the *Franklinia* is a very old species which has finally disappeared, after having perhaps had a very wide distribution, or whether it is a modern species, which has been evolved from the *Gordonia lasianthus*, but did not get the opportunity to spread itself to any great extent before it was swept away, is among the interesting questions still discussed by botanists; many inclining to the idea that it is one of those species which has died in comparative infancy, so far as its native habitat is concerned.

The original trees of William Bartram were living until a few years ago. There are many trees about Philadelphia raised from them, where they are valued as much for their large white and yellow sweet-scented flowers as for the facts connected with the history of the species.

The species called *Gordonia lasianthus* is commonly known as Loblolly Bay, and is a very common plant in the swamps of the maritime portion of the Southern United States. It grows to about 50 feet in height, and 18 inches thick. The bark is used for tanning, though not equal in value to good oak-bark. The timber is useful for furniture, but of no market value in the general timber trade. (T. M.)

FRANZ, ROBERT, a German musical composer, was born at Halle, June 28, 1815. He obtained no instruction in music until he was fourteen years old. After that his passion for it so interfered with his other studies that in 1835 he was placed under the instruction of Schneider at Dessau. In 1837 he returned home and began an earnest study of Bach and other modern composers. He produced a large number of songs, which, from their display of feeling, melody, and originality, obtained wide popularity. Still he pursued his investigation of the works of the great masters, and was very successful in preparing accompaniments for some of the works of Handel, which would otherwise have fallen into neglect. He was organist of a church at Halle, and was very active in the department of church music. He was also professor in the conservatory of music and conducted large concerts. Deafness finally obliged him in 1877 to give up his various positions and to cease from his musical labors.

FRASER, ALEXANDER CAMPBELL, a British metaphysician, was born at Ardchattan, Argyllshire, Scotland, Sept. 3, 1819, where his father was parish minister. His mother was a sister of Sir Duncan Campbell, a baronet of the same county. He was educated at the Universities of Glasgow and Edinburgh, and in 1842 gained the university prize for an essay on toleration. He afterwards became the Free Church minister of Cramond. He early devoted himself to literature and philosophy. He took the chair of logic and metaphysics in the Free Church College in 1846, and from 1850 to 1857 edited the *North British Review*. In 1856 he succeeded Sir William Hamilton as professor of logic and metaphysics in the University of Edinburgh, and in 1859 became Dean of the Arts Faculty. Besides many papers on biographical, educational, and philosophical subjects, he has published *Essays in Philosophy* (1856); a *Collected Edition of the Works of Berkeley* (3 vols., 1871), with a *Life of Berkeley*, and some hitherto unpublished writings of the same philosopher in a fourth volume. This work established Dr. Fraser's fame. He afterwards published *Selections from Berkeley* (1874); a *Monograph on Berkeley* (1881); an annotated edition of Locke's *Essay on Human Understanding*, and a small volume entitled *John Locke*.

FRASER, CHARLES (1782–1860), an American painter, was born at Charleston, S. C., Aug. 20, 1782. After studying law for three years he turned to painting. Becoming discouraged, however, he returned to the law, and was admitted to the bar in 1807. In 1818 he resumed his art-studies, and attained success first as a miniature painter and afterwards in other branches of art. His productions include the portrait of nearly every distinguished person of his native State, besides historical and domestic scenes and still-life. An exhibition of his works was held in Charleston in 1857, in which there were 313 miniatures and 139 oil-paintings. He also contributed to periodical literature and published *Reminiscences of Charleston*. He died at Charleston, Oct. 5, 1860.

FRASER, JAMES (1818–1885), an English bishop, was born at Prestbury, near Cheltenham, in 1818. He was trained at Bridgenorth and Shrewsbury, and graduated in 1839 from Lincoln College, Oxford. In 1840 he became a fellow of Oriel, and was a tutor there. In 1847 he was appointed rector of Cholderton, Wilts, and in 1860 took the living of Ufton Nervet, near Reading. Alike as a college tutor and as a parish priest he was universally beloved, and proved himself very efficient. He took an active part in the educational movements of his time, and was the author of important government reports on that subject. He also served on a royal commission appointed to examine the condition of women and children employed in agricultural labor. In 1870 he was consecrated bishop of Manchester, and was thereafter diligent and zealous in episcopal work. He was Select Preacher at Oxford in 1872 and 1877. In the midst of his labors he died suddenly, Oct. 22, 1885. His only publications were sermons, charges, and reports.

FREDERICK, a city of Maryland, shire-town of Frederick co., Md., is 45 miles N. N. W. of Washington, D. C., and 61 miles by railway W. by N. of Baltimore. It is on a branch of the Baltimore and Ohio Railroad, the original main line of that road being 3½ miles distant. The city is also the terminus of the Frederick and Pennsylvania Line Railroad, operated with a number of accessory lines as the "Frederick Division" of the Pennsylvania Railroad. This latter road connecting with the Western Maryland Railroad, gives the town a competing railway line to Baltimore. The surrounding country is remarkably fertile and beautiful. In the population of this region there is a large and thrifty element of German descent, the immigration dating from colonial times. Frederick College was founded in 1797 by the State, and is undenominational. The Maryland Institution for Deaf Mutes is a State institution, founded in 1868. The city has 1 daily and 5 weekly newspapers, 4 national banks, other banks, and varied manufactures, leather and flour taking the lead. The city has a large local and distributing trade. Population in 1890, 7939.

FREDERICK III., Emperor of Germany. See FRIEDRICH WILHELM.

FREDERICKSBURG, a city of Virginia, in Spottsylvania county, on the right bank of the Rappahannock, at the head of tide, and 100 miles by a tortuous course from its mouth. By the Richmond, Fredericksburg, and Potomac Railroad it is 61 miles N. of Richmond and 55 miles S. S. W. of Washington. The Potomac, Fredericksburg, and Piedmont Railroad (three-foot gauge) extends hence 38 miles westward to Orange, Va. The river here leaves the azoic rock formation of the Piedmont region, passing into the later formation of the tide-water belt; and by its natural fall, supplemented by a dam, affords great water-power, which is utilized in various manufactories. Steamboats ascend the river to this point, though Tappahannock, more than 50 miles below, is the port of entry for the Rappahannock trade. There are churches of all the leading denominations, a national bank, four newspaper offices, and public and private schools.

The town stands at the base and on the lower slope of a high ridge which here limits the river valley. The small town of Falmouth, in Stafford county, is on the opposite bank of the river. The population of the city in 1880 was 5010.

FREDERICKSBURG, BATTLE OF. Gen. Ambrose E. Burnside was, on Nov. 7, 1862, appointed to the command of the Army of the Potomac, superseding Gen. McClellan, who had failed to reap the advantage of his victory at Antietam. Burnside openly declared his inability to command so large an army, but was induced to accept. He divided the army into three grand divisions under Generals Sumner, Hooker, and Franklin, and advanced to Falmouth, opposite Fredericksburg. Had Sumner, who led the van, crossed the Rappahannock at once, he could have seized and held the heights in the rear of the town, but Burnside would not permit the movement. Before he was ready to cross, Lee had massed the Confederate army there and had fortified the heights. Longstreet held the left of the line in the rear of the town and Jackson the right, two miles below, while Stuart's cavalry guarded still farther down. Burnside proposed to cross the river, chiefly with pontoon bridges, in front of Fredericksburg, but although Union batteries severely bombarded the town, sharpshooters who remained were able to prevent laying the bridges. At last, at the suggestion of Gen. Hunt, a small body was rowed across the river, and drove out the Confederates. Sumner and Hooker's divisions then crossed in the evening and Franklin crossed two miles below, where the bridges had been laid without difficulty. The entire crossing had occupied two days, and the Confederate position was so strong that a successful attack seemed almost hopeless. Still Burnside was unwilling to withdraw. On Dec. 13, after the fog lifted from the valley, Franklin moved against Jackson's advanced line, and in spite of a heavy fire pushed across the railroad and up the ridge until he reached a new military road which Lee had constructed to facilitate communications between his wings. Here his force was attacked on all sides and driven back with considerable loss. Jackson followed up his advantage, and, though Meade was reinforced, he was driven still farther back. On the right Sumner had ordered French's division to move from the town against Marye's heights about noon. After crossing a canal they encountered a stone wall occupied by about 1500 men, while the ground in front was completely swept by the batteries on the crest above. Here division after division fell before the deadly fire, and though Burnside refused to countermand the attempt nothing was effected but the sacrifice of thousands of Union soldiers. Even on the next day Burnside wished to renew the assault, but his corps commanders prevailed upon him to desist. During a storm on the night of the 15th the remnant of the Union army was brought back to Falmouth. Its total loss was 12,321, of whom 2078 were missing. The Confederate loss was 5309. A week later, at the unanimous request of the division commanders, Burnside was relieved of his command, and Hooker appointed in his place.

FREEDMEN'S BUREAU. Before the passage of the act of Congress constituting what is usually called the "Freedmen's Bureau," but technically known as "The Bureau of Refugees, Freedmen, and Abandoned Lands," a deplorable state of society, which had resulted from the civil war, confronted the people of the United States. The operations of the various armies, north and south, sundry acts of Congress, and proclamations of the President which were finally made good by amendments to the fundamental law, had set free nearly 5,000,000 slaves, and had disturbed them and also large numbers of the free population of the States in their residence and ordinary means of subsistence. They had followed the moving armies and flocked to the nearest towns seeking safety, food, clothing, and shelter. At the close of the war, May, 1865, the government, through its various agencies, was feeding, by daily issues, 148,000 freedmen and white refugees, and this pauper element seemed to be hopelessly on the increase. The pictures presented throughout the Southern States of men, women, and children herded together promiscuously in abandoned army store-houses and temporary barracks, in want and squalor, beggared description. The ordinary local law was inoperative, and as yet (in 1865) there had been no replacement. The very foundations of social existence were broken up. Meanwhile Congress delayed its decisions upon the new problems presented, such as these: What to do with the enfranchised? What with their masters? How to regulate the new machine? Cannot some temporary measure relieve the people from the shock incident to the sudden emancipation?

The discussion in Congress was earnest and often heated. Finally the House passed, by the very small majority of *two votes*, the "Freedmen's Bureau Act," placing the new division as an attachment to the department of war. This act, dated March 3, 1865, was broad in its scope, covering the control of "all subjects relating to refugees and freedmen" found in any part of the country affected by army movements. The bureau was by subsequent legislation extended to embrace not only the States that had been slave, but any section whatever that contained the beneficiary classes named in the law.

The Commissioner.—The management was given to a commissioner, to be appointed by the President with the advice and consent of the Senate. Assistant commissioners were also authorized by the act of similar appointment. But the President at his option could detail the commissioner and any or all of his helpers from the army. The powers originally conferred were much enlarged in the subsequent acts of Congress with a view to such care and supervision of these wards of the government as to facilitate their becoming self-supporting citizens. The law-makers plainly intended that their new freedom should not be misunderstood nor misdirected, but be a blessing to themselves and to the country which had made them freemen.

A congressional committee said: "The colossal proportions of the work of the bureau will be seen at a glance. Its operations extended over 300,000 square miles of territory devastated by the greatest war of modern times, more than four millions of its people sunk in the lowest depths of ignorance by two centuries of slavery, and suddenly set free amid the fierce animosities of war; free, but poor, helpless, and starving. Here, truly, was a most appalling condition of things. Not only the destiny of the liberated race was in the balance, but the life of the nation itself depended upon the correct solution of this intricate problem."

The President, Abraham Lincoln, for a time delayed the execution of the law; first, because there was no appropriation of money for carrying it out, and further, because he was in doubt as to a person specially fitted for such a difficult and extraordinary task. He had however notified his secretary that he would wait till Gen. Oliver O. Howard, Gen. Sherman's right wing commander, could be spared from the field of military duty in the South, and then assign him as commissioner according to the provisions of the law by which he could detail military officers to that duty. After the death of Mr. Lincoln, upon the suggestion of the secretary, the new President, Andrew Johnson, appointed Gen. Howard to be commissioner, May 12, 1865, and all matters which by a varied correspondence had been accumulating and not settled concerning abandoned property, freedmen, and refugees were at once transferred to him. He entered without delay upon his trust and proposed an organization according to the law.

The secretary of war desired him to select army officers as far as practicable for assistant commissioners and to obtain, by detail, other subordinate helpers from the officers off duty; those who could best be spared from the army and especially from the veteran reserves. These latter were detailed at the will of some immediate army commander.

Assistant Commissioners.—The assistant commissioners at first had a district often embracing more than one State. Col. Orlando Brown, having begun work in care of freedmen's affairs under army rule in a portion of Virginia, was given charge of the entire State, as assistant commissioner, with station at Richmond, Va. His previous experience gave him a special fitness. Col. Eliphalet Whittlesey was assigned to North Carolina, and stationed at Raleigh; Gen. Rufus Saxton, already in charge of the coast of South Carolina, to South Carolina, Georgia, and Florida, with station at Beaufort, S. C.; Col. T. W. Osborne to Alabama, with station at Mobile; Capt. T. W. Conway, who had been put in charge of freedmen's affairs in the South-west by Gen. Banks, to Louisiana, with station at New Orleans; Col. Samuel Thomas to Mississippi, stationed at Vicksburg; Gen. Clinton B. Fisk to Kentucky and Tennessee, stationed at Louisville (later at Nashville); Gen. J. W. Sprague to Missouri and Arkansas, stationed at St. Louis, Mo.; Col. John Eaton, Jr., to whom Gen. Grant had previously given freedmen's affairs along the Mississippi River, was brought to the East and assigned a territory including the District of Columbia, Maryland, and West Virginia, and was stationed at Washington, D. C.

Such were the assistant commissioners named by the commissioner and confirmed by the secretary of war. They soon organized their districts into sub-districts and procured a sub-assistant by detail, as already explained.

Many changes of officers were made during the first summer and fall. We find Gen. Saxton's territory reduced to South Carolina, with station at Charleston; Gen. Davis Tillson sent to Georgia, with station at Augusta; Gen. Wager Swayne to Alabama, station at Mobile; and Col. Osborne transferred to Florida, with station at Tallahassee. Gen. E. M. Gregory was first assigned to Texas, with station at Galveston. In time many of these worthy assistant commissioners were, for a variety of reasons, exchanged for others. The President, in consequence of the numerous complaints of former slave-owners, thought the military commanders—who had been subsequently assigned under acts of Congress applying to reconstruction of the States—would give better satisfaction, by combining in one person the duties of military commander and bureau official in each State or district.

Principally according to this arrangement, Gen. J. M. Schofield and Gen. A. H. Terry became in succession assistant commissioners for Virginia; Gen. Nelson A. Miles and Col. J. V. Bomford likewise for North Carolina; Gen. R. K. Scott for South Carolina; Gen. C. C. Sibley and then Col. J. R. Lewis for Georgia; Gen. W. P. Carlin for Tennessee; Gen. J. C. Davis and, following him, Gen. S. Burbank, for Kentucky; Gen. C. H. Howard for the district which included the District of Columbia; Gens. Absalom Baird, J. H. Mower, Col. W. H. Wood, and Gen. R. C. Buchanan successively for Louisiana; Gen. G. H. Smith for Arkansas; Gens. Charles Griffin, J. B. Kiddoo, and J. J. Reynolds for Texas. Gen. Gregory became after a time assistant commissioner for Maryland, and Gen. Whittlesey passed from North Carolina to aid the commissioner at his head-quarters at Washington.

As the assistant commissioners were already prominent or have since become historic, the mere mention of their names vouches for their character.

The sub-assistant commissioners usually had much of the practical field-work; as holding minor courts, settling contracts, adjusting differences, sustaining schools, making reports, and generally endeavoring to carry out their instructions. At first they came from the existing army; but many of them after the mustering out of our troops were "volunteers retained in service," provided for by law.

The General Head-quarters.—When Gen. Howard took charge of these new duties under the bureau act, he naturally organized his office in Washington according to army usage, the more so because the bureau was in the department of war. Almost the same organization took place with each assistant commissioner who had charge of one State or more. The secretary of war ordered this bureau to have a building or buildings for its general office, separate from the "War Department" proper. This office was first established in Washington at the N. E. corner of 19th and I Streets in a vacant family residence. In time the work grew and caused the occupancy of a house opposite and other buildings at the capital. Finally, after the Howard University had been built, the head-quarters office was located in a part of its largest building. The portions that could, at the time, be spared from the pupils by the trustees were rented to the bureau for its different divisions. Many of the poor students in time became clerks, messengers, or other employés of the bureau and remained so till its close—that is, from 1868 till 1872.

The division of the head-quarters or "Home Office" of the commissioner will afford an insight into the enormous work undertaken by this bureau; a work from its nature necessarily diminishing in its extent till accomplished, except, of course, the educational institutions which it helped into permanent being. These were continued and enlarged.

Adjutant's Division.—The immense bundles of papers, containing suggestions, complaints, petitions, distressing evidences of poverty and suffering now came into the hands of the commissioner. Mr. Stanton, the secretary of war, gave him too a large basket filled to repletion with reports and other communications. It was plain that this work with records and papers would increase, so that he established an adjutant's division in the outset and made it the centre and spring of all the bureau operations. To this division was assigned Lieut.-Col. Saml. L. Taggart, an officer who had had long experience in the adjutant-general's office of the Army of the Tennessee. After a short time he was succeeded by Col. J. S. Fullerton. On his resignation (for the several years of this bureau's existence) Gen. Max Woodhull, Cols. Samuel Thomas and A. P. Ketchum, and Gen. Eliphalet Whittlesey successively filled the chair. The necessary books of record, with a sufficient number of clerks to do the writing, usually fell to the adjutant's division. The officer holding this position was officially denominated adjutant-general of the bureau of R. F. & A. L. He was ever the assistant and confidential adviser of the commissioner, and did all business, like a partner of a commercial firm, in his name when the commissioner was absent, as he frequently was obliged to be on tours of inspections.

Quartermaster's Department.—Though there was at first no appropriation of funds by Congress the bureau had two sources of supply. *First, the abandoned property*—such as abandoned barracks, storehouses, hospitals, sheds, and such structures as had been put up and used by the Confederates before their final surrender to the United States; also all lands with any buildings thereon, which disloyal citizens had deserted and left to the possession of the military occupation; lands ever increasing as the war progressed and very extensive at its conclusion. This class of property included the Sea-islands, which a military necessity had, during his march from the sea, compelled Gen. Sherman to people with some eight or nine thousand freed people that had followed his armies and clogged their operations. These valuable possessions had been long deserted by their owners and many sold at tax sales to Northern men and to freedmen. Unending questions also arose about these fertile and coveted lands, promised by a great commander to the refugees of Georgia and the Carolinas. *Second*, the law and orders permitted the issue of rations and clothing and the giving of shelter to the suffering throngs of destitute whites and swarming blacks. The army, previous to this bureau, had been so supplying 144,000 impoverished people. These were at once transferred to the new bureau. The commissioner designated this part for supply, with its clerks and assistants, the *quartermaster's division*, and first assigned to its charge Lieut.-Col. George W. Balloch, who belonged to the commissary department of the army. He really did for a few months the duty of quartermaster and commissary. An immense host was sheltered, their nakedness covered, and they were fed. At once the hostile cry arose, "That Freedmen's Bureau feeds niggers in idleness!" But the cry did not last long, for every energy was put forth to reduce the pauper class; in fact the number helped by the bureau to food went down in two months from 144,000 to less than 20,000 persons.

During a severe famine which occurred in 1867 among the blacks and whites along the southern coast, a special commissary branch was formed and a direct appropriation of money, $500,000, was made by Congress. A sufficient number of assistants to execute the provisions of the appropriation act were given to Gen. E. Whittlesey, who was placed in charge of this business. The money helped all classes of society where the famine raged; multitudes were saved from starvation. The commissioner closed out this branch as soon as the object of the special appropriation was effected.

Medical Division.—Early in 1865 sickness, more or less severe, set in among the beneficiaries in Washington and almost every Southern town. Aged negroes, both men and women. must be taken care of; and multitudes of children were left without parents or with but one parent not so circumstanced as to support them. The accounts of this suffering were so touching that the benevolent people of the country had organised asylums and put into operation various hospitals. Confederate hospital buildings and abandoned government field-hospitals, many of which had come into disuse, were solicited from the war department and devoted to the relief of the young, the aged, and the sick freed people and refugees. The commissioner as soon as possible started a medical division and gave these helpless recipients of bounty to its keeping. Dr. Caleb W. Horner, of the army, took charge and regulated the supply of medical officers, nurses, food, and medicines. He was succeeded by Dr. L. A. Edwards, U. S. A., and he later by Dr. Robert Reyburn. Little by little, after the reconstruction of society and government had been effected, there was obtained by the bureau, on conditions favorable to the beneficiaries, a transfer of these asylums and hospitals to local authorities. However, many of the old and helpless who could not in the change be provided for in the South were transferred to the permanent Freedmen's Hospital at Washington. A few of these were over a hundred years of age.

The Land Division.—The first officer who took charge of the "abandoned lands" and commenced a systematic record was Major William Fowler. He was succeeded by Gen. A. P. Howe; and the latter by William P. Drew. The books soon showed a large amount of this kind of property, over 800,000 acres of farm-land and 3373 town-lots, besides other species of deserted property that naturally came with the land. It was not long after the records had been made before the policy of the executive rendered it necessary to restore much of this property to the original owners under specific rules established by the President.

Some, however, remained for the bureau revenue in lieu of specific appropriations, none of which were made during the first fiscal year. The commissioner recommended in December, 1865: *First*, that the land-owner agree to set apart and grant title, in fee simple, to each head of family of his former slaves a homestead varying in extent from five to ten acres, to be secured against alienation during the lifetime of the grantee. *Second*, that others (former slave-owners) be like conditioned according to their circumstances, to be determined by a committee appointed by the President.

After consideration, Pres. Johnson overruled this method. A formal pardon was extended to several classes of those who had lost their estates, and on the acceptance of this pardon the lands were given back without further condition. This administrative action practically hindered the operation of the law, so that the commissioner reported: "The uncertainty of the bureau over property, which is the result of the policy of restoration adopted, has rendered the division and assignment of land to refugees and freedmen impracticable."

The commissioner, however, took advantage of the homestead laws and helped many refugees and freedmen to settle on public lands. He met with considerable difficulty here, principally from resistance of the emancipated, they being averse to isolation. Unless a village system obtained the farms were soon deserted. A large number of the very poorest congregated on valuable lands near Washington. In order to remove them the bureau, among other expedients, assigned to each head of family an acre lot and put up for shelter a small house. For gaining a homestead here the family worked in the city for wages and paid the cost by instalments. This course had many good points, promoting as it did thrift and industry. Of course some failed, but schools and churches and happy communities mainly resulted. The vast majority of the Southern freedmen sought out their former occupations, becoming servants, mechanics, and laborers in the cities, or finding work on cotton or rice plantations or other farms in the country, so that the loss of the abandoned lands, even of those assigned to them by Gen. Sherman on the southern coast, though causing much disappointment and crimination and complaint, did not long keep them from securing subsistence and competency.

The Sanitary Commission, a volunteer benevolent organization, had for a time aided various needy families of the beneficiaries, including those of the colored soldiers, sailors, and marines, to collect, without charge, bounties, prize-money, and other government dues. This commission, on closing its operations, transferred this incomplete work to the Freedmen's Bureau, and the commissioner gave it to the land division, which was then fast completing its land records. The chief of this division reported for this claim branch 4000 cases taken up and settled in 1867, and 17,000 cases in 1868. The difficulties of this business will appear from a brief extract taken from the commissioner's report of 1869: "It is not possible by any machinery to furnish absolute security to both the claimants and the government against fraud. The inventions of cupidity are almost infinite, and, when no other scheme is successful, the last resort of baffled dishonesty is to turn upon the bureau agents with false charges in the public prints for the purpose of getting them disgraced and removed."

Self-constituted claim agents were abundant, and

many of them defrauded the ignorant discharged soldiers and marines, getting from them a part or the whole of their just dues.

The Bounty Division was, therefore, established by act of Congress, March 29, 1867. The work of this division was the most difficult of all, and the accusations against the disbursing officials were immediate and constant. The law itself, unfortunately, required that all bounties and other back dues should be paid to the individual claimant *in currency* and never by cheques or drafts. These payments had to be made in every part of the country, though most generally in the former slave States. If any bureau agent became corrupt and withheld a part of the money due a discharged soldier, while he secured from him his signature to a proper and full voucher, there was no effective remedy. It was extremely difficult to discover the fraud in time to recover or punish. But fortunately there were but very few such corrupt officials. A few, however, were found who were hotly pursued and punished by the commissioner. From April, 1867, to 1872, there were $5,831,417.89 paid in bounties and prize-money by the bureau to colored soldiers and sailors; and before the closing of the bureau, bounty- and prize-money payments exceeded $8,000,000. The whole work was carefully systematized, so that there was at all times a complete record, a full history, of each case, so that every essential item concerning it could be traced.

The Financial Division.—Early in the organization all the financial matters proper were gathered into one responsible division. To this after the passage of the Bounty Act in 1867 were also given the bounty- and prize-money payments. George W. Balloch, the commissary before mentioned, who was a lieutenant-colonel in the volunteer army and a brevet brigadier-general, a bonded officer of excellent record during the war, was placed by the commissioner at the head of the finances. He remained in charge from June, 1865, till 1871. The total receipts and expenditures amounted to more than $13,000,000 for the Freedmen's Bureau proper, and, as just said, over $8,000,000 more for bounty- and prize-money to colored soldiers and sailors, making an aggregate of over $21,000,000.

After Gen. Balloch's discharge in 1871, the commissioner, Gen. Howard, himself made the disbursements for a short time and then, at his request, Major J. M. Brown was assigned to this division and remained in charge till the close. Political manœuverers, angry and greedy claim-agents, officials disappointed and discharged for cause, and other malignants, aimed their shafts especially against the disbursing officers of the bureau. Twice was there a lengthy examination, once by a congressional committee, and at the close by a special court of inquiry ordered by Congress. In the first case a majority vindicated the officers and a vote of thanks by the House was awarded the commissioner; and in the second case the court and the President relieved him of the charges and commended his work. It was shown in these investigations that the entire loss to the government in these vast expenditures was within one-eighth of one per cent. of the money disbursed.

General Work.—Much of the work of the Freedmen's Bureau was of a general character and retained by the commissioner under his own eye. A small clerical force kept for him a full record. He had aides and inspectors, such as Lieut.-Col. H. M. Stinson, Capts. Joseph A. Sladen and M. C. Wilkinson, aides, and Gens. W. E. Strong and F. D. Sewall, and later J. M. Langston, Esq., inspectors. The commissioner and these assistants went often over the field, inspecting books and accounts, examining complaints, encouraging the agents who were diligent and faithful, looking into the schools, colleges, and universities, or visiting the hospitals and asylums. Whites and blacks were seen and conferred with. The appeals of employers and employés were heard, and controversies growing out of the new relations adjusted.

Many public addresses were given to mixed multitudes in the interest of industry, frugality, and progress under the new and free system of government. The most important of all subjects were those relating to the schools and the "labor questions." Written contracts succeeded well; and the joint stock companies with capital, encouraged by all the bureau agents who came in contact with the workingmen, gave in the very first year wonderful results. It is remarkable that referring to a single class of products, the cotton, more cotton was produced that year in the cotton States than ever before in any one year under slave-labor. Planters where they had been most fearful began to have hopes of success and the laborers to realize somewhat the value of their freedom.

From "labor questions" arose such a multitude of differences that to meet them some magistracy was demanded. Courts of three, for minor civil cases, were early constituted. The employers nominated one, the freedmen another, and the bureau agent was, ex officio, the third member. These courts did an excellent work. They were the first to receive the testimony of the negroes. These courts were after a time replaced in Alabama by the local justices, on an agreement with the reconstruction governor that all the courts, State and local, should admit the testimony of the colored people, an agreement which the assistant commissioner, Gen. Wager Swayne, negotiated. Finding that this procedure worked well, the same was extended to other States and the bureau courts closed.

School Division.—Mr. J. W. Alvord, a man of education, who had been so employed before and during the war of rebellion as to bring him much in contact with all classes of the Southern people, was made by the commissioner "general superintendent" of the bureau schools. He had his assistant superintendent in each State and district, whose duty it was to aid the assistant commissioner in all things which pertained to the schools, and to make constant and careful reports of what was undertaken and accomplished within the limits assigned him. The commissioner had a consultation with the secretary of war in May, 1865, on the subject of schools for the freedmen and refugees. It was agreed that *the true relief* in the transition period was to be found in education. The first "Bureau circular," dated May 19, 1865, is significant. It promises to all interested that the moral and mental condition of the refugees and freedmen shall not be overlooked. The commissioner declares: "That in all this work it is not my purpose to supersede the benevolent agencies already engaged in it, but to systematize and facilitate them."

After the first enthusiasm of the Northern helpers had subsided, still the bureau educational agencies continued. The decrease of the number of temporary dependents and the amount of intelligent apprehension of their rights and privileges seemed directly correspondent to the knowledge acquired through the schools. Many adults attended, yet much of the important information came from the children whom faithful teachers were instructing.

The commissioner, who was able to save a part of

the funds first devoted to the transportation of refugees and freedmen from places where they were congregated to places of employment, was instructed by subsequent legislation to devote these funds to education. In order to co-operate effectively with church societies and freedmen's commissions he sought first to consolidate them into a less number of agencies. He so far succeeded that from twenty-seven they were so combined as to make but three or four. Then he proposed that, for every dollar this bureau gave, the benevolent agency should add a dollar. It was so done. The agency would find and pay the teacher. The bureau would rent a building for a school and transport the teacher thither. The agency would buy a piece of ground and organize a board of trustees. The bureau would erect structures for teacher's house and for school purposes thereon.

It was thought that the higher grades of schools, like academies, colleges, and universities, were essential to furnish a constant supply of competent teachers. To supply these, six universities and some twenty colleges and normal academies came into being and have been continued with success for many years. The abundant primary and common schools were the nuclei around which the numerous subsequent State, county, and city schools have since formed. To give a slight glimpse into the difficulties of this school work a brief extract from a bureau report of 1869 is inserted, to wit: "Too much praise cannot be bestowed upon the noble band of Christian teachers who have carried on successfully this work of education. Many of them have come from the very best circles of refined and cultivated society, and have been exposed to privations, hardships, and perils which would have discouraged any who were not moved by the spirit of the Divine teacher. To them belongs the credit, in great measure, for all that has been accomplished. They have done the hard work; they have been the rank and file in the long fight with prejudice and ignorance. When they first entered the field as teachers, so general and bitter was the opposition to the education of the blacks that scarcely one white family dared to welcome them with hospitality. When they were insulted and assailed very few had the courage to defend them, but their good conduct finally overcame prejudice and better sentiments have gradually grown up in many parts of the South. Hostility to teachers and schools has in a great measure ceased." (Bureau Report for 1869, p. 12.)

The first year (1865-66) there were 975 of these schools and 96,778 pupils. In 1870, 2118 schools and over 250,000 pupils. In the House resolution, the language is comprehensive: *Resolved*, That the policy pursued by the United States toward four and a half millions of its people suddenly enfranchised by the results of a great civil war, in seeking to provide for them education, to render them independent and self-supporting, and in extending to them civil and political equality, is a source of just national pride. . . . This was done mainly through the agency of the Freedmen's Bureau. To sum up its operations, it may be said: The bureau met the impoverished and helpless classes and aided them either into self-support or provided permanently for their wants. It transferred thousands upon thousands to places of employment. It organized labor upon a permanent basis and demonstrated the practicability of a free system. It brought the freedmen into the courts of law by a gradual and protecting process. It found the marriage relation ignored. Here it brought in and enforced wholesome regulations. In fact as the commissioner has said elsewhere: "Scarcely any subject that has to be legislated upon in civil society failed at one time or another to demand the action of this singular bureau."

The Freedmen's Bank and its branches were instituted under quite another law than that of the Freedmen's Bureau. They had their beginning in a special charter by Congress. The trustees were at first mainly benevolent business men of the North. The bank was attached to no department of the government, and in its management and control had no connection whatever with the Freedmen's Bureau.

In the appropriation bill for 1872 it was provided to discontinue the Freedmen's Bureau, discharging all clerks and employés except such few as the secretary of war should retain for the bounty division. The date of this general closing was June, 1872.

When the years of party strife shall have passed and the student of history is solicitous only for facts, then he will commend the wisdom of the United States legislators of 1865 who so effectually provided for relieving society from the fearful anarchy which sudden emancipation had caused; he will also commend the Freedmen's Bureau officials, commissioners, agents, teachers, and humble employés who, amid ostracism and great danger sometimes attended with loss of life, toiled for years in the interests of humanity and human progress to execute this Freedmen's Bureau law.

(O. O. H.)

FREEMAN, EDWARD AUGUSTUS, an English historian, was born at Harborne, Staffordshire, in 1823. He was the son of a country gentleman and was educated at Trinity College, Oxford, becoming in 1845 a fellow of the college. He devoted himself to historical studies, but his early essays indicated a purpose rather to connect these with the great buildings left as the mark of each succeeding age. His first work was *A History of Architecture* (1849); then followed *An Essay on Window Tracery* (1850), and *The Architecture of Llandaff Cathedral* (1852). The interest aroused by the Crimean war in all matters pertaining to the East was the stimulus which led to his preparation of *A History of the Saracens* (1856), and in a similar way the outbreak of the American civil war led to his incomplete *History of Federal Government* (1863). Freeman is a thorough advocate of constitutional liberty, and a firm believer in that idea of race which has come into prominence in the recent history of the world. His great work on the *History of the Norman Conquest of England, its Causes and Results* (6 vols., 1867-79) serves as an illustration of both these principles. It is marked by the same graphic style as his former works, while it displays abundant evidence of careful research and scrupulous regard for accuracy of fact. Since the completion of his history of the interesting epoch which he had first selected for investigation he has added two volumes on *The Reign of William Rufus and the Accession of Henry I*. (1882). He has also published from time to time historical essays, marked with freshness, originality, and keen insight. Among these may be mentioned *Old English History* (1869); *Growth of the English Constitution* (1872); *Historical and Architectural Sketches, chiefly Italian* (1876); and especially three volumes of *Historical Essays* (1871-79). In the various questions of the day, arising out of general European politics, he has taken great interest, making his deductions from past history bear with great force on the issues of the present time. As has been seen already some of his more important works have been suggested in this way. Another work of similar origin is *The Ottoman Porte in Europe; its Nature, its Growth, and its Decline* (1877). In opposition to the Turkish power he advocated the liberation and nationalization of its subject Christian races. The result of his observations in a journey through the countries on the east side of the Adriatic Sea in 1880 appeared in his *Sketches from the Subject and Neighbor Lands of Venice* (1881). From October, 1881, to April, 1882, he made a journey through the northern-part of the United States delivering lectures, which were afterwards collected into a volume under the title *Lectures to American Audiences* (1882). They comprise two series, one having reference to the development of the English race, the other to the forms of government in Athens, Sparta, Rome, and England. After his return to England he published *Some Impressions of the United States* (1883).

FREEMAN, JAMES (1759-1835), an American Unitarian clergyman, was born at Charlestown, Mass., April 22, 1759. He graduated at Harvard College 1777, and in 1782 was made lay-reader in King's Chapel. The congregation had belonged to the Church of England, but was led by Mr. Freeman's influence to abandon the doctrine of the trinity, as he had done, though still retaining the use of the liturgy with some modifications. He was ordained pastor of the society Nov. 18, 1787, and held this position till his death. He had great influence in the community, and took prominent part in social and philanthropic movements. He received the degree of D. D. from Harvard College in 1811. He died at Newton, Mass., Nov. 14, 1835.

FREEMAN, JAMES EDWARD (d. 1884), an American artist, was born in Nova Scotia, but at an early age was brought by his parents to Otsego, N. Y. With difficulty he made his way to New York city, where he studied in the National Academy of Design, and became an associate in 1831 and a full member in 1833. He married a sister of Claudio Latilla, an Italian artist, who had settled in New York. Freeman painted for a time in Western New York, but about 1840 took up his residence in Rome, though he still occasionally sent pictures to the National Academy. Among his works are The Beggars, The Savoyard Boy in London, Young Italy. He published *Portfolio of Italian Sketches*. He died at Rome Nov. 21, 1884. His wife also devoted herself to sculpture, producing among other works The Culprit Fay.

FREEMASONRY has, as the pages of history show, been cherished and perpetuated by a devoted brotherhood through centuries. Established for the purpose of fraternal deeds of charity and benevolence, it has spread in various shapes over the whole earth, and it has seconded the Christian religion in inculcating morality and the worship of the true God, whose name it has sacredly preserved. Through social vicissitudes and political revolutions the fraternity of freemasons still survives. Its mystic ceremonies have never been divulged, and its numbers have steadily increased, while almost innumerable other associations, patterned more or less after it, have flourished for a season and then disappeared.

See Vol. IX. p. 657 Am. ed. (p. 747 Edin. ed.).

The traditions of Freemasonry have handed down to us the character of many of the fraternity, whose learning and talents were the charm of their own and of all succeeding time. The brethren of the mystic order take pride in seeing inscribed on their rolls the names of so many philosophers, scholars, and statesmen of glorious renown who have mastered their mysteries. Its emblems convey moral lessons, teaching the brethren to feed the hungry, to clothe the naked, to reclaim the wandering, to instruct the ignorant, and to relieve the distressed. The fraternity professes the highest veneration for King Solomon, "the beloved of the Lord," and it adopts as its peculiar pattern St. John the Baptist, the harbinger of Jesus Christ. Every one received into the Masonic order in Christendom is given the Holy Bible as "the rule and guide of his faith and practice."

When the British colonies were established on the Atlantic slope of the continent of North America by adventurous bands of pioneer emigrants, the foundations were laid of a great nation, the people of which would be insured religious, social, and political freedom. Churches and schools were in due time followed by Masonic lodges, and the halls set apart for their accommodation were duly consecrated with corn, wine, and oil, that the brethren therein assembled might be "blessed with the corn of nourishment, the wine of refreshment, and the oil of joy." Some of these lodges were chartered by the Grand Lodge of England, and others by the Mother Kilwinning Grand Lodge of Scotland. When the colonies declared their independence, a large number of the leading citizens were freemasons, and agreed with their brother, George Washington, that "the grand object of Masonry is to perpetuate the happiness of the human race." The order flourished in a land where there was liberty of thought and freedom of conscience, adopting as a tenet, "Honor all men—love the brotherhood." After independence was secured, grand lodges were formed in all of the original States, and an attempt was made to organize a Federal grand lodge, with George Washington as grand master, but it failed.

Freemasonry grew and prospered with the growth of the United States, and received a great impulse in 1825 from the visit of brother Lafayette. Fifty years had elapsed since he had first crossed the Atlantic to peril his life in behalf of freedom, and the descendants of those who had stood shoulder to shoulder with him on hard-fought fields gave a fraternal welcome to the friend, the fellow-soldier, and the brother freemason of George Washington.

In 1826 the assertion that William Morgan had been abducted and drowned because he had revealed the secret of the order raised the storm of anti-masonry, which swept over the country like a tempest. The most outrageous falsehoods and absurdities connected with Freemasonry were circulated for political purposes, and it was in vain that members of the order, of the highest respectability, declared that they had taken no obligation contravening their duties to God, to their country, to society, or to themselves. Many freemasons bowed before the storm of political persecution, and hundreds of lodges were temporarily closed. But after a few years had elapsed, Freemasonry, true to itself and to its principles, arose purified and regenerated. (See ANTI-MASONRY.)

It was the boast of the politicians who had conducted a crusade against Freemasonry that not one stone had been left above another in the walls of the masonic temples throughout the country, and that they had driven the plowshare of ruin through the foundations, so destroying the mystic keystones that the inscriptions on them could not be deciphered. But the "ancient land-marks" remained: the timesonored temples were again gradually re-dedicated; good and true men were initiated, and Freemasonry, with recruited ranks, resumed the discharge of its duties. There is now a Grand Lodge of Masons in every State of the Union, each with its subordinate lodges, with 593,164 regularly affiliated master-masons on their rolls.

Royal Arch Masonry, which exists in English-speaking countries, is supplementary to the universal three first degrees—entered apprentice, fellow-craft, and master-mason. The degrees of Mark Master, Past Master, Most Excellent Master, and Royal Arch Mason, are conferred in Chapters. Delegates from the Chapters in each State constitute a Grand Chapter, and the representatives of the Grand Chapter constitute the General Grand Chapter of the United States, which was organized in 1816. There are now in the different States 44 Grand Chapters, with 140,960 regularly affiliated companions on the rolls of subordinate chapters.

Templar Masonry is a semi-military organization, based on the "valiant and magnanimous order" of the Knights Templar, who are believed to have been initiated into the mysteries of Freemasonry. The Templar degrees are only conferred upon master-masons who have also taken the royal-arch degrees, and it is affiliated with, although totally independent of, those organizations. The only distinction is, that while Hebrews can take those degrees, Knights Templar must believe in the divinity of Jesus Christ. The cross is inscribed on the banners of the order, and under that "sign" they march shoulder to shoulder, to combat intolerance, error, and infidelity. The local commanderies of Knights Templar are dedicated to St. John the Almoner, and in them are conferred the orders of Knight of the Red Cross, Knight Templar, and Knight of Malta. There is a Grand Commandery in almost every State, and its delegates form the Grand Encampment, originally organized in 1816, which meets triennially. The Knights Templar always appear in public, either mounted or on foot, in uniform, and armed. They have a distinctive system of tactics, and since the war of 1861–65 they have received into their ranks so many old soldiers that they march and drill like veterans. There are in the United States 725 Commanderies, with 68,226 regularly affiliated Sir Knights.

The Ancient Accepted Scottish Rite of Freemasonry, which is entirely independent of the organizations of the York rite already mentioned, consists of thirty-three degrees, commencing at the entered apprentice, and ending with that of Sovereign Grand Inspector General. In some countries a Supreme Council, formed of nine Inspectors General, constitute the grand masonic tribunal of the rite, and there are two Supreme Councils. That of the Southern Jurisdiction, the "Mother Council of the World," established in 1801, which has its see at Washington, exercises jurisdiction over the States south of Mason and Dixon's line, and the States and Territories west of the Mississippi River. The other States are under the Supreme Council of the Northern Jurisdiction, organized in 1807, which has its see at New York. Albert Pike is at the head of the Supreme Council for the Southern Jurisdiction, and Henry L. Palmer is at the head of the Northern Jurisdiction. Each State has its bodies of the various "Sublime Degrees," as they are called, with a Grand Consistory. There have been several schisms in the Northern Supreme Council at different times, and there is now a Supreme Council which claims authority from a body organized by Joseph Cerneau in 1813, as "the Supreme Council for the United States of America, its Territories and Dependencies." The number of Scottish Rite bodies is about 13,000, of whom about 10,000 are included in the northern jurisdiction.

In addition to the degrees and rites above mentioned, there have been others invented, from time to time, to gratify those who have desired masonic novelties. Among these have been the "Rite of Memphis," with ninety-five degrees, the "Rite of Misraim," with over one hundred degrees, and a variety of offshoots from the Scottish Rite. There is also a Supreme Council, a Grand Encampment, and a Grand Lodge of Freemasons of African descent, claiming to derive legitimate authority from grand bodies in Great Britain and France. The periodicals in the United States devoted to Freemasonry are: 1 quarterly magazine, 9 monthly publications, 2 semi-monthly and 4 weekly. Nearly all of the "grand bodies" publish their annual transactions, complete collections of which are highly prized; and there is a constant publication of books devoted to Freemasonry, some of which contain much valuable historical information concerning distinguished members of the order. (B. P. P.)

FREEPORT, a city of Illinois, county-seat of Stephenson county, is situated on the Pecatonica River (an affluent of Rock River), 120 miles by rail W. of Chicago. It is on the main line of the Illinois Central R. R., where it crosses the Racine and Southwestern Division of the Chicago, Milwaukee, and St. Paul R. R. It is the western terminus of a branch of the Chicago and North-western Railway, which gives it direct communication with Chicago. It is the seat of active and varied manufactures, has 2 national banks, a large number of churches and schools, 5 weekly newspapers, and a handsome court-house. Freeport College is a Presbyterian institution founded in 1872. The town stands in a highly fertile and well-wooded region, of moderately hilly character. Its population in 1870 was 7889, and in 1890, 10,200.

FREE SOIL PARTY. The anti-slavery movement in the United States was originally and exclusively a movement depending on moral agencies. Its leaders appealed to the moral judgment of mankind against the injustice and inhumanity of slavery, and called on all slave-holders to confess and forsake the wrong with which they were charged. They published no appeals addressed to slaves, as they were absurdly charged with doing, for few of that class could have read them, and they disavowed any thought of invoking force or violence. As slavery was the creature of legislation, and the United States exercised legislation over the District of Columbia and the Territories, petitions numerously signed were sent asking for the abolition of slavery within the territorial jurisdiction of Congress. The refusal to receive such petitions led to a controversy protracted through several sessions (1836–44), in which the right of petition was vindicated by Mr. John Quincy Adams, at length, on Dec. 3, 1844, with success. The House of Representatives was constrained to acknowledge the right of citizens to present and the duty of Congress respectfully to receive their petitions, though the prayer of the petitions could not be granted. Indeed, Mr. Adams himself was not prepared to vote for the legislation asked for. The beginnings of political action were exceedingly modest. Candidates for Congress and the State legislatures were interrogated by abolitionists who voted for such as expressed satisfactory view The Massachusetts Anti-

Slavery Society had from the first declared that it was their duty to be faithful to their convictions "in the church or out of it, at the ballot-box or away from it." But no form of party organization was then thought of. Mr. Garrison, who was at that time their chief leader and protagonist, adopted extreme non-resistant views, which led him to renounce for himself all political activity. But this did not become the badge of his followers until 1843, when the Massachusetts Anti-Slavery Society demanded the dissolution of the Union, and denounced the Constitution as "a covenant with death and an agreement with hell." This position was affirmed the following year by the American Anti-Slavery Society. That society, however, had been sundered by differences on the question of political action and other disputed points. The chief seat of political abolitionism was in Central and Western New York. A local convention held in Albany in 1839 resolved on a presidential nomination, which was offered to Mr. James G. Birney, who, however, declined it. In 1840 a convention representing six States organized the "Liberty Party," nominating Mr. Birney for President, and Thomas Earle, of Pennsylvania, for Vice-President. Not only Mr. Garrison and his followers, but some who were far from his radical position, objected to this organization. They shrewdly contended that it was impolitic for them to stand up to be counted. With their numbers unknown they produced more impression. In their moral warfare they had the sympathy of all who condemned slavery, however measured and restrained might be the expression of their feelings, but as political abolitionists they could gain the support only of the most decided and intense. The new party was also divided on some important questions. Some of them believed that the U. S. Constitution was an anti-slavery instrument, needing only to be fairly and consistently construed to make this evident. Others held that the currently accepted interpretation was sound, but included some forced constructions needing to be reversed, and that for any further amelioration the power of amendment must be relied on. Thus the party was far from embracing the whole number of avowed anti-slavery men, and in the election of 1840 their ticket received a popular vote of less than seven thousand. It must not be assumed that any large portion of the people in the non-slaveholding States were pro-slavery in their feelings. Most of them knew very little on the subject. The country was not linked together as now by railroads and telegraphs. Newspapers had a more limited and local circulation than now. People generally believed slavery to be wrong, but had no very vivid conception of the wrong and what it involved. They admitted what the Southern people constantly asserted, that slavery was a domestic institution, under State laws, with which Congress could not intermeddle. To abolish slavery in the District of Columbia would not free a single slave, but merely cause their removal —from an area ten miles square. In the only Territories in which slavery existed the institution found place by virtue of the Missouri Compromise, a solemn compact which they might regret, but which they felt restrained from breaking. To most people therefore, however sincerely they might sympathise with the anti-slavery spirit, the scope of possible political action was so small as to seem little more than an abstraction. An abolitionist party in politics was up to this time a hopeless undertaking.

The slavery question was introduced into national politics, to become a persistent and commanding issue, not by the opponents but by the friends of the institution. What the abolitionists could not do Mr. Calhoun did. During the administration of John Tyler, after Mr. Webster retired from his cabinet, the question of the annexation of Texas came to be seriously entertained. Negotiations were commenced by Mr. Upshur, then secretary of state, which were interrupted by his sudden death. Mr. Calhoun succeeded to his office and took up the threads of the negotiation. In 1843 a treaty was made with Texas. In a diplomatic dispatch, sent while the ratification of the treaty was pending before the Senate, Mr. Calhoun informed the world that annexation "was made necessary in order to preserve domestic institutions placed under the guaranty of the constitutions of the United States and Texas." He asserted that slavery was a political institution "essential to the peace, safety, and prosperity of those States of the Union in which it exists." The treaty failed of ratification, but the project was still pressed, and with the motives avowed for the measure became a popular issue. The Slavery party had definitely relinquished the defensive position they had so long occupied and now demanded that the powers of the national government should be exerted for the support and propagation of slavery. If this claim were allowed slavery would become not merely a State but a national institution. The nation was called upon to say whether this should be. The first effect of this change of front was the increase of the Liberty party vote from six thousand to sixty thousand. When the annexation was consummated in 1845, and the Mexican war followed, it was easily foreseen that Mexico would be compelled to purchase peace by a cession of territory. To the appropriation for the expense of negotiating a peace a proviso was attached by the House of Representatives, called from the name of its proposer (the Hon. David Wilmot, of Pennsylvania) the "Wilmot Proviso," by which it was provided that slavery should be prohibited in any territory that might be acquired. It was defeated in the Senate, but was taken up with considerable popular enthusiasm in the Northern States. In 1848 the proviso was attempted to be made an issue in the nominating conventions of both the national parties, and in both was thrust aside. A call was made on all who were opposed to the extension of slavery to meet in convention. That convention met at Buffalo, Aug. 9, and constituted the Free Soil party. Into the composition of this party three elements entered—the Liberty party, which recent events had strengthened; seceders from the Democratic and the Whig parties, who had revolted at the resolution to sanction or at least to wink at the opening of free soil to slavery; and the "Barnburners" of New York. The Barnburners claimed to be the regular organization of the Democratic party of the State of New York, who had been unjustly deprived of representation in the Democratic National Convention. They had resisted the annexation of Texas, and supported the Wilmot Proviso, no doubt sincerely, but they were rather allies of the Free Soilers than intimately united with them. The alliance was but temporary. They had held a convention at Utica about a month before, at which they nominated Martin Van Buren for the Presidency. Their delegates to the Baltimore Convention were authorized to attend the Buffalo Convention, and presented there this nomination, which was adopted, and Mr. Van Buren became the Free Soil candidate, with Mr.

Charles Francis Adams, of Massachusetts, as their nominee for the Vice-Presidency. The "platform" of the party disavowed any intention of interfering with slavery in the States; referred to the ordinance of 1787 as evidence that it was the settled policy of the fathers not to extend but to limit slavery; declared that Congress has no more power to make a slave than to make a king; that the national government should relieve itself from all responsibility for the existence of slavery and should prohibit slavery by law in territory now free; and in favor of cheap postage, the free grant of public lands to actual settlers, retrenchment, and a tariff adequate to defray the expenses of an economical administration, and to pay off by instalments the national debt. The campaign opened with a good deal of enthusiasm, but in the election that followed no electoral vote was gained. The contest, however, was not fruitless. In New York State Mr. Van Buren received more votes than his Democratic competitor, Mr. Cass, and a popular vote, all told, of over 300,000. The party gained sufficient strength in several States to hold the balance of power between the two great parties and send to the U. S. Senate two men whose abilities made their cause respected—Charles Sumner, of Massachusetts, and Salmon P. Chase, of Ohio. These were a welcome reinforcement of Mr. John P. Hale, of New Hampshire, who, since 1847, had been the solitary representative of organized anti-slavery in the Senate. Enough members were also elected to the House of Representatives to influence seriously if not to control its action, and for the first time in our political history it was seen that national questions relating to slavery were pressing for solution in such strength as to defy suppression and to menace the Union itself.

What might have been the issue had the territory acquired from Mexico been settled in the moderate and tentative way in which new States had thus far commonly been populated it is useless to conjecture. The discovery of gold had made a State almost in a day, and when the first Congress under the new administration commenced its first session in December, 1849, California was already knocking for admission to the Union as a free State. The more vehement of the Southern extremists insisted on her rejection and the organization of California, Utah, and New Mexico as Territories with no restriction as to slavery. The Free Soilers and many others, both Whigs and Democrats, demanded the immediate admission of California as a State and the territorial organization of Utah and New Mexico with the prohibition of slavery. Further to complicate the problem a bill was introduced to facilitate the recapture of fugitive slaves. Mr. Clay, the hero of two compromises—the Missouri Compromise of 1820 and the Tariff Compromise of 1833—aspired to win new laurels. He proposed to admit California; to organize Utah and New Mexico as Territories without restriction, but acknowledging that slavery had then no legal existence there, having been abolished by Mexico before the cession; to pay Texas for some alleged claim to New Mexico; to forbid the introduction of slaves into the District of Columbia for sale, and to make provision for the recovery of fugitive slaves. Mr. Webster, who had claimed in 1847 the "prior invention" of the Wilmot Proviso, had defended its constitutionality in the Senate, and described its defeat as "portentous," now pronounced it no longer a practical question, while the peril of the Uni— real and imminent. He eloquently adv

promise, including the Fugitive Slave bill, which he pledged himself to support "to the fullest extent," and urged it on the conscience of the Northern people. An "omnibus" bill was drawn up to embrace in one act all the features of the compromise. Such a measure is often the most feasible method of combining the support of parties having distinct interests. But in this case each feature of the bill had so many enemies that it was defeated in detail by successive elisions. Thus far President Taylor had maintained a position of absolute impartiality, except to insist that California could not without injustice be refused immediate admission. His sudden death and the succession of Mr. Fillmore to the Presidency changed the whole aspect of affairs. The appointment of Mr. Webster as secretary of state was taken as an announcement that the Executive was fully committed to the compromise. There followed a long and anxious struggle. Up to the last moment it had more than once seemed that the situation was desperate, but at last the several measures included in the omnibus bill were taken up separately and passed. California was a State in the Union, with a constitution prohibiting slavery. Only the barren privilege of carrying slaves into New Mexico and the doubtful benefit of the Fugitive Slave act (see FUGITIVE SLAVE LAWS) remained to the South of all the aggrandizement hoped for through the annexation of Texas and the war with Mexico.

The territorial question was settled. If slavery was not abolished in the District of Columbia, a certain measure of the scandal involved in it was removed by the prohibition of the slave trade there. The strongest motives for the formation of the Free Soil party no longer existed. But besides the rankling disappointments of the last year there remained the fresh provocation of the Fugitive Slave act which infused new bitterness into the controversy. The enforcement of the law in several cases was accompanied by circumstances adapted to shock men whose feelings, not specially sensitive to descriptions of distant evils, were unable to bear the bringing home of the matter to their very faces. The political element of the Free Soil party was weakened by the diminished stress of merely political motives, but its moral energy was vastly increased, and with decreasing numbers it showed more intense zeal and more energetic determination. But the weight of political, commercial, and social influence in support of the compromise measures was immense and irresistible. It seemed that at last everything was settled; North and South were in harmony; almost everybody said that a "finality" had been reached and agitation must end. In the Presidential Conventions of the Whig and Democratic parties resolutions accepting the compromise as a final and irreversible settlement of the slavery question were passed with practical unanimity. Against this tremendous array the Free Soilers assembled in National Convention, reaffirmed their principles, denounced the compromise—especially the Fugitive Slave act—and nominated John P. Hale, of New Hampshire, for President, and George W. Julian, of Indiana, for Vice-President. It was their last appearance as a party in a national election. The vote for Mr. Hale aggregated 151,000. The Whig party also made its last appearance as a national organization. Franklin Pierce carried all but four States. Scarcely had his administration been installed when, on Jan. 4, 1854, Stephen A. Douglas, of Illinois, introduced into Congress a measure for the organization of the Territory of Nebraska. An amendment was proposed by Mr. Dixon, of Kentucky, to abrogate the Missouri Compromise by which that Territory had been for thirty-three years dedicated to freedom. The Missouri restriction had been treated as having almost the sanctity of the constitution itself. It had been not only acquiesced in by the South, but attempts had been repeatedly made and supported by the whole body of Southern members to extend the compromise line to the Pacific. It was now proposed to open every foot of territory between the Mississippi and the Rocky Mountains to be struggled for by the slave-holding interest. The deed was done. The issue was accepted at the North not by the Free Soil party alone, but by thousands who had reluctantly assented to the Fugitive Slave act, had smothered their convictions and feelings for the sake of peace, and now felt that they had been bitterly deceived. The Whig party was death-struck. The Democratic party lost several leaders and a large following. But the elements of resistance did not crystallize at once. To add to the confusion a secret order, known as "Americans," or "Know-Nothings," a Native-American party under a new name, grew so strong as to carry several States and seemed likely to absorb most of the opposition to the Democratic party. But this was a transient symptom of the prevailing political unrest. In 1855 Free Soilers, Whigs, Democrats, fused by a common spirit of resistance to this last and most audacious aggression of slavery, formed the REPUBLICAN PARTY (*q. v.*).

For authorities on the earlier phases of the anti-slavery movement see article ABOLITIONISTS, and also the *Life of William Lloyd Garrison*, by his sons (1885), a model biography. The history of political anti-slavery is given with fulness by Henry Wilson, *Rise and Fall of the Slave Power*. But for details the only adequate source is the newspapers of the day, so far as they have been preserved.

(L. E. S.)

FREE TRADE. In this article we give first a brief historical statement of the experience of the United States with reference to its alternate periods of free trade and protection. As this experience is seen abundantly to justify the latter policy as most conducive to the interests of the nation, we then proceed to reply to various theoretical arguments which have been brought forward by those who advocate free trade as the only proper system of international intercourse.

See Vol. IX. p. 661 Am. ed. (p. 752 Edin. ed.).

A. *Historical Review.*—Upon the opening of the ports after the war of the Revolution, an immense quantity of foreign manufactures was introduced and the people were tempted by the sudden cheapness of imported goods to purchase beyond their capacity for payment. The bonds of men whose competency to pay their debts was unquestionable could not be negotiated but at a discount of 30, 40, and 50 per cent.; real property was scarcely vendible, and sales of any article for ready money could only be made at a ruinous loss. Property, when brought to sale under execution, sold at so low a price as frequently to ruin the debtor without paying the creditor. A disposition to resist the laws became common. Laws were passed by which property of every kind was made legal tender in the payment of debts, though payable according to contract in gold and silver. Other laws delayed payments, so that of sums already due only a third, and afterwards only a fifth, was annually recordable in the courts of law. Silver and gold departed to pay for the necessary and unnecessary articles imported. In this condition of financial matters the public securities fell to 15, 12, and even 10 cents on the dollar, ruining a large portion of the warmest friends of the Revolution, who had risked their lives and embarked their entire property in its support. In every part of the States the scarcity of money had become a common subject of complaint, and the difficulty of paying debts had become so common that riots and combinations were formed in many places and the operations of civil government were suspended.

Such is the description given by contemporary writers: see Dr. Hugh Williamson, Minot's *History of the Insurrection in Massachusetts*, Marshall's *Life of Washington*, Ramsay's *South Carolina*, and Belknap's *History of New Hampshire*.

This, for several years, had been the experience of the country, when, under the administration of Washington, a report by Alexander Hamilton enumerated the principal circumstances from which may be inferred "that manufacturing establishments not only occasion a positive augmentation of the produce and revenue of society, but that they contribute essentially to rendering them greater than they could possibly be without such establishments." "These circumstances," continued the report, " are, 1. The division of labor 2. An extension of the use of machinery. 3. Additional employment to classes of the community not ordinarily engaged in the business. 4. The immigration from foreign countries. 5. The furnishing greater scope for the diversity of talents and dispositions which discriminate men from each other. 6. The affording a more ample and various field for enterprise. 7. The creating in some instances a new, and securing in all, a more certain and steady demand for the surplus produce of the soil." This last was emphasized as "among the most important. It is the principal means by which the establishment of manufactures contributes to an augmentation of the produce or revenue of a country, and has an immediate and direct relation to the prosperity of agriculture." . . . "It is evident that the exertions of the husbandman will be steady or fluctuating, vigorous or feeble, in proportion to the steadiness or fluctuation, adequateness or inadequateness of the market on which he must depend for the vent of the surplus which may be produced by his labor, and that such surplus, in the ordinary course of things, will be greater or less in the same proportion." . . . "For the purpose of this vent a *domestic market is greatly to be preferred to a foreign one;* because it is, in the nature of things, far more to be relied on." . . . "*To secure such a market there is no other expedient than to promote manufacturing establishments.* Manufacturers, who constitute the most numerous class, after the cultivators of the land, are for that reason the principal consumers of the surplus of their labor." . . . "This idea of an extensive domestic market for the surplus product of the soil is of the first consequence. It is, of all things, that which most effectually conduces to a flourishing state of agriculture."

Such were the arguments which induced the administration of Washington to favor protection to manufactures. The duties were quite inadequate for protection; but this fact, as well as the necessity of encouraging manufactures, was thrown into the shade by the immense demand for our exports which accompanied the wars of the French revolution and of the empire. Then came the period of non-intercourse, embargo, and war with England, ending with 1815, during which our manufactures increased immensely only to be in a great measure destroyed with returning peace. Then came years which resembled closely those which followed the war of the Revolution. The situation was such as forced from Gen. Jackson in 1824 the exclamation, "How and where shall the American farmer find a market for his surplus?" and the conclusion arrived at was the same that Alexander Hamilton had come to in 1791—that he must find it at home, by promoting American manufactures and the allied mechanical arts. Hence the tariffs of 1824 and 1828—followed by years of great prosperity.

But in 1833 the Southern States, which, under the slavery régime, were unable or unwilling to engage in manufactures, caused the tariff to be reduced, and in the ensuing panic of 1837 the lessons of 1786 and 1820 were learned anew, and it became apparent that the farmer absolutely requires the custom of the home manufacturer and mechanic, and that this custom can only be rendered safe by duties sufficiently high to prevent foreign competition, not so much in ordinary times as during periods of financial disturbance abroad. It was seen that any other policy would be as unwise as it would be for Holland to build her dikes only high enough to exclude the ocean in ordinary tides, preferring occasional submergence to a somewhat more expensive security. Nay, it was seen to be even less wise, inasmuch as the higher duty does not entail higher prices; these with regard to such goods as concern the great body of the people being determined by internal competition. They will be as low as they can be under the circumstances of the country, whether the duty be 20 or 60 per cent.—indeed, the higher duty would be more effectual in lowering the cost by giving a greater sense of security, and thereby attracting more capital to the industry. The pernicious experiment of 1837 and subsequent years convinced the people of these truths, and the tariff of 1842 was followed by a period of prosperity. Then came another change in 1846, in which it was decided to cut a foot or two from the top of the dikes; but the stupendous change wrought upon the whole industrial world by the gold discoveries in California and Australia kept the tides within bounds until 1857-60, when another submergence seemed imminent. Then came the civil war and the Morrill tariff. This carried us through the war and its expenditure of over $4,000,000,000; this warded off any collapse similar to those which followed the war of the Revolution, the war of 1812-15, and the collapse of 1837-40, and this gave us eight years of unexampled prosperity until 1873; then a too violent contraction of the currency suddenly throttling a patient in whom the arteries were beating with unusual energy, brought on a panic and a subsequent period of distress and depression. Such occurrences are not altogether avoidable in the present state of our knowledge; but that of 1873 was a far milder case than that of 1837 in the judgment of men who saw them both, and very much milder than those of 1786 and 1820 if we may judge by the contemporary records of those times.

The objects for the promotion of which Hamilton recommended protection in 1791 have all been most efficiently promoted. Such was the predicted result. Such is the result which is seen to have come to pass. The fact is indisputable; but nevertheless those who believe in free trade reply that the events predicted have come to pass, not in consequence of protection, but in spite of it: that the science of political economy demonstrates that no such results could issue from such a cause; that, on the contrary, still greater results would have come to pass under a régime where restriction had no place.

B. *Examination of Arguments for Free Trade.*— Here then we are forced to examine the propositions by which the theory of free trade is supported.

I. It is argued that a protective system is only another form of the mercantile system, which last is alleged to have maintained that the only wealth is gold and silver, and *for that reason* to have watched over the coming and going of treasure, as affected by the balance of trade, with a needless anxiety. It is urged that, as pots and pans are instruments for cooking, so gold and silver are instruments for the exchange of values; that, if more food were produced, a part of it could be exchanged for more pots and pans; and, if more commodities were produced, a portion of these could be exchanged for more gold and silver by which to carry on exchanges among the rest; that no country which has anything to give for either pots and pans, or for gold and silver, will be long without either.

By protectionists this argumentation is not accepted. It is urged in reply that, if anybody ever did suppose that gold and silver alone were wealth, nobody, at all events, supposes so now; but, on the other hand, nobody questions that so long as nations use them as the basis of the machinery of exchange, so long their coming and going will be a matter of vast importance. When they are flowing in, debts are more easily paid, credit more readily transfers capital into hands able to use it advantageously, and the population is more fully employed; first, in converting floating capital into those instruments of production and convenience needed by the continually increasing population, and secondly, in producing additional commodities to supply the augmented demand attending augmented employment. When they are flowing out, the reverse happens in every respect; and when they flow out in excess, one of those panics ensues which keeps for years a vast mass of men and women either partially or absolutely without work, and causes an aggregate of human suffering which entitles such a period to be named with war, pestilence, and famine, in the catalogue of the miseries of mankind.

Pots and pans are instruments; so also are gold and silver! It is easy to find a common name which may be applied to both; shall we then conclude that whatever is true of one class is true of the other? The practical man knows without any argument that, while a growing scarcity of pots and pans has no influence in producing a scarcity of food, a growing scarcity of gold and silver has a most marked influence upon the production of the commodities to be exchanged. The great merchant or banker, so far from being imposed on by the pot-and-pan theory, is even impatient with any one who wastes time in refuting it. The Bank of England to-day watches and governs the out-flow of gold with daily and hourly solicitude, although as a great exporter of manufactures England has comparatively little to apprehend from such a movement. Four times within a century the people of the United States have had experience of the effects of such an out-flow; and although theoretically it is true that the scarcity of gold, by rendering commodities cheap, brings back in time the amount which departed, yet, in the meantime, the industry of the country receives a check, the effects of which may endure for years.

II. It is argued that protective laws establish

monopolies, by which one class of the community is enriched at the expense of the rest. But Adam Smith himself says (*Wealth of Nations*, Book I., chap. x.), that "if in the same neighborhood there was any employment evidently more or less advantageous than the rest, so many people would crowd into it in the one case and so many would desert it in the other, that its advantages would soon return to a level with other employments." Other great economists lay down the same doctrine; and the use of the term monopoly, with respect to industries in which many millions of people are free to enter, seems to show little regard for the intelligence of the reader. Moreover, if there be or should be any industries in which combinations can be made to effect a monopoly, these clearly are the very industries which a nation should possess for itself: because, if the existence of a monopoly be clearly established, the remedy is at hand. A reduction of the duties will keep profits within bounds; but if the monopoly exists abroad we are helpless.

III. A third argument upon which great reliance has been placed is, that industry is limited by capital, so that a protective law which caused capital to be employed in one industry must of necessity have prevented it from being applied to some other. But every industry was commenced because it would yield a satisfactory profit, and the same motive must cause its increase until its products overload the market, bringing down prices and profits and locking up capital in unsold stocks of commodities. Some stock is convenient, in order to meet readily the fluctuations of demand, but the tendency is to go beyond this point; and every stock, whether great or small, is unemployed capital—capital which may be drawn upon to carry out any new undertaking. If a war is to be waged, or a great augmentation of the normal construction of instruments of production or convenience (that is, of fixed capital) be undertaken, in either case the food, clothing, and implements in stock furnish the means. The war or the industrial movement diminishes these stocks, raises the price of the commodities, and stimulates the industries to greater activity. So, too, when a new industry to which a protective law insures the usual profits is introduced, there is a greater demand for the products of the old industries. They are stimulated—not depressed; and their greater activity speedily reproduces the floating capital which is at first converted into mills, forges, or machinery. This must be the effect while the fixed capital necessary for the industry is being formed. Afterwards, if the price of the protected commodity be raised, there are evidently two possible cases. The consumption of the commodity may be diminished more or less than one-half. If it be diminished more than one-half, the gross annual product, which is the same thing as the aggregate of net individual incomes, will be lessened: if it be diminished less than one-half on the contrary, the annual product will be increased; and, if there be no diminution of consumption, the annual product will be increased by the amount of the whole value of the commodities, of which the manufacture has been newly introduced. Here we see at once the fallacy of the dogma, which declares that "if there would be a manifest absurdity in turning towards any employment thirty times more of the capital and industry of the country than would be necessary to purchase from foreign countries an equal quantity of the commodities wanted, there must be an absurdity, though not altogether so glaring, yet *exactly of the same kind*, in turning towards such an employment a thirtieth or even a three-hundredth part more of either." Had industry been limited by capital, as Adam Smith and J. Stuart Mill supposed, the argument would hold; but the moment we discover that in an industrial community normally there is unemployed capital, the premises are changed. Hereafter we see that industry and capital also are limited by the *field of employment*, and this with imported articles includes only the value of the exports, with which the imports are purchased; but with home manufactures it includes the values at each end of the exchange. If then the desire for pineapples or for wine be gratified through commerce, the taste for those articles will cause a production of values to the extent of the cost of the exports with which they are bought. Offer home products obtained with thirty times the expenditure of labor and abstinence, and the consumers will decline to purchase altogether; offer the same products raised at home by one-thirtieth or one three-hundredth part more labor, and the consumers will not diminish but rather increase their demand, for there will be *more able to buy*. The producers of pineapples and of wine will be themselves in condition to consume. That portion then of the field of employment which grows out of the desire for pineapples and wine will in such case be more than doubled, for the consumption of them will be rather increased than diminished even at a slightly higher price, and the commodities which would go abroad in order to procure them through commerce will be consumed at home. Adam Smith's argument then is erroneous in respect to all communities where there is unemployed capital and unemployed labor; and he himself teaches that there is always unemployed labor where there are rent and profits. (See Book I., chap. vi.)

Beneath the *field of employment* and limiting it lie the tastes and desires for the gratification of which the community is willing to work and save. Because the desires of an individual are seen to be never satisfied it has been argued that commodities can never be in oversupply. But commodities are not alone exchanged for commodities and are not the only objects of desire. In the United States (where the population and the gradual extension of the scale of expenditure (caused by new commodities and new services) equals at least 3 per cent. a year) there must upon the average be about one-seventh part of the annual product of commodities passed over to the constructors of instruments of production and of convenience, the possession of which will give a claim upon the increasing annual production of the future. Here commodities are not exchanged for commodities but for fixed property—a vast movement averaging perhaps $1,000,000,000. During periods of confidence and of excitement the call for commodities to satisfy this desire of the savers to better their condition may be much enlarged, and the excitement may extend over a number of years, causing a permanent augmentation of the demand for commodities; it may rise perhaps to $1,500,000,000 a year, accompanied by very full occupation of the population and a very large consumption; but the moment the community is smitten with discouragement—with a conviction that the business of constructing fixed capital has been overdone—the annual demand for commodities to gratify this desire may descend possibly to $500,000,000, with consequent want of employment and a consequent diminution of consumption. Everybody in practical life perceives under such circumstances that the productive energies which had adjusted themselves to satisfy the effective demand of a fully occupied population are in excess where the work to be done is diminished.

The field of employment is limited by the aggregate of the desires which find means of satisfying themselves, and in a community where the division of employments is established, when one desire finds its means of satisfaction impaired the general demand for commodities is curtailed. This accounts for the alternations of periods of very full and of very diminished employment. The effective demand for shoes, for instance, comes from the labor (of every description, both productive and non-productive) which finds a field of employment in satisfying the other desires of the community; and foremost among these other desires is the desire to acquire permanent incomes or a title to a share in future annual products; and this desire can be gratified only to such an extent as the annual product is increased, through the aid of the instruments of production and of convenience constructed directly or indirectly by the savers.

All practical men know that it is possible for the construction of every kind of fixed property to be overdone; overdone to such an extent that the aggregate income it yields does not satisfy the effective desire of accumulation which exists in the country. They know that, when such an event occurs, there must for several years be a diminution of work in this the largest single division of the field of employment, and that a diminution in this necessitates a similar movement in all the other divisions.

IV. A fourth argument which has been urged depends upon the doctrine of international trade. It is argued that the products of the mechanical and manufacturing industries cost the citizens of the United States as much labor and abstinence or nearly as much as they cost the inhabitants of Europe, while the products of agriculture cost us say only two-thirds (in labor and abstinence) what they cost abroad, and that by purchasing the former, which may be denoted by M., with the latter, denoted by A., we may obtain for the same effort half as much more of M. But this is not a universal proposition. It is true only so long as the foreign demand for our A. is equal to our demand for their M. Under our present system we have succeeded in producing say $6,000,000,000 M., and with $700,000,000 A. we purchase abroad tea, coffee, sugar, spices, etc., and such of the fine manufactures as we have not yet learned how to produce. Between ourselves the emoluments of the different employments are equalized with precision if we take an average of years. Between ourselves and the outer world the terms of exchange may be more favorable if we make for ourselves the necessity of buying and selling comparatively little, or it may be less favorable if we put ourselves under the necessity of buying and selling much.

If we now purchase $700,000,000 abroad at an exchange of two-thirds A. for M., it seems as if we might obtain say $300,000,000 more M. for $200,000,000 A. But to sell $1,000,000,000 raw products abroad in place of $700,000,000, we must offer our whole body of exports at a lower price. If there ensue a decline of 20 per cent., then to purchase $1,000,000,000 would require what before was selling for $1,250,000,000. Our $300,000,000 additional imports would then cost $550,000,000 instead of $200,000,000 as expected. At a difference of only 10 per cent. they would cost $400,000,000. The loss would appear to fall upon the producers of raw products chiefly; and it could not stop even at the point named, for the price of what was sold at home would be also diminished. Nor would this necessarily be all. The foreign market might refuse to receive our products to the extent of $1,250,000,000, and prefer to take payment for $100,000,000 or $150,000,000 in the treasure we had succeeded in accumulating while we were obtaining the additional $300,000,000 by our own industry. We should then enter upon one of those periods during which the foundations of our machinery of exchange are gradually being sapped; during which all debts, public and private, become daily more onerous; during which productive industry at each conversion of materials finds itself confronted with loss; and which ends, in the words of Mr. McCulloch (when speaking of 1837 and 1842), "in reducing the country almost to a state of barter, producing a universality of bankruptcy and distress that has no parallel, except perhaps in the denouéments of the Mississippi and assignat schemes in France." Moreover, when our treasure had been so far diminished that no more could be sent abroad, we should be forced *to go without* a portion of the supplies formerly derived from our own industries. After some years, we should discover the futility of endeavering to satisfy from abroad a larger proportion of our needs than will balance the foreign demand for our own products; then the industries would respond to renewed protection; we should construct anew the fixed capital which had gone to decay; we should purchase back, at a higher exchange, the treasure unwisely exported; and after years of misery the country would recover from the effects of a ruinous experiment, which each generation seems eager to repeat for itself.

V. A fifth argument is drawn from analogy. The tailor, it is said, does not make his own shoes, but purchases them with a part of the money which he obtains in the pursuit of his own trade; in which he has a manifest advantage. But the tailor who could find occupation for only a portion of his time would do well to make his own shoes also; and a nation is always in this position. Rent and profit enter into the cost of the great majority of commodities, and are expended partly in supporting the idle and the renderers of services which can be dispensed with. An industrial nation has always both capital lying unused and labor which is not employed in production. Whatever can be produced by these will be clear gain to the nation.

VI. A sixth argument is drawn from the assumed identity of individual and public interests. This was examined and disposed of by John Rowe half a century ago; but it continues, nevertheless, to form one of the main dogmas of free trade. It is represented that free trade simply permits individuals to trade, and that they will cease doing so whenever it becomes unprofitable. But this quietly assumes, without a particle of proof, that what is profitable to the individual must be at the same time profitable to the nation. But if the United States should undertake to satisfy from abroad a larger portion of her desires than balanced the desires of the outer world for her products—as above imagined—the merchants who conducted the exchanges might make their profits and grow rich, while their country was gliding towards the abyss of bankruptcy. They did this at the commencement of the similar movements which followed the war of the Revolution, the war of 1812-15, and the reduction of tariff in 1835-36; and those among them who foresaw the approaching disaster and withdrew in time retained their wealth. The greater portion however were excited by their first success, enlarged their operations, and were overwhelmed in the common ruin. But this only showed that they were by no means better able to judge as to what was for their own interests than "any statesman or lawgiver whatsoever." We may find similar examples in foreign countries. Let us take one from Portugal. In 1703 she was persuaded by the English minister, "that nations who would not buy could not sell—that free buyers were free sellers—that it was better for her to give up attempting to manufacture for herself, and purchase what she required by means of wine, in the production of which she had a natural advantage." She was convinced, and bound herself by the Methuen treaty. This brought about the ruin of her manufactures; after which, as the British merchant grimly describes it, "We brought away so much of their silver as to leave them very little for their necessary occasions, and then we began to bring away their gold." But each cargo of British manufactures gave a profit to the importing merchants. Their interests were promoted, but the interests of the country were sacrificed; and Portugal has remained wretchedly poor from that day to this. According to Mulhall she produces a value of $40 a year for each inhabitant; while France produces $125, and the United States $140. There is not then a particle of evidence that every individual can judge as to his own interests better than any statesman or lawgiver could judge for him, nor a particle of evidence that his own interest (even if he did know it) would be the same as the interests of his country. On the contrary history is full of instances in which individuals mistake their own interests, and also of cases where, though promoting their own interests, they injure that of the country to which they belong.

It is the interest of the nation that fish and game should not be taken or hunted at the breeding season, but it is the immediate interest of each individual to take or hunt these, while the rest of the community abstain; it is the interest of the nation to derive a portion of its revenue from taxes on vanity or ostentation—to sell to vanity that expensiveness which gives the appearance of being rich. Such taxes cost nobody anything; but each individual will evade them if he can.

The nation which produces more of agricultural products than the outer world is able or willing to buy at a fair price has no choice, if it would be wealthy, but to exclude so much of foreign products as will enable it to retain a sufficient metallic basis for its machinery of exchange; and the same is true of the nation whose products salable abroad are not sufficient to pay for whatever else it needs.

Portugal can sell abroad wine only to the value of $1.25 per capita of her population. It was a miscalculation in her to expect to be able to purchase through that article a sufficiency of even cotton and woollen clothing alone, for these in wealthy countries like the United States cost ten times the value named. But the individual trader doubtless made a profit by carrying on the exchanges which ought to have been suppressed.

VII. A seventh argument is, that every man has a right to spend his wages, salary, or income wheresoever he pleases; to exchange his products with anybody anywhere. This proposition regards the rights of property. If it were decided one way or the other, the decision would throw no light upon the question of "how shall the nation become wealthy." Nevertheless, as the argument finds favor with many who do not see its inapplicability to the question, it may be well to record some of the reasons outside of political economy for rejecting such an argument. We claim that both reason and experience have demonstrated that the American people can satisfy their wants from abroad only to an extent which is limited by the foreign demand for our products; and that, to obtain opulence, we must produce by far the greater portion of our commodities at home, and that to do this it is necessary to exclude foreign competition with the certain home industries. In this way the American people can secure abundance, and they cannot secure it by buying a few things at a cheap price, and going without the rest. We have acted upon this system and achieved a success which is the wonder of the world, and which has given to every class unparalleled prosperity; and this arises, we think, solely from the fact that for nine-tenths of our requirements we buy of one another, restricting our foreign purchases to the tea, coffee, spices, etc., which we cannot produce, and to those finer kinds of manufactures which luxury and ostentation will have at any cost. These last we tax with a heavy duty—enough nearly to pay all the expenses of the general government. But this seems unjust to many whom a real or supposed social necessity compels to purchase articles brought from abroad; they think they ought to enjoy not only that share of the general prosperity which demand and supply allot, but also the right to spend their salaries or incomes where they please. A likes to be employed at a high emolument by B, C, D, etc., but does not like employing them in turn. But B, C, D, etc., reply—"Under our system we all prosper, yourself included: under your system we believe all would be impoverished, yourself not excepted." "We, the fifty millions, have a right to say under what conditions A shall share in our prosperity. If he does not like them, he can depart out of our thriving society; and this is the alternative which every moralist from Socrates down has accorded. A may not remain among us, and overrule the rest of the fifty millions in a matter of political economy."

VIII. An eighth argument is drawn from a juggle with the word "obstacle." It is shown that *some* obstacles to exchanges are also obstacles to opulence, and from this undistributed premise is drawn the distributed conclusion that all obstacles to exchanges are obstacles to opulence! Because the United States can sell and buy abroad with advantage to the extent of x, it is assumed that they can do so to the extent of $x + \frac{1}{2}x$, although every attempt to do so has run the country in debt, stripped it of the tools of exchange, and brought on the most deplorable disasters. This is akin to the argument with regard to the identity of individual and public interests. As they are seen to coincide in some cases, they are assumed to do so in all cases, in spite of the most absolute proofs, both deductive and inductive, to the contrary. Such is the logic of free trade as it has appeared to a large part of the American people; but to use such logic

"Non homines, non di, non concessere columnae."

Let us sum up the case in a few words. The administration of Washington urged upon the people the protection of manufactures for reasons which were set forth in the *Report of Alexander Hamilton, Secretary of the Treasury*, Dec. 5, 1791; and whenever this policy has been followed, a very marked prosperity has obtained, with the single exception of 1873-79, when other causes overcame for a time the effects of protection; but those who favor free trade maintain that inductive reasoning is utterly powerless to deal with such questions; that deductive reasoning alone is adequate; and that, although Hamilton's reasoning was deductive, yet it could not have been correct, inasmuch as it led to conclusions at variance with those of free trade. The protectionists then take up one after another the opposing propositions, and show them either to be based upon false premises or to involve logical mistakes of the very worst description, such as the mistaking a part for the whole; the changing of premises in the course of an argument; the reasoning from a conclusion, true in a limited sense and under certain definite circumstances, as if it were true universally under all possible variation of circumstances. We show, in short, a body of doctrine based upon deductive reasoning, and we show its verification by events; and we show that the counter propositions of free trade are in violation of every one of the canons of reasoning which were demonstrated by Aristotle and have been accepted by each succeeding generation for more than two thousand years. (G. B. D.)

FREEZING, the congelation of liquid substances, through reduction of temperature or pressure. The term is mainly applied to the solidification of water, but is also used occasionally with reference to substances which are liquid or gaseous at ordinary temperatures. In addition to congelation from natural causes there are many methods known through which a great degree of cold can be artificially produced, and highly resistant substances congealed. These methods are of practical use in the artificial production of ice, in the freezing of ice-cream and other substances, in artificially chilling the atmosphere, etc. In the liquefaction of a solid, the evaporation of a liquid, or the expansion of a gas, heat is always absorbed from surrounding substances, the latter being chilled. If, in addition to this, a great pressure be exerted on the surface of the chilled substances, the most obdurate gases may be congealed. By such a process oxygen and nitrogen have been liquefied, and even hydrogen is said to have been frozen or solidified.

The simplest method of applying the principle here indicated is the chilling of water through its natural evaporation. This is practised in India and China, the rapid evaporation from shallow pans of water, or from the surface of porous water-jars, absorbing sufficient heat from the remaining water to chill it. Another method of producing the same effect is to greatly compress air or some other gas, cool the vessel containing it, and then suffer it to suddenly expand by removal of the pressure. A considerable chilling effect results. In the many ice-machines now in use the evaporation of some highly volatile liquid is the method employed. Ammonia or the more volatile ethers are used for this purpose. Thus ammonia may be liquefied, or even solidified, by the pressure of its own vapor. If the pressure be then removed the liquid ammonia rapidly evaporates, and absorbs so much heat as to freeze the water in contiguous vessels. In ice-machines, however, the evaporation is usually made to produce its chilling effect upon brine, which flows easily around the water vessels, and congeals their liquid contents. Several methods of producing this effect were known prior to 1850, but the first commercially useful ice-machine was patented in that year, by A. C. Twining, an American inventor. Since then many improvements have been made, the efficiency of machines greatly increased, and the cost of artificial ice lessened, so that it bids fair, ere long, to compete successfully in price with natural ice, even in cold regions.

Of the several volatile liquids employed in ice-machines sulphurous acid, which first came into use in 1876, in the Sictet machine, seems the best. It produces a very intense cold, at a less cost and less injury to the machine than most other agents employ, and it is claimed to be capable of yielding merchantable ice at a cost of one cent per pound. This machine, in which can be used at will sulphurous acid, anhydrous sulphurous acid, sulphurous oxide, or sulphurous anhydride, has come largely into use to make ice for skating-rinks, breweries, etc. But the most recent and in many respects the best system of producing cold artificially is claimed to be the *binary absorption* system of Tessié du Mothay and A. J. Rossi. This is founded on the fact that the ethers formed by the acids, as well as their alcohol radicals, will absorb sulphurous anhydride, some of them to 300 times the volume of the gas employed under certain conditions. In this absorbing power ordinary ether stands first. The liquid employed consists of ether saturated with sulphurous oxide gas, or *Ethylo-sulphurous-dioxide*. This liquid, at temperatures of 60 to 65° Fahr., exerts no pressure. Thus a machine charged with it shows no pressure on the gauges, while with other agents the machines, even when not working, show a pressure which may increase so as to injure the working parts of the apparatus. This liquid, when evaporated under a vacuum, is resolved into its constituents. If afterwards the mixed vapors be subjected to a slight pressure the ether readily liquefies. This absorbs the sulphurous oxide vapor, and the binary liquid is restored. By this means is avoided the strong pressure necessary to liquefy sulphurous oxide when used alone, and a less power and strength of machine become possible. With the advantage of the low pressure of the ether is combined that of the intensity of the cold produced by the volatilization of sulphurous oxide, while the latter acts as a natural lubricant, and no oiling of the working parts is necessary. This removes one of the drawbacks to the ordinary employment of ether. In a machine using this agent, and making 6 tons of ice daily, the average pressure is about 15 pounds, varying from 10 to 23 as conditions grow favorable or unfavorable. This small pressure renders possible the use of simplified machines. The system has been brought into successful operation in the United States.

The great decrease of temperature by which the so-called permanent gases have been liquefied, and in some cases congealed, is produced by great vapor pressure in connection with the chilling methods above epitomized. The most efficacious method is said to be the employment of liquid ethylene as an evaporating medium. In vacuo the boiling point of ethylene is —238° Fahr. It may be liquefied by compression in tubes surrounded by ice, at a pressure of about 750 pounds to the square inch, or at a much lower pressure if a superior chilling process be employed. If it be now evaporated in vacuo in a cylinder surrounding a tube, in which is the gas to be acted upon, such a chill may be produced as to liquefy oxygen, nitrogen, and other highly resistant gases, and even to solidify some of these.

Freezing Mixtures.—In these the liquefaction of solids is the process employed. The best known and most commonly employed of such mixtures is a combination of snow or pounded ice and common salt, in the proportion of two parts of the former to one of the latter. In this mixture the action of the salt on the ice causes it to melt. The water produced dissolves the salt. This double liquefaction causes a considerable absorption of heat sufficient to reduce the thermometer from the freezing-point to $-5°$ F. The process is largely employed in America in the manufacture of ice-cream, the freezing of fruits, etc. A reduction of temperature of more than $20°$ may be maintained for a long time by this means. Of the many other freezing mixtures known a few may be here presented:

Materials.	Parts.	Temperature reduced.
Snow or pounded ice	12	
Common salt	5	$32°$ to $-25°$
Nitrate of ammonia	5	
Water	1	
Nitrate of ammonia	1	$32°$ to $-25°$
Carbonate of soda	1	
Snow	3	$32°$ to $-23°$
Dilute sulphuric acid	2	
Snow	8	$32°$ to $-27°$
Hydrochloric acid	5	
Snow	7	$32°$ to $-30°$
Dilute nitric acid	4	
Snow	4	$32°$ to $-40°$
Calcium chloride	5	
Snow	2	$32°$ to $-50°$
Crystallised calcium chloride	3	
Snow	3	$32°$ to $-51°$
Potash	4	
Sulphate of soda	6	
Nitrate of ammonia	5	$50°$ to $-14°$
Dilute nitric acid	4	
Phosphate of soda	9	$50°$ to $-20°$
Dilute nitric acid	4	

(c. m.)

FRELINGHUYSEN, Frederick T. (1817–1885), an American lawyer and statesman, was born at Milltown, Somerset co., N. J., Aug. 4, 1817, being a nephew and adopted son of Theodore Frelinghuysen. He graduated at Rutgers College in 1836, and was admitted to the bar in 1839. He was distinguished in his profession and was appointed attorney-general of the State in 1861. Soon after, being again called to that position in 1866, he was appointed U. S. senator to fill a vacancy, and continued to hold his seat until December, 1881, when he was called into President Arthur's cabinet as secretary of state. He endeavored to promote commercial intercourse by reciprocity treaties with Mexico, Nicaragua, and other states, and by a new treaty with Spain. Soon after retiring from office he died at Newark, N. J., May 20, 1885.

FRELINGHUYSEN, Theodore (1787–1862), an American statesman, was born at Milltown, Somerset co., N. J., March 28, 1787, being the son of Gen. Frederick Frelinghuysen (1753–1804), who had served with distinction in the revolutionary war, and afterwards was U. S. senator from New Jersey. He graduated at Princeton College in 1804, and was admitted to the bar in 1808. He was captain of a volunteer company in the war of 1812–15. In 1817 he was made attorney-general of the State, and held this position till 1829, when he became U. S. senator. He was a zealous advocate of the measures proposed by Henry Clay. His term expired in 1835, and two years later he was elected mayor of Newark, N. J. In 1838 he was appointed chancellor of the University of the City of New York, and removed to that city. In 1844 he was the Whig candidate for the vice-presidency, Clay being the candidate for president; but they were defeated. In 1850 Frelinghuysen resigned his position in New York to become president of Rutgers College, New Brunswick, N. J. He died at New Brunswick, April 12, 1862. Throughout his career he was prominent in charitable and religious enterprises, and for many years was president of the American Tract Society, temperance and Bible societies, and of the American Board for Foreign Missions. His life has been written by Rev. T. W. Chambers.

FREMONT, a city of Ohio, county-seat of Sandusky county, on the Sandusky River, at the head of navigation, 80 miles W. of Cleveland. It is on the Lake Shore and Michigan Southern, the Wheeling and Lake Erie, and Lake Erie and Western Railroads. The river is here crossed by four bridges. The town has a good local trade, 1 national bank, 1 savings bank, and 1 private bank; 1 daily and 4 weekly papers, a fine city-hall, the Birchard Library, 9 churches and 7 schools, 4 flouring-mills, 2 foundries, engine- and boiler-works, and manufactories of farm-implements, malt-extract, saddlery, harness, and other goods. It has gas- and water-works, and four parks. The public debt is $175,000. The city limits bound a tract of 2 miles square, and the situation is attractive—the city rising upon the hills on either side of the river. Here was Fort Stephenson, where Col. Croghan, in 1813, made his gallant defence against the British and Indians. In 1816 Croghansville was settled on the E. bank, and in 1817 Lower Sandusky was built on the W. side. In 1840 both were incorporated under the name of Lower Sandusky, and in 1846 the name was changed to Fremont. Population in 1870, 5455; in 1880, 8446.

FREMONT, John Charles, an American explorer and general, was born at Savannah, Ga., Jan. 21, 1813, being the son of a French immigrant. His mother, left a widow in 1818, settled at Charleston, and her son John was educated at Charleston College. He afterwards taught mathematics, and became a civil engineer on railroads in the Southern States. In the winter of 1837 he assisted in the military reconnoissance of the Cherokee country in Northern Georgia. He next engaged in the exploration of the Great West, and was thus brought in close contact with Col. Thomas H. Benton. The lieutenant fell in love with the senator's daughter, Jessie, then only fifteen, and was secretly married to her Oct. 19, 1841. Having gained the approval of the government for a thorough exploration of the Rocky Mountain region, in the summer of 1842 he explored the South Pass. The highest peak of the Wind River Mountains being then ascended by him, received the name of Fremont's Peak. The report of this expedition, soon after laid before Congress, established his fame as "the Pathfinder." He now extended his plans of exploration to cover the unknown country beyond the mountains to the Pacific coast. In May, 1843, he started on a new expedition, aiming to reach Oregon by a new route south of the one formerly pursued. In September he arrived at the Great Salt Lake, then imperfectly known. He then crossed to the headwaters of the Columbia, and descended its valley to Fort Vancouver. Returning in November by a more southern route his party was enclosed in a barren region, with little possibility of escape, in the depth of winter. Without guides he crossed the Sierra Nevada, and in March reached Sutter's Fort, on the Sacramento River, in time to save his men, though half of his mules had perished. Undaunted by past perils he returned to explore the desert basin, which was afterwards called by his name. He finally reached the Missouri in July, 1844, and was rewarded for his heroism with a brevet-captaincy. On a third expedition he explored more thoroughly the region which he had discovered, again crossed the Sierra Nevada in winter, and pushed on to Monterey, then the Mexican capital of Alta California. Gen. Castro immediately ordered him to depart from the country, and on his refusal preparations were made for an attack on his little force of 62 men. After a siege of four days Fremont withdrew unmolested, and pushed his way north into Oregon. But early in May, 1846, on account of despatches from Washington, he marched back to the settlements made by Americans on the Sacramento, which were now threatened by Gen. Castro. The settlers rose in revolt against Mexico and proclaimed their independence. Fremont, now lieutenant-colonel, was elected governor of California on July 4. Within a week word was brought that the U. S. fleet had seized Monterey. Fremont hastened thither with about 160 mounted riflemen, and found that Com. Stockton, who had arrived about the same time, had orders to conquer California. Stockton appointed Fremont military commandant and civil governor of the territory. But Gen. Philip Kearny, who also had similar orders to those given to Com. Stockton, arrived soon after, and a dispute ensued between Fremont and Kearny, which was decided in May, 1847, by orders from Washington assigning to Gen. Kearny the supreme authority over the territory. In June the latter returned to the East, ordering Fremont to accompany him, and when he arrived at Fort Leavenworth placed him under arrest and sent him to Washington. Here, being tried by court-martial, he was on Jan. 31, 1848, found guilty of mutiny and disobedience, and sentenced to be dismissed. Pres. Polk approved of the verdict in part, but remitted the penalty. Fremont immediately resigned, but in October following he organized an expedition for the purpose of finding a practicable southern route to California. This was the most disastrous of his expeditions. In his first attempt to cross the mountains all his mules and 11 out of 33 men perished; yet, after being obliged to return to Santa Fé, he renewed the attempt and finally reached the Sacramento in the spring of 1849. Being elected U. S. senator from California he went to Washington, where he took his seat in the Senate as soon as the new State was admitted, Sept. 10, 1850. His term expired in 1851, and as he had opposed the introduction of slavery into the new State he was defeated in the legislature when a candidate for re-election. After a year's visit to Europe, he organized a fifth expedition across the continent to explore the southern route to California. In 1847 Fremont had purchased in California the Mariposa estate, which was afterwards found to contain gold-mines. Lawsuits arose concerning the title, which were not settled until 1855, when the Supreme Court of the United States declared his title valid. He then settled in New York, and was engaged in literary and commercial operations.

The first National Republican Convention at Philadelphia, June 17, 1856, nominated Fremont as its candidate for President of the United States, and W. L. Dayton, of New Jersey, as the candidate for Vice-President. After an animated campaign, James Buchanan, the Democratic nominee, was successful. In the popular vote Buchanan had received 1,838,000 votes; Fremont 1,341,000; and Fillmore 875,000. Fremont afterwards went to California, and in 1860 again visited Europe. When the civil war broke out, Fremont was appointed a major-general in the U. S. army, and was assigned to command of the Western department in July. Reaching St. Louis July 25, he found the State of Missouri almost in the grasp of the Confederates. He issued a proclamation, Aug. 31, placing the State under martial law and declaring the slaves of those who took up arms against the United States free men. This proclamation was modified by Pres. Lincoln, as exceeding the terms prescribed by Congress, but great clamor was raised in many parts of the North for the removal of the general. On Nov. 2, when he thought he was about to secure a victory, he was superseded by Gen. D. Hunter. In the following February he was appointed commander of the mountain district, comprising parts of Virginia and Kentucky. Here he fought a battle at Cross Keys, with Gen. "Stonewall" Jackson, June 8, 1862, but the latter escaped during the night following. Soon after, when Major-Gen. Pope was assigned to the command of the Army of Virginia, Fremont, declining to serve under a general whom he outranked, sent in his resignation, which was accepted. He took no further part in the war. Towards the close of Pres. Lincoln's first term, some dissatisfied Republicans held a convention at Cleveland, Ohio, and nominated Gen. Fremont and Col. John Cochrane for President and Vice-President. The movement failed to obtain support, and the nominees retired from the contest before the election took place. After the war Gen. Fremont was made president of the Memphis, El Paso, and Pacific Railroad, which was intended to traverse the country he had explored in his later expeditions. He spent much time in Europe on its behalf, endeavoring to enlist the aid of European capitalists. But a few years later, the exposure of the transactions of the *Crédit Mobilier* in connection with the Union Pacific Railroad seriously damaged the credit of all such enterprises. The sole guarantee of the bonds which Gen. Fremont had placed on the Paris market was the grant of lands made by Congress, conditioned on completion of the road. On a charge of fraudulent representations concerning them, suit was instituted against Gen. Fremont in Paris, and in his absence he was condemned. He denied all responsibility for the representations made by the brokers, but the failure of his projects reduced him to poverty. In June, 1878, he was made governor of Arizona, which position he held for four years. He died July 13, 1890, having shortly before been restored to the retired list of the U. S. army.

FRENEAU, PHILIP (1752–1832), an American poet, was born in New York city, Jan. 2, 1752, of Huguenot descent. He graduated at Princeton College in 1771, having already written some poems of moderate merit. In 1776 he went to the West Indies on a trading voyage, and was afterwards engaged as a merchant. In 1779 he was a contributor to the *United States Magazine*, established by his class-mate, H. H. Brackenridge, in Philadelphia. In 1780 Freneau was captured at sea by the British, and suffered the horrors of a prison-ship in New York. In 1791 he was editor of the *Daily Advertiser* in New York, but being called to Philadelphia to be clerk in the department of state, he edited there the *National Gazette*, in which he assailed the policy of Washington. In 1793 he removed to New Jersey, where he passed his later years, with occasional visits to New York. He died at Monmouth, N. J., Dec. 18, 1832. A volume of his *Poems* first appeared at Philadelphia in 1786, his *Miscellaneous Works* in 1788, later *Poems* at Mount Pleasant in 1795, and two more volumes at New York in 1815. His early political burlesques are said to have cheered the patriots of the Revolution. His muse ranged over a great variety of subjects, and sometimes rose to a high strain.

FRÈRE, CHARLES THEODORE, a French painter, was born at Paris, June 24, 1815. He studied art with Coignet and Roqueplan, and first exhibited in the Salon of 1834. Two years later he went to Algeria, took part in the siege of Constantine, and afterwards visited the East. His works relate entirely to Eastern subjects. He has a studio in Cairo and another in Paris. Among his more famous pictures are the Halt of the Arabs, which was bought by the French government in 1850, A Harem at Cairo, Ruins of Karnak, The Island of Philæ, The Caravan of Mecca, The Nile—Evening, and The Desert—Noon.

FRERE, SIR HENRY BARTLE EDWARD (1815–1884), an English colonial officer, a nephew of John Hookham Frere (1769–1846), the celebrated wit and diplomatist, was born March 29, 1815. He was educated at Bath and at Haileybury College, and entered the East India Company's civil service in 1834. He was resident and chief-commissioner of Sinde from 1850 to 1859; was made a K. C. B. for services during the mutiny in 1859; was governor of Bombay, 1862–67; a member of the Indian council, 1866–74. In 1872 he was employed on a successful mission to Zanzibar for the suppression of the slave-trade of that sultanate. He was sworn of the privy council, 1873, and was made a baronet in 1876. He was governor of the Cape of Good Hope and high commissioner for South Africa, 1877–80, and was charged with having brought on the Zulu war. Sir Bartle Frere was noted as a philanthropist and an active supporter of Christian missions. An earnest conservative in politics, he enjoyed the special favor of the Queen and of Lord Beaconsfield. His writings were chiefly on the missionary work, and on various philanthropic subjects. With his brother, W. E. Frere, he published, in 1871, the *Memoir of Hookham Frere*, prefixed to the collected works of the latter. He died in London, May 29, 1884.

FRÈRE, PIERRE EDOUARD, a French painter, was born at Paris, Jan. 10, 1819. He studied under Paul Delaroche, and first exhibited in 1843. He painted the amusements and occupations of country children in a way to win the popular heart, and engravings of them were widely circulated. His numerous paintings show careful study and phenomenal success in transferring to canvas the unconscious grace of childhood. Among his works are The Little Gourmand, Boys Going from School, Girls Going from School, The Road to School, The Orphan's First Prayer, and Preparing for Church. The last is in the Corcoran Gallery at Washington.

FRÈRE-ORBAN, HUBERT JOSEPH WALTHER, a Belgian statesman, was born at Liège, April 24, 1812. He received a French education, studied law, and was admitted to the bar in his native city. He was also active as a liberal journalist, and in 1847 was elected to the Chamber of Deputies. Being called to take charge of the public finances he exerted himself to avert a financial crisis after the Revolution of 1848, and organized the national bank of Belgium. Retiring in 1852 he was recalled in 1861, when he opposed the commercial treaty with France. However he remained in the cabinet, and in January, 1868, became its chief. In 1870 the clerical party prevailed and Frère-Orban became the leader of the opposition, the struggle between the two parties turning chiefly on the subject of education. In June, 1878, the liberals prevailed and Frère-Orban became head of the ministry, with the portfolio of foreign affairs. He established a special ministry of public instruction, and by the law of July, 1879, instruction was secularized. The bishops pronounced excommunication against those engaged in these schools, and after an ineffectual appeal to the pope the Belgian embassy to the Vatican was recalled. Frère-Orban maintained his position at the head of the ministry until 1884, when in consequence of the victory of the clerical party at the polls he retired.

FREYCINET, CHARLES LOUIS DE SAULCES DE, a French statesman, was born at Foix, Ariéges, Nov. 14, 1828. He was educated at the École Polytechnique in Paris, and graduated in 1848. He was employed as an engineer on government works until 1855, when, being placed in charge of the railroads of the south of France, he thoroughly reorganized their system. He also published treatises on mechanics, mathematics, and railroad engineering. In 1862 his investigation of the systems of labor in France and other countries led to the amelioration of the condition of workingwomen and children in France. His work on hygiene, *Principes de l'assainissement des villes* (1870), is valuable. In 1870 Gambetta appointed Freycinet chief of the military cabinet at Tours. The fruitless attempt to prolong the struggle against the Germans was afterwards related by him in *La Guerre en province pendant le Siège de Paris* (1871). In 1876 he was elected to the Senate as a supporter of Gambetta, and proved an effective speaker. Even under MacMahon's reactionary administration Freycinet's executive ability caused him to be made minister of public works in December, 1877. The control of public affairs having passed into the hands of the Republicans on Dec. 27, 1879, Freycinet was made chief of the ministry, taking the department of foreign affairs. He did not fulfil the expectations which had been formed and in less than a year he was compelled to resign, Sept. 19, 1880. Gambetta, who had brought about the removal of his old friend and supporter, was for a short time chief of the cabinet. On his death Freycinet, the man of peace and compromise, was again called to the head of affairs, Jan. 31, 1882, and held this position about six months. By preventing France from taking part in the Egyptian war he lost favor. A period of foreign aggression followed, but on Jan. 7, 1886, after the re-election of Pres. Grévy, the peaceful Freycinet was again called to the premiership. When Grévy resigned in Dec., 1887, M. Sadi Carnot was chosen president and Freycinet became minister of war.

FREYTAG, GUSTAV, a German poet and novelist, was born at Kreuzberg, in Silesia, July 13, 1816. He studied at the Universities of Breslau and Berlin, devoting himself especially to German philology, and was made Ph. D. in 1839. Becoming a lecturer on German literature at Breslau he published some volumes of narrative poems, and the dramas, *Die Valentine* (1847) and *Graf Waldemar* (1850). In 1848 he settled at Leipsic, where he edited the *Grenzboten* until 1870. His novel *Soll und Haben* (1855) had now placed him in the front rank of German novelists. In English it has appeared as *Debit and Credit* (1858). Another of his works, *Die verlorene Handschrift* (1864), has been almost equally successful. He began in 1859 a series of picturesque sketches from early German history, which were finally gathered into four volumes, entitled *Bilder aus der deutschen Vorgangenheit* (1862). Among his later works are *Ingo und Ingraban* (1872) and *Die Geschwister* (1878). Freytag is thoroughly imbued with the modern realistic spirit, yet he never loses sight of the necessity of grace in works of true art. His characters are lifelike, and his style graphic. In his dramas he attacks psychologic problems, but presents them with due regard to poetic probability.

FRIEDRICH KARL NIKOLAS, Imperial Prince of Germany, is the eldest son of Prince Karl (1801–1885), the second brother of Emperor Friedrich Wilhelm. He was born March 20, 1828, and received a military education, and when raised to command exerted himself to improve the morale of the army. He was engaged in the Schleswig-Holstein war in 1864, and in the war against Austria in 1866 had command of the First army. On his march through Saxony he won the favor of that people to the cause of Prussia. Entering Bohemia he pushed forward with such boldness that he compelled the Austrian general Benedek to retire to Sadowa. Here by the timely arrival of the Crown Prince Friedrich Wilhelm he gained the great victory which decided the war, and compelled Austria to sue for peace. In the war with France in 1870 he commanded the Second German army, amounting to 250,000 men and 500 guns. He defeated the French general Froissart at Speichorn on Aug. 6, and soon after drove Marshal Bazaine to take refuge in Metz. After a siege of ten weeks Bazaine surrendered his entire force of 150,000 men. The prince was then made a field-marshal. In November he marched against the Army of the Loire, which under Gen. Chanzy had revived the hopes of the French. The prince recaptured Orleans, took Le Mans, and drove Chanzy to the north, where he was unable to effect anything. The prince was married in 1854 to Marie Anhalt, daughter of the Duke of Anhalt, by whom he had four children. He died June 10, 1885.

FRIEDRICH WILHELM NIKOLAS KARL, the only son of Emperor William I., of Germany; was successively Crown Prince of Prussia, Imperial Prince of Germany, and for the brief space of 99 days Emperor of Germany. He was born at Potsdam, Oct. 18, 1831. After receiving a scientific education he entered the military service and rose to the rank of general. In 1866 he had command of three army corps. His army marched from Silesia, and after several very severe engagements reached the field of Sadowa in time to decide the fortune of the day. In the war against France the crown prince had command of the Third German army, comprising about 200,000 men and 500 guns. On Aug. 4 he defeated part of Marshal MacMahon's force at Weissenburg, and on the 6th assailed his entire force of 50,000 men in a strong defensive position at Woerth. After a desperate struggle the French left and centre were completely broken. At the battle of Sedan, Sept. 1, the crown prince again fought with MacMahon, having crossed the river Meuse under specially difficult circumstances. After the battle he took part in the siege of Paris and remained there till peace was declared. In 1871 he was made a field-marshal of Prussia, and Imperial Prince of Germany. He was of liberal inclinations and was fondly called "Unser Fritz." Before his father's death, he was attacked with cancer in the throat, and went to Tyrol and Italy, where the operation of tracheotomy was performed. He returned to be crowned and suffered in silence till his death, June 15, 1888. He was married, Jan. 25, 1858, to Victoria Adelaide, Princess Royal of Great Britain, and had six children. (See WILLIAM II.)

FRINGE TREE, also called *White Fringe* and *Old Man's Beard*, is the *Chionanthus Virginica* of Linnæus. It is a large shrub, about 10 or 12 feet high, though sometimes becoming a small tree of 20 or 30 feet. It belongs to the natural order *Oleaceæ*. The flowers are cut into deep, narrow segments, and the

Chionanthus Virginica (White Fringe).

corolla is rotate, while it is short, salver-form in the olive and generally wanting in the ash. The ash has male and female flowers on separate trees, or at least separate on the same plant, and there is a similar tendency in the white fringe, which often has some individual trees wholly barren. But the fruit is very different in appearance from that of ash, being a purple drupe, having a single stone in the centre, as in the olive. The flowers are borne in axillary slender, drooping panicles, giving the fringe-like character which is expressed by its common name. According to some authors it also bears the name "snow-tree," and the botanical name *Chionanthus* signifies snow-flower. Linnæus tells us he borrowed the name from Royer, a Dutch botanist, who, evidently referring to the species now known as *Chionanthus Zeylonica*, with which *C. Virginica* was once identified, says it was commonly called "sneebaum," or snow-tree. The appearance of *Chionanthus Virginica*, the only American species, would hardly suggest the name. Our snowdrop tree is a very different plant, the *Halesia*. The name *Virginica* is due to the fact that, like so many American plants with the same name, it was first made known to Europeans through the early collections of Clayton from Virginia. It is a comparatively local plant, being confined to the seaboard from Southern Pennsylvania to Florida.

For its rare beauty it is often cultivated in the gardens of the United States and of Europe. It is of no known use in the arts. The aborigines used the bark of the roots, bruised, and applied to obstinate sores and ulcers with very good effect, and an infusion of the roots is still employed with considerable effect in stubborn intermittent fevers. (T. M.)

FRITH, WILLIAM POWELL, an English painter, was born at Studley, Yorkshire, in 1819. His first picture appeared in 1839, and in the next year he exhibited, at the Royal Academy, Malvolio and the Countess Olivia. Many of his earlier works treated in the same way incidents from history and romance and were made widely known by engravings. He became an academician in 1853. In 1858 he achieved a great success with his crowded canvas representing the Derby Day, and another notable work of the same kind, The Railway Station, appeared in 1862. He still continues to depict scenes from Shakespeare, Scott, and others, combining genuine artistic ability with a popular range of subjects.

FROEBEL, JULIUS, a German politician and traveller, was born at Griesheim, July 16, 1805. He was the son of a clergyman and nephew of Friedrich Fröbel, the founder of the Kindergarten system of schools. He studied in the Universities of Munich, Jena, and Berlin. In 1833 he went to Zurich and was appointed professor of mineralogy in the high school there. Engaging in politics as an extreme radical, he resigned his professorship in 1844. In 1848 he was elected to the German Congress at Frankfort, and in October went with Robert Blum to Vienna to excite a revolution. He was arrested and condemned to death, but pardoned by Prince Windischgrätz. Returning to Frankfort he published an account of his attempt (1849). During his years of travel in Central America, Mexico, and California he was a frequent correspondent of the *New York Tribune*. In 1856 he married in New York the Countess Caroline von Armansperg, daughter of the Bavarian minister, and soon after returned to Germany as a naturalized American citizen. In 1862 he was in Vienna advocating by his writings the federal union of the German states. In 1867 he founded in Munich the *Süd-deutsche Presse*, which he edited until 1873. He was then made consul of the German empire at Smyrna, and in 1876 was transferred to Algiers in the same capacity. Among his noteworthy publications is *Theorie der Politik* (1861–64), to which he afterwards added *Die Geschichtspunkte und Aufgaben der Politik* (1878). Besides a German narrative of his travels he published in English *Seven Years' Travel in Central America and the Far West* (1859). He has also published *Die realistische Weltansicht und die utilitarische Civilisation* (1881).

FROG.—The term frog is commonly applied to two distinct groups of amphibians or batrachians, viz., the tree-frogs and burrowing frogs (*Arcifera*) and the true frogs (*Raniformia*). To understand the distinction between these it is necessary to examine the skeleton. In the former group the free diverging ends of the coracoid and pre-coracoid bones of the shoulder girdle are connected by two longitudinal cartilaginous bands with convex borders. These bands permit of a movement which expands and contracts the thoracic cavity. In the Raniformia these cartilages are fused into a narrow median mass which intervenes between the adjacent ends of the nearly parallel coracoid and pre-coracoid bones, the whole structure thus being solid and incapable of expansion and contraction. Tree-frogs, burrowing frogs, and true frogs agree in the possession of teeth, a character distinguishing them from the toads, which have the arciferous shoulder-girdle and no teeth.

See Vol. IX. p. 698 Am. ed. (p. 795 Edin. ed.).

The arcifera are grouped in the families Bufonidæ (see TOAD), Dendrophryniscidæ, natives of the Andes; Discoglossidæ, found in Europe, with one species in New Zealand; Cystignathidæ, an extensive family occurring in Australia and South America, Amphignathontidæ, Hemiphractidæ, and Hylidæ. The last family includes 175 species, most of them South American, though 23 inhabit North America, 20 Australia, and 2 the Old-World continent.

One hundred and sixty species of Cystignathidæ have been described, exhibiting great variety in habit and structure, since some are burrowers, others climbers of trees and rocks, and others adapted for an aquatic life; while some of the forms have bony skulls and breast-bones, and others have these parts of the skeleton cartilaginous. Only a few of those with complete skulls have a bony sternum or breast-bone. Many of the species are of large size. *Cystignathus ocellatus* is the largest, attaining a length of eight inches.

The species of *Lithodytes* inhabit rocky regions, and are abundant north of the Isthmus of Panama, one species occurring in Southern Florida, while another lives in fissures in the limestone precipices of Western Texas. This species is supposed to deposit its eggs in pools of rain-water in the caverns and crevices of the rocks. During the breeding season it is very noisy. The inhabitants usually attribute the noise to a lizard (*Gerrhonotus*).

The genus *Hylides* lives upon the ground, yet has the ends of the toes dilated as in the tree-frogs. *H. martinicensis* is abundant in the West Indies. The eggs are laid between the leaves of living plants, or under fallen leaves or stones. Sometimes the frog sits on them. In about eight days the embryo frog is visible through the transparent substance of the egg, and looks almost like a small salamander. In fourteen days it leaves the egg, and in the course of another day the tail is absorbed. Thus the metamorphosis which in most frogs occupies so long a period is in this species passed through in the egg. The genus *Hylides* is distributed throughout tropical America.

The species of *Ceratophrys* are among the most curious of the family. They are toad-like in shape, and often have horn-like projections from the eyelids and from the muzzle, while some have bony plates set in the skin of the back.

In the genus *Telmatobius*, which inhabits high altitudes in the Andes, the organs of hearing are defective. One species lives in Lake Titicaca. *Pseudis* is remarkable for the very large relative size of the larvæ, and also for the extension of the web of the hind-foot upwards between the external metatarsals or bones of the sole of the hind feet. In most of the tailless batrachians these bones are closely bound together. The species are found in Brazil and southwards.

The family Pelobatidæ may be divided into two sections, the one European, the other North American, distinguished by the structure of the sacrum. The species of *Spea* inhabit the western part of the United States, and extend to the valley of Mexico. Living in an arid region, they take advantage of a summer rain to issue from their burrows and deposit their eggs in the puddles and pools. The larvæ hatch and acquire their legs quickly, and thus some at least become air-breathers in time to escape death by the drying up of their early habitat. *Spea hammondii* inhabits the Pacific region as far south as San Diego, while *S. bombifrons* lives in the central region, that is, in the area included between the Rocky Mountains and the Sierra Nevada. Prof. E. D. Cope found larvæ of this species, though still with toothless jaws and unabsorbed tails, devouring the dead bodies of the Western locust (*Caloptenus spretus*). Most of the species of *Scaphiopus* are found in North-western Mexico and the adjacent parts of the United States, but *S. holbrookii* occurs throughout the Atlantic region. During the greater part of the year it is concealed underground, but in the breeding season (April or May) it appears above ground quite suddenly, and often in considerable numbers, and attracts attention by the loudness of its voice. "The wonder that so great a volume of sound can proceed from so small an animal disappears," says Dr. Abbott, "if we examine the vocal cords." The machinery for producing sounds to equal an ordinary steam-whistle is apparently contained in the throat of this rare and curious batrachian; although the males are most noisy the females are far from voiceless. Dr. Abbott watched the development of this species in the water of a sink-hole in a dry upland field near Trenton, N. J., and found that, notwithstanding the rapidity of their metamorphosis, the greater part of the eggs and newly-hatched larvæ perished by the drying up of the water, so that, if the spade-foot toads habitually lay their eggs in temporary pools, this habit accounts for their rarity. Several specimens were reared in confinement, and it was noted that the tadpoles with large tails and without front legs devoured their more advanced companions with smaller tails and budding front legs. At the latter stage the animal is more defenceless than before or after.

The Hylidæ, or tree-frogs, have the ends of the digits terminated by a disc-like dilatation, thus enabling them to climb. Some true frogs as well as certain Cystignathidæ have similar dilatations, but the structure of the terminal phalanges is different. Although called tree-frogs, many of them live upon the ground, frequently near water. This is the case with the species of *Chorophilus* and *Acris*. Seven kinds of the former genus and two of the latter occur in the United States, principally in the South. Some of the species of *Hyla*, as *H. pickeringii* of the Eastern States, have similar habits, and *H. regilla* of California is usually to be found among grass and herbage. In the genus *Triprion* of Mexico and Central America the ossification of the skull is carried so far that it forms a prominent rim, overhanging the mouth all around. *Triprion* is also exceptional in having a longitudinal row of teeth on the roof of the mouth. Many of the largest Hylidæ are included in the genus *Hypsiboas*, in which the fore-limbs have a thumb ending in a sharp curved spine, enabling the male to hold the female firmly. There is a similar arrangement in some Cystignathidæ. There are ninety-five species of *Hyla*, the largest of which, *H. vasta* of the West Indies, and *H. dolichopsis* of New Guinea, reach a length of five inches. *Phyllomedusa bicolor*, the giant of the family, reaches seven inches. Only one species, *Hyla arborea*, occurs in Europe.

The North American *Hylæ* lay their eggs in the water, in pockets smaller than those of the frogs, and attached to a plant or other fixed object. The young of the common *Hyla versicolor* are gray, and undergo metamorphosis while small. The adults can change their color to that of the object they are upon, passing from pale gray to bright green, and the species of *Acris* and *Chorophyllus*, as well as most Hylidæ, undergo similar changes. The first sounds of spring are the shrill notes of *Hyla pickeringii* and *Acris gryllus* from the swamps. A little later comes the rasping pipe of *Chorophilus triseriatus*. The colors of many Hylidæ are brilliant.

In the genera *Nototrema* and *Opisthodelphys* the eggs are placed upon the back, in a pocket formed by the infolding of the skin which is pushed inwards from the posterior part of the back. This pouch may, when extended with eggs, cover almost the entire dorsal region.

In *Nototrema marsupiatum* the young leave the pouch as tadpoles, but in some other species of this genus they pass through all the stages of their metamorphosis in this position.

The Gastrechmia are a sub-order consisting of only two or three species of African frogs, distinguished by the articulation of the shoulder-blade to the skull. The great firmness of the scapular arch produced by this arrangement, united as it is with the structure of the shoulder-girdle found in the true frogs, enables these species to burrow deftly.

The Firmisternidæ comprise five families, viz.: the Dendrobatidæ of tropical continental America and Madagascar; the Phryniscidæ of the same regions, and also found in Malaysia and New Guinea; the Engystomidæ, common to both continents; the Dyscophidæ, and the extensive family of Ranidæ or true frogs. Sixteen out of the twenty-two species of Phryniscidæ are from tropical America. *Brachycephalus ephippium* is a small bright yellow species common in some parts of Brazil. It looks like a small toad, and has a saddle-like bony plate on its back. *Engystoma carolinense* of the Southern States is the only species of its family found in this country. *Cacopus* and *Glyphoglossus*, Asiatic genera of Engystomidæ, are almost globular when distended with eggs. All the eight species of Discophidæ except one from British Burmah are natives of Madagascar.

About 250 species of Ranidæ are known, of which alone 110 belong to the genus *Rana*. Though the typical forms are aquatic, some species have digital dilatations, and some of these are arboreal. *Rana temporaria* is the most widely spread species, since it extends across the eastern continent from England to Japan, and across the western from California to the Atlantic. It varies widely, so that the diverging forms are sometimes considered species. One well-marked form is found in the Eastern States, another on the Pacific coast, while Europe and Asia have several. Four other species of Rana live in the Eastern United States. These are the leopard frog (*R. halecina*), which extends to Guatemala; the bull-frog (*R. catesbiana*), *R. clamata*, and *R. palustris*. The last but one of these is the common green frog of cold springs, and may be recognized by the enormous size of its ear-drum; *Rana palustris* is inaptly named, since it wanders farther from water and higher into the mountains than *R. halecina*. The species of Rana lay their eggs in more or less globular masses, not in strings like the toads.

In the dry regions of South Africa are several species

of *Rana* which live in holes in the ground, issuing after rains. These have a sort of shovel on their hindfoot, like the Pelobatidæ.

Very few Ranidæ live either in South America or Australia, and the family has its head-quarters in the East Indies. Many of the forms are arboreal in habit. The genus *Rhacophorus* includes the largest and most brilliantly colored of tree-frogs, and comprises some Malaysian species in which the webs connecting the fingers and toes are so large that, like the lateral expansions of the flying-squirrel, they form parachute-like supports for the creature in its long leaps from tree to tree.

Frogs appear to be a desirable article of food, notwithstanding the English prejudice against them. Certain species are eaten in various parts of the civilized world. Thus *Rana esculenta*, the green or edible frog, is a favorite article of food in Central and Southern Europe, and *R. temporaria* is not eaten; while on the Pacific coast of the United States it is the large local variety of *R. temporaria* that is eaten, chiefly by French and Italians. The bull-frog is coming into favor as an article of food in the Eastern States.

(W. N. L.)

FRONTENAC, LOUIS DE BUADE, COUNT DE (1621–1698), a French governor of Canada, was born in France in 1621. Entering the army as colonel in 1638 he served under Maurice of Nassau in Italy, Flanders, and Germany, and in 1669 was made a lieutenant-general. Louis XIV. appointed him governor-general of Canada, where he arrived in September, 1672. To repress the troublesome Iroquois he built Fort Frontenac (now Kingston). He took an active interest in the exploration of the Great West, sending Marquette and Joliet to the Mississippi, and furthering the projects of La Salle. His arbitrary conduct, however, excited the ill-will of Bishop Laval and other officials and caused his recall in 1682. His wife was a court beauty and used her influence to procure his reinstatement that she might be free from his presence. He was again commissioned in 1689, and soon stirred up fresh hostilities against the frontier settlements of New England and New York. He defeated the expedition of Sir William Phips for the capture of Quebec in 1690, and regained for the French their former control of the Indian tribes. Worn out with his labors Frontenac died at Quebec, Nov. 28, 1698. A century later his remains were transferred to the Cathedral of Quebec. His life forms the subject of Parkman's *History of the French Dominion in America*.

FROTHINGHAM, NATHANIEL LANGDON (1793–1870), an American Congregational minister, was born at Boston, July 23, 1793. He graduated at Harvard College in 1811, and afterwards taught there rhetoric and oratory. In 1815 he was ordained pastor of the First Congregational Church of Boston, and retained this charge till 1850. Besides numerous sermons he published *Metrical Pieces, Translated and Original* (1855). He died at Boston, April 4, 1870.

FROTHINGHAM, OCTAVIUS BROOKS, an American clergyman and author, was born in Boston, Nov. 26, 1822. He was the son of the preceding, and on the maternal side a grandson of Peter C. Brooks. He graduated at Harvard College, 1843; became pastor of a Unitarian church at Salem, Mass., 1847; removed in 1855 to Jersey City, N. J., whence in 1857 he went to New York city. Here he became pastor of a congregation of Free Religionists, assuming a position confessedly outside the pale of Christianity. In 1882 he abandoned public speaking and retired to Boston, still continuing his literary activity. Besides many pamphlets and sermons he is author of *Stories from the Lips of the Teacher* (1863); *Stories of the Patriarchs* (1864); a translation of Renan's *Critical Essays* (1864); *Child's Book of Religion* (1866); *The Religion of Humanity* (1873); *Life of Theodore Parker* (1874); *The Safest Creed* (1874); *Beliefs of the Unbelievers* (1876); *History of Transcendentalism in New England* (1876); and a *Life of George Ripley* (1883).

FROTHINGHAM, RICHARD, an American historian, was born at Charlestown, Mass., Jan. 31, 1812. For several years he was connected with the *Boston Post*, and was active in politics as a Democrat. He was six times elected to the Massachusetts assembly and thrice mayor of Charlestown (1851–53). Besides a *History of Charlestown* (1848) and other local histories he published *Life of Gen. Joseph Warren* (1865) and *Rise of the Republic* (1872). He died Jan. 29, 1880.

FROUDE, JAMES ANTHONY, an English historian, was born April 23, 1818, at Totness, Devonshire, where his father was archdeacon. He studied at Oriel College, Oxford, graduating in 1840, and was afterwards chosen a fellow of Exeter College. He was then strongly influenced by the Tractarian movement and took deacon's orders in 1845. But he was soon repelled by the Romanizing tendency of his associates, and turned from theology to literature. He published *Shadows of the Clouds* (1847), a tale, and *Nemesis of Faith* (1849), both of which were condemned by the university. He then gave up his fellowship and devoted himself to writing for *Fraser's Magazine* and the *Westminster Review*. His great work, *The History of England from the Fall of Wolsey to the Defeat of the Spanish Armada*, began to appear in 1856, and was completed in twelve volumes in 1870. By close investigation and abundant use of the statute books and other documents of the time he endeavored to rehabilitate Henry VIII. as the champion of English independence, while he also transferred to Queen Elizabeth's ministers much of the credit which had been assigned to her by former historians. His work throughout is marked by an ultra-Protestant tone, which leads him to severe condemnation of Mary Queen of Scots. In 1869 he was made lord rector of the University of St. Andrews, where he delivered an address on *Calvinism* (1871). In 1872 he visited the United States and delivered a course of lectures on *The English in Ireland in the Eighteenth Century* (enlarged to 3 vols., 1873–74). In these he endeavored to justify the severe repressive measures of the English towards the Irish Roman Catholics on the ground of necessity. Several of Froude's contributions to the magazines were gathered under the title *Short Studies on Great Subjects* (1867), and he has also written biographical sketches of *Cæsar* (1882) and *Becket* (1883), brilliant in style but careless in the statement of fact. Froude was selected by Carlyle to be his literary executor, and in fulfilment of his trust has published *Carlyle's Reminiscences* (1882) and a *Life of Carlyle* (1884). The revelations made in these volumes of Carlyle's cynical judgment of his supposed friends and of his harsh treatment of his devoted wife provoked some censure of the biographer who gave publicity to the unpleasant facts. Yet in obedience to what he considered the interests of truth he persisted in the course which he had marked out.

FRUIT. Of the succulent fruits which constitute so large and important a portion of the food of man and the lower animals the variety is so great that we can here consider only the more important fruits of the temperate zone, with brief reference to the better known products of the torrid zone. Botanically every phanerogamous plant has its fruit, consisting of the seeds and seed-vessels with the other associated parts. But commercially this name is applied only to the succulent fruits, while the edible seeds are usually known as nuts and grains. The fruits of the great mass of plants do not come under either of these categories and have no commercial value. Of the fruits of the northern temperate zone those best known and most important are the apple, the pear, the peach, the apricot, the plum, the cherry, the quince, the fig, the melon, and the grape, with the several familiarly known berries, the strawberry, raspberry, blackberry, gooseberry, currant, whortleberry, cranberry, etc. To these may be added as fruits made very familiar in the North through commerce the orange, lemon, and lime, the banana, pineapple, and olive, most of the remaining fruits of the tropics being too perishable to bear transportation or not being sufficiently desirable to command a profitable sale.

The cultivation of most of these fruits has been extended very far beyond their native regions, and they are now raised wherever the climate and soil render this possible. In this outspreading the apple and pear take the lead, they being capable of cultivation through a very considerable range of climate, extending far into the cold regions of the north, while their geographical range extends around the whole circle of the north temperate zone. They have another quality which gives them great value: their varieties ripen from midsummer until late in the autumn. This quality is as yet shared by few fruits, though the seasonal range of the peach has been greatly increased by recent cultivation and selection.

The succulent fruits, which form so valuable a portion of the food of the human race, are, in their present state, largely a product of intelligent cultivation. In their wild state most of them are small in size and some of them unpleasant in taste, their present great size and luscious flavor being largely due to persistent selection of the best varieties. But this selection has been going on for ages, and, though it was of old mainly effected through hap-hazard choice, it had resulted in producing many improved varieties at the era of the early empires. At the opening of the fourth or fifth centuries of the Christian era we know that figs, peaches, apricots, oranges, citrons, apples, pears, cherries, plums, olives, quinces, grapes, and the principal berries and nuts were in successful cultivation, several varieties of most of them being known, chief among which were thirty-six varieties of the pear. Since that period the dissemination of the hardy fruits has been great, the whole civilized world being occupied. Yet the number of varieties did not greatly increase until after the opening of the present century, though during this century it has been enormously augmented. North America owes most of its cultivated fruits to the French settlers and the Romish missionaries, who were diligent in introducing European varieties. The English settlers also took some share in this work. Though indigenous species of cherries, plums, apples, etc., were found in this country, yet the orchards were early supplied with European varieties, and little effort has been made to develop the native fruits. The French settlers gave much attention to the apple and pear, these being introduced before 1640 and freely cultivated by 1650. The settlers of New England also had apples in bearing by 1639, and a nursery of imported apple-trees in 1640. The grape was introduced by Jesuit missionaries into California and elsewhere in the warmer regions of the country. But the European variety proved unsuitable to the colder climate of the North, and the native species of this fruit have been freely cultivated. The first record of commercial nurseries in America for the growth and sale of fruit-trees is about 1798. Many varieties were then known, especially of the apple, though but few as compared with those now cultivated. Early in the present century fruit-culture became an important agricultural interest, and has developed steadily until the present time. Of the varieties now known the United States enumerates nearly 2400 distinct kinds of apples and about 1300 pears, while peaches, grapes, and strawberries number each over 500. The total number of varieties of apples and pears in existence throughout the civilized world cannot be definitely stated, but has been enormously augmented by the careful and skilful operations of modern fruit-raisers.

The production of new varieties of fruits is now one of the most important of agricultural operations, and very great skill has been attained in its operation. This result is produced by sowing the seeds of carefully selected fruits, while the preservation of any valuable variety is attained by grafting and related processes, it never being sure that a seed will yield a copy of the parent variety. In addition to selecting the seeds of the best and hardiest varieties, the crossing of varieties is also carefully practised, both by growing unlike trees in propinquity in order that natural crossing may take place and by artificially impregnating the stigma of the flower of one tree with pollen taken from another. Probably the best results have arisen from natural impregnation. Of the names specially connected with this art the most prominent are those of Van Mons of Belgium and Knight of England. Van Mons for years constantly selected the best seeds of the pear, beginning with the wild fruit and continuing to select through eight generations, by which time he had produced a great deviation from the original. He had exceptional advantages, having in the early part of his experiments an orchard of as many as 80,000 trees to select from. He thus produced numerous useful varieties. In Knight's operations artificial crossing of varieties was very successfully practised. It is to these various processes that we owe the numerous and highly valuable varieties of the cultivated fruits now in the market. To this, however, must be added the preservation of what are known as *sports*, apparently chance variations, such as that which yielded the nectarine from the peach.

The soil and climate of America are very well adapted to fruit-culture, and it has not been extended as much as is desirable, nor has its practice been generally conducted with that skill that is essential to profitable agriculture. Good soil is needed for fruit-trees as well as for any other vegetable product, and the poor bearing and poor fruit, which many farmers are inclined to charge upon their trees, are really due to themselves. They starve their trees and expect a generous return. Fertilization is necessary for best results, though it must be cor

peach, apricot, and nectarine, for instance, will not bear too high fertilization, since it stimulates them to grow too late in the season and exposes them to damage by frost. Another requisite to the best results is the thinning of fruit in prolific seasons. This is very greatly neglected, yet if the tree be crowded the fruit will be small and deficient in flavor. Where practised it proves very efficacious, the fruit being made finer in quality while the total bulk is not usually reduced. It also permits the removal of the insect-stung or otherwise defective fruit, which, if left on the tree, robs the more perfect fruit of nutriment, while itself of little value. A third necessity is an incessant fight with the insect enemies by which many fruit-trees are attacked and with the diseases to which they are subject. All this entails much labor, but it is not unprofitable labor. The apple, the most easily managed of fruit-trees, yields under ordinary methods of cultivation a product worth from $50 to $100 per acre, yet with skilful culture may be made to yield $200 or $300. With pears, grapes, and strawberries more labor and skill are required, but the results are in accordance. Grapes may be made to yield from $300 to over $500 per acre; pears $500, and sometimes much more; while strawberries, which ordinarily yield $200 to $300, may with exceptional care and skill be pushed well up towards $1000 per acre.

Our ordinary fruits may be divided into the several classes of seed fruits, stone fruits, and berries. The second of these, comprising the plums, peaches, cherries, etc., are distinguished by possessing a single seed, of great size, and protected by a hard covering. They are marked off from the nuts by the fact that their seed is usually of unpleasant flavor, and is enclosed in a soft and juicy outer covering of highly agreeable taste. The seed fruits, the apples, pears, etc., differ from the above by the possession, in a central case, of several small seeds instead of one large one; while in the berries the seeds are disseminated throughout the flesh—a berry constituting usually an aggregation of many small fruits into one large one. Yet the variations of plants in this respect are so great that no strict classification can be made. In such fruits as the melons, for instance, or in the banana, the seeds are arranged in a manner that comes under none of the above categories.

Of the several fruits the apple has long held its own as the favorite fruit of temperate climates. Though less delicious than the pear or peach, its greater hardiness, ease of culture, and long-continued bearing power of the tree, have kept for it a steady reputation. It has also the advantage that it can be kept longer with less care than other fruits, and this forms a valuable addition to the food-supply of winter. With most other fruits preservation in a fresh state is difficult to perform, and is impossible with the more juicy species, with the exception of the grape. The apple and the pear continue to ripen after pulling. This is a notable characteristic of the pear, most varieties of which ripen with a finer flavor if plucked and ripened in the house. This is not the case to any marked extent with most of the fruits, though it is a useful property in several of the imported fruits, such as the orange, banana, and pineapple, which can be plucked unripe, and will ripen on the voyage.

It is not necessary here to enter into any description of the characteristics of our several fruits, either as to their form, flavor, or general character. It may simply be said that they not only vary greatly in size, shape, color, and general appearance, but also in degree of juiciness and of sweetness or acidity, while in certain instances bitterness, astringency, pungency, or some other unpleasant quality, detract from their value. The aroma also varies from pleasant to unpleasant, while nearly every fruit has some characteristic flavor which renders it easily distinguishable, and which may differ in degree of agreeableness. There is thus a great diversity in the characteristics of fruits as articles of diet, and an adaptation to every variety of human taste. As to degree of consistency we may pass from the firm flesh of the apple, through the successively more juicy textures of the pear and peach, to such fruits as the plum, the cherry, the orange, and the melon, with their abundance of juice. As to flavor of this juice the strawberry, cherry, and plum present marked grades of variation from sweetness to tartness, a variation which is strongly marked in the closely related orange and lemon. Many of these fruit acids are of the highest value in the preservation of health; this being particularly the case with the juice of the lemon and lime, while the growing popularity of the cranberry is doubtless due to the same causes. As a rule, indeed, the fruits of summer and autumn form a store of food specially adapted to those seasons, and the health of every community would undoubtedly be bettered by a free consumption of fruits in their proper season.

Within recent years the availability of the fruit supply has been greatly enhanced through several causes. One of these we have already adverted to, the production of earlier and later varieties, so as to extend the duration of the fruit season. This has been most efficient with the apple and pear, though it has been very effective also with the peach. With most other fruits there has been but little extension of the season of bearing. Yet in numerous cases commerce has overcome this difficulty, and the season of certain perishable fruits, such as the strawberry, for instance, has been extended by transport, beginning with the crop of the far South and ending with that of the far North. Commerce in fruits, indeed, has been so greatly developed that now the favorite tropical fruits, formerly scarce and dear in Northern markets, fairly compete with the product of our own trees in cheapness and abundance, and the orange, banana, pineapple, etc., are almost as familiar in our markets as the apple and pear. The ability of transporting the more perishable fruits has been greatly augmented by the use of rapid conveyances and of refrigerating apparatus in cars and vessels, so that the fruits of California are now transported in abundance to the Atlantic States, while the peaches of New Jersey and Delaware, once confined to their immediate neighborhood, are now spread far through the North and West. But we are by no means confined to the consumption of fruits in their seasons, or the preservation of a few species in a fresh state beyond their seasons. The methods of preserving fruits for winter use have greatly extended and improved of late years and to these methods some attention is here demanded.

Fruit Preserving.—The old methods of preserving fruit, beyond that of keeping it in a fresh state, were two, drying by solar heat, and preservation by the curative properties of acids, alcohol, saltpetre, salt, sugar, etc. These gave rise to the pickles, the brandied fruits, the marmalades, the candied and sugar-preserved fruits of old housekeepers, processes which are still largely practised, though not so extensively now as formerly. The drying, as then practised, was a very crude and unsatisfactory process, the sliced fruit, often poorly selected and prepared, being exposed not only to the sun and wind, but to dust and insects, and yielding a hard and blackened product that needed faith and good teeth in its mastication. With care and skill sun-dried fruit was rendered more palatable, yet the process was never a very effectual one as applied to our apples, peaches, etc. With fruits dried whole, such as grapes and plums, it yields better results, and currants, raisins, and prunes are thus produced, though oven-drying is partly employed. The cheapness of the drying process of preservation has brought it into more vogue of late years, and solar heat has been replaced by more rapid artificial agents. The effect of sun-drying is seldom rapid enough to prevent discoloration and some degree of decay, and artificial heat, in closed receptacles, has taken its place. The oven-drying, as at first practised, was ineffective from lack of circulation of the air, the warm, damp air rather cooking than drying the fruit. This was succeeded by placing the cut fruit on trays in a chamber so constructed that a draught of hot air could be sent from the stove up through the chamber. This proved effective if care was taken to change the trays of fruit so that they should dry equally. In the important Alden evaporating process all this is done mechanically, and the temperature and degree of moisture nicely graduated to produce the best results. This apparatus consists of an evaporating chamber, of some 5 feet square by 20 feet high, provided with an endless chain, by whose movement the trays of fruit, which are introduced at the top, sink slowly downwards, and are taken out fully dried at the bottom. There are a steam-coil and a blower below, the current of air from the blower being heated to the desired temperature by the coil, this being generally from 160° to 195° Fahr. The blast is never quite dry, some degree of moisture being considered necessary to prevent too rapid drying. This air enters the chamber at the bottom at maximum heat and dryness, and escapes at the top reduced in temperature and loaded with the moisture which it has extracted from the fruit. Thus the trays of fruit when first introduced meet a moist, warm air, which extracts some moisture, but not with sufficient rapidity to harden or discolor the surface. As the trays descend they meet the air in a warmer and drier state, while they yield their reduced moisture at about the same rate. Reaching the bottom their small remnant of water is extracted by the hot and dry air at this point, and the fruit issues with unchanged color and no induration of the surface. This process has been applied to a great variety of fruits and vegetables, and yields a product which, when again soaked in water, is hardly distinguishable from the original fruit.

Yet the most recent suggestion in relation to fruit drying is that heat is unnecessary and injurious as a curative agent, causing a partial destruction of flavor and some degree of fermentative change in the fruit. This has led to the cold-blast system, in which the fruit is exposed to a current of dry air at a low temperature. The air employed is deprived of its moisture by chemical agents, and kept at a temperature of from 32° to 60° Fahr. The process otherwise resembles the above, but it has a great advantage in economy over the hot-air process, while the dried fruit is said to retain its flavor, color, and other virtues in almost perfection, and to remain good for an indefinite period.

Another and highly valuable preservative process, which has grown to enormous proportions in recent years, is that of canning or preservation in air-tight tin cans or glass jars. This process, applied to every description of perishable food, requires that sufficient heat should be used to destroy all germinal particles capable of setting up fermentation or putrefaction, which the air or the fruit may contain. Being made air-tight while thus heated the causes of decay are effectually removed, and the food may be kept intact for an indefinite period. It is, of course, partly cooked by the heat applied, yet its natural qualities are very well retained, and if cooked on removal from the can it can scarcely be distinguished from fresh viands when cooked. In preserving fruit by this process sugar is generally added, but no more than is necessary to impart an agreeable flavor.

The preservation of fruits and other materials by this method has extended until it is now an industry of great importance, and, as a means of providing vessels with preserved food or of sending the fruits of any country to foreign regions, it is far in advance of any other process employed. We have no statistics as to the value of fruits alone thus preserved, but the canned and preserved fruits and vegetables prepared for sale in the United States in 1880 were valued at $17,599,576. These were in addition to the very great quantities similarly preserved for home use, which, if added, would greatly swell this sum.

In 1870 the value of orchard products in the United States was, reduced from gold rates to ordinary rates, about $38,000,000. In 1880 it amounted to $50,876,154, showing a very marked increase. Of this sum New York is credited with $8,409,794, Pennsylvania with $4,862,826, Ohio with $3,576,242, Illinois with $3,502,583, and Indiana, Michigan, and California with over $2,000,000 each. In some States, particularly in the South, the increase from 1870 to 1880 was in a great percentage, as also in some of the rapidly settling States of the extreme West. (C. M.)

FUEL. The substances employed in America for fuel are mineral coals (anthracite, bituminous, and lignite), coke, wood, charcoal, mineral oils, gas, both natural and manufactured, and to a limited extent peat and residuary products from the distillation of coal, wood, or oils. Indicating the dependence upon mineral fuel is the fact that the mining of coal is the most extensive single industry in the United States.

See Vol. IX. p. 709 Am. ed. (p. 807 Edin. ed.).

The relative consumption of the mineral fuels may be judged from the following statistics. In 1884 there were mined 33,175,756 gross tons of anthracite coal, and 73,730,530 gross tons of bituminous coal, lignite, etc. About ten per cent. of the bituminous coal was made into 4,350,000 gross tons of coke, and a considerable amount is also converted into a gaseous form in producers for consumption in furnaces used in manufacturing industries. Another considerable quantity of bituminous coal is made into illuminating gas, the resultant coke and some of the gas being used as fuel.

For domestic purposes wood and anthracite or bituminous coal are chiefly depended upon, some charcoal, particularly for cooking, is used, and gas is growing in favor for both heating and cooking in the cities. For steam-generation local considerations affect the choice of fuel, and anthracite coal, bituminous coal, and wood are largely used. In manufacturing, all kinds of fuels are utilized. Where a flame is required, bituminous coal, gas made from it, natural gas, or wood are preferred. Where flame is not an object, anthracite coal,

TABLE OF FUEL VALUES.

Common name.	Region.	Fuel Value. By volume—per cubic decimeter.	Fuel Value. By weight—per kilogram.	Order by weight.	Percentage in Dry Woods. Ash.	Hydrogen.	Carbon.	Oxygen.	Hydrogen combined with oxygen.	Excess of hydrogen.	Specific gravity.	Weight of a cubic foot in pounds.
Mountain Mahogany	Interior Pacific	4,234.06	4,052.90	34	1.20	5.45	52.14	41.21	5.15	0.30	1.0447	65.10
Long-Leaved Pine	S. Atlantic Coast	4,113.33	5,545.82	1	0.36	7.41	56.61	32.72	4.21	3.39	0.7617	46.22
Shellbark Hickory	Atlantic	3,851.17	4,078.76	28	0.73	6.49	49.67	43.12	5.39	1.10	0.9442	58.84
Chestnut Oak	Atlantic	3,843.69	3,997.32	38	0.34	6.33	49.50	43.74	5.47	0.86	0.7114	44.33
Pitch Pine	Atlantic Coast	3,472.26	5,491.47	2	1.12	7.19	59.00	32.68	4.07	3.11	0.6323	39.40
Pignut Hickory	Atlantic	3,392.12	3,922.89	43	0.74	6.23	48.98	44.00	5.50	0.73	0.8647	53.88
White Hickory	Atlantic	3,380.57	3,904.11	45	1.04	5.93	49.69	43.35	5.42	0.51	0.8659	53.96
Pitch Pine	S. Atlantic Coast	3,363.40	4,418.55	8	0.16	6.22	53.33	40.29	5.04	1.19	0.7612	47.44
Mesquit	Texas to Cal.	3,291.21	4,352.30	11	2.05	6.61	51.08	40.26	5.03	1.58	0.7562	47.12
Overcup Oak	S. Atlantic	3,268.92	4,105.65	25	0.58	6.75	49.22	43.45	5.43	1.32	0.7962	49.61
White Elm	Atlantic	3,247.02	4,191.87	19	0.74	6.57	50.35	42.34	5.29	1.28	0.7746	48.27
White Oak	Atlantic	3,197.41	4,187.33	21	0.24	6.59	50.44	42.73	5.34	1.25	0.7636	46.58
Spanish Oak	S. Atlantic	3,193.28	4,055.48	33	0.29	6.14	50.58	42.99	5.37	0.77	0.7874	49.07
Cedar	Pacific	3,143.57	4,567.61	6	0.88	6.08	54.97	38.12	4.76	1.27	0.6852	42.70
Bitter Pecan	S. Atlantic	3,140.33	4,073.59	30	1.90	6.60	49.16	43.05	5.38	1.22	0.7709	48.04
Yellow Pine	S. Atlantic	3,091.82	5,062.75	3	0.20	6.91	56.64	36.25	4.53	2.38	0.6107	38.06
Sugar Maple	Atlantic	3,091.37	4,345.48	12	0.56	6.61	51.55	41.28	5.16	1.45	0.7114	44.33
Red Oak	Atlantic	3,062.08	4,075.16	29	0.15	6.62	49.49	43.74	5.47	1.15	0.7514	46.72
Persimmon	Atlantic	2,970.45	3,781.61	50	0.77	6.44	47.37	45.42	5.67	0.77	0.7855	48.96
Larch or Tamarack	N. Atlantic	2,937.46	4,182.04	22	0.37	6.08	51.91	41.79	5.22	0.81	0.7024	43.77
Butternut Hickory	Atlantic	2,868.42	3,903.25	46	1.03	6.91	49.71	42.29	5.41	0.50	0.7336	45.71
Locust	Allegheny Mts.	2,822.99	3,890.02	48	0.23	6.17	49.19	44.41	5.55	0.62	0.7257	45.22
Beech	Atlantic	2,795.34	3,895.04	47	0.54	6.11	49.27	44.08	5.51	0.61	0.7175	44.71
Pecan	S. Atlantic	2,768.72	3,954.75	41	0.95	6.15	49.51	43.39	5.42	0.73	0.7001	43.63
Black-Jack	S. Atlantic	2,693.51	3,713.81	54	1.37	5.73	48.56	44.32	5.54	0.19	0.7280	45.13
Water Oak	S. Atlantic	2,655.62	3,718.07	53	0.53	5.75	48.73	44.69	5.58	0.17	0.7143	44.51
White Ash	Atlantic	2,552.34	4,217.42	17	0.30	6.93	49.73	43.04	5.38	1.55	0.6399	39.19
Black Oak	Atlantic	2,505.04	3,774.60	51	0.15	6.09	48.78	44.96	5.62	0.37	0.6875	43.86
White Oak	N. Pacific Coast	2,594.31	3,667.39	55	0.33	5.73	48.56	45.38	5.67	0.06	0.7074	44.08
Canoe Birch	N. Atlantic	2,583.66	4,101.41	26	0.23	7.12	48.26	44.37	5.55	1.58	0.6297	39.24
White or Gray Birch	N. Atlantic Coast	2,509.00	4,073.05	31	0.29	6.49	49.77	43.45	5.43	1.06	0.6160	38.05
Yellow Pine	Pacific	2,441.24	4,600.04	5	0.31	7.02	52.60	40.77	5.10	2.00	0.5307	33.07
Sycamore	Atlantic	2,406.89	4,071.83	32	0.57	5.83	51.45	42.15	5.27	0.57	0.5911	36.88
Nut Pine	Interior Pacific	2,270.77	4,149.04	23	0.83	6.39	50.48	43.30	5.41	1.10	0.5473	34.11
Sweet or Red Gum	Atlantic	2,255.24	4,016.46	37	0.48	5.85	50.99	42.68	5.33	0.52	0.5615	34.99
Scrub or Gray Pine	N. Atlantic	2,152.66	4,393.18	9	0.19	6.29	52.93	40.59	5.07	1.22	0.4900	30.54
Black Pine	Allegheny Mts.	2,054.73	3,995.80	39	0.30	5.78	51.07	42.85	5.35	0.43	0.5163	32.05
Red or Norway Pine	N. Atlantic	2,051.75	4,226.05	16	0.20	6.07	52.18	41.55	5.19	0.88	0.4855	30.26
Loblolly Pine	S. Atlantic	2,031.75	4,087.20	27	0.25	6.23	50.60	42.92	5.36	0.85	0.4971	30.98
Jersey or Scrub Pine	Atlantic	2,008.20	4,126.15	24	0.26	6.30	50.74	42.70	5.34	0.96	0.4867	30.33
Redwood	California Coast	1,985.50	4,191.47	20	0.13	6.01	52.10	41.70	5.21	0.79	0.4737	29.52
Black Walnut	Atlantic	1,964.56	3,857.26	49	0.56	6.00	49.28	44.16	5.52	0.48	0.5145	32.06
Cypress	S. Atlantic	1,921.63	4,705.27	4	0.40	6.54	54.98	38.08	4.76	1.68	0.4084	24.45
Cottonwood	Atlantic	1,906.42	4,242.15	15	0.65	6.26	51.64	41.45	5.18	1.08	0.4494	28.02
Chestnut	Atlantic	1,868.25	4,042.96	36	0.13	5.70	51.74	42.43	5.30	0.40	0.4621	28.80
Digger or Bull Pine	California	1,804.29	3,982.97	40	0.42	6.04	50.22	43.32	5.41	0.63	0.4530	28.23
Tamarack	Pacific	1,791.33	4,019.13	36	0.37	6.22	50.05	43.36	5.42	0.80	0.4457	27.78
Sugar Pine	California	1,785.49	4,419.31	7	0.19	6.40	52.85	40.56	5.07	1.33	0.4040	25.18
Red or Yellow Fir	Pacific	1,766.32	4,354.84	10	0.03	6.42	52.32	41.23	5.15	1.27	0.4054	25.23
Hemlock	N. Atlantic	1,724.26	4,208.58	18	0.48	5.91	52.38	41.23	5.15	0.76	0.4097	25.52
Aspen	Atlantic & Pacific	1,624.64	4,292.31	13	0.74	6.58	51.13	41.55	5.19	1.39	0.3785	23.59
Black Spruce	N. Atlantic	1,614.11	3,949.37	42	0.30	6.58	48.45	44.67	5.58	1.00	0.4087	25.47
White Pine	N. Atlantic	1,489.03	4,272.69	14	0.12	6.06	52.55	41.25	5.15	0.93	0.3465	21.72
Yellow Poplar	Atlantic	1,425.57	3,744.61	52	0.27	5.43	47.29	46.01	5.75	0.68	0.3807	23.72
Yellow or White Cedar	N. Atlantic	1,411.57	3,917.77	44	0.37	6.37	48.80	44.46	5.56	0.82	0.3603	22.45

See also Marcus Bull's Tables and Chevandier's analysis in the article on CHARCOAL.

coke made from bituminous coal, or charcoal are preferred. In the manufacture of iron, statistics prepared by the American Iron and Steel Association show that in 1884 the consumption of fuel was as follows:

	Gross Tons.
Anthracite coal	1,973,305
Bituminous coal	4,226,986
Coke from bituminous coal	3,833,170
Charcoal (62,110,660 bushels, equivalent to)	517,600
Wood not accounted for.	

In 1884 the estimated consumption of natural gas for fuel purposes was equivalent to the heating capacity of nearly 2,000,000 gross tons of mineral fuel. In cities the residual coke from the manufacture of illuminating gas is purchased for minor industrial purposes.

Artificial fuels are simply fine particles of coal cemented together by clays, by tarry matter, or by heat and pressure. The fine anthracite coal is generally called culm; fine bituminous coal, slack, vreeze, or braize.

The census statistics for 1880 show that 32,375,074 persons used wood for domestic purposes, consuming 140,537,439 cords, and that the total consumption was in that year 145,778,137 cords of wood; probably 7,500,000 cords more were cut and made into charcoal. It is estimated that the annual fuel consumption of the United States is equivalent to from 3 to 4 gross tons of coal per inhabitant, *i. e.*, reducing wood and other fuels to approximate calorific value of coal. The U. S. Census of 1880, Vol. IX., page 489, illustrated by a colored map the predominant character of fuel used in various sections of the United States. The accompanying table of fuel values was prepared by Prof. C. S. Sargent, special agent of the census.

The moisture was determined by drying the wood at 100° C., until its weight becomes sensibly constant, when the calculations were made on the dry wood. The results contain a slight constant error, rarely amounting to one per cent., arising from the fact that the nitrogen in the wood was not determined. The column headed "Hydrogen combined with oxygen" is found by dividing the amount in the column headed "Oxygen" by eight, and represents the hydrogen that may be considered as already combined with oxygen in the form of water, and is therefore useless for fuel.

The woods are arranged in the order of relative value by equal volumes; the figures in the column "Order by weight" show the order of relative value by equal weights.

It is to be regretted that in this table the percentages of water driven off when being dried were not noted, for, as ordinarily obtained, the hygroscopic water in various woods would affect their relative fuel values even more than the theoretical values as given in the table. Experiments by Shindler show that the percentage of water in winter, when the tree was dormant, and in the spring when sap was flowing, was:—Ash, 28.8 and 38.6; sycamore, 33.6 and 40.3; white fir, 52.7 and 61.0. Even after six months' air-drying felled timber frequently contains from 20 to 40 per cent. of hygrometric water.

See CHARCOAL, COAL, COKE, GAS, etc. (J. B.)

FUGITIVE SLAVE LAWS. The Constitution of the United States contains the following provision: "No person held to service or labor in one State, under the laws thereof, escaping into another, shall, in consequence of any law or regulation therein, be discharged from such service or labor, but shall be delivered up on claim of the party to whom such service or labor may be due." Article IV., § 2, ¶ 2.

It is worthy of notice that the word *slave* does not occur either here or in any other part of the Constitution. The terms used apply as properly to indentured apprentices as to slaves. In Northern newspapers, down to 1840 and later, might be seen advertisements of runaway apprentices as conspicuously if not as often as notices of runaway slaves appeared in the Southern newspapers. That slaves were had in view in the framing of the article we know, but care was taken not to avow it. Equally noticeable is the absence of any terms even remotely suggesting the idea that the fugitive might be regarded as property. On the contrary, he is described as a *person* from whom service or labor is *due*.

If a person of good understanding, but without technical knowledge of law, were to read this paragraph of the Constitution, it would hardly occur to him that the words convey any power or impose any duty on Congress. That body is not named nor referred to. The terms used seem to imply only State action, and to define the duty that one State owes to another. Congress, however, at a very early period, assumed jurisdiction over the subject. The first fugitive act, passed in 1793, declared that whenever a person held to service, etc., shall escape into another State or Territory, the person to whom such service may be due, his agent or attorney, may seize or arrest such fugitive and take him before any judge of a court of the United States, or any magistrate of a county, city, or town, and upon proof to the satisfaction of the judge or magistrate, whether by oral testimony or sworn affidavit, that service is owed as claimed, the judge or magistrate shall give a certificate thereof to the claimant, which shall be sufficient warrant to remove the fugitive. This act, it is plain, was framed in the sole interest of masters. It provided no safeguard for the rights of the person claimed as a slave. The Constitution guarantees Amendment V.) that "no person shall be deprived of life, *liberty*, or property without due process of law," *i. e.*, of course, common law; and that (Amendment VI.) in suits at common law, where the matter in controversy shall exceed twenty dollars, the right of trial by jury shall be preserved. But when a man's personal liberty is at stake, no jury-trial is provided. And as jurisdiction was given not only to courts but to petty magistrates, many of whom were ignorant and some corrupt, and the certificate of a Justice Shallow was as conclusive as that of a Justice Story, it was almost inevitable that under cover of this loosely drawn statute free colored people would be kidnapped. There were many complaints of such outrages, especially in Pennsylvania and other border States. Some of the States passed laws in restraint of such abuses. Massachusetts enacted a law to secure trial by jury in all cases in which the right of personal liberty was in question. Pennsylvania passed a law against kidnaping. It was a case arising under that statute which, carried to the Supreme Court of the United States, led to a decision that had important consequences—the case entitled *Prigg* vs. *Pennsylvania*. The opinion of a majority of the court, as given by Justice Story, discarding the cautious reserve of the Constitution, speaks articulately of "slaves," alludes to them as the "property" of their masters, and alleges that the clause of the Constitution on this subject was intended to secure owners of slaves in the possession of their property. It was held that the owner of a slave was clothed with entire authority in every State in the Union to seize and recapture his slave whenever he could do it without a breach of the peace or illegal violence. No legal process was necessary, but the constitutional provision was to that extent self-executing; that the act of 1793 was constitutional, and superceded all State legislation upon the same subject; that the Constitution lays on the States no obligation to provide remedies, and confers on them no power to legislate on the subject. Two of the judges dissented from the doctrine that a claimant could seize his "property" without legal process, and two from the denial of the right and duty of the States in the premises.

It would be out of place here to discuss the merits of this decision. Its effect was soon seen. The States willingly complied with the mandate to keep their hands off this business. Some forbade their courts to hear such claims, forbidding also under severe penalties their officers to arrest and their gaolers to detain alleged fugitives from slavery. An increasing number were equally unofficious, preferring, indeed, to help the fugitive onward in the direction of the North Star, by "the underground railroad." (See ABOLITIONISTS.) These developments caused no small irritation among slaveholders, which led, in connection with other matters of sectional agitation, to the enactment of the Fugitive Slave Act of 1850.

This statute, to fill the vacuum made by the withdrawal of State agencies, conferred on commissioners appointed by the United States courts the powers given to judges and magistrates. Additional commissioners were to be from time to time appointed. Commissioners were given concurrent jurisdiction with judges. Marshals and deputy-marshals were required to obey and execute warrants and other processes, under penalty of one thousand dollars for refusing or neglecting; and, if a fugitive should escape after arrest, the marshal or deputy was subject to be prosecuted on his official bond for the full value of the service or labor claimed to be due—in plain English, for his value as a slave. Commissioners were empowered to appoint other persons to make arrests, having power also to summon bystanders to help. Fugitives arrested under or without warrant were to be taken forthwith before a judge or commissioner, who should hear and determine the case by summary process. It was provided that an affidavit alleging service due, and an escape, with a description of the person, might be sworn to, and certified by any magistrate under seal, and such seal should be sufficient to establish the competency of the proof. Provision was made for military aid to the marshal if needed, and such extraordinary expenses were made a charge upon the public treasury. As a fitting climax to the whole, the commissioner was to be paid a larger fee for a certificate of extradition than for a discharge.

The act, it will have been observed, made the sworn statement of the claimant or his agent conclusive proof. The commissioner was not to inquire whether "labor or service was due." It was enough that the claimant said under oath that it was due. The claimant was his own judge and jury; the commissioner and marshal were his ministerial officers to do his bidding. A curious commentary on the law was made by the first case of its enforcement. The alleged fugitive was surrendered to the agent of the alleged owner. But when he reached his destination in Virginia the claimant discovered that it was a case of mistaken identity, and the man was returned to his Northern home, happy in having to do with a man of justice and honor. To how many would the bait to their cupidity have been a temptation too great to be resisted, especially considering that the kidnapping would have been entirely according to law! In a case that occurred in Boston the alleged fugitive offered to prove his freedom, but the commissioner decided that the evidence could not be admitted. He could only inquire whether the person before him was the person described in the affidavit. That being found, extradition was decreed as of course.

It could not be deemed strange that such a law, enforced with such contempt of all the rules of common justice and of the feelings of humanity, created intense excitement. If more stirring events had not caused a more intense commotion, it may be doubted whether its enforcement would have often called attention to its peculiar features. It was as much the point of honor as the pecuniary grievance that moved men to action. It was observed that the slaveholders of the Gulf States, who very seldom suffered loss from the flight of their "property," were more excited on the subject than they of the border States, who bore the chief brunt of that misfortune. The Fugitive Slave Act bore its part in the prelude of the civil war, and passed away with the system of bondage from which it sprung.

References: *U. S. Statutes at Large*, 1793, 1850; *Prigg vs. Pennsylvania*, 16 *Peters' Reports*, 539; *Sumner's Speech on the Fugitive Slave Bill*; *Wilson's History of the Rise and Fall of the Slave Power*. (L. E. S.)

FULLER, MARGARET. See OSSOLI.

FULLER, RICHARD (1804–1876), an American clergyman, was born at Beaufort, S. C., April 22, 1804. He graduated at Harvard College in 1824, studied law, and, being admitted to the bar, began practice in his native town. In 1832 he was ordained, and became pastor of the Baptist church in Beaufort. He preached also in many parts of South Carolina and Georgia. His eloquence gave him a prominent place in his denomination, and in 1847 he became pastor of a church in Baltimore. Here he labored until his death, Oct. 20, 1876. He published *Letters on the Roman Chancery* (1840), addressed to Bishop England; and *Correspondence on Domestic Slavery* (1845), a controversy with Rev. Dr. Wayland. He also published several sermons, and assisted in editing the *Religious Herald*.

FULTON, JOHN, an American Episcopal clergyman, was born at Glasgow, Scotland, April 2, 1834. He was educated at Aberdeen, and came to the United States in 1853. He was ordained deacon in 1857, and priest in 1858, and became assistant to Bishop L. Polk in Trinity Church, New Orleans. He was banished from that city by Gen. B. F. Butler in 1862, for disobeying orders with reference to church services. After the war he became rector of St. George's Church, St. Louis, Mo. He has frequently been a delegate to the General Convention of the P. E. Church, serving on the committee on canons. In 1868 he received the degree of D. D. from the University of Georgia; and in 1881 that of LL. D. from the University of Alabama. He has published *Letters on Christian Unity* (1868); *Index Canonum* (1873); *Laws of Marriage* (1883); and has in preparation a *Documentary History of the P. E. Church in the Confederate States*.

FUMIGATION (Lat. *fumus*, smoke) is the process by which smoke, or certain gases, are produced and applied, (1) for the destruction of offensive odors; (2) for the extermination of vermin; (3) for the testing of drains or sewers for defects; (4) for the disinfection of ships, rooms, or clothing suspected of being infected with contagious or infectious disease.

(1.) To remove offensive odors, papers or rags may be burned, or pastilles made of charcoal and aromatic barks or spices. This has as a result simply to substitute a pleasant for a disagreeable odor, and has no disinfecting power whatsoever.

(2.) To destroy insects which attack and injure plant-life tobacco-smoke is frequently employed. For the extermination of vermin that infest beds, and out-of-the-way places, the fumes of burning sulphur are best adapted.

(3.) In testing house-drains to discover if any defects exist, the smoke from tarred- or sulphur-paper may be employed. One of the best contrivances for this purpose is the "asphyxiator," which has for a considerable time been in use in Great Britain, and has lately been introduced into the United States. It has enabled health-officers to detect leaks in drains and sewer-pipes, when all other means had failed. It consists of a combustion-chamber in which the prepared paper is ignited, and from which, by the rotation of a fan, the resulting smoke is forced into the pipes to be tested. If defects exist by which sewer-air could escape, they will be discovered by the emitted smoke.

(4.) For the destruction of infectious material, which is the only true disinfection, by fumigation, several substances may be employed. Among these the most important are (a) bromine, (b) iodine, (c) chlorine, and (d) sulphur. (a) *Bromine.* A solution of bromine in bromide of potassium exposed in saucers gives off vapors which are disinfectant in the proportion of 1 part to 500, provided that the air be moist and the exposure to the action of the vapors be continued not less than three hours. This method was employed during the war of the rebellion, but as bromine is a substance which cannot be safely nor easily manipulated, and as its disinfecting power is no greater than that of other substances which are without these disadvantages, it will rarely, if ever, be employed. (b) *Iodine.* The vapor of iodine may be produced by placing it upon a heated plate. It is a true disinfectant in the strength of 1 to 500, and an exposure of two hours. It condenses easily and is not readily diffused, for which reasons it is not well adapted for the disinfection of infected premises. (c) *Chlorine.* This gas may be produced by either of the following methods: First, to 4 parts of common salt and 1 part of binoxide of manganese add 2 parts, by weight, of water, and the same amount of sulphuric acid; second, to 1 part of powdered binoxide of manganese add 4 parts, by weight, of strong hydrochloric acid; third, to 3 parts of chloride of lime (bleaching powder, calx chlorinata) add 1 part of strong sulphuric acid. Chlorine decomposes sulphuretted hydrogen and ammonium sulphide, and destroys all organic matter with which it comes in contact. It is an efficient disinfectant in the proportion of 1 to 100, when the air and the articles to be disinfected are moist, and the exposure lasts one hour. The vigorous bleaching power, however, of chlorine makes its use for the disinfection of colored fabrics impracticable. It has been extensively employed in the disinfection of ships, but its intensely irritating quality, together with its bleaching power, has prevented its general use in household disinfection. (d) *Sulphur.* When sulphur is burned in the presence of an abundance of air, fumes are given off consisting of sulphurous oxide or anhydride (SO_2), also known as sulphurous acid gas. The advantages which this substance possesses are so many that, in fumigation as practised for the destruction of infection, it has almost entirely supplanted all other gaseous disinfectants. Sulphur melts at 111.5° C. (232.7° Fahr.), and takes fire at 260° C. (482° Fahr.), burning with a purplish-blue flame and forming SO_2. In experiments which have been made to test its action upon various fabrics it has been found that in exceptional cases only are the colors faded. So seldom, indeed, does this happen as practically to make it of no moment; fabrics colored with induline seem to be the most altered. Life, whether animal or vegetable, is destroyed by this gas; flies, when confined in traps in closed rooms, being killed in twenty-two minutes, while when at liberty to seek the least exposed places life may be prolonged for one hour and forty-five minutes. Ants and Croton bugs (*Ectobia Germanica*) are killed in about the same time. The temperature of the air of the room is raised 25° or 50° Fahr., according to the amount of sulphur burned. Theoretically, in order to completely burn out all the oxygen of 1000 cubic feet of air, there would be required 15.577 lbs. of sulphur. Experimentally, however, one observer was able to burn only 4.2 lbs., while another succeeded in entirely consuming 18.7 lbs. per 1000 cubic feet. In the latter case the room in which the experiment was conducted could not have been tightly closed. In the process of combustion of sulphur, the SO_2 formed takes up moisture from the air, and a portion of it is converted into sulphuric acid (H_2SO_4), the amount produced depending upon the quantity of moisture present. From the experiments of Koch, Wolffhügel, and Sternberg, it has been definitely ascertained that SO_2 will not destroy spores, and that for all diseases due to spore-bearing germs, therefore, sulphur-fumigation is not an efficient mode of disinfection; while, on the other hand, it will destroy all infectious material not containing spores. Inasmuch as it is the generally accepted theory that the ordinary contagious diseases which affect mankind, small-pox, scarlet fever, measles, diphtheria, etc., depend upon micro-organisms which do not produce spores, and especially in view of the almost unanimous opinion of health-officials throughout the world as to the efficacy of this method of disinfection in the diseases named, we may, in conjunction with other means, cleanliness and the use of germicide solutions, rely upon the gas produced by burning sulphur, as an efficient agent in the destruction of the infection of these diseases; while, for all diseases which depend upon spore-producing germs, chlorine may be employed.

The details of the process of sulphur-fumigation are as follows: All living things, whether plant or animal, should first be removed from the apartment to be fumigated. If it is a room which has been occupied by a patient with a contagious disease, the bedding, body-clothing, carpets, and other articles should be so opened and exposed that the fumes from the burning sulphur can come readily in contact with all portions thereof. All cracks, fire-places, or other openings by which the gases can find an exit must be tightly closed so as to prevent their escape. In an iron pot, or other metallic vessel without soldered joints, should be placed equal parts of brimstone, broken into small pieces, and flowers of sulphur. The quantity of both should be not less than three pounds for every thousand cubic feet of air-space contained in the apartment. If this is of considerable size or length, a number of pots or kettles should be provided, the total amount of sulphur burned to be based upon the proportion of three pounds to each thousand cubic feet of air-space to be fumigated. Everything being in readiness, sufficient alcohol should be poured on the sulphur to moisten it, and a lighted match applied. As soon as it is seen that combustion is well under way, the operator should at once withdraw, as the fumes are exceedingly irritating to the air-passages, and tightly close the door, plugging keyhole and cracks to prevent escape of the gas. At the end of twelve hours the process is completed, and the room may be again opened. This must be done with caution, there being enough of the gas still present to cause suffocation, if breathed deeply into the lungs. If a window can be opened from the outside, the fumes will find their way readily into the open air; if this cannot be done, a cloth wet with water may be held over the mouth and nose, and a hurried entrance made and a window thrown open from the inside; or, if this is impracticable, all the windows of the house may be opened, and then the door of the room, and the fumes will soon escape until the apartment is well freed from the gas; no one entering it should inhale the air, on account of its irritative effects. The same plan of fumigation is to be adopted in the case of ships, care being taken that all planks are removed which are so placed as to prevent full and free admission of the gas to all parts. Yellow-fever has been known to break out in a ship even after this fumigation, owing to the presence of filth between the ship's timbers, doubtless containing the germs of the disease, and the infection was not eradicated until this was removed. At the quarantine grounds of New Orleans sulphurous acid gas is forced into the hold of the ship by a powerful blower, thus, it is claimed, causing the penetration of the gas to parts which, in the ordinary fumigation, would not be reached.

(J. H. R.)

FUR. Since pre-historic times the skins of many of the mammalia of frigid regions, with their cold-defying layer of fine hair, have been worn by the inhabitants of these severe climates as a protection against the wintry chill. Throughout historical times the finer, rarer, and more beautiful of these furs have been articles of luxury or ostentation, and we have abundant records of their use in early China, in the ancient empires of the West, and throughout the Middle Ages down to the present time. The north of Europe and Asia long supplied the principal furs, the Baltic ports being the centres of distribution. But the discovery of America, with its very numerous fur-bearing animals, changed the current of the fur-trade, and very greatly added to the annual supply. Though the highly esteemed sables and ermines came only from Europe and Asia, yet America had the beaver, then held in high estimation, the martin, the mink, several choice varieties of the fox, the raccoon, opossum, muskrat, and other small fur-bearing animals, with the valuable fur-seal, and several larger animals with skins of marketable value, so that it offered a rich field for adventure in this lucrative trade.

See Vol. IX. p. 734 Am. ed. (p. 836 Edin. ed.)

At an early date the Dutch East India Company established an active fur-trade within the limits of the United States, centring at New Amsterdam and some other points. This was maintained from 1609 to nearly the end of that century. During the same period the French of Canada displayed great enterprise in the same trade. The Indians were induced to seek energetically for furs, and to part with them for a trifling compensation. The French themselves became very expert as hunters. There were never more daring and active adventurers than the *voyageurs* and *couriers des bois*, or wood-rangers, of the French fur-trade. They were the pioneers of the settlements of Northern America, penetrating into the wildest regions, braving all perils, and paving the way for more quiet settlers. They adopted the habits of the Indians, grew in time vagrant and vagabondish, and obtained an undesirable reputation. Forts were established in the Indian Territory to protect the trade, the one at Mackinaw becoming an important centre, while the enterprise of the traders extended to Hudson's Bay in the north, far to the west, and southward along the Mississippi Valley.

The British fur-trade in these regions was inaugurated by the charter granted in 1670 by Charles II. to Prince Rupert, the Duke of Albemarle, and others, giving them control of the Hudson's Straits territory. From this originated the Hudson's Bay Company, which for nearly two centuries held a monopoly of the fur-trade of Northern British America. It claimed all the territory north of a line from Hudson's Bay to the Pacific, with the exception of that occupied by the Russians and French, held this territory with a despotic control, and established a highly successful and lucrative business in spite of the persistent opposition of the French fur-hunters. This opposition gave rise in 1783 to an association of Canadian merchants, centring in Montreal, known as the North-west Company. This soon became a powerful competitor, its factories reaching the Pacific coast by 1805. In 1813 it gained possession of Astoria, on the Columbia River, with the property of the Pacific Fur Company. The hostility of the two great companies increased, until for two years they were in a state of actual war. These difficulties ended in 1821, in which year the two companies united into one, under the title of the Hudson's Bay Company. The license of this company expired in 1858. It is still an active competitor for the trade, but its profits are reduced by the activity of private enterprise.

The Russian American Fur Company of Alaska carried on a very extensive trade for a long period, but transferred its rights to the United States on the purchase of Alaska by the latter country in 1867. The most important existing feature of the fur-trade in this region is the hunting of the highly valuable fur-seal. The Aleutian Islands of St. Paul and St. George, greatly frequented by these animals, were leased to the Alaska Company in 1870, the annual catch being strictly limited by the terms of the lease to 100,000 animals. The killing of this number has not perceptibly decreased the stock of seals. There is no restriction on the hunting of other fur-animals in Alaska, and it is open to individual enterprise. The fur-trade of the United States was long conducted by individuals. It led to the early settlement of the Western Territories. This originated in a company formed in New Orleans in 1762, which in 1763 established a trading centre on the site of St. Louis, from which eventually arose the city of that name. Prominent members of this company were Auguste and Pierre Chouteau, whose names long remained identified with the fur-trade of the West. The fur-traders and hunters pushed their way far through the wild regions of the West, despite the opposition of hostile tribes, until they reached the Pacific in 1810. The furs collected throughout this vast region were floated down the streams, shooting the rapids in canoes, or borne on men's backs around shoals and cataracts. The trade was a highly dangerous one, it being stated that of the men employed from 1825 to 1830 two-fifths lost their lives in the service. For the 15 years preceding 1804 the average value of the St. Louis furs was $203,750. In 1806 the Missouri Fur Company was established, but during the war with Great Britain it was dissolved. In 1827 the Rocky Mountain Fur Company was formed. More recently the trade has been in the hands of individuals, and, while the collection of furs has greatly increased, the profits of the trade have considerably diminished. This trade had much to do with the early settlement of the Western Territories. Up to 1848 it was the sole interest of Minnesota, while as late as 1844 Lake Superior was visited only by the agents of the fur companies.

The most prominent name in the fur-trade of the

Eastern United States is that of John Jacob Astor, who engaged in the business in 1784. After a long and highly profitable connection with this trade he founded, in 1808, the American Fur Company, with a capital of $1,000,000. This company in 1811 was merged into the South-west Company. He afterwards became connected with the Pacific Fur Company, which in 1810 founded the town of Astoria, at the mouth of the Columbia, in Oregon. This enterprise did not prove profitable, and the property and settlement were treacherously sold, in 1813, by Mr. Astor's principal Canadian partner, to the North-west Company. After that period his operations were confined to the region east of the Rocky Mountains, and he acquired in time an immense fortune from his profitable trade. Since the settlement of Minnesota, St. Paul has become an important centre for the Western fur-trade. The other important American centres are the cities of New York, Boston, Montreal, and St. Louis. In Europe the cities of London and Leipsic are the best markets for American furs, as they long have been for those of other countries. At the annual fair of Leipsic furs in great quantities and of immense value change hands, while the fur-trade of London is of enormous proportions. Though the market preparation of furs is largely conducted abroad, yet this industry has attained very respectable proportions in the United States, the value of American dressed furs in 1880 being $8,238,712, while the raw materials were valued at $5,338,242.

(C. M.)

FURNESS, HORACE HOWARD, an American lawyer and Shakespearian scholar, was born at Philadelphia, Nov. 2, 1833. He is a son of Rev. W. H. Furness, D. D. He graduated at Harvard College in 1854, and was admitted to the bar in 1859. He has written some legal articles, but is especially known by his valuable Variorum edition of Shakespeare's plays, *Romeo and Juliet* (1871), *Macbeth* (1873), *Hamlet* (1877). His library is one of the best in the world in this department of literature. His wife, who died Oct. 31, 1883, had been his diligent assistant, and published a *Concordance to Shakespeare's Sonnets*.

FURNESS, WILLIAM HENRY, an American Unitarian clergyman, was born at Boston, Mass., April 20, 1802. He graduated at Harvard College in 1820, studied theology at Cambridge, and was ordained pastor of the First Unitarian Church of Philadelphia in 1825. In 1880 he was made pastor emeritus, but he still continued to preach occasionally. During the anti-slavery movement he was noted for his active sympathy with the oppressed. He has published *Family Prayers* (1850), translations from German poets and prose writers, and many sermons. His literary labors, however, have chiefly been concerned with the character of Jesus, and the results of his studies of the Gospels have been set forth in the following works: *Remarks on the Four Gospels* (1836); *Jesus and his Biographers* (1838); *History of Jesus* (1850); *Thoughts on the Life and Character of Jesus of Nazareth* (1859); *The Veil partly Lifted* (1864); *Jesus* (1871). All his works show religious earnestness and a refined literary taste.

FURNITURE. In considering the question of house-furnishing we are obliged, from the very nature of the subject, to observe it from two points of view—that of the fine arts and that of utility. It stands between these two great fields of human endeavor. The effect of furnished apartments is as much injured to the cultivated taste by too strict attention to the ornamental as by rigid confinement to the practical. Of the two sins the latter is the least. The primary purpose of furniture is use. Ornament is a secondary consideration. It is subordinate in function to use and fitness. Yet, these prime necessities being duly attended to, the questions of grace, beauty, and harmonious effect come into the foreground, and a well-furnished apartment should be at once a source of pleasure to the cultivated eye and of comfort to the weary body.

See Vol. IX. p. 745 Am. ed. (p. 847 Edin. ed.).

If we briefly consider the history of furniture in the past it is to find these two ideas gaining successively undue control, now the ornamental, now the practical, rising into supremacy, while only at intervals these essentials became harmoniously combined, and house-decoration became truly artistic. In recent times several false conceptions have dominated in the art of furnishing, greatly to its detriment. The fashion of imitating oriental designs, often with very poor taste and effect, and of reproducing antique and mediæval forms and decorations, has proved injurious to the true development of this art. The methods here alluded to grew naturally in adaptation to the needs of life and character of habitations in the periods and regions referred to, and are out of true harmony with the modes of building and domestic requirements of modern civilized lands. In addition to this a tendency to over-decoration has prevailed, while utility has been thrust somewhat into the background. As a result we have passed through an era of monstrosities, of garish and tricky conceits, eccentric forms and coloring, unartistic in themselves, out of accordance with the purpose of the objects, and with little thought of adaptation to the apartments for which they were intended. More recently the art is passing into a more natural stage, and efforts being made to give to furnished rooms a harmonious and picturesque effect, by due attention to pleasing combinations of color in wall-paper, carpets, and upholstery, to just relations of form, and to subordination of the ornamental character of each article to the general effect, and to the form and character of the apartment furnished. This, however, is rather a tendency than a realization, artistic taste being yet at a low ebb in the community at large, and show and luxury being more regarded than grace and beauty.

The influence of schools of design, exhibitions, etc., has been very important in the education of the public taste, and a rapidly growing attention to the subject of house decoration is being aroused. This has been greatly aided by the efforts of some few originators of artistic furniture, such as the firm of Morris & Co., of London, and the widespread adoption of their designs by other manufacturers; while in the great houses of modern times the details of the furnishing are given into the hands of skilled artists, and each room, as far as possible, is wrought into a harmonious and attractive picture.

All true art in furnishing renders in good taste and pleasant effect the needs of modern life, and even in humble habitations it need not be lost sight of, though the exigencies of the situation necessarily subordinate beauty to utility in the latter case. More than nine-tenths of the supply of modern furniture is made for the use of the poorer and the middle classes, and to these cheapness is a primary requisite. And to the demands of cheapness durability is greatly sacrificed. Furniture of this grade is made by machinery in large factories, its defects being hidden by glue, putty, varnish, and paint. To this may be added a considerable

used in the manufacture of *antique oak* furniture. In this, the log is cut into wedge-shaped quarters, and the boards sawn from these. Other woods are used to a less extent, and several scarce and costly woods, such as satinwood, are employed for inlaid finishing. It may be said here, however, that the great advances in the arts of varnishing and staining have to some extent rendered cabinet-makers independent of material. Ebony, rosewood, and in fact almost any wood, can be imitated so perfectly that only an expert can detect the cheat. Stained rosewood can only be distinguished from the real wood by its lighter weight. The great extension of upholstering has also, while adding to the beauty of furniture, given opportunity for a large use of inferior woods, and, in conjunction with the arts of staining, varnishing, and veneering, has rendered possible the production of artistic effects at a moderate cost and in comparatively humble homes.

The furniture industry of the United States has greatly extended of late years, and it is of rapidly growing importance. In 1850 there were in existence 4242 establishments, with a product valued at $17,663,054. In 1880 the number of establishments had become 5227, while the value of the product had increased to $77,845,725. Of this sum the chair product alone was valued at $9,807,823. Its most noticeable recent feature is the rapid extension of the industry in the West. The chief manufacturing States in 1880 were, New York, $16,615,017, and Massachusetts, $9,332,455, while Illinois equalled Pennsylvania in value of product, each being over $8,000,000, and several other Western States yielded a large product. This is but one indication of the extension of manufacturing facilities in the West, its original devotion to agriculture being now associated with manufacturing enterprise, until it promises ere long to compete with the East on an equal footing,

Folding Furniture.—The crowding of large families into small spaces has considerably developed the "folding" or "combination" furniture. The greatest space occupier in furniture is the bed, and it is naturally desired to change its position from the horizontal to the vertical during the day, thus saving space. By giving it the appearance, when thus vertical, of some other article of furniture, it is easy to convert the living-rooms of the family into

Folding Bedstead Closed.

production of hand-made furniture of more durable and serviceable character, though not very elegant in form and material. Yet a very large supply of comparatively low-priced furniture of a higher grade, and in imitation of superior styles, is now turned out in factories, much of it in form, désign, and coloring of artistic character, and lending itself well to the demands of domestic art. The use of mahogany in the better class of furniture, once so common, has grown more rare of late years through the scarcity of the finer grades of this wood. The Baywood mahogany now largely used is lighter colored and without the handsome grain of the Spanish variety. This once favorite wood was succeeded in public favor by rosewood, and more recently by black walnut, whose fine grain and susceptibility to polish have brought it into high esteem as a cabinet wood. More recently several other woods have come into general use, and the field of choice of the furniture-maker has considerably widened. Prominent among these are ash, cherry, and oak; what is known to the trade as "quartered oak" being largely

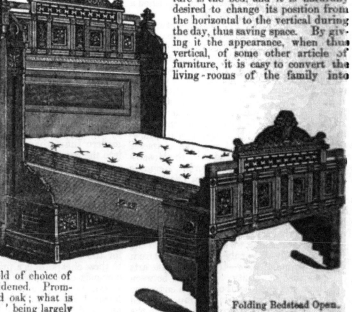

Folding Bedstead Open.

bed-chambers at night, without evidence of this employment during the day.

Folding furniture is made under a variety of patents, all of which embrace one general principle, the difference being in the mode of its application. In one instance the piece of furniture will represent during the day a wardrobe erect against the wall. The front of this seeming wardrobe is movable on hinges at the bottom, and is readily brought forward and downward, revealing the mattress and bed-clothing which have been shut up and concealed from view. By the aid of weights which balance the bed and its support, this movement is easily made. In the morning a slight lifting force throws the bed again into the vertical position, and the seeming wardrobe reappears.

Combination Desk and Washstand.

Many other articles of furniture are thus imitated, frequently a large mirror forming part of the front, and aiding to conceal the true design of the article. Bookcases and writing-desks are thus imitated, neither being a sham, but both capable of use. The inkstand even may be enclosed, being swung in gimbals, so as to remain upright whatever the position of the desk. In all such cases the back portion of the article of furniture serves as the head-board to the bed. In some patents, where the articles represented are low, the front is arranged not only to lower but also to be drawn out, so giving proper length to the bed. Lounges and sofas are also converted into beds. These are made double, and pull open horizontally, the lounge or sofa seat forming half the bed, while an extra mattress has to be supplied to complete its width. Similar combinations in other articles of furniture are quite common. (C. M.)

FURNIVALL, FREDERICK JAMES, an English philologist, born at Egham, Surrey, Feb. 4, 1825. He studied (1841–42) in University College, London, and was matriculated in the London University. He graduated B. A. at Trinity Hall, Cambridge, in 1842. In 1846 he became a zealous and active supporter of F. D. Maurice, in his efforts to improve the condition of the laboring men of London, and for ten years he was engaged in the Working-Men's College. In 1854 he became secretary of the Philological Society. He edited for that society *Early English Poems and Lives of Saints* (1862), and was for a time editor of the society's great English dictionary. In 1864 he founded the Early English Text Society, and was its editor-in-chief. In 1868 he started the Ballad Society and the Chaucer Society. In 1873 he established the New Shakspere Society. He has edited a very large number of early English texts, and through his societies has raised large sums for their publication.

FUTURE STATE. The universal instinct of humanity expects a future life. The Scriptures reveal it. Speculations concerning it have been innumerable. The literature of this subject was very thoroughly indexed by Dr. Ezra Abbot in 1864, and the exhaustive treatise was published as an appendix to W. R. Alger's *Doctrine of a Future Life.*

The future state is the *condition* of the future life. All nations in their creeds have a two-fold condition in the future life—one of happiness and the other of misery. Some have a third condition of purgatory, or purification, as preceding and producing the happiness.

The denial of a future life is an effort of the mind against its natural belief, and but few reach that position. The denial of the two-fold future state seems to be likewise against nature. The ordinary language of men toward virtue and vice asserts a heaven and hell. The doctrines which limit and terminate the hell, and which make a purgatorial vestibule for the heaven, are rather philosophical than natural. They proceed from the desire to remove the dark colors from the universe and from the difficulty in joining closely earth's impurity with heaven's holiness.

Such Scripture expressions as "absent from the body and present with the Lord" (2 Cor. v. 8), "I desire to depart and be with Christ" (Phil. i. 23) seem to show that the heavenly state follows immediately on the body's dissolution. The "spirits in prison" of 1 Peter iii. 19 refer (by any interpretation) to the unbelievers of Noah's day, and by that limitation cannot prove a general purgatory. Moreover, if they were in prison after Christ's crucifixion, they were in the prison of hell as punished sinners, and not in the prison of purgatory as saints undergoing purification. Some hold that they were in the prison of sin in Noah's day and that Christ preached to them through Noah. In any case purgatory cannot be established from that text.

That the bodies of the saved will not be reunited to them till a future resurrection day is clearly taught in Scripture in many places. That a mediate body may be provided for them is argued from 2 Cor. v. 1, and from the presence of Moses with a body on the Mount of Transfiguration.

Those who believe that the saved go directly to heaven on death by parity of reasoning believe that the lost go directly to hell on death.

Many argue that both lost and saved go to an intermediate place (Hades), on one side of which is Paradise, or Abraham's bosom (Luke xvi. 23), and on the other a preliminary place to hell, and that the final disposition to heaven and hell will be made at the general judgment. (H. CR.)

G.

GABORIAU, ÉMILE (1835–1873), a French novelist, was born at Saujon in 1835. He was the son of a notary, but enlisted in a cavalry regiment and was afterwards employed in a carriage-factory in Paris. Writing stories of military and fashionable life for the less important journals, he gradually acquired note by his humorous sketches. Then he turned to elaborate detective stories, which achieved remarkable success. The first of these was *L'Affaire Lerouge* (1866), which was soon followed by *Le Dossier No. 113* (1867), and *Le Crime d' Orcival* (1867). These were his best, though they were followed by several more of the same character. He died at Paris, Sept. 28, 1873.

GACHARD, LOUIS PROSPER, a Belgian historian, was born at Paris, March 12, 1800. He was a journeyman printer and went to Belgium, where, after taking part in the revolution of 1830, he was naturalized. He was placed in charge of the national archives, and not only organized that department but gathered from foreign libraries valuable documents relating to Belgian history. He published *Correspondance de Guillaume le Taciturne* (6 vols., 1847–66); *Correspondance de Philippe II. sur les affaires des Pays Bas* (4 vols., 1848–61), chiefly from the archives of Simancas in Spain; *Correspondance de Marguerite d'Autriche* (3 vols., 1867–81), and several works giving new information concerning Charles V. and Philip II.

GADE, NIELS WILHELM, a Danish composer, was born at Copenhagen, Feb. 22, 1817. At an early age he showed taste for music, and after he had obtained instruction on the piano and violin he was admitted to the royal chapel as a performer. After studying composition, in 1841 he obtained a prize with his overture *Echoes from Ossian*. A royal stipend then enabled him to study at Leipsic, whither he had been invited by Mendelssohn, and where he produced his first symphony in C minor. In the fall of 1844 he was called from Italy to take charge of concerts at Leipsic in Mendelssohn's absence. In 1848 he returned to Copenhagen, where he conducted concerts, and in 1865 became first director of the Conservatory. His works comprise eight symphonies, five overtures, four cantatas, several sonatas, a lyrical drama, *Comala*, and an opera, *Mariotta*. Gade, though inferior to his master, Mendelssohn, in form, excelled him in strength and skilful use of instruments. He died Dec. 22, 1890.

GAD-FLY, also breeze or horse-fly, a name given to many species of *Diptera*, or two-winged insects, from their persistent persecution of horses and other animals. The gad-flies of North America comprise over 100 species of the genus *Tabanus* alone, besides members of other genera. During the hotter parts of the summer, and especially when the sun is shining brightly, these insects appear in multitudes in marshy regions, and on prairie lands, and prove a great annoyance both to man and beast. They do not fly in cloudy weather, and die in the cool nights of September. Our most common species is *Tabanus lineola*, or the green-head fly. Its bite is very painful, its lancet-like jaws being driven deep into the flesh. Horses and cattle are occasionally so harassed by its attacks as to die in consequence. The mouth parts of the horse-fly resemble in a modified form those of the mosquito, and, as in the latter, only the female bites. The golden-eyed flies, of the genus *Chrysops*, are much smaller gad-flies, which cause great annoyance in summer by their buzzing and biting in woods and fields. The *Tsetse* fly of Africa, whose bite is said to poison and kill cattle, is a member of this group. Fortunately i does not attack man.

GADSDEN, CHRISTOPHER (1724–1805), an American patriot, was born at Charleston, S. C., in 1724 He was educated in England and in 1741 returned to Charleston, where by success in mercantile business he recovered the estate which his father had lost in 1733 by gambling. He frequently represented Charleston in the colonial assembly, and was a prominent delegate to the Congress which met at New York in October, 1765. In the Continental Congress in 1774 he advocated American independence. In 1775 he was made colonel and in 1776 brigadier-general of State troops, but resigned in 1779. Being lieutenant-governor of the State in 1780 he remained at Charleston during its siege by Sir Henry Clinton, and signed the capitulation. After the surrender he was for a time prisoner on parole, but soon was transferred to St. Augustine. On his refusing to give another parole he was closely imprisoned for forty-two weeks. After his release he was chosen governor of South Carolina, but declined the office. He died at Charleston, Aug. 28, 1805.

GADSDEN, JAMES (1788–1858), an American statesman, grandson of the preceding, was born at Charleston, S. C., May 15, 1788. Graduating at Yale College in 1806 he engaged in commerce until 1812, when he entered the army as lieutenant and served in Canada. He was an aide to Gen. Jackson in the Seminole campaign of 1818. Leaving the army in 1822 he settled in Florida as a planter, became a member of the territorial council in 1824, and a commissioner to remove the Seminoles to Southern Florida. He afterwards returned to Charleston. In 1853. being appointed minister to Mexico, he negotiated the "Gadsden Purchase," by which the United States acquired for $10,000,000 a large tract now included in Arizona and New Mexico. He died at Charleston, Dec. 26, 1858.

GAGE, MATILDA JOSLYN, an advocate of woman's rights, was born at Cicero, N. Y., March 24, 1826. She was married in 1845 to Henry H. Gage, and first took part in the movement for woman's rights in 1852. Besides lecturing and attending conventions she has written *Woman as Inventor*, and with E. C. Stanton and S. B. Anthony has compiled the *History of Woman Suffrage* (3 vols.).

GAINES, EDMUND PENDLETON (1777–1849), an American general, was born in Culpepper co., Va., March 20, 1777. His father, James, was a captain in the revolutionary war, and a member of the legislature of North Carolina. In 1790 the family removed to Tennessee. Edmund entered the army as ensign in 1799, was major at the beginning of the war of 1812, soon after colonel, and in 1814 brigadier-general. He received the brevet of major-general and other marks of honor for gallantry at Fort Erie, Aug. 15, 1814, where he was severely wounded. While in command on the Southern border he was active against the Seminoles in Florida. When Gen. Jackson took the command Gaines remained and presided over the court-martial which condemned Arbuthnot and Ambrister. He was afterwards in command of the Western district. In 1836 he conducted an expedition against Osceola, but was wounded in an action on the Withlacoochie River, Feb. 29. He died at New Orleans, June 6, 1849.

GAINES, MYRA CLARK (1806–1885), wife of the preceding, was born at New Orleans, Dec. 27, 1806. She was the daughter of Daniel Clark (1766–1813), an Irishman, who had settled in New Orleans and became a millionaire. Her mother, Marie Julie Carriere, at the age of thirteen had married Jerome de Grange, a French nobleman, who had fled from France in 1790. The marriage was not happy, and it was afterwards discovered that he had one or more wives living. Myra's mother, now known as Zulime, had attracted Clark's attention, and he proposed marriage, but she refused to marry until it was proved that she had a right to do so. The two therefore travelled to New York, where de Grange's previous marriage was supposed to have taken place, to get evidence of the fact, but the records of the church had been destroyed before their arrival. Zulime then consented to marriage on condition that it should be kept secret until there was legal evidence of de Grange's bigamy. She was married privately in Philadelphia in 1803 and went to reside near New Orleans. Clark subsequently neglected her, and Myra was brought up in the family of Col. Davis, whom she supposed to be her father until near the time of her marriage to W. W. Whitney, of New York. Davis then stated that Clark had acknowledged Myra as his legitimate daughter, and by a will made in 1813 had bequeathed to her his estate. Clark's partners, however, had already served as executors of a will dated in 1811 which gave the estate chiefly to his mother, Mrs. Mary Clark. Mr. Whitney instituted a search for the missing will; witnesses were found who had seen and read it, and the Supreme Court of Louisiana in February, 1856, decided that the lost or destroyed will, as described, should be received as the last will of Daniel Clark. Mr. Whitney had already suffered imprisonment for libel in charging Clark's partners with destroying this will. Whitney died before the will was established, but in 1839 his widow was married to Gen. E. P. Gaines, who had a fortune of $200,000. Much of this was swept away in the costs of the lawsuits, and he also died, in 1849, before the end was reached. In a later suit evidence was brought to show that Clark himself had destroyed the will, and for a time Mrs. Gaines seemed to have lost all. But she persevered until, in 1861, the Supreme Court of the United States decided in her favor by a vote of four to three. After the civil war, which suspended the proceedings, the Probate Court of New Orleans refused to admit the will, but the U. S. Circuit Court interfered. Part of Clark's estate was by this time the commercial centre of New Orleans, while another part was an entire suburb, St. Johnsburg. The master in chancery to whom the case was referred reported that the city of New Orleans owed Mrs. Gaines over $1,500,000, on account of part of this property. In 1883 Judge Billings granted a mandamus on the city, and ordered the city council to lay a tax of two per cent. to pay the claim. An appeal to the U. S. Supreme Court was afterwards allowed. Up to 1874 Mrs. Gaines was said to have recovered about $6,000,000, but the legal expenses had swallowed up most of this amount. In 1861 the whole estate was valued at $35,000,000, and it afterwards increased in value. Mrs. Gaines died at New Orleans, Jan. 9, 1885. A son-in-law and six grandchildren survived her.

GALENA, a city of Illinois, county-seat of Jo Daviess county, is situated on both sides of Galena River (originally called Fevre River), 6 miles from its junction with the Mississippi; 19 miles S. of Dubuque, Iowa, and 180 miles S. E. of Chicago. Galena River was formerly navigable for any class of boats that could ascend the Mississippi, but owing to the deposit of soil washed from the bluffs on either side it is now rarely navigable. The city is on the Illinois Central Railroad, and is also the southern terminus of a division of the Chicago and North-western Railroad. It was first settled in 1819 as a mining-camp and trading-post; laid off as a town in 1826; incorporated as such in 1835, and as a city in 1839. The ground on which it is built rises abruptly from the river on either side, its streets being laid off in terraces to the tops of the bluffs, giving it a romantic appearance. The highest point in the city is nearly 210 feet above the river. The chief industry is lead-mining, which is carried on to a considerable extent, in the winter seasons principally. As a commercial centre it derived a great portion of its trade from the rich mining and agricultural regions of Southern Wisconsin. Its manufactories and other industries include a foundry and machine-shop, 2 saw-mills, sash-, door-, and blind-factory, pottery, woollen-mill, broom-factory, 2 extensive packing-houses, furniture-factory, and minor industries. Of churches there are Methodist Episcopal, 2; Presbyterian, 2; Lutheran, 2; Episcopal, 1; Catholic, 2. It has a handsome high school building, and substantial public school houses auxiliary thereto. Among the number of private educational buildings in Galena is a Dominican (Catholic) school, also the German-English college, conducted under the auspices of the North-western German M. E. Conference. Its beautiful structure, finely located, was originally the U. S. marine hospital. Galena has a fine court-house and jail, city hall, substantial business blocks, and many beautiful residences. The population of Galena in 1870 was 7019, in 1830, 6406. It was the residence of Gen. Grant at the outbreak of the civil war.

GALES, JOSEPH (1786–1860), an American journalist, was born at Eckington, near Sheffield, England, April 10, 1786. His father (1760–1841), who had conducted a newspaper in Sheffield, came to the United States in 1794, and published the *Independent Gazette* in Philadelphia until 1799, when he removed to Raleigh, N. C., and there published the *Register* until 1839. Joseph graduated at the University of North Carolina, settled in Washington in 1807, and became proprietor of the *National Intelligencer* in 1810. In 1812 he took his brother-in-law, W. W. Seaton, as partner, and in 1813 made the paper a daily. He died at Washington, July 21, 1860. He was an able and influential writer.

GALESBURG, a city of Illinois, county-seat of Knox county, is on the main line of the Chicago, Burlington, and Quincy Railroad, 164 miles W. S. W. of Chicago. This line of railroad extends hence westward to Burlington (Iowa), and to Omaha. From Galesburg a branch runs E. S. E. 52 miles to Peoria. Another branch connects Galesburg with Quincy, while the Fulton County Narrow Gauge Railroad (3 feet wide, 61 miles long) runs southward to Havana, on the Illinois River. The city has 3 national banks, 16 churches, 1 daily and 3 weekly newspapers, and good schools. The leading manufactures are wagons, castings, and farm-implements. There are also shops for railway repairs and construction. Galesburg is the seat of Knox College, founded in 1841 as a Presbyterian institution, but now non-sectarian, and also of Lombard College (Universalist, founded 1852). Besides the college libraries there is a large public library. The population in 1870 was 10,158; in 1880, 11,437; in 1890, 15,184.

GALL OF THE EARTH. This is the common name of *Nabalus Fraseri*, a plant indigenous to the Atlantic portion of the United States. It was one of the Indian remedies for the bite of venomous reptiles. It belongs to the natural order Compositæ, and was referred by Linnæus to the genus *Prenanthes*, from which it differs in the greater number of florets in the head (5–20), the greater number of involucral scales (8–10), as well as in minor particulars. There are ten species of *Nabalus* described, all perennial herbs springing from tuberous roots, with leaves usually varying much on the same plant, and with the mostly nodding flowers on the paniculate branches, of a greenish-white or slightly purple tinge. The roots of all the species are bitter, but those of *N. Fraseri* especially so, whence the common name.

GALLAGHER, WILLIAM D., an American poet and journalist, was born at Philadelphia in 1808. After the death of his father in 1816, his mother removed to Cincinnati where William became a printer. He was editor of the *Backwoodsman* at Xenia, Ohio, in 1830, and afterwards of literary journals in Cincinnati. From 1839 to 1850 he was connected with the *Cincinnati Gazette*. His verses were gathered under the name *Erato* (3 vols., 1835–37), and he also published *Selections from the Poetical Literature of the West* (1841). In 1850 he became confidential clerk of Thomas Corwin, secretary of the U. S. treasury. In 1853 he removed to Louisville, was again an editor, next a farmer, and afterwards again employed in the treasury department.

GALLAUDET, an American family of Huguenot descent, noted for their labors in behalf of deaf-mutes.

I. GALLAUDET, THOMAS HOPKINS (1787–1851), the founder of the first American institution for deaf-mutes, was born at Philadelphia, Dec. 10, 1787. His parents afterwards removed to Hartford and he graduated at Yale College in 1805. He studied theology at Andover, but, as is related in the article on DEAF-MUTES (Vol. II., p. 567), devoted himself to the education of that class. He was principal of the asylum at Hartford until 1830, when he resigned on account of impaired health. In 1838 he became chaplain of the Connecticut Insane Asylum. He died at Hartford, Conn., Sept. 9, 1851. He published several religious works for the young, and edited the *American Annals of the Deaf and Dumb*. See his *Life* by H. Humphrey (N. Y., 1858).

II. GALLAUDET, THOMAS, a son of the preceding, was born at Hartford, Conn., June 3, 1822. After assisting in the Hartford Asylum, he was professor in the New York Institution from 1843 to 1858. In 1850 he was ordained to the Episcopal ministry, and in 1852 founded St. Ann's Church for deaf-mutes. He also assisted in establishing services for deaf-mutes in Albany, Boston, Philadelphia, and Baltimore. He has contributed to the *American Annals of the Deaf and Dumb*.

III. GALLAUDET, EDWARD MINER, brother of the preceding, was born in Hartford, Conn., Feb. 3, 1837. After two years' experience as instructor in the Hartford Asylum, he was, in 1857, made principal of the Columbia Institution at Washington, D. C. (see Vol. II., p. 570). In 1864 he became president of the National Deaf-mute College, which had grown out of his efforts. His further labors are indicated in the article already referred to.

GALLE, JOHANN GOTTFRIED, a German astronomer, was born at Pabsthaus, June 9, 1812. He studied at Wittenberg and Berlin, and became a teacher at Guben and in Berlin. In 1835 he was made assistant in a newly founded observatory in Berlin, and enjoyed Encke's instruction. In three months, about the end of 1839, Galle discovered three new comets, for which he obtained the Lalande prize. On Sept. 23, 1846, he received a letter from Leverrier requesting him to examine a certain part of the sky for an unknown planet, and, by the aid of a map which had just been completed by Dr. Bemicker, was so fortunate as to discover the planet Neptune that very evening. This event marks an era in the history of astronomy. Galle continued to make further discoveries, and since 1851 has been professor of astronomy and director of the observatory at Breslau. He has published many articles in the *Astronomische Nachrichten* and other scientific journals.

GALLITZIN, DEMETRIUS AUGUSTINE (1770–1840), a Russian nobleman who became an American missionary, was born at the Hague, Dec. 22, 1770. His father, Prince Dimitri Gallitsin, while ambassador at Paris, embraced the views of Voltaire, but his mother, after a dangerous illness, became a Roman Catholic in 1784, and three years later Demetrius also professed that faith. He had been destined for military life, and had been commissioned as a captain of the Russian imperial guard. In 1792 he was sent to America, partly to examine the institutions of the country and partly to overcome his natural timidity. He was received with great cordiality by Bishop John Carroll of Baltimore, and soon after his arrival entered the theological seminary of that city. His parents opposed his desire to become a priest but he persevered, and after entering the order of the Sulpitians was ordained, March 18, 1796. He officiated first at Conewango, Pa., then travelled as a missionary, visiting the Catholics scattered through the wilder parts of Pennsylvania and Virginia. In 1799 he determined to take up his abode at Clearfield, Cambria co., Pa., and purchased a large tract of land to be given to Catholic families. Having assumed the name Smith, he was thus naturalized in 1802, but in 1809 was permitted by the legislature to resume his family name. On his father's death he had been declared disqualified to inherit the estate, and though his mother sent him money he was much embarrassed by the expenses incurred for his colony, which he had named Loretto. Still he struggled to hold it, and is said to have spent on it altogether $150,000. The wilderness in which he had settled was before his death transformed into a thrifty community. Besides Loretto, a village named Gallitzin had sprung up. He steadily refused preferment in the church, devoting himself entirely to his colony. He died at Loretto, Pa., May 6, 1840. Ten years later a monument was erected over his remains in front of the church in which he had ministered. During his life he had carried several controversies with surrounding Protestants, and his letters were pubished in pamphlet form. See his *Life* by Sarah M. Brownson (1873).

GALLOWAY, JOSEPH (1730–1803), an American loyalist, was born in Maryland about 1730. He practised law in Philadelphia, and in the Pennsylvania legislature in 1764 he strongly supported the movement for changing the government of the colony from the proprietary to a royal form. (See AMERICAN COLONIES, Vol. II., p. 305.) In 1774 he managed to be elected to the Continental Congress, and there proposed a scheme of government for the United Colonies closely resembling that now in use in Canada. But when the movement for independence grew stronger he became strenuous in opposition. He joined the British troops in New York in 1776 and afterwards returned to Philadelphia, but in 1778 he went to England. Before a committee of the House of Commons in 1779 he made severe strictures upon Sir William Howe and other British officers. He also published pamphlets on the causes and consequences of the American revolution. He was the ablest, most influential, and most violent of the loyalists. He died in England, Aug. 29, 1803.

GALT, SIR ALEXANDER TILLOCH, a Canadian statesman, was born at Chelsea, England, Sept. 6, 1817, being a son of the distinguished novelist, John Galt. From an early age he was in Canada in the employ of the British and American Land Company, and from 1844 to 1856, as the sole manager of its estates, conducted it from insolvency to prosperity. In 1849 he was elected to the Canadian Parliament, and since 1853 he has been the representative of Sherbrooke. Being minister of finance in the Cartier cabinet from 1858 to May, 1862, he arranged a tariff which improved the provincial credit, consolidated the public debt, and negotiated in England an important loan. He again held this position from March, 1864, to August, 1866. He had always advocated the union of the British North American provinces, and in 1866 was sent as a delegate to London to promote the formation of the present Dominion of Canada. He was again minister of finance in 1867–68 under the new government, and soon after was knighted. In 1875 he was appointed a commissioner under the Treaty of Washington, and in 1877 was the representative of Great Britain in the Fishery Commission at Halifax. In 1880 he was appointed the diplomatic representative of Canada at London. His valuable services in behalf of his country have procured for him many marks of honor. He has published *Canada, 1849–1859* (1860).

GALTON, FRANCIS, an English traveller and author, was born in 1822 at Dudderton, near Birmingham. He is a grandson of Dr. Erasmus Darwin. He graduated at Trinity College, Cambridge, in 1844, then travelled in North Africa, visiting the White Nile, and in 1850 explored the western part of South Africa. For this exploration he received in 1852 a gold medal from the Royal Geographical Society, of which he was afterwards secretary for some years. He was general secretary of the British Association from 1863 to 1868; president of its geographical section in 1872, and of its anthropological sub-section in 1877. He has published *Narrative of an Explorer in Tropical South Africa* (1853); *Art of Travel* (1858), a very popular handbook of directions; *Meteorographica* (1863), a weather chart; *Hereditary Genius* (1869); *English Men of Science; their Nature and Nurture* (1874); *Experiments in Pangenesis* (1880).

GALVESTON, the chief city of Texas, county-seat of Galveston county, is on the N. E. end of Galveston Island and at the mouth of Galveston Bay. It is 290 miles W. of New Orleans and 180 miles E. S. E. of Austin. The first census of the population in 1850 gave the number of inhabitants as 4177, in 1860 it was 7307; during the civil war the population was much reduced, but in 1870 it had risen again to 13,817; in 1880 it was 22,253, and by the census of 1890, 29,379. There are two main lines of railway—the Galveston, Houston, and Henderson, now a part of the Missouri Pacific system, and the Gulf, Colorado, and Santa Fé, now operating about 700 miles of main line and branches—reaching the central, northern, and eastern portions of Texas. These two railroads reach the city from the mainland on two trestle bridges, each over 2 miles long. Another road, narrow gauge, the Texas and Mexican, has been built only about 20 miles down the island. The whole length of the island is 33 miles and its breadth from 1 to 4 miles. It is intersected by many bayous, and contains several fresh-water ponds. The beach of the island is smooth and hard, and furnishes a fine drive.

See Vol. X. p. 49 Am. ed. (p. 53 Edin. ed.).

The city of Galveston contains an area of nearly 5000 acres, and is laid off in squares 260 by 300 feet, with wide streets, intersecting each other at right angles. Much attention is paid by householders to shrubbery and trees on sidewalks, and there are many elegant private dwellings, handsome public buildings, and fine business blocks. There are 29 churches of the various denominations, 10 of which belong to the colored people. St. Mary's Cathedral is a fine building, and many of the Protestant denominations have elegant edifices. The Hebrews have a fine synagogue. The public-school system is admirable, controlled by the city, and accommodating all classes. St. Mary's University (Roman Catholic) was founded in 1855 and has about 150 students, chiefly in the preparatory department. There is also a medical school, good libraries, and an orphanage.

Galveston has over 20 hotels, 2 national banks, 3 other banks, and several private banking-houses, with an aggregate capital of $2,000,000. Two daily and 5 weekly newspapers are published here. Owing to the limited supply of fresh water manufactures have not been largely engaged in. The principal are the city gas-works, Brush electric-light works, cottonseed-oil mill, ice-factory, 4 sash- and blind-factories, flouring-mill, brass- and iron-foundries, and 6 cotton-compresses. The principal exports of Galveston are leather, wool, hides, and cottonseed-oil and cake. The principal imports are from South America, Great Britain, and other foreign countries, and include coffee, salt, iron ties, and iron rails; from domestic ports are brought groceries, dry-goods, and general merchandise. The annual exports and imports now amount to $35,000,000, cotton being the chief article of export.

The harbor of Galveston is on the north or bay front of the city, and has capacity for a very large commerce. At the entrance to the harbor from the Gulf of Mexico there is a bar of crescent shape of an average width of ¾ mile, on which bar there is a depth of water on average tides of 13 feet. Efforts have been made by the general government to increase the depth of water on the bar, so as to admit the largest class of sea-going vessels, but little or no effective work has been done.

History.—The progress and condition of Galveston may be divided into four epochs: First, the days of the filibusters and buccaneers from 1816 to 1820, followed by the almost total depopulation of the island for some ten years. Herrera, the minister of the Mexican patriots, having learned the capacity of Galveston harbor, determined to take possession of it. He accordingly sailed to the island and landed on Sept. 1, 1816, having with him Commodore Aury in command of a fleet of 12 vessels of the republics of Mexico, Venezuela, La Plata, and New Grenada. On Sept. 12 a government was organized, and Aury was chosen governor of Texas and Galveston Island, taking an oath of allegiance to the republic of Mexico. Other departments of government were organized and officers elected; and Aury's vessels being sent out to cruise against Spanish commerce swept the whole Gulf of the shipping of the mother country. Meantime Xavier Mina, who had distinguished himself in the Peninsular war against France, entered into an arrangement with Toledo to wrest Florida from Spain; but when Toledo went over to the king of Spain, Mina sailed to Galveston to co-operate with Aury and Perry, landing here on Nov. 24, 1816. Aury's cruisers made Galveston prosperous for the time. Among the prizes taken were many Spanish slavers, but as there was no market for slaves in Texas the captors sought a market for them in the United States. Companies were formed in Louisiana who received them either at Sabine, Point Bolivar, or Galveston, took them to a custom-house officer in Louisiana, denounced them as imported slaves, had them sold under the law by the marshal, and repurchased them, pocketing half of the purchase-money as informers. The forces in Galveston consisted of about 350 men under Aury besides his fleet; and there were 200 under Mina, while Col. Perry commanded 100 men at Bolivar Point on the mainland. They sailed or marched to take part in the war of Mexico against Spain. A few days after Aury and all his men had sailed from Galveston Lafitte and his buccaneers arrived. By the close of 1817 Lafitte's followers in Galveston numbered about 1000 men. The town built by Lafitte on the ruins of that of Aury was called Campeachy. About this time Gen. Lallemand, an artillery officer under Napoleon, came to Galveston with about 100 Frenchmen. Proceeding a short distance up the Trinity he built a fort, intending to cultivate the soil, but was induced to abandon the enterprise owing to the hostility of the Spaniards. His followers returned to Galveston, and a part of them remained with Lafitte. The buccaneers were finally driven away by a U. S. naval vessel. The floating population of the island, during the days of the filibusters, varied from 50 to 1000. Lafitte had established quite a town, mostly of low wooden buildings. The project of establishing a city on the east end of Galveston Island, formed in 1837, first took shape in the winter and spring of 1838. Prior to the battle of San Jacinto, and after the expulsion of the Mexican authorities in 1835, Galveston had no regular commerce, although vessels frequently arrived with immigrants and supplies in aid of the Texas revolution. In 1835 a military post was established by Texas and maintained until after the expulsion of the Mexicans from the country in 1836.

The present site of the city was acquired from the republic of Texas under special grant by M. B. Menard and associates, and its first incorporation as a municipality was in March, 1839. Its population at that time was about 1000. The settlements in this portion of Texas were confined to a few counties contiguous to the coast, and the commerce was correspondingly limited. The foreign trade began in February, 1840, when a French vessel arrived with a cargo, and in the following winter British and German vessels followed. After Texas was annexed to the United States the commerce of Galveston steadily increased. The secession of Texas led to the blockade of the port during the civil war. It was captured by the U. S. forces Oct. 8, 1862, but was regained by the Confederates Jan. 1, 1863. Since the close of the war Galveston has recovered its commercial importance. The greatest conflagration in this city occurred on the night of Nov. 12-13, 1885. It started in a steam planing-mill, and, being spread by a stiff north wind blowing at the rate of 30 miles an hour, it destroyed within 5 hours 47 blocks of the most densely populated portion of the city. The area of the burnt district was about 100 acres and contained 500 dwellings. The property burnt was valued at $2,000,000, on which there was an insurance of $1,200,000, which sum was nearly all paid within a month. This promptness enabled building to be undertaken at once, and the new houses are superior to those which they replace, greatly improving the city.

GALVEZ, BERNARDO DE, COUNT (1756–1786), a Spanish general and colonial governor, was born at Malaga in 1756. He was the son of Don Mathias Galvez, viceroy of Mexico, and his uncle, Don José de Galvez, was president of the council of the Indies. Bernardo, after some military experience in France and Algiers, was appointed colonel and governor of Louisiana in 1776. He assisted the Americans in the revolutionary war, and commanded expeditions, which, in 1779–81, captured from the British various posts from Baton Rouge, as far east as Pensacola. He was made lieutenant-general, with the rank of count, and in 1784 was appointed captain-general of Louisiana and Florida. Early in 1785 Cuba was also placed under his government, and a few months later, on the death of his father, he succeeded to the vice-royalty of Mexico. He built the palace of Chapultepec, but the vastness of this undertaking brought him into suspicion in Spain. He died of vexation in consequence, at Mexico, Nov. 30, 1786.

GAMBETTA, LEON (1838–1882), the greatest of French Republican leaders, was born at Cahors, a small city of the south of France, April 3, 1838. His family was originally from Genoa. Those who seek to mark everywhere the influence of race note in his character a strong dash of Italian strategy and subtlety. His father, who survived him, was a small shop-keeper. His mother, who died only a year before him, was a woman of strong native intelligence, and, though herself denied all opportunity of culture, capable of appreciating its advantages to the full. Accordingly, with her strong will and perseverance, she bent all her efforts to give a superior education to her son, who, from his earliest years, showed a richly endowed nature. He studied at the modest provincial college. Educated in the faith of the majority of his countrymen, he made his first communion in the Catholic Church, though his piety never appeared to be fervent. Later he withdrew entirely from Catholicism, as the enemy of all liberty, and never was able to distinguish between Christianity and Ultramontanism. In this regard he shared the unfortunate error of the great majority of his fellow-countrymen. Philosophical studies never interested him; without close personal examination he accepted the convenient so-

tations of positivism as presented by Auguste Comte and Littré, who discard at the outset the investigation of causes and principles, and concentrate their attention entirely upon the world of phenomena. Such a system permits one to pose as a free thinker by dispensing with thought on the grandest questions which can occupy the human soul.

Gambetta, thanks to the mother who had faith in him and who shrank from no sacrifice to assure his future, went to Paris about 1858 to study law before he attained his twentieth year. He was accompanied by an aged aunt, who kept house for him as long as she lived. To her tender and unwearied care for his wants he returned a great and respectful affection.

Gambetta did not push his study of law very far, but contented himself with what was necessary to his assuming the advocate's robe. His chief study was in the political and historical sciences. His instinct impelled him to action, to direct influence on the spirits of others by his eloquence. Even at this early stage of his career he exercised a veritable fascination on his friends. He dazzled them with his ardent imaginative speech, in which the sallies of a lively and keen wit were mingled with large views and generous and fruitful ideas. Gambetta was the true representative of his generation, the inspired organ of its protest against Napoleonic Cæsarism. Still an opportunity was needed to bring him forward upon the grand stage of contemporary history; this came to him suddenly in the Baudin trial in 1868. This was the prosecution brought against the journals which had opened a subscription to raise a monument to the memory of that heroic representative of the people slain Dec. 4, 1851, while fighting on the barricade against the soldiers of the *coup d'état*. Among the accused appeared the famous Delécluze, destined to so mournful a fate in the days of the Commune, and as his advocate appeared Gambetta. It was really the Empire and the *coup d'état* that were on trial. On that day the young advocate, but yesterday unknown outside of the circle of his intimate friends, rose at once to glory by a speech which was a thunderbolt against the Empire. In that harangue of Nov. 14 the public conscience, long condemned to silence, found utterance, and by its uncompromising verdict rendered amid the frantic applause of a whole people, proclaimed to the usurping government that no statute of limitations covered the deed which had been boldly called a crime before its own tribunal. It was no mere speech that Gambetta made: it was the proclamation of the advent of a new era. It was the first revelation of the causes that were to lead to the fall of the Empire; the moral vote of the country had on that day gone against the government.

The election of 1869 sent Gambetta to the Chamber of Deputies after a prolonged contest at Paris and at Marseilles, in which he took pronounced democratic ground, but without any admixture of socialism. In the debates of the chamber as at the bar of the correctional tribunal he displayed a timely boldness. After the first defeats of the disastrous war of 1870, when the session was resumed Gambetta was ever at the front, urging the arming of the national guard, demanding the formation of a Committee of Defence, pursuing the government with incisive questions on the military situation which they tried to conceal, ever finding words of patriotism adequate to the increasing gravity of the crisis. On Aug. 13, 1870, he pronounced this decisive word: "It must be made clear whether we here (in this house) have made our choice between the salvation of the country and the safety of the dynasty." To the fallaciously optimistic declarations of the ministry, which was endeavoring to delude the people, the orator replied with the terrible apostrophe: "I consider that we have been silent long enough; that for too long a time has the veil of secrecy been cast over the events which are rushing upon us. It is my profound conviction that this country is hurrying towards an abyss and knows it not." When interrupted by the hirelings who dared assert that the situation caused disquiet to none but himself and his friends, with a voice of thunder he turned upon them and put them to silence: "As for you," he cried, "who have never raised your voices but with words of cringing acquiescence, whose effect is but too visible to-day, hold your peace! The only conduct which becomes you now is silence and remorse." Does it not seem that it was the voice of France herself that, with vengeance in its tones, made itself heard in those rapid burning words? They were few indeed, but they struck home.

On Sept. 4, 1870, Gambetta was raised to power, amid circumstances the most tragic. The Second Empire had been crushed by the defeat of Sedan. The Prussians beleaguered Paris. Departing hence by balloon, Gambetta reached Tours and forthwith despatched to the provinces an intensely patriotic proclamation, appealing to the country to put forth all her remaining force to drive out the invader, step by step. Gathering around him helpers as energetic as himself, among whom M. de Freycinet was conspicuous, Gambetta did everything to organize the means of resistance. The Army of the Loire was the first reorganized, and, under the command of the brilliant Chanzy, held in check for two months the Prussian army. In the north Gen. Faidherbe led into action troops hastily raised, who yet bore themselves bravely. Finally the great campaign of the east to turn back the German army was organised with an incredible rapidity. But Bazaine's surrender of Metz and his gallant army neutralized all these efforts. The veteran regiments being thus broken up, the government of national defence had only raw levies to set in array against the most admirable military organization of Europe. Nevertheless we cannot regret that terrible and bloody effort of Gambetta. Honor is worth more than success. France would have been disgraced in the eyes of history and justly, if she had not struggled till the sword broke in her hands to defend her soil, her sons and her daughters that were to be taken from her by the annexation of Alsace and Lorraine. We do not deny that during his dictatorship Gambetta made mistakes, and that in directing the generals whom he had placed in command, removing them at the first check, and imposing on them plans of campaign, he went too far. We recognize that at times he made the weight of his authority too rudely felt, and would not permit himself to be hindered in pursuit of his main object by any local liberty. His greatest error was proclaiming an electoral law which forbade the candidacy of any supporter of the Empire. This measure, published just before the convoking of the National Assembly, was repudiated by the members of the government remaining in Paris, and thus the Republic was threatened with a serious conflict. To judge the matter aright we must transport ourselves to the time. Gambetta believed that the war would be prolonged. He could not bring himself to lay down his arms; he was maddened almost by a patriotic sorrow —a noble sorrow which earned for him the generous forgiveness of all the noble spirits in the nation. In spite of the burning and implacable hatred that his four months' dictatorship had caused, he was none the less, in the eyes of the country, the personification of the national defence, and never ceased to be regarded as the Leonidas of the French Thermopylæ. This more than anything else made him the most powerful man of the Third Republic.

Nevertheless Gambetta seemed more completely defeated on the field of internal politics than on that of war against the invader when the National Assembly, elected Feb. 18, 1871, met at Bordeaux. The majority, largely royalist, was passionately hostile to him, though it also had done its duty in the army. The country, exhausted, wished for peace at any price, demanded it through the organ of its representatives, and denounced the man who pressed for war to the bitter end. Furthermore, the royalist and conservative deputies manifested a sort of furious rage against the democratic dictatorship of the young tribune. Unwilling to take part in the vote on the treaty of peace, he resigned and retired to St. Sébastien. When the commune of Paris let loose the horrible and criminal war which bathed the streets in blood and seemed destined to consummate the ruin of France, irretrievable defeat seemed to be the doom of the Republican party and its eloquent leader. Yet M. Thiers was able to establish the Republic, thanks to his firmness, to his promptness of resolution, to the ability with which he profited by the dissensions of the royalist party. Gambetta, restored to Parliament by Paris through the complementary elections of July 2, 1871, found himself thrust in the background, the leader of a feeble minority. Little by little he regained his influence, speaking on all the great questions where the predominant interests of the country were at stake. He also embraced every opportunity to address the masses of the people in order to maintain and develop in them a love of the new institutions, but carefully steered clear of all compromise with the spirit of disorder and anarchy. As a man and as an orator he daily put forth new strength; the wrongs that were heaped upon him by the royalist and clerical majority served only to increase the authority which he wielded outside of Parliament. Affairs underwent a speedy change after the overthrow of M. Thiers. Within a few months Gambetta became the leader of the entire Republican party —the leader that was to conduct it to victory. Then, indeed, a great change was seen in him, or rather the new circumstances revealed in the man, known only as a popular leader of unsurpassed audacity, a statesman cautious, capable of self-restraint, and able to carry out a far-reaching plan. Thanks to this wisdom Gambetta became really the second founder of the Republic by obtaining from his own party the concessions without which a majority of votes in the Assembly could not have been obtained for the Republican constitution. By the combined efforts of Gambetta and of the Republican adherents of M. Thiers this fundamental measure was passed in February, 1875, by an Assembly which four years before had been controlled by the temporary royalist coalition. On May 16, 1877, with an adroitness equal to his energy, Gambetta led the opposition to the *coup d'état* attempted by Marshal MacMahon and the royalist factions against the Republic. We have now arrived at the debatable period of Gambetta's public career. As he himself said, "The Republic's hour of peril was followed by its hour of difficulties." The most serious of these difficulties was, in truth, the removal of its perils. Danger had united the Republican party and carried it on to victory. When the party found itself master of the country it divided anew. The Chamber of Deputies in 1877 had for its only programme opposition to the attempt of the 16th of May. When that reaction was swept away great divergencies showed themselves. They increased after the elections of August, 1880, to such an extent that the Republicans could no longer form a governing majority. The consequence was a rapid succession of ministries broken on the first caprice. The method by which representatives were chosen to the Chamber of Deputies was certainly an active cause of this governmental disorganization. The deputies, nominated individually by insignificant districts, represented each his arrondissement instead of being placed collectively, as formerly, on a departmental list. Local interests thus prevailed over general interests. The deputy took care above all to serve his little constituency with such fidelity that it was impossible for the Chamber to have a programme marked out on broad lines and to intrust this programme to its chosen ministers. These ministers became merely the clerks of the Chamber, as the deputies themselves were the docile servants of their arrondissements.

On the morrow of the brilliant triumph of the Republic in the elections of October, 1877, the influence of Gambetta was unlimited, especially after Marshal MacMahon had, in 1879, resigned the presidency of the Republic and had been succeeded by M. Jules Grévy. The latter confined himself to the strict discharge of his constitutional duties. The reality of power belonged without reserve to Gambetta, although as long as it was possible he refused to assume the official direction of affairs and remained content with the speakership of the Chamber. Convinced that the Chamber would furnish a real governmental majority and that principles would prevail over selfish interests only when its members should be elected by departmental ballot rather than by separate arrondissements, he resolved to insist upon this cardinal reform before assuming ministerial responsibility. For a moment, in the summer of 1880, he was on the point of obtaining it; he had prevailed over the repugnance of the Chamber, but the project failed in the Senate. When, in consequence of the general elections of August, 1880, he was obliged to accept the presidency of the Council, he made no effort to keep it. By proposing to a Chamber newly elected an electoral reform which should without fail send its members back forthwith to new electors, he exposed himself at once to certain defeat. The few weeks of his ministry furnish therefore no criterion of what he would have been as the premier of the state. But, though fallen from power, in him was still centred, as in its most incontestable representative, the strength of the Republican party, when, on the last day of 1882, the world was startled to hear of his assassination by a woman's hand.

His obsequies were without precedent. All France was there represented. She lamented and eulogized not merely the great orator, one of the chief founders of the Republic, but above all the man who had been her representative and champion in the bloody and direful days of the invasion. The heart of France beat strongly that day in the crowds which followed sadly the hearse of her most illustrious citizen. But, alas! at that service God was not invoked. It was entirely secular. It corresponded too well with the convictions of Gambetta himself, who had never distinguished between Christianity and Ultramontane Catholicism. His famous phrase, "Our enemy is clericalism," was the inspiration of his internal policy, unfortunately followed by many of his political friends with a sectarian narrowness which was foreign to his character. Gambetta may be reproached with having been too faithful to that system of centralization which has been preserved under all the governments of France. Nevertheless he was a man of progress, a true representative of democracy, rejecting the vain dreams of socialism, but earnest and persevering in pursuit of social reform. The heart of the people responded warmly to his own. A thoroughly proved patriot, an orator of matchless power, the loss of Gambetta left in the French Republic an immense void. No leader has been able to take his place, for he surpassed all the men of his generation in the greatness of his eloquence and the grandeur of his political views. (E. DE P.)

GAMBLING, or GAMING. The art or practice of acquiring money or property by hazard or chance; an agreement between two or more to risk money upon a contingency, or chance of any kind, where one must be loser and the other gainer (5 Sneed, 507). "Whenever money or other valuable consideration is hazarded and may be lost, or more than the value obtained by chance, it is gaming, nor will any name or device take it out of this category" (State of Tenn. vs. Smith & Lane, 2 Yer. 272).

See Vol. X. p. 60 Am. ed. (p. 66 Edin. ed.).

Early legislation in England against gaming seemed to be based on the ground that it interfered with the usefulness of servants, laborers, etc.; provoked idleness, and diverted attention from archery. The first statute (12 R. 2, c. 6) in England (1388), prohibiting gaming, applied only to servants of husbandry, artificers, and victuallers—not to servants of gentlemen—and commanded such to refrain from "hand and foot ball, coits, dice, throwing of stone kayles, and such other importune games." The next statute (11 H. 4, c. 4, 1409) enforced the above, with a penalty of six days' imprisonment for each offence. The next act (17 Ed. 4, c. 3, 1477), after naming in a preamble the foregoing games, says, "Contrary to such laws, the said games and divers newly devised games called cloish, kayles, half-bowle, hand-in-and-hand-out, and queekeborde, from day to day are used in divers parts of the land;" then provides that no occupier or master of a house shall voluntarily permit any prohibited person to play at any such game in said house under pain of three years' imprisonment and a forfeiture of £20 for each offence. No prohibited person could play under pain of two years' imprisonment and £10 default. Another act (11 H. 7, c. 2, 1494) provided that no artificer, laborer, or servant should play any unlawful game except at Christmas, while the law (19 H. 7, c. 12) of 1503 absolutely prohibited certain persons named therein from playing at any game. In 1511 (3 H. 8, c. 3) unlawful games were again prohibited, and a still more stringent law was enacted in 1535 (22 H. 8, c. 35).

In 1541 (33 H. 8, c. 25) the manufacturers and dealers in archery petitioned Parliament to prohibit all games and enforce the practice of archery. Accordingly, in 1542, a most stringent act was passed, obliging all able-bodied male citizens between the ages of 17 and 60 years, except ministers and judges, to own bows and arrows, and to practise with the same. Masters were required to see that their servants were provided with bows and arrows and instructed in their uses; if not provided, the master must furnish the same, and was empowered to deduct the price from the servant's wages. This act repeals all other laws concerning gaming, and then prohibits the keeping of any "common house, alley or place of bowlinge, coytinge, cloyshe, cayles, half-bowle, tennys, dysing table, or cardinge, or any other unlawfull new game hereafter to be invented," under a penalty of 40s. for each offence. Magistrates, sheriffs, bailiffs, constables, and head officers of cities, boroughs, and towns were required and authorized to enter all such places at any time and arrest offenders; they must also search at least once a month to discover such places and suppress the same under a monthly penalty of 40s. for every default.

Section 16 of this act then provides that "No manner of artificer, craftsman, husbandman, apprentice, laborer, servant at husbandry, journeyman, or servant of artificer, mariner, fisherman, waterman, or servingman shall play at the tables, tennis, dice, cards, bowles, clash, coyting, logating, or any other unlawful game, out of Christmas, under pain of 20s. for each offence." At Christmas this class could only play in their master's house or presence. This act made no game in itself unlawful. It only became unlawful by being used by certain persons at certain times or certain places. The keeping of a common gambling-house for any unlawful game, for lucre or gain, was prohibited; but no game was made unlawful unless played in such common house. Faro and rouge-et-noir were not then considered unlawful games.

In 1745 faro, bassett, ace of hearts, hazard, passage, roly-poly, roulette, and all games of dice, except backgammon, were prohibited under a penalty to setter-up of £200 and £50 fine for players. The act of 1848 repealed so much of the act of 1542 as prohibits bowling, tennis, and other games of mere skill.

Justices of the peace, at their annual licensing meetings, were empowered to grant a license to persons to keep a room for billiards, bagatelle-boards, and the like; but these were prohibited between the hours of 1 and 8 A. M., and on Sundays, Christmas, Good Friday, or any public fast or thanksgiving day.

Gambling was not indictable at common law.

In England, at common law, it was held, a common gambling-house, kept for lucre or gain, was *per se* a common nuisance, as it tends to draw together idle and evil-disposed persons, to corrupt their morals and ruin their fortunes; being the same reasons given in the case of houses of common prostitution (King vs. Rogers & Humphreys).

New South Wales, in 1850, passed most stringent laws against gaming, naming "billiards, bagatelle, bowles, fives-racket, quoits, skittles, or nine-pins," in addition to banking games. Constables were authorized to enter all suspected places, to arrest all persons keeping any gambling paraphernalia, cards, dice, etc., making the possession of such matters evidence of the house being a common gaming-house, thus throwing the burden of proof upon the occupant. All contracts were void.

In the United States the keeping of a common gambling-house is indictable at common law on account of its evil influence on public morals (1 Bish. Crim. Law, 504; 1 Rus. 3 Eng. Ed. 325; U. S. vs. Dixon, 4 Cranch C. C. 107; State vs. Savannah, T. W. P. Charl. 235; State vs. Doon, R. M. Charl. L)

Gambling has also been almost universally legislated against in the various States and Territories because it contravenes public policy, is destructive of public morals, and creates and fosters other crimes. In Georgia, in 1764, a general act was passed against gambling, yet in 1811, under common law, it was held that "A house where a faro-table is kept for common gambling is *per se* a nuisance, notwithstanding they were subject to taxation by law" (R. M. Charl. I.) In Tennessee, 1785, a tax of £250 was imposed upon every A. B. C. or E. O. table. In 1799 all gaming was prohibited, and all contracts and security in consideration of gaming declared void. No person could institute suit to recover money lost under a penalty. Under the laws of 1817 judges of errors and appeals could debar any practising attorney guilty of violating the law against gaming, while any person convicted of gaming was disqualified to hold any office of trust in the State for five years. In West Virginia the law especially names "faro, keno, wheel of fortune, rolypoly, hop-hazard, alias blink-hazard, alias snick-up, alias sweat, pool, dice, cards, A. B. C. and E. O. tables." New York State, by its penal code, prohibits the occupying, keeping, using, or allowing to be used, any room, tenement, booth, or building, or part thereof, table, device, or apparatus for gambling purposes. It is made the duty of all sheriffs, policemen, constables, district-attorneys, and prosecuting officers to inform against and prosecute all persons whom they have reason to believe guilty of violating these laws. All persons are authorized to arrest, and also empowered and required to seize all articles suitable for gambling purposes, and to bring the same before the magistrate.

The effects of gambling are most vividly described by that eminent jurist, Judge Catron, formerly of the Supreme Court of the United States, in a decision rendered by him. He says:

"Like other passions which agitate the great mass of the community it lies dormant until once aroused, and then, with the contagion and fury of a pestilence, it sweeps morals, motives of honest pursuits and industry into the vortex of vice; unhinges the principles of religion and common honesty; the mind becomes ungovernable, and is destroyed to all useful purposes; chances of successful gambling alone are looked to for prosperity in life, even for the daily means of sustenance; trembling anxiety for success in lotteries, at the faro-bank, or loo-table, exclude all other thoughts" (2 Yer., Tenn., 272).

Notwithstanding stringent State laws and the common law, to the contrary, until 1880, gambling was almost universal throughout the Union—the punishment of gamblers being an exception instead of the rule. Prior to 1880 embezzlements, defalcations, robberies, thefts, breaches of trust, and other crimes were constantly announced by the public press as the direct result of gambling. The gambler's victim, if convicted, received severe penalties, while the gambler could scarcely be brought to justice at all, and if convicted escaped with a nominal fine. It was estimated that the income of these gaming-houses in New York city, including nine lotteries, was upwards of $10,000,000 per year. The principal gamblers ranked high as politicians, and were sought for by the leaders of both political parties, because of the large contributions or assessments they were willing to pay. In return for these assessments they demanded that their business should not be molested. For years it was not, either by police, prosecuting attorneys, or the courts.

In 1877 the New York Society for the Suppression of Vice began a vigorous attack upon these evils. Scores of gamblers were arrested and indicted, their places raided, and their gambling paraphernalia seized. These cases, until the fall of 1880, could not be brought to trial. Gamblers complained that they had paid for protection, and that they were not protected, but were raided and arrested by the agents of the society aforesaid. In August, 1880, Gov. Alonzo P. Cornell issued his proclamation to prosecuting officers, police, and the courts, calling upon them to enforce these laws. So indifferent were the courts, and so powerful the influence of the gambling fraternity, that, in the General Sessions Court, of New York city, 29 gamblers, convicted October, 1880, were sentenced to a total of but $202.50, or less than $7 each. Long and bitter was the conflict. Another society (Society for the Prevention of Crime) bravely seconded the efforts being made. Public sentiment was aroused, and despite all opposition, by the firm, persistent, and relentless efforts of these societies, in 1881-84 scores of these criminals were convicted and sentenced to imprisonment, while thousands of dollars worth of paraphernalia seized was destroyed. In 1885 scarcely a place in New York city was found open to the public, or where a stranger could enter or play, unless vouched for by some one in whom the boss-gambler had confidence. Laws triumphed not only in New York, but her example has been infectious, and in 1885 nearly all the principal cities in the Union waged a bitter warfare against gambling. In Louisville, Ky., long the head-quarters of notorious lotteries, in November and December, 1885, 35 gamblers were convicted and sentenced to a total of 47 months' imprisonment and $16,000 fine—the severest penalties inflicted in any State in the Union upon the same number of gamblers.

The principal games in the United States are faro, poker or roulette, rouge-et-noir, sweat, hazard, baccarat, vantune, monte, three-card-monte, honest-man or twenty-one, odd-and-even, fin-tan or Chinese faro, pool, horse pool, lottery, and policy—the two last most prevalent (See LOTTERY).

Faro is a bet on cards. A layout of green baize cloth has upon it what represents a full deck of cards, arranged about the border, each of the four kinds being grouped together. There are chips or counters of various colors used, each color representing value—white 25 cents, red 50 cents, blue $1, etc., which are sold in stacks of 10 or 20 each to the players. An ordinary whist pack is placed in a metal deal box, which has a spring to keep the cards pressed up to the top. The dealer deals one card at a time from the top of the pack by sliding it out through a slit in one side of the top. The bet is, that a certain card will come out among seven to be dealt. The player places his chips to the amount of his bet upon a certain card. The dealer bets upon the card opposite, on the board. If the card the player has bet upon comes out he wins; if not then at the seventh card dealt the dealer sweeps the board. In an honest game the odds are 85 to 15 in favor of the dealer. With marked or stacked cards the odds are all in favor of the dealer.

Rouge-et-noir is similar to faro: the player bets by placing his chips on a red or black card; if his color is next dealt he wins, if opposite color he loses.

Monte, sweat, honest-man, and twenty-one are all similar games with cards. The dealer deals a card to each player; and one opposite each for himself. The player bets that a certain card will come out first. If it does he wins; if the card opposite to him comes out first he loses.

In odd-and-even the bet is on the card next dealt, to be either an odd number or an even one.

Poker, or bluff, is played with cards. Five cards are dealt each player; the one holding the highest cards wins the bank or pot. Each player bets upon his own hand as against the others. Poker is usually played by not more than four players.

A sweat layout consists of a cloth or board with the numbers "1 2 3 4 5 6" upon it, and is played usually with one and sometimes two dice. The player bets his chips upon a certain number, say on 4, and if 4 appears on the dice he wins; if not he loses.

Three-card-monte is a disreputable trick with three cards, usually employed by sharpers at country fairs, on railroad trains and steamboats, to rob the unwary. The dealer manipulates the cards, after first showing the face of each, throws them down, face downward, and the dupes bet upon the denomination of a certain card.

It must be observed that players exchange their money for chips, then bet their chips against their own money, voluntarily placed by them in the dealer's hand. The dealer manipulates the contingency (cards) upon which the wager depends, with the odds always largely in his favor. Adroitness, cunning, experience at manipulating cards, sleight-of-hand, skill, and practice in trickery, robbery by trick and device, a keen knowledge of human nature, and the weakness of mankind when aroused by greed, contend against ignorance, folly, blinded hopes, clouded judgment, and often distress, desperation, and a brain fired and unbalanced by the wine-cup. (A. C.)

GAMMELL, WILLIAM, an American educator and author, was born at Medfield, Mass., Feb. 10, 1812. He graduated at Brown University in 1831, and was made tutor there. In 1835 he became assistant professor, and in 1836 professor of rhetoric and English literature. In 1850 he was transferred to the chair of history and political economy, and resigned this position in 1864. In 1870 he was made one of the fellows of the corporation. Besides many contributions to reviews and magazines, he has published *Life of Roger Williams* and *Life of Gov. Samuel Ward* in Sparks' *American Biography*, and a *History of American Baptist Missions* (1850).

GANNETT, EZRA STILES (1801-1871), an American Unitarian minister, was born at Cambridge, Mass., May 4, 1801. He was educated at Phillips Academy, Andover, and graduated at Harvard College in 1820. He then studied theology, and in June, 1824, was ordained as colleague to Rev. W. E. Channing, in Boston. Upon Dr. Channing's death in 1842, he became sole pastor and so remained till his death, though he spent two years in Europe on account of his health. He published several sermons, and from 1844 to 1849 was joint editor of the *Christian Examiner*. He was prominent in various benevolent and philanthropic enterprises. He died by a railroad accident near Boston, Aug. 28, 1871.

GARDEN, ALEXANDER (1728-1791), a British naturalist, was born in Scotland in 1728. He graduated at Aberdeen University in 1748, studied medicine and settled at Charleston, S. C., in 1752. On account of his labors in botany and zoölogy he was, in 1773, made a member of the Royal Society, of which he afterwards was vice-president. He was a correspondent of Linnæus, who named the beautiful shrub *Gardenia* in his honor. Being a loyalist, Dr. Garden went to England in 1783, and his property was confiscated, but afterwards was restored to his son. He died at London, April 15, 1791.

GARDEN, ALEXANDER (1757-1829), an American soldier and author, son of the preceding, was born at Charleston, S. C., Dec. 4, 1757. He was educated in England and graduated at Glasgow in 1777. When he returned to South Carolina, he joined the patriot army and served in Henry Lee's light-horse legion In his later years he wrote *Anecdotes of the Revolutionary War* (1822-28; republished, Brooklyn, 2 vols., 1863), which is highly esteemed as an authority for the period. He died at Charleston, S. C., Feb. 29, 1829.

GARDENIA, or CAPE JASMINE. There are numerous species, but those especially thus designated are natives of China and are known in gardening as *Gardenia florida* and *Gardenia radicans*, with some varieties between the two, if, indeed, both of the nominal species be not themselves varieties of one thing. The *Gardenia* belongs to the order *Rubiaceæ*, and to that section of it regarded by Lindley and some other botanists as constituting a distinct order, the name *Cinchonaceæ*, to which the coffee, cinchona, and other tropical plants belong. Beyond the fact that the Chinese are said to prepare from the flowers and fruit an orange or light scarlet dye for silk, the Gardenias have place in none of the arts except that of gardening. The delightful odor of the large waxy-white flowers rendered it a popular favorite on its introduction to England about the year 1754; it fell into the hands of James Gordon, a nurseryman, who from four cuttings in a few years raised and sold plants to the value of $25,000. One of these was sent by Mr. Ellis to Dr. Alexander Garden (q. v.), in whose honor he had named it. From this probably all the American plants spring. It is hardy in the United States wherever the temperature does not go far below the freezing-point in winter, and hence it is one of the most popular plants for out-door gardening in the Southern States. In the North it is a favorite pot-plant, and the flowers in early spring are very much esteemed in florists' work.

The early history of the plant furnishes some of the most fascinating gossip in Smith's *Correspondence of Linnæus*. An East India ship, the Godolphin, Capt. Hutchinson, put in at the Cape of Good Hope. The captain, on shore, was attracted by a sweet odor, and on searching for the source found a small plant in bloom which he put into a tub of earth and carried successfully to England, where it was placed under the care of Mr. Warner. The Dutch were famous florists and had a botanical garden at the Cape. They had exclusive intercourse with China. The plant had been introduced in some way from Asia. But being supposed at that time to belong to the jasmine family, the name "Cape Jasmine" was given to this Chinese plant. After Linnæus' attention had been called to it by Ellis, he found that he had already a dried specimen in his collection which had been received from the East Indies. Ellis had intended to name the plant *Warneria*, but as Miller had so named a ranunculaceous plant (now found to be identical with *Hydrastis*) he gave the name in honor of his friend and correspondent Dr. Garden; but not however without a gentle protest from Linnæus against such honor where the person honored had no connection with the history of the plant. It is used for evergreen hedges in Japan, where it is known as "Kits ginas." In the East Indies it is called "Cotsjopiri." (T. M.)

GARDINER, John (1731-1793), an American lawyer, was born at Boston, Mass., in 1731. He studied law in London, was admitted to the bar in Westminster, and was one of the counsel for John Wilkes in 1764. He was attorney-general in the Island of St. Christopher from 1766, but after the American Revolution returned to Boston, and soon settled at Pownalborough, Me., which he represented in the Massachusetts legislature until his death. Noted for wit and eloquence, he was one of the leaders of the Unitarian movement in 1787. In the legislature he procured the abolition of primogeniture, and the repeal of the laws against theatres. He was drowned off Cape Ann, Oct. 15, 1793.

GARDINER, John Sylvester John, D. D. (1765-1830), an American clergyman, son of the preceding, was born at Haverford West, Wales, in June, 1765. He was taken by his father to the West Indies, was educated in Boston and by Dr. Samuel Parr in England. He returned to America in 1787, and being ordained deacon by Bishop Provoost in New York, had charge of the parish of St. Helena, S. C., until 1791, when he was ordained priest. He became assistant minister of Trinity Church, Boston, in 1792, and rector of the same in 1805. He also conducted a classical school and was a contributor to literary periodicals. He died at Harrowgate, England, July 29, 1830.

GARDINER, Sylvester (1707-1786), an American physician, born at Kingston, R. I., in 1707, studied medicine in London and Paris, but settled at Boston as physician and drug-merchant. On his lands in Maine he established Pittston and Gardiner. Being a loyalist he left Boston with the British troops in 1776, and went to England, but returned to America in 1785, and died at Newport, R. I., Aug. 8, 1786. He was one of the founders of King's Chapel in Boston, and prepared a prayer-book. Much of his property which was confiscated was afterwards restored to his heirs.

GARFIELD, James Abram, twentieth President of the United States, son of Abram and Eliza Garfield, was born in Orange township, Cuyahoga co., Ohio, Nov. 19, 1831. Of his paternal Puritan ancestry, Hon. George F. Hoar says: "Of the seven generations born in America, including the President, not one was born in other than a frontiersman's dwelling. Two of them, father and son, came over with Winthrop in 1630. Each of the six generations who dwelt in Massachusetts has left an honorable record, still preserved. Five in succession bore an honorable military title. Seven were fighters in the Indian wars. At the breaking out of the Revolution the male representatives of the family were two young brothers; one, whose name descended to the President, was in arms at Concord Bridge, at sunrise on April 19, 1775; the other, the President's great-grandfather, dwelling thirty miles off, was on his way to the scene of action before noon." Abram Garfield, father of the President, was born in Otsego co., N. Y., in December, 1799. Two years later his father died. He grew up under the rigid but wholesome discipline of poverty and toil to great physical strength, and formed a good character for industry, courage, persistence, and strong moral and religious principles. His removal in early manhood to Ohio, his marriage with Miss Eliza Ballou, and the planting of their home in the forests of Northern Ohio, bring us to the birthplace of their son, James Abram. Judge Hoar has truly said: "The history of the settlement of Massachusetts, Central New York, and Ohio, is the history of the Garfield race." The hardy virtues of pioneers were theirs. They were patriotic, persevering, heroic, just, and generous; ardent in their devotion to the interests of civil and religious liberty; distinguished for muscular strength, pure morals, and profound religious faith.

Eliza Ballou, daughter of James and Mehitabel Ballou, was born in Richmond, Cheshire co., N. H., Sept. 21, 1801. Maturin Ballou was a Huguenot, who fled from France after the revocation of the edict of Nantes, to a home of freedom in Rhode Island. His descendants in this country were noted for brilliancy of intellect, liberal culture, moral excellence, religious zeal, and superior oratorical power. Several of them were preachers—the most noted of these being the Rev. Hosea Ballou, the founder of the Universalist Church in the United States. Eliza Ballou was his grandniece. From such an ancestry, it may be readily judged what a favorable combination of physical, intellectual, and moral qualities—of brawn and brain and heart—entered into the heritage of James A. Garfield.

In Garfield's child-life there was little that can be called remarkable. He is reported by a friend to have said, after reaching manhood, that his highest ambition, until he was about sixteen years old, was to be captain of a vessel on Lake Erie—certainly a modest ambition compared with the usual dreams and ambitions of childhood and youth. He was the youngest of four children—Mehitabel, Thomas, Mary, and James Abram. Before he was two years old his father died, leaving this family in the log-cabin, with some twenty acres cleared around it, a rude log-barn, a young orchard, and a few farming implements. There were a few straggling debts, but not enough to burden seriously this small inheritance. By dauntless energy and rigid economy the widow succeeded in paying off the debts, in securing a portion of the land for a home, selling twenty of the fifty acres, and in winning a comfortable support for her children. Her immediate neighbors were New Englanders, intelligent, energetic, sociable, and religious. The surroundings of the family were as favorable as those of most pioneer families of New England origin, unblessed with wealth, but combining a good degree of intelligence and strong religious faith with simple tastes, great physical energy, and the sturdy virtues apt to be developed amid the rude scenes and numerous hardships of frontier life. Mrs. Garfield inherited the fine, compact, nervous organization of the Ballous, together with their intellectual tastes and religious fervor. She had been a school-teacher. Although her rude, humble log-cabin held but few books, the Bible being the chief book for the study of the household, her mind was stored with a rich variety of New England lore—with history, tradition, story, and song—and while Bible-reading and prayer were daily exercises in the family her children were also instructed in such knowledge as she possessed, and entertained with the stories and songs with which her memory was enriched. The school-house also was within reach, for instruction in such rudiments as were then taught in the schools of a new country. With such environments the child, James, grew into boyhood, in a pleasant home, with a few agreeable associates from neighboring homes. He inherited a strong, healthy physical constitution. He early learned to read, and, besides the Bible, such books as were within his reach—the old *English Reader*, *Life of Napoleon* and of *Marion*, *Tales of the Sea*, *Plutarch's Lives*, etc., were eagerly devoured. At school he was always forward with his lessons, sometimes puzzling even his teachers by a mastery of his studies beyond their own attainments. Always physically active even to restlessness, manual labor and manly sports were both pleasures to him. Whether toiling on the farm, or chopping cord-wood by the job, or driving horses on the tow-path of the Pennsylvania and Ohio Canal, or working at the carpenter's bench—for, among the rest of his youthful attainments, he had learned how to build houses—he was always diligent and faithful, and uniformly won the respect of his employers. Many a hard-earned dollar was, by such toils, secured for the purchase of books, or to help his mother in the support of the family.

In his sixteenth year a passion for a seafaring life took strong possession of him. This desire had probably been kindled by some of the books he had read, and nurtured by an occasional glimpse of Lake Erie in the distance, dotted with white sails filled with the breeze, and joyously wafting vessels over the blue waters. Gaining his mother's reluctant consent, he went to Cleveland to ship as a sailor on some one of the vessels in port. This was his first serious venture away from home. Disappointed in his applications for service as a sailor, and failing in all his efforts to obtain employment in the city, he hired out to the captain of a canal-boat—one Amos Letcher, a cousin of his—to drive horses on the tow-path. After meeting with various adventures in which were developed great pluck and endurance, it became apparent to him and also to his employer that he was born to higher tasks than this, and he returned to his home preparatory to a search for some worthier employment. After a serious illness of several months, he arose from his sick-bed with a resolution to obtain an education. In his eighteenth year, after perfecting himself in the rudiments taught in the common schools, he entered Geauga Seminary, an academy in Chester, Geauga co., Ohio, under the direction of the Free-Will Baptists. Here he continued his studies between two and three years, with intervals spent in working at his trade as a carpenter and in teaching. Natural philosophy, botany, English grammar, algebra, Latin, and Greek, were the studies pursued at Chester. His studies here occupied four terms, and he taught district-school, at intervals, two terms In the autumn of 1851 he entered the Western Reserve Eclectic Institute—now Hiram College—at Hiram, Portage co., Ohio, an institution under the direction of the body known as DISCIPLES OF CHRIST. Here he pursued his studies until 1854. He was, on his own application, made janitor, that he might earn part of the money needed to pay his way by kindling the fires, sweeping the floors, and ringing the bell. He soon became a general favorite, and his progress in his stuides was such that, ere long, he was employed as tutor during the illness of one of the teachers of science and English literature. He had already taught in district-schools three or four terms, and he now began to develop a peculiar power to impart as well as to receive instruction; so that from this time onward he was constantly employed in teaching from three to six classes a day, as long as he remained at Hiram.

On March 4, 1850, young Garfield was baptized, near his home in Orange, by Evangelist W. A. Lillie, and a week later was received into the church in Orange to which his mother belonged, as had also his father. He had been familiar from childhood with the faith and practice of the Disciples; but he acted, in this matter, on his own conviction of duty, and not until theological difficulties that had arisen in his mind were frankly stated and satisfactorily explained did he make a public confession of his faith. He at once became an earnest worker in the church, frequently speaking in the prayer-meetings, and developing into such force and attractiveness of speech that within a few years the churches in that region were glad to receive visits from him and listen to his discourses. He drew large audiences wherever he went, and it is not unlikely that, for a time, he cherished the idea of devoting his life to the Christian ministry. This, however, was never fully determined, and although he continued for several years to preach with great acceptance whenever his regular employments allowed of it, and, indeed, through all his life was ready to manifest his faith and his interest in spiritual things, by public addresses on suitable occasions, he finally decided that his vocation was in another sphere of life. But this change of pursuit carried with it no change of faith or of fellowship. His ecclesiastical affiliations were never broken; his faith in Christ remained with him, through all changes, to the last

In the fall of 1854 Mr. Garfield entered Williams College, at Williamstown, Mass., then under the presiding care of the eminent Mark Hopkins, D. D., LL. D., to whom he ever after acknowledged great indebtedness for his intellectual and moral growth. Graduating in 1856 he took one of the highest honors of his class. He had obtained a high reputation for thoroughness in study, purity of life, and manly devotion to truth for truth's sake, and won all hearts by his genial spirit and upright ways.

Returning to Hiram, he was elected teacher of ancient languages in the Eclectic Institute. Two years later he became principal. Under his management the institute was eminently prosperous. An enthusiasm for study was kindled among the students, such as is rarely witnessed. His morning lectures—in which not only his book-knowledge but the large store of facts which his quick perceptions and ceaseless inquiry had gathered up from every-day scenes was brought into requisition—were a great inspiration as well as a great source of information to the students. The throng of pupils was held in perfect order by his personal influence.

But the discharge of his duties as principal of the institute was a small part of his work. He kept up a large course of reading and study outside of that which related to educational matters; he delivered lectures and addresses on various subjects; he participated in public debates on questions theological and scientific; he preached almost every Sunday; he engaged in the study of law, and was admitted to the bar by the Supreme Court at Columbus, Ohio: and with all this work on his hands he found time to enter the political arena and make speeches for the Republican party. Nor did all these employments shut him out from the duties and enjoyments of social life. He was cheerful, and even jovial, with his friends, personally familiar with all his pupils, and readily accessible to all that called on him. His position as principal of the Eclectic Institute was held until August, 1861, when he went to the army; though his name was retained in later catalogues, in the hope that he would return to the post from which his patriotism had called him. In the catalogues of 1865 and 1866 his name appears as advisory principal and lecturer, and after that on the list of trustees.

He was married to Miss Lucretia Rudolph, daughter

of Zeb and Arabella Rudolph, Nov. 11, 1858. He first met her at the Geauga Seminary, where they were both students. Subsequently, at Hiram, where Miss Rudolph was one of the first students, she recited in several of the classes taught by Mr. Garfield. An acquaintance thus formed ripened into mutual affection and resulted in their marriage. Miss Rudolph was as remarkable for diligence and success in her studies as for her evenness of disposition, quiet manners, and dignity of character.

To James A. and Lucretia Garfield were born seven children—five sons and two daughters—of whom five are now living. It is due to Mrs. Garfield to say that, having known her husband from the first of his struggles to obtain an education, and having passed with him through several years of student-life, she did not fail, after their marriage, to keep pace with him in intellectual pursuits, or to sympathize with him in the labors and anxieties of his public life. Their home was not only an abode of domestic happiness and social enjoyment but also of refined culture—a centre of attraction to cultivated minds. The neatness and order that ever quietly reigned; the free play of domestic affections; the delightful sympathy between husband and wife in all that pertained to literary and scientific culture; the education of bright, healthy children into sympathy with their parents in intellectual pursuits; and the free, joyous outflow of all this home feeling and sentiment into the social circles that gathered at their fireside, make up a beautiful picture of home-life.

The year of Mr. Garfield's graduation from Williams College (1856) was the year of the first national convention of the Republican party, to nominate candidates for the Presidency and Vice-Presidency. For John C. Fremont, its nominee, Mr. Garfield cast his first vote. From that time until his death he was a steadfast adherent of that party, and rapidly made his way to the front rank of its champions. Constitutionally and educationally, by inheritance and by all his early surroundings, he was the devoted friend of civil and religious liberty, and the determined foe of slavery in all its forms. From the time that the Republican party flung its banner to the breeze, with the inscription, "Resistance to the Spread of Slavery in the National Territories," through all the political conflicts and bloody strifes which ended in the overthrow of slavery in the United States, and thence on through the exciting period of reconstruction unto the consummation of all the measures proposed by the dominant party for the national welfare, Mr. Garfield was the unswerving advocate of Liberty and Union, and, for the most part, a prominent figure in that thrilling period of the history of the government of the United States from 1860 to 1880. We note briefly the steps in his political and military career.

In 1859, in his twenty-eighth year, he was elected to the Ohio Senate from the Summit-Portage district. Although the youngest member of that body, he took a front rank among the State senators, and, along with J. D. Cox and James Monroe, rendered essential service in preparing Ohio for the approaching contest with the forces of the rebellion. These gentlemen were known as "The Radical Triumvirate," whose advanced sentiments, vigilance, and arduous efforts were largely instrumental in preparing the Ohio legislature for a prompt response to Pres. Lincoln's call for 75,000 men—voting in several bills, at different dates, 20,000 men and $3,000,000 for the defence and maintenance of the Union.

Aug. 14, 1861. Mr. Garfield received from Gov. Dennison his commission as Lieut.-Col. of the Forty-second regiment Ohio volunteer infantry, and on the 16th of the same month he was mustered into the service at Camp Chase, near Columbus, Ohio. For four months his time was spent in learning and in teaching the art of war, and in the recruiting service.

Dec. 15, 1861, he was ordered to report for duty to Gen. D. C. Buell, at Louisville, Ky.; and before he had gained the least experience on the battle-field he was placed in command of four regiments of infantry and some eight companies of cavalry, and charged with the duty of driving the forces under Gen. Humphrey Marshall out of Kentucky—forces, as it afterwards appeared, amounting to 4400 infantry and 600 cavalry. On Jan. 10, 1862, the battle of Middle Creek was fought, and Marshall's forces were defeated and driven out of the State. The defeat of Gen. Marshall was followed by the defeat of Zollicoffer's army, at Mill Spring, by Gen. Thomas, Jan. 19. Gen. Zollicoffer was slain, and what remained of his army was chased into Tennessee, as Gen. Marshall's forces had previously been driven into Virginia. These victories were the dawn of a brighter day for the Union. Pres. Lincoln commissioned Col. Garfield a brigadier-general of volunteers, dating his commission Jan. 10, the date of his victory at Middle Creek. He was the youngest general in the army—two months over thirty years of age.

After this, he took part in the battle of Shiloh, under Gen. Buell. Without entering into the details of his military history, it is sufficient to say that his services for some time after the battle of Shiloh were mainly rendered in courts-martial, where his legal knowledge and skill, sound judgment, and strict impartiality were found of great value. The most important and celebrated of these trials was that of Fitz-John Porter, in 1862-3, to bear a part in which Gen. Garfield was ordered to report at Washington City. The trial lasted nearly two months, and involved some complicated questions. The result of the trial was a verdict of guilty. In this verdict, after the most thorough investigation, Garfield heartily joined. Although, since his death, Gen. Grant and others changed their first opinion, and in view of new information declared Gen. Porter justified, it should be recorded here that no subsequent developments made during his lifetime in the least changed Gen. Garfield's conviction as to the righteousness of the verdict.

Disabled for a time by sickness, on his recovery he was made chief of Gen. Rosecrans's staff, succeeding the lamented Col. J. P. Garesché, who was killed in the battle of Stone River. In this important position his services were soon found to be of the highest value. It is sufficient to refer to the language of Gen. Rosecrans in his official report of operations in Middle Tennessee: "All my staff merited my warm approbation for ability and devotion to duty; but I am sure they will not consider it invidious if I especially mention Brig.-Gen. Garfield, ever active, prudent, and sagacious. I feel much indebted to him for both counsel and assistance in the administration of this army. He possesses the energy and instinct of a great commander.

In the battle of Chickamauga, so stubbornly contested, whatever may have been its blunders and disasters, there is no question as to the skill and bravery with which Gen. Garfield performed his difficult duties as chief of staff—skill in the orders he issued directing the movements of the army; heroism in his perilous ride across the battle-field in a terrible crisis, to reach Gen. Thomas, to furnish him with the information he needed to wrest victory from the hand of the enemy, and save the gallant Army of the Cumberland from overwhelming defeat. The official recognition of his meritorious services by Gen. Rosecrans, and the speedy promotion of the brigadier-general to a major-generalship for gallant and meritorious services in this great battle, were but echoes of the general sentiment, among soldiers and civilians, as to the honorable part performed in that terrible conflict by this wise and brave soldier.

In the fall of 1862 Gen. Garfield had been elected to Congress as a representative of the Nineteenth district of Ohio—a district made famous by its enthusiastic support of Joshua R. Giddings in his radical anti-slavery advocacy. The election of Gen. Garfield took place in his absence, and was a spontaneous tribute to his worth by the people of his district. As the seat to which he was elected was not to be occupied until December, 1863, he refrained from a final decision as to his future course until the fortunes of the war should be more fully disclosed. Now, however, the time had arrived when a decision must be made; and after much consultation with distinguished army officers, and with the authorities at Washington, including Pres. Lincoln, he decided to bid adieu to army life in obedience to the urgent demand for his services in the national legislature. From this time forward he gave himself to statesmanship, and for a period of seventeen years his name is identified with all the great measures of the Republican party, in carrying the war to a triumphant issue, in reconstructing the conquered seceding States, in conforming the Constitution and laws of the nation to the new condition of things, and in guarding the country from financial embarrassment and guiding it in the highway of national prosperity. Now in his thirty-third year, possessed already of considerable experience in civil and military affairs, having the advantages of a liberal education and a wide range of reading and study, with well-balanced powers, a robust physical manhood, a peculiar genius for work, oratorical powers of more than ordinary attractiveness and effectiveness, and fixed political, moral, and religious principles, he was eminently fitted for success in the legislative career that opened to him in the most interesting and perilous period of the history of the national government. Whether in committees, originating legislative measures, or on the floor in the House of Representatives advocating and defending these measures, his industry, his encyclopedic knowledge, his comprehensive grasp of the gravest and most difficult subjects, his keen insight, his conservatism, and his enthusiasm in behalf of political justice and constitutional freedom, combined to lift him at once out of the sphere of the mere party politician into that of the Christian statesman. He succeeded from the start in winning that public admiration and confidence which continued to increase throughout his congressional career, and culminated in his election to the Presidency of the United States.

Of his career in Congress Hon. James G. Blaine, in his "Eulogy on James Abram Garfield" before Congress, Feb. 27, 1882, says with just discrimination:

"Those unfamiliar with Garfield's industry, and ignorant of the details of his work, may in some degree measure them by the annals of Congress. No one of the generation of public men to which he belonged has contributed so much that will be valuable for future reference. The speeches are numerous, many of them brilliant, all of them well studied, carefully phrased, and exhaustive of the subject under consideration. Collected from the scattered pages of ninety royal octavo volumes of Congressional Records, they would present an invaluable compendium of the political history of the most important era through which the national government has ever passed. When the history of this period shall be impartially written—when war legislation, measures of reconstruction, protection of human rights, amendments to the Constitution, maintenance of public credit, steps towards specie resumption, true theories of revenue, may be reviewed unsurrounded by prejudice and disconnected from partisanism—the speeches of Garfield will be estimated at their true value, and will be found to comprise a vast magazine of fact and argument, of clear analysis and sound conclusion. Indeed, if no other authority were accessible, his speeches in the House of Representatives from December, 1863, to June, 1880, would give a well-connected history and complete defence of the important legislation of the seventeen eventful years that constitute his parliamentary life. Far beyond that his speeches would be found to forecast many great measures yet to be completed—measures which he knew were beyond the public opinion of the hour, but which he confidently believed would secure popular approval within the period of his own lifetime, and by the aid of his own efforts."

Were we called on to specify any one among the numerous difficult and perplexing subjects discussed by Gen. Garfield in Congress as that in which he showed peculiar mastery, and in handling which he rendered the highest service to his country, we should select that of Finance. As he said in his speech on "Currency and the Public Faith," delivered in the House of Representatives, April 9, 1874: "Next to the great achievements of the nation in putting down the rebellion, destroying its cause, and reuniting the republic on the principle of liberty and equal rights to all, is the task of paying the fabulous expenses of the war, the funding of the debt, the maintenance of public credit, and the launching of the nation on its career of prosperity." He studied financial questions most thoroughly. A reference to his congressional speeches will show with what signal ability and courage he fought against inflation in all forms, and for the maintenance of the public credit, at a time when the popular infatuation for inflation seemed irresistible, and threatened to overwhelm in political ruin any who attempted to resist it. Not only in Congress, but out of Congress, in public speeches, and in essays published in leading periodicals, he sought to educate the public in those views of revenue, public credit, resumption of specie payments, etc., to the adoption of which, after his masterly and unanswerable vindication of them, we are largely indebted for the subsequent national prosperity.

Besides his congressional speeches there were numerous addresses—memorial, historical, educational, and religious; campaign speeches, running through fourteen years, and sometimes numbering sixty or seventy in a single campaign; various legal arguments in important cases; contributions to encyclopædias and literary periodicals; and his speeches after his nomination to the Presidency, during his trip to and from New York city, remarkable for their number, brevity, and variety.

It is proper to add that as an orator, whether in

legislative halls, in the pulpit, on the platform, or on the stump, he was always dignified, argumentative, and didactic. Although justly regarded as one of the most effective campaign orators in the country he despised the tricks of buffoonery and demagogy by which political crowds are often captivated. Refraining from personal and party rancor, never descending to vulgarity, he stood forth rather as a grave and earnest teacher of the public on great public questions. His art was to make plain to the common mind the subject under discussion. He wasted no time in exposing the weak points of an adversary; but, seizing his strongest points, took delight in presenting them in all their strength, that in demolishing them he might put an end to the controversy. His propositions were always clearly stated and logically sustained, and his vast stores of legal, historical, and classic lore furnished him with apt and felicitous allusions and illustrations. On a broad basis of fact and argument he based appeals to the patriotism, justice, and philanthropy of his auditors, in which his eloquence rang out with captivating power. He left his hearers on a higher plane of thought and sentiment than he had found them.

Although prevented by his congressional duties from devoting himself, as he had intended, to the legal profession, he had, in all, about thirty cases in the U. S. courts. It is worthy of note that he made his first appearance as a lawyer before the Supreme Court of the United States. Several of the cases in which he was engaged involved questions of great intricacy and perplexity. His mastery of these questions, and the clearness and strength of his legal arguments, leave no room for doubt as to the eminence he might have reached as a jurist had he devoted himself fully to his favorite profession.

In 1877, after Hon. J. G. Blaine had gone from the House of Representatives to the Senate, Gen. Garfield was left in sole possession of that leadership of the Republican party in the House the honors of which he had previously shared with Mr. Blaine; and this responsible position he continued to occupy as long as he remained in Congress. Though, in a few instances, bitterly assailed with charges affecting his integrity—especially in the years 1872-74—these charges were so manfully met and so entirely disproved that they did not seriously cloud his reputation. As the facts came to be known his character for truthfulness and honesty grew constantly brighter to the public view. Perhaps the best evidence of this is found in the fact that the people of his congressional district stood faithfully by him. He was elected nine times successively to Congress as representative of the Nineteenth district of Ohio. Another evidence is found in the fact that in 1880, without solicitation on his part, he was the unanimous choice of his party in the Ohio legislature for U. S. Senator, and the Democratic minority cordially joined to make his election unanimous. One of his biographers (Major J. M. Bundy) well says: "By this unprecedented vote the State of Ohio, which knew Garfield from the beginning, and had sifted all the slanders that malice and ignorance have combined to invent and keep alive, has cast her broad and protecting mantle over the greatest of her sons."

Before he had resigned his seat in the House of Representatives, or had taken his place in the U. S. Senate, he was, on the 8th of June, 1880, nominated by the National Republican Convention, at Chicago, as the Republican candidate for President of the United States. His election to the Presidency the following November made him, in quick succession, representative in Congress of the Nineteenth Ohio district, U. S. Senator-elect from the State of Ohio, and President-elect of the United States; all these honors unsought and unbought—the spontaneous gifts of the district, the State, and the nation; voluntary tributes to the worth of the man, the patriot, the soldier, and the statesman.

It is proper to say here that Gen. Garfield not only had no aspirations to the Presidency, but that the nomination was forced on him in the face of his most earnest protestations. It is well known to some, at least, of his confidential friends, that the position of U. S. Senator filled, at this time, the measure of his ambition. He regarded himself as best fitted for that place by all his previous training, and anticipated with pleasure a senatorial career in harmony with his cherished tastes, which would open to him a field of usefulness and honor worthy to enlist his highest energies. Moreover, he went to Chicago to represent the interests of Hon. John Sherman, which he did faithfully and ably. But, after two days of undecisive balloting in the convention, in which it became evident that none of the prominent candidates could secure enough votes for a nomination, on the thirty-sixth ballot there burst forth a general and resistless enthusiasm for Gen. Garfield, and, against his earnest expostulations, he received 399 of the 755 votes cast, and his nomination was unanimously confirmed. On Nov. 2 the election resulted in 4,449,053 votes for James A. Garfield, while Winfield Scott Hancock, the rival candidate, received 4,442,035. The electoral votes for the former were 215, for the latter 155. On March 4, 1881, James A. Garfield was inaugurated President of the United States, with the hopes of the nation in an unusual degree centred in him. His broad culture, his large experience in national legislation, his thorough acquaintance with public affairs and with all questions involving our relations to other nations, and his unquestioned integrity and patriotism, created confidence that he would manage justly and wisely the interests of the whole country. But the few months of his administration were insufficient to develop fully its spirit and aims. His career was suddenly ended by the hand of an assassin. Mrs. Garfield, just recovering from a long illness, was at Long Branch, New Jersey; and the President had made arrangements for a brief release from the cares of state, that he might visit his wife at the seaside, and afterwards pay a short visit to the beloved scenes at Williams College, and arrange for the entrance into that institution of two of his sons.

On July 2 he proceeded to execute this purpose, reaching the depot of the Baltimore and Potomac Railroad in Washington at 9.30 A. M. Just after he entered the building, and while passing with Secretary Blaine through the ladies' waiting-room, two pistol-shots were heard in quick succession, and the President tottered and fell to the floor. The assassin was seized and gave his name as Charles Jules Guiteau. The pistol in his hand was found to be of heavy calibre. On examination of the wounded President it was found that the ball had entered the right side of his back, near the spinal column and immediately over the hip-bone, but the ball could not be found. Having been conveyed to the offices of the railroad on the second floor of the depot building, the sufferer, after a consultation of physicians, was borne   to the White House. Mrs. Ga   sent for, at the President's r a notable struggle of eighty days between life and death, which enlisted the sympathies of the world and crowned the sufferer with the sublimest of his honors —that of calm, untrembling faith, and heroic endurance. The best medical and surgical skill, joined to his own unruffled patience and indomitable courage, and the loving ministrations of his devoted wife, failed to rescue him from the grasp of death. A nation in prayers and tears, hoping against hope, appealed to heaven for the recovery of their beloved President. The daily bulletins from the sick-room for a time gave encouragement that his life would be spared; but, as the days and weeks wore anxiously on, it became apparent that the protracted struggle for life was growing weaker, and the "one chance in a hundred" for victory at the start was rapidly diminishing. On Sept. 6, after sixty-six days of suffering in the stifling and malarious atmosphere of Washington, the President was removed in a special railroad train to Elberon, N. J., to the cottage of Mr. Charles P. Francklyn, by the sea—a journey of 233 miles. The longing for the sea, awakened in his early youth, had never entirely died out of him; and now, as death approaches, it revives in all its freshness. Here, on Sept. 19, on the eightieth day of his sufferings, at 10.30 P. M., in the presence of his anguished wife, three of his physicians, and several members of his household, after untold physical suffering, James Abram Garfield calmly drew his last breath and yielded his spirit to God.

A post-mortem examination of the President's body was made on the afternoon of Sept. 20 by the attending and consulting surgeons, assisted by Dr. D. S. Lamb, assistant surgeon of the Medical Museum at Washington, and Dr. A. H. Smith, of Elberon. From the official bulletin prepared by the surgeons, setting forth the results of the autopsy, we quote as follows:

"It was found that the ball, after fracturing the right eleventh rib, had passed through the spinal column in front of the spinal cord, fracturing the body of the first lumbar vertebra, driven a number of small fragments of bone into the adjacent soft parts, and lodging below the pancreas, about two inches and a half to the left of the spine, and behind the peritoneum, where it had become completely encysted.

"The immediate cause of death was secondary hemorrhage from one of the mesenteric arteries adjoining the track of the ball, the blood rupturing the peritoneum, and nearly a pint escaping into the abdominal cavity. This hemorrhage is believed to have been the cause of the severe pain in the lower part of the chest complained of just before death. An abscess cavity, six inches by four in dimensions, was found in the vicinity of the gall bladder, between the liver and the transverse colon, which were strongly adherent. It did not involve the substance of the liver, and no communication was found between it and the wound.

"A long suppurating channel extended from the external wound, between the loin muscles and the right kidney, almost to the right groin. This channel, now known to be due to the burrowing of pus from the wound, was supposed during life to have been the track of the ball.

"On an examination of the organs of the chest evidences of severe bronchitis were found on both sides, with bronchopneumonia of the lower portion of the right lung, and, though to a much less extent, of the left. The lungs contained no abscesses and the heart no clots. The liver was enlarged and fatty, but not from abscesses. Nor were any found in any other organ except the left kidney, which contained near its surface a small abscess about one-third of an inch in diameter."

On September 21 the remains of the President Elberon to Washington, where the rotunda of the capitol for the most part of two days and nights. Funeral services were held in the rotunda, and the remains were then conveyed from Washington to Cleveland by railroad. On the morning of the 26th the burial services were held, and the casket was finally deposited in the tomb prepared for it.

No death ever called forth such general lamentation. It was not only the unparalleled sorrow of a bereaved nation, but a sorrow worldwide in its scope. America, Europe, Asia, Africa, and the islands of the sea united to mourn the death of this illustrious man, all claiming a common kinship with him as a friend of humanity, a noble champion of truth and right. His was a life of scarcely half a century, but the half century in which he lived was, perhaps, the grandest in the history of human progress. In the stirring history of these fifty years James Abram Garfield stands forth a commanding figure—his life opening in a humble log-cabin in the wilderness, made illustrious by its services to his country and to humanity, and closing amid the tears and lamentations of the world.

Eulogies on him were delivered by Senator G. F. Hoar at Worcester, Dec. 30, 1881, and by Hon. J. G. Blaine before Congress, Feb. 27, 1882.

Literature.—The Garfield Family in England, by Wm. P. W. Phillimore, in the *New England Historical and Genealogical Register* (July, 1883); *Ohio in the War: Her Statesmen, her Generals, and Soldiers*, by Whitelaw Reid (Cincinnati, 1868); *The Works of James Abram Garfield*, edited by Burke A. Hinsdale (2 vols., Boston, 1883). (I. E.)

GARIBALDI, GIUSEPPE (1807–1882), the Italian revolutionary leader, was born at Nice, July 4, 1807. He was a sailor, like his father, and, having seen the sufferings of many parts of Italy, became filled with a desire to remove them. His conspiracy at Genoa, in 1834, resulted in his own exile. Taking refuge at Marseilles, he still sailed on the Mediterranean, and then entered the service of the Bey of Tunis. In 1836 he crossed the Atlantic to Rio Janeiro, where he engaged in trade, but without success. Under the influence of Zambeccari, Garibaldi and other Italians sailed in a little vessel, called the Mazzini, to aid in establishing the independence of the republic of Rio Grande. Garibaldi was severely wounded in the neck, and, having landed on neutral ground, was refused permission to leave. Chafing under confinement, he made a desperate effort to escape, but was captured. Though tortured, he refused to disclose the names of those who had given him aid. His next attempt at flight was successful. After some service in a land expedition under President Gonzalez against the Brazilians, he returned to the element with which he was more familiar. At the close of the war he settled at Montevideo, having taken to wife Anita Leonta Crousa, a creole, who henceforth shared all his adventures till her death. When Uruguay was attacked by Buenos Ayres, though the little republic was reduced to desperate straits by the treachery of some of its officers, Garibaldi commanded its naval force. He also organized an Italian legion, by the aid of which Montevideo was saved. It was at this time that, being without an officer's uniform, he first made his red shirt serve as such. In 1848 the movements in his native land seemed to call for his services, and, embarking with his legion in the Speranza, he sailed for Italy. He was received coldly by the king, Charles Albert, and after the defeat of the Sardinians at Novara Garibaldi entered the Sardinian Chamber of Deputies as a member of the opposition. A Roman republic was organised in 1849 by Mazzini and others, who eagerly invited Garibaldi to take command of its army. At first he guarded the frontier towards Naples, but when, in April, Marshal Oudinot led an expedition from France to restore the pope, Garibaldi met him before Rome, and after a vigorous contest of several hours drove him back to Civita Vecchia. Turning then to the south, he defeated the Neapolitans at Velletri. But, in spite of the gallantry which he infused into his troops, the French, with greatly superior numbers, became masters of Rome in July. Garibaldi withdrew towards San Marino, where he found an Austrian army confronting him, while the French pressed on his rear. The Austrians, when he offered to surrender, refused to guarantee the safe dismissal of all his troops. Leaving behind such as chose to accept the terms, he pushed towards the Adriatic with some hundreds of his men. Their attempt to escape in fishing-boats was frustrated by the presence of the Austrian squadron. When Garibaldi landed again, his wife, overcome with the toils and dangers which she had resolutely shared, died on the shore. Having buried her there, he set his face westward and crossed Italy on foot, though proclamations had been issued denouncing the penalty of death to any one who should assist him. He was arrested by Sardinian troops at Chiavari, and after some deliberation was banished by that government.

He sailed for New York, and on his arrival in July, 1850, declined the demonstrations in his honor by those interested in his career. Quickly he settled down as a candle-maker on Staten Island, and was naturalized as an American citizen. Afterwards he took command of a merchant vessel and sailed to the Pacific, where he spent three years. Meantime, under the wise guidance of Count Cavour, Sardinia entered upon a new career. Garibaldi was permitted to return to his native land. The outbreak of the war with Austria in 1859 gave him a fresh opportunity to display the intensity of his hostility to that government and his ability as a leader and inspirer of volunteers. Being appointed major-general and commissioned to raise a corps, he organised the hardy "Hunters of the Alps," who performed prodigies of valor on the plains of Lombardy. After the peace of Villafranca, Garibaldi used his influence to secure the annexation of the Italian duchies to Sardinia, but he was doomed to the grief of seeing his native city ceded to France in spite of his energetic protests.

Though his ardently cherished and openly avowed desire for the unification of Italy was thus wounded by an act which affected him personally, he did not relax his efforts to free other parts of the country from Bourbon rule. The weakness, worthlessness, and wickedness of the Neapolitan government had long been patent to all Europe. Garibaldi determined to free the suffering people from the tyranny which crushed them to the earth. With 1000 devoted followers he sailed on May 6, 1860, from Genoa to Palermo and within a month became dictator of Sicily. The whole structure of Bourbon government crumbled into fragments. In a few weeks a new government was organized, an army and navy provided. He then crossed the Strait of Messina and rested not till he had driven Francis II. from his throne. Dictator now of the Two Sicilies, Garibaldi wished to march to Rome and from the Quirinal proclaim Victor Emmanuel King of Italy. But Napoleon III., distrusting the effect of this movement, interfered and made the Sardinian king rest content with part of the States of the Church. Victor Emmanuel entered the city of Naples in company with Garibaldi, who then resigned his power to the king. Refusing any title or other reward, the true republican retired to the little island of Caprera. Rome and Venice were still wanting to the unification of Italy. To their recovery he gave his thoughts, while the sovereigns of Europe and the leaders of modern democracy listened for his words and noted his actions. In 1861 he was elected to the Chamber of Deputies, and in 1862 he was made general of the National Guard. When he took advantage of his position to raise a Hungarian legion for service against Austria, the Italian government was compelled to disavow his acts and remove him from command. He worked best when untrammelled by the restraints of office. Forming new plans for the capture of Rome, he gathered about 2000 volunteers, and, in spite of several French vessels sent to cruise near Caprera, he crossed to the mainland. But the Italian troops encountered and defeated him at Aspromonte, Aug. 28, 1862. Garibaldi and his son Menotti were wounded and most of his men captured. Only the skill of Dr. Nélaton, who came from Paris, spared Garibaldi the necessity of amputation. After two months' imprisonment at Spezia he returned to his island home. Though still elected to the Chamber of Deputies he took little interest in its proceedings. In the brief Austrian war of 1866 he went to the Tyrol, but the sudden close of the war prevented him from performing any exploit. Yet, when peace was made, he had the satisfaction of seeing Venice ceded to Italy. The veteran patriot now resumed his designs on Rome, which the Italian government for international reasons was obliged to oppose. However, in October, 1867, he succeeded in joining a revolutionary force in the papal territory. After gaining a victory at Monte Rotondo, he was defeated by the French and papal troops at Mentana, Nov. 3. Being arrested he used his American citizenship as a plea for release and was permitted to retire to Caprera. Here he lived quietly for nearly three years, but the desperate situation of the French republic in October, 1870, evoked the sympathies of the chivalrous old man. Offering his services to Gambetta at Tours, he took command in the Vosges for a few weeks, but without effecting anything. Though elected to the French National Assembly he took no part in its deliberations, and soon resigned his seat and his military commission. In 1873 pecuniary embarrassments overtook the old hero, which were aggravated by the faithlessness of a depositary, who fled to America. Garibaldi refused assistance which was offered from many sides, and declined a pension from the government. In 1874 he was elected a representative of Rome in the Chamber of Deputies, and made a triumphal entry in January following. The king and Prince Humbert showed him special marks of respect. Garibaldi proposed in Parliament various plans for the prevention of inundations of the Tiber and the Arno and for the improvement of the campagna. Some of these plans were approved and adopted by the government. Garibaldi did not cease however his opposition to the political course of the government. His dream that all Italian-speaking districts, whether possessed by Austria, Switzerland, or France, should be added to the kingdom of Italy, was not yet realized. Depretis, who became minister in 1876, favored this idea for a time, but afterwards abandoned it.

On account of the state of his health, undermined by hardships, Garibaldi now rarely left Caprera ex-sent to attend the Chamber of Deputies. In 1881 he called on the king at Rome and obtained the release of his son-in-law Canzio. He died at Caprera, June 2, 1882, having only a few weeks earlier assisted in the celebration at Palermo of the 600th anniversary of the Sicilian Vespers. He was buried on the island on June 8, being followed to the grave by prominent representatives of the government as well as delegates of 300 associations. Through all his life he had remained faithful to the dreams of his youth, and aided largely in their accomplishment. To him more than any other belongs the honor of the unification of Italy in a government in which the wishes of the people are heard and obeyed.

In his later years Garibaldi found time to compose two novels, *Cantoni il volontario* (1870) and *Clelia, ovvero il governo monaco* (1870). The latter has been translated into English as *The Rule of the Monk, or Rome in the Nineteenth Century*. He also published *The Thousand* (1876), an account of his expedition to Sicily in 1860. See *Life of Garibaldi, written by himself*, translated by Theodore Dwight (1860). (J. P. L.)

GARLAND, AUGUSTUS HILL, an American statesman, was born near Covington, Tenn., June 11, 1832, but was soon removed to Arkansas. He graduated at St. Joseph's College, Bardstown, Ky., in 1849, studied law and was admitted to the bar at Washington, Ark., in 1853. He removed to Little Rock in 1856, and was a delegate to the convention which passed the ordinance of secession in 1861. He was a member of the Confederate Congress, and when the war closed was a Confederate senator. He was elected to the U. S. Senate for the term beginning in 1867, but was not admitted to a seat. He then practised law until 1874, when he was elected Governor of Arkansas without opposition. In 1876 he was elected to the U. S. Senate and was re-elected in 1883. In March, 1885, he was called into Pres. Cleveland's cabinet as attorney-general. He retired in 1889.

GARNEAU, FRANÇOIS XAVIER (1809–1866), a Canadian historian, was born at Quebec, June 15, 1809. He was admitted as a notary in 1830, was afterwards clerk of the legislative assembly, and in 1845 became clerk of the city of Quebec. He published *Voyage en Angleterre et en France dans les années* 1831–33, and *Histoire du Canada* (3 vols., 1845–52). The latter has been translated into English. Garneau died Feb. 3, 1866.

GARNET, HENRY HIGHLAND (1815–1882), a negro clergyman, was born in Kent co., Md., Dec. 23, 1815. He was a slave and his father George was a slave also; but the grandfather was a Mandingo African chief. George Garnet escaped from slavery in 1824, and went to New York city in 1825. Henry attended the African Free School in Mulberry Street, noted for the number of distinguished men of color who were among its students. Obliged to leave school at an early age, he made two or three voyages as a cook. In early youth he became crippled in his right leg, which left him maimed for life. He early attached himself to the Presbyterian church under Theodore S. Wright, the leading negro preacher of his day. Turning his attention toward the ministry, Garnet in 1835 went to Canaan Academy, N. H., but prejudice against the education of colored children soon broke up the school, and he returned to New York city. He afterward attended the Oneida Institute, Whitesboro, N. Y., one of the seven places in the United States at that time open to colored youth. Rev. Beriah Green was the president. Garnet here pursued his academic studies with profit and zest, and was graduated in 1839. While teaching school at Troy, he still pursued his theological studies. He was licensed to preach in 1842; was pastor of the Liberty Street Presbyterian Church in Troy for ten years, during which time he edited a paper in the interests of the colored people called the *Clarion*. In 1841–42 the colored people of New York State were demanding suffrage, and conventions were held at various places in the State. Garnet became the leading spirit. At the convention of the Liberty Party, at Buffalo, N. Y., 1843, the *Gazette* said of Garnet's speech, "It fairly enchained the audience over whose passions, affections, and actions the speaker appeared to have perfect control." Once entered upon a semi-political career, Garnet became an active worker in different fields. While he retained his connection with the church, he became an anti-slavery orator, a temperance lecturer, the agent of Gerrit Smith in settling the colored people on lands in the State of New York. In 1850 he visited England, and travelled over the United Kingdom preaching and lecturing. He was a delegate while abroad to the Peace Congress at Frankfort. For a brief period he became a missionary and temperance advocate in Jamaica. He returned to the United States and preached successively in New York, Washington, and again in New York city. At the breaking out of the rebellion he promptly called upon colored men to enlist in any capacity, foreseeing the beneficial effects of the war upon his race. He accepted the chaplaincy of a camp of colored soldiers, and was active in organizing a committee for hospital service. He barely escaped with his life during the anti-negro riots in New York in 1863. He was the first colored man who ever spoke in the House of Representatives at Washington. He preached a sermon there Sunday, Feb. 12, 1865, afterwards published in pamphlet form. In the "Exodus" of 1879 he was untiring in his efforts to assist his suffering brethren fleeing from the South. In 1881 he was appointed by Pres. Garfield minister-resident and consul-general at Monrovia, Liberia. He sailed for Africa Nov. 12, 1881, and died Feb. 14, 1882, after a brief illness. Dr. Garnet was an unmixed negro of the best type, an eloquent speaker, bitter and sarcastic when need be, but polished and suave on occasion. In early life he issued an edition of *Walker's Appeal*, and printed numerous pamphlets and sermons. He was always the friend of African civilization, and he was elected an officer of the American Colonization Society. His first wife, Julia Williams, was one of the colored girls driven with Prudence Crandall from Canterbury, Conn., in 1833, for daring to seek the springs of knowledge. His second wife, who survives him, Sarah J. S. Thompson, was a teacher among the colored people in New York city. Dr. Garnet's life illustrates the romance of the American negro—a slave, a partial freeman, enfranchised by war, a preacher, orator, editor, lecturer, and diplomat, driven from New England by prejudice, a graduate of a mixed school in New York State, the friend of Lincoln, Thurlow Weed, Grant, and Garfield, returning after nearly sixty years of active life in America to die in the home of his grandfather, a representative of the government which once denied his right to citizenship and refused him a passport on going abroad in 1850. (R. T. G.)

GARNETT, RICHARD, an English author, born at Lichfield, Feb. 27, 1835. His father, Rev. Richard Garnet, who died in 1850, was an eminent author and philologist and one of the librarians of the British museum. The younger Garnett succeeded his father as assistant keeper of that great library, and in 1875 became superintendent of the reading-room. Among his works are a volume of poems called *Primula* (1858); *Io in Egypt and other Poems* (1859); *Poems from the German* (1862); *Idyls and Epigrams* (1869); and a valuable volume entitled *Relics of Shelley*. He has also edited his father's *Philological Essays* (1858); *Shelley's Minor Poems* (1880), and the *Florilegium Amantis* of Coventry Patmore. Mr. Garnett has written many of the best biographical articles in the ENCYCLOPÆDIA BRITANNICA.

GARNIER-PAGÈS, LOUIS ANTOINE (1803–1878), a French statesman, was born at Marseilles, July 18, 1803. Being engaged in business at Paris, he took part in the revolution of July, 1830, and afterwards was elected to the Chamber of Deputies. He was a Republican and gave special attention to the finances. In the provisional government of 1848 he was minister of finance, and to prevent the national bankruptcy he insisted on an extra taxation, the extreme unpopularity of which drove him soon after into private life. He did not emerge until 1869, though he frequently criticised the financial administration of the empire. On the downfall of this government he took part in the defence of Paris, but had no influence on subsequent events. He died at Paris, Oct. 31, 1878. He published *Histoire de la Revolution de* 1848 (8 vols., 1860–62); *Histoire de la Commission Executive* (1869); *L' Opposition et l' Empire* (2 vols., 1872).

GARRETSON, JAMES EDMUND, an American physician, was born at Wilmington, Del., Oct. 4, 1828. He graduated at the University of Pennsylvania in 1859, and began practice in Philadelphia. He began to lecture on anatomy in 1861; in 1869 was made oral surgeon to the University of Pennsylvania; and in 1880 dean of the Philadelphia Dental College. By his efforts oral surgery has been erected into a surgical system, in which he has performed many noteworthy operations. Besides his *System of Oral Surgery* Dr. Garretson has written several books of practical philosophy in a somewhat humorous vein. These have been published under the name of "John Darby," and comprise *Odd Hours of a Physician, Thinkers and Thinking, Hours with John Darby, Brushland*, and *Two Thousand Years After*.

GAS, ILLUMINATING. The use of inflammable gas as a light-giving agent had its inception in the burning of the gas which rises naturally from the earth in many regions. Its production artificially is of recent date.

See Vol. X. p. 79 Am. ed. (p. 87 Edin. ed.).

Of the gas used in modern cities coal is the principal source, though many other substances have been employed, such as wood, peat, rosin, petroleum, oils, fats, water, and even organic refuse of several kinds. Coal-gas was made and burned as an experiment late in the seventeenth century, and again about 1720. In 1786 Culross Abbey was lighted with gas also, as an experiment. Its first practical employment was in 1792, when William Murdoch used it to light his workshops, at Redruth, in Cornwall. His success led to its extended use. Its first employment in public street lighting was in Pall Mall, London, on Jan. 28, 1807. The first gas company was the "Chartered Gas-Light and Coke Company," chartered in London in 1812. By 1820 it had become more satisfactory as an illuminating agent, had extended to other cities, and had come into use in Paris and some other cities on the Continent. By 1829 there were about 200 gas-works in Great Britain.

In the United States, gas for illumination was first made by David Melville, of Newport, R. I. He lighted his own house and the street in front of it with gas in 1806. In 1813 he took out a patent, and lighted several factories. In 1817 his process was applied to Beaver Tail light-house, being the first use of gas for this purpose. An attempt was made to manufacture gas in Baltimore in 1816, but success was not attained until 1821. In the succeeding year gas was introduced into Boston. In 1823 the New York Gas-Light Company was formed, but the demand was so limited that it was not in active operation until 1827. By 1830 success was assured, and a rival company, the Manhattan, was established. Both companies made their gas from oil and rosin until 1849. In Philadelphia the manufacture of gas has always remained an interest of the corporation, not of private companies. This stood in the way of its early employment, and it was not introduced until 1835. Since these dates, the use of coal-gas has been widely extended throughout the country, in small as well as in large communities, and there are now probably over 500 companies in operation, with an enormous capital, the plant of the New York companies alone being estimated at a value of $45,000,000.

The manufacture of coal-gas has been for many years slowly improving in efficiency, through the invention of new methods and the higher development of old processes. It has made important steps of progress within the last twelve years, partly through the incitement of competition with the electric light. Since about 1873 the tendency in gas-works has been to use higher temperatures and larger retorts. As a result the yield of gas per ton of coal, in the best managed works, has increased from 9500 to 11,420 cubic feet, while the daily yield per retort has advanced from 6000 to 9000 cubic feet. The regenerative principle of the Siemens' furnace has been applied to the production of a more intense heat, with a marked economy in fuel and labor, and a superior yield. The furnace employed is an economical modification of the Siemens' furnace. It comprises a deep fire-place, with a grate of small area. A limited supply of air, sometimes with a little steam, is admitted below, and passes through a thick bed of incandescent coke. Hydrogen and carbonic oxide gases rise, and pass into the oven containing the retorts. Here they meet a new supply of air, which has been previously heated, and a vivid and intensely hot combustion takes place, with a remarkable increase in the heat of the retorts. The hot gases arising from the combustion pass off through flues which run parallel with the flues through which the second air supply enters. They thus heat this air in their passage. In this process we have the Siemens' regenerative principle. The saving in fuel is said to be about 30 per cent.

The charging of the retorts has been simplified and cheapened by the substitution of machine for hand labor. In the latest invention the coal, hauled and placed in front of the door of the retort, is driven into it by the force of jets of steam with a considerable economy in labor. Also the glowing hot coke, taken from the retorts, is at once used in the furnaces, not cooled off and this heat lost as in the old method. Improved and economical processes have been adopted in every other department of the manufacture. It took long to learn, after the introduction of gas, how to deprive it of its ammonia. The *scrubbers* now employed do this completely. The gas is made to rise through coke or other material placed in a tower down which water slowly trickles, absorbing the gaseous ammonia in its descent. Less than a gallon of water suffices to clean 1000 cubic feet of gas, while the ammoniacal liquid obtained is a product of great value. In another system revolving perforated disks are employed, the lower part of which dip into water. The gas passes through the perforations and yields its ammonia to the trickling water. Other improvements in the purification of gas of a less striking character have also been adopted, and the cost of manufacture has been considerably reduced by these various steps towards economy and efficiency.

The manufacture of what is known as water-gas has become an important branch of the industry of late years. Its main principle is the mixture of hydrogen with the vapor of some hydrocarbon for illuminating purposes. The hydrogen-gas is obtained by the decomposition of water, effected by passing steam through highly heated coals. Hydrogen, as is well known, burns with very little light, and the purpose of the hydrocarbon is to increase the brilliancy of the flame. The first patent in which hydrogen is used for purposes of illumination was granted in London, in 1824. Michael Donovan in 1830, George Lowe in 1832, Stephen White in 1847, and other inventors took out patents for improved processes in water-gas manufacture, and for the enriching of coal-gas with hydrogen or hydrocarbon vapors. But none of these methods have been able to compete with coal-gas in cheapness, in England.

In the United States the contrary has been the case, and water-gas manufacture has greatly developed of late years. This is due to the cheapness of petroleum and its products as sources of the hydrocarbon vapors. Several processes are employed, of which the simplest and most economical is the Lowe process, the invention of T. S. C. Lowe, of Norristown, Pa. In this method anthracite coal is charged into a cupola, or blast-furnace, and brought to an intense heat by an air-blast. Then the blast is shut off and superheated steam admitted a little above the grate bars. The steam is decomposed into a mixture of hydrogen and carbonic oxide. At the same time a small stream of naphtha, or crude petroleum, is thrown upon the surface of the burning coal, yielding a vapor which mixes with the preceding gas. Besides this cupola are one or more others filled loosely with fire-bricks, which are heated. Through them the mixed gases pass, and the vapor of naphtha is decomposed into olefiant and other light-giving gases. The remaining processes of scrubbing and purifying are as in coal-gas manufacture. The charge used is about 280 gallons of petroleum to 3600 pounds of anthracite for a yield of 70,000 cubic feet of gas.

The Lowe system was first put into successful operation at Phœnixville, Pa., about 1873. It was afterwards introduced into Utica, N. Y., and in 1876 a larger establishment was operated in Manayunk, Pa. Since these dates it has made its way to a considerable use in the Northern States and Canada. In another method, known as the Strong process, no naphtha is employed, the purpose being to produce a heating instead of an illuminating gas. In this the steam is first passed through the regenerator and introduced in a highly heated state at the top of the furnace, while coal-dust is at the same time showered in at the top. The steam is partly decomposed by contact with the coal-dust, while the process is completed in its passage through the burning coal.

The Municipal Gas-Works of New York, the first to adopt the water-gas process, employ the Tessié du Mothay system. In this the three processes of gas generating, carburetting, and roasting, or fixing, are conducted separately. The *fixing* retorts correspond to the regenerator in the Lowe process, the naphtha vapor being converted into higher hydrocarbons, which make a more stable or *fixed* gas. The system is less economical in theory than the Lowe, but seems to work about as well in practice. In some of the other New York companies an intermediate system is employed, the basis of the manufacture being coal-gas, which is enriched with naphtha vapors.

The American hydrocarbon process, as introduced

Generator in Vault, 50 Feet or more from House.   Air Pump in Cellar of House.

Domestic Gasoline Apparatus.

into the city of Poughkeepsie in 1875, is a simplified application of the same general principles. It yields a gas which it is claimed can be made at the rate of 50 cts. per 1000 feet. The common objection to gases of this character is that the gas is not permanent. The hydrocarbon is not fully gasified, leaves a deposit in the pipes, and smokes when burned. In the Wren process it is claimed that this difficulty is obviated, the oil vapor being so thoroughly heated as to be converted into a permanent gas. The inventor claims that gas can be produced by his process for 36 cts. per 1000 feet.

Gasolene.—In cases where buildings are situated beyond the reach of city gas-mains it becomes necessary to find some substitute for coal-gas, and a very effective one is found in the use of gasolene, a highly volatile liquid distilled from naphtha. The vapor from this is so highly inflammable that it is necessary to keep it in a vault, or bury it underground, at a safe distance from the house to be lighted. For purposes of burning the vapor is mixed with atmospheric air. The apparatus is composed of two parts, a cylinder containing the gasolene, and an air-pump, placed in the cellar of the house. This air-pump is operated by a descending weight, and forces the air through a pipe to the gasolene reservoir. This is a cylinder containing a series of evaporating chambers, partly filled with gasolene, and containing a succession of fibrous webs, which become saturated with the liquid. The air passes successively through these chambers, and winds through their webbed subdivisions, until it becomes thoroughly saturated with the vapor rising from the gasolene, and enters the supply-pipe as a richly carburetted air-gas. This flows back to the building through gas-pipes and is conducted to the burners, where it yields an excellent and agreeable light, without smoke or odor. The machine works automatically, since the closing of the burners checks the air-flow and stops the pump, while it moves again the instant the burners are opened. The supply in the generator usually lasts from 3 to 6 months, while gauges are used to show the height of the liquid in the chambers.

Natural Gas.—Within the United States the gas naturally arising from wells in the petroleum district of Pennsylvania and the adjoining States has been for years past used in some localities as an illuminant, and as a source of heat and power. It is now largely used where gas-wells exist in the vicinity of towns. But a marked advance in its use has taken place within recent years by its conduction through pipes to distant places. In the city of Pittsburg the use of natural gas has grown with such rapidity that it bids fair ere long to completely supplant coal in that city, both for domestic and for manufacturing purposes. It is stated that the disuse of coal in Pittsburg, through the introduction of natural gas into its manufactories and dwellings, amounts at present to about 10,000 tons daily, or more than 3,500,000 tons per year. As a consequence good coal-lands in that vicinity are now offered at $30 per acre, while gas-well privileges have been sold for $5000 per acre. Discoveries of new gas-wells are of not unfrequent occurrence, while some of those now in use have been yielding without diminution for years. The gas can be supplied very cheaply; it is remarkable for its cleanliness and labor-saving as compared with coal, and its use is likely to rapidly extend. Projects are even now on foot to convey it to New York and Philadelphia, and it is possible that, ere many years, these cities will get their light and heat from this earth-born fuel.

The gas-well, however, has one ever-present element of uncertainty, which is, that its supply may give out at any moment, without warning. Its lack of odor is also a dangerous quality, as its escape through leaky joints can only be discovered by an explosion. Yet the use of natural gas has called the attention of manufacturers to the superiority of gaseous over solid fuel, even when artificially produced. Gas-fuel has been employed for some time in several iron-works in and near Philadelphia, with considerable saving, and the glass-works of Ohio are now using it at a saving of 25 per cent. in cost of fuel. This gas is made of coal-slack, of no value at the mines, and existing in great quantities. The time may come, ere many years, when gas-fuel will completely replace coal, as more economical and manageable. The coal may be converted into gas at the mines, and conducted to the cities in pipes, as natural gas now is. Of late years gas-stoves for heating and cooking have come into increased use. Gas is not greatly more expensive than coal as an agent in cooking, while it is far more convenient. Gas-engines have also come into use to some extent. They are cheaper in operation than those run with coal, but more troublesome. Their principal advantage is where the work is intermittent and the power required small. They start at once into full action, and the expense ceases the instant they stop running. Twenty cubic feet of gas per horse-power is as low as the best of them consume.

In consequence of the various improvements in its manufacture the price of gas to consumers has steadily decreased of late years. From a price of some $4 per 1000 feet, or considerably more where the consumption was light, it has declined to prices which range from $2 in some localities to as low as $1 in others. In some of the English cities its cost is considerably less than this, partly through greater cheapness of fuel and labor, and partly through more economical management. The probability is that its price will be still further reduced in this country, and that, if replaced as an illuminant by electricity, it will come into increased use as a source of heat and power. The immense service called for from some gas-works of late years has rendered necessary gas-holders of increased capacity, and some of those recently built are of enormous size. One in London, the largest in the world, has a capacity of 5,500,000 cubic feet. The Municipal Gas Company of New York has one of 2,000,000 feet capacity, and the New York Gas-Light Company has two of 1,500,000 feet each.

The Siemens' Burner.—In relation to gas consumption we need here speak only of the most recent improvement in that direction, the Siemens' regenerative burner, in which the principle of the regenerative furnace has been successfully employed. It differs in principle from ordinary burners in that the gas and the air are not supplied cold, as in ordinary burners, but are heated before combustion. This difference makes a very notable difference in the intensity of the light yielded. In the Siemens' burner the hot products of combustion are not permitted to at once escape, but are carried downwards through a chamber to an escape-flue at the bottom. In so doing they yield heat to the entering air and gas, which are passing upward through adjacent flues. In consequence, when these reach the burners, they are considerably raised in temperature. The consumption is more complete, and the illumination nearly three times that yielded by ordinary burners.

The Siemens' lamps are only suitable for lighting large spaces, for which purpose they are now being rapidly introduced. But several new inventions are in the market, in which this principle is adapted to smaller lamps, suitable for domestic service. In these the flame is inverted, and burns downward. The heat of the products of combustion seems very perfectly taken out by the new entering gas and air, so that the external heating effect is greatly reduced. It seems certain that a lighting effect at least double that now attained in domestic use will be yet gained by the application of this regenerative principle. (C. M.)

GASPARIN, AGÉNOR ÉTIENNE, COMTE DE (1810-1871), a French publicist, was born at Orange, July 10, 1810. His father, Count Adrien E. P. (1783–1862), in 1836 was secretary of the interior. He gave much attention to agriculture, and published some large works on the subject. Agénor was employed under his father while minister, and in 1842 was elected to the Chamber of Deputies. Though classed as a conservative, he favored many liberal measures, being moved thereto by his Protestantism. He was in the East during the Revolution of 1848, and refused to give approval of the republic then established or of the empire which followed. He removed to Switzerland, and lectured at Geneva on historical and religious subjects. He expressed warm friendship for the cause of the Union during the American civil war, and published two works in its behalf: *Les Etats-Unis en 1861*; *Un grand peuple qui se relève* (1861), and *L'Amerique devant l'Europe* (1862). These were translated and published in New York as *The Uprising of a Great People* and *America before Europe*. He was also a frequent contributor to the *Revue des Deux Mondes* and other periodicals. He died at Geneva, May 14, 1871, his death being hastened by his philanthropic labors in behalf of French refugees. Besides the works mentioned above he published others on French Protestantism, Spiritualism, the family, moral liberty. After his death his *Life of Innocent III.* appeared (1874). His wife, VALERIE BOISSIER, born at Geneva, in 1813, has also published several books of travel, and treatises on religious, social, and moral questions.

GASTON, WILLIAM (1778–1844), an American jurist, was born at New Berne, N. C., Sept. 19, 1778. His father, Dr. Alexander Gaston, was of Huguenot descent, and on account of his active efforts in aid of American independence was shot by tories, Aug. 20, 1781. William was brought up by his mother, graduated at Princeton College in 1796, and admitted to the bar in 1798. In 1800 he was chosen to the senate of North Carolina, and afterwards to the lower house, of which he was speaker in 1808. He became a member of Congress in 1813, and was there distinguished by his eloquence and force of argument. This was especially seen in his speech against the Loan Bill, which proposed to place $25,000,000 at the disposal of the President. In 1817 he returned to the practice of his profession in North Carolina, and was soon at the head of the bar. In 1834 he was appointed a judge of the Supreme Court of the State, though he had become a Roman Catholic, and was, therefore, excluded by the State Constitution from holding office—no attempt being made to enforce the provision; and he held this position till his death, at Raleigh, N. C., Jan. 23, 1844. In 1835 he had been prominent in revising the State constitution, and opposed the clause depriving free colored men of the right of suffrage which they had previously enjoyed.

GATLING, RICHARD JORDAN, an American inventor, was born Sept. 12, 1818, near Murfreesborough, N. C. In boyhood he aided his father, Jordan Gatling, in designing a machine for sowing cotton-seed and thinning the young plants; and when 20 years of age he invented a screw for steamers. Among his later inventions were a machine for sowing rice and wheat; a new hemp-brake and a steam-plough. He studied medicine at Laporte, Ind., 1847–48, and in Cincinnati, 1848–49, and took a degree, but never practised his profession. Another of his inventions was one for transmitting power by means of compressed air. But his fame is principally based upon his great invention of the compound repeating or machine gun, known as the Gatling gun; the most original and successful battery or multiple gun yet devised. The invention of this fire-arm was made in 1861 and 1862, while Dr. Gatling was living in Indianapolis, Ind., but it scarcely came into use during the war of the rebellion. It has since been very much improved. It is now made in various forms, and is used by most civilized nations, both as an army and navy arm. (See "Machine-gun" in article "GUN-MAKING" in ENCYCLOPÆDIA BRITANNICA.) Dr. Gatling is a resident of Hartford, Conn.

GAULTHERIA (named by Kalm, the Swedish botanist, in honor of Dr. Gaultier, of Quebec) is a genus of plants belonging to the order *Ericaceæ*, and has numerous representatives in Asia, Java, Tasmania, New Zealand, etc., with three species in the United States. It belongs to the section *Andromedeæ*, which is described by Dr. Gray as having "fruit, a loculicidal chiefly five-celled and many-seeded capsule, the valves usually bearing the partitions, which separate from the persistent placentiferous axis or columella. Corolla gamopetalous, deciduous. Stamens twice the number of the corolla-lobes (mostly 10), more or less included. Leaves mainly alternate." The section *Arbuteæ* has baccate or drupaceous fruit, but though *Gaultheria* has the calyx fleshy and berry-like, it finally opens at the sides as described by Dr. Gray. The species of the Eastern United States is called *Gaultheria procumbens*; but it is not a procumbent plant, though of low growth in comparison with other species. The leaves are evergreen, and this fact has suggested "winter-green" as one of its common names. The pinkish-white flowers appear about the middle of summer, followed by bright red velvet-like berries in autumn, which remain on all winter if undisturbed. The whole plant and the berries have a very pleasant aromatic taste, similar to that of the sweet birch, and, like that, yielding a dark green essential oil, which has a specific gravity of 1.173. It is known as "oil of winter-green." It was known to the Indians in common with other plants of similar character, says Rafinesque, as "Pallom," and a tea made from the plant was used by them as a stimulant. The same author says the Missouri tribes of Indians called it "Moschar," and the Indians of Michigan and Wisconsin gathered and preserved the fruit for culinary uses. During the war of independence the leaves were used by the colonists in the place of Chinese tea, and it is said that they are little inferior to Chinese tea in value and more refreshing. From this use the berries are yet known as "tea-berries." They are somewhat in demand for mixing with beer and other drinks. They also enter considerably into the manufacture of popular tooth-powders and washes. The leaf having some astringency, has been found useful in medicine.

Gaultheria Shallon is the prevailing species along the Pacific coast. It was first described and figured in Pursh's "*Flora of North America*," from specimens collected by Menzies and Lewis and Clarke, who gave it the specific name as the one under which it was known to the Indians of Oregon, though "Salal" is its present name. This is a small shrub, growing two or three feet high, chiefly in places so shaded by other larger plants that nothing else will grow, the fruit being the "Salal-berries" used for food.

Gaultheria Myrsinites is also a native of the more northern districts of the Pacific coast. It is low growing, spreading over the ground in tufts, flowers solitary in the axils of the leaves, and with naked, obscurely four-pointed anthers. Little is known of its economic value, but the *Botany of California* notes that the "fruit is scarlet, aromatic, and said to be delicious."

The Eastern species has had many common names besides those above cited; for instance, "partridge-berry," because game-birds are fond of the fruit, "checker-berry," "ground-holly," and others, which have become almost obsolete. (T. M.)

GAVAZZI, ALESSANDRO, an Italian preacher and agitator, was born at Bologna in 1809. He received minor orders in 1825 and entered the order of the Barnabites. He was afterwards professor of rhetoric at Naples, and became a noted pulpit-orator. On account of his freedom of speech and thought he incurred censure, but on the accession of Pius IX. in 1846, he declared himself a devoted follower of the Pope's policy. In 1848 Gavazzi delivered in the Pantheon a fervid oration on the patriots who had fallen in the struggle against the Austrians at Milan. He continued to harangue the people on their duty as Italians, and the pope made him chaplain-general of the volunteer national army. These troops had reached Vicenza, when the pope, alarmed at the progress of the movement, recalled them to Rome. But Gavazzi, going to Florence, roused the people by his fiery appeals; then expelled from the duchy of Tuscany, he passed to Genoa, but soon returned to the pope's dominions. When the republican government was set up in Rome, Gavazzi as chaplain-general of the army exerted himself to sustain the spirit of the people until they were overwhelmed by the French in July, 1849. A few weeks later, in London, Gavazzi delivered before crowded houses fierce invectives against the Roman Catholic Church. He subsequently visited Scotland, then passed to the United States, and afterwards to Canada, where he encountered great opposition. His *Life, Sermons, and Lessons* were published at London in 1851. Henceforth he devoted himself to furthering the national movement in Italy, and in 1860 he accompanied Garibaldi's expedition to Sicily. In 1870 he again visited England, and in 1873 made a tour in the United States asking aid for a national free church in Italy. He has published *No Union with Rome* (London, 1871), and *The Priest in Absolution* (1877).

GAY, EBENEZER (1696–1787), an American minister, was born at Dedham, Mass., Aug. 26, 1696. He graduated at Harvard College in 1714, and in 1718 was settled as pastor over the church at Hingham, Mass., where he remained till his death, March 18, 1787. On his 85th birthday he preached from the text "Lo, I am this day fourscore and five years old." This sermon, under the title *The Old Man's Calendar*, was frequently reprinted, and other of his sermons were published. Dr. Gay was liberal in his theology, but conservative in his politics, and during the Revolution was ill treated by some of his own parishioners.

GAY, SIDNEY HOWARD, an American journalist, was born at Hingham, May 22, 1814. He graduated at Harvard College in 1833 and began to study law in his father's office. He became an anti-slavery lecturer and for several years was editor of the *Anti-Slavery Standard*. In 1858 he joined the staff of the *New York Tribune*, and was its managing editor from 1862 to 1865. He held a similar position on the *Chicago Tribune* from 1867 to 1871, and then returned to New York to take charge of the *Evening Post*. He is the author of Bryant and Gay's illustrated *History of the United States* (4 vols., 1876–80), and of a *Life of James Madison* (1884). His *History*, though badly proportioned, gives many evidences of careful research, and is marked throughout with a strong love of freedom.

GAY, WINCKWORTH ALLAN, an American painter, brother of the preceding, was born at Hingham, Mass., Aug. 18, 1821. He studied painting under Robert Weir at West Point, N. Y., and under Troyon at Paris. He spent some years in Italy, and has since travelled in Egypt and Eastern Asia. He is noted as a painter of landscapes and especially of sea-coasts. He resides at Boston, where in 1877 he exhibited over a hundred pictures representing his career as an artist.

GAYARRÉ, CHARLES E. ARTHUR, an American lawyer and historian, was born at New Orleans, Jan. 3, 1805. He was educated at the College of New Orleans, studied law at Philadelphia, and was admitted to the bar in 1829. He was elected to the legislature of Louisiana in 1830, was appointed deputy attorney-general in 1831, and presiding judge of the city of New Orleans in 1833. He was elected to the U. S. Senate in 1835, but did not take his seat on account of ill health. He then went to Europe, and on his return in 1846 was made secretary of state in Louisiana, which position he held till 1853. He has published several works on the history of Louisiana, the most important of which is divided into three parts, *Spanish Domination in Louisiana* (1854); *French Domination* (1854); *American Domination* (1857; enlarged edition, 1869). He has also published a satirical sketch, *The School of Politics* (1854), two historical novels, *Fernando de Lemos* (1872), and *Aubert Dubayet* (1882), and a history of *Philip II. of Spain* (1866).

GAY-FEATHER is the most popular common name for plants of the genus *Liatris*, belonging to the eupatoriaceous tribe of *Compositæ*. It has flowers all tubular and perfect; achenia many-ribbed; the slender bristles of the pappus plumose or barbellata; and corollas strongly five-lobed. It comprises about a dozen species, which are mostly confined to that portion of the United States lying east of the Rocky Mountains. The roots of most of the species are tuberous, seldom exceeding a walnut in size, and abound in a balsamic resin, giving the plant, along with so many others, a reputation as a "rattlesnake-master." From this and the form of the root some of the species are known as "button-snake-root." Some of them are found to be diuretic, stimulant, and expectorant, and to have real value in medicine. On the prairies gophers and other rodents store the roots in large quantities under ground for winter use. Besides "gay-feather," the name given to these plants from their plumose habit of growth and inflorescence, some kinds have been called "throatwort," from their use as expectorants; "prairie pine," from the terebinthine odor of the roots; "spike-flower," from the long tapering inflorescence; and "blazing star," from their comet-like appearance when in flower—the heads of purple flowers opening from the apex of the spike downwards. *Liatris odoratissima* is the "Carolina vanilla-plant," or "deer's tongue." When properly cured it has the odor of vanilla, and it has been supposed by the ignorant to be the real vanilla, and chapters have even been written on the culture of vanilla in the South, which really had reference to this plant. It was recently exported to Turkey from Florida to some extent, for the purpose of imparting a good flavor to the finer preparations of tobacco; but the trade did not flourish.

The species of the genus give great beauty to American floral scenery. In the drier portion of the country, just east of the Rocky Mountains, *L. punctata* abounds, with some smaller intermixtures of a dwarf form of *L. scariosa*. As the more grassy regions are reached *L. pycnostachya*, perhaps the original "gay-feather," is the prevailing species. *L. squamosa* and *L. cylindracea* are found in Illinois, while *L. spicata* and *L. graminifolia* are common farther east. A few rarer species occur in the South Atlantic States. (T. M.)

GEARY, JOHN WHITE (1819–1873), an American general, was born at Mount Pleasant, Westmoreland co., Pa., Dec. 30, 1819. He studied at Jefferson College, Canonsburg, became a civil engineer, and was connected with the Allegheny Portage Railroad for several years. In 1846 he was lieutenant-colonel of a volunteer regiment which served in Mexico. He commanded the regiment at Chapultepec, where he was wounded, and was placed in command of the citadel of Mexico after its capture. He removed to San Francisco after the war, and in 1849 was postmaster, then alcalde, and in 1850 was elected the first mayor of that city. In 1852 he returned to his native county, settling on a farm. In 1856 he was appointed governor of Kansas by Pres. Pierce, and held that office till March, 1857. In 1861 he raised and equipped the Twenty-eighth Pennsylvania volunteers, and commanded them in some engagements in Virginia. In April, 1862, he was made brigadier-general. He was severely wounded at Cedar Mountain, Aug. 9, 1862. He commanded a division at Chancellorsville, Gettysburg, and at Lookout Mountain. In Gen. Sherman's campaign through Georgia in 1864, Gen. Geary commanded the Second division of the Twentieth corps. At the close of the war he retired from the army, and from 1867 to 1873 he was governor of Pennsylvania. He died suddenly at Harrisburg, Feb. 9, 1873.

GEFFRARD, FABRE (1806–1879), a Haytian general and president, was born at L'Anse-Veau, Sept. 19, 1806. He was a mulatto and son of Gen. Nicholas Geffrard, one of the founders of Haytian independence. Adopted after his father's death by Gen. Fabre, he entered the army in 1821, was captain in 1843, and assisted Gen. Hérard in overthrowing the government of Pres. Boyer. In the disturbances which followed he displayed great humanity as well as courage, and in 1845 he was made general of a division. Pres. Riche deprived him of his command, but on trial by a military tribunal Geffrard was unanimously acquitted. Soulouque, becoming President in 1849, restored Geffrard to command, and sent him against the Dominicans. When Soulouque assumed imperial dignity he made Geffrard duke of Tabara, but as Soulouque's popularity waned that of Geffrard increased. At last the emperor ordered Geffrard's arrest, Dec. 21, 1858, but he escaped to a neighboring island, and headed an insurrection in the French provinces. Soulouque was overthrown, and Geffrard entered Port-au-Prince in triumph, Jan. 15, 1859. He restored the republic and exercised clemency to the vanquished, allowing Soulouque and his family to go to Jamaica. But Geffrard's political opponents conspired against him, and in an attempt upon his life, his daughter, who had just been married, was assassinated. His attempts at reform met with much opposition, which was heightened by his moderation toward Spain when it took possession of the Dominican republic. In 1864 Salnave started an insurrection which soon became formidable. Although suppressed in 1865 with the aid of the English, it was renewed in July, 1866. Pres. Geffrard declared the abolition of capital punishment for political offences, and tried various conciliatory measures, but in vain. On March 13, 1867, Salnave gained possession of the capital, and Geffrard was obliged to take refuge on a French ship. He went to Jamaica, where he died in February, 1879.

GEIKIE, ARCHIBALD, a Scotch geologist, was born at Edinburgh in 1835. He was educated at the high school and university of that city, and in 1855 was appointed on the Geological Survey of Scotland. In 1867 he was made director of the survey, and in 1870 was appointed professor of mineralogy and geology in the University of Edinburgh. Besides contributing to many scientific and literary periodicals, he has published *The Story of a Boulder* (1858); *Phenomena of the Glacial Drift of Scotland* (1863); *Scenery of Scotland viewed in connection with its Physical Geography* (1865); and some text-books of geology and physical geography. He was associated with Dr. George Wilson in preparing the *Life of Prof. Edward Forbes* (1861), and wrote the *Memoir of Sir Roderick I. Murchison* (2 vols., 1874). In 1881 he was made director-general of the geological survey of the United Kingdom.

GEIKIE, JAMES, a Scottish geologist, brother of Archibald, was born in Edinburgh, Aug. 23, 1839. He was educated at the high school and university of his native town. In 1861 he became assistant geologist in the national survey of Scotland; in 1867 was promoted to be a full geologist, and in 1869 was appointed a district surveyor. Besides many important scientific papers he is the author of *The Great Ice Age and its Relations to the Antiquity of Man* (1874; enlarged, 1876); and *Prehistoric Europe* (1881), a work treating of archæology as well as the pleistocene geology.

GENET, EDMOND CHARLES (1765–1836), a French diplomatist, was born at Versailles, Jan. 8, 1765. His family name was Genest, but after coming to the United States he was generally known as Genet. Though brought up at the French court, he held republican opinions. Appointed *charge d'affaires* at St. Petersburg, in April, 1789, he got into trouble, and was dismissed in July, 1792. In the following December he was appointed minister to the United States. On his arrival at Charleston, S. C., April 8, 1793, popular demonstrations were made in favor of the French republic. Still more enthusiastic was his reception at Philadelphia, May 16. But the government discreetly determined to avoid intermeddling in European affairs. It refused to make further alliance with France, and forbade Genet to grant letters of marque and military commissions, as he had already done. The ambassador fussed and fumed, appealed to the people, and endeavored to stir up Congress against the President. He went so far that, at Washington's request, he was recalled before the end of the year. So imprudent had Genet's conduct been that he preferred to remain in the United States, where he found some warm supporters. He married a daughter of Gov. George Clinton, of New York, in 1794, was naturalized, and proved a useful citizen. After the death of his first wife he married a daughter of Samuel Osgood. He took much interest in improvements in agriculture and the arts. He died at Schodack, Long Island, July 14, 1836.

GENEVA, an incorporated village of New York, in Ontario county, is on the north end of Seneca Lake, 50 miles W. of Syracuse and E. of Rochester. It is on the New York Central Railroad, and has also railroads to Ithaca, Lyons, and Corning. It has 6 hotels, 2 national banks, 1 other bank, 4 weekly newspapers, 11 churches, and 6 schools. Hobart College, an Episcopalian institution, is located here. There are 6 factories, 3 foundries, and several flouring-mills. The town is neat and picturesque; it is lighted with gas and electricity, and has water-works and 2 parks. The property is valued at $3,600,000, and the public debt is $13,000. It was settled in 1790 and incorporated in 1812. Its population in 1890 was 6500.

GENISTA, a genus of plants known as Broom in popular language, although that name covers what are now regarded as two separate genera, *Spartium* and *Genista*, both of the order Leguminosae. The former in classification is distinguished chiefly by the filaments being all united in a simple tube, while they form two sets in *Genista* proper. In *Spartium* the legume is perfectly flat, while it is turgid in *Genista*, and there are some minor differences of interest to the critical botanist. The origin of the name *Genista* is uncertain. It is used by Pliny, who says the flowers are grateful to bees, and that the Greeks call it *Spartion*, but points out that it is distinct from the grass of that name, which we know now as "Esparto grass." The long and leafless branches of *Spartium junceum*, according to Gilbert, were commonly used in French and Spanish vineyards instead of twine for tying the vine, and in the similarity of uses may have originated the similarity of name. In fact, both the esparto grass and the *Spartium* broom furnish fibres now known as *esparto*.

The broom has a historic interest, as being the emblem of the house of Plantagenet, or "Planta-genista," of which King Henry II. was the first representative in England. Some authors incline to the belief that his father Geoffrey, Count of Anjou, was the first who bore the name, from the incident of his wearing a sprig of broom in his helmet during a battle. Another account is that another member of the family, long before, made a penitential voyage to the Holy Land, and used to lash himself for penance every evening with a bunch of broom. *Spartium junceum* seems to have been the *Genista* of the house of Plantagenet. The broom of Scotland is *Spartium sesparium*. The English broom is critically *Genista anglica*, a low, thorny bush, or *G. pilosa*, a low bush with hairy legumes, but probably the most common species in England, and the one which has become naturalized to a considerable extent in the north-eastern part of the United States, is *Genista tinctoria*, known popularly as "Dyers-green weed," and "wood-waxen," or "woad-waxen." A yellow color, prepared from the flowers, was once popular for dyeing wool, but was found of little service in dyeing cotton. Cattle seldom touch it; but it is said that, when cows from hunger are forced to eat it, the milk becomes intensely bitter. It is becoming a bad weed in New England pastures, from the fact that, being rejected by cattle, it is left to perfect seed and spread itself. Broom is used to a considerable extent in medicine. It has especially a reputation for good service in dropsy. (T. M.)

GEORGE, LAKE, one of the most beautiful of American lakes, is in the State of New York. It occupies the bottom of a valley lying between high ridges, and forming, for the principal part of its length of 32 miles, the boundary between Washington county on the E. S. E. side and Warren county on the W. N. W., extending southward into Warren county. The outlet, at the N. N. E. point, is in Essex county. Its elevation is 346 feet above tide-water. The greatest depth exceeds 400 feet. The lake receives several considerable brooks, but no large streams. Its outlet, a copious stream, makes a hurried descent of 99 feet in its course of 5 miles, flowing into Lake Champlain near the ruins of the historic Fort Ticonderoga. At the S. extremity of the lake is the village of Caldwell, and near the outlet is Baldwin, both of which places are reached by branch railways. The lake has 220 islands, some of which are mere rocks. On the shores there are many summer hotels, at most of which steamboats touch several times a day throughout the season. For the most part the shores are bold, rocky, and wooded, and without much cultivated land. After the village of Caldwell (the shire town of Warren county) the principal places on the shores are Bolton and Hague.

Lake George was so named in 1755 by Sir William Johnson, in honor of King George II. The Jesuit missionary Jaques visited it in 1607 and called it Lac du St. Sacrament. The old Indian name is said to be Andia-to-roc-te. The name Lake Horicon appears to have been invented by J. Fenimore Cooper. (See introduction to *The Last of the Mohicans*.) But some writers will have it that Horicon means "the smile of the Great Spirit;" and others translate it "silvery water." The curious identification of this name with that of Oregon appears to be traceable to no higher authority than that of Rafinesque, who translates it "hollow."

During the colonial period the region of this lake was the scene of many important events. The ruins of Fort Wm. Henry (built in 1755 by Sir Wm. Johnson) are at the S. end of the lake, and those of Fort George (built in 1759 by Amherst) are a mile distant. The important battle of Lake George, between the French and Algonkins on the one side and the English and the Iroquois on the other, took place Sept. 8, 1755. In March, 1757, Vaudreuil attempted to take Fort Wm. Henry by surprise, but failed in the attempt. In August following it capitulated to Montcalm, after which his Indian allies fell upon the retreating English garrison and murdered large numbers. Montcalm then destroyed the fort. At Sabbath Day Point Putnam, in 1756, repulsed the French. Lord Howe lost his life (1758) in a skirmish near the N. end of the lake. (C. W. G.)

GEORGE, ENOCH (1768–1828), an American Methodist bishop, was born in Lancaster co., Va., in 1768. He entered the ministry as an itinerant in North Carolina in 1790, was made presiding elder in the Charleston district, S. C., in 1796. Here his labors resulted in a marked revival of religion. In 1801, his health having failed, he opened a school at Winchester, Va. In 1816 he was chosen a bishop

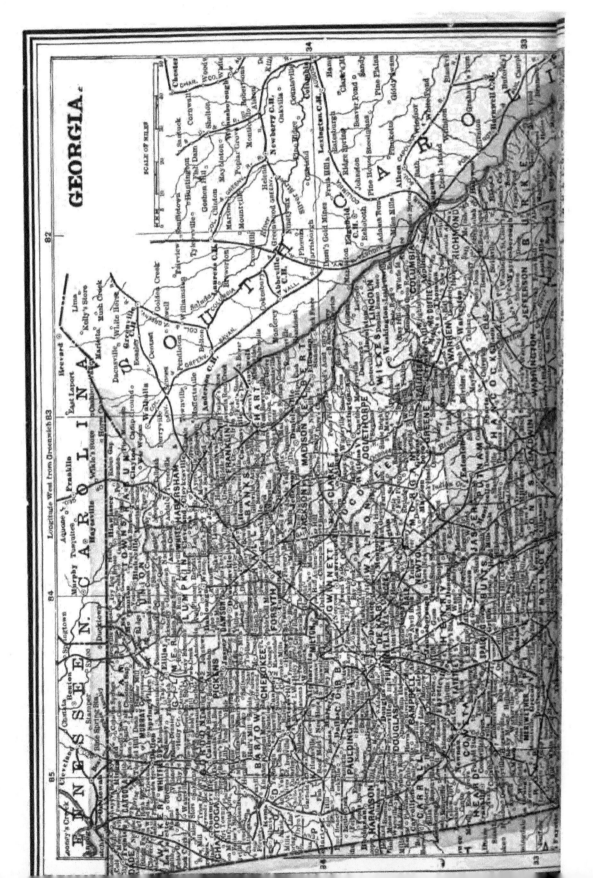

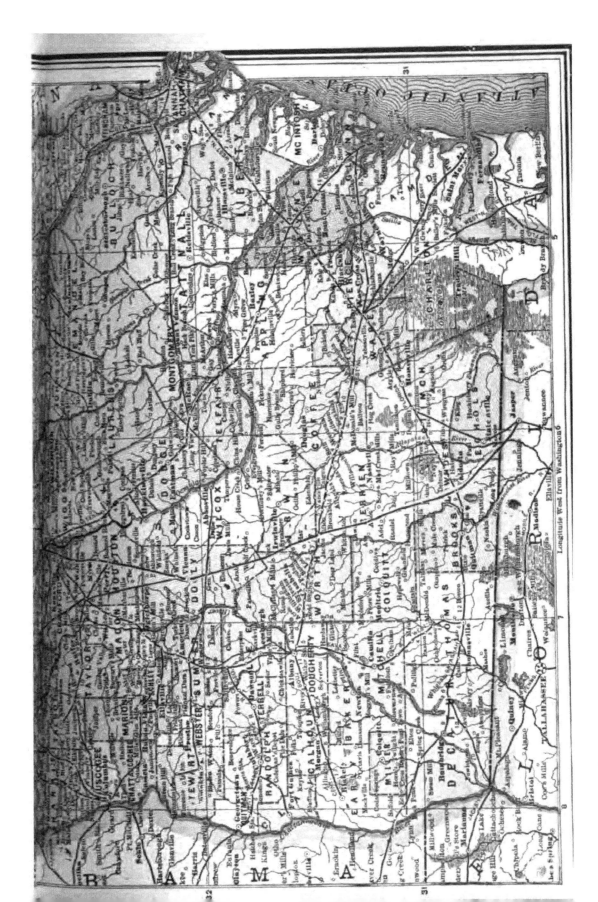

and discharged his duties with great zeal and earnestness. He died at Staunton, Va., Aug. 23, 1828.

GEORGE, HENRY, an American journalist and social economist, was born in Philadelphia, Sept. 2, 1839. Learning the printer's trade he went to California, where, after some experience in mining, he settled down as a journalist. In 1871 he joined with two others in founding the *San Francisco Post*, but his mind was now occupied with the social problem of the distribution of wealth. His first economic publication was *Our Land and Land Policy* (1871). Four years later he retired from editorial work, but he has since continued to write for the newspapers. His principal work, *Progress and Poverty* (1879), attracted considerable attention immediately upon its publication and still more when republished in Europe. It has been translated into several languages, and has been criticised by political economists and social philosophers of all schools. Its main doctrine is that "nothing short of making land common property can permanently relieve poverty and check the tendency of wages to the starvation point." The agitation of the land question in Ireland led him to publish a little book on *The Irish Land Question* (1880), but his views were not approved in the main by the Irish Nationalists. In 1881 Mr. George went to Ireland as a newspaper correspondent to examine the actual condition of the peasantry, and was imprisoned for a time as a suspect, but was afterwards released with ample apologies. He visited England in 1883 and lectured in the principal cities, advocating the theory advanced in his book and causing controversy among the politicians as well as social philosophers. A number of essays treating further of his doctrines were gathered into a volume called *Social Problems* (1883).

GEORGIA, a Southern State of the American Union, lying on the Atlantic Ocean, between South Carolina and Florida. It lies between the meridians of 80° 48' and 85° 38' W. long. from Greenwich and the parallels of 30° 21' 39'' and 35° N. lat. Its area is 59,475 square miles, or 38,064,000 acres, of which 1495 square miles are reckoned as water surface, leaving 57,980 square miles of land area, equal to 37,107,200 acres. Its extreme length from north to south is 320 miles and its extreme breadth from east to west 254 miles. For the purpose of indicating the principal physical features of the State geographers have considered it under five divisions—the Sea Islands, the Swamp Region, the Pine-barren Belt, Middle Georgia, and Cherokee Georgia. A more practical and popular division is, however, that of: the Mountain Region, or Upper Georgia; the Hill Country, or Middle Georgia; and the Low Country, or Lower Georgia.

See Vol. X. p. 390 Am. ed. (p. 434 Edin. ed.).

Upper Georgia has an area of about 10,000 square miles, embracing nearly all the mountains and much hill country. In this region are two distinct chains of mountains—the Blue Ridge, in the north-east, with its lines of separate peaks, of which the Rabun Bald is the highest, 4698 feet above the sea; and the Cumberland Range, a longer and more connected chain of mountains than the Blue Ridge, which enters the State between Rabun and Towns counties and cuts off Towns, Union, and Fannin counties. In this chain are Tray Mountain, 4437 feet; Mount Enotah (Brasstown Bald), 4802 feet; and Blood Mountain, 4460 feet. West and south-west of Fannin county, Cherokee Georgia abounds in mountains and ridges belonging to the western chain of the Appalachian range, though none of their summits are so high as those we have named.

Middle Georgia—the Hill Country—lies between the heads of navigation of the principal rivers of the State and the elevation of 1000 or 1100 feet, and has an area of about 15,000 square miles. The foot-hills, which begin in Middle Georgia, run in nearly parallel ranges and cover a breadth of almost 150 miles, with fertile valleys between them. The southern border of Middle Georgia is a table-land, gradually ascending and reaching in Baldwin county an elevation of 575 feet above the sea.

Lower Georgia—the Low Country—lies below the line joining the heads of navigation of the rivers, and is much the larger part of the State, having an area of nearly 35,000 square miles. It is below the level of 300 feet above the sea.

Rivers.—There are three distinct drainage basins and river systems in Georgia—the *Atlantic basin*, which receives the waters of the Savannah, the Ogeechee, the Altamaha, with its affluents, the Ohoopee, the Oconee, and the Ocmulgee, the Satilla, and the St. Mary's, with their respective tributaries; the *Gulf basin*, which receives the waters of the Chattahoochee, with its great tributary, the Flint, the Ocklockonee, the Suwannee, and several smaller streams, and discharges them into the Mexican Gulf, and the upper waters of the Coosa and its affluents, which also flow into the Gulf; and, third, in the extreme north-west and west, a part of the *Tennessee basin*, into which flow the upper waters of the Tennessee and its affluents, the Hiawassee, the Tacoah, the Notley, the Ocoree, the Catoosa, and Chickamauga Creek. These waters find their way down the Tennessee to the Ohio, and thence to the Mississippi.

The Atlantic and Gulf water-sheds together drain about three-fourths of the State, or about 44,000 square miles. Of this the Coosa, an Alabama river, and its tributaries in Georgia drain 6020 square miles. The Tennessee basin drains somewhat more than 1000 square miles. Of these rivers the Savannah, which has a length of 450 miles, is navigable for 230 miles; the Chattahoochee, which, after its junction with the Flint at the Florida line, is called the Appalachicola, is 550 miles long, is navigable for 350 miles, and the Flint for 300. The Ogeechee, Ocmulgee, Oconee, Satilla, St. Mary's, and the Suwannee are navigable for a considerable distance in Georgia, the total navigable waters of the State exceeding 1500 miles. The sea-coast, extending in a direct line from the St. Mary's to the mouth of the Savannah, is bordered with islands, between which and the mainland are the following sounds, connected with the ocean by numerous inlets: St. Andrew's, St. Simon's, Altamaha, Doboy, Sapelo, St. Catharine's, and Ossabaw Sounds. The whole coast line formed by the islands and sounds is said to be about 480 miles. The islands have a fertile, alluvial soil, and yield large crops of rice and Sea-island cotton.

There are many cataracts and waterfalls of great beauty in Northern and Middle Georgia, the most celebrated of which are Toccoa Falls and the Tallulah

Cataracts; Estatoia Falls, Hiawassee Falls, Amacolola Falls, the Stekoa Falls, the Falls of the Towalaga, the Caledonia Cascade and Oceana Falls, Turner's Point and Indian Arrow Rapids. Most of these are in the extreme northern part of the State.

Geology and Mineralogy.—The geological formations represented in Georgia include almost every known geologic period. We have here, though not in regular succession, the Palæozoic period, represented by the Primordial, Silurian, and Devonian groups and the Carboniferous era; the Mesozoic period, by the Triassic and Cretaceous; the Neozoic, or Tertiary, by the Eocene, Miocene, and Pliocene; and the Quaternary. or Southern drift, by irregular strata of sands and clays, and the still more recent extensive deposits of alluvium. There is also a broad area of metamorphic and crystalline rocks in the middle and northern portions of the State, indicating at some time in the past volcanic action. The rocks of this section are feldspathic granites and gneisses, hornblendic gneisses and schists, mica schists, sandstones, soapstones, and other rocks of the Appalachian region. They are all interpenetrated and crossed at frequent intervals by quartz veins, large and small, and by numerous trap-dikes. Both the veins and dikes are somewhat disintegrated and form part of the local soils. This is the mineral region of the State, and gold and silver are both found in it in considerable quantities. North-west of this metamorphic region we come to the rocks of the Palæozoic period, the Primordial rocks, including the early sandstones, shales, and limestones, followed in turn by the Silurian and Devonian groups, the former extending from the Savannah River above Augusta, through the north-western counties, to the foot of Dugdown Mountain, in Haralson county, on the west line of the State, with occasional outcrops of Devonian. Beyond these, in the north-west corner of the State, the coal measures belonging to the great coal deposit, which occupies Central and North-eastern Alabama, yield an excellent quality of bituminous coal. A very short distance from these coal-beds, in Bartow and Cherokee counties, immense deposits of iron ore are found at the junction of the limestone and Metamorphic rocks, while still nearer, Shinbone Mountain, which runs parallel with Lookout Mountain for forty miles, is simply a mass of fossiliferous iron ore, distant only a mile from the coal-beds. Iron can be produced here cheaper than anywhere else in the United States, and of excellent quality, and many smelting furnaces have been erected and are kept busy.

The triassic formation includes the trap-dikes and clay slates of the metamorphic region and its border. The largest trap-dike in the State lies west of the granite region. The cretaceous group occupies but a small area in the western part of the State, and forms the eastern termination of the chalk beds, which extend from North-eastern Mississippi through Middle Alabama into Georgia. The tertiary beds underlie the most of Southern Georgia and are covered largely by the quaternary deposits of sands and clays on the south and east. The Eocene is most fully represented, but the Miocene and Pliocene also occur on the southeast. The Claiborne, Jackson, and Vicksburg groups of the Eocene are all present, the last named extending northward from Florida. The quaternary (or Southern drift) formation consists of irregular deposits of sands, clays, and ferruginous sandstones over the older strata. These deposits in Georgia are confined to the southern half of the State. The sands are white and deep, and beneath them are variegated clays, mostly plastic.

Besides the veins and lodes of gold and silver in the metamorphic region, and the iron and coal of the carboniferous deposits in the north-west, there are veins of copper ore in Gilmer county, and considerable lead is found with the silver in the argentiferous galena. Gold exists in almost every county north of the central line of the State, but is most plentiful in Cherokee, Carroll, Cobb, and Lumpkin counties. It was first discovered in Habersham county, in 1831. A branch mint was established at Dahlonega, Lumpkin county, in 1837, and in the next 24 years coined $6,121,919, mostly of Georgia gold. It was discontinued in 1861, and the buildings have been given by the government to the North Georgia Agricultural College. Hydraulic mining is now practised extensively in the State in working the placer deposits of free gold. Silver is combined with the gold, and occurs also with sulphuret of lead in the galena ores. The usual minerals found with gold and silver—antimony, zinc, manganese, titanium, tellurium, and graphite—are found here, but are not separated. There are several quarries of excellent marble, one of statuary marble in Cherokee county, building limestone, granite, marls, and burrstones; and gypsum, syenite, talc, soapstone, asbestos, slate, tripoli, fluor-spar, barytes, hydraulic cement of excellent quality and very white in color in Bartow county, and petroleum of good quality are among the mineral products of economic value; while beryls, garnets, agates, amethysts, and perhaps diamonds, have been found in the State. Fossils are numerous and many of them of great importance. Among them are skeletons of the mastodon, megatherium, mylodon, two species of fossil elephant, an extinct ox, and many species of fossil turtles and mollusks. There are many mineral springs in the State, those in the northern counties being mostly chalybeate, while those in the central portion are usually sulphurous. The Indian Springs, in the northern part of Forsyth county, have a deservedly high reputation.

Vegetation.—From the great variety of its soils, almost every production of the temperate and subtropical regions may be successfully cultivated in some part of the State. Its flora and sylva include a large number of genera and species. The forest-trees of the State include 20 species of oak, differing from each other in grain, leaf, texture, strength, and durability; one of them, the live-oak, is the finest ship-timber in the world, and that found in the vicinity of Brunswick is the most valuable grown in the United States. It is an evergreen. There are six species of hickory, and five or six species of pine, but the Georgia yellow- or pitch-pine is the most valuable. The other principal forest-trees are the ash, chestnut, beech, sycamore, dogwood, tulip-tree or American poplar, elm, cottonwood, magnolia, bay, maple (several species), fir, spruce, birch, persimmon, cedar, cypress, black and sweet gum, sassafras, chinquapin, white and black mulberry, haw, black walnut, etc., etc.

The grasses are numerous, but two of them, though valuable for many purposes, are greatly hated and feared by the cotton- and rice-planters. These are the Bermuda grass and the wire grass (*Poa compressa*). (See FORAGE CROPS.)

The *flora* of Georgia includes many beautiful flowering plants, among which the broad-leaved *Kalmia*, the *Magnolia grandiflora*, the dogwood, the azalea, and the wild lilies and roses are most conspicuous.

Climate and Health.—Georgia has three distinct

climates, governed in part by the latitude and in part by the altitude above the sea. Southern and South-eastern Georgia is low, with a rich alluvial soil and extensive swamps; it is sickly during the hot season; malarial, bilious, and typhoid fevers then prevail. Those who are thoroughly acclimated do not find the climate objectionable; but it is dangerous to those from higher and cooler lands. This region has a winter mean temperature of from 48° to 51°, the minimum in the winter months being rarely below 32°. In the exceptional year, 1885–86, it sank to 18°, a lower point than had been reached for fifty years. The maximum temperature of the year is about 95°, but the heat is constant and continued for six months. The summer mean is from 79° to 81°. The rainfall taking the years together is about 57 inches, December and January being the driest months.

In Middle Georgia the rainfall is less, about 41 inches being the average. The driest months are June and September. The yearly temperature ranges from 6° to 102°, though occasionally in very severe winters the mercury sinks to zero. The range is great, but the mean range is much less, the winter mean being about 41°, and the summer 73°. The nights in summer are cool and invigorating. Snow frequently falls, but melts almost as rapidly as it touches the ground.

North-eastern and North-western Georgia have a more varied surface, and a climate as varied as the land. The annual mean temperature ranges from 50° on the highest lands to 60°.3 on those of more moderate elevation. The rainfall ranges from 57 inches to 61. The maximum during the summer months does not usually exceed 95°, and the mean of those months is about 75°; the winter mean is 39°.05, ranging from 45° at Marietta to about 36° at Ringgold; and the winter minimum, ordinarily about 3°, in very severe seasons has been known to drop to —4°. The range is less than in Middle Georgia. Snow falls to a depth of from two to four inches, but usually remains but a short time. The climate is healthy, the winters generally delightful, and many points, not of the highest elevation, are excellent as winter resorts. There is sufficient cold to prevent the enervating effect which is experienced in lower lands. The average mean annual temperature for the whole State is 65°, and the average annual rainfall from 47 to 50 inches.

Agriculture; Crops.—The crops vary with the soil, elevation, and temperature. In the low flatlands, the orange, lemon, banana, olive, and other semi-tropical fruits come to perfection, though at rare intervals affected by frosts. The quality of these fruits is thought to be inferior to those of Central Florida, and they do not command quite so high a price. The principal crops are rice, sugar-cane, Sea-island and some short-staple cotton, sweet potatoes, and a moderate quantity of corn. In Southern Georgia considerable cotton is grown, and rich and succulent grasses, both for pasture and hay. Stock and swine are pastured in the pine woods. Middle Georgia is a fine fruit-region. The peach-tree is hardier, subject to fewer diseases, and yields more abundantly than in any other State. More attention is now given than formerly to the improvement of the quality of the fruit. Apples and pears, especially of the early varieties, are abundant, and many of the seedlings prove excellent. The small fruits are less successful, though the native southern grapes, the Herbemont, Scuppernong, post-oak, etc., do well. Melons, tomatoes, and market vegetables are largely cultivated, and shipped early to Northern ports. Cotton is the staple crop in this section, but Indian corn, wheat, and clover are also important crops, and some rye, oats, and barley are grown. Tobacco, sorghum, and peanuts, or goobers, as they are generally called, are becoming popular crops. The sweet potato is also cultivated largely and exported. North-eastern Georgia is mountainous, but with rich soil in the creek and river lands, where there is heavy timber, and good grass and grain. North-western Georgia is a blue limestone region, with a rich, fertile soil in the river and valley lands. Its crops are wheat, Indian corn, clover, and other grasses; potatoes, apples, pears, peaches, and other fruits; and in the river valleys, where there is sand, cotton. Fruits are from four to five weeks earlier than at the North.

South-western Georgia is the great cotton region of the State, and raises sugar-cane and rice in the bottom lands. Sweet potatoes are grown in great quantities by the negroes, and attempts have been made in tea-culture. This part of the State has a sickly climate in summer.

The returns of 1884 show that the cotton crop reached 760,000 bales, being 58,160 bales larger than the great crop of 1860, but 54,000 bales less than the crop of 1880, and 182,000 bales less than that of 1882, though the bale is steadily growing larger, and now averages at least 485 pounds. The product per acre varies in different sections of the State, being largest on the poorer lands, in consequence of greater care and more abundant fertilization. The statistics of the Sea-island cotton are not given separately. The cotton crop does not average nearly as much as it should, through the carelessness of many of the growers. Of rice production in the State, the statistics of 1880 show a yield of somewhat more than 25,400,000 pounds, about half the crop before the war, but the crop is said to be increasing. Of Indian corn, 28,765,700 bushels were reported in 1884; about an average crop, though showing only 10.6 bushels to the acre. Wheat is never a large crop in Georgia: in 1883 the yield was reported as 2,574,900 bushels; in 1884 it was a little more than 3,500,000 bushels, but the average yield of the State was only 7 bushels to the acre. Oats yielded, in 1884, 6,385,000 bushels, an average yield of 12.02 bushels to the acre. The crop of sugar-cane was 601 hogsheads of sugar and 1,565,784 gallons of molasses in 1880; and of sorghum, 981,152 gallons; of sweet potatoes, 4,397,778 bushels; of hay, 14,469 tons. This product has largely increased.

The numbers and values of farm animals in 1885 were as follows: 105,776 horses, valued at $8,736,040; 143,843 mules, valued at $13,754,268; 344,458 milch cows, valued at $6,028,015; 610,811 oxen and other cattle, valued at $6,566,218; 532,547 sheep, valued at $793,495; 1,597,937 hogs, valued at $5,528,862. Total values, $41,406,898.

Manufactures.—Both manufactures and mining have made a great advance since 1880. In that year the census statistics were: Capital employed, $20,672,410; number of hands employed, 24,875; wages paid, $5,266,152; material used, $24,143,939; annual product, $36,440,948. In 1884 the capital employed was $38,841,822, and the product about $70,000,000. The largest single industry is probably now that of cotton goods, which employs 10,000 hands and $13,000,000 capital, and turns out annually from its 7,834 looms and its more than 340,000 spindles, goods to the amount of $25,000,000, using over 100,000 bales of cotton in the work. There were also, in 1884, 32 woollen-mills, producing over $800,000 of goods; flouring-mills, producing $9,703,898 of flour and meal. The iron and steel interest in the north-western part of the State is nearly equal to the cotton manufacture. Recent statistics are wanting, but the annual product must exceed $20,000,000.

The manufacture of lumber, timber, and naval stores may be reckoned among the great industries of the State. The constantly increasing demand for Georgia yellow-pine lumber keeps hundreds of saw-mills constantly employed, and the market for live-oak and other hard-wood timber is also enlarging with each year. In 1884 the shipment of lumber exceeded 200,000,000 feet, and the timber shipments were also very large. The annual product of lumber and timber in that year was estimated at $7,000,000. Naval stores—tar, pitch, resin, and spirits of turpentine—are produced in great quantities in the pine forests. The shipments of naval stores in 1885 from the ports of Savannah and Brunswick exceeded $3,000,000, of which about $750,000 went to foreign countries. The production has more than doubled since 1880. The manufacture of cotton-seed oil, of tobacco, of iron, cast and wrought, of machinery, paper, etc., etc., make up a grand total, as we have stated, of more than $70,000,000.

Coal-mining, as well as mining for the precious metals, has received a great impulse since 1880, and the coals of North-western Georgia are in large demand for smelting purposes. The present amount of mining products is not known.

Fisheries.—There are extensive and profitable shad-fisheries on the Savannah and Ogeechee rivers, as well as in some of the sounds, and the shad from these are among the earliest brought into Northern markets. There are also fisheries for Spanish mackerel, sea-trout, pompano, grouper, and red snapper, and for green turtle at Brunswick, St. Mary's, etc.

Railroads.—The mileage of railroads in the State in 1884 was 2940 miles, of which 65.5 miles were constructed in 1883. A railway commission, consisting of three members, appointed by the governor, with the advice and consent of the senate, supervise and control all railroad matters in the State. The Central Railroad of Georgia, with its leased lines, is the most potent railway organization in the State. Besides its own lines of 312 miles, it leases 13 other railroads, some of them of great length; it also owns and controls the Ocean Steamship Company, of Savannah. The Savannah, Florida, and Western Railroad has 236 miles of its main line in Georgia, as well as several branches, and owns, leases, and controls in Georgia and Florida over 1000 miles. Other important roads are: the Brunswick and Western, 171 miles long; the Macon and Brunswick, 187 miles long; the Georgia Railroad, uniting Augusta and Atlanta; the Western and Atlantic, the property of the State; the Southwestern; the Marietta and North Georgia, and the Atlanta and West Point. Other roads, mostly belonging to corporations out of the State, are: the Richmond and Danville, with its branches; Alabama Great Southern, East Tennessee, and Georgia; Atlanta and Charlotte Air-line; Georgia Pacific, and Augusta and Knoxville.

There are three canals in the State, but they have a total length of only 37 miles. They are all large enough to admit the passage of steamers, and connect the Savannah and Ogeechee, Brunswick and the Altamaha, and Augusta, above and below the falls of the Savannah.

Ocean Steamship Lines.—The Ocean Steamship line and the Philadelphia line, both owned by the Central Railroad of Georgia, ply between New York and Philadelphia and Savannah. The Boston and Savannah Steamship Company, and the Merchants' and Miners' Transportation Company, of Baltimore, also make Savannah their southern terminus. Several of the West India and New Orleans lines also touch at Savannah, both in going and returning.

Commerce.—The foreign commerce of Georgia is large. She has three ports of entry, viz.: Brunswick, Savannah, and St. Mary's, though the last named is mostly occupied with internal commerce, the coasting trade, and the fisheries. In the year ending June 30, 1885, the exports were $22,142,154, of which Savannah shipped $20,571,446, nineteen-twentieths of it being cotton. The imports for the same year were $654,159, of which $652,625 were brought to Savannah. The coasting trade is very large, and here Brunswick and St. Mary's do much more business. Timber and lumber, especially Georgia pine and live-oak timber, Sea-island and other cotton, early vegetables, tomatoes, Irish and sweet potatoes, fruits large and small, shad, Spanish mackerel and other fish, and naval stores, form the bulk of the shipments. This internal commerce is known to be more than double that to and from foreign ports. There were in the year ending June 30, 1885, 502 vessels which entered these ports from foreign countries, having an aggregate tonnage of 283,867 tons; of these only 27 were American, of 11,365 tons burthen; 569 vessels cleared with 322,081 tons burthen, of which 66 were American, of 27,912 tons. Fifty ocean steamers entered and 63 cleared from Savannah. The total mercantile marine of Georgia in 1885, registered, enrolled, and licensed, was 133 vessels, of 35,830.75 tons, of which 51 were steamers with a tonnage of 24,023.85 tons.

Finances.—The assessed valuation of real and personal estate, which in 1880 was very slightly under $240,000,000, now exceeds $300,000,000, and the real value is probably more than $375,000,000. The recognized bonded indebtedness of the State Oct. 1, 1884, was $8,704,635, and the interest for 1885 was $582,121. The total tax levied in 1884 was $1,165,885.41, and there was collected of this $1,156,244.67. The debt is being gradually reduced by a sinking fund. The current receipts from taxes, licenses, fines, and penalties, exceed the expenditures.

Education.—The latest public school enrolment of children of school age in Georgia gave the total number as 494,411. Of these, 322,144 were enrolled as belonging to the public and private schools, and the number in actual daily average attendance was 188,371. Of those enrolled for the public schools, 175,668 were white and 111,743 colored. About 35,000 were in private schools. The whole number of public schools was 6560; there were about 960 private schools. The whole number of public school teachers was a little more than 6600, and of private school teachers 975. The amount distributed to the schools in 1884, derived from the rental of the State railroad, from dividends of Georgia Railroad, and various taxes, was $488,347. The negroes pay, directly and indirectly, about one-half of this sum. No county is entitled to a share of the fund unless its schools are in operation at least three months of the year. The Peabody fund contributes about $6000 yearly to specified schools, and the John F. Slater fund contributes $3000 or more to the freedmen's schools. Atlanta, Savannah, Augusta, and Macon have excellent high and graded schools, under special city organizations. There are many schools of secondary instruction, academies and seminaries of respectable and some of them of high grade. There are also seven or eight schools of high grade for the education of colored people of both sexes, for teachers and preachers. These are maintained by associations of the different religious denominations; some of them are endowed; they are largely attended, and are doing a good work. There is a State University at Athens, with branches at Dahlonega, Milledgeville, Cuthbert, and Thomasville. The branch at Dahlonega, also called the North Georgia Agricultural College, gives a full scientific course and is empowered to confer degrees. There is also the Mercer University at Macon, under the control of the Baptists. Both these have law and scientific and normal departments. The State University has also medical and agricultural departments, and the Mercer University a school of theology. The number of students in all departments of the State University and its branches was 1097 in 1884. Mercer University

Churches.—There were in 1884 about 3600 churches of all denominations in the State; the Baptists having a membership of 255,067 in the regular Baptist churches, of which more than one-half were negroes; the Disciples, also Baptistic in their ordinances, had about 7000 members; the Methodists came next, divided into Methodist Episcopal Church South, African M. E. Church, Methodist Episcopal Church North, and Methodist Protestant, having in all a membership of 179,850, of whom about one-half were negroes; the Presbyterians had 8228 members, mostly whites; the Protestant Episcopal Church 4569 members, nearly all white; the Congregationalists 1257, and other minor denominations somewhat more than 2000 members in all. The Jewish population is said to be about 7000, and the Roman Catholic is 25,000. These statistics seem to indicate about 1,500,000 as the adherent religious population of the State.

The following table shows the population of Georgia, classified at each enumeration from 1790 to 1880, the rates of growth, and the proportions of males, females, white, free colored, and slaves before the emancipation proclamation, etc. The total population in 1890 was 1,834,366, but the particulars are not yet at hand.

	Total Population.	Males.	Females.	White.	Free Colored.	Slaves.	Natives.	Foreigners.	Density.	Ratio of Increase.	Number of families.	Number of dwellings.	Persons in dwelling.	Of military age.	Of voting age.
1790	82,548			52,866	398	29,264			1.4						
1800	162,686			102,261	1,019	59,406			2.8	97.0					
1810	252,433			145,414	1,801	105,218			4.3	55.1					
1820	340,985			189,566	1,763	149,656			5.8	35.0					
1830	516,823	263,366	253,457	296,806	2,486	217,531			8.7	51.5					
1840	691,392	351,243	340,149	407,695	2,753	280,944			11.7	33.7					
1850	906,185	456,465	449,720	521,572	2,931	381,682	514,566	6,452	15.4	31.0	91,666	91,206	5.75		112,110
1860	1,057,286	41,128	36,519	591,550	3,500	462,198	1,045,615	11,671	17.9	16.6	109,919	109,069	5.46		198,624
1870	1,184,109	311,171	327,755	638,926	545,142	None.	1,172,982	11,127	20.0	11.9	237,850	236,436	5.01	202,573	237,640
1880	1,542,180	403,774	413,162	816,906	725,135	None.	1,531,616	10,564	26.1	30.2	303,060	289,474	5.33	275,815	321,438

has in its several departments a full attendance of students. Emory College, at Oxford, under the control of the Methodist Church South, is a large institution, and has a scientific course in addition to the regular college curriculum. There are also Bowden College, at Bowdon, non-sectarian, and Pio Nono College, at Macon, a Roman Catholic institution. There are six collegiate institutions for freedmen, two of them, Atlanta University and Clark University, both at Atlanta, having the chartered powers of universities. There are 4 or 5 theological schools of the different denominations; 4 medical colleges, 3 regular and 1 eclectic; 2 law schools, connected with the universities; and 14 institutions, some of them liberally endowed, for the superior instruction of women. There are no separate normal schools except for freedmen, but normal instruction is given in some of the colleges, and normal institutes are held in different parts of the State. There is a school for deaf-mutes at Cave Spring, founded in 1847, and one for the blind at Macon, established in 1852. The State has but one insane hospital, situated near Milledgeville, with accommodations for about 1500 patients.

The Georgia penitentiary system is peculiar, the convicts, to the number of nearly 1400, being leased for twenty years to three companies of contractors, who employ them in building railroads, in mines, and at any labor where they can be used.

There are 137 counties in the State, varying in area from 110 to 1160 square miles, in population from 2161 to 46,126, and in valuation from less than $75,000 to $30,736,165.

Principal Cities and Towns.—ATLANTA (the capital) had, in 1890, 65,514 inhabitants; it is a great railroad centre, a thriving, enterprising city, with many manufactories; Savannah, the largest sea-port, also the terminus of several railway lines, had 41,762; Augusta, a fine cotton-market on the Savannah River, 33,150; Macon, noted for its educational institutions, 22,688; Columbus, also a large cotton-market, 18,650; Athens, the seat of the State University, 8627; Milledgeville, the former capital, had 7306.

Recent History.—The history of Georgia in the last few years has been one of material progress. Gov. Colquitt, who held the gubernatorial office from 1877 to 1882, was re-elected to a second term, and at its close elected U. S. Senator. Alexander H. Stephens, who succeeded him in December, 1882, and who was the most eminent statesman the State has produced, lived only three months to enjoy his honors, dying in March, 1883. His term of office was completed by J. S. Baynton and H. D. McDaniel, successively. W. J. Northen, the present governor, took his seat Nov. 2, 1890. The National Exposition of cotton and other products of the Southern States, at Atlanta, in the autumn of 1881, gave a very powerful impulse to the agricultural and manufacturing interests of the State, which still continues, and has been heightened by other Southern expositions which have followed: Since 1880 the State has lost by death several of its eminent political leaders. Among these we may name besides Gov. Stephens, Ex-Govs. C. J. Jenkins and Herschel V. Johnson, Benjamin H. Hill, and Robert Toombs. (L. P. B.)

GERANIUM, a genus of plants, the type of the order *Geraniaceæ*. As usually defined the order contains but four genera, *Erodium*, *Geranium*, *Monsonia*, and *Pelargonium*, but they are represented by more than 500 species, mostly belonging to the genus *Pelargonium*. They are very near the orders represented by the *Oxalis*, *Tropæolum*, and *Impatiens*, and Lindley observes that "the long beak-like torus around which the carpels are arranged, and the presence of membraneous stipules at joints which are usually tumid, are the true marks of this order." Dr. Gray, however, unites the allies cited all under *Geraniaceæ*, making them represent sections only. *Pelargonium* was divided from the original *Geranium*, as the South African species became better known, on account of a lesser number of stamens, more irregular petals, with a calyx spur (free in *Tropæolum*) united with the pedicle. Many of the true *Pelargoniums* still go under their original name of geraniums in gardens. What was known as the "Scarlet Geranium" a quarter of a century ago has been renamed "Zonal Pelargonium" from the dark, horseshoe-like zone which appears on the leaves of many of the varieties. The skill of the florist has now added a great many colors to the original scarlet, and has evolved double flowers of various shades; and, as the plants are continuous bloomers, they are among the most popular of cultivated flowers. They are adapted equally for filling garden-beds during the summer, and affording a supply of flowers f windows and green-houses during the winter season. New races of the African species are continually appearing, and tax the vocabulary of the florist to find suitable names for them.

Most of the true geraniums, as represented by those which have numerous stamens and regular flowers, are natives of cooler climates, and some of them are among the most beautiful of those plants cultivated in the flower-borders of England and America. A number of species are found in the mountainous regions of South America, Asia, and Europe, and in high northern latitudes. England alone has thirteen species, of which one, *G. Robertianum*, is also indigenous to the eastern portion of the United States, though several others have been introduced and are common as harmless weeds. There are among indigenous species two others in the Eastern United States, *G. maculatum*, a very pretty ornament of the woods, and *G. Carolinianum*, partial to exposed places, and often found in rich waste or cultivated ground. *G. Fremontiana*, *Richardsonii*, and *G. Cæspitosum* are found in the Rocky Mountains. Besides the last two and *G. Carolinianum*, *G. incisum* is found on the Pacific coast. Representatives of the genus *Erodium* have also become naturalized in Europe, and one species, *Erodium cicutarium*, thrives so well in California that it has become one of the most esteemed forage-plants of that region, and is popularly known as "Alfilaria" (*Sp. alfilerilla*). Some of the South African species of *Pelargonium* have edible roots, and one in Tasmania is known as the "Parsnep," but their edible character is beneath all proportion to the number of species which the order presents. In medicine, however, *Geranium maculatum* has a fair reputation, especially where powerful astringents are desirable. The roots are said to have considerably more tannin than kino possesses.

Geranium Robertianum is the "Herb Robert" of Europe, the origin of which name is lost in oblivion. Of various surmises Dr. Prior inclines to the one suggested by Adelung that it was so called from Robert, Duke of Normandy, "for whom was written the celebrated medical treatise of the middle ages, *Regimen Sanitatis Salernitanum*." It has, however, been known from early times as "Saint Robert's herb." All the botanical names have been suggested by the beak-like prolongation on which the fruit is borne; *Erodium* from the Greek *Erodios*, a heron; *Geranium*, from *Geranos*, a crane; and *Pelargonium*, from *Pelargos*, a stork. (T. M.)

GERMANY. The history of the German Empire since 1879 is essentially a history of economical and social politics. The internal structure of the empire in its most important relations had been determined, the constitution established, the army and navy organized, the autonomy of the several states of the confederation provided for, a uniform system of coin, weights, and measures, as well as a common administration of justice and a common system of banking, introduced. The next duty was to adjust and regulate the common institutions. During the erection of those foundation-pillars of the constitution the government and the Parliament had for the most part acted in unbroken harmony. The principal party of the imperial diet was the Moderate Liberal, who aimed at the promotion of national power and greatness at least as much as at the development of liberty, and thought to strengthen the new empire most effectually by supporting the policy of Prince Bismarck, to whose genius the country mainly owed its unity. That party, joined with the less numerous Conservative party, who followed Bismarck in every measure, composed the majority in the imperial diet, and the whole legislation of the empire until 1878 bears the stamp of that Liberal-Conservative alliance. The opposition, composed of the Catholic Centre on the one hand and the more radical Liberals (Progressists), together with a small number of Socialists on the other hand, proved ineffectual against the union of the Moderate Liberals with the Conservatives.

[See Vol. X. p. 390 Am. ed. (p. 447 Edin. ed.).]

This state of things underwent an important change when the internal arrangements of the work began to be carried out in detail. Bismarck was convinced that before all things else the financial and custom laws of the empire needed a change. The universal depression of trade, prevailing not only in Germany but also in the other European countries for several years, had revived in the public mind the old and almost forgotten controversy about free-trade and protection. To the government the unsatisfactory state of things became sensible mainly through the deterioration of finances. The indemnity paid by France had made in Germany a great reserve of coin, by means of which it succeeded in substituting the gold-standard for the previously existing silver-standard, and in redeeming loans in the several states. Capital, becoming thereby free, did not fail to stimulate the spirit of enterprise and speculation. Especially railway building was carried on with excessive rapidity. Further, a good part of the means obtained by the indemnity was employed in the construction of military lines, in completing the fortresses, and in other measures of national defence. All this caused a great enhancement of the supply of industrial products, and foreign countries, in particular England, hastened to take advantage of that condition of affairs. Thus it happened that the balance of trade soon turned against Germany, and the billions of the French indemnity, which had diffused all over the country an illusion of inexhaustible wealth, and arrayed especially the finances both of the empire and of the several states in the brightest light, gradually disappeared. Deficits took the place of surpluses, or at least the time when this must happen was seen approaching. At the same time the Free-trade party, whose power in the legislatures and in the administration seemed till now unshaken, proceeded unscrupulously to carry out their principles. The chancellor himself, like the whole conservative party to which he belonged, had once been a partisan of free-trade theories, and a few years before had proclaimed as his plan to reduce all customs to a few profitable financial duties. Indeed, the government of the empire, whose economical policy was almost exclusively guided by Mr. Delbrück, proceeded in the abolition of the existing moderate protective duties even more vehemently than the free-traders of the imperial diet wished, and the total repeal of the duties on iron in 1876 was the work of the government. But this very measure, executed in a time of depression in the iron trade, made the cup overflow. Nothing strengthened the resistance to the tendencies of free-trade among the industrial classes more than that measure. The iron manufacturers were thus roused to the necessity of a conflict; with them the textile manufacturers formed a close connection, and hence arose an agitation against the policy of free-trade, which rapidly spread through the people. The evident distress of trade did not escape the watchful eye of the chancellor. Heretofore he had cared little for economical policy, leaving it confidently and entirely to such men as Delbrück and Camphausen. But now he took the reins himself. The close connection of the commercial depression with the deterioration of the finances gave him the start; and the argument of the protectionists, based on the rapid draining in a few years of the great resources which Germany had received at the establishment of the new empire, seems to have made a strong impression on him. His abandonment of the free-trade policy was decided in 1878, and he delayed not a moment to turn another way. A commission was appointed to inquire into the questions of tariff as regards both the financial and protective effects.

With Prince Bismarck the paramount question was to prevent financial decline. This he sought to attain through combination of a tariff-reform with a reform of finance. Till now the exclusive revenues of the empire, consisting of the produce of the customs and excise duties on beer, spirits, tobacco, sugar, salt, and of stamp-duties, were not sufficient to cover the expenses. Therefore the several states were obliged to make up the difference by means of contributions according to the number of inhabitants (*Matrikularbeiträge*). By that, however, the finances of the various states fell into a dangerous fluctuation, and the states must, eventually, raise loans to pay the *Matrikularbeiträge*. Prince Bismarck aimed therefore to abolish these contributions and to enhance the revenues of the empire so far, that not only this might be done, but also surpluses should be gained, which, being distributed among the states, might enable them also to lessen their direct taxes. In the greatest state of the empire, Prussia, the people had already complained for many years of the pressure of direct taxes. This pressure was so much the more severe since the districts likewise, to supply their wants, depended almost entirely on direct taxes, raised in form of additional payments to the direct taxes of the state. Similar conditions of affairs prevailed in the other states. By this extra taxation especially the country and property were oppressed. The chancellor's plan tended, therefore, to leave to the districts in Prussia the whole or part of the produce of land- and house-taxes, and moreover to relieve them from a part of other burdens, namely, for education and support of the poor. Last but not least he aimed indeed to give a greater measure of protection to home industry and production.

The countries surrounding Germany, as Russia, Austria, France, had lately led the way to better protection of their manufactures. Thus Germany saw herself threatened from two sides, since the Free-trade party, on the one hand, insisted upon more liberal admission of foreign commodities, while, on the other hand, her neighbors endeavored to prohibit or restrict the import of German goods. The chancellor was, therefore, entirely right when he, during the debate on the new tariff, requested that in considering this pure question of interest all questions of politics and oppositional tactics be dropped. The Conservative party, formerly, like Bismarck himself, zealous partisans of the free-trade system, but now, through their master's conversion, totally changed, put themselves at the chancellor's disposal towards accomplishing both his financial and protectional schemes. Of course the conversion of the Conservative party, consisting for the most part of representatives of the landed wealth of the country, required and involved certain concessions; namely, that not only the products of manufactures but also of agriculture should be protected against foreign competition. The proposed customs-duties on corn and cattle were moderate enough. Wheat, rye, oats, and beans, for instance, should pay one mark (25 cents) per 100 kilogr., barley and Indian corn half a mark, etc. Far more considerable was the increase of the customs-duties on manufactures. In the first instance the abolished duties on iron and hardwares were not only restored, but, compared with the old, considerably enhanced. Pig-iron pays 25 cents per 100 kilogr.; bar-iron, 62½ cents; plate-iron, 75 cents; iron-wire, 75 cents; goods of cast-iron, 62½ cents; coarse hardwares, 75 cents to $4.75; fine hardwares, $6 to $15. A character still more distinctly protective is seen in the new duties on yarns and cloths. Cotton-yarn pays, according to the fineness, $3 to $17½ per 100 kilogr.; cotton goods, $20 to $62½; linen-yarn, 75 cents to $9; linen, $1½ to $30; woollen-yarn, 75 cents to $6; woollen goods, $25 to $112½, etc. The foreign competition in the smaller branches of industry being less keen and the financial product of the respective duties being quite trifling, the other duties of the new tariff are of less importance. The imports which produce high financial returns are coffee, petroleum, tobacco, corn, etc., but the entire imperial revenues from customs-duties does not exceed the sum of $50,000,000.

The new tariff passed the imperial diet, July 12, 1879, with 212 against 117 votes. The majority was composed of the Conservatives and the Centre, while the minority consisted of the several factions of Liberals. From this time dates the discord between the Liberals and Prince Bismarck, who now endeavored to rely upon the conservative-clerical coalition which had helped him to put the tariff into effect.

In spite of the insignificance of the duties on agricultural products, the latter encountered on the part of the Liberals a resistance far more violent than the duties on manufactures. They not only predicted the ruin of the German grain-trade, but also protested, above all, against the taxation of the poor man's bread. Hatred between the poor and the landlords, declared the eloquent Lasker, must be the inevitable consequence of duties on the necessaries of life; peace would depart, and the country would be most deeply agitated. Now it may be doubted whether the grain-duties can attain the purpose at which their advocates aimed, or at least pretended to aim—that is, to protect thereby agriculture against foreign competition and to raise its position. Germany has by degrees become a land wherein home agriculture is no longer able to provide for the supply of all its inhabitants. It cannot dispense with the import of foreign breadstuffs and raw materials. Home agriculture, too, suffers less by foreign competition than by the excessive mortgage indebtedness brought on through incessant partitions and changes of possession, which, occurring continually, makes landed property, not only in Germany, but in all Europe, so tributary to mobile capital that the cost of production is, indeed, far greater than in countries wherein such indebtedness as yet does not exist or has not taken the same dimensions. Consequently the true remedy for the European, and especially the German, agriculture is to be found only in the removal of that primary evil. Yet, still, the imposition of so trifling a duty on foreign corn could have by no means the dangerous consequences which the Liberal party showed in a dazzling light. In fact the price of grain in Germany has been scarcely affected by the duty, and the not inconsiderable revenue which the empire gains therefrom (about $5,000,000) works as a pure financial duty felt by nobody.

In close connection with the tendencies to encourage home production by means of an appropriate tariff of duties are similar efforts in the department of railway management. The constitution of the empire allows the government a control of great extent over the railways. Above all it is the prerogative of the empire to control the tariffs of freight. The constitution prescribes to the government explicitly to establish, as much as possible, a uniformity and reduction of tariffs. But while the greatest part of the railways was possessed by private companies, insuperable obstacles were opposed to the efforts of the government to enforce the constitution, and the chancellor became aware that a railway policy directed in the interests of home production was impracticable unless he succeeded in bringing all railways into the possession of the empire. A motion, however, proposed already in 1876 to the federal council, met at once the decided disapproval chiefly of the greater states, several of whom owned the railways laid in their territories and were by no means disposed to resign that possession in favor of the empire. The chancellor, who rather avoids a conflict with the federal governments as with the Parliament, abandoned therefore the idea of imperial railways for a while, and instead of it went the more energetically about a more practicable plan, namely, first of all, in Prussia, to bring the existing railways into this state's possession and here to realize his own ideas of railway policy. Yet still in the empire he tried to do what the constitution directed. He made motions in the federal council with the object of regulating the whole matter of freights according to uniform principles and procuring clearly defined fair tariffs. He proposed also such legal restraints that German railways should promote in the first instance German commerce, German production, and sale of German products, and not give preference to foreign commercial interests. These motions were, to quote the accompanying record, made under the impression "that till now, in management of the German railways, the struggle for financial returns has kept the task of promoting the interests of national economy too far in the background, and that the national interests of commerce fall a victim to a competition which will eventually compromise the solid and regular management of the railways themselves, but at all events hurt the public interests, for the promotion of which the railways have been built and privileged by the governments. I believe that it is correct to assert that the freights for the import of foreign products, on the average, are cheaper than those for the export of home-made or for the transport from one place of Germany to the other. The bounties on the import which in this way are granted to the foreigner, the high charge of the internal German commerce as compared with that of foreign countries to and across Germany, the disadvantages under which the German export to the west suffers by the high tariffs it has to bear in comparison with the cheaper passage from east to west, weigh heavily on our prosperity. . . It lies, according to my judgment, in the task of the governments to remedy these inconveniences as much as possible and to strive for such reform that German goods on German railways, at all events, should be treated at least as favorably and not be carried at dearer rates than foreign." The federal council assigned these motions to a commission, wherein they were speedily buried. No better fate had the chancellor's later steps in the same direction. Undaunted by this resistance on the part of the several governments, Bismarck returned to the prosecution of his railway reforms in Prussia. As the Prussian government, possessing already a greater part of the Prussian lines, could menace the private companies with a very dangerous competition by means of new lines, the plan of bringing them all into the state's possession would meet no great difficulties if the diet could be won for the scheme. Here, of course, the plan met not only the opposition of the Progressists, who occupy almost entirely the position of the Manchester school but are not numerous enough to exercise a weighty influence, but also the resistance of the mighty Catholic Centre, which struggles against every strengthening of the government's power both in Prussia and in the empire. Whilst the new tariff of duties was essentially accomplished by the help of the Centre, they denied to the chancellor's railway policy their assistance, but help was given by the Moderate Liberals. With this parliamentary reinforcement the transfer of the Prussian private lines into the state's possession was executed so rapidly that to-day only a trifling remainder of important private lines yet exists, and this will disappear within a few years. The stockholders were reimbursed with government annuities according to the average produce of the stocks during the last five years; the managers were indemnified, and the officers taken up by the state administration. Although the government in this way has taken upon itself a new debt to the amount of nearly $800,000,000, yet the financial success, notwithstanding the difficulties of the period of transition, is complete, and already annual surpluses of about $30,000,000 over the total interest are gained. Since the amortization of the railway debt is provided by law, the term, after which almost the whole network of railways will be in the unencumbered possession of the country, may be already calculated. The unparalleled advantages thereby secured for the commerce and the finances of the country need no further evidence.

If we inquire for the effects of the protective customs and railway policy inaugurated by Prince Bismarck the answer is, that the situation of industry and the general wealth also are decidedly improved. The productive power of labor is greatly enhanced, wages have risen, the import of many manufactures which are produced in Germany itself in sufficient quantity and high perfection is limited, but the export increased in an unexpected manner, and the revenues from customs-duties as well as the power of taxpaying considerably increased. The common phrases of the free-traders, that such occurrences are not a consequence of protection but would have taken place as well without protection, are refuted in this case by the fact that the main rivals of Germany, England and France, show by no means similar results. France, however, which in consequence of her defeat and her policy of revenge groans under a horrible tax-burden, may be omitted from the comparison. But the circumstance that England's export after the most favorable year, 1881, again decreases, whilst that of Germany continues to rise, may be considered as a conclusive evidence that the manufactures of Germany in many directions gain by degrees the precedence of the English, and that the assertions of free-traders that a protected country must necessarily decrease in power of export, are quite illusory; nay, the direct contrary of the truth. The evidences for these statements of German economical movements the reader will find in the statistics at the close of this article. Meanwhile we continue our account of the political occurrences in the German empire.

As an important part of the policy of completing the unity of the empire must be mentioned the incorporation of the free towns, Hamburg and Bremen, in the Customs' Union. These two small republics, as well as Lübeck, were allowed by the constitution to remain, with their territories, till further orders, out of the Customs' Union. The effect was, that the interests of these great commercial towns were not throughout congruent with those of Germany. They had a stake in promoting the import of foreign goods, without favoring the export from Germany in like measure. Especially did German agriculturalists complain of the exceptional position of Hamburg. While agriculture in Northern Germany owes its prosperity, for a great part, to a highly developed spirits-industry, long ago exceeding the supply of home markets and depending on a large export in the territory of Hamburg, numerous establishments had arisen which imported Russian spirits duty-free, refined it, and thus entered into a very serious competition with the native industry and its export. On the other hand the German textile manufacturers complained likewise, that the free towns did nothing to foster the export of German manufactures. At all events the continuance of these small free-trade territories was an anomaly, which, at the foundation of the Northern German Confederation, had been tolerated only under the supposition that the three towns would soon find it to their own interest to add to the political union an economical one also. To that supposition, indeed, Lübeck responded, but Hamburg and Bremen seemed not at all disposed to sacrifice their exceptional position. They were encouraged therein by the internal free-trade party. Bismarck, however, after the critical turn in the Customs' policy, determined to put an end to that condition also. First of all, he sought in accordance with the right of the federal council, to limit the free-trade territory to a smaller district. The free-trade party in Parliament declared this way unlawful, asserting that the custom limit could not be removed except by law, i. e., with sanction of the imperial diet. Reckless of this opposition Bismarck, in the federal council, made the motion to incorporate the lower Elbe in the Customs' Union, without prejudice of Hamburg's position as a free port. On Hamburg, this movement fell like a stroke of lightning. They well perceived that the chancellor was in earnest, and the case critical. The Progressists in Parliament, indignant at a mode of proceeding so violent, moved a declaration that this procedure was not consistent either with the federal relation or with constitutional right. In the Parliament itself there were excited debates. The chancellor, however, meanwhile seeking to come to an agreement with Hamburg, struck a bargain with the Senate of the republic, by which the territory of free port should be limited to a small district, sufficient only for storehouses, etc., while the federal government pledged itself to bear a great part of the cost arising from the erection of the necessary buildings. While in the Parliament the verbal disputes still continued, the treaty, which was afterwards sanctioned by the legislature of Hamburg, became known, to the great surprise of the opposition. Thus the question of Hamburg's incorporation in the Customs' Union was settled. Similar negotiations took place with Bremen, with the same conclusion, the whole of Germany being now included in the Zollverein.

The question of colonies, too, occupied the federal government and legislature. Of all the great European powers the German Empire alone, in consequence of her former divisions and weakness at sea, possessed no colonies. When the Northern German Confederation, and afterwards the German Empire, was established, public opinion as well as the legislature occasionally took up the question, whether it was advisable for Germany to acquire colonies. While some maintained that establishing colonies was for Germany a matter of national honor, and, in consequence of the continually increasing population, indeed a matter of economical necessity, others urged that the empire must restrict her maritime power to defence, and that the stream of emigration should not be artificially turned in a direction wherein no guarantees could be given for the welfare of emigrants. The federal government hesitated for some time. But when the navy had obtained a respectable strength and peace seemed established, the government aimed at acquisition of stations at sea, and showed a disposition to advance even to real colonial undertakings. Especially did the Pacific attract attention. German enterprise had there created some considerable settlements, and, in the neighborhood of China and Japan, the commerce with which increases every year, it appeared of moment to give to the German navy a strong base in the Pacific. When a Hamburg trading-house, possessing great plantations on the island of Samoa, by several misfortunes had become insolvent, the chancellor, holding this occasion favorable to give to the German sea-trade in the Pacific a strong basis for further enterprises, proposed to establish a joint-stock company with a capital of $2,500,000, which should acquire the respective possessions as well as the privileges therewith joined, while the empire would guarantee a moderate return on the investment. Since this arrangement was made in 1883 there has been great activity in German colonizing in the Pacific Ocean and on the coast of Africa. The German flag has been raised over the northern part of New Guinea, or Papua, and in various islands near Australia. A German protectorate was proclaimed over the Samoa Islands. The Tonga, Gilbert, and Solomon Islands, and finally part of the Caroline group were included in the grand scheme of Germany's colonial empire. In all these instances the claim of Germany is founded on the fact that German merchants and commercial companies have already had large interests in the various islands which needed protection. In South Africa, just north of the Orange River, which is the boundary of the British colonies, the district of Angra Pequeña was proclaimed a German protectorate in 1883. This bold step led to a prolonged diplomatic controversy with Great Britain, in which the substantial victory rested with Germany. Further disputes arose about the annexation of the Cameroons and other places on the West Coast of Africa. But Germany now has assured possession of nearly 800 miles on that side and has gained control of an extensive district in East Africa, stretching the whole length of the coast of Zanzibar, and extending westward to the borders of the Congo Free State. The total area claimed by Germany in Africa is 952,720 square miles, and in the Pacific 92,725 square miles.

Meanwhile, the federal government still endeavored to improve the imperial finances and to increase the special revenues of the empire so far, that the particular states as well as the districts could be assisted by the empire. To this end it proposed an increase of the duty on malt liquor, a taxation of stocks, a defence-tax ("*Wehrsteuer*"), which should be paid by those who were not drafted for military service. Of these propositions the only one approved was that of a moderate taxation of stocks. Then the chancellor contrived to take up his old plan of a tobacco monopoly. The duties and taxes on tobacco had produced heretofore only $9,000,000. In the spring of 1882 Prince Bismarck drew up a scheme by which the net proceeds were calculated to be nearly $42,000,000 annually. The main difficulty of the project was, that all establishments which were then engaged in the manufacture or sale of tobacco must be indemnified by the empire for the loss of their business. The amount necessary for that purpose was estimated at $60,000,000. The Progressists and the moderate Liberals, too, roused the country to defeat the plan, which was denounced as socialistic, while its financial advantages were pronounced doubtful. In fact the repugnance of the Liberal factions was directed less against the monopoly than against the opening of a source of revenue, which might flow more abundantly each year and diminish the dependence of the federal government on the parliamentary grants. The Democratic-Federalist faction feared the monopoly as a step towards centralization, and the Catholic Centre was moved by the same consideration. In the federal council, too, the plan met serious resistance. Bavaria and Saxony, after Prussia the greatest states of the Confederacy, as well as a number of smaller states, voted against it. Prince Bismarck suffered a complete defeat, the plan being rejected by 276 votes against 43.

In financial politics, therefore, the government proceeded in a similar manner as it had formerly done in regard to the railways. Having failed to stir the imperial diet to opening of new and large sources of revenue, Bismarck sought in Prussia to put in motion a financial reform, whereby the opening of new imperial revenues should be made inevitable. We have already told that it was intended by the chancellor to reduce the direct taxes existing in the particular states, respectively, and to throw the produce of some into the hands of the district governments. In Prussia personal taxes include a so-called class-tax, raised gradually to an income of $750, and a so-called income-tax, raised from the larger incomes. At first it was Bismarck's intention to exempt from these taxes all incomes below $1500, and to raise a direct tax only from the larger incomes. This plan, however, is disapproved by all parties, the Liberals as well as the Conservatives and the Centre. It was barely possible, in 1883, to remove at least the first and second grades of the class-tax, reaching to an income of $225 and with a frightful number of seizures. A new proposition of the government to abolish also the third and fourth grades (to $300), wherein likewise the seizures are also numerous, and instead of that to submit the capital-interest to a proper tax, is still undecided. The chancellor prepared still another motion to make education in the primary schools entirely free and put the burden of support of these schools on the state or on the districts, and a similar bill in regard to parish-taxes intended to relieve the parishes. All these projects depend mainly on the correspondent increase of indirect taxes, and since the customs as well as the most lucrative excises belong to the empire, the tax-reform intended by Bismarck in Prussia depends essentially on the success of his projects in the empire.

Another important feature in the internal politics of Germany is the attempt to improve by law the condition of the laboring class. After the outrages against the emperor in 1878, the Parliament passed an exceptional law against the socialistic plots, which were made responsible for those outrages. The newspapers of the socialists were suppressed, their unions dissolved, a number of agitators exiled. The law in question, renewed since the first issue at several times, has had without doubt the effect to frighten away from the surface the revolutionary socialistic tendencies, and thereby to quicken the confidence of the earning classes. So far the recent strengthening of industry and commerce is surely due to a certain point to that law. But the reduction of the socialistic agitation in the laboring classes is quite another question, and we have abundant evidence that it has continued to burn with little diminution. Fearing this result indeed, the government struggled strongly against the repeal of the exceptional condition, while the more radical elements of the Liberals were not willing to prolong it. Besides, from the beginning the federal government was not inclined to rest satisfied with that manner of action. Rather it recognized, even when the exceptional law was introduced, the necessity of meeting by positive laws certain evils from which society suffers, and remedying some grievances of which the laborers complained with good reason. Measures were therefore announced tending to secure by help of the state an effectual insurance of laborers against disasters, disease, and invalidity. The first bill in this direction brought before the Parliament was that regarding the insurance against accident. Heretofore the conductors of factories, mines, and other industrial enterprises have been obliged by law to indemnify injured laborers for accidents, so far as the accident was not due to the fault of the laborer. Even this clause, however, made the benefit of the law in many cases, illusory. The masters who were bound to indemnify, or the companies which had undertaken the insurance for a fixed premium, often replied to the claims of injured laborers or their families that the accident was self-incurred, and then the poor laborer or his family had first to prove the validity of their claim. It is easy to see that the injured, being generally unable to enter upon a prolix and costly process, must either totally abstain from their claim, or content themselves with a trifling indemnity. Numerous cases of this inequitable character are stated. The bill proposed by the government would remedy this evil in such a manner that all laborers must be insured, and all damages without exception indemnified. Insurance should be effectuated by an imperial board, and the greatest part of cost raised from the masters; besides, however, there was proposed an imperial subsidy and a contribution of laborers. The Liberal parties were offended especially at the compulsory insurance and the imperial subsidy, which was stigmatized by them as a socialistic or communistic idea. Others blamed the centralizing tendency of the project. In short neither this nor a second bill, which joined the scheme of accident insurance with a plan of sickness-insurance, could obtain a parliamentary majority. The sickness-insurance was afterwards, May 29, 1883, regulated by a distinct law, according to which all operatives in the empire must be insured either in municipal, or factory, or stock-companies. A third accident-insurance bill, wherein the imperial board and the subsidy are cancelled, met with better sucess than the two former, and is now the law of the land. This law required that workmen should pay from 1½ to 2 per cent. of the normal weekly wages into an insurance fund, from which they were to receive, when sick, treatment, medicines, and half wages for 13 weeks. Sickness-insurance was made compulsory, but did not extend to agriculture, forestry, domestic service, or government employés. The law of accident insurance was strongly contested, but the first part of it passed in June, 1884, its action being restricted to trades where great risks were run. It has since been extended to include the building trades, agriculture, seafaring, and inland boat traffic, while further extensions are contemplated. Under the operation of this law workmen and employers are alike assessed, the latter in proportion to the risks of their industries, and the number and average wages of their workmen. Disabled workmen receive two-thirds of their wages unless these exceed 4 marks daily, in which case the proportion is reduced. In case of death by accident, 20 days' wages are allowed for funeral expenses, and 20 per cent. of the wages are paid to the widow, with 15 per cent. additional for each child under fifteen years of age. The final measure in this system of industrial insurance, insuring against old age and infirmity, passed the Reichstag May 23, 1889, and became a law on June 22d. Its provisions include all workmen of either sex over 16 years of age; the rates of assessment being, for those who earn under 350 marks per annum, 12 pfennigs (about 3 cents) per week; from 350 to 550 marks, 18 pfennigs; from 550 to 850 marks, 24 pfennigs; and over 850 marks, 30 pfennigs. Each person insured is to receive a pension till recovery from disability, or for life if permanently disabled—the state bearing a portion of the burden. Each workman who reaches the age of 70 is to receive an old-age pension whether able to work or not. But no one is to receive a pension until he has made 5 years' payments. The amount of pension varies according to the length of time of payment and other circumstances. It is estimated that about 11,000,000 people come within the scope of this act.

How this complex system of enforced insurance will work remains to be seen. A number of years must pass before its full pressure will be felt, during which a large reserve fund will accumulate. Whether the amount of assessment provided for will then prove sufficient for the drain upon it can be told only by experience. At all events it is the most declared system of state socialism yet devised, and its operation in practice will be looked for with interest. In countries of more liberal institutions private combination does much of what the state here proposes to do, but the German system has this advantage, that the heedless and non-provident class which elsewhere becomes a burden on the community is forced into some provision for the future. From this point of view it is to be hoped that its operation will prove successful.

While the state has been thus organizing socialism, it has strenuously endeavored to bring to an end the activity of private socialism, whose purpose was much less immediate self-help than future political experiment, and whose projects were aimed at the stability of the imperial government. So rapid was the growth of socialistic theory in German society, and so outspoken its advocates against the existing organization of society, that the government made a vigorous effort to suppress it, passing an anti-socialistic law in 1878, which has been renewed from time to time since. This law, which made the advocacy of socialism a misdemeanor, broke up its meetings, suppressed its newspapers, and banished some of its leaders, seemed at first to have a disorganizing effect on the socialistic party. Yet it seems to have grown in secret as actively as it formerly did in public, and has latterly proved that it is stronger in Germany than ever. An active effort was made in 1887 to prolong the anti-socialistic law, which had been renewed annually for five years; but this Bismarckian measure was defeated. In January, 1890, this effort was earnestly renewed, a repressive measure being introduced into the Reichstag which roused general opposition. The proposal to change the temporary coercion act against the socialists into a permanent one was first thrown out, and then the entire bill was defeated. This was in great measure due to the growth of socialism in the Reichstag itself, this political element in Germany being represented by 2 delegates in 1871, by 24 in 1884, and by a much greater number since, the socialistic vote having doubled in the elections of 1890, despite all the difficulties thrown in the way of a free exercise of the franchise and open advocacy of socialistic principles. Of open socialistic movements one of much importance was the great mining strike of 1889, the most serious labor outbreak ever known in Germany, which was induced and organized by socialists. It began on May 3 in the Westphalian and Rhenish coal districts, 100,000 miners being on strike, while violent collisions with the police took place. It soon spread to other mining localities, and several other trades joined the strike. The situation grew so serious that the emperor was appealed to to use his influence to settle the difficulty. He ordered a thorough inquiry to be made, and quickly discovered that the miners had not struck without cause, and that their demands were just and reasonable. He thereupon used his influence with the employers, and on May 20 the strike came to an end, the demands of the miners being granted.

Meanwhile other events of great importance had been taking place in Germany. In 1884 a split took place in the Liberal party in the Reichstag, its advance wing making a coalition with a portion of the National Liberals, for the formation of a new party with a radical platform, whose demands included a responsible ministry, annual budgets, freedom of speech, of meeting, and of the press, and payment of members. The reorganized National Liberal party returned to their old allegiance to Bismarck, and in 1888 they joined the Conservatives in support of the government measures, becoming afterwards part of the Coalition party. The Centre or Ultramontane party became the most determined opponents of Bismarck, yet by a temporary alliance with him in 1879 enabled him to carry his protectionist measures. Among these party changes, the rapid growth of the Social Democrats, the name taken by the socialist delegates, introduced an element of uncertainty in German politics.

The change in the sovereignty of the empire has overshadowed mere parliamentary projects and has altered all the relations of Germany, foreign and internal. On March 9, 1888, the venerable emperor, William I., died. He was succeeded by his son Frederick, from whom a change of government in favor of liberalism had been confidently expected. But he was suffering from a cancerous affection of the throat, which became fatal at the end of three months of his reign. He died on June 15. His son succeeded him as William II. No hope of a liberal policy on his part was entertained, nor did his first actions give any, since they indicated a disposition to adhere to the policy of William I. and Bismarck, and a desire for military glory which seemed to augur ill for the peace of Europe. The remainder of 1888 and the whole of 1889 were spent chiefly in visits to the courts of several of the European sovereigns.

Early in 1890 the emperor addressed a rescript to the Minister of Commerce, in which he affirmed that "It is the duty of the state to so regulate the duration and the nature of labor as to insure the health, the morality, and the supply of all the economic wants of the workingmen." This, the most declared step in favor of socialism ever taken by a modern monarch, created a general sensation; which was increased by a request addressed to the other countries of Europe for a joint conference on the labor question. It was first thought that the leading powers would not accede to this request, but France, England, Italy, and Austria, with most of the smaller powers, finally took part in the conference. The decisions reached by this conference, however, were of little importance. But the emperor's socialistic utterances seemed to have one important effect in giving vitality to socialism in the empire, for in the succeeding election an unexpected number of socialistic delegates were returned to the Reichstag, a sufficient number, in combination with the other liberals, to give a majority against the government in that body. But so far liberalism in the government and liberalism in the Reichstag seem in accord, and political harmony prevails.

The next surprise, which startled the whole world, was the resignation of the Chancellorship by Prince Bismarck in March, 1890. The resignation, which had been instigated by the emperor, was quickly accepted by him, and General Von Caprivi appointed Chancellor in Bismarck's place. This dismissal of the great advocate of imperialism and popular repression in Germany has proved a genuine surprise, to none apparently more than to Bismarck himself, who has spent the succeeding period in a state of agitation and rebellious utterances which show much more spleen than dignity. He is now preparing to return to political life as a delegate to the Reichstag, and Europe waits with some curiosity to learn what course of action he will take in that body. The outcome of the unexpected events which we have here briefly described it is impossible to predict, but that Germany is approaching a period of more liberal government, either as the direct act of the emperor, or as a result of the continued growth of socialism and political liberalism, seems evident. The present emperor would find it no easy matter to restore the stringent imperialism of the epoch of William I.

II. An industrial census which was taken June 5, 1882, and designed to state not so much the number as the distribution of the inhabitants by their employments, has given the striking result that, while a constant increase of the population had been anticipated without doubt, there had really been, since Dec. 1, 1880, a decrease. While the census of 1880 gave the number of 45,234,061, that of June 5, 1882, showed but 45,222,113. The effectual diminution or at least stagnation of numbers is ascertained by the fact, that the number of living births in 1880 had fallen beneath the average by 48,000, and in 1881 by more than 250,000. Since, however, the number of marriages, which showed from 1878 to 1879 a diminution, slowly increases there may be expected a recovery of births. This was shown in the returns of the census taken Dec. 1, 1885, which gave the population at 46,855,704. Emigration, principally to the United States, took from Germany 1,784,871 of her people between 1871 and 1889.

The following table shows the distribution of the inhabitants by their employments in 1882:

Agriculture and stock-raising	18,840,818
Forestry, hunting, and fishing	384,637
Mining and metal-working	16,058,080
Commerce and trade	4,531,080
Hired service	938,294
Professions	2,222,982
Without occupation	2,246,222
Total	45,222,113

The following table shows the chief production of the mines in tons:

	1881.	1882.	1883.
Coal	48,688,161	52,118,595	55,888,490
Lignite	12,818,000	13,259,616	14,334,966
Potassic salts	905,891	1,201,392	
Iron ore	7,600,801	8,263,254	6,160,450
Pig-iron	2,914,009	3,380,806	3,419,635
Cast-iron	560,422	625,478	
Wrought iron and steel	1,421,792	1,586,154	
Other iron	897,425	1,074,807	

The technical efficiency of the high furnaces amounted per workingman and year, in 1877, to about 100 tons; 1881, to 131 tons, and in 1882 reached even 150 tons. Nevertheless, the number of workingmen increased from 15,000 in 1878 to over 20,000 in 1882, and these 20,000 worked almost precisely double as much as the 22,000 occupied in 1874.

As regards the other industries, especially textile manufacture, full statistical reports are wanting; but some local branches give accounts. The celebrated silk industry of Crefeld, for instance, in 1882 exhibited 35,692 power-looms against 32,126 in 1881, the sale advanced from an amount of $19,000,000 to $21,000,000, and the wages paid in the same time increased from $6,400,000 to $7,000,000. Before all the agricultural industries, as sugar, spirits, beer, are constantly increasing. Especially the production of beet-sugar has developed with a rapidity which is beginning to excite apprehensions of a speedy overproduction. Already it amounts to twice that of France. According to the demand of hands, the wages likewise have risen slowly but steadily. In the Westphalian mining districts, for instance, wages rose from 1879 to 1882 by 13.5 per cent., while employment at the same time augmented by 31 per cent.

The merchant fleet of Germany was as follows at the dates indicated: Jan. 1, 1883, sailing vessels, 3855; steamers, 515; total tonnage, 1,226,650. Jan. 1, 1889, sailing vessels, 2779; steamers, 815; total tonnage, 1,320,721. The navy in 1890 consisted of 78 steam and sailing vessels, including 27 iron-clads. The foreign commerce of Germany exhibits the following figures. The total imports in 1880 were valued at $705,000,000; those of 1889 reached a total of $1,003,768,000. The exports of 1880 were $724,000,000; those of 1889, $791,663,750. The national debt of Germany in 1888, the latest date for which we have an official statement, was $307,000,000, this empire possessing the enviable distinction of being practically unburdened by debt. The debt of its rival, France, for instance, is 20 times that of Germany. The budget of income and expenditures for the fiscal year 1890–91 is given at $320,134,000.

The school system of Germany in 1890 embraced 22 universities, with 2437 professors and teachers, and 29,444 students. There were besides 16 polytechnic institutions; 787 gymnasia, realschulen, etc.; numerous technical schools; and nearly 60,000 elementary schools. The proportion of persons who cannot read or write is little over 1 per cent. of the population. In 1887 the empire had 23,634 miles of railroad, three-fourths of which were state roads, 51,148 miles of telegraph, and 19,476 post-offices, the delivery of letters, etc., being 2,322,312,438. (F. S.)

GERM THEORY OF DISEASE, the recently widely adopted view that epidemic diseases are due to vegetable parasites, which gain entrance to the body through the medium of air, water, food, or otherwise, increase enormously, and exhaust the strength of or otherwise injuriously affect their host, while yielding minute and very hardy germs, which may be indefinitely distributed. This theory we may accept as definitely proved in the case of certain diseases of the lower animals. As regards man it is still a subject of controversy. The presumption is strongly in favor of its correctness, both from what we know of the character and life-history of these minute vegetable organisms, and from the close analogy of human epidemic diseases with those of the lower animals. It cannot, however, be considered as proved in the case of any human disease, though the wide-spread investigations now under way can scarcely fail to lead to a definite settlement of this disputed question.

The history of the germ theory may be very briefly told. The idea that epidemic diseases may be due to germs which float in the atmosphere, enter the body, and disturb its conditions by the development of parasitic life, was advanced by Kircher and favored by Linnæus, and has had many adherents since; while the minute organisms now known as Bacteria were observed by Leeuwenhoeck as early as 1675, and were first classified by O. F. Müller, in 1773. Yet the current belief until recently was that epidemic diseases are due to decaying organic matter, which acts as a poison when taken into the body by setting up a similar process of degeneration in the living tissues. Such was supposed to be the action of yeast until 1836, when Cagniard de la Tour discovered that yeast was a living plant. Yet it was still held that fermentation was due to the dead and decaying portions of this plant. About the same time Schwann discovered that putrefaction was due to something in the air which heat could destroy, and that meat would not putrefy in calcined air.

For some thirty years after this period the germ theory remained practically dormant, and it gained new life only in the memorable researches of Pasteur, and of many other active investigators, all of which have taken place since 1860. The most noted early work of Pasteur was in relation to *pebrine*, a disease of silk-worms which threatened to destroy the silk industry of France. He proved conclusively, by researches in 1865 and subsequently, that this disease was due to minute vibratile corpuscles, which filled the body and checked its vital operations, and that it could be overcome by protecting the worms from infection. Another series of experiments, conducted about the same time by Pasteur, in France, and Koch, in Germany, on the terribly destructive disease of the domestic animals known as anthrax, charbon, or splenic fever, led to similar conclusions. It was shown very decisively that in this disease the tissues become filled with a minute bacterial organism, since known as *Bacillus anthracis*, that the disease could be communicated by inoculation with this organism, or by eating food that contained it, and that it never appeared in animals that were rigidly isolated from infectious material. Koch did more than this. He studied the life-history of these organisms, proved that they developed from minute globular spores into rod-like bodies, and that they increased in number with extreme rapidity in an organic infusion, while the dried spores had great resisting powers. Dried blood containing these spores, when kept for four years, communicated the splenic fever to inoculated cattle as readily as fresh material. But the investigations in relation to anthrax went further than this, and yielded exceedingly valuable results. Cultivation of *Bacillus anthracis* in infusions, through several generations, proved to weaken the vitality of the organism through the action of oxygen or other cause. The subsequent inoculation of cattle with this weakened material produced in them a mild form of the disease, which acted to protect them against the fatal effects of subsequent inoculation with the strongest virus. This discovery has proved of the highest industrial importance, thousands of cattle being annually secured against splenic fever by inoculation with these culture germs.

It is not necessary to mention here the various other diseases of the lower animals which seem to be due to bacteria, and may be guarded against by inoculation, or to describe the action of bacteria in inducing the several kinds of fermentation in vegetable products. It will suffice to say that all fermentation and putrefaction seem to be due to chemical changes induced by the nutrient action of minute organisms, with the exception of what is known as "false fermentation," set up by the action of disintegrating organic molecules. The indications are that these organisms play a somewhat similar rôle in living tissues, from which they extract nutriment, inducing pathological changes, and increasing at the expense of the health or life of their host. We need here refer to but one other series of experiments on the lower animals, those recently made by Pasteur into the cause of *rabies*, the "mad dog" disease. It will suffice to say that these experiments were of the same character as those in splenic fever, and yielded similar results. It has been shown that a bacterial organism is present in rabies, that by inoculation with it the disease may be communicated to other animals of various species, and that its energy may be reduced by cultivation and a mild form of rabies produced, which is protective against the most virulent virus.

Investigations of a similar nature have been made into the character of the several epidemic diseases to which man is subject. As a result it may be said that bacterial organisms have been found in nearly every case, though it has not yet been clearly demonstrated that these organisms are the cause of the disease, or that it can be hindered by inoculation with culture germs. The only human disease in which inoculation has proved clearly useful is small-pox, and unluckily for the theory this disease has not yet been traced to the action of any specific bacterium. That such an organism will yet be discovered seems probable from what we know of the conditions of inoculation in the diseases of the lower animals described. Of the human diseases in which the presence of bacteria has been traced *Septicæmia* was the first investigated. There is strong reason to believe that the inflammation of open wounds, and the blood-poisoning thence resulting, are due to the propagation of minute organisms introduced from the air. As a result of this theory the highly valuable preventive process known as *Listerism* was adopted, the wound being permeated with carbolic acid or mercuric chloride spray and lotions to kill the germs present, the instruments used being carefully disinfected, and the wound then dressed with antiseptic dressings and bandages. Some writers, however, question the theory, and claim that the benefit is due to the extra cleanliness and care exercised. Of the other diseases in which bacteria have been discovered, by some of the considerable army of recent investigators, may be named *scarlatina, measles, diphtheria, typhoid, yellow, relapsing,* and *malarial fevers, leprosy,* and, more recently, *tuberculosis* and *cholera.* The studies in the last-named diseases have been made by the indefatigable Koch, who detected in the tubercle of consumption a characteristic and previously unknown bacterium, somewhat resembling that of leprosy. By inoculation with this he succeeded in producing the disease in rabbits and guinea-pigs, a result not yet attained in the case of any other human disease. He studied cholera patients in Egypt and India, and found their organs to swarm with bacteria of many kinds, of which there was one peculiar, comma-shaped form always present, but never found in those not suffering from cholera. This *comma bacillus* soon became the centre of an active controversy, Klein and Lankester, of England, and others, strongly claiming that it had nothing to do with producing cholera, and was perfectly harmless. Inoculation with culture germs of the comma bacillus were made during the outbreak of cholera in France and Spain in 1886, but its efficacy is very doubtful, and as yet, beyond the case of small-pox and possibly of hydrophobia, no human disease has been treated with unquestionable success by the inoculation method so far as evidence shows.

The argument of the opponents of the germ theory is, that the microbes or bacteria found are the result, not the cause, of disease. Dr. Bastian contends that they are "pathological products," generated in the body after it has become diseased through other contagious matter. A similar view is entertained by many other physicians. The evidence in its favor, however, is entirely negative, and is mainly based on the existence of bacteria in healthy organisms. This view is met by the assertion that there are many species of bacteria, each with its own form, habits, and properties; that many of these are innocuous in human bodies, not finding there their natural habitat, and that each distinct disease has its distinct form of bacterium, which always accompanies it. Dr. Koch has made extensive experiments in this direction, and found that he could produce distinct diseases by using bacteria of different appearance and from different sources. His later studies of the consumption bacillus resulted in his producing a "lymph," inoculation with which is claimed to be a specific in the milder stages of consumption and other tubercular diseases. The most recent form of the germ theory is, that the disease effect is not due directly to the presence of the bacteria, but is an indirect result, being produced by chemical excretions, which prove poisonous to their hosts in the case of certain bacterial species, but innocuous in others. Though the germ theory of disease cannot be said at present to be fully demonstrated, its high probability has been shown, and evidence in its favor is accumulating. See BACTERIA. (C.M.)

GÉRÔME, JEAN LÉON, a French painter, was born at Vesoul, May 11, 1824, being the son of a goldsmith. He went to Paris in 1841, and studied under Delaroche, while pursuing the course of the École des Beaux Arts. In 1844 he went with Delaroche to Italy, and in 1847 exhibited his first picture, A Cockfight, gaining thereby a third-class medal. In 1863 he was made professor of painting in the École des Beaux Arts. Gérôme travelled in the East in 1853 and has since often resorted thither for subjects for his canvas. In 1855 he exhibited The Age of Augustus, which was purchased by the French government. His chief works, indeed, have been taken from ancient classic life. Among these are The Gladiators Saluting Cæsar (1859); The Wife of Candaules (1859); Phryne before the Judges (1860); The Death of Cæsar (1867). Among the works derived from his Eastern studies are The Call to Prayer at Cairo (1865); The Clothes Merchant (1868); The Door of the Mosque (1876). Many of his works have become widely known by photographs and engravings. His subjects are often sombre and sometimes indecent, but the drawing is powerful, and gives them a peculiar fascination. The painter's boldness and evident confidence in preparing his work go far to disarm criticism. They are thoroughly thought out and carefully finished, and the choice of subject seems an evidence of the moral corruption and decay of the empire rather than a personal fault.

GERRY, ELBRIDGE (1744-1814), an American statesman, was born at Marblehead, Mass., July 17, 1744. He graduated at Harvard College in 1762, and was a successful merchant in his native town, which in 1772 he was chosen to represent in the State legislature. At his suggestion a law encouraging the fitting out of armed vessels, and establishing a court of admiralty, was passed in November, 1775. Elected to the Continental Congress he took his seat Feb. 9, 1776, and was one of the signers of the Declaration of Independence. He was generally chairman of the committee on finances, and in 1780 was made president of the Treasury Board. The refusal of Congress to adopt efficient measures for raising revenue caused Gerry to withdraw soon after, and he did not return until 1783. Gerry was a delegate to the Constitutional Convention in 1787, but refused to sign the Constitution then framed. He was again a member of Congress from 1789 to 1793. In 1797 Pinckney, Marshall, and Gerry were sent on a special mission to France to obtain compensation for French spoliations. They found Talleyrand the minister of foreign affairs, and had great difficulty in obtaining a hearing. Finally Talleyrand managed to produce division among them; Pinckney and Marshall withdrew, while Gerry remained to afford further diversion to the wily diplomatist. At last finding that there was no prospect of accomplishing anything Gerry returned home in October, 1798. His reputation had suffered, and when the Republicans made him a candidate for governor of Massachusetts he was defeated. After some other attempts he was finally chosen in 1810, and was re-elected in the next year. In order to perpetuate their hard-won control of the State, the Democrats, as his party was now called, made a new arrangement of senatorial districts, and in some instances formed them by townships instead of counties as had heretofore been done. In Essex county the result appeared on the map like a grotesque animal which was speedily known as the "gerrymander," and the word has since prevailed in political vocabulary. Gerry was defeated for governor in 1812, but in the same year he was chosen Vice-President of the United States on the ticket with Madison. He did not live out his term, but died at Washington, D. C., Nov. 23, 1814.

GERSTER, ETELKA, a Hungarian singer, was born at Kaschau, June 16, 1857. The director of the Vienna Conservatory, having chanced to hear her sing in a religious procession, advised that she be placed under the instruction of Madame Marchesi, with whom she studied three years. In January, 1876, she made her *début* in Venice in Verdi's *Rigoletto* with wonderful success. She afterwards took up the parts of Ophelia, Lucia, Amina, and Marguerite. She then went to Berlin, where she had unexampled success. After a brief stay in Buda-Pesth she went to St. Petersburg and Moscow, where she received special marks of favor from the emperor and empress. Returning through Germany she appeared at London in 1877, and remained through the season of 1878, after which she came to the United States. She returned to Europe in 1879, but again visited America in 1880. She was married to M. Carlo Gardini in 1877. Her voice is a pure high soprano.

GETTY, GEORGE WASHINGTON, an American general, was born at Georgetown, D. C., Oct. 2, 1819. He graduated at West Point in 1840, became second lieutenant of artillery, and served on the Canada border. In the Mexican war he was engaged in the battles around the city of Mexico. He afterwards served in Florida against the Seminoles, and from 1857 to 1861 was employed on frontier duty. During the civil war he was connected with the Army of the Potomac. He was a lieutenant-colonel and aide-de-camp to Gen. McClellan in his campaign against Richmond, and was made brigadier-general of volunteers, Sept. 25, 1862. He fought at South Mountain, Antietam, and Fredericksburg. He was severely wounded in the battle of the Wilderness, May 5, 1864; took part in the defence of Washington and in operations in the Shenandoah Valley, and served with distinction from the siege of Petersburg until the surrender of Gen. Lee, attaining the brevet rank of major-general. He commanded various military districts until he was mustered out of the volunteer service in September, 1866. He then returned to the command of his regiment, the Third artillery.

GETTYSBURG, a borough of Pennsylvania, county-seat of Adams county, stands in a picturesque hilly region, 50 miles S. S. W. of Harrisburg, by the Harrisburg and Gettysburg Railroad (35 miles in a direct line). The Hanover and Gettysburg Railroad extends eastward to the Northern Central Railway. To the west are the South Mountain range and the Blue Ridge, the latter 8 miles distant. Gettysburg has a court-house, alms-house, and other county buildings, 2 national banks, 10 churches, 7 hotels, and 2 weekly newspapers. It has manufactures of castings, machinery, flour, boxes, harness, leather, and other goods. The town is neatly yet quaintly built, is gas-lighted, and has water-works. It is the seat of Pennsylvania College (Lutheran, founded 1832) and of a Lutheran Theological Seminary. The population is largely of German origin. Near the town are Round Top Park and Battlefield Park, with numerous monuments commemorating incidents of the great battle fought here, July 1–3, 1863. There is also a large national cemetery in which the dead of that battle are buried, and in which is a fine national monument in honor of the fallen soldiers. Near the town is the well-known Katalysine Spring. Gettysburg was founded in 1800, and was named in honor of James Gettys, its first settler. It was incorporated in 1806.

GETTYSBURG, CAMPAIGN AND BATTLE OF. I. In June, 1863, Gen. Joseph Hooker commanded the Army of the Potomac, then at Falmouth, Va., on the north bank of the Rappahannock, while the Confederate Army of Northern Virginia was under Gen. Robert E. Lee, on the south bank at Fredericksburg. The positions of the two armies were such that neither could be attacked to advantage except by a wide detour. The Confederate commander made the first move with a view to pass as rapidly as possible northward into Maryland and Pennsylvania. Some of the reasons for thus taking the initiative are evident. Lee would relieve the Shenandoah Valley from the devastation of the Union troops, transferring the scene of hostility beyond the Potomac; gain a favorable opportunity to strike Hooker's army in movement; derange the national plan of campaign for the whole summer, thus affording the Confederates time for recuperation and resupply; meet and encourage the prompt rising of secession friends in Maryland, and the co-operation of secret friends farther north.

Lee's army was composed of three army corps. The First corps, under Lieut.-Gen. James Longstreet, had three divisions: (1) Maj.-Gen. McLaws, with 4 brigades and 4 batteries of artillery—19 regiments, aggregate 12,000 men; (2) Maj.-Gen. Pickett, with 4 brigades and 4 batteries—19 regiments, 7000; (3) Maj.-Gen. Hood, with 4 brigades and 4 batteries—

18 regiments, 12,000; and an artillery reserve of ten batteries. The Second corps, under Lieut.-Gen. R. S. Ewell, had three divisions: (1) Maj.-Gen. Early, with 4 brigades and 4 batteries—21 regiments, 9000; (2) Maj.-Gen. Ed. Johnson, with 4 brigades and 4 batteries —22 regiments, 12,000; (3) Maj.-Gen. Rodes, with 5 brigades and 4 batteries—22 regiments, 10,000; and an artillery reserve of 2 battalions—8 batteries. The Third corps, under Lieut.-Gen. A. P. Hill, had also three divisions: (1) Maj.-Gen. Anderson, with 5 brigades and 3 batteries—21 regiments, 15,000; (2) Maj.-Gen. Heth, with 4 brigades and 4 batteries—17 regiments, 10,000; (3) Maj.-Gen. Pender, with 4 brigades and 4 batteries—19 regiments, 10,000; and an artillery reserve of 2 battalions—9 batteries. The cavalry division under Maj.-Gen. J. E. B. Stuart had 6 brigades, a total of 29 regiments, and 6 batteries of horse-artillery. The cavalry, including some reserve artillery detachments under Imboden and Mosby, were estimated by good authority to be 11,000 strong. This aggregates for Lee's army a force of 108,000.

Hooker's army consisted of 8 small army corps as follows: The First corps, under Maj.-Gen. J. F. Reynolds, with 3 divisions: (1) Brig.-Gen. Wadsworth, 2 brigades—11 regiments; (2) Brig.-Gen. Robinson, 2 brigades—11 regiments; (3) Maj.-Gen. Doubleday, 3 brigades—12 regiments; and an artillery brigade, 1 brigade of 5 batteries. The Second corps, under Maj.-Gen. W. S. Hancock, with 3 divisions: (1) Brig.-Gen. Caldwell, 4 brigades—18 regiments; (2) Brig.-Gen. Gibbon, 3 brigades—13 regiments, and a regiment unattached (Andrew's sharpshooters); (3) Brig.-Gen. Alex. Hays, 3 brigades—13 regiments; an artillery brigade of 4 batteries, and a cavalry squadron—2 companies. The Third corps, under Maj.-Gen. Sickles, with 2 divisions: (1) Maj.-Gen. Birney, 3 brigades —18 regiments; (2) Brig.-Gen. Humphreys, 3 brigades —19 regiments; and an artillery brigade of 5 batteries. The Fifth corps, under Maj.-Gen. Sykes, with 3 divisions: (1) Brig.-Gen. Barnes, 3 brigades—12 regiments; (2) Brig.-Gen. Ayres, 3 brigades—13 regiments; (3) Brig.-Gen. Crawford, 2 brigades—9 regiments; and an artillery brigade of 5 batteries. The Sixth corps, under Maj.-Gen. Sedgwick, with 3 divisions: (1) Brig.-Gen. Wright, 3 brigades—12 regiments; (2) Brig.-Gen. Howe, 2 brigades—10 regiments; (3) Brig.-Gen. Wheaton, 3 brigades—14 regiments; an artillery brigade of 8 batteries, and a cavalry detachment—2 companies. The Eleventh corps, under Maj.-Gen. Howard, with 3 divisions: (1) Brig.-Gen. Barlow, 2 brigades—8 regiments; (2) Brig.-Gen. Von Steinwehr, 2 brigades—8 regiments; (3) Maj.-Gen. Schurz, 2 brigades—10 regiments; an artillery brigade of 5 batteries, and a cavalry detachment—3 companies. The Twelfth corps, under Maj.-Gen. Slocum, with 2 divisions: (1) Brig.-Gen. Williams, 3 brigades—14 regiments; (2) Brig.-Gen. Geary, 3 brigades—14 regiments; an artillery brigade of 4 batteries, and a head-quarter guard of 2 companies. The cavalry corps, under Maj.-Gen. Alfred Pleasanton, had 3 divisions: (1) Brig.-Gen. Buford, 3 brigades—10 regiments; (2) Brig.-Gen. Gregg, 3 brigades—12 regiments and 1 detached company; (3) Brig.-Gen. Kilpatrick, 2 brigades—8 regiments; horse-artillery, 2 brigades—9 batteries. The reserve artillery, under Brig.-Gen. Tyler, had 5 brigades—25 batteries. For train-guards, etc., there were 2 regiments and 2 companies. The provost-marshal guard, under Brig.-Gen. Patrick, had 3 regiments—40 companies. The engineer brigade, under Brig.-Gen. Benham, had 2 regiments and 1 company of regulars.

The Confederate army moved by the way of Culpepper Court-House and the Shenandoah Valley, having en route several cavalry encounters, and one considerable battle, defeating about 7600 Nationals, under Brig.-Gen. Milroy, at Winchester. It finished the crossing of the Potomac the 24th of June, at Sharpsburg, Md., and on the 28th Longstreet and Hill were concentrated at Chambersburg, Pa., Ewell, with two divisions, at Carlisle, and one, Early's, farther east at York.

The National army, the instant its commander divined Lee's intention, followed up his movement on interior lines, passing through Warrenton Junction, Thoroughfare Gap, Centreville, Ashby's Gap, and Leesburg, completing its crossing of the Potomac at Edward's Ferry, June 26; and on the 28th its commander with head-quarters was at Frederick, Md., with a line of corps with wide intervals extending westward from that place, through Middletown, to Maryland Heights, opposite Harper's Ferry. When Hooker first had discovered that one of Lee's corps was across the Potomac he proposed to himself to send to Harper's Ferry "a corps or two to sever Ewell from the balance of the rebel army, in case Ewell should make a protracted sojourn with his Pennsylvania neighbors;" Hooker depended upon increasing the force which he intended here to send against Lee, using the garrison of Maryland Heights, which was 11,000 strong; but the instant it was known that Lee's whole force was crossing the river, Hooker changed his plan, designing now, as he declared, "to seize the passes of South Mountain . . . and confine him, Lee, to one line of invasion." While executing this plan, Hooker, on June 27, asked for complete control of the 11,000 men, the garrison of Maryland Heights, under Brig.-Gen. French, intending to move them from their anchorage in support of his columns. His request was refused, and the next day he was relieved from command by Maj.-Gen. Geo. G. Meade.

The excitement caused among the inhabitants by Lee's invasion and wide distribution of forces was intense. The citizens in great numbers fled across the Susquehanna, and the telegraph was surcharged with wild reports from every quarter, which were at once sent to Gen. Meade. Believing from information so gained that Lee's main body was threatening either Harrisburg or Baltimore, Meade at once adopted a new plan: to bring his troops to the Frederick and Harrisburg line of advance, and then move northward and extend his corps so far to the east as to relieve Baltimore.

On June 30 Meade's army was occupying a broken line over 30 miles in extent, the Sixth corps on the right near Manchester, the Fifth near Union Mills, the Twelfth near Littletown on the Hanover road, the Second near Uniontown, Meade's head-quarters at Taneytown, the Third between Taneytown and Emmittsburg, the Eleventh at Emmittsburg, the First 6 miles from Emmittsburg northward. Buford's cavalry held the extreme left at Gettysburg, while the remainder of the cavalry corps went to front and right in vicinity of Hanover. Such was substantially the position of Meade's army on the eve of the great battle. The organization had varied much since Hooker's start from Falmouth; many regiments, by expiration of service, having gone, and others having been brought in from the defences of Washington, from Baltimore, and elsewhere. Meade's morning report, June 30, gives his strength in aggregate: infantry, 77,208; artillery, 6692; cavalry, 12,420; in all, 96,320, with 352 cannon. French's division, 11,000 strong, which had been denied to Hooker, was immediately allowed to Meade, and was in reserve at Frederick, Md. This added, gives a grand aggregate of 107,320. The two armies were very nearly of the same size.

Lee found difficulty in getting information. By a mistake of instructions his cavalry under Stuart, instead of keeping between the two armies, had crossed the Potomac at Seneca below Meade and was making a raid past the rear and right flank of the Army of the Potomac, i. e., between that army and the cities of Washington and Baltimore. Stuart thus cut Meade's communications, and at first did considerable damage, but was obliged to hasten his return. Kilpatrick, supported by infantry, was close upon him, and in fact forced Stuart to a combat near Hanover Junction, Pa., June 30, after which, with all possible speed, Stuart proceeded to join Lee. Meanwhile, during the night of the 28th, Lee learned that the National army had crossed the Potomac and was already at Frederick, Md. Seeing his communications thus endangered, he immediately commenced concentration, ordering Hill's corps to move to Cashtown, 8 miles west of Gettysburg, on June 29, and Longstreet to follow the next day, leaving Pickett's division with his reserve trains at Chambersburg. Ewell was instructed to bring together his divisions at or near Cashtown as soon as he could make the march. On the 29th Heth's division of Hill's corps reached Cashtown, and the next day he sent Pettigrew's brigade to Gettysburg to procure shoes and other supplies. Pettigrew had just arrived at 11 A. M. when he descried the approach of Buford's cavalry. Pettigrew hitherto finding only detachments of militia was surprised thus to meet a portion of Meade's army and so, in haste, withdrew to his division at Cashtown. Buford, who was just in time to seize the town of Gettysburg, immediately pushed out his force so as to cover the approaches from the west, sending his pickets and scouts as far out as possible. Aware that he was in the presence of infantry, he prepared his command to fight on foot. He placed his horse artillery in position so as to sweep the roads and supported it by his two brigades, Gen. Devens holding the right and Gen. Gamble the left. Devens covered the ground from the Mummasburg road to the Chambersburg Railroad, Gamble thence southward as far as the Millerstown road, the whole front from the York around to and beyond the Millerstown road being studded by a good picket-line.

- On the evening of the 30th Lee's command was encamped as follows: Hill's corps—two divisions—Heth and Pender, at Cashtown; Anderson *en route* near Fayetteville; Longstreet's corps—Hood and McLaw's divisions—at Greenwood; Pickett's division at Chambersburg; Ewell's corps, Rodes, at Heidlersburg; Early, 3 miles off on the road to Berlin; and Ed. Johnson, with Brown's reserve artillery, between Greenvillage and Scotland. Four divisions, 39,000 men, were within 10 miles of Gettysburg and it was an easy day's march for Lee's entire force, excepting Pickett's division, to concentrate at or near Cashtown before noon of the next day, so that Lee's army was now substantially massed upon the left flank of Gen. Meade's scattered forces.

II. BATTLE. *First Day.*—The orders of Gen. Meade for July 1 were: "Head-quarters at Taneytown; Third corps to Emmittsburg; Second corps to Taneytown; Fifth corps to Hanover; Twelfth corps to Two Taverns; First corps to Gettysburg; Eleventh corps to Gettysburg (in supporting distance); Sixth corps to Manchester. Cavalry to front and flanks, well out in all directions, giving timely notice of positions and movements of the enemy."

Gettysburg, in 1863, was a town of about 2500 inhabitants. It rests in a sort of highland basin among the somewhat broken parallel ridges which trend north and south, and which westward become steppes toward the South Mountain chain. The environs are occupied by a seminary, a college, almshouse, and commodious farm-houses. The numerous approaches by wagon-roads and a railway, which meet at the town like spokes at the wheel-centre, pass through handsome groves, orchards, and well-watered fertile fields. The first ridge to the west stretches out past the suburbs. Upon it are the Lutheran Seminary and a few residences. It was upon its crest, which is intersected by the Chambersburg Railroad and pike, the Hagerstown and the Mummasburg wagon-roads, that Gen. Buford had established his small division of cavalry. Here the dawn of July 1 found his men in position diligently guarding every entrance to Gettysburg. Toward it the Confederate Gen. A. P. Hill advanced; Heth, with Pegram's battalion of artillery, led; Pender, with McIntosh's battalion, followed, advancing on the Chambersburg pike. Some 2 miles from Gettysburg Heth encountered Buford's advance, and at 9 A. M. quickly formed a line of battle, using Archer's and Davis' brigades in front, with artillery, and Pettigrew's and Brokenborough's in reserve. Buford's skirmishers who had opened fire were soon driven back slowly to the Seminary Ridge. As Buford thus beheld the rapid approach of Hill's command he began to look earnestly for help. The sun was clearing the valleys from the morning mists, and, looking southward, to his joy he discovered Reynolds' head of column. Soon the general himself met him near the Seminary and took command. Wadsworth's division had reached Buford's position, and Doubleday's and Robinson's divisions were some distance behind. By 10 o'clock Wadsworth's men, filing through the woods and fields, were deployed upon a ridge some 800 yards west of the seminary; 15 minutes later Reynolds himself pushed one brigade, Cutler's, into position, so as to hold an important point near the Chambersburg road. This brigade extended north beyond the road, in echelon to the rear, for some distance, the space on the road being occupied by Hall's battery. Meredith soon held the woods to the left of Cutler, and his line ran southward across Willoughby's Run. Meredith was just in time to meet Confederate Archer's first charge, which he promptly repulsed, capturing General Archer himself and 1000 prisoners. Just at this juncture General Reynolds, near his front line, while posting troops at a place now well marked, was killed by a rifle-shot. Here, as the Confederates met stout resistance, A. P. Hill formed new lines. Davis' brigade was put to the left or north of the pike, while Archer's, Pettigrew's, and Brokenborough's were extended to the south. Pender's division, now on the ground, made a second line, several hundred yards to rear, Thomas' brigade to the left, and the brigades of Lane, Scales, and Perrin to the right of the pike. The two accompanying battalions of artillery were distributed to the most favorable positions on high ground. Then again the Confederates advanced, overlapped Meredith's brigade and forced it to retire.

Doubleday, who had preceded his division to the field, now replacing Reynolds, quickly brought up the Sixth Wisconsin, which had been in reserve, and moved it to the right of the pike and into conjunction with two regiments of Cutler's brigade, which had swung back to the railway cut in the same neighborhood. Here Davis' Confederate brigade, pressing too rapidly after our retiring men and driving back Hall's battery, was caught by a front and flank fire, and two of his regiments were forced to surrender. This quick movement released a part of Hall's battery and one of Cutler's regiments, which had been cut off and threatened with capture. Meanwhile the two remaining divisions of the First corps had reached the Seminary. The one now under Gen. Rowley was sent with his batteries in support of Meredith, still holding advance ground south of the pike, and for a time Robinson was kept in column for a reserve nearer town. This was at 11 A. M. Much irregular fighting occurred to both sides on account of the breaking up of the lines. Now we find Biddle's brigade looking north with a line of guns completely at right angles to the main position, and the same is true of two or three Confederate brigades; but by much labor Wadsworth had reorganized his line along the Seminary Ridge, and Doubleday's left was again strongly pressed by the enemy, when a report came that his right was being turned. To meet this Robinson sent Baxter's brigade to the extreme right and went thither in person. He soon brought up Paul's brigade, and with it made as strong a right flank as he could. In this position Robinson's division did grand work, repulsing repeated front attacks and securing almost an entire brigade (Iverson's) as prisoners of war.

The Eleventh corps had left Emmittsburg at 8 A. M. by two roads: Barlow's division on the direct and the other two divisions by Horner's Mill. Gen. Howard, its commander, after setting his corps in motion, had ridden rapidly forward, and was upon Fahnestock's Observatory, in Gettysburg, examining the situation, when Reynolds' death was reported to him. Assuming command of the field he sent word at once to the commanders of his moving columns, also to Gen. Slocum, then several miles back on the Baltimore pike, and to Gen. Sickles at Emmittsburg, that a battle was in progress and urged them to hasten thither; despatches were at the same time sent to Gen. Meade. Gen. Howard went from Gettysburg to a height just south-west of the town, now known as Cemetery Hill, where he had selected a position for his general reserve and one to be held at all hazards in case the Oak Ridge should be forced. Here Gen. Schurz, now commanding the Eleventh corps, hastening up, met him at 11.30 A. M. Schurz was instructed to place Steinwehr's division (the Second) there in support of the reserve batteries of the corps, and to send forward his other two divisions, with the batteries accompanying them, to seize the high ground on the right of the First corps. Between 12 and 1 o'clock these two divisions were hurried through the town, their batteries preceding them at a trot, and formed in lines facing towards the north-west. Two batteries occupied the interval between the First and Eleventh corps. By 2.30 P. M., Gen. Howard having gone along his front, and having established his head-quarters, Steinwehr's division and the reserve batteries defensively on Cemetery Hill, ordered Schurz to advance his front lines and seize a wooded height to the north of Robinson's position. But word was brought from Buford, then on the right near the Harrisburg road, that Ewell's entire corps was coming in from the north, between the Harrisburg and Carlisle roads. Howard notified Doubleday and halted Schurz, whose skirmishers found the high ground in question already occupied by the enemy in force.

To return to Lee's army. The two divisions near Heidlersburg, namely, Rodes' and Early's, set out at daylight directly for Cashtown; but getting part way Rodes was directed by his corps commander, Ewell, to turn southward towards Hill's left flank at Gettysburg. Early set out via Hunterstown; from this point he also took the Gettysburg direction. The two divisions approached each other; Rodes, reaching a place north of Gettysburg, deployed with his right on the Mummasburg and his left touching the Carlisle road about 1 P. M. His left was close by Rock Creek. His order in line was as follows: Iverson's brigade on the right, then O'Neal's and Dole's, Daniels' and Ramseur's brigades, in column of regiments, as reserves. This division then moved forward, and when near enough to the First and Eleventh corps O'Neal and Iverson were ordered to attack, and Daniels brought up to support their flank. O'Neal, encountering a severe fire, seems to have deviated to the left, leaving Iverson's command of three regiments to be overwhelmed by the Nationals under Robinson and himself to be forced back. At 3.30 P. M. Daniels found himself some 1000 yards north of the Chambersburg pike and parallel to it; while Ramseur, with two brigades and a remnant of Iverson's, had swung around, facing Robinson in a line nearly perpendicular to Daniels. Meanwhile, as the contest was going on with Robinson, Dole's and part of O'Neal's brigade faced Schurz's two divisions; when he moved forward the engagement became very severe, especially on the Union right, Barlow's front. About 3 P. M. Dole's men were giving way and Barlow was evidently gaining ground. At this juncture Confederate Early's whole division made its appearance, coming up on the Harrisburg road. Early planted artillery and set it at work, and sent forward Gordon's brigade to the left of Dole's and in his support. This flank movement forced back Ames, who had replaced Barlow, severely wounded, to his second line. A little later Confederate Hays' and Hoke's brigades, in deployed lines, followed Gordon's, and striking the Eleventh corps in flank accomplished its complete displacement.

At 3.30 P. M. the Confederate lines, now extending along Howard's entire front and beyond his flanks, were somewhat readjusted and then pressed forward. The first break in Howard's front was near the centre. Help had been called for by both Doubleday and Schurz; but as it was necessary to hold the Cemetery, but few reinforcements were forwarded. However, Costar's brigade, of Steinwehr's division, was sent to the front of the town, and ordered to barricade so as to cover the anticipated retreat. Finally, when resistance became hopeless, Howard sent positive orders to both Schurz and Doubleday to fall back to the Cemetery as slowly as possible and take post; the Eleventh corps on right and First corps on left of Baltimore pike, and Buford's cavalry to extend the new line leftward with as much show of force as possible. The retreat was made, in front of such odds, with considerable disorder; the two corps, coming together in Gettysburg, and choking up the streets, were much broken up when they reached the Cemetery crest. The majority of Costar's brigade was captured just as the men were reaching the Cemetery gate. Gen. Hancock, who had come from Meade at Taneytown, met Gen. Howard. Hancock, without his corps, was under instructions to assume command of the field. Every effort was made to gather in the stragglers to form the lines along the crest, and to so place the batteries that they could do most service, and these efforts were successful. Gen. Lee made one effort to turn the right flank, but encountered so prompt and so severe a fire from the batteries and from Wadsworth's division, which Hancock had located on Culp's Hill, that he checked and finally withdrew his advance, and decided to postpone further offensive efforts till the next day. The First corps, the Eleventh, and Buford's cavalry, not exceeding all told 23,000 men, having engaged nearly 40,000 at the least, had certainly done a good day's work at Gettysburg. They had fought hard, lost one-third of their numbers, and by so doing had secured an excellent defensive position, and, what was of vital importance, time enough for the scattered Army of the Potomac to come up and occupy it. Gen. Lee at the time overrated the force opposed to him on account of the vigor of its defence, and, beholding the fortification-like appearance of the new line, contented himself with what he had gained. Sickles arrived near sundown to prolong the left, and Slocum's troops were on the ground, with one division beyond Wadsworth and the other, Williams', holding the left near Ziegler's Grove. A little later than Sickles Ewell's division under Ed. Johnson came to reinforce the left of Lee's lines, which were newly formed in front of the National position.

Second Day.—As this day's operation involved nearly the whole force of both armies, it is necessary for the sake of clearness to describe in brief the ground which was to be defended by Meade and attacked by Lee. The shape of Meade's line, as finally taken, is nearly that of a fish-hook : Big Round-Top, at the left and south, is between the Emmittsburg and Taneytown roads, and is the eye of the hook. The shank runs thence north over the crest of Little Round-Top; then through lower ground, afterward gradually ascending by Ziegler's Grove, commences to bend to the east along the Cemetery Ridge; turns more still at Culp's Hill. The point touches McAllister's Mill; and Powers' Hill forms the barb of the hook. The length from eye to around to barb is 5 miles.

Gen. Meade, after having set all his troops in motion, reached the field of battle after midnight. With the earliest light he went with Gen. Howard, hastily examined the position outlined, and planned the further posting of his command. During the forenoon his army, except Sedgwick's Sixth corps, being already at hand, he sent Slocum to hold the uneven, stony, woody slopes, from Culp's Hill across Rock Creek to McAllister's Mill ; Geary's division next to Wadsworth and Williams on Geary's right ; Wadsworth held Culp's Hill and neighborhood ; Meade left Howard's Eleventh corps where it was, Ames' division next to Wadsworth, Schurz' and Von Steinwehr's to the left in order for awhile ; the remainder of Newton's First corps came next ; now, nigh Ziegler's Grove, Hancock's Second was formed, Hays and Gibbon in the front, and Caldwell's near by in temporary reserve ; Sickles had pushed out his Third corps to occupy the Peach Orchard, putting Humphrey's division in echelon with Gibbon, and Birney's next, so drawing back his left as to place the brigades of Graham at the angle, and of Ward back by Little Round-Top or Devil's Den, with De Trobriand's between them. Till afternoon, Sykes' corps, the Fifth, was back of Slocum's right, massed as Slocum's reserve. The artillery was posted on the heights along the lines, with a large reserve parked in rear, between the Baltimore pike and the Taneytown road. The most of Pleasanton's cavalry was on the right, well out ; the left had no cavalry cover till the next day, when Merritt's brigade came. Buford's division had gone to Winchester to protect the trains and get the needed rest. Little Round-Top was occupied for a signal-station, and Big Round-Top as yet was covered only by pickets and a skirmish line. Just before the battle, Meade, finding Sickles in his judgment too far out, brought up Sykes toward Little Round-Top. The weary Sixth corps, having made 35 miles without rest, arrived about 2 P. M., and was massed in rear of the left of Meade's general line.

Meanwhile Lee had been gathering his forces in front of the same general position. Longstreet's corps held the right, making a front of two divisions ; Hood's abreast of Big Round-Top, and McLaws' on his left ; Pickett's had not yet reached the field ; A. P. Hill occupied all the ground from McLaws' left to the Hagerstown road, Anderson and Pender in front, and Heth to their left rear in reserve. Ewell's corps, following the bend of the "fish-hook," makes a right angle with Hill's, continuing a line through the town by Main street, and extending eastward till his left is north-east of McAllister's Mill, in order of divisions from right to left, Rodes', Early's, and Johnson's. Two of Early's brigades were sent out on York pike, and faced to the east, for the purpose of protecting Lee's left flank. From the extreme right to the extreme left along Lee's line the distance was 8 miles. On the Seminary Ridge, the high knobs west of Gettysburg, and the high hills like Brenner's, east of the town, the numerous batteries of Gen. Lee were carefully located, so as to give a concentric fire. But just before the battle a number of batteries were brought together west of Little Round-Top, and within easy range of Sickles' front. The cavalry division of Stuart had returned from its raid, and was placed over against Pleasanton's cavalry to the north-east of the York road.

Meade and his generals had anticipated an attack early in the day, and in fact Lee had for a time contemplated one to be made by Ewell's corps, provided Culp's Hill could be carried without too great loss. Lee visited Ewell during the night. He found Meade's right of great natural strength, and already held in force. Lee now matured a more general plan, and determined that his main attack should be made upon Meade's *apparent* left. Longstreet's corps was to open the battle there, while Hill's was to support it. But Ewell was " to make a simultaneous demonstration, . . . to be converted into a *real attack*, should opportunity offer." It was fortunate for Meade that "the preparations for attack were not completed till the afternoon." Hood formed in two lines—Law's and Robinson's brigades in front, Benning's and G. T. Anderson's in their rear. Everything being ready, at 4 P. M. the signal-guns are slowly discharged ; then all of Lee's batteries within range of the Cemetery commenced firing, but that portion concentrated near Sickles' advanced divisions made the most rapid and terrific discharges. Hood's column, skirmishers well out, was speedily set in motion. His advance was followed up by McLaws, who soon bore off from him somewhat to the left, facing Graham, De Trobriand,

and Ward. The fierce musketry engagement was quickly joined. Longstreet says of this attack: "Our batteries were opened upon his (Sickles') position, Hood's division pressing upon his (Meade's) left, and McLaws upon his front. He (Sickles) was soon dislodged, and driven back upon a commanding hill (Little Round-Top), which is so precipitous and rough as to render it difficult of ascent. Numerous stone fences about its base added greatly to its strength. The enemy taking shelter behind these, held them with great pertinacity." The time covered by the phrase "was soon dislodged and driven back" was two hours and one-half; and in that time, amid a mass of rocks, in the Devil's Den and vicinity, one of the most remarkable and bloody contests of war took place—a contest which was, however, destined to end in a victory to the "driven" troops. As soon as Meade heard the signal-guns he sent to hasten Sykes, already *en route* toward Little Round-Top, and as the battle thickened he ordered Geary and Williams from his right, leaving only Green's brigade to Slocum, beyond Culp's Hill, to hold in check half of Ewell's corps. Soon Sickles, as well as Hood, was badly wounded and taken from the field. Birney replaced him. In twenty minutes after the attack his men at the Peach Orchard began to give way. Sickles' batteries, which were well posted at different points near his line, had their horses and men shot down; one battery, for example, opposite the bend in Graham's front, held on to the very last, continuing firing till the enemy reached the very muzzles of their pieces, and then retired, pulling back the guns with their prolonges. The battery commander was wounded, and 5 non-commissioned officers and 22 men put *hors-de-combat*; he remained, nevertheless, with a portion of his battery, till another from the reserve arrived to relieve him. Other batteries engaged did likewise. Birney now called earnestly for help. First Hancock, having them well in hand and ready, despatched the brigades of Caldwell to the points most needed. Supports came up just in time to drive back portions of McLaws' division, and vigorously to strike the flank of Hood.

General Warren, Meade's chief-engineer, while the contest near Devil's Den was at its height, had gone to the signal-station on Little Round-Top. Catching sight of the approaching Confederates through the trees, he called to the signal-officer to keep the flag in movement till his return, and ran over the brow of the hill, where he met a brigade of Sykes' corps on the way to Birney. From it he detached the One-hundred-and-fortieth New York regiment. About the same time, Sykes being notified, detached Vincent's brigade from Birney's division. It rushed to the left of the same stronghold. These troops promptly met the advancing Confederates, and drove back their front line; both Vincent and the commander of the One-hundred-and-fortieth New York were killed. Under this cover Hazlett's battery soon reached the heights, and was supported by Weed's brigade. Gen. Weed himself was slain, and his friend, Lieut. Hazlett, endeavoring to catch his last words, fell dead across his body. Ayres with his regulars distinguished themselves, being compelled "to fight their way front and flank to the heel of the gorge." A little farther to the right Sweitzer's and Tilton's brigades of Barnes' division were thrown into the same caldron, to come out badly maimed. Lossing says of this point: "Never was there a wilder place for combat, and never was there a combat more fierce than was seen there on that hot July evening, with blazing musketry and hand-to-hand struggles, with clubbed fire-arms and jagged stones." After the contest for Little Round-Top had lasted over half an hour, a charge from Sykes' left routed Hood's remaining troops, and sent them flying to the rear. Meanwhile Fisher's brigade of Barnes' Third division, Fifth corps, had seized Big Round-Top, threatened Hood's right and rear, and secured Meade's flank.

But the contest lasted somewhat longer opposite Humphrey, for the men of A. P. Hill's corps, who had delayed somewhat, as supporting troops do in their advance, finally struck Humphrey's division in front while the movements just described had completely turned his left flank. Little by little he withdrew his left, fighting as he did so. As he wheeled around to the rear, his right flank was the more exposed, so that he finally retired to Hancock's line and took post on his left. When the fragments of the Third corps, with all the broken reinforcements which had been sent, had come back in defeat, closely followed by the victorious Confederates, Meade caused the gap to be filled between Sykes and Gibbon. Thus, Hancock deployed Willard's brigade (and here its commander was killed), and then Doubleday's and Robinson's divisions of the First corps. These were brought in season; some of them, the Vermonters under Stannard, being located in a cluster of trees in such a way as to bring a cross- and flanking-fire upon the advancing enemy. This, with a rapid front discharge from Hancock's men, cleared that part of the field. The last movement was made by Crawford's division of Sykes' corps under Meade's personal observation. Crawford deployed his lines, gave two volleys into such troops of the enemy as were in sight, and then charged across the fields in front of Little Round-Top, and on into and beyond the wheat-field to a strip of woods.

Meade's left was now safe, for the entire Sixth corps, some of whose troops had aided in the final repulse—Wheaton's division for example—was placed in support of the Fifth corps, which we know now strongly held the Round-Tops, and Pleasanton was hastening Kilpatrick's division and Merritt's brigade of Union cavalry to guard the approaches beyond.

But Confederate Gen. Ewell had not yet carried out his instructions. He and his generals had not heard the signals; the portions of Early's division, sent out to the extreme left, promised to return for attacking Howard's front, had not come back in time; and, when finally ready, the woods and rough ground obscured everything, and Ewell could not secure unity of action between his brigades and divisions. But, after a fashion, the work was undertaken. When, late in the afternoon, on Meade's call, Williams' (now Ruger's) division (for Slocum had an added force, a wing, to command, and Williams took the Twelfth corps) had marched off, and Geary's division, though the latter lost its way by the fault of a guide, had crossed beyond Rock Creek, Gen. Green with his one brigade was getting ready to man the barricades and trenches. Then Confederate Johnson was rapidly approaching his front; Green was too late for that. Four Confederate brigades, those of Jones, Stewart, Nichols, and Walker, marched up ready to fight, but were astonished to find no foe in front. So Johnson's men worked along over the logs and stones and through the ravines till they came to the barricades. Then suddenly he met a volley from his right, and

GETTYSBURG.

rapid continuous firing followed. Green touching Wadsworth at Culp's Hill had swung back his right till his lines, hidden by the trees, had become oblique to Johnson's. He was firing fiercely upon Jones and Nichols. It was necessary to dislodge Green, so Johnson turned and faced him, and a most angry and prolonged battle took place; Gen. Jones was slain and the Confederate dead were piled up in front of this stalwart brigade. Wadsworth and Howard rapidly reinforced Green. At 9 P. M. Johnson gave up the blind fight and contented himself with sleeping in Williams' trenches.

Before this, Gordon's brigade, returning from the Confederate left, had rejoined Early's division; and two brigades of the latter having been long in position, lying quietly under the cover of Cemetery Hill on its north side, suddenly, after a new spurt of artillery, at 7 P. M. sprang forward to assault Howard's corps. The Confederates broke through Von Gilsa's brigade, came up into the batteries and a hand-to-hand fight ensued. Reinforcements from Schurz and Von Steinwehr were turned against them, and their advance was soon broken. Gen. Hancock, catching the sound of battle, sent Howard Carroll's brigade, which, with deployed lines and a quick march, regained all the lost ground and filled out again the disordered front. In this contest Early lost a brigade commander, Col. Avery, and many men, so that he, like Ed. Johnson, was forced to give up the strife. By 10 P. M. all was quiet. Meade and his corps commanders were in council; the situation was not encouraging; the Peach-orchard was, with many dead and wounded, in Lee's hands, and Slocum had lost more than half his front by his withdrawal to help Hancock, Birney, and Sykes. Still all voted to stay and fight.

Third Day.—While the night fighting was going on, Ruger worked his way cautiously back to near McAllister's Mill. Some of his flankers wandered within Confederate Johnson's lines and were captured. At last beyond the swale he finds some breastworks not held by the enemy. He seizes them, and puts in an oblique line, like Green's, on the other side of the swale and ravine. Geary, too, by midnight, by careful marching, had come to prolong Green's oblique line; Kane's brigade next to Green, and Canby's next in order. Slocum posted between these oblique lines, supported by Lockwood's brigade and other troops sent from the Sixth corps, as much artillery as could be there used. Geary says: "All these dispositions were made with the utmost silence and secrecy, and within a few rods of the enemy's lines." From 5:30 A. M. till 10.30 A. M. a fearful struggle went on. The Confederate commander was reinforced and began to attack, when Geary and Ruger were already in motion for the same purpose. At last the advantage was with Slocum. After the last charge of the enemy, made with fresh troops, the victory of Slocum's men was so marked that they rushed forward with cheers and completely repossessed themselves of their old barricades and breastworks.

Lee's final effort may be considered in two parts: (1st.) The use of his artillery; (2d.) His infantry assault. This time he chose for his main attack not Little Round-Top, but an interval or lower land, lying between that point and Ziegler's Grove. On a ridge of slight elevation, close by the Emmittsburg road, were some 40 pieces of artillery. Farther south, on ground somewhat higher, was a larger number of guns *en masse*. For the final work Lee concentrated in this neighborhood between 140 and 150 guns. The ranges varied from 1500 to 2000 yards. Other prominent points had batteries which were calculated to divert and scatter the fire of the National guns. Opposite these Confederate cannon the Nationals had 3 groups; on Cemetery Heights, under Osborn, 50 cannon; near Ziegler's Grove, under Hazard, 30 pieces; near Little Round-Top, favorably located, 40 guns, under McGilvray; Hunt, the chief, kept the rest in reserve under shelter, for prompt relief or reinforcement.

Meade's troops to be engaged were little changed. Hancock had general supervision of the threatened points, and at least two corps under his direct command. The Second corps fell to Gibbon. The brigades occupying the lower ground in front and to the left of Ziegler's Grove, and especially exposed, were those of Smyth and Willard (Hay's division); Webb, Hall, and Heath (Harrow's division). Slightly to the left, occupying a point of woods and arranged *en potence*, was again Stannard's large brigade of Vermonters (Doubleday's division); then leftward the shattered brigades of the Third corps and those of the Fifth, all supported by a good second line, with the Sixth corps for a general reserve.

On Lee's side Pickett's division, now up from Chambersburg, was chosen as a sort of forlorn hope. It was formed in brigade lines, Kemper on the right, Garnett on the left, and Armistead in rear. The supporting force on the right rear had 3 brigades: Wilcox's, Perry's, and Wright's. On the left 6 brigades: Posey's, Mahone's, Pettigrew's, Walker's, Law's, and Scales'.

At last Lee sounded his signal-guns, two discharges distinct and clear to both armies. First began the Confederate artillery fire, mainly throwing projectiles upon the interval designated. A little later the National guns concentrated their fire upon the enemy's troublesome artillery. This fire lasted over an hour, till about 2.30 P. M. The whole region resounded as in the heaviest thunder-storm. Fragments of shells killed men everywhere. In one regiment, lying waiting, 27 were killed and wounded by one shot. All buildings in the vicinity were torn and broken; tombstones were crushed, and large numbers of horses killed outright or groaning with painful wounds. Meade stopped his guns to prevent too much heat and to preserve ammunition. Lee's shortly after followed suit. Then came the handsome Confederate advance, with flags waving in the struggling sunlight. Pickett's division went straight to its work. Our artillery opened again, making gaps which were immediately filled. The advance aimed for Ziegler's Grove. Hancock's men, with rifles in hand, covered by the stone walls and slight barricades, were quietly waiting his command. The Vermonters were ready for their oblique fire. Pickett being a little nearer, McGilvray brought his 40 guns to bear. Then instantly the whole of Hancock's front opened its musketry fire, and the choice brigades of Pickett were soon almost annihilated. Garnett was killed. Confederate Peyton, who took his place, says "that the flank fire from the Nationals was fearful, ten men being killed or wounded by a single shot." The fire and the smoke hindered any coherence, the brigades were soon mixed together, and the remnants rushed forward determined "to plant the Southern banner on the walls of the enemy." But here the fighting was soon over. Armistead had but few men left, as wounded to death he surrendered within our lines. When Armistead reached the stone wall the most part of Webb's brigade posted here abandoned their position, but did not retreat entirely, for reinforcements were at hand, coming quickly from Hall's front. There was a momentary breach, so vigorous was this last charge, but it was momentary. To lookers-on the field appeared confused; regiments sprang up and rushed out with their flags flying, gathering in prisoners and battle-memorials, and bringing in the wounded. No panorama can exaggerate the reality of that exciting scene. Crawford sums up the final work a little farther to the left of Meade's line, where some of Lee's supporting troops had wandered and fought: "By this charge of McCandless' brigade and the Eleventh Pennsylvania regiment the whole of the ground lost the previous day was retaken, together with all our wounded, who, mingled with those of the rebels, were lying uncared for." At the time of this attack our cavalry did remarkable service on our left flank, fighting on foot and preventing a turning movement in that direction from Hood. It had previously done similar work on the other flank, near the Hanover road. That night Gen. Lee withdrew behind a defensive cover arranged on the Oak or Seminary Ridge. Meade's soldiers were so weary that no vigorous effort was made to follow up the victory, so that Gen. Lee retreated in comparative security, recrossed the Potomac, and made his way back to Central Virginia.

It is difficult to ascertain Lee's losses. That his official reports (15,234 killed and wounded) are much too small there can be no doubt. Meade had 7262 wounded Confederates on his hands after the battle, and 6359 well prisoners. Lee's reported killed were 2396; his slightly wounded and missing at least 10,000; making Lee's total losses about 26,018. Maj.-Gens. Hood and Heth, Brig.-Gens. Semmes, Barksdale, Kemper, Anderson, Pettigrew, and Scales were wounded. Maj.-Gen. Pender, Brig.-Gens. Garnett, Armistead, and Jones were killed, and several general officers captured.

Meade lost 247 officers killed, 1137 wounded, and 182 captured or missing; enlisted men, 2820 killed, 13,360 wounded, 5255 captured or missing, making an aggregate of 23,001. Some of the Union officers killed were Maj.-Gen. Reynolds, Brig.-Gens. Zook and Weed, Cols. Cross, Willard, Sherrill, and Vincent; wounded, Maj.-Gens. Hancock and Sickles, Brig.-Gens. Meredith, Paul, Gibbon, Graham, Barlow, and Tyler, Cols. Stone, Wistar, and Smyth; also several were captured. (O. O. H.)

GIBBON, JOHN, an American general, was born in Pennsylvania in 1826. He graduated at West Point in 1847, and served in the Mexican war. He was afterwards employed against the Indians until the outbreak of the civil war. He was chief of artillery in Gen. McDowell's army until May, 1862, when he was made brigadier-general of volunteers. He served in the Army of the Potomac, fighting at Bull Run, South Mountain, and Antietam. He commanded a division at Fredericksburg and was wounded. He also took part at Chancellorsville, and at the battle of Gettysburg was severely wounded. On his return to service in May, 1864, he was placed in command of a division of the Second corps, and fought in the battles of the Wilderness and Cold Harbor. He afterwards commanded the Twenty-fourth army corps from the siege of Petersburg to the surrender of Gen. Lee.

He received the brevet of major-general. In 1869 he was placed in command of the Seventh infantry, and in 1886 was promoted brigadier-general.

GIBBONS, JAMES, an American cardinal, was born at Baltimore, July 23, 1834. His parents took him to Ireland at an early age, but in 1853 he returned to Baltimore and was educated at St. Charles College. He was ordained priest June 30, 1864, and in 1868 he was appointed vicar apostolic of North Carolina. In January, 1872, he was made bishop of Richmond, and in May, 1879, became coadjutor to Archbishop Bayley, of Baltimore, whom he succeeded in the same year. In 1883 he was called to Rome to give information of the church in America, and in 1885 he was president of the Third Plenary Council at Baltimore. In 1886 he was raised to the dignity of cardinal, being the second American who has received this honor.

GIBBS, JOSIAH WILLARD (1790-1861), an American philologist, was born at Salem, Mass., April 30, 1790. He graduated at Yale College in 1809, and was tutor there from 1811 to 1815. In 1824 he was made professor of sacred literature in the theological department, and he was also librarian of the college. He translated Storr's *Essay on the Historical Sense of the New Testament* (1817) and Gesenius' *Hebrew Lexicon of the Old Testament* (1824); he also published *Philological Studies* (1857); *Latin Analyst* (1858); and *Teutonic Etymology* (1860). He contributed to the revised edition of Webster's *Dictionary*, to W. C. Fowler's *Grammar*, and to various periodicals. He died at New Haven, March 25, 1861.

GIBBS, OLIVER WOLCOTT, an American chemist, was born at New York, Feb. 21, 1822. He graduated at Columbia College in 1841, and studied chemistry with Prof. Hare at Philadelphia, and medicine at the New York College of Physicians and Surgeons, receiving his degree in 1844. He afterwards studied in Europe under Liebig, and in 1849 was elected professor of chemistry and physics in the New York Free Academy. In 1863 he was called to Harvard College as professor of chemistry. He was appointed by Pres. Grant scientific commissioner to the Vienna Exhibition in 1873. He has contributed to the *American Journal of Science* and other periodicals, and has received marks of honor from European societies.

GIDDINGS, JOSHUA REED (1795-1864), an American statesman, was born at Tioga Point, Pa., Oct. 6, 1795. When he was ten years old his parents removed to Ashtabula county, Ohio. After Gen. Hull's surrender at Detroit in 1812, Giddings enlisted as a volunteer and fought in some engagements with the Indians. He afterwards taught school, then studied law with Elisha Whittlesey, and was admitted to the bar in 1820. He was elected to the Ohio legislature in 1826 and to Congress in 1839, having already acquired a high reputation in his profession. Just before he entered Congress the "Atherton gag" had been passed, which refused to allow any consideration of petitions or papers on the subject of slavery. Giddings at once joined John Quincy Adams' efforts to have the right of petition restored and maintained. A close scrutiny of the Constitution led him to the conclusion that Congress had power to prohibit slavery in the Territories and in the District of Columbia. As a local institution in certain States Congress could not interfere with it, but was under no obligation to countenance or foster it. He therefore opposed the war in Florida on the ground that it was simply an effort to use the U. S. army to catch fugitive slaves. In 1841 some slaves, who were being carried in the Creole, an American vessel, from Virginia to New Orleans, overpowered the crew and took the vessel into the British port of Nassau, N. P., where they were declared free. Daniel Webster, then secretary of state, demanded compensation from the British government. Giddings, in the House of Representatives, March 21, 1842, offered resolutions, declaring that the escaped slaves had exercised their natural rights, and that no wrong had been done for which compensation could be demanded. Great excitement ensued, and, though he withdrew the resolutions at the request of friends, a vote of censure was passed upon him by a vote of 125 to 69. He immediately resigned, and, returning to his constituents, was re-elected by an increased majority. Confirmed in his hostility to the system of slavery, he resisted all its encroachments. He opposed the annexation of Texas as increasing the slave domain. He had acted with the Whigs in favoring a protective tariff, but in 1847 he refused to vote for the Whig candidate for the speaker of the House, and in 1848 he assisted in forming the Liberty party at Buffalo. In 1849 he again refused to vote for R. C. Winthrop for speaker, and thus caused his defeat. Slavery was still the great question of the time, and Giddings steadfastly opposed the compromise measures of Clay, as he did afterwards the Kansas-Nebraska measures of Douglas. In 1856 he was senior member of the House, and as such administered the oath to N. P. Banks, the Republican candidate, who had been elected speaker after a struggle prolonged through two months. Though originally a man of powerful frame, Giddings was now worn out with his excessive toil on behalf of freedom. On May 8, 1856, while addressing the House, he fell to the floor unconscious, and though then he soon revived, he fell again on Jan. 17, 1858. He was compelled to refrain from attendance for some time, and closed his congressional career in 1859. In 1861 he was appointed by President Lincoln consul-general to Canada. He died at Montreal, May 27, 1864. He published a volume of *Speeches* (1853); *The Exiles of Florida* (1858); *Congressional History of Slavery*, and *The Rebellion, its Authors and Causes* (1864).

GIFFORD, ROBERT SWAIN, an American painter, was born on the island of Naushon, Mass., Dec. 23, 1840. His parents soon after removed to New Bedford, where he was educated. He studied painting with Albert Van Beest in New York, and in 1864 opened a studio in Boston, but returned to New York in 1866. He was elected an associate of the National Academy in 1867 and an academician in 1878. He visited Oregon and California in 1869, and went to Europe in 1870. In 1874 he went to Algiers and the Great Desert, and also made a tour through France. His works comprise a wide variety of scene, and are marked by vigor and fine execution. Among his best are Mount Hood, Oregon (1870); Boats on the Nile (1874); Egyptian Caravan (1876); Cedars of New England (1877); Border of the Desert (1878). He has also painted many water-colors and illustrated many fine books. He was president of the New York Etching Club.

GIFFORD, SANFORD ROGERS (1823-1880), an American painter, was born at Greenfield, Saratoga co., N. Y., July 10, 1823. He studied at Brown University, but in 1844 left college to study art in New York. In 1851 he was made an associate of the National Academy, and in 1854 became an academician. He spent the summers of 1855-57 in sketching tours in Europe. He served with the N. Y. Seventh regiment in the civil war. In 1868 he again visited Europe, and in 1870 went to the Rocky Mountains. He died Aug. 29, 1880. His works show great vigor of style and strong sense of color. They aim at an interpretation of the inner sense of nature and are often successful in their object. Among them are Morning in the Adirondacks, San Giorgio, Venice, Venetian Sails, Coming Storm, Lake Geneva, Golden Horn.

GIGNOUX, FRANÇOIS REGIS, a French painter, was born at Lyons in 1816. He studied art at Paris under Delaroche and others. He removed to America in 1840, settling in New York and devoting himself to landscape. In 1851 he was chosen to the Academy of Design, and he was the first president of the Brooklyn Art Academy. In 1870 he returned to France. Among his works are Virginia in Indian Summer, The Four Seasons in America, Niagara in Winter, The Dismal Swamp. His winter landscapes have attracted most attention, but he has depicted with success every aspect of American scenery. He died Aug. 6, 1882.

GIGOUX, JEAN FRANÇOIS, a French painter, was born at Besançon in 1806. He studied at the École des Beaux Arts, and exhibited his first picture in 1831. He devoted himself chiefly to historical and sacred subjects, but has also painted portraits. Among his works are The Death of Cleopatra (1850), The Baptism of Christ, Taking of Ghent, The Last Ecstacy of St. Mary Magdalene. He has been especially successful in his decorations of churches.

GILBERT, JOSEPH HENRY, an English chemist, was born at Hull, Aug. 1, 1817. His mother is known to literature as Ann Taylor, of Ongar. He was educated at Glasgow University, at University College, London, and at Giessen, studying under Graham, A. T. Thomson, Thomas Thomson, and Liebig. He took his doctorate at Giessen, was an instructor in University College, London, 1840-41, and for a time was employed in the Manchester College of Calico-printing. Since 1843 he has been associated with Mr. Lawes (now Sir J. B. Lawes), of Rothamsted, Herts, in a systematic course of experiments and researches in agricultural chemistry, and in the physiology of farm animals. The results of these studies have been given to the world in a long series of papers, everywhere recognized as of the highest value, both to agriculture and to pure science.

GILBERT, WILLIAM SCHWENCK, an English dramatist, was born at London, Nov. 18, 1836. He was educated at Great Ealing School, and received the degree of B. A. from the London University in 1857. He was then employed as a clerk in the privy council office, and was admitted to the bar in 1864. He became a frequent contributor to *Punch* and *Fun*, his verses in the latter being afterwards collected as the *Bab Ballads*. He then turned his attention to writing for the stage; his burlesques, *Dulcamara*, *La Vivandière*, and others, had some success. Then a musical legend, *Ages Ago*, produced in 1868 by Gilbert and F. Clay, gave intimation of the new line of entertainment with which his name is connected. Meantime he produced his first comedy, *An Old Score*, as well as *Pygmalion and Galatea*, and several fairy plays. In 1876 came his comic opera *Trial by Jury*, in which he associated for the first time with Arthur Sullivan. Their joint work was seen again in *The Sorcerer*, and in 1878 they charmed the world with their *H. M. S. Pinafore*, which playfully hit off certain popular foibles. Encouraged by its extraordinary success in the United States, the authors brought out their next work, *The Pirates of Penzance*, in New York, in 1880; but, though well received, it did not attain the popularity of its predecessor. *Patience* followed in 1881, *Iolanthe* in 1883, and the *Mikado* in 1885.

GILDER, WILLIAM HENRY (1812-1864), an American educator, was born in Philadelphia, Sept. 17, 1812. His father, John Gilder (1786-1855), was a leading Methodist layman of that city, served both in the city council and in the State legislature, and was chairman of the building committee of Girard College. The son was educated at Wesleyan University, Connecticut, and entered the Methodist ministry in 1833. He was for a time editor of a Philadelphia literary paper, *The Repository*, and afterwards of *The Literary Register*. He established a young ladies' school at Bordentown, N. J., and was afterwards president of the Female Institute at Flushing, Long Island. In 1862 he entered the army as chaplain of the Fortieth New York volunteers. He died of disease contracted in the discharge of his duty, at Brandy Station, Va., April 13, 1864.

His son, WILLIAM HENRY GILDER, journalist and Arctic traveller, was born in Philadelphia, Aug. 16, 1838. He entered the Union army as a private at the beginning of the civil war, and was a captain (major by brevet) at its close. In Lieut. F. Schwatka's search for Sir John Franklin relics in King William's Land (1878-80), he was *New York Herald* correspondent and second in command. Again he accompanied the Rodgers in St. Lawrence Bay, and joined in the search for the bodies of De Long and his companions in the Lena Delta. He served as correspondent of the *Herald* during the Franco-Chinese war in Tonquin (1883). He is the author of *Schwatka's Search* (1881), and *Ice-Pack and Tundra* (1883), the latter being an account of the search for the Jeannette.

Another son, RICHARD WATSON GILDER, editor and poet, was born at Bordentown, N. J., Feb. 8, 1844. He early became a journalist, and in 1869 was editor of *Hours at Home*. In 1870 he became associate editor of *Scribner's Monthly*, into which *Hours at Home* was merged; and when, in 1881, the title of *Scribner's* was changed to the *Century Magazine*, he succeeded Dr. Holland as its editor-in-chief. Under his management it has been noted for its literary and artistic excellence. Mr. Gilder has published three books of poems: *The New Day* (1875), *The Poet and his Master* (1878), and *Lyrics* (1885).

JEANNETTE LEONARD GILDER, born at Flushing, Long Island, Oct. 3, 1849, and JOSEPH B. GILDER, born June 29, 1858, are also journalists. In January, 1881, they established *The Critic*, New York, which they have since edited.

GILDERSLEEVE, BASIL LANNEAU, an American classical scholar and author, was born at Charleston, S. C., Oct. 23, 1831. He was educated at Charleston and Princeton Colleges, and graduated at the latter in 1849. He pursued further philological studies at Berlin, Bonn, and Göttingen, receiving the degree of Ph. D. at the last named in 1853. He was made professor of Greek in the University of Virginia in 1856, and, after holding this position twenty years, he was called, at the opening of Johns-Hopkins University, Baltimore, to a similar professorship. He has published a series of Latin school-books, including a *Grammar* (1867; revised edition, 1872); and editions of *Persius* (1875); *Justin Martyr* (1877); Pindar's *Olympian and Pythian Odes* (1885). He has been editor of the *American Journal of Philology* since 1880. He received the degree of LL.D. from William and Mary College in 1869.

GILES, HENRY, an American lecturer and essayist, was born at Cranford, county Wexford, Ireland, Nov. 1, 1809. He was educated at Belfast, in the Roman Catholic faith, but after various changes of belief became a Unitarian. He was pastor of a congregation at Greenock for two years, and at Liverpool for three years. In 1840 he came to the United States, where he was chiefly engaged as a lecturer, though he also preached in several parishes. He has published *Lectures and Essays* (1843); *Christian Thoughts on Life* (1850); *Illustrations of Genius* (1854); *Human Life in Shakespeare* (1868). After years of retirement on account of ill health, he died July 10, 1882.

GILES, WILLIAM BRANCH (1762-1830), an American statesman, was born in Amelia co., Va., Aug. 12, 1762. He was educated at Princeton College, N. J., studied law with Chancellor Wythe, and was admitted to the bar at Petersburg. In 1790 he was elected to Congress to fill a vacancy, and he was often re-elected. In December, 1792, he led the attack on Alexander Hamilton's management of the treasury, calling for a complete exposition of the finances, and pointing out a discrepancy of $1,500,000 in the public accounts. Hamilton replied promptly and satisfactorily to every question, and Giles' resolutions of censure on Jan. 23, 1793, were defeated by a large majority. In 1796 he followed Madison in opposing an appropriation to carry into effect Jay's treaty with England. In 1798 he opposed the movement for war against France on account of her depredations on American commerce. He assisted Madison in procuring the passage in the Virginia legislature of the celebrated resolutions of 1798. In 1804 Giles was elected to the National Senate, where he was leader of the Republican party until 1811, when his opposition to the movement for war against England and his feud with Pres. Madison threw him into the background. In 1815 he retired to private life. In 1826 he opposed a revision of the Constitution of Virginia, and was elected first to the legislature and then to the governorship. The project for revision, however, prevailed in 1828, and Giles was prominent in the debates of the Constitutional Convention. He died in Amelia co., Va., Dec. 4, 1830.

GILL, THEODORE NICHOLAS, an American naturalist, was born in New York city, March 21, 1837; was educated in private schools, and has received honorary degrees of Ph. D. and M. D. Dr. Gill has earned a wide reputation as an ichthyologist, and has also given special attention to mammals, reptiles, crustaceans, and mollusks. For many years he has been employed in the Smithsonian Institution, which has published many of his scientific papers. He is one of the most accurate and trustworthy of American systematists, and his varied accomplishments as a man of science are widely recognized in other countries.

GILLEM, ALVAN C. (1830-1875), an American general, was born in Tennessee in 1830. He graduated at West Point in 1851 and entered the artillery service, served in Florida and in garrison and frontier duty until 1861, when he was made captain and assistant-quartermaster. He was engaged at Mill Spring, Shiloh, and Corinth. In May, 1862, he was appointed colonel; in August, 1863, brigadier-general. He was then made adjutant-general of the State of Tennessee, and commanded an expedition in East Tennessee from August, 1864, to March, 1865. He was president of the convention to reorganize the State of Tennessee, Jan. 9, 1865. He afterwards captured Salisbury, N. C., in April, 1865, for which he received the brevet of major-general. In 1867 he commanded the district of Mississippi, and afterwards had commands in the regular army. He was actively engaged against the Indians and was conspicuous in the pursuit of the Modocs in 1873. He died Dec. 2, 1875.

GILLENIA. This plant is best known under its botanical name, though also called "Indian Physic," "Bowman's Root," or "Wild Ipecac." It was employed by the Indians in strong decoctions which operated violently. In small doses it was formerly used as a tonic, and for a long time was considered equal in value to the officinal ipecacuana. The roots were collected in the fall, and the bark only used.

Linnæus and others regarded the plant as a *Spiræa*; but Conrad Moench, a German botanist, discerned its distinct character, and in 1802 named the genus in honor of Dr. Arnold Gillen, a botanist of Cassel. It is distinguished from *Spiræa* readily by its general appearance, and critically by its funnel-shaped calyx, very short stamens, and five carpels combined into a five-celled capsule, with two seeds in each cell. There are only two species known, both natives of the eastern slope of the United States. *Gillenia trifoliata* is distinguished by the narrow pointed stipules from *Gillenia stipulacea*, which has large ovate stipules deeply cut. They grow in rich woods, and, though not often found in great abundance in any one spot, each species is very generally scattered over the area in which it is located.

GILLETT, EZRA HALL (1823–1875), an American clergyman, was born at Colchester, Conn., July 15, 1823. He graduated at Yale College in 1841, and at the Union Theological Seminary in 1844. He was ordained pastor of a Presbyterian church at Harlem in 1845, and gave considerable attention to church history. He published *Life and Times of John Huss* (2 vols., 1861; 3d ed., 1870), and at the request of the Presbyterian Church (New School) prepared an excellent *History of the Presbyterian Church in the United States* (2 vols., 1864; revised ed., 1873). In 1868 he was appointed professor of political economy and history in the University of New York. He died at New York, Sept. 2, 1875. Besides the works mentioned above he published *Ancient Cities*, *England 200 Years Ago*, *Life Lessons*, *God in Human Thought*, and *The Moral System* (1875).

GILLMORE, QUINCY ADAMS, an American general and engineer, was born at Black River, Lorain co., Ohio, Feb. 28, 1825. Graduating at West Point in 1849 at the head of his class, he served three years as assistant engineer in construction of works at Hampton Roads, Va., then became assistant professor of engineering at West Point. He had attained the rank of captain in August, 1861, when he was appointed chief engineer of the expedition to Port Royal, under Gen. T. W. Sherman. He conducted the siege of Fort Pulaski, at the mouth of the Savannah River, and compelled its surrender, after bombardment, on April 11, 1862. In August following Gen. Gillmore held a command in Kentucky, and in January, 1863, he defeated Gen. Pegram, at Somerset. In June he was placed in command of the Department of the South, with the rank of major-general, and thereafter conducted the siege of Charleston, S. C. He effected the capture of Fort Wagner, and the demolition of Fort Sumter. He was transferred to the James River in 1864, where he commanded the Tenth army corps, and was engaged in the battle of Drury's Bluff. He was summoned to Washington in July, when it was threatened by Gen. J. A. Early. In November, 1864, he again had command of the Department of the South, and afterwards had charge of the construction of various fortifications on the Atlantic coast, and in June, 1868, was promoted to be major, and in January, 1874, to be lieutenant-colonel of engineers. He has published *Siege and Reduction of Fort Pulaski* (1863); *Practical Treatise on Limes, Hydraulic Cements, and Mortars* (1863); *Engineer and Artillery Operations Against the Defences of Charleston Harbor in 1863* (1865). He died April 7, 1888.

GILMAN, DANIEL COIT, an American educator and author, was born at Norwich, Conn., July 6, 1831. He graduated at Yale College in 1852, and was superintendent of schools in New Haven, Conn., from 1856 to 1860. He was then appointed professor of physical geography and librarian at Yale College, which positions he held till 1872, being also for two years State superintendent of schools in Connecticut. In 1872 he was called to be president of the University of California, and on the organization of Johns-Hopkins University, at Baltimore, in 1875, was made its president. He has written numerous educational reports, and literary and historical papers. He has also published a *Life of James Monroe* (1883).

GILMAN, SAMUEL (1791–1858), an American clergyman, was born at Gloucester, Mass., Feb. 16, 1791. He graduated at Harvard College in 1811, and was tutor there from 1817 to 1819. He became pastor of the Unitarian church in Charleston, S. C., in December, 1819, and held this relation till his death, which occurred at Kingston, Mass., Feb. 9, 1858. From his writings in the *North American Review* and other periodicals a volume was collected, called *Contributions to American Literature* (1856). He also published *Memoirs of a New England Choir*, and some poems, and translated Boileau's *Satires*. He was an active promoter of the cause of temperance.

His wife, CAROLINE H. GILMAN (1794–1866), was the daughter of Samuel Howard, of Boston, and was born Oct. 8, 1794. At the age of sixteen she wrote religious poems, which were published in the *North American Review*. In 1819 she was married, and removed to Charleston. In 1832 she began to edit the *Rosebud*, a juvenile weekly, afterwards called the *Southern Rose*. From this she afterwards compiled *Recollections of a New England Housekeeper*, *Recollections of a Southern Matron*, and other books. She also published *Oracles from the Poets* (1847), *The Sibyl* (1848), *Verses of a Lifetime* (1849), and contributed to Mrs. Ellett's *Women of the Revolution*. After the death of her husband, she took up her residence in Cambridge, Mass., where she died in 1866.

GILMORE, JOHN R., an American author, was born at Boston, Mass., in 1823. He was trained to business, and became head of a New York firm engaged in the Southern coast-wise trade. On retiring, in 1857, he devoted himself to literature. He assisted in founding the *Continental Monthly*, in 1862. He has published, chiefly under the name "Edmund Kirke," several volumes relating to Southern life, among which are *Among the Pines*, *My Southern Friends*, *Down in Tennessee*, *On the Border*, *Among the Guerrillas*. He is also the author of a *Life of Jesus*, and has contributed to various periodicals.

GINGKO, or MAIDEN-HAIR TREE, was introduced

from Japan. The name is said by Veitch to be of Chinese origin, and to signify "deciduous;" the tree, unlike most *Coniferæ*, losing its leaves in the winter season. It has been found cultivated in both China and Japan, but nowhere indigenous. The Chinese name attached to the tree in Japan would seem to indicate that the first knowledge of the tree in Japan was derived from China. It is generally cultivated in those countries for the sake of the nuts, which are about the size of a filbert, and when roasted in the shell have the flavor of almonds, and are so highly esteemed as to be rarely absent from first-class entertainments. Many travellers speak of the tree's immense size. Bunge is quoted by Hoopes as noting one near Pekin which was forty feet in circumference, and of "prodigious height." Wood from Japan exhibited at the Centennial Exhibition of 1876 was yellowish-white in color, and of such a uniform satiny texture that only by the aid of a pocket-lens could the lines of annual growth be detected. These lines averaged a quarter of an inch apart.

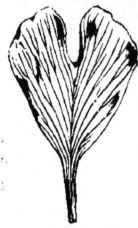

Leaf of Gingko Tree.

This curious tree was made known to Europeans about the beginning of the eighteenth century, through the writings of Kaempfer, but Ellis, in a letter to Linnæus (as published in *Smith's Correspondence*), dated April, 1758, notes it as then being propagated by James Gordon, a nurseryman near London, and botanical chronology fixes 1754 as the date of its introduction to England. This original tree was propagated by layers and cuttings in the absence of seeds, and proved to be a male tree; and it is only in comparatively recent times, probably through seeds from the original countries giving other trees, that fruiting plants have been known in England. The tree is believed in Europe to be diœcious—having males and females on separate trees. In France, where the tree is popularly known as "*L'arbre aux quarante écus*," in consequence of a sharp trick by which the original introducer to that country obtained the first plant from an English tradesman, it is noted by Delile, in *Bull. de la Société ag. du Hérault* for 1835, as having first produced fruit in that part of the world at that time. According to Hoopes (*Book of Evergreens*), it was introduced to America by Alexander Hamilton (no doubt by error for William Hamilton), of Woodlands, near Philadelphia, in 1784. This tree is still standing, and is probably 100 feet high. There are also very large trees in many parts of the United States. The tree is described in most European works as having a conical or pyramidal head, and the early trees—male—from the European original are of that character; but during recent years a number of seedling trees have borne fruit in America, and these have heads spreading like that of an oak. This is the case especially with one growing in the grounds of the Landreths, Bloomsdale, near Philadelphia. These bearing trees are often isolated, and show the two sexes on the same tree. In these examples, at least, the gingko is polygamous, not diœcious, and the genus is not therefore an exception in this respect to *Coniferæ* in general. The yellowish pulp which covers the nut has the odor of rancid butter. It is said to possess considerable astringency. There seem to be no trustworthy records as to the value of the timber. The tree is, however, of immensely rapid growth, and if cheap methods of propagating it were at hand it might become an important tree in American forestry. Even in France, where trees usually grow in a less ratio, a tree planted at Montpelier, in 1788, had reached 52 feet in 1835. Near Philadelphia, the writer has noted 3 feet as a common growth in one year, and a few cases of 5 feet have come under his observation.

In classification the native name "Gingko," as given by Kaempfer, was adopted as the botanical name by Linnæus; but Sir J. E. Smith, in a paper published in the Linnæan Society's *Transactions* for 1796, rejected the name as "barbarous;" and as Mr. R. A. Salisbury, an active member of the Linnæan Society, had recently taken the ground that all names ought to be descriptive, concluded to charge the name from *Gingko biloba* to *Salisburia adiantifolia*, the leaves being merely split down the middle and not bilobed in the strict botanical sense of the word. But these reasons for changing names are not regarded as legitimate by modern botanists, and under the law of priority *Gingko biloba* prevails. Its place in systematic botany is among the Taxineous section of *Coniferæ*, and near the genus *Taxus*, which includes the common yew. In the yew the upper portion of the pedicle enlarges and makes a coral-like cup around the seed. In *Gingko* the seed is wholly enveloped by the orange-colored fleshy covering. The flowers appear in the spring with the leaves, or slightly in advance of them, the male-flowers in narrow catkins, between one and two inches in length, the female in pairs on short peduncles.

It is quite probable that but for the cultivation given it by the people of China and Japan it would have wholly disappeared. A large number of species are found in a fossil condition in the Miocene period, and this one alone is left to modern times, with no very close relation to existing genera. (T. M.)

GINSENG, the root of certain species of *Panax*, largely used in China as a medicine. An American species (*Panax quinquefolium*) now furnishes much of the supply of this article. Its root has been exported to China since colonial times, the export, of late years, being from about 400,000 to 500,000 lbs. yearly. The plant is a perennial herb, found in shady mountain woods from Canada to Carolina. It bears compound leaves of five leaflets, and yellowish-green or white flowers, in a many-flowered umbel. The fruit is a two-celled succulent drupe, of a shining crimson when mature. The root, which is imagined to bear some resemblance to the human form, is slightly stimulant and rather pleasantly aromatic. Its medicinal virtues are very slight, and it is seldom or never prescribed by American physicians. Yet it is highly esteemed in China and Tartary, and enters into nearly every medicine there used. The Chinese consider their native drug the best; Corean ranks second, then American, and last Japanese. In the *U. S. Consular Reports* for October, 1884, a full account of the trade may be found.

GIRARD COLLEGE.—Stephen Girard, a wealthy merchant of Philadelphia, born at Bordeaux, May 20, 1750, died Dec. 26, 1831, having by his will and codicil left his large estate to the city of Philadelphia in trust for the foundation of a college for poor white male orphans. The executors had so far succeeded in the settlement of the estate that early in 1833 they were able to turn over to the city councils sufficient funds to enable them to carry out his intention. Accordingly, on Feb. 11, 1833, the councils elected a board of directors, consisting of 18 prominent citizens, Nicholas Biddle being chairman, to superintend the organization and management of the college in conformity with his will. The councils also, on March 21, appointed a sub-committee of their body, to be called the "building committee," who with eight members of the board of directors and an architect were instructed to prepare a plan for the college buildings. Mr. Thomas U. Walter, the architect employed (who is still living), prepared the plan in accordance with directions laid down in the will of Mr. Girard. This design, substantially the present edifice, was approved by councils on April 29; the excavations for the foundation were begun on May 6, and the corner-stone was laid on July 4, 1833.

(See Vol. X. p. 554 Am. ed. (p. 631 Edin. ed.).)

The college is erected on high ground in the northwestern part of the city of Philadelphia. A tract of 45 acres is devoted to the purpose of the college and is surrounded by a wall 10 feet high, built of gneiss rock, capped with marble slabs. The college building and three out-buildings were completed on the 13th of November, 1847, at a cost of $1,953,821.78, and transferred by the "building committee" to the board of directors. On Dec. 15, 1847, Hon. Joel Jones was elected president. On Jan. 1, 1848, the college was formally opened, with appropriate ceremonies, with a class of 100 orphan boys. There were admitted on Oct. 1 of the same year 100 additional boys, and on April 1, 1849, another class of 100 boys. Since that time, as the income would permit, other buildings have been erected, and additional boys admitted, till there were in January, 1890, within the walls of the college, enjoying the advantages it affords, 1378 boys.

The buildings now number eleven, exclusive of the college building. These are used as dormitories, residences, an infirmary, a chapel, an engine-house, and a mechanical department.

The Pupils.—An orphan is defined by the law of Pennsylvania to be a "fatherless child." The applicant for admission must be a "poor white male orphan," who is above the age of six and under ten years, and who is destitute of means, and without relatives able to maintain and educate him. By the will of Mr. Girard preference is given as follows: 1. To children born in the city of Philadelphia. 2. To those born in the State of Pennsylvania. 3. To those born in the city of New York. 4. To those born in the city of New Orleans. On entering, the orphans are indentured to the college. They are boarded and educated in the college, and are clothed in the prevailing style at the time, each boy, in the spring and fall, being measured for his suit. No distinctive dress is permitted.

The annual cost of maintaining, clothing, and educating each pupil, including current repairs to buildings and furniture and care of grounds, is about $312.

The officers of the college are a president and a vice-president. The officers of instruction consist of 4 professors and 42 teachers. There are 12 prefects and 14 governesses. These officers prevent disorder, and are at hand to attend to any boy who may be taken sick during the night.

The daily routine of duty is as follows:

6 A. M.	Arise	12.30 P.M. to 1	Dinner.
6.30	Breakfast.	1 to 2	Play-ground.
7 to 7.30	Play-ground.	2 to 4	School.
7.30 to 8	Section-room.	4 to 4.15	Evening chapel.
8	Morning chapel.	4.15 to 6	Play-ground.
8.15 to 10	School.	6 to 6.30	Supper.
10 to 10.15	Recess.	6.30 to 7	Play-ground.
10.15 to 12	School.	7 to 8.30	Study hour.
12 to 12.30	Play-ground.	8.45	Retire.

Schools.—The schools are divided into four grades. In the primary children begin with the alphabet. The boys are taught all the branches of a sound English education. In the fourth school the studies correspond to those of high schools. Boys are promoted by merit from one grade to a higher, twice in each year, at the end of the school term.

The department of natural history is liberally supplied with stuffed birds and animals, a cabinet of minerals and fossils, diagrams and models for teaching zoölogy and physiology. The department of chemistry and physics is amply supplied with apparatus for experiments and illustrations. In connection with this department is a technical school, in which about 300 of the older pupils receive instruction. This department of instruction was begun in April, 1882. The experiment was so satisfactory that the board of directors decided to erect a building in which it could be properly carried out. This building was completed in 1884. It was supplied with steam and equipped with the necessary tools and machinery at a cost of about $93,000. Since then a forge has been added, and accommodations for casting materials desired for use in this department. Mechanical drawing is taught here also. The pupil is taught to make a drawing for his proposed casting. In the wood-working department he is taught to make a model. He is then taught moulding, casting, chipping, filing, and scraping. The accommodations are sufficient to make a casting of 500 pounds weight. The boys have made several small engines in this department. In the wood-working department boys are taught to plane, saw, mitre, dovetail, and to make patterns. The pupils attend this department, on an average, 6 hours per week.

There is a battalion of 4 companies, consisting of about 200 of the larger and older boys of the college, and officered by them. They are under a competent instructor, who conducts a drill 4 afternoons in the week after 4 P. M., and a battalion drill every Friday afternoon from May 20 to Nov. 1, except during the months of July and August. A band of 25 pieces, and a drum-corps of 12, composed of the pupils, also have their instructor. Boys of the 3 lower schools receive instruction in vocal music every afternoon in the week except Saturday.

Care-taking.—A resident physician has charge of the infirmary. The death-rate from sickness amounts to about 4 in 1000. When a boy is seriously ill his mother or guardian is notified of it and they are allowed to visit him freely. A dentist is employed one day in each week to attend to the teeth of the boys.

A steward has charge of the purchase of food, clothing, and other necessities; also of the laborers employed in the care of the grounds and buildings. The matron, who has two assistants, has charge of the house-keeping, household supplies, ordering of meals, care of servants, and the multitude of things that usually fall upon a house-keeper. The architect employed is a graduate of the college. A gardener has charge of the trees, ornamentation of the grounds in summer, and of the green-house.

There is a shoe-room, in which some of the pupils are employed and in which the shoes of the boys are soled and mended. Some shoes are made in this department. There is a bakery, in which all the bread used on the premises is baked; a steam-laundry, where the clothes are washed and mangled. The buildings are heated by steam which is conveyed in pipes from the engine-room through a large underground tunnel, and the heat comes from the cellars to the different rooms by means of registers.

As directed by the will of Mr. Girard the food is plain, well cooked, and nutritious. It is served in two large dining-rooms—the one for the younger pupils seating about 350, that for the older boys about 800. Grace is said by an officer before each meal. The meals are inspected daily by the president and vice-president. There is a lavatory in each dormitory. A pool in the cellar serves for the use of the boys for bathing during the winter and cool months. A large pool is located in one corner of the grounds in a depressed place sheltered from observation outside and inside of the enclosure, where the boys bathe and swim during the warm months. Every boy is taught to swim. Amusements are furnished at intervals during the winter months. Lantern-slide exhibitions, legerdemain, singing and oratorical exercises are selected with a view to amuse and entertain all the boys, the small as well as the large ones. They are held in the chapel building, the only assembly-room provided for all occasions. On Sundays the boys are assembled in their section-rooms at 9 A. M. and 2 P. M. for religious reading and instruction. They are taught the Lord's Prayer, the Ten Commandments, and passages of Scripture. At 10.30 A. M. and 3 P. M. they assemble in chapel for religious services, which are conducted by the president or a layman selected by him, or by the vice-president. The exercises consist of reading from the manual prepared by a committee of the board of directors, prayer, singing of hymns, reading of the Scriptures, and an address of a non-sectarian character.

Regulations.—The following extract from Mr. Girard's will is noteworthy:

"I enjoin and require that no ecclesiastic, missionary, or minister of any sect whatever shall ever hold or exercise any station or duty whatever in the said college; nor shall any such person ever be admitted for any purpose or as a visitor within the premises appropriated to the purposes of the said college. My desire is, that all the instructors and teachers in the college shall take pains to instil into the minds of the scholars the purest principles of morality, so that, on their entrance into active life, they may from inclination and habit evince benevolence toward their fellow-creatures, and a love of truth, sobriety, and industry, adopting at the same time such religious tenets as their matured reason may enable them to prefer."

By a law of the college boys are permitted to visit their homes in the city on a day set apart for this purpose once in three months. This day is known as the "third Wednesday holiday." The mothers and guardians are permitted to visit their boys in the college one half-day once in three months. This occurs on a Tuesday afternoon, and the schools are closed for this purpose. This is known as "mothers' day." Boys earning the privilege by good behavior are permitted to visit their homes on Saturday afternoons, there being no school on that day after 10 A. M. They are also permitted to go home on legal holidays.

Stephen Girard's birthday, May 20, is appropriately celebrated on the college grounds. The exercises are participated in by the board of directors and invited guests, the officers and teachers, the alumni of the college, and the pupils. There is a collation at 1 P. M. in the main dining-room, followed by a few short addresses. The alumni celebrate the day with appropriate exercises in the chapel, and the day concludes with a battalion drill of the pupils, which is witnessed by from three to four thousand people.

Schools close July 3 and open again on Sept. 5. In the interval one-half of the teachers and household officers take a vacation of one month, when they return and permit the other portion who have been on duty with the boys during the time to take their vacation. Boys are not required to study during this period. They spend their mornings till 10 A. M. on the playground, and then assemble in chapel for morning prayer, after which they go to their school-rooms and remain till 12. They assemble again at 2 P. M. and remain till 4 P. M., when they go to evening prayer.

A boy whose parent or guardian applies for and agrees to take him out of the city is granted two weeks' leave of absence from July 29. There is usually an annual picnic one day in the month of July, when the boys spend the day on the Wissahickon, a beautiful stream, about 4 miles from the college. There is also an excursion-day in August to the seaside for a day's sport.

A well-selected library of upwards of 9000 volumes has been collected at the college. Upon the tables are to be found nearly all the prominent magazines and reviews published in the United States and in England. The library is opened on Monday and Thursday afternoons after school hours, and on Saturday morning for the use of the officers and older pupils.

The discipline of the college is almost entirely administered through admonition and deprivation of privileges: in extreme cases corporal punishment may be inflicted by order of the president and in his presence. For continued misconduct, a pupil becoming an unfit companion for others, the right to dismiss him summarily is vested in the board of directors by the will of Mr. Girard.

Boys are discharged by binding them out to trades or other occupations or by cancelling their indentures. By the will of Mr. Girard they are to be bound out between the ages of 14 and 18 years. When a boy finally leaves the college he receives an outfit of clothing of the value of $50. An officer is employed to find employment for the boys, to attend to their proper indenture, and to see that they are fairly treated in their positions. The total number of persons employed in the household on Jan. 31, 1886, was 234.

The Girard Estates.—The real estate by which this magnificent charity is supported is located in the city of Philadelphia, Schuylkill and Columbia counties. The total value of the residuary fund, Sept. 30, 1889, is stated in the report of a legislative committee at $14,150,000. The gross revenue for the year was $950,602. The total payment for the college, $941,728. The real estate in Philadelphia includes banking houses, dwellings, stores, wharves, and farms; in Schuylkill and Columbia counties there are also 20,000 acres, the remainder of the estate is in stocks and loans. Coal is mined from the Girard estate under leases of 15 years of the right to mine coal at a fixed rate per ton. The mining is done by the lessee and the royalty is paid the city of Philadelphia, trustee, at the end of each month. The quantity of coal mined from the Girard estate to the end of the year 1883 was 16,953,196 tons. The quantity of coal mined annually from this estate is now 1,500,000 gross tons. The gross revenue derived from the royalty on coal mined is $500,000 annually. One coal seam, the Mammoth vein, has a thickness of 50 feet. (See COAL in Vol. II.)

The board of directors of city trusts has charge of the estate. Twelve of them are appointed by the judges of the courts and serve without remuneration. The mayor of Philadelphia and the presidents of the city councils are also *ex-officio* members of the board.

Presidents.—Alexander Dallas Bache was elected first president of Girard College in July, 1836. Councils finding school could not be established till buildings were erected for the purpose repealed the ordinance which authorized his election. Hon. Joel Jones was elected president by the board of directors in December, 1847, and organized the schools in the college in January, 1848, but resigned June 1, 1849. In November, 1849, William H. Allen, LL. D., then professor of mental philosophy and English literature in Dickinson College, Pennsylvania, was elected president. He was installed Jan. 1, 1850, and remained at the head of the college till 1863, when he was succeeded by Richard Somers Smith, who was inaugurated president June 24, 1863. President Smith was succeeded by President Allen in September, 1867, who occupied the chair till his death occurred Aug. 29, 1882. Adam H. Fetterolf, Ph. D., who had been elected vice-president November, 1880, was elected president Dec. 27, 1882, and Henry D. Gregory, Ph. D., was elected vice-president Jan. 24, 1883. (E. C. H.)

GIRARDIN, EMILE DE (1806-1881), a French journalist, was born at Paris, June 22, 1806. He was the natural son of Count Alexandre de Girardin, and in his youth was known as Émile Delamothe. But in 1827 he claimed his father's name, and ten years later his father acknowledged his right. Educated at the College of Paris, he was employed at the king's court, and afterwards in a broker's office. He began his literary career with a romance, *Émile* (1827), founded on the circumstances of his birth and boyhood. He was afterwards made inspector of the fine arts, and employed his leisure as a journalist. In 1831 he started the monthly *Journal des connaissances utiles*, at four francs a year, which soon attained a circulation of 120,000 copies. Around this paper crystallized various schemes for social improvement, including a model farm, savings banks, and a long list of cheap publications. These professed to be issued by a national society for intellectual emancipation, and had a powerful effect in promoting public instruction. In 1836 Girardin founded the *Presse*, a daily paper, of conservative principles. Its low price brought on Girardin the ill-will of other journalists. His character and every incident of his public and private life were assailed. The fierce controversies of this time led to a duel with Armand Carrel, editor of the *National*, in which the latter was killed. Girardin, who had previously fought three duels, thenceforth refused all challenges. He steadily supported Louis Philippe, but on the establishment of the republic in 1848 he speedily adapted himself to the new order of things and was the first to propose Louis Napoleon for President. But the course of the latter disappointed Girardin, who had now become radical and socialistic. After the *coup d'état* of Dec. 2, 1851, the emperor ordered Girardin out of France, but soon permitted him to return. In 1856 Girardin sold his share of the *Presse* for 800,000 francs, but its prosperity declined until he was recalled to the chief editorship, Dec. 1, 1862. He left it again in June, 1866, to found *La Liberté*. He pursued an independent political course, and gathered around him young and enterprising writers. For his fierce attacks on the administration he was fined and the public sale of the paper was prohibited, yet in the last year of the empire he supported the declaration of war against Prussia. When the Germans came to Paris *La Presse* was removed to the country. During the communist insurrection Girardin published a pamphlet advocating a federal government for France. In 1873 he purchased *Le Petit Journal*, and in 1874 became also chief editor of *La France*. In May, 1877, the ministry of the Duc de Broglie gave him new opportunities to display his ability as a polemical journalist. With his pen he was the champion of the people against the reactionary administration as Gambetta was with his voice. Though recognizing journalism as his proper field, Girardin was at times a member of the Chamber of Deputies. He died at Paris, April 27, 1881. In June, 1831, he had married Delphine Gay (1804-1855), whose writings, in prose and verse, helped to make his name famous. (See GIRARDIN, DELPHINE GAY, in ENCYCLOPÆDIA BRITANNICA.) In October, 1856, he married Guillemette Josephine, Countess Tieffenbach, widow of Prince Frederick of Nassau, but was divorced from her in April, 1872. Girardin from 1834 to 1879 poured forth a stream of pamphlets on political and social questions. Many of his contributions to the *Presse* were collected in twelve volumes, under the title *Questions de mon temps* (1858), and to these he added in later years under various names.

GLACIER. In many mountain districts, notably in the Alps, the accumulation of snow, which gathers on the mountain tops during the winter, and which the heat of summer fails to melt, gives rise to certain interesting phenomena, known as glacial. The snow, increasing in depth, and compacted by pressure, is slowly pushed down to lower levels, gradually changing into ice as it moves onward. It continues to descend, flowing through the mountain valleys like a river of ice, until its further descent is checked by the action of the solar heat, which melts it below to an extent equivalent to its additions above. Such an ice stream is known as a glacier. The causes and peculiarities of its motion present some interesting and puzzling problems, which for many years past have been diligently studied by ardent investigators, the easily accessible glaciers of the Alps presenting a very favorable field for such study. Many theories as to the cause of glacial motion have been advanced, none of which have been accepted as fully satisfactory. The effects of pressure, of gravity, of viscous yielding, of regelation, etc., have been offered in explanation, but none of the causes adduced seems singly sufficient for the observed effects. The probability is that all these influences combine, and that the final result is an aggregate product of several causes.

(See Vol. X. p. 538 Am. ed. (p. 626 Edin. ed.)

A glacier, as seen from above, presents the aspect of a river of ice, filling the mountain valley through which it descends, and conforming to its curves. Its surface becomes more or less cracked and fissured, some of these fissures extending through its whole thickness, and affording a channel for the downflow of water produced by surface melting. A row of stones marks each side of the ice stream, being the droppings and rendings from the sides of its rocky channel. Other rows of stones are seen towards the centre, in cases where two or more glaciers have combined into a single final one, these stone lines marking the limits of the several components. Other stones, sometimes of considerable size, are borne along by the bottom of the ice flow, scratching, polishing, and channelling the rocky bed as they move irresistibly onward, while the abraded materials are ground into pebbles, sand, and impalpable mud. This material is borne onward both by the glacier itself and by the stream of water which flows beneath the outcome of the surface meltings.

The final result of all this is visible at the front of the glacier. What there appears is a rude heap of stones, the accumulation of years, surmounted by rent and dirty ice, steep of face, and deeply furrowed by gullies. If large, a stream of water will issue from beneath it. If the moraine, or stone heap, is cut through, the ice front presents a cavernous, arched opening, from which the steam flows. The water issuing from this cavern is full of sediment, the sands and mud brought downward from above. The lake or river into which this glacial stream flows is often discolored for miles by the accumulation of sediment.

In the temperate regions of Europe and America the glacial stream never reaches the sea, the solar heat being always sufficient to check it at a higher level. In Greenland the contrary is the case. In South Greenland the line of the glacial foot is several hundred feet above sea-level, but farther north it extends to the shore, and pushes out over the sea bottom. In this region immense glaciers exist, no longer conforming to the lines of valleys, but deep enough to cover all the inequalities of the surface. The great Humboldt glacier is said to have an ocean front of 50 miles. As the ice is pushed out into deeper water it is subjected to a lifting action, which breaks off huge masses known as icebergs. The Greenland glaciers advance very slowly, yet their progress is from 100 to 300 feet annually, and the berg ice thus broken off and set afloat may amount to 100 square miles each year.

Glaciers occur abundantly on all the continents except Africa and Australia. In the Alps there are said to be over 1000, of which about 100 are of the "first order" of De Saussure. In Asia the Himalayas bear the largest glaciers known outside the polar regions. Some are said to be between 30 and 40 miles in length. Few exist in Northern Asia, this being a region of moderate precipitation. In America they are found throughout great part of the mountain barrier of the west. In the extreme south of South America the glacier ice extends from the Andes into the fiords of the west coast, and is broken off and floats away as bergs. Northward the Andean glaciers decrease in size, and they vanish near the equator. In Mexico some small ones exist. In the Western United States the most southerly glaciers are those of Mt. Shasta in California, of which the largest is 4½ miles long. Larger ones occur on the Cascade range of Oregon and Washington, one upon Mt. Rainer being described as 4 or 5 miles wide and 10 miles long. In British America the glacial ice reaches the sea-level at Mt. St. Elias. In Alaska glaciers exist of great length and width, pushing out into the ocean bays. Elsewhere in North America the conditions of snowfall and elevation are not favorable to their formation.

The Glacial Period.—The glaciers which now exist are but the remnants of enormous ones which appa-

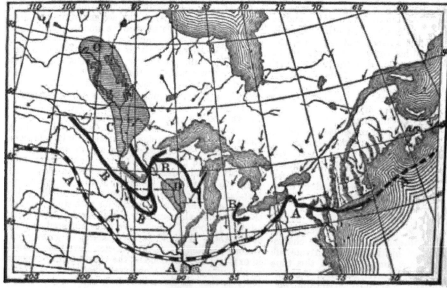

The Glaciated Area of North America.
From Surveys for *Studies in Science and Religion.*

AA. Boundary of glaciated area (the broken line not definitely surveyed).

BB. Special glacial accumulations.

CC. Boundary of Lake Agassiz, once formed by an ice dam.

D. Driftless region.

Arrows show direction of glacial scratches.

rently existed in a late geological era, and which covered Northern Europe and America with vast sheets of ice. It is true that no absolutely positive proofs of such a condition exist, but the evidences in its favor are so numerous, and so inexplicable under any other theory, that no doubt of the former existence of such continental glaciers is now entertained. That of Europe extended south from Scandinavia over Northern Germany and a great part of the British Islands, while the Alps sent out their ice rivers many miles in advance of their present limits. In America the ice-sheet was of enormous proportions. Whether it descended from Greenland, or from the central region of British America, is still a debated question, but its lower limit is somewhat clearly marked out by the line of the moraine which it left behind it. This lower limit extends along the Atlantic coast to Long Island and Perth-Amboy, N. J. Throughout this region the great glacier probably extended into the ocean, and gave rise to bergs. The limiting line extends through New Jersey in a north-westerly direction, and enters Pennsylvania south of the Water Gap. It passes through this State in a somewhat devious course, and leaves it at a point north of Pittsburg. Thence it passes through Ohio, touching the river east of Cincinnati, and extending, for a few miles, into Kentucky. From this point it passes onward through Middle Indiana and Illinois, and the States farther west as far as Dakota. Beyond this point the moraine disappears, and it is probable that in the drier region to the west the glacier-forming conditions were wanting. The movement of this great glacier was not due south. Its direction was south-east over the Atlantic slope. Farther west it was southward and south-westward. Its lines of motion converge northward toward a region north-west of Montreal, which formed its more immediate centre of motion. This immense Atlantic glacier was paralleled by two narrower western ones, which respectively descended along the Pacific coast region, and along the higher ridges of the Rocky Mountains, the latter probably extending very far south.

The thickness of the Atlantic glacier was in due proportion to its extent. It seems to have pushed southward with little conformity to the valley lines, as if every outline of elevation was buried beneath its enormous depth. Indications of its presence are found 5500 feet high on the White Mountains, nearly 3000 feet high in Southern Massachusetts and the Catskill region, and 1000 feet high in Southern Connecticut. These indicate the lowest limit of its depth, which was probably considerably greater, and can scarcely have been less than 6000 or 6500 feet in Upper New England.

The arguments for the former existence of this extraordinary state of affairs are numerous. Throughout the region mentioned the conditions produced by modern glaciers are found to exist on an enormous scale. The whole surface of North America, from the Arctic shores to the latitude of from 40 to 38° south, has been scraped, furrowed, and scoured by ice action. The "barren grounds" bordering on the Polar Seas, as described by Dr. Richardson and others, present "round-backed ridges," "very obtuse conical hillocks," "land-locked sheets of water," furrows and scratchings on the harder rocks, all well-known glacial indications. In Labrador and throughout Canada similar conditions are common. The profusion of lakes spread over the whole drainage area of the St. Lawrence, Hudson's Bay, and the Arctic Ocean, as well as in the Northern United States, leads to the same conclusion. They must owe their existence in great part to ice excavation, for they either rest in rock-bound hollows, or are dammed back by irregular ridges of glacial deposits. The polishing, scratching, and furrowing of the rocks, which exist throughout the region named, wherever the rocks are hard enough to resist weathering, is a condition which can be explained on no other hypothesis than the glacial. These scratchings are often found in closely crowded parallel lines, though grooves of a good yard in depth and several feet wide are sometimes found. The conditions are such as would naturally be produced by an ice plane of enormous weight, a mile or more in thickness, with numerous sharp stones frozen into its bottom and pushed onward with irresistible force over the rocks and earth beneath. Wherever the rocks were soft, or were jointed and fissile, they were broken into fragments and swept forward, thus forming or deepening valleys and lake bottoms. The lines of scratches observed pursue a nearly regular

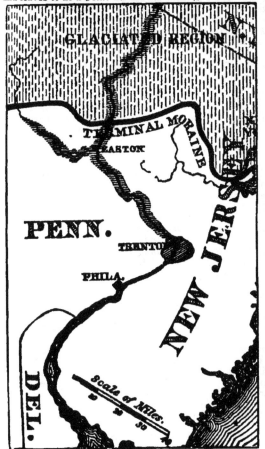

Glaciated Region of Pennsylvania and New Jersey.

course over high and low lands alike, without regard to valley slopes, except in the case of the great valleys of the country, thus proving that no mountain range was sufficiently high to seriously distort the course of the ice-flow. It may here be said that glacial scratches are also found on the boulders by which the scratching is supposed to have been performed. The rocks below reacted upon the rocks above.

An equally significant indication of glacial action is found in certain abundant deposits throughout this region. The lowest of these deposits is the "unstratified boulder clay." This "drift" or "till" is a heterogeneous mixture of gravel, sand, and clay, with subangular stones of all sizes mixed irregularly through it. It is strewed alike over hill and dale to a depth of 30 to 300 feet, its greatest depth being in the valleys. The lowest part is often a stiff clay, enclosing stones, and resting generally on the polished and striated rocks, though in some places it overlies beds of sand and gravel. Over wide regions of the "Barren Grounds" and Labrador this deposit seems entirely absent, or occasionally occupies hollows in small patches. It is plentiful in most of the glaciated Northern States. This result is in accordance with the theory, since, if this material arose from the grinding of the rocks to the north, it would necessarily be deposited in greatest quantities in the more southerly regions. South of the terminal limit of the glacier drift is also found, extending farthest south in the river valleys, and in the Mississippi Valley reaching almost to the Gulf. But this drift, consisting of sand, clay, pebbles, and cobble-stones, is stratified, and is ascribed to water action subsequent to the glacial epoch.

The withdrawal of the ice-sheet was marked by the stranding of the huge blocks of stone, which had been frozen into or borne on the surface of the ice, and by the accumulation of moraine rubbish and diluvial sand and gravel. Numerous mounds of sand and gravel thus formed occur throughout the Northern States, composing hills and ridges of every shape. The ridges are sometimes straight for considerable distances, but are commonly tortuous, while the hills are rounded and even conical, closely resembling what are known as *Kames* in Scotland. Immense multitudes of large erratic boulders cumber the surface in many parts of the Northern States, Canada, and Labrador, and are scattered over the tops and slopes of the mounds and ridges. Similar conditions exist as far north as the Barren Grounds of the Arctic slope. Some of these stones are of immense size, and they may be found from the dimensions of a pebble to blocks of over 40 feet long and 20 feet wide and high. They have been transported usually from 16 to 40 miles, though in some cases more than 200 miles, as learned from research into their localities of origin. The material referred to has been transported not only over the solid surface, but even over the great lakes and Long Island Sound, the land to the south of these being covered with stones from the north.

With the gradual cessation of the intense cold to which this remarkable glacial condition was due, the glacier began a slow retreat, dropping its accumulated foreign materials as it did so. But the retreat seems to have been by no means regular, and to have been attended by occasional protrusions of a more local character. As a consequence new sets of glacial striæ were made in favorable localities, differing in direction from the primary set.

Traces of great local glaciers exist in various localities, as in the valleys of the White Mountains, and those of the Rockies and the Sierra Nevada. Terminal moraines mark the site of these local glaciers, which disappeared as the cold decreased. One of these in the Sierra Nevada filled the Yosemite Valley, and passed down Merced Cañon. Others extended into the basin of Lake Tahoe.

The great glacier here indicated, improbable as its existence may seem, has a partial parallel in the ice-sheet which now covers Greenland. This great island, 1200 miles long and 400 to 500 wide, is covered to a depth of 3000 feet with ice, forming a not inapt parallel to the ancient glacier described. The existence of such a glacier, however, requires conditions of refrigeration of which we have no experience, and whose cause is not of easy discovery. Many theories as to the origin of such an era of intense cold have been promulgated, such as the translation of the solar system into colder regions of space, the change in position of the earth's axis, the redistribution of land and sea, the elevation and depression of the land, the change of land relations in the tropical and frigid zones, etc. None of these are accepted as satisfactory, and the solution now most generally adopted is an astronomical one offered by Mr. Croll. He ascribes the phenomenon to the variation in eccentricity of the earth's orbit, and the cyclical change through which the earth is now nearest to, now farthest from, the sun in winter. This cycle is 21,000 years in length. The most important of these causes is that which produces variation in the eccentricity of the orbit. Within the last three million years three such eras of high ellipticity have occurred, the latest of which began about 240,000 and ended about 80,000 years ago. This, in his theory, was the period of the last great glacial epoch, similar epochs having possibly preceded it. The arguments by which this theory is sustained are too many and lengthy to be here presented, and we can only say that there is a general disposition among geologists to accept it.

The glacial phenomena here considered have produced great changes in the superficial conditions of North America. And these changes are by no means confined to the region actually covered by the glacier. The melting of such a vast body of ice necessarily gave rise to extensive floods, breaking through the terminal moraine in many places, and transporting the glacial mud and sand far to the south. These floods also had much to do with the formation of the *Kames*, or hills and ridges of sand and gravel described. As a general result the surface of the country has been extensively modified, numerous small lakes formed; vast patches of boulders, sand, and gravel deposited; the surface to the north swept of materials to be transported farther south, and great diversities of soil and conditions of fertility from those formerly existing established. Similar results are apparent in Northern Europe, and in other regions where great ancient glaciers existed; but the consideration of the American continental glacier will serve as a fair exemplification of the general results of this powerful geological agency. (C. M.)

GLADSTONE, WILLIAM EWART, the greatest English statesman of the nineteenth century, was born Dec. 29, 1809, in Seaforth House in a suburb of Liverpool. He is of purely Scottish descent. His father, John Gladstone, had begun business in Glasgow, but removed to Liverpool and acquired wealth in the West India trade. He then entered Parliament as a representative of Liverpool, and in 1846 was made a baronet. William, the fourth son, was educated at Eton, and afterwards at Christ Church College, Oxford. At both he gave abundant proof of extraordinary intellectual and oratorical powers and established a high reputation for purity of character. On graduating in 1831 he took the first honors in both classics and mathematics, and became a fellow of All Souls'. He then spent six months in Italy, and in December, 1832, was elected to Parliament from Newark, a borough in the patronage of the Duke of Newcastle. The election address which he issued at this time (Oct. 9, 1832) is a noteworthy document. In it he declares his conviction "that we must watch and resist that uninquiring and undiscriminating desire for change among us, which threatens to produce along with its partial good a melancholy preponderance of evil." Being a devoted follower of Sir Robert Peel, in 1834 he was made a junior lord of the treasury, and in the next year under secretary for colonial affairs, only a few weeks before that ministry was driven from power. In opposition Gladstone displayed the same brilliancy which had been shown at his entrance to Parliament. But he was also inclined to literature, and became a frequent contributor to the *Quarterly Review*, chiefly on literary and ecclesiastical topics. His views at this time are set forth in his work on *The State in Relation to the Church* (1839), which gave Macaulay the opportunity for his famous critique in the *Edinburgh Review*, whose opening sentence runs: "The author of this work is a young man of unblemished character and of distinguished parliamentary talents, the rising hope of the stern and unbending Tories." In 1876 Mr. Gladstone contributed to the *Quarterly Review* an article on Lord Macaulay, a magnanimous return for this criticism of his youthful performance.

In 1841 the Tories came into power, and "handsome Gladstone," as he was called, was appointed vice-president of the board of trade and master of the mint and sworn of the privy council. The revision of the British tariff in 1842 is ascribed to him, and shows his tendency even then towards free trade, which, indeed, he has said he learned first from Canning, his father's friend. In May, 1843, he became president of the board of trade, but two years later he retired from office, when the government took up the measure for the increase of the grant to Maynooth College. But when a new cabinet was formed Mr. Gladstone accepted the position of secretary of the colonies. When the crisis came, and Sir Robert Peel, yielding to the pressure against which he had long struggled, fully accepted the policy of free trade, Gladstone, who was still more profoundly a convert to the new views, felt compelled to resign his seat since his patron, the Duke of Newcastle, remained steadfast in the traditions of the Tory party. This proof of Gladstone's extreme conscientiousness was a matter of amazement to the politicians of the time. Before he re-entered Parliament the battle had been fought and won for free trade—won so decisively that free trade has since been a cardinal principle of every administration.

The interval from the beginning of 1846 to the summer of 1847 is the only break in Mr. Gladstone's parliamentary career. The elections of the latter year gave the University of Oxford an opportunity to choose as her representative the son who had already done her so much honor. He was still a typical High Churchman, yet there were not wanting indications that his mind was moving with the current of the age, and was learning to set a higher value on the principles of human liberty. Although a few years before he had opposed the removal of the civil disabilities of the Jews, he now spoke in favor of admitting them to Parliament. Again, in 1851, he was one of the small band that protested against the futile attempt to prevent the formal institution of a Roman Catholic hierarchy in Great Britain. Personally he is still a devout High Churchman; but he has long recognized the political wisdom, justice, and necessity of according to all citizens the largest measure of religious liberty.

It was Lord Palmerston's effort, by a brilliant foreign policy, to divert attention from troublesome domestic questions. This led him in 1850 to defend the rash British admiral who had blockaded the Piræus and bullied the insecure government of Greece in behalf of a scarcely naturalized British subject. In these Don Pacifico debates he triumphantly declared that he had vindicated for Englishmen abroad the privilege implied in the old Roman boast, *Civis Romanus sum*. Gladstone in reply sought boldly to wrest this very weapon from the veteran's hand and to turn it against him by denouncing in the name of humanity the claim for Englishmen of the exceptional privileges of a conquering race. Palmerston, indeed, won a momentary victory, but the lasting honor of the debate rests with Gladstone. Thenceforth he has been the champion of the application of the fundamental principles of Christianity to all national questions.

Later in the same year he again visited Italy, and while sojourning at Naples became aware of the oppressive cruelty of the government of Francis II. On his return to England he exposed the merciless tyranny of the Bourbon rule. His pamphlet on this subject was widely circulated on the continent and excited an active controversy. Lord Palmerston in Parliament complimented Gladstone on his generous work and sent copies of the pamphlet to all the courts of Europe. Garibaldi declared it to have been "the first trumpet call of Italian liberty."

The death of Sir Robert Peel in 1850 had dissolved the bond which united those members of the Conservative party who had fully gone with him in accepting free trade. Gladstone still remained unattached to either party when, in 1852, Disraeli as chancellor of the exchequer presented his first budget. Disraeli had first established his position as a parliamentary orator by his fierce invectives on Sir Robert Peel, his former leader. Gladstone, faithful to that statesman's memory, now took keen delight in exposing his rival's financial crudities. The memorable debate of that occasion was the opening of the marvellous duel of twenty-five years, which ended only when Disraeli passed into the house of peers. In the first onset Disraeli was defeated and the ministry resigned. Lord Aberdeen, in forming the new cabinet known as the "Coalition Ministry," made Gladstone chancellor of the exchequer, and on April 18, 1853, the latter delivered his first budget speech. Its luminous exposition of finance has been matched only by his subsequent efforts in the same field. Finding himself with a liberal surplus he largely reduced or even totally abolished the duties on hundreds of articles of daily use, and though he somewhat increased the income tax he depended rather on the "elasticity of revenue" to make good the deficiencies immediately accruing. His predictions were accepted with confidence and were abundantly justified by the result effected. Henceforth Gladstone's supremacy as a financier was undisputed, and his budget speeches were the great events of parliamentary sessions. The commercial prosperity of England advanced, to use his own phrase, "by leaps and bounds."

The Crimean war, into which the Aberdeen ministry reluctantly entered, absorbed all the surplus which had accumulated in the few years previous, and likewise the revenue from extra taxation, on which Mr. Gladstone had insisted when war was declared. He has been charged with inconsistency for actively supporting this war yet opposing Disraeli's moral support of Turkey in 1877. It is a sufficient reply to state that in the debate on the terms of the treaty of peace in 1856 he declared that he should condemn a peace which bound Great Britain to maintain the law and institutions of Turkey as a Mohammedan state.

Gladstone was fully committed to the principles of the Liberal party when in 1859 Lord Palmerston made him again chancellor of the exchequer. It was at this time that Mr. Cobden negotiated the famous Anglo-French commercial treaty, and the congenial task of its support in the House of Commons devolved on Mr. Gladstone.

At the outbreak of the civil war in America Mr. Gladstone shared the feeling common to many English statesmen, that the permanent separation of the Northern and Southern States was inevitable, and has been charged with desiring that result. This charge he answered in a letter addressed to Gen. R. E. Schenck, the U. S. minister to Great Britain, which was published in *Harper's Magazine* for November, 1876. On many occasions Mr. Gladstone has expressed a friendly interest in the welfare of the United States. But he has not, as some of the advanced Liberals have done, professed to regard the institutions of the American republic as models for the renovation of those of his own country. He sees without dismay the approaching enlargements of the British constitution, and even hails them with desire. But he seeks these changes only as the voice of the people demands them.

Parliamentary reform, inaugurated in 1832, again came to the front in 1866. It was perhaps unfortunate that the question was presented to a newly elected Parliament. Mr. Gladstone presented a moderate bill, yet he was charged by Mr. Disraeli with an attempt at "Americanizing our institutions." A few Liberals who took the opportunity to secede were wittily described by Mr. Bright as having retired to the Cave of Adullam. Yet their secession was enough to defeat the government, and the Liberals retired from power. The cause of the people could not be stayed, however, and by the time the next Parliament convened Mr. Disraeli had educated his party up to "taking a leap in the dark," and eventually passing a reform bill whose democratic tendency surpassed any proposed by the Liberals. Thus Disraeli "dished the Whigs."

The Conservative ministry formed in 1866 had the support of only a minority, and the genius of Disraeli was taxed to the utmost in maintaining it in equilibrium. The calling up of a truly national question was all that was needed to show its instability. Such a question lay easily at hand. The condition of Ireland was a chronic reproach and menace to England's prosperity. Among its anomalies that of the Established Church was the most flagrant. Mr. Gladstone had learned the practical inapplicability of his youthful arguments in its behalf, and in March, 1868, he struck the first blow for disestablishment. Justice to Ireland was his theme, as it was in many a subsequent struggle, until in 1886 he took the vast responsibility of proposing an Irish Parliament. Though Mr. Gladstone's resolutions in favor of disestablishment obtained large majorities, yet Disraeli tenaciously clung to office and finally dissolved Parliament in November. The most remarkable feature of the election which ensued was the defeat of Mr. Gladstone for South Lancashire. He had ceased to represent Oxford in 1865. But he was now returned for Greenwich, and the new Parliament showed a Liberal majority of 120. Disraeli forthwith resigned and Mr. Gladstone was called to form a new ministry. On March 1, 1869, he introduced his measure for the disestablishment of the Irish Church, unfolding in a speech which won the highest praise even from Disraeli the details of his comprehensive scheme. Earnestly, eloquently, and without hesitation he proceeded to the consummation of his arduous task, while the members were spellbound by his lucid statement and oratorical power. In spite of the utmost efforts of the Opposition, the majority for the government was 118. The passage of the bill, which was carried through the house in less than five months mainly by the unflinching energy of Mr. Gladstone, has been pronounced the most remarkable legislative achievement of modern times.

In this golden age of liberalism other measures of great importance were passed, the Elementary Education Act, the abolition of purchase in the army, the removal of the University tests, and the Trades Union bill. Reform seemed to reach in every direction, to strike at every abuse, social or political. Among the Liberals some differences came to light on foreign questions, on the Irish question, on the educational question. Gradually the Liberal majority fell off, until on the Irish University bill, by which Gladstone hoped to do a further act of justice, it was turned to a minority of three. Mr. Gladstone determined to appeal to the country, and Parliament was dissolved in January, 1874. The answer was decisive, and Disraeli came into power with a majority as strong as that of Gladstone six years before. The pendulum had swung back.

After forty-two years of public life, Gladstone resigned the leadership of his party. Cogent reasons were presented for this action; the Liberals admitted their force, while they deprecated the result. But it was impossible for him, as he had intended, to appear occasionally in Parliament without showing himself the true leader of his party. This interval of self-imposed semi-retirement was filled with new work, the most noted of which was his attack on the Vatican decrees as destructive to civil allegiance. The controversy which ensued involved the ablest representatives of the Roman Catholic communion.

Important as was this controversy its practical effects were less than those of his writings and speeches on the Bulgarian atrocities, which, indeed, involved the whole Eastern question. Disraeli had determined to give the Turkish government moral support against Russia, and during the war of 1877 he fully carried out this plan. A vigorous foreign policy was now the sheet anchor of the Tories as it had been that of the Whigs in Lord Palmerston's time. In Europe, in Asia, and Africa there were wars and rumors of wars in behalf of British interests. Mr. Gladstone entered upon a crusade in behalf of the rights of other nations, which was a concrete fulfilment of what had been an abstract promise in his arraignment of Lord Palmerston's policy. In 1879 Mr. Gladstone accepted the invitation of the Liberal electors of Mid-Lothian to stand as their candidate, though the district was a stronghold of Conservatism and his opponent the son of the Duke of Buccleugh. His aggressive campaign astonished the United Kingdom. Day after day he delivered speeches whose intellectual force was equalled only by the physical endurance of the speaker. A flood of liberalism swept over Scotland, and though Lord Beaconsfield still believed that his hold on England was unshaken, the result of the elections of 1880 proved that his rival's "exuberant verbosity," as he was pleased to term that resistless eloquence, had reached the popular heart and conscience. The Liberal majority in the new Parliament was 114, and the great commoner, to whom the political revolution was due, was justly called to be prime minister.

Unfortunately the outgoing ministry left him a burdensome legacy of war and foreign entanglements. In Afghanistan, in Egypt, in South Africa apparently inextricable confusion prevailed. In settling these troubles on an equitable basis blood was shed, money was sunk, warm friends were alienated, but the veteran "bated not a jot of heart or hope, but still bore up and steered right onward." The wild war-dance of frenzied nations, roused by the British drum, gradually subsided. From England now went forth messages of peace, of hope and sympathy to the down-trodden. But nearer home, in the sister isle of Ireland, there remained the most vexing trouble of all. There a people, wholly dependent upon agriculture, lay at the mercy of their landlords, who were to all intents foreigners. The Irish formed a Land League to obtain three F's—fair rent, fixity of tenure, and free sale. But bad harvests and the oppression of the landlords led to agrarian outrages. Gladstone at once brought forward measures for partial relief, while for repression of disorder a coercion bill was enacted. In 1881 the Irish Home-rulers under Parnell's leadership so obstructed parliamentary business as to compel the adoption of new rules in the House. Gladstone's land law now granted substantially the three F's, but the Home-rulers still demanded the legislative independence of Ireland. They obstructed the operation of the land law, and then for a time Parnell was imprisoned. A "No-Rent" manifesto was then issued, and when Parnell was liberated it was evident that Gladstone had come to an understanding with him. The Home-rulers showed by unmistakable signs that they represented the wishes of the Irish people.

Gladstone had, in 1883, given up the functions of the chancellor of the exchequer, but the government still in every crisis was obliged to depend on his rhetorical genius. But in 1885 the Home-rulers, whose numbers had steadily increased, suddenly combined with the Conservatives, and the Liberal ministry resigned. Such a coalition could not last, and in the next session of Parliament the Conservatives were easily defeated. In February, 1886, Mr. Gladstone became prime minister for the third time, and at once indicated his purpose to accept the course of events as decisive of the Irish question. His former policy of mingled concession and repression was to be laid aside, and the demand of the Irish people for the management of their own affairs was to be granted. The scheme which he proposed for the autonomy of Ireland in insular affairs was unfolded in a speech of marvellous power on April 8, 1886. What will be the decision of Parliament on this momentous question remains to be seen. The very proposal of such a plan is an event of extraordinary magnitude, and may fitly close our brief and imperfect outline of Mr. Gladstone's political career.

At every stage of this career and in every department of statesmanship Mr. Gladstone has given evidence of the highest genius. His return to the leadership of his party after his resolve to retire was a necessity which was recognized by all. Without him the party was unable to satisfy its adherents and to formulate its own principles in practical shape. With him again at its head it was triumphant at the polls and aggressive in Parliament. However great have been the labors of others in an age of unprecedented political activity, yet for more than a generation every important measure in British legislation has been framed on the lines which he had marked out. It is charged that he has not been equally fortunate in winning personal attachment, and has therefore sometimes failed as a mere party leader. Thoroughly in earnest in everything he undertakes, he has disdained to win the support of others on different ground than rational argument. But in every great historical crisis this sincerity and simplicity of purpose have given him the greatest advantage and have increased a hundred-fold the force of his words. His noble appeals to the national conscience have served to raise British legislation to a higher plane of Christian civilization.

What rank shall be assigned to Gladstone as an orator? The almost universal verdict of critics, indorsed by the unanimous popular judgment, places him foremost in nearly every department of eloquence. In some kinds of oratory, that of invective for instance, which his great Tory rival cultivated, Gladstone has rarely indulged, though his refraining may be due to moral rather than to intellectual reasons. Mr. John Bright is the only member of Parliament whose speeches have at times reached such a height of eloquence as to justify a claim to equal rank as an orator. Some critics have compared Bright to Demosthenes and assigned to Gladstone the place of Cicero. While their respective manner of speech furnishes some foundation for such a parallel, it cannot be seriously maintained. The superiority of Gladstone's genius is shown not only in his wider sweep of wing but in his attaining a loftier height. His parliamentary speeches, while preserving the classic traditions of the House of Commons, have been practically effective in winning votes as well as drawing crowds. Before popular assemblages he has always appeared to great advantage. The triumphs of his Mid-Lothian campaign have been unparalleled in English history.

Among the statesmen who have won fame in literature Mr. Gladstone holds a foremost place. His larger literary works have been devoted to Homer, whose poems have furnished him lifelong enjoyment. His *Studies on Homer and the Homeric Age* (3 vols., 1858) show him stanchly conservative in scholarship, yet an able and profound critic. His *Juventus Mundi* (1869) is a popular presentation of the conclusions reached in the former work, and his *Homeric Synchronism* (1876) is an attempt to fix the time and place of Homer and of the events which he recites. Interesting as these treatises are, Mr. Gladstone's briefer articles in various periodicals and on various themes are still more attractive. Many of the most valuable have been collected in his *Gleanings of Past Years* (8 vols., 1879), and his later occasional writings show no diminution of merit or power.

Within our narrow limits it has been impossible to

give an adequate sketch of the life and works of this scholar, orator, and statesman. His words and deeds will ever form an imperishable monument of British greatness. (J. P. L.)

GLASS, a compound of silica with soda or potash, with the addition of an alkaline earth, such as lime or oxide of lead. This compound forms a brittle, transparent substance, unaffected by water or the ordinary solvents, and of the highest value in the arts, since it is employed in an immense variety of industrial and artistic purposes. Its superiority over other transparents consists in its fusibility at a high temperature, and its softness at a red heat, which permit its ready moulding into any desired shape. Its fusibility also enables it to accept many shades of color, which can be added without detriment to its transparency; while, though very hard, it can be readily cut with the diamond, through which its susceptibility to artistic treatment is greatly enhanced.

See Vol. X. p. 576 Am. ed. (p. 647 Edin. ed.).

Glass, as manufactured for various purposes, varies so greatly in composition that it is impossible to give any exact formula of its constituents. Chemically it is a silicate of lime and soda or potash, though the proportions of these elements are so varied that no definite chemical compound can be made out. The silica, for instance, may vary from 50 to 75 per cent., the lime from 5 to 20. Plate-glass contains both soda and potash, while other varieties have but one of these constituents. In lead flint-glass the lime is replaced by a large proportion of oxide of lead, while the common green bottle-glass contains, in addition to these substances, a proportion of alumina and oxide of iron. These latter are impurities in the sand, the greenish hue being due to the iron. The transparency of glass would be gained by the use of silica and soda or potash alone, but the lime or lead are necessary, as making it more resistant to the action of solvents.

It is our purpose here to confine ourselves mainly to the subject of glass as an American industry, and not to enter upon the extensive subject of its history and the details of its various processes of manufacture. In regard to the various ingredients which enter into the composition of glass America stands on a level with other countries, and has a decided advantage in one respect, that of the superior quality of its sand, the source of the silica of glass. This, the basic element of glass, is obtained in some countries from quartz or flint, but only where good sand cannot be procured, the use of the latter being almost universal. The purity and fine quality of American sand is everywhere conceded, and gives to our finer grades of glass a transparency that has excited admiration abroad. The glass made from Berkshire sand was much admired at the London exhibition of 1851, while at the Paris exhibition of 1867 some American flint-glass "surpassed in purity of color all other specimens of glass, whether British or foreign." England, in fact, possesses very little sand suitable for the better grades of glass, and French and German sand is imported for this purpose. Nowhere in Europe, however, is there any parallel to the almost inexhaustible deposits of pure sands in America, suitable for the finest glass. The most important localities now worked are those of Berkshire, Mass.; Juniata co., Pa.; Hancock co., W. Va.; Fox River, Ill.; and Crystal City, Mo.; but there exist immense beds of good sand elsewhere.

Soda of English manufacture enters into the composition of nearly all glass now made. It is extracted from sulphate and carbonate of soda, and is now becoming an article of manufacture in this country, being prepared from common salt. Much of the potash used is extracted from wood-ashes. America has served as an important source of this material, and great tracts of timber have been burnt, in the past history of the country, for the ashes alone. Canada and Russia are now the main source of this material, though potash is supplied to some extent from other sources than wood-ashes. Another important element in the manufacture of glass is pot-clay, which comprises certain very pure and refractory varieties of fire-clay, from which the melting-pots are made. At present the largest proportion of pot-clay is brought from Germany, but American clay is fast superseding it. There are large deposits of excellent pot-clay in many localities of the United States, that now used coming chiefly from Western Pennsylvania, New Jersey, and Missouri. It is purer and more refractory than the German clay, but not so dense. It is also less costly, and will probably in time completely supersede the German.

We can give but brief attention to the history of glass manufacture in the United States. It was tried as an industry in the early period of most of the original colonies, but very little information concerning these attempts is extant. The first known effort at glass-making in this country was in 1608, in the colony of Virginia. In that year eight Poles and Germans were brought to Virginia with intent to make "pitch, tar, glass, mills, and soap-ashes." Some glass was made, and sent aboard on the return of the vessel in 1608 or 1609. Probably this was bottle-glass only, the window-glass needed being imported. In 1621 a subscription was opened in London, for funds to erect a glass-house in Virginia to make glass-beads for the Indian trade. Some Italian workmen were sent over, but we know very little concerning their operations. Nothing further is known of glass-making in Virginia until 1787, in which year glass was exported to the amount of 10,000 lbs., and 500 hands employed. But the industry has been firmly established in that State only since 1815.

In Massachusetts a glass-house was erected in Salem, in 1639. Several slight mentions of similar enterprises occur between that date and 1787, in which year a large glass-house was erected in Boston, where work commenced in 1792. Since then glass-making has been more or less continuous, though the once foremost rank of this State has been lost through a deficiency of fuel. It yet yields, however, some of the best quality of glass made in America. In New York we hear of glass-making early in the history of the city. Of the recorded works there was one built before 1664, one in 1754 which proved unsuccessful, and one in 1786, since which the industry has been continuous. In New Jersey a German established a glass-house in Salem county between 1760 and 1765. This enterprise failed at the beginning of the Revolution, and the workmen removed in 1775 to the place now known as Glassboro. In this locality glass has been made since then without cessation, the Whitney works being the oldest continuous works in the country. In Pennsylvania a letter from Penn of the date of 1683 speaks of the existence of a glass-house in the colony. We know nothing further concerning it. The next mention is of a glass-house built by Baron Steigel in Lancaster, in 1762. In 1771 or 1772 there was one erected in Philadelphia. The Pittsburg glass industry began in

1797, coal being here probably first used as a fuel. There seems to have been little success in these efforts, and it was not until about 1830 that the industry became a flourishing one. In 1831 the Dyottsville factory, then the most extensive in the country, had 4 furnaces, melted about 8000 lbs. of batch daily, and produced about 1200 tons of glass yearly, mainly in bottles and vials. Yet the main seat of the industry in Pennsylvania has moved westward. In 1837 there were 13 factories in Pittsburg, yielding $700,000 in product; in 1857, 33 factories, with a yield of $2,631,990; and 45 factories in 1865, with a product valued at over $6,000,000.

We have not space to describe the progress of the industry in other States, and simply refer to one of its important branches, the manufacture of plate-glass. What was probably the first American attempt in this branch of the glass industry was made at Cheshire, Mass., in 1852-53. After six months' trial the works were removed to Brooklyn, where they ran through 1854 and 1855. Little merchantable glass was made, and the effort was abandoned in 1856. In the same year a second attempt was made at Lenox, Mass., only rough plate being made till 1865, when a polishing-machine invented for marble slabs proved admirably adapted to the polishing of glass. This machine is still in use in an improved shape. The western plate-glass manufacture began in New Albany, Ind., in 1869. The effort proved successful, and works have since been established at Louisville, Jeffersonville, Ind., and Crystal City, Mo., as also at Pittsburg, Pa. It is stated, however, that no plate-glass was made in the United States without loss before 1879.

Of special American contributions to the art of glass-making, far the most important has been the invention of the pressed-glass process, which has added enormously to the scope of the art. Pressed-glass had undoubtedly been made before the invention of the American lever-press, though what is now known as pressed-glass is of unquestionable American origin, despite an English claim to the invention some eight years later in date than the American. It is stated that a carpenter of the town of Sandwich, Mass., in 1827, desiring an article of glassware for some purpose, was informed at the glass-works that such an article could not be made. He asked if a machine could not be made to press glass into any shape. The idea struck the proprietor, and he and the carpenter together fabricated a rude press, which proved successful. A glass tumbler, claimed to be the first article thus made, was shown at the Centennial Exhibition of 1876, where it was unluckily broken. From that time forward the manufacture of pressed-glass rapidly developed, until now the bulk of American glassware is made by this process. It has, in fact, markedly cheapened the manufacture of glass, revolutionized the whole system of flint-glass-making, and enabled manufacturers to offer for common use glassware of a grace of form and beauty of design which formerly only the most wealthy could enjoy.

The varieties of glass now manufactured in the United States may be epitomized as plate-glass, in the several conditions of rough, rolled, ribbed, and polished plate; window-glass; flint-glass, including table and other glassware, both blown and pressed, with a large class of bottles and vials; green-glass, a coarse greenish ware, chiefly used for common bottles, technically hollow-ware; and some other less important varieties, such as water-glass, iridescent-glass, etc.

The glass manufacture of the United States, according to the census of 1880, included 211 establishments with 348 furnaces, and employing 24,177 hands. The total capital was $19,844,699; wages, $9,144,100; value of material, $8,028,621; and value of product, $21,154,571, Pennsylvania being the greatest producer. Of the several varieties of American glass, the plate-glass product is given at 1,700,227 sq. ft., valued at $868,305; the window-glass at 1,864,734 boxes of 50 sq. ft. each, valued at $5,047,313. No estimate is given of the quantity of glassware and green-glass made, but the value of the former is stated at $9,568,520, and of the latter at $5,670,432. Progress since 1880 has been most declared in the plate-glass industry, there being in operation, at latest reports, 8 great works, capable of producing 9,000,000 to 10,000,000 sq. ft. yearly, while work was progressing on new plants, which would greatly increase the output. The industry has thus become one of great importance, and is steadily progressing in the value of its product and in the quality and artistic finish of its ware. (C. M.)

GLEIG, GEORGE ROBERT, a British clergyman and author, was born at Stirling, Scotland, April 20, 1796, being the son of Bishop George Gleig. He was educated at Glasgow and Balliot College, Oxford, received a military commission in 1813 and joined the Duke of Wellington's army in Spain. Serving afterwards in America, he was severely wounded at the capture of Washington in 1814. He then returned to Oxford, graduated and took orders. In 1822 he was made curate of Ash, and afterwards rector of Ivy Church. In 1844 he was appointed chaplain of Chelsea Hospital, and in 1846 chaplain-general of the forces. To carry out his scheme for the education of the soldiers, he was also made inspector-general of military schools. He resigned his office of chaplain general in 1875. His early adventures are recounted in his amusing book, *The Subaltern* (1825). He also wrote *Campaigns at Washington and New Orleans*, a *Family History of England*, and a *Military History of Great Britain*. His *Life of Warren Hastings* was severely criticised by Lord Macaulay for its bulk and general heaviness. His *Life of the Duke of Wellington* (1859) was an improvement on the other. Among his lighter works are *Chelsea Pensioners*, *Country Curate*, and *The Hussar*. From his contributions to the *Edinburgh* and *Quarterly* Reviews two volumes of *Essays* were collected (1858).

GLIDDON, GEORGE ROGERS (1809-1857), an American archæologist, was born in Devonshire, England, in 1809. At an early age he went to Egypt, where his father was a merchant and U. S. consul. He succeeded his father as consul at Cairo, and after spending altogether twenty-three years in Egypt came to the United States with a valuable collection of antiquities. He lectured in New York and other cities on Egypt. He afterwards became agent for the Honduras Inter-oceanic Railway Company, and died at Panama, Nov. 16, 1857. Besides other works he published *Ancient Egypt* (1850), *Types of Mankind* (1854), and *Indigenous Races of the Earth* (1857). Dr. J. C. Nott, of Mobile, assisted in the preparation of the last two, which by their flippant attacks upon the Bible evoked much hostile criticism.

GLOUCESTER, a city of Massachusetts, in Essex county, on the S. shore of the peninsula of Cape Ann, 30 miles N. N. E. of Boston, with which it is connected by a branch of the Eastern Railroad, and by steamboat lines. Its harbor is safe, capacious, and deep enough for all but the largest ships. Gloucester has a fine city-hall and other municipal buildings, a free public library, high and graded schools, several associations for the relief of the widows and orphans of seamen and fishermen, 3 national banks, a savings bank, 2 weekly newspapers, and 14 churches. It is the most important fishing-town in the United States, the cod and mackerel fisheries, with the associated industries, affording the chief business of the place. Its fishery fleet in 1884 was 289 vessels with crews of 3483 men. The total catch was 578,560 quintals of fish. There are within the city limits extensive quarries of granite, numerous establishments for utilizing the by-products of the fisheries, also anchor-works, and manufactures of railroad forgings. The city includes the outlying villages of East Gloucester, West Gloucester, Annisquam (on the north side of Cape Ann), Dogtown, Bay View (whence much granite is shipped), and Lanesville. Gloucester is a port of entry, and hundreds of schooners, mostly engaged in fishing and coasting, are here owned. Around Gloucester the country is high, rocky, and exposed to the ocean winds; it is, hence, a great summer resort, and within the city limits are many summer hotels. The property valuation is $11,203,457; the city debt, $148,000; the yearly expenses are $183,405. Gloucester was settled in 1633, was incorporated as a town and named Gloucester in 1642, was bombarded in 1775 by the British ship Falcon, and in 1814 by the frigate Tenedos. It was incorporated as a city in 1874. Population in 1860, 10,904; in 1880, 19,329; in 1890, 21,262.

GLOUCESTER CITY, a city of New Jersey, in Camden county, is on the east bank of the Delaware, opposite the southern end of Philadelphia, with which it has half-hourly communication by steamboat. It is connected with Camden, 4 miles north, by 2 railroads. It has a foundry and machine-shop and several cotton-factories, 6 churches, and 5 schools. It has water-works and is lighted with gas. Its property is valued at $1,770,000. It was settled about 1700, and incorporated as a city in 1868. Population, 6563.

GLOVERSVILLE, an incorporated village of New York, in Fulton county, 40 miles W. of Albany, is on a branch of the New York Central Railroad, being 7 miles from the main line. It has a town-hall, 4 hotels, 1 national bank, 3 weekly newspapers, and 5 churches. The industry of the town is entirely devoted to the dressing of leather and the manufacture of gloves. The streets are wide and lighted with gas. The property is valued at $3,000,000; the public debt is $92,500. The village was incopororated in 1873, and in 1880 had 7133 inhabitants; and in 1890, 7500.

GLUCOSE. Of recent manufactures in the United States none has sprung more rapidly into activity than that of "glucose," also known in its solid form as "starch sugar." Its production has now become an important American industry, though it is still regarded by many with a measure of distrust, as an unwholesome and impure article of diet. This prejudice, however, is ill-founded, as we shall seek to show further on. This sugar, though known as a constituent of grapes since 1792, was first made from starch by Kirchoff, a Russian chemist, in 1811. In 1819 Braconnet prepared it from wood fibre. It was prepared by boiling the starch or wood in dilute sulphuric acid. It was then believed to be identical with cane sugar, and came into use as an article of food during the English blockade of Continental ports in the Napoleonic wars. After this period its use declined, it being found that it differed from cane sugar, and was less sweet and soluble. Several attempts were made to introduce its manufacture into the United States, but with little success. Recently, syrups and molasses having become more scarce and dear through changes in the methods of sugar-making, the glucose industry has revived, and, aided by improved processes, its manufacture has assumed large proportions. The industry is generally associated with starch-making, the product being used as starch, or converted into glucose, in accordance with the demand of the market.

On Aug. 1, 1880, according to Prof. Wiley, there were 10 glucose-factories in the United States, consuming daily about 20,000 bushels of corn. The product in 1880, by the census report, was valued at $4,324,072, the capital invested being $3,916,750. Of the total product nearly one-half was credited to Pennsylvania. In the year 1885, by the estimate made by the American Glucose Company, of Buffalo, N. Y., there are 13 factories in operation, 5 of which are owned by this company. None of these are in Pennsylvania, they being all in the Western States, except one at Buffalo, and one at Glen Cove, L. I. The aggregate capacity of these works is about 50,000 bushels of corn per day, but the actual daily consumption is from 25,000 to 30,000 bushels, or from 7,500,000 to 10,500,000 bushels per annum. The estimated yield of glucose and starch sugar from this quantity of corn is from 225,000,000 to 315,000,000 pounds, worth from $5,125,000 to $7,875,000. The capital invested in this industry is about $7,500,000, and the annual wages paid nearly $1,000,000. It is claimed that the promotion of the glucose industry has been the main agent in reducing the price of cane sugar to consumers, and that it has thus been an important factor in giving the people cheap sugars.

Commercially the term "glucose" is confined to the thick syrup made from corn-starch, while the solid product from the same source is known as "grape" or "starch sugar." In its manufacture the corn is first soaked for two or three days in warm water, and is then ground on stones over which flows a stream of water. The material thus produced is next washed through a bolting cloth, and the starch separated by proper processes from the gluten. The starch is then beaten up with water until it becomes of a creamy consistency, and is conducted to the converting tubes, where it is treated with dilute sulphuric acid. During the process of conversion, which occupies about two hours, steam is allowed to bubble into the mixture. The acid is then neutralized by the use of marble dust and animal charcoal, and the liquid evaporated to the required concentration. There are other methods employed, but this is the most common.

The glucose thus produced is a thick, tenacious syrup, almost colorless, or of yellowish tinge, its specific gravity at 20° C. being 1.412. The degree of sweetness depends upon the extent of chemical change in the conversion of starch into sugar. If stopped as soon as the starch disappears the glucose has its maximum sweetness. As above mentioned grape sugar was made from wood fibre as early as 1819. Recently this material has been used to some extent in its manufacture, saw-dust and the wood clippings made in the wood-paper-factories being employed. The result is an inferior article of glucose, but not necessarily an unwholesome one.

In 1884 a committee of the National Academy of Sciences submitted a report on glucose, in response to a request made by the Commissioner of Internal Revence. Their report declared that the sweetening power of starch sugar was about two-thirds that of cane sugar. Many experiments were made as to its healthfulness, it being taken internally in its ordinary state, in extracts that retained every ingredient that could be objectionable, and in concentrated extracts from fermented glucose without the slightest deleterious effect. The committee concludes that the present processes by which sugar is made from maize "are unobjectionable in their character, and leave the product uncontaminated." "That the starch sugar thus made and sent into commerce is of exceptional purity and uniformity of composition, and contains no injurious substances." And "that, though having at best only about two-thirds the sweetening power of cane sugar, yet starch sugar is in no way inferior to cane sugar in healthfulness, there being no evidence before the committee that maize starch sugar, either in its normal condition or fermented, has any deleterious effect upon the system, even when taken in large quantities."

Glucose is used chiefly in the manufacture of table syrups and confectionery, in the brewing of ale and beer, and to some extent as food for bees and in the making of artificial honey. No reliable statistics can be had as to the quantity used in brewing, since brewers seek to conceal the fact of its employment. When it is fed to bees the honey yielded by the bees is almost pure glucose. In artificial honey-making the comb is made of paraffine and filled with pure glucose by machinery. For whiteness and beauty it rivals the best white-clover honey, and can be sold at less than half the price. Its one defect is that it is not honey. Glucose is very largely used in candy-making, and has greatly reduced the consumption of cane sugar in this industry, with considerable detriment to the sweetness, though not to the wholesomeness, of the product. For table syrup it is mixed with a small percentage of cane-sugar syrup. In the form of grape sugar it is used to adulterate table sugar. (C. M.)

GNEIST, RUDOLPH, a German jurist, was born at Berlin, Aug. 13, 1816. Educated at Eisleben he studied jurisprudence at Berlin, and in 1833 was made auscultator, in 1841 assessor before the Superior Court, and after journeys in Italy, France, and England in 1844 professor extraordinary. In 1850 he abandoned his judicial career and devoted himself to lecturing, writing, and parliamentary activity. His lectures on English nobility, knighthood, elections, and constitution attracted much attention. Since 1858 he has been a member of the Prussian Chamber of Deputies, acting with the moderate liberals. He advocated the adoption of many ideas taken from British usage, a greater amount of local self-government, attention to the welfare of the working classes, and reform of the judicial and penal systems. In the autumn of 1883 he visited the United States. Besides many smaller works his publications include *Syntagma Institutionum* (1858; 2d ed., 1880); *Das heutige englische Verwaltungsrecht* (1867; 3d ed., 1883); *Englische Verfassungsgeschichte* (1882).

GOAT, ANGORA. This goat (*Capra Angoriensis*), an entirely different species from the common goat, takes its name from the Province of Angora, in Asia Minor, its present most important habitat. It seems most probable the Angora was originally native in the mountains of Thibet. The locality in Asia Minor where the goat husbandry is most successful is from 2000 to 5000 feet above tide-water, with a very dry temperature, hot in summer and cold in winter, with deep snows, commencing from November on, and remaining until March or April, and then going off in a body. The best results in the health and products of the goats are obtained in these elevated districts among the Taurus Mountains. The absence of much humidity in all seasons is an important factor in giving to the fleeces strength, length, fineness, and lustre, and in preventing the shedding or falling off of the hair until the approach of warm weather, when it is natural for the goat to throw off his fleece like an overcoat. The food of the goat in its native ranges, and on which it seems most to thrive, in flesh and fleece, is the bunch-grass and scrub-oak and pines of the region during the summer, and this material is gathered and stored for winter use. The hair of the Angora in its best condition is white, from four to twelve inches long, strong, fine, and lustrous as silk, with an average yield of five pounds to the animal. The average cost of maintenance is about one-half that of sheep, while it is less subject to disease and more hardy every way than that animal. The Angora is tractable, intelligent, easily handled, and can be herded in large flocks with little care and much profit. Yet it is undoubtedly true of the Angora-goat husbandry, as of that of other animals, that intelligent care and seasonable and varied food is an important factor in the attainment of the best and most profitable results. In its purity the fleece of the Angora is white, hanging in wavy or corkscrew ringlets, covering the short and harsh hair of the skin. The flesh, by the testimony of all familiar with its use, is not in any sense inferior to the best mutton. The cross with the Maltese goat has shown remarkable milking qualities.

One of the most remarkable and valuable traits of the Angora is the facility with which the young of the cross, between the thoroughbred Angora male and the female of the common goat, assumes all the marked characteristics of the former. Intelligently bred, good results are obtained at the third cross, and perfection at the fifth and sixth crosses. It is indispensable, however, that thoroughbred Angora bucks be invariably and always used for propagation, as the use of even the highest grade sire gives uncertain results and tends rapidly to a reversion to the common stock.

Mohair, the name by which the fleece of the Angora is known in commerce, is adapted for certain defined uses in the arts, as distinct as silk, wool, or cotton. It has the appearance of silk without its suppleness. It does not felt like wool, is dyed with great facility, taking with equal readiness all colors, and in all the fabrics made from it retaining its fibres distinctly separated. Its qualities of lustre and elasticity with its great durability eminently fit it for the manufacture of braids, hat-bands, bindings, and plushes—especially in the latter for cane-seats and general furniture use. In the works of Bradford and Saltaire in England, and the mills of Lyons and other localities of France, it is very successfully woven with silk, woollen, and cotton, making a distinct and most beautiful class of fabrics. One of the latest of its uses is in the manufacture of imitation furs, in squirrel, seal-skin, etc. It is difficult at a little distance to distinguish the mohair fabric from these materials, while in wearing qualities the product of the Angora fleece is not inferior, and in cost much less. The Angora skin, with the hair on, takes any dye, retaining the lustre, and makes an elegant rug or robe. Tanned, it is the famous

Turkey Morocco of commerce, though in the more extended uses of modern times superseded by the skin of the common goat. The Angora goat is among the most valuable of lanigerous animals. It is not strange, therefore, that the governments of England, France, Germany, and other European nations have expended much labor and money in the effort to plant and foster the husbandry in their various localities during the past century. None of these attempts have in any large sense proved successful, and they have, one after another, been abandoned. The lack of success is attributed by the agricultural authorities of these countries to extreme humidity in England, and lack of range, suitable feed, and intelligent supervision in the other countries. In a limited way the industry has been planted in Australia and the United States within the past thirty years. In the former, largely under the supervision of Sir Samuel Wilson, now the owner of the manor of Hughenden, England, and the residence of the late Earl of Beaconsfield. In the United States, from the first and until now, the industry has thrived under the care and on the lands of Col. Richard Peters, of Atlanta, Ga., who still owns much the largest flock of thoroughbred bucks and ewes in the country. Smaller pure-blood flocks, and larger ones of graded animals, may be found in Kentucky, Tennessee, Texas, California, and some of the Territories west. Renewed attention is now called to the subject by the publication, by Hon. John L. Hayes, secretary of the National Association of Wool Manufacturers, of an elaborate, scientific, and practical treatise upon the *Angora Goat and the Mohair Industry*.

This husbandry has been transplanted and is at present most successful at Cape Colony, South Africa, 600 thoroughbred bucks and ewes having been imported from Asia Minor. In 1865 the mohair product was 6000 pounds of a fair quality. In 1882 the yield of the district was over 3,000,000 pounds, and much of it of a quality that rates as high as the best of Asia Minor. Success there is due to a location in the high table-lands very similar in all respects to those in Angora, with a like climate, to the carefully selected importations, and intelligent supervision in breeding and rearing flocks. Of course such a product could be only from graded flocks. But the sires were and are always thoroughbred, and the grades have been skilfully bred up and maintained by constant selection and the weeding out of inferior animals. As the cost on the average in the Angora flocks is not over two-thirds that for maintenance of a like number of any breed of sheep, while the returns in sales on the mohair of the high grades is fully up to that from the best grades of combing wools, it will be seen the balance is largely in favor of the Angora-goat husbandry.

In the United States there are millions of acres of cheap and unoccupied lands as favorable in soil and location as any in Asia or Africa for this industry. They can be as profitably utilized as that of Cape Colony for an equally well-conducted industry. It becomes, therefore, an important question in the future economy of the country what improvement is made of these industrial resources. Three firms in the country have proved by actual use in their manufactures the superiority of American-grown mohair, and have issued public notice they will take and pay good prices for all the mohair from the first cross to thoroughbred product that can be raised in the country for years to come. We have seen, also, from the hands of an American tanner and dyer, as good results in leather and in the skins cleansed and dyed for rugs and robes as we have ever met in fabrics from the artisans of Turkey or France. One of the uses to which the selected and best products of the Angora flocks in Asia Minor are applied is, as a substitute among the artisans of Persia and India, and also those of France, for silk, in various dress-fabrics, velvets, etc. By its use there is no depreciation in fineness, lustre, or strength in the mingled silk and mohair fabric; but there is a great economy, as standard thoroughbred mohair of the requisite quality can be had, and pay the shepherd richly for his investment, at one-third to one-half the cost of silk that would be required for the same purpose were the whole fabric made of that material. (C. W. J.)

GOBAT, SAMUEL (1799–1879), Anglican bishop of Jerusalem, was born at Cremine, Switzerland, Jan. 26, 1799. In 1821 he entered the Mission House at Basle, and after studying Arabic and Æthiopic in Paris, he entered the service of the Church Missionary Society and was sent to Abyssinia, but on account of wars in that country he spent three years in Cairo. Reaching his field of labor in 1830, he gained the confidence of some princes, who gladly received from him an Amharic translation of the Gospels. Returning to Europe on renewal of the war, he gave the first accurate account of the Æthiopic churches. A second missionary journey, undertaken in 1835, was ineffectual because of his severe illness. In 1839 he became principal of the Missionary College at Malta, where he translated the Bible into Oriental languages. In 1846, in pursuance of an agreement between the governments of England and Prussia, the missionary bishopric of Jerusalem was created, and Dr. Gobat, who was nominated by the king of Prussia to be the first bishop, was consecrated at London, July 5, 1846, and in the following December proceeded to Jerusalem. He took general superintendence of the interests of Protestantism in Palestine and founded schools in connection with many congregations. Though he was personally respected for piety and zeal, the movement was ineffectual in promoting union among the various Christian bodies represented in Palestine. He died at Jerusalem, May 12, 1879.

GOBINEAU, JOSEPH ARTHUR, COMTE DE, a French diplomatist and author, was born at Bordeaux in 1816. At an early age he was employed in the office of foreign affairs and became secretary of legation at Berne in 1851. He was sent as ambassador to Persia in 1861, to Greece in 1864, to Brazil in 1869, to Sweden in 1872, and in 1877, at his own request, was permitted to retire. He was active in anthropological, philosophic, and literary pursuits and used his opportunities in various countries to further his studies. His works comprise *Essai sur l'inégalité des races humaines* (4 vols., 1853–55); *Trois ans en Asie* (1859); *Les Religions et les philosophes dans l'Asie centrale* (1865); *Histoire des Perses* (1869); *Souvenirs de voyage* (1872); *La Renaissance* (1877). Besides other poems he published *Les Cousins d'Isis* (1844), an epic poem, *Amadis* (1876), and a historical novel, translated into English by Dr. C. D. Meigs, *Typhaines Abbey* (1867).

GODFREY, THOMAS (1704–1749), an American inventor, was born near Philadelphia in 1704. He was by trade a glazier, and, being greatly devoted to mathematics, studied Latin that he might read important treatises. In 1730 he communicated to James Logan, secretary of Pennsylvania, the improvements he had made in Davis' quadrant. Logan sent an account of the invention to Edmund Hadley, of London, but, no answer being received, Peter Collinson laid a statement of Godfrey's invention before the Royal Society in 1732. In the meantime Hadley had presented a paper describing a similar improvement as made by himself. The society, upon investigation, decided that both were entitled to the honor, and a reward of £200 was bestowed upon Godfrey. Godfrey was a member of Dr. Franklin's "Junto." He died in Philadelphia in 1749 and was buried on his farm near Germantown, but in 1838 J. F. Watson, the Philadelphia antiquarian, caused his remains to be removed to Laurel Hill Cemetery.

GODKIN, EUGENE LAWRENCE, an American journalist, was born at Moyne, county Wicklow, Ireland, Oct. 2, 1831. He graduated at Queen's College, Belfast, in 1851, and became connected with the London press. During the Crimean war he was correspondent of the London *Daily News*, and at its close came to the United States, and made a journey on horseback through the Southern States, which he described in the same paper. Settling in New York, he was admitted to the bar there in 1858, but continued to contribute to the press. In 1865 he was made editor of the *Nation*, a weekly literary and political paper, of which he was afterwards also proprietor. In 1879 this journal was combined with the New York *Evening Post*, Mr. Godkin retaining a prominent place in its management. He has been in the main a supporter of the Republican party, though criticising severely its leaders and measures. In recent years the movements for civil service reform and of revenue reform have chiefly engaged his attention.

GODMAN, JOHN D. (1794–1830), an American physician and naturalist, was born at Annapolis, Md., Dec. 30, 1794. Left an orphan at an early age, he was apprenticed to a printer, but afterwards studied medicine, and obtained his degree at the University of Maryland in 1818. He practised at New Holland, Pa., Baltimore, and Philadelphia. For a short time in 1821 he was at Cincinnati as professor in the Ohio Medical College. He returned to Philadelphia in 1822, and, amid the requirements of an extensive practice, found time for literary pursuits. In 1826 he was made professor of anatomy in Rutgers Medical College, New York, but his course was interrupted by illness, and he removed to Germantown, Pa., where he died, April 17, 1830. He published *Natural History of American Quadrupeds* (3 vols., 1826); *Rambles of a Naturalist*, and several anatomical treatises.

GODON, SYLVANUS W., an American admiral, was born in Pennsylvania, June 18, 1809. He entered the navy as midshipman, March 1, 1819, and became lieutenant Dec. 17, 1836. He was attached to the bomb-brig Vesuvius in the siege of Vera Cruz, in 1847, and to the steamer Susquehanna in the East Indian squadron, in 1851–53. He commanded the sloop-of-war Powhatan in Commodore Dupont's expedition to Port Royal, S. C., in 1861, and was made captain in July, 1862, and commodore in January, 1863. He commanded a division of Commodore Porter's fleet at Fort Fisher, in December, 1864. After the war he commanded the South American squadron on the coast of Brazil, 1866–67, and had charge of the New York navy yard for two years. He retired from service June 18, 1871.

GODWIN, PARKE, an American journalist and author, was born at Paterson, N. J., Feb. 25, 1816. His father was an officer in the war of 1812, and his grandfather a soldier in the Revolution. Parke graduated at Princeton College in 1834, studied law, and was admitted to the bar in Kentucky. From 1837 to 1853, with the exception of one year, he assisted his father-in-law, W. C. Bryant, in editing the New York *Evening Post*. He was an early advocate of free trade and of the socialist doctrines of Charles Fourier. In 1845 he was appointed a deputy collector in the New York custom-house. In the *Democratic Review* he advocated many reforms, which were afterwards embodied in the constitution and code of New York. In 1853 he was one of the editors of *Putnam's Monthly*, and from his contributions to both series of this magazine (1853–57, and 1867–70) two volumes have been gathered: *Political Essays* (1856), and *Out of the Past* (1870). In 1860 appeared the first volume of his *History of France*, treating of ancient Gaul, down to the reign of Charlemagne. He also published a *Hand-book of Universal Biography* (1851), afterwards enlarged into a *Cyclopædia of Biography* (1865). After 1865 Mr. Godwin was again associated with Bryant in editing the *Evening Post*, until 1873. He has published an excellent *Biography of William Cullen Bryant* (1883).

GOFFE, WILLIAM (c. 1605–1679), an English regicide, was born about 1605, being the son of a Puritan clergyman. He became one of Cromwell's major-generals, and was one of the judges who signed the death-warrant of King Charles I. Before the restoration of Charles II. he came to America with his father-in-law, Gen. Edward Whalley, arriving at Boston in the summer of 1660. They were received courteously by Gov. Endicott, and resided for a time at Cambridge, Mass. But when the king issued a proclamation, offering a liberal reward for their arrest, and officers were sent from England after them, the regicides went to New Haven, where they were favored by Rev. John Davenport, though often compelled to hide in mills and among the rocks. The "Regicides' Cave" is still pointed out near New Haven. In October, 1664, they went to Hadley, Mass., where they lived at the house of Rev. Mr. Russell for many years in seclusion. In 1675 the citizens were called forth from the meeting-house to resist an attack of Indians. Suddenly Goffe put himself at the head of the citizens who were standing irresolute, and led them to victory. But when he disappeared as quickly as he had come, the astonished inhabitants believed that an angel had come to their deliverance.

GOLD, a chemical element belonging to the class of metals, from the remainder of which it is distinguished by its bright yellow color and its unequalled ductility and malleability. Its softness is nearly equal to that of lead. It is soluble to some extent in acids, but is highly resistant to oxidation. Its specific gravity is very high, being about 19, its atomic weight a little over 196, and its melting-point between 1200° and 1400° C., according to different estimates. This metal has been always held in the highest estimation by mankind, from its beauty of color and lustre, its resistance to oxidation, the facility with which it can be wrought into artistic shapes, and its scarcity, which has brought it into use, from an early period, as a medium of exchange. Among the oldest relics of semi-civilized man in Europe articles of gold are prominent, and they were then apparently held in as

See Vol. X. p. 759 Am. ed. (p. 740 Edin. ed.).

high esteem as now. When America was discovered its civilized nations were found to set a like value on gold, and to the present day its costliness and beauty restrict its use to purposes of coinage and ornament, and to the highest class of articles of utility.

Gold, as found in its native state, exists as small grains, spangles, minute crystals, hair-like fibres, and dendritic incrustations. In placer deposits the particles are more or less rounded by friction, and occasionally lumps or nuggets occur, varying from a few ounces to considerably over 100 lbs. weight. According to the opinion of Dr. Genth, these lumps were formed by the gradual aggregation of grains in drift waters. Gold is usually found in the older metamorphic and slaty rocks, mainly in steatitic, talcose or chloritic slates and shales, and in granite or greenstone rocks, ranging from the earliest geological period down to the secondary age. The California gold-bearing shales are among the more recent, being of Jura-Triassic age. It is disseminated finely and sparsely throughout the substance of these rocks in very many regions of the earth, but is found more abundantly in quartz-beds and veins which penetrate them. It is most abundant where iron pyrites, titaniferous iron, or other iron ores prevail, and seems to exist in all sulphurets, but most fully in sulphuret of iron, or iron pyrites. It is never found in solid veins, but usually associated with other metals and minerals, in infiltrated or erupted veins which traverse the fissures of the slates. The grains of gold are often imbedded in masses of quartz, and are usually alloyed with a little silver, which diminishes the value from 15 to 20 per cent. The grains in the Virginia and North Carolina mines are often so small as to be invisible to a strong lens, even when present to the extent of $3 or $4 per bushel of ore.

These facts have led to a theory as to the original mode of deposition of gold, which is of interest, and may be briefly stated. The waters of the ocean now contain gold in very small quantity. How and when they obtained it, we are, of course, unaware, but it is not improbable that this ocean gold may be the main source of the existing rock deposits. The slates which contain it were originally deposited as mud on the ancient sea-bottoms, and it is supposed that this settling mud carried down small quantities of gold, then more abundant in sea-water than now. After the upheaval of the slates, and the various influences to which they were subjected, much of their contained gold was dissolved, and accumulated with silica and metallic sulphides in the fissures of the slates, as the now existing veins. It is quite probable, also, that more or less of this fissure gold came directly from the original source of the ocean gold, the primordial rocks. Here it may have been liquefied, or even vaporized, by the intense heat there prevailing, and driven upwards together with the other contents of the veins, like volcanic lava.

Subsequently to the formation of the veins, the sulphurets, which principally carried the gold, were dissolved by atmospheric action, and left the gold in a still more available form along the backs of the veins. Still later came the action of rains, glaciers, river-water, and other denuding agencies, carrying away the materials of the veins, and depositing the gold in the gravel-beds of ancient and recent streams. Through the gravel it made its way, by its superior weight, to the bottom, where it gained its greatest concentration. This final process took place in the Quaternary era, just before and after man's advent upon the earth. It formed the placer deposits, the source of all the gold known to man until some forty or fifty years ago, when quartz-mining first began. The gold which now exists in sea-water is estimated, from experiments made by Soustadt, at about one grain to the ton. This would make a dollar's worth of gold in twenty-five tons of sea-water. Yet, according to the calculation of Prof. Wurtz, all the gold yet extracted from the earth, which, at the date of his calculation, was estimated at about $2,000,000,000, would give only one dollar for 280,000,000 tons of sea-water. The quantity of gold in existence, therefore, is immensely greater than that possessed by man, and the amount disseminated through the rocks is probably very great. Yet it is only available for mining where accumulated in fissure veins, or washed out into placer deposits. In these veins, whose main mineral is quartz, the gold is almost always associated with pyrites, which usually form from one to three per cent. of the substance of the vein. Of pyrites, the sulphuret of iron is most common, though copper, lead, and arsenical pyrites are common. Above the subterranean water-level the pyrites have largely disappeared, being decomposed by air which penetrates the rocks. This decomposition usually extends to a depth of thirty to sixty feet. The veins to this depth are more easily worked, and the gold, which has been set free, more readily obtained. All such veins, however, do not contain gold, nor possess it in equal quantities. Miners often abandon a lode when they have penetrated to the level of the undecomposed rock, knowing from experience the much greater difficulties of working this hard material.

Gold has been, from a very remote period, extracted by washing or otherwise from the sands and gravels of river-beds, where its yellow, glistening lustre must have early attracted the attention of man. There is scarcely a region of the earth in which it is not found, its wide-spread dissemination through the slates being strong evidence in favor of the theory of its extraction from the ocean waters. There is hardly a country in Europe in which it does not exist in workable quantities; it is found in many Asiatic regions, and it has long been an article of export from Africa. It occurs abundantly in Australia, and is found very widely throughout both North and South America. Whether any very rich deposits, similar to those of California and Australia, will again be discovered, is very doubtful. Yet it is by no means impossible. Gold was sought in California for two or three centuries before the great discovery was made, and there are many localities of the earth which have not yet been "prospected." In addition to the two localities above named, the Siberian slope of the Ural Mountains of Russia is the most prolific locality. Here, several attempts have been made at vein-mining, but they have been abandoned for placer-mining, which yet prevails. The most prolific year was 1847, when 75,000 pounds of gold were obtained.

The earliest known gold deposits of the United States were those found on the slopes of the Appalachian mountain system, at various points, from Nova Scotia to Georgia. Gold-washing seems to have been carried on in very early times by the southern Indians, since an ancient Indian mining village, built on the gold-gravels, and with relics of rude mining-tools, has been found nine feet beneath the surface in Nacooche Valley, Georgia. Gold is also found in strata similar to the Nova Scotian on the northern shore of Lake Superior It has long been mined in the Appalachian region, particularly in Nova Scotia, Virginia, North Carolina, and Georgia. About the beginning of this century, the famous Cabarrus nugget, of 28 pounds' weight, was found at the Reed mine, North Carolina. But the greatest gold excitement in the South followed the discoveries in Georgia, from 1828 to 1830. The maximum product was obtained from 1828 to 1845, probably not more than $600,000 being mined in any one year. Since that period the output has declined, the product of the eastern division in 1880, from Maine to Georgia, being $239,640, of which $200,000 came from Georgia and North Carolina.

The Spaniards, who held California from the sixteenth century, were always in search of the precious metals, yet were not successful in finding any of the important deposits of gold. Cortez knew of the existence of gold in Lower California, and sent an expedition there in 1537, which brought back a small quantity. Its existence in Upper California was discovered by Drake's expedition, in 1577–79, and is noticed in Hakluyt's account of that region. Other mentions of gold-findings were made from time to time, several of them in the first half of the present century. But the earliest discovery of importance was that made by Marshall, in January, 1848, when the first rush of water through Sutter's mill-race washed away the concealing dirt, and revealed the shining particles of gold in the gravels. The report of this discovery gave rise to the first of those mad rushes for wealth which marked the history of the Pacific region for many years afterwards. They had plentiful warrant, for a deposit of gold had been unearthed such as the world had never before known, and which has only been rivalled by the similar Australian discovery of 1851. Of the latter, we can but say here, that it has closely paralleled the California deposit in value, the average gold output of Australia falling but little short of that of the Western United States.

For several years the California mining was confined to washings of the sands and gravels of the surface placer deposits. But it was soon found that the gold beds were not confined to the gravels of recent streams, but also existed in more ancient gravels, in the channels of vanished streams, frequently covered with strata of lava or other material. The working of these deeper gravels necessitated hydraulic mining, which began in a small way in 1854, but did not become important till after the civil war. Vein-mining began in California about 1860. It has not yet become very important in that State, but has been greatly developed in Nevada, though here silver forms the chief volume of the product. The mines of the Comstock lode are worked at an average depth of 2000 feet, though some are nearly half a mile in depth. Gold seems to exist throughout the whole length of the coast-range, from Alaska to Mexico, and in other branches of the Rocky Mountains, and profitable mining has been done in every State from British Columbia southward, though the value of the product is everywhere declining. The largest annual product was that of 1853, amounting to about $65,000,000. The total gold product of the United States, from 1776 to 1847, is variously estimated at from fifteen to twenty millions of dollars. The total output to June 30, 1889, is estimated at $1,804,316,532. The decline in the value of gold obtained, however, steadily holds good, the product of 1877 being estimated at nearly $47,000,000; of 1880, at $36,000,000; of 1881, at $35,000,000; and of 1889. at $32,800,000. The product of the mines of the United States at present is about one-fourth that of the whole world, the Australian product being another fourth. In regard to the cost of producing this gold, various estimates have been advanced, some writers holding that every dollar gained has cost a dollar in labor or machinery. This, however, is somewhat extravagant, and a late writer puts the net profit of working the Pacific mines at $500,000,000. See METALS.   (C. M.)

GOLDEN-ROD is the popular name for the whole genus *Solidago*, which is among the best known of American genera. The genus is closely related to *Aster*, and is described as having either few or many flowers in a head, and the heads radiate, the rays rarely more than 16, and pistillate. The scales of the oblong involucre are oppressed, and, except in one instance, destitute of herbaceous tips so common in *Aster*. The receptacle is small and not chaffy. The achenia are many-ribbed, and nearly terete. The pappus simple, of equal capillary bristles.

The members of the whole order of *Compositæ*, to which this belongs, have so many points in common that it is very difficult to define the genus briefly. When the genus is once known, the species belonging to it are more readily recognized by their appearance than by any written generic character. These more popular features are thus described by Dr. Gray: "Perennial herbs, with mostly wand-like stems, and nearly sessile stem-leaves, never heart-shaped. Heads small, racemed or clustered; flowers of the disk and ray (except rarely) yellow."

There are over a hundred species, inhabiting chiefly the eastern portion of the American continent, extending from the Arctic regions to Mexico and Brasil. A few scattered species are found on the Pacific coast from Unalaska to Chili. One species, *Solidago Virga Aurea*, is found in many varying forms all over the north of Europe, North America, and Northern Asia. This species was famous during the Middle Ages for its supposed medical properties.

Though it has now no known use in the arts, it forms one of the most striking elements in the beautiful autumnal scenery of North America, and is constantly referred to by poets.   (T. M.)

GOLDSBOROUGH, LOUIS MALESHERBES (1805–1878), an American admiral, was born at Washington, D. C., Feb. 18, 1805. He was the son of Charles W. Goldsborough, who was governor of Maryland in 1818–19. Louis entered the navy as midshipman in 1821, became lieutenant in 1825, and in 1827 joined the North Carolina, which was cruising in the Mediterranean. Here, with 35 officers and men, he captured a pirate vessel, after killing 90 of her crew. In 1833 he conducted a colony of Germans to Florida to cultivate lands belonging to his father-in-law, William Wirt, and took part in the Seminole war. In September, 1841, he was promoted to be commander, and at the siege of Vera Cruz in 1847 he was second in command. After the Mexican war he was sent to explore California and Oregon, and was superintendent of the U. S. Naval Academy at Annapolis from 1853 to 1857. In August, 1861, he was flag-officer of the North Atlantic blockading squadron, and was associated with Gen. Burnside in the expedition to Roanoke Island. He dispersed the fleet which had been gathered by Commodore Lynch in Pamlico Sound. In 1862

Goldsborough was made rear-admiral, and after the war he commanded the European squadron. He died at Washington, Feb. 20, 1878.

GOLDSCHMIDT, JENNY, a Swedish vocalist, best known by her maiden name, JENNY LIND, was born at Stockholm, Oct. 6, 1821. She was the daughter of a teacher of languages and at a very early age could sing correctly any piece she had ever heard. When nine years old she was placed under the instruction of Croelius, the best teacher in Stockholm. Soon she appeared on the stage in juvenile parts, showing dramatic ability in addition to her vocal accomplishments. Then the upper notes of her voice lost their sweetness and until she was sixteen she was forbidden to sing, though she studied instrumental music. On one occasion part of Meyerbeer's *Robert le Diable* was to be performed at a concert, and no vocalist could be found to appear as Alice. The director of the academy applied to Jenny Lind, who, taking the place, showed that her voice had recovered its purity and power. The manager then asked her to take the part of Agatha in Weber's *Freischütz*, and for nearly two years she continued to be the prima donna of the Swedish opera. After a series of concerts in Norway and Sweden, she went to Paris to receive the instruction of Garcia, who did not encourage her at first, but she persevered and after a year obtained the approval of Meyerbeer. She returned to Stockholm, where she enjoyed a remarkable triumph, and in 1844, on her appearing at the opening of the opera house in Berlin, her reputation was firmly established. She went to Dresden, Frankfort, Cologne, and Vienna, and sang before the Queen of England, who was visiting Berlin. In May, 1847, for her debut in London she selected the part of Alice, which had first shown the sweetness of her voice. Her répertoire was large, and her success was unprecedented. In her first season she appeared in *Sonnambula*, *La Figlia del Reggimento*, *Norma*, and *Der Freischütz*, and she soon added other parts. In consequence of a popular demand she appeared at Exeter Hall in 1848, in the oratorio of *Elijah*, and she also gave many concerts. In September, 1850, she came to America under the auspices of Mr. P. T. Barnum. Her first concert at New York was preceded and accompanied by scenes of the wildest enthusiasm. The sale of seats was by auction, and hundreds of dollars were bid for the best choice. After giving about one hundred concerts in the principal cities with equal success, and receiving over $300,000 as her share of the proceeds, she withdrew from her contract with Mr. Barnum and gave a series of concerts on her own account. In 1851 she was married to Mr. Otto Goldschmidt, who had accompanied her as pianist. She returned with him to Europe, and having retired from the stage took up her residence at Dresden. Subsequently she made her home in England, where she appeared again in public for brief periods in 1855, 1861, 1863, 1864, 1866, and even later. These have chiefly been for charitable objects, and from the commencement of her career she spent much money in this way. Since 1858 she has resided in England. She was popularly known as the Swedish Nightingale. Her voice was a clear and remarkably sweet soprano, with a register of $2\frac{1}{2}$ octaves. She entered with her soul into whatever she sang, and seemed equally able to express the deepest or lightest emotions, and to gratify the most refined as well as the most simple tastes.

GOLD-THREAD, *Coptis trifolia* of modern botanists, *Helleborus trifolius* of Linnæus. This is a Ranunculaceous plant, differing from the hellebores by having deciduous sepals, and the few-seeded pods set on slender stalks, as well as by some other characters of interest to the critical botanist. It is found from Denmark through Russia to Siberia, and crossing Behring's Straits over the American continent to Iceland. It is a small, creeping plant, the leaves somewhat like those of the strawberry, but much smaller, and evergreen under the snow—the scape not often exceeding five inches high. The flowers are small and white. The name *Coptis* is from the Greek *kopto*, to cut, in allusion to the divided leaves.

As the "gold-thread" it is popularly known in the Northern United States and Canada; the name being given to the underground running root-stocks, which the plant abundantly produces in the bogs and damp places wherein it loves to grow. It was a popular remedy with the Indians of the North for sore mouths and ulcerated throats. It is still used by the French Canadians for the same purposes, and under the name of *Tissa-voyanne jaune* little bundles of the silk-like roots are common in the French markets of Montreal. Bigelow, in his *Medical Botany*, doubts whether it has any real merit in these particulars, but its popularity in the North after so many years of use is somewhat in its favor. It is a pure bitter tonic, free from astringency, and Rafinesque says a tincture made with an ounce of the roots in a pound of diluted alcohol, given in doses of a teaspoonful thrice a day, is of undoubted value as a tonic during convalescence after fever. The Indians made a dye from the stems and leaves, by which they colored skins and other articles a saffron yellow.

GOODE, GEORGE BROWN, an American ichthyologist, was born at New Albany, Ind., Feb. 13, 1851. He graduated at Wesleyan University, Middletown, Conn., in 1870, and having studied also at the Museum of Comparative Zoölogy in Harvard University, was made curator of the museum in the Wesleyan University. In 1874 he was appointed an assistant in the United States Fish Commission, and in 1880 chief of the division of fisheries. His services were called for in connection with the Halifax Fisheries Commission and with the census of 1880. In 1875 he was made assistant curator of the United States National Museum, in 1878 curator-in-chief, and in 1881 assistant director of the same. He has taken part in the Fisheries Exhibitions at Berlin (1880), at London (1883), and at New Orleans (1884). He has published *Fishes of Bermuda* (1876); *History of the Menhaden* (1880); *Game Fishes of the United States* (1879–81); *Food Fishes and Fishery Industries of the United States* (1884); *Bibliography of American Naturalists* (Part I., 1884), and many articles and pamphlets on similar subjects.

GOODELL, WILLIAM (1792–1867), an American missionary, was born at Templeton, Mass., Feb. 14, 1792. He graduated at Dartmouth College in 1817, and at Andover Theological Seminary in 1820. After some missionary work among the Cherokees and Choctaws, he was ordained Sept. 12, 1822, and then, under the direction of the American Board of Commissioners for Foreign Missions, he went to Beyrout, Syria, where he labored five years amid great perils. In 1831 he removed to Constantinople, where he likewise experienced many hardships, being compelled to change his residence thirty-three times in twenty-nine years. He translated the Bible into Armeno-Turkish, completing the work in 1843. After seeing many fruits of his arduous labors, he returned to the United States in 1865, and thereafter lived in retirement at the residence of his son in Philadelphia. Here he died Feb. 18, 1867. His biography was published by his son-in-law, Rev. E. D. G. Prime, under the title *Forty Years in the Turkish Empire* (1883).

GOODRICH, CHAUNCEY ALLEN (1790-1860), an American clergyman and author, was born at New Haven, Conn., Oct. 23, 1790. He was the son of Elizur Goodrich (1761-1849), a distinguished judge and professor of law in Yale College, and grandson of Rev. Elizur Goodrich (1734-1797), who was noted for his fondness for astronomy. Chauncey graduated at Yale College in 1810, served as tutor two years, and was ordained pastor at Middletown in 1816, but soon returned to Yale to be professor of rhetoric, and in 1839 was transferred to the chair of pastoral theology. In 1828 Dr. Noah Webster, his father-in-law, intrusted to him the superintendence of the octavo abridgment of his original quarto dictionary. In 1847 Goodrich issued enlarged and improved editions of both of these dictionaries. In 1856 he published the octavo university edition, and in 1859 the unabridged quarto dictionary, with a valuable supplement. While engaged on the revised edition of 1864 Dr. Goodrich died at New Haven, Feb. 25, 1860. Besides his labors on *Webster's Dictionary*, he published some school textbooks. In 1829 he established the *Christian Quarterly Spectator*, and was its sole editor until 1836.

GOODWIN, WILLIAM WATSON, an American scholar, was born at Concord, Mass., May 9, 1831. He graduated at Harvard College in 1851, afterwards studied philology at Göttingen, Bonn, and Berlin, and received the degree of Ph. D. He was appointed Eliot professor of Greek at Harvard College in 1860. His principal work is *Syntax of the Moods and Tenses of the Greek Verb* (1860), in which he has made valuable elucidations of the principles of the Greek language. He has also published a *Greek Grammar* (1870; revised ed., 1879) and a *Greek Reader* (1871); revised a translation of *Plutarch's Morals* (1870), and contributed to philological publications. He has received the degree of LL. D. from Amherst College (1881), and from the University of Cambridge, England (1883).

GOODYEAR, CHARLES (1800-1860), the inventor of vulcanized India rubber, was born at New Haven, Conn., Dec. 29, 1800. After receiving a common school education he entered into partnership with his father in the manufacture of hardware at Philadelphia. After the failure of the firm in 1830, Charles began to give attention to the manufacture of India rubber, which had already been employed for boots and shoes. His first patent, September, 1835, was for an India rubber cement, which proved of little use, as it melted in warm weather. Goodyear exhausted his means in experiments, but in the midst of dire poverty persevered until he discovered the nitric acid process, by which the surface of the rubber was freed from its adhesiveness. In 1838, having gone to Roxbury, he found Nathaniel Hayward, who had been employed in a rubber-shoe factory, using sulphur to prepare the rubber. A patent for this process was taken out by Goodyear as Hayward's assignee in 1839. But it was still incomplete, and Goodyear continued begging and borrowing to make further experiments. Ten years after he had begun his investigations came an accidental discovery of the advantage of applying a high degree of heat to the sulphurized India rubber. For this vulcanized rubber he took out a patent in France in April, 1844, but his failure to comply with some formalities required by the law rendered his patent void. In England his endeavors to obtain a patent were frustrated by a person who, having received some hints of his process, anticipated him. In the United States vulcanized rubber was first patented by him June 15, 1844. This patent was afterwards renewed and extended, yet, owing to the enormous expenses incurred in maintaining his rights, Goodyear derived little benefit from it. At the World's Fair in London, in 1851 he obtained the great council medal, and at the Paris Exhibition in 1855 the grand medal of honor. Before his death vulcanized rubber was employed for nearly 500 purposes, yet the inventor died in poverty in New York, July 1, 1860.

GOOKIN, DANIEL (1612-1687), an American soldier, was born in Kent, England, in 1612. His father brought him to Virginia in 1621, and during the Indian massacre of the next year held his plantation, now Newport News, against the savages. In May, 1644, Daniel, who had become a Puritan, removed to Cambridge, Mass. There he was cordially received and soon made captain of the militia and member of the house of deputies. In 1651 he was speaker of the house, and in 1652 magistrate. In 1656 he was made superintendent of all the Indians who had submitted to the government of the colony. On his visits to England in 1656 and 1657 he had interviews with Cromwell, then Lord Protector. In 1660 he returned to Massachusetts with the regicides Goffe and Whalley, and afterwards protected them. In 1681 he was made major-general of the colony. He died at Cambridge, Mass., March 19, 1687. His *Historical Collections of the Indians of Massachusetts*, bearing date 1674, was published in 1792, and his *History of the Christian Indians*, written in 1677, was published in 1835. A *History of New England*, also written by him, is lost.

GOOSE. See FOWL.

GOOSEBERRY. The attempts to cultivate the European gooseberry in the United States and Canada have, for the most part, failed. In some cases they succeed for several years after introduction, and reports of success find their way to the agricultural papers; but sooner or later the mildew appears, and when once it appears among the plants it never leaves them. By digging deeply about the plants from year to year, adding salt to attract moisture, covering the whole surface of the ground under the bushes, or by selecting a piece of ground naturally cool and moist, some continued success has been achieved. It has come to be conceded by most American fruit-growers that in limited districts in Nova Scotia and New Brunswick only can the European gooseberry be successfully grown. It would appear that its culture is also practicable in the moister parts of the Pacific region.

See Vol. X. p. 693 Am. ed. (p. 779 Edin. ed.).

But of late years one of the native species, *Ribes oxyacanthoides* of Linnæus (from which *R. hirtellum* of modern botanists is found not to be distinct), and which extends from the Atlantic to the Pacific in the upper portion of the North American continent, has received an improvement which renders the failure of the European species a matter of less importance. The fruit of this species has long been a popular article of food with the Indians. A large-fruited form was brought into cultivation many years ago by Abel Houghton, of Lynn, Mass.; since which some other varieties have been introduced; and now American gooseberries are very popular with American fruit-growers. They are extensively planted in New York, New Jersey, Pennsylvania, Delaware, and Maryland for the markets which look to these territories for their supplies, and are considered among the profitable small fruits. They are not more than half the size of the average European gooseberry, nor are they sweet enough to be particularly desirable to eat in a natural condition, as is the case with its European relative; but they make admirable tarts and preserves. They come into use just as the rhubarb season ends, and thus fill a place in the fruit-market which would be otherwise vacant. They hang so thickly under the pendulous branches as to be easily gathered into sheets by a small rake, and hence can be sold at comparatively low prices. They are not wholly free from mildew, but this attacks them so rarely as not to interfere with their general cultivation. (T. M.)

GOPHER, a word of somewhat varied application in natural history, as it has been given in different regions to several genera of rodents, to a land-tortoise, and to the wood and fruit of certain trees. The animals thus named are all natives of the United States, the genus of rodents best known by this name being the *Geomys*, some species of which are very abundant in the States west of the Mississippi. These are nocturnal, underground animals, the claws on their fore feet being developed into powerful digging implements. They are often called pouched rats, from their large external cheek-pouches. The pouched gopher (*G. bursarius*) is 8 to 10 inches long, of a reddish-brown color above, and ashy-brown beneath, with white feet. It burrows in sandy soils, raising the earth into little mounds. It feeds on grasses, roots, nuts, etc., and does considerable injury to vegetation by its destruction of roots. Another genus, *Thomomys*, mainly belonging to the Pacific coast, has received the same common name, from its close resemblance to *Geomys*. The California gopher, the largest species, is nearly as large as *G. bursarius*. Its root depredations make it very annoying to the farmer, and it is destroyed in considerable numbers by the use of traps and poison.

In some of the Western States the rodent genus *Spermophilus* is also called gopher, though more properly termed "prairie squirrel." It belongs to the marmot family. These animals have a long and squirrel-like tail, and well-developed cheek-pouches. They burrow in the Western prairies, and live on roots and seeds of plants, occasionally injuring the growing corn. The best-known species is the striped prairie squirrel, commonly called gopher in Iowa, Wisconsin, Minnesota, and Northern Illinois.

The tortoise thus called is the large land-tortoise of the Southern States (*Testudo polyphemus*). This animal is about 15 inches long. It has a nearly flat shell, with a thick plastron projecting beyond the carapace in front. The fore limbs are very large and thick, while the nails are strong and well adapted for digging. Its general color is brownish-yellow. It burrows in the ground, mainly in dry, sandy pine-barrens, and does some mischief by destroying roots. The adults are very strong and can move under a weight of 200 lbs. The flesh and eggs are esteemed as food. It is found in Florida, Georgia, and Alabama.

There is a Southern tree (*Cladrastis tinctoria*), which, like the wood of Noah's ark, is called Gopherwood, its wood heavy and very hard, and yielding a clear yellow dye. The gopher plum (*Nyssa capitata*), of the Gulf States, bears a large acid fruit, from which is made a conserve called "Ogeechee limes."

GORDON, Sir Arthur Hamilton, a British colonial governor, was born Nov. 26, 1829, being the youngest son of the fourth earl of Aberdeen. He graduated at Cambridge University and was private secretary to his father during his ministry, 1852-55. From 1854 to 1857 he was member of Parliament for Beverley. In 1858 he was attached to Mr. Gladstone's mission to the Ionian Islands. Since 1861 he has been governor of New Brunswick; of Trinidad (1866); of Mauritius (1870); of the Fiji Islands (1875), then just made into a British colony; governor of New Zealand (1880); and of Ceylon (1883). In all of these positions he displayed administrative abilities of a high order. His niece, Miss C. F. Gordon-Cumming, has given an interesting account of two years spent under his administration under the title *At Home in Fiji* (1880).

GORDON, Charles George (1833-1885), an English general, commonly known as "Chinese Gordon" and "Gordon Pacha," was born Jan. 28, 1833. He was educated in the military academy at Woolwich, and entered the royal engineers as second lieutenant in June, 1852. He served in the Crimean war, and was wounded in the trenches before Sebastopol. After the peace he served on the commission to settle the Turkish and Russian boundary in Asia Minor. In 1857, and again in 1860, he took part in the English and French war against China. At the close of 1861 he journeyed from Pekin to the Chotow and Kalgan passes, on the Great Wall, and returned through Shensi and Tiayuen, a city previously unvisited by Europeans. When the Tai-pings were besieging Shanghai in February, 1863, Gordon offered his services to the Imperialists, and soon after was appointed to the command of the "Ever Victorious Army." After several hard fights he succeeded in rescuing the fertile districts which had fallen into the power of the brigands, and in saving the city of Hangchow from the fate of Nanking, which they had ruined. Towards the close of his campaigns his very name was sufficient to put an army of the rebels to flight. Soo-chow, which was the stronghold of the rebels, surrendered in December, 1863. Gordon was greatly vexed when their leaders were put to death by Li-Hung-Chang, who had the chief command of the Imperialist forces, and who obtained from his own government credit for much of Gordon's success. In May, 1864, Chanchu-Fu was captured, and Gordon, having accomplished his purpose, retired from the Chinese service in July. He resumed his place in the English army, being now lieutenant-colonel. In 1871 he was appointed English consul at the mouth of the Danube, and he remained there until in 1873 he was invited by the Khedive, Ismail Pacha, to carry on the work which had been begun by Sir Samuel Baker in Upper Egypt. Gordon was appointed governor of the Equatorial provinces, and in February, 1874, he marched at the head of 2000 Egyptian and negro troops to Gondokoro, on the White Nile. Here he established his head-quarters, and founded a line of fortified posts as far as the Great Equatorial Lakes. He met with great resistance from the slave-traders, whose nefarious practices he suppressed with a strong hand. The Khedive supported his efforts, raised him to the rank of Pacha, and in 1877 made him governor of all Soudan. In 1879 Gordon, finding his authority not sufficiently supported by Tewfik, the new Khedive, resigned his position. Returning to England he was greeted by the press as the "Uncrowned King," and various important international problems were pointed out as waiting to be solved by him. To the surprise of all he became military secretary to the Marquis of Ripon, who had just been appointed governor-general of India. But he had scarcely reached Bombay when he found that his new position was entirely unsuited to his character, and therefore resigned. He sailed to Hong-Kong and had pleasant interviews with Li-Hung-Chang, with whom he had been associated while crushing the Taiping rebellion. The chief object of his visit, however, was to prevent war between China and Russia, and in this he was happily successful. He returned to England in 1881, and after a brief holiday in Switzerland was ordered to the Mauritius as commanding royal engineer. In March, 1882, he was appointed major-general, and had for some months command of the colonial troops in Cape Colony. He was subsequently selected by the king of Belgium to take military command of the International Congo Region, but before he entered upon this position the successes of El Mahdi in the Soudan and the destruction of Hicks Pacha's army induced him to undertake a mission to Khartoum in the interest of peace. He set out in February, 1884, unattended by European troops, but soon found the difficulties constantly increasing and the British government little disposed to heed the calls he made for aid. El Mahdi steadily advanced, and at last invested Khartoum. Gordon managed to keep up communication with Gen. Wolseley, who moved too slowly to his aid. At last Gen. Stewart with the vanguard of Wolseley's army was cut off, and on Jan. 27, 1885, Gen. Gordon was treacherously slain by an Arab. The gates of Khartoum were then opened to El Mahdi, but in June following he also fell a victim to the storm he had excited.

Gen. Gordon's character was marked by a stern, self-denying, religious fanaticism, mingled with mysticism, which seemed altogether to belong to a Puritan soldier of the seventeenth century, rather than to a man of the nineteenth. He was utterly careless of rewards and honors, but gave himself with enthusiasm to whatever work he undertook, and had the faculty of inspiring the half-civilized tribes among whom his work was carried on with intense personal devotion to himself and faith in his power to accomplish his ends. Yet at last his death was due to failure in this very point.

GORDON, JOHN B., an American general and statesman, was born in Upson co., Ga., Feb. 6, 1832. He graduated at the University of Georgia, studied law, and was admitted to the bar. In 1861 he entered the Confederate army as captain of infantry, and was advanced by successive promotions to the rank of lieutenant-general. He was wounded eight times. In April, 1865, he commanded one wing of Gen. Lee's army when it surrendered at Appomattox. In 1868 he was the Democratic candidate for governor of Georgia, but was unsuccessful. He was elected to the U. S. Senate in 1873, and was re-elected in 1879, but resigned, and engaged in railroad management. In 1888 he was elected governor of Georgia, and in 1891 was again elected to the U. S. Senate.

GÖRGEI, ARTHUR, a Hungarian general, was born at Topporcz, in Hungary, Jan. 30, 1818. He entered the military school at Tuln, and in 1837 was appointed lieutenant in the Royal Life-guards, and subsequently in the Palatine Hussars. But in 1845 he resigned from the army to pursue chemical studies at Prague. In 1848 he offered his services to the National Hungarian government, and was sent against the Croats whom he soon forced to surrender. Kossuth then made him colonel and soon after general of the army defending the frontier against Austria. But his forces being insufficient for the task, he retreated before Windischgrätz, who entered Buda, Jan. 5, 1849. After further disasters and some successes which served to prolong the struggle, Görgei found the chief command given to the Polish general Dembinski. The army officers demanded the removal of the latter and Kossuth yielded. Görgei, though opposed to the unconstitutional actions of the Austrian emperor, was not a Republican, and hence was distrusted by Kossuth's government, while his popularity and military ability compelled them to place him in the most responsible position. In a short time after the campaign opened, Görgei had defeated the Imperial armies and retaken all important places except Buda. Had he neglected the latter and pushed on to Vienna, which was unguarded, he might have closed the war in triumph, but he delayed to press the siege. Buda was taken by storm, May 21, but meantime the Russians had come into the contest. The disputes among the Republican leaders waxed fiercer as their enemies crowded upon them from all sides. On July 12 the Austrians were again masters of Buda. Görgei had fallen back beyond the Theiss, yet he still showed brilliant generalship in his manœuvres against the Russians, but the other generals who had been striving to unite with him were unable to force their way. On Kossuth's resignation Görgei became civil and military dictator. Believing it useless to prolong the war, he surrendered his army of 23,000 men to the Russian general, Rüdiger, at Vilagos, on Aug. 13, 1849. The other generals were executed, but Görgei was carried captive to Klagenfurt, in Austria, where he lived in retirement until 1867, being employed as chemist in a morocco factory. As his defence against a charge of treachery, he wrote *Mein Leben und Wirken in Ungarn in den Jahren* 1848 *und* 1849 (1852), which has been translated into English. Having returned to Hungary in 1867, after it had received a constitutional government, he published anonymously in 1869 a political essay, *Hungary in* 1849 *and after* 1866. In 1872 he was appointed to a position on a railroad.

GORGES, SIR FERDINANDO (d. 1647), lord proprietor of the province of Maine, was born at Ashton Phillips, Somersetshire, England. He took part in the conspiracy of Essex, and testified on his trial in 1601. He served in the navy against Spain, and after the peace in 1604 was appointed governor of Plymouth. Learning something about America from some Indian captives, he and his friends applied to the king for a charter to found colonies. In 1606 two companies, the London and the Plymouth, were incorporated, and between them was divided the territory for 50 miles inland, from 34° to 45° N. lat. The Plymouth company had the northern part called North Virginia, and Gorges sent out an exploring ship, which was captured by the Spaniards. In May, 1607, three ships were sent with 100 men, who began a settlement near the mouth of the Kennebec, but abandoned it in the next spring. In 1614 an attempt by Capt. John Smith was also unsuccessful, but Dr. Richard Vines, sent out in 1616, spent the winter near Saco Bay, and made a good impression on the natives. In 1620, by a new patent, Gorges and others obtained control of the territory from 40° to 48° N. lat., and from sea to sea. In 1622 the land was divided among the incorporators, Gorges and John Mason taking the district between the Kennebec and Merrimack, and calling it Laconia. A settlement was made at Piscataqua in 1623, and in the same year Capt. Robert Gorges, son of Sir Ferdinando, was appointed by the council for New England "general governor of the country." In 1629 Mason and Gorges divided their tract, the former calling his part New Hampshire and the latter his part New Somersetshire, from their respective counties in England. In 1635 the council of New England surrendered their charter to the king, and Gorges obtained a charter constituting him lord proprietary of the province of Maine, as his territory was now called. He divided it into the counties of Agamenticus and Saco, and these were further divided into hundreds and parishes. In 1637 the king commissioned Gorges as governor-general of New England, but the latter never went. In 1640 he sent his nephew, Thomas Gorges, as deputy-governor, who went first to Boston and afterwards to the settlement in Agamenticus, which was now chartered as the city of Gorgeana. Both uncle and nephew were staunch adherents to the Established Church, and, though they showed tolerance to the Puritans, were somewhat distrusted. Hence their settlements were excluded from the confederacy formed in 1643 by the four New England colonies. Sir Ferdinando died at an advanced age in 1647, and, as his territorial rights had been more a source of expense and vexation than of profit, his heirs paid no attention to the letters from the colonists, who now came under the jurisdiction of Massachusetts. In 1677 his grandson, Ferdinando (1629–1718), sold his rights as proprietary to Massachusetts for £1250. He also published *America Painted to the Life* (1659), giving a full account of his grandfather's attempts to settle New England.

GORTSCHAKOFF, Alexander Michailowitsch, Prince (1798–1883), a Russian statesman, was born July 16, 1798, of a family distinguished among the Russian nobility. He was educated at Tsarskoe-Selo and entered upon a diplomatic career. He accompanied Count Nesselrode to the congresses of Laybach and Verona. In 1824 he was secretary of legation at London, and afterwards held diplomatic positions at Florence, Vienna, and Stuttgard. While ambassador at the last named he negotiated the marriage of Princess Olga with Crown Prince Karl of Würtemberg. In 1850 he attended the German imperial diet at Frankfort, and there came into close relations with Prince Bismarck. In 1854 he was sent to Vienna as ambassador, and there guarded the interests of Russia so well during the Crimean war that in April, 1856, he was made minister of foreign affairs. He soon asserted strongly the principle of non-intervention, applying it especially to the case of Naples. He declared as the motto of his policy, "Russia does not sulk, she meditates." Yet in 1860 he favored the French expedition to Syria. In 1861 he showed sympathy with the U. S. government in the American civil war, and repressed the desire of the French emperor for a joint intervention of European powers. He also resented the diplomatic notes of France, England, and Austria with reference to Poland. During the war between France and Germany, Gortschakoff maintained a strict neutrality, but he seized the opportunity to declare that Russia was no longer bound by the treaty of 1856 so far as the navigation of the Black Sea was concerned. In 1871 a conference of the great powers was held in London, in which the demands of Russia were acceded to. Gortschakoff now showed his favor for the ideas of Prince Bismarck, and by interviews between the emperors endeavored to promote cordial relations between Russia and Germany. In Asia he sought continually to extend the power and influence of Russia. His diplomatic skill was especially displayed in connection with the Turkish war of 1877. Russian agents had instigated the people of Bosnia and Herzegovina against Turkey, yet Germany and Austria were induced to keep quiet, while England was almost drawn into war with Turkey. Prince Gortschakoff took part both in the treaty of San Stefano, Feb. 6, 1878, and in the conference at Berlin, July 13, 1878, by which the treaty was somewhat modified to the disadvantage of Russia. Gortschakoff blamed Bismarck for giving favor to Austria, and though the emperors continued on friendly terms the chancellors had serious differences. Bismarck felt that Russian influence under the guise of Pan-Slavism was becoming too strong in the south-east of Europe, while Gortschakoff claimed some return for his friendly neutrality in the French-German war.

Meantime the internal troubles of Russia called for still higher statesmanship. The astute diplomatist, whose skill had so often advanced her interests at the expense of other nations, had no remedy for the disease which was preying on the vitals of the empire. Early in 1882 he retired from the ministry of foreign affairs, and he even withdrew from Russia to Baden-Baden, where he died, March 11, 1883.

GORTON, Samuel (c. 1600–1677), a New England sectary, was born at Gorton, England, about 1600. He was a clothier in London until 1636, when he went to Boston, and afterwards to Plymouth. Being fined and banished for preaching he settled at Aquidneck, again got into dispute with the authorities and was whipped. In 1641 he took refuge with Roger Williams at Providence and soon after bought lands at Pawtuxet, now Cranston. A dispute arose about property and the Massachusetts authorities were called to interfere, which they were ready to do, but Gorton's party, after a protest against the proposed action, abandoned their settlement in September, 1642, and removed to Shawomet, now Warwick, R. I., where they bought land of the sachem Miantonomo. But other claimants appeared and appealed for help to Boston, where the authorities had been offended by the previous protest and by Gorton's heresies, against which even Roger Williams cried out in strong terms. Capt. Cooke with forty soldiers marched to Shawomet, and brought back Gorton's party for trial. They were condemned and sentenced to be dispersed among the towns and kept at hard labor in irons. In the following March (1644) they were set free and ordered to leave the colony. They went to Rhode Island, but Gorton sought redress in England, and by the favor of the Earl of Warwick obtained an order that they should be allowed peaceable possession of their lands at Shawomet. Returning thither in 1648 he named the place Warwick. He held several civil offices and on Sundays preached to the colonists and Indians. He repudiated all outward forms in religion and mingled mysticism with all his views. He died at Warwick, R. I., in November or December, 1677. In vindication of his course he published *Simplicitie's Defence against Seven-headed Policy* (London, 1646; reprinted by the R. I. Historical Society). He also published *An Incorruptible Key composed of the CX Psalm* (1647), and other religious treatises, and left in MS. a commentary on part of the gospel of St. Matthew. Samuel, one of his sons, lived to the age of 94. His sect survived him about a century.

GOSCHEN, GEORGE JOACHIM, an English financier, was born at London, Aug. 10, 1831. He is of German origin, and was educated at Rugby and graduated from Oriel College, Oxford, in 1853. He entered upon a mercantile life, and in 1863 was elected to Parliament from the city of London. The movements for opening the universities to dissenters and for the abolition of religious tests enlisted his support. He was made vice-president of the Board of Trade in November, 1865, and chancellor of the duchy of Lancaster, Jan. 26, 1866, but held this position only until June, when the Russell ministry retired. When Mr. Gladstone became prime-minister in December, 1868, Mr. Goschen was made president of the Poor-Law Board. In March, 1871, he was appointed first lord of the admiralty and held this office until February, 1874. In 1876 the French and English holders of Egyptian bonds appointed Mr. Goschen and M. Joubert to proceed to Egypt on their behalf. The Khedive accepted their plan for the reorganization of finances of that country. Mr. Goschen, in May, 1880, went as ambassador extraordinary to Constantinople, and with the ministers of other nations succeeded in re-adjusting the northern boundary of Greece. After representing Ripon in Parliament he was, in 1885, elected from Edinburgh, but having refused to endorse Gladstone's movement for Home Rule, he was defeated in 1886. But in Feb., 1887, he was elected from a London district, and was then made chancellor of the exchequer.

GOSNOLD, BARTHOLOMEW (d. 1607), an English voyager to America, joined Raleigh in his attempt to colonize Virginia. After the failure of the settlement at Roanoke, he commanded an expedition fitted out by the Earl of Southampton. Sailing from Falmouth, March 26, 1602, with twenty colonists, he steered directly across the Atlantic and reached Massachusetts May 14. He landed on Cape Cod, which he named; then sailing southward around the cape to the mouth of Buzzard's Bay he planted his colony on an island which he called Elizabeth, but which is now known by its Indian name, Cuttyhunk. But, disheartened by the hostility of the Indians and disputes about the division of their profits, the colonists returned to England in a few weeks. They carried a cargo of sassafras roots, cedar, furs, and other goods. Gosnold then organized a company to colonize Virginia, led by Wingfield, Rev. Robert Hunt, and Capt. John Smith, and a charter was obtained April 10, 1606. He set sail Dec. 19, with three vessels and 105 adventurers, and after a tedious voyage was driven into Chesapeake Bay, April 26, 1607. He sailed up the James River about 50 miles, where the colonists founded Jamestown, though Gosnold objected to the site as unhealthy. He himself fell a victim to disease, dying Aug. 22, 1607.

GOSPELS. The Gospels and the Acts of the Apostles constitute the historical portion of the New Testament. The four Gospels give an account of the redemptive work of Christ as wrought in his earthly life, in his death, burial, and resurrection; the Acts presents the work of the Risen Lord in the birth, development, and establishment of the Christian church by the Holy Spirit. The Gospels give the history of redemption in its successive aspects and stages—aspects of the work of Christ and stages of the redemption in process. Each Gospel prepares the way for its successor, each telling afresh the story of the life, death, and resurrection, from its own point of view, each beginning at a higher level than the preceding. The Gospels are vitally related to one another and the four constitute an organic whole.

See Vol. X. p. 702 Am. ed. (p. 789 Edin. ed.).

Matthew is the opening Book—the Genesis—of the New Covenant. The Old Testament closes with the Jewish nation looking for their long-promised King and Messiah, the Jews are the elect people, a kingdom of priests, a holy nation (Ex. xix. 5, 6). In the Christian age, the Jewish nation is discarded; a church exists—an *ecclesia*—whose character and principle of constitution were not revealed in the Old Testament (Rom. xvi. 25, 26; Eph. iii. 3, 5, 6; Col. i. 26, 27). This church is selected out of all nations; in it Jewish rites are abolished; a bond of union heretofore unknown is established, while every existing distinction disappears; in this body the Gentiles form much the larger portion. How has this change been effected? If the promises of God stand, and his gifts and calling are without repentance, how are these astounding facts to be explained and justified? The Gospel according to Matthew answers these questions; it relates the coming of Jesus to the Jews as their King, their rejection of him, his consequent rejection of them, and the prospective establishment of the church and its ordinances. At every step it refers to the Old Testament for the principles on which all this has been done. The Gospel according to Matthew conducts us from the position of the Old Testament to that of the New.

Accordingly, in matter, manner, and style, this Gospel manifests its intimate relationship to the Mosaic dispensation and to the Old Testament. The law is a revelation from God, more real and stable than the outward universe (v. 13); Jerusalem is the holy city (iv. 5); the city of the great king (v. 35); the Jewish temple is God's dwelling-place (xxiii. 21); the holy place (xxiv. 15); the temple of God (xxvi. 61); the temple and altar are sacred and sanctifying (xxiii. 17–21); the altar service furnishes illustrations of obedience to the divine requirements (v. 23, 24); the authority of those who occupy Moses' seat is asserted, and obedience to their official commands enjoined (xxiii. 1–3). The quotations from the Old Testament are numerous, but, with perhaps a single exception, they are not predictions of specific events, but enunciations of great principles. It addresses itself to those who accept the Jewish Scriptures as a revelation of the divine character and conduct. It presents Christ in his character and office as the Jewish King; his forerunner announces that the kingdom of heaven is at hand (iii. 2); Christ repeats this announcement (iv. 17); the apostles are sent to declare the coming kingdom (x. 7); the Gospel which he preaches is the gospel of the kingdom (iv. 23); and his teaching is the word of the kingdom (xiii. 19). The parables in Matthew are all of the kingdom of heaven. Christ sits on the throne of his glory, and applying to himself the august title of The King, gathers before him all the nations and pronounces the sentences of eternity (xxv. 31–46). At his death nature owns his authority, the earth is shaken, the rocks are rent, the graves are opened, the dead are raised (xxvii. 51–53). But the nation rejects its Messiah and King. Perverting the whole purpose and intent of the Mosaic dispensation (xii. 7), refusing to fulfil the office to which they were appointed, they crucified him who was the embodiment of God's purposes for them as a people. At his birth he was doomed to death by the civil authority; as soon as his character was developed the religious guides pursued him with an animosity which would not be satisfied short of his crucifixion. From the beginning his fate is inevitable: "Foxes have holes and birds of the air have nests, but the Son of man hath not where to lay his head" (viii. 20). His life is a continual withdrawal from the Jewish rulers. He withdraws into Egypt (ii. 14); then into Galilee (ii. 22); his public ministry as here told begins with his withdrawal from Judea (iv. 12); the Pharisees follow him and hold a council against him how they may destroy him, but when Jesus knew it, he withdrew himself from thence (xii. 15); still pursued by the Sanhedrim, he withdraws into the borders of Tyre and Sidon (xv. 21); and this course continues until he goes to Jerusalem to die (xix. 1). On the cross, his only word is that desolate wail, "My God, my God, why hast thou forsaken me?" (xxvii. 46). No word of sympathy from any human voice is heard, the passers-by revile him, the chief priests with the elders and scribes mock him (xxvii. 39, 43); while the cry still rings in the air, " His blood be on us, and on our children" (xxvii. 25).

The result of all this is the rejection of the nation. The kingdom of God is taken from them and given to a nation bringing forth the fruits thereof (xxi. 43). Christ declares that the unclean spirit has returned to his former habitation, bringing with him seven other spirits more wicked than himself (xii. 45). All the parables spoken in public after chapter xiii. set forth the national sin and the impending destruction (xxi. 28-33; xxii. 2). The final miracle is the blasting of the fig-tree, the emblem of the nation (xxi. 19). The closing public discourse is an arraignment of the Jewish authorities; portraying their character and history, he bids them fill up the measure of their father's iniquity, and with the inquiry, "Ye serpents, ye generation of vipers, how can ye escape the damnation of hell?" (xxiii.33); pronounces their doom and departs forever from the temple (xxiv. 1). The rejection of the Jews and the acceptance of the Gentiles have not waited until this time for intimation. In the genealogy with which the Gospel begins are found the names of four Gentile women who by faith obtained a place in the royal line (i. 3, 5, 6). At the birth of Christ the Gentile magi recognize and honor him, while the rulers and religious guides of the nation pass him by without notice. Egypt furnishes the refuge which Judea refuses (ii. 14, 15). A Gentile centurion exhibits faith not found in Israel (viii. 10). A Canaanite draws from the Lord the exclamation, "O woman, great is thy faith" (xv. 28). The Roman Pilate cleanses his hands from the blood which the Jews take upon themselves (xxvii. 24); and Pilate's wife warns him to have nothing to do with that just man (xxvii. 19); while the Gentile guards around the cross express their conviction of the blamelessness of the sufferer (xxvii. 54).

To take the place of the nation which has so signally failed to recognize the purpose of its election, a new body is chosen to be God's peculiar people—a holy nation, a kingdom of priests (1 Pet. ii. 9). This body—the church—is founded on the divinely revealed knowledge of Christ (xvi. 17, 18). To it are given a new life, a new covenant, a new constitution, a new commandment, new discipline, new ordinances. It is charged with the duty of discipling all nations, "baptizing them into the name of the Father, and of the Son, and of the Holy Ghost" (xxviii. 19).

At this point the Gospel according to Mark commences. Whatever may be the date of its composition, there can be no question as to its place in the history. It follows logically the Gospel according to Matthew. In it the Christ begins his work. There is no place for kingly character and office here; no one styles him King until he stands before Pilate; even the evangelist does not call him Lord until after the ascension, nor do the disciples give him that title. Here there is no authoritative exposition of law, no adjudication before judgment thrones, no comparison of the doom of the rejecter of the Gospel with that of Sodom and Gomorrah, no mention of the fire with which the Messiah is to baptize. No assertion is there of one greater than the temple, greater than Solomon, greater than Jonah; no argument based on Christ's ownership, as in Matthew and Luke; no ascription of power, such as the centurion utters in both those Gospels. In the other evangelists Christ speaks of his glory, but not in Mark; here it is the glory of the Father (viii. 38), with power and great glory (xiii. 26).

This is "the beginning of the Gospel of the Son of God." It presents the first aspect of sonship and the first aspect and manifestation of redemption. In John the sonship of Christ is that of eternal relationship, in Luke it arises from his conception by the Holy Spirit (Luke i. 35), in Mark's Gospel it is the sonship of consecration, obedience, and service—the privilege and characteristic of all the redeemed. Both as the beginning of the Gospel and as the Gospel of the Son of God, Mark is the Gospel of man—of man in his present constitution and condition, of man irrespective of all distinctions. "The Sabbath was made for man and not man for the Sabbath" (ii. 27); "My house shall be called a house of prayer for all nations" (xi. 17); the distinction between ceremonially clean and unclean food is abrogated: "This he said, making all food clean" (vii. 19); and here is uttered the truth that, "To love God with all the heart, and with all the understanding, and with all the soul, and with all the strength, and to love his neighbor as himself, is more than all burnt offerings and sacrifices" (xii. 32, 33). The transference from the Jewish position of Matthew to the stage of the world occupied by Mark is apparent throughout the Gospel; Jewish customs (vii. 3, 4), Jewish facts (xi. 13), Jewish words (iii. 17; v. 41; vii. 11, 34) are explained. In Matthew the freedom of the nation from its old besetting sin of idolatry is expressly recognized (xii. 43); no instance of any possession by an unclean spirit is recorded. In Mark the cure of the unclean demoniac is the first miracle (i. 23). In Matthew and Luke—Jewish Gospels—repentance is emphasized; in Mark belief and unbelief: "All things are possible to him that believeth" (ix. 23). Our Lord begins his ministry with "Repent ye and believe the gospel" (i. 15), and closes with "He that believeth and is baptized shall be saved" (xvi. 16).

This is the beginning of the Gospel. Called out of Egypt (Matthew ii. 15), the people of God enter here on the first stage of redemption, the journey through the wilderness, in the course of which the old leaven is eliminated and a new and better generation appears. The only parable peculiar to Mark gives the course of Christianity in this dispensation: "So is the kingdom of God, as if a man were to cast seed into the ground, and should sleep and rise night and day, and the seed should spring and grow up he knoweth not how" (iv. 26, 27). To the same purport are the only two miracles peculiar to Mark: the healing of the deaf and dumb (vii. 32-37), and of the blind man at Bethsaida (viii. 22-25). In both of them the person cured is taken aside from the multitude while the cure is wrought; in the second the cure is gradual, as "he took his elect people aside into the wilderness where he would first open their spiritual ears and speak unto them his law, opening their eyes gradually, for not all at once are the old errors and the old confessions put to flight; not all at once do they see clearly; for a while there are many remains of their old blindness which, for a season, still hinder their vision; they see men as trees walking." The same method of dealing finds expression in the statement peculiar to Mark that in the explanation of parables Christ spake the word unto them as they were able to hear it (iv. 33).

The first privilege and requirement of the child of God is service. "Israel is my son, my first-born; let my son go that he may serve me" (Ex. iv. 22) is the demand of God as he begins the redemption of his people. The first sacrifice in the Book of Leviticus is the offering of consecration (Lev. i.). In the New Testament the first duty of those redeemed by the mercies of God is to present their bodies a living sacrifice, holy and acceptable unto God (Rom. xii. 1). Our Lord learns obedience that he may become the author of eternal salvation to all that obey him (Heb. v. 9). His first step is to take on him the form of a servant (Phil. ii. 7). A body is prepared for him, and in that body he comes to do his Father's will (Heb. x. 5, 7). In Mark the bodily actions and gestures of Christ are specially named. This feature occasions what has often been noted as a peculiarity of this Gospel—the minute and vivid details everywhere found. It is not so often noticed that these details relate chiefly to Christ's person, appearance, manner, etc. Equal circumstantiality is found in John, but there the hours of the day and other circumstances connected with the events are recorded. The Gospels that follow Mark emphasize the impartation of the Spirit to Christ. In this Gospel his human emotions are mentioned—anger (iii. 5), compassion (i. 40), wonder (vi. 6), displeasure (x. 14). The effects on the multitude are of the same character. They are astonished (i. 22), amazed (i. 27, ii. 12), beyond measure astonished (vii. 37), greatly amazed (ix. 15), they marvel at him (xii. 17). Only once do we meet the statement, which so frequently occurs in Luke, they glorified God (ii. 12). The sacrifice is spiritual as well as bodily, burning with the unceasing fire of the Holy Ghost. The Spirit driveth him into the wilderness (i. 12); his friends say, "He is beside himself," and wish to put him under restraint (iii. 21); here only are James and John named "Sons of thunder" (iii. 17). The rapid transitions of the Gospel evince its vigor and movement.

In this Gospel Christ is the Son consecrated to his Father's service. This is the one relation and character of the Gospel. It gives no account of Christ's genealogy, birth, infancy, childhood. No sermons or addresses of any length are recorded, and only four parables. In the other Gospels much space is given to his discourses, to his kinsfolk and associates, to the results of his work. This Gospel is occupied with Christ. In Luke we are introduced to the home of his parents; here to his own home (ii. 1; iii. 19). Elsewhere he is the carpenter's son; here he is the carpenter (vi. 3). Not that he is without associates; his human nature is shown in the craving for companionship manifested in the continual notice of the presence of his friends. He ordained twelve that they should be with him (iii. 14). The names of his companions are given by Mark as by no other evangelist (i. 29; xiii. 3). The distinction between Mark and the other Gospels in this respect is that there the persons introduced are objects of interest, exemplifying some working of grace; here they are simply mentioned as being with him. He remains the sole object of attention. The accounts of the cure of the Syro-Phœnician's daughter (vii. 24-30) and of the anointing of Christ (xiv. 3-9) are only apparently inconsistent with this statement; for it is expressly said that the first is given as the reason why Jesus could not find the seclusion he sought, and the second is introduced, out of its chronological place, to account for the arrest of Christ during the feast, contrary to the intention of the chief priests and scribes. Christ's consecration to obedience and service remains the one subject of the Gospel. His place is the characteristic of this dispensation, the privilege and duty of all. Work succeeds work without interruption, until the Gospel closes as it began—"And they went forth and preached everywhere, the Lord working with them" (xvi. 20).

In the Gospel according to Luke we enter on another stage of redemption. We pass from the individual to consider his relations to others, together with the consequent duties and blessings. It is the priestly Gospel, the Gospel of intercession, of redemption, the social Gospel, the ethical Gospel. It opens with the priest in the sanctuary offering incense, the multitude standing without in prayer (i. 8-10); it closes with the disciples "in the temple continually praising and blessing God" (xxiv. 53). From the first word from heaven—"Fear not, Zacharias; thy prayer is heard" (i. 13)—through the parables of the friend rising at midnight (xi. 5-8,) of the importunate widow (xviii. 1-5), of the publican (xviii. 13, 14), to the prayer of the penitent robber (xxiii. 42, 43), instances of successful petition abound; while in all the important crises of our Lord's life his prayers are specially mentioned (iii. 21, vi. 12, ix. 28). The companion of successful prayer is praise, with which this Gospel resounds. The inspired songs of Mary (i. 46-55), of Zacharias (i. 68-79), and of Simeon (ii. 29-32) are still the canticles of the church. At Christ's birth the chorus of the angels sweeps through the midnight sky (ii. 13, 14). The shepherds return, "glorifying and praising God" (ii. 20); the paralytic and all that behold the miracle "glorify God" (v. 25, 26); the blind man at Jericho, as soon as he received sight, glorified God, and "all the people, when they saw it, gave praise unto God" (xviii. 43). The Gospel of relationship from its very nature must have a certain element of restriction. It cannot be—what this Gospel is frequently called—the universal Gospel. We look in vain in Luke for expressions of universality common to all the other evangelists. In Matthew we read, "Ye are the salt of the earth;" "Ye are the light of the world" (v. 13, 14); "The field is the world (xiii. 38);" "Come unto me all ye that labor and are heavy laden" (xi. 28); in Mark, "The Sabbath was made for man" (ii. 27); "My house shall be called a house of prayer for all nations" (xi. 17); in John, "The Lamb of God that taketh away the sin of the world" (i. 29); "God so loved the world that he gave his Son, that whosoever believeth in him should have eternal life" (iii. 16); "The bread which I will give is my flesh, which I will give for the life of the world" (vi. 51); "I, if I be lifted up from the earth, will draw all men unto me" (xii. 32); "I am the light of the world" (viii. 12); "Other sheep I have which are not of this fold" (x. 16); Jesus "should die not for that nation only, but also that he should gather together in one the children of God that are scattered abroad" (xi. 52). Luke is singularly devoid of all such ideas and expressions. The one or two (ii. 32; iii. 6), which at first sight might seem to be in conflict with this statement, will be found on examination to be consistent with it. Only at the close of the Gospel comes the command to preach repentance and remission of sins in his name among all nations (xxiv. 47). In Luke our Lord does not cross the boundary of the Holy Land: nor does any one from beyond its borders come to him for help or grace. No Syro-Phœnician woman, as in Matthew and Mark, daughter of an accursed race, cries to him for succor; no Greeks, as in John, say, "We would see Jesus;" no miracle of feeding the 4000 is here; no blessing comes except through Israel. In the only instance of a Gentile asking a favor from the Lord—that of the Roman centurion—it is expressly stated that the rulers of the Jews were sent to intercede for him with the plea, "He loveth our nation and hath built us a synagogue" (vii. 3-5). The miracles of the Old Testament cited by Christ exhibit the same principle. The widow of Sarepta, in her penury, first makes a cake for the prophet of Israel, and then she and her house eat many days. Naaman, the Syrian, is cured by the interposition of an Israelitish maid, by applying to the king and prophet of Israel, and by dipping seven times—Israel's sacred number—in Israel's sacred river (iv. 25-27). Relationship is often expressly stated as the reason for Christ's action—"Ought not this woman, being a daughter of Abraham, to be loosed from this bond on the Sabbath day?" (xiii. 16); salvation came to the house of Zaccheus because he was a son of Abraham (xix. 9). In chapter xv. it is the *restoration* of the sheep, the coin, and the son that is the ground of rejoicing. The sheep belonged to the flock from which it wandered, the coin was the woman's inheritance, the son was still a son when he took his journey into a far country. In the discussions on the Sabbath it is not, Which of you shall *see*, but, "Which of you shall *have* an ass or an ox fallen into a pit, and will not straightway pull him out on the Sabbath day?" (xiv. 5). "Doth not each of you on the Sabbath loose his ox or his ass from the stall, and lead him away to watering?" (xiii. 15). The widow pleads with the judge to restore what had been taken from her (xviii. 3).

To relationship belongs redemption. Here, first in the New Testament, do we meet the word, "He hath visited and wrought redemption for his people" (i. 68). Anna spake of him to all that looked for the redemption of Jerusalem (ii. 38); and in the sad dialogue after the crucifixion the disciples say, "We trusted it had been he who should have redeemed Israel" (xxiv. 21). The Redeemer, by Israel's law, must be the Kinsman, the Goel. In the genealogy given by Luke Christ is more than the son of Abraham and David, he is the Son of God (iii. 38). Hence appears in this Gospel the primal view of redemption—that presented in the first promise—the personal conflict for man—"He shall bruise thy head and thou shalt bruise his heel" (Gen. iii. 15). Zacharias sings, "We shall be saved from our enemies and from the hand of all that hate us" (i. 71). Christ's opening commission is, "He hath sent me to preach deliverance to the captives" (iv. 18). Here Satan—the arch-enemy of man—says, "All the power and the glory of the kingdoms of the world is delivered to me, and to whomsoever I will I give it" (iv. 6). The woman healed is one whom "Satan has bound these eighteen years" (xiii. 16). In the hour of Christ's joy he beheld "Satan as lightning fallen from heaven" (x. 18). Satan desires to have the disciples that "he may sift them as wheat" (xxii. 31). The whole people and the whole land must be redeemed; if there are any portions of the land under ban, or any outcast classes of people, they will be the objects of Christ's special notice and care. For this reason Samaria and Perea occupy a large space in this Gospel. The rightful position and character of the Samaritan are vindicated (x. 30, 37; xvii. 11, 19).*

The relation of woman to the religious leaders is intimated in John iv. 27. In Luke's Gospel woman is specially honored; before Christ's birth, during Christ's ministry (viii. 2; x. 38-42), at his crucifixion (xxiii. 27, 49, 55), after his resurrection (xxiv. 1, 12). The poor, the publican, the transgressors of the Mosaic law were religious and social outcasts. Christ emphasizes the love of the woman who was a sinner (vii. 36, 50); he places a beggar in Abraham's bosom (xvi. 20, 22); a publican's prayer in the temple is accepted (xviii. 11-14); a publican is declared to be a son of Abraham (xix. 1-10); a malefactor accompanies the Lord to paradise (xxiii. 43).

The Gospel of Luke is the social gospel. The social relations and intercourse of Christ have a place unknown to the other Evangelists. It abounds with instruction as to social duties. John the Baptist directs his disciples, "He that hath two coats let him impart to him that hath none, and he that hath food let him do likewise;" to the publican he says, "Exact no more than that which is appointed you;" and to the soldiers, "Do violence to no man, neither accuse any falsely, but be content with your wages" (iii. 10-14). The Sermon on the Plain is in strong contrast with the Sermon on the Mount reported by Matthew; it covers our social and relative duties, the use that should be made of earthly possessions. "When thou makest a dinner or supper call not thy friends, but call the poor, the maimed, the lame, the blind" (xiv. 12, 13). To the same purport is the parable of the good Samaritan (x. 30-37); that of the rich fool (xii. 16-21); that of the shrewd steward (xvi. 1-9); that of the rich man and Lazarus (xvi. 19-31); the result of the interview with Zaccheus, "Behold, Lord, the half of my goods I give to the poor, and if I have taken anything from any man by false accusation I restore him fourfold" (xix. 8).

This Gospel of Redemption is the gospel of success. In the prophecy quoted when John the Baptist appears Luke adds to the words cited by the other Evangelists:

---

* Indeed Luke sometimes seems to apply the term Judea to the whole of Palestine. In chap. iv. 44 Westcott and Hort read, "He preaching in the synagogues of Judea," and in vi. 17; vii. 17, Judea apparently includes all the Holy Land.

GOSPELS.

"Every valley shall be filled and every mountain and hill shall be brought low, the crooked shall be made straight and the rough way shall be made smooth, and all flesh shall see the salvation of God" (iii. 5, 6). At the call of the first two apostles to their work we have, what we do not find in Matthew or Mark, the wonderful draught of fishes, a prediction of their success in their new calling (v. 4–7). The seventy return again with joy, saying, "Even the devils are subject unto us through thy name" (x. 17), and the Gospel closes as it begins with thanksgiving and praise for what God has done (xxiv. 53).

The Gospel of John is the final Gospel. The opening sentences glow with that ineffable Light which in the Holy of Holies overhung the Mercy Seat between the cherubim; we behold "his glory, the glory as of the only begotten of the Father full of grace and truth" (i. 14). John begins where the other evangelists end, with the rejection of Christ by the Jewish people: "He came unto his own and his own received him not" (i. 11). Throughout the Gospel the Jews and Jesus are arrayed against each other in uncompromising hostility. In the Synoptic Gospels all Christ's intercourse with his disciples until his last journey to Jerusalem is designed to answer the question, Who is the Son of Man (Matt. xvi. 15; Mark viii. 29; Luke ix. 20)? The nature and person of Christ as the Son of the living God having been revealed, he announces for the first time the method of redemption—by his death, burial, and resurrection (Matt. xvi. 21; Mark viii. 31; Luke ix. 22). But John's Gospel begins with the declaration of Christ's divine character and atoning work; in the first chapter he is the Lamb of God that taketh away the sin of the world (i. 29); on him the angels of God are ascending and descending (i. 51); he declares the character and secret actions of Nathanael (i. 47–50); he needs not that any should tell him of man, for he knows what is in man (ii. 25); he is the Son of Man who came down from heaven and is in heaven (iii. 13). The first miracle which John records is the marriage feast (ii. 11); the first public act the cleansing of the Temple (ii. 16); the first discourse the revelation of the heavenlies (iii. 12);—all pertaining to an order of things which comes only at the close of the other Gospels. In Christ's discourses to the Jews, in his prayer recorded in chapter xvii., in the account of the crucifixion, the point of view is that of a finished work. The death on the cross is not so much the process of dying as the results of death; it is not defeat, but victory. In the other Gospels, when Christ speaks to his disciples of his approaching decease, he emphasizes his humiliation and suffering, his delivery to the Gentiles (Matt. xvi. 21; xx. 18; Luke xviii. 32); here his death is voluntary; "No man taketh my life from me but I lay it down of myself" (x. 18); it inheres in the relation he has assumed, "I am the good shepherd, the good shepherd giveth his life for the sheep" (x. 11); it is the reason for his Father's special love, "Therefore doth my Father love me because I lay down my life that I may take it again" (x. 17, 18); and it results in universal appreciation, "And I, if I be lifted up from the earth, will draw all men unto me" (xii. 32). In this Gospel there is no account of the transfiguration with its Moses and Elias, the encouragement for the coming Calvary. There are here no apprehensions of the cross, no Gethsemane; no angels strengthening him. When the band of men and officers approach him in the garden to apprehend him "I am he," they go backward and fall to the ground (xviii. 6). Throughout the whole scene of the crucifixion the same wonderful character is preserved. He does not receive testimony from men; no company of women bewail and lament him; no Judas confesses, "I have betrayed the innocent blood;" no Pilate's wife says, "Have thou nothing to do with this just man;" no dying malefactor testifies, "This man has done nothing amiss;" no Roman centurion says, "Truly this man was the Son of God." And he who needed no help or sympathy or testimony from men or angels would have none from nature; in this Gospel we read nothing of rocks rending, or of the earth quaking, or of the darkness covering the land. From the cross is heard no prayer, no cry, "My God, my God, why hast thou forsaken me?" "Father, into thy hands I commend my Spirit." He speaks but three words—the first, as if on a quiet death-bed, provides for his mother; the second is a fulfilment of Scripture; the third is the shout of the conqueror.

The final Gospel is the personal Gospel. The Divine Persons, Father, Son, and Spirit, are presented in their order, each in his distinct sphere and each in his relation to the others. The personality of Christ, the personal character of the relations he sustains are everywhere emphasized. He speaks rather than acts (viii. 12). His fundamental assertion is, I am—I am the Life, the Truth, the Way, the Vine, the Door, the Shepherd, the Resurrection. Few miracles are recorded, and the discourses are occupied with the nature of God, the essential oneness of Christ with the Father, the mystical union of Christ with his people. In the person of Christ all things find their fulfilment; not only the predictions of the Old Testament but the Old Testament itself; the Shekinah and the tabernacle (i. 14); the temple (ii. 19–21); the ladder on which the angels of God ascend and descend (i. 51); the serpent in the wilderness (iii. 14); the manna (vi. 32); the paschal lamb (i. 20; xix. 36); in him all nature finds its fulfilment —life (i. 4); light (i. 9); water (iv. 10); bread (vi. 50); all offices and relationships—the vine (xv. 1); the door (x. 7); the shepherd (x. 14); the way (xiv. 6). The reason and vindication of all Christ's actions are found in himself. The eight miracles in this Gospel are, with a single exception (iv. 46–53), self-moved—wrought without any request from those to be benefited, and in that exception the cure transcends the faith of the petitioner. In the discussions on the Sabbath there is no argument, as in the Synoptics, from David or the temple, or the conduct of man: his one justification is, "My Father worketh until now, and I work" (v. 17). In the one thought of belief in Christ centre all the requirements of God (vi. 28, 29). A personal relation to a personal Being comprises all that is necessary for perfect conduct and character; this meets every possibility of the soul (i. 4); satisfies every desire (iv. 14); fills every capacity for time and eternity (vi. 35). The personality of the thought moulds the style of John; it shows itself in the avoidance of abstractions, in the absence of all reference to law as now in force, in the continual recurrence of the personal pronoun, in the precision and accuracy with which words are used, in the continual repetition of words which this precision requires, in the ever-recurring antitheses, in the scrupulous restriction of terms. Believers, e. g., are the children of God; only Christ is the Son of God.

It is the universal Gospel, "All things were made by him and without him was not anything made that was made" (i. 2) · he "lighteth every man that cometh into the world" (i. 9); he is "the Lamb of God which taketh away the sin of the world" (i. 29). "The hour is coming in which all that are in the graves shall hear his voice and shall come forth" (v. 28).

The final Gospel is the Gospel of the essential and eternal. There is here no Sermon on the Mount, with its explanation of law; no Sermon on the Plain, with its ethical directions. In the conversations with Nicodemus (iii. 1-21), and with the woman of Samaria (iv. 7-26), in the discussions and controversies with the Jews (chap. vi.-x.), in the farewell discourses with the disciples (chap. xiii.-xvi.), there is no mention of duties which are by their nature restricted to this life. Directions with regard to conduct found in all the other Gospels disappear; the heavenly, the spiritual, and eternal are the subject of discourse. The church is viewed in the same light. Christ institutes no ordinances, ordains no apostles, appoints no officers. He breathes on the disciples the Holy Spirit which is to be the eternal life of the church (xx. 22). The Gospel begins with the declaration of the intrinsic nature of Christ, with his relation on the one hand to the Uncreated and on the other to all that comes into being. The antagonisms are the ultimate and permanent—light and darkness, life and death. The relationships are not historic, but ideal (viii. 39). Times and places disappear; God is Spirit, and is worshipped in spirit and in truth (iv. 21-24); while Christ returns to the glory which he had with the Father before the world was (xvii. 5). (H. G. W.)

GOSSE, EDMUND WILLIAM, an English poet, was born at London, Sept. 21, 1849, being the son of the naturalist P. H. Gosse. He was educated in Devonshire and was made an assistant librarian at the British Museum in 1867. He gave much attention to the languages of Northern Europe and travelled in Sweden, Norway, Denmark, and Holland for the purpose of studying the manners and literature of those countries. He has published *Madrigals, Songs, and Sonnets* (1870); *On Viol and Flute* (1873); *King Erik*, a tragedy (1876); *The Unknown Lover*, a drama (1878); *From Shakespeare to Pope* (1884). He has written largely for periodicals on old English poetry, on Scandinavian and Dutch literature, and has translated several works into English. In 1884 he made a brief visit to the United States and lectured on English literature.

GOSSE, PHILIP HENRY, an English naturalist, was born at Worcester, April 6, 1810. He removed at an early age to Poole, Dorsetshire, where he acquired a taste for natural history. He resided in Newfoundland from 1827 to 1835 in a mercantile capacity, and spent his leisure in collecting insects and making drawings of them. Three years in Lower Canada were spent in the same way. Afterwards travelling through the United States, he made further researches, and in Alabama gave especial attention to the butterflies. Returning to England, he published *The Canadian Naturalist* (1840). In 1844 he went to Jamaica and spent eighteen months, the results of which are seen in his *Birds of Jamaica* with an *Atlas of Illustrations*, and *A Naturalist's Sojourn in Jamaica*. He next wrote some text-books on zoölogy, and, being compelled by ill-health to resort to the sea-coast, he pursued investigations described in *A Naturalist's Rambles on the Devonshire Coast* (1853). He then gave an impulse to the erection of public and private aquariums for the better study of marine life. He took up his residence at Torquay that he might the better prepare his important work on *Actinologia Britannica, A History of the British Sea Anemones and Corals* (1860). Among his other works are *Romance of Natural History*, *A Year at the Shore*, and *Land and Sea*. He died at Torquay, August 23, 1888.

GOTTSCHALK, LOUIS MOREAU (1829-1869), an American pianist and composer, was born at New Orleans, May 8, 1829. He was sent to Paris in 1841 for instruction in music, and made his first public appearance in April, 1845. After several professional tours in Europe he came to the United States in 1853, giving his first concert in New York, Feb. 11. After several very successful tours in American cities, he went, in 1857, to the West Indies, where he spent five years in careless enjoyment of tropical life. Recalled to New York in 1862, he resumed his professional work. Throughout his career his brilliant and effective rendering of his own compositions for the piano won the favor of the public. He composed about fifty pieces, most of which illustrate tropical life. Among them are *Le bananier*, *Marche de nuit*, *Bamboula*, *Chant de Soldat*, *Réponds moi*, *Pastorella e Cavaliere*, and many Cuban dances. He died suddenly near Rio Janeiro, Dec. 18, 1869. He published *Notes of a Pianist* (1865).

GOUGH, JOHN BARTHOLOMEW (1817-1886), an American temperance orator, was born at Sandgate, Kent, England, Aug. 22, 1817. He came to America in 1829 and lived on a farm in Oneida co., N. Y., but in 1831 became a bookbinder's apprentice in New York city. Falling into dissipation he was frequently thrown out of work, and then, to obtain strong drink, sang comic songs in low taverns. He married in 1839, but sank deeper in intemperance and lost his wife and child. When reduced to great misery he was invited by a Quaker to take the temperance pledge, and soon after produced a sensation by telling his story at a public meeting. He became a prominent advocate of the temperance cause, but in 1842 some of his former companions led him to violate his pledge. He subsequently confessed his fault and endeavored to make amends. After ten years of great success as a temperance lecturer he went to England in 1853 and carried on a remarkable work there. But his character was assailed by Dr. F. R. Lees, also a temperance lecturer, and a suit for libel, brought by Mr. Gough, resulted in his complete vindication. He returned to the United States in August, 1860, and soon began to lecture on "Street Life in London." Other subjects were added to his list, and in all he retained his great popularity. In 1873 he announced that he would retire from the lecture field, but he was afterwards prevailed upon to appear on special occasions. In 1878 he again visited England. He died at Philadelphia, Feb. 18, 1886. In 1869 he issued his *Autobiography and Personal Recollections*, and in 1876 *Sunshine and Shadow*, being chiefly passages from his lectures.

GOULBURN, EDWARD MEYRICK, an English clergyman, was born in 1818. He was educated at Eton and at Balliol College, Oxford, graduating in 1839, and was elected fellow of Merton College. He was ordained deacon in 1842 and priest in 1843, and became incumbent of Holywell, Oxford. In 1850 he was Bampton lecturer, and was chosen head-master of Rugby School. In 1858 he was appointed minister of Quebec Chapel and prebendary of St. Paul's Cathedral, London. In 1859 he was appointed one of the Queen's chaplains in ordinary and incumbent of St. John's, Paddington. In 1866 he was made dean of Norwich.

Besides a large number of sermons and lectures, he has published *The Doctrine of the Resurrection of the Body* (1851); *The Idle Word* (1855); *Inspiration of the Holy Scriptures* (1857); *Personal Religion* (1862); *Pursuit of Holiness* (1869); *The Great Commission* (1872); *The Holy Catholic Church* (1873); *The Acts of the Deacons*. He is a high churchman, an earnest preacher, and a vigorous writer.

GOULD, BENJAMIN APTHORP, an American astronomer, was born at Boston, Mass., Sept. 27, 1824. His father, bearing the same name (1787-1859), was for many years the head-master of the Boston Latin High School, and edited school editions of the Latin classics. The son graduated at Harvard in 1844, and afterward studied mathematics and astronomy at Göttingen under Gauss, taking his degree in 1848. After visiting the chief observatories of Europe, he returned to Cambridge, Mass., in December, 1848. Here he founded the *Astronomical Journal*, devoted to original investigations, and edited it from 1849 to 1861. Being called into the service of the coast survey in 1851, Prof. Gould greatly improved the application of the telegraph to the determining of longitudes, and finally, on the laying of the Atlantic cable in 1866, connected the longitude measurements of America with those of Europe. In 1855 Dr. Gould was made director of the Dudley observatory at Albany, superintended the erection and equipment of the building, and introduced many improvements in the instruments and methods of observation and calculation. A controversy, which arose between the trustees of the observatory and the scientific council, who had been placed in charge of its management, terminated Dr. Gould's connection with it in January, 1859, leaving him involved in debt on its account. In 1868 he was appointed by the government of the Argentine Republic to organize and direct a national observatory at Cordova. The building was erected and equipped in 1870, and Dr. Gould, with four assistants, entered upon the work of mapping the southern heavens. The result is given in his *Uranometry of the Southern Heavens*. In 1885 he returned to Cambridge and reestablished his *Astronomical Journal*. He has published many astronomical papers and charts.

GOULD, JOHN (1804-1881), an English ornithologist, was born at Lyme, Dorsetshire, Sept. 14, 1804. He began the study of natural history at an early age, and from 1818 to 1824 resided at the Royal Gardens, Windsor, studying birds and flowers. He then removed to London and was employed in preparing specimens for the museum of the London Zoölogical Society. Having obtained, in 1830, a fine collection from the hill countries of India, he published *A Century of Birds from the Himalaya Mountains*, with illustrations by his wife (1832). The success of this work induced him to undertake a larger one on *The Birds of Europe* (1832-37), and then, in 1838, to go to Australia, where he spent some years in collecting material for his *Birds of Australia* (7 vols., 1842-48); *The Mammals of Australia* (1845-59) soon followed, and in 1865 a *Supplement* was added to his work on the birds, and also a *Hand-book to the Birds of Australia*. He gave much attention to the humming birds, and collected more than 2000 specimens, illustrating 320 species. This collection was the basis of his *Monograph of the Trochilidæ* (1850). He published several other monographs, including one on the *Odontophorinæ, or Partridges of America* (1844-50). His other important works were *The Birds of Great Britain* (5 vols., 1862-73), and *The Birds of New Guinea* (1875). He died at London, Feb. 7, 1881.

GOUNOD, CHARLES FRANÇOIS, a French composer, was born at Paris, June 17, 1818. He was educated at the Paris conservatory and enjoyed the instruction of Halévy and Lesueur. In 1839 he gained the prize which enabled him to go to Rome for further study. Here he devoted himself to old Italian church music, and his love for this branch of the art induced him to enter a priests' seminary. In 1843, returning to Paris, he became musical director at a church, and held this position for six years. Several works of church music were produced in this time, but after his *Messe Solonnelle* (1851), he gave his attention more to secular music, producing the lyric drama *Sappho* and several pastorals, yet for a time without marked results. But his *Faust* (1859) was the first successful opera on a theme which had been essayed by many composers. It captivated the French and even overcame the prejudice of the Germans, who objected to the modifications of Goethe's version of the tragedy. Gounod produced other operas, which did not attain the same popularity. Among these were *La Reine de Saba* (1862); *Mireille* (1864); *Romeo and Juliet* (1867). The war of 1870 drove him to London, but he returned to Paris in 1875. In London he produced the opera *Polyeucte* (1870), and a cantata, *Gallia* (1871). Since his return to Paris his chief works have been the opera *Le tribut de Zamora* (1881), and the oratorio *Redemption* (1882). He has been very successful in songs and minor works, in which he displays complete mastery of the form and elegance of execution. He has been elected a member of the French Institute.

GOURD. This name, while generally given to all members of the genus *Cucurbita*, is more particularly applied to *Lagenaria vulgaris*, a close relative of the *Cucurbitæ*. This is the well-known bottle-gourd or calabash, remarkable for the hard outer layer of its large fruit. It is a climbing annual, with a slender, branching stem, from 10 to 20 feet long, and climbing by aid of 3 to 4 cleft tendrils. The leaves are nearly circular, cordate pubescent, 4 to 8 inches long. The flowers are large and white with green nerves and veins, solitary, axillary, on long peduncles. The fruit is 12 to 18 inches long, unequally biventricose. It is, when mature, nearly hollow, the rind or shell becoming smooth, thin, and hard. The fruit takes different forms in cultivation, the most marked being the *pilgrim's gourd*, in the form of a bottle, the *long-necked gourd*, the *trumpet gourd*, and the *calabash*, large and without a neck. Some rarer varieties have a flattened, very small fruit, like the *snuff-box gourd*. Some of the cultivated varieties are said to become 6 feet long. The great gourd-like fruit, known in the West Indies as the *calabash*, comes from an evergreen tree (*Crescentia cujete*). The shells of this are used by the negroes for various purposes, while the sub-acid pulp is eaten. The flesh of the gourd is sometimes sweet and eatable, sometimes bitter and even purgative.

See Vol. XI. p. 5 Am. ed. (p. 4 Edin. ed.).

Gourds.

The fruit, when ripe, is of a pale yellow color, changing to a pale bay when dried. Its shells are used for various domestic purposes. (C. M.)

GOURKO, JOSEPH VLADIMIROVITSCH, COUNT, a Russian general, was born Nov. 15, 1828. He was trained in the imperial corps of pages at St. Petersburg, and became cornet of the Life-Guard Hussars in 1846. He was captain in the infantry in the Crimean war. In 1857 he returned to the Life-Guards, and became colonel in 1861, brigade-commander in 1873, and division-commander in 1876. At the outbreak of the war with Turkey, in 1877, he was placed in command of the Russian vanguard. After crossing the Danube at the end of June, he pushed on to Tirnova, and beyond the Balkans. But soon meeting the Turkish reserve forces, he was compelled to withdraw, and at the Shipka Pass he joined the Russian main body. In August he was recalled to St. Petersburg to organize a corps of cavalry, which he brought in October to aid in the investment of Plevna, where Osman Pacha was maintaining an unexpectedly gallant struggle. Gourko prevented reinforcements from reaching the besieged Turks, and thus compelled their surrender, Dec. 10. Then taking command of an army of 75,000 men, he crossed the Balkans in the depth of winter, captured Sophia Jan. 4, 1878, Philippopolis on the 16th, and reached Adrianople on the 20th. At the end of the war Gourko was made general of cavalry, and placed on the Czar's staff. In April, 1879, an attempt was made to assassinate the Czar, and Gourko was thereupon made governor-general of St. Petersburg, which was placed under martial law. Yet two further attempts followed, whereupon Gourko was removed from his position, deprived of his command, and banished to his estates. Alexander III. recalled him into active service, and in 1883 made him military governor of Warsaw.

GOVERNMENT. Civil society, government, and law are so closely related that one cannot exist without the other; for civil society is a society which has a government and is held together and regulated by law.

See Vol. XI. p. 9 Am. ed. (p. 9 Edin. ed.).

Without government or without law there can be no civil society. When individuals enter into a voluntary association for hunting, fishing, or mutual sustenance or protection, it is not a civil society if any one of them may, at will, separate himself from the others, and observe or not observe the rules of the association. Civil society can only exist when the rules made for the conduct of its members are forcibly carried out. This can only be done when there is a general consent thereto, and a habitual respect for, and obedience of, those rules on the part of the general body of the members. Without this, all would be confusion and mutual strife.

Why it is that men willingly consent to remain together in civil society, subject to government and law, is a problem which has distressed many inquisitive minds in trying to solve it; and a great many solutions have been given. Some say it is the result of a social contract; some, that it is the desire of mutual security; some, that it is the result of an ordinance of God; and what not. We do not think it necessary to lay it all to any one cause. The fact itself is the most important thing. But if we wish a cause, we may be very well satisfied to believe that it is the nature of mankind to be disposed to society, to order, to government; and that this nature was impressed upon them by the author of their being, as he has impressed upon other orders of his creatures the instinct of herding and flocking and swarming and schooling together, on the land, in the air, and in the sea. At the same time we cannot fail to see that this natural disposition is directly consonant with the other causes that have been suggested; all which tend to cement and strengthen the social union. For perpetual consent and acquiescence is equivalent to a contract; and such perpetual consent and acquiescence are secured by the necessities of men growing out of the circumstances of their situation. They need each other's help in every way. They need rules to protect them in their lives, their liberties, and their property; and they need governors, rulers, magistrates, whatever name we choose to call them, to make and enforce these rules. It is a choice between the condition of savages on the one hand and the benefits of civilization on the other; and men are carried both by their natural instincts, their needs, and their aspirations to the advantages presented by the social state.

But, whatever the cause or causes, civil society, endowed with government and laws as necessary elements of its constitution, is a fact, and as such we are content to deal with it; premising that, as a matter of nomenclature, it is called in its concrete form the body politic, the state, the commonwealth, etc.

The world contains many civil societies of different grades of perfection and development, each independent of the other and constituting an autonomy by itself. Each separate society is a nation or people; and these, according to their respective positions in the scale, are civilized, barbarous, or savage. Amongst the latter the social principle is manifested in a crude and primitive state; it ascends through the other divisions in a gradually improved form until in the highest it reaches a most complicated and artificial refinement.

Each nation, each body politic, each civil society has an organization of its own, adopted or at least used by itself independently of other nations, and each consisting of a people subjected to a government and regulated by an organic and civil law.

Government represents the nation. As such representative it maintains intercourse with other nations, makes and enforces laws, administers justice, suppresses disorder and crime, and promotes the national prosperity by wise regulations and works of public benefit and utility. These are the normal functions of government; though, like all human agencies, they may be imperfectly, unskilfully, or unfaithfully performed.

Governments are of different forms, according to the national preference or to accidental causes in the national history, or to the use of force on the part of those who have obtained the power to govern. The simplest forms are monarchy, aristocracy, and democracy, administered respectively by a single governor or king, by a select few, or by the people themselves. But instances of these simple forms are rarely seen. Most governments are of a mixed character, partaking of two or more of the simple forms, or in which a representation of the people, in lieu of the people themselves, participate; or, they may be, and often are, constituted solely of such representations, different portions of which perform different functions, according to the organic law of the state. Finally, there are federal governments, which are a peculiar combination of all or any of these, and which being the kind of government which prevails in the United States deserves more particular consideration.

FEDERAL GOVERNMENT consists of a union of two

or more States under a common government for national purposes, whilst they remain distinct and independent as to all other purposes. The objects generally sought by such a combination are greater national strength and the mutual convenience and benefit of their citizens in their intercourse with each other.

[margin: See Vol. IX. p. 55 Am. ed. (p. 61 Edin. ed.).]

Of federal governments there are two distinct kinds. One is that in which several independent governments form an alliance or confederation for mutual offence and defence, and the establishment of regulations for their general good, each being represented in a general council which advises or directs for the common welfare within the prescribed limits. An executive head is from time to time appointed by general consent. The old states of Holland, constituting the first Dutch Republic, may be mentioned as an example of this kind of federal government. This, however, is simply a confederation of different governments from which any one may retire at pleasure, and is not, strictly speaking, a constitution or establishment of a new and distinct government. The second form of federal government is of the latter class, namely, a new and distinct government formed for the exercise of certain portions of the sovereign power in and out of two or more separate governments, whose several States become for this purpose united into a single state or commonwealth. The United States of America is of this class. Of all forms of government this is the most complicated in its organization, and requires an exact delimitation of general and local powers between the general and particular states, and a high degree of cultivation in political aptitudes on the part of the people who are the subjects of it. But it is singularly adapted to the needs and energies of an active and enlightened people occupying territories of great extent, since it secures to each portion a local government for its domestic purposes, familiar with its habits, and sympathizing with its wants; and to the united nation a common government sufficiently powerful for its protection against other nations, and clothed with authority to provide general regulations for the mutual good of the whole.

Mr. Edward A. Freeman, in his *History of Federal Government*, speaking of the ideal of such a government, says: "That ideal, in its highest and most elaborate development, is the most finished and the most artificial production of political ingenuity. It is hardly possible that federal government can attain its perfect form except in a highly refined age, and among a people whose political education has already stretched over many generations."

What he adds concerning the true character of a federal government is so germane to the subject in hand that we venture to quote a few more sentences. "Two requisites," says he, "seem necessary to constitute a federal government in this its most perfect form. On the one hand each of the members of the union must be wholly independent in those matters which concern each member only. On the other hand all must be subject to a common power in those matters which concern the whole body of members collectively. Thus each member will fix for itself the laws of its criminal jurisprudence, and even the details of its political constitution. And it will do this, not as a matter of privilege or concession from any higher power, but ... absolute right, by virtue of its inher... endent commonwealth.

But in all matters which concern the general body the sovereignty of the several members will cease. Each member is perfectly independent within its own sphere; but there is another sphere in which its independence, or rather its separate existence, vanishes. It is invested with every right of sovereignty in one class of subjects, but there is another class of subjects on which it is as incapable of separate political action as any province or city of a monarchy or of an indivisible republic. The making of peace and war, the sending and receiving of ambassadors, generally all that comes within the department of international law, will be reserved wholly to the central power. Indeed, the very existence of the several members of the union will be diplomatically unknown to foreign nations, which will never be called upon to deal with any power except the central government. A federal union, in short, will form one state in relation to other powers, but many states as regards its internal administration." (Vol. I., pp. 3, 4.)

The learned author evidently had the government of the United States in view when he portrayed this striking and just ideal of a federal government. Had he imagined it clothed with certain other powers of a general and national character besides those of international relations and personality—powers which will be more particularly specified hereafter—he would have drawn a very perfect outline sketch of the government of the United States and of the several States of which the United States are composed.

The plan of having one general government for the administration of the common affairs of a country or territory, and particular governments for managing the local and domestic concerns of small portions of that territory, is carried out in the United States with much benefit and success in the smaller divisions and subdivisions of the several States; not by establishing small independent sovereignties, but subordinate agencies of the State governments. For this purpose the States are divided into counties, the counties into towns (or townships as they are sometimes called), and, at intervals, cities and other municipal corporations. The legislature of the State (if it is not already done by its constitution) invests the local authorities of these subordinate divisions, who are generally elected by the people of their several districts, with such powers of deliberation, control, and management as are suitable to their limits and necessities, so as to enable the people of these districts, as far as possible, and without interfering with other like districts, to regulate their own domestic affairs. Thus, the counties take due care for the erection and repair of necessary bridges, houses for the poor, asylums for the insane, reformatories for delinquents, high-schools for advanced pupils, etc. The towns are charged with the repair of the common highways, the construction of the smaller class of bridges, the regulation of fences, pounds, and animals, the management of the common schools, and many other minor things that interest the farmers and villagers of the country. The limited legislation exercised in this way by counties is vested in county boards, either elected from the county at large or delegated by the towns. The legislative action of the towns themselves, the last civil division of the State, is usually conducted in the town meetings, consisting of those citizens of the town at large who choose to attend on the regular or special days fixed for that purpose.

The administration of justice in small matters of

controversy is also deputed to local magistrates having county or township jurisdiction, who receive their appointment sometimes from the legislature and sometimes by election of the people. Thus, taking the whole country together, there is a regular gradation of jurisdictions and authority from the local town-meeting to the government of the United States. It is the common belief in our country that this diffusion of the powers of government and its limited participation by the people in their local assemblies is, for most purposes of social advancement, far superior to the centralism which prevails in some countries, where the supreme government intermeddles with the repair of every country road, the management of every parish and common school, and the appointment of all petty local officers and teachers.

This system of popular government by means of representatives, designated by the electoral assemblies of the citizens, involves the postulate that the majority has the right to rule; and this again is grounded on the more fundamental postulate that, in the matter of civil rights, all men are equal, and each one has a right to an equal voice in all that concerns the body politic. The truth of these supposed axioms we do not propose to discuss. It will be assumed. The argument belongs to the field of political philosophy, which has been fully occupied by the ablest thinkers, speakers, and writers. But the right of each citizen to an equal voice at the hustings, and the right of the majority to rule, must be exercised under such safeguards against fraud as the experience of popular elections demonstrates to be necessary. Without such safeguards, sanctioned by the stern rejection of fraudulent votes and fraudulent returns of votes, the system could not stand. Hence, a degraded people, sunk in corruption, are unfitted for the high duties of free government. It requires intelligence and manly virtue. Unless these permeate the mass sufficiently to give it character, despotism is sure to supervene in the end.

Government, it is proper to add, is not the same thing as sovereignty. By sovereignty is meant the ultimate power of the state, to which all final appeals are made. By government is meant the ordinary depositaries of the civil power. In the United States it is a received axiom that the sovereignty resides in the people at large. But the people are not the government. Neither the people of the United States, nor of any single State, can be brought together for consultation, decision, or the execution of measures. They can only meet by representation in what are commonly called "conventions." They never meet, even in convention, except on the extraordinary occasions of framing or amending the constitutional, or fundamental, law, by which the government is created and shaped, its different departments distinguished, their several functions assigned, their powers limited, and the mode of making future constitutional modifications prescribed. At the breaking out of the American Revolution the people of the several States, by their delegates, met in voluntary conventions (or congresses, as they were then called), and instituted State governments, which have continued to the present day, only modified, from time to time, slightly in details by conventions of the people assembled according to the organic law. In this way the great People of the United States, separately assembled in conventions in the several States, adopted and confirmed the Constitution of the United States, which had first been framed by a national convention of all the States.

Thus this great document of national unity and government received the sanction of one of the most august sovereignties that ever stood upon the earth. Its opening words require no adventitious aid to invest them with the dignity due to a nation's utterance: "We, the People of the United States, in order to form a more perfect Union, establish Justice, insure domestic Tranquillity, provide for the common Defence, promote the general Welfare, and secure the blessings of Liberty to ourselves and our posterity, do ORDAIN AND ESTABLISH this CONSTITUTION for the United States of America." (See CONSTITUTION Vol. II.)

This instance is a striking illustration of the distinction between sovereignty and government. To the people of the United States, taken collectively, belongs the sovereignty of the United States; and to the people of each State, in like manner, belongs the sovereignty of that State; whilst the government of the United States and the government of each State are respectively those depositaries of power and authority which preside over, and give law to, the body politic submitted to their respective charge, being thereto elected or appointed, according to the methods prescribed by the respective constitutions.

In other countries this distinction between the sovereignty and the government is not always recognized. In them the sovereignty is often claimed to reside in the government itself. But if it be conceded that the form and structure of a government stand upon the national will or consent, it is difficult to avoid the conclusion that the nation, or people, and not the governmental agency, is really the sovereign power.

We sometimes hear of the *government of the people*. The government of the United States is sometimes so called. But this is only in a figurative sense. It is true, the influence of the people over the government is very great, and this arises from two causes: first, the frequency of elections, by which the persons who are placed in government positions are constantly called to account by the people for the manner in which they have discharged their duties; secondly, the constant influence of public opinion by means of the press. These two causes make the government of the United States, and those of the several States, indirectly governments of the people, but not directly so. It is so near the truth, however, that many inconveniences of a democratic form of government are experienced in the United States; those inconveniences, to wit, which flow from sudden and capricious changes of popular opinion, and from the wild emotions and excitements which designing or reckless demagogues are capable of arousing in the public mind.

The close dependence of the government upon the people under such a Constitution as that of the United States acquires signal importance, not free from peril, when the great conflicting forces of society, such as capital and labor, the rich and the poor, liberty and monopoly, come into active antagonism. Concentrated wealth can, in a thousand unseen ways, move the counsels and hands of those who ostensibly govern the nation; whilst the people, not so sagacious as to what will affect their interests, and not able readily to combine their strength, are overreached and betrayed. Such intrigues may prosper for a time; but, unless some seasonable remedy is applied, a day of reckoning will come at last, when, like an earth-born giant with a million hands, the popular mass will rise up and hurl ruin and desolation broadcast in the land. So, on the other hand, the artful fomenters of discontent may im-cite the operative classes to combinations deleterious to the interests of all, and, for a time, through the ambition of aspiring demagogues, induce a course of mischievous legislation; or the innate jealousy of the people against monopolies and aggregated wealth may operate to bring about a like result, to the serious injury of important public enterprises and great damage to the public.

To such influences, on account of its extreme sensitiveness to the popular will, are free governments occasionally exposed; and it requires not only the constant and sober counsels of the good and great men of the country, but the influences of sound instruction diffused among the masses to counteract them.

But though the evils referred to are, at times, the natural outgrowth of a popular system of government, they may be said to be exceptional, whilst it receives a constant support from certain conservative influences which greatly counterbalance these occasional drawbacks. The close dependence of the government upon the people has a tendency to hold the depositaries of political power to a rigid account, and to prevent the adoption of measures inimical to the public interests. In other words, popular government has its good side and its bad side; but the people of the United States are confidently of opinion that their system is much better calculated than any other to secure personal liberty, and to prevent the operations of government from being carried on for the benefit of the few at the expense of the many.

The close relation between the government and the people in the United States has more especial reference to the legislative and executive branches than to the judicial. The latter is generally one step further removed from popular influence, being mostly appointed or elected by the other departments, either for life or for a long period of time. This gives the judicial department greater independence and stability. But jealousy of this independence has, in several States, brought about a change in the mode of appointment of judges, and has made them elective by the people. This, as far as it goes, has a tendency to make the decisions of the courts, as well as the enactments of the legislature, reflect the popular will—a result to be deplored by right-thinking men.

The division of government into three departments, legislative, executive, and judicial, first emphasized by Montesquieu, has come to be an accepted principle of political philosophy and ethics. It has a foundation in the nature of things, and some faint traces of it are exhibited in the practice of almost all governments. Even the most despotic sovereign employs the services of a council to deliberate upon and prepare proper laws, decrees, or ukases, and appoints judges to attend to the ordinary administration of justice between his subjects. But it has been reserved to modern times and to the United States to exhibit a clear and distinct illustration of the principle. Even the English constitution, from which Montesquieu derived the suggestion, did not do it entirely. First, several of the States, immediately after the Declaration of Independence in 1776, adopted constitutions in which this principle, as well as that of dividing the legislative branch into two houses, was generally adopted. The colonial governments had been of similar form. The Constitution of the United States, however, carried out the principle with greatest distinctness. The first section of Art. I. declares that "All legislative powers herein granted shall be vested in a Congress of the United States, which shall consist of a Senate and House of Representatives." The first section of Art. II. declares that "The executive power shall be vested in a President of the United States of America." The first section of Art. III. declares that "The judicial power of the United States shall be vested in one Supreme Court, and in such inferior courts as the Congress may from time to time ordain and establish." The legislators and president were to hold their offices for limited periods of two, four, and six years; the judges during good behavior; and it is declared that no person, holding any office under the United States, shall be a member of either House [of Congress] during his continuance in office.

The grounds for this threefold division of the departments of government, and the reasons in favor of it, are, that the several functions are essentially different, and that each can be more beneficially discharged for the public good when discharged by separate and independent functionaries specially chosen for their supposed qualifications and fitness for the position assigned them. The legislative department, composed of a large body of direct representatives of the people, and a smaller body of men experienced in public affairs, are most admirably suited to deliberate upon those interests of the body politic which require legislative action; whilst the judges, chosen for their legal acquirements, and sitting in a separate forum, for the calm discussion of questions of doubt and difficulty arising upon the interpretation and application of the laws and the conflicting interests of parties, are supposed capable of bestowing that grave deliberation and calm judgment which their office peculiarly requires; and, lastly, the executive chief of the government, guided by the laws enacted by the legislature, and the exposition they may have received from the judiciary, is enabled to devote himself to their execution and fulfilment, and to the performance of those public acts and duties which the dignity and interests of the commonwealth require to be done. Each department aids the others and acts as a check upon them. Together they work out a most conservative and beneficial result. Political liberty, social progress, material development, have never had such free scope under any other form of government as under this Anglo-American system.

In the United States constitution of government, as we have seen, the legislative department consists of two separate branches, the consent of each of which is necessary to the passage of a law. The Senate is appointed by the State governments, two senators from each State, and for a period of six years. The House of Representatives is elected by the people, one member from each district containing the requisite number of inhabitants, and for a period of two years. The President may veto any act; but if it afterwards receives the vote of two-thirds of each House it becomes a law. It needs only to state this arrangement to see how well calculated it is to prevent hasty and inconsiderate legislation. And after a law has been regularly passed, if any rights should be claimed under it in the courts, the question whether Congress had constitutional power to pass it is still open, and the Supreme Court is the final tribunal to pass upon that question. This operates as a standing barrier against unconstitutional encroachments on the part of Congress.

There is no longer any controversy that the true object of government is the promotion of the happiness of the people governed. The governing class are not made such for their own sakes, but for the advantage of the body politic, whose trustees and servants they are. As was said by the great reformer, Luther—no less statesman than reformer—"Authority was not instituted for its own ends, nor to make use of the persons subjected to it for the accomplishment of its own caprices and ill passions, but for the interests and advantage of the people." This is now a received axiom of politics. The only embarrassment arises in carrying it out in practice; for it often happens that measures greatly demanded by the general interest are injurious to individuals. The erection of public works requires the imposition of taxes; and the suppression of traffic in opium, or intoxicating drinks, or other kinds of merchandise, may work injury to those who have made investments in those articles, or in establishments for their production. In view of the general law that partial evil attends upon universal good, Bentham's method of solution was to pursue the greatest good of the greatest number. Such problems, when they arise, are peculiarly within the province of the legislative department to solve. The representatives in that department are intimately acquainted with the wants, the capabilities, and the resources of the people, with what will be for their benefit and what burdens they can bear.

It may be somewhat difficult to define the exact functions of government and the extent to which it may properly interfere in the development of the material resources and industries of the country and the education and morals of the people. It may attempt too much. It may go too far. It may interfere with the free and unrestrained action of the people themselves and indirectly repress their spontaneous energies and enterprise. This always acts as a retarding and benumbing influence upon social and industrial progress, and should be carefully avoided. But there are certain undertakings which, either from their public character or their magnitude, demand the agency of government. Of course the instrumentalities of government, such as its navy, its fortifications, munitions of war, public buildings, light-houses, seawalls, and the like, will be erected solely by and under the control of the government. Other works for public use, such as railroads, bridges, canals, turnpikes, etc., whilst requiring legislative authority, may be farmed out to private associations, subject always to the public use and to any regulations necessary to secure the people from imposition. The post-office and the mint are regarded in this country as properly under governmental management. Whether telegraphic communication should not also be so is a question for fair consideration. The business of public carriers would seem to be better conducted under private management. In this enumeration of offices and duties we do not distinguish between what belongs to national and what to State jurisdiction. As to the latter, however, we may add that the State legislatures, in matters within their jurisdiction, often descend to minute details. They not only authorize the erection of railroads, canals, turnpikes, and bridges, but they provide for the drainage of lands, authorize the erection of dams for mill-power, and create business, benevolent, educational, religious, and charitable corporations of every kind. In truth, there is hardly an end to the number of interests which they attempt to foster or in some manner to regulate. Legislative interference in private enterprises generally has a tendency to confer exclusive or peculiar privileges on somebody, and the extent to which it has been carried in many States has given so much dissatisfaction that amendments have been made to their constitutions to limit the legislative power. Thus the creation of private corporations has been carried to such an excess in some States that their legislatures have been restrained from creating any private corporations at all, being restricted to the passage of general laws under which private associations might organize themselves into bodies corporate, subject to such wholesome regulations as the interest of the public may require. Turning to one of these constitutional amendments—namely, to that made to the constitution of Illinois in 1870—we find the following provisions, to wit: "The State shall never pay, assume, or become responsible for the debts or liabilities of, or in any manner give, loan, or extend its credit to or in aid of any public or other corporation, association, or individual;" "the general assembly shall not pass local or special laws in any of the following enumerated cases: that is to say, for granting divorces, changing the names of persons or places, laying out, opening, altering, or working roads or highways, vacating roads, town-plats, etc., regulating county and township affairs, . . . granting to any corporation, association, or individual any special or exclusive privilege, immunity, or franchise whatever," etc. . . . "No corporation shall be created by special laws, or its charter extended, changed, or amended, except those for charitable, educational, penal, or reformatory purposes." Instead of special laws for effecting these purposes the legislature is restricted to the passage of general laws on the several subjects enumerated.

The necessity of these restraints upon legislative interference arises from the extreme nearness of the State legislative bodies to the people whom they represent, and the facility with which every petty grievance, want, or wish can be brought to their attention for redress or gratification.

In fine, in popular governments, like those which prevail in the United States, the danger is not that there will be too little legislation but that there will be too much. In one of the States (not a large one, either) the amount of legislation became so great a few years since that the annual volumes of laws grew to the size of nearly 2000 octavo pages; but the adoption of an amendment to the State constitution, limiting the power of the legislature in regard to private laws, has reduced the annual volumes to 400 or 500 pages—still too large by half.

The truth is, Legislation with us is done to death. We can say, in the words of a great statesman, "The world is governed too much." Every new and raw member who can spell his name is seized with an itch to propose a bill. Our laws might well say, as the merchants of France said to Colbert, the great minister of finance under Louis XIV., when he asked what he could do for them, "Let us alone!" Our own conclusion is that the government of the country (considering the national and State governments as a unit) will best perform its duty and best subserve the public good if, after sufficiently protecting its citizens against the withering influence of foreign competition, it leaves them at liberty to pursue their private fortunes in their own way, under the stimulus of those motives which are ever active when the arts of peace are left untrammelled and the rewards of enterprise and honorable ambition are fairly open to all. (J. P. B.)

GRACE. Grace, in theology, is the favor of God to man, which to man as a sinner takes the form of mercy. The *doctrines of grace* are those doctrines which teach the manner and circumstances of the divine favor, as, *e. g.*, the doctrines of the total depravity of man, the incarnation, the atonement, the gift of the spirit, regeneration, sanctification, and glorification.

The word "grace" is also used for that condition which man possesses through the divine favor. He is in a condition of grace, as contrasted with the condition of nature. "Growth in grace" is thus progress in the divine life.

Some distinguish between *general* and *special* grace, the former represented by the light of nature and conscience, and the latter by the Word and Spirit. The holy principles of the soul in a state of grace, such as faith, hope, love, joy, peace, etc., are called "graces."
(H. CR.)

GRAFTING. This process is employed in the propagation of trees, vines, and plants, also in securing early fruiting of new varieties by grafting upon bearing trees and vines, or numerous varieties upon one tree to test the comparative value. Nurserymen secure stocks of the apple, pear, plum, and cherry by sowing seeds in the early spring, or the fall previous. When these seedlings have reached the size of a lead-pencil or larger, which usually occurs in one or two years, they are dug and packed in a cellar. During the leisure of winter the roots, which are often from eight to fifteen inches long, are cut into pieces three to four inches long, and grafted with such varieties as are desired. The process usually employed on such stocks is called whip-grafting, which consists of a slanting cut on the root, a similar one on the scion, with a slit in both root and scion, which enables the parts to fit closely together, and to be held firmly in that position. The grafted root is immediately wound with cotton-yarn that has been drawn through grafting-wax, composed of equal parts of rosin and tallow, and one-fourth part of beeswax. This winding with waxed string is principally intended to hold the parts closely together, and is not intended to prevent the access of air to the parts. In former times it was deemed necessary to envelop the joint between the root and the scion with waxed cloth or paper, to exclude the air, as well as to hold the parts in place, but this method has been discarded, as it is not so expeditious. These grafted roots are placed in layers of moist saw-dust or sand until ready for planting, at the earliest possible moment in the spring, in the nursery rows. *Saddle-grafting* is

Saddle-Grafting.

sometimes employed in grafting roots. It consists in paring the roots in form of a wedge, and by making a saddle-like cleft in the scion, which enables the scion to fit closely over the wedge-like root in the form of a saddle. It is then wound with waxed cotton-yarn as before. In olden times people used wet clay in place of waxed string to protect the graft. *Cleft-grafting* consists in making a deep cleft in the stock or branch. It is held open by a wedge in the centre, while the scion is inserted at one edge, or, in case the stock is large, at both edges of the stock; after which the wound in the stock, and all parts of the scion cut with a knife, are covered with grafting-wax or waxed cloth, so as to exclude moisture or drying influences. If the tops of the scions are covered with wax, it renders success more certain, but is not necessary. Cleft-grafting is usually employed in grafting bearing trees, or where

Cleft-Grafting.

large limbs are grafted. More than one hundred methods of grafting have been practised, but the foregoing methods are principally used at the present date. Twenty methods of grafting were known in the days of the elder Pliny.

Success depends, 1, upon the scions being healthy, fully matured, and full of sap, and of the past season's growth only. Scions are usually cut in the fall, before they have been exposed to the action of severe freezing, which reduces their vitality. As soon as they are cut, they are placed in moist sand in a cellar, and nearly covered with that material until wanted. Where the winters are mild, it is best not to remove the scions from the trees until wanted, unless for very late grafting. In such cases the scions should be inserted before the buds begin to swell in the spring. 2. Only sharp knives and tools should be used, as the parts should be made to fit closely as possible, with the smooth cut of a sharp instrument only. 3. An inner layer of bark, on both scion and stock, should meet or cross at some point, in order to permit the continuous flow of sap from the stock to the scion. 4. The pressure of the stock upon the scion should not be too severe, as it may be in case of cleft-grafting. A strong pressure upon the scion, caused by the removal of the wedge, often holds the scion in too close an embrace. This is avoided by leaving a small wedge between the scion and the stock to bear a portion of the pressure. 5. In planting grafted roots, great care should be taken to have them planted as deep as possible, permitting one bud only to remain above the surface. Compact the soil as firmly as possible about them. In out-door grafting of large stocks, success depends largely upon the season when the work is done, which varies with different species. The plum and cherry require very early grafting. Such work is usually done at the earliest possible moment, often while there are yet traces of snow upon the fields, and before the buds of trees make any growth. The apple and pear may be grafted much later. It has been thought that the best time for grafting the pear or apple is when the leaves are beginning to push forward into growth, providing the scions have been kept retarded in a cool cellar. In no case should the buds of the scion have begun to unfold when grafted.

in nurseries where the buds or grafts have failed the previous season, they are often regrafted in early spring by whip-grafting, the juncture in such cases being protected by waxed cloth or paper. In all cases where the graft is fully exposed to the atmosphere, such protection is necessary, and is only omitted in case of root-grafts, which being buried in the soil, and the soil compacted firmly, are protected by the earth from exposure to the atmosphere. The graft does not take readily upon the peach, therefore the peach is seldom propagated in that manner. Grafts of the pear will grow upon the apple, quince, and thorn, and the plum upon the peach. There are many stocks upon which nearly allied species will thrive for a season, but as connection between different families is usually not permanent nor successful in the end, it is not necessary to go into the details here. The pear grafted upon the apple thrives only for a few years, often giving, however, fine specimens of fruit. The pear upon the quince is one of the most successful of all unions of the kind, forming the dwarf-pear, which is largely cultivated throughout the country with success. Dwarf-trees of the apple, cherry, etc., are secured by grafting upon a slow-growing stock. Thus, dwarf-apples are secured by grafting ordinary varieties upon paradise stock, etc.

Much attention has recently been given to the grafting of the grape, but until lately failure has been so frequently met with as to discourage the vineyardist, and yet, it is exceedingly desirable to make use of strong-growing varieties as stocks for those that grow more feebly. Many of the devices used in grafting the apple and pear have been applied to grafting the grape. It has been found that grafting-wax applied to grape-vines causes failure on account of the rapid escape of the sap from the vine in the spring. There has recently been invented the "Wagner saw," which introduces a new method of grafting the grape that has proved remarkably successful. This saw is composed of two thin blades, placed within one-eighth of an inch of each other, with a sharp chisel-blade between. The earth is removed from the old vine, often as far as the root will permit, exposing the collar. The vine is then cut off with the saw three or four inches below the surface. Cuts are then made in the stub of the vine remaining, cornerwise through the bark and half an inch into the stump, often three or four such clefts being made. Scions of the grape containing from one to three buds, the scions being from four to eight inches long, are inserted. The cuttings should originally be larger than the cut made by the saw, and the length of the cutting is no objection, as it can extend far below the juncture of the cutting with the stock. Our practice has been to pare the cutting on each side near the lower end a little wedge-shaped as usual, and press into the little gap made by the saw, but not too firmly. Often three or more of these cuttings are thus inserted in the root of the old vine. The lower ends of the cuttings extend intact into the soil below the incision made in the stock. The earth is then pressed firmly about the cutting and the stock, leaving only one eye exposed. This is the best method of grafting the grape known.

The effect of the stock upon the scion and the scion upon the stock is worthy of note, and has not received special attention until recently. The effect of the stock upon the scion is plainly shown in the grape. If we graft the Delaware, which is a very slow grower, with small berries, and leaves liable to drop, upon a Concord, which is a vigorous grower, producing large berries, and holding its leaves well, we will thereby secure a more vigorous Delaware vine, inclined to produce larger berries, more of them, and inclined to hold its leaves longer. Those varieties of grapes that are hardly worthy of cultivation upon their own roots, on account of lack of vigor and other constitutional defects, often succeed admirably when grafted upon more vigorous stocks. Where phylloxera has devastated a vineyard, it has been found necessary to graft the desired varieties upon the roots of those varieties that are not affected by the destructive root-insect.

The effect of the scion upon the stock is shown in cases where different varieties in the same nursery are grafted upon seedlings that possess common characteristics. Thus, Fameuse and Red Astrachan apple-scions are grafted upon common seedlings and planted side by side in the nursery row. On digging these trees, after they have grown in the nursery three or four years, it will be discovered that the Fameuse apple-trees have roots characteristic of the Fameuse variety, extending deep into the subsoil with coarse pronged roots, while the Red Astrachan trees will be found to have fibrous roots, branched near the surface as is common with that variety, notwithstanding that the roots of both varieties were originally the same. The effect of the scion upon the stock is further noticed in cases where vigorous pears are grafted upon pear-stocks in the same row in which feeble-growing pears are grafted. After a few years it will be discovered that the pear-roots grafted to the vigorous varieties are nearly double the size of those grafted of feeble varieties, and both the roots were of the same size when first grafted.

The propagation of fruit-trees is now more largely secured by budding than by grafting. When budding is practised the seedlings of the apple, pear, cherry, peach, nectarine, apricot, etc., are planted in the nursery rows, and allowed to grow there, with the best culture, until July, August, or September, when they are budded. Thus new varieties can be propagated much more rapidly from buds than scions, as one scion has several buds, each of which forms a tree when budded. The pear is usually grafted the earliest in the nursery, as it is liable to blight later in the season, which prevents further work. The plum follows next. In fact, the pear and plum cannot be budded much too early, as ripe buds for insertion cannot be secured earlier than July, unless purchased from points farther south, where the buds mature earlier, which method is beginning to be practised with pear-buds. Next come the cherry and apple, and lastly the peach, which is budded last. It has been found that early budding is usually most successful. Budding is accomplished by making a perpendicular slit just above the surface of the soil in a thrifty-growing stock, not smaller than an ordinary lead-pencil. Directly above this slit a cross-cut is made, then the bark is raised at this juncture. The bud is then cut from the scion of the present season's growth, with an inch of bark attached, and a little of the wood directly under the bud, in order to secure all parts of the bud, a portion of the bud often penetrating the wood slightly. This small bit of wood attached to the bud was formerly removed, but is now permitted to remain by most budders. The bud is inserted into the cleft of the bark, and pressed firmly beneath to its full length, after which the wound and bud are bound tightly with a string, usually basswood bark, permitting only a point of the bud to be exposed. At the expiration of two weeks the string is removed. If previous to this time the stock is discovered to be slightly cut by the string, it should be loosened before the expiration of the two weeks. The next spring the stock is cut off above the bud, and the bud only permitted to grow, which forms a tree, all other buds growing upon the stock being removed.

(C. A. G.)

GRAHAM, SYLVESTER (1794-1851), an American vegetarian, was born at Suffield, Conn., in 1794. In early life, being feeble and sickly, he was unable to pursue any employment steadily. In 1823 he entered Amherst College to prepare for the ministry, and was noted there for the fervor of his elocution. In 1826 he married, and soon after was licensed as a Presbyterian preacher. Being employed by the Pennsylvania Temperance Society to lecture, he began to study physiology, and then adopted the views which he afterwards advocated. These were set forth in his *Essay on Cholera* (1832), and more fully in the *Graham Lectures on the Science of Human Life* (1839). In his treatise on *Bread and Bread-Making*, he urged the use of unbolted flour for making bread, and this "Graham" flour and bread have been much used since by dyspeptics. Graham died at Northampton, Mass., Sept. 11, 1851.

GRAHAM, WILLIAM ALEXANDER (1804-1875), an American statesman, was born in Lincoln co., N. C., Sept. 5, 1804. He became a lawyer, and in 1833 was elected to the assembly of his native State. He was several times chosen speaker of that body, and in 1841 was elected to the U. S. Senate. He was governor of the State from 1845 to 1849. Pres. Fillmore appointed him secretary of the navy, which office he resigned when he was nominated by the National Whig Convention for Vice-President in June, 1852. The Whig party was defeated in the next election, and Mr. Graham remained in private life until 1864, when he was a senator in the Confederate Congress. In 1866 he was a delegate to the Union Convention in Philadelphia. He died suddenly at Saratoga, N. Y., Aug. 11, 1875.

GRAHAME, JAMES (1790-1842), a Scotch historian, was born in Glasgow, Dec. 21, 1790. He was educated partly at St. John's College, Cambridge, studied law, and was admitted as an advocate at the Scottish bar in 1812. After practising his profession for some years he removed in 1826 to the south of England for the sake of his health. Here he devoted himself to preparing a *History of the United States*, of which two volumes appeared in 1827. The strong love of American ideas and institutions manifested in it seems to have hindered its success. The author, still in pursuit of health, removed to Nantes, France, where he collected materials for continuing his history, which, however, remains incomplete. Graham also published a *Defence of the Scottish Presbyterians* against Sir Walter Scott. Among his other pamphlets was one on the question of American slavery. He died in London, July 3, 1842. His *History* was republished at Philadelphia in 1846, with a memoir by Josiah Quincy.

GRAMONT, ANTOINE AGÉNOR ALFRED, DUC DE (1819-1880), a French statesman, was born at Paris, Aug. 14, 1819. He was educated at the École Polytechnique. Napoleon III. sent him as minister plenipotentiary to Cassel (1852), Stuttgart (1852), and to Turin (1853), where he assisted in bringing Sardinia into the Anglo-French alliance against Russia. In 1857 he was ambassador to Rome, but after the French recognition of the kingdom of Italy in 1861 he was sent to Vienna. In May, 1870, he was minister of foreign affairs in the Ollivier cabinet. Prince Leopold of Hohenzollern having voluntarily withdrawn his candidacy for the Spanish throne, Gramont insisted that King William of Prussia should declare formally that he would authorize no prince of his house to accept that throne. When the king refused and dismissed the ambassador, Gramont declared in the French Chambers on July 15 that war had begun. The speedy defeat of the army led to the downfall of the Ollivier ministry within a month. Henceforth the duke was the object of fierce attacks by various parties, and in January, 1872, he was summoned before a committee of inquiry into the causes of the disasters of 1870. He afterwards defended his action in various articles in the *Revue der Deux Mondes* and other periodicals. He published also *La France et la Prusse avant la guerre* (1872). He died at Paris, Jan. 18, 1880.

GRAND RAPIDS, a city of Michigan, county-seat of Kent county, is on both banks of the Grand River, 40 miles from where it empties into Lake Michigan and 153 miles W. N. W. of Detroit. Here the river is approached on either side by steep bluffs, and across the river extend the rapids which give name to the town. The river falls 18 feet in one mile. These rapids furnish an excellent motive power, largely utilized in milling and manufacturing, though steam is now used in most of the factories. Here centre several railways, the Chicago and West Michigan, the Grand Rapids and Indiana, one line of the Michigan Central, the Detroit, Grand Haven, and Milwaukee, the Grand Rapids, Newaygo, and Lake Shore, and a branch of the Michigan Southern. Canals for water-power extend along either side of the river, here crossed by six bridges. Above the rapids the river is again navigable for 50 miles. The manufactures include furniture, wagons, wooden wares, machinery, lumber, calcined and land plaster (from gypsum quarried near by), barrels, leather, beer, chemicals, and pale bricks, with a variety of other goods. Grand Rapids is the seat of the U. S. courts for Western Michigan. There are 3 hotels, 4 national banks, 2 other banks, 6 daily and 20 weekly newspapers (1 Dutch, 1 German), a copious water-supply, a system of street railways, good public schools, a city library, and a scientific institution with valuable collections. The police and fire departments are well organized. There are 46 churches, and the city is the see of the P. E. bishop of Western Michigan. It was settled in 1835 from New York and New England, and was incorporated in 1850, when its population was only 2686. In 1870 it had increased to 16,507, and in 1880 to 32,016. By the census of 1890, it was 70,049, making it the second city in the State in population.

GRANGER, GIDEON (1767-1822), an American statesman, was born at Suffield, Conn., July 19, 1767. He graduated at Yale College in 1787, and was admitted to the bar in 1788. He soon acquired a high reputation, and from 1793 was for several years a member of the State legislature. He was noted for his efforts to establish the State school-fund. In 1801 he was appointed postmaster-general of the United States and continued in this office throughout President Jefferson's administration, and under Madison until 1814, when his opposition to the policy of the latter required his removal. He then settled at Canandaigua, N. Y., and he was State senator from 1819 to 1821, and advocated the building of the Erie Canal and other internal improvements. He died at Canandaigua, N.

Y., Dec. 31, 1822. His son, FRANCIS GRANGER (1792-1868), was also a prominent lawyer and was postmaster-general in 1841.

GRANGER, GORDON (1821-1876), an American general, was born at Canandaigua, N. Y., in 1821. He graduated at West Point in 1845 and served in the Mexican war, distinguishing himself at Contreras, Churubusco, and Chapultepec. He was afterwards employed on frontier duty. He was made captain in the Third cavalry May 5, 1861, and served on the staff of Gen. Sturgis in Missouri. He was appointed colonel of the Second Michigan cavalry Sept. 2, 1861, and brigadier-general of volunteers March 26, 1862. He served under Generals Halleck and Grant in the movement to open the Mississippi. In September, 1862, he was promoted to be major-general and commanded in Kentucky and Tennessee, repulsing Van Dorn at Franklin. He was distinguished at the battle of Chickamauga and was afterwards in command of the Fourth army corps at Missionary Ridge. He was engaged in the siege and capture of Mobile, April 12, 1865. After the war he held commands in Texas and Kentucky. He was appointed colonel of the Twenty-fifth infantry in 1866, and transferred to the Fifteenth in 1870, which command he held till his death, Jan. 10, 1876.

GRANGERS. The important association of American agriculturists, commonly known by this name, though formerly called Patrons of Husbandry, originated at the city of Washington, in 1867, through the action of several government employés. In January, 1866, Mr. O. H. Kelly, a clerk in the agricultural department, was sent on a journey through the South in the interests of the department. Finding that agriculture in that section was greatly depressed and disorganized, in consequence of the war, it seemed to him that organization was necessary there, and reason taught him that it might prove as useful to Northern as to Southern farmers. His object was to establish a secret society in the interests of farmers alone. In this he interested William Saunders, J R Thompson and William M Ireland all in the government service. These, with three other persons afterwards associated, devised the scheme, framed the constitution, and organized the ritual of the order and organized the first society at Washington on Dec. 4, 1867, under the name of the "National Grange of the Patrons of Husbandry." Under the scheme of the order it was to be divided into national State, and subordinate assemblies or granges, the officers in all cases having somewhat fanciful names, several derived from the ancient classic mythology. Women were to be admitted to membership on equal standing with men, and others were permitted to share under the titles of Ceres, Pomona, Flora and ...

...

Up to the close of 1871 there were but about 200 granges organized, while the national grange contained only its seven original members. From this time forward its progress was rapid. The farming population began to perceive the advantages of the association and grew as enthusiastic as they had been lethargic. In 1872 there were organized 1160 granges; in 1873, 8669; and in 1874 and 1875 about 11,000 in each year. At the close of 1875 there were about 30,000 granges in existence, said to average about 40 members each, the order being strongest in the West and North-west and well represented in the South. By this time its climax of prosperity had been reached. In the succeeding years jealousy arose between the subordinate and the national granges, and parties with no interest in agriculture beyond that of fleecing the farmers made their way into the order. So far was this carried that one grange was organized on Broadway, New York city, with 45 members, representing a capital of perhaps as many millions, and composed of bank presidents, wholesale dealers, sewing-machine manufacturers, and speculators. Other instances of a similar character might be named. The result of all this was a great depression of the order, from which it is but fairly beginning to recover. It may be said here that one main reason of this partial failure was the lack of discipline in the order, owing to its very rapid progress, and the misconception of many of the members as to its objects and their own true interests. Its more recent revival has been mainly due to an improvement in organization and to a higher realisation of their true interests by the members of the order. As to its present standing it may be said that at the annual session of the national grange, held in Boston, November, 1885, representatives from the State granges of 34 States were present, they representing 24,000 subordinate granges. It is gradually increasing in number of members and of granges and has become generally spread throughout the country, the farmers everywhere beginning to appreciate the advantages of organization. Ten or twelve newspapers are published in its interest. A few years ago a deputy was sent to England who established the order in that country. It has not yet made much progress there.

At the St. Louis session of the national grange, in 1874, the following "Declaration of Purposes" was issued:

"We shall endeavor to advance our cause by laboring to accomplish the following objects:

To secure a better and higher manhood and womanhood among ourselves; to enhance the comforts and attractions of our homes and strengthen our attachments to our pursuits; to foster mutual understanding and co-operation; to maintain inviolate our laws and to embrace each other in labor to hasten the good time coming; to reduce our expenses, both individual and corporate; to buy less and produce more, in order to make our farms self-sustaining; to diversify our crops and crop no more than we can cultivate; to condense the weight of our exports, selling less in the bushel and more in hoof and in fleece, less in lint and more in warp and woof, to systematize our work and calculate intelligently on probabilities; to discountenance the credit system, the mortgage system, the fashion system, and every other system tending to prodigality and bankruptcy.

"To reduce meeting together, talking together, working together, buying together, selling together..."

and, in general, acting together for our mutual protection and advancement, as occasion may require. We shall avoid litigation as much as possible by arbitration in the grange. We shall constantly strive to secure entire harmony, good-will, vital brotherhood among ourselves, and to make our order perpetual."

As to how these objects have been carried out we may briefly epitomize. For the social culture of its members music and literary exercises were introduced at the meetings, and the society has proved of great benefit in educating and entertaining, and in promoting social intercourse and study among the naturally isolated members of the rural community. Books were called for from all quarters, and much money has been invested in select libraries for granges in many of the States. The call for newspapers has been still greater, and one postmaster reports that where there was but one newspaper taken before the establishment of the grange in his vicinity there are now thirty. One clergyman writes: "Since the introduction of the *grange* I have seen a remarkable change in the walk and conversation of my flock; they are more careful in their dress and general appearance and are reading more."

Industrially the grange established agencies with manufacturers for the sale of their products directly to consumers, and at the greatest cash discount. As a consequence they succeeded in securing farming utensils, furniture, books, and all articles needed at a reduction of from 25 to 50 per cent. on former rates. The grange also attempted to institute a series of crop reports with very excellent results. But it was only tried in 1874, proving too expensive for the funds of the order. In addition an effort was made to introduce co-operation on the Rochdale system. But its progress was checked by the opposition of the previously established commission agencies. Yet cooperative stores were organized in many of the States, some of which are yet in profitable existence.

The war in the West against unjust discrimination in railroad freights, which produced restrictive laws in Illinois and Wisconsin in 1873, has been charged upon the granges, but falsely, as they declare. It was organized and sustained by agricultural clubs outside the order, whose constitution did not permit a participation in it, though the members were undoubtedly in strong sympathy with its objects. The result has been a partial removal of the unjust freight discrimination. The Eastern States are now moving actively in the same direction, and Pennsylvania and New York have organizations for this purpose, outside the grange. Other questions which the grange has taken in hand are such as the rapid increase of insects through undue destruction of insectivorous birds, the exposure of attempted swindles to which the isolation of the farmer renders him particularly liable, and of combinations to extort money for the use of articles falsely claimed to be patented, such as the *swing gate*, the *driven well*, etc. We may conclude in the words of Hon. D. Wyatt Aiken: "The harvest of improvement which the American farmers reaped during the prosperous era of the grange, and which is still ripening in every State of this Union, cannot be limited to a monetary valuation. The social elevation, the moral improvement, and the educational advancement have been beyond comprehension." (C. M.)

GRANITE, the name given to a class of igneous rocks, the oldest and most primitive in structure of the known rocks. The structure of the granites, however, seems to indicate that they are resultants of the disruption and reaggregation of still older rocks, since they are compounds of usually three and sometimes four or five constituents; namely, quartz, feldspar in two or three varieties, and mica in two varieties. These minerals are not cemented, but cohere so closely as to form the most compact of rocks, and one which is devoid of stratified structure. The constituents of granite occur often as minute crystals, seldom or never as rounded grains. These particles range from a size indistinguishable to the naked eye, to lumps larger than a walnut, in the so-called giant granites. Where large crystals of feldspar occur in the mass it is called porphyritic granite. Where the mica is replaced by hornblende the stone is called syenite. Granite is of a considerable variety of colors, from pure white, to gray, red, or deep black. Feldspar comprises from a third to a half or a greater proportion of the rock, while its principal chemical constituent is silica, of which it contains from 65 to 81.7 per cent. The feldspar is present in the form of orthoclase or oligoclase, or as albite in the white varieties. It is usually yellowish-white or reddish in color, more rarely gray or greenish, and gives the predominant color to the mass.

Granite gains its principal industrial value from its hardness, compactness, and homogeneous structure, it being uniform in all directions, of great strength and durability, and capable of yielding large blocks from its absence of stratification or parallel joints. These qualities render it suitable for locations where great resisting power is required, such as breakwaters, harbors, light-houses, docks, fortifications, and foundations. It is unsuited for fine sculpture on account of its structure and coarseness, and its resistance to the chisel. It, however, takes a fine polish, and is now much used for monumental purposes. It is subject to a slow decay, particularly in the colder climates, named by Dolomieu *maladie du granit*. This arises from the decomposing action of atmospheric water on feldspar, which is gradually dissolved, the insoluble silicate of alumina remaining as kaolin or clay, through which are mixed the sand grains and mica scales of the granite. If there be any iron present the clay will be red. In some cases this decay extends for many feet below the surface. In warm, dry climates granite may stand intact for thousands of years, as we have evidence in the syenitic obelisks of Egypt. In cold climates there is a gradual but very slow surface exfoliation. But there is a more dangerous weathering inward along lines of weakness, so that a deep disintegration may take place, and large fragments break off by the action of frost.

Commercial granite is not very extensively found in the United States. Its chief occurrence in the Eastern region is in Maine, New Hampshire, Massachusetts, Connecticut, New York, along the Great Lakes, and at points in the Mississippi Valley. It often has crevices or veins filled with foreign material, such as metallic ores and other minerals. The islands off the coast of Maine are chiefly composed of granite, and yield some excellent stone, which is largely used in the Atlantic cities. The red granite now so much used in this country for monuments comes chiefly from near Aberdeen, Scotland, but a similar stone is found in several localities in this country. Nova Scotia and New Brunswick yield a red monumental stone of fine quality, and a similar stone comes from the Red Beach quarries of Maine, which is largely used for polished monumental columns in all our principal cities. A light gray granite from quarries near East Bluehill

Me., has been much used in recent Philadelphia architecture, as in the City Hall and the Pennsylvania Railroad Bridge, as also in the East River Bridge, New York, and elsewhere. From this quarry blocks have been obtained of 90 by 80 by 6 feet dimensions.

Of the many other valuable New England quarries, those of Quincy, Mass., are best known, and the gray Quincy granite has been very largely employed in architectural work in the Eastern States. Granite is largely developed in some parts of the Rocky Mountains, where a red syenite equal to that of Aberdeen is found. Excellent gray and red stone occurs in many localities in the Laurentian area, back of Marquette, Lake Superior. The Sierra Nevada yields a gray granite, which is sometimes nearly white from the presence of albite. Many quarries are worked in California; those in the vicinity of Sacramento yielding blue, black, and gray granite, the black closely resembling the celebrated black granite of Egypt, and very beautiful when highly polished. It is used for monumental purposes. (C. M.)

GRANT. A species of conveyance at common law for transferring the property of incorporeal hereditaments and estates in reversion; it being impossible to give actual *seisin* or corporeal possession of that which had no tangible existence, or which the grantor had not in his possession; therefore such estates passed only by deed of grant. Livery of *seisin*, or delivery of possession, was necessary at common law to transfer an estate of freehold in corporeal hereditaments, and this although there was a written deed. Hence corporeal hereditaments were said to *lie in livery* and incorporeal hereditaments *in grant*. But by statutes 8 and 9 Victoria, c. 106, s. 2, all corporeal hereditaments shall, as regards the conveyance of the immediate freehold thereof, be deemed to lie *in grant* as well as *in livery*. In most of the United States, *livery of seisin* is dispensed with, either by statute or by usage, so that the word *grant* has become a generic term applicable to all transfers of real property.

The word *grant* is also applied to the disposition of personal property, and is distinguished from *gift* in that a grant is based on a consideration or equivalent.

GRANT, SIR ALEXANDER (1826–1884), a Scotch educator, was born at Dalvey in 1826. He was the son of Sir Robert Innes Grant, and the eighth baronet of the line. He was educated at Harrow and Balliol College, Oxford, and in 1849 was elected a fellow of Oriel College. In 1855 he became an examiner for the Indian civil service, and a public examiner in classics at Oxford. In 1858 he was made inspector of schools in the Madras Presidency, and in 1860 professor of history and political economy in Elphinstone College at Madras, to the presidency of which he succeeded in 1862. In the next year he was made vice-chancellor of the University of Bombay, and in 1865 director of public instruction in Bombay Presidency. In 1868 he was called to be vice-chancellor and principal of the University of Edinburgh, and held this position at the celebration of the ter-centenary of that institution in 1883. While at Oxford he gave especial attention to the works of Aristotle and edited the *Nicomachean Ethics of Aristotle* with English notes (1854; 4th ed., 1882). He also prepared sketches of *Xenophon* (1871) and of *Aristotle*, and a *History of the University of Edinburgh* (2 vols., 1884), prepared in view of the ter-centenary celebration. Sir Alexander Grant died Nov. 30, 1884.

GRANT, ULYSSES SIMPSON (1822–1885), the most distinguished American general, eighteenth President of the United States, was born at Point Pleasant, Clermont co., Ohio, April 27, 1822. His ancestry has been traced to Matthew Grant, who came from Dorsetshire, England, in 1630, and settled first at Dorchester, Mass., but afterwards at Windsor, Conn. The family continued to reside in Connecticut until the great westward emigration movement which followed the establishment of the new government of the United States. Then Noah Grant in 1790 removed to Western Pennsylvania, and later his son, Jesse Root Grant, went still farther west, settling on the north bank of the Ohio. He had married Hannah Simpson, and during the infancy of their oldest son, who was named Hiram Ulysses, they removed to Georgetown, Ohio. They were plain, honest, industrious people, belonging to the Methodist Episcopal Church. They both lived to see him President of the United States. Jesse was a tanner, but, finding Ulysses little inclined to follow that occupation, procured for him in 1839 from Thomas L. Hamer, the congressman in whose district he resided, an appointment to the U. S. Military Academy at West Point. By some inadvertence the official document was made out in the name of "Ulysses Sidney Grant," and efforts to have the mistake rectified resulted only in altering the middle name to Simpson. Grant acquiesced in this, but he was generally called by his comrades "Uncle Sam Grant." Though a faithful worker, he was not brilliant nor specially distinguished in any study. When he graduated, June 30, 1843, he was No. 21 in a class of 39, and was made brevet second-lieutenant of infantry. He was assigned to the Fourth regiment, then stationed in Missouri, but in the next year sent to Louisiana, in anticipation of the annexation of Texas. In 1846 the war with Mexico commenced, and Grant, at first under Gen. Zachary Taylor, afterwards under Gen. Winfield Scott, took part in every battle except Buena Vista. At Molino del Rey he won by his gallantry the brevet of first-lieutenant, and later that of captain. Soon after his return from Mexico, on Aug. 22, 1848, Capt. Grant was married to Miss Julia Dent, of St. Louis, and with his wife he spent nearly four years in garrison at Sackett's Harbor and Detroit. In 1852, when he was ordered to the Pacific coast, she was unable to accompany him. After two years of tedious monotony in Oregon and California, Grant resigned his commission and returned to St. Louis, near which his father-in-law gave him a small farm and three negroes. But even hard work on the farm did not produce sufficient for his family, and he sought employment in the neighboring city, and finally in 1860 removed to Galena, Ill., where his brothers took him as partner in the leather trade.

Before twelve months passed several Southern States had seceded, and the war for the Union opened for Grant a new career. Raising a company of volunteers at Galena he led it to Springfield, where his military experience led to his being employed in organizing the Illinois State troops. On June 16, 1861, he was assigned to the command of the Twenty-first regiment, which had become demoralized. Under its new commander, the regiment soon became noted for its thorough discipline and efficiency. In August, through the friendly offices of Elihu B. Washburne, member of Congress from the Galena district, Col. Grant was promoted to the rank of brigadier-general, to date from

May 17, 1861. On Sept. 1, Major-Gen. J. C. Fremont placed him in command of South-eastern Missouri, with head-quarters at Cairo, Ill. Here Grant took John A. Rawlins, a Galena lawyer, as his adjutant-general, and afterwards retained him at the head of his staff throughout his military career. Before a week had passed Grant became aggressive, seized Paducah, Ky., and threatened Columbus. He was also energetic in organizing the regiments which were gathering at Cairo. In November he was ordered by Gen. Fremont to attack a Confederate camp at Belmont, Mo., opposite Columbus, Ky., which the Confederates, under Gen. Leonidas Polk, had now strongly fortified. Taking 3000 troops still imperfectly drilled, in river-steamboats imperfectly iron-clad, Grant sailed 20 miles down the Mississippi; his men clambered up the bank and captured the camp with a large number of prisoners. But meantime 4000 Confederate reinforcements arrived from Columbus, and Grant had to cut his way back through them to reach his transports. The Confederates claimed a victory here, but the substantial success rested with Grant. Gen. Henry W. Halleck having superseded Fremont as commander of the Department of Missouri, Grant spent the winter in drilling his troops while iron-clad gun-boats were constructed to force the passage of the Mississippi, now obstructed by Confederate fortifications. In February he received permission to carry out his plans for the capture of Fort Henry, which commanded the navigation of the Tennessee. The fort was captured Feb. 7, but the garrison escaped to Fort Donelson, which occupied a similar position on the Cumberland, 12 miles distant (see FORT DONELSON). Hastening thither Grant soon compelled its "unconditional surrender." Grant's capture of Fort Donelson on Feb. 16 was the first great success of the Union troops. It opened the way to Nashville, and compelled the evacuation of Columbus.

Pres. Lincoln for this important service promptly conferred on Grant the rank of major-general. Yet at this very time Halleck's displeasure with Grant became manifest, and the latter was for weeks without a command. When at last he was restored to his place, though not fully to the favor of his superiors, Grant prepared for an advance on Corinth, Miss., where the Confederate Gen. Albert Sidney Johnston had gathered a large army. As Gen. D. C. Buell was marching from Nashville to join Grant, Johnston determined to attack the latter before the Union troops could unite. On Sunday, April 6, he reached Grant's out-posts near Shiloh Church, surprised and drove the vanguard from their camp. From his head-quarters at Savannah, on the Tennessee, Grant, still lame from an accidental injury received a few days before, hastened to the fight at Pittsburg Landing, reformed his lines, and infused new vigor into officers and soldiers. The rapid onset of the Confederates was checked. During the afternoon their commander had been killed, and Gen. Beauregard, his successor, did not renew the assault. Gen. Buell's troops were beginning to reinforce Grant's army, and during the night in spite of a heavy rain they were posted. At daybreak the Union troops made a determined advance before which the Confederates gave way, seeking refuge in their intrenchments at Corinth. Again the nation gave due honor to Grant for victory, but Halleck found fault with him for permitting his troops to be surprised. At the time, and long after in his *Personal Memoirs*, Grant denied that there was a surprise, though participants on both sides have admitted it. Halleck now took the field in person, appearing to find it necessary to curb the too adventurous spirit of his subordinate. After a slow and excessively cautious advance for seven weeks, he captured the extensive but now deserted earthworks at CORINTH (*q. v.*), while the army which had been there intrenched escaped to render service elsewhere. In August Halleck, whose theoretic knowledge of strategy had given him high reputation, was summoned to Washington to take command of all the armies of the United States. The magnificent force which he had collected at Corinth was scattered in various directions, and Grant was left in command of the district of West Tennessee.

Grant had not overcome the prejudice which Halleck had formed against him. Yet his patient endurance of slight and his faithful performance of every duty assigned him were beginning to obtain their reward. For a time he was greatly tried by the influx of traders, spies, and camp-followers of all sorts into Northern Mississippi. To preserve the discipline of his army he made stringent regulations and kept his men steadily at work. In September he advanced from Corinth and on the 19th defeated Confederate Gen. Sterling Price at Iuka. Van Dorn's attempt to retake Corinth was also baffled. In November enough troops were gathered to commence the expedition against Vicksburg, "the Gibraltar of the Mississippi," then occupied by Gen. J. C. Pemberton. In the first attempt to capture this stronghold Gen. Sherman commanded the land forces and Commodore Porter the fleet of gun-boats. Entering the Yazoo for the purpose of attacking Vicksburg in the rear, they encountered formidable obstacles in bayous choked with trees and rafts. Sherman was defeated Dec. 28 in a desperate conflict at Chickasaw Bluffs just after a large collection of military stores at Holly Springs had been destroyed by the enemy. Towards the end of January Grant began to dig a canal across the neck of the peninsula which lies opposite Vicksburg. A sudden rise in the river destroyed his works and placed his army in great peril. With indomitable energy and unshaken confidence he persevered in his efforts to gain the Confederate stronghold. Passing below Vicksburg he crossed to the east bank and captured Port Gibson. When Gen. Joseph E. Johnston came from the east to assist Pemberton, Grant swung loose from the river and made a brilliant dash on Jackson, where he captured and destroyed military stores. He then returned and at Champion Hills, May 16, 1863, met and defeated Pemberton, who was now endeavoring to escape from the fate which threatened him if he remained. Pemberton was compelled to return and the siege of Vicksburg commenced on May 19. On both sides the resources of modern warfare were skilfully employed, but the coil of the besiegers steadily closed around the doomed city. Shot and shell fell in all parts, numerous mines were exploded, and the inhabitants began to suffer from famine. On July 3 Gen. Pemberton sent out a flag of truce asking for terms of capitulation, and on July 4 he surrendered his entire force, 31,600 men, with 172 cannon and thousands of small arms. On July 8 Port Hudson was likewise surrendered, and the navigation of the Mississippi was henceforth entirely open to the adherents of the Union, while the domain of the Confederacy was cut in two. Grant now received the rank of major-general in the regular army, and numerous testimonials were bestowed upon him by the grateful people of the loyal

States. Again by dilatory orders of the authorities at Washington much of the fruit of victory was lost. In September General Grant was placed in command of the military division of the Mississippi, and at once hastened to the relief of Chattanooga, where Gen. Rosecrans was cooped up after his defeat at Chickamauga. (See CHATTANOOGA and CHICKAMAUGA.) Grant assigned the command of the town to Gen. Thomas, and soon completed his arrangements for its relief. The battles of Lookout Mountain and Missionary Ridge followed his arrival, and the Confederate Gen. Bragg, who had declared himself certain of capturing Chattanooga, was compelled to withdraw discomfited. The Union army, which under Gen. Burnside had been besieged in Knoxville, was relieved at the same time. In the following session of Congress the grade of lieutenant-general, which had previously been held only by Washington and Winfield Scott, was revived, and President Lincoln carried out the wish of the people in bestowing this rank on Ulysses S. Grant. His complete success in every great object aimed at in the West marked him as the man to accomplish the still more difficult task of overthrowing the military power of the Confederacy in the East.

Gen. Grant was therefore called to Washington in March, 1864, and on the 17th was placed in command of all the armies of the United States. Having arranged plans for their harmonious and simultaneous action in the ensuing campaign he left the details to the discretion of the respective commanders. He decided to move with the Army of the Potomac, while Major-Gen. Meade, the hero of Gettysburg, still retained its immediate command. On May 4 that army crossed the Rapidan and soon encountered the army of Gen. Lee, who had determined to fight at once. On May 5 began the bloody battle of the Wilderness, in which Grant steadily endeavored to outflank the right of the Confederates, but owing to their skill and stubborn bravery was unable to accomplish his purpose. On May 12 he wrote to Washington, "I propose to fight it out on this line, if it takes all summer." Yet he was gradually compelled to diverge from this line, and when at last his desperate assault along the whole line of the rebel fortifications at COLD HARBOR (q. v.) failed he transferred his army to the south side of the James. Want of promptness in his subordinates prevented the immediate seizure of Petersburg, and Gen. Lee divining his new object began to fortify that city. Again, when by prodigious labor a mine had been carried under the fortifications of Petersburg, a like want of promptness and co-operation prevented the explosion from being of service. Yet in spite of such minor failures Gen. Grant's plans for the overthrow of the rebellion were steadily approaching their consummation. Sherman was marching from Atlanta to the sea; the Confederate Gen. Hood, who had made a bold attempt to recall him by attacking Nashville, was repulsed by Gen. Thomas; Sheridan cleared the Shenandoah Valley of the enemy. On Christmas day, 1864, Gen. Sherman entered the city of Savannah, and in January and February, 1865, the Confederates were forced to abandon Charleston and Wilmington sea-ports, which, in spite of the strict blockade, had been of essential service to the Confederacy.

Operations around Richmond and Petersburg were renewed with vigor in February, 1865; Sheridan swept round the north side of Richmond, and after inflicting great damage approached Lynchburg, which he found too strong to be captured. In March he cut off the southern line of retreat from Richmond and won the decisive victory of Five Forks. On April 2 Gen. Longstreet at Petersburg pronounced its further defence impossible, and Lee began to evacuate Richmond, moving westward towards Lynchburg. All Grant's forces were thrown out in vigorous pursuit that the struggle might be brought to a speedy end. Worn out with hunger and the fatigue of incessant marching and fighting, the Confederate Army of Northern Virginia was becoming a mob of stragglers. Gen. Lee with his able lieutenants and brave soldiers had done everything that skill and courage could accomplish. But the end had now come. On April 7 Grant seeking to spare the further sacrifice of life asked Lee for his surrender, and on April 9, 1865, the terms were arranged at a memorable meeting between the two commanders at Appomattox Court-house. Gen. Grant's conduct on this important occasion and his generosity to the conquered foe received universal approval. The terms offered becoming known to the remaining Confederate generals were gladly accepted by all. The great civil war, which had lasted four years, and which had cost 350,000 lives and $4,000,000,000, was brought to a triumphant close. Liberty and union had prevailed over slavery and sectionalism. Yet within a week after the surrender at Appomattox the bitterness of spirit which characterized many adherents of the "lost cause" found expression in the assassination of Pres. Lincoln and the overthrow of the existing administration. But the government, established by the will of the people, and firmly grounded in its affection, survived the shock.

The last scene of the greatest American war was the review of the victorious Union army in Washington City, by Pres. Johnson and Gen. Grant, May 24 and 25, 1865. In his final report Grant summed up the splendid achievements of the various forces with generous criticism of his subordinate generals. Referring to the occasional jealousies of the East and the West he pronounced the verdict, "All have a proud record, and all sections can well congratulate themselves and each other for having done their full share in restoring the supremacy of law over every foot of territory belonging to the United States. Let them hope for perpetual peace and harmony with that enemy, whose manhood, however mistaken the cause, drew forth such Herculean deeds of valor."

As soon as the final victory had been won Grant set about a vigorous reduction of the numbers and expenses of the army. In the bestowal of rewards which accompanied the disbandment of the volunteer forces and the rehabilitation of the regular army, Congress established the rank of general of the United States army, and to this grade Grant was appointed July 25, 1866.

At this time Pres. Johnson was engaged in his unfortunate strife with Congress with regard to the reconstruction of the Southern States. Johnson's policy was baffled by the action of Edwin M. Stanton, who still held the position of secretary of war, to which he had been appointed by Pres. Lincoln. To prevent his removal Congress had passed a tenure-of-office law, but Johnson, while Congress was not in session, suspended Stanton and appointed Grant secretary ad interim. Grant while obeying the orders of the President as his superior carefully refrained from any violation of the letter or spirit of the laws already enacted by Congress. When that body reassembled the Senate refused to approve the removal of Stanton, and Gen. Grant at once relinquished the position. Pres. Johnson, who had used all his arts without avail to get the support of Grant for his policy, now charged Grant with breach of faith and endeavored to find means to humiliate him. But his plans failed; Grant attended faithfully to his duties as general of the army, removing abuses and reducing expenses in that department, and refusing to intermeddle in political affairs.

Yet he could not prevent the minds of the people from turning to him when the time approached for the selection of a President of the nation which his valor had saved. In May, 1868, the Republican National Convention met in Chicago and unanimously nominated Gen. Grant as President. Schuyler Colfax was nominated for Vice-President after an animated contest. In the following November they were elected, receiving a popular vote of 3,015,071, while the rival candidates, Horatio Seymour and Frank P. Blair, Jr., received 2,709,613 votes. In the electoral college the vote stood 214 to 80. In his inaugural address, on March 4, 1869, Pres. Grant declared significantly, "I shall on all subjects have a policy to recommend, but none to enforce against the will of the people." His nominations for the members of his cabinet excited much surprise, as his intentions had been carefully concealed until after his entrance upon his new duties. Mr. E. B. Washburne, Gen. Grant's steadfast friend in the early days of the war, was made secretary of state, but a week later he gave way to Hamilton Fish, of New York, and went as U. S. minister to France. Gen. John A. Rawlins was made secretary of war; Adolph E. Borie, secretary of the navy; Gen. J. D. Cox, secretary of the interior; John A. J. Creswell, postmaster-general, and E. R. Hoar, attorney-general. It had been the President's desire to appoint Alexander T. Stewart secretary of the treasury, but it was discovered that a law enacted at the formation of the government prohibited the appointment of an importer to that position, and, after an ineffectual attempt to secure the repeal of the law, George S. Boutwell was appointed to the position.

Pres. Grant soon made manifest the purpose of his administration to reduce as rapidly as possible the enormous debt incurred during the war, and to secure the resumption of specie payments. The heavy taxes necessary for this purpose were cheerfully borne by the people. During the eight years of Pres. Grant's administration, the public debt was reduced from $2,588,452,213 to $2,180,395,067, showing an average annual payment of over $51,000,000. While thus endeavoring to fulfil strictly all the financial obligations incurred during the war, Grant was not forgetful of what was due to the newly enfranchised colored people of the South. When the Fifteenth Amendment to the Constitution, which conferred on them the right of suffrage, was ratified by three-fourths of the States, in March, 1870, the President sent a special message to Congress, urging it to take all constitutional means to qualify them for their new duties. At a later date the organization in various parts of the South of bands of young men called Ku-Klux-Klan, for the intimidation and oppression of the negroes, obliged the President to call for congressional action. The Force Bill, signed April 21, 1871, enabled him to suppress the outrages to a considerable extent, though still oppression of the negro sheltered itself under State laws.

In the treatment of the Indians residing in the territory of the United States, Pres. Grant's administration showed a marked departure from the methods which had long prevailed. Seeing the need of change, and believing in the efficiency of missionary work, he called upon the prominent religious bodies of the country to take charge of various tribes, and recommended the renewal of the policy which William Penn had used with gratifying results in the settlement of Pennsylvania. This "Quaker" or "Peace policy" is still working for the good of both the red man and the white.

During his first term Pres. Grant brought before Congress the subject of civil service reform, which had already obtained a good degree of popular favor, though it was ridiculed and denounced by politicians of all parties. In 1871 Congress complied so far with his request as to authorize him to appoint an unpaid commission on this subject. The President continued to show favor to the movement throughout his term of office.

The most important event in the foreign relations of the government was the negotiation of the Treaty of Washington in 1870, by which the claims of the United States against Great Britain for infractions of neutrality during the civil war were to be submitted to an international board of arbitration. This board, consisting of distinguished representatives of England, the United States, Italy, Switzerland, and Brazil, met at Geneva in December, 1871, and in the following September gave its judgment, awarding to the United States damages to the amount of $15,500,000. The dispute in regard to the fisheries off the coast of British America was settled in like manner by a commission which met at Halifax, and awarded to the British government the sum of $5,000,000.

Less important, yet fruitful in consequences, were Grant's persistent efforts for the acquisition of San Domingo. In 1869 a treaty ceding this country to the United States failed in the Senate, through the opposition of Senator Sumner, but Pres. Grant continued to urge the project in various ways, though he never obtained congressional approval of his views. Between Pres. Grant and Senator Sumner there came a coldness, which was increased by some misunderstandings, until there was an open rupture. The senator by an intensely bitter speech in the Senate, just before the assembling of the Republican Convention, endeavored to prevent Grant's renomination, but the effort was in vain. Henry Wilson, Sumner's colleague in the Senate, received the nomination for Vice-President. Charles Francis Adams, who, as U. S. minister to England, had honorably maintained the cause of the United States during the critical period of the civil war, had been the original Presidential choice of those Republicans who were disaffected towards Grant; but an attempt to give their movement a more popular character resulted in the nomination of Horace Greeley at Cincinnati, in May, 1872. The Democratic Convention afterwards indorsed this nomination, though some "straight-out" Democrats nominated Charles O'Conor. The Republican ticket was elected by 3,597,070 votes to 2,834,079 for Greeley, and about 35,000 votes for other candidates. Greeley, completely overcome by his defeat, died before the meeting of the electoral colleges in December, and among the mourners at his funeral was Pres. Grant. The electoral vote for Grant was 286 to 63 for other candidates, 17 votes not being counted.

During Gen. Grant's second term occurred a disastrous financial panic, precipitated by the failure of the firm of Jay Cooke & Co., who had been furnishing the means for the building of the Northern Pacific Railroad. The government used its powers under the laws to diminish the evils from which the country was suffering, but the President sternly resisted every measure tending to inflation of the currency. He therefore vetoed a bill passed by Congress which ordered the restoration to the currency of $46,000,000 of greenbacks which had been retired. In 1875, in accordance with his recommendations, Congress passed a bill for the resumption of specie payments on Jan. 1, 1879, and various steps were taken towards the accomplishment of this purpose, which was finally carried out.

In 1875 began what may be called the Centennial movement, in which the hundredth anniversary of each important event connected with the American Revolution was celebrated at the place of its occurrence. On April 19 Gen. Grant attended the celebration of the commencement of the conflict at Concord and Lexington. His next annual message to Congress referred in appropriate terms to the glorious career of the country, from insignificant beginnings to an era of universal freedom and prosperity, and pointed to the lessons of the past and the duties of the present time. The most important centennial celebration was that of the Declaration of Independence, made at Philadelphia, July 4, 1776. To show what the nation had achieved in the hundred years of its existence, it had been determined, with the sanction of Congress, to invite the nations of the world to an industrial exhibition at Philadelphia, from May 10 to Nov. 10. This exhibition, opened by the President at the appointed time, was in the highest degree successful, in spite of an unprecedentedly hot summer. The United States were thereby raised to a still higher place in the estimation of the world, while the American people were greatly benefited by the display of the skill and resources of other nations.

Towards the close of Pres. Grant's administration, the lower House of Congress having passed into the control of the Democratic party, numerous investigations of the management of departments of the government were ordered, and some of Grant's friends were proved to have been faithless to their trust. His own integrity remained untarnished, but his determination to "stick by his friends" gave his political foes opportunities for attacking his method of government. The conflict for the succession to the Presidency, when, according to a custom established by the example of Washington, he should retire at the end of his second term, caused unpleasantness in his cabinet and elsewhere. The Republican National Convention at Cincinnati, in May, 1876, nominated Gov. Rutherford B. Hayes, of Ohio. The Democratic Convention at St. Louis nominated Gov. Samuel J. Tilden, of New York. The contest was so close, and the result so involved in doubt, that Congress, feeling its inability to decide the momentous question, invoked the aid of an electoral commission of fifteen. This commission decided that Hayes had been legally elected President, and Congress accepted and ratified the decision. Pres. Grant, to whose firmness throughout this trying crisis the nation owes the preservation of peace, took the customary part in the inauguration ceremonies of his successor.

Grant's administration was one of the most important in the history of the country. The wounds of the civil war had not yet been healed. Indeed, the disastrous strife between his predecessor and Congress had rudely torn them open. The finances of the country had been in an unhealthy condition. Speculation had been stimulated by the prodigious development of the country, and the uncertain value of the medium of exchange. Political power was gravitating into the hands of leaders who had forfeited it for years by acts of madness without losing their hold on their followers. At such a critical time to guide wisely and safely the ship of state demanded intellectual and executive ability of the highest order. Grant's want of previous political experience may have led him into serious mistakes, yet these were no greater than had been committed by politicians noted for their astuteness and skill in state-craft. He profited by his own mistakes, being careful to avoid a repetition of them. His most vexatious blunder was his quarrel with Senator Sumner, with all its attendant difficulties; yet in this Grant was not chiefly to blame. The exposure of the Credit Mobilier frauds, though one of the most prominent events during his administration, chiefly affected the legislative department of the government. Pres. Grant deserved well of the republic for guarding its dignity in intercourse with foreign nations, preserving its peace at home, and fulfilling strictly all its obligations to every class of citizens and dependents.

When he retired to private life after sixteen years of unremitting and devoted labor in the military and civil service of his country, he determined to spend some time in foreign travel with his wife and some friends. Without deciding beforehand on the extent of his travels, he sailed from Philadelphia on May 17, 1877, on what became eventually a tour around the world. It has been described graphically by Hon. John Russell Young, an experienced journalist, who joined the general's party after it had reached Europe. The decision of Earl Beaconsfield that the ex-President should be received in England with the honors of a sovereign undoubtedly established a precedent which the rulers of other countries gladly followed. After a tour through England and Scotland Grant travelled over the continent of Europe, visited Egypt and the Holy Land, returned to Europe, and then started on a voyage to India, China, and Japan, in each of which countries he was magnificently entertained. Crossing the Pacific Ocean he reached San Francisco, Sept. 20, 1879, and was received with an ovation, which was repeated in several great cities. His tour closed in Philadelphia, the original point of departure, on Dec. 16, 1879.

At once leading members of the Republican party began to urge a third nomination to the Presidency of the distinguished citizen, whose merits had received world-wide recognition, and who, as they argued, was now still better fitted for the post. His claims were urgently pressed, but the power of the unwritten law, forbidding a third term, proved an insurmountable barrier. At the Republican National Convention, at Chicago, in June, 1880, his partisans maintained an unbroken front, but after a severe struggle a majority of votes was given to James A. Garfield, of Ohio, on the thirty-fourth ballot. Gen. Grant gave the nomination hearty support, and Garfield was elected in the following November.

Grant, on retiring from political life, made a visit to Cuba and Mexico. He then settled in New York city, where wealthy friends raised for him a fund of $250,000, the interest of which he was to have during life, while the principal he might dispose of by will. This was intended to offset his relinquishment of the position of general with its assured pension. Gen. Grant entering into business, became a partner in the firm of Grant & Ward, of which his son was already a member. The affairs of the firm were managed entirely by Ferdinand Ward, who had the reputation of being a successful man of business. Eventually it proved that he had engaged in reckless speculation, and while pretending to receive enormous profits had squandered all the money which he could induce his partners and friends to entrust to him. In May, 1884, the startling revelation came that the firm was bankrupt, and Gen. Grant, who had raised money for it on his personal security, was left almost penniless. He had received a severe fall on the ice during the previous winter which for several weeks confined him to his room, and afterwards for a time compelled him to use crutches. In June following a cancerous trouble made its appearance in the roof of his mouth, but little was done for it until October, when the general placed himself under the care of Drs. Fordyce Barker and J. H. Douglas. The location of the cancer was such that no surgical operation could be performed, and it was evident that the disease was malignant and fatal. The general submitted patiently to the treatment prescribed, having already abandoned the use of cigars, to which in some measure his disease was attributable.

During the last year of his life Gen. Grant devoted considerable time to writing reminiscences of his career, beginning at first to write sketches of the war for the *Century Magazine*, and afterwards preparing an autobiography. His statements bear the impress of strict impartiality; he was careful to extenuate nothing, nor set down aught in malice. He tried to do ample justice both to those who served with and under him and to those who fought against him. A few errors that were pointed out in his magazine articles were corrected in his autobiography. His work breathes his earnest desire for the complete reconciliation of all who had been engaged in civil strife, and the full restoration of harmony between all parts of the country.

The misfortunes which had overtaken him led to the effort, during the closing days of the 48th Congress, to restore him to the U. S. army with rank of general on the retired list, which was accomplished on March 4, 1885. Grant's struggle with disease was prolonged for months. On the approach of summer he was removed to the cottage of Mr. J. W. Drexel at Mount McGregor, N. Y. Here his remaining days were passed with the attendance of his family, including his daughter, Mrs. Sartoris, who had come from England to wait upon him. He died on July 23, 1885. An impressive discourse was delivered by Rev. J. P. Newman, D. D., who had been pastor of the church which Gen. Grant attended in Washington, and had been called to his side during his last illness. Grant's body was taken to New York city, and, on Aug. 8, 1885, attended by a memorable military and civic procession, was conducted to its last resting-place in Riverside Park, which had been selected by his family.

Grant was of medium height, with a firm, expressive countenance, well covered by a brown beard. His constitution was remarkably strong, and though throughout the war he often shared the privations of the humblest soldier, he never succumbed to disease. His normal weight was about 160 pounds, but during his Presidency he became stouter. He retained robust health until the appearance of the fatal cancer.

Sprung from seven generations of ancestors born on American soil, Ulysses S. Grant, like Abraham Lincoln and James A. Garfield, is a typical representative of American training and American institutions. His character shows in strongly marked outline that modified Puritan type which prevails wherever New England settlers have formed settlements in the West. Strict integrity with love of freedom and disregard of conventionality are its personal traits. With these is combined a genuine patriotism, an ever-present regard for the welfare of the community and the state. When his country calls for his help, such a man devotes to her service his talents and energies and risks his life to establish and perpetuate her greatness. When the service is finished he retires without regret to the simple station of a private citizen.

Grant's fame will rest chiefly upon his military career. He was the greatest of American generals, not only as having successfully handled the largest armies which had ever been gathered on the Western Continent, but because at every stage of the war he achieved substantial success with the means at his disposal. This success was due to his clear and quick apprehension of the proper object to be aimed at, and the well-balanced judgment which enabled him so to dispose and utilize his resources as to accomplish that end. He learned quickly what his subordinates were able to effect, and more than once during the war of the rebellion he divined what his opponents would do from recollections of their character as displayed in the Mexican war. Though he consulted on proper occasions with his subordinates, he never allowed a council of war to override his own judgment. In the most critical period of the Vicksburg campaign he decided, in opposition to the views of every subordinate commander, to swing loose from the Mississippi, and by this movement, gallantly executed, he gained the desired end, not merely the capture of Vicksburg, but of Pemberton's army. Had he been undisturbed in his command after Fort Donelson, more than a year previous, he would not merely have captured Corinth promptly, but would have rent the Confederacy in twain by leading his victorious army to Mobile or against whatever armed force was gathered to obstruct his way. Armies, not earthworks, were his objective. There was no force then in the South-west which could have effectually resisted his determined attack.

Grant's plans even for great campaigns were simple. Having marked firmly the main outlines, he trusted much of the detail to the discretion of the subordinates who were to carry them out, and knowing his men as he did, he was seldom disappointed. Meantime he and his staff were spared the needless vexation arising from complicated orders, perhaps imperfectly understood. When the time came for action he did all that human might, directed by human skill, could do to accomplish his purpose. In the campaign of 1864, when he first confronted the greatest of the Southern generals, Grant's plans were frustrated rather by a variety of untoward accidents than by the skill of his opponent or the trained valor of the Confederate troops, great as both of these were. Lee was probably better fitted for the defensive than even Grant for the offensive, as was proved by the bloody battle of Cold Harbor, Grant's last attempt to find a weak spot in the guard of Richmond, and by the siege of Petersburg. It became therefore a question of the exhaustion of the resources of either party, and in such a struggle the South must succumb. To Grant was due the unrelaxing firmness with which the grip on Richmond was maintained, the steady narrowing of the field of conflict, and the speedy conclusion of the campaign of 1865.

Grant's vigorous, relentless prosecution of the war caused his character to be misunderstood, even by those who admired the results obtained. Grant was no lover of war; still more was he free from the merciless ambition of Cæsar or Napoleon. He was a sincere patriot, a firm believer in the principles of republican liberty. To these he was willing to sacrifice his wishes as for them he had often imperilled his life. Even when as President he seemed to insist too tenaciously on the carrying out of plans he had framed for his country's welfare, he was but fulfilling in a legitimate way the trust which had been imposed on him. When through want of the necessary co-operation of Congress or the people, his plan was found impracticable, he gave it up without hesitation and without complaint.

As in regard to action, so in regard to speech Grant was often misunderstood. The exigencies of the war had obliged him to be cautious in speaking, and even reticent; yet he was by no means taciturn. On the contrary he was well fitted and well disposed to take part in conversation among friends. But the straightforward simplicity of his nature prevented him from using his words to conceal his thoughts. He had never cultivated the American habit of public speaking, whether from want of opportunity or from positive distaste. Yet from his despatches and public utterances pregnant sentences found their way to become watchwords of public sentiment. The literary work which occupied many hours of the last year of his life bears on every page the impress of his love of truth, honor, and righteousness.

The greatness of Grant's nature is shown in his entire freedom from jealousy. In all his reports, as in his *Personal Memoirs*, he was careful to give all due credit to others, while stating his own plans and their achievement with the utmost modesty. But the results bear witness for themselves. Both in the West and in the East he led the forces of the Union to glorious victory, and finally crushed the rebellion. By his comprehensive genius he extinguished the conflagration which had long threatened the temple of Liberty, and, in obedience to the voice of the people, subsequently directed its restoration in grander and more attractive form. His deeds as general, his statesmanship as President, and his example as an American citizen have raised his country to a still higher position in the regard of the civilized world. (J. P. L.)

GRANVILLE, GRANVILLE GEORGE LEVESON GOWER, EARL, an English statesman, was born in London, May 11, 1815. He is the second Earl of the present line, having succeeded his father Jan. 7, 1846. He was educated at Eton and Christ Church, Oxford, and entered public life in 1835 as an attaché to the embassy at Paris, his father being the ambassador. He was elected to Parliament for Morpeth in 1836, and subsequently sat for Lichfield until he succeeded to his title in 1846. He was under secretary for foreign affairs, 1840–41; vice-president of the board of trade, 1848–51; foreign secretary, 1851–52; lord-president of the council, 1852–54; again, 1855–58, and 1859–66. He was colonial secretary, 1868–70, and secretary of state for foreign affairs, 1870–74, and again from April, 1880, to June, 1885. In February, 1886, when Mr. Gladstone returned to the premiership, Earl Granville was made secretary for the colonies. He was ambassador extraordinary to Russia to attend the coronation of Emperor Alexander II. at Moscow in September, 1856. He has also held other offices and positions of honor. Throughout his political career he has been prominent as a Liberal, being a leader in debate in the House of Lords.

GRAPE, the fruit of the botanical genus *Vitis*, family *Vitaceæ*, comprising shrubs with watery juice, usually climbing by tendrils, with small, regular flowers, a minute calyx, its limb mostly obsolete, and the stamens as many as the valvate petals and opposite them. The berry is two-celled, usually four-seeded. The genus *Vitis* has flowers with five petals, which cohere at the apex into a little cap, shed in flowering. In all the American species the flowers are diœcious, and exhale a fragrance like that of mignonette. The leaves have long petioles, are palmately veined, and often variously lobed, one appearing at each node or joint of the vine, with a tendril or a flower-cluster opposite. The bark is loose, stringy, and dark brown in color.

The Eastern United States are richer in true grapes than any other part of the world, having seven or eight species, four of which have yielded promising cultivated varieties. The cultivated grapes of the Eastern Hemisphere are all varieties of a single species, *Vitis vinifera*, the typical vine. This is generally considered to be of Persian origin, though it is not known in a wild state. It has been domesticated since a very early period, and has given rise to an extraordinary number of varieties. It is said that there are 1400 varieties in the French vineries alone, and 600 in the gardens about Geneva. To it are due all the wines of Europe and the East. The Zante or Corinth currants are the product of a small-fruited variety, or perhaps an allied species. *V. vinifera*, however, will not bear severe cold, and cannot be cultivated, except under glass, in the Northern United States. It grows freely in California, and is the basis of the California wines. The Pacific States have two native species, neither of which have been domesticated. *V. californica* yields large clusters of purple fruit, of a rather pleasant flavor. An allied species, *V. arizonica*, yields a grape of smaller size, but said to be quite luscious. Their value for cultivation has not been tested.

Of the grapes of the Eastern United States the most important species are, *V. labrusca*, the Northern fox-grape; *V. vulpina*, the Muscadine or Southern fox-grape; *V. æstivalis*, the Summer grape; and *V. cordifolia*, the Chicken, Winter, or Frost grape. Of these *V. æstivalis* bears a small fruit, of a bluish-black color, covered with a fine bloom. The berries, ripe in October, have a sprightly, agreeable, acid flavor. It is found in rich woods and thickets, from Connecticut to Florida, and is the highest climber of all our vines. *V. cordifolia*, the common Winter grape, is found from Canada to Florida, in thickets and on river banks. The berries ripen after frosts, and are small, blue or black with a bloom, and too acid for eating. The flowers are very sweet-scented, with a perfume like mignonette.

V. labrusca is common in moist thickets from Canada to the far South; also found in Japan. It is a low-growing vine, straggling over bushes and small trees, the branchlets and young leaves very woolly, the berries large, about ½ inch diameter, dark purple or amber color, with thickish coat and tough pulp of a musky flavor. Flowers in June; fruits, September. The "foxy" flavor disappears in the cultivated varieties, of which many have been produced, such as the well-known Isabella, Catawba, Concord, and many others. These succeed far better in the climate of the Northern States than any foreign varieties, and new seedlings are being constantly produced. *V. vulpina*, the Southern fox-grape, also called Muscadine and Bullet or Bull grape, is found on river banks from Maryland to Florida. It is found also in Japan, Manchuria, and the Himalayas. It is a tall grower, climbing trees to a height of 50 feet, and is peculiar in the close, even texture of its gray bark, which does not separate in strips, like the other species. The fruit is large (½ to ¾ inch diam.), of purple color without bloom, a thick, tough skin, and a musky but not unpleasant flavor. It flowers in May, fruits in July and August. It is the original of the Scuppernong and other cultivated varieties. In the American species the flesh of the berry is separate from the skin; not adherent, as in *V. vinifera*.

Cultivation of the American species has produced many varieties, whose number has been increased by hybridization with each other and with the European grape. Several of these are of great value, from their hardiness and comparative freedom from disease, their fine flavor, and their wine-producing qualities. Of the native species *V. labrusca* has yielded the well-known Isabella, Concord, Catawba, and very many other varieties. To *V. aestivalis* we owe Cynthiana, Norton's Virginia, and Herbemont, all good wine-grapes, and various others. Of the varieties of *V. cordifolia*, Elvira yields an excellent white wine. The most important variety of *V. vulpina* is the Scuppernong. The value of this grape, however, is reduced, by its deficiency in sugar, and its habit of dropping as soon as ripe. The origin of some other cultivated varieties, principal among them the Delaware, is not known. The latter is probably a seedling of the Catawba. To these may be added many hybrids, those known as Rogers' hybrids including several excellent varieties.

The vine grows occasionally to an immense size and attains great age. Some European vines are known to be from 400 to 600 years old, and have attained a circumference of 4 feet. This size is surpassed by some American vines. One at Burlington, N. J., is said to be 6 feet 2½ inches in girth at 2 feet from the ground. At Monticito, Cal., is reported a vine 10 feet in circumference, and bearing 7000 branches, estimated to yield 18,000 lbs. of fruit. The vine is propagated from seeds, layers, cuttings, and by grafting and budding. The production of new varieties is dependant upon seed growth, the other methods being used for various economical purposes. It is subject to several diseases, some so destructive as to prevent the culture of certain varieties, or to check all grape-culture in certain localties. The most dangerous of these are the mildews, which attack the leaves and fruit, and the ravages of the Phylloxera, or root-louse of the vine. The former are fungoid growths which destroy the leaves, so that the berries are unable to ripen, and sometimes attack the grape-clusters. *Phylloxera vastatrix*, an aphid which sucks the juice from the vine-root, has been imported from America to Europe, where it has almost annihilated the vine in some districts of France. In America the *aestivalis* and *cordifolia* varieties are but little subject to its attacks, while those of *Labrusca* are often very susceptible.

The culture of the grape in the United States began at an early period, in an effort to acclimate the European varieties. Vineyards were planted in Virginia as early as 1610, and wine was sent to England in 1612. There were many later efforts made, all of which proved unsuccessful from the severity of our climate, except in the vineyards of North Carolina, where in 1750 wine-making had become a successful though small industry. Early in the present century the culture of the native grape was fairly begun by Maj. John Adlum, of Georgetown, D. C. The introduction of the Catawba to general culture in his vineyards formed an era in our grape history. But its culture became an important industry only in 1849, when Nicholas Longworth, of Cincinnati, after thirty years of experiments with foreign grapes, decided that the native grape must be our reliance. In the year named there were 300 acres of vineyards within 12 miles of Cincinnati, and 50,000 gallons of wine made. In 1850 the American wine-product was 221,249 gallons from seven States. By 1852 there were 1200 acres of vines near Cincinnati. These efforts at grape-culture were attended with many difficulties, through the attacks of vine diseases, yet the wine-making industry has continued, until now it has become of great importance in the United States. In this industry California is now at the head. As early as 1861 this State had 10,500,000 vines, which number has since that date been enormously increased.

Since 1840 the total consumption of wine in the United States has increased about 400 per cent., while the importations have increased but 17½ per cent. From 1870 to 1876 the average annual production of American and importation of foreign wines were each nearly 9,000,000 gallons. From 1877 to 1884 the average annual production was nearly 19,000,000 gallons, and the average importations only about 5,000,000 gallons. Only about one-fifth of the wine now consumed here is imported. In 1880 the acreage of vines in the United States was 181,583 acres, and the wine-product 23,453,827. gallons, valued at $13,426,175. Of this considerably more than one-half was the product of California. The census of 1890 reported as the result of special investigation that in 1889 there were 401,261 acres devoted to grape-growing in the United States; of these 307,575 acres were in bearing, producing 572,139 tons; of which 267,271 tons were table grapes; 240.450 tons were used for producing wine, making 24,306,905 gallons; 41,166 tons in California alone for raisins, making 1,372,195 boxes of 20 pounds each; and 23,252 tons for dried grapes. California had an acreage of 155,272 in 1889, and produced 14,626,000 gallons of wine. The estimate for 1890 in that State was 16,500,000 gallons of wine and 2,197,463 boxes of raisins, with prospect of great increase within five years. The total number of laborers employed in 1889 in the grape industry was 200,780, and the total value of land and plant was $155,661,150.

Of the Eastern wine-producers the Catawba stands first as a white wine grape. The Delaware is also valuable. For red wine the Concord is one of the most useful varieties from its abundant and cheap product. Our native grapes have often a strong flavor, and a deficiency in sugar and consequently in alcoholic property. It is important, therefore, that they should be fully matured before use. Unless so, it is necessary to enrich the mash or mast, rather than to weaken it as in European vineyards. (C. M.)

GRÄSSE, JOHANN GEORG THEODOR (1814–1885), an eminent German bibliographer, was born at Grimma, in Saxony, Jan. 31, 1814. He received his early education in the school of his native town, in which his father was a professor, and studied at Leipsic under Hermann, devoting himself to philology. He was afterwards engaged in teaching in Dresden, but in 1843 was made librarian of King Friedrich August II. In 1848 he was appointed inspector of the mint-cabinet, and in 1852 director of the state porcelain collection. In 1864 he was made one of the directors of the celebrated collection of jewels, etc., known as the "Green Vault," and in 1871 became the sole director. In 1876 he transferred the royal collection of porcelain into the Johanneum. His monumental work, *Lehrbuch einer allgemeinen Literärgeschichte aller bekannten Völker der Welt*, began to appear in 1837, but was not completed till 1860. The remarkable fulness of its bibliographical information and the mass of material collected and arranged in it render this work a unique example of German learning, industry, and patience. His *Handbuch der allgemeinen Literaturgeschichte* (4 vols., 1844–56) is a compendium of his larger work. Among his purely bibliographical works are *Bibliotheca magica* (Leipsic, 1843), *Bibliotheca psychologica* (1845), and *Le Trésor des livres rares et précieux* (1858–67). Grässe gave much attention to the myths and legends of the Middle Ages, publishing a translation of *Gesta Romanorum* (1842), a critical edition of *Legenda aurea* (1840), and essays on *Der ewige Jude* (1844), *Ritter Tannhäuser* (1846), *Sagenschatz des Königreichs Sachsen* (1854), *Sagenbuch des preussischen Staats* (1868), *Freischütz* (1875), *Deutschen Namen-, Geschlechts- und Wappensagen* (1876). He also published popular treatises on hunting, on beer, on ancient coins, on porcelain, besides excellent catalogues of the collections under his charge. His philological essay, *Unsere Vor- und Taufnamen* (1875), gives special prominence to Celtic influence on German proper names. His *Orbis Latinus* (1861) is a list of the Latin names of noted places. He also published in 1876 a popular history of Saxony, which had been prepared to accompany a series of portraits of the Saxon princes. He died at Dresden in September, 1885.

GRASSE, FRANÇOIS JOSEPH PAUL, COMTE DE, also MARQUIS DE GRASSE-TILLY (1723–1788), a French admiral, was born at Valette, Provence, in 1723. He entered the navy of the Knights of Malta in 1734, and was engaged in wars with the Turks. In 1749 he passed into the service of France, but while on a convoy to the East Indies was captured by Admiral Anson and was imprisoned for two years in England. In May, 1754, he was made lieutenant, and in January, 1762, captain. When France came to the assistance of America in 1778, De Grasse was made a rear-admiral, and commanded the second division in the action of July 27, 1778. Being made chief of the squadron in 1779, he sailed from Brest to join the fleet of D'Estaing at Martinique. In the next year he was engaged in three fights with Admiral Rodney. In March, 1781, he set out from Brest with a large fleet, convoying also a large land-force, to the United States. On April 28 he fought with Admirals Hood and Drake in sight of Martinique, but after four hours' fighting they escaped. In June he assisted at the taking of Tobago, and then sailed to the mouth of the Chesapeake in order to assist in the operations against Lord Cornwallis. The English admirals in vain endeavored to drive him from his position, and Cornwallis, shut up in Yorktown, was obliged to surrender to Washington, Oct. 19, 1781. For his part in this decisive victory Comte de Grasse received the thanks of Congress. In January, 1782, he captured from the British the island of St. Christopher, in the West Indies. In April he attacked Rodney near Jamaica, and gained some advantages. But drawn on by his desire to save one of his vessels which had been injured, he became reckless and in spite of his bravery was obliged to surrender, April 12, 1782, after a fight of ten hours. He was taken prisoner to London and there assisted in the negotiations relating to the peace of Sept. 3, 1783, by which the independence of the United States was acknowledged. He had returned to France in August, 1782, and published a defence of his conduct. A court of inquiry was held and he was acquitted, but was no longer employed. He retained the rank of lieutenant-general of the navy till his death at Paris, Jan. 11, 1788. He was brave but rash, and lacked the qualities necessary for the highest commands. His family was ruined by the French Revolution, and his four daughters having come to the United States received assistance from Congress in 1795.

GRASSES. See FORAGE CROPS.

GRASSES, ORNAMENTAL. During the past quarter of a century a taste has arisen for grasses as elements in ornamentation, which has resulted in an enormous trade in them. There are large firms in Germany, France, England, and America which make their collection, preparation, and distribution a specialty in trade, and all leading florists and seedsmen make collections of dried grasses an important part of their stock in hand. Until this comparatively recent time plants were admired and cultivated chiefly for the gayety afforded by their colored flowers. When beauty was recognized in form, expression, and association, as well as in color, the leaves of plants, the fronds of ferns, and the culms of grasses especially, entered largely into human enjoyment. At first bunches of "Quaking Grass" or "Feather Grass" covered every demand, but now some of the larger firms who deal in them offer selection from between 300 and 400 species. Many of these are dried in their natural colors, but others are dyed of various shades of blue, green, orange, pink, purple, red, scarlet, or yellow, and in these forms are largely employed in arranging various parlor-ornaments, or temporary decoration of large halls for festivals. A number of species are crystallized, and then form delicate objects of graceful beauty. The grasses are tied in small bunches and hung from sticks placed across a wide-mouthed vessel into which a pound of alum and a gallon of boiling water have been placed. When the liquid has had time to cool, the immersed grasses will be found covered with frost-like crystals. It often takes 10 or 12 hours before the crystalline deposit commences.

The most popular grasses are of course those which have obtained common names by which they are generally known to the purchasing community. Of these the most esteemed is probably the Pampas Grass, *Gynerium argenteum*. It endures 10 or 12 degrees of frost without injury, but is usually killed when the temperature approaches zero. Its culms are often thrown to the height of 12 feet, with 2 or 3 feet comprising the silvery branching panicles. Very strong plants have been known with 50 of these large culms. It is a diœcious grass, the staminate plant having the finest spikes. Though many grasses have a plumose inflorescence, when a florist speaks of "plumes" he usually refers to the Pampas Grass. Many thousands of these plumes are grown in America for the home-trade and for exportation to Europe. The wholesale price varies from $25 to $100 per 1000. Those grown in California usually bring the best prices. Other popular grasses are the Quaking Grasses, *Briza maxima, media, minima,* natives of the meadows of Europe, and others cultivated from South America; Zebra Grass, *Eulalia japonica,* with variegated leaves, and plumes little inferior in magnificence to the Pampas Grass; Feather Grass, *Stipa pennata;* Hare's-tail Grass, *Lagurus ovatus,* from the south of Europe; Love Grass, *Eragrostis elegans;* Pearl Millet, *Penicillaria spicata;* Squirrel-tail Grass, *Hordeum jubatum,* of the American plains; Animated Oats, *Avena sterilis;* Job's Tears, *Coix lachryma;* Sea Oats, *Uniola latifolia;* and the Florida Sea Oats, *U. paniculata.* These last two grow on drifting sands along the sea-coasts of Carolina, and although not esteemed as highly as the Pampas Grass they are so very popular that the trade in them is enormous. The money value of the trade is probably much larger than that in Pampas plumes. Among grasses largely used in the trade, but which are known only by their botanical names, are many species of *Agrostis, Aira, Andropogon, Arundinaria, Arundo, Bromus, Chloris, Cyperus, Eleusine, Elymus, Eragrostis, Erianthus, Festuca, Leptochloa, Melica, Panicum, Paspalum, Pennisetum, Phlaris, Poa, Polypogon, Saccharum, Setaria, Sorghum, Stipa, Tricholœna, Vulpia.* Grasses have not often much odor; but *Andropogon schœnanthus* is citriodorous, and hence has the common name of Lemon Grass, and the dried flowers of the *Anthoxanthum odoratum* are often known as Vanilla Grass. The last gives the chief odor to new-mown hay. *Hierochloë borealis,* or *Holcus odoratus* of the older botanists, has a very grateful odor when dried, and in some of the northern countries of Europe is gathered into small bundles for placing among clothes and linen to give them a pleasant fragrance. It is also hung over beds in order to aid sleep, but as it is also used to strew before the doors of churches on festivals connected with saints' days, there may be some religious associations connected with its supposed somniferous character aside from its mere fragrance. In countries where it is thus employed it is known as "Holy Grass." It is a native of the Alpine or more northern regions of the American continent, as well as Europe. According to Dr. Gray it should be the true "Vanilla Grass." (T. M.)

GRASSHOPPER, the common name given to various insects of distinct genus and family, and similar only as all belonging to the saltatorial Orthoptera. The term, indeed, has been used with great looseness, and it is now impossible to restrict its application. The scientific names given the saltatores, or jumpers, are also somewhat confused—different writers using different systems. Thus the term *Gryllidæ* is by some writers applied to the grasshoppers, by others to the crickets. We may here, however, consider the grasshoppers as included in the two families *Locustidæ* and *Acrydüdæ,* in both of which the great development of the hind legs gives remarkable leaping powers. Of these the *Locustidæ* have four-jointed legs and long antennæ, the end of the body in the females being provided with a long, sword-shaped ovipositor. The

See Vol. XI. p. 53 Am. ed. (p. 60 Edin. ed.).

wing covers slope downward at the sides of the body, and overlap a little at the top. This portion is provided with strong veins and transparent spaces, and when rubbed together by the males gives the peculiar chirruping sound of this insect family. The color is usually green, and the habit nocturnal. They are mostly solitary, and never migrate in swarms like the *Acrydüdæ.* A large and well-known member of the family is the katydid, famous for its musical powers. The sound it produces may be heard at a distance of a quarter mile. It is peculiar to America.

The *Acrydüdæ* are shorter and stouter, with three-jointed legs, large heads, and short antennæ. They have no long piercer, but four short horny projections. The wing-covers are long and narrow, and the noise of the insect is made by the friction of these against the hind legs. They are social and diurnal in habit, and migrate in voracious and destructive swarms. This family includes the dreaded migratory locust of the Eastern Hemisphere, and *Caloptenus spretus,* the migrating insect which makes such havoc in the States west of the Mississippi. Another species, *Caloptenus femur-rubrum,* the common red-legged grasshopper, has at various times been similarly destructive in the North-eastern States and Canada. Fuller particulars concerning these species will be given under LOCUST. The ravages of the Eastern grasshopper or locust are partly atoned for by their being made an article of diet with the Arabs and Africans. They are roasted and eaten, or dried in hot ashes and stored for future use. The natives grind them to powder, from which they make a kind of soup, said to be more nutritious than palatable. Our Western farmers have not yet begun to revenge the ravages to their grain-fields in this manner.
(C. M.)

GRASSMANN, HERMAN GÜNTHER (1809-1877), a German mathematician, was born at Stettin, April 15, 1809. He studied at Berlin theology, philology, and mathematics. In 1834 he became a teacher in the Otto school at Stettin, and in 1852 succeeded his father as professor of mathematics in the gymnasium of that town. He held this post till his death, Sept. 26, 1877. His chief works are important contributions to modern mathematics. They comprise *Die Wissenschaft der extensiven Grösse* (1844); *Geometrische Analyse* (1847); *Die Ausdehnungslehre* (1862); *Lehrbuch der Arithmetik* (1861-65). He also prepared a Sanskrit dictionary to the *Rig Veda* (1875), and a German translation of this work, with notes (1876-77).

GRASSMANN, ROBERT, a German philosopher, brother of the foregoing, was born at Stettin, March 8, 1815. He studied theology, mathematics, and natural sciences at Berlin, was for a time a teacher, but since 1848 has been a journalist. His works comprise *Die Weltwissenschaft oder Physik* (2 vols., 1862-73); *Die Formenlehre oder Mathematik* (1872); *Die Lebenslehre oder Biologie* (1872); *Die Wissenschaftslehre oder Philosophie* (1876); *Das Weltleben oder Metaphysik* (1881); *Das Gebäude des Wissens* (1883).

GRATRY, AUGUSTE JOSEPH ALPHONSE, ABBÉ (1805-1872), a French theologian, was born at Lille, March 30, 1805. He was educated at the École Polytechnique, and afterwards entered the ecclesiastic state. In 1841 he was appointed director of the College Stanislas, Paris, and in 1846 chaplain of the normal school. Gratry criticised the *Histoire de l'École d' Alexandrie,* by his colleague M. Vacherot, and in consequence of the controversy both resigned their positions. In 1852 Gratry joined the Abbé Petetot in reorganizing the order of the Oratorians of the Immaculate Conception. In 1861 Bishop Dupanloup appointed Gratry vicar-general of Orleans, and in October, 1863, he was made professor of Christian morals at the Sorbonne. He had already published a course of philosophy under the titles *De la Connaissance de Dieu* (1855); *Logique* (1856); and *De la Connaissance de l'âme* (1857); and other works, as *Paix, méditations historiques et religieuses* (1862); *Sources, conseils pour la conduite de l'esprit* (1862). In defence of the truth and authenticity of the Gospels he entered the lists against M. Renan, and his eloquence procured his election to the French Academy in 1867. Being censured by the superior of his order for his connection with Père Hyacinthe and the League of Peace, which advocated religious tolerance, he retired from the Oratorians. In *La morale et la loi de l'histoire* (1868) he had declared the French Revolution to be a true regeneration of human society, and he issued some sharp letters against the Vatican Council, but finally retracted them Nov. 25, 1871. He died at Montreux, Switzerland, Feb. 6, 1872.

GRATTAN, THOMAS COLLEY (1796–1864), an Irish novelist, was born in Dublin in 1796. He studied law and afterwards held a commission in the army, but having married settled at Paris, and adopting literature as his profession contributed to the *Edinburgh Review* and various magazines. He afterwards removed to Brussels, where in the revolution of 1830 he assisted in having Leopold I. called to the throne. In 1839 he was made British consul at Boston, and held this office till 1852, when he accepted a position in the queen's household. He died at London, July 4, 1864. Among his works are *Highways and Byways* (3 series, 1823–27), several novels, histories of Switzerland and the Netherlands, and *Legends of the Rhine* (1849). In his *Civilized America* (1859) he manifested a very bitter spirit towards the United States.

GRAY, ALBERT ZABRISKIE, an American clergyman and author, was born at New York, March 2, 1840. He graduated at the University of the City of New York in 1860, studied theology, and became chaplain in the Fourth Massachusetts cavalry during the latter part of the civil war. He was afterwards rector of several parishes in New Jersey and New York, and in 1883 was made warden of Racine College, Wisconsin. He has published *The Land and the Life, or Sketches and Studies in Palestine* (1876); *Mexico as it is* (1878); *The Words of the Cross* (1880); *Jesus Only, and other sacred songs* (1882).

GRAY, ASA, an American botanist, was born at Paris, Oneida co., N. Y., Nov. 18, 1810. He received his degree of M. D. in 1831 at a medical school at Fairfield, N. Y., studied botany under Prof. Torrey, and was Fisher professor of natural history in Harvard College from 1842 till 1873, when he retired from the more active work of that professorship. He published many works on botany, including *Elements of Botany* (1836); *A Manual of Botany* (1848, subsequently often revised and enlarged); the masterly *Flora of North America* (unfinished; the first volume published in 1838; the earlier volumes prepared conjointly by him and Dr. Torrey); the *Botany of the U. S. Pacific Exploring Expedition* (1st vol., 1854); *Structural and Systematic Botany* (1857); *Lessons in Botany* (1857); *How Plants Grow* (1858); *Field, Forest, and Garden Botany* (1868); *How Plants Behave* (1872); *Synoptical Flora of North America* (1878), and other valuable works. He died at Cambridge, Mass., Jan. 30, 1888.

GRAY, ELISHA, an American inventor, was born at Barnesville, Ohio, Aug. 2, 1835. In his youth he learned carpentry and boat-building, and afterwards attended Oberlin College, supporting himself by his trade. He gave much attention to improvement of the electric telegraph, and engaged in the manufacture of telegraphic apparatus. Since 1872 he has been employed as electrician, and in 1874 he visited Europe for the purpose of study. He has taken out about fifty patents, among which are many relating to the speaking telephone, of which he claims the invention, his first specifications having been filed Feb. 14, 1876. He has also patents for multiplex telegraphy. He has published *Experimental Researches in Electro-Harmonic Telegraphy and Telephony* (1878).

GRAY, HENRY PETERS (1819–1877), an American painter, was born at New York, June 23, 1819. He studied art under Daniel Huntington in 1838, and went to Europe in 1839. He returned to New York in 1843, and from 1846 he devoted himself to *genre* and portrait painting, though occasionally taking historical and sacred subjects. In 1842 he was elected a member of the National Academy, and in 1869 became its president. In 1871 he went to Florence, where he remained till 1874. He died at New York, Nov. 12, 1877. Among his works are The Apple of Discord, Portia, and Bassanio, The Wages of War, and The Birth of Our Flag.

GRAYDON, ALEXANDER (1752–1818), an American author, was born at Bristol, Pa., April 10, 1752. He was educated at Philadelphia and studied law, but became a captain in the Revolutionary army. After carrying a sum of money to Gen. Schuyler at Lake George, he joined the army at New York. He was taken prisoner, and afterwards, being released on parole, went to Reading, Pa. He was prothonotary of Dauphin county from 1785 to 1799, after which he lived on a farm near Harrisburg until 1816, when he returned to Philadelphia, where he died, May 2, 1818. He published in 1811 his entertaining *Memoirs* (republished at Edinburgh in 1822 and at Philadelphia in 1846.)

GRAYLING, a fish of the salmon family, genus *Thymallus*, of which five species are known in the clear cold streams of Northern Europe and America. It is a handsome and lively fish, of a light yellowish-brown color, and of migratory habits, wintering in the sea, and ascending the streams in early spring. It is esteemed for its delicate flavor, so much so that in some countries it is reserved for the tables of the great —the lower orders being prohibited from fishing for it under severe penalties. It is a cautious fish and not readily taken with the line; of elegant form, and 12 to 14 inches, rarely 2 feet, in length. The best known species are the *Poisson bleu*, of the Canadian voyageurs, and the European grayling. In America it is

(See Vol. XI. p. 71 Am. ed. (p. 78 Edin. ed.).)

Grayling (*Thymallus vulgaris.*)

found in the clear cold waters of the Great Bear and

Winter Lakes, and in streams which empty into the Mackenzie River. Back's grayling (*T. signifer*), a large species of this northern region, 17 inches long, is highly esteemed by the voyageurs and Esquimaux. *T. tricolor*, found in some streams of Michigan and in the head-waters of the Yellowstone, is perhaps identical with *T. signifer*.

GREAT BASIN. Between the Rocky Mountains on the east and the Sierra Nevada and Cascade Ranges on the west stretches a vast elevated plateau, or rather series of plateaus, of varying height, and for the most part sufficiently arid to be not improperly termed a desert. The northern portion of this enclosed area is drained by the Columbia and its tributaries into the Pacific Ocean; the eastern and southeastern portions, a region of gigantic cliffs, the escarpments of vast blocks of elevated strata, or the terminations of strata which have been removed by erosion, is penetrated in all directions by the deep cañons of the Colorado and its tributaries, discharging their waters into the Gulf of California, while the remaining portion has no outlet. This last region is the Great Basin. All the rain which falls in this area is evaporated either directly from the soil or after finding its way into some of the small lakes which dot its surface. Most of these lakes are salt, as is usually the case with lakes which have no outlet in consequence of the supply not exceeding the evaporation. The average yearly rainfall of the Great Basin is not more than 12 to 15 inches, and in the more desert parts does not exceed 4 inches.

Desert-like though may be much of the districts drained by the Colorado and Columbia, the Great Basin is even more so. It is, in fact, as true a desert as the Sahara or the deserts of Arabia; scarcely any part is available for agricultural purposes unless rendered so by irrigation, and the streams and lakes within its bounds are so scanty that only a small portion can in this way be reclaimed for human use.

The area thus isolated from the water systems of the world is somewhat greater than that of France, or five times that of Pennsylvania. From its most northern point (in Oregon, north of 44° N. lat.) to its most southern point in the northern part of the peninsula of Lower California, it extends about 800 miles; while its width in the widest part, between 40° and 41° N. lat., is about 500 miles. The calculated area of this region is 208,500 miles, chiefly included within the States and Territories of Oregon, Utah, Nevada, and California, but at its north-eastern angle extending into Idaho and Wyoming. Almost the whole of Nevada is in the Great Basin.

The northern portion of the Great Basin is the more elevated. Here the valleys have a general elevation of 4000 to 5000 feet, while the intervening mountain ranges rise 5000 to 7000 feet above them. Gradually the general level subsides until, at the southern extremity, portions are met with which are even lower than the sea-level. Such are Death and Coahuila Valleys.

The Great Basin is by no means a level plateau, but is diversified with many mountain ranges, some reaching 11,000 or more feet above the sea-level, separated from each other by broad desert valleys. The mountains exhibit a type of structure not described before this region was explored, but now recognized as the "Basin Range" structure. While most mountains have been carved by erosion out of strata which have been by subterranean forces bent into great ridges and hollows (anticlinals and synclinals), the ranges of the Great Basin are composed of huge blocks, which have been broken and tilted up on one side. They thus have one steep face, upon which the broken edges of the beds which compose them are exposed, and one gently sloping side, the slope conformable to the dip of the strata. Most of these ranges run in a north and south direction.

The structure known as "Basin Range" is not confined to the Great Basin, but occupies also that portion of Arizona situated south of the Colorado plateau, and drained by the Colorado and Gila. On the other hand, the basin of the Sevier River is a part of the Great Basin, but the elevations are plateaus of a character similar to those of the Colorado Basin. The valleys between the ridges are more barren than the mountains. Instead of shady vales, or smiling open *vegas*, they are often totally destitute of water, and treeless for many days' journey; the most prominent plant being the grayish-green *Artemisia*, or sage-bush. These valleys are filled with alluvial deposits, and in many cases can be identified as the beds of ancient lakes. In some of the mud plains, left by the evaporation of former lakes, there is scarcely a trace of vegetation, and many parts become covered to a depth of several inches with alkaline salts, which look like drifted snow. Some parts become so baked in the summer sun that a horse's hoof makes scarcely any impression, and so sun-cracked as to look like tessellated pavement. The alkaline dust, caught up by the wind, sometimes forms swaying and bending hollow columns, two or three thousand feet high, and is at all times most trying to the health and eyes of travellers. The Carson and Black Rock Deserts of Northern Nevada, and the desert west of Great Salt Lake, exhibit the extreme of desolation; but they are surpassed in area by the Mojave Desert in Southern California.

Fig. 1.

The accompanying sketch may serve to give an idea of the Basin Range structure, F F being the lines of faults, and the dotted lines representing the dipping strata. The valleys between the tilted blocks have upon one or both sides a cliff formed by the edges of the faulted beds, and are occupied either by alluvial deposits or by lakes; the former predominating in the present era. The depression bounded by the fault upon the left may be taken as a generalized expression of Surprise Valley, Cal., which once held a lake nearly 100 miles long. The central depression, bounded on each side by faults, is a rude diagram of Christmas Lake Valley, Oregon, the sides of which are formed by cliffs 1500 to 2000 feet high. Fault escarpments have in most instances been worn down by erosion, but those of the Great Basin are comparatively recent, and thus remain to testify to the great extent of the displacement.

The geological structure of the Great Basin is very complex. Into the composition of the tilted and faulted mountain blocks enter rocks of all the Palæozoic ages, including the Devonian, which is well represented in and near the White Pine district, Nevada, though as a rule, it is inconspicuous throughout the

Rocky Mountain and Western regions of this country. The various Palæozoic strata are superimposed upon a foundation of Archæan rocks, which are exposed upon the eastern and western boundaries of the Great Basin, and also crop up at isolated points of its surface. Beds belonging to the Jurassic and Triassic ages, which have not in this region been yet well distinguished from each other, are found in Western Nevada. Cretaceous and Eocene strata appear to be absent, but beds of late Tertiary age occur in Eastern Oregon, and recent deposits occupy extensive areas of the valleys and deserts.

Mountains.—The Wahsatch Range forms the eastern boundary of the Great Basin in Utah. Like the Basin Ranges, it is a north and south monoclinal ridge, presenting on the western side a bold abrupt escarpment facing Great Salt Lake, while on the more gently sloping eastern side it is covered by the great Tertiary deposits of the plateau country that drains into the Colorado. Its highest peaks are from 11,000 to 12,000 feet high. In its structure are represented all the principal formations from the Archæan to the latest Tertiaries. South of the Wahsatch Mountains is a region of high plateaus—the highest in America. Geologically they belong to the plateau region, but their drainage is carried by Sevier River into the Great Basin. To the west of the valley of the Sevier lies a range of three high tables, the southernmost, the Markagunt Plateau, about 11,000 feet high. On the opposite side of the Sevier Valley are the Sevier and Paunsagunt Plateaus, the former a table 80 miles long. East of this is the long line of Grass Valley, the waters of which burst through a profound gorge in the Sevier Plateau, and join the Sevier River. East of this valley lie four great plateaus, continuing southward the line of the Wahsatch Mountains. These are the Wahsatch Plateau, nearly as high as the mountains north of it; Fish Lake Plateau, a mesa 11,400 feet high; the Awapa, and the great Aquarius, 35 miles long and 11,600 feet high. The summits of these plateaus are not arid, and the Aquarius bears a forest.

The East Humboldt Range is the main range of Central Nevada, and the most prominent uplift lying between the Sierra Nevada and the Wahsatch. It is a single bold ridge, 80 miles long, terminating at the Humboldt River, with many rugged summits over 10,000 feet above sea-level. Mt. Bonpland, at the northern end, is 11,321 feet high. Its long slopes and glacier-covered cañon-basins are dotted with scattered forests of pines and firs.

Other ranges lying to the east of that just mentioned are the Oquirrh, Aqui, Ibenpah, Wachoe, Gosi-Ute, Egan, Ruby, Ombe, and Peoquop, all of considerable height.

Most of these ranges have the usual nearly north and south direction, and are composed of Palæozoic rocks. The Humboldt Range has an axis of Archæan rocks, upon which Devonian and carboniferous strata rest unconformably. The Wachoe Mountains are an exception to the usual structure, being an irregular group of crystalline rocks.

Westward of the East Humboldt lie the Augusta, Havallah, and Pah-Ute, with other minor ranges, and still farther west the West Humboldt Mountains, culminating in Star Peak, 9925 feet above sea-level. The Virginia Range is the first of the north and south ranges lying to the east of the Sierra Nevada. It is 150 miles long, stretching from 38° 10′ to 40° 15′ N. lat., and is thus one of the longest of the Basin Ranges.

The celebrated Steamboat Springs are situated near the base of a volcanic hill on the western side of the Virginia Range. They cover an area a third of a mile long by 800 to 1000 feet wide. Siliceous sinter covers the ground, formed by the evaporation of the spring-water. Steam, and occasionally jets of hot water, 10 to 15 feet high, are cast up from fissures. Many other thermal springs are found in various parts of the Great Basin.

Other ranges rather farther to the south in Western Utah are the Onaqui, Thomas, Beaver Creek, and House. In Southern Nevada and South-eastern California are the Amargosa and Funeral Mountains, east of Death Valley; the Panamint Range, west of that depression, and the Inyo Range, immediately east of the Sierra Nevada, which it almost rivals in grandeur, and exceeds in loneliness.

South of the Inyo and Panamint Ranges are the Opal, Payute, and Dead Mountains, which are not more than 5000 or 6000 feet high, and south of these the Chocolate, Chucavaila, and Riverside Mountains, which hardly average 4000 feet.

The Stein Mountains, rising 4000 to 5000 feet above Alvord Lake, are the most striking elevations of South-eastern Oregon, and in grandeur of scenery exceed most of the Basin Ranges.

Lakes and Rivers.—Some of the lakes near the borders of the Great Basin have outlets, discharging their waters into a lake or sink at a lower level. These upper lakes, fed by springs and melting snow, are pure and fresh. The finest of them is Lake Tahoe, a beautiful sheet of water, which lies amid the peaks of the Sierra Nevada, at a height of 6247 feet. Its outlet, the Truckee River, flows downward to Pyramid and Winnemucca Lakes, 2400 feet lower; there the water is evaporated, leaving the lakes charged with salts of soda. Lake Tahoe is 21 miles long, and 12 wide in its widest part. It is probably the deepest lake in the United States, since soundings indicate depths of 1385, 1495, 1524, 1600, and 1645 feet. The waters abound in fish, and also in fresh-water entomostraca.

On the opposite or eastern side of the Great Basin lie Utah Lake, which discharges its waters through the Jordan into Great Salt Lake; and Bear Lake, the surplus waters of which are conveyed by Bear River into the same reservoir.

Although all lakes which have no outlet become in time charged with salts, there is great difference in the degree of salinity. Great Salt Lake is exceedingly saline, while Pyramid, Winnemucca, and some others are but slightly so. This may not improbably be due to the entire evaporation of the waters and deposition of the salts, which then become buried under the mud brought down by subsequent storm-waters, so that, on the return of conditions sufficiently humid to permit of the formation of a permanent lake, its waters were comparatively fresh.

Great Salt Lake is a broad, shallow sheet of water, 80 miles long by about 32 wide at its greatest expansion. At its deepest part it is not more than 50 feet deep, and broad belts along the shore-line as well as the inlets have less than 10 feet. It receives its water supply from four rivers: the Bear, Ogden, Weber, and Jordan, which lead into it the drainage of the entire surface of the Wahsatch Range, and much of that of the Uintas. The superficial area of the lake was in 1869 ascertained to be 2360 square miles, while in

GREAT BASIN.

LAHONTAN LAKE BEDS IN HUMBOLDT VALLEY.

PLATE XXVIII.

GREAT BASIN.

PLATE XXIX.

RESERVOIR BUTTE, SHOWING TERRACES OF THE BONNEVILLE SHORE LINES.

Stansbury's map, made in 1849-50, it is shown to cover only 1700 square miles. From the depths of water given on Stansbury's map, and from information given by settlers, it appears that the rise of the lake commenced about 1861. The lake is evidently still rising, and it is the belief of some that the rise has been caused by the agency of man in clearing the forests from the mountains to the eastward, and cultivating the soil, the total effect being to allow more water to enter the lake.

The water of Great Salt Lake is remarkable for its great density and pungent bitterness. The human body floats cork-like on its surface. The water obtained by Stansbury in 1850 contained 22.4 per cent. of mineral matter; but in 1869 the dilution had been so great that only 14.8 per cent. was found. Common salt forms nearly four-fifths of the solid contents, the remainder being chiefly chloride of magnesium, and the sulphates of soda and potash. There is very little sulphate of lime.

Lake Mono, Cal., is 14 miles long and 10 wide. Its waters are strongly charged with sodium carbonate, and contain smaller quantities of lime carbonate, common salt, and borax. The lime carbonate formerly held in solution has been to a great extent deposited in irregular fungoid and coralloid masses of tufa, which stand up thickly on the level shores, and in the shallow marginal waters of the lake. Near the centre of the lake is a group of volcanic islands, in direct line with the extinct volcanic cones, which form a series of twenty or more from the lake margin to a distance of some 15 miles to the southward. These volcanoes vary from 200 to 2700 feet high. There is every probability that they were active since the glacial epoch. Prof. Le-Conte, upon his visit to this lake in 1872, found ample proof that the lake had risen 10 or 12 feet in about as many years.

Pyramid Lake, according to King, rose 9 feet, and Winnemucca Lake 22 feet, in a shorter time. These facts, together with the rise of several lakes in the extreme north of the Great Basin, in one case sufficient to unite two formerly distinct lakes (Malheur and Harney), tend to show that, independently of any interference caused by man, the lakes of the Basin are, on the whole, rising.

Owens Lake has about 110 miles of surface. It is fed by Owens River, about 30 miles long, and is bounded by the Sierra Nevada on the west, and the Inyo Range (10,000 feet high) on the east. The salts of its waters are chiefly sodium carbonate and common salt, in nearly equal quantities, but potassium and sodium sulphates are abundant. The saltness is about twice that of sea-water. A yellowish-green alga abounds in the lake, and is fed upon in great numbers by a curious species of fly not found elsewhere. The larva inhabits the lake, and is considered a delicacy by the Indians.

The longest river of the region is the Humboldt, which, after a course of 300 or more miles, and after receiving Reese River, loses itself in Humboldt Sink, not far from the spot where the Carson loses itself in Carson Sink. The group of lakes and sinks in this part of Nevada are the remains of the former Lake Lahontan. Bear River rises south of Bear Lake, runs with a general northward direction by that lake, with which it communicates by a marsh, and continues northward until it encounters the basalt of Basalt Valley. Here it turns west and then south, flowing through Gentile and Cache Valleys to Great Salt Lake. Its circuitous course is paralleled by that of the Sevier, which, after running northwards for two degrees among the high plateaus, turns south-west, crosses the Sevier Lake Desert, and terminates in Sevier Lake.

In Eastern Oregon there are a number of small lakes, most of which are included in the Great Basin, though some, as the Klamath Lakes, have an outlet. It seems as though during the humid quaternary period the lake which occupied the Klamath Basin cut down its outlet so low that the region became permanently tributary to the ocean. The normal condition of Goose Lake is that of a feeder of the Sacramento, but during recent years it has not overflowed. Some of the lakes are what may be called "playa" lakes, i.e., their waters evaporate to dryness during arid seasons, leaving mud-plains or playas. Many such playa lakes are to be met with in the Great Basin. The only truly fresh-water lake of the group north of Lake Lahontan is Silver Lake, the waters of which are almost without a trace of mineral matter, a fact which is the more singular as it is situated in the midst of a quaternary lake which never overflowed, is itself without outlet, and is not more than ten feet deep. The remaining lakes are somewhat alkaline and brackish, but are in most cases sufficiently pure to afford watering-places for stock, and even to be used for culinary purposes for a while.

Summer and Abert Lakes are strong solutions of potash and soda salts, and are richer in potash than Lake Mono, the potassium salts of the water of Abert Lake amounting to five-sevenths of the total solids. No fishes live in these lakes, but they are tenanted by countless millions of brine-shrimps (*Artemia*).

Alvord, Guano, Massacre, Warner, and Christmas Lakes, as well as those of Surprise and Long Valleys, are playa lakes, and even the larger lakes are very shallow. Goose Lake, the deepest, does not exceed 20 feet.

Quaternary Lakes.—At the time when New England and many of the more Northern States were covered with a sea of ice through the great excess of precipitation over evaporation, a similar excess accompanied by somewhat less frigid conditions caused the Great Basin to be in large part occupied by a number of lakes. Twenty-one of these lakes, the two principal of which have been named Lake Bonneville and Lake Lahontan, have been explored in the northern part of the basin, and at least three of considerable size are known to have existed in the south. The drainage area of the two lakes just mentioned occupied the whole breadth of the Great Basin at 41° N. lat. Perhaps the largest of the southern lakes was that which occupied Death Valley and extended a degree to the southward of it.

The depressed area of the Coahuila Valley was once a lake with an area of over 1000 square miles. Millions of minute fresh-water shells are still to be found among the coarse granite sand of its western shores.

Lake Lahontan.—Lake Lahontan was one of the most eccentrically shaped bodies of water that ever existed. Pyramid and Winnemucca, Humboldt and Walker Lakes, the two Carson Lakes, and Honey Lake in California, were included in its bed, as were also what are now Black Rock and Carson Deserts. Its greatest length was about 260 miles. The actual water area was much inferior to that of Lake Bonneville, for it enclosed an island 126 miles long by 50 wide. The two main bodies of water lay north and south of this island, and were united by a western arm which occupied the valley of Pyramid Lake and part of that of the Truckee River, and by an eastern arm which stretched up the Humboldt Valley. The large central island bore several rugged and lofty mountain ranges, and included in the interior two small lakes which did not overflow into the larger one. Humboldt River and its tributary, Reese River, were the chief feeders of this lake from the east, while on the west it received the waters of Lakes Tahoe and Mono, of Washoe Valley, and of a lake which formerly occupied the Madeline Plains, Lassen county, Cal.

Along the Humboldt River cliffs of clay and marl, sometimes 150 to 200 feet high, show at once the depth of the alluvium and the erosive action of the river since the disappearance of the lake. Carson Desert was once covered with water to a depth of 500 feet, and a large portion of this desert, with some outlying areas, continued to form a lake after the waters had left Black Rock Desert and Quinn River Valley. The area of the drainage basin was about 45,000 square miles. The evidence of the former existence of this lake is unmistakable; the ancient shore-line is clearly defined throughout, and its continuity proves that there was no outlet. The coasts of the lake are scored by several horizontal terraces, each cut by the waves at a period when the lake maintained approximately the same height. The highest wave-cut terrace is not conspicuous, but at a level 30 feet lower is a broad terrace sometimes, as on the south side of Carson Desert, 200 to 300 feet wide, marking a level at which the lake stood for a long period. Four hundred feet below this, and 100 feet above the level of Pyramid Lake, is another distinctly cut terrace. Deposits of carbonate of lime, in the form known as tufa, rise from the alluvial beds of the lake bottom to various heights, and three structurally different kinds of tufa mark three stages in the history

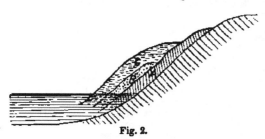

Fig. 2.

of the lake. The most stony and massive form, A, is found from the terrace 30 feet above the highest line to the lake-beds of the bottom; that marked B extends only to the lowest terrace; while that marked C, which is deepest and most abundant, reaches to within about 200 feet of the highest water-line; proving that, after the bed B was deposited, the waters rose again, though they did not remain long enough at one level to score a broad and well-defined terrace. Remains of freshwater shells prove that the lake was fresh at both its high-water periods. Large quantities of salts, chiefly common salt, but including borate, sulphate, and carbonate of soda, and borate of lime, are contained in the lake-beds, and are worked for salt and borax.

Lake Bonneville.—Lake Bonneville is the largest of the ancient lakes of the Great Basin, its surface covering 19,750 square miles, while its drainage basin occupied 52,000 square miles. Its greatest length was more than 300 miles, its greatest width about 150 miles. Not only the existing Great Salt Lake and the broad desert to the west of it were in the Quaternary period covered with water, but Utah and Sevier Lakes were also merged into the sheet, which sent out prolongations in various directions, particularly towards the south, where a long inlet has been named Escalante Bay. The highest water-line is 1000 feet above the level of Great Salt Lake, and evidence of the action of the waves can be found at every foot of the intervening profile. This highest water-line is one of the most conspicuously marked; but the most prominent line of all is 400 feet lower, and has been named the Provo shore-line. Four or five prominent shore-lines can usually be seen between the highest or Bonneville line and the Provo. The prominence of the upper shore-line led to search for an outlet, and this was found at the northern end of Cache Valley, at the northeastern termination of what was once a bay of the lake. The stratum over which the water first discharged was of soft material, and the level at which it was first crossed corresponds to the Bonneville shore-line. The soft sill wore downwards with comparative rapidity, until at length a reef of limestone was reached. This marks the level of the Provo shore-line, and at this level the lake remained until climatic changes diminished the water-supply. The water which escaped from the lake found its way into the Snake branch of the Columbia, so that at this period the basin of Lake Bonneville formed part of that of the Columbia. At the present time there is at the former outlet a marsh, from which a stream flows southward to Bear River and Great Salt Lake, while another passes northward to the Columbia.

The lake-beds consist chiefly of two deposits: yellow clay at the bottom and upon it a layer of white marl from 10 to 20 feet thick. A wedge of gravel interposed between these beds along the mountain margins, together with evidences of erosion upon the surface of the clay, prove that the two beds were deposited at different periods, between which periods the lake partially dried up, and rains washed down the gravels and wore away the surface of the clay. The clay can be traced to 800 feet above Great Salt Lake, while evidences of subsequent wear are found to within 200 feet of the same level. The marl can be traced as high as the clay.

The chief difference between the lower and upper stratum of lake deposits is the larger proportion of the carbonates of lime and magnesia contained in the upper.

Shore-lines must have been level when formed by wave-action, but at the present time neither are the Provo and Bonneville lines horizontal, nor are their deviations from horizontality parallel. These facts prove that there have been earth-movements since the lines were formed, and these movements were apparently of such a nature as to raise the central portion of the ancient lake, and thus to compel the waters of its remnant, Great Salt Lake, to occupy the eastern side of its former basin.

In Quaternary times some of the valleys north of Lake Lahontan contained lakes of great depth. The conspicuous highest beach-line of that which once occupied Surprise Valley is 350 feet above the lake-beds. The long narrow Quaternary lake east of the Stein mountains, of which Lake Alvord is the last remnant, had a depth of 400 feet. Yet neither of these had an outlet.

Zoölogy and Botany.—There are few peculiarities in the animals of the northern part of this region, but the southern portion is nearly related to Northern Mexico as regards its fauna. The buffalo is not now found in the Great Basin, but the big-horn sheep (*Ovis montana*) occurs. The various lakes contain peculiar forms of fishes, most of them belonging to the carp and minnow tribe (*Cyprinidæ*) or to the suckers (*Catostomidæ*), and white-fish and trout occur.

The valleys of the southern portion are the habitat of many lizards and snakes, which do not extend into the northern part.

The flora of the Great Desert is, on the whole, poor. The prevailing plants are undershrubs, such as wormwoods or artemisias, among which the sage-bush is most common, chenopods or goosefoots, and woody small-flowered compositæ. No portion, however, bare of trees or grass, is absolutely without vegetation, unless it be the alkali flats, and even these bear frequently a scattered growth of greasewood (*Sarcobatus*) and *Halostachys*. The characteristics of the vegetation are the wide distribution of a few low shrubs or half-shrubby plants, the want of a grassy green-sward, and the universal dull olive or gray color of the herbage. The sage-bush (*Artemisia tridentata*), though the most widely spread species, does not take kindly to alkaline soil, which is preferred by *Halostachys*. There are but few species peculiar to the basin. The Yucca, and other sub-tropical plants, enter Southern Nevada and the Mohave Desert.

The agriculture of the Great Basin is limited to those areas which can be irrigated. Of more importance, at least at present, is the grazing of sheep and cattle on the bunch grass that abounds in many parts of the mountains, and sometimes grows luxuriantly beneath the sage-bush.

The principal source of wealth, however, and that to which Nevada owes its admission as a State, is mining, and there is also a growing industry in salt, borax, sulphur, and carbonate of soda.

Our knowledge of the Great Basin, as outlined in the foregoing sketch, is due to the explorations and researches of Israel C. Russell, S. F. Emmons, A. Hague, G. K. Gilbert, C. E. Dutton, and O. Loew, who have contributed valuable reports to the *U. S. Geological Survey* (1880–83) and other government documents. (W. N. L.)

GREECE, by the convention of May 24, 1881, acquired from Turkey 5142 square miles of new territory. This acquired area comprised the greater part of ancient Thessaly and a considerable share of South-eastern Epirus. The new boundary line commences at the N. E. on the W. shore of the Gulf of Thessalonica, at a point 4 kilometres S. of Platomona. Its direction in general is irregularly S. W., being mainly determined by mountain crests until the river Arta is reached. From that point the stream is followed southward to the Gulf of Arta; and the town of Arta, with that part of Epirus which lies E. of the river Arta, thus becomes Greek territory. In Thessaly the valley of the Peneus is almost entirely Greek; but its northern tributary, the Xeragis, is still Turkish. The newly acquired lands include some of the very best agricultural tracts in the kingdom.

See Vol. XI. p. 73 Am. ed. (p. 80 Edin. ed.).

The new territories constitute the eparchies of Larissa in the E., and of Trikala in the centre; while W. of the Pindus range is the Epirot district of Arta—the latter a mountainous region, bisected from N. to S. by the river Achelous or Aspropotamo.

The total population of the kingdom in the year 1879 was 1,679,470. The population of the districts annexed in 1881 is given as 299,953, making a total of 1,979,423. This had increased in 1889 to 2,187,208.

The principal cities and towns of Greece are Athens (population, 114,355); Patras (25,494); Hermenopolis (21,245); the Piræus (21,055); Corfu (16,515); Zante (16,250); Tripolis (10,057); Argos (9861); Pyrgos (8788); Argostoli, Kalamata, Chalcis, Spezzia, Hydra, Mesolonghi, Messene, Lixouri, Kranieli, Lamia, Poros, Megara, Vostitza, Agrinion, Ithaka, Nauplia, Sparta, Thebes, etc., and in the new districts Larissa (13,169); Volo (7316); Trikala (5563); Arta (4990); Karditza, Tyrnovo, etc. The chief ports for foreign trade are the Piræus (the chief port for Athens), Hermopolis (Syra), Patras, Corfu, Cephalonia, Nauplia, Kalamata, Chalcis, Engasteria, Volo, Mesolonghi, and Katakolo, the last named being the port for Pyrgos.

The commerce, both in imports and exports, is double what it was twenty years ago. The imports are more than double the exports in valuation, and they have been so for a long term of years. The articles of export are cattle, hides, skins, bones, cheese, honey, cocoons, silk, wool, emery, lead, zinc, ores of zinc and of iron, millstones, barley, wheat, flour, madder, anise seed, sumac, vallonia, tobacco, cotton, yarns, cotton-seed, olives, oil, oranges, lemons, figs, currants, citrons, hemp-seed, sulphur, marble, sponges, wine, soap, spirits, rags, etc. The direct trade with the United States is almost entirely an export of currants, and a much smaller import of petroleum in cases; some wine, soap, oil, tobacco, and goat-skins are shipped to the United States. The country has a large and increasing customs revenue, and the old burdensome levy of one-tenth in kind of all land products was abolished in 1881. Since that time there has been a marked improvement in the Greek finances; but the country is still very far from being in a healthy condition as respects taxation, currency, and balance of trade.

Up to 1883 there were but two railways in Greece, one 5¼ miles long, from Athens to the Piræus, and another of about the same length from the Laurion mines to the port of Ergasteria. In 1883 a railway of 8 miles was opened from Pyrgos to its port, called Katakolo, and a steam-tramway runs from Athens to Phaleron. Since that date the railway system has been much extended, there being in 1889 370 miles of road open, while the telegraph system was 3234 miles in length. The ship-canal across the Corinthian isthmus is now nearing completion. When opened to navigation it must prove of great economic advantage to Greece. Drainage works are going on which are designed to remove the waters of Lake Copais, in Bœotia. This operation will render fertile more than 50,000 acres of marsh and mere. Greece owns 6700 coasting vessels, 5200 sea-going vessels, and some 300 steamers. Many foreign lines of steamers ply the Greek waters, and the Piræus, Syra, Patras, and the other large Greek ports are alive with a spirit of pushing commercial activity. (C. W. G.)

GREEN, ASHBEL (1762–1848), an American clergyman, was born at Hanover, N. J., July 6, 1762. His father, JACOB GREEN (1722–1790), was born at Malden, Mass., Jan. 22, 1722; graduated at Harvard College in 1744; was ordained at Hanover, N. J., in November, 1746; was made vice-president of Princeton College in 1757; was a zealous patriot in Revolutionary times; published some works on church government; and died at Hanover, May 24, 1790. Ashbel graduated at Princeton in 1784, and was tutor in the college until 1786, when he was licensed to preach.

He was ordained as colleague to Rev. Dr. Sproat, in Philadelphia, in 1787, and became pastor in 1793. He was also chaplain of Congress from 1792 to 1800. In 1802, when Princeton College was destroyed by fire, the president, Rev. Dr. Smith, travelled through the States to collect funds, and Dr. Green supplied his place. He also took an active part in establishing the Princeton Theological Seminary in 1812, and was president of its directors until his death. He was also president of Princeton College from 1812 to 1822. He then returned to Philadelphia, where he edited and published the *Christian Advocate*, a religious monthly. He died at Philadelphia, May 19, 1848. He published a *History of Presbyterian Missions, Discourses on the College of New Jersey*, and some other works, including his father's *Autobiography*.

His son, JACOB GREEN (1790-1841), was professor of chemistry in Princeton College, 1818-22, and afterwards till his death professor of chemistry in Jefferson Medical College, Philadelphia. Besides several scientific works he published *Notes of a Traveller through England and Europe* (1831).

GREEN, HORACE (1802-1866), an American physician, was born at Chittenden, Vt., Dec. 24, 1802. He graduated at Middlebury College, Vt., in 1824, and studied medicine at the University of Pennsylvania and in Paris. He practised at Rutland, Vt., but in 1835 removed to New York. In 1840-43 he was professor of the theory and practice of medicine in the Medical College at Castleton, Vt. He assisted in founding the New York Medical College, where he held the same chair from 1850 to 1860. He also assisted in founding and editing the *American Medical Monthly* in 1854. His works relate chiefly to diseases of the throat and air-passages, the last being *Pulmonary Tuberculosis* (1864). He died at Sing Sing, N. Y., Nov. 29, 1866.

GREEN, JOHN RICHARD (1837-1883), an English historian, was born at Oxford, Dec. 12, 1837. He was educated at Magdalen College School and entered Jesus College in 1856. He seems to have found the college and its studies uncongenial, and devoted himself chiefly to historical reading. By some papers on "Oxford in the Eighteenth Century" he attracted the notice of Dean Stanley, and, though trained as a rigid high churchman, he was greatly influenced by the genial dean. This influence led first to Green's taking orders in 1860, when he became curate of St. Barnabas' Church, a poor parish in the east of London. In 1862 he had charge of Hoxton, and in 1865 was made vicar of St. Philip's, Stepney. Overwork, especially during the cholera in 1868, obliged him to retire, and Archbishop Tait made him librarian at Lambeth, in succession to Prof. Stubbs. Green had already become a frequent contributor to the *Saturday Review*, and he now began to work on his *Short History of the English People*. Although obliged to go abroad during the winters on account of the state of his lungs he had his book ready for publication in 1874. It was received with the utmost enthusiasm, as the most lifelike presentation of English history which had yet been prepared. The University of Edinburgh quickly conferred on the author the degree of LL.D. After a time some severe criticisms were made on the inaccuracy of the *History* in minor particulars, but when due allowance is made for the circumstances of its preparation these fade into insignificance. In later editions they have been carefully corrected. The great success of the first work led to an enlargement of the *History* in four volumes (1878-80), the new work being marked by the same characteristics as the former.

Meantime the author had been happily married to a daughter of Archdeacon Stopford, who watched carefully over his precarious health. In 1877 he gathered a number of his essays into a book under the title *Stray Studies*. He also sought to go more deeply into the racial foundation of England's greatness, and in 1882 published a masterly work on *The Making of England*. In continuation of this he was preparing another work, to be called *The Conquest of England*, when his labors were cut short by death. He died at Mentone, Italy, March 7, 1883. Green is noted above all other English historians by his possession of the imaginative faculty. His characters live, move, and act on each other as do men in the world around us. Distant places and times are made to come before us with the distinctness with which we see the lands we journey through. Here or there may be an inaccuracy in detail, but in the main we have in Green's *History* the true picture of the wonderful growth of the English people and their institutions. Such was the fertility of his mind, his friends assure us, that when almost physically incapacitated for further progress in the few noble works he has left, he threw off projects and plans of important works which might have occupied an ordinary lifetime.

GREEN, SETH, an American fish-culturist, was born at Rochester, N. Y., March 19, 1817. He had only a common-school education and became a fisherman. His business steadily increased until he had many persons in his employ along the lakes and rivers of New York. Finding the supply of fish steadily diminishing he turned his attention to fish-culture. In 1838 he carefully observed the habits of salmon when spawning, and was convinced of the practicability of increasing the yield from spawn. By the best methods in vogue he found the yield only 25 per cent. ; but by diminishing the amount of water used he increased the yield to 95 per cent. By invitation of the fish commissioners of four New England States, he restocked the Connecticut River with shad in 1867. He afterwards carried out his plans on the Hudson, Susquehanna, and other rivers, with like favorable results. In 1868 he was appointed on the New York State Fish Commission, and in 1869 was made State superintendent. He published *Trout Culture* (1870) ; *Fish-hatching and Fish-catching* (1879). He died Aug. 20, 1888.

GREEN, WILLIAM HENRY, an American clergyman, was born at Groverville, Burlington co., N. J., Jan. 27, 1825. He graduated at Lafayette College, Easton, Pa., in 1840 ; studied theology at Princeton, and in 1846 became tutor in Hebrew there. He was ordained in 1848, and soon after installed pastor in Philadelphia, but in 1851 he was called to his life-work as professor of Hebrew and Old Testament literature in Princeton Seminary. He has received the degree of D. D. from Princeton College and from the University of Edinburgh, and the degree of LL.D. from Rutgers College. He has published *The Pentateuch Vindicated from the Aspersions of Bishop Colenso ; Hebrew Grammar ; Hebrew Chrestomathy ; The Argument of the Book of Job Unfolded ; Moses and the Prophets*.

GREENBACK PARTY. During the civil war of 1861-65 it was deemed expedient for the Federal government to issue "greenback" notes to a very large amount, and as a consequence the currency of the country became much inflated. As an inevitable result prices went up beyond all recent precedent ; while the supply of the army with the necessaries of subsistence created a great demand for all kinds of farm productions. When the war broke out many Western farms were heavily mortgaged, and their owners were paying ruinous rates of interest. The inflation of the currency gave great relief to land-owners thus burdened, and practically enabled them to pay off their debts for much less than they really owed. When the period of contraction came, after the end of the war, the conditions were reversed. That period helped the creditor class and pinched the debtors. Many persons of the latter class were also much disturbed by the reflection that capitalists were getting the full principal and large interest on bonds for which they had in many cases paid no more than 35 cents on the dollar. What was called in 1868 "the Ohio idea" was the demand that all bonds which did not distinctly call for payment in coin should be redeemed in greenbacks. This "idea" seems to have dominated the Democratic convention of 1868, but was distinctly disavowed by Mr. Tilden and other leading Democrats. Many local and State conventions in the West, chiefly Democratic, endorsed the idea. Its advocates still hoped to bring the entire party to their way of thinking.

The financial crisis of 1873 caused the masses of the people to seek legislative relief for the evils from which they were suffering, and produced a certain disintegration of the established political parties. The pressing questions of the time appeared to require and justify new political organizations. The Greenback convention, held at Indianapolis in 1874, demanded: (1) The withdrawal of the national bank-note currency; (2) That the only currency should be of paper, and that such currency should be made exchangeable for bonds bearing interest at 3.65 per cent.; and (3) That coin might be used for the payment of the interest and principal of such bonds, and such only, as expressly called for coin payments. In 1876 a National Greenback convention was held at Indianapolis, which nominated Peter Cooper, of New York, and Samuel F. Cary, of Ohio, for President and Vice-President of the United States. In the election which followed they received 81,737 popular votes.

To these attempts to found a new party, based on financial issues, a turn in another direction was given by the labor troubles which had culminated in the great railroad strikes of 1877, by which transportation was suspended for two weeks on some prominent lines. When the season came for political action, the Greenback leaders sought and found favor with the laboring classes. In 1878 a "National or Greenback-Labor Convention" was held at Toledo, Ohio, as the result of a coalition between the Labor Reformers and the advocates of a greenback currency. In the following election the Greenback-Labor tickets polled over 1,000,000 votes, and 14 representatives of the party were sent to Congress. But the party was made up of incongruous elements; and although the distresses which gave it such a sudden increase of strength were real, none of the party leaders seem to have had definite ideas as to what was to be done to effect a cure. In 1880 the Greenback-Labor convention, at Chicago, nominated for the offices of President and Vice-President, James B. Weaver, of Iowa, and B. J. Chambers, of Texas. In that year the popular Greenback-Labor vote was 301,867, and 8 of their representatives were elected to Congress. The ticket in 1884 was headed by Gen. B. F. Butler, and received 175,380 votes. In that year the Greenback ticket in Iowa, Michigan, and Nebraska was fused with that of the Democrats, and in Missouri and West Virginia with the Republican ticket.

The Greenback party proper has always had its strongest support in the Western States. In Maine, New York, Vermont, and Massachusetts the Greenback element has been made up of labor-reformers, and its tickets have generally been supported principally by laboring men. But on several occasions the Greenbackers have received much encouragement and support from either one or the other of the two great parties of the country, who have hoped to create a diversion in their own favor by running a third ticket so made up as to draw votes from the opposing party.

The papers of Henry C. Baird and *The Currency Question*, a pamphlet by G. M. Steele, contain moderate and well-considered statements of the views of the Greenback party. The literature of the subject, *pro* and *con*, is large, but much of it is unprofitable reading. (C. W. G.)

GREEN BAY, a city of Wisconsin, county-seat of Brown county, stands at the head or southward extremity of Green Bay, a great inlet of Lake Michigan, nearly 100 miles in length. The town is on the east bank of the navigable Fox or Neenah River, opposite the town of Fort Howard. The city has excellent harborage for lake vessels of the largest class; while the Fox River, the short Portage Canal, and the Wisconsin River give it a steamboat connection with the Mississippi. The Green Bay, Winona, and St. Paul Railroad runs west 214 miles, and the Milwaukee and Northern Railroad gives the city north and south connections. Green Bay is especially prominent as a point for the manufacture and shipment of lumber. Its other manufactures are large and varied. The fisheries are also important, trout, white-fish, and the other species of lake-fish being extensively taken. The streets are paved, and the buildings, public and private, are very generally handsome and substantial. The town is well supplied with schools, churches, banks, and newspapers. It is the see of a Roman Catholic bishop, and has a handsome cathedral. The French settlements in this vicinity date from 1745, or earlier; but the town site was not regularly built upon before 1830. Green Bay was incorporated as a town in 1839, and as a city in 1854. The population in 1870 was 4666, and in 1890, 8922; while Fort Howard, its western suburb, had a population of 4755.

GREENE, GEORGE WASHINGTON (1811–1883), an American author, was born at East Greenwich, R. I., April 8, 1811, being a grandson of Gen. Nathaniel Greene (for whom see ENCYCLOPÆDIA BRITANNICA). He was educated at Brown University, but in 1827 was compelled to leave by ill health. He then went to Europe where he resided until 1847, being U. S. consul at Rome from 1837 to 1845. Returning to America, he was appointed professor of modern languages in Brown University and edited some historical text-books. In 1872 he was made non-resident professor of American history in Cornell University. He died at East Greenwich, R. I., Feb. 8, 1883. He published *Historical Studies* (1850); *Biographical Studies* (1860); *Historical View of the American Revolution* (1865); *Life of Gen. Nathaniel Greene* (3 vols., 1865–76); *The German Element in he War of American Independence* (1876). The last is founded on Friedrich Kapp's researches, but the biography of Gen. Greene is a valuable work from original sources.

GREENE, SAMUEL STILLMAN (1810–1884), an American educator, was born at Belchertown, Mass., May 3, 1810. He graduated at Brown University in

1837, taught school and became superintendent of schools at Springfield, Mass., in 1840. In 1842 he removed to Boston, where he taught in the grammar and English high schools. In 1849 he was agent for the Massachusetts Board of Education. In 1851 he was appointed superintendent of the public schools, Providence, R. I., and was connected with Brown University. In 1855 he became professor of mathematics and civil-engineering in that institution, and in 1864 took the chair of astronomy, which he held till his death, in January, 1884. His chief publications were a series of English grammars, in which he directed special attention to the analysis of sentences.

GREENOUGH, RICHARD S., an American sculptor, was born at Jamaica Plain, Mass., April 27, 1819. He obtained some instruction in sculpture from S. V. Clevenger, and in 1840 went to Italy, where he studied with his brother, Horatio Greenough (for whom see the ENCYCLOPÆDIA BRITANNICA). He soon returned to Boston, where he made portrait busts, but in 1850 went again to Italy, and worked on imaginative subjects in bronze and marble. He also made some statues, including Franklin and Winthrop. He resided in Paris from 1856 to 1868, and then removed to Newport, R. I.

GREENVILLE, a city of South Carolina, county-seat of Greenville county, at the junction of the Greenville and Columbia and the Richmond and Atlanta Railroads, 95 miles (143 by rail) N. W. of Columbia. It is picturesquely situated near Saluda Mountain, in the Blue Ridge, and is on the Reedy River, one of the head-streams of the Saluda. It has a court-house, a city-hall, a national bank, a daily and 2 weekly newspapers, and 7 churches; also a cotton-factory, oil-works, and manufactures of flour, furniture, and machinery. Greenville is the seat of Furman University and Greenville Female College (both Baptist institutions). It is a favorite summer resort. It is lighted with gas. Its property is valued at $1,800,000, and its public debt is $5100. It was settled about 1785, and in 1871 became a city. Population in 1870, 2757; in 1880, 6160; and in 1890, 8340.

GREENWOOD, FRANCIS WILLIAM PITT (1797-1843), an American clergyman, was born at Boston, Mass., Feb. 5, 1797. Graduating at Harvard College in 1814, he studied theology with Rev. Henry Ware. In October, 1818, he became pastor of the new South Church, Boston, but was compelled to desist from preaching a year later. He then went to England, and on his return settled in Baltimore until 1824, when he became colleague to Rev. Dr. James Freeman, pastor of King's Chapel, Boston, under whom he had received his early training, and in 1827 became sole pastor. After his return from a voyage to Cuba in 1837 he published *Sermons of Consolation* (1842). He died at Boston, Aug. 2, 1843. He published a *History of King's Chapel* (1833); *Lives of the Twelve Apostles* (1838), and many sermons. His interest in the natural sciences, especially botany and conchology, was shown by contributions to the *Journal of Natural History* and other periodicals.

GREGG, DAVID MCMURTRIE, an American general, was born at Huntingdon, Pa., April 10, 1833. He graduated at West Point in 1855, and served against the Indians in Oregon in 1858-60. At the outbreak of the civil war he was made captain in the Sixth cavalry, and in January, 1862, became colonel of the Eighth Pennsylvania cavalry. He served with distinction in the Virginia Peninsular campaign, and was made brigadier-general of volunteers on Nov. 29, 1862. He commanded a division of cavalry from this time and was engaged at Gettysburg and other important battles. He commanded the Second cavalry division from April 6, 1864, and was engaged in the Richmond campaign until his resignation, Feb. 3, 1865. In 1874 he was made U. S. consul at Prague.

GREGG, JOHN IRVIN, an American general, was born at Bellefonte, Pa., in 1825. He was made a lieutenant in the U. S. army in 1847 and served in the Mexican war. At the outbreak of the civil war he was made captain in the Sixth U. S. cavalry, and served till the close of McClellan's campaign in 1862. He was then made colonel of the Sixteenth Pennsylvania volunteers, and in 1863 had command of a cavalry brigade. He fought at Gettysburg and throughout Grant's Richmond campaign, but was taken prisoner April 6, 1865. He received various brevets for gallantry, and in 1866 was made colonel of the Eighth U. S. cavalry., and was retired in 1879.

GREGG, MAXCY (1814-1862), a Confederate general, was born at Columbia, S. C., in 1814, his father being an eminent lawyer of that city. He graduated at South Carolina College in 1836, and was admitted to the bar in 1839. He was appointed major of the Twelfth infantry in March, 1847, and served till the close of the Mexican war. He was afterwards colonel of a regiment of State militia, and in 1860 was a prominent member of the State convention and helped to prepare the ordinance of secession. In the civil war he was colonel of the First South Carolina regiment, and in 1861 was made brigadier-general. He was killed at the battle of Fredericksburg, Dec. 13, 1862. At the time of his death he was governor-elect of South Carolina.

GREGOROVIUS, FERDINAND, a German historian, was born at Neidenburg, Jan. 19, 1821. He was educated at Gumbinnen and at the University of Königsberg, where he studied theology and philosophy. He afterwards devoted himself to literature, his first noted wor kbeing *Goethe's Wilhelm Meister in seinem sozialistischen Elementen* (1849). He also wrote some essays on Poland and Polish songs. In 1851 appeared his drama, *Der Todt des Tiberius*, and close after it his first historical work which he has since greatly improved and reconstructed under the title, *Der Kaiser Hadrian* (1884). In 1852 Gregorovius left Königsberg and went to Italy. His books of travel, beginning with *Corsica* (1854) and continued in five volumes of *Wanderjahre in Italien*, are valuable contributions to knowledge. Pompeii was the scene of his hexameter epic *Euphorion* (1858), which has found favor with the book-illustrators. His great historical work is *Die Geschichte der Stadt Rom im Mittelalter* (8 vols., 1859 -72; 3d ed., 1875-82). It is founded on thorough study of original documents in Italy and Germany, and has shed abundant light on many obscure passages in mediæval history. For the sake of his work the author has received the freedom of the city of Rome, being the first Protestant so honored. In connection with his main work he has issued *Die Grabdenkmäler der Päpste* (1857; 2d ed., 1881). He has also published a life of *Lucrezia Borgia* (1874), which has passed through several editions, and has edited the *Letters* of Alexander von Humboldt to his brother Wilhelm (1880). Gregorovius resides alternately in Rome and Munich, and is active in the learned societies of both cities. Besides the works here mentioned he has published several poems and minor historical works.

GREGORA, DANIEL SEELY, an American clergyman and educator, was born at Carmel, Putnam co., N. Y., Aug. 21, 1832. He graduated at Princeton College in 1857 and studied theology at the Princeton Seminary, and during part of his course was instructor in rhetoric and English literature in the college. In 1860 he became pastor of a Presbyterian church at Galena, Ill., and he afterwards had charge of churches in Troy, N. Y., and New Haven, Conn. Compelled to retire from pastoral work in 1869 he recruited his health by farming, and in 1871 he became professor of mental sciences in Wooster University, Ohio, whence in 1878 he was called to be president of Lake Forest University, Ill. He has published *Christian Ethics* (1875); *Why Four Gospels?* (1877); *Practical Logic* (1881).

GRELLET, STEPHEN (1773–1855), a Quaker missionary, was born in France in 1773. He was educated at the military school at Lyons, and in 1790 entered the body-guard of Louis XVI. After the execution of the king, he went to Demerara and thence to New York in 1795. Here he attended a Quaker meeting and was so impressed with that mode of worship that he joined the society. He settled in Philadelphia and was active in benevolent work, especially in the yellow fever epidemic of 1798. He afterwards became a merchant in New York, but in 1800 began to make extended missionary tours in the United States, and in 1807 went to France for the same purpose. In 1818 he travelled over the greater part of Europe and addressed both the Pope and the Czar of Russia. In 1834 he retired to Burlington, N. J., where he died, Nov. 16, 1855. His *Memoirs* were published by B. Seebohm (1868), and other biographies have been issued.

GRÉVY, FRANÇOIS PAUL JULES, a French statesman, was born at Mont-sous-Vaudray, in the Jura, Aug. 5, 1813. The son of a Republican farmer, he was educated at the colleges of Poligny and Besançon, and at Paris. He is said to have fought in the streets of Paris in the Revolution of 1830, but thereafter devoted himself to the study of law, and soon attained an extensive practice. By courageous defence of Republican journalists he obtained also a political reputation, and in 1848 was sent by the provisional government to the Jura to inaugurate the new régime. Being then elected to the Constitutional Assembly from his native district, he was chosen one of the vice-presidents of the Assembly. Dreading the election of Louis Napoleon to the presidency of the Republic, he opposed the plan of choosing a president for four years by universal suffrage, and proposed that the executive power should be intrusted to the president of a ministry, elected by ballot by the Assembly, and liable to be removed in the same way. His project was defeated, and when the Second Empire was established M. Grévy was arrested and imprisoned for months on account of the speeches he had made against Napoleon's presidency. Retiring then to his profession, he held no political position until 1868, when he was again elected to the legislature from the Jura district. On the downfall of the Empire in September, 1870, when the new Republican leaders dissolved the Assembly, Grévy joined in the protest against their action. During the German war he pursued a moderate course, and in 1871 was almost unanimously chosen president of the Assembly. By his impartiality and firmness he did much to prevent outbreaks in that turbulent Assembly, but on April 1, 1873, when some members of the Right protested against one of his decisions, he resigned his place, and though re-elected almost unanimously still refused to take the position. After the retirement of Pres. Thiers, M. Grévy voted constantly with the Left, and opposed the septennate of Marshal MacMahon. He refused to vote for the constitution of 1875, on the ground that the Assembly had no power to make a constitution; he also refused to be a candidate for the Senate, believing that there should be but one legislative chamber. In February, 1876, he was again made president of the Chamber of Deputies. The position was rendered unusually difficult by the religious questions brought before the Chamber, but the president maintained his accustomed impartiality. The Senate, however, had a monarchical majority, and Pres. MacMahon, having forced M. Jules Simon out of the cabinet, called the Duc de Broglie to his place, and prorogued the Chambers for a month, in spite of the protest of 363 delegates against this unconstitutional step. In June the Senate agreed to a dissolution of the Assembly, and in the ensuing election the scheme of the president was defeated. M. Thiers, to whom all sections of the Republican party looked as their choice for president, died on Sept. 4, and M. Grévy, who was the chief speaker at his obsequies, was designated by Victor Hugo and Gambetta as his successor in the electoral district of Paris, and as the future president. Marshal MacMahon, however, continued to hold his place, making such changes in his ministry as he found unavoidable, until Jan. 30, 1879, when he resigned rather than remove some Bonapartist generals. On the same day M. Grévy was elected president for seven years. At this time also the new president received the grand cross of the Legion of Honor, having previously refused any decoration. Pres. Grévy's first cabinet was entirely composed of members of the Left, Waddington being the chief, but Gambetta was the ruling spirit, and, as the progress of events demanded, Waddington was replaced by Freycinet, a friend of Gambetta, in December, 1879, and he, in September, 1880, by Jules Ferry. Fourteen months later Gambetta himself took the responsible position of chief minister, with the portfolio of foreign affairs, but relinquished it in the following January. Up to this time much had been done to secularize education, and on March 30, 1880, Pres. Grévy issued a proclamation ordering the "so-called Society of Jesus" to disband. The Jesuit establishments were closed July 1, and later in the year other unauthorized religious orders were expelled from their cloisters. The military spirit of the French was soon gratified by the campaign against Tunis, which, though more expensive and less glorious than had been expected, resulted in the establishment of a protectorate over that country. In other parts of the world—in Syria, in Madagascar, and especially in Tonquin—a French aggressive policy was manifested, but without results commensurate with the outlay. The yearly expenditure of the Republic has been enormous, exceeding even that of Great Britain, yet the budget steadily shows an excess of receipts; the national debt has been diminished, and the people have been prosperous. The Cobden treaty with England having expired in 1881, was not renewed, and the policy of protection has since prevailed. On Dec. 28, 1885, M. Grévy was re-elected president of France. While he had preserved Republican simplicity and honesty in his high office, his son-in-law, Wilson, was, in 1887, convicted of trafficking in appointments, and M. Grévy, having tried to shield him, was obliged to resign, Dec. 2, 1887.

GRIERSON, BENJAMIN H., an American general, was born at Pittsburg, Pa., July, 1837. In early life he removed to Ohio, and he was afterwards engaged as a produce-dealer at Jacksonville, Ill. At the outbreak of the civil war he served on the staff of Gen. B. M. Prentiss, in Missouri. He was major of the Sixth Illinois cavalry, and became colonel March 28, 1862. In December, 1862, he had command of a cavalry brigade, and was engaged in many raids in Tennessee and Mississippi. To facilitate Gen. Grant's operations against Vicksburg, he made a noted raid from La Grange to Baton Rouge, lasting from April 17 to May 2, 1863. He was then made brigadier-general of volunteers, and at the close of the war was major-general. In July, 1866, he was appointed colonel of the Tenth U. S. cavalry.

GRIFFIN, CHARLES (1826-1867), an American general, was born in Licking co., Ohio, in 1826. He graduated at West Point in 1847, and entered the artillery service. At the outbreak of the civil war he was made captain of the Fifth artillery, and he fought bravely in the battle of Bull Run. He afterwards served with distinction in McClellan's Peninsular campaign, but after Gen. Pope took command was charged with refraining from taking part in the second battle of Bull Run, Aug. 28, 1862. Though arrested for trial on this charge, he was released to join Gen. McClellan in the Maryland campaign, and fought bravely at Antietam. In December he was placed in command of a division, and fought under Burnside, Hooker, and Meade. After Gen. Grant took command of the Army of the Potomac, Gen. Griffin shared in all the engagements from the Wilderness to the Five Forks, April 1, 1865, where he was made commander of the Fifth corps. His commission as major-general of volunteers dated from this battle, and a week later he received the arms and colors of Gen. Lee's army on its surrender. In July, 1866, he was made colonel of the Thirty-fifth infantry, and in the winter following he took command of the department of Texas. He died at Galveston, Texas, Sept. 15, 1867.

GRIFFIN, EDWARD DORR (1770-1837), an American clergyman, was born at East Haddam, Conn., Jan. 6, 1770. He graduated at Yale College in 1790, was licensed to preach in 1792, and held pastorates at Hartford, Conn. (1795-1800), and Newark, N. J. (1801-09). He had acquired fame as a pulpit orator, and in 1809 was made professor of sacred rhetoric at Andover Theological Seminary. In 1811 he returned to pastoral work in Boston, and in 1815 removed to his former charge at Newark. From 1821 to 1836 he was president of Williams College, and labored successfully in its behalf. He died at Newark, N. J., Nov. 8, 1837. He published many sermons, but his most noted work was the *Park Street Lectures* (1813), in which he expounded the Calvinistic system of divinity. Rev. W. B. Sprague edited two volumes of his sermons, with a memoir (1838).

GRIFFIS, WILLIAM ELLIOT, an American educator, was born at Philadelphia, Pa., Sept. 17, 1843. After graduating at the High School of that city in 1859, he spent six years in business pursuits, and then went to Rutgers College, where he graduated in 1869. In the next year he went to Japan to organize schools on the American plan, and for three years was professor of natural science in the Imperial University of Tokio. Returning to the United States, he studied theology at the Union Theological Seminary in 1877, and was ordained pastor of the First Reformed Church, Schenectady, N. Y., and in 1886 accepted a call to a Congregational Church in Boston. Besides some educational works prepared in Japan, he has published *The Mikado's Empire* (1876; 4th ed., 1884); *Japanese Fairy World* (1880); *Corea, the Hermit Nation* (1882); *Corea, Without and Within* (1884).

GRIMES, JAMES WILSON (1816-1872), an American statesman, was born at Deering, N. H., Oct. 20, 1816. He graduated at Dartmouth College in 1835, having already commenced the study of law. He removed to Burlington, Iowa, then in the Territory of Michigan, and became eminent in his profession. He served in the territorial legislature of Iowa in 1838, and afterwards in the State legislature. He belonged to the Whig party, and in 1854 was elected governor of Iowa by a combination of this party with the Free Soil Democrats. During his term he assisted in providing better treatment for the insane, and promoted the construction of railroads in the State. He also contributed to the organization of the Republican party, and in 1858 he was elected to the U. S. Senate. Here he was a prominent member of the committee on the navy, and first suggested the introduction of iron-clad vessels in July, 1861. He was re-elected to the Senate in 1864, and in his second term was conspicuous as one of the few Republicans who refused to sustain the impeachment of Pres. Johnson. During the impeachment trial Senator Grimes was stricken with paralysis, but he continued to discharge the duties of his office until 1869, when he resigned and made a protracted tour in Europe. He died at Burlington, Iowa, Feb. 7, 1872.

GRIMKÉ, THOMAS SMITH (1786-1834), an American lawyer, was born at Charleston, S. C., Sept. 26, 1786. He was the son of John Fancheraud Grimké (d. 1819), who had been a colonel in the Revolutionary army, and was afterwards a judge of the Supreme Court of South Carolina. Thomas graduated at Yale College in 1807, studied law at Charleston, and became eminent in his profession. In the State senate in 1828 he made an able speech, sustaining the national government in the tariff dispute. His most noted legal argument was that on the constitutionality of the South Carolina test oath in 1834. He was a prominent member of the American Peace Society, and earnestly opposed all war, even defensive. He also made addresses on various subjects pertaining to temperance, education, and literature, and attempted to introduce a new system of English spelling. (See Duyckinck's *Cyclopædia of American Literature*, Vol. I., p. 779.) He died near Columbus, Ohio, Oct. 12, 1834. A volume of his addresses was published at New Haven in 1831.

His sister, SARAH MOORE GRIMKÉ (1792-1873), was born at Charleston, S. C., Nov. 6, 1792. From early youth she showed her dislike to slavery, and having inherited some slaves she set them free. In 1821 she removed to Philadelphia, where she joined the Society of Friends. In 1828 she published *An Epistle to the Clergy of the Southern States*, an efficient anti-slavery document. She and her sister Angelina began to lecture against slavery in 1836, and Sarah wrote for Garrison's *Liberator* letters on *The Equality of the Sexes*, which were also published in book-form. After her sister's marriage to Theodore D. Weld, Sarah resided with them and taught in their school, established at Belleville, N. J., in 1840, and afterwards moved to other places. She died at Hyde Park, N. Y., Dec. 23, 1

GRINNELL, HENRY (1790-1874), an American merchant, was born at New Bedford, Mass., Feb. 13, 1799. He was brought up to mercantile pursuits and removing to New York was for thirty years engaged in the whale-oil business. Afterwards he was interested in insurance companies and savings banks. In 1850 he fitted out the Grinnell expedition sent in search of Sir John Franklin. He was the first president of the American Geographical Society. He died at New York, in June, 1874.

GRINNELL, MOSES H. (1803-1877), an American merchant, brother of the preceding, was born at New Bedford, Mass., March 3, 1803. He was associated in business with his brother, and in 1853 actively promoted Dr. E. K. Kane's Arctic expedition. He had been a member of Congress 1839-41, and in 1869 was appointed by Pres. Grant collector of the port of New York. He died at New York, Nov. 24, 1877.

GRISCOM, JOHN HOSKINS (1809-1874), an American physician, was born at New York, Aug. 13, 1809. He was the son of John Griscom (1774-1852), a member of the Society of Friends, noted for his labors in behalf of education in New Jersey, Providence, and New York. John H. Griscom studied medicine at Rutgers Medical College, New York, and at the University of Pennsylvania, where he graduated in 1832. He then became connected with the New York Dispensary and was professor of chemistry in the New York College of Pharmacy, 1836-40; physician to the New York Hospital, 1843-67; and general agent of the commissioners of immigration, 1848-51. He gave much attention to sanitary and hygienic subjects. He died at New York, April 28, 1874. His works include *Animal Mechanism and Physiology* (1839); *Sanitary Condition of the Laboring Classes of New York* (1844); *Uses and Abuses of Air* (1850); *History of the Yellow Fever in New York* (1858); *Sanitary Legislation* (1861); *Use of Tobacco* (1868); and a *Memoir* of his father (1859).

GRISWOLD, ALEXANDER VIETS (1766-1843), an American bishop, was born at Simsbury, Conn., April 22, 1766. He was educated by his uncle, Rev. Roger Viets, who was rector of that parish until 1787, when he went to Nova Scotia. Griswold was ordained June 3, 1795, and ministered in several churches until 1804, when he became rector of St. Michael's Church at Bristol, R. I., and taught a school. When the Eastern diocese was formed, comprising all New England except Connecticut, he was elected bishop and was consecrated by Bishop White, May 29, 1811. He still held the rectorship of the church in Bristol until 1830, when he went to Salem, Mass., and a few years later he removed to Boston. His last public act was, Dec. 29, 1842, to consecrate Rev. Dr. M. Eastburn, who had been chosen his assistant. He died at Boston, Mass., Feb. 15, 1843. His only publications were sermons and addresses. His *Life* was published by Rev. J. S. Stone, D. D.

GRISWOLD, RUFUS WILMOT (1815-1857), an American author, was born at Benson, Rutland co., Vt., Feb. 15, 1815. His early life was spent in voyaging about the world, and before he was twenty he had seen the most interesting parts of America and Europe. He then studied divinity and became a Baptist preacher, but soon turned his attention to journalism. He was connected editorially with weekly newspapers in New York, Boston, and Philadelphia. In 1842-43, as editor of *Graham's Magazine*, he did much to develop American authorship. Of his *International Monthly Magazine* five volumes were issued. He is chiefly known by his collections called *Poets and Poetry of America* (1842); *Prose Writers of America* (1846); *Female Poets of America* (1849). These exhibitions of the literature of this country with his accompanying criticisms had an important influence on its development, and on the reputation of the various authors included. They have passed through many editions and have been revised and enlarged by various editors. Griswold prepared similar volumes on the *Poets and Poetry of England in the Nineteenth Century* and *Sacred Poets of England and America*. Beside popular biographies of *Washington and the Generals of the American Revolution* (1847) and *Napoleon and the Marshals of the Empire* (1847) he published *The Republican Court, or American Society in the Days of Washington* (1854). He was a diligent investigator of American history and literature, and did much to improve and diffuse literary taste among the people. He died at New York city, Aug. 27, 1857. Griswold was Edgar A. Poe's literary executor and took advantage of this position to assail Poe's character in a manner which has roused partisans in defence of the latter.

GROSS, SAMUEL D. (1805-1884), an American surgeon, was born near Easton, Pa., July 8, 1805. After receiving an academic education he studied medicine and graduated at Jefferson Medical College, Philadelphia, 1828. He commenced practice in that city, and being a hard worker devoted much time to translating French and German medical works. His first important work was *Diseases and Injuries of the Bones and Joints* (1830). In 1833 he was appointed demonstrator of anatomy in the Ohio Medical College in Cincinnati, and in 1835 became professor of pathological anatomy in the medical department of Cincinnati College, delivering the first systematic course of lectures on morbid anatomy ever given in the United States. From the lectures delivered here he composed his *Elements of Pathological Anatomy*, the first American treatise on the subject. In 1839 Dr. Gross was appointed professor of surgery in the University of Louisville, Ky. In 1850 he was called to a similar position in the University of New York, but after holding this chair for one year he returned to Louisville. Here he founded and was first president of the Kentucky State Medical Society. In 1856 he was made professor of surgery in Jefferson Medical College and held this position until 1882, when he resigned and was made professor emeritus. He has been a diligent student and voluminous author. His most important work was his *System of Surgery*, which first appeared in 1859 and has since passed through six editions. It has been pronounced the most elaborate work on surgery ever written by one man. Among his later works were *Manual of Military Surgery* (1862); *Practical Treatise on Foreign Bodies in the Air Passages* (1850); *Diseases of the Urinary Organs* (1851); *American Medical Biography* (1861); *History of American Medical Literature*; and *History of the Progress of American Surgery during the last Century*. He was a member of the American Philosophical Society, and of numerous medical societies in all parts of the world. In 1868 the American Medical Association elected him its president. He was also twice a delegate to the British Medical Association, and was unanimously elected president of the International Medical Congress at Philadelphia in 1876. He received the degree of LL. D. from Jefferson College, and in 1872 the degree of D. C. L. from the University of Oxford, and a few days before his death the University of Edinburgh conferred on him the degree of LL. D. He died at Philadelphia, May 6, 1884, having continued at work till a month previous. For forty-eight years he was engaged in the public teaching of surgery. He was noted for his conscientiousness in the discharge of his duty to his patients and his pupils. As an operator he held the foremost rank, being clear in his diagnosis, and quick in deciding the proper treatment. See his *Autobiography* (1888) edited by his sons.

GROVE, GEORGE, an English author, was born at Clapham in 1820. He became a civil-engineer, and erected the first cast-iron light-house ever built, on Morant Point, Jamaica, in 1841. He also erected a similar one on Gibbs' Hill, Bermuda. He was afterwards employed by Robert Stephenson on the Holyhead Railway and the Britannia Bridge. In 1850 he became secretary of the Society of Arts, and in 1852 secretary of the London Crystal Palace Company, which position he held till 1873. For several years he was editor of *MacMillan's Magazine*. His most important work is his *Dictionary of Music and Musicians* (4 vols., 1830-86).

GROVE, SIR WILLIAM ROBERT, an English physicist, was born at Swansea, July 11, 1811. He was educated at Brasenose College, Oxford, graduating in 1830. He was admitted to the bar in 1835; but, having given much attention to the study of electricity, he invented in 1839 a powerful voltaic battery. From 1840 to 1847 he was professor of experimental philosophy at the London Institution. Having resumed the practice of law he became queen's counsel in 1853, and was the leader of the South Wales and Chester circuits. In 1871 he was made justice of the Common Pleas, and soon after received the honor of knighthood. He had continued to prosecute his electrical researches, and in 1866 was president of the British Association at Nottingham. He has made many noteworthy discoveries, but his fame is derived chiefly from the doctrine of the correlation of physical forces, first stated in 1842, and more fully developed in 1846.

GRUNDY, FELIX (1777-1840), an American statesman, was born in Berkeley county, Va., Sept. 11, 1777. His father removed to Kentucky in 1780, and Felix was educated at Bardstown Academy. He studied law, and having begun practice in 1798 became noted as an advocate, especially in criminal cases. In 1799 he was a member of the Kentucky Constitutional Convention and in 1800 was elected to the legislature. In 1806 he was appointed judge in the State Supreme Court, and soon after chief-justice. In 1808 he removed to Nashville, Tenn., where he took a high position at the bar. In 1811 he was elected to Congress and during two terms supported Madison's administration. In 1815 he declined to be made candidate, but in 1829 he was elected to the U. S. Senate. In 1838 Pres. Van Buren appointed him attorney-general of the United States, but in 1840 he was re-elected to the Senate. He died at Nashville, Dec. 19, 1840.

GUARANTY. An undertaking on the part of a person to pay a debt, or perform a duty, upon the failure of another who is in the first instance liable. The English Statute of Frauds, 29 Charles II., c. 3, sect. 4, enacted that such an agreement, to be binding, must be in writing and signed by the party to be charged therewith, or by some other person thereunto by him lawfully authorized; and this statute has been adopted or substantially re-enacted throughout the United States.

See Vol. XI. p. 209 Am. ed. (p. 236 Edin. ed.).

There have been numerous distinctions made under this statute. Where the principal obligation is void by reason of the debtor's incapacity to contract, and this is contemplated by the parties; in such a case the statute does not operate, and the agreement on the part of a third person to answer for such obligation would be enforceable though not in writing and signed. But it seems that if the invalidity of the principal obligation is not contemplated by the parties the case falls within the statute, and the agreement of the third party must be in writing and signed. If a creditor discharge a debtor from liability upon the strength of a promise by a third party to pay the debt such a promise is valid though not in writing. So also where the promisor or guarantor has property in hands belonging to the debtor in consideration of which he promises to pay the debt, or acquires or is benefited by a lien which the creditor had, he is bound although no writing pass. Where exclusive credit is given to the promissor this is treated as an *original* contract, and, of course, does not fall within the statute of frauds; that is to say, the fulfilment of an *original* obligation must be guaranteed by *another* person not the original obligor, in order that the case may be within the statute: in the language of the courts the contract of guaranty must be *collateral*. But if it be collateral only in form and original in substance, the law looks to the substance rather than the form, the question being whose debt is promised to be paid, and not what is the form of the contract.

GUARDIAN. A person having charge, in law, of the person and estate, or either, of a minor. The father is considered, in the first instance, as the guardian *by nature and for nurture* of all his children during minority, and, after him, the mother. The courts will enforce the father's right to the custody of the child as against the claim of the mother; but, if the father be incapable, or unfit for the charge, it will be awarded to the mother; and, in this country, the mother will be awarded the guardianship of a bastard against the claim of its putative father. Guardianship *by nature and for nurture* extends only over the person, and not the estate, of the child. Hence, a mere natural guardian cannot give a valid receipt for a legacy paid him for the child.

By statute 12 Charles II., a father was given power to appoint a guardian for his children during minority. by will. Such a guardian is called a *statutory* or *testamentary* guardian. The English statute has been extensively adopted in this country, and in some States the mother has testamentary powers in respect to the appointment of a guardian. In the absence of a guardian, or in the event of the disability or refusal of a guardian to act, the court of Chancery in England has long exercised the power of appointing a suitable guardian. But the appointment of guardians is generally covered by statute in this country, and, where occasion requires, guardians are generally assigned by probate or other courts, under statutory powers, the chancery courts in some States retaining a general supervision.

If there is no father or mother, the guardian is entitled to the custody of the child. A parent must support his child from his own means, in return for which the child's services belong to him; but a guardian need not supply the wants of his ward except from the latter's own estate; nor is he entitled to the ward's services. The ward must be maintained in a style suitable to his condition in life, but not beyond his means. It is the duty of the guardian to superintend his education, and in general to supply the place of a judicious parent. In managing the ward's property, the following is a summary of the guardian's powers and duties: "To collect all dues and give receipts for the same; to procure such legacies and distributive shares from testators or others as may have accrued; to take and hold all property settled upon the ward by way of gift or purchase, unless some trustee is interposed; to collect dividends and interest, and the income of personal property in general; to receive and receipt for the rents and profits of real estate; to receive moneys due the ward on bond and mortgage; to pay the necessary expenses of the ward's personal protection, education, and support; to invest and reinvest all balances in his hands; to sell the capital of the ward's property, change the character of investments when needful, convert real into personal and personal into real estate, in a suitable exigency, but *not without judicial direction;* to account to the ward, or his legal representatives, at the expiration of his trust."

Guardianship is ended as follows: When the ward, on arriving at fourteen, elects, under the statute, another guardian, and the latter is appointed; when the ward has reached majority; on the expiration of the time limited by testamentary appointment; on the death of the ward, in which case the guardian has simply to settle up his accounts and pay the balance in hand to the ward's representatives, and his trust is ended. On the marriage of the ward, the guardianship ends in so far as it relates to the person. In the case of a male ward, it still continues over his estate until he becomes of age. In case of a female ward, the question is not settled. Guardianship is also terminated upon the death or resignation of the guardian, or upon removal by the court, for cause shown.

GUELPH, a city of Ontario, Canada, county-seat of Wellington county, beautifully situated on the river Speed, which flows through the town. It is on the main line of the Grand Trunk Railway at the junction of 2 branch lines, 45 miles W. S. W. of Toronto. The town is well built and has 6 banks, 2 daily and 2 weekly newspapers, several handsome churches, the county buildings, a high-school, the Ontario Agricultural College, a convent, 5 flour-mills, manufactures of sewing-machines, woollen goods, musical instruments, carpets, carriages, castings, soap, farm-implements, etc., the river affording ample water-power. A large proportion of the buildings are constructed of a handsome white stone, quarried near by. The town is lighted with gas, has water-works and a public park. The total valuation is $3,101,880. Guelph was founded in 1827, and incorporated a city in 1878. Population in 1881 was 9890.

GUERICKE, HEINRICH ERNST FERDINAND (1803-1878), a German theologian, was born at Wettin, Feb. 25, 1803. He studied theology at Halle, where in 1829 he became professor extraordinary. But he strenuously resisted the union of the Lutheran and Reformed Churches of Prussia in 1833, and was ordained pastor of a congregation of Lutheran dissentients. His professorship was then taken from him, but in 1840 it was restored. He then founded a religious journal which he conducted until his death, Feb. 4, 1878. Among his writings are *August Herman Franke* (1827); *Neu-Testamentliche Isagogik* (1854; enlarged from a work published in 1843); *Handbuch der Kirchengeschichte* (2 vols., 1833; 9th ed., 1866-67, translated by Rev. W. G. T. Shedd, 1857-63); *Allgemeine Christliche Symbolik* (1839; 3d ed., 1861); *Lehrbuch der Christlichen Archäologie* (1847; 2d ed., 1859; translated into English, 1851).

GUERRERO, VICENTE (c. 1770-1831) president of Mexico, was a creole mulatto, born at Tixtla about 1770. Being a slave he took part in an insurrection in 1809. In 1818 he became a leader of the liberal troops, and in 1827 was the candidate of the *Yorkino* party for president, but was not elected. War ensued, and in 1829 he was declared president, and when a Spanish invasion occurred he was made dictator. After the defeat of the invaders he showed unwillingness to resign his power, and Vice-Pres. Bustamente marched against him. Guerrero, deserted by his troops, resigned, but a few months later gathered a new force, and was captured and shot at Cailapa, Feb. 14, 1831.

GUESS, GEORGE, also called SEQUOYAH (c. 1770-1843), a Cherokee half-breed, inventor of the Cherokee alphabet, was born about 1770. He occupied a farm in Northern Georgia, and was an ingenious silversmith. Knowing no language but his own, he took the letters found in the English spelling-book as the basis of a syllabic alphabet, which finally had 85 characters. Newspapers and books were afterwards printed in Cherokee with these characters. When his tribe was driven from their possessions, he went with them beyond the Mississippi. He died at San Fernando, in Northern Mexico, in August, 1843.

GUINEA-FOWL. See FOWL.

GULF-WEED, SARGASSO-WEED, in botany *Sargassum bacciferum*. Columbus, in his voyage of discovery, entered on Sept. 15, 1492, an immense plain of sea-weed, in that part of the Atlantic which has been called the Sargasso Sea. Where the plant came from no one knew, and it is not a little remarkable that now, 400 years after, we know but little more of its origin than was known in Columbus' time. Sea-weeds derive all their nourishment from the water which surrounds them. Their attachment to rocks or other objects is for the mere purpose of location. They derive no food from the connection. But this sea-weed has never been found attached anywhere, and some botanists have come to believe that it can exist indefinitely as a floating weed, increasing by bud development and without the agency of sexual products. As, however, there must be a perpetual flow of cold and heavy water to take the place of the water lightened by the tropical sun, and hence a steady stream of water on the surface towards the Arctic Seas to take the place of the heavier waters rolling southward, it is believed that the whole of this floating mass of sea-weed would eventually disappear along the lines of the Gulf Stream, unless there were a fixed source of supply in some tropical location. This is probably in deep water, the exact place as yet undetermined. The weed is usually found in more or less abundance between 20° and 45° N. lat. The true Gulf-weed is *Sargassum bacciferum*, but there are several allied species, some of which have been used as food. In South America the Gulf-weed is used as a remedy in tumors, though some medical men believe that whatever merit it has is simply due to the iodine it contains. Forchammer analyzed the ashes of *Sargassum cocciferum*, and found them to contain of potash 0.09, soda 0.81, magnesia 0.68, lime 5.69, phosphoric acid 0.38, sulphuric acid 2.22, silica 0.19. The total percentage of ash was 11.62. (T. M.)

GUM-PLANT (*Grindelia robusta*). *Grindelia* was named by Willdenow, in 1807, in honor of Dr. Grindel, a German botanist. It is exclusively an American genus, inhabiting the dryer regions of the continent west of the Mississippi, its range extending to the Pacific coast. Some species are found as far north as the Saskatchawan in the British possessions, while Patagonia seems to be the limit on the south. The chief home of the genus seems to be in Texas and Mexico. The genus belongs to the section *Asteroideæ* of the natural order *Compositæ*. It is easily recognized. It differs from other genera in having a pappus composed of from 2 to 8 rigid, horn-like awns, which are early deciduous. The leaves are thickish, and in most species covered by a viscid exudation, and in some instances have a marked tendency to present their edges at a right angle with the horizon. Though so natural a genus, the species are so closely related that there is much difficulty in placing them. California has about 4 recognized species, and one of these, *Grindelia robusta*, is the special one known popularly as the "Gum-Plant" by Californians. It has achieved great popularity in medicine as a remedy in a variety of diseases, concerning the efficiency of which Prof. J. T. Rothrock announces himself as skeptical. It is regarded especially as a remedy for poisoning by the *Rhus diversiloba*, the poison-oak of California. It takes on a number of forms which have been described as species by some botanists, and failure to derive the anticipated benefits from its use has sometimes been charged to employing the wrong variety. (T. M.)

GUM-TREE, a name popularly applied, in various English-speaking countries, to a number of exceedingly diverse kinds of trees. In Australia and Tasmania the Eucalypti are known as gum-trees. The *Bursera gummifera*, or cachiboo gum (order *Amyridaceæ*), is a large tree of Southern Florida and the West Indies. Hog gum, doctor's gum, etc., are trees (or gummy products of trees) of the British West Indies, the names being vaguely and variously applied. A species of wild *Ficus* is locally called gum-tree in South Florida. But the trees generally known as gum-tree in the United States are the following:

I. SOUR GUM, Black gum, Tupelo, Peperidge, are names belonging to trees of the genus *Nyssa*, and order *Cornaceæ*, and which, with the genus *Cornus*—the Dogwoods—constitute the chief portion of the order. They differ much from true Dogwoods in their general appearance, and in a more particular manner in the diœcious or monœcious character of their flowers; in *Cornus* there are but four stamens and four petals; in *Nyssa* there are in the male flower from five to twelve stamens and five petals, and in the female flowers the petals vary from two to five. The chief character would perhaps be the one-celled ovary in *Nyssa*, as against the two or three-celled one of *Cornus*. The various species of *Cornus* are seldom more than large shrubs, while the "Sour gums" (in all the species) are large trees, sometimes among the largest of the forest. They are peculiarly American, and confined to the seaboard of the Atlantic United States. The sour gum was first described by Catesby in his *History of the Carolinas* as a "tree growing in water." The characters are somewhat variable, and in the earlier days of American botany a number of species were distinguished, which in modern times have been reduced to three, namely, *Nyssa multiflora*, which includes all the northern forms, and which extends also south to the Gulf States; *N. uniflora*, which is found from North Carolina to Florida; and *N. capitata*, which grows from Georgia to Florida in swamps near the coast. The last is known as the Ogeechee Lime. The acid fruit evidently suggested the name of "sour gum," in distinction to sweet gum, the wood of the tree, by its intricate fibres, being so much like that of the sweet gum (*Liquidambar Styraciflua*) as to cause the two trees to be classed together by lumbermen, though so very different botanically. The interwoven fibres render the wood extremely difficult to split, and hence it is very valuable for rollers, blocks, and all work where lightness and toughness is desirable. It is the favorite wood for the hubs of wheels. For this purpose the tree is cut in the early part of the winter, the trunk divided into approved lengths, and stored away for two or three years, in the shade, to season. The tree usually grows from 30 to 50 feet high, and about 6 feet in circumference. The writer has measured some on the alluvial soil, known as "the meadows," below Philadelphia, 80 and 90 feet high, and 12 and 13 feet in circumference. As, however, the planks will not plane smooth, it is one of those rare cases in forestry where there is no especial advantage in a large tree. The sub-acid berries are acceptable to birds. In the autumn the leaves turn to a brilliant red, and give a magnificent glow to the American landscape. Some special attention was drawn to the sour gum in 1852, by the exhibition before the Paris Academy of Sciences, by M. Precul, of a part of a trunk brought from Louisiana, which had been deprived of its bark for 16 or 17 inches around its stem, near the ground, and yet made new wood and bark out of the old wood, connecting completely with the bark above and below the wound. It seemed to prove that new wood and bark were formed from the old, and that the cambium layer is but a gummy mucilage provided for the newly forming cells to feed on. But it is now known that a large number of trees, as well as the gum, will make wood and bark in this manner, if care be taken to keep the cambium layer from drying up.

II. SWEET GUM, also called WHITE GUM and BILSTED (*Liquidambar Styraciflua*), is one of the most widely diffused of all the trees of the Atlantic slope of the American continent. It is found sparingly along the line of the Great Lakes, increasing in abundance southwardly to Mexico. The first knowledge Europeans had of it was from the writings of Monardes, a Spanish botanist, who wrote a treatise on Mexican plants. The Mexicans call it *Xochicotozo Quamitl*, according to early authors; and the gum which they prepare from the tree they call *copalm*. This name, according to Micheaux, was also prevalent in his time among the French along the Gulf. The botanical name adopted by Linnæus is evidently derived from the description of Plukenet, who describes it as "Liquidambari arbor seu Styraciflua." In early times the product of the storax of the East was known as "liquid" and "solid," and the product of this tree was classed with the former sort. The Eastern storax is the product of *Styrax officinale*, and was one of the ingredients in the sweet perfumes of the ancients. The gum of the American *Liquidambar* is of much wider utility. It was with the Indians a popular remedy in fevers, and was also employed in healing wounds. It appears from the researches of Dr. F. Peyre Porcher (*Resources of the Southern Fields and Forests*, Charleston, 1869) to have real merit. It is used in Mexico to relieve chronic catarrhs and similar complaints. In the South it is found to be a cordial and stomachic. "A decoction of the inner bark of the gum-tree in a quart of milk, or a tea made with boiling water, is one of the most valuable and useful mucilaginous astringents we possess. It can be employed with advantage in cases of diarrhœa and dysentery" (Porcher). Dr. Lindley remarks, in the *Vegetable Kingdom*, that the produce of *Liquidambar Styraciflua* abounds in benzoic acid; but Dr. Porcher says, "the acid is not benzoic, as the English assert, but cynanic." Michaux and others assert that the trees in the United States yield very little gum; and Dr. Griffith found that the greatest quantity is obtained from young trees, and just before the appearance of the leaves in spring. The gum is about the consistence of honey, of a yellow color, and of a pleasant balsamic taste. Rafinesque says the Cherokees used the gum as a drawing-plaster, and the Mexicans burn it as incense to make a sweet perfume. The name "Bilsted" is a corruption of "Byl-steel," which Dr. Cadwallader Colden, of New York, in an early catalogue of the plants of that State, says was the "name given to it by the Dutch in New York."

As a timber-tree the sweet gum is of little value where the wood is exposed to the weather. As firewood it ranks with poplar or cottonwood, which is about half the value of shell-bark hickory. But where it can be preserved dry, its toughness, lightness, and susceptibility to polish give it many advantages. In these respects it compares favorably with black walnut. It has been employed in buildings, in making coffins, picture-frames, bedsteads, and other furniture. It is much used in making small berry-baskets. It has some advantages over timber more generally useful, in this, that the tree will grow very rapidly in wet places where little else will grow well. In such places trees are sometimes found 12 feet in circumference. Its height is generally about 60 feet. It, however, grows very well on comparatively dry ground, if the soil be not too poor. It is very popular as an ornamental tree. The habit of growth is pleasant, and the lobed, star-like leaves turn to a beautiful crimson purple in the fall of the year. A singular corky excretion often covers the bark, and gives the branches a very picturesque appearance in the winter season. A species closely allied to the American was found growing in China, by Mr. Mavies, but it was not among the large collection of the woods of Japan exhibited at the American Centennial Exhibition. Another species, *Liquidambar imberbe*, is known to botanists, and credited to the Levant. *L. Altingia* grows in the far East.

The exact place of the *Liquidambar* in botanical classification has long been a puzzle to botanists. Dr. Gray refers it to *Hamameliaceæ*, the Witch-Hazel family. This gives three American genera to the order, *Hamamelis*, *Fothergilla*, and *Liquidambar*. From the other two it differs in having monœcious or polygamous flowers, which have no calyx or corolla, and the seed-pods are consolidated into a dense head. The seed-vessels are interesting from the enormous amount of abortive seeds they often contain, in comparison with the few perfect ones. (T. M.)

GÜNTHER, ALBERT KARL LUDWIG GOTTHILF, a German-British zoölogist, was born at Esslingen, Oct. 3, 1830. He was educated at Stuttgart, and studied theology at Tübingen, but afterwards medicine at Berlin and Bonn. In 1855 he obtained the degree of doctor of medicine at Tübingen. Removing then to London he became an assistant in the zoölogical department of the British Museum, and since 1875 has been director of that department. He has published many valuable catalogues and treatises, among which are *Colubrine Snakes* (1857); *Batrachia salientia* (1857); *Reptiles of British India* (1864); *Gigantic Land-Tortoises* (1877); *Introduction to the Study of Fishes* (1880). From 1865 to 1870 he published an annual *Record of Zoölogical Literature*, which has since been issued by others.

GURLEY, RALPH RANDOLPH (1797–1872), an American philanthropist, was born at Lebanon, Conn., May 26, 1797. He graduated at Yale College in 1818, and having settled at Washington, D. C., was licensed as a Presbyterian preacher. In 1822 he became an agent of the American Colonization Society, which position he held till his death. He made three visits to Africa to further the objects of the society, and assisted in organizing the government of Liberia. He also travelled through the United States, making addresses in behalf of the society and edited the *African Repository*, its organ. He prepared biographies of Jehudi Ashmun (1835) and Rev. Sylvester Larned (1844). He died at Washington, D. C., July 30, 1872.

GURNEY, SIR GOLDWORTHY (1793–1875), an English inventor, was born in Cornwall in 1793. He studied medicine, but devoted himself to chemistry, and in 1822 delivered a course of lectures on this subject at the Surrey Institution. He invented the Bude, oil-gas, lime, and magnesium lights, and claimed to have invented the oxy-hydrogen blowpipe, and to have first observed the deflection of the magnetic needle by voltaic cross-currents. He invented the high-pressure steam-jet and the tubular boiler. In 1829 he drove a steam-carriage from London to Bath on a turnpike road, with a speed of 14 miles an hour. His high-pressure steam-jet was used to ventilate and extinguish fires in coal-mines, and to remove poisonous gases from sewers. In 1852 he had charge of the lighting and ventilating of the new Houses of Parliament, which he accomplished by an original method. He was knighted in 1863, but in the same year was paralyzed. He died at Reeds, Cornwall, Feb. 28, 1875.

GURNEY, JOSEPH JOHN (1788–1847), an English philanthropist, was born at Earlham, near Norwich, Aug. 2, 1788. He was educated at Oxford without becoming a member of the University. In 1818 he became a minister in the Society of Friends, and with his sister, Mrs. Elizabeth Fry, took much interest in behalf of prisoners. He travelled extensively in Ireland, the United States, Canada, the West Indies, and on the continent of Europe, examining the condition of prisons, and prosecuting various benevolent enterprises. He was active in the movement of Clarkson and Wilberforce for the abolition of slavery and the slave-trade. He was also an earnest advocate of total abstinence. He died at Earlham, Jan. 4, 1847. Biographies of him were published by Bernard Barton (1847), by J. B. Braithwaite (1854), and by Hodgson (1856). His writings were numerous and include *Notes on Prison Discipline* (1819); *Religious Peculiarities of the Society of Friends* (1824); *Evidences of Christianity* (1827); *History, Authority, and Use of the Sabbath* (1831); *A Winter in the West Indies* (1840); *Thoughts on Habit and Discipline* (1844). A controversy arose in the United States in reference to his doctrinal views, which resulted in a secession of the Wilberites from the Orthodox Friends in 1843.

GUROWSKI, ADAM, COUNT (1805–1866), a Polish-American author, was born at Rusocice in the Palatinate of Kalisz, Sept. 10, 1805. His father, Count Ladislas Gurowski, had lost most of his estates after the insurrection of 1794. Adam was expelled from school for revolutionary demonstrations, and for taking part in the insurrection of 1830 he was condemned to death and his estates confiscated. In Paris he became noted as a writer and agitator in behalf of Poland. But his work, *La vérité sur la Russie* (1835), proved so acceptable to the Russian government by its advocacy of Panslavism, that he was invited to St. Petersburg by the Czar, and employed in his private chancery. He was afterward in the department of public instruction, but in 1844 he went to Germany, and then for two years lectured on political economy in the University of Berne. After a year in Italy he came to the United States in 1849. He wrote for the *New York Tribune* and became deeply interested in American politics. During the civil war he resided in Washington, and was employed in the department of state. He died at Washington, May 4, 1866. His works published in Europe include *La civilisation et la Russie* (1840); *L'Avenir des Polonais* (1841); *Impressions et Souvenirs* (1846); *La Panslavisme* (1848). After he came to the United States he published *Russia as it is* (1854); *America and Europe* (1857); *Slavery in History* (1860); and *My Diary* (3 vols., 1862–66). The last work consisted of notes on the American civil war.

GUTHRIE, JAMES (1792–1869), an American statesman, was born near Bardstown, Ky., Dec. 5, 1792. His father, Gen. Adam Guthrie, had emigrated from Virginia to Kentucky, where he fought with the Indians, and was a member of the legislature for several years. James, after receiving an academical education, became a trader on the Mississippi. Then studying law, he settled in Louisville in 1830 and acquired an extensive practice. He was a member of the State legislature for fifteen years, and was president of the State Constitutional Convention in 1850. He was called to be secretary of the treasury by Pres. Pierce in 1853, and held this position until 1857. When secession was agitated he was a firm friend of the Union, and helped to save Kentucky from joining the Southern Confederacy. In 1864 he was a delegate to the National Democratic Convention at Chicago. In 1865 he was elected to the U. S. Senate, but was compelled by ill health to resign his seat in February, 1866. He died at Louisville, Ky., March 13, 1869.

GUYOT, ARNOLD HENRY (1807–1884), a Swiss-American geographer, was born near Neuchâtel, Switzerland, Sept. 28, 1807, and graduated at the University of Berlin in 1835. He studied theology as well as the natural and physical sciences. He was from 1839 to 1848 professor of history and physical geography in the Neuchâtel Academy, where Agassiz was associated with him. During this time he carried on extensive observations regarding the Alpine glaciers, and announced to the scientific world the laminated structure of glacial ice, and the motion of glaciers by molecular displacement. He also made important observations on boulder transportation by ice. With Agassiz and Desor he published in 1848 the first volume of the *Système Glaciaire*. In 1848 he removed to the United States, and for six years was employed as a lecturer on physical geography in the public schools and teachers' institutes in Massachusetts. In 1855 he became professor of geology and physical geography in the college at Princeton, N. J. Among his works are *The Earth and Man* (translated from the French by Prof. Felton, 1849); *Meteorological and Physical Tables* (1851–59); a series of school geographies and wall-maps; works on physical geography; and numerous reports and papers on hypsometry, meteorology, and other scientific subjects.

GWIN, WILLIAM MCKENDRY (1805–1885), an American politician, was born in Sumner co., Tenn., Oct. 9, 1805. He was educated at Transylvania University, Ky., studied medicine, and settled at Vicksburg, Miss. He was appointed U. S. marshal for Mississippi in 1833, and was elected to Congress in 1841. He was appointed to supervise the erection of the New Orleans custom-house in 1847. He removed to California in 1848, and in the next year was a member of the convention to frame the constitution of that State. He was elected to the U. S. Senate in 1850 and re-elected in 1856. Having advocated the secession of California in 1861 he was arrested for disloyalty, but was released in 1863. Towards the close of the civil war he was active in promoting a scheme for the settlement of Sonora with Confederates, and was reported to have accepted the title of Duke of Sonora from the Emperor Maximilian. He afterwards returned to the United States and lived in obscurity till his death at New York, Sept. 3, 1885.

GWINNETT, BUTTON (c. 1732–1777), a signer of the American Declaration of Independence, was born in England about 1732. He emigrated to Charleston, S. C., in 1770, and after spending two years in trade, purchased land on St. Catharine's Island, Ga., where he devoted himself to agriculture. He was elected a delegate to Congress in February, 1776, and was in 1777 president of the provincial council of Georgia. He planned a military expedition to East Florida which was unsuccessful. He was killed by Gen. McIntosh in a duel, May 27, 1777.

GYPSUM (hydrated sulphate of lime, $CaSO_4$ $2H_2O$,) is a mineral of considerable industrial value, which occurs abundantly in certain localities in the United States and elsewhere. In this country the most extensive deposits are found in the Palæozoic strata, associated with rock-salt, saliferous marls and clays, and limestones. It is mainly amorphous, but frequently crystallized, the latter form often occurring in broad, transparent folia, said to have been used as glass in ancient Rome. Calcined at a low temperature the water of gypsum is driven off, in which state it constitutes plaster of Paris, with its valuable uses in taking impressions, etc. Gypsum is a product of volcanoes, and exists dissolved in sea-water, it being soluble in 400 to 500 parts of water. The principal beds have been deposited by evaporation of sea-water, hence its association with rock-salt.

See Vol. XI. p. 313 Am. ed. (p. 351 Edin. ed.).

In North America gypsum occurs abundantly in Nova Scotia, and in the States of New York, Ohio, Illinois, Virginia, Tennessee, Michigan, Arkansas, Iowa, Kansas, and in the Gulf States from Alabama to Texas. It is also found in large beds and of great purity in many places in Montana, in the Black Hills of Dakota, and throughout Colorado and New Mexico. On the Pacific coast it occurs in considerable abundance, at many points in California, Nevada, and Arizona. In the Mammoth Cave, Ky., it takes the form of rosettes or of flowers, vines, and shrubbery. The New York beds are extensive, stretching across several of the central counties of the State, and in some places 18 feet thick. The annual product in New York and Michigan is about 100,000 tons each, while large quanti-

H.

HABAKKUK. See PROPHETS.

HACKBERRY, the fruit of *Celtis occidentalis*, or the nettle-tree, a name given from the resemblance of its leaves to those of some species of nettles. It is a handsome forest-tree, indigenous to the United States, where it ranges from the valley of the St. Lawrence to Eastern Dakota, and south through the Atlantic region to Florida. It is found also in the valley of the Devil's River, Texas, while a reticulate-leaved variety ranges from Texas to East Oregon. Its height is from 50 to 90 feet, and exceptionally 120 feet, and its trunk from 2 to 4 feet diameter. It is most common and best developed in the Mississippi River basin. In aspect it resembles the elm, and presents an elegant appearance, with its broad and richly-tufted head. The flowers appear before the leaves, and are small, axillary, with five stamens and a calyx of five divisions. Ovary one-celled, with single ovule. Stigmas two. The fruit is a globular drupe with thin flesh, sweet and wholesome, of a dull purple or yellowish-brown color. It ripens in autumn and hangs on the tree through the winter. The leaves vary greatly in size, shape, and texture, but the extremes are connected by intermediate forms. The wood is heavy, compact, coarse-grained, and rather soft, and is of a clear light yellow color. It is largely used for fencing, and occasionally in the manufacture of cheap furniture. The hackberry is also known locally by the names of "sugarberry" and "beaver wood." (C. M.)

[See Vol. XI. p. 322 Am. ed. (p. 360 Edin. ed.).]

HACKLÄNDER, FRIEDRICH WILHELM VON, BARON (1816–1877), a German novelist, was born at Burtscheid, Nov. 1, 1816. He was brought up to mercantile pursuits, but served for a time in the Prussian artillery. This experience he utilized in sketches of soldier-life which attracted the attention of Baron Von Taubenheim, who took him on a journey to the East. After his return, Hackländer became secretary to the Crown Prince of Würtemberg, whom he attended in journeys in Italy. In 1849 he accompanied Marshal Radetzky in his campaign against Piedmont. He afterwards resided at Stuttgart, with the exception of a visit to Spain in 1854, until the Italian war in 1859, when the Emperor of Austria invited him to his head-quarters. In 1861 the emperor conferred on Hackländer a patent of hereditary nobility. On the death of King Wilhelm in 1864 Hackländer lost his position as director of the royal buildings at Stuttgart, but continued to reside there. He died at a villa near Starnberg, July 5, 1877. His prolific pen produced 70 volumes, including books of travel, comedies, stories, and novels. Among these are *Handel und Wandel* (1850); translated into English by Mary Howitt under the title *Behind the Counter*; *Der neue Don Quixote* (1858); *Tag und Nacht* (1860); *Das Geheimniss der Stadt* (1868); *Der letzte Bombardier* (1870); *Der Sturmvogel* (1871); *Verbotene Frucht* (1876). In 1857, in connection with Zoller, he founded the illustrated journal *Über Land und Meer* (1860), in which he published many short stories. His most successful comedies were *Geheimer Agent* (1850), and *Magnetischen Kuren* (1851). Part of an autobiography was published in 1878 under the title *Der Roman meines Lebens*. Hackländer's popularity was well deserved; his humor was rich and healthy, and his varied experience gave him abundant material to draw upon.

HADDOCK. A valuable food-fish belonging to the cod family, and closely related to the cod-fish of commerce. This species, classified as *Gadus aeglefinus*, is distinguished by a stout form in front of the first anal fin, the body gradually diminishing in size posteriorly. It has a prominent snout, the upper jaw projecting, and has several rows of sharp teeth. All the fin-rays are enveloped by a thick, fleshy membrane. Length, one to two feet. The color is dark gray above the lateral line, which is jet black, while the lower portion of the body is of a beautiful silvery gray. On each side there is a large, oblong, dark blotch.

This species is common on the northern Atlantic coasts of Europe and America. It has long been a favorite food-fish in Europe, and vast quantities of it are annually consumed. The Scotch and Irish fisheries are prolific, though the fishermen need to seek it in deeper waters than formerly. Immense quantities are smoke-cured, and sold under the name of "Finnan haddocks." It exists abundantly on our coast from New York to the Arctic seas, accompanying the cod, and is caught in great numbers from spring to autumn, sometimes so abundantly as to be sold at a very low price. The best haddock are caught on rocky bottoms, though in the cold season it is most abundant on clayey bottoms. It is estimated that in the warm season 12 cwt. of haddock are taken to 1 cwt. of cod. In the winter these numbers are reversed, yet the total haddock catch in Massachusetts Bay is three times that of cod. It forms an excellent table-fish, either boiled or as chowder, and is largely eaten by the poorer classes of Boston. It is sometimes taken of 17 lbs. weight, but averages from 2 to 6 lbs. The fishery is conducted in the same manner as the cod-fishery, and forms an important part of the fishing interests of New England and British America. (See COD and FISHERIES.)

The Norway Haddock (*Sebastes Norvegicus*) is of a different family. It is found on our north-east coast, but not eaten, though it is esteemed in Norway. It is taken by the hook from Newfoundland to Greenland, and considered an excellent table-fish. (C. M.)

HADES. This Greek word is doubtfully derived from ἁ and ἰδεῖν, meaning the "unseen." The aspirate seems to make this derivation impossible. It is used by Homer for the god of the under-world, but in later writers it became the name of the under-world itself. It corresponds with the Hebrew word Sheol (which *may* come from Shaal, "to ask," as either asking for men, or asked about by men), and is used in the New Testament for the unseen world. It is contrasted with heaven in Matt. xi. 23, and thus represented as beneath the earth. This may arise from the fact of bodies being buried beneath the earth. In Luke xvi. 23 Hades is represented as in sight of "Abraham's bosom," though far off, and separated from it by a great chasm. Yet in this passage we may suppose both Abraham's bosom and the place of torment as being alike in Hades. In the Revelation (i. 18; vi. 8; xx. 13, 14) Hades seems to be used only in an evil sense. It would seem that the word originally referred to the unseen world in general, and had no determinative meaning as regards the condition of those therein. That unseen world was generally regarded as beneath the earth, because bodies were buried in the earth. Gradually the word came to be used of the unseen world as a place of punishment and sorrow. In the New Testament, the probabilities are that it always has an evil meaning, as opposed to Paradise (comp. Luke xxiii. 43, 2 Cor. xii. 4, "caught *up* into Paradise," and Rev. ii. 7).

In the Old Testament Sheol does not always, if ever, have this determinate character. So, while the two words correspond, it is hardly safe to say that they are synonymous. The Bible teaches that the righteous at death go to Paradise (Luke xxiii. 43), to be present with the Lord (2 Cor. v. 8). This scarcely seems compatible with their going to Hades, as Hades is used in the New Testament (Matt. xi. 23; xvi. 18), and yet in the Old Testament the righteous are represented as going to Sheol (Ps. vi. 5), where Sheol may mean the "grave," as in our English version. (H. CR.)

HÆCKEL, ERNST HEINRICH, the most prominent of living German naturalists, was born at Potsdam, Feb. 16, 1834. His tendency towards biological science was first shown at the gymnasium of Merseburg, where he displayed a fondness for botany. At Berlin he studied the natural sciences and medicine, and at Würzburg he became the assistant of Virchow, of whom he has since become a declared opponent. In order to investigate the lowest forms of animal life he made journeys to Heligoland and to the Mediterranean in 1854 and 1856. He graduated in medicine, and for about a year practised in Berlin, but his increasing inclination toward comparative anatomy and kindred studies led him to make a scientific journey to Italy and Sicily in 1859. The chief result of this was seen in his illustrated monograph *Die Radiolarien* (1862), which appeared after he had been made extraordinary professor of zoölogy at the University of Jena. In this work he not only arranged and described nearly three times as many species of radiolaria as had previously been known, but showed himself already an earnest advocate of the doctrine of evolution. In 1865 a full professorship of zoölogy was specially made for him in the University of Jena, and he began to form the valuable museum which constitutes one of the most important features of that institution. His lectures there extend over comparative anatomy, histology, palæontology, and other branches which he has brought into the closest connection with general zoölogy. In 1866 he published *Generelle Morphologie der Organismen*, a work in which he sought to apply the Darwinian theory of the origin of species to the whole range of organic morphology. The direction of his investigations had already led him towards the theory of development before the publication of Darwin's work, and he has ever since been one of the most radical German advocates of that theory, from which he at once drew conclusions from which Darwin long held aloof. In the work just named he advanced his interesting theory that the lowest forms of life are neither distinctively animal nor vegetable, but should be classed in an intermediate kingdom, to which he gave the name of *Protista*, but scientists have not accepted this conclusion. In 1867 he delivered a series of lectures on evolution, which were published under the title *Natürliche Schöpfungsgeschichte* (1868). This popular work reached a seventh edition in 1879, and was translated into several languages, an English edition appearing in 1874 as the *History of Creation*. A more immediate application of the doctrine of evolution to the origin of man is found in his *Anthropogenie* (1874), translated into English as *The Origin of Man*. Other series of popular lectures were published under the titles of *Ueber die Entstehung und den Stammbaum des Menschengeschlechts* (1868); *Ueber Arbeitstheilung in Natur und Menschenleben* (1869); and other series have since appeared. In 1870 appeared his *Studien über Moneren und andere Protisten*, and in 1872 his important monograph on the calcareous sponges, *Die Kalkschwämme* (2 vols., with atlas). This was the result of five years' consecutive study of this small group, which he found so strikingly variable that he declared they might all be reduced to one genus and seven species, if their resemblances were closely considered, and that they all seemed traceable to a single ancestral form, the Olynthus. This study led to his celebrated *Gastræa Theorie* (1874), his most valuable contribution to speculative science. In this he traces the whole animal kingdom above the Protozoa to an original sac- or stomach-like form, composed of two cell-layers and with a single aperture, which he calls the *Gastræa*, and points out that at an early embryological stage in the development of all animals a similar or a homologous *Gastrula* form appears. This theory has been very generally accepted by biological scientists. In 1880 he published an elaborate monograph on the *Medusæ*. He has made many scientific journeys besides those mentioned, including a tour of three months in the Canary Islands in 1866, a visit to the coast of Norway in 1869, to the eastern coast of the Adriatic in 1871, to the coral islands of the Red Sea in 1873, to Corsica and Sardinia in 1875, and to Ceylon in 1881. Each of these journeys has afforded abundant material, which he has employed in his lectures and writings. His latest publication of interest is an entertaining personal narrative of his visit to Ceylon, with an account of his scientific observations in that tropical island.

Hæckel is one of the most ardent and thoroughgoing advocates of the development theory, which he pushes to extreme conclusions. He sustains, in common with several other German writers, what he names the Monistic philosophy, in opposition to Dualism; that is, he ascribes "an independent soul-life to every organic cell," and maintains that the soul of man is only the sum of a multitude of special cell activities, dependent on the material phenomena of motion, and that the universe contains only matter in motion. The tendency of his mind is toward bold and hasty speculations, and his scientific standing has been somewhat injured thereby. Even his famous Gastræa theory is now said to have originated in an error, though it has proved to be in accordance with fact. He is very combative in his arguments, and wastes no courtesy on his scientific opponents. Of his controversial works may be named *Free Science and Free Teaching* (1878), published in opposition to the views of Virchow on science in education. As a writer—Hæckel is very clear and perspicuous, and though greatly lacking condensation his popular works appeal strongly to the taste of general readers, and have been very widely read. (C. M.)

HAGEN, HERMANN AUGUST, a German-American entomologist, was born at Königsberg, Prussia, May 30, 1817. He graduated at Königsberg University in 1836, studied medicine, and practised his profession until 1867. By the invitation of Prof. L. Agassiz, he removed to Cambridge, Mass., to take charge of the entomological department of the Agassiz Museum, and was afterwards professor of entomology at Harvard University. He has published numerous papers and monographs, chiefly on entomology, and *Bibliotheca Entomologica* (1862).

HAGERSTOWN, a city of Maryland, county-seat of Washington county, is picturesquely situated on Antietam Creek, in the fertile Cumberland Valley, 85 miles W. N. W. of Baltimore and 22 miles N. W. of Frederick. It is an important railway centre. The railways passing through are the Cumberland Valley and the Western Maryland. Hagerstown is the N. terminus of the Shenandoah Valley Railroad and of a branch of the Baltimore and Ohio system. The principal public buildings are a fine court-house, a jail, and an academy of music. The town has a free library, public water-works, 9 hotels, 2 national and 3 other banks, 4 weekly and 2 daily newspapers, 13 churches, a female seminary, and 6 public schools. The chief articles manufactured are furniture, spokes, wheels, castings, doors, sashes, brooms, fertilizers, farm-tools, and cigars. The streets are handsome and are well lighted with gas. The city debt is $20,000, the property valuation, $3,250,000. The population is chiefly of American birth and in large part of German descent. Hagerstown was settled about 1750, and was incorporated in 1790. Owing in part to its secluded situation in a well-wooded mountain valley Hagerstown early became a local centre of high social refinement. Its population in 1870 was 5779; in 1890, 10,172.

HAGGAI. See PROPHETS.

HÄHNEL, ERNST JULIUS, a German sculptor, was born at Dresden, March 9, 1811. He studied architecture under Thürmer, and in 1830 went to Munich, where he became a sculptor. In 1838 he was recalled to Dresden, to prepare sculptures for the new theatre, among which were statues of Sophocles, Aristophanes, Molière, and Shakespeare, and a bas-relief representing the March of Bacchus. He afterwards prepared a statue of Beethoven, erected at Bonn in 1845; a statue of Charles IV. for the University of Prague (1848); and for the new museum at Dresden six statues—Alexander the Great, Lyseppus, Michel Angelo, Dante, Raphael, and Peter von Cornelius. These works and minor decorations occupied him until 1858, when he prepared statues of the Four Evangelists and the Three Kings for the cathedral tower in Dresden. Hähnel has executed other noteworthy statues for his native city; for Vienna, an equestrian statue of Prince Schwartzenberg; and for Leipsic, a bronze statue of Leibnitz. He has been member of the Academy at Dresden since 1842, and professor since 1848.

HAHN-HAHN, IDA MARIE LUISE SOPHIE FRIEDERIKE GUSTAVE, COUNTESS (1805-1880), a German novelist and religious writer, was born June 22, 1805, at Tressow. Her father (1782-1857), through his passion for the theatre, squandered the greater part of his possessions. In 1826 the countess married her cousin, Count Friedrich Wilhelm Adolf von Hahn-Hahn, but was divorced in 1829. Thereafter she resided in Berlin, but made many journeys. Her first publications were some volumes of poems (1835-38), which attracted little attention, but her romances of society, which followed, had remarkable popularity. Among these were *Aus der Gesellschaft* (1838); *Gräfin Faustine* (1841); *Sigismund Forster* (1843); *Cecil* (1844); *Zwei Frauen* (1845). These and others were collected under the title of the first (21 vols., 1844-51). She also published some books of travel, superficial yet attractive. In 1850 she entered the Roman Catholic Church, and thenceforth devoted herself actively to the propagation of her new faith. Her conversion forms the subject of her book, *Von Babylon nach Jerusalem* (1851). In 1852 she retired to a cloister at Angers, but afterwards resided at Mentz, devoting herself to the reformation of fallen women. Here she died, Jan. 12, 1880. Her later works include: *Maria Regina* (1860); *Peregrina* (1864); *Die Glöcknerstochter* (1871); *Die Geschichte eines armen Fräuleins* (1872). Her biography has been published by Haffner (1880), Keiter (1881), and others.

HAIR-TAIL (*Trichiurus*), a genus of tropical marine fishes, remarkable for their compressed and elongated shape, the body being band-like, with a dorsal fin extending the whole length of the back, and having no tail, the body being extended into a slender and compressed cord at its extremity. It is a native of China and America, and is generally found near land, but occasionally wanders far out to sea, and to the waters of the temperate zone. *T. Lepturus*, the silvery hair-tail or ribbon-fish, grows from 2 to 4 feet long, and is caught along the Atlantic shores of the United States. It has a great number of vertebræ, as many as 160 and more. Six species of *Trichiurus* are known.

HALDEMAN, SAMUEL STEHMAN (1812-1880), an American naturalist and philologist, was born near Columbia, Lancaster co., Pa., Aug. 12, 1812. He studied at Dickinson College; in 1836 was appointed an assistant in the New Jersey geological survey, and in 1837 in the Pennsylvania survey. While thus engaged he discovered the oldest fossil then known, *Scolithus linearis*. He was professor of natural history in the University of Pennsylvania from 1851 to 1855, and afterwards in Delaware College. He was well versed in etymology, conchology, and palæontology, and published many papers on these subjects. He also gave much attention to the philosophy of language, and in 1858, by his essay, *Analytic Orthography*, won in England the Trevelyan prize over eighteen competitors. He was made professor of comparative philology in the University of Pennsylvania in 1870. He published *Pennsylvania Dutch* (1872), *Outlines of Etymology* (1873), and some other text-books. He died at Chickie's, Lancaster co., Pa., Sept. 10, 1880.

HALE, BENJAMIN (1797-1863), an American educator, was born at Newbury, Mass., Nov. 23, 1797. He graduated at Bowdoin College in 1818, was principal of Saco Academy, then studied theology at Andover, and was licensed to preach as a Congregationalist in 1822. After a year's service as tutor in Bowdoin

College he established the Gardiner Lyceum, which he conducted until 1827, when he was appointed professor of chemistry and mineralogy in Dartmouth College, where he founded a geological and mineralogical cabinet. Entering the Protestant Episcopal Church he was from 1836 to 1858 president of Hobart College, Geneva, N. Y. He died at Newburyport, Mass., July 15, 1863. He published *Introduction to Mechanical Principles of Carpentry* (1827), *Scripture Illustrations of the Liturgy* (1835), sermons, and educational pamphlets.

HALE, EDWARD EVERETT, an American clergyman and author, was born at Boston, April 3, 1822. He is the son of Nathan Hale, the journalist, and nephew of Edward Everett. He graduated at Harvard College in 1839, studied theology, and became pastor of the Church of the Unity, Worcester, Mass., in 1846. In 1856 he became pastor of the South Congregational Church, Boston, Mass., which position he still holds. He has always been active as a journalist and has been editor at various times of the *Christian Examiner* and the *Sunday School Gazette*, and in 1870 founded the *Old and New*, a literary monthly, which he conducted until 1875. Many of his stories, sketches, and instruction papers have been collected in book form. Among his books are *The Rosary* (1848); *Margaret Percival in America* (1850); *Sketches of Christian History* (1850); *Kansas and Nebraska* (1854); *Ninety Days' Worth of Europe* (1861); *The Ingham Papers* (1869); *How to do it*; *Workingmen's Homes* (1874); *What Career? Mrs. Merriam's Scholars; Seven Spanish Cities; His Level Best*. With his niece he has published several volumes of travel bearing the common title *A Family Flight*. He has also published some volumes of sermons, *Life in Common; Kingdom of God; June to May*. He is specially noted for his skill in giving to romance the appearance of matter of fact, and has been aptly styled "The American Defoe." Perhaps the most notable instance of this quality is his sketch, *The Man without a Country*.

HALE, JOHN PARKER (1806–1873), an American statesman, was born at Rochester, N. H., March 31, 1806. He graduated at Bowdoin College in 1827, and settled at Dover, N. H., where he was admitted to the bar in 1830. He was elected to the State legislature in 1832, and was appointed by President Jackson U. S. Attorney for New Hampshire in 1834, but was removed by President Tyler in 1841. He belonged to the Democratic party, but after being elected to Congress in 1843 opposed the annexation of Texas, although the legislature of New Hampshire sent its congressional delegation instructions to support the measure. Hale appealed to the people, and, when the State Democratic convention removed his name from the ticket, became an independent candidate, but was defeated. In June, 1845, occurred his memorable controversy with Franklin Pierce, at Concord, N. H., in which Hale vindicated his course. He was elected to the State legislature in 1846, and was made speaker of the house. He was also chosen to the U. S. Senate, where he was almost the only anti-slavery member, and maintained his cause with skill and good humor. The Liberty Party convention at Cleveland in 1847 nominated him for President, but he declined and supported Van Buren and Adams, who were nominated at Buffalo in 1848. Nominated again by the Free Soil party at Pittsburg in 1852, Hale received 156,149 votes, but no electoral votes. In 1853 he removed to New York city, where he practised law, but in 1855 he was again elected to the U. S. Senate from New Hampshire for an unexpired term, and in 1858 for a full term. He supported the administration of Lincoln, taking an active part in all the legislation pertaining to the civil war. At the close of his term in March, 1865, he was appointed minister to Spain, but in 1869 was removed in consequence of a violation of the revenue laws of Spain, the blame of which, however, Hale laid on his secretary of legation. After his return from Europe he had a stroke of paralysis in 1870, and he died at Dover, N. H., Nov. 19, 1873.

HALE, NATHAN (1755–1776), an American patriot, was born at Coventry, Conn., June 6, 1755. He graduated at Yale College in 1773 and became a teacher at East Haddam, and afterward at New London. On receiving news of the conflict at Lexington in April, 1775, he entered the army as lieutenant, and before the close of the year was captain. In September, 1776, while at New York he captured a British sloop laden with provisions, taking her from under the guns of a frigate. After the retreat from Long Island Washington was desirous to obtain full information of the number and plans of the enemy, and Hale volunteered to get this. He crossed to the island and having made full notes of the situation was about to return when he was arrested and taken before Sir William Howe, who ordered him to be hanged as a spy the next morning. His execution took place Sept. 22, 1776, his last words being, "I only regret that I have but one life to lose for my country." His *Life* was published by I. W. Stuart (Hartford, 1856).

HALE, NATHAN (1784–1863), an American journalist, nephew of the preceding, was born at Westhampton, Mass., Aug. 16, 1784. He graduated at Williams College in 1804, taught in Exeter Academy for two years, and removed to Boston, where he was admitted to the bar in 1810. While practising his profession he was also editor of the *Weekly Messenger*, and in March, 1814, he purchased the Boston *Daily Advertiser*. In this influential paper he advocated successively the principles of the Federal, Whig, and Republican parties. He opposed the Missouri Compromise in 1820 and the Nebraska Bill in 1854, and gave the start to the free colonization of Kansas in 1856. He was an advocate of a protective tariff and of internal and local improvements. In 1846 he was chairman of the commission to introduce water into the city of Boston, and for nineteen years he was president of the Boston and Worcester Railroad. He was several times elected to the legislature, and was a member of the State Constitutional Conventions of 1853 and 1857. He was one of the founders of the *North American Review* and of the *Christian Examiner*. He died at Brookline, Mass., Feb. 9, 1863.

HALE, SARAH JOSEPHA BUELL (1790–1879), an American author, was born at Newport, N. H., Oct. 24, 1790. In 1814 she was married to David Hale, a lawyer of local note, who died in 1822, leaving her with five children dependent upon her exertions. After publishing *The Genius of Oblivion, and other Poems* (1823) and *Northwood, a Tale* (1827), she removed to Boston, where she edited the *Ladies' Magazine*. In 1837 this magazine was united with *Godey's Lady's Book*, published in Philadelphia, and Mrs. Hale removed to that city in 1841. She continued to act as literary editor until her death, May, 1879. She published many books, among which are *Sketches of American Character* (1830); *Traits of American Life* (1835); *Ladies' Book of Cookery* (1852); *Woman's*

Record (1855). She edited the *Letters* of Madame de Sevigné and Lady Mary Wortley Montagu (1856).

HALÉVY, JOSEPH, a French orientalist, was born at Adrianople, Turkey, Dec. 15, 1827. Devoting himself especially to the study of Semitic languages he taught Jewish schools in Adrianople and Bucharest. His Hebrew poems made his name widely known and in 1868 he was commissioned by the Alliance Israelite Universelle to examine the condition of the Falashas of Abyssinia. His report, dated July 30, 1868, attracted attention throughout the world. In 1869 he was sent by the French government on an archæological exploration of Yemen in Arabia. Here he deciphered 68 inscriptions. He has published several volumes on Oriental antiquities and epigraphy.

HALÉVY, LEON (1802-1883), a French poet and dramatist, was born at Paris, Jan. 14, 1802. He belonged to a Jewish family, and was brother of the distinguished composer Halévy (for whom see ENCYCLOPÆDIA BRITANNICA). While attending the Charlemagne Lyceum, he won a high reputation as a Greek scholar. He afterwards studied law, but becoming a follower of Saint Simon, he assisted in founding *Le Producteur* and furnished the introduction to his master's *Opinions littéraires, philosophiques et industrielles* (1825). He had already published numerous poems, and he soon after issued imitations of the principal poets of Europe, *Poésies européennes* (1827). He also wrote a *Résumé de l'histoire des Juifs* (1828), and later *Histoire résumée de la Littérature Française* (1838). Meantime he had been lecturing on literature in the Polytechnic School, and in 1837 was employed in the bureau of historic monuments in the department of public instruction, where he remained until 1853. He won prizes from the Academy by his *Fables* (1843), *Fables nouvelles* (1855), and *La Grèce tragique* (3 vols., 1845-61). Besides, he published many novels, tales, and translations from ancient and modern languages. His dramatic works include a wide range: beginning with a comedy, *Le Duel* (1826), they include tragedies, among which were *Le Czar Demetrius* (1829) and *Electra* (1845), many dramas, and lighter pieces. He also translated *Macbeth*. He died at St. Germain-en-Laye, Sept. 3, 1883.

HALÉVY, LUDOVIC, a French dramatist, son of the preceding, was born at Paris, Jan. 1, 1834. He was educated at the Lyceum Louis le Grand, and entered the civil service, being attached from 1852 to 1858 to the ministry of state, then until 1861 chief of a bureau in the ministry of Algeria. Afterwards he was employed in the *corps législatif*, but when his success as a dramatist was established he retired from public service. He furnished the librettos for Offenbach's music from *Orphée aux enfers* (1861) to *La Boulangère a des écus* (1875). Among these were *La Barbe bleue* (1866); *La belle Hélène* (1867); *La Périchole* (1868); *Frou frou* (1869). They all breathe the seductive, intoxicating, lustful air of the Second Empire. Halévy has also gathered in a volume some equivocal sketches under the title *Monsieur et Madame Cardinal* (1872), to which he has since added *Les petites Cardinal* (1880). His personal recollections of the siege of Paris were published under the title *L' Invasion* (1872). His latest productions are the romances *L' Abbé Constantin* (1882), and *Criquette* (1883). The former indicates a more healthy tone of morals than his usual productions, and contains sketches of American character remarkable for their truthfulness.

HALL, DOMINICK AUGUSTINE (1765-1820), an American jurist, was born in South Carolina in 1765. He practised law in Charleston until 1809, when he was appointed district judge of Orleans Territory. When this Territory became the State of Louisiana, in 1812, Judge Hall was appointed U. S. Judge of the State, and held this office till his death at New Orleans, Dec. 19, 1820. In 1815, while the city of New Orleans was under martial law by the proclamation of Gen. Jackson, Louis Loniallier was arrested on a charge of exciting mutiny among the troops by publishing on Feb. 10 that a treaty of peace had been signed. Judge Hall granted a writ of habeas corpus, but Jackson, instead of obeying the writ, arrested the judge. Four days later the report was proved correct and the judge, being released, summoned Gen. Jackson before him for contempt of court, and imposed a fine of $1000, which Jackson paid. In 1844 Congress refunded the fine with interest.

HALL, JAMES, an American geologist, was born at Hingham, Mass., Sept. 12, 1811. He studied natural science at the Rensselaer Polytechnic Institute at Troy, N. Y., and in 1836 was appointed one of the geologists in the survey of New York. He published annual reports from 1838 to 1841, and a final report in 1843, which were all marked by thoroughness of research. He was then made palæontologist to the State, and published *Palæontology of New York* (5 vols., 1847, 1852, 1859, 1867, 1874). His investigations have extended far beyond the limits of the State, even to the Rocky Mountains. In 1855 he was appointed also geologist to the State of Iowa, and in connection with Whitney and Worthen published a *Report on the Geology of Iowa*, including also its palæontology (2 vols., 1858-60). He was invited to take charge of the palæontology in the Geological Survey of Canada, but his investigations were limited to the study of the graptolites, on which he published a monograph (1865). In 1857 he was made State surveyor of Wisconsin, and prepared a *Report*. He has also contributed to the reports of several western surveys ordered by the national government. His researches have tended to elucidate the order of formation of the various strata of the American continent.

HALL, JOHN, an American clergyman, was born in the County Armagh, Ireland, July 31, 1829. He graduated at Belfast College in 1846, was licensed to preach in 1849, and was employed as a Presbyterian missionary in the west of Ireland. In 1852 he became pastor of the First Presbyterian Church, Armagh, and in 1858 accepted a call to the church of St. Mary's Abbey, in Dublin. He was appointed commissioner of education for Ireland. In 1867 he was delegate from the Presbyterian Church of Ireland to the Presbyterian Churches of the United States, and soon after his return to Ireland was called to the Fifth Avenue Presbyterian Church, New York. He was installed over this congregation Nov. 3, 1867, and in 1875 a splendid church-edifice was erected at Fifth Avenue and Fifty-fifth Street. He is an earnest and eloquent preacher, a frequent contributor to the religious press, and a diligent promoter of all forms of religious and benevolent work. He has published *Family Prayers for Four Weeks* (1868); *Papers for Home Reading* (1871); *Questions of the Day* (1873); *God's Word through Preaching* (1875).

HALL, LYMAN (1725-1790), a signer of the Declaration of Independence, was born in Connecticut in

1724. He graduated at Yale College in 1747, studied medicine, and settled at Sunbury, Ga., in 1752. He was a member of the colonial convention in 1774–75, and was elected a member of the Continental Congress in 1775. He remained in attendance until 1780, when he was called home by the British invasion. In 1783 he was elected governor of Georgia, and served one term. He died in Burke co., Ga., Oct. 19, 1790.

HALL, NEWMAN, an English Congregational preacher, was born at Maidstone, May 22, 1816. He is the son of John Vine Hall (1774–1860), noted as an advocate of total abstinence, and as the author of the tract *The Sinner's Friend*. Newman was educated at Highbury College, and received the degree of A. B. from the University of London. He also won a law scholarship, and obtained the degree of LL. B. in 1835. He afterwards studied theology, and in 1842 was ordained as a Congregational pastor in Hull. In 1854 he was called to become pastor of Surrey Chapel, Black Friar's Road, London. Although a non-conformist, he uses the liturgy of the Church of England, with slight modifications. During the American civil war he was a warm friend of the Union, and in 1865 he visited the United States in an endeavor to promote a friendly feeling between the American and English peoples. In 1873 he made a second visit and lectured in the principal cities, and again in 1884 he made a brief visit. He has published *The Christian Philosopher* (1849); *Land of the Forum and the Vatican* (1853); *Lectures in America* (1868); *History of Surrey Chapel* (1868); *From Liverpool to St. Louis* (1869); *Pilgrim Songs* (1871). His tract *Come to Jesus* has been widely circulated, and has been translated into 30 languages.

HALL, SAMUEL CARTER, an English author, was born at Waterford, Ireland, May 9, 1800, but was soon taken to the family residence at Topsham, Devon. He studied for the bar, and in 1824 became a barrister of the Inner Temple. In 1823 he undertook, with great success, the profession of a parliamentary reporter for the press. In 1824 he married Anna Maria Fielding, who became his literary partner and associate. In 1830 he became editor of the *New Monthly Magazine*, previously conducted by the poet Thomas Campbell. In 1839 he founded the *Art Union*, afterwards called the *Art Journal*, which he edited for 42 years. Among Mr. Hall's books are *The Royal Gallery of Art*; *The Vernon Gallery*; *The Book of Beauty*; *Gems of European Art*; *The Baronial Halls of England*; *Stately Homes of England* (2 vols., quarto, in part prepared by Llewellyn Jewitt); poems entitled *The Trial of Sir Jasper* and *An Old Story* (1873); and other works. Conjointly with his wife, he produced *Ireland, its Scenes and Characters* (3 vols., 1841–43); *The Book of the Thames* (1859); *A Book of Memories of Great Men and Women* (1871); *Rhymes in Council*, and other writings. He died March 16, 1889.

His wife, ANNA MARIA FIELDING (1800–1881), was born in Dublin, Jan. 6, 1800. Her principal writings are *Sketches of Irish Character* (1829); *Chronicles of the Schoolroom* (1830); *Tales of a Woman's Trials* (1834); *The Outlaw* (1835); *Lights and Shadows of Irish Life* (1838); *Tales of the Irish Peasantry* (1840); *The White-Boy* (1845); *Can Wrong be Right? Pilgrimages to English Shrines* (1850); and many other books. The writings, jointly and separately produced by Mr. and Mrs. Hall, are said to fill over 340 volumes. Mrs. Hall has written much more than her husband. Among her works are several successful plays. She died at East Moulsey, Surrey, Jan. 30, 1881.

HALLIWELL-PHILLIPPS, JAMES ORCHARD, an English critic and antiquarian, was born at Chelsea, June 21, 1820. He was educated at Brighton and Cambridge, and in 1841 took a leading part in organizing the Shakespeare Society. He has published many pamphlets and papers on Shakespearian subjects and early English literature, besides other and larger works, including *The Early History of Free-Masonry* (1843); *The Letters of the Kings of England* (1846); *A Dictionary of Archaic and Provincial Words* (2 vols., 1847); *The Yorkshire Anthology* (1851); *Norfolk Anthology* (1852); *The Evidences of Christianity* (1860); *Notes of Family Excursions in North Wales* (1860); *Rambles in Western Cornwall* (1861); and *An Historical Account of New Place, Stratford* (1804). His folio edition of Shakespeare, in 16 vols., was completed in 1865. In 1873 he assumed his wife's family name of Phillipps. His best work is *Outlines of the Life of Shakspeare* (1874). He died Jan. 3, 1889.

HAMERTON, PHILIP GILBERT, an English writer, born at Laneside, near Shaw, in Lancashire, Sept. 10, 1834, of an old Yorkshire family. His parents died when he was a child, and his education was cared for by an aunt. He gave great attention to landscape-painting, and after 1855 lived much in Paris and in the Scottish highlands. He was for a time art critic for the *Saturday Review*. In 1859 he married a French lady, and took up his residence in France, chiefly at Autun. His paintings have much originality, but though not without technical merits they have failed of popularity. As an etcher he has achieved a reputation, and some important details of the late improvements in the etching process were invented by him. But he is best known by his writings, which show originality of thought on a variety of subjects, and are rendered attractive by a clear and piquant style. Among them are *Isles of Loch Awe*, Poems (1855); *Painter's Camp in the Highlands* (1862); *Thoughts About Art* (1862); *Etching and Etchers* (1866); *Contemporary French Painters* (1867); *The Etchers' Hand-Book* (1868); *Painting in France* (1868); *Wenderholme, a Story* (1869); *The Unknown River* (1870); *The Intellectual Life* (1873); *Chapters on Animals* (1873); *The Sylvan Year* (1876); *The Life of Turner* (1878); *Modern Frenchmen* (1878); *Paris* (1885); *Landscape* (1885).

HAMILTON, a city of Ohio, county-seat of Butler county, is on both sides of the Miami River and canal, 25 miles by rail N. of Cincinnati, and 25 miles S. W. of Dayton. It is on the Cincinnati, Hamilton, and Dayton Railroad, at the junction of lines to Indianapolis and to Chicago, all operated by the same company. It has numerous churches, a public library, an orphanage, a court-house, a high-school, 2 national banks. The manufacturing interests are extensive. The leading articles produced are paper, castings, machinery, farming-implements, woollen goods, and flour. The public-school system is exceptionally good. Manufactures are facilitated by a fine and well-utilized water-power, derived from the Miami by means of a canal. The town was incorporated in 1853. In 1870 the population was 11,081; in 1890, 17,519.

HAMILTON COLLEGE is located in Clinton, Oneida co., N. Y., 9 miles south of Utica, on the Utica and Binghamton Railroad. It was founded in 1793 as an academy, by Rev. Samuel Kirkland, a missionary to the Oneida Indians, and was chartered as a college in 1812, being thus the third college in the

State. Its first president, Dr. Azel Backus, gave diplomas to 33 graduates in 3 classes (1812-16); the second president, Dr. Henry Davis, gave diplomas to 329 graduates in 17 classes (1817-33); the third president, Dr. Sereno F. Dwight, gave diplomas to 39 graduates in 2 classes (1833-35); the fourth president, Dr. Joseph Penney, gave diplomas to 53 graduates in 3 classes (1835-39); Dr. Simeon North, the fifth president, gave diplomas to 622 graduates in 19 classes; Dr. Samuel W. Fisher, the sixth president, gave diplomas to 356 graduates in 9 classes (1858-66); the seventh president, Dr. Samuel G. Brown, gave diplomas to 775 graduates in 15 classes. The administration of Dr. Henry Darling, the eighth president, began in 1881, and he has given diplomas to 171 graduates in 4 classes. Presidents Backus, Davis, Dwight, North, and Fisher were graduates of Yale College. Pres. Penney was a graduate of Dublin University; Pres. Brown, of Dartmouth College, and Pres. Darling, of Amherst College. Hamilton College has educated 685 clergymen, 13 college presidents, 32 foreign missionaries, 5 moderators of the Presbyterian General Assembly, 5 State governors, 27 members of Congress, 25 State senators, 27 Supreme Court judges, 464 lawyers, 76 editors, 72 physicians. The Maynard-Knox Law School, now under the charge of Prof. Francis M. Burdick, has sent out 253 graduates. Its first professor was Hon. Theodore W. Dwight, now warden of the Columbia College Law School. Its excellent law library was bequeathed to the college by William C. Noyes, a distinguished lawyer, who died in 1863. The college has also the valuable working library that was used by Dr. Edward Robinson in preparing his *New Testament Lexicon* and *Biblical Geography*. Dr. C. H. F. Peters, director of the Litchfield Observatory, has discovered 43 asteroids, and made 100,000 zone star observations, which he has published in 20 *Celestial Charts*, and distributed to other observatories and learned societies. Under the auspices of the regents of the State University, Dr. Peters has determined the longitude of Buffalo, Syracuse, Elmira, Ogdensburg; the western boundary of the State of New York, and the longitude of the Detroit Observatory at Ann Arbor, Mich. Hamilton College has 13 professorships, most of which are endowed. Prof. Edward North has occupied the chair of Greek since 1843; Prof. A. G. Hopkins, the chair of Latin since 1869; Prof. A. H. Chester, the chair of chemistry since 1870; Prof. A. P. Kelsey, the chair of natural history since 1878; Prof. Oren Root, the chair of mathematics since 1880; Prof. H. C. G. Brandt, the chair of German and French since 1882; Prof. E. J. Hamilton, the chair of metaphysics since 1883. Rev. Arthur S. Hoyt entered upon his duties as professor of rhetoric and oratory in January, 1886.

Fourteen prize endowments give special encouragement to voluntary work in all departments of study. All candidates for the bachelor's degree have the same required studies until the beginning of the third sophomore term, thenceforward mathematics and modern languages are elective. Other electives are open to juniors and seniors. Special students are received who are not candidates for a degree. Graduates of Hamilton College are in good demand as teachers, and about half of each graduating class make engagements for teaching before leaving college, or soon after. Students of Hamilton College become strongly attached to its rural hillside location, with its far-reaching outlook over the Oriskany Valley. Its campus of fourteen acres is embellished with a great variety of shapely trees, many of them planted by students as class memorials. The pinetum, planted by the late Dr. A. D. Gridley, contains a rich collection of hardy evergreens. The care of the college cemetery is provided for by a permanent fund given by the late S. A. Munson, of Utica. The Memorial Hall is an attractive place for visitors; the history of the college is illustrated by the portraits here seen of many of its benefactors and former officers. Six of these portraits are by Daniel Huntington, a graduate of the college; others are by such artists as Charles L. Elliot, G. A. P. Healy, F. B. Carpenter, E. F. Andrews, and M. E. D. Brown. The portrait bust of the late Edwin C. Litchfield was executed by Hiram Powers near the close of his life.

A college is known to the public mainly through its graduates, and a long list might be given of graduates from Hamilton who have gained distinction in the public service and in various branches of intellectual labor. Much would be lost to American history and American literature with the losing of what we owe to such men as Dr. Edward Robinson, Hon. Gerrit Smith, Rev. Albert Barnes, Dr. Daniel D. Whedon, Dr. Asahel C. Kendrick, of Rochester University; Daniel Huntington, president of the National Academy of Design; Hon. Theodore W. Dwight, of the Columbia College Law School; Dr. Henry Kendall, secretary of the Presbyterian Board of Home Missions; Dr. A. J. Upson and Dr. W. J. Beecher, of Auburn Theological Seminary; Dr. James Eells, of Lane Seminary; Gen. Joseph R. Hawley, of the U. S. Senate; Dr. F. F. Ellinwood, secretary of the Presbyterian Board of Foreign Missions; Pres. D. H. Cochran, of the Brooklyn Polytechnic Institute, Charles Dudley Warner, Dr. Herrick Johnson, and Dr. Arthur T. Pierson.   (E. N.)

HAMILTON, FRANK HASTINGS, an American surgeon, was born at Wilmington, Vt., Sept. 10, 1813. He graduated at the University of Pennsylvania in 1833, and settled at Auburn, N. Y., but in 1844 he removed to Buffalo, as affording a better field for his surgical skill. In 1862 he settled in New York, and in 1863 he was made medical inspector of the U. S. army. He was professor of surgery at Bellevue Medical College until 1875, when he resigned, though he retained his connection with the hospital. He has been noted for his invention and improvement of surgical instruments, among which are a bone-drill and various applications of gutta-percha. He has given special attention to plastic surgery and has frequently performed rhinoplasty, taking the skin from the forehead and from the palm of the hand. His publications include *Military Surgery* (2d ed.); *Fractures and Dislocations* (7th ed.); *General Treatise on Surgery* (2d ed.).

HAMILTON, JAMES (1786-1857), an American statesman, was born at Charleston, S. C., May 8, 1786. He was the son of Major James Hamilton, who served on Washington's staff. Soon after he was admitted to the bar he was a major in the war of 1812, and later was elected mayor of Charleston for several years. In 1822 he detected the plot among the negroes organized by Denmark Vesey. In that year he was elected to Congress, where he advocated free-trade and State rights. Pres. Jackson offered to make him secretary of war and afterwards minister to Mexico, but he declined both positions. He was elected governor of South Carolina in 1830, and urged the passage of the nullification act. Gov. Hayne, his successor, appointed him major-general of the State militia.

Hamilton was afterwards prominent in the affairs of the republic of Texas. In 1841 he was sent to England and France, to procure the recognition of her independence. He also promoted her annexation to the United States in 1845. He was elected to the U. S. Senate from Texas in 1857, but was drowned by the collision of two steamers off the coast of Texas on Oct. 18, 1857.

HAMILTON, JAMES (1814–1867), a British clergyman, was born at Lonend, Paisley, Scotland, Nov. 27, 1814. After being ordained pastor of a church at Abernyte, Scotland, he was removed to Edinburgh, and in 1841 he was called to the National Scotch Church, Regent's Square, London, originally built to accommodate those who flocked to hear the famous Edward Irving. Hamilton also was a master of pulpit oratory, but his aim was to persuade rather than to thrill and denounce. Successful in ministering to a large congregation, he produced no sensation like his predecessor. Dr. Hamilton was a popular religious writer, his books passing through many editions. The two most widely circulated were *Life in Earnest* (1844) and *The Mount of Olives* (1848). He also wrote *The Royal Preacher* (1851), a commentary on Ecclesiastes; *The Light upon the Path; The Prodigal Son;* and *The Church in the House.* His works were collected in 6 volumes in 1873, and a selection in 4 volumes was published at New York, 1875. His *Life* was published by Rev. W. Arnot.

HAMILTON, JAMES (1819–1878), an American artist, was born in Ireland in 1819, but removed to America at an early age and settled at Philadelphia. He was for a time engaged in commercial pursuits, but afterwards studied art. In 1854 he went to England, and on his return furnished the illustrations for Dr. Kane's *Arctic Explorations*, and other works. His oil-paintings are chiefly marine views, in which he displayed great vigor. Among them may be mentioned Capture of the Serapis, Wrecked Hopes, Morning off Atlantic City. He died at Philadelphia, 1878.

HAMILTON, JOHN CHURCH (1792–1882), an American historian, was born at Philadelphia in 1792, being the son of the famous Alexander Hamilton. (See ENCYCLOPÆDIA BRITANNICA.) He graduated at Columbia College, and was admitted to the bar. He was an aide on the staff of Gen. Harrison in the war of 1812. He devoted his life chiefly to the vindication of his father's reputation as a statesman. For this purpose he published *Memoirs of Alexander Hamilton* (2 vols., 1834–40); *History of the Republic*, as traced in the writings of Alexander Hamilton (2 vols., 1850–58), and edited his father's *Works* (7 vols., 1851). He died July 25, 1882.

HAMILTON, SCHUYLER, an American general, son of the preceding, was born at New York, July 25, 1822. He graduated at West Point in 1841, and served with distinction in the Mexican war, being twice wounded. After the war he served on the staff of Gen. Scott until 1855, when he resigned and took up his residence at Branford, Conn. In 1861 he enlisted as a private in the Seventh New York regiment, but soon was made an officer, and rose to be major-general of volunteers in 1862, serving in the West. He resigned from the service in 1863. He published a *History of the National Flag* (1853).

HAMLIN, HANNIBAL, an American statesman, was born at Paris, Maine, Aug. 27, 1809. He was admitted to the bar in 1833, and in 1836 was elected to the legislature, of which he was speaker from 1837 to 1840. In 1842 he was elected to Congress as a Democrat, and served two terms. In 1848 he was elected to the U. S. Senate for an unexpired term, and in 1851 for a full term. When the struggle over the extension of slavery called the Republican party into being, Hamlin joined its fortunes, and in 1856 was its candidate for governor of Maine. Being re-elected U. S. Senator in the same year he resigned the governorship. In 1860 he was elected Vice-President of the United States on the ticket with Abraham Lincoln. In 1865 he was appointed collector of the port of Boston, but soon resigned. He was again elected to the Senate and served from 1869 to 1875.

HAMLINE, LEONIDAS LENT (1797–1865), an American bishop, was born at Burlington, Conn., May 10, 1797. He was educated for the ministry, but studied law, and practised at Zanesville, Ohio. In 1828 he joined the Methodist Episcopal Church, and in 1829 was licensed to preach. In 1832 he was admitted to the Ohio Conference, and in 1834 was stationed at Cincinnati. In 1836 he was made assistant editor of the *Western Christian Advocate*, and in 1841 editor of the *Ladies' Repository*, then established. In 1844 he was a delegate to the General Conference, and drew up the plan of separation, which was required by the division of the church on the subject of slavery. At the same conference he was chosen a bishop, and he continued to discharge this office until 1852, when he resigned on account of ill-health. In 1857 he removed to Mount Pleasant, Iowa, where he died, Feb. 22, 1865. His *Works* were published in 1869.

HAMMOND, JAMES HAMILTON (1807–1864), an American statesman, was born at Newberry, S. C., Nov. 15, 1807. His father, Elisha Hammond (1780–1829), born in Rochester, Mass., graduated at Dartmouth College, became professor of languages in South Carolina College, and afterwards president of that college. James graduated there in 1825, was admitted to the bar, and edited the *Southern Times* at Columbia. He was a strenuous supporter of State rights, advocated nullification, and in 1833 organized the military force which South Carolina raised to resist the national government. He was a member of Congress, 1835–37, and governor of South Carolina, 1842–44. In reply to British attacks on slavery, he wrote letters in its defence, which were collected under the title *The Pro-Slavery Argument* (1853). In 1857 he was elected to the U. S. Senate, where, in a speech delivered March, 1858, he applied to the laboring classes the term "mud-sills," and declared, "Cotton is king, and no power on earth dares make war on it." In September, 1858, in a public speech at Columbia, he opposed the reopening of the slave-trade, which was then agitated. On the secession of South Carolina, in 1860, he withdrew from the Senate, but took no public part in the civil war. In 1861 he was made president of South Carolina College, but the institution was soon suspended. He died at Beach Island, S. C., Nov. 13, 1864.

HAMMOND, SAMUEL (1757–1842), an American soldier and statesman, was born in Richmond co., Va., Sept. 21, 1757. In 1775 he fought at Kenawha and Long Bridge. In 1779 he raised a company of soldiers and joined in the Southern campaign under Gen. Lincoln. He fought at Stono Ferry, and was assistant-quartermaster at the siege of Savannah. In 1781 he was made a colonel of cavalry, and he served under Gen. Greene till the end of the war. He then settled in Georgia, where he was made surveyor-general. In

1793 he led a volunteer corps against the Creek Indians. He was member of Congress from 1803 to 1805, when he was appointed by Pres. Jefferson civil and military commander of Upper Louisiana. In 1824 he removed to South Carolina, when he was appointed surveyor-general in 1827, and secretary of state in 1831. He died near Augusta, Ga., Sept. 11, 1842.

HAMMOND, WILLIAM ALEXANDER, an American physician, was born at Annapolis, Md., Aug. 28, 1828. He graduated in the medical department of New York University in 1848, and entered the U. S. army as assistant surgeon in 1849. In October, 1860, he became professor of anatomy and physiology in the University of Maryland. He was reappointed assistant surgeon in the army, May 28, 1861, and when the medical department was reorganized in April, 1862, he was made surgeon-general. He displayed executive abilities of a high order, but often came in conflict with the secretary of war, and finally was dismissed from the service by order of court-martial in August, 1864. By action of Congress and the President in 1879, he was reinstated and placed on the retired list. He had in the meantime been professor in Bellevue Hospital and was physician to other institutions. He has published many treatises, among which are *Military Hygiene* (1863); *Physiological Memoirs* (1863); *Venereal Diseases* (1864); *Insanity in its Medico-Legal Relations* (1866); *Sleep and its Derangements* (1869); *Physics and Physiology of Spiritualism* (1870); *Diseases of the Nervous System* (1871; new ed., 1881); *Insanity in its Relations to Crime* (1873); *Insanity in its Medical Relations* (1883). He has also published three novels, *Lal* (1882), *Dr. Grattan* (1883), and *Mr. Oldmixon* (1885).

HAMPTON, WADE (1755–1835), an American general, was born in South Carolina in 1755. In the Revolutionary war he served under Sumter and Marion. He was a member of Congress, 1795–97; and again 1803–05. He was appointed colonel in the U. S. army, and in 1809 brigadier-general. He was stationed at New Orleans, but being frequently involved in quarrels with his subordinates he was superseded by Wilkinson in 1812. As major-general in 1813 he was placed in command of an army on the Canada frontier, but his advance was baffled by an inferior force. He also refused to co-operate with Wilkinson in an attempt on Montreal, and in April, 1814, resigned his commission. He had acquired a large fortune by speculation in lands and was said to own more than 3000 slaves. He died at Columbia, S. C., Feb. 4, 1835.

HAMPTON, WADE, an American general and statesman, grandson of the preceding, was born at Columbia, S. C., March 28, 1818. He graduated at South Carolina College in 1838, studied law, and served in both branches of the State legislature, being a senator when the State seceded. He commanded the Hampton Legion of cavalry at the first battle of Bull Run, where he was wounded. Being made brigadier-general he served in the Peninsular campaign, and was wounded at Seven Pines, May 31, 1862. He commanded a cavalry force in the invasion of Maryland and at Antietam. He was also engaged in the invasion of Pennsylvania in 1863, and was severely wounded at Gettysburg, losing a leg. He was made lieutenant-general in 1864, and commanded the cavalry of Lee's army until December, when he was sent to South Carolina. In February, 1865, he commanded the rear-guard of the Confederate army at Columbia, where large quantities of cotton had been stored. When his forces evacuated the city on the approach of Gen. Sherman's army, the cotton took fire and a large part of the city was consumed. At a later period a sharp controversy arose between Hampton and Sherman as to the responsibility for the conflagration, but the fire appears to have been accidental in its origin. Hampton was elected governor of the State in 1876 and again in 1878. He was elected to the U. S. Senate in 1878, and re-elected in 1884, but defeated in 1891.

HANCOCK, WINFIELD SCOTT (1824–1886), an American general, was born near Norristown, Pa., Feb. 14, 1824. He graduated at West Point in 1844 and entering the Sixth infantry served on the frontier until 1846. He was then engaged in the Mexican war and was brevetted first-lieutenant for gallantry at Contreras and Churubusco. After the war he returned to frontier duty until November, 1855, when he was appointed captain in the quartermaster's department and ordered to Florida during a campaign against the Seminoles. In 1859 he served as quartermaster of the southern district of California, and used his influence to oppose secession. In 1861 he was relieved at his own request and sought active duty in the field. He was sent first to Kentucky, and being made a brigadier-general of volunteers, Sept. 23, 1861, organized a brigade at Lewinsville, Va. In McClellan's Peninsular campaign Hancock was with Gen. W. B. Franklin and distinguished himself by a bayonet charge at Williamsburg, May 5, 1862, which won from McClellan the compliment which became proverbial, "Hancock was superb." In the battles around Richmond he rendered valuable service, especially at Frazier's Farm, June 30, 1862. He was active in the Maryland campaign, and at Antietam on the death of Gen. Richardson succeeded to the command of his division. He was promoted major-general of volunteers, Nov. 29, 1862, and at Fredericksburg he took part in the assault on Marye's Heights. Again at Chancellorsville, May 4, 1863, Hancock maintained his well-earned reputation, and soon after was placed in command of the Second corps. At Gettysburg, July 1, 1863, after the death of Gen. Reynolds, he succeeded to the command at the front, and stayed the retreat which had begun. Seizing Culp's Hill, as an advantageous position, he induced Gen. Meade to make the fight there. As commander of the left centre of the Union forces, Hancock on July 3 sustained and repulsed the last determined assault of Lee's army. Having been severely wounded he was debarred from further service in the field for several months, but was engaged in stimulating enlistments in the Northern cities. In 1864 he returned to his command and was conspicuous in the advance under Gen. Grant. At the battle of the Wilderness, May 5–7, Hancock had under his command about 50,000 men; at Spottsylvania, May 12, he captured 4000 prisoners; at the bloody battle of Cold Harbor, June 3, his corps lost over 3000 men. His service was then interrupted by the breaking out of his wound, but he was afterwards engaged in the siege of Petersburg, and in the following winter he organized a veteran corps at Washington. In February, 1865, he was appointed to the command of the Middle Military division, and while he held this position the civil war was brought to a close. In July, 1866, he resigned his commission in the volunteer service, and was made major-general in the regular army. Being transferred to the department of the Missouri he conducted expeditions against the Cheyennes and Sioux. In September 1867 he was ordered to the department of the Gulf. His declaration in "Order No. 40," on taking this command, that the military force was to be used only in subordination to the civil authority, attracted attention throughout the Union, and caused him afterwards to be made the Democratic candidate for President. In March, 1868, he was transferred to the military division of the Atlantic, and a year later to the department of Dakota. After three years' service on the plains he was, on the death of Gen. Meade, recalled to the command of the division of the Atlantic, which he held till his death, which occurred at Governor's Island, New York harbor, Feb. 9, 1886. In the Democratic National Convention, in July, 1868, and again in 1876, he was a prominent but unsuccessful candidate for the Presidential nomination. He was however placed in nomination by the convention which met at Cincinnati in July, 1880, and in the following November received 4,442,035 votes, while Gen. J. A. Garfield received 4,449,053. This result gave Gen. Hancock 155 electoral votes from 19 States, while Gen. Garfield received 214 from 20 States.

Throughout his career Gen. Hancock well deserved the title "superb," being a brave, fearless soldier, ever loyal to his superiors, and entirely free from jealousy. Earnestly patriotic, he gave himself to the duty of defending his government and flag when assailed. Though the choice of many of his fellow-citizens for the Presidency, his ability as a statesman was never fairly tested, but his military record is splendid and untarnished.

HANNIBAL, a city of Missouri, in Marion county, is on the Mississippi River, 111 miles by rail or 150 by water N. N. W. of St. Louis. A grand railway bridge of iron crosses the river to East Hannibal, Ill., where the main line of the Wabash, St. Louis, and Pacific is met by a branch of the Chicago, Burlington, and Quincy. Hannibal is the centre of an important network of railways. Of these the Chicago, Burlington, and Quincy, the Missouri Pacific, the St. Louis, Hannibal, and Keokuk, and the Wabash, St. Louis, and Pacific occupy a passenger-station in common, near which is that of the Hannibal and St. Joseph and the St. Louis, Keokuk, and North-western Railroads. Its extensive connections by rail and river render Hannibal a place of great business activity. It is well supplied with schools (public and private), churches, banks, and newspapers, and has a city-hall and other good public buildings. It carries on a large trade in lumber, flour, meats, tobacco, cattle, and grain, and has important car-works, machine-shops, flour-mills, tobacco-factories, lime-kilns, and other industrial establishments. There are coal-mines in the near vicinity. The bluffs and slopes near the city have many handsome residences. Hannibal College (Methodist Episcopal Church South) was founded in 1868. The population in 1870, 10,125; in 1880, 11,074; in 1890, 12,816.

HARBAUGH, HENRY (1817–1867), an American clergyman, was born near Waynesburg, Pa., Oct. 28, 1817. He worked on a farm until 19 years of age, when he became a carpenter. In 1840 he entered Marshall College, Mercersburg, Pa., and after spending three years there was ordained pastor of a Reformed church at Lewisburg. In 1850 he accepted a call to Lancaster and in 1860 to Lebanon. In 1863 he was made professor of theology in the seminary at Mercersburg, and held this position till his death, Dec. 28, 1867. He was a popular writer on religious topics. He established *The Guardian*, a religious monthly, and edited it for sixteen years. He also edited other denominational periodicals, and during the last year of his life the *Mercersburg Review*. He published *Heaven or the Sainted Dead* (1848); *Heavenly Recognition* (1851); *Heavenly Home* (1853); *Birds of the Bible* (1854); *Life of Michael Schlatter* (1857); *Fathers of the Reformed Church* (1858); *Christological Theology* (1864). He also published some volumes of poems and hymns, and wrote poems in the Pennsylvania German dialect, which were gathered under the title *Harbaugh's Harfe* (1870).

HARBORS AND DOCKS. This article is limited to the harbors of the United States, and for convenience the leading characteristics of these harbors will be considered under the following divisions: (See Vol. XI. p. 406 Am. ed. (p. 455 Edin. ed.).

I. The Atlantic Seaboard. II. The Gulf Coast. III. The Pacific Coast.

I. *Atlantic Seaboard.*—Calais, Me., is the centre of a large lumber trade; population, 7088. There is a bar or ledge at Marks Point, 5 miles from the town. Mean depth over bar at low water is 8 feet. No anchorage in harbor, vessels being obliged to make fast to the wharf. Eastport, Me., dealing in fish and lumber, has a harbor which is not obstructed by ice during the winter. The main entrance to the bay is only 5 miles from the city, which can be approached to within any distance. The other entrance, Lubeck Straits, is crooked and dangerous. The roads are not tenable in a gale from the N. E. In such cases and in winter Brood's Cove is used. Rockland has an open harbor with a depth of 5 fathoms to within half a mile of the wharf, near the centre of the city, and about 3 fathoms to the wharves. Often closed by ice in winter. The best anchorage for protection is under the lee of the breakwater near Jamesson Point.

Frenchman's Bay, 14 miles long and 6 miles wide, is deep and easily accessible. Winter Harbor within its limits is one of the best on the coast. Penobscot Bay extends from Isle au Haut on the east for 20 miles to White Head on the west. From the entrance to the mouth of the Penobscot River is 28 miles. Fort Knox, at the narrows of the Penobscot, defends the harbor. Bangor has an extensive lumber, ice, and ship-building trade. Fourteen feet can be carried to the moorings, but the channel is rapidly filling up with saw-dust and slabs from up the river, and is closed for three months of the year by ice. Can carry 6 to 14 fathoms up to the town of Bucksport, where there is good anchorage, but a very strong current. Limekin's Bay is a deep harbor with a least depth of 5 fathoms, but is used only as a harbor of refuge. The harbor of Wiscasset can hardly be surpassed. It is 14 miles up the Sheepscot River; depth in channel 9 fathoms. Bath has the largest ship-building and ship-owning interests in the State of Maine. Five fathoms can be carried to the city, 12 miles up the Kennebec River; mean rise and fall of tide, 7 feet. The river, owing to the strong current, is seldom closed by ice. Entrance to the river to be defended by Fort Popham, at present unfinished.

Casco Bay is 18 miles long and 12 miles wide. There are 136 islands in the bay, many fertile and nearly all inhabited. Portland, on a peninsula on the west shore, has an extensive foreign and coasting trade, and is the principal shipping port for Canada during the winter, as the harbor is never obstructed by ice. Population, 36,608. Can carry 5 fathoms to within ½ mile of and 16 feet up to the wharves; mean rise and fall of tide, 8.9 feet. There are four entrances to the harbor, but only the most southern can be used by large vessels, owing to the crooked and shallow character of the others. The harbor is defended by Forts Gorges, Preble, Scammell, and a battery on Portland Head. Richmond Island Harbor, being easily entered when vessels cannot get into Portland, is an excellent harbor of refuge, as there is good anchorage in 5 fathoms within ¾ of a mile of the breakwater, except when gales are blowing from south to west. There is no anchorage off Saco, the depth being only 3 feet in some places; mean rise and fall of tide, 8.2 feet. Can anchor in 5 to 7 fathoms 3½ miles from the city in Saco Bay; also in Winter Harbor, at the mouth of the river, 5½ miles from the city.

Portsmouth Harbor is formed by the lower reaches of the Piscataqua River. This is the site of an important naval station—the U. S. navy-yard being opposite the city of Portsmouth, distant ½ mile. The anchorage is good in any except the narrow portions of the bay, where the current is swift, and 6 fathoms can be carried up to the city. The usual anchorage for vessels, not going up to the city or the navy-yard, is at Pepperell's Cove in from 6 to 11 fathoms. The harbor is never closed by ice; mean rise and fall of tide, 8.6 feet. The harbor is defended by Forts Constitution, McClary, and Sullivan, all in a dilapidated condition. Newburyport Harbor is obstructed by a bar with only 6 feet of water at low tide, but this is being deepened. Rockport Harbor forms the best harbor of refuge on the northern shore of Cape Ann. There are 8 fathoms in the inner and 11 fathoms in the outer harbor.

Massachusetts Bay, between the headlands of Cape Ann and Cape Cod, distant 38 miles, contains the important harbors of Gloucester, Salem, Boston, Plymouth, and Provincetown. Gloucester Harbor has good anchorage in 5 fathoms within ¾ of a mile of the shore, and in 3½ fathoms close to the shore. It is frozen over in winter. The city, with a population of 21,262, has the largest fishing industries in the United States. Salem has a large coasting and ice trade, can carry 3½ fathoms into the inner harbor, within ½ mile of the town, and 4½ fathoms to Fort Pickering, 1 mile from the city. The inner harbor is closed by ice during January and February. Forts Lee, Pickering, and Sewall defend the harbor. Marblehead Harbor is rarely obstructed by ice, and 4½ fathoms can be carried to within ½ mile of the town. The channel is clear, and the harbor easy of entry. Lynn Harbor is little used, the nearest anchorage, in 4½ fathoms, being 2 miles from the shore.

Boston has a population of 446,507. At any tide 21 feet can be carried through the main channel with safety; mean rise and fall of tide, 9.4 feet. There are two other channels. The defences are Forts Warren and Independence. The U. S. navy-yard is situated in the district of Charlestown, opposite the city of Boston proper, at the junction of the Rivers Mystic and Charles. The inner harbor of Plymouth is closed by ice during the winter, and the whole harbor is sometimes frozen over. Not more than 21 feet can be carried into the outer harbor. Barnstable Harbor can only be entered by small vessels. Provincetown has one of the finest harbors on the coast, being easy of access, with plenty of water, and good holding ground. It is usually clear of ice, except during severe winters.

Sandwich Harbor, in the south-western part of Cape Cod Bay, has a difficult and narrow entrance, but it is to be the entrance to the ship-canal from Cape Cod Bay to the head of Buzzards Bay. This proposed canal calls for a harbor at Barnstable, formed of two breakwaters, enclosing a basin of 120 acres, to protect the opening of the canal. The northern breakwater is to be 4000 feet long, and the southern one 2000 feet, the opening between the two extremities to be 760 feet. The only work so far is preliminary or prospecting. The harbors of Nantucket Sound are small, poor, and of no importance. There are several good harbors on both shores of Vineyard Sound, viz., Wood's Hole, Edgartown Harbor, and Vineyard Haven. Wood's Hole has a small but good harbor, depth 3½ fathoms. Vineyard Haven has a good harbor, except when the wind is from the north. Edgartown inner harbor is small and narrow, but has excellent anchorage in 17 feet. The outer harbor is open to the north, but has good holding ground in 4 fathoms.

Buzzards Bay, 20 miles long, has deep water throughout. The entrance between Gooseberry Neck and Cuttyhunk Point is 5½ miles across, with a depth of from 9 to 12 fathoms in mid-channel. The most important harbor is that of New Bedford. Can carry 16 feet into the inner harbor through a narrow, crooked channel. The outer harbor, ½ mile from the city, is an open roadstead with 4½ fathoms of water. There are forts at Fort Point and Clark's Point. Up to Fall River 16½ feet can be carried. Newport has a fine harbor with water enough for the largest ships; 19 feet can be carried into the inner harbor. It is the site of the U. S. Torpedo Station, and is defended by Fort Adams and earthworks on Dutch Island. Block Island Basin is an artificial harbor formed by the government for the shelter of small vessels. It is 130 yards in diameter and 7 feet deep, and is protected by a heavy stone breakwater. The anchorage off the lower end of the town of Bristol is 21 feet, and good anchorage can be got in 5 fathoms 2 miles from the town. Twenty-one feet can be carried through a dredged channel 1½ miles long to Providence; the nearest anchorage, in 5 fathoms, is 4½ miles distant. The harbors of Long Island Sound are New London and New Haven, with a number of "tidal" harbors for light-draught coasters on the northern shores. On the southern shores are Greenport and Sag Harbor, Huntington and Oyster Bays, Hampstead and Manhasset Bays, all of which, except the last named, can be entered at low water by vessels drawing 18 feet. The sound is very free from dangers throughout its length, and affords good anchorage in bad weather. New London Harbor, one of the finest in the United States, is formed by the lower portion of the Thames River, and is 3 miles long and 30 feet deep. The entrance is defended by Forts Trumbull and Griswold. Twelve feet can be carried through a very narrow channel to New Haven, and 5 fathoms to within 4 miles of the city. The harbor is defended by Fort Hale. Gardiner's Bay has good anchorage in from 3½ to 8 fathoms. The bay has an average diameter of 6 miles, is protected from all directions, and is singularly free from dangers.

The noble and capacious harbor of New York is entered from Long Island Sound through the East River, the channel between Willet's Point and Throg's Neck being about three-fourths of a mile wide. East River forms a large part of the water front of New York and Brooklyn, and docks stretch along its shores for miles. The removal of some of the obstructions in East River (see Hell Gate Improvement) will have an important bearing on the defence of the harbor, and already a large foreign trade, principally in petroleum, has taken to this route. There are three channels between the reefs, called, respectively, the Main Ship Channel, to the west of the Great and Little Mill Rocks; the Middle Channel, between the Little and Great Mill Rocks and the Middle Reef; and the Eastern Channel, between the Middle Reef and Hallett's Point. The Upper Bay is entered from the ocean through the Narrows, between Staten Island and Long Island. Between 7 and 8 miles below the Upper Bay is Lower New York Bay, a harbor sufficient in capacity for all the fleets of the world.

Perth Amboy has a large coal-trade. Eleven feet of water can be carried up to the town; mean rise and fall of tide, 5.4 feet. During severe winters the harbor is sometimes closed with ice, but steamers can force their way through. Eight feet can be carried over the bar to Little Egg Harbor; rise and fall of tide, 3.4 feet. The channels are very crooked. There is no harbor at Atlantic City except for small vessels, though it can be approached within 3½ miles with 5 to 6 fathoms. Lewes is a small town 2 miles southward and westward of the Delaware Breakwater. Four to 5 fathoms can be carried under the lee of the breakwater; rise and fall of tide, 3.5 feet. Twenty feet can be carried up the Delaware River to Christiana Creek, and 12 feet up the creek to Wilmington, Del.; rise and fall of tide, 5.7 feet.

Hampton Roads, defended by Fortress Monroe, is an excellent rendezvous for a fleet, and there is plenty of water for vessels of any draught from the entrance of Chesapeake Bay to within a short distance of the fort. Twenty-five feet can be carried to Newport News, a growing shipping-town; rise and fall of tide, 2.5 feet. Norfolk, Va., has a large commerce, principally in cotton. Twenty-one feet can be carried to the city through a narrow channel. The U. S. navy-yard is situated at Gosport, on the Elizabeth River, adjoining Portsmouth and nearly opposite to Norfolk. To Annapolis Harbor 19½ feet can be carried over the bar; tide, .9 of a foot. The U. S. Naval Academy is situated here. To the city of Baltimore 24 feet can be carried through a dredged channel 11 miles long; rise and fall of tide, 1 foot. Nineteen feet can be carried to Washington, 200 miles from the ocean. The channel is very narrow above Mt. Vernon. Richmond is 150 miles from the mouth of the James River. Eighteen feet can be carried to City Point, 40 miles below Richmond, and 13 feet to the city; rise and fall of tide, 3.6 feet. Only 8 feet can be carried to the town of Edenton, N. C. Newberne, N. C., ships lumber, tar, and turpentine. Ten feet can be carried to the town, but only 8 feet over the bar from the sea into Pimlico Sound. Ten feet can be carried to Plymouth, but only 8 feet can be brought from the sea. Fourteen feet can be carried over the bar to Beaufort. Inside Fort Macon there are 18½ to 30 feet, with good anchorage, and 9¼ feet can be carried within ¼ mile of the town. Wilmington, N. C., with a population of 20,098, has a considerable trade in lumber, cotton, and turpentine. The city is 30 miles above the mouth of the Cape Fear River. Eight feet can be carried over the outer bar at the mouth of the river, and 7 feet in river channel to the city; tide, 4.5 feet. There is good anchorage off the town of Smithville in from 4 to 6 fathoms, and 14 feet can be carried over the bar; tide, 4.5 feet. Georgetown, S. C., ships lumber and turpentine. The town is 14 miles from the bar at the entrance on Winyaw Bay. Seven and one-half feet can be carried to the town. Charleston, S. C., has a large foreign trade, shipping quantities of cotton, phosphate, and naval stores. Fourteen feet can be carried over the bar to the South Channel, and inside 21 feet can be carried by this channel to the city. Port Royal, S. C., has a fine harbor with 21 feet over bar. Savannah, Ga., ships large quantities of cotton, rice, lumber, and naval stores. Seventeen feet can be carried over the bar at the mouth of the river, and 9 feet to the city; mean rise and fall of tide, 7 feet. Brunswick, population 8403, has one of the best harbors on the coast. Its waters form an arm of the sea, 20 miles long and from 1 to 5 miles wide, with an easy approach through a deep, wide channel; depth on bar, 17 feet; 9 feet can be carried up Brunswick River to the city.

The harbor of St. Mary's, Fla., has several good anchorages inside of the bar in from 3½ to 7 fathoms. Only 11 feet can be carried over the bar, and 17 feet to the town, 10 miles distant. There is 11 feet on the bar at the entrance of the harbor of Fernandina; inside there is good anchorage in from 3½ to 9 fathoms. Principal trade is in lumber. Jacksonville is on the St. John's River, 20 miles from its mouth. Nine feet can be carried over the bar and to the town through a narrow, crooked channel. Saint Augustine has a shifting bar with 10 feet of water, inside of which there is a good harbor to the northward of the town, with from 18 to 20 feet; rise and fall of tide, 6 feet.

II. *Gulf Coast.*—Key West has a trade principally in cigars and sponges. There are several channels entering the harbor, the best being the Main Ship Channel through which 23 feet can be carried; 30 feet can be carried through the S. W. Channel, and 12 feet through the N. W. Channel. There is good anchorage for the largest vessels within 1½ miles of the town. It is defended by Fort Taylor and batteries and two Martello towers. The Dry Tortugas, a group of ten low islets at the S. W. extremity of the chain of Florida reefs, form a large, deep, and commodious harbor. This splendid harbor is defended by Fort Jefferson on Garden Key. If this harbor came into the possession of an enemy it would afford an excellent base for hostile naval operations, but would afford no resources to an enemy beyond good anchorage and a place to rendezvous. Tampa Bay is an extensive estuary from 6 to 10 miles wide, extending from Egmont Island in N. N. E. direction about 22 miles, where it forms two arms. Twenty-one feet can be carried round the east and north sides to a deep lane on the west side. Anchorage in from 4 to 5 fathoms. Cedar Keys is the terminus of the Florida Railroad. There are three channels to the settlement, Sea-Horse Key Channel being the deepest, with 9 feet on its bar.

The Suwanee River has but 5 feet over the bar at its mouth. But this river is likely to become of great importance as the Gulf port of the proposed Florida Ship Canal from Fernandina, on the Atlantic coast, to the St. John's River, up the river to and through Doctor's Lake; thence by cut into the Suwanee River; thence to the Gulf of Mexico. The canal is to be 200 feet wide and 30 feet deep. The harbor on the Atlantic will require but little work to make it of the required depth, but the harbor at the mouth of the Suwanee will cost $1,000,000. The canal will cost $25,000,000, and will take three years to build. Appalachee Bay, a small bight in the N. E. corner of the Gulf of Mexico, is the seaport of Tallahassee, but is very shallow and is seldom visited. Appalachicola is a shipping port for lumber. Fifteen feet can be carried over the bar at

HARBORS AND DOCKS.

THE SIMPSON DRY DOCK, ERIE BASIN, BROOKLYN, N. Y.

PLATE XXX.

the entrance of the bay through the West Pass, but only 4 feet can be carried to the town; rise and fall of tide, 2 feet. St. Joseph's Bay is a large, deep, and commodious bay just north of Cape San Blas. It is easy of access, affords excellent anchorage, and can be entered in a gale or hurricane. The entrance with 19 feet of water is about a mile wide, the depth in the bay varying from 25 to 33 feet. St. Andrew's Bay, with three barred entrances, is only navigable for vessels drawing less than 13 feet. Pensacola Bay is protected by the Santa Rosa Island, a low sandy ridge not more than ⅓ mile broad. The entrance, ⅛ mile wide and 19½ feet deep, is defended by Forts Pickens and McRee, and Fort Barrancas and redoubt on the north side. The city of Pensacola, which ships large quantities of lumber, is 10 miles from the entrance and the U. S. navy-yard 3 miles.

Mobile Bay is an estuary 30 miles long. Just within the entrance, on the east side, is Bon Secours Bay, 10 miles long and 10 miles wide. The Mobile River flows into the N. W. corner of the bay and is navigable for 53 miles. The entrance between Fort Morgan and Dauphin Island is 2¾ miles wide, but is obstructed outside by Pelican and Sand Islands, 3 miles southward, and 2 miles farther out by a narrow bar with 21 feet at low water. Eighteen feet can be carried through a dredged channel 21 miles long to the city of Mobile, the natural outlet of the greatest cotton region of the United States. It is defended by Forts Morgan and Gaines. Mississippi Bay, with only 5 feet of water, is connected with Mobile Bay by Grant's Pass.

New Orleans is on the left bank of the Mississippi, 120 miles from the sea. The extremity of the delta spreads into four prongs between passes termed the South-west, South-east, North-east, and South Pass. The South Pass is 26 feet deep and 300 feet wide. Capt. James B. Eads' famous jetties are at the entrance to this pass. The South-west pass has 15 feet of water, the South-east 7 feet, the North-east 12 feet in its southern channel and 9½ in its northern channel at low water. Forts Jackson and St. Philip are on opposite banks at Plaquemine Bend, 170 miles below the city. The delta and neighboring waters are defended by the following works: Fort Pike, Rigolets; Fort on Ship Island, Mississippi Sound; Fort Macomb, at Chef Menteur Pass, connecting Lake Pontchartrain with Lake Borgne and the Gulf of Mexico; Tower Dupré, Battery Bienvenue, and Tower at Proctorsville, on Lake Borgne; and Fort Livingston, Barataria Bay. Barataria Bay is an extensive lake connecting with the Mississippi, 10 miles above New Orleans, by a canal navigable by light-draught steamers and coasters. Timbalier Bay is only navigable by light-draught vessels. At the outer part of Atchafalaya Bay there is 10 feet of water, but only 7 or 8 feet can be carried by narrow, tortuous channels within the bay. Galveston, Texas, ships large quantities of cotton, and is the most important commercial port in Texas. Eleven feet can be carried over the outer bar and 9½ feet to the city wharves; rise and fall of tide, 1½ feet. Jetties are to be constructed to deepen the entrance to 25 feet. Defended at Fort Point and Bolivar Point by earthen batteries. Brazos Santiagos has 21 feet alongside its wharves; only 6 feet can be carried over the bar.

III. *Pacific Coast.*—Port Townsend, Washington Territory, has a fine harbor, and 5 to 9 fathoms can be carried close to the shore near the centre of the town. Steilacoom has a fine harbor, and 6 to 15 fathoms can be carried within ¼ mile of the town. Seattle has a large trade in lumber. Up to the wharves 4½ fathoms can be carried, and there is plenty of water at the anchorage off the town. Can carry 3¼ fathoms to within 1½ miles of Olympia; inside of that the bay shoals rapidly to a large mud-flat in front of the town, uncovered at low tide; rise and fall of tide, 12 feet. New Dungennes has a good harbor, with 5 to 15 fathoms, but it is open to the eastward. Astoria, Oregon, has large establishments for canning salmon. Sometimes there is 27 feet on the bar at the mouth of the Columbia River, but it is a shifting bar and the depth varies. From the bar to the town (14 miles) there is over 28 feet of water. During winter months there is at times a heavy sea breaking over the bar, delaying passage of all vessels for several days. Reliable information is lacking as to the amount of water that can be carried to the city of Portland. When the river is in good condition 19 feet can be carried to the wharves, but during August and September only 17 feet, according to masters of San Francisco steamers. Nine feet can be carried over the bar at the mouth of the Yaquina River to Newport; rise and fall of tide, 7.8 feet. Ten feet can be carried over the bar to Koos Bay, and 17 feet up to Empire City. Crescent City, California, has a very dangerous harbor and should not be entered without a pilot on account of the numerous shoals and rocks. Twenty-five feet can be carried to the anchorage near Whaler's Island, and 14 feet to the wharf. Trinidad Bay, a small roadstead open to the southward, is a good summer harbor, but is dangerous in winter. Fourteen feet can be carried to the wharves of Trinidad. Mendocino has an open harbor with 5 or 6 fathoms at anchorage, ¾ of a mile from the settlement. Benicia contains a U. S. arsenal and several small factories. Twenty-five feet can be carried up the San Pablo Straits to the town. Drakes Bay is a harbor of refuge from northwest gales. Vallejo is situated on the opposite side of Napa Creek from the U. S. navy-yard, 27 miles north of San Francisco Bay. Twenty-one feet can be carried to the anchorage between the town and the navy-yard; rise and fall of tide, 6 feet. San Francisco, population 297,990, has one of the finest harbors in the world. Twenty-three feet can be carried over the bar to the city and in almost any part of the bay; rise and fall of tide, 3.6 feet. Santa Cruz has a harbor well protected, except from northerly gales. There is good anchorage in from 3½ to 15 fathoms within ½ mile of the shore. The harbor of San Luis Obispo is open to the southward. Good anchorage in 3 to 5 fathoms. Santa Barbara exports large quantities of wood and fruit. The harbor is open to the southward, but is partially protected by a large island. There is 19 feet alongside the wharves. Thick kelp extends out about ½ mile. Inside this the anchorage is good, though it is not safe in winter. San Diego Bay forms the next best harbor on the coast after San Francisco. The port is formed by a bold projecting point of land on the west side, terminating at its southern extremity in Point Lima, and on the east side by a low, flat peninsula, connected by a narrow slip of sand-beach to the mainland, between which the bay winds around and forms an indentation about 6 miles long and 2 miles wide in widest part. The entrance is over a bar with 21 feet of water.

For Lake Harbors, see NAVIGATION, INLAND.

DOCKS may be divided as follows: Wet-docks, or basins, dry- or graving-docks, and floating-docks.

The wet-dock, or basin, is seen on the grandest scale

at places where there is a great rise and fall of tide or where there is not water-front enough to provide wharves sufficient for the unloading of the many ships discharging at a large city. It will be understood that with a rise and fall of tide of as much as 12 feet it is very convenient to have a basin cut off from the influence of the tide, where vessels can lie in water of a fixed level alongside the quays and landing-stages while discharging their cargoes. Such docks are seen on a large scale at London. These are always kept full and have gates or locks which keep in or out the tidal waters as desired, while along the quays are huge landing-stages, packing-yards, cranes, and every kind of apparatus necessary for the loading, unloading, and custody of goods. Vessels can be kept in the docks for undergoing internal repairs, taking in and discharging cargoes, or fitting out for sea. The London docks cover an area of 120 acres. They have four gates on the Thames, and have room for 300 large vessels. The warehouses can stow 220,000 tons of goods, and the cellars will hold 8,316,050 gallons of wine. The Victoria and Albert Docks, farther down the river, are 2¼ miles in length and are lighted by electric lights and provided with every convenience and accommodation for sailing-vessels and steamers of the largest size.

Dry-docks are used for external repairs, and sometimes vessels are built in them. Such docks are built of wood or stone. The entrance is closed by a gate or caisson—a vessel having a projection or keel on the bottom and ends. This vessel is fitted with pumps and is ballasted. When filled with water and in place across the entrance the keel fits into a groove in the masonry at the bottom and sides of the entrance, forming a dam against the passage of the water. The top is wider than the bottom, so that to remove it the water is pumped from it, and it rises and can be towed aside, or else, as in some later docks, is hauled off on a track in direction of its length. When a vessel is to be docked the blocks upon which she is to rest are fixed in place, the filling culverts are then opened, and the water rises to the level outside. The caisson is then floated and removed, as explained above, and the vessel towed in and held by four or more hawsers. The caisson is now placed across the entrance, a valve opened in the bottom, and it sinks into its place. Water is now drained into a well through draining culverts leading from the dock, and the level reduced enough to bring a pressure on the outside of the caisson, fixing it securely in its place. By these culverts command is held over the level of the water as the vessel takes the blocks. Water is now pumped out by means of large pumps and the vessel shored (or propped). Workmen can then get at any point along the outside and make needed repairs. When a vessel is launched she is subjected to strains greater than she is ever likely to be subjected to in service, so that many of the heavy iron-clads of England are built in dry-docks and launching dangers avoided, as the vessel is simply floated out. Advantage is also gained in the handling of heavy weights.

Most of the dry-docks now building in the United States are of wood instead of stone. They are built of spruce pile foundations throughout, upon which are fitted and secured heavy transverse floor timbers of yellow pine, covered with spruce planking to form the floor, and carry the keel blocks, the latter being further supported by rows of piles driven under the floor timbers, and capped with heavy yellow-pine timbers lengthways of the dock, the heads of the piles being cased in a continuous bed of Portland cement. Open box drains on each side of the keelway beneath the floor timbers lead to the drainage culverts at the head of each dock. The sides and heads slope at 45°. The alters are carefully filled in with clay puddle as the sides are built up, and from the level of high water to the top of coping the sides are built of concrete *en masse* faced with Hoope's artificial stone, the alters being continued of the same material to the coping level. The dock is closed by an iron caisson or floating gate, made with sloping ends, corresponding with the slope of the side walls, which bears against the sill and solid timber abutments the whole length of its keel and stem, no grooves being used, the joint being made water-tight by means of a rubber gasket secured to the face of the sills and abutments. The cost of such a dock is from 30 to 40 per cent. of that of a stone dock of the same capacity built upon the same site, and can be built in one-third the time.

The graving-dock is open, and vessels are put in it at high tide to receive repairs on the fall of the tide. Before copper sheathing was introduced they were used to bream or clean the bottoms of ships by fire.

Floating-docks have many merits, and are very useful. They can be employed in deep water, and in situations where from the nature of the ground other docks could not be cut. They are also independent of the action of the tide, and if the demand for their use is diminished at one port they can be moved to another where the demand is greater.

Floating sectional dry-docks consist of several sections joined together by sliding beams. Each section consists of a large rectangular box or tank, at the sides of which are frames formed of four uprights. In each frame a float is made to travel up and down by suitable gearing, rising when lowering the sections and being forced down when raising a vessel.

Balance floating-docks consist of hollow walls built along the two longer sides of a large rectangular tank, the whole looking like a large floating dry-dock without any ends. It is called a balance-dock because it is divided into a number of compartments, and by pumping water into or letting water out the side chambers any level or trim can be got.

The patent tubular floating-docks are very interesting. Both the bottom and vertical sides consist of a number of circular wrought-iron tubes. The bottom is formed of eight circular tubes running longitudinally, and the sides of similar tubes fixed vertically in the two outer longitudinal tubes. The tubes are divided into a great number of water-tight compartments. A certain number of the chambers are sealed, but the others are provided with water valves at the bottom. When it is desired to sink the dock the bottom valves are opened. When it is desired to raise it compressed air is forced into the tubes, and the water expelled through the bottom valves, which are closed as soon as the dock and its vessel are fully raised.

The hydraulic lift-dock is a decided departure, for instead of lifting the vessel into a large reservoir of water and pumping it dry the vessel is lifted bodily out of the water upon a raft-like pontoon that possesses sufficient buoyancy to sustain the weight of the vessel. As soon as the ship is lifted and floated away on its own pontoon the dock is free to be employed on another pontoon to raise a second ship. The pontoon is brought up between two rows of columns extending down to the dock below. These columns carry hydrautic lifts, from the heads of which rods extend and are made fast to lattice girders extending across to the opposite column. On these girders the pontoon rests. When the pontoon is raised the water is let out by the bottom valves and it is floated away.

Dry-docks of more than 58 feet breadth in the ports of the United States.

Port.	Kind.	Length over all.	Width of entrance at top.	Depth over sill at ordinary high water. Spring-tide.	Material.	Location.
Buffalo	Basin.	350	60	10		
Detroit	"	306	65	13		} Foot Orleans St.
"	"	360	75	11.5		
Albina, Oreg.	"	400	72	22		
San Francisco	Floating.	210	60	20	Wood.	
"	Basin.	450	90	24	Stone.	Hunter's Point.
"	"	529	78	25.5	"	Navy-yard.
Portland, Me.	"	425	80	24	Wood.	
Portsmouth, N. H.	Floating.	350	90	23	"	Navy-yard.
Boston	Basin.	379	60	25	Stone.	
"	"	365	64	17.5	Wood.	East Boston.
New York	Balance.	330	90	18.5	"	Foot Rutgers St.
"	Sectional.	360	100	20	"	} Between Pike and Clinton St.
"	"	250	75	15	"	
"	"	170	65	16	"	
Brooklyn	Basin.	350	66	25	Stone.	Navy-yard.
"	"	540	100	22	Wood.	} Erie Basin.
"	"	630	85	25	"	
Jersey City	Balance.	185	62	14	"	Foot Essex St.
Philadelphia	Basin.	434	70	21.5	"	Cramp's Yard.
"	Sectional	200	62	14	"	
Baltimore	Basin.	504	90	23	"	
"	Floating.	320	67	14	"	Locust Point.
Norfolk	Basin.	320	60	......	Stone.	Gosport.
New Orleans	Floating.	315	90	16	Wood.	
"	"	220	75	14	"	
"	"	225	75	16	"	

For the mud-docks at Vizagapatam, India, a deep ditch is dug close to the river and at high tide is filled. The vessel is dragged in and two rows of stakes and mats placed across the entrance and filled in with mud. The mud thrown out from the ditch forms a high wall. Mud is thrown in, raising the level of the water and so elevating the ship. The ship then rests in the mud, and beams are hauled under her and the mud scooped away till her bottom can be got at. To undock, four sets of hawsers are coiled in the shape of cones made solid by filling in with mud. These cones are places under the bilges forward and aft, larger ends out. The dock is dug to the required depth, leaving the ship resting on the beams and cones. The beams are removed and by simultaneously uncoiling the hawsers, beginning at the bases, the cones gradually subside and the vessel with them. (L. N.)

HARCOURT, SIR WILLIAM GEORGE GRANVILLE VENABLES VERNON, an English statesman, was born Oct. 14, 1827. He is the second son of Rev. William Vernon Harcourt, and grandson of Archbishop Harcourt. He graduated with high honors at Trinity College, Cambridge, in 1851, and was called to the bar at the Inner Temple in 1854. He was made queen's counsel in 1866. He had in the meantime acquired high reputation by letters on international law published in the *Times* with the signature *Historicus*. These discussed with great learning and ability the relation of the English government to the American belligerents in the civil war. They were collected and enlarged in a volume in 1863. Mr. Harcourt entered Parliament in 1868 as the representative of the city of Oxford. He was made professor of international law at the University of Cambridge in 1869. He served on the royal commission to amend the neutrality laws and again to amend the naturalization laws. He was made solicitor-general in November, 1873, and received the honor of knighthood. He retired from office with Mr. Gladstone in 1874, and when the Liberals were successful in 1880 Sir Vernon Harcourt was made secretary of state for the home department. He was, however, defeated in the election at Oxford city, but was then elected for Derby, which he still represents. He retired again from the Cabinet in 1885, but was again chancellor of the exchequer in 1886–87.

HARDEE, WILLIAM J. (1815–1873), an American general, was born at Savannah, Ga., Oct. 10, 1815. Graduating at West Point in 1838, he entered the Second dragoons, served in Florida, and was made captain in 1844. He fought in the Mexican war, and was brevetted lieutenant-colonel for bravery. He then served on the frontier until 1856, when he was appointed commandant of cadets and instructor in tactics at West Point. In 1860 he was made lieutenant-colonel of cavalry, but resigned in 1861 and entered the Confederate service as brigadier-general. He commanded in Northern Arkansas, and afterwards fought at Shiloh, April 6, 1862, being promoted major-general for bravery. At Perryville, Oct. 9, 1862, he was again distinguished and was made lieutenant-general. He commanded the Third corps at Stone River, Dec. 29, 1862. He fought at Chickamauga, Chattanooga, and Mission Ridge, and succeeded Gen. Bragg in the chief command, Dec. 2, 1863, until the arrival of Gen. J. E. Johnston. He commanded at Savannah and at Charleston until their surrender to Gen. Sherman. He afterwards fought at Bentonville, N. C., but surrendered with Gen. Johnston's army, April 27, 1865. He died at Wytheville, Va., Nov. 6, 1873.

HARDIE, JAMES ALLEN, an American general, was born at New York, May 5, 1823. He graduated at West Point in 1843, entered the artillery service, and was assistant professor at West Point, 1844–46. He served in the Mexican war as major of the First New York volunteers, and afterwards was employed on the frontier and in garrison duty. He was made lieutenant-colonel and aide-de-camp on Gen. McClellan's staff, Sept. 28, 1861, and served in the Peninsular and Maryland campaigns. He was afterward on the staff of Gen. Burnside and of Gen. Hooker. He was assigned to special duty in the war department and was assistant to Secretary Stanton and his successors in that department until 1870. He died May 5, 1876.

HARDING, CHESTER (1792–1866), an American portrait-painter, was born at Conway, Mass., Sept. 1, 1792. In early life he removed to Western New York, where he worked on a farm. He served in the war of 1812, and afterwards was engaged in various pursuits. While engaged in house-painting at Pittsburg, he had his portrait painted and afterwards endeavored to paint his wife's picture. Having attained some success, he painted many portraits in Kentucky, and then went to Philadelphia for instruction in art. Being successful he bought a farm, but in August, 1823, went to England, where he spent three years. On returning he settled in Boston, and, after another visit to England in 1843, took up his residence at Springfield, Mass., but spent the winters in the West and South. He died at Boston, April 1, 1866. He painted portraits of nearly all the prominent Americans of his time, and also several eminent Englishmen.

HARDY, ARTHUR SHERBURNE, an American mathematician and novelist, was born at Andover, Mass., Aug. 13, 1847. He was educated at Phillips Academy, Andover, at Amherst College, and at West Point, graduating at the latter in 1869. He served for two years as second-lieutenant of artillery, and then resigning became professor of applied mathematics and civil-engineering in Iowa College in 1871. He was professor of civil-engineering in the Chandler Scientific School, Dartmouth College, 1874-78, and has since been professor of mathematics in the same college. His mathematical books include *Elements of Quaternions* (1881); *Imaginary Quantities* (1881); and *Topographical Surveying* (1884). His novels are *Francesca da Rimini* (1878), and *But yet a Woman* (1883).

HARDY, THOMAS, an English novelist, was born in Dorsetshire, June 2, 1840. He studied architecture, and in 1863 gained a prize for an *Essay on Colored Brick and Terra-Cotta Architecture*. But he afterwards turned to novel-writing, his first work being *Desperate Remedies* (1871). Then followed *Under the Greenwood Tree* (1872), *A Pair of Blue Eyes* (1873), *Far from the Madding Crowd* (1874), *The Hand of Ethelberta* (1876), *The Return of Native* (1878), *The Trumpet-major* (1880), *Two on a Tower* (1882). He has succeeded in giving interesting pictures of life among English country-folk, especially in his native Dorsetshire.

HARE, an extensive family of rodent mammalia, comprising many species of the genus *Lepus*, family *Leporidæ*. This genus includes the common hare and rabbit, with many other species, mainly confined to the Northern Hemisphere, and most abundant in North America. It is not easy to divide the hares and rabbits into distinct groups, there being no marked difference of structure. Their main distinction is one of habit, the social and burrowing *Leporidæ* being classed as rabbits, the solitary and non-burrowing as hares. It is the habit of the latter to construct forms or nests on the surface. There are more than 40 species of *Lepus*, nearly half of which belong to North America. The distinguishing feature of the genus is the presence of 4 incisor teeth in the upper jaw, the front pair being well developed, the lateral ones very small. The molar teeth are more numerous than in rodents usually, the upper jaw having 6 on each side, the lower jaw 5. The eyes are large and prominent, the ears very large, the tail short and turned up. The hind legs are usually much longer than the fore ones, which gives the animals great power of leaping. They are all very timid, and depend mainly on their speed for safety.

See Vol. XI. p. 425 Am. ed. (p. 476 Edin. ed.).

The American hares extend into the Polar regions, the Polar hare (*Lepus glacialis*) being the largest of the family, and exceeding a large cat in size. It is two feet long to the root of the tail. In winter it is of a pure white color, in summer of a brownish-gray above, whitish below, with fine, soft, and full fur. The flesh is said to be delicious. It is found in the cold and sterile regions from Newfoundland to the far north, where it feeds on berries, bark, evergreen leaves, etc. It does not usually seek shelter from the Arctic winter by burrowing in the snow, but generally has its lair behind a large stone which partly protects it from the wind. *L. Americanus*, the northern hare, is very widely distributed from Virginia and New Mexico to 68° north. It is a little smaller than the former, whitish in winter and reddish-brown in summer. It is very swift and active, and is said to be able to leap 21 feet at a bound. It frequents thick woods, and winds through tangled wood-paths when pursued until it wears out its pursuer. Its flesh is not much esteemed. Another common species is *L. sylvaticus*, the wood hare, or the ordinary gray rabbit, which is found almost throughout the United States. *L. aquaticus*, the swamp hare, and *L. palustris*, the marsh hare, frequent wet regions, and are excellent swimmers and divers. They belong to the Southern States. There are many other species found in all parts of the United States, while other species, not markedly different from these in character, are abundant in Europe and the other continents. (C. M.)

HARE, AUGUSTUS JOHN CUTHBERT, an English author, was born at Rome, Italy, March 13, 1834. He was the son of Francis G. Hare, but when an infant was adopted by the widow of his uncle, Augustus William Hare. He was educated at Harrow and at University College, Oxford. He has edited *Murray's Hand-books* for some counties of England, but is best known by his interesting books on Italy. Among these are *Walks in Rome* (1870); *Days near Rome* (1874); *Cities of Northern and Central Italy* (1875). He has also published *Wanderings in Spain* (1872), and *Walks in London* (1877). The *Memorials of a Quiet Life* (1872), a record of various members of the Hare family, is a charming biography.

HARE, ROBERT (1781-1858), an American chemist, was born at Philadelphia, Jan. 17, 1781. His father, an English immigrant, had a large brewery, and the son for a time had a share in the business. But led by his fondness for chemistry in 1801 he invented the oxyhydrogen blowpipe, by which he was enabled for the first time to render platinum and some other metals fusible. The American Academy conferred on him the Rumford medal for this invention, Yale College gave him the honorary degree of M. D. in 1806, and Harvard in 1816. He had in that year produced the calorimotor, a form of the galvanic battery, by which intense heat is generated. This was afterwards modified by Prof. Silliman and accepted by Faraday as the best form of apparatus for the purpose. Dr. Hare held the professorship of chemistry in the University of Pennsylvania from 1818 to 1847. He was an excellent instructor in the natural sciences. Late in life he became a believer in spiritualism, and published *Spiritual Manifestations Scientifically Demonstrated* (1855). He died at Philadelphia, May 15, 1858. He had contributed many papers to scientific journals and published some books on Chemistry. His son, JOHN INNES CLARK HARE, was born in 1817, studied law, and has since 1851 been a judge in the District Court of Philadelphia. He was joint author with Horace B. Wallace of *American Leading Cases* (1847), and has annotated several law-treatises.

HARE, WILLIAM HOBART, an American bishop, was born at Princeton, N. J., May 17, 1838, being a son of Rev. Dr. George Emlen Hare. He was educated at the University of Pennsylvania, but did not graduate. He was ordained in the Protestant Episcopal Church in 1859, and had charge of churches in Philadelphia until 1870. He was then made secretary and general agent of the Foreign Committee of the Board of Missions. He was appointed missionary bishop of Niobrara by the House of Bishops in November, 1872, and consecrated Jan. 9, 1873. He has exerted himself for the protection and Christianization of the Indians.

HARLAN, JAMES, an American statesman, was

born in Clarke co., Ill., Aug. 25, 1820. He graduated at Indiana Asbury University in 1845, studied law, and settled in Iowa. He was made State superintendent of instruction in 1847, and was appointed president of Iowa Wesleyan University in 1853. He was elected U. S. Senator from Iowa in 1855, and continued to represent that State until March, 1865, when he was called by President Lincoln, at the beginning of his second term, to be secretary of the interior. He held this position until September, 1866, when he was again elected Senator from Iowa. When his term expired, in 1873, he retired to private life. From the formation of the Republican party he was a moderate but firm supporter of its policy.

HARLESS, GOTTLIEB CHRISTOPH ADOLF (1806–1879), a German Lutheran theologian, was born at Nuremburg, Nov. 21, 1806. He studied theology at Erlangen, graduating in 1829, and afterwards taught there, being full professor from 1836 to 1845. Being then removed from his professorship by the Bavarian government, he accepted a call to Leipsic as professor, and in 1847 was also made pastor of a church there. He exerted great influence on the Lutheran Church in Saxony, and in 1850 was appointed chief court preacher at Dresden. In 1852 he was recalled by the Bavarian government to be president of the Protestant consistory at Munich and member of the state council. In January, 1879, having become completely blind, he retired from all public duty. He died at Munich, Sept. 5, 1879. He was an influential exponent of strict Lutheran orthodoxy. Among his numerous works the most valuable are his *Commentary on Ephesians* (1834; 2d ed., 1858); *Theologische Encyclopädie und Methodologie* (1837); *Die christliche Ethik* (1842; 7th ed., 1875); *Das Verhältniss des Christenthums zu Kultur- und Lebensfragen der Gegenwart* (1863); *Jakob Böhme und die Alchimisten* (1870; 2d ed., 1882); *Staat und Kirche* (1870). He also published an autobiography (1872).

HARMAN, FRANÇOIS JULES (1845–1883), a French explorer, was born in October, 1845, at Saumar. He entered the surgical staff in the navy and took part in various expeditions since 1870. He went to Algeria in the campaign against the Kabyles in 1871, then with Garnier to Tonquin, where he was for some time governor. He returned to France in 1874, but set out for Cambodia in 1875 and pushed his explorations far to the north of that region. In 1881 he returned to Paris seriously ill with consumption, and was made keeper of the Colonial Museum. He died at Florence, April 14, 1883.

HARMS, CLAUS (1778–1855), a German Lutheran theologian, was born at Fahrstedt, Holstein, May 25, 1778. Until he was nineteen years old he assisted his father, who was a miller. Then he began to study at Meldorf, and afterwards at Kiel, and became a private teacher. In 1806 he became deacon at Lunden, and in 1816 archdeacon in the church of St. Nicholas at Kiel. Though frequently called elsewhere, he remained here, and in 1835 he was made chief pastor of this church and provost of Kiel. In 1849 he resigned his office on account of loss of sight, and he died Feb. 1, 1855, at Kiel. On the tercentenary of the Reformation, in 1817, he published 95 theses, in which he opposed rationalism and set forth the strictly orthodox Lutheran doctrines on sin, faith, and grace. A controversy ensued, in which about 200 essays appeared, those of Schleiermacher and Ammon being the most important. The result was a decided revival of orthodox belief. Harms published several volumes of sermons and essays, an *Autobiography* (1852), *Pastoraltheologie* (3d ed., 1878), and some minor treatises. He was a thoroughly popular preacher, and in 1878, on the hundredth anniversary of his birth, a tablet was placed on the house in which he had lived.

HARMS, GEORG LUDWIG DETLEV THEODOR (1808–1865), a German clergyman, was born at Walsrode in Lüneburg, May 5, 1808. He studied theology at Göttingen and taught privately until 1844, when he became assistant to his father, the pastor of Hermannsburg. In 1849, having succeeded to sole charge of the parish, Harms founded an institute, in which manual labor was combined with theological training to fit young men for missionary labor, especially in Africa. Pastor Harms' father had been a rationalist, but he himself was an earnest, spiritual-minded preacher. His sermons reached the hearts of the people and his labors resulted in an extensive revival. Hermannsburg became a strictly religious community, and his missionary institute founded a new Hermannsburg in South Africa. Some volumes of his sermons were widely circulated in Germany. Among these were *Evangelienpredigten* (8th ed., 1877), and *Epistelpredigten* (3d ed., 1875). His brother, Theodor Harms, published his *Lebensbeschreibung* (4th ed., 1874) and his *Briefe* (1879).

HARNACK, THEODOSIUS, a German Lutheran theologian, was born at Petersburg, Jan. 3, 1817. He studied theology at Dorpat, Bonn, and Berlin, and in 1843 became privat-docent of theology at Dorpat. In 1845 he was made extraordinary professor and in 1848 professor of theology in the same place. In 1853 he accepted a call to Erlangen, but in 1866 he returned to Dorpat and in 1873 he retired from his professorship. He is an orthodox Lutheran and has been influential by his works and teaching. He has published *Die Idee der Predigt* (1844); *De theologia practical* (1847); *Der christliche Gemeindegottesdienst* (1854); *Luther's Theologie* (1862); *Die Kirche, ihr Amt, ihr Regiment* (1862); *Practische Theologie* (1877–82). He has contributed to Herzog's *Encyclopædia* and published an edition of *The Teaching of the Apostles*, found by Bryennios (1883).

HARNETT, CORNELIUS (1723–1781), an American patriot, was born in England, April 20, 1723 Having removed to America while young, he became a wealthy planter near Wilmington, N. C. In 1770 he was elected to the provincial assembly, where he was chairman of important committees. Josiah Quincy, who visited him in 1773, called him "the Samuel Adams of North Carolina." Harnett was a member of the provincial Congress in 1776, and prepared the instructions to the North Carolina delegates to the Continental Congress. He also served on the committee to draft the State constitution and bill of rights. Under the new constitution he became a member of the council. In 1778 he was elected to the Continental Congress, and signed the Articles of Confederation when proposed to the States. He was afterwards captured by the British forces in North Carolina, and, while a prisoner, died at Wilmington, N. C., April 20, 1781.

HARNEY, WILLIAM SELBY, an American general, was born in Louisiana in 1798. He entered the army in 1818 as second-lieutenant, in 1833 became major, and in 1836 lieutenant-colonel of dragoons. He served in Florida against the Seminoles, and in 1840 gained the brevet of colonel. In 1846 he become colonel, and served with distinction in the Mexican war, gaining a further brevet at Cerro Gordo. He afterwards served on the plains, where he was noted as an Indian fighter. His athletic strength, skill, and endurance gave him high repute among the tribes. On Sept. 3, 1855, he completely defeated the Sioux on the North Fork of the Nebraska River. In 1858 he was made brigadier-general and commander of the department of Oregon. On July 9, 1859, he took possession of San Juan Island in Puget's Sound, which the English government also claimed as belonging to British Columbia by treaty. The dispute was finally decided in 1875 by the arbitration of the German emperor in favor of the United States, but Gen. Harney's action was premature, and he was recalled. He was placed in command of the department of the West. In April, 1861, while on his way to Washington, he was arrested at Harper's Ferry by Virginia officers and taken to Richmond, where he was promptly released. On his return to St. Louis he warned the people of Missouri against secession. On May 21 he made a truce with Gen. Sterling Price, who commanded the State militia, agreeing to make no military movement as long as the peace was preserved by the State authorities. He was soon after relieved of command and was retired from service in August, 1863. He resided in St. Louis, where he possessed great wealth. In August, 1867, he was member of the Indian Commission. In 1884 he was married a third time.

HARPER, ROBERT GOODLOE (1765-1825), an American statesman, was born near Fredericksburg, Va., in 1765. His parents removed to Granville, N. C., while he was a boy. When only fifteen years of age he joined a troop of horse and took part in Gen. Greene's campaign, acting as quartermaster. After the war, entering the College of New Jersey, he taught the lower classes while studying in the higher. Graduating in 1785, he studied law at Charleston, S. C., and settled in the interior of the State. Having published a series of newspaper articles on proposed changes in the State constitution, he was soon after elected to the State legislature. In 1794 he entered Congress, where he was soon distinguished by his able support of the Federal policy of Washington and Adams. He retired from Congress in 1801, when the Federalists lost their power. He then married the daughter of Charles Carroll, of Carrollton, and settled in Baltimore. He gained further eminence as an advocate, and especially by his successful defence of Judge Samuel Chase when impeached by the House of Representatives. (See CHASE, SAMUEL.) In 1815 the legislature of Maryland elected Harper to the U. S. Senate for an unexpired term. In 1819 he went abroad and made a long sojourn in England, France, and Italy. After his return his public services were in behalf of the Colonization Society, whose plans he ardently advocated. He also promoted canals and internal improvements. He died at Baltimore, Jan. 15, 1825. His widow survived until February, 1861. A volume of Harper's *Speeches* was published in 1814, and he issued political pamphlets at various times.

HARRIS, SAMUEL, an American theologian, was born at East Machias, Maine, June 14, 1814. He graduated at Bowdoin College in 1833, and studied theology at Andover. He was principal of academies in Maine until 1841, then pastor of the Congregational church at Conway, Mass., 1841-51, and at Pittsfield, Mass., 1851-55. He was made professor of systematic theology in Bangor Theological Seminary, Maine, in 1855, president of Bowdoin College in 1867, and professor of systematic theology in Yale Theological School, New Haven, Conn., in 1871. He has published *Zaccheus, or the Scriptural Plan of Benevolence* (1847); *Christ's Prayer for the Death of His Redeemed* (1861); *Christian Doctrine of Human Progress* (1870); *Kingdom of Christ on Earth* (1874); *Philosophical Basis of Theism* (1883).

HARRIS, SAMUEL SMITH, an American bishop, was born in Autauga co., Ala., Sept. 14, 1841. He graduated at the University of Alabama in 1859, was admitted to the bar and practised law at Montgomery, Ala. During the civil war he served with distinction in the Confederate army, and afterwards resumed the practice of law in New York city. He took orders in the Protestant Episcopal Church in 1868, and had charge of churches in Alabama until 1879, when he was elected bishop of Michigan, being consecrated Sept. 17, 1879. He has published *The Relation of Christianity to Civil Society* (1883).

HARRIS, THOMAS LAKE, an American social reformer, was born at Fenny Stratford, England, May 15, 1823. At the age of four he was brought to America by his father, who settled at Utica, N. Y. He was soon compelled to earn his own living, and at seventeen he began to write for newspapers. Having renounced the Calvinistic faith in which he was early trained, he became a Universalist preacher at Minden, N. Y., in 1844. His health failing he went to Charleston, S. C., but from 1845 to 1847 was pastor of a church in New York city. In 1848, having adopted Swedenborgian views, he organized an Independent Christian Society in New York, but in 1850 joined a community at Mountain Cove, Va. He afterwards lectured in many parts of the Union, endeavoring to turn the public interest in spiritualism to what he considered a higher plane of religious thought and life. In 1855 he established the *Herald of Light* to advance his views, and in 1858 he visited England and Scotland, where he gained converts. Returning in 1861 he settled in Amenia, N. Y., where several friends gathered around him and formed the "Brotherhood of the New Life." The settlement was afterwards removed to Brocton, N. Y., where Lady Oliphant and several Japanese of distinction joined the society, which had no written creed or form of government. The property was not held in common; each labored for himself. The Bible and the marriage relation are held in reverence by the "Brotherhood." More than 2000 members, scattered over the world, are said to belong to this unique society. About 1876 Mr. Harris removed to the neighborhood of Los Angeles, Cal., where he lives a retired life. His principal works are *Wisdom of Angels* (1856); *Arcana of Christianity* (1857, 1866); *Modern Spiritualism* (1869); *Millennial Age* (1860). He has also published several volumes of hymns and poems.

HARRIS, THADDEUS WILLIAM (1795-1856), an American entomologist, was born at Dorchester, Mass., Nov. 12, 1795. He was the son of Rev. Thaddeus Mason Harris, D. D. (1768-1842), a Congregational clergyman of considerable note, who was pastor of the church in Dorchester for 46 years. The son graduated at Harvard in 1815, studied medicine and practised in Milton, Mass. He was librarian of Harvard College from 1831 till his death, and also taught botany and natural history in the college. In 1837 he was a member of a commission for the zoölogical and botanical survey of Massachusetts. His collection of

North American insects was purchased by subscription for the Boston Society of Natural History. He took much interest in antiquarian researches. He died at Cambridge, Mass., Jan. 16, 1856. His chief publications were a *Catalogue of the Insects of Massachusetts* (1832); *Insects of New England Injurious to Vegetation* (1841; enlarged editions, 1852, 1862). His *Entomological Correspondence* was published in 1869, with a memoir by T. W. Higginson.

HARRIS, WILLIAM TORREY, an American philosopher and educator, was born at North Killingly, Conn., Sept. 10, 1835. He entered Yale College in 1854 but did not graduate, though in 1869 he received the honorary degree of A. M. In 1857 he became a teacher in St. Louis, and in 1867 was made superintendent of public schools there. In 1875 he was chosen president of the National Educational Association. In 1866 he assisted in founding the Philosophical Society at St. Louis, and in 1867 he founded the *Journal of Speculative Philosophy*, which he has since edited. In 1880 he removed to Cambridge, Mass., where he still resides. His educational articles and reports have been received with marked attention in both Europe and America. In philosophy he is a Christian Hegelian. He has published some school-books, which are extensively used, and prepared for the International Expositions at Vienna and Paris the *Statement of the System of Education of the United States*.

HARRISBURG, the capital of Pennsylvania and county-seat of Dauphin county, is finely situated on the left bank of the Susquehanna River, 106 miles W. by N. of Philadelphia, and 125 miles by rail N. of Washington, D. C. It is on the main line of the Pennsylvania Railroad, here crossed by the Northern Central Railroad. The Cumberland Valley Railroad extends hence southwestward to Martinsburg, W. Va. Harrisburg is also on a branch of the Philadelphia and Reading Railroad. The Harrisburg and Potomac and the Gettysburg and Harrisburg Railroads make connections outside the city limits, and a short branch railway extends from Harrisburg to Steelton. The river, here a mile wide, is crossed by fine railway and other bridges. A park of 12 acres contains the capitol and other State buildings. Harrisburg has a courthouse, county-prison, State arsenal, State insane-asylum, and a hospital. Among the numerous churches is the Roman Catholic Cathedral. The State library, founded before 1777, has over 45,000 volumes. Harrisburg has very large manufacturing interests, especially in the production and working of steel and iron; machinery, boilers, castings, nails, and files, are among the goods produced, as also cotton-goods, brooms, tiles, bricks, shoes, leather, carriages, flour, and lumber. The river and the Pennsylvania Canal bring down large quantities of pine and hemlock lumber, to be distributed from this point. The town was named from John Harris, who settled here in 1726, but Harrisburg was not regularly founded before 1785. It was incorporated in 1791; became the State capital in 1812, and was chartered as a city in 1860. Population in 1870, 23,104; in 1880, 30,782; beside 5000 inhabitants of the close suburbs.

HARRISON, BENJAMIN (1740-1791), an American statesman, was born at City Point, Va., in 1740. He studied at William and Mary College, but did not graduate. He was elected to the State legislature in 1764, and was a member of the committee which prepared the memorials to the king, lords, and commons. He was afterwards speaker of the house. He was a member of all the State conventions held until the government under the Constitution was established. He was a delegate to the Continental Congress of 1774, and was one of the signers of the Declaration of Independence. He served as chairman of the Board of War, but in 1777 resigned his seat in Congress. Being then elected to the Virginia house of burgesses, he was chosen speaker and retained this position till 1782, when he became governor of the State and held this office till 1785. He was a delegate to the State convention of 1788 which ratified the Constitution of the United States, and opposed its adoption unless it should be amended. He died at City Point, Va., April, 1791. His son, William Henry Harrison, became the ninth President of the United States. (See HARRISON, WILLIAM HENRY, in the ENCYCLOPÆDIA BRITANNICA.)

HARRISON, BENJAMIN, twenty-third President of the United States, is the grandson of Pres. W. H. Harrison, and was born at North Bend, on the Miami River, Ohio, Aug. 20, 1833. He graduated at Miami University in 1852, and became a lawyer at Indianapolis in 1854, having already married Miss C. W. Scott, daughter of Dr. John W. Scott, the principal of an academy. In 1860 he was elected reporter of the State Supreme Court, but in July, 1862, he recruited the 70th Indiana regiment and became its colonel Aug. 7th. He joined Gen. Rosecrans' army at Murfreesboro, but was chiefly at Nashville until early in 1864, when he joined Gen. W. T. Sherman's march to Atlanta. His gallantry was conspicuous at Resaca, Kulp's Hill, and Peach Tree Creek. In the fall of 1864 he was renominated as reporter, returned to take part in the political campaign, and was again elected. His next military service was in the defence of Nashville against Hood, but he afterwards rejoined Sherman in North Carolina. He was brevetted brigadier-general March 22, 1865, and mustered out June 8. He returned to the practice of his profession and was also active in political affairs. In 1876 he was Republican candidate for governor of Indiana, but was defeated. In 1880 he was chosen U. S. Senator, but in 1885 he was defeated for re-election. In spite of these defeats he was generally acknowledged to be the leader of his party in the doubtful State of Indiana. In 1888 he was the Republican candidate for President and was elected after an animated campaign.

HART, JOEL T. (1810-1877), an American sculptor, was born in Clark co., Ky., in 1810. He attended school only a few months, but was fond of reading. While working as a stone-cutter at Lebanon, Ky., he began to model busts in clay. He received encouragement from prominent citizens, and in 1849 went to Florence, Italy, where he executed a marble statue of Henry Clay, which was erected in Louisville, Ky. He also produced a bronze statue of Clay, which was set up in New Orleans. His ideal works, Angelica, Woman Triumphant, and Il Penseroso, show delicate perceptions of beauty and skill in expressing them, but he excelled in portrait-busts. He died at Florence, Italy, March 1, 1877.

HART, JOHN (1708-1780), an American patriot, was born at Hopewell, N. J., in 1708. He was the son of a farmer, and followed the same calling. For several years he was a member of the provincial congress, and was distinguished for his patriotism and influence. In June, 1776, he was chosen a delegate to the Continental Congress, in which he signed the Declaration of Independence. In 1777-78 he was a member of the New Jersey council of safety, and suffered much from the loyalists, who drove him from his home. But the capture of the Hessians by Washington enabled him to return and spend the remainder of his life in quiet. He died at Hopewell, N. J., in 1780.

HART, JOHN SEELY (1810-1877), an American author, was born at Stockbridge, Mass., Jan. 28, 1810. His father's family removed to Wilkes-Barre, Pa., where he was brought up. He graduated at Princeton in 1830, and after teaching for a year at Natchez, Miss., became in 1832 tutor of ancient languages at Princeton, and in 1834 adjunct-professor. From 1836 to 1841 he was principal of Edgehill School at Princeton; from 1842 to 1859 principal of the Philadelphia High School. He then resigned, and became editor of the publications of the American Sunday-School Union. In 1863 he was made principal of the New Jersey State Normal School at Trenton. In 1872 he became professor of rhetoric and the English language at Princeton. He died at Philadelphia, March 26, 1877. He was a frequent contributor to periodicals, and edited some literary magazines and illustrated annuals. He published *Spenser and the Faery Queen* (1847), several text-books on English grammar, literature, rhetoric, and composition, and some religious works.

HART, SOLOMON ALEXANDER, an English painter of Jewish descent, was born at Plymouth, in April, 1806. His father, Samuel Hart, had studied painting under Northcote, and in 1820 settled in London. Solomon studied at the Royal Academy, and in 1826 exhibited a miniature of his father, but his first oil-painting, Instructions, was exhibited in 1828. He devoted himself chiefly to historical painting, and in 1840 was made an academician. Visiting Italy in 1841, he made drawings of many places of historical note, which he afterwards used in his paintings. In 1857 he was made professor of painting in the Royal Academy, and in 1865 became its librarian. Among his works are Wolsey and Buckingham (1834); Cœur de Lion and Saladin, Milton Visiting Galileo in Prison, Raphael and Pope Julius II.

HARTE, FRANCIS BRET, an American poet and humorist, was born at Albany, N. Y., in 1837. At the age of 17 he went to California, where, after some experience of life in mining towns, he became editor of a paper in San Francisco. From 1864 to 1870 he was secretary of the U. S. Mint in that city, and in 1868 he was made editor of the newly-founded *Overland Monthly*. In its pages first appeared those vivid, dramatic sketches of California mining-life which have given their author world-wide reputation. The first was "The Luck of Roaring Camp;" then followed "The Outcasts of Poker Camp" and "Tennessee's Partner." Even more widely read were his verses on "The Heathen Chinee," which the author afterwards was reluctant to admit to his *Complete Poetical Works* (1873). In 1871 Mr. Harte removed to Boston, where he was a leading contributor to the *Atlantic Monthly*. He has since been U. S. consul in Germany and Scotland. One of his earliest publications was *Condensed Novels* (1867), containing caricatures of the principal novelists of the time. In later years his poetry has been chiefly in a serious vein, but his idyls of California life still continue his masterpiece.

HARTFORD, the capital of Connecticut and the county-seat of Hartford county, is on the W. bank of Connecticut River, at the head of regular steam-navigation, 50 miles from its mouth. It is on the New Haven, Hartford, and Springfield Railroad, here crossed by the main line of the New York and New England Railroad, of which a branch runs to Springfield. It is also a terminus of the Hartford and Connecticut Valley and the Connecticut Western Railroads. Railway and carriage bridges connect the city with the quaint and sleepy old town of East Hartford, with its wide and densely shaded main street, a typical New England village. Hartford mostly occupies a high and diversified site, and is in the main a remarkably compact and well-built city, the number of fine public and private buildings being unusually large. Among the public buildings and institutions are the splendid marble State-house (a Gothic structure); Trinity College (Episcopal), which occupies very handsome and commodious buildings; the Connecticut Theological Institute (Congregational); the State Asylum for Deaf-mutes; the Connecticut Retreat for the Insane; the city high and grammar school, with a noble building; the Wadsworth Athenæum, containing the Watkinson library of reference (35,000 volumes), the library of the Young Men's Institute (31,000 volumes), and the valuable library (20,000 volumes) and collections of the Connecticut Historical Society, as well as a picture-gallery and a collection of statuary; the city hospital, orphan asylum, State library; the U. S. building, including post-office, court-rooms, etc.; the State arsenal; the county buildings, etc. Many of the banks, stores, insurance companies, and churches have buildings of great architectural merit.

Hartford has an extensive wholesale and retail trade, and is especially distinguished for its large number of companies for life, accident, and fire insurance. It is also a great centre of the subscription-book business. Commercially it is noted as the principal seat in New England of the trade in leaf-tobacco. It has about 40 churches, among them a cathedral, the city being the see of a Roman Catholic bishop. The water-supply is ample, and the principal streets are substantially paved. Hartford is the seat of important and varied manufactures, the principal industrial establishment within the city limits being the extensive works of the Colt fire-arms company. The city is a centre for the offices of the numerous manufacturing establishments of the Connecticut Valley, some of which have handsome warehouses in the city. As a centre of large wealth and social culture, Hartford has attracted many persons of literary distinction.

Hartford was named after Hertford, in England. The Dutch built a fort here in 1633; but in 1635 was occupied by English immigrants from Massachusetts. In 1637 its name was changed from Newtown to Hartford. Its city charter dates from 1784. It shared with New Haven the honor of being the State capital until 1873, when it became the sole capital. The population in 1870 was 37,180; in 1880, 42,015.

HARTINGTON, SPENCER COMPTON CAVENDISH, MARQUIS OF, an English statesman, was born July 23, 1833. He is the eldest surviving son of the seventh Duke of Devonshire, and was educated at Trinity College, Cambridge, where he graduated in 1854. He accompanied Earl Granville to Russia in 1856 to attend the coronation of the Emperor Alexander II. In March, 1857, he entered Parliament as a representative of North Lancashire. He is a Liberal in politics, and in 1859 moved the vote by which Lord Derby lost the control of the government. In March, 1863, Lord Hartington was appointed a lord of the admiralty, and soon after under-secretary of war. In February, 1866, when Lord Russell's ministry was reconstructed, he was made secretary of war, and he went out of office with his colleagues in the following July. In December, 1868, Lord Hartington was defeated in North Lancashire, but being made postmaster-general in Mr. Gladstone's cabinet he was elected from Radnor. In January, 1871, he was made chief-secretary for Ireland, and held that post until 1874, when the Liberals again lost their power. In 1875, when Mr. Gladstone sought to retire from the leadership of that party, the Marquis of Hartington was appointed to succeed him. But when in 1880 the same party was restored to power, chiefly through the remarkable Mid-Lothian campaign of Mr. Gladstone, the latter again took the helm of affairs. Lord Hartington was then made secretary of state for India, and was re-elected from Lancashire. He retired with Mr. Gladstone in 1885, but in February, 1886, did not resume his place, being opposed to the concessions made to Parnell's demands. The Marquis of Hartington is faithful in his devotion to public duty, and earnest in his advocacy of Liberal principles. He has twice been chosen rector of Edinburgh University.

HARTMANN, KARL ROBERT EDUARD VON, a German philosopher, was born at Berlin, Feb. 23, 1842, being the son of Gen. Robert von Hartmann. In 1858, having finished his course at the gymnasium, he entered the artillery service. In consequence of a severe injury to the knee, he was compelled in 1865 to retire from military duty, and henceforth devoted himself to philosophy. His first work, *Die Philosophie des Unbewussten* (1869), has attained a remarkable popularity, having passed through nine editions. Proceeding from Schopenhauer's doctrine of the irrational will and Hegel's of the absolute idea, Hartmann sets forth both as necessary to the true philosophy of the world. Both the will and the idea are attributes or functions of the same unconscious spirit, and the world is their product. Hartmann's works show deep insight into the workings of the human spirit, and constant endeavor to find corroboration for his philosophic theories in the physical sciences. His early acceptance of Schopenhauer's pessimism has been modified somewhat by the doctrine of evolution. His theory of ethics is presented in *Phænomenologie des sittlichen Bewusstseins* (1879), and his philosophy of religion in *Das religiöse Bewusstsein der Menschheit* (1880), and in *Die Religion des Geistes* (1882). Hartmann has been indefatigable as a writer on all the political, educational, and social questions of the day, which he has treated with reference to his philosophical principles. He has also criticised freely the works of other philosophers, and has engaged in many controversies. Among his works are *Dramatische Dichtungen von Karl Robert* (1871).

HARTRANFT, JOHN FREDERIC, an American general, was born at New Hanover, Pa., Dec. 16, 1830. He graduated at Union College, N. Y., in 1853, and was admitted to the bar at Norristown, Pa., in 1859. On the outbreak of the civil war he was colonel of militia, and was made colonel of the Fourth Pennsylvania regiment, which enlisted for three months. He was a volunteer aide to Gen. W. B. Franklin at the first battle of Bull Run. As colonel of the Fifty-first Pennsylvania volunteers he accompanied Gen. Burnside in his expedition to Roanoke Island in February, 1862; in August he commanded a brigade under Gen. Pope, at second Bull Run; in September, under Gen. McClellan, fighting at Antietam; and in December, under Gen. Burnside, at Fredericksburg. He was afterwards transferred to Kentucky, and in June, 1863, commanded a brigade before Vicksburg. Afterwards, at the siege of Knoxville, Tenn., he assisted in repulsing Longstreet. He was commissioned a brigadier-general May 12, 1864, and served through, under Gen. Grant, from the battle of the Wilderness to the capture of Richmond. In October, 1865, he was elected auditor-general of Pennsylvania, and served two terms. In October, 1872, he was elected governor of Pennsylvania, and served two terms. The principal events of his administration were the revision of the State constitution, the celebration of the Centennial anniversary of the Declaration of American Independence by the International Exhibition at Philadelphia, from May 10 to Nov. 10, 1876; and the railroad strike of July 17–Aug. 4, 1877, in which the depot at Pittsburg was destroyed. Gov. Hartranft, who had gone on a summer excursion to the Pacific coast, promptly returned, and ordering out the militia soon restored quiet. On the expiry of his term he settled in Philadelphia, and in 1880 was appointed postmaster of Philadelphia. From 1882 to 1885 he was collector of the port of Philadelphia.

HARTSHORNE, EDWARD (1818–1885), an American physician, was born at Philadelphia, May 14, 1818, being the son of Dr. Joseph Hartshorne (1779–1850), also a distinguished physician. He graduated at Princeton College in 1837, and studied medicine at the University of Pennsylvania. He was resident surgeon at the Pennsylvania Hospital (1841–43), and afterwards physician of the Eastern State Penitentiary at Philadelphia. He then travelled in Europe, observing especially the hospitals, asylums, and prisons, and on his return engaged in general practice in Philadelphia. He became an attending surgeon at the Pennsylvania Hospital, and during the civil war served as consulting surgeon in army hospitals, and in connection with the U. S. Sanitary Commission. He held many offices of trust and honor in his profession. He contributed to the *American Journal of the Medical Sciences* and other medical periodicals, and edited Taylor's *Manual of Medical Jurisprudence*. He died June 22, 1885.

HARTSHORNE, HENRY, an American physician and poet, brother of the preceding, was born at Philadelphia, March 16, 1823. He graduated at Haverford College in 1839, and studied medicine in the University of Pennsylvania. He was professor of the practice of medicine in Pennsylvania College in 1859, and in 1865 was made professor of hygiene in the University of Pennsylvania. He also held other professorships in Haverford College and in the Woman's Medical College of Pennsylvania. He contributed to various medical periodicals, and became editor of the *Friends' Review* in 1874. His professional works include a *Conspectus of the Medical Sciences* and *The Principles and Practice of Medicine*. He also published *Summer Songs* (1865).

HARVARD COLLEGE, in Cambridge, Mass., was founded in 1636, six years after the settlement of Boston. In that year the legislature of the colony of Massachusetts Bay voted £400 to establish a college, and in 1637 chose Newtown, across the Charles River, as a site, because the town was near enough to the capital to be safe against the attacks of the Indians. In 1638 Rev. John Harvard, a Puritan clergyman, who had come to New England in 1637, left

See Vol. XI. p. 447 Am. ed. (p. 500 Edin. ed.).

his will £779 and his library of 300 volumes to aid the proposed college, which as yet existed only on paper. By his generous act the authorities were enabled to open the college at once, and gave it, out of gratitude to its first benefactor, the name of Harvard. At the same time the name of the town was changed to Cambridge, in memory of the university town in England where John Harvard and many of the earlier colonists had received their education.

In 1650, under the first president, Rev. Henry Dunster, the college received its first charter from the legislature. By the terms of this charter the government of the college and the management of its financial affairs were intrusted to the corporation, composed of the president, five fellows, and the treasurer. In certain cases, however, the corporation were obliged to obtain the consent of the board of overseers, which had been in existence for some time before the grant of the charter. This board consisted of the governor, lieutenant-governor, and the magistrates of the jurisdiction, and the elders of the churches of the six neighboring towns. The history of the college has been the effort to rid the board of overseers first of its religious and then of its political element, and to make it, the board, representative of a university. The charter of 1650, with the constitution it enforced, remained in effect with various modifications until 1865.

In the colonial period of its existence the avowed object of Harvard College was to train men for the ministry. A printing-press was early established for the spread of religious books, and here in Cambridge John Eliot printed his Indian translation of the Bible. Of the few Indians, however, who were attracted to the college only one graduated. The Quinquennial Catalogue still contains under the class of 1665 the name of "Caleb Cheeshahteaumuck Indus." In the earlier years the president and two tutors were considered enough to manage the college, and the number of the students was in proportion between 20 and 30. As fully one-half of these became clergymen, the course of study was largely theological in character. From the influence of the clergy at that time throughout New England the college was thus brought into intimate relations with the people. During this colonial period, to the year 1692, the gifts amounted to $32,000 and 1744 acres of land, and the grants of the legislature to $14,000.

In the provincial period, from the end of the colonial government in 1692 to the Revolution, the college gradually underwent a change. It still retained its theological character, but in a more liberal form. It sent forth fewer ministers in proportion to the number of students and altered the course of study to suit the demands for a more secular form of education. Latin was given up as the spoken language of the college. In 1740 Whitefield, the famous Methodist preacher, had no hesitancy in boldly charging the college with a want of religion, so little was the tendency of the age understood. The increasing toleration is well shown in the donations of Thomas Hollis, a London merchant, for the endowment of a professorship of theology in 1722 and of a professorship of mathematics in 1726. A Baptist and a man of liberal views, Hollis required the incumbent of his endowment to accept no particular form of belief beyond the Christian religion. Beside the gifts of Hollis and his family, who deserve to rank among the greatest benefactors of the college, chairs were endowed by Thomas Hancock and three other Boston merchants. From this period date the first college buildings, which are still standing, six in number; one of which was built to replace a building destroyed by fire while occupied by the general court. The number of students gradually increased, until by the time of the Revolution it had reached 160. The corresponding increase in the number of teachers led in 1725 to the formation of all the instructors into a faculty, which had charge of the interior organization of the college. At the outbreak of the war for independence the college was removed to Concord for two years (1774-76), though the number of students was not materially diminished. During the siege of Boston, General Washington occupied Cambridge as the American head-quarters and received from the college the first honorary degree of LL. D. The gifts during the provincial period were about $72,000 in money and 3113 acres of land, and the grants of the legislature amounted to about $100,000.

The national period, from the Revolution to the civil war, represents the final change of the college into a university. The prescribed course of study, which in the earlier years led to the ministry as its end, was gradually widening into a broad field which should teach all the subjects properly belonging to a liberal education. This change was not accomplished without difficulty, and naturally the first reform came in the nature of the governing board. By the charter of 1650 the government was lodged in the hands of the statesmen and ministers of the colony. The time had gone by, however, when these two classes monopolized the best men in the community. In 1810 an amendment to the State constitution allowed the board to consist of 15 laymen and 15 Congregational ministers. But in 1842, after a long struggle, this sectarian distinction was abolished, and ministers belonging to other faiths than the Congregational were made eligible for the board of overseers. Finally, in 1851, all religious restrictions were removed, and the board was allowed to be composed of ministers and laymen alike, one-sixth to be renewed every year.

Hand-in-hand with the abolition of sectarianism went the question of a connection with the State. The same law, in 1851, which threw open the board to laymen, left the election of the overseers in the hands of the legislature. This connection with the State was early found to be an evil, and a law was passed in 1865 by which the election of overseers was placed in the hands of the bachelors of arts of four years' standing. Thus the college severed the last link which bound it to the church and State, and passed under the control of its graduates.

During this national period the transition from a college to a university led to the addition of various departments to the old academical instruction. In 1783 the medical school was founded, and removed to Boston in 1810, in order to take advantage of a wider field for practice. The divinity school, as a separate department, dates from 1815. The law school was opened in 1817. In 1847 a large donation by Abbott Lawrence resulted in the foundation of the Lawrence Scientific School. In 1805 the botanic garden was established, and in 1846 the observatory. One of the notable additions was made in 1859, when the museum of comparative zoölogy was founded, mainly through the efforts of the elder Agassiz. The last grant of the State was made in 1814, when an annual sum of $10,000 was appropriated for 10 years. Since then the university has relied on gifts from private individuals and the tuition-fees. Besides the endowment of many chairs, no less than 16 buildings were added to Harvard during this period (1776–1865), built partly through private gifts, partly by the corporation. From the first catalogue, published in 1819, we find the names of 388 students. During this century the instruction became more liberal.

The period since 1865 marks the existence of the university. During these years the growth has been rapid. Five new departments have been added. In 1866 the Peabody Museum was built from the fund given for that purpose by George Peabody. The dental school, with head-quarters in Boston, was established in 1868, and the Bussey Institution, a school of agriculture in Jamaica Plain, near Boston, in 1871. In 1872 the Arnold Arboretum was founded, as the nucleus of a school of forestry. The last addition is the veterinary school, which was started in Boston in 1882. Thirteen new buildings have been added to the university, besides five dormitories, which are owned by private individuals. Of these buildings two deserve special notice. Memorial Hall, built in 1873 by subscription, commemorates the share which the graduates of the university bore in the war of 1861–65. It contains at one end a large dining-hall, capable of seating over 700 students, which is used as commons; and at the other, Landers Theatre, built after the form of a classic theatre, and seating 1300 persons, which is used for the commencement exercises and other solemnities of the university. The other building is the Hemenway Gymnasium, which is one of the leading institutions of the kind in the country. In 1886, under the presidency of Charles W. Eliot, LL. D., the number of students in all departments of the university is 1662 and the total number of teachers 184, besides 22 librarians, proctors, and other officers.

The treasurer's statement gives the funds of the university at nearly $5,000,000, and the income at over $600,000. The instruction is wholly elective, with the exception of certain prescribed courses in the freshman year. The rest of the work is left to the choice of the student under certain restrictions, and the last vestige of the old theological training has passed away.

(G. R. N.)

HASE, KARL AUGUST, a German theologian, was born at Steinbach, Saxony, Aug. 25, 1800. He was educated at Altenburg and at Leipsic, but being driven thence for taking part in the *Burschenschaft* disturbances, finished his studies at Erlangen. In 1823 he became a *privat docent* of theology at Tübingen, but was brought to trial on account of his old offence as a *Burschenschafter*, and imprisoned for eleven months. In 1830 he settled at Jena as professor of theology, and in 1883, after fifty-three years' service, was permitted to retire with various marks of honor. In 1844 he became one of the editors of the *Protestantische Kirchenzeitung*, the organ of the German rationalists. His numerous works have been directed chiefly to reconciling the Scriptures with the conclusions of modern science. His principal work is *Evangelische Dogmatik* (1825; 6th ed., 1870), to which *Gnosis* (3 vols., 1828; 2d ed., 1870) is a supplement. His *Leben Jesu* (1829) was translated into English by J. Freeman Clarke (1859), and has been enlarged by the author under the name *Geschichte Jesu* (1875). He has also published numerous historical and biographical sketches: *Neue Propheten* (1851); *Franz von Assisi* (1854); *Catarina von Siena* (1862); and has taken part in many controversies. His *Handbuch der protestantischen Polemik gegen die Roman-Katholische Kirche* (1863; 4th ed., 1878) is noteworthy. His *Ideale und Irrthümer* (1872) is an autobiography.

HASE, KARL BENEDICT (1780–1864), a German philologist, was born near Weimar, May 11, 1780. He studied theology and philosophy at Jena and Helmstedt, and in 1801 went to Paris, where in 1805 he obtained a position in the Imperial library. In 1816 he was made professor of Greek palæography and of modern Greek at the *École des langues Orientales*, in 1830 professor of German language and literature at the Polytechnic school, in 1832 keeper of manuscripts in the library, and in 1852 professor of comparative grammar in the University of Paris. He died at Paris, March 21, 1864. He was noted for his knowledge of the Byzantine historians. He edited *Leo Diaconus* (1819), and was the chief editor of a new edition of the Greek Lexicon of Stephanus, which was completed after his death by W. and L. Dinderf.

HASSLER, FERDINAND RUDOLPH (1770–1843), an American scientist, was born at Aarau, Switzerland, Oct. 6, 1770. He early attained a high reputation for mathematical ability, and was engaged in a trigonometrical survey of Switzerland. Removing to the United States, he was brought into notice by his fellow-countryman, Albert Gallatin, and became professor of mathematics at West Point in 1807. In the same year President Jefferson recommended the establishment of a national coast survey; Congress approved the suggestion and made an appropriation, and Secretary Gallatin invited plans for the prosecution of the work. That of Prof. Hassler was accepted, and in 1811 he was sent to Europe to procure the instruments necessary for the undertaking. In consequence of the war with Great Britain he was detained in Europe until 1815, but on his return he was made first superintendent of the survey. He began his operations with a survey of New York harbor, but before he had published the result of his first year's labor the whole work was suspended. He was afterwards made chief of the bureau of weights and measures, and in 1832, when the coast survey was resumed, Hassler was restored to his former position as superintendent. He continued to direct the work until his death, which occurred at Philadelphia, Nov. 20, 1843. He published some text-books on mathematics, *System of the Universe*, and many valuable reports. (See COAST AND GEODETIC SURVEY.)

HAUPT, HERMAN, an American general and engineer, was born at Philadelphia, March 26, 1817. He graduated at West Point in 1835, and entered the infantry service, but soon after resigned and became assistant engineer on the public works of Pennsylvania. In 1844 he was appointed professor of civil-engineering in Pennsylvania College. In 1847 he became principal engineer of the Philadelphia and Columbia Railroad, and in 1849 its superintendent. From 1856 to 1861 he was principal engineer of the Hoosac Tunnel, Mass. In the civil war he served first on the staff of Gen. J. McDowell, and had charge of the transportation service. He was afterwards made chief of the bureau of military railroads. Some of the devices which he put in operation in the army are described under BRIDGES, Vol. II., p. 645. After the war Gen. Haupt returned to the practice of his profession as a railroad engineer, and was connected with railroads in the Southern States and with the Northern Pacific Railroad. He has published several works, among which are *Hints on Bridge Building* (1840); *General Theory of Bridge Construction* (1853); *Military Bridges* (1864).

HAUSSMANN, BARON GEORGES EUGÈNE, a French administrator, was born at Paris, March 27, 1809. After being trained as a musician, he became an advocate. Soon after the Revolution of 1830 he was made sub-prefect of Nérac (1833), and passed thence to St. Girons (1840) and Blaye (1842). Under the presidency of Louis Napoleon he held other prefectures, and after the establishment of the empire he was called to the prefecture of the Seine in June, 1853. He soon entered upon the vast system of public works by which the city of Paris was almost completely transformed. He turned the Bois de Boulogne into a public park, added numerous other parks in different directions, laid out the Boulevard de Sebastopol, then carried twenty boulevards through the old city, tore down old buildings, put up new hospitals, public halls, bridges, churches, theatres, and the gorgeous opera-house. The immense sums required for these purposes were obtained by successive loans contracted by the city of Paris. At last Baron Haussmann's financial administration became the subject of investigation by the *Corps Législatif* in 1869, and it was found that he had issued bonds far in excess of those legally authorized, yet a new issue of bonds was at once authorized, and subscriptions were received for five times the amount asked. On Jan. 5, 1870, he was removed by imperial decree, yet was pensioned. After the fall of the empire in September, he went abroad for some months, but in 1871, having returned, he was made a director of the Crédit Mobilier, and did much to restore its influence. After two failures to gain an entrance to the *Corps Législatif*, he was elected as a Bonapartist from Ajaccio, Corsica, in 1877. He took part only in the discussion of the finances and of public works. The municipal museum which he had established at the Hotel de Ville was destroyed with that building by the Communists in May, 1871. The *Histoire générale de Paris*, which was illustrated by this museum, was published in 16 volumes.

HAÜY, VALENTIN, ABBÉ (1745–1822), a French instructor of the blind, was born at St. Just, Nov. 13, 1745, being a brother of the celebrated mineralogist, R. J. Haüy. (See ENCYCLOPÆDIA BRITANNICA.) He was a man of generous impulses, and becoming acquainted with a blind pianist was led to make the instruction of the blind his life-work. For this purpose he established schools, and though they had little success yet his invention of printing with raised letters for their use has made his name memorable. Although an abbé, he was not a priest, and was twice married. He died at Paris, June 3, 1822. He published an *Essai sur l'éducation des aveugles* (1786) and some other works.

HAVEN, ALICE BRADLEY (1828–1863), an American author, was born at Hudson, N. Y., Sept. 13, 1828. Her name was originally Emily Bradley. While attending school she sent to the *Saturday Gazette*, of Philadelphia, sketches signed "Alice G. Lee." This led to an acquaintance with the editor, Joseph C. Neal, to whom she was married in 1846, having at his request assumed the name Alice. On his death a few months later she took charge of the literary department of the paper, and conducted it successfully until 1853, when she was married to Samuel L. Haven, and removed to Mamaroneck, N. Y. She still continued to write juvenile books, and poems and sketches for the magazines. She died at Mamaroneck, Aug. 23, 1863. Her publications include *The Gossips of Rivertown* (1850); *No Such Word as Fail* (1855); *Out of Debt, Out of Danger* (1861); *Lessons for Lent* (1867); *Home Stories* (1868).

HAVEN, ERASTUS OTIS (1820–1881), an American bishop, was born at Boston, Mass., Nov. 1, 1820. He graduated at Wesleyan University, Conn., in 1842, and engaged in teaching at Sudbury, Mass. He was principal of Amenia Seminary, N. Y., from 1846 to 1848, when he entered the ministry in the Methodist Episcopal Church. After holding pastorates in New York, he was made professor of Latin in the University of Michigan in 1853, but in the next year was transferred to the chair of English literature and history. In 1856 he became editor of *Zion's Herald* at Boston, and held this position till 1863, being also in the meantime a member of the State Board of Education and a State senator. In 1863 he was recalled to the University of Michigan to be its president, and after six years' successful discharge of the duties of that position, was made president of the North-western University, Evanston, Ill., a denominational college. In 1872 he was elected by the General Conference secretary of the board of education, and in 1874 he was made chancellor of Syracuse University. In 1880 he was elected a bishop. While journeying on the Pacific coast in discharge of his duties, he died at Salem, Oregon, Aug. 2, 1881. He was an eloquent preacher and had great executive ability. He had been a member of five general conferences. He published a treatise on *Rhetoric* and other text-books, and after his death his *Autobiography* (1883) was edited by Rev. C. C. Stratton.

HAVEN, GILBERT (1821–1880), an American bishop, was born at Malden, Mass., Sept. 21, 1821. He graduated at Wesleyan University, Conn., in 1846, became professor in Amenia Seminary, N. Y., and then principal from 1848 to 1851. Having joined the New England Conference of the Methodist Episcopal Church, he became noted as a preacher, lecturer, and writer. He was an earnest opponent of slavery and of Romanism. In 1861 he served as chaplain of the Eighth Massachusetts regiment, and in 1862 went to Europe. On account of his interest in the colored people, he was sent on a special mission among the Southern freedmen at the close of the war. He was editor of *Zion's Herald* from 1867 to 1872, and was then elected bishop, with residence at Atlanta, Ga. He travelled extensively in discharge of his duty, visiting especially Mexico and Liberia. On his return from the latter, his health was impaired, and he died at Malden, Mass., Jan. 8, 1880. Besides some volumes of sermons he published *The Pilgrim's Wallet* (1864), relating his travels in Europe, and *Our Next-Door Neighbor* (1874), giving sketches of Mexico.

HAVEN, JOSEPH (1816–1874), an American clergyman, was born at Dennis, Mass., Jan. 4, 1816. He graduated at Amherst College in 1835, and studied in the Union Theological Seminary, New York, and at Andover. He became pastor of the Congregational church at Ashland, Mass., in 1840, and at Brookline, Mass., in 1846. He was appointed professor of moral and mental philosophy in Amherst College in 1850, and was called to be professor of systematic theology in the Chicago Theological Seminary in 1858. On account of ill health he resigned in 1870 and went to Europe. In 1874 he was appointed professor of mental and moral philosophy in the University of Chicago, and died there, May 23, 1874. He published *Mental Philosophy* (1837); *Moral Philosophy* (1859); *Studies in Philosophy and Theology* (1869); and many sermons and essays.

HAVERFORD COLLEGE, in the township of

Haverford, Delaware co., Pa., 9 miles from Philadelphia, was founded in the year 1832 by prominent members of the Society of Friends, whose object was to provide a place for the instruction of their sons in the higher learning and for moral training, which should be healthful, agreeable, and sheltered from temptations. A farm was bought of about 220 acres, at an elevation of nearly 400 feet above tide-water, well furnished with springs and diversified with woods, fields, and meadows. A tract now consisting of upwards of 70 acres was set off by an experienced English landscape-gardener, and planted with a large variety of trees and shrubbery, constituting the academic grove in which the college buildings stand. This park is now the most beautiful which any American college can boast. The "Founders' Hall," a large and well-constructed building of stone, was finished in 1833, and in the autumn of that year Haverford School was opened. This modest title was borne for upwards of twenty years, although a full collegiate course of study was pursued from the beginning. Early in 1856 the institution was incorporated as a college, with the right of conferring academic degrees, which it first exercised at the commencement in that year.

Barclay Hall, built in 1876, a strikingly beautiful building of Port Deposit gneiss, 220 feet in length, and with a tower 110 feet high, furnishes studies and bedrooms. There are two astronomical observatories, one built in 1852, the other in 1884, containing a refracting equatorial telescope of 10 inches aperture, another of $8\frac{1}{4}$ inches aperture, and various instruments and appliances. The students have free access to the observatory, and enjoy opportunities for astronomical observation such as are seldom offered. A tasteful and well-proportioned building, of light-colored gneiss from the neighboring township of Upper Darby, contains the library and a hall used for addresses, society meetings, and the public exercises of the college. Here some 20,000 volumes are always ready for the use of the students, selected with great care in all departments of knowledge. A carpenters' shop was built soon after the opening of the institution, as a place where the students might find profitable exercise and amusement in the use of tools. This was fitted up in 1884 for the department of mechanical engineering then established, and contains a forge, steam-engines, and appropriate machines and tools.

The chemical laboratory was set up in 1833, in a room adjoining Founders' Hall. The present laboratory was built in 1853, and has several times been enlarged and improved. It is amply furnished and under skilful management. In Founders' Hall there is a museum of natural history and geology and a physical laboratory. This hall contains also the recitation-rooms and the dining-hall.

The college has always been famed for its healthiness, the consequence of its fortunate rural situation, the wholesome conditions of the students' lives, and their interest in cricket, foot-ball, and other games and various physical exercises. There is a well-furnished gymnasium, in which exercise is required of all the students under the direction of an experienced physician.

The officers in 1886 are as follows: president, Thomas Chase, LL. D., a graduate of Harvard University, who was a member of the American company of revisers of the translation of the New Testament, is the editor of a series of classical text-books very widely used, and has written many reviews, addresses, and literary articles; dean, Isaac Sharpless, Sc. D., the author of excellent text-books in astronomy, geometry, and physics; Pliny Earle Chase, LL. D., professor of philosophy and logic; Allen Clapp Thomas, A. M., professor of history and political science; Lyman Beecher Hall, Ph. D. of Göttingen, professor of chemistry and physics; Edwin Davenport, A. M. of Harvard, professor of Greek and of English composition; Seth K. Gifford, A. M., professor of Latin and German. There are other professors, distinguished in their respective departments and several assistants.

The college is marked by certain special excellences, such as: First, good moral and religious influences. Endeavors are made to imbue the minds and hearts of the students with the truths of the Christian religion, and to inculcate pure morals under the restraints of a judicious discipline. Second, thorough scholarship. The teaching is of the highest quality. The classes are small enough to secure the regular performance of work and the opportunity for individual instruction. The absence of distractions, and the example and influence of the professors, enable a large amount of honest and fruitful work to be done. Third, the healthfulness and pleasantness of the student life.

In 1885 Jacob P. Jones, a prominent Friend and citizen of Philadelphia, bequeathed the greater part of his large estate to Haverford College, in accordance with a promise made fourteen years before. This endowment gives the assurance of largely increased usefulness and excellence.

HAVERGAL, FRANCES RIDLEY (1836–1879), an English poet, born at Astley, Worcestershire, Dec. 14, 1836, the youngest child of the Rev. Dr. W. H. Havergal (1793–1870), canon of Worcester, and a celebrated composer of church music. Educated in the best English and German schools, she early displayed remarkable talents as a pianist, organist, and singer; but the impulse for the poetical expression of her overmastering religious feelings gradually led her to the adopting the writing of devotional works as her life-work. She died at Caswell Bay, near Swansea, Wales, June 3, 1879. Among her many published books the most are devotional writings in prose and poetry, including *Little Pillows*; *The Ministry of Song*; *Morning Bells*; *Our Work and our Blessings*; *Under His Shadow*; *My King* (1877); *Kept for the Master's Use* (1879); *Swiss Letters* (1882). Miss Havergal's abilities as a poet were great, but in a literary point of view their effect is lessened by the intensity and seriousness of purpose which at all times underlie her writing. Her personal devotion to religious and charitable work was complete and unqualified; and her faith was of the kind that knows no doubts. The *Memorials* (1880) of her life, prepared by her sister, are of great interest.

HAVERHILL, a city of Massachusetts, in Essex county, is on the north side of the Merrimack, at the head of tide-water, 18 miles from its mouth, and 33 miles north of Boston. The city is 11 miles long and 3 miles wide. It is connected with West Newberry, Groveland, and Bradford by iron bridges. Settled in 1639, it was incorporated as a town in 1642, and as a city in 1870. Its principal business is the manufacture of shoes, there being 200 factories; but it has also an iron-foundry, 3 hat-factories, and glass-works. Its principal buildings are the city hall and academy of music. It has 10 hotels, 4 national banks, 2 savings banks, 4 weekly and 3 daily newspapers, 21 churches, a high school, and 29 other schools. It is lighted with gas, and is supplied with water from Keuga Lake and three other small lakes. Its property is valued at $14,293,932, and its debt is $339,696. The thickly settled part has suffered from two large fires in 1873 and 1882.

HAWEIS, HUGH REGINALD, an English clergyman and author, was born at Egham, Surrey, April 3, 1838. He was educated at Trinity College. Cambridge, and graduated in 1859. After serving as curate of churches in London, he was in 1866 appointed incumbent of St. James' Church, Marylebone, where, besides the customary church services, he established others for the benefit of non-church-goers. He has been active in movements to diffuse information among the lower classes, such as "Penny Readings." He has also advocated the opening of museums on Sundays. He has been a frequent contributor to the magazines, and in 1868 was made editor of *Cassell's Magazine*. He visited the United States in 1885 and lectured in the principal cities. He has published *Music and Morals*; *Speech in Season*; *Arrows in the Air*.

HAWES, JOEL (1789–1867), an American clergyman, was born at Medway, Mass., Dec. 22, 1789. He graduated at Brown University in 1813, and studied theology at Andover. He was ordained pastor of the First Congregational Church, Hartford, Conn., in March, 1818, and held that position till his death at Gilead, Conn., June 5, 1867. He was very popular both as preacher and writer. Among his works are *Lectures to Young Men on the Formation of Character* (1828); *The Religion of the East* (1845); *An Offering to Home Missionaries* (1865).

HAWKS, FRANCIS LISTER (1798–1866), an American clergyman, was born at New-Berne, N. C., June 10, 1798. He graduated at the University of North Carolina in 1815, studied law, and was successful in practice. In 1827 he was ordained to the ministry in the Protestant Episcopal Church, and became assistant in churches at New Haven, Conn., and in Philadelphia. In 1830 he was chosen professor of divinity in Washington (afterwards Trinity) College, Hartford. In 1831 he became rector of St. Stephen's Church, New York, and in 1832 of St. Thomas' Church, where he officiated until 1843. Dr. Hawks was, in 1835, appointed by the General Convention historiographer of the American Episcopal Church, and therefore visited England, where he obtained many important documents. In 1839 he established at Flushing, on Long Island, a school for boys, but through its failure became deeply involved in debt. In 1843 he spent some time in Mississippi and was elected bishop of that diocese, but declined the office as he had in 1835 declined that of missionary bishop of the South-west. He was rector of Christ Church, New Orleans, from 1844 to 1849, and was chosen first president of Louisiana University. In 1849 he returned to New York to become rector of Calvary Church, his pecuniary embarrassments having been relieved by subscription. On the outbreak of the civil war Dr. Hawks, on account of his sympathy with the South, resigned his charge and in 1862 became rector of a church in Baltimore. At the close of the war he returned to New York, and was entering upon new work there when he died, Sept. 27, 1866. While practising law he had published some volumes of reports and a digest of cases decided in North Carolina. He afterwards published *Contributions to the Ecclesiastical History of the United States* (2 vols., 1836–41); *Commentary on the Constitution and Canons of the Protestant Episcopal Church* (1841); *Egypt and its Monuments* (1849); and *Documentary History of the Protestant Episcopal Church* (1863). He edited *Commodore Perry's Expedition to Japan* (1856); *Cyclopædia of Biography* (1856); *History of North Carolina* (1857), and other works.

HAWLEY, JOSEPH ROSWELL, an American statesman, was born at Stewartsville, N. C., Oct. 31, 1826. His father, Rev. Francis Hawley, a native of Connecticut, was a Presbyterian minister, and his mother was a native of North Carolina of Scotch descent. In 1837 the family removed to Connecticut, and about 1842 to Central New York. Joseph graduated at Hamilton College in 1847, studied law, and began practice at Hartford, Conn., in 1850. In the spring of 1857 he became editor of the *Hartford Evening Press*, a Republican paper just started. On the outbreak of the civil war he enlisted as a captain in a Connecticut regiment, and rose to the rank of brigadier-general and brevet major-general. He was mustered out of the service Jan. 15, 1866, and was elected governor of Connecticut in 1866. He was president of the Republican National Convention in 1868; secretary of the committee on resolutions in the Convention of 1872, and chairman of the similar committee in 1876. He was president of the U. S. Centennial Commission from its organization, in March, 1873, to the completion of the work of the Centennial Exhibition. He was elected to Congress in 1872 and twice re-elected. In 1881 he was elected to the U. S. Senate.

HAWTHORNE, JULIAN, an American novelist, son of the famous Nathaniel Hawthorne (for whom see ENCYCLOPÆDIA BRITANNICA), was born at Boston, Mass., June 22, 1846. He lived in and near Boston until June, 1852, when his father went to Liverpool, England, as American consul. He remained in Europe till 1860, and then returned to enter Harvard College, where he spent four years, but did not graduate. After another year at Harvard Scientific School, he went to Dresden, Germany, where he studied civil engineering. After his return to America in 1870 he was employed as an engineer in the department of docks, New York, under Gen. McClellan. He now began to contribute short stories to *Harper's Magazine*. While in Dresden in 1872–74 he published his first novels, *Bressant* and *Idolatry*. He resided in England from 1874 until 1882, when he returned to New York. Besides several short stories and a book of sketches called *Saxon Studies* he has published *Garth*; *Sebastian Strome*; *Dust*; *Fortune's Fool* (1883); *Beatrix Randolph* (1884). He has also published a biography, *Nathaniel Hawthorne and his Wife* (1884), and edited some of his father's writings.

HAY, JOHN, an American writer, born at Salem, Ill., Oct. 8, 1839. He graduated at Brown University in 1858; studied law, was admitted to the bar in 1861; was a private secretary, and afterwards aide-decamp to Pres. Lincoln, 1861–65; serving for a time in the field, and attaining the rank of colonel and assistant adjutant-general. He was a secretary of the legation in Paris, 1865–67; *chargé d'affaires* at Vienna, 1867–68; secretary of legation at Madrid, 1869–70; and in 1870 became a member of the editorial staff of the *New York Tribune*. His *Pike County Ballads* (1871), a widely-known series of dialect verses, and *Castilian Days* (1871), a prose work of merit, gave him a high reputation.

HAYDEN, FERDINAND VANDEVEER, an American

geologist, was born at Westfield, Mass., Sept. 7, 1829, removed in early life to Ohio, graduated at Oberlin College in 1850, and took a degree at the Albany Medical College in 1853. In the same year began his career as an explorer of the Western Territories, and as a collector of fossil remains. These explorations were carried on for a time at his own expense. but in 1856 he received a staff appointment as geologist in the Topographical Engineers. In 1861 he entered the army medical service; became an assistant medical inspector in 1864, and was somewhat later made chief medical officer of the forces in the Shenandoah Valley. He was (1865-72) a geological professor in the University of Pennsylvania, still conducting surveys in the West. In 1867 he was placed in charge of the U. S. Geological Survey of the Territories. He published a series of *Reports* embodying the results of this survey.

HAYES, ISAAC ISRAEL (1832-1881), an American explorer, was born at Chester, Pa., March 5, 1832. He studied medicine at the University of Pennsylvania, graduating in 1853. Having become interested in the Arctic explorations of Dr. E. K. Kane, he was appointed surgeon in the second Grinnell expedition, and sailed in the Advance. This vessel was at last hemmed in with ice so that Dr. Kane decided to abandon it and march over the ice to Upernavik. Some of the party, among whom was Dr. Hayes, went to seek help from the Eskimo, spent three months with these people and then returned to the ship. Dr. Hayes had become convinced that there is an "Open Polar Sea," and after his return to the United States in 1855 presented his views in public lectures. With the aid of scientific societies he fitted out a new expedition in July, 1860, taking 14 persons in the schooner United States, 133 tons. He reached Melville Bay, Aug. 23, and spent the winter at Port Foulke on the west coast of Greenland. In the following spring, pushing northward with dog-sledges, he reached on May 18 land in N. lat. 81° 37′, beyond which he saw open water, but his provisions being exhausted was obliged to return. The schooner got free of the ice in the summer, and returned to Boston in October, 1861. The civil war had begun, and Dr. Hayes, entering the army as a surgeon, served till its close. In 1869 he made a voyage to the southern coast of Greenland. In 1875 he was elected to the assembly in New York, and continued to be a member until 1880. He died at New York Dec. 17, 1881. Besides magazine articles Dr. Hayes wrote *An Arctic Boat-Journey* (1860); *The Open Polar Sea* (1867); *Cast Away in the Cold*, a story (1868); and *The Land of Desolation* (1872).

HAYES, RUTHERFORD BIRCHARD, twentieth President of the United States, was born at Delaware, Ohio, Oct. 4, 1822. His father having died, his uncle, Sardis Birchard, gave him the means for a liberal education. Rutherford graduated at Kenyon College in 1842, studied law at Harvard College, and was admitted to the bar at Marietta, Ohio, in 1845. He removed to Cincinnati in 1850, and became prominent in his profession, and was city solicitor from 1859 till 1861. Soon after the outbreak of the civil war he was appointed major of the Twenty-third Ohio infantry, and served in West Virginia. In October, 1861, he was made lieutenant-colonel, and while commanding his regiment was wounded at South Mountain, Sept. 14, 1862. He was then made colonel and soon was in command of a brigade. He fought with great gallantry in the Shenandoah Valley in 1864, and for his services at Cedar Creek he received his commission as brigadier-general. Though then elected to Congress, he served in the field till the close of the war, having been wounded four times. He was re-elected to Congress in 1866, was elected governor of Ohio in 1867, and re-elected by an increased majority in 1869. He declined a nomination for this office in 1871, and in 1872 was defeated as a candidate for Congress. In 1875 he was again made Republican candidate for governor and he was elected. In 1876, at the National Republican Convention at Cincinnati, on the seventh ballot, Gov. Hayes was nominated by a combination of those opposed to Blaine. At the election in November following the popular vote was 4,284,757 for S. J. Tilden, the Democratic candidate, and 4,033,950 for Hayes; but when the electoral votes came to be counted by Congress it appeared that 184 Democratic electors and 172 Republican electors had been regularly certified as chosen, while there were conflicting returns in regard to 13 votes—4 from Florida, 8 from Louisiana, and 1 from Oregon; and there were also objections to the vote of South Carolina. As Congress found itself practically unable to determine the questions involved, it referred the matter to a special electoral commission devised for the occasion. This commission consisted of five Senators, five Representatives, and five Judges of the Supreme Court. After full argument on all the points, the Commission decided in every case by a majority of one that Congress was bound to accept the official returns of the State authorities as final. Congress in accordance with this decision found on March 2, 1877, that Hayes had received 185 electoral votes and Tilden 184. On March 4 Hayes was duly inaugurated as President.

At the outset of his administration he undertook to conciliate the people of the Southern States. As an earnest of this he made D. M. Key of Tennessee postmaster-general. The other positions in the cabinet were filled with prominent conservative Republicans. He appointed a number of Congressmen to visit and report on the measures necessary to restore peace and harmony in the South. In accordance with their advice he withdrew the U. S. troops who had been employed in upholding Republican State officers in South Carolina and Louisiana, and he recognized the Democratic State officers. Throughout his administration Mr. Hayes persevered in his course of conciliation towards the South, though strenuous opposition was made by the recognized leaders of the Republican party in Congress. The latter became known as "Stalwarts," and they applied to those who favored the President's policy the derisive epithet "Half-breeds." Yet the actual result of the President's efforts to allay strife in the South was a gradual restoration of the Republican party to the confidence of the people of the North, as was shown by the results of the elections in the latter part of Mr. Hayes' term and the election of his Republican successor without such dispute as had attended his own. The various branches of the administration had been wisely and economically managed and the country was steadily prosperous. Specie payments, which had been suspended in the first year of the civil war, were resumed on Jan. 1, 1879, without disturbance of the money-market. The laws guarding the public domain in the Territories were strictly enforced against spoliators, and though some troubles with Indians attracted the attention of the country, they were as fairly settled as the nature of the case permitted. Mr. Hayes retired from office with the satisfaction of having done much to promote the best interests of the people in all parts of the Union. Though since living in retirement, he has aided in benevolent work, especially the promotion of education among the freedmen of the Southern States.

HAYNE, ISAAC (1745–1781), an American Revolutionary soldier, was born in South Carolina in 1745. When the British began a campaign in South Carolina in 1780, Hayne, then a senator in the State legislature, became a captain of cavalry. Being made prisoner at the capture of Charleston, May 12, 1780, he was paroled, but early in 1781 he was ordered either to take arms as a British subject or to return to Charleston as a prisoner. On being assured that he would not be required to bear arms against his countrymen, he signed a declaration of allegiance to the king. Afterwards, however, those who had formerly given their parole were required to perform military service, and rather than do this for the British, Hayne went to the American camp, and was commissioned as colonel. In July, 1781, he captured Gen. Williamson, a Scotchman by birth, who had gone over to the British. A large force was immediately sent out from Charleston, by which Hayne was captured. He was confined at Charleston until the arrival of Lord Rawdon, then condemned by a court of inquiry, and executed at Charleston, S. C., Aug. 4, 1781. Gen. Greene issued a proclamation Aug. 26, declaring his determination to make reprisals. The subject was discussed in the British Parliament, and Lord Rawdon published a justification of his conduct, which was afterwards criticised by Robert Y. Hayne in the *Southern Review*, February, 1828.

HAYNE, PAUL HAMILTON, an American poet, was born at Charleston, S. C., Jan. 1, 1831. He was a son of Lieut. Hayne, U. S. N., and nephew of the distinguished statesman, Gov. R. Y. Hayne (for whom see ENCYCLOPÆDIA BRITANNICA). Paul was educated at Charleston, and was a frequent contributor to the *Southern Literary Messenger*. He published a volume of poems in 1855, the longest being "The Temptation of Venus." A second volume, *Sonnets, and other Poems*, followed in 1857, and a third, *Avolio, and other Poems*, in 1859. During the civil war Hayne wrote some fiery poems, which were reprinted in Simms' *War Poetry of the South*. Since that time he has published *Legends and Lyrics* (1872), and has edited the *Poems of Henry Timrod* (1873). Short poems continue to appear from his pen in the prominent literary periodicals. He died July 6, 1886.

HAYS, ISAAC (1796–1879), an American physician, was born at Philadelphia, July 5, 1796. He graduated at the University of Pennsylvania in 1816, where he also received the degree of M. D. in 1820. He had an extensive practice, and was especially noted as an oculist. He became editor of the quarterly *American Journal of the Medical Sciences* in 1820, and had sole charge of it until 1869, when he associated with him his son, Dr. I. Minis Hays, who still edits the periodical. Dr. Hays also established in 1843 a monthly called *Medical News*, and in 1874 the *Monthly Abstract of Medical Science*. He also edited *Wilson's American Ornithology* (1828), and a number of medical works. He framed the code of ethics of the American Medical Association, which has been adopted by every State and county medical society in the Union. He was a member of many learned societies, and president of the Philadelphia Academy of Natural Sciences from 1865 to 1869. He died at Philadelphia, April 12, 1879.

HAZARD, ROWLAND GIBSON, an American manufacturer and philosopher, was born at South Kingston, R. I., Oct. 9, 1801. He has been engaged from his youth in manufacturing pursuits, and has accumulated a large fortune. While in New Orleans, in 1841, he secured the release of a large number of free negroes who, belonging to vessels from the North, had been placed in the chain-gang. He was elected to the State legislature in 1851 and 1854, and to the State senate in 1866. He has published many treatises, among which are *Essay on Language* (1834); *Adaptation of the Universe to the Cultivation of the Mind* (1840); *Decline of Political and National Morality* (1841); *Philosophical Character of Channing* (1844); *Railroad Corporations and the Public* (1849); *Resources of the United States* (1864); *Freedom of the Mind in Willing* (1864); *Causation and Freedom* (1869).

HAZARD, SAMUEL (1784–1870), an American antiquarian, was born at Philadelphia, May 26, 1784, being the son of Ebenezer Hazard (1745–1817), the first postmaster-general of the United States. He was engaged originally in mercantile pursuits, and made many voyages to the East Indies. Afterwards he devoted himself to compiling and editing documents relating to the early history of Pennsylvania. Among these are *Pennsylvania Register* (16 vols., 1828–36); *Annals of Pennsylvania*, 1609–82 (1850); *Pennsylvania Archives*, 1682–1790 (12 vols., 1853). He died at Philadelphia, May 22, 1870.

HAZEN, WILLIAM BABCOCK, an American general, was born at West Hartford, Vt., Sept. 27, 1830. He is a descendant of Gen. Moses Hazen (1733–1803), who served in the French war (1756–63), and afterwards in the Revolutionary war. William's parents removed to Huron, Ohio, in 1833. He graduated at West Point in 1855, and entering the Eighth infantry served against the Indians in California, Oregon, and Texas. In February, 1861, he was appointed assistant professor of infantry tactics at West Point, and in May was made captain. He took command of the Forty-first Ohio regiment, and joined Gen. Buell's army. On Jan. 6, 1862, he was appointed to command a brigade, and was conspicuous at the battle of Shiloh. He accompanied Buell in Alabama, and afterwards drove the Confederates from Danville, Ky. At the battle of Stone River he saved the left wing from being turned. He commanded a brigade in the operations before Chickamauga, and afterwards deprived the Confederates of the advantages they had gained by that battle, and relieved the army at Chattanooga. At Missionary Ridge he captured 18 pieces of artillery. During Sherman's march to the sea he commanded a division, with which he captured Fort McAllister, Dec. 13, 1864, for which he was promoted major-general of volunteers. He took part in the operations resulting in Johnston's surrender, and was appointed to the command of the Fifteenth corps, May 19, 1865. In July, 1866, he was made colonel of the Sixth infantry. On Dec. 8, 1880, he was appointed chief signal officer.

HAZLETON, a borough of Pennsylvania, in Luzerne county, is situated in a picturesque mountain region on the Lehigh Valley Railroad. 80 miles N.N.W. of Philadelphia. The town and vicinity are well known as places of summer resort. Hazleton has a town-hall, an academy, a convent, 10 churches, several banks, daily and weekly newspapers. It has iron-works, lumber-mills, and railway car-shops, but depends mainly for its prosperity upon the neighboring rich and productive mines of anthracite coal. The product is a Lehigh coal of the very best quality. The borough has an important trade, making it the largest town and principal business centre of the Lehigh coal-field. Population in 1870, 4317; in 1880, 7161.

HEADLEY, JOEL TYLER, an American author, was born at Walton, Delaware co., N. Y., Dec. 3, 1814. He graduated at Union College in 1839, and studied theology at the Auburn Theological Seminary. He became pastor of a church at Stockbridge, Mass., but was soon obliged to relinquish pastoral work by ill health. He then went to Europe in 1842, and on his return published *Letters from Italy* (1844), followed soon by *The Alps and the Rhine*. He now devoted himself entirely to authorship, and prepared many popular biographies and historical books, among which were *Napoleon and his Marshals* (1846); *Washington and his Generals* (1847); *History of the War of 1812* (1853); *Chaplains and Clergy of the Revolution* (1861); *Grant and Sherman* (1866); *The Great Rebellion* (1863-66); *The Great Riots of New York* (1873). He has also prepared some volumes of biblical and religious interest, among which are *Sacred Mountains* (1850); *Sacred Scenes and Characters* (1853); *Sacred Heroes and Martyrs* (1870). He resides near Newburg, N. Y., and in 1854 was elected to the State legislature, and in 1855 secretary of the State of New York.

HEADLEY, PHINEAS CAMP, an American author, brother of the preceding, was born at Walton, N. Y., June 24, 1819. He received an academical education and was admitted to the bar in 1847, but afterwards studied theology, graduating at Auburn Theological Seminary in 1851. He has held pastoral charges at Adams, N. Y., and Greenfield, Mass. Among his books are *Women of the Bible* (1850); biographies of *Napoleon* (1855); the *Empress Josephine* (1851); *Mary Queen of Scots* (1853); *Lafayette* (1856); *The Camp and Court of David* (1858); a series of *Heroes of the War* (5 vols., 1863-64); *Massachusetts in the Rebellion* (1866); *Half-hours in Bible Lands* (1867); *Evangelists in the Church* (1873); *Island of Fire*, a description of Iceland (1874); *Public Men of To-day* (1882).

HEALY, GEORGE PETER ALEXANDER, an American painter, was born at Boston, July 15, 1813. After studying art for some time there he went to Paris in 1834, and stayed several years. His American home is at Chicago, but he resides chiefly in Europe. He has executed portraits of the most distinguished men of his time. His historical painting, Webster's Reply to Hayne (1851), now in Faneuil Hall, Boston, contains 130 portraits. His works are acknowledged to be earnest and forcible, but are deficient in carefulness and in sense of color.

HEATH, WILLIAM (1737-1814), an American Revolutionary general, was born at Roxbury, Mass., March 2, 1737. He was brought up a farmer, but in 1770 was commander of the Ancient and Honorable Artillery Company of Boston, was afterwards a member of the committees of correspondence and safety, and in 1774 was a delegate to the provincial Congress. After being appointed brigadier-general and major-general in the provincial army, he was appointed to the same ranks in the Continental army in June, 1775, and August, 1776. He had displayed ability in organizing the army around Boston, and in March, 1776, was ordered to New York, in the vicinity of which he served." In 1779 he had four regiments on the Hudson. At the close of the war he returned to his farm.

He was a member of the Massachusetts convention which ratified the Federal Constitution, and was State senator, 1791-92. In 1793 he was appointed judge of probate for Norfolk county, and in 1806 was elected lieutenant-governor, but declined to serve. He died at Roxbury, Mass., Jan. 24, 1814. He published his *Memoirs* in 1798.

HEAVYSEGE, CHARLES (1816-1876), a Canadian poet, was born of poor parents at Liverpool, England, in 1816. He left school at an early age to become a machinist. In 1843 he married, and in 1853 removed to Montreal, Canada. He had steadily cultivated his talent for poetry, yet not until about 1854 did he venture to print any of his poems, and then only anonymously. Among these were a volume of blank verse, and another containing fifty sonnets. In 1857 his tragedy of *Saul* was published, and its merits were recognized by Emerson, Longfellow, and Hawthorne. In 1860 Heavysege issued a drama called *Count Philippo; or the Unequal Marriage*, and though inferior to his tragedy it brought him employment on the newspapers, which enabled him to give up his trade. He afterwards published an ode for the tercentenary of Shakespeare's birth, and an idyl called *Jephthah's Daughter*.

HEBREWS, EPISTLE TO THE. 1. *Authorship.*— This New Testament writing is anonymous. The question of authorship, which has never been settled, differs therefore from that of the genuineness of the epistles in which Paul is named as the writer. While the current of opinion is at present against the Pauline authorship, it is not in accordance with fact to say that "scarcely any sound scholar will be found to accept Paul as the direct author." (See *Literature*, at close of this article.) The diversity of views respecting the author in the early church furnishes one strong argument against the Pauline authorship. But the style of the epistle, together with a few utterances that apparently disclaim apostleship, presents a more serious objection. The difference between this and the Pauline epistles is rhetorical rather than verbal. It strikes every careful student, and cannot be removed by a mere count of identical words and phrases. Yet evidence of this kind is proverbially precarious. Many, therefore, do not deem this argument of sufficient weight to overbear the early, though partially extended, opinion that the epistle was written by the apostle. It is, moreover, difficult to fix upon any other person in apostolic times as the author. Prof. W. R. Smith himself does not decide between Barnabas and Apollos. The latter name now finds favor, less from positive evidence than from the fact that it is more difficult, in the absence of evidence respecting Apollos, to prove that he did not write the letter. "Not proven" is substantially the verdict in every case. The Pauline authorship has undoubtedly found more support, because it seemed easier to maintain the authority of the epistle by recognising him as the writer. But this proves nothing. In fact, the questions of authorship and canonicity not only may be but ought to be carefully distinguished in a case like this.

(See Vol. XI. p. 538 Am. ed. (p. 602 Edin. ed.).)

2. *Authority.*—The epistle is cited as authoritative by Clemens Romanus, but with no indication that he regarded Paul as the author. In later times doubts existed as to its canonicity, but only partially even among those who doubted that it was the work of the apostle. In the Reformation period the two questions were kept entirely distinct. The Council of Trent

(4th session, April 8, 1546) first made the Pauline authorship an article of faith. Some Protestant symbols class it with Paul's epistles, but the Wesminster Confession expressly leaves the question open. The place of the epistle in the New Testament canon rests, however, on firmer grounds than decrees of councils. The historical evidence, though not so strong as that in support of the Pauline epistles, is overwhelmingly preponderant. The early doubts as to its authority naturally grew out of its anonymous form. These very doubts indicate the care of the early church in its reception of canonical books, so soon as questions arose in regard to the writings properly constituting the rule of faith. The internal evidence is decisive for all who accept the New Testament writings as authoritative (see under 5). In its opening sentence the book exalts the new and perfect revelation of God in his Son above the varied and incomplete methods of the Old Testament times. By implication it asserts its right to form a part of authoritative exposition of this final revelation; its character, like that of the other New Testament writings, justifies this claim, since with the other books it stands apart from all subsequent literature. The more we know of the Christian writings of the second century the wider and deeper does the gulf appear that separates them from the canonical books. No theory respecting the authorship can alter this internal evidence. It may seem easier to account for the character of the epistle by connecting it with the personal gifts of the apostle to the Gentiles; but if Paul did not write it, then it furnishes us a striking proof that the inspiration of the New Testament is a unique fact, not to be confounded with the gifts and graces of the apostles, and not entirely dependent on their personal authority. Moreover, the doubts in the early church serve to show that the authoritative character of these writings grows out of what they are; it may be recognized by ecclesiastical bodies, but cannot be created by decrees of councils. The uncertainty respecting the authorship of this epistle must continue until the (altogether improbable) discovery of further data. So long as it continues, it forces us to discriminate between the authority of Scripture and the personal authority of the apostles.

3. *Destination.*—The class of readers addressed is obviously indicated in the epistle, but the data it furnishes are insufficient to decide the question of original destination. At present the current of opinion tends towards Rome as the home of the believers to whom the letter was sent. Palestine still has, however, numerous advocates, while but few now favor Alexandria. At Rome the epistle was not at first attributed to Paul; hence, this theory of the destination accords best with the non-Pauline authorship. But while the earliest references to it as an authoritative writing come from that city, the uncertainty which existed there respecting the author seems quite singular, if was written for Roman Christians of Jewish birth.

4. *Date of Writing.*—This should, in all fairness, be placed before the destruction of Jerusalem (A. D. 70). It is true, the writer might have used the present tense after that event, in referring to the temple and its ritual, but only positive reasons to the contrary can destroy the force of the implication that the temple was still standing when he thus wrote. Nor is it likely that such a writer would have ignored an event so important in its bearing upon his theme, had it occurred but a few years before. Nothing is gained by assigning a later date. The attempt to place the epistle near the close of the first century is part of a theory which seeks to weaken the authority of the New Testament writings. It seems probable that it was written after the beginning of the persecution under Nero (A. D. 64), and before the beginning of the Jewish war (A. D. 67). Davidson and Schaff, however, assign it to A. D. 63, and Conybeare and Howson to A. D. 68 or 69.

5. *Theme, Contents, and Character of the Epistle.*—The discussions about the uncertain questions, above referred to, not infrequently throw into the background the magnificent thought of the epistle. The argument is, however, intelligible on any theory that recognizes the recipients of the letter as believers of Jewish birth and education, who were tempted by threatening dangers to draw back from Christianity. To warn and encourage them the writer sets forth the superiority of the Christian revelation, because of the superiority of Christ himself, the real High-priest prefigured in the antecedent revelations of God during the Old Testament economy. He is superior to angels, to Moses, to the Levitical priests; that, too, in his person, in the sanctuary and covenant in which he officiates, and, preeminently, in the availing sacrifice he offered. Hortatory passages occur throughout this didactic statement, but they are always interwoven with admirable rhetorical fitness. The latter part is an application, enforcing steadfastness, not only by the main thought, but by the example of the Old Testament heroes of faith, and by the assurance of God's fatherly discipline in their trials.

While the epistle shows great skill in the articulation of its minor details, the progress of thought is less logical, and the arrangement of words and clauses far more rhetorical than is usual in the writings of Paul. The theme calls for the parallels and contrasts of type and anti-type; a task for an imagination of the highest order. The whole letter is poetic in the noblest sense. One peculiarity of the author resembles Wagner's *Leit-motif* in musical composition: a new thought is suggested, to be skilfully elaborated afterwards. The hortatory portions of the epistle are characterized by an arrangement akin to musical modulation: first exhortation, then warning accented almost into censure, then words of encouragement, leading back to the main thought; all skilfully handled so as to perpetuate the movement of the whole. Even in the closing chapter, with its personal notices, the same imaginative power is shown, and few sentences in the New Testament are more touching than the doxology of verses 20, 21.

Another point should not be overlooked: In this epistle we find set forth the unity of Divine revelation in its progressive method. Elsewhere, especially in the letters to the Galatians and Romans, the mutual relations of law and gospel are emphasized, but here the two revelations are shown, with much detail, to be parts of one great redemptive process. It is not so much the universality of the gospel as its completeness. Paul shows that this is the message for all; this epistle shows that it is the message once for all, there being no progress beyond this. The theological point of view is undoubtedly Pauline; but from the nature of the theme the discussion is fuller, and the flight of inspired imagination loftier. Stress is laid upon the sacrificial purpose of the death of Christ; but the resurrection obtains due validity, since only the risen High-priest could enter the true Holy of Holies. As the key to the entire historical movement culminating in the facts of salvation—the death, resurrection, and ascension of Christ—this book agrees with all others, explains all the others. He who believes that God has spoken in the prophets and in the person of his Son will hear his voice throughout this epistle; it will be easy to reckon so masterly a statement of the entire sweep of his revelation among the records of that revelation. Since the Lord promised the Holy Spirit to glorify himself by declaring the truth respecting himself (John xvi. 14), here is a book that stands this test of inspiration, whether it be of Paul, or of Apollos, addressed to Jerusalem or to Rome. Not less does it prove its origin by bringing home its grandest thoughts to the cares, trials, temptations, and needs of the humblest believer. To its authority it is itself the best witness.

Literature.—The most important American commentary is that of Moses Stuart (Andover, 1827, revised by Robbins, 4th ed., 1860), defending the Pauline authorship; so Kay (*Speaker's Commentary*, London and New York, 1880); Angus (Schaff's *Popular Commentary*, New York, 1882). In *Lange's Commentary* (Amer. ed., New York, 1868) Kendrick has made valuable additions to Moll (accepting Apollos as the probable author); S. T. Lowrie (New York, 1884), bases his exposition largely upon that of Von Hofmann, which is thus made accessible to the English reader; Timothy Dwight (New York, 1885) has enriched the English translation of Lünemann (in the Meyer series of commentaries). See also the very full and valuable additions of Ezra Abbot to Davidson's article, "Hebrews," in *Smith's Bible Dictionary* (Amer. ed.), and the revised article of Zahn in the Schaff-Herzog *Encyclopædia* (New York, 1883). (M. B. R.)

HECKER, FRIEDRICH KARL FRANZ (1811–1881), a German-American revolutionist and soldier, was born at Eichtersheim, Baden, Sept. 28, 1811. He was educated at Mannheim, and in 1838 became an advocate in the Superior Court at Mannheim. In 1842 he was elected to the chamber of deputies of Baden, and soon became a prominent member of the opposition. While visiting Prussia in 1845 he was arrested at Berlin and ordered out of the country. In the diet in 1846–47 his extreme views put him in opposition even to the liberals, and for a time he withdrew from its meetings, but he returned and became leader of the extreme left. In the assembly at Heidelberg, in March, 1848, he appeared as a socialist and republican, and he sought with the aid of Struve to unite the South-Germans in a revolutionary movement, which proved a failure. Hecker was obliged to flee to Switzerland. In September, 1848, he emigrated to America, but was recalled by the provisional government erected in Baden in 1849. Before he arrived the government had collapsed and he returned to America, settling as a farmer at Belleville, Ill. In 1856 he was a prominent speaker in behalf of the Republican party. In 1860 he raised the first German Illinois regiment, and while serving under Gen. Fremont was wounded. Afterwards he had command of a brigade under Gen. Howard, and was wounded at the battle of Chancellorsville. In March, 1864, he resigned, and retired to his farm. In the winters he delivered popular lectures to German-Americans, and a selection from these lectures was published in Germany in 1873. He died at St. Louis, March 24, 1881.

HECKER, ISAAC THOMAS, an American clergyman, the founder of the Paulists, was born in New York, Dec. 18, 1819. In 1843 he joined the celebrated Brook Farm Association, near Boston, and afterwards was for a time connected with a similar community at Fruitlands, in Worcester co., Mass. In 1845 he became a Roman Catholic, and in 1847 he joined the Redemptorist fathers in Belgium. In 1849 he was ordained priest by Cardinal Wiseman, in London, and returned to New York in 1851. In 1857, being at Rome, he was, with some of his associates, released by papal authority from connection with the Redemptorists, and in 1858 he founded the new congregation of the missionary priests of St. Paul, having their principal house in New York. He established *The Catholic World*, a monthly periodical, in 1865, and took part in the Vatican Council of 1869 as procurator for Bishop Rosecrans. Among his works are *Questions of the Soul* (1855); *Aspirations of Nature* (1857); and a pamphlet on *Martin Luther* (1883).

HECKEWELDER, JOHN GOTTLIEB ERNEST (1743–1823), an American Moravian missionary to the Indians, was born at Bedford, England, March 12, 1743. His father brought him to America at the age of eleven. In 1762 he accompanied Mr. Post on an expedition to the Indian tribes on the Ohio, and in 1771 he became a missionary to the Delaware Indians. In 1797 he was sent to superintend the Christian Indians on the Muskingum. In 1811 he retired to Bethlehem, Pa., where he afterwards prepared a *History of the Indians of Pennsylvania* (1819), and a *History of the Moravian Missions* among them (1820). He died at Bethlehem, Pa., Jan. 21, 1823.

HEDDING, ELIJAH (1780–1852), an American bishop, was born at Pine Plains, N. Y., June 7, 1780. He was licensed in 1800, and he preached in Northern New York, Vermont, and New Hampshire, enduring great hardships. In 1807 he was presiding elder of New Hampshire, and in 1808 was a delegate to the General Conference at Baltimore. Afterwards he labored in Massachusetts and assisted in founding *Zion's Herald*, the first journal of the Methodist Episcopal Church in the United States. In 1824 he was chosen bishop and was zealous in the discharge of his duty until 1844, when infirmities began to press upon him. Yet in 1848 he was a delegate to the British Wesleyan Conference. He died at Poughkeepsie, N. Y., April 9, 1852. His *Life* was written by D. W. Clark (1855).

HEDGE, FREDERIC HENRY, an American clergyman and author, was born at Cambridge, Mass., Dec. 12, 1805. His father, Levi Hedge (1767–1843), was from 1810 to 1827 professor of logic and metaphysics in Harvard College. Frederic was educated in Germany, returned to America in 1823, and graduated at Harvard in 1825. Having studied theology he became pastor of a church at Cambridge in 1829, removed to Bangor, Me., in 1835, to Providence, R. I., in 1850, and to Brookline, Mass., in 1856. In 1858 he became professor of ecclesiastical history in the Theological Department of Harvard College, and was editor of the *Christian Examiner* from 1857 to 1860. He resigned his pastorate in 1872 to accept the professorship of the German language in Harvard College. Besides many poems, original and translated, and contributions to the *North American Review* and other periodicals, Dr. Hedge has published *The Prose Writers of Germany* (1848); *Reason in Religion* (1865); and *The Primeval World of Hebrew Tradition* (1870). In theology he is a Christian rationalist; as a writer he is noted for the purity of his style and the vigor of his intellect.

HEFELE, KARL JOSEPH VON, a German bishop, was born at Unterkochen, in Würtemberg, March 15, 1809. He graduated at Tübingen in 1834, and in 1840 he was chosen professor of church history, Christian archæology and patrology in the Roman Catholic faculty there. In 1869 he was consecrated bishop of Rottenburg. In the Vatican Council he voted against the declaration of papal infallibility, as being inopportune, but accepted that dogma when definitely announced as of the faith. Among his works are *Die Einführung des Christenthums im südwestlichen Deutschland* (1837); *Patrum Apostolicorum Opera* (1839); *Das Sendschreiben des Apostels Barnabas* (1840); *Der Cardinal Ximenes und die Kirchlichen Zustände Spaniens im 15. Jahrhundert* (1844); *Chrysostomus-Postille* (1845-57). His *Consiliengeschichte* (7 vols., 1855-74) is a work of the first importance. He also published *Beiträge zur Kirchengeschichte Archäologie und Liturgik* (1864-65); and *Causa Honorii Papae* (1870). After the establishment of the new German empire he vigorously maintained the cause of the Roman Church against the repressive legislation of the time.

HEILPRIN, MICHAEL, a Polish-American author, was born at Piotrków, Russian Poland, in March, 1823. His father, Phineas Mendel Heilprin (1801-1863), was a noted Hebrew scholar, who with his family was driven by Russian oppression from his native Poland to Hungary in 1842. In this country the family joined in the Revolutionary movement of 1848. Michael was employed in the literary bureau of the department of the interior under the presidency of Kossuth. In 1856 he removed to America, where he has been engaged in literary work. Besides contributing to periodicals he has been associate editor of Appleton's *American Cyclopædia*, and similar works. He has also prepared *The Historical Poetry of the Ancient Hebrews* (2 vols., 1879-80).

HELL GATE IMPROVEMENTS. The extensive obstructions at Hell Gate in East River, New York Harbor, U. S. A., have been the cause of numerous marine disasters. They consist of dangerous rocks and reefs, both in mid-channel and projecting from the shores of islands washed by a rapid current, which changes with the flood and ebb of the tide, and are designated as the Gridiron, Flood Rock, Hen and Chickens, Negro Head, Bread and Cheese, Hallett's Point, Way's Reef, Pot Rock, Frying Pan, Middle Reef, etc. (See map.) It was estimated that during the two months consumed by the survey of these channels fifty vessels went ashore on the rocks. But it was not until Aug. 18, 1851, that an attempt was made to remove them by introducing M. Maillefert's process of surface-blasting. This consisted of placing large charges of gunpowder, usually 125 lbs., on the surface of the rock and exploding it by a voltaic current. The broken material was not dredged, as it was assumed the currents would carry it away. The rocks operated upon were Pot Rock, which was reduced from 8 feet depth of water to $18\frac{7}{8}$ at a cost of $6837.50, and a consumption of over 34,000 lbs. of powder; the Frying Pan, which was 16 feet long and only 6 inches wide on top, with a depth of 9 feet at low water, and was lowered to 16 feet, at a cost of over $2000 and 12,387 lbs. of powder; Way's Reef, which was conical, with a depth of 5 feet, and was lowered to 14 feet at the same proportional expense; Bald-Headed Billy, a boulder 6 by 6 feet, which was blown into deep water by a single blast, at a cost of $500 and 125 lbs. of powder; Sheldrake Rock, where the depth was increased from 8 to 16 feet; and Diamond Reef,

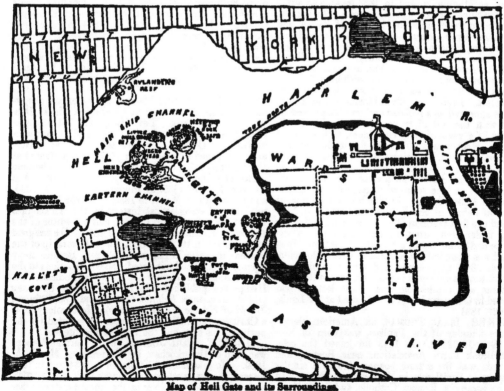

Map of Hell Gate and its Surroundings.

where the depth was increased from 16 to 18 feet. The total cost of these improvements was $13,861, and the total number of pounds of powder used was 74,192, fired in 620 cartridges; all conducted under appropriations made by the citizens of New York. As the depths obtained were insufficient for first-class vessels and numerous other obstructions remained, the U. S. government began making appropriations in 1852, when $20,000 were appropriated, under which Major Frazer, U. S. E., by continuing the Maillefert process, increased the depth over Pot Rock from 18$\frac{7}{12}$ to 20$\frac{7}{12}$ feet, at a cost of $18,000. From this it was inferred that whenever the rock was columnar or conical in form the Maillefert process was very effective and generally cheaper than any other, but when in large masses with flattened surfaces it was very slow and expensive.

For the further improvement of this dangerous passage it was deemed expedient to adopt other methods, and that of drilling under water through diving-bells, the only other method then in use, was not applicable because of the velocity of current, contracted space, and danger from collisions.

No satisfactory plan was devised until 1866, when Gen. John Newton, U. S. E., proposed drilling from a fixed platform through tubes reaching to the surface of the rock. This plan necessitated divers, who were to be protected from the current by movable dams or curtains of iron. This plan was modified until the plant, as used in 1869, consisted of a floating scow having an opening of 32 feet diameter in its centre, through which a large hemispherical iron bell, open both at top and bottom, was lowered to the rock below. This dome or caisson, 30 feet in diameter, made of boiler-iron, affords a frame-work for supporting 21 drill tubes. The drills working through them have a stroke of 18 inches, and weigh from 600 to 900 lbs. The dome has legs which are let out or drawn in to fit the rock and are held in place by cams. This lower open space was intended to be covered by a chain or canvas curtain to break the force of the current, but it was not found to be necessary. The drilling being completed, the holes are filled by a diver who inserts the charges of nitro-glycerine and makes the connections, when the plant is floated off and the blast fired. The broken rock is removed by a Morris & Cummings steam-grapple. It was not until May, 1871, that the steam-drilling scow was first practically introduced on the Diamond Reef, where it was found necessary first to remove by dredging the overlying deposits of sand, gravel, silt, ballast, and boulders, by which it was covered, before the drills could be used. The holes were from 7 to 13 feet deep, 4$\frac{1}{2}$ inches in diameter at the top, tapering to 3$\frac{1}{4}$ at the bottom, and were fired by charges of from 30 to 55 lbs. of nitro-glycerine. The scow ceased work on this reef in January, 1880.

Coenties Reef was operated upon in like manner between 1871 and 1875. During these operations, though the scow encountered numerous collisions, it suffered no other damage than a rupture of the anchor chains. It was also used at the Frying Pan, July 22, 1872, where it drilled 17 holes and made 11 surface blasts; and at Pot Rock, between Aug. 5 and Dec. 28, 1872, when it was struck by vessels 16 times. Four of the colliding vessels were sunk; one was drawn under the scow and carried off the dome, which was recovered in 80 feet of water considerably damaged. Way's Reef was reduced from 17$\frac{1}{2}$ feet to a depth of 26 feet at mean low water by the operations of the scow between Aug. 4, 1874, and Jan. 20 following. The size of the rock at the 26-foot curve is 235 feet long by a maximum width of 115 feet.

But the most extensive of all these operations was the removal of the reef at Hallett's Point. This was accomplished by sinking a large shaft on shore, from which 41 radial and 11 concentric galleries, 25 feet apart and of variable cross-sections, were driven under the reef. The aggregate length of the galleries opened was 7,425.67 feet, and the volume of rock in dump piles on the land was 49,480 cubic yards. This plan was first proposed by Mr. G. C. Reitheimer in the spring of 1868. A similar plan was proposed by Gen. Alexander, of the U. S. corps of engineers, and A. W. Von Schmidt, civil-engineer, Oct. 3, 1868, for the removal of Blossom Rock in the harbor of San Francisco, Cal., where it was successfully applied, April 23, 1870. Work on the shaft at Hallett's Point, 32 feet deep, was commenced in October, 1869, and during its continuance careful records of the progress and cost by various drills gave for the Burleigh drill between 36 and 37 cents per foot of hole, including repairs and all items of expense except first cost and interest. The cost of hammer-drilling was found to be about 95 cents per foot. With 9 Burleigh drills 7 can be kept at work. The number of feet of holes drilled by each machine per shift of 8 hours was 30 feet. The Diamond drill, owing to frequent veins of quartz, did not answer well, but should prove valuable for softer rocks. The Ingersoll rock-drill proved itself fully equal to the others. Owing to the restricted area of the galleries the following data are confined to the experience in the most difficult part of tunneling known as "headings." To blast *one cubic yard* required 10 lineal feet of holes drilled at 37 cents per foot, 1.22 lbs. of nitro-glycerine, 0.39 lbs. of gunpowder; and the following percentages of cost for the various operations were found to exist when the cost of blasting and removing one cubic yard was made the unit of comparison:

Blasting	46. %
Conveying rock to shaft	17.
Hoisting	13.28
Dumping	2.03
Pumping	10.37
Incidentals	21.32
Total	100.00

The estimated amount of rock above the 26-foot curve was 53,971 cubic yards, covering about three acres. The amount to be removed by the explosion was 63,135 cubic yards, which became 86,992 yards after the explosion. The excavations were completed in June, 1875. The actual time, therefore (deducting stoppages), was four years and four months. This was followed by the drilling of holes in piers and roof for the charges, which was completed March 25, 1876, when there had been drilled 5375 3-inch holes in the roof, and 1080 3-inch and 286 2-inch holes in the piers; total length of 3-inch holes 56,548 feet, and of 2-inch 1897 feet. The number of holes charged was 4427; the number of cartridges used, 13,596, many holes containing two of 11 inches each. The charging was commenced Sept. 11, 1876, and completed on the 20th of the same month. The batteries for firing consisted of 40, 43, 44 cells of zinc and carbon, or 960 cells in all, divided into 23 distinct batteries, each one arranged to fire 160 fuses in divided circuits of eight groups of 20 each. Thus there were 3680 mines connected in continuous series with a lead and return wire to close the circuit with the circuit-closer.

Everything being in readiness the mines were tamped by water run in through a syphon, which was started at 12.07 A. M. Sept. 23, 1876, and at 7.30 P. M. of same date the excavations were filled to the level of the tide. The next day, Sunday, 24, the mines were fired at 2.50 P. M., without hurtful shocks to any surrounding objects. The elevation of water and spray reached a height of 123 feet.

Flood Rock.—This dangerous reef, which projects above water, is situated in mid-channel, and at a distance of about 660 feet west of the Astoria shore. Its removal has been accomplished in accordance with the plans of Gen. John Newton, U. S. corps of engineers, and under his immediate supervision, assisted by Lieut.-Col. W. McFarland, Major Wm. Heuer, Capt. Jas. Mercur, Lieut. G. McC. Derby, and others. Work was begun June 7, 1875, by sinking a shaft 10 by 20, and forming an artificial island of the débris to furnish room for the plant.

Suspensions occurred from May 26 to Sept. 30, 1876, and on Dec. 31 of same year the heavy ice in the channel caused work to cease and the mine was filled with water. During the fiscal year ending June 30, 1878, there were no funds available, and during the next year progress was impeded by lack of sufficient machinery, and by the water which had flooded the mine for eighteen months, in consequence of which frequent timbering was required. Another interruption occurred between July 20 and Aug. 21, 1882, and again from March 31 until May 31, 1883, from want of funds, and the next year, 1883–84, no appropriation bill was passed by Congress.

These suspensions added to the cost of the work, in consequence of the pumping, as the mines contained several large seams which at first admitted 737 gallons per minute, but by careful plugging this amount was reduced to 565 gallons per minute on July 22, 1884.

The plant, comprising compressors, pumps, boilers, fans, drills, condensers, hoisting machinery, tugs, and other accessories, was estimated to be worth $125,000. The undermined area covered about 9 acres. The galleries were about 10 feet square, and their total length was 21,670 feet. The shell averaged 18.8 feet thick, and was supported by 467 piers about 15 feet square and 25 feet apart from centre to centre. Twenty-four galleries extended parallel to the axis of the river "and strike of the rock," and 46 at right-angles thereto. To break up the roof and columns 12,561 3-inch holes were drilled, having an average length of 9 feet. In the columns they were placed 5 feet apart, and inclined upward at an angle of 45°. In the roof they were 4 feet apart, and at angles of from 60° to 65°. Their total length was 113,102 feet, or more than 20 miles. Rand & Ingersoll percussion-drills were used, operated by compressed air. The total quantity of rock taken out was 80,166 cubic yards, while the estimated quantity to be ruptured by the blast was 270,717 cubic yards.

In headings 10 by 6 it required 3.62 lbs. of explosive per cubic yard, and for stoping but 1.39 lbs. The total cost of removing one cubic yard of a heading 6 by 4 feet was about $10, and stoping $4.

The following table shows the number of lineal feet of drilling required to remove one cubic yard of rock in the galleries and the price:

Year.	Feet of hole.	Cost per cub. yard for drilling.
1876	9.9	$0.42 per lin. foot.
1877	7.5	2.08
1878		
1879	10.86	2.16
1880	14.66	
1881	14.83	
1882	14.90	0.68 per lin. foot.
1883	19.43	6.652

In charging the holes cartridges 24 inches long and 2¼ inches in diameter were inserted, and held in place by 4 small wire legs. The first one introduced contained 6 lbs. of "rackarock," formed by mixing 79 per cent. of finely ground chlorate of potash with 21 per cent. of dinitro-benzole. Similar cartridges were added until the hole was nearly full, when finally a dynamite cartridge 15 by 2¼ inches, containing 3 lbs. of dynamite, with a 30-grain fulminate of mercury exploder inserted and allowed to project about 6 inches, so that it might receive the full effect of the initial charges connected with the battery. The mine was "fired" by primary charges placed at intervals of 25 feet along the galleries. They consisted of two 24-inch dynamite cartridges of 5 lbs. each, lashed to timbers placed across the gangway. The concussion produced by their explosion ignited the primers in the remaining charges of rackarock, and so exploded the entire mine simultaneously by what is known as the sympathetic method, thus saving a large amount of wiring. The total amount of rackarock used was 240,399 lbs., and of dynamite 42,331 lbs.

The entire mine was divided into 24 independent circuits. So far as possible adjacent charges were put on different circuits to avoid risk of failure. The whole number of primary charges was 591. The battery contained 60 cells coupled in one series. There were 4 carbon and 3 zinc plates, each 6 by 9 inches, in each cell, which were separated by ¼ of an inch. The ordinary bichromate solution was used.

The mine was flooded by 2 syphons of 12 and 16 inches diameter in 15¼ hours, ending at 3.30 A. M., Oct. 10, but the final arrangements for firing could not be completed before 11.13 A. M., same date. As the electric contact was made, an immense mass of water about 1400 feet long by 800 wide rose to some 200 feet, the earth shook, a dull thud was heard, and the whole reef was shattered, but the resulting wave was insignificant. There was no severe shock, and the only damage done was the breaking of a few panes of glass, and shaking down of loose bricks and plaster in Astoria. The resistance to the force of the explosion amounted to about 500,000 tons of rock in place, covered by 200,000 tons of water, which was sufficient to confine the effect to narrow limits. About 1,240,000 cubic feet of gas are estimated to have been liberated.

The velocity of propagation of the shock through earth was found to be 5120 feet per second.

Dredging was immediately commenced by the government scow, which removed from 15 to 30 tons of stone each day. A contract was let in the latter part of October, 1885, for the removal of 30,000 tons of rock at $3.19 per ton, including surface blasting. The removed rock was to be dumped between Hog's Back and Ward's Island. About 120 tons are removed

HELL GATE IMPROVEMENTS.

FLOOD ROCK DURING THE MINING OPERATIONS.
(Perspective and Sectional Views.)

PLATE XXXI.

daily. The total cost of work at Flood Rock, including the final blast, amounted to $2.99 per cubic yard of the whole amount of rock broken. This was 34¼ per cent. less than the cost at Hallett's Point, but there still remains a large amount of work to be done in removing the broken rock above the 26-foot curve. The total cost of the final blast at Hallett's Point was $81,092.24; at Flood Rock it was $106,509.93, although the blast was 5.6 times as large. It will require as much dynamite to reduce the rock to sizes capable of being handled by the grapples as was required in the original blast. The greatest weight that can be lifted is 15 tons, or a cube of 6 feet on edge, 8 cubic yards.

The improvements originally intended for Hell Gate have since been modified to include the rocky obstructions known as Diamond Reef, Coenties Reef, a reef near the North Brothers' Island, and the Pilgrim Rock. These have been removed to a depth of 26 feet at mean low-water, and with the work already done at Hallett's Point, Flood Rock, Way's Reef, and Shelldrake, and the partial removal of the Heel Tap, Frying Pan, and Pot Rock, constitute about four-fifths of the entire project.

The completion of work at Flood Rock will nearly double the width of the principal channel.

The total amount of money expended on these improvements in Hell Gate to the close of the fiscal year, June 30, 1885, has been $3,261,276.06, and the "amount estimated to be required for the entire and permanent completion of the work of improvement, in accordance with the approved and adopted project, is $1,601,340.67," making a total expenditure of $4,862,616.73 for 26 feet of water at mean low-tide through this once very dangerous passage.

Authorities.—Reports, Chief of Engineers, U. S. A.; *Popular Science Monthly, Scientific American, Engineering News*, and local papers. (L. M .H.)

HELMHOLTZ, HERMAN LUDWIG FERDINAND, a German physicist and physiologist, was born Aug. 31, 1821, at Potsdam, where his father was an instructor in the gymnasium. The son studied medicine at Berlin from 1838 to 1842, and for a year after was assistant physician at the Charité hospital. Then he served as a military surgeon, and in 1848 became a lecturer on anatomy at the Berlin Art Academy. In July, 1849, he was called to be professor of physiology in the University of Königsberg, and his researches while holding this position greatly extended his fame. In 1855 he was made professor of anatomy and physiology at Bonn, and in 1858 he removed to Heidelberg, where he held the professorship of physiology. Since 1871 he has been professor of physics in the University of Berlin. In 1870 the French Academy admitted him to foreign membership.

Helmholtz is noted for his investigations of optics, acoustics, and electricity, which have established these sciences on a new basis. In his graduating thesis on the "Nervous System of the Evertebrates" he had shown his ability to make most delicate researches, and other treatises on animal physiology confirmed his growing reputation. His first finished work, *Uber die Erhaltung der Kraft* (1847), caused him to be recognised as one of the foremost champions of the new philosophy of force. This essay was afterwards expanded into *Uber die Wechselwirkung der Naturkraft* (1854), and in the mean time his lectures on the same subject being translated into several languages attracted attention throughout the world. His invention of the ophthalmoscope in 1851 revolutionized both the medical treatment and the physical knowledge of the eye. His *Handbuch der physiologischen Optik* (1856–66) laid a new foundation for the science of vision, as did also his work, *Die Lehre von den Tonempfindungen* (1862: 4th ed., 1877), for the science of music. Throughout these works ingenious experiments are combined with mathematical reasoning and philosophic thought. He has solved many practical questions which have puzzled musicians, as well as suggested reasonable explanations of many perplexing facts in æsthetics and physiology. Besides the main works already mentioned, Helmholtz has published numerous articles of the greatest value in the scientific journals. He has also delivered every year popular lectures, in which he has set forth with admirable clearness and tact the results of many of his most abstruse investigations. Some of these lectures have been published in book-form, and Prof. E. Atkinson has translated two series of them into English.

Of the very numerous and far-reaching discoveries of Prof. Helmholtz in the several distinct branches of science to which he has devoted his attention, only the most striking, and those to which he owes his wide-spread reputation, are here mentioned. In optics, the invention of the ophthalmoscope, the result of a long-continued investigation into the character and conditions of the human eye, has given to the medical profession an instrument which has saved thousands from blindness. Acoustics first became a definite science in his hands. He invented a method of analyzing sound by the use of instruments called resonators, consisting of hollow bodies, whose volume of contained air vibrated in the presence of previously determined sounds. By the aid of this instrument he discovered the cause of musical harmony, and proved that the peculiar tone of every instrument is due to the addition of various overtones and resultant or combination tones to the fundamental, these differing in intensity and pitch with every instrument; that two musical sounds are in harmony when they have one or more common simple sounds; and that the same is the case with two chords when they have one or more compound sounds in common. His researches on *beats* as the cause of dissonance were of equal value. His most striking addition to physiological science was his research into the rapidity of nerve conduction, in which he proved clearly that sensations move with comparative slowness from the surface to the brain, and that an act of will is similarly retarded in producing its effect upon the muscle. This quite disproved the old theory that the agency of nerve action was electricity, since the rate of nerve conduction is excessively slower than that of an electric conductor. In physical science his researches into vortex motion are of extreme interest, and proved that a vortex ring in smoke or vapor has extraordinary qualities previously unsuspected. These discoveries have given rise to the new atomic theory of Sir William Thompson, who advances the idea that atoms are really vortex rings in a non-frictional ether, and as such must be absolutely permanent in shape, substance, and duration. (C. M.)

HEMLOCK, or HEMLOCK SPRUCE, a large and valuable North American conifer, which grows abundantly in the Northern United States and Canada, and whose wood is very largely used for building purposes, railroad ties, etc. The commercial species, *Tsuga (Abies) Canadensis*, grows to a height of from 60 to

100 feet, and from 3 to 4½ feet in diameter of trunk. It frequents dry, rocky ridges, and often forms extensive forests, almost to the exclusion of other species. Less commonly it is found along the borders of swamps, in deep, rich soil. In the United States it extends through several of the Northern States, reaching as far west as Central Wisconsin, and south to Northern Delaware, while it follows the Alleghani as far as Upper Alabama. It grows abundantly throughout Canada, often in vast tracts, and extends to the northern limit of arborescent vegetation. The hemlock differs from the ordinary spruce in having flat, two-ranked leaves, and in the mode of opening of the anther-cells; and from the firs, in having persistent cones, and in some minor characters. It is a handsome, ornamental tree when young, with long, gracefully drooping branches. It is also grown for ornamental hedges. The cones are small, ovate, and terminal, with few scales, their length being about ¾-inch, while the leaves are still shorter. In addition to *T. Canadensis* there are several other species. *T. Caroliniana* is a small tree of the Southern Alleghanies, rare and local. It is closely allied to the above. *T. Mertensiana* is found from Alaska as far south as California. It is a large tree, 100 to 200 feet high, and 4 to 10 feet thick, often forming extensive forests along the base of the Cascade range. Its bark is the principal tanning material of the north-west coast. *T. Pattoniana* is a smaller tree, of Alpine habits, growing on dry slopes and ridges, from an elevation of 2700 feet in British Columbia to 10,000 in Central California, which is nearly the highest limit of tree growth. A variety of the great red fir of the West, *Pseudotsuga Douglassii*, is also known in California as hemlock. The wood of the commercial hemlock is light, soft, brittle, coarse, and crooked-grained, not durable, and is difficult to work. Its color is light-brown, tinged with red, or often nearly white. It is stronger than white pine, and is largely used in construction for outside work. The bark is rich in tannin, and is the principal material used in the Northern States in the tanning of leather. It also yields a fluid extract, sometimes employed in medicine as a powerful astringent. Canada, or hemlock pitch, used for stimulating plasters, is made from this species.

HEMP, *Cannabis sativa*, a member of the *Cannabinaceæ*, a small order containing only two genera, each with a single species, the hemp and the hop plants. The name hemp is given not only to the plant but also to its commercial product, the fibre of the inner bark, which is used to make cordage. There are several other fibre-yielding plants whose product is also known as hemp, but these are of late utilization, while the hemp plant has been cultivated for this purpose since very early times. It is a native of Asia, where it seems to be indigenous over a wide district of the southern region. It is an annual, with a rough, angular stem, from 4 to 12 feet high. The leaves are mostly opposite, digitately divided, with 5 or more serrated leaflets. The flowers are diœcious, without petals, of greenish hue, the staminate flowers in drooping panicles, with 5 sepals and stamens, the pistillate in clustered erect spikes, the ovary with two styles in a calyx of one sepal. The nut is ovoid, greenish, reticulated with whitish veins. Flowers, June; fruits, August. In addition to its valuable fibre it yields two other commercial products. One of these is the seed, which is used as food for cage-birds, and yields a large percentage of oil when pressed. This oil, of which Russia furnishes the principal supply, is used in the manufacture of soaps and varnishes, and also for burning. Its other product is a resinous exudation, which has strong narcotic properties. It is yielded

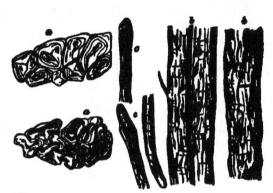

Fibres of Hemp (*Cannabis sativa*) magnified 275 times.
a. a. Sections of groups of fibres. *b.* Fibres seen longitudinally.
c. Ends of fibres.

most fully in hot climates. The leaves, twigs, and flowering heads of the plant produce a similar effect. This narcotic is known as *hasheesh* and by several other names, and is much used in India and some other countries.

Attempts to cultivate hemp in America were made early in the history of the Plymouth and Virginia colonies. In Pennsylvania the colonial government offered bounties for its culture in 1730. These attempts were unsuccessful, though of late years it has become a valuable agricultural product of the United States, particularly in Kentucky. It is cultivated to some extent in all the Northern States, but of the 5025 tons of fibre produced in 1879, 4583 tons were from Kentucky, and 209 from Wisconsin. It is cultivated in Northern New York, mainly for the seed, the yield being from 20 to more than 40 bushels per acre. The export of hemp and its product, in 1880, was valued at $1,272,451.

For the successful cultivation of hemp there is needed a rich alluvial loam, well dried, but not absolutely dry. It yields a full and quick return within the season, being sown as soon as safe from frost, and harvested when the leaves are ready to fall. The staminate plants yield the best fibre immediately after flowering, the seeding plants at a later stage of growth. The plant is now almost always cut, in preference to pulling, as involving less labor and yielding better results. It is then rotted by exposure to the dew, or by steeping in vats for several days, and is afterwards broken in a machine like the flax-breaker. Some further processes are necessary to fully separate the fibre, which is then twisted into bundles for the market. When cultivated for seed-bearing, hemp greatly exhausts the land. Cultivated for the fibre, it is but moderately exhaustive, and grows with such strength as to keep down weeds, so that it may be grown for many seasons on the same land. The hemp plant has escaped from cultivation in the United States and naturalized itself to some extent on waste places and in the vicinity of dwellings.

HENDERSON, a city of Kentucky, county-seat of Henderson county, is on the Ohio River, 10 miles S. of

Evansville, Ind. It is on the St. Louis, Evansville, and Nashville division of the Louisville and Nashville Railroad, 171 miles E. S. E. of St. Louis. It has a court-house, churches of all the leading denominations, several newspapers and banks, and is the seat of a large trade by rail and river. Henderson is especially noted as a great centre of the tobacco business, the country around it being one of the principal seats of tobacco-culture in the United States. In the town there are many tobacco factories and warehouses. It has also railway shops, flouring-mills, saw-mills, and manufactories of farming and household implements and other goods. The country districts near at hand are richly supplied with coal and hard-wood timber, both of them as yet chiefly unwrought. Population, 9500.

HENDERSON, JAMES PINCKNEY (1808–1858), an American soldier, was born in Lincoln co., N. C., March 31, 1808. He removed to Mississippi and practised law. In 1836 he was appointed a brigadier-general in the army of Texas, and when the army was disbanded he was made attorney-general. He was secretary of state of Texas, 1837–39, and then minister to England to procure the recognition of Texan independence. In 1844 he was special minister to the United States to secure the annexation of Texas. In 1845 he was a member of the State Constitutional Convention, and when the constitution was ratified was chosen governor. In the Mexican war which ensued he commanded a division of Texan volunteers. In 1857 he was chosen U. S. Senator, and he died at Washington, D. C., June 4, 1858.

HENDRICKS, THOMAS ANDREWS (1819–1885), an American statesman, was born near Zanesville, Ohio, Sept. 7, 1819. His father soon removed to Indiana, and in 1822 settled in Shelby county. He graduated at Hanover College in 1841, studied law at Chambersburg, Pa., and was admitted to the bar there in 1843. Commencing practice at Shelbyville, Ind., in 1847 he was elected to the State legislature, and in 1850 to the State Constitutional Convention. He was a member of Congress from 1851 to 1855, and in the contest over the Kansas-Nebraska bill followed the leadership of Senator S. A. Douglas. He was commissioner of the U. S. General Land Office, 1855–59, when, as the leader of the Democratic party in Indiana, he was its candidate for governor in 1860, but was defeated by Henry S. Lane. In 1863 Hendricks was elected to the U. S. Senate, where he was conspicuous in the opposition. In 1868 he was a prominent but unsuccessful candidate for the Democratic nomination for President, and he was defeated as candidate for governor of Indiana, but in 1872, although all the rest of the Democratic ticket was defeated, he was elected governor. In 1876 he received the nomination of his party for Vice-President, S. J. Tilden, of New York, being the candidate for President. In the election following this ticket received a majority of the popular vote, but did not secure a majority of the electoral vote. Mr. Hendricks then continued the practice of his profession until 1884, when he was again nominated by the Democratic party for Vice-President, and in November was elected. He was inaugurated on March 4, 1885. He was an effective public speaker and an earnest partisan. He died suddenly at Indianapolis, Nov. 25, 1885.

HENNEPIN, LOUIS (c. 1640–1702), a French explorer of America, was born at Ath, Belgium, about 1640. Entering the Franciscan order, he travelled in Germany and Italy, and was regimental chaplain. In 1675 he was sent to Canada in company with Bishop Laval, and went to the Indian mission at Fort Frontenac, and visited the Mohawks. In 1678, being attached to Sieur La Salle's expedition, he went first to Niagara, where a vessel was built to navigate the upper lakes. By way of Lakes Erie, Huron, and Michigan they reached St. Joseph's River, crossed to the Kankakee, sailed down to the Illinois, and built Fort Crèvecœur, a little below the present site of Peoria. Hence Father Hennepin, by direction of La Salle, set out in a canoe to make further explorations, Feb. 29, 1680. They sailed north on the Mississippi, and on April 11 were captured by the Sioux. In July they were rescued by Daniel Greysolon du Luht, who had come by the way of Lake Superior. Passing down the Mississippi, then up the Wisconsin and down the Fox, they reached Lake Michigan. Hennepin went to Quebec, and thence to France, where he published his *Description de la Louisiane, nouvellement découverte au sudouest de la Nouvelle France* (1683). He was appointed guardian of a convent, but afterwards refusing to return to America he was compelled to leave France. He then sought the favor of William III., and, having laid aside the dress of his order, lived in England, where he published his *New Discovery of a Vast Country in America* (London, 1698). In this he claimed to be the first European who had descended the Mississippi to the Gulf of Mexico. The falseness of his statements was finally exposed by Jared Sparks in his *Life of La Salle*. Hennepin published other works in French, and his books were long held in high esteem. He tried also to recover favor in France and with the superiors of his order, but without success. He died in Holland in 1702.

HENNINGSEN, CHARLES FREDERICK (1815–1877), an English soldier and author, was born in 1815. At the age of nineteen he entered the army of Don Carlos in Spain and became captain of Zumalacarregui's body-guard, afterwards rose to be colonel in command of the cavalry. Being taken prisoner, he was released on parole not to serve again during the war. He then joined the Russian army in Circassia, and on his return to England published *Revelations of Russia* (1845). He proposed a plan of war to the revolutionary leaders of Hungary in 1848, but the struggle ended before the plan was put in operation. He then visited Kossuth at Kutaiyeh, and came to the United States to represent Hungarian interests. In 1856 he was major-general in Walker's Nicaragua expedition. In the American civil war he was a brigadier-general in the Confederate army and served in Virginia. After the war he resided in Washington and gave much attention to the improvement of small arms. He died at Washington, D. C., June 14, 1877. He published *Twelve Months with Zumalacarregui; The White Slave*, a novel; *Eastern Europe; Sixty Years Hence*, a story of Russian life; *Past and Future of Hungary; Analogies and Contrasts*, and other works.

HENRY, CALEB SPRAGUE (1804–1884), an American clergyman, was born at Rutland, Mass., Aug. 2, 1804. He graduated at Dartmouth College in 1825, studied theology at Andover and New Haven, and was ordained as a Congregational minister. In 1833 he took charge of a church at Hartford, Conn., and soon afterward established *The American Advocate of Peace*, which became the organ of the American Peace Society. In 1835 he took orders in the Episcopal Church, and was appointed professor of intellectual and moral philosophy in Bristol College, Pa. In 1837 he went to New York, where, in company with Rev. F. L. Hawks, D. D., he founded the *New York Review*, which they edited until 1840. From 1839 to 1852 Dr. Henry was professor of philosophy and history in the University of New York. In 1857 he removed to Poughkeepsie, and he was afterward rector of a church at Newburg. He died at Stamford, Conn., March 16, 1884. He translated and edited *Cousin's Psychology* (1834); *Guizot's General History of Civilization* (1848), and published *Moral and Philosophical Essays* (1839); *Dr. Oldham at Graystones and his Talk there* (1860); *Elements and Conditions of Social Welfare* (1868).

HERBARIUM. A collection of dried plants, for the purpose of botanical study and reference. Such collections are of the utmost value to botanists, much surpassing in value the most carefully executed drawings in the identification of plants and the study of their characters. If properly prepared and cared for, dried specimens of plants may be kept for centuries, with little loss of value to botanists. The methods of preparation are simple, there being little difficulty in the drying of plants, with the exception of the cellular cryptogams, many of which cannot be satisfactorily preserved.

The plant being gathered, and care taken to secure every part that has any systematic value, it is carefully dried, ordinarily by pressing between layers of bibulous paper, which is changed at first at frequent intervals, and afterwards less frequently, until the plant is completely dry. A wire press has also, of late years, come into use, the plant, enclosed between sheets of drying paper, being hung up in the air to dry, or exposed to the action of artificial heat. As to the value of this method there seem to be differences of opinion. In drying cellular plants, particularly the fungi and algæ, greater difficulty is presented, and it is often impossible to preserve them satisfactorily. In all cases a highly important part of the process is the poisoning of the plant, to secure it from the ravages of insects. A solution of corrosive sublimate in alcohol is the poison generally employed, and is very successful if care be taken to apply it to every part of the plant. In the Harvard herbarium arsenic acid is now used, and is claimed to be of superior value.

The dried specimen is next glued or otherwise fastened to a sheet of stiff white paper, and the name of the genus and species, the locality and date of finding, with any other matter of importance, written beneath. If the dissected parts of a flower be added, the value of the specimen is greatly increased. Thus prepared, the sheets are arranged botanically for ready reference. The species of a genus are usually placed together, and enclosed within a sheet of brown paper, they being ordinarily arranged alphabetically in American herbaria, with a name-card at the lower right-hand corner of the sheet for easy reference. The genera are arranged in their cases either alphabetically or according to their botanical alliances, as suits the taste of the collector. Families, orders, and classes are, of course, arranged in accordance with scientific classification.

The most complete herbarium in the world is that of Kew Gardens, England, which is claimed to contain about 100,000 species, and much more numerous specimens. The British Museum, and most of the more important European cities, also have valuable herbaria. Of the herbaria of the United States, by far the most extensive and important is that of Harvard College, collected by or through the agency of Dr. Gray. This valuable collection is particularly rich in North American species, of which it presents an unequalled representation. Very many of its plants are of particular importance, as being the type specimens of the species. No statement of the number of species possessed has been made public, but it is steadily increasing in extent, both by additions of new American plants and the constant increase of its rich collection of foreign species.

The American herbarium next in importance to this is that of Columbia College, the collection of Dr. Torrey. It has a high value from its numerous types of North American species, and also for the fine drawings, elucidative of structural details, done on the sheets by Dr. Torrey. It is estimated to contain 35,000 species. More recently there has been added to it a very large European collection—the Meisner herbarium—embracing some 30,000 species and the collection of Dr. Chapman; so that the complete herbarium is said now to contain over 70,000 species.

The third in value of American herbaria is the important collection of the Academy of Natural Sciences of Philadelphia. Its value is enhanced by its large number of species of early collectors, and of type specimens of early authors. Of phanerogamous plants and ferns it embraces about 25,000 species, in addition to which there is a large collection of the lower cryptogams, the total herbarium embracing from 40,000 to 45,000 species. Its main special features are the Short herbarium, a splendidly selected and mounted collection, donated by Dr. Charles W. Short, of Louisville, Ky., and a special North American herbarium, illustrative of the botany of the continent. Another Philadelphia collection, small in extent, but valuable for its great age, is that of the American Philosophical Society.

Of the remaining American herbaria there is one of considerable extent at Lafayette College, while the valuable collection of Prof. Eaton, at New Haven, is important as containing the most complete series of ferns in this country. Another large and valuable herbarium is that of the late Dr. Engelmann, of St. Louis. This will probably be deposited in the Shaw Gardens, of that city. Smaller herbaria are possessed by all the colleges of the West, of which we need only mention that of the California Academy of Science, from its rich collection of the plants of the Pacific slope. (C. M.)

HERD-BOOK. A book in which is recorded the name, sex, number, markings, date of birth, pedigree, breeder, and owner of every member of a particular breed of animals. Whenever a family of animals is established as a breed of intrinsic value, a herd-book or register becomes essential to its preservation. The individual breeder finds it necessary to preserve the pedigree and life-record of every animal born in his herd, or otherwise acquired, and his book of record becomes his *private herd-book*. If he has developed in his herd specially valuable features, by reason of which its members excel other herds of the same race of animals, then the sale of members of his herd, and the multiplication of the progeny in the hands of hundreds and thousands of breeders, in different parts of the same country or in others, necessitates the construction of a *common herd-book*, which shall include all members of the same family of pure blood wherever bred.

The herd-book is mainly of value to the breeder of

stock as an evidence of that pedigree which guarantees a fixed family type, and the power of transmitting this type unimpaired to the offspring. Any pure bred family of animals has been preserved from contamination by crossing with animals of the same species, but outside the line of this family, because of some esteemed quality in which the preserved family especially excels. Thus the Arabian horse, and, still more, the English thoroughbred, are of especial value for their speed and endurance; the American trotter for his unequalled capacity for trotting; the English Shire-horse and Clydesdale for their powers of draught; the Shorthorn, Hereford, and Angus cattle for their early maturity and propensity to fatten; the Ayrshire and Holstein cattle for heavy milking; the Jersey, Guernsey, and Alderney for the abundance and quality of their butter; the Leicester sheep for early maturity, long silky wool, and heavy carcass; the different Down-sheep for the excellence of their mutton and medium wool; the Merinos for the fineness and felting quality of their wool; the Manchamp for its exquisite silky fleece; the small Yorkshire, Berkshire, Essex, and Suffolk pigs for early maturity and the delicacy of their pork; and the large Yorkshire and Poland-China for the extent and weight of their "sides." Any such specific quality of a breed is, with very few exceptions, the common property of all members of the breed, so long as the line of descent is pure and uncontaminated by any cross from another family. The greater the number of generations for which the breed has been propagated, without such a cross, the more fixed is this family or race character, and the more rarely will a deviation from it appear. (See HEREDITY.)

Great personal excellence in an animal is of less certain value to the breeder than that fixity of type which comes from purity of blood, and the careful breeding up to this type for many antecedent generations. The first cross, between two different breeds, is often personally larger and better than either of its parents, but he will rarely reproduce his own personal qualities, nor those of either parent with certainty, and if crossed upon an animal of pure blood, but of a race inferior to his parents, will produce offspring more nearly resembling this inferior race than either of the two races from which he himself is sprung. By the cross he has lost the "prepotency" which his parents possessed, and with it much of his value as a breeding animal. Purity of blood guards against this degeneration, and the herd-book will give assurance of this purity.

Again, among animals of valuable breed there appear some of exceptional worth, which it is desirable to perpetuate. This is accomplished by coupling the descendants of one such exceptional animal so far as is compatible with the avoidance of injury from undue consanguinity, and the more numerous the lines on which you can trace the ancestry of a given animal up to some exceptionably valuable progenitor the greater is the proportion of the blood of this progenitor in his veins, and the greater is the certainty that he will reproduce in his progeny the characters of this esteemed ancestor. Thus a colt is valued largely in proportion to the number of lines in which his blood can be traced back to Eclipse, King Herod, Henry Clay, Flora Temple, or other noted performers on turf or track. A shorthorn is valued largely in ratio with the number of lines through which he can be traced to Hubback, or to some special Duke or other valuable animal. Without a herd-book reliable information cannot be obtained.

A breeder striving to establish a special characteristic in his branch of a given breed finds that, to avoid undue consanguinity, he must draw upon another branch of the breed. The herd-book guides him at once to those families and members of the breed most nearly related to his own strain, and where accordingly he will be most likely to find individuals with the qualities he covets. Through the same guidance he can often find animals closely related to his own stock, but which have been bred for a generation or two in a different climate and on different soil, thus acquiring a sexual compatibility with their near relations in his own herd.

Again, in starting a herd, in introducing fresh blood into an old herd, or in purchasing for special personal excellence, the buyer can, by a reference to the herd-book, ascertain what families or strains of the breed have furnished the greatest number of superior animals, and by securing the best he starts with a greatly enhanced prospect of success.

The production, preservation, and improvement of valuable breeds, thus rendered possible by the help of herd-books and stud-books, has received other fostering under the paternal governments of Europe. Over the whole of that continent we find government studs and herds, the purity of which is most sedulously guarded, and the pedigrees of which are recorded in the national stud-books and herd-books. The value of these breeding-farms in distributing thoroughbred sires for the improvement of the native races has been almost beyond computation, but now, when many excellent private establishments of a similar kind have been started, the owners of these feel the pressure of government competition, and are petitioning for the abolition of the state studs. In the United States, as in Great Britain, all such advancement has been left to private enterprise, and by this the demand has been reasonably well met. Yet both countries might profitably learn from Europe, and institute a government control of all herd-books and stud-books. The compilation of such a record by a private individual or an association is confessedly liable to abuse. But our National Bureau of Animal Industry might well undertake this work, and if registration fees were fixed so low as to come within the means of all breeders, a great impetus would be given to the general improvement of live-stock and increase of national wealth.

The following is a list of herd-books, etc., for American stock, at the time of writing:

HORSES.—*Thoroughbreds. English Racer.*—*American Stud Book*, S. D. Bruce, *Turf, Field, and Farm*, New York.

Trotters.—*Wallace's Trotting Register*, Broadway, New York; *Breeders' Trotting Stud Book*, J. H. Sanders, office of *Breeders' Gazette*, Chicago.

Percherons.—*Percheron Stud Book of America*, J. H. Sanders, office of *Breeders' Gazette*, Chicago.

French Draught Horses.—T. Butterworth, Quincy, Ill.

Clydesdales.—*American Clydesdale Stud Book*, C. F. Mills, Springfield, Ill.

Shire-Horses.—*Shire-Horse Stud Book of America*, Charles F. Burgess, Wenona, Ill.

Cleveland Bays.—In preparation.

CATTLE.—*Shorthorns.*—*American Shorthorn Herd Book*, J. H. Pickerell, 27 Montauk Block, Chicago.

Herefords.—*American Hereford Record*, Charles Gudgell, Independence, Mo.

Holstein.—*Holstein Herd Book*, Thos. B. Wales, Jr., Iowa City, Ia.

Dutch-Friesian Herd Book.—S. Hoxie, Whitestown, N. Y. *American Branch of North-Holland Herd Book*, Sanford, Warwick, N. Y.

Aberdeen—Angus.—Charles Gudgell, Independence, Mo.

Galloway.—*American Galloway Herd Book*, W. C. Weedon, Kansas City, Mo.

Jerseys.—*Jersey Herd Register*, T. J. Hand, 3 Broadway, N. Y.; *Jersey Herd Book*, O. B. Hadwen, Worcester, Mass.
Guernseys.—*American Guernsey Herd Register*, E. Norton, Farmington, Conn.
Devons.—*American Devon Record*, James Buckingham, Zanesville, O.
Red Polled.—*American Red Polled Record*, J. C. Murray, Maquokete, Ia.
Ayrshire.—*Ayrshire Record*, C. M. Winslow, Brandon, Vt.
Holderness.—*American Holderness Record*, Truman A. Cole, Salsville, N. Y.
SHEEP.—*Cotswolds.*—*American Cotswold Record*, George Harding, Waukesha, Wis.
Shropshires.—*American Shropshire Record*, Mortimer Levering, La Fayette, Ind.
Southdowns.—*American Southdown Record*, S. E. Prather, Springfield, Ill.
Oxford-Downs.—*American Oxford-Downs Record*, T. W. W. Sunman, Spades, Ind.
Merinos.— *United States Merino Sheep Register*, S. C. Gist, Wellsburg, W. Va.; *Register of the Vermont Merino Sheep-Breeders' Association*, Albert Chapman, Middlebury, Vt.; *Register of the New York State American Merino Sheep-Breeders' Association*, John P. Ray, Hemlock Lake, N. Y.; *Michigan Merino Sheep Register*, W. J. G. Dean, Hanover, Mich.; *Ohio Spanish Merino Sheep Register*, J. G. Blue, Cardington, O.; *Wisconsin Merino Sheep Register*, R. J. Wilkinson, Whitewater, Wis.; *Missouri Merino Sheep Association Register*, H. V. Pugsley, Plattsburg, Mo.; *American Merino Sheep Register*, Asa H. Craig, Caldwell, Wis.; *National Improved Saxony Sheep-Breeders' Association Register*, J. H. Clark, Toledo, Pa.; *Delaine Merino Register*, J. C. McNary, Houstonville, Pa.; *Vermont Attwood Club Register*, George Hammond, Middlebury, Vt.
SWINE.—*Berkshires.*—*American Berkshire Record*, P. M. Springer, Springfield, Ill.
Poland-Chinas.—*American Poland-China Record*, John Gilmore, Vinton, Ia.; *Central Poland-China Record*, W. H. Morris, Indianapolis, Ind.; *Ohio Poland-China Record*, Carl Freigan, Dayton, O.
Small Yorkshires.—*American Yorkshire Record*, G. W. Harris, P. O. Box 3432, New York City.
Chester Whites.—*National Chester White Record*, E. R. Moody, Eminence, Ky.
Duroc-Jerseys.—*Duroc-Jersey Swine Register*, C. H. Holmes, Grinnell, Ia.
(J. L.)

HEREDITAMENTS. See PROPERTY.

HEREDITY. The fact of the persistence of species, the important principle that the offspring of every animal or plant resembles its parents in its general characteristics, is one that has been long recognized, and forms the basis of organic classification. It has given rise to the doctrine of the immutability of species, a doctrine which is attacked by modern evolutionists, who declare that the resemblance of offspring to parents is never complete, and that the slight but incessant deviations may accumulate until a difference of species is established. The controversy which has been long and bitterly waged upon this point is largely based on the facts of heredity. These facts it is our purpose to briefly consider, as established by recent research.

Two things are undisputed: first, that the distinctive characters of a race are repeated in its descendants almost undeviatingly; second, that within the limits of the race individual deviations are of constant occurrence. But close research has been necessary; first, to establish to what degree living beings repeat themselves in their descendants; second, to discover the law of this repetition. We can but give some general results of this research into the facts and principles of heredity. We shall first consider the facts of resemblance, and afterwards those of difference.

The resemblance of children to their parents is a fact of general observation. In some cases the likeness is extraordinarily close, so that, but for difference in age, the child could not be distinguished from one or other of its parents. Usually the likeness is less exact, and while there are traceable resemblances to one or both parents, there are well-marked differences. The most generally observed heredity is of external structure. This embraces resemblance in features, complexion, size, and shape of body, obesity or leanness, and many minor peculiarities of less noticeable character. For instance, such a minor character as a notch or depression in the thumb-nail has been known to be transmitted through several generations of a family. Anomalies of structure are equally persistent. In the case of Edward Lambert, the "porcupine man," whose whole body was covered with horny excrescences, this peculiarity was transmitted to his male descendants for five generations. So the anomaly of six fingers and toes has been transmitted through four generations. Both these features might have been indefinitely persistent but for intermarriage with normal individuals, and the consequent action of normal influences.

A less observable phase of heredity is of internal structure. The proportions of the bones and of the organs of the body are transmissible characters. In some families the heart and the main blood-vessels are very large. In others they are small. Some families are fuller blooded than others. So a great or a small development of the nervous and the muscular systems are transmissible characters. Closely related to this is the hereditary character of certain diseases. These are such as are due to constitutional weaknesses in one or other of the body tissues, these weaknesses, and the consequent liability to the accordant disease, being transmissible. Less directly dependent on structure are other hereditable characteristics, such as fecundity, length of life, and personal idiosyncracies, well-marked instances of each of which are on record. Though the average life of man depends on more general causes, there are families in which both long life and short life are hereditary. In the Turgot family, for instance, the fifty-ninth year was rarely passed; though apparently in good health and strength, the members of that family almost invariably failed and died before reaching that age. In other families, through successive generations, the general life-period will range well up towards the hundred. So we may name among the hereditary qualities immunity from contagious diseases, bodily activity and strength, grace of movement, powers of voice, keenness of sight, or of some other sense, and special peculiarities in these and other characteristics. There are also on record many cases of the inheritance of special habits. Even such a personal peculiarity as a style of handwriting may be transmitted.

If now we consider the mental powers of animals, the influence of heredity is similarly apparent. A striking instance of it is the heredity of instincts in the lower animals. This is remarkably displayed in the long-continued transmission of the highly complex instincts of ants and bees. In like manner newly-gained habits may be transmitted through many generations, as we perceive in the persistence of habits in breeds of trained dogs, etc. In regard to the intellectual qualities the instances of heredity are very numerous. The resemblances of a child to its parents in propensities, passions, mental tendencies, etc., are too numerous and evident to be here dwelt upon. Close observation has traced many instances of inheritance of the higher intellectual powers. Thus, in regard to the imagination, there are long lists extant of poets, painters, musicians, and novelists in whom the faculty descended through two or more generations. The same may be said of general literary or scientific tendency, of logical and mathematical powers, etc. Instructive lists of this kind have been made by Galton and others, with the result of proving that genius may be heritable. Less desirable mental conditions may be similarly transmitted, such as the alcohol habit and the tendency to insanity, of which there are many instances. There are recorded cases where lunacy was transmitted through eight and even through eleven generations. The tendency to commit suicide seems similarly transmissible, as it has been traced through four generations. Aristocratic pride is another inheritable quality, and the list might be extended to cover every phase, minor and major, of the physical and mental characters of animals. In fact, in nations where little or no mingling with external peoples has taken place, peculiar national characters arise, which are transmitted as truly as are family characters. This is strongly manifested in such isolated peoples as the Jews, the Gypsies, and the Chinese, and is manifest in a lesser degree in all distinct nations, members of which can usually be recognized by some peculiarity of body or mind. The same principle strongly applies to the distinct races of mankind, such as the African, the Mongolian, the Aryan, etc. Their distinctive peculiarities are transmitted to millions of descendants, who have "bred true" through very many generations. That this long persistent inheritance is in any sense a result of chance, no sane person will for a moment maintain. That it is due to some principle of heredity, inherent in all organic beings, is too evident to be disputed. Maupertuis cites a case of sexdigitism which was transmitted through four generations. This was in a city of 100,000 inhabitants, in which he found but one other case of this anomaly. Estimating from these data the probability of its transmission by chance to a second generation, he found it to be but 1 in 20,000. The probability of its transmission to the third generation became 1 in 400,000,000; and to the fourth, 1 in 8,000,000,000,000. This calculation removes the problem of heredity from any theory of chance, and relegates it to the domain of natural law.

We have next to consider some other phases of the principle of heredity. As every child has two parents it is simply impossible that he should resemble both. If intermediate in form and character, he can exactly resemble neither. This is one cause of differentiation. In the case of hermaphrodite animals the offspring very closely resemble the single parent. In dual parentage, though the characters of the offspring are very seldom exactly intermediate between those of the parent, and usually strongly deviate towards one parent, an exact resemblance is in nearly every case prevented by some degree of influence from the other parent. Instances of every possible case of transmission of parental characters may be found. Thus the characters of the father sometimes descend to the son, sometimes to the daughter. So the characters of the mother may reappear now in male and now in female children. Cases of this kind are known as direct heredity. Other cases are those of reversional heredity or atavism, and of collateral or indirect heredity. Atavism is a case in which a child resembles one of its grandparents, or a more remote ancestor. Indirect heredity is less common, and applies to resemblance to an aunt or uncle, a nephew or niece, etc. The latter case is, at first sight, puzzling, yet it is probably but a more extended case of atavism, the characters simulated having been derived from some distant ancestor common to both parties. There are cases on record where characters which are traceable to some exceedingly remote ancestor have appeared. These seem to indicate a partial arrest of development in the individual.

Having thus considered the case of resemblance we have next to consider that of difference—the exceptions to heredity, which are as numerous as the accordances. These exceptions are partly due to the influence of both parents upon the child, since a compound of two unlike elements must differ from either. A new combination is also produced by the sexual influence. A female child, for instance, may resemble its father in many particulars of form and mentality, yet it must resemble its mother in certain dominant characters of structure and mental tendency. The principal of differentiation here considered, however, is not the cause of the great diversity in organic beings. If acting alone it would tend to produce homogeneity, the greatest original diversity being gradually obliterated by the constant transmission of intermediate characters to offspring. Under such a principle alone the great homogeneity of hermaphrodite animals could never have become the existing heterogeneity of advanced organisms. There is very evidently some other law of differentiation active, through whose influence all offspring tend to differ from their parents, these differences being usually slight, but occasionally considerable. By their accumulation they overcome the tendency to homogeneity, and produce an increasing heterogeneity. This is added to by the influences already considered in two ways. First by the union of parents of marked differences in organization, whose offspring, even if intermediate, must be strongly individualized. And here two results of experience may be mentioned. If the parents are too greatly unlike in organization no offspring will be produced, or the offspring will be an infertile hybrid. If they are too closely similar in organization, the offspring is liable to be defective in some particular, either of body or mind, as if parental similarity had caused partial or local arrest of development. Thus it has become apparent that a certain degree of difference in temperament and bodily organization, but not too great a difference, is necessary to the best results of sexual union, and that close breeding is apt to yield imperfect offspring, and the union of unlike species to result in infertility. The other general cause of heterogeneity is the gaining of new habits, structural peculiarities, or mental tendencies during the life of the individual, since all such new-gained characters are transmissible, and may produce in the offspring marked changes from the family characteristics. These individual variations, as ordinarily observed, are such as take place during the youth or maturity of the person, and are the results of the action of physical and mental influences upon his body and mind. But it is quite conceivable that similar warping influences may act upon the embryo in its uterine development, and that from the period of fertilization of the germ-cell the growing organism may be subject, even within the body of the mother, to the action of disturbing forces, which produce changes in its organization. Various instances of evident interuterine variations are on record.

That the variations of offspring from parents are due in a considerable measure to the causes above outlined cannot be denied. But that they are due only to these causes cannot be affirmed. There is evidently some principle of variation acting at a lower level in the life history, some force which acts upon the germinal cells of both parents, and so affects these that, while capable of developing into close counterparts of the parental individuals, they have innate tendencies to diverge in certain particulars, and to produce new individuals possessed of characters of organization which are not present in either parent. What this warping principle is remains a mystery. We are confined here to a review of its effects.

A very common divergence in the offspring from its parents is in respect to size and general form. Thus parents of middle height may produce tall children. Others again, of average size, and good health and constitution, may produce offspring of low or dwarfed stature. Thus Bebe, the famous dwarf of King Stanislas, 33 inches high, had well-formed, vigorous parents. The celebrated Polish dwarf, Borwalaski, 28 inches high, had a dwarfed brother and sister, and three other brothers each 5 feet 6 inches high. Other cases of marked differentiation are numerous. Harelip, polydactylism, etc., arise as exceptions, though they afterwards become heritable factors. The case above mentioned, that of Edward Lambert, the porcupine man, arose as an exception from normal parents. Minor exceptions are of every-day occurrence. A remarkable instance of this principle is seen in the case of twins. Here there is often a close resemblance, but often also a strongly marked difference, despite the fact that during gestation they have been exposed to the same influences, and the presumption that the germs must have been formed under similar conditions. Even in double monsters the same differentiation appears. As one instance may be mentioned that of Ritta and Christina, the joined twins of Presburg, of whom one was handsome, gentle, and sedate ; the other ugly, ill-conditioned, and quarrelsome. Chang and Eng, the Siamese twins, were also different in appearance and character, though not to the same extent. As above observed the cause of this difference must have acted upon the germs during their original formation. As to the germinal conditions of joined twins we are greatly in the dark.

Another frequently observed and highly important instance of differentiation is that in the mental powers and faculties. Great intellectual power has frequently arisen as an anomaly. In the case of the great men of the world, in some instances one or both parents were above the average in mind. In other cases there is no evidence of this. And as a rule in such cases the parents have been below their offspring in intellectual powers. Like other anomalies, if it may be regarded as such, this of great intellect is transmissible. But in no instance can it be traced beyond two or three generations. The descendants of great thinkers quickly descend to the common plane in intellect, and often the descent is as sudden and great as was the rise. The greatest men of the earth usually stand alone, with no family link of greatness above or below. We have spoken of extreme intellectuality as an anomaly. And it is certain that children of abnormal brain development, and very active intellect even during childhood, are not infrequent. As a general rule they die young from some brain disease. Yet occasionally such infant prodigies survive to astonish the world

One thing the whole history of mankind and of organic nature teaches us, that divergences from the average condition of a species or race are not persistent. The principle of heredity exerts a stronger force than the opposing principle. We perceive individuals incessantly diverging from the average condition of body or mind, yet their descendants are quickly brought back, and the characters of the race are maintained with a persistence which shows the vigorous influence of heredity. This, of course, is very largely due to the unlimited sexual union of persons of every condition of organization, so that divergence in one direction is overcome by the influence of divergence in another. In consequence, in all the races of organic beings below man and the domesticated animals and plants, the action of heredity is the dominant power, and permanent divergence from the line of a species only appears at long intervals and under exceptional circumstances. In the breeds of domesticated animals and the varieties of cultivated plants the opposite rule holds. Divergent individuals are isolated, promiscuous union prevented, and their peculiarities sustained by close breeding, so that the effects which nature produces after many centuries, and by chance, man produces in a few years, and by design. The numerous persistent breeds of dogs, pigeons, and other domestic animals, and varieties of cultivated plants, are marked results of checking the full action of heredity, and favoring that of divergence, so as to give the latter a supremacy which it does not possess under natural conditions. A similar effect is produced in man, to a lesser degree. The separation of peoples into castes or classes acts as a sort of in-and-in breeding, and yields well-marked varieties. A common instance is the strong difference in body and mind between the members of a nobility and those of the peasantry of the same nation. Yet in nearly every case of a nobility its limitation in numbers and close intermarriage yield the evil effect of too great similarity in organization, with the result of a mental and physical degeneration, and a thinning out in members, so that, in the words of Niebuhr, "aristocracies obliged to recruit their numbers from among themselves become extinct, in the same way often passing through degeneracy, insanity, dementia, and imbecility."

A similar isolation may take place in the case of a nation, with the preservation of special national traits, such as the imaginative intellectuality of the Greeks, the cruelty and warlike spirit of the Romans, the trading tendency of the Jews, and many other characteristics which might be cited. This influence of national heredity is very strong in the older nationalities, and was much stronger in the past than now, from the influence of greater isolation. In these old nations class distinctions are rigidly maintained, the propensities of families are strengthened by legal restriction, prejudices act to check deviations, trades and beliefs are heritable obligations, while sharp hindrances to freedom of thought and action exist. This influence which tends to produce special breeds and varieties of men within the limits of a nation is least active in the United States, where classes, sects, and prejudices have no rigid existence, where the individual is not the slave of old laws and habits, and may change his condition without social or legal restriction, and where the mingling of peoples is not confined to the members of a single nationality, but includes representatives of all the civilized and some of the uncivilized races of mankind. As a consequence strict family heredity is strongly overcome in the United States, and men are not isolated into classes or breeds, while the principle of individual divergence is allowed its fullest exercise, and takes the place of class divergence elsewhere.

The differences between nations in physical and mental character, however, are not of primitive origin. They have been produced by the slow accumulation of divergences of individual origin, and preserved by heredity. If we consider these differences closely it will be to find them more mental than physical, and very largely due to the action of circumstances on the individual. They are not in opposition to the law of heredity, but simply produce new transmissible characters, which, by their slow accumulation, constitute a new national character. But circumstances, education, and natural influences exert less influence upon the body than upon the mind. The physical characters of races are very persistent. They vary slightly but slowly, and while peoples of the same race origin, dwelling under different circumstances, may present observable physical differences, their racial likeness is seldom overcome. The mind is more plastic, is exposed to a greater variety of influences, and special divergences are produced in it by educational training. In consequence separate nations present much stronger mental than physical divergences, and we may perceive growing up in the members of an original race, in a few centuries, such strong mental differences as existed between the Greeks and Romans.

The fact is, heredity acts more vigorously on the body than on the mind. The child receives his complete body from his parents. He receives only the germ of his mind. His individual mental stores must be gathered by himself, and may be of a character to considerably transform his inherited mental strain. Yet the germinal mental tendencies are very vigorous, and yield but slowly to transforming influences. The possible extent of mental development is also strictly limited by hereditary conditions. Thus the brightest offspring of the savage races are incapable of attaining the intellectual development of an average Aryan, despite all efforts at education. "In childhood," says Sir Samuel Baker, "the young negro is more advanced than the white of the same age, but his mind does not bear the fruit of which it gave promise." "In New Zealand," says Thompson, "children of ten years are more intelligent than English; still very few New Zealanders are capable of receiving in their higher faculties a culture equal to that of the English."

To summarize briefly, the influence of heredity on organic beings, while the most powerful of the agencies active in organic nature, is not all-dominant, its action being subject to several opposing agencies which produce steadily increasing divergences, and yield varieties, races, and, as many maintain, species and genera, and all the existing variations in the organic kingdoms. Of these diverging influences a very strong one is the action of natural agencies on the individual, both before and after birth, with the effect of producing new inheritable qualities. Another is the sexual union of individuals of bodily and mental divergence, yielding young who are specialized by the combination of characters derived from two unlike individuals. A third is the action of some untraced principle of divergence which acts on the germ cell during its original formation, side by side with the principle of heredity, so that, while there is instilled a strong inherent tendency to repeat the characters of the parent, there is instilled a like inherent tendency to diverge in certain particulars, and to produce characters in the offspring not existent in either parent.

The influences here considered are those which have controlled the whole evolution of organic nature, in the creed of modern evolutionists, and have produced the extraordinary variety of living beings which now exist side by side with the strong persistence of family and race characteristics. The plastic life substance and mental faculties of organic beings have steadily yielded to the force of influences internal and external, and have gained new forms and conditions despite the action of a highly vigorous principle of heredity.

(C. M.)

HERING, CONSTANTINE (1800–1880), an American physician, was born at Oschatz, Saxony, Jan. 1, 1800. He studied medicine at Leipsic and Dresden and in 1826 received his degree at Würzburg. He was afterwards sent on a scientific expedition to Dutch Guiana, and in 1834 he settled in Philadelphia, where he gained an extensive practice. He was the first to introduce homœopathy in the United States and was long the most prominent advocate of that system. His first work was *The Rise and Progress of Homœopathy* (1834), which has been translated into several languages. He also published *The Domestic Physician* and *American Drug-Provings*, which were also issued in Germany. Dr. Hering also contributed to homœopathic reviews and journals. He died at Philadelphia, July 23, 1880.

HERKIMER, NICHOLAS (c. 1725–1777), an American Revolutionary soldier, was the eldest son of J. J. Herkimer, a Palatine, and one of the original patentees of Burnet's Field in what is now Herkimer co., N. Y. He was appointed lieutenant of militia, Jan. 5, 1758, and commanded Fort Herkimer during the attack of the French and Indians in that year. In 1775 he was colonel of a battalion and chairman of Tryon county committee of safety. In September, 1776, he was made brigadier-general, and when Col. St. Leger, sent out by Gen. Burgoyne, was besieging Fort Schuyler, Herkimer with 800 militia marched to its relief. At first he proceeded cautiously, but being urged to proceed more rapidly he fell into an ambuscade at Oriskany, Aug. 6, 1777. He was soon wounded, but continued to direct the fight for five hours. A sortie from Fort Schuyler relieved his men after a loss of 200. Herkimer died from the effects of his wound, Aug. 11, 1777. At the centennial anniversary of Oriskany his statue was ordered to be erected.

HERKOMER, HUBERT, an English painter, was born in Waal, Bavaria, in 1849. His father was a wood-carver, who, after a residence of six years in the United States, settled in 1857 at Southampton, England. After studying in the art school there and at South Kensington Hubert settled at Hythe in 1868, and exhibited two pictures in the Dudley gallery in 1869. The *London Graphic* in 1873 published the first sketch of his Chelsea Pensioners, the oil-painting of which was highly successful when exhibited in 1875. Eventide, showing a group of old women at the workhouse, may be considered a companion piece. He has executed other pictures in which he shows the same combination of pathos and humor in delineations of the aged.

HERNDON, WILLIAM LEWIS (1813–1857), an American naval officer, was born at Fredericksburg, Va., Oct. 25, 1813. He entered the navy in 1828, served on various cruises and in the Mexican war, and was afterwards engaged for three years in the observatory at Washington with his brother-in-law, Lieut. M. F. Maury. In 1851 he was sent to explore the Amazon River, and reaching its headwaters by crossing the Andes from Lima, he sailed down it in a canoe. Two volumes were published by the U. S. Government, the first by Herndon and the second by his associate Lieut. Lardner Gibbon, under the title, *Exploration of the Valley of the Amazon* (1853-54). Herndon was commander of the steamer Central America, which sailed from Havana for New York, Sept. 8, 1857, with 474 passengers, 105 sailors, and about $2,000,000 in gold. During a violent storm she sprang a leak, and sank on Sept. 12 in the Gulf stream in N. lat. 31° 44'. All the women and children were put in boats and with a few men were saved. Herndon and 426 men sank with the vessel. Pres. Arthur's wife was a daughter of Capt. Herndon.

HERON, the name generally applied to a large series of wading birds, of the family *Ardeidæ*, which includes many species, and is found in all the tropical and temperate regions of the earth. The true herons belong to the sub-family *Ardeidæ*, and in particular to the genus *Ardea*. They are tall birds, with very long neck and legs, and a long, sharp-pointed bill. The neck contains from 15 to 17 vertebræ. As a rule the head is partly or wholly naked. The tibia is naked below, the toes long and slender, and never fully webbed. The tail is short, and contains 12 broad and stiff feathers. The wings are long, broad, and ample. The peculiar feathers known as powder-down find their highest development on the herons.

See Vol. XI.
p. 679 Am.
ed. (p. 760
Edin. ed.).

Heron—Egret (*Ardea egretta*).

They occur on some other birds in a single pair, while *Ardea* has three pairs of powder-down tracts. The bill is longer than the head, straight, or nearly so, and with sharp-cutting edges. It is used to grasp their prey, the birds standing solitary and motionless for hours by the water, watching for passing fish, which are caught by the darting bill. They often perch on trees, where their nests are usually built. The birds sometimes breed singly, but oftener in great heronries, to which they return year after year.

In ordinary language the various types of *Ardeida* are known as herons, egrets, bitterns, night herons, and boatbills. These have been variously subdivided into genera, some writers retaining all but the boatbills in the genus *Ardea*, while others divide them up into several genera, and even separate the bitterns as a distinct sub-family. There is, in fact, very little variation in form between the species, and it is a difficult matter to classify them properly.

The herons are well represented in North America, comprising several large and abundant species. Among the most marked of these is *A. herodias*, the great blue heron, a species 4 feet in length, and nearly 6 feet in spread of wing. It extends throughout North America and into Central and South America. A still larger species, which belongs to the group of egrets, is *A. occidentalis*, the great white or Florida heron. It is 4½ feet long, with 7 feet extent of wings. A somewhat smaller species, *A. egretta*, or *Herodias egretta*, the great white egret, of 36 to 42 inches long, is of interest from its magnificent train of very long plumes of decomposed feathers, which droop far over the tail. *A. candidissima*, or *Garzetta candidissima*, the little white egret, has similar plumes, as also a long occipital crest of the same character, Both these species inhabit the Southern States, though occasionally straggling to the north. There are several other American forms, belonging to the different groups, but the above-named species are the most important.

HERRING, a highly important food-fish, comprising several species of the genus *Clupea*, a genus with considerable analogy to the *Salmonidæ*, yet differing in the absence of an adipose dorsal fin. The body is well scaled, the scales being sometimes very large. The jaw is formed as in the trout, in the middle by intermaxillary, and on the sides by the maxillary bones. The mouth is variously provided with teeth, these occurring sometimes on the pectinated tongue. The family comprises several of the most useful and indispensable of food-fishes, including the sardine, anchovy, sprat, shad, and various herring, all of which are very abundant. In the genus *Culpea* the body is compressed, the scales large, thin, and deciduous, the head compressed, the teeth minute or lacking. It has a single dorsal fin. The abdominal line forms a sharp, keel-like edge. The common herring is a beautiful fish, being highly iridescent when first taken from the water. Its back is deep-blue tinged with yellow, the side silvery with metallic reflections, the lower portion silvery. The body is elongated, fusiform, compressed, the eyes large and circular; length 12 to 15 inches. Its distinguishing feature is a patch of very small teeth on the vomer, or centre of the palate. The common American herring has been classified as a distinct species, under the name of *Clupea elongata*, but is now considered to be identical with *C. harengus*, the European species. Jordan, in his synopsis, date 1883, gives the American species of *Clupea* as *C. ha-*

See Vol. XI.
p. 683 Am.
ed. (p. 764
Edin. ed.).

rengus (the common herring); *C. mediocris* (hickory shad, tailor herring, fall herring); *C. vernalis* (alewife); *C. æstivalis* (blue-back, glut herring); and *C. sapidissima* (shad). But it must be noted that earlier writers do not include all these in one genus.

As to the natural history of the herring great uncertainty prevails. It was formerly supposed that they were a migratory species, descending annually in enormous shoals from the Arctic Seas to the shores of Northern Europe and America. This is now known to be an error. Herring are found in no abundance in the Arctic Seas. It is also found that those which visit each coast have some peculiarity, as of size, fatness, etc., tending to show that each is a separate brood. It is now believed that their habitat is the deep-sea region, off the immediate coast, which they visit annually for the purpose of spawning, and for other purposes, since shoals frequently appear which are not in spawning condition. They can, in fact, be caught all the year round on the British coasts, and on the Northern American shores, though the great shoals come in only at fixed periods.

These shoals sometimes contain enormous multitudes of fish. Their dense ranks have been traced to a length of 8 to 10 miles, by 2 to 4 miles wide, and of unknown depth. Yet great variations take place in the numbers in different years, they being in some seasons countless, in others very limited; while the individuals will now be very lean, now large and fat. This may be partly due to annual differences in the food-supply, though perhaps principally to destruction of spawn and young fish by the many enemies of the herring. A seeming scarcity is also often caused by a change of habitat, the shoals deserting old and seeking new spawning-grounds—a habit which belongs to nearly all migrating food-fishes.

The food of the herring consists of small fish and crustaceans, and other minor ocean-life forms. Its variation in quality in different localities is probably mainly due to differences in the character of its food. Herrings breed with great rapidity, and are so prolific that their numbers do not seem to be reduced by the annual raids made upon them. They are less exposed to destruction in their deep-sea life, and enough of the young escape to repair the annual ravages. Thus the herring serves as a means of rendering available as food the abundant stores of minor life of the ocean, which otherwise would be useless to man. The catch of herrings by man is frequently enormous. In some cases as many as 50,000 have been taken in one cast of the net. The total catch of 1873, by the boats of Yarmouth and Lomestofft, was 422,400,000. Yet the whole number taken by man is insignificant as compared with their destruction by their other enemies. On the approach of the shoals to land they are usually followed by hordes of hungry foes. Whales of several species rush through and make havoc in their ranks. The dog-fish and other voracious fish assail them. Great flocks of fishing-birds hover above, and dart down for their finny prey. But the most destructive of their enemies in American waters is the blue-fish, which kills ten times as many fish as it needs, and, according to Prof. Baird's calculation, must destroy 300,000,000,000 food-fish yearly. Compared with this the destruction by man is trifling.

The European herring-fisheries extend from the most northerly extremity of Scandinavia to the British Islands and the coast of Normandy, south of which the herring is seldom found. In Great Britain 100,000 men are employed in this industry, with 3000 vessels and a great number of small boats. The Dutch fishery, which once supplied Europe with cured herrings, has now greatly declined, while the Scotch fishery,

The Herring.

which was unimportant a century ago, has taken its place. The Dutch do not cure now more than 20,000 barrels, while the Scotch cure annually more than 500,000 barrels. These vary greatly in quality according to the season of the catch, the spring herrings being very poor, the midsummer run larger and fatter, while the true "harvest of the sea" is that which begins in September and lasts till Christmas. In addition to the localities named the herring-fishery is an important industry of England, Ireland, France, Denmark, Norway, and recently of Iceland.

On the Atlantic coast of North America, and particularly in the waters of Maine and Nova Scotia, the herring-fishery is important, being only surpassed by those of the cod and the mackerel. *C. harengus* is mainly confined to the northerly locality, where it is caught in great numbers. The fishing is done with nets, both drift or gill nets and seine nets being used. In this region the annual shoal makes its first appearance in the month of March, the product of the early catch being principally consumed as bait for the cod and other line fisheries. The more important market fishing does not commence until May. In this month a run of large fat herring is taken in nets on the banks, which lie 10 to 15 miles seaward and are about 75 fathoms deep. The nets used are 30 fathoms long and 3 deep. They are passed out from the anchored boat, the free end drifting backward and forward with the tide from evening till morning. The ordinary nightly catch is from 20 to 100 dozen per net. This fishing is very precarious, from the distance from shore and the need of fair weather. The inshore run of smaller-sized fish is taken in nets set to a buoy and left to drift, or else moored from one buoy to another across a creek or small bay. A small but very fat variety of herring visits the Bay of Fundy in the month of May, and is caught by the aid of herring weirs, a fish-gate over a shallow, which permits the fish to enter at high tide, but is bare at low tide. The extraordinary tides of this bay render this method very successful, and from 150 to 250 hogsheads of herring are frequently captured in a single tide. A considerable variety of such weirs is in use on the north-east coast of America, and a great multitude of herrings thus caught.

The herring catch of the States south of Maine is also very considerable, and consists mainly of the species known as the alewife, which differs from *C. harengus* in ascending the rivers to spawn. This species (*C. vernalis*) is from 8 to 12 inches long, and in no sense inferior to the common herring, which it much resembles. It is found plentifully in the rivers from New England to North Carolina, and very abundantly in the southerly part of this region. It was formerly so abundant on the coast of North Carolina that, according to Pennant, the inhabitants flung it ashore by shovelfuls. It left the salt water in March and ran up the rivers and over the shallow fords in such multitudes that travellers trampled many under foot while crossing the fords. In Maryland and Virginia it has been caught so abundantly as to be used for manure. A seine at the mouth of the Chowan River, N. C., 1½ miles long, and worked by steam, has taken as many as 300,000 herring in a day, together with 1000 to 2000 shad. It is still the custom of the North Carolina and Virginia farmers from the back counties to visit the coast annually for a supply of herrings to salt down. A large portion of the catch is thus disposed of. (See ALEWIFE.)

On the Pacific coast the principal species of herring is *C. mirabilis*. In size, appearance, and habits this species closely resembles the common herring, differing in some anatomical points. It is somewhat smaller, but is said to be of equal flavor. It occurs in great abundance, and the fishery promises to soon become important. At present it is most actively prosecuted in British America. The product of the American sea-herring-fishery for the year ending June 30, 1885, is given at 109,701 cwts. of cured fish, valued at $150,097. This is in addition to the very large number consumed fresh. The Canadian fisheries are considerably more prolific, the value of the Nova Scotia catch in 1876 being given at $4,128,000.

Herrings are largely consumed fresh, or partly cured for immediate use, in which state they are known as *bloaters*. But the principal part of the catch is cured, either by salting or by smoke-drying. In the former state they are known as white, in the latter as red herrings. Thus preserved they form a highly important part of the food of man, and one that is not likely to be exhausted, since the habits of the herring save it from danger of serious reduction by human fisheries. Its finny enemies are a hundred-fold more destructive than man, though they probably do less injury to the spawn. The name *herring* is said by Pennant to be derived from German *heer*, an army, a title significant of their extensive migrations. (C. M.)

HESSIAN FLY (*Cecidomyia destructor*, Say). It

See Vol. XI. p. 697 Am. ed. (p. 781 Edin. ed.).

is quite generally accepted by entomological writers that the Hessian fly was originally an European insect and was first introduced into this country at the time of the Revolutionary war, yet some consider the species indigenous, and at this late date the question cannot well be decided. At present it occurs throughout all the Northern States, as far west as Kansas and Minnesota, and as far south as the northern portion of the Gulf States. The adult is a delicate, two-winged midge, and the larva an orange-colored, footless maggot from 2 mm. to 3 mm. in length. There are two broods in the course of a year throughout the great wheat-section of the country, but a third, or an attempt at a third, in the more Southern States. The eggs of the first brood are laid in April or May, and those of the second usually in September. Each female lays about thirty eggs on the leaves of the wheat, and the larvæ, after four days, hatch and make their way down between the stalk and its sheath, near the base, causing the plant to swell, turn yellow, and die. At the end of from four to six or seven weeks, according to the temperature, the larvæ assume what is called the "flaxseed" state, in which the larva hardens so as to form what has been known as the coarctate pupa, but which is more correctly termed the coarctate larva. Within the shell the final larva lives for a while, and then transforms to the pupa and finally to the imago state. Hibernation takes place in the "flaxseed" state.

Hessian Fly.

a, larva; *b*, pupa; *c*, stalk showing "flaxseed" state; *d*, female fly—all enlarged but *c*. (After Fitch.)

Five parasites have been mentioned as attacking the Hessian fly, and these are said to destroy about nine-tenths of the larvæ hatched. But one of these—*Semiotellus destructor* (Say)—has been identified. Packard claims, in an egg-parasite, to have discovered the *Platygaster error*, Fitch; but this is doubtful, as Fitch's description is very scant.

Remedies.—Late sowing (after Sept. 20) has been recommended, and this is improved upon by sowing early a small patch or a narrow belt around the field to act as a trap. Where the field is only partly affected, careful cultivation and the use of fertilizers will cause it to recuperate. Pasturing with sheep in November and early December will cause the destruction of many of the hibernating puparia. The *Lancaster*, *Clawson*, *Diehl*, *Underhill*, and *Mediterranean* varieties resist the work of the Hessian fly more effectually than do the more delicate varieties. (C. V. R.)

HETH, HENRY, an American general, was born in Virginia in 1825. He graduated at West Point in 1847, and entered the Sixth infantry. He rose to be captain in March, 1855. On the secession of Virginia he resigned and entered the service of that State as a brigadier-general. He was promoted major-general in May, 1863, and commanded a division in Gen. A. P. Hill's corps in Virginia. He fought at Chancellorsville, Gettysburg, and in the campaigns of 1864-65. He surrendered with Gen. Lee.

HEWES, JOSEPH (1730–1779), an American patriot, was born at Kingston, N. J., in 1730, of Quaker parentage. He was educated at Princeton, and was a merchant at Philadelphia, and also at Edenton, N. C. In 1763 he was elected to the colonial legislature of New Jersey, and in 1774 was sent to the Continental Congress. In 1776 he was one of the signers of the Declaration of Independence, and was at the head of the naval committee. In 1777 he declined a re-election, but resumed his seat in July, 1779. His health failing, he resigned Oct. 29, and died at Philadelphia, Nov. 10, 1779.

HEWIT, Augustine Francis, an American clergyman, son of Rev. Nathaniel Hewit, D. D. (1788–1867), was born at Fairfield, Conn., in 1820. He graduated at Amherst College in 1839, studied theology at East Windsor, Conn., and entered the Episcopalian ministry. While holding a charge in North Carolina in 1846, he became a Roman Catholic, and was ordained in that church in 1847. He joined the order of the Paulists in 1858, and was appointed professor of philosophy, theology, and Holy Scripture in the Paulist Seminary in New York city. He edited the *Catholic World* from 1869 to 1874, and published *Problems of the Age; Light in Darkness*, and other works.

HEWITT, Abram Stevens, an American statesman, was born at Haverstraw, N. Y., July 31, 1822. He graduated at Columbia College in 1842, and studied law, but, his eyesight failing, became a manufacturer of iron at Trenton, N. J. He was a commissioner to the French Exhibition of 1867, and made a report on "Iron and Steel." He married a daughter of Peter Cooper, his partner, and has been secretary of the Cooper Union for the Advancement of Science and Art since its incorporation in 1859. He was elected to Congress in 1874 as a Democrat from the Tenth district of New York, and served two terms, declining a nomination in 1878. He was again elected in 1880, and served till 1886, when he was elected mayor of New York. After an administration of conspicuous ability he retired to private life.

HEYWARD, Thomas (1746–1809), an American statesman, was born at St. Lukes, S. C., in 1746, being the son of Col. Daniel Heyward, a wealthy planter. He was educated in London, and studied law. Returning home, he was elected to the Continental Congress of 1775, and was one of the signers of the Declaration of Independence. In 1778 he was appointed a State judge, and in 1779 served again in Congress. He was captured at the surrender of Charleston in 1780, and was sent prisoner to St. Augustine, Florida. After he was released he resumed his office as judge until 1798. He died in March, 1809.

HICKOK, Laurens Perseus (1798–1876), an American philosopher, was born at Bethel, Conn., Dec. 29, 1798. He graduated at Union College in 1820, studied theology and held pastorates successively at Newtown, Kent, and Litchfield, Conn. He was appointed professor of theology in Western Reserve College in 1836, and in Auburn Theological Seminary in 1844. He was made vice-president of Union College, Schenectady, N. Y., in 1852; being also professor of moral and mental philosophy. From 1860 Dr. Hickok had sole charge of the college, although he was not formally inducted into the presidency until the death of Rev. Dr. Eliphalet Nott, the former president, in 1866. At the age of seventy Dr. Hickok retired from public work and took up his residence at Amherst, Mass., where he devoted himself to philosophical study. He died June 10, 1876. He published many theological and philosophical articles in the *Bibliotheca Sacra, Princeton Review*, and other reviews. His works comprise *Rational Psychology* (1848); *Moral Science* (1853); *Empirical Psychology* (1854); *Creator and Creation* (1872); *Humanity Immortal* (1872); *Logic of Reason* (1875). His philosophy is distinguished by the pre-eminence which it assigns to reason, placing it as far above and beyond the understanding in its comprehensiveness as the understanding is above sensual perception. Human reason has a consciousness of its own activity, and it also knows the absolute reason as its own necessary source. These fundamental principles Dr. Hickok applied in his successive works to the whole range of human thought.

HICKORY, a genus of valuable trees peculiar to North America, and belonging to the *Juglandaceæ* or Walnut family. There are in all 9 or 10 species included in the genus *Carya*. The hickories are distinguished by their large compound leaves, 5 to 15 in number of leaflets, but generally not more than 11. They bear male and female flowers; the former in compound catkins with 4 to 8 stamens; the latter solitary, or in small groups at the ends of the branches. The nut of the hickory is enveloped in a hard husk which splits into 4 regular valves. The nut has a smooth shell, though with 4 or more ridges running from end to end. Internally it is divided by partitions of the shell as in the walnut. These partitions are lacking in the Pecan nut, the most highly esteemed of the hickory nuts.

See Vol. XI. p. 705 Am. ed. (p 790 Edin. ed.).

C. olivæformis, the Pecan nut hickory, is a large, showy tree, 60 to 70 feet high, and in exceptional cases much higher. Its locality is in the river bottoms of the Mississippi Valley, from Illinois southward. The nut is of an olive shape and delicious flavor. The wood is less valuable than that of some other species. The most esteemed of the eastern hickories is *C. alba*, the shell-bark or shag-bark. It is well marked by its shaggy bark which exfoliates in rough strips or plates. It is a large and handsome tree, furnishing most valuable wood. The leaf is divided into 5 leaflets. The nut is white, of flattish globular form, with a rather thin shell, and of sweet and delicious flavor. It is the principal hickory nut of the market. This species is found from Massachusetts to Nebraska and southward. *C. sulcata*, the western shell-bark, has 7 to 9 leaflets, and a small, oval, thick-shelled nut, with very thick husk and strongly pointed at each end. It ranges from Pennsylvania to Wisconsin and southward. Both these species form large trees, occasionally from 80 to 100 feet high and 3 feet diameter.

Of the remaining species may be named *C. amara*, the bitter nut or swamp hickory, a common species, with a thin-shelled but extremely bitter nut; *C. porcina*, the pig nut or broom hickory, also common, its nut thick-shelled and bitterish, its very tough fibres sometimes made into brooms; and *C. tomentosa*, the mocker nut, a tree with rough but not shaggy bark, extending from New England to Nebraska, with very thick and hard husk and very thick-shelled fruit. There are several other species, but those named are the most important.

The wood of the hickories is, as a rule, exceedingly valuable, it being generally heavy, hard, close-grained, and remarkably tough and elastic. As fuel they rank higher than any other of our native woods. They are confined to the region east of the Rocky Mountains, where they furnish timber of high industrial value. The wood of *C. alba* is of a brown color, the thin and more valuable sap-wood being nearly white. It is largely used for agricultural implements, carriages, axe-handles, baskets, etc. The wood of *C. sulcata, porcina*, and *tomentosa* is of the same character and used for the same purposes. *C. amara* furnishes material for hoops, ox-yokes, etc. *C. aquatica*, the swamp hickory of the South, yields timber suitable for fencing and fuel. *C. ovæformis* is used only for fuel. The wood of the hickory is subject to attacks of insects, and decays rapidly when exposed. (C. M.)

HICKS, EDWARD (d. 1883), a British soldier, known as Hicks-Pasha, entered the British service at an early age, and rose in India to the rank of colonel. About the beginning of 1883 the British government sent Col. Hicks as chief of staff to the Egyptian army in Soudan. He arrived at Khartoum, March 9, 1883, organized a force of 5000 men, then proceeded by steamboat to Gowo, where he brought together over 6000 Egyptians and formed a train of 6000 camels. On April 29 he was attacked by 45,000 Arabs, chiefly cavalry, and repulsed them. Leaving part of his troops on the White Nile, he returned to Khartoum, which had meanwhile been besieged. Then he formed in camp opposite Khartoum a new expedition, and in August was placed in command of all the Egyptian troops in the Soudan, amounting to 14,000 men. After fortifying several camps he had still 8000 men, well supplied with artillery, when about the middle of October he began his march towards El Obeid. At the same time El Mahdi, the Mohammedan prophet, had set out from the Soudan, but only with the intention of harassing the march of the Egyptians. On Nov. 1, near El Obeid, Hicks attacked the vanguard of the Soudanese host, and after a struggle, prolonged through four days, his army was annihilated, though the enemy had suffered a loss of 60,000 men. Hicks fell at the head of the Egyptian infantry, while leading a bayonet charge, on Nov. 4, 1883. This victory made El Mahdi master of the Soudan:

HICKS, GEORGE EDGAR, an English painter, was born at Lymington in 1824. He began to study medicine at the University of London, but turned his attention to art and entered the Royal Academy in 1844. In 1855 he exhibited at the Academy his Lark at Heaven's Gate, and in 1859 he established his reputation by his Dividend Day at the Bank. The success of this picture brought from him other paintings, showing power in depicting groups of varied character. But he also painted pathetic incidents with fewer figures. Among his works are Changing Homes (1862); The Return from the Gleaning (1876); Fisherman's Wife, Woodman's Daughter, Faith, Hope, and Charity.

HICKS-BEACH, SIR MICHAEL EDWARD, an English statesman, was born at London, Oct. 23, 1837, the descendant of a long line of Gloucestershire baronets. He was educated at Eton and Christ Church, Oxford; graduated with honors in 1858; was chosen to Parliament in 1864 for East Gloucestershire, a constituency he has constantly represented since that time. In 1868 he was parliamentary secretary for the poor-law board, and for a time an under secretary for the home department. He was chief secretary for Ireland (1874-78) under Beaconsfield, and in that difficult position displayed great tact and capacity for business, and his moderation and skill even won the praise of the Home-Rule members. He was secretary of state for the colonies, 1878-80, and in 1885.

HIGGINSON, THOMAS WENTWORTH, an American author, descended from Rev. Francis Higginson (1587-1630), was born at Cambridge, Mass., Dec. 22, 1823. He graduated at Harvard in 1841, studied theology at Cambridge, and was ordained pastor at Newburyport, Mass., in 1847. He took an active part in the anti-slavery movement, and in 1850 was a Free-Soil candidate for Congress. His congregation became dissatisfied and he resigned his charge. In 1852 he became minister of a free church at Worcester, Mass. In 1853 he led an attack on the Boston Court-house to rescue Anthony Burns, a fugitive slave then in custody of the U. S. marshal, and was wounded in the face. A man having been killed in the conflict, Higginson was afterwards indicted for murder, but escaped through a flaw in the indictment. He went to Kansas in 1856, and was conspicuous in the movement to make it a free State. He then definitely retired from the ministry. On the outbreak of the civil war he recruited several companies of volunteers, and he was made captain in the Fifty-first Massachusetts regiment. In November, 1862, he became colonel of the First South Carolina volunteers (afterwards Thirty-third U. S. colored infantry), the first regiment of former slaves mustered into the service of the United States. With these troops he served in various expeditions in South Carolina and Florida, but being wounded in August, 1863, was compelled to retire in October, 1864. He afterwards resided at Newport, R. I., and engaged in literary pursuits. Returning to Cambridge, Mass., he was elected to the legislature for 1880-81, and has since been a member of the State Board of Education. He has delivered many lectures on historical and social topics, and has taken a prominent part in advocating woman suffrage and the higher education of both sexes. He has published *Out-Door Papers* (1863); *Harvard Memorial Biographies* (1866); *Malbone, an Oldport Romance* (1869); *Army Life in a Black Regiment* (1870); *Atlantic Essays* (1871); *Oldport Days* (1873); *Young Folks' History of the United States* (1875); *Young Folks' Book of American Explorers* (1878); *Short Studies of American Authors* (1880); *Common Sense about Women* (1881); *Margaret Fuller* (1884); *Larger History of the United States* (1884).

HIGH CHURCH. This is a phrase used to designate an adherence to church precedent and ecclesiastical authority. It is used as an adjective. Thus we say a high-church party or a high-church Christian. It has not so much relation to doctrine as to the outward church-life, yet it involves the doctrine of selected channels for the divine grace. High-church views are chiefly found in the prelatical churches, and yet the non-prelatical churches hold many who lay great stress on the efficacy of church order in service and sacraments, and who can be called advocates of high-church views. Low-church views emphasize the spiritual doctrines of the gospel, and make but little of ecclesiastical rules, beyond the decent order that avoids confusion. (H. CR.)

HILGARD, EUGENE WALDEMAR, an American geologist, was born at Zweibrücken, Bavaria, Jan. 5, 1831. He is a son of Theodor Erasmus Hilgard (1790-1873), a German jurist, who removed with his family to the United States in 1835, but in 1850 returned to Germany. Eugene studied at the Academy of Mines, Freiberg, and at the Universities of Zürich and Heidelberg, graduating in 1853. He returned to the United States in 1855, and became assistant State geologist of Mississippi. In 1857 he had charge of the laboratory at the Smithsonian Institution at Washington, and from 1858 to 1873 he was State geologist of Mississippi, being also professor of chemistry in the University of Mississippi from 1866 to 1873. He was appointed professor of geology in the University of Michigan in 1873, and professor of agriculture in the University of California in 1875. He had charge of the statistics of cotton production for the census of

1880. He has also published reports on the geology and agriculture of Mississippi, and numerous articles in scientific journals.

HILGARD, JULIUS ERASMUS, an American engineer, brother of the preceding, was born at Zweibrücken, Bavaria, Jan. 7, 1825. He received a classical education from his father, and studied civil engineering at Philadelphia. In 1845 he entered the service of the coast survey, and became in 1862 head of its office, and in 1881 superintendent. He gave especial attention to the construction of standard weights and measures. In 1872 he was a member of the international metric commission at Paris. In 1874 he was president of the American Association for the Advancement of Science. In 1885 he resigned his position in the coast survey.

HILL, AMBROSE POWELL (1825-1865), an American general, was born in Culpeper co., Va., in 1825. He graduated at West Point in 1847, and became second lieutenant of artillery. He served for a short time in the Mexican war, and afterwards on the frontier and in Florida. He was engaged in duty in the coast survey office from 1855 until the outbreak of the civil war, when he resigned. When Virginia seceded Hill was appointed colonel of a regiment, and he took part in the first battle of Bull Run. He was promoted to be brigadier-general, and for his services at Williamsburg he was made major-general. He was conspicuous during the seven days' fighting around Richmond in June, 1862. He was next attached to Gen. Jackson's force in Northern Virginia, and fought at Cedar Mountain, Second Bull Run, and Chantilly. Pushing on to the north he captured Harper's Ferry, and fought at Antietam. In December, 1862, he held the right of Jackson's force at Fredericksburg, and repulsed the attack of Meade. At Chancellorsville, in May, 1863, he took part in Jackson's daring march and unexpected assault on Howard's division. On the death of Jackson Hill succeeded to his command, but was soon disabled by a wound. He was then promoted to be lieutenant-general, and fought at Gettysburg in July. In the desperate conflicts of 1864 Hill displayed the same skill and gallantry as before. In 1865 he commanded the city of Petersburg during its siege, and on April 2, 1865, while reconnoitring, was killed by a rifle-shot.

HILL, BENJAMIN HARVEY (1823-1882), an American statesman, was born in Jasper co., Ga., Sept. 14, 1823. He graduated at the University of Georgia in 1844, and was admitted to the bar at La Grange, Ga., in 1845. He was successful in his profession, and in 1851 was elected to the State legislature. After the dissolution of the Whig party he was a favorite candidate with the American party, but was not elected either to Congress or to the governorship for which he had been nominated. In 1859, when secession was agitated, he was elected to the State senate as a Union man. In January, 1861, in the State convention he earnestly advocated remaining in the Union, but afterwards voted for the ordinance of secession. He was elected to the provisional Confederate Congress which met at Montgomery, Feb. 4, 1861, and afterwards to the Confederate Senate at Richmond, where he remained till the close of the war. In May, 1865, he was arrested at his home at La Grange, Ga., and confined for six weeks at Fort Lafayette, New York, being then released on parole. In 1867 he assisted in reorganizing the Democratic party in Georgia, and opposed the Reconstruction measures of Congress. In 1870 he advocated hearty acceptance by the Southern people of the issues of the war, and in 1872 warmly supported Horace Greeley as the Democratic candidate. In January, 1873, he was unsuccessful in his candidacy for the U. S. Senatorship. In 1875 he was elected to Congress, and was re-elected, but resigned on being chosen U. S. Senator in 1877. He died at Atlanta Aug. 16, 1882.

HILL, DANIEL HARVEY, an American general, was born in South Carolina in 1821. He graduated at West Point in 1842 and entered the artillery, but in 1847 was made first-lieutenant of infantry. He served throughout the Mexican war and by his gallantry attained the brevet rank of major. Resigning his commission in 1849 he was professor of mathematics in Washington College, Va., in 1849-54, then in Davidson College, N. C., until 1859, when he was made president of the Military Institute at Charlotte. On the outbreak of the civil war he was made colonel of the First N. C. volunteers, and he was engaged in the fight at Big Bethel, Va., June, 1861. He was soon raised to the rank of major-general and commanded a division during the Seven Days' fight around Richmond in June, 1862. He fought afterwards at South Mountain, Antietam, Fredericksburg, and in 1863 was sent to command in North and South Carolina. He fought at Chickamauga in September, 1863, and was afterwards recalled to Virginia, but at the surrender of the Confederate armies his division was with Gen. J. E. Johnston. After the war Gen. Hill returned to Charlotte, N. C., where he published a monthly magazine *The Land We Love*, (1867-69). He died there Sept. 24, 1889. He was a brother-in-law of Stonewall Jackson, and like him a man of strong religious principle, and an able general. He has published *Elements of Algebra, Consideration of The Sermon on the Mount*, and *The Crucifixion of Christ*.

HILL, THOMAS, an American clergyman and educator, was born at New Brunswick, N. J., Jan. 7, 1818. He graduated at Harvard College in 1843, studied theology, and was ordained pastor at Waltham, Mass., in 1845. He succeeded Horace Mann as president of Antioch College in 1859. In 1862 he was called to be president of Harvard College, but he resigned in 1868 on account of ill health. In 1871 he was botanist in the Hassler expedition around the coasts of South America under Prof. Agassis. In 1872 he became pastor of a church at Portland, Me. He is well versed in the natural sciences and is especially fond of mathematics, in the methods of which he has made some improvements. He also aims to make all science tributary to religion. He has published besides some elementary mathematical books: *Geometry and Faith* (1849; 2d ed., 1874); *Liberal Education* (1855); *True Order of Studies, Jesus the Interpreter of Nature* (1859); *Natural Sources of Theology* (1875).

HILLIARD, HENRY WASHINGTON, an American statesman, was born in Cumberland co., N. C., Aug. 8, 1808. He graduated at South Carolina College in 1826, was admitted to the bar at Athens, Ga., in 1829, and was appointed professor in the State University of Alabama in 1831; but in 1834 resumed the practice of his profession at Montgomery, Ala. He was elected to the State legislature in 1838 as a Whig. In 1842 he was sent by Pres. Tyler as minister to Belgium. From 1845 to 1851 he was a member of Congress, when he supported Clay's compromise of 1850. After being an earnest advocate of the Union cause he cast in his lot with the Confederacy. He was sent as commissioner to Tennessee to secure the secession of that State. He held nominal rank as a brigadier-general in the

Confederate army At the close of the war he resumed the practice of law at Augusta, Ga., and afterwards at Atlanta. He was U. S. minister to Brazil from 1877 to 1880. He published a volume of *Speeches* (1855), and a novel, *De Vane*.

HINCKS, EDWARD (1792–1866), an Irish clergyman and Assyriologist, was born at Cork, in August 1792. He was the son of Rev. T. D. Hincks, LL.D., professor of Oriental languages in the Belfast Academical Institution, and inherited a fondness for the study of languages. He graduated at Trinity College, Dublin, and received a fellowship. He took orders in the Established Church of Ireland and became rector of Ardtrea, and in 1826 of Killyleagh. Though having but little means to procure books he took great interest in the study of Egyptian and Assyrian archæology and laid the foundation of Assyrian grammar. He also discovered the key to the Assyrian numeral system. He died at Killyleagh, Dec. 3, 1866.

HINCKS, SIR FRANCIS, a Canadian statesman, brother of the preceding, was born at Cork, Ireland, in 1805. He was educated at Fermoy and Belfast, and became a merchant. In 1832 he settled at Toronto, when he entered into politics and edited the *Examiner* with great vigor. In 1841 he was elected to the Dominion Parliament and was soon after appointed inspector-general. He was a prominent advocate of "responsible government," and by persistent effort obtained the recognition of this principle in the administration of Canadian affairs. In 1851 he was made prime minister of Canada and held this post until 1854. In 1855 he was appointed governor and commander-in-chief of the Windward Islands, and from 1860 to 1866 he was governor of British Guiana. He then returned to Canada and took part in the union of the British provinces in the Dominion of Canada. He received the honor of knighthood in 1869, and from that time until 1873 he was the finance minister of Canada. In 1878 he was one of the commissioners to settle the northern and western boundary of Ontario.

HIND, JOHN RUSSELL, an English astronomer, was born at Nottingham, May 12, 1823. From an early age he was devoted to the study of the stars, and when sixteen years old contributed astronomical notes to a local paper. He was sent to London in 1840 as an assistant to a civil-engineer, but through the influence of Prof. Wheatstone he was soon employed in the royal observatory. Nearly four years later his talents caused Prof. G. B. Airy to recommend him for the position of observer in Mr. G. Bishop's observatory, at Regent's Park. From the series of observations which he conducted here, Hind calculated the orbits and declinations of 70 planets and comets; he also noted 16 movable stars and 3 nebulæ, and discovered 10 asteroids. The dates of the latter extend from Aug. 13, 1847, when Iris was discovered, to July 22, 1854, when Urania was discovered. In December, 1844, Mr. Hind was elected a member of the Royal Astronomical Society, and in 1847 he was appointed its foreign secretary. In 1852 the British government bestowed on him a pension of £200, and many marks of honor have been bestowed on him by foreign governments and societies. He is the superintendent of the British Nautical Almanac, which, under his direction, has become of the highest authority for astronomical as well as for nautical use. He has published *The Solar System* (1846); *Illustrated London Astronomy* (1853); *Elements of Algebra* (1855); *Descriptive Treatise on Comets* (1857).

HINDMAN, THOMAS C. (1818–1868), an American general, was born in Tennessee in 1818. He served in the Mexican war as second-lieutenant of Mississippi volunteers. Elected to Congress from Arkansas in 1859, he served until secession began, being also a member of the Democratic Convention at Charleston, S. C., in 1860. On the outbreak of the civil war he was made a brigadier-general in the Confederate army, and served under Gen. S. B. Buckner in Kentucky, and afterwards had command at Memphis. He was engaged at the battle of Shiloh, and was commissioned as major-general. He was then transferred to Arkansas, where he had the chief command. He commanded a division in Gen. Polk's army at Chickamauga. After the close of the war he went to Mexico, but returned in 1867 to Helena, Ark., where he was killed by one of his former soldiers, Sept. 27, 1868.

HINSDALE, BURKE AARON, an American educator and author, was born at Wadsworth, Ohio, March 31, 1837. He was educated at the Elective Institute, and became a minister of the Christian (or Campbellite) Church in 1861. He was pastor of a church at Solon, 1864–66, and at Cleveland, 1866–68. He was then appointed professor of history and English literature in Hiram College, and became its president in 1870. He was assistant editor of the *Christian Standard* from 1866 to 1869, and has since been assistant editor of the *Christian Quarterly*, Cincinnati. He has published *Genuineness and Authenticity of the Gospels* (1873); *Evolution of the Theological and Doctrinal Systems of the Ancient Church* (1876); *Life of President Garfield* (1882); *Schools and Studies* (1884). He has edited Pres. Garfield's *Works* (1883).

HITCHCOCK, ETHAN ALLEN (1798–1870), an American general and author, was born at Vergennes, Vt., May 18, 1798. He was a son of Judge Samuel Hitchcock and a grandson of Col. Ethan Allen. He graduated at West Point in 1817, and was assistant instructor in tactics there in 1824, and from 1829 to 1833 was commandant of cadets. He volunteered his services in the Florida war, and was inspector-general in Gaines' campaign in 1836. He was afterwards employed on the frontier, and in the Mexican war he was inspector-general under Scott, receiving the brevet of brigadier-general. He then made a tour in Europe and the East, and in 1851, having attained the rank of colonel, was placed in command on the Pacific coast. In October, 1855, he resigned his commission because Jefferson Davis, then secretary of war, refused to confirm a leave of absence which Gen. Scott had granted. Gen. Hitchcock afterwards resided in St. Louis, and engaged in philosophical and literary pursuits. When the civil war broke out he offered his services to the government, and was appointed major-general of volunteers, Feb. 10, 1862. He was placed on duty in the war department, and was afterwards commissioner for the exchange of prisoners, and commissary-general of prisoners. He retired from service in October, 1867, and died at Sparta, Ga., Aug. 5, 1870. Among his published works are *The Doctrines of Swedenborg and Spinoza Identified* (1846); *Alchemy and the Alchemists* (1857); *Swedenborg a Hermetic Philosopher* (1858); *Christ the Spirit* (1861); *Remarks on the Sonnets of Shakespeare, Colin Clout Explained* (1865); *Remarks on the Vita Nuova of Dante* (1866).

HITCHCOCK, ROSWELL DWIGHT, an American theologian, was born at East Machias, Maine, Aug. 15, 1817. He graduated at Amherst in 1836, and studied theology at Andover. He was tutor at Amherst from

1839 to 1842, and then resident licentiate at Andover until 1844, when he went to Waterville, Maine. He was ordained pastor of the First Congregational Church, Exeter, N. H., Nov. 19, 1845, and held this office until 1852, though spending a year in Germany at the Universities of Halle and Berlin. In 1852 he was appointed professor of natural and revealed religion at Bowdoin College. In 1855 he was made professor of church history in Union Theological Seminary, New York, and in 1880 president of that seminary. During the civil war he earnestly advocated the cause of the Union. In 1866 he visited Italy and Greece, and in 1869-70 Egypt and Palestine. He then assisted in organizing the Palestine Exploration Society, and in 1871 was elected its president. In 1885 he again went abroad. He was a frequent contributor to the *Presbyterian Quarterly*, and from 1863 to 1870 was one of the editors of the *American Theological Review*. Besides numerous addresses and sermons he published a *Complete Analysis of the Bible* (1869), and *Socialism* (1878). He edited *Life and Writings of Edward Robinson* (1864), and several hymn-books, including *Carmina Sanctorum* (1885). He died June 16, 1887.

HOAR, EBENEZER ROCKWOOD, an American jurist, was born at Concord, Mass., Feb. 21, 1816, being a son of Judge Samuel Hoar (1778-1856). He graduated at Harvard College in 1835, studied law at Cambridge, and was admitted to the bar in 1840. He was appointed judge of the court of common pleas in 1849, but resigned in 1855, and resumed practice in Boston. He was appointed a judge of the Supreme Court of Massachusetts, and held this office until 1869, when Pres. Grant appointed him U. S. attorney-general. This office was then constituted the department of justice. In 1870 Judge Hoar was nominated a justice of the Supreme Court of the United States, but was not confirmed. He was a member of the Joint High Commission which negotiated the treaty of Washington in 1871. He was a member of Congress from Massachusetts from 1873 to 1875. He is noted for his fine culture, wit, and social qualities, as well as his professional attainments.

HOAR, GEORGE FRISBIE, an American statesman, brother of the preceding, was born at Concord, Mass., Aug. 29, 1826. He graduated at Harvard College in 1846, studied law at Cambridge, and was admitted to the bar in 1849. He settled at Worcester, Mass., and became a member of the legislature in 1852, and of the State senate in 1857. He took a prominent part in organizing the Republican party in Massachusetts. He was elected to Congress in 1868, and served four terms. He was a member of the Electoral Commission of 1877, since which time he has been U. S. Senator. He has been a delegate to each Republican National Convention since 1876, and presided over the Convention of 1880. He is the author of *Memoir of Samuel Hoar*, *Memoir of A. H. Bullock*, and has published many speeches and addresses.

HOAR, SAMUEL (1778-1856), an American statesman, was born at Lincoln, Mass., May 18, 1778. His father, Samuel, was a captain in the Revolutionary army, and served many years in the State legislature. The son graduated at Harvard in 1802, and was admitted to the bar in 1805. He became eminent in his profession, and in 1820 was a member of the State Constitutional Convention. He was a State senator in 1825 and 1833, a member of Congress in 1835-37, and a State councillor in 1845-46. In 1844 he was sent by the State of Massachusetts to South Carolina to test the constitutionality of acts of the latter State by which free negro sailors were seized and imprisoned on entering its ports. On Dec. 5, 1844, he was driven from Charleston by a mob, and the State legislature on the same day authorized the governor to expel him. Mr. Hoar was active in religious and charitable work. He died at Concord, Mass., Nov. 2, 1856.

HOBART, AUGUSTUS CHARLES, known as HOBART PASHA, a Turkish admiral, was born in England, April 1, 1822, being the third son of the Earl of Buckinghamshire. He entered the British navy in 1836, and while a midshipman gained distinction by his zeal in the suppression of the Brazilian slave-trade. In 1845-46 he served in the queen's yacht. He had command of the Driver in the Baltic Sea in 1854, and was commended for gallantry. He then retired on half-pay, and during the American civil war he commanded the Don, a blockade-runner. An account of his experiences appeared under the name of Captain Roberts. He became a post-captain in 1862, and in 1867 he offered his services to the Turkish government. He was employed to stop the Greek blockade-runners at Crete during the Cretan insurrection. His great success in this service and in negotiations caused him to be made pasha and admiral. The Greek minister, however, had complained to the British government of his conduct, and his name was struck off the navy list. In 1874 he appealed to Lord Derby for reinstatement, acknowledged his breach of discipline in accepting service under the Turkish government without leave, but pleaded in extenuation his services in organizing and strengthening the navy of an ally, establishing training schools, maintaining the reputation of England, and preventing bloodshed and a general war. His request was granted on the ground of "imperial policy." At the outbreak of the Russo-Turkish war, in 1877, he was placed in command of the Black Sea fleet of Turkey, and his name was again removed from the British navy list. Hobart Pasha sailed down the Danube under a heavy fire from the Russians, but effected nothing. After the war he was inspector-general of the Turkish navy. He returned to England and died in June, 1886.

HOBART, JOHN HENRY (1775-1830), an American bishop, was born at Philadelphia, Sept. 14, 1775. He graduated at Princeton College in 1793, and was tutor there from 1796 to 1798. In the meantime he studied theology, and was ordained deacon in June, 1798, and priest in 1801, being the assistant minister of Trinity Church, New York. Here he became assistant rector in 1812 and rector in 1816. Before 1800 he had been secretary of the House of Bishops, and was deputy to the General Convention of 1801, and secretary of the lower House in 1804 and 1808. He was chosen assistant bishop of New York in February, 1811, and bishop in 1816. He was one of the founders of the General Theological Seminary in New York, and in 1821 became professor of pastoral theology and pulpit eloquence in it. In 1823 he visited Europe, and while in England published two volumes of sermons (1824). He denied the validity of any but episcopal orders, and opposed the formation of Bible and tract societies composed of Christians of different denominations. He died at Auburn, N. Y., Sept. 10, 1830. He published *Companion for the Altar* (1804; 13th ed. 1840); *Apology for Apostolic Order* (1807); *State of the Departed* (1816; new ed., 1843). His posthumous works with a memoir were edited by Rev. W. Berrian, D. D. (1833). Other memoirs were published by Schroeder (1833) and McVickar (1834-36).

HOBOKEN, a city of New Jersey, in Hudson county,

is immediately adjacent to Jersey City on the north. Being on the Hudson River opposite New York, it is one of the suburbs of the metropolis. To the westward a steep rocky escarpment separates it from West Hoboken. It is the seat of a large shipping trade, especially in coal, and is the place whence several lines of European steamers start. The Delaware, Lackawanna, and Western Railroad has its eastern terminus at this place. Lead-pencils and iron-castings are among the leading articles manufactured. The most noteworthy public institution is the Stevens Institute of Technology, which ranks among the principal schools of its class in the United States. Hoboken is well provided with churches, schools, newspapers, and street railways, and has several banks; but its business interests are in the main subsidiary to those of New York. Population in 1870, 20,297; in 1880, 30,999.

HODGE, ARCHIBALD ALEXANDER, an American theologian, son of Rev. Charles Hodge, D. D. (for whom see ENCYCLOPÆDIA BRITANNICA), was born at Princeton, N. J., July 18, 1823. He graduated at Princeton College in 1841, was tutor there from 1844 to 1846, and graduated at Princeton Theological Seminary in 1847. He went as a missionary to Allahabad, India, but returned in 1850 on account of his wife's impaired health. He was pastor of a Presbyterian church at Lower West Nottingham, Md., from 1851 to 1855, then at Fredericksburg, Va., until 1861, and afterwards at Wilkes-Barre, Pa., for a year. In 1864 he was chosen by the Presbyterian General Assembly to the chair of didactic, historical, and polemic theology in the Western Theological Seminary, Allegheny, Pa. In 1866 he became also pastor of the North Presbyterian Church of that city. In 1872 he was called to Princeton Theological Seminary to be assistant to his father, and after the latter's death, in 1878, succeeded him as professor of dogmatic theology, while his brother, Rev. Charles W. Hodge, became professor of exegetical theology. He has published *Outlines of Theology* (1860); *The Atonement* (1867); *Commentary on the Confession of Faith* (1869); *Presbyterian Doctrine briefly Stated* (1869); *Life of Charles Hodge* (1880). He died Nov. 11, 1886.

HODGE, HUGH LENOX (1796–1873), an American physician, was born at Philadelphia, June 27, 1796, being brother of the theologian, Rev. Charles Hodge, D. D., and son of Dr. Hugh Hodge, an eminent physician. He graduated at Princeton in 1814, studied medicine at the University of Pennsylvania, taking his degree in 1817. He acquired an extensive practice, and in 1835 was made professor of obstetrics in the University of Pennsylvania. After a service of twenty-eight years he became professor emeritus in 1863. He died at Philadelphia, Feb. 23, 1873. He published *System of Obstetrics* and *Diseases Peculiar to Women*, both of which passed through several editions. He also contributed frequently to professional journals. His son, HUGH LENOX HODGE (1833–1882), was a noted surgeon.

HOFFMAN, CHARLES FENNO (1806–1884), an American author, was born at New York city in 1806. He was the son of Judge J. Ogden Hoffman. When he was eleven years old his leg was crushed between a steamboat and a wharf on which he was sitting, and had to be amputated above the knee. He attended Columbia College for two years, and was admitted to the bar in 1827. He then became associate editor of the *New York American*, and in 1833 was the first editor of the *Knickerbocker Magazine*. A trip to the prairies furnished the material for *A Winter in the West* (1834), and *Wild Scenes in the Forest and the Prairie* (1837), and also for his novel, *Greyslaer* (1840). His poems, which had been widely circulated, were first collected in a volume called *The Vigil of Faith and other Poems* (1842). A second volume appeared in 1844, under the title *Borrowed Notes for Home Circulation* (1844). In 1849 he was unfortunately attacked by a mental disorder, which closed his literary career. He died at Harrisburg in 1884. His *Poems* were edited with notes by his nephew, Edward Fenno Hoffman, in 1873.

HOFFMAN, DAVID (1784–1854), an American jurist, was born at Baltimore, Dec. 25, 1784. He became an eminent lawyer, and in 1817, being chosen professor of law in the University of Maryland, published a *Course of Legal Study*, which has been approved by the highest authorities. In 1836 he resigned his professorship, and spent two years in Europe. He then practised law in Philadelphia until 1847, when he made another visit to Europe. He returned in 1853, and died suddenly at New York, Nov. 11, 1854. He had received the degree of LL. D. from the University of Maryland, and from the University of Oxford, England, and that of J. U. D. from the University of Göttingen. His publications were *Legal Outlines* (1836); *Thoughts on Men, Manners, and Things, by Anthony Grumbler* (1837); *Viator, or A Peep in My Note-book* (1840); *Legal Hints* (1846), which included his *Course of Legal Study*; and *Chronicles Selected from the Originals of Cartaphilus, the Wandering Jew* (2 vols., 1853–55). The last was intended to be a summary of modern history, and to comprise six volumes, but only two were published.

HOFFMANN, LUDWIG FRIEDRICH WILHELM (1806–1873), a German clergyman, was born at Leonberg, Würtemberg, Oct. 30, 1806. He studied theology at Tübingen, became in 1830 vicar at Heumaden, and in 1833 at Stuttgart. In 1834 he was pastor at Wienenden, and in 1839 was made director of the Missionary Institute at Basle. Here he labored with great zeal, and was also for some years professor of theology at the Basle University. In 1850 he was recalled as professor to Tübingen, and in 1852 he was made court-preacher at Berlin by King Frederick William IV. Over the king Hoffmann had great influence, and he used it to promote ecclesiastical union between the two great Protestant churches. He also labored earnestly to unite all Germany. He died at Berlin, Aug. 28, 1873. His writings include *Missionsstunden und Vorträge* (1847–53); *Epochen der Kirchengeschichte Indiens* (1853); *Franz Xavier* (1869); *Ruf zum Herrn* (1854–58); *Die Haustafel* (1859–63); *Ein Jahr der Gnade* (1864).

HOFMANN, AUGUST WILHELM, a German chemist, was born at Giessen, April 8, 1818. He studied philology and law, and graduated Ph. D. in 1842, but then devoted himself to chemistry, as assistant to Liebig. In 1845 he was made professor of chemistry at Bonn, and in 1848 he was called to the newly founded Royal College of Chemistry at London. He did much to promote the study of his favorite science, and a chemical class which he instructed was in 1853 included in the Royal School of Mines. In 1855 he was also made assayer at the Mint. In 1864 he was called to Bonn as professor of chemistry, and proceeded to organize an excellent laboratory, but before he could use it he was called to Berlin, where another well-equipped laboratory was erected under his supervision. He has devoted special attention to the investigation of ammonium compounds, and of aniline colors. His researches have had great influence upon industrial as well as analytical chemistry. His publications include *Hand-book of Organic Analysis* (1853); *Einleitung in die Moderne Chemie* (6th ed., 1877). Since the death of Liebig, Hofmann has edited the *Annalen der Chemie*. In the controversy about University studies in 1881 Hofmann took the classical side.

HOLBROOK, JOHN EDWARDS (1794–1871), an American naturalist, was born at Beaufort, S. C., Dec. 31, 1794. He was taken to Massachusetts while an infant by his parents. He graduated at Brown University in 1815, and after receiving the degree of M. D. from the University of Pennsylvania went to Europe, where he continued his professional studies. While at Paris he resided at the *Jardin des Plantes*. In 1822 he settled at Charleston, S. C., and in 1824 he was made professor of anatomy in the Medical College of South Carolina, which position he held for more than thirty years. His most important work is *American Herpetology, or a Description of the Reptiles of the United States* (5 vols., 1842). He began a work on *Southern Ichthyology*, but finding the field too extensive he confined himself to the *Ichthyology of South Carolina*, of which 10 numbers had been issued before the civil war. He was compelled to serve as surgeon in a South Carolina regiment, though while professor he had refrained from performing any surgical operations. He died at Norfolk, Mass., Sept. 8, 1871.

HOLDER, JOSEPH BASSETT, an American naturalist, was born at Lynn, Mass., Oct. 26, 1824. He was educated at Friends' College, Providence, R. I., and studied medicine. Entering the U. S. service, he was acting-post-surgeon at Fort Jefferson, Florida, in 1858–59, and surgeon, 1860–65; assistant-post-surgeon at Fortress Monroe, Va., 1866–70. He then resigned, and joined Prof. A. S. Bickmore in establishing the American Museum of Natural History in New York. He is a member of several scientific societies. He has published *History of American Fauna* (1878); *History of the Atlantic Right Whales* (1883), and many papers on natural history.

HOLLAND, a minor country of Europe, which formerly occupied a prominent position in European politics, but has now greatly declined in importance. We shall here deal with it only in its most recent aspects.

See Vol. XII. p. 61 Am. ed. (p. 59 Edin. ed.).

This country, with one or two small outlying provinces, constitutes the kingdom of the Netherlands, a limited monarchy, now under King William III., who was born Feb. 19, 1817, and succeeded William II. on March 17, 1849. The area of the Netherlands is 12,648 square miles, with a population, in 1888, of 4,719,215. The population, under the census of 1879, comprised 2,469,814 Protestants, 1,439,137 Catholics, 81,693 Jews, and 22,049 of other beliefs. The principal cities are Amsterdam, with 399,424 inhabitants; Rotterdam, with 197,722; and the Hague, with 153,340, by the census of 1889.

The commerce of Holland in 1889 reached a total import trade of $459,455,415; while the total exports were $395,620,400. The total revenue, by the budget of 1889, was $50,920,790, with an expenditure of $51,781,245. The deficiency in the revenue has been considerable for several years past. It is met provisionally by the issue of treasury bills, but efforts are being made to overcome it. A considerable portion of the expenditure is on account of the public debt, which amounts altogether to $452,437,600, most of which is funded at 2½ per cent. interest. The colonial provinces of Holland have a surface extent of 659,126 square miles, with a population of about 28,333,000. The principal part is in the island of Java. The remaining colonies embrace the greater part of Sumatra and other islands in the Malaysian archipelago, several places in New Guinea and Dutch Guiana and the Dutch Antilles in America. The colonial budget for 1885 estimates the expenditure at $57,200,000, which exceeds the estimated receipts by $500,000. The principal exports from these colonies are coffee, sugar, indigo, cloves, nutmegs, rice, tobacco, tea, gutta-percha, pepper, tin, etc. The principal imports are cotton cloth, petroleum, beer, wine, liquors, butter, flour, iron wares, glass, crockery, paper, etc. The government of Java has been until recently administered under a species of serfdom, known as the "culture system." This was abolished in 1882 in respect to the cultivation of indigo, pepper, tobacco, tea, etc., but retained in respect to sugar and coffee. The forced labor in sugar cultivation is to end in 1890. Nearly all the soil is claimed as government property, and forced labor for the government without pay may be exacted one day out of seven. The natives in the coffee districts must plant a certain number of coffee plants annually and sell the product to the government at the rate of 14 guilders ($5.60) per pecul of 133 pounds. In January, 1884, Otto Van Rees was appointed governor-general of the East India colonies, in pursuance of the liberal colonial policy, under which the natives in the coffee districts are given the option to continue to hold their lands in common, as now, or to be given them as individual property.

The total tonnage of sailing vessels entered in Holland for 1883 was 2,246,927 cubic meters, of which 797,000 was under the Dutch flag. Steam-tonnage entered, 8,750,949; under Dutch flag, 2,417,435. The railroad mileage on Jan. 1, 1890, was about 1520 miles, of which more than half belonged to the state. The length of colonial railroads was about 400 miles. The state telegraph lines on Jan. 1, 1890, were 3002 miles in length. The telegraphic despatches in 1889 numbered 4,084,188. The number of letters sent by the postal service in 1888 was 187,782,345, there being 277 chief postal and 27 minor offices.

The navy in 1890 consisted of 147 vessels, of which 24 were iron-clad, with 78 guns. These vessels were manned by over 11,000 sailors and marines. The army on the war footing embraced 2342 officers and 63,391 men, with a militia or reserve force of 118,000. The German military system has been adopted, but the army is partly recruited by voluntary enlistment. The army of the East Indies is composed of about 33,000, more than half of whom are natives.

The fisheries of Holland, though they have greatly declined, are still of considerable value, employing some 12,000 hands and over 3000 vessels. In 1887 the North Sea fisheries yielded 3,769,841 barrels of salted herring, while over 35,000,000 oysters were taken. The annual value of the fisheries is estimated at $15,000,000. Of the other industries, there were, in 1888, 12 sugar-refining establishments, 30 beet-root sugar factories, 57 salt works, 87 soap works, and about 400 gin distilleries.

Historical.—In 1873 a war broke out between Holland and the province of Acheen in Sumatra, which has continued until the present time. The unpleasant relations of Acheen with European states have existed for a long time. In 1824 Holland was forced by England to assent to a guarantee of independence to the Sultan of Acheen. England withdrew this guarantee in 1871, in consequence of the insults to foreign flags by the fanatical sultan. An effort was made to form a treaty with Acheen, but, as it became evident that the sultan was negotiating with the Italian and United States consuls, the authorities of Java, fearing foreign intervention, declared war against Acheen on March 26, 1873. The first expedition proved an entire failure. The commander-in-chief was killed, and his troops had great difficulty in re-embarking. A second expedition landed about Dec. 11, 1873, and quickly captured the Kraton, the fortress and capital of the sultan, who shortly afterwards died of cholera. Many of the coast rajahs submitted, and the governor-general decided to annex Acheen as the best policy, since a treaty would be useless. This annexation has been bitterly resisted. In 1877, after a feeble protraction of the war, Gen. Van der Heyden took command, and in two brilliant campaigns brought the war to a temporary close. He remained in control of the country as a kind of military dictator. But despite the efficiency of his administration a home pressure was brought against this dictatorial rule, and he was removed in 1881, and succeeded by a new civil administration. Immediately a revolt broke out, and the Acheenese still continue defiant, though recently the Dutch military operations have been more energetic. The trouble was complicated in 1883 by the capture of the crew of a wrecked English merchant ship called the Nisero, by the Acheenese rajah of Lenom. He tried every means to embroil Holland and England, and though his country was ravaged by an army he held his captives for a year, and only released them on payment of an indemnity of 100,000 guilders ($40,000). Only 20 of them still lived, the others having died of starvation and other privations. The war with Acheen has cost more than $120,000,000, and the lives of over 60,000 Dutch soldiers. The population of Great Acheen, of 300,000 or 400,000, had been reduced in 1880 to 50,000.

The most important home question in Holland has been that of the succession to the throne. The death of the Prince of Orange left the royal line without male descendants. The Princess Wilhelmina, the only surviving child of the king, born in 1880, became heiress to the throne, to which she succeeded on the death of her father, Nov. 23, 1890. The prospect of a long regency caused the Chambers, in December, 1883, to adopt a bill to modify the constitution in such a manner as to remove the restriction which forbade a revision of the constitution during a regency. Other important measures were adopted, and efforts made to extend the franchise. The existing election laws gave the franchise to only a select portion of the people, and only a fraction of these voted, so that there were usually not more than 25,000 votes polled in the whole country. This important question of state politics was finally settled by the adoption of a new constitution, promulgated Nov. 30, 1887, under which 200,000 voters were added to the electorate, and other valuable reforms introduced.

In July, 1884, a syndicate was given the task of raising a new 4 per cent. loan of 60,000,000 guilders to cover past deficiencies. There was also a bill passed to reorganize the state lottery, so as to increase the revenue. Other important late events in Holland are the abolition of the death-penalty in 1870, the opening of the great Amsterdam ship-canal in 1876, and the preliminary measures toward the project of draining the Zuyder Zee. If this should be accomplished it would add an area of 650 square miles to the country. The draining of the Harlem Lake, from 1840 to 1853, added 70 square miles of highly fertile land, now thickly populated.

HOLLAND, JOSIAH GILBERT (1819–1881), an American journalist, editor, and author, was born at Belchertown, Mass., July 24, 1819. He graduated at Berkshire Medical College, Pittsfield, Mass., and after some practice as a physician went to Vicksburg, Miss., where he was superintendent of public schools for a year. In May, 1849, he became associate editor of the *Springfield Republican*, to the success of which he contributed much. In 1855 Dr. Holland published a *History of Western Massachusetts*, and in 1857 *The Bay-Path*, a tale giving some romantic aspects of life in a Puritan community. *Bitter Sweet* (1857), his first poem, was a more ambitious attempt to combine romance with modern New England life. *Miss Gilbert's Career* (1860), a realistic novel, gave the author scope for his propensity to point a moral. This ingrained moralizing tendency marks all his writings, and has probably contributed to their success. *Timothy Titcomb's Letters to Young People* (1858), *Gold Foil Hammered from Popular Proverbs* (1859), *Letters to the Joneses* (1863), and other books of the same kind, are ingenious essays in giving youth the results of experience, without the trouble or danger of going through it for themselves. Dr. Holland's aim was to be a moral instructor to American people, especially to American youth; and, trained in the school of journalism to get the attention of his readers, he succeeded admirably in his purpose. With a moderate talent for humor, he maintained in general a cheerful gravity, as became a teacher of the people. His teaching was not confined to his books; he was also in demand as a popular lecturer. In 1860 he retired from the *Springfield Republican*, and until 1870 his literary work was confined to his books, though he spent two years in travelling in Europe. Then with mind enriched by observation abroad, he returned to become editor-in-chief of *Scribner's Monthly*, a new magazine, which proved a success from the start. In it he published another novel, *Arthur Bonnicastle* (1874), showing the training of an American boy to genuine manhood. Dr. Holland published a complete edition of his poems, under the title *Garnered Sheaves* (1873). Still later he published *The Mistress of the Manse* (1874). He died Oct. 12, 1881.

HOLMES, ABIEL (1763–1837), an American clergyman, was born at Woodstock, Conn., Dec. 24, 1763. He was a son of Dr. David Holmes, who served as a captain in the French and in the Revolutionary war. Abiel graduated at Yale College in 1783, and was tutor there in 1786–87. He had in the meantime studied theology, and in 1788 was ordained pastor of a congregation at Midway, Ga. In 1790 he married Mary, daughter of Rev. Dr. Ezra Stiles, president of Yale College. Being obliged to return to the North on account of his health he became in 1792 pastor of the First Congregational Church at Cambridge, Mass. In 1832 the congregation divided on account of the Unitarian controversy, and Dr. Holmes remained pastor of the orthodox portion, being assisted in his duties by a colleague. He died at Cambridge, June 4, 1837. His first wife had died in 1795, and in 1800 he married Sarah, daughter of the Hon. Oliver Wendell, of Boston. Dr. Holmes wrote the *Life of President Stiles* (1796); and he afterwards devoted much time to historical and antiquarian research. He published *American Annals* (2 vols., 1805; 2d ed., 1829), which gained high commendation for its accuracy. He also published sermons, and contributed to the *Massachusetts Historical Collections* a *Memoir of the French Protestants*, and a *History of Cambridge*.

HOLMES, GEORGE FREDERICK, an American educator, was born in Georgetown, Demerara, Guiana, Aug. 21, 1820. He was early sent to England, and was educated at the University of Durham. He removed to the United States in 1838, and taught in classical schools in Virginia, Georgia, and South Carolina. In 1842, although not naturalized, he was licensed by special act of the South Carolina legislature to practice law. In 1845 he was appointed professor of ancient languages in Richmond College, Va., and in 1847 professor of history, political economy, and international law in William and Mary College. In 1857 he became professor of history and literature in the University of Virginia, and since 1882 has been professor of historical science in the same institution. He has contributed articles to the *North British Review*, and many other periodicals, has prepared a series of text-books for schools in the Southern States, and a *New History of the United States*.

HOLMES, OLIVER WENDELL, an American author, was born at Cambridge, Mass., Aug. 29, 1809, being the son of Rev. Dr. Abiel Holmes (*q. v.*). He was educated at Phillips Academy, Exeter, and at Harvard College. Graduating at the latter in 1829 he began to study law, but soon turned to medicine. In 1832 he went to Europe, and pursued professional studies for nearly three years in Paris and other cities. In 1836 he obtained the degree of M. D., and in 1838 was elected professor of anatomy and physiology in Dartmouth College. In 1840 he established himself as a practitioner in Boston, and in 1847 he was made Parkman professor of anatomy and physiology in the medical school of Harvard College.

While still an undergraduate Holmes had displayed a knack for humorous poetry, and in 1830, with a few kindred spirits, prepared the sparkling paper called *The Collegian*. Six numbers only were issued, but out of the twenty-five pieces which Holmes supplied five or six have been thought worthy of a place in his latest collections. In 1836, after his return from Europe, he delivered his metrical essay on *Poetry* before the Phi Beta Kappa Society, and on numerous similar occasions since that time he has presented appropriate poems of lasting merit. His "Old Ironsides," which he used as an illustration in that first essay, had already become a national lyric. Dr. Holmes is a sworn foe of humbug, but he assails it not with denunciation but with the barbed arrows of ridicule. He has not hesitated to expose the quackeries and foibles of the learned profession, including his own. Yet behind all his fun and humorous extravagance there is a sound and healthy sympathy with what is true to nature and genuine in art. His occasional poems, delivered before gatherings of professional and college friends, are charming with their grace and polished wit.

In November, 1857, the *Atlantic Monthly* was founded, and Dr. Holmes was engaged to furnish some articles of general interest. Taking up a title which he used twenty-five years before, he gave to the world the genial observations of *The Autocrat of the Breakfast Table*. The mingled wit, shrewdness, and good humor of the comments, as well as the witty and pathetic poems introduced, created a strong public demand for their continuance. The characters dimly suggested were by a few strokes made more vivid, and the talk even took the form of a story. This tendency was still more manifest in the series called *The Professor at the Breakfast Table*. This in turn was succeeded by *The Professor's Story*, afterwards called *Elsie Venner; a Romance of Destiny*. In this Dr. Holmes at times crosses the border line from the region of facts into a region of physiological and psychological mystery, for which he has elsewhere shown strong predilection. Less weird in its effect, yet belonging to the same class, mingling medical truth and fancies with able delineations of character, is *The Guardian Angel* (1867). These stories had appeared in the *Atlantic Monthly*, and some other contributions were collected under the title *Soundings from the Atlantic* (1864). Still later another series appeared under the title *The Poet at the Breakfast Table* (1873), in which there was more discussion of books than in his earlier papers.

Dr. Holmes had also published some volumes of professional papers, in which his wit, good humor, and literary skill are seen as plainly as in his books for general readers. *Currents and Counter-Currents in Medical Science, Border Lines in Some Provinces of Medical Science* (1867), *Mechanism in Thought and Morals* (1871), indicate by their titles the range of subjects which he delights to treat. His poems, grave and gay, have been gathered in various volumes as *Songs in Many Keys* and *Songs of Many Seasons*. He has also published memoirs of his friends, John Lothrop Motley and Ralph Waldo Emerson.

Dr. Holmes gave his most popular book the subtitle, "Every Man his own Boswell." In his various publications, as well as in his attractive recitations of his poems, he has indeed made a full display of his own character. He has been the sympathetic connecting link between the self-limited culture of early New England and the unsparing critical tendency of the present day.

HOLST, HERMAN EDUARD VON, a German historian, was born at Fellin, Livonia, June 19, 1841. He was educated at Dorpat and Heidelberg, studying especially political economy and history. In 1867 he settled in New York, when he was correspondent of various newspapers, and also an editor of the *Deutsch-Americanisches Conversations-Lexicon*. In 1872 he was appointed professor of history in the University of Strassburg, and in 1874 he was called to a similar position at Freiburg. He has obtained a high reputation by his works *Verfassung und Demokratie der Vereinigten Staaten von Nord Amerika* (1873) and by his *Constitutional History of the United States* (4 vols. German, 1878-85; 5 vols. English, 1880-85). He also prepared a *Life of John C. Calhoun* (1884).

HOLT, JOSEPH, an American statesman, was born in Breckinridge co., Ky., Jan. 6, 1807. He was educated at St. Joseph's College, Bardstown, Ky., and at Centre College, Danville, Ky. In 1828 he began to practice law at Elizabethtown, Ky., but in 1832 removed to Louisville, and in 1835 to Port Gibson, Miss. Returning to Louisville in 1842, he acquired an extensive and lucrative practice. In 1857 he was appointed commissioner of patents, and in 1859 was called into Pres. Buchanan's cabinet as postmaster-general. He succeeded John B. Floyd as secretary of war in January, 1861, while the cabinet was embarrassed by the secession movement. Holt firmly maintained the right and duty of the national government to resist attacks on its existence and property. At the close of Buchanan's administration Holt retired from the war department, but afterwards served in civil departments until September, 1862, when he was appointed judge-advocate-general of the army. In 1864 he was placed at the head of the bureau of military justice, and declined the appointment of attorney-general. In March, 1865, he was made brevet major-general.

HOLTZENDORFF, FRANZ VON, a German jurist, was born at Vietmannsdorf, Prussia, Oct. 14, 1829. He attended the gymnasium at Schulpforta and studied jurisprudence at Berlin, Heidelberg, and Bonn, taking his degree as doctor in 1852. He became privat-docent at Berlin in 1857, professor extraordinary in 1861, and full professor in 1873. In the same year he was made professor of jurisprudence at Munich. He was a member of the North German Parliament in 1867. He has devoted himself especially to the reform in the treatment of criminals, opposing capital punishment and laboring for the establishment of reformatory institutions, and has visited other countries of Europe to examine the penal systems. He has also labored for the improvement of public education. From 1861 to 1874 he edited the *Allgemeine deutsche Strafrechtszeitung*; since 1866, in company with Virchow, the *Sammlung gemeinverständlicher wissenschaftlicher Vorträge*; since 1872, with W. Oncken, the *Deutschen Zeit- und Streitfragen*, and since 1871 the *Jahrbuch für Gesetzgebung, Verwaltung und Rechtspflege des Deutschen Reichs*. He was president of the International Prison Congress at London in 1872, and of Institute of International Law at Munich in 1883. He has founded and assisted in many charitable and philanthropical societies. Among his numerous publications are *Französische Rechtszustände* (1859); *Die Reform der Staatsanwaltschaft in Deutschland* (1864); *Die Grundsätze und Ergebnisse des irischen Strafvollzugs* (1865); *Die Principien der Politik* (2d ed., 1879); *Encyklopädie der Rechtswissenschaft* (4 vols., 4th ed., 1882); *Handbuch des deutschen Strafrechts* (4 vols., 1871–77); *Zeitglossen des gesunden Menschenverstandes* (1884). He died Feb. 5, 1889.

HOLYOAKE, GEORGE JACOB, an English secularist, was born at Birmingham, April 13, 1817. He was educated in the workingmen's schools of that city and afterwards became a teacher in them. In 1842 he published a tract which brought upon him a charge of blasphemy and atheism, and was imprisoned on account of it. In 1846 he founded a journal called *The Reasoner*, in which he advocated secularism as "the practical philosophy of the people." He has published many essays, among which are *A Logic of Facts* (1848); *Secularism* (1854–55); *The Limits of Atheism* (1861); *History of Co-operation in Rochdale* (1858); *Life of Robert Owen* (1859); *History of Co-operation in England* (2 vols., 1875–77). About 1857 he removed to London, where he opened a book store for the publication and sale of books on free-thinking and social reform. Since 1874 he has published the *Secular Review*. In 1880 he made a visit to the United States, and on his return published *Among the Americans*.

HOLYOKE, a city of Massachusetts, in Hampden county, is on the W. bank of the Connecticut River, and on the Connecticut River Railroad, 8 miles N. of Springfield and 105 miles W. of Boston. It is the terminus of the Holyoke and Westfield Railroad. In 1849 a dam was here constructed 1018 feet in length, which furnishes immense water power. The fall is 60 feet, and the river 2 mile. There are 20 paper-mills, 10 cotton and woolen mills, and several planing- and grist-mills. The city has a fine city hall, built of granite, 15 churches, 3 national banks, 2 savings banks, 3 convents, an orphanage, a Roman Catholic home for girls, 3 hotels, 4 weekly newspapers, and 2 monthly trade journals. The school system is excellent. There are 13 school buildings besides the Roman Catholic parish school-houses. There is also a free public library. Holyoke is one of the largest seats of the paper-making business in the United States, or, indeed, in the world. The river is here the seat of a considerable shad-fishery in the spring of the year. Holyoke is connected by bridge with South Hadley on the east side of the Connecticut, beyond which, at some distance to the north, is Mount Holyoke, rising 1120 feet above the sea level and about 7 miles long. Much nearer the town, and on the same side of the river, is Mount Tom, a sharp crest of trap, rising to a somewhat greater height. The population of Holyoke in 1870 was 10,733; in 1880, 21,915; and in 1890, 35,526.

HOMER, WINSLOW, an American painter, was born at Boston, Feb. 24, 1836. He early evinced a talent for drawing, and after spending two years in a lithograph establishment began to make wood-engravings. In 1859 he settled in New York, working on *Harper's Weekly* and studying in the Academy of Design. In 1861 he drew many scenes of the war for *Harper's Weekly*. His experiences also furnished subjects for oil-paintings exhibited at the National Academy. Among these were many pictures of negro life, and especially Home, Sweet Home (1863), and Prisoners to the Front (1865). The latter attracted much attention when exhibited at Paris in 1867. Homer resided in New York, where he was made a member of the National Academy in 1865.

HOMESTEAD LEGISLATION. The Homestead act was approved by Pres. Lincoln on May 20, 1862. Since that time there have been occasional changes in its provisions, but these changes have been generally in the direction of extending rather than restricting the privileges it confers. The intent of the original law was to give to every citizen who would accept it as a home a farm of 160 acres, to be selected at will from any of the unappropriated public lands of the United States, and such is the effect of all the statutes on the subject as they now exist. The essential condition attached by the government to the grant of the homestead privilege is that the land shall be taken in good faith as a home. All the requirements of the law and the regulations prescribed by the General Land Office are based upon this theory. The homestead right is not conferred upon persons temporarily residing in the United States, nor upon minors, but an alien may acquire the right to initiate an entry by declaring his intention to become a citizen of the United States, and a minor who is in fact the head of a family is allowed the homestead privilege.

(See Vol. XII. p. 125 Am. ed. (p. 122 Edin. ed.).)

An applicant, having selected the land he desires to enter, should satisfy himself before taking any further steps that no improvements have been made upon it which might become the basis of a pre-emption claim, or, if such improvements exist, that they have been abandoned. The right of a pre-emptor dates from the time he begins improvement of the land, and he is allowed in some cases three months in which to appear at the local office and make entry. If the land is free from such adverse claim the homestead applicant may then proceed to the land office for the district which the land is located and ascertain whether the records of that office show any prior entry. If none is found he may appear before the register or receiver and make the prescribed affidavit as to age and citizenship, and that the entry is made for his own exclusive use and benefit and for actual settlement and cultivation. Then, upon payment of the fees and commissions, which vary, according to circumstances, from $1 to $12, the entry is complete, and the applicant receives as his evidence of title the receiver's duplicate receipt. This paper contains the full description of the land by section, township, and range, and must be surrendered or its loss accounted for when final proof is made.

The initiatory steps toward the acquirement of title to the homestead are thus taken, and they give to the entryman what is called an "inceptive right" only. To secure a patent he must proceed to establish, within 6 months, his residence upon the land, and he must reside upon and cultivate it continuously for 5 years. During this period he must have no other home; but the fact that he is the owner of land elsewhere does not at all affect his right of homestead entry. If in active service in the army or navy, the residence of the applicant's family upon the land is considered sufficient; and in favor of soldiers of the war of the rebellion it is provided that the term of their service during the war, to the extent of 4 years, may be deducted from the 5 years' residence required by law; and a soldier honorably discharged by reason of wounds or disability contracted in the service may be so credited with the entire term of his enlistment. Therefore patent may be issued to a person claiming the benefit of these provisions, and who is entitled to credit for 4 years' service in the army, upon proof of one year's residence upon the land.

As the area of the unappropriated public lands diminishes from year to year, the interpretation of the laws regarding residence and cultivation become more strict. At the present time the government keeps in the field a force of special agents and inspectors, whose duty it is to examine into the validity of entries suspected of being fraudulent and to report to the commissioner of the General Land Office at Washington for cancellation all entries where the law has not been complied with in good faith.

At this stage in the progress of a homestead entry the title to the land remains in the government. The settler may relinquish to the United States, but he has no title which he can convey to another; and, since the entry may never be completed, no act of the entryman can fix upon the land any obligation. Neither the land nor the improvements upon it are subject to execution for debt, nor can they be taxed. This immunity continues until the settler has received his patent from the government, and in most of the States and Territories local laws provide that the homestead may not be levied upon under execution after patent has issued.

In addition to making his residence upon the land the homestead claimant must cultivate it and must make such improvements as will satisfy the register and receiver of the perfect good faith of the entry. A habitable house must be built, with such appurtenances as are usually considered essential to a home in the region in which the land is situated. As a rule a reasonable portion of the quarter-section must be brought under cultivation. In grazing districts the establishment of a dairy upon the land has been held sufficient.

If the homestead settler does not wish to remain 5 years upon the land he may pay for it with cash or scrip or land warrants at the rate of $1.25 per acre, or, if the land is situated within the limits of a railroad land-grant, at the rate of $2.50 per acre. This privilege of commutation is by present rulings restricted to homestead claimants who have never exercised their right of pre-emption.

Final proof must be made within 7 years from the date of the homestead entry. This proof consists in the affidavit of the settler that he is a citizen of the United States and that he has complied with the requirements of the homestead laws in every particular. A full description of his improvements must be given, and his statements must be corroborated by the affidavits of two disinterested witnesses. Public notice by advertisement in a newspaper in the land district must be given by the settler that he intends to make final proof on a date named before the register and receiver, or some other officer authorized by law to receive such proof, and the local land officers must also be notified. These provisions are intended to afford an opportunity to any one who may desire to contest the claim to be present with adverse evidence.

Where application is made to contest the validity of a homestead entry on the ground of abandonment, the contestant must file his affidavit with the district land officers, accompanied by the affidavits of one or more witnesses in support of the allegations made, setting forth the facts on which his application is founded, describing the tract and giving the name of the settler. Upon this the officers will set apart a day for hearing, giving all the parties in interest due notice of the time and place of trial. The contestant must defray the expenses incident to such a contest. If he succeeds in the contest, and procures the cancellation of the entry, he will be notified thereof, and for a period of 30 days from such notice will be allowed a preference right over any other person to institute a claim to the land.

As the law allows but one homestead privilege, a settler relinquishing or abandoning his claim cannot thereafter make a second entry; although where the entry is cancelled as invalid for some reason other than abandonment, and not the wilful act of the party, he is not thereby debarred from entering again, if in other respects entitled, and may have the fee and commissions paid on the cancelled entry refunded on proper application. Where a party makes a selection of land for a homestead, he must, as a general rule, abide by his choice. If he has neglected to examine the character of the land prior to entry and it proves to be infertile or otherwise unsatisfactory, he must suffer the consequences of his own neglect. In some cases, however, where obstacles which could not have been foreseen, and which render it impracticable to cultivate the land, are discovered subsequently to entry (such as the impossibility of obtaining water by digging wells or otherwise), the entry may, in the discretion of the commissioner of the General Land Office, be cancelled and a second entry allowed. But in the event of a new entry, the party will be required to show the same compliance with law in connection therewith as though he had not made a previous entry, and must pay the proper fees and commissions upon the same.

If the homestead claimant's proof is satisfactory to the register and receiver the final fees and commissions are paid and the applicant receives his final certificate, which constitutes his sole evidence of title until the papers can be forwarded to Washington and patent issued by the President.

During the fiscal year ending June 30, 1890, 5,531,678 acres were entered under the homestead laws, during the fiscal year 1888 the entries amounted to 6,076,616 acres, and during the fiscal year 1886 to 9,145,136 acres. The marked decrease seems to show that the

HOMŒOPATHY, compounded of the Greek words, ὅμοιον, like, similar, and πάθος, disease, or condition, denotes a similarity or correspondence of disease or condition as opposed to Allopathy (ἄλλον, other, different, and πάθος), signifying a dissimilarity of disease or condition. The name was applied to a system of therapeutics by its chief expositor, Dr. Samuel Hahnemann. The law of this system is tersely expressed, "*Similia similibus curantur*"—"Like diseases are cured by like remedies." The enunciation of this law, as governing isolated cases, dates from Hippocrates, but its universality, united to a method of its application in therapeutics, was first promulgated by Hahnemann, who was led to a belief in its truth very slowly and as a result of painstaking experiment. It was while translating, in 1790, from the English into German, Cullen's *Materia Medica*, that Hahnemann met with the assertion by Cullen, under the article on *Cinchona*, that "it is established as a fact that both astringents and bitters, in their simple and separate estates, have proved often sufficient to prevent the recurrence of intermittent fever;" to this Hahnemann added in a footnote that "much more bitter and astringent substances than Peruvian bark might be prepared from the extracts of quassia and nut-gall, but that the compound cannot cure any intermittent fever of six months' duration." Cullen further says; "Whilst it is allowed to be a very safe and powerful remedy, the only question, which remains respecting it, is : In what circumstances may it be most properly employed?" This question Hahnemann set himself to answer. Knowing that Cinchona when administered to persons in health produces febrile symptoms, Hahnemann prepared an alcoholic tincture of *Cinchona officinalis* and took a dose of it himself, whereupon he felt symptoms which were, in a remarkable degree, *similar* to those of the peculiar fever for which the bark was pre-eminently the cure, and in which its administration had been successful. Was this then the test? Does the cure of a disease reside in that drug which when administered in health produces a *similar* disease, just as similar waves of light or of sound will neutralize each other? Many experiments could alone verify this law, if such it were, and to this verification Hahnemann devoted himself, in the course of which it was proved beyond a doubt that Cinchona when administered to healthy persons effected peculiar changes in the system ; and a careful comparison of these changes, or symptoms, with the symptoms of intermittent fevers which had been cured by doses of Peruvian bark, revealed their similarity in all cases. Thus, for instance, to cite some of the leading distinctions which should guide a physician in the administration of Cinchona, Hahnemann discovered that this drug should be given when the attack begins with some preliminary symptoms before the occurrence of the chill, such as palpitation of the heart ; or when there is no thirst either during the chill or the fever ; or when there is much determination of blood to the head during the fever, etc. In short, only those cases demand this medicine wherein all the morbid symptoms which occur during the apyrexia, as well as those of the paroxysm, most closely correspond to those produced in health by the bark itself. Having satisfied himself that *Similia similibus curantur* held good with regard to Cinchona, Hahnemann undertook a similar investigation of other remedies, and in each case with corresponding results. The specific virtue of Mercury in cases of syphilis had long been known, but it became clear from Hahnemann's investigations that the change of organization produced by Mercury in healthy persons manifested great similarity to syphilis. Sulphur, the well-known specific against itch, produces on the healthy subject an eruption similar to that disease. Jenner's discovery may be also cited in confirmation, where inoculation of the cow-pox destroys the susceptibility to the small-pox. Early in his investigations Hahnemann observed that children who had been poisoned by the berries of *Belladonna* were sometimes attacked by an eruption resembling that of scarlet fever, and he found by experiment that this same Belladonna, when given as a remedy in the scarlet fever of that day, cured the disease, and that it likewise served as a prophylactic.

Having convinced himself that he had discovered a law of nature, he set to work to find out the method of its application. It is clear that all drugs produce disease ; that is, deviations from the standard of health. It is to be presumed that every drug produces a peculiar, characteristic disease, which may be termed an artificial disease. If, then, artificial drug diseases are to be employed in counteracting natural diseases, we must have a knowledge of drug diseases commensurate with the infinite variety of natural diseases. He therefore applied himself to form a new *Materia Medica*, based on the recorded effects of drugs upon the healthy human subject, a work which he continued to the end of his life.

At the very outset of his practice under the new law Hahnemann encountered an obstacle which might have proved insurmountable to a less practical mind. To a patient suffering from an acute disease the administration, in the ordinary dose, of a drug which creates a similar disease, so far from effecting an immediate cure, produced, very naturally, an aggravation of all the characteristic symptoms. The reason of this was not far to seek. Diseased organs are extremely sensitive, and the medicine, homœopathically administered, affected the very organs already suffering from a natural disease. To this aggravation of the disease there usually followed, to be sure, a crisis and a rapid recovery, yet the aggravation sometimes proved so alarming as to demand the use of antidotes. This unhappy result threatened to render the discovery of the new law barren, until it occurred to Hahnemann that the ordinary dose was too large. Instead, therefore, of administering a whole drop of the tincture of Belladonna (which was the first drug with which he experimented) he diluted one drop with ninety-nine drops of alcohol, and of this dilution he gave one drop as a dose. To his astonishment even this one-hundredth of a drop of the tincture produced excessive aggravation. Again he diluted this one-hundredth of a drop with ninety-nine drops of alcohol, and administered as a dose one drop of this second dilution, but with no expectation that it would produce more than a very insignificant effect. In the majority of cases, however, a more rapid cure followed, but to his intense astonishment the same aggravation of symptoms invariably ensued. Again he diluted, as before, this ten-thousandth of a drop, but so far from the sequent aggravation being greatly diminished the medicinal energy seemed actually to have developed, so that a dose of this, the millionth of a drop of the tincture, when given to very sensitive children, demanded an antidote. Rather encouraged than discouraged Hahnemann continued his dilutions until he found that while the aggravating effects of the drug gradually diminished, its curative powers remained fully the same, nay, were hastened by no longer having the cure delayed by the excessive aggravation. Even up to the thirtieth dilution he found, in highly sensitive temperaments, an inconvenient increase of symptoms, and he therefore diminished the dose of one drop by saturating with the liquid of the final dilution one hundred small pills of sugar of milk, and, with these, obtained satisfactory results.

From time to time Hahnemann published the results of his experiments, asking for them merely a fair trial, which is after all their only and ultimate test. He demanded the acceptance of no theory; he had none to offer during the development of his system, but having been led, step by step, by actual experience, all he requested was that his brother physicians should candidly test his results and verify his facts. In 1810 he published the *Organon of Homœopathic Medicine*, wherein his system was at last set forth. Thirteen years later he issued a fifth edition, and from this, the last from his hand, the following abstracts are made, as affording the best exposition of Homœopathic practice:—

Great stress is laid on the rule that it is against the symptoms in their combined sum that the physician's art is to be directed. These symptoms are the deviations from the standard of health, and constitute the disease as far as the prescriber is concerned, who has nothing else to guide him but what is manifest to his senses. With the subtle cause of the disease he need not be concerned; the cause is always of an immaterial nature; about it, even if it could be discovered, there might exist a difference of opinion; but let the perceptible manifestations of that cause be removed and the disease is cured. The sum of the symptoms, therefore, and that alone, must guide the physician in the choice of his remedy.

Since the only curative effect of drugs lies in their power to produce changes in the human system, it behooves us to learn by experiment the exact nature and quality of the changes which each drug causes. The exact nature of these changes can be measured only by its symptomatic departure from a fixed standard, which must be, necessarily, that of health. All other standards cannot but be fluctuating and fallacious. The character of the symptoms produced by drugs having been thus most exactly ascertained, it follows that drugs will become medicinal only by creating an *artificial* disease which will counteract the disease already present, or, if it may be so termed, the *natural* disease. Wherefore, in practice, we must select a medicine which will create symptoms either similar or opposite to those already present; whichever experience shows to be the easier, safer, and more enduring means of restoring health. Other than these two methods of treating disease, viz., by creating, artificially, similar symptoms, or opposite symptoms, there exists only a third, viz., the Allopathic method; whereby remedies are given which bear to the natural disease no correlation whatever, but which create symptoms neither similar nor opposite, but wholly dissimilar.

As it is not the province of this article to enter into the polemics of therapeutics, it suffices to say that Hahnemann proves to the entire satisfaction of himself and of his followers that, of these three methods, Homœopathy, or the Law of the Similar Remedy, is alone capable of effecting a speedy, safe, and enduring cure. To disprove the efficacy of *Contraria contrariis curantur* he adduces the homely instances, drawn from common experience, of burns which are not cured by cold but by heat, of frost-bitten limbs which are exposed not to heat but to cold. To disprove the utility of Allopathy he denies that diverting a disease to organs not diseased effects a permanent cure, though it may give temporary relief; equally futile is it to follow nature, as it is termed, for nature is blind and unintelligent; nature cannot tie an artery, or draw together the gaping lips of a wound, or heal a stricture; nor will getting rid of the secretions produced by disease effect a cure any more than blowing the nose will cure a cold in the head; nor is it necessary, in cases which are not surgical, to attempt to remove the supposed cause of a disease; the cause, which is often very occult, if not utterly beyond our ken, expresses itself in the symptoms, and if these be cured the cause is removed. There remains, accordingly, "no other method of profitably applying medicines than the Homœopathic, whereby we select that medicine the action whereof upon persons in health is known, and which produces an artificial disease [not identical, be it observed, but] the closest in resemblance to the entire sum of the symptoms of the natural disease." This result, Hahnemann maintains, is founded upon the Therapeutic Law of Nature that a disease in man is permanently extinguished only by one that is most similar but artificially produced. This is maintained to be an irreversible, infallible Law of Nature, not a theory nor a dogma, but a law inviolable. In thus founding his system of therapeutics upon a Law of Nature Hahnemann elevates medicine to a science, and removes from it the reproach of empiricism. If his law be not a law, of course his whole system topples headlong, but he claims that it is a law inductively founded upon innumerable instances, "however unsatisfactory may be the theory of the manner in which it acts." Hahnemann asserts that he attaches no value whatever to any explanation, his own included, that can be given of this phenomenon. After this assertion it is not worth while to state at length the explanation which, in default of a better, Hahnemann himself suggests, more especially since it has been rejected by some of his most eminent followers. But for the sake of any explanation which may be attempted he calls attention to the facts upon which he founded his own theory, viz.: that the human system is more sensitive to the action of a drug than to the assaults of a natural disease arising from miasm, etc. This is proved by the fact that all men are not smitten by an epidemic even when all are equally exposed to it, whereas all men, at all times, and under all circumstances, are affected by drugs or poisons; or, in other words, natural morbific influences exert only conditional power, while medicinal influences exert a power which is absolute, direct, and greatly superior to that of the former, yet at the same time running commonly a more brief and rapid course. When therefore to the natural disease the similar drug disease has been added (the same organs in each case being thereby affected), the greater intensity of the drug disease has full scope and gives the power of overriding and of obliterating the natural disease. Without this resemblance between the two diseases the mere intensity of the drug will not effect a cure. Nature herself cannot effect a genuine cure by the excitement of a new yet dissimilar disease, be the intensity of the latter ever so great. Hahnemann then illustrates this law of nature by reference to the three following instances:

First: If a patient be exposed to two *dissimilar* diseases which have an *unequal* power, or if he be already attacked by one which is more violent or more pronounced in its character, the weaker or newer will be repelled or expelled by the stronger or older, and will not be able to obtain a lodgment. Thus a patient suffering from a severe chronic disease will never be subject to an attack of autumnal dysentery or any other mild epidemic disease. According to Larrey, the plague peculiar to the Levant never breaks out where scurvy prevails, nor does it ever attack those who are suffering from herpetic ailments. According to Jenner, the rickets prevents vaccination from taking effect, and Hildebrand informs us that persons suffering from phthisis are never attacked by epidemic fevers unless the latter are extremely violent.

Secondly: If the *new* disease, which is *dissimilar* to the old, be the *more powerful*, it will cause the suspension of the old disease, until the new has either run its course or is cured; then the old disease reappears. Where the measles and the small-pox exist together and have both attacked the same infant, it is usual for the measles, even after they have already declared themselves, to be arrested by the small-pox, and not to resume their course until after the cure of the small-pox. On the other hand Manget has seen the small-pox, which had fully developed itself after inoculation, suspended during four days by the measles, and after the desquamation of which it revived, to run its course. It is the same with all diseases which are *dissimilar:* the stronger suspends the weaker (except in cases where they blend together, which rarely occurs in acute diseases), but they never cure each other reciprocally.

Thirdly: It sometimes occurs that the new disease, after having acted for some time in the system, joins itself finally to the old and dissimilar disease, and thence results a complication of two different maladies, both of them incapable of annihilating or curing the other. Venereal symptoms are effaced and suspended in the first instances whenever a psoric eruption commences, but in process of time the venereal affection, being at least quite as powerful as the psoric, the two unite—that is, each seizes upon those parts of the organism which are its especial field, whereby the patient is rendered worse and the cure more difficult.

But the result is far different when two *similar* diseases meet. They n neither *repel* each other, as in the first of the three instances just given, nor *suspend* each other, as in the second; nor, as in the third, can they *co-exist* and form a double or complicated disease; but they always destroy each other. The stronger defeats the weaker, and puts it to flight. Violent inflammation of the eyes, even to blindness, is caused, as is well known, by small-pox, and yet by inoculation with small-pox chronic inflammations of the eyes have been perfectly cured, as reported by Dezoteux and Leroy. Deafness and asthma have been removed in the same way, according to Closs. The fever attendant upon cow-pox cured intermittent fever in two cases, as observed by Hardige the younger, a confirmation of John Hunter's remark that two fevers [being similar] cannot co-exist in the same patient.

It is upon the foregoing propositions that Hahnemann grounds his division of the healing art into three branches. First, stands the *Homœopathic*, the only true method, following nature in her most lawful mood, by inducing, through medicines, diseases most *similar* in their symptoms to the disease to be cured. Secondly, the *Antipathic*, which by exciting an opposite state to that which exists, is only palliative, ending in chronic diseases by making matters far worse. And lastly, the *Allopathic*, hitherto the commonest method, which aims at cure by exciting *dissimilar* affections. It is a proof of Hahnemann's fame that he has made these learned appellations current in men's mouths, and that the two leading medical sects are now generally known as *Homœopaths* and *Allopaths*.

In addition to the "law of the similars" there are two practical rules which Homœopaths maintain to be of essential importance. The first is "The Single Remedy." Great stress is laid on this rule. Even if the exact effects of a drug on the healthy be accurately known we are still ignorant of the effect upon an invalid of a combination of drugs which might oppose, and would certainly modify, each other. Hence, also, every drug homœopathically prescribed must be permitted to exhaust its power before another is given.

The second rule is "The Minimum Dose." What the smallest dose may be in every individual case must be left to the wisdom and experience of the practitioner, guided by close observation, regard being always had to the fact that too strong a dose injures the patient; and the injury is the greater the more homœopathic, or similar, the medicine, because, in the main, those organs only are affected by it which are already attacked by the natural disease. The result of Hahnemann's experience was that the dose should be graduated to such a degree of minuteness as to produce, at first, an almost imperceptible aggravation of the disease. As a corollary, he insists, naturally, that a dose must not be repeated until after its effect is ended. It is not infrequently alleged that the minute doses administered by Homœopathic physicians are not an essential part of their system, but that patients can be treated homœopathically—that is, by the law of the similars—and yet that large doses may be administered. This is true only in theory; in practice it is found that a large dose thus given defeats its purpose and instead of healing aggravates the disease. It was this fact, as we have seen, that led Hahnemann to diminish the dose, and to continue to diminish it until it no longer produced undue aggravation. If, as it is argued, disease is of a spiritual or immaterial, dynamic origin, the action of drugs, which is also disease, must be of a spiritual nature also. The material substance of a drug, it may be supposed, is merely the physical expression of the hidden power; the material substance is "the muddy vesture of decay which hems" the essence in, and the more we free the essence from the grosser body the more freedom of action it develops. This process of elimination Hahnemann called *potentizing*, and in order that all drugs at each stage of elimination may have a uniform degree of potency he laid down certain rules to be followed in the preparation of medicines. Obviously the simplest way of attenuating solid substances is by trituration, but as the minute particles of most substances, when reduced to fine dust, have an attraction for each other, and a tendency to cohere, it becomes necessary to triturate with a foreign substance, which will not only prevent this cohesion but assist in the continued mechanical subdivision. Hahnemann selected sugar of milk as this foreign substance on account of its innocuousness and its capacity of extremely minute subdivision. One grain of the drug therefore is mixed with 99 grains of sugar of milk; this proportion is arbitrary: some physicians prefer the decimal ratio of one to nine; all that Hahnemann aimed at was uniformity, and, to this end also, he directed that the trituration should be carried on for one-half hour; whereupon one grain of this mixture is again triturated with other 99 grains of milk. This is called the second potency. This process is to be continued until the number of triturations has been deemed sufficient. In the case of tinctures the medium for greater mechanical subdivision instead of being sugar of milk is alcohol, and shaking is substituted for trituration. Again, for the sake of uniformity, Hahnemann lays down certain rules for the preparation of dilutions, namely: that they must be shaken a certain number of times, etc., and the shaking, or *succussion*, as it is called, imparts a higher curative power to the medicine by immaterializing it. This process of potentizing drugs by continuous trituration and dilution has been carried to an extent whereat it would seem physically impossible that any material trace of the original substance can survive, and yet so far from losing thereby their curative powers many Homœopathic physicians maintain that these are very greatly increased. Certain it is, however, that the microscope and spectroscope reveal material traces of the original substance in some of the triturations and dilutions far beyond the point where we might reasonably expect it to have utterly vanished. Mayrhofer, with a magnifying power of 300 diameters, observed distinct signs of the presence of platina, of gold, in the tenth trituration, as also of metallic mercury. Metallic iron is still visible under a magnifying power of 300 diameters in the seventh and eighth attenuation. A patient therefore who takes a grain of the third centesimal trituration of tin or arsenic swallows the amazing number of 115,200,000 particles of the medicine, and, if it be prepared according to the decimal scale, no less than 576,000,000 particles, each of which necessarily possesses all the properties of the metal. While the diameter of the smallest metallic particles thus observed is shown to be from $\frac{1}{30}$ to $\frac{1}{100}$ of a line, the diameter of the blood globule is only $\frac{1}{80}$ of a line; there is therefore no part of the system into which these drugs thus prepared may not freely penetrate. By means of this trituration and dilution many substances, such as vegetable Charcoal, Lime, Silica, Lycopodium, etc., which in their crude state possess no medicinal properties, become prominent in the Homœopathic *Materia Medica* for their curative power.

Hahnemann's methods of preparing medicines have not been formerly followed; subsequent investigators have claimed greater efficacy for certain modifications of the original processes, and machines have been invented whereby the physical labor of preparing triturations and dilutions has been greatly abbreviated.

In ascertaining or proving the effects of drugs upon the healthy, the Homœopathic school, with unceasing vigilance, has endeavored so to conduct the experiments that the results shall be absolutely trustworthy. To attain this it has been deemed requisite to make as many experiments on as many individuals as possible, of all ages and of both sexes, of different constitutions and temperaments, of all habits and peculiarities, in different climates, at different seasons, in different states of the weather, etc., etc. As diversities of constitution and disposition are required, perfect health is not demanded, provided the prover has the ability to distinguish his habitual abnormal symptoms from any unusual or new symptoms. The substance to be proved must be of the very purest, and one dose only, according to Hahnemann, is to be taken, but such a dose as is sufficient to produce an effect without seriously endangering health. Hahnemann's general rule, in regard to drugs already known and used, was to take such a dose as in most cases of illness had been considered efficacious by the Allopathic school. Great stress is laid upon all symptoms of effects upon the *mind*, and the greatest accuracy, in this regard, enjoined upon the provers. The symptoms which are common to all the provers are considered characteristic of the drug. Some extremely characteristic symptoms often serve as a so-called "key-note" to a whole train of drug effects. In short, the exactest rules are laid down that ingenuity, quickened by search after facts, can devise.

The law of Therapeutics laid bare by Homœopathy is of so recent discovery that the wisest of its adherents shrink from the assertion that all its relations and bearings have yet been fathomed. Thus far, however, the fact that it is in harmony with the known laws of Light, and of Heat, and of Motion, gives assurance that it will be eventually acknowledged by all as a factor in the awful formula of the universe. In the present tendency of the age to accept the mightiest effects as springing from immaterial causes, when the basis of modern science is laid on atoms and molecules that no human eye has ever seen or can see, and which require almost a poet's brain to imagine, the believers in infinitesimal doses discern the final recognition of their system. In the meantime, Homœopathy is fairly entitled to the praise which even its bitterest opponents accord to it, that if it does not effect good it certainly works no harm—no small praise, negative though it be, when the infinitely complex and delicate structure of the mysterious human organization is in question.

Homœopathy was introduced into the United States in 1825 by Dr. Gram, a native of Boston, but educated in Copenhagen. His success attracted the attention of Gray, Channing, and a few others. Constantine Hering (*q. v.*) soon became the recognized leader of the new school of therapeutics in the United States. There are from 10,000 to 12,500 practitioners of Homœopathy in the United States, with an estimated clientèle of 10,000,000 persons. The hospitals number 62, in which, during 1890, 35,242 patients received treatment. There are 13 colleges, which had, in 1890, students, 1175; graduates, 369; professors and lecturers, 254. The American Institute of Homœopathy, organized in 1844, is the national society. There are four sectional societies, 29 State societies, 122 local societies, a publishing society, and several miscellaneous ones. The medical journals devoted to Homœopathy number 22. Many works have been issued, the literature on practical subjects being particularly rich for a school so young. See MEDICAL SCHOOLS. (H. H. F.)

HOOD, EDWIN PAXTON (1820–1885), an English preacher and author, was born at Westminster in 1820. He became a minister among the Independents, and had a church in London. He was busily engaged in literary work, and for several years was editor of the *Eclectic Review*, and again of the *Preacher's Lantern*. He published many minor works, a volume on the preacher's vocation under the quaint title, *Lamps, Pitchers, and Trumpets*; *The Villages of the Bible*; *Life of Rev. Thomas Binney*; *The Genius and Phi-*

losophy of Thomas Carlyle; Oliver Cromwell, and other popular books. He edited *The World of Anecdote* and *The World of Religious Anecdote*. He died at London, June 15, 1885.

HOOD, JOHN BELL, an American general, was born at Owingsville, Ky., June 29, 1831. He graduated at West Point in 1853, and entered the infantry, but was transferred to the cavalry in 1855. He was severely wounded in a fight with the Comanches and Lipans in Texas, July 20, 1857. He was made first-lieutenant Aug. 18, 1858, and was chiefly engaged in frontier duty until the outbreak of the civil war, when he assisted in handing over the U. S. troops in Texas to the secessionists. He resigned his commission, April 16, 1861, and raised a regiment of Kentuckians for the Confederate army. He commanded a brigade under Gen. A. S. Johnston, and afterwards under Gen. Bragg, but joined the Army of Virginia in the spring of 1862. He assisted in the defence of Richmond against McClellan, and fought at the second battle of Bull Run. He was promoted major-general, and at Antietam, in September, 1862, he commanded a division; he also fought at Fredericksburg, and at Gettysburg, where he was severely wounded, July 2, 1863. Rejoining his command in Georgia, he fought again at Chickamauga, where he lost a leg, and was made lieutenant-general. From the command of a corps in the army of Gen. J. E. Johnston, whom Sherman had forced back into Atlanta, Hood was raised, in obedience to a popular demand, to the full command. Three bold but unsuccessful attempts were then made to drive Sherman off, but on Sept. 1 Gen. Hood was compelled to evacuate the city. Then he made a rash attempt to cut Sherman's communications, fought the battle of Franklin, Nov. 30, and pushed as far north as Nashville, where he was repulsed by Gen. G. H. Thomas, Dec. 17, 1864. Having entirely failed to check Gen. Sherman's progress, he was relieved of his command in January, 1865, by Gen. Richard Taylor. After the war Gen. Hood settled in New Orleans, and died there Aug. 30, 1879.

HOOKER, SIR JOSEPH DALTON, a British botanist, was born at Glasgow in 1817, being the son of the distinguished botanist, Sir William Jackson Hooker. He studied medicine and accompanied Capt. James Ross in his Antarctic exploring expedition (1839–43) as assistant-surgeon, and on his return published *Flora Antarctica* (2 vols., 1845–48), a valuable contribution to the knowledge of distribution of plant-life. He was afterwards employed as botanist in the geological survey of Great Britain, and in 1847 he made a botanical exploration of the Himalaya Mountains. In 1855 he became assistant to his father, then director of the Kew Gardens, and in 1865, on his father's death, succeeded him in this post. In 1871 Dr. Hooker visited Morocco and explored some of the Atlas Mountains. In 1868 he was president of the British Association for the Advancement of Science. In 1877 he visited the United States. He has received degrees from the Universities of Oxford and Dublin, and many marks of honor from foreign societies. His publications include *The Rhododendrons of the Sikkim Himalaya* (1849–51); *Himalayan Journals* (2 vols., 1854); *Flora of New Zealand* (2 vols., 1853–55); *Flora Tasmaniae* (1859); *Student's Flora of the British Islands* (1870); *Flora of British India* (1872). He has also published, in conjunction with G. Bentham, *Genera Plantarum*, 3 vols., 1862–83).

HOOKER, WORTHINGTON (1806–1867), an American physician, was born at Springfield, Mass., March 2, 1806. He was educated at Yale College, and received the degree of M. D. from Harvard Medical College in 1829. He settled in Norwich, Conn., and in 1852 was made professor of the theory and practice of medicine at Yale College. In 1864 he was vice-president of the American Medical Association. He died at New Haven, Conn., Nov. 6, 1867. His publications include *Physician and Patient* (1849); *Lessons from the History of Medical Delusions* (1850); and a series of text-books in physiology, chemistry, and natural history.

HOPKINS, EDWARD (1600–1657), colonial governor of Connecticut, was born at Shrewsbury, England, in 1600. He was a merchant in London, and came to Boston with Rev. Mr. Davenport in 1637. Then removing to Hartford he was chosen a magistrate in 1639, and from 1640 to 1654 was governor of Connecticut alternately with Haynes. In 1643 he helped to form the union of the New England colonies. Having returned to England, he became warden of the fleet, commissioner of the admiralty, and member of Parliament. He still gave assistance to his friends in New England, and at his death left his estate there for support of schools in New Haven and Hartford, besides a bequest of £500, which was by decree of chancery paid to Harvard College in 1710.

HOPKINS, ESEK (1718–1802), first commander of the American navy, was born at Scituate, R. I., in 1718. At the commencement of the Revolutionary war he was commissioned by Gov. Cooke as brigadier-general, and in December, 1775, by Congress, as commodore and commander-in-chief of the navy. Putting to sea in February, 1776, with a squadron of four ships and three sloops, he sailed to the Bahamas, and captured the forts at New Providence with 80 cannon and stores of ammunition. Off Block Island on his return he captured a British schooner and bomb-brig, but two days later, having attacked the Glasgow, of 29 guns, allowed it to escape. In June, 1776, he was ordered by Congress to appear before the naval committee for not annoying the enemy's ships off the southern coast, and being defended by John Adams was acquitted, but was finally dismissed, Jan. 2, 1777. He resided near Providence, and was often a member of the Rhode Island general assembly. He died at North Providence, R. I., Feb. 26, 1802.

HOPKINS, JOHN HENRY (1792–1868), an American bishop, was born at Dublin, Ireland, Jan. 30, 1792. He came to America with his parents in 1800, and received a classical education. He spent a year in a counting-room in Philadelphia, and assisted Wilson, the ornithologist, in preparing the plates of his work. About 1810 he engaged in iron manufacture in the western part of Pennsylvania, but becoming bankrupt in October, 1817, studied law and was admitted to the bar in Pittsburg. In November, 1823, he took deacon's orders in the Episcopal Church, and priest's orders in May, 1824, and became rector of Trinity Church, Pittsburg. When a new building was needed, he studied Gothic architecture, in order to become its architect. In 1831 he was called to Trinity Church, Boston, as assistant minister, and he became also professor of systematic divinity in a newly established theological seminary. He was elected the first bishop of Vermont, and was consecrated in New York, Oct. 31, 1832. He became at the same time rector of St. Paul's Church, Burlington, and also established a boys' school. The expense of buildings for the latter involved him in pecuniary difficulties, and compelled him to sacrifice his property. In 1856 he resigned his rectorship, in order to devote himself to diocesan work and the building up of the Vermont Episcopal Institute. He was an able preacher, a vigorous and thoughtful writer, an earnest defender of high-church principles. He was presiding bishop of the United States after the death of Bishop Brownell in 1865. As such he took a prominent part in the Pan-Anglican Synod at Lambeth in 1867, and at that time received from the University of Oxford the degree of D. C. L. He died at Rock Point, Vt., Jan. 9, 1868. Among his numerous publications, besides sermons, were: *Christianity Vindicated* (1833); *The Primitive Creed Examined and Explained* (1834); *The Primitive Church* (1835); *The Church of Rome in her Primitive Purity* (1837); *Twelve Canzonets*, words and music (1839); *Refutation of Milner's End of Controversy* (2 vols., 1854); *The American Citizen* (1857); *Vindication of Slavery* (1860); *Law of Ritualism Examined* (1867). His *Life*, by his son, Rev. Dr. J. H. Hopkins, appeared in 1872.

HOPKINS, MARK, an American clergyman and educator, was born at Stockbridge, Mass., Feb. 4, 1802, being a grandson of Mark Hopkins, an officer in the Revolutionary army. He graduated at Williams College in 1824, and was tutor there for two years. Then studying medicine he received the degree of M. D. in 1828, and began the practice of medicine in New York. In 1830 he was made professor of moral philosophy and rhetoric in Williams College, and in 1836 he became president of that institution. After discharging the duties of this position with great fidelity and success for thirty-six years, he resigned in 1872, but remained professor of mental and moral philosophy until 1882, when he was made emeritus professor. He was also pastor of the College Church, and throughout his career exerted a marked influence on those under his tuition. He was also active in the American Board of Commissioners of Foreign Missions, and in 1857 was elected its president. Among his publications are *Lectures on the Evidences of Christianity* (1846; new ed., 1864); *Miscellaneous Essays* (1847); *Lectures on Moral Science* (1862); *Baccalaureate Sermons* (1863); *Law of Love, Love as a Law* (1869); *Outline Study of Man* (1873). He died June 17, 1887.

HOPKINS, SAMUEL (1721–1803), an American theologian, was born at Waterbury, Conn., Sept. 17, 1721. He graduated at Yale College in 1741, and studied divinity with Jonathan Edwards. In 1743 he was ordained pastor of the church in Housatonnac (now Great Barrington), Mass. He was also a zealous missionary to the Indians in that neighborhood. His ministry was often interrupted by the French and Indian wars, and sometimes his family had to flee to other towns for safety. He was dismissed in January, 1769, and began to preach at Newport, R. I., where he became pastor in April, 1770. When the British took possession of Newport in 1776 he left the town and preached in various places. Returning in 1780 he found his parish so impoverished that for the remainder of his life he depended on weekly contributions and the aid of a few friends. In 1799 he had a paralytic stroke, from which he never fully recovered, though he was able to preach occasionally. He died at Newport, R. I., Dec. 20, 1803. Dr. Hopkins earnestly opposed domestic slavery and the slave-trade, which then flourished at Newport. By his sermons, letters to influential men, newspaper essays, and especially by his famous *Dialogues*, he aroused public sentiment against the system. In 1774 a law was passed forbidding the importation of negroes into Rhode Island. In 1784 the legislature enacted that all children of slaves born after the following March should be free. Dr. Hopkins had early formed a plan for evangelizing Africa, and colonizing it with free negroes from America, which was afterward the basis of the American Colonization Society. He was also noted as the founder of "Hopkinsian divinity," a modification of Calvinism, which is expounded in his *System of Doctrines* (1793). It is really the full development of the theology of Dr. Jonathan Edwards, by whom Hopkins was trained, whose manuscripts he had studied, and several of whose treatises and sermons he had edited and published. Dr. Hopkins also wrote *The Wisdom of God in the Permission of Sin* (1759); *True State and Character of the Unregenerate* (1769); *Nature of True Holiness* (1773); and other theological treatises and religious biographies. Most of his works were republished in 1805, and again at Boston in 1854. His *Autobiography* was published in 1805, and *Memoirs* of him have been published by Prof. E. A. Park (1854) and others. Dr. Hopkins is the hero of Mrs. H. B. Stowe's *Minister's Wooing*.

HOPKINS, STEPHEN (1707–1785), an American statesman, was born at Scituate, R. I., March 7, 1707, being brother of Com. Esek Hopkins. Removing to Providence in 1731, he became a merchant, and in 1732 was elected to the assembly, where he was made speaker. He was a delegate to Congress at Albany in 1754, and served on the committee to prepare a plan of union for the colonies. In the same year he was governor of Rhode Island, and so continued until 1768, except for four years. In 1773 he was a member of the committee of correspondence, and in 1774 was sent to the Continental Congress, where in 1776 he signed the Declaration of Independence. He was a member of the naval committee, and also of the committee which drafted the Articles of Confederation. He died at Providence, R. I., July 19, 1785. He published an account of Providence and *The Rights of the Colonies Examined* (1765).

HOPKINSON, FRANCIS (1738–1791), an American judge and author, was born at Philadelphia in 1738. His father, Thomas, was a native of England, and held the office of judge at Philadelphia. The son was educated at the College of Pennsylvania, and studied law. In 1761 he was secretary of a treaty conference with the Indians of Pennsylvania. On his return from England in 1767 he settled at Bordentown, N. J., having married Ann Borden. In 1776 he was a delegate from New Jersey to the Continental Congress, in which he signed the Declaration of Independence. He was already noted for his witty and satirical writings. In 1779 he was made a judge of the admiralty of Pennsylvania, and held this office until it was abolished by the adoption of the Federal Constitution. Pres. Washington appointed him U. S. judge for Pennsylvania. Hopkinson died at Philadelphia, May 9, 1791. His political writings include *The Pretty Story* (1774); *The Prophecy* (1776); and *The Political Catechism* (1777). But more noted are *The Battle of the Kegs* (1777) and *The New Roof* (1788). He had collected for publication his *Miscellaneous Essays and Occasional Writings* (1792).

HOPKINSON, JOSEPH (1770–1842), an American jurist, son of the preceding, was born at Philadelphia, Nov. 12, 1770. He graduated at the University of

Pennsylvania in 1789, and became a lawyer first at Easton, Pa., but soon returned to Philadelphia, where he was counsel for Dr. B. Rush in his libel suit against Cobbett in 1799, and for Fries in his trial for treason before Judge Chase. When Chase was afterwards impeached before the U. S. Senate, Hopkinson was chosen to defend him. In 1815 he was elected to Congress, but in 1819 he removed to Bordentown, N. J. In 1823 he resumed the practice of his profession in Philadelphia, and in 1828 Pres. J. Q. Adams appointed him U. S. judge for the eastern district of Pennsylvania. He was a prominent member of the State Constitutional Convention of 1834. He assisted in founding the Philadelphia Academy of Fine Arts, and was its first president. Many of his addresses before literary societies were published, but he is best known as the author of "Hail Columbia," which was composed in 1798 for the benefit of an actor. Hopkinson was a confidential friend of Joseph Bonaparte, who resided at Bordentown from 1815 to 1832. He died at Philadelphia, Jan. 15, 1842.

HOPPIN, JAMES MASON, an American clergyman and author, was born at Providence, R. I., Jan. 17, 1820. He graduated at Yale College in 1840, studied law at Harvard Law School, and theology at Andover Theological Seminary, graduating in 1845. In March, 1850, he became pastor of a Congregational church in Salem, Mass., and held this charge until 1859. In 1861 he was appointed professor of homiletics in the theological department of Yale College, and in 1879 he became in the same college professor of the history of art. He has published *Notes of a Theological Student* (1854); *Old England: its Art, Scenery, and People* (1867); *The Office and Work of the Christian Ministry* (1869); *Life of Admiral A. H. Foote* (1874); *Life of Henry Armitt Brown* (1880); *Homiletics* (1881).

HOPS. The Hop (*Humulus Lupulus*) is a member of the botanical order *Cannabinaceæ*, which has but one other species, *Cannabis Sativa*, or hemp. It is a common wild plant in the south of England, and occurs throughout Europe and parts of Asia. It is common in the Northern United States, and is considered by Gray as "truly indigenous," though this has been doubted by other botanists. It has been cultivated from a very early era, and may have escaped from cultivation in many places where now found wild. It is a hardy plant, with rough angular stem from 10 to 20 feet long, which climbs by twining around the stems of other plants. Its leaves are opposite, heart-shaped, 3 to 5 lobed. The flowers are diœcious, and non-petalous. The staminate flowers have 5 sepals and stamens, and grow in loose axillary panicles. The fertile flowers grow in short catkins of leafy scales, each with 2 flowers, the calyx of a single sepal embracing the ovary, which has a style with 2 stigmas. The plant has a perennial root, which sends up numerous annual stems. The fruit is a roundish ovoid nut, enclosed in the persistent calyx. The scales of the strobiles are covered at their base with an aromatic resinous substance called *lupulin*, which forms the commercially valuable product of the plant. It composes about $\frac{1}{8}$ the weight of the dried catkin.

The hop is a common plant on the banks of streams in the Northern United States, and is very commonly cultivated in gardens for culinary purposes. For commercial purposes it is raised on sunny hill-slopes, a well-drained soil being necessary. It is subject to blights, and to a species of aphis which is sometimes very destructive. The plant is twined around poles, the vines being cut near the ground and the poles pulled up, in the harvest-season, and the strobiles gathered. These are dried in kilns, and bleached at the same time by the fumes of burning sulphur. They are packed for transport so tightly that they may be cut into blocks with a knife. In this state they will keep for years, if kept dry and well aired.

The value of hops is due to a bitter principle and a volatile oil in the *lupulin*, whose virtues are imparted to water and alcohol. They are used to flavor malt liquors, and also as a medicinal tonic. Their use gives a tonic effect to malt liquors, though this is modified by the alcohol and other ingredients. They are also credited with narcotic and sedative properties, though these are very slight.

Although the culture of the hop was begun in this country at an early period of colonial history, it did not become extensive until the present century. The hop has now become an agricultural product of great value, and is extended over most of the States. The main product is that of Western New York, where it is cultivated on a large scale. Wisconsin and California come next in importance, its commercial culture in the latter being of recent date. According to the census of 1880 the total hop-product of 1879 was 26,546,378 pounds, raised on 46,800 acres. Of this product New York is credited with 21,628,931 pounds, Wisconsin with 1,966,827 pounds, and California with 1,444,077 pounds. The export was 9,739,566 pounds, valued at $2,573,292. In 1889 the export was 12,589,262 pounds; in 1890, 7,540,854 pounds; the amount varying with the crop, and there is sometimes a large importation. The hop-plant also yields a fibre similar to that of hemp, and is employed to some extent for this purpose. Ordinarily only the female plant is cultivated, it yielding sufficient male flowers for fertilization. The male plant is of little importance, and scarcely known except to botanists. (C. M.)

Hops, showing Vine and Stem.

HORNE, RICHARD HENGIST (1803–1884), an English author, was born at London, Jan. 1, 1803. He was educated at the military college, Sandhurst, then entered the Mexican navy as a midshipman, and served till the close of the war of independence. He sailed to New York, visited Canada, and after a variety of adventures round his way back to England. Here he devoted himself to literature, and produced some tragedies founded on Elizabethan models, among which were *The Death of Marlowe, Cosmo de Medici,* and *Gregory VII.* His epic poem, *Orion* (1843), was sold on its first appearance at a farthing a copy, this ridiculous price being intended as a sarcasm on the public estimate of epic poetry. Then, following in the footsteps of Hazlitt, Horne published *A New Spirit of the Age* (1846), being criticisms on living British authors. Next came *Spirit of Peers and People* (1846), then *The Poor Artist* (1850), and other books. In 1852 Horne went to the gold-fields of Australia in company with William Howitt. There he became chief of police, commissioner of the gold-fields, mining registrar, and held other offices. He published *Australian Facts and Principles* (1859). Returning to England in 1859 he again contributed frequently to periodicals, and in 1874 a pension from the civil list was awarded to him by Lord Beaconsfield. His latest works were *Bible Tragedies* (1881) and *Sithron, the Star-stricken* (1883). In his old age he lost his sight entirely. He died at Margate, England, March 13, 1884.

HORSE. Of the genus *Equus*, of large, herbivorous mammalia, to which the horse belongs, there are at present known seven species, and several varieties which some writers have classed as species. Of this genus the most marked anatomical peculiarity is the character of the foot. This consists of a single developed toe, two of the others being completely and two very nearly aborted. The animal walks on the nail of this toe, which has become a large, tough, horny hoof. As an organ of swift movement the foot of the equine genus has no equal in the limbs of any other inhabitant of the hard, level plains which form its native habitat.

See Vol. XII.
p. 176 Am.
ed. (p. 172 Edin. ed.).

The horse differs from the asses and zebras in having the long hairs of its tail developed over the whole surface, in its longer mane, shorter ears, longer limbs, and smaller head. It also has a small bare callosity on both fore and hindlegs, while the asses and zebras have this mark only on the forelegs. In Thibet, which is the home of the variety of the ass which most nearly approaches the horse, there has been recently discovered a new species of *Equus*, which is closely related to the horse, since it has the warts on its hindlegs, and the broad hoofs of the horse. It differs from the horse, and approaches the ass in the long hairs of the tail being confined to its lower half. The mane is short and erect, and there is no forelock. It is of small stature, with thick and strong legs, a large and heavy head, and ears smaller than those of the ass. This species, discovered in 1881 by the traveller Przevalsky, has been named *E. Przevalsky*. It inhabits the Dzungarian Desert, between the Altai and Tianshan Mountains; is very active, shy, and difficult to approach, and seems able to do without water for long periods, so that it can only be hunted in the winter, when melted snow can be obtained by the hunters.

No description of the general form and size of the domestic horse is here requisite, these particulars being familiar to all readers. We need simply say that it varies very considerably in size in different localities, partly as a result of selection and partly through the influence of climate. Between the small breeds of Canada and the Shetland Islands, which are apparently stunted by extreme cold, and the huge draught-horses of the Flemish and other stocks, the difference is almost as marked as that between the larger and smaller varieties of the dog. In form also there is as marked a difference between the slender-limbed and clean-cut bodies of racers and the elephantine proportions of draught-horses, with their sturdy limbs and solid frames. All this, however, is mainly the result of selection, and has no bearing on the characteristics of the horse as a species.

The domestic horse is probably native to Europe, Asia, and Northern Africa. Its exact habitat, however, cannot be positively ascertained, as all existing wild herds may have escaped from domestication. We know that it was abundant in a wild state in early Europe, and was apparently used as food by the inhabitants, to judge from the condition of the remains found. The horse also formerly existed in great abundance in America, as is proved by its fossil remains, found almost throughout the whole extent of that continent. In fact, if we might judge from geological evidence, America has truer claims than Europe or Asia to be the native home of the horse. A highly interesting series of fossil animals has been recently exhumed in the Western Territories, in which nearly every step of development from an original five-toed to the existing one-toed animal can be traced. The size also gradually increases from an animal little larger than a fox to the noble proportions of the existing horse. Various other changes have taken place: in the number and position of the teeth, the form of the limbs, and other anatomical points which we cannot particularize. In Europe some members of this fossil series have been found, but the complete and direct series is as yet confined to America.

It is somewhat singular that an animal so capable of self-preservation as the horse, which evolved through long ages from an original five-toed animal on this continent, and long survived here in a form not anatomically distinct from the horse of Europe, should have utterly disappeared. That our climate and conditions are still suitable to it is proved by its rapid multiplication in a wild state when brought here by the Spaniards, and it is a puzzling geological problem to understand what causes could have annihilated such a species throughout the whole length of the American continent. A doubtful theory has been recently advanced, to the effect that the horse was not extinct on this continent when first visited by Europeans. One of the first navigators who visited the coast of Buenos Ayres speaks of horses among the animals seen there. The date was anterior to that of the invasion of Peru by the Spaniards, and too early for any escaped Spanish horse to have possibly reached this locality. The mention, however, is too vague and indefinite to serve as a basis for any conclusion, and while it is not impossible that the horse may have survived in the region of the pampas, it is, for various reasons, exceedingly improbable.

The Spaniards introduced the horse into this continent not long after the discovery of America. In addition to those brought over by Spanish cavaliers, and used by them in the conquest of Mexico and Peru, some of which may have escaped, there is mention of several shipments of horses from Spain to America. Azara remarks that a few were introduced into America in 1535, and that several were shipped to Paraguay in 1537. These seem to have been the origin of the vast herds of wild horses now found on the South American plains, where the conditions of nature appear to have highly favored their increase. These extensive plains, so widely spread through the territory of the Argentine Republic, are now the habitat of myriads of wild horses. Herds containing several thousand each may be there met, each led by a master stallion, whom the others obey. These wild horses greatly resemble their Spanish ancestors in shape. They have fair but not high speed and great powers of endurance.

North America has also its herds of wild horses, which exist abundantly in Mexico and northward. Those of Mexico, California, and Texas are known as *Mustangs*, and are probably of Spanish stock. These are small but spirited horses, of good speed and endurance. The wild horse of the prairie region of the north and north-west is known as the "Indian Pony." It is impossible to ascertain its source. It may have been derived from the mustang, with a probable mixture of northern blood. It is very small, being seldom or never over 13 hands high, so that its rider's feet nearly touch the ground. Yet it is strongly built in body and legs, and has great strength and activity, so that it carries its rider with ease. It has a high crest, a flowing tail and mane, and a proud carriage of the head. Many of these horses have been brought into use in Canada. The other portions of the earth where the wild horse abounds are the plains of Central Asia and Siberia, of interior Africa, and of Australia, where it has multiplied abundantly. Its powers of increase and self-preservation are so great on dry, level, grassy plains, that its extinction in America is a very remarkable phenomenon.

The horse has been domesticated since a very early period. It is specially fitted by its compact, close-knit frame, its muscular limbs, easy and rapid stride, and general structure and habits, for the use of man, both in draught and carriage, and its powers were early availed of. Rude tribes have used its flesh for food, and with the modern Tartars it is the most highly esteemed of all animal food. The Tartars also use its milk, which they make into an intoxicating beverage called *Koumiss*. But among civilized peoples, as a rule, it is used only for labor and carriage, for both of which it is so well adapted.

Of the domestic horse, the most celebrated race is that of Arabia, which has now spread throughout the Mohammedan world. It is plentiful in Turkey and in Barbary, where it is specially known as the *Barb*. This breed is of beautiful form, having fine legs and feet, small heads, and small, shapely bodies, usually not over 15 hands high. This horse, as Strabo asserts, did not flourish in Arabia in his time, about the beginning of the Christian era. If so, it has been remarkably developed since, attaining a wonderful agility, tractability, lightness, and endurance. Of the other well-marked races may be named the Flanders horse, a large-bodied, heavy, coarse-legged, slow-moving animal, the basis of the modern draught-horse; and the Tartar horse, a small, bony, rough animal, with shaggy mane and tail, large head, and great endurance. The characteristics of this horse seem to repeat those of the wild horse of Neolithic Europe, and it may be the most direct representative of the original stock.

The best modern horses of Europe and America quite possibly came from mixtures of these three breeds. The Barbs of Barbary, introduced into Spain and Italy, seem there to have met the Tartar horse, which had spread westward through Russia and Hungary, and the Flanders horse, which had extended southward. From various crosses of these breeds, and perhaps of others, we have the many valuable stocks of modern horses, from the thoroughbred racers to the huge and vigorous modern draught-horses. Several importations of Arabians to England were made between 1600 and 1700, and numerous ones after 1700. It is to the tempering of the original English stock by this fine foreign strain that the modern English racer, and its American descendant, are due; horses which surpass their Eastern relatives in speed, strength, and endurance, as has been proved by tests of English racers with fine-blooded Arabians.

The English thoroughbred surpasses all other horses in beauty and speed. By the title thoroughbred is meant a horse whose ancestry for five generations is recorded in the Stud Book—a record of racers instituted about the beginning of this century, but which gives pedigrees dating back to 1700, and complete ones from about 1759. Of the other varieties of English horses, which, however, are not special breeds, may be named the hunter, the hack- or saddle-horse, the troop-horse or charger, the carriage-horse, and the cart-horse, which, in the London dray-horse, has become a huge animal of enormous strength.

The importation of horses of fine breed into the United States began early in colonial history, and races took place in Maryland and Virginia by the middle of the seventeenth century. The first recorded importation of an English thoroughbred was a horse called Bully Rock, a son of the Darby Arabian, brought over in 1730. The first imported thoroughbred mare was Bonny Lass, a granddaughter of the same Arabian, brought over about 1740. From that time forward the importation of thoroughbreds increased, and became common after the Revolutionary period. Of these importations of prime horses a list of some 300 might be given, among them several winners of the Derby. Through this means the original American stock was greatly improved. Though these and their descendants were kept principally for racing purposes, yet the cross with imported blood has improved horses kept for all purposes. The American racer as a rule is stouter and stronger than his English representative, through the custom of longer races in this country.

Of the importations of thoroughbred stallions the most important was that of Messenger. This noted horse was foaled in 1780 and imported in 1788. He died in 1808. He stood for many years in New York and in the vicinity of Philadelphia, and the best horses of the neighboring States have more or less traces of his blood. Among his noted descendants may be named the stallions Potomac, Hambletonian, Bay Figure, Engineer, Mambrino, Tippo Saib, and in particular his unsurpassed grandson, American Eclipse. Importations of Arabians have also been made, but the experience of the United States favors the best English blood in preference. We have had but one Arabian of capital excellence. This was the white barb Ranger, which reached here as the result of an accident some time before 1770, and became the parent of much fine stock. No other of the many imported Arabians has left descendants of special reputation. The improvement of the horse in this country has not been a matter of definite record until recently, the American Stud Book beginning at a much later date than that of the English. Yet improvement has been going on for considerably more than a century, till now we have a race of horses which equal those of any other country for draught, road, or saddle. The preference of horses to oxen for farm-work before the Revolution led to greater rapidity of operation and the use of lighter machinery and has had a beneficial effect on all our agricultural operations. As for the number of horses in use in this country, it was supposed that it would be greatly decreased by the wide-spread introduction of railroads, and the consequent disuse of horse-power. Yet such has not been the result, but horses have increased in number, being needed for increased farming operations and goods transportation.

None of the foreign breeds seem to have taken root in this country, unless, as many claim, the Canadian horse is a stunted representative of the Norman. This horse is small, generally 14 to 14½ hands high. It is remarkably hardy, and has good temper and great endurance. It has admirable legs and feet, full and broad breast, strong shoulders, a lofty crest, with mane and tail abundant and of wavy habit. It is not high in speed, yet adds speed to its other good qualities when crossed with thoroughbred stock.

Another noted American breed is the Morgan of Vermont. These horses are claimed to have originated in an animal of doubtful pedigree, owned by Justin Morgan, a Vermont schoolmaster, about the beginning of this century. Some claim that a race of such horses existed at that period, made up of crosses between the English thoroughbred and the Canadian. However that may be, the special ancestor of the Morgan stock was not remarkably fast, yet he has given origin to some excellent trotters, among them Black Hawk, Ethan Allen, American Eagle, and a host of others. The Morgan horses are undoubtedly a fine race, spirited, docile, hardy, with an easy, rapid trot, and most excellent as roadsters. They have thick and long manes and tails, with considerable curl in both. They seldom exceed 15 hands high, and have few of the marks of thoroughbred blood.

Another American stock, once highly esteemed, but now nearly or quite extinct, is the Narraganset pacer. This beautiful breed seems to have descended from a Spanish horse, probably of Barb ancestry, introduced into New England from Andalusia by Gov. Robinson. The breed was long kept up to supply a demand from Cuba, but has been allowed to die out since the cessation of this demand. They were natural pacers, of good size, and of remarkably easy motion as compared with modern pacers. They had great reputation for spirit, endurance, and speed. No pure descendant of the race is now known.

In the extreme South and West the favorite horse is of Spanish origin, a descendant of the domesticated breed of Mexico, Louisiana, and Florida. These horses are diversified in character, and generally of medium size and merit. Another breed of marked individuality is a race of partly wild horses on the seaboard islands of Maryland and Virginia, where they have existed since long before the Revolution. These, called beach horses, run wild through the year, and are never fed. They are very diminutive in size, yet often of perfect symmetry and great powers of action and endurance. They are said to be able to trot fifteen miles in an hour. They probably are descendants of animals escaped from the racing stock which has, from early colonial times, been kept up in Virginia, Kentucky, and the South generally.

Of draught-horses the only peculiar American breed is that known as the Conestoga, from its being produced in the valley of Conestoga, Pa. It is a very large and muscular horse, often of 17 hands and upwards in height, and closely resembles the heaviest breed of German and Flemish cart-horses. No record of its origin is kept, but its ancestors may have been brought over by the early German settlers of this region, or selected by them from native stock. It closely resembles the London dray-horse, having similar heavy outline of body with comparatively light limbs, but is not buried under a similar mountain of flesh. In color it follows the Flemish horse, except that black is more rare, and bay, brown, and iron-gray colors predominate. These animals, which have grown somewhat scarce of late, are used chiefly for wagons, and though of slow motion are quicker and lighter than their weight promises.

Nearly all the recent valuable varieties of European draught-horses have been introduced into this country, with considerable improvement to the older stock. This old draught-stock is largely made up of the English cart-horse, which was long since introduced into this country. There have been, recently, new importations of the same breed, and also of the Clydesdale horse of Scotland. Of other importations from England may be mentioned the Cleveland Bay, a large and showy coach-horse, much esteemed in England. The more notable of recent introductions are several improved breeds of French stock. The old Norman has been succeeded by the modern Norman, an animal of much power and endurance, with thick head, short, heavy neck, large breast and shoulders, and strong limbs, with much wavy mane, tail, and fetlocks. A valuable variety of this stock is the Percheron, now very much esteemed among our horse-fanciers. This animal perhaps springs from a tempering of the Norman blood with Andalusian stock. It is rather smaller than the Norman, and a quicker stepper, and is used in France as a *diligence* horse. It is the basis of the large iron-gray stock used in express wagons in our cities. From a mingling of these various breeds we may look for a great improvement in our future draught-horses.

Of distinctive breeds of American horses, however, the most marked and notable is the trotter, an animal whose special gait has been developed in this country to an extent not equalled elsewhere in the world. The trotter, indeed, is everywhere acknowledged as peculiarly of American origin, and its superior qualities conceded. The early gait of our racers was the run, like that of their English ancestors, the trot being of comparatively recent introduction. Racing was early indulged in at the South. About the beginning of the present century New York and other Northern States joined in the same amusement. But it has fallen into decadence since the middle of the century, being replaced by trotting, which has become the fever of the American turf. Racing, however, has not quite died out, and American runners have recently beat the best English thoroughbreds on their own soil. Mr. F. A. Walker, the late superintendent of the Census, says: "Receiving the running horse from England, we have so improved the strain that, in spite of disadvantages (recently), the honors of the British turf have been gathered in a degree almost unprecedented in the history of British racing by three American horses; and while Iroquois was winning his unprecedented series of victories, two, if not three, American three-year-olds, generally believed to be better than Iroquois, were contesting the supremacy at home."

We may further quote from the same article. "The trotting horse we have created, certainly the most useful variety of the equine species, and we have improved that variety in a degree unprecedented, I believe, in natural history. Two generations ago the trotting of a horse in 2 minutes and 40 seconds was so rare as to give rise to a proverbial phrase signifying something extraordinary. It is now a common occurrence. 'But a few years ago,' wrote Prof. Brewer in 1876, 'the speed of a mile in 2.30 was unheard of; now perhaps five or six hundred horses are known to have trotted a mile in that time.' The number is to-day perhaps nearer 1000 than 500. Steadily onward have American horses pressed the limit of mile-speed till, within the last three seasons, the amazing figures 2.10 have been reached by one trotter and closely approached by another.''

We may here say that since 1879, the date of the article quoted from, the record of 2.08¾ has been made by Maud S., and a half-mile record of 1.03¼. It is confidently predicted by trainers that the limit of trotting speed will yet be brought down to 2 minutes. In regard to other gaits it may be here remarked that the best pacing record, a faster gait than the trot, is 2.06¼ in harness, and 2.01¾ with running mate; and the best running record of American horses 1.39¼.

Many consider the American trotter a distinct strain or breed of horses. It is more probably a result of constant practice on suitable roads, since good trotters have come from several distinct stocks, as the Canadian, the Morgan, the Indian Pony, and the thoroughbred. Yet it is certain we have developed a variety of the horse not found in like perfection elsewhere. No English thoroughbred could venture to compete as trotters with many American horses of very low record, yet the root of our trotting stock cannot be traced to the English Stud Book or to Arabian ancestry, but seems of home make. Dutchman, one of our best trotters, was taken out of a clay-yard, and put on the turf from a Pennsylvania wagon team. The American trotter is simply a remarkable instance of the effect of keeping an animal to one kind of work, and breeding from the best specimens.

In the early part of our racing history three- and four-mile heats were the American fashion, and longer heats were occasionally made. This has had the effect to add to the strength and endurance of American horses, as compared with the English racer, with his short bursts of a mile or less. More recently the length of races has been reduced, and mile heats, best three out of five, are the prevalent fashion. The trotting horse is less delicate in form and needs less training than the high-bred racer, and is of superior value to the latter in that his gait is adapted to ordinary road driving.

The number of horses on farms in the United States, according to the census of 1880, is 10,357,488. Of these Illinois is credited with 1,023,082; Texas with 805,606; Iowa, 792,322; Ohio, 736,478; Missouri, 667,776; New York, 610,358; Indiana, 581,444; Pennsylvania, 533,587; and the other States in diminishing proportions. (C. M.)

HORSE-SHOEING. All the standard authorities in farriery admit that the bane of the shod hoof is too often a crippled foot. Despite all empirical science these authorities further admit that hoof maladies would be largely avoided and obviated if the horse's hoof was unpared and unrasped, and he could travel without excessive wear of the horn on hard roads without shoes. But in the domesticated state these conditions are impracticable. Just in proportion as the draught burden he is compelled to overcome is increased beyond his own weight, or his gait is quickened beyond his voluntary speed, his unshod hoofs break and wear away more rapidly than they are renewed by recuperative growth. In consequence they become so tender and sore that the average horse, in daily use upon hard roads, is rendered a more confirmed cripple than when his feet are subjected to iron shoes. So that, by universal consent, horse-shoes are accepted as an absolute necessity just as certainly as paring the hoof and nailing on iron plates cause the many ailments of the feet and limbs to which the domesticated horse is subject. This is a full and fair statement of the dilemma presented by the present advanced stage of farriery.

Now, whether these foot and limb diseases arise mainly from improper dressing of the hoof, or whether they are more directly caused by its being confined to the iron band, called the shoe, or whether the formation of the different patterns of shoes place the position of the foot and the bearings upon the iron contrary to the mechanical action of the foot and limb, is the complex question that has divided the various systems of farriery which have obtained in Italy, Germany, France, England, and America.

These diverse systems can be grouped into two comprehensive classes, namely: 1. Those who agree with the great French farrier, La Fosse, and his greater English disciple, Fleming, and his American follower, Goodenough, that the frog is the main weight-bearer in connection with the wall, and should, therefore, be placed squarely and firmly upon the ground; and 2. Those who contend with the great Italian farrier, Fiaschi, and the greater English professor, Gamgee, and the still more original Roberge and Bonner of America, that the frog is not a primary weight-bearer, and, therefore, should not be placed upon the ground on a level with the inferior surface of the shoe at the heels.

Modern horse-shoeing, therefore, admits that the science of the whole subject revolves upon these two problems: 1. How must the hoof be dressed so as to bring those portions of its inferior surface upon the shoe and the ground that nature designed to be the primary weight-bearers? 2. How must the shoe be fashioned and applied so as to place the weight only upon those portions of the hoof that should bear the pressure and the primary concussion, and thus insure the perfect articulation of the foot and limb? Upon the correct solution of these vital propositions depend not only the soundness of the horse's foot but the true progress of modern farriery.

The only true starting-point in the investigation has been an exhaustive examination of the unpared, unrasped, unshod hoof. The feet of colts, in the various stages of development, from foals to matured horses, have been carefully noted. When they have never been rasped, or pared, or shod, but have been subjected to severe friction, they have been accepted as the correct means of ascertaining the primary evidence of the weight-bearing portions of the hoof. This has reference only to the average sound, normal hoof. Any variations from this form are abnormal, and not only are unsuited as the bases of scientific deductions, but require peculiar treatment both in paring and shoeing.

The normal hoof that has never been shod or pared invariably shows that the wall grows down lower than the sole and the frog; much lower than the sole, not so much lower than the frog. The colt's foot always furnishes this testimony when it is perfect and subjected to the wear of an ordinary pasture. To insure a perfect foot he must range over upland pastures. Then his hoof is dense, tough, though comparatively small. It is marked with quite a downward growth at the heels, a less active growth at the quarters, and a much more rapid growth at the toes. The upturned hoof plainly reveals the facts that the wall at the heels on landing bears the weight, and on springing from the ground the wall at the toes performs the same function at every footstep. The quarters are elevated above the pressure, just as the hollow of the human foot is arched above the ground. When the horse is confined to low, marshy grounds, on the contrary, the hoof becomes softer, more spongy, wider, and weaker, with the entire bottom surface, embracing the wall, sole, and frog, upon the ground. Such a hoof is called a flat foot. When shod it is liable to have a "drop sole" and to such soreness that it is predisposed to many foot maladies. It is universally dreaded by farriers and generally discarded by intelligent horsemen. The colt's foot, raised upon an upland pasture, is, therefore, accepted as the only sound, healthy, normal foot. Upon the intelligent observation of its laws of growth, pressure, and mechanical action is based the advancement of modern horse-shoeing.

It plainly reveals that the wall to its termination at the anterior points of the bars is the only primary weight-bearer. When the foot is sound and healthy its action is a beautiful illustration of the perfect adaptation of means to ends, for the limitation of the primary pressure upon the inferior surface of the wall is in exact accord with the revelations of the mechanical action of its internal structure.

To illustrate: The terminal bone of the limb and foot, called the coffin-bone, because it is encased by the hard wall, is semilunar in shape in front. It is supplied with two posterior arms, reaching downwards and backwards, beyond the centre of the quarters, called the wings. To this coffin-bone are attached the extensor tendon in front, and the flexor tendon behind. These flex the foot, the latter drawing it back and elevating it, while the former throws it forward, thus completing the revolution of every footstep. This coffin-bone is furnished, on its superior surface, with striated, longitudinal ridges of bone, to which are attached cartilaginous leaves, exceedingly tenacious, yet moderately expansive. The inner surface of the encasing wall is likewise furnished with leaves, made of horn, that perfectly dovetail into the cartilaginous leaves of the coffin-bone. These two sets of leaves are called the sensitive and insensitive laminæ. Their union is so strong that the entire weight of the horse is thereupon suspended. This was the first important discovery of modern farriery. It was proven by the great Dr. Coleman, leading professor of the Royal Veterinary College of London, as early as 1799. His demonstration was complete. He removed the entire bottom of a horse's front feet—sole, bars, and frog—and then walked and trotted him, and even caused him to kick, with both hind feet in the air, so that the entire weight was violently concentrated upon the front feet; yet the internal structure did not descend to the least perceptible degree.

The union of the sensitive and insensitive laminæ was, therefore, admitted by modern farriery to be the means by which the superincumbent weight was sustained. The wall, therefore, was accepted by advanced horse-shoers as the primary weight-bearer. Its excessive growth at the heels and toes was accepted as evidence that the greatest wear and friction and pressure were concentrated at these two points at every footfall. These two conclusions mark the first practical step in the advancement of modern farriery.

They led to further important deductions upon a more intelligent examination of the colt's foot from this advanced standpoint. From the inspection of many feet it was found that the frog is located nearer to the ground than the sole. Moreover the frog is more spongy in texture, and much more expansive when subjected to pressure. It is very delicately connected with the sole by thin grooves of horn, called the commissures. In the colt's foot these semi-translucent commissures are so thin that, in the live state, as well as in the green specimen, the hoof can be expanded by the thumbs and fingers when applied to forcing them apart at the bulbs of the heels. It was thereby discovered that there is a natural expansion of the hoof, at the heels, when subjected to ground pressure, followed by a contraction to the normal dimensions when the hoof is lifted and freed from pressure. When these commissures, on the contrary, grow thick and firm, the natural elasticity of the hoof is materially lessened, and in extreme cases completely destroyed.

Modern farriery then began to investigate the connection between this lateral expansion of the hoof, when subjected to pressure, and the suspension of the weight by the sensitive and insensitive laminæ, and the slight elevation of the frog above the ground surface of the wall. The result was a marvellous discovery. The sensitive laminæ were subjected to extreme pressure in the green foot, and found to have an elasticity equal to at least ¼ inch. The object of this elasticity became manifest. It has been estimated that, in the case of a horse weighing 1000 pounds, the pressure upon the bottom of each one of his front feet, when trotting, at the rate of 2 minutes and 40 seconds to the mile, is equal to 1000 pounds to the square inch. In order, therefore, to break the force of this tremendous concussion, the superincumbent weight was not only suspended to the sensitive and insensitive laminæ, but they were provided with an elasticity to break the force of every blow caused by each footstep, especially in rapid motion. There are 700 of these sensitive laminæ, each one being provided with an elasticity equal to ¼ inch of elongation, both laterally and longitudinally. The aggregate elasticity of these sensitive laminæ, therefore, amounts to 700 quarters of an inch, or to 175 inches when reduced to a single lamina. These 700 springs evince the wonderful design of nature to break the force of concussion resulting from every footfall. But these provisions of nature do not end with the action of the laminæ. The lateral expansion of the hoof, at the heels, when the foot is placed upon the ground, is still another means of breaking the concussion. This lateral expansion co-operates with the elasticity of the sensitive laminæ to destroy the tremendous force of every step upon the ground. It amounts to at least ¼ inch at each heel, lessening towards the toes, where it is not requisite. Now, it is a well-established law of mechanics that the sole must descend just one-half the distance of the lateral expansion of the wall at the heels. This descent of the sole, aggregating ¼ inch at both heels, is sufficient to enable the slightly elevated frog to come in contact with the ground. There was revealed to modern farriery the complicated yet beautiful mechanical action of the foot to break the concussion at every footfall. Nothing could be devised more effective, more enduring, more complete. It worked a revolution in discarding the ingenious devices of man to soften the hoof and to break the force of each footstep. The wall should not be made soft by lotions, or poultices, or wet swabs, simply because these laminæ require firm supports on the sides of both the wall and the coffin-bone, just as the full action of springs require the unyielding attachments of the axle and the bed of the vehicle. No leather, or rubber, or sponge, or felt, or any other intervening cushion should be placed between the shoe and bottom of the foot. For, in addition to the fact that the foot should not be exposed to these dampened and decaying substances, but requires cleanliness and exposure as the conditions of vigorous health, the elasticity and expansion of the foot so far transcend those afforded by these meagre pads that they are entirely unnecessary. This mechanical action of the foot to destroy concussion can be epitomized in the following resumé: The wall is the primary weight-bearer. The sensitive and insensitive laminæ, by suspending the bones of the foot and limb to the wall, in connection with their elasticity, mainly destroy the concussion of every footfall. The expansion of the wall at the heels operates as a secondary means of dissipating the concussion. If any jar still remains, then the descent of the sole enables the frog to rest upon the ground, and its yielding, spongy texture destroys the last vestige of concussion, so that none can be transmitted into the sensitive regions of the navicular joint; for the slightest abrasion of the surface of the navicular bone, resulting from concussion, produces that hitherto incurable lameness called navicular thritis.

These discoveries belong exclusively to the triumphs of modern farriery, and they furnish the only correct data for properly paring and shoeing both the normal and the abnormal hoof.

1. The first absolute condition for the perfect mechanical action of the foot is that the wall shall be perfectly level. By this term is meant that the heels should measure the same distance from the ground surface to the coronet, where the hair and hoof unite. Then, at equidistant points, on the ground surface of the wall, from the heels, the quarters should measure the same height from the ground to the coronet. Then the wall, around the forward arches of the toe, should measure, at corresponding points, the same from the ground surface to the coronet. Then, and only then, will the foot measurements be mathematically level, and the action will be comfortable and perfect. For then will the hoof land squarely upon even heels, revolve evenly over equal quarters, and spring straight and true from the toes. This precision of action alone insures the correct descent of the coffin-bone between the equally taxed springs of the sensitive laminæ on either side of the wall, the perfect articulation of all the joints of the foot and limb in their journals, and that full, free, straightforward movement of the foot and limb, without either twisting or turning, that prevents strains, and ruptures, and ankle-cuffing, and tendon-striking, and knee-banging in the vast majority of horses.

2. The hoof must be balanced. By this term is meant that the heels and quarters should be equidistant, at corresponding points of the frog, which is the centre line or axis of the ground surface of the foot. Balancing the foot prevents undue weight on either side, and, therefore, enables the tendons to carry the hoof straight, both in elevating it from the ground and carrying it out straight and true without the least interference with the companion foot and limb. Moreover it equally distributes the pressure by equalizing the sections of the foot on either side of the frog, and, therefore, materially assists the sensible laminæ in the perfect performance of their functions.

3. The wall must be pared with reference to the proper length of the toe and the correct height of the heels. Modern farriery has detected the fact that the vast majority of foot-maladies resulting from horse-shoeing must be attributed to an uneven and an unbalanced wall, in connection with the undue height of the heels and the excessive length of the toes. If the heels are permitted to grow too high, then the preponderance of weight is thrown forward upon the bone structure of the limbs. Moreover the bones of the feet are forced forward against the wall in front. Inflammation in the feet and soreness in the joints and bones speedily follow, which the ignorant smith generally mistakes for shoulder lameness. If the toes, on the contrary, are allowed to grow too long, then the preponderance of weight is thrown upon the flexor tendons, which excites acute inflammation in them, and in extreme cases produces a rupture of the sheath that binds them to the cannon-bone, resulting in an incurable "let down." The foot must be pared so that the weight is equally distributed between the tendons and the bones, and then no undue strain can be forced upon either part. When one heel is permitted to grow higher than the other, bruises in the high heel, called corns, invariably result. When the toe grows too long, then the toe of the coffin-bone is unduly elevated, and the wings of the coffin-bone, at their inferior points, are forced down upon the fleshy floor of the foot, and extravasation of the minute blood-vessels that cover the sensible floor of the foot occurs, thereby producing bruises and blood-spots by seepage through the porous sole at both heels in the angle formed by the wall and the bars, ordinarily called corns.

It has been discovered, quite recently, that the proper height of the heels and length of the toes can be determined only by the inclination of the pastern-joints. No arbitrary law, such as an inclination of 45 degrees, insisted upon by the older authorities, can be laid down. This can be made plainly manifest from the mechanical conditions present. The weight in the front limb, for instance, descends perpendicularly from the carcass to the ankle. At that point it is deflected. According to the law of the resolution of forces, one-half of the force continues in the perpendicular line to the ground. The other half is deflected, and passes through the axis of the pastern-bones to the hoof. Now if the inclination of the axis of the hoof coincides with the inclination of the axis of the pasterns, then the force is transmitted, with the least possible injury or disturbance, in a direct line to the ground. But if the axis of the hoof does not coincide with the axis of the pasterns, then the force is again divided in the hoof, one-half passing to the ground in the line of the axis of the pasterns, and the other half being deflected in the line of the axis of the hoof. This division of the force in the hoof results in an unnatural jar or disturbance, to the manifest injury of its sensitive parts and interference with its mechanical action. Now if the inclination of the axis of the pasterns and that of the hoof coincide, then the deflected force from the ankle is transmitted in a direct line, without undue disturbance, from the ankle through the pastern-bones and the hoof to the ground. The heels, therefore, should be lowered and the toe foreshortened, having reference to the normal strength of the hoof to perform its functions, till the line of inclination or descent is continuous, measured in front of the pasterns and the wall, from the ankle to the ground. In paring the hoof, nothing is more important than the proper foreshortening of the toe with reference to the normal height of the heels. It means the full expansion of the hoof at the quarters, where the coffin-bone must have free play in the perfect articulation of the foot. It means the absence of contraction, thrush, corns, or the ossification of the lateral cartilages. It means perfect freedom from soreness of the flexor and extensor tendons, and it insures that springy action of colthood and that length of stride consonant with the shape of the carcass and the muscular capacity of the propelling powers.

4. *Paring the Sole and Frog.*—Herein, till quite recently, the teachings of farriery were in inextricable confusion. The older authorities insisted that the sole should be pared till it yielded to the pressure of the thumb, in order to insure the elasticity of the hoof. This was directed without reference to the shape or condition of the hoof. Mayhew may be mentioned as the head of this school of farriers. More recent masters, like Mr. George Fleming, insist that neither the sole nor the frog should ever be touched : that the frog is shed by nature at the proper seasons, and the sole exfoliates as it passes from the live to the dead state. However erroneous the latter position may be, very few authorities advise paring the frog unless it may be to remove its ragged edges. But it has been recently demonstrated that the sole is much more liable to abnormal growths. It is dominated by the wall, and answers to its encroachments or recessions. If the wall contracts, the sole becomes cramped and grows too thick. If the wall is wide-spread, as in flat foot, the sole becomes exceedingly thin. Its natural thickness varies from ¼ to ⅜ inch. It sometimes becomes abnormal and grows an inch thick. This is always due to the encroachments of the wall. If the wall wires in at the heels, the sole will inevitably become thickened at the heels and quarters. If the wall becomes unduly rounded at the toe, bending under and backwards, then the sole around the forward arch of the toe will invariably become abnormally thick. The result is exceedingly destructive. Undue thickness of the sole cramps the mechanical action of the bones of the foot, and often excites an active local inflammation that produces waste or atrophy of adjacent parts. When the narrowed quarters or the rounded, bent-under wall at the toes are present, the sole must be pared to its usual thickness, as it will never exfoliate to its normal condition. In all cases, except that of an unusually thin, weak wall, the sole should be pared so as to approximate to the concave form it preserves in colthood. In no instance should the sole press upon the shoe, except where the wall is so thin and weak as not to be able to bear the weight of the horse without pain. Then the sole, for hospital purposes only, should be so pared that its outer margin, where it joins to the wall, and about the thickness of the wall, should bear the weight equally with the wall. These are the generally accepted directions of advanced farriery for dressing normal feet.

5. *Preparation of Abnormal Feet for Shoeing.*—Abnormally shaped feet can generally be detected by the general contour of the wall and sole, as hereinbefore noted. But they can be more definitely determined by the direction of the bars. If the bars are parallel with the commissures, then the wall is neither unduly expanded nor contracted, but normal in width. If the bars turn inwardly and point sharply towards the commissures, then the wall is unduly contracted and the sole is correspondingly thickened. If, on the contrary, the bars point outwardly, then the wall is unduly expanded, the sole thin and excessively low and convex, and the condition of general weakness prevails. Abnormal feet may, therefore, be comprehensively grouped into contracted, flat, concave, and convex feet.

A. *Contracted Hoofs.*—These are either narrow at the quarters or drawn in at one or both heels. When narrow at the quarters the wall must be sharply foreshortened at the toe. Then the heels must be lowered and the bars pared down thin, while the sole must be concaved, care being taken to pare out the commissures so thin that the hoof can be expanded by the pressure of the thumbs and fingers at the heels. This method insures the free action of the hoof at every footfall, so that its own restored lateral movement will gradually expand the hoof to its normal dimensions, provided, always, the nails are driven in anterior to the middle of the quarters, and the toes are kept constantly foreshortened. When the contraction is only on one side, then the bar and commissure, on that side, should be pared out, and the contracted side during the treatment should be left slightly higher than the other side. When the heels are drawn, or wired in, then, in addition to the treatment above indicated, the knife should be drawn through the angle of the heels, and where they have grown abnormally high they should be sharply lowered, and both the heels and frog placed squarely upon the ground. When the wall is sunken on one side, generally at the forward arch of the foot, the wall of the full side should be slightly narrowed and thinned with the rasp, and the margin of the shoe set as full on the shrunken side as the hoof is required to expand. Gradually the shrunken side will expand to the full measure of the shoe.

B. *Flat Feet.*—These are as much too wide as the average of contracted feet are too narrow. Either too wide or too narrow means positive weakness and discomfort to the horse; for the wall, allowing for its bell-shaped curves from the coronet to the ground surface, should be perpendicular in effect from the coronet to the ground, like the foundation of a house, and directly under the superstructure. Flat feet are always accompanied by a drop sole, which indicates that the sole has either become flat, or, in severe cases of founder, so convex, instead of being concave, that it receives the ground pressure before the wall takes the bearing. The wall in front then separates from the coffin-bone, and grows out to an extreme length. Frequently between the wall and the coffin-bone is a fungus growth, of partly honey-combed horn in structure, that often degenerates into "seedy toe." In such cases the wall, in front, must be rasped back, or foreshortened, until the excess of horn is removed. Then the wall must be pared down from the anterior points of the quarters to the extreme heels, but the sole, bars, and frog must be left intact, as the hoof is already too wide-spread, and consequently very weak. All pressure must be taken from the toe, and the nails must be driven into the wall at the quarters and heels. Then, at every shoeing, it will be found that the sole, in front of the point of the frog, can be gradually concaved, until it assumes the arched form of the normal sole; because the coffin-bone has been changed from a comparatively upright position where it was pressing the sole downwards, and, by exciting inflammation, causing atrophy in both its own substance and the sole, to a more inclined normal position, that enables the sole to rise to its proper concavity, or arched-like shape.

C. *Convex Feet.*—By this term is meant that rounded form of the wall in front, from the coronet to the ground surface, which causes the wall to bend under at the anterior ground surface. This pressure forces the sole anterior to the point of the frog upwards. The sole thus grows to an undue thickness, which, in turn, forces the coffin-bone upwards at the toe, out of its position, so that only the upper portion of its journal articulates with the navicular and lower coronal bones. This partial articulation produces a short, painful step, that seriously cripples the action of the horse. The convex toe is always attended with an abnormally low heel. The result is the same in effect as if several toe-calkins had been welded upon the shoe, thus tilting the foot up, beyond its true level, and practically making the horse walk constantly up-hill, even on level ground. The treatment is as effective as it is simple. The sole, in front of the toe of the frog, must be severely pared as far back as the middle of the quarters, in the concave form, until it is quite thin. The wall, from the forward arch of the quarters, around the toe, must also be pared down, leaving the quarters and heels intact. The hoof should then be armed with a shoe, provided with oblong heel-calkins, and, to insure a more perfect articulation, two more oblong calkins should be placed on the inner margin of the web of the shoe at the forward arches of the quarters. These forward calkins should be made less in height than the posterior ones, and then the involuntary articulation of the foot is decidedly increased. The repetition of this treatment through four or five shoeings, at intervals of a month apart, will restore the hoof to its normal shape.

D. *Concave Feet.*—These are the reverse of the convex. The walls, in front, sink, or bend in, midway between the coronet and the lower edge, and then flare outward at the ground surface. They are sometimes called "sunken walls." They are always attended with abnormally high heels. The treatment must be the reverse of that indicated for convex feet. The heels must be severely lowered, the walls foreshortened and a plain shoe used, drawn to advantage, thinner at the heels than at the toes.

The most common foot maladies resulting from bad shoeing are thrush, quarter-crack, bruised heels, and sore toes. These come directly under the care of the smith, while quitter and grease heels are too complicated for the treatment of the average farrier, and should be relegated to the supervision of the veterinary surgeon. Both thrush and quarter-crack are the results of contraction of the wall, the former being frequently attended with an unduly brittle wall, and the latter with an uncleanliness on the stable floor upon which the horse stands. Expansion of the wall will remedy both. The crevice of the quarter-crack must be cleaned out by the knife of the farrier, and its downward growth from the coronet checked by a lateral incision that separates the new growth from the fractured wall. The thrush must be kept clean and dry by frequent swabbings of the cleft of the frog. Local caustic applications, such as sulphate of zinc, must first be applied to check fungus growth, and then healing remedies, such as vaseline, must be used to heal it up from the bottom.

Bruised heels, other than corns, are produced either by permitting the shoes to remain on too long, thereby springing from the wall at the heels, and becoming embedded in the angle between the wall and bars, or by gravel or stone contusion. These will yield readily to poultice applications and rest. The shoe must be removed, and stoppings of flaxseed, applied warm, resorted to until the inflammation has subsided.

Sore toes are as numerous and even more painful than bruised heels. They are produced by the undue pressure of the shoe upon the wall, resulting from permitting the shoes to remain on too long and the toes to grow to an excessive length. The pressure is frequently so severe that a line of contused blood can be plainly seen between the wall and the sole all around the toe. The toe must be lowered and foreshortened, and the removal of pressure of the shoe around the toe is attended with immediate relief.

This epitome of modern horse-shoeing properly concludes with a review of the different patterns of recently devised horse-shoes. The older forms need only a cursory mention. These are "tips," which cover only the wall generally around the toes, and sometimes only one quarter in connection with the toe, leaving the posterior parts of the hoof bare upon the ground; the plain shoe, either with or without heel- and toe-calkins, that rests upon the wall from one heel around the toe to the other heel, generally flat upon the ground surface, and concaved from the wall so as to avoid sole pressure on the foot surface; and the bar shoe, that is provided with a bar of iron, extending across form one heel to the other, upon which the frog rests. All of these patterns, subject to numerous fanciful variations, have been advocated in turn as the very perfection of horse-shoes. They have been in constant use ever since their respective invention in Italy, France, and England centuries ago. They all have their uses. Under certain conditions differently shaped feet require their employment. The work-horse cannot overcome heavy draught burdens unless his feet are armed with heel- and toe-calkins. The horse afflicted with weak heels or quarter-cracks upon both the inside and outside quarters has been benefited by the use of tips if for light harness purposes, or the use of bar shoes if for draft purposes; while Prof. Gamgee insists that navicular thritis, even when accompanied with transverse fractures of the navicular bone, can be permanently cured, and the sections of the bone again firmly united, simply by the use of the ordinary shoe armed with heel-calkins.

But the newest patterns of horse-shoes are the Peri-planter of Charlier, the four-calkin of Mr. Robert Bonner, the rolling motion ball shoe of Dr. David Roberge, and the wing-heeled Centennial shoe of Mr. S. T. Harris.

The Peri-planter is based upon the theory that the entire base of the hoof-walls, bars, frog, and sole should come upon the ground at the same instant. It is a narrow rim of iron forged just as wide as the wall. The wall is cut away at its lower margin, in depth precisely equal to the thickness of this iron rim, which is neatly inserted in the groove thus made. Its design is simply to prevent the wear of the wall by contact with hard roads. If the frog and sole are primary weight-bearers with the wall and bars, then this shoe is practical, but actual test has demonstrated that it is as fanciful as it is an ingenious pattern.

The four-calkin shoe, invented by Mr. Robert Bonner, is one of the greatest improvements of modern farriery. It answers more completely on the front foot than the French rolling motion shoe in articulating the coffin-joint, and operates, on the hind feet, as a marvellous cure for spavin when the outside calkins are made higher than the inside ones. Two of the calkins, made oblong, are welded on to the web at the heels of a plain shoe, while the other two are placed at the inner edges of the forward arches of the quarters. Thus the flexor tendons are protected while the danger of slipping is prevented, and the articulation of the foot increased at the same time.

The rolling-ball shoe of Dr. David Roberge is another valuable hospital shoe. It is solid at the bottom, being round or convex in shape at the base. It corresponds to the ball-and-socket joints of the shoulder and hip. If there is anchylosis of any of the intermediate joints, or if there is any soreness in the joints, muscles, or tendons, the rolling-ball shoe, co-operating with the ball-and-socket joint, will enable the afflicted horse to revolve and ease the foot in such a position as will relieve the strain upon the injured part. Horses with stiff joints, that have been regarded as useless, have been enabled to do excellent service by the aid of this ingenious shoe.

The wing-heeled Centennial shoe follows the wall to the heels, and then turns with the inflexion of the wall and covers the bars. It is based upon the fact that the bar grows down to the level of the wall, and is a powerful agent both in preventing the wall from unduly expanding or contracting, and in assisting the wall to obviate slipping by preserving the effectual check presented by the angle at the heel formed by the wall and bar of the unshod hoof. The wings of this shoe, furthermore, preserve the division of pressure between the wall and bar at the heel just as do the uncovered wall and bar. It has been found to relieve horses with weak heels or quarter-cracks, and especially valuable for saddle-horses that have to bear, forehanded, the extra weight of the rider.

There are various other patterns, especially of rimmed shoes, some plain like the English blank, and some corrugated like the American form of Mr. Goodenough, but they present nothing novel either in theory or design. They are simply the productions of ingenious patentees, and have nothing new to offer as to the position or the weight-bearing portions of the hoof that have not already been recognized in the literature of farriery.

Two other requisites are now demanded by modern scientific horse-shoeing as necessary. One is the greatest possible lightness of the shoe consistent with the use of the horse, and the other is the smallest size and the least possible number of nails consistent with its secure fastening to the wall. The honor of first forcibly presenting these requisites belongs to the English farrier, William Miles. The greatest French hippopathologist, M. Boulèy, has demonstrated that an ounce of artificial weight at the foot is equal to a pound at the shoulder, and that a horse who carries on his four feet shoes weighing two pounds each, and walks four hours in his daily routine, is compelled to lift 114 pounds of extra weight upon his four feet. From this calculation may be realized the tremendous strain imposed upon the strength of the horse by reason of shoes of unnecessary weight. Besides it has been found that light shoes not only wear as long as heavy ones but they retain their position on the foot more tenaciously.

The nails, too, should be light, smooth, highly finished, hot-forged, and driven so as to have a short, thick, transverse hold, rather than extending high up, which splits the wall and crowds upon the sensitive internal structure. Heavy draught shoes can be retained on the feet by 7 nails instead of 9, which was the old practice, and 5 will answer for the shoes of saddle- and light-harness-horses.

Since modern farriery has recognized the important fact that the hoof grows unequally, in some instances more rapidly at the heels than at the toes, and the reverse, and in other instances more rapidly on one side than on the other, the necessity of more frequently dressing the feet and resetting the shoes has been acknowledged. Moreover, the cruel practice of overheating the shoe, and burning the hoof for a close fit, till the smithy is filled with the fumes of the destroyed horn, has been discarded as a serious injury to the texture of the horn. The shoe, in most cases, is now only slightly heated to destroy the inequalities between the wall and the shoe, and in many cases, where the shoe is carefully made and finished, it is perfectly fitted entirely cold. This humane practice is daily gaining public favor and authoritative sanction.

It will now be obvious to the general reader that modern farriery has made great advancement over the older practice and attainments of the Italian methods of horse-shoeing as set forth in the works of Fiaschi, and of the French methods as taught by La Fosse, and of the English rules as laid down by Prof. Coleman. (S. T. H.)

HOSACK, DAVID (1769–1835), an American physician and naturalist, was born at New York, Aug. 31, 1769. He graduated at Princeton College in 1789, studied medicine, and received his degree of M. D. at the University of Pennsylvania in 1791. He then spent three years in further study in Europe, and returned with a large collection of plants and minerals. In 1795 he was made professor of botany in Columbia College, New York, and in 1797 professor of materia medica. In 1807 he became professor of materia medica and of midwifery in the College of Physicians and Surgeons then founded. In 1811 he became professor of the theory and practice of medicine in the same institution, and after its union with the medical school of Columbia College in 1813 retained his position. In 1826 Dr. Hosack, with the rest of the faculty, resigned, and took part in founding the Rutgers Medical School, which was closed in 1830. He also held many important professional positions, and was a fellow of the Royal Societies of London and Edinburgh. He established the Elgin Botanic Garden, and was one of the founders of the New York Historical Society, of which he was president (1820–28). His medical treatises, especially those on fevers and contagious disorders, long had a standard value. He died at New York, Dec. 23, 1835. Besides medical works he published memoirs of Dr. Hugh Williamson (1820) and of De Witt Clinton (1829).

HOSMER, HARRIET G., an American sculptor, was born at Watertown, Mass., Oct. 9, 1830. As she was naturally of delicate constitution, her father, a physician, gave her rather a boy's training. At an early age she began modelling in clay, and after completing her school education studied anatomy at the Medical College of St. Louis. In 1852 she exhibited at Boston a marble bust, Hesper, and then, by the advice of Charlotte Cushman, her father placed her under the instruction of Gibson, the sculptor, at Rome. Here she produced busts of Daphne, Medusa, and Aenone, and for the Public Library of St. Louis the statue of Beatrice Cenci. She also made a bronze statue of Thomas H. Benton for that city. Her best-known works are Puck, a spirited conception (1855); Zenobia in Chains, a colossal statue (1859); The Sleeping Faun (1867); and The Pompeian Sentinel (1878). Her works show great power both in thought and execution.

HOSPITALS IN THE UNITED STATES. With the increase of schools for medical education, the subject of clinical teaching has come to demand more and more largely the attention of the medical profession. Where such schools are located so as to avail themselves of the opportunity afforded by the public hospitals, this has been seized upon by the professors, and thus they have been enabled to teach their students by means of the bedside instruction thus presented. But, as schools multiplied in a city, other means became necessary, and hence medical colleges at first organized hospitals on a small scale, within their own buildings, or in close proximity thereto. These accommodations becoming inadequate, buildings were erected by each college for its own use. Thus, in Philadelphia, there are the hospitals of the University of Pennsylvania, the Jefferson Medical College, the Women's Medical College, the Hahnemann Medical College, occupying large and stately structures, equipped with all the most recent appliances known to the profession. The same holds good in New York, where are the Bellevue Hospital, the Long Island Hospital, etc. In

(See Vol. XII. p. 314 Am. ed. (p. 301 Edin. ed.).

short, every medical college now organized in America is regarded as not fully prepared for its task as an instructor in medicine unless it has its own hospital, or has the right to teach its students in the wards of the public institution usually provided for the sick poor, etc. Special hospitals are also rapidly being erected, as for cancer, consumptives, diseases of the eye and ear, of the throat, of the skin, orthopædics, and recently there have been added hospitals for incurables and for convalescents. Hospitals, sometimes preferably called asylums for the insane, have long been a distinctive feature throughout the United States. It has been found that so many insane persons were kept without proper care or any form of treatment at their homes, or in prisons as criminal insane, or in almshouses, that recently a new impetus has been given to the erection of institutions for the care of the indigent insane. (See INSANITY.)

Hospitals or asylums for inebriates have also been organized, and have met with greater or less success in relieving the intemperate of their diseased condition. Similarly, hospitals for opium habitues, and those addicted to the use of other forms of narcotics, have been opened in many parts of the United States, but these are yet a subject of consideration as to how much value they have proved to be to the unfortunate victims of such degrading appetites. While it may be thought that the idea of hospitals for every form or phase of illness has run wild, but little attention has been given to one class, who perhaps demand it more earnestly than any other. But few institutions for the special care of sick children have been provided. It is of great importance that children when sick should at once be placed in the best possible condition for restoration to health. It is rarely advisable that they should be mixed up with adults, or those near puberty, as they too readily are indoctrinated with the follies and vices of their older associates, and this is particularly the case within the walls and surroundings of a hospital during the period of convalescence, when, for want of occupation, they are readily attracted by anything which promises amusement or employment.

Nor is this the only reason for such a separation. If the mortality of children in the ordinary hospitals is compared with that of a similar number, even of the poorest and least cared for elsewhere, it will be found that the excess of the former is frightful. Thus, at one time in a well-known and at one time infamously notorious hospital, the mortality was 100 per cent. of the foundlings that were brought under its roof. This has recently given origin to the organization of a hospital for foundlings, called The Sheltering Arms, in Philadelphia, where, even though under very unfavorable conditions, the mortality of the self-same class was reduced nearly to 31 per cent.

In New York similar hospitals have been organized, and have met with equal and even better results. In this connection it may be added that the United States yet lacks hospitals which will care for the infant children of mothers, widows, or it may be worse, who are compelled to labor hard all day for the poorest pittance, and who are often tempted in their sore need to desert the child or even take its life, and thus be free of what is purely a burden to them.

The subject of the proper training of nurses has recently largely occupied the minds of sanitarians. Training schools have been organized in connection with a number of the larger American hospitals, particularly in the cities of Philadelphia and New York. Good results have followed this agitation, as shown by the largely diminished mortality of the hospitals which have enjoyed the advantage of these trained nurses, and of the improved methods of ventilation, sewerage, and general construction.

An additional point has lately been brought into prominence in connection with hospitals—that is, the dispensary service. Recently it has become a fixed fact that there are few hospitals, save those in the country and those devoted to special treatment, as for insanity, intemperance, and the like, which have not a dispensary department, where the sick poor are enabled to apply for and receive medical advice and medicine free, for such cases as are still able to be brought away from their homes. In many large cities, indeed, this department completely overshadows the real hospital work, and the whole time of the hospital staff is devoted to the care of these walking cases. (See DISPENSARY.)

Construction.—In the construction of a hospital, it must ever be borne in mind that the great, the important points to be considered are an abundance of light and air. These desiderata are almost invariably so deficient in the places from whence the sick are brought that they thus prove the great factors in disease production. Again, cheapness and even ready destructibility are required. The latter is too often of greater importance than one at first would imagine. Thus, when an epidemic of infectious disease, as puerperal or child-bed fever, causes death after death, the ward or wards need purification as by fire.

In fact, in more than one instance, the burning of such a hospital has proved as though a direct interposition of Providence to teach men how to deal with the germs of disease. In certain cases the wards have been stripped of perishable articles, and huge furnaces have been kept at an intense heat for days, with the windows and doors almost hermetically sealed, in order to destroy such germs. Where a ward, as of the pavilion or hut form, is inexpensive in construction, it may readily be destroyed.

In the war of the rebellion, when hospital gangrene made its appearance in the wards of the army hospitals, much benefit was obtained by the erection of large tents, and the removal of cases to this shelter. It is reported that almost invariably a check was at once put upon the progress or spread of the trouble. Again, where a larger or more substantial building has been erected, in cases of infection of the wards by the presence of disease, the plaster may be entirely removed, and also the flooring; and these being renewed, the building is again placed in a healthful condition.

The important data for such a building will be about 100 feet square of space for each bed, and 1200 cubic feet at least of air-space for each patient. Not to exceed thirty patients, to be under the care of one head-nurse and in one ward. Crowding under no circumstances should be permitted, whether of patients in the wards, or of wards upon other wards, as thus much of the value of a hospital is sure to be interfered with if not positively destroyed. In diseases of an infectious nature there should be every opportunity for the most positive isolation. The means for ventilation here will prove a great source of benefit. In this connection we may refer to the report of the building committee of the Pennsylvania Institution for the Deaf and Dumb, located in Philadelphia. It may be mentioned in passing, that, prior to the erection of the additional buildings, fully equal in capacity to the original institution, rats had proved a great source of annoyance. "The old buildings were so overrun with such vermin that, on the removal of plaster ceilings under the main floors, the stench was so offensive as to sicken the workmen, and to reveal the danger of a pestilence that had been ignorantly incurred. After ascertaining the fact that rats will not inhabit buildings when their access to the ground is wholly cut off, the committee remedied this so thoroughly that not a rat is to be found about the existing institution. The floors of the basement are made of lithogen cement, the upper stratum of which is composed of white sand and Portland cement in equal quantities." In the basement are four reservoirs of pure air, forced down from the roof by an inexpensive contrivance that gives a pressure when the wind blows, superior to any resistance on the windward side of the building. Thus there is a steady flow of air, warmed by the furnaces, into each school-room. During warm weather this method will supply the rooms with pure air at a low temperature. The ventilation of the various dormitories, sitting- and school-rooms, is further promoted by a number of ventilating shafts, nine of which are 4½ feet in the clear and 60 feet high. "The products of combustion are conveyed up these shafts in iron pipes, which terminate 3 feet below the top of the chimney, which is reduced in size by a gradual slope to quicken the exit both of the foul and the heated air. These shafts ventilate the kitchen, sitting-rooms, playrooms, and especially the dormitories. In the latter there are four large openings at the floor adjoining the external walls at each end of the building. The beds are arranged head to head in the middle of the room, because the breath, being 30° warmer than the surrounding air, ascends to the ceiling and passes over to the cold external walls on each side of the room; it then descends, and is immediately drawn off by the large shafts, in which an active upward current is induced by the hot iron pipes, and also by the peculiar arrangement at the top of the shaft, which is capped in a manner highly promotive of ventilation. This arrangement of beds favors the use of the windows, which would otherwise let the cold air fall upon the heads of the children." "The water-closets are perfectly free from all offensive odors, as the draught is downwards into ventilating shafts, and the water is drawn off from the closets twice every day."

Again, with its own proper ventilation and warming apparatus, each ward must be perfect in itself, so that it will prove a matter of impossibility for infection to be transmitted from one to the other. Warming and ventilation go side by side, and hence, no matter what system of heating is adopted, much will depend upon the care with which the currents are compelled to enter in a pure condition, and after collecting in their course the odors, etc., to pass off without any obstruction. Hence is required the most constant vigilance as to cleanliness, proper working of all the machinery, whether human or artificial; and thus is avoided the opportunity for any part of the establishment to become tainted, which, though imperceptible to the senses, yet in due time makes its presence known and felt by the increase in mortality. Cracks in plastering, open seams or the like in any part of the ward, become a nest in which may germinate the most fatal forms of filth disease. It has been frequently observed that these diseases result from or are produced by decay of flooring or plastering, as from dampness, or where, owing to the urgency of the case or parsimony in building, inferior material has been employed in construction. In all such instances cremation of the building is the only positive remedy.

Where possible, sufficient space should be secured around a hospital building to secure full circulation of pure air. While it may be necessary in order to prevent intrusion to have some form of enclosure, in many instances this is a high stone or brick wall, which is highly objectionable as giving too much the appearance of a penal institution. Better will be a low wall with a railing on top of sufficient height to fulfil the indications. The enclosed grounds are to be graded and planted with appropriate trees and shrubbery, avoiding any forms which would give either too dense a shade or, when in the process of fructification, an unpleasant odor. As a hospital should ever be surrounded with all that is calculated to aid the return to health, so its style of building should be cheerful and attractive, not dark and gloomy, nor, on the other hand, needlessly ornamented or glaring to the eye. It has been found by observation that the inner walls when plastered with a finishing coat of very hard material have proved least liable to allow of the retention of disease-germs. This coat should be perfectly smooth, as a rough coating affords abundant opportunity for the collecting of dust as it floats in the air, and undoubtedly germs of all kinds would find this a very suitable place for lodgment and propagation. Floors should be of cement, or hard, close-grained wood laid with great care, and for the same reason as that stated relative to the plastering. As it is always objectionable to cover them with carpets of any kind, wood floors should be stained and oiled. A moment's thought will show the advantage of this plan, as cleansing a soiled floor by scrubbing in the manner usually adopted gives dampness and its consequent injurious results to the inmates.

In all apartments, as the laundry, etc., where water inevitably must be freely used, the floor should be of slate or flag of some material, so as to prevent the absorption of the dampness. Too much stress cannot be laid upon the importance of the water-closets. They should be easy of access, and in every way provided with means for self-purification. It is too much to expect that all or even a majority of the inmates of any institution, but especially a hospital, can be so imbued with the value of care and cleanliness as to be painstaking when using a water-closet, and therefore these should be as much automatic in their action as may be, and should always be regarded as a source of possible contagion and subjected to the most careful observation. A very interesting experiment as to purification of all such places is found in Mouat and Snell's work on *Hospital Construction:* "The Hindoos of every part of India from time immemorial have possessed a means of purifying the atmosphere of their rooms and huts, by spreading a light coating of a mixture of earth containing organic materials on their walls and floors, which enables them to dispense, to a considerable degree, with ordinary ventilation. The process is called 'leoping,' and is usually performed by the women of the household. With a view to submit this proceeding to a practical test, I had four cells, each containing 480 cubic feet of air, and practically unventilated, carefully prepared. Two of them were lime-washed and the two others leoped. I had four healthy prisoners locked up in them at night, one in each cell. On opening the cells next morning the two which were lime-washed were stuffy and offensive, redolent of the peculiar animal odor exhaled by native prisoners in such circumstances. The two others were as fresh and as pure as if no one had slept in them. This led me, as head of the prison department, to direct the application of the principle generally in all the jails under my administrative control, so far as it was susceptible of direct application to walls, floors, and earthen beds. I also employed charcoal extensively for the same purpose—the purification of the air of prison wards from animal exhalations—and I had reason to believe with success." The same authority says: "Associated with the purity of person and place is that of the disinfection and cleansing of all clothing and bedding, and the immediate destruction of all dressings, etc., for which, as a rule, due and proper provision is or requires to be made."

The drainage and water-supply are equally important matters. The water should be in great abundance and known to be pure. Wells or stored water, as in reservoirs, should be examined frequently and with great care. In a large city the manner of drainage will depend largely upon that which is furnished by the municipal authorities. In the country, or where isolated, the excreta should be cared for on the dry system. Earth will always constitute the best deodorizer and disinfectant. The subject of drainage requires a special consideration and therefore cannot be given here in detail.

Kitchens and laundries, as well as any other departments of a hospital which are likely to produce an atmosphere injurious to the sick, should be completely separated from the wards containing the patients; never beneath the sick-wards if possible to avoid it. The kitchen and laundry should be so separated that by no possibility could the air of the latter be carried to that of the former. While the tendency to combination of a series of wards, and hence an increase in the number of inmates, is reasonable with the remembrance of the importance of thus reducing the running expenses by placing a larger number under one management, etc., yet it must not be forgotten that this must not be carried on without limit. The best authorities regard that limit as 600, say about 20 wards with 30 patients in each. In all cases surgical wards will demand additional amounts of floor-space and cubic feet of air, and also where disease prevails which causes deterioration of the air to an unusual extent. Beds should never be less than nine feet apart. The furniture should be of the simplest character; there should be no curtains or hangings of any kind, and closets only for very particular purposes, as the necessitated locking up of medicine, etc. Recently it has become quite customary in some localities to introduce pictures, flowers, and a variety of decorations, with a view to lend cheerfulness and break the fearful monotony of blank space which is often regarded as detrimental to the convalescent. These are good only so far as they are not allowed to interfere with the air of the ward.

One point necessary for hospital constructors to bear strongly in mind is that they must equally be careful to protect the surrounding air from vitiation. Of course, this more particularly applies to large cities where such institutions are usually necessarily located in the midst of dwellings, stores, etc. Especially has this been demanded with hospitals for cholera and small-pox cases, and so dangerous have these been regarded that an imperious public clamor has compelled their location in the rural suburbs. But there are other causes of vitiation incident to the aggregation of large numbers of cases of disease. Hence, provision must be made that the ventilating shafts shall carry their foul air away from the atmospheric supply of the neighborhood, and that antiseptic precautions be taken that will destroy germs of infection from every source.

In order to avoid the vitiation of the air by tobacco-smoke, which unfortunately has become a necessary evil of the day, an appropriate separate place must be provided for convalescents who may be allowed to return to such a habit. This place must be so arranged that the smoke, etc., cannot be carried into the wards. Again, as convalescents are greatly aided in their recovery by fresh air and exercise, here galleries easily reached from the wards have been utilized. Better, however, will be open verandas with a southern exposure. These may be enclosed with glass, and shut off by doors from the corridors or halls. In every hospital there should be provided small apartments for use in cases where it might become necessary to remove a patient from his fellows. For the same purpose, movable screens should be an adjunct of every ward, that at a moment's notice privacy may be obtained for a patient.

Soiled garments, etc., are never allowed to accumulate, but are thrown into a shaft which carries them at once to the basement, whence they are removed to the laundry. This shaft is coated with smooth, hard plaster and open, not into the wards but into the stairway.

Where clinical teaching is designed to be connected with a hospital an appropriate amphitheatre is necessitated, capable of comfortably seating the students, and so arranged that patients may readily and without fatigue be brought to the arena. Here, placed on the revolving table, or it may be seated in a rolling-chair, one may be exhibited to the class, or the requisite operation be performed. It is better to have this room as much away from the wards as may be. An excellent example may be seen in the Pennsylvania Hospital of Philadelphia. Where the amphitheatre is located in the midst of the wards, as is too often the case, it becomes impossible to prevent disturbance of patients by the noise and clamor of the class. In fact, the mere tramping of the students as they disperse after the clinic is apt to strike terror to many of the inmates, who are keenly alive to the dangers of fire, etc., and their inability to aid themselves in making their escape. Or, where this may not obtain, the cries and struggles of patients are too often plainly heard by others who may be dreading their turn, and thus are excited and their nervous system so shocked that injurious results might follow an operation.

As there will be constant need of splints and orthopedic apparatus, both for convenience and economy, a machine-shop within the grounds should be erected, and appropriate machinery placed therein. By this means much time and great expense will be saved, and often an ingenious convalescent will be enabled to work out a valuable apparatus, under the direct supervision of the surgeon desiring it, and with the patient close at hand upon whom to test its fitness. An example of such a shop and its value may be seen at the hospital of the University of Pennsylvania.

No hospital can be regarded as complete without the best form of ambulance to carry accident or other cases most safely to the buildings. For many cases, and those at no great distance, stretchers may be employed, and a number of these should always be at hand that no delay may occur when they are required. A point that seems greatly to be lost sight of is the fact that very many cases are better conveyed upon the rudest form of stretchers, as seen in the door unhinged for the purpose, or the settee which is found in nearly every house, and properly supplied with quilts or blankets to protect projecting points. In the usually rough streets of our large cities, and with the constant obstructions to which they are subjected, the stretcher will be found preferable as avoiding the jarring which is so liable to occur, and which, in many instances, has added vastly to the complications of the injury, or the shock and consequent depression of the sick man. It would be well if the general public could be instructed on this point, as their officious, perhaps well-meant, efforts frequently are productive of great harm. It need only be remembered that broken bones are very apt to be driven through the flesh and skin until their splintered ends protrude, by the worse than useless efforts of the bystanders to carry a wounded person in the arms of several, without some form of apparatus to keep the injured parts from further displacement. Hence the value of the recent ambulance system now established in most of our large cities, by which the hospitals are notified and can send an ambulance with a physician provided with apparatus and medicine to meet an emergency. Thus, hemorrhage may be stanched, broken bones supported, shock prevented; in short, the work for which the institution is created is materially aided.

In recently erected hospitals it has been found wise to build large bay-windows in all the wards, which serve greatly to relieve the monotony of the straight corridors, and are always regarded by the inmates as pleasant places to sit during convalescence. These, with the first floor on iron beams and brick arches wherever there are steam-pipes and radiators in the cellar beneath, making the attic floor of a similar fire-proof construction, with metal cornices, have been regarded as the latest improvements.

Protection of the most thorough kind against fire should hold a first place. Inner plugs and hose may prove valuable in the early stages of a conflagration, but added to these there should be a good supply of hose and plugs on the outside, as otherwise, when the fire-apparatus on the inside is rendered useless, there is no alternative but to watch the progress of destruction. A recent fire at an insane hospital where this order obtained gives rise to this suggestion.

Army Hospitals.—By *Circular No.* 10 of the Surgeon-general's Office the following specifications have been given for this important class of hospitals, which may serve also as a guide for others:

A hospital of 24 beds consists of a central administration building and two wards arranged as wings, each wing 45 feet 8 inches long by 25 feet 4 inches wide and 15 feet high in the clear from floor to ceiling. In very cold climates the height may be 12 feet with a length of 50 feet. Attached to each ward, and at the outer end and behind, will be room for earth-closets. The administration building will be 36 feet 4 inches front by 40 feet 4 inches deep, and 2 stories high, with a back building of 43 feet 8 inches by 15 feet 4 inches. Each story 13 feet from floor to ceiling. A veranda 10 feet wide will surround the hospital. In hot climates the wards will be detached from the main building, connected with it by the veranda. The back building will also be separated.

In malarious climates it is desirable that a ward shall be in the second story, hence the building will be 2 stories high, 78 feet 10 inches long, 26 feet 4 inches wide, with a veranda as before.

The regulation hospitals will usually be built of wood, but brick, stone, or other material may be used. A provisional hospital may be constructed of logs, lumber, or adobe. This is where no delay can be allowed.

In the mason work all sills will be supported on stone or brick piers or timber posts. Stone piers should be 2 feet by 1 foot 4 inches, of large flat-bedded stones, laid to break joints. If brick they shall have a stone footing 2 by 2 feet and 6 inches thick. The brickwork shall be 18 by 18 inches, of hard-burnt brick. All piers to be built in good lime-mortar. Wooden posts should be of cedar or locust, no less than 8 by 8 inches. Piers to be carried deep enough to secure from frost. Frame a balloon frame, sills 6 by 8 inches. All sills will be mortised, tenoned, and pinned to each other. Studs framed or notched into the sills and with the joists strongly and securely nailed to the sills. The studs for exterior walls will be notched at ends to fit the sill mortise, and will be 2 by 6 inches, placed 16 inches from centres, doubled at all corners and openings, and well braced and bridged where necessary, being braced at the corners at least 5 feet upon the studs and bridged over all openings. Joists of second floor will be carried on a ribbon, 1 by 4 inches, let into and strongly nailed to studs. Partition studs 2 by 4 inches, 16 inches from centres. All joists 2 by 10 inches, 16 inches from centres, spiked to studs, with three rows of herring-bones, 1 by 1½ inches, bridging in the width of ward building, and one row in width in other spans. Ceiling joists will rest on a wall plate, spiked to the studs in two thicknesses of 2 by 4 inch stuff, put on to break joints. Roofs will be of 2 by 8 inch stuff, back building of 2 by 6 inch. Roof of administration building will have 3 by 12 inch hip-rafters resting inside on partitions. Rafters 2 feet apart. Rafters for wards 2 feet 8 inches apart. Roofs of verandas will have 2 by 6 inch rafters, 2 feet apart. All roofs sheathed. Roofs shingled, laid ⅓ to the weather. Ventilation on the ridge of 2 by 4 inch stuff, covered with shingles and lined with ⅞ matched, tongued, and beaded stuff to form inside ceiling. Veranda posts will be 7 by 7 inches, braces 4 by 4 inches, all framed together. All exterior walls will be rough-boarded with inch boarding, in which will be laid a covering of tar paper or felt, and finished with clean siding, each lapped 1½ inches on the other. All windows double hung. Exterior doors 3 feet by 7 feet 6 inches by 1¾ inches, hung with 3 hinges to each door. Transoms over each door hung on swivels.

In all cases the ground-floor must be raised at least 18 inches from the ground. In warm climates and malarious regions the ground-floor should be raised at least 3 feet above the ground, on piers or open arches. To insure cleanliness the space between piers or arches should be filled with lattice work sufficiently open to allow free ventilation. A good cistern of suitable capacity is to be constructed and connected with the gutters and eave spouts of the roof. In northern climates, where the nature of the ground is suitable, a good cellar, well drained and ventilated, is to be constructed under the kitchen. The dispensary is to be neatly fitted with shelving, drawers, and counter, and the store-rooms with shelving, which, for bedding and clothing, will be open racks with slat bottoms. The windows of the administration building, both above and below, will be furnished with outside shutters, and will be 6 feet 6 inches high by 3 feet 3 inches wide.

The windows of the isolation ward should be made secure with a frame containing an iron grating, this room being intended to receive sick prisoners, cases of *delirium tremens*, etc., when not in use for cases of low fever, etc. Contagious diseases, as small-pox, should be treated in hospital tents when the weather permits, and the isolation ward should not be used for such cases. The dimensions given each room must be attained in the clear. At posts where the mean temperature of the winter is liable to fall to 28° Fahr., the ceiling of the ward being 12 feet from the floor, the windows will be double and 9 feet high by 3 feet 3 inches wide.

The arrangements for ventilation of the wards will vary according to climate. On the Gulf coast and in Arizona the wards will not be ceiled and will have ridge ventilation their whole length. At all posts where continuous artificial heat is required for three months in the year, the wards will be ceiled and have boxed openings carried from the centre of the ceiling to the ridge for summer ventilation. There will be two of these openings, each 10 feet long by 2½ feet wide, and 10 feet apart, each filled below with lattice work and above with movable shutters. A ventilating shaft 6 inches square will be placed in each earth-closet room, and the lamp or gas-burner of this room should be directly beneath this shaft. The chimney of the kitchen will be built with two flues, one of which will open near the ceiling and be used exclusively for ventilation.

In hospitals built of brick, the walls will be 12 inches in thickness, built hollow, a space of not less than 3 inches being left between the inner and outer shells, which will be tied together at intervals of not less than 2 feet by banders; the air-chambers thus formed must be made as nearly air-tight as possible by closing them at top and bottom, and laying the brick carefully in full mortar. (W. B. A.)

HOTELS (from Latin *hospitalis*, through the Old French form *hostel*) are a mark of advanced civilization which accords with the railway and steamship. In former times, when 30 or 40 miles was the rate of a day's journey, inns were numerous, but the restricted travel neither urged their enlargement nor pushed their display beyond comfort. Now, that travel can be so planned as to end the day in a city or large town, and as its extent and ease have been so greatly augmented, the needs and competition of innkeeping have developed the hotel to a degree which merits the term "palatial."

Although certain demands may control their scope, nearly all the recently built hotels of America and Europe have in common so many principles of design and operation that the points of difference are few and need only be described as they are reached; thus the great hostelries built over and in conjunction with railway termini, the best commercial and the so-called elegant and fashionable hotels, are so little different in appointments and service that they may be grouped, forming a type. In a hotel of this class there are usually from 400 to 800 rooms, including the dining-halls, public chambers, and parlors. In the basement are the machinery spaces, the mechanics' shops, wine-cellars, servants' dining-room, laundry, wash-rooms, public closets, and storage-rooms. Upon the ground floor the halls and entrances usually open into the shops of an outfitter, a barber, and a druggist, the public reading- and writing-rooms, the telegraph and passage ticket-offices, the wine-room, or bar (in America usually large and exceedingly ornate), the coffee-room and restaurant, and the hotel-office. In Europe the latter is quite small, and often in charge of women, being devoted chiefly to the allotment of rooms, the posting of charges as they come in from the eating- and wine-rooms, and the care of mails; whereas in America the office is the resort of the male population of the hotel; and, in addition to the duties above described, the clerks are expected personally to care for the comfort of each guest, as the client is called, to give him information he may ask, and to secure for him such introductions and favors that his business and pleasure may be promoted. The breakfast-, supper-, and dining-rooms are usually upon the second story, where are also the public parlors, the large chambers used for balls, banquets, and assemblies, and a few special suites of rooms. Upon the upper floors (the hotel having from 5 to 8 stories) are the living-rooms, for the most part in suites combining parlor and bath- and bed-rooms. Running through these floors at convenient points are the lift or elevator shafts, and distinct from the rest and with its own ventilation is the so-called back of the house, in which on convenient stories are the kitchens, pantries, bakery, the ice-room, sinks, and servants' quarters. Although the many divisions compel a large use of wood, the modern hotel is built with some regard to fire-proof effect. The walls are of stone and brick, the girders and many of the stairways are iron, the basement and ground floors are of concrete and tiling, and in some cases the upper floors are cemented. Generally the stokers, watchmen, and a certain number of the night porters are drilled as a fire-brigade. Ample lines of hose are hung near standpipes upon the several stories, and special steam-pumps are always kept in readiness. So efficient are the precautions against fire and its damage that hotel insurance is often effected at rates lower than those of other risks in which hazards of the same class are met. Abundant light is secured to the inner halls and rooms through the wings and courts, and there are sky-lights over the lower and unbroken floors. Ventilation is generally excellent. Much is done by the elevator-shaft, aided by the heating of the halls, which draws and expels air through the many open places, and a judicious arrangement of the baths and closets makes quite efficient their system of pipes and flues running to the roofs. In many cases the city's supply of water is unsatisfactory, and artesian wells have been sunk. Then the water is usually pumped into large tanks on the roofs, whence it is distributed, and a certain supply which has been heated by passage over the exhaust- and other steam-pipes is forced to all the baths and chambers. The arc form of the electric light is much used in the lower halls and larger rooms, but the incandescent form at present appears to have certain disadvantages for general use in hotels, and gas is not yet superseded. Steam-heat is usual in the corridors and large spaces, but the public parlors, the meeting and other rooms are furnished with fire-places.

The service is the test of the hotel's quality, and it receives great attention. The working management is usually dual, the superintendent (often one of the proprietors) directing the office and its functions, and the steward having charge of the marketing, the eating-rooms, the kitchens, and their branches. The office force (in America made up of room clerks, answering clerks, and cashiers) is divided into two watches, alternately serving 6 hours one day and 12 hours the next, and there is a night clerk with important duties who serves from midnight until 7 A. M. The bellmen, grouped near the office in America and in Europe distributed throughout the hotel, answer the electric calls which are in each room, and are likewise detailed in alternate day-watches and night service. Each public entrance of the hotel has its attendant. The house-keeper oversees the chambermaids and the force of cleaners and scrubbers, and is expected to secure nurses in case of illness and to act as the female representative of the management. Each chambermaid has the care of from 10 to 20 rooms, her work varying with the population of the hotel. She is allotted and is answerable for a certain supply of bed and toilet furniture, and is required to report to the inspector any leak, breakage, or damage; and, since her work keeps her about the rooms and halls throughout the day, to guard the property of the hotel and its guests. The inspector's duty is to visit each room as soon as it is vacated, to report its condition to the office, and to patrol the corridors as a check to mischievous or thievish intrusion. At night the watchmen, usually three, make the rounds of the hotel, visiting every half-hour each connection of the electric watch-clock, which should present to the night clerk a complete record of the patrol. At 2 A. M. the scrubbers take possession of the lower halls and public rooms, and thoroughly clean the tiled floors, stairways, and woodwork; then, after daybreak and until noon, when their work stops, these women scrub and clean the floors and painted surfaces in different parts of the hotel with such system that twice a week every part is visited. Shortly after midnight a count is made, and the exact number of guests is sent to the night steward, and the bakers begin to work up the breakfast rolls and muffins and the bread which will be required during the day. The night steward now inventories the larder and ice-room and prepares the day's marketing-slips for the buyer, who starts out at 6 A. M. The average of the season shows that the larder is generally stocked with provisions for 2½ days, and of dry and preserved stuff there is usually a week's supply. After 3 A. M. the morning cooks report for duty. These are known as broilers, stewers, and friers, and with the rest of the kitchen force are under the orders of the *chef*, who has entire charge of them. All wages are paid to him, and he has the power to hire and discharge. When a new *chef* is engaged he appears with his own force of from 8 to 12 men, the former cooks leaving to a man. The individual pay of a *chef* ranges from $1500 to $5000 a year, and a daily supply of wine for himself and staff is included. These cooks are helped by 7 or 8 women, who dress the fowls and prepare the ordinary vegetables. The soups and made dishes, especially the latter, are the work of the *chef*, who, with the steward, prepares the *menu*, in which, although there are certain constant features, there will be daily a distinct character that the bill of fare may please the refined and epicurean as well as the unexacting tastes. At 5 A. M. the waiters appear, the urn-keeper prepares the coffee, tea, and chocolate, and breakfast is served to those who will leave by early trains. This meal lasts until noon, when another force of waiters sets forth the luncheon. This is followed at 2 P. M. by the dinner, which is served until 8 o'clock. Tea, beginning at 6 P. M., is merged at 7.30 into supper, which then goes on till 12.45 A. M. Meanwhile in the coffee-room and restaurant there is maintained an informal service of meals from 7 A. M. till midnight.

A point of difference between the American and European plans of meal service may be here mentioned. By the former each meal has a fixed price, while the latter means a charge for each dish ordered; however, there are concessions from these plans in either form of hotel. Thus in Europe there is always a dinner called *table d' hôte* which is served complete at a certain sum, and in most of the American hotels a guest may arrange to be served after the European plan. The variety of food furnished in hotels is great, and the quantity may be judged from this statement, which presumes the daily supply for 400 guests: 672 lbs. beef, 200 lbs. mutton, 540 lbs. poultry, 143 doz. eggs, 252 qts. milk, 75 lbs. table-butter, 3 bbls. of flour. These figures of course include the food consumption of the servants, and to a population as above there are usually, of clerks and foremen and their assistants, 25; of cooks and pastrymen, waiters, bellmen, ushers, and porters, 150; of chambermaids, scrubbers, laundry and kitchen girls, 110; a total of 285. As the supplies come in the storekeeper receipts for them, and they are only dealt out upon an order signed by the chief of the department in which they are needed; every day these orders are filed with the bookkeepers, and every week they are made to tally with the storekeeper's report and the bills against the hotel; then the number of guests is brought into comparison, and the management may thus determine exactly the expenses *per diem* and *per capita*. Though a high class of service is required the wages are comparatively good, and they are paid monthly. Every 30 days a complete account of stock is taken: the loss and breakage are great, despite a system of fines, for the ware is constantly handled and a piece may be used more than twice during one meal. In Europe the hotel's washing is usually done by contract, but American hotels as a rule contain a laundry in which also is taken the washing for guests. As the bed and table linen is changed after each use and as a great supply of towels and small pieces is necessary, the daily laundry work is large and demands the best features for facilitating and expediting the labor, such as steam-wash-tubs, wringers, and drying-rooms.

In the large scope of a hotel the daily wear and accidents are such that a carpenter, upholsterer, mason, painter, plumber, and their helpers are in regular service and constantly employed. The carpets are generally renewed every three years, and at the end of a like period the interior of the hotel will have been entirely repainted. The hotel furniture, which is substantial and often lavishly rich, is constantly under repair and replacement. A map of the flues, drains, and pipes provides for the stoppage of a leak or break with very slight disturbance of fixtures.

The charges are varied and are always controlled by the stay of the guest and the position and extent of his quarters. In Europe a certain daily fee is charged for attendance; in America this personal service is gratuitous, and there are no other extra charges save for fire and the private service of meals and other refreshments. The fee-system in Europe is omnipresent and seems to be ineradicable in hotels, although honest attempts to suppress it are made by most innkeepers, as they cannot scale their pay-rolls in consideration of this extra profit to their servants without incurring the inattention of these to such of the guests as may be careless of or insensible to this sort of levy. Of this, however, American hotels are almost free. The property of the guest is always under guard, which inn-keepers maintain is a matter of courtesy, not obligation, and quote a statute defining their liability as not for loss of property which has not been deposited in their safes. (E. C.)

HOUDIN, ROBERT (1805–1871), a French conjuror, was born at Blois in 1805. After he was educated at the College of Orleans his aptitude for mechanics led him to follow his father's trade of watch-making, and he also learned something of natural magic. After he went to Paris, his mind, overtasked, gave way. On regaining his mental powers he made mechanical toys and automata, for which he won a medal at the Paris exhibition of 1844. He conducted magical soirées in the Palais Royal from 1845 to 1855, which became famous throughout Europe. He then retired to Blois with a large fortune, but in 1856 was sent by the French government to Algeria to compete with the marabouts or priests in performance of pretended miracles. After many singular adventures he succeeded in breaking down the influence of these impostors on their countrymen. Returning to France he published *Robert Houdin, sa vie, ses œuvres, et son théâtre* (1857); afterwards his *Confidences* (1859; translated into English 1859); and finally *Les tricheries des Grecs dévoilées* (1861). He died at Blois, June, 1871.

HOUGH, Franklin Benjamin, an American author, was born at Martinsburg, N. Y., July 20, 1822, being the son of Dr. Horatio G. Hough. He graduated at Union College, Schenectady, N. Y., in 1843, and studied medicine, taking his degree at Cleveland Medical College in 1848. He practised his profession for four years at Somerville, N. Y., and has since been engaged in literary and scientific pursuits. He was superintendent of the New York State Census in 1855 and 1865; surgeon of the Ninety-seventh New York volunteers, 1862–63, and has been employed in forestry investigations under the department of agriculture since 1876. He has published histories of St. Lawrence, Franklin, Jefferson, and Lewis counties, N. Y.; *Indian Treaties of New York* (1861); *Pouchot's Memoirs* (1866); *Washingtoniana* (2 vols., 1865); *New York State Gazetteer* (1872); *American Constitutions* (1871); *Cultivation of Timber and Preservation of Forests* (1874); *Elements of Forestry* (1882); and treatises on meteorology, hospitals, and the early history of New York. He died June 11, 1885.

HOUGHTON, Richard Monckton Milnes, Baron (1809–1885), an English author, was born at Fryston Hall, Yorkshire, June 19, 1809. He graduated at Trinity College, Cambridge, in 1831, and spent much time in travel in Southern Europe and the East. In 1857 he entered Parliament as member for Pontefract, and represented that constituency until 1863, when he was raised to the peerage as Baron Houghton. He was at first a conservative but afterwards a liberal, advocating popular education and religious equality. He published political pamphlets and speeches, and several volumes of travels, but was best known as a poet and as the friend and biographer of Keats. Many of his poems relate to oriental scenes and subjects. His style is graceful, and his tone of thought subdued, yet cheerful rather than melancholy. He died Aug. 11, 1885. His publications include *Memorials of a Tour in Greece* (1833); *Memorials of a Residence on the Continent* (1838); *Poetry for the People* (1840); *Memorials of Many Scenes* (1843); *Palm Leaves* (1844); *Poems, Legendary and Historical* (1844); *Good Night and Good Morning* (1859); *Monographs, Personal and Social* (1873); *Poetical Works* (1874).

HOUSSAYE, Arsène, a French author, was born at Bruyères, near Laon, March 28, 1815. At an early age he went to Paris, and there began his literary career in 1836, with two novels, *La Couronne de bluets* and *La Pécheresse*. The friendship of Jules Janin and Théophile Gautier and his co-operation with Jules Sandeau gave him an assured place among the authors of the time. He was especially noted as an art critic and historian. His *Galerie de portraits du XVIIIe Siècle* (1844) and his *Histoire de la peinture flamande et hollandaise* (1846) were received with marked favor. In November, 1849, he was appointed manager of the Théâtre Français, which became a means of promoting the policy of Louis Napoleon. In 1856 the loss of his wife gave Houssaye an excuse for withdrawing from a charge which brought upon him a heavy burden of scandals. He was then made inspector-general of the provincial museums. In 1861 he became one of the proprietors of *La Presse* and its managing editor. He has used a variety of pseudonyms, and has published *Le Roi Voltaire* (1858), and many sketches of writers of the eighteenth century; three series of *Les Grandes Dames* (1868–70), and numerous novels, some of which are historical. His volumes of poems issued at various times have been collected under the title *Poésies complètes* (1877). His few plays are of little account, but his critical and biographical sketches are animated, witty, and graceful.

HOUSTON, a city of Texas, seat of justice of Harris county, and the second city of the State in commerce and population, is situated on the navigable Buffalo Bayou, 49 miles by rail north-west of Galveston. Vessels drawing 9 feet of water can reach the town; larger craft load and discharge freights at Clinton, 8 miles distant. Houston has become a great railway-centre; the principal roads being the Southern Pacific (running from New Orleans to Southern California); the Galveston, Harrisburg, and San Antonio; the Galveston, Houston, and Henderson, which here connects with the International and Great Northern Railroad; the Houston branch of the Gulf, Colorado, and Santa Fé Railway; the Houston and Texas Central; the Houston, East, and West Texas; and the Texas Western Railway. The city has six passenger railway stations. It stands in a pleasantly undulating region, and its principal streets are well shaded and are traversed by horse railroads. It is the centre of commerce for a large and very fertile district, which ships here a great quantity of grain, provisions, meats, and cotton. It is also the chief point for the preparation and distribution of the products of the great-pine forests of South-eastern Texas. Among the leading articles of manufacture are fertilizers, cement, cottonseed-oil, soap, flour, lumber, railway rolling-stock, wagons, farm and household utensils, castings and other metallic wares, machinery, etc. The city has churches of all the prominent denominations, and is well provided with schools (public, parochial, and private), newspapers, hotels, and banks. Among the finest buildings are the city-hall and market, and the Masonic temple. The population in 1870 was 9382; in 1880, 18,646, and in 1890, 27,598.

HOVEY, Alvah, an American clergyman, was born at Greene, N. Y., March 5, 1820. He graduated at Dartmouth College in 1844 and at Newton Theological Institution in 1848. He was then ordained pastor of a Baptist church at North Gloucester, Mass. In 1850 he became instructor in Biblical literature at Newton Theological Institution, in 1853 professor of ecclesiastical history, in 1856 professor of Christian theology, and in 1868 president of the institution. He has published *Life and Times of Isaac Backus* (1858), *State of the Impenitent Dead* (1859), *Miracles of Christ* (1864), *Scriptural Law of Divorce* (1868), *God with Us* (1872), *Religion and the State* (1874).

HOWARD, John Eager (1752–1827), an American soldier and statesman, was born in Baltimore co., Md., June 4, 1752. He became a captain in a Maryland regiment in 1776, and fought in the battle of White Plains, N. Y. His corps was dismissed in December, but he rejoined the army as major in April, 1777, and distinguished himself at Germantown, where he commanded his regiment. His commission as lieutenant-colonel dated from March 11, 1778. He was present at the battle of Monmouth in June, 1778. He went to the South with the Maryland troops in April, 1780, and served under Gates at Camden, S. C., Aug. 16. At the battle of Cowpens, Jan. 17, 1781, Col. Howard commanded the Continentals, and led them in a bayonet-charge which decided the fortune of the day. His troops again showed their courage and discipline at Guilford Court-house, March 15, and at Hobkirk's Hill, April 25. At Eutaw Springs, Sept. 8, Col. Howard was severely wounded. After the war he married Margaret, daughter of Chief-Justice Chew, of Pennsylvania. He was a member of Congress in 1787-88, and governor of Maryland from 1789 to 1792. Pres. Washington offered him the secretaryship of war, but he declined. He was a State senator of Maryland in 1795, and U. S. Senator from 1795 to 1803. Thereafter he held no official position, but in 1814, after the capture of Washington by the British, he strenuously resisted the evacuation of Baltimore proposed by some citizens. He died at Baltimore, Oct. 12, 1827.

HOWARD, OLIVER OTIS, an American general, was born at Leeds, Maine, Nov. 8, 1830. He graduated at Bowdoin College in 1850 and at West Point in 1854. He entered the ordnance corps, and in 1857 was made instructor in mathematics at West Point. After the civil war broke out he became colonel of the Third regiment of Maine volunteers, and at the battle of Bull Run, July 21, 1861, he commanded a brigade. He was made brigadier-general of volunteers Sept. 3, 1861, and fought in McClellan's Peninsular campaign. At the battle of Fair Oaks, June 1, 1862, he lost his right arm. At Antietam, September, 1862, he had command of the Second corps, and at Chancellorsville, May 1, 1863, of the Eleventh, which was routed by the fierceness of Stonewall Jackson's attack. At Gettysburg, July 1, 1863, after the death of Gen. Reynolds, Howard succeeded to the command at the front. He was transferred with his command to Tennessee in October, 1863, and was engaged in the battles of Lookout Valley and Missionary Ridge, Oct. 29, at Chattanooga, Nov. 23, and in the operations for the relief of Knoxville in December. In April, 1864, Gen. Howard took command of the Fourth corps, Army of the Cumberland, and in July following was placed in command of the Army of the Tennessee. He fought in most of the battles from that of Chattanooga to Atlanta, and commanded the right wing of Sherman's army during its march to the sea and through the Carolinas. His commission as brigadier-general dated from Dec. 21, 1864, and he received the brevet of major-general March 13, 1865. He was appointed commissioner of the Freedmen's Bureau May 12, 1865, and held that office until June 30, 1872, when its operations closed. He was also made, in March, 1867, a trustee of Howard University, which was established at Washington for the higher education of the colored race. He was made president of that university April 6, 1869, but resigned in 1874. He conducted a campaign against the Nez Percés from May to November, 1877. His pursuit of these Indians for 1300 miles is related in his book, *Chief Joseph* (1880). He also defeated the Bannocks and Piutes in 1878. In 1881 he was made superintendent of the U. S. Military Academy, at West Point. In March, 1886, he was promoted to be major-general, and took command of the division of the Pacific. In January 1889, he was transferred to the division of the Atlantic.

HOWARD UNIVERSITY, situated in Washington, D. C., was chartered by Congress in 1867 for the education of youth in the liberal arts and sciences. The charter provides "that the university shall consist of the following departments and such others as the board of trustees may establish: first, normal; second, collegiate; third, theological; fourth, law; fifth, medicine; sixth, agriculture." It originated in the Christian and philanthropic plans, in behalf of the colored population of the country, which were occasioned by the result of the civil war, which had just come to an end. Far-sighted patriots, who knew the degradation of the millions of the freedmen but foresaw also the prominent part which they must play in the future, felt that, while common schools were the prime necessity, care must also be taken to found institutions for the higher education of a portion of the negro race. This would be necessary to deliver them from undue dependence on the whites and on ignorant and incapable leaders of their own race, and to provide variety of employment for those of good natural ability who might aspire to become teachers, clergymen, lawyers, physicians, civil-engineers, architects, editors, and authors. It was further believed that no location for such an institution of varied learning would be so favorable as the national metropolis. It was easily accessible from all parts of the country, and presented special attractions to students and professors in a multitude of auxiliary instrumentalities and forces additional to the university itself, such as galleries of art, museums, libraries, hospitals, courts of law, especially the Supreme Court, the sessions of Congress, the capitol, the numerous public buildings and monuments, the several administrative departments, the churches and clergymen of various denominations, and the meetings of scientific, literary, religious, and political conventions. A residence in Washington is itself an education. There, also, it might be expected that the nation would conspicuously show to the world its purpose to redress the wrongs of the negro, not the least of which had been the denial to him of education. But, while it was planned to provide for the negro full opportunity of intellectual and moral culture, it was not deemed best to place the institution on a race basis by naming him as its object. Hence the charter only speaks of "the education of youth," and its doors have ever stood open to all qualified to enter, irrespective of race or sex. The Caucasian, the Mongolian, the North American Indian, and the negro have actually been numbered among its students, and ladies have graduated from its normal, college, law, and medical departments.

A site was selected on the northern edge of the city, commanding an extensive view of Washington and its suburbs. Commodious and tasteful buildings for lectures, dormitories, and professors' residences were erected through the aid of the Freedmen's Bureau, surrounded by a campus of 20 acres and facing on a park of 11 acres. The university was named in honor of Maj.-Gen. Oliver O. Howard, then head of the Freedmen's Bureau, who also became its president, and successfully promoted its interests in many ways, till, on the abolition of this bureau and his return to army service, he resigned in 1874. In December, 1875, Hon. Edward P. Smith accepted the position, but died a few months later on a voyage to the coast of Africa. In May, 1877, Rev. William W. Patton, D. D., LL. D., was elected president. He has been succeeded by Rev. J. E. Rankin, D. D., LL. D. The instructors in the various departments number 55, and the students in attendance about 400. Seven departments are now in successful operation. The *normal course*, occupying from 3 to 5 years, according to the previous attainments of those entering it, fits for general business and domestic life, and especially for the work of teaching, giving an education in English branches, with the rudiments of Latin. The *preparatory course*, of 3 years, pays attention to the Latin and Greek classics, and fits for college. The *college course*, of 4 years,

usual curriculum of reputable American colleges in the study of Latin, Greek, science, philosophy, history, mathematics, and English literature, with something of the modern languages. The *theological course*, of 3 years, provides a training in natural and revealed theology, exegetical study of the Scriptures in English and in the Hebrew and Greek, ecclesiastical and Biblical history, archæology, homiletics, and elocution. This course is evangelical but undenominational; the professors are of different ecclesiastical connections, and the students enter the ministry of various Christian churches. The *medical course*, of 3 years, has 3 branches, medicine proper, pharmacy, and dentistry, and the excellence of the instruction, the free access to the large hospital on the ground adjacent, and the cheapness of the terms have drawn large numbers of white students. The *law course*, also of 3 years, gives the usual preparation for legal practice. No charge for tuition is made in any educational department but those of medicine and law. The *industrial* department, lately opened, enables students to add a knowledge of the rudiments of several branches of manual industry. It is hoped that ultimately it may grow into a technological school.

The property of the university of all kinds may be valued at about $650,000, and is the gift of the government and of many private benefactors. The annual expenses are met partly from the income of a few endowments, partly from donations of individuals and charitable organizations, partly from tuition fees and room-rents, and partly from Congressional appropriations. Its numerous graduates are teaching and laboring in this and in other lands. The library and cabinet are yet small and inadequate. Its future is bright with promise. (W. W. P.)

HOWE, ELIAS (1819–1867), an American inventor, was born at Spencer, Mass., July 9, 1819. He was the son of a farmer and miller, and received a common-school education. In 1835 he went to Lowell and was employed in a machine-shop. Afterwards, while working in Boston, he developed his invention of the sewing-machine, and having constructed the first machine in May, 1845, obtained a patent Sept. 10, 1846. Though very poor, he went to England to introduce his invention, but meeting no success he returned to Boston in 1847. His patent had been infringed, and although he found some friends to assist him yet he was engaged for nearly seven years in litigation to protect his rights. At last, in 1854, the principal manufacturers, defeated in the courts, agreed to pay him royalties on the machines made by them. Under this arrangement his annual income increased to $200,000, and the total fortune obtained from his invention was $2,000,000. During the civil war he enlisted as a private in the Seventeenth Connecticut regiment, and served for some time. He received many marks of distinction for his invention. He died at Brooklyn, N. Y., Oct. 3, 1867.

HOWE, JOSEPH (1804–1873), governor of Nova Scotia, was born at Halifax, Dec. 13, 1804. His father, John Howe, had been a printer at Boston before the Revolution, but being a loyalist went with the British troops to Halifax, where he became postmaster-general. Joseph followed his father's trade, and in 1827 became part proprietor of the *Acadian*, and in January, 1828, sole editor and proprietor of the *Nova Scotian*. He was a liberal in politics, and by his opposition to the local government brought upon himself a libel-suit, in which he was acquitted. He also had a duel with Mr. T. C. Haliburton. Eventually, through the efforts of Howe and his friends, Halifax received a municipal charter. In 1840 he became a member of the provincial cabinet; he was also frequently elected to the provincial parliament, and was colonial agent in England for many years. In 1854 he resigned his position as provincial secretary to superintend the construction of the first railroad in Nova Scotia. When the formation of the Dominion of Canada was proposed, Howe insisted upon proper guaranties for the interests of Nova Scotia. After the federal government was fully established, he was secretary of state for the provinces from 1869 to 1872. He was also superintendent of Indian affairs. He was afterwards lieutenant-governor of Nova Scotia. He died at Halifax, June 1, 1873. His *Speeches and Public Letters* appeared in two volumes (1858).

HOWE, JULIA WARD, an American poet, wife of Dr. S. G. Howe, was born at New York, May 27, 1819. Her father, Samuel Ward, was a banker, noted for his liberality and public spirit. Her mother was a lady of poetic culture. After receiving a careful education, of unusual range, Miss Ward was married in 1843 to Dr. S. G. Howe and made an extended tour in Europe. In 1850 she again went abroad and spent nearly a year in Rome. She took a deep interest in her husband's philanthropic labors, and was a warm friend of the anti-slavery cause. During the civil war she was a prominent worker in the U. S. Sanitary Commission. She contributed by voice and pen to many social reforms. Her administrative ability also led to her being selected as the chief of the women's department of the New Orleans World's Fair in 1885. Some of the poems written in her youth appeared in print, but her first volume, *Passion Flowers*, was published in 1854. Then came *Words for the Hour* (1856); then two tragedies, *The World's Own* (1857), and *Hippolytus* (1858); but her best were in *Later Lyrics* (1866), which comprised "Poems of the War; Lyrics of the Street; Parables; and Poems of Study." Her whole nature was deeply stirred by the terrible facts of the war; her great mental powers then found adequate occasion for making themselves felt. Of all her poems the most memorable is the "Battle-Hymn of the Republic," which, founded on the soldier's refrain called "John Brown's Hymn," gave expression to the deep moral purpose of the war. The fervor of the anti-slavery crusade and of war time she afterwards carried into her labors in behalf of woman's rights. Besides her poems she has published *A Trip to Cuba* (1858), and *From the Oak to the Olive* (1868), which is a record of her journey from London to Athens in 1867.

HOWE, SAMUEL GRIDLEY (1801–1876), an American philanthropist, was born at Boston, Nov. 10, 1801. He was educated at the Boston Grammar School and Brown University, graduating at the latter in 1821. After studying medicine, he went to Greece in 1824, where he served as surgeon in the war for independence, and was placed at the head of the surgical service. In 1831, when he returned to the United States, he took part in the project for establishing an institution for the blind in Boston. Being appointed superintendent, he went to Europe to examine the schools for the blind. At Paris he was appointed president of the Polish committee, and as such he endeavored to carry aid to part of the Polish army which had crossed into Prussia. On going there he was arrested, imprisoned for six weeks, and then taken back to

France. For his noble work in connection with the training of the blind see articles BLIND and BRIDGMAN, LAURA DEWEY, in Vol. I. He was also prominent in the work of the anti-slavery party in Massachusetts, and in 1846 was a Free-soil candidate for Congress. He assisted in founding a school for the training of idiots, which was afterwards organized as the Massachusetts School for Idiotic and Feeble-minded Youth. During the civil war he was an active and earnest supporter of the U. S. Sanitary Commission and its work for the soldiers. In 1867 he went to Greece in behalf of the Cretans, then struggling for independence. In 1871 he was sent by Pres. Grant as a member of the commission to visit San Domingo and report upon the advisability of its annexation to the United States. He died at Boston, Jan. 9, 1876. He published a *Historical Sketch of the Greek Revolution* (1828) and a *Reader for the Blind* (1839).

HOWELLS, WILLIAM DEAN, an American author, was born at Martinsville, Ohio, March 1, 1837. His father soon after became the publisher of a paper at Hamilton, Ohio, and the son learned the printer's trade. But he soon began to write for the papers both prose and verse, and in 1858 he was editor of the *Ohio State Journal*. Two years later, in company with John James Piatt, he published a little volume called *Poems of Two Friends* (1860), having edited, about the same time, a *Life of Abraham Lincoln* (1860). He was, in 1861, appointed U. S. consul at Venice, and there he remained until 1865, having in the meantime married Miss Eleanor Meade, sister of the sculptor, Larkin J. Meade. His *Venetian Life* (1865) and *Italian Journeys* (1867) record some of the impressions made upon his intellect and imagination by this long sojourn in a land so favorable to romance. When Mr. Howells returned to the United States he became an editorial writer for *The Nation*. He had already been a contributor to the *Atlantic Monthly*; in 1865 he became its assistant-editor, and removed to Cambridge, and in 1871 he succeeded Mr. J. T. Fields as editor-in-chief. A complete collection of his *Poems* was made in 1873. But Mr. Howells had now turned his attention to the faithful analytic portrayal of American character of the present day. Beginning with *Their Wedding Journey* (1872), this was continued in *A Chance Acquaintance* (1873); *The Lady of the Aroostook* (1875); *The Undiscovered Country* (1880); *Doctor Breen's Practice* (1881); *A Modern Instance* (1882); and culminated in *The Rise of Silas Lapham* (1885). Mr. Howells' skill in the delineation of character is only equalled by the ease of his style and his apt use of every-day incidents. Several comedies for parlor-theatricals have been added to Mr. Howells' publications in recent years. In 1885 he removed to New York city to take charge of an editorial department in *Harper's Magazine*.

HOWSON, JOHN SAUL (1816–1885), an English clergyman, was born in 1816. He was educated at Trinity College, Cambridge, graduating with honors in 1837. After taking orders in 1845, he became senior classical master, and in 1849 principal of Liverpool College, which position he held till 1865. He was then appointed vicar of Wisbech, and in 1867 dean of Chester. He is especially noted as joint author with Rev. W. J. Conybeare of *The Life and Epistles of St. Paul* (1850–52). Besides many sermons and lectures he published an essay on *Deaconesses* and the Hulsean lectures on *The Character of St. Paul* (1862). In 1880 he visited the United States and delivered lectures. Among his publications are *The Metaphors of St. Paul* (1868); *The Companions of St. Paul* (1871); *Meditations on the Miracles of Christ* (1871–77); *Chester as it was* (1872); and *The River Dee* (1875). He died at Bournemouth, Dec. 15, 1885.

HUBER, JOHANNES NEPOMUK (1830–1879), a German theologian, was born at Munich, Aug. 18, 1830. He was educated in that city, studying theology and philosophy, and obtained the degree of doctor in 1854. In 1855 he became professor extraordinary, and in 1864 full professor of philosophy at Munich. His *Philosophie der Kirchenväter* (1859) gave offence to the Jesuits, and was placed on the Index. Huber then became a strenuous opponent of Ultramontanism, and afterwards of the Vatican Council. He was one of the writers of *Janus* (1869), and was the author of *Quirinus* (1870). He then became an active leader of the Old Catholic movement. He died at Munich, March 19, 1879. He published *Johannes Scotus Erigena* (1861); *Das Papstthum und der Staat* (1876); *Der Jesuitenorden* (1873), and some philosophical essays.

HÜBNER, JOSEPH ALEXANDER, BARON VON, an Austrian diplomatist, was born at Vienna, Nov. 26, 1811. He was educated at the University of that city, and in 1833 entered the government service. In 1835 he was made an attaché of the Austrian embassy at Paris, and in 1841 chief-secretary of the embassy at Lisbon. After the establishment of the French Republic, in 1848, Hübner was sent to Paris, and remained there as minister plenipotentiary until 1859. He was then recalled to Vienna on account of the outbreak of the war in Italy. He went on special missions to Naples and Rome, and was for a short time member of the Austrian cabinet. In 1865 he was again ambassador at Rome, and in 1868 he retired from public service. He visited the United States in 1870, and in 1871 he undertook a journey round the world, which he afterwards described very pleasantly in his *Promenade autour du Monde* (1873), which has been translated into English and German. In October, 1879, he became a member of the Austrian House of Lords. His great work on *Pope Sixtus V*. appeared in 1871, and has been translated into several languages.

HUDSON, HENRY NORMAN (1814–1886), an American essayist, born at Cornwall, Vt., Jan. 28, 1814. He was brought up on a farm and apprenticed to a coachmaker, but fitted himself for college. He graduated at Middlebury College in 1840, and then taught in Kentucky, Alabama, and elsewhere. Having devoted himself especially to the study of Shakespeare, he delivered lectures on the great dramatist in many parts of the country. These were published in 1848, and established his reputation as a learned, discerning, and philosophic critic of the school of Coleridge. In 1844 Mr. Hudson had become a member of the Protestant Episcopal Church, and in 1849 he was ordained priest. On Jan. 1, 1853, he became editor of *The Churchman*, which he conducted for nearly two years. He afterwards edited the *American Church Monthly* in 1857–58, and was rector of the Episcopal church at Litchfield, Conn., in 1859–60. During the civil war he was a chaplain in the army, serving chiefly in South Carolina and with Gen. Butler on the James. He afterwards conducted a young ladies' school at Boston. Throughout his career he has continued his labors in Shakespearian criticism. His complete edition, with carefully revised text, notes, and biography, appeared in 11 volumes (1850-56). A school edition in 2 volumes was issued in 1871; and in 1873 he published *Shakespeare: His Life, Art, and Character* (2 vols.). He died Jan. 16, 1886.

HUDSON'S BAY is a large but shallow enclosed sea in British America, extending over about 13° of latitude from its southern extremity (James Bay) to the coast between Chesterfield Inlet and Southampton Island, and of nearly equal breadth. With the exception of a small area near the centre, but somewhat nearer to the eastern shore, the whole of the bay is less than 100 fathoms deep. Situated to the north and north-east of Manitoba, with which it communicates, not only by the large River Nelson, bearing the surplus waters poured into Lake Winnipeg by the Saskatchewan and Red River of the North, but also by the Severn and the Albany Rivers, Hudson's Bay would become the natural outlet for the productions of that province, could the navigability of Hudson's Straits be clearly demonstrated.

The expedition sent by the Canadian government to Hudson's Bay in 1884 seems to have proved that this outlet can be utilized. The icebergs met with at the western end of Hudson's Straits come from the glaciers in Fox Channel, and in August and September would form no greater barrier to navigation than do those met with in the Straits of Belleisle. The ordinary field-ice, though declared by the Esquimaux to be unusually abundant, offered no obstruction to the ship's course, though the heavy Arctic ice coming down from Fox Channel compelled a detour southward. No icebergs were met with in Hudson's Bay, nor were there reports of any. No difficulty was met with in navigating south of Dudley Digges Island, north-west to Chesterfield Inlet, south to Fort Churchill and York Factory, on the western coast, and then across the bay. Temperature observations taken during 15 months seem to show that the climate of Hudson's Bay is less severe than in many other parts of the dominion; and the ice observations show that Hudson's Bay and Straits are navigable for properly built and equipped vessels from July to October.

HUGER, the name of a Huguenot family settled in South Carolina, some of whose members have attained eminence. 1. HUGER, ISAAC (1742-1797), an American general, was born at Limerick Plantation, S. C., March 19, 1742. He served under Col. Middleton in an expedition against the Cherokees in 1760. On the outbreak of the Revolution he was made lieutenant-colonel of the First South Carolina regiment, and afterwards colonel of the Fifth regiment. He opposed the British invasion of Georgia in 1778, but was obliged to retire before a superior force. He was appointed brigadier-general, Jan. 19, 1779, and commanded the left wing at Stono, June 20, where he was wounded. During the siege of Charleston, in 1780, he commanded a body of light troops, but was surprised and defeated by Tarleton at Monk's Corner. He joined Gen. Greene's army, and commanded the Virginia brigade at the battle of Guilford Court-House, March 15, 1781, where he was again wounded. At Hobkirk's Hill, April 25, 1781, he was again in command, and exerted himself to regain the day. At the close of the war he retired to his estates. He died at Charleston, November, 1797. His brothers, Daniel, John, Francis, and Benjamin, were also active in the Revolutionary movements, and Maj. Benjamin Huger was killed at the siege of Charleston, May 11, 1780.

2. HUGER, FRANCIS KINLOCH (1774-1855), was born near Georgetown, S. C., in 1774. He was the son of Maj. Benjamin Huger, on whose plantation Lafayette first landed in 1777. He studied medicine and was a pupil of the celebrated John Hunter, of London. While at Vienna, in 1798, he took part in Dr. Eric Bollman's attempt to liberate Lafayette from imprisonment at Olmutz. This attempt having miscarried, Huger was himself imprisoned, but was soon released. Returning to the United States he was made a captain in the army. He afterwards served in both branches of the State legislature. In 1812 he was appointed lieutenant-colonel of an artillery regiment, and in 1813 adjutant-general. He died at Charleston, S. C., Feb. 15, 1855.

3. HUGER, BENJAMIN, an American general, son of the preceding, was born at Charleston, S. C., in 1806. He graduated at West Point in 1825, entered the artillery service, and became captain of ordnance, May 30, 1832. He was chief of ordnance to Gen. Scott's army in the Mexican war, and received several brevets. He became major, Feb. 15, 1855, and resigned April 22, 1861. Entering the Confederate service he was made brigadier-general, and employed at and near Richmond. When McClellan entered on his Peninsular campaign, Huger, now major-general, held Norfolk. A few regiments were sent from Fortress Monroe to capture the place, and Huger quickly withdrew, May 10, 1862, having first fired the navy-yard, the Merrimac, and other vessels. Huger commanded a division at Fair Oaks, May 31, and at Malvern Hill, July 1, 1862. An inquiry having been instituted into his abandonment of Norfolk, he was retired from service. After the war he became a farmer in Virginia. He died Dec. 7, 1877.

HUGGINS, WILLIAM, an English astronomer, was born at London, Feb. 7, 1824. He was educated in that city and became proficient in natural science. He devoted himself for some years to the study of physiology with the aid of the microscope. In 1855 he erected and equipped an observatory at his residence at Upper Tulse Hill, with a view of applying to astronomy his practical knowledge of other branches of physics. Obtaining in 1858 a telescope of 8 inches aperture from Alvan Clark, he made careful observations of double stars and accurate drawings of planets; then in 1862, having mapped the spectra of 26 chemical elements, observed the spectra of the planets, stars, and nebulæ. By comparison of these spectra he discovered the nature of these bodies, showing that certain nebulæ are chiefly composed of hydrogen, and that certain comets have the same spectrum as carbon. He went on to determine by the spectroscope whether the fixed stars are approaching or receding from the earth, and with what velocity, and even to measure the heat received from them. His remarkable and valuable researches obtained for him in 1870 the degree of LL. D. from the University of Cambridge, and that of D. C. L. from the University of Oxford. The Royal Society showed its appreciation of his labors by presenting him with a telescope of 15 inches aperture. Every learned society in Europe has conferred on him marks of honor. From 1876 to 1878 he was president of the Royal Astronomical Society of Great Britain.

HUGHES, JOHN (1797-1864), an American Archbishop, was born at Annaboghan, County Tyrone, Ireland, June 24, 1797. He emigrated to America in 1817, and was employed for a time as a gardener. He was educated at Mount St. Mary's College, Emmitsburg, Md., supporting himself by taking care of the college garden for a time, and afterwards was a teacher in the institution. He was ordained both deacon and priest in 1825, and had charge of churches in Philadelphia until 1838. During this time he founded St. John's Orphan Asylum (1828), established the *Catholic Herald* (1833), and conducted noted controversies with Rev. John Breckinridge, D. D., in 1830 and 1834. These discussions were published by both parties. In 1838 Dr. Hughes was made coadjutor to Bishop Dubois, of New York, with the title of bishop of Basilopolis *in partibus*, and in 1842 he became bishop of New York. In 1839 he visited France, Austria, and Italy to obtain pecuniary aid for his diocese. He purchased property at Fordham, in Westchester county, and opened there in 1841 St. John's College and the Theological Seminary of St. Joseph. He had already made open attacks on the public-school system of New York as sectarian. He now organized the Roman Catholic population against it, and instituted a complete system of parochial schools. He also used great exertions to effect a change in the tenure of church property. Previously the property of all religious denominations had been held by lay trustees, but in spite of opposition Bishop Hughes succeeded in having the title to that of the Roman Catholic Church vested in the bishop. The archbishop collected and published the letters of the controversy which he had had with Hon. Erastus Brooks in regard to this change. In 1850 the diocese of New York had been so increased by immigration and other causes that Bishop Hughes was made archbishop, and suffragan bishops were appointed to assist in the administration of affairs. In 1854 the first provincial council of New York was held, attended by seven suffragan bishops. In 1861 Archbishop Hughes and Thurlow Weed were sent by Secretary Seward as special commissioners to Europe to counteract the representations of secession agents in influential circles, and to set fairly before foreign governments the true object of the United States in conducting the war. The archbishop continued to use his influence in behalf of the integrity of the Union. In 1863, when draft-riots broke out in New York, he urged upon the excited people the duty of submission to the government. He died at New York, Jan. 3, 1864. His *Writings* have been published in 2 volumes, and his *Life* was written by J. G. R. Hassard (1866).

HUGHES, ROBERT BALL (1806–1868), an English-American sculptor, was born at London, Jan. 19, 1806. At a very early age he showed aptitude for art, and while a student with E. H. Bailey won several prizes and medals. He made busts of George IV. and the Dukes of York, Sussex, and Cambridge. In 1829 he removed to New York, where he made a marble statue of Hamilton, the first work of the kind in America. It was placed in the Merchants' Exchange, New York, and was destroyed in the great fire of 1835. He made the monumental alto-relief of Bishop Hobart, in Trinity Church, New York, and a bronze statue of Dr. N. Bowditch, at Mount Auburn Cemetery, Boston. He also made a bust of Washington Irving, a statuette of Gen. Warren, a model for an equestrian statue of Washington, and several minor works. He died at Boston, March 5, 1868.

HUGHES, THOMAS, an English author, was born at Donnington, near Newbury, Berkshire, Oct. 20, 1823. He was educated at Rugby and Oriel College, Oxford, where he graduated in 1845. He studied at Lincoln's Inn, and was called to the bar in 1848, and practised as an advocate. His story, *Tom Brown's School-Days* (1856), gave him immediate fame. It is an admirable picture of life in the great English public schools, and an affectionate tribute of the author to the memory of his own instructor, the great Thomas Arnold, of Rugby. Hughes continued his story in *Tom Brown at Oxford* (1861), but this, though well done, was less successful. Between the two he published *The Scouring of the White Horse* (1858). Pursuing his profession he became queen's counsel in 1869. He also took part in politics as a liberal, and became a member of Parliament, representing Lambeth from 1865 to 1868, and Frome from 1869 to 1874. He has always taken great interest in movements for the improvement of the working classes and was principal of the Workingmen's College in London, in which instruction is given in the evenings. In 1880 he established in a remote district of Tennessee a colony called Rugby; intended especially as a haven for young persons from the English middle classes who found difficulty in obtaining employment at home. But it has failed to accomplish its chief object, life in the wilderness having but few attractions for those accustomed to the comforts of civilization. The basis of Mr. Hughes' character, manifest in all his acts and writings, is a profound belief in Christ and an earnest endeavor to apply Christ's teachings in every-day life. He has published in enforcement of his views *The Manliness of Christ* (1879), and as an example of a Christian life *A Memoir of Daniel MacMillan* (1882).

HUGO, VICTOR MARIE (1802–1885), was born at Besançon, in the Maison Barette, Place St. Quentin, Feb. 26, 1802. His father was Joseph Léopold Sigisbert Hugo (1774–1828), and although Victor Hugo has hinted at the antiquity of his family, even suggesting that Hougoumont on the field of Waterloo was originally *Hugo mons*, and belonged to his ancestors, there is no record by which these hints can be verified. His mother, Sophie Trébuchet, was the daughter of a ship-owner of Nantes. Victor, at birth, was so small and sickly that it was thought he would not live. His father's military career took him first to Italy, where he served under Joseph Bonaparte, was governor of Arellino, and captured the brigand Fra Diavolo, and then to Spain. His wife and children followed him, and those early impressions of Italy and Spain seem never to have left the poet. Thus the first Spanish town in which he stopped on the way to Madrid was Ernani, and among the instructors at the College of Nobles, which he and his brothers attended at Madrid, was a hunchback named Corcova, from whom grew *Quasimodo* and *Triboulet*. In 1812 Madame Hugo returned to Paris and settled again at the deserted convent of the Feuillantines, where during 1808–11 Victor's childhood had been spent, and where he had had for instructor General Lahorie, a proscribed conspirator who was finally tracked to this hiding-place and shot. Larivière, a former priest, also had a share in Victor's education at that time. The downfall of the Bonapartists in Spain cut off the salary of General Hugo, who had been created count and aide of King Joseph, and obliged his family to move into smaller quarters. Victor was a great reader, taking especial delight in Capt. Cook's *Voyages*, and, like the youthful Goethe, amused himself with mimic theatrical performances. In 1815 he entered the boarding-school of M. Decotte, where he remained for three years, attending also lectures at the Collège Louis-le-Grand. Many copy-books filled with poems on many subjects and in many styles—including a drama, *Irtamène*, written at fourteen, and *Inez de Castro* at sixteen—prove that the boy was already instinct with poetic emotions. The author of the *Génie du Christianisme* was then Victor's hero: "Je veux être Châteaubriand ou rien," he wrote in his diary, July 12, 1816, and he preferred reading that heavy work rather than studying mathematics. In 1817 he competed for the prize offered by the Academy for the best poem on "The Advantages of Study." The Immortals hardly believed that his 320 verses were the work of a boy of fifteen; his precocity astonished literary Paris and earned him the acquaintance of many literary magnates. Châteaubriand called him "a sublime child" and invited him to his house; Neufchâteau, another Academician, petted him, and appropriated a criticism prepared by him on *Gil Blas*. In 1819 Hugo took two prizes for poetry at the Floral Games of the Academy of Toulouse, writing upon *The Virgins of Verdun* and *The Statue of Henry IV.*; the next year his *Moses on the Nile* was also successful.

By this time he was fairly launched in literature. After the Restoration his mother and he lived permanently at Paris, and he echoed her strong royalist and Vendean politics; Comte Hugo, whose previous republican and Bonapartist record deprived him of Bourbon favors, lived in retreat at Blois. Victor, in 1820, joined his brother Abel in editing *Le Conservateur Littéraire*, in which first appeared *Bug-Jargal*. He was already in love with Adèle Foucher, but both were too poor to think of marrying. Just at this time the death of his mother, to whom he was devotedly attached, wrought a gradual change in his views, political and religious, although it must be admitted that in religion that admirable and strong woman wished her sons to think for themselves. For a year Victor lived in great straits, having only 700 francs. Then the publication of *Hans d' Islande* (1823), a grotesque novel, preceded by the collection of *Odes* (1822), assured him a prominent position among the young generation of writers. In October, 1822, he had married, and shortly after Louis XVIII. bestowed upon him an annual pension of 1500 francs, thereby encouraging, as he thought, talents which should bring glory to Bourbonism. But Hugo was hurrying towards opposite opinions. He felt the inspiration of Romanticism more deeply than any of his associates, and was soon looked up to as their leader. In 1826, when *Bug Jargal* was published, it was extolled by *Le Globe*, the organ of the Romantics, which had then a corps of contributors of unrivalled strength, who were pushing the war upon the "Classics" to a crisis. This vast literary movement cannot be more than referred to here. It represented the reassertion of the individual; the refusal to bow before authority based only on tradition; the declaration that the nineteenth century should choose its own methods and use its own voice instead of mimicking the methods and voices of other ages. In Germany, Goethe, Lessing, and Schiller had already emancipated their literature; in England, Wordsworth and Coleridge, followed by Byron and Shelley, had at last got the mastery over the imitators of the imitative Pope, but in France the contest was still undecided. The "Golden Age" of French literature belonged to the artificial reign of Louis XIV., so that the models to be followed—especially in the drama—required obsequious observance of the "three unities," of time, of place, of theme. Moreover, the French Academy, always ready to place an elephantine foot upon non-academic productions, was particularly conservative in the first decade of this century. Finally the political reaction after the fall of Napoleon extended to literature, and delayed by several years the expression in literary form of the spirit which had impelled the Revolution of 1789. To these causes may be attributed the retardation in France. Although Victor Hugo's early poems had proceeded from no conscious rebellion against the old school, and although he was a legitimist at heart, it is easy now to see in their grace, variety, and naturalness an intuitive predilection for Romanticism. Another instalment of *Odes* and the *Ballades* in 1826 fixed the impression made by his earlier works. By this time he was an open and vigorous champion of the new school. In a long preface to *Cromwell* (December, 1827,) he boldly preached the new gospel. We have the account of a dinner at which Hugo sat beside Talma and recited to him scenes from this then unpublished drama, which converted the great actor to the young poet's views; but Talma died too soon to act in any of Hugo's plays. *Cromwell* was not intended for the stage. *Amy Robsart* (1828), based upon *Kenilworth*, and written in collaboration with Ancelot, was hissed after one representation at the Odeon.

Then follow three years of wonderful fertility and triumph. In January, 1829, appeared *Les Orientales*, a volume of lyrics in which the poet's rich genius is fully developed. Three weeks later a pamphlet, *Le Dernier Jour d'un Condamné*, contained the first of many vehement protests against capital punishment. In twenty-four days of June he wrote his third drama, *Marion de Lorme* (first entitled *Un Duel sous Richelieu*). An imposing gathering, in which were Balzac, Dumas, and Alfred de Musset, listened to Hugo's reading of this piece, and applauded without reserve. The chance of presenting it on the stage was not lacking, but the Polignac Ministry and Charles X. then ruled. M. Hugo was invited to confer with the censor, Martignac, who pretended to discover disloyal allusions in the 4th act. Hugo declared that the words used by the king in the drama had no political significance. Nevertheless, Charles X., who also summoned the poet to an interview, prohibited the representation, but tried to conciliate Hugo by offering to increase his pension to 6000 francs—an offer which he refused. Not discouraged, Hugo soon produced another drama, *Hernani, ou l'Honneur Castillan*, which was performed at the Théâtre Français, February 25, 1830. The story of that Saturday night has been often told. "Classics" and "Romantics" foresaw that the supreme hour was at hand. The former rallied to hiss; the latter, wearing red badges with the watchword *hierro*, which Hugo had distributed among them, crowded to applaud. The boxes were filled by persons distinguished in rank, letters, or art, who joined in the tumult of the partisans in the pit. Many of the "Romantics" decked themselves in extravagant costumes—Théophile Gautiér's scarlet waistcoat became famous—and as the piece proceeded and the champions of Hugo and *Jeune France* were victorious the disorder grew. In the entr'actes verbal quarrels led to blows. Mlle. Mars, then 51 years old and not in sympathy with Romanticism, played Doña Sol; Firmin was Hernani. The press, with the exception of the *Jour*-

nal des Débats, condemned the drama, but it could not be crushed, and for two months it was repeated, often amid storms like that of the first night. The Cénacle, or club of "Romantics," now ruled French literature and Victor Hugo ruled the Cénacle, whose head-quarters were his rooms in the Place Royale. He and his colleagues were called barbarians by the "Classics." "We accept the comparison," rejoined P. de Saint-Victor. "Where Attila passed, the grass grew no more; where Victor Hugo, Lamartine, Saint Beuve, Théophile Gautier, George Sand, Alfred de Musset have passed the mournful thistles and the artificial flowers of the pseudo-classics will never sprout again." Almost immediately another volume of poems, *Les Feuilles d'Automne*, appeared to widen Hugo's fame. Victorious in lyric and dramatic poetry he next conquered the headship in romance. On July 27, 1830—just before the Revolution exploded which blew Charles X. into exile—he began a semi-historical novel, placing the scene at Paris in the reign of Louis XI. On Jan. 14, 1831, his story and the bottle of ink he had used in writing it were ended together—a coincidence which suggested the title, *Ce qu'il y a dans une bouteille d'encre*. A month later the work was published under the name *Notre Dame de Paris*. This great work fairly represents the strength and weakness of Victor Hugo's genius. Here are chapters of tempestuous passion followed by chapters of dry and inaccurate history or archæology. Here is the tremendous guilt of the villain, Frollo, contrasted with the exquisite simplicity and naiveté of Esmeralda. The shadows are all the blacker from the intense light. No one but Victor Hugo would have hazarded the minute description of Frollo's death, and no one but him could have created Quasimodo, that reformed Caliban to whose brutal instinct of ferocity has been added the instinct of love. In *Notre Dame de Paris*, as in all of Hugo's characteristic work, we find amazing instances of his lack of humor—that safeguard against extravagance and bombast. In one place he describes one of the characters as pulling out his hair by handfuls to see if it was turning white in the agony he was suffering! In another place an unfortunate attempts to wrench his head from his shoulders in order to dash it to the ground! Evidently, the author sometimes misses the sublime and plunges into the ridiculous. But in spite of its defects there are few novels that make so deep an impression on the reader as *Notre Dame de Paris*: it is one of the books about which it is impossible to remain indifferent. Critics gave it but faint praise when it appeared, but it sold rapidly and has long been familiar wherever European languages are read. In 1832, in the 8th edition, Hugo added the chapters, "Impopularité," "Abbas Beati Martini," and "Ceci tuera cela."

Thus successful in the field of romance, Hugo now devoted himself once more to the theatre. Under the new king the censorship was relaxed and *Marion de Lorme* was produced at the Porte St. Martin Theatre, Aug. 11, 1831. Madame Dorval played the part of the heroine; M. Bocage that of Didier. The tumultuous scenes of 1830 were repeated: "Classics" hissed and groaned; "Romantics" applauded and cheered. *Marion de Lorme* was successful—having a run of 63 nights—although in a smaller degree than *Hernani*. On June 1, 1832, Hugo began *Le Roi s'Amuse* and, writing with his usual speed, it was soon finished and given to M. Taylor, director of the Comédie Française, where it was at once put in rehearsal. The parts were distributed as follows: Triboulet, M. Ligier; St. Vallier, M. Joanny; François I., M. Perrier; Blanche, Mlle Anaïs. Shortly before the opening performance, M. d'Argout, Minister of Public Works, informed Hugo that certain passages in the drama savored of disloyalty. Hugo replied that what he had written had no reference to Louis Philippe but to Francis I. On Nov. 22, 1832, the play was produced. The author's partisans sang the "Marseillaise" and the "Carmagnole." His enemies were louder than ever. To add to the confusion the report spread that the king had been shot. On the morrow critics denounced *Le Roi s'Amuse* as indecent, monstrous, horrible, seditious. Louis Philippe was worked upon by politicians and academic "Classics," and an order was issued forbidding a repetition. Victor Hugo then replied in a manifesto, defending his play against the charge of immorality. Two lawsuits were brought, one by him against the Comédie Française for failing to fulfil its contract; the other by the management of the theatre against the Minister of Public Works for compensation. Needless to say, when freedom of speech is controlled by government censorship, the government will take care that courts of justice shall support itself: judgment was rendered against the poet and the theatre. This rebuff discouraged neither Hugo nor his friends, and in a few weeks his prose drama *Lucrèce Borgia* was in rehearsal at the Port St. Martin Theatre under the direction of M. Harel. The cast on the first night (Feb. 2, 1833) included M. Frédéric Lemaître as Gennaro; M. Delafosse as Alfonse d'Este; Mlle. Georges as Lucrèce Borgia, and Mlle. Juliette as Princesse Negroni. Victor Hugo has written as follows in regard to these two plays which were begotten almost simultaneously in 1832: "Embody a mother even within a monster, and the monster will not fail to excite interest, and perhaps sympathy. Physical deformity, sanctified by paternal love, this is what you have in *Le Roi s'Amuse*; moral deformity, purified by maternal love, this is what you find in *Lucrèce Borgia*." At the same theatre, on Nov. 6, 1833, was presented *Marie Tudor* (originally entitled *Marie d'Angleterre, ou Souvent Femme Varie*), with Mlle. Georges again in the leading part. That admirable actress, although 47 years old, still divided with her elder rival, Mlle. Mars, the honors of the Parisian stage; it was in this very year that the Jewish girl who was destined to succeed and surpass them both entered the Conservatory. *Marie Tudor* was successful, and was followed on April 28, 1835, by *Angélo, Tyran de Padoue*, at the Théâtre Français, Mlle. Mars and Mme. Dorval appearing in the chief rôles. Victor Hugo now returned to verse—*Marie Tudor* and *Angélo* are in prose—and wrote the libretto of an opera called *Esmeralda*, the story being borrowed from *Notre Dame de Paris*. Mlle. Bertin, daughter of the editor of the *Journal des Débats*, composed the music for this piece, which failed at its production at the Royal Academy, Nov. 14, 1836. At the new theatre of the Renaissance, on Nov. 8, 1838, was brought out the last of Hugo's successful dramas, *Ruy Blas*, which ran for fifty nights, with Lemaître as the lackey-lover. His vogue began to grow dim; the public was used to his victories, and younger men, taught in his school, received attention. He tried once more, however, in his trilogy, *Les Burgraves*, to compel admiration. This work was produced at the Comédie Française, March 8, 1843, and withdrawn after 30 representations. Thenceforward, Victor Hugo invariably refused to give any new piece to be performed during his life, although he did not relinquish dramatic writing. *Torquemada, La Grand' mère, L' Épée, Peut-être Frère de Gavroche*, and a pantomime in which trees and flowers talk, *La Forêt Mouillée*, must be added to his work as a dramatist. Of these *Torquemada* was published in 1882.

During this remarkable period of fifteen years between the publication of *Cromwell* and the production of *Les Burgraves*, Victor Hugo's energy was incessant. Besides the works mentioned, he published in 1834 an essay upon Mirabeau. In 1835 *Les Chants du Crépuscule* appeared. The lyrics in this volume are less glowing and fanciful than those in *Les Orientales*; the poet has left the East, where his imagination wandered freely among gorgeous colors and beautiful objects, and he now faces the realities of life in a period when doubt prevails, and no man can say whether the twilight will deepen into night or brighten into morning. Two years later, in *Les Voix Intérieures*, he offered variations on this theme. He dedicated the volume to his father, "Joseph Léopold Sigisbert, Count Hugo, a name inscribed on the Arch of Triumph de l'Étoile." *Les Rayons et les Ombres* (1840) completes what has been called his *gray* manner. These volumes of lyrics cannot be matched in French poetry, either for variety or melody, for power or delicacy. A tour into Germany resulted in a book of travel, *Le Rhin* (1842).

In France, since 1789, all paths lead to politics; the poet, the artist, the general, the journalist, if he achieve but the smallest success in his calling, is almost sure to be drawn into the whirlpool of public affairs. It is not surprising that Victor Hugo, whose plays had kindled political as well as literary wrangling, and who was ambitious to shine as a statesman, hailed the opportunity by which he expected to take his place among his country's law-makers. After his mother's death he outgrew the Bourbon doctrines in which he had been brought up, but not before he had addressed an eulogistic ode to Charles X., whom he subsequently despised. Then followed a period during which he fell under the spell of the Napoleonic legend, when he admired the glory which Frenchmen, while serving Napoleon, had won for France, but this admiration for the past did not prevent him from accepting the reign of Louis Philippe. In 1836 Victor Hugo was a candidate to the French Academy, not only because his election to that body would confer an official recognition upon his literary fame, but also because it was the stepping-stone to the peerage. He was defeated by Dupaty, an obscure person, whose qualifications were meagre. "I always thought," said Hugo, "that the way to the Academy was across the Pont des Arts; I find that it is across the Pont Neuf." In 1839 he was defeated by Molé, ex-premier, and in 1840 by Flourens, now forgotten. At length, in 1841, he was elected in place of Népomucène Lemercier. Among those who voted against him were Delavigne and Scribe. Balzac retired from the candidacy, rather than lessen the chances of his friend, and was never made an "immortal." Victor Hugo took his seat June 3, 1841. Four years later, April 13, 1845, he was made a peer. In the Chamber he spoke in favor of literary and artistic copyright; in behalf of Poland, of coast defences, of the petition of Jerome Napoleon Bonaparte to be allowed to return to France. When the Revolution of 1848 sent Louis Philippe into exile, Victor Hugo supported the republic as a means to liberty. In June he was elected to the assembly, his name standing on the list between those of Leroux and Louis Napoleon. Although nominally a member of the Moderate party, he soon discovered democratic preferences to which he had long been tending. Of the insurrection of June he wrote afterwards: "The very thing that made it terrible was that it demanded respect. It was the outcome of a people's despair. The first duty of the Republic was to suppress the revolt; the next was to pardon it." This was the attitude held by Victor Hugo towards the Communists of 1871. On August 1, 1848, he started *L'Événement*, P. Meurice, Théophile Gautier, Vacquerie, A. Vitu, and Charles and François Hugo being its foremost contributors. This journal hinted at Victor Hugo as the proper candidate for the presidency. In the Legislative Assembly he came out boldly as a democrat and socialist. As president of the Peace Congress—Cobden was vice-president—(Aug. 21, 1849), he denounced French intervention at Rome. Frequent were his oratorical contests during the next three years, memorable among them being his replies to Montalembert, (who charged him with deserting the principles of his younger days, and taunted him by quoting from Hugo's Bourbon odes,) and his stubborn opposition to the re-election of Louis Napoleon. The *coup d'état* put Hugo's name at the head of the proscribed; 25,000 francs were offered for his capture, dead or alive; and, after being concealed for five days in the house of a royalist marquis, he escaped to Brussels in the disguise of a workman.

There began an exile which proved the genuine nobility of Hugo's character. Between December, 1851, and May, 1852, he wrote *L'Histoire d'un Crime* (published in 1877), and *Napoléon le Petit* soon followed it. The publication of this terrific satire caused the passage of the Faider law, by which Hugo was compelled to leave Belgium. On Aug. 5, 1852, he landed at Jersey, where his home was, at Marine Terrace, until 1855, when the English government—then in alliance with Napoleon III.—requested him to depart. He settled at Hauteville House, on the island of Guernsey. In 1853 *Les Châtiments* renewed in verse the attack upon the emperor. In spite of police scrutiny thousands of copies of this work were introduced into France. Hugo's income was reduced to 7000 francs at the time of his exile, and in spite of the large sale of these satires he realized little from them; but in 1856 he was more fortunate with *Les Contemplations*, a poetical record in two volumes of the poet's life, chiefly previous to 1843. In 1859 came the first part of *La Légende des Siècles*, a vast epic work whose aim it is to describe the progress of the human race from the days of Adam to the French Revolution, by presenting typical pictures of each epoch. In 1862 *Les Misérables* was issued simultaneously in Paris, Brussels, London, New York, Milan, Leipsic, Antwerp, Madrid, Warsaw, Pesth, and Rio Janeiro. This is Hugo's master-piece in prose. It consists of five volumes, entitled: *Fantine, Cosette, Marius, L'Idylle Rue Plumet et l'Épopée Rue Saint-Denis*, and *Jean Valjean*. The author wrote: "It is a sort of planetary system, making the circuit about one giant mind that is the personification of all social evil." The success of this colossal work was instantaneous; no other book has since created so immediate and profound an international sensation. In 1866 *Les Travailleurs de la Mer*, with Guernsey and fisher-folk for its background and characters, appeared. In 1869 *L'Homme Qui Rit* followed, but it fell far below its predecessors. Whilst engaged with these productions

Hugo was also writing his prose rhapsody on *William Shakespeare*, which served as a preface to his son's translation of Shakespeare into French (1864), and his *Chansons des Rues et des Bois* (1865), a collection of light and beautiful verse. From his retreat Hugo's voice was often heard in behalf of the oppressed. He appealed to the United States to save John Brown's life; to Juarez to spare Maximilian; to Europe to aid the Cretans; to the Spaniards to cease persecuting the Cubans. His life-long opposition to capital punishment evoked many passionate pleas from him. Besides *Le Dernier Jour d'un Condamné* (published in 1829; reprinted with a preface in 1832), he published *Claude Gueux* (1834); interceded for A. Barbès, 1839; for Joseph Henry, 1846, and Lecomte, 1847, who had fired at the king; spoke in favor of the abolition of capital punishment, in the Assembly, 1848; defended his son Charles, who had been arrested for condemning, in his newspaper, an execution, 1851—this being one of Hugo's finest orations. More recently he begged for the lives of nihilists, socialists, anarchists, and Irish invincibles. At the time of the Universal Exposition at Paris the emperor allowed *Hernani* to be performed at the Théâtre Français, and the occasion was made a triumph of the exiled poet by his friends. The popularity of the drama proved its vitality. In 1869 the Empire was beginning to be sensible of the hostility of its republican enemies, whom Hugo encouraged from his island refuge. *Le Rappel* newspaper was founded by the men who had managed *L'Événement* in 1848, assisted by Henri Rochefort and by contributions from Hugo.

At last the ignominy of Sédan recalled the patriot from banishment. On Sept. 5, 1870, he re-entered Paris. He issued almost immediately an address to the Germans, bidding them to come to Paris, but as friends. "This war does not proceed from us," he wrote. "It was the Empire that willed the war; it was the Empire that prosecuted it. But now the Empire is dead, and a good thing, too! We have nothing to do with its corpse; it is all the past; we are the future.... Pause awhile before you present to the world the spectacle of Germans becoming Vandals, and of barbarism decapitating civilization. Victory will not be for your honor." But the Germans did not pause; their armies rapidly conquered French territory and invested Paris. On Sept. 17 Hugo issued an appeal to his countrymen to rise and arm. At the general election on Feb. 8, 1871, he was elected representative for the department of the Seine, being second among 43 candidates. He acted with the extreme Left; opposed the ratification of peace and the cession of Alsace and Lorraine; and, on March 8, being interrupted in the tribune whilst defending Garibaldi, he resigned from the assembly. Ten days later he escorted to Paris the body of his son Charles, who had suddenly died, and thence proceeded to Brussels, where he abode during the Reign of Terror. When the Communists were worsted by the troops from Versailles, Hugo offered them a refuge in his house—an offer which caused a Brussels mob to attack his dwelling. Expelled from Belgium he shortly returned to Paris. At the election in July, and again in December, he was beaten at the polls, but his active sympathy was constantly given to the Radicals. In 1876 he was elected life-senator, sitting with the extreme Left. He supported a measure for extending amnesty to the condemned Communists, which was rejected, and favored civilization. When it became evident that Mr. ...

was intriguing with Bonapartists for a return of the Empire, he published *L'Histoire d'un Crime* to refresh the memory of the Napoleonic crime of 1851. During the last years of his life Victor Hugo was the idol of Paris. Placed above political parties and literary cliques, his countrymen accepted him as their national hero. If his views upon public affairs were too vague or extravagant to be followed, the patriotism that inspired them was unassailable. His later works were *Actes et Paroles* (1876), a further contribution in prose to the understanding of his political career and creed; *L'Année Terrible* (1872), a record in verse of the horrors of the war and of the siege of Paris; *La Libération du Territoire* (September, 1873), a poem, and *Pour un Soldat* (1875), a pamphlet, for the benefit of the people of Lorraine and Alsace; *Quatre-vingt-treize* (1874), his last powerful romance, dealing with Britany in 1793, published simultaneously in seven or eight languages; the second part of *La Légende des Siècles* and *L'Art d'être Grand-père* (1877), a charming volume of verse, in which the poet's love for children is immortalized; *Le Pape* (1878), a picture of an ideal spiritual sovereign; *La Pitié Suprême* (1880), a further plea for tolerance; *L'Ane* (1880), a satire aimed at pedantry; *Les Quatre Vents de l'Esprit* (1881-83); *Torquemada* (1882), a drama; and *L'Archipel de la Manche*. On the fiftieth anniversary of *Hernani* (Feb. 25, 1880), a jubilee performance was given at the Comédie Française, Hugo's bust being crowned by Sarah Bernhardt, who enacted Doña Sol. Again, at the completion of his 79th year, Feb. 27, 1881, the poet was fêted by multitudes of his admirers, including a procession of children, at his residence in the Avenue d'Eylau. He retained his health and activity until within a few days of his death, which occurred Friday, May 22, 1885, of congestion of the lungs. He was given a state burial at the Pantheon ten days later, and not even Paris, the home of vast pageants, ever conducted so stupendous a public spectacle. Victor Hugo left 100,000 francs to the poor of Paris, and bequeathed his manuscripts to the Bibliothèque Nationale. His fortune was estimated at 5,000,000 francs. It is understood that several volumes of his posthumous works will eventually be published.

Of Victor Hugo's place in the world's literature it is still too early to speak. No other author while living—not even Petrarch, or Voltaire, or Goethe—achieved such unbounded national popularity as his. In romance he stood first, although his rivals were George Sand and Balzac; in lyrical poetry he stood first, in spite of Lamartine and Alfred de Musset; in the drama he had no near competitor. He gave to French rhythm a strength and variety it had never known, and invented a prose style which is singularly effective when used by him. His range of character-creation is very broad. He depicts the immensity of the ocean, the battle of Waterloo, the horrors of the Vendée, the innocent prattle of little children, with equal mastery. He possessed the genius of emotion to the highest degree; of reflection, of wisdom, he had but little. Hence the strange unevenness in his works, their inaccuracy and exaggeration. Controlled wholly by impulse, he lacked a corrective sense of humor, which might have dissipated his egotism. He seems the supreme embodiment of the Gallic type; versatile, mercurial, enthusiastic, delighting in the half-truths of the epigram, demanding brilliance at any cost, readily ...ng new ideas and embarking on new schemes.

sympathizing with those who suffer, and sincerely rhetorical. In his works he is always the eloquent and fearless advocate pleading in behalf of the downtrodden—the champion of the outcast against society which has cast them out. He has the brilliance and eloquence and sometimes the sophistry of the special pleader. A true orator, he knows the magic which sways the heart, if not the head. Whatever may be the value of this power as compared with the impersonal majesty of Shakespeare or Sophocles, Victor Hugo's endowment of it is unmatched. Be it further recorded that his impulses were ever noble: he refused pensions from Bourbons and soft promises of amnesty from Napoleon III. rather than sell his freedom of speech; he succored the distressed; and forgave all enemies except those of liberty. And in an age when his ablest contemporaries treated chastity and the ties of family with contempt, he was steadfastly on the side of morality. His creed was deistic—he believed in immortality. He belongs with Montaigne and Molière at the head of French literature.

Victor Hugo's father died in 1828; his wife in 1868. He had two brothers: Abel (1798-1855), a writer upon historical and literary subjects, and Eugène (1801-1837), who wrote verse. Victor Hugo had three children: Leopoldine, who was drowned with her husband, Charles Vacquerie, at Villequier, Sept. 4, 1843, a few months after their marriage; Charles (1826-1871), and François (1828-1873), whose *Ile de Jersey* (1857) and *Œuvres Complètes de Shakespeare* (1864) entitle him to a place among the less conspicuous French writers of the last generation. Victor Hugo's living descendants are his grandson, Georges, and his granddaughter, Jeanne, children of Charles Hugo, whose widow married M. Charles Lockroy.

A vast amount of material exists for the study of Hugo's career. Besides his autobiographic works, above mentioned, his wife wrote *Victor Hugo Raconté par un Témoin de sa Vie* (2 vols.), in which the first forty years of his life are related; *Victor Hugo et Son Temps*, by Alfred Barbon, and *Victor Hugo chez lui*, by Gustave Rivet, are the works of Hugolaters. The works of Sainte-Beuve, Jules Janin, Lamartine, and, indeed, of all the participators in the romantic movement, may be consulted. In English there are essays by G. H. Lewes, F. H. W. Myers, John Morley, Lady Pollock, A. C. Swinburne, A. R. Spofford, Leslie Stephen, Henry James, E, Dowden, G. Saintsbury, John Burroughs, H. H. Boyesen, and many others. In Spanish Castelar, in Italian Edmondo dé Amicis, etc. Hugo's dramas and romances have furnished the plots of many libretti. (W. R. T.)

HULL, ISAAC (1775-1843), an American commodore, was born at Derby, Conn., March 9, 1775. His father had been an officer in the Revolution. Isaac having entered the merchant service, had command of a vessel to London at the age of 19. In 1798 he entered the U. S. navy as lieutenant. In 1800 he manned a small sloop from the U. S. ship Constitution, ran into Port Platte, Hayti, and captured a French letter-of-marque. He then landed and spiked the guns of a battery on shore, before its commander could prepare for defence. He afterwards distinguished himself in the attacks on Tripoli, assisted Gen. Eaton in capturing Derne, and in the Bay of Naples protected American vessels against the French. In April, 1806, he was made captain. When the war of 1812 opened Hull had command of the frigate Constitution of 54 guns, and in July, while cruising off New York, was pursued by a British squadron of five vessels, but by splendid seamanship escaped them, after a chase of nearly three days and nights. Spending a few days in Boston harbor, he sailed again on Aug. 2, and on Aug. 19 encountered the British frigate Guerriere of 49 guns, Capt. Dacres. The latter hove to for an engagement, and commenced firing at 5 P. M. An hour later the ships grappled, and after half an hour's hard fighting the Guerriere surrendered, having been reduced to a wreck. When she began to sink on the next day the prisoners were removed, and the vessel being set on fire soon blew up. In this action the Constitution suffered chiefly in her rigging; her loss in killed and wounded was only 14, while that of the Guerriere was 79. This being the first naval action of the war, created a great sensation. Capt. Hull was enthusiastically received on his arrival in Boston. Congress ordered a gold medal to be presented to Capt. Hull, silver medals to each commissioned officer under him, and $50,000 to the crew. After the war Hull was a naval commissioner, and also had command of the navy-yards at Boston, Portsmouth, and Washington. In October, 1842, he took up his residence at Philadelphia, and died there Feb. 13, 1843.

HULL, WILLIAM (1753-1825), an American general, was born at Derby, Conn., June 24, 1753. He graduated at Yale College in 1772, studied divinity for a year, then turned to law, and was admitted to the bar in 1775. He was appointed captain in a Connecticut regiment, and joined the American army at Cambridge. He fought at White Plains, Trenton, and Princeton, and after the latter was promoted to be major of a Massachusetts regiment. He was afterwards engaged at Ticonderoga, Stillwater, Saratoga, Monmouth, and Stony Point. He was made lieutenant-colonel in 1779, and was an inspector under Baron Steuben. For his expedition against Morrisania in January, 1781, he received the thanks of Congress. He was present at the surrender of Cornwallis, and was afterwards sent to Quebec to demand the surrender of Niagara, Detroit, and other Western posts. After the war he practised law at Newton, Mass., and was prominent in the Massachusetts legislature. He was also major-general of the State militia, and in Shays' rebellion commanded the left wing of Lincoln's troops. By a forced march through a snow-storm he surprised the insurgents in their camp and dispersed them. In 1798, on his return from a visit to Europe, he was appointed judge of the court of common pleas. In 1805 he was appointed governor of Michigan Territory, and at the outbreak of the war of 1812 he was made brigadier-general and commander of the Northwestern army, with orders to invade Canada. By mismanagement on the part of the government, the declaration of war had reached the British general, Brock, in Canada, before Hull had received it. The British then surprised and seized the fort at Michilimackinac, and thus brought the hesitating Indian tribes to their side. Hull had crossed into Canada, but afterwards, through distrust of the raw militia who composed his army, retired to Detroit. While half of Hull's force was away getting supplies, Brock crossed the river with over 2000 regulars and Indians and demanded the surrender of Detroit, declaring that he would be unable to restrain the Indians if the place were carried by assault. Hull, knowing the instability of the militia, yielded to his humane feelings and surrendered, thus giving up not only Detroit but also the entire North-west. Col. Lewis Cass, who had commanded a regiment from Ohio, hastened to Washington with the news, and by exaggerated statements produced strong feeling against Hull. The latter was tried by court-martial and condemned to be shot, but Pres. Madison pardoned him in consideration of his past services. In 1814 Gen. Hull published a defence of his conduct, and still later a history of the *Campaign of the North-west Army*, 1812 (1824). He died at Newton, Mass., Nov. 25, 1825. His *Life* was published by his daughter, Mrs. M. Campbell, and by his grandson, Rev. J. Freeman Clarke, in 1848.

HULLAH, JOHN (1812-1884), an English teacher of singing, born at Worcester, June 27, 1812. He studied under Horsley and Crevelli, and in 1836 composed the music for Dickens' opera, *The Village Coquettes*. In 1840, in an effort to popularize the study of music, he established at Exeter Hall his system of singing. St. Martin's Hall was afterwards built for him, but unfortunately was burnt down in 1860. He was professor of vocal music and of harmony in King's College from 1844 to 1874, and in other institutions, and was conductor of the orchestra and chorus at the Royal Academy of Music from 1870 to 1873. From 1872 to 1881 he was musical inspector in the schools of Great Britain. He has done much to improve musical taste and to cultivate a love of music among the people. He, however, opposed the tonic Sol-fa system, which was introduced as an aid for that purpose. Among Mr. Hullah's publications are *A Grammar of Harmony, Grammar of Counterpoint, History of Modern Music, Transition Period of Musical History*. As an acknowledgment of his services in popularizing music, the University of Edinburgh in 1876 conferred on him the degree of LL. D. He died Feb. 21, 1884.

HUMBERT I., RENIER CHARLES EMMANUEL JEAN MARIE FERDINAND EUGENE, King of Italy, was born March 14, 1844, being the son of Victor Emmanuel II. (1820-1878) and of Queen Adelaide (1822-1855). He attended his father during the war of Italian independence in 1859, and took part in the reorganization of the government of the two Sicilies, visiting Naples and Palermo in July, 1862. Before war was declared against Austria in 1866 Prince Humbert visited Paris to sound the French government with regard to Italy's alliance with Prussia. When hostilities commenced he took the field, having command of a division in Gen. Cialdini's army, and was present at the disastrous battle of Custozza, June 23, 1866. He was married at Turin, April 22, 1868, to his cousin, Princess Marie Marguerite Thérèse Jeanne of Savoy. His eldest son, born Nov. 11, 1869, is Victor Emmanuel Ferdinand Mary Januarius, and bears the title Prince of Naples. After Rome was occupied in 1870 by the Italian troops, Prince Humbert took up his residence in Rome. He succeeded to the throne of Italy on the death of his father, Jan. 9, 1878. In November of that year an unsuccessful attempt was made to assassinate him, and when the assassin was afterwards condemned to death, the king commuted the sentence to imprisonment at hard labor. By other actions, showing a kind and gentle disposition, he has won the affection of the people, and especially by his sympathy manifested during the epidemic of cholera at Naples in 1884.

HUMPHREY, HEMAN (1779-1861), an American clergyman, was born at West Simsbury, Conn., March 26, 1779. Having obtained a common-school education he began to teach at the age of sixteen, and afterwards went to Yale College, where he graduated in 1805. He studied theology under Pres. Dwight and was ordained pastor of the Congregational Church at Fairfield in April, 1807. Here he continued ten years and then became pastor of the church in Pittsfield. He was president of Amherst College from October, 1823, to 1845. (See AMHERST COLLEGE, Vol. I.) He then retired to private life, but was a frequent contributor to religious periodicals. He had been one of the pioneers in the temperance reformation, and was a promoter of religious revivals. Among his publications were *A Tour in France, Great Britain, and Belgium* (2 vols., 1838); *Domestic Education* (1840); *Sketches of the History of Revivals* (1859). He died at Pittsfield, Mass., April 3, 1861.

HUMPHREYS, ANDREW ATKINSON, an American general and engineer, was born at Philadelphia, Nov. 2, 1810. He graduated at West Point in 1831, and entered the artillery service. He distinguished himself in the Florida war and became first lieutenant in August, 1832. He resigned his commission, Sept. 30, 1836, but in July, 1838, was appointed first-lieutenant of topographical engineers. He had charge of the coast survey office from 1845 to 1849, and afterwards began the topographic and hydrographic survey of the delta of the Mississippi. In 1854 he took charge of the office of explorations and surveys in the war department, and gave special attention to the selection of a route for a railroad from the Mississippi to the Pacific. He became major Aug. 6, 1861, and in December, 1861, was placed in the staff of Gen. McClellan. Soon after he was made brigadier-general of volunteers, and in September, 1862, commanded a division at Antietam. He was engaged at the battles of Fredericksburg, Chancellorsville, and Gettysburg, and was chief of staff to Gen. Meade. Being placed in command of the Second corps he was engaged in the siege and capture of Petersburg and the pursuit and capture of Lee's army. At the close of the war he received the brevet of major-general, and in 1866 was again engaged in engineering work on the Mississippi. He was appointed chief of engineers, U. S. A., Aug. 8, 1866. He has served on many important commissions, and has published *The Physics and Hydraulics of the Mississippi River* (1867) and other reports. He died Dec. 27, 1883.

HUMPHREYS, DAVID (1752-1818), an American general, was born at Derby, Conn., in July, 1752, being son of Rev. Daniel Humphreys. At the outbreak of the Revolutionary war he entered the army as captain, was aide to Gen. Putnam in 1778, and to Washington in 1780, being then lieutenant-colonel. He distinguished himself at the siege of Yorktown, and being appointed to bear the captured standards to Congress received from it a sword as a testimonial of his services. At the close of the war he accompanied Gen. Washington to Virginia, and in July, 1784, went to France as secretary of legation to Jefferson. Returning to his native town in 1786 he was elected to the legislature, and while at Hartford, in company with Joel Barlow, Hopkins, and Trumbull, published the *Anarchiad*. He was appointed to the command of a regiment for the Western service, and when the troops were not required he visited Washington at Mount Vernon. While here, in 1790, he was appointed minister to Portugal, where he stayed till 1794. After his return to Lisbon in 1797 he was appointed also minister to Spain, and he made treaties with Tripoli and Algiers. Returning to America in 1802 he introduced into this country merino sheep, and established a woollen- and cotton-factory at Derby. As a member of the legislature he was active in 1812 in providing for the defence of the State; he also took command of the State militia. He died at New Haven, Feb. 21, 1818. He was somewhat noted in his day as a poet, publishing among other poems *An Address to the Armies of the United States* (1782), which was translated into French by Chastellux. His writings were collected and published at New York in 1790 and again in 1804.

HUNT, RICHARD MORRIS, an American architect,

was born at Brattleboro, Vt., Oct. 28, 1828. He went to Europe in 1843 and studied at Paris in the school of fine arts. He also made a tour through Europe, Asia Minor, and Egypt, and was employed under Lefuel in the erection of the building connecting the palaces of the Tuileries and the Louvre. Returning to America in 1855 he was engaged on the extension of the capitol at Washington. Among the buildings since designed by him are the Lenox Library, the Stuyvesant building, and the Tribune building, New York; the Yale Divinity College, New Haven; and many residences in Boston, Newport, and elsewhere.

His brother, WILLIAM MORRIS HUNT, an American painter, was born at Brattleboro, Vt., March 31, 1824. He studied for a time at Harvard College, then went to Europe, and in 1846 began to study sculpture at Düsseldorf; soon afterwards he removed to Paris, where he studied painting under Couture. He returned to the United States in 1855, opened studios both at Boston and Newport, though he also made frequent visits to Europe. Besides many portraits he painted sketches of types of street life in Paris, and incidents of the American civil war, as The Drummer Boy, The Bugle Call. His allegorical paintings in the State capitol at Albany are the finest mural paintings in the United States. His landscapes are admirable for their truth, force, and refinement. He died Sept. 8, 1879, at Isles of Shoals, N. H.

HUNT, THOMAS STERRY, an American chemist and geologist, was born at Norwich, Conn., Sept. 5, 1826. After entering on the study of medicine he devoted himself to chemistry, under the direction of Prof. B. Silliman at Yale College. In 1847 he was called to be chemist and mineralogist in the geological survey of Canada under Sir William Logan. While holding this position he was also for some years professor of chemistry in McGill College, Montreal, and in the University of Quebec. In 1872 he became professor of geology in the Massachusetts Institute of Technology. In 1855 and again in 1867 he was a member of the international jury at the Paris exhibitions, and is a member of many learned societies. He has published many important papers on theoretical chemistry, mineralogy, and dynamic geology. These have appeared in the *American Journal of Science* and the scientific journals of both Europe and America.

HUNT, WILLIAM HOLMAN, an English painter, was born at London in 1827. He studied in the school of the Royal Academy, and in 1846 exhibited his first picture, Hark. He then painted some scenes from Sir Walter Scott, Keats, and Bulwer, but in 1850 he exhibited his Converted British Family Sheltering a Christian Missionary from the Persecution of the Druids. This was the public announcement of the new school of Pre-Raphaelitism which had been formed by Hunt, Millais, and D. G. Rossetti. A strong current of thought and feeling had been directed towards study of the Middle Ages. These young painters, moved by this pervading influence, thought they had discovered in the painters preceding Raphael a closer study of nature than afterwards prevailed in art. They determined in their own work to copy nature's works with the utmost minuteness and accuracy. Hunt was the true leader and exponent of the school. Among his earlier works are Valentine Rescuing Sylvia from Proteus (1851) and Hireling Shepherd (1853). Then came in 1855 two powerful pictures, The Awakened Conscience and The Light of the World. These brought the discussion of the theory of Pre-Raphaelitism to a crisis, and Ruskin entered the lists on their behalf. Henceforth the painters were left free to follow the bent of their inclinations, the result in each case being judged on its own merits without reference to the method exemplified. Determining to paint sacred subjects Hunt went to Palestine and, as the result of a summer's study on the shores of the Dead Sea, gave to the world in 1856 The Scapegoat. He afterwards made his home at Jerusalem and only rarely visited England. His Christ Discovered in the Temple is one of the noblest results of his devotion to transcendentalism in art. It has been followed by The Flight into Egypt and The Shadow of Death, which show the same marvellous combination of intense energy of conception with minute realism in details.

HUNTER, DAVID (1802–1886), an American general, was born at Washington, D. C., July 21, 1802. He graduated at West Point in 1822, and after being long engaged on frontier duty resigned in 1836. In 1842 he was made paymaster with rank of major, and so continued until the outbreak of the civil war. On May 14, 1861, he was made colonel of the Sixth U. S. cavalry, and on May 17 brigadier-general of volunteers. He commanded a division at Bull Run, where he was wounded. In August he became major-general of volunteers and in November succeeded Gen. Fremont in command of the Western department. On March 31, 1862, he was transferred to the department of the South, and soon after issued a general order declaring free all slaves in Georgia, Florida, and South Carolina. But on May 19 Pres. Lincoln issued a proclamation, annulling this order, and postponing for the present the decision of the question of granting freedom to slaves. An unsuccessful expedition against Charleston followed. In order to provide for the slaves who had been left on the island plantations by fugitive masters Gen. Hunter organized the First South Carolia volunteers, and Jefferson Davis thereupon issued a proclamation declaring Hunter an outlaw, who if captured should be treated as a felon. The government soon after appointed Gen. Rufus Saxton to superintend the freedmen and employ them in cultivating the abandoned lands. In September Hunter was recalled to Washington. In May, 1864, he was placed in command of the department of West Virginia, and set out on an expedition against Lynchburg. Before he reached that city a large Confederate force arrived and compelled him to retreat. He received the brevet of major-general March 13, 1865, and was retired July 31, 1866. He died at Washington, Feb. 2, 1886.

HUNTER, ROBERT MERCER TALIAFERRO, an American statesman, was born in Essex co., Va., April 21, 1809. He was educated at the University of Virginia, and having studied law at the Virginia Law-School was admitted to the bar in 1830. He was elected to the House of Delegates in 1834, and to Congress in 1837. He was chosen speaker in 1839, after a memorable struggle in which the venerable John Quincy Adams had organized the House, when the clerk refused to do his duty. Hunter was again returned to Congress in 1845, where he supported the tariff bill of 1846, and originated the warehouse system. In 1847 he entered the U. S. Senate and took a leading part in its debates, as an advocate of States' rights, until July, 1861. He strenuously resisted any interference by the general government with the institution of slavery, and maintained the right of the slaveholder to carry his slaves to any Territory. He was chairman of the finance committee from 1849 to

1861, and to prevent the exportation of silver he initiated the reduction in actual value of the subsidiary coins of the country. He opposed the homestead bill and the river and harbor bill, and framed the tariff act of 1857, which lowered the duties and reduced the revenues. In 1860 he was a prominent candidate for the presidential nomination at the Democratic National Convention in Charleston. He was active in the secession movement, and it is said that, according to the original plan of the leaders, Hunter was to be president of the Confederacy, while Jefferson Davis was to be commander-in-chief of the army. The delay in the secession of Virginia prevented this, and in July, 1861, Hunter was expelled from the U. S. Senate. He became secretary of state in the Confederate cabinet, but was afterwards superseded by J. P. Benjamin. Hunter, being elected to the Confederate Senate, became an opponent of Davis' administration. In February, 1865, Hunter, in company with A. H. Stephens and Campbell, met Pres. Lincoln and Seward in a conference at Hampton Roads, to consider the possibility of terminating the war. Pres. Lincoln absolutely refused to recognize the independence of the Confederacy, which the Southern leaders proposed as a basis of negotiation. When Gen. Lee and others asked for the arming of negroes as soldiers in the Confederate service, Hunter resisted the proposal, although when instructed by the legislature of Virginia to vote for it he did so. At the close of the war he was arrested but released on parole, and in 1867 he was pardoned by Pres. Johnson. In 1874 he was a candidate for U. S. Senator, but was not elected. In 1885 he was appointed a collector of customs. He died July 18, 1887.

HUNTINGTON, DANIEL, an American painter, was born at New York, Oct. 14, 1816. He was educated at Hamilton College, and studied painting under Prof. S. F. B. Morse and Henry Inman. Among his early works are The Bar-Room Politician, The Toper Asleep, and some landscapes. He went to Italy in 1839, and there painted The Sibyl, Early Christian Prisoner, and other works. Returning to New York he painted portraits, and Mercy's Dream, and Christiana and her Children. Owing to inflammation of the eyes he relinquished his work, but afterwards resumed it in Italy. After returning to New York in 1846, he painted many portraits, but also historical scenes, such as Queen Mary Signing the Death warrant of Lady Jane Grey. He became a member of the National Academy in 1840, was its president from 1862 to 1869, and was again elected in 1877. He has worked in various departments of painting, and in all has shown great skill, true feeling, and rare simplicity. His Republican Court in the Time of Washington contains 64 careful portraits.

HUNTINGTON, FREDERICK DAN, an American bishop, was born at Hadley, Mass., May 28, 1819. He graduated at Amherst College in 1839, and studied theology in the Cambridge Divinity School. In 1842 he was ordained pastor of the South Church, Boston, being then a Unitarian. In 1855 he was chosen preacher in Harvard College, and professor of Christian morals. His theological views underwent a gradual change, and finally, having become a Trinitarian, he entered the Episcopal Church. In 1860 he was admitted to its ministry, and in 1864 resigned his office at Harvard. He then became rector of Emmanuel Church, Boston, and in 1869 he was elected and consecrated bishop of Central New York. He was one of the founders of the *Church Monthly*, and he has published some volumes of sermons: *Human Society* (1860); *Lessons on the Parables* (1865); *Steps to Living Faith* (1873).

HUNTINGTON, SAMUEL (1732-1796), an American statesman, was born at Windham, Conn., July 3, 1732. He was originally a cooper, but became a lawyer in 1758, and was made king's attorney and associate judge of the superior court of Connecticut. In January, 1776, he was sent as delegate to the Continental Congress, and signed the Declaration of Independence. In September, 1779, he became president of Congress, and filled that office until 1781. He still retained his office of State judge, and in 1784 he was made chief-justice. In 1785 he was elected lieutenant-governor, and in 1786 governor of Connecticut. He retained this office until his death, which occurred at Norwich, Conn., Jan. 5, 1796.

HUNTSVILLE, a city of Alabama, the county-seat of Madison county, is in the valley of the Tennessee River, on the Memphis and Charleston Railroad, 212 miles E. S. E. of Memphis, and 100 miles S. of Nashville. It is 10 miles N. of the river, and is surrounded by the Cumberland Mountains. It has 4 hotels, 1 national bank and 1 other bank, 1 daily and 6 weekly newspapers, 11 churches, and 10 schools. The industrial works comprise a cotton-factory, ice-factory, cottonseed-oil-mill, and cotton-press. The city is lighted with gas, has finely macadamized and well-shaded streets, water-works, and a park. A spring in the centre yields 15,000,000 gallons of water daily. The city was settled in 1808 by people from the Carolinas, and was incorporated in 1818. Here the first State convention of Alabama was held, and the first meeting of the legislature. The population in 1880 was 4977, and in 1890, 4635.

HURON, LAKE, one of the Great Lakes of the St. Lawrence basin, is bounded on the N. and E. by the Province of Ontario, Canada, and on the W. by the State of Michigan. It extends from 43° to 46° 20′ N. lat., and from 79° 40′ to 84° 40′ W. long. Exclusive of its bays, the lake has a maximum breadth of 105 miles, but the average breadth is less than 75 miles. The extremest length measured as nearly as possible in a straight line falls short of 200 statute miles. The area is usually given as 21,000 sq. miles; but if Georgian Bay (its great eastern gulf) be added, the total area, exclusive of islands, will not fall below 25,000 sq. miles. It is smaller than Lake Michigan. The main body of the lake has a crescentic outline, with the convexity towards the E. On the W. or Michigan side are Saginaw Bay and Thunder Bay; while on the E. is the vast expanse of Georgian Bay, nearly enclosed by Canadian territory, being cut off from the main lake by the island of Grand Manitoulin and the Cabot's Head peninsula. The mean elevation is 589 feet above sea-level, or 49 feet less than that of Lake Superior, and 16 more than that of Lake Erie. It is stated that the average depth is over 1000 feet and the maximum about 1800 feet, making it far deeper than either of the other Great Lakes.

The boundary line between the United States and the Canadian jurisdiction takes a curved direction in such a way as to divide equally the water-surface of the main lake, without reference to the bays.

Lake Huron is remarkable among the Great Lakes for the number and size of its islands. Of these, numbering altogether 3000, nearly all are Canadian, Drummond Island and Bois Blanc being the only considerable islands belonging to the United States. Of the Canadian islands, Grand Manitoulin (80 miles long, area 1600 sq. miles) is by far the largest. The principal islands are well timbered, but very rocky, and have a surface much broken. They are chiefly disposed in a line along the N. shore, forming with its aid the safe and commodious North Channel, well sheltered from the violence of the storms which render the ordinary navigation of the lakes so hazardous. The waters of Lake Superior enter the N. N. W. end of Lake Huron through St. Mary's River, which falls 49 feet in the 75 miles of its course, but is rendered navigable by a canal and locks. Lake Michigan is on nearly a level with Lake Huron, the two lakes communicating by the Straits of Mackinaw. The outlet of Lake Huron is called St. Clair River above the expansion called Lake St. Clair; from that lake to Lake Erie it is called Detroit River.

From Michigan Lake Huron receives many small streams, including Pine, Cheboygan, Thunder Bay, Au Sable, Rifle, Saginaw, and Black Rivers, some of them navigable to a small extent. The Canadian tributaries are larger and more numerous; among them are Winnesauqua, Spanish, White-Fish, French, Maganetawan, Muskoka, Severn, Notawasaga, Saugeen, Maitland, and Aux Sables Rivers, some of them fine streams, giving exit to the waters of noble lakes.

The commerce of Lake Huron is facilitated by the very considerable number of good harbors and roadsteads, chiefly on the Canadian side. At Sand Beach, Mich., the U. S. government has constructed an artificial harbor of refuge, having a breakwater parallel to the shore, and a pier or mole at the N. end, reaching out from the land. The principal natural ports on the United Sates side are those of Hammond's Bay, Michael Bay, Presque Isle, False Presque Isle, Thunder Bay, and Saginaw Bay. Among the towns on the lake are (in Michigan) Mackinaw City, Cheboygan, Alpena, Bay City, and Port Huron. On the Canadian shore are Collingwood, Southampton, Kincardine, Port Albert, and Goderich.

The N. shore of the lake is a region of rich mineral promise; the other shores produce much grain and timber. The regions on the E. and W. are rich in salt, the Michigan side being at present more productive, but not naturally any more abundantly stocked with this commodity than the Canadian side. The fisheries of Lake Huron are considerable.

(C. W. G.)

HURST, JOHN FLETCHER, an American bishop, was born near Salem, Md., Aug. 17, 1834. He graduated at Dickinson College in 1853, taught for two years at Ashland, N. Y., and then went to Germany, where he studied theology at Halle and Heidelberg. From 1858 to 1866 he was pastor of Methodist churches in Passaic and Elizabeth, N. J. In 1866 he took charge of a Methodist missionary institute at Bremen, Germany, which was afterwards removed to Frankfort. While holding this charge he travelled extensively in Europe and the East. In 1871 he became professor of historical theology at Drew Theological Seminary, Madison, N. J., and in 1873 was made president of that institution. In 1880 he was elected bishop at the General Conference at Cincinnati. He has been a frequent contributor to the periodical press, and has published a *History of Rationalism* (1865); *Outlines of Bible History* (1873); *Martyrs of the Tract Cause* (1873); *Life and Literature in the Fatherland* (1874); *Outlines of Church History* (1876); *Bibliotheca Theologica* (1883). He has also translated and edited important works from the German.

HUSBAND AND WIFE. The law of husband and wife was brought to America from England, and adopted in the several colonies with little or no modification. The wife, by the marriage, lost her capacity to make contracts or act independently, her personal property passed to the husband, her choses in action might be collected, sold, or otherwise reduced to possession by him, for his own use; her chattel interests in land he might in like manner appropriate, and by the birth of issue of the marriage, which might inherit any estate of inheritance possessed by her, the husband became tenant by the curtesy in respect to such estate, and thereby was vested with a disposable life-interest. For all that the wife thus lost the law was supposed to make compensation, which consisted in an obligation on his part for the discharge of her debts, in an equity to a settlement from the property she brought him, in a right to be supported by him, and in a right to certain defined interests in his property at his death in case she survived him. The equity to a settlement from the property she brought to him was one springing originally from the necessity the husband was often under of seeking the aid of chancery to reduce to possession choses in action, or other rights or interests, in which case the court might, as a condition to its assistance, require him, if he had not made proper settlement before, to make it now to such extent as under the circumstances should appear reasonable. At length the right to have such allowance made in an original suit by her was recognized. The right to a support was to be claimed only at her husband's home unless, by his misconduct, he drove her away from it, or gave full justification for her separating herself from him. What circumstances would justify her leaving him might be open to some question: certainly great cruelty; the bringing of depraved persons to the house as associates; the refusal of proper support, and any such misbehavior as would by law entitle her to divorce or judicial separation. As to what was suitable support, however, the husband rather than the wife was to be judge, and it would only be in an extreme case that she would be held justifiable in law in leaving him. While living with him the wife had an implied agency to act in his behalf in the purchase of family necessaries, but this might be terminated by notice to dealers not to give her credit on his account. If, however, he drove her from his home by misbehavior or otherwise, she took with her the agency so far as necessary to her reasonable support, and the husband's notification to dealers would not protect him from liability for necessaries.

On the death of the husband, leaving her surviving, she was entitled to a life-interest in one-third in value of any estates of inheritance of which he may have been seized during the marriage, unless barred by accepting jointure or some provision made for her by will of the husband, or unless she had joined with him in disposing of it. From early times the joining of the wife in the husband's conveyance was held a good bar to dower. If the husband had failed to reduce to possession any of her choses in action or chattel interests in land, the right to these survived to her. Then the wife was entitled to both her own and her husband's paraphernalia, and statutes very generally made provision for further allowances from personal property, and for her support from his estate while it was in process of settlement, or at least for some definite time. About the year 1844 great changes in the legal position of the wife in respect to property began to be made by statute. The most important of these was generally embodied in a legislative declaration that the real and personal property of the wife, which belonged to her at the time of the marriage or to which she might afterwards become entitled by gift, grant, inheritance, or otherwise, should be and remain hers to the same extent as if she were a *feme sole*. The terms of some of the statutes were so broad as to cut off altogether any possible estate by the curtesy not already initiate, but others saved the right either in express terms or by judicial construction. Some of the early statutes did not give her the power to dispose of real property except with the husband's assent or by order of a competent court; but legislation soon went further, and gave her full power to make contracts of all sorts in respect to her individual property as she might if *feme sole*, including conveyances of lands. Statutes also gave her full testamentary capacity, which she might exercise independent of the husband's assent, and to his exclusion from the estate if she saw fit. Since these statutes it has not been uncommon for married women to carry on business in their own names, with full personal responsibility, and with the same power to enforce contracts that would be possessed by other persons. Meanwhile the common law dower has in some States been converted into an estate of inheritance, and in some the testamentary power of the husband has been so limited that he cannot bequeath more than a certain proportion away from his wife and family. The wife's right to property has been generally held to extend to any sum which she may recover at law for a wrong done to her in estate or person.

How far the old English law which recognized the right of the husband to govern and restrain the movements of the wife, and even to inflict moderate corporal punishment, was ever in force in America it is not easy to say. Its existence has often been assumed, but on slender grounds. The husband's battery of the wife would be a criminal offence, not to be excused by his opinion that she needed correction, though her misconduct might go in mitigation of punishment. And his attempt to restrain her movements, and to compel her, against her will, to reside where he might direct would not be aided by the law. In fine, the law has come to recognize the existence of two wills in husband and wife, neither of which can be subordinated to the other and forced into submission by legal compulsion or penalties. The old rule, however, that the services of the wife belong to the husband is generally left in force, but she employs them in his behalf only as she may choose. The wife having power to make contracts on her own behalf may make them with her husband, and may sue him upon them. In some States she may sue him at law, in others she would be compelled to sue in equity by guardian or trustee. In some States she may receive conveyances directly from her husband, but probably this rule is not universal.

At common law the right of the husband to the custody and control of children of the marriage was best, and he might, by deed or will, appoint guardians for them. The first of these rights must probably be recognized as still existing, except that, if the parties are living apart, the courts would give the custody of infant children to one or the other, according as under the circumstances should seem best for the children, irrespective of claims; and in some States there are statutes which make the mother's claim best in the very early infancy of children, or, perhaps, for female children. The father's right to appoint guardians has also been modified in some States, so as not to leave it absolute regardless of the mother's will. It will be seen from the foregoing that very little of the common law disabilities of the married woman remains, and her control of property is very generally made at least as complete as it could have been formerly by a settlement made upon her as and for her separate estate, with express power of disposition.

Simultaneously with these statutory changes in the law has been going on an agitation for concession of political rights to women, which has had some success, but, as it has not concerned married women specially, it would be out of place to consider it in detail here. The same may be said of the claim for women to participate freely in many avocations from which they were formerly excluded, and especially in the learned professions—a claim that has met with much more general favor than that for political privileges.

It is difficult to say how far the sweeping statutory changes have affected the common law of the States, but it will probably be found hereafter, as from time to time judicial decisions are made, that the changes are by no means unimportant. No doubt the great increase in divorce is to some extent attributable to the more independent position of woman, and probably agreements for separation without divorce would now be viewed with less disfavor than formerly. The old rule, that a crime committed by the wife in the presence of the husband is presumed to have been committed under duress, and therefore to be his crime, is still in force, and he is still in general left responsible for her torts. (T. M. C.)

HUTCHINSON, ANNE (1591-1643), an American religious enthusiast, was born at Alford, Lincolnshire, England, in 1591. She was a daughter of Francis Marbury, a parish clergyman, and was married to Edward Hutchinson. She removed to New England in 1634 with her husband and her brother-in-law, Rev. John Wheelwright, being attracted by the preaching of Rev. John Cotton, who had come over in 1633. She was well versed in the Scriptures and in theology, and stoutly maintained that those who were in the covenant of grace were entirely freed from the covenant of works. She gave lectures twice a week, which were attended by nearly a hundred women. Her adherents, called antinomians, included Sir Henry Vane and other prominent men, and when Cotton did not approve her extreme views they tried to elect Wheelwright as his associate. But the imprudence of the latter brought on his banishment, and in May, 1637, at the annual election, Winthrop and Dudley, who had opposed Mrs. Hutchinson, were elected, though the people of Boston were favorable to her party. In August an ecclesiastical synod at Newtown condemned her views, and in November the general court brought her to trial for not discontinuing her meetings as had been ordered. She was banished after two days' trial, but was allowed to pass the winter at Roxbury. Seventy-six of her adherents were required to surrender their arms. Wheelwright had gone to Exeter, N. H., but Mrs. Hutchinson accompanied Coddington's colony, which settled on Aquidneck, now Rhode Island, in 1638, and formed a theocracy. In the next year, however, there was some trouble at the election. Edward Hutchinson was chosen magistrate, and in 1640 Coddington withdrew to Newport at the other end of the island. After wards the two settlements were united under one government, Coddington being chief magistrate and Hutchinson one of the assistants. Great dislike of them was still entertained at Boston, and in 1641 Hutchinson's son and son-in-law, Collins, when on a visit to that city, were arrested and imprisoned. In 1642 Hutchinson died, and Mrs. Hutchinson went to the Dutch territory of New Netherland, settling near New Rochelle. But in 1643 an Indian outbreak occurred, in which she and all her family were murdered, except one granddaughter, who was carried away captive.

HUXLEY, THOMAS HENRY, an eminent English naturalist, was born at Ealing, near London, May 4, 1825. His father was one of the teachers in the school at Ealing, but his education was chiefly acquired at home, where his range of studies included medicine and German scientific literature. In 1842 he engaged in the study of medicine at Charing Cross Hospital, and in 1845 received his degree from the University of London. He had already displayed remarkable powers of investigation, and had described in the *Medical Times and Gazette* a layer in the rootsheath of hair, which has since borne his name. In 1846 he entered the medical service of the navy, and after a short stay at the Haslar Hospital was sent, in the winter of that year, as assistant surgeon on the Rattlesnake with Capt. Strachey's expedition to the Southern Pacific Ocean. This expedition surveyed the east coasts of Australia and Papua, and returned to England in November, 1850, after circumnavigating the globe. The opportunity for original investigation in this voyage was embraced by the ardent young naturalist with a diligence only equalled by that of Darwin in his similar voyage. He studied particularly the invertebrate surface-life of the ocean, and sent home several communications, the first published of which was "On the Anatomy and Affinities of the Family of Medusæ." In this he called attention to the important fact that the bodies of the Medusæ consist of two cell-layers, which he compared with the germinal layers of the higher animals. The most important result of this voyage, however, was his splendid work on *Oceanic Hydrozoa* (1859), which greatly extended our knowledge of the Zoöphytes. His important papers having brought him into scientific repute, he was elected a fellow of the Royal Society in June, 1851. He resigned from the navy in 1853, and in the next year was appointed professor of natural history in the Royal School of Mines. He also received the appointment of naturalist on the Geological Survey of Great Britain. Since that period he has lived mainly in London, engaged in incessant scientific labors. To his regular lectures at the School of Mines, and his persistent investigations, he has added many popular lectures and has filled a variety of important positions. In 1855 he was appointed Fullerian Professor of Physiology to the Royal Institution, and Examiner in Physiology and Comparative Anatomy to the University of London. In 1858 he delivered the Croomian lecture to the Royal Society, taking for his subject the *Theory of the Vertebrate Skull*, a problem which he handled with great ability. After the publication of Darwin's work on *Natural Selection*, Huxley became an ardent supporter of the theory, and was the first to apply it to the problem of the evolution of the human race. In his lectures to workingmen, at the Museum of Practical Geology, in 1860, he dealt with *The Relations of Man to the Lower Animals*. These lectures gave rise to warm controversies in the British Association in that and subsequent years. The whole matter was summed up in his *Evidence of Man's Place in Nature* (1863), in which he endeavored to trace the ancestry of man to the anthropoid apes. This work attracted strong interest and gave rise to much discussion. He continued to lecture to the workingmen on Darwin's views in 1862, and published his lectures under the title *On our Knowledge of the Causes of the Phenomena of Organic Nature*. He delivered lecture courses also on the *Elements of Comparative Anatomy*; the *Classification of Animals*, etc. From 1863 to 1869 he was Hunterian professor in the Royal College of Surgeons, was made president of the Geological Survey in 1869, and in 1870 was president of the British Association for the Advancement of Science in its meeting at Liverpool. After the education act of 1870 went into force Prof. Huxley served on the London school board for two years, and was chairman of the committee which drew up the scheme of education adopted in the board schools. He took an active part in the discussion of educational systems, and was conspicuous for his opposition to denominational teaching and for his vigorous denunciation of the doctrines of the Roman Catholic Church. He was elected lord rector of Aberdeen University for three years in December, 1872, and installed Feb. 27, 1874. In 1873 he was elected secretary of the Royal Society, and in the summers of 1875 and 1876 was acting professor of natural science at the University of Edinburgh during Prof. Thomson's absence with the Challenger expedition. In June, 1879, he was elected corresponding member of the French Academy of Science in the sections of anatomy and zoölogy, in the place of the Russian naturalist Baer. In 1881 he was made inspector of fisheries, to succeed Frank Buckland, deceased, and in July, 1883, he was chosen president of the Royal Society. In the same year he was elected a foreign member of the American National Academy, and delivered the Rede lecture at Cambridge on *The Origin of the Existing Forms of Life—Construction or Evolution*. In 1876 he visited the United States, where he delivered a series of popular lectures since published.

Prof. Huxley ranks to-day as the first zoölogist among his countrymen and has a world-wide reputation, unsurpassed by that of any other living scientist. This reputation is due to the breadth of the field which his researches have covered—the word zoölogy with him embracing the whole range of animal biology—his extensive knowledge, his clear, incisive, and brilliant style of writing, his quick perception of scientific principles, and in particular to his outspoken advocacy of certain radical and startling doctrines, which have brought his name into notice in all ranks of society. One of these doctrines, already mentioned, is that in which he advocated the descent of man from the apes. Another was his theory of the *Physical Basis of Life*, which formed one of his *Lay Sermons* (1870). In this he combats the prevailing idea that life is a principle distinct from organization, and holds that it is but the outcome of the qualities of protoplasm, a substance found in every part of every organism, and which he considers to be the physical basis of life. This doctrine, advanced in his trenchant style and with his felicity of illustration and vigor of argument, attracted very wide-spread attention at the time. It was followed by a yet more startling doctrine, advocated before the British Association at Belfast in 1874, and based on the phenomena of certain cases of brain injury, to the effect that the seeming voluntary movements of animals, and even those of man, are really automatic and independent of will, and to some extent of consciousness. It embraced the definite declaration that an animal is a machine, a sort of highly complex clock, wound up to run for a certain period, and that such consciousness as exists is but a side-product of its activities and has no actual controlling influence over these activities.

Apart from these side-issues of a vividly active mind, and from a strong tendency to generalization, Prof. Huxley is one of the most exact and indefatigable of scientists, and has pursued his studies with an intensity injurious to his health. His researches have covered the various fields of comparative anatomy, morphology, physiology, embryology, palæontology, etc., and in addition to much exact knowledge have led to many valuable generalizations in the affinities and classification of animals. He was the first to remove the echinoderms from the radiates, and to prove their affinity to the vermes; he has made important advances in our knowledge of the morphology of the mollusca and arthropoda, and has offered many valuable suggestions in classification. His *Manual of the Anatomy of Vertebrated Animals* (1871) favorably compares with the splendid works of Gegenbaur on this subject, while its brilliant handling of the problems of comparative anatomy was completed in 1877 by his *Anatomy of Invertebrate Animals*. In his dealing with the vertebrates he has been as suggestive and happy as in his handling of the lower orders of life, and has displayed a marked power of scientific foresight in his almost prophetic conceptions of the character of the early birds and of the progenitors of the horse, conceptions which have been strikingly verified in the discovery of toothed birds by Prof. Marsh, and of the tertiary ancestors of the horse. Of his services in classification may be mentioned his discovery of the close affinities of birds and reptiles, his grouping of them in one class under the name Sauropsida, and his like combination of batrachians and fishes into the single class Ichthyopsida. He has, in fact, an unusually broad and clear discernment of the laws and affinities of organic nature, and can be credited with the high honor of scarcely ever making a mistake in a scientific deduction, despite the voluminous character of his work. Prof. Huxley has by no means confined his attention strictly to biological science. He strays to the fields of physical geography in his *Physiography, an Introduction to the Study of Nature* (1877), while he keeps himself well acquainted with the poetry, fiction, and other literary work of the day. One example of his interest in general topics we possess in his biography of *Hume* (1879), in which are displayed all that vigorous command of language and literary richness of style which have done so much to give popularity to his works on abstruse scientific subjects. Other illustrations of the same ability may be found in his *Lay Sermons*, his *Critiques and Addresses*, his *Lectures to Workingmen*, etc. As a public speaker he is quiet, deliberate, fluent, almost colloquial in manner. By his numerous lectures and his many popular works he has done much towards spreading the modern conceptions of biological science among the general public. And he has accomplished the difficult task of rendering intelligible to educated people generally some of the most difficult of scientific problems. He has been elected a corresponding member of numerous scientific societies, has received the Wollaston medal of the Geological Society, the honorary title of LL. D. from the Universities of Edinburgh, Dublin, and Cambridge, and other marks of high appreciation both from foreign and home sources. Recently his health has been so affected by his arduous labors that he has been obliged to resign the several positions which he held, those of naturalist of the Geological Survey, inspector of Fisheries, president of the Royal Society, and professor of the Royal School of Mines. In the latter institution, with which he has been so long connected, he still retains an honorary position. In consequence of these resignations a pension has been granted to him by the government based on the general plea of his services to literature.

In addition to the works already named Prof. Huxley is the author of *Lessons in Elementary Physiology* (1866); *An Introduction to the Classification of Animals* (1869); *The Crayfish, an Introduction to the study of Zoölogy* (1879); *Science Culture and other Essays* (1882); together with numerous valuable papers published in the *Transactions* and *Journal* of the Royal, Linnæan, Geological, and Zoölogical Societies, the *Memoirs of the Geological Survey of Great Britain*, and in several popular periodicals. More recently he has written a number of controversial articles, on Biblical interpretation and other subjects, in reply to Mr. Gladstone and others, in which he has shown much ability as a literary combatant. (c. m.)

HYACINTH, the name of a favorite cultivated species of liliaceous plants of the genus *Hyacinthus*. They possess bulbous roots, bell-shaped flowers, with a 6-cleft perianth, and dry capsular fruit. *H. orientalis*, the cultivated species, is a native of Persia, Asia Minor, and Syria, and is naturalized in some parts of Southern Europe. It has a whorl of broad linear leaves, rising from the bulb, and a flower-stem with many flowers arranged linearly or in a raceme. The hyacinth occurs abundantly in its native locality in form not unlike the common harebell. It has long been cultivated, with a remarkable change in its conditions, the cultivated form being one of the most beautiful and fragrant of our garden-flowers. This cultivation has been principally conducted in Holland, which has become a centre of export for hyacinth bulbs and where more than 2000 varieties have been named. They are grown there in such profusion as to give a gorgeous aspect to some of the Dutch towns. In the wild state the hyacinth flower is blue and single. As cultivated, both single and double varieties are common, while many shades of color are produced, principally red, white, and blue. The yellow varieties seem a greater deviation from the original and their bulbs are delicate.

(See Vol. XII. p. 435 Am. ed. (p. 419 Edin. ed.).)

An immense number of bulbs are annually imported into this country from Holland and are thrown by or allowed to depreciate by neglect after once blooming. Great care is needed for their proper cultivation. They should be planted in a rich, light, sandy soil, the beds being covered with decayed tan-bark or the like material and protected by mats in severe weather. The time of blooming is early spring, the hyacinth flowers immediately following those of the crocus. To preserve the bulbs the flower-stem is broken when the flowering is over, but the leaves are left till they turn yellow. Then the bulb is taken from the ground in May or June and carefully dried in the shade. There are few flowers better adapted to house-culture than the hyacinth. For this purpose the bulb is potted in the autumn, and may be brought into bloom as early as Christmas if potted early and forced. By potting from September to November a continuous winter bloom may be assured. The hyacinth will grow well in wet sand, and even in water. The bulb should be kept a week or two in damp sand or moss before being placed in the water. After the roots are an inch or two long it is placed in a vase-shaped glass, preferably dark-colored and opaque, filled with rain-water, with a lump of charcoal, and kept in the dark for a few days before exposure to sunlight. November is the proper month for this. (C. M.)

HYDROPHOBIA. This word, signifying "dread of water," from its most marked symptom is the name given to a specific disease. "Rabies" is frequently used as a synonym. It is produced by a specific poison or virus. The virus exists in the salivary glands and the central nervous system of the dog, horse, wolf, fox, pig, cat, and a number of other lower animals. It can be communicated from one animal to another, and from any of these animals to man. Up to the present time no evidence exists that it has ever been communicated from one human being to another. How the disease originates, whether spontaneously or only by inoculation from one animal to another, has not yet been settled. The more reasonable view seems to be that it originates only by inoculation.

See Vol. XII. p. 578 Am. ed. (p. 545 Edin. ed.).

The principal seat of the poison is unquestionably in the saliva or spittle of animals. The curious experiments of Dr. Sternberg, of the U. S. Navy, have shown that even normal human saliva is not without danger, if not actually poisonous, and have given a new interest to the study of the effects of the saliva of animals. But they are so recent that they have not yet been sufficiently studied to warrant a definite opinion on the subject. The researches of M. Pasteur and others have apparently shown that while the virus resides in the saliva, it is even more intense in the central nervous system, that is the brain and spinal cord. While its existence in the saliva is a constant menace to man, yet it has its advantages, since when an animal bites a human being it is frequently apt to be at a point that is covered by the clothing, and so the teeth are wiped clean in penetrating the clothes, the bite being thus often rendered harmless.

As it is all important to be able to recognize the symptoms of rabies in suspected dogs, the following is a summary description, chiefly from Virchow, whose portrayal is perhaps the most vivid. It exists in three stages, the melancholic, the furious, and the paralytic. The first is often unnoticed at its onset. There is restlessness and change of place, sudden waking from sleep, irritability and loss of appetite. The specific symptoms soon develop. There is great sensitiveness in the scar if one exists; the dog laps his own urine and eats the fæces of other dogs, with a peculiar appetite for unnatural articles of diet, such as straw, paper, wood, etc.; much sexual excitement exists; he seems friendly to the cat, but exhibits a marked change in his usual affection for his master, becomes shy and backward, and avoids observation. The organs of swallowing and breathing soon become involved as if something were sticking in his throat, the voice is altered, the saliva is arrested; he licks cold surfaces, such as stone, iron, etc., and there is marked debility.

The furious stage generally sets in from 1 to 3 days, and is rarely delayed after the eighth day. The dog is restless and irritable, runs out of the house, attempts to bite, not by systematic and vicious attacks but aimlessly, goes from place to place without thought or reason, endeavors to break his chain or destroy his kennel, his inability to do so increasing his rage, and if he gets loose he will run great distances. Then follows sometimes a period of remission, which is deceptive and against which we should be on our guard.

After the acute mania of this stage and its dangerous snappishness, there follows the third stage of paralysis. The paroxysms become weaker and remittent, the coat falls off, the flanks sink in, the legs are weak and lame, he lies on one side in great prostration, but when roused still snaps and bites. If able to walk, he totters and drags himself about, the eyes are sunken and dull, the mouth open and dry, the tongue hanging out and hard, the heart weak, irregular, and intermittent, the breathing oppressed, and convulsions may occur. Death takes place from exhaustion or during a paroxysm in from 5 to 8 days from the beginning of the attack.

When a person has been bitten by a supposed rabid dog the most senseless thing to do is nearly always done, viz.—to kill the dog. The proper thing to do is to determine the fact whether the dog is really mad, and this can only be done by preserving it under observation for a definite time. If the dog is proved to be not mad the fear that must always exist that the bitten person will suffer from hydrophobia will be seen to be without any foundation, and if the dog is really mad the precautions to be named later should be taken at once. Pasteur's very sensible advice is as follows: "Every mad dog, whether it eats or not, dies from rabies in a few days. If it eats, death takes place more slowly, but this time never exceeds 8 or 10 days. In the interval it exhibits rabid symptoms. Confine the dog to his kennel, where he must be fed with precaution for at least 12 days. This had better be done under the supervision of a veterinary surgeon. If the dog lives after the time indicated you may be assured that it is not mad."

After a person has been bitten by a dog that is really mad there is a period of "incubation" or development during which the victim shows no symptoms of the disease. This period, in 89 cases analyzed by Blatchford and Spoor, of Troy, was on the average 70 days, a period fortunately sufficiently long for prevention, if such means, as now seems probable, really exist. In 23 cases it was 30 days and under, and the maximum in 6 was 200 days. There seems to be, however, little doubt that this period may be much longer. It may extend to 18 months or even $3\frac{1}{2}$ years. Those cases in which many years have elapsed, as is alleged, between the bite and the development of the disease, in most cases are unreliable.

No age, sex, country, climate, or season seems to be exempt from the disorder. Europe has, however, furnished the greatest number of cases. It is more common in Canada and New England than in the South in this country. The general opinion that it is a disease of summer is erroneous. Of 2550 cases noted, 1704 occurred in the spring, 621 in summer, 608 in the autumn, and 587 in the winter. Of all persons bitten only about one in six develop the disease.

The wound inflicted by a rabid dog generally heals as kindly as any other. When the disease is about to break out the scar begins to itch, burn, and smart. It becomes sore and irritable, the pain radiating to some distance. The wound reopens and the absorbent vessels leading from it towards the trunk become reddish lines. Soon a general feeling of discomfort is experienced, with headache, disturbed sleep, a melancholy feeling, and more or less chilliness. In from 12 to 24 hours any attempt to swallow is accompanied by a spasm of the throat so severe that the patient dashes away the cup, and though tormented with thirst will touch no liquid, or if he does so he is oppressed by a sense of impending suffocation and jumps from the bed or couch panting for breath. There is severe pain located in the throat, with a sense of constriction of the chest, difficulty of breathing, sighing respiration, and the thickened ropy saliva and mucus accumulate and aggravate the already existing thirst which he cannot relieve by drinking. His fruitless attempts to swallow end only in renewed spasm and fright. Meanwhile he becomes sensitive in a high degree to the slightest movement, the faintest noise, and the lightest breath of air. All these provoke the most fearful spasms not unlike those of lock-jaw. His irritability increases till it amounts to a veritable and often violent delirium. The last stage is the most deplorable. His eyes are glaring, the pupils are dilated, his tongue is dry and parched, his voice shrill, his appearance haggard and horror-struck, the breathing is panting, the pulse 140 to 160 and feeble, and he is exhausted to the last degree. After 2 or 3 days from the onset of the malady he dies, exhausted by the paroxysms, either suddenly by suffocation or in a final calm produced by the weakness. No cases of recovery, that are reliable from a scientific point of view, have been reported.

Post-mortem examinations have shed but little light on the essential nature of the malady. Forster asserts that there is congestion of the spinal cord with many points at which the blood has escaped in small amounts. Congestion of the throat has also been observed. That it is an intense nervous malady is not to be doubted. It is not probably propagated through the blood itself, as is shown by the long period of latency, nor by the absorbent vessels, else the absorbent glands would be involved.

The treatment is not an easy matter to determine. Youatt, from an experience in some 400 cases and four times upon himself, states his belief that cauterization with nitrate of silver ("lunar caustic") is a specific. This is strong evidence, yet it would seem that cutting out the part, if that be practicable, and cupping, if the means are at hand at the moment, should precede the caustic. Even at a comparatively late period excision of the part is not to be neglected, as it not only may prevent the action of the poison, but does very much to relieve the patient's mind of the fearful dread of the malady, which is a large element of the mental torture during the disease and possibly of its production. If the disease has been actually developed, of course it will do no good. Other treatment will unhappily do little or nothing to cure, but something may be done which will relieve the patient's sufferings. Inhalations of the nitrite of amyl, ether, or chloroform, with sufficient doses of morphia hypodermatically, will give some relief. The nitrite of amyl seems to hold out the best promise of relief, especially as to the inability to swallow liquids. The room should be kept dark and warm, and the utmost quiet should prevail. A fearless and judicious doctor and an efficient nurse are among the best means of assuaging the terrors and sufferings of the victim of this dread disease.

M. Louis Pasteur, of Paris, who has done so much by his researches on fermentation, pébrine or silkworm disease, splenic fever, and chicken cholera, etc., has of late turned his attention to hydrophobia. Should his claims prove true we shall owe him a debt not easily appreciated, and one that can never be adequately discharged. Sufficient time has not yet elapsed, and a sufficient number of experiments on the lower animals has not yet been made, nor has a sufficient trial been made in man to allow a positive opinion to be expressed on the validity of his claims. But it is certainly true also, that both his past reputation for scientific accuracy and acumen, and the results so far obtained, present a strong evidence of the probable truth of his present assertions.

Pasteur states that by passing the virus through a number of monkeys successively it loses its virulence, but that by passing it through a number of rabbits in succession it gains greatly in power. This transmission is effected by inoculating one animal from a rabid dog, the second animal from the first, the third from the second, and so on—the inoculations being made chiefly by trephining the skull, a much more certain plan than by inoculations under the skin. He also asserts (and this is his most recent method) that if he inoculates a number of rabbits from one to another in a series, and then exposes the spinal cords of these rabbits in glass jars, entirely free from moisture (by caustic potash), and at a constant temperature of 20° (centigrade), they lose in virulence with each day of such exposure until, after a period of fourteen days after death, no poisonous effect results from their inoculation into a healthy rabbit or dog. The result of numerous experiments has been that a spinal cord so kept has, as a rule, a certainty of action dependent entirely upon the time of such exposure. That is, while the cord of a dog that has died of rabies, if inoculated when fresh, will produce rabies in a rabbit in 14 days; that of a rabbit dead of rabies is more virulent, and will cause rabies in 7 days if inoculated when fresh. But if this rabbit-cord be kept as above described, it will produce by inoculation milder and milder symptoms, in proportion to the length of time it has been kept, till at last, when it has been kept for 14 days, it will produce no symptoms whatever.

Next he inoculated these modified cords on healthy rabbits, beginning with the weakest, and he found that daily inoculation of the same rabbit with more and more virulent cords produced no ill effects, immunity apparently being produced by the preceding inoculations. At the end of the series, inoculations even of perfectly fresh cords that should produce the disease in 7 days were followed by no ill results whatever, if preceded by such graduated inoculations. He communicated his results to the French Academy of Sciences, and a commission was appointed to examine the results. Pasteur furnished them with 23 protected dogs, and these dogs with 19 others unprotected, were all vaccinated with the fresh virus. Of the 19 unprotected, 14 died of rabies; of the 23 protected, 1 died of diarrhœa, and all the others escaped.

Feeling now sure of his ground, Pasteur was ready to try it on human beings, and did not hesitate on July 7, 1885, when a boy recently bitten presented himself at his laboratory, to inoculate him. This historic boy—Joseph Meister—was subjected to 12 inoculations, beginning on the seventh and ending on the 16th. Each inoculation was tested or "controlled" by making at the same time an inoculation from the same cord upon a healthy rabbit. Those from a number of the fresher cords produced rabies in the rabbits, but none of them had any effect upon the boy, so that at the end of the inoculations he was considered by Pasteur not only proof against canine rabies but against rabbit rabies, which he considers much more virulent. Since that date a large number of inoculations have been practiced by Pasteur, persons coming from other European countries, and even from the United States, to be treated. The results seem highly favorable. Of persons bitten by mad dogs 20 per cent. or more are said to die of hydrophobia, while in the Pasteur Institute the rate of mortality is said to have fallen to less than ½ per cent.

Of a number of wolf-bitten Russians, however, several have died of rabies, but the wolf virus is said to be much more virulent than that of the dog, and their cases may therefore be exceptional. In 1889 a Mansion House Fund was raised in London, to enable poor English sufferers to be taken to the institute. Dr. Paul Gibier, an assistant of M. Pasteur, has opened a Pasteur Institute in New York, in which several hundred persons have been operated upon, and with encouraging success.

It must not be ignored that some medical men of such attainments as to challenge our respect, assert that there is no such disorder as hydrophobia. The general consensus of the medical profession, not only men who have given no critical study to the alleged disease but of those of the greatest eminence, is strongly in favor of the real existence of hydrophobia.

(w. w. k.)

HYMNS. The use of hymns other than versifications of Scripture began somewhat later in this country than in England. Until near the close of the last century versions of the Psalms held the field. The so-called "Bay Psalm Book" went through many editions from 1640 to 1762, and was much used in New England; the revision of it by T. Prince, 1758, met with little favor. About 1750 the English *New Version* of Tate and Brady, with a small supplement of hymns from Watts, began to be used in and near Boston. In other parts Watts, Tate and Brady, with perhaps here and there the Scotch version and that of Sternhold and Hopkins, must have supplied the wants of our ancestors during colonial times. After the Revolution imported editions and reprints were less relied on, and homemade books multiplied. Under the auspices of the Association of Connecticut, Joel Barlow in 1785, and Timothy Dwight in 1800, severally completed and revised Watts' version of the Psalms, adapting it to American use, and adding each a selection of hymns. Their books were much used during the first years of the present century (Barlow's in and about Philadelphia especially), and some of Dwight's paraphrases, or rather hymns based on parts of psalms, are still valued and familiar.

See Vol. XII. p. 612 Am. ed. (p. 577 Edin. ed.)

Our first important hymn-writer was Samuel Davies (1723-61), president of what is now Princeton College. His MSS. were intrusted to Dr. Gibbons, who published therefrom in London five volumes of sermons, and 16 hymns in his book of 1769; some of these are still in use. So are a fragment from Mather Byles (1706-88); one or two pieces ascribed by unconfirmed tradition to Samson Occom, the Indian preacher (1723-92), and one by Benjamin Cleveland, before 1792. Henry Alline (1748-84), the founder of a peculiar sect, left 486 hymns (3d ed., 1797), some of which were considerably used for a while.

Toward the end of the last century, and later, appeared in New England and elsewhere sundry collections which reflected the revivalistic spirit of the time, and contained much new material. Rude, often illiterate, but ardent, and not without flashes of real poetry, these effusions were mainly anonymous, but some of them came from John A. Granade and Caleb J. Taylor, Methodists, and John Leland (1754-1841), a well-known Baptist. Among the most important of these curious works were the so-called "Baltimore Collection," ab. 1800; that of Joshua Smith, 9th ed., 1799, and that of Elias Smith and Abner Jones, 1805-10. This last was the earliest compilation for the sect called Christians, and is of no little interest and value. They are all scarce now, and it is probable that several books of this class and era either have perished or are so rare as to be unknown to students.

From this point onward the progress of American hymnody, both in writing and in compiling, may best be traced on denominational lines. With no desire to emphasize these, the subject cannot be presented accurately or clearly if they are ignored.

The Episcopal Church adopted in 1789 Tate and Brady entire, with 27 hymns, to which 30 were added in 1808. In 1827 appeared the 212 hymns long bound up with the Prayer Book, including important originals by H. U. Onderdonk, W. A. Muhlenberg, and F. S. Key, and earlier lyrics from G. W. Doane and J. W. Eastburn; a number of these were very widely copied. The book was influenced by Muhlenberg's *Church Poetry* (1823). In 1833 an abridged Version of Psalms, with a few from other quarters, superseded Tate entire. This provision lasted, with some license in the sixties, till 1871, when the present Hymnal appeared: it received slight revision in 1874. The chief Episcopal writers of later years are Bishop Coxe, Bishop Burgess, and Dr. Crosswell.

The Lutherans put forth English hymn books in 1795, 1797, and 1806, all in New York. Their *New York Collection* (so called), 1814-34, was long and widely used. The General Synod issued a collection in 1828, revised, 1841 and 1850, and another, 1871: the General Council in 1865, revised, 1868. The Tennessee and Ohio Synods have put forth several books, the last of which from Ohio, 1880, contains numerous originals and translations from the German, by M. Loy, E. Cronenwett, C. H. L. Schuette, and others. The German Reformed body has issued no very notable collections, but has had in Drs. H. Harbaugh and E. H. Nevin two writers of repute.

The Methodists began with a *Pocket Hymn Book*, whose origin was long a mystery: Rev. C. S. Nutter has lately proved it to be a reprint of that of T. Spence, strangely enough the very book that John Wesley preached against. From this grew by degrees the collections of 1836 and 1849, whose contents were mainly from C. Wesley. In 1878 came the present Hymnal. There are also various collections for semi-private use, and of other societies, as the Southern Methodist Episcopal of 1847, and several of the Methodist Protestants and Wesleyan Methodists. Leading names are those of Drs. W. Hunter, T. O. Summers, and T. H. Stockton.

The Universalists began early, issuing two books (Philadelphia and Boston) in 1792, and were for a while very active. One of their first workers was George Richards (c. 1755-1816), one or two of whose 75 hymns survive, and are among the few of theirs which have travelled beyond the denomination. In

1808-10 appeared 415, "composed at the request of the General Convention," by Hosea Ballou, Abner Kneeland, S. Streeter, etc. Later, books were compiled by S. and R. Streeter (1829); H. Ballou, 2d (1837); A. C. Thomas (1839); Adams and Chapin (1846); J. G. Adams (1861); H. C. Leonard (1865). All these contain originals, by the editors and others.

Both in writing and in compiling, the Unitarians have done a work which for quantity and quality alike is proportioned to their advantages of education and position rather than to their numbers. Dr. Putnam's *Singers and Songs of the Liberal Faith* (1874) bears witness to the extent of this field without exhausting it, and is a monograph such as no other religious body in America as yet possesses. Their earliest books (in substance, though perhaps not in name) were issued in Boston, by Jeremy Belknap (1795); James Freeman (1799); and the West Society (1803). Notable later collections were prepared in Philadelphia (1812); by H. D. Sewall in New York (1820), Bryant and the Gilmans contributing; by W. B. O. Peabody in Springfield (1835); by F. W. P. Greenwood (1830), enlarged by R. C. Waterston (1835); by W. P. Lunt (1841); by J. Freeman Clarke (1844-55); by G. W. Briggs, G. E. Ellis, and the Connecticut Cheshire Association, severally, in 1845; by Chandler Robbins, in 1843-54; by S. Longfellow and S. Johnson, 1846-48 and 1864; by C. A. Bartol (1849;) by Drs. Hedge and Huntingdon (1853); by Dr. S. Osgood (1862); and L. J. Livermore, *Hymn and Tune Book* (1868). Among the writers for these are many distinguished names: Andrews Norton, Henry Ware, Jr., Dr. S. Gilman and his wife, Mrs. Follen, John Pierpont, John Quincy Adams, Drs. Furness, Peabody, Frothingham, and Hedge, Mrs. Miles, Theodore Parker, Bryant, Emerson, the Longfellows, Samuel Johnson, E. H. Sears, J. F. Clarke, W. H. Burleigh, C. T. Brooks, S. G. Bulfinch, Jones Very, T. W. Higginson. Many of their hymns are favorites in other bodies, and some of them are widely used in England as well as here.

The Baptists have produced a greater number of books than any other home denomination, though most of these are small in size and revivalistic in character. They have also many writers, but only one of marked importance. Among the former may be mentioned the Boston Collection (1808); Parkinson's (1809-17); Maclay's (1816); Winchell's *Supplement to Watts* (1819-32); several by A. Broaddus (1828-42); Mercer's *Cluster* (1835); Linsley and Davis' *Select Hymns* (1836-41); *The Psalmist* (1843); Banvard's *Christian Melodist* (1849); Manly's Southern *Baptist Psalmody* (1850); *Baptist Harp* (1849); *Devotional Hymn Book* (1864); *Baptist Hymn Book*, *Praise Book*, and *Service of Song* (1871). The most valuable and widely circulated of these, *The Psalmist* (1843), includes numerous originals by S. F. Smith, one of the compilers, and a few by S. S. Cutting, H. S. Washburn, G. Robins, and others. Among earlier writers are Dr. T. Baldwin, J. Leland, O. Holden, Mrs. Sigourney, and the Judsons. Dr. Smith, both for number and quality, stands at the head. Besides their own compilations, there have been Baptist editions of the leading Congregational books for the last 55 years. Several minor Baptist sects have their own collections.

The first important and meritorious Congregational book—apart from Psalm versions by Barlow—was *The Hartford Selection* (1799) by N. Strong and others, with some originals. Then came Worcester's *Watts and Select Hymns* (1815-34); this had a great circulation. So had Nettleton's *Village Hymns* (1824), which derived part of its missionary spirit from a little volume, *Hymns for the Monthly Concert* (1823), prepared by L. Bacon while a student at Andover, and now very rare. In these two first appeared the hymns of W. B. Tappan, Mrs. Sigourney, Mrs. A. B. Hyde, and Mrs. P. H. Brown. Mason and Greene's *Church Psalmody* (1831) was long and widely used. The Connecticut Association's *Psalms and Hymns* (1845) contained some originals by Drs. Bacon and Fitch, two of the compilers. Henry Ward Beecher's *Plymouth Collection* (1855) and the Andover *Sabbath Hymn Book* (1858) marked an advance in range of materials and standards of taste. L. W. Bacon has issued *The Book of Worship* (1866) and *The Church Book* (1883). The Oberlin *Manual of Praise* (1880) was prepared by Profs. Mead and Rice. E. Nason's *Congregational Hymn Book* (1857) took more pains than was usual at that day to give authors' names correctly.

The Presbyterians appear to have been content for some time with Watts. In 1828-29, at Princeton, appeared their first *Psalms and Hymns*, which, revised in 1830 and 1834, culminated in the volume of 1843, long used by the Old School branch. More variety was found in Joshua Leavitt's *Christian Lyre* (1830-31), containing originals by J. B. Waterbury, W. Mitchell, J. Hopkins, D. Dutton, and others; and in T. Hastings' *Spiritual Songs* (1831-33), with many of his own lyrics, and several by S. F. Smith and R. Palmer; the three leading American writers thus making what seems their first appearance in the same book. These two had music, then a novelty in a hymn book proper. Dr. Hastings, by far the most voluminous of our singers, continued his work in *The Christian Psalmist* (1836), and with his son in *Church Melodies* (1858), besides contributing to other collections. Dr. Beman's *Sacred Lyrics* (1832) gave its name to his much larger book of 1841, which, as the *Church Psalmist*, was adopted by the New School Assembly in 1843. The same year appeared in Philadelphia *Parish Hymns*, enlarged, 1844, as *Parish Psalmody*, both containing originals by Mrs. J. L. Gray and others. Abner Jones' *Melodies of the Church* (1832), and his son's *Temple Melodies* (1851), and *Songs for the New Life* (1869), had some success. The *Hymnal of the Presbyterian Church*, and a similar Southern book, both 1867, were on the old lines; more modern in spirit and scope is *The Presbyterian Hymnal* (1874). *The Sacrifice of Praise* appeared 1869. The most active and popular of recent compilers is Dr. C. S. Robinson, whose compilations, *Songs of the Sanctuary*, etc., range from 1862 to 1884; the most careful and studious are Dr. Hatfield (1872), Drs. Hitchcock, Schaff, and Eddy (1874), and Messrs. Lasar and Hall (1880). Dr. C. H. Richards, of Wisconsin, has produced two noteworthy books (1880-83).

The lines between Presbyterian and Congregational have not been strictly drawn; the same books are often used by societies of both kinds, and bear no certain mark of affiliation. The same is true, in later years and less degree, of the (Dutch) Reformed. They had their own version of Psalms before the Revolution, and editions of *Psalms and Hymns* dated 1789, 1814, 1831, and 1849. *Hymns of the Church* (1869) is a great improvement on its predecessors. To this body belong Dr. Bethune and Dr. A. R. Thompson.

The very popular *Gospel Hymns*, and many of similar character, fall under no denominational head; they gave currency to the verses of P. P. Bliss, Fanny Crosby (Mrs. Van Alstyne), and many others. The increasing flood of juvenile hymns likewise transcends bounds and defies description. Mrs. G. C. Smith's *Woman in Sacred Song* (1886) contains immense missionary and temperance departments, and brings out hundreds of writers hitherto little known.

No extended account of American hymns and writers as yet exists in permanent form, though the subject has been handled in the columns of the *New York Independent* (1880-84), and in those of the forthcoming *Dictionary of Hymnology*, to be published in London. Prof. Cleveland's *Lyra Sacra Americana* (1868), a volume of selections, by no means covers the whole ground, and is more valued in England than here. Of selections from all sources, intended for home reading, among the most important are Dr. Schaff's *Christ in Song* (1868) and *Library of Religious Poetry* (1880).

In translating, we have done no work to compete with that of Neale, Caswall, and Chandler, of J. Wesley and Miss Winkworth. Dr. H. Mills' *Horæ Germanicæ* (1845-56) is valuable rather for good intention than successful execution. Dr. N. L. Frothingham also has rendered many German hymns. Bishop Doane in 1824 anticipated the era of popular versions from the Latin, and Bishop J. Williams, in *Ancient Hymns of Holy Church* (1845), made a larger attempt. A few valued hymns from foreign sources have been made by Drs. J. W. Alexander, Bethune, Hedge, Palmer, and Prof. R. P. Dunn; and M. W. Stryker and S. W. Duffield are working at this vein.

All our collections for public worship, of course, are filled mainly with hymns of British origin, though those born on American soil occupy increasing space in books of the last thirty years. Here, as elsewhere, we command the vast literature of the mother-land; and we have as yet no Watts, Wesley, Montgomery, Bonar, or Neale of our own. But Ray Palmer is in the rank next to these, and particular pieces by a few who have written less stand with the best. "I Love Thy Kingdom, Lord;" "I Love to Steal Awhile Away," "Thou Art the Way," "My Faith Looks Up to Thee," and "O Sacred Head, Now Wounded," are known everywhere. The youngest of these is 55 years old; a hymn must have time to find its place and fame. The loveliness of Dr. Sears' two Christmas songs is widely recognized, and a missionary hymn of Bishop Coxe, though not much known here, is among the sweetest in *Hymns Ancient and Modern*.

Advancing standards of taste have made a marked improvement in our hymnals; and though less attention has been paid to hymnology here than in England, some of our recent hymnals are as carefully edited, as accurate in matters of text, authorship, and date, as any. The pioneer worker in this department was David Creamer, of Baltimore (1848); his work has been followed up by Rev. C. S. Nutter for the *Methodist Hymnal*, and by Dr. Putnam for the Unitarians. Whether we do our share in producing original material or not, there is little question that the art of compilation will continue to be cultivated with diligence, and loving care be bestowed on the service of song in the Lord's house. (F. M. B.)

HYPOTHECATION (from Greek *Hypotheca*, a pledge) is the right to satisfy a debt that is due and unpaid by a sale of the property pledged for it, and, strictly speaking, it differs from the pawn or pledge in that possession of the security is not given to the creditor; but this form only survives in the mechanic's lien or a seaman's claim for wages; for the term hypothecation is currently applied to many forms of pledge, and may be defined, according to Domat, as an appropriation of the thing given for the security of the engagement. However, there is distinction in the names used to describe the pledging of various property: thus, the pledge of tools, furniture, utensils, or apparel, is called a pawn; the pledge of real property, such as lands and buildings, is called a mortgage; and, generally speaking, hypothecation is the pledge of negotiable instruments, bonds, certificates of stock, and evidences of value or property in which the title is complete. To make the title complete when there cannot be strict possession of the property, there are certain convenient forms: thus, in the case of goods on shipboard, or otherwise in transit, the transfer to the pledgee of the bills of lading makes title to the property. So of merchandise on storage or in bond, does the warehouseman's receipt form the usual understanding of possession. With these transfers to the pledge also goes the written obligation of the debtor pledging the property, and describing the conditions and agreements of the pledge, which may be for a fixed time or for an indefinite period, in which latter case the debt is to be paid and the possession delivered back upon the call of either pledgeor or pledgee; this call provides such notice as may be agreed upon. Thus pledges or loans are currently spoken of as being in 1, 2, or 10 days' call, which means that the contract will determine 1 day, or 2, or 10 days after the call has been made; frequently it is agreed that the pledge shall be payable within an hour, or a number of hours from the call; again, it may be agreed that a contract shall run 30 or 60 days, or more, and thereafter continue on call.

The hypothecation is not narrowed to a mere contract for the payment of money, for it may apply to any other lawful engagement where value is pledged for the performance of an undertaking, and it is open to all persons who are not incapable of contract by law, which debars idiots and lunatics, married women, persons under disabilities, and those incompetent by reason of age or weakness; minors, however, may hypothecate, for their contracts are not void but simply voidable, and then only by their act and choice; and factors may pledge goods in their hands for the amount of their lien upon them but not more, as the law only gives them that degree of possession and title. And the pledge applies not only to the principal but to the interest of the debt, even after it has become due while it remains unpaid, through an improper delay of the debtor. Pledges or loans for a fixed time are usually discounted, but the interest on "call" loans, although not due until the loan is paid, is, in many cases, collected at intervals. The pledge applies also to any charges that may be fairly made for the care and maintenance of the security, such as for storage, repairs, or insurance, and the pledgee cannot be held, but he may hold the debtor, for any loss or destruction of the security through unavoidable accident; and in the case of such loss of a part, the rest of the security may be held for the whole debt. All increase of the collateral security, such as interest, dividends, or other profit, may be kept by the pledgee as further security for the debt; an indulgent custom, however, permits the claim of this income by the debtor, and although the pledgee cannot be compelled to release any part of the security by the payment of a portion of the debt, yet it is usually agreed that if certain parts of the collateral are sold, or are required by the debtor, he may regain possession of them from the pledgee (for delivery to the purchaser or other purpose) by payment of their rated portion of the debt. Unless it is so stipulated, the pledgee cannot hold the collateral for a former debt due him by the pledgeor, nor can it be held for a subsequent debt, unless it should appear that the new loan was made upon the security of the former pledge, in which case the collateral could be made by the pledgee to apply to all the debts. And the pledgee may hypothecate securities that have been hypothecated with him; provided, always, that his pledge of them is not for a greater debt than they represent to him.

An important feature of the usual form of hypothecation is the provision made for the protection of the pledgee, should the fluctuation of values during the term of the pledge destroy any part of the security which the contract bore at the time of making; this is called the margin, and it is the difference by which the property pledged is superior in value to the debt or loan. This margin is gauged by the character of the collateral, being small or large in the proportion that the price of the security is stable or varying. And there is usually an agreement in the contract that if the fixed rate of margin be not maintained, and the impairment of the margin through a decline in the price of the collateral, not supplied after a certain agreed upon notice, the contract shall determine. And in such a case, or if the engagement has not been otherwise properly carried out, or if the pledge be not redeemed when it has become due (either by the lapse of its term or by the call of the creditor), then the pledgee has the right to recover his debt by the sale of the security for it, and by a sale only; for the debt cannot be satisfied by the pledgee's retention of the pledge; and, unless it is otherwise stipulated, this sale must be judicial and after formal notice to the debtor, who in this case has still the right to redeem his property. But it is usually agreed that these privileges shall be waived, and that the sale may be in the open market or privately, and without notice to the debtor.

And at this sale the pledgee cannot become a purchaser of the pledge or any part of it, unless it is expressly stipulated in the contract that he may, provided he shall be the highest bidder; usually, however, pledges are sold at public auction or in the exchanges, as the courts scrutinize closely all private sales, and their validity is open to attack. Where several things are pledged, each with its increment may be sold to extinguish the debt, but the sale must stop when the debt is satisfied, and the remainder unsold or arising from the sale of a part must be turned over to the debtor.

Creditors of the pledgeor who have so-called privileged debts may precede the pledgee; generally, however, creditors take place according to the date of their claims, but a point of law is that any creditor who has a superior claim "may maintain it and receive full compensation from the fund before the creditor who holds under a mere contract of pledge from the debtor." The debtor may hold the pledgee responsible for any neglect or failure to do his whole duty, and where negotiable instruments, such as notes, are pledged, for any compromise the pledgee may effect with their makers; and when the terms of the contract give the pledgeor the right to cancel the debt by tender of its payment after proper notice to the pledgee, then the pledgee must deliver back the possession of the pledge and its increment, upon satisfaction of his claim; but the debtor cannot recover the title to his property from a *bona fide* purchaser, when by a breach of trust the pledgee thus disposes of the security. The common law requires a pledgee to satisfy himself fully as to the integrity of the pledge, and the debtor's title to it; thus great care is used in exactly determining the right of the debtor to pledge property of which he is agent or trustee; also the right to pledge of a husband acting for his wife, for the law is not inclined to protect a pledgee, if, unknown to him, there is a fatal flaw in the collateral. (E. C.)

I.

IBERVILLE, PIERRE LE MOYNE, SIEUR D' (1661-1706), a Canadian commander, founder of Louisiana, was born at Montreal, July 10, 1661. He was one of eleven brothers, named Le Moyne, several of whom attained distinction in the French service. Pierre entered the navy as a midshipman in 1675, and served in the overland expedition of 1686 against the English forts on Hudson Bay. In 1688 he went again and captured two English vessels, and in October, 1694, he captured Fort Nelson. He had now attained the rank of captain of a frigate, and in 1696 with three vessels he entered the Bay of Fundy, defeated three English ships, captured St. John's, and destroyed Fort Pemaquid. In 1697 he again went to Hudson Bay, defeated three English vessels, and reduced Fort Bourbon. In 1698, being sent from Brest to occupy the mouth of the Mississippi, he set sail Oct. 24, found Pensacola occupied by Spaniards, and on Jan. 31, 1699, anchored in Mobile Bay. Then taking his brother BIENVILLE (see Vol. I.) and 50 men, he proceeded in two barges to the mouth of the Mississippi, which he reached on March 2. After ascending the river for some distance he received from the Indians a letter which had been left by Tonty in 1686 for La Salle. He built Fort Biloxi, and sailed for France in May, 1699. Returning early in the next year he built a new fort some distance up the Mississippi, and sent a party under Le Sueur to the copper mines of Lake Superior. In December, 1701, his colony, having suffered from fevers, was transferred to Mobile. In 1706 he captured the Isle of Nevis, and he was preparing to attack the coast of Carolina when he died at Havana, July 9, 1706.

IBSEN, HENRIK, a Norwegian poet and dramatist, was born at Skien, March 20, 1828. He was a druggist, but having gained renown by his drama *Catilina*, went to Christiania, in 1850, for the purpose of further study. In 1851 he was called to take charge of the National Theatre at Bergen, founded by Ole Bull. In 1857 he accepted a similar position at Christiania; and in 1863, having obtained a travelling pension, he went as far as Rome. Since 1866 he has lived at Dresden and Munich, being in receipt of an annual pension. Among his earlier dramas were *Gildet på Solhoug* (1856); *Fru Inger til Östrat* (1857); *Härmändene på Helgeland* (1858). Later came *Kongs-emnerne* (1864); *Brand* (1866); *De Unges Forbund* (1869); *Keiser og Galiläer* (1873); *Samfundets Stötter* (1877); *Gjengangere* (1881); and *En Folkefjende* (1882).

ICE, the solid form assumed by water at the temperature of 32° Fahr. When reduced to this temperature water solidifies, expanding as it does so with such extreme force as to rend thick iron receptacles in which it may be confined. In freezing it loses much of its contained heat. In returning to the liquid state this lost heat must be regained, and the melting of ice is considerably retarded by this necessity. The congelation of water takes place under several conditions. In the form of hail it is due to the exposure of condensed moisture to low temperatures in the upper air. If the moisture is frozen before condensation, it yields snow, a form due to the loose aggregation of minute ice crystals. By compression in mountain valleys or ravines snow is reduced to ice, and takes the glacier form. More ordinarily ice is produced by the freezing of the surface-layers of streams, ponds, and lakes, or their congelation to the bottom if the cold be sufficiently intense. In more northerly regions the freezing extends to open bays and gulfs, and in the Arctic seas to the whole surface of the ocean. On Arctic lands glaciers of enormous extent are formed, and the masses which are broken from the front of these and drop into the ocean constitute the icebergs which are drifted into the temperate seas by polar currents. One important property of freezing ice is that it discards impurities and dissolved matters. This may be experimentally proved by the mixture of coloring matters in water. If now frozen, the ice will be found to be colorless and transparent, while the coloring matter is concentrated in the remaining water. Thus very impure water may furnish pure and wholesome ice. Bubbles of gas, or water included in the ice through irregular freezing, may contain impurities, yet the ice itself is free from them. Thus the best ice is that which is least porous, which renders the steadily freezing, compact, and dense ice of the colder regions of superior commercial value. It is also affirmed that the ice of the more northern localities melts more slowly, from its superior density, but that is questionable. The same quantity of actual ice must take the same time to melt, whether porous or not.

See Vol. XII. p. 646 Am. ed. (p. 611 Edin. ed.).

Ice has been used for domestic purposes since an early era, its first employment being in the form of snow gathered from the mountains. This commercial use of snow is still practised in Italy, Spain, and some other countries. Ice has also been long used by the wealthy, being gathered from ponds on their estates, and stored for summer use. It has become a commercial article only within the present century, and that mainly in America. In London it was not sold to private consumers until 1845, though it had been previously in demand by fishmongers and confectioners. In the Middle States of America it has been stored for domestic use for nearly two centuries, in deep cellars, in which the ice was surrounded by sawdust or some other non-conductor. It became an article of commerce much later, and up to 1820 it was a scarce and dear commodity in the Northern cities, and not used in the South—deep wells and spring-houses partly obviating its necessity. It was sold on a small scale to consumers in Boston early in the century, but in New York there was no private demand before 1825, though it was much used previously by butchers, fishmongers, and probably in some other industries.

The first attempt to transport ice to tropical America was made by Mr. Frederick Tudor, of Boston, in 1805, in which year he took a cargo of 130 tons to Martinique. He continued in this business without opposition and with little profit for many years. In 1815 he obtained a monopoly of the Havana trade, and afterwards extended his enterprise to Charleston, Savannah, and New Orleans. Yet in 1832 his total shipments amounted to 4352 tons, all taken from Fresh Pond, Cambridge. In addition to the above-named places he sent ice to Brazil and to the East Indies, in which latter country he sold it at half the price of the ice collected by the natives. Until 1836 the whole shipping trade remained in his hands. Then competition entered, and the ice commerce rapidly increased. The total shipments from Boston to all ports, from 1805 to 1856, were 230,000 tons, of which 146,000 tons were shipped in the latter year. From 1856 to 1872 the total trade covered 2,768,000 tons, there being 225,000 tons shipped in 1872. Since then the Boston trade has met with opposition from other quarters, and has fallen in importance—New York and Maine coming into active competition. In 1874 the total export to foreign ports was 20,000 tons. In the year ending June 30, 1885, it was 38,901 tons, thus showing a considerable increase. Very little of this ice is sent to England, the English market being more cheaply supplied from Norway.

In Europe, indeed, there is a very small ice consumption as compared with that of America, in which country it has grown very large. In addition to the very large quantity stored by the cities of the North for their own consumption, much ice is sent South, both from the Atlantic seaboard and from the cities bordering on the great lakes, such as Chicago, Cleveland, Buffalo, etc., which ship ice by rail, or by boat down the Mississippi. It may be said here, however, that the Southern trade is lately much reduced, through the growing use of ice-making machines, and is now mainly confined to cities easily reached by water.

Of the principal Northern cities the ice supply of New York is mainly taken from the Hudson; that of Philadelphia from the Schuylkill, Delaware, and Lehigh, and from the Kennebec River and other localities of Maine; and that of Boston from Fresh Pond, Wenham Lake, and other neighboring bodies of fresh water; while the cities of the West draw their main supply from the great lakes. The ice is stored in huge ice-houses, generally of wood, with double, triple, or quadruple walls, the interspaces filled with sawdust or some other non-conductor of heat. These ice-houses vary greatly in size, some being great clusters of buildings, capable of holding from 20,000 to nearly 80,000 tons. As for the consumption of the several cities, it may be stated that the ice at present cut for the supply of Philadelphia averages about 700,000 tons annually, and of New York and the surrounding cities about 1,200,000 tons. These estimates will apply to other cities, with a variation in proportion to population—the estimated use of ice in the Middle States being 1600 pounds annually per individual. In addition to that collected for sale, there is a very large private collection by brewers, butchers, and others, but principally by farmers and dairymen in rural regions, so that the total consumption of ice in America would foot up an enormous sum.

Of the eastern ice supply the two great sources are the Hudson and Kennebec Rivers—the great bulk of the ice-trade being in the hands of the Knickerbocker Ice Companies of New York and Philadelphia, these being separate organizations, though bearing the same title. The Kennebec ice is claimed to be the clearest

Ice-cutting Scene, with the Endless Elevating Chain in Operation.

and finest gathered anywhere in the world. This furnishes a large part of the Philadelphia supply and of the foreign shipments.

The methods of gathering the ice-crop are wholly of American origin. The requisite thickness of ice for the home market is from 9 to 12 inches, and for exportation 20 inches. In collecting it the surface is first cleared of snow and porous ice by the Snow Plane, which is drawn by horses. The surface of the ice-field is then mapped out into large squares by the Marker, which, after cutting its first groove, is directed in parallel lines by a permanent guide attached to it. The Plow, adapted for various thicknesses of ice, then cuts the shallow grooves made by the Marker two-thirds through the ice. Plows are made with or without guides, as may be desired. Some blocks being sawed out and removed so as to leave a space of open water near the elevator, other blocks are then floated into

Snow Plane.

Ice Saw.

position by the help of ice poles, and are split off into sizes convenient for handling by means of a Splitting Chisel or Bar thrust into the plow-grooves. These detached masses are floated to the foot of the inclined

Splitting Bars.

plane, up which moves by steam-power an endless chain, with shelves at intervals, which carry up the blocks of ice, separated as they here are into the required size for storage. A late attachment to the elevator planes the ice as it passes to the storehouse, so dispensing with the Snow Plane, though cleaning the ice before it is cut has obvious advantages in some of its superficial conditions. These squared blocks are laid side by side in the building, so as to leave no spaces. The cost of labor in ice-gathering has been reduced by the use of improved machinery, until it is not more than 8 or 10 cents per ton in favorable seasons. The great cost is in the wastage by melting and the expense of delivery. The cost to large consumers was formerly $20 to $25 per ton, but has been reduced to about $5 per ton to large users, and $9 per ton to householders, the difference being due to increased wastage and expense in delivering in the latter case.

For many years past machines for the artificial manufacture of ice have been in operation. These have become now very effective, and their use is rapidly extending in warm regions. As yet they have not been able to compete with natural ice in Northern cities, since the ice made by them has cost from $4 to $8 per ton. But in the South they are coming more and more into use, and reducing the ice commerce. In 1880 there were 35 establishments in the United States engaged in the manufacture of machine-made ice, with a capital of $1,251,200, and an annual product valued

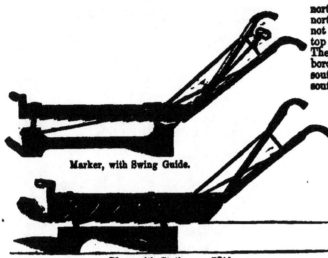

Marker, with Swing Guide.

Plow, with Stationary Guide.

at $544,763. The main seats of this industry were Louisiana and Texas, while Georgia and California came next in order. More recently it is claimed that machines are in existence which will make ice at a cost of from $1 to $1.50 per ton, and a Chicago company has proposed to the ice-gathering companies to furnish them with machine-made ice at a cheaper rate than river ice can be furnished. This claim, however, remains to be practically proved, and there is an unwarranted prejudice against machine-made ice to be overcome ere it can be generally used.

Until within recent times the only use made of ice was in the cooling of drinks. It is now very largely employed in the preservation of meats and other perishable articles of food, while the employment of refrigerating cars and vessels has enabled great quantities of meats, tropical fruits, etc., to be transported for long distances, and delivered in a fresh state to consumers. Large quantities of ice are also used by brewers, and by other industries that require a low temperature. In many instances ice-machines are employed to produce cold without making ice, the required effect being thus gained at reduced cost. Another important recent use is the preservation of dead bodies until ready for burial. The use of ice in medical and surgical operations is equally important, it being employed in fevers to cool the mouth and reduce the internal temperature, while it is applied externally in other cases, and locally to produce partial insensibility of the tissues in surgical operations. Its value in the preservation of the public health renders it one of the most important of industrial products.

(C. M.)

IDAHO. This State was organized by Congress as a separate Territory, March 3, 1863, from portions of Nebraska, Dakota, and Washington. At this time it included all of what is now Montana and the larger part of Wyoming, and had an area of over 375,000 square miles. In 1863 it was reduced to its present limits. It was declared a State July 3, 1890. This new State is of very irregular shape, long from north to south, and very narrow on the northern boundary. On the map it appears not unlike a gigantic easy-chair, with the top towards the north and fronting the east. The length, north and south, on the western border, is 485 miles; east and west, on the southern border, it is 300 miles; from the south-eastern corner it extends north along the border of Wyoming for a distance of 130 miles, and then follows the ridge of the Rocky Mountains irregularly in a north-westerly direction to the northern boundary, where it is only 45 miles wide.

See Vol. XII. p. 736 Am. ed. (p. 697 Edin. ed.).

The State is estimated to contain an area of 84,800 square miles, or 54,272,000 acres, and ranks twelfth in area of the political divisions of the United States. It is nearly as large as Pennsylvania and Ohio combined. The lands of the State have not been fully explored and surveyed, and the classification is only approximately made. These lands are defined as agricultural, desert, timber, and mineral. As now found, and without artificial aids, all the lands suitable for agricultural purposes are estimated at from 12,000,000 to 15,000,000 acres, and are mostly found in the valleys of the larger streams. That which is capable of being reclaimed for agricultural uses by irrigation with the available water now flowing in the rivers and larger streams is put at from 10,000,000 to 12,000,000 acres more; a considerable portion of this land is now considered as grazing lands. The natural grazing lands, unfit for agricultural use by any practicable means, are estimated at 5,000,000 acres. The timbered lands are almost wholly in the northern part, and are estimated at 10,000,000 acres. The mineral lands comprise about 8,000,000 acres, while fully 5,000,000 acres are totally unfitted for any use, so far as is now known.

The population in 1880, excluding Indians on the reservation, was 32,810. The report of the governor for 1884 placed the population at that time at 80,000. The report of another governor for 1885 estimated the population at 75,000. The development of certain minerals and the large influx of miners account for the differences of estimate. The most reliable statistics are those which were gathered by the general government. These show the population in 1890 to have been 84,229. For further particulars see Table I.

Statistics.—Table II. exhibits the farm areas and farm values by counties for the year 1880.

The assessed valuation and taxation of the Territory in recent years appears in the subjoined table:

	Valuation.	Receipts.
1880	$6,408,089	$100,826
1881	8,066,366	56,526
1882	9,108,450	47,103
1883	13,938,412	51,801
1884	15,497,598	50,909
1885	15,973,601	

The mining property of the Territory is not taxable; if it were, the above showing would be more than doubled. The indebtedness of the Territory was, in 1872, $132,217.71. On Jan. 1, 1885, it was $69,268.60. On Jan. 1, 1886, it was $46,268.60, with cash in the public treasury to the amount of $52,261.30.

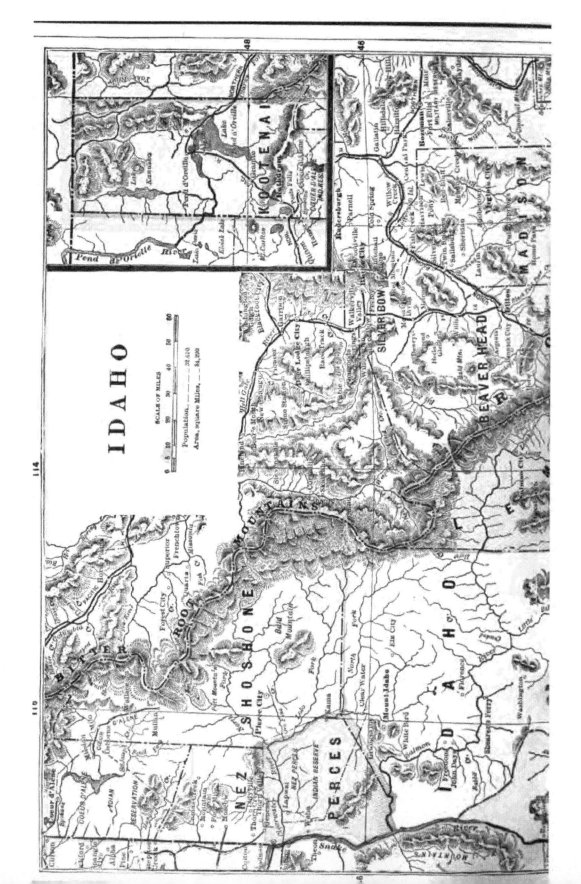

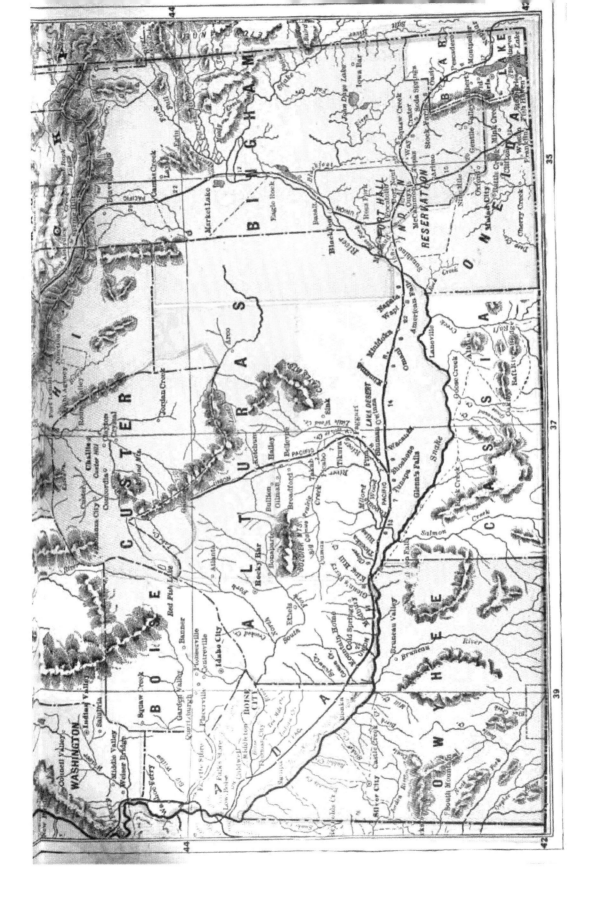

IDAHO.

TABLE I.—POPULATION.

Counties.	White.		Colored.		Chinese.		Indians.		Native.		Foreign.	
	1880.	1870.	1880.	1870.	1880.	1870.	1880.	1870.	1880.	1870.	1880.	1870.
Ada	4,674	2,675	4,447	2,569	16	20	203	78	8	8	3,948	2,178	726	497
Alturas	1,698	689	1,554	369	1	5	128	314	10	1	1,202	286	491	403
Bear Lake	3,235	.....	3,234	.....	.....	.....	.....	.....	1	.....	2,250	.....	985	.....
Boisé	3,214	3,834	1,970	2,057	10	15	1,225	1,754	9	8	1,347	1,183	1,867	2,651
Cassia	1,312	.....	1,289	.....	.....	.....	22	.....	1	.....	1,135	.....	177	.....
Idaho	2,031	849	1,271	415	.....	2	736	425	22	7	1,001	205	1,030	644
Kootenai	518	.....	493	.....	3	.....	7	.....	15	.....	373	.....	145	.....
Lemhi	2,230	988	1,950	864	5	2	262	120	13	2	1,423	509	807	479
Nez Percé	3,965	1,607	3,684	837	6	4	198	747	77	19	3,184	609	781	998
Oneida	6,964	1,922	6,892	1,921	3	1	61	.....	8	.....	5,036	1,189	1,928	733
Owyhee	1,426	1,713	1,179	1,334	7	9	239	368	1	2	809	862	617	851
Shoshone	469	722	171	252	2	2	296	468	.....	.....	113	93	356	629
Washington	579	.....	579	.....	.....	.....	.....	.....	.....	.....	515	.....	64	.....
The Territory	32,610	14,999	29,013	10,618	53	60	3,370	4,274	165	47	22,636	7,114	9,974	7,885

TABLE II.—LAND.

Counties.	Farms.	Average size.	Total acres.	Improved land.			Unimproved land.		Value of farms (land, fences, and buildings).	Value of implements and machinery.	Value of live-stock.	Value of products.
				Total acres.	Tilled.	Permanent meadows, pastures, etc.	Total acres.	Forest.				
Ada	256	316	80,853	62,842	49,235	13,607	18,011	6,091	$800,475	$84,545	$522,264	$517,809
Alturas	90	16	1,444	919	632	287	525	295	28,050	3,225	11,870	34,550
Bear Lake	169	70	11,794	11,604	3,668	7,936	190	.....	138,050	23,380	51,781	52,865
Boisé	64	157	10,061	4,444	3,503	941	5,617	788	116,050	12,710	71,079	97,664
Cassia	143	142	20,248	7,336	4,086	3,250	12,912	.....	110,900	15,963	106,319	44,122
Idaho	155	199	30,914	22,830	11,515	11,315	8,084	1,000	254,225	30,370	170,838	140,816
Kootenai	20	187	3,740	1,100	339	761	2,640	1,014	14,290	2,877	7,117	8,080
Lemhi	88	240	21,150	17,750	3,100	14,650	3,400	617	135,850	18,460	164,460	110,930
Nez Percé	258	141	36,377	18,992	14,679	4,313	17,385	180	546,460	70,240	260,067	210,500
Oneida	422	161	67,790	30,148	20,042	10,106	37,642	462	359,890	63,785	349,588	117,315
Owyhee	66	231	15,230	4,897	2,122	2,775	10,333	.....	117,000	12,865	237,405	64,695
Shoshone	5	172	859	699	562	137	160	160	12,100	830	6,250	5,500
Washington	149	183	27,338	13,846	7,771	6,075	13,492	1,285	196,650	24,680	257,812	110,318
The Territory	1,885	174	327,798	197,407	121,254	76,153	130,391	11,892	2,832,890	363,930	2,246,800	1,515,314

TABLE III.—GOLD AND SILVER.

Counties.	Ore raised. Tons.	Total assay value of ore raised.				Ore raised and treated. Tons.	Average yield per ton.	
		Gold (ounces).		Silver (ounces).		Total.		Gold.	Silver.
Alturas	4,077.75	7,185.4	$148,535	145,477	$188,087	$336,622	908.00	$53.13	$65.45
Boisé	16,605.00	13,594.3	281,019	83,684	108,195	389,214	15,645.00	13.44	5.39
Idaho	500.00	604.7	12,500	.....	.....	12,500	500.00	20.00	
Lemhi	5,000.00	14,512.5	300,000	232,036	299,999	599,999	2,500.00	50.00	50.00
Nez Percé	300.00	290.3	6,001	.....	.....	6,001	300.00	15.00	
Oneida	500.00	604.7	12,500	.....	.....	12,500	500.00	20.00	
Owyhee	8,342.75	13,057.7	269,927	218,190	282,098	552,025	7,176.75	25.09	24.68
Washington	500.00	362.8	7,500	.....	.....	7,500	500.00	10.00	
Total	35,825.50	50,212.4	1,037,982	679,387	878,379	1,916,361	28,029.75	21.16	15.91

The manufacturing interests of the Territory are yet in their infancy. The mining interest, grazing, and latterly agricultural have absorbed the attention of the settlers. The manufactures in 1880 furnished the following statistics:

Establishments	162
Capital	$677,215
Hands employed	388
Wages for year	$136,326
Value of materials	$844,874
Value of products	$1,271,317

The number of live-stock, with their production, in 1880 was as follows: horses, 24,300; mules and asses, 610; working oxen, 737; milch cows, 12,838; other cattle, 71,292; sheep, 27,326; swine, 14,178. The wool produced was 127,149 pounds; milk, 15,627 gallons; butter, 310,644 pounds; cheese, 20,295 pounds. The estimates made from local reports for the year 1885 are as follows: horses and cattle, 400,000 head, with a value of $15,000,000; sheep, 200,000 head, with a wool-crop of 1,000,000 pounds, worth about 13 cents per pound; the number of swine is placed at 40,000 head. The vegetable and cereal productions of the Territory for the year 1885 are as follows: barley, 274,750 bushels; Indian corn, 41,000; oats, 1,032,000; rye, 24,341; wheat, 1,154,000; hay, 140,053 tons; Irish potatoes, 457,307 bushels; tobacco, 1400 pounds; value of orchard products, $923,147.

Minerals.—The mineral resources of Idaho constitute one of its chief sources of wealth. The most extensive belt of the precious minerals, gold and silver, lies on the western slope and the spurs of the Rocky Mountains that enter the Territory in Oneida county, and run the entire length of it to Lake Pend d'Oreille, a distance of 410 miles. The mines have not been developed as greatly nor as rapidly as in other Territories; many difficulties have had to be overcome by the miners, not the least of which were the long and severe winters with short working seasons, and the great distance from railroad communication until quite recently. The annual output from 1883 to 1885 was about $7,000,000. Some of the richest placer mines of the country are in this Territory. There are also mines of copper, mica, etc. The production of the deep mines for the year 1880 is shown in Table III. The amount of bullion produced in the Territory is given in the following table:

Counties.	Gold (ounces).		Silver (ounces).		Total.
Alturas	250.3	$51,743	48,678	$62,936	$114,678
Boisé	19,336.1	213,666	65,330	84,465	294,695
Idaho	483.7	9,999			9,999
Lemhi	6,046.9	125,001	96,683	125,001	250,002
Nez Percé	217.7	4,500			4,500
Oneida	483.7	9,999			9,999
Owyhee	3,712.4	180,101	136,985	177,108	357,209
Washington	241.9	5,001			5,001
Total	29,025.5	600,010	347,676	449,510	1,049,519

Education.—The public-school system of the Territory is modelled after that of all the Western States of the Union. A great pride is manifested in projecting the best system possible for the education of the youth. The 16th and 36th sections of each township were set aside for school purposes, aggregating over 3,000,000 acres. This land is productive of little revenue up to this time, and the schools are supported by local taxation. The following table exhibits the school statistics for several years:

	1871.	1874.	1877.	1880.	1882.
Youth of school age (5–21)	1,592	4,010	4,026	6,000	9,850
Scholars enrolled	905	2,030	2,631	6,758	6,090
School districts	35	77	96	149	183
Schools	28		74	155	
Receipts	$18,295	$23,515	$23,366	$51,530	$54,609
Expenditure	19,003	21,787	18,764	38,812	44,840

In 1884 the number of children was 12,000, distributed among 300 districts. The annexed report of the territorial superintendent of public instruction for 1885 exhibits the state of the schools for that year:

Counties.	Districts.	School-houses.	Schools.	Scholars.	Length of school year.	Youth of school age.	Total expense.
					Days.		
Ada	36	33	33	1,468	144	2,082	$26,921.46
Alturas	34	7	26	1,230	127	1,305	25,660.32
Bear Lake	12	12	12	724	84	1,523	4,431.90
Bingham	25	23	23	822	115	2,302	5,212.72
Boisé	13	13	14	327	67	462	6,507.84
Cassia	22	16	17	618	75	1,030	3,391.27
Center	5	1	5	135	36	292	4,136.14
Idaho	13	10	13	160	36	432	1,689.81
Kootenai	4	4	4	179	22	179	1,468.77
Lemhi	9	7	10	189	39	340	3,205.65
Nez Percé	45	34	47	1,490	208	2,045	16,338.53
Oneida	22	23	24	1,939	145	2,127	4,486.27
Owyhee	7	9	9	166	47	166	5,365.41
Shoshone	5	1	4	67	18	188	1,729.25
Washington	21	12	17	523	73	836	3,651.62
Totals	273	205	248	10,037	1,240	15,399	$115,097.84

Railroads.—There are three railroads through the Territory, aggregating 820 miles within its limits. These are the Utah and Northern, 208 miles; Oregon Short Line—main line 452 miles, Wood River branch 70 miles—together 522 miles, and the Northern Pacific, 90 miles. Notwithstanding its high altitudes and rough surface, the facilities afforded by the valleys and mountain passes for railroad-making are equal to those of any Territory on the plateau. (A. G. M.)

IDEALISM is a term applied to the doctrine of those schools of philosophy which find their basis in consciousness as distinguished from those which fix their beginning in sensations. It stands in marked contrast with sensationalism because of the fact that the latter bases its reasonings and results upon the facts of an external world, while the former relies upon an analysis of self (*Ego*). This indicates the normal use of the word in its application chiefly to modern philosophy. The same title however is applied to all systems which deny reality to the outer world and its impressions, or which find their starting ground in abstract conceptions.

Idealism is usually regarded by metaphysicians as developing itself in two phases, viz.: subjective and objective idealism. When the innate faculties of the human mind are made the primary subject of investigation, and from their intuitions and relations a philosophical system is predicated, we have *subjective idealism*. If, however, a step higher is taken, and Being in the abstract is the theme of contemplation, when the thinker and the world on which he gazes are lost in a higher and eternal principle, the limited and conditioned in the unlimited and unconditioned, and this is the starting-point of theory and reasoning, we have what is called *objective idealism*. This term, however, is used by philosophers generally rather as a convenient form of phraseology than because it is defensible on the ground of accurate definition; some contending that "the proper association of the absolute is with the *not me*" and that on this account objective idealism is a misnomer.

The ideal philosophy is to be traced as far back as the Eleatics. Among these, Parmenides, of Elea (fl. 500 B. C.) seems to be the first to justify this appellation. He united with the early Greek philosophers in the continuous search for the primitive force or origin of things. Instead of accepting the modes of matter as explaining the existent order, he sought for some abstract conception of power. Rejecting the anthropomorphic representations of his predecessors he insisted that "Only being is, non-being is not, there is no becoming." Plurality and change were declared to be only appearances. We cannot know anything except as it has been the subject of thought and this is the proof of its reality, for only that which exists is thinkable. The senses he claimed are perpetually vehicles of deception by which men are seduced into deceitful and rhetorical discourse about things which are plural and changing. This marked advance on the earlier philosophy, which had been based entirely on sensuous perceptions, prepared the way for Zeno, who led the way into more abstract realms of investigation, and who was followed in like endeavor by Melissus, of Samos.

The nearest approach among the Greeks to the spirit of modern idealism is found in Plato. His philosophy turns mainly upon his theory of ideas. To him the idea was the archetype according to the pattern of which all individuals, properly belonging to its class, were made. At times, indeed, he seems to call in question the individual and localized object as a real existence; it is merely a phenomenon, or appearance, while real being is affirmed of the idea. When you have thought, for example, of all kinds of trees, and then have removed from your conception everything that differs among them, there remains to you an idea of a tree which is not contingent or accidental, but which has real and unconditional existence. So of all things. The highest of all ideas is the idea of the Good. This, in contravention of the Eleatics, he affirmed is higher than the idea of Being. The Good becomes a personality in Plato's thought, and is regarded as an ultimate source of power. Before God made the world he made its soul of three elements: the indivisible and unchangeable was one, the divisible and changeable was another, to which was added an intermediate substance between the other two; then the body or the visible world was made. Thus all apparent physical facts are accounted for by their precedent and governing or archetypal ideas.

Modern idealism had its rise with the powerful advance of the philosophy of Descartes (1596–1650). Starting with the statement that consciousness gives testimony to a number of impressions, some of which are apparently contradictory of others, he declares that he is incapable of making any other affirmative statement with certainty than this one, "I doubt." Instead of passing from this to downright scepticism, he proceeds to the recognition of the thoughts which this process has involved, and finally lays down his positive postulate from which an entire philosophical system is developed: "*Cogito ergo sum.*" The existence of mind as totally distinct from matter is regarded by him as a subject of positive proof. The property of the mind is in the possession of ideas, and these ideas are determined to be true on the sole basis of their distinctness or clearness. Since the idea of God is the clearest of all, the idea of an all-perfect infinite being, our consciousness itself furnishes direct proof of the divine existence. From this second point of departure Descartes ranges over the whole field of human knowledge. God has so created us that we shall not be deceived in the deductions of abstract science. Likewise our perceptions are affirmed to be true because a Being of infinite veracity could not have so formed us that our minds and senses would move in a constant realm of falsehood. The proof of the reality of the external world is contingent in this system upon the prior proof of the existence of God. The universe depends not only for its first existence upon the productive power of God, but equally so for its continued being. Creation is perpetual. This is very near objective idealism, to which indeed it was soon carried. Baruch Spinoza (1632–1677) seized upon that feature of the philosophy of Descartes which made the perceptions of the finite mind contingent upon the interposition of the divine power. Absolute perfection is only an attribute, he insists, of some perfect Being. The fundamental idea, therefore, is the idea of Being; that is, self-existent substance. God enshrines in himself all reality. Thought and extension are simply attributes. Substance, he declares, is that which exists in itself, and is conceived by itself, and which needs nothing else for its existence. God is indeed the only substance. All ideas are true so far as they are referable to God; for all ideas which are in God agree perfectly with their objects. The human mind so far as it knows things truly is a part of the infinite divine intellect. Reason apprehends things under a certain form of eternity. True and final knowledge is not of sensation or perception, but is in the apprehension of the essence of things. Thus we see that objective idealism has its legitimate end in pantheism.

In England pure idealism was carried to extreme conclusions by Bishop Berkeley (1684–1753). He declared that the supposed existence of a material world was not only incapable of proof but was positively false. He contended that we are immediately conscious and certain of the existence of our thoughts. We infer also that bodies different from our thoughts exist. This, however, is merely an inference, and is erroneous. There is no law of nature; what we mistake for it is the order of succession of our ideas. In short, as we can never get beyond our ideas, these ideas are the real objects of knowledge. He did not reject a phenomenal world, but denied that it was material. Arthur Collier (1680–1732), following Malebranche, developed a similar theory. Reid, of Scotland (1710–1796), based a system of philosophy upon consciousness, which has been termed "the philosophy of common-sense," in which he denied the representative character of ideas, and insisted upon the validity of our perceptions and of the observed facts of our consciousness. He was followed in methods and conclusions by Dugald Stewart (1753–1828), who carried the work to more satisfactory and scientific conclusion. The effect of their work was to destroy the sceptical conclusions of previous idealists. Unquestionably the most learned of English idealists was Sir William Hamilton (1788–1856). Adopting largely the method and terminology of Reid, he rescued this system from much that was inaccurate and misleading. He denies that we have any direct consciousness of the *Ego* or self. Our knowledge of mind as of matter is limited to its phenomena. The reality, or the being developing the phenomena would be suggested by them. Of the outward world and of the categories of matter we have a direct and not a representative knowledge; but as to the nature of this *Non Ego*, whether it is made up of phenomena only, or whether it involves substantial being, seems to have been left by him in such doubt that his followers are by no means agreed in their interpretation of him.

Idealism was borne to its highest visions and most perfect realizations in Germany. The author from whom its greatest influence was derived was Gottfried Wilhelm Leibnitz (1646-1716). Originally a disciple of Descartes, he subsequently incorporated into his writings more of the spirit of Aristotle and Plato. It is exceedingly difficult, in a brief space, to give any adequate idea of his ideal philosophy. He developed a theory of monads, concerning which he claimed that everything is composed of an infinite number of them. A monad is simple unextended substance. These monads are not conceived of as atoms but as forces or ideas, each idea being a force. All monads are percipient; some are consciously so, and these he called appercipient. He who should know perfectly one single monad would in it know perfectly the world whose mirror it is. But these monads differ in the point from which they reflect the world, hence there are not in all the universe two monads precisely alike. It is not possible, he affirms, that the soul, or any other true substance, should receive anything from without unless through Divine omnipotence. The soul is the governing monad of the body. Matter, with its continuous extension, exists only in the confused apprehension of the senses. It is only a "well-founded phenomenon;" which does not deceive the inquirer who is guided by the higher rules of reason. He affirmed the immortality and indestructibility of the soul, and at first declared that God was not the author of the harmony of the universe but was that harmony itself. Subsequently, however, he changed the latter statement. His writings constituted a controlling element in almost all subsequent philosophical thought in his own country. Immanuel Kant (1724-1804), the first prominent philosopher to follow Leibnitz, was an idealist so far as to give to his doctrine of the world a subjective origin, but his insistence upon the truth that the material of thought is in the external world seems to class his philosophy as of a dual character. His idealistic tendency culminated in Fichte, Schelling, and Hegel. Fichte (1762-1814) affirmed that "the matter of representations was not derived, as Kant had affirmed, from the action of things in themselves on the agent of representation, or the percipient subject, but that both matter and form were the result of the *Ego*, and that they were furnished by the same synthetic act which produces the forms of intuition and the categories." The contents of our experience are not the consequence of outward phenomena but are the product of our own creative faculty. This power of creation is the ground of all consciousness. The *Ego* posits itself and the *Non-ego*. This *Ego* is not the individual but the absolute. Friedrich Wilhelm J. Schelling (1775-1854) combined the methods of Fichte and Spinoza, and produced what is known as a system of identity. The absolute involves every individual and every category. Here the real and the ideal, the object and the subject, nature and spirit merge into one. He insists that the necessary tendency of all science is to pass from nature into intelligence. The perfect theory of nature would be the resolution of all nature into intelligence. Nature, therefore, finds her highest end and her real existence in reason. Matter, he affirms, is extinct mind, and all the forces of nature are reducible in the last resort to powers of ideal representation. But George W. F. Hegel (1770-1831) developed from this principle of identity, suggested by Schelling, in combination with Fichte's methods, a system of absolute idealism. He contended that phenomena do not exist simply in the consciousness of the individual *Ego*, but are phenomena *per se, i. e.*, that they have an existence in the divine idea. This idea, or the absolute reason, is revealed in nature and spirit, and, having reproduced itself in human thought, returns after this alienation to itself. A "thing in itself" is an abstraction, it is the mere reflection of the thing into itself, in distinction from a reflection of itself into others. Hence the final reality must be sought apart from a world of mere phenomena. Rudolph H. Lotze (1817-1881), a more recent idealist, proclaimed, with slight modification, a similar view, contending, however, that goodness is the ultimate idea, and that everything exists only because it has a necessary place in its expression.

For idealism it is claimed that it is the true method in philosophy, since the mind can only be known by an investigation of its own phenomena, and that it emancipates men from the gross and sensuous by determining the reality of that which is super-sensuous and spiritual. Under its influence legislation is said to have taken higher ground, by recognizing the inherent claims that lie in the nobility of human nature, while religion recognizes in this mode of philosophic thought a congenial handmaid.

References: Heinrich Stein, *Fragment des Parmenides* περὶ φύσεως *in the Sym. Phil. Bonn. coll.* (Leipsic, 1867, pp. 763-806); Schleiermacher, *Introductions to the Dialogues of Plato*, translated by W. Dobson (Cambridge, 1836); Heinrich Ritter, *Ueber den Einfluss Descartes auf die Ausbildung des Spinozismus* (Leipsic, 1816); Erdman, *Leibnitz und die Entwickelung des Idealismus vor Kant* (Leipsic, 1842); A. E. Kroeger, *Kant's System of Transcendentalism*, in *Journal of Spec. Philos.* (1869); *Kant's Critique of the Pure Reason* (London, 1870); Jacobi, *David Hume Ueber den Glauben, oder Idealismus und Realismus* (Breslau, 1787); Fichte, J. G., *Sämmtliche Werke* (Berlin, 1845-46); *Fichte's Popular Works*, translated with Memoir by W. Smith (London, 1848); Fleming, W., *Vocabulary of Philosophy* (N. Y., 1879); Lewes, G. H., *Biographical History of Philosophy* (N. Y., 1867); Ueberweg, F., *History of Philosophy*, translated by G. S. Morris (1874); A. Schwegler, *History of Philosophy in Epitome*, translated by J. H. Seelye (1860); Arthur Collier, *Demonstration of the Non-existence of an External World*; *Metaphysical Tracts* (London, 1837); George Berkeley, *Works, with prefaces, life, etc.*, by A. C. Fraser (Oxford, 1871); H. L. Mansel, *Letters, Lectures, and Reviews* (London, 1873), in which may be found an interesting essay on the Idealism of Berkeley; F. W. J. von Schelling, *Werke* (Stuttgart, 1858); Schelling's *Introduction to Idealism* is translated by T. Davidson, in *Journal of Spec. Philos.*, vol. 1, pp. 159-164.

(T. A. K. G.)

IDIOCY. See INSANITY.

IGNATIEFF, NIKOLAS PAULOVITSCH, a Russian general and diplomatist, was born at St. Petersburg, Jan. 29, 1832. His father, a captain of infantry, had been the first army officer to acknowledge Czar Nicholas on his accession to the Russian throne in 1825, and hence was an object of imperial favor. The son had the czar as god-father, and was educated in the corps of pages and in the Nicholas Academy. In 1849 he entered the Imperial Guard, and during the Crimean war he served on the staff of Gen. Berg in the Baltic provinces. After the war Ignatieff was made military

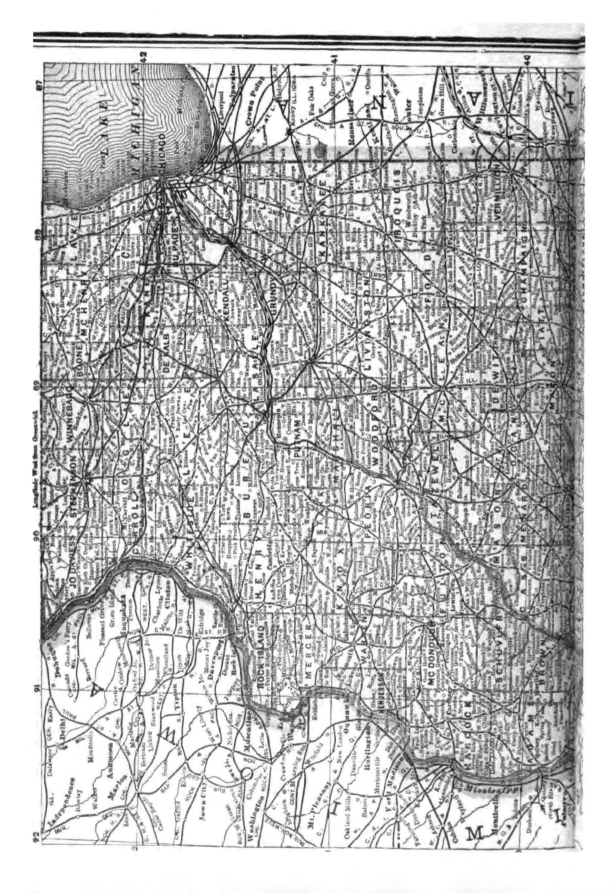

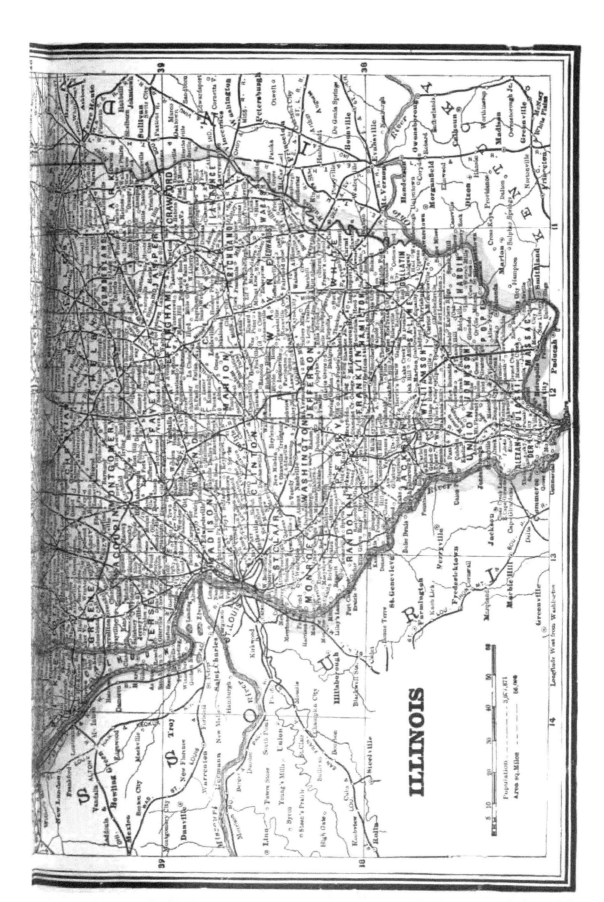

attaché to the Russian embassy at London, and his report on England's military position in India attracted the attention of Alexander II. In 1858, being now a colonel and aide-de-camp to the emperor, he was sent on a special mission to Khiva and Bokhara. In 1860 he was a major-general, and was sent as plenipotentiary to Pekin, where he negotiated a commercial treaty with China, and also obtained the cession of Ussuri. On his return to St. Petersburg Ignatieff took charge of the Asiatic department in the ministry of foreign affairs. On July 26, 1864, he was appointed minister to Constantinople, and in 1867 was raised to the dignity of ambassador. He directed himself steadily to the advancement of Russian interests, moved cautiously during the Cretan insurrection, protected the Bulgarian church party in their contest with the Greek patriarch, and acquired a strong personal influence with the sultan, as well as general popularity. But in 1876 the troubles in Servia gave to Russia a pretext for armed interference, while England gave Turkey encouragement in resisting such action. A change in the Turkish ministry transferred to Sir Henry Elliot, the British ambassador, the influence long wielded by Ignatieff. Servia was defeated in her struggle with the Turkish empire and compelled to sue for peace, yet the threats of Ignatieff enabled her to get two months' truce, while representatives of the Great Powers held a conference on the situation. The conference, however, failed to obtain satisfaction from Turkey, and in March, 1877, Ignatieff visited Berlin, Paris, Vienna, and London, ostensibly on account of his eyes, but really to ascertain the disposition of the other Great Powers with reference to the war which Russia was now determined to wage. After the war Ignatieff was the chief representative of Russia in negotiating the treaty of San Stefano, March 3, 1878, and then went to Vienna, where he effected an understanding with the Austrian government. He took no part in the Congress of Berlin, and in the last two years of Alexander II.'s reign resided at Nice. On the accession of Alexander III., in March, 1881, he was called to be minister of public lands, and in May to be minister of the interior. This position he held for one year only.

ILLINOIS was the eighth State admitted into the Union under the Federal Constitution. Congress passed the act April 18, 1818, and the Territory was admitted on Dec. 3, 1818. It contained at that time a population of 40,000. It ranks twenty-first among the States in area, having, by the latest surveys, 56,650 square miles, or 36,256,000 acres. In 1870 it reached the fourth rank in population, and remained the same in 1880. Its population in the latter year was 3,077,871, classified as follows: males, 1,526,523; females, 1,491,348; native, 2,494,295; foreign, 583,576; white, 3,031,151; colored, 40,720. The population in 1890 was 3,801,285, of which 1,086,000, or nearly one-third, was in the city of Chicago. In 1884 the rank of the State was first in corn, wheat, oats, meat-packing, lumber traffic, horses, malt and distilled liquors, and in the number of miles of railway operated. It ranked second in rye, coal, agricultural implements, and soap. It ranked fourth in hay, potatoes, iron and steel products, mules, milch-cows, and in oxen and other cattle.

See Vol. XII.
p. 742 Am.
ed. (p. 703
Edin. ed.).

Topography.—The greater part of the State is a high, grassy plain. Except Delaware and Louisiana, it has the most level surface of any State in the Union. In the central and eastern parts the surface is level, often stretching out into what is termed "flat prairies." The highest point in the State is in the north-western part, between Freeport and Galena, where the elevation reaches 1,150 feet above the level of the sea. At the extreme southern part the elevation is only 350 feet, and the average for the entire State is less than 500 feet. The interior is traversed by numerous streams, along the borders of which are bluffs and broken land, so that the surface is not one vast prairie but is composed of many small prairies, separated from each other by these streams, along which growths of timber are found. The State lies midway in the Great Central Plain of the continent, and contains some of the richest lands of the valley. The soil is a heavy, black loam, of great depth and inexhaustible fertility.

Climate.—The climate is as nearly that of season and latitude as can be found on the continent. The modifying influences are not many nor great. Yet among these must be noted the general fact that the topography of the Mississippi Valley, open, as it is, at both ends, and with an Arctic region on the north and the warm waters of the large gulf on the south, is favorable to sudden and violent changes of temperature. No mountain ranges intervene at either north or south, to check or modify the extremes of heat and cold which come from beyond. The State of Illinois is too far removed from either extreme to be subject to the severest of the changes, and yet sufficiently near to both to be influenced by them. In the north-eastern part of the State the presence of the lakes has some modifying influence on the climate, making it warmer in winter and cooler in summer than in corresponding latitudes outside the lake region. In other respects the climate conforms to latitude and seasonal changes. On the whole, it is salubrious, bracing, and pleasant. The malaria, which was once found here, has disappeared with the cultivation of the soil. The atmosphere on the prairies is almost constantly in motion, making even the highest temperature endurable. On the 40th parallel the mean temperature for the summer season is 77°; for the winter it is 33° 30′, while the mean annual temperature is 54°. The annual rainfall at the same latitude is 35 inches.

Minerals.—The State is underlaid in more than three-fourths of its extent by beds of bituminous coal of excellent quality and workable depth. The coal area is little short of 37,000 square miles, and is about one-seventh of the entire known coal-area of North America. The first coal-mine opened in America of which any record exists was at Ottawa in this State in 1669. The average annual coal-product for five years ending with 1885 was about 10,000,000 tons. (See COAL in Vol. II.) Along the Fox and Des Plaines Rivers are found vast quantities of limestone of a superior quality. It is quarried extensively for building purposes, and the well-known "La Salle stone" was used largely in rebuilding the city of Chicago after the destructive conflagration in 1871. The great central lead-deposit which is found in Wisconsin, Iowa, and Minnesota, extends into the north-western parts of Illinois. It constitutes an important mineral of the State. The richest and most extensive lead-diggings of the country are found near Galena. In Saline and Gallatin counties are found salt-wells, so rich that 75 gallons of the water produce 50 pounds of salt.

Agricultural.—All the factors necessary to successful agriculture conspire to give this State the pre-eminence. The soil is rich, level, free from stones and gravel, easily tilled and highly fertile. Every ingenuity of modern machinery is readily applied here. The rainfall is abundant and seasonable. The seasons are long enough and come with such regularity that little danger is experienced by the skilful farmer in managing any crop he may choose to cultivate. The State lies almost entirely within the celebrated "corn-belt" of the country, and this cereal is produced here with the greatest ease and abundance. Wheat and the other cereals can be raised in all parts, and wheat is cultivated extensively in the southern portions. According to the latest official reports the farms and farm values of the State are as follows: The number of farms of 3 acres and upwards is 235,741; the improved or cultivated land reaches 26,115,154 acres; the value of the farms, including land, fences, and buildings, is $1,009,594,580; the value of farming implements and machinery is $33,739,951; the value of live-stock as found on the farms on July 1, 1880, is $132,437,762; the total cost of all fertilizers used during the previous year was only $174,277, and this was chiefly in localities near the cities where market gardening was done; the estimated value of all farm-products sold, consumed, or on hand for the year previous to the census was $203,980,137. The following table shows the average product of the State for nine years, ending with 1880, in the principal cereals and vegetables. The column on the left shows the rank the State held among the other States:

Rank	Crop.	Number of acres.	Number of bushels.	Yield per acre.	Value per acre.	Total value of crop.
1	Corn	7,879,399	234,499,337	28.60	$8.97	$70,749,491
2	Wheat	2,326,591	30,438,354	13.2	13.15	30,034,369
3	Oats	1,688,238	49,558,899	30.2	7.61	12,740,356
3	Potatoes	133,616	10,273,875	78.	40.92	5,467,423
4	Hay	2,114,303	(a) 2,897,162	(a) 1.36	10.92	22,678,771
9	Buckwheat	10,709	151,362	14.2	11.03	118,132
12	Tobacco	10,018	(b) 7,357,857	(b) 73.4	53.11	515,907

(a) Tons. (b) Pounds.

The following table shows the product for 1889:

	Acres.	Bushels.	Value.
Corn	6,988,267	247,980,589	$58,337,049
Oats	3,633,936	142,150,811	28,981,064
Wheat	2,052,388	37,201,916	26,093,250
Rye	204,873	3,803,419	1,466,229
Barley	40,088	1,207,157	511,994
Potatoes	123,758	15,855,006	4,145,823
Hay	3,176,281	(tons 4,910,544)	26,819,871
Total	16,219,591	448,198,898	$146,355,280

The live-stock in the State for the same year was as follows:

Cattle	2,448,262
Horses	1,005,474
Mules	88,245
Hogs	2,172,322
Sheep	546,496

Commerce.—Few States in the Union are more favorably located or possess greater facilities for commerce. The State has a river navigation of over 4000 miles, while Lake Michigan on the north-east gives free connection with the Atlantic ports. Lines of railway form a network in every section of the State. The commerce upon the lake is chiefly from the port of Chicago. The following exhibit of the water traffic of a single year will give some conception of the extent of this branch of commerce:

	Number of vessels.	Tonnage.	Number of crew.	Value of vessels.	Capital invested.	Gross earnings.
Lake	115	16,035.35	908	$970,300	$1,342,135	$1,263,975
River	56	6,510.77	439	256,500	540,050	437,360
	171	22,546.12	1,347	1,226,800	1,882,185	1,701,335

The State has the greatest number of miles of railway of any State in the Union, Pennsylvania coming second and New York third. These run in every direction and reach every point of commercial interest. Over fifty distinct roads are found in the State, while the number of branch roads added makes the number ninety-five. The level and unobstructed surface of the State makes it exceedingly favorable for railroad building and operating, and the cost of construction and the labor necessary are comparatively trifling and easy. The State has over 10,000 miles of railway track. The capital invested is more than $400,000,000; the funded debts over $250,000,000, other debts about $50,000,000. The total cost of construction and equipment was about $450,000,000. The freight traffic of all the roads is upwards of 35,000,000 tons annually, while the number of passengers transported rarely falls below 25,000,000 each year. The net earnings of the roads is about $80,000,000 annually. These roads all pay a tax to the State upon their assessed valuation, except the Illinois Central, which pays seven per cent. of its gross earnings.

Finances.—Illinois ranks among the six States of the Union which are free of debt. The total value of assessed property in the State was $800,771,626, of which the railroad property was estimated at $68,799,061. Merchandise was assessed at $25,555,028. The total mortgage debt on farming property was $123,733,098. The State charitable institutions include 4 hospitals for the insane, at Elgin. Jacksonville, Anna, and Kankakee; a deaf and dumb, and a blind asylum, at Jacksonville; one for the feeble-minded, at Lincoln; a soldiers' orphans' home, at Normal, a soldiers' and sailors' home, at Quincy; an eye and ear infirmary, at Chicago; and a reform school for boys, at Pontiac. These institutions had in all 6024 inmates in 1889, their expenses being $1,005,617. Education is compulsory, all children between seven and fourteen being required to attend day school for at least sixteen weeks in the year. In 1889 the public schools of the State had 23,089 teachers, with an average attendance of 763,411 pupils; the total expense of the schools being $11,730,895. The State maintains two normal schools, an agricultural college, and an industrial university.

Manufactures.—Grazing and agriculture obtained the attention of the first settlers, but after the State was fully settled attention was turned to the development of the manufacturing industries. In 1880 the number of establishments was 15,549, with a capital of $140,652,066. The average number of persons engaged in manufactures was as follows: males over 16 years of age, 120,558; females over 15 years, 15,233; children and youth, 8936. The total wages paid the employés in 1880 was $57,429,085, and the total value of the products, $414,864,670. The largest and most extensive manufactories of the country in the line of agricultural implements are found in this State, chiefly in Chicago. Extensive manufactories of wagons, plows, buckets, and other wooden wares are found at Moline.

The centre of the live-stock traffic and of lumber is found in Chicago, and statistics have been given in the article on that city (see CHICAGO, in Vol. II.).

Religion.—Almost every denomination of the Christian faith is found in the State. Some of these are large and flourishing; most all of them have denominational schools and colleges for the higher education of their youth, while almost all are represented by one or more newspapers or other periodicals. The larger of the denominations have branch departments of their publishing houses in Chicago. The following table exhibits the number of the ministers and communicants in the several denominations found in the State, according to the official figures furnished in 1880:

Denomination.	Ministers.	Members.
Roman Catholic	409	390,000
Methodist Episcopal	790	128,181
Christian	650	82,250
Lutheran	345	76,000
Baptist, Regular	687	68,186
Presbyterian	405	42,889
United Evangelical	102	27,155
Congregational	251	23,115
United Brethren	254	15,482
Evangelical Association	178	12,100
Presbyterian, Cumberland	138	10,903
Protestant Episcopal	107	8,123
Dunkards	152	7,500
United Presbyterian	64	6,394
Methodist Episcopal, South	48	5,186
Methodist Protestant	114	4,900
Free Will Baptist	78	4,788
Second Advent	30	3,750
Reformed in U. S. (German)	18	3,726
Universalist	41	3,253
Anti-Mission Baptist	63	2,800
Friends	18	2,619
Reformed in America (Dutch)	22	2,106
Reformed Episcopal	11	1,950
Free Methodist	85	1,638
Winebrennarian	38	1,415
Reformed Presbyterian	6	1,200
Unitarian, Congregational	11	1,000
Wesleyan Methodist	34	875
Seventh Day Adventist	10	760
Moravian	4	611
Jews (total pop. 12,443)	8	570
Swedenborgian	8	456
Seventh Day Baptist	13	391
Primitive Methodist	4	250
Presbyterian, South	3	60
New Mennonites	2	150

Historical.—The early history of this State is somewhat similar to that of most frontier States, in the troubles with the Indians, and with lawless gangs driven from the Eastern States. The most notable of the Indian wars was that which commenced with the burning of Fort Dearborn and the massacre of the garrison, in 1812, by the Pottawatomies, and the Black Hawk war of 1831–32. This war culminated in the expulsion of the Indians from the State. A few years after this, trouble began with the Mormons in Hancock county. The Mormons had settled on the river, founded the town of Nauvoo, and erected a magnificent temple. Their doctrines, and especially their practices and their interference with the civil polity of the county, were very distasteful to other settlers. From 1839 to 1844 there was constant conflict and trouble between the Mormons and the settlers. In 1844 the destruction of a press by the Mormons in Nauvoo led to the suing out of warrants for the arrest of Joseph and Hiram Smith, the founders of the sect. The Mormons armed to resist the arrest, and the "Nauvoo Legion," a body of cavalry 2000 strong, was called to arms. A mob was raised at Warsaw, a few miles up the river, and the State militia of the county called out. Before anything was done leading to bloodshed, the Smiths went over to Carthage, the seat of justice, and delivered themselves up to the civil authorities. When the Warsaw mob learned of this, they turned aside from the road to Nauvoo and came to Carthage, where the two Smiths were shot and killed in the jail. These troubles resulted in the emigration of the Mormons to Salt Lake. During the Mexican war Illinois raised and equipped six regiments for the service. In the civil war of 1861–65 the State contributed largely of men and means for the struggle. The first call of Pres. Lincoln for 75,000 volunteers was made on April 15, 1861. In ten days after that the State had 10,000 volunteers enlisted, although her quota was but 6000. During the progress of the war the State contributed 259,092 men. Of these, 5888 were killed in battle, 3032 died of wounds received in action, 19,496 died of disease, 967 died in prison, and 205 were lost at sea, making a total loss of 29,588 in the war.

The State has sent two men to the Presidential chair, Abraham Lincoln and Ulysses S. Grant, both of whom were re-elected. She has furnished many prominent men in civil, military, and judicial positions.
(A. G. M.)

IMMIGRATION is the act of removal into a country of which one is not a native, for the purpose of permanent residence. The same act with reference to the country from which the removal is made is emigration. The migrations of individuals or communities have been almost first among the means by which countries have been developed, civilization spread abroad, and the wealth of the world increased.

See Vol. VIII. p. 159 Am. ed. (p. 173 Edin. ed.).

The history of immigration to the lands now included in the United States is largely a history of the nation itself. The aboriginal element in the population is insignificant in numbers and influence, and practically every civilized resident of the United States is either an immigrant or the descendant of persons who immigrated to this land at some time within the last three centuries.

Early in the seventeenth century the great movements of population from Europe began. English colonists settled in Virginia, Massachusetts, and subsequently at many points on the coast from Canada to Georgia. The Dutch established settlements along the Hudson and in New Jersey. Louisiana was claimed by the French. Many colonists of that nation settled along the Lower Mississippi and established forts connecting their possessions there with the colonies in Canada. Spanish adventurers founded, after repeated unsuccessful attempts, permanent settlements in Florida, though the province was afterwards ceded to the English and remained under their control for twenty years. Pennsylvania received early in the eighteenth century large accessions of population from the German districts along the Rhine. The descendants of the European colonists, with the slave population, numbered when the Revolutionary war had closed about 3,000,000 persons. These constituted the infant nation, and subsequent additions to the inhabitants by immigration, though from the same sources, constitute the foreign-born element of the population of the United States considered as a political body.

The Revolutionary war, creating a strong enmity between the new nation and the country from which its colonists had been principally drawn, discouraged immigration, and subsequent events in European history were influential in the same direction. The wars which the French Revolution and the conquests of Napoleon Bonaparte engendered attracted the adventurous spirits who might otherwise have sought the new republic established in the Western continent. The government of the United States by the constitutional provision forbidding any immediate attempts by Congress to suppress immigration, and by its early enactments providing for naturalization, encouraged settlers from all parts of the world. The laws at first provided that only two years' residence in the United States was necessary before an alien could become a naturalized citizen. The period of residence preliminary to citizenship was increased to five years in 1795, and in 1798, in a sudden fit of opposition to the incoming of aliens, to fourteen years. The present period of five years was again fixed in 1802. All the offices in the republic except those of president and vice-president are entirely open to the foreign-born citizen.

No record of the number of immigrants was kept until after the passage of the law of 1819, and estimates as to the number who came to this country before that time have greatly differed. The most generally accepted estimate is that of Dr. Young, of the Bureau of Statistics, who placed the number of those who arrived between 1776 and 1820 at 250,000. Other estimates have been: Mr. Blodget, 4000 a year from 1789 to 1794; Dr. Seybert, 6000 a year from 1790 to 1810; Prof. Tucker, 50,000 from 1790 to 1800; 70,000 from 1800 to 1810, and 114,000 from 1810 to 1820; making 234,000 from 1790 to 1820.

The condition of many of the immigrants who came to the United States before 1819 had excited much sympathy. They were crowded between the lower decks of emigrant vessels by agents who had hired the space from the ship-owners. The long voyages in slow sailing vessels and the crowding in insufficient space resulted in a mortality which frequently exceeded 10 per cent. of the number of passengers. Nor was the condition of the immigrants, when they had landed, greatly improved. The passage-money of nearly all of the immigrants had been paid in advance by agents, and the labor of the newly arrived foreigners was relied on to reimburse the agent and to secure for him an exorbitant commission. The immigrants—children as well as adults—were made "indented servants," and their labor for periods of from three to ten years was sold at public auction to the highest bidder. The system led to cruelty, and prevented the immigrants from gaining the full benefit of their change of residence. The evils of the system of importing aliens for indenture were for the most part remedied by the act of Congress passed in 1819.

Immigration in the early years after 1820 was largely from England and Ireland, the British Isles supplying two-thirds of the immigrants for several years. The Irish immigration increased rapidly, and in 1825 and the few years immediately following was about one-half of the whole foreign addition to the population. German immigration in large numbers began in 1832, and from that time Germany has furnished a large part—frequently a third and sometimes nearly a half—of the yearly number of new residents. The Irish immigration in 1832 was also large. The years 1838-39 showed a decline in immigration, probably caused by the financial crisis of 1837 in this country. A return of comparative prosperity here, the famine in Ireland in 1846-47, and political disturbances in Russia and other parts of Europe, led to a gradual but great increase in immigration, which continued with hardly a backward step for fifteen years, until the number of alien passengers reached in 1854 a total of 427,833 persons, a number which was not equalled for nearly twenty years afterwards.

While the causes which have led to the increase and decrease in immigration at successive periods are not always exactly ascertainable, the most important influences can be determined by noticing the conditions of the countries to which and from which the migrations are made. Religious or political persecutions, famine, general business depression, the imposition of unusually heavy taxes, and the requirement of extra military duty are powerful inducements to emigration, while prosperous business conditions and popular governmental acts encourage the residents of a country to remain at home. On the other hand the condition of the country which is the destination of the intending emigrants is no less a factor in determining their number. When there is no threat of war and no unjust oppression is to be feared, when business is active and wages are high, the favorable circumstances are quickly known in countries less happily situated. Former immigrants, finding plenty of profitable employment, send accounts of their prosperity to their friends at home, and frequently assist them to enjoy the same advantages in new homes. An unfavorable condition of business affairs, or public disturbances in the intended home of the alien purposing a change of residence, will often suffice to keep him in his native country. The causes thus noted have had effects that can often be traced in examining the course of American immigration.

The tide of immigration, nearly at its height in 1854, began to ebb in the succeeding years under the combined influences of an improved condition of affairs in Ireland, which had been relieved by emigration from an apparent overplus of population, the discovery of gold in Australia, and the war with Russia. The panic of 1857 had a still greater influence in reducing the number of immigrants, so that in 1858-59 the number was only a third of that reached in several years previous to 1855. Just as the effect of the financial depression was beginning to pass away came the civil war, which, in the early disturbance of established industries and in the vague terror which rumors of it carried to distant lands, was powerful in preventing immigration. The number of alien passengers fell in 1860 and 1861 to about 89,000 a year—less than at any other time after 1844. The Irish immigration was resumed in large numbers in 1863, when the inflation of the currency and the demand for labor in many kinds of business made a period of temporary prosperity.

The immigration from Germany, if it felt less quickly

the effect of renewed business activity, resumed in 1865 the first place in numbers, which it has since held. The number of English immigrants also rapidly increased. Sweden, which had previously given only a small number of permanent residents to the United States, sent over large numbers in 1868 and the five succeeding years. The effect of the Franco-German war was shown in a decreased emigration from Germany in 1870 and 1871, while in 1872 and 1873 the French, usually a home-loving race, but then despairing at the misfortunes of their country, gave almost their only important contribution to the crowd of newcomers.

By 1873 the number of aliens seeking new homes in this land had again reached a number over 400,000 in a year, but the financial panic of that year quickly affected the flow of immigration. The succeeding years of business depression continued to affect the numbers of the incoming population until in 1877 the point was reached from which a reaction began. The increase was rapid and was remarkable in the large number of nations which felt the inspiration of the influences tending to augment emigration. Hungary, Bohemia, Russia, and, in an especial degree, the Scandinavian countries, suddenly increased the numbers of their emigrants in 1880. Local influences, such as the Eastern troubles affecting several of the nations and an unpopular government in Denmark, added to the hopefulness as to business prospects in this country, were influential in causing these changes. The religious persecution to which the Hebrew population in Russia were subjected was also an important influence in increasing emigration. The year 1882 brought a larger number of immigrants to the United States than had arrived in any preceding year; the total reaching 730,349. The immigration since 1882 has decreased from various causes, that of 1890 being 455,302.

The total number of immigrants who, up to the middle of the year 1890, had arrived in this country since the foundation of the republic—estimating 250,000 arrivals in the period preceding 1820—is given as 15,631,000.

The following table shows the number of immigrants from the principal foreign countries unto 1885, as far as the official figures are a correct guide. Before 1856 the reports from the collectors of the various ports furnished only the number of alien passengers, which included some transient visitors. Between 1856 and 1868 a deduction was made in the totals of the number of alien passengers, not immigrants, but all alien passengers were included in the returns of the arrivals from specified countries. The figures in the columns under the names of particular countries in those years in the following table will not be accurate, while the totals will be more exact. A deduction of nearly 2 per cent. should be made from the number of alien passengers, to estimate the number of immigrants. Since 1868 the immigrants have been separately counted. The number of immigrants who arrive by railroads from British America is not reported, but the number is probably not large. The totals of the British Isles in the table on page 386, besides including natives of Wales, contain the only enumeration of a large number of Irish and Scotch who previous to 1871 were not fully recorded separately.

Not only have the United States welcomed to their shores the throngs of aliens seeking homes in this country, but their safety and health while on the voyage hither, their protection from imposition upon landing, and their care in sickness or distress until they had a fair opportunity to become self-supporting, have all been subjects of State or national legislation. The act of Congress, approved March 2, 1819, provided, that if the master of any vessel should take on board or transport between the United States and any foreign port a greater number of passengers than 2 for every 5 tons of measurement, he should forfeit $150 for each passenger above that number. Children under 1 year of age were not counted, and 2 children under 8 years of age were counted as 1 passenger. The vessel itself was forfeited if the number of passengers in excess of that allowed by law amounted to 20. The law also required that an allowance should be made for a voyage between this country and Europe of at least 60 gallons of water, 100 pounds of salted provisions, 1 gallon of vinegar, and 100 pounds of wholesome ship-bread for each passenger, and a proportionate amount for a shorter or longer voyage. In case the passengers were put on short allowance at any time, a payment of $3 a day for each passenger for every day of the restricted allowance must be made. Ship captains were required to make under oath lists of passengers arriving on their vessels, designating in each list the age, sex, occupation, and nationality of each passenger, and setting forth the number of deaths on the voyage.

The national legislature hoped in this way to do away with the evils which had existed in the overcrowding of vessels and in the insufficient provision that was made for the sustenance of immigrants on the long voyages made in slow sailing vessels. The substitution of steam for sails, and the influence of competition between the various lines of steamers, have been, perhaps, as powerful as legislation in the suppression of many of the evils to which immigrants were formerly subjected. Congress has continued to enact laws which, under the general name of "passenger acts," form an important part of national legislation.

Several of these laws were enacted in 1847 and 1848. One, approved Feb. 22, 1847, provided, that the space allotted to each passenger should not be less than fourteen superficial feet on the lower deck, if the vessel was not to pass within the tropics. If it was to pass within the tropics, twenty superficial feet were to be allowed to each passenger, or thirty feet on an "orlop" deck. A year later, legislation compelled the proper ventilation of passenger vessels and the victualling of them so that each passenger might have on his voyage, if needful, 15 pounds of good navy-bread, 10 pounds of rice, 10 pounds of oatmeal, 10 pounds of wheat flour, 10 pounds of potatoes, 1 pint of vinegar, 60 gallons of fresh water, and 10 pounds of salted pork; which was considered provision for 10 weeks. The space allowed to each passenger was increased, and regulations made respecting cleanliness and good discipline.

The provisions of previous laws were partly superseded by the elaborate act of 1855, which after providing that only 1 passenger shall be carried for every 2 tons of vessel, fixes the space that shall be appropriated to each passenger at not less than 16 superficial feet on the main or poop decks, or in the deck houses, and 18 superficial feet on the lower deck—no passenger to be carried on any other deck, nor where the height or distance between the decks is less than 6 feet. A hospital must be provided, berths constructed of sufficient width, and not occupied by more than 2 passengers. Ventilation must be secured by the erection of wooden houses or booby-hatches. Each vessel must have a sufficiently large cooking range, and an ample supply of provisions—nearly as fixed by the law of 1855—must be placed on board. Discipline and cleanliness must be maintained. The captains of vessels who shall fail to furnish sufficient well-cooked provisions shall be subject to a fine

IMMIGRATION.

IMMIGRATION TO THE UNITED STATES.

		England.	Ireland.	Scotland.	Total British Isles.	Germany (including Prussia).	Sweden and Norway.	France.	Switzerland.	Italy.	Spain and Portugal.	Netherlands.	British America.	Total.
Years ending September 30.	1820	1,782	3,614	268	6,024	968	3	371	31	25	174	49	209	8,385
	1821	3,073	1,518	293	4,728	383	12	370	93	62	209	56	184	9,127
	1822	856	2,267	196	3,488	148	10	351	110	32	180	51	204	6,911
	1823	851	1,908	180	3,008	183	1	460	47	32	244	19	167	6,354
	1824	713	2,345	257	3,609	230	9	377	253	41	372	40	155	7,912
	1825	1,002	4,888	113	6,983	450	4	515	166	58	286	37	314	10,199
	1826	1,459	5,408	230	7,727	511	16	545	245	50	452	176	223	10,837
	1827	2,521	9,766	460	13,952	432	13	1,280	207	35	421	245	165	18,875
	1828	2,735	12,488	1,041	17,840	1,851	10	2,843	1,592	30	223	263	267	27,382
	1829	2,149	7,415	111	10,574	597	13	582	314	16	211	189	409	22,520
Calendar Year.	1830	733	2,721	29	3,874	1,976	3	1,174	109	8	24	22	189	23,322
	1831	251	5,772	226	8,247	2,413	13	2,038	63	28	37	175	176	22,633
	*1832	944	12,436	158	17,767	10,194	313	5,361	129	2	111	205	608	60,482
	1833	2,966	8,648	1,921	13,564	6,968	16	4,662	634	1,693	1,149	39	1,194	58,640
	1834	1,129	24,474	110	34,964	17,686	42	2,989	1,359	105	151	87	1,020	65,365
	1835	468	20,927	63	29,897	8,311	31	2,696	548	56	212	124	1,193	45,374
	1836	420	30,578	106	43,684	20,707	57	4,443	445	107	209	301	2,514	76,242
	1837	896	28,508	14	40,726	23,740	290	5,074	353	36	264	312	1,279	79,340
	1838	157	12,645	48	18,065	11,683	60	3,675	128	52	226	27	1,476	38,914
	1839	62	23,963	..	34,234	21,028	324	7,198	607	76	447	85	1,926	68,069
Years ending Sept. 30.	1840	318	29,430	21	42,043	29,704	55	7,419	500	28	148	57	1,938	84,066
	1841	147	37,772	35	53,960	15,291	195	5,006	751	166	222	214	1,816	80,289
	1842	1,743	51,342	24	73,347	20,370	553	4,504	483	93	137	330	2,078	104,565
	‡1843	3,517	19,670	41	28,100	14,441	1,748	3,346	553	108	177	330	1,502	52,496
	1844	1,357	33,490	28	47,543	20,731	1,311	3,155	839	79	286	184	2,711	78,615
	1845	1,710	44,821	368	64,031	34,355	928	7,663	471	63	213	721	3,195	114,371
	1846	2,854	51,752	305	73,982	57,561	1,916	10,583	696	88	75	979	3,855	154,416
	1847	3,476	105,536	337	128,838	74,281	1,307	20,040	192	100	163	2,631	3,827	234,968
	1848	4,455	112,934	659	148,098	58,465	903	7,743	319	219	231	918	6,473	226,527
	1849	6,036	159,398	1,080	214,530	60,235	3,473	5,841	13	208	355	1,190	6,890	297,024
	†1850	6,797	164,004	850	215,089	78,896	1,569	9,381	325	406	795	684	9,276	369,980
	1851	5,306	221,213	966	272,740	72,482	2,424	20,126	427	447	485	352	7,436	379,466
	1852	30,007	159,548	3,148	200,247	145,918	4,103	6,763	2,788	351	459	1,719	6,262	371,603
	1853	28,867	162,649	6,006	200,235	141,946	2,364	10,770	2,748	555	1,186	600	5,424	368,645
	1854	43,901	101,606	4,605	160,253	215,009	3,531	13,317	7,953	1,263	1,505	1,534	6,091	427,833
	1855	38,871	49,627	5,275	97,199	71,918	521	6,044	4,433	1,052	1,156	2,588	7,761	200,877
	1856	25,904	54,349	3,297	99,007	71,028	1,157	7,246	1,780	1,365	914	1,395	6,488	195,857
	1857	27,804	54,361	4,182	112,840	91,781	1,712	3,897	2,080	1,007	806	1,775	5,670	246,945
	1858	14,638	26,873	1,946	55,829	45,310	2,430	3,155	1,056	1,240	1,459	185	4,902	119,501
	1859	13,826	35,216	2,293	61,379	40,784	1,091	2,879	833	932	1,329	290	4,163	118,616
	1860	13,001	48,637	1,613	78,374	54,491	296	3,961	913	1,019	1,054	351	4,514	150,237
	1861	8,970	23,797	767	43,472	31,661	616	2,326	1,007	811	495	283	2,069	89,724
	1862	10,947	23,351	657	47,990	27,529	892	3,142	643	566	420	432	3,375	89,007
	1863	24,065	55,916	1,940	122,798	33,162	1,627	1,888	690	547	586	416	3,464	174,524
	1864	26,096	63,523	3,476	116,951	57,276	2,249	3,128	1,396	600	1,157	708	3,636	193,196
	1865	15,038	29,772	3,087	112,237	83,424	6,109	3,583	2,869	924	1,057	779	21,536	247,053
	¶1866	3,559	36,690	1,088	131,614	115,892	12,683	6,855	3,823	1,362	1,062	1,716	32,150	314,917
	1867	36,972	72,879	7,582	125,520	133,426	7,055	5,237	4,168	1,624	1,030	2,223	23,378	310,965
	1868	11,107	43,747	1,949	107,583	123,070	20,490	3,936	3,261	1,406	1,061	652	10,894	289,145
	1869	55,046	51,290	12,415	147,716	124,788	41,833	4,118	3,488	2,182	1,377	1,360	20,921	385,357
	1870	59,488	56,628	11,820	151,069	91,779	24,365	3,586	2,474	2,940	802	970	53,340	356,302
	1871	61,174	61,463	12,135	143,937	107,201	22,966	5,760	2,894	2,940	677	1,122	39,939	346,938
	1872	72,810	69,761	14,565	157,905	155,595	24,993	13,782	4,081	7,321	923	2,006	40,288	437,750
	1873	69,600	75,845	13,008	159,355	133,141	39,458	10,813	3,223	7,507	520	4,640	39,508	422,545
	1874	43,396	47,586	8,765	100,422	56,927	10,917	8,741	2,436	5,867	623	1,533	30,596	260,514
	1875	30,040	29,969	5,739	66,179	36,565	10,496	8,607	1,641	3,344	1,741	1,073	23,420	191,231
	1876	21,051	16,506	4,383	42,243	31,322	11,235	6,723	1,572	2,979	1,413	709	21,218	157,449
	1877	18,193	13,791	3,405	35,554	27,417	9,107	5,127	1,612	3,659	1,094	572	22,131	130,508
	1878	19,581	17,113	5,700	40,706	31,958	11,392	4,668	2,051	5,391	1,080	652	30,102	153,207
	1879	40,997	27,651	8,728	78,424	43,531	26,147	4,121	3,634	9,041	1,110	1,199	53,267	250,565
	1880	64,190	64,799	14,495	164,438	134,040	69,777	4,939	5,498	12,781	581	3,730	139,781	563,708
	1881	76,547	70,909	16,451	165,230	249,572	82,859	5,653	11,628	20,101	11,687	10,812	95,188	720,045
	1882	70,893	72,937	15,957	161,428	232,269	87,610	5,580	11,433	29,348	11,928	7,880	86,908	730,342
	1883	61,432	83,554	10,539	157,361	184,389	53,891	4,016	11,433	29,512	12,063	6,928	66,950	570,316
	1884	53,270	58,589	8,791	121,756	155,529	37,923	3,690	8,215	14,441	520	3,731	47,886	461,346
	§1885	45,385	49,356	10,163	104,904	106,910	31,591	3,135	5,126	15,680	......	2,499	......	325,411
		1,304,478	3,093,144	243,698	5,557,686	7,054,880	684,090	341,167	141,535	196,325	73,894	78,902	1,029,000	13,347,462

* And last quarter of 1831. † First three quarters. ‡ And last quarter of 1849. (The remaining years are calendar years.) § The figures for 1885 are from a preliminary report of the Bureau of Statistics and comprise about 90 per cent. of the immigration for that year.

of not more than $1000, and imprisonment for not more than one year. Money penalties may be collected for other violations of the act. A payment of $10 must be made for each death on board during the voyage. Vessels are subject to inspection and examination, and lists of passengers, with designations of age, sex, occupation, nationality, etc., must be delivered on the arrival of the vessel.

This act forms the basis of the provisions in the U. S. Revised Statutes, and in the later passenger act of 1882, which contains additional provisions for the separation of passengers of different sexes, and of passengers from the members of the crew, and for exercise on the upper deck by immigrant passengers. Other legislation, providing for the inspection of steam and other passenger vessels, has been directed mainly to preserving the lives of the passengers, by regulations as to fire appliances, life-preservers, and the testing of boilers, engines, and hulls.

The division between the duties and powers of the national government and those of the State governments has always been clearly marked. The right of regulating the carriage of alien passengers, up to the time of their landing, has been within the scope of national legislation, but as soon as they had landed their protection became a matter of State concern. The State of New York had, as early as 1788, a law by which the masters of vessels were required, within 24 hours of their arrival, to report to the mayor or recorder the names and occupations of every person brought into port on their vessels, under a penalty of £20 for each person, or £30 for each foreigner not reported. The law further provided, "That if any master of any ship or other vessel shall bring or land within this State any person who cannot give a good account of himself or herself to the mayor or recorder of the said city for the time being, as aforesaid, or who is likely to be a charge to the said city, such master shall within one month carry or send the person so imported by him back again to the place from whence he or she came." Similar provisions were made in some of the other States. The principal burden of the care and protection of immigrants has fallen upon the State of New York. Three-fourths of the emigrants from countries other than British America arrive at the port of New York. Over 9,000,000 alien passengers have been received at that port in the forty-four years since 1847. In the six years, 1880-85, the number of alien passengers arriving at New York was:

1880	327,371	1883	405,909
1881	455,681	1884	330,030
1882	476,086	1885	273,594

The proportionate importance of the various ports at which immigrants are received may be seen from the following table of the number who arrived in the several districts in 1884:

Districts.	Immigrants.	Districts.	Immigrants.
Aroostook, Me.	191	New Bedford, Mass.	503
Baltimore, Md.	30,740	Newburyport, Mass.	3
Boston and Charlestown, Mass.	31,491	New Haven, Conn.	9
		New Orleans, La.	2,954
Buffalo Creek, N. Y.	842	New York, N. Y.	322,781
Cape Vincent, N. Y.	167	Oswego, N. Y.	17
Chicago, Ill.	42	Passamaquoddy, Me.	1,499
Corpus Christi, Tex.	1	Pearl River, Miss.	28
Cuyahoga, Ohio.	20	Pensacola, Fla.	24
Detroit, Mich.	22,594	Philadelphia, Pa.	19,064
Duluth, Minn.	240	Portland and Falmouth, Me.	1,539
Fairfield, Conn.	2	Providence, R. I.	2
Galveston, Tex.	962	Salem and Beverly, Mass.	3
Gloucester, Mass.	145		
Huron, Mich.	20,418		
Key West, Fla.	1,972	San Francisco, Cal.	1,528
Machias, Me.	1	Savannah, Ga.	1
Michigan, Mich.	3	Superior, Mich.	501
Minnesota, Minn.	924	Teche, La.	135

Total..........461,346

The New York legislature in 1847 passed an act which initiated the system which has since been carried out at New York city for the reception and care of emigrant passengers. Important amendments and additions were made to the provisions of the original law by acts passed in 1848, 1849, 1853, 1855, 1857, 1868, 1881, and 1883. The present system has become so far perfected that the reception of the enormous numbers of alien passengers of the last few years has been accomplished without friction.

When a vessel arrives at New York harbor from a foreign port it is boarded by quarantine officers and by an officer of the Commissioners of Emigration. The quarantine regulations must first be complied with. The emigration officer then examines as to the cleanliness of the vessel and receives a report of the number of steerage passengers, the record of births or deaths on the voyage, and the particulars of any cases of sickness, and receives complaints from the steerage passengers if any are dissatisfied. The master of the vessel is required to make a sworn report of the name, place of birth, last legal residence, age, and occupation of each alien passenger. The report must also specify whether any of the passengers are lunatic, idiotic, deaf, dumb, blind, infirm, maimed, above the age of 60 years, under the age of 13 years, or a widow having a family, or a woman with a family and without a husband. The names of those who have died on the voyage must also be reported.

The immigrants, after their baggage has been examined, are transferred to the landing-depot, which the Commissioners of Emigration are required to designate. This landing-place was for over 30 years at Castle Garden. A fortification known as Castle Clinton had been erected at that place, and was used in 1814 during the war of 1812. The reception of the Marquis de Lafayette at Castle Garden in 1824, and the use of the great enclosure for the concerts of Jenny Lind in 1850, connected the place with two of the important local celebrations of New York city. The main structure which served as the immigrant station was encircled by the walls of the old Castle. It was large enough to accommodate 3000 immigrants, while provision was made to enable the inmates to obtain all the articles necessary for subsistence without leaving the building. Yet, in a structure so easy of access and exit, it proved no easy matter to protect the inmates from extortion and fraud, and this and other evils caused the authorities in 1890 to remove the immigrant station to Governor's Island in the harbor, where they can be kept under better control, and secured against the frauds and evil solicitations of extortionists.

Immigrants who have friends may await them at the Information Bureau. Those who wish to remain for a time in New York city may make arrangements with licensed boarding-house keepers, who are admitted to the building on agreeing to furnish board and lodging on terms approved by the commissioners. Those who wish to go immediately to some other part of the United States may procure tickets from representatives of the several railroads without leaving the building, and they and their baggage are conveyed without extra charge to the railway-stations. Interpreters are provided, who can speak and write every European language; brokers, whose responsibility is approved by the commissioners, exchange foreign money for that of the United States.

Immigrants who are sick are received at a temporary hospital, whence they are transferred to the emigrant institutions on Ward's Island, where from 2000 to 4000 persons are under treatment each year. The Commissioners of Emigration have established a free labor-bureau for those of the immigrants who desire employment, and the German and Irish emigrant societies now pay the expenses of the bureau. In 1884 the bureau procured employment for 23,687 immigrants, of whom 8385 were females. The female immigrants were for the most part engaged for domestic service. The males, to the number of 11,768, found employment as laborers, and over 3000 in skilled occupations.

The immigrant reception station presents a curious scene after the arrival of one or more large emigrant vessels. In various parts of the room are groups of foreigners, many of them dressed in the costumes of their native countries, gesticulating earnestly, and talking excitedly in their various languages. Many families are among them, with children in the quaint apparel, perhaps, of Italy or of Switzerland. Sometimes, on a wintry day, when the large room is cold and damp, a group of Arabs or of natives of India gather about the stove, shivering even under heavy cloaks that are lent to them, their own loose robes being ill-adapted to the climate, and their stockingless feet half frozen in touching the cold soil instead of the warm sands of the desert. Or, on a sultry day, Russians may swelter under the fur costume suited for their own wintry climate.

The throngs of immigrants are now so safely watched over by the officers appointed by the State and nation that complaints of ill-treatment on the voyage or of swindling after their arrival are rare. The relief of immigrants who were incapable of their own support was formerly continued by New York State for five years after the arrival of the immigrant. The Commissioners of Emigration in 1882 strongly recommended a reduction of this period to one year, saying in their report, "This long period of provisional support tends to encourage pauperism, and to increase the number in the almshouses and charitable institutions of New York by many immigrants who first settled in other States. A recent census shows that nearly one-half of the inmates of this department applied for aid and care after having been in this country one year or more, while nearly one-fourth came from or have resided in other States." On these representations the legislature reduced the period for which the State assumed the care of sick and destitute immigrants to one year from the time of arrival.

The Commissioners of Emigration of New York are nine in number, six being appointed by the governor and confirmed by the senate. The mayor of the city of New York, the president of the German society, and the president of the Irish Emigrant society are also members of the commission, though the representatives of the societies have restricted powers as to the appointment of employés. A change in the law, providing for three commissioners, has not been carried into effect, owing to differences between the governor and the senate as to the selection of a commissioner. Laws somewhat similar to those in New York exist in Massachusetts and other States.

The payment of the expense of caring for and protecting alien passengers intending to reside in the United States has usually been made at New York directly by the owners or consignees of the vessels on which they arrived, though the cost has indirectly fallen probably on the passengers themselves in the increased charge for transportation. The New York city authorities were permitted from the formation of the State to demand a bond from the master of a vessel that the alien passengers brought by him would not be a charge upon the county. The bond might be compounded for under the early statutes, and in 1830 it was provided by law that a commutation might be made by the payment of a sum of money for each passenger. The act establishing the Emigrant Commission in New York in 1847 provided for a bond of $300 from the captain, owner, or consignee of an immigrant vessel to indemnify the cities, counties, and towns of this State for the support of any immigrant who became a public charge within five years of his arrival, or, in place of such a bond, a tax for each immigrant was to be paid. This tax, or "head-money," which varied between $1.50 and $2.50, amounted at New York from 1847 to 1876 to $11,229,329.46.

The payment of this tax was finally resisted by the steamship companies, and in 1876 the New York law was declared unconstitutional, as encroaching on the prerogative of Congress to legislate concerning commerce. No tax was collected from the steamship companies from 1876 to 1882. A new law, called an inspection law, but imposing a tax of $1 for each alien passenger, was also declared unconstitutional. Suits were begun by the steamship companies for the recovery of the amount paid as "head-money," but these suits were finally dismissed. A law permitting the Commissioners of Emigration to close Castle Garden and the emigrant hospitals to such steamship companies as did not pay for the privilege and levy a fee for each alien passenger led to a dispute which convinced the steamship companies that the privileges of the landing-depot would be cheaply purchased at the fee imposed. They voluntarily paid a fee of 50 cents for each alien passenger, and soon after, in 1882, Congress passed a law which put an end to the troubles in New York as well as in other States about the collection of "head-money."

This law, which has been sustained by a decision of the U. S. supreme court, provides for the payment of 50 cents for each alien passenger by the owner or master of the vessel in which he arrives. The money thus collected forms an immigrant fund, to be used by the secretary of the treasury, who may contract with a State board, or officer designated by the governor, in each seaboard or lake State, for the relief and protection of immigrants, the expense being paid out of the immigrant fund. The amount thus collected from the steamship companies has generally been sufficient to pay the expenses of the State commissioners.

The immigrants, who come from countries widely separated, who are protected on their way to this country by the national laws, and are guarded on their arrival and relieved in distress or sickness by State officers, are distributed in various proportions among the States of the Union. No statistics of the place of birth of the inhabitants of the United States were gathered at any national census before 1850, and no approximate estimate can be made of the number of inhabitants of foreign birth, or the distribution of the foreign-born population, before that time. At the various enumerations since and including 1850 the number of foreign-born inhabitants have been as follows:

Year.	Total population.	Persons of foreign-birth.	Per cent. of foreign-born.
1850	23,191,876	2,244,602	9.68
1860	31,443,321	4,138,697	13.16
1870	38,558,371	5,567,229	14.44
1880	50,155,783	6,679,943	13.32

The several nationalities, as reported in the census of 1880, were represented as follows:

Country of birth.	Foreign-born population.	Per cent. of foreign-born population.	Per cent. of total population.
England and Wales	745,978	11.17	1.49
Ireland	1,854,571	27.76	3.70
Scotland	170,136	2.55	0.34
Germany	1,966,742	29.44	3.92
France	106,971	1.60	0.21
British America	717,157	10.74	1.43
Sweden, Norway, and Denmark	440,262	6.59	0.88
Other foreign countries	678,126	10.15	1.35

The following table shows how the principal elements of the foreign-born population have changed in proportion to the total foreign-born population at various enumerations:

Place of birth.	Per cent. of foreign-born population.			
	1850.	1860.	1870.	1880.
Ireland	42.85	38.93	33.33	27.76
Germany	26.01	30.83	30.37	29.44
England and Wales	13.75	11.54	11.24	11.17
British America	6.58	6.04	8.86	10.74
Sweden, Norway, and Denmark	0.80	1.75	4.34	6.59

No State or Territory has a larger foreign-born than native population. The Southern States, except Florida, Louisiana, and Texas, have practically no foreign-born population. The proportion of foreign-born to native population decreased in the ten years between 1870 and 1880, except in Dakota, Oregon, Michigan, and Washington, where the agricultural lands have attracted settlers; Colorado and New Mexico, where the mining industry has greatly developed; New Hampshire, Rhode Island, and Massachusetts, where factories have been established in large numbers; and in Florida and Arkansas, where a beginning has been made in attracting immigrants to the Southern States.

The following table shows the total native and foreign-born population in each of the States in 1880, and the ratio per cent., except where that is less than 1:

States and Territories.	Native.	Foreign-born.	Per cent.
Alabama	1,252,771	9,734	
Arizona	24,391	16,049	66
Arkansas	792,175	10,850	1
California	571,820	292,874	51
Colorado	154,537	39,790	26
Connecticut	492,708	129,992	26
Dakota	83,382	51,795	62
Delaware	137,140	9,468	7
District of Columbia	160,502	17,122	11
Florida	259,584	9,909	4
Georgia	1,531,616	10,564	
Idaho	22,636	9,974	44
Illinois	2,494,295	583,576	24
Indiana	1,834,123	144,178	8
Iowa	1,362,965	261,650	19
Kansas	886,010	110,086	14
Kentucky	1,589,173	59,517	4
Louisiana	885,800	54,146	6
Maine	590,053	58,883	10
Maryland	852,137	82,806	10
Massachusetts	1,339,594	443,491	33
Michigan	1,248,429	388,508	31
Minnesota	513,097	267,676	52
Mississippi	1,122,388	9,209	
Missouri	1,956,802	211,578	11
Montana	27,638	11,521	42
Nebraska	354,988	97,414	27
Nevada	36,613	25,653	70
New Hampshire	300,697	46,294	15
New Jersey	909,416	221,700	24
New Mexico	111,514	8,051	7
New York	3,871,492	1,211,379	31
North Carolina	1,396,008	3,742	
Ohio	2,803,119	394,943	14
Oregon	144,265	30,503	21
Pennsylvania	3,695,062	587,829	16
Rhode Island	202,536	73,993	36
South Carolina	987,891	7,686	
Tennessee	1,525,657	16,702	1
Texas	1,477,133	114,616	8
Utah	99,969	43,994	44
Vermont	291,327	40,959	14
Virginia	1,497,869	14,696	
Washington	59,313	15,803	27
West Virginia	600,192	18,265	3
Wisconsin	910,072	405,425	45
Wyoming	14,939	5,850	39

In the decade 1880–1890 emigration considerably increased from Italy, Hungary, and some other nations not before largely represented. Italy sent large contingents of laborers, the number in 1890 being 52,003.

There is a large British American population in Maine, New Hampshire, and Vermont, besides that in the States mentioned in the table, and the Scandinavians have large settlements in Dakota and Nebraska. About two-thirds of the Mexicans in the United States are to be found in Texas, and three-fourths of all the Chinese are in California.

States.	Ireland.	Germany.	England and Wales.	British America.	Scandinavia.
California	62,962	42,532	26,577	16,889	9,723
Connecticut	20,638	15,627	15,860	16,444	2,682
Illinois	117,543	235,786	60,012	34,043	65,414
Indiana	25,741	80,756	12,020	5,569	3,886
Iowa	44,061	88,268	25,550	21,097	46,046
Kansas	14,993	28,034	16,260	12,536	14,402
Massachusetts	226,700	16,872	48,136	119,229	5,971
Michigan	43,413	89,085	44,032	148,866	16,445
Minnesota	25,942	66,592	9,598	29,631	107,768
Missouri	48,898	106,800	17,564	8,685	4,517
New Jersey	93,079	64,935	32,148	3,536	3,115
New York	499,445	355,913	123,585	84,182	16,494
Ohio	78,927	192,597	55,318	16,146	2,006
Pennsylvania	236,505	168,426	109,649	12,376	8,901
Texas	8,103	35,347	6,749	2,472	2,662
Wisconsin	41,907	184,328	30,268	28,965	66,284

A computation by the Census Bureau indicates that if a line were drawn north and south through Pittsburg, one-third of the Germans and two-thirds of the Irish residents would be eastward of the line, and two-thirds of the Germans and one-third of the Irish to the westward. The Swiss are mainly found in Ohio, New York, Illinois, Pennsylvania, Wisconsin, Missouri, California, and Iowa. A large majority of the Russians are in Kansas, New York, and Dakota. The Bohemians are most numerous in Wisconsin, Illinois, and Iowa, and the Poles in New York. One-third of the Belgians are found in Wisconsin, and more than half the Portuguese in California. The Austrians are widely scattered. Nearly a third of the French are in New York and Ohio, and one-half of the remainder are in Louisiana, California, Illinois, Pennsylvania, Missouri, and Indiana. The Chinese abound in the Pacific States and Territories. The Hollanders are most numerous in Michigan—which has nearly one-third of the number of that nationality—New York, Wisconsin, Illinois, and Iowa.

The immigrants of almost every nationality have been received with favor here, and the policy of the government has been to foster immigration. There have been slight restrictions on immigration in other cases, but the laws respecting the importation of Chinese laborers form the only important exception to the general rule. The inhabitants of China had been, up to thirty years ago, so averse to leave their native land that Chinese immigration had scarcely been a factor in the development of the population. The total number of natives of China reported as having arrived in the United States before 1851 was 46. In 1854 the number of arrivals of this race increased from 42 in the previous year to over 13,000. The yearly immigration of the Chinese has since been—

Year.	Chinese Immigrants.	Year.	Chinese Immigrants.
1854	13,100	1870	11,943
1855	3,526	1871	6,030
1856	4,733	1872	10,642
1857	5,944	1873	18,154
1858	5,128	1874	16,651
1859	3,457	1875	19,033
1860	5,467	1876	16,879
1861	7,518	1877	10,379
1862	3,633	1878	8,468
1863	7,214	1879	9,189
1864	2,975	1880	7,011
1865	2,942	1881	20,711
1866	2,385	1882	35,614
1867	3,863	1883	381
1868	10,684	1884	84
1869	14,902		

The increasing number of Chinese laborers who came into the United States excited fear and aroused opposition on the Pacific coast, where almost all of these immigrants had landed and settled. The system under which a limited servitude was kept up by the contractors who imported Chinese laborers was distasteful to the community.

Some of the objections to the Chinese as permanent residents of this country were stated by Justice Field of the United States Supreme Court in a judicial opinion delivered in California in September, 1882. He said: "It was discovered that the physical characteristics and habits of the Chinese prevented their assimilation with our people. Conflicts between them and our people, disturbing to the peace of the country, followed as a matter of course, and were of frequent occurrence. Chinese laborers, including in that designation not merely those engaged in manual labor but those skilled in some art or trade, in a special manner interfered with the industries and business of this State. Their frugal habits, the absence of families, their ability to live in narrow quarters without apparent injury to health, their contentment with small gains and the simplest fare gave them great advantages in the struggle with our laborers and mechanics, who always and properly seek something more from their labors than sufficient for a bare livelihood, and must have and should have something for the comforts of a home and the education of their children. A restriction upon the immigration of such laborers was therefore felt throughout this State to be necessary if we would prevent the degradation of labor and preserve all the benefits of our civilization."

Other objections to the presence of the Chinese on the Pacific coast were offered. Allegations of unhealthful, vicious, and corrupting practices were freely made. Public feeling was aroused, and many attacks on them by street boys and men occurred in San Francisco and other cities. Restrictive measures were adopted by the city authorities designed to prevent the Chinese from carrying on freely their usual avocations. Some of these measures were oppressive enough to be rebuked by the local courts. A wide difference of opinion existed in various parts of the country as to the justness of some of the complaints, and the necessity of forbidding the further importation of Chinese laborers.

A committee of the U. S. Senate and House of Representatives investigated the subject in 1876 and 1877, and made a report recommending legislation to restrain the incoming of Asiatic populations. The Chinese government had never greatly favored the emigration of its subjects, and little difficulty in modifying the treaty with China was experienced in 1880, when in response to the urgent appeals from the inhabitants of the Pacific coast an effort was made to limit the immigration of Chinese laborers. The Burlingame Treaty of 1868 had provided for free emigration and immigration, but the modified treaty permitted the limitation or suspension by the United States government of the coming or residence in the United States of Chinese laborers, but the absolute prohibition of such immigration was forbidden.

After excited discussion Congress passed in 1882 a bill suspending for twenty years the coming into the United States of Chinese laborers. The bill was vetoed by President Arthur, but a modified act fixing the limit of suspension at ten years became a law. The Chinese who had already become residents of the country were not disturbed, and those who wished to make visits to China with the intention of returning hither were furnished with passports. The suspension of immigration related only to laborers, a term which has been construed to include skilled workmen. The results hoped for from the law by its advocates have for the most part been accomplished already. The open immigration of natives of China has practically ceased, the number reported as arriving in 1884 being 84. Statements are made that large numbers of Chinese laborers land on the Pacific coast at ports in British North America and make their way across the border into the United States. The number of such immigrants is, however, probably not large, and the number of Chinese returning to their own country greatly exceeds the number of reported arrivals. The Chinese population is probably declining, as there are almost no Chinese families here.

The value of the Chinese as immigrants has been a disputed matter. In the Pacific States, where they abound, their presence has certainly proved a disturbing element, and in some places the inhabitants have resorted to violence to drive them out, while in many Eastern cities they form an industrious, useful, and law-abiding portion of the community.

Immigrants who have met with even more general disfavor than the Chinese are the members of the pauper and criminal classes. Laws to restrain the immigration of such persons have been framed in almost every State at which an alien could enter the United States. The enforcement of these laws has not always been easy. Some European governments have favored the policy of deportation to America as a means of getting rid of criminals. This custom prevailed in Switzerland a few years ago, and it was only on representations of the strongest character by our government that the practice was abandoned.

The English law has for many years recognized assisted emigration as a mode of relief under the Poor Laws of that country. The Poor Law Commissioners have charge of the fund which is raised annually from the poor rates. In times of unusual distress Parliament has voted large amounts to assist emigration, especially among the Irish peasantry. The purpose of these acts is not criticised, but it has been found in practice that in some districts the local authorities have chosen old, decrepit, or helpless persons, who were likely soon to become public charges, as emigrants, and have paid their passage to the United States, expecting thus to save the expense of their maintenance. In 1883, when a large sum was appropriated to assist Irish emigration, the New York Commissioners of Emigration found that many of the emigrants were unable to support themselves even if employment was given to them. Affidavits of many of the emigrants showed that they belonged to the pauper class. Three hundred of such emigrants arrived on one vessel in the summer of 1883. Many of them were returned to the country from which they came by the steamship companies. The importation of criminals and paupers is guarded against so carefully that no organised immigration of persons of those classes has been successful, though many individuals who are incapable or criminal doubtless find a refuge here.

The act of Congress controlling this matter, passed Aug. 3, 1882, provides that no idiot, lunatic, convict, or person unable to take care of himself, shall be permitted to land in the United States, but shall be returned at the expense of the vessel bringing him. A rule was adopted in 1885 providing for strict search of emigrant-bearing vessels for such persons; yet despite all efforts the law has been so frequently evaded that more stringent regulations seem necessary. The steamship companies make emigration a mere matter of business, employing brokers to induce poor and ignorant persons to emigrate, whom they bring to this country without regard to their character or condition. This is particularly the case at present as regards Italy, though it may be said of other European countries. As a result many of the immigrants now reaching the United States are of the most undesirable kind, being convicts, anarchists, paupers, and others much more likely to become elements of disturbance or burdens upon charity than useful citizens of the commonwealth. Another evil which had grown to large proportions, the bringing over of assisted immigrants, pledged to work out the cost of their passage, created so much dissatisfaction among the laboring classes that a law prohibiting it was passed Feb. 26, 1885. The effect of this contract immigration was shown most decidedly in the mining regions, which were filled with Hungarians, Poles, and others of the lowest peasantry of Europe, whose willingness to work for low wages and to live under debased conditions, has greatly disturbed the economic conditions of those localities. The public feeling upon the subject is daily becoming more strongly awakened, and should force Congress to take definite action. The diplomatic difficulty with Italy, regarding the lynching of the Mafia assassins in New Orleans in 1891, the trouble with the Hungarian and Polish coke-burners in western Pennsylvania in the same year, and other minor occurrences, have roused an active opposition to the present state of affairs. The industrial classes of the country are growing bitterly opposed to the constant disturbance of their wage rates and other economic conditions by the influx of European artisans to whom privation is normal; the press is unanimous in its demand for some check to the free inflow of the lowest European peasantry. The bills which have been presented to Congress propose that all persons desiring to emigrate to the United States shall be obliged to declare their intention in advance, filing at the consular office of the port of embarkation, a statement of their place of birth, age, pursuit, purpose in emigration, and other needed particulars; this being done 30, 60, or 90 days before the date of the intended emigration, that the consul may have the time to investigate each special case; and he is required to refuse the privilege to all who in any way are likely to become undesirable residents of the United States. The strict observance of such a law would probably reduce the evils which now surround the whole subject of immigration, and give us in the future freedom from all those who are not likely to become useful citizens and desirable additions to our population.

Of the inmates of the almshouses in 1880 44,106 were natives and 22,961 were foreign-born. The percentage of paupers to inhabitants among natives was 0.10 and among foreign-born 0.34. The native paupers and criminals according to statistics in several States include a large proportion of persons whose parents were born aliens. The persons confined in prisons in 1880 numbered 59,255, of whom 46,338 were natives and 12,917 were of foreign birth. The percentage of foreign-born criminals to foreign-born population is larger than that of native criminals to the native population.

These results might naturally be expected when it is remembered that vicious persons may often be compelled to leave their native countries for causes which are not sufficiently serious to demand extradition. The crowding of masses of foreigners into the tenement houses of the great cities is one of the principal agencies in promoting crime in the immediate descendants of immigrants. The cities, and especially New York city, are peculiarly affected by these evil influences. The New York Commissioners of Emigration, in their report for the year 1882, say, "The largest and most vigorous and valuable part of immigration merely passes through New York to those parts of our country where cheap and fertile lands and comfortable homes may be obtained, while the less valuable portion remains in the city of New York, unable from want of means to go farther, or, attracted by the fascinations of a great city, attempt a fortune among the vicissitudes of a populous metropolis."

The beneficial effects, however, of the immigration, which alone has rendered the rapid development of the United States possible, are still further beyond estimate. Every kind of skilled and unskilled labor has been introduced to add to the productive power of the country. The records of the Bureau of Statistics show that in the years from 1873 to 1883 the principal occupations of the immigrants were:

Professional.		*Professional.*	
Actors	953	Physicians	1,747
Artists	1,725	Teachers	3,616
Clergymen	3,957	*Skilled.*	
Lawyers	856	Bakers	13,830
Musicians	4,815	Blacksmiths	21,009
Skilled.		*Skilled.*	
Butchers	12,779	Painters	8,531
Carpenters	63,406	Shoemakers	22,174
Clerks	23,875	Tailors	20,990
Engineers	8,958	Weavers	11,150
Mariners	16,893	*Miscellaneous.*	
Masons	28,424	Farmers	350,847
Mechanics (not specified)	21,312	Laborers	943,581
		Merchants	67,937
Miners	45,288	Servants	152,777

The totals, including many other occupations, are:

Professional occupations	25,343
Skilled occupations	455,949
Miscellaneous occupations	1,588,246
Occupations not stated	81,223
Without occupations	1,997,019
Total immigration	4,147,780

The laborers of every class are scattered throughout the land. The Lake States of the North-west have no population more industrious and more efficient in agricultural pursuits than the Scandinavians, who form a large proportion of the community. Much of the railroad building, which has been a chief instrument in developing the country, would have been impossible but for the labor of immigrants, who endure drudgery that the natives of this country are unable or unwilling to undergo. The quick invention and adaptability of the Irish, the economy and industry of the Germans, the sturdy qualities of the Scandinavian character, and the varied excellencies of the other component parts of our vast foreign-born population have been of incalculable advantage. Without the added population and wealth which immigration has brought the growth of the country would have been slow indeed.

The bibliography of American immigration deserves only the briefest mention. The reports of the U. S. Bureau of Statistics contain the figures which form the basis of all the calculations on this subject. Dr. Edward Young, of that Bureau, compiled a useful pamphlet on *Immigration* (1871). Friedrich Kapp's thoughtful discussion of the subject is in the published transactions of the American Social Science Association. Dr. Schade has written on *Immigration since 1790*, and W. J. Bromwell has collected many of the statistics in a *History of Immigration to the United States.* There are several magazine articles on the subject, of which those of Dr. Jarvis in the *Atlantic Monthly* and Mr. Self in the *North American Review* are noteworthy. An article on Immigration in Vol. I. of the Tenth Census gives valuable statistics and deductions. The Annual Reports of the New York Commissioners of Emigration frequently contain valuable information on special topics relating to immigration, as well as full and accurate statistics of the work of the commission.

(J. P. D.)

IMPEACHMENT. The Constitution of the United States provides that the President, Vice-President, and all civil officers of the United States shall be removed from office for and on conviction of treason, bribery, or other high crimes or misdemeanors (Art. 2, § 4). The House of Representatives has the sole power of impeachment (Art. I, § 2), but the Senate tries the charges, and no conviction can take place without the concurrence of two-thirds of the members present. The chief-justice must preside on the trial of the President. Judgment in case of conviction cannot extend further than to removal from office, and disqualification to hold and enjoy any office of honor, trust, or profit under the United States; but the party convicted is nevertheless liable and subject to indictment, trial, judgment, and punishment according to law. Provisions similar to these are incorporated in the constitutions of the several States. Under these provisions several questions of importance have arisen in case of impeachments by the Federal House of Representatives, of which the following are most important:

(See Vol. XII. p. 755 Am. ed. (p. 717 Edin. ed.).)

1. Who is to be deemed a civil officer within the meaning of the clause first quoted from the Constitution? This question would only be raised in regard to the members of the legislative department of the government. Executive and judicial officers are unquestionably included in the term civil officers as here used; but whether members of the two Houses of Congress are also included has always been matter of dispute. In 1797 William Blount, a senator from Tennessee, was impeached by the House of Representatives for alleged participation in a conspiracy to transfer New Orleans from Spain to Great Britain by the aid of military and naval forces, but his counsel pleaded to the jurisdiction that the office of senator was not such a civil office as was intended by the Constitution, and also that he had been expelled by the Senate, and was therefore no longer an officer, and no longer subject to the process whether so before or not. The Senate sustained the plea, but without distinctly placing its decision on either ground, so that no question of law was settled by the decision.

2. The second question, Whether by ceasing to be an officer the party accused ceased to be amenable to this process, was raised again in the case of William W. Belknap, who, in 1876, was impeached by the House for a corrupt use of his power of appointment as secretary of the war department. A few hours before the impeachment the secretary resigned, and his resignation was accepted by the President. When the impeachment came on for trial it was contended on his behalf that as he was only a private citizen when impeached the process failed for want of jurisdiction, but the Senate decided by a vote of 37 to 29 that an accused party could not thus evade a trial, and that the liability concerned the status at the time of the offence

alleged, and not at the time of the accusation. Unfortunately this vote, though it determined that the cause should proceed, was nevertheless conclusive against conviction, since the senators who held to want of jurisdiction, and who constituted more than a third of the body, must on the same ground vote on the final submission against conviction; and the final result was that the accused was acquitted for want of jurisdiction, though the plea to the jurisdiction had been overruled. It can hardly be said under these circumstances that the question of jurisdiction for such cases has been authoritatively determined.

3. A further very important question is, What, within the intent of the Constitution, are such high crimes and misdemeanors as are impeachable? A subordinate question is, whether the terms crimes and misdemeanors are used in the Constitution in their ordinary legal sense—a sense which would exclude any case not punishable by law, if the accused was a private person—or in some broader and more general sense. If employed in their legal sense, the scope of impeachment is restricted on the one side, but not on the other; for the descriptive words are accompanied by a qualifying term, which, while it implies an exclusion of some crimes and misdemeanors, does not by specification exclude any, and as a consequence the impeaching body and the trial court must determine upon the special facts of particular cases, whether they are or are not within the constitutional intent. But there is scarcely room for reasonable doubt that the descriptive terms in the Constitution were employed in a popular rather than in the legal sense. Many acts may constitute misdemeanors in an officer unfitting him for his position, which in a private citizen would be only breaches of good morals or of decency. The case of Judge Pickering, the district judge for the federal district of New Hampshire, will furnish an illustration. He was impeached in 1803 on charges the chief of which were drunkenness and profanity on the bench, and was convicted and removed from office. The charges, if sustained, were of such a nature as made his further continuance in office a great public evil, and the power of impeachment would be very seriously defective if it did not embrace such a case. But the constitutional provision was necessarily left vague and very much at large in view of the absolute impossibility of specifying by enumeration or description in advance the infinite variety of ways in which public officers may so conduct themselves as to render their further continuance in office a public scandal or a public danger. This would be particularly true in the case of officers whose duties are political, who would generally escape punishment if it were necessary to define impeachable offences in advance as in the case of ordinary criminal laws.

Few cases of impeachment of federal officers have so far occurred. Three have been mentioned: the others are the following: In 1804 Judge Samuel Chase, of the federal Supreme Court, was impeached on charges of arbitrary and overbearing conduct on the trial of certain political cases, of improperly urging certain indictments upon the grand-jury, and of indulging in highly indecent and extra-judicial reflections before another grand-jury upon the government of the United States, then administered by Mr. Jefferson. Judge Chase had been a signer of the Declaration of Independence, and was a very able judge; but he was also a very ardent Federalist, and like most judges of the day took liberties in his judicial action, and especially in his charges to grand-juries, which at this time would be regarded as highly improper and wholly out of place. But the party feeling of the day ran so high that it was impossible to convict him; the trial took on a party character, and the Federal senators, who constituted more than a third of the body, voted for acquittal.

In 1830 Judge Peck, the federal district judge for the district of Missouri, was impeached for arbitrary and illegal conduct in punishing a member of the bar as for contempt of court for a severe criticism in a newspaper of one of his judicial opinions. He was not convicted, a small majority of the Senate voting in his favor. On the breaking out of the civil war in 1861 Judge Humphreys, the federal district judge for the district of Tennessee, repudiated his allegiance to the United States and accepted a commission from the Confederacy, and for this was impeached, convicted, and removed from office, making no defence.

The most important trial of impeachment was that of Pres. Johnson in 1868. The charges were eleven in number, but only three were voted upon. Two of these were based upon alleged violations of the tenure-of-office law, in an attempted removal of Secretary Stanton from the department of war and the substitution of Lorenzo Thomas in his place. The other was founded on language made use of by him in a public speech, in which Congress was characterized as a Congress of only a part of the States, and not a constitutional Congress, with intent, as was charged, of denying that its legislation was obligatory upon him, or that it had any power to propose amendments to the Constitution. The trial of this case also to some extent assumed a party character, the Republican party having strongly condemned the action complained of, while the Democratic party approved; but seven of the Republican Senators refused to vote for conviction, and an acquittal followed, on a vote of 35 guilty to 19 not guilty. A question of importance on the trial was, whether the president pro tem. of the Senate, who in the event of conviction would become President, had a right to vote; but he claimed and exercised the right.

It is apparent from the foregoing statement that the power of impeachment has been used very sparingly in the national system, and has resulted in conviction in those cases only in respect to which there could be no fair ground for dissent. Impeachment has been a rare proceeding in State government, and none of the cases which have arisen is sufficiently important to be specially mentioned here. (T. M. C.)

IMPUTATION, in theology, is the gracious grant of Christ's righteousness to believers, by which God accepts them as holy. This imputation is conditioned on faith, and involves the impartation of the Holy Spirit with the new sanctified nature in the believer. Man has thus, through faith, the righteousness of God and not his own (Rom. x. 3), but made his own, on which his holy character, life, and destiny are built. There is also an imputation of man's sins to Christ, who bears them and becomes a curse under them (Gal. iii. 13; 2 Cor. v. 21; 1 Pet. ii. 24). These two imputations are possible because of the Word becoming flesh (John i. 14). Christ entered fully into humanity and the believer and Christ are thus identified. (See John vi. 56 and xvii. 23.) (S. G.)

INCARNATION, in theology, is the appearance of the Deity upon the earth in animate form. The heathen nations believed that their _____ as beasts or as men at different times.

to Europa as a bull. Apollo served Admetus as a man-slave. Probably every heathen nation believed that a divine being could, when he pleased, adopt a visible form, but it is certain that they did not regard the god as assuming an animal or human nature in such appearance. It was a mere metamorphosis, not a change of nature. Here the Christian idea of incarnation differs altogether from the heathen notion. Christ was God incarnate, not merely as a theophany but as a human being. The Word became flesh. The Divine and human were united in him. The appearances of God to Abraham were theophanies, but the Christ of Bethlehem was a real babe; Jesus of Nazareth was a real youth, a real man, although the Son of God. How the human and the Divine were united in Christ has been a speculative problem causing great contests in the church. Some have denied the human, like the Docetæ, the Patripassians, and the Eutychians, and others have denied the Divine, like the Arians. The various theories that unite the human and Divine are very numerous, some emphasizing the human and some the Divine, while still others recognize a single theanthropic condition as constituting the union. (For details, see article JESUS CHRIST in the ENCYCLOPÆDIA BRITANNICA.) (H. CR.)

INDEPENDENCE, DECLARATION OF AMERICAN. The instrument known by this name, the adoption of which on the 4th of July, 1776, has made that day memorable as the birthday of a nation, was but the formal, diplomatic publication of what had been a virtual fact for several months. While it is undoubtedly true that the great body of the people of the thirteen colonies entered into the contest with the mother country with no purpose of separation, it is equally certain that John Adams, from the outbreak of hostilities in 1775, and Samuel Adams, from a still earlier period, looked forward to independence. Washington and other army officers were unequivocally committed in favor of it as early as the beginning of 1776, about which time Thomas Paine's pamphlet, *Common Sense*, was widely diffusing this sentiment among the people. As early as in November, 1775, the Congress had recommended to the people of New Hampshire, South Carolina, and Virginia to establish governments suited to their condition. North Carolina followed their example, and in May, 1776, the Congress voted that each one of the united colonies, where no government sufficient to the exigencies of their affairs had as yet been established, should adopt such government as would in the opinion of the representatives of the people best conduce to the happiness and safety of their constituents in particular and of America in general. The preamble to this resolution, after reciting the act of Parliament which purported to exclude the Americans from the protection of the crown, the king's neglect to answer their petition, and the employment of "the whole force of the kingdom, aided by foreign mercenaries, for the destruction of the good people of these colonies," declared that it was "absolutely irreconcilable with reason and good conscience for the people of these colonies now to take the oaths necessary for the support of any government under the crown of Great Britain, and that it was necessary that the exercise of every kind of authority under the crown should be totally suppressed, and all the powers of government exerted under the authority of the people of the colonies." This was a virtual assertion of independence. The vote was not unanimous, but it committed the Congress and the most important of the colonies—Pennsylvania excepted—to that full extent.

Other acts had implied as much. In March, 1776, privateers were authorized to cruise against British ships, and in April the commerce of the thirteen colonies was thrown open to all the world not subject to the king of Great Britain. The only difference between these measures and that which was consummated on the 4th of July is that they were provisional, while the Declaration proclaimed a final and irrevocable act. The provincial congress of North Carolina on April 12 unanimously "empowered their delegates in the Continental Congress to concur with the delegates of the other colonies in declaring independency and forming foreign alliances." On May 4 the general assembly of Rhode Island discharged the inhabitants of that colony from all allegiance to the king of Great Britain, and authorized its delegates in Congress to join in treating with any prince, state, or potentate for the security of the colonies, and directed them to favor the most proper measures for confirming the strictest union. The Virginia convention, on May 15, unanimously resolved that they had "no alternative but an abject submission or a total separation," and therefore voted "that their delegates in Congress be instructed to propose to that body to declare the united colonies free and independent States, absolved from all allegiance or dependence upon the crown or Parliament of Great Britain; and that they give the assent of this colony to such declaration and to measures for forming foreign alliances and a confederation of the colonies." In accordance with these instructions, on June 7, Richard Henry Lee, in the name of Virginia, proposed in Congress, "That these united colonies are, and of right ought to be, free and independent States; that they are absolved from all allegiance to the British crown, and that all political connection between them and the state of Great Britain is, and ought to be, totally dissolved; that it is expedient forthwith to take the most effectual measures for forming foreign alliances; and that a plan of confederation be prepared, and transmitted to the respective colonies for their consideration and adoption." The resolution was seconded by John Adams. On the following day the debate was begun, and continued two days with great earnestness on both sides. It appeared that a majority of colonies was for independence, but a postponement of the question for three weeks was agreed to in order, if possible, to secure unanimity. To save time a committee consisting of Jefferson, Adams, Franklin, Roger Sherman, and Robert R. Livingston was appointed to prepare a declaration. In the meantime, on June 14, Connecticut instructed her delegates in favor of independence, foreign alliances, and a permanent union of the colonies; and on the same day the Delaware assembly abolished the royal government and authorized her delegates to vote for independence. The question on Lee's resolution came to a vote in Congress on July 2, and delegates from twelve colonies (New York being unable to vote) unanimously declared that "these united colonies are, and of right ought to be, free and independent States." "The 2d of July, 1776," John Adams wrote, "will be the most memorable epocha in the history of America; to be celebrated by succeeding generations as the great anniversary festival, commemorated as the day of deliverance . . . . from one end of the continent to the other, from this time forward for evermore." But as the Declaration was not reported and adopted until the 4th, the anniversary of independence was fixed upon that day. The Declaration was drawn up by Jefferson, who was deficient in power as a debater, but was a master in the use of the pen. His draft was adopted with a few slight amendments suggested by his colleagues of the committee. The only considerable change was the striking out of an eloquent denunciation of the slave-trade, and of Great Britain for forcing the traffic on the colonies. Unhappily it was but too clear that the colonies were not unanimous on this subject. The declaration was adopted and authenticated by the signatures of the president and the secretary of the Congress, was published, and was proclaimed at the head of the army. On the 2d of August the members of Congress signed the declaration, which had been engrossed on parchment. The body was somewhat changed since the 4th of July by the retirement of members and the election of successors. The changes made the body unanimous. It was in a season of gloom and anxiety that the young nation threw down the gage of defiance to the most puissant empire then in the world, and more than five years of conflict and endurance were required to translate the bold word into accomplished fact. For upward of half a century "Independence Day" was celebrated with national enthusiasm, and the public reading of the Declaration of Independence was an essential part of the celebration. Then came the period of self-criticism. Our history, our achievements, our institutions, it seemed, had perhaps been too enthusiastically magnified. Fourth-of-July oratory was another name for bombast. Rufus Choate allowed himself to indulge in something like a sneer at the "glittering generalities" of the Declaration. At length our government was submitted to the crucial test of a titanic civil war, and now again our institutions are a subject of pride and rejoicing. Again, the Fourth of July and the Declaration of Independence have their honors, and they will not improbably recover the enthusiastic recognition they enjoyed "sixty years since."

The facts concerning the Declaration are given in sufficient detail by Bancroft, *History of the United States*. In Jefferson's *Works* will be found a fac-simile of his draft, with the corrections of the committee. Fuller details of the measure are exhibited in the *Lives* of John and Samuel Adams and Jefferson. (L. E. S.)

INDIA, OR THE EAST INDIES. Under this general term are comprehended the two great peninsulas of Hindostan and Farther India, or, as it is now usually styled, Indo-China, as well as the East India or Sunda Islands. The western peninsula, that of Hindostan, to which the name of India is often restricted, is by far the more important, better known, and more populous, but has already been fully treated in the ENCYCLOPÆDIA BRITANNICA. Some recent facts are here noted.

Since the first mention of India in history it has had a teeming population, but the division of the peninsula into numerous states, regarding each other as a foreign power, and constantly at war with each other, kept the population within the bounds of production until the ascendancy of British power practically welded the whole into one empire.

Since that date the increase of population has been immense, and, as improvements in agriculture, the reclamation of waste lands, and the growth of manufactures have not kept pace with that of population, periodical famines occur, taxing to the utmost the resources of the entire country. There are districts so thickly peopled that, though they bear two crops annually, this is not sufficient to save the people from starvation.

In the endeavor to remedy this evil to some extent, the Indian government has caused the execution of a vast series of irrigation works—undoubtedly the most remarkable and extensive that have been constructed in modern times. India has always been a land of irrigation. The plains of Northern India, away from the foot-hills of the Himalaya, and the tableland of Southern India, would without irrigation support but a sparse population, and the former rulers, Brahminical, Buddhist, and Mohammedan alike, perpetuated their power by the erection of dams and tanks to supply the fields of their subjects with water. Many of these works had with the lapse of time and the disappearance of dynasties fallen into ruin or disuse, and their complete restoration would have been insufficient for the needs of agriculture. The execution of these great works has doubtless somewhat alleviated the condition of the people, but population seems to increase beyond the limits of any effort that can be made by government, and the people have as yet not learned to emigrate to any appreciable extent.

The population and area of Hindostan at the present time may be set down approximately as follows:

	Sq. miles.	Population.
Ajmeer, Berar, and Coorg	22,005	3,480,000
Assam	46,341	5,100,000
Bengal	193,198	72,800,000
Bombay Presidency	124,122	16,800,000
Central provinces	84,445	10,300,000
North-west provinces and Oude	106,111	45,000,000
Madras	141,001	31,200,000
Punjab	106,632	20,000,000
Hyderabad (native)	81,807	10,200,000
Rajputana (native)	129,750	10,700,000
Mysore, Travancore, Baroda	116,463	19,400,000
Tributary States, etc. (native)	143,529	13,700,000
French and Portuguese possessions	1,491	800,000
Himalayan States	90,350	3,300,000
Ceylon	24,700	2,890,000
	1,411,745	265,670,000

Out of this vast population more than 50,000,000 are Mohammedans, and Islamism is continually on the increase at the expense of Brahminism, which is still the prevailing faith.

During the last twenty-five years a special state department has administered the Indian forests. The need of conservators educated in forestry soon became apparent, and in 1866 an arrangement was made by which candidates were trained in forestry in France. In 1878 a central forest school was established to prepare natives of India for the executive charge of forest ranges. The total area of the forests of British India was computed in 1883 at 75,270 square miles, of which about 48,000 have been acquired by the forest department. These forests owe their escape from destruction to their inaccessibility or the unsuitability of the ground for irrigation. Many of them are upon the Himalayas up to heights of 8000 to 9000 feet. A survey is in progress on a scale of 4 inches to the mile.

The trigonometrical survey of Hindostan, the last chain of the principal triangulation of which was completed in 1882, was probably the greatest of modern surveys. A project for the general triangulation of Southern India was drawn up by Major Lambton. In 1818 the survey had reached the northern limits of the Madras Presidency, and was transferred to the supreme government. Lambton was succeeded by Everest who devised a system of meridional chains of triangulation about 1° apart, tied together by longitudinal

INDIA

... the work
... these lines
... and jungle,
... The mortal-
... lying ... longitudinal
... ... deadly malarial
... ... Himalayas, was
... ... famous battle.
... ... The peninsula of
... ... one of the least
... ... and cannot even now, great
... ... to our knowledge of it, be
... ... explored. The geography of
... ... to render exploration difficult,
... ... of the peninsula into a num-
... ... which are separated by almost
... ... From the mountain-mass of
... ... may be regarded as an eastward pro-
... ... Himalayan system, descend several
... ... mountains dividing the peninsula into a
... ... north and south valleys, each watered
... ... great river. These great rivers are, proceeding
... west to east, the Irawadi, Salween, Meinam, Me-
... and Songka or Red River of Tonquin. There
... many other rivers of less importance, but these are
the main arteries.

The source of the Irawadi is unknown, and its upper
course, though it may be marked upon maps, is unex-
plored. About its head-waters lies a mountainous
country, inhabited by tribes which, though claimed as
a portion of Burmah, are not under the control of any
regular government. Throughout its lower course it
is the river of Burmah, and it finally forms an extensive delta upon the western side of the Bay of Martaban. The Salween flows through the Shan states,
and across the British possessions on the eastern shore
of the Bay of Bengal, finally entering the sea at Moul-
mein. The Mekong descends to the China Sea by a
circuitous course through the Shan states, those of the
Lao Shans tributary to Siam, Cambodia, and French Cochin China. The last two of these rivers are believed
to rise in the mountains of Eastern Thibet, and it is
believed by some that the Irawadi has its origin in the
same region. The Meinam runs a comparatively short
course, watering the fertile land of Siam, and entering
the bay of that name a little below Bangkok. The
Songka enters the Bay of Tonquin far to the north
and east of the Mekong, and east of the mountains
which separate Anam from the Laos states. It rises
somewhere among the mountains of Yunnan and thus
cannot compare in length of course with the Salween
or Mekong. The Donnai, Saigon, and other smaller
but more or less navigable rivers form a second fluvial
system in French Cochin-China. The Sittang, which
flows into the head of the Bay of Martaban, has a
course almost as long as that of the Meinam. The
tide rushes up its mouth in a great bore.

The arguments in favor of the rise of the Irawadi far to
the north of the limits of Indo-China are briefly as follows:
(1) The great volume of the Irawadi, which has an average
discharge of 521,794,000,000 cubic yards of water annually, or three-fourths that of the Mississippi, and thus
must, to all appearances, need a larger drainage basin than
the ... Mekong, which bear down a much smaller
... (2) Chinese geographical annals extend-
... and corroborated by the reports of
... and others, by Chinese maps, and by
... ... all go to prove that the Sanpo
... course of the Irawadi, and not that
... usually supposed. (3) The water-
shed of the Brahmaputra, without that of the Sanpo, is
sufficiently extensive to account for the volume of that river.
Against these arguments can be arrayed the fact that there
does not appear to be, from the conformation of the country,
any possibility for the Sanpo to make its way around the
Brahmaputra to the Irawadi.

The frontier between Indo-China and China proper
is by no means well defined, and the districts along
that frontier are almost unknown to Europeans.

Peoples and History.—The ruling peoples of Indo-
China appear to consist for the most part of the descendants of successive hordes of Chinese who, at
various dates, have spread southward from the over-
populated parts of Southern China, or have fled their
country from political reasons. These semi-Chinese
races, who for the most part are considerably behind
the Chinese in culture and the arts of civilization, are
superimposed upon an older population inhabiting the
mountains, forests, and jungles, and maintaining themselves more or less independent. Around the coasts
and in the peninsula of Malacca the Malay race predominates. Hindostan gave to the peninsula its prevailing creed of Buddhism, and the now tottering kingdom of Cambodia or Khmer was largely tinctured
with Hindu civilization, as evidenced in the architecture of its famous ruined temples, which are in the
bounds of the present kingdom of Siam.

The modern Chinese are now spreading throughout
much of the peninsula. They are almost dominant
in Siam, they are making their way from Yunnan
along the Mekong Valley, they swarm in Tonquin
under the black and yellow flag, and they are numerous
in Malacca and Singapore.

Previous to the irruption of the more or less sini-
cised races of Southern China Indo-China seems to
have been peopled by aborigines of the same stock as
those which inhabited the former region. Among
these were the Trao, now represented by a people of
the same name in Cochin-China, who are among the
smallest of men; by the Mincopies of the Andaman
Islands, the Simangs of Malacca, and one or two communities within the bounds of the Chinese Empire.
This race was, in fact, Negrito. Another tattooed race
known to the early Chinese was that of Tchang Rioh,
or long-legged people, whose descendants are probably
to be met with in the Mois of Cochin-China, the
Phnongs, and the Khas.

The predominant race, however, from the region
around the great bend of the Yellow River, southward over Southern China and Indo-China, at the date
of the appearance of the more cultured Chinese from
the west, was that known as Mon, Ngu, or Man.
These people were also called by the Chinese the Great
Bowmen or Y. They tattooed, cropped their hair, and
were good potters. Though, in the course of time,
overpowered by the culture and finally by the administrative power of the Chinese, and also mixed with
Chinese blood to a considerable extent, the Mon appear to have been an important ingredient of the race
of the Shans, or, as they call themselves, Tai, which
has from time to time poured down upon Indo-China.
Other intrusive races beside the Chinese were the
Tek or Teh, and the Tok or Tchou. These finally
gave a dynasty to the Chinese, and also founded a rival
great kingdom in the south, known as Teru or Tsv.
The Tek seem to have had some connection with
Turkish hordes, and were to some extent the ancestors
of the Karens.

The Chinese Emperor Yaou, who came to the

throne B. C. 2356, sent the tribe of Hi to take the government of the country south of the Yang-tse. From this period forward the Chinese emperor, whether of Chinese race or not, claimed suzerainty over the districts to the south of the Yang-tse, and though the claim seems for the most part to have been unaccompanied with any real power, the Chinese colonists prepared the way for unification. The great state of Teru remained the rival of the empire until B. C. 224. Every political change seems to have forced southwards a portion of the nations of Southern China, each successive immigration more imbued with Chinese customs and blood than the one which preceded it. The Karens seem to have been the earliest immigrants from Southern China. For a long period the Karen kingdom of Lin-y Youe-chang, or Lam-ap, blocked the path of the invading Yun Shans, and the Mau Shans by treachery put an end to a Karen kingdom west of the Salween. Three bodies of Shans seem to be distinguishable, viz.: the Yun Shans, Mau Shans, and Laos Shans. The cradle of the Tai, or Shan, seems to have been the Kiu-lung Mountains.

About 543 B. C. the Yun Shans had founded towns to the south of Yunnan, and were pushing down the Mekong to the Karen country. In A. D. 431 they founded cities in the Meinam Valley and overran and occupied the northern part of Cambodia.

Early in the sixth century B. C. the Mau Shans entered the valley of the Irawadi, drove the Burmese southward, by 1220 annexed Assam, and in 1293 became predominant over the Shan states to the east and west of the Salween as far as Zimmé. By the end of the thirteenth century they had shattered the Burmese Empire, driven the Yun Shans southward, attacked Java, Malacca, and Cambodia, annexed part of Pegu, and extended their sway over the Malay Peninsula as far south as Tavoy. From this time to A. D. 1554 Shan princes were ruling in the valleys of the Irawadi, Sittang, and Salween, as well as in the country south of Yunnan as far east as Cochin-China. The Yun Shans, driven southward by the Mau Shans, founded the kingdom of Siam.

The Laos Shans were settled in the country west of Tonquin at a very early date, and had wedged themselves as far south as Vien-Chang before the arrival of the Yun Shans; these are therefore known to their neighbors as Lau or Lao, which means old.

The kingdom of Vien-Chang was at the height of its power in the fourteenth century, was flourishing in the seventeenth, and did not succumb to the Siamese until 1827.

The Anamese, who have the unenviable reputation of being the ugliest race in Indo-China, seem to have been a mixture of Mau and Chinese, who spread southward from Tonquin, and have been but little intercrossed with the Shans. They are squat, less vigorous than the other races, and are noted for the deformity of the big toe, which sticks out separate from the others.

The Burmese are of Thibetan origin. Their kingdom was contracted by the irruption of the Mau Shans in the sixth century B. C. In the thirteenth century the whole of Burmah except Pegu fell into the hands of the Mau Shans, and notwithstanding the disruption of the Mau Empire was governed by Shans until 1554, when the emperor of Pegu annexed it to his dominions.

Cambodia, or Khmer, is the oldest empire of the peninsula. It is first mentioned in 1109 B. C. In the third century it traded with Rome. It seems to have received its civilization from India, and tradition states that an immigration of Hindus took place B. C. 254. The Karen wave extended into Cambodia, which in the fourth century was ruled by Karen princes. Buddhism was not introduced until A. D. 422, and the Indian dynasty in Cambodia ended in 581 A. D. Since that date the state has gradually declined in extent and importance.

Whatever the older natives of Siam may have been, the term Siam is the equivalent of Shan, and the present Siamese Empire commences with the founding of Ayuthia in 1350. The history of Indo-China is a confused mass of struggles between the more or less distinct races; or rather, the constantly varying political agglomerations which occupied it. These struggles seem to have been more sanguinary and incessant since the rise of the Siamese and Peguan or modern Burmese Empire than they were previously. Burmah, Siam, Cambodia, and Vien-Chang were engaged in constant warfare, during which the Burmese were more than once at Ayuthia, and Siamese power seemed to be broken, only to rise again, and finally to become predominant over a large part of Cambodia, over the Zimmé Shans, who for a while were ruled by Pegu, and over the Laos. The Portuguese annals furnish lively pictures of the wars of the sixteenth century, in which Portugal took part.

Present Condition.—The principal political divisions of Indo-China are Anam, including Tonquin, the original seat of Anamese power, Cochin-China (see COCHIN-CHINA in Vol. II.), and French Cochin-China; Cambodia, once the seat of a powerful kingdom, but now under the protection of France; Siam, which occupies a large area with undetermined boundaries in the centre of the peninsula, as well as a portion of its southern prolongation, the peninsula of Malacca; and the British possessions, which may, since the taking of Mandelay, and the deposition of King Theebaw in 1885, be considered to comprehend what has before been known as the Burmese Empire, as well as the districts of Lower Burmah and Tenasserim, and the Straits settlements of Pulo Penang, Wellesley, and Singapore, etc. The northern Shan tribes, once subject to Burmah, are now independent, and many of the hill-tribes, remnants of states which were formerly powerful, still maintain a practical independence. Several small independent Malay states exist in the peninsula of Malacca—as Johore, Selângor, Pahang, Perak, Negri Sembilan, and Sungei Ujong. Those named are all situated in the southern part of the peninsula between 2° and 5° N. lat. The Pahang is one of the largest rivers of Malacca, rising nearer to the western than the eastern coast; it runs north-west into the China Sea. The little state of Perak is famous for its tin-mines, which are to a great extent worked by Chinese. The River Perak runs nearly north and south for about 150 miles, and then turns abruptly westward to the Straits of Malacca.

The population of Indo-China is greater than has been supposed. M. R. du Caillaud estimates that of Tonquin alone at 18,000,000, and it cannot certainly fall short of 15,000,000. Cochin-China proper is less populous, but the valley of the Mekong is densely peopled. The following is as close an approximation to the population of the various states as can well be obtained:

	Sq. miles.	Population.
Anam { Tonquin	63,780	15,000,000
Cochin China	101,660	6,000,000
French Cochin China, Cambodia	59,970	3,100,000
Siam, including the Siamese Shans	280,640	7,000,000
Lower Burmah and Tenasserim	87,220	4,050,000
Upper Burmah and Independent tribes	209,600	4,400,000
Singapore and Straits settlements	1,445	470,000
Independent Malacca	31,500	500,000
	835,815	40,520,000

These figures, with the exception of those relating to English and French possessions, are but rough approximations. The interior of Siam is well peopled, and the figures given may be below the truth.

The productions are vast and varied. The mountains abound in metals. Gold is plentiful, and can be found in the basins of all the rivers. The taxes are paid by the princes tributary to Siam in gold; gold is used without stint on the Burmese pagodas, and travellers mention its existence in Tonquin, Siam, Burmah—in whatever part they journeyed. Silver, argentiferous galena, lead, iron, copper, antimony, are known to exist; and tin occurs in Cambodia, and is probably mined in Perak. Upon the plains between Chantabun and Battambong sapphires are found of a quality not inferior to those of Ceylon.

The forests furnish many valuable timbers, including teak. Gutta-percha, pepper, coffee, rice, cotton, sugar-cane, and indigo are among the vegetable products; and the best tea used by the Chinese is grown at Puerh, within the Shan states.

Ivory and silk are among the most important animal products. Most of the mammals of Hindostan are found here, together with others peculiar to the region. The rich valleys and deltas of the Irawadi, Meinam, Mekong, and Song-ka teem with life of every kind, the birds and insects being especially numerous and beautiful.

Siam is the largest political agglomeration of the peninsula. The reigning family are Siamese, but that branch of the Shans is probably inferior in numbers to the other races of the empire. In all the centres of trade, especially in the sea-ports, Chinese are predominant, while the Laos and other Shan princes are only nominally subjected, paying an annual tribute, but ruling their own subjects. The most south-western Laos are those who inhabit the provinces of Pachim and Nayok-nayok, and who were transported thither by the king of Siam after the destruction of Vien-Chang. These Laos are exceedingly indolent, scarcely raising rice enough to maintain themselves. Those nearer Korat are more active, and devote more attention to agriculture, especially to sericulture. Indolence, however, seems to be the curse of both Siamese and Laos, and is causing them to give way, on the one hand, before the "black-bellied" or body-tattooing northern Shans, and on the other before the ever-active and pushing Chinese.

Besides Bang-kok, the Venice of the East, with its floating houses on the Meinam, and a population of perhaps 500,000, Siam contains many other large cities, as Zinmé or Cheng-Mai, an entrepôt of trade between British Burmah and Siam, and the capital cities of the Laos states. The seaport of Chantabun has a population of 30,000.

The power of Burmah has been on the decline of recent times, so that not only the hill-tribes of the north and east, i. e., of the parts bordering on China on the one hand and those west of the Salween on the other, are practically independent, but the once tributary Shan states have become entirely so.

The Burmese are in indolence equal to the Siamese and Laos, and seem certainly inferior in manliness to the northern Shans. They are an exceedingly polished and courteous race, conceited to excess, loquacious and boasting. It must be conceded that in the graces of civilization they are in advance of all other Indo-Chinese. Pegu and the western sea-coast still contains a remnant of the Talains or Mon race, who were probably the aboriginal inhabitants.

The Karens are one of the most interesting races of the peninsula. They include a large number of tribes, principally resident in what was once Burmah, but found also on the other side of the Mekong. The white Karens of Lower Burmah have been for ages overridden and persecuted by the Shans and Burmese, and are an excessively timid race. They have been taken in hand by the American Mission, and have proved specially amenable to Christianity. Colquhoun states that there are 457 Christian Karen churches in British Burmah.

The Karen-nees or Red Karens, so called from their short red breeches, are very different. Kidnappers by profession, their country cannot be passed through by traders, and blocks trade between the Shan states and British Burmah. The Kachyens of the north of Burmah seem to be allied to the Karens. There are a great number of hill-tribes bearing separate names, some of them remains of the former Karen agglomeration, but some, as the Lawas, apparently even of older date. The hill-tribes behind the delta of Tonquin, called by the Anamites Muongs, are Shans. The difficulty of arriving at a clear idea of the distribution of the peoples of Indo-China is enhanced by the fact that each has a different name for the other.

The prevailing religion of the ruling races of the peninsula is Buddhism, but Buddhistic beliefs and practices are strangely mixed up with the original nature-worship of Mongolian peoples. There is also a belief in a Supreme God, called Tie, Brā, and Phya-Then by different peoples. The worship of "nats" or genii is still the sole religion of these hill-tribes, whose residence in the country is older than the introduction of Buddhism.

European Possessions.—The valleys of Indo-China have of late years assumed great importance in the eyes of Europeans, not only on account of their own great fertility and capabilities, but as furnishing a high-road into Southern China, by which the productions and manufactures of that country can be brought to the markets of the rest of the world more readily than they now are. The chief claimants to power in the peninsula are the English and the French. The latter hold the delta of the Mekong, and have acquired a protectorate over Cambodia and the whole of Anam.

England has held Tenasserim and Arracan since 1826; Lower Burmah and the mouths of the Irawadi since 1852; and, at the end of 1885, in consequence of the arbitrary conduct of King Theebaw, sent an expedition to Mandalay, the result of which was the dethronement and captivity of Theebaw, and the annexation of Burmah to the Empire of India. W. N. L.

CPSIA information can be obtained
at www.ICGtesting.com
Printed in the USA
LVHW060155200921
698234LV00009B/170